BARENTS SEA
WHITE SEA
FINLAND
LADOGA
Helsingfors
Viborg
GULF OF FINLAND
Leningrad (Petrograd)
Hango
Reval
Baltiski
Hungerburg
Narva
Rakvere
ESTHONIA
Luga
Novgorod
Parnu
Dorpat
Pskov
GULF OF RIGA
Riga
LATVIA
Siauliai
Dvinsk
Polotsk
Vitebsk
LITHUANIA
Kovno
Wilno
Minsk
Grodno
Bialystok
Pinsk
Brześć nad Bugiem
Kowel
Chelm
Równe
Lwów
Cernăuţi
Mukačevo
UNION OF SOVIET SOCIALIST REPUBLICS
RUSSIAN SOCIALIST FEDERAL SOVIET REPUBLIC
WHITE RUSSIAN S.S.R.
UKRAINIAN S. S. R.
UNION ASIATIC TERRITORY
Yaroslavl
VOLGA
Nijni Novgorod
Kazan
Tver
Moscow
Smolensk
Simbirsk
Samara
Penza
Perm
Ekaterinburg
Cheliabinsk
Ufa
Orenburg
Gomel
Kursk
Voronezh
Saratov
Kiev
Kharkov
DON
DNIEPER
DNIESTER
BUG
Stalingrad
Astrakhan
Zinovievsk (Elizabethgrad)
Dnepropetrovsk (Ekaterinoslav)
Zaporozhe (Alexandrovsk)
Mariupol
Rostov
Nikolaev
Odessa
Chisinău
Bacau
ROUMANIA
Braşov
Focşani
Galatz
Brăila
Sulina
Bucharest
DANUBE
Constanza
BALKANS
Varna
BULGARIA
Burgas
SEA OF AZOV
CRIMEA
Simferopol
Sevastopol
Theodosia
Novorossisk
KOUBAN
CAUCASUS
DAGHESTAN
BLACK SEA
TRANSCAUCASIAN S.F.S.R.
Poti
Batoum
GEORGIA
Tiflis
AZERBAIJAN
Baku
KURA
ARMENIA
Erivan
CASPIAN SEA
Istanbul (Constantinople)
Scutari
MARMARA
Derindje
Dardanelles
Angora
TURKEY
AEGEAN SEA
Izmir
Athens

AMERICAN FOOD IN THE WORLD WAR AND RECONSTRUCTION PERIOD

AMERICAN FOOD IN THE WORLD WAR AND RECONSTRUCTION PERIOD

Operations of the Organizations Under the Direction of Herbert Hoover 1914 to 1924

•

By

FRANK M. SURFACE

and

RAYMOND L. BLAND

1931

STANFORD UNIVERSITY PRESS

STANFORD UNIVERSITY, CALIFORNIA

PRINTED AND BOUND IN THE UNITED STATES
OF AMERICA BY STANFORD UNIVERSITY PRESS

TO

HERBERT HOOVER

CHIEF—LOYAL FRIEND

YOUR FORMER ASSOCIATES DURING THE PERIOD OF THE GREAT WAR AND ITS AFTERMATH PRESENT THIS FIRST COMPLETE RECORD OF THE WORK OF THE MANY ORGANIZATIONS UNDER YOUR ACTIVE DIRECTION AND DEDICATE IT TO YOU. AS EVIDENCE OF THEIR AFFECTION AND AS A MEMORIAL OF THOSE DAYS OF COMMON SERVICE THEY SUBSCRIBE THEIR NAMES HEREWITH AS A TOKEN OF THEIR APPRECIATION OF THE PRIVILEGE OF SERVING UNDER YOUR INSPIRING LEADERSHIP.

THE ABOVE DEDICATION, FOLLOWED BY MORE THAN ELEVEN HUNDRED ORIGINAL SIGNATURES, APPEARS IN THE FIRST PRINTED COPY OF THIS BOOK PRESENTED TO PRESIDENT HOOVER AT WASHINGTON

FOREWORD

In 1914, when the Commission for Relief in Belgium was formed, Herbert Hoover demanded that there should be maintained a most complete accounting of financial transactions, including accurate statistical records covering the movement of all commodities. This policy, which was strictly followed in all the organizations under his leadership, resulted in many published accounting and statistical documents covering separately and completely the various activities from 1914 to the end of operations in 1924. Although this information has been available, the individual operations were so intertwined that no accurate picture of the work as a whole could be given without co-ordination of all this material.

The authors of this book are unusually well qualified to undertake the vast compilation necessary to make this presentation. Frank M. Surface, now assistant director of the Bureau of Foreign and Domestic Commerce, served as statistician for the Food Administration in Washington, was assigned to assist Mr. Hoover in the Supreme Economic Council in Paris, and was statistician for the United States Grain Corporation in London and in New York. Raymond L. Bland served as a statistician with the American Relief Administration practically from the beginning of that organization, and has carried on his work not only at headquarters in New York, but also in the field in Europe. The authors have approached and executed this difficult task in a fine spirit of service.

It has appeared important that this composite presentation should be published with an explanatory text because

1. Herbert Hoover during these ten years accepted responsibility and has accounted for $375,000,000 in benevolent contributions from individuals and groups. This represents unprecedented generosity and the results should be better known.

2. In one way or another—by contributions in money, gifts of commodities in form of food and clothing, in saving food, in personal service—practically every American was involved in these enterprises. For instance, over twelve million American women signed a pledge to co-operate fully with Hoover, the United States Food Administrator, in his plans to conserve food for overseas shipments, and every producer, manufacturer, and distributor of food products, every hotel, restaurant, and home, large or small, participated. The ultimate result in tons and dollars of this effort to make effective the slogan "Food will win the war" should have a place in history.

3. Well over a half-million American men and women were enrolled and gave their entire time, largely without remuneration, for periods extending from a few months to several years, in service with the Food Administration and Grain Corporation or with the relief organizations engaged in the actual distribution of food. This fine service should not be forgotten.

4. There was no precedent to guide Herbert Hoover in these gigantic enterprises, which involved furnishing to Europe food and related supplies to the value of more than $5,234,000,000, but should mass relief operations again be required, this book will be a guide and inspiration.

5. This is not a history, and the text is nothing more than a statistician's interpretation of facts and figures. There has been no effort to evaluate what might have happened if this work had not been undertaken and carried through with efficiency. It was a super-preventive measure, contributing to an earlier rehabilitation of Europe than would otherwise have been possible, and it takes but little imagination to conjure up the horrors of famine and disease averted before and after the Armistice.

6. Although Herbert Hoover would reject the assertion, this book is the story of a one-man job. His associates dedicate this book to him; it is impossible to lay too great stress upon his stupendous achievement.

Any one of the foregoing six points is a sufficient justification for this book.

EDGAR RICKARD
Administrative Assistant
to Herbert Hoover, 1914–1924

PREFACE

From the beginning of the World War in August, 1914, up to the close of the Russian Relief work in 1924, Herbert Hoover created and directed organizations which were responsible for securing and delivering vast quantities of foodstuffs to the peoples of various European countries. The importance and magnitude of this work and the results accomplished can hardly be overestimated. To mention only a few of the possibilities, it may be pointed out that a large portion of the 10,000,000 people in the occupied regions of Belgium and Northern France might have perished. The results of the World War might have been far different, for the final decision depended as much upon food as it did upon armed forces. In the Armistice Period the peoples of Central and Eastern Europe would have died by millions in the greatest famine the world had seen in three hundred years. Millions of young men and women in Europe today owe their very lives and their present physical fitness to the child-feeding work carried on from 1919 to 1923, and finally, still further millions of the Russian people owe their lives to the relief work in the terrible famine of 1921–1922.

These outstanding achievements in that decade of service were accomplished in the face of world-wide disorganization and the desire of every nation to concentrate on its own problems of reconstruction.

During the ten years, 1914 to 1924, operations were carried on under Mr. Hoover's direction and by the organizations which he headed involving the expenditure of the enormous sum of almost five and a quarter billions of dollars ($5,234,028,208.56). Part of these funds came from charitable donations, part were funds from the United States Treasury donated for relief or loaned to other governments, part came from other countries or from other organizations.

For this sum there were delivered to the people of Europe more than thirty-three million (33,841,307) tons of commodities, mostly American foodstuffs but including some clothing and medical supplies.

Much of this relief work was carried on under the stress of great emergency and under pressure to make food available at a definite place in a limited space of time in order to save human life. Through it all, detailed records were kept of every ton of supplies from the moment of their purchase until they left the hands of the American organization. Considering the magnitude of the work and the conditions under which it was carried on, the statistical records are remarkably complete, with no serious gaps.

It is these records, including the audited reports from the accounting departments, supplemented by the operating commodity statements, which form the basis of this volume. Although this is not an accountant's report, all of the values reported are in reconciliation with audited figures. In order to bring out the details for the non-technical reader and to render the tables more intelligible from the standpoint of the separate operations, the accountant's set-up has often had to be dissected and recombined.

No attempt has been made here to write a popular history of the various projects. Such an undertaking would run into many volumes the size of this. The story of several distinct phases of these operations has already been published, such as *America and Germany,* by Sidney Brooks; *America and the New Poland,* by H. H. Fisher; *American Pork Production in the World War,* by Frank M. Surface; *The Grain Trade during the World War,* by Frank M. Surface; *On the Trail of the Russian Famine,* by Frank A. Golder and Lincoln Hutchinson; *The Famine in Soviet Russia,* by H. H. Fisher; *The Commission for Relief in Belgium, a Statistical Review of Relief Operations,* by George I. Gay; *Public Relations of the Commission for Relief in Belgium —Documents,* in two volumes by Gay and Fisher; bulletins of the American Relief Administration covering seven years.[1] These works, and many pamphlets, are to be found in the Library of Congress, the Hoover War Library, and many public libraries.

Other volumes will no doubt appear in the future as the work of those best qualified to

[1] For further reference to these and to other publications see Bibliography, pages 989–98.

cover particular subjects. Such text as has been included in this report is designed only to give background material necessary for an understanding of the statistical data. It is hoped that this text will make it possible for the reader to obtain a picture of the various undertakings and some idea of their magnitude and significance.

The authors desire to express their appreciation to many individuals and organizations for assistance in making this report possible. To Edgar Rickard, Director General of the American Relief Administration in later years, has fallen the task of supplying many details and furnishing constructive criticism of the results. Edward M. Flesh has also furnished invaluable assistance throughout the preparation of this report. Acknowledgment is also due to Harry Hyslop, in New York, and to the staffs of the Hoover War Library and of Stanford University Library, at Stanford University, California. The manuscript has been read by and many helpful suggestions received from Mr. Rickard, H. H. Fisher of Stanford University, and Perrin C. Galpin and George Barr Baker, of New York.

Frank M. Surface
Raymond L. Bland

January, 1931

CONTENTS

PART II

RELIEF BY COUNTRIES OF DESTINATION

APPENDIX TABLES

BIBLIOGRAPHY

INDEX

LIST OF ILLUSTRATIONS

LIST OF TEXT TABLES

(See page xxi for List of Appendix Tables)

LIST OF APPENDIX TABLES

(See page xvii for List of Text Tables)

EXPLANATORY NOTES

ACT OF CONGRESS

Act appropriating $100,000,000 for relief (Public, No. 274, 65th Congress). This Act was approved February 25, 1919 (40 Stat. L., page 1161). However, the Executive Order was signed by President Wilson upon his arrival at Boston, Massachusetts, on February 24, 1919.

APPENDIX TABLES

All of the summary tables in the Appendix contain a column headed "Table No." where reference is made to the table which contains a further segregation of the information given under that title. For example, in Table 101 there is a summary of the total relief delivered by major operations. On the third line of that table, after "Armistice Period," the reader is directed to Table 107, which divides the total relief in this period under organizations, or groups of organizations. Under "American Relief Administration" in this table, reference is made to Table 109. This latter table divides the A.R.A. relief by methods of finance, one of which is the "U.S. Congressional Appropriation for Relief," and, under this, reference is made to Table 112, which in turn shows the relief from this appropriation delivered to each country. Under "Armenia," the first country in this table, reference is made to Table 201, where one will find the detail by steamers of all relief delivered to Armenia from the Congressional Appropriation. All other items may be followed with the same or greater detail by this method of table reference.

A.R.A.—A.R.A.E.C.F.—A.R.A.

The original American Relief Administration was organized to handle the official relief under the $100,000,000 appropriation from the United States Treasury (Act of February 25, 1919). The period of operation was from February to August 1, 1919. The equipment and unconsumed stocks of the A.R.A. were turned over to the child-feeding organization, supported chiefly by private charity, known as the A.R.A.-European Children's Fund. Later (August, 1921), when the A.R.A.E.C.F. started operation in Russia, a shorter name was desired. The organization then shortened the name to the A.R.A. (For further explanation see pages 73–74, 872 n.)

A.R.A.W. AND A.R.A.E.C.F.

Food Remittances and Bulk Sales for Central Europe

The stocks of the American Relief Administration Warehouses were pooled with those of the European Children's Fund on November 1, 1920. However, in order to distinguish between the commercial organization (A.R.A.W.) and the child-feeding organization (A.R.A.E.C.F.), the A.R.A.W. has been given credit for all food remittance and bulk sale operations.

NAMES OF CITIES CHANGED

Alexandrovsk *to* Zaporozhe.
Constantinople *to* Istanbul.
Ekaterinoslav *to* Dnepropetrovsk.
Elizabethgrad *to* Zinovievsk.
St. Petersburg *to* Petrograd *to* Leningrad.
Tzaritzin *to* Stalingrad.

COUNTRIES

Czechoslovakia

During the Armistice Period this country was generally spelled as two words and hyphenated. All Appendix tables referring to this country will be listed under Czecho-Slovakia. The text, which is of a later date, will show the country spelled as one word, Czechoslovakia.

Jugoslavia

The name of this country has been changed rather frequently. Jugoslavia, being the accepted term today, has been used throughout this book to embrace Serbia, Greater Servia, the Kingdom of S.H.S., and Jugo-Slavia.

LIST OF ABBREVIATIONS

A.C.R.N.E.	American Committee for Relief in the Near East
A.F.S.C.	American Friends Service Committee
A.K.H.A.	Amerikanische Kinderhilfsaktion [Austria] (American Aid for Children. An organization of Austrians)
A.P.	Armistice Period
A.P.E.C.	Allied Purchasing Executive Committee
A.R.A.	American Relief Administration
A.R.A.E.C.F.	American Relief Administration European Children's Fund
A.R.A.W.	American Relief Administration Warehouses
A.R.C.	American Red Cross
C.A.	Congressional Appropriation
C.I.F.	"Cost, insurance, and freight" (cost of goods, transportation, and shipping expenses included)
C.N.	Comité National (National Committee. An organization of Belgians)
C.R.	Children's relief
C.R.B.	Commission for Relief in Belgium
C.R.B.P.	Commission for Relief in Belgium Period
C.S.	Cash settlement (used in referring to A.R.A. cash sales)
E.C.F.	European Children's Fund (contracted form for A.R.A.E.C.F.)
E.R.C.	European Relief Council
E.T.A.	European Technical Advisers
Eurelcon	European Relief Council (this term was used to designate sales in Russia to members of the council)
F.A.G.C.	Food Administration Grain Corporation
F.A.P.	United States Food Administration Period
F.E.W.V.-R.C.	Friends Emergency and War Victims Relief Committee
F.O.B.	"Free on board" (transportation and shipping expenses included)
G.C.	Grain Corporation (contracted form for F.A.G.C. and U.S.G.C.)
J.D.C.	American Jewish or Jewish Joint Distribution Committee
N.E.R.	Near East Relief
N.Y.	New York
Paiok	Primarily meant an allowance of food as for soldiers in the trenches, but later was used for any stipulated allowance, as money to a soldier's wife at home. It was used by the A.R.A. as a monthly food package.
P.A.K.P.D.	Polsko-Amerykański Komitet Pomocy Dzieciom [Poland] (Polish-American Children's Relief Committee. An organization of Poles)
Phila.	Philadelphia
P.K.P.D.	Państwowy Komitet Pomocy Dzieciom [Poland] (State Children's Relief Committee. An organization of Poles)
P.O.D.	Péče o Dítě [Czechoslovakia] (Children's Relief organization. An organization of Czechoslovakians)
President's N.S.D.F.	President's National Security and Defense Fund
Puzapp	Państwowy Urzad Zakupu Artykułów Pierwszej Potrzeby [Poland] (Government Purchasing Office for Articles of Prime Necessity. A Polish agency used in forwarding relief supplies)
Q.	Quakers
Q.M.	Quartermaster (used in referring to Quartermaster invoices for Army supplies)
R.P.	Reconstruction Period
R.S.F.S.R.	Russian Socialist Federative Soviet Republic
S.E.C.	Supreme Economic Council
T.L.	Treasury Loans (U.S.)
U.K.	United Kingdom
U.S.F.A.	United States Food Administration
U.S.G.C.	United States Grain Corporation
U.S. Liq. Com.	United States Liquidation Commission
U.S.R.	Ukrainian Soviet Republic
V.A.	Volunteer Army (Russian)
W.E. Co.	Wheat Export Company
W.S.C.F.	World's Student Christian Federation
Y.M.C.A.	Young Men's Christian Association
Y.W.C.A.	Young Women's Christian Association

PART I

INTRODUCTION

In August, 1914, some 200,000 panic-stricken American tourists were stranded in the meshes of the Great War that had so suddenly enveloped continental Europe. At the first opportunity these Americans piled into England by tens of thousands, most of them without available funds because of the moratorium, and all of them without transportation home. In this emergency, the Honorable Walter Hines Page, the American Ambassador to Great Britain, persuaded Herbert Hoover, a mining engineer with an international reputation in his profession, to organize these chaotic groups of tourists and direct their homeward movement. Accustomed to co-ordinating big engineering projects, he soon reduced these confused groups to something like order. With ten other Americans he guaranteed an American Bank in London against loss and announced that all sorts of American paper, even personal checks, would be exchanged for currency. He arranged transportation with the steamship companies and soon the stream of tourists was homeward bound in an orderly fashion. Five thousand or more Americans a day passed through the hands of this organization during these first six weeks of the war. And although Hoover's Committee accepted checks and other evidences of credit to the extent of $1,500,000, with little opportunity to scrutinize the security, they lost in all only $150.

Hoover himself had engaged passage home for the last week in September, 1914. But the gods had another fate in store for him. Before he could sail, the German armies had invaded Belgium and left the people of that little country in a desperate situation. American and Belgian representatives importuned him to undertake the delicate and difficult task of organizing some means of saving the lives of these ten million people within the occupied territories. Hoover knew what this decision meant. He knew it was a long and difficult job and that if he undertook it he must sever his connections with all commercial activities. At that time, by reason of his numerous mining connections, he was in a position to control a large share of the world's supply of base metals, particularly zinc and lead. These were bound to be enormously valuable if the war continued and if he held on to these it was certain to result in a very large fortune. For three days he sat with Mr. Page and the Belgians, discussing details and imagining possibilities. And for three nights he weighed his own perplexities before he finally decided to cast his lot with the relief for the Belgians.

With that decision was born the Commission for Relief in Belgium—a decision of supreme importance for himself and for the world.

The story of the Commission for Relief in Belgium has been told many times:[1] of how this organization, beginning as a purely philanthropic enterprise, soon received the financial support of the Allied and American Governments; of how the C.R.B. without incorporation or definite legal status came to have many attributes of a government, flying its own flag, issuing its own passports, operating its own fleet under agreed immunity from all belligerent powers, and operating to feed a civilian population within its enemy lines. In April, 1917, the United States entered the war and it was necessary to delegate the distribution in Belgium and France to a neutral Spanish-Dutch committee. Mr. Hoover, now U.S. Food Administrator, continued as chairman of the Commission and arranged for financing the purchase and transport of the food supplies.

In the meantime President Wilson had asked Mr. Hoover to take charge of the food situation, which was rapidly approaching a crisis, in this country. Mr. Hoover arrived in the United States on May 19, 1917, and immediately initiated the preparatory work which led to the establishment of the United States Food Administration. Under the authority of the Food Control Act, which became a law on August 10, 1917, Mr. Hoover was appointed United States Food

[1] Among other publications see *The Commission for Relief in Belgium—Statistical Review of Relief Operations,* by George I. Gay, Stanford University Press, 1925, and *Public Relations of the Commission for Relief in Belgium—Documents,* by George I. Gay, with the collaboration of H. H. Fisher, Stanford University Press, 1929.

Administrator. From that time until after the Armistice, he directed all measures relating to the conservation and distribution of food in this country to insure an adequate supply to support our own needs and those of the Allies in Europe.

In the summer of 1918, Mr. Hoover, anticipating the distress in the liberated and enemy countries on the cessation of hostilities, caused a survey to be made of world food resources and prepared a definite plan for initiating relief measures. Immediately after the Armistice had been signed, President Wilson requested Mr. Hoover to go to Europe and represent the United States in such measures as had to be taken according to the plans already prepared, in order to relieve the impending suffering. He sailed from the United States on November 18, 1918, only seven days after the signing of the Armistice, having arranged before his departure for the dispatch of large quantities of food supplies. From that time until the following September was the most strenuous, the most difficult, but probably the most fruitful period of Mr. Hoover's relief activities. As Director General of Relief for the Allied Governments during these nine months he secured the finance and directed the delivery of more than 4,000,000 tons of food valued at more than one billion dollars.

With the 1919 harvest it was possible to bring this form of relief in Central and Eastern Europe to a close, but in the meantime it had been found that there were millions of children in these countries, many of them orphans, suffering from under-nutrition, many facing death, but all certain of permanent disability unless some means of relief were found. Mr. Hoover immediately set about perfecting an organization which could take care of this need. For three years the American Relief Administration European Children's Fund raised money and fed some 10,000,000 children in these stricken countries.

Before this work was entirely completed, the great famine in Russia again raised the need for "mass feeding" relief on a tremendous scale. The A.R.A. organization, although ready to liquidate, again responded to the call, and under Mr. Hoover's direction, relief to the value of more than $63,000,000 was furnished to these stricken people.

With the close of the Russian relief and the withdrawal of the child-feeding operations in Central Europe, this vast work extending over ten years came to a close.

Scope of Report

The present volume attempts to give a statistical summary and a brief outline of relief activities by the organizations with which Mr. Hoover was connected, and also of the activities of other organizations in respect to their co-operation in this work. This is by no means a complete summary of all the relief work in Europe during this period. Many of the relief organizations mentioned in this volume spent millions, even hundreds of millions of dollars, entirely on their own activities, of which no account is taken in this report. To mention a few of these organizations: The American Red Cross spent upwards of $200,000,000 in relief activities in Europe during this period,[1] yet in this report we have included less than $7,300,000 (Table 33, page 58) as the amount spent by the Red Cross in activities in co-operation with the American Relief Administration. The Near East Relief, the Jewish Joint Distribution Committee, the American Friends Service Committee, the Knights of Columbus, and many other organizations each spent vast sums which had no relation to the work of the organizations which Mr. Hoover was then directing and, hence, are not included in this report. These facts are pointed out in the discussion of the work of each of these organizations but it is important that the reader bear in mind that the volume of relief attributed to many of these organizations in this report is only that portion carried on in co-operation with the American Relief Administration or its subsidiaries and often is only a small fraction of the total activities of those organizations during this period.

Organizations Involved

Because of the large number of activities which were carried on at various times during these ten years and because at different times the same name was applied to totally separate organizations, the terminology used in this report is likely to be confusing. In the following paragraphs an attempt will be made to explain

[1] *Annual Reports of the American National Red Cross*, 1919 to 1923.

briefly the relationship between the major organizations involved. Because of the lengthy names of some of the organizations and in accordance with the usage which grew up during the work, many of these organizations are referred to by their initials, such as C.R.B. for Commission for Relief in Belgium; A.R.A. for American Relief Administration, etc. Some of these are indicated below, while others will be found in the List of Abbreviations on page xxiii.

The Commission for Relief in Belgium (C.R.B.) was established October 22, 1914, and was the buying and shipping organization for all relief supplies to the occupied regions of Belgium and Northern France for the entire duration of the war. Until the United States entered the war the C.R.B. was responsible to the belligerent governments for the execution of the agreements relative to the distribution of the relief in occupied territories. The Commission remained in active operation until August 31, 1919, by which time both the Belgian and French Governments were in a position to take care of their own people and the Commission had liquidated its stock of commodities.

Operating under the C.R.B. were two committees: one composed of Belgians and known as the "Comité National de Secours et d'Alimentation"; the other the corresponding committee of Frenchmen known as the "Comité d'Alimentation du Nord de la France." These two committees carried out the actual internal distribution of relief supplies within the respective countries. Under these committees there were numerous district and local committees through which the supplies moved to the people.

The United States Food Administration was created by Executive Order of President Wilson on August 14, 1917, to carry out the provisions of the Food Control Act of August 10, 1917. Under the United States Food Administration there were several organizations set up to carry out particular functions. The first of these referred to in this volume is the Food Administration Grain Corporation, which was charged with the responsibility of maintaining the guaranteed price of wheat and which engaged in buying and selling wheat, flour, and other cereals and was the source from which the Allied Governments secured their supplies of these commodities during the remainder of the war. The Food Administration came to a close officially on June 30, 1919, and in order to maintain President Wilson's guaranty of the minimum price of wheat to the producer for the 1919–1920 crop, the President directed a new corporation to be formed, known as the United States Grain Corporation, which was the successor to the preceding corporation.

The second organization under the Food Administration was the Sugar Equalization Board, which was incorporated, and purchased both the Cuban and the United States crops of sugar in 1918 and attended to the distribution of the available supplies, both to the Allied countries and internally in the United States.

The third organization under the Food Administration was the Division of Co-ordination of Purchases, through which all food purchases by the Allies, except cereals and sugar, were allocated (cf. page 21).

Immediately after the signing of the Armistice, Mr. Hoover went to Europe at President Wilson's request and through his efforts there was formed an Interallied Council of Supply and Relief, which later became the Food Section of the Supreme Economic Council. Mr. Hoover was made Director General of Relief for the Allied Governments and was given direct charge of all official relief work during the Armistice Period.

In order to handle the official relief from the United States, particularly the supplies furnished under the Congressional Appropriation of $100,000,000 for Relief in Europe (Act of February 25, 1919), President Wilson directed Mr. Hoover to form the American Relief Administration (frequently designated A.R.A.), which was an official organization to handle the allocation and distribution of relief furnished by the United States Government. In addition to the relief paid for from the specific Congressional appropriation, the A.R.A. handled relief furnished from United States Treasury loans direct to certain of the newly established governments, supplies furnished from the President's National Security and Defense Fund and certain relief furnished against cash payment.

Under authorization of President Wilson, the Food Administration Grain Corporation co-operated in the buying and shipping of all relief supplies distributed by the American Relief Administration. The Grain Corporation established a London office which took care of all shipping activities in European waters, handled all the accounting work, and made all settlements with the European governments. In the present report all relief deliveries are referred to as handled by the A.R.A., although to be exact the Grain Corporation should receive joint credit.

With the signing of the Treaty of Versailles on June 28, 1919, the Armistice Period ended and with it all official relief from the United States. From that time on the A.R.A. and the Grain Corporation were engaged solely in liquidating commitments.

In order to render further aid to the millions of destitute children in Europe, Mr. Hoover proposed the organization of an association which could mobilize charitable contributions from the United States. With the approval of President Wilson, it was arranged that any surplus which might have been earned by the Grain Corporation on the relief shipment in the Armistice Period should be turned over to this new organization for the relief of European children. The name of this new organization was the American Relief Administration European Children's Fund. In the present report this is usually referred to as the European Children's Fund or simply as the E.C.F. This was a purely private charitable organization and should not be confused with the American Relief Administration of the Armistice Period which was a semi-official organization.

At a somewhat later period, a separate but correlated organization was set up and known as the American Relief Administration Warehouses (sometimes designated by A.R.A.W.), which handled all food draft and bulk sale operations during its existence. (Cf. page 90.)

During this period there was also set up the European Relief Council (E.R.C.), which was an association of a number of charitable organizations under the leadership of Mr. Hoover which pooled their appeal for charitable contributions from the American public.

Finally, when it became necessary to expand an organization to take care of the crisis in the great Russian famine, the name American Relief Administration was again adopted. This latter organization was an outgrowth of the American Relief Administration European Children's Fund, but since the Russian relief included both adult and child feeding the latter name was regarded as inappropriate. In this book this new organization is frequently referred to as the "American Relief Administration, Russian Unit," or as "A.R.A., Russian Unit." It should not be confused with the A.R.A. of the Armistice Period.

The origin and work of each of the above organizations is fully explained in the appropriate section of this volume but perhaps the above brief discussion will make clear some of the interrelations which might otherwise prove to be confusing.

Total Relief Deliveries

As indicated in the preceding brief summary, this decade of relief work may be divided into four major operations or periods of activities. Although even these were often overlapping and graded one into the other, they stand out as four distinct major developments in the work with which Mr. Hoover was connected. The first of these was the work of the Commission for Relief in Belgium, which took care of the food supply of the occupied territories of Belgium and Northern France during the war. This work was started in November, 1914, and continued during the Armistice Period and up to August 31, 1919, before the respective governments were in a position entirely to take care of their people.

The second major activity was that of the United States Food Administration, which among other things was charged with the responsibility of furnishing the Allied nations with such food supplies as could be spared from the United States. Although the Food Administration was not definitely established until August, 1917, yet for many months prior to that, Mr. Hoover, under authority from President Wilson, was directing the work of furnishing food to the Allies. In this report we have included all food supplies furnished to the Allied Governments which were paid for from United States Treasury loans from April 6, 1917, to June 30, 1919, when the Food Administration passed out of existence.

The third major activity was the relief to European countries during the period from the signing of the Armistice on November 11, 1918, to the signing of the Treaty of Versailles on June 28, 1919. This was the period of official relief during which Mr. Hoover was Director

TABLE 1

GRAND TOTAL OF ALL FOOD AND OTHER RELIEF DELIVERED DURING THE WORLD WAR AND THE RECONSTRUCTION PERIOD —BY MAJOR OPERATIONS, 1914 TO 1924

Major Relief Operation	Duration	Total Metric Tons	Total Value
Commission for Relief in Belgium	November, 1914, to August, 1919	4,988,059.0	$ 861,340,244.21
U.S. Food Administration	April, 1917, to June, 1919	23,103,266.2	3,050,496,599.23
Armistice Period (Director General of Relief)	November, 1918, to August, 1919	4,178,447.7	1,101,486,783.34
Reconstruction Period	August, 1919, to July, 1923	1,571,534.1	220,704,581.78
Grand total net deliveries	November, 1914, to July, 1923	33,841,307.0	$5,234,028,208.56

General of Relief and had direct charge of all relief activities of the Allied Governments. Deliveries of relief commitments made during this Armistice Period were completed by the end of August, 1919.

The fourth and final period of relief activities considered in this report is that of the Reconstruction Period, which began with the work of the American Relief Administration European Children's Fund, in August, 1919, and included many phases of charitable relief, ending with the work in Russia in 1922 and 1923. The major portion of this relief was in the nature of child feeding, but it also includes many phases of adult relief, such as the food draft and bulk sale operations, intelligentsia relief, and much of the Russian work.

Table 1 summarizes the grand total of all relief work accounted for in this report under these four major operations. Table 101 (Appendix) gives additional detail of these deliveries by commodities.

This table shows that the total deliveries accounted for in this report reached the enormous amount of 33,841,307.0 metric tons[1] with a net delivered value of $5,234,028,208.56. Some idea of the volume of these activities may be had by considering that this tonnage would have filled more than 500,000 American freight cars and would require more than 6,700 vessels of 5,000 tons each for its transatlantic transportation.

Table 1 shows further that some 60 per cent of these deliveries represent food supplies furnished to the Allied Governments during the Food Administration Period. As will be pointed out later (cf. page 15), the exigencies of the Allied food and shipping situation resulted in throwing almost the entire burden of feeding these countries during the last two years of the war upon the United States. By the extraordinary increase in the total production by the American farmers and by strict conservation measures, the latter under the guidance of the Food Administration, this country was able to export more than three times the amount of foodstuffs which had been sent abroad during the pre-war years. To a very considerable extent this was due to measures inaugurated under Mr. Hoover's guidance.

Table 2 (page 9) shows the division by commodity groups[2] of the total tonnage delivered under each of the four major operations. It will

[1] All quantities in this report, unless otherwise specified, are given in metric tons, which is a common unit of measurement in continental Europe and on which all accounting was based. A metric ton contains 1,000 kilos (kilograms) and is the equivalent of 2,204.6 avoirdupois pounds as used in the United States. The metric ton is thus slightly smaller than the long ton of 2,240 pounds used very largely in Great Britain and to some extent in this country, and it is roughly 10 per cent larger than the short ton of 2,000 pounds. In the majority of tables quantities are given to the nearest tenth of a ton.

[2] In this and in all summary tables in the Appendix a uniform classification of commodities has been followed. This results in grouping together many closely related commodities under a single heading. Thus flour includes wheat, rye, and all other cereal flours. Grain includes all bread grains and substitutes, such as wheat, rye, corn, and barley. Rice is shown separately. Pork products is used to designate all meats and fats including bacon, hams, shoulders, lard, and also such small amounts of beef or other meats as were occasionally handled. Vegetable oils are also included under pork products because they were used as substitutes for lard. Milk includes both evaporated and condensed milk. Miscellaneous food includes a great variety of items most of which were individually small in tonnage. Examples are cod liver oil, hard-tack, etc. The detail tables of arrivals and particularly of internal deliveries of relief supplies show these separate commodities in greater detail. These summary groups have been used to bring the tables into reasonable size and to avoid much unnecessary detail.

be noted that flour and grain in the total constitute by far the major tonnage. These two groups make up approximately 22,000,000 tons, or roughly 65 per cent of the total quantity. Pork products, including all fats, totaled approximately 2,000,000 tons, but in value this was a relatively much more important item than the tonnage figures indicate.

Table 3 gives the grand total deliveries of all food and relief by countries of destination.

Deliveries were made to 23 separate countries exclusive of sundry accounts, which in-

CHART I

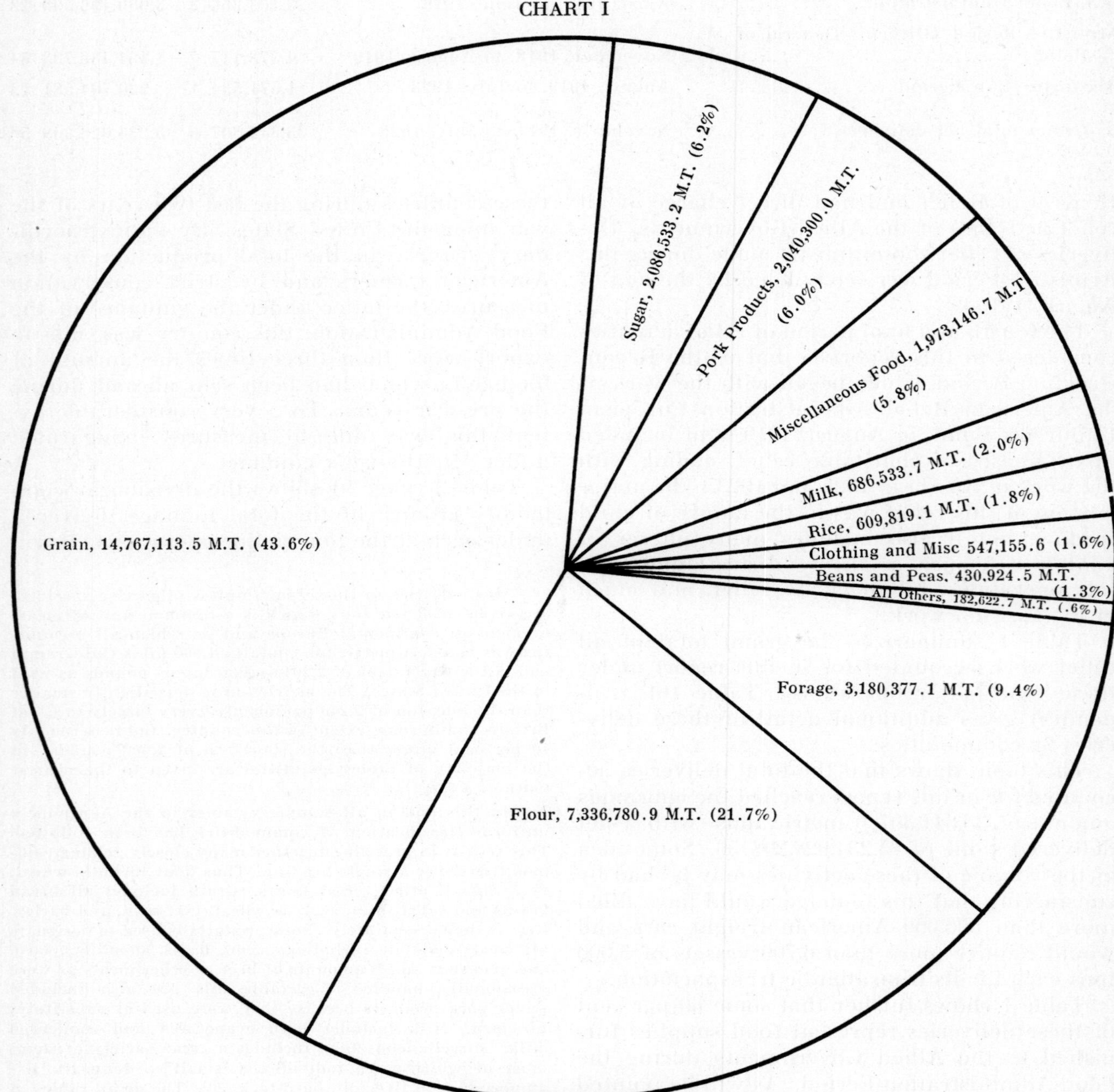

Segregation, by major commodity groups, of the grand total metric tons of all food and other relief deliveries during the World War and the Reconstruction Period—1914–1924. The detail of "all other" commodities may be obtained from Table 2, page 9.

TABLE 2

GRAND TOTAL OF ALL FOOD AND RELIEF DELIVERED DURING THE WORLD WAR AND THE RECONSTRUCTION PERIOD — BY COMMODITIES AND MAJOR OPERATIONS

(Metric Tons)

Commodity	C.R.B.	United States Food Administration	Armistice Period	Reconstruction Period	Total
Flour	411,421.0	4,904,600.4	1,253,568.0	767,191.5	7,336,780.9
Grain	3,310,898.0	10,083,228.8	983,979.6	389,007.1	14,767,113.5
Rice	317,455.0	143,514.0	99,039.1	49,811.0	609,819.1
Beans and peas	171,434.0	108,860.4	104,833.6	45,796.5	430,924.5
Corn grits	....	....	....	103,301.1	103,301.1
Pork products	379,926.0	1,363,799.6	266,979.6	29,594.8	2,040,300.0
Milk	80,921.0	451,346.9	50,653.7	103,612.1	686,533.7
Cocoa	12,870.0	....	511.5	10,762.6	24,144.1
Sugar	51,024.0	1,947,936.8	43,276.7	44,295.7	2,086,533.2
Misc. food	173,272.0	922,736.5	873,062.2	4,076.0	1,973,146.7
Forage	....	3,177,242.8	....	3,134.3	3,180,377.1
Soap	39,129.0	....	1,110.5	2,276.6	42,516.1
Medical supplies	....	....	4,377.5	8,283.9	12,661.4
Clothing and misc.	39,709.0	....	497,055.7	10,390.9	547,155.6
Grand total	4,988,059.0	23,103,266.2	4,178,447.7	1,571,534.1	33,841,307.0

clude chiefly local cash sales and deliveries to prisoners of war or refugees from one country but located in another so that it was difficult to allocate the relief.

The largest deliveries were made to the United Kingdom and France, both of which obtained supplies in excess of one and a quarter billions of dollars. Deliveries to Italy were nearly 800 million dollars. These were the three major Allies which received the bulk of food delivered during the war under the United States Food Administration.

Deliveries to Belgium amounted to nearly 700 million dollars, the major portion of which came from the C.R.B. A portion of the Belgian supplies was furnished under the Food Administration on direct loans from the United States Treasury.

Of the countries receiving relief after the Armistice only, the deliveries to Germany of nearly 300 million dollars were the largest. The major portion of these were sold for cash and paid for by German gold during the Armistice Period. Deliveries to Poland exceeded 200 million dollars. Those to Austria were more than 145 million dollars and to Czechoslovakia they exceeded 115 million. Other countries received smaller amounts, some of the largest of which were those to Russia, Roumania, Jugoslavia, Finland, and Armenia.

TABLE 3

THE GRAND TOTAL OF ALL FOOD AND RELIEF DELIVERED DURING THE WORLD WAR AND THE RECONSTRUCTION PERIOD—BY COUNTRIES OF DESTINATION

1914 TO 1924

Country	Total Metric Tons	Total Value
Armenia	135,764.1	$ 28,795,426.49
Austria	822,200.1	145,481,222.30
Belgium	4,198,856.3	697,140,348.91
Bulgaria	22,862.4	4,856,647.53
Czechoslovakia	545,134.6	115,438,351.98
Danzig Free State	573.2	127,700.69
Denmark	19,912.0	2,147,059.30
Esthonia	67,358.5	21,017,263.56
Finland	188,520.9	30,282,047.90
France	8,425,699.7	1,289,488,622.47
Germany	1,272,934.1	294,373,692.75
Greece	20,374.0	1,211,949.95
Hungary	21,393.5	4,607,139.37
Italy	7,479,780.7	799,608,264.01
Jugoslavia	127,359.0	45,898,651.43
Latvia	26,366.6	7,550,021.69
Lithuania	12,877.7	5,980,781.39
Netherlands	25,027.4	4,219,498.41
Poland	751,135.6	200,864,857.73
Roumania	229,202.8	53,637,311.31
Russia	768,159.9	78,305,318.49
Turkey	20,278.3	4,369,404.30
United Kingdom	8,652,668.6	1,386,102,780.05
Sundry Accounts	56,529.2	23,654,740.07
Grand total	33,890,969.2	$5,245,159,102.08
Less duplication	49,662.2	11,130,893.52
Grand total net	33,841,307.0	$5,234,028,208.56

In the following pages each of the four major operations will be reviewed as independent operations and where applicable these will be broken up into their subsidiary operations, each of which will be discussed separately. After these have been covered each country will be treated independently, giving a brief picture of the conditions making the relief necessary, and a detailed discussion of the relief furnished, allocating it to each of the major and subsidiary operations involved.

The tables given in connection with the text

CHART II

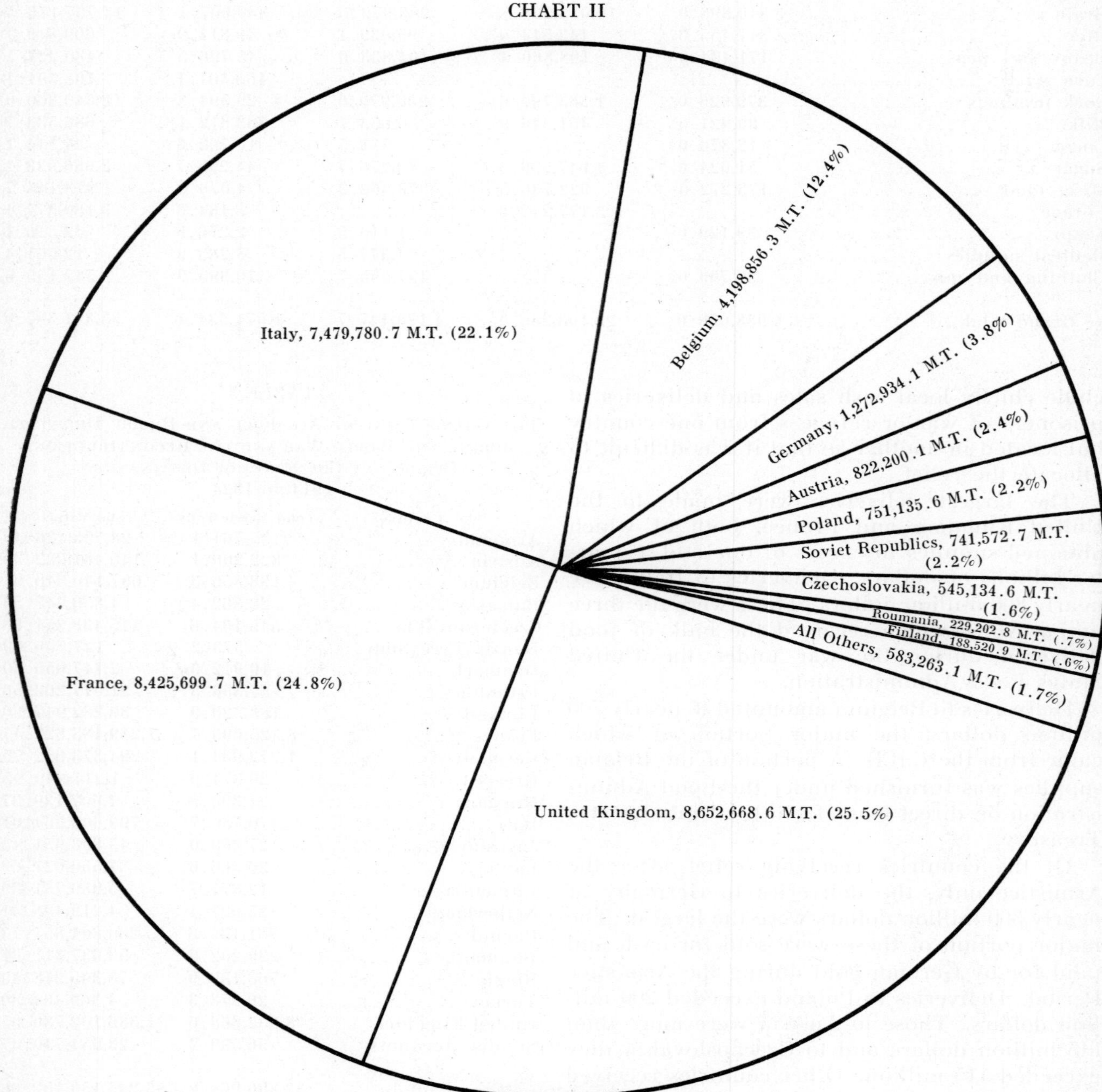

Grand total metric tons and percentage of deliveries, by countries, during the World War and the Reconstruction Period—1914–1924. The totals may be obtained from Table 3, page 9, and greater detail for all countries is shown in Table 102, pages 274–75.

are all of a summary nature. The details are all given in the Appendix with the tables so arranged and cross-referenced as to enable every angle to be followed conveniently. In most instances the supplies are traced from the time the relief was loaded on the vessel in the United States until it was delivered to its final destination, which in some cases was a European government and in others a local feeding kitchen in an isolated village.

CHART III

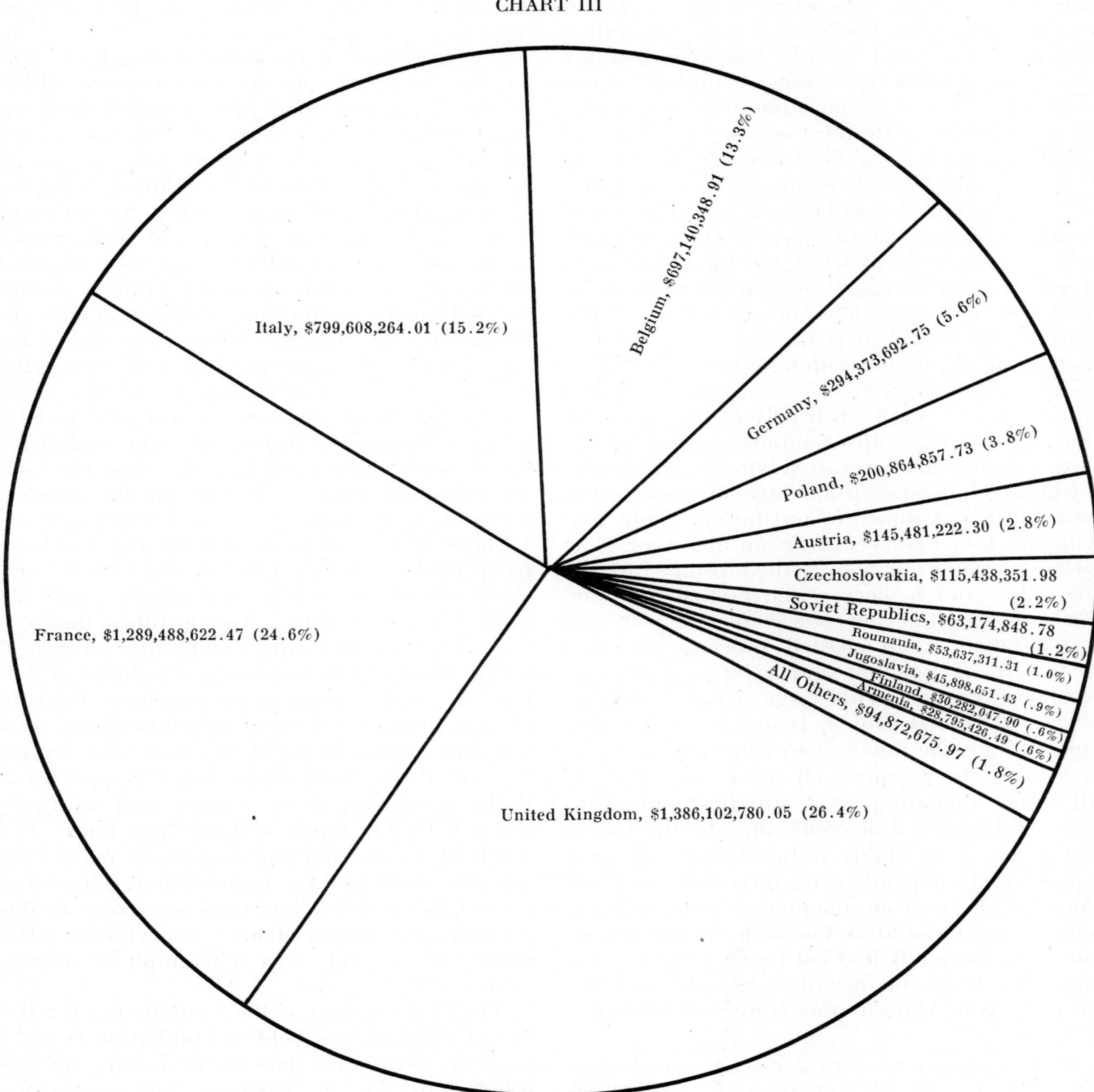

Grand total value and percentage of deliveries, by countries, during the World War and the Reconstruction Period—1914–1924. The totals may be obtained from Table 3, page 9, and greater detail for all countries is shown in Table 102, pages 274–75.

COMMISSION FOR RELIEF IN BELGIUM PERIOD

The first of the major operations discussed in the preceding pages is the Commission for Relief in Belgium. The work of this Commission has been presented in a detailed statistical report by George I. Gay.[1] The same author has also published a very complete documentary history of the Commission's work.[2] These, together with many minor bulletins and other publications, make it unnecessary to present any detailed discussion or statistical material regarding the relief work in Belgium and Northern France in this report. Our purpose here is merely to pick up the total deliveries from Mr. Gay's report so that these may be included in a complete picture of the relief activities of those ten years.

The origin of the Commission for Relief in Belgium and Mr. Hoover's connection with this work has been outlined briefly in the introduction. The work of the Commission was of the most delicate character, involving as it did very intimate relations with the German Government and Military Authorities on the one hand and with the Allied Governments on the other. The German attempt to destroy the military force of the Allies and to occupy the English Channel ports in the first few weeks of the war had failed, but they did succeed in occupying practically all of Belgium and a large portion of Northern France. This large area, containing nearly 10,000,000 people, remained under German rule for the four years of the war.

During the German offensive, materials of all kinds including food supplies and crops were requisitioned or confiscated by the invading army. This highly industrialized area, always largely dependent on imported food was thus cut off from any communication with the outside and in addition had lost its own meager supplies. Germany had her hands full to secure sufficient food for her own people and her armies. The Allies immediately established a blockade of the Central Powers and naturally they were in no mood to allow food supplies into Belgium which might find their way to Germany.

The first task of the newly formed committee was to secure permission from the Allied Powers to import food into occupied Belgium and Northern France. This in itself was no easy task, but permission was finally given providing adequate assurance could be obtained that none of this food would reach either the German people or the German Army, and further providing assurance could be given that all food produced within the occupied territory would be used for the civilian population and not confiscated by the German Army. The successful negotiation of these delicate agreements and the maintenance of strict observance of the terms during four years of a terrible war was in itself no mean triumph of diplomacy. The confidence which both sides placed in the sincerity and ability of Mr. Hoover was by far the greatest factor in the success of this undertaking.

But even after diplomatic authority had been secured, the difficulties facing the Relief Commission were stupendous, and failure was freely predicted on all sides. Among other things it was necessary to secure finance for an undertaking running into hundreds of millions of dollars. It was necessary to purchase food in already limited and disorganized markets. Vessels had to be chartered to cross mine-strewn seas and through naval blockades. Supplies had to be transshipped by barges and railroads through hostile naval and military lines. The whole of the Belgian crops had to be taken over and distributed by the Commission. These and many other hazards had to be overcome in this gigantic and unprecedented undertaking. The successful outcome was a triumph of organization.

The first meeting of the Commission for Relief in Belgium was held in London on October 22, 1914. Within ten days the first of the Belgian relief ships, the SS. "Coblenz," had crossed the channel and its cargo of flour, beans, and peas was being distributed to starving Belgians. This was the first of 2,313 cargoes, of which 993 came

[1] *The Commission for Relief in Belgium—Statistical Review of Relief Operations,* by George I. Gay. Stanford University Press, 1925.

[2] *Public Relations of the Commission for Relief in Belgium—Documents,* by George I. Gay, with the collaboration of H. H. Fisher. Stanford University Press, 1929.

from overseas, and which carried more than 5,000,000 tons of relief supplies during the next five years.

The period of active operation of the C.R.B. extended from November 1, 1914, to August 31, 1919. By this latter date, eight and one-half months after the Armistice, the Belgian and French governments were in a position to secure their own supplies, and international trade had again become sufficiently normal so that the Commission could close its operations.

In the present report all deliveries to Belgium and to Northern France by the C.R.B. from the beginning to the end of the Commission's operations are regarded as constituting the Commission for Relief in Belgium Period. These deliveries may be summarized in the following tabulation:

Deliveries to	Total Metric Tons	Total Value
Belgium	3,896,180.0	$641,056,693.69
Northern France	1,091,879.0	220,283,550.52
Total	4,988,059.0	$861,340,244.21

In addition to these operations the C.R.B. sold to Germany and certain other destinations a considerable volume of supplies during the Armistice Period. In this report these are accounted for under the Armistice Period where they constitute a portion of the work of the Director General of Relief. These latter deliveries may be summarized here as follows:

Deliveries to	Total Metric Tons	Total Value
Germany	134,980.0	$44,350,810.47
Sundry Accounts	51,392.0	21,990,430.40
Total	186,372.0	$66,341,240.87

Together these two constitute the entire commodity operations of the Commission for Relief in Belgium, which during the five years of its active operation imported and distributed 5,174,431 metric tons of food and other supplies, which reached the value of $927,681,485.08. This does not include the distribution of the native Belgian crops which were also handled by the Commission.

Table 4 summarizes by commodities the total deliveries to Belgium and France by the C.R.B., while Table 5 (page 14) summarizes the total deliveries by fiscal years as reported by the Commission.

Tables 103 to 105 (Appendix) summarize other of the more important aspects of these gigantic operations. The detailed statistics of these operations are given in Mr. Gay's report, which shows among other things the arrival of supplies by vessels, by ports, by commodities, and the distribution of these commodities by

TABLE 4

Summary by Commodities of Relief Deliveries to Belgium and France by the Commission for Relief in Belgium—1914 to 1919

(Metric Tons)

Commodity	Belgium	France	Total
Flour	335,608.0	75,813.0	411,421.0
Grain	2,801,887.0	509,011.0	3,310,898.0
Rice	215,411.0	102,044.0	317,455.0
Beans and peas	122,105.0	49,329.0	171,434.0
Pork products	242,517.0	137,409.0	379,926.0
Milk	27,169.0	53,752.0	80,921.0
Cocoa	5,882.0	6,988.0	12,870.0
Sugar	1,517.0	49,507.0	51,024.0
Miscellaneous food	108,258.0	65,014.0	173,272.0
Soap	14,490.0	24,639.0	39,129.0
Clothing and miscellaneous	21,336.0	18,373.0	39,709.0
Total tons	3,896,180.0	1,091,879.0	4,988,059.0
Total value	$641,056,693.69	$220,283,550.52	$861,340,244.21

TABLE 5

SUMMARY BY FISCAL YEARS OF THE RELIEF DELIVERIES TO BELGIUM AND FRANCE BY THE COMMISSION FOR RELIEF IN BELGIUM—1914 TO 1919

(*Metric Tons*)

Fiscal Year	Belgium	France
Nov. 1, 1914, to Oct. 31, 1915	802,103.0	129,195.0*
Nov. 1, 1915, to Oct. 31, 1916	905,946.0	373,000.0
Nov. 1, 1916, to Oct. 31, 1917	576,394.0	191,501.0
Nov. 1, 1917, to Oct. 31, 1918	751,874.0	289,383.0
Nov. 1, 1918, to Aug. 31, 1919	858,624.0	108,501.0
Total	3,894,941.0	1,091,580.0
Five years (for refugees in Holland)	883.0	299.0
Five years (for refugees in Havre)	356.0	....
Total tons	3,896,180.0	1,091,879.0
Total value	$641,056,693.69	$220,283,550.52

* Deliveries from April 1, 1915, to Oct. 31, 1915.

provinces and communes for each year of operation. The reader is referred to the volumes cited for these and many other details.

The question of financing such vast operations was obviously one of the most difficult which had to be solved. The program at the outset of the Commission's work called for the expenditure of about $5,000,000 per month, but due to increased prices and greater need this was increased to as high as $30,000,000 per month in 1918. It was obvious that such vast sums could not be expected from charitable contributions and that the only hopes of success was in securing government subsidies. This was arranged and in the early years the principal source of funds were loans to the Belgian Government from England and France. With the entrance of the United States into the war in 1917 our own Treasury began making direct advances to Belgium for expenditures through the C.R.B.

In addition to these government subsidies, charitable contributions were organized on a world-wide scale and more than $52,000,000 were contributed from such sources.

The work of the Commission was organized on a business basis, and for accounting purposes the Belgian Government was charged with food delivered at a price sufficient to cover cost and some measure of the hazards involved in transporting and distributing the various commodities. Through good management the Commission thus accumulated a surplus which was used to supply additional relief.

Table 105 shows the source of the Commission's basic capital for the entire period and the division between Belgium, France, and other destinations.

UNITED STATES FOOD ADMINISTRATION PERIOD

The United States entered the World War on April 6, 1917. Even prior to that date President Wilson had cabled to Mr. Hoover asking him to return to this country in order that the government might have the benefit of his experience and expert knowledge in handling war-time food problems. Mr. Hoover at that time was in London directing the work of the Commission for Relief in Belgium. He began immediately to put the affairs of the Commission in shape to leave and arrived in this country early in May, 1917.

Even at that time the food situation in this country was becoming precarious. The heavy and uncontrolled demand by the Allies, and the neutral countries as well, was fast drawing the food supplies out of this country, and prices were rising rapidly with evident demoralization of markets in many quarters.[1] It was evident that, for the safety of the Allied cause and for the protection of our own food requirements, some immediate steps must be undertaken to conserve supplies. Congress already had under consideration some form of legislation which would enable the President to conserve food, protect producers and consumers, and enable us to be of the greatest assistance to the Allies. Such legislation, much of it revolutionary in the extent of control of private business, required prolonged discussion in Congress. The Food Control Act, under which the United States Food Administration was created, did not become a law until August 10, 1917. In the meantime it was absolutely necessary to take some action to control the food situation.

Under the war powers of the President, Mr. Hoover was authorized to take such steps as were possible to organize the voluntary conservation of food, to co-operate with business organizations on a voluntary basis to secure both conservation and direction of movement of supplies to the Allies. Under the newly organized Council of National Defense and the Exports Administrative Board (the predecessor of the War Trade Board), it was possible to exert considerable control on the export movement of food and to direct these supplies to the Allied countries.

Under the Act of Congress of April 24, 1917, the Treasury was authorized to establish credits in favor of the Allied Governments to the extent of $3,000,000,000 for the purchase of supplies in this country. In connection with the granting of these loans the Treasury required that all purchases should be made with the permission of the Treasury so as not to demoralize American markets. At a later time (August, 1917), a Purchasing Commission was appointed by the Treasury to co-ordinate all Allied purchasing.[2] But even before this commission was established all food purchases by the Allies were made in consultation with Mr. Hoover as the President's representative in all matters pertaining to food supplies. Thus, almost from the time we entered the war, Mr. Hoover took an important part in determining our food policies toward the Allied Governments and in directing all possible supplies to their needs.

With the passage of the Food Control Act and the appointment of Mr. Hoover as United States Food Administrator on August 10, 1917, it was possible to exert much more definite control on food supplies. The chief problems of the Food Administrator were first to eke out the exceedingly short crop in this country in 1917 by the most rigid conservation and prevention of waste, to see that hoarding of supplies and profiteering by dealers was prevented, to maintain sufficient supplies to feed our own population and at the same time to direct the largest possible amount of food to the Allied Governments. In its final essence the United States Food Administrator was charged with the stupendous duty of anticipating and preventing a world food shortage during the war.

Space does not permit us to go into a discussion of the numerous measures which were taken to accomplish these several purposes. It is sufficient to state that they were accomplished and largely through the voluntary co-operation

[1] For a further discussion of the food situation at this time see *American Pork Production in the World War,* F. M. Surface, A. W. Shaw Co., 1925, and *The Grain Trade during the World War,* F. M. Surface, Macmillan Co., 1928.

[2] For discussion of this see *The Grain Trade during the World War,* pages 174–177.

TABLE 6

PROGRAM AND EXPORTS OF THE PRINCIPAL GROUPS OF FOODSTUFFS IN 1918–1919, COMPARED WITH EXPORTS FOR THE PRECEDING YEAR AND PRE-WAR

(Net Metric Tons)

Groups of Foodstuffs	Three-Year Pre-War Average	1917–1918 Exports	1918–1919	
			Program	Actual Exports
Breadstuffs (wheat and substitutes in terms of grain)	3,320,000	6,800,000	10,400,000	10,566,165
Meats and fats (beef, pork, dairy, poultry, and vegetable oil products)	645,000	1,550,000	2,600,000	2,369,630
Sugar (from United States and West Indies)	618,000	1,520,000	1,850,000	1,704,523
Feed grain (mostly army oats)	950,000	1,950,000	2,700,000	1,660,743
Total	5,533,000	11,820,000	17,550,000	16,301,061

of the American people and American business under Mr. Hoover's leadership.

Too much emphasis cannot be placed upon the importance of this in assisting to bring about a successful termination of the war. There were times, particularly in the early spring of 1918, when the fate of the Allied cause depended upon the successful fulfillment of food shipments from the United States. And this program had to be fulfilled in spite of the fact that our own food crops were barely sufficient for our own normal consumption. The Allied food situation at that time has been discussed in previous publications.[1] Perhaps the seriousness of the situation that developed can be made clear by a few extracts from a letter written to Mr. Hoover on February 22, 1918, by the highest representatives in this country of the three Allied Powers. This letter, signed by Lord Reading, Ambassador from Great Britain, Count V. Macchi di Cellere, Ambassador from Italy, and André Tardieu, the French High Commissioner, read in part as follows:

> We feel that every endeavor must be made to ship at least 1,100,000 tons in March and more if possible. With that object in view we have got together the necessary shipping and we are now met with the probability of being unable to procure sufficient grain to load full cargoes. A situation such as that would be nothing short of a calamity and we most earnestly seek your assistance..... You are so familiar with the grave urgency of this problem that we do not recapitulate the facts, but we *must* meet and overcome the present crisis. .... Our excuse for our insistence is the fact, which is well known to you, that a failure to make adequate shipments in March may produce events of incalculable gravity in both Europe and America.

[1] See *The Grain Trade during the World War*, pp. 184–203.

Ambassadors of foreign governments are not given to using such language in their official correspondence unless the urgency of the situation demands it. Many other letters and cables might be quoted to show how serious the Allied food situation was at this time. These all make it clear that the slightest failure in food supplies from the United States was fraught with the greatest danger, even to jeopardizing the Allied cause itself.

Owing to our extremely short crops, to the breakdown in rail transportation, and the shortage in shipping, it was only with the greatest difficulty that the Food Administration could meet these demands by the Allies. Although it was necessary to make many substitutions and there were many annoying delays, nevertheless enough food was moved to seaboard and shipped to enable the Allies to "carry on" during this critical period.

Some idea of the supreme effort made by this country in supplying the Allies with food during the war is shown by the accompanying comparison of pre-war exports, and the war-time program and export movement. The 1918–1919 program for food exports called for more than three times our pre-war average exports, and this program was fulfilled.

Three agencies of the United States Food Administration organization were of particular importance in assisting with the food supply of the Allied countries. These were the Food Administration Grain Corporation, the Sugar Equalization Board, and the Division of Coordination of Purchase.

Food Administration Grain Corporation

The problems of cereal supplies were the ones most urgent both for this country and for the Allies, and attention was first directed to these. Through numerous conferences, plans had been perfected for the control of cereal marketing prior to the passage of the Food Control Act. Under the authority of this Act, President Wilson issued an Executive Order on August 14, 1917, creating the Food Administration Grain Corporation as an agency of the government for the purpose of buying, selling, and storing grain and cereal products. This Executive Order directed that the Corporation be incorporated under the laws of the State of Delaware with a capital stock of $50,000,000 to be paid for by the United States Treasury and that this stock should be held for the use and benefit of the United States.

Mr. Hoover was chairman of the Board of Directors and Julius H. Barnes was made president of the Corporation.[1] The organization was perfected by the end of August, and active operation was begun on September 4, 1917.

The primary purpose of the Grain Corporation was to provide a method of putting into effect the congressional guaranty of a price for wheat to the producer, which should not be less than $2.00 per bushel for the 1918 crop. By presidential proclamation a basic fair price of $2.20 per bushel for No. 1 Northern wheat at Chicago for the 1917 crop was established on the recommendation of a special wheat price committee.[2] This basic price was increased to $2.26 for the 1918 and 1919 crops. Appropriate differentials were established for other grades and other markets. The Grain Corporation established buying agencies at all important markets and stood ready to purchase all wheat offered at the established price, thus maintaining this as the minimum price throughout the period of its active existence, which was from September 4, 1917, to May 31, 1920.[3]

The Grain Corporation throughout the duration of the war also undertook to see that an equitable distribution of wheat supplies was made to American mills, and to control the prices at which flour and other products were sold by the mills and to the consumer. The Corporation was also charged with the control of all cereal supplies for export, i.e., those to the Allied and Neutral Governments. The authority for this control came, first from the War Trade Board, which refused to furnish an export license for any food commodity unless approved by the Food Administration, and second from the Treasury, which appointed a purchasing committee to co-ordinate all Allied buying in the United States.

The Allied Governments were being loaned vast sums by the United States Treasury, and as a condition of these loans the Treasury reserved the right to direct their purchasing so as not to dislocate unnecessarily the trade and industry of this country. This committee, consisting of Bernard M. Baruch, Robert S. Lovett, and Robert S. Brookings, authorized the Food Administrator to act for them in regard to the purchase of all food and feeding stuffs by any of the Allied Governments. So far as cereals and cereal products were concerned this authority was exercised by the Food Administration Grain Corporation.

Just prior to our entrance into the war the Allied Governments had pooled their cereal-buying efforts in one organization known as the Allied Wheat Executive with headquarters in London. The Wheat Executive established buying organizations in all important wheat exporting countries. In the United States this buying organization was known as the Wheat Export Company, Incorporated, with offices at 27 Beaver St., New York City. The Wheat Export Company thus became the organization to which the Grain Corporation sold its cereals and cereal products which could be spared for the Allied countries.

The total gross sales of the Grain Corporation during the 33 months of its active existence totaled $3,763,800,246.40. Of this amount, a considerable proportion represented inter-agency transaction within the Corporation. The total

[1] Following is a list of the officers of the corporation at the time of its organization: President, Julius H. Barnes; First Vice-President, Frank G. Crowell; Second Vice-President, Watson S. Moore; Treasurer, Gates W. McGarrah; General Counsel, Curtis H. Lindley; New York City Counsel, Edwin P. Shattuck; Transport Executive, Edward Chambers; Second Vice-Presidents, Edw. M. Flesh, M. H. Houser, C. B. Fox, H. D. Irwin, P. H. Ginder, Frank L. Carey, Geo. S. Jackson, Howard B. Jackson, Charles Kennedy, R. A. Lewin, D. F. Piazzek, Charles T. Neal, and E. F. Newing.

[2] See *Grain Trade during the World War*, pages 64–75.

[3] On July 1, 1919, the name of the corporation was changed to United States Grain Corporation.

value of net sales to organizations outside the Corporation amounted to $2,127,127,659.41. Of this latter amount, the total sales to the Wheat Export Company were valued at $952,091,853.71. Table 7 summarizes these sales to the Wheat

TABLE 7

SUMMARY OF SALES TO THE WHEAT EXPORT COMPANY BY THE FOOD ADMINISTRATION GRAIN CORPORATION AND ITS SUCCESSOR, THE UNITED STATES GRAIN CORPORATION—SEPTEMBER, 1917, TO JANUARY 31, 1921

Commodity	Total Metric Tons	Total Value
Wheat flour	3,120,203.3	$376,516,811.55
Cereal flour	32,749.5	3,222,194.83
Wheat grain	6,238,617.2	549,185,139.28
Rye grain	57,646.7	4,262,599.41
Barley grain	79,880.9	4,765,390.15
Corn grain	5,527.4	325,628.84
Beans and peas	67,556.3	13,753,007.09
Rolled oats	502.4	61,082.56
Total	9,602,683.7	$952,091,853.71

Export Company as shown by the books of the Grain Corporation.[1] These figures, however, do not represent the total cereal supplies obtained by the Allied Governments from the United States during our participation in the war and the immediate post-war period. In the first place the Grain Corporation did not begin operations until September, 1917, or five months after our entrance into the war. In the second place the Grain Corporation did not attempt to handle any coarse grains or coarse grain products until after July, 1918, and even then it permitted the Wheat Export Company to purchase a large proportion of its supplies in the open market. The Grain Corporation never undertook to handle feed oats or many other important cereal supplies.

It should be possible to determine from export and import figures for the several countries, the details of food movement during the war and the post-war period. However, several difficulties are encountered here. Exports of cereals from the United States to Allied countries were handled by the Wheat Export Company as noted above. Because of the submarine activities and also because of the exigencies of the various programs, vessels were frequently re-allocated en route and did not discharge their cargo in the country for which the ship's manifest was made out and which formed the basis of our export statistics. Thus a food ship might leave New York bound for Liverpool, and export statistics would show the cargo going to England, but the vessel may have been instructed en route to proceed to Marseilles and the cargo thus finally have been consigned to France. The import statistics of most European countries cannot be relied upon for details covering the war period.

In order to get some measure of the assistance rendered to the Allied countries through food supplies during the war and the immediate post-war period, it has seemed best to depend primarily upon Treasury statistics showing the amount of money loaned to each of the Allied countries for food purchases in the United States.

Under the acts of Congress of April 24, 1917, September 24, 1917, April 4, 1918, and July 9, 1918, the Treasury was authorized to establish credits in favor of foreign governments engaged in war with enemies of the United States to the extent of $10,000,000,000.00. The total net cash advanced under these acts amounted to $9,466,283,171.25 according to the Treasury report.[2] The Treasury figures also show that of this total amount the sum of $3,050,496,599.23 was definitely ear-marked for the purchase of foodstuffs for the governments of Great Britain, France, Italy, and Belgium.[3] The total expenditures from these loans for the purchase of cereals and cereal products amounted to $1,438,419,102.99. The final allocation of these purchases to the country receiving the supplies is somewhat involved, because in the majority of cases the original credit was established in favor of Great Britain, and later, if the supplies were allocated to another country, Great Britain was reimbursed through credits, transferred to the other governments. It is perfectly easy to get the totals of such reimbursing credits, but it has not always been so easy to

[1] For further details see *The Grain Trade during the World War,* pages 423–435.

[2] *Annual Report of the Secretary of the Treasury for the Fiscal Year Ending June 30, 1920,* page 338.

[3] This is exclusive of the advances made to Belgium, France, and other countries for relief work. These advances, totaling $538,188,490.99, were also used chiefly for food and in this report are accounted for under the Commission for Relief in Belgium (pages 12–14) and under the work of the Director General of Relief (pages 23–72).

TABLE 8

SUMMARY OF THE SALES OF AMERICAN CEREALS AND CEREAL PRODUCTS TO THE ALLIED GOVERNMENTS, FINANCED BY UNITED STATES TREASURY CREDITS—APRIL, 1917, TO DECEMBER 31, 1919

(Net Metric Tons)

Allied Governments	Flour and Meals	Grains	Total	Value
Belgium*	11,687.0	219,565.0	231,252.0	$ 21,247,631.42
France*	1,738,079.8	1,549,746.1	3,287,825.9	344,641,786.44
Great Britain	1,350,580.8	3,274,037.9	4,624,618.7	421,788,930.45
Italy	1,804,252.8	5,039,879.8	6,844,132.6	650,740,754.68
Total	4,904,600.4	10,083,228.8	14,987,829.2	$1,438,419,102.99

* Exclusive of relief supplies.

determine the division of such reimbursements between the several categories of purchases. By using the published reports and the document files in the Treasury Department it has been possible to allocate most of the food credits to the proper government.

The Treasury files contain little information on the physical quantities of the various commodities purchased with the credits established. However, by using the export figures for the period under consideration and re-allocating these in accordance with the Treasury loans, it has been possible to arrive at estimated tonnage figures which went to the several countries under the food credits established by the Treasury.

Even these figures do not represent the total amounts of food which were supplied to the Allied countries from the United States, for in many instances, particularly in the early period of our participation in the war and again in the post-Armistice periods, large supplies were purchased with credits other than those supplied by the United States Government. The figures here considered, therefore, are rather the minimum shipments of foodstuffs all of which were purchased with American Treasury credits. Furthermore, these foodstuffs were all either purchased through agencies of the United States Food Administration or else with the permission and co-operation of the Food Administrator.

The total purchases of cereals by the several governments determined according to the methods discussed above are shown in Table 8.

THE SUGAR EQUALIZATION BOARD

The second important commodity problem faced by the United States Food Administrator had to do with sugar. In the pre-war years the United States produced in the form of beet sugar and Louisiana cane sugar about one-fifth of our total consumption, which averaged about 4,000,000 tons per year. The balance of the supply for the United States was imported from Cuba, with lesser amounts from Hawaii, Porto Rico, and the Philippines. Before the war Europe depended almost entirely upon domestic beet sugar produced chiefly in France, Germany, and parts of the old Austro-Hungarian Empire. Great Britain produced little sugar but secured about 54 per cent of her supply from Germany and Austro-Hungary, with about 6 per cent from France and Belgium.

The war had practically destroyed the sugar-beet industry of Europe. Great Britain, France, and Italy had turned largely to Cuba to make up for the decreased supplies at home and from their normal sources in the Central Empires. In 1916 these three nations had imported, either from Cuba direct or from the United States, a total of 1,242,750 tons, as compared with only 272,516 tons from the same sources in 1913. The United States was dependent upon Cuba for the major portion of its domestic supply of sugar, and with the Allies increasing their demands by more than 1,000,000 tons per year from this source it was evident that our supply was in danger. With the increasing intensity of the war it was clear that the Allied demands for Cuban sugar would increase.

Mr. Hoover immediately sensed this serious situation and long before the Food Control Act became a law he was holding innumerable conferences with beet-sugar producers, refiners, and others in order to reach some solution which would protect our own supply and yet give the Allies the maximum that could be spared from the Western Hemisphere.

Arrangements were finally perfected for the organization of an International Sugar Committee,[1] which was to undertake the distribution of our domestic beet sugar and which later on was able to effect an agreement with the Cuban Government by which three-fourths of the Cuban crop was to be handled by the committee. This arrangement gave the Food Administrator a chance to control the principal supplies for our own needs and to prevent the threatened demoralization of this market.

It was evident, however, that this control by a committee based upon voluntary agreement was not sufficient to cope with the situation which might arise the next year. In the early part of 1918 Mr. Hoover proposed to President Wilson that a new organization should be incorporated with capital supplied by the Treasury, and which should undertake to purchase and distribute both to the domestic market and to the Allies the whole of our domestic production and the whole of the Cuban sugar crop. There were many other reasons behind this proposal which space does not permit us to discuss here.[2] For one thing there was a very difficult price situation which had to be met. In order to stimulate domestic beet production it was deemed necessary to raise the wholesale price of beet sugar to nine cents per pound, which was far above the price necessary to pay for Cuban sugar. Through the Sugar Equalization Board it was possible to pay the higher price for domestic sugar, which could then be equalized by the lower price of Cuban, thus protecting the price to the consumer, and if any profits should be realized on the operations they would be returned to the United States Treasury.

The President approved Mr. Hoover's proposal and the Sugar Equalization Board[3] was incorporated under the laws of the State of Delaware on July 11, 1918, with a capital of $5,000,000. The Board made the advance purchase of the 1918–1919 Cuban crop and carried out its distribution and the control of sugar prices. Because of the urgent needs of the Allies which could not be supplied from other sources it was necessary to make rather drastic restrictions on sugar consumption in this country. The Board undertook to allocate supplies to industrial users and domestic consumers were limited to two pounds per person per month. It has been estimated that the conservation policies of the Food Administration reduced consumption in this country by more than 1,300,000,000 pounds (650,000 tons) in 1918, thus making this amount available for the Allies.

In connection with the purchase of the Cuban crop, the Sugar Equalization Board entered into an agreement with the Royal Commission on Sugar Supplies, acting for the Allied Powers, by which the Commission was to have one-third of the total Cuban crop. The Royal Commission was to have the privilege of bringing a portion of this raw sugar into the United States to be refined if it desired. In fact a considerable proportion of this sugar was handled in this way, thus relieving the labor situation abroad.

The United States Treasury agreed to finance the purchases of sugar for the Allied Governments and, according to the Treasury figures referred to above, a total of $303,191,544.71 was loaned to Great Britain, France, and Italy for sugar purchases. Table 9 gives the allocation of sugar credits to the three countries as shown by the Treasury reports, together with the estimated tonnage to each.

TABLE 9

SUMMARY OF THE SALES OF SUGAR TO THE ALLIED GOVERNMENTS FINANCED BY UNITED STATES TREASURY CREDITS—APRIL, 1917, TO DECEMBER 31, 1919

Allied Governments	Metric Tons	Value
France	378,018.0	$ 58,741,487.85
Great Britain	1,539,236.7	239,853,538.86
Italy	30,682.1	4,596,518.00
Total	1,947,936.8	$303,191,544.71

[1] This committee consisted of five members: two of which, Sir Joseph White-Todd and John Ramsay Drake, represented the English, French, and Italian Governments; two members, Earl D. Babst and Wm. A. Jamison, represented American refiners; one member, George M. Rolph, represented the United States Food Administration. Final agreement for the purchase of the 1918 Cuban crop was signed December 24, 1917, at a price of $4.60 per hundred pounds, f.o.b. Cuban ports. One-third of the amount bought was to go to the Royal Commission on Sugar Supplies for the Allies.

[2] For complete discussion of war-time sugar problems, see Joshua Bernhardt, *Government Control of the Sugar Industry in the United States* (Macmillan, New York, 1920).

[3] The officers of the Sugar Equalization Board were as follows: Chairman of Board, Herbert Hoover; President, George M. Rolph; Treasurer, Theodore F. Whitmarsh; Secretary, Robert A. Taft; other Directors, George A. Zabriskie, Clarence M. Wooley, Wm. A. Glasgow, and F. W. Taussig.

Division of Co-ordination of Purchase

As stated earlier the great problem constantly before the United States Food Administrator was to anticipate and prevent a world shortage of food during the war. In order to do this it was necessary also to prevent the demoralization of the food markets, especially in the United States, which formed the basis of the Allied supply. We had already witnessed in the spring of 1917 something of what the unco-ordinated and unguided demand of the Allies could do to our markets, especially in wheat and flour. Mr. Hoover was determined there should be no repetition of this if it could be prevented. The Allies had already pooled their purchases of grain supplies with one buying agency, the Wheat Export Company, in this country. Mr. Hoover now asked that similar action be taken with regard to other food supplies and that the Allied Governments each indicate their needs through a single agency. For this purpose there was created a joint Allied commission known as the Allied Provisions Export Commission, to which each government submitted its food requirements with the exceptions of grains, flours, and meals. This Commission was in turn to give notice to the Food Administration of these requirements.

To take care of this business the Food Administration organized a Division of Co-ordination of Purchase. Upon receipt of notice from the Allied Provisions Export Commission it was the function of this division to indicate the method of purchase which should be followed in securing these requirements in order that market conditions might be disturbed as little as possible. Such purchases were made either by allocation throughout the industry concerned or on bids secured and passed to the purchaser for approval, or the purchaser was advised to buy direct in the open market. In the case of allocation of purchases or of bids, the Division of Co-ordination of Purchase exercised general supervision in co-operation with a committee from the industry.

The Division of Co-ordination of Purchase was organized on October 24, 1917. Shortly after that there was also organized a Food Purchase Board, composed of a representative each from the Secretary of War, Secretary of the Navy, Federal Trade Commission, and the Food Administrator. The purpose of this board was to co-ordinate the food purchases of the Army, the Navy, and the Marine Corps. Other large food purchasers, such as the Commission for Relief in Belgium, the American Red Cross, the Salvation Army, and the Y.M.C.A., also submitted their requirements through the Division of Co-ordination of Purchase.

For a considerable part of the war this division was supervising business amounting to more than $200,000,000 per month. No complete record of the purchases handled through this division are available, although for the eight months from May to December, 1918, the Division of Co-ordination of Purchase cleared transactions totaling $1,069,370,419.00. Of this amount $715,000,000 were for the Allied Governments; $206,000,000 were for the Army, Navy, and Marine Corps, and the remainder for the miscellaneous organizations noted above. The commodities purchased through the Division of Co-ordination of Purchase included meats and pork products, canned foods, vegetable oils, dairy products, dried fruits, and vegetables, as well as many other miscellaneous foods.[1]

Statistics as to the detailed purchases of particular commodities by the Allied countries are not available. However, by using the allocation of Treasury credits discussed above it is possible to arrive at some approximation of the amounts going to the several countries. The division between the several groups of miscellaneous foods has been based largely on export figures for the period, allocated in accordance with Treasury loans. Even here it is probable that the proportion of miscellaneous foods going to Great Britain is unduly large because many of the purchases were made in the name of Great Britain and subsequently diverted to either France or Italy. It has been impossible to be certain that all of the reimbursing credits have been properly allocated to this group of food purchases.

Table 10 (page 22) summarizes the food purchases of the Allied countries, as shown by the allocation of United States Treasury credits for this purpose. The estimated tonnage figures are based on the relation of the shipments to these countries, as shown by official export figures for

[1] For a discussion of the efforts made to stimulate pork production in the United States to supplement the Allied supply of meats and fats and of the difficulties encountered in carrying out this program, see F. M. Surface, *American Pork Production in the World War.*

TABLE 10

TOTAL SALES OF FOODSTUFFS TO THE ALLIED GOVERNMENTS FINANCED BY UNITED STATES TREASURY CREDITS*—APRIL, 1917 TO DECEMBER 31, 1919

(*Net Metric Tons*)

Foodstuffs	Belgium	France	Great Britain	Italy	Total
Flour	11,687.0	1,738,079.8	1,350,580.8	1,804,252.8	4,904,600.4
Grain	218,565.0	1,549,746.1	3,274,037.9	5,039,879.8	10,083,228.8
Rice	.....	104,589.9	24,289.4	14,634.7	143,514.0
Beans and peas	.....	78,625.8	23,878.9	6,355.7	108,860.4
Meats and meat products	.....	264,290.4	957,641.3	141,867.9	1,363,799.6
Milk, evaporated and condensed	20,650.3	235,657.7	181,886.2	13,152.7	451,346.9
Sugar	.....	378,018.0	1,539,236.7	30,682.1	1,947,936.8
Oats for forage	.....	2,042,715.2	813,945.6	320,582.0	3,177,242.8
Miscellaneous foods	.....	389,594.7	439,799.9	93,341.9	922,736.5
Total tons	251,902.3	6,781,317.6	8,605,296.7	7,464,749.6	23,103,266.2
Total value	$27,533,982.47	$850,714,632.84	$1,375,484,734.33	$796,762,249.59	$3,050,496,599.23

* Values based upon records in the United States Treasury, with tonnage allocated according to record of food exports to these countries during the war period.

the war and immediate post-war period. Table 10 includes the cereal and sugar purchases already set forth in Tables 8 and 9.

According to these figures, the total exports of foodstuffs to the Allied Governments paid for through United States Treasury credits amounted to more than 23,000,000 metric tons, with a total value of $3,050,496,599.23. Even this enormous total does not represent all the foodstuffs sold to these countries from the United States. As pointed out in an earlier paragraph, large purchases were made, particularly in the early part of 1917 and after the Armistice, with credits other than those provided by the United States Treasury. No effort has been made to include these here.

The purchases credited to Belgium are only relatively minor purchases made by the Belgian Government in 1919 after the Commission for Relief in Belgium had begun to close its operations. The C.R.B. purchases are treated elsewhere in this volume. (See pages 12–14.)

ARMISTICE PERIOD—DIRECTOR GENERAL OF RELIEF

November, 1918, to September, 1919

The terrible suffering which the peoples of Central and Southern Europe were undergoing because of military requisitions and the ebb and flow of belligerent armies was well known in official circles long before the close of the war. For example, the suffering of the Polish people became intense within a few months after the beginning of the war. Sections of Congress Poland near the German frontier and a large portion of the eastern half of Austrian Poland were the scene of destructive military operations in 1914. In 1915 came the great German-Austrian drive and the retreat of the Russians, who systematically destroyed everything that would be of use to the Germans. By the end of 1915 practically all of the present Poland was cut off from Russia and because of the destruction of crops and factories was in great distress.

Through the dense curtain of war-time censorship there gradually filtered some inkling of this suffering. These reports came to the ears of Mr. Hoover in connection with his relief work in Belgium. The Relief Commission had its hands full in caring for the total population of Belgium and Northern France, but such impassioned appeals could not be ignored. Mr. Hoover had a special investigation of Polish conditions made and attempted to get the belligerents to agree to the organization of some form of relief similar to that in Belgium. In spite of repeated attempts, the belligerents could never be brought to agree to any terms by which relief could be carried on. The Poles suffered all that Belgium would have experienced without the Relief Commission, and it was impossible to offer any outside help.

Nor was Poland the only country which experienced these distressing effects of war. Someone has spoken of "the rivalry in martyrdom of Belgium, Poland, Serbia, and Armenia." Besides these, various classes within the combatant countries such as Roumania, Bulgaria, Russia, as well as the Czechs, the Hungarians, and the Jugoslavs suffered equally or at best in but slightly less degree.

When the Armistice came and the curtain was lifted on this great territory of Eastern and Southern Europe, there was displayed to an astonished world a population of some 200,000,000 people on the verge of starvation. Besides the task of relieving these people, the relief of the 10,000,000 people of Belgium and Northern France seemed mere child's play.

There was no chance that these peoples could help themselves or could by their own efforts improve their condition before the next harvest. If help in vast amounts was not immediately forthcoming, it seemed as if fifty per cent or more of this great population must perish before the next spring. No catastrophe of such great proportions had faced the Western World since the Thirty Years' War, three centuries before.

The problem of succoring this large population was far too big for public charity, too big even for any one government; it must of necessity be a responsibility upon the Allied and Associated Governments.

These facts were recognized by the officials of the United States and of the Allied countries long before the Armistice, although the full extent of the enormous suffering and need did not become apparent until later. Even as early as October, 1918, the Allied and Associated Powers were discussing the terms of a possible armistice and in this connection were drafting various recommendations to deal with food relief to these countries. Cables from Mr. Hoover's representatives began to tell of the arrangements which the Allies wanted to make by which all such relief supplies would be handled through the already existing Allied food agencies. Mr. Hoover consistently opposed this method, and his reasons are clearly stated in his many letters and cables at this time. Thus the following extract from his cable, November 7, 1918, to Joseph C. Cotton, the Food Administration's representative in London, is typical:

> For your general advice this government will not agree to any program that even looks like Inter-Allied control of our economic resources after peace. After peace, over one-half of the whole export food supplies of the world will come from the United States and for

the buyers of these supplies to sit in majority in dictation to us as to prices and distribution is wholly inconceivable. The same applies to raw materials. Our only hope of securing justice in distribution, proper appreciation abroad of the effort we make to assist foreign nations, and proper return for the service that we will perform will revolve around complete independence of commitment to joint action on our part.

Again on November 11, 1918, the day of the Armistice, Mr. Hoover wrote President Wilson setting forth his views in somewhat greater detail. This letter was as follows:

I enclose herewith two cables which I would be grateful if you could find time to peruse.

The first, with regard to our entering into a joint Inter-Allied pool for the purpose of distributing all of the world's wheat until the middle of 1920 fills me with complete horror. Of all of the import wheat in the world, seventy per cent must come from the Western Hemisphere and I assume that we would be called upon to finance it and to place the distribution of it in the hands of a body that we could not control.

I can see no objective in such a plan, as I believe there is sufficient wheat for the world to get through with, unless it is the intention to use this control of the prime necessity of life to dominate other measures in the world.

As to the second telegram on the subject of arrangements which the English may set up in London for provisioning the world with our foodstuffs and on our credit, I have a similar reaction.

Both of these telegrams bring me to express to you the urgency of a definition of our principles in these matters, to be conveyed to the Allied Governments in order that I and the other agents of the government in Europe may be able to act in entire unison with your own views.

If I might make a suggestion in this direction, it would be on the line that we consider ourselves as trustees of our surplus production of all kinds for the benefit of the most necessitous and the most deserving. We feel that we must ourselves execute this trusteeship; that we are not unmindful of the obligation which we have to the sustenance of those who have fought with us against Germany and that, together with the necessities of those populations released from the German yoke, we feel that they may well deserve a priority in our distribution. On the other hand, we cannot undertake any co-operative arrangements that look to the control of our exports after peace and furthermore—and equally important—that the Inter-Allied councils hitherto set up in Europe were entirely for the purpose of guiding Inter-Allied relations during the period of the war and that any extension of their functions either by way of their control of our relations to other nations or the extension of their present functions beyond peace, cannot be entertained by us; that all relationship involving the use of American food or credit for the people of other nations than the Allies themselves must await Mr. Hoover's arrival in Europe, so far as any such supplies or interest of the United States is concerned.

I believe that the settlement of this question requires some specific statement from you.

Yours faithfully,

As indicated in the letter above, arrangements had already been made for Mr. Hoover to go to Europe immediately after the Armistice to direct the work of the United States in the matter of relief to these countries. These and certain other arrangements were definitely authorized in a memorandum approved by the President on November 12, 1918. This memorandum was as follows:

MEMORANDUM OF ARRANGEMENTS WITH REGARD TO PROVISIONING THE POPULATIONS WHICH ARE NOW OR HAVE BEEN UNDER THE DOMINATION OF THE CENTRAL EMPIRES.

1. Mr. Hoover, as United States Food Administrator, will proceed at once to Europe to determine what action is required from the United States and what extensions of the Food Administration organization or otherwise are necessary in order to carry out the work of the participation of the United States Government in this matter, and to take such steps as are necessary in temporary relief.

2. In order to expedite the movement of foodstuffs toward Europe, the War Department will undertake to purchase, in the usual co-ordination through the Food Administration during the next twenty days, 120,000 tons of flour and from 30,000,000 to 40,000,000 pounds of pork products. These foodstuffs to be shipped by the diversion of Army tonnage at the earliest possible moment that the Shipping Board arranges and to be consigned to French ports for re-consignment or storage.

3. This foodstuff and any other suitable surplus supplies of the Quartermaster in Europe to be made available for distribution at Mr. Hoover's direction, it being understood that if it proves infeasible to re-ship or re-direct the steamers to the territories lately held by the Central Empires, Mr. Hoover will make arrangements for the resale of the foodstuffs to the Allied Governments or, alternatively, to the Belgian Relief.

4. In order to facilitate administration in Washington, Mr. Hoover will set up a preliminary committee to assist the Food Administration, comprising: Mr. Theodore Whitmarsh, of the Food Administration, who will act as Chairman in Mr. Hoover's absence; Mr. F. S. Snyder, of the Meat Division of the Food Administration; Mr. Julius H. Barnes, of the Cereal Division of the Food Administration; General R. E. Wood, Quartermaster General, representing the War Department; Mr. John Beaver White, representing the War Trade Board; Mr. Prentiss N. Gray, representing the Shipping Board. These gentlemen to take in hand the general directions of these operations through the various government agencies concerned.

5. The War Department is to purchase, inspect, pay for, load, and ship these foodstuffs in the usual manner of transmission of Quartermaster's supplies, and upon transfer from the Quartermaster's Department in Europe they are to be paid for by the buyer.

6. The American representatives in Europe are to be at once instructed by cable that the whole of the matter of the American food supplies and the establishment of a more permanent organization are to be settled by Mr. Hoover on his arrival in Europe and that the United States will take no participation in any arrangements made pending that time.

INTER-ALLIED RELIEF ORGANIZATION

Under these arrangements, Mr. Hoover sailed for Europe on November 18, 1918, only seven days after the signing of the Armistice. Before leaving he had made arrangements as indicated by the memorandum above for the shipment of about 140,000 tons of foodstuffs, to be transported and financed by the War Department and, in addition, he had also arranged for the Food Administration Grain Corporation to ship and finance up to the time of its sale a further amount of some 120,000 tons. Thus arrangements were made for something more than 250,000 tons of American foodstuffs to be shipped immediately to European ports. This food was to form the nucleus of American relief and was to be available for delivery as quickly as plans for this work could be perfected. The wisdom of shipping these advance supplies was amply demonstrated in the strenuous months which followed. Without these readily available supplies, the suffering in these countries would have been vastly greater during the early months of 1919. Yet it is necessary to remember that it took a high degree of courage and foresight to arrange for the advance shipment of these vast supplies costing many millions of dollars. It was many weeks before any methods were devised by which these supplies could finally be financed and in the meantime there was much uncertainty as to the course events might take.

It was no easy task that confronted Mr. Hoover on this trip to Europe. In the first place, it was necessary to effect some agreement with the Allies which would be acceptable to the United States. Mr. Hoover was determined that we should enter into no arrangements by which we should lose control of supplies which had to come from and be financed by the United States. On the other hand, the relief of Europe had to be handled as a joint responsibility of the Allied and Associated Governments. This was necessary, first, because the task was too large to be undertaken by any one government and, second, because of the many political and economic questions such as blockade, finance, transportation, etc., which could only be solved by international co-operation.

In the second place, Mr. Hoover's task involved finding methods of financing and transporting these enormous quantities of food. The newly liberated countries had no funds which could be used to purchase these supplies, and for the most part they had no liquid assets which could be used. Congress at that time had made no appropriation which could be used in furnishing this food on credit. Even if financial arrangements were completed, there still remained the difficulty of securing shipping for overseas transportation and the even greater difficulty of securing internal distribution within the countries of Europe. The war had reduced the world's available shipping far below the normal needs, and tonnage was extremely difficult to charter while rail transportation throughout Europe was almost completely disorganized.

Mr. Hoover's first task was to secure some form of Inter-Allied co-operation so that the necessary organization for relief could be set up. Following Mr. Hoover's views and at his instance, President Wilson directed Colonel E. M. House, who was then in Europe, to present a memorandum from him to the Allied Governments. This memorandum dated December 1, 1918, was as follows:

The President has requested me to communicate to you for the consideration of your government the following memorandum containing his views respecting the general question of furnishing relief to the civilian population of the European countries affected by the war:

I have given much thought to the formulation of the most practicable means of carrying into effect the resolution presented by Colonel House at the last meeting of the Supreme War Council at Versailles to the effect that the Supreme War Council in a spirit of humanity desired to co-operate in making available, as far as possible, supplies necessary for the relief of the civilian populations of the European countries affected by the war.

In considering this matter I have had constantly in mind the urgent necessity of the case and the fact that it is essential in the working out of relief of this character on a large scale, that there be a unity of direction similar in character to that which has proved so successful under French and British Chief Command in the operations of the Allies on the land and on sea respectively. I suggest that the Supreme War Council proceed along the following lines:

In order to secure effective administration there should be created a Director General of Relief whose field of activities will cover not only enemy populations but also the whole of the populations liberated from enemy yoke and the neutrals contiguous to these territories.

It is obvious that present Inter-Allied administrative arrangements cover the Allied countries themselves and if the whole of the world's food supplies could be made available through sufficient shipping, there appears to be sufficiency to take effective care of these other populations provided that these supplies are administered with care, with economy, and with single direction.

The one essential to this plan in order that all world supplies may be brought into play is that enemy tonnage shall be brought into service at the earliest possible moment. It would appear to me entirely just that the enemy shipping in consideration of relief of enemy territory should be placed in the general food service of all the populations released from the enemy yoke as well as enemy territory.

I have carefully considered the suggestion made by Mr. Balfour to the Supreme War Council at the time the terms of armistice to be offered the enemy were under discussion to the effect that the enemy should be required to place under the operation and control of the Allied Maritime Transport Council the enemy mercantile fleet in enemy and neutral ports. It appears to me that in practice there would be many embarrassments presented by this plan, and that the principle should be maintained that this fleet be used as to its carrying capacity for purposes of relief and be under the direction of the Director General of Relief. In order to secure its adequate operation, the Director General should assign appropriate portions of this tonnage, first for operations individually by Italy, France, and Belgium sufficient to transport the relief to actually liberated nationals of these nations. The administration of relief in the three above instances would then naturally fall entirely under the three governments mentioned, and would not further interest the Director General of Relief. Second: the remainder of enemy cargo tonnage or such part of it as is necessary should be placed under the operation of the British Ministry of Shipping and the United States Shipping Board in equal portions. These two institutions agreeing with the Director General of Relief to deliver a quantity of cargo equal to the carrying capacity of these two fleets from such sources to such destinations as the Director General of Relief may direct in supplying the balance of population to be relieved. Third: the passenger tonnage or so much of it as may be required by the United States Shipping Board should be assigned to them, they giving the equivalent cargo capacity delivery to the Director General of Relief. Under this plan it does not follow that enemy shipping would be employed directly in the transportation of this cargo but that equivalent cargo should be delivered. This plan enables the use of enemy passenger tonnage in the transportation of the United States Armies homeward. This arrangement would in effect add materially to the volume of the world's shipping and release tonnage for the particular purposes of the individual countries.

In the operations of the Director General of Relief, he would, of course, purchase and sell foodstuffs to enemy populations and therefore not require financial assistance in this particular further than working capital. In the relief of newly liberated peoples such as Belgium, Poland, Servia (including Jugoslavia) and Bohemia, it will no doubt be necessary to provide temporary advances from the Associated Governments to these recuperating nationalities with which they can purchase supplies from the Director General, such arrangements to be worked out by the Associated Treasuries. In some cases public charity may have to be mobilized.

In the Director General's dealings with neutrals they of course would provide their own shipping and financial resources and probably some tonnage and food, either directly or indirectly for the purposes of the Director General, they acting under his direction and authorization as to supplies and sources thereof. The Director General, of course, acting in these matters in co-operation with the blockade authorities of the Allies and the United States.

In order to prevent profiteering the Director General must make his purchases directly from the respective Food Administrations of the Associated Governments where his supplies arise from their territories and where purchasing in neutral markets he should act in co-operation with the established Inter-Allied agencies.

It is evident that after the Allies have supplied themselves from their own territories at home and abroad and the balance from other sources, the only effective source of surplus supplies available for relief lies to a minor extent in the Argentine but to a vast preponderance in the United States. The Director General will have a large command of American resources and markets and will require the undivided support of the American people in saving and productive activities.

Owing to the political necessity of American control over American resources and the greater co-ordination and efficiency to be obtained thereby, I am sure that you will agree with me that the Office of Director General of Relief must be held initially by the United States Food Administrator and in case of necessity by such a successor as may be nominated by me. I would suggest, however, that the policies of the Director General should be determined by the Supreme War Council, to whom he should report, it being our united policies in these matters not only to save life but also to stabilize governments.

All these arrangements to be for the period of emergency and it is highly desirable for them to be liquidated as fast as practicable.

I shall be grateful to you if you will advise me as

soon as practicable the views of the British Government concerning this matter.

Faithfully yours,

(*Signed*) E. M. House

This proposal did not meet with the immediate approval of the Allied Governments. It was their point of view that the Central Powers were a common foe and that all the resources of the Allied and Associated Governments should be pooled. They wished first of all to use their already existing and functioning Inter-Allied agencies as those through which the relief should be handled. From their point of view, such a desire was not unreasonable. Here were agencies already organized and working smoothly and handling many millions of dollars' worth of supplies. It would be a simple matter for these to expand their scope of operations sufficiently to take care of this additional work. Why should it be necessary to set up new agencies with the additional expense and the confusion which would result, as they argued? Furthermore, in place of centralizing the direction of the relief work in the hands of a Director General of Relief, they proposed the establishment of an Inter-Allied Board consisting of two members from each of the four Associated Governments.

Under the leadership of Mr. Hoover these proposals were strongly opposed by the American representatives. The chief reasons for this opposition have been set forth in the letters and memoranda quoted above. Mr. Hoover felt that the only hope of accomplishing the difficult tasks ahead would be to have the executive power centralized in a single hand. This, of course, is only the elementary essential of executive efficiency. A board or commission is always inefficient in executive control, although useful in advisory or semi-judicial capacities. Here was a task that required prompt executive action and no doubt frequent changes in policy as the work developed. Such action could never be obtained from an international board of eight men.

Furthermore, the United States did not propose to enter any organization in which the distribution of its supplies and finances could be determined by a majority vote of representatives of foreign countries.

Mr. Hoover arrived in London at the end of November, 1918. Three weeks were spent in fruitless endeavor to come to some agreement with the Allied Governments. They were insistent that their views be accepted and Mr. Hoover was just as obstinate in his contention for the rights of the United States. Finally, near the middle of December, Mr. Hoover moved his office to Paris and established his headquarters in the Hotel Crillon in connection with the American Commission to Negotiate Peace.

In the meantime, while carrying on these negotiations with the Allies, Mr. Hoover had not been idle in other directions. With a small group of trained associates chosen largely from the Belgian Relief he had begun immediately an investigation of the actual food conditions in the newly liberated territories. Missions had been sent to Poland, Czechoslovakia, Austria, Jugoslavia, Roumania, and other countries. Preliminary reports from some of these missions began to come in about the middle of December and they revealed a situation so serious, so much worse than had been realized, that it called for some immediate action. With men, women, and children actually starving, there was no longer time to argue with foreign diplomats as to the best formula for relief. What was needed was the actual movement of food toward these people and that Mr. Hoover decided to start without delay.

Accordingly on December 16, 1918, he addressed a memorandum to President Wilson, who was then in Paris, pointing out the serious condition of the people in Serbia and Austria and suggesting that the American Government take immediate and independent action to relieve this situation, but that they invite the Allies to join with them if they would. The President accepted this suggestion and on the same day directed Colonel House to address another letter to the Allied Governments. The text of this letter is as follows:

Dear Mr. Balfour:

The President requests me to say that the discussions of his proposal of December 1 submitted through me, for the creation of a European Relief Administration and the appointment of a Director General of Relief, have been reported to him. He entertains no doubt but that he will receive in due course from the Allied Governments a reply to that note, but it appears from the discussions that some time will be required to reconcile the differences of view involved in the undertaking.

The objects of the United States Government in connection with food supply—which concern only the

Armistice—are to save lives, to preserve order throughout the liberated, neutral, and enemy territories, and to create an efficient organization to accomplish these purposes. In these purposes he feels assured of your entire sympathy and co-operation.

Pending further discussions of the entire problem, however, the situation in certain areas is of so critical a nature, and requires such immediate emergency action, that he wishes me to inform you that he is instructing the United States Food Administration to take measures at once to furnish food supplies and to establish an organization to this end in certain places outside of Germany.

Taking it for granted that you will also be anxious to undertake immediate action in these matters through your various food departments and in order that there shall be full co-ordination in this task, he has asked Mr. Hoover to indicate to you these situations and points at which he proposes to establish representatives for the administration of relief measures, so that if you see fit, you may also send your representatives to these points and these gentlemen may mutually co-ordinate their various efforts.

Mr. Hoover proceeded at once to put these arrangements into operation. On December 11 he sent a representative to Germany, and on December 20, 1918, a mission in charge of Colonel W. G. Atwood of the United States Army was dispatched to Belgrade to set up relations with the Serbian Government and to make arrangements for the delivery of food supplies which were then on passage from the United States. Spurred on by this concrete example of activity the British and French decided to join forces in this operation and each sent representatives to Belgrade to co-operate with Colonel Atwood. A similar mission under Captain T. T. C. Gregory and with similar Allied co-operation was dispatched to Vienna, and another under Dr. Vernon Kellogg and Colonel W. R. Grove to Warsaw.

These activities inaugurated by Mr. Hoover, as well as the concrete reports on the terrible condition in Central and Southern Europe which began to come in from all sides, materially hastened the negotiations with the Allies for the establishment of the necessary relief machinery. Thus, on December 31, 1918, the four Associated Governments agreed upon the establishment of a Supreme Council of Supply and Relief, to which each government was to appoint two delegates.

Although the relief situation was serious and urgent, it proved impossible to arrange the first meeting of this Supreme Council before January 11, 1919. At this meeting, which was held in Paris, Mr. Hoover was made Director General of Relief in Europe. The Supreme Council of Supply and Relief was established for the purpose of investigating the relief requirements of Europe, their relation to the general supply of the Allied and neutral countries, to determine the general policies and measures which should be carried out, and to co-ordinate the relief efforts of the several governments. The Council decided at its first meeting that these objects could best be carried out by a permanent committee, which was established.

This Permanent Committee of the Supreme Council of Supply and Relief held its first meeting on January 19, 1919, under the chairmanship of Mr. Hoover. This committee continued to meet until February 24, 1919, having held a total of twelve meetings. By this time it had become clear that the question of relief to Europe was too complicated to be handled by an isolated body with only the meager powers accorded to the Supreme Council of Supply and Relief. The question of relief was not alone one of allotting food to needy nations. It involved questions of finance, shipping, inland transportation, blockade, and many other problems, all of which must be closely co-ordinated.

SUPREME ECONOMIC COUNCIL

In the early part of February, 1919, the Supreme War Council had, at the request of the American representatives, set up a body known as the Supreme Economic Council. This latter organization was authorized to have final supervision over all economic activities of the Allied and Associated Governments in connection with the Armistice. Its decisions were final, subject only to review by the Supreme War Council itself.

The Supreme Economic Council was directed to absorb whatever Inter-Allied organizations and whatever powers of such organizations it might deem necessary and also to establish new organizations under it whenever such action seemed essential to the accomplishments of its purposes.

At the first meeting of the Supreme Economic Council, held on February 24, 1919, it was voted to establish under itself Sections on Finance, Blockade, Communications, Raw Materials, Food, and Maritime Transport. The work of the Permanent Committee of the Supreme Council of Supply and Relief was absorbed, and this body now became the Food Section of the Supreme Economic Council. The functions of the Inter-Allied Food Council were also assumed by the Food Section. The first meeting of the Food Section was held on February 27, 1918, and it continued to meet weekly or bi-weekly under the chairmanship of Mr. Hoover until the early part of August, 1919, at which time the Supreme Economic Council was dissolved.

The co-ordination of efforts accomplished under the Supreme Economic Council very materially aided the relief work and made possible many things which had previously been impossible, or at most, possible only with great difficulty.

The personnel of the Food Section changed from time to time but the following persons represented their respective governments either throughout the period or at various times.

Director General of Relief and Chairman of the Food Section: Herbert Hoover
American Representatives: Robert A. Taft, Colonel James A. Logan, Jr.
British Representatives: Sir John Beale, Sir William Goode, E. F. Wise
French Representatives: M. J. May, Jean Monnet, Major R. Fillioux, J. M. Carpentier
Italian Representatives: Professor Attolico, Count Zucchini, Captain Caetani
Belgian Representative: Baron de Cartier de Marchienne

At the meetings of the Food Section as well as those of its predecessor, the Permanent Committee, all matters pertaining to relief needs or requests, relief programs, deliveries, and reports from missions were presented, discussed, and acted upon. Through the Supreme Economic Council, questions involving financial relation, transportation, blockade, etc., were referred to their respective sections, where it was possible to secure prompt consideration.

ORGANIZATION OF THE WORK OF THE DIRECTOR GENERAL OF RELIEF

Almost immediately after his arrival in Europe, Mr. Hoover dispatched missions to various sections of Europe to study at first-hand their needs and requirements. In December, 1918, Dr. Alonzo E. Taylor headed a mission to Vienna and various parts of the old Austro-Hungarian Empire as well as to a portion of the Balkan States. At the same time Dr. Vernon Kellogg headed a mission to Poland. Preliminary reports from these expeditions were received by the middle of December and showed the alarming shortage of food supplies of all kinds in many parts of these countries. Drs. Taylor and Kellogg returned to Paris early in January and their reports formed the first basis for relief programs to these countries.

The next step was to establish resident missions in each country which should have charge of receiving the relief shipments and, in cooperation with the authorities of that country, to see that these were distributed to the people who were most in need. The further duty of these missions was, of course, to study the changing food situation within each of these countries and to keep the Director General of Relief informed as to the immediate and probable future needs.

With the establishment of Inter-Allied cooperation in the relief work these missions at the more important points were composed of representatives of the several governments. Each government through its representative was responsible for receiving and accounting for its own supplies. All programs were co-ordinated through the Food Section in Paris. Each government made its own financial arrangements as to payment or obligations received for their relief deliveries, although these were co-ordinated and approved by the Finance Section of the Supreme Economic Council.

COUNTRIES IN NEED OF RELIEF

At the time of the Armistice it was known that Poland, Serbia, and many sections of the old Austro-Hungarian Empire were in dire need of food and other relief. These countries had in many instances been the battleground for contending armies or these armies had swept through their territories en route to the several battle fronts. Native food supplies had been requisitioned by the military authorities even to the last obtainable pound. There was no way in which these people could increase their native food supply before the next harvest, some nine months away. The breakdown in internal transportation made it impossible to move any surpluses which might be in one part of a country to another part where they were so badly needed. In general, the peasants had succeeded in secreting a fair supply of food from the authorities sufficient for their own use for some months, but in the industrial districts the suffering was most acute.

The upheaval in Europe after more than four years of war had resulted in the birth of many new nations. These new governments were necessarily feeble and without financial resources. If they were to succeed in maintaining order within their territories it was imperative that their people should be fed. However, the new national boundaries with their new military and customs barriers supported by the age-old racial hatreds between the different peoples of Eastern Europe presented a serious obstacle to the interchange of food, raw material, or manufactured products.

The Allied nations were on record as supporting the development of these new nationalities along lines to be determined by the peoples of those territories. If these new governments were to succeed, their people must be fed and enabled to get to work. If this were not done revolution and Bolshevism were threatened throughout this territory, with the possibility that it might spread over the rest of Europe, including the Allies themselves. There were, therefore, many urgent political, as well as humanitarian, reasons why relief should be given to these countries.

The rigid censorship of the war had prevented any intimate knowledge of the extent of the needs of these countries reaching the Allied or Associated Powers. As pointed out above, one of Mr. Hoover's first acts after his arrival in Europe late in November, 1918, was to dispatch missions to Poland, Vienna, and Serbia to determine the extent of their needs. The reports of these missions revealed situations much more serious and distressing than had hitherto been recognized. Mr. Hoover took immediate steps to get relief supplies moving toward these countries. At the same time he extended his investigation of the needs of Europe by sending other missions to the new Baltic countries, to Germany, to Jugoslavia, and to the several Balkan countries. Reports were received from still other countries, such as Finland, Armenia, and various sections of Russia, showing urgent need for help.

Gradually as these reports came in and the extent of the needs in different countries were realized, monthly programs of the requirements to each country were prepared.

In addition to the so-called liberated countries, which included Belgium and the invaded regions of Northern France, it was found that certain neutrals and even Allied countries were in need of assistance in securing food supplies for their people. Also the enemy countries, particularly Austria and Germany, were in almost if not quite as serious need of food relief as any of the liberated countries. It was not without a long struggle that the Allies consented to allowing these enemy countries to secure additional food, but if this had not been done they would undoubtedly have been overrun by Bolshevism and the peace of all Europe would have been threatened.

Altogether more than twenty different countries of Europe were furnished food supplies under the direction of the Director General of Relief. These countries, as shown in Table 11, comprised an area of some 1,400,000 square miles, an area nearly half the size of continental United States, and with a total population of more than 200,000,000 people. The countries and territories included in this relief area are shown on the endsheet map.

Naturally not the whole of the 230 million people in these countries were suffering for food, yet it is safe to say that few of the 100 million people included within the liberated countries could have gone until the next harvest without great privation, and the same is true of the populations of Austria and Germany. Certainly more than one hundred and fifty million people were in real need of relief and if that relief had not been forthcoming many millions would have died of actual starvation.

RELIEF PROGRAMS

Obviously one of the first things that had to be done in planning the relief work was to make out programs for each country based both on the needs of the country and on the finances that could be secured to carry it through. The first programs were of a tentative nature, based on incomplete reports of conditions within the countries. Gradually these monthly programs were modified as the conditions for each country became better known, but at all times these programs remained essentially tentative, and

TABLE 11

AREA AND POPULATION OF COUNTRIES REQUIRING ASSISTANCE FROM THE DIRECTOR GENERAL OF RELIEF IN 1919

Liberated Countries	Area, Square Miles	Population
Poland	149,220	27,179,000
Lithuania	20,390	2,011,000
Latvia	25,402	1,851,000
Esthonia	18,355	1,111,000
Northwest Russia	......	....
Finland	149,639	3,403,000
Belgium (occupied area)	11,355	7,290,000
Northern France (occupied area)	8,100	1,795,000
Czechoslovakia	54,190	13,611,000
Jugoslavia	96,134	12,017,000
Roumania (new boundary)	113,608	16,262,000
South Russia	......	....
Armenia	15,240	1,214,000
Total	661,633	87,744,000
Enemy Countries	**Area, Square Miles**	**Population**
Germany	182,264	59,856,000
Austria	32,395	6,423,000
Hungary	35,832	7,951,000
Bulgaria	39,825	4,861,000
Turkey	282,144	14,549,000
Total	572,460	93,640,000
Neutral and Allied Countries	**Area, Square Miles**	**Population**
Italy	119,991	38,835,000
Holland	13,205	6,977,000
Denmark	17,149	3,290,000
Total	150,345	49,102,000
Grand total	1,384,438	230,486,000

new developments within a given country required frequent shifts of program and often the re-allotment of cargoes en route so that the points of most serious suffering should receive relief.

The first comprehensive although tentative relief program was prepared by Mr. Hoover and submitted to the Supreme Council of Supply and Relief about February 1, 1919. This program was as follows:

TABLE 12

PRELIMINARY RELIEF PROGRAM—ARMISTICE PERIOD, 1919

Country	Monthly Requirements Tons of Food	Monthly Requirements Estimated Cost
Liberated countries		
Poland	60,000	$13,000,000
Czechoslovakia	55,000	12,000,000
Roumania	35,000	7,500,000
Jugoslavia	35,000	8,000,000
Armenia	20,000	5,000,000
Enemy countries		
Austria	40,000	12,000,000
Hungary	4,000	2,000,000
Turkey	10,000	2,500,000
Total	259,000	$62,000,000

Something of the magnitude of the relief task can be gathered from these early figures, which indicated a monthly requirement of 259,000 tons of food at an estimated cost of $62,000,000. This program alone would require upward of fifty shiploads of supplies each month, and if it were continued until the next harvest its total cost would be in the neighborhood of $400,000,000.

Yet, as was found out later, this program was by no means complete. It contained no provision for the Baltic countries, which later were found to be in such dire distress. It contained no provision for Germany, which at this time was not permitted to secure outside supplies. It did not contain provision for Belgium and Northern France, which were being cared for by the Commission for the Relief of Belgium.

In making up the programs and estimating the requirements for these countries, four principal groups of staple food commodities were considered, viz: (1) Breadstuffs, consisting chiefly of wheat and cereal flour, and wheat and rye grain; (2) Peas, beans, and rice; (3) Milk, consisting of both evaporated and condensed milk, and (4) Fats, including pork products (meats), lard, lard substitute, and other vegetable oils. Other commodities were delivered in small amounts in some cases to meet special demands. In general the relief countries possessed sufficient supplies of vegetables with which to supplement the above-mentioned staples.

Of the foregoing commodities, breadstuffs were by far the most important and constituted more than three-fourths of the total tonnage delivered. Peas, beans, and rice were delivered

TABLE 13

Monthly Relief Programs—Armistice Period, 1919

(Metric Tons)

Country	February	March	April	May	June	July	Total Tonnage	Total Calories *(in millions)*
			Breadstuffs					
Finland	.....	.....	....	20,000	20,000	20,000	60,000	196,761
Esthonia	.....	2,000	2,000	2,000	2,000	2,000	10,000	32,793
Latvia	.....	.....	2,000	200	2,000	2,000	6,200	20,332
Lithuania	.....	.....	2,000	2,000	....	....	4,000	13,117
Poland	24,000	25,000	35,000	50,000	50,000	40,000	224,000	734,573
Germany	.....	.....	250,000	250,000	250,000	250,000	1,000,000	3,279,342
Belgium *	312,000	104,000	90,000	90,000	90,000	90,000	776,000	3,544,769
Northern France *	.....	.....	....	.....	.....	.....	.....	.....
Austria	35,000	40,000	50,000	50,000	50,000	50,000	275,000	901,819
Czechoslovakia	15,000	40,000	45,000	55,000	45,000	45,000	245,000	803,439
Jugoslavia (S.H.S.)	12,000	15,000	10,000	9,000	9,000	.....	55,000	180,364
Roumania	20,000	20,000	40,000	40,000	40,000	40,000	200,000	655,868
Armenia	5,000	5,000	5,000	5,000	5,000	5,000	30,000	93,380
Turkey	.....	5,000	5,000	5,000	5,000	5,000	25,000	81,984
Bulgaria	.....	.....	6,000	6,000	4,000	.....	16,000	52,469
Total	423,000	256,000	542,000	584,200	572,000	549,000	2,926,200	10,596,010
			Peas, Beans, and Rice					
Finland	.....	.....	....	1,000	1,000	1,000	3,000	10,780
Esthonia	.....	.....	200	10	200	200	610	2,158
Latvia	.....	.....	200	200	200	200	800	2,831
Lithuania	.....	.....	200	200	.....	.....	400	1,415
Poland	.....	5,000	3,000	7,000	5,000	.....	20,000	71,098
Germany	.....	.....	50,000	50,000	50,000	50,000	200,000	707,677
Belgium *	12,000	12,000	7,600	7,600	7,600	7,600	54,400	194,273
Northern France *	22,986	7,662	7,662	7,662	7,662	7,662	61,296	218,915
Austria	.....	.....	3,000	3,000	3,000	3,000	12,000	42,461
Jugoslavia (S.H.S.)	.....	2,500	....	2,500	.....	.....	5,000	17,692
Total	34,986	27,162	71,862	79,172	74,662	69,662	357,506	1,269,300
			Milk					
Finland	.....	.....	....	500	500	500	1,500	3,638
Esthonia	.....	.....	100	100	100	100	400	970
Latvia	.....	.....	100	100	100	100	400	970
Lithuania	.....	.....	100	100	.....	.....	200	485
Poland	1,000	1,000	1,000	1,000	1,000	.....	5,000	12,125
Germany	.....	.....	....	10,000	10,000	10,000	30,000	72,752
Belgium *	9,000	3,000	2,670	2,670	2,670	2,670	22,680	55,000
Northern France *	6,435	2,145	2,145	2,145	2,145	2,145	17,160	41,614
Austria	.....	.....	1,000	1,000	1,000	1,000	4,000	9,700
Czechoslovakia	400	500	2,000	1,500	.....	.....	4,400	10,670
Jugoslavia (S.H.S.)	500	500	700	700	700	.....	3,100	7,518
Roumania	500	500	1,000	1,000	1,000	1,000	5,000	12,125
Armenia	500	.....	....	200	.....	.....	700	1,698
Total	18,335	7,645	10,815	21,015	19,215	17,515	94,540	229,265

* The programs for Belgium and Northern France date from December, 1918. The programs given here for February include the three months, December, January, and February.

TABLE 13—*Continued*

(*Metric Tons*)

Country	February	March	April	May	June	July	Total Tonnage	Total Calories (*in millions*)
			FATS					
Finland	.....	.....	....	1,500	1,500	1,500	4,500	33,975
Esthonia	.....	.....	200	200	200	200	800	6,040
Latvia	.....	.....	200	200	200	200	800	6,040
Lithuania	.....	.....	200	200	.....	.....	400	3,020
Poland	4,000	4,000	2,000	6,000	4,000	4,000	24,000	181,200
Germany	.....	.....	60,000	60,000	60,000	60,000	240,000	1,812,000
Belgium *	54,000	18,000	18,000	5,000	5,000	5,000	105,000	792,750
Northern France *	15,078	5,026	5,026	5,026	5,026	5,026	40,208	303,570
Austria	.....	.....	4,000	4,000	4,000	4,000	16,000	120,800
Czechoslovakia	8,000	1,000	5,000	4,000	2,000	.....	20,000	153,265
Jugoslavia (S.H.S.)	.....	2,500	300	300	300	.....	3,400	25,670
Roumania	.....	.....	1,000	1,000	1,000	1,000	4,000	30,200
Total	81,078	30,526	95,926	87,426	83,226	80,926	459,108	3,468,530
			TOTAL FOOD					
Finland	.....	.....	....	23,000	23,000	23,000	69,000	245,154
Esthonia	.....	2,000	2,500	2,310	2,500	2,500	11,810	41,961
Latvia	.....	.....	2,500	700	2,500	2,500	8,200	30,173
Lithuania	.....	.....	2,500	2,500	.....	.....	5,000	18,037
Poland	29,000	35,000	41,000	64,000	60,000	44,000	273,000	998,996
Germany	.....	.....	360,000	370,000	370,000	370,000	1,470,000	5,871,771
Belgium *	387,000	137,000	118,270	105,270	105,270	105,270	958,080	4,586,792
Northern France *	44,499	14,833	14,833	14,833	14,833	14,833	118,664	564,099
Austria	35,000	40,000	58,000	58,000	58,000	58,000	307,000	1,074,780
Czechoslovakia	23,400	41,500	52,000	60,500	47,000	45,000	269,400	967,374
Jugoslavia (S.H.S.)	12,500	20,500	11,000	12,500	10,000	.....	66,500	231,244
Roumania	20,500	20,500	42,000	42,000	42,000	42,000	209,000	698,193
Armenia	5,500	5,000	5,000	5,200	5,000	5,000	30,700	100,078
Turkey	.....	5,000	5,000	5,000	5,000	5,000	25,000	81,984
Bulgaria	.....	.....	6,000	6,000	4,000	.....	16,000	52,469
Grand total	557,399	321,333	720,603	771,813	749,103	717,103	3,837,354	15,563,105

* The programs for Belgium and Northern France date from December, 1918. The programs given here for February include the three months, December, January, and February.

largely as substitutes for other and more expensive commodities. Owing to the decrease in the number of dairy cows and the decreased production of those remaining, there were many places in Europe where absolutely no milk could be obtained. Preserved milk, particularly for children and invalids, was therefore a very important commodity, although in number of tons delivered it amounted to less than any of the other principal groups.

The shortage of fats throughout Europe had made itself evident in many diseases which follow a fat-deficient diet. It was very important that a large quantity of fat-containing food should be delivered to remedy this deficiency. Fortunately, the United States possessed a large supply of pork products created under stimulation of the war demand and which the Allies no longer wanted. These supplies proved to be a godsend to these famished people, and their disposal in this way relieved a serious oversupply of a perishable product in the hands of American farmers.[1]

Relief programs for each country (Table 13) were calculated from reports sent in by special and permanent missions in these countries. These reports covered, as far as possible, estimates of production, available stocks of food, population in need of relief, as well as general economic conditions. Naturally the disorganization of the war had upset all statistical activities within these territories so that no reliable estimates of production and supplies could be furnished by these governments. The relief missions were therefore forced to make many estimates themselves. These had to be regarded as

[1] For a detailed discussion of this subject see F. M. Surface, *American Pork Production in the World War.*

tentative and were revised at frequent intervals as experience showed the need. Tentative relief programs were based on these early estimates and their adequacy tested by the cut-and-try method. It frequently happened that the estimates for a given country proved to be too low and the missions reported that supplies were not adequate to meet the urgent needs. Wherever these requirements were sufficiently urgent, vessels on passage for other countries were reallocated to the one most in need. In some instances, the estimated requirements were too high and later deliveries were cut down below the original estimate. Table 13 gives the monthly relief programs for each country as they were originally made out for the shipment of overseas supplies. These programs served as a basis for the ordering of supplies which had to be done from a month to six weeks in advance of the date of delivery.

RELIEF FINANCES

Not the least of the many difficult tasks which faced Mr. Hoover as Director General of Relief was that of finding means by which these much-needed food supplies could be financed. The situation as it appeared after the Armistice was as follows: The Allied countries were already receiving advances from the United States Treasury to cover their food and other purchases in the United States. It was anticipated that these would be continued for a time at least. The neutral countries had been much restricted in their food purchases both because of the world shortage under war conditions and also in order to prevent supplies leaking through to the enemy. It was assumed that their rations under the blockade would be increased. They had sufficient funds to pay cash for their purchases but they might need some help in securing supplies and shipping. The newly liberated countries were almost totally without available financial assets. On the whole, they were in greater need than any of the other countries but some means would have to be found by which supplies could be furnished to them on credit. The enemy countries would be in great need of food before the next harvest, but with the exception of Austria they had sufficient tangible assets which could be used to pay for their requirements.

The immediate and urgent problem was to find some means of financing deliveries to the liberated countries and to Austria. Shortly after the Armistice, and at Mr. Hoover's request, a bill had been introduced in the United States Congress appropriating $100,000,000 for relief to the liberated countries, but specifically excluding all ex-enemy countries. This, like most legislation, pursued a leisurely course through Congress and did not become a law until February 25, 1919. In the meantime, men, women, and children were starving, and something had to be done. Mr. Hoover's first move was to ask for and receive an allotment of $5,000,000 from the President's National Security and Defense Fund. Although relatively insignificant compared with the total needs, this furnished a nucleus for the relief. He next took up with President Wilson the possibility of granting United States Treasury loans to certain of the liberated countries which were technically Allies and would thus come under the war powers by which Congress had authorized the President to make loans to the Allies (Acts of April 24, 1917; September 24, 1917; April 4, 1918; and July 9, 1918). Under these powers relief loans were made to Czechoslovakia, Roumania, and Jugoslavia (Kingdom of the Serbs, Croats, and Slovenes). Before the end of the operations these loans totaled upward of $87,000,000.

Methods of financing relief to Austria offered a serious obstacle. Austria was technically an enemy country and, hence, the United States could neither give her a direct Treasury loan nor furnish supplies from the $100,000,000 relief appropriation by Congress. Mr. Hoover tried to persuade the Allies to take care of the Austrian requirements, but this they were both unwilling and unable to do. This difficulty was finally overcome by a joint financial arrangement by which the United States advanced $16,000,000 to each of the three Allies, Great Britain, France, and Italy, to be used in purchasing American food for Austria, the Allies in turn agreeing to furnish transportation and take Austrian obligations for the repayment of the total amounts.

In addition to the arrangements above, the relief of Belgium and Northern France was continued as during the war, largely through loans from the United States and Allied treasuries. Also through Mr. Hoover's efforts the United States Liquidation Commission (War Department) sold large quantities of surplus army food and other commodities on credit to these countries.

Great Britain provided a relief credit of £12,500,000 (about $59,500,000) which they used largely to supplement the deliveries made by the United States. Neither France nor Italy established definite relief credits, but from time to time they did furnish supplies or other assistance to certain groups and countries.

In addition to the foregoing operations which were on a credit basis, the Director General of Relief arranged the sale of large quantities of supplies for cash or on the basis of exchange of commodities, which was the equivalent of cash.[1]

In addition to the various sources of official relief provided through Treasury funds, the Director General of Relief undertook to co-ordinate the work of the various charitable organizations which were furnishing non-medical relief to the European countries. The co-operation thus effected was of very material help in providing certain kinds of relief which could not well be undertaken under the government operations. Thus, the feeding of German children by the American Friends Service Committee, the work of the Joint Distribution Committee for Jewish Relief, and other similar work supplemented that done by the governments and accomplished much greater good than would have been possible with each organization working independently.

Among the American charitable organizations thus co-operating with the Director General of Relief were the following: American Friends Service Committee; American Jewish Joint Distribution Committee; American Committee for Relief of the Near East; American Red Cross (non-medical relief), and, of course, the Commission for Relief in Belgium, part of which was supported by public charity. A number of British charitable societies also contributed to this work, including: Friends' Emergency Relief Committee in Vienna; Friends' War Victims Relief Committee in Poland; the British Red Cross; Lady Muriel Paget's Mission in Czechoslovakia; "Save the Children" Fund; Scottish Women's Hospitals; and the Vienna Emergency Relief Fund in London.

[1] For further discussion of the relief finances provided by each government see pages 142–44.

[2] See Appendix Tables 107 and 108.

TOTAL DELIVERIES UNDER THE DIRECTION OF THE DIRECTOR GENERAL OF RELIEF[2]

As indicated in the preceding paragraphs Mr. Hoover, as Director General of Relief for the Allied and Associated Governments, was responsible not only for the official relief delivered from the United States but also for the co-ordination of the relief work of other governments and of many charitable organizations. During the nine months from the end of November, 1918, to the first of September, 1919, there were delivered under his direction a total of 4,178,447.7 metric tons of food and other relief, valued at $1,101,486,783.34. Table 14 summarizes under four major categories these total deliveries, while Table 107 (Appendix) gives further details regarding these operations.

TABLE 14

Total Relief Deliveries under the Direction of the Director General of Relief, by Major Operations—Armistice Period, 1919*

Major Operation	Total Metric Tons	Total Value
American Relief Administration	1,684,456.6	$ 363,211,835.48
Other American organizations	1,058,770.9	462,622,804.46
Joint Allied Finance	345,839.8	48,000,000.00
Countries other than United States	1,139,042.6	238,783,036.92
Total	4,228,109.9	$1,112,617,676.86
Less duplications	49,662.2	11,130,893.52
Grand total net deliveries	4,178,447.7	$1,101,486,783.34

* See Table 107 for details.

The deliveries under each of these major operations are discussed in detail in the following pages. It may be pointed out here that the American Relief Administration was the official organization set up to handle in particular the relief furnished by the United States Government. Under "Other American Organizations" are included a number of charitable societies in so far as their work was directly co-ordinated with the Director General of Relief. It should be remembered that each of these organizations carried on a large amount of other work on their own responsibility which is not included in the present report. Under this category are also included the relief deliveries from the United States Liquidation Commission (War Department) which while official in character was entirely separate from the work of the American Relief Administration.

Under Joint Allied Finance is included the relief to Austria for which the United States Treasury furnished the money but for which the three major Allies accepted the credit risk (cf. pages 59–60).

The duplications which are deducted to obtain the net total arise through deliveries from one organization to another. The most important duplication arises from the sale of certain supplies to the United Kingdom by the A.R.A. which were then delivered to Austria as part of the Joint Allied Finance (see page 60).

The supplies furnished under the direction of the Director General of Relief during the Armistice Period[1] were delivered to 21 different countries of Europe. Table 15 summarizes the deliveries to each of these countries.

It will be noted that the largest deliveries to any country during the Armistice Period were those to Germany. These supplies were paid for by the transfer of German gold and other assets as explained elsewhere (cf. page 194). France also received a large volume of supplies which is accounted for largely through the transfer of material by the United States Liquidation Commission (cf. page 53). Poland, Czechoslovakia, Austria, and Jugoslavia were other countries receiving large quantities of relief. These deliveries will be discussed in more detail in connection with the separate operations.

TABLE 15

Total Relief Deliveries under the Direction of the Director General of Relief, by Countries of Destination—Armistice Period, 1919*

Country	Total Metric Tons	Total Value
Armenia	83,964.3	$ 20,231,455.01
Austria	561,705.7	98,771,595.93
Belgium	50,774.0	28,549,672.75
Bulgaria	22,862.4	4,856,647.53
Czechoslovakia	503,230.0	105,545,794.40
Denmark	19,912.0	2,147,059.30
Esthonia	61,510.8	19,347,812.47
Finland	185,033.7	29,172,056.10
France	552,503.1	218,489,439.11
Germany	1,215,217.8	282,410,999.21
Hungary	319.1	245,519.96
Italy	15,031.1	2,846,014.42
Jugoslavia	121,249.8	43,596,570.69
Latvia	19,609.7	5,961,851.35
Lithuania	11,677.0	5,517,004.47
Netherlands	25,027.4	4,219,498.41
Poland	403,184.2	135,023,140.98
Roumania	225,443.5	52,135,716.29
Russia	26,236.9	15,006,260.98
Turkey	20,278.3	4,369,404.30
United Kingdom	47,371.9	10,618,045.72
Sundry Accounts	55,967.2	23,556,117.48
Total	4,228,109.9	$1,112,617,676.86
Less duplications	49,662.2	11,130,893.52
Grand total net deliveries	4,178,447.7	$1,101,486,783.34

* See Table 108 for further details.

THE AMERICAN RELIEF ADMINISTRATION

When Mr. Hoover went to Europe immediately after the Armistice, there was no organization in the United States through which the relief activities of this country could be handled. It is true that the Commission for Relief in Belgium had received official recognition as the agency through which United States Treasury loans to Belgium were being expended, but it is also true that similar recognition and official patronage had been extended to this Commission by Great Britain, France, and Belgium.

In the memorandum approved by President Wilson on November 12, 1918 (see pages 24–25), he had directed Mr. Hoover to determine "what extensions of the Food Administration organization or otherwise are necessary in order to carry out the work of the participation of the United States Government in this matter."

What was needed immediately was some organization which could purchase, ship, and finance food supplies up to the point of delivery to the relief countries. It still remained, of course, to arrange methods by which these countries could pay for the supplies thus delivered.

Before sailing for Europe, Mr. Hoover had already arranged for an initial service of purchasing, shipping, and financing of foodstuffs for relief by the United States Army as was

[1] The Armistice Period was officially from November 11, 1918, to the signing of the Treaty of Versailles on June 28, 1919. However, it required until September, 1919, to complete the deliveries on commitment made prior to the first of July and, hence, this is regarded as the duration of the Armistice Period in this report.

CHART IV

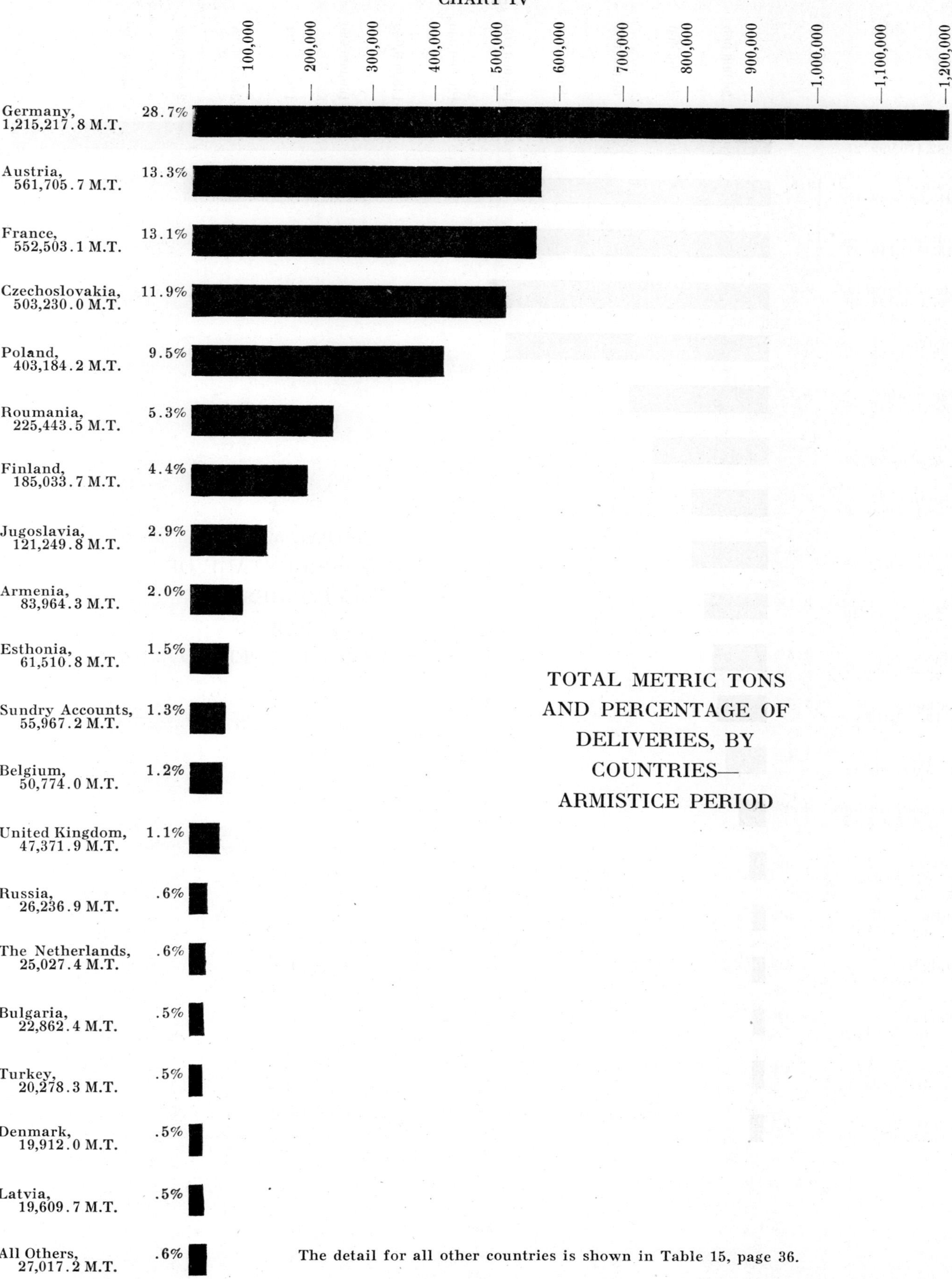

TOTAL METRIC TONS AND PERCENTAGE OF DELIVERIES, BY COUNTRIES—ARMISTICE PERIOD

The detail for all other countries is shown in Table 15, page 36.

CHART V

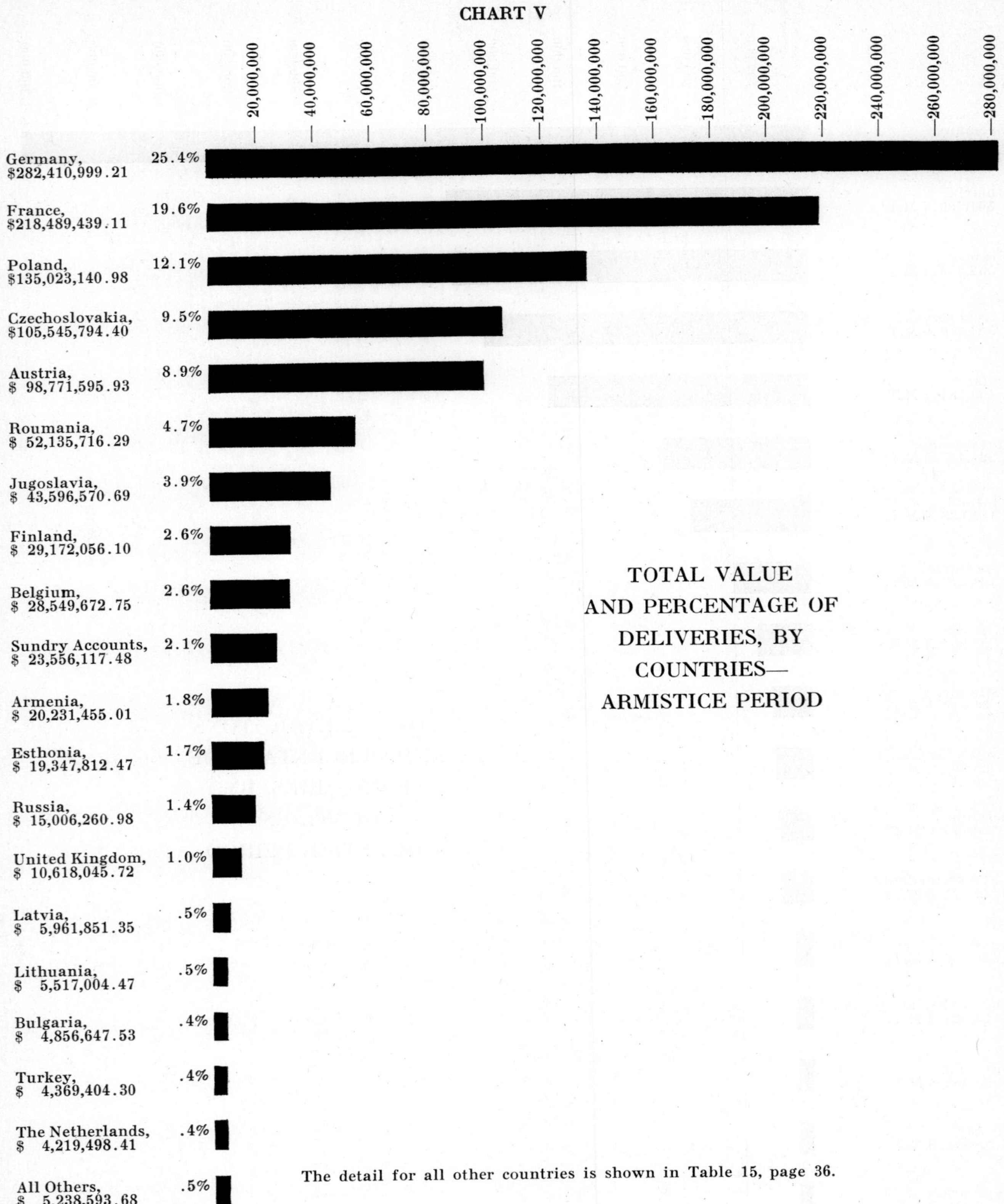

TOTAL VALUE AND PERCENTAGE OF DELIVERIES, BY COUNTRIES—ARMISTICE PERIOD

The detail for all other countries is shown in Table 15, page 36.

provided in the memorandum of November 12, 1918, referred to above. This service was supplemented by arrangements for the Food Administration Grain Corporation also to purchase and transport an initial program for this work.

If there was to be an extension of the Food Administration organization to handle this work, the logical thing to do was to extend the operation of the Grain Corporation to include European transactions. The Food Administration Grain Corporation was a commercial organization incorporated by direction of the President under the laws of Delaware and with a capital, at this time, of $150,000,000 from the United States Treasury as provided in the Food Control Act of August 10, 1917. The Grain Corporation had been established for the purpose of making effective the Congressional guaranty as to the price of wheat to American farmers.[1] This Corporation was engaged in buying and selling grain and flour, and thus possessed the commercial organization which could readily purchase and ship relief supplies. However, the Food Control Act, under which authority the Grain Corporation had been established, had not contemplated operations in foreign countries. There was some question as to whether the President had the authority to extend the operation of the Corporation to countries outside of the United States. After some consideration of this and possible alternatives, Mr. Hoover asked President Wilson to approve this extension of the scope of the Grain Corporation's activities, which he did on December 23, 1918.[2]

In the meantime, a bill had been introduced into Congress appropriating $100,000,000 to be used for the relief of non-enemy countries of Europe, which became a law February 25, 1919.[3]

[1] For further discussion of this subject see F. M. Surface, *The Stabilization of the Price of Wheat during the War and Its Effect upon the Returns to the Producer,* United States Grain Corporation, Washington, D.C. (May, 1925) and *The Grain Trade during the World War.*

[2] Following is the text of the memorandum from Mr. Hoover to President Wilson which the latter approved:

"In order to adequately handle the problem of European food relief, it is necessary that we should establish stocks of food, particularly cereals and fats, at certain strategic ports, these stocks to be drawn upon for the supply of different countries from time to time. Such an arrangement enables us to maintain constant transporting and a regular drain of our food supplies from the United States. This arrangement, together with many political considerations involved, requires that the foodstuffs in transit and in storage at these bases should be in the name and possession of the United States Government. The War Department, with your approval, is now performing this function in respect to certain stocks in the Adriatic, but I assume that their action is only for the emergency, and beyond this it is necessary for us to establish further such stocks at points like Rotterdam, possibly at Gutenberg, and even at German ports as well. The United States Food Administration has the right to buy and sell foodstuffs as may be required in the common defense. The appropriation to the Food Administration for these purposes lies entirely in the Food Administration Grain Corporation, of which you are the sole stockholder. The directors of the Grain Corporation feel that, as a corporation, they should have your approval for extending their operations outside of United States territory.

"There is no reason either in the intention or in the purpose of the United States to maintain the common defense that does not warrant such action, and there is abundant actual reason why this action should be taken as a part of the necessity of the United States to maintain tranquillity in Europe while its armies are entangled here.

"It is not proposed to part with any of the foodstuffs thus belonging to the Grain Corporation without prior payment. There is, of course, some commercial risk in the matter, also there might be further outbreak of hostilities in Europe and some of our bases might be involved. This, however, I regard as a risk of war that cannot be avoided.

"I would, therefore, be glad to know if you will authorize the Grain Corporation to extend its operations to the extent of establishing these stocks and carrying them on the capital and credit which it possesses.

"Yours faithfully,
(*Signed*) "HERBERT HOOVER"

[3] Following is the text of this Act (Public, No. 274, 65th Congress):

"An Act Providing for the relief of such populations in Europe, and countries contiguous thereto, outside of Germany, German-Austria, Hungary, Bulgaria, and Turkey, as may be determined upon by the President as necessary.

"Be it enacted by the Senate and House of Representatives of the United States of America in Congress assembled, That for the participation by the Government of the United States in the furnishing of foodstuffs and other urgent supplies, and for the transportation, distribution, and administration thereof to such populations in Europe, and countries contiguous thereto, outside of Germany, German-Austria, Hungary, Bulgaria, and Turkey: Provided, however, That Armenians, Syrians, Greeks, and other Christian and Jewish populations of Asia Minor, now or formerly subjects of Turkey may be included within the populations to receive relief under this Act, as may be determined upon by the President from time to time as necessary, and for each and every purpose connected therewith, in the discretion of the President, there is appropriated out of any money in the Treasury not otherwise appropriated $100,000,000, which may be used as a revolving fund until June thirtieth, nineteen hundred and nineteen, and which shall be audited in the same manner as other expenditures of the Government: Provided, That expenditures hereunder shall be reimbursed so far as possible by the Governments or subdivisions thereof or the peoples to whom relief is furnished: Provided further, That a report of the receipts, expenditures, and an itemized statement of such receipts and expenditures made under this appropriation shall be submitted to Congress not later than the first day of the next regular session: And provided further, That so far as said fund shall be expended for the purchase of wheat to be donated, preference shall be given to grain grown in the United States."

This act, besides appropriating money, also resulted in providing definite Congressional authority for the relief work, and thus permitted the President to authorize definitely the establishment of the American Relief Administration, and authorized the employment of the Grain Corporation as the commercial and fiscal agent of the Relief Administration. This the President did by issuing the following Executive Order on February 24,[1] 1919:

In pursuance of an Act entitled "An Act providing for the relief of such populations in Europe and countries contiguous thereto, outside of Germany, German-Austria, Hungary, Bulgaria and Turkey, as may be determined upon by the President as necessary," approved February 24, 1919, I hereby direct that the furnishing of foodstuffs and other urgent supplies, and the transportation, distributing, and administration thereof, provided for in said Act, shall be conducted under the direction of Herbert Hoover who is hereby appointed Director General of the American Relief Administration with full power to determine to which of the populations named in said Act the supplies shall be furnished and in what quantities, and further to arrange for reimbursement so far as possible as in said Act provided.

He is hereby authorized to establish the American Relief Administration for the purpose of carrying out the provisions of said Act and to employ such persons and incur such expenses as may be necessary for such purpose, to disburse all sums appropriated under the aforesaid Act or appoint a disbursing officer with that power; and particularly to employ the Food Administration Grain Corporation, organized under the provisions of the Food Control Act of August 10, 1917, as an agency for the purchase, transportation, and distribution of foodstuffs and supplies to the populations requiring relief.

He is hereby further authorized in the carrying out of the aforesaid Act of February twenty-fourth, 1919, to contract with the Food Administration Grain Corporation or any other person or corporation, that such person or corporation shall carry stocks of food in transit to Europe, and at points in Europe, in such quantities as may be agreed upon and as are required to meet relief needs, and that there shall be paid to such person or corporation in advance from the appropriation made in the aforesaid Act of February twenty-fourth, 1919, any sums which may be required for the purchase and transportation of foodstuffs and maintenance of stocks.

Food Administration Grain Corporation—London Office

In the meantime, under the authority of the memorandum of December 23, 1918, the Grain Corporation had established an office in London and had built up stocks of food in foreign ports as well as having carried on a considerable amount of actual distribution of relief supplies.

The work accomplished by the American Relief Administration in 1919 would have been impossible had it not been able to call upon some going commercial organization like the Grain Corporation to carry on this phase of its work.

The London office of the Food Administration Grain Corporation was established at 12 Grosvenor Garden, London, early in January, 1919. Edward M. Flesh, who throughout the war had acted as second vice-president of the Grain Corporation in charge of the St. Louis office, was asked by Mr. Hoover to come to London and organize this work. The London office had complete charge of the movement of all American relief ships while in European waters. It also acted as fiscal agent for the American Relief Administration and, as such, established agencies in each of the important European ports used in the relief work. Through these agencies the London office kept accurate account of all relief arrivals, saw to it that all deliveries were properly receipted for and, finally, made all settlements with the foreign governments or others to which relief supplies were delivered.

The New York office of the Grain Corporation was the purchasing and shipping agency for the American Relief Administration, and for this purpose organized a special division called the Miscellaneous Commodities Division.

Briefly the method of operation was as follows: The American Relief Administration with headquarters in Paris outlined all relief programs. These were made out on the basis of reports to the Director General of Relief from the relief missions in the various countries, supplemented by information and reports from other sources. The programs were all cleared through the Supreme Council of Supply and Relief, and later the Food Section of the Supreme Economic Council which kept the American activities co-ordinated with those of the Allies and of other relief organizations. These programs were cabled to the New York office of the Food Administration Grain Corporation as far in advance as possible. There they served as warrants for the purchase and shipment of commodities. These programs were made out in two sections, known respectively as Northern

[1] See note regarding date of Act, page xxii.

and Southern Relief. The former included all supplies destined for Northern European ports between Rotterdam and Helsingfors, while the Southern Relief program included shipments destined to Adriatic and Black Sea ports.

As the ships were loaded at American ports, those designed for the Northern Relief program were dispatched to Falmouth, England, for orders, and those for Southern Relief cleared for Gibraltar for orders. Immediately after each ship sailed, the London office of the Grain Corporation and the Paris office of the Relief Administration were advised of the name of the vessel, port, and date of sailing, the contents of the cargo, and whether for Falmouth or Gibraltar. Before the vessel arrived within wireless range of its port of call, it was allocated to the relief program of some country and to a final port of discharge. This allocation was made by the Paris office and advice sent to London. All orders and directions to ships were handled by the London office of the Grain Corporation. When the vessel arrived in its port of discharge, it was, in most cases, turned over to officials of the receiving government or other recipient on a c.i.f. basis, but in some instances it was necessary to unload the cargo in warehouses and to make deliveries from stock. In either case, the London office of the Grain Corporation through its port agencies obtained properly executed receipts from the receiving officials, attended to the details of checking cargoes, etc.

In the case of deliveries to governments all the details and expenses of handling and distributing the supplies from the ports were handled by the receiving governments. However, the American Relief Administration officials assigned to that country followed these distributions to make sure that the relief supplies actually reached the people who were in distress. This provision was one of the conditions under which the supplies were furnished by the American Relief Administration. In the Children's Relief and some other deliveries as discussed later, the Administration followed the distribution in considerably greater detail.

As fast as the relief supplies were shipped from American ports by the New York office they were invoiced to the London office of the Grain Corporation. The latter office was thus made responsible for the accounting on all relief commodities, and for carrying through all settlements, both in payment for commodities to the New York office, for shipping and other costs, and for the settlement with the ultimate receivers of these supplies. The task of the London office as the shipping and financial agent of the American Relief Administration was one of the most important and exacting. It is a remarkable tribute to the personnel of the London office that this vast program of handling the shipping and accounting for supplies delivered within a period of nine months, valued at $363,271,835.48, was carried through without a single serious error. These results are to be attributed to the efficient organization established in London by Edward M. Flesh, in which the shipping operations were under the immediate direction of Captain Rodger D. Lapham and the accounting work under George K. Hyslop.

In acting as commercial and fiscal agent for the Relief Administration, the Food Administration Grain Corporation must of necessity protect itself against possible losses. The Grain Corporation had at this time a capital from the United States Treasury of only $150,000,000, which was far too small to carry on its normal operations of protecting the guaranteed price of wheat. At one time before the Armistice, the Corporation had found it necessary to borrow money from outside sources to the extent of $385,000,000, and even during 1919 its borrowing ran into hundreds of millions. It, therefore, had no funds which it could tie up for any length of time in relief supplies, unless it could secure their return along with costs including interest and overhead.

Furthermore, commercial operations in European waters during the Armistice Period were particularly hazardous. Many of these waters were still mined and hence a serious menace to shipping. Furthermore, conditions within many of these countries were extremely precarious. New governments had been established, often with the support of a bare majority of the population. The spirit of unrest and revolution was everywhere apparent. With populations hungry, or on the verge of starvation, no one knew when the governments might be overthrown and stocks of commodities, particularly food, confiscated. In addition, there was the very real threat of a Bolshevist invasion from the east, with uprising and warfare throughout this whole territory.

The risks were so great that no private organization could engage in trade with many of these countries, and certainly could not undertake to establish stocks of food in these ports. No insurance company could afford to underwrite these risks except at almost confiscatory premiums.

It was under such conditions that the Grain Corporation was asked to make deliveries to these countries and to build up port stocks. Yet the Grain Corporation had no capital which it could afford to lose without endangering its ability to carry out its primary purpose of protecting the guaranteed price of wheat in the United States. The only protection which the Grain Corporation could secure in its European operations was to recognize these risks and to make its prices high enough to cover some portion of the hazards thus imposed upon it.

One of the first tasks of the London office after its establishment was to work out definite arbitraries for each European port which could be added to the f.o.b. cost of the commodities, and thus arrive at a c.i.f. or delivered price at which the relief supplies should be invoiced. These arbitraries had to include allowance for marine freight and insurance, war risk insurance, and handling charges, as well as for the added hazards discussed above.

The Grain Corporation had no desire to make any profit out of these relief operations but it felt it would be seriously remiss in the trust which had been imposed upon it if it did not use the ordinary business methods of protecting the integrity of its capital. Fortunately, the Grain Corporation experienced no serious losses in these operations, and as a result, the 1919 relief work was completed with a fair surplus over and above all expenditures. Inasmuch as this work had been undertaken for purely humanitarian reasons, it was felt that it would be entirely unjust for the Grain Corporation, and hence the United States Government, to retain this surplus. Several ways were available by which this surplus could be returned to the countries from which it was received in protection of the Grain Corporation against possible loss. This could be done by a direct cash rebate, or by a credit on the account of those governments which were indebted to the United States.

A survey of the European food situation late in the summer of 1919 convinced Mr. Hoover that there would be serious suffering in many countries during the coming year. On the other hand, it was obviously desirable that further governmental or official relief should be withdrawn after the arrival of the 1919 harvest. This harvest would be sufficient to feed these countries for several months, during which time, if placed on their own responsibility, they should be able to make their own arrangements for further supplies. However, certain classes of these populations, and particularly the children, were likely to suffer because of the lack of sufficient quantity, and especially the proper kind, of food. After consulting with the representatives of the several governments to which relief had been supplied, as well as with President Wilson, it was determined that the best way in which this surplus from the 1919 operations could be returned to these countries would be in the form of further food relief for the children. Accordingly at the express request of these governments, and at the direction of the President, Mr. Hoover organized the American Relief Adiministration European Children's Fund, incorporated under the laws of Delaware, as a charitable institution which continued to feed the undernourished children of these countries for another three years. The surplus above cost of operation on the 1919 European relief operations of the Grain Corporation was turned over to this new organization. This formed the nucleus of the fund for later child-feeding operations in Europe. This fund was greatly increased by charitable contribution in the United States and by contributions from European governments and elsewhere.

The account of the child-feeding work carried on by the American Relief Administration European Children's Fund, after August 1, 1919, is given in detail in a subsequent section of this volume (see pages 73–90).

Source of Finance

References have been made to the difficulties which faced the Director General of Relief in securing finance for the relief that must be furnished to these countries.

The sources of the relief finances for the Armistice Period as a whole have been briefly outlined (pages 32–35), but it will be advantageous to set forth here the finance that was available to the American Relief Administration as one of the agencies under the Director General of Relief.

Table 16 summarizes the total finance available to the A.R.A. and indicates the value of the supplies delivered from each of these sources.

TABLE 16

SUMMARY OF FINANCES AVAILABLE TO THE AMERICAN RELIEF ADMINISTRATION FOR COMMODITY PURCHASES AND THE SALES VALUE OF RELIEF SUPPLIES DELIVERED—ARMISTICE PERIOD, 1919

Source of Finance	Funds Available	Sales Value of Relief Supplies Delivered
Act of Congress, February 25, 1919	$100,000,000.00	$120,566,195.32*
U.S. Treasury Loans	89,450,000.00	86,743,158.36
President's National Security and Defense Fund	5,000,000.00	3,339,426.26
Cash sales, commodities	168,946,191.10	168,946,191.10
Total	$363,396,191.10	$379,594,971.04

* For explanation of deliveries in excess of funds available, see text page 45.

The total finance thus available for the American Relief Administration in 1919 amounted to $363,396,191.10 including cash sales at their actual value. Against this the Grain Corporation delivered commodities having a sales value of $379,594,971.04. The difference represents, in part, the commodities paid for out of the Grain Corporation surplus.

In all of these operations the Food Administration Grain Corporation acted as the fiscal agent of the American Relief Administration, purchasing the commodities, attending to their transportation and handling, and collecting all accounts. The books of the London office of the Grain Corporation have been audited and a detailed report covering all phases of these operations has been made by certified accountants. All of the operating expenses of the American Relief Administration, including the expenses of the Paris office and the Relief Missions in various parts of Europe, were paid by the Grain Corporation. Thus none of the expenses of the relief operations were charged directly against the relief appropriations or other relief funds. The total operating expenses of the American Relief Administration were $1,551,173.42. The expenses of the London office of the Grain Corporation, including its European Agencies, totaled $444,144.29, making the grand total of all expenses connected with the 1919 relief operation $1,995,317.71. This represents 0.5273 per cent or approximately 53/100 of one per cent of the total sales value of all supplies delivered by the organization in 1919. These expenses included many other items than those actually connected with the food deliveries, as, for example, the expenses of the coal and railway missions in Austria, Czechoslovakia, Jugoslavia, and elsewhere, the expenses of establishing and maintaining telegraphic and other communications over large areas, the expenses of conducting exchange operations for these countries, etc. Many of these operations are discussed briefly in other parts of this volume.[1]

DELIVERIES BY THE AMERICAN RELIEF ADMINISTRATION—ARMISTICE PERIOD, 1919[2]

Table 17 summarizes the total deliveries made by the American Relief Administration

TABLE 17

DELIVERIES BY THE AMERICAN RELIEF ADMINISTRATION BY METHODS OF FINANCE—ARMISTICE PERIOD, 1919

Method of Finance	Total Metric Tons	Total Value
Congressional Appropriation	485,558.1*	$107,132,276.99*
U.S. Treasury Loan...	417,024.6	86,743,158.36
President's National Security and Defense Fund	1,622.0†	390,209.03†
Cash Settlement	780,251.9	168,946,191.10
Total	1,684,456.6‡	$363,211,835.48‡

* Does not include 36,002.1 metric tons valued at $13,433,918.33, representing children's relief which in this report is accounted for under European Children's Fund. See Table 150.

† Does not include 7,823.1 metric tons, valued at $2,949,217.23, used for children's relief in Austria and in this report accounted for under the European Children's Fund. See Table 150.

‡ If the children's relief referred to in the two preceding notes were included, the deliveries made by the American Relief Administration in the Armistice Period would amount to a total of 1,728,281.8 metric tons and a total value of $379,594,971.04 which agrees with the sales value of relief supplied by the A.R.A. as shown in Table 16. For the reasons for treatment of the children's relief under the Reconstruction Period, see text, page 44.

during the Armistice Period under four headings representing the methods by which these deliveries were financed. As indicated else-

[1] See also section on Sources of Relief Finances, pages 142–46.

[2] See Appendix Tables 109 to 120.

where (cf. page 82), this table does not include the deliveries for children's relief paid for from the Congressional Appropriation for Relief, and which in this report are accounted for under the Reconstruction Period, because the major portion of the deliveries were actually made in this latter period. Likewise the children's relief to Austria, paid for from the President's National Security and Defense Fund, is also accounted for under the European Children's Fund in the Reconstruction Period.

While it is true that the arrangements for these children's relief supplies were all made by the Director General of Relief and most of the foodstuffs were shipped and received in Europe during the Armistice Period, a considerable portion was regarded as stocks for child-feeding work after August, 1919, and hence were in reality actually distributed by the European Children's Fund. The real reason for accounting for these supplies in the Reconstruction Period is that the feeding-station receipts are almost inextricably tied up with other child-feeding supplies furnished by the E.C.F. In many instances, the same receipt contains commodities paid for from the Congressional Appropriation and other commodities from other sources. Hence, it has seemed that the data could be presented much more simply by regarding these child-feeding operations as part of the work of the European Children's Fund.

This method has, of course, the effect of reducing the amount of relief credited to the American Relief Administration during the Armistice Period by 43,825.2 metric tons and $16,383,135.56 divided as follows:

	Metric Tons	Value
Congressional Appropriation	36,002.1	$13,433,918.33
President's National Security and Defense Fund	7,823.1	2,949,217.23
Total	43,825.2	$16,383,135.56

However, these amounts are fully accounted for elsewhere in this report (cf. Tables 53, 150, pages 82 and 334–35) and, hence, are included in the total relief supplied. If the above-mentioned amounts were included in the deliveries by the American Relief Administration in the Armistice Period, it would bring the total to 1,728,281.8 metric tons and a value of $379,594,971.04, as shown in Table 16.

Table 18 gives the division of the total relief credited to the American Relief Administration in the Armistice Period by country of destination. Altogether deliveries were made to twenty different countries in addition to the sundry accounts which could not well be credited to any one country. It will be noted that the largest deliveries were made to Germany, Poland, Czechoslovakia, Finland, and Roumania. Relatively large amounts also went to Jugoslavia, Armenia, and the United Kingdom.

TABLE 18

Deliveries by the American Relief Administration by Countries of Destination—Armistice Period, 1919*

Country	Total Metric Tons	Total Value
Armenia	52,553.2	$ 11,189,983.01
Austria	8,325.3	3,293,470.93
Bulgaria	22,862.4	4,856,647.53
Czechoslovakia	311,360.7	58,602,496.13
Denmark	19,912.0	2,147,059.30
Esthonia	21,991.9	4,617,625.56
Finland	166,842.7	25,876,576.10
France	32,728.1	5,422,039.11
Germany	483,155.8	113,758,637.74
Hungary	319.1	245,519.96
Italy	15,031.1	2,846,014.42
Jugoslavia	55,077.2	13,272,387.44
Latvia	13,313.7	3,323,978.51
Lithuania	3,357.0	1,045,023.08
Netherlands	25,027.4	4,219,498.41
Poland	260,843.2	63,735,352.01
Roumania	102,942.5	23,438,339.29
Russia	19,259.9	5,868,966.85
Turkey	20,278.3	4,369,404.30
United Kingdom	47,371.9	10,618,045.72
Sundry Accounts	1,903.2	464,770.08
Total	1,684,456.6	$363,211,835.48

* For details see Table 110, Appendix.

Deliveries to Russia include three separate operations as follows:

	Metric Tons	Value
Northwest Russia	17,950.4	$5,337,568.35
Southern Russia (Kouban)	915.5	444,718.50
Volunteer Army (Russian)	394.0	86,680.00
Total	19,259.9	$5,868,966.85

Congressional Appropriation for Relief

(Act of February 25, 1919)

Reference has been made (page 39) to the Act of Congress of February 25, 1919, which appropriated $100,000,000 "for the relief of such populations in Europe, and countries contiguous thereto, outside of Germany, German-Austria, Hungary, Bulgaria, and Turkey, as may be determined upon by the President as necessary." The act provided that this money could be used as a revolving fund and that as far as possible expenditures should be reimbursed by the government or peoples to whom relief was furnished.

By the executive order previously quoted (page 40), President Wilson placed the administration of this relief in Mr. Hoover's hands. Mr. Hoover proposed to use this fund for three purposes. The major portion was to be used to furnish foodstuffs to the newly liberated governments of Central and Eastern Europe on credit. Since these governments had no funds available it was impossible to obtain cash payment and, hence, their notes to repay the United States Treasury were to be accepted. Smaller portions of this fund were to be used to furnish special foods for child-feeding programs in certain of these countries, and these were to be delivered as gifts from the American people without any obligation for repayment. The third activity undertaken with funds from the Congressional Appropriation was the payment of transportation charges on supplies which were furnished to these liberated governments from other sources, but which were useless in relieving the people until transported to these countries. A portion of these freight and insurance costs was charged against the respective countries and included in the notes which they gave to the United States Treasury, while a smaller portion, representing charges on charitable gifts, was furnished to the respective countries without obligation on their part.

The total activities carried on under the Congressional Appropriation may be summarized under these headings:

Congressional Appropriation

	Metric Tons	Value
Deliveries to governments (credit)	485,558.1	$105,915,038.72
Freight, insurance, etc. (credit)	....	733,247.86
Freight, insurance, etc. (gift)	....	483,990.41
Sub-total	485,558.1	$107,132,276.99
Children's Relief (gift)	36,002.1	13,433,918.33
Grand total	521,560.2	$120,566,195.32

It will be noted that the total value of the relief furnished under the Congressional Appropriation was $120,566,195.32, although the appropriation was for only $100,000,000. This apparent anomaly arose from the fact that the Comptroller of the Treasury refused to allow payment for any of the costs of the operations, and required detailed vouchers for each cargo of relief showing the f.o.b. cost of the foodstuffs in the United States and separate vouchers showing the ocean transportation costs and certain handling charges. No allowance was permitted for any overhead costs, such as the cost of purchasing, directing the operation, checking the delivery, or making settlement with the receiving government. Therefore, in order to obtain the use of the major portion of the Congressional Appropriation, it was necessary to deliver commodities, the sales value of which was far in excess of the amount of the reimbursement received from the Treasury. The difference had to be absorbed by the Food Administration Grain Corporation out of surplus derived from other operations.

Reference has been made to the fact that the Food Administration Grain Corporation was made the purchasing and fiscal agent for the American Relief Administration, under the authority of the Executive Order of February 24, 1919. A contract between the American Relief Administration and the Grain Corporation was drawn up and signed on March 15, 1919.[1]

[1] This contract was as follows:

"The Grain Corporation will, by constant contact with the American Relief Administration in America and Europe, endeavor to maintain, in suitable European ports and en route thereto, sufficient food stocks, so that the American Relief Administration may be assured of adequate supplies for its requirements; and the American Relief Administration agrees to take from the Grain Corporation, at European ports or elsewhere, a total of foodstuffs as indicated by the American Relief Administration to the Grain Corporation from time to time.

"The American Relief Administration has the right to draw from any of the present stocks of the Grain Corporation in European ports, or en route thereto, and from such additional quantities as may be put afloat by the Grain Corporation for European destinations after joint conference and discussion; and the American Relief Administration will take delivery of such foodstuffs at such European destinations or as otherwise mutually arranged, and at such prices as may be mutually agreed on from time to time.

"The Grain Corporation shall so arrange its accounting system that, on commodities actually afterwards sold to the American Relief Administration in European ports or elsewhere, any profit between such European sale prices and

Under this contract it was expected that duly executed invoices together with receipts from the governments to which deliveries were made would be accepted by the Treasury as warrants for payments from the appropriation. However, the Comptroller ruled otherwise after a considerable period of delay and, as stated above, required the detailed vouchers without any allowance for any of the necessary items of overhead expense. Under this ruling it would have been impossible to have made any deliveries under the appropriation had there not been available the services of a public commercial organization like the Grain Corporation, which not only did not demand payment for the services rendered, but which, also, was able to absorb the very heavy expenses and the risk incident to these operations.

Under these rulings of the Comptroller, it was deemed necessary to draw up a new contract between the American Relief Administration and the Grain Corporation to take the place of the one signed on March 15, 1919. This new contract, signed on June 11, 1919,[1] provided that the overhead expense of the American Relief Administration would be paid by the Grain Corporation out of a margin to be charged on supplies delivered for the A.R.A. other than those for the Congressional Appropriation, and further that the Grain Corporation would turn over any balance of such margins on its European operations to the Director General of Relief, or to institutions or governments named by him.

The ruling by the Comptroller worked a great hardship on the Grain Corporation because of the long delay in securing any of the funds from the Congressional Appropriation. Although the

the f.o.b. American price, after deduction of all proper and necessary expenses and losses, shall be for account of the American Relief Administration and accounted for to the American Relief Administration.

"The Grain Corporation agrees to accept payment either directly from the American Relief Administration or from such Governments or Agencies as may be designated by the Director General of the American Relief Administration; but not later than actual delivery of the goods, as evidenced by proper invoices, for which payment the American Relief Administration remains responsible.

"American Relief Administration,
"By Edgar Rickard,
"Theo. F. Whitmarsh

"Accepted,
"Food Administration Grain Corporation,
"Julius H. Barnes, *President*"

---

1 The text of this contract was as follows:

"1. Grain Corporation will endeavor to maintain in suitable European ports and en route thereto sufficient food stocks so that Director General of Relief may be assured of adequate supplies for all operations conducted under his direction.

"2. Director General of Relief shall have right to draw from any of present stocks of Grain Corporation in European ports or en route thereto and from such additional quantities as may be put afloat by Grain Corporation for European destinations after joint conversation and discussion. Director General of Relief will arrange either that American Relief Administration takes delivery of such foodstuffs at such European destinations or that other persons or governments designated by Director General of Relief take delivery after paying cash for such cargoes.

"3. To extent such foodstuffs are turned over to American Relief Administration to be ultimately charged against hundred million dollar appropriation settlement shall be made directly between American Relief Administration and Grain Corporation in accordance with such regulations as may be prescribed by the Comptroller of the Treasury. Where ships intended for relief purposes and invoiced by Grain Corporation to American Relief Administration to be charged against the hundred million dollar appropriation are subsequently by agreement diverted for other purposes Grain Corporation agrees to credit American Relief Administration with the amount previously paid by American Relief Administration or repay it in such manner as may be directed by the Director General of Relief.

"4. Except for foodstuffs referred to in paragraph 3 prices of such foodstuffs shall be agreed upon from time to time between Grain Corporation and Director General of Relief.

"5. Grain Corporation agrees to pay all expenses of American Relief Administration in Europe.

"6. It is the intention of this contract that the Grain Corporation shall make no profit from its relief operations and shall suffer no losses. It therefore agrees that it will deduct from its gross receipts on all supplies, other than those delivered to American Relief Administration for payment from hundred million dollar appropriation, all items of cost and expense on such sales including expenses paid under paragraph 5 of this contract and will hold balance as special fund. From this fund shall be paid First any items of insurance or expense relating to the cargoes delivered against the hundred million dollar appropriation and not repaid from United States Treasury. The balance, if any, shall be paid to Director General of Relief or his successor or such person, institution or government as he or his successor may direct for charitable purposes in Europe. In case there should be no Director General of Relief such direction shall be made by United States Wheat Director.

"7. Director General of Relief agrees that in case operations of Grain Corporation in Europe should result in loss to it he will pay to Grain Corporation sufficient sum to make good such loss to extent that he has funds available from special allocation of five million dollars made by the President of the United States for relief purposes from his National Security and Defense Fund.

"8. Grain Corporation agrees to accept payment either directly from American Relief Administration or from such governments or agencies as may be designated by Director General of Relief but not later than actual delivery of goods as evidenced by proper invoices for which payment American Relief Administration remains responsible."

Act authorized the use of this money as a revolving fund, it was impossible to secure any of these funds from the Treasury until late in the fall of 1919, after the relief operations had been entirely closed. In the meantime, the Grain Corporation had to carry the burden of these operations out of its own meager capital and on funds which it could borrow from the banks.

In the final settlement with the United States Treasury, the Grain Corporation received a total of $94,938,417.05, against which it had made deliveries of commodities and services valued at $119,832,947.86. The Grain Corporation thus had to absorb a total of $24,894,530.81 on this operation. In addition to the foregoing the Grain Corporation made disbursements, which were billed to, or collected from, other organizations, in the amount of $733,247.86. This amount represented freight, insurance, and other transportation charges on relief supplies forwarded for other organizations. Following is a comparison of the sales value and the amounts received from the Treasury and other organizations under the main headings under which this appropriation was expended.

Sales Value and Reimbursements on Deliveries under the Congressional Appropriation

	Treasury Reimbursement	Sales Value
Deliveries to governments	$84,014,527.92	$105,915,038.72
Freight, insurance, etc.	385,749.83	483,990.81
Children's Relief	10,538,139.30	13,433,918.33
Total	$94,938,417.05	$119,832,947.86

	Other Reimbursements	Sales Value
Freight, insurance, etc., billed and/or collected	$ 733,247.86	$ 733,247.86
Total	$95,671,664.91	$120,566,195.72

Deliveries to Governments

Table 19 summarizes the deliveries made to governments, under the Congressional Appropriation, by country of destination. As pointed out earlier, these deliveries were made on credit and notes from each government were taken covering the amount of the Treasury reimbursement. The difference between the Treasury reimbursement and the sales value had to be absorbed by the Food Administration Grain Corporation.

It will be noted that by far the largest deliveries to any one government from the Congressional Appropriation were those to Poland, where the whole of A.R.A. relief of the Armistice Period, as shown in Table 18, was paid for from this source, if we include the freight and insurance costs discussed below. The same is true of the deliveries to Latvia, Lithuania, and Russia. In the case of the other countries, the A.R.A. deliveries from the Congressional Appropriation were supplemented by supplies financed from other sources. Large amounts

Drying pine bark in Finland. The Finns used pulverized pine bark for flour prior to arrival of A.R.A. relief supplies.

TABLE 19

Deliveries of Relief Supplies to European Governments under the Congressional Appropriation for Relief, by Countries of Destination—Armistice Period, 1919*

Country	Total Metric Tons	Total Treasury Reimbursement	Total Sales Value
Armenia	50,558.9	$ 8,028,412.15	$ 10,630,872.19
Czechoslovakia	52,285.3	6,348,653.56	8,251,639.28
Esthonia	21,129.9	1,785,767.72	4,299,650.87
Finland	65,725.7	8,281,926.17	9,849,587.73
Latvia	13,313.7	2,610,417.82	3,323,818.79
Lithuania	3,357.0	822,136.07	996,093.08
Poland	260,843.2	51,671,749.36	63,191,316.61
Russia			
Northwest Russia	17,950.4	4,390,638.69	5,285,380.17
Volunteer Army	394.0	74,826.38	86,680.00
Total	485,558.1	$84,014,527.92	$105,915,038.72

* For further details see Table 112, Appendix.

were furnished for Czechoslovakia from direct loans from the United States Treasury, while for the other countries listed in Table 18, the supplemental deliveries were chiefly from sales for cash.

Payment of Freight and Insurance

The payment of freight and insurance charges on supplies furnished from organizations other than the A.R.A. is discussed in some detail in the section on transportation (pages 135–38). As indicated above, a portion of these charges was included as additional credit extended to these governments, while the remainder was furnished as direct gifts to the people of these countries. The latter represented freight and insurance paid on commodities which were given to these countries by other organizations.

TABLE 20

Freight and Insurance Charges Paid from the Congressional Appropriation, by Countries of Destination—Armistice Period, 1919

Country	Credit	Direct Gift	Total
Armenia	....	$ 47,688.48	$ 47,688.48
Austria	$ 15,224.11	178.47	15,402.58
Czechoslovakia	184,606.63	18,898.99	203,505.62
Esthonia	151,113.05	50,490.02	201,603.07
Finland	....	22,584.24	22,584.24
Jugoslavia	....	81,140.98	81,140.98
Latvia	....	159.72	159.72
Lithuania	48,930.00	......	48,930.00
Northwest Russia	52,188.18	......	52,188.18
Poland	281,185.89	262,849.51	544,035.40
Total	$733,247.86	$483,990.41	$1,217,238.27

Table 20 summarizes the freight and insurance charges paid from the Congressional Appropriation, showing the country for which the charges were incurred, and whether a credit or a benevolent operation.

Children's Relief

As pointed out in an earlier section, the Children's Relief deliveries paid for from the Congressional Appropriation are considered in this report as part of the relief during the Reconstruction Period, because a large portion of the supplies were actually used during that period and because the records of these deliveries are closely interwoven with the records of other operations by the American Relief Administration European Children's Fund. The reader, therefore, is referred to that section of this report (pages 84 to 88) for a discussion of the deliveries for Children's Relief.

Table 21 summarizes the operations under the Congressional Appropriation for Relief in the Armistice Period, as accounted for in this report, by the countries receiving the relief.

TABLE 21

Summary of Total Relief under the Congressional Appropriation, Accounted for in This Report, in the Armistice Period*

Country	Value of Commodities Delivered	Value of Freight and Insurance	Total Value
Armenia	$ 10,630,872.19	$ 47,688.48	$ 10,678,560.67
Austria	....	15,402.58	15,402.58
Czechoslovakia	8,251,639.28	203,505.62	8,455,144.90
Esthonia	4,299,650.87	201,603.07	4,501,253.94
Finland	9,849,587.73	22,584.24	9,872,171.97
Jugoslavia	....	81,140.98	81,140.98
Latvia	3,323,818.79	159.72	3,323,978.51
Lithuania	996,093.08	48,930.00	1,045,023.08
Poland	63,191,316.61	544,035.40	63,735,352.01
Russia			
Northwest Russia	5,285,380.17	52,188.18	5,337,568.35
Volunteer Army	86,680.00	....	86,680.00
Total	$105,915,038.72	$1,217,238.27	$107,132,276.99

* Does not include deliveries for children's relief, see pages 84–88.

RELIEF DELIVERIES UNDER UNITED STATES TREASURY LOANS DURING THE ARMISTICE PERIOD

As shown in Table 17, the second important source of finance for relief handled by the American Relief Administration during the Armistice Period was direct loans from the United States Treasury to certain of the newly established European governments. These loans were made under the authority granted by Congress for the Treasury to loan money to countries at war with the enemies of the United States (Acts of April 24, 1917; September 24, 1917; April 4, 1918; and July 9, 1918). Certain of these countries, like Roumania and Serbia, had been fighting on the side of the Allied nations, while the newly established governments in Central Europe had declared war against Germany and Austria and, hence, were technically on the side of the Allies.

Realizing the great need of food to prevent not only great suffering, but actual starvation, Mr. Hoover, through President Wilson, made arrangements for the Treasury to establish credits for three countries, viz., Czechoslovakia, Jugoslavia (then called Greater Serbia or the Kingdom of the Serbs, Croats, and Slovenes), and Roumania. Against these credits, the American Relief Administration was able to deliver relief supplies, and to secure direct payment from the United States Treasury upon authorization from the respective governments.

Table 22 summarizes the deliveries made under these Treasury loans by countries receiving the relief. Further details showing the commodities delivered to each country are given in Table 119 (Appendix).

TABLE 22

Relief Deliveries Paid for from United States Treasury Loans, by Countries of Destination—Armistice Period, 1919

Country	Total Metric Tons	Total Value
Czechoslovakia	259,004.9	$50,113,572.61
Jugoslavia	55,077.2	13,191,246.46
Roumania	102,942.5	23,438,339.29
Total	417,024.6	$86,743,158.36

The total deliveries under these Treasury loans amounted to 417,024.6 metric tons, valued at $86,743,158.36. For this full amount the American Relief Administration through the Grain Corporation turned over duly executed notes of the respective governments. It will be noted that about 60 per cent of the deliveries under this heading went to Czechoslovakia. It will also be recalled that Czechoslovakia participated in the relief from the Congressional Appropriation to the extent of $8,455,144.90 (Table 21), so that the total relief to that country from these two sources amounted to $58,568,717.51. In addition to this, there were some minor cash sales credited to Czechoslovakia, which makes up the total from the American Relief Administration as shown in Table 18.

RELIEF DELIVERIES FROM THE PRESIDENT'S NATIONAL SECURITY AND DEFENSE FUND DURING THE ARMISTICE PERIOD

As recorded on page 32, President Wilson turned over to Mr. Hoover $5,000,000 from the President's National Security and Defense Fund, to be used as a nucleus for relief and for the payment of expenses of the administration of the relief work. As a matter of fact, none of this fund was used for expenses, since all of these were paid by the Grain Corporation, and only $3,339,426.26 out of the $5,000,000 were actually expended, the remainder being turned back to the President.

This fund was used to finance relief operations for which it was impossible to use money from other sources. Two operations of this kind were paid for from the President's Fund. One was for children's relief in Austria where the Congressional Appropriation could not be used, and the other was for the relief of Russian prisoners of war in Germany. Table 23 (page 50) shows relief furnished for these two purposes.

The children's relief deliveries from the President's Fund are considered in connection with the work of the European Children's Fund in the Reconstruction Period and, hence, in this report is not regarded as part of the relief in the Armistice Period. The reasons for considering this relief in the Reconstruction Period are the same as those discussed under the Congressional Appropriation.

Consequently, as indicated in Table 17, the

only relief from the President's National Security and Defense Fund considered in this report as an Armistice Period delivery is that to the Russian prisoners of war who were being held in Germany.

TABLE 23

RELIEF DELIVERIES PAID FOR FROM THE PRESIDENT'S NATIONAL SECURITY AND DEFENSE FUND

Delivered to	Total Metric Tons	Total Value
Austrian Children's Relief*	7,823.1	$2,949,217.23
Russian prisoners of war in Germany	1,622.0	390,209.03
Total	9,445.1	$3,339,426.26

* In the final allocation of these supplies by the European Children's Fund, a portion was delivered to Hungary. See page 89.

Reports were received by the Director General of Relief showing the very serious condition of these war prisoners. Germany did not have sufficient food to feed her own people who, as pointed out elsewhere (pages 189 ff.), were suffering greatly. These war prisoners could not be repatriated at this time, nor was there sufficient food for them. Mr. Hoover persuaded the French Government that they should take the responsibility of furnishing relief to these Russian war prisoners, but at the time the French Government had no supplies which could be used for this purpose. Accordingly, the American Relief Administration undertook to advance these supplies, to be later reimbursed by the French Government. No free funds were available to the American Relief Administration except from the President's National Security and Defense Fund. Supplies to the extent of 1,622.0 metric tons of flour, sugar, and miscellaneous food, with a total value of $390,209.03, were turned over to the French for these prisoners. At a later time, notes were obtained from the French Government to repay this amount to the United States Treasury.

RELIEF DELIVERIES AGAINST CASH SETTLEMENT DURING THE ARMISTICE PERIOD

It was necessary to mobilize every available source of finance to take care of vast and urgent needs for food in the period following the Armistice. Many of the European governments possessed some cash or available assets which could be used for this purpose. In other cases, it was possible to sell food for cash to local organizations or to commercial establishments, which agreed to handle this on a minimum margin in order to relieve the suffering people. It must be remembered that during this time practically all ordinary commercial operations had ceased, blockade restrictions were still in force, and, hence, the relief organizations had to perform many functions which would ordinarily be carried on by commercial establishments.

It was Mr. Hoover's principle that, wherever possible, food should be sold for cash payment, and as pointed out in an earlier section, a very considerable proportion, 46.5 per cent, of the relief delivered under the Director General of Relief was sold for cash. In this connection, the American Relief Administration, acting through its fiscal agent, the Food Administration Grain Corporation, played an important part. As shown in Table 17, one of the four main divisions of the work of the American Relief Administration was sales against cash settlement. The total deliveries made during the Armistice Period under this category amounted to 780,251.9 metric tons, valued at $168,946,191.10. These supplies were delivered to fifteen different countries in addition to sundry accounts.

Table 24 summarizes these cash sales by country of destination, while Table 120 (Appendix) gives further details regarding these operations.

The conditions surrounding these cash sales are discussed in detail under each of the countries to which deliveries were made. Only a few of the important points regarding these deliveries will be discussed here.

The deliveries to Germany, totaling 483,155.8 metric tons, valued at $113,758,637.74, far exceeded those to any other country. These supplies were furnished to Germany under the terms of the Brussels agreement and were paid for through the deposit of German gold in Rotterdam and Brussels to the credit of the Director General of Relief. Sales to Bulgaria were also paid for by gold deposits. In both instances, the Grain Corporation later sold this gold to the Federal Reserve Bank of New York.

Deliveries to Italy represented emergency supplies furnished because of a deficiency in the Allied program. Deliveries to the United Kingdom represented supplies which were furnished to Austria by the British under the Joint Allied Finance plan. Deliveries to countries like Denmark, Finland, and the Netherlands represented direct sales to supplement the greatly diminished food supply of these countries. Sales to Turkey were made through a commercial organization which then undertook to supplement the bread supply in Istanbul (Constantinople). Deliveries to Armenia represent cash sales to the Near East Relief, while the sales to France represent a transaction involving flour sold to Esthonia by the United States Liquidation Commission, but which France refused to allow to be moved out of the country (cf. page 68).

TABLE 24

SUMMARY OF RELIEF DELIVERIES BY THE AMERICAN RELIEF ADMINISTRATION AGAINST CASH SETTLEMENT—ARMISTICE PERIOD, 1919

Country of Destination	Total Metric Tons	Total Value
Armenia	1,994.3	$ 511,422.34
Austria	8,325.3	3,278,068.35
Bulgaria	22,862.4	4,856,647.53
Czechoslovakia	70.5	33,778.62
Denmark	19,912.0	2,147,059.30
Esthonia	862.0	116,371.62
Finland	101,117.0	16,004,404.13
France	31,106.1	5,031,830.08
Germany	483,155.8	113,758,637.74
Hungary	319.1	245,519.96
Italy	15,031.1	2,846,014.42
Netherlands	25,027.4	4,219,498.41
Russia (Southern Russia)	915.5	444,718.50
Turkey	20,278.3	4,369,404.30
United Kingdom	47,371.9	10,618,045.72
Sundry Accounts	1,903.2	464,770.08
Total	780,251.9	$168,946,191.10

RELIEF DELIVERIES DURING THE ARMISTICE PERIOD BY AMERICAN ORGANIZATIONS OTHER THAN THE AMERICAN RELIEF ADMINISTRATION

Table 14 (page 35), shows the second major division under the work of the Director General of Relief as deliveries by American organizations other than the American Relief Administration. The total deliveries under this heading is given as 1,058,770.9 metric tons, valued at $462,622,804.46. This includes the work of five separate organizations operating during the Armistice Period, and which worked in close co-operation with the Director General of Relief. Table 25 summarizes these deliveries by the separate organizations.

It should be pointed out again that, with each of those organizations, the operations recorded here form only a portion of their total activities.

TABLE 25

RELIEF DELIVERIES BY AMERICAN ORGANIZATIONS OTHER THAN THE AMERICAN RELIEF ADMINISTRATION—ARMISTICE PERIOD, 1919

Organization	Total Metric Tons	Total Value
U.S. Liquidation Commission	823,202.0	$381,721,094.59
Commission for Relief in Belgium	186,372.0	66,341,240.87
Near East Relief	30,657.0	8,711,472.00
Joint Distribution Committee	11,029.1	4,107,257.00
American Red Cross	7,510.8	1,741,740.00
Total	1,058,770.9	$462,622,804.46

The United States Liquidation Commission (War Department) disposed of vast quantities of munitions, railroad and industrial equipment, and other supplies which were not regarded as relief within the meaning of this report, and which are not included in the table above.

The deliveries by the C.R.B. do not include any of the supplies going to Belgium or Northern France during the Armistice Period, which are accounted for elsewhere. The three other organizations were each spending vast sums for relief, which was not directly co-ordinated with the work of the Director General of Relief and, hence, are not included in this report.

Table 26 (page 52) shows total deliveries from these five organizations tabulated by the countries receiving the relief. France heads the list because of the large amount of supplies turned over to that country by the United States Liquidation Commission. Other countries receiving substantial amounts of relief from these sources were Poland, Germany, Belgium, Jugoslavia, and Czechoslovakia. In the following pages, the deliveries by each of these organizations will be discussed.

TABLE 26

TOTAL RELIEF DELIVERIES BY AMERICAN ORGANIZATIONS OTHER THAN THE AMERICAN RELIEF ADMINISTRATION, BY COUNTRIES OF DESTINATION—ARMISTICE PERIOD, 1919

Country	Total Metric Tons	Total Value
Armenia	31,411.1	$ 8,970,072.00
Austria	901.3	363,760.00
Belgium	50,774.0	28,549,672.75
Czechoslovakia	41,225.2	19,273,914.27
Esthonia	30,432.3	12,352,618.99
Finland	282.0	56,400.00
France	519,775.0	213,067,400.00
Germany	134,980.0	44,350,810.47
Jugoslavia	32,517.6	20,688,991.25
Latvia	6,296.0	2,556,952.84
Lithuania	8,320.0	4,414,861.39
Poland	120,874.4	63,591,408.97
Roumania	22,713.0	13,268,689.00
Russia	6,877.0	9,126,822.13
Sundry	51,392.0	21,990,430.40
Total	1,058,770.9	$462,622,804.46

UNITED STATES LIQUIDATION COMMISSION—WAR DEPARTMENT

Under an Act of Congress approved May 10, 1918, the President was authorized, during the war-time emergency, to sell supplies, material, equipment, or other properties which had previously been purchased or acquired in connection with the prosecution of the war. Under these powers, there was created by General Orders No. 24 of the War Department, dated February 11, 1919, the "United States Liquidation Commission (War Department)" as a central agency (1) to dispose of America's surplus war stocks in Europe, and (2) to settle all claims and accounts between Allied Governments and their nationals on the one side and the United States War Department on the other side. The powers thus granted to this Commission were further confirmed by Section 3 of an Act of Congress approved March 2, 1919, which directly empowered the Secretary of War to make such sales and settlements.

The Liquidation Commission was composed of Judge Edwin B. Parker, Chairman, Brigadier General Charles G. Dawes, H. H. Johnson, and Henry F. Hollis. The Commission entered immediately upon its task, with its principal office established in Paris.

The signing of the Armistice had naturally found the American Army with vast stores of commodities, equipment, and establishments in several countries of Europe. With more than 2,000,000 men in overseas service at this time, and with an equal number rapidly moving toward or preparing to move toward the war zone, it was necessary to have enormous supplies of all kinds of material and equipment on hand. The assets of the War Department consisted of both installations and stocks. Under installations were included warehouses, cold storage plants, barracks, hospitals, railway yards, docks, telephone and telegraph lines, etc. These structures had been erected upon land for the most part requisitioned for war purposes and involved claims for rent, damages, etc., from more than 150,000 individual owners.

Stocks of supplies and equipment included clothing, food and subsistence, machinery, tools, lumber, transport equipment, ordnance, hospital supplies, office fixtures, etc. Most of this material could not be salvaged and returned to the United States without costing more than could possibly be received for it. Furthermore, for a large part of these war supplies, there would be little or no demand in the United States.

On the other hand, many of these supplies were urgently needed to assist the hungry and demoralized peoples of Europe. After much consideration, it was decided that the bulk of these supplies should be sold in Europe as speedily as possible and under the best obtainable terms. It was hoped that the sale of these commodities and installations could be made to offset all, or most, of the claims against the War Department arising in the several European countries.

The United States Liquidation Commission (War Department) has issued a final report prepared by its chairman, Edwin B. Parker.[1] This report discusses the scope of the Commission's activities, the many difficulties encountered, and the results obtained. The following summary taken from this report gives some idea of the extent of the Commission's work:

[1] *Final Report of the United States Liquidation Commission (War Department)* (Government Printing Office, Washington, D.C., 1920). See also *Report of the War Department* (1920).

SUMMARY OF SETTLEMENTS NEGOTIATED AND SALES EFFECTED BY THE UNITED STATES LIQUIDATION COMMISSION (WAR DEPARTMENT)—FEBRUARY 11, 1919, TO MAY 31, 1920

Amounts Involved in Settlements	
Settlement with France	$748,392,004.82
Settlement with Great Britain	112,996,912.16
Settlement with Belgium	2,279,827.12
Settlement with Italy	12,620,173.75
Settlements with individuals, associations, and others	17,427,175.41
Total	$893,716,093.26
Amounts of Sales	
Bulk sale to France	$400,000,000.00
Other sales, stated in dollars	377,905,193.23
Other sales, stated in francs and converted	45,018,032.59
Total	$822,923,225.82

The distribution of these sales to the various countries of Europe is shown by the following table. This table also gives, separately, the values of the groups of commodities which were of most interest in the relief work, viz., clothing and subsistence.

The largest single item in these operations was the so-called "bulk sale" to France by which all remaining stocks, equipment, and installations in France were turned over to the French Government for the lump sum of $400,000,000 in ten-year five per cent bonds and the agreement of the French Government to assume all responsibility for claims against the United States War Department for rents, damages, etc., and also for the waiver by France of all claims for taxes or custom duties on properties imported and sold in France after our entrance into the war. Although the stocks and properties thus turned over to France had cost several times the amount realized, this sale undoubtedly was of advantage to the United States. It enabled us to dispose of possessions, many of which could be sold only to France, and others of which had little or no commercial value elsewhere; it enabled us to expedite the return of the American Army; and, in particular, it avoided the necessity of making individual settlements with many thousands of individual claimants in these foreign countries. Such settlements would undoubtedly have led to long-

TABLE 27

SUMMARY OF DISTRIBUTION OF TOTAL SALES BY UNITED STATES LIQUIDATION COMMISSION (WAR DEPARTMENT)

Sales Made To	Clothing and Textiles	Subsistence Supplies	All Other Commodities	Total Value
France	$ 5,820,612.39	$ 36,590,339.54	$ 90,255,045.00	$132,665,996.93
Great Britain	204,109.72	1,464,706.16	507,670.39	2,176,486.27
Italy	54.03	12,356.57	484,421.50	496,832.10
Belgium	15,346,255.31	9,370,277.94	3,833,139.50	28,549,672.75
Russia	45,540.72	379.86	382,378.88	428,299.46
Poland	20,288,155.42	13,855,252.62	25,221,703.93	59,365,111.97
Esthonia	3,929,042.80	7,214,397.33	1,119,378.86	12,262,818.99
Latvia	1,364,738.28	1,075,771.80	116,442.76	2,556,952.84
Lithuania	2,141,163.84	1,006,404.74	1,267,292.81	4,414,861.39
Ukraine	7,335,832.41	....	1,164,390.26	8,500,222.67
Greece	....	1,965.67	101,868.40	103,834.07
Serbia	11,321,149.68	3,204,717.07	5,938,324.50	20,464,191.25
Roumania	8,435,608.44	4,399,165.17	177,915.39	13,012,689.00
Czechoslovakia	8,734,301.14	9,105,616.47	1,258,956.66	19,098,874.27
Portugal	34,500.00	195,914.14	....	230,414.14
Spain	....	292,600.94	....	292,600.94
Sociedad Espanola	474,452.00	3,412,528.50	579,539.27	4,466,519.77
Holland	....	....	36,083.10	36,083.10
Associations, corporations and individuals	20,439,349.67	31,375,267.07	61,986,147.17	113,800,763.91
Total	$105,914,865.85	$122,577,661.59	$194,430,698.38	$422,923,225.82
France, bulk sale	....	....	....	400,000,000.00
Grand total	$105,914,865.85	$122,577,661.59	$194,430,698.38	$822,923,225.82

drawn-out negotiations and litigation, and would inevitably have left in their wake much bitterness and hard-feeling toward the United States which it was hoped could be avoided.

Much of the work of the United States Liquidation Commission (War Department) could not be considered as relief to Europe and had no connection with the Office of the Director General of Relief or with any of the American agencies engaged in relief work. On the other hand, a considerable portion of the sales were made either at the direct instance of the Director General of Relief, or through his immediate assistance.

On March 17, 1919, Mr. Hoover wrote to Judge Parker, Chairman of the Liquidation Commission, pointing out the serious needs of additional supplies of both clothing and subsistence in the newly liberated countries. He suggested that many of the surplus Army supplies could be disposed of to these countries, provided the prices were reasonable and the Commission was willing to accept the obligations of these countries in lieu of cash payment.

On March 24, 1919, President Wilson wrote the Commission, seconding Mr. Hoover's suggestion and adding, "I would be glad, therefore, if the Commission could accept as its guiding principle in these negotiations the fact that it is not only securing a rapid liquidation of materials that may otherwise prove unsalable but also that it is an opportunity to perform a fine human service by approaching the matter in the most sympathetic mind, and I would be glad if the Commission could see its way to very largely accept Mr. Hoover's views as to the terms upon which dealings should be undertaken with the liberated peoples."

These suggestions were accepted by the Commission and as a result large quantities of clothing, food, and reconstruction materials were made available to these distressed countries.

The final report of the Liquidation Commission gives, for the most part, dollar values only for the sales which it effected. These transactions have been closed so long that it is practically impossible to obtain further details on these operations at this late date. Based upon information which was available in the Paris office of the American Relief Administration at the time these transactions took place, we have compiled a table which gives an approximation of the tonnage of commodities delivered to these several countries by the Liquidation Commission. In compiling this table the total deliveries by the Commission to the liberated countries, including Belgium, and in addition, those deliveries to France which comprised food, clothing, and the more important reconstruction material have been regarded as relief. In the case of France, these categories amounted to approximately 40 per cent of the total value of all sales to that country by the Commission. All of the foregoing transactions were carried out with the collaboration and assistance of the Director General of Relief. Other sales by the Commission, such as those to Great Britain, Italy, Spain, Holland, Greece, and Portugal, have not been considered as relief transactions, although in many instances they might well have been so regarded.

Table 28 summarizes the relief sales made directly by the Liquidation Commission, and for which they accepted the obligations of the countries to which the commodities were sold.

As shown by this table, there was a total of approximately 823,202 metric tons, valued at $381,721,094.59, delivered to these countries, and here considered as European relief. This amounts to less than one-half of the total value of all sales by the Commission which, as shown above, amounted to nearly $823,000,000.

In addition to the relief deliveries shown in Table 28, page 55, the American Relief Administration purchased outright from the Commission, food commodities to the value of $18,308,655.58. The commodities thus purchased consisted of cereals, beans, pork products, evaporated milk, and a small quantity of medical supplies. The American Relief Administration paid cash for these commodities which were priced on a basis to justify their purchase in France rather than their shipment from the United States. These commodities are accounted for under the deliveries by the American Relief Administration. A portion of the commodities thus taken over were sold to the French Government as shown in Table 47, page 69. The remainder was delivered to various liberated countries. The details of this distribution are shown in Table 141B, pages 324–25.

The direct sales of commodities by the Liquidation Commission to many of these newly established governments involved serious diffi-

TABLE 28

RELIEF SUPPLIES FURNISHED BY THE UNITED STATES LIQUIDATION COMMISSION (WAR DEPARTMENT)—ARMISTICE PERIOD, 1919

(Approximate quantities stated in metric tons of 2,204.6 pounds each)

Country	Food	Clothing	Other Non-food Commodities	Total Tons	Total Value
France	370,285.0	129,490.0	20,000.0	519,775.0	$213,067,400.00
Belgium	37,480.0	8,184.0	5,110.0	50,774.0	28,549,672.75
Poland	44,360.0	13,719.0	49,047.0	107,126.0	59,365,111.97
Esthonia	26,000.0	2,620.0	1,500.0	30,120.0	12,262,818.99
Latvia	5,378.0	758.0	160.0	6,296.0	2,556,952.84
Lithuania	4,700.0	2,220.0	1,400.0	8,320.0	4,414,861.39
Czechoslovakia	34,500.0	4,550.0	1,300.0	40,350.0	19,098,874.27
Jugoslavia (Serbia)	16,300.0	5,400.0	10,150.0	31,850.0	20,464,191.25
Roumania	17,596.0	4,500.0	235.0	22,331.0	13,012,689.00
Russia (Northern Government)	....	200.0	510.0	710.0	428,299.46
Russia (Ukraine)	....	4,000.0	1,550.0	5,550.0	8,500,222.67
Total	556,599.0	175,641.0	90,962.0	823,202.0	$381,721,094.59

culties in transportation. Most of these supplies were located in France and these new countries possessed no shipping, nor did they have acceptable funds with which to pay for this transportation. Consequently, it looked as if many of these supplies would remain inaccessible to these suffering people even after their governments had purchased them. This problem was solved largely through the co-operation of the American and British Relief agencies.

The American Relief Administration undertook to transport a large portion of the pork sold by the Liquidation Commission, and these charges were finally paid from the Congressional Appropriation for Relief. The details of these coastwise shipments are given in Table 144 and the transactions are further discussed on pages 67–69 and 137.

The transportation on these commodities by Great Britain is included in Table 41.

DELIVERIES BY THE COMMISSION FOR RELIEF IN BELGIUM DURING THE ARMISTICE PERIOD

The work of the Commission for Relief in Belgium has been discussed and the deliveries by that organization to Belgium and Northern France have been presented (page 13). In addition to those activities the Commission also co-operated with the Director General of Relief during the Armistice Period in furnishing supplies which went to other countries in Europe. These deliveries may be considered under two categories, viz., sales to Germany, and sundry activities.

For purposes of clarity it may be well to summarize, in Table 29, the total operations of the C.R.B., divided between the two periods to which they apply.[1]

The deliveries to Belgium and Northern France have been treated elsewhere, and at this point we are concerned only with the deliveries from this organization, which are credited in Table 25 to the Armistice Period, and

TABLE 29

TOTAL OPERATIONS OF THE COMMISSION FOR RELIEF IN BELGIUM

Period and Country	Total Metric Tons	Total Value
Commission for Relief in Belgium Period		
Belgium	3,896,180.0	$641,056,693.69
Northern France	1,091,879.0	220,283,550.52
Sub-total	4,988,059.0	$861,340,244.21
Armistice Period		
Germany	134,980.0	44,350,810.47
Sundry Activities	51,392.0	21,990,430.40
Sub-total	186,372.0	$ 66,341,240.87
Grand total	5,174,431.0	$927,681,485.08

[1] All of the statistics relating to the operations of the C.R.B. are taken from the statistical report on the work of that organization, by G. I. Gay, to which the reader is referred for further details.

which total 186,372.0 metric tons, valued at $66,341,240.87.

Approximately two-thirds of this amount represents deliveries to Germany under the terms of the Brussels Agreement.[1] In March, 1919, Germany was in a serious condition with regard to food. When the Brussels Agreement was finally signed permitting her to purchase limited quantities of foodstuffs, it was impossible to make immediate delivery of sufficient quantities from A.R.A. stocks. Mr. Hoover, therefore, arranged with the Commission for Relief in Belgium to sell to Germany such supplies as could be spared from stocks in Rotterdam and Antwerp. These sales, totaling 134,980.0 metric tons, worth $44,350,810.47, were of the greatest importance in relieving the acute situation in Germany at this time.

These supplies were paid for out of the gold which Germany deposited to the credit of the Director General of Relief in designated banks in Belgium and the Netherlands. These operations are discussed in more detail under deliveries to Germany.

The work of the C.R.B., classified in Table 29 as Sundry Activities during the Armistice Period, includes a great variety of operations, not all of which occurred during the Armistice, but which have been grouped here for convenience. Of the total amount, nearly $4,500,000 represent commodities purchased from the C.R.B. by the American Relief Administration. An almost equal amount applies to the distribution of some twenty million British Army rations. Other miscellaneous sales include recovery from underwriters on commodities damaged or lost in transit, and also the sale of surplus or other damaged commodities not required for the work of the Commission. Further details regarding these operations are given in Table 103, Appendix, and in Mr. Gay's report.

Deliveries by the Near East Relief in the Armistice Period

The work of the Near East Relief is referred to in some detail in the section dealing with deliveries to Armenia. As has been pointed out repeatedly, this report deals only with that small portion of the work of the Near East Relief, which was directly co-ordinated with the work of the Director General of Relief in the Armistice Period and with certain other operations in the Reconstruction Period.

Although at the moment we are concerned only with the deliveries of the Near East Relief during the Armistice Period, it will be more convenient to refer, at this point, to all of the Near East Relief work reported on in this volume. This is summarized in Table 30.

TABLE 30

Relief Deliveries to Armenia by the Near East Relief as Covered by This Report

Period of Delivery	Total Metric Tons	Total Value
Armistice Period	30,657.0	$ 8,711,472.00
Reconstruction Period		
Relief deliveries	7,404.3	$ 1,411,329.90
Freight and miscellaneous	......	532,790.01
Sub-total Reconstruction Period	7,404.3	$ 1,944,119.91
Grand total	38,061.3	$10,655,591.91

According to this table, the Near East Relief delivered during the Armistice Period a total of 30,657.0 metric tons of supplies, with a total value of $8,711,472.00. In addition to this amount, the American Relief Administration sold to the Near East Relief 1,994.3 metric tons of food, worth $511,422.34. The Near East Relief paid cash for this food and were responsible for its delivery. For the purpose of this report this latter delivery is credited to the American Relief Administration under cash sales. The credit also belongs to the Near East Relief, which would bring their total deliveries during this period as reported here up to 32,651.3 metric tons, with a value of $9,222,894.34.

The work of the Near East Relief in the Reconstruction Period will be discussed in a later section (page 122).

Jewish Joint Distribution Committee

At the very outbreak of the war in 1914, American Jewry recognized there would be need for alleviating the inevitable suffering of war. At that time, American Jews were primarily interested in bringing relief to the suffering Jews in Palestine. Early in 1915 there was organized the Joint Distribution Committee for General

[1] Cf. pages 194–95, and Table 326, pages 616–25.

Relief in Palestine, and during the period up to the Armistice approximately $1,750,000.00 was raised by American Jews and expended for relief work in the Holy Land.

When the Armistice raised the curtain of censorship on Central and Eastern Europe, it disclosed the appalling sight of millions of persons facing starvation and the ravages of disease. The American Jewish Joint Distribution Committee was one of the several organizations which immediately went to work to alleviate such of this suffering as they could. Throughout the terrible winter of 1919–1920 and the succeeding years, this organization worked in all the countries of Europe and finally did valiant service in fighting the famine in Russia in 1921, 1922, and 1923. Throughout this work its relief was administered without prejudice to the race, religion, or politics of the recipient. Naturally, its effort was directed largely to countries where there was a considerable proportion of Jews in the population, but its relief was on the basis of need, not religion.

During the period from 1914 to 1924, the Joint Distribution Committee collected in America, and expended in Europe and contiguous territory, the enormous sum of more than $60,000,000. Its relief work was carried on in forty-one different countries.

Throughout the whole period the Joint Distribution Committee worked in close co-operation with the American Relief Administration. It is our purpose in these pages to refer only to those operations in which the two organizations were involved as shown by the records and accounts of the American Relief Administration.

This co-operation began early in 1919, or almost immediately after the Armistice, and extended to the close of the Russian operations in 1923. Table 31 presents in summary form the extent of the co-operation between these two organizations, and includes work done during both the Armistice and the Reconstruction periods. The work of the Committee during the Armistice will be discussed in the following pages, while the work after August, 1919, will be referred to in a later section (page 121).

The first co-operation between the two organizations occurred early in the relief work of 1919. It will be remembered that Mr. Hoover, before sailing from the United States in November, 1918, had arranged for the immediate shipment of large quantities of food supplies to be financed temporarily by the War Department and by the Food Administration Grain Corporation. Mr. Hoover proposed, if necessary, to place these foodstuffs in store in strategic points in Europe pending the settlement of some means of financing these to the stricken countries. Among the first cargoes to be loaded by the Grain Corporation was that of the "Westward Ho," which

TABLE 31

Summary of Total Relief Operations of the Joint Distribution Committee Carried on in Co-operation with the American Relief Administration

Country	Armistice Period	Reconstruction Period	Total Value
Austria	$ 363,760.00	$ 200,000.00	$ 563,760.00
Poland	3,412,497.00	323,555.00	3,736,052.00
Roumania ..	256,000.00	....	256,000.00
Siberia	75,000.00	....	75,000.00
Russia	....	4,396,129.34	4,396,129.34
Total ...	$4,107,257.00	$4,919,684.34	$9,026,941.34

sailed from New York January 26, 1919, with a cargo of flour, milk, and fats, totaling 6,486 metric tons and valued at $2,000,000. Prior to this, the Joint Distribution Committee had sent investigators into Poland, and their reports, together with those obtained by the American Relief Administration, indicated the urgent need of immediate help. In the meantime, Mr. Hoover had not been able to perfect satisfactory arrangements with the Allies, nor to secure definite finance for the relief to Poland. He therefore proposed to the Joint Distribution Committee that they purchase and distribute the cargo of the "Westward Ho."

Although this was relief on a larger scale than hitherto contemplated by the J.D.C., they were able to raise immediately the money for the purchase of one-half of this cargo, and to arrange with the Polish National Department, a Polish-American organization, to donate the other half. The "Westward Ho," I,[1] arrived in Danzig, February 25, 1919, and arrangements were made for its immediate distribution in Poland, thus constituting one of the first large pieces of actual relief work in the Armistice Period.

The Joint Distribution Committee undertook many phases of the relief work on their own

[1] Roman numerals refer to the voyage number.

responsibility. So far as direct co-operation with the Director General of Relief in 1919 was concerned, the principal J.D.C. deliveries were made to Poland and consisted besides the "Westward Ho," I, mentioned above, of a portion of the cargo of the "Westward Ho," II, and of the "Schwarzenfels" as well as Army Liquidation supplies transported from France in the "Kerowlee," "Lake Clear," IV, "Lake Clear," V, "Lake Eckhart," V, and "Democracy," II. Smaller amounts were also delivered to Roumania, Austria, and Siberia during this period.

Table 32 gives the total tons and value of these deliveries, while Table 125 (Appendix) gives the details by cargoes and countries.

TABLE 32

SUMMARY OF RELIEF DELIVERIES BY THE JOINT DISTRIBUTION COMMITTEE IN CO-OPERATION WITH THE DIRECTOR GENERAL OF RELIEF—ARMISTICE PERIOD, 1919

Country	Total Metric Tons	Total Value
Austria	901.3	$ 363,760.00
Poland	9,705.8	3,412,497.00
Roumania	382.0	256,000.00
Siberia	40.0	75,000.00
Total	11,029.1	$4,107,257.00

THE AMERICAN NATIONAL RED CROSS

The splendid work of the American Red Cross is too well known to call for extended comment here. During the war this organization collected and expended vast sums of money. After the Armistice and during the Reconstruction Period, it maintained relief activities in nearly every country in Europe. From 1914 to the end of 1923, the American Red Cross collected and expended some $350,000,000. A very considerable portion of this was used for work in Europe, both during the war and afterward. It is impossible, readily, to extract from the Annual Reports of the American Red Cross a definite figure, which would represent the expenditures for purely relief work in Europe during these years. It is evident, however, from an examination of these reports, that such expenditures would exceed $200,000,000.

Naturally, the work of the American Red Cross was largely in the field of medical relief and related activities. However, like any versatile organization, they not infrequently found that food and clothing relief was essential to supplement any relief from disease which they might render. A very substantial portion of the Red Cross expenditures in Europe were for food and clothing.

In addition they carried on an active campaign for children's relief in these countries. Again they stressed the medical phase of relief, but by no means neglected food and clothing, where these were essential.

The major portion of the activities of the American Red Cross was carried on quite independently of the American Relief Administration, although where there was any reason for co-operation, these two organizations worked hand-in-hand for the common cause. As in the case of other charitable organizations, we have included in this report only those activities of the American Red Cross which were conducted in close co-operation with the organizations which Mr. Hoover directed. Table 33 sum-

TABLE 33

SUMMARY OF TOTAL RELIEF OPERATIONS BY THE AMERICAN RED CROSS, CARRIED ON IN CO-OPERATION WITH THE AMERICAN RELIEF ADMINISTRATION

Country	Armistice Period	Reconstruction Period	Total Value
Armenia	$ 258,600.00	$ 500,000.00	$ 758,600.00
Czechoslovakia	175,040.00	....	175,040.00
Esthonia	89,800.00	....	89,800.00
Finland	56,400.00	....	56,400.00
Greece	....	1,211,949.95	1,211,949.95
Jugoslavia	224,800.00	....	224,800.00
Poland	813,800.00	....	813,800.00
South Russia	123,300.00	....	123,300.00
Soviet Republics	....	3,804,863.15	3,804,863.15
Total	$1,741,740.00	$5,516,813.10	$7,258,553.10

TABLE 34

SUMMARY OF RELIEF DELIVERIES BY THE AMERICAN RED CROSS IN CO-OPERATION WITH THE DIRECTOR GENERAL OF RELIEF—ARMISTICE PERIOD, 1919

Country	Metric Tons Transported by A.R.A.	Metric Tons Transported by A.R.C.	Total Metric Tons	Total Value
Armenia	754.1	......	754.1	$ 258,600.00
Czechoslovakia	301.2	574.0	875.2	175,040.00
Esthonia	312.3*	......	312.3	89,800.00
Finland	282.0	......	282.0	56,400.00
Jugoslavia	667.6	......	667.6	224,800.00
Poland	2,177.6*	1,865.0†	4,042.6	813,800.00
South Russia	.....	577.0*	577.0	123,300.00
Total	4,494.8‡	3,016.0	7,510.8	$1,741,740.00

* Medical supplies only.
† Includes 415.0 tons of medical supplies.
‡ Transportation costs of $369,404.95 paid by A.R.A. (Table 143, page 328), not included in total value shown in this table.

marizes these activities as divided between the Armistice and the Reconstruction periods.

Of the total of $7,258,553.10 accounted for in Table 33, only $1,741,740.00 represented relief carried on during the Armistice Period. This latter consisted entirely of clothing and medical relief. A large portion of the former represented second-hand clothing collected in the United States, and transported to Europe by the American Relief Administration. These transportation costs were paid for from the Congressional Appropriation for Relief, as a direct gift to these countries.[1] Table 34 summarizes the American Red Cross deliveries during the Armistice Period, and separates those on which the A.R.A. paid the transportation costs. As shown in Table 126 (Appendix), 4,028.9 tons of the American Red Cross supplies consisted of clothing, and 3,481.9 tons were medical and hospital supplies.

Through numerous conferences between the officials of the American Relief Administration and the American Red Cross, much of the other work of the latter organization was co-ordinated with the work of the Director General of Relief, but the operations discussed here were the only ones where the relations were close enough to be reported through the Paris office of the Director General of Relief.

The work of the American Red Cross in co-operation with the European Children's Fund and other organizations in the Reconstruction Period is discussed in a later section. (Page 116.)

[1] Cf. pages 48 and 135.

JOINT ALLIED FINANCE

Table 14 (page 35) shows the third major operation under the Director General of Relief, in the Armistice Period, as deliveries under Joint Allied Finance. The Act of Congress, approved February 25, 1919, by which a revolving fund of $100,000,000 was created for European relief, expressly stated that this money would be available for the assistance of such population in Europe and contiguous countries as may be determined upon by the President, except Germany, German-Austria, Hungary, Bulgaria, and Mohammedan Turkey. Likewise, it was impossible for the United States Treasury to loan money to these countries which were technically at war with the United States.

These areas were as much in need of relief as the rest of Europe, although perhaps not subject, at that time, to such sympathetic attention. But, as one of the primary objects of the relief work was to prevent anarchy and its spread, and to encourage the establishment of good government, some means had to be found for furnishing relief to these enemies, as well as to our friends.

So far as Germany, Bulgaria, and Turkey were concerned, payment could be effected by the transfer of gold or other forms of securities. Hungary had formed a Communistic government under Bela Kuhn, in close association with the Soviet régime in Russia. Therefore, under the ruling of the Supreme War Council, relief could not be delivered to her in any event.

Austria, on the other hand, was prostrate. The need for relief there was certainly as great as anywhere else in Europe. Some means had to be found by which this situation could be relieved, or else the revolution which must follow in Austria might well render all relief and reconstruction in other parts of Europe of no avail.

After much difficulty, Mr. Hoover, in the latter part of February, 1919, arranged through the United States Treasury, that loans should be made to England, France, and Italy for the purchase of food in the United States, and that these countries in turn would accept Austrian securities for the food delivered. Through this plan the relief to Austria was financed jointly by the United States, United Kingdom, France, and Italy.

TABLE 35

SUMMARY OF DELIVERIES TO AUSTRIA UNDER JOINT ALLIED FINANCE—ARMISTICE PERIOD, 1919

(*Metric Tons*)

Commodity	By United Kingdom	By France	By Italy	Total
Wheat flour...	64,454.3	72,409.5	3,225.0	140,088.8
Cereal flour ..	7,718.2	22,480.4	10,076.0	40,274.6
Wheat grain ..	24,309.8	44,904.3	71,855.0	141,069.1
Rye grain	......	10,190.3	......	10,190.3
Pork products.	......	....	11,374.0	11,374.0
Milk	1,998.0	....	845.0	2,843.0
Total	98,480.3	149,984.5	97,375.0	345,839.8

The preliminary arrangements contemplated the advance of $10,000,000 to each of the three Allies, but it was later found that this would be insufficient, and the amount was increased to $16,000,000 to each country, or a total of $48,000,000 in all. The three Allies agreed that this money should all be available for the purchase of food, and that they would finance the overseas transportation out of separate funds.

The total supplies delivered to Austria for this $48,000,000, as shown in Table 35, amounted to 345,839.8 metric tons, chiefly breadstuffs, but including some 14,000 tons of pork and milk. In addition to the cost of this food in America, the Allies advanced the freight charges amounting to approximately $11,281,250.00.

DELIVERIES BY GREAT BRITAIN

At the time the original arrangement was made, the Austrian food situation was very serious. It was predicted by competent observers that the Austrian Republic could not remain in control much longer unless relief was received. The American Relief Administration therefore arranged to sell to England, against this Treasury loan, 46,283.9 tons of flour and 1,088 tons of milk, then in stock at Trieste. (This transaction by the A.R.A. is accounted for under cash sales in Table 120.) This arrangement, which avoided the long delay necessary in transporting supplies from America, was able to save the situation, and once more tide Austria over the danger point. The details of these deliveries by the American Relief Administration to the United Kingdom for Austria are shown in Table 131 (Appendix).

During August and September, 1919, five steamers with 25,888.6 metric tons of American flour for Austria were delivered at Trieste by the British (Table 130). During this period, the United Kingdom also delivered 910 tons of American milk from surplus stocks in Great Britain. Owing to the delay in turning over the Austrian tonnage to the Allies, it was impossible to complete the British deliveries during September. Five cargoes of wheat grain shipped in former Austrian tonnage were delivered to Austria by the British after September, 1919. No details of these shipments by steamers are available.

Table 36 summarizes the total deliveries to Austria by the United Kingdom under the Joint

TABLE 36

SUMMARY OF DELIVERIES TO AUSTRIA BY GREAT BRITAIN, FINANCED BY UNITED STATES TREASURY LOANS TO GREAT BRITAIN

(*Commodities in Metric Tons*)

	Wheat Flour	Cereal Flour	Wheat	Milk	Total Tons	Total Value
American stocks at Trieste.................	46,283.9	......	....	1,088.0	47,371.9	$10,618,045.72
Direct shipment from America.............	18,170.4	7,718.2	....	......	25,888.6	2,845,451.28
Supplies from Great Britain................	....	......	....	910.0	910.0	300,000.00
Delivered after September	....	......	24,309.8	......	24,309.8	2,236,503.00
Total	64,454.3	7,718.2	24,309.8	1,998.0	98,480.3	$16,000,000.00

Allied Finance arrangement. Further details are shown in Tables 130 and 131.

Deliveries by France

The deliveries to Austria by France under the Joint Allied financial arrangements were all shipped direct from the United States in ex-Austrian steamers, with the exception of three cargoes. These three cargoes were from Australia and destined for Italy under the direction of the Allied Wheat Executive. In May, 1919, the Austrian food supply was so dangerously low that Mr. Hoover succeeded in arranging with the Italians to have these three cargoes diverted to Austria on the French account, and later replaced to Italy by three similar cargoes from America. By this act another serious food crisis in Austria was averted.

The total French deliveries were not completed up to the close of September, but some 18,000 tons of wheat, valued at $1,662,958, were shipped from America at a later date to complete the program.

The details of the French deliveries on the joint finance account are given in Table 129.

The total deliveries by commodities are summarized in Table 35.

Deliveries by Italy

No complete statement has ever been obtained of the actual amounts of American supplies delivered to Austria as the Italian portion of the Joint Allied Finance. Throughout the Armistice Period, the Italians were delivering supplies to Austria, part of which were of Italian origin and part were imported from America. In spite of repeated requests, no separation of these supplies could be obtained. Finally, Mr. Hoover, in a conference with the Italian representative in Paris, came to an agreement on the amount of American foods which they had shipped to Austria. This statement, submitted to the Supreme Economic Council by Mr. Hoover in July, 1919, was as follows:

Commodity	Total Tons	Value F.O.B. New York
Wheat	82,724	$ 7,610,608
Wheat flour	3,225	407,962
Maize flour	10,076	886,688
Lard	12,343	7,405,800
Pork	3,394	2,445,680
Vegetable oil	524	209,600
Condensed milk	845	316,793
Total	113,131	$19,283,131

Inasmuch as the f.o.b. New York value of the above amount totaled more than the $16,000,000 loaned by the United States Treasury, it is clear that some $3,000,000 of this was delivered by the Italians under their own financial arrangements with Austria. Accordingly, we have arbitrarily reduced the amounts in the statement above so that the f.o.b. value totals $16,000,000, and the remainder is added to the direct Italian deliveries.

Table 37 gives a summary of the total supplies which are regarded as having been delivered to Austria, by the Italians, under the joint financial arrangement. The Italians have never submitted a detailed statement to the Director General of Relief showing the ships on which these cargoes were carried.

TABLE 37

Summary of Deliveries to Austria by Italy, Financed by United States Treasury Loan to Italy—Armistice Period, 1919

Commodity	Metric Tons
Wheat	71,855
Wheat flour	3,225
Maize flour	10,076
Pork products	10,850
Vegetable oils	524
Milk	845
Total tons	97,375
Total value, f.o.b. New York	$16,000,000

DELIVERIES BY COUNTRIES OTHER THAN THE UNITED STATES—ARMISTICE PERIOD, 1919[1]

Table 14 (page 35) shows that the fourth and final major operation under the Director General of Relief in the Armistice Period consisted of relief deliveries by countries other than the United States. It will be remembered that the office of Director General of Relief was established by the Inter-Allied Supreme Council of Supply and Relief. One of the chief functions of the Director General was to co-ordinate the relief activities of all the Allied nations in order to secure an equitable distribution of the supplies available in accordance with the needs of

[1] See Appendix Tables 132 to 136.

the various countries. As explained elsewhere (page 28), this co-ordination was accomplished first through the Permanent Committee on Supply and Relief, and later, through the Food Section of the Supreme Economic Council.

While it is true that the United States possessed the bulk of the supplies available for relief, and was also in a position to furnish the major portion of the finance, yet the contributions from other countries totaled to an imposing figure. Table 38 (also Table 107) shows that the total relief deliveries during the Armistice Period from countries other than the United States amounted to 1,139,042.6 metric tons, valued at $238,783,036.92. As in the case of the United States, this includes supplies furnished on credit or as gifts from funds appropriated by various governments, supplies furnished from benevolent funds, as well as cash sales or their equivalent. Furthermore, as in the case of the United States, this is not a complete statement of all relief furnished from these various countries, but only that portion which was handled in co-operation with the Director General of Relief and, hence, was reported to his office.

Approximately three-fourths of the relief accounted for under this heading came from the three major Allies in Europe, the United Kingdom, France, and Italy. The United Kingdom alone contributed about one-half of the value of the total relief from these countries. The supplies furnished by the other countries represented largely commodity exchanges between the several countries, which were arranged through the Director General of Relief.

Table 38 summarizes the deliveries by countries other than the United States, by the countries which furnished the relief, while Table 39 summarizes these same deliveries by the countries to which the supplies were delivered. Further details are shown in Tables 132 *A* and 132 *B* in the Appendix. These tables do not include the supplies handled under the Joint Allied Finance, which has been discussed separately.

TABLE 38

RELIEF DELIVERIES FROM COUNTRIES OTHER THAN THE UNITED STATES, BY COUNTRIES OF ORIGIN*—ARMISTICE PERIOD, 1919

Country	Total Metric Tons	Total Value
Major Allies		
British Empire	491,372.0	$120,171,279.00
France	88,647.0	29,404,724.00†
Italy	139,922.0	37,532,042.00‡
Sub-total, Major Allies	719,941.0	$187,108,045.00
Other Countries		
Argentina	155,000.0	16,774,000.00
Austria	520.0	281,600.00
Czechoslovakia	62,898.0	9,914,858.00
Denmark	10,481.6	1,187,015.92
Germany	330.0	13,200.00
Hungary	8,878.0	805,063.00
Jugoslavia	34,436.0	3,051,611.00
Norway	4,467.0	1,192,130.00
Netherlands	47,458.0	9,897,389.00
Poland	54,026.0	1,204,896.00
Switzerland	40,609.0	7,355,349.00
Polish League of Women	4.1	1,640.00
Russo Carpathian Committee	.5	200.00
Sub-total, Other Countries	419,108.2	$ 51,678,951.92
Total, gross	1,139,049.2	$238,786,996.92
Less transfers to Reconstruction Period	6.6	3,960.00
Grand total, net deliveries	1,139,042.6	$238,783,036.92

* Exclusive of Joint Allied Finance.
† Includes finance on freight for $4,500,000.00.
‡ Includes finance on freight for $2,021,250.00.

TABLE 39

RELIEF DELIVERIES FROM COUNTRIES OTHER THAN THE UNITED STATES, BY COUNTRIES OF DESTINATION—ARMISTICE PERIOD, 1919

Country	Total Metric Tons	Total Value
Armenia	....	$ 71,400.00*
Austria	206,639.3	47,114,365.00
Czechoslovakia	150,644.1	27,669,384.00
Esthonia	9,086.6	2,377,567.92
Finland	17,909.0	3,239,080.00
Germany	597,082.0	124,301,551.00
Jugoslavia	33,655.0	9,635,192.00
Latvia	....	80,920.00*
Lithuania	....	57,120.00*
Poland	21,466.6	7,696,380.00
Roumania	99,788.0	15,428,688.00
Russia (Kouban)	100.0	10,472.00
Sundry Accounts	2,672.0	1,100,917.00
Grand total	1,139,042.6	$238,783,036.92

* Freight payments only.

Deliveries from the British Empire

Early in 1919, the British Treasury voted a credit of £12,000,000 sterling, approximately $59,000,000, for European relief. In addition to this, many private and charitable organizations in the United Kingdom furnished large quantities of supplies either as direct gifts or in return for cash or credit and, finally, the British Government participated in furnishing relief to Germany against cash settlement as in the case of the United States. In addition to the relief from the United Kingdom, Canada and Newfoundland each furnished substantial quantities of relief to Roumania on credit. Canada established a credit of $5,000,000 in favor of Roumania, against which wheat, flour, and agricultural implements to the value of $3,836,600.00 were delivered during the Armistice Period. Newfoundland furnished to Roumania a cargo of fish, valued at $1,566,040. The total relief deliveries from the British Empire, as accounted for in this report for the Armistice Period, may be summarized as in Table 40.

TABLE 40

Summary of Relief Deliveries from the British Empire—Armistice Period, 1919

Furnished by	Total Metric Tons	Total Value
United Kingdom	450,832.0	$114,768,639.00
Canada	38,184.0	3,836,600.00
Newfoundland	2,356.0	1,566,040.00
Total	491,372.0	$120,171,279.00

As pointed out above, the relief from Canada and Newfoundland was furnished to Roumania. Table 41 summarizes the deliveries from the United Kingdom, by country of destination.

It will be noted that the United Kingdom financed the freight and other charges on relief supplies to the extent of $7,063,820.00, leaving the value of commodities furnished as $107,704,810.00. Included in the finance on freight is $4,760,000 for Austria, which represents the freight and other charges on the supplies delivered under the Joint Allied Finance as discussed elsewhere. The remainder of the freight finance consisted chiefly of the cost of transporting from French ports supplies sold to the liberated countries by the United States Liquidation Commission. The United Kingdom transported more than 80,000 tons of these supplies, and thus contributed very materially to the relief of these countries. In addition to these direct contributions, the United Kingdom furnished large amounts of shipping for both the liberated and enemy countries as indicated in Table 184, page 392. In this period of world shortage of shipping, Great Britain bore also the burden of supplementing the tonnage required for transporting to France and Italy their share of the Allied cereal program and other necessary foodstuffs.

TABLE 41

Summary of Relief Deliveries from the United Kingdom, by Countries of Destination—Armistice Period, 1919

Country	Finance On Freight	Total Metric Tons	Total Value Including Freight
Armenia	$ 71,400.00	....	$ 71,400.00
Austria	4,760,000.00	18,000.0	6,676,640.00
Czechoslovakia ...	....	7,132.0	1,599,836.00
Esthonia	309,400.00	8,624.0	2,342,360.00
Finland	....	3,467.0	920,250.00
Germany ...	....	299,144.0	75,653,861.00
Jugoslavia ..	373,660.00	33,655.0	9,635,192.00
Latvia	80,920.00	....	80,920.00
Lithuania ...	57,120.00	....	57,120.00
Poland	1,389,920.00	21,462.0	7,694,540.00
Roumania ..	21,420.00	59,248.0	10,026,048.00
Russia (Kouban)	....	100.0	10,472.00
Total	$7,063,840.00	450,832.0	$114,768,639.00

Of the 450,832.0 metric tons of relief supplies furnished by the United Kingdom in cooperation with the Director General of Relief, the major portion, 299,144.0 tons, valued at $75,653,861.00, represented cash sales to Germany under the Brussels agreement. The remaining 151,688.0 tons, with a sales value of $32,050,949.00, represents almost entirely relief furnished on credit. The freight finance was also a credit transaction, making a total of $39,114,778.00, which was largely furnished during the Armistice Period out of the British Treasury credits. The remainder of the British credits of $59,500,000 was used chiefly in assistance to Central European countries after the Armistice Period and are not included here.[1]

[1] For an account of the British relief work, the reader is referred to reports by Sir William Goode, *Economic Conditions in Central Europe,* Miscellaneous Series No. 1 (1920), Cmd. 521, and Miscellaneous No. 6 (1920), Cmd. 641.

It should also be said that some of the deliveries accounted for above represent sales for cash by British dealers, and some benevolent deliveries by British charitable organizations. No complete separation of these operations was ever furnished to the Director General of Relief, but from the information available it seems certain that such deliveries included in these figures would amount to less than $3,000,000. They include, chiefly, certain cash sales to Finland and certain benevolent deliveries in Jugoslavia.

In addition to any figures included in this report, there were many British organizations which carried on important relief operations during the Armistice Period, but which, like many American organizations, were working quite independently of the Director General of Relief. Among these organizations may be mentioned the British Red Cross, Friends' Emergency and War Victims' Relief Committee, and the Lady Muriel Paget's Mission.

Deliveries by France

France had suffered severely in the war. The whole of Northern France had been devastated. Her own people were in need of all the assistance which the French Government could furnish. Under these circumstances, it was not expected that France could play the same part in the relief of other countries that the United States or Great Britain could undertake. Nevertheless, during the Armistice Period, France furnished a total of 88,647.0 metric tons of relief supplies of a total value of $29,404,724.00 (Table 38). The latter includes $4,500,000 as finance on the freight and insurance of supplies to Austria furnished under Joint Allied Finance.

Table 42 summarizes the total deliveries by France exclusive of the Joint Allied Finance.

Of the total deliveries by France, 69,404.0 metric tons, valued at $16,262,889.00, represented sales to Germany under the Brussels agreement. Germany paid for these supplies chiefly through the exchange of commodities and not through the transfer of gold as in the case of supplies furnished by the United States and Great Britain. Of the supplies furnished to Germany by France, 55,000 tons consisted of oil seeds from French provinces in Africa. The remainder consisted of flour, pork products, and miscellaneous foods, chiefly army rations.[1]

[1] See Table 134, Appendix.

French deliveries to Czechoslovakia consisted chiefly of rice, beans, and pork products. Of this amount, 20 tons of flour and 20 tons of rice represented a gift from the French Government to Czechoslovakian children's relief, while the remainder was exchanged for 20,000 tons of sugar.

TABLE 42

Summary of Relief Deliveries from France, by Countries of Destination—Armistice Period, 1919

Country	Total Metric Tons	Total Value
Austria	....	$ 4,500,000.00
Czechoslovakia	16,571.0	7,540,918.00
Germany	69,404.0	16,262,889.00
Sundry (Russian prisoners)	2,672.0	1,100,917.00
Total	88,647.0	$29,404,724.00

The deliveries under Sundry Activities represent supplies furnished by France for Russian prisoners of war in Germany. These prisoners were in a pitiful condition because of the food shortage in Germany. France undertook to assist them pending their repatriation. Of the 2,672 tons furnished to these prisoners, 1,622 tons represent commodities delivered by the American Relief Administration from the President's National Security and Defense Fund, but which were subsequently paid for by France (cf. page 49). The whole of the relief to the Russian prisoners represents a benevolent gift from France.

Deliveries by Italy

Italy, like France, was in no position to render a large amount of assistance in the relief of other European countries. However, as shown in Table 38, Italy did furnish a total of 139,922.0 metric tons of a total value of $37,532,042.00. This is exclusive of Italy's share in the commodity deliveries to Austria under the Joint Allied Finance, but it does include $2,021,250.00 paid by Italy as freight and insurance on the Joint Allied Finance deliveries. As summarized in Table 43, Italy's contributions during the Armistice Period were confined to deliveries to Austria and Czechoslovakia. With the exception of the freight referred to above, all of these operations were in the nature of cash transactions. The commodities furnished by Italy to these countries were paid for through the exchange of other commodities or by concessions.

TABLE 43

SUMMARY OF RELIEF DELIVERIES FROM ITALY, BY COUNTRIES OF DESTINATION—ARMISTICE PERIOD, 1919*

Country	Total Metric Tons	Total Value
Austria	64,061.0	$20,878,122.00†
Czechoslovakia	75,861.0	16,653,920.00
Total	139,922.0	$37,532,042.00

* See Table 135 for details.
† Includes $2,021,250.00 as freight on commodities delivered under Joint Allied Finance.

DELIVERIES BY COUNTRIES OTHER THAN THE MAJOR ALLIES

Table 38 shows a total of 419,108.2 metric tons, valued at $51,678,951.92, delivered during the Armistice Period by countries other than the three major Allies. Of the amounts shown in that table, the delivery of 155,000.0 tons, valued at $16,774,000.00, from Argentina, represents wheat for which Germany was able to negotiate credit. The deliveries by the Polish League of Women, the Russo Carpathian Committee, and 25 tons of codliver oil from Norway represent benevolent gifts. All of the remainder represents barter transactions involving the exchange of commodities between these countries and, in principal, were cash transactions. These exchanges were arranged, through the Director General of Relief, to take care of surpluses of certain commodities in one country and shortages in others. The trade barriers between these newly established nations had not yet been adjusted so that such transactions could take place between the normal commercial agencies, and the intervention of the Director General of Relief was necessary to bring about these exchanges, which were mutually advantageous to both sides. Table 44 summarizes the total deliveries from these thirteen sources, by the countries of destination. Table 136 (Appendix) shows the destination of the deliveries from each country of origin.

TABLE 44

SUMMARY OF RELIEF DELIVERIES FROM COUNTRIES OTHER THAN THE MAJOR ALLIES, BY COUNTRIES OF DESTINATION*—ARMISTICE PERIOD, 1919

Country	Total Metric Tons	Total Value
Austria	124,578.3	$15,059,603.00
Czechoslovakia	51,080.1	1,874,710.00
Esthonia	462.6	35,207.92
Finland	14,442.0	2,318,830.00
Germany	228,534.0	32,384,801.00
Poland	4.6	1,840.00
Total	419,101.6	$51,674,991.92
Accounted for in Reconstruction Period	6.6	3,960.00
Grand total	419,108.2	$51,678,951.92

* It should be pointed out that only food and related relief commodities concerned in these transactions were reported to the Director General of Relief. Very often food supplies from one country would be paid for by coal, machinery, or manufactured goods from the other. In general, these latter commodities are not included in these tables.

PURCHASES OF UNITED STATES ARMY SUPPLIES[1]—ARMISTICE PERIOD, 1919

Before Mr. Hoover sailed from the United States in November, 1918, he had arranged with the War Department, upon the authorization of President Wilson, that the United States Army Quartermaster should ship from army stocks in the United States approximately 120,000 short tons (108,863 metric tons) of wheat flour, 20,000 short tons (18,144 metric tons) of pork products, and 4,000 short tons (3,629 metric tons) of milk. These supplies were shipped by the Army in its own tonnage and constituted what was known as the Southern Relief Program. The ships, twenty-one in number, all sailed for Gibraltar as a port of call, and from there were directed to Adriatic or Black Sea ports for discharge. For the most part these cargoes were unloaded into warehouses by the Army, and were then invoiced to the American Relief Administration, at a c.i.f. price, as they were needed in the relief operations. In all of these transactions, the London office of the Food Administration Grain Corporation acted as the fiscal agent, undertaking the settlement with the Army, and in turn, securing either cash or obligations from the governments to which the supplies were delivered.

The Army ships which sailed on this first Southern Relief program and were discharged under this agreement were as follows:

[1] See Appendix Tables 138 to 142 inclusive.

Southern Relief Army Ships

Discharged at Adriatic Ports

Canoga	West Alcasco
Cape Lookout	Westerner
Durham	Western Hope
East Wind	Western Plains (part)
Mount Shasta	Western Scout
Nantahala	West Kyska, I
Oregonian	West Lashaway, I
Sudbury	Williamantic

Discharged at Black Sea Ports

Englewood	West Mahomet
Maine	Western Plains (part)
West Eldara	West Mount

The total tonnage delivered from these Army cargoes amounted to 124,709.2 metric tons, for which the invoiced value amounted to $35,111,425.34. The charges on these shipments, including the actual cost of the commodities plus all transportation and handling charges, were paid to the Army Quartermaster by the Grain Corporation.

The American Relief Administration, also, purchased from the United States Liquidation Commission, large quantities of supplies from surplus Army stocks at French ports. The total direct purchases from the Liquidation Commission amounted to 69,624.1 metric tons of a total value of $18,308,655.58.

The total purchases of relief supplies from the United States Army are summarized in Table 138, showing a total of 194,323.3 metric tons, with a value of $53,420,080.92.

Adriatic Ports

Table 139 (Appendix) gives the details of purchases from the United States Army Quartermaster at Trieste and Adriatic ports, by Quartermaster (Q.M.) invoices and by cargoes. The total purchase, as shown by this table, consisted of the following:

Commodities	Metric Tons
Flour	77,446.5
Pork products	7,230.8
Lard	2,470.8
Lard substitute	1,116.7
Milk	1,361.0
Total tons	89,625.8
Total value	$25,428,013.84

These commodities were delivered to the various countries and for various relief purposes, including sales to governments, children's relief, and miscellaneous cash sales. Table 45 summarizes the total quantities and values delivered to each country, and for each relief project. The details of these deliveries are given in the Appendix Tables for the respective countries.

TABLE 45

Summary of Relief Deliveries of Army Stocks from Adriatic Ports—Armistice Period, 1919

Delivered to	Total Metric Tons	Total Value
Austria, Children's Relief	50.8	$ 37,679.59
Jugoslavia, Children's Relief	200.3	86,930.55
Czechoslovakia, Children's Relief	54.4	38,605.26
Jugoslavia	24,092.9	6,652,118.60
Czechoslovakia	34,591.1	10,360,307.47
Austria	3,680.6	2,047,811.35
Great Britain	21,349.5	4,706,713.64
Italy	4,686.4	1,033,158.45
Hungary	319.1	245,519.96
Miscellaneous cash sales	600.7	219,168.97
Total	89,625.8	$25,428,013.84

The Children's Relief deliveries to Jugoslavia and Czechoslovakia were paid for out of the $100,000,000 Congressional appropriation, while those to Austria were paid for from the President's National Security and Defense Fund. The deliveries to the governments of Czechoslovakia and Jugoslavia were paid from United States Treasury loans. The deliveries to Austria and Hungary were paid for in cash. Deliveries to Italy represent a relief cargo turned over to Italy to avert a serious food shortage. This was paid for through the Wheat Executive in London. The deliveries to Great Britain represent part of the Joint Allied Finance for the Relief of Austria (see page 60). The miscellaneous cash sales represented small sales to individuals or local organizations, or to United States Army or Navy officers' messes in these localities.

Constantinople and Black Sea Ports

Table 140 (Appendix) gives the details of the American Relief Administration purchases from the Army Quartermaster at Constantinople (Istanbul) and Black Sea Ports, by cargoes, and by countries or agencies to which the supplies were delivered. These purchases consisted of the following:

Commodities	Metric Tons
Wheat flour	31,136.9
Pork products	1,972.2
Lard	986.9
Milk	977.4
Total tons	35,073.4
Total value	$9,683,411.50

Table 46 summarizes these deliveries according to destination and use.

TABLE 46

SUMMARY OF RELIEF DELIVERIES FROM ARMY STOCKS AT CONSTANTINOPLE AND BLACK SEA PORTS—ARMISTICE PERIOD, 1919

Delivered to	Total Metric Tons	Total Value
Roumania, Children's Relief..	40.0	$ 28,750.00
Roumania	19,405.7	5,905,760.02
Armenia	464.9	145,527.00
American Commission for Relief in Near East	1,217.4	340,503.68
J. W. Whittall & Co. (Turkey)	8,591.1	2,083,437.80
Bulgaria	4,010.9	882,387.00
French Army	907.2	200,000.00
Russian Volunteer Army	394.0	86,680.00
Miscellaneous cash sales	42.2	10,366.00
Total	35,073.4	$9,683,411.50

The deliveries for Roumanian Children's Relief and to the Government of Armenia were paid for from the $100,000,000 Congressional appropriation. For the Armenian deliveries the Relief Administration took notes which were turned over to the Treasury. The Children's Relief was a direct gift as explained elsewhere. The deliveries to the American Commission for Relief in the Near East were destined for Armenia, but represent supplies which were purchased for cash from the American Relief Administration.

The sales to J. W. Whittall and Company represent purchases by a British syndicate in Turkey, which was organized to purchase and sell foodstuffs to the Turkish population at a nominal profit in order to relieve some of the distress in that country (see page 265). The deliveries to Bulgaria were paid for in gold as discussed elsewhere (page 164). The other deliveries were all sales, for cash, of supplies which were urgently needed, but which could not be secured locally because of the breakdown in commercial operations.

In the majority of instances, the sales from these Army stocks represent only a fraction of the deliveries made to the respective countries or agencies, and the reader is referred to other sections of this report for further details regarding these.

PURCHASES FROM THE UNITED STATES LIQUIDATION COMMISSION

As discussed elsewhere in this report, the United States Liquidation Commission, in 1919, made large sales of American Army surplus stock in France to many European countries. These transactions, in so far as they related to food and relief supplies, were carried on in close co-operation with the American Relief Administration. It was found that certain of these surplus stocks could be used to advantage in some of the A.R.A. relief programs and that they could be purchased at prices which would permit their transportation from French ports in competition with supplies direct from the United States. As shown in Table 141 (Appendix), the American Relief Administration purchased from the Liquidation Commission a total of 69,624.1 metric tons of these supplies, with a total delivered sales value of $18,308,655.58.

These purchases consisted of the following:

Commodities	Metric Tons
Wheat flour	54,336.1
Cereal flour	1,376.3
Rice	2,691.1
Beans and peas	434.9
Pork products	6,982.5
Milk	2,723.4
Clothing	52.0
Miscellaneous commodities	1,023.2
Soap	4.6
Total tons	69,624.1
Total sales value	$18,308,655.58

These supplies as sold by the Commission were in store in various French ports, and for the most part, they had to be transported by the American Relief Administration to North Baltic, or other ports, where they could be delivered on the relief programs to the several countries. This transportation was handled chiefly by a fleet of "Lake" boats, which the Grain Corporation had chartered from the United States Shipping Board in order to transport supplies from Rotterdam and other North Sea and Channel ports up to the Baltic countries.[1]

The supplies purchased were stored principally at the three French ports of Bordeaux, Marseilles, and St. Nazaire, although considerable amounts of flour were turned over at interior warehouses.

Table 142 (Appendix) shows the detail of the total purchases at the several locations, and shows that the principal supplies were at Bordeaux and St. Nazaire.

This table also shows the total deliveries of these supplies to the country of destination and by the French ports from which they were shipped. The deliveries from internal warehouses in France are lumped together in this table and will be discussed later.

The same table also gives the movement of these supplies by vessels, and by destination. With the exception of the flour deliveries to France, all of the supplies from Bordeaux and St. Nazaire were moved by vessels chartered by the American Relief Administration. From Bordeaux, 12,512.3 metric tons were moved in eight cargoes to the ports of Hamburg, Libau, Riga, and Reval. The bulk of these supplies were delivered to the governments of Czechoslovakia and Latvia, with smaller amounts going to Esthonia, Lithuania, and Northwest Russia. Many of these commodities were also used for child feeding in Austria, Czechoslovakia, Esthonia, Latvia, and Jugoslavia. The remaining 16,250.1 tons from Bordeaux represents flour delivered to France.

Ten cargoes, carrying 19,041.8 tons of flour, pork, and milk, were shipped from St. Nazaire to the ports of Hamburg, Danzig, Viborg, and Reval. The bulk of these supplies were delivered to the governments of Poland, Northwest Russia, and Czechoslovakia. Relatively large amounts of these supplies were also used for child feeding in Poland, and smaller amounts in Esthonia and Czechoslovakia. The remainder of the supplies from St. Nazaire, consisting of 2,098.2 tons of flour, were delivered to the French Government.

The American Relief Administration had no vessels on the Mediterranean, and it was necessary to handle the shipments from Marseilles in a different manner. Mr. Hoover learned that the Roumanians had some small vessels available and suggested that they should send these to Marseilles and undertake themselves to transport such supplies as could be made available to them. Three Roumanian vessels were sent to Marseilles under this arrangement, and transported a total of 6,742.3 metric tons of Army food, of which 300 tons were used for Roumanian Children's Relief and the remainder went to the government. The Roumanian Government financed the transportation of these supplies, which were sold to them at Marseilles on United States Treasury credit.

The fourth cargo of supplies from Marseilles was that of the "Kickapoo," a United States Shipping Board vessel which the American Relief Administration chartered for this voyage. As discussed elsewhere (see page 150), this vessel carried chiefly agricultural implements and miscellaneous supplies, which were bartered to the peasants in the Kouban (South Russia) for surplus wheat, which in turn was delivered to Armenia.

Of the deliveries of Army supplies at interior French warehouses, 52.0 tons of clothing and 4.6 tons of soap were obtained at Montoir in northwestern France, and were shipped to Czechoslovakia by rail. Here they were used in connection with the Children's Relief operations.

The remainder of the supplies from interior warehouses represented flour, which the United States Liquidation Commission had sold to the Esthonian Government, but which the French Government refused to permit them to move out of France because of the severe flour shortage there at that time. Mr. Hoover finally solved the difficulty by arranging for the French to pay the American Relief Administration for this flour, and the latter organization delivered other foodstuffs to Esthonia in place of the flour for which Esthonia had given notes to the United Stated Liquidation Commission. The 9,996.7 tons of flour delivered to France from interior warehouses represents the flour originally sold to Esthonia.

The total sales of Army flour to France by the American Relief Administration are shown by United States Army Quartermaster invoices in Table 47.

[1] See pages 130–33 for further details.

TABLE 47

SALES OF AMERICAN ARMY FLOUR TO FRANCE BY THE AMERICAN RELIEF ADMINISTRATION—ARMISTICE PERIOD, 1919

Q.M.C. Invoices (Paris Division) Invoice No.	Metric Tons	Value
12	6,797.844	$1,087,655.04
17	2,587.142	413,942.72
25	1,877.756	300,440.96
28	1,177.472	188,395.55
29	2,851.039	456,166.24
30	360.737	57,717.92
43	536.001	85,760.16
44	67.668	10,826.88
45	451.441	72,230.56
71 (Replaces No. 54)	336.804	53,888.64
56	1,905.647	304,903.52
57	2,370.896	379,343.36
58	2,125.842	340,134.72
60	286.029	45,764.64
61	715.689	114,510.24
62	345.142	55,222.72
63	4,721.453	755,432.45
64	684.336	109,493.76
Total	30,198.938	$4,831,830.08

Table 48 shows the sources of these deliveries, by warehouses. Of the deliveries from interior warehouses, the bulk of the flour for France came from Montierchaume, and the remainder from scattered warehouses in different parts of the country.

TABLE 48

SUMMARY OF FLOUR DELIVERIES TO FRANCE FROM AMERICAN ARMY WAREHOUSES—ARMISTICE PERIOD, 1919

Location of Warehouse	Metric Tons	Total Value
St. Nazaire	2,098.244	$ 335,719.04
Bordeaux	16,250.130	2,600,020.80
Marseilles	1,853.900	296,604.52
Interior warehouses	9,996.664	1,599,485.72
Total	30,198.938	$4,831,830.08

EXCHANGE REMITTANCES

The urgent need for greater food supplies in the war-torn countries of Central and Eastern Europe, in 1919, has already been emphasized. This food was needed not only to save lives, but also to stabilize the newly formed governments in these liberated countries. A hungry and starving population forms fertile soil for the spread of anarchy and bolshevism. To provide even the most necessary relief for these peoples required the mobilization of every form of credit which could be obtained. Public and private charity and government loans were being utilized to the utmost, but still there was not enough.

It was well known that there were thousands of Americans who had relatives or friends in Central and Eastern Europe, whom they would be glad to assist, but since all forms of communication had been severed during the war and in most instances had not been re-established, they had no way of transmitting that assistance.

Mr. Hoover conceived that here was a relatively large reservoir of credit which might be mobilized to assist in the relief work. Accordingly negotiations were entered into with the Federal Reserve Board, and with the several European governments, which terminated in plans to facilitate exchange remittances. Under the plan worked out, the Federal Reserve Board issued an order prohibiting the purchase of foreign exchange by dealers in the United States for certain specifically named countries, except from the American Relief Administration. The Relief Administration undertook to secure the needed local currency from the government in which the payee was located. The A.R.A. then retained the dollar value, which was placed to the credit of the government to be used in purchasing food supplies, or for other purposes which the government might indicate.

In the practical operation of the plan, a banker in an American city would receive an application from an individual to transmit a sum of money to a friend or relative in Poland, for example. The banker would remit this sum together with the application to the American Relief Administration in New York. The New York office cabled Mr. Hoover's office in Paris daily the total amount of the remittances received for each country. The Paris office forwarded this information to the A.R.A. Missions in the respective countries, and they, in turn, notified the governments of the amounts of currency which would be required when the schedules arrived by mail. On the arrival of the schedules, the A.R.A. saw to it that the local governments deposited the required currency in the designated banks, where it was available to the payee. It was certain that a considerable number of remittances would be made for persons who could not be found by the disbursing bank. The Relief Administration undertook to see that these sums were returned to the remitting bank, but without interest. There were many safeguards to insure safety and accuracy in handling these remittances, which space will not permit us to discuss here.

The Exchange Remittance plan was put into operation on April 23, 1919, and continued until June 30, 1919, by which time conditions had become more stable, and the general relief operations were drawing to a close. During this short period of less than ten weeks the total number of remittances sold was 17,216, with a total value of $8,900,676.29. Of this amount remittances to the value of $2,428,820.14 were refunded either because the payee could not be located, or because satisfactory arrangements could not be made with the government of the designated country.

There were also remittances to the amount of $111,715.26, which were executed by the United States Grain Corporation, either because they had facilities for handling them, or because these countries needed special credits to meet obligations due to the Grain Corporation. There remained therefore a net total of $6,360,140.89 in executed remittances, which were accounted for on the books of the American Relief Administration.

In the beginning, arrangements were made to put the exchange remittance plan in operation in eight countries, namely: Bulgaria, Czechoslovakia, Finland, Austria, Jugoslavia, Poland, Roumania, and Turkey. Later on, the arrangements with Bulgaria and Turkey were canceled, all remittances to those countries returned, and Germany was added to the list.

As indicated above, the dollar credits arising from these exchange transactions were held by the American Relief Administration for the credit of the respective governments. The major portion of these credits were turned over by the governments to the A.R.A., European Children's Fund for child-feeding work. A portion was drawn upon by the respective governments for the purchase of food supplies in the United States, and a portion was used for the European Technical Advisers in connection with the rehabilitation of the industry and commerce of these countries. The following summary shows the disposition of the Exchange Remittance Fund according to these several requirements.

Summary of Disposition of Exchange Remittance Credits

A.R.A., E.C.F., for child feeding	$3,824,683.35
Account of governments	1,775,005.53
European Technical Advisers	759,997.72
Refund adjustments	454.29
Total	$6,360,140.89

The detailed summaries of the Exchange Remittance operations showing remittance by countries of destination, sources of remittances, and the disposition of funds by countries are shown in Tables 179–182.

EUROPEAN TECHNICAL ADVISERS

Throughout the entire relief work, and particularly in 1919, Mr. Hoover was constantly bending his efforts toward the economic rehabilitation of the war-torn countries. The immediate job was to get food to these people to prevent actual starvation, but Mr. Hoover perceived that charitable relief could only be temporary and that the solution of their difficulties lay in the revival of industry and commerce. If the people could be put to work they would have money with which to buy the food they needed. Consequently, we find, time after time, that Mr. Hoover was making concrete suggestions to these governments as to how they might stimulate industry and trade, and put it on a firm foundation. Through the reorganization of the transport and communication systems in these countries, the A.R.A. was itself laying the foundations for such revival.

As early as March, 1919, Mr. Hoover suggested to Mr. Paderewski, the Prime Minister of Poland, that a Commission of Polish business men should be set up and provided with local and foreign credits as a revolving fund for the purpose of buying such commodities as Poland needed from foreign countries, and of selling in foreign markets the products of Polish industry and agriculture. It proved impossible to put such a plan into operation at that time, but after the peace treaty M. Paderewski requested Mr. Hoover to outline this plan. Mr. Hoover did this in a long letter addresesd to the Prime Minister under date of August 17, 1919.[1] Many of the features of this plan were put into actual operation by Poland, and were of great assistance in starting the wheels of industry and commerce in this new country.

Mr. Hoover also made many similar suggestions to the governments of other Central and Eastern European states, all of which were of material help in the period following the peace treaty. Among these suggestions was one to the effect that they should employ certain technical advisers, particularly American engineers, who could assist in the rehabilitation of trade and industry. It was Mr. Hoover's belief that, in addition to the technical help which such an engineer could render, the presence of a prominent American on the staffs of these governments would inspire confidence and greatly facilitate trade negotiations. Since most of the finance and the supplies needed would have to be obtained in the United States, it was important that such an adviser should be an American.

The following quotations from a letter which Mr. Hoover addressed to Dr. Edouard Beneš, the representative of the Czechoslovakian Government in Paris, will make clear the objects which it was hoped would be accomplished by this plan. This letter, dated July 11, 1919, read in part as follows:

Dear Doctor Beneš:

The suggestion that I made to you this morning in connection with transportation matters in Czecho-Slovakia is as follows:

It appears to us from the experience we have had with transportation questions in Central Europe that Czecho-Slovakia is in vital need of securing an eminent American Engineer, with a few assistants, to act as Transportation Advisor of the government. Aside from the intrinsic advantage of the skill of such a gentleman, there are other reasons which appear to me are pertinent for taking such an action during the forthcoming year.

First, the Czecho-Slovak Government will probably be in need of railway material and finance from the United States and, if their Transportation Advisor is an American Engineer of standing, his reports will be of the greatest possible use in negotiations for such finance.

Second, the Czecho-Slovak Government will need to continue to set up further railway relationship with the surrounding governments and, in view of the antagonistic feeling in many of these countries, an eminent American could be of a great deal of use in conduct of such negotiations. All of these governments will be seeking American assistance and the presence of an eminent American on the Czecho-Slovak Government staff would contribute, I am sure, towards practical and amiable settlement of transportation problems outside of Czecho-Slovakia. As you know, during the last six months we have carried on a general transportation service throughout Europe in the conduct of co-ordination of railway systems of different States, traffic on the Elbe, etc., and as I am compelled to withdraw these services with the demobilization of the American Army they will necessarily come to an end.

The ideal man for such a position would be Colonel Ryan, who has had charge of the Food Administration's distribution, formerly in Serbia and since that time in Germany. Before the war he was the Manager of an important railway. I do not know that Colonel Ryan would accept such a position, but I feel that he might do so.

Such a Transportation Advisor would require two or three assistants, for instance, to maintain a representative at Hamburg and another at Trieste, with possibly a third to maintain relationships with Polish and Austrian railways. I imagine that such a Commission might cost, for salaries and expenses, perhaps One Hundred Thousand Dollars for the twelve months. The problem of how to finance this in American dollars would at once occur to you, and I could make the following suggestion in this particular:

We have in our hands some unexpended balance of exchange remittances made to Czecho-Slovakia and, if the Czecho-Slovak Government would authorize me, acting under your guidance, to engage this staff, I would undertake to act as a trustee for the deposit of $100,000.00 and engage that my New York office would attend to the details of paying salaries, etc., of such a staff, and would, of course, furnish the accounts to the Czecho-Slovak Government.

The matter is somewhat pressing as we are compelled to take steps at an early moment to the demobilization of our staff and these men will be returning to the United States and are already making arrangements to set up their pre-war relationships. I would be glad if you could let me know whether the Czecho-Slovak Government desires that I should proceed in the matter as above outlined.

Faithfully yours,

(*Signed*) Herbert Hoover

Letters making similar proposals for technical advisers were sent to the governments of Austria, Poland, and Jugoslavia (Kingdom S.H.S.). Each of these four governments readily accepted the proposal and the following Americans were appointed as chiefs of the Technical Adviser Missions to the respective governments: Austria, Col. W. B. Causey; Czechoslo-

[1] This letter is quoted in full in *America and the New Poland* by H. H. Fisher (Macmillan), pp. 267–271.

vakia, Lt. Col. W. B. Ryan, followed by Dr. Lincoln Hutchinson; Poland, Col. A. B. Barber; Jugoslavia, Col. Wm. G. Atwood.

Each of these men took with him a small staff of trained engineers and experts. In addition certain of the governments employed other American experts for special problems. For example, Dr. E. Dana Durand, an economist of world-wide reputation, became the Food Adviser to the Polish Government, and Mr. Irving Shuman was engaged by Mr. Paderewski, as Commercial Adviser.

In order to assist the Technical Advisers with contacts in America and particularly in the purchase of supplies, Messrs. Edgar Rickard and W. B. Poland maintained offices in New York in connection with the A.R.A., and were able also to assist greatly the various agents which came to the United States from these countries on important economic missions.

The Technical Advisers and their staffs remained in the respective countries from one to three years and were able to render invaluable service, particularly, in reorganizing the transportation systems, securing needed equipment, and in negotiating satisfactory agreements between neighboring countries with regard to through transportation, interchange of equipment, etc. They also assisted in re-establishing trade routes and the interchange of commodities.[1] The following letter to Col. Barber from Arthur Sliwinski, President of the Council of Ministers of Poland, dated July 29, 1922, shows something of the appreciation which these countries felt for the service rendered.

Dear Colonel:

In the name of the Polish Government I feel that I must express to you, before you quit the soil of our country, the gratitude which Poland owes you for what you have accomplished during the three years that you have spent among us.

You arrived in Poland at the moment when the state, which had just been reconstituted after a century of foreign oppression and a war of long duration, was still struggling with a thousand political and economic difficulties. Under these difficult circumstances you brought to bear the effective aid of your experienced ability in the organization of the state railways. It was due to the normal functioning of the railways, to which your advice and intervention largely contributed, that Poland, during very perilous times, was able to avoid disaster due to lack of coal and food and to develop uninterruptedly her reborn commerce and industry. Neither would I fail to mention the services which you rendered to Poland both at Genoa and at Geneva during the various conferences dealing with the economic reconstruction of Europe and the organization of the economic system of Upper Silesia.

The rôle which you have played in all political and economic questions relating to Poland cannot but contribute to the maintenance and strengthening of the excellent friendly relations which exist between Poland and the United States of America, and I am sure that your departure will not in any way break the ties which you have formed with us and that you will remain always a true bond of union between our two countries.

Arthur Sliwinski
President of the Council of Ministers

As indicated in Mr. Hoover's letter (page 71) it was proposed to the several governments that the Technical Advisers should be paid out of credits arising from the A.R.A. exchange operations. This the governments agreed to and as shown in Table 180 the following amounts were expended for this work:

Austria	$184,997.72
Czechoslovakia	100,000.00
Poland	325,000.00
Jugoslavia	150,000.00
Total	$759,997.72

[1] For complete statement of accomplishments, see *Report of European Technical Advisers Mission to Poland, 1919–1922* by A. B. Barber (New York, 1923), and manuscript reports from other missions in Hoover War Library, Stanford University.

RECONSTRUCTION PERIOD

As presented in Table 1 (page 7), the fourth and final major division of this decade of relief is designated as the Reconstruction Period. With the signing of the peace treaty at Versailles on June 28, 1919, the period of official relief in Europe came to a close. The months of July and August, 1919, were occupied in completing the deliveries of relief supplies contracted for prior to July 1 and in closing up the relief operations. During the first seven months of 1919 the primary purpose of the Director General of Relief had been fulfilled, viz., that of furnishing foodstuffs to the newly constituted countries until the next harvest. With the new harvest in sight these countries would be able to take care of themselves for some months at least.

However, long before this time Mr. Hoover realized that Europe could not get through the next winter without serious suffering unless she received some outside assistance. Obviously, it could not be expected that either the United States or any other government could continue indefinitely to furnish food to these countries either on credit or as charity. Furthermore, such continuing relief would be good for neither the receiving governments nor their peoples. If these nations were to survive they must make their own arrangements to take care of their own people. The arrival of the new harvest therefore formed an opportune time at which to withdraw all official relief and to put the responsibility for future food supplies squarely up to the respective governments.

On June 10, 1919, the Director General of Relief submitted a memorandum to the Supreme Economic Council which read in part:

> . . . . We are notifying the various governments that, while American intervention in the distribution of overseas foodstuffs in the present form will cease with harvest, we will be glad to receive an estimate from each of the governments under relief in respect to the assistance which they will need during the coming year from the United States. Further that we consider it desirable that these estimates should be presented in the United States by a Commission fully empowered to handle credit, shipping, and collateral questions. Under this arrangement there will therefore be no break in American interest and helpfulness, and, on the other hand, a definite step will have been attained in advancement from sheer relief to economic measures in co-operation with the countries concerned. . . . .

CHILDREN'S RELIEF

As pointed out in a preceding section of this report, the pitiful situation of the children in the newly liberated countries had attracted Mr. Hoover's attention soon after his arrival in Europe. By the end of February, 1919, a special Children's Relief Bureau had been organized in the American Relief Administration and definite programs for child feeding were carried out in most of the countries.[1] As the period of official relief came to a close it became evident that the children would be heavy sufferers in the food shortage that was certain to develop during the next year. Many of the children who were being cared for were war orphans; all of them had suffered from undernourishment during the war and many of them were just beginning to show signs of improvement under the influence of these increased rations. Mr. Hoover could not leave these children to their fate and he accordingly began to make plans for the continuance of children's relief under a charitable foundation.

On July 7, 1919, Mr. Hoover sent a long cable from Paris to the New York office of the American Relief Administration, which read in part as follows:

> In order to meet all the various complexions of the problem of winding up the Government's relief measures and of continuing the Children's Relief, of applying any residuum of the contingent funds to this purpose, with the approval of the various governments in Europe, and of handling and developing private charity, we believe it is critically necessary that we should at once set up a new and wholly private organization, which we propose to call the American Relief Administration European Children's Fund. . . . .

In this cable Mr. Hoover further suggested that there should be a committee formed in the United States consisting of some of the leading men in the Food Administration and the Relief Administration and that they should incorporate at once as a private charitable organization under the laws of the state of New York.

[1] See page 84.

This proposal met with the approval of the men in New York and the organization was perfected. Although an outgrowth of the American Relief Administration, which acted as an agent of the United States Government, the new organization, the A.R.A. European Children's Fund, was purely a voluntary private organization for the promotion of charitable purposes. It had no official charter although it did enjoy the confidence of the Government and assumed responsibility for the distribution of the remaining food supplies donated from the Congressional Appropriation and the President's National Security and Defense Fund. As the American Relief Administration and the Grain Corporation withdrew from the various countries the European Children's Fund took over the remaining equipment and continued their work without a break in the program.

EUROPEAN CHILDREN'S FUND

The headquarters of the E.C.F. were in New York and the European branch was in London. Mr. Hoover was chairman, Edgar Rickard was director for America, and Walter Lyman Brown was director for Europe. Field missions were located at Helsingfors, Finland; Reval, Esthonia; Jamburg, Northwest Russia; Riga, Latvia; Kovno, Lithuania; Warsaw, Poland; Prague, Czechoslovakia; Vienna, Austria; Budapest, Hungary; Bucharest, Roumania; and Belgrade, Jugoslavia.

The New York office controlled policy and arranged finances, purchases, and shipping. The London office carried out the policies by supervision of the work of each mission, made such purchases in Europe as were necessary, prepared programs, directed shipments, and handled such accounts, statistics, and records as were needed.

All commodities purchased in the United States were charged to the London office as shipped and these in turn were charged against the various relief operations as and when distributed. All expenditures or deliveries in each country were reported weekly to London with properly approved and receipted vouchers for every expenditure or delivery. The books of both the New York and London offices were audited monthly by recognized chartered accountants. These records and receipts form the basis of the statistics contained in this report, all of which are in reconciliation with the accountants' figures.

When the European Children's Fund began operations in August, 1919, it was expected that these could be discontinued in the summer of 1920 at the time the new harvest became available. However, economic recovery was slower than had been anticipated. The 1920 crops were less in many countries than had been hoped for, and milk and fat supplies, due to the continued shortage of cattle feeds, were still entirely inadequate. Furthermore, the Bolshevist invasions had again prostrated the Polish people. It seemed necessary, therefore, that some assistance should be continued to the children of certain of these countries. It was estimated that there were still some 2,500,000 children who would need help in 1920–1921. In the summer of 1920 child feeding was entirely discontinued in Finland and in Jugoslavia, with important reductions in Czechoslovakia and a few other countries.

In the summer of 1921 it was found that some child feeding would still be necessary, although it was possible to discontinue all work in Czechoslovakia and Hungary. In the spring of 1922 child feeding was discontinued in Poland and Austria and the operations in Central Europe were practically closed during the year.

In the meantime, however, the terrible famine in Russia had broken out in the summer of 1921. This required the remobilization of the relief organization on a scale larger than ever, and continued until late in 1923 before the whole of these operations could be discontinued.

During the course of the five years 1919 to 1924 the A.R.A. E.C.F. found it necessary to undertake many subsidiary operations and to cooperate with many other relief organizations, often for the relief of certain portions of the adult population as well as for child feeding. Among the more important of these undertakings were the A.R.A.W. operations, including food drafts and bulk sales;[1] the various special programs, including intelligentsia and student feeding; the handling of the United States Grain Corporation deliveries to Russia; the European Relief Council drive; and the co-operation with the Red Cross, the Joint Distribution Committee, American Friends Service Committee, the Y.M.C.A., and many other organizations.

[1] See pages 90–95.

The European Children's Fund began to function about August 1, 1919. As fast as the American Relief Administration and the United States Grain Corporation withdrew from a country or locality where child feeding was being carried on, the new organization stepped in and continued the work without any break in its continuity, and often with the same personnel. The change in organization involved no change in policies inaugurated by the Children's Relief Bureau under the old American Relief Administration.[1]

Each field mission was charged with the duty of maintaining a continual check upon conditions in each community within its territory and to make such adjustments as were needed in required supplies. In this way it was possible to reduce excessive stocks in one community and to increase supplies to another where the needs were greater. Each month the local committees forwarded a statement showing the number of children needing relief during the coming month. These statements were assembled by each field mission and forwarded to the London office with notes and recommendations for modifications in the respective local requirements. These statements formed the basis on which advance supplies were ordered by the London office through New York. Additional checks on the equitable distribution of supplies were assured through the reports of American inspectors, who were constantly in the field summarizing conditions, visiting kitchens, and reporting special needs or suggesting changes in requirements.

A system of central and regional warehouses was maintained at strategic points,[2] and as requisitions were approved the commodities needed were issued to the local kitchens.

There were three steps in the selection of children needing aid: first, their registration, usually through school teachers; second, an investigation by the local committee; and third, a physical examination by a local physician. These examinations were repeated at regular intervals and any child reaching a fair state of nourishment was taken off the list to make way for another whose condition was worse.

All child feeding was carried on in special kitchens set up for that purpose or in institutions such as orphanages or hospitals. In most countries a noonday meal was served six days a week. Each child admitted to feeding received a card which was punched for each meal received. These meals were prepared by the local committees which bore all the expense of preparing and serving the meal. In some instances a small charge, amounting to about one cent per meal, was made by the local committee to defray the necessary expenses. However, it was an unvarying rule that no child was refused admittance because of inability to pay. At other places these expenses were met by local donations and no charges were paid by the children or their parents. The services of the local committees were always voluntary, and in most instances rentals for kitchens and equipment were also donated.

Finance for European Children's Fund

The basis of the work of the A.R.A. European Children's Fund consisted of the undistributed stocks of child-feeding supplies which had been furnished by the American Relief Administration during the summer of 1919. These supplies had been paid for out of the Congressional Appropriation and the President's National Security and Defense Fund.[3] All child-feeding work was based upon furnishing actual meals under supervision. The programs had been planned to carry this work through the fall of 1919 until after the new harvest had been completed and was available. When the American Relief Administration decided to withdraw its official work after the peace treaty, these supplies were already in stock, or en route. Mr. Hoover secured the consent of President Wilson to have the distribution of these supplies administered by the European Children's Fund. The total stocks of child-feeding commodities which were thus distributed under the direction of the European Children's Fund are shown in Table 147 and total to 17,585.0 metric tons, valued at $6,625,051.36. The distribution of these commodities to the final country of destination is accounted for under the European Children's Fund.[4]

The presence of these supplies in European ports or en route made it possible for the European Children's Fund to begin functioning at once. However, the program which the E.C.F.

[1] See pages 84–86 for description of these policies and methods used in child feeding.

[2] See page 93.

[3] See pages 49–50 and 88–90.

[4] See pages 86–88.

contemplated involved the expenditure of much larger sums of money.

The first source of additional funds for this work came from the surplus accumulated by the London office of the Food Administration Grain Corporation in connection with the handling of American Relief Administration supplies. In the contract[1] drawn up between the American Relief Administration and the Food Administration Grain Corporation there was the following paragraph:

> 6. It is the intention of this contract that the Grain Corporation shall make no profit from its relief operations and shall suffer no losses. It therefore agrees that it will deduct from its gross receipts on all supplies, other than those delivered to the American Relief Administration for payment from the hundred million dollar appropriation, all items of cost and expense on such sales, including expenses paid under paragraph 5 of this contract [expenses of A.R.A. in Europe], and will hold balance as a special fund. From this fund shall be paid, first, any items of insurance or expense relating to the cargoes delivered against the hundred million dollar appropriation and not repaid from the United States Treasury. The balance, if any, shall be paid to the Director General of Relief or his successor, or such person, institution, or government as he or his successor may direct, for charitable purposes in Europe. In case there should be no Director General of Relief such direction shall be made by the United States Wheat Director. . . . .

It has already been pointed out[2] that, due to the extraordinary hazards of conducting shipping and commercial operations in Europe immediately after the Armistice, the Grain Corporation felt it necessary to add a sufficient margin to protect it against any unusual loss. This margin had to be higher than usual because no insurance company would take the risk on this business. Furthermore, the Grain Corporation had very definite responsibilities in connection with the marketing of the American wheat crop. If it should risk the impairment of its capital through its connection with the European relief work it might cause serious apprehension at home and would most certainly make the Corporation liable for serious criticism. Therefore, to assure against this risk, which no commercial concern would assume at any price, larger margins above cost were carried than would normally be deemed essential.

Fortunately, the losses actually suffered by the Grain Corporation on its European business were smaller than had been anticipated and, consequently, the operation showed a rather large net remainder. This remainder under the arrangements finally made was turned over to the European Children's Fund to be used in child feeding in the several liberated countries.

As soon as Mr. Hoover had determined upon the establishment of a charitable organization for children's relief, he addressed a letter to each of the countries to which relief supplies had been delivered, outlining the plan of using such profits as might develop and asking their approval of this action. Following is the letter addressed to the Czechoslovakian Minister of Foreign Affairs, which is similar to those addressed to the other governments:

51, Avenue Montaigne
Paris, France
June 12, 1919

M. Edouard Benes
Minister Foreign Affairs
Czecho-Slovak Republic
18, rue Bonaparte, Paris

Sir:

In the course of supplying foodstuffs to the Republic of Czecho-Slovakia under our arrangement of February 28, 1919, the American Relief Administration has delivered all foodstuffs at fixed prices as near to the actual outlay as could be determined, with a sufficient margin to protect the Relief Administration against loss arising from the unknown factors in the continuing state of war where every commercial service had been destroyed, and private capital did not dare to venture.

The whole operation of relief to Europe has been by a coordination of shipping, finance and administration conducted as one operation and it has of course been impossible in advance to determine the exact cost for the contingent liabilities inherent in the operation. It is possible therefore that with the closing of the program in the month of July, and a final calculation of cost and liabilities incurred, there may be some profit accruing to the Relief Administration or its agencies.

Under the agreement of February 28, 1919, possible profits could of course be retained by the Relief Administration, but it is our earnest desire that no profits should be earned from the relief operations in Czecho-Slovakia. If such a profit should exist, it will represent partially the saving effected through the sacrifice of the representatives of the United States Food Administration, the American Relief Administration and the Grain Corporation, whose services are partially or wholly voluntary. Even when salaries are received they are usually paid by other departments of the United States Government without being calculated in the price of the foodstuffs. The prices fixed have therefore been

[1] For text of this contract see page 46 n.

[2] See page 41.

less than commercial prices in a free market. Therefore such margins represent a gift of service to Czecho-Slovakia by these gentlemen.

In these lights I propose that any such total residual sum as may be determined by the Food Administration or its agencies to be in fact a profit after the completion of our total operations should be lodged with me or such organizations as I may erect in New York to be added to public charity for the continued support of child relief in Czecho-Slovakia as a contribution representing service.

It is my intention to organize the supply of further funds by public charity in the United States and the addition of such residual amounts as above would give a substantial substratum and endurance to this effort.

It is very desirable however that such action should have the full approval of the Czech-Slovak Government, and I would be glad if you would indicate that this course would meet with their approval. It is my intention to personally direct the organization and extension of such work in the United States if the above plan can be adhered to. It has been accepted by the other Governments to which it has been submitted.

Faithfully yours,

(*Signed*) Herbert Hoover

This proposal was enthusiastically endorsed by each of the liberated governments to which relief deliveries had been made and thus gave official approval to the turning over of these funds to the European Children's Fund when it was created.

Other important sources of funds for the European Children's Fund were the contributions from other charitable and national organizations in the United States, the funds collected in the European Relief Council campaign, the proceeds of the exchange remittances, the sale of food drafts and bulk sales, the donations by such organizations as the Commonwealth Fund, the Laura Spelman Rockefeller Memorial, the American Red Cross, the American Friends Society, the Jewish Joint Distribution Committee, the Y.M.C.A., and many others.

For the Russian relief operations special funds were made available through the Congressional appropriation of money from the capital of the Grain Corporation, Soviet gold, United States Government surplus, and American Red Cross medical supplies, and from many other sources.[1]

EUROPEAN RELIEF COUNCIL

As shown on page 145, one of the important sources of finance for work in the Reconstruction Period was the fund collected by the European Relief Council.

[1] For further detail see pages 245–47.

In the latter part of 1919 and in 1920, it was clearly recognized by the relief workers in Central Europe that there was an enormous need for charitable aid to these countries, covering many months and even years. These war-torn countries and their newly organized governments were not in a position to restore anything approaching normal economic conditions for a long time. In the meantime, the impoverished population *must* eat if anarchy and rebellion were not to gain the upper hand. There were a number of well-organized American relief agencies already in the field doing their utmost to alleviate the terrible suffering on every hand. Each of these organizations was constantly appealing to its constituents and to the American public for the urgently needed funds with which to continue this work.

Realizing the enormity of the need and also the fact the such unco-ordinated efforts were not likely to secure the necessary funds for this work, Mr. Hoover called together the leaders of many of these relief organizations and proposed that their efforts, particularly as applied to child relief, should be co-ordinated. It was only by such co-ordination and by a joint appeal to the American public that there seemed any chance of obtaining the staggering sums of money needed for this work.

As a result of Mr. Hoover's efforts there was organized in the fall of 1920 the European Relief Council, which comprised nine organizations, as follows: American Friends Service Committee, American Red Cross, American Relief Administration, Federal Council of the Churches of Christ in America, Jewish Joint Distribution Committee, Knights of Columbus, National Catholic Welfare Council, Young Men's Christian Association, and Young Women's Christian Association.

An executive committee was organized with Herbert Hoover, chairman; Franklin K. Lane, treasurer; Christian A. Herter, secretary; and the following representatives of the nine organizations in the order named above: Dr. Rufus M. Jones, Dr. Livingston Farrand, Edgar Rickard, Dr. Arthur J. Brown, Felix M. Warburg, James A. Flaherty, Michael J. Slattery, C. V. Hibbard, and Miss Sarah S. Lyon.

It was decided by the Council that child relief in Eastern and Central Europe should have priority over any other form of European relief until the next harvest. On the basis of careful surveys it was estimated that a total 3,500,000 ill, undernourished, and orphan children would require support until the harvest of 1921. It was further estimated that $33,000,000 would be required for this work, of which $10,000,000 would be needed for medical service and care and $23,000,000 for mass child-feeding and clothing requirements. This vast program contemplated the greatest collection from the American public for charitable purposes ever undertaken by any organization. Furthermore, it came in a period of financial depression and at a time when the community at large was just emerging from generous and repeated financial support of various war activities.

The success of this undertaking was due largely to the thorough organization for the work and its support by leading citizens in every state. This support in turn was secured because of the prestige and the confidence in the Chairman, because the appeal was for children and because of the consolidated appeal of nine relief organizations all recognized for ability and integrity.

The Chairman appointed four committees upon which the burden of organization fell. These were the Executive, Control, Publicity, and Finance committees.

Voluntary state organizations were perfected in every state, often headed by the governor or, if not, by another out-standing citizen. Local committees were formed in nearly every city and many smaller places. Organizations were also perfected in Alaska, Hawaii, the Philippines, and the Canal Zone, which turned in substantial subscriptions. The success of the drive for funds which began December 19, 1920, and ended April 1, 1921, was due largely to the energetic efforts of the local chairmen and their co-workers and to the assistance rendered by local banks, newspapers, and other businesses, and by such nation-wide organizations as that of the *Literary Digest* and the many charitable foundations. It would be far beyond the scope of this report to attempt to name the hundreds of organizations and the thousands of individuals, who by their untiring efforts made this campaign a success.

Various publications of the European Relief Council and of the American Relief Administration have given these and many other facts regarding this campaign.[1] The summary pre-

TABLE 49

EUROPEAN RELIEF COUNCIL, SOURCES OF CONTRIBUTIONS BY ORGANIZATIONS

Organization	Amount
Various states, territories, national headquarters, and sundry	$10,645,510.40
American Red Cross	5,000,000.00
American Relief Administration	3,200,000.00
*Literary Digest**	2,516,000.00
Joint Distribution Committee	2,200,000.00
John D. Rockefeller, Jr.	1,000,000.00
The Rockefeller Foundation	1,000,000.00
Laura Spelman Rockefeller Memorial	1,000,000.00
American Friends Service Committee	861,022.31
Commodity contributions	351,440.51
Cleveland Community Fund	300,000.00
Detroit War Chest	200,000.00
Contributions of Securities†	192,487.50
Cincinnati War Chest	179,180.82
Motion Picture Campaign‡	169,187.76
Rochester Patriotic and Community Fund	149,100.00
Twenty-four community funds§	112,000.00
The Commonwealth Fund	100,000.00
School children, New York City¶	100,000.00
Interest received on contributed funds	88,092.52
Young Women's Christian Association	52,204.52
National Polish Committee	50,000.00
Miami County (Ohio) War Chest	35,000.00
American Express Company	29,845.56
Youngstown Community Fund	25,000.00
Total contributions	$29,556,071.90

* It is impossible to estimate the total influence of this publication upon the whole campaign in this appeal, as in others of the Hoover appeals, because of its special efforts, which covered the entire United States to the benefit of local efforts of all the constituent bodies.

† This represents donations of United States Treasury Certificates of Indebtedness, Liberty Loan Bonds, and other securities at par value.

‡ The proceeds of the Motion Picture Campaign were turned over by the Motion Picture Campaign headquarters, to the various state depositories and national headquarters of the European Relief Council. While it is estimated that more than $1,000,000 were brought in from this campaign, they are credited here with the amount of $169,187.76, which they turned over directly to the Relief Council.

§ The various Community Chests and funds, of which there were thirty in number, contributed upward of $1,000,000. However, since only those contributions in excess of $25,000 are listed separately, the remaining twenty-four community funds were totaled and entered as one item in the amount of $112,000.

¶ The school children of New York City contributed $100,000 to the drive. It is also estimated that more than $500,000 was contributed by school children of the United States and Territories, but New York was the only state that segregated the donations as between school children and other donors.

[1] See *National Collection of European Relief Council, 1920–21* (New York), *Interim Report of European Relief Council* (New York, May 31, 1921), and *Final Report of European Relief Council* (May 31, 1922), issued by the American Relief Administration as Liquidators of European Relief Council.

sented herewith based on the audited accounts of the Council will show the origin and disposition of the funds collected.

The contributions received by the European Relief Council totaled $29,556,071.90, or approximately three and a half million dollars less than the mark set at the beginning of the campaign. Considering the difficulties of collecting funds during this particular period of economic and financial stress, the outcome can only be regarded as highly successful. Because of the considerable fall in the price of food, clothing, and transportation between the time that plans were made for the campaign and its completion, it was believed that the funds collected would accomplish all the work the Council had planned. According to the audited statement the total cost of conducting the campaign amounted to only $677,929.22, or 2.31 per cent of the total contributions. These expenses were paid by the American Relief Administration out of credits arising from their food draft operations (see page 95) so that every dollar contributed to the European Relief Council was available for relief purposes.

Table 49 shows the sources of the larger contributions to this fund. Throughout the campaign emphasis was placed upon the small contributions by individuals, and results show that over $10,000,000, or more than one-third of the total, was made up of such contributions to state and national headquarters. The final reports of the European Relief Council show that more than 3,000 persons gave their time and energies to this service and it is estimated that more than 7,000,000 persons contributed to the funds.

Table 50 gives an analysis of the Relief Council contributions by state of origin so far as this could be determined.

The allocation of European Relief Council

TABLE 50

EUROPEAN RELIEF COUNCIL, SOURCES OF CONTRIBUTIONS BY STATES, COUNTRIES, ORGANIZATIONS

State, Country, Organization	Amount of Contribution	State, Country, Organization	Amount of Contribution
Alaska	$ 21,707.11	Nevada	14,548.55
Alabama	158,341.99	New Hampshire	105,687.30
Arizona	49,047.11	New Jersey	911,744.53
Arkansas	40,783.45	New Mexico	20,166.59
California	950,053.95	New York	7,255,350.44
Canada	2,472.18	North Carolina	153,816.02
Canal Zone	15,080.91	North Dakota	35,355.29
Colorado	108,650.75	Ohio	1,235,714.36
Connecticut	668,074.06	Oklahoma	63,185.96
Delaware	161,172.31	Oregon	253,010.81
District of Columbia	190,839.95	Pennsylvania	1,486,752.24
Florida	86,792.73	Philippine Islands	22,544.00
Foreign	5,416.22	Porto Rico	19.85
Georgia	123,387.70	Rhode Island	251,180.54
Hawaii	67,843.20	South Carolina	76,590.45
Idaho	37,717.37	South Dakota	88,767.37
Illinois	1,284,222.25	Tennessee	232,002.08
Indiana	292,777.39	Texas	370,517.32
Iowa	362,870.50	Utah	110,298.49
Kansas	62,499.51	Vermont	42,790.12
Kentucky	138,580.65	Virginia	170,820.57
Louisiana	166,286.71	Washington	264,726.88
Maine	167,555.29	West Virginia	83,338.84
Maryland	226,885.32	Wisconsin	110,180.08
Massachusetts	1,109,818.32	Wyoming	6,437.71
Michigan	833,160.23	Miscellaneous	566,979.98
Minnesota	530,684.65	American Red Cross	5,000,000.00
Mississippi	48,989.92	Joint Distribution Committee	2,200,000.00
Missouri	281,041.88		
Montana	33,076.65		
Nebraska	197,715.27	Total contributions	$29,556,071.90

funds among the several relief organizations was as follows:

A.R.A. European Children's Fund.....	$15,669,899.59
American Red Cross................	10,000,150.00
Joint Distribution Committee.........	3,000,000.00
American Friends Service Committee..	861,022.31
National Polish Committee...........	25,000.00
Total contributions	$29,556,071.90

The European Children's Fund was therefore responsible for the distribution of $15,669,899.59, which is shown in the table on page 145 as one source of relief funds in the Reconstruction Period. Various other allocations of funds to other relief organizations were made by the A.R.A. from its share of the Relief Council funds. However, these were made for special purposes, such as the student relief discussed on pages 110–11, which was carried on in close co-operation with the Y.M.C.A. organization, but which for the most part was directed by the European Children's Fund.

TOTAL RELIEF DELIVERIES DURING THE RECONSTRUCTION PERIOD

Table 1 (page 7) shows that during the Reconstruction Period the total relief furnished to Europe, within the scope of this report, amounted to 1,571,534.1 metric tons and a total value of $220,704,581.78. Although considerably smaller in volume than the relief furnished during any of the three preceding periods, it is to be remembered that dependence for finance in this latter period was more largely upon benevolent contributions, and also that the character of the relief furnished was quite different. During each of the three preceding periods relief was being delivered to governments and the responsibility was for feeding whole nations. During the Reconstruction Period, relief was largely restricted to the furnishing of supplementary meals to children and to a few other special classes of the population. With the exception of the Russian relief, it represented largely the tapering off of the vast operations which were necessary during the war and the Armistice Period.

Table 51 summarizes the total relief deliveries accounted for during this period, under the three principal categories of relief organizations involved. Table 148 (Appendix) gives the detail of the commodities supplied under each of these categories.

The deliveries under each of these categories will be discussed in the following pages. It may be pointed out here that the American Relief Administration European Children's Fund was the central organization for the work of this period. Under "Other American Organizations" is included the work of a large number of charitable societies so far as their activities were carried on in direct co-operation with the European Children's Fund. Under this heading there are also included the deliveries by the United States Grain Corporation under the authority of Congress both to Central Europe and to Russia. Also the United States Government surplus medical supplies for Russia are included here.

TABLE 51

Summary of Total Relief Deliveries in the Reconstruction Period, by Principal Operations

Deliveries by	Total Metric Tons	Total Value
European Children's Fund	422,098.2	$ 84,639,241.40
Other American organizations	942,267.0	96,506,869.36
Countries other than United States	266,229.1	44,222,231.22
Total	1,630,594.3	$225,368,341.98
Less duplication *	59,060.2	4,663,760.20
Grand total, net......	1,571,534.1	$220,704,581.78

* These duplications include (1) expenditures for advance deliveries against Soviet gold which are covered both under "E.C.F." and "Countries other than the United States" and (2) certain warehouse sales to the American Friends Service Committee which are included both in the A.R.A.W. operations and in the deliveries by the Friends Committee under "Other American organizations." The amounts involved in these two duplications are:

	Tons	Value
Soviet gold	57,823.0	$4,322,450.83
Sale to Friends...........	1,237.2	341,309.37
Total	59,060.2	$4,663,760.20

These transactions are more fully discussed in the text; cf. pages 120 and 246.

The duplications deducted to obtain the net total in Table 51 are caused by inter-organization deliveries. The most important of these in the Reconstruction Period concerns certain supplies delivered to Russia by the American Relief Administration but subsequently paid for by a portion of the Russian gold.

The supplies furnished during the Reconstruction Period were delivered to sixteen countries of Europe, in addition to sundry accounts. Table 52 (page 82) summarizes the total deliveries during this period from all sources by countries of destination.

The largest deliveries to any one country in point of value were those to Poland, while the supplies furnished to the Soviet Republics represented a much larger tonnage but a slightly smaller value. The Russian supplies consisted to a large extent of grain and corn grits, which were much cheaper per ton than the type of supplies

CHART VI

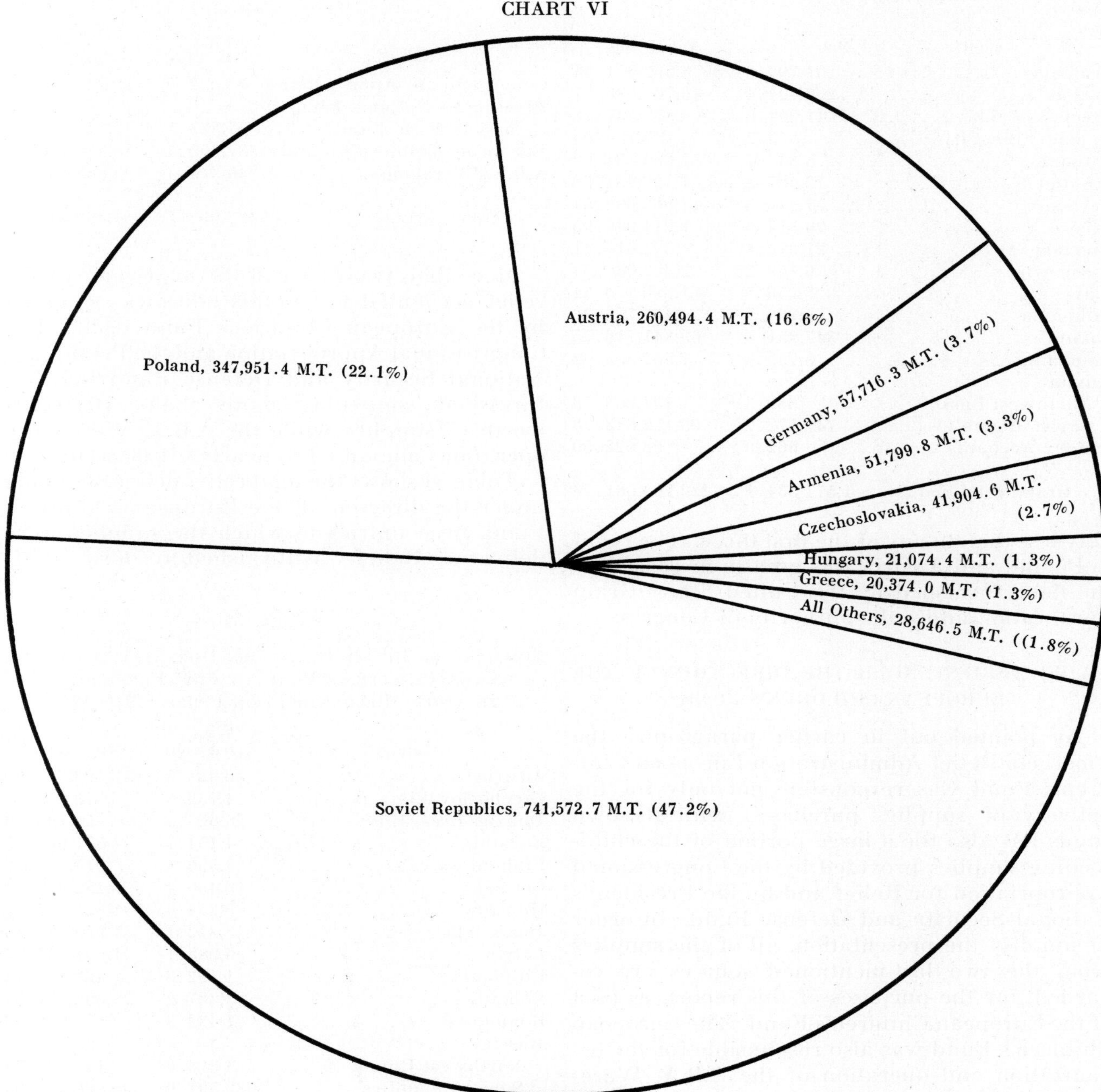

Total metric tons and percentage of deliveries, by countries—Reconstruction Period. The detail for all other countries is shown in Table 52, page 82.

furnished to the other countries. The third country in point of value of relief received was Austria, with Germany fourth, although considerably less than to any of the first three. The relief to Poland and Austria was greatly increased by the flour furnished by the United States Grain Corporation under the authority of Congress.

TABLE 52

SUMMARY OF ALL RELIEF DELIVERIES DURING THE RECONSTRUCTION PERIOD, BY COUNTRIES OF DESTINATION, 1919–1924

Country	Total Metric Tons	Total Value
Armenia	51,799.8	$ 8,563,971.48
Austria	260,494.4	46,709,626.37
Czechoslovakia	41,904.6	9,892,557.58
Danzig Free City	573.2	127,700.69
Esthonia	5,847.7	1,669,451.09
Finland	3,487.2	1,109,991.80
Germany	57,716.3	11,962,693.54
Greece	20,374.0	1,211,949.95
Hungary	21,074.4	4,361,619.41
Jugoslavia	6,109.2	2,302,080.74
Latvia	6,756.9	1,588,170.34
Lithuania	1,200.7	463,776.92
Poland	347,951.4	65,841,716.75
Roumania	3,759.3	1,501,595.02
Russia		
Northwest Russia	350.3	124,208.73
Soviet Republics	741,572.7	63,174,848.78
Sundry Accounts	562.0	98,622.59
Grand total, net	1,571,534.1	$220,704,581.78

I. DELIVERIES UNDER THE DIRECTION OF THE EUROPEAN CHILDREN'S FUND

As pointed out in earlier paragraphs, the American Relief Administration European Children's Fund was responsible not only for the delivery of supplies purchased with its own funds but also for a large portion of the child-feeding supplies provided by the Congressional Appropriation for Relief and by the President's National Security and Defense Fund. In order to simplify the presentation, all of the supplies from the two last-mentioned sources are regarded, for the purposes of this report, as part of the European Children's Fund. The European Children's Fund was also responsible for the organization and operation of the A.R.A. Warehouses, through which the food and clothing drafts and bulk sale operations were carried on.

The deliveries credited to the European Children's Fund in Table 51 may, therefore, be divided under four heads, as summarized in Table 53.

TABLE 53

SUMMARY OF RELIEF DELIVERIES DIRECTED BY THE EUROPEAN CHILDREN'S FUND—RECONSTRUCTION PERIOD, 1919–1924

Source	Total Metric Tons	Total Value
Congressional Appropriation	36,002.1	$13,433,918.33
President's National Security and Defense Fund	7,823.1	2,949,217.23
European Children's Fund	337,953.5	58,370,700.11
A.R.A. Warehouses	40,319.5	9,885,405.73
Total	422,098.2	$84,639,241.40

More than two-thirds of the total value of the relief accounted for in this table was supplied by the European Children's Fund itself. The Congressional Appropriation and the President's National Security and Defense Fund together furnished something more than $16,000,000 worth of supplies while the A.R.A. Warehouse operations amounted to nearly $10,000,000.

Table 54 shows the total relief deliveries made under the direction of the European Children's Fund, by countries to which the supplies were delivered. Relief was furnished to fourteen dif-

TABLE 54

SUMMARY OF RELIEF DELIVERIES DIRECTED BY THE EUROPEAN CHILDREN'S FUND, BY COUNTRIES OF DESTINATION—RECONSTRUCTION PERIOD, 1919–1924

Country	Total Metric Tons	Total Value
Austria	46,934.5	$13,193,794.30
Czechoslovakia	14,139.8	5,373,858.23
Danzig Free City	8,061.2	953,397.39
Esthonia	4,154.7	1,371,006.45
Finland	2,550.8	914,042.80
Germany	13,400.4	3,182,991.74
Hungary	5,214.9	1,820,887.77
Jugoslavia	3,372.1	1,655,322.45
Latvia	6,280.1	1,524,257.57
Lithuania	1,192.3	462,850.14
Poland	83,887.2	24,500,251.54
Roumania	1,432.3	477,272.76
Russia		
Northwest Russia	318.0	117,928.73
Soviet Republics	230,597.9	28,992,756.94
Sundry accounts	562.0	98,622.59
Total	422,098.2	$84,639,241.40

ferent countries, in addition to sundry accounts. Deliveries to the Soviet Republics of Russia during the great famine of 1922 and 1923 accounted for 230,597.9 metric tons of supplies valued at $28,992,756.94. The next largest deliveries were to Poland, totaling $24,500,251.54. Although this amount was less than $4,500,000 below the value of the deliveries to the Soviet Republics, the tonnage going to Poland was only a little more than one-third that supplied to Russia. This is accounted for by the much greater value per ton of child-feeding supplies, including

CHART VII

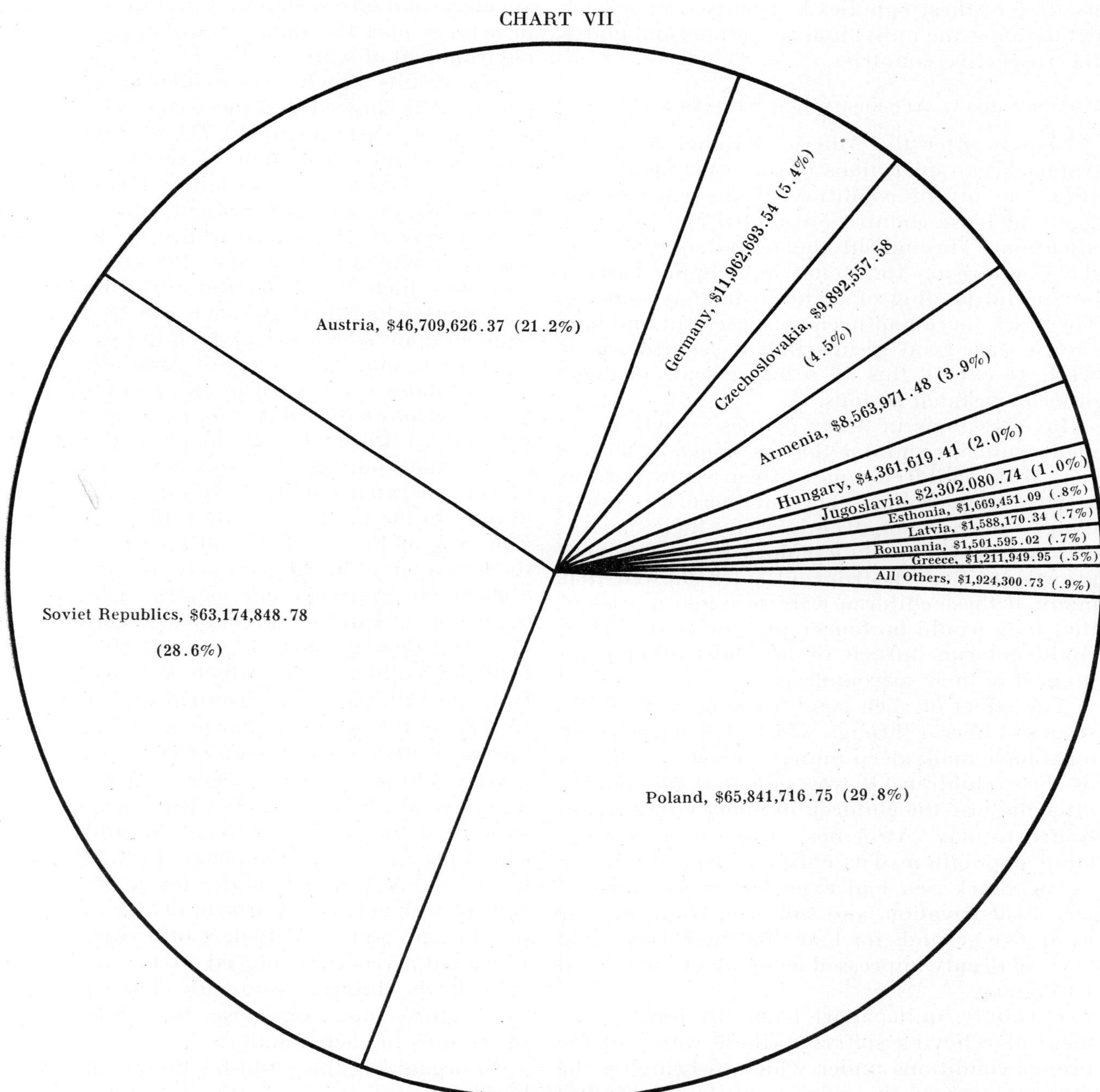

Total value and percentage of deliveries, by countries—Reconstruction Period. The detail for all other countries is shown in Table 52, page 82.

chiefly milk, cocoa, and fats compared with the flour, meal, and corn grits which made up a large part of the Russian famine relief. The country receiving the third largest amount of relief under E.C.F. direction was Austria, with $13,193,794.30. Other countries received smaller amounts in proportion to their needs. The allocation of these supplies is discussed in greater detail under the individual operations and under the respective countries.

Congressional Appropriation, Children's Relief

Shortly after the American Relief Administration began operations in the early months of 1919, the pitiful condition of the children in many of these countries attracted Mr. Hoover's attention. Throughout the period of the war, the Commission for Relief in Belgium carried on special feeding of children in that country. The work there had been so successful and had shown such good results that it seemed worth while to extend this on a larger scale to these other devastated regions.

Investigations in many of these newly liberated countries showed that as many as 90 per cent of the children under fifteen years were so seriously undernourished that there was grave danger of permanent injury to their health. Rickets, scurvy, and tuberculosis were extremely prevalent. Reports from all sides showed that many of these children were so undernourished that they would no longer play or smile. They could not run but sat or lay down, taking no interest in their surroundings.

The effect of such conditions, as well as the scenes of horror through which they had passed, must have made deep impressions on the minds of these children. It was said that for months after the war the children in many villages continued to play "Atrocities" to the horror of the adult population. The children from the Baltic to the Black Sea had experienced so much of terror, deprivation, and suffering from the war as to give grounds for fear that their minds had been so deeply impressed as to affect their adult psychology.

Certainly, quite apart from the human element of relieving suffering, these were not the proper conditions under which to bring up the men and women that were to control the future destinies of Europe, and perhaps the world.

It was these considerations which led Mr. Hoover to inaugurate the first child-feeding program. It was proposed to make this a direct gift from the American people to the children of these countries. It was hoped that the effect of food arriving suddenly from a distance, by an unseen hand, without price or compensation, would do much to develop their ideals of justice, altruism, and citizenship and perhaps obliterate in a large part the influences of the degrading environment of war.

The results which were evident in the latter part of 1919 showed that these contentions were in part, at least, justified. The demonstration upon Mr. Hoover's visit to Warsaw in August, 1919, and the hundreds of letters from individuals, societies, and government officials which were received, showed how deeply this work was appreciated at that time. Probably there is nothing which the American Government has ever done which brought such heartfelt thanks from so many persons, or which did so much at the time to make the name of America and the United States reverenced in all parts of Europe.

Organization of A.R.A. Children's Relief.—By February, 1919, Mr. Hoover had received reports of the conditions in sufficient detail from most of the liberated countries to cause him to act at once in the matter of child relief. The Act of Congress of February 25, 1919, had authorized the President at his discretion to use parts of the $100,000,000 appropriation as gifts to the suffering people of Europe. Mr. Hoover secured President Wilson's approval to use a portion of this fund for child feeding, which was to be a gift from the American Government and quite distinct from the general relief program, for which the respective governments were required by Congress to pay either in cash or by notes.

A special Children's Relief Bureau was set up as part of the American Relief Administration. This Bureau, with headquarters in the Paris office of the A.R.A., was under the joint supervision of Colonel A. J. Carlson, of the University of Chicago, and E. A. Peden, of Texas. Special representatives were placed in the relief missions in the different countries. Their duty was to organize and supervise the child-feeding operations in each country.

In organizing this child-feeding work, several basic principles were outlined and strictly adhered to. These were, first, that no children's relief should be extended to countries which were able to care for their own people; second, that the selection of children should be based solely on their state of undernourishment, preferably as determined by medical examination, and that no preference was to be given because of race, nationality, creed, politics, or class; third, that one of the factors in determining the extent of the relief furnished must be the willingness of the people to help themselves by such material contributions as they were able to make; fourth, that all distribution was to be carried out by local organizations under the supervision and control of the A.R.A.; fifth, that all children were to be fed in public kitchens and that no food was to be taken from the premises unless exceptional conditions made it necessary to make such arrangements; and, finally, that the A.R.A. representatives must refrain from any participation in political, military, racial, or other controversial questions and must abstain from personal business activities.

The rule requiring food to be consumed on the premises was necessary to make certain that the rations intended for a child did not go to others. This was strictly adhered to except in certain parts of Finland, Jugoslavia, Northwest Russia, and Esthonia, where the most needy children often lived miles away from the nearest village, and it would have been a severe hardship to require them to come to a central kitchen.

The first duty of the local Children's Relief representative of the A.R.A. was to determine some approximation of the number of children that would require relief and thus give a basis for a program of importation. Next, it was his duty to acquaint the local government with the aims of the Administration and, with their assistance, to organize a national committee to arrange the details of the internal distribution. This committee, with the assistance of the A.R.A. representative, was then to organize the network of subsidiary organizations necessary to distribute the food to needy children in the form of cooked meals.

The national committee operated by dispatching representatives to local areas to organize a committee in each town or district where feeding was to be undertaken. Upon arriving at a town this representative interviewed a few influential persons, usually the mayor or a priest, and asked to have assembled at once a small gathering of leading men and women, such as the head of any local charitable organization, a physician, a prominent Jew, a member of the school board, and others. The proposed work was first described to this gathering and the requirements regarding a local committee outlined. One of the important rules regarding such local committees was that they must be representative of all prevailing races, religions, and classes. Where local conflicts existed between such groups, they were induced by all means possible to subordinate such differences to the higher purposes of this work. The records of the Administration show that in many instances this influence, exerted solely in the interest of child welfare, often brought about mutual understandings which seemed to augur well for future co-operation between these groups.

Although methods necessarily differed somewhat in different countries, there were three steps in selecting the children to be fed which were followed in all cases where possible. These were: first, their registration, which was generally made through the school teachers; second, an investigation of each case by the local committee; and, third, a physical examination by a local physician. These examinations were repeated at regular intervals, and at each examination those children who had reached a fair state of nourishment were taken off the list to make way for others whose condition was worse and who had not been receiving rations.

The child-feeding work was carried on by furnishing a supplementary meal to each child admitted to the feeding. In most places these meals were served at noon, six days a week, in special kitchens set up for the purpose or in existing institutions, such as orphanages or hospitals. Expectant mothers also were provided with food either in hospitals or at special dining-rooms, or in exceptional cases in their own homes. All children upon being admitted to the feeding received a card which was punched for each meal.

The national committees arranged to take care of the internal transportation of all children's relief supplies and, in addition, to arrange for national and local contributions of additional supplies, such as flour, vegetables, etc. The local committees always provided the kitchen facilities, including quarters for offices and kitchens, cooking utensils, dishes, fuel and light, as well as local supplies of vegetables and other food. The local committees also undertook to see that the meals were prepared and served.

By means of this decentralization of efforts, it required a relatively small American personnel to guide and direct these vast operations.

This policy of organizing the relief as a step in self-help had a decided constructive influence upon these local and national groups. It was not unusual to find these groups extending their activities in other directions of their own accord, and many of the organizations continued long after the American child feeding ceased. Benevolence which merely maintains an individual or a group without an incentive for self-help too often tends to lower self-reliance and aggravates the very condition it sought to remedy.

However, the tasks of the American representatives in these countries were by no means easy. The general political turmoil of new governments and their conflicting personalities, frequent ministerial changes, long periods with no responsible government due to inability to form a cabinet, and the feeling in many quarters that there must be some ulterior motive behind these free gifts, all tended to make the work more difficult. Furthermore, the general demoralization of railroad transportation and of all communication systems caused incessant troubles in the moving of supplies from the ports to internal points where they were needed.

Child-feeding programs.—As pointed out above, the first duty of the American representatives was to make some approximation of the number of children in each country needing relief. These first estimates could not be very accurate but they served as a basis for the first relief programs. The first children's relief program by the American Relief Administration was made up early in March, 1919, and contemplated the expenditure of some $2,000,000, allotted chiefly to Austria, the Baltic States, Czechoslovakia, Jugoslavia, Poland, and Roumania. Even before these commodities had arrived, it was found that this was hopelessly inadequate to meet even the most urgent needs for this work. A second program was prepared involving approximately double the amount called for by the first program. Before the close of the American Relief Administration's work, it became clear that many of these children would need to be fed at least to the end of 1919, and a third program was made up in June, 1919, providing sufficient food to feed some 3,000,000 children to the first of 1920. None of the commodities on the third A.R.A. program arrived until after the close of the American Relief Administration in July, 1919. These, together with the remaining stocks from the first and second programs, were turned over to the European Children's Fund for distribution.

Table 55 gives the three relief programs as originally made out by the American Relief Administration. These programs were modified considerably by further knowledge of local needs and the re-allocation of supplies to countries where the requirements were more urgent. In these programs the children's relief for Austria was to be paid for from the President's National Security and Defense Fund since the Congressional Appropriation expressly forbade its use for countries regarded as enemy territory.

Relief from Congressional Appropriation.—As pointed out above, the Children's Relief Bureau of the American Relief Administration was organized in February, 1919. The first child-feeding operations were started early in March and were continued by that organization until the end of July, 1919. By the first of August the American Relief Administration had practically withdrawn and the work had been taken over by the European Children's Fund. A large portion of the children's relief supplies purchased by the A.R.A. from the Congressional Appropriation was designed for use during the latter half of 1919. These supplies either were in store in European ports or warehouses or were still on passage when the work of further distribution was taken over by the E.C.F. For purposes of its records and accounting, all of the child-feeding supplies had been allocated to individual countries in accordance with the indicated needs. Table 113 (Appendix) shows in detail the original allocation of these supplies by countries of destination as given in the records of the American Relief Administration. These allocations are summarized in Table 56.

TABLE 55

AMERICAN RELIEF ADMINISTRATION CHILDREN'S RELIEF PROGRAMS

(Metric Tons)

Country	Flour	Rice	Beans, Peas	Fats	Milk	Sugar	Cocoa	Codliver Oil	Total
			FIRST PROGRAM						
Austria	425	..	45	90	300	180	90	15	1,145
Baltic States	230	23	22	30	105	124	65	..	599
Czechoslovakia	500	117	62	8	455	215	110	10	1,477
Jugoslavia	...	80	..	..	651	173	88	..	992
Poland	850	400	150	..	640	203	228	35*	2,506
Roumania	250	..	30	40	185	202	104	..	811
Total	2,255	620	309	168	2,336	1,097	685	60*	7,530
			SECOND PROGRAM						
Austria	600	450	360	250	675	465	99	..	2,899
Baltic States	298	120	100	40	215	142	97	..	1,012
Czechoslovakia	700	150	184	300	300	...	69	..	1,703
Jugoslavia	760	150	90	90	90	250	158	..	1,588
Poland	...	1,670	1,170	750	1,450	750	440	..	6,230
Roumania	...	170	100	30	250	200	120	..	870
Total	2,358	2,710	2,004	1,460	2,980	1,807	983	..	14,302
			THIRD PROGRAM						
Baltic States	270	180	180	90	1,080	360	180	..	2,340
Czechoslovakia	300	200	200	100	1,200	400	200	..	2,600
Jugoslavia	180	48	120	60	680	240	130	..	1,458
Poland	480	320	320	160	1,680	360	280	..	3,600
Total	1,230	748	820	410	4,640	1,360	790	..	9,998

* Includes 15.0 metric tons of prunes.

When the European Children's Fund came to actually distribute some of these supplies it was found much more economical and convenient to use certain commodities from these stocks for other countries than the ones for which they had been designated. The European Children's Fund was distributing similar commodities purchased with other funds and they not infrequently substituted supplies from these latter sources for the ones allocated from the Congressional Appropriation stocks. Thus, when we come to actually trace the deliveries of the commodities purchased from the Congressional Fund for children's relief we find they were distributed somewhat differently from that shown above in the table of allocations.

TABLE 56

SUMMARY OF ORIGINAL ALLOCATION OF CHILDREN'S RELIEF SUPPLIES PAID FOR FROM THE CONGRESSIONAL APPROPRIATION FOR RELIEF

(For detail see Table 113, Appendix)

Country	Total Metric Tons	Total Value
Czechoslovakia	6,831.4	$ 2,986,054.64
Esthonia	1,444.5	481,381.79
Finland	2,272.1	696,412.22
Jugoslavia	3,445.4	1,335,783.36
Latvia	1,763.3	632,826.90
Lithuania	1,000.4	350,518.35
Poland	16,584.9	6,025,682.03
Roumania	1,432.3	477,272.76
Russia		
Northwest Russia	1,261.9	447,986.28
Total	36,036.2	$13,433,918.33

Table 114 (Appendix) gives the actual distribution of these supplies as totaled from the delivery receipts. These deliveries are summarized in Table 57 (page 88).

The difference between the allocation and actual delivery of these supplies is of no material consequence because, in the case of most of the countries, the E.C.F. furnished supplies to several times the value of those obtained from the Congressional Appropriation. The difference is discussed here because the reports of the American Relief Administration show one set of figures and those of the European Children's Fund show a different set, which might lead to confusion unless explained.

TABLE 57

SUMMARY OF DELIVERIES OF CHILDREN'S RELIEF SUPPLIES PAID FOR FROM THE CONGRESSIONAL APPROPRIATION FOR RELIEF BY COUNTRIES OF DESTINATION

(For detail see Table 114, Appendix)

Country	Total Metric Tons	Total Value
Austria	746.3	$ 319,471.90
Czechoslovakia	6,476.2	2,837,748.69
Esthonia	2,029.9	701,520.82
Finland	2,109.3	660,175.34
Jugoslavia	3,054.3	1,164,617.41
Latvia	2,142.3	753,774.72
Lithuania	1,005.4	351,789.53
Poland	16,700.9	6,055,842.03
Roumania	1,432.3	477,272.76
Russia		
Northwest Russia	305.2	111,705.13
Grand total	36,002.1	$13,433,918.33

All of the children's relief supplies paid for from the Congressional Appropriation were furnished as a gift from the American Government to the children of these respective countries and no obligations for repayment for these supplies were requested. The arrival of these children's relief supplies in European ports is shown in detail in Table 115 (Appendix).

The distribution of other portions of the Congressional Appropriation for Relief has been discussed under the Armistice Period (cf. pages 44–48).

THE PRESIDENT'S NATIONAL SECURITY AND DEFENSE FUND

When Mr. Hoover went to Europe after the Armistice to take charge of the relief activities, President Wilson turned over to him the sum of $5,000,000 from the President's National Security and Defense Fund. This sum was intended as a nucleus for starting such work as was urgently needed and to pay the expenses of such organization as was deemed necessary. The National Security and Defense Fund was an appropriation of $50,000,000 which Congress made available to the President during the war for such emergencies as might arise from time to time, and for which it would be undesirable to await the delays incident to a special appropriation.

Mr. Hoover found it possible to take care of all of the necessary expenses of the relief work from other sources and the $5,000,000 allocated from this fund was used for only two purposes which could not be paid for out of other funds. As pointed out on pages 49–50 these two purposes were supplies for Russian prisoners of war in Germany, and for children's relief to Austria. In summary form the expenditures from the National Security and Defense Fund were as follows (cf. Table 23, page 50):

	Total Metric Tons	Total Value
Russian prisoners of war	1,622.0	$ 390,209.03
Austrian children's relief	7,823.1	2,949,217.23
Total expended	9,445.1	$3,339,426.26
Returned to the President		1,660,573.74
Total		$5,000,000.00

The deliveries to the Russian prisoners of war in Germany have been discussed under the relief work in the Armistice Period.

The children's relief furnished from this fund, although purchased and partly delivered during the Armistice Period, is considered in this report along with other children's relief work in the Reconstruction Period. The reason for the use of this fund for children's relief to Austria was that the Act of Congress making available the $100,000,000 for relief work (Act of February 25, 1919, cf. page 39 n.) expressly forbade its use in Austria or other countries then regarded as enemies of the United States. Yet Austrian children were suffering as much as those of any other country and the new Government had no resources which could be used to purchase supplies. With the approval of President Wilson, Mr. Hoover arranged to furnish urgently needed assistance to Austrian children from this fund.

The children's relief work in Austria was started early in March, 1919, under the Children's Relief Bureau of the American Relief Administration. As in the case of the children's relief deliveries from the Congressional Appropriation, this work was taken over by the European Children's Fund in August, 1919, and a large proportion of the actual deliveries of supplies from the National Security and Defense Fund were made under the direction of the E.C.F.

According to the allocation of supplies made by the American Relief Administration, all of the food purchased from this fund was intended for Austrian children. However, in the actual delivery of these supplies by the E.C.F. a small portion was used for children's relief in Hungary. This change in destination was made only because of convenience and the availability of supplies urgently needed in Hungary. The E.C.F. delivered large quantities of similar food for Austrian children paid for from other funds, which replaced many times the supplies diverted to Hungary.

Table 116 (Appendix) shows in detail the deliveries from the President's National Security and Defense Fund. Table 58 summarizes the children's relief deliveries from this fund as shown by the feeding-station receipts obtained by the European Children's Fund.

TABLE 58

Summary of Children's Relief Deliveries Paid for from the President's National Security and Defense Fund

Country	Total Metric Tons	Total Value
Austria	7,536.1	$2,847,892.23
Hungary	287.0	101,325.00
Total	7,823.1	$2,949,217.23

Relief Supplied by the European Children's Fund

Table 53 (page 82) shows that the European Children's Fund furnished supplies for relief which totaled to 337,953.5 metric tons, valued at $58,370,700.11. This amount includes the relief furnished to the Soviet Republics in the great Russian famine, which in reality was handled by the American Relief Administration Russian Unit.[1] By far the major portion of the relief supplied by the E.C.F. was for child feeding. Of the total shown above, 235,533.1 metric tons, valued at $41,390,238.98, were specifically earmarked as children's relief. This includes 131,412.6 metric tons, valued at $12,347,924.55, for children's relief in Soviet Russia, a part of which, however, was used for adult relief. The children's relief figures include 5,616.1 tons of clothing and 1,000.4 tons of soap. The remainder represented food supplies. Table 59 (page 90) shows total deliveries by the European Children's Fund segregated as children's relief and for other purposes. The detail of the total deliveries is given in Table 156 and in the several tables under the individual countries.

The children's relief deliveries were used to provide supplementary meals for undernourished children in accordance with the methods already described. The particular arrangements varied somewhat from country to country. These differences are set forth in the discussion of deliveries to individual countries.

It will be noted that by far the largest tonnage of children's relief supplies from the E.C.F. went to the Soviet Republics, although the value of these supplies was considerably less than the value of those furnished to Poland. This difference is accounted for by the type of commodities furnished. Those going to Russia consisted to a large extent of flour, meals, corn grits, and other foods with a lower value per ton than that of the type of commodities furnished to Poland. Outside of Russia and Poland the next largest deliveries by the E.C.F. were to Austria, where the suffering was very great. Czechoslovakia, Hungary, and Latvia also received relatively large amounts of these children's relief supplies. The deliveries to Germany were handled through the American Friends Service Committee and represent contributions of commodities to the Friends Committee by the E.C.F. (see pages 117–18).

The relief deliveries by the E.C.F. for purposes other than children's relief were inconsequential, except in the case of Russia. In the other countries these represented chiefly the sale of child-feeding or other commodities to governmental organizations, many of which were donated for the relief work by these governments.

In the case of Russia the relief other than that designated for children and adults was

[1] See discussion on page 6.

TABLE 59

SUMMARY OF RELIEF SUPPLIED BY THE EUROPEAN CHILDREN'S FUND—RECONSTRUCTION PERIOD, 1919–1924

Country of Destination	Children's Relief		Other Relief		Total	
	Metric Tons	Value	Metric Tons	Value	Metric Tons	Value
Austria	25,963.4	$ 6,695,693.43	892.9*	$ 101.26*	26,856.3	$ 6,695,794.69
Czechoslovakia	4,995.0	1,906,945.54	1,292.1†	195,731.31†	6,287.1	2,102,676.85
Danzig Free City	108.0	17,749.51	......	......	108.0	17,749.51
Esthonia	1,831.3	522,929.39	......	......	1,831.3	522,929.39
Finland	91.4	216,205.33	350.1‡	37,662.13‡	441.5	253,867.46
Germany	4,053.0	362,571.27	......	......	4,053.0	362,571.27
Hungary	3,298.1	1,190,832.53	.2§	790.83§	3,298.3	1,191,623.36
Jugoslavia	317.8	490,705.04	......	......	317.8	490,705.04
Latvia	4,020.3	752,076.08	33.5**	2,720.62**	4,053.8	754,796.70
Lithuania	186.9	111,060.61	......	......	186.9	111,060.61
Poland	59,242.5	16,769,322.10	......	......	59,242.5	16,769,322.10
Russia						
Northwest Russia	12.8	6,223.60	......	......	12.8	6,223.60
Soviet Republics	131,412.6	12,347,924.55	99,185.3††	16,644,832.39††	230,597.9	28,992,756.94
Sundry accounts	....	....	562.0‡‡	98,622.59‡‡	562.0	98,622.59
Total	235,533.1	$41,390,238.98	102,316.1	$16,980,461.13	337,849.2	$58,370,700.11

* Includes 892.8 tons obtained in exchange for other commodities and also a sale of 1/10 ton of surplus clothing.
† Bulk sales to Czechoslovakian Government and to the State Fat Institute.
‡ Represents commodities purchased through exchange of surplus stock.
§ Sale of surplus clothing.
** Sale to the Latvian Government.
†† Represents the following items (see Table 511, Russia, for detail):

	Total Metric Tons	Total Value
Clothing deliveries	1,723.4	$ 1,700,795.00
Employees paiok	3,687.5	375,312.38
Food remittance sales	54,316.3	9,305,300.00
Clothing—remittance and bulk sales	350.0	737,317.12
Food—bulk, Eurelcon, and internal sales	34,570.5	4,374,893.28
Sale of damaged commodities	4,537.6	151,214.61
Total	99,185.3	$16,644,832.39

‡‡ Represents deliveries made for the Laura Spelman Rockefeller Memorial.

increased chiefly because of the food and clothing remittances and the bulk sales to other organizations.[1] These transactions are described in detail in the text covering deliveries to the Soviet Republics. In the case of the other countries the bulk sales and remittances were handled by a separate organization of the A.R.A. Warehouses, described elsewhere.

The finance for the relief supplies furnished by the European Children's Fund came from a number of sources. The nucleus of this was furnished by the surplus from the European operations of the Food Administration Grain Corporation.[2] This was greatly increased by the funds obtained through the European Relief Council,[3] and also by funds supplied by various charitable and relief organizations. Also, the profits on the food and clothing remittances and particularly on the bulk sales handled through the A.R.A. Warehouses helped to increase the amount available for charitable relief. Further details of sources of the relief finances are given in another section of this report (pages 142–46).

[1] See footnote †† to Table 59.
[2] Cf. page 76.
[3] Cf. pages 77–80.

AMERICAN RELIEF ADMINISTRATION WAREHOUSES

The last of the four major operations under the immediate supervision of the European Children's Fund is that of the American Relief Administration Warehouses, which handled all of the food and clothing remittance business and the bulk sales of commodities for Central European countries. As shown in Table 53 (page 82) the total supplies handled by this organization amounted to 40,319.5 metric tons with a total value of $9,885,405.73.

Shortly after the European Children's Fund had begun operations in the latter part of 1919, it became evident that in addition to the child-feeding work there was also need for additional adult relief because the supplies of food from the 1919 harvest were insufficient to take care of all requirements. Furthermore, the newly formed governments were not yet in a position to make satisfactory arrangements for imported supplies. Food supplies were being requisitioned and rationed by the governments, but the rations were inadequate and the cost of food outside the rations was exorbitant.

The A.R.A. had had considerable experience in appealing to the residents of America who had emigrated from Central and Eastern Europe. It was known that these people were receiving urgent requests for help from relatives, friends, and acquaintances in the mother countries. These were willing and anxious to render this help but their unorganized efforts largely were meeting with disappointment. If they sent money, this was largely useless because food was not available except at such exorbitant prices that little could be secured with the money sent. If they attempted to send packages of food, these all too often went astray or were looted en route under the chaotic conditions prevailing in most of these countries immediately after the war.

Realizing this condition, Mr. Hoover in November, 1919, proposed to his associates that a scheme of food draft deliveries from warehouses should be put into operation. He proposed to sell through American bankers "food drafts" to persons in this country. These drafts were to be mailed to their relatives or friends in Europe. The receiver could then "cash" the drafts for definite amounts of food at warehouses to be established at designated places in Europe. The operation was to be much the same as the cashing of a foreign bank draft except that the recipient would obtain a package of food instead of money.

For three months the officials of the American Relief Administration worked over the details of this plan, trying to foresee every difficulty and to perfect the machinery for this new experiment to make it both simple and foolproof. Finally, in January, 1920, the scheme was launched. Perhaps no better statement of the purpose and object to be accomplished can be given than the following letter from Mr. Hoover which was sent to American bankers at this time:

To the Bankers of America:

Owing to the slow economic recovery of Europe, the depreciation and exhaustion of its securities, and the shortage of export commodity production, due to the lack of raw material, the only hope of large sections passing the winter without going into sheer anarchy lies in their again obtaining food supplies on some basis of support from America.

Throughout the whole of Central and Eastern Europe the food supply of the people falls into two classes: first, the ration issued by the government; second, illicit circulation of food available to those who have a sufficient amount of money. The government ration is necessarily meagre and nowhere near sufficient to properly maintain life, and must be supplemented. Under these circumstances, the scramble for such supplementary margin has placed the price of the illicit food supplies entirely beyond the reach of the great bulk of the population. To illustrate: A single ham outside the ration system sells for as high as one hundred and fifty dollars.

In groping for a solution of this problem we have decided to undertake a measure on the following basis, as we believe it will contribute largely to relieve the situation:

There are three to four million families in the United States with family affiliations in Eastern and Central Europe. Many of them are desirous of giving direct personal assistance to these relatives and friends. Some are endeavoring to perform this service by preparing or purchasing packages of food for overseas shipment. In some cases the packing and extra freight involved adds one hundred per cent to the cost. We are proposing to solve this difficulty by establishing warehouses to carry stocks of staple foodstuffs in European cities where distress is particularly acute. We propose to sell, in America, orders upon these warehouses in the form of food drafts which can be transmitted to friends or relatives in Europe. We propose to charge the buyer of the food draft the factory cost of the food plus a reasonable margin to cover cost of transportation and insurance. Profits, if any accrue, will be turned over to the European Children's Fund.

The object of this plan is to add to the total stock of available food supplies in Central and Eastern European countries. Under an arrangement set up with the governments of these countries, this food will be allowed to revolve outside the rationing system, with the hope that enough food will be injected to reduce the pressure on the narrow marginal supplies. The officials of these new governments are endeavoring to impress upon the American people that it is useless to remit money to a family in Central or Eastern Europe with the hope of improving its food situation. The sum total of food now available in Central Europe is insufficient to keep the population alive, and under these circumstances money thus becomes that much paper so far as nutrition is concerned. A hungry man wants food, not money, and under the arrangements outlined above we can meet his need. I feel that you will agree that such an enterprise, organized on a thoroughly business basis, will effect a considerable amount of actual relief abroad. I am informed that the President of the American Bankers' Association states that the Association will co-operate in all possible ways in the plan as above outlined. I do not believe, under the system which we have devised, that this will entail any great effort on the part of the banks, and the plan is one of such sympathetic character that the banks can well entertain it to aid the distressed people of Europe.

Faithfully,

(*Signed*) HERBERT HOOVER

The working out of the detailed plans for this undertaking brought up many difficult problems. First, it was necessary to insure the co-operation of the banks all over the United States; it was necessary that instructions to these banks be simple and should not require revision. The food packages must be simple and unvarying in content, although five nations and two classes of consumers, Christian and Jew, had to be served. The price of the packages would have to remain unchanged for at least a year. It was necessary to build up these stocks of foods and establish the warehouses, together with the personnel to operate them. Steps had to be taken to insure that the food furnished was of the highest quality; and to make certain of this the A.R.A. established its own inspectors in every factory where this food was purchased.

The careful attention which was given to these and many other details based upon experience in Belgium and other countries was responsible very largely for the success of this undertaking. Another important element in this success was the whole-hearted co-operation of the banks throughout the United States and in many other countries. Food drafts were sold by 4,827 banks located in every state in the United States and in Alaska, the Hawaiian Islands, Canada, Central and South American countries, Mexico, England, France, Denmark, and Australia. This service was performed by the banks without any remuneration whatever.

ORIGINAL NOT TRANSFERABLE — GOOD ONLY IF PRESENTED WITHIN 90 DAYS FROM DATE OF ISSUE

No. 744684

FOOD DRAFT

ADMINISTERED BY AND FOR THE PROFIT OF THE EUROPEAN CHILDREN'S FUND

To American Relief Administration Warehouse at Hamburg

Date NOV 3 1920

Please deliver on presentation to Johanna Bellinger

Or his properly constituted representative one Packages

Designated as letter A Hereon, being the equivalent of $10#

IN CASE OF EMERGENCY WE RESERVE THE RIGHT TO SUBSTITUTE COMMODITIES OF EQUAL FOOD VALUE

A	B	C	D
24½ lbs. Flour 10 lbs. Beans 8 lbs. Bacon 8 cans Milk	140 lbs. Flour 50 lbs. Beans 16 lbs. Bacon 15 lbs. Lard 12 lbs. Corned Beef 48 cans Milk	24½ lbs. Flour 10 lbs. Beans 7½ lbs. C'ttnseed Oil 12 cans Milk	140 lbs. Flour 50 lbs. Beans 45 lbs. C'ttnseed Oil 48 cans Milk
$10	$50	$10	$50

American Relief Administration

Herbert Hoover, CHAIRMAN — Edgar Rickard, DIRECTOR

THE CORN EXCHANGE BANK, UNIVERSITY BRANCH.

COUNTERSIGNING BANK

AT New York City

The Gift of Franz Bellinger

Address 50 [illegible] N.Y. City

Signature [illegible] Ass't Manager

THE COST OF THIS FOOD DRAFT AS SHOWN ABOVE COVERS ALL EXPENSE TO PURCHASER INCLUDING ANY BANKING CHARGES

Facsimile of food draft drawn on American Relief Administration Warehouse at Hamburg.

Central warehouses were established in important cities in five countries as follows: Prague, Czechoslovakia; Warsaw, Poland; Hamburg, Germany; Budapest, Hungary; and Vienna, Austria. It was soon found that because of transportation and other difficulties it would be necessary to establish branch warehouses in many other cities. Altogether, sixty-four such branch warehouses were established, located as follows:

Czechoslovakia
- *Central Warehouse*
  - Praha (Prague)
- *Branch Warehouses*
  - Brno (Brünn)
  - Opava (Troppau)
  - Bratislava (Pressburg)
  - Mukačevo (Munkácz)
  - Košice (Kaschau)
  - Karlovy Vary (Karlsbad)
  - Ústi n/Labem (Aussig)
  - Plzeň (Pilsen)
  - Liberec (Reichenberg)

Poland
- *Central Warehouse*
  - Warszawa (Warsaw)
- *Branch Warehouses*
  - Białystok
  - Kraków (Cracow)
  - Łódź
  - Lwów (Lemberg)
  - Chelm
  - Brześć Litewski (Brest Litovsk)
  - Sosnowiec
  - Wilno (Vilna)
  - Kowel
  - Danzig
  - Bedzin (Bendzin)
  - Stanisławów
  - Tarnopol
  - Przemyśl

Germany
- *Central Warehouse*
  - Hamburg
- *Branch Warehouses*
  - Berlin
  - Frankfurt a/Main
  - München (Munich)
  - Stuttgart
  - Dresden
  - Leipzig

Hungary
- *Central Warehouse*
  - Budapest

Austria
- *Central Warehouse*
  - Wien (Vienna)
- *Branch Warehouses*
  - Wiener Neustadt
  - Eggenberg
  - St. Pölten
  - Amstetten
  - Linz
  - Wels
  - Steyr
  - Gmunden
  - Kirchdorf
  - Graz
  - Mürzzuschlag
  - Bruck a/Mur
  - Leoben
  - Selzthal
  - Salzburg
  - Schwarzach
  - Klagenfurt
  - St. Veit
  - Villach
  - Innsbrück
  - Wörgl
  - Lienz
  - Feldkirch
  - Bregenz
  - Vorarlberg
  - Aussee
  - Knittelfeld
  - Krems
  - Voitsberg
  - Admont
  - Melk

The location of these warehouses and the territory served by the food draft operations are shown in the map on page 132.

The foods were shipped in bulk from the United States either to Hamburg or Danzig and then transported to the several warehouses, where they were made up into the standard packages ready for delivery upon presentation of the drafts by the recipients.

The contents of the food packages were carefully standardized by food experts to contain the maximum nutrient value consistent with bulk and price. Drafts were sold for four different types of packages at two different prices. Packages "A" and "B" were sold at $10 and $50, respectively, and contained foods for consumption by Christians. Packages "C" and "D" at the same respective prices contained food for Jewish consumption.

The contents of the four types of packages were as follows:

Package "A" $10.00	Package "B" $50.00
24½ lbs. flour	140 lbs. flour
10 lbs. beans	50 lbs. beans
8 lbs. bacon	16 lbs. bacon
8 cans milk	15 lbs. lard
	12 lbs. corned beef
	48 cans milk

Package "C" $10.00	Package "D" $50.00
24½ lbs. flour	140 lbs. flour
10 lbs. beans	50 lbs. beans
7½ lbs. cottonseed oil	45 lbs. cottonseed oil
12 cans milk	48 cans milk

In November, 1920, due to the decrease in the cost of food, each $10 package was augmented by 2 and 1/5 pounds sugar and 1 pound cocoa, and each $50 package by 13 pounds of sugar and 3 and 1/3 pounds of cocoa, in addition to the commodities listed.

Food drafts were primarily designed for the convenience of persons having friends or relatives in Central Europe. However, provision was also made for anyone charitably inclined to purchase drafts for "General Relief" if there were no individual to whom they wished to send food. Many thousands of dollars of "General Relief" drafts were purchased. The American Relief Administration undertook to see that all such packages were delivered to worthy and needy individuals. The selection of recipients was usually made by local committees, but in some instances selections were made from lists of those who had applied for relief. The final selection was made only after careful investigation.

Soon after the Warehouses had begun operations it was found that many organizations conducting relief in Europe desired to purchase supplies from these Warehouses, rather than to take the trouble and risk of importing directly relatively small lots of food. Arrangements were therefore perfected by which so-called "bulk sales" could be made from warehouse stocks. Each warehouse was stocked with the following commodities:

Cocoa	Flour	Pure lard
Sugar	Peas	Lard substitute
Evaporated milk	Beans	Vegetable oil
Condensed milk	Rice	Corned beef
		Bacon

Bulk sales were limited to a minimum of $500 value, but any relief organization could purchase supplies made up of any of the above commodities at definitely determined prices. Advantage was also taken of this plan by many European governments to purchase food for relief purposes. This plan proved to be of great assistance to many organizations, and almost four million dollars' worth of food supplies were sold in these bulk sales.

Although it was not intended that the warehouse operations should yield a profit, yet it was necessary that a sufficient protective allowance be made for fluctuating food prices, administrative expenses, transportation, port charges, insurance, etc. Because of the experience with the Belgian Relief Commission it was possible to arrive at fairly definite overhead charges to cover the expenses and the risks involved. However, owing to the unforeseen decline in food prices, the warehouse operations resulted in fairly large profits. As indicated in Mr. Hoover's letter to the bankers, and in the agreement with the respective countries, these profits were all turned over to the European Children's Fund to be used for child feeding in the countries to which the drafts had been sent. The surplus from A.R.A.W. operations, totaling $605,194.61, was divided between the several countries as follows:

Distribution of Surplus of A.R.A. Warehouses

Austria	$289,222.50
Czechoslovakia	44,481.81
Hungary	45,813.23
Poland	80,914.52
Sub-total	$460,432.06
Germany	144,762.55
Total	$605,194.61

Of this amount, $460,432.06 was turned over to the European Children's Fund and used for child feeding in the countries indicated. The $144,762.55 for Germany was turned over to the American Friends Service Committee for use in German child feeding, since the A.R.A. had no organization for that purpose in Germany.

TABLE 60

Summary of Food Draft and Bulk Sale Deliveries by the American Relief Administration Warehouses—Reconstruction Period, 1919–1924

Country of Destination	Food Drafts		Bulk Sales		Total	
	Metric Tons	Value	Metric Tons	Value	Metric Tons	Value
Austria	6,030.7	$2,444,510.00	5,765.1	$ 886,125.48	11,795.8	$3,330,635.48
Czechoslovakia	815.1	347,750.00	561.4	85,682.69	1,376.5	433,432.69
Danzig Free City	63.6	25,920.00	169.3	45,165.48	232.9	71,085.48
Esthonia	.....	....	293.5	146,556.24	293.5	146,556.24
Germany	5,242.8	2,096,410.00	4,104.6	724,010.47	9,347.4	2,820,420.47
Hungary	912.6	373,850.00	717.0	154,089.41	1,629.6	527,939.41
Latvia	.....*	20.00	84.0	15,666.15	84.0	15,686.15
Poland	1,571.3	624,910.00	13,988.5†	1,914,739.81†	15,559.8†	2,539,649.81†
Total	14,636.1	$5,913,370.00	25,683.4	$3,972,035.73	40,319.5	$9,885,405.73

* Only two drafts sold, amounting to less than 1/10 ton.
† Includes 7,720.3 metric tons, worth $864,562.40, purchased through the warehouse at Danzig.

The sales of food drafts which were begun in January, 1920, were continued until April 30, 1921, at which time all banks were notified to stop selling. This operation was discontinued because a survey of the several countries showed that food conditions were becoming much more normal and the Central European governments were planning to decontrol all food supplies. The arrangements were that the Warehouses would honor all drafts sold prior to April 30, 1921, and presented to the Warehouses, before July 31, 1921. During the period of warehouse operation a total of 403,037 food drafts of all kinds were sold and delivered, amounting to $5,913,370. A summary of these deliveries is given in Table 60. Further details will be found in Tables 153 and 154 in the Appendix.

The bulk sales operations were proving so helpful to the relief work of the various governments and relief organizations that it was decided to continue the warehouse operations after the sale of food drafts had been discontinued. These Warehouses were also useful in connection with the child-feeding operations as centers from which to make deliveries to feeding stations.

The bulk sales were continued up until June, 1923, during which time 25,683.4 metric tons of food, valued at $3,972,035.73, were delivered in this way. A summary of these operations also is given in Table 60 and further details are shown in the Appendix Tables 153–155.

Further profits originating from the bulk sales and other warehouse operations amounted to $630,969.07 and were used to defray the expenses of the European Relief Council campaign.[1]

Special Programs

Outside of the warehouse and food draft operations the work of the European Children's Fund in Central Europe was connected chiefly with child relief. As a matter of fact, contributions to its funds were given with the definite understanding that they would be used only for child feeding, a restriction which was always very carefully observed. The aftermath of the war, however, left a considerable portion of the adult population in extreme distress. This was particularly true of the educated and professional classes. With the vanishing purchasing power of their former income, if they were so fortunate as to have even this, college professors, teachers, lawyers, doctors, actors, engineers, and many others were often unable to secure sufficient food for mere existence. The appeal to the educated classes in the United States and in other countries resulted in a considerable volume of food drafts designated for college professors and teachers, but these were far too limited to meet the widespread needs.

Intelligentsia Dining Room, Lwów University, Poland.

Appeals were therefore made to a number of charitable foundations in the United States to render special assistance in connection with these problems of adult feeding in Central Europe. These organizations responded freely, and during the period from 1919 to 1923 considerable sums of money were contributed mainly for this purpose. The books of the E.C.F. accounted for the donations under the heading of "Special programs." In addition, certain contributions obtained during the European Relief Council drive were designated for or were available for adult relief. The total contributions accounted for under the heading of "Special programs," together with the sources of these funds, are shown in Table 61 (page 96). These sums have already been accounted for in connection with relief furnished by the European Children's Fund, or by other organizations, but it is desirable to include some further description of this work at this point.

[1] See page 79.

TABLE 61

Source of Funds for the Special Programs (Chiefly Intelligentsia Relief)

The Commonwealth Fund	$2,165,211.20
The Joint Distribution Committee	250,000.00
The Laura Spelman Rockefeller Memorial	98,622.59
American Relief Administration	695,323.76
Refugee Relief	302,300.00
Total	$3,511,457.55

The Commonwealth Fund.—The Commonwealth Fund was incorporated under the laws of the state of New York on October 17, 1918. The purpose of the organization as stated in the articles of incorporation was "the application to charitable purposes of the income or the principal of such property as from time to time the corporation shall possess." The organization had its inception in the offer of a very considerable gift from Mrs. Stephen V. Harkness, which was later supplemented by further gifts from the same source. The appropriations from the fund have largely been used for the purposes of aiding child welfare, the promotion of health and hygienic activities, and for educational research. In general, the appropriations have been made in the form of grants to organizations already in existence, rather than to establish new organizations to carry out the purposes of the corporation.

During the first year of its existence the directors of the Fund became convinced that the critical condition of many of the peoples of Europe, as a result of the long continued war, was a matter to which they should give attention. As a result of these inquiries, negotiations were entered into with the American Relief Administration European Children's Fund, by which very considerable donations were made to the latter organization during the period from 1919 to 1923. Following is a summary of these appropriations as shown by the annual reports of the Commonwealth Fund:

Appropriations by the Commonwealth Fund to the European Children's Fund

Fiscal Year	Total Appropriation
1919–1920	$1,250,000
1920–1921	600,000
1921–1922	149,000
1922–1923	150,000
Total	$2,149,000

In addition to these appropriations, there should be added the sum of $16,211.20, which represents the amount received by the American Relief Administration from the sale of flour in Armenia, an amount which was used for subsequent relief deliveries by the European Children's Fund and credited to the Commonwealth Fund. The total amount to be accounted for by the American Relief Administration is therefore $2,165,211.20.

Certain of these funds were appropriated with the understanding that they would be used for definite purposes, while other funds were given for the general relief activities in Central Europe. The appropriations from this fund were especially valuable in furnishing relief to the intelligentsia classes in Central Europe, especially university professors, many of whom were in dire distress during these years.

The records of the American Relief Administration show the following allocation of these funds by countries and by types of relief:

Distribution by European Children's Fund of Appropriations Received from the Commonwealth Fund, 1919–1923

Country	Food Drafts	Intelligentsia General Relief	Professors' Relief	Child Feeding	Total
Armenia	....	....	....	$746,107.12*	$ 746,107.12*
Austria	$200,000.00	$470,868.38	$20,464.66	....	691,333.04
Czechoslovakia	62,500.00	20,001.10	....	....	82,501.10
Danzig Free City	9,752.84	5,000.00	....	....	14,752.84
Hungary	62,500.00	64,494.30	....	....	126,994.30
Poland	175,000.00	226,532.38	....	....	401,532.38
To E.C.F. general fund	....	1,639.18	....	351.24	1,990.42
To E.C.F. for E.R.C. fund	....	....	....	100,000.00	100,000.00
Total	$509,752.84	$788,535.34	$20,464.66	$846,458.36	$2,165,211.20

* This sum is accounted for under the Commonwealth Fund. See page 121.

The contributions from the Commonwealth Fund for European relief were made in nine separate appropriations. Thus the contribution in 1919–1920, totaling $1,250,000, consisted of three separate appropriations. The first appropriation of $750,000 was to assist the feeding of Armenian children during the winter of 1919–1920, while the second and third appropriations of $250,000 each were for the purchase of food drafts to be distributed by the American Relief Administration to individuals of the intellectual classes in Central Europe.

The contribution of $600,000 in 1920–1921 was made in four separate appropriations. The first of these, or the fourth in the total appropriations, consisted of $100,000 given to the European Relief Council. This gift, made on November 30, 1920, formed part of the large funds raised during the Relief Council drive. No separate segregation of this particular fund to countries can be made, but it is included in the relief furnished by the European Children's Fund, previously discussed.

The fifth appropriation from the Commonwealth Fund consisted of $250,000 given to supply food for the intellectual classes in Central Europe. The sixth appropriation of $150,000 was given in response to the urgent need for clothing by the suffering intelligentsia of these countries. With the exception of $5,464.66, this latter appropriation was used for clothing in Austria, Hungary, and Poland. The latter sum was used for special food relief to Austrian university professors, as discussed later.

The seventh appropriation from the Commonwealth Fund made near the end of June, 1921, consisted of an additional $100,000 for intelligentsia relief. This money was received so late in the fiscal year that it was carried over and distributed in 1921–1922, along with the $149,000 contained in the eighth Commonwealth Fund appropriation. These two appropriations were used to supply food to the intellectual classes in Austria and Poland.

The ninth and last appropriation from the Commonwealth Fund was made in 1922–1923 and consisted of $150,000 for the intellectual classes in Austria, where there was still great suffering.

In order to defray the costs of port operations, inland freight, and other sundry expenses connected with the delivery of the relief supplies in Armenia, it was found necessary from time to time to sell small amounts of flour in Constantinople for cash. As a result of these operations, there remained $16,211.20 as a cash balance, which was credited to the Commonwealth Fund. This balance plus $3,892.88 of the original appropriation not spent for Armenian food ($750,000.00 − $746,107.12 = $3,892.88) made a total of $20,104.08 remaining to the credit of the Commonwealth Fund. This sum was later used to purchase food drafts for destitute intelligentsia in Austria and Danzig Free City. The actual allocation of this balance was as follows:

Danzig Free City	$ 9,752.84
Austria—Graz	5,000.00
Austria—Vienna	5,000.00
E.C.F. general feeding balance	351.24
Total	$20,104.08

The distribution of the funds from each of the Commonwealth appropriations as shown by the records of the American Relief Administration is given in the accompanying table (Table 62), which also includes the allocation of the cash received from the sale of flour in Armenia.

There was also the sum of $1,639.18 remaining from the fifth Commonwealth appropriation which was turned into unallocated general funds of the European Children's Fund and is accounted for under Special Programs as shown on page 112. As a matter of fact, this money was used along with other funds for additional food relief to the intelligentsia in Poland, but in order to tie this up with the actual delivery of food it is necessary to account for it under other operations of the American Relief Administration.

a) *Armenian Relief:* The Commonwealth Fund contribution formed part of the funds expended under the direction of Colonel (now Major General) William N. Haskell, Allied High Commissioner to Armenia.[1] The contribution from the Commonwealth Fund was used to purchase four cargoes of foodstuffs in the United States, which were shipped from New York late in 1919 and early in 1920. These four cargoes, carried on the "Chincha," "Massillon Bridge,"

[1] See pages 151–52 for discussion of the work of Colonel Haskell's mission.

TABLE

DISTRIBUTION BY APPROPRIATIONS OF THE

Country	1919–1920			1920–1921	
	First	Second	Third	Fourth	Fifth
Armenia	$746,107.12	....	....	....	....
Austria	....	$125,000.00	$ 75,000.00	....	$ 93,393.12
Czechoslovakia	....	25,000.00	37,500.00	....	20,001.10
Danzig Free City	3,892.88	....	....	....	5,000.00
Hungary	....	37,500.00	25,000.00	....	39,966.71
Poland	....	62,500.00	112,500.00	....	89,999.89
European Relief Council and general	....	....	....	$100,000.00	1,639.18
Total	$750,000.00	$250,000.00	$250,000.00	$100,000.00	$250,000.00

"Lake Fiscus," and "River Araxes" (see arrival table, pages 410–11), consisted of the following commodities for the child-feeding program:

Commodity	Metric Tons
Flour	2,679.3
Milk, condensed	102.8
Sugar	96.5
Cocoa	61.0
Beans	404.6
Rice	366.9
Fats	50.9
Total	3,762.0

The total cost of these four cargoes delivered in Near East ports amounted to $746,107.12.

No detail of the internal distribution of these foodstuffs in Armenia is available, but Colonel Haskell reported that this contribution enabled the relief mission to reach nearly all the undernourished Armenian children, as well as some of other nationalities. At the height of the work more than 75,000 children were being fed daily. When Colonel Haskell left Armenia in July, 1920, he reported that there were sufficient quantities of these foods remaining to continue the child-feeding program, as taken over by the Near East Relief, for at least four months. In the meantime, the Near East Relief made provision for continuing the work which had been inaugurated through the Commonwealth Fund appropriation.

b) *Austria:* Probably in no country of Central Europe were the post-war conditions of the intellectual classes so deplorable as in the new republic of Austria. Vienna, once the great center of art, drama, and learning, presented a sorry spectacle in the period from 1920 to 1923. Thousands of individuals of the former wealthy and intellectual classes were existing by trading for food such remnants of former prosperous days as remained in their hands. It was not unusual to see families take an old coat or an old pair of shoes into the country to trade for a few potatoes or other vegetables. And still other thousands had nothing left to trade.

It was conditions such as these which influenced the trustees of the Commonwealth Fund to make their appropriations for the relief of the suffering intellectuals. As shown in Table 61, a total of $691,333.04 from the Commonwealth Fund was expended in Austria. Of this amount, $62,475.26, from the sixth appropriation, was for clothing. The remainder of the Commonwealth appropriations was spent for food. The latter was distributed both as packages to individuals and as bulk food to intelligentsia kitchens and to students' and professors' messes.

As in the other countries, this relief was distributed in co-operation with, and on the recommendation of, local committees. An Austrian national committee was formed, headed by Karl Seitz, then president of the Austrian Republic. Under the direction of this organization, numerous local committees were formed representing the various professions. Approximately 70 per cent of the intelligentsia relief in Austria was distributed in Vienna. The remainder went to the provinces, particularly to the Universities of Innsbruck, Graz, and Loeben.

Table 63 (pages 100–101) shows distribution of food supplies made available from each of the Commonwealth appropriations, by occupation of the beneficiary so far as this was known. This food was supplied to a total of more than 150,000 separate beneficiaries and represented the equivalent of almost 11,000,000 meals.

62

Commonwealth Fund Contributions to European Relief

1920–1921		1921–22	1922–1923	Cash from Flour Sales	Total	Country
Sixth	Seventh	Eighth	Ninth			
....	....	....	....	....	$ 746,107.12	Armenia
$ 67,939.92	$ 45,000.00	$125,000.00	$150,000.00	$10,000.00	691,333.04	Austria
....	....	....	....	....	82,501.10	Czechoslovakia
....	....	....	....	5,859.96	14,752.84	Danzig Free City
24,527.59	....	....	....	....	126,994.30	Hungary
57,532.49	55,000.00	24,000.00	....	....	401,532.38	Poland
....	....	....	....	351.24	101,990.42	European Relief Council and general
$150,000.00	$100,000.00	$149,000.00	$150,000.00	$16,211.20	$2,165,211.20	Total

In addition to the distribution of food detailed above, a total of $62,475.26 from the sixth Commonwealth appropriation was expended for clothing for the intellectual classes in Austria. This sum was used to purchase the following commodities:

Commodity	Quantity	
Shoes	5,800	pairs
Socks and stockings	11,600	pairs
Woolen cloth	20,913	yards
Lining	28,156½	yards
Pocketing	9,883	yards
Combination underwear	2,800	suits
Undershirts	8,800	each
Underdrawers	8,800	pairs
Needles	5,000	number
Thread	3,000	cops
Buckles	8,800	each
Ivory buttons	68,544	number
Metal buttons	53,568	number
Hooks and eyes	6,912	pairs
Snap fasteners	12,096	pairs
Total value	$62,475.26	

This material was arranged in packages as follows:

Men's outfits:
- Cloth with accessories for 1 suit
- 2 pairs of socks
- 2 suits of underwear
- 1 pair shoes

Women's outfits:
- Cloth with accessories for 1 dress
- 2 pairs of stockings
- 2 suits of underwear
- 1 pair shoes

At the time these outfits were distributed in the winter of 1921–1922 the local prices of clothing had increased some 600 per cent over prewar prices. The value of such an outfit in the local shops approximated 100,000 Kronen.

Following is the distribution of these clothing outfits by districts. All packages were distributed to the intellectual classes, but no complete statistics are available as to the distribution to different classes in the population.

Distribution of Commonwealth Fund Clothing in Austria

(Number of Outfits)

Province	Men	Women	Total
Vienna	2,772	882	3,654
Lower Austria	220	70	290
Upper Austria	264	84	348
Salzburg	176	56	732
Tyrol	308	98	406
Vorarlberg	44	14	58
Styria	440	140	580
Carinthia	176	56	232
Total	4,400	1,400	5,800

The total relief delivered to the Austrian intelligentsia from the Commonwealth Fund appropriations may be summarized as follows:

	Food	Clothing	Total
Value of relief distributed	$628,857.78	$62,475.26	$691,333.04
Number of beneficiaries	150,038	5,800	158,838
Equivalent number of meals	10,889,778	....	10,889,778
Average cost per beneficiary	$4.24	$10.77	....
Average cost per meal	$0.0584	....	....

TABLE

DISTRIBUTION OF
FROM THE SEVERAL COMMON-
FOR INTELLECTUAL

Occupation	Appropriation No. 2 No. of Benefi- ciaries	Appropriation No. 2 Value	Appropriation No. 3 No. of Benefi- ciaries	Appropriation No. 3 Value	Appropriation No. 5 No. of Benefi- ciaries	Appropriation No. 5 Value
Professors	1,192	$ 6,000.00	1,000	$ 8,350.00	1,553	$20,407.12
Students	3,008	15,000.00	3,280	8,200.00	...	......
Physicians	407	2,000.00	1,030	8,617.00	309	8,448.00
Lawyers	5,173	25,900.00	435	3,674.00	207	5,632.00
Teachers	4,694	23,500.00	966	8,083.00	534	14,502.00
Engineers and architects	1,506	7,500.00	308	2,538.00	...	......
Army officers	2,409	12,000.00	795	6,613.00	...	......
Authors	....	......	...	......	229	6,248.00
Musicians	....	......	...	......	173	4,664.00
Artists	1,991‡	10,000.00	636‡	5,277.00	...	......
Actors	....	......	...	......	416	11,264.00
Clergy	1,765	8,800.00	163	1,403.00	89	2,428.00
Public employees	....	......	...	......	...	......
Private employees	....	......	...	......	...	......
Small pensioners	....	......	...	......	...	......
Welfare institutions	287	1,500.00	...	......	...	......
Social workers	....	......	...	......	...	......
Retired officials	2,396	12,000.00	...	......	...	......
Chemists	164	800.00	...	......	...	......
Clerks	....	......	1,335	11,156.00	...	......
Civil servants	....	......	...	......	729	19,800.00
Miscellaneous, not segregated	....	......	1,329	11,089.00	...	......
Total	24,992	$125,000.00	11,277	$75,000.00	4,239	$93,393.12
Equivalent number of meals	1,752,665		1,051,600		1,402,584	

* Proceeds from sale of surplus flour.

† Includes $5,464.66 from the sixth Commonwealth appropriation. This appropriation was intended for clothing relief, but $5,000 of this was utilized for the purchase of additional food and $464.66 was turned over to Dr. C. Pirquet for the purchase of kitchen equipment to facilitate the distribution of food in the professors' and students' messes. Included in this item was $15,000 from the seventh appropriation which was given by the Common-

c) *Czechoslovakia:* In Czechoslovakia a national committee was formed in 1920, consisting of representatives of various professional societies, which recommended the cases of individuals or families among the intellectual classes which were in most serious need of relief.

As shown by Table 62 (pages 98–99), the total amount from the Commonwealth Fund distributed in Czechoslovakia was $82,501.10, which represented parts of the second, third, and fifth appropriations. The second and third appropriations were used entirely for food drafts, and

DISTRIBUTION OF FOOD DRAFTS FROM THE COMMONWEALTH FUND IN CZECHOSLOVAKIA

Type of Beneficiary	Number of Individuals	Sales Value
College professors	354	$ 1,282
School teachers	3,733	13,525
High-school teachers	34	125
Clergymen	972	3,524
Physicians	497	1,800
Lawyers	248	900
Engineers and architects	373	1,350
Musicians	1,923	6,966
Actors	310	1,121
Artists	197	712
Authors	231	836
Journalists	195	$ 709
Jewish students	2,760	10,000
Families of disabled and fallen officers	1,546	5,600
Intellectuals in Karlsbad district	28	100
Pensioned officials	3,105	11,250
Miscellaneous	745	2,700
Total	17,251	$62,500
Equivalent number of meals		400,000

63

FOOD RELIEF
WEALTH FUND APPROPRIATIONS
CLASSES IN AUSTRIA

Appropriations Nos. 6, 7		Appropriation No. 8		Appropriation No. 9		Cash Receipts *		Total	
No. of Beneficiaries	Value	No. of Beneficiaries	Value	No. of Beneficiaries	Value	No. of Beneficiaries	Value	Total No. of Beneficiaries	Total Value
12,399	$50,464.66†	737	$ 1,792.60	1,004	$ 2,859.92	1,523	$10,000.00	19,408	$ 99,874.30†
.....	....	...	....	3,920	22,693.47	....	....	10,208	45,893.47
.....	....	796	2,101.53	993	2,266.61	....	....	3,535	23,433.14
.....	....	769	2,038.84	835	2,062.71	....	....	7,419	39,307.55
.....	....	2,581	7,034.72	2,824	6,799.20	....	....	11,599	59,918.92
.....	....	810	2,258.87	1,152	2,675.65	....	....	3,776	14,972.52
.....	....	3,163	8,891.84	2,955	7,696.01	....	....	9,322	35,200.85
.....	....	424	1,124.13	660	1,937.90	....	....	}	}
.....	....	1,124	3,187.91	1,313	3,162.49	....	....	} 9,390	} 53,387.63
.....	....	764	2,180.82	833	2,116.79	....	....	}	}
.....	....	382	1,038.99	445	1,185.60	....	....	}	}
.....	....	132	295.51	315	636.79	....	....	2,464	13,563.30
.....	....	12,804	38,617.24	13,531	34,459.01	....	....	26,335	73,076.25
.....	....	5,928	17,352.48	7,809	20,253.92	....	....	13,737	37,606.40
.....	....	3,436	9,916.35	4,039	10,281.41	....	....	7,475	20,197.76
.....	....	1,363	4,854.14	1,267	4,375.98	....	....	2,917	10,730.12
.....	....	982	2,809.39	1,339	3,418.41	....	....	2,321	6,227.80
.....	....	...	....	....	......	....	....	2,396	12,000.00
.....	....	...	....	....	......	....	....	164	800.00
.....	....	...	....	....	......	....	....	1,335	11,156.00
.....	....	...	....	....	......	....	....	729	19,800.00
.....	....	7,870	19,504.64	6,309	21,118.13	....	....	15,508	51,711.77
12,399	$50,464.66	44,065	$125,000.00	51,543	$150,000.00	1,523	$10,000.00	150,038	$628,857.78
560,321		2,013,013		3,969,381		140,214		10,889,778	

wealth Fund as a Christmas gift to Austrian professors in December, 1921. The remaining $30,000 from the seventh appropriation was utilized partly for student relief and partly for professors. The statistics do not show the complete separation between these two classes and the total has been included here under professors, although a part of the 9,881 beneficiaries fed from this sum were university students.

‡ Includes authors, musicians, and actors.

of these Czechoslovakia received $62,500, representing approximately 400,000 meals. These food drafts were distributed to 17,251 individuals, at an average cost of $3.62 per person. The accompanying table shows the distribution of the food drafts among the several types of beneficiaries.

From the fifth Commonwealth appropriation, the sum of $20,001.10 was distributed in Czechoslovakia to assist college professors and their families in the universities of Prague and Brünn. From this fund, 2,420 individuals were given a total of 145,200 meals.

The total Commonwealth relief in Czechoslovakia thus supplied the equivalent of 545,200 meals to 19,671 individuals, with a total value of $82,501.10.

d) Danzig Free City: As in other sections of Central Europe, the professional and intellectual classes in Danzig Free City were in serious need in 1921 and 1922. No specific mention had been made of Danzig in the Commonwealth Fund appropriations, but, with the surplus derived from the sale of Armenian flour and certain surplus stocks accumulated in other Central European countries, the European Children's Fund was able to take care of a portion of the suffering in that country. Relief amounting to $14,752.84 was furnished to the educated classes in Danzig from the Commonwealth Fund. Of this amount, the sum of $9,752.84 was delivered in 1921 and 1922 in the form of food drafts, which supplied the equivalent of 122,964 meals to 3,351 beneficiaries distributed among the different classes of the population as shown in the table on page 102.

When the Commonwealth Fund decided to continue intelligentsia relief in Poland to June, 1923, as provided in their fifth appropriation, an appeal was made on behalf of the Free City of Danzig. Early in January, 1923, the sum of $5,000 was set aside for additional intelli-

Distribution of Food Drafts from the Commonwealth Fund in Danzig Free City

Type of Beneficiary	Number of Individuals	Sales Value
Professors	7	$ 20.37
Teachers	643	1,871.41
Clergymen	114	331.79
Lawyers	21	61.12
Musicians	149	433.65
Retired officers	208	605.37
Students	132	384.17
Sea captains	114	331.79
Pensioned higher officials	889	2,587.37
Engineers	73	212.46
Widows of prominent merchants	303	881.86
Miscellaneous	698	2,031.48
Total	3,351	$9,752.84
Equivalent number of meals		122,964

gentsia feeding in that city. These funds were used for the purchase of the following commodities from the Relief Administration supplies:

Commodity	Metric Tons
Flour	16.9
Sugar	3.1
Rice	4.9
Corn grits	3.0
Cocoa	1.0
Lard substitute	2.8
Vegetable oil	1.4
Milk, evaporated	8.0
Milk, condensed	2.0
Total	43.1

Three kitchens were opened, one in the Wiebenkaserne and two in the suburb of Langfuhr. Approximately 800 persons were served one meal a day from these kitchens for a period of six months, making a total of approximately 144,000 meals, costing $5,000, or an average of 3.47 cents per meal.

The total relief to Danzig from the Commonwealth Fund, totaling $14,752.84, supplied 4,151 beneficiaries with an equivalent of 266,964 meals.

The appreciation of this gift is perhaps best expressed in a letter to the American Relief Administration from President H. Sahm of the Free City of Danzig, in which he says in part:

It has caused us great joy to note the interest which America has always evinced in the fate of our suffering population, and in the well-being of our tiny state. But this gift for our intellectuals brings special gladness to our heart; it will appease the hunger of many of our unfortunate citizens whom the Free City would like to, but is powerless to help.

Please accept our thanks and the thanks of our people for your organization and for your generous country which has not forgotten us in our need.

e) *Hungary:* In Hungary the distribution of food packages from gifts of the Commonwealth Fund began in July, 1920, and food relief ended in January, 1921. As in other countries, a Hungarian committee of representatives of professional societies was formed to aid in the investigation and selection of the most needy cases. Food relief, totaling $102,466.71, was supplied to Hungary from the second, third, and fifth Commonwealth appropriations and, in addition, $24,527.59 worth of clothing from the sixth appropriation. Thus, the relief to Hungarian intellectuals from this source totaled $126,994.30.

The second and third appropriations were used in the form of food drafts, with a total value of $62,500, which represented the equivalent of about 660,000 meals and were distributed to families and individuals totaling approximately 25,000 beneficiaries. The distribution of these food drafts among the several classes of the population is shown in the accompanying table.

Distribution of Food Drafts in Hungary to Intellectual Classes by Type of Beneficiary

Type of Beneficiary	Number of Individuals	Sales Value
Normal school teachers	3,924	$ 9,810
High-school teachers	2,356	5,890
Kindergarten teachers	356	890
University professors	232	580
Actors and actresses	612	1,530
Writers, journalists	828	2,070
Painters, sculptors, composers	948	2,370
Judges, attorneys	612	1,530
Lawyers	832	2,080
Physicians	292	730
Engineers, architects	1,032	2,580
Clergymen, rabbis	692	1,730
State officials	4,296	10,740
Municipal officials	660	1,650
Widows and orphans	1,964	4,910
Pensioned people	536	1,340
Miscellaneous cases	1,628	4,070
Four university mensas	3,200	8,000
Total	25,000	$62,500
Equivalent number of meals		660,000

In addition to these food drafts, there was allotted to Hungary a total of $40,000 out of the fifth Commonwealth Fund appropriation. Of this amount, $39,966.71 was actually expended in Hungary. This was used to supply food to professors' and students' "mensas," or dining-rooms, where meals were served at a nominal price far below the actual cost and, in the case of particularly needy individuals, were furnished free. In all, the equivalent of 403,400 meals to 15,900 individual beneficiaries were furnished from this appropriation.

The total food relief to Hungarian intellectuals from the Commonwealth Fund thus totaled $102,466.71, representing 1,063,400 meals distributed among approximately 40,900 individual beneficiaries.

From the sixth Commonwealth appropriation for clothing relief the sum of $25,000 was allocated to Hungary and the records show that $24,527.29 was actually spent. This sum was used to purchase the following commodities:

Commodities	Quantity
Shoes	2,500 pairs
Socks and stockings	4,984 pairs
Woolen cloth	9,392 yards
Lining	12,077 yards
Pocketing	3,630 yards
Underdrawers	3,400 pairs
Combination underwear	1,600 suits

For distribution, this was divided into two types of packages: "A"—Woolen, lining, etc., for 1 suit or costume; "B"—1 pair shoes, 2 pairs stockings, 2 suits underwear. A small charge was made for each package sufficient to cover the incidental cost of distribution. This money was placed in a special fund and was later used to purchase 9,000 meters of linen, sufficient to supply 1,800 persons with outfits.

In all, the European Children's Fund was able to supply 5,000 clothing packages in Hungary from this Commonwealth appropriation. The distribution of these gifts by type of beneficiary is given in the accompanying tabulation.

Altogether, the $126,994.30 from the Commonwealth Fund which was used in Hungary benefited a total of approximately 45,900 individuals.

f) Poland: The situation in Poland was rendered particularly difficult because of the large number of refugees from Russia and the war-stricken districts of eastern Poland. It was estimated that in the five larger cities of Poland there were at least 65,000 Russian refugee intellectuals in urgent need, as well as other thousands in the smaller cities.

Distribution of Clothing Packages to Intellectual Classes in Hungary by Type of Beneficiary

Type of Beneficiary	Number of Individuals
Teachers and professors	1,412
State employees	508
Clerks	453
Widows and orphans	452
Pensioners	310
Architects and engineers	235
Refugees	220
University students	185
Physicians	180
Unemployed	147
Attorneys, ex-judges, and lawyers	156
Journalists	107
Actors	97
Musicians	78
Law students	78
Pharmacists	59
Sculptors	55
Ex-army officers	55
Writers and authors	44
Invalid war veterans	42
Painters	41
Priests, various faiths	33
Ex-police staff	29
Applied art	24
Total beneficiaries	5,000
Total value	$24,527.59

The contributions from the Commonwealth Fund formed an important means of relieving many thousands of these Polish and Russian intellectuals. As shown in Table 62 (pages 98–99), the total contributions from the Commonwealth Fund used in Poland amounted to $401,532.38. Of this amount $57,532.49 came from the sixth contribution and was used for the purchase of clothing. This left $343,999.89 from the second, third, fifth, seventh, and eighth appropriations, all of which was used for food relief.

The distribution of the Commonwealth food was in the form of food packages, except in certain cities where kitchens were operated for professors, students, and other needy intelligentsia. In each instance, investigations were carried out by local committees representing the various professions or organizations and the distributions were made after recommendation by these committees. In certain instances the final distribution was made through well-established local relief organizations.

The following table gives an analysis of the Commonwealth Fund food distribution in Poland.

The food distributed to these 85,187 beneficiaries was equivalent to approximately 3,920,348 meals, making the average cost per meal $0.088 and the cost per beneficiary $4.04.

In addition to the food relief, the sixth Commonwealth Fund appropriation provided for an intelligentsia clothing program, of which a total of $57,532.49 was expended for beneficiaries in Poland. This sum provided for the following commodities:

Commodity	Quantity	
Shoes	5,800	pairs
Socks and stockings	11,600	pairs
Cloth	20,938⅝	yards
Lining	24,252	yards
Pocketing	2,503	yards
Undershirts	2,000	each
Drawers	2,000	pairs
Combination underwear	9,600	suits
Ivory buttons	70,704	number
Metal buttons	12,096	number
Hooks and eyes	86,400	pairs
Thread, needles, and other accessories		

Distribution of Food from the Commonwealth Fund to Intellectual Classes in Poland

Kitchen or Type of Beneficiary	Number of Individuals	Sales Value
Intelligentsia kitchens		
Warsaw	19,458	$ 78,577.00
Lemberg	9,336	37,700.00
Wilno	4,925	19,888.00
Lwów	3,092	12,485.00
Kraków	6,872	27,749.00
Poznań	1,888	7,626.00
Równe	1,388	5,606.00
Lublin	1,521	6,143.00
Łódź	4,550	18,373.00
Krzemieniec	266	1,075.00
Biała-Podlaska	124	500.00
Białystok	991	4,000.00
Brest-Litovsk	276	1,117.00
Chełm	248	1,000.00
Chorzele	22	90.00
Ciechanów	248	1,000.00
Częstochowa	421	1,700.00
Hrubieszów	371	1,500.00
Kalisz	309	1,250.00
Kielce	248	1,000.00
Kowel	215	870.00
Krasnystaw	495	2,000.00
Kutno	62	250.00
Lenczyca	94	380.00
Łomża	371	1,500.00
Mińsk-Mazowiecki	42	169.00
Mława	248	1,000.00
Northeast Poland		
Białystok, Brest-Litovsk, Grodno, Vilna, Pińsk, Mińsk	196	790.00
Novo-Podomsk	322	1,300.00
Ostrołeka	124	500.00
Ostrów	248	1,000.00
Piotrków	248	1,000.00
Płock	248	1,000.00
Pułtusk	248	1,000.00
Radom	124	500.00
Intelligentsia kitchens		
Sanok	99	$ 400.00
Siedlce	210	850.00
Sokołów	80	324.00
Tomaszów	38	152.00
Zdulecyna	310	1,250.00
Przasnysz	35	140.00
Teachers	5,901	23,828.00
Students and faculty		
Warsaw University	1,840	7,432.00
University of Lemberg	1,238	5,000.00
University of Kraków	619	2,500.00
Other professors	82	333.00
Russian prisoner camp near Kraków	495	2,000.00
Russian intelligentsia homes		
Wołomin	440	1,778.00
Ostrów	293	1,182.00
Falenica	146	590.00
Authors—Warsaw	250	1,010.00
Engineers	486	1,961.00
Institutions		
Hospitals, clinics, asylums, convents	186	750.00
Girls' boarding houses	62	250.00
J.D.C. for Jewish war sufferers	4,457	18,000.00
Russian Red Cross	2,972	12,000.00
Old Teachers' Home—Zielonka	78	314.00
Old People's Home—Sulejowek	52	210.00
Widows of lawyers—Lemberg	30	120.00
Professions undesignated	639	2,579.00
Through other relief organizations	3,912	15,799.00
Miscellaneous	398	1,609.89
Total	85,187	$343,999.89

Distribution of Clothing Outfits to Intellectual Classes in Poland

City and Organization	Number of Beneficiaries Men	Women
Warsaw		
Society of Women's Protection	2	83
Committee of Aid to Ukrainian Refugees	66	226
Polish White Cross	47	158
"Bratnia Pomoc," students' organization	112	40
Committee for Aid to White Russian Refugees	14	60
Polish Red Cross	..	27
Russian Red Cross	46	191
Polish National Red Cross	41	222
Society for Relief to Blind War Victims	23	2
Old Ladies' Home	1	15
Emergency Relief of Polish Women	8	27
National Club Jewish Deputies to Diet	34	5
University assistants	20	..
Polish intelligentsia kitchens	130	540
Direct distribution	86	243
Total to Warsaw	630	1,840
Łódź		
Direct distribution	..	25
Kraków		
Association Catholic Women	153	737
Poznań		
Society "Caritas"	7	52
Society of Help to Refugees	25	113
Lemberg		
Jewish Intelligentsia Relief Commission	30	70
Catholic Society of Women	151	837
Ukrainian Commission for Help to War Victims	30	120
Direct distribution	10	30
Total to Lemberg	221	1,057
Wilno		
Association Catholic Women	70	315
Association of Russians	45	300
Jewish Community	5	85
Association of Lithuanians	5	45
White Russian National Commission	5	30
Ukrainian Committee	4	8
German Community	5	25
Direct distribution	31	22
Total to Wilno	170	830
Kowel		
Direct distribution	36	180
Lublin		
Direct distribution	42	162
Grand total	1,284	4,996

It was estimated that this material would supply 5,800 complete outfits, of which 1,000 were allotted to men and 4,800 to women. Certain savings which were effected in the actual manufacture of this material made it possible to increase the number of outfits distributed to 6,280, including 1,284 for men and 4,996 for women. The preceding table shows the distribution of these clothing outfits by cities and the organizations through which distribution was effected. Direct distribution where indicated was through the European Children's Fund.

Joint Distribution Committee contributions.—As pointed out in another section of this report the American Jewish Joint Distribution Committee played a very important part in the post-war relief in Central Europe. In addition to large funds spent on their own responsibility, this organization through, or in co-operation with, the A.R.A.E.C.F. made relief contributions totaling $8,161,941.34. Of this amount, we are concerned, here, only with the $250,000 contributed by the J.D.C. to the special programs for intelligentsia feeding. This sum of money was turned over to the E.C.F. in 1922 with the instructions that it was to be used in Austria and Poland without regard to the race or religion of the beneficiary. As in the case of other intelligentsia feeding, this relief was administered in co-operation with local relief organizations, which investigated needy cases and recommended relief. The relief was applied through food packages to individuals, through meals served in kitchens, food deliveries to homes, and that supplied to students' and professors' messes.

Of the total amount, $200,000 was distributed in Austria and $50,000 in Poland. The following table summarizes these deliveries.

Summary of J.D.C. Intelligentsia Relief on Special Programs

Country	Number of Beneficiaries	Equivalent Number of Meals	Sales Value of Food Distributed
Austria	72,339	4,352,771	$200,000.00
Poland	10,900	1,958,174	50,000.00
Total	83,239	6,310,945	$250,000.00

TABLE 64

DETAIL OF DELIVERIES OF J.D.C. INTELLIGENTSIA RELIEF TO AUSTRIA

Profession	Packages: Number of Beneficiaries	Packages: Value	Kitchens: Number of Beneficiaries	Kitchens: Value	Home and Student Messes: Number of Beneficiaries	Home and Student Messes: Value	Total Number of Beneficiaries	Total Value
Students	...	......	...	......	3,739	$17,074.25	3,739	$ 17,074.25
Physicians	413	$ 989.46	186	$ 749.02	....	....	599	1,738.48
Lawyers	576	1,379.98	221	855.58	....	....	797	2,235.56
Teachers	3,237	7,755.19	1,546	5,921.70	....	....	4,783	13,676.89
Engineers and architects	641	1,535.71	488	1,888.71	....	....	1,129	3,424.42
Officers, old army	3,403	8,152.90	1,398	5,421.74	....	....	4,801	13,574.64
Authors, journalists	531	1,272.17	347	1,293.71	....	....	878	2,565.88
Painters and sculptors	507	1,214.67	328	1,223.66	....	....	835	2,438.33
Musicians	1,824	4,369.93	513	1,922.44	....	....	2,337	6,292.37
Actors and other artists	500	1,197.90	233	864.45	....	....	733	2,062.35
Clergy	193	462.39	26	104.52	....	....	219	566.91
State and public employees	12,220	29,276.63	5,946	22,605.36	....	....	18,166	51,881.99
Private employees	3,044	7,292.81	2,196	8,369.69	....	....	5,240	15,932.50
Small pensioners	1,970	4,719.72	1,213	4,936.75	....	....	3,183	9,656.47
Welfare institutions	3,077	7,371.87	2,410	8,799.56	....	....	5,487	16,171.43
Nurses	1,041	2,494.05	340	1,241.43	....	....	1,381	3,735.48
Miscellaneous, not segregated to professions	2,346	5,620.54	2,385	8,937.83	13,301	72,413.68	18,032	36,972.05
Total	35,523	$85,105.92	19,776	$75,406.15	17,040	$89,487.93	72,339	$200,000.00

The detail of the Austrian deliveries is shown in Table 64, which gives the number of beneficiaries and the value of deliveries by types of relief and by professions of recipients.

The relief to the intellectual classes in Poland from the Joint Distribution Committee funds was used entirely for supplementary rations in intelligentsia kitchens. The Farmers' Union in Poland co-operated in furnishing certain supplies for these kitchens, particularly vegetables, and these were also supplemented by local government contributions. As a result, the supplies furnished by the European Children's Fund were distributed to a much larger number of persons and over a longer period than would otherwise have been possible. As shown in the summary table given on this page, the $50,000 spent in Poland was distributed in 1,958,174 meals, making the average cost of this food only $0.0255 per meal. In Austria, where local donations could not be supplied so freely, the cost per meal was approximately $0.0459, or nearly double that in Poland.

The accompanying table shows the number of beneficiaries in each of the fourteen Polish cities where this fund was distributed. No statistics are available to show the division by professions of the beneficiaries of this particular fund. However, they were in all cases selected on the same basis as were those for other intelligentsia feeding.

J.D.C. INTELLIGENTSIA RELIEF TO POLISH CITIES

Location of Kitchens	Number of Beneficiaries
Falenica	60
Kowel	200
Kraków	1,100
Krzemieniec	100
Łódź	200
Lublin	430
Lwów	1,500
Ostrów	120
Poznań	1,200
Równe	400
Sulejowek	20
Vilna	2,500
Warsaw	2,700
Warsaw for Russian students	150
Wołomin	220
Total number of beneficiaries	10,900
Total value of relief	$50,000.00
Estimated number of meals	1,958,174

Laura Spelman Rockefeller Memorial.—Following the revolution in Russia, approximately 2,000,000 Russian citizens were forced to leave their native country. A considerable number of these refugees, especially from Odessa, Novorossisk, and Crimea, were forced into Turkey and particularly into Constantinople. The plight of these refugees, many of them from the educated classes, was particularly deplorable. It soon became evident that there was no immediate possibility of these Russians becoming permanently established in Turkey and little chance of their returning to Russia. The solution of the problem therefore involved their evacuation to other countries. The next difficulty, in view of their destitute and demoralized condition, was to find countries which would permit their entry. In the meantime it was urgently necessary that they be fed.

In the fall of 1921 Dr. Fridtjof Nansen, High Commissioner for Russian Refugee Relief of the League of Nations, visited Constantinople and from that time the League took an active interest in expediting the evacuations of these Russians from Constantinople. However, relatively little was accomplished, and the condition of the refugees was becoming worse in the summer of that year.

In the meantime the European Children's Fund had attempted to alleviate some of the worst suffering, but the lack of funds available for adult relief permitted little activity there. Besides, it would be an enormous drain on any relief funds to attempt to feed these refugees indefinitely. Therefore it was decided that steps must be taken to solve this problem permanently.

In the meantime the E.C.F. had interested the trustees of the Laura Spelman Rockefeller Memorial in the pitiful condition of these refugees. In March, 1922, the E.C.F. at the request of this Fund, sent Arthur Ringland to Constantinople. As a result of Mr. Ringland's efforts, an agreement between the League of Nations and the E.C.F. was drawn up which provided that if the League would appropriate $150,000 (£30,000 sterling) for the evacuation of the dependent refugees the E.C.F., on behalf of the Laura Spelman Rockefeller Memorial, would undertake their feeding during the period of evacuation, estimated to require four months, commencing July 1, 1922. The League accepted the proposal and invited the member nations to subscribe the necessary funds. Late in June contributions, totaling approximately $90,000, had been received from Belgium, Brazil, China, Czechoslovakia, Great Britain, Japan, and Switzerland. To this amount the American Red Cross generously contributed approximately $60,000 to complete the necessary fund.

The Laura Spelman Rockefeller Memorial made available to the E.C.F. the sum of $100,000 to take care of the feeding operations. Although it was estimated that there were approximately 27,000 Russian refugees in the vicinity of Constantinople, the Relief Administration could only undertake the support of those who were wholly dependent. A special registration showed 11,407 refugees in this class, divided as follows:

Class of Refugee	Number of Refugees
Children from four to fifteen, inclusive	1,378
Hospital patients	1,159
Convalescent invalids	3,568
Able-bodied adults	3,558
Children under four, and nursing and expectant mothers	1,744
Total	11,407

The complete evacuation of the Russian refugees from Constantinople was not accomplished until May 1, 1923. During this period about 22,000 refugees were evacuated, of which 1,847 were sent to the United States. The expense of evacuating those sent to the United States was shared equally by the E.C.F., the League of Nations, and the Red Cross fund.

The final accounting for the $100,000 contribution from the Laura Spelman Rockefeller Memorial is shown by the records of the E.C.F., as follows:

Value of food purchased	$62,957.64
Cost of warehousing	3,581.60
Cost of transportation	4,982.81
Cost of kitchens and bakeries	5,841.79
Total cost of feeding operations	$77,363.84
Cost of evacuation operations	21,402.18
Total cost	$98,766.02
Received from sale of equipment	143.43
Total expended	$98,622.59
Balance returned to Memorial Fund by check dated February 8, 1924	1,377.41
Total fund	$100,000.00

It will be noted that the expenses for warehousing, transportation, and for kitchens and bakeries total $14,406.20. This extra cost was made necessary because the operations were carried on with little assistance from the local governments or other organizations and also because facilities in the vicinity of Constantinople were scarce and costly. The overhead cost of the operations was borne by the E.C.F.

Because of the various needs of the refugees it was necessary to establish special rations for each class. These rations varied in caloric value from 1,133 calories for the able-bodied to 2,000 calories for the hospital patients. Altogether, 1,357,632 meals were served with a total cost of $77,363.84, or approximately 5.7 cents per meal.

The food purchased for the refugee relief in Constantinople is summarized in the accompanying table.

Summary of Food Distributed in Refugee Relief in Constantinople

(Paid for from the Laura Spelman Rockefeller Memorial Appropriation)

Commodity	Metric Tons	Value
Cocoa	11.0	$ 980.15
Sugar	19.0	1,755.71
Milk, evaporated	87.0	18,023.13
Milk, condensed	35.0	8,212.47
Flour	257.0	18,085.26
Rice	55.0	4,010.25
Lard substitute	28.0	8,131.96
Corned beef	1.0	878.52
Corn grits	23.0	931.92
Beans	38.0	1,693.08
Salt	8.0	255.19
Total	562.0	$62,957.64

European Children's Fund contribution.—As pointed out in an earlier paragraph, a large portion of the money available to the E.C.F. had been contributed for particular purposes and hence was not available for many needs for which relief was urgently required. In some instances the Administration was able to secure special appropriations from other organizations to take care of these particular needs, as in the case of the intelligentsia relief discussed in the preceding pages. On the other hand, there were also other relief organizations which were in a particularly strategic position to carry out certain kinds of needed relief and these not infrequently asked for contributions from the E.C.F. In only a few instances could these requests for funds be granted, and then it frequently became a trade by which the other organization undertook a form of relief for which the E.C.F. was not organized.

These contributions by the E.C.F. to other relief organizations were handled under the heading of "Special programs." Such contributions, totaling $696,962.94, were made to two organizations as follows:

American Friends Service Committee	$326,962.94
World's Student Christian Federation	370,000.00
Total	$696,962.94

The contribution to the American Friends Service Committee was made for work in three countries, viz., Russia, Poland, and Austria.

American Friends Service Committee.—*(a) Russia:* Early in 1921 Russia was suffering from the terrible effects of the revolution, but the E.C.F. at that time had effected no arrangements with the Soviet Government which would permit them to undertake relief work there. The Friends Emergency and War Victims' Relief Committee, one of the organizations of international Quaker relief, was already established in Russia. The severe suffering there led the Quakers to appeal for help from many sources. The American Friends Service Committee, with headquarters in Philadelphia, appealed to the E.C.F., who in May, 1921, agreed to turn over to the Friends Committee food supplies to the value of $100,000.

Although the American Relief Administration (Russian Unit) began its own relief work in Russia in the latter part of 1921, they made a further agreement to turn over a second $100,000 worth of food to the Quakers in 1922. The work of the Friends Committee was serving such a useful purpose that it seemed much better to support this organization than to attempt to duplicate the work they were already carrying out.

Under these agreements a total of 468.2 metric tons of food, valued at $196,672.20, was furnished to the Quaker organization. The commodities delivered are shown in the accompanying table.

COMMODITIES DELIVERED TO THE FRIENDS SERVICE COMMITTEE FOR RELIEF IN RUSSIA

Commodity	Metric Tons	Value
Rice	98.9	$ 13,256.62
Lard substitute	5.6	1,833.82
Milk, condensed	113.0	49,884.04
Milk, evaporated	107.7	46,675.74
Cottonseed oil (tins)	43.2	28,007.98
Cottonseed oil (bulk)	75.8	49,996.46
Soap	24.0	7,017.54
Total	468.2	$196,672.20

b) *Poland:* Almost immediately after the close of hostilities a committee of the Friends relief organization made a visit to Poland. The suffering they found there induced them to undertake various relief activities, including a considerable amount of child feeding. By 1921 the E.C.F. was engaged in extensive child feeding in Poland, but it was found that the Quakers were reaching certain types of the population and certain localities which the E.C.F. could not duplicate without great expense. Rather than attempt this duplication the E.C.F. undertook to assist the Friends in certain of their special programs.

Altogether, commodities to the value of $80,290.74 were turned over to the Friends Committee in Poland. These deliveries were effected by two transactions: first, a bulk sale from warehouse stock at Warsaw of 106.7 metric tons of foodstuffs, valued at approximately $50,000; and, second, three cargoes of cottonseed meal shipped from Galveston, Texas, to Hamburg and then transshipped to Danzig. This cottonseed meal, amounting to 633.3 metric tons valued at $30,291.26, was to supplement the cattle feed and thus to increase the local milk supply. This was in line with the policy of the E.C.F. to help the various countries help themselves, and to build up their industries.

The commodities turned over to the Quakers under the bulk sale transactions are shown in Table 65.

The cottonseed meal was delivered in three cargoes, as shown below.

Date (1921)	Galveston to Hamburg via	Hamburg to Danzig via	Metric Tons
May	King City	Mottlau	152.4
June	Alness	Aeolus, VII	289.1
August	Hans	Adele, IV	191.8
Total tons			633.3
Total value			$30,291.26

The total deliveries of all commodities to the Friends for Polish relief thus amounted to 740.0 metric tons, valued at $80,290.74.

TABLE 65

COMMODITIES DELIVERED FROM A.R.A. WAREHOUSE STOCKS TO THE AMERICAN FRIENDS SERVICE COMMITTEE FOR RELIEF IN POLAND

Commodity	Metric Tons	Value
Flour	16.4	$ 2,375.35
Beans	7.6	1,244.50
Rice	15.3	2,244.69
Milk, condensed	10.4	4,719.70
Lard	9.7	7,472.84
Cottonseed oil	3.2	2,334.24
Bacon	22.6	20,193.41
Cocoa	10.9	1,972.90
Corned beef	10.6	7,441.85
Total	106.7	$49,999.48

c) *Austria:* As in other countries of Central Europe, the Quakers established their relief work in Vienna and certain other sections of Austria shortly after the Armistice. A certain proportion of this work was child feeding, and among other things they were feeding in the homes a large number of undernourished younger children, i.e., those between the ages of three and six years who were not able to come to the kitchens.

The E.C.F. was carrying on a large child-feeding program in Austria, but all of its feeding was being done in kitchens and they had no organization to adequately supervise home feeding of this character. The Quakers asked that either the E.C.F. should take over this home feeding or else furnish the Friends organization with supplies.

The E.C.F. agreed to turn over $50,000 worth of food to the Quaker organization for feeding these younger children, with the understanding that this should be known as E.C.F. feeding, but handled entirely by the Friends personnel. This food was used to feed approximately 40,000 children, each of whom was furnished with half the regular child-feeding ration. These funds thus provided for approximately 3,000,000 supplementary meals for these younger children.

This transfer of food to the Quaker organization took place in six bulk sale deliveries from the Vienna warehouse. The detail of these deliveries is given in Table 66 (page 110).

TABLE 66

Deliveries from Vienna A.R.A. Warehouse to Friends Service Committee for Child Feeding in Austria

(Commodities in Metric Tons)

Date (1921)	Receipt Number	Cocoa	Sugar	Milk	Flour	Lard Substitute	Total Tons	Total Value
Mar. 11	66	....	3.0	....	....	....	3.0	$ 703.08
Mar. 14	68	....	3.0	....	....	....	3.0	703.08
Mar. 21	89	....	4.0	....	....	....	4.0	937.44
Mar. 22	91	....	20.0	....	29.9	....	49.9	9,403.76
Apr. 22	118	....	...	....	....	20.0	20.0	7,100.00
Apr. 28	121	20.0	...	83.9	....	....	103.9	31,152.64
Total tons		20.0	30.0	83.9	29.9	20.0	183.8	....
Total value		$3,619.60	$7,030.80	$27,533.04	$4,716.56	$7,100.00	.....	$50,000.00

Student feeding.—In connection with the campaign for the European Relief Council fund (see pages 77–80), efforts were made in co-operation with the American Y.M.C.A. to have special gifts designated for the relief of students in Central European universities. The condition of many of the students in these universities was particularly distressing. This appeal had particular weight with many American universities and considerable sums of money were contributed by American students to assist their distressed brothers in Europe.

As a result of the Relief Council drive, Mr. Hoover was able to allocate the sum of $370,000 for this student feeding, which sum was to be spent in co-operation with the American Y.M.C.A. and Y.W.C.A. and their suborganization, the World's Student Christian Federation.

Of this total, the sum of $80,000 was turned over to the World's Student Christian Federation in cash to be expended for general relief other than feeding. This arrangement was in accordance with an agreement entered into with the Y.M.C.A. at the time the funds were collected. The reports of the Student Federation show that this money was spent for relief in Austria, Czechoslovakia, Poland, Hungary, and the Baltic countries. This money was expended for such things as textbooks, scientific apparatus, bedding, room rent, fuel, and many other necessaries in the life of these destitute students. However, the reports of the World's Student Christian Federation show no details as to these expenditures nor their exact allocation to the several countries. For the purposes of this report this $80,000 will have to be carried as unallocated relief.

Of the remaining $290,000, £4,000 sterling, or $16,755.98, was expended for clothing purchased in London. This clothing was distributed to needy students in the universities in Central Europe. This purchase and distribution was handled entirely by the World's Student Christian Federation, and no details of the type of clothing, the number of beneficiaries, or the countries in which the clothing was distributed are available at this date.

With these expenditures deducted, there remained from the student-feeding fund a total of $273,244.02, all of which was used for feeding purposes. The distribution of this food was handled by the E.C.F. working in close co-operation with the World's Student Christian Federation and through them with the well-organized local students' committees in the various schools. The personnel of the W.S.C.F. was used largely to assist in this distribution.

The general policy of the student-feeding work was to furnish or contribute toward the supply of one relief meal a day to needy students. The size of the ration varied somewhat according to needs, but the average meal was planned to consist of about 1,000 calories. In most cases the feeding was done at the local student messes, which were going concerns, usually under faculty supervision. Usually a nominal charge of a few cents was made for each meal; however, one of the conditions imposed by the Relief Administration was that no student should be excluded on account of inability to pay or on account of race, religion, or politics. In some places, as in Graz and Innsbruck, it was necessary to establish completely new kitchens and to furnish all the food requirements for the relief meal.

Table 67 shows the allocation of this student-

TABLE 67

DISTRIBUTION OF STUDENT RELIEF CARRIED ON IN CO-OPERATION WITH WORLD'S STUDENT CHRISTIAN FEDERATION

Country	Time of Delivery	Maximum Number Students Fed	Estimated Number Meals Served	Value of Commodities Donated
Austria	Mar., 1921—Jan., 1923	9,500	2,998,524	$ 95,147.34
Czechoslovakia	Mar., 1921—Sept., 1921	2,819	245,907	23,511.71
Esthonia	Apr., 1921—May, 1921	600	31,200	1,271.02
Hungary	May, 1921—Dec., 1921	3,385	672,040	28,300.16
Latvia	Apr., 1921—Feb., 1922	1,000	208,600	8,497.95
Lithuania	Apr., 1921—May, 1921	745	22,750	926.78
Poland	Mar., 1921—June, 1922	11,695	2,586,839	115,589.06
Sub-total		29,744	6,765,860	$273,244.02
Unallocated expenditures:				
General purposes, W.S.C.F.				$ 80,000.00
General relief:				
Clothing purchased by W.S.C.F.				16,755.98
Sub-total				$ 96,755.98
Grand total				$370,000.00

feeding fund, by countries, together with the number of beneficiaries, and the estimated number of meals in each.

Refugee relief in Poland.—On July 12, 1920, the London office of the E.C.F. relayed the following message from Warsaw to New York:

Thousands destitute refugees coming into Poland as result Bolshevik advance. Great need food relief, especially warehouse packages. General relief food drafts almost exhausted. Cannot some philanthropic organization be persuaded to help in this emergency?

Mr. Hoover replied immediately by allotting $50,000 from E.C.F. funds for this purpose and by making an immediate appeal to other organizations for assistance. Within ten days after this cable was received the A.R.A. European Children's Fund had secured contributions of $200,000 to care for this emergency.

The extreme urgency of the refugee situation is clearly shown in the cables and reports from the Warsaw office at this time. Thus, a cable from Warsaw dated July 24, 1920, contains the following:

Freight cars in train loads reach our eastern feeding stations filled with refugee families, frequently days without food. Crowded into same cars are several families with such belongings as they could rescue, often including cow, pig, or few chickens.

On July 13, 1920, Hugh Gibson, American Minister to Poland, gave an interview to the press asking for assistance in this emergency. He said in part:

Reports from various sources indicate that thousands of refugees are pouring westward before the Soviet Army under conditions of desperate suffering and distress. The food situation, already bad, has been aggravated by this influx of refugees and by the effect of the crisis on transportation and distribution. If suffering and starvation are to be averted there must be immediate help from this country.

Much is now being done but not enough to meet the crisis. The European Children's Fund is feeding 1,200,000 children every day in Poland. Various other relief bodies are working to the limit of their resources. . . . . It is to be hoped that the acute suffering of the present crisis will awaken practical sympathy and that our splendid corps of relief workers in Poland may be enabled to meet the crisis through adequate support from their own country.

The refugee relief work is especially noteworthy for the speed with which it was put into execution. As pointed out above, the first cable regarding this situation was sent to New York on July 12, 1920. By July 16, the London office had been authorized to deliver food on this program to the extent of $50,000. On July 24, 1920, W. P. Fuller, Jr., chief of the E.C.F. Warsaw Mission, cabled in part as follows:

. . . . Within 48 hours of notice of donation our food was actually being fed to refugees in Warsaw, Białystok, Brest, and Lwów, which are most important stations. Shortly afterwards we were also feeding at Chełm, Kraków, and Łódź, as well as on smaller scale at many roadside points. Large-scale operations now beginning at Thorn, where permanent refugee camps are being arranged. . . . .

The quickness with which this work was started was of course possible because of the warehouse stock of food and the ability of the E.C.F. personnel to meet emergencies of this character.

The total of the special refugee relief fund amounted to $302,000. The sources of these contributions were as follows:

European Children's Fund—General funds..	$125,000
National Polish Committee................	50,000
Joint Distribution Committee..............	25,000
Edward W. Harkness......................	75,000
William Bingham II.......................	27,000
Total	$302,000

The contribution from the E.C.F. general fund includes a number of small donations especially earmarked for refugee relief.

This money was used to purchase food packages and bulk deliveries to the refugee kitchens. The total amount delivered was 809.9 metric tons. The warehouse records account for these deliveries as shown in Table 68.

The meals furnished by the refugee kitchens consisted of an average of 280 grams per person. On this basis the estimated number of meals provided by the relief deliveries would amount to 2,892,572, and the average cost per meal was 10.44 cents.

The distribution of this food in the refugee camps and kitchens was greatly aided by many existing relief organizations, such as the National Refugee Commission, Joint Distribution Committee, the Red Cross, and others. These organizations had already established feeding stations, railroad station canteens, or central kitchens, on the eastern border of Poland and were thus able to render great assistance in getting food to the refugees.

No accurate figures of the number of refugees fed are available. Many hundreds of thousands, even millions, of refugees crossed the Polish border during these trying times. There were times when the E.C.F. kitchens in Warsaw served as many as 10,000 dinners a day to these unfortunates.

In addition to the relief meals furnished to adult refugees discussed above, the E.C.F. fed vast numbers of refugee children at its regular child-feeding kitchens. No separate report on the number of these children is available, but it was estimated that more than 150,000 refugee children under fifteen years were actually being fed in the 2,000 kitchens and institutions oper-

TABLE 68

DETAIL OF FOOD DELIVERIES TO KITCHENS FOR REFUGEE RELIEF IN POLAND

Report No. (A.R.A.W.)	Deliveries Made Week Ending (1920)	Unit	Flour M.T.	Rice M.T.	Beans M.T.	Milk Case	Corned Beef 6-lb. Tin	Bacon 8-lb. Piece	Bacon 16-lb. Piece	Lard 5-lb. Tin	Lard 10-lb. Tin	Lard Substitute M.T.	Oil 1-gal. Tin	Oil 5-gal. Tin	Total Metric Tons	Sales Value
13.......	July 23	....	11.9	4.5	....	192	98	353	49	49	49	...	159	59	.....	$ 9,930.00*
13.......	July 23	....	41.7	2.3	17.7	320	904	...	320	120	120	...	...	380	.....	30,000.62
14.......	July 30	....	4.2	.5	.8	32	312	...	11	...	...	...	2	62	.....	3,416.86
15.......	Aug. 6	....	39.8	1.6	20.9	341	208	1	341	...	217	...	...	199	.....	26,676.24
16.......	Sept. 17	....	159.0	31.1	95.6	1,280	1,803	310	2,171	213	685	1.8	16	1,336	.....	135,592.00
17.......	Sept. 24	....	24.2	11.0	13.2	101	260	4	443	...	142	...	835	44	.....	21,764.73
18.......	Oct. 1	....	14.2	7.1	7.1	85	427	...	186	2	84	...	5	127	.....	13,163.97
19.......	Oct. 8	....	14.1	6.9	6.9	84	482	1	207	1	96	...	10	98	.....	12,949.01
21.......	Oct. 22	....	17.3	8.7	8.7	103	533	...	232	...	65	.2	6	151	.....	16,105.72
22.......	Oct. 31	....	4.2	2.1	2.1	31	110	...	48	...	22	...	...	44	.....	3,958.57
(E.C.F.† Form S6)																
5.......	July	....	3.2	1.9	1.0	306	...	34	...	...	...	1.8	...	1	.....	6,587.31
5.......	August	....	24.7	4.8	7.4	430	...	...	...	...	...	2.4	...	1	.....	16,155.45
5.......	September	....	8.1	2.5	3.3	118	...	...	...	...	...	.8	...	...	.....	5,699.52
Total deliveries		Unit	366.6	85.0	184.7	3,423	5,137	703	4,008	385	1,480	7.0	1,033	2,502	.....	....
		M.T.	366.6	85.0	184.7	67.2	14.0	2.6	29.1	.9	6.7	7.0	3.5	42.6	809.9	$302,000.00

* Represents value of package deliveries to kitchens, to-wit: 353 "A," 49 "B," 100 "C," 59 "D." All other deliveries were made from bulk stock.

† Owing to the Bolshevik invasion, the A.R.A. Warehouses were unable to make deliveries in eastern Poland. The following deliveries were taken care of by the E.C.F. from surplus child-feeding stocks, which were later returned to the E.C.F. by the A.R.A.W.

ated in Poland by the E.C.F. All of this child feeding was in addition to the refugee relief discussed above.

The files of the Hoover War Library at Stanford University contain hundreds of letters from Polish officials and private citizens expressing appreciation and thanks for the help rendered at a time when it looked as if Poland would be overrun by this horde of refugees from the east.

II. AMERICAN ORGANIZATIONS OTHER THAN THE EUROPEAN CHILDREN'S FUND—RECONSTRUCTION PERIOD, 1919–1924

Table 51 (page 80) shows that aside from the work under the immediate direction of the European Children's Fund there were other American organizations which, in co-operation with the E.C.F., furnished relief supplies amounting to 942,267.0 metric tons and valued at

TABLE 69

RELIEF DELIVERIES BY AMERICAN ORGANIZATIONS OTHER THAN THE EUROPEAN CHILDREN'S FUND—RECONSTRUCTION PERIOD, 1919–1924

Organization	Total Metric Tons	Total Value
U. S. Grain Corporation	868,016.1	$76,444,298.20
U. S. Government (surplus medical supplies)	3,107.6	4,267,392.88
American Red Cross	25,548.3	5,516,813.10
American Friends Service Committee	33,713.9	7,056,966.68
Commonwealth Fund	3,836.7	890,642.46
Joint Distribution Committee	537.0	273,555.00
Near East Relief	7,404.3	1,944,119.91
Serbian Child Welfare Association	79.3	77,869.94
American Women's Hospital (Jugoslavia)	23.8	35,211.19
Total	942,267.0	$96,506,869.36

$96,506,869.36, during the Reconstruction Period. Two of these organizations, the United States Grain Corporation and the "United States Government,"[1] were governmental bodies and the deliveries made by them were with the authority of Congress. The other American organizations were private charitable bodies. In addition to the organizations included here, there were certain other American organizations where the co-operation with the European Children's Fund was of a more involved nature; these have been discussed under Special Programs. Records of such deliveries have for the most part been included with those of the E.C.F.

Table 69 summarizes the deliveries by organizations other than the E.C.F. which will be discussed in this section.

UNITED STATES GRAIN CORPORATION

The relief deliveries to European countries by the United States Grain Corporation during the Reconstruction Period were made under the authority of two acts of Congress. The first was the Act of March 30, 1920,[2] which authorized the Grain Corporation to sell to these countries, for cash or credit, up to 5,000,000 barrels of surplus flour which the Corporation had acquired in connection with its operations in maintaining the guaranteed price of wheat.[3] The second was the Act of December 22, 1921,[2] which appropriated $20,000,000 of the Grain Corporation's capital to be used to purchase American corn, milk, and seed grain for the relief of the Russian people during the great famine.

Surplus flour.—With the approach of the end of the 1919–1920 crop year, the United States Grain Corporation found that it had accumulated a considerable stock of soft winter-wheat straight flour which had been acquired in connection with maintaining the guaranteed price of wheat under the Act of March 4, 1919. This flour was not readily salable in such large quantities either in this country or to the Allies. In the spring of 1920, Mr. Barnes wrote to President Wilson pointing out that the Corporation had some 500,000 tons of this flour which it was feared might spoil with the advent of warmer weather. In reply to this, the President wrote:

> It is desirable that you should take steps to dispose of these accumulated stocks on credit, if you cannot do so for cash, to such buyers and on such terms and conditions as best protect the interest of our Government.
>
> On these points, it is desirable that the views of our own Department of State and of our National Treasury should be secured.

[1] In accordance with the executive order of President Harding, dated January 24, 1922, the surplus medical and hospital supplies were to be delivered by the War, Navy, and Treasury departments and by the United States Shipping Board.

[2] For text of this Act, see *The Grain Trade during the World War*, by F. M. Surface, page 514.

[3] For further discussion of this, see Surface, *loc. cit.*

Before any action was taken on this, it was deemed best to place the whole situation before Congress for such action as it might care to take. Congress promptly passed an act (approved March 30, 1920) which directly authorized the Grain Corporation to dispose of its remaining stock of flour up to 5,000,000 barrels for cash, or on credit, for the purpose of providing relief for the distressed population in the countries of Europe or countries contiguous thereto.

Under this direct authorization the Grain Corporation made sales of flour on credit to Armenia, Austria, Czechoslovakia, Hungary, and Poland. The Grain Corporation secured treasury notes from each of these governments covering the sums involved. These notes, payable in eighteen months, with 5 per cent interest payable semiannually, were turned over to the United States Treasury as part of the assets of the Grain Corporation.

The deliveries of flour to these countries under this Act, totaling 481,945.3 metric tons, valued at $57,782,118.20, are summarized in Table 70 (page 115).

It should be pointed out that the foregoing value represents the f.o.b. value of this flour in the United States. The Grain Corporation had no funds and no authority to pay for the transportation from American ports to Europe. The countries to which the flour was sold likewise had no facilities for overseas transportation and were also without funds with which to pay for its movement. The European Children's Fund was able to persuade the British Government to pay the major portion of freight, insurance, and other charges for the overseas transportation of this flour (cf. page 123). The freight for the flour going to Armenia was paid in part by the American Red Cross and the Near East Relief.

Soviet Republics.—In December, 1921, Congress, upon recommendation of President Harding and Secretary of Commerce Hoover, passed an act (approved December 22, 1921) which authorized the President to cause to be spent out of the capital of the United States Grain Corporation a sum not exceeding $20,000,000. This was to be used to purchase in the United States, and to transport and distribute in Russia, corn, seed grain, and preserved milk for the relief of the Russian people. Corn was specified as the only food grain to be purchased because of the large surplus in this country and the low price which it was bringing.

To carry out this Act, President Harding issued an Executive Order on December 24, 1921, creating a "Purchasing Commission for Russian Relief," and naming the U.S. Grain Corporation as the fiscal agent of the Commission, while the American Relief Administration was directed to accept these commodities in Russia and to attend to their distribution in that country.[1]

The members of this Purchasing Commission named in the Executive Order were the Secretary of Commerce; James P. Goodrich, of Indiana; Edward M. Flesh, of Missouri; Edgar Rickard, of New York; and Don Livingston, of South Dakota.

Because of the terrible conditions existing in Russia at this time it was necessary for the Commission to act quickly if they were to save any considerable portion of the population. The Purchasing Commission was fortunate enough to be able to buy four cargoes of corn grits and milk which were already on their way to Europe, one having sailed as early as December 10, 1921. These early cargoes enabled the relief work to get under way early in January, which would otherwise have been delayed a full month.

The Purchasing Commission at once advertised for bids on corn for immediate shipment and before the end of December had purchased upward of 1,000,000 bushels. The bulk of the commodities paid for from the Grain Corporation funds were purchased and shipped during the period from January to April, 1922, although some purchases were made as late as August, 1922.

Owing to the very large crop of corn in the United States in 1921, the price had fallen to disastrously low levels. According to the figures compiled by the Department of Agriculture, the average price paid to the producer for corn in Nebraska was twenty-five cents a bushel in November, 1921, and instances are known where the price fell as low as eleven cents a bushel. Many farmers were using corn for fuel. Largely as a result of President Harding's Purchasing Committee for Russian Relief entering the mar-

[1] For the text of this Executive Order, see Surface, *loc. cit.*, page 545.

Summary of Commodities Purchased for Soviet Russia and Paid for by the United States Grain Corporation

Commodity	Unit	Quantity	Equivalent Metric Tons	Total Value
Mixed corn, No. 2	Bushel	8,147,294	206,953.6	$ 5,196,359.10
Amber durum seed wheat	Bushel	1,357,234	36,938.6	1,725,100.07
Corn grits	Long ton	82,633	83,960.4	2,976,948.07
Seed corn	Bushel	724,760	18,410.0	735,251.79
Seed rye, No. 2	Bushel	752,660	19,118.6	889,880.61
Evaporated milk	Cases	870,143	18,945.9	3,163,477.45
Condensed milk	Cases	33,788	643.7	170,577.74
Miscellaneous		.....	1,100.0	....
Total f.o.b. value			386,070.8	$14,857,594.83
Total transportation cost				3,804,585.17
Total c.i.f. value				$18,662,180.00

ket, the average price to the producer rose to fifty cents a bushel in February, 1922, and shortly afterward was above sixty cents. This indirect result of the Russian relief added hundreds of millions of dollars to the value of the corn crop for the American farmers.

The Act of Congress authorized the payment of transportation charges as well as the cost of the food and seed grain. In order to handle the work, the Grain Corporation had to reorganize its purchasing and shipping departments, which had been practically demobilized preparatory to liquidation, and it had also to build up its accounting department. In spite of these handicaps the supplies were handled with dispatch, and a total of 386,070.8 metric tons of food and seed grain, with a total value of $18,662,180, were shipped. The preceding tabulation summarizes the detail of these purchases, while Tables 511 and 517 give further details of their shipment and distribution.

The supplies furnished from the Grain Corporation funds were of the greatest help in alleviating some of the worst suffering during that terrible winter of 1921–1922. Furthermore, without the seed grain furnished in time for planting, Russia would have been even worse off the year following, because in many regions the peasants had eaten the last of their grain and it would have been impossible to have planted another crop.[1]

The total deliveries by the Grain Corporation in the Reconstruction Period summarized by operation and country of destination are given in Table 70. Further detail will be found in Appendix tables, and in discussion of relief to the respective countries.

TABLE 70

Summary of Relief Deliveries by the United States Grain Corporation—Reconstruction Period, 1920–1924

Country of Destination	Total Metric Tons	Total Value
Act of March 30, 1920		
Armenia	40,633.5	$ 4,813,744.45
Austria	200,824.8	24,055,708.92
Czechoslovakia	23,809.0	2,873,238.25
Hungary	14,114.0	1,685,835.61
Poland	202,564.0	24,353,590.97
Subtotal	481,945.3	$57,782,118.20
Act of December 22, 1921		
Russia, Soviet Republics	386,070.8	18,662,180.00
Grand total	868,016.1	$76,444,298.20

U.S. Government Surplus Medical Supplies

One of the difficult conditions which faced the Russian unit of the American Relief Administration in its work in Soviet Russia was the rapid spread of disease and the lack of facilities with which to combat it. Russian cities and provinces were found to be reasonably well supplied with hospital facilities, but these were almost entirely denuded of equipment, including drugs, medicines, instruments, bedding, etc. In order to help remedy this situation, Mr. Hoover first interested the American Red Cross in the Russian situation, with the result that they turned over to the A.R.A. large quantities of

[1] For further discussion, see page 255, but especially H. H. Fisher, *The Famine in Soviet Russia,* Macmillan Company, 1927.

supplies which are discussed in a later section of this report. At the same time he undertook to secure from the United States Government certain supplies which they had accumulated in Europe during the war and which were in store in Germany in connection with the Army of Occupation. The Army was willing to release these supplies but was lacking in authority to do so. At Mr. Hoover's instance the matter was presented to Congress and an act was passed (Act of January 20, 1922) authorizing these supplies to be turned over to the American Relief Administration for use in Russia.

The medical and hospital supplies obtained from the Government totaled approximately 3,107.6 metric tons, valued at $4,000,000.00. The Laura Spelman Rockefeller Memorial contributed $267,392.88 to pay the freight charges on transporting these supplies to Russian ports. A portion of these supplies was turned over to the Near East Relief for distribution and use in the Caucasus. The remainder was distributed by the A.R.A. Russian Medical Unit, which was organized for this purpose. The following tabulation summarizes the distribution of these supplies.

U.S. Government Surplus Medical Supplies

	Metric Tons	Value
Distributed by A.R.A.		
Soviet Russia	2,892.4	$3,790,268.37
Distributed by Near East Relief		
Caucasus	215.2	209,731.63
Total	3,107.6	$4,000,000.00
Freight on supplies to Soviet Russia contributed by Laura Spelman Rockefeller Memorial	.....	$ 267,392.88
Grand total	3,107.6	$4,267,392.88

The distribution of these supplies to the eighteen districts of Soviet Russia is shown in detail in Medical Tables 2 and 3 (pages 946–86). The work of the A.R.A. Medical Unit is also further described in the section on Russian relief (pages 251–53).

American Red Cross

In connection with relief deliveries during the Armistice Period reference has been made to the work of the American Red Cross in Europe (cf. page 58). The major portion of the work of the American Red Cross was carried on quite independently of any of the organizations which form the basis of this report. Only those operations of the Red Cross which were in close co-operation with the A.R.A. or the E.C.F. are reported in this volume. Table 33 (page 58) shows that the total operations of the Red Cross coming in this category amounted to $7,258,553.10, of which $1,741,740.00 represented relief during the Armistice Period and has been reported upon elsewhere. This leaves $5,516,813.10 as the relief furnished by the American Red Cross in co-operation with the European Children's Fund and affiliated organizations during the Reconstruction Period. As shown by Table 69, this represented a total of 25,548.3 metric tons of relief supplies. The following tabulation shows the distribution of this relief by countries of destination.

Summary of Relief Furnished by the American Red Cross during the Reconstruction Period

Country	Total Tons	Total Value
Armenia (freight)	....	$ 500,000.00
Greece	20,374.0	1,211,949.95
Russia, Soviet Republics	5,174.3	3,804,863.15
Total	25,548.3	$5,516,813.10

The relief furnished to Armenia was toward the payment of freight on flour sold by the U.S. Grain Corporation. This contribution by the Red Cross, together with contributions by the Near East Relief and the United Kingdom, made it possible for this flour to be delivered to Armenia at a time when these people were in urgent need.

The relief to Greece was to render aid to the panic-stricken Greek refugees from Turkey in the fall of 1922. As described elsewhere (page 201), a special emergency fund was collected for this purpose in the United States. The American Relief Administration undertook to act as purchasing agent for the American Red Cross for the supplies needed. Between November, 1922, and May, 1923, the A.R.A. purchased and shipped 20,374.0 metric tons of foodstuffs, chiefly cereal supplies. The total f.o.b. value of these commodities at New York City was $1,178,163.85. In addition, the A.R.A. paid out $33,786.10 for freight and other charges, making a total of $1,211,949.95. The American Red Cross reimbursed the A.R.A. for this full amount and paid out of other funds all additional freight and miscellaneous charges. The distribution of these supplies in Greece was entirely in the hands of the Red Cross.

The relief furnished to the Soviet Republics of Russia by the Red Cross represents medical and hospital supplies turned over to the American Relief Administration for distribution in Russia. As discussed earlier in connection with the U.S. Government surplus medical supplies, there was urgent need for medical relief in Russia in 1922. The Red Cross had no organization in Russia which could handle this, but agreed to furnish these supplies if the A.R.A. would undertake their distribution.

As shown in the table on page 116 the total amount of the medical and hospital supplies turned over by the Red Cross was 5,174.3 metric tons, valued at $3,804,863.15. Medical Table 1 (pages 936–45) shows the distribution of these supplies in detail, and further facts regarding the work of the A.R.A. Medical Unit in Soviet Russia are given in connection with the discussion of the relief to that country.

American Friends Service Committee

As is well known, the Quaker religion teaches that all war is wrong. History is replete with incidents wherein the members of this faith have suffered disgrace, ignominy, and imprisonment at the hands of their own governments rather than take an active part in that which was against their conscience. When the war broke out in 1914, the Quakers in England were divided in opinion. Some felt that the special circumstances of this war justified them in joining the army, and, since the basis of the Quaker religion is individual responsibility according to the dictates of one's own conscience, they did so. Others joined the Red Cross or ambulance work in the field. Still others, believing that any direct participation in the war was wrong, devoted themselves to the alleviation of the suffering which the war brought to the civilian populations. It was this latter group which in September, 1914, formed the Friends War Victims Relief Committee, which later became known as the Friends Emergency and War Victims Relief Committee.

This organization began at once its relief work among the civilians in the occupied territory of France and Belgium. Helping to rehabilitate homes, building temporary houses, securing needed furniture, distributing clothing and food, and alleviating suffering among the peasants were among the self-imposed duties of these bands of Friends from England. Throughout this period the American Quakers co-operated with the English Friends in this work.

In June, 1917, after the United States had entered the war, there was organized the American Friends Service Committee which represented all Quaker organizations in America. This organization continued to co-operate with the English Friends and joined with them in relief activities in Russia prior to the Armistice.

Following the Armistice the American Friends Service Committee began immediately to send out little bands of relief workers. These went to Poland, Syria, Serbia, and other countries, and as soon as conditions permitted into Germany and Austria. The Friends thus sought to heal the wounds of war by extending a helping hand to these peoples in their time of need.

In the summer of 1919, Mr. Hoover asked the Friends to extend this relief work into Germany, where the need was great but where American public opinion would not yet permit official relief to be extended.[1]

In the meantime, the Friends made a survey of German conditions and found that 75 per cent or more of the German children were suffering from undernourishment and were in need of outside help. A beginning was made in the summer of 1919 when the Friends Committee purchased from the American Relief Administration 60.9 tons of fats, milk, cocoa, and clothing for $29,687.25, with which they began the program of German child feeding under the direction of Carolena M. Wood, Jane Addams, and Dr. Alice Hamilton.

In November, 1919, Mr. Hoover asked the American Friends Service Committee to extend their work over the whole of Germany, and to carry this on along the lines being followed by

[1] Congress in making the appropriation of $100,000,000 for European Relief (Act of February 25, 1919) specifically excepted all former enemy countries from its benefits.

By the Armistice extension agreement, dated January 16, 1919, Germany was permitted to buy food in large quantities, for cash (cf. pages 193 ff.).

the European Children's Fund in other countries. This the Friends Committee gladly undertook.

Under the agreement between the two organizations, the European Children's Fund attended to the purchasing and shipping of all commodities originating with the E.C.F. for German child feeding. These commodities were turned over to the American Friends Service Committee in German ports, chiefly at Hamburg, and all details of the distribution within the country were handled by the Friends Committee.[1] Under these arrangements shipments of food were started in January, 1920, and actual feeding began on February 26, 1920.

During the early period of this relief the purchase and shipment of supplies were financed by the European Children's Fund out of such profits as had been realized by the Grain Corporation on cash sales of food to Germany in 1919.

In the winter of 1920–1921 the American Friends Service Committee participated in the European Relief Council drive and, as shown on page 80, the Friends Committee were credited with a total of $861,022.31 from the proceeds of this campaign. The major portion of this amount was expended through the European Children's Fund for supplies for German child feeding. In addition to this, the E.C.F. from time to time set up further large credits for the Friends work in Germany. Up to the end of 1922 when the Quakers officially withdrew from Germany, the European Children's Fund had furnished supplies for German child feeding amounting to 28,720.1 tons, valued at $6,728,989.92.

The sources of the finance for these operations were as follows:

Direct contributions from E.C.F.	$5,031,582.14
Allotment from European Relief Council	861,022.31
Cash collected by A.F.S.C.	836,385.47
Total	$6,728,989.92

Because of the urgent need for additional child feeding in Germany beyond anything that could be done with the funds already collected, the Friends Committee called a meeting of a group of Americans, of German descent, at Philadelphia in April, 1921. At this meeting it was agreed to organize a campaign for a fund of three million dollars, to be solicited from Americans of German descent. By July, 1922, approximately $1,500,000 had been raised, which was sufficient to continue the child-feeding program from January, 1922, to September 30, 1922. The supplies for this latter program were purchased chiefly in America by the Friends Service Committee, in co-operation with the purchasing committee of the E.C.F. From these latter funds also the sum of $100,000 was used to purchase clothing in Germany, which was distributed to needy children.

In addition to its principal work of child feeding, the Friends Committee also handled the distribution of clothing and materials for clothing which were contributed from various American sources. During 1921 and 1922, 416 bales of clothing and 989 bales of flannels were donated to the Friends and were distributed to children and needy mothers in Germany. Of the flannels, 547 bales were the gift of the American Red Cross. The estimated tonnage of this clothing and cloth amounted to 175.6 metric tons, with a total estimated value of $287,000.

In the early part of 1922 the Friends Committee considered that the most urgent need for German child relief would be over with the next harvest and they made plans to withdraw from further operations. This was accomplished by the end of July, 1922, but they left in the hands of the Deutscher Zentralausschuss für die Auslandshilfe (the German Central Committee for Foreign Relief) in Berlin sufficient supplies to continue the feeding until the end of September, 1922.

Throughout the whole of these operations the German Government had co-operated closely with the child-feeding work and had made very substantial contributions both in commodities and in services. The German Food Ministry undertook to furnish free of charge all flour and sugar used in the child-feeding work from October, 1920, to September 30, 1922. The total contribution of the German Government of these two commodities amounted to:

	Metric Tons	Total Value
Flour	12,663.0	$1,627,005.56
Sugar	4,170.0	765,015.69
Total	16,833.0	$2,392,021.25

[1] The methods of distribution were similar to those used by the E.C.F. described on pages 84–86. Also see discussion of relief in Germany, pages 198–99, for further details.

In addition, the German Government undertook to furnish free transportation and express service for all internal shipments of relief supplies; to supply warehouse and handling services; to furnish free transportation to members of the Friends Mission when on relief business; and to furnish preferential telephone service. In addition, the preparation and serving of the meals and all costs of operating the local kitchens were taken care of by local committees and by volunteer services. The value of these contributions by the German Government and the German people exceeded $2,500,000.

Although the Quakers withdrew from Germany in the middle of 1922 it soon became evident that conditions had not yet become sufficiently normal to avoid much serious suffering among German children. In 1923, recurring reports of the condition of these children aroused the sympathies of a number of prominent Americans. Under the leadership of the late Major General Henry T. Allen, formerly commander of the American Army of Occupation in Germany, a committee was formed to undertake the collection of funds to feed 1,000,000 German children through the winter of 1923–1924. This committee, known as the American Committee for Relief of German Children, was sponsored by more than 100 Americans prominent in all walks of life. Their appeal for funds was backed by President Coolidge, Mrs. Woodrow Wilson, Cardinal Dougherty, Rabbi Wise, Mr. Hoover, and many others. Unsuccessful efforts were made to get Congress to appropriate funds for this work. However, the Committee was successful in raising more than $4,300,000 in the United States for this relief. This made it possible to feed more than 1,000,000 German children until the end of 1924 and to arrange a program for feeding several hundred thousand children during the winter of 1924–1925. Although the European Children's Fund had completed most of its work and had exhausted most of its available funds in the Russian relief before the work of this committee was started, it made a cash contribution of $50,000 to the Committee's fund.

The American Friends Service Committee played a prominent part in collecting the funds for General Allen's American Committee for Relief of German Children, and this committee turned over to the Quakers the work of purchasing all supplies and the supervision of the relief work in Germany. The actual distribution in Germany was carried out by the German Central Committee for Foreign Relief (Deutscher Zentralausschuss für die Auslandshilfe), which had co-operated in the earlier work undertaken by the Quakers.

In connection with the work of General Allen's Committee a food draft service similar to that formerly conducted by the A.R.A. Warehouses and the E.C.F. was organized. This service, under the directorship of W. Gordon Brown, made sales totaling 17,200 packages, valued at $172,000.

The total child relief work in Germany under the direction of the American Friends Service Committee may be summarized as follows:

Summary of American Friends Service Committee Relief to German Children

Source of Relief	Total Metric Tons	Total Value
Purchases in 1919 by A.F.S.C.	60.9	$ 29,687.25
In co-operation with E.C.F.	28,720.1	6,728,989.92
German-American contribution	.....	1,500,000.00
American Committee for Relief of German Children	.....	4,300,000.00
Food draft service	495.5	172,000.00
Clothing distribution	175.6	287,000.00
Total from America		$13,017,677.17
German Government commodities	16,833.0	$ 2,392,021.25
German Government service	.....	2,500,000.00
Grand total		$17,909,698.42

In addition to work in Germany, the American Friends Service Committee conducted extensive post-Armistice relief operations in Austria, Poland, Russia, Danzig Free City, and in Jugoslavia. Many of these operations were not connected with the American Relief Administration. Such, for example, were the building of houses for Serbian families, the improvement of agricultural conditions in Jugoslavia, Poland, and Austria, and the anti-typhus work in Poland.

The A.F.S.C. worked jointly with the English Quakers in most countries, pooling supplies and personnel. According to the reports of these committees the total amount actually handled by them for relief purposes totaled considerably more than $50,000,000.[1]

However, the food relief work by the American Friends Service Committee was very closely co-ordinated with the work of the European Children's Fund. The latter organization attended to the purchasing and shipping of a considerable portion of these supplies from the United States.

Table 69 shows the total deliveries during the Reconstruction Period credited to the American Friends Service Committee in this report as 33,713.9 metric tons, valued at $7,056,966.68. The distribution of these commodities by countries of destination is given in Table 71.

TABLE 71

Relief Furnished by American Friends Service Committee in Co-operation with the European Children's Fund—Reconstruction Period, 1919–1924

Country of Destination	Total Metric Tons	Total Value
Danzig Free City	158.3	$ 30,291.26
Germany	28,720.1	6,728,989.92
Poland	633.3	30,291.26
Russia, Soviet Republics	4,202.2	267,394.24
Total	33,713.9	$7,056,966.68

This, however, does not cover all of the work in which the American Friends Service Committee was associated with the E.C.F. But in the case of the other operations, credit had already been given to the A.R.A. Warehouses for bulk sales or to the European Children's Fund on special programs so that to include these deliveries here would mean a duplication. For the sake of completeness the tabulation in the next column shows the deliveries by the Friends organization for which credit is given elsewhere. (See also Table 159, pages 340–41.)

Of the relief definitely credited to the American Friends Service Committee in Table 71, the deliveries to the Free City of Danzig represent child-feeding operations carried on there by the Friends which were taken over by the E.C.F. in April, 1921. The relief to Poland represents cottonseed meal which was turned over to the Friends by the E.C.F. These operations, which are somewhat involved, are described more in detail under Special Programs and under the discussion of relief deliveries to Danzig and to Poland.

Country	Total Metric Tons	Total Value
Austria	248.6*	$ 62,112.08*
Poland	106.7†	49,999.48†
Russia, Soviet Republics	468.2‡	196,672.20‡
Total	823.5	$ 308,783.76
Total from Table 71	33,713.9	7,056,966.68
Grand total	34,537.4	$7,365,750.44

* Of this amount, 183.8 tons, valued at $50,000, is included in Special Programs. The remainder represents bulk sales from A.R.A. Warehouses.

† Represents part of the special program operation as discussed on page 109.

‡ Special program for Russia described on page 108.

The delivery of 28,720.1 tons of supplies to Germany, valued at $6,728,989.92, represents the child-feeding work carried on there in co-operation with the E.C.F. as described above. Of this amount, 1,237.2 metric tons, with a value of $341,309.7, represent bulk sales from the A.R.A. Warehouses and has been included in the warehouse reports. This duplication is included here to give full credit to the Friends for their German operations. This is included in the deduction to arrive at the net total relief delivered as in Table 51 (page 80).

The relief for Soviet Russia shown in Table 71 represents commodities which the European Children's Fund transported for the Friends from Hamburg to Baltic ports in 1922. The detail of these shipments is given in Table 525.

In addition to all of the operations by the Friends referred to here, it is to be remembered that they carried on much additional work entirely independent of the E.C.F. or affiliated organizations, which is not included in this report.

The total contribution to the Quaker relief work from the European Children's Fund, including the European Relief Council, may be summarized as follows:

Direct contribution for German child feeding	$5,031,583.14
Allotment from European Relief Council	861,022.31
Special programs (Austria, Poland, and Russia)	326,962.94
Contribution to General Allen's Committee	50,000.00
Total	$6,269,567.39

[1] For a description of this work, see *A Quaker Adventure*, by A. Ruth Fry; *Service of Love in War Time*, by Rufus M. Jones; *Quakers in Action*, by Lester M. Jones; and *Quaker Adventures*, by Edward Thomas.

The Commonwealth Fund

The origin of the Commonwealth Fund and its activities in European relief have been discussed under Special Programs. It is shown there that the Commonwealth Fund made nine separate appropriations to the European Children's Fund for special relief in Europe. These nine appropriations totaled $2,149,000, of which seven, amounting to $1,249,000, were earmarked for food relief to the intellectual classes in Central European countries. These latter appropriations were used either to purchase food drafts or bulk food from the A.R.A. Warehouses. These transactions are, therefore, accounted for under the A.R.A. Warehouse operations and in this report are not again specifically credited to the Commonwealth Fund.

Of the two remaining appropriations by the Commonwealth Fund, one, the first to be made, was for $750,000 to be used for children's relief in Armenia. The other, the sixth Commonwealth Fund appropriation, was for $150,000 to be used to furnish clothing for the intellectual classes in Central European countries. These two appropriations, totaling $900,000, involved special purchases of commodities by the E.C.F. and are not accounted for elsewhere in this report.

Table 69 (page 113) gives the Commonwealth Fund credit for 3,836.7 metric tons of supplies, valued at $890,642.46. The difference between this amount and the $900,000.00 appropriated was used to purchase food through the A.R.A. Warehouses, as explained below.

The following table summarizes the distribution of the commodities credited to the Commonwealth Fund by countries to which they were distributed. Further details are given in Table 160 and in the discussion under Special Programs.

Summary of Relief Deliveries Credited to the Commonwealth Fund—Reconstruction Period, 1919–1924

Country of Destination	Total Tons	Total Value
Armenia (child feeding)	3,762.0	$746,107.12
Austria (clothing)	31.8	62,475.26
Hungary (clothing)	12.5	24,527.59
Poland (clothing)	30.4	57,532.49
Total	3,836.7	$890,642.46

The deliveries to Armenia of 3,762.0 metric tons, worth $746,107.12, were child-feeding supplies purchased from the first Commonwealth appropriation of $750,000.00. The balance of $3,892.88 from this appropriation was later used to purchase food drafts for destitute intelligentsia in Austria and Danzig Free City, as explained on page 97.

The clothing relief to Austria, Hungary, and Poland, totaling 74.7 metric tons valued at $144,535.34, was from the sixth Commonwealth Fund appropriation of $150,000.00, which was designated for the purchase of clothing for the intellectual classes in these countries. Of the balance of this appropriation, $5,000.00 was used for the purchase of greatly needed food supplies for Austrian intelligentsia and $464.66 was used to purchase kitchen equipment for professors' and students' messes. These transactions, together with further detail regarding the clothing distribution, are given in the section under Special Programs.

Jewish Joint Distribution Committee

Reference has been made to the work of the American Jewish Joint Distribution Committee and the important part which it played in the relief work in the Armistice Period. This organization continued its work throughout the Reconstruction Period, but for the most part these later operations were entirely separate from the work of the European Children's Fund, although at all times the two organizations worked in close co-operation. The J.D.C. made extended use of the A.R.A. Warehouses and a large portion of the bulk and food draft sales in certain countries was made to this committee. Unfortunately, no tabulation is available showing the amount of these purchases, which are all credited under the A.R.A.W. operations (page 94) by countries to which they were delivered. Some indication of the purchases made by the J.D.C. is given in connection with the discussion of relief to Poland and Russia.

Table 69 (page 113) shows that only 537.0 metric tons of relief supplies, valued at $273,555, are credited to the J.D.C. in this report for the Reconstruction Period. This represents a contribution of milk and soap made to the European Children's Fund for the children's relief work in Poland.

Reference should also be made here to the part taken by the J.D.C. in the intelligentsia relief to Austria and Poland by which they contributed the sum of $250,000 for the purchase of food packages and bulk food. This money was expended through the A.R.A. Warehouses and is included in the report of those operations. This work is discussed in more detail under Special Programs.

Near East Relief

The work of the Near East Relief has been discussed briefly under the Armistice Period and is referred to in more detail in the discussion of relief to Armenia. As in the case of other similar organizations, this report covers only that small portion of the work of the Near East Relief which was carried on in close affiliation with the A.R.A. or the E.C.F.

Table 69 (page 113) shows that during the Reconstruction Period the Near East Relief is credited in this report with the delivery of 7,404.3 metric tons of supplies, and with a total money expenditure of $1,944,119.91. All of this relief was for Armenia.

Table 30 (page 56) shows that of this total amount expended in the Reconstruction Period $532,790.01 was for the payment of freight and other miscellaneous charges. This represented the payment of a portion of the freight on flour furnished to Armenia by the U.S. Grain Corporation under the Act of Congress of March 30, 1920.

The remainder of the relief credited in this report to the Near East Relief during the Reconstruction Period consisted of 7,404.3 metric tons of food and clothing shipped to Armenia by the European Children's Fund in 1920 and 1922 and paid for by the Near East Relief. The total delivered value of these supplies was $1,411,329.90 (see Table 205).

Reference should also be made here to the work of distributing 215.2 tons of U.S. Government surplus medical supplies in the Caucasus, which was handled by the Near East Relief. Many other activities carried on by the Near East Relief are beyond the scope of this report.

Other American Organizations

While there were numerous other American organizations which rendered important assistance to these European countries during the difficult period of reconstruction, the work of most of these lies entirely outside the scope of this report. Some phases of the work of the Y.M.C.A. and the Y.W.C.A., together with the World's Student Christian Federation, are referred to under Special Programs. Many others might be mentioned, but even then the list would be incomplete, and except for purchases of supplies through the A.R.A. Warehouses the work of these bodies was quite independent of the organizations which form the basis of this report.

Table 69 (page 113) shows small deliveries by two American organizations operating in Jugoslavia which are not accounted for elsewhere in this report. These are the Serbian Child Welfare Association of America and the American Women's Hospital in Serbia. These two organizations purchased clothing supplies from the stocks imported by the European Children's Fund and attended to the internal distribution of these. The total amount of these supplies for the two organizations was 103.1 metric tons, valued at $113,081.13. The distribution between the two organizations was as follows:

Organization	Metric Tons	Total Value
Serbian Child Welfare Association*	79.3	$ 77,869.94
American Women's Hospital......	23.8	35,211.19
Total	103.1	$113,081.13

* Included 1,000 blouses or 1.6 metric tons, valued at $1,303.12, for Dr. Reeder of the Welfare Association.

The details of these operations are given in Tables 361 and 362.

III. RELIEF FROM COUNTRIES OTHER THAN THE UNITED STATES—RECONSTRUCTION PERIOD, 1919–1924

Much of the relief work of the Reconstruction Period discussed in this report was of the nature of private charitable operations and, consequently, there was no occasion for the type of international co-operation which was found in the Armistice Period. This, of course, does not mean that other nations were not undertaking important relief measures but rather that these were carried on quite independently of the organizations which form the basis of this report.

It should also be pointed out that individuals in many countries contributed to the funds which were available to the European Children's Fund and its affiliated organizations. This was particularly true of the purchases of food remittances and also of the sales of bulk food to foreign relief organizations. These sales are included in the A.R.A. Warehouse operations and it is impossible to make any separate tabulation.

Throughout its work in Central Europe and Russia the European Children's Fund made it a condition of supplying relief that each country should contribute in accordance with its ability. As a result, these countries furnished large quantities of food in addition to transportation, warehousing, and the personal services which made this work possible.

Table 51 (page 80) shows the total contributions from countries other than the United States during the Reconstruction Period as 266,229.1 metric tons with a total value of $44,222,231.22. Table 72 segregates this by sources of the contributions.

TABLE 72

SUMMARY OF RELIEF SUPPLIED FROM COUNTRIES OTHER THAN THE UNITED STATES—RECONSTRUCTION PERIOD, 1919–1924

Source	Total Metric Tons	Total Value
United Kingdom (freight)	....	$18,212,473.88
Central European Governments	96,540.2	14,652,432.21
Russia, Soviet Republics	169,688.9	11,357,325.13
Total	266,229.1	$44,222,231.22

RELIEF FROM THE UNITED KINGDOM

After Congress passed the Act of March 30, 1920, authorizing the U.S. Grain Corporation to sell up to 5,000,000 barrels of flour for the relief of Europe, there arose the important problem as to how this flour was to be transported from the United States to countries which needed it. The Grain Corporation was prepared to sell the flour to these countries on credit but it had no authority and no funds to pay for the ocean transportation. None of these countries were themselves able to finance these transportation charges. In this emergency the European Children's Fund sought the aid of the British Government, which had available some unexpended funds for relief work. The British Treasury was finally persuaded to undertake the payment of the freight and other charges on these flour shipments, and in return to accept the obligations of the Central European governments for payment. As a result, the United Kingdom paid out a total of $18,212,473.88 for such freight, insurance, and miscellaneous charges. These were divided among the several countries as follows:

FREIGHT PAYMENT BY THE UNITED KINGDOM—RECONSTRUCTION PERIOD, 1919–1924

Country	Amount Paid
Armenia	$ 560,000.00*
Austria	8,032,991.88
Czechoslovakia	952,362.08
Hungary	564,561.60
Poland	8,102,558.32
Total	$18,212,473.88

* Represents approximately one-third of the transportation charges on Armenian flour; remainder paid by the American Red Cross and the Near East Relief. See footnote to Table 203.

Further details of these freight and transportation charges will be found in Table 162 and in the discussion of the relief to the separate countries.

The United Kingdom carried on various other relief activities during the Reconstruction Period which form no proper part of this report.[1]

RELIEF SUPPLIED BY CENTRAL EUROPEAN GOVERNMENTS

As indicated above, one of the conditions under which the European Children's Fund undertook relief work in any country was that the government of the country should undertake to render all the assistance possible. This meant in addition to transportation, warehousing, and personal services in preparing meals, etc., that the governments should contribute such food supplies as they were able to furnish. These contributions came both from the Central governments and from local governmental bodies. The most important commodities donated from these sources were flour, sugar, and fresh vegetables.

Table 72 shows that the total of such contri-

[1] See *Economic Conditions in Central Europe,* Misc. Series (I), 1920 [Cmd. 521], LI, 173; and *Economic Conditions in Central Europe,* Misc. Series (II), 1920 [Cmd. 641], LI, 189.

butions amounted to 96,540.2 metric tons, with a total equivalent value of $14,652,432.21. Table 73 summarizes these donations by the countries from which they came. Such donations were naturally used within the country contributing the supplies with the exceptions noted.

TABLE 73

Summary of Relief Contributed by Central European Governments, Including Local Donations—Reconstruction Period, 1919–1924

Country	Total Metric Tons	Total Value
Austria	12,703.3	$ 1,364,656.01
Czechoslovakia	3,955.8	693,099.02
Danzig Free City	74.0	8,574.44
Esthonia*	1,693.0	299,547.58
Finland	936.4	195,949.00
Germany	16,833.0	2,392,021.25
Hungary	1,733.0	265,806.84
Jugoslavia	2,634.0	533,677.16
Latvia*	478.6	85,137.24
Norway†	6.6	3,960.00
Poland*	52,579.2	7,749,374.77
Roumania	2,327.0	1,024,322.26
Northwest Russia	32.3	6,280.00
Russia, Soviet Republics	554.0	30,026.64
Total	96,540.2	$14,652,432.21

* All commodities were distributed within the country making the contributions in these instances with the following exceptions: Esthonia, Latvia, and Poland donated warehouse space for supplies going to Soviet Russia of which the estimated value was:

Esthonia	$ 1,102.94
Latvia	24,257.69
Poland	90,000.00

† The contribution of 6.6 tons of miscellaneous food from Norway was delivered to Latvia.

Further details of these contributions are given in Table 161 and in the discussion of the relief to the respective countries.

In addition to the commodities donated by these Central European governments and accounted for above, each country made valuable contributions in the form of intangible services and facilities, including local transportation of supplies and personnel, warehousing, handling, office facilities and supplies, kitchen facilities and equipment, fuel, and the personal services of many thousands of individuals in preparing and serving the daily meals for children. It is impossible to make even approximate estimates of the total value of such contributions. It was estimated by many of the E.C.F. men in the field that the money value of such contributions if they had been paid for would have equaled the contributions from the European Children's Fund, which totaled nearly $85,000,000. No attempt is made to estimate the total value of these intangible contributions from all countries, although in the discussion of relief to certain individual countries some estimates made by the E.C.F. representatives in the field have been included.

Relief Contributed by the Soviet Republics

Shortly after the relief work had started in the great famine-stricken regions of Soviet Russia, Mr. Hoover learned that the Soviet authorities had several million dollars' worth of gold and platinum, and he immediately suggested that this should be used for the purchase of food and seed grain. The Soviet officials were not antagonistic to this suggestion but it required several months of negotiations before this gold was placed at the disposition of the American Relief Administration on December 30, 1921. The total value of this gold was estimated at $10,000,000. A few days later the Ukrainian Soviet Republic turned over nearly $2,000,000 additional gold, making a total of nearly $12,000,000.

The food situation had become so serious in Russia before this was received that the A.R.A. had found it necessary to anticipate its receipt and had delivered food to the value of $4,322,450.83 (57,823.0 metric tons) against the expected receipt of this gold. This delivery has been carried in the record as part of the work of the European Children's Fund and is also included in deliveries by the Soviet Republics. In Table 51 (page 80) this duplication is deducted to arrive at a net total of the relief delivered in the Reconstruction Period.

Table 72 shows the total relief furnished by the Soviet Republics as 169,688.9 metric tons, valued at $11,357,325.13. This is made up of two operations, as follows:

Operation	Total Tons	Total Value
Food delivered in advance by A.R.A.	57,823.0	$ 4,322,450.83
Seed grain handled by A.R.A.	111,865.9	7,034,874.30
Total	169,688.9	$11,357,325.13

Further details of the deliveries against these credits are given in Tables 165 and 519, and in the discussion of the relief deliveries to Russia.

TRANSPORTATION, COMMUNICATION, AND FINANCE

TRANSPORTATION AND COMMUNICATION

Of the many problems which had to be met in connection with the furnishing of relief to Europe during and after the war, one of the most serious was that of adequate transportation, both overseas and overland. The problems were different in the several operations reported in this volume and can best be covered under the four major groups of activities.

C.R.B. Period

Transportation was one of the major problems in the Belgian relief work. This has been discussed so fully in previous publications[1] that only a few of the more important points are referred to here.

In the first months of the relief, i.e., the latter part of 1914 and the early months of 1915, no difficulty arose as tonnage was readily available and could be chartered through the usual commercial channels. The Commission gradually secured, under a continuous charter, a fleet of some twenty-three Belgian vessels totaling to 117,355 dead weight tons. This fleet was entirely inadequate to handle the necessary food imports and the Commission was continuously in the market for something like 179,000 dead weight tons in order to fulfil its minimum program. By the end of 1915 the growing world shortage of tonnage began to make itself felt. Charters began to be more difficult to obtain and their costs rose rapidly. In December, 1916, the Germans announced their proposed policy of unrestricted submarine warfare. This immediately altered the whole shipping situation. The Allies were threatened with imminent starvation and disaster; they needed every available ton of shipping for their own purposes. But the most immediate effect upon the Commission was the withdrawal of all neutral shipping from the seas. The Commission was left with only the Belgian vessels, which also had to be moved with extreme caution. Of necessity all cross-Channel service from the United Kingdom was suspended.

During all of 1917 the greatest problem for the relief work was to secure necessary tonnage. The Allies had by this time instituted a complete control of all shipping, including neutral charters, and it was only by appeal to the Allied Governments that the Commission could obtain any tonnage. Finally on December 5, 1917, at an Inter-Allied conference in Paris it was decided that the Commission's needs should be placed on a priority list. Even then it was the end of April, 1918, before this decision could be put into effect.

Of course, all shipping operations required the agreement of all the belligerent governments to exempt the Commission's vessels from attack. All C.R.B. vessels were plainly marked, and flew the Commission's own distinctive flag. Nevertheless, the Commission's vessels had to pass through the most dangerous areas of the English Channel and the North Sea, both of which were filled with mine-strewn areas and German submarines. Safe conduct passes had to be secured for every vessel. Notwithstanding all these guaranties, the Commission lost a total of thirty-eight cargoes, of which twenty were torpedoed, fourteen sunk by mines, three sunk by submarine fire, and one by collision. Fourteen other vessels and cargoes were damaged. The total cargo lost through these fifty-two accidents amounted to 114,000 tons.

Rotterdam in neutral Holland, with its excellent harbor and equipment, and its direct canal connections with both Belgium and Northern France, was used as the principal port from which the relief commodities were transshipped to the interior. Antwerp, Dunkirk, and Lille were also used, but to a minor extent. The tabulation on the following page shows the total tonnage of Belgian relief supplies which passed through these four Northern European ports.

[1] George I. Gay, *Commission for Relief in Belgium—Statistical Review of Relief Operations* (Stanford University Press, 1925), pages 28–44; and, by the same author, *Public Relations of the Commission for Relief in Belgium—Documents,* 2 volumes (Stanford University Press, 1929).

Port	Metric Tons
Rotterdam	4,686,359
Antwerp	462,502
Dunkirk	15,826
Lille	9,744
Total	5,174,431

The internal distribution of supplies in Belgium was greatly facilitated by the excellent system of canals. However, during the German invasion in 1914, many of these canals had been destroyed, locks blown up, or the canals obstructed by destroyed bridges, sunken lighters, etc. The Germans had requisitioned most of the serviceable lighters, as well as the railroad rolling stock. Much preliminary work had to be accomplished in putting the most necessary canals in shape to operate and in securing equipment. In the early work the Commission chartered such Dutch- and Belgian-owned equipment as could be obtained, but, later on, the Commission began to purchase both tugs and lighters, and before the close of the work it had acquired a fleet of 495 lighters and 36 tugs.

The Commission also made use of rail shipments, particularly to move supplies to provinces not reached by the canal system and for emergency shipments when the canals were frozen.

In addition to the internal movement of relief supplies, the Commission also had to transport bunker coal for its vessels to the extent of some 20,000 tons per month, and an additional 12,000 tons per month from Belgian mines for the flour mills which the Commission operated in various parts of Belgium.

It was only natural that, with the Allied food blockade firmly clamped down on the Netherlands, there should occasionally be some difficulty because of the large volume of food going into Belgium through Rotterdam. Walter L. Brown[1] tells of a midnight visit to his apartment by two dignitaries of the city of Rotterdam to inform him that the Dutch Food Minister had instructed the Mayor of Rotterdam to stop all C.R.B. shipments to the Belgians until arrangements had been made to share supplies with the Dutch. Reinforced by the representatives of the American, British, French, and Belgian embassies, Mr. Brown called at the Dutch Foreign Office the next morning and the embargo was soon lifted. At another time a strike of the Dutch stevedores threatened the whole program, until arrangements were made to have Belgian stevedores who were interned in Holland do the work under the protection of Dutch soldiers, with the result that the Rotterdam stevedores soon resumed their duties.

It is of interest to record that the development of the "dispatch" clause in ships' charters originated in the Rotterdam office of the C.R.B. Charters had always provided for demurrage, permitting a certain number of days for loading or unloading and charging a specified sum for each day in excess of the number allowed. Rotterdam was breaking all records in unloading, and the C.R.B. officials conceived the idea that the ship should pay for every day that could be saved out of the minimum allowed. While the vessel owners objected at first, such a plan was finally put into operation with practically all C.R.B. ship charters. Since then a "dispatch" clause has appeared in many charters. By this arrangement the C.R.B. effected a saving of more than $1,250,000 and set a new pace for the turn-around of cargo vessels between Atlantic ports and Rotterdam.

The paragraphs above describe very inadequately a few of the many transportation difficulties experienced in the Belgian relief work.

U.S.F.A. Period

The problem of supplying the Allied countries with food during the period of our participation in the war was to a large extent a problem of marine transportation. The sinking of food and passenger ships, in the unrestricted submarine campaign of Germany, more than any other one thing, was responsible for bringing the United States into the war at the time she entered. It was this same submarine campaign that had reduced the world's available shipping tonnage to a minimum, and that prevented the Allied Governments from sending vessels on the longer voyages to the Southern Hemisphere and the East where surplus food supplies existed. Instead, it concentrated the demand for food upon North America, where the ocean voyage required only one-half to one-third the time necessary to make a round trip to South America or Australia. Besides, the Allies urgently

[1] *C.R.B. Bulletin,* October 22, 1930, page 16.

required munitions equipment and American soldiers, all of which were competing for ocean transport space. The Allies had already found it necessary to pool their shipping interests, which were controlled by the Allied Maritime Transport Council. Through this organization all Allied tonnage was allotted to the respective needs so far as these could be met.

One of the first requests which the Allies made of the United States in 1917 was for more ships. This was responsible for the organization of the Emergency Fleet Corporation and our vast shipbuilding program. It was not until the latter part of 1918 that this gigantic program began to bear significant fruit. If the war had continued a few months longer, the United States would have been able to replace with emergency vessels much of the tonnage destroyed by the war. During all of 1917 and the first half of 1918, the Allies had to depend upon their own tonnage and such neutral vessels as they could persuade, with exorbitant rates, to risk the hazards of the submarine-infested and mine-strewn passages.

Thus, during the war period, the problem of overseas transportation was almost entirely a responsibility of the Allied Governments. The United States Food Administration through its several agencies arranged for the sale of such foodstuffs as could be spared to the Allied buying organizations in this country. Our direct responsibility ceased when these commodities had been moved to seaboard. However, the Food Administration co-operated with the Allied agencies, as far as possible, to insure proper junctions between rail and water shipments, and to provide those commodities which could be handled with the least delay of the vessels in port. By these measures the rate of "turn around" of the available vessels was increased.

However, we had many problems of internal transportation which taxed our ability to the utmost. The great industrial activity in the United States, due to the Allied demand for munitions and supplies, together with the rapidly expanding war operations of the Government itself, had placed a heavy strain on our internal transportation system, for which it was totally unprepared.

Difficulties in securing deliveries began to appear by the middle of 1917. By fall they had become serious. The Government began to use its authority for priority movement not only for strictly army and navy movements but for many commercial activities connected with the war. These priority requests resulted in upsetting whatever plans the transportation companies had devised for handling the traffic and conditions became chaotic.

The Food Administration could no longer secure movement of foodstuffs either for the Allies or for domestic needs. Embargoes were placed on loadings from certain territories in an effort to straighten out conditions, but such measures merely temporized with a vitally serious problem. Finally, on December 29, 1917, President Wilson directed that the Government take over the management of all railroads, and appointed William G. McAdoo, then Secretary of the Treasury, as director general of railroads.

This action, designed to bring unity of control and the formulation of a consistent policy for all rail transportation lines, might have been successful had the new administration not been met with the most severe adverse operating conditions. January, 1918, was a month of extremely severe blizzards, heavy snows, and unusually low temperatures. With the transportation situation already at the breaking point, this severe weather became the last straw. These conditions resulted in drastic freight embargoes and still more drastic fuel embargoes. Industries closed and conditions became chaotic.

In the meantime, the war program of the Allied countries was on the verge of collapse, due to inadequate supplies of food.[1] The United States was unable to bring the full measure of its assistance to them because of this transportation breakdown, which prevented movement of foodstuffs both from the farms to terminal markets and from these terminals to seaboard.

On January 6, 1918, Mr. Hoover wrote the Director General of Railroads[2] pointing out the extremely urgent needs of the Allies and suggesting a plan by which these needs could be met. This plan was not adopted until much later, and in the meantime it was only with the very greatest difficulty that the Food Administration was able to meet the Allied minimum demand.

[1] Compare letters from Allied officials cited on page 16.

[2] For copy of this letter and further details of transportation difficulties, see F. M. Surface, *The Grain Trade during the World War*, chapter 13.

It was not until March, 1918, that conditions improved perceptibly. By that time the Director General of Railroads had met the crisis by arranging with the Grain Corporation to operate under a permit system for grain movements, and this greatly simplified the whole problem.

Throughout the war and in the immediate post-war period transportation remained inadequate to meet the needs of the country during this period of accelerated activity.

Armistice Period

Of the many major problems which faced the Director General of Relief in the Armistice Period there were none more serious than that of transportation. This was true of both overseas shipping and of overland internal transportation in Europe.

Overseas transportation.—The Armistice resulted in some relief to world shipping since it was no longer necessary to transport a vast tonnage of munitions and war supplies. However, Europe was filled with the armies and navies of the Allies and these still required a large tonnage for their support and for their repatriation. The food supply of the Allied countries had been on a hand-to-mouth basis for many months, and still required a vast tonnage, particularly if normal stocks were to be accumulated. These needs were more than enough to occupy all available mercantile tonnage for many months to come.

For a few months immediately after the Armistice no special difficulty was experienced in obtaining tonnage, but by February, 1919, the freight market had tightened so that it was only with great difficulty that the Grain Corporation was able to secure the required shipping for relief work. In many instances serious delays in forwarding supplies were caused by this factor.

It was because of this acute shortage in shipping that the Allies insisted that Germany and Austria must turn over all their merchant tonnage to be operated by the Allies, as a precedent to the delivery of any food to these countries. After the German and Austrian vessels were placed in commission the situation eased somewhat, but this did not appreciably affect the tonnage position until near the end of the official relief operations in 1919.

Throughout the work of the American Relief Administration, the uncertainty as to whether the provisional programs for a given country were adequate, as well as the uncertainty of internal conditions, rendered it impractical to allocate vessels at the time they left American ports. Consequently, the great majority of relief ships sailed with orders to report either at Gibraltar or at Falmouth, England, and were then directed to the ports where their cargoes were most needed at that time. In this way there was established what was known as the Southern Relief through Gibraltar, and the Northern Relief through Falmouth.

Mr. Hoover foresaw the probable difficulty in securing adequate shipping, and before he left the United States in November, 1918, used the authority granted him by President Wilson to make definite arrangements for two large relief programs, totaling approximately 240,000 tons of foodstuffs with definite commitments that shipping for these would be available. One of these programs was to be carried out and financed by the United States Army Quartermaster while the other was to be handled and financed by the Food Administration Grain Corporation. The shipping for both programs was to be supplied by the War Department with vessels no longer needed for the movement of munitions or troops from the United States.

a) Grain Corporation shipment — First program: The program undertaken by the Grain Corporation, also known as the First Northern Relief Program, consisted of some nineteen cargoes loaded in vessels furnished by the War Department. The first ship on this program, the "Ossineke," sailed from New York on December 15, 1918, or long before any definite arrangements for the relief work had been perfected. These Northern Relief vessels all left the United States bound for Falmouth, England, as a port of call. Before they arrived they were directed by wireless to final destinations.

Inasmuch as no definite relief programs for the various countries had been agreed upon when these vessels began to arrive in European waters, it was decided to store these early cargoes in Rotterdam. Owing to disturbed conditions it was not considered safe to build up stocks of foodstuffs in other Northern European ports during January and February, 1919. During January nearly 80,000 metric tons of food were unloaded into warehouses in Rotterdam.

Of the nineteen vessels which were loaded by the Grain Corporation on this first program, one, the "Piave," was sunk en route and the cargo sold for insurance. Of the other eighteen, all but two, the "Westward Ho," I, and the "West Humhaw," I, discharged at Rotterdam. The two last-mentioned vessels proceeded to Danzig, where the cargo of the "Westward Ho," I, was sold to the Jewish Joint Distribution Committee, while that of the "West Humhaw," I, consisting entirely of fats and milk, was delivered to the Government of Poland.

The tabulation below lists the steamers which sailed on the First Northern Relief Program, together with date of arrival and total cargo. The 115,059 metric tons shown here, together with the cargo of the "Piave," made approximately 120,000 tons as originally planned.

Steamer	Date of Arrival 1919	Cargo in Metric Tons
Fairmont	January 4	6,283.0
West Shore	January 4	6,482.0
Ossineke	January 5	6,085.0
West Madaket	January 8	6,683.0
Absaroka, I	January 14	6,370.0
Western Hero	January 14	6,945.0
Indianapolis	January 16	9,439.0
Nantasket	January 21	6,422.0
Western Sea	January 25	6,756.0
West Mead	January 26	6,936.0
Western Maid, I	January 31	6,263.0
Eastern Star	January 31	4,672.0
Morristown	February 3	4,829.0
Western Light	February 10	6,153.0
Pequot	February 18	6,591.0
Newburg	February 18	6,331.0
Westward Ho, I	February 25	6,486.0*
West Humhaw, I	March 5	5,333.0*
Total		115,059.0†

* "Westward Ho," I, and "West Humhaw," I, discharged at Danzig; other vessels at Rotterdam. The cargo of the "Westward Ho," I, was sold to the Joint Distribution Committee and distributed by them and the American Polish Committee.

† This tonnage (except "Westward Ho" and "West Humhaw") went into storage in Rotterdam. Shipments were made ex-stock. Therefore, few of these steamers appear in the Appendix tables.

b) U.S. Army shipments: As noted above, Mr. Hoover, before he sailed for Europe in November, 1918, had arranged with the War Department for the United States Army Quartermaster to ship from Army stocks in the United States approximately 120,000 metric tons of foodstuffs for the relief work. The arrangements made were to ship approximately 120,000 short tons of wheat flour, 20,000 short tons of pork products, and 4,000 short tons of preserved milk. These supplies were shipped by the Army in its own tonnage and constituted what was known as the First Southern Relief Program. These ships all sailed for Gibraltar as a port of call and from there were directed to Adriatic or Black Sea ports. These vessels arrived in January, February, and March, 1919, for the most part before definite relief programs had been arranged for the individual countries. Most of the cargoes were unloaded into warehouses by the Army and were then invoiced by the Quartermaster to the Food Administration Grain Corporation at a c.i.f. price, as they were needed for the relief work. In all of these transactions the London office of the Grain Corporation acted as the business agent of the American Relief Administration, attending to all details of receipts and settlements from the receiving governments and the settlement with the Army Quartermaster.

U.S. Army Shipments, First Southern Relief Program

	Date of Arrival 1919	Cargo in Metric Tons
Discharged at Adriatic ports		
West Lashaway, I	January 3	7,174.0
West Alcasca	January 22	6,953.0
Western Scout	January 25	7,346.0
Sudbury	February 4	4,533.0
Oregonian	February 8	4,183.0
Nantahala	February 10	6,500.0
Westerner	February 13	5,705.0
Cape Lookout	February 19	5,302.0
Williamantic	February 21	6,093.0
Mount Shasta	February 25	5,538.0
East Wind, I	February 26	7,344.0
West Kyska, I	February 27	7,335.0
Western Hope	February 28	7,320.0
Durham	March 5	2,663.0
Canoga	March 31	4,761.0
Total		88,750.0*
Discharged at Black Sea ports		
Western Plains	January 21	7,426.0
Maine	January 28	5,898.0
West Mahomet	February 17	7,103.0
Western Belle	February 19	7,326.0
West Eldara	February 22	7,112.0
West Mount	March 1	5,252.0
West Leda	March 7	6,681.0
Englewood	April 21	3,667.0
Total		50,465.0*

* This tonnage went into storage in Adriatic and Black Sea ports and was delivered to the A.R.A. on Q.M. invoices, ex-Army stock. Therefore, but few of these steamers appear in the Appendix tables.

These reserve supplies built up in Southern European ports proved to be extremely important in relieving famine conditions in those countries.

The Army ships which sailed on this First Southern Relief Program and which were discharged under this agreement are shown in the list on page 129, together with their dates of arrival and total cargoes. Further details will be found in Table 111, pages 282–99.

c) Grain Corporation shipment—Later programs: After the completion of the original programs by the Grain Corporation and the Quartermaster General, the American Relief Administration sent to the New York office, each month in advance, an estimate of the amount and of the kind of supplies that would be required. The New York office of the Grain Corporation then arranged for the purchase of the supplies, the chartering of the ships, and attended to their dispatch. As each ship sailed, the Paris office of the Relief Administration was advised by cable of the fact, and of the approximate cargo, also whether sailing for Falmouth or Gibraltar.

The allocation of the ships to the various countries and relief programs was done in the Paris office. Before a ship was due at its port of call, the Paris office advised the London office of the Grain Corporation of the final destination. The Grain Corporation then transmitted the order to the ship and directed its course.

In the matter of communication with the ships at sea the co-operation of the American Navy was of inestimable service. Admiral Sims placed all Navy wires and means of communication at the disposal of Mr. Hoover, and made the statement that he could reach any vessel at any time and in any European waters. This statement was upheld by over seven months' operation. The facility with which supplies were diverted from a port jammed with excessive freight, as was Trieste during the third week in March, to more open ports in Roumania, or by which the program of one nation was decreased and another immediately increased by the change of destination of vessels in passage, testifies to the efficiency of our Naval communications.

During the period between December, 1918, and August, 1919, more than three hundred cargoes from America were handled and, at the peak of the operation, as many as seventy relief cargoes were on passage at one time.

In all, the American Relief Administration delivered supplies at thirty-seven different European ports. Nineteen of these were in Northern Europe and eighteen on the Southern route. The map on page 132 shows the location of these ports and the main lines of internal transportation.

At each of these ports the Grain Corporation had an agent who, ordinarily, was also the agent of the United States Shipping Board. It was the duty of these agents to look after the discharge of the ship, to check its cargo, and to forward the supplies, or to obtain a receipt from the purchasing government.

Many difficulties were encountered by these agents. In some instances, owing to the demoralization of internal transportation, it was necessary to use ports unaccustomed to discharging large ships. This was the case at Gravosa (Ragusa), Cattaro, and Spalato. In other ports, such as Trieste and Danzig, the discharge was complicated by political differences and jealousies.

The table on the opposite page shows a summary of the weekly sailings from the United States, and the weekly arrivals in European ports, of the shipments made during the 1919 relief operations.

Transshipping operations.—One other phase of the marine transportation remains to be discussed. It has already been noted that the early relief shipments to the north were discharged at Rotterdam because other ports could not be used for storage. During January, February, and March, 1919, approximately 120,000 metric tons were discharged there. In order to deliver these supplies to the liberated countries, it was necessary to transship the major portion by sea. Small amounts were sold to Holland and some was sold to Finland, for which the Finns provided their own transportation.

In February, 1919, the recognition of the serious food scarcity in Poland rendered it necessary to send some of these supplies to that country. To do this, ten American ships of the Lake-boat type (a boat of 2,000 to 3,000 tons, developed for use on the Great Lakes) were chartered from the United States Shipping

American Relief Administration, 1919 Operation

(Weekly Sailings from United States and Arrivals in Europe)

Week Ending	Sailing from U.S.		Arrivals in European Ports: Northern Relief		Arrivals in European Ports: Southern Relief	
	Number of Ships	Cargo Tons Cumulative	Number of Ships	Cargo Tons Cumulative	Number of Ships	Cargo Tons Cumulative
1918						
November 16	1	7,320	..	.....	..	....
November 23	..	7,320	..	.....	..	....
November 30	1	14,494	..	.....	..	....
December 7	2	29,266	..	.....	..	....
December 14	1	36,219	..	.....	..	....
December 21	7	81,794	..	.....	..	....
December 28	2	98,178	..	.....	..	....
1919						
January 4	1	104,600	2	12,765	1	7,174
January 11	5	133,634	2	25,533	..	7,174
January 18	5	164,252	3	48,287	..	7,174
January 25	5	186,022	2	61,445	2	21,473
February 1	10	248,206	3	81,318	2	34,788
February 8	2	260,715	1	86,147	2	43,504
February 15	7	314,362	2	98,891	2	56,356
February 22	7	358,849	1	105,222	5	89,014
March 1	7	403,637	1	111,708	5	121,803
March 8	10	454,950	4	141,635	1	128,484
March 15	10	515,784	1	142,225	3	146,563
March 22	10	575,008	7	194,441	1	151,527
March 29	7	614,707	6	226,675	3	165,997
April 5	7	644,267	6	261,043	3	183,624
April 12	10	696,852	10	316,976	2	198,113
April 19	11	763,507	4	339,147	4	220,661
April 26	23	889,996	3	354,202	6	251,722
May 3	14	961,738	6	381,329	4	270,810
May 10	15	1,044,562	11	443,588	3	288,296
May 17	18	1,143,677	11	505,517	2	302,818
May 24	21	1,254,169	14	580,278	4	326,211
May 31	12	1,309,624	13	665,184	4	348,621
June 7	7	1,334,344	15	758,847	2	358,260
June 14	11	1,419,777	12	816,910	1	365,258
June 21	5	1,442,040	10	867,668	2	372,103
June 28	9	1,492,379	17	952,209	1	375,362
July 5	5	1,531,179	11	1,023,176	..	375,362
July 12	1	1,538,497	14	1,095,705	..	375,362
July 19	2	1,553,269	3	1,111,773	..	375,362
July 26	8	1,594,696	4	1,137,109	1	381,805
August 2	3	1,614,417	2	1,148,736	1	382,440
August 9	5	1,634,129	2	1,163,508	1	383,257
August 16	1	1,641,760	3	1,184,873	2	385,294
August 23	1	1,643,660	3	1,204,594	..	385,294
August 30	..	......	4	1,233,855	3	391,917
September 6	..	......	..	......	2	407,905
September 13	..	......	..	......	1	409,805

Board, at $600 a day for the bare boat, and arrangements made with the Navy to furnish the crews at cost. These boats were used to move the accumulated stocks from Rotterdam to Danzig and other northern ports. Later on, some of them were used to transport United States Liquidation Commission supplies from French ports.

Early in March, two more boats of this type were added to the American Relief fleet. The

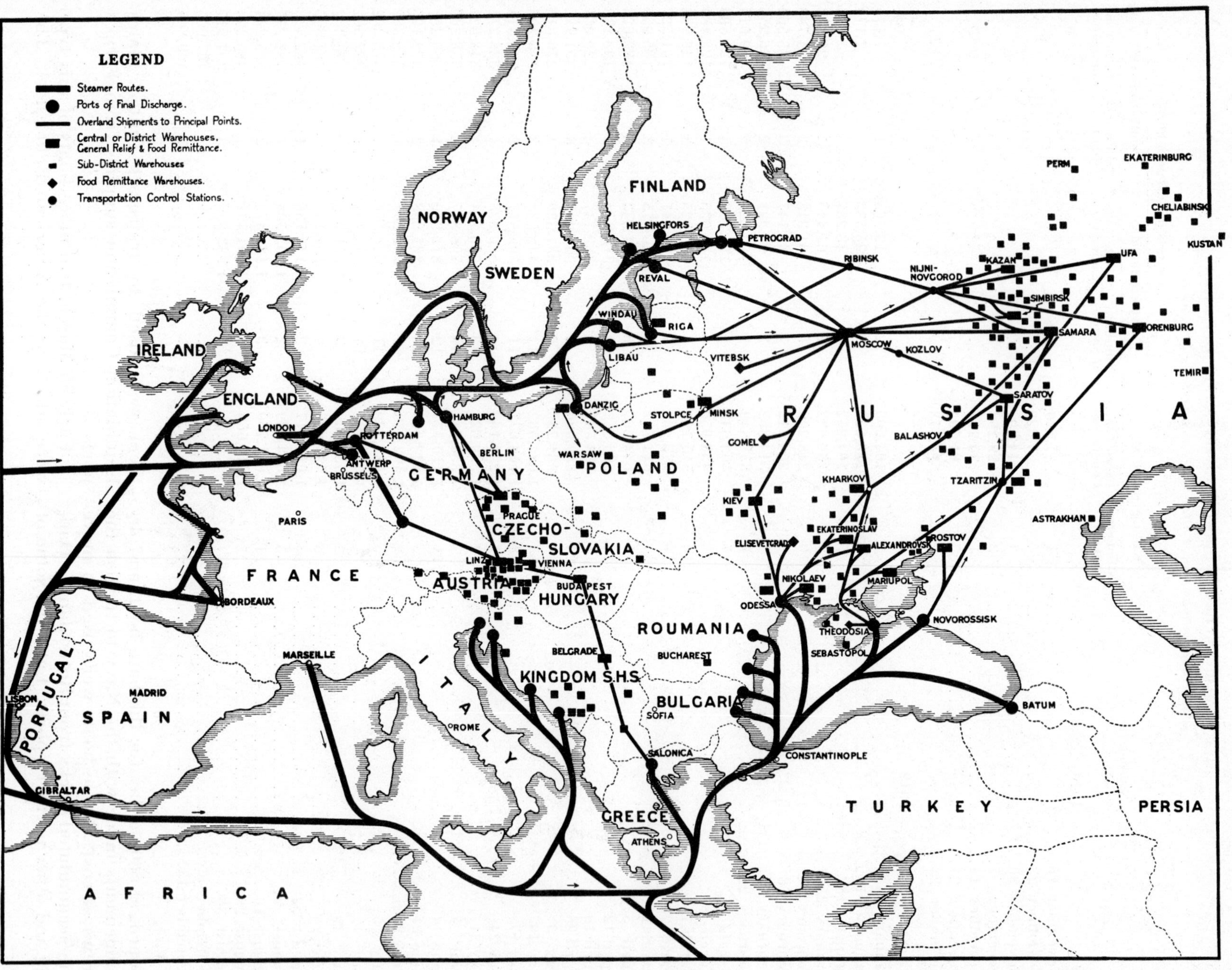

Map showing movement of A.R.A. relief supplies, 1919–1923, steamer routes, ports, overland shipments, and warehouses.

twelve Lake boats finally put in use for this work were:

Lake Mary	Lake Catherine
Lake Clear	Lake Dancey
Lake Traverse	Lake Eckhart
Lake Wimico	Lake Tulare
Lake St. Clair	Democracy
Lake St. Regis	Kerowlee

By employing Lake boats in this movement, eight days were cut off of the voyage of trans-Atlantic liners, which otherwise would have had to proceed direct to Danzig and other Baltic ports. It was also possible to ship to Danzig considerable quantities of supplies purchased from the C.R.B., which were urgently needed in Poland. The additional cost of transshipment was charged against the purchasing government. In all, more than 160,000 tons of food and other supplies were moved by these Lake boats.

It is perhaps not generally realized that the freight movements under the direction of the American Relief Administration and the Grain Corporation were possibly the largest ever carried on under a single operating head. It is extraordinary that there was not a single serious error in execution of any of the programs outlined at Paris, in spite of the frequent changes required by the state of affairs in Europe.

Much credit for this accomplishment is due to Colonel A. B. Barber and his assistant, Captain H. L. Bodman, who were in charge of the allocation of ships in the Paris office, but more especially to Edward M. Flesh, in charge of the London office of the Grain Corporation, and his able assistant, Captain Roger D. Lapham. To these latter gentlemen fell the responsibility of issuing all orders to all ships and of seeing that they followed these instructions.

Table 137 shows a summary of the monthly arrivals at each port, giving both the number of ships and the total cargo tons. The shipments from American ports, and the transshipments from European ports, are shown separately.

Overland transportation.—Among other serious difficulties encountered in 1919 were those connected with the overland transportation of relief supplies in the devastated territories. Mention has already been made of the chaotic political and economic conditions which prevailed in Central Europe after the Armistice. The transportation systems had suffered particularly. In old Serbia, for example, practically all railroads were destroyed and to put these in operation would require the construction of bridges, tracks, etc., as well as the acquisition of rolling stock. In Roumania, out of 900 locomotives remaining after the Armistice, only 160 were in working order. The number of tank and freight cars had been very much reduced.

Overland transportation of American Relief supplies. Transporting American flour from Lieksa, Finland, into Russian Karelia for a distance of one hundred kilometers.

Even in such regions as Czechoslovakia, Austria, and Poland, where the actual destruction had not been so complete, there was practically no rolling stock worth the name. Added to this were the serious political difficulties caused by the breaking up of the former Austro-Hungarian Empire and the existing national and racial animosities. Practically all boundary lines of the new states were closed to traffic.

Nevertheless, the problem of the maintenance of human life and the preservation of order through adequate food supplies depended fully as much upon its proper internal distribution as it did on the proper amount of imports.

In view of these difficulties, Mr. Hoover in a memorandum to the Supreme War Council, March 5, 1919, proposed the following solution:

> The solution which I propose, after elaborate investigation by American Railway Engineers, is one that I not only believe is feasible but will meet the various exigencies of the political situation. To this end the following plan is proposed: (*a*) All the states of the old Austrian Empire, including the areas held by the Italians on the Adriatic, should be called upon to furnish a definite contribution of railway rolling stock;

(*b*) This rolling stock should be marked as belonging to the Relief Administration and used solely for its purposes; (*c*) The Director General of Relief should be made the mandatory for the disposition of this rolling stock; (*d*) A regular train service should be established under his direction that will carry out the necessary programmes of food to the different localities; (*e*) This service should have entire freedom of movement over all railways regardless of political boundaries and in complete priority to other services; (*f*) The railway servants of any nationality may be employed in operations over any territory regardless of nationality or political boundaries; (*g*) Definite portions of port facilities should be assigned to the Relief Administration at Trieste and Fiume for the consummation of these ends; (*h*) The rolling stock should not be demanded by any of the Allied Governments until this service is completely equipped; (*i*) That the railway officials of each state and port officials in each port should be called upon to co-operate in maintenance of this service.

Transporting American flour above the Arctic Circle, Finland.

The Supreme War Council approved this plan on March 7, 1919, and directed each of the Central European states to contribute its quota of cars and locomotives. The organization of an Inter-Allied mission, known as the "Allied Railway Mission," with broad powers to control the movement of relief traffic in Central Europe, was also approved.

This Mission was organized under the direction of Mr. Hoover with an American, Lieutenant Colonel William B. Ryan, T.C., U.S.A., at its head. Later, it was necessary to relieve Colonel Ryan for other work, and Lieutenant Colonel W. B. Causey, Engineers, U.S.A., was designated to replace him. Colonel William G. Atwood was the American representative on the Communication Section of the Supreme Economic Council and under Mr. Hoover was in charge of the communication work at the Paris office.

The first work initiated by the Allied Railway Mission was the opening of through freight service from Trieste to German Austria and Czechoslovakia. When the Mission commenced its operations in March, there were some 40,000 tons of supplies in Trieste and 12,000 in Fiume, and the average daily movement was only 700 tons out of Trieste, and nothing out of Fiume. From March 23 to June 15, under the operation of the Allied Railway Mission, a total of 178,200 tons, or a daily average, including holidays, which are numerous in Italy, of 2,121 tons, was moved from Trieste. On several days during this period, the daily movement exceeded 4,000 tons.

A study of the transportation systems showed that supplies for Czechoslovakia could be handled with greater economy and expediency through the German port of Hamburg, and then by barge down the Elbe. As soon as the necessary transportation and political arrangements could be made, supplies for Czechoslovakia were routed this way. The first barge left Hamburg on April 1, and arrived at Schandau near the Czechoslovakian border April 9. To the end of August more than 240,000 tons of supplies were shipped by the Elbe. (Cf. Table 240.)

The Mission also exercised general supervision over the transportation systems of the several Central European states. In particular, they assisted in the distribution of the available coal supply and assisted in obtaining an increased production of coal.

Communications.—Another important problem for the Director General of Relief was that of overland communication between the different countries in which relief missions were established. Following the political upheavals after the Armistice, all forms of communication including the postal service were interrupted between many of these Central European nations. Yet, if relief operations were to be directed in these countries, it was necessary to have an adequate means of communication between Paris and the field offices. At first, this had to be maintained entirely by the A.R.A.

courier service, and more than twenty courier routes were established and maintained between Paris and various European points. Even here great difficulty was experienced in maintaining schedules because of the irregular and intermittent train service between many points.

Telegraphic and telephone communications between most of the newly established governments had been interrupted and there seemed no likelihood of any early resumption of such service. Even where telegraph lines were established, international complications made the service almost impossible. For example, between Trieste and Vienna, the telegraph lines were controlled part of the distance by the Italian Government, part by Jugoslavia, and part by Austria. Deliveries were slow and uncertain. It was not unusual for the confirmation copy to be delivered by courier, before the message itself arrived.

Because of these conditions Mr. Hoover secured the services of a group of officers from the U.S. Army Signal Corps and undertook to establish a workable communication system. In some places the A.R.A. had to build new telegraph lines, but in most cases they were able to secure the lease or control of already existing lines and by negotiations with adjoining countries were able to establish satisfactory circuits throughout most of Central and Southern Europe. American operators, secured either from the Army Signal Corps or from the U.S. Navy, were installed at all points and the lines operated entirely by the A.R.A. Before the close of the relief work in July, 1919, upward of 10,000 miles of telephone and telegraph lines were being operated in this manner. The communication work was in charge of Major Frank H. Fay, Signal Corps, in the Paris office, while the negotiations for, and the establishment of, most of the circuits in Central and Southern Europe were handled by Captain Paul S. Clapp, Signal Corps, with headquarters in Vienna.

The map on page 136 shows the principal lines under the control of, or affiliated with, the American Relief Administration.

Freight and insurance charges paid by American Relief Administration.—

a) Red Cross shipments: The question of transportation of relief supplies for other relief organizations was of particular importance during the Armistice Period. For example, the American Red Cross assembled large quantities of secondhand clothing in the United States but had no way of sending this to the countries in Europe where it was needed. Since practically no commercial vessels were running to continental ports during the Armistice Period, the A.R.A. undertook to transport a large portion of this clothing and also other miscellaneous supplies, chiefly medical and hospital materials, from the United States and to superintend their distribution in the countries where they were urgently needed.

During the period of the Armistice the A.R.A. transported a total of 4,494.8 metric tons of Red Cross clothing and medical and hospital supplies, on which the freight charges amounted to $369,404.95. The following tabulation shows the quantities of these commodities going to each of the relief countries, with total freight charges. Table 143 gives the detail of these shipments.

Freight on American Red Cross Clothing and Other Supplies Paid by American Relief Administration

Country	Type of Commodity	Metric Tons	Freight and Other Charges
Armenia	Clothing	754.1	$ 47,688.48
Czechoslovakia	Clothing	301.2	18,681.81
Esthonia	Medical	312.3	50,490.02
Finland	Clothing	282.0	22,584.24
Jugoslavia	Clothing	667.6	81,140.98
Poland	Medical	2,177.6	148,819.42
Total		4,494.8	$369,404.95

In addition to the transportation of these Red Cross supplies, the A.R.A. also transported and distributed minor donations from other organizations, including 25.0 metric tons of cod-liver oil which was a gift from the Norwegian Government. These transactions, showing the countries to which they were distributed and the value of the transportation charges, are given in detail in Tables 143 *A* and *B*, and may be summarized as follows:

Freight on Other Miscellaneous Charity Shipments Paid by American Relief Administration

Country	Commodities Donated by	Metric Tons	Misc. Charges
Poland	Polish League of Women	4.1	$216.56
Poland	Russo Carpathian Committee	0.5	28.01
Austria	Norwegian Government	8.3	178.47
Czechoslovakia	Norwegian Government	10.1	217.18
Latvia	Norwegian Government	6.6	159.72
Total		29.6	$799.94

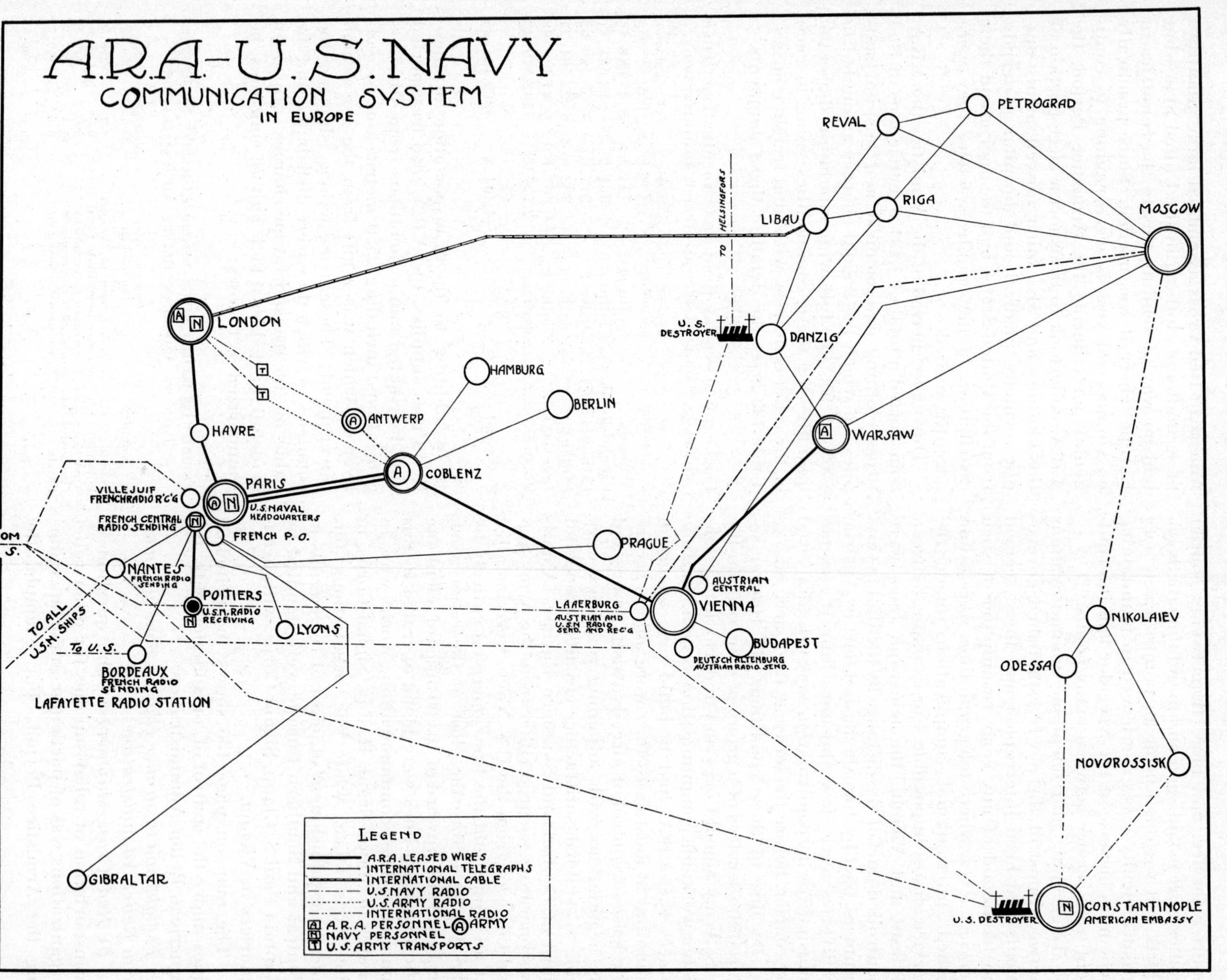

Map showing communication system of the A.R.A. and the United States Navy, in Europe.

The total freight and other charges on the Red Cross and other miscellaneous charity shipments thus totaled to $370,204.89, which was paid by the A.R.A. and charged against the Congressional Appropriation for European Relief as a gift to these countries from the American people.

b) *Supplies sold direct by the U.S. Liquidation Commission:* As pointed out elsewhere (see page 52) the U.S. Liquidation Commission (War Department) sold large quantities of food, clothing, and miscellaneous supplies from surplus stocks to various European governments, including the newly liberated countries. These supplies were sold on credit, f.o.b. the warehouses where they were located, chiefly in France, at the ports of Bordeaux and St. Nazaire. The newly formed governments were without shipping facilities of their own, and under the conditions during the Armistice Period they found great difficulty in getting these supplies transported to their own borders. The American Relief Administration therefore undertook to transport a portion of these commodities, which consisted of pork products and miscellaneous Army and medical supplies. Altogether, 26,777.6 metric tons of such supplies were transported, on which the freight and insurance charges amounted to $765,455.15. The value of these supplies, exclusive of transportation, is included in the sales by the U.S. Liquidation Commission shown in Table 122. The details of the tonnage moved and the freight and insurance paid by the American Relief Administration are given in Tables 144 and 145. The following tabulation summarizes these transportation charges by the countries to which the supplies were delivered.

Of the supplies going to Poland, 10,000 tons of typhus equipment were sold on credit by the U.S. Liquidation Commission and the shipment by rail from Coblenz to Warsaw was attended to, and paid for, by the A.R.A. The total freight charges on this shipment, of approximately 900 carloads, amounted to $113,785.52, which was charged against the Congressional Appropriation as a gift to Poland from the American people.

The freight and insurance costs against the other commodities, totaling $651,659.63, were charged against the respective governments, and notes covering these costs were obtained by the American Relief Administration.

c) *Jewish Joint Distribution Committee supplies:* As shown elsewhere in this report (see pages 56–58) the J.D.C. worked very closely with the Director General of Relief throughout the Armistice Period. From time to time the A.R.A. was able to assist the J.D.C. by transporting supplies which they had purchased but for which they could not readily furnish transportation. This was particularly true of supplies purchased from the U.S. Liquidation Commission which the J.D.C. wished to move to Hamburg and Danzig. The A.R.A. handled a total of 1,112.1 metric tons of such supplies for this organization at a total cost of $81,588.23 for freight and insurance. The value of the commodities purchased from the Liquidation Commission, but without transportation costs, is included in Table 125. The detail of this movement, together with the cost of freight and insurance, is shown in Table 146. The summary at the top of page 138 shows the transportation cost by countries to which the supplies were delivered.

The J.D.C. later reimbursed the A.R.A. for these charges.

FREIGHT AND INSURANCE PAID BY THE A.R.A. ON SUPPLIES SOLD BY THE U.S. LIQUIDATION COMMISSION

Distributed to	Total Metric Tons*	Cost of Insurance	Cost of Freight	Total Freight and Insurance
Czechoslovakia	4,954.5	$18,613.70	$165,992.93	$184,606.63
Esthonia	2,020.4	10,881.95	140,231.10	151,113.05
Lithuania	6,096.3	....	48,930.00	48,930.00
Northwest Russia	349.2	3,351.18	48,837.00	52,188.18
Poland	13,357.2	17,295.71	311,311.58	328,607.29
Total	26,777.6	$50,142.54	$715,302.61	$765,445.15

* The supplies to Czechoslovakia, Esthonia, and 3,357.2 tons to Poland consisted of pork products. All other supplies are listed as miscellaneous Army supplies, except the 10,000 tons of typhus equipment shipped to the American Typhus Commission in Poland.

Freight and Insurance on Supplies Purchased by Joint Distribution Committee from U.S. Liquidation Commission and Transported by American Relief Administration

Distributed to	Total Metric Tons	Cost of Insurance	Cost of Freight	Total Freight and Insurance
Austria ...	319.3	$ 410.96	$14,813.15	$15,224.11
Poland ...	792.8	2,824.12	63,540.00	66,364.12
Total ..	1,112.1	$3,235.08	$78,353.15	$81,588.23

The following tabulation summarizes the total amounts paid for freight and insurance in relief shipments for various governments and other relief organizations which are not accounted for in any of the regular commodity movements shown in this report. Of the total of $1,217,238.27, the sum of $651,659.63 was furnished on credit to the liberated governments while the remainder of $565,578.64 was furnished as a gift. Of this latter amount, $493,990.41 was supplied by the American Relief Administration and $81,588.23 by the Jewish Joint Distribution Committee.

Reconstruction Period

European Children's Fund.—The problems of overseas shipment of the supplies for child feeding after August 1, 1919, were by no means so difficult as those of the preceding period. This was due partly to the fact that the world tonnage situation had become somewhat easier, and as the operation was on a smaller scale no special difficulty in securing tonnage was experienced. The supplies were purchased by the New York office and shipped as either full or partial cargo on ordinary liner terms. Hamburg and Danzig were the principal ports of discharge for the child-feeding supplies for Central Europe. A small portion of the shipments was sent direct to north Baltic ports and a few shipments of clothing for Jugoslavia were discharged at Salonica. For the Russian operations, the ports of Reval in the north and Novorossisk in the south were the most important, although relatively large shipments were also handled at several other ports.

The children's relief work was carried on entirely through feeding kitchens. In order to keep these kitchens supplied with current needs, it was necessary to maintain warehouse stocks in near-by positions. The Relief Administration therefore established a system of central or district warehouses to which supplies were shipped in large quantities and also a series of subdistrict warehouses which in turn were kept supplied from the district warehouses. One of the conditions of the relief work was that the several governments would handle and finance the transportation of supplies from the port of arrival to the district warehouses and to the feeding stations. No serious difficulties arose in connection with the internal transportation although there were annoying details from time to time. The shipment of food supplies through countries in which people were actually suffering for lack of food naturally made these supplies subject to pilfering or other unaccountable losses. This frequently resulted in shortages which disturbed the plans for the feeding work. Finally, the Relief Administration negotiated agreements with each of the governments in Central Europe by which the latter agreed to make good any losses in relief supplies whether suffered en route or in the warehouses. For ex-

Summary of Amounts Paid for Freight and Insurance by American Relief Administration, Not Elsewhere Shown

Delivered to	Red Cross Shipments	Charity Shipments	U.S. Liquidation Commission Shipments	Joint Distribution Committee Shipments	Total Amount Paid
Armenia	$ 47,688.48	.....	....	....	$ 47,688.48
Austria	....	$178.47	....	$15,224.11	15,402.58
Czechoslovakia	18,681.81	217.18	$184,606.63	....	203,505.62
Esthonia	50,490.02	.....	151,113.05	....	201,603.07
Finland	22,584.24	.....	....	....	22,584.24
Jugoslavia	81,140.98	.....	....	....	81,140.98
Latvia	....	159.72	....	....	159.72
Lithuania	....	.....	48,930.00	....	48,930.00
Northwest Russia	....	.....	52,188.18	....	52,188.18
Poland	148,819.42	244.57	328,607.29	66,364.12	544,035.40
Total	$369,404.95	$799.94	$765,445.15	$81,588.23	$1,217,238.27

ample, in August, 1922, the Polish Government assigned credits for the purchase of flour and beans to make up for shortages of 1,159.5 metric tons of foodstuffs which had occurred during the preceding year.

Russian Relief.—The pouring of more than 700,000 tons of relief supplies into Russia in a relatively short period during the famine of 1921–1922 brought forth a vast array of difficulties which could not be foreseen. At times, these difficulties became so serious as to threaten the success of the whole operation, but by some means or other they were overcome and the work carried through with only annoying and threatening delays.

The first problem was to secure satisfactory ports with accompanying rail facilities and connections. The major portion of the supplies had to go through northern ports on the Baltic. None of the Baltic ports had sufficient equipment to handle all of the supplies, and in many cases facilities were so limited as to make it very expensive to send ocean-going vessels to them, where demurrage costs were likely to become prohibitive before the vessels could be unloaded. It was soon found that considerable savings could be effected by discharging trans-Atlantic cargoes at Hamburg and then reshipping these to the Baltic on small steamers. Consequently, the American Relief Administration maintained a large warehouse at Hamburg throughout this operation, and altogether more than 101,000 metric tons of supplies were transshipped in this manner. Tables 513, 517, 519, 521, 523, and 525 give some indication of the extent to which Hamburg and some other North Sea ports were used for the primary discharge of these cargoes.

Altogether, ten ports were used as final points of discharge for the Russian supplies. Six of these, Petrograd (Leningrad), Reval, Riga, Windau, Libau, and Danzig, were on the Baltic Sea, while four, Odessa, Theodosia, Novorossisk, and Batoum, were on the Black Sea and were used for supplies to Southern Russia and the Ukraine. The heaviest tonnages were handled through Riga and Novorossisk.

The majority of these ports, particularly those in the south, had remained inactive for so many years of the war that it was with difficulty that local officials, and particularly the railroad officials, could be brought to believe that a period of renewed activity was at hand. The rapid handling of a large tonnage of supplies required adequate preparations, including the overhauling of discharging equipment, the renovation of warehouses long unused or filled with all sorts of débris, the provision for stevedoring, checks against pilferage, arrangements for the handling of bulk grain, etc.

All these could be accomplished through the perseverance and persistence of the A.R.A. port officials, but the thing they could not do was to provide freight cars and locomotives where none existed and that was where the great difficulty came. When a program of relief and seed amounting to 100,000 tons and more per month was projected, the Russian officials expressed entire confidence in their ability to handle the rail movement. The first cargoes were moved promptly and then difficulties began to pile up. When the first lot of empty cars were filled, the roads were unable to get these emptied and returned in time, and port stocks began to mount, reaching more than 120,000 tons in March, 1922. Train movement was incredibly slow. The first train of forty-three cars of food out of Odessa took a month to reach Simbirsk, fifteen hundred miles away. Trains from Baltic ports to Moscow took from one to four weeks to cover a distance made by a passenger train in fourteen hours.

Petrograd port canal with 250-ton floating crane. Transshipping A.R.A. food for relief of Russian famine sufferers. Scene taken last week in March, when winter's ice nearly blocked the harbor.

This situation was due first to the run-down

condition of the railway equipment, but also to the ineffective method of administration in those early days of the Soviet Government, and finally to the underpaid and undernourished railway employees. The latter situation was remedied in a measure through the loan of some 5,000 tons of corn and rye to the Soviets for special relief of the railway workers (cf. page 250). This had a marked effect upon railway movement and upon conditions generally.

The spring months of 1922 were dark days for the A.R.A. officials, who had to witness men and women on the verge of starvation with the knowledge that thousands of tons of food were in Russian ports which could not be moved to the famine areas. Yet constant pressure on the Soviet authorities finally overcame the difficulties and the food came in time to save millions of lives and the seed arrived in time for planting.

As soon as the ice was out of the Volga this great river was used to supplement the rail transportation, but even here the equipment was so depleted that great difficulties were experienced. However, the river movement speeded up distribution greatly.

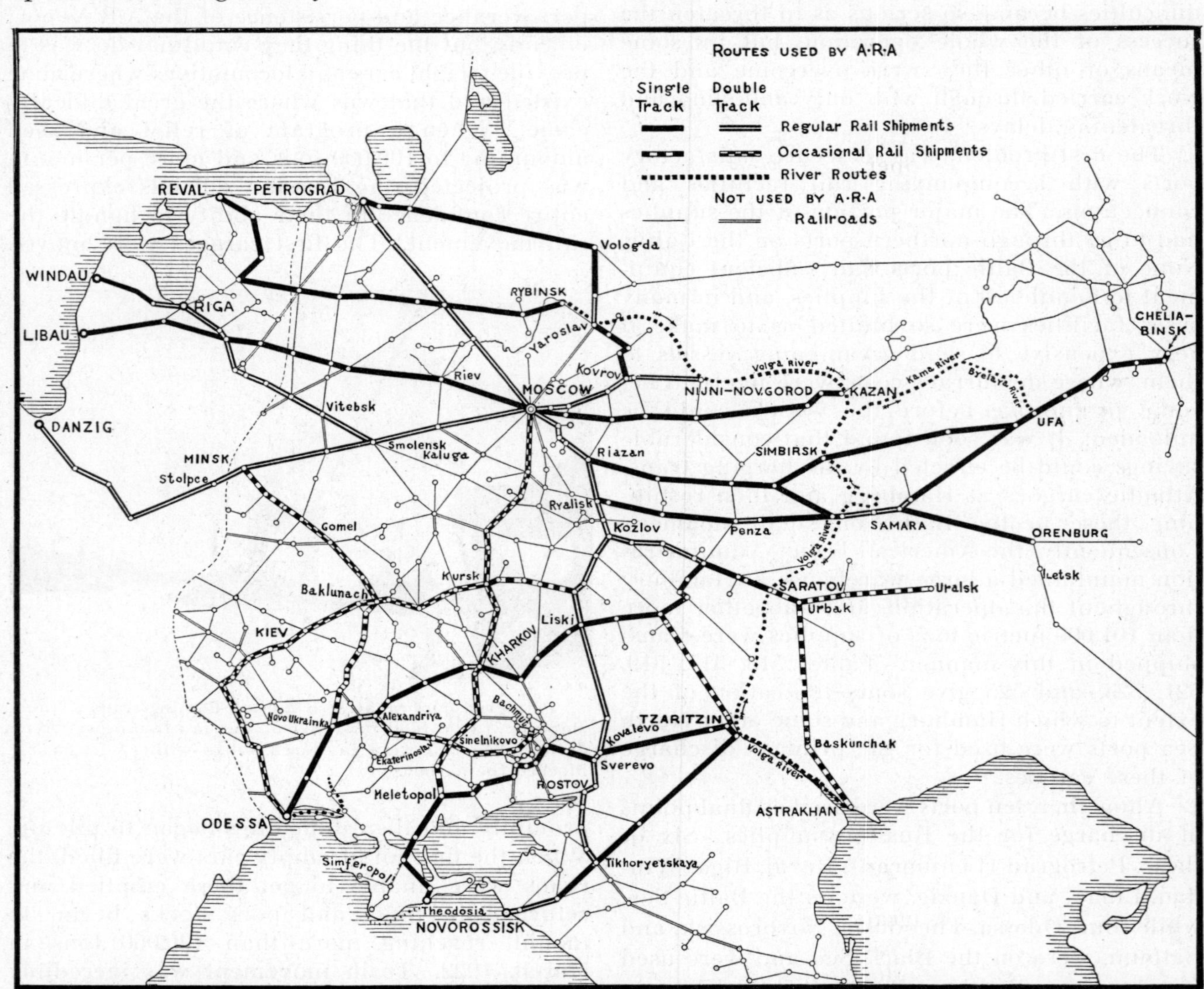

Map showing Russian transport lines used by A.R.A.

The spring months of 1922 were dark days for the A.R.A. officials, who had to witness men and women on the verge of starvation with the knowledge that thousands of tons of food were in Russian ports which could not be moved to

Other problems of transportation in Russia involved the movement of supplies from railhead to the famine districts. This was a matter mainly of man and animal power. Pack animals, droskies, camel caravans, and other

A peasants' camel caravan crossing the frozen Volga in Saratov District, returning to the village with relief supplies.

methods were used to get this food to areas remote from rail or water connections.[1]

SOURCES OF RELIEF FINANCE

To secure the enormous sums required for these vast relief operations was no small undertaking. It will be worth while at this point to tabulate the sources from which the money was secured, although the detail involved in securing particular sums has been discussed when the operations themselves were being considered.

The financial structure of the several undertakings can best be presented from the standpoint of gross basic capital. It will be understood that on many of these operations, where sales were made to governments or organizations, it was possible to charge a margin to cover the cost of operation and some measure of the commercial risk involved. In some instances, these resulted in surpluses which were used to supply still further relief to the countries concerned. These surpluses are discussed in connection with the several operations.

Dividing the relief work into the four major periods, it is possible to tabulate the total gross basic capital for each, as shown in the following table:

Total Gross Basic Capital for European Relief by Major Periods of Operation—1914 to 1924

Major Period	Total Basic Capital
Commission for Relief in Belgium	$ 759,159,607.19
U.S. Food Administration	3,050,496,599.23
Armistice Period	1,135,131,158.68
Reconstruction Period	212,385,557.59
Grand total	$5,157,172,922.69

It will be noted that the total basic capital amounted to $5,157,172,922.69 for the entire period, whereas the total deliveries (Table 1) amounted to $5,234,028,208.56. The difference as discussed above was covered by the surplus earning on certain of the operations.

C.R.B. Period

Taking each of the major periods separately, it is possible to show the sources of the basic capital for the various operations. The following tabulation summarizes the source of the funds available for the Commission for Relief in Belgium.

Commission for Relief in Belgium—Source of Basic Capital

Source of Capital		Total Basic Capital
Government subsidies		
United States	$386,632,260.44	
United Kingdom	109,045,328.73	
France	204,862,854.21	
Total subsidies		$700,540,443.38
Benevolence		
United States	34,521,026.99	
United Kingdom	16,641,034.85	
Other countries	1,128,773.67	
Total benevolence		52,290,835.51
Commercial exchange		6,328,328.30
Grand total		$759,159,607.19

U.S.F.A. Period

For the deliveries to the Allied Governments during the Food Administration Period we have taken only the actual expenditures for food paid for from U.S. Treasury loans. These expenditures by fiscal-year periods, as shown by the records of the United States Treasury,[2] may be summarized as follows:

United States Food Administration—Expenditures by Allied Governments for Foodstuffs, from U.S. Treasury Loans

Period	For Cereals	For Other Food	Total
Apr. 6, 1917, to Dec. 31, 1917	$ 362,761,098.41	$ 175,661,662.66	$ 538,422,761.07
Jan. 1, 1918, to June 30, 1918	386,921,956.94	484,893,090.59	871,815,047.53
July 1, 1918, to Dec. 31, 1918	467,901,495.91	367,904,188.12	835,805,684.03
Jan. 1, 1919, to June 30, 1919	165,384,156.38	519,695,805.12	685,079,961.50
July, 1, 1919, to Nov. 1, 1920	39,507,998.50	79,865,146.60	119,373,145.10
Total	$1,422,476,706.14	$1,628,019,893.09	$3,050,496,599.23

Armistice Period

During the Armistice Period funds for the relief work were obtained from government subsidies and credits, from the sale of commodities for cash or its equivalent, and from benevolence.

[1] For further detail regarding transportation in Russia, see *A.R.A. Bulletin*, Series 2, No. 42, November 1923.

[2] *Annual Report of the Secretary of the Treasury for 1920*, pages 330 ff.

The sources of the basic capital for the work during this period, under these headings, and by the countries from which the funds were supplied, were as follows:

Sources of Basic Capital for Relief Operations—Armistice Period, 1919

Source of Capital		Total Basic Capital
Government subsidies and credits		
United States	$624,171,094.59	
United Kingdom	59,500,000.00	
Canada	5,000,000.00	
Newfoundland	1,500,000.00	
France	5,600,000.00	
Italy	2,100,000.00	
Total subsidies		$ 697,871,094.59
Sales for cash or barter		
United States	$234,377,089.09	
United Kingdom	77,187,500.00	
France	23,800,000.00	
Italy	35,511,000.00	
Other countries	51,666,000.00	
Total cash		422,541,589.09
Benevolence		
United States	$ 14,560,469.00	
United Kingdom	149,006.00	
Norway	9,000.00	
Total benevolence		14,718,475.00
Grand total		$1,135,131,158.68

The funds supplied by the United States Government for relief work during the Armistice Period amounted to $624,171,094.59. The detail of the sources of these funds is given below:

Detail of U.S. Government Subsidies and Credits for Relief—Armistice Period, 1919

Source of Capital	Total
Act of Congress, February 25, 1919	$100,000,000.00
Direct Treasury Loans	89,450,000.00
Joint Allied Finance *	48,000,000.00
President's National Security and Defense Fund	5,000,000.00
U.S. Liquidation Commission (credits)	381,721,094.59
Total	$624,171,094.59

* Represents U.S. Treasury loans to the United Kingdom, France, and Italy of $16,000,000 each, with which they in turn furnished relief supplies to Austria on credit.

Early in 1919 the British Treasury voted relief credits of £12,500,000, which was equivalent to $59,500,000. This was used to supply relief to a number of countries in Central and Southern Europe, as shown in Table 133.

Canada and Newfoundland each granted credit to Roumania for the purchase of urgently needed supplies. The French and Italian credits were for the payment of freight on supplies for Austria and in the case of France also for relief to Russian war prisoners in Germany.

Under sales for cash or barter there are included those transactions where the receiving country made immediate payment for the supplies furnished, either in the form of cash or by the exchange of other commodities or concessions. All of the relief furnished to Germany during the Armistice Period comes under this heading and accounts for the major portion of the deliveries from the United Kingdom, France, and Italy. The deliveries from "Other countries" were all in the nature of barter.

In the case of the United States, the sum shown includes sales made to Germany and to such organizations as the Near East Relief, the Jewish Joint Distribution Committee, and to certain commercial establishments like J. W. Whittall and Company, in Turkey. In addition to the sums received as actual payment for the commodities, there is also included cash advanced by these governments to cover certain expenses of distribution under the Congressional Appropriation. These receipts had the effect of decreasing the expenses of the American Relief Administration, which otherwise would have required other funds.

Under benevolence during the Armistice Period, there is included such operations of various charitable organizations as were carried out in co-operation with the Director General of Relief. The contribution from Norway covers the value of 25 tons of cod liver oil which the Norwegian Government contributed to the children's relief work.

Reconstruction Period

The sources of the funds for relief work during the Reconstruction Period may be divided under two general headings, government subsidies and benevolence. Under the former are included all direct contributions by governmental authority and under the latter all funds contributed by either individuals or organizations. The following tabulation summarizes the source of the basic capital available in this period under these two heads and by the countries from which the contributions came:

SOURCES OF BASIC CAPITAL FOR RELIEF OPERATIONS—RECONSTRUCTION PERIOD

Source of Capital		Total Basic Capital
Government subsidies		
United States	$81,782,118.20	
United Kingdom	18,212,473.88	
Central European governments	14,652,432.21	
Soviet Republics	11,464,948.18	
Total subsidies		$126,111,972.47
Benevolence		
United States	$57,586,406.01	
World charity	28,687,179.11	
Total benevolence		86,273,585.12
Grand total		$212,385,557.59

Subsidies from the United States were provided by three separate acts of Congress, as follows:

Act of Congress, March 30, 1920 *	$57,782,118.20
Act of Congress, December 22, 1921 †	20,000,000.00
Act of Congress, January 20, 1922 ‡	4,000,000.00
Total	$81,782,118.20

* Authorizing the U.S. Grain Corporation to sell 5,000,000 barrels of flour on credit to relieve the food famine in Central Europe.

† Appropriating $20,000,000 of the capital of the U.S. Grain Corporation for the relief of Russia.

‡ Authorizing the gift of surplus medical supplies to Russia.

Subsidies from the United Kingdom were used for the payment of freight and insurance charges on the flour furnished by the United States Grain Corporation under the Act of Congress of March 30, 1920.

Subsidies from Central European governments include the donations of commodities for the child-feeding programs in their own countries and also contributions of services in connection with the relief of Russia. This statement does not include any allowance for services and facilities contributed by each country in connection with the child-feeding work in that particular country. It does, however, include commodity donations from local as well as national governmental organizations.

The contribution from each country as accounted for under this heading was as follows:

CONTRIBUTIONS BY CENTRAL EUROPEAN GOVERNMENTS—RECONSTRUCTION PERIOD

Country	Commodities for Child Feeding	Facilities for Russia	Total
Austria	$ 1,364,656.01	....	$ 1,364,656.01
Czechoslovakia	693,099.02	....	693,099.02
Danzig Free City	8,574.44	....	8,574.44
Esthonia	298,444.64	$ 1,102.94	299,547.58
Finland	195,949.00	....	195,949.00
Germany	2,392,021.25	....	2,392,021.25
Hungary	265,806.84	....	265,806.84
Jugoslavia	533,677.16	....	533,677.16
Latvia	64,839.55	24,257.69	89,097.24*
Poland	7,659,374.77	90,000.00	7,749,374.77
Roumania	1,024,322.26	....	1,024,322.26
Russia			
Northwest Russia	6,280.00	....	6,280.00
Soviet Republics	30,026.64	....	30,026.64
Total	$14,537,071.58	$115,360.63	$14,652,432.21

* Includes $3,960, value of cod liver oil donated by Norwegian Government.

A large proportion of the contributions by these Central European governments consisted of flour which in most instances they agreed to furnish as their contribution to the child-feeding work. In many instances, they contributed other commodities as well. In addition to those commodity contributions which can readily be evaluated, these countries also made large contributions to the child-feeding work of a more intangible nature which are not included in these tables. These contributions consisted of the services of thousands of volunteer workers in conducting the feeding kitchens, of free transportation, handling, and warehousing of relief supplies. Some estimates of these contributions are given in the discussion of the relief work in the separate countries.

In the above tabulation the contribution of $30,026.64 from the Soviet Republics represents commodities contributed for the child-feeding work in Russia.

The first table in column one on this page shows as a subsidy from the Soviet Republics the sum of $11,464,948.18, which represents a direct contribution of Soviet gold to the American Relief Administration for the purchase of seed and food during the famine of 1921 and 1922.

Benevolence from the United States during the Reconstruction Period includes the charitable contributions from a large number of organizations and individuals in this country. The following tabulation summarizes the contributions from the principal sources.

Benevolent Contributions for Relief from the United States—Reconstruction Period

Source	Amount
Director General of Relief	$25,109,988.64
Commission for Relief in Belgium	25,000.00
European Relief Council	15,669,899.59
Jewish Joint Distribution Committee	4,209,684.34
American Red Cross	3,754,587.38
American Friends Service Committee	1,964,802.02
The Commonwealth Fund	1,565,211.20
Near East Relief	1,944,119.91
Laura Spelman Rockefeller Memorial	367,392.88
All other American organizations	113,081.13
Sundry cash donations (individuals)	2,862,638.92
Total	$57,586,406.01

The funds listed under the Director General of Relief represent the surplus accumulated by the Food Administration Grain Corporation under the terms of the agreement between that organization and the American Relief Administration. Under this agreement as quoted on page 46, any surplus developed by the Grain Corporation in its European operations was to be turned over to the Director General of Relief, or his successor, to be used for additional relief in the respective countries. (See also agreement with individual countries as referred to on pages 76–77.)

Contributions of these various organizations are discussed in detail in other sections of this report and need no further reference at this point.

Under "World charity" in the first table on page 144 are included two operations for which the funds were derived from a number of different countries. These operations were as follows:

Exchange remittances	$ 6,360,140.89
Food drafts and bulk sales, net *	22,327,038.22
Total	$28,687,179.11

* Food drafts and bulk sales to organizations listed in the preceding table have been deducted from the total of these sales and credited to the respective organizations.

Exchange remittances carried on by the A.R.A. during the Armistice Period are discussed in a separate section (cf. pages 69–70). While the major portion of these remittances came from the United States, individuals in other countries also participated. The same comment may be made with regard to sale of food drafts and the bulk sale operations. These represented purchases by individuals all over the world.

At the end of these activities the problem which confronted the directors of the Administration was a dual one. In the first instance the stupendous operations carried on in "Food Remittance" transactions and in transportation of food supplies for distribution to children involved large liabilities for shipping, for maintenance of insurance on food stocks, reserve for bank guaranties, etc. Of necessity there was distinct responsibility to safeguard the integrity of the organization by insuring that there should be no default on any of those liabilities and righteous claims which might arise in respect to the several hundred million dollars for which it had been responsible.

The liquidation of these matters required a period of some two or three years, and then it was found that the residue of funds in hand amounted to less than one per cent of the charitable and other income of the organization, indicating the close margin between income and disbursements with which the operations were conducted and the liquidation consummated.

As final liquidation approached, the directors were faced with the problem of allocating this residue, which gave indications of approaching $5,000,000. As monies had been provided by the efforts of various committees and large donors, a plan was presented to them to hold these funds in reserve for a few years, to be expended on children should further calamities occur similar to that growing out of the World War, and ultimately, the funds being entirely in origin from American charity, to distribute them for the benefit of American children. In the interim it was further suggested that the income should be expended on the study of children's problems in the United States, utilizing the vast experience gained by the organization in handling such problems. Unanimous approval was given to this plan.

There was thereupon created the A.R.A. Children's Fund, into which all sums remaining after liquidation were paid. In accordance with the plan, the funds were held intact for over five years and the income expended largely through the American Child Health Association. Finally, large gifts of the capital were made to such agencies as the Girl Scouts, Boy Scouts, Conference on Child Health, Red Cross relief for American children, Porto Rican children and various subsidiary gifts for the benefit of American children.

It is expected that the whole of this fund will be distributed at an early date to agencies actively interested in child health problems, including the American Child Health Association, and the fund closed out.

As indicating the time and patience required in the liquidation work, deferred payments are still being received on insurance claims instituted ten years previously.

Deliveries for Credit, Cash, and Benevolence

It has been pointed out that in order effectively to relieve the distress in Europe during the war and afterward, it was necessary to take advantage of every possible method of financing the operations. Wherever funds or the equivalent were available, the relief supplies were sold for cash or bartered for other commodities or services. Where this was not possible, arrangements could frequently be made to extend credit from some other government. Where neither of these methods was possible, it was necessary to mobilize charitable contributions and to furnish supplies as a direct gift.

Tables 188–89, pages 398–401, show in detail the segregation of the relief deliveries to each country and by major periods, on the basis of deliveries for credit, cash, and benevolence.

Table 74 A summarizes these deliveries under these three headings and by major operations, while Table 74 B shows the percentage of relief furnished for credit, cash and benevolence under each of the four major periods and the total.

From these tables it will be noted, considering the total, that 85.3 per cent of the supplies were furnished on credit, 8.5 per cent for cash, and only 6.2 per cent as benevolence. This total is, of course, very greatly influenced by the large deliveries to the Allied Governments by the U.S. Food Administration, all of which were furnished on United States Treasury credits.

However, in two other periods, viz., the Commission for Relief in Belgium and the Armistice, the major portion of the relief supplies was furnished on government credits. During the Armistice Period, cash sales represented 37.3 per cent of the total, whereas benevolent deliveries were relatively unimportant, accounting for only 1.5 per cent of the total.

During the Reconstruction Period benevolent deliveries represented a much larger proportion and accounted for 53.1 per cent of the total.

It should be noted that for the entire period benevolent deliveries amounted to the very large sum of $325,829,202.38. The mobilization of charitable contributions on such a vast scale represents in itself a noteworthy accomplishment and gives a measure of the public interest in the European relief work and of the confidence in the operating organization.

For further detail of the deliveries for credit, cash, and benevolence, the reader is referred to Tables 188–89 and the discussion under the separate countries.

TABLE 74 A

Summary of Relief Operations Segregated as to Deliveries for Credit, Cash, and Benevolence

Period	Credit	Cash	Benevolence	Total
Commission for Relief in Belgium	$ 663,248,935.33	$ 6,328,328.30	$191,762,980.58	$ 861,340,244.21
U.S. Food Administration	3,050,496,599.23	....	....	3,050,496,599.23
Armistice Period	673,745,376.82	410,909,621.81	16,831,784.71	1,101,486,783.34
Reconstruction Period	75,994,592.08	27,475,552.61	117,234,437.09	220,704,581.78
Total	$4,463,485,503.46	$444,713,502.72	$325,829,202.38	$5,234,028,208.56

TABLE 74 B

Summary of Relief Operations Showing the Percentage of the Deliveries for Credit, Cash, and Benevolence

Period	Credit Percentage	Cash Percentage	Benevolence Percentage	Total Percentage
Commission for Relief in Belgium	77.0	0.7	22.3	100.0
U.S. Food Administration	100.0	...	...	100.0
Armistice Period	61.2	37.3	1.5	100.0
Reconstruction Period	34.4	12.5	53.1	100.0
Total	85.3	8.5	6.2	100.0

PART II

ARMENIA

(Appendix Tables 200–205)

ARMISTICE PERIOD

The American public is familiar in general with the conditions in Christian Armenia. For many years before the war these people had suffered from the Mohammedan Turks. With the entrance of Turkey into the war on the side of the Central Powers, all restraint was removed from the Turkish forces. The terrible conditions that resulted in Armenia have been described by Henry Morganthau and others. It is not necessary to repeat them here. Hundreds of thousands of Armenians were driven from their homes, a large majority of the able-bodied men were killed, and the women, children, and old men were driven out as refugees.

The condition of these refugees was terrible beyond description. A report from a member of the American Committee for Armenian and Syrian Relief in March, 1919, reads as follows:

> There is no bread anywhere; the Government has not a pound. Forty-five thousand in Erivan are without bread. The orphanages and troops throughout Erivan are in terrible condition. Not a dog, cat, camel, or any living thing is to be found in all the Igdir region. I have seen refugee women stripping flesh from dead horses with their bare hands today. Thirty deaths a day are reported from Ashtarag; twenty-five from Etchmiadsin. Another week will score ten thousand lives lost. We have enough food now in the country at Bakou and Batoum to keep the starving people alive for a time, and the railways are doing all they possibly can to get food to the people. We hope to weather the storm, but snow is our enemy at present.

The first relief to this stricken territory was undertaken by the American Committee for Armenian and Syrian Relief, which was the outgrowth of an effort started by Henry Morganthau, American ambassador to Turkey, to secure some relief for the suffering in the Near East during the war. This committee was later reorganized and incorporated under the name of the "Near East Relief." As such, it has done a wonderful work to relieve the suffering in this territory. However, neither their funds nor their personnel were sufficient to care for this enormous problem in 1919.

A report to Mr. Hoover by Howard Heinz, who was in charge of the American Relief Administration work in the Near East, showed still further evidence of the terrible conditions in that country. Mr. Heinz reported that in many parts of the country there was absolutely no food and the people were existing on grass roots and bark. Even cannibalism was reported as not uncommon in some sections. Mr. Heinz estimated that there were at least 500,000 refugees in need of food and that 200,000 to 250,000 of these were at the point of starvation.

The former Turkish provinces of Armenia and Kurdistan occupied an area of about 72,000 square miles, with a population of approximately 2,500,000 persons. Of this, probably half the area and somewhat more than half the population belonged to Armenia. The principal products of this territory were tobacco, wheat and other cereals, some cotton, nuts, and fruit. Agriculture was in a very primitive state, but, if unmolested, these people were industrious and produced more than sufficient food for their own requirements.

Estimates indicated that at least 6,000 tons of breadstuffs per month, or between 30,000 and 40,000 tons, would be required until the 1919 harvest. The Near East Relief was able to take care of a part of these requirements. The cargo of the "Western Belle," one of the early ships to sail on the Southern Relief Program, was purchased by the Near East Relief through the New York office of the Grain Corporation. Two other cargoes of relief supplies, on the "Mercurius" and the "Pensacola" (see Table 123) were shipped from New York in January, 1919, by the Near East Relief and formed a substantial nucleus of relief.

The A.R.A. had no means of financing relief to Armenia until the Congressional Appropriation for Relief in Europe became available at the end of February, 1919. It was then planned that the A.R.A. would make a total contribution of about 20,000 tons of flour and small quantities of milk for Armenia. It was proposed to send one cargo of about 5,000 tons during each month from March to June. During this period the American Relief Administration actually delivered 22,202.8 metric tons of food for Armenia (Table 201). It was then found that the 1919 harvest in Armenia would be far from adequate to care for the population; consequently, additional shipments were made, making a further contribution of more than 28,000 tons. Altogether, the A.R.A. furnished 50,558.9 metric tons of food for Armenia, with a total value of $10,630,872.19 (Table 201). This food was paid for by funds from the Congressional Appropriation for Relief; however, the A.R.A. secured notes from the Armenian Government which were turned over to the U.S. Treasury.

As shown by Table 201 these supplies were all shipped from the United States with the exception of the cargo of the "Kickapoo," which carried 49 tons of pork and 107.7 tons of miscellaneous supplies for Armenia from Marseilles. These supplies were purchased from the U.S. Liquidation Commission. The "Kickapoo" also carried 915.5 metric tons of miscellaneous supplies, chiefly hardware and agricultural implements, from Marseilles to Novorossisk in Southern Russia (see Table 508) to be bartered for wheat for Armenia.

The conditions which led to this latter transaction were as follows. In the early summer of 1919, it became apparent that the lack of seed in Armenia would seriously decrease the 1920 harvest unless some immediate steps were taken to relieve this shortage. Reports from the Caucasus indicated that there was considerable surplus wheat in certain parts of Southern Russia, particularly in the Kouban. Lack of transportation to the seaboard prevented the distribution of much of this, but it was ascertained that considerable amounts could be obtained near the coast if some method of finance could be devised. This grain was in the hands of the peasants, and they absolutely refused to part with it for any kind of currency. Most of the currency with which they were familiar was so depreciated as to be of little value, but more important than this was the fact that nothing could be purchased with the money. As in so many other parts of Europe, the supply of manufactured articles, clothing, hardware, implements, etc., was entirely exhausted.

Reports from A.R.A. officials in this part of Europe indicated that by bringing in commercial articles for barter much larger supplies of grain could be obtained for the same money value than if purchased in the regular markets. Accordingly, the A.R.A. purchased a cargo of hardware, clothing, implements, etc., amounting roughly to 915 tons and costing, together with transportation charges, approximately $500,000. These supplies were loaded on the S.S. "Kickapoo" at Marseilles and sent to Novorossisk on the far eastern edge of the Black Sea. An American Relief Administration Mission accompanied the cargo and superintended the exchange of these supplies for Kouban wheat. In all, approximately 8,000 tons of wheat were secured for the $500,000 cargo.

By this operation more than twice as much wheat was made available for Armenia for the same money as would have been the case if it had been purchased in America and shipped to the Black Sea. Furthermore, it saved both shipping and food at a time when there was a serious scarcity of both.

A portion of the wheat thus secured was carried directly to an Armenian port by the "Kickapoo." The remainder was shipped on Russian boats. The cargo of the "Kickapoo" was of material assistance to the peasants of the Kouban, who, although not suffering for food, were in serious need of the articles supplied.

In addition to the deliveries to Armenia, the A.R.A. sold 1,994.3 tons of foodstuffs from Constantinople stocks to the Near East Relief for a total value of $511,422.34.

During the period of the Armistice the Near East Relief delivered a total of 32,651.3 metric tons of relief supplies to Armenia, with a total value of $9,222,894.34. This included the supplies purchased from the A.R.A. as shown above. If the supplies paid for by the A.C.R.N.E. are deducted from the total to avoid duplication, the net deliveries by the Near East Relief made in co-operation with the Director General of Relief but exclusive of commodities handled by the A.R.A., totaled 30,657.0 metric tons valued at $8,711,472.00, as shown in Table 123.

The American Red Cross furnished 754.1 metric tons of clothing, with a total estimated value in New York of $258,600.00. The A.R.A. undertook to transport this clothing from New York to Armenia. The total cost of this freight charge was $47,688.48, which was charged against the Congressional Appropriation for Re-

TABLE 75

SUMMARY OF TOTAL RELIEF DELIVERIES TO ARMENIA
(For detail see Table 200)

Operation	Total Metric Tons	Total Value
Armistice Period (Director General of Relief)		
American Relief Administration (Congressional Appropriation)	50,558.9	$10,630,872.19
American Relief Administration (cash sales)	1,994.3	511,422.34
American Relief Administration (freight finance)	......	47,688.48
Near East Relief	30,657.0	8,711,472.00
American Red Cross	754.1	258,600.00
Total relief from the United States	83,964.3	$20,160,055.01
United Kingdom (freight finance)	......	71,400.00
Total, Armistice Period	83,964.3	$20,231,455.01
Reconstruction Period		
The Commonwealth Fund (children's feeding)	3,762.0	$ 746,107.12
Near East Relief	7,404.3	1,411,329.90
Near East Relief (freight and miscellaneous charges)	......	532,790.01
American Red Cross (freight and miscellaneous charges)	......	500,000.00
U.S. Grain Corporation (Act of Congress, March 30, 1920)	40,633.5	4,813,744.45
Total relief from the United States	51,799.8	$ 8,003,971.48
United Kingdom (freight and miscellaneous charges)	......	560,000.00
Total, Reconstruction Period	51,799.8	$ 8,563,971.48
Grand total relief deliveries	135,764.1	$28,795,426.49

lief as a gift to Armenia from the United States Government. (Cf. Table 20, page 48).

The total relief to Armenia from the United States during the Armistice Period amounted to 83,964.3 metric tons, with a total value of $20,160,055.01. Of this amount, $10,630,872.19 represented a sale on credit, while the remaining $9,529,182.82 was, in the last analysis, a benevolent gift to Armenia.

No other governments contributed directly to the relief of Armenia during the Armistice Period. Nevertheless, the British army, which occupied this territory, did much to assist the Armenians. At one time it was stated that the British Intelligence Service was spending between $30,000 and $40,000 per month for the relief of Armenian sufferers. No definite report was received as to the amount actually spent by the British military forces in this work. The British Government assisted in transportation of relief supplies to Armenia to the extent of about £15,000 ($71,400), as shown in Table 133.

The relief of Armenia was in the nature of benevolence to alleviate actual suffering. It was impossible to do much toward putting the Armenian people on their feet, thus enabling them to take care of themselves. The most serious drawback to this latter object, which is the real purpose of all constructive relief work, was the lack of an established government and the absence of stable currency.

The total value of all relief to Armenia during the Armistice Period, as accounted for in this report, amounted to $20,231,455.01, as summarized in Table 75.

RECONSTRUCTION PERIOD

COLONEL HASKELL'S MISSION

In the period following the Armistice, the political and military situation in the Caucasus was particularly difficult and confused. The American public had become interested in the fate of the Armenian people and numerous requests reached President Wilson and other American officials urging that some steps be taken to continue relief to Armenia after the Armistice. As a result of conferences between Henry Morganthau and Mr. Hoover, a joint recommendation was made to President Wilson that an Allied resident commissioner be appointed to Armenia through which the Allied and Associated governments could direct their assistance to Armenia and make some attempt toward its economic rehabilitation. This recommendation bore fruit in the appointment of Colonel William N. Haskell as Allied High Commissioner to Armenia by the Supreme Council of the Allied and Associated Powers, on July 5, 1919. Under the terms of his appointment Colonel Haskell was to act not only as High Commissioner, but also as the agent for the various relief organizations working in Armenia. The Near East Relief agreed to pay for local purchases, salaries of personnel, and the administrative and operating expenses of the relief in Armenia after August 1, which were estimated at $500,000 per month. The personnel of the Haskell Mission consisted chiefly of officers and enlisted men from the U.S. Army and Navy.

Colonel Haskell had charge of the distribution of a portion of the American relief supplies which had been purchased from the Congressional Appropriation as outlined above, but had not yet been distributed. In October, 1919, the Commonwealth Fund made an appropriation of $750,000 to the European Children's Fund for child feeding in Armenia. With this money the European Children's Fund sent four cargoes (Table 204) of child-feeding supplies to Armenia, which were distributed under Colonel Haskell's direction. At one time more than 75,000 Armenians were being fed daily from these supplies.

In March, 1920, Congress passed an act authorizing the U.S. Grain Corporation to sell up to 5,000,000 barrels of flour for cash or credit to relieve famine conditions in Europe and contiguous territory. Of this, 40,633.7 metric tons, valued at $4,813,744.45 f.o.b. New York, were sold to Armenia for which notes of the Republic of Armenia were taken in payment. The Near East Relief agreed to finance the freight and other charges on this flour and for this purpose they received from the American Red Cross a donation of $500,000. The freight and other charges on three cargoes of the Armenian flour, viz., "River Araxes," "Sheafmead," and "Poldemnis" (Table 203), were paid by Great Britain, at a cost of about $560,000. The balance of the freight, approximately $533,000, was paid by the Near East Relief. This latter amount was in addition to the Red Cross contribution. (See note to Table 203.)

The distribution of the Grain Corporation flour in Armenia was handled by the Haskell Mission. No details of the internal distribution of this flour are available, but the comprehensive reports by Colonel Haskell show that the distribution of this flour to the Armenian population was strictly supervised by his organization, with the assistance of the Near East Relief personnel.

Colonel Haskell's Mission also superintended the distribution of contributions for Armenian relief from other countries, including the Canadian Fund of $50,000 which was used to buy oxen to facilitate the planting of crops; the Manchester (England) Clothing Fund, by which several consignments of clothing were sent for distribution in Armenia; the Lord Mayor's Fund of approximately $5,000, and the Friends of Armenia Society, in England, which also donated approximately $5,000. These funds and contributions are included in the Near East Relief Contributions through which they were expended, but under the direction of Colonel Haskell.

Colonel Haskell's Mission withdrew from Armenia on July 1, 1920, leaving all further relief to that country in the hands of the Near East Relief.

The present report accounts for a total expenditure in Armenia during the Reconstruction Period of $8,563,971.48, including 51,799.8 metric tons of relief supplies. This by no means includes all of the relief extended to Armenia, even up to the closing of Colonel Haskell's Mission, but it accounts for that portion which was handled in close co-operation with the American Relief Administration and its associated organizations. The Near East Relief on its own responsibility has expended large sums for Armenian relief which are not taken into account here. It is also probable that a portion of the supplies credited to Southern Russia (see page 250) through the U.S. Grain Corporation Russian Relief, and through the Surplus Medical Supplies (page 252), were used in Armenia, but no exact record of these can be obtained.

The total relief to Armenia during the whole period from January, 1919, to July, 1920, as accounted for in this report, amounted to 135,764.1 metric tons, with a total value of $28,795,426.49.

On the basis of the conditions on which these supplies were furnished to Armenia, they may be divided as follows:

Delivered on credit	$16,076,016.64
Benevolence	12,719,409.85
Total	$28,795,426.49

AUSTRIA

(Appendix Tables 206–232)

ARMISTICE PERIOD

Perhaps no one of the new countries of Central Europe was in such a serious plight after the Armistice as was the Republic of Austria. This country comprised the provinces of old Austria, known as Upper and Lower Austria, Salzburg, Vorarlberg, Carinthia, and parts of Styria and Tyrol. These provinces, with a total area of about 35,000 square miles, compose less than 15 per cent of the former Austro-Hungarian territory. The total population of this territory was approximately 6,500,000, of which 2,500,000 lived in Vienna.

Vienna, as the capital of the old Empire, comprised the business, financial, educational, and social center of the 242,000 square miles of territory formerly ruled by the Hapsburgs. In the days before the war, Vienna ranked as the third city of Europe and second only to Paris in beauty and social splendor. In 1915, Vienna, with less than 5 per cent of the total population of the Austro-Hungarian Empire, paid fully 50 per cent of the corporate taxes and between 40 and 50 per cent of the business and industrial taxes. For the most part these enterprises represented business outside of Vienna, that is, located in what is now Czechoslovakia, Hungary, Jugoslavia, etc. With the loss of the war, all of these outside properties were confiscated and their former owners were left in Vienna with no income.

To a large extent, the territory left to Austria is mountainous and non-productive. It was estimated after the Armistice that only 1,500,000, or less than 20 per cent of the population, were producers of breadstuffs, leaving nearly 5,000,000 inside the bread ration.

In 1918, the entire crop of wheat, rye, and barley, exclusive of seed and the allowance of 120 kilograms for each producer, amounted to only 145,000 tons. Imports and contributions from Hungary before the Armistice amounted to about 75,000 tons. This made a total cereal supply of only 220,000 tons, or less than 40 kilograms (88 pounds) per person for the year, provided equal distribution could be obtained. Compare this with a normal ration of, say, 150 kilograms (330 pounds) of breadstuffs per year and we have some idea of the depleted supply.

After the Armistice, the Austrian ration cards called for a total of about 1,200 tons of flour per day, with a minimum ration of 165 grams of bread per person. This demand was equivalent to some 500,000 tons of grain for the year, of which they possessed only about 200,000 tons. This would require the importation of 25,000 tons per month, but the ration was far too low, and really needed to be raised to 60,000 tons per month to give a daily ration of something like 240 grams of flour.

The fat ration had been 40 grams per week, but in January, 1919, this was raised to 60 grams. The potato ration was 1½ kilos per week, but no one received more than 1 kilo, and the majority of the people none. Ninety-seven thousand tons of potatoes had been promised from Galicia, but only 18,000 tons were delivered. Milk, eggs, and meat could be obtained only with great difficulty and then at prices so high that the majority of the people made no attempt to secure them. Throughout all these early days of the Republic, Vienna lived from hand to mouth, never with more than two or three weeks' minimum allowance of food in sight and often much less. The death-rate rose from 14 to 38 per thousand. Suffering was as great as anywhere in Europe.

The problem of supplying food to Austria was the most difficult of all Central European countries. Yet it was self-evident that food must be supplied, not only to prevent starvation, but to prevent the establishment of a hot-bed of bolshevism in the very center of Europe.

Austria was regarded as the remnant of the old Hapsburg Empire. For this reason she was doomed to bear much of the burden of the Austro-Hungarian war debt, although her resources were only a fraction of those of the former Empire. Under the terms of the Armistice it was impossible for her, an enemy country, to dispose of such securities as she might possess. Her depreciated kronen would buy but little in the world's markets. Further, the appropriations for relief, both by the United States and by England, had been so worded that none of these funds could be used for Austria. The United States Treasury could not loan money to Austria, as it did to various liberated countries, because of Austria's status as an enemy country. The financial condition of England, France, and Italy precluded the idea that they could of themselves finance any large portion of Austria's requirements.

Under these difficult conditions, Mr. Hoover finally succeeded in making a joint financial arrangement between the United States and England, France, and Italy, by which our Treasury agreed to advance $10,000,000 to each of the three Allies to be used for the purchase of food in America for Austria. The Allies, in turn, agreed to finance the overseas transportation and to accept German-Austrian credit in payment for both food and transportation. The amounts of the Treasury loans to England, France, and Italy for this purpose were later increased to $48,000,000 in all, or $16,000,000 to each Ally (cf. pages 59–61).

In addition to this, the American Relief Administration sold over 8,000.0 metric tons of supplies to Austria for cash. Italy delivered relatively large amounts outside the Joint Allied Finance program, for which she secured concessions equivalent to cash payment. Also through the efforts of Mr. Hoover, comparatively large amounts of food and other materials were delivered to Austria from the other Central European states.

Table 76 shows that the total relief deliveries to Austria during the Armistice Period under the direction of the Director General of Relief amounted to 561,705.7 metric tons, with a value of $98,771,595.93. Of this amount, only 9,226.6 tons, with a value of $3,657,230.93, was furnished directly by the United States. The major portion of this consisted of miscellaneous cash sales to the Austrian Government by the A.R.A. from stocks at Trieste. The detail of these sales is shown in Table 207. The remainder of the direct relief from the United States consisted of 901.3 tons of supplies furnished by the Jewish Joint Distribution Committee, the detail of which is given in Table 208. Of this amount, 319.3 metric tons were purchased by the Joint Distribution Committee from the U.S. Liquidation Commission in France. These supplies were transported by the A.R.A. from Bordeaux to Hamburg on the "Lake Clear," V, and the "Coperas." (See note to Table 208.) The cost of freight, insurance, and other charges on these cargoes amounted to $15,224.11. The A.R.A. also transported 8.3 tons of cod liver oil given to Austria by the Norwegian Government. The charges on this, amounting to $178.47, were paid by the American Relief Administration as a gift to Austria.

Although the amount of relief furnished directly to Austria by the A.R.A. in the Armistice Period was relatively small, nevertheless it was Mr. Hoover's exertion and the co-operation of the United States Treasury that made possible the delivery of $48,000,000 worth of supplies under the Joint Allied Finance as pointed out above. The Allies, on the other hand, accepted Austrian notes in payment for these deliveries in lieu of notes given by them to the U.S. Treasury. Each of the three Allies financed the freight on the supplies delivered by them under this arrangement and accepted Austrian notes for this amount also.

The total deliveries under the Joint Allied Finance plan consisted of 345,839.8 metric tons of food, chiefly flour and bread grain, as follows:

Commodity	Metric Tons
Flour	180,363.4
Grain	151,259.4
Pork products	11,374.0
Milk	2,843.0
Total	345,839.8

At the time these arrangements with the Allies were completed, the food situation in Austria was so serious that Mr. Hoover arranged to turn over to the United Kingdom 47,371.9 metric tons of foodstuffs which the American Relief Administration had in store at Trieste. This enabled the British to begin deliveries to Austria immediately.[1] The remainder of the British deliveries to Austria, as well as those by France and Italy, consisted chiefly of foodstuffs transported from the United States in tonnage turned over to the Allies by Austria for this purpose.

In addition to the operations under the Joint Allied Finance, both the United Kingdom and

[1] For further details regarding this transaction see page 60 and Tables 128–131.

TABLE 76

SUMMARY OF TOTAL RELIEF DELIVERIES TO AUSTRIA
(For detail see Table 206)

Operation	Total Metric Tons	Total Value
Armistice Period (Director General of Relief)		
American Relief Administration (cash sales)	8,325.3	$ 3,278,068.35
American Relief Administration (freight finance)	......	15,402.58
Joint Distribution Committee	901.3	363,760.00
Total American Relief—direct	9,226.6	$ 3,657,230.93
Joint Allied Finance	345,839.8	$ 48,000,000.00
United Kingdom (commodities)	18,000.0	1,916,640.00
United Kingdom (freight finance)	......	4,760,000.00
France (freight finance)		4,500,000.00
Italy (commodities)	64,061.0	18,856,872.00
Italy (freight finance)		2,021,250.00
Other European countries (Table 209)	124,578.3	15,059,603.00
Total countries other than United States	552,479.1	$ 95,114,365.00
Total, Armistice Period	561,705.7	$ 98,771,595.93
Reconstruction Period		
American Relief Administration (President's National Security and Defense Fund)	7,536.1	$ 2,847,892.23
American Relief Administration (Congressional Appropriation)	746.3	319,471.90
European Children's Fund	25,963.4	6,695,693.43
Austrian Government donations	10,816.0	1,323,948.55
Provincial Government donations	1,887.3	40,707.46
Total children's relief	46,949.1	$ 11,227,713.57
American Relief Administration Warehouses (food drafts and bulk sales)	11,795.8	$ 3,330,635.48
E.C.F. (surplus clothing sale)	.1	101.26
The Commonwealth Fund (intelligentsia clothing)	31.8	62,475.26
E.C.F. (commodity exchange)	892.8	....
U.S. Grain Corporation (Act of Congress, March 30, 1920)	200,824.8	24,055,708.92
United Kingdom (freight finance)	....	8,032,991.88
Total other than children's relief	213,545.3	$ 35,481,912.80
Total, Reconstruction Period	260,494.4	$ 46,709,626.37
Grand total relief deliveries	822,200.1	$145,481,222.30

Italy delivered large amounts of relief supplies to Austria. The deliveries by the United Kingdom amounted to approximately 18,000 metric tons, with a total value of $1,916,640, made up as follows:

Commodity	Metric Tons
Bread grains	1,000.0
Pork products	500.0
Potatoes	10,000.0
Non-foods	6,500.0
Total	18,000.0

Italy furnished large quantities of food supplies to Austria during the Armistice Period. The total tonnage of these foodstuffs, as reported to the Director General of Relief, amounted to 64,061.0 metric tons, valued at $18,856,872. These supplies were financed chiefly by the surrender of commodities and other concessions to Italy by Austria. These transactions, therefore, essentially were sales for cash. The commodities delivered to Austria during this period according to the Italian reports were as follows:

Commodity	Metric Tons
Flour	12,808.0
Grain	16,761.0
Rice	9,852.0
Beans and peas	4,209.0
Pork products	18,168.0
Milk	728.0
Miscellaneous foods	1,535.0
Total	64,061.0

These, of course, are in addition to the deliveries under the Joint Allied Finance.

Deliveries by Other Countries

As pointed out on page 65, Mr. Hoover made every effort to re-establish some portion of the pre-war trade between the several territories of the former Austro-Hungarian Empire and other contiguous countries. Because of the distressing situation in Austria, special efforts were made to secure commodities from neighboring countries. In this the Director General of Relief was particularly successful, and according to reports submitted to the Supreme Economic Council a total of 124,578.3 metric tons of relief supplies, with an estimated value of $15,059,603, were furnished to Austria by countries other than the major Allies. Czechoslovakia furnished large quantities of sugar and coal, Jugoslavia supplied large quantities of wheat and other foods from the Banat region, and important assistance was rendered by many other countries. The following table summarizes the deliveries from each of these countries. Further details may be obtained from Tables 136, 206, and 209.

Summary of Deliveries to Austria by Countries Other than the United States and the Major Allies—Armistice Period, 1919

Country	Total Metric Tons	Total Value
Czechoslovakia	62,898.0	$ 9,914,858.00
Denmark	19.0	10,108.00
Germany	330.0	13,200.00
Hungary	8,878.0	805,063.00
Jugoslavia	33,886.0	2,464,561.00
Netherlands	2,810.0	112,400.00
Norway	8.3	4,980.00
Poland	4,026.0	204,896.00
Switzerland	11,723.0	1,529,537.00
Total	124,578.3	$15,059,603.00

In the main these deliveries were made in exchange for manufactured articles or for concessions from Austria to the various governments. In principle they were deliveries against cash payment. However, the delivery of 8.3 tons of cod liver oil by Norway was a direct gift from the Norwegian Government for children's relief.

The total relief supplies furnished to Austria during the Armistice Period and under the direction of the Director General of Relief (exclusive of children's relief) may be summarized according to the basis upon which they were furnished, as follows:

Sold for cash	$37,189,563.35
Delivered on credit	61,197,890.00
Benevolence	384,142.58
Total	$98,771,595.93

The successful fulfillment of this Austrian food program in the face of almost overwhelming financial difficulties marks this as probably the greatest triumph of the Director General of Relief in the entire Armistice Period.

RECONSTRUCTION PERIOD

Children's Relief

It was inevitable that with food conditions so serious in Austria the children should be the greatest sufferers. In 1919 Dr. August Bohm, chief of the Vienna Board of Health, reported that, "as a consequence of the War and particularly of the lack of food, children between the ages of six and eighteen have suffered considerably, and in many cases irreparable damage has been done. Their physical development has been practically arrested. Children of twelve and fourteen are developed physically only to the extent of the normal child of eight and ten years." It was estimated that 80 to 85 per cent of the children up to three years of age, from the middle and working classes, were more or less affected from rickets, and many had tuberculosis because of the prolonged undernourishment.

Yet the Lodge Amendment to the Congressional Appropriation for Relief (Act of February 25, 1919) had been so worded as to exclude the use of any of these funds for ex-enemy countries. Consequently, children's relief could not be furnished to Austria from this fund, as was being done in other Central European countries. There was never any question in Mr. Hoover's mind but that some form of relief must be supplied to the Austrian children. Consequently, in the spring of 1919 he obtained President Wilson's consent to use a portion of the allotment of $5,000,000 from the President's National Security and Defense Fund for child relief in Austria.

The first program for relief of Austrian children provided for one meal a day for 60,000 children for a period of about four months. This was found to be totally inadequate, and the second program provided for approximately double that number. Later on, due to political difficulties in certain countries, and to the improvement of conditions in others, it was possible to divert certain child-feeding supplies to Austria which had been ordered and allocated originally for those countries. The first two programs for Austrian children's relief as originally made out were as follows:

Austrian Children's Relief Programs—1919

(Metric Tons)

Commodity	First Program	Second Program
Wheat flour	425	600
Rice	...	450
Beans and peas	45	360
Pork products	90	250
Milk	300	675
Sugar	180	465
Cocoa	90	99
Cod liver oil	15	...
Total	1,145	2,899

Child-feeding operations were begun in Austria on May 5, 1919, with 15,500 children receiving a daily ration. The number of children rapidly increased until 213,600 were on the lists in November, 1919. Even then, only a small proportion of the undernourished were being fed. On August 1, 1919, the European Children's Fund took over the administration of the Austrian children's relief, and it was under their direction that most of the supplies allotted during the Armistice Period were actually delivered.

The total children's relief for Austria paid for from the President's National Security and Defense Fund amounted to 7,536.1 metric tons, valued at $2,847,892.23. In addition to these supplies, it happened that under the administration of the European Children's Fund a portion of the supplies purchased by the Congressional Appropriation was actually used in Austria, although this was forbidden by the act of Congress. In reality, these supplies were merely substituted in place of other commodities which the European Children's Fund furnished from charitable contributions. Altogether, 746.3 metric tons of supplies from the Congressional Appropriation, valued at $319,471.90, were delivered in Austria. These supplies had been originally ordered for Jugoslavia and Czechoslovakia, but conditions had changed in the former country so that all of these supplies were not needed there. The need was still urgent in Czechoslovakia, but with the location of these supplies it was more economical for the European Children's Fund to send them to Austria and supply other commodities in their place to Czechoslovakia.

The commodities delivered under the two funds are shown in detail in Tables 211 and 212. They may be summarized as follows:

Summary of Commodities for Austrian Children's Relief Paid for from U.S. Government Funds

(Metric Tons)

Commodity	President's National Security and Defense Fund	Congressional Appropriation	Total
Flour	1,503.7	....	1,503.7
Rice	1,079.5	....	1,079.5
Beans and peas	815.4	....	815.4
Pork products	323.6	....	323.6
Milk	2,805.0	553.7	3,358.7
Cocoa	367.3	76.6	443.9
Sugar	517.4	116.0	633.4
Cod liver oil	14.0	....	14.0
Soap	110.2	....	110.2
Total	7,536.1	746.3	8,282.4

Deliveries by European Children's Fund.—The children's relief supplies furnished from U.S. Government funds as listed above were sufficient to carry on this work until the early spring of 1920. In April, 1920, a careful medical survey of child health was made by the Austrian National Committee. The deplorable situation even after a year of mass child feeding is shown by the following figures:

	Austria, Including Vienna	Percentage	Vienna Alone	Percentage
Total child population under 15 years.....	1,182,000	100	340,000	100
Undernourished children	930,000	78	327,000	96
Undernourished children receiving American meals	300,000	32	160,000	49

Under these conditions it was necessary that redoubled efforts should be made to improve the health of these children. The European Children's Fund entered upon an enlarged program which extended over the next three years. The number of children fed increased until a maximum of 356,214 was reached in June, 1921. This increase occurred in spite of the fact that a close control was kept on the condition of all children at the feeding stations and only those urgently requiring additional food were permitted to remain.

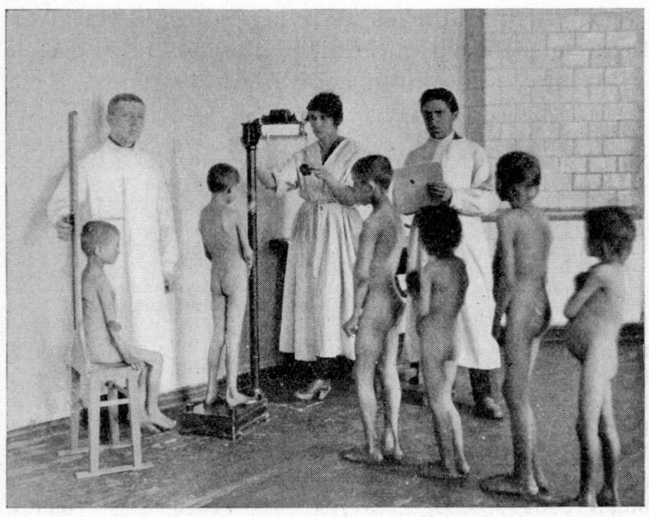

Selecting children by the Pelidisi system who should receive relief, in Austria.

The method of selecting children who should receive relief was developed in a highly scientific manner in Austria, under the direction of Dr. Clemens Pirquet of Vienna University Children's Hospital. Dr. Pirquet's method, known as the Pelidisi formula, consisted in determining the ratio between the sitting height and the weight of the child. With adults the normal Pelidisi[1] was expressed as 100, but with children who do not carry as much fat the normal Pelidisi is 94.5. Children with a Pelidisi of 94 were considered underfed and those showing 93 or less were admitted to feeding at once. This method, which eliminated all personal opinion and all local influence, proved extremely simple and satisfactory. The examinations were repeated at frequent intervals and all children showing sufficient improvement were eliminated to make room for those whose needs were greater.

Dr. Pirquet also devised a simple method of calculating the nutritive value of the feeding rations used. This was called the "Nem" system (an abbreviation for the expression "Nutritive Element Milk" or the German "Nahrungs-Einheit-Milch). A "Nem" represented the quantity of any food which had the same nutritive value as one gram of average human milk. One kilonem, therefore, represented a meal with the equivalent nutritive value of a liter (a little more than a quart) of milk. All allocations of child-feeding supplies were made on the "Nem" basis, which greatly simplified all operations.

During the period from 1920 to 1923 the European Children's Fund furnished 25,963.4 metric tons of food and other supplies for children's relief in Austria. The total value of these supplies was $6,695,693.43 (cf. Table 76).

Throughout this period the Austrian Government co-operated wholeheartedly in the child-feeding work. Among other things, the central government and many of the provincial governments made important contributions of supplies. The donations from the central government totaled 10,816.0 metric tons, with a value of $1,323,948.55, while those from the several provincial governments amounted to 1,887.3 tons, with a value of $40,707.46.

In order to assist in the expense of distribution a small charge, which never exceeded the value of one cent a meal, was made by the local

[1] Of a normal adult the cube of the sitting height, measured in centimeters, equals the 10-fold weight in grams. This is computed as follows: divide the weight in grams, multiplied by 10, by the cube of the sitting height in centimeters. Thus, an adult weighing 72.9 kilograms, or 72,900 grams, with a sitting height of 90 centimeters, would have a normal Pelidisi of 100, computed as follows: 72,900 (grams) $\times$ 10 $\div$ 90^3 = 729,000 $\div$ 729,000 = 1, or the equivalent of 100 Pelidisi.

A complete explanation of this can be found in *An Outline of the Pirquet System of Nutrition*, by Dr. Clemens Pirquet (W. B. Saunders Company, Philadelphia, 1922).

committees against the parents of the children. As elsewhere, however, no child was excluded because its parents were unable to make this contribution.

In addition to the donation of tangible commodities, the Austrian Government and people made many very important contributions, both in facilities and services, which it is difficult to evaluate. It has been estimated by those in charge of the Austrian work that these intangible contributions amounted to more than $2,500,000, which may be divided as follows:

Contribution	Estimated Value
Parents contributions	$ 418,555.00
Quarters furnished	204,092.00
Light and heat	102,497.00
Transportation	300,551.00
Miscellaneous donations	692,566.00
Volunteer services (7,800 workers)	782,969.00
Total	$2,501,230.00

The commodities delivered by the European Children's Fund and the Austrian Government donations are shown in detail in Tables 213, 215, and 216. The totals of these deliveries in metric tons may be summarized as follows:

Commodity	European Children's Fund	Government Donations, Including Provincial Governments	Total
Flour	5,030.7	10,389.8	15,420.5
Rice	3,743.1	......	3,743.1
Beans and peas	3,417.8	......	3,417.8
Corn grits	970.3	......	970.3
Pork products	1,806.6	......	1,806.6
Milk	6,232.9	......	6,232.9
Cocoa	640.7	......	640.7
Sugar	2,773.7	638.0	3,411.7
Miscellaneous foods	418.9	......	418.9
Soap	98.7	......	98.7
Clothing	830.0	......	830.0
Coal	.....	1,675.5	1,675.5
Total	25,963.4	12,703.3	38,666.7

The total children's relief supplies delivered to Austria from May, 1919, to the close of operations in 1923 amounted to 46,949.1 metric tons, valued at $11,227,713.57, including supplies for more than 200,000,000 meals served to Austrian children. Of this amount, $9,863,057.56 came from the United States as a benevolent donation to the Austrian children.

Tables 211–216 show the detail of the arrivals of these supplies by steamers and ports. Tables 222–231 show in detail the distribution from Austrian warehouses to the local feeding kitchens by receipt numbers. The total distribution of the food supplies by provinces, as shown by the receipts, may be summarized as follows (cf. Table 218):

Province	Warehouse	Total Metric Tons
Lower Austria	Vienna	28,888.4
Upper Austria	Linz	3,912.9
Carinthia	St. Veit	1,604.2
Salzburg	Salzburg	1,753.6
Styria	Graz	5,214.9
Tyrol	Lienz Innsbrûck	2,225.4
Vorarlberg	Bregenz	850.8
Turnover to committees	....	1,668.9
Total		46,119.1

The files of the American Relief Administration contain abundant evidence of the deep appreciation of the Austrian Government and the Austrian people for this work. A national Austrian commission was appointed by the government to co-operate in this work, and before the close of the child-feeding operations the Austrian Legislature passed an act (Act of June 2, 1922) providing for the permanent continuation of child feeding. This law created an organization known as "Amerikanisch-Österreichisches Kinderhilfswerk" (the "American-Austrian Children's Relief") in recognition of the aid given Austria by America. The law provides for the periodic examination and feeding of school children through the co-operation of the central government and the provinces.

Warehouse and Bulk Sales

As may be evident from the preceding discussion the distress in Austria was by no means confined to the children. There was terrible suffering in the post-Armistice years, particularly among the educated and upper classes. In 1920 the adults of the cities were living from hand to mouth upon a ration scarcely more than enough to maintain emaciated individuals in a resting condition. Physical labor was out of the question. The country was barely able to exist on supplies furnished through Allied credits.

Under these conditions the A.R.A. undertook to secure such assistance for Austrian adult relief as it could muster without making appeal to American public charity, which was already contributing heavily to the children's relief work. Among other things, the plans for food drafts were put into operation and these proved of great assistance to Austria. The sale of drafts for Austria far exceeded those for any other Central European country. Through these drafts, 6,030.7 metric tons of food, with a total value of $2,444,510, was provided for more than 150,000 Austrian families. The detail of these deliveries is shown in Table 219.

In order to provide still further aid to needy adults the A.R.A. undertook to interest various philanthropic organizations in Austrian relief, particularly for the educated classes. Among the organizations which made noteworthy contributions to Austrian relief in this period were the Commonwealth Fund, Jewish Joint Distribution Committee, American Friends Service Committee, and the World's Student Christian Federation. The work of these organizations has been discussed under the heading of Special Programs. Their contributions were used chiefly to make bulk purchases of food from the American Relief Administration Warehouses.

The Commonwealth Fund made a total contribution of $691,333.04 toward Austrian relief. Of this amount, $200,000 was used to purchase food drafts and is included under that heading above. Another item of $62,475.26 was used for clothing for Austria and is referred to below. This left a total of $428,857.79 from the Commonwealth Fund which was used to purchase bulk food for Austria. The other three organizations used their funds entirely for bulk food purchases from A.R.A. Warehouses. These purchases may be summarized as follows:

Bulk Food Purchases for Austria

Commonwealth Fund	$428,857.79
Joint Distribution Committee	200,000.00
American Friends Service Committee	50,000.00
Student feeding—W.S.C.F. and A.R.A.*	95,147.34
Total	$774,005.13
Bulk sale purchases by other organizations	112,120.35
Total bulk sales to Austria	$886,125.48

* See A.R.A. contribution to Special Programs.

As shown in detail in Table 220 the total net bulk sales for Austria from the A.R.A. Warehouses amounted to 5,765.1 metric tons of food, with a total value of $886,125.48.

Altogether, the food drafts and bulk sales operations resulted in making available to the Austrian people 11,795.8 metric tons of food, with a total value of $3,330,635.48 (Table 76 above).

Commonwealth Fund Clothing

Reference has been made to the efforts of the Commonwealth Fund to relieve the suffering in Austria. The sixth Commonwealth Fund appropriation of $150,000 was to be used for clothing for the intellectual classes. Of this amount, $62,475.26 was used for the purchase of 31.8 tons of clothing materials for Austria. The detail of the items purchased and their distribution within Austria are given in Tables 221 and 222.

Other Relief

Other items shown on the Summary Table 76 (also Table 206, Appendix) include the cash sale of approximately 1/10 ton of surplus clothing from the children's relief operations for $101.26 and needs no further comment.

The item on commodity exchange is shown in detail in Table 218 C. It results from the fact that in the children's relief work there was a surplus of certain commodities and a shortage of others. Arrangements were made whereby 800.0 metric tons of flour were exchanged for 600.0 metric tons of sugar, while 38.2 tons of milk and 54.6 tons of cocoa were exchanged for 243.0 metric tons of other commodities consisting of 84.1 tons of beans, 30.7 tons of pork products, and 128.2 tons of sugar (cf. Tables 213 and 218). No money was involved in these exchanges.

U.S. Grain Corporation Flour

The circumstances under which Congress passed an act (Act of March 30, 1920) authorizing the United States Grain Corporation to sell up to 5,000,000 barrels of flour to relieve the food shortage in Europe have been set forth in an earlier section (page 113). In no part of Europe were conditions worse than in Austria and, consequently, that country received a large portion of this flour. The total deliveries to Austria under this Act amounted to 2,258,867 barrels of flour, equivalent to 200,824.8 metric tons, with a total value f.o.b. New York of $24,055,708.92. Notes of the Republic of Austria were taken for this amount and turned over to the United States Treasury by the Grain Corporation.

The Grain Corporation was not authorized to finance the freight and other transportation charges on this flour from American ports to Europe, nor was the Austrian Government in a position to do this. The European Children's Fund was successful in getting Great Britain to finance the freight and other charges on this flour which amounted to $8,032,991.88, as shown in Tables 162 and 217. The United Kingdom accepted Austrian notes for this amount. The detail of these flour deliveries is shown in Table 217.

This flour enabled the Austrian people to pass the difficult food crisis in the spring and summer of 1920 and saved untold suffering during that period.

Total Relief Deliveries

Total relief deliveries to Austria during the Reconstruction Period amounted to 260,494.4 tons of food and other supplies, with a delivered value of $46,709,626.37, as shown in Table 206. This, together with the relief furnished during the Armistice Period, made a grand total of 822,200.1 metric tons, with a value of $145,481,222.30. In no country of Europe, with the possible exception of Poland, was the post-war distress so severe or relief measures of such vital importance. The total deliveries to Austria during the period from 1919 to 1923 may be summarized, according to the basis on which they were furnished, as follows:

Sold for cash	$ 38,554,320.62
Delivered on credit	93,286,590.80
Benevolence	13,640,310.88
Total	$145,481,222.30

BELGIUM

(Appendix Table 233)

C.R.B. PERIOD

The work of the Commission for Relief in Belgium has been discussed in earlier sections of this report (cf. pages 12–14 and 55) and references have been given to the detailed statistics of this operation. What this Commission did for Belgium is so well known that little needs to be added here. In spite of the many almost insuperable obstacles the Commission carried on its work for nearly five years (November 1, 1914, to August 31, 1919). During most of this time the Commission stood between the warring powers as the only gateway through which food could flow to nearly 10,000,000 people in the occupied territory of Belgium and Northern France.

Table 77 shows that the total deliveries to Belgium[1] by the Commission for Relief in Belgium, including the deliveries to Belgian refugees in Holland and at Le Havre, amounted to 3,896,180.0 metric tons, with a total value of $641,056,693.69. Of this amount, 3,036,317 metric tons were delivered in the period from November 1, 1914, to the Armistice. During this whole period of the war, the function of the Commission was to keep the destitute people of this country from starvation. After the signing of the Armistice and the evacuation of this territory by the Germans, the character of the work changed somewhat, the object then becoming the organization of the Belgian people and their industries so that they could take care of themselves. At the time of the Armistice both the Belgian and French governments requested the Commission to continue in charge of the food and relief supplies until the governments themselves could organize and take it over. The Commission therefore continued its shipments of supplies until May, 1919. By this time, through the insistence of Mr. Hoover, the Belgian and French governments had made arrangements to take charge of delivering these supplies to their respective territories. After May the Commission was engaged in liquidating its stocks, a portion of which was sold to Germany (cf. page 197) and the remainder distributed in the relief territories.

[1] Deliveries to Northern France by the C.R.B. are given in the section on France.

The following tabulation summarized from Mr. Gay's report (*loc. cit.*) shows the total tonnage of relief supplies delivered to Belgium each year by the Commission.

Time of Delivery	Total Metric Tons
Nov. 1, 1914, to Oct. 31, 1915	802,103.0
Nov. 1, 1915, to Oct. 31, 1916	905,946.0
Nov. 1, 1916, to Oct. 31, 1917	576,394.0
Nov. 1, 1917, to Oct. 31, 1918	751,874.0
Total prior to Armistice	3,036,317.0
Nov. 1, 1918, to Aug. 31, 1919	858,624.0
Grand total	3,894,941.0

Throughout its whole work, the Commission devoted special attention to the feeding of undernourished children. Canteens were established in all parts of the occupied territory at which children secured one meal a day, consisting largely of cocoa, milk, bread, and fats. In order that this work could go on without interruption until more stable food conditions were established, the Commission agreed to continue the child feeding after May 1 until the beginning of the next harvest. The supplies for this work were in stock on May 1, and required no further shipments.

U.S.F.A. PERIOD

In accordance with his plans to place the responsibility on each government of caring for its own people as soon as possible, Mr. Hoover made arrangements in May, 1919, by which the U.S. Treasury extended loans to the Belgian Government direct instead of through the C.R.B. Under this arrangement the Belgian Government purchased food supplies in the United States totaling 251,902.3 metric tons, for which the Treasury extended credits totaling $27,533,982.47. Although all of these purchases were made from May to September, 1919, they formed a part of the program of the United States

TABLE 77

Summary of Total Relief Deliveries to Belgium
(For detail see Table 233)

Operation	Total Metric Tons	Total Value
C.R.B. Period		
Occupied Belgium	3,894,941.0	$639,692,817.25
Belgium refugees in Holland and Le Havre	1,239.0	1,363,876.44
Total C.R.B. deliveries	3,896,180.0	$641,056,693.69
U.S.F.A. Period		
U.S. Treasury loans—direct	251,902.3	27,533,982.47
Armistice Period		
U.S. Liquidation Commission	50,774.0	28,549,672.75
Grand total relief deliveries	4,198,856.3	$697,140,348.91

Food Administration for supplying the Allies with food during the war. In the case of all the Allies, these purchases were continued during the Armistice Period. As shown in Table 106, these purchases by the Belgian Government consisted chiefly of flour and bread grains which were obtained through the U.S. Grain Corporation.

ARMISTICE PERIOD

The relief to Belgium listed in Tables 77 and 233 under the Armistice Period includes only the sale to the Belgian Government of 50,774.0 metric tons of food and clothing by the United States Liquidation Commission from surplus Army stocks in France. These supplies, valued at $28,549,672.75, were sold to Belgium on credit; notes covering this amount were taken by the Liquidation Commission.

From a strictly chronological standpoint the relief to Belgium during the Armistice Period should include the following:

	Metric Tons
Post-Armistice deliveries by C.R.B.	858,624.0
Belgian Government purchases (U.S. Treasury credits)	251,902.3
U.S. Liquidation Commission	50,774.0
Total	1,161,300.3

For the purpose of tying these to the various relief operations it is simpler to regard them as deliveries under the headings given in Table 77.

Table 540 shows a cash sale by the American Relief Administration of 668.3 metric tons of flour for $122,638.77 which was used for relief in Belgium. This is accounted for under the C.R.B. sales and hence is omitted from the summary in Tables 77 and 233, where it would constitute a duplication.

The total relief deliveries to Belgium as summarized in Table 77 include 4,198,856.3 metric tons, valued at $697,140,348.91. All of the operations during the Food Administration and the Armistice periods represent purchases on credit. The deliveries by the C.R.B. were partly on government credit and partly as benevolence, while a total of $6,328,328.30, representing exchange remittances to individuals in Belgium (Table 105), may be regarded as cash purchases. On this basis the total relief to Belgium may be summarized as follows:

Sold for cash	$ 6,328,328.30
Delivered on credit	504,078,737.22
Benevolence	186,733,283.39
Total	$697,140,348.91

Of the total credits extended to Belgium during this period, $315,715,915.66 came from the United States and the remainder from Great Britain and France (cf. Table 105).

BULGARIA

(Appendix Tables 234–235)

ARMISTICE PERIOD

Bulgaria, like the other Central and Eastern European states, had an acute food situation in 1919, the result not only of the World War, but also of the Balkan wars from which Bulgaria had not recovered in 1914. As an ex-enemy state, Bulgaria was excluded from the benefits of the Congressional Appropriation for Relief, but this, of course, did not keep the Director General of Relief from taking steps to prevent suffering among women and children in that country.

Before the war, Bulgaria was able to export considerable amounts of wheat, maize, and live stock. Detailed statistics are lacking for the war years, but production of wheat, which in 1913 was about 1,300,000 tons, fell below 900,000 tons in 1918. The production of other crops probably suffered more in proportion. It was estimated by British authorities in Bulgaria that about 50,000 tons would be needed before the 1919 harvest. At any rate, there can be no question of the severe suffering in certain internal sections.

In February, the Bulgarian Government requested assistance. It was finally arranged that some $2,000,000 worth of Bulgarian gold should be delivered to the Director General of Relief and in return he agreed to deliver American flour to its full value.

In all, 22,862.4 metric tons of flour for Bulgaria were delivered at Varna by the American Relief Administration. Additional amounts of Bulgarian gold were later deposited to cover the cost of the foodstuffs delivered. This gold was placed aboard an American destroyer and held at Constantinople with the idea of allowing the Bulgarian Government to buy it back, if foreign credits could be obtained. Bulgaria was unable to realize these credits by the time the A.R.A. closed its operations, and at the direction of the U.S. Grain Corporation this gold was transported to New York by an American destroyer, where it was sold to the Federal Reserve Bank. The total sum realized from the sale of this gold was $5,210,357.57. After paying all expenses incident to the transaction, the balance above the cost of the flour was returned to the Bulgarian Government by the U.S. Grain Corporation.

This transaction represented a cash sale of 22,862.4 metric tons of flour for $4,856,647.53 delivered at Bulgarian ports. For detail of these deliveries see Tables 234 and 235.

CZECHOSLOVAKIA

(Appendix Tables 236–279)

POST-ARMISTICE NEEDS

Of the six territorial divisions resulting from the succession states of the Austro-Hungarian Empire, the Republic of Czechoslovakia possessed the greatest resources. However, the division of the old Empire was along national rather than industrial or economic lines. Czechoslovakia was fortunate in that she possessed some of the best coal mines of the old monarchy. This meant that she also possessed large manufacturing and industrial plants, but she was dependent, to some extent, on outside sources for agricultural products and raw materials. For example, while most of the beet sugar factories of the old Empire were located in Czechoslovakia, on account of the coal, the beets which supplied these factories were, to a large extent, grown in Hungary. Under normal conditions it would have been easy to exchange coal for beets, or sugar for potatoes or grain. However, after the Armistice, the innumerable restrictions in the form of embargoes upon the operation of trade, finance, and travel prevented all this.

As a matter of fact, Czechoslovakia at this time was actively continuing military operations on two sides of the Republic. These operations were against the Hungarians on the south, and the Poles in Teschen on the north. Although Czechoslovakia recognized that the final determination of her boundaries would be made by the Peace Conference in Paris, she was acting on the old adage that possession is nine points of the law. She was particularly anxious to extend her boundaries to the south, in order to secure more agricultural land to balance her industrial facilities.

The Republic of Czechoslovakia embraces Bohemia, Moravia, Slovakia, Ruthenia, and a portion of Silesia. The population of the territory thus outlined was approximately 13,000,000. Of this number, probably 7,000,000 would be classed as non-producers of food. This includes some 110,000 miners and their dependents, or a total of, say, 450,000; about 400,000 soldiers; some 2,000,000 so-called heavy workers; and 4,000,000 to 5,000,000 light workers, including their dependents. Of this total number, excluding the soldiers, about 4,500,000 were in Bohemia, 1,500,000 in Moravia, 500,000 in Silesia, and the remainder in Slovakia. The district of Silesia, for which but few statistics are available, was considered able to take care of its own population.

The following table shows the approximate figures for the production of some of the more important crops in Bohemia, Moravia, and Silesia prior to the war. All figures are in metric tons.

The normal cereal supply, excluding oats, from this territory was thus approximately 3,000,000 tons.

The war had seriously interfered with agricultural production. According to information furnished by our secret service during the war, the crops of the old Empire in 1918 were between 50 and 60 per cent of normal. These figures were later confirmed in general by data presented to the A.R.A. by the authorities at Prague. According to the Czechoslovakia military authorities, the available supply of bread grains from Bohemia and Moravia in February, 1919, would total to only 560,000 tons. The conditions in Slovakia and Silesia were such that they were

Approximate Pre-War Production of the More Important Commodities

(Metric Tons)

District	Wheat	Rye	Maize	Barley	Oats	Potatoes
Bohemia	461,800	990,700	300	644,300	846,900	3,050,000
Moravia	169,800	329,300	16,900	328,900	260,700	1,600,000
Silesia	13,000	61,800	.....	29,800	71,900	270,000
Total	644,600	1,381,800	17,200	1,003,000	1,179,500	4,920,000

compelled to regard these simply as self-supporting. It was the experience of the authorities that not over 70 per cent of these supplies could be requisitioned. This would amount to only 390,000 tons of grain, equivalent to some 300,000 tons of flour.

Counting the population to be supplied as 7,000,000, an average ration of 12 kilograms of flour per month would require at least 550,000 tons of flour before the next harvest. Of this, 250,000 to 275,000 tons must be imported. This amounted to an average monthly requirement of about 45,000 tons until the 1919 harvest.

A serious defect in the food supply of Czechoslovakia after the Armistice was the failure of the potato crop. A considerable portion of the population depended upon this commodity for their main food. Normally Bohemia imported its potatoes from Galicia, but this was now impossible. In January, 1919, it was impossible to procure potatoes in the public markets in Prague. The health of the people in the districts which depend largely upon potatoes for food was in a very deplorable condition.

Live stock, with the exception of sheep and goats, had decreased greatly. In April, 1918, the number of cattle was 25 per cent less than in 1910, and the number of swine 70 per cent below the pre-war figure. By 1919 the numbers were undoubtedly much lower, because the army had combed the country again in July, 1918.

While food conditions in Czechoslovakia were not so absolutely terrible as in Poland and some other liberated territories, this does not mean that the people were not suffering. Furthermore, in no other section of Europe was food so important for combating the spread of bolshevism. Work was available in the mines and foundries, and upon the output of these depended to a critical extent not only the fate of Czechoslovakia, but that of the other countries of Central Europe as well.

Another district whose final affiliations were not determined at this time was that around Mährisch Ostrau, in the Teschen-Silesian coal region. This district, with a population of 1,450,000, was in serious need not only of food, but of clothing and other supplies. With the exception of a special child-feeding program, discussed later, provisions for this region were supplied through Czechoslovakia.

The final program for the general relief of Czechoslovakia in the Armistice Period consisted of 45,000 tons of breadstuffs per month, 4,000 tons of fats, and about 1,000 tons of milk. As shown in Table 13 on pages 32–33, this program was frequently changed, either because of available supply or because of special requirements.

Difficulties Encountered

Like the other newly established governments of Central Europe, Czechoslovakia had no funds with which to purchase these needed foodstuffs. The first task which faced the Director General of Relief was to find some means of financing these relief supplies. This was accomplished by arranging for credits to Czechoslovakia from the United States Treasury under the acts of Congress authorizing credits to countries engaged in war with the enemies of the United States. The first of these Treasury loans was established in January, 1919, and shipments of foodstuffs from stocks at Trieste were started at once. The demoralized condition of the railroads leading out of Trieste made this movement slower than had been anticipated. Up to the end of February, 1919, only 6,594 tons of foodstuffs had been delivered.

Thus the provisioning of Czechoslovakia, with no access to the sea, offered special difficulties, because of the complete demoralization of the transportation systems of Central Europe. It was originally intended to send all supplies by way of the southern route to Adriatic ports and then overland to Prague and other centers. It soon became apparent that the rail facilities from this port would not be adequate, even under the most favorable conditions, to handle these supplies, together with the shipments to Austria and other more southern regions. By the end of March, the Brussels Agreement had been signed, by which food supplies were to be sold to Germany. One of the conditions of this agreement was that supplies to Czechoslovakia and other countries should be landed at Hamburg and shipped by barge down the Elbe to Prague. This arrangement, although requiring much diplomacy and constant watchfulness, worked very satisfactorily. In all, more than 240,000 tons of relief supplies were delivered at Hamburg for the Czechs, and transported by the Elbe. Table 240 gives the weekly barge movements from Hamburg for Czechoslovakia and gives some idea of the task carried out by the American Relief Mission at Hamburg.

At no time, however, were the shipments to Czechoslovakia from Trieste abandoned. In all, nearly 80,000 tons of American supplies were shipped to the Czechs from the south. Table 241 gives the summary of the monthly shipments from Trieste to Prague.

In addition to the delivery of food supplies, the Director General of Relief took an active part in reorganizing and establishing economic relations between Czechoslovakia and the neighboring nations as well as other foreign countries. Through the assistance of the American Relief Administration a contract was signed in April, 1919, between the Polish and Czechoslovakian governments whereby the Poles agreed to exchange 4,000 cars of potatoes from Poznań for 215 carloads of sugar. Other exchanges of this character were also initiated by which the Czechs were able to exchange their sugar and coal for much-needed supplies.

March 11, 1919, Mr. Hoover addressed a letter to the Czechoslovakian Minister of Foreign Affairs in which he pointed out certain steps which he believed the government ought to undertake in order to rehabilitate their normal economic life, and promised the co-operation of the United States Government to that end.[1] This was part of the general program of getting these newly formed governments started on a firmly established basis so that they would be in a position to care for their own people.

ARMISTICE PERIOD

As shown in Table 78 (page 168), total relief deliveries to the Government of Czechoslovakia during the Armistice Period under the Director General of Relief amounted to 503,230.0 metric tons, with a total value of $105,545,794.40. Of this amount, 352,585.59 tons, with a value of $77,876,410.40, were furnished from the United States, thus constituting 73.8 per cent of the value of all relief delivered during this period. In addition to this amount the 6,476.2 metric tons (valued at $2,837,748.69), of children's relief from the A.R.A. was delivered during the Armistice Period, but since a large portion of this was consumed after the peace treaty this is accounted for under child feeding in the Reconstruction Period.

The deliveries to the Government of Czechoslovakia by the A.R.A. during the Armistice Period totaled 311,360.7 tons, with a total value of $58,602,496.13. Of this amount, 70.5 tons, worth $33,778.62, represented cash sales by the A.R.A. from supplies purchased from U.S. Army Stocks in Trieste, the detail of which is shown in Table 239.

The sum of $203,505.62 represents charges for insurance and freight, partly on the transportation of commodities purchased from the U.S. Liquidation Commission in France and transported by the A.R.A., and partly for the transportation of American Red Cross clothing and of Norwegian cod liver oil as explained elsewhere. The detail of these transshipments is shown in Tables 143 and 144. Of these charges, the sum of $18,898.99 was a direct gift to Czechoslovakia and the remainder charged against the government as a credit operation.

The remainder of the supplies from the A.R.A. totaling 311,290.2 metric tons and valued at $58,365,211.89, were delivered on credit to the Czechoslovakian Government. The major portion of this credit of $50,113,572.61, as indicated in Table 78, was obtained by direct U.S. Treasury loans to the Government of Czechoslovakia, while the remainder was delivered on credit authorized by Congress in the Act for the Relief of Europe (approved February 25, 1919).

The detail of the shipments of these supplies by vessels, and cargoes of each, is given in Tables 237 and 238. The movement of these supplies from the ports to Czechoslovakia is summarized in Tables 240 and 241. Deliveries of these supplies were made to the Government of Czechoslovakia upon arrival in the country, and receipts, signed by authorized government officials, were obtained for each shipment. The internal distribution of these supplies was entirely in the hands of the Czechoslovakian Government, although officials of the A.R.A. kept a general oversight of these operations. No further details are available on the internal distribution of these supplies.

Deliveries to Czechoslovakia by the United States Liquidation Commission amounted to 40,350.0 metric tons of food, clothing, and miscellaneous supplies, valued at $19,098,874.27 (see Table 122). These supplies were sold to

[1] Quoted in *American Relief Administration Bulletin* No. 2, March 24, 1919.

TABLE 78

SUMMARY OF TOTAL RELIEF DELIVERIES TO CZECHOSLOVAKIA

(For detail see Table 236)

Operation	Total Metric Tons	Total Value
Armistice Period		
A.R.A.—Treasury loan	259,004.9	$ 50,113,572.61
A.R.A.—Congressional Appropriation	52,285.3	8,251,639.28
A.R.A.—Cash sales	70.5	33,778.62
A.R.A.—Payment on freight	....	203,505.62
U.S. Liquidation Commission (War Department)	40,350.0	19,098,874.27
American Red Cross	875.2	175,040.00
Total from United States	352,585.9	$ 77,876,410.40
United Kingdom	7,132.0	$ 1,599,836.00
France	16,571.0	7,540,918.00
Italy	75,861.0	16,653,920.00
Austria	520.0	281,600.00
Jugoslavia	550.0	587,050.00
Norway	10.1	6,060.00
Poland	50,000.0	1,000,000.00
Total from countries other than United States	150,644.1	$ 27,669,384.00
Grand total, Armistice Period	503,230.0	$105,545,794.40
Reconstruction Period		
A.R.A.—Congressional Appropriation	6,476.2	$ 2,837,748.69
European Children's Fund	4,995.0	1,906,945.54
Government donations (commodities)	3,955.8	693,099.02
Total children's relief	15,427.0	$ 5,437,793.25
A.R.A. Warehouses—food drafts and bulk sales	1,376.5	$ 433,432.69
E.C.F.—sale to Government of Czechoslovakia	1,264.1	174,549.84
E.C.F.—sale to State Fat Institute (Czechoslovakia)	28.0	21,181.47
Total warehouse and bulk sales	2,668.6	$ 629,164.00
Total children's relief, warehouse and bulk sales	18,095.6	$ 6,066,957.25
U.S. Grain Corporation (Act of Congress, March 30, 193	23,809.0	2,873,238.25
United Kingdom—freight finance	....	952,362.08
Grand total, Reconstruction Period	41,904.6	$ 9,892,557.58
Grand total relief deliveries	545,134.6	$115,438,351.98

Czechoslovakia on credit, and notes for the foregoing amount were obtained by the Liquidation Commission.

The American Red Cross furnished 875.2 metric tons of clothing for Czechoslovakia. The estimated value of these supplies, exclusive of transportation charges, was $175,040.00. Of this amount, 301.2 tons were transported from the United States by the American Relief Administration at a cost of $18,681.81 included in payments on freight discussed above. Table 127 shows the detail of the Red Cross shipments.

Table 78 shows a total of 150,644.1 metric tons of relief supplies, valued at $27,669,384, which were furnished to Czechoslovakia during the Armistice Period by countries other than the United States. Of this amount, the three principal Allies, United Kingdom, France, and Italy, contributed 99,564.0 metric tons, with a total value of $25,794,674. Of the 7,132.0 metric tons delivered from the United Kingdom, 300 tons of milk were given by the Lady Muriel Padget Mission, and 70 tons of flour, rice, and miscellaneous supplies were furnished as a gift by the British

Red Cross. These two gifts of 370 tons were valued at approximately $149,006. The remaining 6,762 tons, valued at $1,450,830 represented commodities sold on credit by the British Government and paid for from British relief funds. For detail of the commodities delivered by the United Kingdom, see Table 242.

The deliveries from France to Czechoslovakia amounted to 16,571.0 metric tons, valued at $7,540,918. Of this amount, 20 tons of flour and 20 tons of rice, valued at approximately $5,138, represented a gift from the French Government to the Czechoslovakian children's relief. The remainder of the supplies from France, consisting chiefly of rice, beans, and pork products, were sold for cash and in exchange for 20,000 tons of sugar. For detail of commodities delivered by France, see Table 236.

The deliveries from Italy to Czechoslovakia during the Armistice Period consisted of 75,861.0 metric tons of foodstuffs, including flour, rice, pork products, and milk, with a total value of $16,653,920. These supplies were practically all exchanged for other commodities on a barter basis. Coal and sugar were the two principal commodities exchanged by Czechoslovakia. In principle, these deliveries may be regarded as cash sales. The detail of the commodities delivered by Italy is given in Table 135.

Of the other deliveries of foodstuffs to Czechoslovakia during the Armistice Period, the most important was 50,000 tons of miscellaneous food, chiefly potatoes, from Poland in return for coal and sugar. Small quantities of fats and miscellaneous food were also furnished by Austria and Jugoslavia in exchange for coal and other commodities. The 10.1 tons of cod liver oil from Norway was a direct gift of the Norwegian Government to Czechoslovakian children's relief. For further detail of these deliveries see Table 136.

The total relief supplies furnished to Czechoslovakia during the Armistice Period and under the direction of the Director General of Relief (exclusive of the children's relief) may be divided, according to the basis upon which they were furnished, as follows:

Sold for cash	$ 26,092,128.62
Delivered on credit	79,099,522.79
Benevolence	354,142.99
Total	$105,545,794.40

RECONSTRUCTION PERIOD

The Czechoslovak Republic began its existence after the Armistice with a staggering national debt, including a third of the Austro-Hungarian pre-war debt, a portion of the reparation fund, and debts incurred by military operations and by the purchases of relief supplies and raw materials during the Armistice Period. The country had suffered comparatively slightly from actual war devastation, but the economic stagnation of Europe in 1919 and 1920 had disorganized its industries and trade, resulting in serious unemployment, increased prices, and scarcity of such necessities as food and clothing. These conditions affected particularly the urban and industrial population and were reflected in the undernourished condition of the children. The government was in no position to take care of these needs and it was imperative that some outside help should be extended.

Children's Relief

The A.R.A. had begun its child-feeding work in Czechoslovakia in the spring of 1919 and in co-operation with the government had created an organization known as the Czechoslovak Péče o Dítě (P.O.D.), or National Child Welfare Committee, under the patronage of the President of the Republic. This organization provided for close co-operation with the government.

At the start, the active direction of the details of child feeding was carried out by the A.R.A. officials, but it soon became possible to turn this over to the National Committee, and the American representatives acted only in an advisory capacity.

Child feeding in Czechoslovakia was started in April, 1919, with about 4,000 children in the vicinity of Prague. The demands rapidly increased, and the first child relief program provided for the feeding of about 60,000 children until September, 1919. It soon became apparent that this was not sufficient, and a second program provided for nearly 80,000 additional children up to September 1. A third program was prepared by the A.R.A. designed to furnish sufficient food to feed about 140,000 children from September 1 to December 31, 1919.

These three programs prepared by the A.R.A. were as follows:

A.R.A. Proposed Programs

(*Metric Tons*)

Commodity	First Program	Second Program	Third Program	Total
Wheat flour	500	700	300	1,500
Rice	100	150	200	450
Beans and peas	45	184	200	429
Pork products	...	300	100	400
Milk	425	300	1,200	1,925
Sugar	200	...	400	600
Cocoa	100	69	200	369
Cod liver oil	10	...	...	10
Total	1,380	1,703	2,600	5,683

In addition to these programs, special arrangements were made for feeding the children of the coal miners in Mährisch Ostrau. These mines were being operated by an Interallied Coal Commission, and it was found that food conditions there were especially serious before the arrival of the American mission.

Before the close of the official relief work in 1919, reports indicated that still further child feeding would be needed in Czechoslovakia. Arrangements were made with the Czechoslovakian Government to donate supplies of flour and sugar, and the A.R.A. agreed to increase its supplies of fats and milk. As a result, the A.R.A. delivered a total of 6,476.2 tons of foodstuffs for Czechoslovakian child feeding which were paid for out of the Congressional Appropriation for Relief, and were a direct gift from the American Government to Czechoslovakia. The value of these supplies amounted to $2,837,748.69, as shown in Tables 78 and 236.

The urgent need for these supplies was clearly demonstrated in the winter of 1919–1920. By December, 1919, more than 465,000 children were being fed, and this was continued until May, 1920.

In April, 1920, a very careful food survey was carried out by the National Child Welfare Committee, which disclosed serious undernourishment in large classes of the population. The European Children's Fund was urgently appealed to for a continuation of the child-feeding work. With the funds which were available, this organization furnished supplies to enable them to continue the work until the end of the year. From April, 1919, to the end of 1921 the total number of meals for which supplies were distributed amounted to approximately 151,522,000.

Internal deliveries of child-feeding supplies. —As shown by Table 78, the total deliveries for child feeding in Czechoslovakia from April, 1919, to the close of operations in September, 1921, amounted to 15,427.0 metric tons of food and clothing. Of this amount, 6,476.2 tons came from the A.R.A., paid for from the Congressional Appropriation for the Relief of Europe (Act of February 25, 1919) and represented a gift from the American Government to Czechoslovakia to the value of $2,837,748.69. The European Children's Fund furnished 4,995.0 tons of food and clothing, with a value of $1,906,945.54, while the Czechoslovakian Government made donations of commodities, chiefly flour and sugar, which totaled to 3,955.8 metric tons, valued at $693,099.02.

The delivery of these commodities for child feeding under the A.R.A. was started during the Armistice Period in April, 1919. At that time the urge for help for these suffering children was very great, and deliveries had to be started with relatively inexperienced organizations in each country. During this period all commodities were receipted for by the P.O.D., but no receipts were required for the commodities turned over to each feeding station. Later on and particularly with the organization of the European Children's Fund, the P.O.D. not only receipted for the foodstuffs as received in bulk but also secured receipts for commodities turned over to each feeding station. Altogether, seventeen zone warehouses were operated in Czechoslovakia which served 2,623 kitchens operated by 2,445 local committees and supervised by 161 district committees. Table 250 shows the tabulation from the receipts of the total deliveries from each zone warehouse.[1] These receipts account for 11,543.1 metric tons of food, or approximately 75 per cent of the total children's relief deliveries. The remainder is accounted for partly by supplies delivered before the institution of feeding-station receipts, partly by government donations, the receipts for which were turned over to Czechoslovakian officials, and by the commodities turned over to the Péče o Dítě at the time the E.C.F. withdrew from Czechoslovakia. The detail of these operations is shown in Table 250 and may be summarized as follows:

[1] Tables 255–279 give the detail of these deliveries in each district by receipts.

Summary of Child-Feeding Deliveries

Operation	Total Metric Tons
Deliveries by A.R.A. in Armistice Period (no feeding-station receipts)	1,607.7
Deliveries accounted for by feeding-station receipts	11,543.1
Government donations (receipts to government)	982.2
Stock turned over to Péče o Dítě	1,074.7
Deliveries of clothing by E.C.F.	210.7
Warehouse adjustment	8.6
Total	15,427.0

In connection with its child-feeding operations the P.O.D. made arrangements with local bakers, to whom they turned over flour and other ingredients and received, without charge, an equivalent amount of biscuits. The total number of biscuits thus received was 29,707,476, with a total weight of 753.2 metric tons (see Table 250 and supporting tables in Appendix). The amount of flour turned over to the bakers to produce these biscuits was 702.2 metric tons. Salt, sugar, baking powder, and other ingredients were supplied as part of the donations by the Czechoslovakian Government.

Food drafts and bulk sales.—The sales of food drafts for delivery in Czechoslovakia were not as large as those for many other countries. As shown in Table 251 (see also page 94), the total number of food packages delivered in Czechoslovakia was 21,231, amounting to 815.0 metric tons and valued at $347,750. Table 251 shows the detail of these deliveries by months and that the period of heaviest delivery was from May to August, 1920. After the early months of 1921 the number of packages declined sharply, reflecting the somewhat less urgent need after that period.

Under bulk sales operations the total net deliveries for use in Czechoslovakia, as shown in Table 252, amounted to 561.4 metric tons, with a total value of $85,682.69. Table 252 also gives the detail of the bulk sales in Czechoslovakia by months. The intelligentsia feeding from the Commonwealth Fund for $82,501.10 (cf. page 100) and the student-feeding program for $23,511.71 (cf. page 111) are included in the food draft and bulk sales operations. The food draft sales also include relatively large purchases by various Czechoslovakian organizations in the United States, such as The Sokols, The National Lutheran Council, and others.

In addition to the bulk sales accounted for above, the European Children's Fund sold 1,018.4 metric tons of flour to the Czechoslovakian Government and received in payment 472.0 metric tons of sugar which were used for child feeding, 443.0 in Poland and 29.0 in Austria (cf. Tables 400 and 213). Also, 245.7 tons of milk were sold to Czechoslovakia, making total sales to the government of 1,264.1 metric tons, valued at $174,549.84. A further sale of 28.0 tons of pork products was made to the Czechoslovakian State Fat Institute.

As shown in Table 78, the total warehouse and bulk sale operations in Czechoslovakia amounted to 2,668.6 metric tons, with a value of $629,164. These transactions were all cash sales in principle. As explained previously, such profits as were realized of the food draft and bulk sale operations were used to extend the child-feeding work in that country.

The total deliveries of child feeding, warehouse and bulk sale operations during the Reconstruction Period amounted to 18,095.6 metric tons, valued at $6,066,957.25 (Table 78). As shown by data given in Table 243, the total arrivals of commodities for child feeding, warehouse and bulk sales, amounted to 18,068.3 metric tons, with a value of $5,965,279.78. The excess of deliveries over arrivals of 27.3 metric tons is apparently accounted for by the increase in the weight of biscuits due to water and other ingredients added by the bakers. The excess in value is due to profits on the bulk sale operations, which as stated above were turned back into child feeding (cf. page 94). Detail of the arrivals by steamers and cargoes for Czechoslovakian child feeding, warehouse and bulk sale operations is given in Tables 244–248.

Czechoslovakian contributions to children's relief.—Reference has been made to the commodities donated by the Czechoslovakian Government for children's relief which totaled $693,099.02. In addition to tangible gifts, the people of Czechoslovakia rendered much other valuable aid to the European Children's Fund, without which it could not have accomplished its work. For the most part this assistance was of an intangible nature difficult to evaluate properly. The following tabulation represents estimates by those in charge of the children's relief work in Czechoslovakia of the more important contributions. It does not, however, make any allowance for supplies and equipment contributed locally for kitchens or for the quarters occupied by the kitchens, which frequently were donated.

Czechoslovakian Contributions to Child Relief

Transportation, insurance, and warehousing	$ 537,362.00
Expenses of E.C.F. Mission	4,437.00
Contributions from citizens	229,920.00
Special charges	8,376.00
Estimated value of volunteer services (9,246 workers)	1,529,816.00
Total non-commodity contributions	$2,309,911.00
Commodity contributions (Table 78)	693,099.02
Grand total	$3,003,010.02

Continuation of child feeding.—The work of the American Relief Administration European Children's Fund in Czechoslovakia did more than merely relieve the suffering of these children during this difficult Reconstruction Period. By working in close co-operation with the government it brought about a recognition by the government, and by the people, that it was a public duty to provide for the physical development of the child, as well as for his mental development. The country was so impressed with the results of this child-feeding work that a law was passed providing for a continuation of the work on a permanent basis through co-operation of the national government with individual cities which cared to avail themselves of the opportunity. This has had a marked influence on child health in the Republic.

U.S. Grain Corporation Deliveries

The Act of Congress approved March 30, 1920 (cf. page 113), authorized the United States Grain Corporation to sell for cash or credit up to 5,000,000 barrels of flour to European countries to relieve the severe food shortage from which they were suffering at that time. As shown in detail in Table 249, a total of 267,803 barrels of flour, equal to 23,809.0 metric tons, was sold to Czechoslovakia. This flour was sold on credit, and notes to the extent of $2,873,238.25 were obtained by the Grain Corporation and turned over to the United States Treasury.

The Act of Congress provided only for the sale of this flour f.o.b. American ports and made no provision for its overseas transportation. Czechoslovakia had no shipping of its own and was not in a position to pay the costs of transportation at that time. The American Relief Administration undertook negotiations with the United Kingdom which resulted in their granting credits to cover the freight and insurance on this flour. These freight and other charges amounted to approximately $952,362.08, for which the British Government accepted Czechoslovakian notes.

Total Deliveries

As shown in Table 78 (details in Table 236, Appendix), the total deliveries of relief supplies to Czechoslovakia during the period from 1919 to 1922 amounted to 545,134.6 metric tons, with a total value of $115,438,351.98. Of this amount, $82,925,123.12, or 71.8 per cent, represented sales on credit; $26,980,958.95, or 23.4 per cent, represented sales for cash; and $5,532,269.91, or 4.8 per cent of the total, constituted gifts from public and private benevolence. The officials of the Czechoslovakian Government have given evidence on many occasions of their appreciation of the help rendered during the dark and distressing days which followed the birth of this new Republic.

THE FREE CITY OF DANZIG

(Appendix Tables 280–289)

RECONSTRUCTION PERIOD

The Free City of Danzig was established by the Treaty of Versailles. Danzig, which before the war was a part of Germany, was made a free city by the treaty as a compromise between the claims by Poland for an outlet to the sea and the opposition of the German inhabitants to become a part of Poland. The Free City of Danzig comprises an area of about 754 square miles and a total population of 386,000, most of which is concentrated in the city of Danzig and its environs. The Free City is, of course, not self-supporting and must import the major portion of its food supplies from its neighbors or from overseas through its very excellent port.

Like other sections of Europe the food situation was extremely bad in Danzig territory after the Armistice. At that time a separate government had not been created, and it was necessary to provide food for the Danzig population through one of the other nations. A portion of the relief food delivered to Poland during the Armistice Period was used in Danzig, but since this was all credited to Poland it is impossible to set up any separate statement of the Danzig deliveries.

The port of Danzig was used almost exclusively as the gateway through which Polish food moved. It was of importance to Poland, therefore, that the Danzig people should be taken care of, and she assumed that responsibility.

Children's Relief

No special provisions were made for Danzig child feeding by the European's Children's Fund at the beginning of their operations after the Armistice Period. Instead, the American Friends Service Committee, which was operating in Germany, assumed responsibility for the Danzig territory also. They continued to care for undernourished children in this region until April, 1921, and during this time were feeding about 3,000 children. As shown in Table 79 (page 174), the Friends delivered during this period a total of 158.3 metric tons of child feeding supplies, valued at $30,291.26.

In the spring of 1921 an acute situation developed in Poland due to the refugees from the Bolshevist invasion. The European Children's Fund had no money which could be used for adult relief and, in order to take care of the Polish situation, it was proposed by the Friends that the E.C.F. take over the Danzig child feeding and thus free the Quakers' funds for refugee relief in Poland. This was agreed to and the European Children's Fund took over this work on April 11, 1921.

In taking over this work the E.C.F. undertook to reimburse the Friends for the child-feeding supplies they had used in Danzig. In order to do this they turned over to the Friends 633.0 metric tons of cottonseed meal, which the Friends delivered to Poland.[1] In the present report the American Friends Service Committee is given credit for the child-feeding supplies used in Danzig and for the cottonseed meal for Poland, while the E.C.F. is credited with a donation of $30,291.26 to the Friends, under Special Programs. This is in accordance with the way these transactions have been handled in the accounts.

A careful physical examination of Danzig children in the spring of 1921 indicated that there were many who needed relief but who were not being reached by the program in effect. By July, 1921, the number of children fed had been increased to 7,274, in addition to a small amount of feeding in schools by the local organization for which the E.C.F. furnished the supplies.

Danzig child feeding was continued until April, 1922, when the E.C.F. withdrew. During the year in which they operated in Danzig, the E.C.F. furnished 108.0 metric tons of foodstuffs, valued at $17,749.51. To this the Free City of Danzig added 74.0 tons of flour and sugar worth $8,574.44. The total number of meals furnished to Danzig children was 957,374.

The Free City of Danzig co-operated liberally in this relief work and, in addition to the

[1] See discussion under Special Programs, page 109, and also under American Friends Service Committee, page 120.

supplies furnished as noted above, it assumed all expenses of distribution and maintenance of kitchens, as well as donations of vegetables and other commodities to local feeding stations. It has been estimated that the value of these services and commodities aside from those accounted for in Table 79 would have amounted to $5,758.

The total children's relief for the Free City of Danzig amounted to 340.3 metric tons, with a total value of $56,615.21. The detail of the arrivals and of the internal distribution of these supplies is shown in Tables 280–289.

TABLE 79

SUMMARY OF TOTAL RELIEF DELIVERIES TO THE FREE CITY OF DANZIG

(For detail see table 280)

Operation	Total Metric Tons	Total Value
Reconstruction Period		
American Friends Service Committee	158.3	$ 30,291.26
European Children's Fund	108.0	17,749.51
Donation from the Free City of Danzig	74.0	8,574.44
Total children's relief	340.3	$ 56,615.21
A.R.A. Warehouses (food drafts and bulk sales)	232.9	71,085.48
Grand total relief deliveries	573.2	$127,700.69

OTHER RELIEF

In addition to the children's relief work, the American Relief Administration maintained a warehouse in Danzig through which a relatively large volume of relief, both as food drafts and as bulk sales, was supplied.

The total volume of food drafts and bulk sales for the Free City of Danzig was 232.9 metric tons, valued at $71,085.48. These were divided as follows:

Operation	Metric Tons	Total Value
Food drafts	63.6	$25,920.00
Bulk sales	169.3	45,165.48
Total	232.9	$71,085.48

In addition to the above-listed bulk sales for the Free City of Danzig, the Danzig warehouse handled sales to the Government of Poland totaling 7,720.3 metric tons, valued at $864,562.40 (cf. Table 394, Poland, and page 231).

Included in the bulk sales and food drafts for the Free City of Danzig are the purchases by the Commonwealth Fund, totaling $14,752.84, for intelligentsia relief discussed under Special Programs. Bulk sale purchases by the Jewish Joint Distribution Committee and other charitable organizations accounted for most of the remaining supplies furnished from the A.R.A.W. operations.

Although the A.R.A.W. operations represented cash sales so far as the A.R.A. was concerned, the commodities for the most part were donated as gifts to the Danzig people by the purchasers. From this standpoint, therefore, the whole of the Free City of Danzig operations, with the exception of the government donation, may be regarded as benevolence, giving the following division:

Sold for cash	$ 8,574.44
Benevolence	119,126.25
Total	$127,700.69

DENMARK

(Appendix Tables 290–291)

ARMISTICE PERIOD

In March, 1919, the supplies of grain in Denmark reached a dangerously low level, and the Danish Government appealed to the Director General of Relief for assistance. Inasmuch as the American Relief Administration was using Copenhagen as a storage port for certain supplies intended for the north Baltic countries, it was considered advisable to deliver sufficient supplies to provide against suffering by the Danish population. Accordingly, arrangements were made by which the Danish Government purchased 10,000 tons of rye grain for cash.

In the latter part of April, the cereal situation became serious in Finland, and, since the American Relief Administration had no near-by cargoes, Mr. Hoover appealed to the Danish Government to help out the situation by furnishing 10,000 tons of barley to Finland (cf. page 183). The American Relief Administration promised to replace this barley to Denmark at an early date;[1] consequently, the cargo of barley of 9,912.0 metric tons on the S.S. "Talabot" was delivered to Denmark in the latter part of May. In reality, this transaction represented an advance delivery of American supplies to Finland, but is treated here as a separate transaction.

The total deliveries of rye and barley grain to Denmark during the Armistice Period, as shown in Tables 290–291, amounted to 19,912.0 metric tons, with a total value of $2,147,059.30. This was entirely a cash transaction.

Food conditions in Denmark were never such as to require any other assistance from the relief organizations. Like other countries of Europe, Denmark suffered during the Reconstruction Period but was always able to take care of her own people.

[1] At the request of the Director General of Relief, Denmark also furnished 1,989 tons of barley and oats seed grain to Esthonia in May, 1919. Denmark was paid for this in cash. (See pages 177–78.)

ESTHONIA

(Appendix Tables 292–305)

ARMISTICE PERIOD

The western edge of Russia where it formerly bordered on the Baltic Sea and the Gulf of Finland is fringed by a series of new independent countries which arose as a result of the Russian debacle. This territory, crossed and recrossed by the German and Russian armies, suffered untold miseries during the war. Following the Armistice three provisional governments, Esthonia, Latvia, and Lithuania, were formed from this territory.

Esthonia, the smallest of the three Baltic countries, has an area of 18,358 square miles and possesses a population of about 1,100,000 people. Approximately 50 per cent of the population are engaged in agriculture, of which dairying and grain and flax raising form important parts.

Following the Russian revolution the country had been occupied by German troops. When they withdrew after the Armistice, they took with them almost all readily movable goods, including agricultural machinery, live stock, etc. A provisional government was formed immediately after the Armistice and by February, 1919, they had succeeded in driving out the Bolshevist troops which had attempted to occupy the country. In this process, however, still more food supplies had been carried away by the retreating army.

In response to reports of the deplorable conditions in these countries, Mr. Hoover sent representatives of the American Relief Administration to the Baltic states. Arriving in Reval (Tallin), Esthonia, on April 19, 1919, the A.R.A. representatives found that conditions were even worse than had been reported. This was true not only in the cities, but in the outlying districts as well. The population had existed during the winter chiefly on a meager supply of potatoes which the invading armies had left. These were now practically exhausted and the de facto government, with a worthless currency, dismantled industrial plants, and without seed for the spring planting, was facing a serious situation.

On the receipt of a report on the conditions in this country, Mr. Hoover immediately arranged a relief program for Esthonia of approximately 5,000 tons of food per month to be sold to Esthonia on credit and paid for out of the Congressional Appropriations for Relief. Deliveries were begun immediately from A.R.A. stocks in store in Copenhagen and from supplies purchased from the U.S. Liquidation Commission in France. Later on, cargoes direct from the United States were directed to Reval. Table 80 shows that under the Congressional Appropriation a total of 21,129.9 metric tons of foodstuffs were furnished to Esthonia, with a total value of $4,299,650.87. Table 293 shows the detail of these deliveries by steamers and source of supplies. In addition to these deliveries, the A.R.A. sold to the Esthonian Government 862.0 tons of rye grain for which they paid $116,371.62 in cash (cf. Table 294). This grain was urgently needed to provide for the spring planting. The commodities furnished to the Esthonian Government by the A.R.A. during the Armistice Period may be summarized as follows:

Commodity	Total Metric Tons
Flour	15,649.9
Grain	5,328.5*
Rice	91.6
Pork products	725.3
Milk	127.5
Sugar	55.0
Prunes	14.1
Total	21,991.9*

* Included 862.0 tons sold for cash.

At Mr. Hoover's request the U.S. Liquidation Commission sold to Esthonia on credit 30,120.0 metric tons of supplies, including 26,000 tons of miscellaneous food, and 4,120.0 tons principally clothing, for $12,262,818.99. Esthonia had no means of transporting these supplies from the French ports where they were located, and the A.R.A. undertook to transport 2,020.4 tons of pork products on which the freight and insurance charges amounted to $151,113.05 (cf. Table 144 for details). This was paid for from the Congressional Appropriation for Relief and was covered by notes from the Esthonian Government.

The American Red Cross had accumulated certain medical and hospital supplies in New York in 1919, a portion of which were needed in Esthonia. The A.R.A. undertook to transport 312.3 tons of these supplies to Esthonia, on which the freight and other charges amounted to $50,490.02. This freight charge was paid for from the Congressional Appropriation as a gift to Esthonia from the American people. The Red Cross supplies, valued at $89,800.00, also constituted a benevolent donation by that organization.

Early in February, 1919, the United Kingdom had undertaken to afford some relief to Esthonia and had negotiated the sale of certain foodstuffs in return for Esthonian flax. Under this arrangement approximately 1,000 tons of herring, a quantity of salt, and 600 tons of wheat were delivered and paid for in flax. The estimated value of these shipments was $500,000, representing a cash transaction.

The United Kingdom also made certain grants to Esthonia from the British Relief Fund, from which three cargoes, the "Baltonia," "Kajax," and the "George Fisher," carried 5,574.0 tons of relief supplies, valued at $1,003,000. This, together with the deliveries ex-stock, made a total of 6,274.0 tons, valued at $1,532,960, which was sold to Esthonia on credit. As shown in Table 295, the total relief deliveries to Esthonia by Great Britain during the Armistice Period amounted to 8,624.0 metric tons, worth $2,032,960.

In addition to these deliveries of commodities, the United Kingdom financed the movement of a large portion of the supplies sold to Esthonia by the U.S. Liquidation Commission. The total value of the freight and other charges amounted to $309,400, making the total British contribution to Esthonian relief $2,342,360.

Under arrangements entered into between the A.R.A. and the Danish Government, the latter delivered to Esthonia 1,983.4 metric tons of barley and oats seed grain to the value of

TABLE 80

Summary of Total Relief Deliveries to Esthonia

(For detail see Table 292)

Operation	Total Metric Tons	Total Value
Armistice Period (Director General of Relief)		
A.R.A. (Congressional Appropriation)	21,129.9	$ 4,299,650.87
A.R.A. (cash sales)	862.0	116,371.62
A.R.A. (freight finance)	.....	201,603.07
U.S. Liquidation Commission	30,120.0	12,262,818.99
American Red Cross	312.3	89,800.00
Total from the United States	52,424.2	$16,970,244.55
United Kingdom (commodities)	8,624.0	$ 2,032,960.00
United Kingdom (freight finance)	.....	309,400.00
Denmark	462.6	35,207.92
Total from other countries	9,086.6	$ 2,377,567.92
Total relief, Armistice Period	61,510.8	$19,347,812.47
Reconstruction Period		
A.R.A. (Congressional Appropriation)	2,029.9	$ 701,520.82
European Children's Fund	1,831.3	522,929.39
Esthonian Government donation	1,693.0	298,444.64
Total children's relief	5,554.2	$ 1,522,894.85
A.R.A. Warehouses (bulk sales)	293.5	146,556.24
Total relief, Reconstruction Period	5,847.7	$ 1,669,451.09
Grand total relief deliveries	67,358.5	$21,017,263.56

$150,955.90. In part settlement for this delivery, the Government of Esthonia made a cash payment to the Danish Government of the equivalent of $35,207.92, representing the value of 462.6 metric tons of grain. This represents a cash sale to Esthonia by Denmark, but the A.R.A. paid the Danish Government for the balance of this cargo and charged the amount to Esthonia as part of the deliveries under the Congressional Appropriation.

Small amounts of supplies were delivered to Esthonia during the Armistice Period by Finland and Sweden, but on account of the incompleteness of the record these are not included in the tables.

The total relief deliveries to Esthonia during the Armistice Period, exclusive of children's relief, amounted to 61,510.8 metric tons, valued at $19,347,812.47. This may be divided as follows according to the basis upon which it was delivered:

Sold for cash	$ 651,579.54
Delivered on credit	18,555,942.91
Benevolence	140,290.02
Total	$19,347,812.47

RECONSTRUCTION PERIOD

Children's Relief

The relief work in Esthonia and the other Baltic countries did not get started until after similar work had been well organized in most of the Central European countries. Shortly after the arrival of the A.R.A. representatives, a preliminary survey was made which showed the urgent need for some special relief for the children. A central committee on child feeding was formed in Reval known as the Esthonian Children's Relief Association. Later on, the Esthonian legislature passed a law making this one of the permanent government departments.

The A.R.A. prepared a preliminary child-feeding program, designed to furnish one meal a day to about 20,000 children for three months. As in the other countries, this soon proved inadequate, and a second program nearly twice as large as the first was prepared. Later, a third program was planned to continue the child-feeding work until the end of 1919. These three programs as originally outlined were as follows:

Children's Relief Programs

(Metric Tons)

Commodity	First	Second	Third	Total
Wheat flour	90	120	60	270
Rice	10	55	40	105
Beans and peas	10	40	40	90
Pork products	12	17	20	49
Milk	60	85	240	385
Sugar	40	55	80	175
Cocoa	20	40	40	100
Total	242	412	520	1,174

Even these programs proved quite inadequate, and before the close of the official relief work in 1919 the Esthonian Government offered to donate relatively large amounts of flour and other commodities for this work if the A.R.A. would increase its contribution of milk and certain other commodities. As a result, the total deliveries for Esthonian child feeding by the A.R.A. were nearly double the amount originally planned in the child-feeding programs. As shown by Table 80, these deliveries totaled 2,029.9 metric tons, valued at $701,520.82, all of which was paid for from the Congressional Appropriation for Relief as a gift to Esthonian children from the United States Government.

The European Children's Fund took over the distribution of the children's relief supplies in August, 1919, and continued that work until June, 1920. With the coming of the 1920 harvest it was believed that Esthonia would be able to take care of her own food supply. The records of the Government Health Office showed that child mortality, which had been constantly increasing since 1914, began to decline in the fall of 1919 and by the middle of 1920 had almost reached normal. The E.C.F. therefore closed its operations, leaving sufficient food in the hands of the local organization to continue the feeding until the fall of 1920.

However, the 1920 harvest again proved to be short of requirements, and by December it was seen that supplies would not last through the winter. An investigation made in January, 1921, disclosed great need among the children. This condition was aggravated by the large number of Russian refugees which pressed into Esthonia from areas to the east. It was estimated some 43,000 children would need to receive supplementary feeding during the winter and spring. Consequently, a new program for the feeding of this number was undertaken in February, 1921, and continued until August, 1922. After August, 1921, the amount of feeding was greatly reduced.

As shown in Table 80 the total children's relief delivered to Esthonia amounted to 5,554.2 metric tons, valued at $1,522,894.85. Of this amount, the A.R.A. furnished 2,029.9 tons, valued at $701,520.82; the E.C.F. furnished 1,831.3 tons worth $522,929.39; while the donations by the Esthonian Government totaled 1,693.0 tons, valued at $298,444.64.

The commodities delivered from each of these sources is shown in Table 292 and may be summarized as follows:

Esthonian Children's Relief Deliveries

(Metric Tons)

Commodity	A.R.A. Congressional Appropriation	E.C.F.	Esthonian Government Donation	Total
Flour	288.0	551.3	1,504.0	2,343.3
Rice	250.1	266.7	15.0	531.8
Beans and peas	222.4	225.1	.....	447.5
Pork products	61.6	169.0	1.0	231.6
Milk	787.7	408.0	153.0	1,348.7
Cocoa	104.4	39.4	.....	143.8
Sugar	284.6	104.6	10.0	399.2
Miscellaneous foods	.....	.....	10.0	10.0
Soap	31.1	7.3	.....	38.4
Clothing	.....	59.9	.....	59.9
Total	2,029.9	1,831.3	1,693.0	5,554.2

Tables 297–301 show the arrival of these supplies by steamer and source, while Tables 304–305 show the internal deliveries of clothing by committees, and of child-feeding supplies by kitchens or districts, by months, as compiled from the local committee receipts.

The method of child feeding was to furnish a supplementary meal daily, including Sunday, to all undernourished children. Children over six years were fed in public kitchens, while the younger children were fed in their homes. During December, 1919, and January, 1920, about 1,700 Russian refugee children in camps near the Esthonian border were fed two meals a day. The maximum number of children for whom supplies were provided at any one time was 84,000. It is estimated that the total number of meals provided was 35,935,350.

The Esthonian winters are particularly cold, and in the early days of the operation it was found that many children suffered severely in making the daily trip from their homes to the feeding kitchens. Many of them came in oddly assorted outfits, coats belonging to older relatives, shawls, blankets, boots many sizes too large, etc. On November 3, 1919, it was decided that in addition to the food program the E.C.F. would supply shoes, stockings, and cloth for heavy coats for some 40,000 Esthonian children. As shown in Table 299, there were 59.9 metric tons of shoes and clothing materials delivered to Esthonia. The detail of the internal distribution of these supplies is shown in Table 304. The total supplies furnished may be summarized as follows:

Clothing Deliveries for Esthonian Children

Commodity	Quantity	
Shoes	50,012	pairs
Shoe laces	41,840	pairs
Stockings	52,426	pairs
Woolens	60,638	yards
Thread	6,799	spools
Needles	35,000	number
Buttons	139,600	number
Total (metric tons)	59.9	

The Esthonian Government co-operated in the children's relief work in every way possible. In addition to the commodities donated for this work, the Esthonian Government undertook to furnish storage and transportation for all supplies and the expenses incurred in handling the feeding operations. District and local committees were composed entirely of volunteers, as was much of the service in the kitchens. It has been estimated by those in charge of the Esthonian child feeding that these intangible contributions amounted to approximately $432,632. These may be divided as follows:

Esthonian Contributions* to Children's Relief

Rail transportation	$ 23,086.00
Warehousing and handling	14,399.00
Administration expense	21,556.00
Kitchen expense	49,522.00
Paid personnel	45,071.00
Volunteer services	278,998.00
Total	$432,632.00
Commodity donations (Table 80)	298,444.64
Grand total	$731,076.64

* In addition to these contributions toward the relief of its own people, Esthonia also furnished warehouse facilities valued at $1,102.94 in connection with relief deliveries to Soviet Russia in 1922. (See page 263.)

Other Relief

No food drafts were sold for delivery in Esthonia, but certain small bulk sales were made to organizations engaged in Esthonian relief. Table 80 shows that the total bulk sales were 293.5 metric tons, valued at $146,556.24. The detail of these sales is shown in Table 303. Of the total, approximately 10 tons were sold for student feeding at Dorpat (Tartu) University (see Special Programs), while the remainder was sold to the British Quaker organization, the Friends Emergency and War Victims Relief Committee.

The total relief supplied to Esthonia during the Armistice and Reconstruction periods, as summarized in Table 80, amounted to 67,358.5 metric tons, valued at $21,017,263.56. Segregated according to the basis on which the supplies were furnished, this relief may be summarized as follows:

Sold for cash	$ 950,024.18
Delivered on credit	18,555,942.91
Benevolence	1,511,296.47
Total	$21,017,263.56

FINLAND

(Appendix Tables 306–319)

ARMISTICE PERIOD

Finland, geographically isolated in the northwest section of Europe, had suffered relatively much less than other liberated territories. She had been subject to no direct invasion by the German Army, nor had Bolshevist military forces been able to penetrate more than a short distance into her territory. She had, however, not wholly escaped. During the later years of the war she suffered a food shortage because of the growing disorganization in Russia, and in 1918 Finland was the scene of a short but devastating civil war between the Reds, supported by the Russian Bolshevists, and the Whites, aided by the German forces of General von der Goltz.

The population of Finland was approximately 3,275,000, of whom about 50 per cent were engaged in agriculture. Her total area is some 82,000,000 acres, but less than 5 per cent of this is under cultivation. The people live to a large extent upon fish, but have to depend upon outside sources for from one-fourth to one-third of their cereal supply. The average pre-war net imports of cereals and potatoes amounted to about 650,000 metric tons. To a very large extent, this had been cut off during the war. At the time of the signing of the Armistice, the situation in Finland with regard to breadstuffs was very serious. There had already been much suffering and, if outside supplies had not been available, there would have been actual starvation before spring.

A survey of the food situation showed that, while undoubtedly the want in the cities was great, it was not so severe as in the timberlands of the eastern and northeastern districts.

Finland had to her credit several million dollars deposited in the National City Bank in New York before the Russian revolution. However, there was no way in which this money could be drawn until there was some recognition of the new Finnish Government. The United States and England recognized the de facto Government of Finland in May, 1919, but until this time their American credits were useless.

The emergency caused by this situation was taken care of by the A.R.A. Early in January, wheat and cereal flour and some fats were sold on credit to Finland from Rotterdam stocks. Finland had sufficient shipping of her own, which was sent to Rotterdam and transported these supplies to Finnish ports. In all, 23,244.8 metric tons were delivered to Finland at Rotterdam.

At about the same time arrangements were made to ship cereal supplies from United States ports direct to Finland. Finland had her own flour mills, which were well distributed in the various provinces. A considerable saving was therefore effected by shipping unmilled rye grain to them. In all, nineteen ships, carrying 103,039.0 tons of rye and barley grain, were discharged at Finnish ports. (See Tables 81 and 306).

Nearly 23,000 tons of food were sold to Finland from Copenhagen stocks, and a small amount from the stores at Danzig. A total of 166,842.7 tons of food, valued at $25,853,991.86, were delivered to the Government of Finland by the A.R.A. These were all sold on credit, but later a considerable portion was paid for from the Finnish credits in America. Supplies to the value of $9,849,587.73 were paid for from the Congressional Appropriation for Relief. Obliga-

American Relief Administration Deliveries to the Government of Finland during the Armistice Period

Port of Delivery	Congressional Appropriation Metric Tons	Congressional Appropriation Value	Cash Sales Metric Tons	Cash Sales Value	Total Metric Tons	Total Value
Rotterdam	....	....	23,244.8	$ 4,991,875.83	23,244.8	$ 4,991,875.83
Copenhagen	13,923.1	$2,893,174.09	8,743.8	2,001,164.52	22,666.9	4,894,338.61
Plymouth	....	....	5,597.3	643,689.16	5,597.3	643,689.16
Finnish ports *	51,802.6	6,956,413.64	63,531.1	8,367,674.62	115,333.7	15,324,088.26
Total	65,725.7	$9,849,587.73	101,117.0	$16,004,404.13	166,842.7	$25,853,991.86

* Helsingfors, Hango, Abo, and Mantyluoto.

tions were obtained from the Finnish Government to repay this amount to the United States at a later date. The total operation with Finland was on a credit basis, but a portion of this debt, amounting to $16,004,404.13, was discharged prior to the close of the relief work.

The tabulation on page 181 summarizes the deliveries of relief supplies to the Government of Finland by the A.R.A. by ports of delivery. The detail of these arrivals by steamers and by commodities will be found in Tables 307 and 308.

As indicated above, Finland's greatest need was for cereal supplies and these made up the great bulk of the commodities furnished by the A.R.A. The tabulation to the right summarizes these deliveries, the details of which are shown in the tables cited above.

In addition to the deliveries to Finland by the A.R.A. in the Armistice Period, the American Red Cross collected a quantity of clothing in New York, a portion of which they wished to send to Finland because of the suffering reported there. The A.R.A. undertook to transport 282 tons of this clothing on the "Lake Hemlock," which arrived at Hango on July 12, 1919. The estimated value of this clothing was $56,400.00, and cost for freight and other charges amounted to $22,584.24. The A.R.A. charged this freight cost against the Congressional Appropriation for Relief as a gift from the United States to the Finnish people. The Red Cross of course donated the clothing.

Summary of American Relief Administration Deliveries to Finland

(Metric Tons)

Commodity	Congressional Appropriation	Cash Sales	Total
Wheat flour	9,955.9	34,208.3	44,164.2
Cereal flour	11,014.8	4,138.5	15,153.3
Rye grain	43,880.6	59,158.4*	103,039.0
Beans and peas	121.5	1,685.5	1,807.0
Pork products	.....	744.1	744.1
Lard	714.1	1,182.2	1,896.3
Milk	38.8	.....	38.8
Total	65,725.7	101,117.0	166,842.7

* Includes 7,532.4 metric tons of barley grain.

Table 81 summarizes the total deliveries of

TABLE 81

Summary of Total Relief Deliveries to Finland

(For detail see Table 306)

Operation	Total Metric Tons	Total Value
Armistice Period (Director General of Relief)		
A.R.A. (Congressional Appropriation)	65,725.7	$ 9,849,587.73
A.R.A. (cash sales)	101,117.0	16,004,404.13
A.R.A. (freight finance)	......	22,584.24
American Red Cross	282.0	56,400.00
Total from United States	167,124.7	$25,932,976.10
United Kingdom	3,467.0	$ 920,250.00
Denmark	10,000.0	1,141,700.00
Norway	4,442.0	1,177,130.00
Total from other countries	17,909.0	$ 3,239,080.00
Grand total, Armistice Period	185,033.7	$29,172,056.10
Reconstruction Period		
A.R.A. (Congressional Appropriation)	2,109.3	$ 660,175.34
European Children's Fund	91.4	216,205.33
E.C.F.—Purchased by local committee *	350.1	37,662.13
Government donation (Finland)	936.4	195,949.00
Total deliveries, Reconstruction Period	3,487.2	$ 1,109,991.80
Grand total relief deliveries	188,520.9	$30,282,047.90

* This transaction represents, in a sense, a duplication in value. The A.R.A. had shipped cocoa, sugar, and milk to Finland in excess of the requirements for these commodities, and they authorized the local committee to dispose of these supplies (112.2 metric tons, valued at $37,662.13—E.C.F. sale in local market) and replace them by an equivalent value of flour.

relief to Finland during both the Armistice and Reconstruction Periods. This table shows that the total deliveries to Finland from the United States during the Armistice Period amounted to 167,124.7 metric tons with a total value of $25,932,976.10.

Under the direction of the Director General of Relief, supplies were furnished to Finland from certain other countries. Thus, 3,467.0 metric tons of beans, rice, milk, sugar, and miscellaneous foods were sent to Finland from Great Britain in return for cash payments. These transactions were handled by private English firms at the solicitation of the Director General of Relief in order to meet urgent needs.

The delivery of 4,442.0 tons of rice and pulses from Norway in March, 1919, represents a cash transaction similar to that carried out by British exporters referred to above. The delivery of 10,000.0 tons of barley by Denmark represents a transaction carried out at the urgent request of Mr. Hoover in order to tide over an acute food shortage in Finland in March, 1919. Denmark herself had no surplus food, and she undertook this delivery only after the specific promise that it would be replaced by a later cargo of grain from the United States. This was done by the cargo of the S.S. "Talabot," which arrived in Copenhagen May 29, 1919. This later transaction in reality represents an advance delivery to Finland by the United States.

As shown in Table 81 the total relief deliveries to Finland during the Armistice Period by countries other than the United States amounted to 17,909.0 metric tons with a value of $3,239,080.00. The grand total of all relief delivered during this period under the direction of the Director General of Relief, exclusive of children's relief, amounted to 185,033.7 metric tons, valued at $29,172,056.10. The detail of these deliveries is shown in Table 306 and supporting tables.

RECONSTRUCTION PERIOD

Children's Relief

It was always difficult in any country to obtain accurate information on the number of children who actually required relief. This difficulty was especially marked in Finland because so large a proportion of the worst distress was in the timberlands of the eastern and north-eastern districts where distances are great and the means of travel limited. There was also a large amount of suffering in the industrial cities. A survey of conditions in Finland was made by the A.R.A. in February, 1919, and it was estimated that 50,000 children were in need of relief which could not be supplied from native sources. On this basis it was decided to include Finland in the list of countries to which children's relief should be furnished. The first children's relief program was based on the needs of 50,000 children until the next harvest, but it was soon found that this was inadequate, and a second program was arranged to supplement the first. A third program was prepared before the close of the A.R.A. which was designed to continue the child-feeding work until the end of 1919 under the direction of the European Children's Fund. These three programs as originally prepared were as follows:

American Relief Administration—Children's Relief Programs for Finland
(Metric Tons)

Commodity	First	Second	Third	Total
Wheat flour	670	310	150*	1,130
Rice	75	125	100*	300
Beans and peas	75	90	100*	265
Pork	85	20	50*	155
Lard	15	...	...	15
Milk	140	200	600	940
Sugar	85	115	200	400
Cocoa	40	...	100	140
Total	1,185	860	1,300	3,345

* To be furnished by Finland.

The actual allocation of supplies varied somewhat from these programs, and of the supplies actually delivered to Finland it was found necessary to exchange certain items for others which were more suitable. For example, it was found that the Finnish people were totally unaccustomed to cocoa, which formed an important part of the child-feeding ration in other territory. As a result, certain of these commodities were exchanged through a local committee for flour which was needed to balance the ration. Also, it was found that conditions improved more rapidly than had been anticipated, and at a later time it was possible to transfer certain child-feeding supplies from Finland to Esthonia and to Northwest Russia where they were more urgently needed. However, in order to balance the child-feeding supplies in Finland the Euro-

Summary of Child Feeding Commodity Operations by A.R.A. and E.C.F. in Finland

(Metric Tons)

Commodity	By A.R.A.	Supplies Delivered By E.C.F.	Total Gross	Supplies Transferred To Local Committee	Supplies Transferred To Esthonia and Northwest Russia	Total Net Deliveries
Wheat flour	560.0	...	560.0	....	....	560.0
Cereal flour	200.0	...	200.0	....	60.0	140.0
Rice	221.9	9.5	231.4	....	....	231.4
Beans and peas	253.9	2.4	256.3	....	....	256.3
Pork products	104.0	...	104.0	....	8.7	95.3
Milk	658.3	18.3	676.6	54.1	....	622.5
Cocoa	35.0	...	35.0	9.6	25.0	.4
Sugar	204.9	5.2	210.1	48.5	35.0	126.6
Clothing	.....	56.0	56.0	....	....	56.0
Total tons	2,238.0	91.4	2,329.4	112.2	128.7	2,088.5
Total value	$696,412.22	$216,205.33	$912,617.55	$37,662.13	$36,236.88	$838,718.54

pean Children's Fund furnished 35.4 metric tons of food and also 56.0 tons of clothing. A summary of these transactions by commodities is shown in the preceding tabulation.

In return for the 112.2 metric tons of supplies turned over to the local Finnish committee they furnished 350.1 metric tons of wheat flour which was the equivalent value of the foodstuffs turned over to them, viz., $37,662.13. The total tonnage and value of the children's relief supplies furnished by the American Relief Administration and the European Children's Fund should therefore be increased by these amounts, making a total of 2,438.6 metric tons with a value of $876,380.67.

The Government of Finland co-operated wholeheartedly in these child-feeding operations. For a number of years there had been organized societies in Finland whose purpose it was to look after the welfare of children. Early in 1919 the government organized the Central Children's Relief Committee of Finland under the direction of Professor Robert Tigerstedt, an eminent physiologist. The committee functioned very efficiently, and among other things made possible the difficult task of getting relief to the suffering children in isolated districts. As shown in Table 81 (cf. also Table 306), the Government of Finland made substantial donations of commodities for the child-feeding work. The total of these commodity donations amounted to 936.4 metric tons, chiefly flour, with a value of $195,949.

In addition to these tangible donations, the Finnish Government and people made substantial contributions of services and facilities for which no exact accounting can be rendered. It was estimated by those in charge of the relief work in Finland that these intangible contributions, exclusive of many local services, would have cost approximately $685,000. These may be summarized as follows:

Shipping, transportation, and handling costs	$ 70,570.00
Administration and distribution costs	39,870.00
Establishment and maintenance of school kitchens	293,880.00
Volunteer services (700 volunteers)	280,000.00
Total	$684,320.00

Child-feeding operations in Finland were begun in March, 1919. In the first month, approximately 19,000 children were receiving rations. This number was gradually increased until the maximum number of 127,770 was reached in January, 1920. From this time on conditions improved, and the number was gradually reduced until June, 1920, when the European Children's Fund withdrew from Finland. Altogether, approximately 35,000,000 meals, averaging about 600 calories each, were provided through this relief. The detail of the internal deliveries of all child-feeding supplies in Finland, by districts and kitchens, as shown by the receipts, is given in Tables 316 to 318.

In addition, it was found imperative to provide some assistance in the form of warm clothing in this rigorous climate if the health of the children was to be preserved. Altogether, 56.0 metric tons of clothing material was supplied which was sufficient for more than 40,000 outfits, each consisting of material for one heavy coat, pants or dress, one pair of stockings, and one pair of boots. The detail of the distribution of this clothing is given in Table 319.

As shown in Table 81, the net grand total of all relief deliveries to Finland during both the Armistice and Reconstruction periods amounted to 188,520.9 metric tons with a total value of $30,282,047.90. Divided according to the method on which these supplies were furnished to Finland, these may be summarized as follows:

Sold for cash	$18,335,395.26
Delivered on credit	10,991,287.73
Benevolence	955,364.91
Total	$30,282,047.90

FRANCE

(Appendix Tables 320–322)

C.R.B. PERIOD

The tragic fate of Belgium in the early days of the war was shared equally by the northern provinces of France, which were invaded early in September, 1914, by the German Army and were occupied continually for more than four years. As soon as the Commission for Relief in Belgium had organized its work in that country, it was found necessary to extend it to these provinces of Northern France. This extension of the Commission's activities occurred in March, 1915, and at that time there was formed an organization known as "The Comité d'Alimentation du Nord de la France," also called the "Comité Français," which was responsible, under the direction of the Commission for Relief in Belgium, for the internal administration of relief in occupied sections of France.

The invaded area in Northern France for which relief was supplied comprised six districts, with 2,133 communes having a total area of 8,100 square miles and 1,794,506 in population. The administration of relief in this area was similar to that in Belgium and has been described in many publications of the Commission for Relief in Belgium.[1]

As shown in Tables 82 and 320, summarized from Mr. Gay's report, the *Statistical Review of Relief Operations* of the C.R.B., there was a total of 1,091,580.0 metric tons of relief supplies furnished to the invaded districts of Northern France during the five years that the Commission operated. The total value of these supplies was $220,203,521.62, of which the French Government paid $110,681,443.43. Of the remainder, $104,572,409.90 may be regarded as paid from credit extended to France by the United States and Great Britain. The balance of $4,949,668.29 represents relief supplies paid for from benevolent contributions.

The deliveries of relief supplies to the invaded districts of Northern France may be summarized from Mr. Gay's report by years as follows:

C.R.B. Deliveries to Northern France by Years
(*Metric Tons*)

	Total
Mar. 1, 1915, to Oct. 31, 1915	129,195.0
Nov. 1, 1915, to Oct. 31, 1916	373,000.0
Nov. 1, 1916, to Oct. 31, 1917	191,501.0
Nov. 1, 1917, to Oct. 31, 1918	289,383.0
Total to Armistice	983,079.0
Nov. 1, 1918, to Aug. 31, 1919	108,501.0
Grand total	1,091,580.0

In addition to the deliveries to Northern France, the Commission also furnished 299.0 tons of relief supplies, valued at $80,028.90, for French refugees in Holland, which included not only interned adults, but also children and French prisoners of war (cf. Table 103). These were paid for from benevolent contributions.

The total deliveries of relief commodities by the Commission for the French account therefore amounted to 1,091,879.0 metric tons, valued at $220,283,550.52. These deliveries may be summarized by commodity groups as follows:

Commission for Relief in Belgium
Deliveries for the French Account,
1914–1919
(*Metric Tons*)

Commodity	Total
Flour	75,813.0
Grain	509,011.0
Rice	102,044.0
Beans and peas	49,329.0
Pork products	137,409.0
Milk	53,752.0
Cocoa	6,988.0
Sugar	49,507.0
Miscellaneous food	65,014.0
Soap	24,639.0
Clothing and miscellaneous	18,373.0
Total	1,091,879.0

[1] See Bibliography, pages 989–90.

U.S.F.A. PERIOD

With the entrance of the United States into the World War in April, 1917, one of the most important contributions expected by the Allied countries was additional food supplies. As discussed in an earlier section of this report (page 15), the United States Government began immediately to grant large loans to the Allies for the purchase of various commodities needed in the prosecution of the war, including foodstuffs. The duty of seeing that the Allied countries obtained the food supplies needed was delegated to Mr. Hoover as United States Food Administrator. Some of the difficulties encountered in this work have been outlined in previous sections of this report and in the publications there referred to (cf. page 16).

As summarized in Table 82 (page 188), a total of 6,781,317.6 metric tons of foodstuffs were furnished to France during the period from April, 1917, to the middle of 1919, all of which was financed by U.S. Treasury loans to France to the extent of $850,715,632.84. These commodities were all sold f.o.b. American ports to the Allied buying organizations and no details as to their shipment or distribution are available. Table 320 shows the types of food commodities furnished and the quantities of each. These may be summarized as follows:

U.S. Food Administration Deliveries to France, 1917–1919

Commodity	Total Metric Tons
Flour	1,738,079.8
Grain	1,549,746.1
Rice	104,589.9
Beans and peas	78,625.8
Pork products	264,290.4
Milk	235,657.7
Sugar	378,018.0
Miscellaneous food	389,594.7
Forage (oats)	2,042,715.2
Total	6,781,317.6

ARMISTICE PERIOD

Table 82 (see also Table 320) shows that the American Relief Administration made a cash sale of 31,106.1 metric tons of flour to France for a total value of $5,031,830.08. As explained elsewhere (pages 68–69), this transaction came about because the U.S. Liquidation Commission (War Department) had sold this flour from surplus Army stocks in France to Esthonia. But because of the shortage of food supplies in France at that time, the French Government refused to permit this flour to be shipped out of the country. The A.R.A. solved this difficulty by agreeing to accept cash payment for this flour from France, and in turn undertaking to deliver an equivalent amount of food to Esthonia from the United States. The detail of the deliveries of this flour to France is shown in Table 322.

In closing out the operations of the American Expeditionary Forces the U.S. Liquidation Commission disposed of large quantities of supplies to France. A brief description of the work of the Liquidation Commission has been given in an earlier section (pages 52–55). It was pointed out there that specific commodities were sold on credit to the Government of France to the value of $132,665,996.93 (Table 27), and that, in addition, a bulk sale of equipment of all kinds, with an estimated value of $400,000,000.00, was turned over to France to offset French claims for supplies used by the American Army, claims for damages, etc. The total sales to France were thus in the neighborhood of $533,000,000.00. But many of these commodities were in the nature of munitions, machinery, telephone lines, etc., which could not be considered relief supplies in the sense used in this report. Making a careful segregation of the foods, clothing, and miscellaneous items to be used for the relief of the French people, particularly in the devastated areas, we have included a total of 519,775.0 metric tons of supplies, valued at $213,067,400.00, as the portion of these transactions which should be included and for the sale of which Mr. Hoover was in part responsible. The whole of this operation was a credit transaction.

One other item included in the Armistice Period deliveries to France has to do with relief to Russian prisoners of war held in Germany. France had assumed the responsibility of furnishing food to these prisoners pending their repatriation, but at the time of urgent need France did not have this food to spare. Mr. Hoover arranged to furnish 1,622.0 metric tons of supplies, valued at $390,209.03, and paid for out of the President's National Security and Defense Fund. This was advanced as a loan to France and was later paid by the French Gov-

TABLE 82

SUMMARY OF TOTAL RELIEF DELIVERIES TO FRANCE

Operation	Total Metric Tons	Total Value
C.R.B. Period		
C.R.B.—Northern France	1,091,580.0	$ 220,203,521.62
C.R.B.—French Refugees in Holland	299.0	80,028.90
Total C.R.B. deliveries	1,091,879.0	$ 220,283,550.52
U.S.F.A. Period		
U.S. Treasury Loans	6,781,317.6	$ 850,715,632.84
Armistice Period		
A.R.A.—President's National Security and Defense Fund	1,622.0	$ 390,209.03
A.R.A. (cash sales)	31,106.1	5,031,830.08
U.S. Liquidation Commission	519,775.0	213,067,400.00
Total, Armistice Period	552,503.1	$ 218,489,439.11
Grand total relief deliveries	8,425,699.7	$1,289,488,622.47

ernment. This transaction, which forms part of the total relief to Russian prisoners of war from France, is included here as a delivery to France by the American Relief Administration and later under Sundry Accounts (page 269) as a delivery to the Russian prisoners. This duplication is deducted in arriving at the total relief furnished in the Armistice Period (Table 14).

Table 82 shows that the total deliveries to France from the beginning of the war in 1914 to the close of the Armistice Period, accounted for in this report, amounted to 8,425,699.7 metric tons, valued at $1,289,488,622.47. Considering the basis upon which these supplies were originally delivered, this may be divided as follows:

Sold for cash	$ 5,031,830.08
Delivered on credit	1,279,427,095.20
Benevolence	5,029,697.19
Total	$1,289,488,622.47

However, inasmuch as the French Government contributed $110,681,443.43 toward the work of the Commission for Relief in Belgium, this would increase the deliveries for cash to $115,713,273.51 and reduce the amount furnished on credit to $1,168,745,651.77.

GERMANY

(Appendix Tables 323–333)

ARMISTICE PERIOD

Food Conditions in 1919

In December, 1918, Mr. Hoover asked the Germans for a complete statement of their food situation as a preliminary to the furnishing of any supplies. A special commission was appointed by the Germans, which submitted a detailed report in January, 1919, showing their supplies for the three crop years 1916, 1917, and 1918, together with much other relevant data.

After the receipt of this report, Mr. Hoover sent a mission consisting of Dr. A. E. Taylor and Dr. Vernon Kellogg to Berlin and elsewhere in Germany to study the conditions and to determine as far as possible the accuracy of the data submitted. The results of this investigation showed that apparently the Germans had placed all their cards on the table, and that the statement of their requirements was approximately correct.

It is of interest to note that, in explaining certain discrepancies between the crop figures submitted and the official war-period returns for previous years, the Germans stated that the earlier crop returns had been systematically increased from 10 to 20 per cent to make it appear that Germany was self-supporting.

The data which were made available showed very clearly how great a part the food situation had played in the collapse of the German military régime. In the light of these figures it appears that the slogan, "Food will win the war," was not so far from the truth.

The accompanying table gives the approximate production of cereals in Germany for the years 1913 to 1918, inclusive. This shows that the total cereal production decreased from over 30,000,000 metric tons in 1913 to only 15,000,000 in 1917 and 16,500,000 in 1918. The average pre-war consumption of these four cereals in Germany was approximately 32,500,000 tons, of which on the average about 4,500,000 tons were imported.[1] The principal import was barley, used for brewing purposes.

Approximate Production of the Principal Cereals in Germany

(Thousand Metric Tons)

	1913	1914	1915	1916	1917	1918
Wheat	4,656	3,972	3,886	3,288	2,386	2,590
Rye	12,222	10,427	9,152	9,109	6,591	7,447
Barley	3,673	3,138	2,484	2,797	2,003	2,085
Oats	9,714	9,038	5,986	7,696	4,038	4,459
Total	30,265	26,575	21,508	22,890	15,018	16,581

The pre-war consumption of bread grains (wheat and rye), including seed and those for industrial uses, was, according to German figures, approximately 16,850,000 tons. Of this amount, the average net imports supplied about 1;150,000 tons. Thus, on this showing Germany normally produced about 93 per cent of her required bread grains.

For the three years 1916, 1917, and 1918, the total production of wheat and rye was only 30,500,000 tons, or an average of 10,200,000 tons per year. This was only 60 per cent of her pre-war consumption. After deducting seed and the absolutely necessary industrial requirements, which would amount to approximately 2,000,000 tons, there were on the average only about 8,200,000 tons available for food. Calculating a ration of 12 kilograms per month for 70,000,000 persons would require for bread alone more than 10,000,000 tons.

During 1917–1918 and 1918–1919 the ration was reduced far below 12 kilograms per month. In 1918–1919 the rations may be taken as follows: for "self-producers," 9 kilograms of grain per month, while the regular ration for persons entitled to receive supplies was 260 grams of flour per day milled to 94 per cent extraction, equivalent to about 8⅓ kilograms of grain per month. From the data submitted by the Germans it is possible to determine the approxi-

[1] The 1913 crop was considerably above the average.

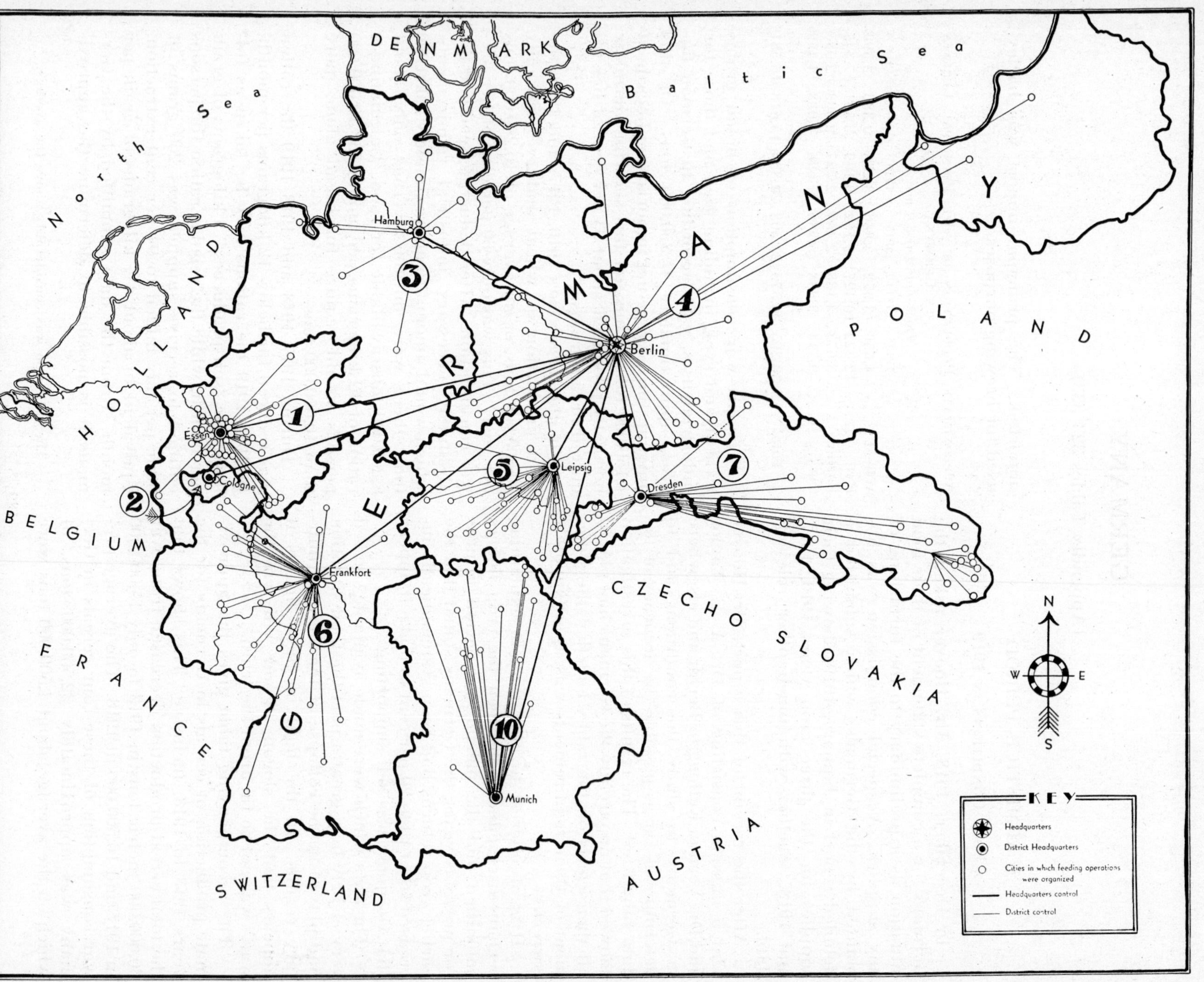

Map of Germany showing headquarters of American Friends Service Committee for cities in which feeding operations were organized, by districts.

mate requirements for the year 1918–1919 as follows:

Approximate Bread-Grain Requirement in Germany for the Crop Year Beginning August 15, 1918

	Metric Tons
16,000,000 self-producers at 9 kilograms per month	1,728,000
49,000,000 persons rationed at 8⅓ kilograms per month	4,900,000
Seed	1,400,000
Army and navy	1,000,000
Additional rations for heavy workers and other industrial classes	1,200,000
Industrial uses, dealers' stocks, and illicit trading	500,000
Total	10,728,000
Crop, less amount used previous to August 15, 1918	9,520,000
Deficit	1,208,000

On this calculation, which represents almost the minimum requirement, Germany had a deficit of 1,208,000 tons of bread grains. The Germans argued that their people had been undernourished for so long that they should be given an increased ration. If the ration were to be raised to 12 kilograms per month after January, another million tons would be required. It was on this basis that they asked for 400,000 tons of breadstuffs per month, or a total of 2,400,000 tons. In view of the world food situation and the needs of the Allies and the liberated territories it was impossible to meet this demand and, consequently, this sort of ration had to be refused.

The Germans were worse off in regard to their supply of meats, and particularly of fats, than of cereals. Chart VIII, copied from a diagram submitted with the report of the Germans to Mr. Hoover, shows a comparison of the civilian rations in 1917–1918 with the consumption in 1912–1913.

Expressed in another way, the 1917–1918 ration shows the following percentages of the pre-war consumption:

	Percentage
Cereal products	64
Meats	18
Fats	12

Thus, while the consumption of cereals was only 36 per cent less than normal, the consumption of fats was reduced by 88 per cent. This reduction in fat consumption was due largely to the decline in the number of hogs and to the lack of imports. With the exception of hogs, Germany's supply of animals did not decrease as much during the war as might be expected.

CHART VIII

PER CAPITA YEARLY CONSUMPTION OF IMPORTANT FOODS IN GERMANY 1912-13 AND 1917-18

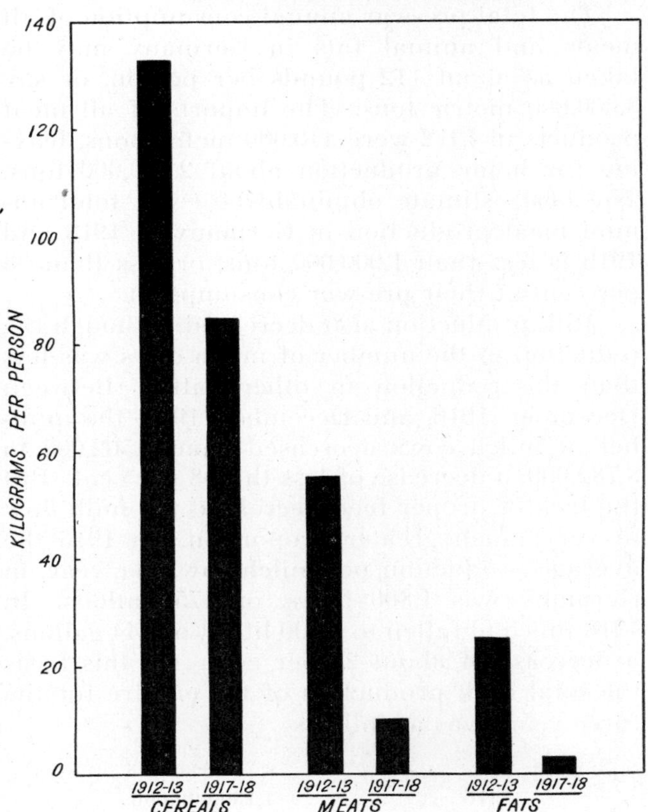

The decrease in the number of cattle in 1918 compared with 1913 was only a little over 11 per cent, but for swine the decrease was nearly 58 per cent, or if we take the low point in the hog supply in March, 1918, the decrease was almost 80 per cent of the pre-war number.

A comparison of the number of animals does not, however, give a true picture of the possible supply of meats and fats. The shortage in feeding stuffs (particularly concentrated feeds) had seriously reduced the weight per head. The following table, compiled from the report of the Germans, shows the extent of this reduction in the dressed weight per head.

	Average Pre-War Weight in Kilograms	Average Weight in Kilograms for First 9 Months of 1918	Percentage Decrease
Cattle	250	137	45
Calves	40	29	27
Swine	85	55	35
Sheep	22	17	22

Naturally, this decrease in weight per animal resulted in a very much greater decrease in the fat content.

The total pre-war annual consumption of all meats and animal fats in Germany may be taken as about 112 pounds per person, or say 3,300,000 metric tons. The imports of all meat products in 1912 were 440,000 metric tons, leaving for home production about 2,860,000 tons. The best estimate obtainable for the total annual meat production in Germany in 1918 and 1919 is less than 1,000,000 tons, or less than 33 per cent of their pre-war consumption.

Milk production also decreased, although the reduction in the number of milch cows was less than the reduction in other cattle. Between December, 1916, and December, 1918, the number of milch cows decreased from 9,502,000 to 8,782,000, a decrease of less than 8 per cent. But the lack of proper feed decreased the milk flow in very much greater proportion. In 1916 the average production per milch cow, per year, in Germany was 1,800 liters, or 475 gallons. In 1918 this had fallen to 1,300 liters, or 344 gallons, a decrease of about 28 per cent. On this basis the total milk production of the empire for the three years was as follows:

	Gallons
1916	4,130,000,000
1917	3,510,000,000
1918	3,010,000,000

The serious reduction in the food supply was evident in the appearance of the German population. It was estimated that the population as a whole was 20 per cent under weight, and travelers in Germany after the Armistice say that this reduction was very evident to the eye.

Of far more importance than this was the reported increase in the death-rate and the increasing prevalence of constitutional diseases. This, according to the post-Armistice report of the Germans, was due to the lack of sufficient and proper food. The figures which they submitted in support of these claims were indeed startling. The increase in the death-rate and the decrease in births is shown strikingly by the figures for the city of Berlin between 1913 and 1917, as follows:

Year	Per 1,000 Population Births	Deaths	Excess of Births	Deaths
1913	19.6	13.5	6.1	...
1914	18.5	14.6	3.9	...
1915	16.5	15.2	1.3	...
1916	12.6	15.1	...	2.5
1917	10.1	19.6	...	9.5

Chart IX, copied from the German report, shows the absolute figures for births and deaths in Berlin for each year since 1913.

CHART IX

BIRTHS AND DEATHS IN THE CITY OF BERLIN

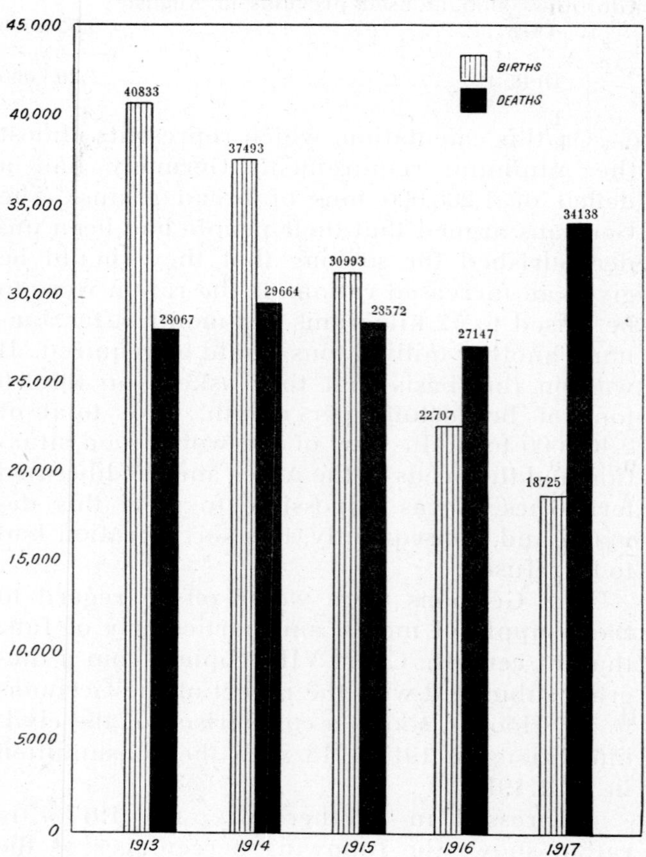

The death-rate was highest in young children and in persons over sixty years of age. The death-rate in 1918 was even greater than in 1917, largely because of the influenza epidemic. In December, 1918, it was stated that on the average over 800 persons were dying daily in Germany because of undernourishment and the diseases resulting therefrom.

The chief cause of the increased death-rate, according to the German physicians, was the lowered resistance against infectious diseases, especially tuberculosis, caused by insufficient and improper food. Other causes were diseases of the alimentary canal, and such diseases as oedema, caused particularly by the lack of fats.

Chart X presents graphically some figures showing the increase in the death-rate from tuberculosis.

CHART X

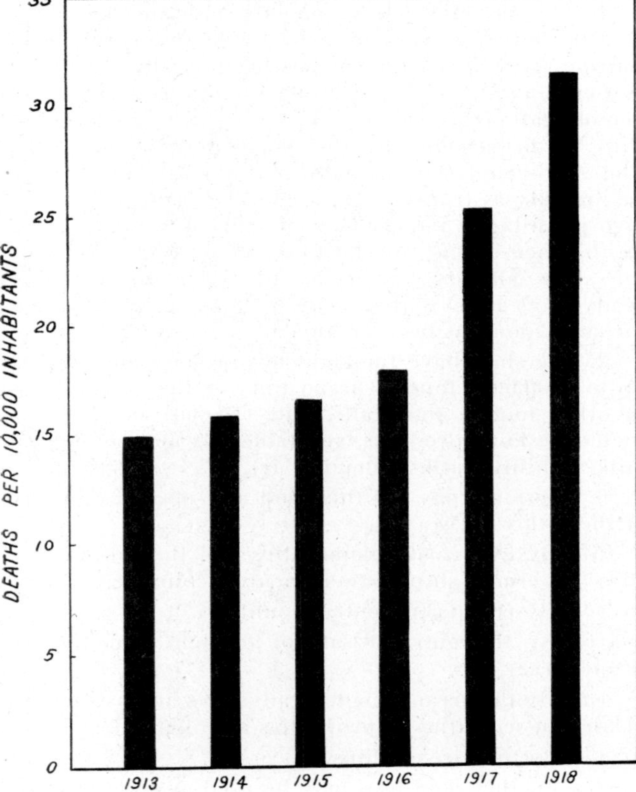

The Allied Blockade

With a knowledge of these conditions Mr. Hoover urged the Allies to provide some arrangements by which Germany could secure the food she needed so badly.[1] Article XXVI of the Armistice Convention of November 11, 1918,[2] read as follows:

> The existing blockade conditions set up by the Allied and Associated Powers are to remain unchanged, and all German merchant ships found at sea are to remain liable to capture. The Allies and United States contemplate the provisioning of Germany during the Armistice as shall be found necessary.

By this article the Allied and Associated Powers expressed their conviction that it was impossible to establish peace with a section of Europe in serious want of food, even though this section contained a powerful enemy. Quite apart from its political aspects, modern civilization could not permit actual, preventable starvation to take place.

On the other hand, the Allies were equally convinced that it was the first duty of the world to see that the food supply was assured to the liberated and Allied territories. If there was any food left, the question of feeding Germany should then be considered.

No move was made toward the provisioning of Germany until the Armistice Convention at Treves, on January 16, 1919. At this convention the Armistice was extended from January 17 to February 17, 1919. The Associated Governments stated that it must be regarded as a condition precedent to the importation of food into Germany that the German mercantile shipping should be placed at the disposal of the Associated Powers. Article VIII of this Armistice extension[3] stated that:

> In order to secure the provisioning of Germany and of the rest of Europe, the German Government shall take all necessary steps to place the German fleet, for the duration of the Armistice, under the control and the flags of the Allied Powers and the United States, who shall be assisted by a German delegate. . . . .

The Associated Powers also informed Germany at this convention that, in the first instance, they would permit the importation of 200,000 tons of breadstuffs, and 70,000 tons of pork per month in such manner and from such places as the Associated Governments might prescribe.

No movement was made by Germany toward placing her ships at the Allies' disposal and, consequently, no arrangements were made for the

[1] For a further discussion of Mr. Hoover's point of view, and of the steps taken by him at this time, see Frank M. Surface, *American Pork Production in the World War* (Chicago, A. W. Shaw Company, 1926), pp. 123–158; and Sidney Brooks, *America and Germany, 1918–1925*, Second Edition, revised (Macmillan Company, 1927), pages 144 ff.

[2] See H. W. V. Temperley, *A History of the Peace Conference of Paris* (London, 1920), I, 467–468.

[3] *Loc. cit.*, pages 479–480.

shipment of food until the conference called at Spa on the sixth of February, 1919. At this conference it was arranged that the British authorities should supply certain foodstuffs to Germany, up to the value of 6,000,000 pounds sterling, this being the approximate value of 100,000,000 German gold marks and 25,000,000 gold francs, florins, and kroner which Germany agreed to deposit at the Nederlandsche Bank in Rotterdam for British credit. The quantities and prices of the foodstuffs to be furnished were 30,000 metric tons of pork products, at 180 pounds sterling per ton c.i.f. Rotterdam; 250,000 cases (4,763 metric tons) condensed milk, at 32 shillings per case c.i.f. Rotterdam; and such additional pork as the balance of the gold would buy.

The delivery of the first consignment of these commodities was delayed until the end of March, both because of Germany's reluctance to part with her ships and because of her delay in sending the gold to Rotterdam.

At the Spa Conference, Germany stated that her requirements for each month from March to August, 1919, inclusive, were 400,000 tons of wheat, 170,000 tons of maize, and 100,000 tons of fats and meats.

This quantity was far beyond the ability of the Allied Powers to supply from available stocks, or to transport with the available shipping. Germany was therefore told that she would have to get along with much smaller amounts. The maximum quantities which would be allowed were later fixed by the Brussels Agreement.

The Brussels Agreement

Several other conferences were held with the German representatives, ending in the Brussels Conference of March 13 and 14, 1919. At this conference it was made clear to Germany that no food would be delivered to her until she had first complied with her agreement to turn over that part of her merchant fleet specified by the Naval Armistice Commission and, in addition, had deposited with the Director General of Relief sufficient gold to cover the value of the food.

Germany was very loathe to part with her merchant ships, inasmuch as she regarded these as her last card and was determined to secure all the advantages possible with them. But, after having sidestepped the issue for over two months, she finally accepted the inevitable, signed the Brussels Agreement, began the delivery of her ships, and on March 22 made the first deposit of gold.

The following is the memorandum from the Supreme Economic Council[1] which was read at the Brussels Conference and which was accepted by Germany. All food deliveries to Germany during the Armistice Period were made under the terms of this Agreement:

Memorandum of the Supreme Economic Council Stating the Intentions of the Associated Powers

1. The Associated Governments reiterate their decision to deliver to Germany the food now available in Europe for which payment has been arranged as soon as Germany shows her genuine intention to carry out her obligations, by sending to sea for that purpose the ships to be selected by the Associated Governments. The Associated Governments will themselves provide (as quickly as transportation can be arranged) or will give permits for import from neighboring neutrals for the balance of the 270,000 tons agreed on, as soon as the ships already named by the Germans as being ready have been sent to sea and as soon as payment for such food has been arranged.

2. She shall have the right to purchase and import up to (300,000) tons of breadstuffs or their equivalent in other human foodstuffs, and (70,000) tons of fats including Pork products, vegetable oils and condensed milk monthly until September 1st.

3. She must pay for this food and may pay in any of the following ways:—

(*a*) By export of commodities and the sale of cargoes of German ships now in neutral countries.

(*b*) By credits in neutral countries.

(*c*) By the outright sale of foreign securities or properties.

(*d*) By the arrangement of advances against the use of foreign securities or properties as collateral.

(*e*) By the hire of ships.

(*f*) Further gold also may be used as collateral for loans to be released as other means of payment provide means of liquidating such loans. The outright sale of gold can only be permitted in the event of its being agreed by the Associated Powers that the above named means of payment are inadequate.

4. She may export commodities (except those that will be enumerated in a prohibited list) to any neutral or other approved destination. The proceeds from these exports must, however, be converted into payments for foodstuffs.

[1] Food Document 128 of Supreme Economic Council, Appendix II, Paris, 1919.

5. When the German ships are delivered, and subject to continuous performance by Germany of the whole of her obligations in relation to the subject matter of this memorandum the carriage of German supplies, up to the amount specified above for the period to 1st. September, will be a first charge upon their use.

6. She may purchase and import foodstuffs within the limits above stated, from neutrals who will, when necessary, be allowed to re-import equivalent quantities.

7. It is understood that the declaration of the Associated Governments under this communication will be null and void, should Germany break the terms of the Armistice, or in any way fail to carry out her obligation as respects the delivery of her mercantile marine.

Food deliveries under the Brussels Agreement.—Under the terms of the Brussels Agreement, Germany was to be allowed to purchase and import food up to 300,000 tons of breadstuffs and 70,000 tons of fats, including milk, per month. In other words, the Allied blockade was raised to this extent. It was clear that such quantities could not be purchased by Germany without the assistance of the Associated Governments. Germany, however, had the right to refuse or accept any particular lot of food offered by the Allies or other nations.

In order to facilitate the operations with Germany, the Associated Governments established a commission at Rotterdam, known as the Rotterdam Food Commission. This Commission was charged particularly with seeing that Germany's purchase of food did not exceed the total monthly ration allowed to her, and also to facilitate commercial transactions in foods between Germany and the outside world.

The Germans appointed a delegate to work with the Rotterdam Commission. This delegate was empowered to accept or refuse particular lots of food offered for sale to Germany.

Under the terms of the Brussels Agreement, Germany was to pay for all food purchased from the Allies by deposits of gold in banks in Allied or neutral countries, which were to be placed to the credit of the Director General of Relief. This gold was to be used as collateral and Germany was to be given the opportunity to repurchase it from the proceeds of exports or the sale of securities. Under the original agreement, 125,000,000 gold marks were to be sent to the Nederlandsche Bank in Rotterdam for British credit, and 220,000,000 gold marks deposited at the Banque Nationale in Brussels for American credit. These amounts proved inadequate to cover the quantities needed, and from time to time further deposits of gold were required to cover the cost of food ordered.

The gold deposits were received as follows:

Date of Receipt 1919	British Account, Marks	American Account, Marks	Place Received
Mar. 22...	50,000,000	....	Rotterdam
Mar. 25...	50,000,000	....	Rotterdam
Mar. 26...	....	220,000,000	Brussels
Apr. 1...	25,000,000	....	Rotterdam
Apr. 15...	80,000,000*	70,000,000*	Brussels
May 21...	....	200,000,000	Amsterdam
June 4...	....	210,000,000	Amsterdam
June 11...	120,000,000	30,000,000	Amsterdam
Total marks	325,000,000	730,000,000	
Equivalent in dollars	$77,187,500	$173,645,000	

* This total of 150,000,000 marks was originally deposited for American credit, but 80,000,000 marks were later transferred to the British account.

In all, Germany deposited 1,055,000,000 gold marks, worth approximately $250,000,000 to cover the value of food delivered by the A.R.A., the Commission for Relief in Belgium, and the British Government. An examination of the gold deposited showed that it was worth approximately 23.75 cents per mark. In spite of the fact that this was gold, it proved exceedingly difficult to realize American dollars for it. The gold deposited for American credit was finally sold to the Federal Reserve Bank in New York for dollar credit in New York. The cost of melting and distributing the gold meant a considerable reduction on the pure gold value.

Immediately on receipt of the first indication that the Germans would carry out their agreements, the Director General of Relief diverted to Hamburg the S.S. "West Carnifax," then afloat for relief purposes. This steamer carried a cargo of 6,626.7 tons of wheat flour and arrived in Hamburg on March 25, anticipating by one day the arrival of the first consignment of gold for American credit.

Immediately after the signing of the Brussels Agreement, the Associated Governments indicated the following amounts of food available, all of which were accepted by the Germans:

From the A.R.A. stocks, and near-by afloat:

Commodity	Metric Tons
Wheat flour	35,000
Cereal flour	14,000
Rye grain	25,000

From C.R.B. stocks:

Commodity	Metric Tons
Cereal flour	15,000
Rice	10,000
Peas and beans	15,000
Barreled beef	4,000
Lard substitute	1,000

From the British Government:

Commodity	Metric Tons
Bacon	30,000
Condensed milk	10,000
Vegetable oil	20,000
Margarine	2,000
Drippings	2,000
Rice	35,000
Rangoon beans	50,000
Oatmeal	15,000
Cereal flour	10,000

From the French Government:

Commodity	Metric Tons
Palm kernels *	50,000

* In addition to the palm kernels, which were estimated to contain 15,000 tons of palm kernel oil, smaller amounts of mandioca flour, codfish, etc., were available.

In addition, the A.R.A. indicated their willingness to load for May delivery 25,000 tons of cereal flour and 100,000 tons of rye grain, beans, and peas. As a matter of fact, this provisional program was changed several times because of the supplies available in the home markets.

Furthermore, Germany was allowed to purchase supplies in any markets she chose, up to the limits of the allowed ration per month, provided she could make satisfactory financial arrangements. Considerable quantities were purchased from the Netherlands and other nearby countries and, in addition, arrangements were made to purchase grain from Argentina.

Table 83 summarizes the total supplies furnished to Germany from the time of the Brussels Agreement to September, 1919. As shown by this table, 1,215,217.8 metric tons, valued at $282,410,999.21, were delivered during the Armistice Period under the direction of the Director General of Relief. Of this total, 618,135.8 metric tons, worth $158,109,448.21, were furnished by American organizations.

The deliveries by the A.R.A. amounted to 483,094.9 metric tons, for which Germany paid $113,728,950.49. The detail of these deliveries by steamers and the commodities carried on each is given in Table 324. The C.R.B. also made substantial deliveries to Germany, partly from surplus stocks in Antwerp, and partly by direct shipments from the United States. The total deliveries to Germany by the C.R.B. included 134,980.0 metric tons, for which they received cash from the proceeds of the German gold in the amount of $44,350,810.47. The detail of these deliveries is given in Table 326. This operation made it possible to supply, immediately, fats which were so badly needed in Germany. The supplies from the C.R.B. were sold to Germany for the most part f.o.b. Antwerp and Rotterdam and were transported to German ports in their own ships.

The total deliveries from the United States in the Armistice Period may be summarized by commodities as follows:

Deliveries to Germany from the United States
Armistice Period, 1919
(Metric Tons)

Commodity	American Relief Administration Cash Sales	American Relief Administration Quakers	Commission for Relief in Belgium	Total
Flour	241,865.1	....	16,065.0	257,930.1
Grain	131,748.3	....	44,581.0	176,329.3
Rice	9,209.6	....	21,245.0	30,454.6
Beans and peas	42,200.0	....	19,567.0	61,767.0
Pork products	46,956.1	10.0	32,995.0	79,961.1
Milk	11,115.8	26.7	......	11,142.5
Cocoa	......	13.2	......	13.2
Miscellaneous food	......	....	527.0	527.0
Clothing and miscellaneous	......	11.0	......	11.0
Total	483,094.9	60.9	134,980.0	618,135.8

The A.R.A. made a further sale of 60.9 metric tons to the American Friends Service Committee (cf. page 117) which undertook to furnish benevolent relief to German children. This was used for supplementary meals to children under the direction of the Quaker personnel in much the same manner as the child feeding carried on by the A.R.A. in other countries. In a sense this was the forerunner of the extensive child-feeding operations under the Quakers in the Reconstruction Period as discussed below. The details of this sale are shown in Table 325. In the present report this is regarded as a sale by the A.R.A., but the American Friends Service Committee is given credit with a cash donation of this amount.

TABLE 83

SUMMARY OF TOTAL RELIEF DELIVERIES TO GERMANY
(For detail see Table 323)

Operation	Total Metric Tons	Total Value
Armistice Period		
American Relief Administration (cash sales)	483,094.9	$113,728,950.49
American Friends Service Committee	60.9	29,687.25
Commission for Relief in Belgium (cash sales)	134,980.0	44,350,810.47
Total from United States	618,135.8	$158,109,448.21
United Kingdom	299,144.0	$ 75,653,861.00
France	69,404.0	16,262,889.00
Argentina	155,000.0	16,774,000.00
Netherlands	44,648.0	9,784,989.00
Switzerland	28,886.0	5,825,812.00
Total from countries other than United States	597,082.0	$124,301,551.00
Total, Armistice Period	1,215,217.8	$282,410,999.21
Reconstruction Period		
American Friends Service Committee	28,720.1	$ 6,728,989.92
German Government donation	16,833.0	2,392,021.25
Total children's relief	45,553.1	$ 9,121,011.17
American Relief Administration Warehouses, food drafts and bulk sales	9,347.4	$ 2,820,420.47
E.C.F. (sundry sales, liquidation Hamburg warehouses)	4,053.0	362,571.27
Total other than children's relief	13,400.4	$ 3,182,991.74
Total, Reconstruction Period	58,953.5	$ 12,304,002.91
Deduct duplication, bulk sales included in children's relief	1,237.2	341,309.37
Total net, Reconstruction Period	57,716.3	$ 11,962,693.54
Grand total relief deliveries	1,272,934.1	$294,373,692.75

DELIVERIES FROM OTHER COUNTRIES

The total deliveries to Germany during the Armistice Period from countries other than the United States amounted to 597,082.0 metric tons, valued at $124,301,551. Of this amount, the United Kingdom furnished 299,144.0 tons for a total of $75,653,861. These deliveries were for the most part made from surplus stocks of food which Great Britain had accumulated during the latter period of the war, but which, with the rearrangement of her food supply, were not so readily disposed of in England. Part of the British deliveries were from Canada and Australia, and, in addition, approximately 100,000 tons of potatoes were from England. No detailed record of the shipment of these supplies was furnished to the Director General of Relief, but Table 327 shows the deliveries by months. All deliveries to Germany by the United Kingdom were paid for in cash from the German deposits of gold.

The French Government undertook to deliver to Germany certain quantities of French Colonial products, consisting of 55,000 tons of palm kernels and 6,000 tons of pork and other fats. Smaller quantities of other Colonial products were also offered for sale. These supplies were not paid for by German gold, as in the case of the United States and England, but instead, German commodities, including iron ore and coal, were imported into France to cover their value. Table 83 shows the total deliveries from France as 69,404.0 metric tons, with a valuation of $16,262,889. The only detail available regarding these transactions is the record of the deliveries, by months, as shown in Table 328.

Germany purchased small quantities of food from neighboring neutrals, such as Holland and

Deliveries to Germany from Countries Other than the United States
Armistice Period, 1919
(Metric Tons)

Commodity	United Kingdom	France	Argentina	The Netherlands	Switzerland	Total
Flour	21,045.0	1,402.0	....	....	....	22,447.0
Grain	......	......	135,000.0	....	....	135,000.0
Rice, beans, peas	37,658.0	......	....	....	....	37,658.0
Pork products	49,228.0	6,488.0	....	13,650.0	....	69,366.0
Milk	17,018.0	......	....	....	....	17,018.0
Miscellaneous food	145,699.0	6,514.0	....	24,695.0	28,886.0	205,794.0
Miscellaneous non-foods	28,496.0	55,000.0	20,000.0	6,303.0	....	109,799.0
Total	299,144.0	69,404.0	155,000.0	44,648.0	28,886.0	597,082.0

Switzerland. The chief supplies received from Holland were lard and potatoes. In May, Germany was able to contract for the purchase of 200,000 tons of wheat and linseed from Argentina. To take care of the transportation of these supplies the Freight Committee of the Supreme Economic Council allocated German tonnage to go to the Plate region. Up to September, 1919, Germany had received 135,000 tons of wheat and 20,000 tons of linseed from Argentina.

These supplies from neutral countries were financed by the surrender of German securities or by the sale of ships and cargoes in neutral ports, and therefore represent cash transactions.

The total deliveries from these countries are shown above, and available details are given in Table 329. The tabulation above summarizes deliveries to Germany during the Armistice Period from countries other than the United States.

The total supplies delivered to Germany in terms of breadstuffs and fats amounted to approximately 600,000 tons of the former and 175,000 tons of the latter. These deliveries cover a period of five months. Under the terms of the Brussels Agreement, Germany would have been allowed to import in five months 1,500,000 tons of cereals and 350,000 tons of fats. Her importations were thus far below the allowed ration. She did, however, purchase all that the world supply of food and shipping would permit and all for which she could provide finance.

There can be no question but that the delivery of these supplies to Germany saved that country from the fate of Russia. We have already pointed out that food conditions in Germany after the Armistice had reached a point where deaths resulting from starvation were of daily occurrence among the civilian population. No country could long resist bolshevism under such conditions. From the middle of February and well into the month of March, Germany was staggering on the verge of this curse. It is significant that soon after the first food ship arrived the political situation made a decided change and, after that time, steadily improved.

If bolshevism had secured a position in the center of Europe it must have seriously threatened all other Western European countries, and it is only a step from the Eastern to the Western Hemisphere.

RECONSTRUCTION PERIOD

Children's Relief

Reference has been made to the work in Germany by the American Friends Service Committee (cf. pages 117–20) and other Quaker organizations. This work was begun almost immediately after the Armistice. A survey made by the Friends at that time indicated that 75 per cent of the children in Germany were undernourished and in need of supplementary feeding. It was impossible to undertake much of this work during the Armistice Period, partly because the Allied Powers were unwilling to permit it and partly because public opinion in America and the Allied countries was not ready to approve of it. However, with the peace treaty definitely signed public opinion was no longer willing to see women and children suffer needlessly. As expressed by Mr. Hoover[1] in a memorable statement during the Armistice Period, when asked why we were feeding Germany:

> From the point of view of my Western upbringing, I would say at once, because we do not kick a man in the stomach after we have licked him. . . . .

[1] For complete statement see Sidney Brooks, *America and Germany*, Second Edition, revised (Macmillan, 1927), pages 73 ff.

> From the point of view of a humanitarian, I would say that we have not been fighting with women and children and we are not beginning now. . . .
>
> Taking it by and large, our face is forward, not backward on history. We and our children must live with these seventy millions of Germans. No matter how deeply we may feel at the present moment our vision must stretch over the next hundred years, and we must write now into history such acts as will stand creditably in the minds of our grandchildren.

In November, 1919, Mr. Hoover asked the A.F.S.C. to undertake the responsibility for German child-feeding and promised full co-operation from the E.C.F. An agreement was drawn up between the two organizations by which the E.C.F. undertook to attend to the purchasing and shipping of commodities required in the child-feeding work in Germany while the A.F.S.C. was to handle all details of distribution within the country. The funds for this work were provided from the proceeds of the European Relief Council drive, and from the nominal surplus derived from the food draft sales in Germany referred to below. The overhead expenses of the Quaker mission were paid out of other funds. In addition to this work by the American Friends, the British Quakers undertook similar work in the part of Germany occupied by the British Army. This was handled entirely by funds collected in Great Britain and by British personnel and is not included in this report.

The original mission from the A.F.S.C. was composed of fifteen volunteers who arrived in Germany in January, 1920. The first shipment of child-feeding supplies under these arrangements arrived in Hamburg on February 13, 1920 (Table 167), and child feeding was started on February 26. By the first of July, 1920, the Quakers were feeding 632,000 children from 3,392 feeding stations, in 88 German cities and districts. The number of children fed reached its peak a year later in June, 1921, when 1,026,856 were receiving the supplementary meal.

The methods employed by the Quakers were almost identical with those used in other countries by the E.C.F. One meal a day (excluding Sundays) was furnished to undernourished children, and to expectant and nursing mothers. Children over six were fed mostly in schools, while the younger children and mothers obtained their meals at kindergartens or similar institutions. The details of cooking and distribution were handled chiefly by local German committees. In crowded localities the food was cooked in large central kitchens, and distributed to feeding centers in large thermos kettles. Thus, two kitchens in Berlin cooked for 35,000 and 25,000, respectively.

Children and mothers to be fed were selected in accordance with regulations prepared by an advisory committee of the leading child specialists in Germany. No distinction was made on account of race, religion, politics, or social position.

Very strict regulations were enforced by the Quakers requiring that all food furnished to each kitchen must be accounted for by the proper number of meals actually served as recorded by meal-ticket attendance. Weekly reports were rendered by each local committee.

The total supplies furnished to the Friends by the E.C.F. for German child feeding amounted to 28,720.1 metric tons, valued at $6,728,989.92 (Tables 83 and 323). The detail of the arrival of these supplies in Germany and their delivery to the Friends Committee is shown in Tables 167 and 331. The records of the internal deliveries of these supplies are in the archives of the A.F.S.C. in the Haverford College Library at Haverford, Pennsylvania.

The map on page 190 shows the location of the district offices and the feeding stations maintained by the Quakers.

Co-operation of the German Government.—Throughout this work the German Government co-operated in a wholehearted manner with the A.F.S.C. A committee was formed, known as the German Central Committee for Foreign Relief (Deutscher Zentralausschuss für die Auslandshilfe), headed by Dr. Bose of the German Food Ministry, which co-ordinated the work of all welfare organizations in Germany. The German Government made substantial contributions of commodities (flour and sugar) for the children's relief work to the extent of 16,833.0 metric tons, valued at $2,392,021.25. In addition to these amounts, Germany also paid for the transportation, handling, and warehousing of all relief supplies, and through volunteer services for the cooking and distribution of the food. On the next page is a rough estimate of the total German contribution to this work.

German Contribution to Child Feeding

Transportation, warehousing, etc.	$ 175,000.00
Volunteer services (30,000 workers)	2,375,000.00
Total services	$2,550,000.00
Commodity donations (Table 83)	2,392,021.25
Total	$4,942,021.25

The Friends withdrew from German child-feeding operations at the end of 1922, but, as previously related, they later returned to Germany to continue their child-feeding operations with funds raised through a committee headed by Major General Henry T. Allen. This work lies outside the scope of the present report. It should also be pointed out that in addition to the relief work discussed here the American Friends Service Committee and other Quaker organizations carried on a large amount of relief work in Germany, as well as elsewhere, entirely on their own responsibility, which we have not attempted to cover. For information regarding this the reader is referred to the publications of the A.F.S.C. and also to an interesting book by Ruth Fry,[1] which deals particularly with the work of the English Quakers.

Food Drafts and Bulk Sales

The food draft plan was inaugurated in 1920, as a means of supplying the people of Central Europe with food which their relatives and friends in America wished to provide. The large German population in the United States quickly availed themselves of this method of assisting their relatives in Germany. The sale of food drafts for delivery in Germany was the second largest in Central Europe, being exceeded only by the sale of drafts for Austria. As shown in Table 332, the number of food drafts for Germany was 142,873, representing 5,242.8 metric tons of food with a total value of $2,096,410.

Extensive bulk sales of food were also made from the Hamburg warehouse for Germany. Table 333 shows that these sales amounted to 4,104.6 metric tons of food with a total value of $724,010.47. These sales were made to various organizations in Germany, including local relief bodies, and also to certain commercial houses which undertook to resell the commodities at a nominal profit. Included in this amount are 1,237.2 metric tons, valued at $341,309.37, which were delivered to the A.F.S.C. for child feeding and represents the profits by the E.C.F. on the total food draft and bulk sale business in Germany. As pointed out in an earlier section (page 94), all profits from the warehouse operations were returned for child feeding in the countries in which these sales were made. The only way this could be done in Germany was to turn over commodities to the Quaker organization.

Table 83 shows that the total food draft and bulk sales operation in Germany amounted to 9,347.4 metric tons, valued at $2,820,420.47. Inasmuch as the deliveries to the Quakers for child feeding discussed above are included in this and also in the Friends child-feeding operations, it has been necessary to deduct the bulk sale to the Quakers to obtain the figure for net deliveries to Germany (cf. Table 83 and Table 323).

Table 83 also shows an item of sundry sales for the liquidation of the stock in Hamburg warehouses. This represents the final closing of the Hamburg warehouses in the late summer of 1923. Hamburg had been used as a transshipping point for supplies going into Russia, since it was cheaper to unload trans-Atlantic steamers there and forward supplies by small ships than to direct the large steamers to the Baltic ports. After the completion of the Russian operations there were certain stocks of supplies remaining which could not be used in Russia, and since all other relief operations had ceased these stocks were sold for cash to German dealers. The total quantity sold was 4,053.0 metric tons (including some damaged commodities) for which the Administration received $362,571.27.

The total net relief deliveries to Germany during the Reconstruction Period was 57,716.3 metric tons, valued at $11,962,693.54. Adding this to the deliveries during the Armistice Period gives a grand total of all relief to Germany accounted for in this report of 1,272,934.1 metric tons with a total value of $294,373,692.75. This may be summarized as follows:

Sold for cash	$285,135,904.48
Benevolence	9,237,788.27
Total	$294,373,692.75

As pointed out above there were still other relief deliveries to Germany by the Quakers, the Red Cross, and other organizations which are not included in this report.

[1] A. Ruth Fry, *A Quaker Adventure*, Nisbet and Company, London, 1926.

GREECE

(Appendix Tables 334–335)

RECONSTRUCTION PERIOD

The end of the World War in Europe did not mean the end of fighting in European and Anatolian territories formerly a part of the Turkish Empire. There were complex and bitter struggles in which the Great Powers, Greece and Turkish nationalists, were involved. The conflict reached its climax in the Greco-Turkish War of 1920–1922. After early successes the Greeks were finally defeated in the autumn of 1922, and were forced to retire from Anatolia. After these military disasters, great numbers of Greek residents of Eastern Thrace and Anatolia were forced to leave the Turkish territories.

By the early part of October these panic-stricken refugees began to arrive in Greek territory in enormous numbers. The majority of the refugees traveled by ox cart or on foot, with only meager supplies. By the time they reached Greek territory, they were a mass of exhausted and starving men, women, and children, which presented a tremendous relief problem calling for prompt and decisive action.

The Near East Emergency Fund was organized as a co-ordinating committee to reinforce the appeal of the American Red Cross and the Near East Relief for money with which to meet this Greco-Turkish emergency. These two relief organizations were already operating in the Near East field and were in a position to administer the relief if funds were available. President Harding issued an appeal to the American people for contributions, and Mr. Hoover, then Secretary of Commerce, supported the movement. The American Relief Administration offered the facilities of its experienced purchasing and shipping organization in handling the supplies. The funds contributed were handled and accounted for by the American Red Cross.

Between November, 1922, and May, 1923, the American Relief Administration purchased and shipped 20,374.0 metric tons of foodstuffs which were paid for by the American Red Cross. Table 334 shows the summary of these deliveries, while Table 335 gives the detail of the shipments by steamers. The total amount of money provided by the American Red Cross was $1,211,949.95, which included the f.o.b. value of these commodities at New York and $33,786.10 in payment of freight and miscellaneous charges. All insurance and the balance of the freight and other charges were paid directly by the American Red Cross. Of this we have no record.

The total commodities handled for the American Red Cross in this operation may be summarized as follows:

Summary of Relief Shipments for the American Red Cross for Greece

Commodities	Total Metric Tons
Flour	12,886.0
Grain	2,451.0
Rice	203.0
Beans and peas	1,269.0
Corn grits	2,642.0
Pork products	102.0
Milk	162.0
Cocoa	409.0
Sugar	203.0
Miscellaneous food	45.0
Soap	2.0
Total	20,374.0

During this operation, the relief organization cared for and fed more than 1,000,000 refugees. In addition to the food relief accounted for here, the American Red Cross and other relief organizations provided large amounts of medical and sanitary relief, housing facilities, etc., with which the American Relief Administration had no connection.

HUNGARY

(Appendix Tables 336–351)

ARMISTICE PERIOD

Pre-war Hungary was an exporter of foodstuffs. After the war, large sections of the kingdom, exercising the right of self-determination, broke away and attached themselves to the neighboring states of Czechoslovakia, Roumania, and Jugoslavia. Even in the territory that remained to Hungary there were considerable stocks of supplies in 1919, but as many regions were the scene of armed conflict, and as transportation was broken down and the revolutionary government in confusion, there was acute suffering in the large centers, particularly in Budapest.

As in the case of other ex-enemy countries in Central Europe, the Director General of Relief arranged to sell needed supplies to the Hungarians. Negotiations were begun for the sale of some 2,000 tons of fats and some milk for delivery to the Karolyi Government, which had taken over the power when the old régime fell in November, 1918. On March 21, 1919, the Karolyi Government fell, and a new government under Bela Kun took the power with the program of setting up a soviet government on the Russian model. The supplies contracted for by Karolyi were delivered, to the extent of 114.7 tons of pork products and 204.4 tons of lard and substitutes with a total value of $245,519.96, all of which was paid for in cash. No further deliveries were made, as the Supreme Council set up a blockade against Soviet Hungary.

The soviet régime under Bela Kun attempted to establish a system of communism, which involved the complete overthrow of individual production and which, in addition, became involved in war-like maneuvers. The latter finally led to the occupation of Hungary by Roumanian troops in August, 1919, which lasted until November of that year. All of these operations tended to increase state expenditures, without introducing constructive measures for finding funds with which to meet these burdens.

When the new Hungarian Government took control in November, 1919, it was necessary for them to take possession of all food supplies and to issue rations to the people. Even if each inhabitant had been able to obtain the full amount called for on the ration card, it would have provided less than 1,300 calories, compared with 1,800 calories necessary to maintain a motionless man, or 2,700 calories as the minimum for the ordinary light worker.

The conditions in Budapest were particularly bad. In addition to its normal population of some 880,000, the city was filled with refugees from Bukovina and Galicia, which with the returning soldiers brought the population to more than 1,000,000. Industry was at a standstill, no work could be obtained, and, with the depreciated currency, prices of the few commodities that were available rose to prohibitive levels. Health conditions were bad, contagious diseases prevalent, and the death-rate far exceeded the birth-rate. As always, the infants and children were heavy sufferers.

RECONSTRUCTION PERIOD

Children's Relief

Immediately following the downfall of the Soviet Government, the A.R.A. sent a representative to Budapest. He arrived on August 7, 1919, and found conditions so serious that supplies were shipped immediately from stocks in Vienna, and feeding for the neediest children and for expectant mothers was started on August 13. During the first month approximately 36,000 children received the supplementary daily meal.

Hungary, like Austria, being regarded as an enemy country, could not participate in the food furnished from the Congressional Appropriation. Mr. Hoover, with the permission of President Wilson, allotted certain child-feeding supplies to Hungary from the stocks purchased with the President's National Security and Defense Fund. Table 84 shows that a total of 287.0 metric tons of food, valued at $101,325, were furnished to Hungary from this source. These supplies, however, were sufficient to last only until the end of September, 1919, when child feeding in Hungary had to cease because no other funds were available for use in that country.

Because of the distressing conditions in Budapest, an effort was made to raise funds for feeding children in that city. This effort was successful chiefly through contributions by Hungarians in the United States, and by November, 1919, it was again possible to resume the feeding. This new operation started with nearly 45,000 children, which was gradually increased to a maximum of 110,000 in April, 1920. With improved conditions, this number was reduced to 32,000 in June, and after the harvest in September to only 8,000. A survey made in January, 1921, showed that again there was great suffering among the children for lack of essential food, and the program was therefore increased to 47,000. The number was again reduced in the summer of 1921 to about 18,000, and from then on the number receiving relief gradually fell off until May, 1922, when all feeding from American supplies was finally discontinued.

Table 84 shows that during this period the European Children's Fund supplied 3,298.1 metric tons of relief supplies, with a value of $1,190,832.53, to which the Hungarian Government added 1,733.0 tons of flour, beans, and pork with a value of $265,806.84. The total children's relief furnished to Hungary, including the President's National Security and Defense Fund, amounted to 5,318.1 metric tons, valued at $1,557,964.37, all of which was a direct gift to Hungarian children. The total number of meals provided from these supplies was approximately 28,500,000.

The detail of the child-feeding supplies for Hungary is summarized in Table 336 and may be set forth briefly as follows:

Children's Relief Supplies for Hungary
(*Metric Tons*)

Commodity	President's National Security and Defense Fund	European Children's Fund	Hungarian Government Donation	Total
Flour	98.0	459.2	1,441.0	1,998.2
Rice	....	430.2	.....	430.2
Beans and peas	....	326.9	242.0	568.9
Corn grits	....	23.4	.....	23.4
Pork products	....	135.0	50.0	185.0
Milk	95.0	1,049.0	.....	1,144.0
Cocoa	27.0	125.6	.....	152.6
Sugar	30.0	476.3	.....	506.3
Misc. food	....	55.2	.....	55.2
Clothing	....	217.3	.....	217.3
Soap	37.0	.....	.....	37.0
Total	287.0	3,298.1	1,733.0	5,318.1

No Hungarian organization existed which was in a position to manage the child-feeding operations. It was necessary, therefore, for the E.C.F. to exercise close supervision over all of this work. A number of committees were formed, composed of prominent Hungarians of

TABLE 84

Summary of Total Relief Deliveries to Hungary
(For detail see Table 336)

Operation	Total Metric Tons	Total Value
Armistice Period		
American Relief Administration (cash sales)	319.1	$ 245,519.96
Reconstruction Period		
American Relief Administration (President's National Security and Defense Fund)	287.0	$ 101,325.00
European Children's Fund	3,298.1	1,190,832.53
Hungarian Government donation	1,733.0	265,806.84
Total children's relief	5,318.1	$1,557,964.37
A.R.A. Warehouses (food drafts and bulk sales)	1,629.6	$ 527,939.41
European Children's Fund (surplus clothing sale)	.2	790.83
Commonwealth Fund (clothing)	12.5	24,527.59
U.S. Grain Corporation (Act of Congress, March 30, 1920)	14,114.0	1,685,835.61
United Kingdom (freight finance)	....	564,561.60
Total, other than children's relief	15,756.3	$2,803,655.04
Total, Reconstruction Period	21,074.4	$4,361,619.41
Grand total relief deliveries	21,393.5	$4,607,139.37

all faiths and parties, who greatly assisted in this work. All feeding was confined to the city of Budapest and its suburbs. Great assistance was rendered by a group of retired Hungarian army officers of high rank who acted as inspectors of the various kitchens, and thus gave the relief mission a direct control on all operations.

Hungarian Government co-operation.—Officials of the Hungarian Government showed every desire to co-operate in the child-feeding work, although frequent changes in the ministry made this co-operation more difficult. At all times, however, they provided funds for transporting, warehousing, and administering the relief supplies. It is undoubtedly true that the Hungarian Government contributed more funds for the relief work than it could well afford under the circumstances. The following estimates give some idea of the Hungarian contribution to this work.

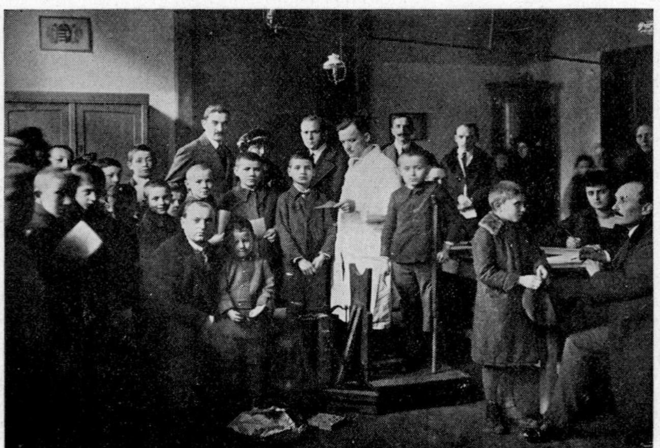

Selecting children who should receive relief in Hungary.

Hungarian Contributions to Children's Relief

Transportation, warehousing, etc.	$ 55,528.00
Administration and kitchen expense	21,982.00
Volunteer services (1,190 workers)	98,976.00
Clothing contribution	8,044.00
Cash contributed by the government	23,912.00
Total	$208,442.00
Commodity contributions (Table 84)	265,806.84
Grand total	$474,248.84

Warehouses and Miscellaneous Sales

Table 84 shows that the total food draft and bulk sale operation in Hungary amounted to 1,629.6 metric tons, valued at $527,939.41. About three-fourths of this consisted of food drafts purchased chiefly by Hungarians in the United States for relatives and friends in the old country. Table 349 shows that 26,129 food drafts were delivered in Hungary, furnishing 912.6 metric tons of food and valued at $373,850.00.

Bulk sales in Hungary totaled 717.0 metric tons with a sales value of $154,089.41 (Table 350). These sales were made chiefly to a number of charitable organizations, including the International Red Cross, the Jewish Joint Distribution Committee, the World's Student Christian Federation, and others.

A portion of the contributions by the Commonwealth Fund were used for food relief in Hungary. The total amount of this relief was $102,466.71, of which $62,500.00 was used to purchase food drafts, and the remainder in bulk sales, all of which was used for relief to the intellectual classes.

In co-operation with the European Children's Fund, the World's Student Christian Federation used $28,300.16 of the funds turned over to them by the European Relief Council for the purchase of bulk food for student feeding in Hungary.

Table 84 shows that 12.5 tons of clothing, valued at $24,527.59, were distributed in Hungary from the Commonwealth Fund. The detail of this contribution to Hungarian intelligentsia is discussed under the Commonwealth Fund (pages 102–3). The sale of 0.2 tons of surplus clothing for $790.83 represents a cash transaction in closing out the children's relief operations.

The E.C.F. recognized the necessity of furnishing suitable clothing to maintain the health of the needy children they were feeding. Early in 1920 they began to supply shoes, stockings, and cloth for coats and dresses. Altogether, 217.3 metric tons of shoes and clothing were furnished for Hungarian children. The detail of the distribution of these commodities to the Hungarian committee is shown in Table 347. This clothing distribution may be summarized as follows:

Commodity	Quantity	
Shoes	101,261	pairs
Laces	66,000	pairs
Stockings	98,426	pairs
Woolen cloth	248,976	yards
Thread	7,052	spools
Needles	53,000	number
Buttons	759,600	number
Blouses	3,926	number

Grain Corporation Flour

The conditions under which Congress passed the Act of March 30, 1920, authorizing the U.S. Grain Corporation to sell surplus flour on credit for the relief of European countries, has been set forth in an earlier section of this report. Hungary, or in particular the city of Budapest, was suffering from a severe food shortage in the spring of 1920. The Grain Corporation therefore sold to the Hungarian Government on credit 158,754 barrels of flour, or 14,114.0 metric tons, with a total value of $1,685,835.61 at American ports. Hungary had no means of transporting this flour, or of paying for its transportation in cash. Through the auspices of the American Relief Administration, Great Britain was persuaded to undertake the movement of this flour from the United States to Hungary, at a cost of approximately $564,561.60. The United Kingdom accepted Hungarian notes in payment for this freight and other charges.

As shown in Table 84, the total relief extended to Hungary, as covered by this report, amounted to 21,393.5 metric tons of supplies, valued at $4,607,139.37. On the basis of the conditions under which these supplies were delivered, the total may be divided as follows:

Sold for cash	$ 512,117.63
Delivered on credit	2,250,397.21
Benevolence	1,844,624.53
Total	$4,607,139.37

This is by no means a complete statement of all the relief furnished to Hungary from foreign countries during this period. Medical and hospital supplies were furnished from British naval and military stocks in Italy and from American Army stocks in France, and by the American Red Cross. The International Red Cross, the Jewish Joint Distribution Committee, and others were also active in Hungarian relief. Many of these organizations secured such food supplies as they distributed from the A.R.A. Warehouses and this is included in the total above. Other operations were entirely independent of the A.R.A. or E.C.F. and no authoritative report of these is available.

ITALY

(Appendix Tables 352–353)

U.S.F.A. PERIOD

Italy, as one of the major Allies in the war against the Central Empires, received large grants of credit from the United States Treasury in the period between April, 1917, and the end of 1919. These credits were used for the purchase in the United States of supplies which were needed in the prosecution of the war and included, of course, foodstuffs. Italy purchased these supplies through the Allied buying organizations such as the Wheat Executive, the Interallied Meats and Fats Executive, the Royal Commission on Sugar Supplies, etc. The foregoing organizations in turn secured their American supplies through the United States Food Administration.

The total loans granted to Italy by the United States Treasury for the purchase of foodstuffs amounted to $796,762,249.59, for which they were furnished approximately 7,464,749.6 metric tons of supplies (Tables 85 and 352). These supplies were sold to Allied organizations f.o.b. American ports and no further information is available regarding their transportation or distribution.

The following tabulation summarizes the commodities furnished to Italy:

U.S. Food Administration Deliveries to Italy, 1917 to 1919

Commodity	Total Metric Tons
Flour	1,804,252.8
Grain	5,039,879.8
Rice	14,634.7
Beans and peas	6,355.7
Pork products	141,867.9
Milk	13,152.7
Sugar	30,682.1
Miscellaneous food	93,341.9
Forage (oats)	320,582.0
Total	7,464,749.6

ARMISTICE PERIOD

Throughout the Armistice Period the food supplies for the Allied countries were taken care of through the Allied buying organizations as outlined above. Consequently, the Director General of Relief was not concerned with shipments to these countries. However, in April, 1919, the supply of cereals for Italy reached an alarmingly low level. Due to the world shortage of commercial shipping, the Wheat Executive had been able to furnish Italy only 70,000 tons of wheat in March, 1919, against a minimum monthly import requirement of approximately 250,000 tons. From the allocation of ships, then loading, there was little hope of immediate relief. In response to urgent requests from Italy, the Director General of Relief turned over to the Italian Government 5,000 tons of flour from American stocks at Trieste and also diverted two near-by American cargoes of flour to Italian ports. The 15,031.1 metric tons of flour thus delivered to Italy served to prevent the threatened serious suffering by the Italian population. The Italian Government paid $2,846,014.42 for this flour, which may be regarded as a cash transaction.

Table 353 shows the detail of the delivery of this flour from American Relief Administration supplies.

The total deliveries to Italy accounted for in this report (Table 85) amounted to 7,479,780.7 metric tons, valued at $799,608,264.01. Of this, the sum of $2,846,014.42 represents sales for cash, and the remainder, sales on credit.

TABLE 85

Summary of Total Relief Deliveries to Italy
(For detail see Table 352)

Operation	Total Metric Tons	Total Value
U.S.F.A. Period		
U.S. Treasury loans	7,464,749.6	$796,762,249.59
Armistice Period		
American Relief Administration (cash sales)	15,031.1	2,846,014.42
Grand total relief deliveries	7,479,780.7	$799,608,264.01

JUGOSLAVIA

(Appendix Tables 354–368)

ARMISTICE PERIOD

The map of the Balkan peninsula has had many vicissitudes in recent years, but the changes wrought as a result of the world war were most profound. Of the seven independent governments, exclusive of Turkey, which occupied this region in 1914 but five now remain. Montenegro and Serbia united with the Balkan possessions of the old Austro-Hungarian Empire to form the Kingdom of Jugoslavia (formerly the Kingdom of the Serbs, Croats [Hroatia], and the Slovenes and sometimes referred to as Greater Serbia). The Balkan possessions of the Austro-Hungarian Empire were divided between Jugoslavia and Roumania, so that these two countries now overshadow in area and population the remaining Balkan states. The former Austro-Hungarian provinces which have been included in Jugoslavia are Bosnia and Herzegovina, Dalmatia, Slavic Carinthia, Slavic Styria, Carniola, Croatia-Slavonia, and a portion of the Banat, including parts of Batchka and Baranya. The following table gives the approximate areas and population by districts of the Kingdom of Jugoslavia.

APPROXIMATE AREA AND POPULATION OF JUGOSLAVIA

District	Area in Square Miles	Population
Serbia	33,891	4,500,000
Montenegro	5,603	400,000
Bosnia and Herzegovina	19,768	2,000,000
Slavic Carinthia	900	85,000
Slavic Styria	3,000	450,000
Carniola	3,845	524,000
Dalmatia	4,956	655,000
Croatia and Slavonia	16,421	2,680,000
Banat, Batchka, and Baranya	10,000	1,500,000
Total	98,384	12,794,000

From a relief point of view, Jugoslavia presented a peculiar situation in 1919. In common with the other countries of Central Europe, a large part of this territory was suffering from semi-starvation, almost total lack of internal transportation, scarcity of coal, financial chaos, and industrial disorganization. This imposing array of economic disorders, together with several others not mentioned, were sufficient cause for worry over the future. Yet, within the confines of Jugoslavia there are some of the richest agricultural lands of Europe. The territory of the old Banat had been practically untouched by the war. Travelers reported that in this region the granaries were full, the fields were in a high state of cultivation, and the landscape was literally dotted with fattening cattle, sheep, and swine. That there should be starvation in a country with these resources may seem strange until one considers the transportation and coal facilities. The situation in southern and western Jugoslavia was somewhat similar to what might happen in the United States if the flow of supplies from the Mississippi Valley to the Atlantic States was interrupted through railroad disorganization.

The market place in historic Sarajevo, Bosnia, Jugoslavia.

The normal pre-war production of that portion of the Banat on either side of the Tisza River and now included in Jugoslavia was about 3,500,000 tons of grains and large amounts of live stock. The 1918 crop in this region was estimated by the Hungarian authorities to be about 2,500,000 tons of grain. Prior to the Armistice, only 200,000 tons had been removed from this territory. There should have been at the beginning of 1919 between 600,000 and 800,000 tons of exportable surplus still remaining. The Serbian authorities denied the existence of such large supplies but did not deny that at least 200,000 tons of grain could be obtained. Normally, this would go to Roumania, Hungary, and Austria. Transportation facilities were never well developed to the south unless supplies could be moved by barge down the Danube and up the Save.

The fact that these movements did not take place is due, in the first instance, to lack of coal and other transportation facilities, but perhaps more than anything else to the political condition in the new government. Mr. Hoover, both through the American Relief officials, and through the Interallied Supreme Economic Council, repeatedly had to insist that some means must be found by which this food could be used to provision those areas in serious need.

As a result of these measures, a considerable portion of these supplies were finally moved, and in addition to shipments to northern Jugoslavia large quantities were forwarded to Austria to provide for the starving masses in Vienna.

Regardless of these supplies from northern Jugoslavia, those sections in southern Serbia and along the Dalmatian coast could not be supplied from inland points. The first survey of this territory indicated that southern Serbia would require between 3,000 and 5,000 tons of flour per month; central Serbia would need an equal amount; while Dalmatia, Montenegro, Bosnia, and Herzegovina would require 12,000 to 15,000 tons per month. A portion of these supplies could be sent from the Banat surplus. The original program for overseas relief shipments to Serbia included 12,000 tons of breadstuffs, 2,500 tons of beans and peas, and 500 tons of milk per month. This program was very much modified by later developments.

Arrangements were made whereby the British Government agreed to furnish supplies to southern Serbia through Salonica, and the United States would thus have only the Dalmatian coast and contiguous territory to supply. Owing to shortage in the arrivals from the United Kingdom, it was necessary to send a few American cargoes to Salonica to insure a continuous supply.

Table 86 gives a summary of all relief deliveries to Greater Serbia. This table shows that the total relief deliveries to Jugoslavia during the Armistice Period consisted of 121,249.8 metric tons of food and relief supplies with a total value of $43,596,570.69. Of this total, the United States furnished 87,594.8 tons, valued at $33,961,378.69, while the United Kingdom sup-

TABLE 86

Summary of Total Relief Deliveries to Jugoslavia

(For detail see Table 354)

Operation	Total Metric Tons	Total Value
Armistice Period		
American Relief Administration (Treasury loan)	55,077.2	$13,191,246.46
American Relief Administration (freight finance)	....	81,140.98
U.S. Liquidation Commission	31,850.0	20,464,191.25
American Red Cross	667.6	224,800.00
Total from United States	87,594.8	$33,961,378.69
United Kingdom (relief credit)	33,655.0	$ 9,261,532.00
United Kingdom (freight finance)	....	373,660.00
Total from United Kingdom	33,655.0	$ 9,635,192.00
Total relief, Armistice Period	121,249.8	$43,596,570.69
Reconstruction Period		
American Relief Administration (Congressional Appropriation)	3,054.3	$ 1,164,617.41
European Children's Fund	317.8	490,705.04
Jugoslavian Government donation	2,634.0	533,677.16
Total children's relief	6,006.1	$ 2,188,999.61
Serbian Child Welfare Association	77.7	$ 76,566.82
Serbian Child Welfare Association (Dr. Reeder)	1.6	1,303.12
American Women's Hospital	23.8	35,211.19
Total other than children's relief	103.1	$ 113,081.13
Total relief, Reconstruction Period	6,109.2	$ 2,302,080.74
Grand total relief deliveries	127,359.0	$45,898,651.43

Relief Deliveries to Jugoslavia during the Armistice Period
(*Metric Tons*)

Commodities	American Relief Administration	United Kingdom	U.S. Liquidation Commission	American Red Cross	Total
Flour	50,199.4	10,197.0	....	.....	60,396.4
Grain	....	4,116.0	....	.....	4,116.0
Rice	58.2	......	....	.....	58.2
Beans and peas	1,469.9	3,788.0	....	.....	5,257.9
Pork products	2,714.0	985.0	....	.....	3,699.0
Milk	469.8	381.0	....	.....	850.8
Sugar	....	52.0	....	.....	52.0
Miscellaneous food	....	48.0	16,300.0	.....	16,348.0
Clothing and miscellaneous	165.9	14,088.0	15,550.0	667.6	30,471.5
Total	55,077.2	33,655.0	31,850.0	667.6	121,249.8

plied the remaining 33,655.0 tons with a value of $9,635,192.00.

Of the supplies coming from the United States, the A.R.A. furnished 55,077.2 metric tons, worth $13,191,246.46, which were paid for by direct loans to Serbia (Jugoslavia) from the United States Treasury. For the most part these supplies were delivered at the Adriatic ports of Trieste, Fiume, Gravosa, Spalato, Zeleneke, and Cattaro, but three cargoes were discharged at Salonica for southern Serbia, while one small lot of flour was moved from Constantinople by local shipping. The details of these arrivals, by steamer, and the cargo of each are shown in Table 355. A large portion of these supplies represents cargoes shipped by the U.S. Army Quartermaster under the arrangements made by Mr. Hoover in November, 1918 (cf. page 129). Serbian Government officials signed receipts for all of these supplies, but no further detail of their internal distribution is available.

The A.R.A. also spent the sum of $81,140.98 in transporting the 667.6 tons of clothing donated to Jugoslavia by the American Red Cross. This charge for freight and insurance from the United States to Adriatic ports was made against the Congressional Appropriation for Relief as a gift to the people of Jugoslavia from the United States. The Red Cross supplies, valued at $224,800.00 were also a gift from that organization.

As pointed out in connection with other countries, the U.S. Liquidation Commission made extensive sales of surplus Army stocks to numerous European countries. These sales were all made on credit. The sales to Serbia (Jugoslavia) consisted chiefly of clothing and subsistence materials and totaled approximately 31,850.0 metric tons with a total value, at French ports, of $20,464,191.25. Jugoslavia had no facilities for transporting this material to her own borders, and, at the suggestion of Mr. Hoover, the United Kingdom undertook to move a large portion of this material at a cost of $373,660.00, which was paid for out of the British relief credits.

In addition to the finance on freight referred to above, the United Kingdom furnished a large quantity of relief supplies to Jugoslavia, which was also sold on credit and paid for out of the British appropriation for relief. Table 86 shows the total quantity of this material as 33,655.0 metric tons, valued at $9,261,532.00. The tonnage of the various types of commodities furnished by the United Kingdom is shown in Table 354, while the detail by steamers is given in Table 356.

The total relief tonnage furnished to Jugoslavia during the Armistice Period, exclusive of children's relief discussed below, is summarized by commodities in the table above.

RECONSTRUCTION PERIOD

Children's Relief

In southern Serbia and in the territory reached from the Dalmatian coast the suffering of the children was as great as anywhere in Europe. The story of the suffering of old Serbia and of Montenegro during the invasion of Austro-Hungarian and German armies is well known. The occupation of this country by the enemy forces had left it destitute of supplies. The demoralization of the transportation systems had prevented such supplies being replenished. The same reasons that made it necessary to furnish general relief supplies to these sections of Jugoslavia, also made it necessary to furnish some special relief for the children.

It was estimated that 150,000 children in Greater Serbia were seriously in need of relief. Since Serbia had been associated with the Allied Powers in the war, it was possible to utilize funds from the Congressional Appropriation for Relief for child feeding in this country. The first program for this work in Jugoslavia was made out

Returning Serbian war prisoners, Jugoslavia.

in April, 1919, and contemplated sufficient food to give 70,000 children one meal a day for three months. This was later supplemented by a second program providing for nearly twice as many children up to September 1, 1919. A third program was designed to carry this work to the end of 1919. The accompanying tabulation shows these three programs as originally planned by the A.R.A.

CHILDREN'S RELIEF PROGRAMS FOR JUGOSLAVIA
(*Metric Tons*)

Commodity	First	Second	Third	Total
Flour	..	760	180	940
Rice	80	150	48	278
Beans and peas	..	90	120	210
Pork products	..	90	60	150
Milk	651	90	680	1,421
Sugar	173	250	240	663
Cocoa	88	158	130	376
Total	992	1,588	1,458	4,038

The difficulties of conducting children's relief in Jugoslavia were probably greater than in any other country of Europe. This was due chiefly to the lack of transportation and communication facilities, making much of the population almost inaccessible, and, also, to the disorganization and inexperience of the government officials.

The Kingdom of Jugoslavia was an aggregation of territories which had previously had little economic communication. Such transportation systems as were available had been designed to serve another economic territorial scheme. All of these transportation lines were in so dilapidated a condition that they could scarcely function at all. Many places were accessible only by extremely poor mountain roads, some of which could only be traversed by pack animals. Motor transportation was extremely scarce and gasoline difficult to obtain. Telegraphic service was almost useless and mail often took weeks for delivery.

Conditions were somewhat better in the provinces taken over from the old Austro-Hungarian Empire for some attempt had been made there to build better roads and there were available some forms of child welfare organizations which could be used as a basis for this work.

In old Serbia and in Montenegro conditions were far worse. It was estimated that in Serbia alone half of the adult male population had been lost in the two years of the Balkan War and the four years of the World War. This had left some 500,000 fatherless children, of whom many were entirely destitute. The population had always been poor and the officials had difficulty in comprehending the necessity of furnishing any relief.

The lack of local physicians made it impossible to put into effect any policy of selecting children for feeding through medical examination. Similarly, it was impossible to enforce any rigid policy of conducting feeding in central kitchens. Many of the children in greatest need lived in mountain homes miles from the nearest village. Feeding in cities and villages was always conducted in central kitchens where the children were required to eat their meals on the premises. Many of these kitchens consisted only of a huge outdoor kettle to which the children brought their own utensils, and consumed their meals while seated on near-by stones.

In Serbia and Montenegro practically no child welfare organizations existed, and the American officials were required to organize committees and to supervise the feeding in detail. In Bosnia and along the Dalmatian coast it was possible to make somewhat greater use of local organizations.

The first American supplies for child feeding arrived in the latter part of April, 1919, and feeding was started the first of May. The number of children cared for rapidly increased to approximately 200,000 by September, 1919. The results of the new harvest permitted the number to be reduced to 150,000, but this number had to be continued until May, 1920, when it was possible to make a further reduction to 50,000. The 1919 harvest was disappointing in many respects and, consequently, a much greater amount of feeding was required than had been originally anticipated. The 1920 harvest was much better and it was believed that the country could take care of its own problems after that. The E.C.F., which had taken over the child-feeding work in August, 1919, was able to close its mission in Jugoslavia in August, 1920, but it left sufficient food to continue the feeding up to the end of September of that year. The children's relief work in Jugoslavia supplied a total of approximately 56,500,000 meals.

Jugoslavian Government co-operation.—The indifference and inexperience of some of the Jugoslavian Government officials in the early part of the relief work placed many obstacles in the path of the A.R.A. representatives. But later on, most of these officials became much interested and ably assisted in the work. The government was induced to contribute certain foodstuffs for the child feeding and to pay all warehousing and transportation charges and other local expenses. Table 86 shows that the Jugoslavian Government donated a total of 2,634.0 metric tons of food, chiefly flour, for this work with a total value of $533,677.16.

Excellent co-operation was also secured from volunteer workers, chiefly teachers and priests, who understood the value of this work for their people. While it is impossible to evaluate accurately many of these intangible services, the estimates in the next column made by those in charge of the Jugoslav Mission give some idea of the contributions by the government and the people of that country.

Table 86 shows that the total supplies used for children's relief in Jugoslavia amounted to 6,006.1 metric tons, valued at $2,188,999.61. Of this, the Jugoslavian Government furnished 2,634.0 tons, while the A.R.A. supplied 3,054.3 tons, worth $1,164,617.41, paid for from the Congressional Appropriation for Relief as a direct gift to the children of Jugoslavia. The original allocation of child-feeding supplies to Jugoslavia from the Congressional Appropriation amounted to 3,445.4 metric tons, valued at $1,335,783.36, but in the latter part of 1919 conditions became so much worse in Austria than in the other countries that a portion of these supplies was transferred there (cf. page 157). The total transfer to Austria from Jugoslavian supplies amounted to 391.1 tons, valued at $171,165.95.

The European Children's Fund found it necessary to furnish only 317.8 metric tons of supplies to Jugoslavia. These supplies, chiefly sugar and clothing, were valued at $490,705.04.

The detail of the supplies used for children's relief in Jugoslavia is shown in Table 357, and the further details of arrivals by steamers and sources are shown in Tables 358 to 360. The accompanying summary shows the commodities delivered from each of the three sources.

Contribution by Jugoslavia to the Child-Feeding Operations

Transportation	$ 270,113.00
Warehousing and kitchen expenses	45,000.00
Fuel and light	25,000.00
Miscellaneous	527.00
Volunteer services (5,000 workers)	452,000.00
Total services	$ 792,640.00
Commodity contribution (Table 86)	533,677.16
Grand total	$1,326,317.16

Summary of Children's Relief Supplies for Jugoslavia

(*Metric Tons*)

Commodity	American Relief Administration	European Children's Fund	Jugoslavia Government Donation	Total
Flour	.....	...	2,551.0	2,551.0
Rice	477.3	5.7	58.0	541.0
Beans and peas	287.9	...	5.0	292.9
Pork products	30.0	...	20.0	50.0
Milk	1,623.3	1.6	.....	1,624.9
Cocoa	239.0	...	.....	239.0
Sugar	327.7	127.8	.....	455.5
Soap	69.1	2.7	.....	71.8
Clothing	.....	180.0	.....	180.0
Total	3,054.3	317.8	2,634.0	6,006.1

Tables 364 to 368 show the details of the internal distribution of these supplies as given by the feeding-station receipts from the district warehouses. Receipts for commodities donated by the Jugoslavian Government were turned over to their officials and hence are not given in detail here. The distribution of American supplies to the three large divisions of the Kingdom may be summarized as follows:

SUMMARY OF INTERNAL DISTRIBUTION OF AMERICAN CHILD-FEEDING SUPPLIES IN JUGOSLAVIA

(Metric Tons)

Commodity	Southern	Southwestern	Northern	Total
Rice	78.7	322.6	139.7	541.0
Beans and peas	181.6	54.0	52.3	287.9
Pork products	11.5	17.0	1.5	30.0
Milk	453.4	789.1	521.5	1,764.0
Cocoa	60.8	105.8	72.4	239.0
Sugar	150.2	176.6	128.7	455.5
Soap	0.3	45.1	26.4	71.8
Clothing	180.0*	....	....	180.0
Total	1,116.5	1,510.2	942.5	3,569.2
Deduct adjustment on weight of milk..........				139.1
Deduct rice supplied by government..........				58.0
Total net deliveries from American supplies				3,372.1

* Delivered to all sections of Jugoslavia; added here to include in cross-total.

During the fall of 1919 the field reports showed a great need for children's clothing, particularly in the mountain districts. The American Red Cross, the British Relief, and the activities of many other organizations had helped to furnish clothing to the adult population, but many of the children were still unprovided for. The European Children's Fund, therefore, decided to ship in material for some 70,000 outfits consisting of shoes, stockings, and cloth for coats or suits. The latter were to be made up locally. Unfortunately, this material did not arrive until the first of 1920, and then, through port delays and the difficulties in making up the garments, part could not be delivered before spring. It was then decided to hold the remainder over and distribute it the following autumn.

A further investigation in the fall of 1920 showed that there was still great need for clothing, in addition to the material which the E.C.F. had held over. Arrangements were made by which the Serbian Child Welfare Association and the American Women's Hospital purchased a quantity of clothing and material from the stocks held by the E.C.F., which they distributed. As shown in Table 86, the total quantity purchased by these organizations was 103.1 metric tons, valued at $113,081.13. The details of these clothing operations are shown in Tables 360–362 and may be summarized as follows:

CLOTHING DELIVERIES FOR JUGOSLAVIA BY THE EUROPEAN CHILDREN'S FUND

Commodity	European Children's Fund	Serbian Child Welfare Association	American Women's Hospital	Total
Shoes (pairs)	69,932	19,000	9,991	98,923
Laces (pairs)	69,932	.....	....	69,932
Stockings (pairs)	70,362	.....	10,000	80,362
Woolens (yards)	158,288	70,058	60,613	288,959
Linings (yards)	.....	21,186	....	21,186
Muslin (yards)	.....	94,000	....	94,000
Thread (1,000 yards)...	13,776	.....	....	13,776
Thread (cops)	.....	14,400	312	14,712
Buttons (number)	390,528	94,608	250,128	735,264
Needles (number)	66,000	100,000	....	166,000
Sewing machines (number)	30	100	....	130
Woolen yarn (pounds)	.....	6,924	....	6,924
Leather (pounds)	.....	716	....	716
Overcoats (number) ..	4,030	.....	....	4,030
Blouses (number)	.....	1,000*	....	1,000
Total (metric tons)	180.0	79.3	23.8	283.1

* Special purchase by Dr. Reeder of the Serbian Child Welfare Association.

The relief work in Jugoslavia, during both the Armistice and the Reconstruction Periods was greatly assisted by various charitable organizations operating in Serbia. These included the Serbian Child Welfare Association (an association of foreign child welfare missions operating in Serbia), the Serbian Relief Fund (British), the Society of Friends, the American Red Cross, the American Commission to Serbia for Restoration of Serbian Youth, the Society of Serbian Mothers, the American Women's Hospital, the Dutch Mission, and many other private and public organizations. Without the co-operation of these organizations it would have been impossible to establish and maintain the child-feeding and other relief activities.

As shown by Table 86, the total relief deliveries to Jugoslavia from the Armistice until 1921, as accounted for in this report, amounted to 127,359.0 metric tons of supplies with a total value of $45,898,651.43. This may be divided, according to the basis upon which it was delivered to Jugoslavia, as follows:

Sold for cash	$ 533,677.16
Delivered on credit...........	43,290,629.71
Benevolence	2,074,344.56
Total	$45,898,651.43

Other Relief

The record above is by no means complete with regard to all of the relief furnished to Jugoslavia during this period. All of the organizations referred to above and many others were making contributions to Jugoslavian relief on their own account. Many commodities were also supplied to Jugoslavia from neighboring countries, such as coal and some foodstuffs from Roumania, Czechoslovakia, and Austria, as well as supplies from Hungary and Italy. No comprehensive report on the extent of such transactions was ever furnished to the Director General of Relief or to the other organizations considered in this report. The supplies obtained from these countries were paid for chiefly by the shipment of foodstuffs from the Banat region. Every effort was made by the interallied relief missions to encourage private trading. The demoralization of the currency systems in these countries practically reduced such operations to the level of bartering. Producers were unwilling to sell their products for currency, when none of the things which they wanted were to be had in return for this money. Lack of manufactured articles, or of surplus raw material, hindered even this kind of trading.

The military occupation of this country by the Allied armies was also a hindrance to open trading because of the lack of free communication, the strict censorship, and the uncertainty of the future. Under the direction of the relief missions considerable progress was made toward the re-establishment of normal commercial operations.

LATVIA

(Appendix Tables 369–381)

ARMISTICE PERIOD

The Republic of Latvia, made up of the former Russian provinces of Courland and part of Livonia, comprises an area of 25,402 square miles, with a population in 1920 of about 1,600,000. This territory, lying in the pathway between northern Russia and Germany, had been fought over seven times during the World War. The hardships which these people had suffered had left them and their country destitute. The death-rate had more than doubled during the winter of 1918–1919, and it looked as if many more must perish before new supplies of food could be produced.

Although the Armistice was signed in November, 1918, the war in these northern countries did not cease. The Russian Bolshevists were ever pressing westward and the Letts and Germans were in conflict with each other, and with the Russians. Even on April 9, 1919, when the first American Relief Administration representative arrived at Riga, he found the larger part of this country in the hands of German troops, and the city of Riga itself in the possession of the Bolshevists. The provisional government which had been formed in November, 1918, had been driven out of Riga, and had even been forced to leave the country for a time, but had recently returned and set up the government at Libau. During the next nine months, Latvia was the scene of many bitter armed conflicts between the contending nationalities.

Throughout all of this, the civilian population suffered untold agonies. How badly they suffered may perhaps be illustrated by the following extracts from reports by A.R.A. representatives in Riga. One report written by Captain Evan H. Foreman, May 27, 1919, contains the following:

> Freed from Bolshevism, after four months of "Red Terror," the city of Riga, hungry and helpless, without national or city government, turned yesterday to the American Relief Administration as the only barrier against famine. The story of what this once prosperous old Russian port has undergone during the years of the war and the months of the more horrible Bolshevism, when the social structure of the city was turned topsy-turvy, is incredible to one who is not here on the ground to see what the "red" handiwork has wrought. Although the Bolshevist Army has now been cleared from the environs of the city, the red flag has left Riga only a shell of a city. The people, feeble and foodless, counting themselves fortunate to have survived, stalk the silent streets in a ghastly sort of a way, and hundreds of emaciated children besiege the food kitchens for scraps. Corpses are being cleared from the prison yards, which were strewn with the bodies of intelligent, well-dressed citizens, including seven pastors and many women, all murdered by the Bolshevists. . . .

Another report from this same city in the early part of June, written by Lieutenant Colonel A. J. Carlson, serves to bring home to us the indescribable suffering of these people.

> . . . 5. Scores of children and old people lined up on the quay all day long before the American food ship "Lake Mary" and the British destroyer "Vancouver" in mute appeal for food. They fought for garbage from the ships' kitchens. With old tin cans tied to a stick they picked up the garbage that was thrown overboard, even to raw potato peelings, a piece of gristle or a crust of bread. Children and old women begged for the privilege of sweeping the quay where American flour was being unloaded and put in the warehouse. With their bare hands, or with a rag, they would sweep the stones for the little flour that dusted through the sacks, then pick out the larger particles of dust or dirt and put the remaining meagre gleanings into their pockets, in a handkerchief, or even directly into their mouths. After viewing these distressing scenes, I could not help thinking of my home city (Chicago), where enough good food to support more than half the population of Riga is thrown out as garbage every day. . . .

It was under conditions such as these that Mr. Hoover determined to do what he could to relieve the suffering of these people. The vessel which carried the first A.R.A. representative to Latvia, "Lake Wimico," III, unloaded at Libau 1,166.3 tons of flour, which were turned over to the Latvian authorities. Other commodities were rushed from stocks at Copenhagen, and as soon as the Bolshevist forces were driven from Riga other steamers were directed to that port.

As shown by Table 370, 13,313.7 metric tons of food, valued at $3,323,818.79, were delivered to the Latvian Government, and paid for out of the Congressional Appropriation. This food was sold to Latvia on credit, for the general relief of the population.

In order still further to supplement the food supply of Latvia, Mr. Hoover arranged for the U.S. Liquidation Commission to sell the Latvian Government 6,296.0 tons of supplies from surplus Army stocks in France, and he further arranged with the British Government to transport these supplies to Latvian ports. As shown by Table 369, the value of the Liquidation Commission supplies at French ports was $2,556,952.84, and the United Kingdom expended $80,920.00 in transporting these. Both transactions were on a credit basis with the Latvian Government.

The A.R.A. undertook to transport 6.6 tons of cod liver oil which were donated for children's relief in Latvia by the Government of Norway.

The total deliveries of relief to Latvia during the Armistice Period, as accounted for in this report, amounted to 19,609.7 metric tons, valued at $5,961,851.35.

RECONSTRUCTION PERIOD

Children's Relief

The conditions which made it so imperative to furnish assistance to the Latvian people made it doubly important to render special aid to the suffering children who could not stand these hardships as well as the adults. The early estimates indicated that some 30,000 children needed to be fed immediately, and the first program was designed to carry them through the month of May, 1919. Before this was completed a second program was established to supply these children until September and a third program to continue until the end of 1919. The three programs as originally planned by the American Relief Administration were as follows:

Children's Relief Programs for Latvia
(*Metric Tons*)

Commodity	First	Second	Third	Total
Flour	50	58	60	168
Rice	5	30	40	75
Beans and peas	4	30	40	74
Pork products	6	8	20	34
Milk	30	45	240	315
Sugar	24	27	80	131
Cocoa	9	17	40	66
Total	128	215	520	863

The needs of the Latvian children proved to be much greater than these programs provided. At a later time it was possible to transfer to Latvia a considerable portion of the supplies originally allotted for children's relief in Northwest Russia, which could not be used there owing to political developments.

Table 87 shows that the total of children's

TABLE 87

Summary of Total Relief Deliveries to Latvia

(For detail see Table 369)

Operation	Total Metric Tons	Total Value
Armistice Period		
American Relief Administration (Congressional Appropriation)	13,313.7	$3,323,818.79
American Relief Administration (freight finance)	......	159.72
U.S. Liquidation Commission	6,296.0	2,556,952.84
Total American Relief	19,609.7	$5,880,931.35
United Kingdom (freight finance)	......	80,920.00
Total, Armistice Period	19,609.7	$5,961,851.35
Reconstruction Period		
American Relief Administration (Congressional Appropriation)	2,142.3	$ 753,774.72
European Children's Fund	4,020.3	752,076.08
Norwegian Government donation	6.6	3,960.00
Latvian Government donation	478.6	60,879.55
Total children's relief	6,647.8	$1,570,690.35
A.R.A. Warehouses (food drafts and bulk sales)	75.6	$ 14,759.37
European Children's Fund (sale to Latvian Government)	33.5	2,720.62
Total other than children's relief	109.1	$ 17,479.99
Total, Reconstruction Period	6,756.9	$1,588,170.34
Grand total relief deliveries	26,366.6	$7,550,021.69

relief in Latvia from the Congressional Appropriation amounted to 2,142.3 metric tons, valued at $753,774.72. Table 113 shows that the original allocation from the Congressional Appropriation to Latvia was only 1,763.3 tons, valued at $632,826.90. Consequently, there was transferred from other allocated destinations a net total of 379.0 metric tons, worth $120,947.82.

These commodities were received in Latvia from stock originally allocated to Northwest Russia, Esthonia, and Finland. The detail of the various transfers is shown in the arrival statements for the several countries.

Conditions in Latvia continued to be such that the European Children's Fund had to supply relatively large amounts of relief supplies in 1920 and again in 1921. As shown in Table 87, the total deliveries by the E.C.F. comprised 4,020.3 metric tons, worth $752,076.08.

The Latvian Government was not in a position to render extensive aid in this work, although they did contribute commodities to the extent of 478.6 metric tons, valued at $60,879.55. Also the Norwegian Government made a contribution of 25.0 tons of cod liver oil for child feeding, of which 6.6 tons were sent to Latvia.

The total supplies used for children's relief in Latvia amounted to 6,647.8 metric tons, worth $1,570,690.35. With the exception of the relatively small government donations, this all represented a benevolent gift to Latvian children from the United States. The details of these deliveries are shown in Tables 380–381, and may be summarized by commodities as follows:

Children's Relief Deliveries in Latvia

(*Metric Tons*)

Commodity	A.R.A.	E.C.F.	Government Donation	Total
Flour	260.2	2,114.3	....	2,374.5
Rice	310.0	505.9	28.9	844.8
Beans and peas	447.0	205.9	342.0	994.9
Pork products	43.3	122.7	76.5	242.5
Milk	814.0	670.7	31.2	1,515.9
Cocoa	83.2	71.4	....	154.6
Sugar	147.9	263.8	....	411.7
Cod liver oil	.....	....	6.6*	6.6*
Soap	36.7	7.9	....	44.6
Clothing	....	57.7	....	57.7
Total	2,142.3	4,020.3	485.2	6,647.8

* Gift from the Government of Norway.

It was the original plan to continue child feeding in Latvia only to the middle of 1920, when it was expected that the new crops would enable the people to take care of themselves. The feeding was discontinued in June, 1920, but the new harvest proved to be insufficient, and, since the provisional government was unsuccessful in arranging foreign credits for food, the children's situation again became very bad in the winter of 1920–1921. In February, 1921, the E.C.F. resumed child feeding in Latvia, furnishing a supplementary meal to about 40,000 children. This was continued until June, 1922, when it was possible finally to withdraw from Latvia.

The peak of the operations in Latvia occurred in June, 1920, when 81,000 children were being fed at the relief kitchens. During the whole period of child feeding approximately 39,616,000 meals were furnished.

Latvian Government co-operation.—Although handicapped by lack of funds, the Latvian Government co-operated splendidly throughout this work. They assisted greatly in organizing committees, furnishing quarters, and taking care of the warehousing and transportation of supplies. The estimated value of these contributions may be summarized as follows:

Contributions to Children's Relief by Latvia

Warehousing, transportation, etc.	$136,925.00
Kitchens and administration	13,160.00
Paid personnel	22,942.00
Volunteer services (840 workers)	117,946.00
Total services	$290,973.00
Food donations	60,879.55
Total*	$351,852.55

* In addition to these contributions, the Latvian Government donated warehouse space for the storage of relief supplies in transit to Russia, from June, 1922, to June, 1923. Estimated value of contribution, $24,257.69.

The severe Latvian winters and the ragged clothing of many of the children induced the E.C.F. to plan an extensive clothing program. The major portion of this distribution was carried out in the winter of 1919–1920, but some additional outfits were supplied in 1921. The details of the arrival and the internal distribution of the 57.7 tons of clothing allotted to Latvia are shown in Tables 374 and 381. This distribution may be summarized as follows:

Clothing Distribution to Latvian Children

Commodity	Quantity
Shoes	48,736 pairs
Shoe laces	35,208 pairs
Stockings	45,049 pairs
Woolens	80,564 yards
Thread	800 pounds
Thread	1,000,000 yards
Needles	50,000 number
Buttons	140,832 number
Total (metric tons)	57.7
Total value	$198,763.64

Warehouses Operation

Food draft sales for Latvia were negligible, amounting to only two drafts for a total of $20. The A.R.A. Warehouses, located at Riga, made bulk sales of 84.0 metric tons of food, valued at $15,666.15. Of this amount, 8.4 tons were sold for $926.78 for student feeding in Lithuania (cf. page 219). Of the 75.6 metric tons remaining in Latvia and accounted for in Table 378, approximately 40.0 tons were sold for student feeding in Latvia as discussed under Special Programs, pages 110–11. The remainder represents sales to the Latvian Government and to a few charitable organizations.

Table 87 shows a further sale to the Latvian Government of 33.5 metric tons of food, chiefly rice, for $2,720.62 by the E.C.F. This transaction represented a cash sale and was made after the Warehouses operation had been discontinued.

The total relief deliveries to Latvia during the Reconstruction Period amounted to 6,756.9 metric tons, valued at $1,588,170.34. Adding this amount to the deliveries during the Armistice Period gives a grand total of all relief to Latvia accounted for in this report of 26,366.6 metric tons, valued at $7,550,021.69. These deliveries may also be summarized as follows:

Sold for cash	$ 69,215.62
Delivered on credit	5,961,691.63
Benevolence	1,519,114.44
Total	$7,550,021.69

LITHUANIA

(Appendix Tables 382–391)

ARMISTICE PERIOD

Lithuania, like the other Baltic countries, had served as the pathway for the contending armies during the conflict between Germany and Russia and in the subsequent encounters with the Bolshevists. As in the case of Latvia, German troops were in possession of much of the country during the early part of 1919, and their requisitions served still further to deplete the supplies of food. Notwithstanding the great suffering caused by the war, Lithuania was in a better position with respect to food supplies than any of the other Baltic countries. This was due largely to the predominantly agricultural character of the country, with its comparatively rich soil, normally abundant crops, and the absence of large cities or any industrial population of consequence.

The area of present Lithuania is 21,440 square miles, with a population in 1923 of 2,028,971. However, in 1919 the provisional government laid claims to a considerably larger area, with an estimated population of over 3,000,000, of which nearly two-thirds were under Bolshevist domination. The devastation had been greatest in the east and northeast sections of the country, and in those regions as well as some others there was an acute lack of foodstuffs. The insecure position of the provisional Lithuanian Government and its lack of resources made it difficult to render much assistance.

The first American Relief Administration representative arrived in Memel in March, 1919, and after a tour of investigation reported the need for some relief to prevent acute suffering and starvation. Based on this and the appeal for assistance from the provisional government, Mr. Hoover arranged to deliver a small amount of food to the Lithuanian Government on credit from the Congressional Appropriation for Relief. The "Lake Wimico," III, which had been sent to the Baltic countries, discharged 1,078.5 tons of flour at Memel on April 15, 1919. This was followed by several smaller shipments during May to July, making a total delivery from

TABLE 88

SUMMARY OF TOTAL RELIEF DELIVERIES TO LITHUANIA
(For detail see Table 382)

Operation	Total Metric Tons	Total Value
Armistice Period		
American Relief Administration (Congressional Appropriation)	3,357.0	$ 996,093.08
American Relief Administration (freight finance)	......	48,930.00
U.S. Liquidation Commission	8,320.0	4,414,861.39
Total from United States	11,677.0	$5,459,884.47
United Kingdom (freight finance)	......	57,120.00
Total relief, Armistice Period	11,677.0	$5,517,004.47
Reconstruction Period		
American Relief Administration (Congressional Appropriation)	1,005.4	$ 351,789.53
European Children's Fund	186.9	111,060.61
Total children's relief	1,192.3	$ 462,850.14
Student relief	8.4	926.78
Total relief, Reconstruction Period	1,200.7	$ 463,776.92
Grand total relief deliveries	12,877.7	$5,980,781.39

the Congressional Appropriation of 3,357.0 metric tons, valued at $996,093.08. As shown by Table 383, these supplies consisted of 2,565.9 tons of flour, 84.2 tons of rice, 185.1 tons of beans and peas, 425.0 tons of pork products, and 96.8 tons of milk. All supplies were receipted for by Lithuanian officials and were distributed by them under the direction of the A.R.A. officials, but no records of the internal deliveries are available.

In addition to these deliveries, Mr. Hoover arranged with the U.S. Liquidation Commission to sell surplus stock of Army food and clothing to Lithuania to the extent of 8,320.0 metric tons, valued at $4,414,861.39 at French ports. As in the case of the other liberated countries, the transportation of these Army supplies was a difficult problem. The A.R.A. undertook to transport a portion of these supplies, consisting of 6,096.3 metric tons (cf. page 137), at a cost of $48,930.00, which was charged against the Lithuanian Government as a further credit from the Congressional Appropriation. Mr. Hoover arranged with the British Government to transport the remainder of these supplies. As shown in Table 88, the total charges for freight and insurance on relief commodities transported for Lithuania by the United Kingdom amounted to approximately $57,120.00, which was also made on a credit basis and paid from the British relief credits.

The total of all relief supplies furnished to Lithuania under the Director General of Relief amounted to 11,677.0 metric tons, valued at $5,517,004.47, all of which was furnished on credit.

RECONSTRUCTION PERIOD

Children's Relief

The reports from Lithuania showed that in many districts the people were existing on black bread and thin soup. This diet, at its best, was sapping the health of infants and children. It seemed important, therefore, that some attempt should be made to maintain child health. Programs for child feeding were therefore outlined similar to those for Esthonia. The first shipment of child-feeding supplies for Lithuania arrived at Pillau about the middle of April, 1919, and feeding was started during that month. Considerable difficulty was experienced in organizing this work because of the limited number of citizens able and willing to take charge of the local committees. It was therefore found impossible to organize the child-feeding work in the manner used for most other countries. The government, however, stood ready to assist in every way possible, and the Department of Social Affairs, of the Ministry of the Interior, undertook general direction of the work from the Lithuanian side. For this work the government established four warehouses, located at Mažeikiai, Šiauliai, Panėvežys and Kaunas (Kovno). Relief supplies were transported from the ports to these warehouses by the Lithuanian Government. From these warehouses, supplies were distributed to the towns and districts included in the feeding scheme. This distribution was under the control of the Department of Social Affairs, but deliveries were made only on orders stamped and approved by the A.R.A. representative.

All feeding was conducted in school kitchens, or specially arranged public kitchens, financed and managed by the state or a municipality. In many towns this was the first time in history that the people had been aroused to a sense of their responsibility for their own poor children. One meal a day was served, excluding Sundays.

Table 88 shows that the total deliveries for Lithuanian children's relief amounted to 1,192.3 metric tons, valued at $462,850.14. Of this amount 1,005.4 tons, worth $351,789.53, were paid for out of the Congressional Appropriation, and as in the case of children's relief to other countries was a direct gift from the United States. The remainder of the child-feeding supplies, amounting to 186.9 tons and worth $111,060.61, was furnished by the European Children's Fund. In addition to these amounts, 8.4 tons, valued at $926.78, were used for student feeding. This represents a bulk sale from the Riga (Latvia) warehouse, and forms part of the student-feeding operations discussed under Special Programs (pages 110–11).

The total supplies furnished to Lithuania during the Reconstruction Period amounted to 1,200.7 metric tons, with a value of $463,776.92. The details of the arrivals of these supplies at Lithuanian ports are shown in Tables 385–387, while Tables 389–391 show the details of the distribution of these commodities by districts and towns as shown by the feeding-station receipts.

The maximum number of children fed with American rations was 22,900 in August, 1919. In May, 1920, conditions had improved, and the E.C.F. believed it would be possible to withdraw from further work in Lithuania. Feeding ceased at the end of May, 1920, but in the winter of 1920–1921 considerable suffering developed in certain parts of the country and feeding on a restricted scale was again undertaken in March, 1921. Owing to the lack of funds of the Lithuanian Government, it was necessary for the E.C.F. to finance and manage the feeding kitchens during April and May of that year. The small quantity of food remaining at the end of May, 1921, was turned over to orphanages and children's hospitals in Kaunas (Kovno) which had sufficient endowment to insure their operation during the summer. All operations were completed and the American aid withdrawn from Lithuania by August, 1921.

The total deliveries of children's relief supplies and those for student feeding may be summarized as follows:

Lithuanian Relief in the Reconstruction Period
(*Metric Tons*)

Commodity	Children's Relief A.R.A.	Children's Relief E.C.F.	Students' Relief	Total
Flour	351.0	42.6	3.2	396.8
Rice	83.0	15.9	.8	99.7
Beans and peas	77.8	25.4	1.7	104.9
Pork products	28.0	19.1	.5	47.6
Milk	307.5	58.2	1.3	367.0
Cocoa	57.2	3.4	.2	60.8
Sugar	95.9	9.3	.7	105.9
Soap	5.0	....	...	5.0
Clothing	....	13.0	...	13.0
Total	1,005.4	186.9	8.4	1,200.7

Lithuanian Government co-operation.—It will be noted that the Lithuanian Government made no donation of supplies to the child-feeding work such as occurred in most of the other countries. This was due to the very difficult situation in which the government found itself during this period and its lack of finance. The government did, however, do everything possible to encourage and assist in this work and as in other countries made substantial contributions in intangible services which are difficult to evaluate, including, however, a cash contribution of $1,000 toward the expenses of the operations. The following estimate was prepared by those in charge of the Lithuanian child feeding:

Estimate of Lithuanian Contributions to Child Feeding

Cash contribution	$ 1,000.00
Transportation, warehousing, etc.	13,443.00
Distribution and kitchen expense	18,148.00
Administration and personal services	20,164.00
Total	$52,755.00

Clothing.—In the fall of 1919, the distressing appearance of many of the children attending the feeding kitchens showed that there would be great suffering from cold unless some means were found to supply needed clothing. The E.C.F. allocated approximately 12,500 clothing outfits to Lithuania. These were distributed during the winter of 1919–1920. The total clothing distribution may be summarized as follows:

Clothing Distributed to Lithuanian Children

Commodity	Quantity	
Shoes	13,939	pairs
Shoe laces	12,528	pairs
Stockings	12,588	pairs
Woolens	19,044	yards
Thread	5,034	spools*
Needles	15,000	number
Buttons	49,680	number
Total (metric tons)	13.0	

* Equivalent to 350 pounds.

Total Relief

The total deliveries for Lithuanian relief from 1919 to 1921, as shown by Table 88, comprised 12,877.7 metric tons, valued at $5,980,781.39. This may be divided as follows, according to the basis upon which it was furnished:

Delivered on credit	$5,517,004.47
Benevolence	463,776.92
Total	$5,980,781.39

THE NETHERLANDS

(Appendix Tables 392–393)

ARMISTICE PERIOD

The responsibility for the food supply of the Allied and Neutral countries during the Armistice Period rested with the Wheat Executive and the other organizations of the Interallied Food Council. However, the extreme shortage in world tonnage immediately after the Armistice frequently made it impossible for the Allied organizations to furnish supplies in time to prevent serious shortages in some countries. As also pointed out on page 128, Mr. Hoover had arranged to have relief supplies shipped from American stocks in advance of arrangements for their distribution, knowing that there would be need for all the food that could be delivered. The early vessels that sailed on the Northern Relief Program were directed to Rotterdam and the cargoes put into storage there until further arrangements had been perfected.

Late in January, 1919, it was found that the Wheat Executive was delayed in making deliveries of flour and grain to the Netherlands, and that a serious shortage would develop in that country unless some assistance could be furnished. The Netherlands Government approached Mr. Hoover asking that they be permitted to obtain a portion of the flour then stored in Rotterdam by the American Relief Administration. They offered to buy this flour for cash and, if necessary, to replace it later from other arrivals.

Mr. Hoover acceded to this request, partly to prevent suffering, and partly to insure stability in the Netherlands, which had to be depended upon to handle many of the relief supplies which were being forwarded through their ports to other European countries.

Altogether, 25,027.4 metric tons of flour were sold to the Netherlands Government for which the American Relief Administration received $4,219,498.41 in cash. The details of these deliveries by steamers and cargoes are given in Table 393.

POLAND

(Appendix Tables 394–490)

ARMISTICE PERIOD

Conditions in Poland

Of the many countries of Europe in dire need of relief, perhaps none appealed so strongly to the imagination as Poland. This country, famous for its heroic struggles for freedom, had emerged from the chaos of the World War a united and free nation. Under the leadership of M. Paderewski, the foremost pianist of the world, and of the great leader of the Polish Legions, Pilsudski, this little nation was struggling against the almost insuperable odds of famine, bolshevism, unemployment, and financial chaos. Poland had endured all that Belgium would have suffered without the relief work. While the Belgian relief was in progress Mr. Hoover attempted to bring aid to Poland under a similar arrangement with the belligerents. This, however, proved to be impossible because of the attitude of the hostile groups. Nothing could be done until after the Armistice, when the curtain of censorship was raised, exposing the terrible suffering that Poland had endured.

Yet, with it all, the indomitable spirit of this people was unbroken. One little story from an A.R.A. representative is typical of the courage of the common people. A poor woman at Łódź was asked how the people managed to hold out, and she replied: "It is very hard, but give us a little better bread, and a little more bread, and we'll manage for Poland." The meaning of this is better understood when one considers what they were living on. Take, for example, the Polish soldiers: they had very little clothing, often no shoes, and received a daily ration of coffee made from substitutes and a slice of black, stinking bread for breakfast; for dinner a liter of cabbage and potato soup, with occasionally a little piece of meat and another slice of that unthinkable bread; for supper, more so-called coffee and bread. On this they were fighting the Bolshevists.

The civilian population fared even worse. In Łódź, 300,000 people were out of work, because the Germans had destroyed all the machinery in the cotton mills. In other cities, conditions were similar. Hundreds of thousands were being fed, if it can be called that, at public soup kitchens, where they received a little vegetable soup and a little of the mixture which passed for bread. They were getting just enough to exist; the death-rate was double or triple the normal rate for adults, and among the children it was four or five times the normal.

Almost immediately after his arrival in Europe, Mr. Hoover arranged to send a mission to Poland to ascertain the needs of the people and to make arrangements for sending supplies. This mission consisted of Dr. Vernon Kellogg, Colonel W. R. Grove, and Captain Chauncey McCormick. From every side they heard the same story: a country devastated by the contending armies, drained of its material resources, and despoiled by the retreating Germans. This committee reported to Mr. Hoover in January, 1919, and immediately steps were taken to alleviate some of the most serious conditions. It was clearly apparent that the greatest distress was in the cities.

The situation in Lemberg was probably the most critical. The city was then under fire from the Bolshevists, being contested by the Poles and Ukrainians. Only one outlet was maintained, and that by the most strenuous exertions. Trains could be run only at night, and were almost always fired upon. It was not unusual for passengers to be killed or wounded. Food supplies were almost exhausted. The city had been without a drop of milk for weeks, and the children and babies who had survived were in a terrible condition.

General Relief

Pending the arrival of shipments in quantities, arrangements were made to purchase some supplies in Switzerland from the American and British Red Cross, to be shipped by rail. A trainload of flour and condensed milk arrived the first week in February, and a portion was rushed to Lemberg, arriving there on the morning after the municipal stocks were completely exhausted. One can, perhaps, hardly imagine what a carload of condensed milk means to the children of a city which has had no milk of any kind for many weeks.

It was apparent, from the preliminary investigation, that the only route by which supplies could reach Poland in quantity was from the port of Danzig and then through Germany to the Polish border. By the terms of the Armistice, Germany had agreed that supplies to the Polish population could be sent from Danzig. Nevertheless, it required considerable diplomacy, and some threats from the Supreme War Council, to get this provision actually carried out.

The A.R.A. already had a supply of food at Rotterdam and, in order to avoid the long delay necessary in shipping directly from America, it was decided to transship some of these stocks. Accordingly, ten ships of the "Lake" type were chartered from the United States Shipping Board (cf. page 130) and put to work transshipping these supplies to Danzig. During February and March practically all shipments to Poland were from Rotterdam to Danzig. Subsequently, direct shipments from American ports to Danzig were established. Three lake boats arrived in Danzig on February 19, and to the end of that month over 13,000.0 metric tons of American food arrived for the Poles. Although handicapped by the disorganized conditions of the railroads, the scarcity and poor condition of the rolling stock, and especially the numerous annoyances caused by the Germans, through whose territory it must pass, this food was promptly shipped from Danzig to Warsaw and other Polish cities.

The effect on the Poles of such prompt relief from America was wonderful. Food trains were all plainly marked and their passage through the country was triumphal. One prominent Pole remarked: "This is the first time in history that any government has made a promise to Poland and kept it."

The boundaries of the present Poland were not definitely determined, at this time, but for purposes of the relief work it consisted of the following six provinces or districts: the old Kingdom of Poland, the district of Białystok (Province of Grodno), Silesia, Galicia, Poznania (Posen), and West Prussia. This territory contained a population of approximately 27,000,000 people, and had normally perhaps 25,000,000 acres of land under cultivation. Normally, this territory produced about 8,000,000 tons of bread grains, about 2,500,000 tons of oats, and a similar quantity of potatoes. The production had, of course, been seriously decreased by the war. However, the preliminary investigation brought out the fact that the peasants had sufficient supplies to carry them through on a limited ration, and that it was only in the cities and industrial centers that serious suffering would ensue. It was further estimated that probably not more than 6,000,000 persons would be entirely dependent on relief. These were divided somewhat as follows: in the old Kingdom of Poland, about 2,750,000, of which 1,125,000 were in the Warsaw district; in Upper Silesia, about 1,250,000; in Galicia and Silesia approximately 1,000,000; while Posen and the remaining districts contained at least 1,000,000 more persons requiring relief.

On the basis of these estimates, a program for Poland was made up requiring about 55,000 tons of food per month. This was divided as follows: 45,000 tons of breadstuffs, 4,000 tons of beans and rice, 5,000 tons of fats, and 1,000 tons of milk. These supplies, while by no means sufficient to completely ration 6,000,000 people, did supply their cereal and fat requirements to a very large extent. Poland still had rather generous amounts of potatoes and certain vegetables with which to supplement these relief supplies.

This program, made out by the Director General of Relief in February, 1919, called for the delivery of 385,000 metric tons of supplies during the seven months from February to August, 1919. Table 89 shows that the total deliveries of supplies to Poland from all sources during the Armistice Period were 403,184.2 metric tons, exclusive of 16,700.9 metric tons of children's relief supplies from the A.R.A. which were also delivered during the Armistice Period but for reasons explained elsewhere are considered here with the Reconstruction Period.

The total deliveries of 403,184.2 metric tons during the Armistice Period were valued at $135,023,140.98. The finding of the finance for this enormous operation, when the Polish Government was unable to pay for any of it in cash, was no small undertaking. The $100,000,000.00 Congressional Appropriation for Relief in Europe (Act of February 25, 1919) was, of course, available for use in Poland, and was called upon to bear a large portion of the Polish burden. The total amount furnished to Poland from this Appropriation amounted to $69,724,829.92, and may be summarized as follows:

General relief (credit)	$63,191,316.61
Freight finance (credit)	328,607.29
Freight finance (gift)	149,063.99
Children's relief (gift)	6,055,842.03
Total	$69,724,829.92

The deliveries to the Polish Government for general relief from the Congressional Appropriation totaled 260,843.2 metric tons, worth $63,191,316.61 (Table 89). The detail of these deliveries by steamers and cargoes is given in Table 395. In addition to this, the A.R.A. financed the freight and other charges on various shipments of commodities to Poland to the total value of $544,035.40. These freight charges, as shown in Tables 143, 144, and 146, may be summarized as follows:

Organization or Source of Supplies	Total Freight
American Red Cross and other benevolent organizations	$149,063.99
U.S. Liquidation Commission	328,607.29
Joint Distribution Committee	66,364.12
Total	$544,035.40

The A.R.A. paid the freight and other charges on 2,177.6 metric tons of medical supplies furnished by the American Red Cross. The cost of transporting these supplies from New York to Danzig amounted to $148,819.42. The Administration also paid the freight on the shipments of clothing from New York for the Polish League of Women and the Russo-Carpathian Commission to the amount of $244.57, making the total transportation charges of Red Cross and other benevolent shipments of $149,063.99, as shown above. This amount was charged against the Congressional Appropriation as a gift to Poland from the United States Government.

Transportation charges on the shipment of 13,357.2 metric tons of supplies secured by Poland from the U.S. Liquidation Commission amounted to $328,607.29 which was paid out of the Congressional Appropriation, but as a credit operation with Poland. As explained elsewhere these shipments included 3,357.2 metric tons of pork products from French ports and 10,000 tons of typhus equipment shipped by rail from Coblenz to Warsaw for the American Typhus Commission in Poland.

The third item of freight charges paid by the A.R.A. includes the cost of shipping 802.8 metric tons of supplies purchased by the Jewish Joint Distribution Committee from the U.S. Liquidation Commission. The detail of this transaction is discussed on page 137 and shown in Table 146. The total cost of this movement was $66,364.12, which was later paid by the Jewish Joint Distribution Committee.

In order to supplement the supplies going to Poland during the Armistice Period, Mr. Hoover arranged for the U.S. Liquidation Commission (War Department) to sell to the Polish Government on credit 107,126.0 metric tons of surplus Army food, clothing, and other supplies, the total value of which was approximately $59,365,111.97. As shown by Table 122, the total sales to Poland by the Commission included 44,360.0 tons of foodstuffs, 13,719.0 tons of clothing, and 49,047.0 tons of other non-food commodities, among which were the 10,000.0 tons of typhus equipment and other badly needed hospital and medical supplies.

The Jewish Joint Distribution Committee was one of the relief organizations which began work in Poland immediately after the Armistice. They carried on a large portion of their work in this country on their own account, and of it we have no complete record. As explained elsewhere, this report takes into account only that portion of the Committee's work which was done in close co-operation with the Director General of Relief. The total deliveries to Poland during the Armistice Period by the J.D.C., made under the conditions outlined, amounted to 9,705.8 metric tons, with a total value of $3,412,497. Table 125 shows the detail by steamers of these deliveries. As noted above, 802.8 metric tons of the supplies delivered by the J.D.C. were purchased from the U.S. Liquidation Commission and transported by the American Relief Administration. All of the Joint Distribution Committee's deliveries to Poland were benevolent gifts.

The American Red Cross donated 4,042.6 metric tons of clothing and medical supplies to Poland, on which the value was approximately $813,800.00. As shown in Table 394, this consisted of 2,592.6 tons of medical supplies and

SUMMARY OF COMMODITY DELIVERIES FROM THE UNITED STATES TO POLAND DURING THE ARMISTICE PERIOD*

(Net Metric Tons)

Commodity	American Relief Administration	U.S. Liquidation Commission	Jewish Joint Distribution Committee	American Red Cross	Total
Flour	132,619.5	......	3,663.0	......	136,282.5
Grain	81,871.5	......	......	......	81,871.5
Rice	8,041.2	......	......	......	8,041.2
Beans and peas	8,586.3	......	......	......	8,586.3
Pork products	21,797.3	......	2,267.0	......	24,064.3
Milk	2,100.8	......	1,707.0	......	3,807.8
Cocoa	47.6	......	......	......	47.6
Sugar	1.6	......	......	......	1.6
Miscellaneous food	......	44,360.0	90.2	......	44,450.2
Soap	......	......	75.0	......	75.0
Medical supplies	......	......	525.6	2,592.6	3,118.2
Clothing, etc	5,777.4	62,766.0	1,378.0	1,450.0	71,371.4
Total	260,843.2	107,126.0	9,705.8	4,042.6	381,717.6

* Exclusive of children's relief.

1,450.0 tons of clothing. The A.R.A. transported 2,177.6 tons of these supplies as a gift to Poland.

The total deliveries from the United States to Poland during the Armistice Period, as recorded in this report, amounted to 381,717.6 metric tons, valued at $127,326,760.98. The detail of these deliveries is shown in Table 394 and related tables in the Appendix, and may be summarized by commodities as shown above.

Great Britain undertook to assist in the relief of Poland and early in February, 1919, dispatched a relief mission to Warsaw. The work of the United Kingdom, while not so extensive as that of the United States because of her own economic situation, served admirably to fill in the gaps with materials and assistance which the United States could not supply. The total supplies furnished by the United Kingdom during the Armistice Period, according to reports to the Director General of Relief, amounted to 21,462.0 metric tons, valued at approximately $6,304,620. In addition to these supplies furnished from the British Relief Credits, the United Kingdom also undertook to finance on credit the freight and insurance charges on some 35,000.0 tons of the supplies sold to Poland by the U.S. Liquidation Commission. These supplies, located in French ports, could scarcely have been made available for consumption in Poland except for this British assistance. The total freight and other charges on this movement amounted to $1,389,920, which was also furnished to Poland on credit.

The small amounts of clothing for use by the Polish League of Women and the Russo-Carpathian Commission (Table 89, page 226) were benevolent donations from these organizations, for which the A.R.A. provided transportation from the United States.

The commodities furnished to Poland by Great Britain are shown in Table 394, and by steamers, so far as this information is available, in Table 396. The total deliveries may be summarized as follows:

DELIVERIES TO POLAND BY UNITED KINGDOM DURING THE ARMISTICE PERIOD

(Metric Tons)

Commodity	Total
Flour	3,239.0
Grain (including oats and seed)	5,813.0
Beans and peas	1,362.0
Pork products	1,255.0
Miscellaneous food (Army biscuits, etc.)	541.0
Soap	568.0
Medical supplies	370.0
Clothing	1,054.0
Miscellaneous and railroad equipment	7,260.0
Total	21,462.0

The total relief deliveries to Poland during the Armistice Period, as accounted for in this report, may be summarized as follows:

Delivered on credit	$130,579,575.87
Benevolence	4,443,565.11
Total	$135,023,140.98

TABLE 89

SUMMARY OF TOTAL RELIEF DELIVERIES TO POLAND

(For detail see Table 394)

Operation	Total Metric Tons	Total Value
Armistice Period		
American Relief Administration (Congressional Appropriation)	260,843.2	$ 63,191,316.61
American Relief Administration (freight finance)	......	544,035.40
U.S. Liquidation Commission	107,126.0	59,365,111.97
Jewish Joint Distribution Committee	9,705.8	3,412,497.00
American Red Cross	4,042.6	813,800.00
Total from United States	381,717.6	$127,326,760.98
United Kingdom (commodities)	21,462.0	$ 6,304,620.00
United Kingdom (freight finance)	......	1,389,920.00
Polish League of Women	4.1	1,640.00
Russo-Carpathian Commission	.5	200.00
Total other than United States	21,466.6	$ 7,696,380.00
Total, Armistice Period	403,184.2	$135,023,140.98
Reconstruction Period		
American Relief Administration (Congressional Appropriation)	16,700.9	$ 6,055,842.03
European Children's Fund	59,242.5	16,769,322.10
Polish Government donation	44,569.9	6,702,221.02
Other Polish donations	1,040.9	40,094.51
Jewish Joint Distribution Committee	537.0	273,555.00
Total children's relief	122,091.2	$ 29,841,034.66
A.R.A. Warehouses (food drafts and bulk sales)	7,839.5	$ 1,675,087.41
A.R.A. Warehouses (Danzig sale to Polish Government)	7,720.3	864,562.40
Polish Government donation (adult relief)	7,072.7	917,059.24
The Commonwealth Fund (intelligentsia clothing)	30.4	57,532.49
American Friends Service Committee	633.3	30,291.26
U.S. Grain Corporation (Act of Congress, March 30, 1920)	202,564.0	24,353,590.97
United Kingdom (freight finance)	......	8,102,558.32
Total other than children's relief	225,861.2	$ 36,000,682.09
Total, Reconstruction Period	347,951.4	$ 65,841,716.75
Grand total relief deliveries	751,135.6	$200,864,857.73

RECONSTRUCTION PERIOD

CHILDREN'S RELIEF

From this brief description of the food condition in Poland, it may well be imagined that the conditions for growing children were very bad. Rickets, scurvy, and tuberculosis ran riot. Where municipal soup kitchens were maintained, no especial attention could be paid to the needs of children, because the proper supplies were not available. Here, in common with other devastated countries, the children more than the adults showed the effects of undernourishment. Their faces reflected the haunted look of unsatisfied hunger, they refused to play, or even to smile, but simply sat quietly, showing no interest in anything.

It was obvious that such conditions did not augur well for the future of Poland, nor of Europe. For these reasons, Mr. Hoover arranged to supply certain kinds of food to these children. The first program for the Polish children's relief was arranged the latter part of March, 1919, and the first supplies arrived early in April. This program consisted of 2,506.0 tons of food, worth about $760,000, and capable of furnishing one meal a day to 175,000 children for three months. After the work was well organized in the field, it was found that the original program was by no means sufficient to take care of the requirements; consequently, the second program, consisting of 6,230.0 tons of food, was arranged. The Polish Government had become so impressed with this work that it agreed to contribute a similar amount of food from the government supplies. By the middle of July, 500,000 Polish children were receiving one meal a day from the child welfare kitchens.

These two programs were regarded as sufficient to carry the work to the end of August. Before this time the American Relief Administration European Children's Fund had been organized to carry on this work, after the withdrawal of other relief from Europe. A third program was therefore prepared, which, with the aid given by the Polish Government, it was expected would carry the work to the end of 1919.

The detail of these three programs, as originally arranged for Poland, is given in the following table:

Children's Relief Programs for Poland

(Metric Tons)

Commodity	First	Second	Third	Total
Flour	850	....	480*	1,330
Rice	400	1,670	320*	2,390
Beans and peas	150	1,170	320*	1,640
Pork	...	750	160*	910
Milk	640	1,450	1,680	3,770
Sugar	203	750	360	1,313
Cocoa	228	440	280	948
Cod liver oil	20	...	...	20
Prunes	15	...	...	15
Total	2,506	6,230	3,600	12,336

* To be furnished by the Polish Government.

Polish Government co-operation.—From the beginning, the Polish Government took a deep interest in the children's relief work. On March 23, 1919, at a conference between the Polish premier, M. Paderewski, and A.R.A. officials, arrangements were made for the formation of the Central Children's Relief Committee (Centralny Komitet Pomocy Dzieciom), of which Madame Paderewski accepted the presidency. This committee, which functioned under the general direction of the Ministry of Health, was later (June, 1919) increased in size and the name changed to the National Children's Committee (Panstwowy Komitet Pomocy Dzieciom). Finally, in 1920, at the request of the Polish people, a statute was passed designating this the Polish-American Children's Relief Committee, often referred to in the relief work as the P.A.K.P.D. from the initials of its Polish name (Polsko-Amerykanski Komitet Pomocy Dzieciom).

This committee played a most important part in the extensive children's relief work in Poland. They operated a complete system of interior administration, distribution, and control over all supplies received for children's relief. A thorough and regular system of inspection and control was carried out over each unit of the organization, including regional warehouses, regional inspection offices, district committees, subcommittee kitchens, and institutions. The various district and local committees were entirely nonpartisan in character, including Christians and Jews, representatives of the various nationalities and social classes. The faithful work of this organization deserves the very greatest praise.

Children of the Zydaczow Orphan Asylum, Poland, having Easter dinner under supervision of Catholic Sisters.

The selection of children to be fed was left to local committees of which one member, at least, had to be a physician. The principle that "food was to go only to the neediest children" was so thoroughly impressed upon the committee and the public that the pressure of public opinion was almost sufficient to insure that the children who most needed the food received it.

Table 89 shows that the total deliveries for children's relief in Poland from the Congressional Appropriation amounted to 16,700.9 metric tons, valued at $6,055,842.03. This quantity, nearly 4,400.0 tons more than the original programs, fell far short of the terrible needs in this country. The E.C.F., which took over the distribution of these supplies on August 1, 1919, also made vast contributions to the relief program. The E.C.F. furnished a total of 59,242.5 metric tons of relief supplies for Poland, at a total cost of $16,769,322.10. To this, the Polish Government itself donated commodities to the extent of 44,569.9 metric tons, worth $6,702,221.02. Various provincial and city governments made further donations of commodities to the extent of 1,040.9 tons, worth $40,094.51, while

One of the Jewish milk stations in Poland.

the J.D.C. contributed 537.0 tons of milk and soap, worth $273,555.00.

As shown in Table 89, the total commodities used for children's relief in Poland from 1919 to the close of operations in May, 1922, amounted to 122,091.2 metric tons, valued at $29,841,034.66. Vast as was this program of public and private charity, it was barely enough to mitigate the most severe suffering.

In the first month of child feeding (May, 1919), approximately 125,000 children were on the rationing list. This number rapidly increased, exceeding the 1,000,000 mark in December, 1919, and reaching its peak in May, 1920, when 1,315,500 children were receiving one meal a day. At this time there were 7,650 feeding stations operating in Poland, of which 6,289 were community kitchens and 1,361 were in children's institutions. Of the total number, 1,492 were operated exclusively for Jewish children.

After May, 1920, conditions improved and the number being fed was reduced to 327,000, but the prolongations of post-war conditions and the Bolshevist invasion made it necessary again to increase the program to 1,246,900 by April, 1921. From then on, the number of children admitted to feeding was gradually reduced, until June, 1922, when all feeding in Poland by the E.C.F. was discontinued. It is estimated that approximately 640,000,000 meals were provided during the thirty-eight months in which child-feeding work was carried on.

The Bolshevist offensive against Poland, which began in May, 1920, imposed a severe strain on the field organization of the child-relief work. During the invasion it was necessary to evacuate the relief supplies in advance of the Bolshevist army. At the beginning of the invasion supplies from the regional warehouses at Minsk, Vilna, Białystok, Brest, Chelm, Kowel, Lwów (Lemberg) were moved to a special depot at Modlin. This evacuation had no sooner been completed than the supplies had to be moved again to Thorn and Danzig. Thorn itself was threatened, and the supplies stored there had to be moved a third time to Danzig. Stocks from Warsaw and Lemberg were also evacuated to Działoszice and Krakow near the Czechoslovakian border. In August, 1920, when the final attack of the Bolshevists was repulsed, 6 of the 11 regional warehouses, 6 of the 15 regional offices, and 93 of the 207 district offices were in the hands of the invading army. Due to the heroic work of both Polish and American members of the relief organization, the loss of child-feeding supplies was negligible. However, the occupation of nearly one-half of Poland and the wanton destruction of food and other supplies set back the reconstruction work in Poland by nearly a year's time. This made it necessary for the relief organization to redouble its efforts in the winter of 1920–1921, and introduced the further problem of caring for Russian and Polish refugees (cf. pages 111–13).

Reference has already been made to the whole-hearted way in which the Polish people and the Polish Government co-operated in this work of child relief. The total contributions of commodities by the national and local Polish governments amounted to 45,610.8 metric tons, valued at $6,742,315.53 (Table 89). But in addition to this, the contributions of services and other assistance made the conduct of this work possible. It is impossible to make other than a rough approximation of the value of these intangible services. But the following tabulation, made by men intimately connected with the Polish work, will serve to give some indication of the extent of the Polish co-operation.

Polish Contributions to Child Relief
1919 to 1922

Contribution	Value
Rail transportation	$ 1,127,627.00
Storage and handling	292,983.00
Administrative expenses	129,719.00
Private and local donations	1,632,892.00
Motor transportation	46,620.00
Telegraph facilities	7,016.00
Volunteer services (14,654 workers)	1,343,370.00
Total services	$ 4,580,227.00
Commodities donated	6,742,315.53
Total*	$11,322,542.53

* In addition to the above, the Polish Government donated railway and transportation facilities for forwarding relief supplies to Russia, with an estimated value of $90,000.

Before the E.C.F. withdrew from Poland in June, 1922, the Polish Government had adopted a plan for a permanent national organization to take charge of the development of child welfare work. Both the E.C.F. and the American Red Cross co-operated with the Polish Government in getting this work established on a permanent basis.

Many other foreign charitable organizations assisted in the children's relief work in Poland. The most important of these was the Jewish Joint Distribution Committee, which, in addition to the general relief during the Armistice Period discussed above, made important contributions of commodities and money for this work. Table 89 shows a contribution to the E.C.F. of 537.0 tons of milk and soap, with a value of $273,555.00, which was in addition to important distribution of commodities on their own account, some of which are referred to under Special Programs (page 105) and in the account of the work of the J.D.C. (pages 56–58).

Jewish war orphans of Sambor, Poland, proudly displaying clothing outfits received from the A.R.A.

Other Relief Work during Reconstruction Period

Food drafts and bulk sales from the American Relief Administration Warehouses (A.R.A.W) in Poland formed an important part of the food relief to that country. Table 89 shows the total food drafts and bulk sales by the A.R.A.W. in Poland as 7,839.5 metric tons, valued at $1,675,087.41. These were divided as follows:

	Metric Tons	Total Value
Food drafts	1,571.3	$ 624,910.00
Bulk sales	6,268.2	1,050,177.44
Total	7,839.5	$1,675,087.44

The total number of food drafts of all sizes amounted to 48,643 (Table 400). These represented chiefly purchases by relatives and friends of Polish people in the United States. Some purchases by charitable organizations, such as the $175,000 from the Commonwealth Fund for food drafts in Poland, were also included.

Bulk sales were made chiefly to other charitable organizations, which used this method of obtaining supplies rather than attempting to import them with their own organizations. Of the $401,532.38 supplied for Poland by the

CHART XI

Total Number Children and Nursing Mothers Fed, Month by Month, from Beginning of Operations to August 1, 1922 (cf. Table 410)

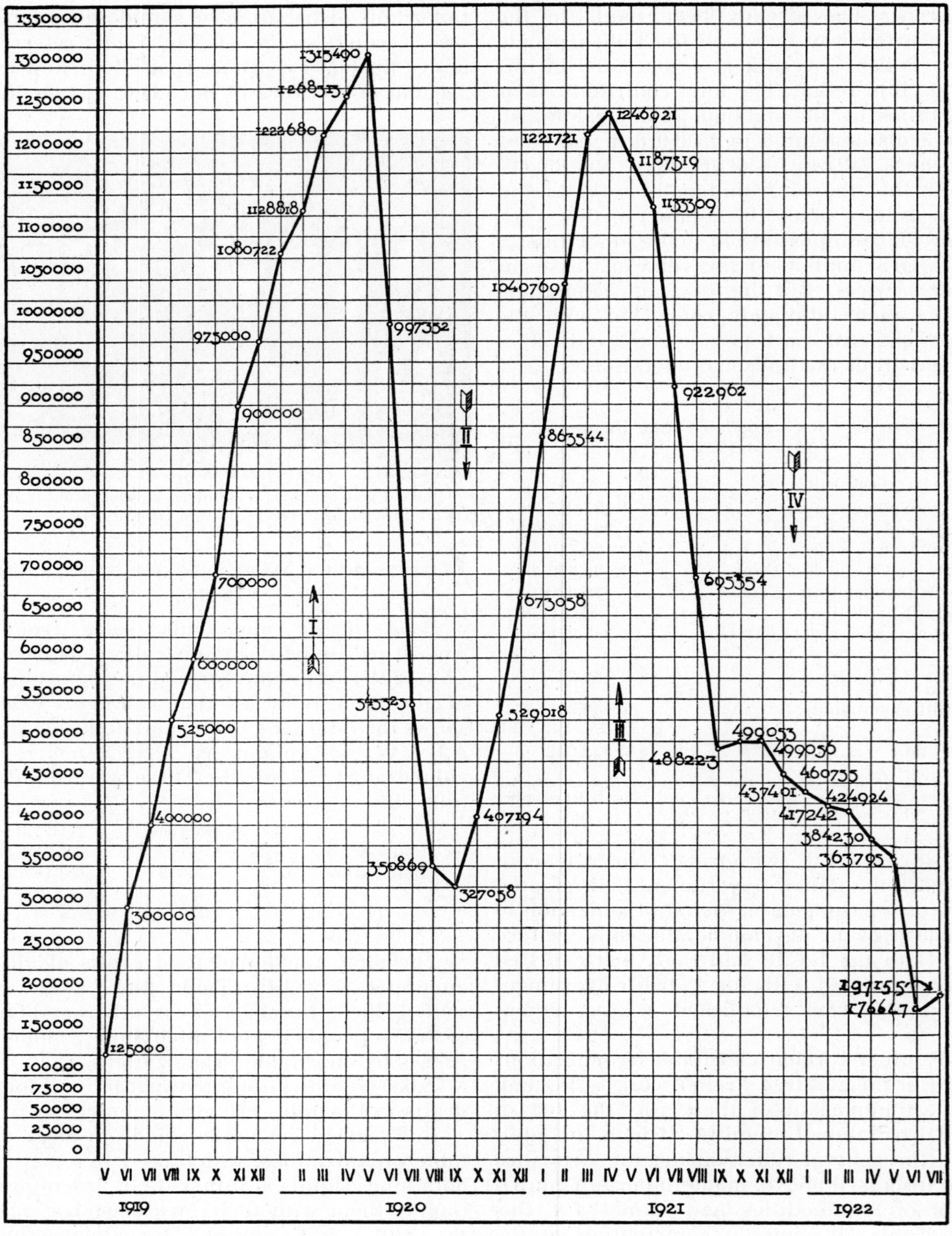

—I— *Period of Organization*

—II— *Bolshevik Invasion*

—III— *Reorganization after Bolshevik Invasion*

—IV— *Systematic Reduction following Improvement in General Economic Situation*

Commonwealth Fund, a total of $168,999.89 (excluding food drafts and clothing) was used for the purchase of bulk food from the A.R.A.W. for intelligentsia feeding. The Jewish Joint Distribution Committee also expended $50,000 for food relief in Poland as discussed under Special Program. This food was purchased from the A.R.A. Warehouses. Another $50,000 worth of food was purchased from the A.R.A.W. for Poland by the American Friends Service Committee. Other large sums were used in bulk food purchases by the World's Student Christian Federation, and for refugee relief in Poland after the Bolshevist invasion. These purchases are all discussed under Special Programs.

Some bulk sales of food were also made to the Polish Government to cover certain immediate needs. The most important sale of this nature is that of 7,720.3 metric tons by the A.R.A.W. at Danzig. Of the flour donated by the Polish Government for children's relief (Table 404), there was a total of 7,072.7 metric tons, valued at $917,059.24, which was later transferred for use as adult relief.

Other items of relief deliveries shown in Table 394 include 30.4 tons of clothing for Polish intelligentsia, distributed through money supplied by the Commonwealth Fund. The detail of this distribution, amounting to $57,532.49, has been discussed under the Commonwealth Fund. The transaction with the American Friends Service Committee, involving the delivery of 633.3 metric tons of cottonseed meal to Poland, has also been discussed elsewhere.

The details of all arrivals of relief supplies for child feeding, A.R.A.W. operations, and special programs in Poland are given in Tables 398–404. The distribution of all child-feeding supplies through the regional warehouses to the ultimate feeding stations, as shown by the receipts, is given in Tables 407–490.

Tables 408 and 409 give the details of the food draft and bulk sale deliveries to Poland.

U.S. Grain Corporation

The plight of Poland in the spring of 1920 had much to do with the passage of the Act of Congress of March 30, 1920, which authorized the United States Grain Corporation to sell up to 5,000,000 barrels of flour to European governments for cash or on credit in order to relieve the acute food shortage (page 113). Under this authorization and that contained in the letter from President Wilson of November 14, 1919, the Grain Corporation sold to Poland 2,278,429 barrels of wheat flour (202,564.0 metric tons) for $24,353,590.97, for which Polish notes were accepted and turned over to the United States Treasury. The Polish Government had no means of providing for the transportation of this flour from American ports and the United Kingdom undertook to provide the freight and other costs connected with this movement. The total value of the freight finance advanced to Poland on credit by the United Kingdom in connection with this transaction was approximately $8,102,558.32 (Table 89).

This brief account of the major relief activities for Poland shows that a total of 225,861.2 metric tons, valued at $36,000,682.09, was delivered during the Reconstruction Period outside of the children's relief work. Taking these two activities together gives a total for the entire Reconstruction Period of 347,951.4 metric tons, worth $65,841,716.75. The major portion of this vast program was either furnished to Poland on credit or given as benevolence. That it has had an enormous influence upon the later development of Poland, and that this assistance was greatly appreciated by the Polish people is clear from innumerable letters and communications from the Polish people and the government.

The human interest connected with this story of tons and dollars has been clearly portrayed by H. H. Fisher in his book on *America and the New Poland*,[1] to which the reader is referred for further details of this effort to assist a struggling and courageous nation in a period of dire distress.

Table 89 shows that the total relief deliveries accounted for in this report, including both the Armistice and the Reconstruction Periods, amounted to 751,135.6 metric tons, valued at the enormous sum of $200,864,857.73. On the basis of method on which these supplies were furnished to Poland, this total may be divided approximately as follows:

Sold for cash	$ 8,523,937.17
Delivered on credit	163,035,725.16
Benevolence	29,305,195.40
Total	$200,864,857.73

[1] Macmillan Company, New York, 1928. 403 pages.

ROUMANIA

(Appendix Tables 491–495)

ARMISTICE PERIOD

Conditions in Roumania

Roumania entered the list of belligerents in the World War at the end of August, 1916. During the fall and early winter of that year the Austro-Germans succeeded in occupying a large part of the country. On December 6, 1916, the capital, Bucharest, was captured and the government moved to Jassy. At the close of the 1916 campaign, the Austro-Germans occupied Wallachia and the Bulgarians occupied the Dobrudja. Behind the Roumanian army, in Moldavia, were vast numbers of Roumanian and Russian refugees. The collapse of Russia in 1917 left Roumania at the mercy of the Central Powers, and in May, 1918, she was obliged to sign the onerous Treaty of Bucharest. Germany remained master of the country until a few weeks before the Armistice of 1918.

In the areas occupied by the Germans all kinds of supplies were extorted from the inhabitants. In the territory retained by the Roumanians the supplies were exhausted because of the excessive population, including, besides the native population, the Roumanian refugees, the Roumanian army, part of the Russian army, and Russian refugees. Transportation was entirely disorganized, and the little rolling stock not taken by the enemy was in a deplorable condition.

With the signing of the Armistice, Roumania laid claim to large areas outside her old domain. In 1914, Roumania consisted of the provinces of Moldavia, Grand Wallachia, Oltenia, Dobrudja, and the department of Durostor. The latter province, including Caliacra, was acquired from Bulgaria during the Balkan War (Treaty of Bucharest, August, 1913). Old Roumania contained 53,489 square miles and had a population of approximately 7,500,000. The present Roumania contains, in addition, the province of Bukovina from Austria, a portion of the Banat and Transylvania from Hungary, and Bessarabia from Russia. This newly added territory more than doubled the area of former Roumania, and added some 8,000,000 to its population.

The following table gives approximate areas and estimated population of the principal provinces at the time of the Armistice.

Approximate Area and Population of Roumania by Provinces

Provinces	Area in Square Miles	Population
Moldavia	15,200	2,145,464
Grand Wallachia	22,000	3,298,394
Oltenia	10,080	1,413,897
Dobrudja	3,240	381,306
Durostor and Caliacra	2,969	273,090
Total old Roumania	53,489	7,512,151
Banat and Transylvania	35,000	5,000,000
Bukovina	4,033	818,328
Bessarabia	17,143	2,686,600
Total present Roumania	109,665	16,017,079

The population of Roumania is essentially agricultural. Of the 7,500,000 people in old Roumania, only about 1,500,000 lived in cities. Only two classes of society existed: one, the small capitalistic ruling class; the other, a large peasant class with a very small income and a very low standard of living. Little in the way of organized charitable relief had ever been attempted by the upper class and if it had not been for the Allied missions it is unlikely that any adequate relief for the suffering peasants would have been undertaken. It should be said that King Ferdinand and particularly Queen Marie always took the greatest interest in the relief of their people. They worked honestly and tirelessly to improve the condition of the country.

The normal annual consumption of cereals in old Roumania, including seed, amounted to about 4,000,000 tons. The peasants lived largely upon corn, supplemented by some dairy and meat products. Roumania was thus able to export from 1,500,000 to 2,500,000 tons of cereals each year. Nearly one-half of this was wheat. Prior to the war, Roumania ranked sixth among the nations in the export of wheat, and second in the export of corn.

For the three years 1916, 1917, and 1918, the combined grain crop amounted to less than 12,000,000 tons. Of this, the Central Powers are known to have exported 2,540,000 tons. At least 1,000,000 tons would be needed for seed, leaving at best but 8,500,000 tons for the support of the country for the three years. Their normal consumption, during these three years, would amount to at least 11,000,000 tons. There was thus a mean yearly deficit of nearly 900,000 tons, or almost 25 per cent of their requirement.

The live stock presented even a more serious problem. A reduction of more than 80 per cent in the number of domestic animals in old Roumania in 1919 compared with 1916 shows something of the destitution of the country. Conditions in Transylvania were almost as bad as in old Roumania. These facts, together with the appalling shortage of agricultural implements, made the situation very serious. In many places, plows and other implements were totally lacking, and the peasants were forced to cultivate the land with hoes. From such cultivation, it did not seem that much could be expected for the 1919 harvest. The work of the Allied missions in bringing in seed and agricultural implements did much toward increasing the Roumanian crops in that year.

At the time of the Armistice, the Roumanians were among the most destitute peoples in Europe. In many places the peasants had eaten all their seed and were forced to subsist on grass, leaves, and roots. They were without shoes or stockings, and had only patched and ragged clothing.

Dr. A. E. Taylor, who made several trips to Roumania to determine the needs of the people, has the following to say regarding the effect of the German occupation on the food supply:

> . . . The Germans established a definite system of controlled agriculture. Out of the crop a ration of 300–350 grammes of native grain per person per day was allowed, a seed ration set aside and all other grain confiscated. More than this, for the crop of 1917 and 1918, the Germans decided exactly what acreage should be planted to the different grains, and in particular forbade the planting of clover and lucerne seed, the entire stock of which was shipped to Germany. In addition, each German soldier was permitted, or indeed instructed, to ship home a five-kilo food parcel per week. This came in part out of the 350 gramme ration. All animal products, meats, oils and poultry products were reserved to the Central Powers. This placed the Roumanians theoretically on vegetarianism. . . . When the Roumanians recovered the rule of their country in November, 1918, they faced a greater relative and absolute depletion of the food production of the country than occurred in any other nation at war. . . .

In addition, the Germans had requistioned agricultural equipment, work animals, and household equipment, until the Roumanian peasant had little left to work with.

Under such conditions there could be no question of the urgent need of relief. From the preliminary survey in January, 1919, the first program for the relief of Roumania was made out. It consisted of 20,000.0 tons of breadstuffs, and 500.0 tons of milk per month. The fulfilment of this program was shared between England, Canada, and the United States. By these deliveries the most serious deficiencies were met.

General Relief

Early in January, 1919, the Director General of Relief arranged for the British authorities to undertake a portion of the Roumanian relief and as far as possible to send supplies from Australia. At the same time, two cargoes of flour then on passage from American army stocks in the United States were directed to Constanza. The first of these cargoes arrived at the end of January, and the second by the middle of February. The British also sent in two cargoes of flour in February. The 27,000 tons of flour thus delivered to Roumania before the first of March saved untold suffering in the Dobrudja and along the Danube.

Relief from the United States.—In order to finance the delivering of supplies from the United States, Mr. Hoover arranged for Roumania to secure a direct loan from the United States Treasury, under the authority granted by Congress in connection with the Allied countries. Under this authority the American Relief Administration delivered a total of 102,942.5 metric tons of foodstuffs, with a total value of $23,438,339.29 (Table 90). The detail of these deliveries by steamers and commodities is given in Table 492. These supplies were for the most part delivered at the Roumanian ports of Constanza, Galatz, and Braila. The Roumanians had some shipping, and Mr. Hoover arranged for them to secure two cargoes ("Bucegi," I and "Regele Carol") from A.R.A. stocks at Constantinople and Derindje. He also arranged for them to send three small vessels to Marseilles and to transport certain supplies which the American Relief Administration had purchased from the U.S. Liquidation Commission. The total deliveries direct to Roumania from United States ports amounted to 93,655.7 metric tons. All of the supplies delivered by the A.R.A. were receipted for by Roumanian Government officials. The internal distribution was taken care of by the Roumanian Government but under general supervision of the A.R.A., who saw to it that the supplies reached the people in distress. No detail of the internal distribution of these supplies is available.

As in the case of other countries seriously needing relief, arrangements were made by which the U.S. Liquidation Commission sold surplus United States Army stocks to Roumania on credit. Table 90 shows the total of these sales to be 22,331.0 metric tons, worth $13,012,689. Of this amount, 17,596.0 tons were food supplies, 4,500.0 tons were clothing, and 235.0 tons were miscellaneous non-foods (Table 122).

The Jewish Joint Distribution Committee made certain deliveries of commodities for Roumanian relief in co-operation with the Director General of Relief. The total of these deliveries, according to reports received, amounted to 382.0 metric tons of food, clothing, and soap, valued at $256,000. The detail of these shipments is shown in Table 124.

The total deliveries to Roumania in the Armistice Period from all American sources working in co-operation with the Director General of Relief amounted to 125,655.5 metric tons, worth $36,707,028.29.

Relief from the British Empire.—The United Kingdom assumed a relatively large responsibility for Roumanian relief. Early in 1919, in response to the reports of the serious food conditions in that country, the United Kingdom directed two cargoes of flour to Constanza. These two cargoes were unloaded early in February and were among the first relief cargoes to be actually distributed to any of the relief territories. During April, May, and June, 1919, the United Kingdom sent eight other cargoes to Roumania. These cargoes consisted chiefly of wheat and flour from Australia and from Indian ports. The total deliveries by the United Kingdom amounted to 59,248.0 metric tons, with a total value of approximately $10,004,628. Of this amount, 7,000.0 tons were non-food material, chiefly railroad supplies, which were so badly needed in Roumania.

The detail of these deliveries by the United Kingdom is given in Table 493. Included in these supplies were 300.0 tons of meats and 5,240.0 tons of miscellaneous foods from British army stocks in Eastern Europe.

In addition to the delivery of these commodities, the United Kingdom financed the freight and other charges on a large portion of the commodities sold to Roumania by the U.S. Liquidation Commission. The expenditures for this purpose amounted to approximately $21,420, making the total contribution to Roumanian relief by the United Kingdom $10,026,048. This relief was extended on a credit basis and paid for from the British Relief Credit.

In March, 1919, Canada agreed to loan Roumania the sum of $5,000,000 with which to purchase Canadian food supplies. To the end of August, 1919, 38,184.0 metric tons had been shipped from Canada. The value of these commodities was approximately $3,836,600. The supplies from Canada consisted of wheat and wheat flour, and a partial cargo of agricultural implements, estimated at about 4,100.0 tons. Newfoundland also sent one cargo of fish, with a value of $1,566,040. The detail of these shipments is given in Table 493.

The total relief sent to Roumania by the British Empire during the Armistice Period amounted to 99,788.0 metric tons, with a total value of $15,428,688.

The combined relief from the United States and the British Empire during the Armistice Period, as accounted for in this report, amounted to 225,443.5 metric tons, valued at $52,135,716.29.

Other relief for Roumania.—Aside from Great Britain, none of the other Allied countries assisted in the relief of Roumania. The Director General of Relief, adopting the same principles used with the other relief territories, made every effort to re-establish trade with the neighboring states. Early in 1919, it was seen that the best solution of the Roumanian food situation was the shipment of supplies from the Banat region, a part of which was already occupied by Roumania with the remainder claimed by Jugoslavia. The chief difficulty here was the lack of transportation facilities. Another difficulty was the arrangement of satisfactory payment. The peasants, who held the surplus supplies of the Banat, were unwilling to part with them in return for the depreciated currency. What they wanted in return for their food was shoes, clothing, and implements. None of these were available. Many efforts were made to promote the exchange of Roumanian salt, petroleum, and other products for food from Serbia. Owing to friction between the two nations and the difficulties of transportation, only partial success attended these efforts. No satisfactory record has been obtained as to the amount of commodities received by Roumania through these exchanges, but it is known that several thousand tons of food were actually secured.

In March, Mr. Hoover proposed a Roumanian Commission for Food and Credit, similar to those described for other countries. By these and other means, very definite steps were taken to re-establish Roumanian trade and to place the country upon a stable commercial basis.

It should, of course, be borne in mind that here, as in most of the other European countries, large quantities of materials and other forms of relief were supplied by other organizations not necessarily co-ordinated with the Director General of Relief. In Roumania, for example, the American Red Cross and the British Red Cross distributed large quantities of food and clothing, in addition to the medical and hospital relief. The same was true of many other organizations which did not report through the office of the Director General of Relief, and hence are not included here.

RECONSTRUCTION PERIOD

Children's Relief

In many regions the diet almost exclusively of corn and the lack of dairy products had resulted in numerous cases of pellagra. Everywhere evidence of malnutrition in children was

TABLE 90

Summary of Total Relief Deliveries to Roumania

(For detail see Table 491)

Operation	Total Metric Tons	Total Value
Armistice Period		
American Relief Administration (U.S. Treasury Loan)	102,942.5	$23,438,339.29
U.S. Liquidation Commission	22,331.0	13,012,689.00
Jewish Joint Distribution Committee	382.0	256,000.00
Total from United States	125,655.5	$36,707,028.29
United Kingdom (commodities)	59,248.0	$10,004,628.00
United Kingdom (freight finance)	....	21,420.00
Canada	38,184.0	3,836,600.00
Newfoundland	2,356.0	1,566,040.00
Total from British Empire	99,788.0	$15,428,688.00
Total, Armistice Period	225,443.5	$52,135,716.29
Reconstruction Period		
American Relief Administration (Congressional Appropriation)	1,432.3	$ 477,272.76
Roumanian Government donation	2,327.0	1,024,322.26
Total children's relief	3,759.3	$ 1,501,595.02
Grand total relief deliveries	229,202.8	$53,637,311.31

to be found and reports showed that thousands had died from lack of nourishment.

The first report indicated that in Wallachia there were 60,000 children in need of assistance, while in Moldavia there were 40,000 more, with large numbers in the Dobrudja.

Mr. Hoover's plan for the relief of the children in Roumania met with the hearty response of the Queen. Owing to her tireless efforts, this movement was organized on a sound basis. An influential committee was formed, known as the Roumanian Children's Relief Association. The Queen secured the co-operation of the Roumanian Government which appropriated currency for local expenses and transportation. She also obtained their promise to supplement the American children's relief supplies with large quantities of foodstuffs. The Queen also issued a proclamation requesting each family to refrain from one meal per month and to contribute the proceeds to the relief of the suffering children.

The first program for children's relief in Roumania contemplated feeding about 70,000 children for three months. The second program contained supplies for 200,000 children. Supplies to cover both of these programs were shipped from America, but, owing to the rapid recovery of the country, a portion of these supplies was diverted to other destinations.

Many difficulties had to be overcome in the distribution of these children's relief supplies in Roumania. In the first place, the total disorganization of the railroad system rendered it difficult to get the supplies away from the ports. At the time of the Armistice, Roumania had only 216 locomotives left in the country. Of these, only 62 were in actual operation in April, 1919. The others could not be used because the copper, tin, nickel, etc., needed for their repair could not be obtained.

Other difficulties were encountered in securing transportation from rail distributing points to small places. The peasants were not accustomed to gifts or benevolence in any form and were suspicious. They could not understand that Americans were coming to their country to help them in their difficulty without the expectation of any return. A report, dated June 10, 1919, from Colonel W. N. Haskell, in charge of the Roumanian relief work says:

> . . . . The people in the country have no notion of charity and will not furnish ox-teams, kettles, wood, or even axes to chop the wood for the establishment of canteens in their own villages to feed their own children. It is a most remarkable country. . . . .

In one way or another, these difficulties were overcome and by July, 1919, there were 530 canteens in operation, giving one meal a day to over 200,000 undernourished children. The food delivered for the relief of the Roumanian children amounted to 1,432.3 tons, valued at $477,272.76. These supplies were paid for from the Congressional Appropriation for Relief and were given to the Roumanian people without any obligation on the part of Roumania toward the United States. The detail of the arrivals of supplies for child feeding is shown by steamers and commodities in Table 494, while the detail of the internal deliveries is given in Table 495.

Central warehouses for child-feeding supplies were established at Constanza, Braila, and Bucharest, from which distribution was made to interior points. All food sent to subcommittees was convoyed by an officer of the Roumanian army. He was held strictly responsible to the A.R.A. officials for each kilo turned over to him, and was required to return receipts signed jointly by the prefect of the district and the subcommittee for child feeding. All district committees were required to account for receipts and issues weekly. One meal of approximately 750 calories was given to each child daily except Sunday.

Roumanian Government co-operation.—As indicated above, the Queen had been able to secure the co-operation of the Roumanian Government in this work, and they made very substantial contributions of commodities for the child-feeding work. Table 90 shows the total commodity donation by the government as 2,327.0 metric tons, worth $1,024,322.26. This large contribution was made possible because Roumania is a surplus food-producing area, and with the harvest of 1919, meager though it was, conditions in the country improved very greatly.

In addition to these commodity donations, the Roumanian Government paid for transporting and warehousing the supplies, and local committees carried on the work of the canteens. The following is an estimate of the value of these services:

Roumanian Contributions to Child Feeding

Transportation and warehousing	$ 25,648.00
Administrative expenses	15,000.00
Local donations (towns and districts)	151,000.00
Donation from Princess Cantacuzene	378.00
Volunteer services (3,000 workers)	90,000.00
Total	$ 282,026.00
Commodity donations	1,024,322.26
Grand total	$1,306,348.26

The details of the commodities used in Roumanian child feeding may be summarized as follows:

Roumanian Children's Relief
May to November, 1919
(*Metric Tons*)

Commodities	American Relief Administration	Roumanian Government	Total
Flour	250.0	492.0	742.0
Rice	170.0	.....	170.0
Beans and peas	130.0	492.0	622.0
Pork products	70.0	161.0	231.0
Milk	185.0	1,090.0	1,275.0
Cocoa	220.9	.....	220.9
Sugar	406.4	.....	406.4
Miscellaneous food	.....	92.0	92.0
Total	1,432.3	2,327.0	3,759.3

Owing to the fact that food conditions improved greatly in Roumania after the 1919 harvest and that imported food was needed so much more in other countries, it was decided to discontinue child-feeding work in Roumania after November, 1919. The European Children's Fund took over the work of distributing children's relief in August, 1919, but they made no further contributions of commodities beyond the shipments made during the Armistice Period, paid for out of the Congressional Appropriation as a gift to Roumanian children. During the seven months of the child-feeding work in Roumania supplies for approximately 24,515,000 meals were distributed, which prevented great suffering among these children.

As shown in Table 90, the total relief deliveries to Roumania during the Armistice and the Reconstruction Periods, as accounted for in this report, amounted to 229,202.8 metric tons, valued at $53,637,311.31. Considering the basis on which this relief was furnished to Roumania, the total may be divided as follows:

Sold for cash	$ 1,024,322.26
Delivered on credit	51,879,716.29
Benevolence	733,272.76
Total	$53,637,311.31

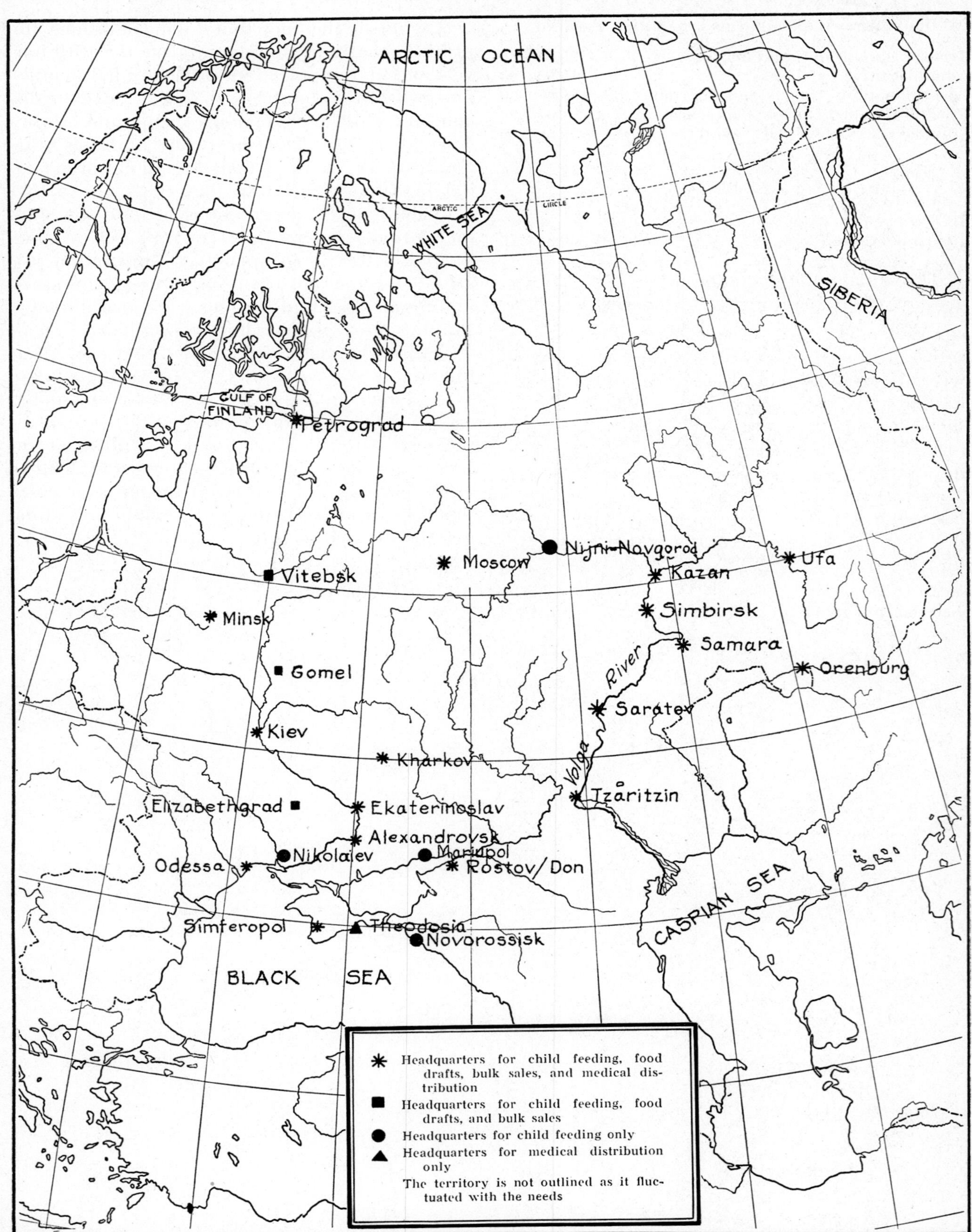

Map of Russia showing principal warehouses, feeding and distributing centers.

RUSSIA

ARMISTICE PERIOD

Conditions in Russia

Relief deliveries to Russia, or to different portions of that great country, were made at various times and for various reasons between 1919 and 1924. By far the most important of these operations was the relief furnished to Soviet Russia during the terrible famine which afflicted that country in 1922 and 1923. The earlier deliveries, some of them relatively large and important, were all made during the Armistice Period or immediately thereafter. Table 91 summarizes the several Russian relief operations considered in this report and shows that the total deliveries for that account amounted to 768,159.9 metric tons, valued at $78,305,318.49. This is by no means all of the relief supplied to Russia during this period. As explained in other sections of this report, such organizations as the Jewish Joint Distribution Committee, the American Red Cross, the American Friends Service Committee, and a great many other organizations were furnishing food and medical relief to Russia on their own responsibility—relief which is not reported in the present volume.

TABLE 91

Summary of Total Relief Deliveries to Russia, 1919–1924

(For detail see Table 496)

Accounts	Total Metric Tons	Total Value
Northwest Russia	19,010.7	$ 5,890,076.54
Kouban	1,592.5	578,490.50
Siberia	40.0	75,000.00
Ukraine	5,550.0	8,500,222.67
Volunteer Army	394.0	86,680.00
Soviet Republics	741,572.7	63,174,848.78
Total	768,159.9	$78,305,318.49

The problem of Russian relief was complicated by the fact that in 1919 civil wars raged throughout the former Russian Empire. The Bolshevist seizure of power in November, 1917, their dispersion of the All-Russian Constituent Assembly, their repudiation of foreign loans and expropriation of property, their separate peace with the Central Powers, their program of world revolution, brought on conflict with national groups which demanded complete separation from Soviet Russia, with political groups opposed to the Bolshevist program, and finally with the Entente Powers. By the time the Peace Conference met, Allied representatives had been withdrawn from Soviet territory and Allied troops were in conflict with Red forces in different parts of Russia. At the same time the Allies were giving moral and material support to the national and anti-Bolshevist governments which had repudiated the Bolshevist external and internal program. During the early weeks of the Peace Conference three attempts were made to re-establish relations with the Soviets, and to put an end to the civil wars. The proposal to have all the Russian governments meet representatives of the Allies at Prinkipo, and the visit of Bullitt and Steffens to Moscow to find out the peace terms of the Bolshevists came to nothing.[1] In March, 1919, Mr. Hoover proposed to the Allied Supreme Council a plan of relief to all Russia, Bolshevist and non-Bolshevist alike, under the direction of Dr. Nansen. This plan encountered strong opposition in Paris and elsewhere. The Bolshevist conditional acceptance, long delayed, had a hostile reception in the Supreme Council, and Mr. Hoover's efforts to save the plan failed. (Cf. page 244.) The failure of this plan did not affect relations between the Supreme Council and the non-Bolshevist governments of the Baltic States, the Ukraine, the Kouban, and Siberia, and it was to these territories where suffering was intense that relief was given in 1919.

[1] H. W. V. Temperley, *A History of the Peace Conference of Paris* (London, 1924), Vol. VI; *Russian-American Relations* (New York, 1920), Documents 129–133; W. C. Bullitt, *The Bullitt Mission to Russia* (New York, 1919).

NORTHWEST RUSSIA

(Appendix Tables 497–506)

ARMISTICE PERIOD

Reference has been made in preceding sections of this report to the condition of the population in the northern Baltic countries of Esthonia, Latvia, and Lithuania in the spring of 1919. The terrible situations pictured there were not confined to those countries but were even worse in the sections of Russia between the Esthonian border and the Petrograd - Moscow railway. Most of this territory had been occupied by German troops prior to the Armistice of November 11, 1918, after which the German troops withdrew. Later, in addition to the local forces a Russian anti-Bolshevist military force was organized in this region under the leadership of General Yudenitch. In May and June, 1919, this army succeeded in driving the Soviet forces out of a considerable area and in taking Narva and Jamburg.

The retreating Soviet troops had sacked the towns, destroyed property, and carried off most of the already scanty stocks of food. Reports which came to the Director General of Relief indicated that food conditions in this area were as bad as or worse than anywhere else in Europe.

By virtue of the relations existing between the Northwest Government and the Allied and Associated Powers it was possible to deliver relief to civilians in this area. Contracts similar to those made with the other governments of the liberated regions of Central and Eastern Europe were made with the representatives of the Russian Northwest Government. The first cargo delivered under this arrangement was that of the "Lake Strabo," which arrived at Reval, June 16, 1919, with 633.3 tons of flour. From that time until the first of August, 1919, a total of 17,950.4 metric tons of food, valued at $5,285,380.17, was delivered to the Northwest Government and assisted in alleviating some of the suffering of the people in this region. The details of these deliveries by steamers and commodities are shown in Table 498.

The condition of these people with regard to clothing was little better than that with regard to the food supply. Mr. Hoover arranged with the U.S. Liquidation Commission to sell the Russian Northwest Government 200.0 tons of clothing and 510.0 tons of miscellaneous supplies, for which they agreed to pay $428,299.46 (Table 92). The A.R.A. transported the major portion of these commodities from France to northern Russian ports at a cost of $52,188.18. This made the total relief delivered to Northwest Russia during the Armistice Period 18,660.4 metric tons, with a value of $5,765,867.81. The Russian Northwest Government gave notes for this amount to the organizations making deliveries, all of which were turned over to the U.S. Treasury. At the end of 1919, the fortunes of war turned against General Yudenitch, and this territory again came into the possession of the Soviet authorities.

TABLE 92

SUMMARY OF TOTAL RELIEF TO NORTHWEST RUSSIA

(For detail see Table 497)

Operation	Total Metric Tons	Total Value
Armistice Period		
American Relief Administration (Congressional Appropriation)	17,950.4	$5,285,380.17
American Relief Administration (freight finance)	.....	52,188.18
U.S. Liquidation Commission	710.0	428,299.46
Total, Armistice Period	18,660.4	$5,765,867.81
Reconstruction Period		
American Relief Administration (Congressional Appropriation)	305.2	$ 111,705.13
European Children's Fund	12.8	6,223.60
Northwest Russian Government donation	32.3	6,280.00
Total, children's relief and Reconstruction Period	350.3	$ 124,208.73
Grand total relief deliveries	19,010.7	$5,890,076.54

RECONSTRUCTION PERIOD

Children's Relief

The terrible condition of the children in this Northwest territory led the A.R.A. to undertake a child-feeding program similar to those in the other Baltic countries. A central committee was formed of leading citizens and under their guidance local committees were organized. Feeding began on July 4, 1919, and continued under the European Children's Fund until after this territory was captured by the Bolshevists.

The A.R.A. delivered a total of 305.2 metric tons of food for child feeding, with a total value of $111,705.13. This was paid for out of the Congressional Appropriation for Relief as a gift from the United States Government to Russian children. The E.C.F. supplemented these supplies with 12.8 tons of food and clothing, worth $6,223.60, while the Russian Northwest Government contributed 32.0 tons of flour and 0.3 tons of pork products, thus making a total of 350.3 metric tons of supplies for children's relief with a total value of $124,208.73.

The maximum number of children fed in this territory reached 8,000 in July and again in October, 1919. During the eight months of feeding, the estimated number of meals provided was 1,286,000. In addition, the E.C.F. provided shoes, stockings, and overcoats for some 1,500 Russian children.

With the retreat of the Northwest army in October, 1919, a vast number of refugees fled across the Esthonian border, where their condition was extremely pitiful. The E.C.F. persuaded the Esthonian Government to provide camps for these refugees. The children were fed under the direction of the Esthonian children's relief committee.

The children's relief in this part of Russia was accomplished with extreme difficulty, due to the rapid movement of troops, the shifting of the children from place to place, and the general disorder in which the work had to be carried on. At times, the food issued was woefully insufficient for proper nourishment, and often the parents were unable to supplement the ration with other food, but at all times it represented at least the margin which prevented actual starvation.

The details of the arrivals of relief supplies for child feeding in Northwest Russia are given in Tables 500 to 503, while Table 505 gives the internal distribution of these supplies as shown by feeding-station receipts. Table 93 shows the commodities delivered in this territory during the whole of the relief operations.

As shown by Table 92, the total deliveries to Northwest Russia during the existence of the provisional government amounted to 19,010.7 metric tons, valued at $5,890,076.54. The major portion of this was furnished on credit for which payment will probably never be made, but having regard to the basis on which it was supplied the total may be divided as follows:

Sold for cash	$ 6,280.00
Delivered on credit	5,765,867.81
Benevolence	117,928.73
Total	$5,890,076.54

TABLE 93

Commodities Delivered to Northwest Russia

(*Metric Tons*)

Commodity	General Relief: American Relief Administration	General Relief: U.S. Liquidation Commission	Child Feeding: American Relief Administration	Child Feeding: European Children's Fund	Child Feeding: Northwest Russian Government	Total
Flour	14,248.4	.....	39.4	3.3	32.0	14,323.1
Rice	......	.....	64.0	...	....	64.0
Beans and peas	379.8	.....	27.9	...	....	407.7
Pork products	2,266.6	.....	20.0	3.0	.3	2,289.9
Milk	1,055.6	.....	129.4	3.9	....	1,188.9
Cocoa	......	.....	5.0	.2	....	5.2
Sugar	......	.....	9.0	.1	....	9.1
Soap	......	.....	10.5	...	....	10.5
Clothing and miscellaneous	......	710.0	....	2.3	....	712.3
Total	17,950.4	710.0	305.2	12.8	32.3	19,010.7

THE KOUBAN

(Appendix Tables 507–509)

ARMISTICE PERIOD

The Kouban in southern Russia is one of the great surplus food-producing areas of Russia. Even in this region, however, there was considerable suffering in the cities after the Armistice, because of unemployment and because the peasants refused to sell their food for the local currency. The war had depleted the country of all manufactured articles, such as clothing, tools, implements, etc. The peasants found that none of the things they wanted were to be purchased with the currency, and hence preferred to keep their grain.

Partly in order to supply this demand of the peasants, and partly to secure cheaper grain for Armenia, the A.R.A. chartered the steamship "Kickapoo" and loaded a cargo of miscellaneous supplies, including hardware, implements, clothing, etc., purchased from the U.S. Liquidation Commission at Marseilles. The "Kickapoo" proceeded to Novorossisk on the Black Sea, where 915.5 tons of these miscellaneous supplies, worth $444,718.50, were traded to the peasants for wheat which was sent to Armenia (cf. page 150). In this way the A.R.A. was able to secure some 8,000.0 tons of wheat for Armenia at a cost of less than $500,000, while at the same time the peasants of the Kouban were supplied with materials they needed so badly. To have supplied 8,000.0 tons of wheat for Armenian relief from the United States would have cost upward of $1,500,000. The transaction thus resulted in a very significant saving.

In addition, the "Kickapoo" carried 577.0 tons of clothing for the Kouban, which represented a donation by the American Red Cross. The value of this clothing was approximately $123,300.

The United Kingdom also donated 100.0 tons of clothing and miscellaneous supplies to the people of the Kouban. The value of these commodities was approximately $10,472.

The total relief to the Kouban amounted to 1,592.5 metric tons, valued at $578,490.50. Of this, $444,718.50 may be regarded as a cash transaction, while $133,772.00 represented direct gifts.

These transactions are summarized in the following table.

TABLE 94

SUMMARY OF TOTAL RELIEF DELIVERIES TO THE KOUBAN

(For detail see Table 507)

Operation	Total Metric Tons	Total Value
Armistice Period		
American Relief Administration (cash settlement)	915.5	$444,718.50
American Red Cross.........	577.0	123,300.00
Total American relief....	1,492.5	$568,018.50
United Kingdom	100.0	10,472.00
Grand total relief deliveries	1,592.5	$578,490.50

SIBERIA

(Appendix Table 510)

ARMISTICE PERIOD

In the middle of 1919, the American Jewish Joint Distribution Committee sent 40.0 tons of clothing to Siberia by way of Vladivostok to relieve some of the distress reported there. This shipment was reported to the office of the Director General of Relief and hence is included here, although it was undertaken entirely on the responsibility of the Joint Distribution Committee. The total value of this shipment was $75,000. (Cf. Table 124.)

UKRAINE

(Appendix Table 537)

ARMISTICE PERIOD

Reports received by the Director General of Relief during the Armistice Period indicated that the peasants in Ukraine, like those in the Kouban, were suffering for lack of clothing and manufactured articles. A sale to the Ukrainian Government of 5,550.0 tons of miscellaneous commodities was arranged with the U.S. Liquidation Commission. This transaction included 4,000.0 tons of surplus Army clothing, and 1,550.0 tons of other non-foods which included medical supplies, motor trucks, and building materials. The total value of the commodities sold to Ukraine was $8,500,222.67. This sale was handled through a co-operative society known as *Ukrailian,* which operated for the government and which turned over notes of the Ukrainian Government in payment to the U.S. Liquidation Commission.

VOLUNTEER ARMY

(Appendix Table 538)

ARMISTICE PERIOD

In spite of the fact that the Kouban had a large surplus of grain, there was great suffering in the cities, because the peasants would not part with their grain for the local currencies. In May, 1919, reports to the Director General of Relief showed the need for some assistance to these people. Great Britain had established a military mission with headquarters at Ekaterinodar, some seventy miles northeast of Novorossisk, and were co-operating with General Denikin, who had organized a volunteer army in southern Russia and had established a provisional government. The British supported a request from the Denikin Government for supplies of flour to relieve some of the civilian suffering in this territory.

Acting upon the request of the Supreme War Council, the A.R.A. sent 394.0 metric tons of flour from stocks at Constantinople to Novorossisk on the British transport "War Pointer." This flour was turned over to the Russian Volunteer Army (Denikin Government), from whom obligations to pay the United States were obtained. This sale for $86,680, like those to other newly formed governments, was a credit transaction, paid for out of the $100,000,000 appropriation for European relief.

SOVIET REPUBLICS

(Appendix Tables 511–536)

RECONSTRUCTION PERIOD

The story of the food crisis in Soviet Russia and the attempt made by the United States and others to alleviate the suffering there in 1921 to 1923 has been told by many competent writers, including Fisher,[1] Golder and Hutchinson,[2] and others. No attempt will be made to repeat this story here, but a few of the outstanding events will be discussed briefly in order to give some basis for understanding the necessity which caused the American Relief Administration to pour hundreds of thousands of tons of food and millions of dollars into this territory.

In the first place, it must be understood that food difficulties in Russia began long before the autumn of 1921. As a matter of fact, they began almost immediately after the declaration of war in 1914. These early difficulties were not due to

[1] H. H. Fisher, *The Famine in Soviet Russia, 1919–1923* (Macmillan, 1927).

[2] Frank A. Golder and Lincoln Hutchinson, *On the Trail of the Russian Famine* (Stanford University Press, 1927).

a food shortage, for Russia was always a surplus food-producing region. But the disturbance of the war was sufficient to upset the transportation and financial systems of the country. This, together with the corruption and incompetence of the administration, soon resulted in a deficient supply to the cities and in rising prices. The revolution of March, 1917, which overthrew the Czar, was hastened at least, if not actually precipitated, by "bread riots" in Petrograd and Moscow. The inability of the provisional government to handle the food situation, as much as anything else, made possible the *coup d'état* of October 25, 1917, known as the Bolshevist Revolution. Lenin and his grimly competent associates were abler and more determined than their predecessors. But they, too, failed to solve the food situation, although they did control distribution, and thus used food as a weapon to compel support and to thwart opposition.

Russian food was a problem of no small moment at the Peace Conference in Paris. The Supreme Council made several attempts to grapple with the Russian question, but all were unsuccessful. The last of these attempts was inspired by Mr. Hoover, who, as Director General of Relief, had received disquieting reports about the Russian food situation. In a letter to President Wilson on March 28, 1919, Mr. Hoover described the dangers to the rest of Europe and to the world in the fomenting caldron on the east. He pointed out the suffering which the Russian people were enduring, and, with the thought that the Soviet Government would welcome assistance in their difficulties, he proposed that a neutral international food commission should be organized, patterned after the Belgian relief, which could assist the Russian people and thus perhaps give them an opportunity to work out their social re-organization. This plan was approved by President Wilson, and at Mr. Hoover's request Dr. Fridtjof Nansen, of Norway, undertook to organize such a commission. Nansen's proposal was given formal approval by the Council of Four on April 9, 1919, and the plan was transmitted to the Soviet authorities for their views. The Bolshevist reply was a bitter criticism of the Allied policy toward Russia and a refusal either to cease hostilities or to divorce political control from the distribution of foodstuffs. Since the Allied Powers would not consider turning over vast quantities of foodstuffs to any country in a state of civil war without retaining power to see that the relief went actually to the civilian population, this reply ended any further attempt to furnish relief to Russia during the Armistice Period.

In the summer of 1920, during the Russian invasion of Poland the European Children's Fund sought permission from the Soviet Government to continue the operation of the child-feeding stations in eastern Poland, occupied by the Bolshevists, and offered to extend the child-feeding work to such Russian cities as might require assistance, providing that assurance be given that all feeding should be carried on "without regard to race, politics, or religion." The reply from the Soviet Government declared that the government had departments fully adequate to take special care of children, and that any relief brought in from the outside must be placed under control of the Soviet relief organization. This rebuff effectively closed the door to any further negotiations.

The Great Famine

In the spring of 1921, Russia suffered an exceptionally severe drought which totally ruined the crops in the Volga region and in the districts to the east. Vast areas of that fertile country failed to return the seed that had been used in planting. The news of this disaster was carefully hidden behind the wall of censorship, which permitted only dissemination of news that the authorities believed desirable for the world to know. By June, 1921, however, the situation began to get beyond control. The hunger and panic of the peasants threatened to depopulate the villages and overwhelm the cities with starving and diseased refugees. The censorship had to be relaxed, and an official statement admitted that famine raged among a population of "about 25,000,000." The European press began to publish grim rumors of horrors, but the Soviet authorities did not bring themselves to the point of making an appeal for help until July 11. Even then, the Soviet Government did not ask directly, but permitted Maxim Gorky to issue his famous appeal, dated July 13, 1921, which told of the crop failure, the threatened starvation of millions of Russians, and asked for prompt aid from Europe and America. This appeal did not appear in the press until July 23, 1921. On the same day, Mr. Hoover sent a telegram to Gorky offering the assistance of the A.R.A. on condition that the Soviet authorities must ask for this relief and agree to its distribution under the same terms accepted by other countries.

On July 31, the acceptance of Mr. Hoover's offer by the Soviet Government was received, and on August 20, 1921, a formal agreement was signed at Riga by Maxim Litvinov for the Soviets and by Walter Lyman Brown for the American Relief Administration.[1] This agreement set forth the conditions under which food would be distributed, and provided that the costs of internal distribution should be borne by the Soviet Government.

Among other things, the Soviet authorities agreed to fully protect supplies imported by the A.R.A. and affiliated organizations and to replace or pay for any supplies lost or stolen; to permit full control by the A.R.A. of distribution up to the time of consumption; to bear the entire cost of unloading, storage, and inland transportation of commodities, as well as the overhead expenses of the necessary distributive organization in Russia; to furnish necessary office space and living quarters for American personnel; to allow full freedom of movement to the American personnel in Russia, as well as freedom from search; to furnish free telephone and telegraph communications, and other necessary guaranties. In return, the A.R.A. agreed to feed children and adults in the famine area to the extent of their capability and gave formal assurances regarding the non-participation of American personnel in political questions.

On August 27, 1921, seven days after the signing of the Riga agreement, the first contingent of the A.R.A. Russian Unit arrived in Moscow and began preparations for what proved to be two long years of strenuous work. On September 1, the S.S. "Phoenix" docked at Petrograd with 700.0 tons of balanced rations, and on September 7 the first relief kitchen was opened.

Finance for Relief

In the fall of 1921, the immensity and urgency of the Russian debacle were verified, and the necessity for immediate relief was apparent. Securing funds for such an enormous undertaking presented the most difficult problem which had ever faced the officials of the American Relief Administration. Less than $5,000,000 remained from the European Relief Council drive, and commitments for child-feeding programs in other countries had not yet been fulfilled. It seemed impossible to make a successful campaign for benevolent funds in the United States, following so closely the European Relief Council drive for $30,000,000. The depression of 1921 throughout America was at its peak, and American benevolence had been extended to its limit. Furthermore, a campaign of this character would require months of preparation and there was no time to lose, as the famine was a reality; people were dying, and it would be too late before a campaign really got into effective operation. Part of this urgency was due to the necessity for supplying seed grain, without which the following year would record a still more appalling catastrophe. A meeting of the European Relief Council was held at Washington at the end of August, 1921, when the Riga Agreement was accepted as a working charter and the several organizations incorporated in the European Relief Council agreed to give support to the relief work in Russia.

The only alternative of benevolent support to meet the financial requirements was federal aid. Mr. Hoover placed the problem before President Harding, calling his attention to the difficulties of our own farmers at this time, particularly as regards the enormous surplus of corn and the fact that this cereal was selling at 14 cents per bushel and was actually being burned. President Harding was sympathetic and recommended legislation in his message of December 6, 1921, and, after hearings, a bill was passed (Act of December 22, 1921), which authorized the Congress to cause to be expended out of the capital of the United States Grain Corporation a sum not exceeding $20,000,000 for corn, seed grain, and milk for the starving people of Russia. Corn was specifically mentioned as it was a distressed product in the United States and at the same time the Russians were familiar with its use as food.[2]

[1] Cf. pages 926–27 for copy of this agreement.

[2] As shown on page 114 there was a significant increase in the price of corn in the United States between November, 1921, and the spring of 1922. This result was due largely to the effect of the heavy purchases of this commodity for the Russian relief work, and was of substantial benefit to thousands of American farmers.

With this $20,000,000 as a nucleus, immediate efforts were made to supply the balance of approximately $40,000,000 to complete the estimated requirements. The American Red Cross, although desirous of giving the medical aid, did not have the personnel actually to pursue the work in Russia on such a large scale. They agreed, however, that they would provide medical supplies to the extent of $3,600,000, which generous gift fell far short of the estimated medical needs in Russia. The War Department had a considerable surplus stock of hospital and medical supplies and, through Mr. Hoover's efforts, a resolution was introduced in Congress, authorizing the President to transfer to the American Relief Administration medical and hospital supplies not to exceed $4,000,000 cost value, without further charge. This Act was finally passed by both houses and approved by the President on January 20, 1922.

Following the policy pursued in other countries, Mr. Hoover urged the Soviet authorities to do their share, as he was aware of the fact that they had several million dollars in gold coin in their treasury, and he proposed that a large portion of this reserve should be used for the purpose of purchasing seed grain and food supplies. The Soviet authorities were not averse to this suggestion, but the agreement to transfer the gold was not completed until December 30, 1921, when the Soviet Government placed gold, chiefly gold rubles, of an approximate value of $10,000,000 at the disposal of the American Relief Administration. This action was followed within a very few days by a similar agreement with the Ukrainian Soviet Republic, which placed approximately $2,000,000 in the form of gold at the disposal of the American Relief Administration.

This made a total of approximately $12,000,000 of Russian gold for the purchase of relief supplies. The realization of credit for this gold was no simple matter. It had to be transported from Russia to the United States, permission had to be secured for its entry into this country, and many other obstacles had to be overcome, all of which involved long delays, while Russian people starved. Plans were finally worked out by which credits for the major part of this gold were established in advance of its receipt. The A.R.A. began buying for the Soviet account on January 10, 1922, although the first shipment of gold was not received until February 7. This enabled the A.R.A. to get seed grain to Russia in time for the spring planting.

Shortly after the meeting of the European Relief Council referred to above, a number of other relief organizations which proposed to work in Russia made arrangements to conduct their work in co-operation with the A.R.A. Among these organizations may be mentioned the following: the Volga Relief Society, the National Lutheran Council, the American Mennonite Relief, and the Southern Baptist Convention. Other organizations affiliated with the European Relief Council were: the American Friends Service Committee, American Red Cross, Federal Council of Churches, American Jewish Joint Distribution Committee, National Catholic Welfare Association, Knights of Columbus, the Y.M.C.A., and the Y.W.C.A.

Each of these organizations undertook to collect funds on its own account, but agreed to co-ordinate its work with the A.R.A. The A.R.A., on the other hand, undertook to leave as much freedom as possible to each organization, but to assist and protect their work in every way possible.

In Central Europe it had been found that the work of these charitable organizations had been facilitated by the A.R.A. Warehouses, which carried stocks of supplies suitable for relief work. The supplies were sold to these organizations at a small profit, but at considerably less than these organizations could purchase and ship in small quantities on their own account. It was decided to adopt the same plan for Russia, and bulk food sales of this character accounted for more than $4,000,000 worth of relief to Russia, while clothing sales represented nearly three-quarters of a million dollars in addition (Table 96, page 248).

In connection with the Warehouse operations the A.R.A. established a food remittance service in which food drafts, similar to those used successfully elsewhere in Europe, were sold. Food draft sales for Russia amounted to more than $9,000,000, a considerable portion of which was purchased by co-operating relief organizations in a manner similar to the bulk sales.

In addition to the sources of finance listed above, the Laura Spelman Rockefeller Memorial paid for the transportation of the government medical supplies in the amount of $267,392.38. The American Friends Service Committee purchased supplies for direct shipment to the extent of $267,394.24. The governments of Poland, Latvia, and Esthonia donated transportation and warehouse facilities for Russian supplies valued at $115,360.63, while the Soviet Government contributed commodities for child feeding worth $30,026.64.

By these various means, the A.R.A. was able to mobilize finance for the relief of the Russian famine to the extent of $63,174,848.78. The sources of this finance, as outlined above, are shown in tabular form in Table 95. The contribution of $10,252,795.71 from the American Relief Administration includes cash donations to the A.R.A. funds by the Jewish Joint Distribution Committee to the extent of $3,686,129.24 (cf. page 145). The remainder of this fund came from money contributed through the European Relief Council, and from such profits as were realized on the remittance and bulk sale operations in Russia.

TABLE 95

SOURCES OF FINANCE FOR RELIEF TO THE SOVIET REPUBLICS*

U.S. Grain Corporation (Congressional Appropriation)	$18,662,180.00
American Relief Administration	10,252,795.71
Soviet gold	11,357,325.13
U.S. Government medical supplies	4,000,000.00
Laura Spelman Rockefeller Memorial (freight finance)	267,392.88
American Red Cross medical supplies	3,804,863.15
Remittances and bulk sales	14,417,510.40
American Friends Service Committee	267,394.24
Soviet Government donation (commodities)	30,026.64
Facilities donated by European governments	115,360.63
Total	$63,174,848.78

* This table represents the total and final figures for all relief to the Soviet Republics handled under the direction of the A.R.A. The figures quoted by H. H. Fisher in *The Famine in Soviet Russia* do not include under "Charitable distribution" the following contributions and donations: clothing for general relief; clothing deliveries to institutions; food distributed to employees in lieu of pay (*paioks*); accounting adjustments directly chargeable to relief applied; and the donation of facilities by European governments.

RELIEF DELIVERIES

Table 96 shows that from the beginning of these operations in August, 1921, to their close in 1923, the A.R.A. was instrumental in delivering to Russia a total of 741,572.7 metric tons of relief supplies, with a total value, including the contribution of facilities by other European governments, of $63,174,848.78. For purposes of discussion, the relief to the Soviet Republics may be divided into three principal groups: (1) child and adult relief; (2) seed grain; and (3) remittances and bulk sales from warehouses. Table 526 shows the distribution of total relief by districts within Russia.

Child and adult relief.—The famine conditions made it necessary to include adults in the relief work as well as children. The experience of the A.R.A. in Central Europe during the Reconstruction Period had been chiefly with child relief, and the appeal for funds for Central Europe were largely restricted to children. However, for Russia, contributions were requested which made it possible to extend the work to adults. For the most part, the records do not permit a segregation of relief given to children from that for adults.

Table 96 shows the total deliveries for child and adult relief as 471,567.1 metric tons, valued at $38,216,887.24. A portion of this, 131,966.6 tons, valued at $12,377,951.19, was definitely allocated for children's relief and used through child-feeding kitchens in the same manner as similar relief in Central Europe. The remainder of this relief, including supplies from the Grain Corporation, medical relief, etc., was used for both children and adults.

a) Children's relief: The sources of the finance for the specific children's relief, referred to above, may be summarized as follows:

Soviet gold	$ 4,322,450.83
Soviet Government contribution (commodities)	30,026.64
Joint Distribution Committee	3,686,129.24
American Relief Administration	4,339,345.48
Total	$12,377,951.19

The child-feeding operations followed closely the methods successfully developed in Belgium and in Central Europe. Local volunteer committees were organized, but the work required close supervision by the two hundred members of the American staff, assisted by a large number of Russian employees furnished by the Soviet Government. By August, 1922, more than 4,000,000 children were being fed in some 28,000 kitchens located in 18,000 cities, towns, and villages.

TABLE 96

SUMMARY OF TOTAL RELIEF DELIVERIES TO THE SOVIET REPUBLICS, AUGUST, 1921—JUNE, 1923

(For detail see Table 511)

Operation	Total Metric Tons	Total Value
Reconstruction Period		
Child and adult relief		
American Relief Administration (children's relief)	131,412.6	$12,347,924.55
Soviet Government donation	554.0	30,026.64
American Relief Administration (clothing deliveries)	1,723.4	1,700,795.00
American Relief Administration (employees paiok)	3,687.5	375,312.38
U.S. Grain Corporation (delivered by A.R.A.)	310,673.7	14,865,303.45
U.S. Grain Corporation (delivered by Near East Relief)	11,031.8	557,874.95
Medical Supplies		
U.S. Government surplus and American Red Cross (delivered by A.R.A.)	8,066.7	7,862,524.40
U.S. Government surplus (delivered by Near East Relief	215.2	209,731.63
American Friends Service Committee	4,202.2	267,394.24
Total child and adult relief	471,567.1	$38,216,887.24
Seed Grain		
American Relief Administration (Grain Corporation)	55,107.6	$ 2,948,485.24
American Relief Administration (Soviet gold)	111,865.9	7,034,874.30
Total seed grain	166,973.5	$ 9,983,359.54
Remittances and bulk sales		
American Relief Administration (food remittances)	54,316.3	$ 9,305,300.00
American Relief Administration (bulk, Eurelcon,* and internal sales)	34,570.5	4,374,893.28
American Relief Administration (clothing)	350.0	737,317.12
Total remittances and bulk sales	89,236.8	$14,417,510.40
Sale damaged commodities and other adjustments	13,795.3	$ 441,730.97
Total relief from United States	741,572.7	$63,059,488.15
Relief from other countries		
Esthonian Government (warehouse facilities)	....	$ 1,102.94
Latvian Government (warehouse facilities)	....	24,257.69
Polish Government (railroad transportation, etc.)	....	90,000.00
Total from other countries	....	$ 115,360.63
Grand total relief deliveries	741,572.7	$63,174,848.78

* Abbreviation refers to sales to organizations belonging to the European Relief Council.

The actual work of feeding was controlled by the segregation of the famine zone into districts; each in charge of an American district supervisor (cf. map, page 238), with one or two American assistants and an American district physician. Allocation of supplies was made from the A.R.A. headquarters in Moscow, based on the reports of conditions received from the district supervisors. It was the supervisor's responsibility to organize committees and kitchens, allocate supplies to towns and villages, arrange transportation, inspect and control distribution, and to account for every pound of food with receipts from the local committees. This gave an absolute control on all American supplies, which was deemed essential. The results accomplished by these supervisors and their assistants deserves the very highest praise. It was work under great pressure, much of it under very difficult and discouraging conditions. But through their loyalty and devotion and their ability to overcome all obstacles, the work succeeded, millions of lives were saved, and much suffering was mitigated.

All of the direct child-feeding operations were carried on under the immediate supervision of the A.R.A. with the exception of 1,401.3 tons of supplies, valued at $127,305.00, which were turned over in sixteen different districts to the Joint Distribution Committee, who themselves handled the feeding. Table 527 shows the detail of these deliveries to the J.D.C. by districts. The same table also shows the detail of the internal deliveries, by districts and by commodities, of the 130,539.0 metric tons ($12,250,646.19) of supplies fed by the A.R.A. through kitchens to Russian children. The commodities delivered on the child-feeding program are summarized in Table 97.

b) *Child and adult relief:* Table 96 shows a total of 310,673.7 metric tons of food, valued at $14,865,303.45, purchased with U.S. Grain Corporation funds, as authorized by Congress, and distributed by the A.R.A. This table also shows a total of 11,031.8 metric tons of supplies, worth $557,874.95, turned over to the Near East Relief for distribution in the Caucasus district of southern Russia. These two allotments represent the portion of the Grain Corporation funds used for food, while the remainder was used for the purchase of seed, as discussed below. The total accounting for the Grain Corporation fund may be summarized as follows:

Food for child and adult relief	
Accounted for by districts	$14,627,294.12
Special relief to railroad workers	238,009.33
Total	$14,865,303.45
Seed for planting	2,948,485.24
Total distributed by A.R.A.	$17,813,788.69
To Near East Relief for Caucasus	557,874.95
Sales of damaged goods, pilferage, etc.	290,516.36
Grand total	$18,662,180.00

The detail of the distribution of these supplies is shown by districts and by commodities in Table 530.

In carrying out the terms of the Act of Congress of December 22, 1921, President Harding issued an executive order creating the Purchasing Commission for Russian Relief, consisting of the following members: Secretary of Commerce Herbert Hoover; James P. Goodrich of Indiana; Edward M. Flesh of Missouri, vice-president and

TABLE 97

Summary of Commodities Delivered for Child Feeding in the Soviet Republics, August, 1921—June, 1923

(*Metric Tons*)

Commodity	A.R.A.*	J.D.C.*	Total
Flour	85,372.5	615.1	85,987.6
Rice	6,968.9	322.6	7,291.5
Beans and peas	3,221.2	.....	3,221.2
Corn grits	821.7	106.7	928.4
Pork products	7,627.9	59.8	7,687.7
Milk	9,271.7	188.2	9,459.9
Cocoa	3,301.9	23.5	3,325.4
Sugar	12,804.7	85.6	12,890.3
Miscellaneous food	578.9	....	578.9
Soap	569.6	....	569.6
Total	130,539.0	1,401.5	131,940.5

* Organizations in charge of distribution through kitchens.

treasurer of the U.S. Grain Corporation; Edgar Rickard of New York, director general of the A.R.A.; and Don Livingston, formerly commissioner of agriculture for South Dakota. This commission was charged with the duty of purchasing, transporting, and delivering in Russia the commodities authorized by the Act. The President also designated that the Purchasing Commission should deliver these commodities

A.R.A. child and adult dining room at Ufa, Russia. Note mess equipment on table at right.

to the American Relief Administration in Russia, which was to have full charge of the internal distribution within Russia.

Authority was also granted to the A.R.A. to designate other organizations to distribute a portion of these commodities, which permitted them to turn over 11,031.8 metric tons to the Near East Relief for the Caucasus, where the latter organization was in much better position to secure adequate distribution than was the A.R.A. No detail of the internal distribution of these supplies in the Caucasus has been received from the Near East Relief. Details of the shipments of all supplies handled by the Purchasing Commission for Russian Relief, showing steamers and cargoes, are given in Tables 517 and 518.

The supplies to be purchased from the Grain Corporation fund were restricted by the Act of Congress to corn, seed grain, and preserved milk. These commodities, including the seed grain[1] purchased from this fund, may be summarized as follows:

Distribution of Commodities Purchased for Russia from the Grain Corporation Funds
(*Metric Tons*)

Commodity	A.R.A. Seed Grain	A.R.A. Food	N.E.R. Food	Damaged Commodities and Other Adjustments	Total
Seed wheat	35,713.3	......	......	1,225.3	36,938.6
Seed corn	18,294.3	......	......	115.7	18,410.0
No. 2 corn	......	201,395.3	......	5,558.3	206,953.6
Corn grits	......	76,415.0	6,103.9	1,441.5	83,960.4
Rye	......	13,315.1	4,927.9	875.6	19,118.6
Milk	......	19,548.3	......	41.3	19,589.6
Miscellaneous	1,100.0	......	......	......	1,100.0
Total	55,107.6	310,673.7	11,031.8	9,257.7	386,070.8

Table 530 shows that of the Grain Corporation food delivered by the A.R.A., 5,757.0 metric tons of rye and corn, worth $238,009.33, were supplied as special relief to Russian railroad workers. This was connected with the breakdown of Russian transportation, in the spring of 1922, which in part was due to the inability of the Soviet Government to pay its railroad employees a living wage. The government was requiring these workers to transport vast quantities of food for the benefit of other people, but did not supply sufficient food for the workers and their families. The situation promised to get out of hand unless the railroad workers' demands for satisfactory rations were fulfilled. The A.R.A. agreed to loan a small amount of corn to the government to feed the railroad workers, on condition that it should be paid back. As a matter of fact, repayment was never made, and the matter was not adjusted until the final liquidation agreement in 1923. But the railroad workers secured food which they badly needed and this, no doubt, contributed greatly toward speeding up the movement of supplies to the famine areas.

[1] Additional seed grain was purchased with Soviet gold as discussed on page 255.

When the $20,000,000 appropriation from the Grain Corporation Fund was made by Congress, the Near East Relief asked that a portion of this relief be allocated to Russian famine sufferers in the Caucasus. In order to determine the need in this area, in comparison with other parts of Russia, Lincoln Hutchinson, who had made a study of conditions in the Volga and Ukraine districts, was sent to the Caucasus. Based on Mr. Hutchinson's recommendations, a total of 11,031.8 metric tons of food, consisting of corn grits and rye grain, was shipped to Batoum, on the SS. "Deepwater," II, and turned over to the Near East Relief for internal distribution. No further detail is available on this shipment.

Likewise, when the Act of Congress was passed, making $4,000,000 worth of medical supplies available for Russia, the Near East Relief requested a portion of these for the Caucasus. A total of 215.2 metric tons of these supplies, valued at $209,731.63, was delivered and turned over to the Near East Relief at New York by the A.R.A. Medical Table 3 (pages 977–86) furnishes a detailed inventory of the medical and hospital supplies receipted for by the Near East Relief at New York. No further details are available regarding the distribution of these supplies which were shipped and handled entirely by the Near East Relief and at their expense.

c) *Clothing relief:* The need for clothing in many parts of Russia during the famine was only a little less acute than the need for food. In a large measure, this was due to the almost complete stagnation of industry during the early years of the Soviet régime and, of course, to the lack of funds with which to purchase such garments as might be available.

During the early period of operation, the relief work, of necessity, consisted in efforts to get food to the starving people. However, the A.R.A. began in the late fall of 1921 to send in shoes, stockings, and woolen goods for children's relief. With the cold winters in the greater part of Russia, it was necessary to provide clothing to enable the children to come to the feeding stations.

The question of clothing to the adult popula- was still unsolved. Consideration was given to plans for clothing remittances similar to the food remittances which had operated so successfully. This plan had to be abandoned for 1921–1922, largely because of the transportation difficulties within Russia. The plan was revived and carried through in the fall of 1922.

Table 511 shows that the total deliveries of clothing by the A.R.A. for children and adults amounted to 1,447.8 metric tons, valued at $1,700,795.00. This is divided into three parts in the records of the relief work: (1) children's relief, including shoes and stockings only; (2) general relief, including cloth and accessories for garments distributed to both children and adults; and (3) miscellaneous deliveries, which includes material furnished to children's homes and similar institutions. The deliveries under (1) and (2) are shown in Table 529, segregated by districts. Table 98 summarizes the commodities which were delivered under each of these categories and includes also the clothing remittances and bulk sales which are discussed on pages 259–61.

d) *Medical relief:* One of the striking features of Russian famine conditions was the almost complete exhaustion of supplies necessary for the prevention and treatment of diseases. With the population undernourished, and with congestion in the medical institutions, the spread of sickness and infectious diseases was especially serious. These conditions made medical relief next in importance to food relief. As a practical matter, there was little use in spending energy and resources to feed people who were almost certain to die later from epidemics of cholera, typhus, or other diseases.

As stated in an earlier paragraph, the American Red Cross was not in a position to go into Russia itself, but agreed to donate medical supplies to the value of some $3,600,000, an amount which was later increased. Mr. Hoover succeeded in obtaining surplus medical and hospital supplies, worth $4,000,000, from the U.S. Government through an Act of Congress. The Laura Spelman Rockefeller Memorial contributed funds to cover the cost of transporting the government supplies to Russian ports. The problem presented to the A.R.A. was that of providing for the distribution and the utilization of some eight million dollars' worth of medical supplies. The American Relief Administration had never carried on medical relief in other countries.

Upon the advice of the American Red Cross, Colonel Henry Beeuwkes, Medical Corps, U.S.A., was selected to head the medical division of the A.R.A. His function was to distribute these supplies to Russian hospitals and institutions and to render all assistance possible to Russian physicians, who were carrying on a heroic struggle under great difficulties.

The medical unit found that cities and towns in Russia were adequately supplied with hospitals and institutions which were well organized, but unable to function effectively, due to the extreme shortage of drugs and dependable supplies. Blankets, bedding, and clothing were worn out or entirely lacking. Rubber goods, such as hot-water bags, syringes, sheeting, etc., simply did not exist; quinine, aspirin, salvarsan, and

TABLE 98

SUMMARY OF CLOTHING DELIVERIES IN SOVIET RUSSIA

Commodity	General Relief	Children's Relief	Institutions	Remittances and Bulk Sales
Woolens (yards)	117,585	......	637,107	191,561
Linings (yards)	153,298	......	......	163,800
Flannel (yards)	311,796	......	......	327,600
Muslin (yards)	638,559	......	......	655,202
Buttons (1,000 cases)	1,809	......	33	1,966
Thread (1,000 yards)	30,329	......	6,600	32,760
Thread (cases)	.....	......	17	.....
Needles (number)	.....	......	20,736	.....
Needles (cases)	.....	......	2	.....
Miscellaneous (pieces)	.....	......	12,990*	.....
Shoes (pairs)	.....	586,991	......	.....
Stockings (pairs)	.....	771,827	......	.....
Total value	$301,758.79	$971,670.96	$427,365.25	$737,000.00

* Includes 9,920 overcoats, 2,890 bales of old clothing, and 180 barrels of overcoats.

similar common drugs, not to mention sera or rarer products, were seldom to be had.

The need, therefore, was not for new first-aid stations, but for a distribution of the supplies to already existing institutions. Distribution was made throughout Russia and Ukraine, as far north as Karelia and as far south as the Black Sea.

The total quantity of medical and hospital supplies furnished to Russia amounted to 8,291.9 metric tons, valued at $8,072,256.03, of which 215.2 tons, worth $209,731.63, were turned over to the Near East Relief for the Caucasus (cf. page 116). This left 8,066.7 metric tons, valued at $7,862,524.40, to be distributed by the A.R.A. Table 99 summarizes the source of the entire medical program for Russia.

TABLE 99

Summary of Medical Supplies for Soviet Russia

Source	Total Metric Tons	Total Value
Distributed by American Relief Administration		
American Red Cross supplies	5,174.3	$3,804,863.15
U.S. Government surplus medical and hospital supplies	2,892.4	3,790,268.37
Laura Spelman Rockefeller Memorial (freight finance)	.....	267,392.88
Total	8,066.7	$7,862,524.40
Distributed by Near East Relief		
U.S. Government surplus medical and hospital supplies	215.2	209,731.63
Grand total	8,281.9	$8,072,256.03

If one has any misconception as to the diversity which can be exhibited by 8,000.0 tons of medical and hospital supplies, he will do well to examine Medical Tables 1, 2, and 3, pages 936–86, which show in detail the distribution of these supplies by districts in Russia. Among other items, there were 357 kinds of medicines, 627 kinds of surgical instruments, and hundreds of kinds of laboratory supplies, disinfectants, vaccines, etc. In quantity, too, these supplies ran into enormous numbers.[1]

[1] A complete description of the work of the medical division in Russia has been issued by Dr. Beeuwkes under the title of "American Medical and Sanitary Relief in the Russian Famine, 1921–1923," in the A.R.A. *Bulletin Series 2*, No. 45.

Some idea of the magnitude of the work of distributing these thousands of different kinds of articles can be obtained from the following tabulation, showing the number of institutions to which they were sent.

Russian Institutions Furnished with Medical and Hospital Supplies

Kind of Institution	Number of Institutions	Total Capacity
Hospitals	5,764	352,332
Dispensaries, etc.	4,123	247,087
Children's homes	4,760	326,821
Day nurseries	372	25,259
Schools, etc.	165	17,999
Homes for aged, etc.	248	59,237
Unclassified	987	11,000
Total	16,419	1,039,735

The following summary includes the estimated tonnage and the value of the supplies to each of the eighteen districts, and to the Caucasus through the Near East Relief.

Summary of the Distribution of Medical and Hospital Supplies by Districts

District	Estimated Metric Tons	Value
Ekaterinoslav	484.0	$ 471,751.46
Kazan	484.0	471,751.46
Kharkov	484.0	471,751.47
Kiev	645.3	629,001.95
Minsk	484.0	471,751.46
Moscow	887.3	864,877.68
Odessa	484.0	471,751.46
Orenberg	161.3	157,250.49
Petrograd	726.0	707,627.20
Rostov/Don	645.4	629,001.95
Samara	484.0	471,751.47
Sanitary Train No. 1	121.0	117,937.87
Sanitary Train No. 2	121.0	117,937.86
Saratov	484.0	471,751.46
Simbirsk	484.0	471,751.47
Theodosia	161.3	157,250.49
Tzaritzan	161.4	157,250.49
Ufa	564.7	550,376.71
Caucasus (N.E.R.)	215.2	209,731.63
Total	8,281.9	$8,072,256.03

Among other things accomplished by the A.R.A. medical unit was the completion of a program by which approximately 10,000,000 Russians were inoculated against five different epidemic diseases: viz., typhoid fever, two types of paratyphoid, smallpox, and diphtheria. In another effort to stamp out disease, able-bodied refugees in the cities were organized into clean-up gangs. The receipt of food was conditioned on this work. These gangs cleaned out sewers, drains, and depositories of rubbish and litter where disease germs might collect.

e) *Paiok for employees:* The Russian word *paiok* means "allowance." The A.R.A. had to employ a large number of Russians, including office employees, chauffeurs, warehouse managers and assistants, food and clothing remittance employees engaged in making up and delivering remittance packages, etc. These employees were paid by the A.R.A. It was soon found, however, that the employees had difficulty in purchasing food supplies with the money paid to them, and that they would much prefer to have part of their pay in the form of food commodities. Efforts were made to induce the Soviet Government to provide such rations at reduced prices, as was done for employees of Soviet institutions, but it proved impossible to secure action on this request. With the rapidly rising prices, it became impossible for anyone to support a family on the rate of pay which had been agreed upon with the government, and the A.R.A. employees became dissatisfied. In order to provide adequate support, and also to remove some of the temptation for pilfering, the A.R.A. decided in December, 1921, to supplement the pay of their employees with a definite food package. Strict regulations were drawn up as to the class of employees entitled to this paiok, which did not include laborers, port workers, servants, local committees, or kitchen personnel, all of whom were furnished and paid by the Soviet Government under the Riga agreement.

The authorized paiok to be issued on the last working day of each month included the following:

Corn grits	30 pounds
Cocoa	3 pounds
Evaporated milk	10 cans
Bulk lard	10 pounds
Flour	45 pounds
Sugar	10 pounds

At times, certain other commodities were substituted in accordance with the available supplies.

As shown by Table 96, the total deliveries of food in the form of employees' paioks amounted to 3,687.5 metric tons, valued at $375,312.38. Table 532 shows the detail of these deliveries by commodities and by districts. These deliveries represent relief applied, but in principle are sales for cash, since they were delivered in lieu of cash payments.

The commodities delivered under employee paiok may be summarized as follows:

Employee Paiok

Commodity	Metric Tons
Flour	1,603.5
Rice	693.2
Beans and peas	10.0
Corn grits	273.8
Pork products	278.5
Milk	345.6
Cocoa	66.1
Sugar	373.8
Miscellaneous food	15.2
Soap	27.8
Total	3,687.5

f) *American Friends Service Committee:* Reference has been made in earlier sections of this report (cf. pages 117–20) to the relief work of the Quakers, and a brief indication has been given of their co-operation in Russia. The Quakers were in Russia before the Riga agreement, and the A.R.A. had contributed certain commodities to their work there, as discussed under Special Programs. With the signing of the Riga agreement and its adoption by the European Relief Council, of which the American Friends Service Committee was a member, they enlarged their Russian program. Among other things, the Friends had assembled certain relief supplies at Hamburg intended for German relief. With conditions so much more serious in Russia, they sought the co-operation of the A.R.A. in transporting certain of these commodities from Hamburg to Baltic ports, for use in that country. Between January and August, 1922, the A.R.A. forwarded for the Friends a total of 4,202.2 metric tons of supplies, valued at $267,394.24. These commodities were delivered to the A.F.S.C. at Russian ports, and the further handling and internal distribution was taken care of by the American Friends Service Committee. The detail of these shipments by steamers and commodities is given in Table 525.

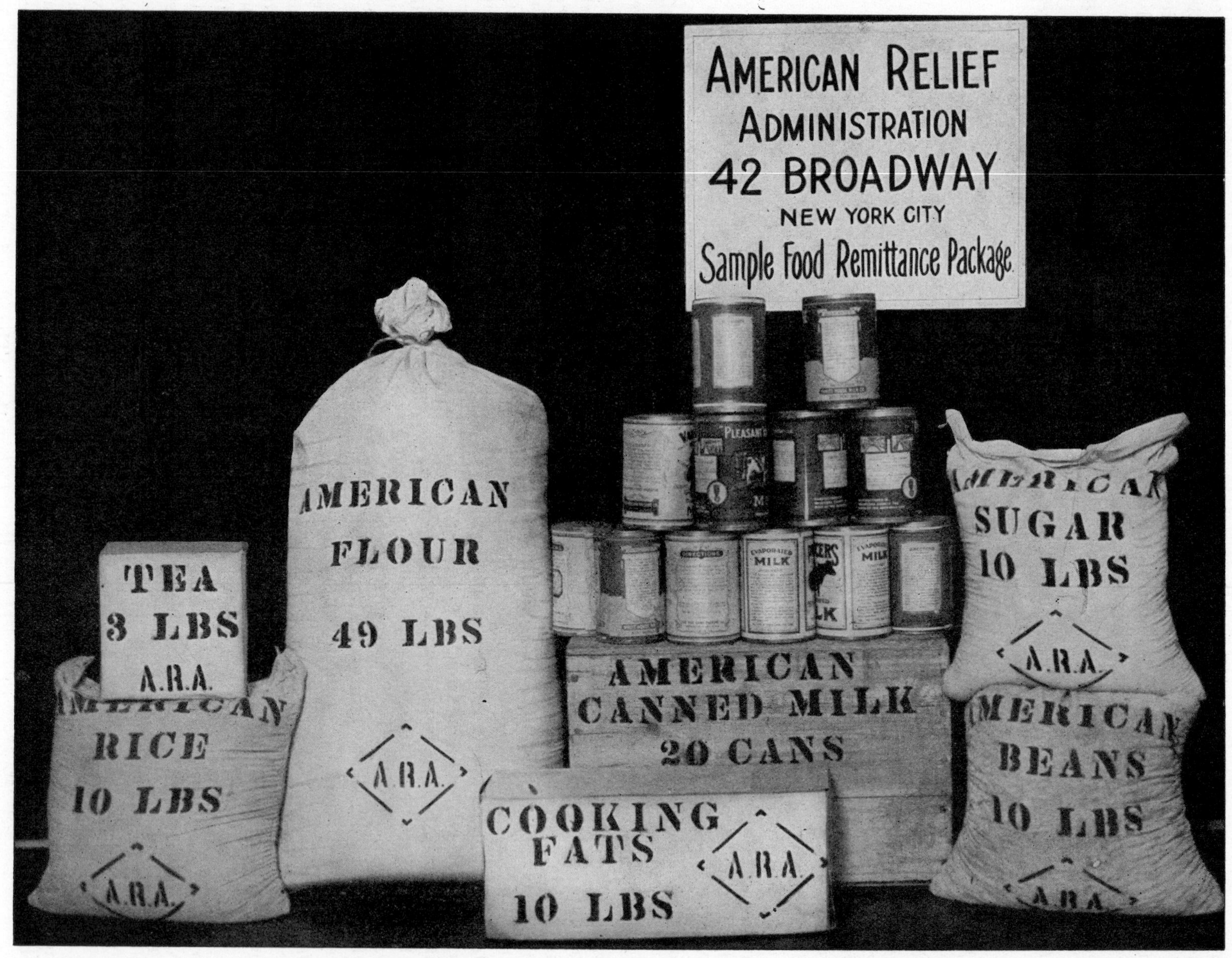

Contents of an A.R.A. Russian food remittance package

The following tabulation summarizes the commodities handled by the A.R.A. for the Friends on this operation.

Commodities Handled by A.R.A. for American Friends Service Committee

Commodities	Metric Tons
Flour	3,037.3
Rice	71.9
Beans and peas	90.6
Corn grits	917.8
Pork products	16.6
Sugar	67.6
Clothing	.4
Total	4,202.2

In addition to this work, the Friends purchased substantial quantities of commodities from the A.R.A. Warehouses, either as bulk or Eurelcon sales, and they carried on substantial relief programs on their own account, quite apart from the work done in direct co-operation with the A.R.A. and referred to in this report.

Seed grain.—The second major division of relief for the Soviet Republics was that of grain for seeding purposes. The early investigations of the A.R.A. disclosed the fact that in vast territories along the Volga, in eastern and southern Russia, and in Ukraine not only was there no food, but there would be no grain for planting the next year and consequently the famine conditions in 1922–1923 would only be aggravated. This was one of the main arguments placed before Congress for the appropriation of the Grain Corporation funds. The Act of Congress specifically mentioned that seed grain should be supplied.

The Soviet Government also was deeply concerned about seed and specified that the major portion of their appropriation for relief should be for seed grain. This fund, like that of the Grain Corporation, did not become available until January, 1922, and it was with the very greatest difficulty that the purchases were made and the grain transported and distributed to the peasants in time for the spring planting. These difficulties were greatly increased by the breakdown of railroads and all internal distribution in Russia. But these difficulties were overcome, and the seed grain was distributed and planted by the peasants. This was the big factor in relieving the distress in 1922.

Table 96 shows that the total deliveries of seed grain amounted to 166,973.5 metric tons, worth $9,983,359.54. This was divided between the two funds as follows:

Fund	Metric Tons	Total Value
Grain Corporation	55,107.6	$2,948,485.24
Soviet gold	111,865.9	7,034,874.30
Total	166,973.5	$9,983,359.54

The purchases from the Grain Corporation Fund were all made in the United States,[1] as required by the law. The seed was shipped to Russia and distributed to districts, where it was delivered to authorized representatives of the Soviet Government and receipted for by them. The final distribution to the peasants was made by the Soviet authorities. Table 530 shows the distribution of this grain to districts as compiled from the receipts, while Table 517 shows the detail of the shipment of these supplies from the United States.

The purchases of seed grain, from the Soviet gold, were made in the United States, excepting the oats which was purchased in Esthonia and Sweden. This oats was for forage, rather than seed, and was required to feed the horses in order that the land might be prepared for planting. The famine had naturally greatly decreased the number of work animals available, and it was important that those remaining should be maintained in working condition.

The grain purchased with the Soviet gold was delivered to the Russian authorities at Baltic ports, and all responsibility of the A.R.A. ceased at that point. The Soviet officials attended to the internal distribution of the grain, and no detailed information is available regarding these operations, except that it is known to have been distributed in the famine areas.

The detail of the shipment of the grain, purchased for the Soviet account, is shown in Table 519.

[1] It is of interest to note that in selecting seed adaptable to Russian conditions, purchases were made of grain produced in some of our Northwestern states from seed originally imported from the Russian famine districts. This was true also of purchases from the Soviet gold.

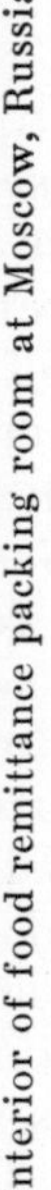

Interior of food remittance packing room at Moscow, Russia

The following tabulation summarizes the seed grain purchases under these two funds:

Summary of Seed Grain Deliveries in Russia
(*Metric Tons*)

Commodity	Grain Corporation	Soviet Gold	Total
Seed wheat	35,713.3	101,321.0	137,034.3
Seed corn	18,294.3	4.1	18,298.4
Seed rye	.....	3,810.2	3,810.2
Beans and peas	.....	4,229.6	4,229.6
Grass seed	.....	142.0	142.0
Forage oats	.....	2,359.0	2,359.0
Shipping material	1,100.0	.....	1,100.0
Total	55,107.6	111.865.9	166,973.5

Remittances and bulk sales.—The third group of relief activities in the Soviet Republics had to do with remittances and bulk sales. As in the countries of Central Europe, these represented sales of relief commodities to organizations or individuals and were used as a means of mobilizing certain types of charity funds and of facilitating the work of other organizations.

The total remittances and bulk sales in Russia amounted to 89,236.8 metric tons, valued at $14,417,510.40, and were divided as follows:

Operation	Metric Tons	Value
Food remittances	54,316.3	$ 9,305,300.00
Bulk sales	34,570.5	4,374,893.28
Clothing remittances	350.0	737,317.12
Total	89,236.8	$14,417,510.40

a) *Food remittances*: The food remittance operation of the A.R.A. Warehouses in Central Europe (cf. page 90) had been successful in mobilizing relief funds which would not ordinarily have been contributed to any general fund. Since no public appeal had been made for funds for Russia, and since the need was so great, a similar plan was put into operation there. By these means thousands of Americans purchased food drafts in the United States which, when sent to their friends and relatives in Russia, enabled the latter to obtain packages of American food at far less cost than the same food could be purchased and shipped by the donor. No special warehouse operation was set up, but the remittances and bulk sales were handled by the A.R.A. organization, although for the most part from supplies shipped specially for that purpose.

The Russian food remittances were sold in $10 units only, and were offered for sale not only in America, but in all the principal countries of central and western Europe and in Siberia.

The food parcels were made up in Russia from imported supplies, and deliveries were made direct to beneficiaries at the nineteen different district headquarters where A.R.A. Warehouses were located. Deliveries to outlying districts were made from these stations, using the Russian parcel post under the terms of a special agreement with the Soviet authorities with regard to remittances. Each package was sent fully insured for its gold value, in favor of the beneficiary.

The contents of the Russian food remittance were as follows (cf. page 254):

Flour	49 pounds
Rice	25 pounds
Tea	3 pounds
Fats	10 pounds
Sugar	10 pounds
Milk	20 tins

In order to provide additional funds for child feeding in Russia, it was decided to allow a rather large margin of profit on the food remittance business. The food making up the standard package, purchased in large quantities, cost the A.R.A. about $6.75. Transportation, insurance, packing, etc., amounted to about $1.00, so that on the average there was a margin of about $2.25 per package. Inasmuch as the cost of similar food in Russia varied from $60 to $16 in different cities, and at different times, the price of the package was not excessive, and all who purchased Russian remittances were advised of this margin, and the intentions of the A.R.A. to use the surplus for child feeding.

The sales of individual Russian remittances as distinct from "bulk sales" ran to a very large volume, reaching a total not far from 1,000,000 packages. Table 96 shows that the food remittances distributed amounted to 54,316.3 metric tons of supplies, valued at $9,305,300. Table 533 shows the distribution of these remittances by districts within Russia and by commodities. A summary of the commodities delivered through the food remittances is shown on page 259.

A considerable portion of the food remittance business was due to large purchases of remittances by other relief organizations, such as the

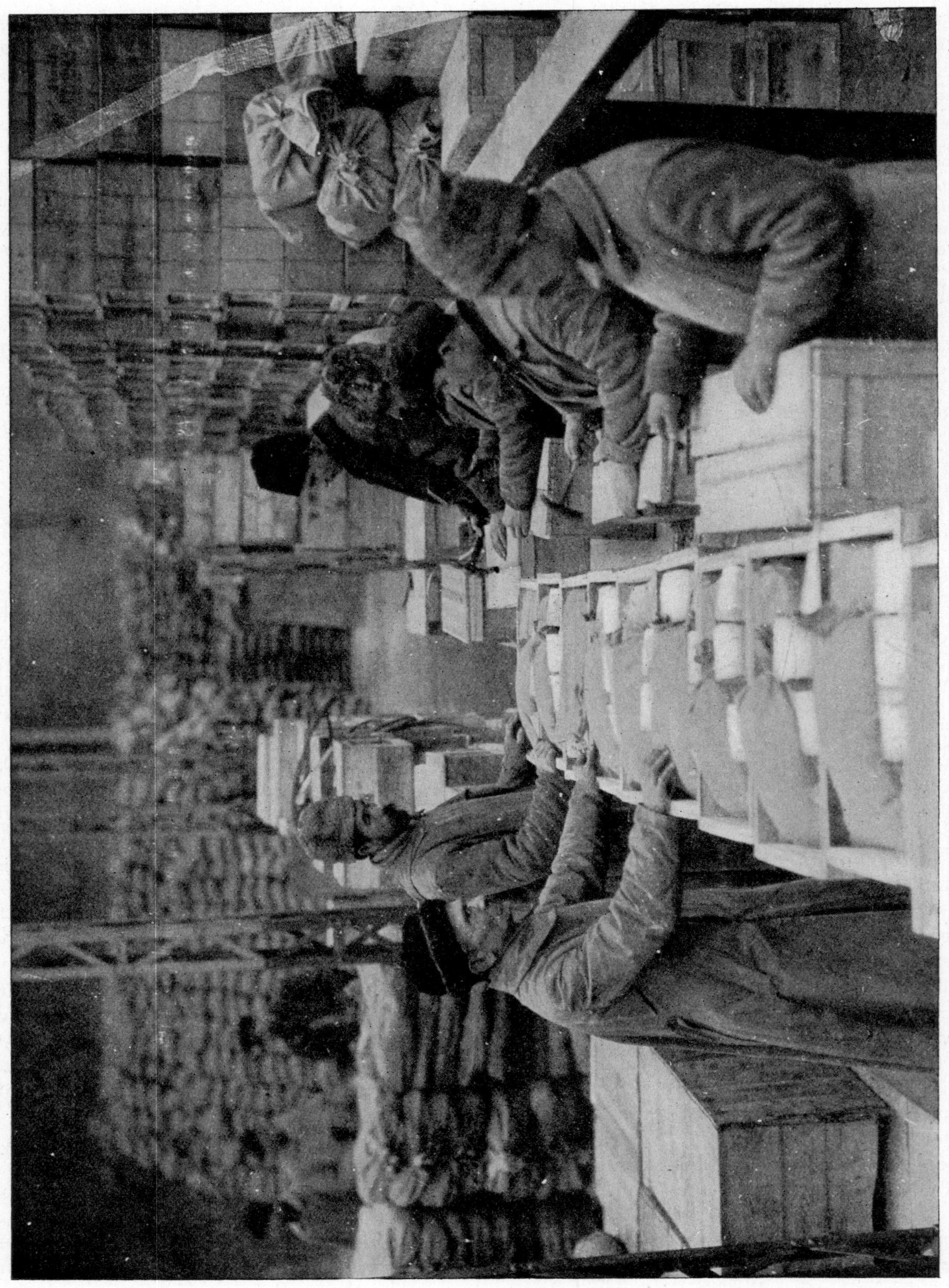

Food remittances being packed for delivery by post, Moscow warehouse

Jewish Joint Distribution Committee, which often found it more convenient to purchase these packages than to use the bulk commodities. A large number were used also in the intelligentsia relief (cf. page 261).

b) *Bulk sales:* In an earlier section, reference is made to the A.R.A. warehouse stocks of relief supplies in Russia from which sales could be made to any of the co-operating relief organizations who cared to avail themselves of the opportunity. These commodities were sold by the A.R.A. at cost, plus a sufficient margin to insure the organization against loss, with the understanding that profits, if any, would be used for child feeding in Russia.

The total food bulk sales of all kinds in Russia amounted to 34,570.5 metric tons, with a sales value of $4,374,893.28 (Table 96). These sales were handled under three different heads. The first group was known as Eurelcon sales, meaning sales to organizations belonging to the European Relief Council, according to the agreement signed in August, 1921. The second group was designated as bulk sales, and included sales to relief organizations not belonging to the European Relief Council. The third group, known as internal sales, included sales to organizations and individuals within Russia. The total volume of business was as follows:

	Metric Tons	Value
Eurelcon sales	15,840.8	$1,812,726.02
Bulk sales	13,886.2	2,148,457.28
Internal sales	4,843.7	413,709.98
Total bulk sales	34,570.7*	$4,374,893.28

* Difference of .2 metric ton between this total and that in Table 96 (see reference in paragraph above) is due to detail being carried to three decimals.

Many of the co-operating organizations also made large purchases of food remittances in addition to bulk sale purchases.

No tabulation is possible from the receipts for bulk sales and remittances which will show the total purchases by different organizations. However, the following tabulation adapted from data contained in the *Annual Report of the Executive Committee of the American Relief Administration* of April 4, 1923, shows the approximate contributions from various organizations which were available for the purchase of bulk food and clothing, and food and clothing remittances.

Approximate Sums Used to Purchase Food and Clothing Remittances and Bulk Commodities by Relief Organizations

American Jewish Joint Distribution Committee	$1,314,000
American Friends Service Committee	415,000
Apostolic Delegation (Catholics)	750,000
Federal Council of the Churches of Christ in America	90,000
Laura Spelman Rockefeller Memorial	830,000
Mennonite Central Committee	400,000
National Lutheran Council	300,000
Seventh-Day Adventists	50,000
Various Protestant churches	25,000
Volga Relief Society	220,000
Y.M.C.A. and Y.W.C.A. (student relief)	200,000
Total	$4,594,000

In addition to these sums from organizations, there were many large contributions from private sources, such as $95,000 from William Bingham, II, for relief of doctors and $5,000 from the Rochester (New York) Community Chest for the same purpose, as well as many others.[1]

The following tabulation summarizes the commodities delivered through the food remittances and various types of bulk sales:

Summary of Food Commodities Delivered on Russian Remittances and Bulk Sales

(*Metric Tons*)

Commodity	Food Remittances	Bulk Sales	Eurelcon Sales	Internal Sales
Flour	27,199.1	6,740.6	6,718.0	2,324.7
Rice	6,690.0	1,826.6	1,545.9	344.4
Beans and peas	.....	0.1	217.8	31.6
Corn grits	3,737.1	894.5	2,707.1	635.7
Pork products	2,741.0	853.2	638.4	210.1
Milk	8,428.5	2,104.8	2,536.9	705.3
Cocoa	69.2	62.6	306.5	115.2
Sugar	4,919.1	1,292.5	1,151.0	463.3
Tea	532.1	111.3	.....	5.3
Miscellaneous foods	.....	.....	19.1	5.8
Soap	0.2	.....	.....	2.2
Total	54,316.3	13,886.2	15,840.7	4,843.6

c) *Clothing remittances:* Reference has been made to a proposed plan for clothing remittances, similar to the food remittances discussed

[1] In addition to the references cited, much additional information regarding the remittance and bulk sale operations is contained in numerous issues of the American Relief Administration *Bulletins.* See particularly "The Carriage of Philanthropy," by J. R. Ellingston, A.R.A. *Bulletin Series 2,* No. 43.

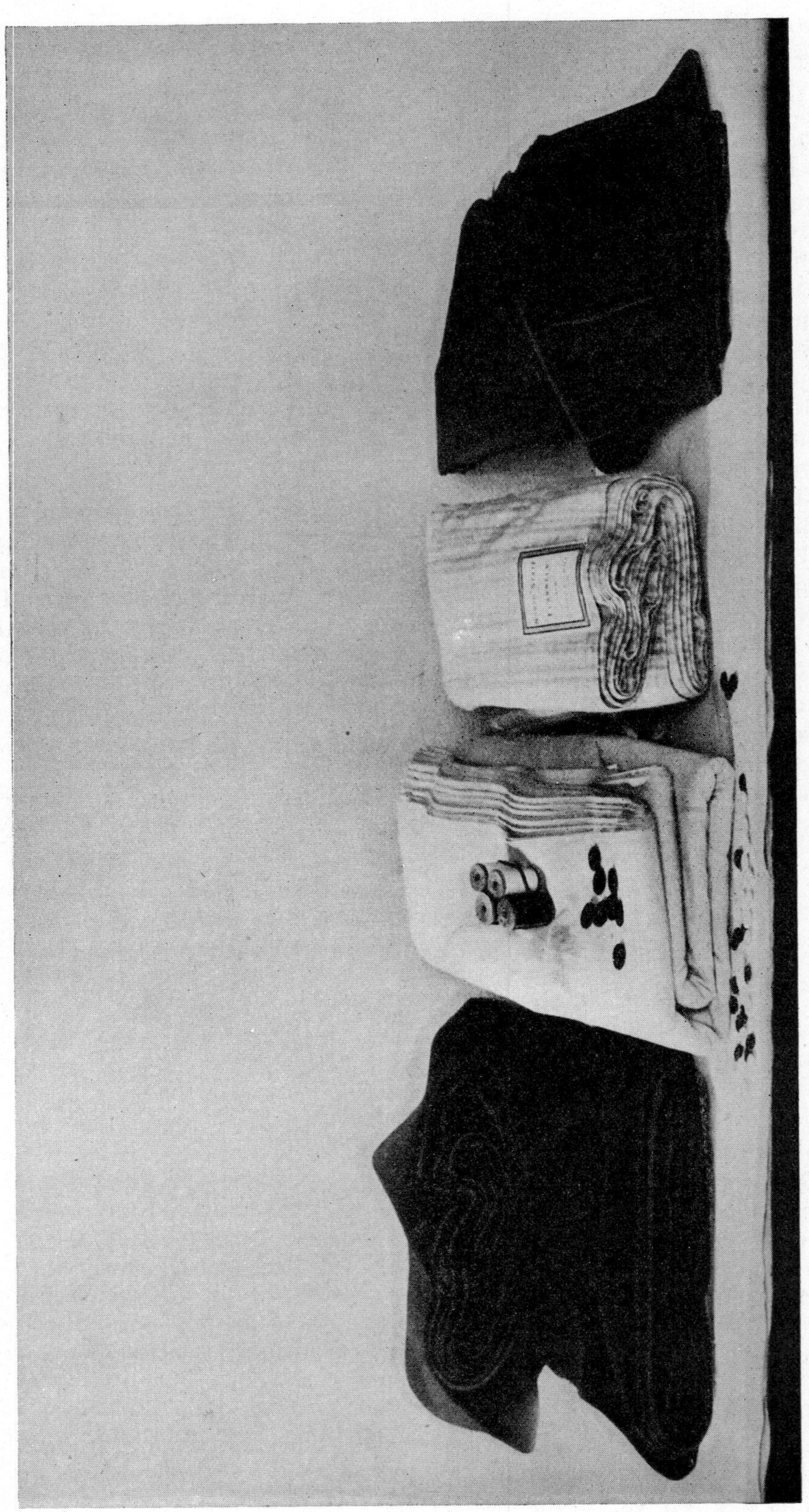

Sample of clothing remittance package for Russia (contents quoted in text on opposite page).

above. The urgent need for clothing in Russia in the winter of 1921–1922 caused the plan to be proposed, but it had to be abandoned because of the severe internal transportation difficulties in Russia. In the fall of 1922, the need for clothing was still urgent, and the remittance plan was revived. A clothing remittance agreement was signed with the Soviet Government on October 26, 1922, and the plan was put into effect during the next few months. The fact that both food and clothing remittance sales were discontinued in March, 1923, gave this plan only a few months' operation. During that period, the total sales of clothing amounted to 350.0 metric tons, valued at $737,317.12.

The perfecting of plans for the clothing remittance offered many difficulties. It was necessary that the package should be acceptable to both men and women, and to all ages and sizes. This made it impossible to include shoes, stockings, or ready-made garments. The package finally adopted consisted of 4⅔ yards of woolen cloth, 4 yards of linings, 16 yards of muslin, 8 yards of flannelette, 4 spools of thread, and 48 buttons of different sizes. By buying in large quantities, the A.R.A. was able to sell this package, delivered in Russia, for $20.00, with a small margin of profit for safety. The same package would have retailed in New York for about $21.50, and in Russia was worth from $30.00 to $40.00.

Although in no way comparable in extent with the food remittance operation, the clothing remittances formed a very useful supplement to the other phases of Russian relief. Both the sales and the gift packages came at an opportune time to meet a need strongly emphasized by the changing economic conditions in Russia.

The details of the clothing remittance deliveries are given in Table 529 and the commodities delivered are summarized in Table 98, page 251.

d) Intelligentsia relief: Although not forming a special section of the Russian relief, some reference should be made to the relief provided for the intellectual classes through the contributions from organizations and individuals, used especially to purchase food and clothing remittances.

It would be impossible to describe the hardships through which the educated classes in Russia passed during the revolution and the famine. Nor is it possible to estimate what Russia and the world lost through the untimely death of thousands of scholars and artists who could not survive these difficulties. Physically, the intelligentsia were worse off than the peasants during the famine, for the former had no hidden reserves of food and they were looked upon with too great disfavor by the new government to receive the ration which went to the common laborer. In a land where the sole interest of practically everyone was to secure bread for the day, the educated and professional groups were ill adapted to hold their own. Many broke under the burden, and it looked as if the whole of the intellectual class of Russia might meet extinction. Ellingston[1] quotes from a letter written by a Russian in Petrograd from which the following is extracted:

Special or intelligentsia relief packages being given to the priests of the Russian Orthodox Church at Ufa, February, 1922.

> Death was now more in evidence than life. Before my eyes there died Feodor Batiushkov, the famous professor of philology, poisoned from eating uneatably filthy cabbage. Another one to die from hunger was S. Bengerov, professor of history and literature, he who gave to the Russian people entire editions of Shakespeare, of Schiller and of Pushkin. . . . . I saw the talented critic A. A. Ismailov die of hunger. At the same period the philosopher V. V. Rosanov succumbed to starvation in Moscow. Before his death the latter roamed the streets in search of cigarette ends with which to appease his hunger. . . . . Try to visualize your own Emerson in tatters, wandering about the streets of Boston, snatching with frozen fingers some crumb from the highway mud. . . . .

[1] "The Carriage of Philanthropy," *A.R.A. Bulletin*, Series 2, No. 43 (December, 1923), page 107.

Peasants waiting for packages at delivery station at Simbirsk, Russia

For many, the conditions were more than they could bear, and thousands committed suicide.

With the establishment of the food remittance plan in November, 1921, the way was open to supply relief to special classes of the population. Special appeals were made by various groups of Russian intelligentsia to similar groups in America. In time these bore fruit.

The first contribution for intelligentsia relief was for doctors and was the result of an appeal by the A.R.A. personnel, who had seen the heroic fight that Russian physicians were making against the ravages of disease, although they themselves often had little to eat or wear. This first contribution totaled $67,500, including a gift of $35,000 from William Bingham, II., of Maine (later increased by another $60,000); $25,000 from the Jewish Joint Distribution Committee; $5,000 from the Rochester Community Fund; and many others.

The largest contribution for intelligentsia relief was $830,000 from the Laura Spelman Rockefeller Memorial. The funds administered for this purpose were distributed in several different categories, with the approximate amounts for each as follows:

University professors and other teachers	$ 527,659
Physicians, nurses, and attendants	123,587
Artists and musicians	13,791
Ballet schools	2,900
Writers	4,100
Religious bodies	10,000
General intelligentsia	330,000
Individual relief, not specified	194,000
Total	$1,206,037

In addition to the above, there were hundreds of thousands of dollars worth of supplies distributed to intelligentsia by organizations affiliated with the A.R.A.

Damaged Commodities and Adjustments

Table 96 shows under the sale of damaged commodities and other adjustments in the Russian operation an item of 13,795.3 metric tons, worth $441,730.97. This includes a number of categories, among which were 9,257.7 tons, worth $290,516.36, from the Grain Corporation supplies which were damaged or lost in transit. The Grain Corporation sold the damaged supplies for what they would bring and collected for the lost supplies from underwriters and ocean carriers. The principal item in the Grain Corporation adjustment was the loss of the S.S. "West Munham," which grounded off Heligoland on March 9, 1922, with the result that the cargo was badly damaged.

Adjustments on the A.R.A. shipment included a total of 4,537.6 metric tons, with a value of $138,528.60. This included port outturn, overages and shortages, losses in transit, and pilferage. In addition, there was a loss of $12,686.01 in handling, cutting, and other shortages in connection with the clothing operations. These adjustments are all shown in the detailed distribution tables in the Appendix to this report.

When one considers that these food commodities all had to be transported through large areas where the population was on the verge of starvation, it is remarkable that the pilferage losses were not larger. In any event, the stolen articles were no doubt consumed, probably by individuals who needed them as badly as those to whom they were destined.

Donations from European Governments

Table 96 shows facilities and services donated to the Russian relief by the governments of Esthonia, Latvia, and Poland, to the value of $115,360.63. The donations consisted of warehouse space for A.R.A. Russian supplies in Esthonia and Latvia, and of railroad transportation for similar supplies in Poland. These contributions were of material assistance to the A.R.A. and, had they not been donated, it would have been necessary for the A.R.A. to pay out these sums, thereby reducing by that much the commodities which were sent into Russia.

The Soviet Government itself made very large contributions to the relief work in the form of cash, services, and facilities. A careful estimate of the value of these contributions at the completion of the A.R.A. work in Russia placed the value of these donations at $13,960,850.00, which is exclusive of the $11,357,325.13 in gold and of the $30,026.64 in commodity donations accounted for elsewhere. This contribution includes such items as stevedoring and other port services, rail and water freights, handling, warehousing, motor and wagon handling, light, water, fuel, baking, telephone and telegraph, travel and housing for A.R.A. personnel.

Liquidation

In the early spring of 1923, Mr. Hoover asked that a careful survey of Russian food conditions be made to determine the need, if any, for a continuation of the relief work. On May 14, 1923, Lincoln Hutchinson reported the results of a careful study of Russian crops and needs which indicated that Russia should have a surplus of grain and other foods after the new harvest. This conclusion was supported by much other evidence, including the rapidly declining price of foodstuffs, and by the unanimous opinion of the A.R.A. district supervisors.

Food and clothing remittance sales had been closed on March 15, 1923, and plans were made to liquidate the other activities as rapidly as possible. On June 15, 1923, a liquidation agreement was signed between the A.R.A. and the Soviet officials by which all responsibilities of the A.R.A. in Russia were terminated, and the Soviet Government agreed to accept the A.R.A. accounting for all supplies without question. By July 4, 1923, the last of the district headquarters had been closed, and after the inevitable festivities, in which the Soviet Government expressed its sincere appreciation of the work of the A.R.A., the relief personnel was on its way home.

TURKEY

(Appendix Tables 541–542)

ARMISTICE PERIOD

In the early months of 1919, the supply of wheat flour in Constantinople was exhausted, and the poor were existing chiefly on bread called *vecika,* of a very inferior quality, and sold at exorbitant prices. Samples of this bread revealed that it contained all sorts of refuse matter, including large amounts of chopped straw.

In February, the price of flour jumped from the government's buying price of 3½ piasters per 2½ pounds to a selling price of 250 and 300 piasters. Small chocolate-colored loaves of bread, containing just enough flour to amalgamate their adulteration of sawdust and straw, were retailed on the streets at prices equivalent to 30 cents in American money.

The Ottoman Empire had no credits, and there was practically nothing to be exported in payment for Allied supplies. Obviously, credit could not be granted to Turkey, which was still considered an enemy country. Finally, arrangements were made with a syndicate composed of officials of the National Bank of Turkey, a British institution. This syndicate, in possession of foreign credits, was able to purchase flour and resell it to the Turkish population at a nominal profit. These transactions were carried on through the commercial organization of J. W. Whittall and Company. In all, the American Relief Administration sold against cash settlement 20,278.3 metric tons of flour, valued at $4,369,404.30, through this syndicate for Turkish consumption. No other relief to Turkey during the Armistice Period was reported through the office of the Director General of Relief.

The effect of these deliveries on the food situation in Constantinople was most beneficial. Wide publicity was given to the arrival of each American cargo, and it finally became known that this American flour was to be sold at a price to undercut the wholesalers, and thus eliminate the inflated prices of the speculators.

The effect was almost instantaneous. The wholesalers became frightened, and flour dropped over 50 per cent. The street speculator in bread disappeared, and white loaves made from American flour were placed on sale at reasonable prices.

UNITED KINGDOM

(Appendix Table 543)

U.S.F.A. PERIOD

The United Kingdom is always dependent upon overseas imports for the major portion of the food supply of her people. Between 40 and 45 per cent of the total imports into the country are in the classification of food, drinks, and tobacco. In the pre-war years, the average imports of the United Kingdom were equivalent to approximately 220,000,000 bushels of wheat, as against domestic production of less than 60,000,000 bushels. Nearly 80 per cent of the nation's bread supply had to come by ships from overseas points. Nearly half of the normal meat supply, all of the sugar, and a large portion of the dairy products consumed in the United Kingdom had to be imported. Consequently, when Germany announced her plan of unrestricted submarine warfare and began to put it into effect, Great Britain was seriously concerned as to her food supply. The entrance of the United States into the World War, in the spring of 1917, was welcomed by Great Britain more for the assurance of our great agricultural resources to support her food requirements than for any immediate assistance on the battle field.

With the continuation of the submarine warfare, and the resulting shortage in world shipping, the Allied nations and Great Britain, in particular, came to depend more and more upon the United States for their food supply. Reference has been made in an earlier section to the great expansion of food production in this country under the demands of the Allies.[1] Reference has also been made (page 16) to the serious shortage of the food supply in the United Kingdom in the early months of 1918 and the almost desperate efforts made by the United States Food Administration to meet these demands which for a time threatened the whole success of the Allied cause.

Almost immediately after our declaration of war against Germany, Congress passed an act (Act of April 24, 1917) establishing a credit of $3,000,000,000 in favor of the foreign governments engaged in war with the enemies of the United States. These credits were extended to a total of $10,000,000,000 by later acts (Acts of September 24, 1917; April 4, 1918; and July 9, 1918). Under these authorizations, the U.S. Treasury loaned vast sums to the Allied countries.

The total net credits established in favor of Great Britain under these authorizations amounted to $4,196,818,358.44.[2] Of this amount, according to the records in the United States Treasury, $1,375,484,734.33 was for the purpose of purchasing foodstuffs in the United States.

As explained on page 19, it has been necessary to partially estimate the tonnage of foodstuffs which were purchased with these credits, since the records in the Treasury are incomplete in this respect. Using the methods outlined, a grand total of 8,605,296.7 metric tons is obtained as the quantity of foodstuffs, including oats, purchased by the United Kingdom with these credits. The commodities purchased are shown in Table 543 and may be summarized as follows:

FOOD PURCHASES BY THE UNITED KINGDOM FINANCED BY U.S. TREASURY CREDITS, 1917 TO 1919

Commodities	Metric Tons
Flour	1,350,580.8
Grain	3,274,037.9
Rice	24,289.4
Beans and peas	23,878.9
Pork products	957,641.3
Milk	181,886.2
Sugar	1,539,236.7
Miscellaneous food	439,799.9
Forage (oats)	813,945.6
Total	8,605,296.7

[1] See also F. M. Surface, *American Pork Production in the World War* and *The Grain Trade during the World War.*

[2] *Annual Report of the Secretary of the Treasury for the Fiscal Year Ending June 30, 1920*, page 338.

ARMISTICE PERIOD

As in the case of all Allied and neutral countries, the food purchases for Great Britain during the Armistice Period were made through the the Interallied purchasing organizations, and had no direct relationship to the Director General of Relief (cf. page 17). In fact, a portion of the food supply for the United Kingdom during the Armistice Period is included in the sales during the U.S.F.A. Period, since the U.S. Treasury continued to grant credits to the Allies during a portion of the Armistice Period.

However, in connection with the relief of Austria under the Joint Allied Finance arrangement, it became important to make immediate deliveries which could not be financed directly by the American Relief Administration. Mr. Hoover, therefore, arranged a sale of 47,371.9 tons of food, valued at $10,618,045.72, to the United Kingdom, which they in turn delivered to Austria as part of the $16,000,000 worth of food which the United Kingdom was to furnish that country under the terms of the Joint Allied Finance. From the standpoint of the American Relief Administration this represented a cash sale, but in reality it represented a credit sale to Austria by the United Kingdom, financed by a loan to the latter country from the United States Treasury for that purpose.

As shown in the footnote to Table 543, the commodities and value involved in this transaction are accounted for under Joint Allied Finance for Austria (cf. page 60), and for purposes of the general summary of all relief deliveries this transaction is deducted to obtain a net total of the relief furnished.

SUNDRY ACTIVITIES

(Appendix Tables 539–540)

ARMISTICE PERIOD

Among the varied operations carried on by the several organizations included in this report, there were certain activities that cannot well be classified as relief to any special country. For example, when, under the direction of the Director General of Relief, France furnished food supplies to Russian prisoners of war interned in Germany, it is difficult to decide whether this should be classed as relief to Russia or to Germany. These and certain other inter-organization operations have been included under "Sundry Activities" as outlined in Table 539.

The total volume of relief classified under this heading amounts to 56,529.2 metric tons, with a value of $23,654,740.07. Inasmuch as these sundry operations represent less than two-tenths of one per cent of the total tonnage, and less than one-half of one per cent of the value of the operations included in this report (cf. Table 3), they cannot be regarded as excessive. Table 100 summarizes the operations included under Sundry Activities.

TABLE 100

SUMMARY OF DELIVERIES CLASSED UNDER SUNDRY ACTIVITIES
(For detail see Table 539)

Operation	Metric Tons	Total Value
Armistice Period		
C.R.B. (sundry sales)	51,392.0	$21,990,430.40
A.R.A. (cash sales)	1,903.2	464,770.08
Total from United States	53,295.2	$22,455,200.48
France (Russian prisoners of war in Germany)	2,672.0	1,100,917.00
Total, Armistice Period	55,967.2	$23,556,117.48
Reconstruction Period		
E.C.F.–Laura Spelman Rockefeller Memorial (Russian refugees in Constantinople)	562.0	98,622.59
Grand total	56,529.2	$23,654,740.07

SUNDRY SALES BY THE C.R.B.

The details of these sundry operations are shown in the statistical report on the work of the Commission for Relief in Belgium.[1] As some of the major items, these sales include commodities transferred to the American Relief Administration, to the value of $4,486,570.10 (cf. Table 103); also the distribution in Belgium of some twenty million British army rations, valued at $4,377,650.26; and miscellaneous sales, including recovery from underwriters and the sale of damaged commodities.

A.R.A. CASH SALES

These activities include a group of sundry cash sales made to various organizations or individuals from American Relief Administration stocks during the Armistice Period. These sales in many respects are similar to the A.R.A.W. sales carried on during the Reconstruction Period. With the great shortage of food supplies in many of these countries, it was often possible to effect needed relief by selling these supplies for cash, either to organizations which expected to use them as relief, or to employees or even to tradesmen, providing sufficient precautions against profiteering in their further sale were taken. As shown in detail in Table 540, these sundry sales are grouped in several categories which may be summarized as follows:

SUMMARY OF SUNDRY CASH SALES BY THE AMERICAN RELIEF ADMINISTRATION—ARMISTICE PERIOD

	Metric Tons	Total Value
Commission for Relief in Belgium	668.3	$122,638.77
Jadranska Bank—Trieste	326.3	156,975.28
U.S. Navy—Adriatic ports	16.7	6,325.33
Viborg sales	373.7	79,515.01
Miscellaneous sales, all ports	518.2	99,315.69
Total	1,903.2	$464,770.08

[1] George I. Gay, *The Commission for Relief in Belgium, Statistical Review of Relief Operations.*

The sales to the Commission for Relief in Belgium represent commodities from American Relief Administration stocks at Rotterdam which were taken over by the Commission to meet special needs and which were settled for either by cash or by the return of commodities as indicated above.

Sales to the Jadranska Bank in Trieste were for supplies to employees and others who were experiencing difficulty in securing adequate amounts of food. The sale to the U.S. Navy in the Adriatic, and the Viborg sales, were for supplies to Americans or American government personnel in the respective regions.

Miscellaneous sales include sales to commercial organizations, such as the Magazzini Generali in Trieste, to army officers and Red Cross officials, and commodities used to pay for services, etc.

Russian Prisoners of War in Germany

The deliveries of 2,672.0 metric tons of food to Russian prisoners of war in Germany have been commented upon elsewhere (cf. page 187). This represented a benevolent gift by France, with a value of $1,100,917. Owing to the difficulties Germany was experiencing with food supplies for her own people during the Armistice, the war prisoners were suffering severely, and this gift by France was of great assistance in relieving a very distressing situation.

RECONSTRUCTION PERIOD

Russian Refugees in Constantinople

The remaining relief, to be accounted for under Sundry Activities, relates to the food furnished to Russian refugees in Constantinople (Istanbul) in 1922. This relief, which was handled by the European Children's Fund, was made possible by a special donation of $100,000 from the Laura Spelman Rockefeller Memorial. The need for this relief and its character have already been discussed under Special Programs and need not be repeated here. This relief, because of its special character, referring again to nationals of a country located on foreign soil, has not been included under any of the other relief activities accounted for in this report. The total supplies of food furnished to these refugees amounted to 562.0 metric tons, valued at $98,622.59.

Of the total deliveries under Sundry Accounts, the major portion, $22,455,200.48, represented sales for cash or its equivalent, and $1,199,539.59 consisted of benevolent contributions. The latter category includes the deliveries to the Russian prisoners of war in Germany and to the Russian refugees in Constantinople.

APPENDIX TABLES

NOTE TO APPENDIX TABLES

Parentheses ( ) in the Port of Sailing or Port of Arrival column have been used to designate geographical divisions or cities other than recognized ports. Cf. Table 111, page 284 (Berne), (Lemberg), (U.S.A.), (Paris), etc.

APPENDIX I

GENERAL TABLES

GRAND TOTAL OF FOOD AND RELIEF SUPPLIES

By Major Operations

Table 101

Major Operation	Table No.	Commodities					
		Flour	Grain	Rice	Beans, Peas	Corn Grits	Pork Products
Commission for Relief in Belgium Period	103	411,421.0	3,310,898.0	317,455.0	171,434.0	....	379,926.0
U.S. Food Administration Period	106	4,904,600.4	10,083,228.8	143,514.0	108,860.4	....	1,363,799.6
Armistice Period	107	1,253,568.0	983,979.6	99,039.1	104,833.6	....	266,979.6
Reconstruction Period	148	767,191.5	389,007.1	49,811.0	45,796.5	103,301.1	29,594.8
Grand Total, Net Deliveries	...	**7,336,780.9**	**14,767,113.5**	**609,819.1**	**430,924.5**	**103,301.1**	**2,040,300.0**

GRAND TOTAL OF FOOD AND RELIEF SUPPLIES

By Countries o

Table 102

Country	Table No.	Commoditie					
		Flour	Grain	Rice	Beans, Peas	Corn Grits	Pork Products
Armenia	200	91,248.8	8,000.0	2,427.6	3,066.4	......	339.9
Austria	206	428,767.0	184,464.4	19,187.6	11,537.6	1,491.9	36,963.1
Belgium	233	347,295.0	3,021,452.0	215,411.0	122,105.0	......	242,517.0
Bulgaria	234	22,862.4	....	......	......	......	......
Czecho-Slovakia	236	207,527.3	175,638.0	8,236.8	7,107.8	77.3	41,852.2
Danzig Free City	280	131.7	....	69.2	78.6	2.8	49.8
Denmark	290	....	19,912.0	......	......	......	......
Esthonia	292	22,596.9	6,462.1	624.9	752.4	......	1,033.2
Finland	306	61,256.0	113,039.0	231.4	7,675.3	......	2,747.7
France	320	1,845,958.5	2,058,757.1	206,633.9	127,954.8	......	401,699.4
Germany	323	304,022.8	311,329.3	73,254.1	67,814.6	1,149.0	152,990.2
Greece	334	12,886.0	2,451.0	203.0	1,269.0	2,642.0	102.0
Hungary	336	16,784.5	....	638.6	642.4	23.4	678.0
Italy	352	1,819,283.9	5,039,879.8	14,634.7	6,355.7	......	141,867.9
Jugoslavia	354	62,947.4	4,116.0	599.2	5,550.8	......	3,749.0
Latvia	369	13,637.1	....	1,112.1	1,565.8	......	1,039.3
Lithuania	382	2,962.7	....	183.9	290.0	......	472.6
Netherlands	392	25,027.4	....	......	......	......	......
Poland	394	407,607.5	87,684.5	21,528.8	30,098.3	1,689.4	31,939.6
Roumania	491	121,731.8	53,838.3	544.3	3,298.1	......	3,812.1
Russia							
Northwest Russia	497	14,323.1	....	64.0	407.7	......	2,289.9
Kouban	507	....	....	......	......	......	......
Siberia	510	....	....	......	......	......	......
Soviet Republics	511	134,781.2	386,556.1	18,914.6	7,895.5	96,202.3	12,425.5
Ukraine	537	....	....	......	......	......	......
Volunteer Army (Russian)	538	394.0	....	......	......	......	......
Sundry Accounts	539	3,516.7	19,496.0	1,030.0	1,579.8	23.0	4,090.3
Turkey	541	20,278.3	....	......	......	......	......
United Kingdom	543	1,396,864.7	3,274,037.9	24,289.4	23,878.9	......	957,641.3
Total, Gross Deliveries	....	**7,384,692.7**	**14,767,113.5**	**609,819.1**	**430,924.5**	**103,301.1**	**2,040,300.0**
Less Duplications	....	47,911.8	....	......	......	......	.....
Grand Total, Net Deliveries	....	**7,336,780.9**	**14,767,113.5**	**609,819.1**	**430,924.5**	**103,301.1**	**2,040,300.0**

DELIVERED DURING WORLD WAR AND RECONSTRUCTION PERIOD

1914–1924

In Net Metric Tons of 1,000 Kilograms or 2,204.6 Pounds

Milk	Cocoa	Sugar	Miscellaneous Food	Forage	Soap	Medical and Hospital Supplies	Clothing and Misc.	Total Tons	Total Value
80,921.0	12,870.0	51,024.0	173,272.0	....	39,129.0	......	39,709.0	4,988,059.0	$ 861,340,244.21
451,346.9	....	1,947,936.8	922,736.5	3,177,242.8	......	......	....	23,103,266.2	3,050,496,599.23
50,653.7	511.5	43,276.7	873,062.2	....	1,110.5	4,377.5	497,055.7	4,178,447.7	1,101,486,783.34
103,612.1	10,762.6	44,295.7	4,076.0	3,134.3	2,276.6	8,283.9	10,390.9	1,571,534.1	220,704,581.78
686,533.7	**24,144.1**	**2,086,533.2**	**1,973,146.7**	**3,180,377.1**	**42,516.1**	**12,661.4**	**547,155.6**	**33,841,307.0**	**$5,234,028,208.56**

DELIVERED DURING WORLD WAR AND RECONSTRUCTION PERIOD

Destination, 1914–1924

In Net Metric Tons of 1,000 Kilograms or 2,204.6 Pounds

Milk	Cocoa	Sugar	Miscellaneous Food	Forage	Soap	Medical and Hospital Supplies	Clothing and Misc.	Total Tons	Total Value
4,996.5	355.9	1,392.9	6,586.9	......	732.3	2.0	16,614.9	135,764.1	$ 28,795,426.49
15,712.9	1,337.0	44,535.1	41,938.8	......	208.9	.....	36,055.8	822,200.1	145,481,222.30
47,819.3	5,882.0	1,517.0	145,738.0	......	14,490.0	.....	34,630.0	4,198,856.3	697,140,348.91
......	.....	......	......	......	.....	.....	......	22,862.4	4,856,647.53
9,392.0	813.3	848.1	85,230.0	......	171.5	.....	8,240.3	545,134.6	115,438,351.98
191.8	16.7	28.5	2.5	......	.....	.....	1.6	573.2	127,700.69
......	.....	......	......	......	.....	.....	......	19,912.0	2,147,059.30
1,685.2	144.0	1,355.1	27,774.1	......	38.4	312.3	4,579.9	67,358.5	21,017,263.56
791.4	10.0	1,590.1	842.0	......	.....	.....	338.0	188,520.9	30,282,047.90
289,409.7	6,988.0	427,706.3	825,374.8	2,042,715.2	24,639.0	.....	167,863.0	8,425,699.7	1,289,488,622.47
39,657.8	1,037.2	5,185.1	206,520.8	......	50.0	.....	109,923.2	1,272,934.1	294,373,692.75
162.0	409.0	203.0	45.0	......	2.0	.....	......	20,374.0	1,211,949.95
1,441.9	173.0	627.9	105.8	......	37.0	.....	241.0	21,393.5	4,607,139.37
13,152.7	.....	30,682.1	93,341.9	320,582.0	.....	.....	......	7,479,780.7	799,608,264.01
2,475.7	239.0	507.5	16,348.0	......	71.8	.....	30,754.6	127,359.0	45,898,651.43
2,035.7	155.7	415.7	5,384.9	......	44.6	.....	975.7	26,366.6	7,550,021.69
463.8	60.8	105.9	4,700.0	......	5.0	.....	3,633.0	12,877.7	5,980,781.39
......	.....	.....	......	......	.....	.....	......	25,027.4	4,219,498.41
25,719.7	2,079.4	8,385.8	46,396.8	633.3	1,379.3	3,488.2	82,505.0	751,135.6	200,864,857.73
4,099.9	220.9	406.4	25,309.0	......	25.0	.....	15,917.0	229,202.8	53,637,311.31
1,188.9	5.2	9.1	......	......	10.5	.....	712.3	19,010.7	5,890,076.54
......	.....	......	......	......	.....	577.0	1,015.5	1,592.5	578,490.50
......	.....	......	......	......	.....	.....	40.0	40.0	75,000.00
43,362.6	3,945.0	21,555.9	1,351.5	2,501.0	599.8	8,281.9	3,199.8	741,572.7	63,174,848.78
......	.....	......	......	......	.....	.....	5,550.0	5,550.0	8,500,222.67
......	.....	......	......	......	.....	.....	......	394.0	86,680.00
888.0	272.0	420.3	837.1	......	11.0	.....	24,365.0	56,529.2	23,654,740.07
......	.....	......	......	......	.....	.....	......	20,278.3	4,369,404.30
182,974.2	.....	1,539,236.7	439,799.9	813,945.6	.....	.....	......	8,652,668.6	1,386,102,780.05
687,621.7	**24,144.1**	**2,086,714.5**	**1,973,627.8**	**3,180,377.1**	**42,516.1**	**12,661.4**	**547,155.6**	**33,890,969.2**	**$5,245,159,102.08**
1,088.0	.....	181.3	481.1	......	.....	.....	......	49,662.2	11,130,893.52
686,533.7	**24,144.1**	**2,086,533.2**	**1,973,146.7**	**3,180,377.1**	**42,516.1**	**12,661.4**	**547,155.6**	**33,841,307.0**	**$5,234,028,208.56**

Table No. 103

Delivered to	Table No.	Flour Wheat, Cereal	Grain Wheat, Corn, Rye, Barley, Breadstuffs, and Seed	Rice	Beans, Peas
		COMMISSION FOR RELIEF			
Occupied Belgium	233	335,608.0	2,801,887.0	215,411.0	122,105.0
Belgian Refugees, Holland	233	....	....	....	....
Belgian Refugees, Havre	233	....	....	....	....
Invaded Northern France	320	75,788.0	508,861.0	102,030.0	49,312.0
French Refugees, Holland	320	....	150.0	1.0	....
French Children, Holland	320	25.0	....	10.0	12.0
French Prisoners of War, Holland	320	....	....	3.0	5.0
Total, C.R.B. Period	101	**411,421.0**	**3,310,898.0**	**317,455.0**	**171,434.0**
		ARMISTICE			
Sales to German Government Ex-C.R.B. Stock	326	1,039.0	44,581.0	16,181.0	9,645.0
Sales to German Government Ex-Comité National Stock	326	15,026.0	....	5,064.0	9,922.0
Transfers to G.C. and A.R.A.—1919	539	....	....	....	1,128.0
Miscellaneous Transactions	539	618.0	19,496.0	975.0	370.0
Total, Armistice Period	....	**16,683.0**	**64,077.0**	**22,220.0**	**21,065.0**
Grand Total Relief Deliveries	....	**428,104.0**	**3,374,975.0**	**339,675.0**	**192,499.0**

* For detail see Gay, "The Commission for Relief in Belgium—Statistical Review of Relief Operations," Stanford University Press, 1925.

† This value represents (a) sale of damaged commodities, $2,429.77; (b) 20,000,000 rations supplied through British War office, $4,377,650.26; (c) credit balances from foodstuffs sunk en route, $7,634,673.21; (d) credit balances from foodstuffs sold en route, $2,913,076.27; (e) credit balances from sundry operations, interest, exchange, etc., $2,576,030.79.

‡ Includes 23,769.0 metric tons of clothing; details in Table 104.

COMMISSION FOR

Detail of Clothin

Table 104*

Distributed to	Cloth (Yards)	Cloth (Square Yards)	Outer Garments: Blouses (Each)	Breeches (Pairs)	Coats (Each)	Garments (Each)
Belgium	9,165,700	5,464,207	90,089	94,253	2,970	1,586,347
Northern France	5,602,121	3,016,900	6,040	5,900	....	908,030
The Hague	......	....	....	....	....	......
Refugee Camps, Holland	7,092	....	....	....	....	25,085
U.S. Food Administration	......	....	....	....	....	......
Harve	......	....	....	....	....	......
Oeuvre de Soutiens	......	....	....	....	....	......
Total	**14,774,913**	**8,481,107**	**96,129**	**100,153**	**2,970**	**2,519,462**

* See ‡ note in Table 103.

COMMISSION FO

Detail of Clothir

Table 104—*Continued*

Distributed to	CLOTHING PURCHASED—(Continued) Leather: Heels (Pairs)	Soles (Pairs)	Repair Leather (Pieces)	Accessories: Buckles, Buttons, Hooks, Eyes (Dozen)	Press Stud (Dozen)
Belgium	670,320	864,218	397,882	5,544,912	55,000
Northen France	336,960	840,248	149,189	23,937,528	82,762
The Hague	......	......	......	....	.....
Refugee Camps, Holland	......	......	......	....	.....
U.S. Food Administration	......	......	......	....	.....
Harve	......	......	......	....	.....
Oeuvre de Soutiens	......	......	......	....	.....
Total	**1,007,280**	**1,704,466**	**547,071**	**29,482,440**	**137,762**

† Delivered to children in Poland and Czecho-Slovakia by the A.R.A.

RELIEF IN BELGIUM*

November 1, 1914 to August 31, 1919

Pork Products Bacon, Lard, Lard Subst., Vegetable Oils	Milk Evap., Cond.	Cocoa	Sugar	Miscellaneous Food	Soap	Clothing, Miscellaneous	Total Tons	Total Value
Commodities in Net Metric Tons of 1,000 Kilograms or 2,204.6 Pounds								
N BELGIUM PERIOD								
242,460.0	26,890.0	5,882.0	1,517.0	108,258.0	14,490.0	20,433.0	3,894,941.0	$639,692,817.25
57.0	.....	.....	.....	.....	....	826.0	883.0	1,363,876.44
....	279.0	.....	.....	.....	....	77.0	356.0	
137,280.0	53,731.0	6,988.0	49,505.0	65,009.0	24,621.0	18,355.0	1,091,580.0	220,203,521.62
6.0	12.0	.....	.....	.....	14.0	18.0	201.0	
20.0	7.0	.....	.....	1.0	2.0	.....	77.0	80,028.90
3.0	2.0	.....	2.0	4.0	2.0	.....	21.0	
379,926.0	**80,921.0**	**12,870.0**	**51,024.0**	**173,272.0**	**39,129.0**	**39,709.0**	**4,988,059.0**	**$861,340,244.21**
PERIOD, 1919								
17,171.0	.....	.....	.....	527.0	....	.....	89,144.0	$ 44,350,810.47
15,824.0	.....	.....	.....	.....	....	.....	45,836.0	
1,821.0	743.0	261.0	139.0	54.0	....	940.0	5,086.0	4,486,570.10
1,024.0	13.0	.....	81.0	293.0	11.0	23,425.0	46,306.0	17,503,860.30†
35,840.0	**756.0**	**261.0**	**220.0**	**874.0**	**11.0**	**24,365.0**	**186,372.0**	**$ 66,341,240.87**
415,766.0	**81,677.0**	**13,131.0**	**51,244.0**	**174,146.0**	**39,140.0**	**64,074.0‡**	**5,174,431.0**	**$927,681,485.08**

RELIEF IN BELGIUM

Deliveries, 1914–1919

CLOTHING PURCHASED									
Under Garments		Hose	Shoes		Bed Clothes		Miscellaneous		
Drawers (Pairs)	Shirts (Each)	(Pairs)	New (Pairs)	Repaired Army (Pairs)	Blankets (Each)	Pillows (Each)	Sweaters (Each)	Gloves (Pairs)	Shoe Laces (Pairs)
315,639	281,302	596,623	1,499,311	264,701	372,812	....	14,979	127,400	596,258
261,316	304,830	400,100	1,636,226	......	414,674	7,765	43,000	74,318	1,148,791
......	......	......	....	......	.....	....	.....	.....	......
......	......	......	....	......	1,157	....	.....	.....	......
......	......	......	....	......	.....	....	.....	.....	......
......	......	......	....	......	.....	....	.....	.....	......
......	......	......	....	......	.....	....	.....	.....	......
576,955	**586,132**	**996,723**	**3,135,537**	**264,701**	**788,643**	**7,765**	**57,979**	**201,718**	**1,745,049**

RELIEF IN BELGIUM

Deliveries, 1914–1919

Accessories		CLOTHING DONATED					Total Weight of Clothing Purchased and Donated
Thread (Spools)	Wool Knitting (Pounds)	Blankets, Quilts (Each)	Garments New Made up (Each)	Garments Second-Hand Made Up (Each)	Shoes (Pairs)	Hose (Pairs)	
2,974,614	132,400	6,287	571,967	19,298,840	799,916	144,515	15,870.0
1,641,661	97,170	11,136	308,229	4,874,416	255,858	134,464	6,639.0
......	......	.....	......	768,955	......	......	180.0
12,390	......	.....	......	67,812	3,655	......	53.0
......	......	.....	......	2,130,812	114,883	......	938.0†
......	......	.....	......	191,015	......	......	77.0
......	......	.....	......	......	......	......	12.0
4,628,665	**229,570**	**17,423**	**880,196**	**27,331,850**	**1,174,312**	**278,979**	**23,769.0**

COMMISSION FOR RELIEF IN BELGIUM

Summary of Source of Finance

Table 105 — November 1, 1914—August 31, 1919

Source	Belgium	France	Central Europe	Total
Government Subsidies				
From the United States Government	$259,632,260.44	$127,000,000.00	....	$386,632,260.44
From the British Government	94,181,410.78*	14,863,917.95	....	109,045,328.73
From the French Government	94,181,410.78*	110,681,443.43	....	204,862,854.21
Total Subsidies	**$447,995,082.00**	**$252,545,361.38**	....	**$700,540,443.38**
World Charity				
From the United States	**$ 27,423,641.85**	**$ 5,029,697.19**	**$2,067,687.95†**	**$ 34,521,026.99**
From the British Empire				
United Kingdom	$ 5,739,349.10	....	....	$ 5,739,349.10
Australia	6,210,288.08	....	....	6,210,288.08
New Zealand	2,462,272.07	....	....	2,462,272.07
Canada	1,742,560.57	....	....	1,742,560.57
India	197,692.22	....	....	197,692.22
South Africa	175,294.84	....	....	175,294.84
British West Indies	36,209.98	....	....	36,209.98
Sundry British Colonies	77,367.99	....	....	77,367.99
Total, British Empire	**$ 16,641,034.85**	....	....	**$ 16,641,034.85**

* The distribution of these amounts between the British and French governments is subject to adjustments between the two governments.

† Value of clothing distributed in Central Europe by A.R.A.

U.S. FOOD

Table 106 — Total Sales of Foodstuffs to the Allied Governments during

Country	Table No.	Flour	Grain	Rice
Belgium	233	11,687.0	219,565.0	....
France	320	1,738,079.8	1,549,746.1	104,589.9
Great Britain	543	1,350,580.8	3,274,037.9	24,289.4
Italy	352	1,804,252.8	5,039,879.8	14,634.7
Total	101	**4,904,600.4**	**10,083,228.8**	**143,514.0**

* Values based upon records in the United States Treasury with tonnage allocated according to record of food exports to these countries during the war period. See text.

SUMMARY OF TOTAL DELIVERIES UNDER THE

Table 107 — By Operations—

Operation	Table No.	Flour	Grain	Rice	Beans, Peas
American Relief Administration	109	936,747.8	531,082.6	22,120.1	60,100.6
American Organizations, Other than A.R.A.	121	28,000.0	64,077.0	22,220.0	21,165.0
Joint Allied Finance	128	180,363.4	151,259.4	....	....
Countries Other than United States	132A	156,368.6	237,560.6	54,699.0	23,568.0
Total, Gross Deliveries	...	**1,301,479.8**	**983,979.6**	**99,039.1**	**104,833.6**
Less Duplications	...	47,911.8	....	....	....
Grand Total, Net Deliveries	101	**1,253,568.0**	**983,979.6**	**99,039.1**	**104,833.6**

COMMISSION FOR RELIEF IN BELGIUM

Summary of Source of Finance

Table 105—*Continued* November 1, 1914—August 31, 1919

Source	Belgium	France	Central Europe	Total
From Other Countries				
Belgium ‡	$ 606,865.89	....	....	$ 606,865.89
Argentina	200,608.77	....	....	200,608.77
Holland	168,662.63	....	....	168,662.63
Spain	39,455.13	....	....	39,455.13
Italy	34,993.66	....	....	34,993.66
China	20,724.13	....	....	20,724.13
Brazil	16,233.33	....	....	16,233.33
Sundry	41,230.13	....	....	41,230.13
Total, Other Countries	**$ 1,128,773.67**	....	....	**$ 1,128,773.67**
Total, World Charity	**$ 45,193,450.37**	**$ 5,029,697.19**	**$2,067,687.95**	**$ 52,290,835.51**
ommercial Exchange	**$ 6,328,328.30**	....	....	**$ 6,328,328.30**
Grand Total	**$499,516,860.67**	**$257,575,058.57**	**$2,067,687.95**	**$759,159,607.19**

‡ Includes Belgian Relief Fund, $485,000.00 and Belgian Orphans' Fund, 5,475.00. Chiefly American and British contributors.

DMINISTRATION

e World War, Financed by U.S. Treasury Credits, 1917–1919

ommodities in Net Metric Tons of 1,000 Kilograms or 2,204.6 Pounds							Total Value *
Beans, Peas	Meats, Meat Products	Milk, Evap., Cond.	Sugar	Forage Oats	Miscellaneous Food	Total Tons	
....	....	20,650.3	....	....	....	251,902.3	$ 27,533,982.47
78,625.8	264,290.4	235,657.7	378,018.0	2,042,715.2	389,594.7	6,781,317.6	850,715,632.84
23,878.9	957,641.3	181,886.2	1,539,236.7	813,945.6	439,799.9	8,605,296.7	1,375,484,734.33
6,355.7	141,867.9	13,152.7	30,682.1	320,582.0	93,341.9	7,464,749.6	796,762,249.59
108,860.4	**1,363,799.6**	**451,346.9**	**1,947,936.8**	**3,177,242.8**	**922,736.5**	**23,103,266.2**	**$3,050,496,599.23**

IRECTION OF THE DIRECTOR GENERAL OF RELIEF

rmistice Period, 1919

ommodities in Net Metric Tons of 1,000 Kilograms or 2,204.6 Pounds									Total Value
Pork Products	Milk	Cocoa	Sugar	Miscellaneous Food	Soap	Medical and Hospital Supplies	Clothing and Miscellaneous	Total Tons	
100,516.6	24,683.5	250.5	1,050.7	495.2	431.5	......	6,977.5	1,684,456.6	$ 363,211,835.48
38,789.0	3,811.2	261.0	220.0	564,402.6	111.0	4,007.5	311,706.6	1,058,770.9	462,622,804.46
11,374.0	2,843.0	.....	.....	....	.....	......	....	345,839.8	48,000,000.00
116,300.0	20,404.0	.....	42,187.3	308,645.5	568.0	370.0	178,371.6	1,139,042.6	238,783,036.92
266,979.6	**51,741.7**	**511.5**	**43,458.0**	**873,543.3**	**1,110.5**	**4,377.5**	**497,055.7**	**4,228,109.9**	**$1,112,617,676.86**
....	1,088.0	.....	181.3	481.1	.....	......	....	49,662.2	11,130,893.52
266,979.6	**50,653.7**	**511.5**	**43,276.7**	**873,062.2**	**1,110.5**	**4,377.5**	**497,055.7**	**4,178,447.7**	**$1,101,486,783.34**

SUMMARY OF TOTAL DELIVERIES UNDER THE

Table 108

By Countries of Destination—

Country of Destination	Table No.	Flour	Grain	Rice	Beans, Peas
Armenia	200	43,430.5	8,000.0	1,022.3	2,661.8
Austria	206	205,097.4	184,464.4	13,122.0	6,639.6
Belgium	233	....	......	.....	.....
Bulgaria	234	22,862.4	......	.....	.....
Czecho-Slovakia	236	178,838.3	175,638.0	6,924.2	5,489.9
Denmark	290	....	19,912.0	.....	.....
Esthonia	292	20,249.9	6,462.1	91.6	303.0
Finland	306	59,317.5	113,039.0	.....	7,419.0
France	320	32,065.7	......	.....	.....
Germany	323	280,377.1	311,329.3	68,112.6	61,767.0
Hungary	337	....	......	.....	.....
Italy	352	15,031.1	......	.....	.....
Jugoslavia	354	60,396.4	4,116.0	58.2	5,257.9
Latvia	369	11,244.6	......	233.5	564.3
Lithuania	382	2,565.9	......	84.2	185.1
The Netherlands	392	25,027.4	......	.....	.....
Poland	394	139,521.5	87,684.5	8,041.2	9,948.3
Roumania	491	120,989.8	53,838.3	374.3	2,676.1
Russia					
Northwest Russia	497	14,248.4	......	.....	379.8
Kouban	507	....	......	.....	.....
Siberia	510	....	......	.....	.....
Ukraine	537	....	......	.....	.....
Volunteer Army (Russian)	538	394.0	......	.....	.....
Sundry Accounts	539	3,259.7	19,496.0	975.0	1,541.8
Turkey	541	20,278.3	......	.....	.....
United Kingdom	543	46,283.9	......	.....	.....
Total, Gross Deliveries	...	**1,301,479.8**	**983,979.6**	**99,039.1**	**104,833.6**
Less Duplications	...	47,911.8	......	.....	.....
Grand Total, Net Deliveries	107	**1,253,568.0**	**983,979.6**	**99,039.1**	**104,833.6**

AMERICAN RELIEF

Table 109

Summary of Total Deliveries, by Method

Method of Finance	Table No.	Flour	Grain	Rice	Beans, Peas
U.S. Congressional Appropriation for Relief	112	266,706.6	155,657.4	9,472.8	12,498.8
Cash Settlement	120	446,973.9	211,680.7	11,238.6	44,957.9
U.S. Treasury Loans	119	222,107.7	163,744.5	1,408.7	2,643.9
President's National Security and Defense Fund	117	959.6	....	......	......
Total Deliveries	107	**936,747.8**	**531,082.6**	**22,120.1**	**60,100.6**

DIRECTION OF THE DIRECTOR GENERAL OF RELIEF

Armistice Period, 1919

Commodities in Net Metric Tons of 1,000 Kilograms or 2,204.6 Pounds									
Pork Products	Milk	Cocoa	Sugar	Miscellaneous Food	Soap	Medical and Hospital Supplies	Clothing and Miscellaneous	Total Tons	Total Value
49.0	4,715.7	186.9	812.8	6,585.0	431.5	.....	16,068.8	83,964.3	$ 20,231,455.01
33,710.3	4,293.8	2.8	39,639.0	41,287.7	....	.....	33,448.7	561,705.7	98,771,595.93
......	.....	....	.....	37,480.0	....	.....	13,294.0	50,774.0	28,549,672.75
......	.....	....	.....	.....	....	.....	......	22,862.4	4,856,647.53
40,084.0	3,375.3	....	.....	85,035.1	....	.....	7,845.2	503,230.0	105,545,794.40
......	.....	....	.....	.....	....	.....	......	19,912.0	2,147,059.30
725.3	127.5	....	955.0	27,764.1	....	312.3	4,520.0	61,510.8	19,347,812.47
2,640.4	78.8	....	1,415.0	842.0	....	.....	282.0	185,033.7	29,172,056.10
......	.....	....	181.3	370,766.1	....	.....	149,490.0	552,503.1	218,489,439.11
149,327.1	28,160.5	13.2	.....	206,321.0	....	.....	109,810.0	1,215,217.8	282,410,999.21
319.1	.....	....	.....	.....	....	.....	......	319.1	245,519.96
......	.....	....	.....	.....	....	.....	......	15,031.1	2,846,014.42
3,699.0	850.8	....	52.0	16,348.0	....	.....	30,471.5	121,249.8	43,596,570.69
771.1	500.2	....	.....	5,378.0	....	.....	918.0	19,609.7	5,961,851.35
425.0	96.8	....	.....	4,700.0	....	.....	3,620.0	11,677.0	5,517,004.47
......	.....	....	.....	.....	....	.....	......	25,027.4	4,219,498.41
25,319.3	3,807.8	47.6	1.6	44,991.2	643.0	3,488.2	79,690.0	403,184.2	135,023,140.98
3,581.1	2,824.9	....	.....	25,217.0	25.0	.....	15,917.0	225,443.5	52,135,716.29
2,266.6	1,055.6	....	.....	.....	....	.....	710.0	18,660.4	5,765,867.81
......	.....	....	.....	.....	....	577.0	1,015.5	1,592.5	578,490.50
......	.....	....	.....	.....	....	.....	40.0	40.0	75,000.00
......	.....	....	.....	.....	....	.....	5,550.0	5,550.0	8,500,222.67
......	.....	....	.....	.....	....	.....	......	394.0	86,680.00
4,062.3	766.0	261.0	401.3	828.1	11.0	.....	24,365.0	55,967.2	23,556,117.48
......	.....	....	.....	.....	....	.....	......	20,278.3	4,369,404.30
......	1,088.0	....	.....	.....	....	.....	......	47,371.9	10,618,045.72
266,979.6	**51,741.7**	**511.5**	**43,458.0**	**873,543.3**	**1,110.5**	**4,377.5**	**497,055.7**	**4,228,109.9**	**$1,112,617,676.86**
......	1,088.0	....	181.3	481.1	....	.....	......	49,662.2	11,130,893.52
266,979.6	**50,653.7**	**511.5**	**43,276.7**	**873,062.2**	**1,110.5**	**4,377.5**	**497,055.7**	**4,178,447.7**	**$1,101,486,783.34**

ADMINISTRATION

of Finance—Armistice Period, 1919

Commodities in Net Metric Tons of 1,000 Kilograms or 2,204.6 Pounds								
Pork Products	Milk	Cocoa	Sugar	Miscellaneous Food	Soap	Clothing and Miscellaneous	Total Tons	Total Value
26,748.4	7,039.5	234.5	869.4	14.1	431.5	5,885.1	485,558.1	$107,132,276.99
51,613.7	12,844.6	16.0	.....	....	.....	926.5	780,251.9	168,946,191.10
22,154.5	4,799.4	.....	.....	....	.....	165.9	417,024.6	86,743,158.36
....	......	.....	181.3	481.1	.....	.....	1,622.0	390,209.03
100,516.6	**24,683.5**	**250.5**	**1,050.7**	**495.2**	**431.5**	**6,977.5**	**1,684,456.6**	**$363,211,835.48**

AMERICAN RELIEF

Table 110 — Summary of Total Deliveries, by Countries

Country of Destination	Table No.	Flour	Grain	Rice	Beans, Peas
Armenia	200	35,818.5	8,000.0	1,022.3	2,661.8
Austria	206	2,837.0	......	2,029.0	1,028.6
Bulgaria	234	22,862.4	......	.....	.....
Czecho-Slovakia	236	116,112.3	175,638.0	976.2	489.9
Denmark	290	......	19,912.0	.....	.....
Esthonia	292	15,649.9	5,328.5	91.6	.....
Finland	306	59,317.5	103,039.0	.....	1,807.0
France	320	32,065.7	......	.....	.....
Germany	323	241,865.1	131,748.3	9,209.6	42,200.0
Hungary	336	......	......	.....	.....
Italy	352	15,031.1	......	.....	.....
Jugoslavia	354	50,199.4	......	58.2	1,469.9
Latvia	369	11,244.6	......	233.5	564.3
Lithuania	382	2,565.9	......	84.2	185.1
The Netherlands	392	25,027.4	......	.....	.....
Poland	394	132,619.5	81,871.5	8,041.2	8,586.3
Roumania	491	90,644.8	5,545.3	374.3	684.1
Russia					
Northwest Russia	497	14,248.4	......	.....	379.8
Kouban	508	......	......	.....	.....
Volunteer Army (Russian)	538	394.0	......	.....	.....
Sundry Accounts	540	1,682.1	......	.....	43.8
Turkey	542	20,278.3	......	.....	.....
United Kingdom	543	46,283.9	......	.....	.....
Total Deliveries	109	**936,747.8**	**531,082.6**	**22,120.1**	**60,100.6**

AMERICAN RELIEF

Table 111 — Detail of Arrivals by Steamers, Excluding Children's Relief

Arrival No.	Steamer or Source	Port of Sailing	Date of Arrival	Port of† Arrival	Allocated to	Fund *	Flour Wheat
			1919				
1	West Lashaway, I.	New York	Jan. 3	Trieste	United Kingdom	C.S.	7,173.8
2	West Shore	New York	Jan. 4	Rotterdam	Netherlands	C.S.	3,793.7
3	Ossineke	New York	Jan. 5	Rotterdam	Netherlands	C.S.	2,442.6
4	Absaroka, I.	New York	Jan. 14	Rotterdam	Germany	C.S.	828.6
5	Western Hero	New York	Jan. 14	Rotterdam	Netherlands	C.S.	3,491.7
5	Western Hero	New York	Jan. 14	Rotterdam	Germany	C.S.	425.2
6	Western Plains	New York	Jan. 14	Cattaro	Jugoslavia	T.L.	598.1
7	Indianapolis	Philadelphia	Jan. 16	Rotterdam	Germany	C.S.	303.8
8	Nantasket	New York	Jan. 21	Rotterdam	Germany	C.S.	24.7
9	Western Plains	New York	Jan. 21	Constanza	Roumania	T.L.	6,637.6
10	West Alcasca	New York	Jan. 22	Trieste	United Kingdom	C.S.	6,952.9
11	Western Scout	New York	Jan. 25	Trieste	United Kingdom	C.S.	7,222.8
11	Western Scout	New York	Jan. 25	Trieste	Czecho-Slovakia	T.L.	5,000.0
12	Western Sea	New York	Jan. 25	Rotterdam	Germany	C.S.	5,570.9
13	Maine	New York	Jan. 28	Constantinople	Turkey	C.S.	4,069.4
13	Maine	New York	Jan. 28	Constantinople	Armenia	C.A.	300.0
13	Maine	New York	Jan. 28	Constantinople	Armenia	C.S.	185.5
13	Maine	New York	Jan. 28	Constantinople	Russian V.A.‡	C.A.	394.0
13	Maine	New York	Jan. 28	Constantinople	France	C.S.	907.2
14	Western Plains	New York	Jan. 28	Zeleneke	Jugoslavia	T.L.	190.1
15	Eastern Star	Philadelphia	Jan. 31	Rotterdam	Netherlands	C.S.	2,985.8
	Total for January	....	....	....	....	......	**59,498.4**

* This table includes steamers applying against three funds—C.A., Congressional Appropriation; C.S., Cash Sales; T.L., Treasury Loan (U.S.).

† Detail of grain and miscellaneous commodities indicated by th following indexes: ᵇ, barley; ᶜ, corn; ᵈ, cotton; ᵉ, soap; ᵍ, oil; ᵏ, clothin and other miscellaneous items; ᵖ, prunes; ʳ, rye; ˢ, seed grain; ʷ, wheat See end of Table 111, page 298, for complete detail.

ADMINISTRATION

of Destination—Armistice Period, 1919

Pork Products	Milk	Cocoa	Sugar	Miscellaneous Food	Soap	Clothing and Miscellaneous	Total Tons	Total Value
Commodities in Net Metric Tons of 1,000 Kilograms or 2,204.6 Pounds								
49.0	3,462.7	186.9	812.8	....	431.5	107.7	52,553.2	$ 11,189,983.01
2,223.3	204.6	2.8	....	....	.....	.....	8,325.3	3,293,470.93
.....	.....	....	....	....	.....	.....	22,862.4	4,856,647.53
16,533.0	1,611.3	....	....	....	.....	.....	311,360.7	58,602,496.13
.....	.....	....	....	....	.....	.....	19,912.0	2,147,059.30
725.3	127.5	....	55.0	14.1	.....	.....	21,991.9	4,617,625.56
2,640.4	38.8	....	....	....	.....	.....	166,842.7	25,876,576.10
.....	.....	....	181.3	481.1	.....	.....	32,728.1	5,422,039.11
46,966.1	11,142.5	13.2	....	....	.....	11.0	483,155.8	113,758,637.74
319.1	.....	....	....	....	.....	.....	319.1	245,519.96
.....	.....	....	....	....	.....	.....	15,031.1	2,846,014.42
2,714.0	469.8	....	....	....	.....	165.9	55,077.2	13,272,387.44
771.1	500.2	....	....	....	.....	.....	13,313.7	3,323,978.51
425.0	96.8	....	....	....	.....	.....	3,357.0	1,045,023.08
.....	.....	....	....	....	.....	.....	25,027.4	4,219,498.41
21,797.3	2,100.8	47.6	1.6	....	.....	5,777.4	260,843.2	63,735,352.01
2,919.1	2,774.9	....	....	....	.....	.....	102,942.5	23,438,339.29
2,266.6	1,055.6	....	....	....	.....	.....	17,950.4	5,337,568.35
.....	.....	....	....	....	.....	915.5	915.5	444,718.50
.....	.....	....	....	....	.....	.....	394.0	86,680.00
167.3	10.0	....	....	....	.....	.....	1,903.2	464,770.08
.....	.....	....	....	....	.....	.....	20,278.3	4,369,404.30
.....	1,088.0	....	....	....	.....	.....	47,371.9	10,618,045.72
100,516.6	**24,683.5**	**250.5**	**1,050.7**	**495.2**	**431.5**	**6,977.5**	**1,684,456.6**	**$363,211,835.48**

ADMINISTRATION

and Russian Prisoners of War—Armistice Period, 1919

Flour Cereal	Grain †	Rice	Beans, Peas	Pork Products: Pork	Pork Products: Lard	Pork Products: Lard Substitute	Milk	Cocoa	Sugar	Misc.†	Total Tons	Total Value
Contents of Cargoes in Net Metric Tons of 1,000 Kilograms or 2,204.6 Pounds												
......	......	......	......	......	......	......	......	.....	.....	......	7,173.8	$ 1,581,536.91
2,687.9	......	......	......	......	......	......	......	.....	.....	......	6,481.6	1,091,011.77
3,451.7	......	......	......	......	......	......	......	.....	.....	......	5,894.3	982,713.91
591.2	......	......	......	......	......	......	......	.....	.....	......	1,419.8	270,573.88
1,632.3	......	......	......	......	......	......	......	.....	.....	......	5,124.0	874,772.67
......	......	......	......	......	......	......	......	.....	.....	......	425.2	84,441.60
......	......	......	......	......	......	......	......	.....	.....	......	598.1	131,855.47
......	......	......	......	......	......	......	......	.....	.....	......	303.8	56,919.65
.2	......	......	......	......	......	......	......	.....	.....	......	24.9	4,977.34
......	......	......	......	......	......	......	......	.....	.....	......	6,637.6	1,390,187.74
......	......	......	......	......	......	......	......	.....	.....	......	6,952.9	1,532,837.28
......	......	......	......	......	......	......	......	.....	.....	......	7,222.8	1,592,339.45
......	......	......	......	......	......	......	......	.....	.....	......	5,000.0	1,102,300.00
1,184.9	......	......	......	......	......	......	......	.....	.....	......	6,755.8	1,324,686.72
......	......	......	......	......	......	......	......	.....	.....	......	4,069.4	985,325.00
......	......	......	......	......	......	......	......	.....	.....	......	300.0	66,000.00
......	......	......	......	......	......	......	......	.....	.....	......	185.5	40,880.80
......	......	......	......	......	......	......	......	.....	.....	......	394.0	86,680.00
......	......	......	......	......	......	......	......	.....	.....	......	907.2	200,000.00
......	......	......	......	......	......	......	......	.....	.....	......	190.1	41,912.60
1,686.1	......	......	......	......	......	......	......	.....	.....	......	4,671.9	792,996.54
11,234.3	......	......	......	......	......	......	......	.....	.....	......	**70,732.7**	**$ 14,234,949.33**

‡ V.A., abbreviation for Volunteer Army.

[*Continued on next page*]

Table 111—*Continued*

Detail of Arrivals by Steamers, Excluding

Arrival No.	Steamer or Source	Port of Sailing	Date of Arrival	Port of Arrival	Allocated to	Fund *	Flour Wheat
			1919				
16	Western Hope	New York	Feb. 2	Gravosa	Jugoslavia	T.L.	7,319.9
17	Morristown	New York	Feb. 3	Rotterdam	Germany	C.S.	669.6
18	Sudbury	Philadelphia	Feb. 4	Trieste	Czecho-Slovakia	T.L.	......
19	Via Rail (purchase from R. Cross)	(Berne)	Feb. 5	(Lemberg)	Poland	C.A.	......
20	Durham	New York	Feb. 6	Zeleneke	Jugoslavia	T.L.	......
21	Oregonian	New York	Feb. 8	Trieste	Czecho-Slovakia	T.L.	......
22	Nantahala	New York	Feb. 10	Fiume	Jugoslavia	T.L.	7,146.8
23	Western Light	New York	Feb. 10	Rotterdam	Netherlands	C.S.	1,190.8
24	Westerner	Norfolk	Feb. 13	Trieste	Czecho-Slovakia	T.L.	10,000.0
25	West Mohamet	New York	Feb. 17	Constanza	Roumania	T.L.	7,053.5
26	Newburg	New York	Feb. 18	Rotterdam	Netherlands	C.S.	......
27	Pequot	New York	Feb. 18	Rotterdam	Netherlands	C.S.	13.0
28	Western Belle	New York	Feb. 19	Derindje	....	......	......
29	Bucegi	Derindje	......	Galatz	Roumania	T.L.	2,326.0
30	Cape Lookout, I	Norfolk	Feb. 19	Trieste	Czecho-Slovakia	T.L.	......
31	Lake Dancey, I	Rotterdam	Feb. 19	Danzig	Poland	C.A.	2,646.8
32	Lake Mary, I	Rotterdam	Feb. 19	Danzig	Poland	C.A.	2,448.6
33	Lake Wimico, I	Rotterdam	Feb. 19	Danzig	Poland	C.A.	1,995.3
34	Merfax	Rotterdam	Feb. 20	Helsingfors	Finland	C.S.	1,414.2
35	Vesta	Rotterdam	Feb. 20	Helsingfors	Finland	C.S.	881.7
36	West Mount	New York	Feb. 21	Derindje	Turkey	C.S.	4,521.7
36	West Mount	New York	Feb. 21	Derindje	Armenia	C.S.	......
36	West Mount	New York	Feb. 21	Derindje	Armenia	C.A.	......
37	Williamantic	New York	Feb. 21	Fiume	Jugoslavia	T.L.	5,446.0
38	Markab	Rotterdam	Feb. 22	Helsingfors	Finland	C.S.	1,108.6
39	West Eldara	New York	Feb. 22	Constantinople	Armenia	C.S.	689.0
39	West Eldara	New York	Feb. 22	Constantinople	....	......	......
40	Constantia	Constantinople	......	Varna	Bulgaria	C.S.	4,010.9
41	Hero	Rotterdam	Feb. 24	Helsingfors	Finland	C.S.	1,391.1
42	Lake Clear, I	Rotterdam	Feb. 25	Danzig	Poland	C.A.	1,452.6
43	Lake Eckhart	Rotterdam	Feb. 25	Danzig	Poland	C.A.	2,352.6
44	Mount Shasta	Norfolk	Feb. 25	Trieste	Czecho-Slovakia	T.L.	5,000.0
45	East Wind, I	New York	Feb. 26	Trieste	Czecho-Slovakia	T.L.	5,000.0
46	Lake St. Regis, I	Rotterdam	Feb. 27	Danzig	Poland	C.A.	2,068.4
47	West Kyska, I	New York	Feb. 27	Trieste	Czecho-Slovakia	T.L.	......
47	West Kyska, I	New York	Feb. 27	Trieste	Jugoslavia	T.L.	433.4
48	Hollandish Diep	Rotterdam	Feb. 28	Helsingfors	Finland	C.S.	1,211.0
	Total for February	....	....	....	....	....	**79,791.5**
49	Lake St. Clair	Rotterdam	Mar. 2	Danzig	Poland	C.A.	793.5
50	Canoga	New York	Mar. 3	Trieste	Czecho-Slovakia	T.L.	......
51	Army Stock	(U.S.A.)	....	Trieste	Czecho-Slovakia	T.L.	3,565.5
52	Durham	New York	Mar. 5	Spalato	Jugoslavia	T.L.	......
53	West Humhaw, I	New York	Mar. 5	Danzig	Poland	C.A.	......
54	Lake Catherine, I	Rotterdam	Mar. 6	Danzig	Poland	C.A.	1,447.4
55	West Zeda	New York	Mar. 7	Constanza	Roumania	T.L.	6,681.2
56	Bali	New York	Mar. 7	Copenhagen	Finland	C.A.	5,398.[illegible]
57	Durham	New York	Mar. 10	Gravosa	Jugoslavia	T.L.	......
58	Tjisondari	Philadelphia	Mar. 10	Copenhagen	Finland	C.S.	6,797.[illegible]
59	Lake Tulare, I	Rotterdam	Mar. 11	Danzig	Poland	C.A.	1,623.[illegible]
60	West Cressey	Norfolk	Mar. 11	Constanza	Roumania	T.L.	7,117.[illegible]
61–2	Mirach and Besoeki	New York	Mar. 13	Copenhagen	Finland	C.A.	503.2
61–2	Mirach and Besoeki	New York	Mar. 13	Copenhagen	Finland	C.S.	......
63	Eastern Shore	New York	Mar. 14	Constanza	Roumania	T.L.	8,298.3
64	Leda	Rotterdam	Mar. 14	Helsingfors	Finland	C.S.	1,416.3
65	By Rail (to Polish White Cross)	(Paris)	Mar. 15	(Warsaw)	Poland	C.A.	......
66	Edgecombe	Norfolk	Mar. 17	Rotterdam	Germany	C.S.	17.[illegible]
67	Edgefield	Norfolk	Mar. 17	Rotterdam	Germany	C.S.	11.[illegible]

‡ Beef, 37.4.

ADMINISTRATION

Children's Relief, and Russian Prisoners of War

Contents of Cargoes in Net Metric Tons of 1,000 Kilograms or 2,204.6 Pounds												
				Pork Products								
Flour Cereal	Grain †	Rice	Beans, Peas	Pork	Lard	Lard Substitute	Milk	Cocoa	Sugar	M'sc.†	Total Tons	Total Value
......	......	......	......	......	......	......	......	.....	.....	......	7,319.9	$ 1,613,739.40
398.1	......	......	......	......	......	......	......	.....	.....	......	1,067.7	204,910.94
......	......	......	......	......	......	......	400.0	.....	.....	......	400.0	164,227.80
......	......	......	......	......	......	......	38.0	.....	.....	2.0*	40.0	14,709.49
......	......	......	......	......	301.0	......	27.0	.....	.....	......	328.0	240,539.90
......	......	......	......	3,279.4	903.4	......	......	.....	.....	......	4,182.8	2,950,820.44
......	......	......	......	......	......	......	......	.....	.....	......	7,146.8	1,572,009.30
1,181.3	......	......	......	......	......	......	......	.....	.....	......	2,372.1	401,790.39
......	......	......	......	......	......	......	......	.....	.....	......	10,000.0	2,204,600.00
......	......	......	......	......	......	......	......	.....	.....	......	7,053.5	1,477,301.38
219.1	......	......	......	......	......	......	......	.....	.....	......	219.1	35,738.29
251.4	......	......	......	......	......	......	......	.....	.....	......	264.4	40,474.84
......	......	......	......	......	......	......	......	.....	.....	......	......	....
......	......	......	......	......	......	......	217.8	.....	.....	......	2,543.8	606,220.00
......	......	......	......	......	......	......	200.0	.....	.....	......	200.0	82,113.90
......	......	......	......	......	......	......	......	.....	.....	......	2,646.8	554,348.73
......	......	......	......	......	......	......	......	.....	.....	......	2,448.6	512,840.44
......	......	......	......	......	......	......	......	.....	.....	......	1,995.3	417,887.46
283.3	......	......	......	......	73.6	......	......	.....	.....	......	1,771.1	368,665.78
176.6	......	......	......	......	......	......	......	.....	.....	......	1,058.3	194,429.08
......	......	......	......	......	......	......	......	.....	.....	......	4,521.7	1,098,112.80
......	......	......	......	......	......	......	342.9	.....	.....	......	342.9	148,031.00
......	......	......	......	......	......	......	164.9	.....	.....	......	164.9	79,527.00
......	......	......	......	......	......	......	......	.....	.....	......	5,446.0	1,197,901.40
222.1	......	......	......	6.5	251.4	......	......	.....	.....	......	1,588.6	442,825.46
......	......	......	......	......	......	......	......	.....	.....	......	689.0	151,591.88
......	......	......	......	......	......	......	......	.....	.....	......	......	....
......	......	......	......	......	......	......	......	.....	.....	......	4,010.9	882,387.00
278.7	......	......	......	......	78.9	......	......	.....	.....	......	1,748.7	367,631.53
......	......	......	......	......	339.2	......	......	.....	.....	......	1,791.8	573,467.78
......	......	......	......	......	143.2	......	......	.....	.....	......	2,495.8	606,432.50
......	......	......	......	......	......	......	......	.....	.....	......	5,000.0	1,102,300.00
......	......	......	......	......	......	......	......	.....	.....	......	5,000.0	1,102,300.00
......	......	......	......	37.4‡	275.5	......	......	.....	.....	......	2,381.3	675,703.10
......	......	......	......	......	......	68.0	......	.....	.....	......	68.0	44,630.44
......	......	......	......	......	......	......	......	.....	.....	......	433.4	95,544.00
83.5	......	......	......	22.1	292.0	......	......	.....	.....	......	1,608.6	481,141.58
3,094.1	......	......	......	**3,345.4**	**2,658.2**	**68.0**	**1,390.6**	.....	.....	**2.0**	**90,349.8**	**$ 22,706,895.03**
......	......	......	......	214.6	928.1	......	197.9	.....	.....	......	2,134.1	$ 1,158,510.70
......	......	......	......	340.2	......	......	......	.....	.....	......	340.2	242,506.01
......	......	......	......	388.4	5.4	370.3	......	.....	.....	......	4,329.6	1,330,730.26
......	......	......	......	19.0	......	......	......	.....	.....	......	19.0	12,417.00
......	......	......	......	2,196.1	2,679.5	......	457.6	.....	.....	......	5,333.2	3,911,290.08
......	......	......	......	351.8	99.2	......	......	.....	.....	......	1,898.4	634,440.26
......	......	......	......	......	......	......	......	.....	.....	......	6,681.2	1,399,302.36
2,134.5	......	......	121.5	......	......	......	......	.....	.....	......	7,654.6	1,378,686.95
......	......	......	......	1,031.7	1,002.5	......	294.9	.....	.....	......	2,329.1	1,558,289.87
1,230.7	......	......	......	......	......	......	......	.....	.....	......	8,028.3	1,455,150.50
......	......	......	......	304.2	54.2	......	......	.....	.....	......	1,981.8	607,446.22
......	......	......	......	......	......	......	......	.....	.....	......	7,117.7	1,490,725.22
5,012.4	......	......	......	......	714.1	......	38.8	.....	.....	......	6,268.5	1,514,487.14
......	......	......	......	715.5	......	......	......	.....	.....	......	715.5	546,014.02
......	......	......	......	......	......	......	......	.....	.....	......	8,298.3	1,738,001.19
......	......	......	......	......	16.2	......	......	.....	.....	......	1,432.5	277,917.95
......	......	54.4	......	......	......	......	......	.....	.....	......	54.4	11,297.56
......	......	......	......	......	......	......	......	.....	.....	......	17.8	3,297.48
......	......	......	......	......	......	......	......	.....	.....	......	11.0	2,127.40

[*Continued on next page*]

Table 111—*Continued*

Detail of Arrivals by Steamers, Excluding

Arrival No.	Steamer or Source	Port of Sailing	Date of Arrival	Port of Arrival	Allocated to	Fund *	Flour Wheat
68	West Cobalt	Norfolk	Mar. 17	Danzig	Poland	C.A.	7,086.2
69	Lake Mary, II	Rotterdam	Mar. 18	Danzig	Poland	C.A.	1,460.2
70	Lake Wimico, II	Rotterdam	Mar. 18	Danzig	Poland	C.A.	1,169.0
71	Maartensdijk	New York	Mar. 18	Copenhagen	Denmark	C.S.	......
72	Tijkembang	New York	Mar. 18	Copenhagen	Denmark	C.S.	......
72 73	Tijkembang and Maartensdijk	New York New York	Mar. 18 and Mar. 23	Copenhagen	Esthonia	C.S.	......
74	Lake Dancey, II	Rotterdam	Mar. 19	Danzig	Poland	C.A.	1,954.5
75	Lake Traverse, I	Rotterdam	Mar. 19	Danzig	Poland	C.A.	1,450.5
76	Lydia	Baltimore	Mar. 19	Constanza	Roumania	T.L.	4,963.7
77	Zaca	Norfolk	Mar. 19	Danzig	Poland	C.A.	7,996.1
78	Dubhe	Philadelphia	Mar. 20	Helsingfors	Finland	C.A.	......
79	Lake Clear, II	Rotterdam	Mar. 20	Danzig	Poland	C.A.	1,291.0
80	Edenton	Baltimore	Mar. 22	Spalato	Jugoslavia	T.L.	3,859.8
81	Lahta	Rotterdam	Mar. 22	Helsingfors	Finland	C.S.	2,233.1
82	Yessel, I	Rotterdam	Mar. 22	Helsingfors	Finland	C.S.	1,383.3
73	Maartensdijk	New York	Mar. 23	Copenhagen	Esthonia	C.S.	......
73	Maartensdijk	New York	Mar. 23	Copenhagen	Esthonia	C.A.	......
83	Orion	New York	Mar. 23	Salonica	Jugoslavia	T.L.	4,435.9
84	Arakan, I	New York	Mar. 24	Danzig	Poland	C.A.	......
85	Alkaid	Baltimore	Mar. 25	Helsingfors	Finland	C.S.	......
86	Garfield	Baltimore	Mar. 25	Helsingfors	Finland	C.S.	......
87	Lake St. Clair, II	Rotterdam	Mar. 25	Danzig	Poland	C.A.	2,393.5
88	West Carnifax	Norfolk	Mar. 25	Hamburg	Germany	C.S.	6,626.7
89	Bjarmia	Rotterdam	Mar. 26	Helsingfors	Finland	C.S.	1,090.5
90	Callabasas	Norfolk	Mar. 27	Messina	Italy	C.S.	2,914.4
91	Democracy, I	Rotterdam	Mar. 27	Danzig	Poland	C.A.	3,077.6
92	Lake St. Catherine, II	Rotterdam	Mar. 27	Danzig	Poland	C.A.	2,211.5
93	Lake St. Regis, II	Rotterdam	Mar. 27	Danzig	Poland	C.A.	2,397.2
94	Sapinero	(U.S.A.)	Mar. 28	Plymouth	Finland	C.S.	......
95	Watonwah	Philadelphia	Mar. 28	Genoa	Italy	C.S.	2,894.1
96	Lake Tulare, II	Rotterdam	Mar. 30	Hamburg	Czecho-Slovakia	T.L.	2,139.3
97	Canoga	New York	Mar. 31	Trieste	Jugoslavia	T.L.	......
98	Edenton	New York	Mar. 31	Trieste	Czecho-Slovakia	T.L.	4,422.9
	Total for March	....	....	....	....	......	**113,122.5**
99	Lake Eckhart, II	Rotterdam	Apr. 1	Hamburg	Germany	C.S.	......
99	Lake Eckhart, II	Rotterdam	Apr. 1	Hamburg	Czecho-Slovakia	T.L.	2,364.2
100	Manitowoc, I	New York	Apr. 1	Danzig	Poland	C.A.	......
101	West Wauna	Norfolk	Apr. 1	Hamburg	Germany	C.S.	7,218.8
102	West Waumeke	Norfolk	Apr. 2	Hamburg	Czecho-Slovakia	T.L.	7,298.2
103	Sverre	New York	Apr. 2	Helsingfors	Finland	C.S.	......
104	Melang	New York	Apr. 3	Helsingfors	Finland	C.S.	......
105	Ascutney	New York	Apr. 4	Trieste	Czecho-Slovakia	T.L.	3,323.1
106	Regulus	New Orleans	Apr. 4	Rotterdam	Germany	C.S.	......
107	Lake Yelverton	Philadelphia	Apr. 6	Helsingfors	Finland	C.A.	......
108	Mirach and Besoeki§	New York	Apr. 8	Copenhagen	Latvia	C.A.	......
109	Samarinda	New York	Apr. 8	Hamburg	Czecho-Slovakia	T.L.	2,250.3
110	West Elcajohn	Baltimore	Apr. 8	Trieste	Czecho-Slovakia	T.L.	7,260.1
111	Wierington	New York	Apr. 8	Helsingfors	Finland	C.A.	......
112	Lake Wimico, III	Rotterdam	Apr. 9	Libau	Latvia	C.A.	1,166.3
113	Selandia, I	New York	Apr. 9	Danzig	Poland	C.A.	3,839.7
114	West Compo	Baltimore	Apr. 9	Trieste	United Kingdom	C.S.	5,606.8
114	West Compo	Baltimore	Apr. 9	Trieste	Austria	C.S.	118.4
114	West Compo	Baltimore	Apr. 9	Trieste	Czecho-Slovakia	T.L.	1,617.1
115	Oostdijk	Philadelphia	Apr. 10	Amsterdam	Germany	C.S.	1,404.4
116	Hoxie	Baltimore	Apr. 11	Hamburg	Czecho-Slovakia	T.L.	......
117	Canton, I	Baltimore	Apr. 12	Danzig	Poland	C.A.	......
118	Franklin	Philadelphia	Apr. 12	Bremerhaven	Germany	C.S.	255.5

§ Name of transshipping steamer and date of arrival at final port of discharge not known.

ADMINISTRATION

Children's Relief, and Russian Prisoners of War

Contents of Cargoes in Net Metric Tons of 1,000 Kilograms or 2,204.6 Pounds												
				Pork Products								
Flour Cereal	Grain †	Rice	Beans, Peas	Pork	Lard	Lard Substitute	Milk	Cocoa	Sugar	Misc.†	Total Tons	Total Value
......	......	......	......	......	......	......	......	......	......	......	7,086.2	$ 1,269,346.17
......	......	......	......	615.9	19.2	......	......	......	......	......	2,095.3	745,364.81
......	......	......	......	571.3	......	......	......	......	......	......	1,740.3	664,363.31
......	2,253.0r	......	......	......	......	......	......	......	......	......	2,253.0	257,225.00
......	7,747.0r	......	......	......	......	......	......	......	......	......	7,747.0	884,475.00
......	520.0r	......	......	......	......	......	......	......	......	......	520.0	70,200.00
......	......	......	......	366.6	259.3	......	......	......	......	......	2,580.4	928,292.01
......	......	......	......	355.3	......	......	......	......	......	......	1,805.8	548,572.19
......	......	......	......	......	......	......	......	......	......	......	4,963.7	1,039,596.07
......	......	......	......	......	......	......	......	......	......	......	7,996.1	1,432,345.33
......	4,070.0r	......	......	......	......	......	......	......	......	......	4,070.0	496,710.09
......	......	......	......	271.8	276.1	......	......	......	......	......	1,838.9	717,349.23
......	......	......	......	......	......	......	......	......	......	......	3,859.8	808,391.49
310.1	......	......	127.9	......	82.4	......	......	......	......	......	2,753.5	561,581.16
56.3	......	......	......	......	106.4	......	......	......	......	......	1,546.0	346,988.83
......	342.0r	......	......	......	......	......	......	......	......	......	342.0	46,171.62
......	2,000.0r	......	......	......	......	......	......	......	......	......	2,000.0	270,000.00
......	......	......	......	......	......	......	......	......	......	......	4,435.9	929,058.20
......	......	......	......	2,364.4	1,722.9	......	861.1	......	......	......	4,948.4	3,500,577.33
......	3,986.6r	......	......	......	......	......	......	......	......	......	3,986.6	486,526.62
......	2,898.3r	......	......	......	......	......	......	......	......	......	2,898.3	353,710.00
......	......	......	......	......	......	......	......	......	......	......	2,393.5	501,288.15
......	......	......	......	......	......	......	......	......	......	......	6,626.7	1,325,340.00
193.2	......	......	......	......	69.4	......	......	......	......	......	1,353.1	287,522.47
......	......	......	......	......	......	......	......	......	......	......	2,914.4	543,087.93
......	......	......	......	232.8	412.7	......	......	......	......	......	3,723.1	1,161,673.46
......	......	......	......	......	......	......	......	......	......	......	2,211.5	463,184.52
......	......	......	......	......	......	......	......	......	......	......	2,397.2	502,068.94
......	5,597.3r	......	......	......	......	......	......	......	......	......	5,597.3	643,689.16
4,222.6	......	......	......	......	......	......	......	......	......	......	7,116.7	1,200,631.34
......	......	......	......	......	......	......	......	......	......	......	2,139.3	427,847.97
......	......	......	......	144.6	......	137.9	......	......	......	......	282.5	187,909.66
......	......	......	......	......	......	......	......	......	......	......	4,422.9	926,324.42
13,159.8	**29,414.2**	**54.4**	**249.4**	**10,484.2**	**8,447.6**	**508.2**	**1,850.3**	......	......	......	**177,290.6**	**$ 43,800,050.65**
......	......	......	......	......	63.5	......	......	......	......	......	63.5	$ 47,727.38
155.7	......	......	......	......	......	......	......	......	......	......	2,519.9	500,436.63
......	6,299.2r	......	......	......	......	......	......	......	......	......	6,299.2	744,000.00
......	......	......	......	......	......	......	......	......	......	......	7,218.8	1,443,754.40
......	......	......	......	......	......	......	......	......	......	......	7,298.2	1,459,645.40
......	5,116.8r	......	......	......	......	......	......	......	......	......	5,116.8	624,459.57
......	3,713.2r	......	......	......	......	......	......	......	......	......	3,713.2	453,161.10
......	......	......	......	508.8	140.8	......	557.6	......	......	......	4,530.3	1,445,400.25
......	......	592.4	......	......	......	......	......	......	......	......	592.4	150,319.22
......	2,995.1r	......	......	......	......	......	......	......	......	......	2,995.1	365,530.30
500.0	......	......	......	65.0	20.0	......	4.8	......	......	......	589.8	140,458.44
......	......	......	......	2,821.9	1,099.6	......	......	......	......	......	6,171.8	3,445,846.41
......	......	......	......	......	......	......	......	......	......	......	7,260.1	1,520,556.18
......	4,074.3r	......	......	......	......	......	......	......	......	......	4,074.3	497,230.99
......	......	......	......	......	......	......	......	......	......	......	1,166.3	247,707.91
......	......	......	846.7	687.5	32.2	......	212.4	......	......	......	5,618.5	1,612,629.32
......	......	......	......	......	......	......	......	......	......	......	5,606.8	1,222,221.36
......	......	......	......	......	......	......	......	......	......	......	118.4	25,454.07
......	......	......	......	......	......	......	......	......	......	......	1,617.1	355,689.39
2,175.8	......	......	......	......	......	......	......	......	......	......	3,580.2	652,891.37
......	6,031.1r	......	......	......	......	......	......	......	......	......	6,031.1	723,729.36
......	2,804.2r	......	......	......	......	......	......	......	......	......	2,804.2	347,743.63
5,978.9	......	......	......	......	......	......	......	......	......	......	6,234.4	1,127,298.90

[*Continued on next page*]

Table 111—*Continued*

Detail of Arrivals by Steamers, Excluding

Arrival No.	Steamer or Source	Port of Sailing	Date of Arrival	Port of Arrival	Allocated to	Fund *	Flour Wheat
			1919				
119	Lambs	New York	Apr. 12	Bremerhaven	Germany	C.S.	6,002.3
120	Victorius	New York	Apr. 12	Hamburg	Germany	C.S.	......
121	Cape Henry	New York	Apr. 13	Danzig	Germany	C.S.	......
122	Cape Henry, I	New York	Apr. 13	Danzig	Poland	C.A.	1,690.7
123	West Grama	Norfolk	Apr. 13	Varna	Bulgaria	C.S.	7,049.0
124	Lake Traverse, II	Rotterdam	Apr. 14	Danzig	Poland	C.A.	2,188.5
125	Lake Tulare, III	Rotterdam	Apr. 14	Danzig	Poland	C.A.	2,229.3
126	Lake Wimico, III	Rotterdam	Apr. 14	Memel	Lithuania	C.A.	1,078.5
127	Constantia	Boston	Apr. 15	Stettin	Germany	C.S.	414.3
128	Merauke	Philadelphia	Apr. 15	Hamburg	Germany	C.S.	......
129	Cabegon	Philadelphia	Apr. 16	Hamburg	Czecho-Slovakia	T.L.	......
130	Lake Catherine, III	Rotterdam	Apr. 16	Danzig	Poland	C.A.	2,245.4
131	Lake Clear, III	Rotterdam	Apr. 16	Danzig	Poland	C.A.	2,257.9
132	Lake Mary, III	Rotterdam	Apr. 16	Danzig	Poland	C.A.	2,397.8
133	Laurel	Baltimore	Apr. 16	Trieste	Czecho-Slovakia	T.L.	......
134	East Cape	Norfolk	Apr. 17	Constanza	Roumania	T.L.	7,300.2
135	Lake Eckhart, III	Rotterdam	Apr. 17	Danzig	Poland	C.A.	884.7
136	Lake St. Regis, III	Rotterdam	Apr. 17	Danzig	Poland	C.A.	2,156.1
137	Sicilia	Rotterdam	Apr. 17	Helsingfors	Finland	C.S.	1,729.4
138	Orangepolder	Rotterdam	Apr. 18	Helsingfors	Finland	C.S.	410.0
139	Lake Fostoria	Norfolk	Apr. 19	Trieste	Czecho-Slovakia	T.L.	......
140	Thordis	New York	Apr. 20	Hamburg	Germany	C.S.	3,121.1
141	Waalhaven	New Orleans	Apr. 20	Stettin	Germany	C.S.	1,487.1
142	West Corum	New York	Apr. 20	Constanza	Roumania	T.L.	7,352.6
143	Bussum	Baltimore	Apr. 21	Helsingfors	Finland	C.A.	......
144	Englewood	New York	Apr. 21	Constanza	Roumania	T.L.	......
145	Lake St. Clair, III	Rotterdam	Apr. 21	Hamburg	Czecho-Slovakia	T.L.	1,948.7
146	Easterling	Norfolk	Apr. 23	Trieste	Czecho-Slovakia	T.L.	7,437.4
147	Lake Farge	New York	Apr. 23	Trieste	Czecho-Slovakia	T.L.	......
147	Lake Farge	New York	Apr. 23	Trieste	Austria	C.S.	......
148	Neuse	New York	Apr. 23	Trieste	Czecho-Slovakia	T.L.	......
148	Neuse	New York	Apr. 23	Trieste	Austria	C.S.	......
148	Neuse	New York	Apr. 23	Trieste	United Kingdom	C.S.	2,031.0
148	Neuse	New York	Apr. 23	Trieste	Jugoslavia	T.L.	......
149	Yssel, II	Rotterdam	Apr. 23	Helsingfors	Finland	C.S.	1,448.1
150	Tordenskjold	Baltimore	Apr. 26	Gravosa	Jugoslavia	T.L.	4,747.3
151	Andalusia	Philadelphia	Apr. 27	Hamburg	Czecho-Slovakia	T.L.	......
152	Gorontalo	New York	Apr. 27	Hamburg	Germany	C.S.	4,581.7
153	Jan Van Nassau	Boston	Apr. 27	Danzig	Poland	C.A.	3,271.0
154	Lake Eckhart, III	Rotterdam	Apr. 30	Memel	Lithuania	C.A.	929.5
155	Lake Tulare, IV	Rotterdam	Apr. 30	Danzig	Poland	C.A.	......
156	Mirach and Besoeki§	New York	Apr. 30	Copenhagen	Esthonia	C.A.	......
	Total for April	....	....	....	....	......	**122,112.5**
157	Absaroka, II	New York	May 1	Rotterdam	Germany	C.S.	1,938.
158	Agnes, I	Rotterdam	May 1	Helsingfors	Finland	C.S.	622.
159	Coastwise	Philadelphia	May 1	Constanza	Roumania	T.L.	.....
160	Sigyn	Antwerp	May 1	Hamburg	Czecho-Slovakia	T.L.	.....
161	Harold	New York	May 2	Trieste	United Kingdom	C.S.	2,650.
162	Everett	New York	May 3	Constanza	Roumania	T.L.	3,870.
163	Tabor	New York	May 3	Trieste	United Kingdom	C.S.	443.
163	Tabor	New York	May 3	Trieste	Austria	C.S.	.....
163	Tabor	New York	May 3	Trieste	Czecho-Slovakia	T.L.	.....
164	Lake Linden	Philadelphia	May 3	Hamburg	Czecho-Slovakia	T.L.	1,499.
165	Bjornefjord	New York	May 5	Rotterdam	Germany	C.S.	3,354.
166	Volunteer	New York	May 5	Hamburg	Germany	C.S.	1.
167	Democracy, II	St. Nazaire	May 6	Danzig	Poland	C.A.	4,312.
168	Ingold	New York	May 6	Rotterdam	Germany	C.S.	1,095.

ADMINISTRATION

Children's Relief, and Russian Prisoners of War

Contents of Cargoes in Net Metric Tons of 1,000 Kilograms or 2,204.6 Pounds

Flour Cereal	Grain †	Rice	Beans, Peas	Pork Products		Lard Substitute	Milk	Cocoa	Sugar	Misc. †	Total Tons	Total Value
				Pork	Lard							
......	......	......	1,447.1	255.6	106.8	......	255.3	......	......	......	8,067.1	$ 2,009,616.82
......	10,020.5[r]	......	......	......	......	......	......	......	......	......	10,020.5	1,202,459.64
......	......	......	......	1,055.0	......	......	......	......	......	......	1,055.0	885,321.97
......	829.4[r]	......	......	19.1	359.2	......	333.8	47.6	.8	......	3,280.6	993,607.58
......	......	......	......	......	......	......	......	......	......	......	7,049.0	1,495,744.14
......	......	......	......	......	......	......	......	......	......	......	2,188.5	458,366.77
......	......	......	......	......	......	......	......	......	......	......	2,229.3	466,900.19
......	......	......	......	......	......	......	......	......	......	......	1,078.5	229,053.26
2,324.8	......	......	......	......	......	......	......	......	......	......	2,739.1	501,324.08
......	7,248.4[r]	......	......	......	......	......	......	......	......	......	7,248.4	869,812.92
......	7,497.6[r]	......	......	......	......	......	......	......	......	......	7,497.6	899,715.00
......	......	......	......	......	......	......	......	......	......	......	2,245.4	470,273.02
......	......	......	......	......	......	......	......	......	......	......	2,257.9	472,887.04
......	......	......	......	......	......	......	......	......	......	......	2,397.8	502,188.11
......	4,895.9[r]	......	......	......	......	......	......	......	......	......	4,895.9	660,953.12
......	......	......	......	......	......	......	......	......	......	......	7,300.2	1,528,962.06
......	......	......	......	......	......	......	......	......	......	......	884.7	185,286.12
350.8	......	......	......	......	......	......	......	......	......	......	2,156.1	451,579.03
87.1	......	......	......	......	104.5	......	......	......	......	......	2,184.7	459,268.31
......	......	......	......	......	......	......	......	......	......	......	497.1	91,230.96
......	3,302.6[r]	......	......	......	......	......	......	......	......	......	3,302.6	445,854.51
......	......	......	1,017.3	613.1	......	239.5	266.0	......	......	......	5,257.0	1,707,940.07
3,406.8	......	......	......	......	......	......	......	......	......	......	4,893.9	910,635.50
......	......	......	......	......	......	......	......	......	......	......	7,352.6	1,539,922.68
......	4,906.3[r]	......	......	......	......	......	......	......	......	......	4,906.3	598,769.98
......	......	......	......	1,932.2	986.9	......	962.0	......	......	......	3,881.1	2,732,860.90
......	......	......	......	......	......	......	......	......	......	......	1,948.7	390,983.16
......	......	......	......	......	......	......	......	......	......	......	7,437.4	1,557,688.84
......	......	......	......	290.3	......	......	......	......	......	......	290.3	248,214.93
......	......	2,029.0	......	......	......	......	4.3	......	......	......	2,033.3	580,124.61
......	......	......	......	678.3	9.9	......	243.7	......	......	......	931.9	696,711.23
......	......	......	......	......	......	......	......	2.8	......	......	2.8	1,223.31
......	......	......	......	......	......	......	......	......	......	......	2,031.0	442,735.89
......	......	......	......	......	......	......	......	......	......	165.9[g]	165.9	31,950.00
85.9	......	......	......	......	80.8	......	......	......	......	......	1,614.8	345,221.42
......	......	......	......	......	......	......	......	......	......	......	4,747.3	994,282.38
......	5,936.6[r]	......	......	......	......	......	......	......	......	......	5,936.6	712,387.56
1,070.0	......	1,353.0	......	......	......	......	......	......	......	......	7,004.7	1,494,566.11
......	......	......	......	......	......	......	......	......	......	......	3,271.0	585,934.23
......	......	......	......	......	......	......	......	......	......	......	929.5	202,114.18
......	......	1,645.3	......	......	......	......	......	......	......	......	1,645.3	460,693.52
......	......	......	......	147.7	10.0	......	......	......	......	......	157.7	116,592.28
16,135.8	**75,671.2**	**5,619.7**	**3,311.1**	**9,074.5**	**3,014.2**	**239.5**	**2,839.9**	**50.4**	**.8**	**165.9**	**238,235.5**	**$ 50,785,849.01**
1,456.3	......	......	954.5	1,224.9	115.0	......	346.7	......	......	......	6,036.0	$ 2,083,468.42
132.1	......	......	......	......	1.3	......	......	......	......	......	755.4	139,351.90
......	5,545.3[rc]	......	......	......	......	......	......	......	......	......	5,545.3	774,291.59
......	2,338.2[w]	......	......	......	......	......	......	......	......	......	2,338.2	315,659.70
......	......	......	......	......	......	......	1,088.0	......	......	......	3,738.0	1,053,580.95
22.2	......	......	501.4	......	......	......	590.8	......	......	......	4,985.0	1,224,443.37
......	......	......	......	......	......	......	......	......	......	......	443.0	96,569.17
......	......	......	1,028.6	......	......	......	......	......	......	......	1,028.6	303,437.00
......	......	......	......	2,107.8	337.6	......	......	......	......	......	2,445.4	2,152,769.91
1,041.9	......	......	......	......	......	......	......	......	......	......	2,541.8	487,520.48
......	......	......	......	332.5	51.3	234.1	721.9	......	......	......	4,693.9	1,378,052.60
9,954.6	......	......	......	......	......	......	......	......	......	......	9,956.2	1,792,153.34
......	......	......	......	......	......	......	......	......	......	......	4,312.7	884,093.25
......	......	......	......	......	......	......	2,111.0	......	......	......	3,206.9	1,036,930.58

[*Continued on next page*]

Table 111—*Continued*

Detail of Arrivals by Steamers, Excluding

Arrival No.	Steamer or Source	Port of Sailing	Date of Arrival	Port of Arrival	Allocated to	Fund *	Flour Wheat
			1919				
169	Osterland	Antwerp	May 6	Hamburg	Czecho-Slovakia	T.L.	......
170	Lake Traverse, III	Rotterdam	May 7	Danzig	Poland	C.A.	......
171	Magdala	Antwerp	May 7	Hamburg	Czecho-Slovakia	T.L.	......
172	Western Ally	Norfolk	May 8	Sulina	Roumania	T.L.	6,666.3
173	West Modus	Norfolk	May 8	Trieste	United Kingdom	C.S.	7,486.8
174	Absecon	New York	May 9	Constanza	Roumania	T.L.	2,329.2
175	August	New York	May 9	Hamburg	Germany	C.S.	758.7
176	Galesburg	Philadelphia	May 9	Rotterdam	Germany	C.S.	3,575.2
177	Jethou	New York	May 9	Rotterdam	Germany	C.S.	892.9
178	Lake Dancey, III	Cardiff	May 9	Danzig	Poland	C.A.	108.0
179	Thorjerd	New York	May 10	Hamburg	Germany	C.S.	......
180	Western Pride	Philadelphia	May 10	Hamburg	Czecho-Slovakia	T.L.	......
181	Wico	Philadelphia	May 10	Danzig	Poland	C.A.	3,835.3
182	Agwidale	New York	May 11	Rotterdam	Germany	C.S.	4,053.5
183	Lake St. Regis, IV	Copenhagen	May 11	Danzig	Poland	C.A.	......
184	New Windsor	New York	May 11	Hamburg	Germany	C.S.	3,225.6
185	West Armagosa	Newport News	May 11	Rotterdam	Germany	C.S.	2,220.1
186	Western Chief	Baltimore	May 11	Danzig	Poland	C.A.	7,133.1
187	West Humhaw, II	New York	May 11	Hamburg	Germany	C.S.	......
188	Lake Berdan	Philadelphia	May 12	Hamburg	Czecho-Slovakia	T.L.	2,204.2
189	Ardgroom	St. Johns	May 13	Hamburg	Germany	C.S.	581.4
190	Kerowlee, I	St. Nazaire	May 13	Danzig	Poland	C.A.	4,339.9
191	Lake Clear, IV	St. Nazaire	May 13	Danzig	Poland	C.A.	153.6
192	Navarino	(Canada)	May 14	Danzig	Poland	C.A.	6,142.1
193	Eastern Sun	Philadelphia	May 15	Constantinople	Armenia	C.S.	776.9
193	Eastern Sun	Philadelphia	May 15	Constantinople	Jugoslavia	T.L.	600.0
193	Eastern Sun	Philadelphia	May 15	Constantinople	Turkey	C.S.	5,244.3
194	Hatteras	Philadelphia	May 15	Rotterdam	Germany	C.S.	2,110.9
195	Lake St. Clair, IV	Bordeaux	May 15	Hamburg	Czecho-Slovakia	T.L.	......
196	Masuda	New York	May 15	Hamburg	Germany	C.S.	1,095.4
197	Morristown, II	Philadelphia	May 15	Hamburg	Czecho-Slovakia	T.L.	......
198	Balli, II	New York	May 16	Hamburg	Germany	C.S.	1,612.7
199	West Harcuvar	Newport News	May 16	Constanza	Roumania	T.L.	7,551.4
200	Eastern Queen	Baltimore	May 18	Danzig	Poland	C.A.	7,345.0
201	Guardo	New York	May 19	Bremerhaven	Germany	C.S.	......
202	Lake Catherine, IV	St. Nazaire	May 19	Hamburg	Czecho-Slovakia	T.L.	......
203	Saco	Philadelphia	May 19	Danzig	Poland	C.A.	......
204	Ternate	New York	May 19	Emdem	Germany	C.S.	3,757.8
205	West Loquassuck	Boston	May 19	Rotterdam	Germany	C.S.	7,146.[illegible]
206	Aila	U.S.A.	May 20	Hamburg	Czecho-Slovakia	T.L.	......
207	Groenloo	Rotterdam	May 20	Helsingfors	Finland	C.S.	1,373.[illegible]
208	Mirach, II	Philadelphia	May 20	Brake	Germany	C.S.	3,077.[illegible]
209	Mystic	Philadelphia	May 20	Helsingfors	Finland	C.S.	......
210	Oshkosh	New York	May 20	Batoum	Armenia	C.A.	3,929.[illegible]
211	Saucon	Philadelphia	May 20	Constanza	Roumania	T.L.	6,288.[illegible]
212	Themisto	Boston	May 20	Hamburg	Czecho-Slovakia	T.L.	.....
213	Ceres	Rotterdam	May 21	Helsingfors	Finland	C.S.	549.[illegible]
214	Ida	New York	May 21	Gravosa	Jugoslavia	T.L.	3,910.[illegible]
215	Lake Dancey, III	Cardiff, Danzig	May 21	Reval	Esthonia	C.A.	1,360.[illegible]
216	Ribe	Antwerp	May 21	Hamburg	Czecho-Slovakia	T.L.	.....
217	Casco	New York	May 22	Hamburg	Czecho-Slovakia	T.L.	.....
218	Alwina	Rotterdam	May 24	Helsingfors	Finland	C.S.	917.[illegible]
219	Athenic	St. John	May 24	Danzig	Poland	C.A.	.....
220	Eastern Star, II	Philadelphia	May 24	Hamburg	Czecho-Slovakia	T.L.	.....
221	West Lashaway, II	New York	May 24	Trieste	United Kingdom	C.S.	6,716.[illegible]
222	Winnebago	New Orleans	May 24	Hamburg	Germany	C.S.	2,013.[illegible]
223	Point Bonita	New York	May 25	Varna	Bulgaria	C.S.	2,501.[illegible]
224	Queen Alexandra	Portland	May 25	Danzig	Poland	C.A.	.....

ADMINISTRATION

Children's Relief, and Russian Prisoners of War

Flour Cereal	Grain †	Rice	Beans, Peas	Pork Products: Pork	Pork Products: Lard	Pork Products: Lard Substitute	Milk	Cocoa	Sugar	Misc.†	Total Tons	Total Value
				Contents of Cargoes in Net Metric Tons of 1,000 Kilograms or 2,204.6 Pounds								
......	5,996.0[w]	......	......	......	......	......	......	......	......	......	5,996.0	$ 809,467.29
......	......	1,941.0	......	......	......	......	......	......	......	......	1,941.0	543,482.24
......	6,666.4[w]	......	......	......	......	......	......	......	......	......	6,666.4	899,961.17
......	......	......	......	......	......	......	......	......	......	......	6,666.3	1,399,932.66
......	......	......	......	......	......	......	......	......	......	......	7,486.8	1,632,035.44
......	......	......	......	......	......	......	1,004.3	......	......	......	3,333.5	923,666.89
3,201.9	......	......	937.1	909.8	605.5	809.5	......	......	......	......	7,222.5	2,681,678.75
1,126.9	......	......	664.5	......	......	......	......	......	......	......	5,366.6	1,006,559.91
211.5	......	2,597.5	2,570.0	......	......	......	......	......	......	......	6,271.9	1,623,103.30
......	......	......	......	......	......	......	......	......	......	......	108.0	20,520.00
......	......	......	......	1,466.2	644.3	52.6	......	......	......	......	2,163.1	1,624,947.09
......	7,045.3[r]	......	......	......	......	......	......	......	......	......	7,045.3	845,432.28
......	......	......	......	......	......	......	......	......	......	......	3,835.3	728,706.62
60.5	......	......	875.9	......	......	974.1	......	......	......	......	5,964.0	1,623,105.16
......	2,400.0[r]	......	......	......	......	......	......	......	......	......	2,400.0	372,000.00
......	......	......	......	175.0	151.0	977.9	1,902.8	......	......	......	6,432.3	2,347,508.37
4,528.7	......	......	......	......	......	......	......	......	......	......	6,748.8	1,124,205.10
......	......	......	29.0	......	......	......	......	......	......	......	7,162.1	1,363,118.68
......	......	......	......	......	......	4,692.4	......	......	......	......	4,692.4	3,143,890.58
657.8	......	......	......	......	......	......	......	......	......	......	2,862.0	516,323.76
......	6,039.7[w]	......	......	......	......	......	......	......	......	......	6,621.1	922,917.39
......	......	......	......	......	......	......	......	......	......	......	4,339.9	889,682.78
......	......	......	......	282.7	......	......	......	......	......	......	436.3	268,979.95
......	......	......	......	......	......	......	......	......	......	......	6,142.1	921,310.05
......	......	......	......	......	......	......	......	......	......	......	776.9	170,918.66
......	......	......	......	......	......	......	......	......	......	......	600.0	132,000.00
......	......	......	......	......	......	......	......	......	......	......	5,244.3	1,002,178.83
59.4	......	......	......	......	......	1,705.0	812.0	......	......	......	4,687.3	1,833,506.94
......	......	......	......	1,396.0	......	......	......	......	......	......	1,396.0	1,165,694.24
......	......	783.9	2,607.4	852.6	376.1	22.8	......	......	......	......	5,738.2	2,168,787.36
......	5,781.4[r]	......	......	......	......	......	......	......	......	......	5,781.4	693,765.36
140.1	......	......	257.7	666.9	92.4	2,506.3	......	......	......	......	5,276.1	2,596,315.09
......	......	......	......	......	......	......	......	......	......	......	7,551.4	1,585,788.96
......	......	......	......	......	......	......	......	......	......	......	7,345.0	1,395,552.85
......	......	......	......	......	......	2,272.4	......	......	......	......	2,272.4	1,522,494.60
......	......	......	......	1,128.1	......	......	153.4	......	......	......	1,281.5	1,000,105.63
......	6,127.5[r]	......	......	......	......	......	......	......	......	......	6,127.5	796,576.95
29.7	......	......	......	......	......	1,276.8	955.2	......	......	......	6,019.5	1,980,777.70
......	......	......	......	......	......	......	......	......	......	......	7,146.5	1,286,370.36
......	2,316.3[r]	......	......	......	......	......	......	......	......	......	2,316.3	277,960.68
238.3	......	......	......	......	25.3	......	......	......	......	......	1,637.2	315,469.42
635.9	......	......	......	104.3	1,116.0	......	......	......	......	......	4,933.8	1,613,617.66
......	7,532.4[b]	......	......	......	......	......	......	......	......	......	7,532.4	902,946.35
......	......	......	619.2	......	......	......	......	......	......	......	4,548.5	1,004,717.49
......	......	......	......	......	......	......	......	......	......	......	6,288.3	1,320,532.92
......	4,755.2[r]	......	......	......	......	......	......	......	......	......	4,755.2	570,618.84
88.3	......	......	......	......	......	......	......	......	......	......	637.8	117,573.82
......	......	......	1,469.9	......	......	......	......	......	......	......	5,380.3	1,193,650.08
......	......	27.2	......	334.3	......	......	45.5	......	55.0	14.1[p]	1,836.7	609,006.70
......	3,345.5[r]	......	......	......	......	......	......	......	......	......	3,345.5	401,461.68
......	6,026.2[r]	......	......	......	......	......	......	......	......	......	6,026.2	723,148.32
139.7	......	......	......	......	......	......	......	......	......	......	1,057.4	195,056.16
......	6,167.1[w]	......	......	......	......	......	......	......	......	......	6,167.1	616,710.50
......	4,987.4[r]	......	......	......	......	......	......	......	......	......	4,987.4	598,487.88
......	......	......	......	......	......	......	......	......	......	......	6,716.8	1,464,189.27
27.2	......	918.1	2,840.7	......	......	......	......	......	......	......	5,799.4	1,429,418.45
......	......	......	......	......	......	......	......	......	......	......	2,501.2	525,241.92
......	6,226.4[w]	......	......	......	......	......	......	......	......	......	6,226.4	933,959.85

[*Continued on next page*]

Table 111—*Continued*

Detail of Arrivals by Steamers, Excluding

Arrival No.	Steamer or Source	Port of Sailing	Date of Arrival	Port of Arrival	Allocated to	Fund *	Flour Wheat
			1919				
225	West Ekonk	New York	May 25	Hamburg	Czecho-Slovakia	T.L.	......
226	Chimo	Norfolk	May 26	Hamburg	Germany	C.S.	......
227	Lake Larga	Philadelphia	May 26	Danzig	Poland	C.A.	......
228	Lake Wimico, IV	Bordeaux	May 26	Libau	Lativa	C.A.	462.2
229	Cape Lookout, II	Baltimore	May 27	Batoum	Armenia	C.A.	6,017.0
230	Santa Cruz	Norfolk	May 27	Rotterdam	Germany	C.S.	......
231	West Arrow	Norfolk	May 27	Varna	Bulgaria	C.S.	7,287.9
232	Williamantic, II	New York	May 27	Hamburg	Germany	C.S.	1,387.2
233	Western Maid, II	Baltimore	May 29	Rotterdam	Germany	C.S.	128.9
233	Western, Maid, II	Baltimore	May 29	Rotterdam	Sundry Accts.	C.S.	551.2
234	Kronenfels	Philadelphia	May 30	Hamburg	Germany	C.S.	......
235	Lake Mary, IV	Bordeaux	May 30	Libau	Latvia	C.A.	1,151.5
236	Lake Mary, IV	Bordeaux	May 30	Riga	Latvia	C.A.	847.5
237	Quistconck	Norfolk	May 30	Salonica	Jugoslavia	T.L.	6,285.0
238	Wauconda	Philadelphia	May 30	Hamburg	Czecho-Slovakia	T.L.	......
239	Lake Wimico, IV	Bordeaux	May 31	Reval	Esthonia	C.A.	1,409.0
240	Talabot	Newport News	May 31	Copenhagen	Denmark	C.S.	......
241	Western Spirit	Baltimore	May 31	Hamburg	Czecho-Slovakia	T.L.	......
242	U.S. Army Stock	(U.S.A.)	....	Trieste	Czecho-Slovakia	C.S.	2.3
	Total for May	....	....	....	....	......	**170,903.3**
243	Forster	Norfolk	June 1	Danzig	Poland	C.A.	......
244	Galahad	Baltimore	June 1	Hamburg	Czecho-Slovakia	T.L.	......
245	Honolulu	New York	June 1	Hamburg	Czecho-Slovakia	T.L.	......
246	Lake Eckhart, IV	St. Nazaire	June 1	Danzig	Poland	C.A.	111.[illegible]
247	Maine, II	Baltimore	June 1	Rotterdam	Germany	C.S.	......
248	Wakanna	Newport News	June 1	Danzig	Poland	C.A.	......
249	Rondo	New York	June 2	Hamburg	Czecho-Slovakia	T.L.	......
250	Calvert	Baltimore	June 4	Rotterdam	Germany	C.S.	5,169.[illegible]
251	Challenger	Baltimore	June 4	Rotterdam	Germany	C.S.	9,953.[illegible]
252	Decatur Bridge	New York	June 4	Hamburg	Germany	C.S.	852.[illegible]
253	East Wind, II	New York	June 4	Hamburg	Czecho-Slovakia	T.L.	.....
254	Edgecombe, II	New Orleans	June 4	Hamburg	Germany	C.S.	8,480.
255	Fort Pitt Bridge	New York	June 4	Batoum	Armenia	C.A.	3,973.[illegible]
256	Weissenfels	New York	June 4	Hamburg	Germany	C.S.	2,302.[illegible]
257	Woonsocket	New York	June 4	Hango	Finland	C.A.	.....
258	Lake St. Regis, V	Rotterdam	June 5	Hamburg	Czecho-Slovakia	T.L.	.....
259	Agwistar	New York	June 6	Trieste	Czecho-Slovakia	T.L.	3,083.
259	Agwistar	New York	June 6	Trieste	Austria	C.S.	123.
260	Arakan, II	New York	June 6	Hamburg	Czecho-Slovakia	T.L.	.....
261	Clio	New York	June 6	Rotterdam	Germany	C.S.	1,325.
262	Bellatrix	Philadelphia	June 8	Hamburg	Czecho-Slovakia	T.L.	.....
263	Maartensdijk, II	New York	June 8	Hamburg	Czecho-Slovakia	T.L.	.....
264	Wondrichen	Baltimore	June 9	Bremerhaven	Germany	C.S.	3,870.
265	Milcovul	Marseilles	June 10	Galatz	Roumania	T.L.	5,386.
266	Panola	New York	June 10	Danzig	Poland	C.A.	.....
267	West Erral	New York	June 10	Danzig	Poland	C.A.	.....
268	Catawba	Havre	June 11	Danzig	Poland	C.A.	.....
269	Flint	New York	June 11	Hamburg	Czecho-Slovakia	T.L.	.....
270	West Togus	Norfolk	June 11	Trieste	Austria	C.S.	1,318.
270	West Togus	Norfolk	June 11	Trieste.Spalato	Jugoslavia	T.L.	428.
270	West Togus	Norfolk	June 11	Trieste	Italy	C.S.	313.
271	U.S. Army Stock	(U.S.A.)	....	Trieste	Italy	C.S.	4,686
272	Coperas	Montreal	June 12	Rotterdam	Germany	C.S.	2,552.
273	Tyr	New York	June 12	Libau	Latvia	C.A.	397
274	Tyr	New York	June 12	Memel	Lithuania	C.A.	551.
275	West Kyska, II	New York	June 12	Hamburg	Germany	C.S.	2,136
276	Ocland	New York	June 13	Salonica	Jugoslavia	T.L.	....

ADMINISTRATION

Children's Relief, and Russian Prisoners of War

Contents of Cargoes in Net Metric Tons of 1,000 Kilograms or 2,204.6 Pounds				Pork Products								
Flour Cereal	Grain †	Rice	Beans, Peas	Pork	Lard	Lard Substitute	Milk	Cocoa	Sugar	Misc.†	Total Tons	Total Value
......	6,915.7[r]	......	......	......	......	......	......	......	......	......	6,915.7	$ 829,886.16
......	......	2,742.6	......	......	......	......	......	......	......	......	2,742.6	685,657.25
......	2,924.6[r]	......	......	......	......	......	......	......	......	......	2,924.6	380,226.99
......	......	......	......	......	......	......	......	......	......	......	462.2	97,066.62
......	......	......	......	......	......	......	......	......	......	......	6,017.0	1,263,562.65
......	6,493.8[r]	......	......	......	......	......	......	......	......	......	6,493.8	746,789.53
......	......	......	......	......	......	......	......	......	......	......	7,287.9	1,530,451.02
......	......	......	517.4	1,058.1	......	1,733.7	......	......	......	......	4,696.4	2,386,359.26
1,633.8	5,265.3[r]	......	......	......	......	......	......	......	......	......	7,028.0	886,382.87
117.1	......	......	......	......	......	......	......	......	......	......	668.3	122,638.77
......	10,745.2[r]	......	......	......	......	......	......	......	......	......	10,745.2	1,289,425.20
......	......	......	......	......	......	......	......	......	......	......	1,151.5	241,812.27
......	......	......	......	132.4	......	......	104.0	......	......	......	1,083.9	336,575.88
......	......	......	......	......	......	......	......	......	......	......	6,285.0	1,225,568.76
......	7,413.0[r]	......	......	......	......	......	......	......	......	......	7,413.0	889,556.76
......	......	......	......	56.7	......	......	.5	......	......	......	1,466.2	351,301.16
......	9,912.0[b]	......	......	......	......	......	......	......	......	......	9,912.0	1,005,359.30
......	6,366.2[r]	......	......	......	......	......	......	......	......	......	6,366.2	763,943.16
......	......	......	......	8.3	3.3	......	56.6	......	......	......	70.5	33,778.62
25,503.9	**145,332.1**	**9,010.3**	**15,873.3**	**12,236.6**	**3,519.1**	**17,257.6**	**9,892.7**	......	**55.0**	**14.1**	**409,598.0**	**$ 91,165,801.47**
......	......	2,788.7	......	......	......	......	......	......	......	......	2,788.7	$ 725,065.90
340.8	7,378.1[r]	......	......	......	......	......	......	......	......	......	7,718.9	941,599.35
......	6,567.2[r]	......	......	......	......	......	......	......	......	......	6,567.2	788,059.08
......	......	......	......	217.1	......	......	......	......	......	......	328.1	205,112.37
......	7,190.7[r]	......	......	......	......	......	......	......	......	......	7,190.7	882,900.14
......	......	......	618.6	......	......	......	......	......	......	......	618.6	167,031.99
......	8,776.2[r]	......	......	......	......	......	......	......	......	......	8,776.2	1,053,143.40
......	......	......	......	......	......	......	......	......	......	......	5,169.3	930,479.04
210.8	......	......	......	......	......	......	......	......	......	......	10,164.5	1,825,391.34
167.6	......	......	......	157.5	161.3	1,839.8	......	......	......	......	3,178.7	1,672,429.47
......	7,462.0[r]	......	......	......	......	......	......	......	......	......	7,462.0	895,440.12
......	......	......	......	......	......	......	......	......	......	......	8,480.8	1,568,943.74
33.8	......	......	......	......	......	......	......	115.8	203.2	......	4,326.3	942,913.43
......	......	......	......	6,487.6	......	123.0	......	......	......	......	8,912.6	5,901,270.59
......	7,496.5[r]	......	......	......	......	......	......	......	......	......	7,496.5	930,882.81
......	......	......	337.7	......	......	......	......	......	......	......	337.7	94,543.40
......	......	......	......	......	......	......	......	......	......	......	3,083.1	662,857.90
......	......	......	......	......	......	......	19.6	......	......	......	142.8	36,480.95
......	6,182.6[r]	......	......	......	......	......	......	......	......	......	6,182.6	741,908.16
......	......	......	......	......	......	1,271.4	......	......	......	......	2,597.2	1,077,755.22
......	4,787.7[r]	......	......	......	......	......	......	......	......	......	4,787.7	574,407.84
......	7,550.1[r]	......	......	......	......	......	......	......	......	......	7,550.1	906,014.64
......	......	......	......	......	......	......	......	......	......	......	3,870.0	715,944.82
......	......	......	......	......	......	......	......	......	......	......	5,386.1	969,502.14
......	3,810.2[r]	......	......	......	......	......	......	......	......	......	3,810.2	495,327.95
......	6,667.8[r]	......	......	......	......	......	......	......	......	265.8[a]	6,933.6	1,075,479.56
......	......	......	......	......	......	......	......	......	......	1,281.7[d]	1,281.7	1,148,851.21
......	6,345.5[r]	......	......	......	......	......	......	......	......	......	6,345.5	761,454.60
......	......	......	......	......	......	......	......	......	......	......	1,318.8	283,537.06
......	......	......	......	......	......	......	......	......	......	......	428.6	92,158.24
......	......	......	......	......	......	......	......	......	......	......	313.6	69,136.70
......	......	......	......	......	......	......	......	......	......	......	4,686.4	1,033,158.45
......	......	......	......	......	......	......	......	......	......	......	2,552.8	459,500.58
......	......	......	149.2	......	......	15.3	......	......	......	......	562.4	131,388.86
......	......	......	1.1	......	......	101.3	50.6	......	......	......	704.6	200,091.10
......	......	222.1	1,094.0	1,683.5	65.8	718.5	536.6	......	......	......	6,456.8	2,933,825.74
......	......	58.2	......	......	......	77.3	147.9	......	......	......	283.4	147,683.79

[*Continued on next page*]

Table 111—*Continued*

Detail of Arrivals by Steamers, Excluding

Arrival No.	Steamer or Source	Port of Sailing	Date of Arrival	Port of Arrival	Allocated to	Fund *	Flour Wheat
			1919				
277	Sacandago	New Orleans	June 13	Danzig	Poland	C.A.	1,900.1
278	Yakima	Baltimore	June 13	Danzig	Poland	C.A.	80.0
279	Westward Ho, II	New York	June 14	Danzig	Poland	C.A.	......
280	Western Belle, II	New York	June 14	Danzig	Poland	C.A.	......
281	Adelheid	New York	June 15	Hamburg	Czecho-Slovakia	T.L.	......
282	Westford	New York	June 15	Abo	Finland	C.A.	......
283	Lake Strabo	Montreal	June 16	Reval	Esthonia	C.A.	2,059.7
284	Lake Charlottesville	Montreal	June 16	Hungerburg	Russia N.W.R.	C.A.	2,774.3
285	Lake Strabo	Montreal	June 16	Reval	Russia N.W.R.	C.A.	633.7
286	Sangamon	Philadelphia	June 16	Hamburg	Czecho-Slovakia	T.L.	......
287	Solfels	Philadelphia	June 16	Bremerhaven	Germany	C.S.	1,709.2
288	Sahale	Philadelphia	June 17	Mantyluoto	Finland	C.A.	......
289	Western Plains, II	Philadelphia	June 17	Hango	Finland	C.S.	......
290	Agawan	New York	June 18	Batoum	Armenia	C.A.	188.1
291	Schodack	Philadelphia	June 18	Danzig	Poland	C.A.	......
292	West Togus	Norfolk	June 18	Gravosa	Jugoslavia	T.L.	4,798.1
293	Bavaria	New York	June 20	Batoum	Armenia	C.A.	2,661.8
294	Python	Montreal	June 20	Hamburg	Germany	C.S.	2,540.8
295	Dio	New York	June 22	Viborg	Sundry Accts.	C.S.	162.4
295	Dio	New York	June 22	Viborg	Russia N.W.R.	C.A.	3,973.9
296	Coquinor	Montreal	June 23	Danzig	Poland	C.A.	2,520.1
297	Erfurt	Philadelphia	June 23	Hamburg	Czecho-Slovakia	C.A.	......
298	Lake Licoco	Montreal	June 23	Danzig	Poland	C.A.	2,754.3
299	Regele Carol	Constantinople	June 23	Galatz	Roumania	T.L.	300.7
300	Shooters Island	Philadelphia	June 23	Danzig	Poland	C.A.	2,998.0
301	West Cressey, II	New York	June 23	Danzig	Poland	C.A.	......
302	West Chester	New York	June 24	Danzig	Poland	C.S.	......
303	Democracy, III	St. Nazaire	June 25	Viborg	Sundry Accts.	C.S.	167.5
303	Democracy, III	St. Nazaire	June 25	Viborg	Russia N.W.R.	C.A.	3,381.1
304	Lake Calvenia	Montreal	June 25	Reval	Russia N.W.R.	C.A.	2,731.7
305	Lake Gravity	Montreal	June 25	Bremerhaven	Germany	C.S.	3,107.3
306	Ocland	New York	June 25	Varna	Burgaria	C.S.	2,013.4
307	West Durfee	Boston	June 25	Mantyluoto	Finland	C.S.	......
308	Ceralvo	Montreal	June 26	Danzig	Poland	C.A.	1,272.3
309	Lake Foxboro	Montreal	June 26	Stettin	Germany	C.S.	2,991.5
310	Phoenix Bridge	Philadelphia	June 26	Danzig	Poland	C.A.	......
311	Gertrud	Baltimore	June 27	Emdem	Germany	C.S.	......
312	Lake Gretna	Montreal	June 27	Hamburg	Czecho-Slovakia	C.A.	2,397.6
313	Lake Corapeak	Montreal	June 28	Hamburg	Germany	C.S.	2,520.9
314	Artemisia	Philadelphia	June 29	Hamburg	Germany	C.S.	......
315	Bermuda	Philadelphia	June 29	Hamburg	Czecho-Slovakia	C.A.	847.4
316	Franziska	New York	June 29	Hamburg	Germany	C.S.	559.8
317	Lake Catherine, V	Bordeaux	June 29	Hamburg	Czecho-Slovakia	T.L.	......
318	Altenfels	New York	June 30	Hamburg	Germany	C.S.	......
319	U.S. Army Stock	(U.S.A.)	....	Trieste	Austria	C.S.	1,276.6
319	U.S. Army Stock	(U.S.A.)	....	Trieste	Hungary	C.S.	......
	Total for June	....	....	....	....	......	**112,339.**
320	Lake Lilicusum	Montreal	July 1	Danzig	Poland	C.A.	2,781.
321	Lake Traverse, IV	St. Nazaire	July 1	Reval	Russia N.W.R.	C.A.	.....
322	Lake Tulare, V	Bordeaux	July 1	Riga	Latvia	C.A.	1,465.
323	Augsburg	New York	July 2	Bremerhaven	Germany	C.S.	.....
324	Cerosco	Montreal	July 2	Hamburg	Czecho-Slovakia	C.A.	2,789.
325	Charlot	New York	July 2	Riga	Latvia	C.A.	2,525.
326	Charlot	New York	July 2	Libau	Lithuania	C.A.	.....
327	Lake Clear, V	Bordeaux	July 2	Hamburg	Czecho-Slovakia	T.L.	.....
328	Lake Foxcroft	Montreal	July 2	Hamburg	Germany	C.S.	2,985.
329	Lipsos	Rotterdam	July 2	Danzig	Poland	C.A.	.....

ADMINISTRATION

Children's Relief, and Russian Prisoners of War

Contents of Cargoes in Net Metric Tons of 1,000 Kilograms or 2,204.6 Pounds												
				Pork Products								
Flour Cereal	Grain †	Rice	Beans, Peas	Pork	Lard	Lard Substitute	Milk	Cocoa	Sugar	Misc. †	Total Tons	Total Value
......	......	......	4,400.6	......	......	......	......	......	......	......	6,300.7	$ 1,549,196.75
......	......	115.8	1,909.4	......	......	......	......	......	......	......	2,105.2	560,823.85
......	4,063.6[r]	......	......	......	......	......	......	......	......	......	4,063.6	528,266.05
......	......	......	......	......	......	4,688.8	......	......	......	......	4,688.8	3,188,360.20
2,019.8	......	......	......	......	......	616.8	......	......	......	......	2,636.6	746,487.87
......	7,214.0[r]	......	......	......	......	......	......	......	......	......	7,214.0	895,807.00
......	......	......	......	......	......	......	......	......	......	......	2,059.7	401,648.13
......	......	......	......	......	......	......	......	......	......	......	2,774.3	540,984.80
......	......	......	......	......	......	......	......	......	......	......	633.7	123,573.84
1,139.1	5,533.2[r]	......	......	......	......	......	......	......	......	......	6,672.3	851,941.39
......	......	......	......	4,605.6	41.0	......	......	......	......	......	6,355.8	4,225,845.36
......	6,256.5[r]	......	......	......	......	......	......	......	......	......	6,256.5	776,903.03
......	7,145.7[r]	......	......	......	......	......	......	......	......	......	7,145.7	887,325.46
......	......	......	1,606.2	......	......	......	1,950.5	......	......	......	3,744.8	1,565,693.73
......	6,140.7[r]	......	82.2	......	......	......	......	......	......	......	6,222.9	820,493.97
......	......	......	......	......	......	......	......	......	......	......	4,798.1	984,384.92
......	......	3.1	436.4	......	......	......	......	......	......	......	3,101.3	686,408.77
......	......	......	......	......	......	......	......	......	......	......	2,540.8	470,054.11
......	......	......	43.8	......	......	......	......	......	......	......	206.2	43,492.83
57.9	......	......	379.8	......	......	420.7	364.3	......	......	......	5,196.6	1,373,227.60
......	......	......	......	......	......	......	......	......	......	......	2,520.1	478,826.60
3,572.9	6,769.7[r]	......	......	......	......	......	......	......	......	......	10,342.6	1,401,894.26
......	......	......	......	......	......	......	......	......	......	......	2,754.3	523,324.79
......	......	......	......	......	......	......	......	......	......	......	300.7	66,151.58
67.5	......	744.8	699.8	......	......	419.4	......	......	......	......	4,929.5	1,250,367.70
......	5,751.8[r]	......	......	......	......	......	......	......	......	1,007.7[d]	6,759.5	1,538,776.68
......	6,198.0[r]	......	......	......	......	......	......	......	......	913.9[d]	7,111.9	1,523,141.08
......	......	......	......	......	......	......	......	......	......	......	167.5	36,022.18
......	......	......	......	498.7	......	......	450.3	......	......	......	4,330.1	1,331,826.86
......	......	......	......	......	......	......	......	......	......	......	2,731.7	532,688.13
......	......	......	......	......	......	......	......	......	......	......	3,107.3	574,846.06
......	......	......	......	......	......	......	......	......	......	......	2,013.4	422,823.45
......	6,953.2[r]	......	......	......	......	......	......	......	......	......	6,953.2	863,424.12
......	......	......	......	......	......	......	......	......	......	......	1,272.3	241,737.76
......	......	......	......	......	......	......	......	......	......	......	2,991.5	553,420.66
......	4,334.0[r]	......	......	......	......	......	......	......	......	......	4,334.0	563,419.09
......	6,772.9[r]	......	......	......	......	......	......	......	......	......	6,772.9	812,753.16
......	......	......	......	......	......	......	......	......	......	......	2,397.6	443,563.59
......	......	......	......	......	......	......	......	......	......	......	2,520.9	466,365.21
1,667.9	5,815.9[r]	......	......	......	......	......	......	......	......	......	7,483.8	973,110.47
1.991.7	6,977.2[r]	......	......	......	......	......	......	......	......	......	9,816.3	1,322,664.58
1,059.1	5,040.1[r]	......	279.6	13.8	......	......	221.0	......	......	......	7,173.4	1,080,567.61
494.4	......	181.4	152.2	......	......	......	......	......	......	......	828.0	185,330.62
362.5	8,019.9[r]	......	......	39.5	......	......	792.8	......	......	......	9,214.7	1,432,348.71
......	......	......	......	1,763.1	......	460.2	180.7	......	......	......	3,680.6	2,047,811.35
......	......	......	......	114.7	196.3	8.1	......	......	......	......	319.1	245,519.96
13,185.8	**179,201.0**	**4,114.1**	**12,190.6**	**15,581.1**	**464.4**	**10,760.6**	**4,714.3**	**115.8**	**203.2**	**3,469.1**	**356,339.3**	**$ 76,175,317.60**
......	......	......	......	......	......	......	......	......	......	......	2,781.3	$ 528,452.70
......	......	......	......	961.8	......	......	......	......	......	......	961.8	817,514.45
......	......	161.2	......	127.5	......	......	55.5	......	......	......	1,809.5	487,620.56
548.5	7,426.8[r]	......	1,973.6	177.5	16.9	......	184.6	......	......	......	10,327.9	1,723,009.04
......	......	......	......	......	......	......	......	......	......	......	2,789.7	516,096.72
......	......	......	415.1	......	......	410.9	335.9	......	......	......	3,687.7	1,057,548.94
......	......	......	59.7	......	......	......	......	......	......	......	59.7	16,131.15
......	......	26.4	......	30.4	......	......	......	......	......	......	56.8	32,009.48
......	......	......	......	......	......	......	......	......	......	......	2,985.7	552,351.54
......	5,341.2[r]	......	......	......	......	......	......	......	......	......	5,341.2	827,890.81

[*Continued on next page*]

Table 111—*Continued*

Detail of Arrivals by Steamers, Excluding

Arrival No.	Steamer or Source	Port of Sailing	Date of Arrival	Port of Arrival	Allocated to	Fund *	Flour Wheat
			1919				
330	Greiffenfels	New York	July 3	Bremerhaven	Germany	C.S.	13.4
331	Lake Grampian	Montreal	July 3	Emden	Germany	C.S.	3,099.9
332	Pasadena	Philadelphia	July 5	Helsingfors	Finland	C.S.	......
333	Hornfels	Philadelphia	July 6	Stettin	Germany	C.S.	1,495.6
334	Lake Fray	Montreal	July 6	Hamburg	Czecho-Slovakia	C.A.	3,171.0
335	Hilda	Rotterdam	July 7	Danzig	Poland	C.A.	......
336	Lake Fontanet	Montreal	July 7	Hamburg	Czecho-Slovakia	C.A.	3,097.0
337	Kybfels	Philadelphia	July 8	Bremerhaven	Germany	C.S.	3,670.8
338	Gundomar	New York	July 9	Hamburg	Germany	C.S.	1,682.5
339	Lake Fraichur	Montreal	July 9	Hamburg	Czecho-Slovakia	C.A.	2,972.9
340	Lippe	Philadelphia	July 9	Bremerhaven	Germany	C.S.	2,080.6
341	Dessau	Boston	July 10	Bremerhaven	Germany	C.S.	1,943.7
342	Lake St. Clair, V	Bordeaux	July 10	Reval	Esthonia	C.A.	......
342	Lake St. Clair, V	Bordeaux	July 10	Reval	Russia N.W.R.	C.A.	......
343	Lake St. Clair, V	Bordeaux	July 10	Libau	Lithuania	C.A.	......
344	Lake Gravella	Montreal	July 11	Bremerhaven	Germany	C.S.	3,126.7
345	Gallipoli	Philadelphia	July 12	Hamburg	Germany	C.S.	637.6
346	Lake Hemlock	New York	July 12	Hango	Finland	C.S.	......
347	Tyr	New York	July 12	Libau	Lithuania	C.A.	6.3
348	Waldenburg	Philadelphia	July 12	Hamburg	Germany	C.S.	4,593.7
349	Garabaldi	Liverpool	July 14	Danzig	Poland	C.A.	......
350	Hansa	Liverpool	July 25	Danzig	Poland	C.A.	......
351	Jadden	(U.S.A.)	....	Helsingfors	Finland	C.S.	8,230.6
352	U.S. Army Stock	(U.S.A.)	....	All Ports	Sundry Accts.	C.S.	683.9
353	Lake Fraley	Montreal	July 16	Hamburg	Czecho-Slovakia	C.A.	2,986.8
354	Isis	New York	July 18	Hamburg	Germany	C.S.	474.6
354	Isis	New York	July 18	Hamburg	Germany A.F.S.C.	C.S.	......
355	Faraby	New York	July 19	Danzig	Poland	C.A.	......
356	Bucegi, II	Marseilles	July 20	Braili	Roumania	T.L.	......
357	Elbing	Philadelphia	July 20	Constantinople	Turkey	C.S.	3,976.6
358	Meiningen	Philadelphia	July 20	Bremerhaven	Germany	C.S.	7,825.8
359	Theresa Horn	New York	July 20	Reval	Esthonia	C.A.	4,572.0
360	Lake Connoton	New York	July 21	Hamburg	Germany	C.S.	2,624.1
361	Constanza	Marseilles	July 25	Galatz	Roumania	T.L.	......
362	Coperas	Bordeaux	July 25	Hamburg	Czecho-Slovakia	T.L.	......
363	Lake Dancey, IV	Danzig	July 25	Libau	Latvia	C.A.	228.1
363	Lake Dancey, IV	Danzig	July 25	Libau	Lithuania	C.A.	......
364	Mannheim	Philadelphia	July 26	Hamburg	Germany	C.S.	3,762.2
365	Wolfsburgh	Baltimore	July 26	Helsingfors	Finland	C.S.	......
366	Hannau	New York	July 31	Helsingfors	Finland	C.A.	......
367	U.S. Army Stock	(U.S.A.)	....	(Various)	France	C.S.	30,198.9
	Total for July	....	....	....	....	....	**109,703.1**
368	Slavonia	New York	Aug. 2	Reval	Russia N.W.R.	C.A.	415.6
368	Slavonia	New York	Aug. 2	Reval	Esthonia	C.A.	4,108.6
369	Crostafels	New York	Aug. 5	Hamburg	Czecho-Slovakia	C.A.	2,203.7
370	Wolfram	New York	Aug. 7	Hamburg	Germany	C.S.	541.7
371	Schwarzenfels	New York	Aug. 12	Danzig	Poland	C.A.	......
372	Wachtfels	New York	Aug. 12	Hamburg	Germany	C.S.	537.4
373	Ehrenfels	New York	Aug. 13	Hamburg	Germany	C.S.	1,850.2
374	Belgravia	New York	Aug. 18	Rotterdam	Germany	C.S.	3,444.6
375	Gerfreid	New York	Aug. 19	Danzig	Poland	C.A.	284.4
376	Kagera	New York	Aug. 21	Danzig	Latvia	C.A.	2,500.0
376	Kagera	New York	Aug. 21	Danzig	Poland	C.A.	2,866.2
377	Remschied	New York	Aug. 21	Rotterdam	Germany	C.S.	1,275.7
377	Remschied	New York	Aug. 21	Rotterdam	Germany A.F.S.C.	C.S.	......
378	Lake Fray	Montreal	Aug. 25	Hamburg	Germany A.F.S.C.	C.S.	......
379	Plitvice	New York	Aug. 25	Hamburg	Germany	C.S.	2,567.8

ADMINISTRATION

Children's Relief, and Russian Prisoners of War

Flour Cereal	Grain †	Rice	Beans, Peas	Pork Products: Pork	Pork Products: Lard	Pork Products: Lard Substitute	Milk	Cocoa	Sugar	Misc. †	Total Tons	Total Value
Contents of Cargoes in Net Metric Tons of 1,000 Kilograms or 2,204.6 Pounds												
172.9	6,918.6[r]	......	......	......	......	......	458.5	......	......	......	7,563.4	$ 1,075,813.62
......	......	......	......	......	......	......	......	......	......	......	3,099.9	573,474.84
......	7,729.8[r]	......	......	......	......	......	......	......	......	......	7,729.8	959,853.69
2,117.9	1,651.1[r]	......	......	......	......	......	......	......	......	......	5,264.6	824,265.87
......	......	......	......	......	......	......	......	......	......	......	3,171.0	586,627.79
......	5,785.8[r]	......	......	......	......	......	......	......	......	......	5,785.8	896,804.27
......	......	......	......	......	......	......	......	......	......	......	3,097.0	572,947.77
2,859.4	......	......	......	......	......	......	......	......	......	......	6,530.2	1,150,892.82
28.4	3,037.5[r]	......	......	......	20.4	......	179.0	......	......	......	4,947.8	781,925.62
......	......	......	......	......	......	......	......	......	......	......	2,972.9	549,978.55
427.6	7,074.5[r]	......	......	......	......	......	......	......	......	......	9,582.7	1,304,403.02
969.5	6,865.0[r]	......	......	......	......	......	......	......	......	......	9,778.2	1,343,328.32
102.5	......	......	......	......	......	......	81.5	......	......	......	184.0	54,809.91
280.2	......	......	......	385.4	......	......	241.0	......	......	......	906.6	484,516.64
......	......	......	......	278.2	......	......	......	......	......	......	278.2	235,041.82
......	......	......	......	......	......	......	......	......	......	......	3,126.7	578,432.47
36.0	5,061.8[r]	......	......	......	......	......	......	......	......	......	5,735.4	731,306.89
181.8	......	......	1,557.6	......	......	......	......	......	......	......	1,739.4	437,070.29
......	......	......	124.3	......	......	45.5	46.2	......	......	......	222.3	89,234.00
3,791.0	......	......	......	......	......	......	......	......	......	......	8,384.7	1,475,346.16
......	......	......	......	......	......	......	......	......	......	1,002.0[d]	1,002.0	986,150.90
......	......	......	......	......	......	......	......	......	......	......	8,230.6	1,345,548.64
......	......	......	......	109.9	39.6	17.8	10.0	......	......	......	861.2	262,616.30
......	......	......	......	......	......	......	......	......	......	......	2,986.8	552,551.34
1,841.5	6,066.9[r]	......	824.2	......	......	......	1,372.4	......	......	......	10,579.6	1,997,291.47
......	......	......	......	......	......	......	26.7	......	......	......	26.7	12,156.00
......	......	751.2	......	......	......	......	......	......	......	415.2[d]	1,166.4	521,235.84
481.3	......	363.8	156.8	......	......	......	......	......	......	......	1,001.9	218,364.68
2,466.3	......	......	......	......	......	......	......	......	......	......	6,442.9	1,283,787.67
1,902.6	......	......	......	......	......	......	......	......	......	......	9,728.4	1,761,701.36
......	945.6[r]	......	......	......	......	......	......	......	......	......	5,517.6	1,019,195.06
......	......	......	......	......	......	......	......	......	......	......	2,624.1	485,450.92
17.9	......	10.5	25.9	......	......	......	......	......	......	......	54.3	12,584.90
......	......	768.4	......	......	......	......	......	......	......	......	768.4	192,098.25
......	......	72.3	......	......	......	......	......	......	......	......	300.4	71,139.31
......	......	84.2	......	......	......	......	......	......	......	......	84.2	24,427.57
......	3,556.2[r]	......	......	......	......	......	......	......	......	......	7,318.4	1,122,743.91
......	8,485.1[r]	......	......	......	......	......	......	......	......	......	8,485.1	1,053,648.78
3,023.6	3,224.7[r]	......	......	......	......	......	......	......	......	......	6,248.3	964,458.54
......	......	......	......	......	......	......	......	......	......	......	30,198.9	4,831,830.08
[illegible]1,248.9	**79,170.6**	**2,238.0**	**5,137.2**	**2,070.7**	**76.9**	**474.2**	**2,991.3**	......	......	**1,417.2**	**224,528.1**	**$ 39,983,681.27**
......	......	......	......	......	......	......	......	......	......	......	415.6	$ 81,047.85
853.4	......	......	......	......	......	......	......	......	......	......	4,962.0	950,520.64
598.2	3,691.9[r]	......	......	......	......	......	......	......	......	......	6,493.8	949,409.69
......	......	......	7,735.9	......	......	......	......	......	......	......	8,277.6	2,111,563.55
266.0	......	......	......	......	......	......	......	......	......	889.1[d]	1,155.1	743,202.38
......	......	......	6,996.3	......	......	......	......	......	......	......	7,533.7	1,918,450.30
......	......	......	4,265.1	......	......	......	......	......	......	......	6,115.3	1,451,202.19
......	5,437.5[r]	......	......	......	......	......	......	......	......	......	8,882.1	1,245,343.74
8,012.2	......	......	......	......	......	......	......	......	......	......	8,296.6	1,416,107.51
......	......	......	......	......	......	......	......	......	......	......	2,500.0	512,500.00
......	......	......	......	......	......	......	......	......	......	......	2,866.2	544,586.36
......	......	......	......	......	......	......	......	......	......	......	1,275.7	229,623.48
......	......	......	......	......	......	......	......	13.2	......	......	13.2	8,276.01
......	......	......	......	10.0	......	......	......	......	......	......	10.0	8,344.66
206.2	......	......	2,076.3	......	......	......	......	......	......	......	4,850.3	1,048,911.24

[*Concluded on next page*]

AMERICAN RELIE[F]

Table 111—*Concluded*

Detail of Arrivals by Steamers, Excludin[g]

Arrival No.	Steamer or Source	Port of Sailing	Date of Arrival	Port of Arrival	Allocated to	Fund *	Flour Wheat
			1919				
380	Rudelsberg	New York	Aug. 25	Helsingfors	Finland	C.A.	4,054.
381	Huberfels	New York	Aug. 30	Hamburg	Czecho-Slovakia	C.A.	.....
381	Huberfels	New York	Aug. 30	Hamburg	Germany A.F.S.C.	C.S.	.....
382	Kagera	New York	Aug. 30	Hamburg	Germany	C.S.	.....
383	Kickapoo	Marseilles	Aug. 30	Novorossisk	Russia Kouban	C.S.	.....
384	Sonnenfels	New York	Aug. 30	Batoum	Armenia	C.A.	1,336.
385	Kickapoo	Marseilles	Aug. 30	Batoum	Armenia	C.A.	.....
385	Kickapoo	Novorossisk	Aug. 30	Batoum	Armenia	C.A.	.....
386	Aschenburg	New York	Aug. 31	Batoum	Armenia	C.A.	2,005.
387	Naimes	Philadelphia	Aug. 31	Batoum	Armenia	C.A.	5,378.
388	Lake Dancey, V	Danzig	Aug. 31	Reval	Esthonia	C.A.	1,184.
...	Danzig Stock	(U.S.A.)	....	Danzig	Poland	C.A.	859.
...	Danish Seed Grain	....	....	Reval	Esthonia	C.A.	.....
...	Misc. Charges	....	....	....	Armenia	C.A.	.....
	Total for August	....	....	....	....	....	**37,414.**
	Grand Total Arrivals	....	....	....	....	....	**804,884.**

† Detail of grain totals: [c], corn, 2,977.8; [b], barley, 17,444.4; [r], rye, 467,705.7; [s], seed grain, 1,520.9; [w], wheat, 41,433.8; grand total, 531,082.6. Detail of miscellaneous commodity totals: [d], cotton, 5,775.4; [e], soap, 431.5; [p], prunes, 14.1; [g], oil, 165.9; [k], clothing and other miscellaneo[us] commodities, 1,036.2; grand total, 7,423.1.

‡ Freight only.

AMERICAN RELIE[F]

Table 112

Summary of Deliveries to Governments under Congressional Appropriatio[n]

Country of Destination	Table No.	Flour	Grain	Rice	Beans, Peas
Armenia	201	34,167.1	8,000.0	1,022.3	2,661.8
Czecho-Slovakia	237	34,846.5	17,438.8	.....	.....
Esthonia	293	15.649.9	4,466.5	91.6	.....
Finland	307	20,970.7	43,880.6	.....	121.5
Latvia	370	11,244.6	....	233.5	564.3
Lithuania	383	2,565.9	....	84.2	185.1
Poland	395	132,619.5	81,871.5	8,041.2	8,586.3
Russia					
Northwest Russia	498	14,248.4	....	.....	379.8
Volunteer Army (Russian)	538	394.0	....	.....	.....
Freight, Insurance, Etc.	...*	.....	....	.....	.....
Total Deliveries	109	**266,706.6**	**155,657.4**	**9,472.8**	**12,498.8**

* Cf. Tables 143, 144, 146.

DMINISTRATION

ildren's Relief, and Russian Prisoners of War

Contents of Cargoes in Net Metric Tons of 1,000 Kilograms or 2,204.6 Pounds												Total Value
				Pork Products								
Flour Cereal	Grain †	Rice	Beans, Peas	Pork	Lard	Lard Substitute	Milk	Cocoa	Sugar	Misc.†	Total Tons	
844.3	3,643.2[r]	......	......	......	......	......	......	......	......	......	8,541.6	$ 1,430,120.90
8,217.6	......	......	......	......	......	......	......	......	......	......	8,217.6	1,355,904.99
......	......	......	......	......	......	......	......	......	......	11.0[k]	11.0	910.58‡
......	......	......	2,265.4	......	......	......	......	......	......	......	2,265.4	588,999.84
......	......	......	......	......	......	......	......	......	......	915.5[k]	915.5	444,718.50
......	......	1,019.2	......	......	......	......	1,004.4	71.1	609.6	431.5[e]	4,472.7	1,343,972.79
......	......	......	......	49.0	......	......	......	......	......	107.7[k]	156.7	94,816.97
......	8,000.0[w]	......	......	......	......	......	......	......	......	......	8,000.0	444,718.50
6,399.5	......	......	......	......	......	......	......	......	......	......	8,404.8	1,637,008.32
1,943.5	......	......	......	......	......	......	......	......	......	......	7,321.9	1,498,735.43
......	......	64.4	......	......	......	176.6	......	......	......	......	1,425.1	410,829.01
......	......	......	......	......	......	......	......	......	.8	......	860.2	163,473.30
......	1,520.9[s]	......	......	......	......	......	......	......	......	......	1,520.9	115,747.98
......	......	......	......	......	......	......	......	......	......	......	......	2,797.11
7,340.9	**22,293.5**	**1,083.6**	**23,339.0**	**59.0**	......	**176.6**	**1,004.4**	**84.3**	**610.4**	**2,354.8**	**115,760.6**	**$ 22,751,843.82**
),903.5	**531,082.6†**	**22,120.1**	**60,100.6**	**52,851.5**	**18,180.4**	**29,484.7**	**24,683.5**	**250.5**	**869.4**	**7,423.1†**	**1,682,834.6**	**$361,604,388.18**

DMINISTRATION

r Relief, by Countries of Destination—Armistice Period, 1919

Commodities in Net Metric Tons of 1,000 Kilograms or 2,204.6 Pounds								Total Value
Pork Products	Milk	Cocoa	Sugar	Miscellaneous Food	Soap	Clothing and Miscellaneous	Total Tons	
49.0	3,119.8	186.9	812.8	....	431.5	107.7	50,558.9	$ 10,630,872.19
.....	.....	.....	.....	....	.....	.....	52,285.3	8,251,639.28
725.3	127.5	.....	55.0	14.1	.....	.....	21,129.9	4,299,650.87
714.1	38.8	.....	.....	....	.....	.....	65,725.7	9,849,587.73
771.1	500.2	.....	.....	....	.....	.....	13,313.7	3,323,818.79
425.0	96.8	.....	.....	....	.....	.....	3,357.0	996,093.08
21,797.3	2,100.8	47.6	1.6	....	.....	5,777.4	260,843.2	63,191,316.61
2,266.6	1,055.6	.....	.....	....	.....	.....	17,950.4	5,285,380.17
.....	.....	.....	.....	....	.....	.....	394.0	86,680.00
.....	.....	.....	.....	....	.....	.....	.....	1,217,238.27
26,748.4	**7,039.5**	**234.5**	**869.4**	**14.1**	**431.5**	**5,885.1**	**485,558.1**	**$107,132,276.99**

AMERICAN RELIEF

Summary of Original Allocation,† by Countries of Destination, of Child Feeding Supplies

Table 113*

Country	Commodities i					
	Wheat Flour	Rye Flour	Rice	Beans, Peas	Pork	Lard
Czecho-Slovakia	700.0	.....	318.9	271.3	374.0	26.1
Esthonia	207.0	.....	273.2	151.8	20.0	....
Finland	560.0	200.0	221.9	253.9	76.0	28.0
Jugoslavia	.....	.....	477.3	287.9	....	....
Latvia	260.2	.....	160.0	341.0	35.3	6.0
Lithuania	351.0	.....	83.0	77.8	....	12.0
Poland	858.2	.....	2,077.3	2,898.2	765.0	....
Roumania	250.0	.....	170.0	130.0	60.0	10.0
Russia						
Northwest Russia	60.4	.....	306.9	204.5	20.0	....
Total	**3,246.8**	**200.0**	**4,088.5**	**4,616.4**	**1,350.3**	**82.1**

† This allocation is in accord with report to the President of the United States.

* Cf. Table 114 for final net weights of deliveries per country.

AMERICAN RELIEF

Summary of Final Deliveries, by Countries of Destination, of Child Feeding Supplies, Pai

Table 114†

Country	Table No.	Flour	Rice	Beans, Peas	Pork Products
Austria	212	.....	.....	.....	.....
Czecho-Slovakia	244–45	700.0	318.9	271.3	454.5
Esthonia	297	288.0	250.1	222.4	61.6
Finland	310	700.0	221.9	253.9	95.3
Jugoslavia	358	.....	477.3	287.9	30.0
Latvia	372	260.2	310.0	447.0	43.3
Lithuania	385	351.0	83.0	77.8	28.0
Poland	398–99	858.2	2,193.3	2,898.2	765.0
Roumania	494	250.0	170.0	130.0	70.0
Russia					
Northwest Russia	500	39.4	64.0	27.9	20.0
Total	...	**3,446.8**	**4,088.5**	**4,616.4**	**1,567.7**

† Table 113 shows the allocation of these child feeding supplies as originally determined by the American Relief Administration, and as reported to the President and Congress. In order to meet urgent needs in certain countries, the European Children's Fund found it necessary shift some of these supplies to other countries. Table 114 shows t final destination by countries in which the supplies were consumed.

ADMINISTRATION

Paid for by Funds from the Congressional Appropriation for Relief—Armistice Period, 1919

Net Metric Tons of 1,000 Kilograms or 2,204.6 Pounds								
Lard Substitute	Milk	Cocoa	Sugar	Miscellaneous Food	Soap	Clothing	Total Tons	Total Value
54.4	4,020.2	742.0	.....	10.1	151.2	163.2	6,831.4	$ 2,986,054.64
32.9	443.8	89.4	205.6	....	20.8	.....	1,444.5	481,381.79
....	687.4	40.0	204.9	....	....	.....	2,272.1	696,412.22
30.0	1,900.1	295.3	385.7	....	69.1	.....	3,445.4	1,335,783.36
2.0	711.0	58.2	147.9	....	41.7	.....	1,763.3	632,826.90
16.0	307.5	57.2	95.9	....	....	.....	1,000.4	350,518.35
....	6,284.2	766.3	1,647.1	20.3	441.6	826.7	16,584.9	6,025,682.03
....	185.0	220.9	406.4	....	....	.....	1,432.3	477,272.76
....	576.3	20.0	53.0	....	20.8	.....	1,261.9	447,986.28
135.3	**15,115.5**	**2,289.3**	**3,146.5**	**30.4**	**745.2**	**989.9**	**36,036.2**	**$13,433,918.33**

ADMINISTRATION

for by Funds from the Congressional Appropriation for Relief—Armistice Period, 1919

Commodities in Net Metric Tons of 1,000 Kilograms or 2,204.6 Pounds							
Milk *	Cocoa *	Sugar *	Miscellaneous Food	Soap	Clothing	Total Tons	Total Value
553.7	76.6	116.0	....	....	.....	746.3	$ 319,471.90
3,743.3	663.7	.....	10.1	151.2	163.2	6,476.2	2,837,748.69
787.7	104.4	284.6	....	31.1	.....	2,029.9	701,520.82
658.3	10.0	169.9	....	....	.....	2,109.3	660,175.34
1,623.3	239.0	327.7	....	69.1	.....	3,054.3	1,164,617.41
814.0	83.2	147.9	....	36.7	.....	2,142.3	753,774.72
307.5	57.2	95.9	....	5.0	.....	1,005.4	351,789.53
6,284.2	766.3	1,647.1	20.3	441.6	826.7	16,700.9	6,055,842.03
185.0	220.9	406.4	....	....	.....	1,432.3	477,272.76
129.4	5.0	9.0	....	10.5	.....	305.2	111,705.13
15,086.4	**2,226.3**	**3,204.5**	**30.4**	**745.2**	**989.9**	**36,002.1**	**$13,433,918.33**

* Figures in this table differ from those listed in Table 113 for the following reasons: 58.0 metric tons originally invoiced as cocoa were found to be sugar. In tabulating internal deliveries for Finland, several deliveries of milk and cocoa were found to be gross weight. The tare on the milk was 29.1 metric tons, on cocoa 5.0. The final net figures are listed in this table.

Table 115*

Detail of Arrivals by Steamers of Children's Relief Supplies, Paid for by

Steamer or Source	Port of Sailing	Date of Arrival	Port of Arrival	Flour
		1919		
Copenhagen Stock				
Besoeki and Mirach	New York	Mar. 13	Copenhagen	760.0
Edgefield	Norfolk	Mar. 17	Rotterdam	90.0
Regulus	New York	Apr. 4	Rotterdam	.....
Cape Henry	New York	Apr. 13	Danzig	.....
Englewood	New York	Apr. 21	Constanza	.....
Lake Farge	New York	Apr. 23	Trieste	.....
Neuse	New York	Apr. 23	Trieste	.....
Point Bonita	New York	Apr. 25	Braila	.....
Everett	New York	May 3	Constanza	250.0
Tabor	New York	May 3	Trieste	.....
Ida	New York	May 21	Gravosa	.....
West Lashaway, II	New York	May 24	Trieste	.....
Siretul	London	May 27	Salonica	.....
Wakanna	Newport News	June 1	Danzig	.....
Agwistar	New York	June 6	Trieste	.....
Tyr	New York	June 12	Libau	309.6
Ocland	New York	June 13	Salonica	.....
Yakima	Baltimore	June 13	Danzig	.....
Westward Ho, II	New York	June 14	Danzig	.....
Adelheid	New York	June 15	Hamburg	.....
Lake Strabo	Montreal	June 16	Reval	60.4
Dio	Montreal	June 22	Viborg	.....
Shooters Island	Philadelphia	June 23	Danzig	.....
West Cressey, II	New York	June 23	Danzig	.....
Lake Gretna	Montreal	June 27	Hamburg	700.0
Charlot	New York	July 2 July 9	Libau Riga	.....
Isis	New York	July 18	Hamburg	.....
Faraby	New York	July 19	Danzig	.....
Theresa Horn	(U.S.A.)	July 20	Reval	147.0
Augusta Foherczegno	New York	July 29	Trieste	.....
Szent Istvan	New York	Aug. 8	Trieste	.....
Marianne	New York	Aug. 10	Trieste	.....
Schwarzenfels	New York	Aug. 12	Danzig	.....
Frederica	New York	Aug. 15	Trieste	.....
Remschied	New York	Aug. 21	Rotterdam	.....
Sonnenfels	New York	Aug. 25	Trieste	.....
Brisgravia	New York	Aug. 27	Trieste	.....
Quarter Master Invoice No. 9	(U.S.A.)	June ..	France	.....
Quarter Master Invoice No. 10	(U.S.A.)	June ..	France	.....
Quarter Master Invoice No. 51	New York Philadelphia	Mar. 3 Feb. 4	Trieste Trieste	.....
Quarter Master Invoice No. 54	Philadelphia	Feb. 4	Trieste	.....
Danzig Stock				
Edgefield, Ceralvo, Regulus, Lonoke, Cape Henry, Ponola, Schwarzenfels	New York	......	Danzig	180.0
Purchased from U.S. Army Stock, France	(U.S.A.)	......	St. Nazaire, Bordeaux	949.8
Purchased from C.R.B. Stock	(U.S.A.)	......	Rotterdam	.....
Freight, Insurance, and Sundry Charges	(Poland)	......	....	.....
Total †	....	....	....	**3,446.8**

* For detail of deliveries to countries, and transshipping steamers, cf. Tables 212, 244–45, 297, 310, 358, 372, 385, 398–99, 494, and 500.

† Cf. Table 114 for summary of delivered net weights per country.
‡ Of the total, 30.4 metric tons are cod liver oil; 989.9 are clothing.

ADMINISTRATION

Funds from the Congressional Appropriation for Relief—Armistice Period, 1919

Contents of Cargoes in Net Metric Tons of 1,000 Kilograms or 2,204.6 Pounds									
Rice	Beans, Peas	Pork Products	Milk	Cocoa	Sugar	Soap	Clothing and Misc.	Total Tons	Total Value
.....	....	104.0	7.6	....	.....	....	....	871.6	$ 219,701.90
.....	....	....	....	....	.....	....	....	90.0	19,115.10
493.6	....	....	....	....	.....	....	....	493.6	136,624.76
.....	8.0	12.0	45.6	54.0	201.1	....	....	320.7	106,407.14
.....	....	40.0	....	....	.....	....	....	40.0	28,750.00
204.8	....	....	211.6	69.8	.....	....	....	486.2	180,245.15
.....	....	91.9	237.6	8.7	.....	....	....	338.2	193,589.13
.....	....	....	....	116.9	203.2	....	....	320.1	102,536.32
.....	30.0	....	185.0	104.0	203.2	....	....	772.2	252,996.56
.....	94.0	....	....	....	.....	....	....	94.0	27,719.68
.....	60.0	....	....	....	.....	....	....	60.0	16,800.00
.....	....	....	....	60.3	.....	....	....	60.3	25,908.44
27.5	....	....	216.5	27.4	55.9	....	....	327.3	121,490.31
778.6	1,263.0	....	....	....	.....	....	....	2,041.6	543,451.14
.....	....	....	847.2	101.5	.....	....	....	948.7	495,072.26
.....	9.3	48.9	284.7	....	.....	....	....	652.5	251,779.81
50.0	197.2	30.0	90.0	50.8	101.6	....	....	519.6	181,945.86
551.0	....	....	....	....	.....	....	....	551.0	143,260.00
.....	....	....	....	274.5	101.6	....	....	376.1	134,169.44
.....	....	....	....	102.9	.....	....	....	102.9	40,641.55
.....	....	....	....	....	.....	....	....	60.4	11,775.47
.....	71.7	....	25.0	....	.....	....	....	96.7	32,807.00
.....	....	....	784.9	....	.....	....	....	784.9	393,550.00
.....	....	....	....	81.2	.....	....	....	81.2	32,473.20
.....	....	....	....	....	.....	....	....	700.0	129,500.00
.....	15.0	2.0	18.5	....	.....	....	....	35.5	12,869.44
.....	....	....	152.1	....	.....	....	....	152.1	73,053.00
.....	....	....	....	45.6	.....	....	....	45.6	18,248.40
.....	....	....	....	....	.....	....	....	147.0	28,665.00
.....	....	....	330.6	181.5	.....	....	....	512.1	290,375.07
.....	....	....	271.7	....	.....	....	....	271.7	112,797.00
.....	....	....	341.0	....	.....	....	....	341.0	140,931.00
.....	....	....	1,490.0	100.0	200.0	150.0	....	1,940.0	797,191.58
.....	....	....	108.0	....	.....	121.1	....	229.1	91,429.55
.....	....	....	5,213.0	199.1	1,032.8	218.8	....	6,663.7	2,697,246.96
.....	....	....	157.5	60.8	.....	30.0	....	248.3	111,834.29
246.5	36.6	....	245.9	16.5	99.7	64.6	....	709.8	236,690.18
.....	....	....	....	....	.....	....	52.0	52.0	72,760.30
.....	....	....	....	....	.....	4.6	....	4.6	2,116.80
.....	....	54.4	107.6	....	.....	....	....	162.0	85,297.71
.....	....	....	92.7	....	.....	....	....	92.7	40,238.10
1,258.1	2,393.0	6.0	1,537.9	271.7	866.5	156.1	....	6,669.3	2,146,555.73
478.4	100.0	1,178.5	1,637.2	....	.....	....	....	4,343.9	1,972,388.70
.....	338.6	....	476.1	304.1	138.9	....	968.3	2,226.0	658,916.30
.....	....	....	....	....	.....	....	....	....	22,003.00
4,088.5	**4,616.4**	**1,567.7**	**15,115.5**	**2,231.3**	**3,204.5**	**745.2**	**1,020.3‡**	**36,036.2**	**$13,433,918.33**

AMERICAN RELIEF ADMINISTRATION
PRESIDENT'S NATIONAL SECURITY AND DEFENSE FUND

Summary of Original Allocations, by Operations and Countries
Armistice Period, 1919

Table 116

Operation and Country	Commodities in Net Metric Tons of 1,000 Kilograms or 2,204.6 Pounds										Total Value
	Flour	Rice	Beans, Peas	Pork Products	Milk	Cocoa	Sugar	Misc. Food	Soap	Total Tons	
Children's Relief—Austria	1,601.7	1,079.5	815.4	323.6	2,900.0	394.3	547.4	14.0	147.2	7,823.1	$2,949,217.2
Russian Prisoners of War in Germany—France	959.6	......	.....	.....	......	.....	181.3	481.1	.....	1,622.0	390,209.0
Total Allocations	**2,561.3**	**1,079.5**	**815.4**	**323.6**	**2,900.0**	**394.3**	**728.7**	**495.1**	**147.2**	**9,445.1**	**$3,339,426.2**

AMERICAN RELIEF ADMINISTRATION
PRESIDENT'S NATIONAL SECURITY AND DEFENSE FUND

Summary of Deliveries, by Operations and Countries
Armistice Period, 1919

Table 117

Operation and Country	Table No.	Commodities in Net Metric Tons of 1,000 Kilograms or 2,204.6 Pounds										Total Value
		Flour	Rice	Beans, Peas	Pork Products	Milk	Cocoa	Sugar	Misc. Food	Soap	Total Tons	
Children's Relief—Austria	211	1,503.7	1,079.5	815.4	323.6	2,805.0	367.3	517.4	14.0	110.2	7,536.1	$2,847,892.2
Children's Relief—Hungary	339	98.0	......	.....	.....	95.0	27.0	30.0	.....	37.0	287.0	101,325.0
Russian Prisoners of War in Germany—France	321	959.6	......	.....	.....	.....	.....	181.3	481.1	.....	1,622.0	390,209.0
Total Deliveries *	109	**2,561.3**	**1,079.5**	**815.4**	**323.6**	**2,900.0**	**394.3**	**728.7**	**495.1**	**147.2**	**9,445.1**	**$3,339,426.2**

* The children's relief commodities, 7,823.1 metric tons, valued at $2,949,217.23, are transferred to the Reconstruction Period where all children's relief will be discussed in detail. The balance, 1,622.0 metric tons valued at $390,209.03, will be discussed in the Armistice Period.

AMERICAN RELIEF ADMINISTRATION
PRESIDENT'S NATIONAL SECURITY AND DEFENSE FUND

Detail of Arrivals, by Q.M. Invoices, of Supplies for Russian Prisoners of War in Germany—Armistice Period, 1919

Table 118

Quartermaster Invoice No.*	Date of Delivery	Commodities in Net Metric Tons of 1,000 Kilograms or 2,204.6 Pounds					Total Value
		Flour	Sugar	Miscellaneous Food		Total Tons	
				Tea	Hard Bread		
	1919						
40............	Mar. 17	288.0	45.4	6.1	127.1	466.6	$111,290.
34............	Mar. 18	84.9	44.9	2.3	109.4	241.5	60,612.
65............	Mar. 18	562.7	90.7	6.1	54.6	714.1	161,642.
68............	Mar. 19	....	....	6.1	....	6.1	5,347.
33............	Mar. 19	24.0	.3	2.3	167.1	193.7	51,316.
Total	....	**959.6**	**181.3**	**22.9**	**458.2**	**1,622.0**	**$390,209.**

* Supplies purchased by A.R.A. from U.S. Army Quartermaster in France.

AMERICAN RELIEF ADMINISTRATION
UNITED STATES TREASURY LOANS
Summary of Relief Deliveries, by Countries of Destination
Armistice Period, 1919

Table 119

Country of Destination	Table No.	Commodities in Net Metric Tons of 1,000 Kilograms or 2,204.6 Pounds								Total Value
		Flour	Grain	Rice	Beans, Peas	Pork Products	Milk	Clothing and Misc.	Total Tons	
Czecho-Slovakia	238	81,263.5	158,199.2	976.2	489.9	16,521.4	1,554.7	.....	259,004.9	$50,113,572.61
Jugoslavia	355	50,199.4	......	58.2	1,469.9	2,714.0	469.8	165.9	55,077.2	13,191,246.46
Roumania	492	90,644.8	5,545.3	374.3	684.1	2,919.1	2,774.9	.....	102,942.5	23,438,339.29
Total Deliveries	109	**222,107.7**	**163,744.5**	**1,408.7**	**2,643.9**	**22,154.5**	**4,799.4**	**165.9**	**417,024.6**	**$86,743,158.36**

AMERICAN RELIEF ADMINISTRATION
CASH SALES
Summary of Deliveries, by Countries of Destination and Sundry Accounts
Armistice Period, 1919

Table 120

Country of Destination and Sundry Accounts	Table No.	Commodities in Net Metric Tons of 1,000 Kilograms or 2,204.6 Pounds									Total Value
		Flour	Grain	Rice	Beans, Peas	Pork Products	Milk	Cocoa	Clothing and Misc.	Total Tons	
Armenia	202	1,651.4	....	......	......	.....	342.9	....	....	1,994.3	$ 511,422.34
Austria	207	2,837.0	....	2,029.0	1,028.6	2,223.3	204.6	2.8	....	8,325.3	3,278,068.35
Bulgaria	235	22,862.4	....	......	......	.....	.....	....	....	22,862.4	4,856,647.53
Czecho-Slovakia	239	2.3	....	......	......	11.6	56.6	....	....	70.5	33,778.62
Denmark	291	......	19,912.0	......	......	.....	.....	....	....	19,912.0	2,147,059.30
Esthonia	294	......	862.0	......	......	.....	.....	....	....	862.0	116,371.62
Finland	308	38,346.8	59,158.4	......	1,685.5	1,926.3	.....	....	....	101,117.0	16,004,404.13
France	322	31,106.1	....	......	......	.....	.....	....	....	31,106.1	5,031,830.08
Germany	324–5	241,865.1	131,748.3	9,209.6	42,200.0	46,966.1	11,142.5	13.2	11.0	483,155.8	113,758,637.74
Hungary	337	......	....	......	......	319.1	.....	....	....	319.1	245,519.96
Italy	353	15,031.1	....	......	......	.....	.....	....	....	15,031.1	2,846,014.42
The Netherlands	393	25,027.4	....	......	......	.....	.....	....	....	25,027.4	4,219,498.41
Russia											
Kouban	508	......	....	......	......	.....	.....	....	915.5	915.5	444,718.50
Sundry Accounts	540	1,682.1	....	......	43.8	167.3	10.0	....	....	1,903.2	464,770.08
Turkey	542	20,278.3	....	......	......	.....	.....	....	....	20,278.3	4,369,404.30
United Kingdom	543	46,283.9	....	......	......	.....	1,088.0	....	....	47,371.9	10,618,045.72
Total Sales	109	**446,973.9**	**211,680.7**	**11,238.6**	**44,957.9**	**51,613.7**	**12,844.6**	**16.0**	**926.5**	**780,251.9**	**$168,946,191.10**

AMERICAN ORGANIZATIONS, OTHER THAN
OPERATIONS CARRIED ON IN CO-OPERATION

Table 121

Summary of Relief Deliveries, by

Operation	Table No.	Flour	Grain	Rice	Beans, Peas
United States Liquidation Commission, War Department	122	......	....	....	.....
Commission for Relief in Belgium	103	16,683.0	64,077.0	22,220.0	21,065.0
Near East Relief	123	7,612.0	....	....	.....
Joint Distribution Committee	124	3,705.0	....	....	100.0
American Red Cross	126	......	....	....	.....
Total Deliveries	107	**28,000.0**	**64,077.0**	**22,220.0**	**21,165.0**

THE UNITED STATES LIQUIDATION COMMISSION (WAR DEPARTMENT)

Detail of Relief Deliveries, by Countries of Destination

Table 122†

Armistice Period, 1919

Country of Destination	Table No.	Commodities in Net Metric Tons of 1,000 Kilograms or 2,204.6 Pounds				Total Value *
		Miscellaneous Food	Clothing	Other Miscellaneous	Total Tons	
Belgium	233	37,480.0	8,184.0	5,110.0	50,774.0	$ 28,549,672.75
Czecho-Slovakia	236	34,500.0	4,550.0	1,300.0	40,350.0	19,098,874.27
Esthonia	292	26,000.0	2,620.0	1,500.0	30,120.0	12,262,818.99
France	320	370,285.0	129,490.0	20,000.0	519,775.0	213,067,400.00
Jugoslavia (Kingdom of S.H.S.)	354	16,300.0	5,400.0	10,150.0	31,850.0	20,464,191.25
Latvia	369	5,378.0	758.0	160.0	6,296.0	2,556,952.84
Lithuania	382	4,700.0	2,220.0	1,400.0	8,320.0	4,414,861.39
Poland	394	44,360.0	13,719.0	49,047.0	107,126.0	59,365,111.97
Roumania	491	17,596.0	4,500.0	235.0	22,331.0	13,012,689.00
Russia						
Northwest Russia	497	....	200.0	510.0	710.0	428,299.46
Ukraine	537	....	4,000.0	1,550.0	5,550.0	8,500,222.67
Total Deliveries	...	**556,599.0**	**175,641.0**	**90,962.0**	**823,202.0**	**$381,721,094.59**

† See Tables 144 and 145. Further details may be obtained from "Final Report of United States Liquidation Commission (War Department)," by Edwin B. Parker, chairman, Washington Government Printing Office, 1920.

* F.O.B. at point of sale.

JEWISH JOINT

Table 124*

Summary of Relief Deliveries, by Countries

Country of Destination	Table No.	Cereal Flour	Beans, Peas	Pork and Beef	Lard
Austria	208	42.0	.....	518.0	....
Poland	394	3,663.0	.....	1,622.0	67.0
Roumania	491	......	100.0	50.0	....
Russia (Siberia)	510	......	.....	....	....
Total	121	**3,705.0**	**100.0**	**2,190.0**	**67.0**

* Cf. Table 125.

THE AMERICAN RELIEF ADMINISTRATION WITH THE DIRECTOR GENERAL OF RELIEF

)perations—Armistice Period, 1919

Commodities in Net Metric Tons of 1,000 Kilograms or 2,204.6 Pounds									Total Value
Pork Products	Milk	Cocoa	Sugar	Miscellaneous Food	Soap	Medical and Hospital Supplies	Clothing and Misc.	Total Tons	
......	......	.....	.....	556,599.0	....	.....	266,603.0	823,202.0	$381,721,094.59
35,840.0	756.0	261.0	220.0	874.0	11.0	.....	24,365.0	186,372.0	66,341,240.87
......	1,253.0	.....	.....	6,585.0	....	.....	15,207.0	30,657.0	8,711,472.00
2,949.0	1,802.2	.....	.....	344.6	100.0	525.6	1,502.7	11,029.1	4,107,257.00
......	......	.....	.....	.....	....	3,481.9	4,028.9	7,510.8	1,741,740.00
38,789.0	**3,811.2**	**261.0**	**220.0**	**564,402.6**	**111.0**	**4,007.5**	**311,706.6**	**1,058,770.9**	**$462,622,804.46**

NEAR EAST RELIEF

Detail of Relief Deliveries, by Steamers Armistice Period, 1919

Table 123

Steamer or Source	Port of Sailing	Date of Arrival	Port of Arrival	Contents of Cargoes in Net Metric Tons of 1,000 Kilograms or 2,204.6 Pounds						Total Value *
				Wheat Flour	Milk	Clothing	Misc. Foods	Misc. Non-Foods	Total Tons	
		1919								
Iercurius	New York	Feb. 12	Constantinople	......	125.0	107.0	......	316.0	548.0	$ 917,517.00
Vestern Belle	New York	Feb. 19	Constantinople	7,326.0	......	......	......	......	7,326.0	1,524,418.00
'ensacola	New York	Feb. 20	Beirut	......	33.0	11.0	1,000.0	80.0	1,124.0	266,125.00
'ensacola	New York	Mar. 1	Constantinople	......	......	1,000.0	2,000.0	1,138.0	4,138.0	1,033,023.00
Iewport News	New York	May 20	Constantinople	......	......	1,500.0	......	2,000.0	3,500.0	1,370,000.00
'arthian	New York	Sept...	Constantinople	......	218.0	1,000.0	1,000.0	4.0	2,222.0	728,716.00
Vest Catanace	New York	....	....	......	877.0	......	......	14.0	891.0	334,695.00
:ittegaum	....	....	....	31.0	......	7.0	......	......	38.0	5,390.00
Iurona	....	....	....	255.0	......	30.0	85.0	......	370.0	298,919.00
'urchased from Red Cross	....	....	....	......	......	8,000.0	......	......	8,000.0	1,600,000.00
'urchased through Constantinople Office †	....	....	....	1,651.4	342.9	......	......	......	1,994.3	511,422.34
'urchased from U.S. Army Liquidation Com.	....	....	....	......	......	......	2,500.0	......	2,500.0	632,669.00
Total	....	....	....	**9,263.4**	**1,595.9**	**11,655.0**	**6,585.0**	**3,552.0**	**32,651.3**	**$9,222,894.34**
,ess duplication under A.R.A.	....	....	....	1,651.4	342.9	......	......	......	1,994.3	511,422.34
Net Deliveries	....	....	....	**7,612.0**	**1,253.0**	**11,655.0**	**6,585.0**	**3,552.0**	**30,657.0**	**$8,711,472.00**

* Partly estimated.

† Cash sale to Near East Relief by A.R.A. Table 202.

)ISTRIBUTION COMMITTEE

f Destination—Armistice Period, 1919

ommodities in Net Metric Tons of 1,000 Kilograms or 2,204.6 Pounds								Total Value
Vegetable Oils	Milk	Miscellaneous Food	Soap	Medical Supplies	Clothing	Other Miscellaneous	Total Tons	
64.0	45.2	229.4	....	.....	.....	2.7	901.3	$ 363,760.00
578.0	1,707.0	90.2	75.0	525.6	730.0	648.0	9,705.8	3,412,497.00
50.0	50.0	25.0	25.0	.....	82.0	.....	382.0	256,000.00
....	....	....	....	.....	40.0	.....	40.0	75,000.00
692.0	**1,802.2**	**344.6**	**100.0**	**525.6**	**852.0**	**650.7**	**11,029.1**	**$4,107,257.00**

Table 125

Detail by Steamers of Relief

Arrival No.*	Steamer	Port of Sailing	Date of Arrival	Port of Arrival	Allocated to	Cereal Flour	Beans, Peas
			1919				
1	Westward Ho, I	New York	Feb. 25	Danzig	Poland	3,663.0	.....
2	Democracy	St. Nazaire	Mar. 7	Danzig	Poland	....	.....
3	Kerowlee	St. Nazaire	May 13	Danzig	Poland	....	.....
4	Lake Clear, IV	St. Nazaire	May 13	Danzig	Poland	....	.....
5	Lake Eckhart	St. Nazaire	June 1	Danzig	Poland	....	.....
6	Westward Ho, II	New York	June 14	Danzig	Poland	....	.....
7	Karpathos	Bordeaux	June 20	Danzig	Poland	....	.....
8	Lake Clear, V	Bordeaux	July 2	Hamburg	Austria	42.0	.....
9	Coperas	Bordeaux	July 25	Hamburg	Austria	....	.....
10	Tenyo Maru	....	July ..	Vladivostok	Russia (Siberia)	....	.....
11	Schwarzenfels	New York	Aug. 12	Danzig	Poland	....	.....
12	Ashburn	....	Aug. ..	Danzig	Poland	....	.....
13	Thala	....	Sept. ..	Danzig	Poland	....	.....
14	Polybius	....	Sept. ..	....	Austria	....	.....
15	Jacona	....	Sept. ..	....	Roumania	....	100.0
16	Kitteguano	....	Sept. ..	....	Roumania	....	.....
	Total					**3,705.0**	**100.0**

* Arrival Nos. 2, 3, 4, 5, 7, 8, and 9 were purchased from the United States Liquidation Commission (War Department); a total of 1,112.1 metric tons so purchased was paid for by the J.D.C. Freight and insurance on these arrivals was paid by the A.R.A. and billed to the J.D.C. See Table 146.

† Detail of miscellaneous commodities is indicated by the following indexes: [a], hard bread; [b], oil; [c], autos and trucks; [d], molasses.

AMERICAN RED CROSS

Summary of Relief Deliveries by Countries of Destination

Armistice Period, 1919

Table 126†

Country	Commodities in Net Metric Tons of 1,000 Kilograms or 2,204.6 Pounds			Total Value *
	Clothing	Medical Supplies	Total Tons	
Armenia	754.1	.....	754.1	$ 258,600.0
Czecho-Slovakia	875.2	.....	875.2	175,040.0
Esthonia	.....	312.3	312.3	89,800.0
Finland	282.0	.....	282.0	56,400.0
Jugoslavia (S.H.S.)	667.6	.....	667.6	224,800.0
Poland	1,450.0	2,592.6	4,042.6	813,800.0
Russia				
Kouban	.....	577.0	577.0	123,300.0
Total	**4,028.9**	**3,481.9**	**7,510.8**	**$1,741,740.0**

† Cf. Tables 127, 143.

* Partially estimated.

ISTRIBUTION COMMITTEE

eliveries—Armistice Period, 1919

Pork and Beef	Lard	Vegetable Oils	Milk	Misc. Food †	Soap	Medical Supplies	Clothing	Other Misc. †	Total Tons	Total Value
Contents of Cargoes in Net Metric Tons of 1,000 Kilograms or 2,204.6 Pounds										
1,117.0	67.0	578.0	1,023.0	....	....	....	38.0	....	6,486.0	$2,000,000.00
.....	....	....	....	....	....	4.9	102.0	....	106.9	76,700.00
.....	....	....	....	....	....	22.6	....	....	22.6	9,200.00
.....	....	....	....	....	....	450.6	....	....	450.6	135,300.00
.....	....	....	....	90.2[a]	....	47.5	....	....	137.7	37,200.00
.....	....	....	684.0	....	....	....	579.0	573.0[b]	1,836.0	700,000.00
.....	....	....	....	....	....	....	....	75.0[c]	75.0	150,000.00
.....	....	....	45.2	229.4	....	....	....	....	316.6	70,310.00
.....	....	....	....	....	....	....	....	2.7[c]	2.7	5,000.00
.....	....	....	....	....	....	....	40.0	....	40.0	75,000.00
.....	....	....	....	....	....	....	11.0	....	11.0	2,200.00
505.0	....	....	....	....	....	....	....	....	505.0	286,648.00
.....	....	....	....	....	75.0	....	....	....	75.0	15,249.00
518.0	....	64.0	....	....	....	....	....	....	582.0	288,450.00
50.0	....	50.0	50.0	15.0[d]	25.0	....	81.0	....	371.0	250,000.00
.....	....	....	....	10.0	....	....	1.0	....	11.0	6,000.00
2,190.0	**67.0**	**692.0**	**1,802.2**	**344.6**	**100.0**	**525.6**	**852.0**	**650.7**	**11,029.1**	**$4,107,257.00**

AMERICAN RED CROSS

Detail by Steamers of Relief Deliveries—Armistice Period, 1919

Table 127

ival o.	Steamer	Port of Sailing	Date of Arrival	Port of Arrival	Allocated to	Contents of Cargoes in Net Metric Tons of 1,000 Kilograms or 2,204.6 Pounds: Clothing	Hospital, Medical Supplies	Total Tons	Total Value *
			1919						
1	Lake St. Regis, III.....	Rotterdam	April 17	Danzig	Poland	950.0	.....	950.0	$ 190,000.00
2	Neuse	New York	April 23	Trieste	Czecho-Slovakia	450.0	.....	450.0	90,000.00
3	Lake Traverse, III....	Rotterdam	May 7	Danzig	Poland	500.0	.....	500.0	100,000.00
4	Ida	New York	May 21	Gravosa	Jugoslavia	218.3	.....	218.3	48,000.00
5	Ocland	New York	June 13	Salonica	Jugoslavia	449.3	.....	449.3	176,800.00
6	Westward Ho, II.....	New York	June 14	Danzig	Poland	.....	415.0	415.0	166,000.00
7	Karpathos	Bordeaux	June 20	Danzig	Poland	.....	29.1	29.1	9,200.00
8	Lake Hemlock	New York	July 12	Hango	Finland	282.0	.....	282.0	56,400.00
9	Faraby	New York	July 19	Danzig	Poland	.....	1,110.0	1,110.0	222,000.00
0	Lake Dancey, V.......	Danzig	Aug. 1	Reval	Esthonia	.....	24.5	24.5	9,800.00
1	Lake Fray	New York	Aug. 7	Reval	Esthonia	.....	287.8	287.8	80,000.00
2	Schwarzenfels	New York	Aug. 12	Danzig	Poland	.....	1,038.5	1,038.5	126,600.00
3	Sonnenfels	New York	Aug. 25	Trieste	Czecho-Slovakia	301.2	.....	301.2	60,240.00
4	Sonnenfels	New York †	Aug. 30	Batoum	Armenia	488.3	.....	488.3	206,200.00
5	Huberfels	New York	Aug. 30	Hamburg	Czecho-Slovakia	10.0	.....	10.0	2,000.00
6	Kickapoo	Marseilles	Aug. 30	Novorossisk	Kouban	.....	577.0	577.0	123,300.00
7	Aschenburg	New York	Aug. 31	Batoum	Armenia	265.8	.....	265.8	52,400.00
8	Naval Ship	....	....	....	Czecho-Slovakia	114.0	.....	114.0	22,800.00
	Total	....	....	....	....	**4,028.9**	**3,481.9**	**7,510.8‡**	**$1,741,740.00**

Partially estimated.
First port of arrival was Trieste.

‡ The transportation of 4,494.8 tons was handled by the A.R.A. Freight and other charges on charity shipments by A.R.A. paid for by funds from the Congressional appropriation for relief. See Table 143.

JOINT ALLIED FINANCE†

Summary of Relief to Austria, by Countries Making Deliveries
Armistice Period, 1919

Table 128

Country Making Delivery	Table No.	Commodities in Net Metric Tons of 1,000 Kilograms or 2,204.6 Pounds								Total Value *
		Wheat Flour	Cereal Flour	Wheat Grain	Rye Grain	Pork Products	Vegetable Oil	Milk	**Total Tons**	
France	129	72,409.5	22,480.4	44,904.3	10,190.3	....	.....	.....	149,984.5	$16,000,000.
Italy	...‡	3,225.0	10,076.0	71,855.0	....	10,850.0	524.0	845.0	97,375.0	16,000,000.
United Kingdom	130	64,454.3	7,718.2	24,309.8	....	....	.....	1,998.0	98,480.3	16,000,000.
Total	107	**140,088.8**	**40,274.6**	**141,069.1**	**10,190.3**	**10,850.0**	**524.0**	**2,843.0**	**345,839.8**	**$48,000,000.**

† Financed by U. S. Treasury Loan of $48,000,000, allocated to countries as noted above, for the benefit of Austria.
* Value quoted f.o.b. New York.

‡ No complete statement has been obtained of actual amounts American supplies delivered to Austria. Cf. text on J.A.F., page These commodities prorated from total deliveries by Italy.

JOINT ALLIED FINANCE

Detail by Steamers of Relief Deliveries to Austria, by France†
Armistice Period, 1919

Table 129

Steamer or Source	Date of Arrival	Port of Arrival	Contents of Cargoes in Net Metric Tons of 1,000 Kilograms or 2,204.6 Pounds					Total Value *
			Wheat Flour	Cereal Flour	Wheat Grain	Rye Grain	Total Tons	
	1919							
Hungaria	Apr. 30	Trieste	......	......	4,289.9	......	4,289.9	$ 388,488.
Africana	May ..	Trieste	......	......	4,694.2	......	4,694.2	428,972.
War Earl ‡	May ..	Trieste	6,018.0	......	......	......	6,018.0	752,852.
Porsanger ‡	May 15	Trieste	6,361.3	......	......	......	6,361.3	795,799.
Perserveranza, I	May 15	Trieste	4,769.5	......	......	......	4,769.5	604,031.
War Cowslip ‡	May 22	Trieste	7,240.0	......	......	......	7,240.0	905,266.
Dubac, I	June 2	Trieste	515.3	1,015.2	2,541.3	......	4,071.8	468,414.
Caterino Gerolimich	June 10	Trieste	980.9	977.9	4,672.9	......	6,631.7	644,960.
Sztereny	June 10	Trieste	2,510.9	1,662.4	......	......	4,173.3	466,179.
Adriatico	June 10	Trieste	3,202.3	1,814.9	......	......	5,017.2	566,917.
Maria Immaculata	June 16	Trieste	4,244.6	674.9	......	......	4,919.5	599,146.
Kossuth Ferencz	June 28	Trieste	4,587.3	1,271.3	......	......	5,858.6	693,712.
Boheme	July 7	Trieste	6,329.6	......	......	......	6,329.6	776,767.
Emelia	July 9	Trieste	4,184.1	......	......	......	4,184.1	530,348.
Lapad	July 11	Trieste	3,485.4	......	......	......	3,485.4	442,241
Georgia, I	July 11	Trieste	230.6	......	......	......	230.6	29,995
Izvor	July 15	Trieste	......	......	5,399.7	......	5,399.7	480,074
Dardania	July 15	Trieste	4,556.0	127.0	......	......	4,683.0	592,037
Ellenia	July 18	Trieste	826.3	4,615.0	......	......	5,441.3	516,435
Istina	July 23	Trieste	172.8	931.9	......	4,064.2	5,168.9	378,883
Erdely	July 26	Trieste	6,021.3	579.3	......	......	6,600.6	830,695
Perserveranza, II	July 30	Trieste	......	2,766.9	......	1,651.0	4,417.9	364,602
Clumecky	July 31	Trieste	3,836.8	......	......	771.9	4,608.7	550,942
Atlantico	Aug. 2	Trieste	175.6	2,809.5	......	......	2,985.1	274,749
Szent Istvan	Aug. 10	Trieste	784.5	1,548.2	......	......	2,332.7	242,350
Marianne	Aug. 10	Trieste	365.8	1,557.8	......	......	1,923.6	177,639
Proteo	Aug. 17	Trieste	1,010.6	128.2	......	3,703.2	4,842.0	369,439
Georgia, II	....	....	......	......	5,230.7	......	5,230.7	465,110
Supplies delivered after September 1	....	....	......	......	18,075.6	......	18,075.6	1,662,958
Total	....	....	**72,409.5**	**22,480.4**	**44,904.3**	**10,190.3**	**149,984.5**	**$16,000,000**

† Financed by U.S. Treasury loan to France.
* F.O.B. New York.

‡ Cargoes of Australian flour diverted from Italy and later replaced shipment from New York.

JOINT ALLIED FINANCE

Detail by Steamers of Relief Deliveries to Austria, by the United Kingdom*

Table 130 Armistice Period, 1919

Steamer or Source	Date of Arrival	Port of Arrival	Contents of Cargoes in Net Metric Tons of 1,000 Kilograms or 2,204.6 Pounds					Total Value
			Wheat Flour	Cereal Flour	Wheat Grain	Milk	Total Tons	
	1919							
R.A. Stocks (Table 131)	....	Trieste	46,283.9	....	....	1,088.0	47,371.9	$10,618,045.72
rederica	Aug. 25	Trieste	22.2	1,557.9	....	.....	1,580.1	136,840.71
ubac, II	Aug. 27	Trieste	1,459.9	1,646.7	....	.....	3,106.6	308,644.40
isgravia	Aug. 27	Trieste	2,126.7	4,486.3	....	.....	6,613.0	678,292.59
hildturn	Sept. ..	Trieste	6,780.7	27.3	....	.....	6,808.0	833,355.30
andelfels	Sept. 8	Trieste	7,780.9	....	....	.....	7,780.9	888,318.28
pplies from United Kingdom	....	....	......	....	....	910.0	910.0	300,000.00
elivered after September	....	....	......	....	24,309.8	.....	24,309.8	2,236,503.00
Total	....	....	**64,454.3**	**7,718.2**	**24,309.8**	**1,998.0**	**98,480.3**	**$16,000,000.00**

* Financed by the U.S. Treasury loan to United Kingdom.

JOINT ALLIED FINANCE

Detail by Steamers of American Relief Administration Cash Sales to United Kingdom, for Austria—Armistice Period, 1919

Table 131†

ival o.*	Steamer	Port of Sailing	Date of Arrival	Port of Arrival	Contents of Cargoes in Net Metric Tons of 1,000 Kilograms or 2,204.6 Pounds			Total Value
					Wheat Flour	Milk	Total Tons	
			1919					
1	West Lashaway, I	New York	Jan. 3	Trieste	7,173.8	......	7,173.8	$ 1,581,536.91
10	West Alcasco	New York	Jan. 22	Trieste	6,952.9	......	6,952.9	1,532,837.28
11	Western Scout	New York	Jan. 25	Trieste	7,222.8	......	7,222.8	1,592,339.45
14	West Compo	Baltimore	Apr. 9	Trieste	5,606.8	......	5,606.8	1,222,221.36
48	Neuse	New York	Apr. 23	Trieste	2,031.0	......	2,031.0	442,735.89
61	Harold	New York	May 2	Trieste	2,650.0	1,088.0	3,738.0	1,053,580.95
63	Tabor	New York	May 3	Trieste	443.0	......	443.0	96,569.17
73	West Modus	Norfolk	May 8	Trieste	7,486.8	......	7,486.8	1,632,035.44
21	West Lashaway, II	New York	May 24	Trieste	6,716.8	......	6,716.8	1,464,189.27
	Total Sales—to Table 120	....	....	....	**46,283.9**	**1,088.0**	**47,371.9**	**$10,618,045.72**

† Cf. Table 130.

* Arrival numbers from Table 111. Arrival Nos. 1, 10, and 11 are from U.S. Army stock, Trieste, billed to A.R.A. on Q.M. invoices Nos. 22 and 40.

COUNTRIES OTHER

Table 132 A

Summary of Relief Deliveries b

Country of Origin	Table No.	Flour	Grain	Rice	Beans, Peas
United Kingdom	133	71,055.0	59,893.0	41,741.0	8,515.0
France	134	2,411.6	......	1,542.0	5,000.0
Italy	135	73,825.0	16,761.0	10,175.0	4,209.0
Argentina	136	......	135,000.0	......	......
Austria	136	......	......	......	......
Czecho-Slovakia	136	......	......	......	......
Denmark	136	......	10,462.6	......	......
Germany	136	......	......	......	......
Hungary	136	1,287.0	2,473.0	......	......
Jugoslavia	136	235.0	12,433.0	......	1,402.0
Norway	136	......	......	......	4,442.0
The Netherlands	136	......	......	......	......
Poland	136	......	......	......	......
Switzerland	136	7,555.0	538.0	1,241.0	......
Polish League of Women	136	......	......	......	......
Russo-Carpathian Commission	136	......	......	......	......
Total, Gross Deliveries	...	**156,368.6**	**237,560.6**	**54,699.0**	**23,568.0**
Less Transfer to Reconstruction Period	369	......	......	......	......
Total, Net Deliveries	107	**156,368.6**	**237,560.6**	**54,699.0**	**23,568.0**

* Excluding Joint Allied Finance.
† Including finance on freight, $4,500,000.00.
‡ Including finance on freight, $2,021,250.00.

COUNTRIES OTHER

Table 132 B

Summary of Relief Deliveries b

Country of Destination	Table No.	Flour	Grain	Rice	Beans, Peas
Armenia	200	......	......	......	......
Austria	206	21,855.0	33,205.0	11,093.0	5,611.0
Czecho-Slovakia	236	62,726.0	......	5,948.0	5,000.0
Esthonia	292	4,600.0	1,133.6	......	303.0
Finland	306	......	10,000.0	......	5,612.0
Germany	323	22,447.0	135,000.0	37,658.0	......
Jugoslavia	354	10,197.0	4,116.0	......	3,788.0
Latvia	369	......	......	......	......
Lithuania	382	......	......	......	......
Poland	394	3,239.0	5,813.0	......	1,362.0
Roumania	133, 493	30,345.0	48,293.0	......	1,892.0
Russia					
Kouban	507	......	......	......	......
Sundry Accounts	134, 539	959.6	......	......	......
Total, Net Deliveries	...	**156,368.6**	**237,560.6**	**54,699.0**	**23,568.0**

* Excluding Joint Allied Finance.

THAN UNITED STATES*

Countries of Origin—Armistice Period, 1919

Commodities in Net Metric Tons of 1,000 Kilograms or 2,204.6 Pounds								Total Value
Pork Products	Milk	Sugar	Miscellaneous Food	Soap	Medical and Hospital Supplies	Clothing and Misc.	Total Tons	
52,530.0	17,739.0	2,367.0	166,476.0	568.0	370.0	70,118.0	491,372.0	$120,171,279.00
17,508.0	.....	181.3	7,004.1	.....	.....	55,000.0	88,647.0	29,404,724.00†
31,029.0	2,192.0	.....	1,731.0	.....	.....	.....	139,922.0	37,532,042.00‡
.....	.....	.....	.....	.....	.....	20,000.0	155,000.0	16,774,000.00
200.0	.....	.....	320.0	.....	.....	.....	520.0	281,600.00
234.0	.....	39,639.0	.....	.....	.....	23,025.0	62,898.0	9,914,858.00
19.0	.....	.....	.....	.....	.....	.....	10,481.6	1,187,015.92
.....	.....	.....	330.0	.....	.....	.....	330.0	13,200.00
10.0	.....	.....	5,108.0	.....	.....	.....	8,878.0	805,063.00
852.0	.....	.....	19,514.0	.....	.....	.....	34,436.0	3,051,611.00
.....	.....	.....	25.0	.....	.....	.....	4,467.0	1,192,130.00
13,650.0	.....	.....	27,505.0	.....	.....	6,303.0	47,458.0	9,897,389.00
105.0	.....	.....	50,000.0	.....	.....	3,921.0	54,026.0	1,204,896.00
163.0	473.0	.....	30,639.0	.....	.....	.....	40,609.0	7,355,349.00
.....	.....	.....	.....	.....	.....	4.1	4.1	1,640.00
.....	.....	.....	.....	.....	.....	.5	.5	200.00
116,300.0	**20,404.0**	**42,187.3**	**308,652.1**	**568.0**	**370.0**	**178,371.6**	**1,139,049.2**	**$238,786,996.92**
.....	.....	.....	6.6	.....	.....	.....	6.6	3,960.00
116,300.0	**20,404.0**	**42,187.3**	**308,645.5**	**568.0**	**370.0**	**178,371.6**	**1,139,042.6**	**$238,783,036.92**

THAN UNITED STATES*

Countries of Destination—Armistice Period, 1919

Commodities in Net Metric Tons of 1,000 Kilograms or 2,204.6 Pounds								Total Value
Pork Products	Milk	Sugar	Miscellaneous Food	Soap	Medical and Hospital Supplies	Clothing and Misc.	Total Tons	
.....	.....	.....	.....	.....	.....	.....	....	$ 71,400.00
19,531.0	1,201.0	39,639.0	41,058.3	.....	.....	33,446.0	206,639.3	47,114,365.00
23,551.0	1,764.0	.....	50,535.1	.....	.....	1,120.0	150,644.1	27,669,384.00
.....	.....	900.0	1,750.0	.....	.....	400.0	9,086.6	2,377,567.92
.....	40.0	1,415.0	842.0	.....	.....	.....	17,909.0	3,239,080.00
69,366.0	17,018.0	.....	205,794.0	.....	.....	109,799.0	597,082.0	124,301,551.00
985.0	381.0	52.0	48.0	.....	.....	14,088.0	33,655.0	9,635,192.00
.....	.....	.....	.....	.....	.....	.....	....	80,920.00
.....	.....	.....	.....	.....	.....	.....	....	57,120.00
1,255.0	.....	.....	541.0	568.0	370.0	8,318.6	21,466.6	7,696,380.00
562.0	.....	.....	7,596.0	.....	.....	11,100.0	99,788.0	15,428,688.00
.....	.....	.....	.....	.....	.....	100.0	100.0	10,472.00
1,050.0	.....	181.3	481.1	.....	.....	.....	2,672.0	1,100,917.00
116,300.0	**20,404.0**	**42,187.3**	**308,645.5**	**568.0**	**370.0**	**178,371.6**	**1,139,042.6**	**$238,783,036.92**

Table 133

Detail of Relief Deliveries by the British Empire,*

Country of Destination	Table No.	Commoditie						
		Wheat Flour	Cereal Flour	Wheat, Rye Grain	Rice	Beans, Peas	Pork Products	Lard
Armenia	200	......	......	.....	......	.....	.....	.....
Austria †	206	......	......	1,000.0	......	.....	.....	.....
Czecho-Slovakia	242	20.0	1,609.0	.....	4,083.0	.....	.....	.....
Esthonia	295	1,400.0	3,200.0	671.0	......	303.0	.....	.....
Finland	306	......	......	.....	......	1,170.0	.....	.....
Germany	327	......	21,045.0	.....	37,658.0	.....	43,657.0	2,571.0
Jugoslavia (S.H.S.)	356	10,197.0	......	4,116.0§	......	3,788.0	15.0	970.0
Latvia	369	......	......	.....	......	.....	.....	.....
Lithuania	382	......	......	.....	......	.....	.....	.....
Poland	396	......	3,239.0	5,813.0§	......	1,362.0	1,255.0	.....
Roumania	493	13,200.0	9,443.0	21,911.0	......	1,892.0	262.0	.....
Russia								
Kouban	507	......	......	.....	......	.....	.....	.....
Total Deliveries	...	**24,817.0**	**38,536.0**	**33,511.0**	**41,741.0**	**8,515.0**	**45,189.0**	**3,541.0**
Roumania	493	**7,702.0**	......	**26,382.0**	......	.....	.....	.....
Roumania	493	......	......	.....	......	.....	.....	.....
Grand Total, British Empire	132A	**32,519.0**	**38,536.0**	**59,893.0**	**41,741.0**	**8,515.0**	**45,189.0**	**3,541.0**

* Based on records in the office of the Director General of Relief, supplemented by Sir William Goode's report on "Economic Conditions in Central Europe" (I) and (II) Miscellaneous Series Nos. 1, 6 (1920), Command Papers 521, 641, London, 1920.

† Exclusive of deliveries under Joint Allied Finance. See Table 128.
‡ Potatoes.
§ Partly seed grains.

COUNTRIES OTHER THAN UNITED STATES

Detail of Relief Deliveries by France,* by Countries of Destination Armistice Period, 1919

Table 134

Country of Destination	Table No.	Commodities in Net Metric Tons of 1,000 Kilograms or 2,204.6 Pounds											Total Value
		Wheat Flour	Cereal Flour	Rice	Beans, Peas	Pork Products	Lard	Sugar	Miscellaneous Foods	Miscellaneous Non-Foods	Finance on Freight	Total Tons	
Austria †	206	....	....	......	......	......	.....	.....	...	....	$4,500,000.00	....	$ 4,500,000.0
Czecho-Slovakia	236	50.0	....	1,542.0	5,000.0	9,970.0	.....	.....	9.0	....	....	16,571.0	7,540,918.0
Germany	328	1,318.0	84.0	......	......	6,488.0	.....	.....	6,514.0	55,000.0	....	69,404.0	16,262,889.0
Russian Prisoners of War in Germany	539	959.6‡	....	......	......	900.0	150.0	181.3‡	481.1‡	....	....	2,672.0	1,100,917.0
Total	132A	**2,327.6**	**84.0**	**1,542.0**	**5,000.0**	**17,358.0**	**150.0**	**181.3**	**7,004.1**	**55,000.0**	**$4,500,000.00**	**88,647.0**	**$29,404,724.0**

* Based on records in the office of the Director General of Relief in Paris.
† Exclusive of deliveries under Joint Allied Finance. See Table 128, page 310.

‡ Commodities purchased by A.R.A. from U.S. Army Quartermaste in France, accounted for in Tables 118 and 321. See text, page 187.

'HAN UNITED STATES

y Countries of Destination—Armistice Period, 1919

Net Metric Tons of 1,000 Kilograms or 2,204.6 Pounds										Total Value
Lard Substitute	Milk	Sugar	Misc. Food	Soap	Cloth and Clothing	Medical and Hospital Supplies	Other Non-Foods	Finance on Freight	Total Tons	
DELIVERIES BY THE UNITED KINGDOM										
.....	.....	.....	.....	.....	.....	.....	.....	$ 71,400.00	....	$ 71,400.00
500.0	.....	.....	10,000.0	.....	.....	.....	6,500.0	4,760,000.00	18,000.0	6,676,640.00
.....	300.0	.....	.....	.....	50.0	.....	1,070.0	....	7,132.0	1,599,836.00
.....	.....	900.0	1,750.0	.....	300.0	.....	100.0	309,400.00	8,624.0	2,342,360.00
.....	40.0	1,415.0	842.0	.....	.....	.....	.....	....	3,467.0	920,250.00
3,000.0	17,018.0	.....	145,699.0‡	.....	.....	.....	28,496.0	....	299,144.0	75,653,861.00
.....	381.0	52.0	48.0	.....	1,532.0	.....	12,556.0	373,660.00	33,655.0	9,635,192.00
.....	.....	.....	.....	.....	.....	.....	.....	80,920.00	....	80,920.00
.....	.....	.....	.....	.....	.....	.....	.....	57,120.00	....	57,120.00
.....	.....	.....	541.0	568.0	1,054.0	370.0	7,260.0	1,389,920.00	21,462.0	7,694,540.00
300.0	.....	.....	5,240.0	.....	.....	.....	7,000.0	21,420.00	59,248.0	10,026,048.00
.....	.....	.....	.....	.....	.....	.....	100.0	....	100.0	10,472.00
3,800.0	**17,739.0**	**2,367.0**	**164,120.0**	**568.0**	**2,936.0**	**370.0**	**63,082.0**	**$7,063,840.00**	**450,832.0**	**$114,768,639.00**
DELIVERIES BY CANADA										
.....	.....	.....	.....	.....	.....	.....	**4,100.0**	....	**38,184.0**	**$ 3,836,600.00**
DELIVERIES BY NEWFOUNDLAND										
.....	.....	.....	**2,356.0**	.....	.....	.....	.....	....	**2,356.0**	**$ 1,566,040.00**
3,800.0	**17,739.0**	**2,367.0**	**166,476.0**	**568.0**	**2,936.0**	**370.0**	**67,182.0**	**$7,063,840.00**	**491,372.0**	**$120,171,279.00**

COUNTRIES OTHER THAN UNITED STATES

Detail of Relief Deliveries by Italy,* by Countries of Destination
Armistice Period, 1919

Table 135

Country of Destination	Table No.	Commodities in Net Metric Tons of 1,000 Kilograms or 2,204.6 Pounds									Total Value
		Wheat Flour	Wheat	Beans, Peas	Rice	Pork Products	Milk	Misc. Food	Finance on Freight	Total Tons	
ıstria †	206	12,808.0	16,761.0	4,209.0	9,852.0	18,168.0	728.0	1,535.0	$2,021,250.00	64,061.0	$20,878,122.00
echo-Slovakia	236	61,017.0	....	......	323.0	12,861.0	1,464.0	196.0	....	75,861.0	16,653,920.00
Total	132A	**73,825.0**	**16,761.0**	**4,209.0**	**10,175.0**	**31,029.0**	**2,192.0**	**1,731.0**	**$2,021,250.00**	**139,922.0**	**$37,532,042.00**

* Based on records in the office of the Director General of Relief in ris.

† Exclusive of deliveries under Joint Allied Finance. Cf. Table 128.

COUNTRIES OTHER THAN UNITED STATES

Table 136*

Detail of Relief Deliveries by Countries of

Country of Origin	Country of Destination	Table No.	Wheat Flour	Barley, Oats, Wheat Grain	Beans, Peas
Argentina	Germany	329	.....	**135,000.0**	......
Austria	Czecho-Slovakia	236	.....	.....	......
Czecho-Slovakia	Austria	209	.....	.....	......
Denmark	Austria	209	.....	.....	......
Denmark	Esthonia	292	.....	462.6	......
Denmark	Finland	306	.....	10,000.0	......
Total Ex-Denmark	......	......	.....	**10,462.6**	......
Germany	Austria	209	.....	.....	......
Hungary	Austria	209	**1,287.0**	**2,473.0**	......
Jugoslavia	Czecho-Slovakia	236	30.0	.....	......
Jugoslavia	Austria	209	205.0	12,433.0	1,402.0
Total Ex-Jugoslavia	......	......	**235.0**	**12,433.0**	**1,402.0**
The Netherlands	Austria	209	.....	.....	......
The Netherlands	Germany	329	.....	.....	......
Total Ex-Netherlands	......	......	.....	.....	......
Norway	Austria	209	.....	.....	......
Norway	Czecho-Slovakia	236	.....	.....	......
Norway	Finland	306	.....	.....	4,442.0
Norway	Latvia	371	.....	.....	......
Total Ex-Norway	......	......	.....	.....	**4,442.0**
Poland	Czecho-Slovakia	236	.....	.....	......
Poland	Austria	209	.....	.....	......
Total Ex-Poland	......	......	.....	.....	......
Switzerland	Austria	209	7,555.0	538.0	......
Switzerland	Germany	329	.....	.....	......
Total Ex-Switzerland	......	......	**7,555.0**	**538.0**	......
Polish League of Women	Poland	394	.....	.....	......
Russo-Carpathian Commission	Poland	394	.....	.....	......
Total, Gross	......	......	**9,077.0**	**160,906.6**	**5,844.0**
Less Transfer	......	......	.....	.....	......
Grand Total, Net	......	......	**9,077.0**	**160,906.6**	**5,844.0**

* Cf. Table 132.

† Transferred to Reconstruction Period and accounted for with oth child-feeding supplies.

EXCLUSIVE OF THE THREE MAJOR ALLIES)

rigin and Destination—Armistice Period, 1919

Commodities in Net Metric Tons of 1,000 Kilograms or 2,204.6 Pounds									Total Value
Rice	Pork Products	Lard	Lard Substitute	Milk	Sugar	Misc. Foods	Other Miscellaneous	Total Tons	
.....	.....	.....	.....	.....	.....	.....	**20,000.0**	**155,000.0**	**$16,774,000.00**
.....	**200.0**	.....	.....	.....	.....	**320.0**	.....	**520.0**	**281,600.00**
.....	**34.0**	.....	**200.0**	.....	**39,639.0**	.....	**23,025.0**	**62,898.0**	**9,914,858.00**
.....	19.0	.....	.....	.....	.....	.....	.....	19.0	10,108.00
.....	.....	.....	.....	.....	.....	.....	.....	462.6	35,207.92
.....	.....	.....	.....	.....	.....	.....	.....	10,000.0	1,141,700.00
.....	**19.0**	.....	.....	.....	.....	.....	.....	**10,481.6**	**$ 1,187,015.92**
.....	.....	.....	.....	.....	.....	**330.0**	.....	**330.0**	**13,200.00**
.....	.....	.....	**10.0**	.....	.....	**5,108.0**	.....	**8,878.0**	**805,063.00**
.....	520.0	.....	.....	.....	.....	.....	.....	*550.0	587,050.00
.....	187.0	.....	145.0	.....	.....	19,514.0	.....	33,886.0	2,464,561.00
.....	**707.0**	.....	**145.0**	.....	.....	**19,514.0**	.....	**34,436.0**	**$ 3,051,611.00**
.....	.....	.....	.....	.....	.....	2,810.0	.....	2,810.0	112,400.00
.....	981.0	12,669.0	.....	.....	.....	24,695.0	6,303.0	44,648.0	9,784,989.00
.....	**981.0**	**12,669.0**	.....	.....	.....	**27,505.0**	**6,303.0**	**47,458.0**	**$ 9,897,389.00**
.....	.....	.....	.....	.....	.....	8.3	.....	8.3	4,980.00
.....	.....	.....	.....	.....	.....	10.1	.....	10.1	6,060.00
.....	.....	.....	.....	.....	.....	.....	.....	4,442.0	1,177,130.00
.....	.....	.....	.....	.....	.....	6.6†	.....	6.6	3,960.00
.....	.....	.....	.....	.....	.....	**25.0**	.....	**4,467.0**	**$ 1,192,130.00**
.....	.....	.....	.....	.....	.....	50,000.0	.....	50,000.0	1,000,000.00
.....	105.0	.....	.....	.....	.....	.....	3,921.0	4,026.0	204,896.00
.....	**105.0**	.....	.....	.....	.....	**50,000.0**	**3,921.0**	**54,026.0**	**$ 1,204,896.00**
1,241.0	163.0	.....	.....	473.0	.....	1,753.0	.....	11,723.0	1,529,537.00
.....	.....	.....	.....	.....	.....	28,886.0	.....	28,886.0	5,825,812.00
1,241.0	**163.0**	.....	.....	**473.0**	.....	**30,639.0**	.....	**40,609.0**	**$ 7,355,349.00**
.....	.....	.....	.....	.....	.....	.....	**4.1**	**4.1**	**1,640.00**
.....	.....	.....	.....	.....	.....	.....	**.5**	**.5**	**200.00**
1,241.0	**2,209.0**	**12,669.0**	**355.0**	**473.0**	**39,639.0**	**133,441.0**	**53,253.6**	**419,108.2**	**$51,678,951.92**
.....	.....	.....	.....	.....	.....	6.6†	.....	6.6	3,960.00
1,241.0	**2,209.0**	**12,669.0**	**355.0**	**473.0**	**39,639.0**	**133,434.4**	**53,253.6**	**419,101.6**	**$51,674,991.92**

Table 137*

Detail by Months of Number of Steamers and Net Metric Tons of

Final Port of Arrival	January		February		March		April
	Number of Steamers	Total Tons Carried	Number of Steamers	Total Tons Carried	Number of Steamers	Total Tons Carried	Number of Steamers
Abo	..	.....	..	.....	..	......	..
Amsterdam	..	.....	..	.....	..	......	1
Batoum	..	.....	..	.....	..	......	..
Braila	..	.....	..	.....	..	......	..
Brake	..	.....	..	.....	..	......	..
Bremerhaven	..	.....	..	.....	..	......	2
Cattaro	1	598.1	..	.....	..	......	..
Constantinople	1	5,856.1	1	689.0	..	......	..
Constanza	1	6,637.6	1	7,053.5	4	27,060.9	3
Copenhagen	..	.....	..	.....	7	35,528.9	2
Danzig	..	.....	6	13,759.6	16	52,164.2	14
Derindje	..	.....	1	5,029.5	..	......	..
Emdem	..	.....	..	.....	..	......	..
Fiume	..	.....	2	12,592.8	..	......	..
Galatz	..	.....	1	2,543.8	..	......	..
Genoa	..	.....	..	.....	1	7,116.7	..
Gravosa (Ragusa)	..	.....	1	7,319.9	1	2,329.1	1
Hamburg	..	.....	..	.....	2	8,766.0	12
Hango	..	.....	..	.....	..	......	..
Helsingfors	..	.....	5	7,775.3	7	18,040.0	8
Hungerburg	..	.....	..	.....	..	......	..
Libau	..	.....	..	.....	..	......	1
Mantyluoto	..	.....	..	.....	..	......	..
Memel	..	.....	..	.....	..	......	2
Messina	..	.....	..	.....	1	2,914.4	..
Novorossisk	..	.....	..	.....	..	......	..
Plymouth	..	.....	..	.....	1	5,597.3	..
Reval	..	.....	..	.....	..	......	..
Riga	..	.....	..	.....	..	......	..
Rotterdam †	8	31,101.3	4	3,923.3	2	28.8	1
Salonica	..	.....	..	.....	1	4,435.9	..
Spalato	..	.....	..	.....	2	3,878.8	..
Stettin	..	.....	..	.....	..	......	2
Sulina	..	.....	..	.....	..	......	..
Trieste	3	26,349.5	7	25,284.2	3	5,045.6	8
Varna	..	.....	1	4,010.9	..	......	1
Viborg	..	.....	..	.....	..	......	..
Zelenika	1	190.1	1	328.0	..	......	..
Total	**15**	**70,732.7**	**31**	**90,309.8**	**48**	**172,906.6**	**58**
Less Duplications ‡	1	.....	..	.....	..	......	..
Total (Identified to Steamers)	**14**	**70,732.7**	**31**	**90,309.8**	**48**	**172,906.6**	**58**
Arrivals Ex-Stock							
Danzig	..	.....	..	.....	..	......	..
Reval	..	.....	..	.....	..	......	..
Sundry Ports	..	.....	..	40.0	..	54.4	..
Trieste	..	.....	..	.....	..	4,329.6	..
Grand Total	**14**	**70,732.7**	**31**	**90,349.8**	**48**	**177,290.6**	**58**

* Compiled from data contained in Table 111.

† Rotterdam was used extensively as a storage and forwarding port. Had the figures been compiled on first port of arrival basis, Rotterdam would have been credited with 255,000 tons. In this table the tonnage has been transshipped to final port of arrival and therefore is reflect in the figures of the other ports.

‡ Due to steamers discharging at more than one port.

ADMINISTRATION

Cargo Carried to Final Ports of Arrival—Armistice Period, 1919

April	May		June		July		August		Grand Total	
Total Tons Carried	Number of Steamers	Total Tons Carried	Number of Steamers	Total Tons Carried	Number of Steamers	Total Tons Carried	Number of Steamers	Total Tons Carried	Number of Steamers	Tons Carried
......	..	......	1	7,214.0	..	......	..	......	1	7,214.0
3,580.2	..	......	..	......	..	......	..	......	1	3,580.2
......	2	10,565.5	3	11,172.4	..	......	4	28,356.1	9	50,094.0
......	..	......	..	......	1	1,001.9	..	......	1	1,001.9
......	1	4,933.8	..	......	..	......	..	......	1	4,933.8
14,301.5	1	2,272.4	3	13,333.1	7	56,637.5	..	......	13	86,544.5
......	..	......	..	......	..	......	..	......	1	598.1
......	1	6,621.2	..	......	1	6,442.9	..	......	4	19,609.2
18,533.9	5	27,703.5	..	......	..	......	..	......	14	86,989.4
747.5	1	9,912.0	..	......	..	......	..	......	10	46,188.4
38,333.5	14	59,468.0	18	68,823.7	6	16,076.7	3	14,817.9	77	263,443.6
......	..	......	..	......	..	......	..	......	1	5,029.5
......	1	6,019.5	1	6,772.9	1	3,099.9	..	......	3	15,892.3
......	..	......	..	......	..	......	..	......	2	12,592.8
......	..	......	2	5,686.8	1	54.3	..	......	4	8,284.9
......	..	......	..	......	..	......	..	......	1	7,116.7
4,747.3	1	5,380.3	1	4,798.1	..	......	..	......	5	24,574.7
74,216.8	29	150,119.6	24	144,383.8	14	58,445.0	8	43,774.7	89	479,705.9
......	..	......	2	14,642.2	1	1,739.4	..	......	3	16,381.6
25,102.3	5	11,620.2	..	......	4	30,693.8	1	8,541.6	30	101,773.2
......	..	......	1	2,774.3	..	......	..	......	1	2,774.3
1,166.3	2	1,613.7	1	562.4	4	944.8	..	......	8	4,287.2
......	..	......	2	13,209.7	..	......	..	......	2	13,209.7
2,008.0	..	......	1	704.6	..	......	..	......	3	2,712.6
......	..	......	..	......	..	......	..	......	1	2,914.4
......	..	......	..	......	..	......	1	915.5	1	915.5
......	..	......	..	......	..	......	..	......	1	5,597.3
......	2	3,302.9	3	5,425.1	3	7,570.0	2	6,802.7	10	23,100.7
......	1	1,083.9	..	......	2	5,497.2	..	......	3	6,581.1
592.4	11	64,312.0	5	27,674.5	..	......	2	10,171.0	33	137,803.3
......	1	6,285.0	1	283.4	..	......	..	......	3	11,004.3
......	..	......	..	......	..	......	..	......	2	3,878.8
7,633.0	..	......	1	2,991.5	1	5,264.6	..	......	4	15,889.1
......	1	6,666.3	..	......	..	......	..	......	1	6,666.3
40,223.8	4	21,858.6	2	5,286.9	..	......	..	......	27	124,048.6
7,049.0	2	9,789.1	1	2,013.4	..	......	..	......	5	22,862.4
......	..	......	2	9,900.4	..	......	..	......	2	9,900.4
......	..	......	..	......	..	......	..	......	2	518.1
238,235.5	**85**	**409,527.5**	**75**	**347,653.2**	**46**	**193,468.0**	**21**	**113,379.5**	**379**	**1,636,212.8**
......	2	......	3	......	2	......	..	......	8	....
238,235.5	**83**	**409,527.5**	**72**	**347,653.2**	**44**	**193,468.0**	**21**	**113,379.5**	**371**	**1,636,212.8**
......	..	......	..	......	..	......	..	860.2	..	860.2
......	..	......	..	......	..	......	..	1,520.9	..	1,520.9
......	..	......	..	......	..	31,060.1	..	......	..	31,154.5
......	..	70.5	..	8,686.1	..	......	..	......	..	13,086.2
238,235.5	**83**	**409,598.0**	**72**	**356,339.3**	**44**	**224,528.1**	**21**	**115,760.6**	**371**	**1,682,834.6**

Table 138

Summary of Purchases of Relief Supplies

Source of Purchases	Table No.	Wheat Flour	Cereal Flour	Rice	Beans, Peas
U.S. Army Quartermaster—Trieste and Adriatic Ports	139	77,446.5	......	......	.....
U.S. Army Quartermaster—Constantinople and Black Sea Ports	140	31,136.9	......	......	.....
U.S. Liquidation Commission (War Department)—France	141A	54,336.1	1,376.3	2,691.1	434.9
Total	...	**162,919.5**	**1,376.3**	**2,691.1**	**434.9**

AMERICAN RELIEF

Table 139

Detail of Purchases of Relief Supplies from U.S. Army Quartermaster

Steamer or Source	Q.M. Invoice	Port of Sailing	Date of Arrival	Port of Arrival
			1919	
Canoga	51	New York	Mar. 3	Trieste
Canoga	52	New York	Mar. 3	Trieste
Sudbury	51	Philadelphia	Feb. 4	Trieste
Sudbury	54	Philadelphia	Feb. 4	Trieste
Canoga, I	51	New York	Mar. 3	Trieste
Canoga, II	50	New York	Mar. 31	Trieste
Western Plains	8, 12	New York	Jan. 14	Cattaro
Western Plains	41	New York	Jan. 28	Zelenika
Western Hope	46	New York	Feb. 2	Gravosa
Nantahala	38	New York	Feb. 10	Fiume
Williamantic	38	New York	Feb. 21	Fiume
West Kyska, I	16	New York	Feb. 27	Trieste
Durham	53	New York	Feb. 6	Zelenika
Durham	53	New York	Mar. 5	Spalato
Durham	53	New York	Mar. 10	Gravosa
Oregonian	36, 51	New York	Feb. 8	Trieste
Western Scout	15	New York	Jan. 25	Trieste
Sudbury	17	Philadelphia	Feb. 4	Trieste
Westerner	18	Norfolk	Feb. 13	Trieste
Cape Lookout, I	23	Norfolk	Feb. 19	Trieste
Mount Shasta	26	Norfolk	Feb. 25	Trieste
East Wind, I	27	New York	Feb. 26	Trieste
West Kyska, I	28	New York	Feb. 27	Trieste
Canoga	50	New York	Mar. 3	Trieste
Army Stock	56	(U.S.A.)	....	Trieste
Army Stock	59	(U.S.A.)	....	Trieste
Army Stock	60	(U.S.A.)	....	Trieste
Army Stock	19, 25, 29, 34	(U.S.A.)	....	Trieste
Canoga	33, 35	New York	Mar. 3	Trieste
Army Stock	39	(U.S.A.)	....	Trieste
Army Stock	43	(U.S.A.)	....	Trieste
Army Stock	49	(U.S.A.)	....	Trieste
Army Stock	55, 60	(U.S.A.)	....	Trieste
Army Stock	..‡	(U.S.A.)	....	Trieste
Army Stock	20	(U.S.A.)	....	Trieste
West Kyska, I	9	New York	Feb. 27	Trieste
Canoga	52	New York	Mar. 3	Trieste
Army Stock	58	(U.S.A.)	....	Trieste
West Lashaway, I	32, 40	New York	Jan. 3	Trieste
West Alcasca	32, 40	New York	Jan. 22	Trieste
Western Scout	32, 40	New York	Jan. 25	Trieste

* C.R. designates Children's Relief, all other allocations for government accounts.

† Recorded as local cash sales at Trieste.

‡ Recorded on Trieste Grain Corporation invoice No. 71. No Q.M invoice number given.

ADMINISTRATION

'rom U.S. Army—Armistice Period, 1919

Commodities in Net Metric Tons of 1,000 Kilograms or 2,204.6 Pounds								
Pork Products	Lard	Lard Substitute	Milk	Miscellaneous Food	Clothing	Soap	Total Tons	Total Value
7,230.8	2,470.8	1,116.7	1,361.0	......	....	...	89,625.8	$25,428,013.84
1,972.2	986.9	......	977.4	......	....	...	35,073.4	9,683,411.50
6,982.5	.....	......	2,723.4	1,023.2	52.0	4.6	69,624.1	18,308,655.58
16,185.5	**3,457.7**	**1,116.7**	**5,061.8**	**1,023.2**	**52.0**	**4.6**	**194,323.3**	**$53,420,080.92**

ADMINISTRATION

t Trieste and Adriatic Ports—Armistice Period, 1919

Allocated To *	Contents of Cargoes in Net Metric Tons of 1,000 Kilograms or 2,204.6 Pounds						Total Value
	Wheat Flour	Pork Products	Lard	Lard Substitute	Milk	Total Tons	
Austria C.R.	.....	7.1	6.1	....	....	13.2	$ 10,132.06
Austria C.R.	.....	24.4	13.2	....	....	37.6	27,547.53
Jugoslavia (S.H.S.) C.R.	.....	....	....	....	107.6	107.6	46,692.45
Jugoslavia (S.H.S.) C.R.	.....	....	....	....	92.7	92.7	40,238.10
Czecho-Slovakia C.R.	.....	....	....	54.4	....	54.4	38,605.26
Jugoslavia	.....	144.6	....	137.9	....	282.5	187,909.66
Jugoslavia	598.1	....	....	....	....	598.1	131,855.47
Jugoslavia	190.1	....	....	....	....	190.1	41,912.60
Jugoslavia	7,319.9	....	....	....	....	7,319.9	1,613,739.40
Jugoslavia	7,146.8	....	....	....	....	7,146.8	1,572,009.30
Jugoslavia	5,446.0	....	....	....	....	5,446.0	1,197,901.40
Jugoslavia	433.4	....	....	....	....	433.4	95,544.00
Jugoslavia	.....	....	301.0	....	27.0	328.0	240,539.90
Jugoslavia	.....	19.0	....	....	....	19.0	12,417.00
Jugoslavia	.....	1,031.7	1,002.5	....	294.9	2,329.1	1,558,289.87
Czecho-Slovakia	.....	3,279.4	903.4	....	....	4,182.8	2,950,820.44
Czecho-Slovakia	5,000.0	....	....	....	....	5,000.0	1,102,300.00
Czecho-Slovakia	.....	....	....	....	400.0	400.0	164,227.80
Czecho-Slovakia	10,000.0	....	....	....	....	10,000.0	2,204,600.00
Czecho-Slovakia	.....	....	....	....	200.0	200.0	82,113.90
Czecho-Slovakia	5,000.0	....	....	....	....	5,000.0	1,102,300.00
Czecho-Slovakia	5,000.0	....	....	....	....	5,000.0	1,102,300.00
Czecho-Slovakia	.....	....	....	68.0	....	68.0	44,630.44
Czecho-Slovakia	.....	340.2	....	....	....	340.2	242,506.01
Czecho-Slovakia	3,565.5	....	....	....	....	3,565.5	786,043.18
Czecho-Slovakia	.....	185.6	....	129.0	....	314.6	226,887.46
Czecho-Slovakia	.....	202.8	5.4	241.3	....	449.5	317,799.62
Czecho-Slovakia †	2.3	8.3	3.3	....	56.6	70.5	33,778.62
Austria	.....	198.2	....	78.8	150.0	427.0	272,541.73
Austria	.....	755.2	....	....	....	755.2	595,434.86
Austria	.....	700.3	....	....	....	700.3	532,581.88
Austria	.....	4.5	....	....	....	4.5	3,838.21
Austria	.....	104.1	....	....	....	104.1	76,386.61
Austria	5.7	.8	....	1.5	....	8.0	2,854.88
Austria	.....	....	....	....	19.2	19.2	9,240.00
Austria	1,270.9	....	....	....	....	1,270.9	280,191.65
Austria	.....	....	....	379.9	....	379.9	269,761.38
Austria	.....	....	....	....	11.5	11.5	4,980.15
United Kingdom	7,173.8	....	....	....	....	7,173.8	1,581,536.91
United Kingdom	6,952.9	....	....	....	....	6,952.9	1,532,837.28
United Kingdom	7,222.8	....	....	....	....	7,222.8	1,592,339.45

[*Continued on next page*]

AMERICAN RELIEF

Table 139—*Continued* — Detail of Purchases of Relief Supplies from U.S. Army Quartermaster

Steamer or Source	Q.M. Invoice	Port of Sailing	Date of Arrival	Port of Arrival
			1919	
Army Stock	32	(U.S.A.)	....	Trieste
Army Stock	47	(U.S.A.)	....	Trieste
Army Stock	22	(U.S.A.)	....	Trieste
Army Stock	30, 58	(U.S.A.)	....	Trieste, Gravosa
Army Stock	20, 31	(U.S.A.)	....	Trieste
Army Stock	..	(U.S.A.)	....	Sundry
Total	....	....	....	....

AMERICAN RELIEF

Table 140 — Detail of Purchases of Relief Supplies from U.S. Army Quartermaster

Steamer or Source	Port of Sailing	Date of Arrival	Port of Arrival
		1919	
Western Plains	New York	Jan. 21	Constanza
Maine	New York	Jan. 28	Constantinople
Maine	New York	Jan. 28	Constantinople
Maine	New York	Jan. 28	Constantinople
Maine	New York	Jan. 28	Constantinople
Maine	New York	Jan. 28	Constantinople
West Mohamet	New York	Feb. 17	Constanza
West Mount	New York	Feb. 21	Derindje
West Mount	New York	Feb. 21	Derindje
West Mount	New York	Feb. 21	Derindje
West Eldara	New York	Feb. 22	Constantinople
Western Belle			
Bucegi, I	Derindje	....	Galatz
West Eldara			
Constantia	Constantinople	....	Varna
Englewood	New York	Apr. 21	Constanza
Englewood	New York	Apr. 21	Constanza
Miscellaneous Sales and Sundry Charges	(U.S.A.)	....	....
Total	....	....	....

* Delivered to and paid for by J. W. Whittall and Company.

† Delivered to and paid for by American Commission for Relief i Near East.

AMERICAN RELIEF ADMINISTRATION

Table 141 A — Summary by Ports and Warehouses of Purchases from the U.S. Liquidation Commission (War Department), France—Armistice Period, 1919

Port and Warehouse	Table No.	Commodities in Net Metric Tons of 1,000 Kilograms or 2,204.6 Pounds										Total Value
		Wheat Flour	Cereal Flour	Rice	Beans	Pork Products	Milk	Misc. Food	Clothing	Soap	Total Tons	
Bordeaux	142A	21,677.2	877.1	2,146.8	152.2	3,000.1	909.0	......	....	...	28,762.4	$ 7,399,288.2
Marseilles	142B	7,240.0	499.2	544.3	282.7	79.0	......	1,023.2	....	...	9,668.4	2,129,581.5
St. Nazaire	142C	15,422.2	.....	.....	.....	3,903.4	1,814.4	......	....	...	21,140.0	7,105,422.9
Deliveries ex-Interior Warehouses— France	...*	9,996.7	.....	.....	.....	....	......	......	52.0	4.6	10,053.3	1,674,362.8
Total Purchases	138	**54,336.1**	**1,376.3**	**2,691.1**	**434.9**	**6,982.5**	**2,723.4**	**1,023.2**	**52.0**	**4.6**	**69,624.1**	**$18,308,655.5**

* Flour deliveries covered in Table 322 n; soap, Table 244; clothing, Table 245.

DMINISTRATION

Trieste and Adriatic Ports—Armistice Period, 1919

Allocated To *	Contents of Cargoes in Net Metric Tons of 1,000 Kilograms or 2,204.6 Pounds						Total Value
	Wheat Flour	Pork Products	Lard	Lard Substitute	Milk	Total Tons	
Hungary	.....	98.7	192.2	8.1	....	299.0	$ 230,792.69
Hungary	.....	16.0	4.1	....	....	20.1	14,727.27
Italy	4,686.4	....	....	....	....	4,686.4	1,033,158.45
U.S. Navy in Adriatic	10.6	.9	....	.7	1.5	13.7	5,037.79
Jadranska Bank	160.6	109.0	39.6	17.1	....	326.3	156,975.28
Sundry Sales	260.7	....	....	....	....	260.7	57,155.90
....	**77,446.5**	**7,230.8**	**2,470.8**	**1,116.7**	**1,361.0**	**89,625.8**	**$25,428,013.84**

DMINISTRATION

Constantinople and Black Sea Ports—Armistice Period, 1919

Allocated To	Contents of Cargoes in Net Metric Tons of 1,000 Kilograms or 2,204.6 Pounds					Total Value
	Wheat Flour	Pork Products	Lard	Milk	Total Tons	
Roumania	6,637.6	....	.....	.....	6,637.6	$1,390,187.74
Armenia	300.0	....	.....	.....	300.0	66,000.00
Turkey *	4,069.4	....	.....	.....	4,069.4	985,325.00
Armenia †	185.5	....	.....	.....	185.5	40,880.80
France (French Army)	907.2	....	.....	.....	907.2	200,000.00
Russia (Volunteer Army)	394.0	....	.....	.....	394.0	86,680.00
Roumania	7,053.4	....	.....	.....	7,053.4	1,477,301.38
Armenia	.....	....	.....	164.9	164.9	79,527.00
Turkey *	4,521.7	....	.....	.....	4,521.7	1,098,112.80
Armenia †	.....	....	.....	342.9	342.9	148,031.00
Armenia †	689.0	....	.....	.....	689.0	151,591.88
Roumania	2,326.0	....	.....	217.8	2,543.8	606,220.00
Bulgaria	4,010.9	....	.....	.....	4,010.9	882,387.00
Roumania C.R.	.....	40.0	.....	.....	40.0	28,750.00
Roumania	.....	1,932.2	986.9	251.8	3,170.9	2,432,050.90
Sundry Activities	42.2	....	.....	.....	42.2	10,366.00
....	**31,136.9**	**1,972.2**	**986.9**	**977.4**	**35,073.4**	**$9,683,411.50**

AMERICAN RELIEF

Table 141 B

Summary of Deliveries from Army Supplies Purchased from U.S. Liquidation

Country of Destination	Bordeaux Tons	Bordeaux Value	Marseilles Tons
Armenia	.....	....	156.7
Austria Children's Relief	951.0	$ 384,012.93	.....
American Friends' Service Committee	.....	....	.....
Czecho-Slovakia Children's Relief	668.2	372,140.70	.....
Czecho-Slovakia	3,049.2	1,575,132.59	.....
Esthonia Children's Relief	184.3	74,060.00	.....
Esthonia	1,650.2	406,111.07	.....
France	16,250.1	2,600,020.80	1,853.9
Jugoslavia Children's Relief	100.0	25,004.50	.....
Latvia Children's Relief	217.5	80,171.86	.....
Latvia	4,507.1	1,163,075.33	.....
Lithuania	278.2	235,041.82	.....
Russia (Northwest Russia) Children's Relief	.....	....	.....
Russia (Northwest Russia)	906.6	484,516.64	.....
Poland Children's Relief	.....	....	.....
Poland	.....	....	.....
Roumania Children's Relief	.....	....	300.0
Roumania	.....	....	6,442.3
Russia (Kouban)	.....	....	915.5
Miscellaneous Cash Sales	.....	....	.....
Total	**28,762.4**	**$7,399,288.24**	**9,668.4**

AMERICAN RELIE

Detail of Deliveries of Relief Supplies Purchased from the U.S. Liquidatic

Table 142 A

Deliveries fro

Steamer or Source	Port of Arrival	Date of Arrival	Table No.	Allocated To*
		1919		
Lake St. Clair, IV	Hamburg	May 15	238	Czecho-Slovakia
Lake Wimico, IV	Libau	May 26	370	Latvia
Lake Wimico, IV	Libau	May 26	372	Latvia C.R.
Lake Mary, IV	Libau	May 30	372	Latvia C.R.
Lake Mary, IV	Libau	May 30	370	Latvia
Lake Mary, IV	Riga	May 30	370	Latvia
Lake Wimico, IV	Reval	May 31	293	Esthonia
Lake Catherine, V	Hamburg	June 29	244	Czecho-Slovakia C.R.
Lake Catherine, V	Hamburg	June 29	238	Czecho-Slovakia
Lake Tulare, V	Riga	July 1	372	Latvia C.R.
Lake Tulare, V	Riga	July 1	370	Latvia
Lake Clear, V	Hamburg	July 2	238	Czecho-Slovakia
Lake Clear, V	Hamburg	July 2	358	Jugoslavia C.R.
Lake Clear, V	Hamburg	July 2	211	Austria C.R.
Lake St. Clair, V	Reval	July 10	297	Esthonia C.R.
Lake St. Clair, V	Libau	July 10	383	Lithuania
Lake St. Clair, V	Reval	July 10	498	Russia (Northwest Russia)
Lake St. Clair, V	Reval	July 10	293	Esthonia
Coperas	Hamburg	July 25	244	Czecho-Slovakia C.R.
Coperas	Hamburg	July 25	238	Czecho-Slovakia
U.S. Army Stock	Bordeaux	....	322n	France
Total	....	....	....	....

* C.R. designates Children's Relief; other allocations for account of governments.

DMINISTRATION

ommission, by Countries of Destination and Ports of Shipment—Armistice Period, 1919

Marseilles	St. Nazaire		Interior Warehouses		Total Tons	Total Value
Value	Tons	Value	Tons	Value		
$ 94,816.97	.....	....	......	....	156.7	$ 94,816.97
....	.....	....	......	....	951.0	384,012.93
....	10.0	$ 8,344.66	......	....	10.0	8,344.66
....	107.1	40,573.50	56.6	$ 74,877.10	831.9	487,591.30
....	1,281.5	1,000,105.63	......	....	4,330.7	2,575,238.22
....	135.2	63,287.50	......	....	1,319.5	137,347.50
....	.....	....	......	....	1,650.2	406,111.07
296,604.52	2,098.2	335,719.04	9,996.7	1,599,485.72	30,198.9	4,831,830.08
....	.....	....	......	....	100.0	25,004.50
....	.....	....	......	....	217.5	80,171.86
....	.....	....	......	....	4,507.1	1,163,075.33
....	.....	....	......	....	278.2	235,041.82
....	260.3	113,556.25	......	....	260.3	113,556.25
....	5,291.9	2,149,341.31	......	....	6,198.5	2,633,857.95
....	2,371.3	1,110,604.51	......	....	2,371.3	1,110,604.51
....	9,417.0	2,247,868.35	......	....	9,417.0	2,247,868.35
92,989.88	.....	....	......	....	300.0	92,989.88
1,200,451.72	.....	....	......	....	6,442.3	1,200,451.72
444,718.50	.....	....	......	....	915.5	444,718.50
....	167.5	36,022.18	......	....	167.5	36,022.18
$2,129,581.59	**21,140.0**	**$7,105,422.93**	**10,053.3**	**$1,674,362.82**	**69,624.1**	**$18,308,655.58**

DMINISTRATION

ommission (War Department), France—Armistice Period, 1919

ordeaux

Contents of Cargoes in Net Metric Tons of 1,000 Kilograms or 2,204.6 Pounds							Total Value
Wheat Flour	Cereal Flour	Rice	Beans	Pork Products	Milk	Total Tons	
.....	.....	.....	.....	1,396.0	....	1,396.0	$1,165,694.24
462.2	.....	.....	.....	.....	....	462.2	97,066.62
.....	.....	.....	.....	15.2	29.6	44.8	24,687.63
1.6	.....	.....	.....	.1	....	1.7	452.78
1,151.5	.....	.....	.....	.....	....	1,151.5	241,812.27
847.5	.....	.....	.....	132.4	104.0	1,083.9	336,575.88
1,409.0	.....	.....	.....	56.7	.5	1,466.2	351,301.16
.....	.....	167.4	.....	308.2	30.2	505.8	310,612.20
.....	494.4	181.4	152.2	.....	....	828.0	185,330.62
90.0	.....	41.0	.....	20.0	20.0	171.0	55,031.45
1,465.3	.....	161.2	.....	127.5	55.5	1,809.5	487,620.56
.....	.....	26.4	.....	30.4	....	56.8	32,009.48
.....	.....	100.0	.....	.....	....	100.0	25,004.50
.....	.....	701.0	.....	250.0	....	951.0	384,012.93
.....	.....	.....	.....	.....	184.3	184.3	74,060.00
.....	.....	.....	.....	278.2	....	278.2	235,041.82
.....	280.2	.....	.....	385.4	241.0	906.6	484.516.64
.....	102.5	.....	.....	.....	81.5	184.0	54,809.91
.....	.....	.....	.....	.....	162.4	162.4	61,528.50
.....	.....	768.4	.....	.....	....	768.4	192,098.25
16.250.1	.....	.....	.....	.....	....	16,250.1	2,600,020.80
21,677.2	**877.1**	**2,146.8**	**152.2**	**3,000.1**	**909.0**	**28,762.4**	**$7,399,288.24**

AMERICAN RELIEF

Detail of Deliveries of Relief Supplies Purchased from the U.S

Table 142 B

Deliveries from

Steamer or Source	Port of Sailing	Date of Arrival	Port of Arrival	Table No.	Allocated To *
		1919			
Milcovul	Marseilles	June 10	Galatz	492	Roumania
Bucegi, II	Marseilles	July 20	Braila	492	Roumania
Bucegi, II	Marseilles	July 20	Braila	494	Roumania C.R.
Constanza	Marseilles	July 25	Galatz	492	Roumania
Kickapoo	Marseilles	Aug. ..	Novorossisk	201	Russia (Kouban
Kickapoo	Marseilles	Aug. 30	Batoum	201	Armenia
U.S. Army Stock	(U.S.A.)	....	Marseilles	322n	France
Total Deliveries	....	....	....	....	....

* C.R. means Children's Relief; all other deliveries for account of governments.

AMERICAN RELIEF ADMINISTRATION

Detail of Deliveries of Relief Supplies Purchased from the U.S. Liquidation Commission (War Department), France—Armistice Period, 1919

Table 142 C

Deliveries from St. Nazaire

Steamer or Source	Port of Sailing	Date of Arrival	Table No.	Allocated To *	Contents of Cargoes in Net Metric Tons of 1,000 Kilograms or 2,204.6 Pounds				Total Value
					Wheat Flour	Pork Products	Milk	Total Tons	
		1919							
Democracy, II	Danzig	May 6	395	Poland	4,312.7	.....	.....	4,312.7	$ 884,093.
Democracy, II	Danzig	May 6	398	Poland C.R.	858.2	.....	.....	858.2	175,927.
Kerowlee, I	Danzig	May 13	395	Poland	4,339.9	.....	.....	4,339.9	889,682.
Lake Clear, IV	Danzig	May 13	395	Poland	153.6	282.7	.....	436.3	268,979.
Lake Clear, IV	Danzig	May 13	398	Poland C.R.	.....	.....	474.1	474.1	185,104.
Lake Catherine, IV	Hamburg	May 19	238	Czecho-Slovakia	.....	1,128.1	153.4	1,281.5	1,000,105.
Lake Eckhart, IV	Danzig	June 1	395	Poland	111.0	217.1	.....	328.1	205,112.
Lake Eckhart, IV	Danzig	June 1	398	Poland C.R.	.....	765.0	274.0	1,039.0	749,572.
Democracy, III	Viborg	June 25	498	Russia (Northwest Russia)	3,381.1	498.7	450.3	4,330.1	1,331,826.
Democracy, III	Viborg	June 25	540	Sundry Sales (Viborg)	167.5	.....	.....	167.5	36,022.
Roma	Hamburg	June 26	244	Czecho-Slovakia C.R.	.....	.....	74.4	74.4	28,182.
Lake Traverse, IV	Reval	July 1	297	Esthonia C.R.	.....	20.0	115.2	135.2	63,287.
Lake Traverse, IV	Reval	July 1	500	Russia (Northwest Russia) C.R.	.....	20.0	240.3	260.3	113,556.
Lake Traverse, IV	Reval	July 1	498	Russia (Northwest Russia)	.....	961.8	.....	961.8	817,514.
Coperas	Hamburg	July 25	244	Czecho-Slovakia C.R.	.....	.....	32.7	32.7	12,391.
Lake Fray	Hamburg	Aug. 25	325	American Friends Service Committee	.....	10.0	.....	10.0	8,344.
U.S. Army Stock	St. Nazaire	....	322n	France	2,098.2	.....	.....	2,098.2	335,719.
Total	....	....	.....	....	**15,422.2**	**3,903.4**	**1,814.4**	**21,140.0**	**$7,105,422.**

* C.R. designates Children's Relief; other allocations are for account of governments.

ADMINISTRATION

Liquidation Commission (War Department), France—Armistice Period, 1919
Marseilles

Contents of Cargoes in Net Metric Tons of 1,000 Kilograms or 2,204.6 Pounds							
Wheat Flour	Cereal Flour	Rice	Beans	Pork Products	Miscellaneous	Total Tons	Total Value
5,386.1	.....	.....	.....	....	.....	5,386.1	$ 969,502.14
......	481.3	363.8	156.8	....	.....	1,001.9	218,364.68
......	.....	170.0	100.0	30.0	.....	300.0	92,989.88
......	17.9	10.5	25.9	....	.....	54.3	12,584.90
......	.....	.....	.....	....	915.5	915.5†	444,718.50
......	.....	.....	.....	49.0	107.7	156.7	94,816.97
1,853.9	.....	.....	.....	....	.....	1,853.9	296,604.52
7,240.0	**499.2**	**544.3**	**282.7**	**79.0**	**1,023.2**	**9,668.4**	**$2,129,581.59**

† Bartered in Russia (Kouban) for wheat to be sent to Armenia. Cf. Table 201, and text page 242.

AMERICAN RELIEF ADMINISTRATION

Summary of Freight and Other Charges Paid on Charity Shipments, by Countries of Destination*
Armistice Period, 1919

Table 143 A

Country of Destination	Metric Tons	Freight and Charges Paid
AMERICAN RED CROSS SHIPMENTS		
Armenia	754.1	$ 47,688.48
Czecho-Slovakia	301.2	18,681.81
Esthonia	312.3	50,490.02
Finland	282.0	22,584.24
Jugoslavia	667.6	81,140.98
Poland	2,177.6	148,819.42
Total, Red Cross	**4,494.8**	**$369,404.95**
POLISH LEAGUE OF WOMEN		
Poland	**4.1**	**$ 216.56**
NORWEGIAN GOVERNMENT DONATION		
Austria	8.3	$ 178.47
Czecho-Slovakia	10.1	217.18
Latvia	6.6	159.72
Total, Norwegian Government	**25.0**	**$ 555.37**
RUSSO-CARPATHIAN COMMITTEE		
Poland	**.5**	**$ 28.01**
Total Shipment Handled by A.R.A.	**4,524.4**	**$370,204.89**

* Details in Table 143 B.

AMERICAN RELIEF ADMINISTRATION

Detail by Steamers of Freight and Other Charges on Charity Shipments Paid for by Funds from Congressional Appropriations for Relief*

Table 143 B

Armistice Period, 1919

Arrival No.	Steamer	Port of Sailing	Date of Arrival	Port of Arrival	Allocated To	Contents of Cargoes in Net Metric Tons of 1,000 Kilograms or 2,204.6 Pounds			Total Charges Paid by A.R.A.
						Clothing	Hospital and Medical Supplies	Total Tons	
						AMERICAN RED CROSS			
			1919						
4	Ida	New York	May 21	Gravosa	Jugoslavia	218.3	......	218.3	$ 23,112.5
5	Ocland	New York	June 13	Salonica	Jugoslavia	449.3	......	449.3	58,028.4
7	Karpathos	Bordeaux	June 20	Danzig	Poland	.....	29.1	29.1	3,029.2
8	Lake Hemlock	New York	July 12	Hango	Finland	282.0	......	282.0	22,584.2
9	Faraby	New York	July 19	Danzig	Poland	.....	1,110.0	1,110.0	89,439.9
10	Lake Dancey, V	Danzig	Aug. 1	Reval	Esthonia	.....	24.5	24.5	490.0
12	Lake Fray	New York	Aug. 7	Reval	Esthonia	.....	287.8	287.8	50,000.0
11	Schwarzenfels	New York	Aug. 12	Danzig	Poland	.....	1,038.5	1,038.5	55,388.9
13	Sonnenfels	New York	Aug. 25	Trieste	Czecho-Slovakia	301.2	......	301.2	18,681.8
14	Sonnenfels	New York	Aug. 30	Batoum	Armenia	488.3	......	488.3	30,282.0
17	Aschenburg	New York	Aug. 31	Batoum	Armenia	265.8	......	265.8	17,406.4
...	Miscellaneous Expenses †	....	....	....	Poland	.....	......	......	961.3
	Total Transp. Charges	....	....	....	....	**2,004.9**	**2,489.9**	**4,494.8**	**$369,404.9**
						POLISH LEAGUE OF WOMEN			
...	Schwarzenfels	New York	Aug. 12	Danzig	Poland	4.1	......	4.1	$ 216.5
						GIFT FROM GOVERNMENT OF NORWAY‡			
...	Lake Wimico, IV	Rotterdam	May 18	Hamburg	Czecho-Slovakia	.....	10.1	10.1	$ 217.1
...	Lake St. Regis, V	Rotterdam	June 5	Hamburg	Austria	.....	8.3	8.3	178.4
...	Lake Dancey, V	Danzig	July 25	Libau	Latvia	.....	6.6	6.6	159.7
	Total Transp. Charges	....	....	....	....	.....	**25.0**	**25.0**	**$ 555.3**
						RUSSO-CARPATHIAN COMMITTEE			
...	Schwarzenfels	New York	Aug. 12	Danzig	Poland	.5	......	.5	$ 28.0
	Total Transp. Charges	....	....	....	....	**2,009.5**	**2,514.9**	**4,524.4**	**$370,204.[illegible]**

* See Table 127.
† Expenses paid on supplies carried by Lake Dancey, V, Karpathos, and Schwarzenfels.
‡ Codliver oil.

AMERICAN RELIEF ADMINISTRATION

Summary by Countries of Destination of Supplies Sold by U.S. Liquidation Commission (War Department) on which Freight and Insurance Were Paid by the A.R.A.—Armistice Period, 1919

Table 144

Country	Pork Products	Miscellaneous Army Supplies	Total Tons *	Insurance	Freight	Total Insurance and Freight
Czecho-Slovakia	4,954.5	......	4,954.5	$18,613.70	$165,992.93	$184,606.63
Esthonia	2,020.4	......	2,020.4	10,881.95	140,231.10	151,113.05
Lithuania	......	6,096.3	6,096.3	....	48,930.00	48,930.00
Russia (Northwest Russia)	......	349.2	349.2	3,351.18	48,837.00	52,188.18
Poland	3,357.2	10,000.0	13,357.2	17,295.71	311,311.58	328,607.29
Total	**10,332.1**	**16,445.5**	**26,777.6**	**$50,142.54**	**$715,302.61**	**$765,445.15**

* Commodities in net metric tons of 1,000 kilograms or 2,204.6 pounds.

Detail of Shipments of Supplies Sold by U.S. Liquidatio
Were Paid for by the A.R.A

Table 145

Steamer	Port of Sailing	Date of Arrival	Port of Arrival
		1919	
Schwinge	St. Nazaire	June 18	Danzig
Karpathos	Bordeaux	June 20	Danzig
Roma	St. Nazaire	June 26	Hamburg
Lake Catherine, V	Bordeaux	June 29	Hamburg
Lake Clear, V	Bordeaux	July 2	Hamburg
Antwerpen	Bordeaux	July 4	Reval
Coperas	St. Nazaire	July 25	Hamburg
Coperas	Bordeaux	July 25	Hamburg
Cerosco	St. Nazaire	July 31	Hamburg
Lake Fray	St. Nazaire	Aug. 15	Hamburg
Lake Fray	St. Nazaire	Aug. 17	Reval
Lake Fray	Bordeaux	Aug. 17	Reval
Karpathos, August Wilke	....	....	Memel
Rail Shipment (900 cars)	Coblenz	Mar.–Oct.	Warsaw
Total	....	....	....

* Contents of cargoes in net metric tons of 1,000 kilograms or 2,204.6 pounds.

† For American Typhus Commission.

AMERICAN RELIE

Detail of Shipments of Supplies Sold to the Jewish Joint Distributic
on which Freight and Insurance Were Pa

Table 146†

Steamer	Port of Sailing	Date of Arrival	Port of Arrival	Allocated To *	Cereal Flour
		1919			
Democracy	St. Nazaire	Mar. 7	Danzig	Poland	....
Kerowlee	St. Nazaire	May 13	Danzig	Poland	....
Lake Clear, IV	St. Nazaire	May 13	Danzig	Poland	....
Lake Eckhart	St. Nazaire	June 1	Danzig	Poland	....
Karpathos	Bordeaux	June 20	Danzig	Poland	....
Lake Clear, V	Bordeaux	July 2	Hamburg	Austria	42.0
Coperas	Bordeaux	July 25	Hamburg	Austria	....
Total	....	....	....	....	**42.0**

† See Table 125.
* For Poland cf. Table 394; Austria, Table 208 n.

‡ Freight and insurance paid on supplies for Austria, $15,224.11; Poland, $66,364.12; total, $81,588.23.

DMINISTRATION

mmission (War Department) on which Freight and Insurance Armistice Period, 1919

Allocated To	Pork Products	Miscellaneous Army Supplies	Total Tons *	Insurance	Freight	Total Insurance and Freight
Poland	1,624.2	.....	1,624.2	$ 8,632.03	$ 64,966.56	$ 73,598.59
Poland	1,733.0	.....	1,733.0	8,663.68	132,559.50	141,223.18
Czecho-Slovakia	1,483.7	.....	1,483.7	8,546.55	44,511.91	53,058.46
Czecho-Slovakia	126.2	.....	126.2	361.73	4,417.04	4,778.77
Czecho-Slovakia	230.5	.....	230.5	661.48	8,066.59	8,728.07
Esthonia	2,020.4	.....	2,020.4	10,881.95	140,231.10	151,113.05
Czecho-Slovakia	512.0	.....	512.0	1,480.55	17,921.47	19,402.02
Czecho-Slovakia	353.3	.....	353.3	974.05	12,365.64	13,339.69
Czecho-Slovakia	1,725.7	.....	1,725.7	5,128.96	60,400.67	65,529.63
Czecho-Slovakia	523.1	.....	523.1	1,460.38	18,309.61	19,769.99
Russia (Northwest Russia)	.....	2.3	2.3	13.84	267.00	280.84
Russia (Northwest Russia)	.....	346.9	346.9	3,337.34	48,570.00	51,907.34
Lithuania	.....	6,096.3	6,096.3	....	48,930.00	48,930.00
Poland †	.....	10,000.0	10,000.0	....	113,785.52	113,785.52
....	**10,332.1**	**16,445.5**	**26,777.6**	**$50,142.54**	**$715,302.61**	**$765,445.15**

DMINISTRATION

mmittee by the U.S. Liquidation Commission (War Department) the A.R.A.—Armistice Period, 1919

Contents of Cargoes in Net Metric Tons of 1,000 Kilograms or 2,204.6 Pounds						Freight	Insurance	Total Payments
Milk	Miscellaneous Food	Medical Supplies	Clothing	Other Miscellaneous	Total Tons			
....	....	4.9	102.0	....	106.9	$ 6,000.00	$ 418.37	$ 6,418.37
....	....	22.6	.....	....	22.6	1,350.00	103.55	1,453.55
....	....	450.6	.....	....	450.6	31,530.00	1,183.73	32,713.73
....	90.2	47.5	.....	....	137.7	16,560.00	533.33	17,093.33
....	....	....	.....	75.0	75.0	8,100.00	585.14	8,685.14
45.2	229.4	....	.....	....	316.6	14,520.00	401.18	14,921.18
....	....	....	.....	2.7	2.7	293.15	9.78	302.93
45.2	**319.6**	**525.6**	**102.0**	**77.7**	**1,112.1**	**$78,353.15**	**$3,235.08**	**$81,588.23‡**

AMERICAN RELIEF

Detail by Steamers or Source of Relief Supplies Turned over to
Paid for by Funds from the Congressiona

Table 147

Steamer or Source	Port of Sailing	Date of Arrival	Port of Arrival	Flour
		1919		
Augusta Foherczegno	New York	July 29	Trieste	....
Szent Istvan	New York	Aug. 8	Trieste	....
Marianne	New York	Aug. 10	Trieste	....
Schwarzenfels	New York	Aug. 12	Danzig	....
Frederica	New York	Aug. 15	Trieste	....
Remschied	New York	Aug. 21	Rotterdam	....
Sonnenfels	New York	Aug. 25	Trieste	....
Brisgravia	New York	Aug. 27	Trieste	....
Danzig Stock				
Edgefield, Ceralvo, Regulus, Lonoke, Cape Henry, Ponola, and part of Schwarzenfels	New York	....	Danzig	180.0
Total *	....	....	....	**180.0**

* These supplies were allocated to countries by the A.R.A., but arrived too late to be distributed prior to August 1, the withdrawal date for all A.R.A. personnel. Therefore, the distribution was supervised b the A.R.A.-E.C.F.

SUMMARY OF FOOD AND RELIEF SUPPLIES DELIVEREI

Table 148

By Majo

Major Operation	Table No.	Flour	Grain	Rice	Beans, Peas	Corn Grits
A.R.A.-European Children's Fund	150	176,574.0	....	43,525.7	32,706.7	15,703.6
American Organizations Other than A.R.A.-E.C.F.	151	509,916.8	283,871.8	6,052.5	7,230.9	87,520.2
Countries Other than United States	152	119,447.7	105,135.3	6,298.9	6,038.6	77.3
Total Gross Deliveries	....	**805,938.5**	**389,007.1**	**55,877.1**	**45,976.2**	**103,301.1**
Less Duplications	...*	38,747.0	....	6,066.1	179.7	....
Total Net Deliveries	....	**767,191.5**	**389,007.1**	**49,811.0**	**45,796.5**	**103,301.1**

* Represents 57,823.0 metric tons, value $4,322,450.83, included in Soviet Republic accounts (cf. Table 165); also 1,237.2 metric tons, value $341,309.37, bulk sales under A.R.A. Warehouses, delivered to Ame can Friends Service Committee (cf. Table 323).

.DMINISTRATION

ıe American Relief Administration European Children's Fund, ppropriation for Relief—August, 1919

Commodities in Net Metric Tons of 1,000 Kilograms or 2,204.6 Pounds								Total Value
Rice	Beans, Peas	Pork Products	Milk	Cocoa	Sugar	Soap	Total Tons	
.....	....	...	330.6	181.5	.....	.....	512.1	$ 290,375.07
.....	....	...	271.7	.....	.....	.....	271.7	112,797.00
.....	....	...	341.0	.....	.....	.....	341.0	140,931.00
.....	....	...	1,490.0	100.0	200.0	150.0	1,940.0	797,191.58
.....	....	...	108.0	.....	.....	121.1	229.1	91,429.55
.....	....	...	5,213.0	199.1	1,032.8	218.8	6,663.7	2,697,246.96
.....	....	...	157.5	60.8	.....	30.0	248.3	111,834.29
246.5	36.6	...	245.9	16.5	99.7	64.6	709.8	236,690.18
1,258.1	2,393.0	6.0	1,537.9	271.7	866.5	156.1	6,669.3	2,146,555.73
1,504.6	**2,429.6**	**6.0**	**9,695.6**	**829.6**	**2,199.0**	**740.6**	**17,585.0**	**$6,625,051.36**

·URING THE RECONSTRUCTION PERIOD, 1919–1924

perations

ommodities in Net Metric Tons of 1,000 Kilograms or 2,204.6 Pounds										Total Value
Pork Products	Milk	Cocoa	Sugar	Misc. Food	Forage	Soap	Medical and Hospital Supplies	Clothing and Misc.	Total Tons	
25,182.3	72,530.8	9,163.9	35,564.5	2,397.8	.....	1,892.8	......	6,856.1	422,098.2	$ 84,639,241.40
3,227.2	29,822.4	1,570.3	1,758.7	161.9	633.3	383.8	8,283.9	1,833.3	942,267.0	96,506,869.36
5,019.6	2,280.9	1,476.4	14,408.6	1,516.3	2,501.0	327.0	......	1,701.5	266,229.1	44,222,231.22
33,429.1	**104,634.1**	**12,210.6**	**51,731.8**	**4,076.0**	**3,134.3**	**2,603.6**	**8,283.9**	**10,390.9**	**1,630,594.3**	**$225,368,341.98**
3,834.3	1,022.0	1,448.0	7,436.1	......	.....	327.0	......	......	59,060.2	4,663,760.20
29,594.8	**103,612.1**	**10,762.6**	**44,295.7**	**4,076.0**	**3,134.3**	**2,276.6**	**8,283.9**	**10,390.9**	**1,571,534.1**	**$220,704,581.78**

SUMMARY OF FOOD AND RELIEF SUPPLIES DELIVERED

Table 149

By Countries of

Country of Destination	Table No.	Flour	Grain	Rice	Beans, Peas	Corn Grits
Armenia	200	47,818.3	......	1,405.3	404.6	......
Austria	206	223,669.6	......	6,065.6	4,898.0	1,491.9
Czecho-Slovakia	236	28,689.0	......	1,312.6	1,617.9	77.3
Danzig Free City	280	131.7	......	69.2	78.6	2.8
Esthonia	292	2,347.0	......	533.3	449.4	......
Finland	306	1,938.5	......	231.4	256.3	......
Germany	323	23,645.7	......	5,141.5	6,047.6	1,149.0
Greece	334	12,886.0	2,451.0	203.0	1,269.0	2,642.0
Hungary	336	16,784.5	......	638.6	642.4	23.4
Jugoslavia	354	2,551.0	......	541.0	292.9	......
Latvia	369	2,392.5	......	878.6	1,001.5	......
Lithuania	382	396.8	......	99.7	104.9	......
Poland	394	268,086.0	......	13,487.6	20,150.0	1,689.4
Roumania	491	742.0	......	170.0	622.0	......
Russia						
Northwest Russia	497	74.7	......	64.0	27.9	......
Soviet Republics	511	134,781.2	386,556.1	18,914.6	7,895.5	96,202.3
Sundry Accounts	539	257.0	......	55.0	38.0	23.0
Total Net Deliveries	......	**767,191.5**	**389,007.1**	**49,811.0**	**45,796.5**	**103,301.1**

A.R.A.-EUROPEAN

Table 150

Summary of Deliveries under Direction of the A.R.A.-E.C.F.

Operation	Table No.	Flour	Rice	Beans, Peas	Corn Grits
U.S. Congressional Appropriation for Relief	114	3,446.8	4,088.5	4,616.4	.....
President's National Security and Defense Fund	116B	1,601.7	1,079.5	815.4	.....
A.R.A. Warehouses—Central Europe	153	23,295.4	3,271.2	2,217.8	556.0
A.R.A.-European Children's Fund	156	148,230.1	35,086.5	25,057.1	15,147.6
Total Deliveries	......	**176,574.0**	**43,525.7**	**32,706.7**	**15,703.6**

AMERICAN ORGANIZATIONS OTHER THAN

Table 151

Summary of Deliveries by

Operation	Table No.	Flour	Grain	Rice	Beans, Peas	Corn Grits
U.S. Grain Corporation (Act of Congress, March 30, 1920)	157	481,945.3	......	.....	.....	.....
U.S. Grain Corporation (Act of Congress, December 22, 1921)	517	......	281,420.8	.....	.....	83,960.4
U.S. Government Surplus Medical (Act of Congress, January 16, 1922)	521	......	......	.....	.....	.....
Laura Spelman Rockefeller Memorial—Freight and Other Charges Paid	521n	......	......	.....	.....	.....
American Red Cross	158	12,886.0	2,451.0	203.0	1,269.0	2,642.0
American Friends Service Committee	159	7,900.7	......	4,444.2	5,557.3	917.8
Commonwealth Fund	160	2,679.3	......	366.9	404.6	.....
Joint Distribution Committee	397	......	......	.....	.....	.....
Near East Relief—Armenia	200	4,505.5	......	1,038.4	.....	.....
Sundry Accounts—Jugoslavia	354	......	......	.....	.....	.....
Total Deliveries	.....	**509,916.8**	**283,871.8**	**6,052.5**	**7,230.9**	**87,520.2**

URING THE RECONSTRUCTION PERIOD, 1919–1924

stination

mmodities in Net Metric Tons of 1,000 Kilograms or 2,204.6 Pounds

Pork Products	Milk	Cocoa	Sugar	Misc. Food	Forage	Soap	Medical and Hospital Supplies	Clothing and Misc.	Total Tons	Total Value
290.9	280.8	169.0	580.1	1.9	.....	300.8	2.0	546.1	51,799.8	$ 8,563,971.48
3,252.8	11,419.1	1,334.2	4,896.1	651.1	.....	208.9	...	2,607.1	260,494.4	46,709,626.37
1,768.2	6,016.7	813.3	848.1	194.9	.....	171.5	...	395.1	41,904.6	9,892,557.58
49.8	191.8	16.7	28.5	2.5	.....	....	...	1.6	573.2	127,700.69
307.9	1,557.7	144.0	400.1	10.0	.....	38.4	...	59.9	5,847.7	1,669,451.09
107.3	712.6	10.0	175.1	.....	.....	....	...	56.0	3,487.2	1,109,991.80
3,663.1	11,497.3	1,024.0	5,185.1	199.8	.....	50.0	...	113.2	57,716.3	11,962,693.54
102.0	162.0	409.0	203.0	45.0	.....	2.0	...	.....	20,374.0	1,211,949.95
358.9	1,441.9	173.0	627.9	105.8	.....	37.0	...	241.0	21,074.4	4,361,619.41
50.0	1,624.9	239.0	455.5	.....	.....	71.8	...	283.1	6,109.2	2,302,080.74
268.2	1,535.5	155.7	415.7	6.9	.....	44.6	...	57.7	6,756.9	1,588,170.34
47.6	367.0	60.8	105.9	.....	.....	5.0	...	13.0	1,200.7	463,776.92
6,620.3	21,911.9	2,031.8	8,384.2	1,405.6	633.3	736.3	...	2,815.0	347.951.4	65,841,716.75
231.0	1,275.0	220.9	406.4	92.0	.....	....	...	.....	3,759.3	1,501,595.02
23.3	133.3	5.2	9.1	.....	.....	10.5	...	2.3	350.3	124,208.73
2,425.5	43,362.6	3,945.0	21,555.9	1,351.5	2,501.0	599.8	8,281.9	3,199.8	741,572.7	63,174,848.78
28.0	122.0	11.0	19.0	9.0	.....	....	...	.....	562.0	98,622.59
9,594.8	**103,612.1**	**10,762.6**	**44,295.7**	**4,076.0**	**3,134.3**	**2,276.6**	**8,283.9**	**10,390.9**	**1,571,534.1**	**$220,704,581.78**

HILDREN'S FUND

Operations—Reconstruction Period, 1919–1924

Commodities in Net Metric Tons of 1,000 Kilograms or 2,204.6 Pounds

Pork Products	Milk	Cocoa	Sugar	Miscellaneous Food	Soap	Clothing and Misc.	Total Tons	Total Value
1,567.7	15,086.4	2,226.3	3,204.5	30.4	745.2	989.9	36,002.1	$13,433,918.33
323.6	2,900.0	394.3	547.4	14.0	147.2	.....	7,823.1	2,949,217.23
2,930.8	5,548.0	349.9	1,325.0	575.3	.....	250.1	40,319.5	9,885,405.73
20,360.2	48,996.4	6,193.4	30,487.6	1,778.1	1,000.4	5,616.1	337,953.5	58,370,700.11
25,182.3	**72,530.8**	**9,163.9**	**35,564.5**	**2,397.8**	**1,892.8**	**6,856.1**	**422,098.2**	**$84,639,241.40**

.R.A.-EUROPEAN CHILDREN'S FUND

perations—Reconstruction Period, 1919–1924

Commodities in Net Metric Tons of 1,000 Kilograms or 2,204.6 Pounds

Pork Products	Milk	Cocoa	Sugar	Misc. Food	Forage	Soap	Medical and Hospital Supplies	Clothing and Misc.	Total Tons	Total Value
.....	.....	.....	.....	....	.....	....	....	.....	481.945.3	$57,782,118.20
.....	19,589.6	.....	.....	....	.....	....	....	1,100.0	386,070.8	18,662,180.00
.....	.....	.....	.....	....	.....	....	3,107.6	.....	3,107.6	4,000,000.00
.....	.....	.....	.....	....	.....	....	....	.....	......	267,392.88
102.0	162.0	409.0	203.0	45.0	.....	2.0	5,174.3	.....	25,548.3	5,516,813.10
2,834.3	9,284.0	992.3	975.6	115.0	633.3	50.0	....	9.4	33,713.9	7,056,966.68
50.9	102.8	61.0	96.5	....	.....	....	....	74.7	3,836.7	890,642.46
.....	506.0	.....	.....	....	.....	31.0	.....	.....	537.0	273,555.00
240.0	178.0	108.0	483.6	1.9	.....	300.8	2.0	546.1	7,404.3	1,944,119.91
.....	.....	.....	.....	....	.....	....	....	103.1	103.1	113,081.13
3,227.2	**29,822.4**	**1,570.3**	**1,758.7**	**161.9**	**633.3**	**383.8**	**8,283.9**	**1,833.3**	**942,267.0**	**$96,506,869.36**

COUNTRIES OTHER THAN

Table 152

Summary of Deliveries by Operations

Operation	Table No.	Flour	Grain	Rice	Beans, Peas	Corn Grits
European Government and Local Donations for Relief	161	80,700.7	....	632.9	1,809.0	77.3
R.S.F.S.R. and U.S.R. Donation*	519	38,747.0	105,135.3	5,666.0	4,229.6	....
United Kingdom—Finance on Freight	162	....	....	......	......	....
Total Deliveries	.....	**119,447.7**	**105,135.3**	**6,298.9**	**6,038.6**	**77.3**

* Russian Socialist Federative Soviet Republic and Ukranian Soviet Republic (R.S.F.S.R. and U.S.R.) donated gold rubles, the equivalent of $11,357,325.13, with which the A.R.A.-E.C.F. purchased seed grain in the amount of $7,034,874.30, and child-feeding supplies in the amoun of $4,322.450.83. The latter supplies were turned over to the Soviet Re publics from child-feeding stocks in Russia. (Cf. Table 165.)

A.R.A. WAREHOUSES AND A.R.A.

Table 153

Summary of Food Draft and Bulk Sales, Exclusive of Russia, by

Country	Commodities in Net Metric Tons of 1,000 Kilograms or 2,204.6 Pounds											Total Value
	Flour	Rice	Beans, Peas	Corn Grits	Pork Products	Milk	Cocoa	Sugar	Misc. Food	Misc.*	Total Tons	
Austria	5,120.6	1,243.0	664.8	521.6	1,122.6	1,789.3	195.0	851.0	218.2	69.7	11,795.8	$3,330,635.4
Czecho-Slovakia	694.3	112.3	85.2	....	122.3	263.9	8.7	16.3	52.3	21.2	1,376.5	433,432.6
Danzig Free City	7,799.7	18.5	13.2	2.8	16.9	89.9	2.5	5.6	2.5	1.6	7,953.2	935,647.8
Esthonia	3.7	1.5	1.9	....	76.3	209.0	.2	.9	....	....	293.5	146,556.2
Germany	4,020.7	1,166.7	801.0	....	864.7	2,154.6	43.6	107.1	84.8	104.2	9,347.4	2,820,420.4
Hungary	672.3	208.4	73.5	....	173.9	297.9	20.4	121.6	50.6	11.0	1,629.6	527,939.4
Latvia	18.9	4.7	7.3	....	26.2	20.8	1.3	4.5	.3	....	84.0	15,686.1
Poland	4,965.2	516.1	570.9	31.6	527.9	722.6	78.2	218.0	166.6	42.4	7,839.5	1,675,087.4
Total Deliveries	**23,295.4**	**3,271.2**	**2,217.8**	**556.0**	**2,930.8**	**5,548.0**	**349.9**	**1,325.0**	**575.3**	**250.1**	**40,319.5**	**$9,885,405.7**

* Sacks and containers for packing, etc.

A.R.A. WAREHOUSES AND A.R.A.

Table 154

Summary of Food Draft Deliveries, Exclusive of Russia, by

Country	Date of Delivery	Table No.	Number of Drafts Delivered				Total Packages Delivered
			A $10.00	B $50.00	C $10.00	D $50.00	
Austria	Mar., 1920–July, 1921	219	115,801	18,875	26,130	1,629	162,435
Czecho-Slovakia	Mar., 1920–July, 1921	251	15,160	3,269	2,685	117	21,231
Danzig Free City	Mar., 1920–July, 1921	288	1,375	205	132	12	1,724
Germany	Mar., 1920–July, 1921	322	109,356	15,379	16,825	1,313	142,873
Hungary	Mar., 1920–July, 1921	349	17,415	2,442	5,900	372	26,129
Latvia	Feb., 1921	378	2	....	.....	...	2
Poland	Apr., 1920–July, 1921	408	33,792	2,756	11,389	706	48,643
Total Deliveries	Mar., 1920–July, 1921	....	**292,901**	**42,926**	**63,061**	**4,149**	**403,037**

HE UNITED STATES

-Reconstruction Period, 1919–1924

ommodities in Net Metric Tons of 1,000 Kilograms or 2,204.6 Pounds									Total Value
Pork Products	Milk	Cocoa	Sugar	Miscellaneous Food	Forage	Soap	Clothing and Miscellaneous	Total Tons	
1,361.6	1,736.9	31.4	6,972.6	1,516.3	......	.....	1,701.5	96,540.2	$14,652,432.21
3,658.0	544.0	1,445.0	7,436.0	......	2,501.0	327.0	......	169,688.9	11,357,325.13
......	.....	......	......	......	......	.....	......	....	18,212,473.88
5,019.6	**2,280.9**	**1,476.4**	**14,408.6**	**1,516.3**	**2,501.0**	**327.0**	**1,701.5**	**266,229.1**	**$44,222,231.22**

UROPEAN CHILDREN'S FUND

ountries of Destination—Reconstruction Period, 1919–1924

UROPEAN CHILDREN'S FUND

ountries of Destination—Reconstruction Period, 1919–1924

Commodities in Net Metric Tons of 1,000 Kilograms or 2,204.6 Pounds									Total Tons	Total Value
				Milk			Miscellaneous			
Flour	Rice	Beans, Peas	Pork Products	Evap., Cond., Powdered	Cocoa	Sugar	Food	Sacks, Containers		
2,952.959	614.111	467.550	790.802	933.528	33.176	60.986	111.577	65.992	6,030.681	$2,444,510.00
393.529	85.178	62.148	111.643	122.673	2.625	6.324	16.455	14.433	815.008	347,750.00
30.510	5.367	6.342	8.563	9.485	.422	1.039	1.119	.786	63.633	25,920.00
2,462.549	723.515	220.009	693.367	825.214	41.794	101.093	83.808	91.433	5,242.782	2,096,410.00
452.692	89.266	73.463	120.892	142.564	3.076	7.620	15.279	7.776	912.628	373,850.00
.022	....	.009	....	.014	.001	.002	......	......	.048	20.00
721.669	203.466	89.157	213.596	231.657	16.394	38.008	14.968	42.436	1,571.351	624,910.00
7,013.930	**1,720.903**	**918.678**	**1,938.863**	**2,265.135**	**97.488**	**215.072**	**243.206**	**222.856**	**14,636.131**	**$5,913,370.00**

A.R.A. WAREHOUSES AND A.R.A.-

Table 155

Summary of Net Bulk Sale Deliveries, Exclusive of Russia,

Country	Date of Delivery	Table No.	Flour	Rice
Austria	Mar., 1920—May, 1923	220	2,167.706	628.944
Czecho-Slovakia	June, 1920—Nov., 1921	252	300.791	27.152
Danzig Free City *	July, 1920—Sept., 1922	289	7,769.156	13.084
Esthonia	May, 1921—Oct., 1921	303	3.654	1.464
Germany	Feb., 1920—Mar., 1922	333	1,558.135	443.179
Hungary	Oct., 1920—June, 1922	350	219.598	119.142
Latvia †	Apr., 1921—June, 1922	378	18.900	4.662
Poland	Apr., 1920—June, 1923	409	4,243.548	312.603
Total Net Deliveries	Feb., 1920—June, 1923	...	**16,281.488**	**1,550.230**

* Total bulk sales handled by Danzig Mission are listed in this table. Cf. Table 289 for net deliveries actually consumed in Danzig territory.

† Of the total, 8.4 metric tons, value $926.78, were transferred and used in Lithuania.

A.R.A.-EUROPEAN

Table 156

Summary of A.R.A.-E.C.F. Commodities Purchased and Delivered,

Country	Table No.	Flour	Rice	Beans, Peas	Corn Grits
Austria	206	5,830.7	3,743.1	3,417.8	970.3
Czecho-Slovakia	236	1,082.7	881.4	1,261.4	.....
Danzig Free City	280	.8	20.3	25.1	.....
Esthonia	292	551.3	266.7	225.1	.....
Finland	306	350.1	9.5	2.4	.....
Germany	323	2,099.0	33.0	.....	1,149.0
Hungary	336	459.2	430.2	326.9	23.4
Jugoslavia	354	.....	5.7	.....	.....
Latvia	369	2,116.6	535.8	206.8	.....
Lithuania	382	42.6	15.9	25.4	.....
Poland	394	3,652.6	10,247.2	15,952.9	1,657.8
Russia					
Northwest Russia	497	3.3	......	.....	.....
Soviet Republics	511	131,679.9	18,842.7	3,575.3	11,324.1
Sundry Accounts	539	257.0	55.0	38.0	23.0
Total Deliveries *	....	**148,125.8**	**35,086.5**	**25,057.1**	**15,147.6**

* Excludes commodities purchased and used for draft and bulk sales operation, which are summarized under the A.R.A. Warehouses.

UNITED STATES GRAIN CORPORATION

Table 157

Summary of Deliveries under Act of Congress, March 30, 1920,* by Countries of Destination—Reconstruction Period, 1919–1924

Country	Table No.	Flour		F.O.B. Value	Freight and Transportation Charges	Total Value
		Total Barrels	Total Metric Tons			
Armenia	203	457,043	40,633.5	$ 4,813,744.45	$ 1,592,790.01	$ 6,406,534.4
Austria	217	2,258,867	200,824.8	24,055,708.92	8,032,991.88	32,088,700.8
Czecho-Slovakia	249	267,803	23,809.0	2,873,238.25	952,362.08	3,825,600.3
Hungary	343	158,754	14,114.0	1,685,835.61	564,561.60	2,250,397.2
Poland	405	2,278,429	202,564.0	24,353,590.97	8,102,558.32	32,456,149.2
Total	151	**5,420,896**	**481,945.3**	**$57,782,118.20**†	**$19,245,263.89**‡	**$77,027,382.0**

* H.R. 12954, Public 167, Sixty-sixth Congress, entitled "An Act providing for the relief of populations of Europe and in countries contiguous thereto suffering for want of food.

† Value of supplies handled by U.S. Grain Corporation.

‡ United Kingdom paid freight and transportation charges in th amount of $18,212,473.88; Near East Relief, in the amount of $532,790.0 American Red Cross, in the amount of $500,000.00.

EUROPEAN CHILDREN'S FUND

by Countries of Destination—Reconstruction Period, 1919–1924

Commodities in Net Metric Tons of 1,000 Kilograms or 2,204.6 Pounds									
			Milk			Miscellaneous			
Beans, Peas	Corn Grits	Pork Products	Evap., Cond., Powdered	Cocoa	Sugar	Food	Sacks, Containers	Total Tons	Total Value
197.214	521.614	331.706	855.756	161.861	790.001	106.634	3.713	5,765.149	$ 886,125.48
23.036	.....	10.665	141.237	6.080	9.973	35.798	6.699	561.431	85,682.69
6.862	2.790	8.345	80.453	2.054	4.621	1.415	.817	7,889.597	909,727.88
1.914	.....	76.318	208.983	.244	.870	.....	.....	293.447	146,556.24
581.062	.....	171.326	1,329.355	1.783	6.034	.957	12.782	4,104.613	724,010.47
.....	.....	53.058	155.333	17.275	113.956	35.368	3.250	716.980	154,089.41
7.305	.....	26.213	20.783	1.297	4.500	.299	.....	83.959	15,666.15
481.753	31.603	314.313	490.922	61.830	180.004	151.612	.....	6,268.188	1,050,177.41
1,299.146	**556.007**	**991.944**	**3,282.822**	**252.424**	**1,109.959**	**332.083**	**27.261**	**25,683.364**	**$3,972,035.73**

CHILDREN'S FUND

by Countries of Destination—Reconstruction Period, 1919–1924

Commodities in Net Metric Tons of 1,000 Kilograms or 2,204.6 Pounds								
Pork Products	Milk	Cocoa	Sugar	Miscellaneous Food	Soap	Clothing and Misc.	Total Tons	Total Value
1,806.6	6,271.1	695.3	2,773.7	418.9	98.7	830.1	26,856.3	$ 6,695,794.69
1,002.6	1,582.8	140.9	1.8	102.5	20.3	210.7	6,287.1	2,102,676.85
12.8	43.7	5.3	.....	.....	....	.....	108.0	17,749.51
169.0	408.0	39.4	104.6	.....	7.3	59.9	1,831.3	522,929.39
.....	18.3	....	5.2	.....	....	56.0	441.5	253,867.46
177.0	595.0	....	.....	.....	....	.....	4,053.0	362,571.27
135.0	1,049.0	125.6	476.3	55.2	....	217.5	3,298.3	1,191,623.36
.....	1.6	....	127.8	.....	2.7	180.0	317.8	490,705.04
122.8	670.7	71.4	264.1	.....	7.9	57.7	4,053.8	754,796.70
19.1	58.2	3.4	9.3	.....	....	13.0	186.9	111,060.61
4,475.4	14,399.1	1,155.9	5,217.4	305.0	263.7	1,915.5	59,242.5	16,769,322.10
3.0	3.9	.2	.1	.....	....	2.3	12.8	6,223.60
12,408.9	23,773.0	3,945.0	21,488.3	887.5	599.8	2,073.4	230,597.9	28,992,756.94
28.0	122.0	11.0	19.0	9.0	....	.....	562.0	98,622.59
20,360.2	**48,996.4**	**6,193.4**	**30,487.6**	**1,778.1**	**1,000.4**	**5,616.1**	**337,849.2**	**$58,370,700.11**

AMERICAN

Table 158

Summary of Relief Supplies Furnished by A.R.C. in Co-operation wit

Country	Table No.	Commoditie				
		Flour	Grain	Rice	Beans, Peas	Corn Grits
Armenia*	200	......	......	.....	......	......
Greece	335	12,886.0	2,451.0	203.0	1,269.0	2,642.0
Russia						
Soviet Republics	523	......	......	.....	......	......
Total Deliveries	151	**12,886.0**	**2,451.0**	**203.0**	**1,269.0**	**2,642.0**

* Cf. Table 157n.

AMERICAN FRIEND

Table 159

Summary of Relief Supplies Delivered in Co-operation with th

Country	Table No.	Commoditi				
		Flour	Rice	Beans, Peas	Corn Grits	Pork Products
Danzig Free City	287	.4	30.4	40.3	.....	20.1
Germany	330	4,863.0	4,341.9	5,426.4	.....	2,797.6
Poland	394	......	....	....	.....	....
Russia						
Soviet Republics	525	3,037.3	71.9	90.6	917.8	16.6
Total Deliveries	151	**7,900.7**	**4,444.2**	**5,557.3**	**917.8**	**2,834.3**

COMMONWEALTH FUND*

Summary of Relief Supplies, not Otherwise Shown, Delivered in Co-operation with the A.R.A.-E.C.F., by Countries of Destination—Reconstruction Period, 1919–1924

Table 160

Country	Table No.	Commodities in Net Metric Tons of 1,000 Kilograms or 2,204.6 Pounds									Total Value
		Flour	Rice	Beans, Peas	Pork Products	Milk	Cocoa	Sugar	Clothing and Misc.	Total Tons	
Armenia	204	2,679.3	366.9	404.6	50.9	102.8	61.0	96.5	....	3,762.0	$746,107.
Austria	221	......	.....	.....	....	.....	....	....	31.8	31.8	62,475.
Hungary	346	......	.....	.....	....	.....	....	....	12.5	12.5	24,527.
Poland	403	......	.....	.....	....	.....	....	....	30.4	30.4	57,532.
Total Deliveries	151	**2,679.3**	**366.9**	**404.6**	**50.9**	**102.8**	**61.0**	**96.5**	**74.7**	**3,836.7**	**$890,642.**

* Total contributions by the Commonwealth Fund, amounting to $2,165,211.20, are shown under Special Programs, page 96. The portion not included in this table ($1,274,568.74) was used for bulk sale purcha from A.R.A. Warehouses and is accounted for under that heading.

RED CROSS

.R.A.-E.C.F., by Countries of Destination—Reconstruction Period, 1919–1924

Pork Products	Milk	Cocoa	Sugar	Miscellaneous Food	Soap	Medical and Hospital Supplies	Total Tons	Total Value
.....	.....	.....	.....	....	...	......	....	$ 500,000.00
102.0	162.0	409.0	203.0	45.0	2.0	......	20,374.0	1,211,949.95
.....	.....	.....	.....	....	...	5,174.3	5,174.3	3,804,863.15
102.0	**162.0**	**409.0**	**203.0**	**45.0**	**2.0**	**5,174.3**	**25,548.3**	**$5,516,813.10**

(n Net Metric Tons of 1,000 Kilograms or 2,204.6 Pounds)

ERVICE COMMITTEE

.R.A.-E.C.F., by Countries of Destination—Reconstruction Period, 1919–1924

Milk	Cocoa	Sugar	Miscellaneous Food	Forage	Soap	Clothing and Misc.	Total Tons	Total Value
58.2	8.9	.....	.....	.....	....	...	158.3	$ 30,291.26
9,225.8	983.4	908.0	115.0	.....	50.0	9.0	28,720.1	6,728,989.92
......	.....	.....	.....	633.3	....	...	633.3	30,291.26
......	.....	67.6	.....	.....	....	.4	4,202.2	267,394.24
9,284.4	**992.3**	**975.6**	**115.0**	**633.3**	**50.0**	**9.4**	**33,713.9**	**$7,056,966.68**

(Net Metric Tons of 1,000 Kilograms or 2,204.6 Pounds)

SUMMARY OF EUROPEAN GOVERNMEN

Table 161

By Countries of Origin*-

Country of Origin	Table No.	Flour	Rice	Beans Peas	Corn Grits
Austria	215–16	10,389.8	....	.....	....
Czecho-Slovakia	248	2,403.0	....	.....	77.3
Danzig Free City	282	51.1	....	.....	....
Esthonia	300	1,504.0	15.0	.....	....
Finland	313	888.4	....	.....	....
Germany	330n	12,663.0	....	.....	....
Hungary	342	1,441.0	....	242.0	....
Jugoslavia	363	2,551.0	58.0	5.0	....
Latvia	369	......	28.9	342.0	....
Norway	...	......	....	.....	....
Poland	394	48,221.4	531.0	728.0	....
Roumania	494n	492.0	....	492.0	....
Russia					
Northwest Russia	503	32.0	....	.....	....
Soviet Republics	520	64.0	....	.....	....
Total Donations †	....	**80,700.7**	**632.9**	**1,809.0**	**77.3**

* Quantities and values for country of destination remain the same as for country of origin with the following exceptions: Norway donation used for Latvian child feeding; Esthonia and Latvia donated, respectively, warehouse space for storage of transit supplies en route to Russia, the estimated value of the donations being $1,102.94 and $24,257.69; Poland donated railway transportation and other facilit for the same purpose, valued at $90,000.00. These amounts to be add to Soviet Republic's account, and deducted from Esthonia, Latvia, a Poland.

† Cf. discussion on countries for value of service donations.

UNITED STATES GRAIN CORPORATION

Summary of Finance on Freight and Transportation Charges on Flour Sold by U.S. Grain Corporation, under Act of Congress, March 30, 1920—Reconstruction Period, 1919–1924

Table 162

Paid by	Receiving Country	Table No.	Freight, Insurance Misc. Charges
Near East Relief	Armenia	203	**$ 532,790.**
American Red Cross	Armenia	203	**500,000.**
United Kingdom	Armenia	203	560,000.
United Kingdom	Austria	217	8,032,991.
United Kingdom	Czecho-Slovakia	249	952,362.
United Kingdom	Hungary	343	564,561.
United Kingdom	Poland	405	8,102,558.
Total by United Kingdom		152	**$18,212,473.**
Grand Total		....	**$19,245,263.**

AND LOCAL DONATIONS FOR RELIEF

Reconstruction Period, 1919–1924

Commodities in Net Metric Tons of 1,000 Kilograms or 2,204.6 Pounds							
Pork Products	Milk	Cocoa	Sugar	Miscellaneous Food	Clothing and Misc.	Total Tons	Total Value
....	....	....	638.0	....	1,675.5	12,703.3	$ 1,364,656.01
188.8	426.7	....	830.0	30.0	....	3,955.8	693,099.02
....	....	....	22.9	....	....	74.0	8,574.44
1.0	153.0	....	10.0	10.0	....	1,693.0	299,547.58
12.0	36.0	....	.....	....	....	936.4	195,949.00
....	....	....	4,170.0	....	....	16,833.0	2,392,021.25
50.0	....	....	.....	....	....	1,733.0	265,806.84
20.0	....	....	.....	....	....	2,634.0	533,677.16
76.5	31.2	....	.....	....	....	478.6	85,137.24
....	....	....	.....	6.6	....	6.6	3,960.00
852.0	....	31.4	1,301.7	913.7	....	52,579.2	7,749,374.77
161.0	1,090.0	....	.....	92.0	....	2,327.0	1,024,322.26
.3	....	....	.....	....	....	32.3	6,280.00
....	....	....	.....	464.0	26.0	554.0	30,026.64
1,361.6	**1,736.9**	**31.4**	**6,972.6**	**1,516.3**	**1,701.5**	**96,540.2**	**$14,652,432.21**

SUMMARY OF DELIVERIES FOR CHILDREN'S RELIEF IN

Table 163† Handled under the Direction of the American Relief

Country	Table No.	Commodities					
		Flour	Grain	Rice	Beans, Peas	Corn Grits	Pork Products
Austria	206	16,924.2	....	4,822.6	4,233.2	970.3	2,130.2
Czecho-Slovakia	236	3,167.3	....	1,200.3	1,532.7	77.3	1,617.9
Danzig Free City	280	52.3	....	50.7	65.4	....	32.9
Esthonia	292	2,343.3	....	531.8	447.5	....	231.6
Finland	306	1,938.5	....	231.4	256.3	....	107.3
Germany	323	17,526.0	....	4,341.9	5,426.4	....	2,797.6
Hungary	336	1,998.2	....	430.2	568.9	23.4	185.0
Jugoslavia	354	2,551.0	....	541.0	292.9	....	50.0
Latvia	369	2,374.5	....	844.8	994.9	....	242.5
Lithuania	382	393.6	....	98.9	103.2	....	47.1
Poland	394	45,763.8	....	12,971.5	19,579.1	1,657.8	6,092.4
Roumania	491	742.0	....	170.0	622.0	....	231.0
Russia							
Northwest Russia	497	74.7	....	64.0	27.9	....	23.3
Soviet Republics	511	90,628.4	219,638.3	8,056.6	3,321.8	84,638.9	7,982.8
Total Deliveries	....	**186,477.8**	**219,638.3**	**34,355.7**	**37,472.2**	**87,367.7**	**21,771.6**

* All the German children's relief was administered by the American Friends Service Committee.

† Cf. Table 164 for number of persons fed.

ENTRAL EUROPE, CHILD AND ADULT RELIEF IN RUSSIA

dministration and A.R.A.-European Children's Fund,* 1919–1924

Net Metric Tons of 1,000 Kilograms or 2,204.6 Pounds								Total Value
Milk	Cocoa	Sugar	Miscellaneous Food	Soap	Medical and Hospital Supplies	Clothing and Miscellaneous	Total Tons	
9,591.6	1,084.6	4,045.1	432.9	208.9	......	2,505.5	46,949.1	$ 11,227,713.57
5,507.1	804.6	831.8	142.6	171.5	......	373.9	15,427.0	5,437,793.25
101.9	14.2	22.9	....	....	......	....	340.3	56,615.21
1,348.7	143.8	399.2	10.0	38.4	......	59.9	5,554.2	1,522,894.85
658.5	.4	126.6	....	....	......	56.0	3,375.0	1,072,329.67
9,225.8	983.4	5,078.0	115.0	50.0	......	9.0	45,553.1	9,121,011.17
1,144.0	152.6	506.3	55.2	37.0	......	217.3	5,318.1	1,557,964.37
1,624.9	239.0	455.5	....	71.8	......	180.0	6,006.1	2,188,999.61
1,515.9	154.6	411.7	6.6	44.6	......	57.7	6,647.8	1,570,690.35
365.7	60.6	105.2	....	5.0	......	13.0	1,192.3	462,850.14
21,189.3	1,953.6	8,166.2	1,239.0	736.3	......	2,742.2	122.091.2	29,841,034.66
1,275.0	220.9	406.4	92.0	....	......	....	3,759.3	1,501,595.02
133.3	5.2	9.1	....	10.5	......	2.3	350.3	124.208.73
29,353.8	3,391.5	13,331.8	594.1	597.4	8.281.9	1,749.8	471,567.1	38,216,887.24
83,035.5	**9,209.0**	**33,895.8**	**2,687.4**	**1,971.4**	**8,281.9**	**7,966.6**	**734,130.9**	**$103,902,587.84**

Table 164A‡

Summary, by Countries and by Months, of Numbe

Month	Central Europe-					
	Finland	Esthonia	Latvia	Lithuania	Poland	Czecho-Slovakia
1919						
April	.....	.....	.....	.....	......	4,000
May	19,291	.....	.....	13,200	125,000	63,000
June	50,945	81,374	8,000	18,275	300,000	97,000
July	52,010	54,821	19,000	12,945	400,000	166,000
August	79,394	59,950	21,000	22,905	525,000	365,660
September	98,260	54,950	22,840	17,875	600,000	412,775
October	94,535	54,950	59,000	16,945	700,000	547,786
November	96,015	66,050	59,400	18,870	900,000	547,786
December	97,315	66,050	80,000	15,990	975,000	547,786
1920						
January	127,770	73,050	81,000	16,000	1,080,722	547,786
February	127,525	77,550	81,000	17,500	1,128,818	547,786
March	126,220	84,000	81,000	17,500	1,222,680	547,786
April	66,524	84,000	81,000	17,500	1,268,313	547,786
May	66,420	84,000	81,000	17,500	1,315,490	394,149
June	50,000	.....	.....	1,000	997,352	394,149
July	.....	.....	.....	1,000	545,325	394,149
August	.....	.....	.....	.....	350,869	394,149
September	.....	.....	.....	.....	327,058	106,010
October	.....	.....	.....	.....	407,194	106,010
November	.....	.....	.....	.....	529,018	106,010
December	.....	.....	.....	.....	673,058	106,010
1921						
January	.....	.....	.....	.....	863,544	106,010
February	.....	43,000	24,026	.....	1,040,769	82,050
March	.....	43,000	24,428	5,000	1,221,721	89,650
April	.....	43,000	44,539	5,000	1,246,921	133,840
May	.....	30,695	41,153	5,000	1,187,319	158,310
June	5,000	22,879	31,980	5,000	1,133,309	131,385
July	5,000	27,435	46,548	5,000	922,962	57,698
August	5,000	20,000	21,700	5,000	695,354	55,000
September	5,000	12,000	42,700	.....	488,223	.....
October	5,000	20,000	41,800	.....	499,053	.....
November	5,000	10,000	39,600	.....	499,056	.....
December	5,000	10,000	41,200	.....	460,755	.....
1922						
January	.....	10,000	40,378	.....	437,401	.....
February	.....	10,000	41,519	.....	424,924	.....
March	.....	10,000	39,600	.....	417,242	.....
April	.....	10,000	46,900	.....	384,230	.....
May	.....	10,000	41,503	.....	363,795	.....
June	.....	10,000	40,490	.....	176,647	.....
July	.....	10,000	21,830	.....	197,155	.....
August	.....	10,000	19,574	.....	......	.....
September	.....	.....	.....	.....	......	.....
October	.....	.....	.....	.....	......	.....
November	.....	.....	.....	.....	......	.....
December	.....	.....	.....	.....	......	.....
1923						
January	.....	.....	.....	.....	......	.....
February	.....	.....	.....	.....	......	.....
March	.....	.....	.....	.....	......	.....
April	.....	.....	.....	.....	......	.....
May	.....	.....	.....	.....	......	.....
June	.....	.....	.....	.....	......	.....

‡ Cf. Table 163 for food supplies and value.

* Administered by American Friends Service Committee.

.R.A.-EUROPEAN CHILDREN'S FUND

Persons Fed Daily—April, 1919–July, 1923

Children's Relief						Total for Central Europe	Child and Adult	Grand Total for All Europe
Austria	Hungary	Roumania	Jugoslavia	Germany *	Danzig Free City		Total for Russia **	
.....	.....	.....	.....	.....	....	4,000	....	4,000
15,000	.....	11,100	100,000	.....	....	346,591	....	346,591
63,534	.....	74,000	200,000	.....	....	893,128	....	893,128
116,735	.....	125,000	200,000	.....	....	1,146,511	8,000	1,154,511
141,855	35,900	150,000	200,000	.....	....	1,601,664	6,000	1,607,664
180,217	36,000	42,100	150,000	.....	....	1,615,017	7,000	1,622,017
186,915	36,000	8,600	150,000	.....	....	1,854,731	8,000	1,862,731
213,616	44,710	.....	150,000	.....	....	2,096,447	1,000	2,097,447
211,654	73,992	.....	150,000	.....	....	2,217,787	1,900	2,219,687
216,267	89,302	.....	150,000	.....	....	2,381,897	1,800	2,383,697
227,521	106,328	.....	150,000	.....	....	2,464,028	1,800	2,465,828
249,884	107,706	.....	150,000	708,589	....	3,295,365	....	3,295,365
269,838	110,357	.....	150,000	708,589	....	3,303,907	....	3,303,907
294,887	65,300	.....	150,000	708,589	....	3,177,335	....	3,177,335
296,376	31,670	.....	50,000	708,589	....	2,529,136	....	2,529,136
265,619	31,499	.....	50,000	708,589	....	1,996,181	....	1,996,181
226,655	34,657	.....	30,000	708,589	....	1,744,919	....	1,744,919
199,777	7,651	.....	20,000	346,933	....	1,007,429	....	1,007,429
219,843	7,651	.....	.....	390,629	....	1,131,327	....	1,131,327
245,568	7,651	.....	.....	465,893	....	1,354,140	....	1,354,140
274,829	7,651	.....	.....	569,165	....	1,630,713	....	1,630,713
284,679	10,447	.....	.....	653,316	....	1,917,996	....	1,917,996
288,588	21,107	.....	.....	672,000	....	2,171,540	....	2,171,540
307,619	31,084	.....	.....	736,001	....	2,458,503	....	2,458,503
360,267	34,751	.....	.....	736,000	4,501	2,608,819	....	2,608,819
357,615	35,264	.....	20,000	820,000	6,542	2,661,898	....	2,661,898
362,309	33,637	.....	20,000	997,000	7,250	2,749,749	....	2,749,749
276,476	15,472	.....	20,000	800,000	7,274	2,183,865	....	2,183,865
214,000	8,000	.....	20,000	177,000	1,900	1,222,954	....	1,222,954
160,900	10,900	.....	20,000	130,000	2,200	871,923	200	872,123
164,000	16,900	.....	20,000	360,500	3,300	1,130,553	68,598	1,199,151
180,500	13,000	.....	.....	500,000	3,300	1,250,456	183,961 1,371	1,435,788
190,600	19,200	.....	.....	500,000	3,200	1,229,955	565,555 2,465	1,797,975
173,700	11,875	.....	.....	.....	4,351	677,705	992,151 7,464	1,677,320
168,999	17,871	.....	.....	.....	4,250	667,563	1,313,027 7,924	1,988,514
165,190	17,500	.....	.....	.....	4,330	653,862	1,548,938 9,709	2,212,509
157,700	17,200	.....	.....	.....	4,130	620,160	1,739,968 681,795	3,041,923
142,461	18,100	.....	.....	.....	....	575,859	1,997,501 2,993,728	5,567,088
72,405	.....	.....	.....	.....	....	299,542	2,821,331 4,500,660	7,621,533
45,474	.....	.....	.....	.....	....	274,459	3,613,174 5,353,718	9,241,351
20,476	.....	.....	.....	.....	....	50,050	4,173,339 6,317,958	10,541,347
16,604	.....	.....	.....	.....	4,000	20,604	3,295,876 5,005,618	8,322,098
.....	.....	.....	.....	.....	4,000	4,000	1,086,905 103,838	1,194,743
.....	.....	.....	.....	.....	4,000	4,000	743,453 62,050	809,503
.....	.....	.....	.....	.....	4,000	4,000	832,380 63,509	899,889
.....	.....	.....	.....	.....	....	....	919,217 63,780	982,997
.....	.....	.....	.....	.....	....	....	1,036,428 67,146	1,103,574
.....	.....	.....	.....	.....	....	....	1,442,155 78,005	1,520,160
.....	.....	.....	.....	.....	....	....	2,033,492 121,358	2,154,850
.....	.....	.....	.....	.....	....	....	2,484,025 139,027	2,623,052
.....	.....	.....	.....	.....	....	....	2,767,598 142,227	2,909,825

** Cf. Table 164B for Russian detail.

Table 164B†

Summary, by Districts and by Months, of Numbe

Month	Russia—				
	Moscow	Petrograd	Kazan	Samara	Saratov
1919					
July	....	....	.....	....	....
August	....	....	.....	....	....
September	....	....	.....	....	....
October	....	....	.....	....	....
November	....	....	.....	....	....
December	....	....	.....	....	....
1920					
January	....	....	.....	....	....
February	....	....	.....	....	....
1921					
September	....	200	.....	....	....
	....	....	.....	....	....
October	....	200	67,290	1,108	....
	....	....	.....	....	....
November	905	35,100	105,508	36,381	1,280
	....	1,200	.....	....	....
December	13,514	35,137	156,743	185,625	82,010
	....	1,628	.....	....	....
1922					
January	32,080	34,138	201,662	252,300	146,062
	....	1,550	4,720	....	....
February	34,491	34,549	301,075	257,994	173,979
	....	204	4,720	....	....
March	36,635	35,075	338,665	298,651	186,998
	....	1,293	4,720	....	176
April	35,869	36,955	339,705	329,756	185,256
	....	3,029	4,720	....	55,618
May	36,798	35,601	361,383	347,690	199,428
	9,655	3,757	197,022	561,321	468,211
June	40,678	32,875	508,384	440,218	287,093
	14,747	6,776	791,530	770,688	738,662
July	36,094	35,602	664,174	433,801	332,611
	18,863	5,519	1,089,014	789,749	748,803
August	42,117	36,639	700,638	477,653	338,023
	16,511	5,815	1,093,329	811,681	529,231
September	41,570	41,983	462,683	333,357	303,076
	16,669	3,985	818,164	813,836	553,118
October	34,950	36,751	148,045	94,422	5,948
	7,685	4,338	4,611	934	51,481
November	27,971	38,829	133,461	97,368	8,666
	9,100	4,508	4,318	1,268	6,043
December	33,503	30,665	142,988	113,070	51,057
	10,149	4,585	4,720	1,739	4,444
1923					
January	32,177	27,608	156,433	80,173	119,980
	10,542	2,510	4,937	1,531	4,878
February	32,507	29,767	169,009	88,969	121,909
	11,061	2,803	4,896	1,601	4,912
March	33,272	30,902	253,824	146,478	159,458
	11,944	10,983	5,666	2,043	4,260
April	32,895	36,114	392,722	160,052	201,762
	14,604	13,655	6,505	3,169	4,425
May	35,171	35,746	543,399	185,092	219,032
	14,743	11,401	7,179	4,319	4,246
June	35,291	35,835	642,096	193,111	273,066
	14,556	11,477	7,486	4,368	5,762

† Cf. Table 164A for Central European detail.
* Two figures are given for each month. The upper figure in each case represents the number of children fed, and the lower the number of adults. The adult feeding figures largely indicate the "Corn Distrib tion" by U.S.G.C. The total for Russia from July, 1919, to Februa 1920, represents feeding in Northwest Russia.

A.R.A.-EUROPEAN CHILDREN'S FUND

of Persons Fed Daily in Russia—July, 1919–July, 1923

Child and Adult Relief *

Simbirsk	Rostov, Tzaritzin	Ufa	Orenburg	Crimea	Minsk, Vitebsk, Gomel	Ukraine	Total for Russia
....	....	.....	....	.....	....	....	8,000
....	....	.....	....	.....	....	....	6,000
....	....	.....	....	.....	....	....	7,000
....	....	.....	....	.....	....	....	8,000
....	....	.....	....	.....	....	....	1,000
....	....	.....	....	.....	....	....	1,900
....	....	.....	....	.....	....	....	1,800
....	....	.....	....	.....	....	....	1,800
....	....	.....	....	.....	....	....	200
....	....	.....	....	.....	....	....	....
....	....	.....	....	.....	....	....	68,598
....	....	.....	....	.....	....	....	....
2,499	2,288	.....	....	.....	....	....	183,961
171	....	.....	....	.....	....	....	1,371
59,235	8,500	17,732	7,059	.....	....	....	565,555
837	....	.....	....	.....	....	....	2,465
165,158	80,000	34,000	46,751	.....	....	....	992,151
....	....	.....	1,194	.....	....	....	7,464
201,908	111,732	90,349	106,950	.....	....	....	1,313,027
....	....	.....	3,000	.....	....	....	7,924
238,244	139,550	135,037	140,083	.....	....	....	1,548,938
2,575	....	.....	945	.....	....	....	9,709
244,226	201,932	144,624	221,645	.....	....	....	1,739,968
2,758	352,225	260,294	3,151	.....	....	....	681,795
264,565	246,117	158,469	340,450	.....	....	7,000	1,997,501
373,261	432,271	473,570	474,660	.....	....	....	2,993,728
323,441	346,673	281,624	330,345	.....	....	230,000	2,821,331
397,898	489,770	619,460	666,112	.....	5,017	....	4,500,660
386,494	434,816	393,985	326,620	.....	2,000	566,977	3,613,174
404,775	609,102	648,988	668,832	95,300	7,500	267,273	5,353,718
390,759	358,871	504,989	339,508	3,100	2,100	978,942	4,173,339
292,007	612,517	1,021,727	860,041	91,000	8,527	975,572	6,317,958
403,622	197,570	521,767	335,615	43,269	1,520	609,844	3,295,876
301,227	233,602	1,074,595	788,808	92,000	6,115	303,499	5,005,618
120,401	108,519	38,601	231,387	56,047	5,025	206,809	1,086,905
2,413	2,032	7,225	4,950	2,119	7,621	8,429	103,838
57,980	40,560	59,960	....	61,089	3,650	213,919	743,453
2,337	2,417	10,040	....	1,671	6,325	14,023	62,050
74,336	53,602	63,361	....	31,756	19,587	218,455	832,380
1,943	2,249	11,639	....	1,745	6,184	14,112	63,509
76,421	40,902	86,668	....	44,267	19,887	234,701	919,217
2,113	1,728	9,518	....	3,433	5,856	16,734	63,780
92,958	79,554	114,777	....	46,396	21,466	239,116	1,036,428
2,243	4,533	10,023	....	3,174	5,900	16,000	67,146
122,208	113,060	177,853	13,920	69,506	23,170	298,504	1,442,155
2,427	3,297	9,986	....	3,077	6,450	17,872	78,005
164,088	125,709	236,061	139,825	118,105	23,671	402,488	2,033,492
2,512	4,176	27,808	15,740	6,758	6,206	15,800	121,358
199,806	150,982	291,506	172,585	132,254	23,610	494,842	2,484,025
4,297	4,165	28,635	23,855	13,952	6,354	15,881	139,027
255,001	153,472	370,040	175,890	92,575	32,904	508,317	2,767,598
4,370	4,308	30,506	24,275	9,956	7,969	17,194	142,227

Table 165† **Detail of Arrivals by Steamers—**

Arrival No.	Steamer or Source	Port of Sailing	Date of Arrival	Port of Arrival	Contents of Cargoes in Net				
					Flour	Rice	Beans, Peas	Corn Grits	Pork Products
			1919						
1	Lother Bohlen, Ex-C.R.B. . .	(U.S.A.)	Aug. . .	Antwerp	.....	.....	....	....	**219.3**
2	Lita, I	London	Nov. 15	Danzig	.....	.....	....	....	.....
3	Modesta, Ex-Comité National	Rotterdam	Nov. 15	Hamburg	.....	.....	....	....	283.7
4	Reval, I	London	Nov. 18	Danzig	.....	.....	....	....	.....
5	St. Croix, I	London	Nov. 19	Danzig	.....	.....	....	....	.....
6	Akershus, I	London	Nov. 24	Danzig	.....	.....	....	....	.....
7	Leda, I	London	Nov. 30	Danzig	.....	.....	....	....	.....
8	E. H. Stinnes, Ex-Comité National	Rotterdam	Nov. 30	Danzig	.....	.....	....	....	285.2
9	Batavier 3, I	London	Nov. 30	Rotterdam	.....	.....	....	....	.....
	Total for November . . .	....	....	....	.....	.....	....	....	**568.9**
10	Batavier 6, I	London	Dec. 4	Rotterdam	.....	.....	....	....	.....
11	Commercial, Ex-Comité National	Rotterdam	Dec. 4	Danzig	.....	.....	1,166.1	....	247.3
12	National, Ex-Comité National	Rotterdam	Dec. 5	Danzig	.....	.....	233.9	....	243.4
13	Keresan, I	New York	Dec. 6	Hamburg	.....	.....	....	....	.....
14	Gustav Salling, Ex-Comité National	Rotterdam	Dec. 6	Hamburg	.....	.....	400.0	....	284.7
15	Batavier 3, II	London	Dec. 7	Rotterdam	.....	.....	....	....	.....
16	Ozaukee, I	New York	Dec. 8	Danzig	.....	.....	....	....	.....
17	Noordam	New York	Dec. 9	Rotterdam	.....	.....	....	....	.....
18	Nieuw Amsterdam	New York	Dec. 9	Rotterdam	.....	.....	....	....	.....
19	Batavier 4, I	London	Dec. 9	Rotterdam	.....	.....	....	....	.....
20	St. Croix, II	London	Dec. 10	Danzig	.....	.....	....	....	.....
21	Batavier 6, II	London	Dec. 11	Rotterdam	.....	.....	....	....	....
22	Rotterdam	New York	Dec. 13	Rotterdam	.....	.....	....	....	....
23	Batavier 3, III	London	Dec. 14	Rotterdam	.....	.....	....	....	....
24	Juno, I	Hull	Dec. 15	Hamburg	.....	.....	....	....	....
25	Batavier 6, III	London	Dec. 18	Rotterdam	.....	.....	....	....	....
26	Reval, II	London	Dec. 19	Libau	.....	.....	....	....	....
27	Asam 19, Ex-Comité National	Antwerp	Dec. 20	Mannheim	200.0	.....	....	....	68.
28	Batavier 3, IV	London	Dec. 21	Rotterdam	.....	.....	....	....	....
29	Continental Purchase	Antwerp	Dec. 22	Mannheim	.....	.....	....	....	....
30	Bonn, I, Ex-Comité National	Antwerp	Dec. 22	Hamburg	1,018.4	.....	....	....	....
31	Jolly Kate	London	Dec. 24	Danzig	.....	.....	....	....	....
32	Batavier 6, IV	London	Dec. 25	Rotterdam	.....	.....	....	....	....
33	Asam 12, Ex-Comité National	Antwerp	Dec. 27	Mannheim	192.0	.....	....	....	....
34	Julia Luckenbach	New York	Dec. 28	Rotterdam	.....	.....	....	....	....
35	Continental Purchase	Antwerp	Dec. 29	Rotterdam	.....	.....	....	....	....
36	Morlais	(United Kingdom)	Dec. 29	Hamburg	.....	.....	....	200.1	....
37	Barmen, Ex-Comité National	Antwerp	Dec. 31	Danzig	1,994.1	.....	....	....	....
38	Admiral, Ex-Comité National	Rotterdam	Dec. 31	Danzig	.....	.....	....	....	427.
	Total for December . . .	....	....	....	**3,404.5**	.....	**1,800.0**	**200.1**	**1,271.**
			1920						
39	Batavier 6, V	London	Jan. 1	Rotterdam	.....	.....	....	....	....
40	Koningen Den Netherlanden	New York	Jan. 2	Rotterdam	.....	.....	369.4	....	....
41	Kosciuszko	Philadelphia	Jan. 3	Danzig	.....	.....	....	....	....
42	Batavier 3, V	London	Jan. 4	Rotterdam	.....	.....	....	....	....
43	Hero, I	Hull	Jan. 5	Hamburg	.....	.....	....	....	....
44	Continental Purchase	Antwerp	Jan. 5	Mannheim	.....	.....	....	....	....
45	Maine	New York	Jan. 6	Rotterdam	.....	.....	....	....	....
46	Bonn, II, Ex-Comité National	Antwerp	Jan. 7	Hamburg	.....	.....	176.4	....	....

† This table includes relief supplies for child feeding, N.E.R., and balance of A.R.A. Warehouses and A.F.S.C. deliveries.

* Detail of miscellaneous food indicated by the following indexes: [a], whalemeat; [b], soup; [c], codliver oil; [d], chocolate; [e], herring; [g], salmon; [h], dried fruit; [i], fish; [k], dehydrated potatoes; [l], powdered and dri[ed] milk; [m], salt; [n], biscuits; [o], dates; [p], tea; [q], rice and milk; and [r], corne[d] beef; [s], groceries. See end of Table 165 (page 374) for complete detail.

CHILDREN'S FUND

Reconstruction Period, 1919–1924

Metric Tons of 1,000 Kilograms or 2,204.6 Pounds											
Milk	Cocoa	Sugar	Misc. Food *	Soap	Clothing and Misc.	Total Tons	F.O.B. Value	Freight	Insurance	Miscellaneous Charges	Total C.I.F. Value
....	....	....	**9.4**[c]	....	....	**228.7**	**$ 151,917.68**	......	......	....	**$ 151,917.68**
....	....	....	....	....	83.0	83.0	$ 324,976.42	......	......	....	$ 324,976.42
....	....	....	....	....	....	283.7	116,165.41	......	......	....	116,165.41
....	....	....	....	....	25.0	25.0	105,074.78	......	......	....	105,074.78
....	....	....	....	....	10.0	10.0	44,072.95	......	......	....	44,072.95
....	....	....	....	....	59.0	59.0	198,613.06	......	......	....	198,613.06
....	....	....	....	....	33.0	33.0	121,858.69	......	......	....	121,858.69
....	....	....	....	....	....	285.2	112,130.00	$ 6,431.05	$ 1,024.01	....	119,585.06
....	....	....	....	....	1.0	1.0	814.87	......	......	....	814.87
....	....	....	....	....	**211.0**	**779.9**	**$ 1,023,706.18**	**$ 6,431.05**	**$ 1,024.01**	....	**$ 1,031,161.24**
....	....	....	....	....	3.0	3.0	$ 8,747.81	......	......	....	$ 8,747.81
....	....	....	....	....	....	1,413.4	183,516.84	$ 20,053.90	$ 2,695.21	....	206,265.95
....	....	....	....	....	....	477.3	112,986.66	5,926.58	1,030.53	....	119,943.77
381.0	....	....	....	....	....	381.0	162,355.64	15,796.65	1,271.95	....	179,424.24
....	....	....	....	....	....	684.7	151,537.86	......	......	....	151,537.86
....	....	....	....	....	8.0	8.0	24,665.17	......	......	....	24,665.17
....	....	....	....	....	354.5	354.5	787,024.11	39,951.27	5,734.23	....	832,709.61
238.1	....	....	....	....	....	238.1	100,092.96	8,740.90	515.39	....	109,349.25
29.1	....	....	....	....	....	29.1	12,432.78	1,032.75	62.95	....	13,528.48
....	....	....	....	....	9.0	9.0	34,054.63	......	......	....	34,054.63
....	....	....	....	....	17.0	17.0	95,059.26	......	......	....	95,059.26
....	....	....	....	....	22.0	22.0	95,233.51	......	......	....	95,233.51
313.8	....	....	....	....	....	313.8	132,729.23	11,472.75	679.25	....	144,881.23
....	....	....	....	....	15.0	15.0	52,762.86	......	......	....	52,762.86
....	....	....	....	....	55.8	55.8	124,464.33	......	......	....	124,464.33
....	....	....	....	....	32.0	32.0	118,237.42	......	......	....	118,237.42
....	....	....	....	....	17.0	17.0	58,859.31	......	......	....	58,859.31
....	....	....	....	....	....	268.1	45,608.03	......	......	....	45,608.03
....	....	....	....	....	12.0	12.0	44,611.15	......	......	....	44,611.15
....	....	....	....	....	0.6	.6	5,671.50	......	......	....	5,671.50
....	44.4	....	....	....	....	1,062.8	115,754.68	......	......	....	115,754.68
....	....	....	....	....	80.0	80.0	285,618.02	......	......	....	285,618.02
....	....	....	....	....	6.1	6.1	25,540.89	......	......	....	25,540.89
....	....	....	....	....	....	192.0	17,764.00	......	......	....	17,764.00
....	....	....	....	....	47.0	47.0	114,203.96	3,756.61	1,462.50	$ 1.50	119,423.97
....	....	....	....	....	1.0	1.0	5,551.80	......	......	....	5,551.80
....	....	....	....	....	....	200.1	17,928.41	1,463.50	111.90	....	19,503.81
....	....	....	....	....	....	1,994.1	173,606.32	15,017.75	2,067.42	....	190,691.49
....	....	....	....	....	....	427.8	168,184.51	7,063.66	1,030.19	....	176,278.36
962.0	**44.4**	....	....	....	**680.0**	**8,362.3**	**$ 3,274,803.65**	**$ 130,275.72**	**$ 16,661.52**	**$ 1.50**	**$ 3,421,742.39**
....	....	....	....	....	7.1	7.1	$ 27,044.56	......	......	....	$ 27,044.56
....	41.0	....	....	....	....	410.4	76,804.86	$ 9,348.93	$ 1,029.37	$ 75.00	87,258.16
....	....	....	....	....	105.0	105.0	214,403.09	14,007.15	1,645.00	132.08	230,187.32
....	....	....	....	....	.4	.4	839.16	......	......	....	839.16
....	....	....	....	....	62.4	62.4	149,935.25	......	......	....	149,935.25
....	....	....	....	....	.6	.6	6,050.55	......	......	....	6,050.55
....	....	....	....	....	29.5	29.5	57,301.65	2,462.20	708.75	....	60,472.60
....	....	....	....	....	....	176.4	14,973.07	......	......	....	14,973.07

[*Continued on next page*]

Table 165—*Continued*

Detail of Arrival

Arrival No.	Steamer or Source	Port of Sailing	Date of Arrival	Port of Arrival	Contents of Cargoes in N				
					Flour	Rice	Beans, Peas	Corn Grits	Pork Product
			1920						
47	Carib, I	New York	Jan. 7	Hamburg	.....	.....	....	....	...
48	Batavier 6, VI	London	Jan. 8	Rotterdam	.....	.....	....	....	...
49	Suffolk	New York	Jan. 9	Rotterdam	2,900.6	.....	998.9	....	...
50	St. Croix, III	London	Jan. 10	Danzig	.....	.....	....	....	...
51	Kajak	London	Jan. 10	Reval	.....	.....	....	....	...
52	Kerkenna	New York	Jan. 11	Hamburg	.....	.....	....	....	...
53	Continental Purchase	Antwerp	Jan. 13	Mannheim	.....	.....	....	....	...
54	Bonn, III, Ex-Comité National	Antwerp	Jan. 13	Danzig	1,985.7	.....	....	....	...
55	Amsteldijk	New Orleans	Jan. 13	Rotterdam	.....	558.7	....	....	...
56	Bellingham	New York	Jan. 13	Rotterdam	.....	.....	....	....	...
57	Edward Luckenbach	New York	Jan. 14	Rotterdam	.....	.....	....	....	...
58	St. Thomas, I	London Danzig	Jan. 16 Jan. 19	Danzig Riga	.....	250.1	....	....	...
59	Jolly George, I	London	Jan. 17	Danzig	.....	250.1	....	....	...
60	Desdemonia, I	(United Kingdom)	Jan. 19	Hamburg	.....	150.0	....	....	...
61	River Orontes	Boston	Jan. 19	Salonica	.....	.....	....	....	...
62	Continental Purchase	Antwerp	Jan. 20	Rotterdam	.....	.....	....	....	...
63	Akershus, II	London	Jan. 20	Danzig	.....	.....	....	....	...
64	Batavier 4, II	London	Jan. 25	Rotterdam	.....	.....	....	....	...
65	Pollux	London	Jan. 25	Helsingfors	.....	.....	....	....	...
66	Continental Purchase	Antwerp	Jan. 26	Mannheim	.....	.....	....	....	...
67	Angelica Maersk	Liverpool	Jan. 26	Danzig	.....	.....	....	....	...
68	Rail, Ex-Comité National	Antwerp	Jan. 27	Mannheim	.....	.....	....	....	100.
69	Vesta	London	Jan. 27	Helsingfors	.....	.....	....	....	...
70	Leda, II	London	Jan. 28	Helsingfors	.....	.....	....	....	...
71	Asam 14, Ex-Comité National	Antwerp	Jan. 29	Mannheim	.....	.....	200.0	....	...
72	Batavier 6, III	London	Jan. 29	Rotterdam	.....	.....	....	....	...
73	Risquons Tout, Ex-Comité National	Antwerp	Jan. 31	Hamburg	200.1	.....	....	....	...
	Total for January				**5,086.4**	**1,208.9**	**1,744.7**	....	**100**
74	F. J. Luckenbach	New York	Feb. 1	Rotterdam	.....	.....	....	....	...
75	Hero, II	Hull	Feb. 2	Hamburg	.....	.....	....	....	...
76	Continental Purchase	Antwerp	Feb. 2	Mannheim	.....	.....	....	....	...
77	Continental Purchase (Schenker & Co.)	Antwerp	Feb. 2	Hamburg	.....	.....	....	....	...
78	Capella, I	London	Feb. 5	Helsingfors	.....	.....	....	....	...
79	Reval, III	London	Feb. 6	Libau	.....	.....	....	....	...
80	Desdemonia, II	(United Kingdom)	Feb. 8	Hamburg	.....	150.0	....	....	...
81	Batavier 4, III	London	Feb. 8	Rotterdam	.....	.....	....	....	...
82	Continental Purchase (Schenker & Co.)	Antwerp	Feb. 9	Hamburg	.....	.....	....	....	...
83	Shortsville	New York	Feb. 9	Danzig	.....	.....	....	....	...
84	Bavaria, II, Ex-Comité National	Antwerp	Feb. 9	Libau	686.1	.....	....	....	...
85	Romeo	New York	Feb. 10	Salonica	.....	.....	....	....	...
86	Steywell 9, Ex-Comité National	Antwerp	Feb. 13	Mannheim	.....	.....	97.6	....	...
87	Local Purchase, Poland	(Warsaw)	Feb. 14	(Warsaw)	.....	.....	....	....	...
88	Wisla	New York	Feb. 16	Danzig	.....	.....	....	....	...
89	Agnes, I, Ex-Bridges & Co. Purchase	Hamburg	Feb. 16	Danzig	.....	.....	....	....	...
90	Continental Purchase (Schenker & Co.)	Antwerp	Feb. 16	Hamburg	.....	.....	....	....	...
91	Jolly George, II	London	Feb. 16	Danzig	.....	.....	....	....	...
92	Indianola	London	Feb. 17	Salonica	.....	.....	....	....	...
93	Bridges & Co. Purchase	Antwerp	Feb. 18	Rotterdam	.....	.....	....	....	...
94	St. Thomas, II, Purchase from Frazier & Co.	London Danzig	Feb. 19 Feb. 29	Danzig Riga	.....	76.0	54.6	....	...
95	Chincha	New York	Feb. 21	Batoum	.....	.....	....	....	...
96	Manchuria, I	New York	Feb. 26	Hamburg	.....	.....	....	....	...
97	Local Purchase, Poland	(Warsaw)	Feb. 27	(Warsaw)	.....	.....	....	....	...
98	Keresan, II	New York	Feb. 27	Hamburg	.....	.....	....	....	...
99	Hero, III	London	Feb. 29	Hamburg	.....	.....	....	....	...

CHILDREN'S FUND

by Steamers

Milk	Cocoa	Sugar	Misc. Food	Soap	Clothing and Misc.	Total Tons	F.O.B. Value	Freight	Insurance	Miscellaneous Charges	Total C.I.F. Value
Metric Tons of 1,000 Kilograms or 2,204.6 Pounds											
.....	....	....	....	....	49.1	**49.1**	$ 108,110.14	$ 3,921.11	$ 1,711.88	$ .75	$ 113,743.88
.....	....	....	....	....	1.3	1.3	6,704.46	......	......	....	6,704.46
.....	....	....	....	....	....	3,899.5	490,661.21	87,310.63	6,784.88	16,244.91	601,001.63
.....	....	....	....	....	9.0	9.0	33,889.58	......	......	....	33,889.58
.....	....	....	....	....	47.0	47.0	186,323.21	......	......	....	186,323.21
.....	....	....	....	....	22.6	22.6	56,983.16	2,107.29	825.00	....	59,915.45
.....	....	....	....	....	.8	0.8	8,122.50	......	......	....	8,122.50
.....	....	....	....	....	....	1,985.7	178,024.07	16,020.17	1,729.35	....	195,773.59
.....	....	....	....	....	....	558.7	146,717.96	17,476.70	2,150.00	61.64	166,406.30
.....	....	....	....	....	16.0	16.0	28,444.26	1,309.95	353.25	....	30,107.46
.....	....	....	....	....	24.5	24.5	97,034.29	5,047.55	1,222.82	4.00	103,308.66
.....	....	....	....	....	16.0	266.1	98,425.44	......	......	....	98,425.44
.....	....	....	....	....	94.0	344.1	486,933.39	......	......	....	486,933.39
.....	....	....	....	....	....	150.0	13,450.03	1,416.53	59.38	....	14,925.94
.....	....	....	....	....	39.0	39.0	94,000.28	5,861.48	801.32	.75	100,663.83
.....	....	....	....	....	1.6	1.6	8,140.06	......	......	....	8,140.06
.....	....	....	....	....	74.0	74.0	287,184.17	......	......	....	287,184.17
.....	....	....	....	....	1.4	1.4	3,710.35	......	......	....	3,710.35
.....	....	....	....	....	11.0	11.0	32,180.23	......	......	....	32,180.23
.....	....	....	....	....	10.0	10.0	7,193.86	......	......	....	7,193.86
.....	....	....	....	....	.7	.7	1,259.36	......	......	....	1,259.36
.....	....	....	....	....	....	100.3	39,938.49	......	......	....	39,938.49
.....	....	....	....	....	5.0	5.0	19,009.02	......	......	....	19,009.02
.....	....	....	....	....	1.0	1.0	3,934.51	......	......	....	3,934.51
.....	....	....	....	....	....	200.0	15,704.33	......	......	....	15,704.33
.....	....	....	....	....	2.4	2.4	8,121.66	......	......	....	8,121.66
.....	....	....	....	....	....	200.1	18,511.56	......	......	....	18,511.56
.....	**41.0**	**....**	**....**	**....**	**631.4**	**8,812.7**	**$ 3,026,063.77**	**$ 166,289.69**	**$ 19,021.00**	**$ 16,519.13**	**$ 3,227,893.59**
.....	....	....	....	....	2.0	2.0	$ 1,749.60	$ 66.88	$ 16.10	$ 31.57	$ 1,864.15
.....	....	....	....	....	13.8	13.8	39,746.31	......	......	....	39,746.31
.....	....	....	....	....	1.3	1.3	5,131.81	......	......	....	5,131.81
.....	....	....	....	....	1.0	1.0	2.512.36	......	......	....	2,512.36
.....	....	....	....	....	5.0	5.0	21,834.95	......	......	....	21,834.95
.....	....	....	....	....	2.0	2.0	10,241.02	......	......	....	10,241.02
.....	....	....	....	....	....	150.0	13,450.03	1,416.54	59.37	....	14,925.94
.....	....	....	....	....	1.1	1.1	2,030.22	......	......	....	2,030.22
.....	....	....	....	....	2.2	2.2	10,201.03	......	......	....	10,201.03
.....	....	....	....	....	99.7	99.7	228,652.58	14,068.78	3,500.40	532.18	246,753.94
.....	....	....	....	....	....	686.1	74,443.63	......	......	....	74,443.63
.....	....	....	....	....	78.0	78.0	194,292.50	10,496.26	2,343.75	.75	207,133.26
.....	32.0	....	....	....	....	129.6	18,436.23	157.81	109.40	....	18,703.44
.....	....	....	....	....	.0	.0	144.26	......	......	....	144.26
158.7	....	....	....	....	36.0	194.7	109,054.07	12,625.07	1,837.50	875.71	124,392.35
380.1	....	....	....	....	....	380.1	189,675.66	......	......	....	189,675.66
.....	....	....	....	....	1.0	1.0	4,607.80	......	......	....	4,607.80
.....	....	....	....	....	78.0	78.0	298,100.88	......	......	....	298,100.88
.....	....	....	....	....	4.0	4.0	21,647.60	......	......	....	21,647.60
302.8	....	....	....	....	....	302.8	145,130.44	......	......	....	145,130.44
.....	....	....	....	....	1.9	132.5	23,718.74	......	......	....	23,718.74
.....	....	....	1.9[s]	....	75.1	77.0	57,203.00	......	......	3,080.00	60,283.00
.....	....	227.5	....	....	....	227.5	52,876.80	5,000.00	707.00	....	58,583.80
.....	....	....	....	....	.0	.0	165.65	......	......	....	165.65
183.9	....	....	....	....	....	183.9	51,936.75	5,489.25	675.00	8.00	58,109.00
.....	....	....	....	....	2.5	2.5	8,381.64	......	......	....	8,381.64

[*Continued on next page*]

Table 165—*Continued*

Detail of Arrivals

Arrival No.	Steamer or Source	Port of Sailing	Date of Arrival	Port of Arrival	Contents of Cargoes in Ne				
					Flour	Rice	Beans, Peas	Corn Grits	Pork Products
			1920						
100	Elizabeth, Ex-Comité National	Antwerp	Feb. 29	Mannheim	515.5	.....	104.1	....	....
101	Purchase from Foekel & Werner	Hamburg	Feb. 29	Hamburg	.....	.....	....	....	....
	Total for February	....	....	....	**1,201.6**	**226.0**	**256.3**	....	....
102	Clauseus, I	San Francisco	Mar. 2	Hamburg	.....	.....	500.0	....	....
103	Local Purchase, Poland	(Warsaw)	Mar. 2	(Warsaw)	.....	.....	....	....	....
104	Krakow	New York	Mar. 3	Danzig	.....	.....	....	....	....
105	Reval, IV, Purchase from Frazier & Co.	London	Mar. 6	Libau	.....	.....	25.8	....	....
106	Severn, Purchase from Frazier & Co.	Brazil	Mar. 7	Hamburg	.....	324.7	....	....	....
107	Mar Caspio, I	New York	Mar. 7	Hamburg	.....	.....	....	....	51.
108	Neptune, I	London	Mar. 8	Danzig	.....	.....	....	....	....
109	Clauseus, I	San Francisco	Mar. 9	Danzig	.....	.....	3,474.0	....	....
110	Aleppo	New York	Mar. 14	Salonica	.....	.....	....	....	....
111	Vardulia	New York	Mar. 15	Danzig	.....	868.6	....	....	....
112	Echo, I	Antwerp	Mar. 15	Danzig	.....	400.0	....	....	....
113	Willdomino	New York	Mar. 20	Danzig	.....	1,706.0	2,045.0	....	346.
114	Carib, II	New York	Mar. 26	Hamburg	.....	.....	....	....	....
115	Capella, II	London	Mar. 26	Helsingfors	.....	.....	....	....	....
116	Local Purchase, Vienna	(Vienna)	Mar. 30	(Vienna)	.....	.....	....	....	....
117	Local Purchase, Ex-Polish Government	(Poland)	Mar. 31	(Poland)	.....	.....	....	....	....
118	Englebert Purchase	Antwerp	Mar. 31	Rotterdam	.....	301.3	....	....	....
	Total for March	....	....	....	.....	**3,600.6**	**6,044.8**	....	**397.**
119	Kermanshah	New York	Apr. 3	Hamburg	.....	.....	....	....	....
120	Lake Freeborn	New York	Apr. 3	Poti	.....	.....	....	....	....
121	Neptune, II	London	Apr. 4	Danzig	.....	.....	....	....	....
122	Valacia	New York	Apr. 5	Danzig	.....	164.0	....	....	203.
123	Vasconia	New York	Apr. 5	Danzig	.....	.....	....	....	....
124	Manchuria, II	New York	Apr. 8	Hamburg	.....	.....	....	....	186.
125	Kermoor, II	New York	Apr. 11	Hamburg	.....	.....	....	....	....
126	Purchase from Foekel & Werner	Hamburg	Apr. 12	Hamburg	.....	.....	....	....	....
127	Claro	London	Apr. 12	Salonica	.....	.....	....	....	....
128	Jomar	Philadelphia	Apr. 13	Poti	2,031.4	.....	....	....	....
129	Mexico, I	New York	Apr. 14	Danzig	.....	.....	....	....	....
130	Purchase from Pickard & Co.	Antwerp	Apr. 21	Rotterdam	.....	.....	....	....	....
131	Ozaukee, II	New York	Apr. 24	Danzig	.....	.....	....	....	....
132	Walter Luckenbach	New York	Apr. 26	Rotterdam	.....	.....	....	....	....
133	Jessica, Ex-British Ministry of Food	(United Kingdom)	Apr. 26	Hamburg	.....	94.0	....	....	....
	Total for April	....	....	....	**2,031.4**	**258.0**	....	....	**389.**
134	Warszawa, I	London	May 4	Danzig	.....	345.0	....	....	....
135	St. Antoine, Ex-Comité National	Antwerp	May 11	Hamburg	408.0	.....	....	....	87.
136	Purchase from Wilson & Co.	Rotterdam	May 13	Hamburg	.....	.....	....	....	152.
137	Manchuria, III	New York	May 20	Hamburg	.....	.....	....	....	....
138	Purchase from Frazier & Co.	Rotterdam	May 20	Rotterdam	.....	300.0	....	....	....
139	Carib, III	New York	May 23	Hamburg	.....	.....	....	....	18
140	Purchase from Frazier & Co.	Rotterdam	May 24	Rotterdam	.....	90.0	....	....	....
141	Keresan, III	N.Y., Phila.	May 27	Hamburg	.....	.....	104.0	....	....
	Total for May	....	....	....	**408.0**	**735.0**	**104.0**	....	**257**

CHILDREN'S FUND

y Steamers

etric Tons of 1,000 Kilograms or 2,204.6 Pounds							F.O.B. Value	Freight	Insurance	Miscellaneous Charges	Total C.I.F. Value
Milk	Cocoa	Sugar	Misc. Food	Soap	Clothing and Misc.	Total Tons					
.....	40.4	....	....	....	....	660.0	$ 65,972.58	......	......	....	$ 65,972.58
12.0	....	....	....	....	....	12.0	4,247.44	......	......	....	4,247.44
1,037.5	**72.4**	**227.5**	**1.9**	....	**404.6**	**3,427.8**	**$ 1,655,585.58**	**$ 49,320.59**	**$ 9,248.52**	**$ 4,528.21**	**$ 1,718,682.90**
.....	....	....	....	....	....	500.0	$ 102,686.59	......	$ 439.98	....	$ 103,126.57
.....	....	....	....	....	.0	.0	133.86	......	......	....	133.86
37.0	....	....	....	....	10.0	47.0	24,413.83	$ 3,030.88	395.32	$ 168.34	28,008.37
.....	....	....	....	....	.5	26.3	6,402.04	......	......	....	6,402.04
.....	....	....	....	....	....	324.7	88,513.55	......	......	....	88,513.55
109.0	101.6	....	....	....	....	262.0	103,435.57	7,319.33	1,305.00	33.31	112,093.21
.....	....	....	....	....	23.0	23.0	65,065.85	......	......	....	65,065.85
.....	....	....	....	....	....	3,474.0	706,413.19	......	3,079.85	....	709,493.04
.....	....	....	....	....	56.0	56.0	107,921.48	6,642.20	2,134.00	....	116,697.68
1,776.0	51.8	....	....	....	15.0	2,711.4	958,961.14	92,070.03	12,450.87	1,992.34	1,065,474.38
.....	....	....	....	....	....	400.0	105,569.18	3,730.50	111.10	....	109,410.78
430.8	....	454.0	....	....	....	4,981.8	1,232,324.09	178,990.06	19,903.05	4,222.05	1,435,439.25
85.0	....	....	....	....	....	85.0	23,777.67	3,167.94	449.06	....	27,394.67
.....	....	....	....	....	1.0	1.0	3,009.59	......	......	....	3,009.59
.....	....	....	....	....	.5	.5	132.52	......	......	....	132.52
.....	....	1,001.5	....	....	....	1,001.5	250,364.25	......	......	....	250,364.25
.....	....	....	....	....	....	301.3	79,728.33	......	......	....	79,728.33
2,437.8	**153.4**	**1,455.5**	....	....	**106.0**	**14,195.5**	**$ 3,858,852.73**	**$ 294,950.94**	**$ 40,268.23**	**$ 6,416.04**	**$ 4,200,487.94**
100.0	....	....	....	....	....	100.0	$ 28,047.80	$ 3,735.88	$ 451.00	$ 17.78	$ 32,252.46
.....	....	....	....	....	338.9	338.9	24,033.00	......	......	13,566.00	37,599.00
.....	....	....	....	....	27.0	27.0	74,143.52	......	......	....	74,143.52
779.0	151.0	....	....	....	25.0	1,322.0	536,547.97	47,553.43	6,878.22	575.23	591,554.85
230.0	....	....	....	....	....	230.0	73,937.55	8,560.00	975.19	10.00	83,482.74
.....	....	....	....	....	....	186.5	92,245.72	4,150.90	1,136.25	....	97,532.87
244.0	102.0	....	....	....	....	346.0	102,915.95	11,286.99	1,643.13	63.75	115,909.82
232.4	....	....	....	....	....	232.4	82,082.74	......	......	....	82,082.74
.....	....	....	....	....	3.0	3.0	12,636.47	......	......	....	12,636.47
.....	....	....	....	....	....	2,031.4	245,625.99	......	......	81,256.00	326,881.99
86.0	....	....	....	....	12.0	98.0	52,630.69	3,377.04	804.38	35.33	56,847.44
306.2	....	....	....	....	....	306.2	113,508.89	......	......	....	113,508.89
.....	....	....	....	....	(.02)	.0	65.55	7.50	1.50	1.37	75.92
.....	....	....	....	....	1.0	1.0	47.50	10.00	.44	2.25	60.19
.....	....	....	....	....	.1	94.1	16,698.31	3,656.13	204.85	....	20,559.29
1,977.6	**253.0**	....	....	....	**407.0**	**5,316.5**	**$ 1,455,167.65**	**$ 82,337.87**	**$ 12,094.96**	**$ 95,527.71**	**$ 1,645,128.19**
.....	....	....	....	....	....	345.0	$ 61,245.79	$ 4,719.09	$ 280.60	....	$ 66,245.48
.....	....	....	....	....	....	495.1	71,970.35	405.12	43.16	....	72,418.63
.....	....	....	....	....	....	152.1	83,796.84	......	......	....	83,796.84
.....	....	....	29.6[b]	....	....	29.6	4,200.00	571.20	56.25	$ 450.55	5,278.00
.....	....	....	....	....	....	300.0	79,592.59	......	......	....	79,592.59
.....	....	....	....	....	....	18.3	9,005.02	413.89	136.13	....	9,555.04
.....	....	....	....	....	....	90.0	23,478.64	......	......	....	23,478.64
.....	....	....	....	....	....	104.0	14,788.43	2,439.11	202.50	530.94	17,960.98
.....	....	....	**29.6**	....	....	**1,534.1**	**$ 348,077.66**	**$ 8,548.41**	**$ 718.64**	**$ 981.49**	**$ 358,326.20**

[*Continued on next page*]

Table 165—*Continued*

Detail of Arrivals

Arrival No.	Steamer or Source	Port of Sailing	Date of Arrival	Port of Arrival	Contents of Cargoes in Ne				
					Flour	Rice	Beans, Peas	Corn Grits	Pork Products
			1920						
142	Mongolia, III	New York	June 3	Hamburg	....	....	....	....	....
143	Kermit, I	New York	June 5	Hamburg	....	....	63.0	....	45.
144	Corson, I	New York	June 10	Danzig	....	....	776.0	....	88.
145	Kerlew, II	Norfolk	June 24	Hamburg	....	....	178.9	....	....
146	Bird City	New York	June 26	Danzig	....	....	....	....	....
	Total for June	....	....	....	....	....	**1,017.9**	....	**133.**
147	Mar Blanco, I	New York	July 2	Hamburg	....	....	35.0	....	....
148	Kermoor, III	New York	July 3	Hamburg	....	....	294.0	....	....
149	Monticello, I	New York	July 9	Hamburg	....	....	....	....	....
150	Poznan, I	New York	July 13	Danzig	....	....	....	....	....
151	Mar Caspio, II	New York	July 16	Hamburg	....	....	....	....	175.
152	Charlot	Philadelphia	July 21	Hamburg	....	....	....	....	....
153	Mar Mediterraneo, II	New York	July 22	Hamburg	....	....	....	....	372.
154	Wheeling Mold	New York	July 22	Danzig	....	....	....	....	....
155	Verbania, I	New York Hamburg	July 26 Aug. 1	Hamburg Danzig	....	....	....	....	17.
156	Purchase from Paul Stuppel	Hamburg	July 27	Hamburg	....	....	406.0	....	....
157	Purchase from Frazier & Co.	Rotterdam	July 27	Rotterdam	....	....	575.0	....	....
158	Belgic	New York	July 27	Hamburg	....	....	....	....	50.
	Total for July	....	....	....	....	....	**1,310.0**	....	**616.**
159	Purchase from Rosenberg	Hamburg	Aug. 9	Hamburg	....	....	506.0	....	....
160	Herefordshire	Rangoon	Aug. 18	Hamburg	....	1,880.0	....	....	....
161	Kermit, II	New York	Aug. 21	Hamburg	....	....	....	....	....
162	Mette Jensen, I	New York	Aug. 22	Hamburg	....	....	....	....	16.
163	Susquehanna, I	New York	Aug. 23	Danzig	....	....	....	....	....
164	Mar Blanco, II	New York	Aug. 24	Hamburg	....	....	....	....	193.
165	Monticello, II	New York	Aug. 28	Hamburg	....	....	....	....	....
166	Warszawa, III	Philadelphia	Aug. 30	Danzig	....	....	70.0	....	89.
	Total for August	....	....	....	....	**1,880.0**	**576.0**	....	**298**
167	Mar Caribe, I	New York	Sept. 4	Hamburg	....	....	....	....	...
168	Germar, I	London	Sept. 16	Hamburg	....	....	....	....	...
169	Mar Rojo	New York	Sept. 16	Hamburg	....	....	....	....	...
170	Corson, II	Philadelphia	Sept. 19	Hamburg	....	....	61.0	....	...
171	Mar Cantabrico	New York	Sept. 22	Hamburg	....	....	....	....	...
172	Gerrat, II	London	Sept. 22	Hamburg	....	....	....	....	...
173	Maja, I	Copenhagen	Sept. 29	Hamburg	....	....	....	....	...
174	Akershus, III	London	Sept. 29	Danzig	....	....	....	....	...
	Total for September	....	....	....	....	....	**61.0**	....	...
175	Vittorio Emmanuelle, III	New York	Oct. 1	Hamburg	....	....	....	....	...
176	Kerlew, III	New York	Oct. 6	Hamburg	....	....	....	....	...
177	Minnekahda	New York	Oct. 6	London	....	....	....	....	...
178	Hansa, I	London	Oct. 6	Danzig	....	....	....	....	...
179	Agnes, II	Copenhagen	Oct. 10	Hamburg	....	....	....	....	...
180	Maja, II	Copenhagen	Oct. 10	Hamburg	....	....	....	....	...
181	Susquehanna, II	New York	Oct. 13	Danzig	....	....	....	....	...
182	Schoharie, I	New York	Oct. 13	Hamburg	....	....	....	....	...
183	Hermodia	London	Oct. 18	Danzig	....	....	....	....	...
184	Polar Bear	New York	Oct. 19	Batoum	....	....	....	....	...
185	Mette Jensen, II	New York	Oct. 20	Hamburg	....	....	....	....	...
186	Satartia	New York	Oct. 22	Hamburg	....	....	....	....	...
187	Stonehenge	London	Oct. 24	Hamburg	....	....	....	....	...
188	Mystic, I	New York	Oct. 26	Hamburg	....	....	....	....	...
189	Hulda Maersk	London	Oct. 28	Danzig	....	....	....	....	...
	Total for October	....	....	....	....	....	....	....	...

:HILDREN'S FUND

y Steamers

etric Tons of 1,000 Kilograms or 2,204.6 Pounds											
Milk	Cocoa	Sugar	Misc. Food	Soap	Clothing and Misc.	Total Tons	F.O.B. Value	Freight	Insurance	Miscellaneous Charges	Total C.I.F. Value
108.4	....	....	....	....	....	108.4	$ 31,597.60	$ 2,749.79	$ 405.00	$ 1,722.20	$ 36,474.59
122.0	....	....	....	....	....	230.0	65,014.35	6,528.08	937.50	8.50	72,488.43
815.0	....	....	....	....	3.0	1,682.0	365,246.04	44,399.45	4,829.63	3,582.70	418,057.82
75.7	....	....	....	....	....	254.6	50,138.62	6,492.52	669.38	50.08	57,350.60
.....	....	....	....	....	4.0	4.0	8,838.32	310.95	112.50	143.62	9,405.39
1,121.1	....	....	....	....	**7.0**	**2,279.0**	**$ 520,834.93**	**$ 60,480.79**	**$ 6,954.01**	**$ 5,507.10**	**$ 593,776.83**
238.3	127.0	....	1.0[a]	....	.0	401.3	$ 120,585.24	$ 11,674.42	$ 1,560.16	$ 64.18	$ 133,884.00
105.0	....	....	....	....	....	399.0	63,266.97	10,135.27	977.86	34.00	74,414.10
50.0	15.1	....	....	....	....	65.1	24,618.47	1,863.01	323.09	....	26,804.57
.....	152.0	....	....	....	28.0	180.0	61,960.00	4,532.22	778.58	2,695.87	69,966.67
140.0	....	....	....	....	....	315.5	135,479.59	9,282.33	1,709.45	7.93	146,479.30
9.9	....	....	....	....	....	9.9	5,102.20	294.56	64.13	16.00	5,476.89
121.5	152.0	....	....	....	....	646.4	272,814.14	20,025.84	3,634.45	157.00	296,631.43
.....	....	....	....	....	4.0	4.0	6,630.97	259.60	84.38	52.64	7,027.59
156.3	....	....	....	....	1.0	174.3	90,067.30	5,278.23	1,156.99	19.17	96,521.69
.....	....	....	....	....	....	406.0	35,839.12	......	......	....	35,839.12
.....	....	....	....	....	....	575.0	57,579.88	......	......	....	57,579.88
.....	....	....	....	....	....	50.9	24,119.35	1,319.14	300.37	239.87	25,978.73
821.0	**446.1**	....	**1.0**	....	**33.0**	**3,227.4**	**$ 898,063.23**	**$ 64,664.62**	**$ 10,589.46**	**$ 3,286.66**	**$ 976,603.97**
.....	....	....	....	....	....	506.0	$ 40,946.24	......	......	....	$ 40,946.24
.....	....	....	....	....	....	1,880.0	246,893.76	......	......	....	246,893.76
429.0	....	....	....	....	....	429.0	223,534.16	$ 13,249.44	$ 2,849.07	$ 36.19	239,668.86
316.3	....	....	8.4[b]	....	....	341.4	162,575.86	10,308.76	2,149.41	106.26	175,140.29
.....	....	....	....	....	16.8	16.8	20,516.46	1,291.54	309.23	652.60	22,769.83
97.6	....	....	....	....	9.5	300.2	141,028.37	9,392.12	1,928.05	11.33	152,359.87
144.5	....	....	....	....	....	144.5	68,728.50	4,981.72	1,131.58	30.78	74,872.58
.....	....	....	....	....	....	159.0	50,607.23	4,081.51	711.88	58.16	55,458.78
987.4	....	....	**8.4**	....	**26.3**	**3,776.9**	**$ 954,830.58**	**$ 43,305.09**	**$ 9,079.22**	**$ 895.32**	**$ 1,008,110.21**
148.0	....	....	....	....	....	148.0	$ 75,312.50	$ 4,340.00	$ 939.38	....	$ 80,591.88
.....	....	....	....	....	6.2	6.2	18,105.00	82.04	71.14	....	18,258.18
243.3	....	....	....	....	....	243.3	103,004.50	8,109.06	1,307.26	$ 6.72	112,427.54
.....	....	....	....	....	....	61.0	7,262.63	1,417.29	122.10	88.60	8,890.62
18.7	....	....	....	....	....	18.7	9,757.24	562.50	162.00	....	10,481.74
.....	....	....	....	....	6.1	6.1	17,395.00	79.00	50.09	....	17,524.09
.....	....	....	....	....	9.8	9.8	18,359.26	......	......	....	18,359.26
.....	....	....	....	....	34.0	34.0	63,715.70	460.99	564.35	....	64,741.04
410.0	....	....	....	....	**56.1**	**527.1**	**$ 312,911.83**	**$ 15,050.88**	**$ 3,216.32**	**$ 95.32**	**$ 331,274.35**
122.8	....	....	....	....	....	122.8	$ 70,787.42	$ 3,638.88	$ 882.00	....	$ 75,308.30
105.0	....	....	....	....	....	105.0	59,909.85	3,080.00	650.98	....	63,640.83
.....	....	....	....	....	.0	.0	11.10	2.50	......	$ 2.00	15.60
.....	....	....	....	....	26.0	26.0	44,460.92	334.34	332.40	....	45,127.66
.....	....	....	....	....	3.1	3.1	5,787.30	......	......	....	5,787.30
.....	....	....	....	....	.8	.8	1,745.10	......	......	....	1,745.10
.....	....	....	....	....	.7	.7	1,980.30	29.96	28.75	37.77	2,076.78
132.1	....	....	....	....	148.3	280.4	325,419.08	15,274.75	4,299.76	11.30	345,004.89
.....	....	....	....	....	9.0	9.0	14,894.92	164.33	258.53	....	15,317.78
.....	....	....	....	....	134.1	134.1	384,792.00	......	......	5,364.00	390,156.00
48.0	....	....	....	....	....	48.0	27,455.95	840.00	309.38	....	28,605.33
18.6	....	....	....	....	....	18.6	10,893.72	560.00	124.88	5.70	11,584.30
.....	....	....	....	....	6.3	6.3	9,884.45	......	......	....	9,884.45
229.0	....	....	....	....	1.3	230.3	136,564.72	6,784.70	2,114.22	11.50	145,475.14
.....	....	....	....	....	1.0	1.0	2,471.30	25.13	27.67	....	2,524.10
655.5	....	....	....	....	**330.6**	**986.1**	**$ 1,097,058.13**	**$ 30,734.59**	**$ 9,028.57**	**$ 5,432.27**	**$ 1,142,253.56**

[*Continued on next page*]

Table 165—*Continued*

Arrival No.	Steamer or Source	Port of Sailing	Date of Arrival	Port of Arrival	Contents of Cargoes in N				
					Flour	Rice	Beans, Peas	Corn Grits	Pork Product
			1920						
190	Beursplein, I	New York	Nov. 1	Hamburg	.....	.....	....	....	...
191	Purchase from Meunster & Sisman	Hamburg	Nov. 3	Hamburg	.....	.....	....	....	...
192	Iowan, I	New York	Nov. 6	Hamburg	.....	.....	....	....	...
193	Germar, II	London	Nov. 8	Hamburg	.....	.....	....	....	...
194	Via Courier, London Purchase	London	Nov. 12	Hamburg	.....	.....	....	....	...
195	Wheeling Mold	New York	Nov. 13	Batoum	.....	239.8	....	....	...
196	Prutan, I	(United Kingdom)	Nov. 13	Hamburg	.....	.....	....	....	...
197	Purchase from Meunster & Sisman	Hamburg	Nov. 13	Hamburg	.....	.....	....	....	...
198	American, I	New York	Nov. 15	Hamburg	.....	.....	....	....	...
199	Purchase from Meunster & Sisman	Hamburg	Nov. 19	Hamburg	.....	.....	....	....	...
200	Gul Djemal	New York	Nov. 20	Batoum	444.0	264.2	....	....	...
201	Local Purchase, Ex-Czecho-Slovakian Gov't.	(Prague)	Nov. 21	(Vienna)	.....	.....	....	....	...
202	Mopang	New York	Nov. 22	Derindje	578.1	149.4	....	....	...
203	Texan	New York	Nov. 22	Hamburg	.....	.....	....	....	...
204	Orlando	(United Kingdom)	Nov. 26	Danzig	.....	.....	....	....	...
205	Susquehanna, III	New York	Nov. 26	Danzig	.....	.....	....	....	...
206	Local Purchase, Ex-Czecho-Slovakian Gov't.	(Prague)	Nov. 30	(Vienna)	.....	.....	....	....	...
	Total for November	....	....	....	**1,022.1**	**653.4**	....	....	...
207	Purchase from Meunster & Sisman	Hamburg	Dec. 4	Hamburg	.....	.....	....	....	...
208	Via Parcel Post	New York	Dec. 5	London	.....	.....	....	....	...
209	Local Purchase, Ex-Czecho-Slovakian Gov't.	(Czecho-Slovakia)	Dec. 6	(Czecho-Slovakia)	.....	.....	....	....	...
210	Mystic	New York	Dec. 17	Hamburg	.....	.....	....	....	...
211	Homer City, I	New York	Dec. 19	Hamburg	.....	.....	....	....	...
212	Iowan, II	New York	Dec. 21	Hamburg	.....	.....	....	....	...
213	Purchase from Phillips	Hamburg	Dec. 22	Hamburg	.....	.....	105.7	....	...
214	Mar Del Norte	New York	Dec. 22	Hamburg	.....	.....	157.4	....	101
215	Newburgh	New Orleans	Dec. 24	Hamburg	.....	406.4	....	....	...
216	Beursplein, II	New York	Dec. 27	Hamburg	.....	.....	....	....	...
217	Cornish City, I	New York	Dec. 31	Danzig	.....	.....	3,065.6	....	34
218	Manhattan	New York	Dec. 31	London	.....	.....	....	....	..
	Total for December	....	....	....	.....	**406.4**	**3,328.7**	....	**44**
			1921						
219	Juno, II	(United Kingdom)	Jan. 3	Hamburg	.....	.....	....	....	..
220	Gerrat, III	(United Kingdom)	Jan. 4	Hamburg	.....	.....	....	....	..
221	Roath	New Orleans	Jan. 5	Hamburg	.....	1,058.0	....	....	..
222	Paz de Epalza	New York	Jan. 9	Hamburg	1,528.2	.....	....	....	15
223	Billung, Ex-London Purchase	London	Jan. 10	Hamburg	.....	.....	....	....	..
224	Sirrus, Purchase from Franis Kanow	Bergen	Jan. 11	Hamburg	.....	.....	....	....	..
225	Norwich City	New York	Jan. 11	Hamburg	.....	.....	44.8	....	..
226	American, II	New York	Jan. 12	Hamburg	.....	.....	....	....	..
227	Modlin Purchase	(Poland)	Jan. 13	Danzig	.....	.....	....	....	..
228	Bradclyde, I	New York	Jan. 15	Hamburg	.....	.....	....	....	..
229	Breiz Izel	New Orleans	Jan. 17	Hamburg	.....	37.6	....	....	..
230	Mount Clay, I	New York	Jan. 18	Hamburg	.....	.....	....	....	..
231	Clarksburg, I	New York	Jan. 18	Hamburg	.....	80.1	....	....	..
232	Susquehanna, IV	New York	Jan. 18	Danzig	.....	.....	....	....	..
233	Mount Sterling, III (Formerly Kerowlee)	Philadelphia	Jan. 22	Hamburg	.....	.....	....	....	1
234	Ipswich, I	New York	Jan. 25	Hamburg	.....	225.5	....	....	..
235	Eastern City, I	New York	Jan. 25	Danzig	3,829.1	.....	....	....	..
236	Leeds City, I	New York	Jan. 26	Hamburg	.....	.....	....	....	20
237	Purchase from Staude	Hamburg	Jan. 31	Hamburg	.....	.....	10.0	....	..
	Total for January	....	....	....	**5,357.3**	**1,401.2**	**54.8**	....	**37**

HILDREN'S FUND

Steamers

...ric Tons of 1,000 Kilograms or 2,204.6 Pounds							F.O.B. Value	Freight	Insurance	Miscellaneous Charges	Total C.I.F. Value
Milk	Cocoa	Sugar	Misc. Food	Soap	Clothing and Misc.	Total Tons					
181.0	....	....	....	....	....	181.0	$ 104,524.93	$ 5,142.78	$ 1,558.90	....	$ 111,226.61
.....	....	10.0	....	....	....	10.0	2,685.04	......	......	....	2,685.04
148.9	....	....	....	....	48.0	196.9	159,766.43	7,390.20	2,206.14	....	169,362.77
.....	....	....	....	....	1.8	1.8	2,277.40	18.44	8.14	....	2,303.98
.....	....	....	....	....	.0	.0	36.72	......	......	....	36.72
.....	....	76.2	....	300.8	....	616.8	75,068.00	......	......	$ 24,672.00	99,740.00
.....	....	....	....	....	.3	.3	411.61	......	......	....	411.61
.....	3.0	....	....	....	....	3.0	636.66	......	......	....	636.66
155.7	....	304.7	....	....	....	460.4	155,513.36	10,291.39	2,206.25	20.58	168,031.58
.....	10.3	....	....	....	....	10.3	2,767.56	......	......	....	2,767.56
.....	....	59.7	....	....	....	767.9	82,081.00	......	......	30,716.00	112,797.00
.....	....	433.0	....	....	....	433.0	94,875.00	......	......	....	94,875.00
.....	....	42.7	....	....	....	770.2	84,032.00	......	......	30,808.00	114,840.00
.....	....	....	....	....	32.0	32.0	46,353.65	2,144.10	558.23	....	49,055.98
.....	....	....	10.0[c]	....	....	10.0	3,842.78	104.84	15.52	....	3,963.14
.....	....	....	....	....	17.0	17.0	39,692.66	1,529.95	595.38	....	41,817.99
.....	....	320.1	....	....	....	320.1	70,125.00	......	......	....	70,125.00
485.6	**13.3**	**1,246.4**	**10.0**	**300.8**	**99.1**	**3,830.7**	**$ 924,689.80**	**$ 26,621.70**	**$ 7,148.56**	**$ 86,216.58**	**$ 1,044,676.64**
.....	13.4	....	....	....	....	13.4	$ 3,398.05	......	......	....	$ 3,398.05
.....	....	....	....	....	.0	.0	9.83	......	......	....	9.83
.....	....	2,130.0	....	....	....	2,130.0	436,643.03	......	......	....	436,643.03
.....	....	....	....	....	1.0	1.0	5.10	$ 7.50	$ .39	$ .65	13.64
.....	....	....	....	....	19.0	19.0	19,391.59	2,239.25	346.95	1.50	21,979.29
.....	....	....	....	....	(.02)	(.02)	(Donation)	5.00	.43	1.25	6.68
.....	....	....	....	....	....	105.7	7,030.00	......	......	....	7,030.00
.....	99.1	....	....	....	....	358.1	50,795.26	3,945.57	615.98	512.18	55,868.99
.....	....	....	....	....	....	406.4	58,240.00	6,272.00	843.75	67.20	65,422.95
65.3	....	....	....	....	.9	66.2	16,851.13	938.34	211.77	....	18,001.24
,469.9	127.0	....	....	....	....	5,007.8	742,851.99	67,930.78	11,554.13	12,857.03	835,193.93
.....	....	....	....	....	(.03)	(.03)	33.30	5.00	.47	2.50	41.27
,535.2	**239.5**	**2,130.0**	....	....	**20.9**	**8,107.6**	**$ 1,335,249.28**	**$ 81,343.44**	**$ 13,573.87**	**$ 13,442.31**	**$ 1,443,608.90**
.....	....	....	6.1[c]	....	....	6.1	$ 1,715.59	$ 58.85	$ 8.24	....	$ 1,782.68
.....	....	....	5.8[c]	....	....	5.8	2,073.11	27.85	9.78	....	2,110.74
.....	....	....	....	....	....	1,058.0	121,477.20	13,994.18	1,699.20	$ 65.11	137,235.69
.....	....	....	....	....	....	1,681.4	191,510.69	13,400.49	2,574.00	240.65	207,725.83
.....	....	....	11.1[c]	....	....	11.1	3,203.53	78.33	14.27	....	3,296.13
.....	....	....	12.1[c]	....	....	12.1	3,375.23	......	......	....	3,375.23
.....	140.2	....	....	....	.2	185.2	16,105.31	1,933.08	202.64	229.35	18,470.38
224.5	....	....	....	....	....	224.5	58,006.95	3,644.07	998.20	....	62,649.22
.....	....	521.0	....	....	....	521.0	92,827.00	......	......	....	92,827.00
.....	33.0	....	....	....	....	33.0	3,640.00	401.32	53.13	....	4,094.45
.....	....	....	....	....	....	37.6	4,938.00	497.50	75.53	....	5,511.03
143.7	....	....	....	....	....	143.7	43,898.21	1,866.63	514.92	....	46,279.76
478.7	....	....	....	....	21.0	579.8	149,753.88	7,827.71	1,955.84	110.32	159,647.75
.....	....	....	....	....	1.0	1.0	1,446.96	24.11	24.03	13.60	1,508.70
.....	....	....	....	....	....	10.7	3,844.64	99.74	44.61	....	3,988.99
150.1	....	....	....	....	9.4	385.0	70,896.49	4,827.38	1,181.76	214.92	77,120.55
394.8	....	....	6.0[b]	....	....	4,229.9	440,510.71	42,428.98	7,824.40	59.79	490,823.88
63.7	40.6	....	....	....	....	314.0	68,112.66	3,009.01	801.41	....	71,923.08
.....	....	....	....	....	....	10.0	701.70	......	......	....	701.70
,455.5	**213.8**	**521.0**	**41.1**	....	**31.6**	**9,449.9**	**$ 1,278,037.86**	**$ 94,119.23**	**$ 17,981.96**	**$ 933.74**	**$ 1,391,072.79**

[*Continued on next page*]

Table 165—*Continued*

Arrival No.	Steamer or Source	Port of Sailing	Date of Arrival	Port of Arrival	Contents of Cargoes in Ne				
					Flour	Rice	Beans, Peas	Corn Grits	Pork Products
			1921						
238	Gothland	New York	Feb. 5	Danzig	11.0	.....	....	....	....
239	Moerdijk	Portland	Feb. 6	Hamburg	1,016.0	.....	....	....	....
240	Lowenburg Purchase, 1B	Hamburg	Feb. 7	Hamburg	.....	.....	....	....	....
241	Bradford City, I	New York	Feb. 7	Hamburg	.....	.....	....	....	....
242	Leeds City, I	New York	Feb. 7	Danzig	1,343.0	.....	....	....	....
243	Purchase from Abraham	Hamburg	Feb. 14	Hamburg	.....	.....	90.4	....	....
244	Phoenix Bridge	New Orleans	Feb. 21	Hamburg	.....	1,452.7	....	....	....
245	Purchase from Borga	Hamburg	Feb. 24	Hamburg	.....	.....	274.6	....	....
246	Homer City, II	New York	Feb. 25	Hamburg	.....	.....	329.3	....	476.
247	Haimon	New York	Feb. 25	Hamburg	.....	.....	54.7	....	....
248	Sophie Rickmers	New Orleans	Feb. 26	Hamburg	.....	823.8	....	....	....
249	Hawaiian, I	New York	Feb. 28	Hamburg	414.3	.....	....	....	....
250	Oregonian, I	New York	Feb. 28	Hamburg	406.0	.....	....	....	....
	Total for February	....	....	....	**3,190.3**	**2,276.5**	**749.0**	**....**	**476.**
251	Bradavon	New York	Mar. 3	Hamburg	.....	.....	....	....	150.
252	Loewenberg Purchase, 2A	Hamburg	Mar. 3	Hamburg	.....	.....	....	....	....
253	Borga	New York	Mar. 4	Hamburg	195.3	.....	....	....	....
254	Mount Clay, II	New York	Mar. 5	Hamburg	.....	.....	....	....	....
255	Watsness, I	New York	Mar. 5	Danzig	.....	.....	....	....	203.
256	Poland	New York	Mar. 8	Danzig	17.8	.....	....	....	....
257	Andrea F. Luckenbach	New York	Mar. 12	Hamburg	.....	.....	21.5	....	....
258	Mystic, III	New York	Mar. 14	Hamburg	.....	.....	....	....	....
259	Purchase from Marcus, 1A	Hamburg	Mar. 19	Hamburg	.....	.....	64.4	....	....
260	Kenowis	New Orleans	Mar. 21	Hamburg	.....	873.3	....	....	....
261	Bradclyde, II	New Orleans Hamburg	Mar. 23 Apr. 2	Hamburg Danzig	.....	.....	....	....	....
262	Harry Luckenbach	New York	Mar. 23	Hamburg	.....	.....	....	....	....
263	Eastern City, II	New York	Mar. 27	Hamburg	.....	.....	....	....	203.
264	Pomona	Portland	Mar. 28	Hamburg	108.0	.....	....	....	....
265	Purchase from Marcus, 1B	Hamburg	Mar. 29	Hamburg	.....	.....	31.7	....	....
	Total for March	....	....	....	**321.1**	**873.3**	**117.6**	**....**	**557.**
266	Purchase from Marcus, 1C	Hamburg	Apr. 2	Hamburg	.....	.....	43.3	....	....
267	Oregonian, II	New York	Apr. 5	Hamburg	.....	.....	....	50.8	....
268	Purchase from Staude, No. 2	Hamburg	Apr. 6	Hamburg	.....	.....	55.6	....	....
269	Naamhok	Philadelphia	Apr. 6	Hamburg	.....	.....	....	....	....
270	Purchase from Staude, 3A	Hamburg	Apr. 9	Hamburg	.....	.....	20.0	....	....
271	Purchase from Staude, 3B	Hamburg	Apr. 9	Hamburg	.....	.....	10.7	....	....
272	Westbrook	New Orleans	Apr. 9	Hamburg	.....	358.4	....	....	....
273	Leeds City, II	New York	Apr. 12	Hamburg	.....	.....	358.4	....	403.
274	Minnekahda, III	Boston	Apr. 12	Hamburg	.....	.....	....	....	....
275	Fairmont	New York	Apr. 13	Hamburg	.....	.....	....	....	....
276	Osawatomie	Boston	Apr. 17	Hamburg	.....	.....	....	....	....
277	Leeds City, II	New York	Apr. 19	Danzig	99.6	.....	52.7	....	357.
278	Grandon, I	(United Kingdom)	Apr. 20	Hamburg	.....	.....	....	....	....
279	Eemdijk	Seattle	Apr. 22	Hamburg	.....	.....	....	....	....
280	Purchase in Budapest	(Budapest)	Apr. 22	(Budapest)	29.0	.....	....	....	....
281	Bradford City, II	New York	Apr. 23	Hamburg	.....	.....	367.4	....	134.
282	West Raritans	New Orleans	Apr. 25	Hamburg	.....	617.9	....	....	....
283	Schoharie, II	New Orleans	Apr. 27	Hamburg	.....	948.6	....	....	....
284	King City	Galveston	Apr. 29	Hamburg	.....	965.0	....	....	....
285	Ipswich, Local Purchase	Hamburg	Apr. 30	Hamburg	.....	.....	106.9	....	....
	Total for April	....	....	....	**128.6**	**2,889.9**	**1,015.0**	**50.8**	**895.**
286	East Cape	New York	May 2	Danzig	.....	.....	140.7	88.4	156
287	Mystic, IV	New York	May 9	Hamburg	.....	.....	....	....	....
288	Geron Bean Purchase, 7H, London	Hamburg	May 10	Hamburg	.....	.....	100.0	....	....
289	West Katan	Portland	May 12	Hamburg	.....	.....	....	....	....
290	Watsness, II	New York	May 13	Danzig	.....	.....	368.2	318.1	203
291	Strathlorne	New Orleans	May 14	Hamburg	.....	.....	15.7	....	....
292	Cornish City, II	New York	May 14	Hamburg	.....	.....	....	....	....

CHILDREN'S FUND

by Steamers

Milk	Cocoa	Sugar	Misc. Food	Soap	Clothing and Misc.	Total Tons	F.O.B. Value	Freight	Insurance	Miscellaneous Charges	Total C.I.F. Value
Metric Tons of 1,000 Kilograms or 2,204.6 Pounds											
.....	....	....	....	....	....	11.0	$ 1,000.00	$ 84.28	$ 17.10	$ 39.56	$ 1,140.94
.....	....	....	....	....	....	1,016.0	95,428.57	......	1,728.00	....	97,156.57
.....	....	....	....	....	6.0	6.0	2,319.84	......	......	....	2,319.84
924.4	....	....	....	....	.1	924.5	193,752.43	9,663.76	2,291.09	....	205,707.28
.....	....	....	....	....	....	1,343.0	116,098.05	12,583.66	2,084.75	....	130,766.46
.....	....	....	....	....	....	90.4	6,500.93	......	......	....	6,500.93
.....	....	....	....	....	....	1,452.7	82,645.71	25,614.68	1,881.02	10,558.29	120,699.70
.....	....	....	....	....	....	274.6	19,399.90	......	......	....	19,399.90
949.5	271.9	....	....	....	....	2,026.8	406,132.97	18,005.79	4,789.13	913.47	429,841.36
226.2	....	....	....	....	....	280.9	72,365.90	2,354.55	842.80	7.00	75,570.25
.....	....	....	....	....	....	823.8	54,872.79	6,811.19	931.72	24.94	62,640.64
.....	....	....	....	....	....	414.3	19,396.38	3,804.43	375.10	32.00	23,607.91
.....	....	....	....	....	....	406.0	18,922.09	3,881.78	380.80	32.62	23,217.29
2,100.1	**271.9**	....	....	....	**6.1**	**9,070.0**	**$ 1,088,835.56**	**$ 82,804.12**	**$ 15,321.51**	**$ 11,607.88**	**$ 1,198,569.07**
134.1	....	....	....	....	....	285.0	$ 74,462.96	$ 2,108.58	$ 863.23	....	$ 77,434.77
.....	....	....	....	....	5.4	5.4	7,559.89	......	......	....	7,559.89
.....	....	....	....	....	....	195.3	8,785.18	1,830.22	177.60	$ 15.42	10,808.42
108.9	....	....	....	....	....	108.9	22,275.00	893.75	264.45	....	23,433.20
176.0	....	....	....	....	....	379.1	87.393.38	3,693.32	1,480.25	....	92,566.95
.....	....	....	....	....	....	17.8	1,600.00	118.44	27.76	145.02	1,891.22
111.2	....	....	....	....	....	132.7	24,663.75	865.50	288.11	117.90	25,935.26
201.4	....	....	....	....	....	201.4	41,489.06	1,653.44	486.98	....	43,629.48
.....	....	....	....	....	....	64.4	4,373.52	......	......	....	4,373.52
.....	....	....	....	....	....	873.3	52,041.10	5,776.07	727.20	....	58,544.37
956.3	....	....	....	71.0	....	1,027.3	224,797.61	10,310.00	3,702.83	....	238,810.44
212.5	....	....	....	....	....	212.5	46,359.51	1,427.54	539.65	....	48,326.70
758.0	81.3	....	....	....	....	1,042.5	219,903.14	7,525.68	2,563.88	....	229,992.70
.....	....	....	....	....	....	108.0	12,587.00	1,701.00	240.00	148.83	14,676.83
.....	....	....	....	....	....	31.7	2,355.77	......	......	....	2,355.77
2,658.4	**81.3**	....	....	**71.0**	**5.4**	**4,685.3**	**$ 830,646.87**	**$ 37,903.54**	**$ 11,361.94**	**$ 427.17**	**$ 880,339.52**
.....	....	....	....	....	....	43.3	$ 2,692.06	......	......	....	$ 2,692.06
.....	....	....	....	....	8.2	59.0	6,060.00	$ 765.10	$ 90.41	....	6,915.51
.....	....	....	....	....	....	55.6	2,988.44	......	......	....	2,988.44
.....	....	....	73.5[d]	....	....	73.5	24,498.00	489.96	288.63	$ 592.35	25,868.94
.....	....	....	....	....	....	20.0	909.40	......	......	....	909.40
.....	....	....	....	....	....	10.7	473.01	......	......	....	473.01
.....	....	....	....	....	....	358.4	23,870.98	3,555.36	484.07	....	27,910.41
690.6	51.3	5.6	....	30.5	....	1,539.7	322,011.02	10,463.90	3,780.24	40.33	336,295.49
.....	66.0	....	....	15.2	....	81.2	9,553.60	743.00	117.18	80.00	10,493.78
.....	....	....	54.0[e]	....	....	54.0	8,400.00	416.50	99.98	266.60	9,183.08
.....	....	....	....	15.0	....	15.0	3,948.00	124.20	46.22	20.00	4,138.42
302.3	127.0	....	....	17.9	.4	957.2	166,602.30	8,244.79	2,839.60	1,083.93	178,770.62
.....	....	....	....	....	.1	.1	118.39	......	......	....	118.39
.....	....	....	573.8[g]	....	....	573.8	91,432.07	......	......	....	91,432.07
.....	....	....	....	....	....	29.0	1,740.00	......	......	....	1,740.00
761.4	....	....	....	....	....	1,263.6	261,533.70	8,583.18	3,186.00	574.94	273,877.82
.....	....	....	....	....	....	617.9	33,591.60	4,087.19	474.00	....	38,152.79
.....	....	....	....	....	....	948.6	46,603.60	8,975.72	809.51	4.83	56,393.66
.....	....	....	....	....	152.4	1,117.4	62,907.28	8,745.46	1,058.60	....	72,711.34
.....	....	....	....	....	....	106.9	6,547.67	......	......	....	6,547.67
1,754.3	**244.3**	**5.6**	**701.3**	**78.6**	**161.1**	**7,924.9**	**$ 1,076,481.12**	**$ 55,194.36**	**$ 13,274.44**	**$ 2,662.98**	**$ 1,147,612.90**
346.2	....	....	....	53.3	....	784.7	$ 138,681.48	$ 6,611.62	$ 2,362.20	$ 38.33	$ 147,693.63
.....	....	....	....	30.5	32.6	63.1	27,869.38	2,165.23	348.30	1,064.05	31,446.96
.....	....	....	....	....	....	100.0	3,296.96	......	......	....	3,296.96
.....	....	....	57.8[g]	....	....	57.8	7,462.00	1,486.40	192.70	....	9,141.10
585.4	42.3	....	....	....	....	1,517.2	231,962.67	12,357.64	2,880.00	76.43	247,276.74
.....	....	....	....	....	....	15.7	1,065.00	107.57	20.40	399.89	1,592.86
239.9	....	....	....	....	....	239.9	55,022.76	1,790.59	670.50	....	57,483.85

[*Continued on next page*]

Table 165—*Continued*

Detail of Arrivals

Arrival No.	Steamer or Source	Port of Sailing	Date of Arrival	Port of Arrival	Contents of Cargoes in Net: Flour	Rice	Beans, Peas	Corn Grits	Pork Products
			1921						
293	Nemaha	Philadelphia	May 15	Hamburg	.....	.....	....	....	.....
294	Vittorio Emmanuelle, IV	New York Hamburg	May 15 May 24	Hamburg Danzig	52.1	.....	....	....	50.8
295	Hawaiian, II	New York	May 17	Hamburg	62.2	.....	....	....	.....
296	Delavan	New York	May 17	Danzig	697.0	.....	....	....	.....
297	Massilon Bridge	New York	May 23	Salonica	.....	.....	....	....	.....
298	Chile	San Francisco	May 26	Hamburg	.....	.....	1,290.9	....	.....
299	American, IV	New York	May 27	Hamburg	.....	.....	....	....	.....
300	Amassia	New Orleans	May 27	Hamburg	.....	212.0	....	....	.....
301	Oregonian, III	New York	May 29	Hamburg	806.8	.....	....	419.9	399.3
302	Grandon, II	London	May 29	Hamburg	.....	.....	....	....	.....
303	Mount Carroll, I	New York	May 30	Hamburg	.....	.....	....	....	.....
304	Purchase by Warsaw Mission, II	(Warsaw)	May 30	Danzig	.....	.....	....	....	.....
305	Norrtelje	London	May ..	Danzig	.....	.....	....	....	.....
	Total for May				**1,618.1**	**212.0**	**1,915.5**	**826.4**	**809.4**
306	Orbita, I	New York	June 2	Hamburg	.....	.....	101.9	....	103.3
307	Walter A. Luckenbach	Philadelphia	June 12	Hamburg	203.2	.....	....	....	.....
308	Clarksburg, II	New York	June 13	Hamburg	.....	.....	....	....	.....
309	Corson, III	New York	June 17	Hamburg	.....	.....	....	....	.....
310	Oropesa	New York	June 17	Hamburg	.....	.....	203.1	....	.....
311	Ruurle	New York	June 18	Hamburg	.....	136.1	....	....	.....
312	Alness	Galveston	June 21	Hamburg	.....	.....	....	....	.....
313	American, V	New York	June 21	Hamburg	.....	.....	....	....	.....
314	West Camak	San Francisco	June 24	Hamburg	.....	.....	168.9	....	.....
315	Mexico, II	New Orleans	June 25	Hamburg	.....	171.3	.2	....	.....
316	Chickamauga	New York	June 25	Danzig	303.8	.....	....	....	.....
317	Purchase from Polish Government	(Poland)	June 30	(Poland)	.....	.....	....	....	.....
	Total for June				**507.0**	**307.4**	**474.1**	....	**103.3**
318	Orduna, I	New York	July 1	Hamburg	.....	.....	....	....	98.
319	Mystic, V	New York	July 2	Hamburg	.....	.....	....	....	.....
320	Bakersfield	San Francisco	July 3	Hamburg	.....	.....	....	....	.....
321	Hawaiian, III	New York	July 4	Hamburg	156.5	.....	....	539.3	.....
322	Mount Clay, III	New York	July 5	Hamburg	.....	.....	....	....	.....
323	Bradclyde, III	New York	July 5	Danzig	.....	.....	120.5	....	.....
324	Croxteth Hall	New York	July 6	Hamburg	.....	.....	....	....	151.
325	Potomac, I	New York	July 6	Danzig	.....	.....	....	351.4	193.
326	Blair	New York	July 9	Salonica	.....	.....	....	....	....
327	Oregonian, IV	New York	July 11	Hamburg	114.4	.....	....	662.9	....
328	Mount Carroll, II	New York	July 12	Hamburg	.....	.....	....	....	....
329	Westbrook, II	New York	July 12	Danzig	.....	.....	354.6	....	....
330	Orbita, II	New York	July 14	Hamburg	.....	.....	....	....	49.
331	Mount Clinton, I	New York	July 19	Hamburg	.....	.....	....	....	....
332	Michigan	New Orleans	July 20	Bremen, Hamburg	.....	636.5	....	....	....
333	Jacques Cartier, II	New Orleans	July 20	le Havre	.....	373.8	....	....	....
334	Sudbury, I	New York	July 24	Hamburg	106.0	.....	....	232.6	....
335	Ipswich, II	New York	July 28	Hamburg	.....	.....	....	....	....
	Total for July				**376.9**	**1,010.3**	**475.1**	**1,786.2**	**493.**
336	Panama, I	San Francisco	Aug. 7	Hamburg	1,016.1	.....	....	....	....
337	Clarksburg, III	New York	Aug. 9	Hamburg	.....	.....	....	....	....
338	Panama, I	San Francisco	Aug. 13	Danzig	1,981.3	2,031.5	755.4	....	....
339	Oronoke	New York	Aug. 14	Danzig	.....	.....	....	....	....
340	West Kedron, I	San Francisco	Aug. 14	Hamburg	.....	.....	893.3	....	....
341	Mystic, VI	New York	Aug. 15	Hamburg	.....	.....	....	....	250.
342	Guernsey, I	New York	Aug. 16	Danzig	.....	.....	....	253.6	....
343	West Kedron, I	San Francisco	Aug. 19	Danzig	34.8	308.9	1,017.0	....	....
344	Latvia, I	New York	Aug. 19	Danzig	.....	.....	....	....	....

CHILDREN'S FUND

by Steamers

Metric Tons of 1,000 Kilograms or 2,204.6 Pounds											
Milk	Cocoa	Sugar	Misc. Food	Soap	Clothing and Misc.	Total Tons	F.O.B. Value	Freight	Insurance	Miscellaneous Charges	Total C.I.F. Value
348.0	....	....	....	....	....	348.0	$ 82,273.23	$ 2,827.31	$ 1,091.68	$ 128.00	$ 86,320.22
764.4	84.7	....	....	60.9	....	1,012.9	232,098.59	8,869.12	3,070.51	555.03	244,593.25
.....	....	....	....	50.9	34.0	147.1	37,163.25	2,935.22	474.43	1,070.25	41,643.15
.....	....	....	....	....	....	697.0	52,920.00	4,609.92	677.25	64.12	58,271.29
.....	....	....	....	....	65.2	65.2	58,397.14	4,251.50	688.80	395.86	63,733.30
.....	....	....	....	....	....	1,290.9	100,420.48	21,343.64	2,979.80	....	124,743.92
.....	....	....	....	30.4	....	30.4	7,495.85	482.66	119.70	....	8,098.21
.....	....	....	....	....	....	212.0	11,540.00	1,869.10	200.21	35.05	13,644.36
.....	....	....	....	30.4	32.6	1,689.0	171,138.33	17,852.96	5,483.48	1,204.04	195,678.81
.....	....	....	....	....	1.0	1.0	170.04	......	......	....	170.04
.....	....	....	....	....	31.6	31.6	18,081.87	1,814.85	588.60	1,067.69	21,553.01
.....	....	40.0	....	....	....	40.0	8,765.43	......	......	....	8,765.43
.....	....	....	....	4 cases	.0	.0	1,724.44	......	......	....	1,724.44
2,283.9	**127.0**	**40.0**	**57.8**	**256.4**	**197.0**	**8,343.5**	**$ 1,247,548.90**	**$ 91,375.33**	**$ 21,848.56**	**$ 6,098.74**	**$ 1,366,871.53**
99.8	116.8	....	....	....	....	421.8	$ 67,258.46	$ 7,260.32	$ 2,214.90	$ 93.73	$ 76,827.41
.....	....	....	....	....	....	203.2	14,624.49	1,456.00	456.30	20.00	16,556.79
.....	....	....	....	....	31.1	31.1	19,111.45	1,815.30	618.30	1,070.67	22,615.72
104.1	....	....	....	....	....	104.1	24,593.10	776.75	718.20	....	26,088.05
371.3	....	....	....	....	....	574.4	126,146.17	9,066.50	4,003.43	96.60	139,312.70
.....	....	....	....	....	....	136.1	4,890.37	1,350.59	201.30	....	6,442.26
.....	....	....	....	....	289.1	289.1	9,532.96	2,868.43	393.45	27.00	12,821.84
117.3	89.4	....	....	....	48.5	255.2	71,984.95	6,462.89	2,254.50	1,608.29	82,310.63
.....	....	....	79.9[h,i]	....	....	248.8	21,509.00	3,306.71	569.80	193.57	25,579.08
.....	....	....	....	....	....	171.5	6,344.99	1,698.60	257.05	15.78	8,316.42
.....	....	....	....	....	....	303.8	23,065.71	2,009.28	723.25	27.54	25,825.78
.....	....	2,666.0	....	....	....	2,666.0	430,074.54	......	......	....	430,074.54
692.5	**206.2**	**2,666.0**	**79.9**	**....**	**368.7**	**5,405.1**	**$ 819,136.19**	**$ 38,071.37**	**$ 12,410.48**	**$ 3,153.18**	**$ 872,771.22**
462.6	....	....	....	....	....	561.5	$ 118,581.93	$ 10,044.52	$ 3,996.23	....	$ 132,622.68
323.5	....	....	....	....	34.0	357.5	96,543.46	7,048.81	3,029.40	$ 1,074.89	107,696.56
.....	....	....	4.1[h]	....	....	4.1	385.00	55.14	16.00	48.02	504.16
35.6	259.1	....	....	....	65.1	1,055.6	113,473.07	14,080.15	3,852.45	1,186.59	132,592.26
108.8	....	....	....	....	....	108.8	25,078.60	1,782.04	780.30	....	27,640.94
205.5	....	....	....	....	....	326.0	72,247.49	5,057.33	2,430.68	130.12	79,865.62
.....	....	....	....	....	....	151.8	28,059.09	2,538.70	1,040.00	....	31,637.79
.....	....	....	....	....	....	544.8	46,898.75	6,144.03	1,586.75	55.34	54,684.87
.....	....	....	....	....	6.1	6.1	3,366.48	429.55	122.00	24.49	3,942.52
424.6	....	....	....	....	24.0	1,225.9	147,377.97	14,315.33	4,847.85	929.20	167,470.35
548.1	....	....	....	....	24.8	572.9	156,096.19	10,406.31	4,950.68	....	171,453.18
190.5	....	....	....	....	....	545.1	79,599.58	7,064.52	2,723.18	239.80	89,627.08
27.2	....	....	....	....	....	76.5	14,940.64	1,224.18	485.44	....	16,650.26
88.4	....	....	....	....	11.2	99.6	24,513.43	2,268.74	824.85	398.08	28,005.10
.....	....	....	....	....	....	636.5	28,770.75	6,314.72	1,119.35	29.68	36,234.50
.....	....	....	....	....	....	373.8	17,455.40	3,707.70	674.05	....	21,837.15
65.3	....	....	....	....	10.2	414.1	39,357.17	3,878.04	1,313.55	53.32	44,602.08
196.0	....	....	....	....	....	196.0	41,400.00	3,656.25	1,415.70	....	46,471.95
2,676.1	**259.1**	**....**	**4.1**	**....**	**175.4**	**7,256.6**	**$ 1,054,145.00**	**$ 100,016.06**	**$ 35,208.46**	**$ 4,169.53**	**$ 1,193,539.05**
.....	....	....	....	....	....	1,016.1	$ 77,000.00	......	$ 2,530.73	....	$ 79,530.73
.....	104.7	....	....	....	....	104.7	7,498.40	$ 2,164.55	278.10	....	9,941.05
.....	....	....	....	....	....	4,768.2	269,469.58	42,578.38	10,956.00	....	323,003.96
.....	....	....	....	....	77.1	77.1	87,566.80	3,617.50	2,700.99	....	93,885.29
.....	....	....	....	....	....	893.3	61,118.79	11,816.15	2,395.43	....	75,330.37
.....	....	....	....	....	20.1	270.2	78,645.86	4,268.97	2,411.10	....	85,325.93
1,108.5	....	....	....	....	152.7	1,514.8	436,478.44	26,443.19	14,314.63	$ 39.94	477,276.20
.....	....	....	....	....	....	1,360.7	79,794.55	20,874.61	3,527.70	63.80	104,260.66
.....	....	....	....	....	93.0	93.0	124,825.39	5,116.12	3,850.00	....	133,791.51

[*Continued on next page*]

Table 165—*Continued*

Detail of Arrivals

Arrival No.	Steamer or Source	Port of Sailing	Date of Arrival	Port of Arrival	Contents of Cargoes in Net: Flour	Rice	Beans, Peas	Corn Grits	Pork Products
			1921						
345	Hawaiian, IV	New York	Aug. 22	Hamburg	....	....	....	....	....
346	Oronoke	New York, Danzig	Aug. 22	Riga	....	....	....	....	....
347	Galileo	New York	Aug. 24	Hull	....	....	....	....	232.3
348	Keilehaven	New Orleans	Aug. 24	Hamburg	....	510.8	....	....	....
349	Wachsmuth Purchase, I	(Czecho-Slovakia)	Aug. 26	Hamburg	....	....	....	....	....
350	Oregonian, V	New York	Aug. 28	Hamburg	....	....	....	....	....
351	Hansa	Galveston	Aug. 29	Hamburg	....	....	....	....	....
352	Adalia	New Orleans	Aug. 29	Hamburg	....	....	16.2	....	....
353	Lizzie	Amsterdam	Aug. 29	Hamburg	....	....	....	....	....
354	Mount Carroll, III	New York	Aug. 30	Hamburg	....	....	....	....	....
355	Estonia	New York	Aug. 30	Danzig	22.2	....	....	....	....
	Total for August	....	....	....	**3,054.4**	**2,851.2**	**2,681.9**	**253.6**	**482.4**
356	Lackawanna Valley	New York	Sept. 3	Reval	....	....	....	....	....
357	Polonia, I	New York	Sept. 7	Danzig	248.7	....	....	....	....
358	Samland, I	Philadelphia	Sept. 7	Danzig	1,016.1	....	....	....	....
359	Via Parcel Post	New York	Sept. 8	London	....	....	....	....	....
360	Chile, II	San Francisco	Sept. 8	Hamburg	....	....	567.1	....	....
361	Sudbury, II	New York	Sept. 13	Hamburg	....	....	....	....	....
362	Crewe Hall	New York	Sept. 14	Salonica	....	....	....	....	....
363	Noruega	New York	Sept. 15	Hamburg	....	....	....	....	....
364	Idefjord	Philadelphia	Sept. 18	Danzig	1,524.4	....	....	....	....
365	Ipswich, III	New York	Sept. 19	Hamburg	....	....	....	....	....
366	Lituania, I	New York	Sept. 21	Danzig	....	....	....	....	....
367	Werra	London	Sept. 21	Hamburg	....	....	....	....	....
368	West Nerranus, I	New Orleans	Sept. 23	Hamburg	....	441.7	....	....	....
369	Dakotan, I	New York	Sept. 24	Hamburg	....	....	....	....	....
370	Mount Clay, IV	New York	Sept. 26	Hamburg	....	....	....	....	149.2
	Total for September	....	....	....	**2,789.2**	**441.7**	**567.1**	....	**149.2**
371	Virginian, I	New York	Oct. 1	Hamburg	....	....	....	....	54.6
372	Moravia Bridge	Philadelphia	Oct. 3	Riga	2,032.6	....	....	....	....
373	Massick	New York	Oct. 3	Riga	....	....	....	....	....
374	Latvia, II	New York	Oct. 5	Danzig	....	....	....	260.7	....
375	Clarksburg, IV	Baltimore	Oct. 8	Hamburg	1,345.1	....	....	....	395.1
376	Hawaiian, V	New York	Oct. 10	Hamburg	....	....	....	....	....
377	Mount Carroll, IV	New York	Oct. 11	Hamburg	....	....	....	....	....
378	Potomac, II	New York	Oct. 12	Danzig	....	....	....	....	....
379	City of Flint, II	Philadelphia	Oct. 12	Hamburg	394.8	....	....	....	....
380	Winfried	New York	Oct. 12	Hamburg	....	....	....	260.7	....
381	Tonesit	Baltimore	Oct. 13	Copenhagen	186.7	....	....	....	....
382	Westbrook, III	New York	Oct. 13	Hamburg	535.3	....	....	....	....
383	Estonia, II	New York	Oct. 18	Danzig	....	....	....	....	....
384	Tordenskjold	New York	Oct. 19	Hamburg	....	....	....	....	....
385	Oregonian, VI	New York	Oct. 19	Hamburg	....	....	....	....	....
386	Bayern	New York	Oct. 19	Hamburg	....	....	....	....	....
387	Manchuria, V	New York	Oct. 23	Hamburg	308.4	....	....	190.5	....
388	New England	Baltimore	Oct. 25	Copenhagen	438.2	....	....	....	....
389	Guernsey, II	Norfolk	Oct. 26	Hamburg	80.1	....	....	....	....
390	Bradford City, III	New York	Oct. 26	Hamburg	378.1	....	....	595.9	....
391	Deutschfeld	Norfolk	Oct. 29	Hamburg	511.2	....	....	....	....
392	Orla, I	New York	Oct. 29	Hamburg	....	....	....	....	....
393	Samland, II	Philadelphia	Oct. 31	Danzig	1,016.1	....	....	....	....
	Total for October	....	....	....	**7,226.6**	....	....	**1,307.8**	**449.1**

:HILDREN'S FUND

y Steamers

etric Tons of 1,000 Kilograms or 2,204.6 Pounds							F.O.B. Value	Freight	Insurance	Miscellaneous Charges	Total C.I.F. Value
Milk	Cocoa	Sugar	Misc. Food	Soap	Clothing and Misc.	Total Tons					
....	....	....	....	....	35.0	35.0	$ 51,182.50	$ 1,749.60	$ 1,541.70	....	$ 54,473.80
....	....	....	....	....	19.0	19.0	26,311.44	1,129.16	850.49	....	28,291.09
....	....	....	....	....	....	232.3	42,087.42	3,810.64	1,602.25	....	47,500.31
....	....	....	....	....	....	510.8	27,256.25	4,785.85	1,049.20	$ 69.09	33,160.39
....	....	65.0	....	....	....	65.0	5,102.32	......	......	....	5,102.32
....	....	....	....	....	45.5	45.5	67,151.11	2,214.95	2,019.60	....	71,385.66
....	....	....	....	....	191.8	191.8	7,362.50	2,114.36	333.30	....	9,810.16
....	....	....	....	....	....	16.2	1,074.42	268.61	61.00	404.95	1,808.98
....	....	101.8	....	....	....	101.8	10,230.00	......	......	....	10,230.00
....	....	....	....	....	16.0	16.0	25,532.50	776.25	766.80	....	27,075.55
32.8	....	205.2	....	....	9.7	269.9	45,327.83	2,977.70	1,430.00	5.25	49,740.78
1,141.3	**104.7**	**372.0**	....	....	**659.9**	**11,601.4**	**$ 1,531,016.10**	**$ 136,706.59**	**$ 52,619.02**	**$ 583.03**	**$ 1,720,924.74**
....	....	....	....	....	15.0	15.0	$ 16,341.66	$ 593.43	$ 594.75	....	$ 17,529.84
....	....	496.5	....	....	....	745.2	66,048.34	6,023.33	2,263.95	$ 26.60	74,362.22
....	....	....	....	....	....	1,016.1	68,571.49	6,720.00	2,383.80	10.50	77,685.79
....	....	....	....	....	.0	.0	6.44	......	......	....	6.44
....	....	....	....	....	....	567.1	40,240.16	8,664.99	1,634.38	....	50,539.53
....	....	....	....	....	97.2	97.2	147,276.08	4,994.90	4,541.63	....	156,812.61
....	....	....	....	....	12.3	12.3	17,356.10	692.90	594.75	116.52	18,760.27
1,175.0	....	....	....	....	104.9	1,279.9	357,641.42	20,187.96	11,889.81	....	389,719.19
....	....	....	....	....	....	1,524.4	102,115.04	9,746.03	3,566.55	29.00	115,456.62
....	....	....	....	....	7.6	7.6	9,946.93	431.98	302.36	....	10,681.27
....	....	304.8	....	....	46.4	351.2	96,813.50	4,733.81	3,060.75	....	104,608.06
....	....	....	....	....	.2	.2	1,009.00	......	......	....	1,009.00
....	....	....	....	....	....	441.7	29,810.46	3,895.36	1,022.65	56.03	34,784.50
430.0	239.8	312.1	....	....	8.8	990.7	162,904.18	15,672.52	5,278.05	....	183,854.75
....	....	....	....	....	....	149.2	33,617.68	2,193.53	1,058.40	....	36,869.61
1,605.0	**239.8**	**1,113.4**	....	....	**292.4**	**7,197.8**	**$ 1,149,698.48**	**$ 84,550.74**	**$ 38,191.83**	**$ 238.65**	**$ 1,272,679.70**
815.4	....	90.0	....	....	....	959.4	$ 206,599.20	$ 15,274.57	$ 6,635.03	$ 24.00	$ 228,532.80
....	....	....	....	....	....	2,032.6	134,857.23	17,472.00	4,728.15	31.50	157,088.88
....	....	....	.9[k]	....	....	.9	2.00	20.10	2.07	6.52	30.69
....	....	....	....	....	111.2	371.9	155,843.36	6,441.91	4,897.75	38.99	167,222.01
....	....	....	....	....	....	1,740.2	176,332.34	15,263.26	5,814.00	105.91	197,515.51
1,149.0	....	....	....	....	....	1,149.0	257,655.10	21,012.60	8,802.00	....	287,469.70
21.8	....	....	....	....	....	21.8	4,650.00	406.25	162.34	....	5,218.59
....	99.6	....	....	....	....	99.6	7,606.37	1,940.40	301.28	....	9,848.05
....	....	....	....	....	....	394.8	26,097.11	2,611.14	847.80	5.50	29,561.55
....	....	....	....	....	....	260.7	10,627.50	1,437.10	355.05	20.54	12,440.19
....	....	....	....	....	....	186.7	12,075.00	1,440.60	407.00	14.70	13,937.30
....	....	....	....	....	....	535.3	35,754.42	3,540.18	1,158.30	42.16	40,495.06
....	....	....	....	....	20.7	20.7	29,978.00	970.07	1,020.00	....	31,968.07
....	....	....	....	....	11.3	11.3	16,520.83	677.09	551.36	....	17,749.28
329.6	....	....	....	....	1.0	330.6	72,613.20	5,627.27	2,437.60	....	80,678.07
200.1	....	....	....	....	....	200.1	42,528.85	3,285.06	1,352.70	....	47,166.61
....	....	....	....	....	....	498.9	27,325.71	3,299.94	1,060.45	39.29	31,725.39
....	....	....	....	....	....	438.2	28,392.97	3,381.00	1,106.25	34.50	32,914.72
....	....	....	....	....	....	80.1	5,257.08	529.62	173.25	6.28	5,966.23
....	....	....	....	....	11.7	985.7	62,371.43	7,063.33	2,315.45	80.89	71,831.10
....	....	....	....	....	....	511.2	33,925.00	3,944.50	1,311.28	40.25	39,221.03
....	....	....	....	....	2.1	2.1	3,596.37	75.95	108.00	....	3,780.32
....	....	....	....	....	....	1,016.1	67,416.21	6,720.00	2,568.57	11.00	76,715.78
2,515.9	**99.6**	**90.0**	**.9**	....	**158.0**	**11,847.9**	**$ 1,418,025.28**	**$ 122,433.94**	**$ 48,115.68**	**$ 502.03**	**$ 1,589,076.93**

[*Continued on next page*]

Table 165—*Continued*

Detail of Arrival

Arrival No.	Steamer or Source	Port of Sailing	Date of Arrival	Port of Arrival	Contents of Cargoes in N				
					Flour	Rice	Beans, Peas	Corn Grits	Pork Product
			1921						
394	Glentworth	New Orleans	Nov. 1	Hamburg	.....	464.6	....	....	....
395	Panola	Philadelphia Danzig	Nov. 2 Nov. 5	Danzig Riga	1,613.0	.....	....	....	....
396	Polonia, II	New York	Nov. 2	Danzig	.....	.....	....	....	....
397	Hudson	New York	Nov. 3	Bremerhaven	.....	.....	....	....	....
398	Mexico, III	New Orleans	Nov. 3	Hamburg	.....	1,008.4	....	....	....
399	William A. McKenney	New York	Nov. 5	Hamburg	.....	.....	....	....	....
400	Chester Valley	New York	Nov. 7	Salonica	.....	.....	....	....	....
401	Guernsey, II	Norfolk	Nov. 9	Riga	.....	.....	....	....	590.
402	Buchanness	New York	Nov. 10	Hamburg	.....	.....	....	101.5	....
403	Lituania, II	New York	Nov. 15	Danzig	106.7	.....	....	....	....
404	Mount Carroll, V	New York	Nov. 21	Hamburg	.....	.....	....	....	....
405	Manitowac	New York	Nov. 22	Danzig	427.5	.....	103.5	441.8	....
406	Elzasier, I	New York	Nov. 23	Danzig	.....	.....	56.4	....	....
407	Samnanger	New Orleans	Nov. 25	Hamburg	.....	257.0	....	....	....
408	Sachsenwald	New Orleans	Nov. 25	Hamburg	.....	309.7	....	....	....
409	Tancred	New York	Nov. 25	Hamburg	.....	.....	....	....	....
410	Manitowac	New York	Nov. 27	Riga	2,263.9	478.4	183.5	311.1	247.
	Total for November	....	....	....	**4,411.1**	**2,518.1**	**343.4**	**854.4**	**837.**
411	Elzasier, I	New York, Danzig	Dec. 1	Riga	.....	.....	....	....	....
412	Chickasaw	New York	Dec. 4	Hamburg	.....	.....	....	....	....
413	Natirar	New York	Dec. 5	Riga	.....	.....	....	....	....
414	Mount Clinton, II	New York	Dec. 7	Hamburg	.....	.....	....	....	....
415	Floridian	Portland	Dec. 11	Hamburg	2,011.8	.....	....	....	....
416	Clarksburg, V	Norfolk	Dec. 12	Hamburg	.....	.....	....	....	448.
417	Mongolia, V	New York	Dec. 12	Danzig	.....	.....	....	....	74.
418	Via Parcel Post	New York	Dec. 14	Danzig	.....	.....	....	....	....
419	Mount Clay, V	New York	Dec. 19	Hamburg	.....	.....	....	....	....
420	Polonia, III	New York	Dec. 20	Danzig	.....	.....	....	....	....
421	Westbrook, IV	New York	Dec. 22	Hamburg	.....	.....	....	....	....
422	Gdansk	New York	Dec. 23	Danzig	.....	.....	....	....	....
423	Eastport, I	New York	Dec. 24	Riga	.....	.....	....	....	....
424	Edna, Ex-Siberian Z. Co.	London	Dec. 25	Riga	.....	.....	....	....	....
425	Minnekahda, III	New York	Dec. 26	Hamburg	.....	.....	....	....	90.
	Total for December	....	....	....	**2,011.8**	.....	....	....	**613.**
			1922						
426	Mount Carroll, VI	New York	Jan. 3	Hamburg	.....	.....	153.0	....	....
427	Mercator, Ex-Siberian Z. Co.	London	Jan. 6	Riga	.....	.....	....	....	....
428	Orleans	New Orleans	Jan. 8	Hamburg	.....	179.0	....	....	....
429	City of Weatherford	New Orleans	Jan. 10	Hamburg	.....	514.7	....	....	....
430	Purchased Ex-Auk	Hamburg	Jan. 13	Hamburg	.....	.....	....	....	....
431	Corson, IV	New York	Jan 13	Hamburg	.....	.....	....	....	....
432	Mount Clinton, III	New York	Jan. 17	Hamburg	.....	.....	27.4	....	....
433	Texan, II	Portland	Jan. 19	Hamburg	2,600.0	.....	....	....	...
434	Potomac, III	New York	Jan. 20	Hamburg	.....	.....	164.2	....	...
435	Conejos, I	New York	Jan. 22	Reval	.....	.....	....	....	...
436	Oregonian, VII	New York	Jan. 24	Hamburg	.1	.....	320.3	....	...
437	Gasconier, I	New York	Jan. 26	Hamburg	.....	.....	274.1	....	...
438	Eastern Coast	New York	Jan. 26	Danzig	.....	.....	137.2	....	...
439	Mongolia, VI	New York	Jan. 29	Hamburg	.....	.....	....	....	...
440	Hickman	New York	Jan. 31	Hamburg	.....	.....	....	....	...
441	European Purchases	....	Jan. 31	....	.....	.....	....	....	...
	Total for January	....	....	....	**2,600.1**	**693.7**	**1,076.2**	....	...

CHILDREN'S FUND

by Steamers

Milk	Cocoa	Sugar	Misc. Food	Soap	Clothing and Misc.	Total Tons	F.O.B. Value	Freight	Insurance	Miscellaneous Charges	Total C.I.F. Value
Metric Tons of 1,000 Kilograms or 2,204.6 Pounds											
....	....	....	....	....	....	464.6	$ 24,889.41	$ 4,096.67	$ 891.29	$ 27.34	$ 29,904.71
....	....	....	....	....	....	1,613.0	107,042.95	14,462.24	4,231.50	19.00	125,755.69
....	....	....	....	....	.8	.8	1,540.00	25.87	52.51	....	1,618.38
....	20.3	....	....	....	....	20.3	1,552.32	396.00	68.26	....	2,016.58
....	....	....	....	....	....	1,008.4	62,950.33	9,640.74	2,291.03	131.32	75,013.42
....	....	....	....	....	4.2	4.2	5,083.33	168.58	156.60	....	5,408.51
....	....	....	....	....	17.9	17.9	22,658.47	892.14	796.05	152.18	24,498.84
....	....	....	....	....	....	590.1	149,602.82	9,605.86	5,966.35	....	165,175.03
....	....	447.1	....	....	....	548.6	37,872.37	3,920.53	1,279.26	8.00	43,080.16
....	....	....	....	....	1.9	108.6	11,336.97	700.83	396.00	105.20	12,539.00
108.9	....	....	....	....	....	108.9	20,000.00	1,015.63	595.88	22.00	21,633.51
169.3	11.5	....	....	....	....	1,153.6	88,056.90	8,454.71	3,386.25	431.90	100,329.76
1,158.1	86.9	....	....	....	....	1,301.4	244,196.98	15,808.07	8,534.23	106.25	268,645.53
....	....	....	....	....	....	257.0	14,549.93	2,549.76	623.10	24.91	17,747.70
....	....	....	....	....	....	309.7	16,459.46	3,072.60	699.60	51.21	20,282.87
....	....	....	....	57.3	....	57.3	11,349.90	379.31	354.76	....	12,083.97
832.2	100.3	....	....	20.4	....	4,437.0	450,085.37	33,291.79	16,986.75	857.63	501,221.54
2,268.5	**219.0**	**447.1**	....	**77.7**	**24.8**	**12,001.4**	**$ 1,269,227.51**	**$ 108,481.33**	**$ 47,309.42**	**$ 1,936.94**	**$ 1,426,955.20**
....	....	....	....	123.1	....	123.1	$ 28,664.25	$ 1,559.08	$ 1,092.30	....	$ 31,315.63
108.9	39.6	....	....	....	....	148.5	22,498.72	1,858.02	684.98	$ 98.00	25,139.72
....	....	....	....	....	10.9	10.9	15,365.00	457.20	552.75	....	16,374.95
242.8	....	....	....	....	....	242.8	44,600.00	2,542.23	1,624.01	64.00	48,830.24
....	....	....	....	....	....	2,011.8	129,674.00	......	4,154.38	8.80	133,837.18
....	....	....	....	....	....	448.2	95,829.21	4,439.05	3,041.93	....	103,310.19
87.1	....	....	....	....	....	161.8	32,880.73	1,512.89	975.07	20.00	35,388.69
....	....	....	....	....	.0	.0	10.94	......	......	....	10.94
90.4	50.8	....	.1[l]	....	64.1	205.4	95,179.43	4,397.54	2,823.60	20.00	102,420.57
....	....	....	....	....	.8	.8	73.93	5.00	2.71	....	81.64
305.7	....	....	....	....	18.7	324.4	78,171.82	3,870.95	2,336.87	80.00	84,459.64
726.7	....	....	....	....	140.1	866.8	316,192.38	12,063.81	10,635.62	229.60	339,121.41
....	127.0	....	....	....	....	127.0	8,260.00	1,605.71	351.78	35.00	10,252.49
....	....	....	49.0[m]	....	....	49.0	1,326.00	......	......	....	1,326.00
130.6	....	....	....	....	....	221.2	44,475.82	2,065.29	1,319.59	42.00	47,902.70
1,692.2	**217.4**	....	**49.1**	**123.1**	**234.6**	**4,941.7**	**$ 913,202.23**	**$ 36,376.77**	**$ 29,595.59**	**$ 597.40**	**$ 979,771.99**
26.4	70.1	....	....	....	67.5	317.0	$ 102,760.49	$ 5,877.39	$ 3,088.03	$ 367.92	$ 112,093.83
....	....	....	49.0[m]	....	....	49.0	1,795.75	......	......	....	1,795.75
....	....	....	....	....	....	179.0	6,952.39	1,382.55	247.50	....	8,582.44
....	....	....	....	....	....	514.7	19,956.62	3,971.15	828.55	....	24,756.32
28.5	....	....	....	....	....	28.5	7,764.75	......	......	....	7,764.75
....	50.8	501.6	.8[n]	....	....	553.2	39,631.05	4,196.63	1,264.05	35.00	45,126.73
....	....	....	....	1.7	107.1	136.2	84,884.69	6,534.47	1,333.01	41.94	92,794.11
....	....	....	....	....	....	2,600.0	125,750.43	15,122.94	4,183.99	....	145,057.36
....	....	....	....	....	109.0	273.2	165,638.50	4,839.20	3,590.44	101.66	174,169.80
....	49.8	....	....	....	....	49.8	2,963.52	637.21	132.27	35.00	3,768.00
....	....	....	....	.5	18.3	339.2	39,293.91	2,688.83	585.50	200.14	42,768.38
28.5	45.2	....	....	126.1	....	473.9	65,378.49	5,126.57	2,462.59	649.86	73,617.51
....	....	....	....	....	88.7	225.9	129,906.89	4,048.09	4,484.94	84.89	138,524.81
....	....	....	....	....	17.7	17.7	6,310.74	589.88	80.10	....	6,980.72
....	....	....	....	....	3.0	3.0	3,983.25	125.55	59.40	....	4,168.20
4.0	.8	495.0	136.7[mp]	....	4.0	640.5	78,534.96	......	......	....	78,534.96
87.4	**216.7**	**996.6**	**186.5**	**128.3**	**415.3**	**6,400.8**	**$ 881,506.43**	**$ 55,140.46**	**$ 22,340.37**	**$ 1,516.41**	**$ 960,503.67**

[*Continued on next page*]

Table 165—*Continued*

Detail of Arrival

Arrival No.	Steamer or Source	Port of Sailing	Date of Arrival	Port of Arrival	Contents of Cargoes in Ne: Flour	Rice	Beans, Peas	Corn Grits	Pork Product
			1922						
442	Dakotan, II	Portland	Feb. 6	Hamburg	3,767.7	.....	....	....	....
443	Mount Clay, VI	New York	Feb. 7	Hamburg	26.6	.....	71.9	....	203.
444	Minnekahda, IV	New York	Feb. 8	Hamburg	1,467.1	.....	....	....	....
445	Sudbury, III	Norfolk	Feb. 9	Hamburg	.....	.....	....	....	203.
446	Nobles, I	New Orleans	Feb. 9	Hamburg	.....	443.3	....	....	....
447	Dallas	New York	Feb. 9	Hamburg	813.1	.....	....	....	....
448	Bayern, II	New York	Feb. 11	Hamburg	508.6	.....	....	....	....
449	Mount Carroll, VII	New York	Feb. 15	Hamburg	71.1	.....	....	....	....
450	Minnesotan	Portland	Feb. 19	Hamburg	1,882.6	.....	....	....	....
451	Hansa	New York	Feb. 20	Hamburg	296.4	.....	....	....	....
452	Georgian	New York	Feb. 21	Hamburg	527.9	.....	....	....	59.
453	Chappaqua, I	Norfolk	Feb. 21	Hamburg	.....	.....	....	....	585.
454	Stonewall	Baltimore	Feb. 21	Novorossisk	.....	.....	....	....	....
455	Haverford	New York	Feb. 23	Hamburg	2,071.2	.....	....	....	....
456	Chickasaw, II	New York	Feb. 24	Hamburg	2,432.2	.....	....	....	....
457	Waxahachie	Galveston	Feb. 25	Hamburg	.....	25.8	....	....	....
	Total for February	....	....	....	**13,864.5**	**469.1**	**71.9**	....	**1,051.**
458	West Neris	Baltimore	Mar. 1	Libau	.....	.....	....	....	....
459	Potomac, IV	New York	Mar. 3	Hamburg	.....	.....	....	....	....
460	Mount Clinton, IV	New York	Mar. 7	Hamburg	667.4	.....	84.2	....	42.
461	Bradford City, IV	New York	Mar. 7	Hamburg	.....	.....	....	....	....
462	Lloyd	Boston	Mar. 7	Novorossisk	.....	.....	....	....	....
463	Western Ocean	New Orleans	Mar. 7	Hamburg	.....	863.3	....	....	....
464	Württemberg	New York	Mar. 9	Hamburg	342.9	.....	....	....	....
465	Peninsular State	New York	Mar. 10	Hamburg	.....	.....	....	....	....
466	Morristown, I	Philadelphia, New York	Mar. 12	Hamburg	933.3	.....	....	40.6	....
467	Mira **	Bergen	Mar. 13	Hamburg	.....	.....	....	....	....
468	Orduna, II	New York	Mar. 15	Hamburg	1,000.0	.....	....	....	....
469	Alaska	Portland	Mar. 16	Hamburg	1,016.1	.....	....	....	....
470	Huronian	New York	Mar. 18	Hamburg	1,475.2	.....	....	....	....
471	Cody, I	New Orleans	Mar. 23	Hamburg	.....	1,195.5	....	....	76.
472	Oregonian, VIII	New York	Mar. 23	Hamburg	313.0	.....	....	....	698.
473	West Norranus, II	Galveston	Mar. 25	Hamburg	270.3	308.8	....	....	....
474	Minnekahda, V	New York	Mar. 26	Hamburg	1,582.3	.....	....	33.0	....
475	Siam City	New York	Mar. 26	Hamburg	865.9	.....	....	....	....
476	Mount Carroll, VIII	New York	Mar. 26	Hamburg	.....	.....	27.0	....	....
477	City of Flint, III	Norfolk	Mar. 26	Hamburg	.....	.....	....	....	294
478	Clontarf, I	New York	Mar. 27	Odessa	448.6	.....	....	....	....
479	Cragness	New York	Mar. 28	Hamburg	1,036.8	.....	....	....	....
480	Noccalula, I	New Orleans	Mar. 30	Hamburg	.....	464.4	....	....	226
481	Corson, V	New York	Mar. 31	Hamburg	1,330.0	.....	....	231.6	....
482	European Purchases	....	Mar. 31	....	.....	.....	....	....	....
	Total for March	....	....	....	**11,281.8**	**2,832.0**	**111.2**	**305.2**	**1,338**
483	Schoharie, III	New York	Apr. 1	Hamburg	1,631.3	.....	....	38.4	...
484	Gaffney, I	New York	Apr. 3	Odessa	2,248.6	475.4	....	....	...
485	Hawaiian VI	New York	Apr. 5	Hamburg	.....	.....	....	....	508
486	Haverford, II	New York	Apr. 7	Hamburg	172.9	.....	....	....	...
487	Jacona	New York	Apr. 12	Odessa	.....	.....	....	....	304
488	Mount Clinton, V	New York	Apr. 12	Hamburg	201.7	.....	....	....	...
489	Nobles, II	New Orleans	Apr. 15	Hamburg	.....	1,312.3	....	....	...
490	Georgian, II	New York	Apr. 20	Hamburg	.....	.....	....	....	...
491	Saugus	New York	Apr. 22	Odessa	154.4	147.9	....	....	96
492	Chickasaw, III	Philadelphia	Apr. 25	Hamburg	93.4	.....	....	....	...
493	Western Scout	New York	Apr. 26	Hamburg	3,152.8	.....	....	....	...
494	Chappaqua, II	Norfolk	Apr. 28	Hamburg	.....	.....	....	....	739
495	Mount Clay, VII	New York	Apr. 29	Hamburg	.....	.....	....	....	...
496	Sunewco	New York	Apr. 29	Odessa	1,780.9	.....	....	....	...
497	Chester Valley	Beaumont	Apr. 30	Hamburg	.....	619.9	....	....	...
498	Minnekahda, VI	New York	Apr. 30	Hamburg	.....	.....	....	....	...
499	European Purchases	....	Apr. 30	....	.....	.....	....	....	...
	Total for April	....	....	....	**9,436.0**	**2,555.5**	....	**38.4**	**1,648**

** Commodities donated by Vladimar Goriachovsky.

CHILDREN'S FUND

y Steamers

etric Tons of 1,000 Kilograms or 2,204.6 Pounds

Milk	Cocoa	Sugar	Misc. Food	Soap	Clothing and Misc.	Total Tons	F.O.B. Value	Freight	Insurance	Miscellaneous Charges	Total C.I.F. Value
.....	....	....	....	....	....	3,767.7	$ 184,679.28	$ 21,915.26	$ 6,138.00	$ 10.00	$ 212,742.54
367.6	99.6	....	.7[o]	....	27.9	797.6	150,243.86	7,857.93	2,264.37	169.30	160,535.46
.....	181.9	....	....	....	....	1,649.0	83,350.37	8,515.51	1,079.83	136.95	93,082.66
.....	....	....	....	....	....	203.3	43,611.81	1,888.30	657.25	....	46,157.36
.....	....	....	....	....	....	443.3	15,842.68	3,420.80	306.80	5.00	19,575.28
.....	....	511.8	....	....	....	1,324.9	74,756.03	7,252.53	1,185.71	71.86	83,266.13
.....	....	....	....	....	....	508.6	25,740.77	2,242.31	329.51	41.57	28,354.16
.....	....	1,023.7	....	11.1	....	1,105.9	71,074.94	7,804.71	928.51	35.35	79,843.51
.....	....	....	....	....	....	1,882.6	93,170.00	10,950.13	1,911.65	....	106,031.78
.....	....	204.7	....	....	....	501.1	27,993.07	2,773.68	362.18	30.33	31,159.26
.....	....	....	....	11.4	23.4	622.3	46,364.22	3,744.66	591.23	273.68	50,973.79
.....	....	....	....	....	....	585.6	125,113.89	5,400.76	1,547.26	....	132,061.91
.....	....	....	....	....	.1	.1	324.48	......	7.80	2.13	334.41
.....	....	....	....	....	....	2,071.2	104,448.46	9,133.70	1,337.66	173.38	115,093.20
.....	....	266.2	....	....	35.7	2,734.1	173,807.98	15,338.17	2,233.50	196.91	191,576.56
.....	....	....	....	....	....	25.8	1,053.36	184.86	17.15	....	1,255.37
367.6	**281.5**	**2,006.4**	**.7**	**22.5**	**87.1**	**18,223.1**	**$ 1,221,575.20**	**$ 108,423.31**	**$ 20,898.41**	**$ 1,146.46**	**$ 1,352,043.38**
.....	....	....	....	....	.1	.1	$ 486.72	$ 1.05	$ 13.20	$ 3.20	$ 504.17
21.0	....	....	....	....	....	21.0	4,950.00	211.72	96.68	8.00	5,266.40
227.3	....	511.8	....	47.2	10.3	1,590.3	146,143.09	11,106.46	1,900.10	204.07	159,353.72
.....	181.9	....	....	....	....	181.9	9,430.58	1,591.31	129.80	17.50	11,169.19
.....	....	....	....	....	1.5	1.5	993.47	156.00	28.35	....	1,177.82
.....	....	....	....	....	....	863.3	33,191.02	6,326.83	539.26	....	40,057.11
.....	....	....	....	....	....	342.9	17,354.26	1,511.75	289.14	28.50	19,183.65
80.6	....	....	....	....	....	80.6	13,135.00	835.28	269.19	26.00	14,265.47
.....	203.2	511.8	....	11.7	1.9	1,702.5	97,801.01	10,754.72	1,520.34	212.73	110,288.80
.....	....	....	53.0[n]	....	....	53.0	7,799.04	......	......	....	7,799.04
.....	....	....	....	....	....	1,000.0	49,896.34	4,629.60	846.01	125.78	55,497.73
.....	....	....	....	....	....	1,016.1	50,285.71	5,910.00	962.08	....	57,157.79
.....	....	....	....	....	....	1,475.2	70,662.19	6,504.45	1,248.89	191.88	78,607.41
.....	....	....	....	....	....	1,272.2	66,635.09	9,521.15	1,091.24	....	77,247.48
16.5	....	255.9	....	28.3	7.4	1,319.3	190,038.39	10,283.58	3,181.91	38.41	203,542.29
.....	....	....	....	....	....	579.1	27,211.56	3,556.21	457.67	....	31,225.44
.....	....	....	15.5[l]	30.6	.1	1,661.5	92,653.84	7,994.01	1,560.69	214.76	102,423.30
.....	....	....	....	....	....	865.9	43,469.00	3,817.72	719.46	156.55	48,162.73
.....	....	481.1	....	51.0	....	559.1	47,398.01	4,330.48	660.57	60.70	52,449.76
.....	....	....	....	....	....	294.8	62,745.85	2,753.98	1,076.52	....	66,576.35
108.8	25.4	273.3	81.2[p]	....	1.5	938.8	85,651.23	10,861.96	2,095.77	335.99	98,944.95
.....	....	....	....	....	....	1,036.8	51,265.63	4,342.93	870.72	113.15	56,592.43
.....	....	....	....	....	....	691.3	66,264.92	6,276.73	1,226.48	....	73,768.13
.....	....	255.9	....	....	....	1,817.5	92,913.98	8,770.01	1,504.21	226.20	103,414.40
14.0	....	....	23.9[c]	....	2.0	39.9	49,241.10	......	......	....	49,241.10
468.2	**410.5**	**2,289.8**	**173.6**	**168.8**	**24.8**	**19,404.6**	**$ 1,377,617.03**	**$ 122,047.93**	**$ 22,288.28**	**$ 1,963.42**	**$ 1,523,916.66**
.....	128.5	....	....	71.4	....	1,869.6	$ 109,742.21	$ 9,759.57	$ 1,749.60	$ 312.86	$ 121,564.24
.....	15.2	244.6	....	....	28.0	3,011.8	177,498.06	26,493.47	4,831.02	287.98	209,110.53
.....	....	....	....	....	....	508.0	108,081.06	4,718.56	1,918.60	....	114,718.22
.....	....	....	....	....	....	172.9	9,270.28	800.38	152.58	15.12	10,238.36
283.0	20.3	....	....	....	....	608.0	125,966.85	11,773.50	3,256.21	114.67	141,111.23
.....	....	511.8	....	....	....	713.5	46,530.59	4,600.94	649.68	20.64	51,801.85
.....	....	....	....	....	....	1,312.3	55,101.29	9,387.61	848.26	....	65,337.16
.....	....	502.9	....	....	....	502.9	35,212.80	3,603.13	528.11	5.00	39,349.04
152.4	....	....	....	....	....	550.7	67,170.56	7,434.59	1,651.75	64.24	76,321.14
.....	.8	....	....	....	....	94.2	5,112.49	441.65	83.00	5.00	5,642.14
136.7	100.8	....	15.2[l]	65.4	4.0	3,473.9	225,552.36	17,766.70	3,509.42	381.74	247,210.22
.....	....	....	....	....	....	739.9	170,919.17	5,359.51	2,536.88	....	178,815.56
12.7	146.3	260.0	....	....	....	419.0	29,975.22	3,517.70	417.79	44.00	33,954.71
43.5	....	972.6	....	....	15.7	2,812.7	218,029.28	30,278.78	3,948.47	1,054.86	253,311.39
.....	....	....	....	....	....	619.9	28,894.14	4,099.87	450.21	....	33,444.22
153.0	....	220.1	46.7[l]	....	....	419.8	75,790.06	3,399.33	932.14	111.00	80,232.53
.....	7.0	....	....	....	152.0	159.0	12,474.49	......	......	....	12,474.49
781.3	**418.9**	**2,712.0**	**61.9**	**135.8**	**199.7**	**17,988.1**	**$ 1,501,320.91**	**$ 143,435.29**	**$ 27,463.72**	**$ 2,417.11**	**$ 1,674,637.03**

[*Continued on next page*]

Table 165—*Continued*

Arrival No.	Steamer or Source	Port of Sailing	Date of Arrival	Port of Arrival	Flour	Rice	Beans, Peas	Corn Grits	Pork Produc
			1922						
500	Emergency Aid, I	New Orleans	May 1	Hamburg	1,284.6	1,134.7	....	....	...
501	Rodondo	New York	May 5	Riga	.....	.....	....	....	...
502	Manchuria, VI	New York	May 8	Hamburg	.....	.....	....	....	...
503	Sutransco	New York Odessa	May 13 May 27	Odessa Novorossisk	1,498.6	.....	....	381.5	857
504	Virginian, II	Portland	May 14	Hamburg	447.7	.....	....	....	...
505	Sapinero, I	New Orleans	May 14	Hamburg	462.3	118.1	....	....	134
506	St. Paul, I	New York	May 14	Hamburg	98.6	.....	....	....	...
507	Bremerton	New York	May 14	Riga	.....	.....	....	....	...
508	Surico	Boston	May 16	Petrograd	953.5	.....	....	....	...
509	Sunelseco	New York	May 19	Petrograd	2,396.2	.....	....	....	...
510	Sutorpco	New York	May 19	Odessa	1,619.3	.....	....	396.3	50
511	City of Flint, IV	Norfolk	May 21	Hamburg	.....	.....	....	....	249
512	Suholco	Newark Odessa	May 22 June ..	Odessa Novorossisk	1,542.3	.....	....	347.6	...
513	Menominee	New York	May 22	Hamburg	338.4	.....	....	....	...
514	Mount Clinton, VI	New York	May 23	Hamburg	232.9	.....	....	....	...
515	Casey, I	New Orleans	May 25	Odessa	.....	1,495.9	....	....	...
516	Mailand **	Copenhagen	May 25	Riga	.....	.....	....	....	...
517	Dakotan, III	New York	May 26	Hamburg	889.1	.....	....	....	...
518	Morristown, II	Philadelphia	May 28	Hamburg	.....	.....	....	....	...
519	Cody, II	New Orleans	May 31	Hamburg	1,138.2	.....	....	....	...
520	European Purchases	....	May 31	....	.....	.....	....	....	...
	Total for May				**12,901.7**	**2,748.7**	....	**1,125.4**	**1,291**
521	Texan, III	Tacoma	June 1	Hamburg	2,222.6	.....	....	....	...
522	Conejos, II	New York	June 1	Odessa	.....	77.2	....	803.9	...
523	Minnekahda, VII	New York	June 3	Hamburg	365.7	.....	....	....	...
524	Casey, I	New Orleans	June 5	Novorossisk	1,860.6	.....	....	....	...
525	Corson, VI	Philadelphia	June 7	Hamburg	.....	.....	....	....	...
526	Noccalula, II	New York	June 9	Hamburg	1,650.1	.....	....	....	...
527	Manchuria, VII	New York	June 11	Hamburg	.....	.....	....	....	...
528	Eastport, II	New York	June 16	Riga	284.9	.....	....	....	...
529	St. Paul, II	New York	June 18	Hamburg	.....	.....	....	....	...
530	Gaffney, II	New York	June 19	Odessa	637.4	.....	....	....	136
531	Mount Carroll, IX	New York	June 20	Hamburg	.....	.....	....	182.6	...
532	West Helix	Norfolk	June 24	Hamburg	.....	.....	....	....	33
533	Belvidere, II	New York	June 24	Riga	654.3	.....	....	....	...
534	Clontarf, II	New York	June 29	Constantinople	159.4	78.3	....	....	2
	Total for June				**7,835.0**	**155.5**	....	**986.5**	**189**
535	Nobles, III	New Orleans	July 2	Hamburg	.....	103.4	....	....	...
536	Emergency Aid, II	New Orleans	July 9	Hamburg	.....	690.0	....	....	...
537	Clontarf, II	New York	July 10	Odessa	983.6	.....	....	....	...
538	Allaguash, I	New York	July 25	Petrograd	1,935.8	.....	....	....	26
539	Saugus, II	New York	July 26	Odessa	31.1	922.4	....	....	18
540	Irene	New York	July 29	Odessa	1,541.8	.....	....	243.5	8
	Total for July				**4,492.3**	**1,715.8**	....	**243.5**	**54**
541	Nevadan	Norfolk	Aug. 6	Hamburg	.....	.....	....	....	23
542	George W. Allen	New York	Aug. 13	Odessa	6,900.8	.....	....	....	8
543	Manitowac, I	New York	Aug. 22	Petrograd	4,831.7	.....	....	....	..
544	St. Paul	New York	Aug. 27	Hamburg	.....	.....	....	....	..
545	Eastern Star	New York	Aug. 31	Petrograd	370.7	.....	....	....	..
	Total for August				**12,103.2**	.....	....	....	**32**
546	Conejos, III	New York	Sept. 1	Odessa	334.0	.....	....	....	..
547	Chebaulip	New York	Sept. 10	Petrograd	587.7	.....	....	....	..
548	Norlina	New York	Sept. 11	Petrograd	3,647.8	.....	....	....	..
549	Sagaporack	New York	Sept. 21	Odessa	.....	.....	....	....	..
550	Eastern Coast, III	New York	Sept. 26	Petrograd	165.4	.....	....	....	..
551	Emergency Aid, III	New Orleans	Sept. 28	Hamburg	.....	466.1	....	....	..
552	James B. Duke	New York	Sept. 29	Petrograd	4,645.5	.....	....	....	..
553	Clontarf, III	New York	Sept. 30	Constantinople	209.0	385.0	....	....	24
	Total for September				**9,589.4**	**851.1**	....	....	**24**

** Commodities donated by Vladimir Goriachovsky.

ILDREN'S FUND

Steamers

c Tons of 1,000 Kilograms or 2,204.6 Pounds											
ilk	Cocoa	Sugar	Misc. Food	Soap	Clothing and Misc.	Total Tons	F.O.B. Value	Freight	Insurance	Miscellaneous Charges	Total C.I.F. Value
....	....	395.3	....	....	....	2,814.6	$ 142,393.27	$ 17,363.98	$ 2,511.87	$ 160.72	$ 162,429.84
....	....	309.9	....	....	....	309.9	23,052.00	2,459.11	432.68	4.00	25,947.79
91.4	....	....	....	....	....	91.4	14,385.00	800.10	178.75	23.00	15,386.85
65.3	240.9	588.5	....	....	....	3,631.8	430,973.95	40,200.67	9,187.82	2,256.19	482,618.63
....	....	....	....	....	....	447.7	23,000.00	3,333.33	445.77	....	26,779.10
....	....	....	....	....	....	714.5	66,836.87	5,038.88	1,016.22	59.74	72,951.71
71.9	....	....	....	....	....	170.5	16,874.38	1,187.12	287.41	36.60	18,385.51
....	....	597.2	....	....	....	597.2	44,427.80	4,739.40	833.82	8.00	50,009.02
....	....	....	....	....	.5	954.0	51,309.07	6,837.55	1,110.49	215.42	59,472.53
....	101.6	....	....	....	20.9	2,518.7	153,536.34	17,063.43	3,129.84	81.34	173,810.95
74.7	....	....	....	....	7.0	3,247.7	338,094.44	38,066.87	6,070.20	3,036.62	385,268.13
....	....	....	....	....	....	249.9	72,311.96	2,086.73	1,253.94	....	75,652.63
'46.2	119.9	....	30.8[p]	....	1.0	2,787.8	257,032.02	32,876.02	4,500.51	1,276.22	295,684.77
....	....	....	....	....	....	338.4	18,390.55	1,566.66	299.10	8.90	20,265.21
....	....	....	....	....	....	232.9	13,029.12	1,283.56	286.66	3.25	14,602.59
....	....	....	....	....	....	1,495.9	75,434.00	19,226.06	1,648.09	....	96,308.15
....	....	....	8.6[q]	....	....	8.6	1,183.96	......	......	....	1,183.96
....	....	....	....	....	....	889.1	50,823.27	7,231.05	891.82	....	58,946.14
....	320.1	....	....	....	....	320.1	17,342.08	3,969.00	262.66	40.00	21,613.74
....	....	....	....	....	....	1,138.2	65,780.06	6,147.47	1,087.56	124.38	73,139.47
....	....	....	122.1[pr]	....	30.0	152.1	18,884.26	......	......	....	18,884.26
49.5	**782.5**	**1,890.9**	**161.5**	....	**59.4**	**23,111.0**	**$ 1,895,094.40**	**$ 211,476.99**	**$ 35,435.21**	**$ 7,334.38**	**$ 2,149,340.98**
....	....	....	....	....	....	2,222.6	$ 130,000.00	$ 16,666.70	$ 2,281.17	....	$ 148,947.87
38.8	....	....	....	....	16.8	1,036.7	75,383.72	13,380.80	1,380.37	$ 114.70	90,259.59
08.8	15.7	....	....	....	....	490.2	42,317.21	2,584.93	620.81	82.54	45,605.49
....	....	....	....	....	....	1,860.6	124,543.67	18,311.60	2,646.67	330.25	145,832.19
....	76.2	....	....	....	....	76.2	4,280.64	945.00	61.55	35.00	5,322.19
....	....	....	....	....	....	1,650.1	105,159.57	8,587.12	1,601.27	256.65	115,604.61
33.7	....	100.4	....	....	....	434.1	65,163.06	3,568.07	1,021.05	106.00	69,858.18
.6	....	....	....	....	5.0	290.5	19,692.76	1,697.47	399.11	4.47	21,793.81
19.8	....	....	....	....	....	119.8	18,920.00	1,041.75	363.20	42.00	20,366.95
72.2	....	138.2	40.8[p]	....	15.0	1,239.8	157,472.88	17,562.49	2,715.85	309.26	178,060.48
83.8	....	....	....	....	3.3	269.7	20,317.22	1,522.59	256.40	47.65	22,143.86
....	....	....	....	....	....	33.1	8,656.54	219.36	102.08	....	8,977.98
....	....	....	....	....	2.0	656.3	41,694.99	3,685.18	807.23	3.48	46,190.88
71.1	8.1	44.1	....	....	....	381.3	37,745.90	3,806.92	644.97	66.05	42,263.84
28.8	**100.0**	**282.7**	**40.8**	....	**42.1**	**10,761.0**	**$ 851,348.16**	**$ 93,579.98**	**$ 14,901.73**	**$ 1,398.05**	**$ 961,227.92**
....	....	....	....	....	....	103.4	$ 5,052.59	$ 631.59	$ 74.55	....	$ 5,758.73
....	....	....	....	....	....	690.0	33,602.28	4,182.98	499.74	....	38,285.00
....	....	....	....	....	....	983.6	65,659.45	8,542.20	1,148.04	$ 81.19	75,430.88
557.4	101.6	990.0	53.4[p]	....	13.1	3,921.0	410,025.19	31,165.47	9,366.30	579.88	451,136.84
....	....	248.3	....	....	12.5	1,399.5	128,998.28	13,892.75	2,217.34	6,715.95	151,824.32
566.1	20.3	101.0	81.8[p]	....	3.3	2,643.9	270,931.15	29,202.63	4,673.48	533.57	305,340.83
123.5	**121.9**	**1,339.3**	**135.2**	....	**28.9**	**9,741.4**	**$ 914,268.94**	**$ 87,617.62**	**$ 17,979.45**	**$ 7,910.59**	**$ 1,027,776.60**
....	....	....	....	....	....	236.8	$ 62,525.07	$ 1,898.57	$ 1,464.87	....	$ 65,888.51
142.8	....	....	....	....	1.0	7,128.5	475,667.16	60,137.35	8,325.41	$ 573.48	544,703.40
405.5	211.3	487.3	....	....	....	5,935.8	432,622.07	38,941.17	10,220.29	636.64	482,420.17
....	....	....	....	....	.0	.0	20.00	5.00	.37	1.50	26.87
....	....	....	....	....	....	370.7	23,876.24	2,125.05	542.78	4.20	26,548.27
548.3	**211.3**	**487.3**	....	....	**1.0**	**13,671.8**	**$ 994,710.54**	**$ 103,107.14**	**$ 20,553.72**	**$ 1,215.82**	**$ 1,119,587.22**
....	....	....	....	....	....	334.0	$ 20,386.85	$ 2,958.51	$ 362.29	$ 22.55	$ 23,730.20
....	....	....	....	....	....	587.7	37,342.46	3,368.47	914.86	18.79	41,644.58
....	....	573.3	....	....	33.2	4,254.3	282,233.83	26,046.42	6,405.40	270.62	314,956.27
398.4	....	....	....	....	....	398.4	68,613.37	6,738.36	1,169.12	120.00	76,640.85
65.3	....	....	....	....	....	230.7	21,466.90	1,581.88	481.07	30.13	23,559.98
....	....	....	....	....	....	466.1	21,165.01	2,568.93	311.15	....	24,045.09
834.4	117.4	1,504.1	16.2[p]	....	....	7,117.6	571,901.38	46,333.22	12,900.63	722.57	631,857.80
178.0	108.0	305.0	....	....	....	1,425.0	160,255.83	......	......	17,254.59	177,510.42
476.1	**225.4**	**2,382.4**	**16.2**	....	**33.2**	**14,813.8**	**$ 1,183,365.63**	**$ 89,595.79**	**$ 22,544.52**	**$ 18,439.25**	**$ 1,313,945.19**

[*Continued on next page*]

Table 165—*Continued*

Detail of Arriva[ls]

Arrival No.	Steamer or Source	Port of Sailing	Date of Arrival	Port of Arrival	Flour	Rice	Beans, Peas	Corn Grits	Pork Produc[ts]
					Contents of Cargoes in N[et Metric Tons]				
			1922						
554	Western Scout	Norfolk	Oct. 9	Hamburg	.....	.....	....	....	359
555	West Islay	New York	Oct. 16	Petrograd	4,377.2	126.0	....	404.7	374
556	West Hematite	New Orleans	Oct. 18	Hamburg	.....	103.4	....	....	...
557	European Purchases	....	Oct. 27	Constantinople	.....	.....	....	....	...
558	Orient	New York	Oct. 29	Odessa	2,375.6	3.0	....	733.7	158
	Total for October				**6,752.8**	**232.4**	....	**1,138.4**	**892**
559	Cliffwood	New Orleans	Nov. 11	Hamburg	.....	76.4	....	....	...
560	Helmo Hemsoth	London	Nov. 18	Petrograd	.....	.....	....	....	...
561	Allaguash, II	New York	Nov. 24	Petrograd	3,769.4	52.8	....	485.3	144
562	Aquarius	New Orleans	Nov. 26	Hamburg	.....	883.1	....	....	...
	Total for November				**3,769.4**	**1,012.3**	....	**485.3**	**144**
563	Mount Carroll, X	New York	Dec. 4	Hamburg	156.2	.....	....	....	22
564	Emergency Aid, IV	New Orleans	Dec. 17	Hamburg	.....	309.2	....	....	...
565	Mount Clinton, VII	New York	Dec. 20	Hamburg	71.0	.....	....	....	40
566	Muskegon	New York	Dec. 22	Odessa	1,486.7	289.5	....	....	640
567	Stuyvesant	New York	Dec. 24	Odessa	22.2	826.2	....	....	379
568	Winnebago	New York	Dec. 25	Riga	2,083.9	34.6	....	149.7	217
569	Chester Valley, II	New Orleans	Dec. 31	Hamburg	.....	188.9	....	....	...
	Total for December				**3,820.0**	**1,648.4**	....	**149.7**	**1,300**
			1923						
570	Mount Clay, X	New York	Jan. 1	Hamburg	97.7	.....	20.5	....	...
571	Mount Carroll, XI	New York	Jan. 25	Hamburg	.....	.....	....	....	...
572	Manitowac, II	New York	Jan. 28	Odessa	1,107.1	259.2	....	....	...
573	Belvidere	New York	Jan. 29	Riga	.....	.....	....	....	...
	Total for January				**1,204.8**	**259.2**	**20.5**	....	...
574	Mount Clay, XI	New York	Feb. 14	Hamburg	425.7	.....	....	....	60
575	West Maximus	New York	Feb. 17	Riga	.....	.....	....	....	...
576	Saugus	New York, Norfolk	Feb. 26	Odessa	.....	.....	....	....	59
577	West Ira	New Orleans	Feb. 28	Hamburg	.....	865.2	....	....	...
	Total for February				**425.7**	**865.2**	....	....	**65**
578	Tomalva	Galveston	Mar. 3	Hamburg	.....	132.4	....	....	..
579	Winneconne	New York	Mar. 10	Odessa	3,002.6	.....	....	....	..
580	Emergency Aid, V	New Orleans	Mar. 14	Hamburg	.....	212.5	....	....	..
581	Allaguash, III	New York	Mar. 24	Windau	4,132.8	.....	....	....	..
582	Bayern, III	New York	Mar. 26	Hamburg	.....	.....	....	19.3	..
583	Rockaway Park	New York	Mar. 28	Windau	4,089.1	.....	....	....	..
	Total for March				**11,224.5**	**344.9**	....	**19.3**	..
584	Cold Water	Norfolk	Apr. 5	Hamburg	.....	.....	....	....	75
585	Eastern Star	New York	Apr. 11	Windau	2,072.8	.....	....	31.8	..
586	Suruga	New York Hamburg	Apr. 12 May 3	Hamburg Riga	2,763.2	.....	....	2,186.4	..
587	Eastern Coast	Philadelphia	Apr. 14	Riga	198.8	.....	....	749.1	..
588	President Harding	New York	Apr. 16	Hamburg	76.1	.....	....	358.0	..
589	Springfield	Norfolk	Apr. 18	Hamburg	.....	.....	....	....	75
590	Coeur d'Alene	New York	Apr. 24	Odessa	.....	.....	....	....	..
591	Conejos, IV	New York	Apr. 24	Odessa	.....	.....	....	....	..
592	Local Purchase	Riga	Apr. 24	Riga	.....	.....	....	....	..
593	George Washington	New York	Apr. 24	Bremen	.....	.....	....	269.6	..
594	Andalusia, III ‡	New York	Apr. 25	Riga	294.9	.....	....	532.6	..
595	Satsuma	New York	Apr. 26	Libau	2,825.9	.....	....	2,012.0	..
596	Local Purchase	Riga	Apr. 30	Riga	.....	.....	....	....	..
	Total for April				**8,231.7**	.....	....	**6,139.5**	**1,50**

‡ This steamer sailed from Hamburg to Riga, transshipping commodities shipped on through B/L New York–Riga, ex-"Mount Carroll," XII, "Reliance," and "Hansa," which arrived at Hamburg April 2, 11, and [...] 1923, respectively.

HILDREN'S FUND

Steamers

ric Tons of 1,000 Kilograms or 2,204.6 Pounds							F.O.B. Value	Freight	Insurance	Miscellaneous Charges	Total C.I.F. Value
Milk	Cocoa	Sugar	Misc. Food	Soap	Clothing and Misc.	Total Tons					
.....	....	....	....	....	....	359.7	$ 79,697.71	$ 1,934.80	$ 960.91	....	$ 82,593.42
,313.3	54.9	....	....	....	18.7	6,668.9	598,005.75	45,130.65	13,410.91	$ 724.38	657,271.69
.....	....	....	....	....	....	103.4	4,682.39	570.10	68.91	....	5,321.40
39.0	....	....	....	....	....	39.0	7,521.05	......	......	....	7,521.05
,050.1	108.3	870.1	15.7p	....	8.8	5,323.8	484,562.13	36,197.56	7,930.64	11,902.47	540,592.80
,402.4	**163.2**	**870.1**	**15.7**	....	**27.5**	**12,494.8**	**$ 1,174,469.03**	**$ 83,833.11**	**$ 22,371.37**	**$ 12,626.85**	**$ 1,293,300.36**
.....	....	....	....	....	....	76.4	$ 2,912.23	$ 370.73	$ 43.06	....	$ 3,326.02
.....	....	....	5.0p	....	....	5.0	2,573.82	......	......	....	2,573.82
670.9	....	....	6.8p	....	35.8	5,165.2	410,803.33	33,323.78	11,091.85	$ 417.95	455,636.91
.....	....	....	....	....	....	883.1	39,497.32	4,283.19	495.29	....	44,275.80
670.9	....	....	**11.8**	....	**35.8**	**6,129.7**	**$ 455,786.70**	**$ 37,977.70**	**$ 11,630.20**	**$ 417.95**	**$ 505,812.55**
21.8	28.5	132.1	....	....	....	360.9	$ 34,856.35	$ 1,695.28	$ 560.99	$ 44.30	$ 37,156.92
.....	....	....	....	....	....	309.2	15,135.55	1,499.72	173.40	....	16,808.67
62.8	....	....	....	....	47.8	222.3	98,974.56	2,154.76	2,231.02	37.60	103,397.94
525.3	107.7	888.5	54.6p	....	11.4	4,004.1	467,822.57	37,603.67	9,797.26	505.93	515,729.43
661.6	....	....	....	....	....	1,889.3	242,185.60	12,936.28	5,186.34	192.25	260,500.47
522.6	....	789.3	32.2p	....	472.5	4,302.6	1,030,791.76	38,874.32	19,816.22	459.43	1,089,941.73
.....	....	....	....	....	....	188.9	6,921.70	916.12	102.85	....	7,940.67
,794.1	**136.2**	**1,809.9**	**86.8**	....	**531.7**	**11,277.3**	**$ 1,896,688.09**	**$ 95,680.15**	**$ 37,868.08**	**$ 1,239.51**	**$ 2,031,475.83**
15.2	....	....	....	....	200.4	333.8	$ 239,574.70	$ 5,192.72	$ 4,871.68	$ 19.70	$ 249,658.80
217.7	....	....	....	91.5	....	309.2	65,759.74	2,353.40	1,293.71	40.00	69,446.85
396.2	....	....	....	....	101.4	1,863.9	162,514.54	18,217.54	3,302.86	133.39	184,168.33
.....	....	....	....	....	80.2	80.2	152,893.85	2,185.21	2,928.20	....	158,007.26
629.1	....	....	....	**91.5**	**382.0**	**2,587.1**	**$ 620,742.83**	**$ 27,948.87**	**$ 12,396.45**	**$ 193.09**	**$ 661,281.24**
34.8	32.6	....	....	....	....	553.6	$ 52,517.94	$ 2,452.64	$ 780.79	$ 65.00	$ 55,816.37
140.3	....	....	....	42.4	....	182.7	38,422.25	1,274.68	700.93	81.00	40,478.86
296.1	....	....	....	....	....	892.4	220,984.06	15,156.24	4,295.47	65.00	240,500.77
.....	....	....	....	....	....	865.2	36,758.66	4,768.87	547.03	....	42,074.56
471.2	**32.6**	....	....	**42.4**	....	**2,493.9**	**$ 348,682.91**	**$ 23,652.43**	**$ 6,324.22**	**$ 211.00**	**$ 378,870.56**
.....	....	....	....	....	....	132.4	$ 5,538.34	$ 729.41	$ 82.20	....	$ 6,349.95
489.9	....	350.5	....	....	....	3,843.0	328,189.21	33,416.05	6,561.02	$ 254.50	368,420.78
.....	....	....	....	....	....	212.5	8,932.07	1,171.16	134.33	....	10,237.56
796.5	....	512.5	....	81.0	27.8	5,550.6	495,769.45	36,908.54	9,324.40	339.70	542,342.09
140.3	....	182.7	....	....	....	342.3	53,330.53	1,700.44	787.21	49.52	55,867.70
339.0	382.5	176.3	....	....	1.0	4,987.9	369,219.04	35,525.19	7,145.49	300.58	412,190.30
,765.7	**382.5**	**1,222.0**	....	**81.0**	**28.8**	**15,068.7**	**$ 1,260,978.64**	**$ 109,450.79**	**$ 24,034.65**	**$ 944.30**	**$ 1,395,408.38**
.....	....	....	....	....	....	754.1	$ 205,324.93	$ 4,064.89	$ 2,464.50	$ 10.00	$ 211,864.32
.....	....	....	....	....	....	2,104.6	130,398.73	12,062.99	2,515.45	61.22	145,038.39
934.4	....	312.0	....	....	....	6,196.0	497,502.51	43,530.21	7,015.23	488.15	548,536.10
700.0	13.6	568.8	....	....	5.2	2,235.5	262,835.42	14,327.77	4,885.71	237.03	282,285.93
.....	....	....	....	....	....	434.1	19,792.15	1,530.29	368.27	34.21	21,724.92
.....	....	....	....	....	....	751.6	213,240.48	4,752.34	2,565.86	15.00	220,573.68
214.9	....	....	....	....	....	214.9	46,453.66	3,568.09	1,110.65	65.00	51,197.40
21.8	....	....	....	....	....	21.8	4,600.00	348.21	83.40	8.00	5,039.61
.....	....	304.6	....	....	....	304.6	45,880.05	......	......	....	45,880.05
.....	....	....	....	....	....	269.6	11,470.38	950.91	202.68	21.24	12,645.21
428.6	....	....	....	....	....	1,256.1	127,801.51	9,312.58	3,358.25	183.49	140,655.83
,297.1	....	22.7	....	....	.2	6,157.9	526,158.99	43,764.56	10,978.75	558.77	581,461.07
.....	....	155.0	....	....	....	155.0	20,428.38	......	......	....	20,428.38
596.8	**13.6**	**1,363.1**	....	....	**5.4**	**20,855.8**	**$ 2,111,887.19**	**$ 138,212.84**	**$ 35,548.75**	**$ 1,682.11**	**$ 2,287,330.89**

[*Concluded on next page*]

Table 165—*Concluded*

Detail of Arrival

Arrival No.	Steamer or Source	Port of Sailing	Date of Arrival	Port of Arrival	Contents of Cargoes in Ne — Flour	Rice	Beans, Peas	Corn Grits	Pork Product
			1923						
597	Local Purchase	Riga	May 4	Riga	.....	.....	....	....	....
598	Local Purchase	Riga	May 25	Riga	.....	.....	....	....	....
599	Baltannic	London	May 28	Libau	.....	.....	....	....	....
	Total for May........	....	....	....	.....	.....	....	....	....
	Grand Total, Gross....	....	....	....	**163,679.3**	**40,133.7**	**25,916.7**	**15,910.5**	**22,060.**
	Deduct Cargoes Transferred to Soviet Republics §....	....	....	....	38,747.0	5,666.0	....	....	3,658.
	Grand Total, Net......	....	....	....	**124,932.3**	**34,467.7**	**25,916.7**	**15,910.5**	**18,402.**

* The total, 1,885.2 metric tons, is composed of: [a], whalemeat, 1.0; [b], soup, 44.0; [c], codliver oil, 78.4; [d], chocolate, 73.5; [e], herring, 54.0; [g], salmon, 631.6; [h], dried fruit, 79.0; [i], fish, 5.0; [k], dehydrated potatoes, .9; [l], powdered and dried milk, 77.5; [m], salt, 148.0; [n], biscuits, 53. [o], dates, .7; [p], tea, 618.2; [q], rice and milk, 8.6; [r], corned beef, 9.1; [s], gr ceries, 1.9.

AMERICAN RELIE

Table 166

Detail of Arrivals by Steamers-

Arrival No.	Steamer or Source	Port of Sailing	Date of Arrival	Port of Arrival	Contents — Flour	Rice	Beans, Peas
			1920				
1	Cripple Creek	New York	Jan. 4	Hamburg	8,138.8	.....	.....
2	Inverawe	Liverpool	Jan. 23	Hamburg	.....	.....	.....
	Total for January...............	....	....	....	**8,138.8**	.....	.....
3	Kermoor, I	New York	Feb. 2	Hamburg	.....	.....	.....
4	Shortsville	New York	Feb. 9	Danzig	.....	.....	588.
5	Zeeland	Liverpool	Feb. 10	Hamburg	.....	.....	.....
6	Borderland	Liverpool	Feb. 14	Hamburg	.....	.....	.....
7	Wisla	New York	Feb. 16	Danzig	.....	.....	.....
8	Manchuria, I	New York	Feb. 26	Hamburg	.....	.....	.....
9	Keresan, II	New York	Feb. 27	Hamburg	.....	.....	84.
10	Pawnee	Philadelphia	Feb. 28	Danzig	1,561.0	.....	.....
	Total for February..............	....	....	....	**1,561.0**	.....	**672.**
11	Clauseus, I	San Francisco	Mar. 2	Hamburg	.....	.....	2,032.
12	Ina Blumenthal	Liverpool	Mar. 4	Danzig	.....	.....	....
13	Mar Caspio, I	New York	Mar. 7	Hamburg	.....	.....	....
14	Clauseus	San Francisco	Mar. 9	Danzig	.....	.....	615.
15	Mongolia, I	New York	Mar. 10	Hamburg	.....	.....	....
16	Stock Purchase from Bridges.........	Hamburg	Mar. 11	Hamburg	.....	.....	....
17	Vardulia	New York	Mar. 15	Danzig	326.3	.....	....
18	Kerowlee, II	New York	Mar. 29	Hamburg	.....	.....	....
	Total for March.................	....	....	....	**326.3**	.....	**2,647.**
19	Kermanshah	New York	Apr. 3	Hamburg	.....	.....	....
20	Vasconia	New York	Apr. 5	Danzig	.....	.....	....
21	Valacia	New York	Apr. 5	Danzig	.....	.....	75.
22	Manchuria, II	New York	Apr. 8	Hamburg	.....	.....	....
	Total for April..................	....	....	....			**75.**
23	Carib	New York	May 23	Hamburg	.....	.....	....
24	Keresan, II	Philadelphia	May 27	Hamburg	.....	.....	....
25	Mar Mediterraneo	New York	May 31	Hamburg	.....	.....	....
	Total for May....................	....	....	....	.....	.....	....

† Balance of deliveries from E.C.F. arrivals, Table 165.
* All corned beef.
‡ Bags, containers, etc.
§ Commodities delivered c.i.f.

HILDREN'S FUND

Steamers

tric Tons of 1,000 Kilograms or 2,204.6 Pounds											
Milk	Cocoa	Sugar	Misc. Food *	Soap	Clothing and Misc.	Total Tons	F.O.B. Value	Freight	Insurance	Miscellaneous Charges	Total C.I.F. Value
.....	....	195.4	....	....	....	195.4	$ 29,431.93	......	......	....	$ 29,431.93
.....	....	100.0	....	....	....	100.0	15,062.41	......	......	....	15,062.41
.....	....	....	....	....	1.0	1.0	390.00	$ 25.00	$ 5.00	....	420.00
.....	....	**295.4**	....	....	**1.0**	**296.4**	**$ 44,884.34**	**$ 25.00**	**$ 5.00**	....	**$ 44,914.34**
,735.3	**7,044.0**	**30,262.4**	**1,885.2***	**1,577.9**	**7,231.7**	**370,437.1**	**$53,248,740.75**	**$3,579,594.16**	**$856,449.91**	**$332,417.21**	**$58,017,202.03**
544.0	1,445.0	7,436.0	....	327.0	....	57,823.0	3,869,365.00	381,761.15	67,391.11	3,933.57	4,322,450.83
,191.3	**5,599.0**	**22,826.4**	**1,885.2***	**1,250.9**	**7,231.7**	**312,614.1**	**$49,379,375.75**	**$3,197,833.01**	**$789,058.80**	**$328,483.64**	**$53,694,751.20**

§ These supplies were purchased with Soviet gold. Cf. Tables 513
519.

DMINISTRATION WAREHOUSES†

econstruction Period, 1919–1924

rgoes in Net Metric Tons of 1,000 Kilograms or 2,204.6 Pounds											
Pork roducts	Milk	Cocoa	Sugar	Misc. Food *	Misc.‡	Total Tons	F.O.B. Value	Freight	Insurance	Miscellaneous Charges	Total C.I.F. Value
.....	.....	....	....	.....	2.3	8,141.1	$ 967,122.50	$185,869.03	$17,191.16	....	$1,170,182.69
.....	.....	....	....	106.0	....	106.0	61,688.55§	....	....	....	61,688.55
.....	.....	....	....	**106.0**	**2.3**	**8,247.1**	**$1,028,811.05**	**$185,869.03**	**$17,191.16**	....	**$1,231,871.24**
.....	.....	....	....	.....	1.2	1.2	$ 2,993.75	$ 70.31	$ 36.57	....	$ 3,100.63
.....	.....	....	....	.....	....	588.1	99,218.72	20,273.27	1,711.88	....	121,203.87
.....	.....	....	....	169.6	....	169.6	98,999.25§	....	....	....	98,999.25
.....	.....	....	....	30.6	....	30.6	18,140.33§	....	....	....	18,140.33
.....	.....	....	....	.....	2.7	2.7	3,065.60	93.71	52.50	....	3,211.81
340.2	.....	....	....	.....	....	340.2	223,538.81	9,731.32	2,733.75	....	236,003.88
.....	.....	....	....	.....	8.5	92.7	17,794.51	2,466.41	241.88	....	20,502.80
.....	.....	....	....	.....	....	1,561.0	184,335.00	53,764.38	4,828.13	....	242,927.51
340.2	.....	....	....	**200.2**	**12.4**	**2,786.1**	**$ 648,085.97**	**$ 86,399.40**	**$ 9,604.71**	....	**$ 744,090.08**
.....	.....	....	....	.....	....	2,032.0	$ 328,169.12	$ 64,943.87	$ 4,931.52	....	$ 398,044.51
.....	.....	....	....	102.0	....	102.0	59,359.38§	....	....	....	59,359.38
.....	430.0	....	....	.....	20.9	450.9	136,207.24	14,256.75	1,771.88	....	152,235.87
.....	.....	....	....	.....	....	615.0	117,614.69	21,647.96	2,462.07	....	141,724.72
172.9	71.9	....	....	.....	....	244.8	150,570.00	6,864.24	1,859.63	....	159,293.87
.....	1,368.0	....	....	.....	....	1,368.0	675,347.51§	....	....	....	675,347.51
465.0	190.1	....	....	.....	....	981.4	444,078.60	32,619.06	5,859.07	....	482,556.73
842.5	187.0	....	....	.....	....	1,029.5	624,570.55	29,958.93	8,575.00	....	663,104.48
,480.4	**2,247.0**	....	....	**102.0**	**20.9**	**6,823.6**	**$2,535,917.09**	**$170,290.81**	**$25,459.17**	....	**$2,731,667.07**
96.1	230.8	....	....	.....	....	326.9	$ 135,910.20	$ 9,666.58	$ 1,715.63	....	$ 147,292.41
.....	106.7	....	....	.....	....	106.7	29,890.00	3,981.25	201.68	....	34,072.93
15.5	236.0	....	....	.....	7.1	334.4	124,634.10	11,407.75	1,542.80	....	137,584.65
.....	.....	....	....	.....	9.1	9.1	3,250.00	220.00	41.63	....	3,511.63
111.6	**573.5**	....	....	.....	**16.2**	**777.1**	**$ 293,684.30**	**$ 25,275.58**	**$ 3,501.74**	....	**$ 322,461.62**
.....	.....	....	....	.....	11.8	11.8	$ 18,138.17	$ 708.95	$ 325.00	....	$ 19,172.12
37.0	.....	....	....	.....	....	37.0	28,644.00	882.77	349.88	....	29,876.65
.....	50.0	....	....	.....	....	50.0	14,030.00	1,270.75	180.00	....	15,480.75
37.0	**50.0**	....	....	.....	**11.8**	**98.8**	**$ 60,812.17**	**$ 2,862.47**	**$ 854.88**	....	**$ 64,529.52**

[*Continued on next page*]

AMERICAN RELIE[F]

Table 166—*Continued*

Detail of Arrival[s]

Arrival No.	Steamer or Source	Port of Sailing	Date of Arrival	Port of Arrival	Contents o[f Cargoes] Flour	Rice	Beans, Peas
			1920				
26	West Isleta	Boston	June 18	Hamburg	.....	.....	.....
27	Gerrat	London	June 28	Hamburg	.....	253.2	.....
	Total for June				.....	**253.2**	.....
28	Belgic	New York	July 27	Hamburg	.....	.....	.....
29	Minnekahda, I	New York	July 31	Hamburg	.....	.....	.....
	Total for July				.....	.....	.....
30	Bellerose	Philadelphia	Aug. 2	Hamburg	.....	.....	.....
31	West Ekonk	Boston	Aug. 15	Hamburg	.....	.....	.....
32	Purchase from Koch	Hamburg	Aug. 18	Hamburg	.....	.....	.....
33	Kermit, II	New York	Aug. 21	Hamburg	56.0	.....	.....
34	Mette Jensen, I	New York	Aug. 22	Hamburg	63.5	.....	.....
35	Susquehanna, I	New York	Aug. 23	Danzig	.....	.....	.....
36	Mar Blanco, II	New York	Aug. 24	Hamburg	86.7	.....	.....
37	Mongolia, IV	New York	Aug. 26	Hamburg	.....	.....	.....
38	Monticello, II	New York	Aug. 28	Hamburg	394.0	.....	.....
	Total for August				**600.2**	.....	.....
39	Mar Caribe, I	New York	Sept. 4	Hamburg	128.5	.....	.....
40	Jacques Cartier	New York	Sept. 7	Hamburg	.....	.....	.....
41	Sacandaga	New Orleans	Sept. 9	Hamburg	223.7	.....	.....
42	Mar de Irlanda	Baltimore	Sept. 12	Hamburg	177.8	.....	.....
43	Westford	New Orleans	Sept. 13	Hamburg	1,398.0	.....	.....
44	Mar Rojo	New York	Sept. 16	Hamburg	120.9	.....	.....
45	Herefordshire	Rangoon	Sept. 18	Hamburg	.....	1,174.7	.....
46	Mar Cantabrico	New York	Sept. 22	Hamburg	.....	.....	.....
	Total for September				**2,048.9**	**1,174.7**	.....
47	Vittorio Emmanuelle, III	New York	Oct. 1	Hamburg	31.6	.....	.....
48	Kerlew, III	New York	Oct. 6	Hamburg	.....	.....	.....
49	Purchase from Bobsein	Hamburg	Oct. 23–29	Hamburg	.....	.....	.....
50	Schoharie, I	New York	Oct. 13	Hamburg	.....	.....	.....
	Total for October				**31.6**	.....	.....
	U.S. Handling Charges—Not Allocated to Steamer				.....	.....	.....
	Grand Total				**12,706.8**	**1,427.9**	**3,395.1**

§ Commodities delivered c.i.f.

AMERICAN FRIEND[S]

Table 167

Detail of Arrivals by Steamers[—]

Arrival No.	Steamer or Source	Port of Sailing	Date of Arrival	Port of Arrival	Contents of Cargoes Flour	Rice	Beans, Peas	Pork Product[s]
			1919					
1	Kerowlee, I	New York	Dec. 26	Hamburg	.....	....	....	...
			1920					
2	Cripple Creek	New York	Jan. 4	Hamburg	**565.0**	....	....	...
3	Sark	New York	Feb. 13	Hamburg	.....	84.0	225.0	...
4	Manchuria, I	New York	Feb. 26	Hamburg	.....	....	171.0	...
5	Keresan, II	New York	Feb. 27	Hamburg	.....	....	50.0	61.[0]
	Total for February				.....	**84.0**	**446.0**	**61.0**

† Balance of deliveries from E.C.F. arrivals, Table 165.
* Detail of miscellaneous food indicated by the following indexes: ^{c}, codliver oil; ^{l}, dried milk. See end of Table 167 (page 380) for co[m]plete detail.

DMINISTRATION WAREHOUSES

Steamers

goes in Net Metric Tons of 1,000 Kilograms or 2,204.6 Pounds							F.O.B. Value	Freight	Insurance	Miscellaneous Charges	Total C.I.F. Value
Pork roducts	Milk	Cocoa	Sugar	Misc. Food	Misc.	Total Tons					
157.4	.....	....	....	.....	....	157.4	$ 121,584.40	$ 4,375.24	$ 1,485.00	....	$ 127,444.64
.....	.....	....	....	.....	....	253.2	51,319.00§	....	....	....	51,319.00
157.4	.....	....	....	.....	....	**410.6**	**$ 172,903.40**	**$ 4,375.24**	**$ 1,485.00**	....	**$ 178,763.64**
10.2	.....	....	....	.....	....	10.2	$ 5,675.00	$ 70.88	$ 332.50	....	$ 6,078.38
136.0	.....	....	....	.....	....	136.0	75,511.00	4,415.84	939.38	....	80,866.22
146.2	.....	....	....	.....	....	**146.2**	**$ 81,186.00**	**$ 4,486.72**	**$ 1,271.88**	....	**$ 86,944.60**
366.8	.....	....	....	.....	....	366.8	$ 283,018.40	$ 10,117.24	$ 3,457.23	....	$ 296,592.87
.....	106.3	....	....	.....	....	106.3	29,280.00	3,172.00	382.50	....	32,834.50
.....	.....	....	....	.....	4.0	4.0	1,330.85§	....	....	....	1,330.85
130.2	55.7	....	....	.....	....	241.9	100,006.33	6,635.90	1,347.51	....	107,989.74
15.9	....	....	....	.....	29.3	108.7	27,839.00	3,706.65	378.96	....	31,924.61
.....	.....	....	....	.....	2.4	2.4	750.00	176.15	11.66	....	937.81
.....	174.2	....	....	.....	....	260.9	59,937.75	6,823.70	785.25	....	67,546.70
157.9	.....	....	....	.....	....	157.9	102,707.20	4,222.52	1,261.13	....	108,190.85
61.2	95.2	....	....	.....	5.9	556.3	155,217.16	12,231.68	1,974.38	....	169,423.22
732.0	**431.4**	....	....	.....	**41.6**	**1,805.2**	**$ 760,086.69**	**$ 47,085.84**	**$ 9,598.62**	....	**$ 816,771.15**
.....	21.8	....	....	.....	....	150.3	$ 23,824.75	$ 3,057.37	$ 313.88	....	$ 27,196.00
152.5	.....	....	....	.....	....	152.5	99,157.76	3,473.79	1,210.50	....	103,842.05
.....	.....	....	....	.....	9.4	233.1	34,524.70	4,969.57	468.68	....	39,962.95
.....	.....	....	....	.....	....	177.8	24,267.65	3,332.00	396.69	....	27,996.34
.....	.....	....	....	.....	....	1,398.0	182,827.14	27,730.08	2,471.63	....	213,028.85
.....	.....	....	....	.....	....	120.9	16,671.00	2,265.76	272.25	....	19,209.01
.....	.....	....	....	.....	....	1,174.7	152,948.50§	....	....	....	152,948.50
12.8	.....	....	....	.....	....	12.8	8,684.80	358.07	125.09	....	9,167.96
165.3	**21.8**	....	....	.....	**9.4**	**3,420.1**	**$ 542,906.30**	**$ 45,186.64**	**$ 5,258.72**	....	**$ 593,351.66**
.....	43.5	....	....	.....	....	75.1	$ 16,384.25	$ 1,891.43	$ 232.75	....	$ 18,508.43
.....	43.5	....	....	.....	....	43.5	12,000.00	1,300.00	170.28	....	13,470.28
.....	.....	20.0	44.0	.....	....	64.0	12,677.32§	....	....	....	12,677.32
.....	43.5	....	....	.....	....	43.5	12,000.00	1,300.00	169.05	....	13,469.05
.....	**130.5**	**20.0**	**44.0**	.....	....	**226.1**	**$ 53,061.57**	**$ 4,491.43**	**$ 572.08**	....	**$ 58,125.08**
.....	.....	....	....	.....	....	.....	....	....	....	**$134,053.46**	**$ 134,053.46**
,170.1	**3,454.2**	**20.0**	**44.0**	**408.2**	**114.6**	**24,740.9**	**$6,177,454.54**	**$576,323.16**	**$74,797.96**	**$134,053.46**	**$6,962,629.12**

ERVICE COMMITTEE†

econstruction Period, 1919–1924

Metric Tons of 1,000 Kilograms or 2,204.6 Pounds							F.O.B. Value	Freight	Insurance	Miscellaneous Charges	Total C.I.F. Value
Milk	Cocoa	Sugar	Misc. Food *	Soap	Misc.‡	Total Tons					
....	....	....	....	....	**1.0**	**1.0**	....	**$ 149.10**	**$ 26.12**	**$ 13.17**	**$ 188.39**
....	....	....	....	....	...	**565.0**	**$ 66,765.53**	**$ 13,909.50**	**$ 1,184.89**	**$ 514.21**	**$ 82,374.13**
136.0	14.0	....	....	....	...	459.0	$ 118,423.77	$ 14,052.05	$ 1,625.63	$ 2,178.17	$ 136,279.62
....	....	102.0	....	....	...	273.0	49,923.70	6,007.94	648.63	1,162.34	57,742.61
....	....	....	....	....	...	111.0	38,753.48	2,675.11	492.75	522.97	42,444.31
136.0	**14.0**	**102.0**	....	....	...	**843.0**	**$ 207,100.95**	**$ 22,735.10**	**$ 2,767.01**	**$ 3,863.48**	**$ 236,466.54**

‡ Clothing and accessories.

[*Continued on next page*]

Table 167—*Continued*

Detail of Arrival

Arrival No.	Steamer or Source	Port of Sailing	Date of Arrival	Port of Arrival	Contents of Cargoes: Flour	Rice	Beans, Peas	Pork Products
			1920					
6	Mar Caspio, I	New York	Mar. 7	Hamburg	329.0	133.0	30.0	....
7	Mongolia, I	New York	Mar. 10	Hamburg	.....	....	....	....
8	Carib, II	New York	Mar. 26	Hamburg	.....	....	....	....
9	Kerowlee, II	New York	Mar. 29	Hamburg	.....	....	40.0	45.0
	Total for March	....	....	....	**329.0**	**133.0**	**70.0**	**45.0**
10	Kermanshah	New York	Apr. 3	Hamburg	703.0	....	101.0	51.0
11	Manchuria, II	New York	Apr. 8	Hamburg	1,618.0	....	492.0	99.0
12	Kermoor, II	New York	Apr. 11	Hamburg	58.0	151.0	508.0	88.0
13	Mongolia, II	New York	Apr. 22	Hamburg	.....	....	....	....
14	Kerlew, I	New York	Apr. 23	Hamburg	.....	....	20.0	....
15	Jessica, Ex-British Ministry of Food	(United Kingdom)	Apr. 26	Hamburg	.....	264.0	....	....
	Total for April	....	....	....	**2,379.0**	**415.0**	**1,121.0**	**238.0**
16	West Ekonk, I	New York	May 11	Hamburg	1,062.0	....	....	....
17	Manchuria, III	New York	May 20	Hamburg	528.0	....	188.0	....
18	Carib, III	New York	May 23	Hamburg	.....	250.0	....	....
19	Keresan, III	New York	May 27	Hamburg	.....	....	....	38.0
20	Mar Mediterraneo, I	New York	May 31	Hamburg	.....	66.0	....	102.0
	Total for May	....	....	....	**1,590.0**	**316.0**	**188.0**	**140.0**
21	Mongolia, III	New York	June 3	Hamburg	.....	....	10.0	....
22	Kermit, I	New York	June 5	Hamburg	.....	....	....	35.0
23	Kerlew, II	Norfolk	June 24	Hamburg	.....	....	....	....
	Total for June	....	....	....	.....	....	**10.0**	**35.0**
24	Mar Blanco, I	New York	July 2	Hamburg	.....	....	....	....
25	Kermoor, III	New York	July 3	Hamburg	.....	....	....	154.0
26	Monticello	New York	July 9	Hamburg	.....	....	....	....
27	Mar Caspio, II	New York	July 16	Hamburg	.....	....	....	....
28	Mar Mediterraneo, II	New York	July 22	Hamburg	.....	....	....	....
29	Verbania, I	New York	July 26	Hamburg	.....	....	....	80.0
30	Belgic	New York	July 27	Hamburg	.....	....	....	54.0
31	Purchase from Stuppel	Hamburg	July 27	Hamburg	.....	....	181.0	....
32	Minnekahda, I	New York	July 31	Hamburg	.....	....	410.0	155.0
	Total for July	....	....	....	.....	....	**591.0**	**443.0**
33	Bellerose	Boston	Aug. 2	Hamburg	.....	....	....	86.0
34	Mississippi	Baltimore	Aug. 9	Hamburg	.....	....	....	34.0
35	Manchuria, IV	New York	Aug. 12	Hamburg	.....	....	191.0	....
36	Herefordshire	Rangoon	Aug. 18	Hamburg	.....	1,010.0	....	....
37	Kermit, II	New York	Aug. 21	Hamburg	.....	....	....	35.0
38	Mette Jensen, I	New York	Aug. 22	Hamburg	.....	....	....	....
39	Mar Blanco, II	New York	Aug. 24	Hamburg	.....	....	....	104.0
40	East Indian	Baltimore	Aug. 24	Hamburg	.....	....	....	87.0
41	Mongolia, IV	New York	Aug. 26	Hamburg	.....	....	....	17.0
42	City of Flint	Philadelphia	Aug. 28	Hamburg	.....	....	....	....
43	Monticello, II	New York	Aug. 28	Hamburg	.....	....	....	....
	Total for August	....	....	....	.....	**1,010.0**	**191.0**	**363.0**
44	Mar Caribe, I	New York	Sept. 4	Hamburg	.....	....	....	....
45	Mar Rojo	New York	Sept. 16	Hamburg	.....	....	....	37.0
46	Mar Cantabrico	New York	Sept. 22	Hamburg	.....	....	....	....
	Total for September	....	....	....	.....	....	....	**37.0**
47	Vittorio Emmanuelle, III	New York	Oct. 1	Hamburg	.....	....	....	....
48	Schoharie, I	New York	Oct. 13	Hamburg	.....	....	....	....
49	Satartia	New York	Oct. 22	Hamburg	.....	....	....	....
	Total for October	....	....	....	.....	....	....	....

§ Commodities delivered c.i.f.

ERVICE COMMITTEE

Steamers

Metric Tons of 1,000 Kilograms or 2,204.6 Pounds							F.O.B. Value	Freight	Insurance	Miscellaneous Charges	Total C.I.F. Value
Milk	Cocoa	Sugar	Misc. Food	Soap	Misc.	Total Tons					
....	....	....	....	....	...	492.0	$ 78,288.16	$ 10,897.07	$ 1,051.88	$ 840.73	$ 91,077.84
....	....	....	....	....	1.0	1.0	....	....	11.25	.07	11.32
36.0	61.0	....	....	....	7.0	104.0	28,881.00	2,444.10	460.19	1,062.29	32,847.58
....	31.0	76.0	19.0[c]	....	...	211.0	71,613.61	5,086.23	1,006.25	736.60	78,442.69
36.0	**92.0**	**76.0**	**19.0**	....	**8.0**	**808.0**	**$ 178,782.77**	**$ 18,427.40**	**$ 2,529.57**	**$ 2,639.69**	**$ 202,379.43**
148.0	....	130.0	....	....	...	1,133.0	$ 208,597.93	$ 24,048.18	$ 2,722.50	$ 2,195.82	$ 237,564.43
864.0	146.0	....	....	....	...	3,219.0	587,971.68	61,282.47	7,650.03	10,139.34	667,043.52
....	....	....	....	....	...	805.0	154,493.77	16,359.63	2,036.25	4,108.84	176,998.49
....	16.0	....	....	....	...	16.0	5,017.60	345.44	63.57	104.44	5,531.05
211.0	5.0	....	....	....	...	236.0	64,668.63	5,820.42	832.50	1,115.77	72,437.32
....	....	....	....	....	...	264.0	51,359.42§	....	......	......	51,359.42
,223.0	**167.0**	**130.0**	....	....	...	**5,673.0**	**$1,072,109.03**	**$107,856.14**	**$13,304.85**	**$17,664.21**	**$1,210,934.23**
436.0	....	....	....	....	...	1,498.0	$ 237,236.07	$ 27,452.65	$ 3,116.25	$ 4,695.48	$ 272,500.45
134.0	34.0	....	....	....	...	884.0	131,155.44	16,397.98	1,738.12	3,024.00	152,315.54
155.0	....	....	....	....	...	405.0	118,710.81	8,391.66	1,849.37	1,857.25	130,809.09
....	....	....	5.0[c]	....	...	43.0	18,329.30	1,141.53	407.25	198.78	20,076.86
....	....	....	....	....	...	168.0	65,555.82	3,414.12	815.63	1,148.90	70,934.47
725.0	**34.0**	....	**5.0**	....	...	**2,998.0**	**$ 570,987.44**	**$ 56,797.94**	**$ 7,926.62**	**$10,924.41**	**$ 646,636.41**
140.0	....	....	....	....	...	150.0	$ 61,052.62	$ 3,699.15	$ 765.00	$ 1,283.81	$ 66,800.58
38.0	....	....	....	....	...	73.0	30,741.20	1,704.75	382.50	635.68	33,464.13
19.0	....	....	....	....	...	19.0	8,450.00	476.00	105.75	251.29	9,283.04
197.0	....	....	....	....	...	**242.0**	**$ 100,243.82**	**$ 5,879.90**	**$ 1,253.25**	**$ 2,170.78**	**$ 109,547.75**
26.0	....	....	....	....	...	26.0	$ 9,502.00	$ 640.22	$ 120.38	$ 172.42	$ 10,435.02
78.0	....	....	....	....	...	232.0	90,185.81	5,364.03	1,125.00	1,639.06	98,313.90
21.0	....	....	....	....	...	21.0	7,998.89	547.40	137.04	166.82	8,850.15
16.0	....	....	....	....	...	16.0	5,793.98	396.51	93.38	120.78	6,404.65
38.0	152.0	....	....	....	...	190.0	42,464.17	5,333.02	618.75	956.48	49,372.42
59.0	....	....	....	....	...	139.0	68,889.03	3,808.06	846.00	1,470.86	75,013.95
....	....	....	....	....	...	54.0	25,555.12	1,397.53	318.37	545.42	27,816.44
....	....	....	....	....	...	181.0	17,942.36§	....	......	......	17,942.36
....	....	....	....	....	...	565.0	106,972.30	12,153.45	1,440.01	2,781.36	123,347.12
238.0	**152.0**	....	....	....	...	**1,424.0**	**$ 375,303.66**	**$ 29,640.22**	**$ 4,698.93**	**$ 7,853.20**	**$ 417,496.01**
....	....	....	....	....	...	86.0	$ 39,736.83	$ 2,226.65	$ 497.15	$ 481.73	$ 42,942.36
....	....	....	....	....	...	34.0	15,732.05	889.94	196.88	336.37	17,155.24
....	....	....	....	....	...	191.0	15,585.18	3,790.99	227.25	511.84	20,115.26
....	....	....	....	....	...	1,010.0	132,639.70§	....	......	......	132,639.70
582.0	....	....	....	....	...	617.0	319,135.57	18,037.36	3,948.75	6,878.14	347,999.82
301.0	91.0	....	6.0[c]	....	...	398.0	168,478.70	11,610.44	2,193.75	3,653.33	185,936.22
334.0	....	....	....	....	...	438.0	221,260.03	12,508.86	2,751.75	4,756.22	241,276.86
....	....	....	....	....	...	87.0	41,432.44	2,271.93	515.25	884.38	45,104.00
....	....	....	....	....	...	17.0	7,756.89	433.14	96.75	165.74	8,452.52
76.0	....	....	....	....	...	76.0	28,000.00	1,963.50	354.37	520.22	30,838.09
427.0	....	....	....	....	...	427.0	221,995.51	12,545.12	2,739.38	4,816.70	242,096.71
1,720.0	**91.0**	....	**6.0**	....	...	**3,381.0**	**$1,211,752.90**	**$ 66,277.93**	**$13,521.28**	**$23,004.67**	**$1,314,556.78**
295.0	....	....	....	....	...	295.0	$ 154,838.03	$ 8,680.00	$ 1,896.75	$ 3,236.22	$ 168,651.00
80.0	....	....	....	....	...	117.0	58,049.24	3,294.26	723.38	1,253.11	63,319.99
23.0	....	....	....	....	...	23.0	11,800.30	670.88	166.16	259.73	12,897.07
398.0	....	....	....	....	...	**435.0**	**$ 224,687.57**	**$ 12,645.14**	**$ 2,786.29**	**$ 4,749.06**	**$ 244,868.06**
19.0	....	....	....	....	...	19.0	$ 10,000.00	$ 560.00	$ 135.98	$ 213.92	$ 10,909.90
28.0	....	....	....	....	...	28.0	14,207.50	812.00	194.78	314.41	15,528.69
6.0	....	....	....	....	...	6.0	2,955.00	168.00	37.13	63.20	3,223.33
53.0	....	....	....	....	...	**53.0**	**$ 27,162.50**	**$ 1,540.00**	**$ 367.89**	**$ 591.53**	**$ 29,661.92**

[*Concluded on next page*]

AMERICAN FRIEND

Detail of Arriva

Table 167—*Concluded*

Arrival No.	Steamer or Source	Port of Sailing	Date of Arrival	Port of Arrival	Contents of Cargoes: Flour	Rice	Beans, Peas	Pork Products
			1921					
50	Triumph	New York	Feb. 17	Hamburg	.....	....	....	....
51	American	New York	Feb. 23	Hamburg	.....	....	....	....
	Total for February	....	....	....	.....	....	....	....
52	Naamhok	New York	Apr. 6	Hamburg	.....	....	....	....
53	Leeds City, II	New York	Apr. 12	Hamburg	.....	....	....	....
	Total for April	....	....	....	.....	....	....	....
54	Mount Carroll, V	New York	Nov. 21	Hamburg	.....	....	....	....
55	Chickasaw	New York	Dec. 4	Hamburg	.....	....	....	....
56	Westbrook, IV	New York	Dec. 22	Hamburg	.....	....	....	....
	Total for December	....	....	....	.....	....	....	....
	Grand Total	....	....	....	**4,863.0**	**1,958.0**	**2,617.0**	**1,362.0**

* The total, 115.0 metric tons, is composed of: [c], codliver oil, 30.0; [l], dried milk, 85.0.

COMMONWEALT

Table 168*

Detail of Arrivals, Not Otherwise Shown, Delivered

Steamer	Port of Sailing	Date of Arrival	Port of Arrival	Contents of Cargo: Flour	Rice	Beans, Peas
		1920				
Chincha	New York	Feb. 21	Batoum	845.2	366.9	377.4
Massillon Bridge	New York	Mar. 12	Constantinople	.....	.....	27.2
Lake Fiscus	New York	May 23	Constantinople	1,015.2	.....	.....
River Araxes	New York	June 8	Piraeus	818.9	.....	.....
		1921				
King City, II	New York	Sept. 1	Hamburg	.....	.....	.....
Noruega	New York	Sept. 15	Hamburg	.....	.....	.....
Ipswich, III	New York	Sept. 19	Hamburg, Danzig	.....	.....	.....
Virginian, I	New York	Oct. 1	Hamburg	.....	.....	.....
Latvia, II	New York	Oct. 5	Danzig	.....	.....	.....
Orla, I	New York	Oct. 29	Hamburg	.....	.....	.....
Total Deliveries *	....	....	....	**2,679.3**	**366.9**	**404.6**

† Balance of deliveries taken from E.C.F. arrivals (Table 165) and A.R.A.W. arrivals (Table 166).

* Cf. Table 160.

A.R.A.-EUROPEAN CHILDREN'S FUND

Detail by Countries of Commodities Received Through Exchange*

Reconstruction Period, 1919–1924

Table 169

Country	Table No.	Commodities in Net Metric Tons of 1,000 Kilograms or 2,204.6 Pounds: Flour	Rice	Beans, Peas	Pork Products	Sugar	Total Tons	Total Value
Austria	213	.....	....	84.1	30.7	728.2	843.0	.....
Czecho-Slovakia	.	.....	....	....	....	472.0	472.0	.....
Finland	306	350.1	....	....	....	.....	350.1	.....
Hungary (Local Purchase)	340	.....	26.6	....	....	.....	26.6	$3,999.
Hungary	340	.....	....	....	18.4	.....	18.4	.....
Poland	...	.....	....	....	....	938.0	938.0	.....
Total	....	**350.1**	**26.6**	**84.1**	**48.8**	**2,138.2**	**2,647.8**	**$3,999.**

* The E.C.F. turned various relief supplies over to these countries and received in exchange the commodities listed in this table, without any money being involved except in Hungary.

:RVICE COMMITTEE

Steamers

Metric Tons of 1,000 Kilograms or 2,204.6 Pounds							F.O.B. Value	Freight	Insurance	Miscellaneous Charges	Total C.I.F. Value
ilk	Cocoa	Sugar	Misc. Food	Soap	Misc.	Total Tons					
....	....	....	16.0[l]	....	...	16.0	(Donations)	....	......	$ 2,155.19	$ 2,155.19
....	....	....	1.0[l]	....	...	1.0	(Donations)	....	......	235.79	235.79
....	**....**	**....**	**17.0**	**....**	**...**	**17.0**	**........**	**.......**	**......**	**$ 2,390.98**	**$ 2,390.98**
....	....	....	43.0[l]	....	...	43.0	(Donations)	....	......	$ 4,632.52	$ 4,632.52
....	....	....	5.0[l]	....	...	5.0	(Donations)	....	......	1,470.56	1,470.56
....	**....**	**....**	**48.0**	**....**	**...**	**48.0**	**........**	**.......**	**......**	**$ 6,103.08**	**$ 6,103.08**
....	**....**	**....**	**20.0[l]**	**....**	**...**	**20.0**	**$ 15,168.38**	**$ 268.80**	**$ 437.72**	**$ 344.00**	**$ 16,218.90**
....	....	....	....	25.0	...	25.0	$ 2,447.50	$ 338.80	$ 86.77	$ 600.00	$ 3,473.07
....	....	....	....	25.0	...	25.0	2,301.98	353.93	73.17	600.00	3,329.08
....	**....**	**....**	**....**	**50.0**	**...**	**50.0**	**$ 4,749.48**	**$ 692.73**	**$ 159.94**	**$ 1,200.00**	**$ 6,802.15**
726.0	**550.0**	**308.0**	**115.0***	**50.0**	**9.0**	**16,558.0**	**$4,054,814.03**	**$336,819.90**	**$50,964.36**	**$84,026.47**	**$4,526,624.76**

JND†

-operation with the E.C.F.—Reconstruction Period, 1919–1924

et Metric Tons of 1,000 Kilograms or 2,204.6 Pounds						F.O.B. Value	Freight	Insurance	Miscellaneous Charges	Total C.I.F. Value
Pork roducts	Milk	Cocoa	Sugar	Clothing	Total Tons					
....	.....	....	96.5	....	1,686.0	$273,324.09	$ 64,836.26	$ 5,182.50	$ 6,009.57	$349,352.42
50.9	102.8	61.0	....	....	241.9	103,837.67	13,019.16	1,815.00	1,390.68	120,062.51
....	.....	....	....	....	1,015.2	122,752.66	25,000.00	2,464.50	1,775.67	151,992.83
....	.....	....	....	....	818.9	99,022.86	22,508.40	1,873.10	1,295.00	124,699.36
....	.....	....	....	14.7	14.7	18,675.00	863.76	569.70	125.68	20,234.14
....	.....	....	....	9.9	9.9	13,050.00	471.47	87.18	85.06	13,693.71
....	.....	....	....	36.7	36.7	77,590.07	1,501.42	2,428.24	509.50	82,029.23
....	.....	....	....	1.7	1.7	3,575.00	94.05	110.70	23.62	3,803.37
....	.....	....	....	5.8	5.8	10,300.00	240.00	319.00	67.87	10,926.87
....	.....	....	....	5.9	5.9	13,125.00	240.11	396.90	86.01	13,848.02
50.9	**102.8**	**61.0**	**96.5**	**74.7**	**3,836.7**	**$735,252.35**	**$128,774.63**	**$15,246.82**	**$11,368.66**	**$890,642.46**

AMERICAN RELIEF ADMINISTRATION

Table 170

Summary by Operations of Shipments Handled by Abov

Operation	Table No.	Flour	Grain	Rice	Beans, Peas
A.R.A.—$100,000,000 Fund Congressional Appropriation	114	3,446.8	......	4,088.5	4,616.4
A.R.A.—President's National Security and Defense Fund	116	1,601.7	......	1,079.5	815.4
U.S. Grain Corporation (Act of Congress, March 30, 1920)	157	481,945.3	......	.....	.....
Finance on Freight and Other Charges for U.S.G.C. Flour	157	......	......	.....	.....
U.S. Grain Corporation—$20,000,000 Appropriation (Russia)	517	......	281,420.8	.....	.....
Soviet Gold Purchases—Supplies Delivered ex-Stocks in Russia	165	38,747.0	......	5,666.0	.....
Soviet Gold Purchases—Direct Shipments	519	......	105,135.3	.....	4,229.6
U.S. Government Surplus Medical Supplies (Russia)	521	......	......	.....	.....
Laura Spelman Rockefeller Memorial—Finance on Freight, etc	521	......	......	.....	.....
American Red Cross Medical Supplies (Russia)	523	......	......	.....	.....
American Red Cross (Greece)	335	12,886.0	2,451.0	203.0	1,269.0
European Children's Fund, Less Transfer of Soviet Gold Purchases	165	124,932.3	......	34,467.7	25,916.7
American Relief Administration Warehouses	166	12,706.8	......	1,427.9	3,395.1
European Governments' Donations	161	80,700.7	......	632.9	1,809.0
Commonwealth Fund	168	2,679.3	......	366.9	404.6
American Friends Service Committee (Russia)	525	3,037.3	......	71.9	90.6
American Friends Service Committee (Principally Germany)	167	4,863.0	......	1,958.0	2,617.0
Jewish Joint Distribution Committee (Poland)	394	......	......	......	.....
Commodities Received through Exchange	169	350.1	......	26.6	84.1
Total	...	**767,896.3**	**389,007.1**	**49,988.9**	**45,247.5**

* In Table 165, 2.0 metric tons of medical supplies and 633.3 metric tons of forage are included in the clothing and miscellaneous column.

AMERICAN RELIEF ADMINISTRATION

Table 171

Reconciliation of Deliveries and Shipments-

Reconstruction Period	Table No.	Flour	Grain	Rice	Beans, Peas
Total Deliveries	149	767,191.5	389,007.1	49,811.0	45,796.5
Add Shortages	...	704.8	....	177.9	....
Total	...	**767,896.3**	**389,007.1**	**49,988.9**	**45,796.5**
Deduct Overages	...	....	....	....	549.0
Total Shipments	170	**767,896.3**	**389,007.1**	**49,988.9**	**45,247.5**
Total Net Difference (between Deliveries and Shipments)	...	704.8	....	177.9	*—549.0*

AND A.R.A.-EUROPEAN CHILDREN'S FUND

rganizations—Reconstruction Period, 1919–1924

	Commodities in Net Metric Tons of 1,000 Kilograms or 2,204.6 Pounds											
	Corn Grits	Pork Products	Milk	Cocoa	Sugar	Misc. Food	Forage	Soap	Medical Supplies	Clothing and Misc.	Total Tons	Total C.I.F. Value
	.....	1,567.7	15,086.4	2,284.3	3,146.5	30.4	.....	745.2	.....	989.9	36,002.1	$ 13,433,918.33
	.....	323.6	2,900.0	394.3	547.4	14.0	.....	147.2	.....	.....	7,823.1	2,949,217.23
	.....	.....	.....	.....	.....	....	.....	.....	.....	.....	481,945.3	57,782,118.20
	.....	.....	.....	.....	.....	....	.....	.....	.....	.....	......	19,245,263.89
	83,960.4	.....	19,589.6	.....	.....	....	.....	.....	.....	1,100.0	386,070.8	18,662,180.00
	.....	3,658.0	544.0	1,445.0	7,436.0	....	.....	327.0	.....	.....	57,823.0	4,322,450.83
	.....	.....	.....	.....	.....	....	2,501.0	.....	.....	.....	111,865.9	7,034,874.30
	.....	.....	.....	.....	.....	....	.....	.....	3,107.6	.....	3,107.6	4,000,000.00
	.....	.....	.....	.....	.....	....	.....	.....	.....	.....	......	267,392.88
	.....	.....	.....	.....	.....	....	.....	.....	5,174.3	.....	5,174.3	3,804,863.15
	2,642.0	102.0	162.0	409.0	203.0	45.0	.....	2.0	.....	.....	20,374.0	1,211,949.95
	15,910.5	18,402.4	54,191.3	5,599.0	22,826.4	1,885.2	633.3*	1,250.9	2.0*	6,596.4	312,614.1	53,694,751.20
	.....	3,170.1	3,454.2	20.0	44.0	408.2	.....	.....	.....	114.6	24,740.9	6,962,629.12
	77.3	1,361.6	1,736.9	31.4	6,972.6	1,516.3	.....	.....	.....	1,701.5	96,540.2	14,652,432.21
	.....	50.9	102.8	61.0	96.5	....	.....	.....	.....	74.7	3,836.7	890,642.46
	917.8	16.6	.....	.....	67.6	....	.....	.....	.....	.4	4,202.2	267,394.24
	.....	1,362.0	4,726.0	550.0	308.0	115.0	.....	50.0	.....	9.0	16,558.0	4,526,624.76
	.....	.....	506.0	.....	.....	....	.....	31.0	.....	.....	537.0	273,555.00
	.....	48.8	.....	.....	2,138.2	....	.....	.....	.....	.....	2,647.8	3,999.05
	103,508.0	**30,063.7**	**102,999.2**	**10,794.0**	**43,786.2**	**4,014.1**	**3,134.3**	**2,553.3**	**8,283.9**	**10,586.5**	**1,571,863.0**	**$213,986,256.80**

ND A.R.A.-EUROPEAN CHILDREN'S FUND

econstruction Period, 1919–1924

	Commodities in Net Metric Tons of 1,000 Kilograms or 2,204.6 Pounds										
	Corn Grits	Pork Products	Milk	Cocoa	Sugar	Misc. Food	Forage	Soap	Medical Supplies	Clothing and Misc.	Total Tons
	103,301.1	29,594.8	103,612.1	10,762.6	44,295.7	4,076.0	3,134.3	2,276.6	8,283.9	10,390.9	1,571,534.1
	206.9	468.9	....	31.4	....	......	......	276.7	......	195.6	2,062.2
	103,508.0	**30,063.7**	**103,612.1**	**10,794.0**	**44,295.7**	**4,076.0**	**3,134.3**	**2,553.3**	**8,283.9**	**10,586.5**	**1,573,596.3**
	....	....	612.9	....	509.5	61.9	......	......	......	....	1,733.3
	103,508.0	**30,063.7**	**102,999.2**	**10,794.0**	**43,786.2**	**4,014.1**	**3,134.3**	**2,553.3**	**8,283.9**	**10,586.5**	**1,571,863.0**
	206.9	468.9	*—612.9*	31.4	*—509.5*	*—61.9*	......	276.7	......	195.6	328.9

AMERICAN RELIEF ADMINISTRATION AND A.R.A.-EUROPEAN CHILDREN'S FUND

Summary by Ports of the Total Number of Steamers and Tons Arrived at First Port, Number of Transshipping Steamers and Tons Carried, and Grand Total†—Reconstruction Period, 1919–1924

Table 172

Port	First Port of Arrival *		Transshipments		Grand Total	
	Number of Steamers	Tons Carried	Number of Steamers	Tons Carried	Number of Steamers	Tons Carrie
Abo	..	.....	2	230.9	2	230.
Antwerp	1	228.7	..	.....	1	228.
Batoum	14	54,947.1	..	.....	14	54,947.
Braila	1	320.1	..	.....	1	320.
Constantinople (Istanbul)	5	3,102.4	..	.....	5	3,102.
Constanza	2	812.2	..	.....	2	812.
Copenhagen	4	1,496.5	..	.....	4	1,496.
Danzig	115	84,156.7	213	48,054.9	328	132,211.
Derindje	1	770.2	..	.....	1	770.
French Ports	3	4,774.3	..	.....	3	4,774.
Gravosa (Ragusa)	1	60.0	..	.....	1	60.
Hamburg	537‡	213,136.7‡	6	2,461.5	543	215,598.
Hango	..	.....	5	1,889.7	5	1,889
Helsingfors, Viborg	6	119.7	5§	329.9§	11	449.
Hull	1	232.3	..	.....	1	232
Libau	18	38,617.5	9	4,980.2	27	43,597
Mannheim	11	1,563.3	7	1,696.5	18	3,259
Novorossisk	26	125,902.3	..	.....	26	125,902
Odessa	39	112,943.4	..	.....	39	112,943
Petrograd (Leningrad)	42	92,479.7	29	16,561.2	71	109,040
Piraeus	17	21,192.9	..	.....	17	21,192
Poti	2	2,370.3	..	.....	2	2,370
Reval	34	146,514.7	12	3,703.5	46	150,218
Riga	67	25,459.4	123	48,431.3	190	73,890
Rotterdam	39	17,008.5	..	.....	39	17,008
Salonica	11	1,128.4	..	.....	11	1,128
Sundry **	103	449,983.4	..	.....	103	449,983
Theodosia	9	47,904.8	..	.....	9	47,904
Trieste	27	11,038.2	..	.....	27	11,038
Windau	16	13,874.3	73	30,856.7	89	44,731
Total	**1,152**	**1,472,138.0**	**484**	**159,196.3**	**1,636**	**1,631,334**

† Exclusive of government donations, J.D.C., and Exchange commodities. Cf. Table 173, † footnote.

* Cf. Table 173.

‡ Bremen and Bremerhaven arrivals included with Hamburg.

§ All Helsingfors arrivals.

** Includes all shipments f.o.b. U.S.A. ports. Records do not refl
ports of arrival.

AMERICAN RELIEF ADMINISTRATION AND A.R.A.-EUROPEAN CHILDREN'S FUND

Summary by Years of Total Number of Steamers and Metric Tons Carried to First Port of Arrival—Reconstruction Period, 1919–1924

Table 173*

First Port of Arrival	Total for 1919		Total for 1920		Total for 1921		Total for 1922		Total for 1923		Grand Total	
	No. of Steamers	Tons Carried	No. of Steamers	Tons Carried	No. of Steamers	Tons Carried	No. of Steamers	Tons Carried	No. of Steamers	Tons Carried	No. of Steamers	Tons Carried
Antwerp	1	228.7	..	....	..	....	..	....	..	....	1	228.7
Batoum	3	18,408.4	10	25,506.9	..	....	1	11,031.8	..	....	14	54,947.1
Braila	1	320.1	..	....	..	....	..	....	..	....	1	320.1
Constantinople (Istanbul)	..	....	2	1,257.1	..	....	3	1,845.3	..	....	5	3,102.4
Constanza	2	812.2	..	....	..	....	..	....	..	....	2	812.2
Copenhagen	2	871.6	..	....	2	624.9	..	....	..	....	4	1,496.5
Danzig	24	18,069.7	47	28,773.9	41	30,660.1	3	6,653.0	..	....	115	84,156.7
Derindje	..	....	1	770.2	..	....	..	....	..	....	1	770.2
French Ports	2	4,400.5	..	....	1	373.8	..	....	..	....	3	4,774.3
Gravosa (Ragusa)	1	60.0	..	....	..	....	..	....	..	....	1	60.0
Hamburg	13	4,903.1	170	50,889.8	103	58,035.4	177	88,010.8	14	11,297.6	537	213,136.7
Helsingfors, Viborg	1	96.7	5	23.0	..	....	..	....	..	....	6	119.7
Hull	..	....	..	....	1	232.3	..	....	..	....	1	232.3
Libau	3	705.0	3	714.4	..	....	9	31,031.9	3	6,166.2	18	38,617.5
Mannheim	3	460.7	8	1,102.6	..	....	..	....	..	....	11	1,563.3
Novorossisk	..	....	..	....	..	....	26	125,902.3	..	....	26	125,902.3
Odessa	..	....	..	....	..	....	34	106,107.4	5	6,836.0	39	112,943.4
Petrograd (Leningrad)	..	....	..	....	..	....	42	92,479.7	..	....	42	92,479.7
Piraeus	..	....	1	818.9	..	....	4	5,249.0	12	15,125.0	17	21,192.9
Poti	..	....	2	2,370.3	..	....	..	....	..	....	2	2,370.3
Reval	2	207.4	1	47.0	1	15.0	29	146,180.7	1	64.6	34	146,514.7
Riga	..	....	..	....	21	7,864.9	26	12,908.0	20	4,686.5	67	25,459.4
Rotterdam	18	10,176.3	21	6,832.2	..	....	..	....	..	....	39	17,008.5
Salonica	2	846.9	5	180.0	4	101.5	..	....	..	....	11	1,128.4
Sundry	2	7,017.4	94	438,179.5	2	2,695.0	5	2,091.5	..	....	103	449,983.4
Theodosia	..	....	..	....	..	....	9	47,904.8	..	....	9	47,904.8
Trieste	27	11,038.2	..	....	..	....	..	....	..	....	27	11,038.2
Windau	..	....	..	....	..	....	11	1,064.3	5	12,810.0	16	13,874.3
Total	**107**	**78,622.9**	**370**	**557,465.8**	**236**	**100,602.9**	**379**	**678,460.5**	**60**	**56,985.9**	**1,152**	**1,472,138.0†**

* For detail of deliveries see Table 174 for 1919, Table 175 for 1920, Table 176 for 1921, Table 177 for 1922, Table 178 for 1923.

† In addition to cargo carried by steamers to first port of arrival, the following items in net metric tons should be added in order to reconcile this statement with the total arrivals per operation during the Reconstruction Period: European government donations, 96,540.2; J.D.C., 537.0; Exchange commodities, 2,647.8.

AMERICAN RELIEF ADMINISTRATION

Table 174

Detail by Months of Number of Steamers and Net Metri

First Port of Arrival	February		March		April		May	
	No. of Steamers	Total Tons Carried	No. of Steamers	Total Tons Carried	No. of Steamers	Total Tons Carried	No. of Steamers	Total Tons Carried
Antwerp	..	.....	..	.....	..	.....	..	.....
Batoum	..	.....	..	.....	..	.....	..	.....
Braila	..	.....	..	.....	1	320.1	..	.....
Constanza	..	.....	..	.....	1	40.0	1	772.2
Copenhagen	..	.....	2	871.6	..	.....	..	.....
Danzig	..	.....	..	.....	4	6,990.0	..	.....
French Ports	..	.....	..	.....	..	.....	1	4,343.9
Gravosa (Ragusa)	..	.....	..	.....	..	.....	1	60.0
Hamburg	..	.....	..	.....	..	.....	..	.....
Helsingfors, Viborg	..	.....	..	.....	..	.....	..	.....
Libau	..	.....	..	.....	..	.....	..	.....
Mannheim	..	.....	..	.....	..	.....	..	.....
Reval	..	.....	..	.....	..	.....	..	.....
Rotterdam	..	.....	1	90.0	1	459.5	1	2,226.0
Salonica	..	.....	..	.....	..	.....	1	327.3
Sundry	..	.....	..	.....	..	.....	..	.....
Trieste	2	254.7	1	50.8	5	1,663.0	4	297.6
Total	**2**	**254.7**	**4**	**1,012.4**	**12**	**9,472.6**	**9**	**8,027.0**

* Arrivals at Viborg.

AMERICAN RELIEF ADMINISTRATIO

Table 175

Detail by Months of Number of Steamers and Net Metri

First Port of Arrival	January		February		March		April		May		June	
	No. of Steamers	Total Tons Carried	No. of Steamers	Total Tons Carried	No. of Steamers	Total Tons Carried	No. of Steamers	Total Tons Carried	No. of Steamers	Total Tons Carried	No. of Steamers	Total To Carried
Batoum	2	7,435.3	2	1,763.0	..	.....	..	.....	2	9,153.1	1	5,636.
Constantinople (Istanbul)	..	.....	..	.....	1	241.9	..	.....	1	1,015.2	..	....
Danzig	7	2,784.6	8	3,036.9	9	13,335.6	7	2,118.1	1	345.0	2	1,686.
Derindje	..	.....	..	.....	..	.....	..	.....	..	.....	..	....
Hamburg	9	9,472.7	17	2,071.1	13	7,104.9	13	6,968.0	13	3,895.9	8	1,245.
Helsingfors, Viborg	3†	17.0†	1†	5.0†	1†	1.0†	..	.....	..	.....	..	....
Libau	..	.....	2	688.1	1	26.3	..	.....	..	.....	..	....
Mannheim	5	311.7	3	790.9	..	.....	..	.....	..	.....	..	....
Piraeus	..	.....	..	.....	..	.....	..	.....	..	.....	1	818.
Poti	..	.....	..	.....	..	.....	2	2,370.3	..	.....	..	....
Reval	1	47.0	..	.....	..	.....	..	.....	..	.....	..	....
Rotterdam	12	4,952.8	3	305.9	1	301.3	2	307.2	2	390.0	..	....
Salonica	1	39.0	2	82.0	1	56.0	1	3.0	..	.....	..	....
Sundry	..	.....	6	10,492.1	14	49,245.9	13	82,948.2	25	118,057.8	18	86,547.
Total	**40**	**25,060.1**	**44**	**19,235.0**	**41**	**70,312.9**	**38**	**94,714.8**	**44**	**132,857.0**	**30**	**95,934.**

† Arrivals at Helsingfors.

ND A.R.A.-EUROPEAN CHILDREN'S FUND

ns of Cargo carried to First Port of Arrival—1919

June		July		August		November		December		Total for 1919	
o. of amers	Total Tons Carried	No. of Steamers	Total Tons Carried	No. of Steamers	Total Tons Carried	No. of Steamers	Total Tons Carried	No. of Steamers	Total Tons Carried	No. of Steamers	Tons Carried
..	.....	..	.....	1	228.7	..	.....	..	.....	1	228.7
..	.....	..	.....	..	.....	2	11,379.1	1	7,029.3	3	18,408.4
..	.....	..	.....	..	.....	..	.....	..	.....	1	320.1
..	.....	..	.....	..	.....	..	.....	..	.....	2	812.2
..	.....	..	.....	..	.....	..	.....	..	.....	2	871.6
5	3,834.8	1	45.6	1	1,940.0	6	495.2	7	4,764.1	24	18,069.7
1	56.6	..	.....	..	.....	..	.....	..	.....	2	4,400.5
..	.....	..	.....	..	.....	..	.....	..	.....	1	60.0
4	1,130.9	2	1,103.1	..	.....	1	283.7	6	2,385.4	13	4,903.1
1*	96.7*	..	.....	..	.....	..	.....	..	.....	1	96.7
1	652.5	1	35.5	..	.....	..	.....	1	17.0	3	705.0
..	.....	..	.....	..	.....	..	.....	3	460.7	3	460.7
1	60.4	1	147.0	..	.....	..	.....	..	.....	2	207.4
..	.....	..	.....	1	6,663.7	1	1.0	13	736.1	18	10,176.3
1	519.6	..	.....	..	.....	..	.....	..	.....	2	846.9
..	.....	..	.....	..	.....	1	1,241.6	1	5,775.8	2	7,017.4
2	2,229.1	2	636.1	11	5,906.9	..	.....	..	.....	27	11,038.2
16	**8,580.6**	**7**	**1,967.3**	**14**	**14,739.3**	**11**	**13,400.6**	**32**	**21,168.4**	**107**	**78,622.9**

ND A.R.A.-EUROPEAN CHILDREN'S FUND

ns of Cargo Carried to First Port of Arrival—1920

July		August		September		October		November		December		Total for 1920	
. of amers	Total Tons Carried	No. of Steamers	Total Tons Carried	No. of Steamers	Total Tons Carried	No. of Steamers	Total Tons Carried	No. of Steamers	Total Tons Carried	No. of Steamers	Total Tons Carried	No. of Steamers	Tons Carried
..	.....	..	.....	..	.....	1	134.1	2	1,384.7	..	.....	10	25,506.9
..	.....	..	.....	..	.....	..	.....	..	.....	..	.....	2	1,257.1
2	184.0	3	178.2	1	34.0	4	36.7	2	27.0	1	5,007.8	47	28,773.9
..	.....	..	.....	..	.....	..	.....	1	770.2	..	.....	1	770.2
20	4,038.6	25	8,784.9	18	4,348.2	16	1,094.4	10	895.7	8	969.8	170	50,889.8
..	.....	..	.....	..	.....	..	.....	..	.....	..	.....	5†	23.0†
..	.....	..	.....	..	.....	..	.....	..	.....	..	.....	3	714.4
..	.....	..	.....	..	.....	..	.....	..	.....	..	.....	8	1,102.6
..	.....	..	.....	..	.....	..	.....	..	.....	..	.....	1	818.9
..	.....	..	.....	..	.....	..	.....	..	.....	..	.....	2	2,370.3
..	.....	..	.....	..	.....	..	.....	..	.....	..	.....	1	47.0
1	575.0	..	.....	..	.....	..	.....	..	.....	..	.....	21	6,832.2
..	.....	..	.....	..	.....	..	.....	..	.....	..	.....	5	180.0
13	73,888.0	1	7,095.8	1	7,021.0	..	.....	2	753.1	1	2,130.0	94	438,179.5
36	**78,685.6**	**29**	**16,058.9**	**20**	**11,403.2**	**21**	**1,265.2**	**17**	**3,830.7**	**10**	**8,107.6**	**370**	**557,465.8**

AMERICAN RELIEF ADMINISTRATION

Detail by Months of Number of Steamers and Net Metri

Table 176

First Port of Arrival	January		February		March		April		May		June	
	No. of Steamers	Total Tons Carried	No. of Steamers	Total Tons Carried	No. of Steamers	Total Tons Carried	No.of Steamers	Total Tons Carried	No. of Steamers	Total Tons Carried	No. of Steamers	Total Tons Carried
Copenhagen	..	.....	..	.....	..	.....	..	.....	..	.....	..	.....
Danzig	3	4,751.9	2	1,354.0	2	396.9	1	957.2	5	3,038.9	1	303.8
French Ports	..	.....	..	.....	..	.....	..	.....	..	.....	..	.....
Hamburg*	16	4,698.0	13	7,733.0	13	4,288.4	20	6,986.7	14	5,239.4	10	2,435.3
Hull	..	.....	..	.....	..	.....	..	.....	..	.....	..	.....
Reval	..	.....	..	.....	..	.....	..	.....	..	.....	..	.....
Riga	..	.....	..	.....	..	.....	..	.....	..	.....	..	.....
Salonica	..	.....	..	.....	..	.....	..	.....	1	65.2	..	.....
Sundry	..	.....	..	.....	..	.....	1	29.0	..	.....	1	2,666.0
Total	**19**	**9,449.9**	**15**	**9,087.0**	**15**	**4,685.3**	**22**	**7,972.9**	**20**	**8,343.5**	**12**	**5,405.1**

* Includes [a], one steamer carrying 636.5 metric tons, and [b], one steamer carrying 20.3 metric tons, which arrived at Bremerhaven.

AMERICAN RELIEF ADMINISTRATION

Detail by Months of Number of Steamers and Net Metri

Table 177

First Port of Arrival	January		February		March		April		May		June	
	No. of Steamers	Total Tons Carried	No. of Steamers	Total Tons Carried	No. of Steamers	Total Tons Carried	No.of Steamers	Total Tons Carried	No. of Steamers	Total Tons Carried	No. of Steamers	Total Tons Carried
Batoum	..	.....	..	.....	..	.....	..	.....	..	.....	1	11,031.8
Constantinople (Istanbul)	..	.....	..	.....	..	.....	..	.....	..	.....	1	381.3
Danzig	2	291.4	..	.....	..	.....	1	6,361.6	..	.....	..	.....
Hamburg	28	9,494.8	22	812.2	35	26,954.9	29	12,686.4	24	8,994.7	17	6,318.9
Libau	..	.....	..	.....	5	23,019.2	4	8,012.7	..	.....	..	.....
Novorossisk	..	.....	8	46,651.7	9	41,224.7	6	33,864.0	1	1,219.6	2	2,942.3
Odessa	..	.....	2	17,235.3	5	22,809.2	7	7,514.8	7	26,996.3	2	2,276.5
Petrograd (Leningrad)	1	110.5	..	.....	..	.....	..	.....	13	28,167.9	5	12,527.5
Piraeus	..	.....	..	.....	..	.....	..	.....	..	.....	..	.....
Reval	2	1,339.8	..	.....	9	57,071.4	16	86,007.0	2	1,762.5	..	.....
Riga	1	49.0	..	.....	1	163.4	..	.....	7	3,950.5	10	4,125.8
Sundry	1	640.5	..	.....	1	39.9	2	1,259.0	1	152.1	..	.....
Theodosia	..	.....	1	5,927.3	4	23,468.3	3	11,430.9	..	.....	1	7,078.3
Windau	2	.5	1	.7	3	40.3	5	1,022.8	..	.....	..	.....
Total	**37**	**11,926.5**	**34**	**88,627.2**	**72**	**194,791.3**	**73**	**168,159.2**	**55**	**71,243.6**	**39**	**46,682.**

AMERICAN RELIEF ADMINISTRATION AND A.R.A.-EUROPEAN CHILDREN'S FUND

Detail by Months of Number of Steamers and Net Metric Tons of Cargo Carried to First Port of Arrival—1923

Table 178

First Port of Arrival	January		February		March		April		May		June		Total for 1923	
	Number of Steamers	Total Tons Carried	Number of Steamers	Total Tons Carried	Number of Steamers	Total Tons Carried	Number of Steamers	Total Tons Carried	Number of Steamers	Total Tons Carried	Number of Steamers	Total Tons Carried	Number of Steamers	Tons Carried
Hamburg	4	786.2	2	1,418.8	3	687.2	5	8,405.4*	..	.....	..	..	14	11,297
Libau	..	.....	..	.....	..	.....	2	6,165.2	1	1.0	..	..	3	6,16
Odessa	1	1,863.9	1	892.4	1	3,843.0	2	236.7	..	.....	..	..	5	6,83
Piraeus	2	3,436.0	2	6,378.0	1	2,904.0	2	1,100.0	5	1,307.0	..	..	12	15,12
Reval	..	.....	1	64.6	..	.....	..	.....	..	.....	..	..	1	6
Riga	3	153.8	2	214.6	3	52.3	6	3,968.3	5	296.8	1	.7	20	4,68
Windau	..	.....	..	.....	4	10,705.4	1	2,104.6	..	.....	..	..	5	12,81
Total	**10**	**6,239.9**	**8**	**8,968.4**	**12**	**18,191.9**	**18**	**21,980.2**	**11**	**1,604.8**	**1**	**.7**	**60**	**56,98**

* Includes one steamer carrying 269.6 metric tons which arrived at Bremen.

ND A.R.A.-EUROPEAN CHILDREN'S FUND

ons of Cargo Carried to First Port of Arrival—1921

July		August		September		October		November		December		Total for 1921	
o. of amers	Total Tons Carried	No. of Steamers	Total Tons Carried	No. of Steamers	Total Tons Carried	No. of Steamers	Total Tons Carried	No. of Steamers	Total Tons Carried	No. of Steamers	Total Tons Carried	No. of Steamers	Tons Carried
..	.....	..	.....	..	.....	2	624.9	..	.....	..	.....	2	624.9
3	1,415.9	6	8,083.7	4	3,636.9	5	1,514.1	5	4,177.4	4	1,029.4	41	30,660.1
1	373.8	..	.....	..	.....	..	.....	..	.....	..	.....	1	373.8
13[a]	5,460.8[a]	12	3,266.4	11	3,594.9	18	7,699.9	10[b]	2,799.0[b]	13	3,833.6	103	58,035.4
..	.....	1	232.3	..	.....	..	.....	..	.....	..	.....	1	232.3
..	.....	..	.....	1	15.0	..	.....	..	.....	..	.....	1	15.0
..	.....	1	19.0	3	30.0	5	2,264.8	4	5,068.5	8	482.6	21	7,864.9
1	6.1	..	.....	1	12.3	..	.....	1	17.9	..	.....	4	101.5
..	.....	..	.....	..	.....	..	.....	..	.....	..	.....	2	2,695.0
18	**7,256.6**	**20**	**11,601.4**	**20**	**7,289.1**	**30**	**12,103.7**	**20**	**12,062.8**	**25**	**5,345.6**	**236**	**100,602.9**

ND A.R.A.-EUROPEAN CHILDREN'S FUND

ons of Cargo Carried to First Port of Arrival—1922

July		August		September		October		November		December		Total for 1922	
o. of eamers	Total Tons Carried	No. of Steamers	Total Tons Carried	No. of Steamers	Total Tons Carried	No. of Steamers	Total Tons Carried	No. of Steamers	Total Tons Carried	No. of Steamers	Total Tons Carried	No. of Steamers	Tons Carried
..	.....	..	.....	..	.....	..	.....	..	.....	..	.....	1	11,031.8
..	.....	..	.....	1	1,425.0	1	39.0	..	.....	..	.....	3	1,845.3
..	.....	..	.....	..	.....	..	.....	..	.....	..	.....	3	6,653.0
4	912.3	6	470.8	2	508.2	2	463.1	2	959.5	6	1,435.0	177	88,010.8
..	.....	..	.....	..	.....	..	.....	..	.....	..	.....	9	31,031.9
..	.....	..	.....	..	.....	..	.....	..	.....	..	.....	26	125,902.3
3	5,027.0	1	7,128.5	2	732.4	1	5,323.8	2	5,170.2	2	5,893.4	34	106,107.4
5	14,744.6	6	11,182.7	8	18,890.5	3	6,700.7	1	155.3	..	.....	42	92,479.7
..	.....	..	.....	..	.....	..	.....	..	.....	4	5,249.0	4	5,249.0
..	.....	..	.....	..	.....	..	.....	..	.....	..	.....	29	146,180.7
..	.....	2	8.6	..	.....	1	2.0	1	114.9	3	4,493.8	26	12,908.0
..	.....	..	.....	..	.....	..	.....	..	.....	..	.....	5	2,091.5
..	.....	..	.....	..	.....	..	.....	..	.....	..	.....	9	47,904.8
..	.....	..	.....	..	.....	..	.....	..	.....	..	.....	11	1,064.3
12	**20,683.9**	**15**	**18,790.6**	**13**	**21,556.1**	**8**	**12,528.6**	**6**	**6,399.9**	**15**	**17,071.2**	**379**	**678,460.5**

Table 179

Summary of Exchange Remittance Receipts, b

Receipts, Refunds, Etc.	Bulgaria	Czecho-Slovakia	Finland	Austria
Receipts				
General Remittances	$5,695.50	$ 121,635.87	$ 36,808.60	$142,947.86
Mail Transfers	300.00	308,655.37	125,583.19	34,708.32
Cable Transfers	1,000.00	733,639.61	250,556.04	465,195.28
Import Transfers *	....	....	....	....
Miscellaneous *	....	....	....	....
Total receipts	**$6,995.50**	**$1,163,930.85**	**$412,947.83**	**$642,851.46**
Refunds				
General Remittances	$5,695.50	$ 17,559.89	$ 2,698.89	$ 5,503.27
Mail Transfers	300.00	17,806.45	30,725.38	15,833.33
Cable Transfers	1,000.00	86,000.00	....	25,000.00
Import Transfers *	....	....	....	....
Miscellaneous *	....	....	....	....
Total refunds	**$6,995.50**	**$ 121,366.34**	**$ 33,424.27**	**$ 46,336.60**
Executed by U.S.G.C.	....	....	42,105.26	....
Total deductions from receipts	**$6,995.50**	**$ 121,366.34**	**$ 75,529.53**	**$ 46,336.60**
Total net remittances	....	**$1,042,564.51**	**$337,418.30**	**$596,514.86**

* All import transfers and miscellaneous remittances were canceled due to the discontinuance of the transfer of funds through the A.R.A.

AMERICAN RELIEF ADMINISTRATION

Summary of the Disposition of Exchange Remittance Funds
Armistice Period, 1919

Table 180

Country of Destination	Child Feeding	Account of Government	European Technical Advisers	Refund Adjustment	Total
Austria	$ 400,000.00	$ 11,517.14	$184,997.72	......	$ 596,514.
Czecho-Slovakia	887,000.00	55,564.51	100,000.00	......	1,042,564.
Finland	105,033.00	232,385.30	....	......	337,418.
Germany	....	391,363.43	....	......	391,363.
Jugoslavia	172,650.35	....	150,000.00	$300.00	332,950.
Poland	2,260,000.00	8,107.42	325,000.00	154.29	2,593,261.
Roumania	....	1,076,067.73	....	......	1,076,067.
Total	**$3,824,683.35**	**$1,775,005.53**	**$759,997.72**	**$454.29**	**$6,360,140.**

ADMINISTRATION

Countries of Destination—Armistice Period, 1919

Germany	Jugoslavia	Poland	Roumania	Turkey	Unallocated	Total
$ 531,721.10	$ 80,916.22	$ 443,386.44	$ 240,275.67	$19,056.58	....	$1,622,443.84
14,427.05	100,241.90	80,248.35	371,163.06	....	....	1,035,327.24
400,342.32	382,568.74	2,537,972.67	735,112.22	21,640.00	....	5,528,026.88
547,459.61	....	....	....	....	....	547,459.61
....	....	....	....	....	$167,418.72	167,418.72
$1,493,950.08	**$563,726.86**	**$3,061,607.46**	**$1,346,550.95**	**$40,696.58**	**$167,418.72**	**$8,900,676.29**
$ 142,929.22	$ 40,193.73	$ 128,132.00	$ 140,804.08	$16,956.58	....	$ 500,473.16
14,427.05	23,408.87	44,343.75	24,679.14	....	....	171,523.97
397,770.77	177,173.91	250,000.00	105,000.00	....	....	1,041,944.68
547,459.61	....	....	....	....	....	547,459.61
....	....	....	....	....	$167,418.72	167,418.72
$1,102,586.65	**$240,776.51**	**$ 422,475.75**	**$ 270,483.22**	**$16,956.58**	**$167,418.72**	**$2,428,820.14**
....	....	45,870.00	....	23,740.00	....	111,715.26
$1,102,586.65	**$240,776.51**	**$ 468,345.75**	**$ 270,483.22**	**$40,696.58**	**$167,418.72**	**$2,540,535.40**
$ 391,363.43	**$322,950.35**	**$2,593,261.71**	**$1,076,067.73**	....	....	**$6,360,140.89**

AMERICAN RELIEF ADMINISTRATION

umber of Exchange Remittance Sales, by States or Countries of Origin

Armistice Period, 1919

Table 181

State or Country	General Remittances	Mail Transfers	Cable Transfers	Total
alifornia	3	..	..	3
anada	2	..	..	2
istrict of Columbia	..	..	1	1
ance	2	..	..	2
linois	792	17	12	821
diana	8	..	..	8
ansas	..	..	5	5
ouisiana	1	..	..	1
aryland	..	..	1	1
assachusetts	47	7	..	54
ichigan	12	..	3	15
innesota	41	..	..	41
issouri	75	..	1	76
ebraska	2	..	..	2
ew Jersey	349	3	..	352
ew York	14,376	52	175	14,603
hio	240	4	4	248
regon	7	..	..	7
ennsylvania	795	36	4	835
exas	3	..	..	3
rginia	1	..	..	1
ashington	30	3	..	33
est Virginia	1	..	..	1
isconsin	101	..	..	101
Total	**16,888**	**122**	**206**	**17,216**

AMERICAN RELIEF ADMINISTRATION

Number of Exchange Remittance Sales, by Countries of Destination

Armistice Period, 1919

Table 182

Country	General Remittances	Mail Transfers	Cable Transfers	Total
Bulgaria	....*	..*	..*	....*
Czecho-Slovakia	1,118	37	31	1,186
Finland	230	14	14	258
Austria	233	12	41	286
Germany	3,644	8	17	3,669
Jugoslavia	740	18	38	796
Poland	10,284	17	31	10,332
Roumania	637	16	32	685
Turkey	2	..	2	4
Total	**16,888**	**122**	**206**	**17,216**

* All remittances canceled.

A.R.A.-EUROPEAN CHILDREN'S FUND

Summary by Months Showing the Revenue Derived from Sale of Empty Food Containers in Poland, August, 1919–June, 1922

Table 183*

Month	Sacks and Bales (Number)	Barrels (Number)	Wooden Milk Cases (Number)	Misc. Wooden Cases (Number)	Milk Tins (Number)	Misc. Metal Cases (Number)	Value of Misc. Containers Sold (Polish Marks)	Total Value Containers Sold (Polish Marks)	Rate of Exchange (Marks to Dollars)	Total Value Containers Sold (Dollars)
1919										
Aug.-Dec.	.....	...	....	...	......	....	....	176,443.25	60	$ 2,947.7
1920										
January	12,731	167	6,532	787	383,448	5,638	....	192,233.66	136	1,413.4
February	7,485	107	9,447	829	589,125	8,796	....	206,749.36	156	1,325.3
March	19,444	113	15,265	1,911	767,989	7,789	....	551,539.56	157	3,512.9
April	19,063	158	11,042	1,257	802,312	8,728	....	386,529.43	174	2,221.4
May	19,081	102	11,394	812	679,146	7,560	....	517,420.41	188	2,752.2
June	20,814	201	27,328	1,005	719,545	2,050	....	542,454.46	157	3,455.1
July	9,911	72	8,719	558	274,486	916	422,038.38	731,334.39	170	4,301.9
August	9,286	235	12,932	1,457	791,841	3,606	16,456.45	487,501.72	211	2,310.4
September	29,147	380	8,448	1,063	482,107	2,994	304,84[illegible].54	1,076,831.84	252	4,273.1
October	30,591	301	10,264	395	471,067	2,508	6,808.80	1,019,930.84	288	3,541.4
November	35,807	462	16,399	1,272	622,807	2,230	7,970.00	1,327,518.48	437	3,037.8
December	16,813	253	10,394	802	516,196	2,034	249,727.44	1,218,799.90	595	2,048.4
1921										
January	21,066	307	9,986	840	525,990	1,475	112,175.58	1,349,088.25	771	1,749.7
February	26,839	581	19,597	731	1,180,354	1,945	53,093.90	2,761,871.87	837	3,299.7
March	33,105	1,029	27,773	1,519	1,347,886	4,602	8,422.40	2,585,214.02	792	3,264.1
April	21,154	486	14,978	1,123	738,934	1,454	90,000.00	2,782,050.74	809	3,438.8
May	14,653	560	9,911	627	617,309	1,026	160,562.50	2,558,578.75	940	2,721.8
June	11,301	365	18,376	757	925,818	761	199,426.00	3,211,760.87	1,458	2,202.8
July	58,233	1,279	24,651	2,241	1,544,926	1,308	70,303.00	7,549,164.70	1,968	3,835.9
August	87,996	2,006	21,350	770	1,085,258	1,305	553,370.20	10,525,152.10	2,331	4,515.2
September	151,135	2,435	35,441	1,540	1,580,432	792	149,898.00	19,523,186.38	4,789	4,076.6
October	51,033	1,429	43,130	1,286	1,913,648	884	211,447.00	12,319,487.40	4,562	2,700.4
November	48,218	1,186	31,605	1,832	1,291,662	6,501	477,919.95	9,097,257.95	3,370	2,699.4
December	11,729	419	8,629	702	365,187	3,779	388,687.40	4,354,166.20	3,052	1,425.6
1922										
January	14,019	551	12,298	1,390	611,122	38,769	127,637.10	5,431,677.73	3,013	1,802.7
February	8,186	310	15,262	2,942	707,037	24,812	567,532.00	5,392,352.20	3,793	1,421.6
March	7,758	624	15,841	712	780,197	3,344	2,145,682.36	8,111,419.01	4,099	1,978.8
April	26,737	575	18,087	1,595	840,307	3,413	403,125.30	8,485,036.36	3,895	2,178.4
May	21,901	1,100	36,994	1,497	1,716,393	2,744	1,141,179.74	12,042,402.24	4,002	3,009.1
Total	**845,236**	**17,793**	**512,073**	**34,252**	**24,872,529**	**153,763**	**7,868,305.04**	**126,515,154.07**	....	**$83,464.**

* This table is inserted to show economy practiced by each of the E.C.F. missions. The figures are taken from a report compiled by the Revenues Department, P.A.K.P.D.

UNITED KINGDOM

Summary of Tonnage Provided for Liberated and Enemy Countries Armistice Period, 1919

Table 184

Country	Chartered British Steamers		Requisitioned British Steamers		Chartered Neutral Steamers		German Steamers		Austrian Steamers		Polish Steamers		Roumanian Steamers		Total	
	No.	Tons	No.	Tons	No.	Tons	No.	Tons	No.	Tons	No.	Tons	No.	Tons	No.	Tons
Austria	19	9,575	3	19,598	1	1,077	..	.....	17	83,958	..	....	..	...	40	114.2
Czecho-Slovakia	1	2,032	..	.....	3	4,000	..	.....	..	.....	..	....	..	...	4	6,0
Esthonia	1	1,200	..	.....	..	....	6	20,700	..	.....	1	5,000	1	600	9	27.5
Finland	..	....	..	.....	..	....	1	8,485	..	.....	..	....	..	...	1	8,4
Germany	117	55,724	..	.....	86	34,920	28	215,399	..	.....	..	....	..	...	231	306.0
Jugoslavia *	3	6,497	4	20,842	..	....	..	.....	..	.....	..	....	..	...	7	27,3
Latvia	..	....	..	.....	..	....	2	11,042	..	.....	..	....	..	...	2	11.0
Poland	6	12,046	3	19,726	2	1,582	12	46,767	..	.....	..	....	..	...	23	80,1
Roumania	1	217	9	49,130	1	2,350	..	.....	5	26,841	..	....	4	20,040	20	98.5
Russia																
Northwest Russia	..	....	..	.....	..	....	1	6,376	..	.....	..	....	..	...	1	6.3
Total	**148**	**87,291**	**19**	**109,296**	**93**	**43,929**	**50**	**308,769**	**22**	**110,799**	**1**	**5,000**	**5**	**20,640**	**338**	**685,7**

* Includes Greater Serbia.

SUMMARY OF FOOD AND RELIEF SUPPLIES DELIVERED, 1914–1924

Table 185† By Periods and Countries of Destination

Country		(37) Grand Total (Table 102)	(1) C.R.B. Period (Table 103)	(2) U.S.F.A. Period (Table 106)	(3)* Armistice Period (Table 108)	(21)** Reconstruction Period (Table 149)
rmenia	Tons	135,764.1	....	....	83,964.3	51,799.8
	Value	$ 28,795,426.49	....	....	$ 20,231,455.01	$ 8,563,971.48
ıstria	Tons	822,200.1	....	....	561,705.7	260,494.4
	Value	$ 145,481,222.30	....	....	$ 98,771,595.93	$ 46,709,626.37
lgium	Tons	4,198,856.3	3,896,180.0	251,902.3	50,774.0	....
	Value	$ 697,140,348.91	$641,056,693.69	$ 27,533,982.47	$ 28,549,672.75	....
ılgaria	Tons	22,862.4	....	....	22,862.4	....
	Value	$ 4,856,647.53	....	....	$ 4,856,647.53	....
echo-Slovakia	Tons	545,134.6	....	....	503,230.0	41,904.6
	Value	$ 115,438,351.98	....	....	$ 105,545,794.40	$ 9,892,557.58
ınzig Free City	Tons	573.2	....	....	....	573.2
	Value	$ 127,700.69	....	....	....	$ 127,700.69
nmark	Tons	19,912.0	....	....	19,912.0	....
	Value	$ 2,147,059.30	....	....	$ 2,147,059.30	....
thonia	Tons	67,358.5	....	....	61,510.8	5,847.7
	Value	$ 21,017,263.56	....	....	$ 19,347,812.47	$ 1,669,451.09
nland	Tons	188,520.9	....	....	185,033.7	3,487.2
	Value	$ 30,282,047.90	....	....	$ 29,172,056.10	$ 1,109,991.80
ance	Tons	8,425,699.7	1,091,879.0	6,781,317.6	552,503.1	....
	Value	$1,289,488,622.47	$220,283,550.52	$ 850,715,632.84	$ 218,489,439.11	....
rmany	Tons	1,272,934.1	....	....	1,215,217.8	57,716.3
	Value	$ 294,373,692.75	....	....	$ 282,410,999.21	$ 11,962,693.54
eece	Tons	20,374.0	....	....	....	20,374.0
	Value	$ 1,211,949.95	....	....	....	$ 1,211,949.95
ıngary	Tons	21,393.5	....	....	319.1	21,074.4
	Value	$ 4,607,139.37	....	....	$ 245,519.96	$ 4,361,619.41
ly	Tons	7,479,780.7	....	7,464,749.6	15,031.1	....
	Value	$ 799,608,264.01	....	$ 796,762,249.59	$ 2,846,014.42	....
goslavia	Tons	127,359.0	....	....	121,249.8	6,109.2
	Value	$ 45,898,651.43	....	....	$ 43,596,570.69	$ 2,302,080.74
tvia	Tons	26,366.6	....	....	19,609.7	6,756.9
	Value	$ 7,550,021.69	....	....	$ 5,961,851.35	$ 1,588,170.34
huania	Tons	12,877.7	....	....	11,677.0	1,200.7
	Value	$ 5,980,781.39	....	....	$ 5,517,004.47	$ 463,776.92
e Netherlands	Tons	25,027.4	....	....	25,027.4	....
	Value	$ 4,219,498.41	....	....	$ 4,219,498.41	....
land	Tons	751,135.6	....	....	403,184.2	347,951.4
	Value	$ 200,864,857.73	....	....	$ 135,023,140.98	$ 65,841,716.75
umania	Tons	229,202.8	....	....	225,443.5	3,759.3
	Value	$ 53,637,311.31	....	....	$ 52,135,716.29	$ 1,501,595.02
ssia						
orthwest Russia	Tons	19,010.7	....	....	18,660.4	350.3
	Value	$ 5,890,076.54	....	....	$ 5,765,867.81	$ 124,208.73
iberia	Tons	40.0	....	....	40.0	....
	Value	$ 75,000.00	....	....	$ 75,000.00	....
ouban	Tons	1,592.5	....	....	1,592.5	....
	Value	$ 578,490.50	....	....	$ 578,490.50	....
oviet Republics	Tons	741,572.7	....	....	....	741,572.7
	Value	$ 63,174,848.78	....	....	....	$ 63,174,848.78
kraine	Tons	5,550.0	....	....	5,550.0	....
	Value	$ 8,500,222.67	....	....	$ 8,500,222.67	....
olunteer Army	Tons	394.0	....	....	394.0	....
	Value	$ 86,680.00	....	....	$ 86,680.00	....
ndry Accounts	Tons	56,529.2	....	....	55,967.2	562.0
	Value	$ 23,654,740.07	....	....	$ 23,556,117.48	$ 98,622.59
rkey	Tons	20,278.3	....	....	20,278.3	....
	Value	$ 4,369,404.30	....	....	$ 4,369,404.30	....
ited Kingdom	Tons	8,652,668.6	....	8,605,296.7	47,371.9	....
	Value	$1,386,102,780.05	....	$1,375,484,734.33	$ 10,618,045.72	....
Total Gross	Tons	33,890,969.2	4,988,059.0	23,103,266.2	4,228,109.9	1,571,534.1
	Value	**$5,245,159,102.08**	**$861,340,244.21**	**$3,050,496,599.23**	**$1,112,617,676.86**	**$220,704,581.78**
s Duplications	Tons	49,662.2	....	....	49,662.2	....
	Value	$ 11,130,893.52	....	....	$ 11,130,893.52	....
Grand Total Net	Tons	33,841,307.0	4,988,059.0‡	23,103,266.2	4,178,447.7	1,571,534.1
	Value	**$5,234,028,208.56**	**$861,340,244.21‡**	**$3,050,496,599.23**	**$1,101,486,783.34**	**$220,704,581.78**

In Tables 185, 186, and 187 the columns are numbered consecutively boldface figures in parentheses. In this summary table only the mns representing totals are given.

Cf. Table 186 for detail of Column 3.

** Cf. Table 187 for detail of Column 21.

‡ Total for the C.R.B. Period only. Cf. Table 186, Column 11, for balance of deliveries handled under the direction of the C.R.B.

DETAIL OF ARMISTICE PERIOD RELIEF DELIVERIE

Table 186

By Operations or Funds and b

Country		(3) Total (Table 108)	(4) Congressional Appropriation Government Account (Table 112)	(5) Congressional Appropriation Freight, Insurance Paid (Tables 143–44)	(6) Congressional Appropriation Freight, Insurance Billed (Table 146)	(7) U.S. Treasury Loan (Table 119)	(8) Cash Sales (Table 120)	(9) President's National Security and Defense Fund[a] (Table 117)	(10) U.S. Liquidation Commission (Table 122)
Armenia	Tons	*83,964.3*	*50,558.9*				*1,994.3*		
	Value	$ 20,231,455.01	$ 10,630,872.19	$ 47,688.48			$ 511,422.34		
Austria	Tons	*561,705.7*					*8,325.3*		
	Value	$ 98,771,595.93		$ 178.47	$15,224.11		$ 3,278,068.35		
Belgium	Tons	*50,774.0*							*50,774*
	Value	$ 28,549,672.75							$ 28,549,672
Bulgaria	Tons	*22,862.4*					*22,862.4*		
	Value	$ 4,856,647.53					$ 4,856,647.53		
Czecho-Slovakia	Tons	*503,230.0*	*52,285.3*			*259,004.9*	*70.5*		*40,350*
	Value	$ 105,545,794.40	$ 8,251,639.28	$ 203,505.62		$50,113,572.61	$ 33,778.62		$ 19,098,874
Denmark	Tons	*19,912.0*					*19,912.0*		
	Value	$ 2,147,059.30					$ 2,147,059.30		
Esthonia	Tons	*61,510.8*	*21,129.9*				*862.0*		*30,120*
	Value	$ 19,347,812.47	$ 4,299,650.87	$ 201,603.07			$ 116,371.62		$ 12,262,818
Finland	Tons	*185,033.7*	*65,725.7*				*101,117.0*		
	Value	$ 29,172,056.10	$ 9,849,587.73	$ 22,584.24			$ 16,004,404.13		
France	Tons	*552,503.1*					*31,106.1*	*1,622.0*	*519,775*
	Value	$ 218,489,439.11					$ 5,031,830.08	$390,209.03	$213,067,400
Germany	Tons	*1,215,217.8*					*483,155.8*		
	Value	$ 282,410,999.21					$113,758,637.74		
Hungary	Tons	*319.1*					*319.1*		
	Value	$ 245,519.96					$ 245,519.96		
Italy	Tons	*15,031.1*					*15,031.1*		
	Value	$ 2,846,014.42					$ 2,846,014.42		
Jugoslavia	Tons	*121,249.8*				*55,077.2*			*31,850*
	Value	$ 43,596,570.69		$ 81,140.98		$13,191,246.46			$ 20,464,191
Latvia	Tons	*19,609.7*	*13,313.7*						*6,296*
	Value	$ 5,961,851.35	$ 3,323,818.79	$ 159.72					$ 2,556,952
Lithuania	Tons	11,677.0	*3,357.0*						*8,320*
	Value	$ 5,517,004.47	$ 996,093.08	$ 48,930.00					$ 4,414,861
Netherlands	Tons	*25,027.4*					*25,027.4*		
	Value	$ 4,219,498.41					$ 4,219,498.41		
Poland	Tons	*403,184.2*	*260,843.2*						*107,126*
	Value	$ 135,023,140.98	$ 63,191,316.61	$ 477,671.28	$66,364.12				$ 59,365,111
Roumania	Tons	*225,443.5*				*102,942.5*			*22,331*
	Value	$ 52,135,716.29				$23,438,339.29			$ 13,012,689
Russia									
Northwest Russia	Tons	*18,660.4*	*17,950.4*						*710*
	Value	$ 5,765,867.81	$ 5,285,380.17	$ 52,188.18					$ 428,299
Siberia	Tons	*40.0*							
	Value	$ 75,000.00							
Kouban	Tons	*1,592.5*					*915.5*		
	Value	$ 578,490.50					$ 444,718.50		
Ukraine	Tons	*5,550.0*							*5,550*
	Value	$ 8,500,222.67							$ 8,500,222
Volunteer Army	Tons	*394.0*	*394.0*						
	Value	$ 86,680.00	$ 86,680.00						
Sundry Accounts	Tons	*55,967.2*					*1,903.2*		
	Value	$ 23,556,117.48					$ 464,770.08		
Turkey	Tons	*20,278.3*					*20,278.3*		
	Value	$ 4,369,404.30					$ 4,369,404.30		
United Kingdom	Tons	*47,371.9*					*47,371.9*		
	Value	$ 10,618,045.72					$ 10,618,045.72		
Grand Total Gross	Tons	*4,228,109.9*	*485,558.1*			*417,024.6*	*780,251.9*[h]	*1,622.0*	*823,202*
	Value	**$1,112,617,676.86**	**$105,915,038.72**[f]	**$1,135,650.04**	**$81,588.23**[g]	**$86,743,158.36**	**$168,946,191.10**[h]	**$390,209.03**	**$381,721,094**
Less Duplications	Tons	*49,662.2*					*48,040.2*	*1,622.0*[i]	
	Value	$ 11,130,893.52					$ 10,740,684.49	$390,209.03[i]	
Grand Total Net	Tons	*4,178,447.7*	*485,558.1*			*417,024.6*	*732,211.7*		*823,202*
	Value	**$1,101,486,783.34**	**$105,915,038.72**[f]	**$1,135,650.04**	**$81,588.23**[g]	**$86,743,158.36**	**$158,205,506.61**		**$381,721,094**

[a] Deliveries from this fund for children's relief are accounted for in Column 23, Table 187.

[b] Includes the total deliveries listed to the United Kingdom in Column 8.

[c] Represents freight paid by France on relief supplies delivered by the A.R.A.

[d] Includes $2,021,250.00, representing freight and transportation cha paid by Italy on relief supplies delivered by the A.R.A.

[e] Includes total deduction listed in Column 9.

[f] The detail of $1,217,238.27, which is in addition to the above t and represents freight, insurance, etc., is shown in Columns 5 and 6

[g] This sum was paid for by the A.R.A. but billed to the J.D.C.

NDER THE DIRECTION OF THE DIRECTOR GENERAL OF RELIEF

ountries of Destination—1919

(11) Commission for Relief in Belgium (Table 103)	(12) Near East Relief (Table 123)	(13) Jewish Joint Distribution Committee (Table 124)	(14) American Red Cross (Table 126)	(15) Joint Allied Finance (Table 128)	(16) United Kingdom (Table 133)	(17) United Kingdom Freight (Table 133)	(18) France (Table 134)	(19) Italy (Table 135)	(20) All Other Countries (Table 136)
....	30,657.0	....	754.1	....	....	....	....	....	....
....	$8,711,472.00	....	$ 258,600.00	....	....	$ 71,400.00	....	....	....
....	....	901.3	....	345,839.8[b]	18,000.0	....	....	64,061.0	124,578.3
....	....	$ 363,760.00	....	$48,000,000.00[b]	$ 1,916,640.00	$4,760,000.00	$ 4,500,000.00[c]	$20,878,122.00[d]	$15,059,603.00
....	....	....	....	....	....	....	....	....	....
....	....	....	....	....	....	....	....	....	....
....	....	....	....	....	....	....	....	....	....
....	....	....	....	....	....	....	....	....	....
....	....	....	875.2	....	7,132.0	....	16,571.0	75,861.0	51,080.1
....	....	....	$ 175,040.00	....	$ 1,599,836.00	....	$ 7,540,918.00	$16,653,920.00	$ 1,874,710.00
....	....	....	....	....	....	....	....	....	....
....	....	....	....	....	....	....	....	....	....
....	....	....	312.3	....	8,624.0	....	....	....	462.6
....	....	....	$ 89,800.00	....	$ 2,032,960.00	$ 309,400.00	....	....	$ 35,207.92
....	....	....	282.0	....	3,467.0	....	....	....	14,442.0
....	....	....	$ 56,400.00	....	$ 920,250.00	....	....	....	$ 2,318,830.00
....	....	....	....	....	....	....	....	....	....
....	....	....	....	....	....	....	....	....	....
134,980.0	....	....	....	....	299,144.0	....	69,404.0	....	228,534.0
4,350,810.47	....	....	....	....	$ 75,653,861.00	....	$16,262,889.00	....	$32,384,801.00
....	....	....	....	....	....	....	....	....	....
....	....	....	....	....	....	....	....	....	....
....	....	....	....	....	....	....	....	....	....
....	....	....	....	....	....	....	....	....	....
....	....	....	667.6	....	33,655.0	....	....	....	....
....	....	....	$ 224,800.00	....	$ 9,261,532.00	$ 373,660.00	....	....	....
....	....	....	....	....	....	....	....	....	....
....	....	....	....	....	....	$ 80,920.00	....	....	....
....	....	....	....	....	....	....	....	....	....
....	....	....	....	....	....	$ 57,120.00	....	....	....
....	....	....	....	....	....	....	....	....	....
....	....	....	....	....	....	....	....	....	....
....	....	9,705.8	4,042.6	....	21,462.0	....	....	....	4.6
....	....	$3,412,497.00	$ 813,800.00	....	$ 6,304,620.00	$1,389,920.00	....	....	$ 1,840.00
....	....	382.0	....	....	99,788.0	....	....	....	....
....	....	$ 256,000.00	....	....	$ 15,407,268.00	$ 21,420.00	....	....	....
....	....	....	....	....	....	....	....	....	....
....	....	....	....	....	....	....	....	....	....
....	....	40.0	....	....	....	....	....	....	....
....	....	$ 75,000.00	....	....	....	....	....	....	....
....	....	....	577.0	....	100.0	....	....	....	....
....	....	....	$ 123,300.00	....	$ 10,472.00	....	....	....	....
....	....	....	....	....	....	....	....	....	....
....	....	....	....	....	....	....	....	....	....
....	....	....	....	....	....	....	....	....	....
....	....	....	....	....	....	....	....	....	....
51,392.0	....	....	....	....	....	....	2,672.0[e]	....	....
1,990,430.40	....	....	....	....	....	....	$ 1,100,917.00[e]	....	....
....	....	....	....	....	....	....	....	....	....
....	....	....	....	....	....	....	....	....	....
....	....	....	....	....	....	....	....	....	....
....	....	....	....	....	....	....	....	....	....
186,372.0	30,657.0	11,029.1	7,510.8	345,839.8	491,372.0	....	88,647.0	139,922.0	419,101.6
,341,240.87	**$8,711,472.00**	**$4,107,257.00**	**$1,741,740.00**	**$48,000,000.00**	**$113,107,439.00**	**$7,063,840.00**[k]	**$29,404,724.00**	**$37,532,042.00**[d]	**$51,674,991.92**
....	....	....	....	....	....	....	....	....	....
....	....	....	....	....	....	....	....	....	....
186,372.0[j]	30,657.0	11,029.1	7,510.8	345,839.8	491,372.0	....	88,647.0	139,922.0	419,101.6
,341,240.87[j]	**$8,711,472.00**	**$4,107,257.00**	**$1,741,740.00**	**$48,000,000.00**	**$113,107,439.00**	**$7,063,840.00**	**$29,404,724.00**	**$37,532,042.00**[d]	**$51,674,991.92**

These totals actually represent net deliveries under Cash Sales. wever, 668.3 metric tons, valued at $122,638.77, are reflected in Col- 1 1, Belgian deliveries; and the entire deliveries to the United Kingdom d in Column 8 are also reflected in the deliveries to Austria, Col- 15. These two items total 48,040.2 metric tons, valued at $10,740,- 49, which have been deducted from Column 8 totals in order to avoid lication.

[i] Although deliveries were actually made to France for benefit of Russian prisoners of war in Germany, they have been deducted from Column 9 (in order to avoid duplication) and listed in Column 18 under Sundry Accounts.

[j] Cf. Column 1, Table 185, for balance of deliveries handled under the direction of the C.R.B.

[k] Paid on relief supplies delivered by the A.R.A.

DETAIL OF RECONSTRUCTIO

Table 187

By Operations or Funds and b

Country		(21) Total Net (Table 149)	(22) Congressional Appropriation Children's Relief (Table 114)	(23) President's National Security and Defense Fund[a] Children's Relief (Table 117)	(24) European Children's Fund (Table 156)	(25) American Relief Administration Warehouses (Table 153)	(26) U.S. Grain Corporation (Tables 157, 517
Armenia	Tons	*51,799.8*	....	....	....	....	*40,633.5*
	Value	$ 8,563,971.48	....	....	....	....	$ 4,813,744.4
Austria	Tons	*260,494.4*	*746.3*	*7,536.1*	*26,856.3*	*11,795.8*	*200,824.8*
	Value	$ 46,709,626.37	$ 319,471.90	$2,847,892.23	$ 6,695,794.69	$3,330,635.48	$24,055,708.9
Czecho-Slovakia	Tons	*41,904.6*	*6,476.2*	....	*6,287.1*	*1,376.5*	*23,809.0*
	Value	$ 9,892,557.58	$ 2,837,748.69	....	$ 2,102,676.85	$ 433,432.69	$ 2,873,238.2
Danzig Free City	Tons	*573.2*	....	....	*108.0*	*232.9*[c]	....
	Value	$ 127,700.69	....	....	$ 17,749.51	$ 71,085.48[c]	....
Esthonia	Tons	*5,847.7*	*2,029.9*	....	*1,831.3*	*293.5*	....
	Value	$ 1,669,451.09	$ 701,520.82	....	$ 522,929.39	$ 146,556.24	....
Finland	Tons	*3,487.2*	*2,109.3*	....	*441.5*	....	....
	Value	$ 1,109,991.80	$ 660,175.34	....	$ 253,867.46	....	....
Germany	Tons	*57,716.3*[e]	....	....	*4,053.0*	*9,347.4*	....
	Value	$ 11,962,693.54[e]	....	....	$ 362,571.27	$2,820,420.47	....
Greece	Tons	*20,374.0*	....	....	....	....	....
	Value	$ 1,211,949.95	....	....	....	....	....
Hungary	Tons	*21,074.4*	....	*287.0*	*3,298.3*	*1,629.6*	*14,114.0*
	Value	$ 4,361,619.41	....	$ 101,325.00	$ 1,191,623.36	$ 527,939.41	$ 1,685,835.6
Jugoslavia	Tons	*6,109.2*	*3,054.3*	....	*317.8*	....	....
	Value	$ 2,302,080.74	$ 1,164,617.41	....	$ 490,705.04	....	....
Latvia	Tons	*6,756.9*	*2,142.3*	....	*4,053.8*	*75.6*[f]	....
	Value	$ 1,588,170.34	$ 753,774.72	....	$ 754,796.70	$ 14,759.37[f]	....
Lithuania	Tons	*1,200.7*	*1,005.4*	....	*186.9*	*8.4*[h]	....
	Value	$ 463,776.92	$ 351,789.53	....	$ 111,060.61	$ 926.78[h]	....
Poland	Tons	*347,951.4*	*16,700.9*	....	*59,242.5*	*15,559.8*[i]	*202,564.0*
	Value	$ 65,841,716.75	$ 6,055,842.03	....	$16,769,322.10	$2,539,649.81[i]	$24,353,590.9
Roumania	Tons	*3,759.3*	*1,432.3*	....	....	....	....
	Value	$ 1,501,595.02	$ 477,272.76	....	....	....	....
Russia							
Northwest Russia	Tons	*350.3*	*305.2*	....	*12.8*	....	....
	Value	$ 124,208.73	$ 111,705.13	....	$ 6,223.60	....	....
Soviet Republics	Tons	*741,572.7*[k]	....	....	*230,597.9*	....	*386,070.8*
	Value	$ 63,174,848.78[k]	....	....	$28,992,756.94	....	$18,662,180.0
Sundry Accounts	Tons	*562.0*	....	....	*562.0*	....	....
	Value	$ 98,622.59	....	....	$ 98,622.59	....	....
Grand Total	Tons	*1,571,534.1*	*36,002.1*	*7,823.1*	*337,849.2*	*40,319.5*	*868,016.1*
	Value	**$220,704,581.78**	**$13,433,918.33**	**$2,949,217.23**	**$58,370,700.11**	**$9,885,405.73**	**$76,444,298.2**

[a] Deliveries from this fund for Russian prisoners of war are accounted for in Column 9, Table 186.
[b] This value includes $532,790.01, which represents freight and insurance charges on Grain Corporation flour listed in Column 26.
[c] In order to show the food and the country where it was consumed, 7,720.3 metric tons, valued at $864,562.40, have been transferred to Poland. (Cf. footnote [i].)
[d] See value for Soviet Republics.
[e] The gross total has been reduced to a net figure by deducting 1,237.2 metric tons and $341,309.37, which figures appear as duplications in Columns 25 and 29.

[f] These are net quantities consumed in Latvia. Table 153 inclu the Lithuanian deliveries in the Latvian total because the sales w made in that country.
[g] These figures include a Norwegian Government donation of c liver oil in the amount of 6.6 metric tons, valued at $3,960.00.
[h] This represents net supplies delivered to Lithuania. (Cf. footnote
[i] This total includes the supplies transferred from Danzig and us in Poland. (Cf. footnote [c].)
[j] See value for Soviet Republics.

ERIOD RELIEF DELIVERIES

ountries of Destination—1919–1924

(27) U.S. Government Surplus Medical Supplies (Table 521)	(28) American Red Cross (Table 158)	(29) American Friends Service Committee (Table 159)	(30) Common-wealth Fund (Table 160)	(31) Jewish Joint Distribution Committee (Table 406)	(32) Near East Relief (Tables 203n, 205)	(33) Other American Organizations (Table 354)	(34) United Kingdom (Table 162)	(35) European Governments (Table 161)	(36) Soviet Republics (Tables 165, 519)
....	....	....	*3,762.0*	....	*7,404.3*	....	....	....	....
....	$500,000.00	....	$746,107.12	....	$1,944,119.91[b]	....	$560,000.00	....	....
....	....	....	*31.8*	....	....	....	....	*12,703.3*	....
....	....	....	$62,475.26	....	....	....	$8,032,991.88	$1,364,656.01	....
....	....	....	....	....	....	....	....	*3,955.8*	....
....	....	....	....	....	....	....	$952,362.08	$693,099.02	....
....	....	*158.3*	....	....	....	....	....	*74.0*	....
....	....	$30,291.26	....	....	....	....	....	$8,574.44	....
....	....	....	....	....	....	....	....	*1,693.0*	....
....	....	....	....	....	....	....	....	$298,444.64[d]	....
....	....	....	....	....	....	....	....	*936.4*	....
....	....	....	....	....	....	....	....	$195,949.00	....
....	....	*28,720.1*	....	....	....	....	....	*16,833.0*	....
....	....	$6,728,989.92	....	....	....	....	....	$2,392,021.25	....
....	*20,374.0*	....	....	....	....	....	....	....	....
....	$1,211,949.95	....	....	....	....	....	....	....	....
....	....	....	*12.5*	....	....	....	....	*1,733.0*	....
....	....	....	$24,527.59	....	....	....	$564,561.60	$265,806.84	....
....	....	....	....	....	....	*103.1*	....	*2,634.0*	....
....	....	....	....	....	....	$113,081.13	....	$533,677.16	....
....	....	....	....	....	....	....	....	*485.2*[g]	....
....	....	....	....	....	....	....	....	$64,839.55[g]	....
....	....	....	....	....	....	....	....	....	....
....	....	....	....	....	....	....	....	....	....
....	....	*633.3*	*30.4*	*537.0*	....	....	....	*52,579.2*	....
....	....	$30,291.26	$57,532.49	$273,555.00	....	....	$8,102,558.32	$7,659,374.77[j]	....
....	....	....	....	....	....	....	....	*2,327.0*	....
....	....	....	....	....	....	....	....	$1,024,322.26	....
....	....	....	....	....	....	....	....	*32.3*	....
....	....	....	....	....	....	....	....	$6,280.00	....
3,107.6	*5,174.3*	*4,202.2*	....	....	....	....	....	*554.0*	*169,688.9*
4,267,392.88	$3,804,863.15	$267,394.24	....	....	....	....	....	$145,387.27[l]	$11,357,325.13
....	....	....	....	....	....	....	....	....	....
....	....	....	....	....	....	....	....	....	....
3,107.6	*25,548.3*	*33,713.9*	*3,836.7*[o]	*537.0*	*7,404.3*	*103.1*	....	*96,540.2*	*169,688.9*
4,267,392.88[n]	**$5,516,813.10**	**$7,056,966.68**	**$890,642.46**[o]	**$273,555.00**	**$1,944,119.91**[b]	**$113,081.13**	**$18,212,473.88**[p]	**$14,652,432.21**	**$11,357,325.13**

[k] The gross total has been reduced to a net figure by deducting ,823.0 metric tons and $4,322,450.83, which figures appear as duplications Columns 24 and 36.

[l] This value represents donations by: Soviet Republics of $30,026.64; olish Government, $90,000.00; Latvian Government, $24,257.69; Estho-an Government, $1,102.94.

[m] This total includes 481,945.3 metric tons of flour, f.o.b. value 7,782,118.20, sold under Act of Congress, March 30, 1920, and 586,070.8 etric tons, valued at $18,662,180.00, delivered to Russia under Act of ongress, December 22, 1921.

[n] This total includes $267,392.88, representing transportation charges paid by Laura Spelman Rockefeller Memorial.

[o] This total includes 3,762.0 metric tons of food, valued at $746,107.12, which were delivered to Armenia. The balance of 74.7 metric tons, valued at $144,535.34, represents clothing deliveries for the intelligentsia.

[p] This value represents finance on freight paid on tonnage listed in Column 26.

SUMMARY, BY COUNTRIES, OF FINANCE FOR FOOD AND RELIEF SUPPLIES DELIVERED, 1914–1924

Table 188* Segregated as to Deliveries for Credit, Cash or Barter, and Benevolence

Country	Total	Credit	Cash or Barter	Benevolence
Armenia	$ 28,795,426.49	$ 16,076,016.64	....	$ 12,719,409.8
Austria	145,481,222.30	93,286,590.80	$ 38,554,320.62	13,640,310.8
Belgium	697,140,348.91	504,078,737.22	6,328,328.30	186,733,283.3
Bulgaria	4,856,647.53	....	4,856,647.53	....
Czecho-Slovakia	115,438,351.98	82,925,123.12	26,980,958.95	5,532,269.9
Danzig Free City	127,700.69	....	8,574.44	119,126.2
Denmark	2,147,059.30	....	2,147,059.30	....
Esthonia	21,017,263.56	18,555,942.91	950,024.18	1,511,296.4
Finland	30,282,047.90	10,991,287.73	18,335,395.26	955,364.9
France	1,289,488,622.47	1,279,427,095.20	5,031,830.08	5,029,697.1
Germany	294,373,692.75	....	285,135,904.48	9,237,788.2
Greece	1,211,949.95	....	....	1,211,949.9
Hungary	4,607,139.37	2,250,397.21	512,117.63	1,844,624.5
Italy	799,608,264.01	796,762,249.59	2,846,014.42	....
Jugoslavia	45,898,651.43	43,290,629.71	533,677.16	2,074,344.5
Latvia	7,550,021.69	5,961,691.63	69,215.62	1,519,114.4
Lithuania	5,980,781.39	5,517,004.47	....	463,776.9
Netherlands	4,219,498.41	....	4,219,498.41	....
Poland	200,864,857.73	163,035,725.16	8,523,937.17	29,305,195.4
Roumania	53,637,311.31	51,879,716.29	1,024,322.26	733,272.7
Russia				
Northwest Russia	5,890,076.54	5,765,867.81	6,280.00	117,928.7
Siberia	75,000.00	....	....	75,000.0
Kouban	578,490.50	....	444,718.50	133,772.0
Soviet Republics	63,174,848.78	....	11,502,712.40	51,672,136.3
Ukraine	8,500,222.67	8,500,222.67	....	....
Volunteer Army	86,680.00	86,680.00	....	....
Sundry Accounts	23,654,740.07	....	22,455,200.48	1,199,539.5
Turkey	4,369,404.30	....	4,369,404.30	....
United Kingdom	1,386,102,780.05	1,375,484,734.33	10,618,045.72	....
Grand Total Gross	**$5,245,159,102.08**	**$4,463,875,712.49**	**$455,454,187.21**	**$325,829,202.3**
Less Duplications	11,130,893.52	390,209.03	10,740,684.49	....
Grand Total Net	**$5,234,028,208.56**	**$4,463,485,503.46**	**$444,713,502.72**	**$325,829,202.3**

* Cf. Table 189 for detail by Major Periods.

DETAIL, BY COUNTRIES AND PERIODS, OF FINANCE FOR FOO

Table 189

Segregated as to Deliveries for Credi

Country	C.R.B. Period				U.S.F.A. Period	
	Total	Credit	Cash or Barter	Benevolence	Total	Credit
Armenia	....	....	....	....	....	....
Austria	....	....	....	....	....	....
Belgium	$641,056,693.69	$447,995,082.00	$6,328,328.30	$186,733,283.39	$ 27,533,982.47	$ 27,533,982.4
Bulgaria	....	....	....	....	....	....
Czecho-Slovakia	....	....	....	....	....	....
Danzig Free City	....	....	....	....	....	....
Denmark	....	....	....	....	....	....
Esthonia	....	....	....	....	....	....
Finland	....	....	....	....	....	....
France	220,283,550.52	215,253,853.33	....	5,029,697.19	850,715,632.84	850,715,632.8
Germany	....	....	....	....	....	....
Greece	....	....	....	....	....	....
Hungary	....	....	....	....	....	....
Italy	....	....	....	....	796,762,249.59	796,762,249.5
Jugoslavia	....	....	....	....	....	....
Latvia	....	....	....	....	....	....
Lithuania	....	....	....	....	....	....
Netherlands	....	....	....	....	....	....
Poland	....	....	....	....	....	....
Roumania	....	....	....	....	....	....
Russia						
Northwest Russia	....	....	....	....	....	....
Siberia	....	....	....	....	....	....
Kouban	....	....	....	....	....	....
Soviet Republics	....	....	....	....	....	....
Ukraine	....	....	....	....	....	....
Volunteer Army	....	....	....	....	....	....
Sundry Accounts	....	....	....	....	....	....
Turkey	....	....	....	....	....	....
United Kingdom	....	....	....	....	1,375,484,734.33	1,375,484,734.3
Grand Total Gross	**$861,340,244.21**	**$663,248,935.33**	**$6,328,328.30**	**$191,762,980.58**	**$3,050,496,599.23**	**$3,050,496,599.2**
Less Duplications	....	....	....	....	....	....
Grand Total Net	**$861,340,244.21**	**$663,248,935.33**	**$6,328,328.30**	**$191,762,980.58**	**$3,050,496,599.23**	**$3,050,496,599.2**

AND RELIEF SUPPLIES DELIVERED, 1914–1924

Cash or Barter, and Benevolence

Armistice Period				Reconstruction Period			
Total	Credit	Cash or Barter	Benevolence	Total	Credit	Cash or Barter	Benevolence
$ 20,231,455.01	$ 10,702,272.19	....	$ 9,529,182.82	$ 8,563,971.48	$ 5,373,744.45	....	$ 3,190,227.03
98,771,595.93	61,197,890.00	$ 37,189,563.35	384,142.58	46,709,626.37	32,088,700.80	$ 1,364,757.27	13,256,168.30
28,549,672.75	28,549,672.75	....	....	....	....	....	....
4,856,647.53	....	4,856,647.53	....	....	....	....	....
105,545,794.40	79,099,522.79	26,092,128.62	354,142.99	9,892,557.58	3,825,600.33	888,830.33	5,178,126.92
....	....	....	....	127,700.69	....	8,574.44	119,126.25
2,147,059.30	....	2,147,059.30	....	....	....	....	....
19,347,812.47	18,555,942.91	651,579.54	140,290.02	1,669,451.09	....	298,444.64	1,371,006.45
29,172,056.10	10,991,287.73	18,101,784.13	78,984.24	1,109,991.80	....	233,611.13	876,380.67
218,489,439.11	213,457,609.03	5,031,830.08	....	....	....	....	....
282,410,999.21	....	282,381,311.96	29,687.25	11,962,693.54	....	2,754,592.52	9,208,101.02
....	....	....	....	1,211,949.95	....	....	1,211,949.95
245,519.96	....	245,519.96	....	4,361,619.41	2,250,397.21	266,597.67	1,844,624.53
2,846,014.42	....	2,846,014.42	....	....	....	....	....
43,596,570.69	43,290,629.71	....	305,940.98	2,302,080.74	....	533,677.16	1,768,403.58
5,961,851.35	5,961,691.63	....	159.72	1,588,170.34	....	69,215.62	1,518,954.72
5,517,004.47	5,517,004.47	....	....	463,776.92	....	....	463,776.92
4,219,498.41	....	4,219,498.41	....	....	....	....	....
135,023,140.98	130,579,575.87	....	4,443,565.11	65,841,716.75	32,456,149.29	8,523,937.17	24,861,630.29
52,135,716.29	51,879,716.29	....	256,000.00	1,501,595.02	....	1,024,322.26	477,272.76
5,765,867.81	5,765,867.81	....	....	124,208.73	....	6,280.00	117,928.73
75,000.00	....	....	75,000.00	....	....	....	....
578,490.50	....	444,718.50	133,772.00	....	....	....	....
....	....	....	....	63,174,848.78	....	11,502,712.40	51,672,136.38
8,500,222.67	8,500,222.67	....	....	....	....	....	....
86,680.00	86,680.00	....	....	....	....	....	....
23,556,117.48	....	22,455,200.48	1,100,917.00	98,622.59	....	....	98,622.59
4,369,404.30	....	4,369,404.30	....	....	....	....	....
10,618,045.72	....	10,618,045.72	....	....	....	....	....
$1,112,617,676.86	**$674,135,585.85**	**$421,650,306.30**	**$16,831,784.71**	**$220,704,581.78**	**$75,994,592.08**	**$27,475,552.61**	**$117,234,437.09**
11,130,893.52	390,209.03	10,740,684.49	....	....	....	....	....
$1,101,486,783.34	**$673,745,376.82**	**$410,909,621.81**	**$16,831,784.71**	**$220,704,581.78**	**$75,994,592.08**	**$27,475,552.61**	**$117,234,437.09**

A.R.A.-EUROPEAN CHILDREN'S FUND

Table 190 Austrian Children—The Weekly Menu by Days and by Rations

Day	Menu *	Unit	Flour	Rice	Beans, Peas	Corn Grits	Pork Products	Milk	Cocoa	Sugar	Misc. Food	Total
Monday	Milk and rice	Nem	...	300	...	...	...	200	..	200	...	700
		Grams	...	60	...	...	...	100	..	33.3	...	193.
	Bread	Nem	300	...	...	...	...	...	..	...	...	300
		Grams	75	...	...	...	...	...	..	...	...	75
Tuesday	Maize grits stewed in fats	Nem	...	...	...	330	220	90	..	60	...	700
		Grams	...	...	...	66	16.5	45	..	10	...	137.
	Cocoa	Nem	...	...	...	...	...	60	40	200	...	300
		Grams	...	...	...	...	...	30	6.6	33.3	...	69.
Wednesday	Stewed rice	Nem	...	306	...	...	90	...	..	...	4	400
		Grams	...	61.2	...	...	6.8	...	..	...	8†	76
	Bread	......	(Same ration as Monday)									
	Cocoa	......	(Same ration as Tuesday)									
Thursday	Cornmeal mush	Nem	...	...	...	200	...	250	..	250	...	700
		Grams	...	...	...	40	...	125	..	41.8	...	206.
	Cocoa	......	(Same ration as Tuesday)									
Friday	Bread Dumpling	Nem	160	...	...	...	100	...	..	...	340‡	600
		Grams	32	...	...	...	7.5	...	..	...	83	122.
	Milk soup	Nem	80	...	...	...	100	220	..	...	...	400
		Grams	16	...	...	...	7.5	110	..	...	...	133.
Saturday	Cake	Nem	350	...	...	...	120	50	..	80	...	600
		Grams	70	...	...	...	9	25	..	13.3	...	117.
	Cocoa	Nem	...	...	...	...	...	80	60	260	...	400
		Grams	...	...	...	...	...	40	10	43.3	...	93.

* All kitchens are required to issue the food supplies on the basis of a standard menu. This menu has been changed from time to time with a view to obtaining the maximum of variety with the available foodstuffs. The basic daily ration is 10 hectonem (1,000 nem) or the equivalent of 667 calories.

† Onions.

‡ Consisting of bread, 300 nem, 75 grams; bread crumbs, 40 ner
8 grams.

A.R.A.-EUROPEAN CHILDREN'S FUND

Table 191 Czecho-Slovakian Children—The Weekly Menu by Days and by Rations

Day	Menu *	Quantities in Grams						
		Flour	Rice	Beans, Peas	Pork Products	Milk	Cocoa	Suga
Monday and Thursday	Rice pudding, ½ liter	10.0	50.0	....	7.0	20.0	....	10
Tuesday and Friday	Bean soup, ½ liter	10.0	....	62.5	7.5	20.0	....	..
Wednesday	Cocoa pudding, ½ liter	15.0	....	....	...	60.0	12.5	32
Saturday	Cocoa, ½ liter	....	....	....	...	45.0	10.0	20

* Each daily menu was supplemented by a 75.0 gram roll or biscuit, which included the following commodities in grams: flour, 50; pork products, 6; sugar, 5.

A.R.A.-EUROPEAN CHILDREN'S FUND

Table 192 Hungarian Children—The Weekly Menu by Days and Rations*

Day	Menu	Unit	Flour	Rice	Beans, Peas	Pork Products	Milk	Cocoa	Sugar	Bread	Total
nday	Rice in Milk....................	Nem	...	500	...	100	100	..	100	...	800
		Grams	...	100	...	8	20	..	17	...	145
	Cocoa	Nem	...	...	...	..	100	42	60	...	202
		Grams	...	...	...	..	20	7	10	...	37
sday	Bean Soup	Nem	100	...	600	100	..	..	..	...	800
		Grams	20	...	150	8	..	..	..	...	178
	White Bread	Nem	200	...	...	..	..	..	..	...	200
		Grams	50	...	...	..	..	..	..	...	50
dnesday ..	Noodles in Milk.................	Nem	650	...	...	50	180	60	60	...	1,000
		Grams	130	...	...	4	90	10	10	...	244
rsday	Rice and Beans..................	Nem	...	400	200	200	..	..	..	...	800
		Grams	...	80	75	8	..	..	..	...	163
	White Bread.....................	....	(Same ration as Tuesday)								
day	Roll Dumpling	Nem	400	...	...	200	..	..	..	200	800
		Grams	80	...	...	15	..	..	..	50	145
	Cocoa	....	(Same ration as Monday)								
urday	Baked Pastry or Coffee Cake....	Nem	575	...	...	50	50	..	25	...	700
		Grams	115	...	...	4	10	..	4	...	133
	Cocoa	Nem	...	...	...	..	150	72	78	...	300
		Grams	...	...	...	..	30	12	13	...	55

The basic daily ration is 10 hectonem (1,000 nem) or the equivalent
67 calories.

A.R.A.-EUROPEAN CHILDREN'S FUND

Table 193* Polish Children—The Weekly Menu by Days and Rations

Day	Menu	Quantities in Grams								
		Flour	Rice	Beans, Peas	Pork Products	Milk	Cocoa	Sugar	Misc. Food **	Salt
nday	Milk and rice.....................	...	60	....	..	60†	..	14.8	...	1
esday	Dumplings with pork products....	164	..	....	12	..	..	..	9.2	8
dnesday ..	Dumplings with rice.............	92	30	....	12	..	..	..	9.2	8
ursday	Beans and rice..................	12	30	10.5	12	..	..	..	9.2	8
day	Cocoa	12	..	....	..	72‡	12	16	...	..
turday	Dumplings with beans...........	92	..	10.5	12	..	..	..	9.2	8

This table represents the standard ration. The ration for Jewish
dren included 8 grams of vegetable oil, whereas the Christian chil-
ı were given 8 grams of lard or lard substitute. The small children
e fed on a milk ration consisting of 120 grams of milk.

** Principally vegetables: onions, carrots, and parsley.
† One part condensed, two parts evaporated.
‡ Equal portions of condensed and evaporated.

AMERICAN RELIEF ADMINISTRATION

Russian Unit*—Detail of Hospital Ration by Commodities, Grams, and Calories. Requirements for One Child for One Day

Table 194

Commodity	Grams	Calories
our	218.4	797.2
culent	54.6	196.6
rk products	10.2	89.8
lk	105.9	180.0
coa	8.5	40.0
gar	20.5	84.0
Total	**418.1**	**1,387.6**

* See note following Table 198.

AMERICAN RELIEF ADMINISTRATION

Russian Unit*—Detail of First Ration by Commodities, Grams, and Calories. Requirements for One Child for One Day

Table 195

Commodity	Grams	Calories
Flour	100.00	365.0
Feculent	54.30	195.5
Pork products	8.57	75.4
Milk	36.00	61.2
Cocoa	4.00	18.8
Sugar	16.00	65.6
Total	**218.87**	**781.5**

* See note following Table 198.

AMERICAN RELIEF ADMINISTRATION

Russian Unit*—Detail of Second Ration by Commodities, Grams, and Calories. Requirements for One Child for One Day

Table 196

Commodity	Grams	Calories
Flour	65.0	237.25
Feculent	36.0	129.60
Pork products	6.0	52.80
Milk	24.0	40.80
Cocoa	3.0	14.10
Sugar	11.0	45.10
Total	**145.0**	**519.65**

* See note following Table 198.

AMERICAN RELIEF ADMINISTRATION

Russian Unit*—The Weekly Menu by Days and Rations

Table 197

Day	Menu	Flour	Feculent	Pork Products	Milk	Cocoa	Sugar
Sunday, Wednesday, Friday	Corn grits with fats, rolls, or noodles	65	50	10	14	....	....
Monday, Thursday	Cocoa and rolls	65	..	..	50	10.5	25.0
Tuesday, Saturday	Corn grits and sugar	65	51	6	13	....	13.5

* See note following Table 198.

AMERICAN RELIEF ADMINISTRATION

Russian Unit*—Detail of Third Ration by Commodities, Grams, and Calories. Requirements for One Child for One Day

Table 198

Commodity	Grams	Calories
Flour	80.0	292.
Feculent	56.0	201.
Pork products	7.5	66.
Milk	24.0	40.
Cocoa	3.0	14.
Sugar	11.0	45.
Total	**181.5**	**659.**

* Russian Unit—The menus for the Russian child-feeding program varied in proportion to the demands of the community and the malnutrition of the children. The details of the rations are set forth i Tables 194–198, inclusive.

Table 194 shows the ration for children confined in hospitals.

Table 195 shows the first or famine ration, or the supplies delivere to the kitchens when conditions were at their worst.

Table 196 shows the ration when local conditions had improved t the extent that the local institutions were able to assist in the child feeding operation, thereby making the A.R.A. feeding purely a supple mental ration. The corresponding menu is shown in Table 197.

Table 198 shows the A.R.A. ration as it was increased to care fo the greater demands of the communities. The increased demands we due to local food shortages prior to the spring harvesting.

Feculent, though technically an incorrect term, was used to designat rice, beans, peas, and corn grits. These commodities were interchang able, depending upon the available stocks. The interchanging of thes commodities materially assisted in varying the menu as rice and mil bean soup, maize gruel, maize pudding, etc.

AMERICAN RELIEF ADMINISTRATION

Statement Showing the Number of Pairs, per Size, of Shoes and Stockings Ordered for Russian Children, in 100 Lots

Table 199

	Shoes		Stockings	
	Size	Number of Pairs	Size	Number of Pairs
Little gent's	9	2	6½	2
	10	4	7	10
	11	6		
	12	6	7½	12
	13	6		
Youths'	1	8	8	8
	2	8	8½	18
Boys'	3	10		
	4	12	9	12
	5	12	9½	12
Men's	6	12	10	12
	7	10	10½	10
	8	4	10½, 11	4
	..	100	..	100

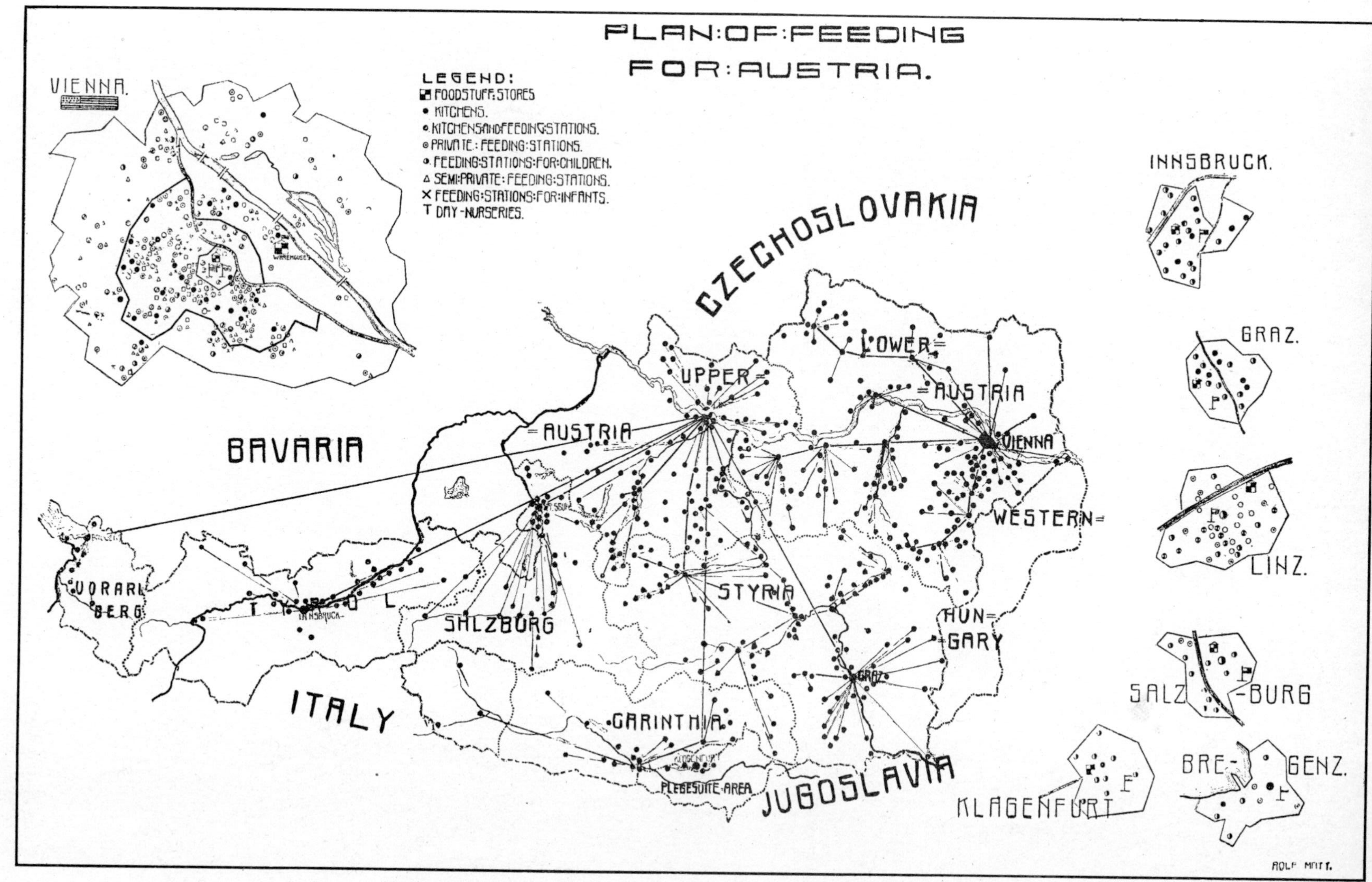

Map of Austria showing principal warehouses and child-feeding centers

APPENDIX II
COUNTRY TABLES

Table 200

ARMENIA—

Operation	Table No.	Flour	Grain	Rice	Beans, Peas
		ARMISTIC			
A.R.A.—Congressional Appropriation, $100,000,000 Fund	201	34,167.1	8,000.0	1,022.3	2,661.8
A.R.A.—Cash Settlement (through A.C.R.N.E.)	202	1,651.4	......	......	......
A.R.A.—Freight on Charity Shipments	143	......	......	......	......
Near East Relief	123	7,612.0	......	......	......
American Red Cross	126	......	......	......	......
Total American Relief	...	**43,430.5**	**8,000.0**	**1,022.3**	**2,661.8**
United Kingdom—Finance on Freight	133	......	......	......	......
Total, Armistice Period	...	**43,430.5**	**8,000.0**	**1,022.3**	**2,661.8**
		RECONSTRUCTIO			
U.S. Grain Corporation (Act of Congress, March 30, 1920)	203	40,633.5	......	......	......
Near East Relief—Freight, Insurance, Misc. Charges	203n	......	......	......	......
American Red Cross—Freight, Insurance, Misc. Charges	203n	......	......	......	......
United Kingdom—Freight, Insurance, Misc. Charges	203n	......	......	......	......
Commonwealth Fund	204	2,679.3	......	366.9	404.6
Near East Relief	205	4,505.5	......	1,038.4	......
Total, Reconstruction Period	...	**47,818.3**	......	**1,405.3**	**404.6**
Grand Total Relief Deliveries	...	**91,248.8**	**8,000.0**	**2,427.6**	**3,066.4**

ARMENIA—

Table 201

Detail by Steamers of Relief Deliveries Paid for from th

Arrival No.*	Steamer	Port of Sailing	Date of Arrival	Port of Arrival	Wheat Flour	Cereal Flour
			1919			
13	Maine	New York	Jan. 28	Constantinople	300.0	......
36	West Mount	New York	Feb. 21	Derindje	......	......
210	Oshkosh	New York	May 20	Batoum	3,929.3	......
229	Cape Lookout, II	Baltimore	May 27	Batoum	6,017.0	......
255	Fort Pitt Bridge	New York	June 4	Batoum	3,973.5	33.8
290	Agawan	New York	June 18	Batoum	188.1	......
293	Bavaria	New York	June 20	Batoum	2,661.8	......
384	Sonnenfels	New York	Aug. 30	Batoum	1,336.9	......
385	Kickapoo ‡	Marseilles	Aug. 30	Batoum	......	......
385	Kickapoo	Novorossisk	Aug. 30	Batoum	......	......
387	Naimes	Philadelphia	Aug. 31	Batoum	5,378.4	1,943.5
386	Aschenburg	New York	Aug. 31	Batoum	2,005.3	6,399.5
	Miscellaneous Charges	....	....	....	......	......
	Total	....	....	....	**25,790.3**	**8,376.8**

§ Cf. Table 112.
* Arrival numbers from Table 111.

‡ Army stocks in France purchased by the American Relief Admin tration from U.S. Liquidation Commission.

nmary of Relief Deliveries

ork oducts	Milk	Cocoa	Sugar	Miscellaneous Food	Soap	Medical and Hospital Supplies	Clothing and Miscellaneous	Total Tons	Total Value
Commodities in Net Metric Tons of 1,000 Kilograms or 2,204.6 Pounds									
RIOD									
49.0	3,119.8	186.9	812.8	......	431.5	...	107.7	50,558.9	$10,630,872.19
....	342.9	.....	.....	......	.....	...	....	1,994.3	511,422.34
....	......	.....	.....	......	.....	...	....	....	47,688.48
....	1,253.0	.....	.....	6,585.0	.....	...	15,207.0	30,657.0	8,711,472.00
....	......	.....	.....	......	.....	...	754.1	754.1	258,600.00
49.0	**4,715.7**	**186.9**	**812.8**	**6,585.0**	**431.5**	...	**16,068.8**	**83,964.3**	**$20,160,055.01**
....	......	.....	.....	......	.....	...	....	....	71,400.00
49.0	**4,715.7**	**186.9**	**812.8**	**6,585.0**	**431.5**	...	**16,068.8**	**83,964.3**	**$20,231,455.01**
RIOD									
....	......	.....	.....	......	.....	...	....	40,633.5	$ 4,813,744.45
....	......	.....	.....	......	.....	...	....	....	532,790.01
....	......	.....	.....	......	.....	...	....	....	500,000.00
....	......	.....	.....	......	.....	...	....	....	560,000.00
50.9	102.8	61.0	96.5	......	.....	...	....	3,762.0	746,107.12
240.0	178.0	108.0	483.6	1.9	300.8	2.0	546.1	7,404.3	1,411,329.90
290.9	**280.8**	**169.0**	**580.1**	**1.9**	**300.8**	**2.0**	**546.1**	**51,799.8**	**$ 8,563,971.48**
339.9	**4,996.5**	**355.9**	**1,392.9**	**6,586.9**	**732.3**	**2.0**	**16,614.9**	**135,764.1**	**$28,795,426.49**

nerican Relief Administration

ngressional Appropriation for Relief§—Armistice Period, 1919

Vheat Grain	Beans, Peas	Rice	Pork Products	Milk	Sugar	Cocoa	Soap	Misc.	Total Tons	Total Value
Contents of Cargoes in Net Metric Tons of 1,000 Kilograms or 2,204.6 Pounds										
.....	......	......	....	......	.....	....	.....	.....	300.0	$ 66,000.00
.....	......	......	....	164.9	.....	....	.....	.....	164.9	79,527.00
.....	619.2	......	....	......	.....	....	.....	.....	4,548.5	1,004,717.49
.....	......	......	....	......	.....	....	.....	.....	6,017.0	1,263,562.65
.....	......	......	....	......	203.2	115.8	.....	.....	4,326.3	942,913.43
.....	1,606.2	......	....	1,950.5	.....	....	.....	.....	3,744.8	1,565,693.73
.....	436.4	3.1	....	......	.....	....	.....	.....	3,101.3	686,408.77
.....	......	1,019.2	....	1,004.4	609.6	71.1	431.5	.....	4,472.7	1,343,972.79
.....	......	......	49.0	......	.....	....	.....	107.7	156.7	94,816.97
,000.0†	......	......	....	......	.....	....	.....	.....	8,000.0	444,718.50
.....	......	......	....	......	.....	....	.....	.....	7,321.9	1,498,735.43
.....	......	......	....	......	.....	....	.....	.....	8,404.8	1,637,008.32
.....	......	......	....	......	.....	....	.....	.....	....	2,797.11
,000.0	**2,661.8**	**1,022.3**	**49.0**	**3,119.8**	**812.8**	**186.9**	**431.5**	**107.7**	**50,558.9**	**$10,630,872.19**

† Wheat grain received from the Kouban Government (South Russia) xchange for 915.5 M.T. miscellaneous army supplies with a total e of $444,718.50. (See page 242.)

ARMENIA-

Table 202

Detail by Steamers of Relief Deliveries Paid for by America

Arrival No.*	Steamer	Port of Sailing	Date of Arrival	Port of Arrival	Contents of Cargoes in Net Metric Tons of 1,000 Kilograms or 2,204.6 Pounds			Total Value
					Wheat Flour	Milk	Total Tons	
			1919					
13	Maine	New York	Jan. 28	Constantinople	185.5	.....	185.5	$ 40,880.
36	West Mount	New York	Feb. 21	Derindje	......	342.9	342.9	148,031.
39	West Eldara	New York	Feb. 22	Constantinople	689.0	.....	689.0	151,591.
193	Eastern Sun	Philadelphia	May 15	Constantinople	776.9	.....	776.9	170,918.
	Total Deliveries				**1,651.4**	**342.9**	**1,994.3**	**$511,422.**

† Later Near East Relief.

* Arrival numbers from Table 111.

ARMENIA-

Table 203

Detail by Steamers of Flour Deliveries, under Act

Arrival No.	Steamer	Port of Sailing	Date of Sailing or Arrival	Port of Arrival	Flour	Rice	Pork Products
			1919				
1	West Raritan	Baltimore	Nov. 26	Batoum	7,270.0	......	.....
2	Delisle	New York	Nov. 29	Batoum	4,109.1	......	.....
3	West Pocasset	New York	Dec. 10	Batoum	7,029.3	......	.....
			1920				
4	Chincha	New York	Jan. 17	Batoum	1,095.7	......	.....
5	Gaffney	New York	Jan. 26	Batoum	6,339.6	......	.....
6	Sheafmead	Philadelphia	May 20	Batoum	6,412.5	......	.....
7	River Araxes	N. Y.-Phila.	May 20	Batoum	2,740.6	......	.....
8	Poldennis	New York	June 14	Batoum	5,636.7	......	.....
	Total Deliveries				**40,633.5**	......	.....

* Freight, Insurance, and Misc. Charges Paid by Near East Relief $ 532,790.01 on arrivals No. 1, 2, and part of 3
Freight, Insurance, and Misc. Charges Paid by American Red Cross 500,000.00 on arrivals No. 4, 5, and part of 3
Freight, Insurance, and Misc. Charges Paid by United Kingdom 560,000.00 on arrivals No. 6, 7, and 8

Total $1,592,790.01

ARMENIA-

Table 204

Detail by Steamers of Relief Deliveries in Co-operation with th

Steamer	Port of Sailing	Date of Arrival	Port of Arrival	Contents of Cargoes		
				Flour	Rice	Beans, Peas
		1920				
Chincha	New York	Feb. 21	Batoum	845.2	366.9	377.4
Massillon Bridge	New York	Mar. 12	Constantinople	......	.....	27.2
Lake Fiscus	New York	May 23	Constantinople	1,015.2	.....	.....
River Araxes	New York	June 8	Piraeus	818.9	.....	.....
Total				**2,679.3**	**366.9**	**404.6**

nerican Relief Administration

mmission for Relief in the Near East†—Armistice Period, 1919

nited States Grain Corporation

ngress, March 30, 1920—Reconstruction Period, 1919–1924

ntents of Cargoes in Net Metric Tons of 1,000 Kilograms or 2,204.6 Pounds								F.O.B. Value	Freight, Insurance, Miscellaneous Charges *	Total Value
Milk	Cocoa	Sugar	Misc. Food	Soap	Medical and Hospital Supplies	Clothing and Misc.	Total Tons			
.....	.....	.....	...	.....	...	.....	7,270.0	$ 858,615.00	$ 292,173.71	$1,150,788.71
.....	.....	.....	...	.....	...	.....	4,109.1	485,295.00	164,943.87	650,238.87
.....	.....	.....	...	.....	...	.....	7,029.3	830,190.00	292,348.15	1,122,538.15
.....	.....	.....	...	.....	...	.....	1,095.7	129,405.00	41,032.24	170,437.24
.....	.....	.....	...	.....	...	.....	6,339.6	748,725.00	242,292.04	991,017.04
.....	.....	.....	...	.....	...	.....	6,412.5	757,051.34	242,801.30	999,852.64
.....	.....	.....	...	.....	...	.....	2,740.6	323,441.25	103,770.76	427,212.01
.....	.....	.....	...	.....	...	.....	5,636.7	681,021.86	213,427.94	894,449.80
.....	.....	.....	...	.....	...	.....	**40,633.5**	**$4,813,744.45**	**$1,592,790.01**	**$6,406,534.46**

mmonwealth Fund

R.A.-European Children's Fund—Reconstruction Period, 1919–1924

Metric Tons of 1,000 Kilograms or 2,204.6 Pounds					F.O.B. Value	Freight	Insurance	Miscellaneous Charges	Total Value
Pork Products	Milk	Cocoa	Sugar	Total Tons					
....	.....	....	96.5	1,686.0	$273,324.09	$ 64,836.26	$ 5,182.50	$ 6,009.57	$349,352.42
50.9	102.8	61.0	....	241.9	103,837.67	13,019.16	1,815.00	1,390.68	120,062.51
....	.....	....	....	1,015.2	122,752.66	25,000.00	2,464.50	1,775.67	151,992.83
....	.....	....	....	818.9	99,022.86	22,508.40	1,873.10	1,295.00	124,699.36
50.9	**102.8**	**61.0**	**96.5**	**3,762.0**	**$598,937.28**	**$125,363.82**	**$11,335.10**	**$10,470.92**	**$746,107.12**

Table 205

Detail by Steamers of Relief Deliveries in Co-operation with th

Arrival No.	Steamer	Port of Sailing	Date of Sailing or Arrival	Port of Arrival	Flour	Rice	Pork Products
			1920				
1	Chincha	New York	Feb. 21	Batoum	......	......	.....
2	Lake Freeborn	New York	Apr. 3	Poti	......	......	.....
3	Jomar	Philadelphia	Apr. 13	Poti	2,031.4	......	.....
4	Polar Bear	New York	Oct. 19	Batoum	......	......	.....
5	Wheeling Mold	New York	Nov. 13	Batoum	......	239.8	.....
6	Gul Djemal	New York	Nov. 20	Batoum	444.0	264.2	.....
7	Mopang	New York	Nov. 22	Derindje	578.1	149.4	.....
			1922				
8	Clontarf, III	New York	Sept. 30	Constantinople	209.0	385.0	240.0
9	Orient	New York	Oct. 29	Odessa	1,243.0	......	.....
	Total Deliveries	....	....	....	**4,505.5**	**1,038.4**	**240.0**

* Groceries.

ear East Relief

.R.A.-European Children's Fund—Reconstruction Period, 1919–1924

ntents of Cargoes in Net Metric Tons of 1,000 Kilograms or 2,204.6 Pounds								F.O.B. Value	Freight, Insurance, Miscellaneous Charges	Total Value
Milk	Cocoa	Sugar	Misc. Food	Soap	Medical and Hospital Supplies	Clothing and Misc.	Total Tons			
.....	.....	.....	1.9*	.....	2.0	73.1	77.0	$ 57,203.00	$ 3,080.00	$ 60,283.00
.....	.....	.....	...	.....	...	338.9	338.9	24,033.00	13,566.00	37,599.00
.....	.....	.....	...	.....	...	.....	2,031.4	245,625.99	81,256.00	326,881.99
.....	.....	.....	...	.....	...	134.1	134.1	384,792.00	5,364.00	390,156.00
.....	.....	76.2	...	300.8	...	.....	616.8	75,068.00	24,672.00	99,740.00
.....	.....	59.7	...	.....	...	.....	767.9	82,081.00	30,716.00	112,797.00
.....	.....	42.7	...	.....	...	.....	770.2	84,032.00	30,808.00	114,840.00
178.0	108.0	305.0	...	.....	...	.....	1,425.0	160,255.83	17,254.59	177,510.42
.....	.....	.....	...	.....	...	.....	1,243.0	80,393.22	11,129.27	91,522.49
178.0	**108.0**	**483.6**	**1.9**	**300.8**	**2.0**	**546.1**	**7,404.3**	**$1,193,484.04**	**$ 217,845.86**	**$1,411,329.90**

Table 206

Operation	Table No.	Flour	Grain	Rice	Beans, Peas	Corn Grits
						ARMISTICE
A.R.A.—Cash Settlement	207	2,837.0	....	2,029.0	1,028.6	....
A.R.A.—Freight on Charity Shipments	143	....	....	....	....	....
A.R.A.—Freight and Ins. on U.S. Liq. Com. Sales to J.D.C.	208n	....	....	....	....	....
Joint Distribution Committee	208	42.0	....	....	....	....
Total American Relief	....	**2,879.0**	....	**2,029.0**	**1,028.6**	....
JOINT ALLIED FINANCE						
France	129	94,889.9	55,094.6	....	....	....
Italy	128	13,301.0	71,855.0	....	....	....
United Kingdom	130	72,172.5	24,309.8	....	....	....
Total Deliveries against Joint Allied Finance	128	**180,363.4**	**151,259.4**	....	....	....
COUNTRIES OTHER THAN UNITED STATES AND JOINT ALLIED FINANCE						
United Kingdom	133	....	1,000.0	....	....	....
United Kingdom—Finance on Freight	133	....	....	....	....	....
France—Finance on Freight	134	....	....	....	....	....
Italy—Finance on Freight	135	....	....	....	....	....
Italy	135	12,808.0	16,761.0	9,852.0	4,209.0	....
Czecho-Slovakia	209	....	....	....	....	....
Denmark	209	....	....	....	....	....
Germany	209	....	....	....	....	....
Hungary	209	1,287.0	2,473.0	....	....	....
Jugoslavia	209	205.0	12,433.0	....	1,402.0	....
Netherlands	209	....	....	....	....	....
Norway	209	....	....	....	....	....
Poland	209	....	....	....	....	....
Switzerland	209	7,555.0	538.0	1,241.0	....	....
Total from Countries other than U.S. and Joint Allied Finance	....	**21,855.0**	**33,205.0**	**11,093.0**	**5,611.0**	....
Total for Armistice Period	108	**205,097.4**	**184,464.4**	**13,122.0**	**6,639.6**	....
						RECONSTRUCTION
A.R.A.—President's National Security and Defense Fund	211	1,503.7	....	1,079.5	815.4	....
A.R.A.—Congressional Appropriation, $100,000,000 Fund	212	....	....	....	....	....
A.R.A.-European Children's Fund	213–18	5,030.7	....	3,743.1	3,417.8	970.
Austrian Government Donations	215	10,178.0	....	....	....	....
Austrian Provincial Government Donations	216	211.8	....	....	....	....
Total Children's Relief	218	**16,924.2**	....	**4,822.6**	**4,233.2**	**970.**
U.S. Grain Corporation (Act of Congress, March 30, 1920)	217	200,824.8	....	....	....	....
United Kingdom—Freight, Insurance, Misc. Charges	217n	....	....	....	....	....
A.R.A. Warehouses—Food Drafts and Bulk Sales	218	5,120.6	....	1,243.0	664.8	521.
Sale of Clothing Surplus	221	....	....	....	....	....
Commonwealth Fund—Intelligentsia Clothing Deliveries	221	....	....	....	....	....
Exchange of Commodities	218c	800.0	....	....	....	....
Total Other Than Children's Relief	....	**206,745.4**	....	**1,243.0**	**664.8**	**521.**
Total for Reconstruction Period	....	**223,669.6**	....	**6,065.6**	**4,898.0**	**1,491.**
Grand Total Relief Deliveries	....	**428,767.0**	**184,464.4**	**19,187.6**	**11,537.6**	**1,491.**

* See Arrival 843.0 M.T. Sugar, Beans, Pork Products, Table No. 213.

ummary of Relief Deliveries

Commodities in Net Metric Tons of 1,000 Kilograms or 2,204.6 Pounds

Pork Products	Milk	Cocoa	Sugar	Misc. Food	Forage	Soap	Medical and Hospital Supplies	Clothing and Misc.	Total Tons	Total Value
ERIOD										
2,223.3	204.6	2.8	......	......	......	....	......	......	8,325.3	$ 3,278,068.35
......	......	.....	......	......	......	....	......	......	....	178.47
......	......	.....	......	......	......	....	......	......	....	15,224.11
582.0	45.2	.....	......	229.4	......	....	......	2.7	901.3	363,760.00
2,805.3	**249.8**	**2.8**	......	**229.4**	......	....	......	**2.7**	**9,226.6**	**$ 3,657,230.93**
......	......	.....	......	......	......	....	......	......	149,984.5	$ 16,000,000.00
1,374.0	845.0	.....	......	......	......	....	......	......	97,375.0	16,000,000.00
......	1,998.0	.....	......	......	......	....	......	......	98,480.3	16,000,000.00
1,374.0	**2,843.0**	.....	......	......	......	....	......	......	**345,839.8**	**$ 48,000,000.00**
500.0	......	.....	......	10,000.0	......	....	......	6,500.0	18,000.0	$ 1,916,640.00
......	......	.....	......	......	......	....	......	......	....	4,760,000.00
......	......	.....	......	......	......	....	......	......	....	4,500,000.00
......	......	.....	......	......	......	....	......	......	....	2,021,250.00
8,168.0	728.0	.....	......	1,535.0	......	....	......	......	64,061.0	18,856,872.00
234.0	......	.....	39,639.0	......	......	....	......	23,025.0	62,898.0	9,914,858.00
19.0	......	.....	......	......	......	....	......	......	19.0	10,108.00
......	......	.....	......	330.0	......	....	......	......	330.0	13,200.00
10.0	......	.....	......	5,108.0	......	....	......	......	8,878.0	805,063.00
332.0	......	.....	......	19,514.0	......	....	......	......	33,886.0	2,464,561.00
......	......	.....	......	2,810.0	......	....	......	......	2,810.0	112,400.00
......	......	.....	......	8.3	......	....	......	......	8.3	4,980.00
105.0	......	.....	......	......	......	....	......	3,921.0	4,026.0	204,896.00
163.0	473.0	.....	......	1,753.0	......	....	......	......	11,723.0	1,529,537.00
9,531.0	**1,201.0**	.....	**39,639.0**	**41,058.3**	......	....	......	**33,446.0**	**206,639.3**	**$ 47,114,365.00**
3,710.3	**4,293.8**	**2.8**	**39,639.0**	**41,287.7**	......	....	......	**33,448.7**	**561,705.7**	**$ 98,771,595.93**
ERIOD										
323.6	2,805.0	367.3	517.4	14.0	......	110.2	......	......	7,536.1	$ 2,847,892.23
......	553.7	76.6	116.0	......	......	....	......	......	746.3	319,471.90
1,806.6	6,232.9	640.7	2,773.7	418.9	......	98.7	......	830.0	25,963.4	6,695,693.43
......	......	.....	638.0	......	......	....	......	......	10,816.0	1,323,948.55
......	......	.....	......	......	......	....	......	1,675.5	1,887.3	40,707.46
2,130.2	**9,591.6**	**1,084.6**	**4,045.1**	**432.9**	......	**208.9**	......	**2,505.5**	**46,949.1**	**$ 11,227,713.57**
......	......	.....	......	......	......	....	......	......	200,824.8	$ 24,055,708.92
......	......	.....	......	......	......	....	......	......	....	8,032,991.88
1,122.6	1,789.3	195.0	851.0	218.2	......	....	......	69.7	11,795.8	3,330,635.48
......	......	.....	......	......	......	....	......	.1	.1	101.26
......	......	.....	......	......	......	....	......	31.8	31.8	62,475.26
......	38.2	54.6	......	......	......	....	......	......	892.8	...........*
1,122.6	**1,827.5**	**249.6**	**851.0**	**218.2**	......	....	......	**101.6**	**213,545.3**	**$ 35,481,912.80**
3,252.8	**11,419.1**	**1,334.2**	**4,896.1**	**651.1**	......	**208.9**	......	**2,607.1**	**260,494.4**	**$ 46,709,626.37**
6,963.1	**15,712.9**	**1,337.0**	**44,535.1**	**41,938.8**	......	**208.9**	......	**36,055.8**	**822,200.1**	**$145,481,222.30**

AUSTRIA—American Relief Administration

Table 207

Detail by Steamers or Source, of Commodities Sold for Cash—Armistice Period, 1919

Arrival No.*	Steamer or Source†	Port of Origin	Date of Arrival	Port of Arrival	Contents of Cargoes in Net Metric Tons of 1,000 Kilograms or 2,204.6 Pounds: Wheat Flour	Beans, Peas	Rice	Pork Products	Lard Substitute	Milk	Cocoa	Total Tons	Total Value
			1919										
319	Q.M. 33, 35	(U.S.A.)	......	Trieste	......	......	......	198.2	78.8	150.0	...	427.0	$ 272,541.
319	Q.M. 39	(U.S.A.)	......	Trieste	......	......	......	755.2	.....	.....	...	755.2	595,434.
319	Q.M. 43	(U.S.A.)	......	Trieste	......	......	......	700.3	.....	.....	...	700.3	532,581.
319	Q.M. 49	(U.S.A.)	......	Trieste	......	......	......	4.5	.....	.....	...	4.5	3,838.
319	Q.M. 55, 60	(U.S.A.)	......	Trieste	......	......	......	104.1	.....	.....	...	104.1	76,386.
319	Q.M. 20	(U.S.A.)	......	Trieste	......	......	......	......	.....	19.2	...	19.2	9,240.
319	Q.M. 9	(U.S.A.)	......	Trieste	1,270.9	......	......	......	.....	.....	...	1,270.9	280,191.
319	Q.M. 52	(U.S.A.)	......	Trieste	......	......	......	......	379.9	.....	...	379.9	269,761.
319	Q.M. 58	(U.S.A.)	......	Trieste	5.7	......	......	.8	1.5	11.5	...	19.5	7,835.
114	West Compo.	Baltimore	Apr. 9	Trieste	118.4	......	......	......	.....	.....	...	118.4	25,454.
148	Neuse	New York	Apr. 23	Trieste	......	......	......	......	.....	.....	2.8	2.8	1,223.
147	Lake Farge	New York	Apr. 23	Trieste	......	......	2,029.0	......	.....	4.3	...	2,033.3	580,124.
163	Tabor	New York	May 3	Trieste	......	1,028.6	......	......	.....	.....	...	1,028.6	303,437.
259	Agwistar	New York	June 6	Trieste	123.2	......	......	......	.....	19.6	...	142.8	36,480.
270	West Togus	Norfolk	June 11	Trieste	1,318.8	......	......	......	.....	.....	...	1,318.8	283,537.
	Total Sales (to Table 120)	....	....	....	**2,837.0**	**1,028.6**	**2,029.0**	**1,763.1**	**460.2**	**204.6**	**2.8**	**8,325.3**	**$3,278,068.**

* Arrival numbers from Table 111.

† Q.M. refers to quartermaster invoice number on commodities p[urchased] and transported by U.S. Army.

AUSTRIA—

Table 209

Detail of Monthly Deliveries

Month	Commodities in Net Met[ric Tons]: Wheat Flour	Grain	Rice	Beans	Pork Products	Lard and Lard Substitutes
						DELIVERIES
1919						
January	......	....	......	......	.....	.....
February	......	....	......	......	.....	.....
March	......	....	......	......	.....	.....
April	......	....	......	......	.....	.....
May	......	....	......	......	34.0	200.0
June	......	....	......	......	.....	.....
July	......	....	......	......	.....	.....
Total Deliveries	......	....	......	......	**34.0**	**200.0**
						DELIVERIES
May	......	....	......	......	**19.0**	.....
						DELIVERIES
May	......	....	......	......	.....	.....
						DELIVERIES
January	282.0	1,389.0	......	......	.....	10.0
February	1,005.0	203.0	......	......	.....	.....
March	......	....	......	......	.....	.....
April	......	881.0	......	......	.....	.....
May	......	....	......	......	.....	.....
June	......	....	......	......	.....	.....
Total Deliveries	**1,287.0**	**2,473.0**	......	......	.....	**10.0**

AUSTRIA—Joint Distribution Committee

Detail by Steamers of Relief Deliveries in Co-operation with A.R.A.

Table 208

Armistice Period, 1919

Steamer	Date of Arrival	Port of Arrival	Contents of Cargoes in Net Metric Tons of 1,000 Kilograms or 2,204.6 Pounds							Total Value
			Cereal Flour	Pork Products	Vegetable Oil	Milk	Misc. Foods	Autos	Total Tons	
	1919									
ake Clear, V.......	July 2	Hamburg	42.0	.....	....	45.2	229.4	...	316.6	$ 70,310.00*
peras	July 25	Hamburg	....	.....	....	....	.....	2.7	2.7	5,000.00*
lybius	Sept. ..	....	....	518.0	64.0	....	.....	...	582.0	288,450.00
Total	....	....	**42.0**	**518.0**	**64.0**	**45.2**	**229.4**	**2.7**	**901.3**	**$363,760.00**

* In addition to these amounts, freight and insurance to the total of ,224.11 was paid by A.R.A. and billed to J.D.C. (cf. page 154).

ountries Other than United States and Major Allies

ountries of Origin—Armistice Period, 1919

ns of 1,000 Kilograms or 2,204.6 Pounds						Total Value
Milk	Sugar	Miscellaneous Food	Live Animals	Miscellaneous Non-Foods	Total Tons	
ZECHO-SLOVAKIA						
.....	6,943.0	....	......	4,315.0	11,258.0	$1,801,280.00
.....	1,900.0	....	......	403.0	2,303.0	368,480.00
.....	3,941.0	....	......	2,926.0	6,867.0	1,098,720.00
.....	4,708.0	....	......	4,309.0	9,017.0	1,381,620.00
.....	6,446.0	....	......	3,774.0	10,454.0	1,634,318.00
.....	3,955.0	....	......	1,931.0	5,886.0	892,360.00
.....	11,746.0	....	......	5,367.0	17,113.0	2,738,080.00
.....	**39,639.0**	....	......	**23,025.0**	**62,898.0**	**$9,914,858.00**
ENMARK						
.....	....	....	......	....	**19.0**	**$ 10,108.00**
ERMANY						
.....	....	**330.0**	......	....	**330.0**	**$ 13,200.00**
UNGARY						
.....	....	....	903.0	....	2,584.0	$ 305,526.00
.....	....	1,800.0	878.0	....	3,886.0	338,171.00
.....	....	635.0	60.0	....	695.0	34,218.00
.....	....	586.0	31.0	....	1,498.0	115,368.00
.....	....	160.0	15.0	....	175.0	10,180.00
.....	....	40.0	......	....	40.0	1,600.00
.....	....	**3,221.0**	**1,887.0**	....	**8,878.0**	**$ 805,063.00**

[*Continued on next page*]

Table 209—*Continued*

Detail of Monthly Deliveries

Month	Commodities in Net Metri					
	Wheat Flour	Grain	Rice	Beans	Pork Products	Lard and Lard Substitutes
						DELIVERIES BY
1919						
March	205.0	2,714.0	......	51.0	.....	.....
April	......	2,650.0	......	......	.....	.....
May	......	4,112.0	......	......	38.0	25.0
June	......	2,010.0	......	39.0	113.0	31.0
July	......	947.0	......	1,312.0	36.0	89.0
Total Deliveries	**205.0**	**12,433.0**	......	**1,402.0**	**187.0**	**145.0**
						DELIVERIES BY
May	......	....	......	......	.....	.....
						DELIVERIES BY
June	......	....	......	......	.....	.....
						DELIVERIES BY
January	......	....	......	......	.....	21.0
February	......	....	......	......	.....	.....
March	......	....	......	......	.....	.....
April	......	....	......	......	.....	20.0
May	......	....	......	......	.....	32.0
June	......	....	......	......	.....	22.0
July	......	....	......	......	.....	10.0
Total Deliveries	......	....	......	......	.....	**105.0**
						DELIVERIES BY
January	2,128.0	....	421.0	......	.....	97.0
February	1,609.0	488.0	248.0	......	.....	66.0
March	2,868.0	....	324.0	......	.....	.....
April	950.0	50.0	248.0	......	.....	.....
May	......	....	......	......	.....	.....
June	......	....	......	......	.....	.....
Total Deliveries	**7,555.0**	**538.0**	**1,241.0**	......	.....	**163.0**

* Includes 356 cattle and 530 horses.

† Includes 683 cattle, 935 horses, and 236 pigs.

AUSTRIA—

Table 210†

Summary of Arrivals by Operations—

Operation	Table No.	Flour	Rice	Beans, Peas	Corn Grits
A.R.A.—President's National Security, and Defense Fund	211	1,503.7	1,079.5	815.4	......
A.R.A.—Congressional Appropriation	212	....	......	......	......
A.R.A.-European Children's Fund (Food)	213	10,951.3	4,986.1	4,082.6	1,491.9
A.R.A.-European Children's Fund (Clothing)	214	....	......	......	......
Austrian Government Donations	215	10,178.0	......	......	......
Austrian Provincial Government Donations	216	211.8	......	......	......
U.S. Grain Corporation (Act of Congress, March 30, 1920)	217	200,824.8	......	......	......
United Kingdom—Finance on Freight, etc	217n	....	......	......	......
Total Arrivals, Reconstruction Period	......	**223,669.6**	**6,065.6**	**4,898.0**	**1,491.9**

† Cf. Tables 206, 218. The value quoted in this table is c.i.f. European ports, whereas Table 206 shows value of commodities delivered in Austria.

* The total 38,683.9 metric tons was delivered as follows: E.C.F., f children's relief, 25,963.4; A.R.A.W., food drafts and bulk sales, 11,795. clothing other than children's relief, 31.9; exchanged commodities, 892.

Countries Other than United States and Major Allies

y Countries of Origin

ons of 1,000 Kilograms or 2,204.6 Pounds						
Milk	Sugar	Miscellaneous Food	Live Animals	Miscellaneous Non-Foods	Total Tons	Total Value
UGOSLAVIA						
.....	....	....	......	....	2,970.0	$ 312,716.00
.....	....	2,341.0	......	....	4,991.0	363,940.00
.....	....	4,832.0	......	....	9,007.0	593,100.00
.....	....	9,220.0	466.0*	....	11,879.0	633,283.00
.....	....	1,797.0	858.0†	....	5,039.0	561,522.00
.....	....	**18,190.0**	**1,324.0**	....	**33,886.0**	**$2,464,561.00**
ETHERLANDS						
.....	....	**2,810.0**	......	....	**2,810.0**	**$ 112,400.00**
ORWAY						
.....	....	**8.3**	......	....	**8.3**	**$ 4,980.00**
OLAND						
.....	....	....	......	....	21.0	$ 11,172.00
.....	....	....	......	....	....	....
.....	....	....	......	1,025.0	1,025.0	41,000.00
.....	....	....	......	1,222.0	1,242.0	59,528.00
.....	....	....	......	840.0	872.0	50,624.00
.....	....	....	......	778.0	800.0	42,824.00
.....	....	....	56.0	....	66.0	10,920.00
.....	....	....	**56.0**	**3,865.0**	**4,026.0**	**$ 204,896.00**
WITZERLAND						
341.0	....	20.0	......	....	3,007.0	$ 503,186.00
132.0	....	....	......	....	2,543.0	375,097.00
.....	....	....	......	....	3,192.0	423,372.00
.....	....	329.0	......	....	1,577.0	171,722.00
.....	....	355.0	......	....	355.0	14,200.00
.....	....	1,049.0	......	....	1,049.0	41,960.00
473.0	....	**1,753.0**	......	....	**11,723.0**	**$1,529,537.00**

ummary of Arrivals

econstruction Period, 1919–1924

Commodities in Net Metric Tons of 1,000 Kilograms or 2,204.6 Pounds									
Pork Products	Milk	Cocoa	Sugar	Miscellaneous Food	Soap	Clothing and Miscellaneous	Coal	Total Tons	Total Value
323.6	2,805.0	367.3	517.4	14.0	110.2	.....	......	7,536.1	$ 2,847,892.23
......	553.7	76.6	116.0	.....	.....	.....	......	746.3	319,471.90
2,929.2	8,060.4	890.3	3,624.7	637.1	98.7	69.7	......	37,822.0*	7,650,877.75
......	....	......	......	.....	.....	861.9	......	861.9*	1,504,523.05
......	....	......	638.0	.....	.....	.....	......	10,816.0	1,323,948.55
......	....	......	......	.....	.....	.....	1,675.5	1,887.3	40,707.46
......	....	......	......	.....	.....	.....	......	200,824.8	24,055,708.92
......	....	......	......	.....	.....	.....	......	....	8,032,991.88
3,252.8	**11,419.1**	**1,334.2**	**4,896.1**	**651.1**	**208.9**	**931.6**	**1,675.5**	**260,494.4**	**$45,776,121.74**

Table 211

Detail by Steamers of Children's Relief Deliveries Paid for from th

Steamer or Source	Port of Sailing	Date of Arrival	Port of Arrival	Wheat Flour	Rice
		1919			
Q.M. Inv. 51 (ex Canoga)	New York	Mar. 3	Trieste	......	......
Q.M. Inv. 52 (ex Canoga)	New York	Mar. 3	Trieste	......	......
West Compo	Norfolk	Apr. 9	Trieste	4.8	......
Lake Farge	New York	Apr. 23	Trieste	......	3.5
Neuse	New York	Apr. 23	Trieste	426.0	12.5
Tabor	New York	May 3	Trieste	......	......
West Lashaway, II	New York	May 24	Trieste	......	......
Lake St. Regis, IV	Rotterdam	June 5	Hamburg	......	......
Agwistar	New York	June 6	Trieste	605.6	......
Adelheid	New York	June 15	Hamburg	......	......
Lake Clear, V	Bordeaux	July 2	Hamburg	......	701.0
Augusta Foherczegno	New York	July 29	Trieste	......	......
Szent Istvan	New York	Aug. 8	Trieste	......	......
Marianne	New York	Aug. 10	Trieste	......	......
Frederica	New York	Aug. 15	Trieste	......	279.7
Sonnenfels	New York	Aug. 25	Trieste	......	......
Brisgravia	New York	Aug. 27	Trieste	534.2	82.8
Dubac	New York	Aug. 27	Trieste	31.1	......
River Elbe handling charges	......	......	......	......	......
Total Deliveries	......	......	......	**1,601.7**	**1,079.5**
Deduct transfer to Hungary	......	......	......	98.0	......
Net Deliveries to Austria	......	......	......	**1,503.7**	**1,079.5**

† Cf. Tables 116 A and 116 B.

* Codliver oil.

AUSTRIA—American Relief Administration

Detail by Steamers of Children's Relief Deliveries, Paid for from Congressional Appropriation for Relief—Armistice Period, 1919

Table 212

Steamer	Transshipped on*	Port of Sailing	Date of Arrival	Port of Arrival	Contents of Cargoes in Net Metric Tons of 1,000 Kilograms or 2,204.6 Pounds				Total Value
					Milk	Cocoa	Sugar	Total Tons	
			1919						
Remschied	Allemania	New York	Aug. 21	Rotterdam	217.8	40.6	.....	258.4	$107,064.
Remschied	Anna Jacobus	New York	Aug. 21	Rotterdam	.....	....	116.0	116.0	26,096.
Remschied	Rail shipment	New York	Aug. 21	Rotterdam	335.9	....	.....	335.9	163,451.
Stock†		(U.S.A.)		(Vienna)	.....	36.0	.....	36.0	22,860.
Total Arrivals	......	......	......	......	**553.7**	**76.6**	**116.0**	**746.3**	**$319,471.**

* All transshipments from Rotterdam to Mannheim, thence via rail to Vienna in February, 1920.

† Transferred from Jugoslavia to Austria.

ierican Relief Administration

sident's National Security and Defense Fund,†—Armistice Period, 1919

Contents of Cargoes in Net Metric Tons of 1,000 Kilograms or 2,204.6 Pounds									
eans, Peas	Pork Products	Lard	Milk	Cocoa	Sugar	Miscellaneous Food	Soap	Total Tons	Total Value
....	7.1	6.1	......	.....	.....	....	.....	13.2	$ 10,132.06
....	24.4	13.2	......	.....	.....	....	.....	37.6	27,547.53
....	.....	....	......	.....	.....	....	.....	4.8	1,060.41
....	.....	....	......	31.8	.....	....	.....	35.3	14,673.43
....	22.8	....	277.7	59.5	.....	....	.....	798.5	293,842.97
44.3	.....	....	......	.....	.....	....	.....	44.3	13,082.07
....	.....	....	......	99.0	.....	....	.....	99.0	42,554.52
34.0	.....	....	......	.....	.....	14.0*	.....	248.0	74,250.78
....	.....	....	674.8	.....	.....	....	.....	1,280.4	469,953.30
....	.....	....	......	80.0	.....	....	.....	80.0	31,600.00
....	250.0	....	......	.....	.....	....	.....	951.0	384,012.93
....	.....	....	......	124.0	.....	....	.....	124.0	78,713.33
....	.....	....	570.4	.....	.....	....	.....	570.4	293,437.00
....	.....	....	387.2	.....	.....	....	.....	387.2	194,637.25
59.4	.....	....	239.1	.....	.....	....	82.4	1,060.6	330,854.35
....	.....	....	589.2	.....	241.5	....	27.7	858.4	371,877.69
77.7	.....	....	161.6	.....	305.9	....	37.1	1,199.3	308,957.91
....	.....	....	......	.....	.....	....	.....	31.1	6,223.40
....	.....	....	......	.....	.....	....	.....	......	1,806.30
15.4	**304.3**	**19.3**	**2,900.0**	**394.3**	**547.4**	**14.0**	**147.2**	**7,823.1**	**$2,949,217.23**
....	.....	....	95.0	27.0	30.0	....	37.0	287.0	101,325.00
15.4	**304.3**	**19.3**	**2,805.0**	**367.3**	**517.4**	**14.0**	**110.2**	**7,536.1**	**$2,847,892.23**

AUSTRIA-

Table 213

Detail by Steamers of Arrivals of Reli

Steamer or Source	Port of Sailing	Date of Arrival	Port of Arrival	Flour	Rice	Beans, Peas
		1919				
C.R.B., Lother Bohlen	United States	Aug. ..	Antwerp	.....	.....	.....
Nieuw Amsterdam†	New York	Dec. 9	Rotterdam	.....	.....	.....
Noordam‡	New York	Dec. 9	Rotterdam	.....	.....	.....
Rotterdam	New York	Dec. 13	Rotterdam	.....	.....	.....
Comité National, Asam 19	Antwerp	Dec. 20	Mannheim	200.0	.....	.....
Comité National, Asam 12	Antwerp	Dec. 27	Mannheim	192.0	.....	.....
Morlais	(United Kingdom)	Dec. 29	Hamburg	.....	200.1	.....
		1920				
Koningen den Netherlanden	New York	Jan. 2	Rotterdam	.....	.....	369.4
Cripple Creek	New York	Jan. 4	Hamburg	2,500.3	.....	.....
Suffolk	New York	Jan. 9	Rotterdam	2,900.6	.....	998.9
Amsteldijk§	New Orleans	Jan. 13	Rotterdam	.....	400.7	.....
Inverawe	Liverpool	Jan. 23	Hamburg	.....	.....	.....
Comité National, rail	Antwerp	Jan. 27	Mannheim	.....	.....	.....
Comité National, Asam 14	Antwerp	Jan. 29	Mannheim	.....	.....	200.0
Comité National, Risquons Tout	Antwerp	Jan. 31	Hamburg	200.1	.....	.....
Kermoor, I	New York	Feb. 2	Hamburg	.....	.....	.....
Zealand	Liverpool	Feb. 10	Hamburg	.....	.....	.....
Comité National, Steywell 9	Antwerp	Feb. 13	Mannheim	.....	.....	97.6
Bridges & Co. Purchase	Antwerp	Feb. 18	Rotterdam	.....	.....	.....
Manchuria, I	New York	Feb. 26	Hamburg	.....	.....	.....
Keresan, II	New York	Feb. 27	Hamburg	.....	.....	78.9
Comité National, Elizabeth	Antwerp	Feb. 29	Mannheim	515.5	.....	104.1
Clauseus	San Francisco	Mar. 2	Hamburg	.....	.....	971.3
Mar Caspio, I	New York	Mar. 7	Hamburg	.....	.....	.....
Severn	Brazil	Mar. 7	Hamburg	.....	124.6	.....
Mongolia, I	New York	Mar. 10	Hamburg	.....	.....	.....
Bridges Stock Purchase	Hamburg	Mar. 11	Hamburg	.....	.....	.....
Kerowlee	New York	Mar. 29	Hamburg	.....	.....	.....
Englebert Purchase	Antwerp	Mar. 31	Rotterdam	.....	301.3	.....
Kermanshaw	New York	Apr. 3	Hamburg	.....	.....	.....
Manchuria, II	New York	Apr. 8	Hamburg	.....	.....	.....
Forkel & Werner	Hamburg	Apr. 12	Hamburg	.....	.....	.....
Pickard & Co. Purchase, rail	Antwerp	Apr. 21	Rotterdam	.....	.....	.....
Jessica	(United Kingdom)	Apr. 26	Hamburg	.....	91.4	.....
Comité National, St. Antoine	Antwerp	May 11	Hamburg	408.0	.....	.....
Frazier & Co. Purchase, rail	Rotterdam	May 20	Rotterdam	.....	300.0	.....
Manchuria, III	New York	May 20	Hamburg	.....	.....	.....
Carib, III	New York	May 23	Hamburg	.....	.....	.....
Frazier & Co., rail	Rotterdam	May 24	Rotterdam	.....	90.0	.....
Keresan, III	Philadelphia	May 27	Hamburg	.....	.....	.....
Danzig Stock, Susanne	Danzig	May ..	Hamburg	.....	.....	.....
Mongolia, III	New York	June 3	Hamburg	.....	.....	.....
West Isleta	Boston	June 18	Hamburg	.....	.....	.....
Gerrat	London	June 28	Hamburg	.....	100.1	.....
Mar Blanco, I	New York	July 2	Hamburg	.....	.....	.....
Monticello, I	New York	July 9	Hamburg	.....	.....	.....
Mar Caspio, II	New York	July 16	Hamburg	.....	.....	.....
Charlot	Philadelphia	July 21	Hamburg	.....	.....	.....
Mar Mediterraneo, II	New York	July 22	Hamburg	.....	.....	.....
Verbania	New York	July 26	Hamburg	.....	.....	.....
Belgic	New York	July 27	Hamburg	.....	.....	.....
Frazier & Co., Alster	Rotterdam	July 27	Hamburg	.....	.....	273.8
Bellerose	Philadelphia	Aug. 2	Hamburg	.....	.....	.....
Rosenberg Purchase	Hamburg	Aug. 9	Hamburg	.....	.....	504.9
West Ekonk	Boston	Aug. 15	Hamburg	.....	.....	.....
Herefordshire	Rangoon	Aug. 18	Hamburg	.....	1,266.5	.....
Kermit, II	New York	Aug. 21	Hamburg	.....	.....	.....
Mette Jensen, I	New York	Aug. 22	Hamburg	.....	.....	.....

* These arrivals include relief supplies for child feeding and American Relief Administration Warehouses, draft, and bulk sale business.

† Shipped from Rotterdam to Mannheim via lighter Henri.
‡ Shipped from Rotterdam to Mannheim via lighter Bogaerts.

A.R.A.-European Children's Fund

upplies*—Reconstruction Period, 1919–1924

Corn Grits	Pork Products	Milk	Cocoa	Sugar	Miscellaneous Food	Soap	Other Misc. Sacks, Containers, Etc.	Total Tons	Total Value
Contents of Cargoes in Net Metric Tons of 1,000 Kilograms or 2,204.6 Pounds									
.....	....	....	....	....	4.7	....	....	4.7	$ 2,853.22
.....	....	29.1	....	....	....	....	....	29.1	13,528.48
.....	....	238.1	....	....	....	....	....	238.1	109,349.25
.....	....	20.4	....	....	....	....	....	20.4	9,404.81
.....	68.1	....	....	....	....	....	....	268.1	45,608.03
.....	....	....	....	....	....	....	....	192.0	17,764.00
.....	....	....	....	....	....	....	....	200.1	19,503.81
.....	....	....	41.0	....	....	....	....	410.4	87,258.16
.....	....	....	....	....	....	....	.7	2,501.0	359,445.56
.....	....	....	....	....	....	....	....	3,899.5	601,001.63
.....	....	....	....	....	....	....	....	400.7	118,975.63
.....	....	....	....	....	50.3	....	....	50.3	29,272.97
.....	100.3	....	....	....	....	....	....	100.3	39,938.49
.....	....	....	....	....	....	....	....	200.0	15,704.33
.....	....	....	....	....	....	....	....	200.1	18,511.56
.....	....	....	....	....	....	....	1.2	1.2	3,100.63
.....	....	....	....	....	113.0	....	....	113.0	65,980.43
.....	....	....	32.0	....	....	....	....	129.6	18,703.44
.....	....	302.8	....	....	....	....	....	302.8	145,130.44
.....	174.2	....	....	227.5	....	....	....	401.7	181,708.28
.....	....	183.9	....	....	....	....	1.8	264.6	74,668.17
.....	....	....	40.4	....	....	....	....	660.0	65,972.58
.....	....	....	....	....	....	....	....	971.3	197,699.95
.....	51.4	476.3	50.8	....	....	....	9.9	588.4	212,911.92
.....	....	....	....	....	....	....	....	124.6	33,966.08
.....	70.6	....	....	....	22.8	....	....	93.4	93,805.83
.....	....	595.4	....	....	....	....	....	595.4	293,740.60
.....	137.4	3.7	....	....	....	....	....	141.1	91,912.43
.....	....	....	....	....	....	....	....	301.3	79,728.33
.....	63.0	105.3	....	....	....	....	....	168.3	81,370.07
.....	186.5	....	....	....	....	....	....	186.5	97,532.87
.....	....	232.4	....	....	....	....	....	232.4	82,082.74
.....	....	306.2	....	....	....	....	....	306.2	113,508.89
.....	....	....	....	....	....	....	....	91.4	20,559.29
.....	87.1	....	....	....	....	....	....	495.1	72,418.63
.....	....	....	....	....	....	....	....	300.0	79,592.59
.....	....	....	....	....	29.6	....	....	29.6	5,278.00
.....	18.3	....	....	....	....	....	4.7	23.0	17,223.89
.....	....	....	....	....	....	....	....	90.0	23,478.64
.....	7.6	....	....	....	....	....	....	7.6	6,136.83
.....	63.1	....	....	....	....	....	....	63.1	51,504.00
.....	....	108.4	....	....	....	....	....	108.4	36,474.59
.....	106.7	....	....	....	....	....	....	106.7	86,393.50
.....	....	....	....	....	....	....	....	100.1	20,288.47
.....	....	....	127.0	....	....	....	....	127.0	31,683.15
.....	....	....	15.1	....	....	....	....	15.1	3,649.27
.....	70.7	....	....	....	....	....	....	70.7	36,402.91
.....	....	9.9	....	....	....	....	....	9.9	5,476.89
.....	168.6	56.8	....	....	....	....	....	225.4	116,180.65
.....	....	38.7	....	....	....	....	....	38.7	21,029.21
.....	58.8	....	....	....	....	....	....	58.8	30,686.50
.....	....	....	....	....	....	....	....	273.8	27,743.69
.....	179.6	....	....	....	....	....	....	179.6	145,223.84
.....	....	....	....	....	....	....	....	504.9	40,946.24
.....	....	47.4	....	....	....	....	....	47.4	14,647.73
.....	....	....	....	....	....	....	....	1,266.5	166,316.78
.....	....	448.1	....	....	....	....	....	448.1	246,300.50
.....	....	246.3	....	....	8.4	....	....	254.7	129,758.66

§ Shipped from Rotterdam to Hamburg via Fredrick Karl.

[*Continued on next page*]

Table 213—*Continued*

Detail by Steamers c

Steamer or Source	Port of Sailing	Date of Arrival	Port of Arrival	Flour	Rice	Beans, Peas
		1920				
Mar Blanco, II	New York	Aug. 24	Hamburg	.....	.....	.....
Mongolia, IV	New York	Aug. 26	Hamburg	.....	.....	.....
Monticello, II	New York	Aug. 28	Hamburg	.....	.....	.....
Mar Caribe, I	New York	Sept. 4	Hamburg	.....	.....	.....
Porta†	Hamburg	Sept. 6	Hamburg	200.0	.....	.....
Jacques Cartier	New York	Sept. 7	Hamburg	.....	.....	.....
Sacandaga	New Orleans	Sept. 9	Hamburg	.....	.....	.....
Mar de Irlanda	Baltimore	Sept. 12	Hamburg	173.8	.....	.....
Mar Cantabrico	New York	Sept. 22	Hamburg	.....	.....	.....
Vittorio Emmanuelle, III	New York	Oct. 1	Hamburg	.....	.....	.....
Kerlew, III	New York	Oct. 6	Hamburg	.....	.....	.....
Schoharie, I	New York	Oct. 13	Hamburg	.....	.....	.....
Mette Jensen, II	New York	Oct. 20	Hamburg	.....	.....	.....
Satartia	New York	Oct. 22	Hamburg	.....	.....	.....
Beursplein	New York	Nov. 1	Hamburg	.....	.....	.....
American, I	New York	Nov. 15	Hamburg	.....	.....	.....
Czecho-Slovakia, local purchase	(Prague)	Nov. 21	(Vienna)	.....	.....	.....
Czecho-Slovakia, local purchase	(Prague)	Nov. 30	(Vienna)	.....	.....	.....
Iowan, II	New York	Dec. 21	Hamburg	.....	.....	.....
Mar del Norte	New York	Dec. 22	Hamburg	.....	.....	.....
Newburgh	New Orleans	Dec. 24	Hamburg	.....	200.8	.....
		1921				
Juno, II	(United Kingdom)	Jan. 3	Hamburg	.....	.....	.....
Gerratt, III	(United Kingdom)	Jan. 4	Hamburg	.....	.....	.....
Roath	New Orleans	Jan. 5	Hamburg	.....	369.0	.....
Paz de Epalza	New York	Jan. 9	Hamburg	500.2	.....	.....
Billung	London	Jan. 10	Hamburg	.....	.....	.....
Norwich City	New York	Jan. 11	Hamburg	.....	.....	.....
Sirrus, purch. fr. Francis Kanow	Bergen	Jan. 11	Hamburg	.....	.....	.....
Bradclyde, I	New York	Jan. 15	Hamburg	.....	.....	.....
Clarksburg, I	New York	Jan. 18	Hamburg	.....	.....	.....
Mount Clay, I	New York	Jan. 18	Hamburg	.....	.....	.....
Ipswich, I	New York	Jan. 25	Hamburg	.....	.....	.....
Leeds City, I	New York	Jan. 26	Hamburg	.....	.....	.....
Moerdijk	Portland	Feb. 6	Hamburg	400.0	.....	.....
Bradford City, I	New York	Feb. 7	Hamburg	.....	.....	.....
Haimon	New York	Feb. 25	Hamburg	.....	.....	.....
Homer City, II	New York	Feb. 25	Hamburg	.....	.....	235.0
Sophie Rickmers	New Orleans	Feb. 26	Hamburg	.....	298.3	.....
Bradavon	New York	Mar. 3	Hamburg	.....	.....	.....
Loewenberg Purchases, 1-B, 2-A, 2-D	Hamburg	Mar. 3	Hamburg	.....	.....	.....
Mystic, III	New York	Mar. 14	Hamburg	.....	.....	.....
Czecho-Slovakia, local purchase	(Prague)	Mar. 18	(Vienna)	.....	.....	.....
Kenowis	New Orleans	Mar. 21	Hamburg	.....	541.1	.....
Harry Luckenbach	New York	Mar. 23	Hamburg	.....	.....	.....
Czecho-Slovakia, local purchase	(Prague)	Mar. 25	(Vienna)	.....	.....	.....
Eastern City, II	New York	Mar. 27	Hamburg	.....	.....	.....
Naamhok	Philadelphia	Apr. 6	Hamburg	.....	.....	.....
Leeds City, II	New York	Apr. 12	Hamburg	.....	.....	.....
Minnekahda, III	Boston	Apr. 12	Hamburg	.....	.....	.....
Fairmont	New York	Apr. 13	Hamburg	.....	.....	.....
Osawatomie	Boston	Apr. 17	Hamburg	.....	.....	.....
Eemdijk	Seattle	Apr. 22	Hamburg	.....	.....	.....
Bradford City, II	New York	Apr. 23	Hamburg	.....	.....	.....
Schoharie, II	New Orleans	Apr. 27	Hamburg	.....	130.1	.....
King City	Galveston	Apr. 29	Hamburg	.....	486.6	.....
Cornish City, II	New York	May 14	Hamburg	.....	.....	.....
Vittorio Emmanuelle, IV	New York	May 15	Hamburg	.....	.....	.....
Hawaiian, II	New York	May 17	Hamburg	61.8	.....	.....
Transfer from Cz.-S., rail, P.-V., I.*	(U.S.–Prague)	May 27	(Vienna)	.....	.....	.....
Oregonian, III	New York	May 29	Hamburg	383.9	.....	.....

†Czecho-Slovakia government replacement at Hamburg.

* P.-V., I. is Prague to Vienna shipment No. 1.

A.R.A.-European Children's Fund
Arrivals of Relief Supplies

Corn Grits	Pork Products	Milk	Cocoa	Sugar	Miscellaneous Food	Soap	Other Misc. Sacks, Containers, Etc.	Total Tons	Total Value
Contents of Cargoes in Net Metric Tons of 1,000 Kilograms or 2,204.6 Pounds									
.....	....	117.0	....	....	....	....	....	117.0	$ 53,749.47
.....	16.8	....	....	....	....	....	....	16.8	11,511.12
.....	14.5	104.7	....	....	....	....	2.0	121.2	67,300.75
.....	....	167.6	....	....	....	....	....	167.6	87,321.72
.....	....	....	....	....	....	....	....	200.0	28,608.20
.....	77.6	....	....	....	....	....	....	77.6	52,840.32
.....	....	....	....	....	....	....	4.5	4.5	2,705.35
.....	....	....	....	....	....	....	....	173.8	27,996.34
.....	....	18.7	....	....	....	....	....	18.7	10,481.74
.....	....	122.8	....	....	....	....	....	122.8	75,308.30
.....	....	104.0	....	....	....	....	....	104.0	63,640.43
.....	....	132.1	....	....	....	....	....	132.1	80,796.40
.....	....	47.0	....	....	....	....	....	47.0	28,605.33
.....	....	18.6	....	....	....	....	....	18.6	11,584.30
.....	....	15.5	....	....	....	....	....	15.5	9,477.40
.....	....	....	....	200.0	....	....	....	200.0	47,277.60
.....	....	....	....	433.0	....	....	....	433.0	94,875.00
.....	....	....	....	320.1	....	....	....	320.1	70,125.00
.....	....	....	....	....	....	....	(.02)‡	.0	6.68
.....	47.1	....	38.2	....	....	....	....	85.3	19,408.96
.....	....	....	....	....	....	....	....	200.8	32,356.91
.....	....	....	....	....	6.1	....	(1 Cs. Taps)	6.1	1,782.68
.....	....	....	....	....	5.8	....	(1 Cs. Taps)	5.8	2,110.74
.....	....	....	....	....	....	....	....	369.0	47,863.73
.....	123.2	....	....	....	....	....	....	623.4	91,188.52
.....	....	....	....	....	11.1	....	....	11.1	3,296.13
.....	....	....	100.8	....	....	....	....	100.8	10,164.77
.....	....	....	....	....	12.1	....	....	12.1	3,375.23
.....	....	....	30.0	....	....	....	....	30.0	4,095.45
.....	....	226.7	....	....	....	....	....	226.7	70,019.81
.....	....	92.6	....	....	....	....	....	92.6	33,790.54
.....	....	4.0	....	....	....	....	....	4.0	910.13
.....	49.8	62.5	....	....	....	....	....	112.3	27,149.57
.....	....	....	....	....	....	....	....	400.0	38,250.80
.....	....	420.9	....	....	....	....	....	420.9	93,611.53
.....	....	139.1	....	....	....	....	....	139.1	50,874.50
.....	180.7	433.3	60.0	....	....	....	....	909.0	185,964.64
.....	....	....	....	....	....	....	....	298.3	23,175.63
.....	91.9	68.8	....	....	....	....	....	160.7	48,167.15
.....	....	....	....	....	....	....	2.4	2.4	2,945.97
.....	....	199.1	....	....	....	....	....	199.1	43,629.48
.....	....	.....	....	172.0	....	....	....	172.0	35,420.99
.....	....	.....	....	....	....	....	....	541.1	39,289.51
.....	....	103.1	....	....	....	....	....	103.1	23,450.30
.....	....	.....	....	828.0	....	....	....	828.0	170,515.01
.....	....	262.1	....	....	....	....	....	262.1	65,111.19
.....	....	.....	....	....	51.2	....	....	51.2	18,020.28
.....	....	216.6	....	5.5	....	30.3	....	252.4	59,049.14
.....	....	.....	....	....	....	15.2	....	15.2	4,134.07
.....	....	.....	....	....	54.0	....	....	54.0	9,183.08
.....	....	.....	....	....	....	15.2	....	15.2	4,138.42
.....	....	.....	....	....	172.7	....	....	172.7	27,518.88
.....	20.0	96.2	....	....	....	....	....	116.2	26,532.01
.....	....	.....	....	....	....	....	....	130.1	8,137.45
.....	....	.....	....	....	....	....	....	486.6	29,123.96
.....	....	43.4	....	....	....	....	....	43.4	10,394.73
.....	....	108.5	....	....	....	....	....	108.5	26,734.97
.....	....	.....	....	....	....	30.5	....	92.3	12,944.61
.....	....	.....	50.2	....	....	....	....	50.2	5,017.24
208.5	153.6	.....	....	....	....	....	....	746.0	69,787.69

‡ One case games for Dr. Pirquet.

[*Continued on next page*]

Table 213—*Continued*

Detail by Steamers o[f]

Steamer or Source	Port of Sailing	Date of Arrival	Port of Arrival	Flour	Rice	Beans, Peas
		1921				
Orbita	New York	June 2	Hamburg	.....	.....	100.6
Corson, III	New York	June 17	Hamburg	.....	.....	.....
Oropesa	New York	June 17	Hamburg	.....	.....	199.6
American, V	New York	June 21	Hamburg	.....	.....	.....
West Camak	San Francisco	June 24	Hamburg	.....	.....	.....
Hamburg Packing House Stock	United States	June ..	Hamburg	.....	72.1	.....
Orduna	New York	July 1	Hamburg	.....	.....	.....
Mystic, V	New York	July 2	Hamburg	.....	.....	.....
Bakersfield	San Francisco	July 3	Hamburg	.....	.....	.....
Hawaiian, III	New York	July 4	Hamburg	145.6	.....	.....
Oregonian, IV	New York	July 11	Hamburg	114.4	.....	.....
Panama	San Francisco	Aug. 7	Hamburg	473.0	.....	.....
Dakotan, I	New York	Sept. 24	Hamburg	.....	.....	.....
Virginian	New York	Oct. 1	Hamburg	.....	.....	.....
Clarksburg, IV	Baltimore	Oct. 8	Hamburg	.....	.....	.....
Chickasaw	New York	Dec. 4	Hamburg	.....	.....	.....
Clarksburg, V	Norfolk	Dec. 12	Hamburg	.....	.....	.....
Mount Clay, V	New York	Dec. 19	Hamburg	.....	.....	.....
Westbrook, IV	New York	Dec. 22	Hamburg	.....	.....	.....
		1922				
Mount Carroll, VI	New York	Jan. 3	Hamburg	.....	.....	.....
Mount Clay, VI	New York	Feb. 7	Hamburg	.....	.....	.....
Dallas	New York	Feb. 9	Hamburg	14.3	.....	.....
Nobles, I	New Orleans	Feb. 9	Hamburg	.....	130.9	.....
Sudbury, III	Norfolk	Feb. 9	Hamburg	.....	.....	.....
Mount Carroll, VII	New York	Feb. 15	Hamburg	.....	.....	.....
Haverford	New York	Feb. 23	Hamburg	603.8	.....	.....
Bradford City, IV	New York	Mar. 7	Hamburg	.....	.....	.....
Mount Clinton, IV	New York	Mar. 7	Hamburg	.....	.....	.....
Württemberg	New York	Mar. 9	Hamburg	76.1	.....	.....
Morristown, I	Phila.-New York	Mar. 12	Hamburg	.....	.....	.....
Oregonian, VIII	New York	Mar. 23	Hamburg	.....	.....	.....
Local Purchase, Austria	(Vienna)	Mar. 24	(Vienna)	.....	.....	.....
Minnekahda, V	New York	Mar. 26	Hamburg	.....	.....	.....
Noccalula	New Orleans	Mar. 30	Hamburg	.....	.....	.....
Corson, V	New York	Mar. 31	Hamburg	.....	.....	.....
Juno, III	(United Kingdom)	Mar. 31	Hamburg	.....	.....	.....
Otto	(United Kingdom)	Mar. 31	Hamburg	.....	.....	.....
Schoharie, III	New York	Apr. 1	Hamburg	.....	.....	.....
Western Scout	New York	Apr. 26	Hamburg	.....	.....	.....
Chappaqua, II	Norfolk	Apr. 28	Hamburg	.....	.....	.....
Mount Clay, VII	New York	Apr. 29	Hamburg	.....	.....	.....
Minnekahda, VI	New York	Apr. 30	Hamburg	.....	.....	.....
Manchuria, VI	New York *	May 8	Hamburg	.....	.....	.....
Sapinero	New Orleans	May 14	Hamburg	.....	.....	.....
St. Paul	New York	May 14	Hamburg	.....	.....	.....
Local Purchase	(Vienna)	May 26	(Vienna)	.....	.....	.....
Morristown, II	Philadelphia	May 28	Hamburg	.....	.....	.....
Minnekahda, VII	New York	June 3	Hamburg	365.7	.....	.....
Manchuria, VII	New York	June 11	Hamburg	.....	.....	.....
Mount Carroll, IX	New York	June 20	Hamburg	.....	.....	.....
Nobles, III	New Orleans	July 2	Hamburg	.....	103.4	.....
Emergency Aid, II	New Orleans	July 9	Hamburg	.....	286.4	.....
Mount Carroll, X	New York	Dec. 4	Hamburg	74.6	.....	.....
Mount Clinton, VII	New York	Dec. 20	Hamburg	71.2	.....	.....
Chester Valley, II	New Orleans	Dec. 31	Hamburg	.....	150.3	.....
		1923				
Mount Clay, X	New York	Jan. 1	Hamburg	53.3	.....	.....
Mount Clay, XI	New York	Feb. 14	Hamburg	309.3	.....	.....
West Ira	New Orleans	Feb. 28	Hamburg	.....	152.6	.....
Emergency Aid, V	New Orleans	Mar. 14	Hamburg	.....	3.9	.....
Bayern, III	New York	Mar. 26	Hamburg	.....	.....	.....
Suruga	New York	Apr. 12	Hamburg	395.4	.....	.....
Springfield	Norfolk	Apr. 18	Hamburg	.....	.....	.....

* For Dr. Pirquet.

R.A.-European Children's Fund

rivals of Relief Supplies

Corn Grits	Pork Products	Milk	Cocoa	Sugar	Miscellaneous Food	Soap	Other Misc. Sacks, Containers, Etc.	Total Tons	Total Value
Contents of Cargoes in Net Metric Tons of 1,000 Kilograms or 2,204.6 Pounds									
....	....	37.5	40.4	....	....	....	....	178.5	$ 27,927.60
....	....	102.4	....	....	....	....	....	102.4	26,088.05
....	....	111.8	....	....	....	....	....	311.4	61,725.40
....	....	116.7	88.9	....	....	....	....	205.6	48,419.89
....	....	....	....	....	79.9	....	....	79.9	10,475.08
....	....	....	....	....	....	....	....	72.1	5,889.85
....	70.3	....	....	....	....	....	....	70.3	13,953.57
....	....	298.4	....	....	....	....	....	298.4	76,283.31
....	....	....	....	....	4.1	....	....	4.1	504.16
545.1	....	35.1	5.1	....	....	....	....	730.9	48,635.36
252.5	....	....	....	....	....	....	....	366.9	19,144.17
....	....	....	....	....	....	....	....	473.0	37,021.99
....	....	151.4	20.0	....	....	....	....	171.4	49,552.80
....	4.2	387.3	....	....	....	....	....	391.5	102,522.12
....	115.1	....	....	....	....	....	....	115.1	28,048.83
....	....	....	39.5	....	....	....	....	39.5	3,558.20
....	93.6	....	....	....	....	....	....	93.6	21,491.12
....	....	.1*	....	....	....	....	....	.1	84.16
....	....	107.6	....	....	....	....	....	107.6	23,604.02
....	....	24.6	....	....	....	....	....	24.6	7,056.75
....	....	234.3	....	....	....	....	....	234.3	54,110.58
....	....	....	....	....	....	....	....	14.3	799.44
....	....	....	....	....	....	....	....	130.9	5,780.28
....	32.0	....	....	....	....	....	....	32.0	7,265.31
....	....	....	....	178.4	....	....	....	178.4	12,747.75
....	....	....	....	....	....	....	....	603.8	33,552.20
....	....	....	26.9	....	....	....	....	26.9	1,651.74
....	....	157.8	....	165.3	....	....	....	323.1	47,573.09
....	....	....	....	....	....	....	....	76.1	4,257.41
40.1	....	....	4.1	20.9	....	....	....	65.1	3,370.38
....	....	16.5	....	....	....	....	....	16.5	4,110.17
....	....	13.9	....	....	....	....	....	13.9	3,003.30
32.5	....	15.5	....	....	....	....	....	48.0	11,100.83
....	89.9	....	....	....	....	....	....	89.9	20,451.35
231.5	....	....	....	....	....	....	....	231.5	8,418.24
....	....	....	....	....	11.9	....	(2 Cs. Taps)	11.9	1,715.70
....	....	....	....	....	12.0	....	(1 Cs. Taps)	12.0	1,730.10
37.3	....	....	....	....	....	....	....	37.3	1,371.82
....	....	94.1	5.8	....	....	....	....	99.9	28,436.02
....	4.0	....	....	....	....	....	....	4.0	890.15
....	....	12.7	....	5.1	....	....	....	17.8	3,374.76
....	....	184.4	....	216.6	....	....	....	401.0	77,882.59
....	....	77.5	....	....	....	....	....	77.5	13,036.51
....	132.8	....	....	....	....	....	....	132.8	38,532.72
....	....	71.6	....	....	....	....	....	71.6	12,101.81
....	....	....	....	....	9.1	....	....	9.1	1,723.00
....	....	....	110.4	....	....	....	....	110.4	7,454.43
....	....	....	15.7	....	....	....	....	381.4	27,139.25
....	....	....	....	49.9	....	....	....	49.9	4,420.04
182.5	....	....	....	....	....	....	....	182.5	7,547.42
....	....	....	....	....	....	....	....	103.4	5,758.73
....	....	....	....	....	....	....	....	286.4	15,891.19
....	....	....	20.3	109.7	....	....	....	204.6	18,743.07
....	40.7	46.2	....	....	....	....	....	158.1	26,879.79
....	....	....	....	....	....	....	....	150.3	6,349.08
....	....	15.1	....	....	....	....	....	68.4	8,340.89
....	37.0	18.3	25.4	....	....	....	....	390.0	36,949.54
....	....	....	....	....	....	....	....	152.6	7,657.28
....	....	....	....	....	....	....	....	3.9	187.89
....	....	72.5	....	161.0	....	....	....	233.5	36,919.65
....	....	60.0	....	....	....	....	....	455.4	40,479.78
....	90.1	....	....	....	....	....	....	90.1	26,441.83

[*Concluded on next page*]

Table 213—*Concluded*

Detail by Steamers of

Steamer or Source	Port of Sailing	Date of Arrival	Port of Arrival	Flour	Rice	Beans, Peas
						SUNDRY
		1920				
Czecho-Slovakia Purchase.........	(Prague)	....	(Vienna)	.....	.....	.....
Stock.........................	(U.S.A.)	July 9	(Vienna)	.....	.....	.....
Stock.........................	(U.S.A.)	Sept. 24	(Vienna)			
Czecho-Slovakia Purchase.........	(C.-S.)	Oct.	(Vienna)	.....	.....	.....
Hungarian Stock	(U.S.A.)	Aug. 13–17	(Vienna)	.....	.....	169.7
		1921				
Stock.........................	(U.S.A.)	May 27	(Vienna)	.....	.....	.....
Czecho-Slovakia Stock...........	(U.S.A.)	....	(Vienna)	.....	.....	.....
Local Exchange	(Austria)	....	(Vienna)	.....	.....	.....
Local Exchange.................	(Austria)	....	(Vienna)	.....	.....	84.1
Warehouse Overages and Commodity Charges	....	....	....	.....	.8	14.7
Total Arrivals	....	....	....	**11,332.9**	**5,801.0**	**4,402.6**
Deduct deliveries to:						
Czecho-Slovakia	....	....	....	.....	222.2	.....
Hamburg for Russia............	....	....	....	.....	.....	.....
Hungary	....	....	....	381.6	592.7	320.0
Poland	....	....	....	.....	.....	.....
Warehouse and handling adjustments	....	....	....	.....	.....	.....
Total Deductions	....	....	....	**381.6**	**814.9**	**320.0**
Net Arrivals—to Table 210..	....	....	....	**10,951.3**	**4,986.1**	**4,082.6**

* No money involved. Sugar received in lieu 800.0 metric tons flour listed on Table 218C.

† No money involved. Beans, pork products, sugar received in li milk and cocoa listed on Table 218C.

AUSTRIA—

Table 214

Detail by Steamers of Clothing Arrivals for Children'

Steamer or Source	Port of Sailing	Date of Arrival	Port of Arrival	Shoes (Pairs)	Laces (Pairs)	Stockings (Pairs)	Woolens (Yards)	Flannel (Yards)
		1919						
Batavier 3, I............	London	Nov. 30	Rotterdam	....	50,400	....	....	....
Batavier 6.............	London	Dec. 4	Rotterdam	....	....	....	6,707.25	....
Batavier 3, II..........	London	Dec. 7	Rotterdam	1,440	....	....	15,615.25	....
Batavier 4, I............	London	Dec. 9	Rotterdam	19,100	....	....	....	....
Batavier 6, II...........	London	Dec. 11	Rotterdam	32,229	50,400	....	8,914.00	....
Batavier 3, III..........	London	Dec. 14	Rotterdam	1,478	....	....	22,670.00	....
Batavier 6, III..........	London	Dec. 18	Rotterdam	2,137	....	....	24,362.75	....
Batavier 3, IV..........	London	Dec. 21	Rotterdam	17,812	....	....	4,399.50	....
Continental Purchase....	Antwerp	Dec. 22	Mannheim	....	....	12,000	....	....
Batavier 6, IV..........	London	Dec. 25	Rotterdam	....	....	....	11,064.25	....
Julia Luckenbach	New York	Dec. 28	Rotterdam	....	....	....	....	....
		1920						
Batavier 6, V...........	London	Jan. 1	Rotterdam	1,648	....	14,880	12,546.75	....
Batavier 3, V...........	London	Jan. 4	Rotterdam	....	....	....	633.75	....
Continental Purchase	Antwerp	Jan. 5	Mannheim	....	....	13,200	....	....
Maine	New York	Jan. 6	Rotterdam	22,000	22,000	....	....	....
Batavier 6, VI..........	London	Jan. 8	Rotterdam	....	....	8,400	....	....
Continental Purchase....	Antwerp	Jan. 13	Mannheim	....	....	18,000	....	....
Edward Luckenbach	New York	Jan. 14	Rotterdam	....	....	....	67,351.375	....
Continental Purchase....	Antwerp	Jan. 20	Mannheim	....	....	2,400	....	....
Batavier 4, II...........	London	Jan. 25	Rotterdam	1,542	....	....	....	....
Continental Purchase....	Antwerp	Jan. 26	Mannheim	....	....	22,800	....	....

R.A.-European Children's Fund

·ivals of Relief Supplies

Corn Grits	Pork Products	Milk	Cocoa	Sugar	Miscellaneous Food	Soap	Other Misc. Sacks, Containers, Etc.	Total Tons	Total Value
Contents of Cargoes in Net Metric Tons of 1,000 Kilograms or 2,204.6 Pounds									
LIVERIES									
....	....	....	....	29.0	....	....	....	29.0	$ 5,906.14
....	7.4	....	....	....	....	....	....	7.4	5,340.13
....	....	....	....	380.2	....	....	....	380.2	78,296.87
....	....	57.2	....	....	....	....	....	226.9	62,509.06
....	....	....	48.4	....	....	....	....	48.4	4,837.34
....	....	....	....	....	....	10.2	....	10.2	2,753.11
....	....	....	....	600.0	....	....	....	600.0	.......*
....	30.7	....	....	128.2	....	....	....	243.0	.......†
....	.1	....	....	....	11.4	....	42.5	69.5	25,787.48
,530.0	**3,135.1**	**9,294.6**	**1,036.4**	**4,230.4**	**670.2**	**101.4**	**69.7**	**41,604.3**	**$ 8,633,449.58**
....	....	....	....	....	....	....	....	222.2	$ 55,649.09
....	70.3	....	....	....	....	....	....	70.3	48,638.13
23.4	135.6	1,234.2	146.0	605.7	17.8	2.7	....	3,459.7	867,911.21
....	....	....	....	....	15.3	....	....	15.3	10,373.40
14.7	....	....	.1	....	....	....	....	14.8	....
38.1	**205.9**	**1,234.2**	**146.1**	**605.7**	**33.1**	**2.7**	....	**3,782.3**	**$ 982,571.83**
,491.9	**2,929.2**	**8,060.4**	**890.3**	**3,624.7**	**637.1**	**98.7**	**69.7**	**37,822.0‡**	**$ 7,650,877.75**

This tonnage includes: 11,795.8 metric tons delivered against draft sales, 892.8 metric tons delivered against exchange of commodities, ;.4 metric tons delivered for child feeding operation.

R.A.-European Children's Fund

lief, Etc.—Reconstruction Period, 1919–1924

Thread ·ards)	Thread (Reels)	Needles (No.)	Underwear (Suits)	Buttons (No.)	Snap Fasteners (Pairs)	Hooks and Eyes (Pairs)	Trousers Buckles (No.)	Woolen Jackets (No.)	Lining (Yards)	Cotton Tape (Yards)	Total Metric Tons	Total Value
.....	.....	.....	.....	.....	.....	.....	.....	...	.....	.....	.7	$ 575.86
.....	.....	.....	.....	.....	.....	.....	.....	...	.....	.....	3.0	8,747.81
.....	.....	.....	.....	.....	.....	.....	.....	...	.....	.....	8.0	24,665.17
.....	.....	.....	.....	.....	.....	.....	.....	...	.....	.....	9.0	34,054.63
.....	.....	.....	.....	.....	.....	.....	.....	...	.....	.....	17.8	83,829.10
.....	.....	.....	.....	.....	.....	.....	.....	...	.....	.....	10.5	36,189.55
.....	.....	.....	.....	.....	.....	.....	.....	...	.....	.....	10.8	40,355.55
.....	.....	.....	.....	.....	.....	.....	.....	...	.....	.....	10.7	38,932.03
.....	.....	.....	.....	.....	.....	.....	.....	...	.....	.....	.6	5,671.50
.....	.....	.....	.....	.....	.....	.....	.....	...	.....	.....	3.8	16,191.22
)00,000	.....	100,000	.....	126,144	.....	.....	.....	...	.....	.....	1.8	2,985.99
.....	.....	.....	.....	.....	.....	.....	.....	...	.....	.....	6.9	25,643.47
.....	.....	.....	.....	.....	.....	.....	.....	...	.....	.....	.4	839.16
.....	.....	.....	.....	.....	.....	.....	.....	...	.....	.....	.6	6,050.55
.....	.....	.....	.....	.....	.....	.....	.....	...	.....	.....	29.4	59,989.68
.....	.....	.....	.....	.....	.....	.....	.....	...	.....	.....	.4	3,676.91
.....	.....	.....	.....	.....	.....	.....	.....	...	.....	.....	.8	8,122.50
)84,000	.....	.....	.....	383,616	.....	.....	.....	...	.....	.....	24.1	102,289.53
.....	.....	.....	.....	.....	.....	.....	.....	...	.....	.....	.2	1,096.68
.....	.....	.....	.....	.....	.....	.....	.....	...	.....	.....	1.4	3,710.35
.....	.....	.....	.....	.....	.....	.....	.....	...	.....	.....	10.0	7,193.86

[*Continued on next page*]

Table 214—*Continued*

Detail by Steamers of Clothin

Steamer or Source	Port of Sailing	Date of Arrival	Port of Arrival	Shoes (Pairs)	Laces (Pairs)	Stockings (Pairs)	Woolens (Yards)	Flannel (Yards)
		1920						
Batavier 6, VII	London	Jan. 29	Rotterdam	2,704	....	....	....	....
Continental Purchase	Antwerp	Feb. 2	Mannheim	....	....	8,344	....	....
Batavier 4, III	London	Feb. 8	Rotterdam	....	....	....	....	....
Local Purchase	(Vienna)	Mar. 30	(Vienna)	....	....	....	....	....
Germar, I	London	Sept. 16	Hamburg	....	....	51,000	....	....
Gerratt, II	London	Sept. 22	Hamburg	....	....	49,000	....	....
Maja, I	Copenhagen	Sept. 29	Hamburg	....	....	....	....	65,395.55
Agnes, II	Copenhagen	Oct. 10	Hamburg	....	....	....	....	20,614.40
Maja, II	Copenhagen	Oct. 10	Hamburg	....	....	....	....	6,216.00
Schoharie, I	New York	Oct. 13	Hamburg	35,936	35,936	....	....	554,034.00
Mystic, I	New York	Oct. 26	Hamburg	....	....	....	....	....
Beursplein, I	New York	Nov. 1	Hamburg	....	....	....	....	....
Iowan, I	New York	Nov. 6	Hamburg	39,877	39,877	....	....	....
Germar, II	London	Nov. 8	Hamburg	....	....	....	....	....
Courier	(U.K.)	Nov. 12	Hamburg	....	....	....	....	....
Prutan, I	(U.K.)	Nov. 13	Hamburg	....	....	....	....	....
Texan	New York	Nov. 22	Hamburg	24,240	24,240	....	....	....
Beursplein, II	New York	Dec. 27	Hamburg	....	....	....	....	9,444.50
Mrs. Halsted, donation	....	Dec. ..	....	....	....	96	....	....
		1921						
Mystic, IV	New York	May 9	Hamburg	....	....	....	61,486.25	....
Hawaiian, II	New York	May 17	Hamburg	....	....	....	61,486.25	....
Oregonian, III	New York	May 29	Hamburg	....	....	....	60,269.50	....
American, V	New York	June 21	Hamburg	....	....	....	88,514.25	....
Mystic, V	New York	July 2	Hamburg	....	....	....	59,597.50	....
Hawaiian, III	New York	July 4	Hamburg	....	....	....	128,454.50	....
Mount Carroll, II	New York	July 12	Hamburg	....	....	....	66,727.00	....
Mystic, VI	New York	Aug. 15	Hamburg	....	....	....	....	....
Hawaiian, IV	New York	Aug. 22	Hamburg	19,951	....	....	....	....
Oregonian, V	New York	Aug. 28	Hamburg	42,396	....	....	....	....
Mount Carroll, III	New York	Aug. 30	Hamburg	10,881	....	....	....	....
King City, II*	New York	Sept. 1	Hamburg	5,732	....	....	....	....
Sudbury, II	New York	Sept. 13	Hamburg	66,372	....	....	....	....
Ipswich, III*	New York	Sept. 19	Hamburg	....	....	85,704	20,913.00	....
Dakotan	New York	Sept. 24	Hamburg	....	....	49,605	....	....
Orla*	New York	Sept. 29	Hamburg	....	....	14,496	....	....
Virginian*	New York	Oct. 1	Hamburg	....	....	....	....	....
Poland Stock	(Warsaw)	Nov. ..	(Vienna)	....	....	724	....	....
Total Deliveries	....	....	....	**347,475**	**222,853**	**350,649**	**721,713.25**	**655,705.0**
Less Deliveries to Hungary	....	....	....	....	....	....	....	....
Net Deliveries, Austria	....	....	....	**347,475**	**222,853**	**350,649**	**721,713.25**	**655,705.0**

* Designates steamers carrying Commonwealth Fund clothing for Intelligentsia.

.R.A.-European Children's Fund

rrivals for Children's Relief, Etc.

Thread (Yards)	Thread (Reels)	Needles (No.)	Under-wear (Suits)	Buttons (No.)	Snap Fasteners (Pairs)	Hooks and Eyes (Pairs)	Trousers Buckles (No.)	Woolen Jackets (No.)	Lining (Yards)	Cotton Tape (Yards)	Total Metric Tons	Total Value
......	......	......	......	......	......	......	.....	...	......	.....	2.3	$ 6,936.38
......	......	......	......	......	......	......	.....	...	......	.....	1.0	2,512.36
......	......	......	......	......	......	......	.....	664	......	.....	.5	3.05
......	......	......	......	110,448	......	......	.....	...	......	.....	.5	132.52
......	......	......	......	......	......	......	.....	...	......	.....	6.2	18,258.18
......	......	......	......	......	......	......	.....	...	......	.....	6.1	17,524.09
......	......	......	......	......	......	......	.....	...	......	.....	9.8	18,359.26
......	......	......	......	......	......	......	.....	...	......	.....	3.1	5,787.30
......	......	......	......	......	......	......	.....	...	......	.....	.8	1,745.10
......	......	......	......	......	......	......	.....	...	......	.....	148.3	264,208.49
......	15,000	6,000	......	862,272	......	......	.....	...	......	40,320	1.3	4,966.13
......	......	......	......	74,304	......	......	.....	...	......	.....	(.03)	114.25
......	......	......	......	......	......	......	.....	...	......	.....	45.2	77,929.84
......	76,000	75,000	......	......	......	......	.....	...	......	.....	1.8	2,303.98
......	......	2,200	......	......	......	......	.....	...	......	.....	.0	36.72
......	14,000	......	......	......	......	......	.....	...	......	.....	.3	411.61
......	......	......	......	......	......	......	.....	...	......	.....	26.4	47,176.08
......	......	......	......	......	......	......	.....	...	......	.....	.9	1,939.63
......	......	......	......	......	......	......	.....	...	......	.....	.....	....
......	......	......	......	......	......	......	.....	...	......	.....	32.6	23,419.04
......	......	......	......	......	......	......	.....	...	......	.....	34.0	23,269.12
......	......	......	......	......	......	......	.....	...	......	.....	32.6	22,836.82
......	......	......	......	......	......	......	.....	...	......	.....	48.5	33,890.74
......	......	......	......	......	......	......	.....	...	......	.....	31.0	23,482.81
......	......	......	......	......	......	......	.....	...	......	.....	52.9	45,930.31
......	......	......	......	......	......	......	.....	...	......	.....	16.8	18,894.42
......	30,000	14,000	......	1,417,392	141,696	177,984	84,960	...	127,237	.....	20.1	26,789.27
......	......	......	......	......	......	......	.....	...	......	.....	21.5	32,216.60
......	7,648	5,000	......	672,912	......	......	.....	...	......	.....	45.5	71,385.66
......	......	......	......	......	......	......	.....	...	......	.....	10.6	17,109.77
......	......	......	......	......	......	......	.....	...	......	.....	10.3	14,143.23
......	......	......	......	......	......	......	.....	...	......	.....	68.1	105,657.35
......	3,000	5,000	......	122,112	12,096	6,912	8,784	...	38,039	.....	22.6	44,589.44
......	......	......	......	......	......	......	.....	...	......	.....	4.7	6,965.90
......	......	......	8,552½	......	......	......	.....	...	......	.....	5.1	13,848.02
......	......	......	2,800	......	......	......	.....	...	......	.....	1.1	2,416.00
......	......	......	......	......	......	......	.....	...	......	.....	.1	97.59
,884,000	**145,648**	**207,200**	**11,352½**	**3,769,200**	**153,792**	**184,896**	**93,744**	**664**	**165,276**	**40,320**	**863.5**	**$1,508,098.16**
......	7,648	5,000	......	672,912	......	......	.....	...	......	.....	1.6	3,575.11
,884,000	**138,000†**	**202,200**	**11,352½**	**3,096,288**	**153,792**	**184,896**	**93,744**	**664**	**165,276**	**40,320**	**861.9**	**$1,504,523.05**

† This 138,000 reels is equivalent to 23,000,000 yards.

AUSTRIA—A.R.A.-E. C. F.

Detail of Government Donations for Child Feeding, by Months—Reconstruction Period, 1919–1924

Table 215

Month	Flour	Sugar	Total Tons*	Total Value
1920				
June	.....	638.0	638.0	$ 172,898.00
July	209.0	.....	209.0	33,165.10
August	682.0	.....	682.0	108,892.84
September	571.0	.....	571.0	91,334.28
October	1,014.0	.....	1,014.0	156,427.38
November	348.0	.....	348.0	53,655.68
December	705.0	.....	705.0	108,727.14
1921				
January	692.0	.....	692.0	90,859.55
February	255.0	.....	255.0	22,947.35
March	564.0	.....	564.0	53,234.14
April	729.0	.....	729.0	70,045.63
May	972.0	.....	972.0	74,985.70
June	1,348.0	.....	1,348.0	104,881.06
July	229.0	.....	229.0	17,216.14
August	414.0	.....	414.0	31,098.28
September	189.0	.....	189.0	20,584.91
October	17.0	.....	17.0	1,346.35
November	377.0	.....	377.0	29,525.86
December	18.0	.....	18.0	1,410.62
1922				
January	37.0	.....	37.0	2,906.81
February	485.0	.....	485.0	58,951.44
March	.....	.....	.....	....
April	107.0	.....	107.0	6,094.16
May	204.0	.....	204.0	11,976.46
June	12.0	.....	12.0	783.67
Total	**10,178.0**	**638.0**	**10,816.0**	**$1,323,948.55**

* Quantities net metric tons of 1,000 kilograms or 2,204.6 pounds.

AUSTRIA—A.R.A.-E. C. F.

Provincial Government Donations for Child Feeding—Reconstruction Period, 1919–1924

Table 216

	Flour	Coal	Total Metric Tons†	Estimated Value*
Total	**211.8**	**1,675.5**	**1,887.3**	**$40,707.4[illegible]**

† Quantities net metric tons of 1,000 kilograms or 2,204.6 pounds.
* Flour value estimated at $113.09, average price of 10,178.0 metri[c] tons, listed in Table 215. Coal value estimated at $10.00 per metric ton

AUSTRIA—

Summary of Internal Deliveries, by Provinces—

Table 218*

Receipt No.	Province	Zone Warehouse	Period of Delivery	Table No.	Flour	Rice	Beans, Peas
					(A) INTERNA		
1st Series 1–153, 2d Series 1–157, 3d Series 1–38	Lower Austria	Vienna	May, 1919 – June, 1922	224	9,984.7	2,852.9	2,776.0
	Upper Austria	Linz	June, 1922	225	1,598.9	415.2	388.1
	Carinthia	St. Veit	June, 1922	226	678.3	158.4	135.4
	Salzburg	Salzburg	June, 1922	227	722.0	175.4	158.7
	Styria	Graz	June, 1922	228	2,202.3	519.3	437.9
	Tyrol	Lienz, Innsbrûck	June, 1922	229	868.9	217.3	231.7
	Vorarlberg	Bregenz	June, 1922	230	351.0	79.7	94.0
39	Turnover to Committees	....	Aug., 1922	231	518.1	404.4	11.4
	Clothing for Children	....	1919–1922	222	.....	.....	.....
	Total Deliveries	....	....	206	**16,924.2**	**4,822.6**	**4,233.2**

* For value of commodities and division to organizations furnishing the finance, cf. Table 206.

AUSTRIA—United States Grain Corporation

Detail by Steamers of Deliveries under Act of Congress, March 30, 1920*

Table 217

Reconstruction Period, 1919–1924

Steamer	Date of Sailing	Flour Barrels	Flour Pounds	Total Tons†	Total Value‡
	1920				
ıemore	Apr. 1	86,846	84	7,721.1	$ 933,347.56
peranza de Larrinaga	Apr. 12	77,382	98	6,879.7	751,159.78
oria de Larrinaga	Apr. 17	80,367	168	7,145.1	863,487.99
yncote	Apr. 17	76,223	112	6,776.7	818,821.46
rcedes de Larrinaga	Apr. 23	68,022	28	6,047.5	730,946.52
mon de Larrinaga	Apr. 29	93,359	56	8,300.1	964,128.21
limba	Apr. 30	75,950	...	6,752.3	816,344.30
rnfield	May 8	41,759	56	3,712.6	448,912.32
lmede	May 10	66,647	28	5,925.3	716,172.13
ilsby	May 11	62,832	168	5,586.1	666,328.03
ıziristan	May 17	72,802	168	6,472.5	782,350.72
ient City	May 20	68,361	80	6,077.7	734,626.26
kbridge	May 22	56,896	84	5,058.4	611,279.08
mbov	May 22	35,257	28	3,134.5	378,692.95
elrosa	May 30	48,734	56	4,332.7	523,388.39
erdale	June 3	55,532	28	4,937.1	596,821.08
elstone	June 4	71,430	140	6,350.5	767,731.03
ıuen	June 8	57,117	168	5,078.1	613,355.13
rst	June 11	75,977	28	6,754.8	816,298.52
nnonia	June 19	33,392	168	2,968.8	356,707.11
ry Horlock	June 19	73,358	112	6,522.0	788,153.77
lglass Castle	June 21	58,715	140	5,220.1	631,088.54
lda	June 25	61,600	...	5,476.6	661,975.96
menetz Podolsk	June 28	60,715	...	5,397.9	652,339.84
hsfeld	July 3	60,862	28	5,411.0	654,088.64
drun	July 10	61,135	35	5,435.2	588,011.39
een Elizabeth	July 16	62,052	168	5,516.8	662,829.69
lgowan	July 17	66,385	...	5,902.0	710,866.73
ndomar	July 24	52,742	168	4,689.1	563,321.78
lkenfels	July 24	120,315	140	10,696.7	1,292,936.51
gsburg	July 30	117,305	...	10,429.0	1,255,422.43
seric	Aug. 25	79,812	168	7,095.8	855,957.28
peranza de Larrinaga	Sept. 4	78,972	28	7,021.0	847,817.79
Total Deliveries	....	**2,258,866**	**185**	**200,824.8**	**$24,055,708.92**

* Cf. Table 157.

† Contents of cargoes in net metric tons of 1,000 kilograms or 2,204.6 nds.

‡ Value quoted f.o.b. U.S.A. ports. Freight and other transportation charges were paid by the United Kingdom in the amount of $8,032,991.88.

.R.A. and A.R.A.-European Children's Fund

construction Period, 1919–1924

Commodities in Net Metric Tons of 1,000 Kilograms or 2,204.6 Pounds

Corn Grits	Pork Products	Milk Evaporated, Condensed, Dried, Powdered	Cocoa	Sugar	Miscellaneous Food	Miscellaneous Sacks, Containers, Clothing, Etc.	Soap	Coal	Total Tons
LIVERIES, BY PROVINCES, FOR CHILD FEEDING									
591.8	1,322.8	6,120.5	630.7	2,476.8	327.9	.....	128.8	1,675.5	28,888.4
92.2	180.5	780.8	85.9	321.8	32.9	.....	16.6	......	3,912.9
48.7	72.8	318.7	29.8	147.8	9.7	.....	4.6	......	1,604.2
54.6	81.4	340.3	35.6	168.6	12.4	.....	4.6	......	1,753.6
105.8	231.1	1,065.3	123.6	477.6	30.5	.....	21.5	......	5,214.9
58.1	104.3	465.8	47.3	213.1	13.5	.....	5.4	......	2,225.4
19.1	35.1	171.1	15.6	77.0	6.0	.....	2.2	......	850.8
....	102.2	329.1	116.1	162.4	.....	.....	25.2	......	1,668.9
....	.....	.....	....	......	.....	830.0	.....	......	830.0
970.3	**2,130.2**	**9,591.6**	**1,084.6**	**4,045.1**	**432.9**	**830.0**	**208.9**	**1,675.5**	**46,949.1**

[*Continued on next page*]

Table 218—*Continued*

Receipt No.	Province	Zone Warehouse	Period of Delivery	Table No.	Flour	Rice	Beans, Peas
						(B) DELIVERIE	
	Total	....	....	153	**5,120.6**	**1,243.0**	**664.8**
						(C) DELIVERIE	
	Exchanged for 600.0 M.T. Sugar	....	....	213	800.0	.....	.....
	Exchanged for 243.0 M.T. Beans, Pork Products, Sugar	....	....	213	.....	.....	.....
	Total Commodities Exchanged	....	....	...	**800.0**	.....	.....
						(D) DELIVERIE	
	Clothing	....	....	221	.....	.....	.....
						(E) U.S. GRAI	
	Flour Deliveries (F.O.B.) New York	....	....	217	200,824.8	.....	.....
	Total Deliveries	....	....	206	**223,669.6**	**6,065.6**	**4,898.0**

‡ Tables 219 and 220.

AUSTRIA-

Table 219

Detail by Months of Food Draft Deliveries

Time of Delivery	Number of Drafts Delivered* A $10.00	B $50.00	C $10.00	D $50.00	Unit	Flour M.T.	Rice M.T.	Beans, Peas M.T.
1920								
March	2,369½	607	164	17	...	114.366	......	......
April	7,262	1,631	2,222	126	...	234.434	......	83.094
May	27,090	4,516	6,503	430	...	686.132	......	262.620
June	11,449	2,117	2,778	242	...	318.345	......	121.836
July	10,806½	1,594	2,285	198	...	258.755	99.412	......
August	6,792	794	2,429	71	...	157.108	61.044	......
September	6,951½	1,521	1,554	63	...	194.678	74.073	......
October	8,283½	1,688	1,438	100	...	224.254	84.156	......
November	3,209	715	1,123	72	...	97.903	37.279	......
December	8,586	932	1,865	66	...	179.180	69.584	......
1921								
January	8,076	779	1,255	79	...	157.885	61.380	......
February	4,425	568	707	40	...	95.450	36.834	......
March	3,602	318	689	33	...	69.849	27.242	......
April	3,388	367	497	41	...	68.950	26.704	......
May	1,636	439	385	28	...	51.994	19.649	......
June	1,022	193	162	15	...	26.338	10.030	......
July	853	96	74	8	...	17.338	6.724	......
Total Deliveries in Units	**115,801**	**18,875**	**26,130**	**1,629**	Unit	**2,952.959**	**614.111**	**467.550**
Total Deliveries in Metric Tons	....	....	....	....	M.T.	**2,952.959**	**614.111**	**467.550**

* Values: A, $1,158,010; B, $943,750; C, $261,300; D, $81,450. Total, $2,444,510 (see Table 154).

† Corned beef.

R.A.-European Children's Fund

liveries, by Provinces

Corn Grits	Pork Products	Milk—Evaporated, Condensed, Dried, Powdered	Cocoa	Sugar	Miscellaneous: Food	Miscellaneous: Sacks, Containers, Clothing, Etc.	Soap	Coal	Total Tons
Commodities in Net Metric Tons of 1,000 Kilograms or 2,204.6 Pounds									
AFTS AND BULK SALES‡									
521.6	**1,122.6**	**1,789.3**	**195.0**	**851.0**	**218.2**	**69.7**	.....	......	**11,795.8**
COMMODITIES EXCHANGED									
....	.....	.....	....	......	.....	.....	.....	......	800.00
....	.....	38.2	54.6	......	.....	.....	.....	......	92.8
....	.....	**38.2**	**54.6**	......	.....	.....	.....	......	**892.8**
CLOTHING OTHER THAN CHILDREN'S RELIEF									
....	.....	.....	....	......	.....	**31.9**	.....	......	**31.9**
RPORATION, ACT OF CONGRESS, MARCH 30, 1920									
									200,824.8
,491.9	**3,252.8**	**11,419.1**	**1,334.2**	**4,896.1**	**651.1**	**931.6**	**208.9**	**1,675.5**	**260,494.4**

R.A. Warehouses and A.R.A.-European Children's Fund

construction Period, 1919–1924

Bacon: 8-Ib. Piece	Bacon: 16-Lb. Piece	Lard: 5-Lb. Tin	Lard: 10-Lb. Tin	Oil: 1-Gal. Tin	Oil: 5-Gal. Tin	Milk: Cond. Evap. Case	Cocoa M.T.	Sugar M.T.	Misc. Food† Case	Misc. Containers, Sacks No.	Total Metric Tons
.....	.....	....	....	....	...	1,280	.....	......	348	.....	....
10,143	.....	1,152	1,938	2,038	188	3,568	.....	......	289	.....	....
13,461	11,473	3,541	5,025	6,219	575	11,087	.....	......	753	.....	....
5,345	5,192	1,561	2,395	2,725	301	5,128	.....	......	353	.....	....
11,822	1,089	1,272	1,755	2,123	270	4,188	.....	......	266	.....	....
8,380	.....	584	899	2,505	70	2,604	.....	......	132	.....	....
8,525	734	693	1,935	1,517	83	3,131	.....	......	253	.....	....
7,558	2,097	1,158	2,019	1,498	109	3,529	.....	......	288	.....	....
2,303	1,168	397	874	1,050	101	1,603	.....	......	119	.....	....
5,880	2,285	918	939	1,786	95	2,895	6.622	16.117	155	.....	....
5,464	2,085	679	829	1,329	80	2,518	5.964	14.507	130	.....	....
3,447	1,057	544	580	727	44	1,522	3.478	8.780	95	233,350	....
3,744	274	230	362	697	38	1,124	2.671	6.397	53	.....	....
2,183	941	307	397	511	47	1,097	2.554	6.333	61	23,125	....
2,038	238	139	589	413	28	836	1.711	4.823	73	5,637	....
1,268	70	159	210	177	15	419	.904	2.432	32	3,060	....
925	60	96	96	122	8	275	9.272	1.597	16	2,950	....
92,486	**28,763**	**13,430**	**20,842**	**25,437**	**2,052**	**46,804**	**33.176**	**60.986**	**3,416**	**268,122‡**	....
35.610	**208.755**	**30.457**	**94.540**	**86.536**	**34.904**	**933.528**	**33.176**	**60.986**	**111.577**	**65.992**	**6,030.681**

The total represents containers, 5,000, and sacks: Flour A, 122,835;
n A, 122,435; Bean B, 17,852.

AUSTRIA—

Detail by Months of Bulk Sale Deliveries—

Table 220

Time of Delivery	Unit	Flour M.T.	Rice M.T.	Beans M.T.	Corn Grits M.T.	Bacon A 8-Lb. Piece	Bacon B 16-Lb. Piece	Lard A 5-Lb. Tin	Lard B 10-Lb. Tin	Lard and Lard Substitute M.T.	Oil A 1-Gal. Tin	Oil B 5-Gal. Tin
1920												
March	...	7.009	......	......	......	....	....	....	...	....	...	...
May	...	3.165	......	......	......	....	....	....	...	....	...	...
June	...	......	......	......	......	....	2,404	....	...	....	...	...
July	...	......	......	......	......	....	....	....	...	....	...	...
September	...	......	......	......	......	....	....	....	48	....	75	52
October	...	1.199	36.415	......	......	....	....	....	...	....	...	...
November	...	16.378	......	......	......	....	....	....	...	....	...	...
December	...	20.996	.100	......	......	....	....	....	...	....	...	6
1921												
January	...	5.315	......	150.314	......	....	....	....	...	....	...	...
February	...	36.267	......	......	......	....	....	....	...	....	...	...
March	...	854.441	18.593	......	......	30	100	3,120	120	.100	...	500
April	...	24.313	56.656	.312	......	839	....	358	358	24.175	...	...
May	...	1.768	......	......	......	6	1	1	1	....	34	...
June	...	11.027	3.993	......	......	1,214	2	510	4	....	464	...
July-October	...	173.835	59.574	40.255	......	10,546	1	5,564	13	....	3,303	432
Nov.-Jan. 1922	...	76.721	11.337	.280	.010	....	....	....	2	8.989	...	...
1922												
February	...	78.548	10.539	6.013	4.144	....	....	....	...	20.114	...	...
March	...	142.381	.130	.040	76.886	....	....	....	...	19.700	...	...
April	...	107.020	.010	......	60.691	....	....	....	...	4.161	...	...
May	...	166.633	.152	......	52.421	....	....	....	...	11.706	...	...
June	...	164.429	8.010	......	80.778	....	....	....	...	16.806	...	...
July	...	230.493	27.316	......	86.767	....	....	....	...	16.853	...	...
August	...	97.174	13.122	......	33.680	....	....	....	...	9.381	...	...
September	...	131.539	37.400	......	66.100	....	....	....	...	5.531	...	...
October	...	63.111	21.080	......	26.863	....	....	....	...	6.782	...	...
November	...	60.263	17.587	......	33.274	....	....	....	...	8.371	...	...
1923												
January	...	130.963	95.701	......	......	....	....	....	...	29.192	...	...
February	...	198.431	114.322	......	......	....	....	....	...	29.049	...	...
March	...	76.594	55.083	......	......	....	....	....	...	7.113	...	...
April	...	92.944	35.184	......	......	....	....	....	...	9.876	...	...
May	...	9.600	6.640	......	......	....	....	....	...	.901	...	...
Total	Unit	**2,982.557**	**628.944**	**197.214**	**521.614**	**12,635**	**2,508**	**9,553**	**546**	**228.800**	**3,876**	**990**
	M.T.	**2,982.557**	**628.944**	**197.214**	**521.614**	**45.850**	**18.202**	**21.666**	**2.471**	**228.800**	**13.186**	**16.840**
Less Food Accounted for in Child Feeding Program	Unit	......	......	......	......	....	....	3,000	...	....	...	500
	M.T.	814.851	......	......	......	....	....	6.804	...	....	...	8.505
Bulk Sale deliveries, Net	Unit	......	......	......	......	....	....	**6,553**	**546**	....	**3,876**	**490**
	M.T.	**2,167.706**	**628.944**	**197.214**	**521.614**	**45.850**	**18.202**	**14.862**	**2.471**	**228.800**	**13.186**	**8.335**

* Sacks: Flour A, 7,785; Bean A, 7,785; Bean B, 400.

AUSTRIA—

Summary of Clothing Deliveries

Table 221†

Account	Table No.	Shoes* (Pairs)	Stockings (Pairs)	Woolens (Yards)	Flannel (Yards)	Thread (Yards)	Thread (Reels)
Children's Relief‡	222	341,415	337,523	669,193	655,705	19,884,000	134,712
Commonwealth Fund, intelligentsia	...	5,732	11,960	20,913	......	......	3,000
Sale of surplus stock	...	......	......	277.5	......	......	......
Shortage and adjustments	...	328	1,166	1,329.75	......	......	288
Total deliveries	...	**347,475**	**350,649**	**721,713.25**	**655,705**	**19,884,000**	**138,000**

† See Table 214.
* Including laces.

‡ Cloth and accessories itemized here were used in the manufacture clothing outfits itemized in detail in Table 222.

.R.A. Warehouses and A.R.A.-European Children's Fund

econstruction Period, 1919–1924

Milk				Miscellaneous Foods								
Evap., Cond. Case	Powdered M.T.	Cocoa M.T.	Sugar M.T.	Corned Beef Case	Salmon Case	Herring Keg	Canned Fish Case	Dried Fruit M.T.	Codliver Oil M.T.	Misc. Sacks No.	Total Metric Tons	Total Value
280	.....	......	......	...	....	...	....	....	....	....	....	....
...	.....	......	......	...	....	...	....	....	....	....	....	....
...	.....	......	......	...	....	...	....	....	....	....	....	....
24	.....	......	......	...	....	...	....	....	....	....	....	....
...	.....	......	......	...	....	...	....	....	....	....	....	....
...	.....	......	......	...	....	...	....	....	....	....	....	....
2,146	.....	......	9.892	...	....	...	....	....	....	....	....	....
170	.....	.207	10.418	...	....	...	....	....	....	....	....	....
155	.....	8.020	.035	...	....	...	....	....	....	....	....	....
204	.....	10.180	10.030	...	....	...	....	....	....	....	....	....
10,889	.....	10.506	41.582	20	....	...	....	....	....	....	....	....
5,518	.....	8.037	32.428	61	....	...	....	....	....	540	....	....
3,887	.....	22.153	.178	1	....	...	....	....	....	....	....	....
123	.....	.497	2.653	69	85	...	....	....	....	1,800	....	....
2,275	.....	.030	35.113	748	1,347	370	380	....	....	13,630	....	....
1,390	.....	2.094	67.312	...	....	...	....	17.746	.001	....	....	....
1,387	.....	1.965	15.400	...	....	...	....	....	....	....	....	....
3,440	.....	6.927	42.291	...	....	...	....	....	....	....	....	....
2,233	.....	6.733	36.106	...	....	...	....	....	....	....	....	....
1,098	7.024	3.061	34.527	278	....	...	....	....	....	....	....	....
434	13.446	10.801	41.502	...	....	...	....	....	....	....	....	....
1,424	10.195	8.717	52.127	...	....	...	....	....	....	....	....	....
720	5.816	5.749	25.864	...	....	...	....	....	....	....	....	....
783	12.643	4.792	19.632	...	....	...	....	....	....	....	....	....
886	4.183	2.965	19.022	...	....	...	....	....	....	....	....	....
1,564	2.313	3.218	23.368	...	....	...	....	....	....	....	....	....
2,795	.....	14.042	73.085	...	....	...	....	....	....	....	....	....
2,904	.....	16.127	85.726	...	....	...	....	....	....	....	....	....
955	.....	7.106	30.258	...	....	...	....	....	....	....	....	....
730	.....	7.238	74.155	...	....	...	....	....	....	....	....	....
88	.....	.696	7.297	...	....	...						
48,502	**55.620**	**161.861**	**790.001**	**1,177**	**1,432**	**370**	**380**	**17.746**	**.001**	**15,970***	....	....
94.018	**55.620**	**161.861**	**790.001**	**38.424**	**31.188**	**14.266**	**5.009**	**17.746**	**.001**	**3.713**	**6,789.191**	**$1,175,347.98**
10,177	.....	......	......	...	....	...	....	....	....	....	....	....
93.882	.....	......	......	...	....	...	....	....	....	....	1,024.042	289,222.50
38,325	.....	......	......	**1,177**	**1,432**	**370**	**380**	......	....	**15,970**	....	....
00.136	**55.620**	**161.861**	**790.001**	**38.424**	**31.188**	**14.266**	**5.009**	**17.746**	**.001**	**3.713**	**5,765.149**	**$ 886,125.48**

.R.A.-European Children's Fund

econstruction Period, 1919–1924

Needles (No.)	Underwear (Suits)	Buttons (No.)	Snap Fasteners (Pairs)	Hooks and Eyes (Pairs)	Trousers Buckles (No.)	Woolen Jackets (No.)	Lining (Yards)	Cotton Tape (Yards)	Total Metric Tons	Total Value
197,200	.....	2,974,176	141,696	177,984	84,960	664	126.379	40,320	830.0	$1,441,946.53
5,000	11,352½	122,112	12,096	6,912	8,784	...	38,039	.....	31.8	62,475.26
......	....	......	......	......	.....	...	......	.....	.1	101.26
......	....	......	......	......	.....	...	858	.....	.....	..........§
202,200	**11,352½**	**3,096,288**	**153,792**	**184,896**	**93,744**	**664**	**165,276**	**40,320**	**861.9**	**$1,504,523.05**

§ Weight and value included in Commonwealth Fund and Children's
lief deliveries.

Table 222

Detail by Programs and Provinces of Clothing Deliverie

Program and Province	Program	Shoes (Pairs)	Stockings (Pairs)	Overcoats (Each)	Caps (Each)
A—Program					
Winter 1919–1920	1	100,056	99,528	100,680	2,553
Winter 1920–1921	2	102,037	100,500	......	....
Winter 1921–1922	3	139,322†	137,495	......	....
Total deliveries	..	**341,415**	**337,523**	**100,680**	**2,553**
					DETAI
B—Province					
Lower Austria (including Vienna)	1	68,038	67,679	68,462	1,737
Lower Austria (including Vienna)	2	69,032	67,408	......	....
Lower Austria (including Vienna)	3	86,820	85,595	......	....
Total	..	**223,890**	**220,682**	**68,462**	**1,737**
Upper Austria	1	8,405	8,360	8,457	214
Upper Austria	2	8,400	8,566	......	....
Upper Austria	3	12,600	12,458	......	....
Total	..	**29,405**	**29,384**	**8,457**	**214**
Salzburg	1	4,102	4,081	4,128	105
Salzburg	2	4,100	4,285	......	....
Salzburg	3	7,000	6,922	......	....
Total	..	**15,202**	**15,288**	**4,128**	**105**
Tyrol	1	3,802	3,782	3,826	97
Tyrol	2	3,641	3,738	......	....
Tyrol	3	7,000	6,922	......	....
Total	..	**14,443**	**14,442**	**3,826**	**97**
Vorarlberg	1	1,501	1,493	1,510	38
Vorarlberg	2	1,500	1,558	......	....
Vorarlberg	3	2,800	2,769	......	....
Total	..	**5,801**	**5,820**	**1,510**	**38**
Carinthia	1	2,802	2,787	2,819	71
Carinthia	2	2,958	3,064	......	....
Carinthia	3	7,000	6,919	......	....
Total	..	**12,760**	**12,770**	**2,819**	**71**
Styria	1	11,406	11,346	11,478	291
Styria	2	12,400	11,881	......	....
Styria	3	16,102	15,910	......	....
Total	..	**39,908**	**39,137**	**11,478**	**291**
Samples	2	**6**	......	......	....
Total deliveries	..	**341,415**	**337,523**	**100,680**	**2,553**

† See Table 223 for further detail on internal deliveries of shoes on third program.

* Made from surplus lining and issued in Vienna only, due to sm number available.

.R.A.-European Children's Fund

r Children's Relief—Reconstruction Period, 1919–1924

BOYS'			GIRLS'				
Suits (Each)	Shirts (Each)	Underwear (Suits)	Dresses (Each)	Blouses (Each)	Underwear (Suits)	Aprons (Each)	Bloomers (Each)
......	......	......	1,614	......	.....	.....	.....
......	154,525	110,230	......	107,715	82,165	.....	.....
92,273	......	1,140	48,180	......	17,488	10,659	17,488
92,273	**154,525**	**111,370**	**49,794**	**107,715**	**99,653**	**10,659**	**17,488**
F INTERNAL DELIVERIES							
......	......	......	1,097	......	.....	.....	.....
......	101,806	74,956	......	74,410	54,965	.....	.....
63,393	......	775	32,335	......	11,892	10,659*	17,488*
63,393	**101,806**	**75,731**	**33,432**	**74,410**	**66,857**	**10,659**	**17,488**
......	......	......	136	......	.....	.....	.....
......	13,842	9,259	......	8,474	6,898	.....	.....
6,932	......	96	3,802	......	1,469	.....	.....
6,932	**13,842**	**9,355**	**3,938**	**8,474**	**8,367**	.....	.....
......	......	......	66	......	.....	.....	.....
......	6,713	4,519	......	4,122	3,361	.....	.....
3,849	......	47	2,114	......	717	.....	.....
3,849	**6,713**	**4,566**	**2,180**	**4,122**	**4,078**	.....	.....
......	......	......	61	......	.....	.....	.....
......	5,927	4,189	......	3,692	3,003	.....	.....
3,849	......	43	2,114	......	664	.....	.....
3,849	**5,927**	**4,232**	**2,175**	**3,692**	**3,667**	.....	.....
......	......	......	24	......	.....	.....	.....
......	2,402	1,653	......	1,513	1,232	.....	.....
1,539	......	20	843	......	257	.....	.....
1,539	**2,402**	**1,673**	**867**	**1,513**	**1,489**	.....	.....
......	......	......	45	......	.....	.....	.....
......	5,827	3,086	......	3,968	3,347	.....	.....
3,849	......	45	2,114	......	590	.....	.....
3,849	**5,827**	**3,131**	**2,159**	**3,968**	**3,937**	.....	.....
......	......	......	185	......	.....	.....	.....
......	18,008	12,568	......	11,536	9,359	.....	.....
8,862	......	114	4,858	......	1,899	.....	.....
8,862	**18,008**	**12,682**	**5,043**	**11,536**	**11,258**	.....	.....
......	......	......	......	......	.....	.....	.....
92,273	**154,525**	**111,370**	**49,794**	**107,715**	**99,653**	**10,659**	**17,488**

Table 223

Detail by Provinces of Internal Deliveries

Province	Size 11	Size 11½	Size 12	Size 13	Size 1
Vienna and Lower Austria	5,231	2,700	5,710	5,638	8,285
Upper Austria	567	567	819	819	1,197
Salzburg	315	315	455	455	665
Tyrol	315	315	455	455	665
Vorarlberg	126	126	182	182	266
CARINTHIA					
Klagenfurt	126	126	182	182	266
Villach	95	95	136	136	200
St. Veit-on-Glan	63	63	91	91	133
Wolfsberg	15	16	23	23	33
Lienz-in-Tyrol	16	15	23	23	33
STYRIA					
Graz	352	352	508	508	742
Muerzzuschlag	72	72	104	104	151
Bruck-on-Mur	57	57	83	83	121
Donawitz	91	91	132	132	193
Zeltweg	62	62	90	90	131
Steinach	34	34	49	49	72
Selztal	57	57	81	81	119
Total	**7,594**	**5,063**	**9,123**	**9,051**	**13,272**

* Space will not permit the quotation of complete detail for all clothing deliveries. Since Austria is the first one of the countries appearing in the Appendix, to which clothing for children was delivered, this table covering the distribution of shoes delivered on third program is quoted as evidence of the detail manner in which the records were kept for each article issued. This applies not only to Austria but in ea country where operations were carried on under the supervision of t ARAECF. Individual receipts, supporting this table, were signed each child as the articles of clothing were issued.

AUSTRIA-

Detail of Internal Deliveries for Children's Reli

(Tables 22

Table 224

Province of LOWER AUSTRI

Receipt No.	Zone Warehouse	Date of Receipt	Flour	Rice	Beans, Peas	Corn Grits
Series 1		1919				
4	Vienna	Aug. 1	170.671	....	14.698	....
8	Vienna	Aug. 15	438.955	12.319	125.060	....
	Total for August	....	**609.626**	**12.319**	**139.758**	....
9	Vienna	Aug.-Oct.	643.094	394.464	326.810	....
16	Vienna	November	632.823	127.870	106.655	....
24	Vienna	December	....	....	87.355	....
28	Vienna	Sept.-Jan.	....	....	....	....
		1920				
29	Vienna	Jan. 1-7	75.515	....	....	....
30	Vienna	Jan. 8-14	150.426	....	....	....
31	Vienna	Jan. 15-21	15.165	....	....	....
32	Vienna	Jan. 22-31	15.350	31.933	.183	....
	Total for January	....	**256.456**	**31.933**	**.183**	....
40	Vienna	Feb. 1-7	70.045	....	24.710	....
41	Vienna	Feb. 8-14	....	....	....	....
42	Vienna	Feb. 15-21	37.374	31.581	.250	....
43	Vienna	Feb. 22-29	140.500	21.370	69.004	....
	Total for February	....	**247.919**	**52.951**	**93.964**	....

..R.A.-European Children's Fund

' Shoes—Reconstruction Period, 1919–1924

Number of Pairs Receipted for								
Size 2	Size 3½	Size 4	Size 5	Size 6	Size 7	Size 8	Size 9	Total Pairs
8,275	10,825	11,018	7,791	7,892	6,773	5,115	1,567	86,820
1,197	1,575	1,575	1,134	1,134	1,008	756	252	12,600
665	875	875	630	630	560	420	140	7,000
665	875	875	630	630	560	420	140	7,000
266	350	350	252	252	224	168	56	2,800
266	350	350	252	252	224	168	56	2,800
200	262	262	189	189	168	126	42	2,100
133	175	175	126	126	112	84	28	1,400
33	44	44	32	31	28	21	7	350
33	44	44	31	32	28	21	7	350
742	976	976	702	702	625	468	156	7,809
151	200	200	142	142	128	96	32	1,594
121	159	159	114	114	102	76	25	1,271
193	254	254	183	183	162	122	40	2,030
131	173	173	125	125	111	83	27	1,383
72	95	95	68	68	60	45	15	756
119	157	157	114	114	100	76	27	1,259
13,262	**17,389**	**17,582**	**12,515**	**12,616**	**10,973**	**8,265**	**2,617**	**139,322**

.R.A. and A.R.A.-European Children's Fund

om Zone Warehouses—Reconstruction Period, 1919–1924
1, Inclusive)
Jiederösterreich)

Commodities in Net Metric Tons of 1,000 Kilograms or 2,204.6 Pounds								
	Milk							
Pork Products	Evaporated	Condensed	Cocoa	Sugar	Miscellaneous Food	Soap	Coal	Total Tons
17.702	....	69.924	17.034	54.835	.775	....	....	....
31.216	....	330.228	74.258	218.855	27.636	....	....	....
48.918	....	**400.152**	**91.292**	**273.690**	**28.411**	....	....	**1,604.166**
123.012	894.902	....	122.272	319.151	2.650	....	....	**2,826.355**
50.070	101.662	....	....	20.305	....	....	....	**1,039.385**
27.513	....	....	....	25.125	....	....	....	**139.993**
....	....	....	....	....	10.625	31.150	....	**41.775**
39.025	....	....	....	....	....	....	....	....
9.395	....	....	....	....	....	....	....	....
....	....	....	....	....	....	....	....	....
.086	65.480	....	10.420	11.765	....	....	....	....
48.506	**65.480**	....	**10.420**	**11.765**	....	....	....	**424.743**
....	1.950	....	....	12.025	....	....	....	....
....	11.394	....	6.687	....	....	....	....	....
....	39.754	....	2.955	14.536	....	....	....	....
20.996	164.343	....	3.987	22.005	....	2.544	....	....
20.996	**217.441**	....	**13.629**	**48.566**	....	**2.544**	....	**698.010**

[*Continued on next page*]

Table 224—*Continued*

Receipt No.	Zone Warehouse	Date of Receipt	Flour	Rice	Beans, Peas	Corn Grits
Series 1		1920				
53	Vienna	Mar. 1-7	84.220	15.045	1.480	....
54	Vienna	Mar. 8-14	46.993	26.225	50.380	....
55	Vienna	Mar. 15-21	123.835	15.000	18.416	....
56	Vienna	Mar. 22-31	176.065	52.140	52.155	....
	Total for March	....	**431.113**	**108.410**	**122.431**	....
69	Vienna	Apr. 22-30	218.767	11.820	47.246	....
70	Vienna	Apr. 15-21	85.185	19.795	22.970	....
71	Vienna	Apr. 8-14	115.135	59.000	36.100	....
72	Vienna	Apr. 1-7	85.830	17.345	28.055	....
	Total for April	....	**504.917**	**107.960**	**134.371**	....
73	Vienna	May 1-7	59.563	12.755	....	....
74	Vienna	May 8-14	110.581	19.260	48.527	....
75	Vienna	May 15-21	122.115	39.555	38.655	....
76	Vienna	May 22-31	109.355	27.455	10.855	....
	Total for May	....	**401.614**	**99.025**	**98.037**	....
95	Vienna	June 1-7	87.170	21.890	37.020	....
96	Vienna	June 8-14	99.605	58.545	49.095	....
97	Vienna	June 15-21	106.170	....	24.570	....
98	Vienna	June 22-30	127.795	14.075	23.115	....
	Total for June	....	**420.740**	**94.510**	**133.800**	....
106	Vienna	July 1-7	119.270	14.510	32.220	....
107	Vienna	July 8-14	108.065	58.380	76.830	....
108	Vienna	July 15-21	130.406	32.309	61.639	....
109	Vienna	July 22-31	109.350	49.330	....	....
	Total for July	....	**467.091**	**154.529**	**170.689**	....
117	Vienna	Aug. 1-7	21.055	17.660	....	....
118	Vienna	Aug. 8-14	39.283	34.522	....	....
119	Vienna	Aug. 15-21	61.070	32.600	11.490	....
120	Vienna	Aug. 22-31	195.976	9.935	....	....
	Total for August	....	**317.384**	**94.717**	**11.490**	....
127	Vienna	Sept. 1-7	70.760	....	9.950	....
128	Vienna	Sept. 8-14	.935	....	70.730	....
129	Vienna	Sept. 15-21	49.512	26.085	77.750	....
130	Vienna	Sept. 22-30	14.845	47.765	28.265	....
131	Vienna	September	24.728	20.826	26.308	....
	Total for September	....	**160.780**	**94.676**	**213.003**	....
138	Vienna	Oct. 1-7	55.367	15.087	51.435	....
139	Vienna	Oct. 8-14	70.655	19.210	29.105	....
140	Vienna	Oct. 15-21	111.997	....	....	....
141	Vienna	Oct. 22-31	....	.102	.433	....
	Total for October	....	**238.019**	**34.399**	**80.973**	....
Series 2						
1	Vienna	Nov. 1-7	61.315	....	19.645	....
2	Vienna	Nov. 8-14	80.645	13.915	47.745	....
3	Vienna	Nov. 15-21	99.430	20.495	10.240	....
4	Vienna	Nov. 22-30	94.025	38.287	30.693	....
	Total for November	....	**335.415**	**72.697**	**108.323**	....
11	Vienna	Dec. 1-6	109.419	17.217	....	....
12	Vienna	Dec. 7-13	71.003	6.555	80.745	....
13	Vienna	Dec. 14-20	47.127	21.921	....	....
14	Vienna	Dec. 21-31	219.856	67.600	45.925	....
15	Vienna	Dec. 14	25.139	6.182	24.206	....
	Total for December	....	**472.544**	**119.475**	**150.876**	....

ıternal Deliveries
OWER AUSTRIA

Commodities in Net Metric Tons of 1,000 Kilograms or 2,204.6 Pounds

Pork Products	Milk		Cocoa	Sugar	Miscellaneous Food	Soap	Coal	Total Tons
	Evaporated	Condensed						
15.940	48.015	....	2.100	27.490	....	7.448	....	....
5.644	76.078	....	13.296	....	....	....	....	....
33.871	59.699	....	8.096	....	....	....	....	....
....	23.610	....	....	22.280	....	....	....	....
55.455	**207.402**	....	**23.492**	**49.770**	....	**7.448**	....	**1,005.521**
16.959	10.823	34.548	....	15.095	....	....	....	....
....	14.584	....	11.117	.617	....	....	....	....
11.719	90.518	....	6.345	14.860	....	....	....	....
....	68.651	....	....	13.840	....	....	....	....
28.678	**184.576**	**34.548**	**17.462**	**44.412**	....	....	....	**1,056.924**
8.939	34.500	....	4.611	11.675	....	....	....	....
8.528	51.214	....	3.670	15.860	....	....	....	....
9.459	....	53.861	....	18.175	....	....	....	....
13.890	58.389	68.670	10.017	13.540	....	....	....	....
40.816	**144.103**	**122.531**	**18.298**	**59.250**	....	....	....	**983.674**
13.379	27.986	44.370	....	12.940	....	....	....	....
14.120	18.049	74.840	13.454	18.420	....	....	....	....
7.777	31.609	13.822	.887	18.055	....	....	....	....
8.300	5.865	43.583	3.784	11.555	....	....	....	....
43.576	**83.509**	**176.615**	**18.125**	**60.970**	....	....	....	**1,031.845**
9.112	4.043	35.892	11.768	8.845	....	....	200.300	....
15.177	....	37.246	....	11.425	....	....	187.200	....
5.598	57.509	39.433	2.666	18.272	2.135	....	....	....
....	20.966	30.409	9.231	30.970	....	....	....	....
29.887	**82.518**	**142.980**	**23.665**	**69.512**	**2.135**	....	**387.500**	**1,530.506**
11.553	....	27.458	....	....	16.014	....	....	....
....	31.578	10.203	.808	....	....	....	....	....
15.072	55.571	27.056	3.996	....	....	....	....	....
11.533	28.992	....	6.720	19.600	....	....	....	....
38.158	**116.141**	**64.717**	**11.524**	**19.600**	**16.014**	....	....	**689.745**
....	37.630	....	....	14.890	....	....	....	....
6.449	....	50.369	....	11.770	....	....	....	....
16.367	11.577	7.530	6.565	....	....	....	....	....
....	19.073	....	....	14.390	....	....	....	....
11.203	....	36.058	3.222	14.457	....	....	....	....
34.019	**68.280**	**93.957**	**9.787**	**55.507**	....	....	....	**730.009**
....	....	39.928	5.015	14.765	....	....	....	....
....	....	24.902	7.169	7.490	....	....	....	....
....	....	2.452	....	....	....	....	....	....
11.306	....	.452	....	9.870	....	....	....	....
11.306	....	**67.734**	**12.184**	**32.125**	....	....	....	**476.740**
9.263	....	....	....	5.870	....	....	....	....
12.885	....	17.828	9.891	6.270	....	....	....	....
....	....	31.600	....	9.445	....	....	....	....
11.077	....	26.543	4.898	30.156	....	....	....	....
33.225	....	**75.971**	**14.789**	**51.741**	....	....	....	**692.161**
13.270	61.957	....	6.913	....	5.588	10.943	....	....
6.962	13.335	....	6.594	10.519	....	9.563	....	....
8.961	28.850	....	3.154	12.548	....	4.642	....	....
12.176	100.062	....	9.798	24.526	....	....	....	....
2.015	24.211	....	1.272	2.488	....	....	....	....
43.384	**228.415**	....	**27.731**	**50.081**	**5.588**	**25.148**	....	**1,123.242**

[*Continued on next page*]

Table 224—*Continued*

Receipt No.	Zone Warehouse	Date of Receipt	Flour	Rice	Beans, Peas	Corn Grits
Series 2		1921				
19	Vienna	Jan. 1–7	37.676	11.888	59.597	....
20	Vienna	Jan. 8–14	115.452	17.070	....	....
21	Vienna	Jan. 15–21	42.646	24.364	64.547	....
22	Forwarded from Linz	Jan. 21	44.235	10.710	11.455	....
23	Vienna	Jan. 22–31	125.208	....	22.276	....
	Total for January	....	**365.217**	**64.032**	**157.875**	....
30	Vienna	Feb. 1–4	....	....	13.051	....
31	Vienna	Feb. 5–11	72.488	40.840	31.479	....
32	Vienna	Feb. 12–18	194.872	15.440	2.177	....
33	Vienna	Feb. 19–25	55.214	24.565	34.903	....
34	Vienna	Feb. 26–28	45.216	....	6.939	....
35	Forwarded from Linz	Feb. 19–25	38.686	11.177	8.904	....
	Total for February	....	**406.476**	**92.022**	**97.453**	....
42	Vienna	Mar. 1–4	26.728	15.041	27.949	....
43	Vienna	Mar. 5–11	94.326	24.837	42.749	....
44	Vienna	Mar. 12–18	87.261	31.712	43.803	....
45	Vienna	Mar. 19–25	41.051	....	....	....
46	Vienna	Mar. 26–31	292.330	....	33.549	....
47	Forwarded from Linz	Mar. 1–25	3.537	1.105	1.391	....
	Total for March	....	**545.233**	**72.695**	**149.441**	....
52	Vienna	Apr. 1	3.773	....	....	....
53	Vienna	Apr. 2–8	11.321	40.891	13.263	....
54	Vienna	Apr. 9–15	65.007	65.396	45.031	....
55	Vienna	Apr. 16–22	148.641	26.875	....	....
56	Vienna	Apr. 23–30	170.534	15.395	30.741	....
57	Forwarded from Linz	Apr. 1–30	49.628	13.987	16.801	....
	Total for April	....	**448.904**	**162.544**	**105.836**	....
64	Vienna	May 1–6	11.633	29.373	30.244	....
65	Vienna	May 7–13	49.289	32.354	47.758	....
66	Vienna	May 14–20	69.595	37.243	24.128	....
67	Forwarded from Linz	May 1–20	60.080	26.200	....	....
68	Vienna	May 21–27	61.998	40.533	23.621	....
69	Vienna	May 28–31	288.966	18.710	....	....
	Total for May	....	**541.561**	**184.413**	**125.751**	....
78	Vienna	June 1–3	30.080	50.963	....	....
79	Vienna	June 4–10	18.575	32.803	....	....
80	Vienna	June 11–17	241.561	96.471	....	....
81	Vienna	June 18–24	51.120	....	13.995	....
82	Vienna	June 25–30	221.213	....	....	....
83	Forwarded from Linz	June 1–24	42.403	24.599	....	....
	Total for June	....	**604.952**	**204.836**	**13.995**	....
91	Vienna	July 1	17.135	15.309	....	....
92	Vienna	July 2–8	18.212	60.645	....	17.370
93	Vienna	July 9–15	262.920	45.035	....	32.958
94	Forwarded from Linz	July 1–22	7.191	26.233	....	17.331
95	Vienna	July 16–22	28.847	....	....	15.060
96	Vienna	July 23–31	43.045	....	....	....
	Total for July	....	**377.350**	**147.222**	....	**82.719**
104	Vienna	Aug. 1–5	27.800	29.545	....	16.800
105	Vienna	Aug. 6–12	84.609	....	....	....
106	Vienna	Aug. 13–19	8.680	179.751	.088	....
107	Vienna	Aug. 19	13.420	....	....	....
108	Vienna	Aug. 20–26	91.785	14.955	....	4.350
109	Vienna	Aug. 27–31	46.610	....	....	8.600
	Total for August	....	**272.904**	**224.251**	**.088**	**29.750**

ternal Deliveries

OWER AUSTRIA

Commodities in Net Metric Tons of 1,000 Kilograms or 2,204.6 Pounds

Pork Products	Milk		Cocoa	Sugar	Miscellaneous Food	Soap	Coal	Total Tons
	Evaporated	Condensed						
15.248	48.536	....	....	9.495	....	....	....	....
10.828	89.595	....	3.729	8.559	....	....	....	....
20.386	25.738	....	....	9.229	....	....	....	....
4.140	20.823	....	2.348	7.214	....	....	....	....
3.186	26.328	....	4.473	6.501	....	....	....	....
53.788	**211.020**	....	**10.550**	**40.998**	....	....	....	**903.480**
....	....	....	....	1.177	....	....	....	....
12.529	55.924	....	4.166	23.343	....	....	....	....
25.986	18.460	....	4.064	12.160	20.958	....	....	....
....	70.377	....	5.182	19.621	....	....	....	....
....	8.265	....	....	.852	....	....	....	....
3.975	16.551	....	2.032	5.856	....	....	....	....
42.490	**169.577**	....	**15.444**	**63.009**	**20.958**	....	....	**907.429**
13.368	....	7.810	13.208	2.453	....	....	....	....
10.208	....	71.542	....	29.349	....	....	....	....
10.038	....	41.335	....	21.512	....	....	....	....
24.690	41.185	13.366	3.353	13.099	....	....	....	....
15.100	11.322	....	....	16.273	....	....	511.000	....
1.831	....	1.029	....	.571	....	....	....	....
75.235	**52.507**	**135.082**	**16.561**	**83.257**	....	....	**511.000**	**1,641.011**
2.480	....	....	....	....	....	....	....	....
6.424	....	56.012	13.310	32.638	1.795	....	....	....
4.158	130.643	....	6.502	48.855	....	....	....	....
22.882	42.053	....	6.909	66.057	....	....	....	....
20.937	48.937	3.048	....	51.189	....	....	169.000	....
4.893	....	22.859	1,829	7.160	....	....	....	....
61.774	**221.633**	**81.919**	**28.550**	**205.899**	**1.795**	....	**169.000**	**1,487.854**
12.541	68.162	....	10.262	51.720	....	....	....	....
24.339	59.194	8.335	....	52.539	1.958	11.435	....	....
....	42.120	....	5.080	22.600	15.705	10.000	....	....
7.533	26.021	....	1.829	18.859	....	2.672	....	....
11.174	37.159	....	3.962	35.295	....	....	....	....
5.928	38.792	....	....	28.847	12.288	....	388.000	....
61.515	**271.448**	**8.335**	**21.133**	**209.860**	**29.951**	**24.107**	**388.000**	**1,866.074**
2.594	39.435	....	3.048	25.286	....	....	....	....
18.615	47.645	....	8.941	40.683	62.373	....	....	....
13.253	47.425	.021	10.160	18.545	19.149	....	....	....
9.743	69.908	....	10.160	44.603	24.378	....	....	....
16.351	23.410	....	....	57.533	17.815	....	220.000	....
4.543	22.532	....	1.524	19.436	8.861	....	....	....
65.099	**250.355**	**.021**	**33.833**	**206.086**	**132.576**	....	**220.000**	**1,731.753**
....	24.923	....	....	....	....	....	....	....
....	22.818	....	1.524	27.668	....	....	....	....
14.487	5.430	45.672	11.582	18.832	3.157	....	....	....
9.022	13.598	24.357	3.150	14.818	....	....	....	....
3.410	....	11.679	6.096	27.092	....	....	....	....
5.961	....	26.390	5.181	14.634	37.157	....	....	....
32.880	**66.769**	**108.098**	**27.533**	**103.044**	**40.314**	....	....	**985.929**
....	....	34.819	....	18.580	22.100	....	....	....
13.316	....	36.403	....	10.375	....	....	....	....
19.967	24.626	11.900	2.067	28.024	.441	32.927	....	....
....	....	31.250	....	....	....	5.442	....	....
....	....	3.986	....	....	....	....	....	....
13.384	....	22.170	....	....	....	....	....	....
46.667	**24.626**	**140.528**	**2.067**	**56.979**	**22.541**	**38.369**	....	**858.770**

[*Concluded on next page*]

Table 224—*Concluded*

Receipt No.	Zone Warehouse	Date of Receipt	Flour	Rice	Beans, Peas	Corn Grits
Series 2		1921				
121	Vienna	Sept. 10–16	.048	....	....	46.002
122	Vienna	Sept. 17–23	222.370	....	....	53.765
123	Vienna	Sept. 24–31	71.670	....	....	17.270
123a	Vienna	Sept. 1–9	....	....	....	....
	Total for September	....	**294.088**	....	....	**117.037**
129	Forwarded from Lager Burg	Oct. 1–14	....	....	....	....
130	Vienna	Oct. 15–21	....	....	....	....
131	Forwarded from Linz	Oct. 15–21	9.406	.363	....	12.525
132	Vienna	Oct. 22–28	20.000	....	....	....
133	Vienna	Oct. 29–31	....	....	....	....
	Total for October	....	**29.406**	**.363**	....	**12.525**
139	Vienna	Nov. 1–4	5.000	....	....	....
140	Vienna	Nov. 5–11	30.000	....	....	10.000
141	Vienna	Nov. 12–17	13.000	....	....	....
142	Vienna	Nov. 18–25	6.000	....	....	....
143	Vienna	Nov. 26–30	13.000	....	....	10.000
144	Forwarded from Linz	Nov. 30	11.422	....	....	7.140
	Total for November	....	**78.422**	....	....	**27.140**
151	Vienna	Dec. 2	30.000	....	....	10.000
152	Vienna	Dec. 3–9	65.555	....	....	14.600
153	Vienna	Dec. 10–16	26.500	....	....	7,200
154	Vienna	Dec. 17–23	58.800	....	....	12.500
155	Vienna	Dec. 24–31	30.400	....	....	14.672
	Total for December	....	**211.255**	....	....	**58.972**
Series 3		1922				
7	Forwarded from Linz	January	22.469	....	7.893	10.655
8	Vienna	January	153.211	10.445	18.364	26.491
	Total for January	....	**175.680**	**10.445**	**26.257**	**37.146**
12	Vienna	February	124.841	11.799	21.296	42.165
13	Vienna	March	183.895	18.797	32.395	59.193
20	Vienna	April	182.717	25.289	25.964	8.247
31	Vienna	May	256.155	19.545	40.906	97.902
32	Vienna	June	25.708	14.700	....	19.000
	Total Internal Deliveries for Lower Austria	....	**11,264.299***	**2,852.888**	**2,775.975**	**591.796**

* Of the 11,264.3 metric tons of flour, only 9,984.7 tons were used for child feeding. The difference, amounting to 1,279.6 metric tons, was accounted for by 800.0 tons being exchanged for 600.0 tons of sugar (Table 213) and 479.6 tons being shipped to Hungary. Of this latter amount, 98.0 tons came from A.R.A. stock and 381.6 tons from E.C.F supplies. These adjustments involve a change in the total tonnage use for child feeding, reducing this from 30,168.0 metric tons, as shown, t 28,888.4 metric tons.

AUSTRIA—

Table 225

Province of UPPER AUSTRI

Receipt No.	Zone Warehouse	Date of Receipt	Flour	Rice	Beans, Peas
Series 1		1919			
5	Linz	August 1	77.496	......	20.615
11	Linz	August–October	10.093	30.870	......
17	Linz	October–November	60.415	21.620	21.250
26	Linz	December	50.630	12.460	16.365
		1920			
33	Linz	January	42.263	10.200	......
44	Linz	February	21.985	4.140	7.240
57	Linz	March	......	11.968	22.747

ternal Deliveries
OWER AUSTRIA

Commodities in Net Metric Tons of 1,000 Kilograms or 2,204.6 Pounds

Pork Products	Milk		Cocoa	Sugar	Miscellaneous Food	Soap	Coal	Total Tons
	Evaporated	Condensed						
....	....	11.422	....	....	....	....	....	....
....	....	13.818	....	....	....	....	....	....
....	....	51.025	....	39.209	....	....	....	....
....	....	11.675	....	....	....	....	....	....
....	....	**81.940**	....	**39.209**	....	....	....	**532.274**
....	.146	....	....	....	....	....	....	....
....	1.424	13.184	....	....	....	....	....	....
1.072	....	19.642	.407	....	....	....	....	....
6.338	1.366	16.349	....	....	....	....	....	....
....	....	1.690	....	....	....	....	....	....
7.410	**2.936**	**50.865**	**.407**	....	....	....	....	**103.912**
6.647	....	16.820	....	....	....	....	....	....
9.924	.450	37.374	....	....	....	....	....	....
3.287	.734	20.354	....	....	....	....	....	....
6.008	.274	15.286	....	....	....	....	....	....
2.991	....	9.400	.674	....	....	....	....	....
3.319	10.625	....	.610	1.985	....	....	....	....
32.176	**12.083**	**99.234**	**1.284**	**1.985**	....	....	....	**252.324**
2.873	....	9.718	1.000	....	....	....	....	....
10.094	....	38.256	3.360	....	....	....	....	....
6.751	....	13.815	1.438	....	....	....	....	....
6.177	.268	21.604	2.148	5.200	....	....	....	....
2.890	.339	27.318	2.722	5.110	....	....	....	....
28.785	**.607**	**110.711**	**10.668**	**10.310**	....	....	....	**431.308**
3.696	1.002	....	1.422	9.200	....	....	....	....
24.991	18.277	76.942	9.633	36.108	....	....	....	....
28.687	**19.279**	**76.942**	**11.055**	**45.308**	....	....	....	**430.799**
18.714	85.459	.552	7.305	59.752	14.390	....	....	**386.273**
31.223	47.182	42.465	10.338	61.165	....	....	....	**486.653**
21.954	17.984	57.915	7.265	30.896	....	....	....	**378.231**
36.884	21.555	64.268	12.050	67.429	....	....	....	**616.694**
....	9.097	3.963	....	....	....	....	....	**72.468**
1,322.800	**3,878.546**	**2,242.043**	**630.713**	**2,476.756**	**327.948†**	**128.766**	**1,675.500**	**30,168.030‡**

† Codliver oil, 53.792; fruit, 50.665; corned beef, 33.643; chocolate, 16; salmon, 100.998; herring, 25.765; soup, 30.469. Total, 327.948.

‡ See first footnote. Net total to child feeding is 28,888.4.

ternal Deliveries
berösterreich)

Commodities in Net Metric Tons of 1,000 Kilograms or 2,204.6 Pounds

Corn Grits	Pork Products	Milk		Cocoa	Sugar	Miscellaneous Food	Soap	Total Tons
		Evaporated	Condensed					
......	2.061	50.032	......	20.094	38.780	.365	......	209.443
......	13.273	19.478	......	2.240	4.000	......	......	79.954
......	8.934	37.684	......	2.000	6.100	......	......	158.003
......	7.483	22.845	......	2.333	7.172	......	......	119.288
......	3.760	18.795	......	1.872	5.241	......	.054	82.185
......	1.517	7.140	......	3.046	3.441	......	......	48.509
......	5.430	21.810	......	.995	6.802	......	2.227	71.979

[*Continued on next page*]

AUSTRIA—

Table 225—*Continued*

Province o

Receipt No.	Zone Warehouse	Date of Receipt	Flour	Rice	Beans, Peas
Series 1		1920			
64	Linz	April	98.426	11.982	15.500
83	Linz	May	68.230	15.262	19.273
99	Linz	June	48.266	13.413	......
110	Linz	July	19.423	5.997	31.184
121	Linz	August	57.661	13.340	31.355
132	Linz	September	30.031	14.449	10.676
142	Linz	October	93.599	11.306	9.851
148	Linz	November	46.521	14.120	14.250
Series 2					
5	Linz	December	82.608	31.620	40.720
		1921			
24	Linz	January	100.392	18.981	24.054
36	Linz	February	95.190	18.280	23.080
48	Linz	March	16.105	3.070	5.120
58	Linz	April	42.361	20.318	33.176
70	Linz	May	65.352	14.500	......
84	Linz	June	97.138	46.876	......
97	Linz	July	92.252	37.378	......
110	Forwarded from Vienna	August	3.801	1.435	......
111	Linz	August	30.629	......	......
124	Linz	September	22.010	......	......
134	Linz	October	4.649	......	......
145	Linz	November	39.378	6.684	......
156	Linz	December	......	4.193	......
Series 3		1922			
6	Linz	January	29.327	8.348	10.651
11	Linz	February	42.068	......	1.359
14	Linz	March	43.436	......	6.319
21	Linz	April	12.023	......	......
30	Linz	May	2.597	.270	1.265
33	Linz	June	52.606	12.168	22.012
	Total Deliveries, Upper Austria	....	**1,598.961**	**415.248**	**388.062**

* Codliver oil, 7.465; fruits, 5.036; corned beef, .180; chocolate, 3.252; salmon, 9.469; soup, 7.458.

AUSTRIA—

Table 226

Province of CARINTHI

Receipt No.	Zone Warehouse	Date of Receipt	Flour	Rice	Beans, Peas
Series 1		1919			
3	St. Viet	August 1	13.083	......	10.225
13	St. Viet	Aug.-Oct.	25.060	8.105	8.130
20	St. Viet	Oct.-Nov.	14.500	8.395	.092
25	St. Viet	December	17.823	4.375	5.790
		1920			
39	St. Viet	January	16.310	3.870	3.185
50	St. Viet	February	15.600	1.845	4.815
60	St. Viet	March	......	4.793	8.200
67	St. Viet	April	40.821	4.797	6.200
77	St. Viet	May	14.609	......	.380
105	St. Viet	June	23.451	5.351	4.543
116	St. Viet	July	5.188	1.124	4.234
126	St. Viet	August	12.751	4.047	5.431
137	Forwarded from Lienz	September	36.837	4.572	6.065
147	St. Viet	October	2.698	4.857	5.106
153	Forwarded from Lienz	November	26.477	4.924	5.562
Series 2					
10	St. Viet	December	33.917	12.256	16.953
18	St. Viet	December	10.755	2.663	3.415

ernal Deliveries

PER AUSTRIA

Commodities in Net Metric Tons of 1,000 Kilograms or 2,204.6 Pounds

Corn Grits	Pork Products	Milk		Cocoa	Sugar	Miscellaneous Food	Soap	Total Tons
		Evaporated	Condensed					
......	4.389	21.491	......	.740	6.800	......	2.430	161.758
......	5.836	26.845	......	3.219	6.108	......	1.213	145.986
......	5.452	32.400	6.775	2.091	7.585	......	1.120	117.102
......	2.140	16.677	10.500	.985	4.334	......	1.120	92.360
......	6.026	25.658	13.853	2.582	8.357	1.743	1.120	161.695
......	7.435	......	16.811	2.763	11.508	7.458	1.120	101.651
......	15.539	......	29.380	3.014	5.384	......	.667	168.740
......	......	......	24.193	1.976	8.073	.183	......	109.316
......	8.175	......	56.252	5.258	17.130	......	......	241.763
......	7.762	31.434	......	3.466	12.411	......	......	198.500
......	8.787	27.180	......	3.454	10.824	3.012	......	189.807
......	1.736	15.873	......	.831	2.246	......	......	44.981
......	8.001	......	35.798	3.759	12.983	......	......	156.396
......	3.474	12.098	.019	.406	11.032	......	3.908	110.789
......	6.586	56.088	.019	3.759	36.780	12.721	......	259.967
22.459	12.465	9.924	13.173	5.182	5.216	......	......	198.049
......	1.017	1.312	......	.125	.352	.180	......	8.222
......	......	......	......	......	25.091	......	......	55.720
8.160	......	......	3.486	......	......	5.036	......	38.692
7.805	5.453	......	34.369	1.016	......	......	......	53.292
21.176	7.418	8.712	.057	2.438	5.123	......	......	90.986
......	.791	15.263	......	.813	4.967	......	......	26.027
18.106	9.663	23.784	......	3.454	29.600	2.162	......	135.095
.011	.153	8.274	......	......	......	......	......	51.865
6.753	4.147	23.232	.010	1.328	10.737	......	1.008	96.970
......	......	......	......	......	......	......	......	12.023
7.771	3.612	2.112	......	1.219	7.579	......	.567	26.992
......	1.980	......	......	......	......	......	......	88.766
92.241	**180.495**	**536.141**	**244.695**	**85.858**	**321.756**	**32.860***	**16.554**	**3,912.871**

ternal Deliveries

aernten)

Commodities in Net Metric Tons of 1,000 Kilograms or 2,204.6 Pounds

Corn Grits	Pork Products	Milk		Cocoa	Sugar	Miscellaneous Food	Soap	Total Tons
		Evaporated	Condensed					
......	2.050	11.552	......	3.120	4.900	.097	......	45.027
......	3.276	14.812	......	1.000	2.000	......	......	62.383
......	3.107	8.467	......	1.224	3.105	......	......	38.890
......	1.977	8.108	......	.829	2.470	......	......	41.372
......	2.000	7.815	......	.834	3.770	......	......	37.784
......	.300	3.919	......	.950	2.721	......	.393	30.543
......	2.064	8.606	......	......	......	......	......	23.663
......	1.576	8.535	......	.950	2.737	......	.213	65.829
......	1.381	5.906	......	......	1.648	......	.183	24.107
......	2.836	13.964	3.150	1.213	3.045	......	.186	57.739
......	.312	13.000	1.125	.100	.300	......	.181	25.564
......	.678	3.192	3.748	.208	.822	.879	.186	31.942
......	2.532	......	9.419	.383	2.645	......	.179	62.632
......	1.146	......	8.187	.401	1.427	......	.187	24.009
......	1.623	......	7.980	.736	3.133	......	......	50.435
......	5.663	......	23.295	2.124	7.659	......	......	101.867
......	1.150	4.876	......	.489	1.508	......	......	24.856

[*Continued on next page*]

Table 226—*Continued*

Receipt No.	Zone Warehouse	Date of Receipt	Flour	Rice	Beans, Peas
Series 2		1921			
29	Forwarded from Linz	January	29.906	7.250	7.861
41	Forwarded from Linz	February	20.525	7.658	9.546
51	St. Viet	March	4.975	......	......
61	Forwarded from Linz	April	65.872	7.765	8.825
77	Forwarded from Linz	May	20.939	18.284	......
90	Forwarded from Linz	June	34.194	17.853	......
103	Forwarded from Linz	July	57.654	18.840	......
119	Forwarded from Vienna	August	1.351	.488	......
120	Forwarded from Linz	August	......	......	......
128	Forwarded from Linz	September	27.502	.176	......
138	Forwarded from Linz	October	23.033	.316	......
150	Forwarded from Linz	November	23.726	2.089	......
157	Forwarded from Linz	December	3.023	......	......
Series 3		1922			
5	Forwarded from Linz	January	5.956	.450	5.670
16	St. Viet	March	24.978	......	2.740
26	Forwarded from Linz	April	11.556	.045	.586
28	St. Viet	May	3.212	......	......
37	St. Viet	June	10.080	1.181	1.816
	Total Deliveries for Carinthia	....	**678.362**	**158.369**	**135.370**

* Codliver oil, 2.834; salmon, 4.874; chocolate, 1.673; corned beef, .082; fruits, .216.

AUSTRIA-

Province of SALZBUR

Table 227

Receipt No.	Zone Warehouse	Date of Receipt	Flour	Rice	Beans, Peas
Series 1		1919			
6	Salzburg	August 1	19.352	......	10.560
10	Salzburg	Aug.-Oct.	7.500	10.540	......
19	Salzburg	Oct.-Nov.	18.390	4.150	3.980
27	Salzburg	December	19.655	4.840	6.320
		1920			
34	Salzburg	January	15.100	3.755	4.545
45	Salzburg	February	6.870	.850	1.690
58	Salzburg	March	......	3.589	6.340
65	Salzburg	April	29.570	4.600	4.650
82	Salzburg	May	33.740	4.444	6.374
100	Salzburg	June	11.271	3.892	4.551
111	Salzburg	July	1.000	3.048	4.124
122	Salzburg	August	13.513	3.641	7.221
133	Salzburg	September	35.695	9.562	11.347
143	Salzburg	October	6.772	6.035	6.901
149	Salzburg	November	43.477	5.742	6.874
Series 2					
6	Salzburg	December	5.526	15.351	19.815
16	Forwarded from Linz	December	19.850	......	......
		1921			
25	Forwarded from Linz	January	24.667	10.087	11.492
37	Forwarded from Linz	February	42.282	9.167	11.227
49	Flour Forwarded from Linz, balance from Vienna	March	19.622	.016	......
59	Forwarded from Linz	April	48.613	12.473	14.883
71	Salzburg	May	32.850	14.383	......
85	Forwarded from Linz	June	31.853	20.601	......
98	Forwarded from Linz	July	62.120	18.732	......
112	Forwarded from Vienna	August	2.330	.910	......
113	Forwarded from Linz	August	......	......	......
125	Forwarded from Linz	September	15.000	......	......
137	Forwarded from Linz	October	27.370	......	......
146	Forwarded from Linz	November	3.933	......	......

ternal Deliveries
ARINTHIA

Commodities in Net Metric Tons of 1,000 Kilograms or 2,204.6 Pounds

Corn Grits	Pork Products	Milk: Evaporated	Milk: Condensed	Cocoa	Sugar	Miscellaneous Food	Soap	Total Tons
......	1.153	11.424	......	1.457	3.673	......	......	62.724
......	3.948	14.655	......	1.423	4.738	1.016	......	63.509
......	......	......	......	......	......	......	......	4.975
......	3.919	......	12.971	1.524	4.795	......	......	105.671
......	4.151	29.467	......	1.626	12.820	......	2.117	89.404
......	3.238	11.940	......	1.320	15.128	6.547	......	90.220
12.123	6.807	32.290	......	3.150	16.342	......	......	147.206
......	.337	.477	......	.035	.127	.082	......	2.897
......	......	......	......	......	9.986	......	......	9.986
.509	.153	2.024	......	.102	......	.216	......	30.682
9.918	2.527	5.487	......	.407	3.418	......	......	45.106
10.165	3.915	7.267	......	1.219	9.964	......	......	58.345
......	......	......	......	......	......	......	......	3.023
8.187	3.974	11.569	......	1.727	12.197	.361	......	50.091
4.135	1.745	5.509	.010	.716	6.188	.362	.504	46.887
3.636	1.489	3.919	......	.508	3.876	.119	.304	26.038
......	......	......	......	......	......	......	......	3.212
......	1.816	......	......	......	.633	......	......	15.526
48.673	**72.843**	**248.780**	**69.885**	**29.775**	**147.775**	**9.679***	**4.633**	**1,604.144**

ternal Deliveries
alzburg)

Commodities in Net Metric Tons of 1,000 Kilograms or 2,204.6 Pounds

Corn Grits	Pork Products	Milk: Evaporated	Milk: Condensed	Cocoa	Sugar	Miscellaneous Food	Soap	Total Tons
......	1.031	17.421	......	5.916	17.042	....	....	71.322
......	5.100	7.762	......	1.000	3.350	....	....	35.252
......	1.253	9.263	......	....	......	....	....	37.036
......	2.900	8.846	......	....	......	....	....	42.561
......	1.665	7.651	......	....	1.850	....	....	34.566
......	.162	.394	......	.500	1.183	....	....	11.649
......	1.681	6.450	......	.718	2.040	....	.421	21.239
......	1.223	6.939	......	.715	2.240	....	.213	50.150
......	2.440	8.850	......	.936	2.837	....	.213	59.834
......	1.821	10.470	1.838	.650	2.035	....	.213	36.741
......	.909	5.002	3.281	.767	1.899	....	.213	20.243
......	1.249	8.793	4.800	.691	2.461	....	.213	42.582
......	3.684	......	17.602	1.850	6.469	.466	.213	86.888
......	3.576	......	10.125	1.279	3.233	....	.134	38.055
......	2.284	......	9.420	.940	2.475	....	....	71.212
......	6.911	......	27.225	2.315	8.866	....	....	86.009
......	......	......	......	....	......	....	....	19.850
......	3.614	15.168	......	1.860	4.932	....	....	71.820
......	3.861	16.579	......	1.727	5.222	1.218	....	91.283
......	.055	......	......	....	.082	....	....	19.775
......	5.280	......	21.129	2.235	6.223	....	....	110.836
......	3.018	14.675	......	1.422	11.068	....	1.869	79.285
......	3.382	19.571	......	1.219	14.927	6.396	....	97.949
11.610	6.276	30.263	......	2.642	14.483	....	....	146.126
......	.697	.785	......	.090	.213	.048	....	5.073
......	......	......	......	....	8.708	....	....	8.708
7.127	......	......	......	....	......	2.842	....	24.969
1.087	2.977	......	......	.711	......	....	....	32.145
11.858	4.538	10.843	......	1.727	12.672	....	....	45.571

[*Continued on next page*]

Province o

Table 227—*Continued*

Receipt No.	Zone Warehouse	Date of Receipt	Flour	Rice	Beans, Peas
Series 2		1922			
4	Forwarded from Linz	January	27.115	2.802	6.665
10	Salzburg	February	15.126	......	......
17	Salzburg	March	28.726	......	3.111
23	Salzburg	April	30.313	......	......
27	Salzburg	May	.673	.135	2.299
34	Salzburg	June	22.215	2.074	3.685
	Total Deliveries for Salzburg	....	**722.089**	**175.419**	**158.654**

* Codliver oil, 3.126; salmon, 4.723; chocolate, 1.673; corned beef, .048; fruits, 2.842.

AUSTRIA—

Province of STYRI

Table 228

Receipt No.	Zone Warehouse	Date of Receipt	Flour	Rice	Beans, Peas
Series 1		1919			
1	Graz	August 1	165.735	3.500	10.865
15	Graz	Aug.-Nov.	30.372	46.505	......
23	Graz	December	14.950	4.787	6.270
		1920			
35	Graz	January	10.492	.252	11.290
36	Graz	January	45.075	16.221	12.913
49	Graz	February	24.868	6.395	18.134
62	Graz	March	170.235	17.970	33.104
63	Graz	April	14.206	18.011	13.606
78	Graz	May	103.927	23.660	24.832
104	Graz	June	76.691	14.820	21.797
115	Graz	July	45.210	15.636	19.469
125	Graz	August	75.364	18.625	33.242
136	Graz	September	64.063	17.687	19.169
146	Graz	October	123.100	22.180	16.905
152	Graz	November	50.123	17.124	26.301
Series 2					
9	Graz	Dec.-Jan. '21	109.771	40.951	55.356
17	Graz	December	15.070	......	......
		1921			
28	Forwarded from Linz	January	133.039	50.326	60.954
40	Forwarded from Linz	February	72.592	9.024	12.034
50	Forwarded from Linz	March	9.841	......	......
60	Forwarded from Linz	April	145.311	13.263	12.947
75	Forwarded from Linz	May	109.492	48.452	......
76	Forwarded from Vienna	May	4.374	1.320	.897
88	Forwarded from Vienna	June	4.013	1.204	.786
89	Forwarded from Linz	June	139.525	54.793	......
100	Forwarded from Linz	July	220.038	54.856	......
101	Forwarded from Vienna	July	......	......	......
117	Forwarded from Vienna	August	1.745	.662	......
118	Forwarded from Linz	August	......	......	......
149	Forwarded from Linz	November	53.762	......	......
Series 3		1922			
2	Forwarded from Linz	January	9.257	......	14.275
9	Graz	February	15.783	......	......
18	Forwarded from Linz	March	61.546	......	9.612
22	Forwarded from Linz	April	72.639	......	1.361
29	Graz	May	......	......	......
38	Graz	June	10.100	1.093	1.805
	Total Deliveries to Styria	....	**2,202.309**	**519.317**	**437.924**

* Codliver oil, 9.995; corned beef, .838; herring, 1.120; salmon, 14,269; chocolate, 4.345.

ternal Deliveries
LZBURG

Corn Grits	Pork Products	Milk: Evaporated	Milk: Condensed	Cocoa	Sugar	Miscellaneous Food	Soap	Total Tons
		Commodities in Net Metric Tons of 1,000 Kilograms or 2,204.6 Pounds						
12.607	2.897	22.673	......	2.134	18.414	1.320	.....	96.627
......	......	......	......	.....	......	.....	.....	15.126
5.784	2.397	8.949	.010	.820	9.830	.....	.504	60.131
......	......	......	......	.....	......	.....	.....	30.313
4.499	2.267	7.403	.095	.780	3.270	.122	.363	21.906
......	2.277	......	......	.....	.546	.....	.....	30.797
54.572	**81.425**	**244.750**	**95.525**	**35.644**	**168.570**	**12.412***	**4.569**	**1,753.629**

ternal Deliveries
teiermark)

Corn Grits	Pork Products	Milk: Evaporated	Milk: Condensed	Cocoa	Sugar	Miscellaneous Food	Soap	Total Tons
		Commodities in Net Metric Tons of 1,000 Kilograms or 2,204.6 Pounds						
......	12.075	115.033	......	37.600	75.100	.626	.....	420.534
......	10.368	73.805	......	10.000	16.220	......	.....	187.270
......	2.265	9.008	......	.924	2.580	......	.....	40.784
......	1.115	7.658	......	......	.536	......	..... }	
......	6.350	21.861	......	2.706	8.571	1.631	6.029 }	152.700
......	3.087	14.846	......	1.621	5.344	......	.....	74.295
......	8.102	33.038	......	3.334	10.298	......	1.883	277.964
......	7.123	33.134	......	3.345	10.209	......	.960	100.594
......	13.203	44.032	......	2.349	13.706	......	1.013	226.722
......	6.936	51.086	7.556	1.896	10.163	......	.933	191.878
......	6.618	29.207	14.616	3.052	6.917	......	.933	141.658
......	7.500	39.866	17.016	2.881	11.366	1.721	.933	208.514
......	9.732	......	41.800	2.824	15.352	......	.933	171.560
......	8.535	......	28.241	3.985	10.401	......	.....	213.347
......	6.252	......	29.177	3.770	8.510	......	.453	141.710
......	19.539	......	81.525	6.683	25.562	......	.....	339.387
......	......	......	......	......	......	......	.....	15.070
......	21.576	89.556	......	9.207	15.917	......	.....	380.575
......	4.266	10.937	......	1.727	15.576	3.012	.....	129.168
......	......	......	......	......	......	......	.....	9.841
......	5.202	1.720	14.936	3.454	12.214	.188	.....	209.235
......	11.288	49.319	......	4.572	36.288	......	5.105	264.516
......	.472	2.540	......	.225	.777	.272	.....	10.877
......	.755	.454	......	.200	.708	1.134	.....	9.254
......	9.770	48.268	......	4.267	39.854	13.950	.....	310.427
31.096	17.186	89.037	......	6.626	44.791	4.345	.....	467.975
......	......	......	......	......	......	.607	.....	.607
......	.470	.630	......	.060	.161	.076	.....	3.804
......	......	.007	......	......	16.600	......	.....	16.607
39.509	9.774	2.036	......	.508	9.347	......	1.102	116.038
19.784	12.076	36.875	......	5.489	30.630	2.765	.....	131.151
......	......	......	......	......	......	......	.....	15.783
12.551	6.674	20.880	.005	.312	19.827	......	.720	132.127
2.821	......	5.595	.010	.008	4.033	.240	.538	87.245
......	1.480	......	......	......	......	......	.....	1.480
......	1.314	......	......	......	......	......	.....	14.312
105.761	**231.103**	**830.428**	**234.882**	**123.625**	**477.558**	**30.567***	**21.535**	**5,215.009**

Table 229

Receipt No.	Zone Warehouse	Date of Receipt	Flour	Rice	Beans, Peas
Series 1		1919			
2	Innsbrück	August 1	40.780	......	20.830
12	Innsbrück	Aug.-Oct.	12.640	23.535	......
18	Innsbrück	Oct.-Nov.	34.560	13.730	12.700
21	Tirol u Lienz	December	37.146	9.430	11.857
21	From Bregenz	December	......	......	......
		1920			
37	Tirol u Lienz	January	.342	3.412	6.505
37	From Bregenz	January	......	......	......
46	Innsbrück	February	......	......	3.400
48	Forwarded from Lienz	February	.610	.220	.190
59	Tirol u Lienz	March	......	8.405	28.840
68	Tirol u Lienz	April	72.707	9.305	12.018
80	Forwarded from Lienz	May	2.268	......	.020
81	Innsbrück	May	28.300	5.099	7.605
101	Innsbrück	June	24.761	8.036	10.676
102	Forwarded from Lienz	June	.187	......	.251
112	Innsbrück	July	22.674	5.766	8.857
113	Forwarded from Lienz	July	......	.137	.190
123	Innsbrück	August	34.206	7.708	4.306
134	Innsbrück	September	18.760	5.023	18.947
144	Innsbrück	October	24.966	3.898	1.232
150	Innsbrück	November	18.650	4.625	3.629
Series 2					
7	Innsbrück	December	57.320	13.552	17.326
		1921			
26	Forwarded from Linz	January	32.428	7.920	10.113
38	Forwarded from Linz	February	32.886	7.890	10.100
63	Forwarded from Linz	April	49.553	12.614	15.401
72	Forwarded from Vienna	May	6.009	1.803	1.217
73	Forwarded from Linz	May	29.826	13.202	......
86	Forwarded from Linz	June	36.946	20.233	......
99	Forwarded from Linz	July	62.830	17.815	......
114	Forwarded from Vienna	August	2.196	.798	.023
115	Forwarded from Linz	August	......	......	......
126	Forwarded from Linz	September	5.659	......	......
135	Forwarded from Linz	October	22.468	......	......
147	Forwarded from Linz	November	33.708	2.830	......
Series 3		1922			
3	Forwarded from Linz	January	52.953	2.269	7.417
15	Forwarded from Linz	March	21.921	......	2.872
24	Forwarded from Linz	April	28.312	.812	2.400
35	Innsbrück	June	20.330	7.218	12.780
	Total Deliveries to Tyrol	....	**868.902**	**217.285**	**231.702**

* Codliver oil, 3.785; corned beef, .481; salmon, 4.724; chocolate, 1.673; fruits, 2.821.

iternal Deliveries

Tirol)

Commodities in Net Metric Tons of 1,000 Kilograms or 2,204.6 Pounds								
Corn Grits	Pork Products	Milk Evaporated	Milk Condensed	Cocoa	Sugar	Miscellaneous Food	Soap	Total Tons
......	2.061	35.749	......	12.342	16.901	.245	.....	128.908
......	13.517	17.966	......	1.224	10.125	.....	.....	79.007
......	4.867	23.295	......	.300	.670	.....	.....	90.122
......	5.387	16.886	......	......	3.102	.....	.....	83.808
......	......	......	......	1.727	2.160	.....	.....	3.887
......	.130	30.875	......	.099	13.301	.....	.....	54.664
......	......	......	......	1.320	4.000	.....	.....	5.320
......	......	1.630	......	......	......	.....	.....	5.030
......	.142	.262	......	......	.092	.....	.....	1.516
......	3.767	15.401	......	1.623	4.770	.....	.392	63.198
......	3.167	16.624	......	1.863	10.271	.....	.409	126.364
......	......	......	......	......	.172	.....	.....	2.460
......	1.951	10.215	......	1.038	......	.....	.267	54.475
......	4.424	21.971	5.602	1.261	4.100	.....	.258	81.089
......	.163	.761	......	......	.161	.....	.....	1.523
......	2.759	9.902	7.359	1.160	5.045	.....	.267	63.789
......	......	.367	.638	.110	.067	.....	.....	1.509
......	1.072	20.310	6.450	1.433	4.900	.....	.267	80.652
......	2.272	......	15.224	.852	5.758	.806	.266	67.908
......	2.790	......	.787	.706	1.474	.....	.133	35.986
......	1.954	......	7.238	.727	1.561	.....	.....	38.384
......	6.430	......	30.149	2.242	8.320	.....	.....	135.339
......	3.178	10.925	......	1.626	4.810	.....	.....	71.000
......	3.245	10.931	......	1.422	4.999	1.110	.....	72.583
......	5.242	......	22.543	2.235	7.049	.....	.....	114.637
......	.635	3.466	......	.306	1.059	.384	.....	14.879
......	3.110	14.022	......	1.219	9.748	.....	1.869	72.996
......	3.698	20.640	......	1.420	16.695	6.397	.....	106.029
11.680	6.663	27.440	......	2.337	13.346	.....	.....	142.111
......	.457	.769	......	.067	.198	.165	.068	4.741
......	......	......	......	......	9.749	.....	.....	9.749
3.845	.319	......	......	.203	......	2.821	.....	12.847
7.805	3.593	.610	......	1.016	2.406	.....	.....	37.898
12.524	4.799	17.975	......	1.727	14.528	.....	.360	88.451
11.419	6.042	22.740	......	2.032	17.600	1.316	.....	123.788
6.258	2.493	9.275	.010	.922	9.462	.....	.504	53.717
4.540	2.200	8.731	......	.759	3.930	.240	.380	52.304
......	1.808	......	......	......	.547	.....	.....	42.683
58.071	**104.335**	**369.738**	**96.000**	**47.318**	**213.076**	**13.484***	**5.440**	**2,225.351**

Table 230

Province of VORARLBER(

Receipt No.	Zone Warehouse	Date of Receipt	Flour	Rice	Beans, Peas
Series 1		1919			
7	Bregenz	August 1	14.335	......	10.355
14	Bregenz	Oct.-Nov.	18.190	3.005	6.140
22	Bregenz	December	13.335	3.380	4.245
		1920			
38	Bregenz	January	11.430	2.750	3.870
47	Bregenz	February	......	.400	.660
61	Bregenz	March	......	3.043	9.080
66	Bregenz	April	25.830	3.019	3.885
79	Bregenz	May	16.894	2.285	2.730
103	Bregenz	June	8.836	2.529	3.511
114	Bregenz	July	4.056	2.040	3.347
124	Bregenz	August	11.225	2.394	2.138
135	Bregenz	September	6.595	.947	4.091
145	Bregenz	October	16.077	3.989	4.106
151	Bregenz	November	10.201	2.929	3.322
Series 2					
8	Bregenz	December	24.973	5.959	7.769
		1921			
27	Forwarded from Linz	January	15.187	3.732	4.319
39	Forwarded from Linz	February	13.574	3.357	3.856
62	Forwarded from Linz	April	17.383	4.383	4.734
74	Forwarded from Linz	May	16.615	7.360	......
87	Forwarded from Linz	June	11.917	6.998	......
102	Forwarded from Linz	July	25.545	7.272	......
116	Forwarded from Vienna	August	1.484	.542	......
127	Forwarded from Linz	September	2.540	......	......
136	Forwarded from Linz	October	7.420	......	......
148	Forwarded from Linz	November	13.788	1.961	......
Series 3		1922			
1	Forwarded from Linz	January	21.077	1.101	2.606
19	Forwarded from Linz	March	7.340	......	1.174
25	Forwarded from Linz	April	5.087	.318	.629
36	Bregenz	June	10.110	4.030	7.444
	Total Deliveries to Vorarlberg	....	**351.044**	**79.723**	**94.011**

* Codliver oil, 1.778; corned beef, .093; salmon, 2.089; chocolate, .780; fruits, 1.218.

AUSTRIA-

(Tables 22-

Table 231

Local Committees-

Receipt No.	Zone Warehouse	Date of Receipt	Flour	Rice	Beans, Peas
		1922			
39	Final Turnover	August 1	**518.068**	**404.440**	**11.388**

* Deliveries to local committees were made by the Central Committee, which was known as A.K.H.A. or Amerikanische Kinderhilfsaktion.

orarlberg)

Commodities in Net Metric Tons of 1,000 Kilograms or 2,204.6 Pounds

Corn Grits	Pork Products	Milk Evaporated	Milk Condensed	Cocoa	Sugar	Miscellaneous Food	Soap	Total Tons
......	......	15.675	......	4.181	15.000	.097	....	59.643
......	.490	9.300	......	.....	......	.....	....	37.125
......	1.996	6.032	......	.....	......	.....	....	28.988
......	2.874	5.438	......	.....	......	.....	....	26.362
......	......	1.275	......	.....	.225	.....	....	2.560
......	1.415	5.569	......	.592	1.700	.....	.106	21.505
......	1.042	5.362	......	.704	1.680	.....	.160	41.682
......	.754	3.450	......	.....	.733	.....	.080	26.926
......	1.589	7.757	1.409	.522	1.497	.....	.080	27.730
......	.622	3.677	2.212	.382	1.098	.....	.080	17.514
......	.748	6.305	2.185	.461	.560	.....	.080	26.096
......	.459	......	3.630	.209	2.470	.392	.080	18.873
......	1.955	......	5.100	.681	1.900	.....	.080	33.888
......	1.148	......	4.275	.518	.860	.....	....	23.253
......	2.650	......	11.704	1.073	3.630	.....	....	57.758
......	1.323	6.153	......	.659	1.864	.....	....	33.237
......	1.077	5.715	......	.711	1.754	.714	....	30.758
......	1.840	......	8.508	.610	2.443	.....	....	39.901
......	1.715	8.705	......	.610	6.009	.....	.792	41.806
......	1.191	5.165	.019	.610	4.681	2.869	....	33.450
4.705	2.477	12.647	......	.892	9.300	.....	....	62.838
......	.366	.530	......	.041	.139	.093	....	3.195
4.030	.166	......	......	.102	......	1.218	....	8.056
......	1.092	2.177	......	.305	1.958	.....	....	12.952
3.933	1.556	7.096	......	.610	5.501	.....	.194	34.639
4.208	2.071	8.274	......	.813	6.891	.473	....	47.514
1.354	.652	3.250	.015	.256	2.690	.....	.288	17.019
.914	.658	2.482	......	.102	2.023	.102	.172	12.487
......	1.143	......	......	.....	.406	.....	....	23.133
19.144	**35.069**	**132.034**	**39.057**	**15.644**	**77.012**	**5.958***	**2.192**	**850.888**

ternal Deliveries

, Concluded)

K.H.A.*

Commodities in Net Metric Tons of 1,000 Kilograms or 2,204.6 Pounds

Corn Grits	Pork Products	Milk Evaporated	Milk Condensed	Cocoa	Sugar	Miscellaneous Food	Soap	Total Tons
......	**102.212**	**149.864**	**179.239**	**116.053**	**162.432**	......	**25.200**	**1,668.896**

Table 232

Detail of Internal Deliverie

Receipt No.	Institutions	Date	Flour	Rice	Beans, Peas	Pork Products
		1921				
1	Mensa Academica	Apr. 14	11.520	3.456	2.330	1.206
2	Mensa Judaica	Apr. 14	4.722	1.418	.958	.462
3	Mensa Technica	Apr. 14	2.639	.792	.534	.277
4	Bodenkultur College Mensa	Apr. 14	2.854	.858	.575	.301
5	Mensa Hochschule für Welthandel	Apr. 14	4.448	1.332	.899	.459
6	Mensa Tierärztliche Hochschule	Apr. 14	1.868	.562	.377	.197
	Total for April	....	**28.051**	**8.418**	**5.673**	**2.902**
7	Welthandelshochschule	May 6	1.480	.443	.300	.151
8	Mensa Academica Judaica ritualis	May 14	.075	.022	.015	.....
9	Mensa Juedischer Studenten aus S.H.S.	May 24	.114	.030	.024	.017
10	Mensa Juedischer Studenten aus S.H.S.	May 24	.495	.150	.096	.085
11	Acad. Juedischer Unterstützungsverein	May 24	1.076	.324	.212	.204
12	Mensa Acad. Juedischer Unterstützungsverein	May 24	.160	.048	.032	.017
13	Mensa Academica	May 24	7.345	2.200	1.435	1.367
14	Mensa Judaica	May 24	3.312	.992	.648	.544
15	Mensa Hochschule für Bodenkultür	May 24	2.319	.694	.453	.432
16	Mensa Hochschule für Welthandel	May 24	2.555	.768	.502	.484
17	Mensa Judaica Studenten aus S.H.S.	May 24	4.547	1.364	.892	.853
18	Mensa der Universität, Graz	May 24	.343	.100	.065	.051
19	Mensa der Hochschule	May 24	.075	.022	.015	.017
20	Mensa Academica Judaica ritualis	May 24	.114	.030	.024	.017
21	Mensa Academica Judaica ritualis	May 24	4.440	1.340	.910	.472
22	Mensa Technica	May 27	3.000	.900	.606	.310
	Total for May	....	**31.450**	**9.427**	**6.229**	**5.021**
23	Mensa Universität, Graz	June 27	4.013	1.204	.786	.753
24	Mensa Academica	June 28	13.200	3.960	2.588	2.476
25	Mensa Judaica	June 28	5.026	1.500	.980	.816
26	Mensa Technica	June 28	2.997	.900	.587	.564
27	Hochschule für Bodenkultür	June 28	2.997	.900	.587	.564
28	Hochschule für Welthandel	June 28	5.153	1.560	1.018	1.012
29	Mensa Judaica ritualis	June 28	.396	.120	.078	.068
30	Mensa Jüdischer Studenten aus S.H.S.	June 28	.593	.180	.118	.102
31	Mensa des Jugoslav. Unterstützungsverein	June 28	1.208	.360	.235	.222
	Total for June	....	**35.583**	**10.684**	**6.977**	**6.577**
32	Mensa Acad. der Universität Innsbrück	July 13	6.100	1.830	1.235	.637
	Total Deliveries for Students' Relief	....	**101.184**	**30.359**	**20.114**	**15.137**
		1922				
	Professors' Relief, Vienna	Feb. 16	42.896	6.219	5.321	7.081
	Deliveries to Committees for Students' Relief	Feb.-May	......	130.900	......	......
	Grand Total	....	**144.080**	**167.478**	**25.435**	**22.218**

* Rice, ex-Nobles, I (Arr. Feb. 9, 1922), milk, ex-St. Paul (Arr. May 14, 1922), and cocoa, ex-Morristown, II (Arr. May 28, 1922), were turned over to the committees for the continuation of the student feeding program.

R.A.-European Children's Fund

Institutions, for Student Feeding

Commodities in Net Metric Tons of 1,000 Kilograms or 2,204.6 Pounds										Total Value
Milk		Cocoa	Sugar	Corned Beef	Herring	Salmon	Soap	Total Tons		
aporated	Condensed									
6.532	.....	.576	2.029	.718	......	......	......	28.367		....
2.680	.....	.236	.833	.294	......	......	......	11.603		....
1.497	.....	.132	.465	.166	......	......	......	6.502		....
1.619	.....	.143	.503	.177	......	......	......	7.030		....
2.517	.....	.223	.783	.280	......	......	......	10.941		....
1.061	.....	.094	.331	.119	......	......	......	4.609		....
15.906	.....	**1.404**	**4.944**	**1.754**	......	......	......	**69.052**		....
.835	.....	.074	.260	.019	......	......	......	3.562		....
.044	.....	.004	.014	.005	......	......	......	.179		....
.068	.....	.006	.021	.006	......	......	......	.286		....
.054	.....	.024	.089	.041	......	......	......	1.034		....
.122	.....	.054	.190	.082	......	......	......	2.264		....
.091	.....	.008	.028	.011	......	......	......	.395		....
.830	.....	.366	1.292	.549	......	......	......	15.384		....
.375	.....	.165	.583	.248	......	......	......	6.867		....
.263	.....	.116	.408	.174	......	......	......	4.859		....
.290	.....	.128	.451	.190	......	......	......	5.368		....
.517	.....	.227	.800	.408	......	......	......	9.608		....
.036	.....	.017	.059	.027	......	......	......	.698		....
.044	.....	.004	.014	.005	......	......	......	.196		....
.068	.....	.006	.021	.005	......	......	......	.285		....
2.540	.....	.225	.788	.272	......	......	......	10.987		....
1.698	.....	.150	.529	.188	......	......	......	7.381		....
7.875	.....	**1.574**	**5.547**	**2.230**	......	......	......	**69.353**		....
.457	.....	.200	.708	.302	.800	1.023	......	10.246		....
1.579	.....	.633	2.326	.979	5.152	5.596	......	38.489		....
.598	.....	.240	.880	.373	2.016	2.547	......	14.976		....
.358	.....	.144	.530	.223	1.024	1.274	......	8.601		....
.358	.....	.144	.530	.223	1.024	1.274	......	8.601		....
.758	.....	.060	1.000	.389	1.760	2.210	......	14.920		....
.048	.....	.020	.070	.027	.128	.174	......	1.129		....
.073	.....	.029	.105	.044	.192	.250	......	1.686		....
.144	.....	.058	.211	.090	.416	.501	......	3.445		....
4.373	.....	**1.528**	**6.360**	**2.650**	**12.512**	**14.849**	......	**102.093**		....
3.465	.....	.306	1.075	.384	......	......	......	15.032		....
31.619	.....	**4.812**	**17.926**	**7.018**	**12.512**	**14.849**	......	**255.530**		**$60,327.61**
22.927	.....	1.438	7.527	.....	......	......	......	93.409		15,002.22
53.700	.....	55.200	......	.....	......	......	......	239.800		19,817.51*
108.246	.....	**61.450**	**25.453**	**7.018**	**12.512**	**14.849**	......	**588.739**		**$95,147.34**

Table 233*

Operation	Table No.	Flour	Grain	Rice
		COMMISSIO		
Deliveries to Occupied Belgium	103	335,608.0	2,801,887.0	215,411.0
Deliveries to Belgian Refugees, Holland and Havre	103	....	....	....
Total Deliveries, C.R.B. Period	...	**335,608.0**	**2,801,887.0**	**215,411.0**
		UNITED STATE		
Sales—Financed by U.S. Treasury Credit	106	11,687.0	219,565.0	....
		ARMISTIC		
Sales—U.S. Liquidation Commission (War Dept.)	122	....	....	....
Grand Total Relief Deliveries	102	**347,295.0**	**3,021,452.0**	**215,411.0**

* For complete statement of C.R.B. activities, including deliveries to northern France and other countries, cf. Table 103.

ummary of Relief Deliveries

Beans, Peas	Pork Products	Milk	Cocoa	Sugar	Misc. Food	Soap	Clothing and Misc.	Total Tons	Total Value
Commodities in Net Metric Tons of 1,000 Kilograms or 2,204.6 Pounds									
OR RELIEF IN BELGIUM PERIOD									
122,105.0	242,460.0	26,890.0	5,882.0	1,517.0	108,258.0	14,490.0	20,433.0	3,894,941.0	$639,692,817.25
....	57.0	279.0	......	......	....	....	903.0	1,239.0	1,363,876.44
122,105.0	**242,517.0**	**27,169.0**	**5,882.0**	**1,517.0**	**108,258.0**	**14,490.0**	**21,336.0**	**3,896,180.0**	**$641,056,693.69**
OOD ADMINISTRATION PERIOD									
....	....	20,650.3	......	......	....	....	....	251,902.3	$ 27,533,982.47
ERIOD									
....	....	....	......	......	37,480.0	....	13,294.0	50,774.0	$ 28,549.672.75
122,105.0	**242,517.0**	**47,819.3**	**5,882.0**	**1,517.0**	**145,738.0**	**14,490.0**	**34,630.0**	**4,198,856.3**	**$697,140,348.91**

BULGARIA—Summary of Relief Deliveries

Table 234

Operation	Table No.	Wheat Flour *	Total Value
A.R.A.—Cash Settlement	235	22,862.4	$4,856,647.5
Grand Total Relief Deliveries	102	**22,862.4**	**$4,856,647.5**

* Commodities in net metric tons of 1,000 kilograms or 2,204.6 pounds.

BULGARIA—American Relief Administration

Detail by Steamers of Flour Sold for Cash
Armistice Period, 1919

Table 235

Arrival No.*	Steamer	Port of Sailing	Date of Arrival	Port of Arrival	Wheat Flour‡	Total Value
			1919			
123	West Grama	Norfolk	Apr. 13	Varna	7,049.0	$1,495,744.1
223	Point Bonita	New York	May 25	Varna	2,501.2	525,241.9
231	West Arrow	Norfolk	May 27	Varna	7,287.9	1,530,451.0
306	Ocland	New York	June 25	Varna	2,013.4	422,823.4
40	Constantia †	Constantinople	......	Varna	4,010.9	882,387.0
	Total Sales—To Table 120				**22,862.4**	**$4,856,647.5**

* Arrival numbers from Table 111.
† Ex West Eldara, New York, February 22, Constantinople; purchased from United States Army stocks.
‡ Contents of cargoes in net metric tons of 1,000 kilograms or 2,204 pounds.

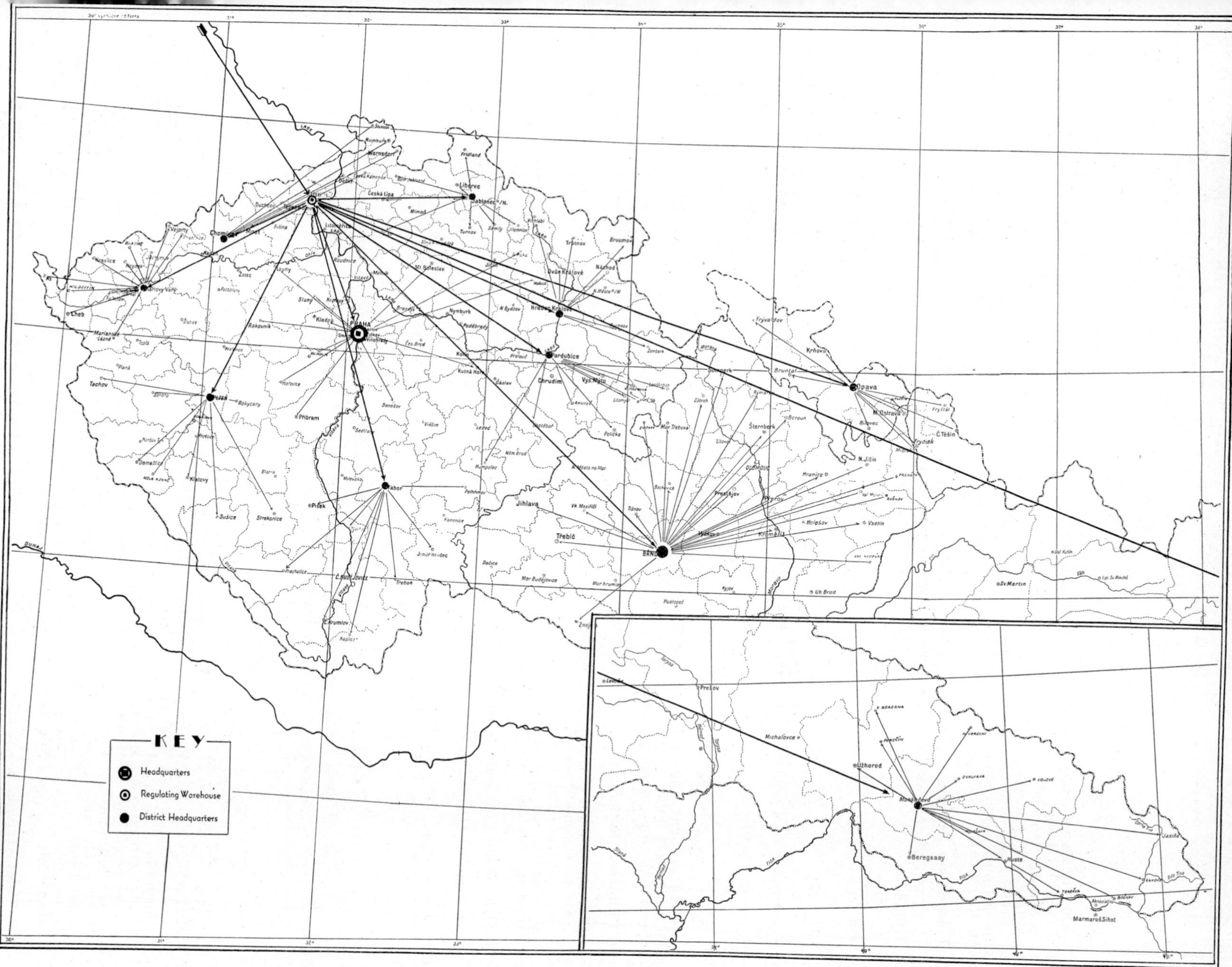

Map of Czechoslovakia showing headquarters, regulating and district warehouses

Table 236 **CZECHO-SLOVAKIA—**

Operation	Table No.	Flour	Grain	Rice
A.R.A.—Congressional Appropriation, $100,000,000 Fund	237	34,846.5	17,438.8	.....
A.R.A.—Treasury Loan	238	81,263.5	158,199.2	976.2
A.R.A.—Cash Settlement	239	2.3	....	.....
A.R.A.—Freight on Charity Shipments	143	....	....	.....
A.R.A.—Freight and Insurance, U.S. Liquidation Commission Supplies	144	....	....	.....
U.S. Liquidation Commission (War Dept.)—Sales	122	....	....	.....
American Red Cross	126–27	....	....	.....
Total American Relief	....	**116,112.3**	**175,638.0**	**976.2**
DELIVERIES BY COUNTRIES OTHER THAN UNITED STATES				
United Kingdom	242	1,629.0	....	4,083.0
France	134	50.0	....	1,542.0
Italy	135	61,017.0	....	323.0
Jugoslavia	136	30.0	....	.....
Norway	136	....	....	.....
Poland	136	....	....	.....
Austria	136	....	....	.....
Total Deliveries by Countries Other than United States	132B	**62,726.0**	....	**5,948.0**
Total, Armistice Period	108	**178,838.3**	**175,638.0**	**6,924.2**
A.R.A.—Congressional Appropriation, $100,000,000 Fund, Children's Relief	244–45	700.0	....	318.9
European Children's Fund	246–47	64.3	....	881.4
Czecho-Slovakian Government Donation	248	2,403.0	....	.....
Total Children's Relief	250	**3,167.3**	....	**1,200.3**
A.R.A. Warehouses—Food Drafts and Bulk Sales	251–52	694.3	....	112.3
E.C.F.—Sale to Czecho-Slovakian Government	250	1,018.4	....	.....
E.C.F.—Sale to State Fat Institute (Czecho-Slovakia)	250	....	....	.....
U.S. Grain Corporation (Act of Congress, Approved March 30, 1920)	249	23,809.0	....	.....
United Kingdom—Freight, Insurance, Etc.	249n	....	....	.....
Total Other than Children's Relief	....	**25,521.7**	....	**112.3**
Total, Reconstruction Period	149	**28,689.0**	....	**1,312.6**
Grand Total Relief Deliveries	102	**207,527.3**	**175,638.0**	**8,236.8**

CZECHO-SLOVAKIA—American Relief Administration

Detail by Steamers of Relief Deliveries Paid for by Funds from the Congressional Appropriation for Relief—Armistice Period, 1919

Table 237

Arrival No.*	Steamer	Port of Sailing	Date of Arrival	Port of Arrival	Contents of Cargoes in Net Metric Tons of 1,000 Kilograms or 2,204.6 Pounds				Total Value
					Wheat Flour	Cereal Flour	Rye Grain	Total Tons	
			1919						
297	Erfurt	Philadelphia	June 23	Hamburg	......	3,572.9	6,769.7	10,342.6	$1,401,894
312	Lake Gretna	Montreal	June 27	Hamburg	2,397.6	......	......	2,397.6	443,563
315	Bermuda	Philadelphia	June 29	Hamburg	847.4	1,991.7	6,977.2	9,816.3	1,322,664
324	Lake Cerosco	Montreal	July 2	Hamburg	2,789.7	......	......	2,789.7	516,096
334	Lake Fray	Montreal	July 6	Hamburg	3,171.0	......	......	3,171.0	586,627
336	Lake Fontanet	Montreal	July 7	Hamburg	3,097.0	......	......	3,097.0	572,947
339	Lake Fraichur	Montreal	July 9	Hamburg	2,972.9	......	......	2,972.9	549,978
353	Lake Fraley	Montreal	July 16	Hamburg	2,986.8	......	......	2,986.8	552,551
369	Crostafels	New York	Aug. 5	Hamburg	2,203.7	598.2	3,691.9	6,493.8	949,409
381	Huberfels	New York	Aug. 30	Hamburg	......	8,217.6	......	8,217.6	1,355,904
	Total Arrivals	....	....	....	**20,466.1**	**14,380.4**	**17,438.8**	**52,285.3**	**$8,251,639**

* Arrival numbers from Table 111.

ummary of Relief Deliveries

Beans, Peas	Corn Grits	Pork Products	Milk	Cocoa	Sugar	Misc. Food	Soap	Clothing and Misc.	Total Tons	Total Value
Commodities in Net Metric Tons of 1,000 Kilograms or 2,204.6 Pounds										
RMISTICE PERIOD										
.....	....	....	......	.....	.....	....	.....	......	52,285.3	$ 8,251,639.28
489.9	....	16,521.4	1,554.7	.....	.....	....	.....	......	259,004.9	50,113,572.61
.....	....	11.6	56.6	.....	.....	....	.....	......	70.5	33,778.62
.....	....	....	......	.....	.....	....	.....	......	....	18,898.99
.....	....	....	......	.....	.....	....	.....	......	....	184,606.63
.....	....	....	......	.....	.....	34,500.0	.....	5,850.0	40,350.0	19,098,874.27
.....	....	....	......	.....	.....	....	.....	875.2	875.2	175,040.00
489.9	....	**16,533.0**	**1,611.3**	.....	.....	**34,500.0**	.....	**6,725.2**	**352,585.9**	**$ 77,876,410.40**
.....	....	....	300.0	.....	.....	....	.....	1,120.0	7,132.0	$ 1,599,836.00
5,000.0	....	9,970.0	......	.....	.....	9.0	.....	......	16,571.0	7,540,918.00
.....	....	12,861.0	1,464.0	.....	.....	196.0	.....	......	75,861.0	16,653,920.00
.....	....	520.0	......	.....	.....	....	.....	......	550.0	587,050.00
.....	....	....	......	.....	.....	10.1	.....	......	10.1	6,060.00
.....	....	....	......	.....	.....	50,000.0	.....	......	50,000.0	1,000,000.00
.....	....	200.0	......	.....	.....	320.0	.....	......	520.0	281,600.00
5,000.0	....	**23,551.0**	**1,764.0**	.....	.....	**50,535.1**	.....	**1,120.0**	**150,644.1**	**$ 27,669,384.00**
5,489.9	....	**40,084.0**	**3,375.3**	.....	.....	**85,035.1**	.....	**7,845.2**	**503,230.0**	**$105,545,794.40**
ECONSTRUCTION PERIOD										
271.3	....	454.5	3,743.3	663.7	.....	10.1	151.2	163.2	6,476.2	$ 2,837,748.69
1,261.4	....	974.6	1,337.1	140.9	1.8	102.5	20.3	210.7	4,995.0	1,906,945.54
.....	77.3	188.8	426.7	.....	830.0	30.0	.....	......	3,955.8	693,099.02
1,532.7	**77.3**	**1,617.9**	**5,507.1**	**804.6**	**831.8**	**142.6**	**171.5**	**373.9**	**15,427.0**	**$ 5,437,793.25**
85.2	....	122.3	263.9	8.7	16.3	52.3	.....	21.2	1,376.5	$ 433,432.69
.....	....	....	245.7	.....	.....	....	.....	......	1,264.1	174,549.84
.....	....	28.0	......	.....	.....	....	.....	......	28.0	21,181.47
.....	....	....	......	.....	.....	....	.....	......	23,809.0	2,873,238.25
.....	....	....	......	.....	.....	....	.....	......	....	952,362.08
85.2	....	**150.3**	**509.6**	**8.7**	**16.3**	**52.3**	.....	**21.2**	**26,477.6**	**$ 4,454,764.33**
1,617.9	**77.3**	**1,768.2**	**6,016.7**	**813.3**	**848.1**	**194.9**	**171.5**	**395.1**	**41,904.6**	**$ 9,892,557.58**
7,107.8	**77.3**	**41,852.2**	**9,392.0**	**813.3**	**848.1**	**85,230.0**	**171.5**	**8,240.3**	**545,134.6**	**$115,438,351.98**

CZECHO-SLOVAKIA—

Table 238

Detail by Steamers of Relief Deliveries Paid for by Fund

Arrival No.*	Steamer or Source	Port of Sailing	Date of Arrival	Port of Arrival	Wheat Flour	Cereal Flour	Rye Grain
			1919				
11	Western Scout, QM. 15......	New York	Jan. 25	Trieste	5,000.0	.....	......
18	Sudbury, QM. 17...........	Philadelphia	Feb. 4	Trieste	......	.....	......
24	Westerner, QM. 18.........	Norfolk	Feb. 13	Trieste	10,000.0	.....	......
30	Cape Lookout, I, QM. 23....	Norfolk	Feb. 19	Trieste	......	.....	......
44	Mount Shasta, QM. 26......	Norfolk	Feb. 25	Trieste	5,000.0	.....	......
45	East Wind, I, QM. 27.......	New York	Feb. 26	Trieste	5,000.0	.....	......
47	West Kyska, I, QM. 28......	New York	Feb. 27	Trieste	......	.....	......
50	Canoga, QM. 50............	New York	Mar. 3	Trieste	......	.....	......
51	Army Stock, QM. 56........	(U.S.A.)	....	Trieste	3,565.5	.....	......
51	Army Stock, QM. 59........	(U.S.A.)	....	Trieste	......	.....	......
51	Army Stock, QM. 60........	(U.S.A.)	....	Trieste	......	.....	......
21	Oregonian, QM. 36 and 51...	New York	Feb. 8	Trieste	......	.....	......
96	Lake Tulare, II............	Rotterdam	Mar. 30	Hamburg	2,139.3	.....	......
98	Edenton	New York	Mar. 31	Trieste	4,422.9	.....	......
99	Lake Eckhard, II...........	Rotterdam	Apr. 1	Hamburg	2,364.2	155.7	......
102	West Waumeke	Norfolk	Apr. 2	Hamburg	7,298.2	.....	......
105	Ascutney	New York	Apr. 4	Trieste	3,323.1	.....	......
109	Samarinda	New York	Apr. 8	Hamburg	2,250.3	.....	......
110	West Elcajohn	Baltimore	Apr. 8	Trieste	7,260.1	.....	......
114	West Compo	Baltimore	Apr. 9	Trieste	1,617.1	.....	......
116	Hoxie	Baltimore	Apr. 11	Hamburg	......	.....	6,031.1
129	Cabegon	Philadelphia	Apr. 16	Hamburg	......	.....	7,497.6
133	Laurel	Baltimore	Apr. 16	Trieste	......	.....	4,895.9
139	Lake Fostoria	Norfolk	Apr. 19	Trieste	......	.....	3,302.6
145	Lake St. Clair, III..........	Rotterdam	Apr. 21	Hamburg	1,948.7	.....	......
146	Easterling	Norfolk	Apr. 23	Trieste	7,437.4	.....	......
151	Andalusia	Philadelphia	Apr. 27	Hamburg	......	.....	5,936.6
148	Neuse	New York	Apr. 23	Trieste	......	.....	......
147	Lake Farge	New York	Apr. 23	Trieste	......	.....	......
160	Sigyn, C.R.B.	Antwerp	May 1	Hamburg	......	.....	......
164	Lake Linden	Philadelphia	May 3	Hamburg	1,499.9	1,041.9	......
163	Tabor	New York	May 3	Trieste	......	.....	......
169	Osterland, C.R.B.	Antwerp	May 6	Hamburg	......	.....	......
171	Magdala, C.R.B.	Antwerp	May 7	Hamburg	......	.....	......
216	Ribe, C.R.B.	Antwerp	May 21	Hamburg	......	.....	3,345.5
180	Western Pride	Philadelphia	May 10	Hamburg	......	.....	7,045.3
188	Lake Berdan	Philadelphia	May 12	Hamburg	2,204.2	657.8	......
197	Morristown, II	Philadelphia	May 15	Hamburg	......	.....	5,781.4
195	Lake St. Clair, IV..........	Bordeaux	May 15	Hamburg	......	.....	......
202	Lake Catherine, IV.........	St. Nazaire	May 19	Hamburg	......	.....	......
206	Aila, C.R.B.	(U.S.A.)	May 20	Hamburg	......	.....	2,316.3
212	Themisto	Boston	May 20	Hamburg	......	.....	4,755.2
238	Wauconda	Philadelphia	May 30	Hamburg	......	.....	7,413.0
241	Western Spirit	Baltimore	May 31	Hamburg	......	.....	6,366.2
217	Casco	New York	May 22	Hamburg	......	.....	6,026.2
220	Eastern Star, II...........	Philadelphia	May 24	Hamburg	......	.....	4,987.4
225	West Ekonk	New York	May 25	Hamburg	......	.....	6,915.7
244	Galahad	Baltimore	June 1	Hamburg	......	340.8	7,378.1
245	Honolulu	New York	June 1	Hamburg	......	.....	6,567.2
249	Rondo	New York	June 2	Hamburg	......	.....	8,776.2
253	East Wind, II.............	New York	June 4	Hamburg	......	.....	7,462.0
258	Lake St. Regis, V..........	Rotterdam	June 5	Hamburg	......	.....	......
259	Agwistar	New York	June 6	Trieste	3,083.1	.....	......
262	Bellatrix	Philadelphia	June 8	Hamburg	......	.....	4,787.7

* Arrival numbers from Table 111.

American Relief Administration

Loaned by the United States Treasury—Armistice Period, 1919

Contents of Cargoes in Net Metric Tons of 1,000 Kilograms or 2,204.6 Pounds								
Wheat Grain	Beans, Peas	Rice	Pork Products			Milk	Total Tons	Total Value
			Pork	Lard	Lard Substitute			
......	.....	.....	.....	.....	.....	.....	5,000.0	$ 1,102,300.00
......	.....	.....	.....	.....	.....	400.0	400.0	164,227.80
......	.....	.....	.....	.....	.....	.....	10,000.0	2,204,600.00
......	.....	.....	.....	.....	.....	200.0	200.0	82,113.90
......	.....	.....	.....	.....	.....	.....	5,000.0	1,102,300.00
......	.....	.....	.....	.....	.....	.....	5,000.0	1,102,300.00
......	.....	.....	.....	.....	68.0	.....	68.0	44,630.44
......	.....	.....	340.2	.....	.....	.....	340.2	242,506.01
......	.....	.....	.....	.....	.....	.....	3,565.5	786,043.18
......	.....	.....	185.6	.....	129.0	.....	314.6	226,887.46
......	.....	.....	202.8	5.4	241.3	.....	449.5	317,799.62
......	.....	.....	3,279.4	903.4	.....	.....	4,182.8	2,950,820.44
......	.....	.....	.....	.....	.....	.....	2,139.3	427,847.97
......	.....	.....	.....	.....	.....	.....	4,422.9	926,324.42
......	.....	.....	.....	.....	.....	.....	2,519.9	500,436.63
......	.....	.....	.....	.....	.....	.....	7,298.2	1,459,645.40
......	.....	.....	508.8	140.8	.....	557.6	4,530.3	1,445,400.25
......	.....	.....	2,821.9	1,099.6	.....	.....	6,171.8	3,445,846.41
......	.....	.....	.....	.....	.....	.....	7,260.1	1,520,556.18
......	.....	.....	.....	.....	.....	.....	1,617.1	355,689.39
......	.....	.....	.....	.....	.....	.....	6,031.1	723,729.36
......	.....	.....	.....	.....	.....	.....	7,497.6	899,715.00
......	.....	.....	.....	.....	.....	.....	4,895.9	660,953.12
......	.....	.....	.....	.....	.....	.....	3,302.6	445,854.51
......	.....	.....	.....	.....	.....	.....	1,948.7	390,983.16
......	.....	.....	.....	.....	.....	.....	7,437.4	1,557,688.84
......	.....	.....	.....	.....	.....	.....	5,936.6	712,387.56
......	.....	.....	678.3	9.9	.....	243.7	931.9	696,711.23
......	.....	.....	290.3	.....	.....	.....	290.3	248,214.93
2,338.2	.....	.....	.....	.....	.....	.....	2,338.2	315,659.70
......	.....	.....	.....	.....	.....	.....	2,541.8	487,520.48
......	.....	.....	2,107.8	337.6	.....	.....	2,445.4	2,152,769.91
5,996.0	.....	.....	.....	.....	.....	.....	5,996.0	809,467.29
6,666.4	.....	.....	.....	.....	.....	.....	6,666.4	899,961.17
......	.....	.....	.....	.....	.....	.....	3,345.5	401,461.68
......	.....	.....	.....	.....	.....	.....	7,045.3	845,432.28
......	.....	.....	.....	.....	.....	.....	2,862.0	516,323.76
......	.....	.....	.....	.....	.....	.....	5,781.4	693,765.36
......	.....	.....	1,396.0	.....	.....	.....	1,396.0	1,165,694.24
......	.....	.....	1,128.1	.....	.....	153.4	1,281.5	1,000,105.63
......	.....	.....	.....	.....	.....	.....	2,316.3	277,960.68
......	.....	.....	.....	.....	.....	.....	4,755.2	570,618.84
......	.....	.....	.....	.....	.....	.....	7,413.0	889,556.76
......	.....	.....	.....	.....	.....	.....	6,366.2	763,943.16
......	.....	.....	.....	.....	.....	.....	6,026.2	723,148.32
......	.....	.....	.....	.....	.....	.....	4,987.4	598,487.88
......	.....	.....	.....	.....	.....	.....	6,915.7	829,886.16
......	.....	.....	.....	.....	.....	.....	7,718.9	941,599.35
......	.....	.....	.....	.....	.....	.....	6,567.2	788,059.08
......	.....	.....	.....	.....	.....	.....	8,776.2	1,053,143.40
......	.....	.....	.....	.....	.....	.....	7,462.0	895,440.12
......	337.7	.....	.....	.....	.....	.....	337.7	94,543.40
......	.....	.....	.....	.....	.....	.....	3,083.1	662,857.90
......	.....	.....	.....	.....	.....	.....	4,787.7	574,407.84

[*Continued on next page*]

Table 238—*Continued*

Detail by Steamers of Relief Deliveries Paid for by

Arrival No.*	Steamer or Source	Port of Sailing	Date of Arrival	Port of Arrival	Wheat Flour	Cereal Flour	Rye Grain
			1919				
260	Arakan, II	New York	June 6	Hamburg	......	.....	6,182.6
263	Maartensdijk, II	New York	June 8	Hamburg	......	.....	7,550.1
269	Flint	New York	June 11	Hamburg	......	.....	6,345.5
281	Adelheid	New York	June 15	Hamburg	......	2,019.8	......
286	Sangamon	Philadelphia	June 16	Hamburg	......	1,139.1	5,533.2
317	Lake Catherine, V	Bordeaux	June 29	Hamburg	......	494.4	......
327	Lake Clear, V	Bordeaux	July 2	Hamburg	......	.....	......
362	Coperas	Bordeaux	July 25	Hamburg	......	.....	......
	Total Arrivals				**75,414.0**	**5,849.5**	**143,198.6**

* Arrival numbers from Table 111.

CZECHO-SLOVAKIA—

Table 239

Detail by Source of Commodities

Arrival No.*	Source	Port of Arrival	Wheat Flour	Pork Products	Lard	Milk	Total† Tons	Total Value
242	Q.M. Inv. 19, 25, 29, 34..	Trieste	2.3	8.3	3.3	56.6	70.5	$33,778.

* Arrival number from Table 111, United States Army Stock.

† Contents of cargoes in net metric tons of 1,000 kilograms or 2,204 pounds.

CZECHO-SLOVAKIA—

Table 240†

Detail of Barge Movements from Hamburg v

Week Ending	Number of Barges	Wheat Flour	Rye Flour	Rye Grain	Wheat Grain	Rice
1919						
Apr. 7	3	1,466	.....	.....	.....	...
Apr. 14	18	4,736	.....	5,973	.....	...
Apr. 21	17	6,416	.....	3,100	.....	...
Apr. 28	18	1,501	.....	4,795	.....	...
May 5	20	1,777	.....	6,169	1,718	...
May 12	24	1,774	1,314	330	9,113	...
May 19	33	943	481	8,780	2,650	...
May 26	35	1,712	371	12,271	.....	...
June 2	66	489	287	22,019	.....	...
June 9	76	.....	170	25,057	8	...
June 16	47	.....	169	14,706	.....	...
June 23	34	.....	638	8,827	.....	...
June 30	46	.....	978	10,974	.....	...
July 7	35	1,858	1,233	9,325	1,511	...
July 14	45	3,246	1,671	12,189	.....	...
July 21	31	7,508	3,978	.....	.....	405
July 28	7	1,604	578	.....	.....	371
Aug.*	..	5,840	8,363	7,924	.....	368
Total	**555**	**40,870**	**20,231**	**152,439**	**15,000**	**1,144**

† Cf. Table 241. These two tables show the movement of supplies quoted in Tables 237, 238, 239, 244, and 245. Cased goods in gross tons.

* Weekly reports were not received after August 1.

nerican Relief Administration

nds Loaned by the United States Treasury

Wheat Grain	Beans, Peas	Rice	Pork Products: Pork	Pork Products: Lard	Pork Products: Lard Substitute	Milk	Total Tons	Total Value
	Contents of Cargoes in Net Metric Tons of 1,000 Kilograms or 2,204.6 Pounds							
......	.....	.....	.....	.....	.....	.....	6,182.6	$ 741,908.16
......	.....	.....	.....	.....	.....	.....	7,550.1	906,014.64
......	.....	.....	.....	.....	.....	.....	6,345.5	761,454.60
......	.....	.....	.....	.....	616.8	.....	2,636.6	746,487.87
......	.....	.....	.....	.....	.....	.....	6,672.3	851,941.39
......	152.2	181.4	.....	.....	.....	.....	828.0	185,330.62
......	.....	26.4	30.4	.....	.....	.....	56.8	32,009.48
......	.....	768.4	.....	.....	.....	.....	768.4	192,098.25
5,000.6	**489.9**	**976.2**	**12,969.6**	**2,496.7**	**1,055.1**	**1,554.7**	**259,004.9**	**$50,113,572.61**

nerican Relief Administration

d for Cash—Armistice Period, 1919

nerican Relief Administration

Elbe, by Weeks—Armistice Period, 1919

Beans, Peas	Pork Products	Lard	Lard Substitutes	Milk	Cocoa	Codliver Oil	Clothing	Total Tons
modities in Net Metric Tons of 1,000 Kilograms or 2,204.6 Pounds								
...	.....	...	...	...	...	..	...	1,466
...	.....	...	...	...	...	..	...	10,709
...	.....	...	...	...	...	..	...	9,516
...	3,251	868	117	...	...	..	...	10,532
...	648	...	...	196	...	..	...	10,508
...	.....	...	...	...	...	..	...	12,531
...	.....	...	...	...	...	..	...	12,854
...	50	...	...	...	...	..	...	14,404
...	2,152	...	...	...	...	10	...	24,957
...	1,311	...	...	193	...	..	...	26,739
...	.....	...	...	...	...	..	...	14,875
490	.....	...	...	...	...	..	111	10,066
...	.....	232	500	...	203	15	...	12,902
...	.....	...	...	...	...	..	...	13,927
...	900	...	...	39	...	..	...	18,045
...	1,503	...	...	47	...	..	...	13,441
...	391	...	...	36	...	..	...	2,980
...	395	...	...	293	...	..	...	23,183
490	**10,601**	**1,100**	**617**	**804**	**203**	**25**	**111**	**243,635**

CZECHO-SLOVAKIA–

Table 241*

Shipment of Relief Supplies from Triest

Months	Commodities			
	Wheat Flour	Rye Grain	Rice	Beans, Peas
February	5,000	.....	...	...
March	20,000	.....	...	...
April	24,527	8,199	...	...
May	....	.....	100	94
June	5,582	.....	...	...
July and August	602	.....	51	177
Total Deliveries	**55,711**	**8,199**	**151**	**271**

* Cf. Table 240. The two tables show the movement of supplies quoted in Tables 237, 238, 239, 244, and 245. Cased goods in gross tons.

CZECHO-SLOVAKIA–

Table 242

Detail of Deliveries by the Unit

Steamer or Source	Origin of Cargo	Date of Arrival	Port of Arrival
		1919	
St. Patrick	United Kingdom	Feb. 6	Hamburg
Greenbatt	United Kingdom	June 4	Hamburg
British Stock	United Kingdom	June ..	....
British Red Cross	United Kingdom	....	....
British Stock	United Kingdom	....	....
Total Deliveries	....	....	....

* Donation by Lady Muriel Padget Mission.

CZECHO-SLOVAKIA

Table 243*

Summary of Arrivals by Operations

Operation	Table No.	Flour	Rice	Beans, Peas
A.R.A.—Congressional Appropriation, $100,000,000 Fund (Food)	244	700.0	318.9	271.
A.R.A.—Congressional Appropriation, $100,000,000 Fund (Clothing)	245	......	.....	.....
European Children's Fund (Food)	246	1,777.0	993.7	1,346.
European Children's Fund (Clothing)	247	......	.....	.....
Czecho-Slovakian Government Donations	248	2,403.0	.....	.....
U.S. Grain Corporation (Act of Congress, March 30, 1920)	249	23,809.0	.....	.....
United Kingdom—Finance on Freight, etc	249n	......	.....	.....
Total Arrivals	......	**28,689.0**	**1,312.6**	**1,617.**

* Cf. Tables 236 and 250. The difference in metric tons is explained in Table 250n. The value shown in this table is c.i.f. European ports, whereas the other tables quote value of commodities delivered in Czecho-Slovakia.

nerican Relief Administration

Rail, by Months—Armistice Period, 1919

ric Tons of 1,000 Kilograms or 2,204.6 Pounds

Pork Products	Lard	Lard Substitutes	Milk	Cocoa	Soap	Total Tons
1,594	...	...	.....	...	...	6,594
1,823	454	368	600	...	...	23,245
1,521	141	...	1,012	...	...	35,400
2,436	...	...	.....	10	...	2,640
.....	...	...	257	64	...	5,903
283	830	124	1,068	154	130	3,419
7,657	**1,425**	**492**	**2,937**	**228**	**130**	**77,201**

untries Other than the United States

ngdom—Armistice Period, 1919

Commodities in Net Metric Tons of 1,000 Kilograms or 2,204.6 Pounds							Total Value
Wheat Flour	Cereal Flour	Rice	Milk	Clothing	Other Miscellaneous	Total Tons	
....	......	......	300.0	....	......	300.0	$ 118,906.00*
....	1,609.0	......	.....	....	......	1,609.0	295,609.00
....	......	4,043.0	.....	....	......	4,043.0	860,463.00
20.0	......	40.0	.....	10.0	......	70.0	30,100.00
....	......	......	.....	40.0	1,070.0	1,110.0	294,758.00
20.0	**1,609.0**	**4,083.0**	**300.0**	**50.0**	**1,070.0**	**7,132.0**	**$1,599,836.00**

mmary of Arrivals

construction Period, 1919–1924

Commodities in Net Metric Tons of 1,000 Kilograms or 2,204.6 Pounds									Total Value
Corn Grits	Pork Products	Milk	Cocoa	Sugar	Misc. Food	Soap	Clothing and Misc.	Total Tons	
....	454.5	3,743.3	663.7	.....	10.1	151.2	.....	6,313.0	$2,737,176.06
....	......	......	.....	.....	.....	.....	163.2	163.2	100,572.63
....	1,124.9	1,846.7	149.6	18.1	127.5	20.3	21.2	7,425.6	1,918,304.57
....	......	......	.....	.....	.....	.....	210.7	210.7	516,127.50
77.3	188.8	426.7	.....	830.0	30.0	.....	.....	3,955.8	693,099.02
....	......	......	.....	.....	.....	.....	.....	23,809.0	2,873,238.25
....	......	......	.....	.....	.....	.....	.....	......	952,362.08
77.3	**1,768.2**	**6,016.7**	**813.3**	**848.1**	**167.6**	**171.5**	**395.1**	**41,877.3**	**$9,790,880.11**

CZECHO-SLOVAKIA–

Table 244

Detail by Steamers of Children's Relief Arrivals, Paid for fro

Steamer or Source	Port of Sailing	Date of Arrival	Port of Arrival	Wheat Flour	Rice	Beans, Peas
		1919				
Canoga, Q.M. 51	New York	Mar. 3	Trieste	.....	.....	....
Lake St. Clair, III	Rotterdam	Apr. 21	Hamburg	.....	.....	....
Lake Farge	New York	Apr. 23	Trieste	.....	151.5	....
Neuse	New York	Apr. 23	Trieste	.....	.....	....
Tabor	New York	May 3	Trieste	.....	.....	94.0
Lake Wimico, IV	Rotterdam	May 15	Hamburg	.....	.....	....
West Lashaway, II	New York	May 24	Trieste	.....	.....	....
Lake St. Regis, V	Rotterdam	June 5	Hamburg	.....	.....	171.4
Agwistar	New York	June 6	Trieste	.....	.....	....
Adelheid	New York	June 15	Hamburg	.....	.....	....
Roma	St. Nazaire	June 26	Hamburg	.....	.....	....
Lake Gretna	Montreal	June 27	Hamburg	700.0	.....	....
Lake Catherine, V	Bordeaux	June 29	Hamburg	.....	167.4	....
Isis	New York	July 18	Hamburg	.....	.....	....
Coperas	St. Nazaire & Bordeaux	July 25	Hamburg	.....	.....	....
Augusta Foherczegno	New York	July 29	Trieste	.....	.....	....
Szent Istvan	New York	Aug. 8	Trieste	.....	.....	....
Marianne	New York	Aug. 10	Trieste	.....	.....	....
Frederica	New York	Aug. 15	Trieste	.....	.....	....
Remschied †	New York	Aug. 21	Rotterdam	.....	.....	....
Remschied ‡	New York	Aug. 21	Rotterdam	.....	.....	....
Montoir Warehouse, France, Q.M. 10	(U.S.A.)	....	(Prague)	.....	.....	....
Sonnenfels	New York	Aug. 25	Trieste	.....	.....	....
Brisgravia	New York	Aug. 27	Trieste	.....	.....	5.9
Total	....	....	....	**700.0**	**318.9**	**271.3**

* Codliver oil.
† Transshipped from Rotterdam on Gretchen Muller, arriving Hamburg, October 25.
‡ Transshipped from Rotterdam on Gustav Salling, arriving Ha-burg, December 9.

CZECHO-SLOVAKIA–

Table 245

Detail by Steamers of Clothing Arrivals, Paid for from Congression

Steamer or Source	Port of Sailing	Date of Arrival	Port of Arrival	Shoes (Pairs)	Laces (Pairs)
		1919			
Montoir, Warehouse, Q.M. Inv. 9, Rail	(U.S.A.)	June	Bordeaux	.....	......
Lake St. Regis, V, from C.R.B.	Rotterdam	June	Hamburg	14,016	......
Total Arrivals	....	....	....	**14,016**	......

* See Tables 247–254.

CZECHO-SLOVAKIA

Table 246

Detail by Steamers of Arrivals of Rel

Steamer or Source	Port of Sailing	Date of Arrival	Port of Arrival	Flour
		1919		
C.R.B., Lother Bohlen	(U.S.A.)	Aug. ..	Antwerp	.....
Gift from Norway	......	Aug. ..	....	.....
Comité National, Modesta	Rotterdam	Nov. 15	Hamburg	.....
Austrian Stock, from Lake Clear, V	Vienna	Nov. ..	(Prague)	.....
Comité National, Commercial	Rotterdam (Warsaw)	Dec. 4	Danzig (Prague)	.....
Comité National, Gustav Salling	Rotterdam	Dec. 6	Hamburg	.....
Keresan, I	New York	Dec. 6	Hamburg	.....
Rotterdam, Borussia †	New York	Dec. 13	Rotterdam	.....
Comité National, Bonn, I	Antwerp	Dec. 22	Hamburg	1,018.

* These arrivals include relief supplies for children's relief and for drafts and bulk sales by American Relief Administration Warehouses.

‡ Codliver oil.

nerican Relief Administration

gressional Appropriation for Relief—Reconstruction Period, 1919–1924

Contents of Cargoes in Net Metric Tons of 1,000 Kilograms or 2,204.6 Pounds									Total Value
Pork oducts	Lard	Lard Substitute	Milk	Cocoa	Misc. Food	Soap	Clothing and Misc.	Total Tons	
....	....	54.4	.....	.....	....	.....	.....	54.4	$ 38,605.26
....	....	....	200.0	100.0	....	.....	.....	300.0	107,996.96
....	....	....	.....	.....	....	.....	.....	151.5	43,175.50
65.8	26.1	....	237.6	.....	....	.....	.....	329.5	189,831.75
....	....	....	.....	.....	....	.....	.....	94.0	27,719.68
....	....	....	.....	.....	10.1*	.....	.....	10.1	6,307.50
....	....	....	.....	10.0	....	.....	.....	10.0	4,281.68
....	....	....	.....	.....	....	.....	.....	171.4	47,989.48
....	....	....	549.9	68.5	....	.....	.....	618.4	316,243.94
....	....	....	.....	102.9	....	.....	.....	102.9	40,641.55
....	....	....	74.4	.....	....	.....	.....	74.4	28,182.00
....	....	....	.....	.....	....	.....	.....	700.0	129,500.00
308.2	....	....	30.2	.....	....	.....	.....	505.8	310,612.20
....	....	....	152.1	.....	....	.....	.....	152.1	73,053.00
....	....	....	195.1	.....	....	.....	.....	195.1	73,920.00
....	....	....	330.6	163.0	....	.....	.....	493.6	278,632.65
....	....	....	4.9	.....	....	.....	.....	4.9	2,529.00
....	....	....	.2	.....	....	.....	.....	.2	72.00
....	....	....	108.0	.....	....	63.1	.....	171.1	68,801.52
....	....	....	1,065.0	101.6	....	.....	.....	1,166.6	528,186.27
....	....	....	391.9	56.9	....	.....	.....	448.8	182,911.80
....	....	....	.....	.....	....	4.6	.....	4.6	2,116.80
....	....	....	157.5	60.8	....	27.7	.....	246.0	111,221.93
....	....	....	245.9	.....	....	55.8	.....	307.6	124,643.59
374.0	**26.1**	**54.4**	**3,743.3**	**663.7**	**10.1**	**151.2**	.....	**6,313.0**	**$2,737,176.06**

nerican Relief Administration

propriation for Relief*—Reconstruction Period, 1919–1924

ockings Pairs)	Woolens (Yards)	Thread (Yards)	Needles (No.)	Buttons (No.)	Garments (Each)	Drawers, Woolen (Pairs)	Undershirts, Woolen (Each)	Shirts, O.D., Woolen (Each)	Total Metric Tons	Total Value
99,812	......	....	......	......	......	40,380	39,938	10,074	52.0	$ 72,760.30
.....	......	....	......	......	259,959	.....	.....	.....	111.2	27,812.33
99,812	......	....	......	......	**259,959**	**40,380**	**39,938**	**10,074**	**163.2**	**$100,572.63**

R.A.-European Children's Fund

plies*—Reconstruction Period, 1919–1924

Contents of Cargoes in Net Metric Tons of 1,000 Kilograms or 2,204.6 Pounds										Total Value
Rice	Beans, Peas	Pork Products	Milk	Cocoa	Sugar	Misc. Food	Soap	Misc.	Total Tons	
....	.....	219.3	.....	....	....	4.7	....	....	224.0	$ 149,064.46
....	.....	.....	.....	....	....	17.8‡	....	....	17.8	....
....	.....	283.7	.....	....	....	....	....	....	283.7	116,165.41
162.2	.....	.....	.....	....	....	....	....	....	162.2	40,622.33
....	300.0	.....	.....	....	....	....	....	....	300.0	45,141.12
....	400.0	284.7	.....	....	....	....	....	....	684.7	151,537.86
....	.....	.....	381.0	....	....	....	....	....	381.0	179,424.24
....	.....	.....	293.4	....	....	....	....	....	293.4	135,476.42
....	.....	.....	.....	44.4	....	....	....	....	1,062.8	115,754.68

* Transshipped from Rotterdam to Mannheim on Borussia.

[*Continued on next page*]

CZECHO-SLOVAKIA-

Table 246—*Continued*

Detail by Steamers of Arriva

Steamer or Source	Port of Sailing	Date of Arrival	Port of Arrival	Flour
		1920		
Cripple Creek	New York	Jan. 4	Hamburg	1,030.8
Comité National, Bonn, II	Antwerp	Jan. 7	Hamburg	......
Desdemonia	(U.K.)	Jan. 19	Hamburg	......
Inverawe	Liverpool	Jan. 23	Hamburg	......
Desdemonia, II	(U.K.)	Feb. 8	Hamburg	......
Manchuria, I	New York	Feb. 26	Hamburg	......
Keresan, II	New York	Feb. 27	Hamburg	......
Clauseus	San Francisco	Mar. 2	Hamburg	......
Mar Caspio, I	New York	Mar. 7	Hamburg	......
Purchase from Frazier & Co., Severn	Brazil	Mar. 7	Hamburg	......
Mongolia, I	New York	Mar. 10	Hamburg	......
Purchased from Bridges & Co., Henrietta	Hamburg	Mar. 11	Hamburg	......
Kerowlee	New York	Mar. 29	Hamburg	......
Purchased from Wilson & Co., Mont Cervin	Rotterdam	May 13	Hamburg	......
Purchased from Wilson & Co., Sephora Worms	Rotterdam	May 13	Hamburg	......
Carib, III	New York	May 23	Hamburg	......
Keresan, III	New York	May 27	Hamburg	......
Mar Mediterraneo	New York	May 31	Hamburg	......
West Isleta	Boston	June 18	Hamburg	......
Mar Blanco, I	New York	July 2	Hamburg	......
Monticello	New York	July 9	Hamburg	......
Mar Caspio, II	New York	July 16	Hamburg	......
Minnekahda, I	New York	July 31	Hamburg	......
Bellerose	Philadelphia	Aug. 2	Hamburg	......
Herefordshire	Rangoon	Aug. 18	Hamburg	......
Kermit, II	New York	Aug. 21	Hamburg	......
Mette Jensen	New York	Aug. 22	Hamburg	......
Mar Blanco, II	New York	Aug. 24	Hamburg	......
Mongolia, IV	New York	Aug. 26	Hamburg	......
Monticello, II	New York	Aug. 28	Hamburg	......
Jacques Cartier	New York	Sept. 7	Hamburg	......
Sacandaga	New Orleans	Sept. 9	Hamburg	......
Mar Rojo	New York	Sept. 16	Hamburg	20.
Vittorio Emmanuelle, III	New York	Oct. 1	Hamburg	......
Kerlew, III	New York	Oct. 6	Hamburg	......
Schoharie	New York	Oct. 13	Hamburg	......
Local Purchase	(Prague)	Dec. 6	(Prague)	......
Mar del Norte	New York	Dec. 22	Hamburg	......
		1921		
Roath	New Orleans	Jan. 5	Hamburg	.....
Paz de Epalza	New York	Jan. 9	Hamburg	100.1
Mount Clay, I	New York	Jan. 18	Hamburg	.....
Bradford City, I	New York	Feb. 7	Hamburg	.....
Haimon	New York	Feb. 25	Hamburg	.....
Homer City, II	New York	Feb. 25	Hamburg	.....
Andrea F. Luckenbach	New York	Mar. 12	Hamburg	.....
Kenowis	New Orleans	Mar. 21	Hamburg	.....
Local Purchase	(Prague)	Mar. ..	(Prague)	.....
Naamhok	Philadelphia	Apr. 6	Hamburg	.....
Eemdijk	Seattle	Apr. 22	Hamburg	.....
Bradford City, II	New York	Apr. 23	Hamburg	.....
Mystic, IV	New York	May 9	Hamburg	.....
Noruega	New York	Sept. 15	Hamburg	.....
Dakotan, I	New York	Sept. 24	Hamburg	.....
Westbrook, IV (for P.O.D.)	New York	Dec. 22	Hamburg	.....
		1922		
Purchase from Czecho-Slovakian Government	(Prague)	Jan. 30	(Prague)	.....
Warehouse Overage	....	....	....	.....
Total Arrivals				2,169.
Deduct Transfer, etc.				392.
Total Net Arrivals ‡				1,777.

* The European Children's Fund loaned the State Grain Institute at Prague 356.298 metric tons of flour, which was returned by 392.3 metric tons of flour ex-S.S. Porta at Hamburg. The difference in the tonnage is due to the difference in the price of flour at the time of the loan time of replacement.

† Shipped to Vienna for Austrian program. See Austrian Table 2

R.A.-European Children's Fund
Relief Supplies

Contents of Cargoes in Net Metric Tons of 1,000 Kilograms or 2,204.6 Pounds										
Rice	Beans, Peas	Pork Products	Milk	Cocoa	Sugar	Misc. Food	Soap	Misc.	Total Tons	Total Value
....	.....	.....	.....	....	....	....	....	1.1	1,031.9	$ 148,046.71
....	176.4	.....	.....	....	....	....	....	....	176.4	14,973.07
50.0	.....	.....	.....	....	....	....	....	....	150.0	14,925.94
....	.....	.....	.....	....	....	32.7	....	....	32.7	19,030.34
50.0	.....	.....	.....	....	....	....	....	....	150.0	14,925.94
....	.....	40.1	.....	....	....	....	....	....	40.1	26,822.99
....	.....	.....	.....	....	....	....	....	.9	.9	352.94
....	380.0	.....	.....	....	....	....	....	....	380.0	77,546.98
....	.....	.....	37.4	50.8	....	....	....	3.4	91.6	36,394.41
00.1	.....	.....	.....	....	....	....	....	....	200.1	54,547.47
....	.....	23.8	.....	....	....	....	....	....	23.8	19,219.67
....	.....	.....	119.1	....	....	....	....	....	119.1	58,796.69
....	.....	21.3	61.4	....	....	....	....	....	82.7	34,634.65
....	.....	126.4	.....	....	....	....	....	....	126.4	69,637.88
....	.....	25.7	.....	....	....	....	....	....	25.7	14,158.96
....	.....	.....	.....	....	....	....	....	7.4	7.4	3,020.31
....	.....	1.5	.....	....	....	....	....	....	1.5	1,211.22
....	.....	.....	39.4	....	....	....	....	....	39.4	12,198.83
....	.....	7.6	.....	....	....	....	....	....	7.6	6,153.61
....	.....	.....	37.2	....	....	....	....	....	37.2	15,960.39
....	.....	.....	21.4	....	....	....	....	....	21.4	11,259.92
....	.....	.....	76.8	....	....	....	....	....	76.8	41,097.98
....	.....	15.2	.....	....	....	....	....	....	15.2	9,038.00
....	.....	32.4	.....	....	....	....	....	....	32.4	26,198.51
60.0	.....	.....	.....	....	....	....	....	....	60.0	7,879.20
....	.....	4.1	54.7	....	....	....	....	....	58.8	19,863.65
....	.....	.....	.....	....	....	....	....	2.3	2.3	779.73
....	.....	.....	25.6	....	....	....	....	....	25.6	7,909.43
....	.....	5.5	.....	....	....	....	....	....	5.5	3,768.52
....	.....	.....	.....	....	....	....	....	2.3	2.3	1,402.25
....	.....	3.7	.....	....	....	....	....	....	3.7	2,519.45
....	.....	.....	.....	....	....	....	....	.7	.7	139.33
....	.....	.....	.....	....	....	....	....	....	20.0	3,177.68
....	.....	.....	18.7	....	....	....	....	....	18.7	5,790.40
....	.....	.....	42.5	....	....	....	....	....	42.5	13,470.28
....	.....	.....	31.4	....	....	....	....	....	31.4	9,722.51
....	.....	.....	.....	....	5.0	....	....	....	5.0	1,029.68
....	.....	.....	.....	4.9	....	....	....	....	4.9	571.98
146.8	.....	.....	.....	....	....	....	....	....	146.8	19,041.72
.....	.....	37.3	.....	....	....	....	....	....	137.4	22,263.88
.....	.....	.....	10.9	....	....	....	....	....	10.9	2,603.82
.....	.....	.....	61.0	....	....	....	....	....	61.0	13,566.89
.....	.....	.....	86.1	....	....	....	....	....	86.1	19,123.20
.....	90.2	.....	76.6	87.9	....	....	....	....	254.7	35,195.80
.....	.....	.....	110.2	....	....	....	....	....	110.2	24,210.33
124.6	.....	.....	.....	....	....	....	....	....	124.6	8,363.01
.....	.....	.....	.....	....	10.0	....	....	....	10.0	2,059.36
.....	.....	.....	.....	....	....	22.3	....	....	22.3	7,848.66
.....	.....	.....	.....	....	....	50.0	....	....	50.0	5,967.25
.....	.....	.....	100.0	....	....	....	....	....	100.0	23,290.30
.....	.....	.....	.....	....	....	....	30.5	....	30.5	8,027.92
.....	.....	.....	100.0	....	....	....	....	....	100.0	19,980.20
.....	.....	.....	.....	10.0	....	....	....	....	10.0	998.35
.....	.....	.....	61.9	....	....	....	....	....	61.9	12,312.10
.....	.....	.....	.....	....	3.1	....	....	....	3.1	352.77
.....	.....	.....	.....	....	....	....	....	3.1	3.1	....
993.7	**1,346.6**	**1,132.3**	**1,846.7**	**198.0**	**18.1**	**127.5**	**30.5**	**21.2**	**7,883.9**	**$1,966,569.58**
.....	.....	7.4†	.....	48.4†	....	....	10.2†	....	458.3	48,265.01
993.7	**1,346.6**	**1,124.9**	**1,846.7**	**149.6**	**18.1**	**127.5**	**20.3**	**21.2**	**7,425.6**	**$1,918,304.57**

In addition to the above the following steamers arrived at Ham-
r. Cargo was United States flags and auto parts. They are not in-
ed in this table because value is charged to expenses. Jessica, from
ed Kingdom, arrived Apr. 26, 1920; Homer City, I, from New York, arrived Dec. 19, 1920; Norwich City, from New York, arrived Jan. 11, 1921; Grandon, I, from United Kingdom, arrived Apr. 20, 1921; Grandon, II, from London, arrived May 29, 1921.

CZECHO-SLOVAKIA-

Table 247

Detail by Steamers of Clothing Arrivals f

Steamer or Source	Port of Sailing	Date of Arrival	Port of Arrival	Shoes (Pairs)	Laces (Pairs)
		1919			
Juno, I	Hull	Dec. 15	Hamburg	40,500	100,800
		1920			
Hero, I	Hull	Jan. 5	Hamburg	60,796	......
Carib	New York	Jan. 7	Hamburg	.....	......
Kerkenna	New York	Jan. 11	Hamburg	.....	......
Hero, II	Hull	Feb. 2	Hamburg	.....	......
Continental Purchase (Schenker & Co.)	Antwerp	Feb. 2	Hamburg	.....	......
Continental Purchase (Schenker & Co.)	Antwerp	Feb. 9	Hamburg	.....	......
Continental Purchase (Schenker & Co.)	Antwerp	Feb. 16	Hamburg	.....	......
Hero, III	London	Feb. 29	Hamburg	.....	......
Total Arrivals	....	....	....	**101,296**	**100,800**

CZECHO-SLOVAKIA—A.R.A. and A.R.A.-European Children's Fund

Table 248

Detail by Months of Czecho-Slovakian Government Donations for Child Feeding—Reconstruction Period, 1919–1924

Time of Delivery	Commodities in Net Metric Tons of 1,000 Kilograms or 2,204.6 Pounds							Total Value
	Flour	Corn Grits	Pork Products	Milk	Sugar	Misc. Food	Total Tons	
1919								
June	.....	63.0	.....	.....	.....	....	63.0	$ 3,136
July	.....	3.0	.....	.....	.....	....	3.0	150
August, September, October	.....	....	.....	.....	.....	....	.....	.....
November	30.0	....	.....	.....	.....	....	30.0	4,322
December	537.0	....	.....	.....	158.0	....	695.0	117,753
1920								
January	300.0	....	.....	.....	33.0	....	333.0	52,337
February	.....	11.3	.....	.....	.....	....	11.3	563
March	.....	....	.....	.....	113.0	30.0*	143.0	40,384
April	10.0	....	.....	.....	96.0	....	106.0	24,096
May	30.0	....	.....	.....	110.0	....	140.0	30,250
June	145.0	....	.....	.....	97.0	....	242.0	43,434
July	183.0	....	.....	.....	.....	....	183.0	29,025
August	201.0	....	.....	.....	.....	....	201.0	32,050
September	108.0	....	.....	.....	.....	....	108.0	17,228
October	.....	....	.....	.....	.....	....	.....	.....
November	.....	....	.....	245.7	.....	....	245.7	75,948
December	.....	....	34.0	.....	.....	....	34.0	10,684
1921								
January	.....	....	.....	5.0	15.0	....	20.0	4,239
February	.....	....	.....	100.0	8.0	....	108.0	23,873
March	460.0	....	154.8	54.0	.....	....	668.8	92,564
April	380.0	....	.....	22.0	200.0	....	602.0	89,625
May, June	.....	....	.....	.....	.....	....	.....	.....
July	19.0	....	.....	.....	.....	....	19.0	1,428
Total	**2,403.0**	**77.3**	**188.8**	**426.7**	**830.0**	**30.0**	**3,955.8**	**$693,099**

* Baking powder.

R.A.-European Children's Fund

ildren's Relief—Reconstruction Period, 1919–1924

ɔckings (Pairs)	Woolens (Yards)	Thread (Yards)	Needles (No.)	Buttons (No.)	Garments (Each)	Drawers, Woolen (Pairs)	Undershirts, Woolen (Each)	Shirts, O.D., Woolen (Each)	Total Metric Tons	Total Value
5,520	30,473	....	......	......	......	.....	.....	.....	55.8	$124,464.33
18,474	17,680	....	......	......	......	.....	.....	.....	62.4	149,935.25
.....	76,440⅛	20,096,000	100,000	537,408	......	.....	.....	.....	49.1	113,743.88
.....	57,136⅜	....	......	......	......	.....	.....	.....	22.6	59,915.45
18,958	24,695¾	....	......	......	......	.....	.....	.....	13.8	39,746.31
15,600	.....	....	......	......	......	.....	.....	.....	1.3	5,131.81
26,400	.....	....	......	......	......	.....	.....	.....	2.2	10,201.03
11,200	.....	....	......	......	......	.....	.....	.....	1.0	4,607.80
3,336	5,479¼	....	......	......	......	.....	.....	.....	2.5	8,381.64
99,488	**211,904½**	**20,096,000**	**100,000**	**537,408**	......	.....	.....	.....	**210.7**	**$516,127.50**

CZECHO-SLOVAKIA—United States Grain Corporation

Detail by Steamers of Deliveries under Act of Congress, March 30, 1920*

Table 249

Reconstruction Period, 1919–1924

Steamer	Date of Sailing	Flour		Total Tons†	Total Value‡
		Barrels	Pounds		
	1920				
ɾdulia	May 13	19,412	28	1,725.8	$ 208,173.81
nnonia	June 15	13,220	...	1,175.3	141,816.35
ɾta	July 17	110,917	168	9,861.2	1,191,937.23
s	July 29	124,252	168	11,046.7	1,331,310.86
Total Deliveries	....	**267,802**	**168**	**23,809.0**	**$2,873,238.25**

* Cf. Table 157.
† Contents of cargoes in net metric tons of 1,000 kilograms or 2,204.6 nds.
‡ Value quoted, f.o.b. U.S.A. ports; freight and other transportation charges were paid by the United Kingdom in the amount of $952,362.08.

Table 250

Summary by Zone Warehouses and Major Operations

Zone Warehouse	Table No.	Date of Delivery	Flour	Rice	Beans, Peas	Corn Grits
Bratislava	256	Nov. 4, '19–July 12, '20	72.320	49.085	66.990	......
Brno, etc.	257	Sept. 10, '19–June 26, '21	342.048	168.692	186.065	......
Chomůtov	258	Sept. 11, '19–July 9, '21	149.661	99.904	114.183	......
Budweis	259	Sept. 5, '19–Nov. 20, '19	12.658	3.171	3.157	......
Dejvice	260	Sept. 9, '19–July 30, '21	226.036	159.023	165.309	......
Jablonec	261	Sept. 10, '19–July 19, '21	161.169	97.534	101.309	......
Karlsbad	262	Sept. 5, '19–July 23, '21	228.886	141.332	146.419	......
Smíchov	263	May 2, '19–July 9, '19	191.342	49.970	37.360	......
Užhorod	264	Aug. 27, '19–June 10, '20	8.382	6.147	7.376	.066
Tábor	265	Dec. 1, '19–June 28, '21	39.846	26.745	33.677	......
Prague	266	Sept. 5, '19–Oct. 27, '19	23.405	5.852	5.847	......
Pilsen	267	Sept. 5, '19–July 9, '21	89.147	47.543	52.752	......
Pardubice	268	Sept. 16, '19–July 15, '21	86.185	49.072	55.354	......
Opava, etc.	269	Oct. 2, '19–July 28, '21	194.820	104.246	118.542	......
Mukačevo	270	Apr. 16, '20–July 19, '21	71.655	29.573	25.862	12.765
Hradec Králové	271	June 10, '19–July 26, '21	129.286	68.301	76.178	.340
Dejvice (Province Bohemia)	272	Oct. 26, '19–June 20, '21	....	....	....	......
Bratislava (Province Slovakia)	273	Jan., 1920	....	....	....	......
Opava (Province Silesia)	274	Jan., 1920	....	....	....	......
Brno (Province Moravia)	275	Jan., '20–Feb. 26, '21	....	....	....	......
Brno (Province Moravia)	276	June, 1921	....	....	....	......
Opava (Province Silesia)	277	May–June, 1921	....	....	....	......
Dejvice (Province Bohemia)	278	May–June, 1921	....	....	....	......
Aussig (Ústí n/Labem)	279	June–July, 1921	....	....	....	......
Total, per Itemized Receipts	......	......	**2,026.846**	**1,106.190**	**1,196.380**	**13.171**
Receipts to Czecho-Slovakian Government	...	......	....	....	....	64.100
Turned over to P.O.D.*	...	July 1–Sept. 1, 1921	438.244	65.713	44.107	......
A.R.A. (Not Segregated to Committee)	...	......	....	28.400	292.200	......
E.C.F. Clothing	255	......	....	....	....	......
Warehouse Adjustment	...	......	....	....	....	......
Total	......	......	**2,465.090**	**1,200.303**	**1,532.687**	**77.271**
Transfer Flour Used in Misc. Food to Flour	...	......	702.200	....	....	......
Net Total, Children's Relief	......	......	**3,167.290**	**1,200.303**	**1,532.687**	**77.271**
A.R.A.W. and A.R.A., E.C.F., Food Drafts and Bulk Sales	251–52	......	694.300	112.300	85.200	......
E.C.F.—Sale to Czecho-Slovakian Govt.	...	......	1,018.400†	....	....	......
E.C.F.—Sale to State Fat Institute	...	......	....	....	....	......
U.S. Grain Corp. (Act of Congress, March 30, 1920)	...	......	23,809.000	....	....	......
United Kingdom—Freight, Insurance, etc.	...	......	....	....	....	......
Total, Reconstruction Period	......	......	**28,688.990**	**1,312.603**	**1,617.887**	**77.271**

* Pece O Dite or Czecho-Slovakian Children's Relief Bureau.

‡ 702.2 metric tons of flour was turned over to the bakeries, which was returned to the local committees as biscuits. The miscellaneous food deliveries are in excess of arrivals by 27.3 metric tons, which increase weight is due to moisture or other ingredients added by the bakers.

R.A. and A.R.A.-European Children's Fund

Relief Deliveries—Reconstruction Period, 1919–1914

Commodities in Net Metric Tons of 1,000 Kilograms or 2,204.6 Pounds									Total Value
Pork Products	Milk Evap. and Cond.	Cocoa	Sugar	Misc. Food	No. of Biscuits	Soap	Clothing and Misc.	Total Tons	
53.649	158.971	17.607	13.889	8.062	94,000	.012	....	440.585	....
195.616	684.799	88.791	76.978	101.217	3,683,983	.250	....	1,844.456	....
91.119	315.664	38.571	40.049	89.450	3,557,000	.031	....	938.632	....
12.946	41.227	5.759	......	.198	....	......	....	79.116	....
124.992	531.424	68.709	77.844	122.085	4,791,200	9.858	....	1,485.280	....
80.101	261.926	32.948	40.995	81.275	3,227,800	......	....	857.257	....
113.835	375.179	46.003	54.755	123.316	4,921,358	......	....	1,229.725	....
174.635	410.579	44.556	......	....	....	......	....	908.442	....
6.166	40.767	2.673	.372	....	....	.040	....	71.989	....
21.942	85.342	10.311	13.344	26.072	1,005,000	.379	....	257.658	....
23.521	73.986	10.199	......	....	....	......	....	142.810	....
50.042	182.823	25.705	23.305	29.098	1,152,000	1.162	....	501.577	....
56.392	215.262	29.728	22.062	37.279	1,476,160	1.750	....	553.084	....
95.500	363.576	45.892	52.399	111.420	4,200,400	......	....	1,086.395	....
17.680	91.326	12.790	6.186	31.532	1,201,955	.133	....	299.502	....
85.440	272.075	34.384	27.648	10.479	396,620	2.075	....	106.206	....
......	....	......	......	....	....	50.702	....	50.702	....
......	....	......	......	....	....	4.996	....	4.996	....
......	....	......	......	....	....	3.757	....	3.757	....
......	....	......	......	....	....	9.436	....	9.436	....
......	10.620	......	......	....	....	......	....	10.620	....
......	7.118	......	......	....	....	......	....	7.118	....
......	44.754	......	......	....	....	......	....	44.754	....
......	....	......	......	9.020	....	......	....	9.020	....
,203.576	**4,167.418**	**514.626**	**449.826**	**780.503**	**29,707,476**	**84.581**	....	**11,543.117**	....
188.800	426.700	......	302.600	....	....	......	....	982.200	....
112.645	218.327	41.738	79.373	40.700	....	33.846	....	1,074.693	....
104.300	694.600	248.300	......	23.600	....	53.100	163.200	1.607.700	....
......	....	......	......	....	....	......	210.700	210.700	....
8.600	....	......	......	....	....	......	....	8.600	....
,617.921	**5,507.045**	**804.664**	**831.799**	**844.803**	**29,707,476**	**171.527**	**373.900**	**15,427.010**	....
......	....	......	......	*—702.200*	....	......	....	.........‡	....
,617.921	**5,507.045**	**804.664**	**831.799**	**142.603**	**29,707,476**	**171.527**	**373.900**	**15,427.010**	**$5,437,793.25§**
122.300	263.900	8.700	16.300	52.300	....	......	21.200	1,376.500	433,432.69
......	245.700	......	......	....	....	......	....	1,264.100	174,549.84
28.000	....	......	......	....	....	......	....	28.000	21,181.47
......	....	......	......	....	....	......	....	23,809.000	2,873,238.25¶
......	....	......	......	....	....	......	....	....	952,362.08
,768.221	**6,016.645**	**813.364**	**848.099**	**194.903**	**29,707,476**	**171.527**	**395.100**	**41,904.610**	**$9,892,557.58**

§ For division to operations see Table 236.
† Proceeds of the flour sale were used to purchase sugar, which was
vered to Poland and Austria.

¶ Delivered f.o.b. U.S ports, therefore no detail of internal deliveries.

CZECHO-SLOVAKIA—

Table 251 — Detail by Months of Food Draf

Time of Delivery	Number of Drafts Delivered ‡ A $10.00	B $50.00	C $10.00	D $50.00	Unit	Flour M.T.*	Rice M.T.	Beans, Peas M.T.	Bacon A 8-Lb. Piece	Bacon B 16-Lb. Piece
1920										
March	25	1	5	0	....	.793	......	......	....	...
April	147	47	50	4	....	6.963	......	1.444	126	102
May	2,029½	243	236	28	....	42.430	......	16.163	2,025	243
June	2,632	564	210	14	....	68.423	......	25.808	2,632	564
July	2,475	316	233	26	....	51.776	5.449	14.468	2,475	316
August	1,178	194	155	8	....	27.623	9.576	.988	1,178	194
September	735	102	125	6	....	17.467	5.460	.546	694	94
October	919	164	98	3	....	21.894	7.771	.582	919	164
November	615	97	94	6	....	44.916	10.865	.280	615	347
December	1,071	92	577	8	....	37.891	15.625	1.640	1,434	394
1921										
January	1,293	71	86	3	....	20.006	7.783	.098	344	546
February	601	1,147	644	1	....	20.147	10.046	.032	600	167
March	728	113	74	3	....	16.268	6.203	.027	728	113
April	301	36	30	5	....	6.279	2.344	.072	301	36
May	187	40	54	1	....	5.280	2.012	......	187	40
June	119	17	8	1	....	2.553	.979	......	119	17
July	105	25	6	..	....	2.820	1.065	......	105	25
Grand Total	**15,160**	**3,269**	**2,685**	**117**	Unit†	**393.529**	**85.178**	**62.148**	**14,482**	**3,362**
					M.T.	**393.529**	**85.178**	**62.148**	**52.552**	**24.400**

‡ Values: A, $151,600.00; B, $163,450.00; C, $26,850.00; D, $5,850.00; total $347,750.00.
* M.T. means metric tons of 1,000 kilograms or 2,204.6 pounds.

† Unit in the total carries the quantity of each commodity; for e ample, 14,482 represents the number of pieces of Bacon A, or 8-pou

CZECHO-SLOVAKIA-

Table 252 — Detail by Months of Bulk Sale Deliveries-

Time of Delivery	Unit	Flour M.T.*	Rice M.T.	Beans, Peas M.T.	Bacon A 8-Lb. Pc.	Bacon B 16-Lb. Pc.	Lard A 5-Lb. Tin	Lard B 10-Lb. Tin
1920	....							
June	....	140.015	.....	20.025	...	...	....	..
July	....	50.038	.....	......	...	...	....	..
October	....	29.758	8.256	......	455	19	619	19
November	....	.542	.....	......	...	...	....	..
1921	....							
January	....	.823	.....	......	...	...	....	..
February	....	3.990	1.900	......	...	...	573	..
March	....	.751	.288	.323	...	...	....	..
April	....	1.468	.182	.195	...	...	....	..
May	....	17.219	3.138	1.664	...	16	48	..
June	....	36.083	7.618	......	...	214	261	..
July–October	....	20.104	5.770	.829	376	91	2,648	12
Total Deliveries	Unit†	**300.791**	**27.152**	**23.036**	**831**	**340**	**4,149**	**31**
	M.T	**300.791**	**27.152**	**23.036**	**3.015**	**2.468**	**9.410**	**.140**
Less Food Accounted for in Child Feeding Program (A.R.A.W. Surplus)	Unit†	....	.....	......	...	...	3,000	..
	M.T.	....	.....	......	...	...	6.804	..
Net Deliveries against Bulk Sales	Unit†	**300.791**	**27.152**	**23.036**	**831**	**340**	**1,149**	**31**
	M.T.	**300.791**	**27.152**	**23.036**	**3.015**	**2.468**	**2.606**	**.140**

* M.T. means metric tons of 1,000 kilograms or 2,204.6 pounds.

† Unit in the total carries the quantity of each commodity; for ample, 831 represents the number of pieces of Bacon A, or 8-pound pie

R.A. Warehouses, and A.R.A.-European Children's Fund

liveries—Reconstruction Period, 1919–1924

Lard A 5-Lb. Tin	Lard B 10-Lb. Tin	Oil A 1-Gal. Tin	Oil B 5-Gal. Tin	Milk Condensed Evaporated Case	Cocoa M.T.	Sugar M.T.	Miscellaneous Food Case	Miscellaneous Sacks and Containers No.	Total Metric Tons
...	...	...	..	9	....	.....	2	62	....
43	39	37	4	98	....	.....	18	755	....
243	243	263	28	668	....	.....	41	7,093	....
564	564	219	14	1,070	....	.....	95	9,483	....
316	316	281	26	813	....	.....	53	6,571	....
194	194	163	8	437	....	.....	32	3,070	....
94	94	122	6	266	....	.....	22	1,936	....
164	164	101	3	345	....	.....	27	2,559	....
297	297	100	6	479	....	.....	100	....	....
155	565	926	8	753	.304	.734	37	5,015	....
71	71	89	3	311	.803	1.823	12	....	....
265	455	300	1	513	.429	1.012	26	8,069	....
241	49	77	3	256	.513	1.252	19	2,447	....
46	31	35	5	99	.228	.573	6	1,004	....
120	...	55	1	86	.162	.434	7	710	....
51	...	9	1	40	.092	.235	3	391	....
29	23	6	152	44	.094	.261	4	349	....
2,893	**3,105**	**2,783**	**269**	**6,287**	**2.625**	**6.324**	**504**	**49,514**	....
6.563	**14.084**	**9.468**	**4.576**	**122.673**	**2.625**	**6.324**	**16.455**	**14.433**	**815.008**

es, whereas the figure immediately under the unit total converts the
nber of pieces to net metric tons.

R.A. Warehouses, and A.R.A.-European Children's Fund

construction Period, 1919–1924

Oil A 1-Gal. Tin	Oil B 5-Gal. Tin	Milk Evap. Case	Milk Cond. Case	Cocoa M.T.	Sugar M.T.	Misc. Food Corned Beef Case	Misc. Food Salmon Case	Misc., Sacks and Containers No.	Total Metric Tons	Total Value
...	...	.....	200	.....	.....	250	...	1,418	....	....
...	...	.....	...	.....	.....	...	...	788	....	....
4	...	.....	372	.....	.....	3	...	.....	....	....
...	...	.....	...	.....	.....	...	...	.....	....	....
...	3	.....	43	.....	.....	...	...	.....	....	....
...	...	2,300	...	1.250	2.300	...	...	.....	....	....
...	...	48	...	.168	.....	3	...	.....	....	....
...	100	2,332	...	.102	.225	19	...	.....	....	....
...	...	365	...	1.185	1.046	46	3	16	....	....
13	52	476	...	1.558	1.284	99	296	309	....	....
424	...	5,005	...	1.817	5.118	86	587	20,732	....	....
441	**155**	**10,526**	**615**	**6.080**	**9.973**	**506**	**886**	**23,263**	....	....
1.500	**2.637**	**229.180**	**11.710**	**6.080**	**9.973**	**16.520**	**19.278**	**6.699**	**669.589**	**$130,164.50**
...	100	4,577	...	.....	.....	...	...	.....	....	....
...	1.701	99.653	...	.....	.....	...	...	.....	108.158	44,481.81
441	**55**	**5,949**	**615**	**6.080**	**9.973**	**506**	**886**	**23,263**	....	....
1.500	**.936**	**129.527**	**11.710**	**6.080**	**9.973**	**16.520**	**19.278**	**6.699**	**561.431**	**$ 85,682.69**

ereas the figure immediately under the unit total converts the number
pieces to net metric tons.

CZECHO-SLOVAKIA—

Table 253

Detail of Internal Deliveries by

Receipt No.	Local Committee (Mistni Komitét)	Date	Flour	Rice
			A. DELIVERIE	
		1921		
1	Prague	Mar. 31	2.000	.....
2	Prague—Albertov	Mar. 15	.375	.065
3	Prague—Albertov	Mar. 27	.100	.....
4	Prague—Albertov	Apr. 5	1.280	.223
5	Albertov	Apr. 24	.....	.....
6	Prague II—Albertov	Apr. 20	1.024	.182
7	Prague—Albertov	Apr. 20	.....	.....
8	Příbram	Apr. 27	.719	.125
10	Prague—Albertov	May 11	2.397	.410
11	Prague—Albertov	May 14	.....	.....
12	Prague—Albertov	May 18	1.873	.325
14	Prague II—Albertov	May 21	3.912	.742
15	Prague—Albertov	May 28	3.983	.364
16	Prague—Albertov	June 7	4.057	.774
17	Prague—Albertov	June 22	4.224	.797
18	Příbram	June 18	.240	.091
21	Prague—Albertov	June 22	4.224	.797
22	Prague—Letná	June 15	.896	.330
23	Prague II—Albertov	July 2	4.224	.797
24	Prague—Albertov	July 16	.....	.797
25	Prague—Albertov	July 16	.....	.....
	Total	....	**35.528**	**6.819**
			B. DELIVERIE	
9	Brno	Apr. 26	1.498	.260
11	Brno	May 17	1.498	.550
19	Brno	June 18	1.498	.550
20	Brno	June 17	1.049	.385
	Total	....	**5.543**	**1.745**
			C. DELIVERIE	
26	Prague—Albertov	July 28	.538	.212
27	Prague—Letná	July 30	.234	.348
28	Prague—Albertov	Aug. 2	.470	.696
29	Prague—Albertov	Aug. 6	.382	.148
	Total	....	**1.624**	**1.404**
			D. DELIVERIE	
30	Prague—Albertov	Aug. 16	.....	.....
	Grand Total	....	**42.695**	**9.968**

* Cf. text, Special Programs. These deliveries, valued at $23,511.71, are included in bulk sales.

† Corned beef, 4.450; salmon, 2.197.
‡ Corned beef, .995; salmon, .485.

CZECHO-SLOVAKIA-

Table 254

Summary of Clothing Deliveries, by Operations-

Operation	Table No.	Shoes (Pairs)	Laces (Pairs)
American Relief Administration	245*	14,016	......
A.R.A.-European Children's Fund	247†	101,296	100,800
Total	....	**115,312**	**100,800**

* The Czecho-Slovakian P.O.D. acknowledged receipt of the clothing listed, by signing for entire cargoes. No data available on internal deliveries.

† The woolens and other clothing accessories were used in the ma facture of overcoats for boys, and topcoats or dresses for girls. T

.R.A.-European Children's Fund

ɔcal Committees for Student Feeding*

Beans	Pork Products	Milk	Cocoa	Sugar	Miscellaneous Food	Total Tons
Commodities in Net Metric Tons of 1,000 Kilograms or 2,204.6 Pounds						
ꓤOM DEJVICE WAREHOUSE						
.....	.300	.....	.....	.200	.....	2.500
.075	.....	.235	.040	.....	.098	.888
.....	.012	.....	.....	.010	.....	.122
.249	.099	.805	.129	.....	.343	3.128
.....	.200	.....	.....	.....	.....	.200
.195	.100	.631	.102	.....	.270	2.504
.....	.....	.....	.....	.200	.....	.200
.137	.....	.457	.072	.....	.192	1.702
.....	.....	1.480	.236	.448	.640	5.611
.....	.500	.....	.....	.....	.....	.500
.827	.....	1.175	.204	.500	.500	5.404
.....	.....	1.263	.204	.....	.540	6.661
.410	.....	1.284	.144	.....	.550	6.735
.....	.....	1.089	.204	.....	.560	6.684
.....	.....	1.350	.217	.....	.580	7.168
.....	.....	.152	.024	.....	.064	.571
.....	.....	1.350	.217	.....	.580	7.168
.....	.....	.566	.102	.....	.240	2.134
.....	.....	1.350	.217	.....	.580	7.168
.....	.....	.....	.217	.....	.580	1.594
.....	.....	1.355	.050	.....	.330	1.735
1.893	**1.211**	**14.542**	**2.379**	**1.358**	**6.647†**	**70.377**
ꓤOM BRNO WAREHOUSE						
.290	.....	.930	.150	.....	.400	3.528
.....	.....	.929	.150	.....	.400	3.527
.....	.....	.929	.150	.....	.400	3.527
.....	.....	.650	.105	.....	.280	2.469
.290	.....	**3.438**	**.555**	.....	**1.480‡**	**13.051**
ꓤOM PRAGUE, KINSKÝ PALACE WAREHOUSE						
.....	.162	.185	.022	.049	.011	1.179
.....	.270	.392	.132	.123	.348	1.847
.....	2.342	.766	.990	2.114	.552	7.930
.....	.109	.130	.014	.035	.011	.829
.....	**2.883**	**1.473**	**1.158**	**2.321**	**.922§**	**11.785**
ꓤOM MASARYK ÚSTÍ N/L STATION WAREHOUSE						
.....	.....	.....	.....	.....	**1.307****	**1.307**
2.183	**4.094**	**19.453**	**4.092**	**3.679**	**10.356††**	**96.520**

§ Corned beef, .748; salmon, .174.
** Salmon, 1.307.

†† Corned beef, 6.193; salmon, 4.163.

.R.A. and A.R.A.-European Children's Fund

ɐconstruction Period, 1919–1924

ꓢtockings (Pairs)	Woolens (Yards)	Thread (Yards)	Needles (No.)	Buttons (No.)	Garments (Each)	Drawers, Woolen (Pairs)	Undershirts, Woolen (Each)	Shirts, O.D., Woolen (Each)	Total Metric Tons	Total Value
99,812	......	....	......	......	259,959	40,380	39,938	10,074	163.2	$100,572.63
99,488	211,904½	20,096,000	100,000	537,408	......	.....	.....	.....	210.7	516,127.50
199,300	**211,904½**	**20,096,000**	**100,000**	**537,408**	**259,959**	**40,380**	**39,938**	**10,074**	**373.9**	**$616,700.13**

ult is that 101,296 pairs of shoes, 99,488 pairs of stockings, and 115,142
ɐrcoats, topcoats, and dresses are to be accounted for (see Table 255).

CZECHO-SLOVAKIA—

Table 255

A. Detail of Internal Deliveries of Clothing

Receipt No.	Local Committee (Mistni Komitét)	Number of Clothing Outfits	Receipt No.	Local Committee (Mistni Komitét)	Number of Clothing Outfits	Receipt No.	Local Committee (Mistni Komitét)	Number of Clothing Outfits
1	Smíchov	2	64	Praha VIII	821	127	Vyškov	85
2	Hlubočepy	34	65	Vršovice	337	128	Znojmo	11
3	Hlubočepy	13	66	Slovensko	3,300	129	Moravské Budějovice	1
4	Břevnov	173	67	Praha I a V	242	130	Beroun	11
5	Bráník	43	68	Praha	163	131	Kroměříž	9
6	Bráník	8	69	Praha II	25	132	Frenštát	13
7	Dejvice	94	70	Praha II	46	133	Holešov	39
8	Dejvice	36	71	Praha IV	38	134	Litovel	10
9	Chuchle M. a V.	12	72	Praha II	67	135	Nový Jičín	52
10	Chuchle M. a V.	27	73	Praha I	100	136	Olomouc	40
11	Radotín	23	74	Praha III	129	137	Prostějov	54
12	Radotín	22	75	Praha III	4	138	Prostějov	2
13	Selce	9	76	Bubeneč	488	139	Přerov	15
14	Selce	25	77	Praha II	11	140	Rožnov	14
15	Vinoř	24	78	Praha IV	61	141	Rýmařov	14
16	Vinoř	35	79	Česká Třebová	742	142	Šternberk	38
17	Záběhlice	32	80	Staňkov	28	143	Šumperk	33
18	Záběhlice	24	81	Praha II	10	144	Valašské Meziříčí	24
19	Dobrovíz	10	82	Aš	856	145	Všetín	34
20	Dobrovíz	36	83	Praha III	1,000	146	Zábřeh	17
21	Hloubětín	34	84	Něm. Brod	469	147	Louny	13
22	Hodkovičky	8	85	Domažlice	189	148	Benešov	7
23	Hostivař	29	86	Warnsdorf	246	149	Brandýs n/L.	16
24	Vinohrady	300	87	Kadaň	77	150	Náchod	99
25	Karlín	191	88	Čáslav	132	151	Roudnice	11
26	Karlín	120	89	Žamberk	758	152	Nusle	32
27	Bohnice	15	90	Litomyšl	350	153	Bílovec	13
28	Košíře	198	91	Královice	100	154	Jägerndorf	46
29	Košíře	500	92	Přísečnice	198	155	Freiwaldau	29
30	Praha	24	93	Pelhřimov	337	156	Freudenthal	34
31	Břevnov	15	94	Dobřany	317	157	Frýdek	39
32	Jinonice	56	95	Chomutov	509	158	Hnojník	24
33	Liboce	15	96	Polička	355	159	Místek	61
34	Libšice	23	97	Hradec Králové	377	160	Troppau	77
35	Lysoleje	8	98	Bilina	143	161	Kamenice n/L.	21
36	Modřany	19	99	Rychnov	390	162	Karlsbad	42
37	Podkarpatská Rus	1,600	100	Dubá	94	163	Karlín	10
38	Malešice	9	101	Stříbro	117	164	Dobříš	14
39	Vysočany	91	102	Příbram	262	165	Říčany	11
40	Kbely	32	103	Výprty	107	166	Neudek	42
41	Keje	31	104	Třeboň	97	167	Kladno	96
42	Michle	426	105	Wildstein	333	168	Kralupy n/Vlt.	19
43	Podolí Dvorce	87	106	Strakonice	258	169	Praha VII	3
44	Prosek	28	107	Podbořany	65	170	Humpolec	1
45	Radlice	65	108	České Budějovice	581	171	Graslitz	4
46	Roztoky	8	109	Mariánské Lázně	254	172	Falkenau	61
47	Střešovice	20	110	Rumburk	719	173	Saaz	[illegible]
48	Sukdol	10	111	Cheb	635	174	Slaný	31
49	Vokovice-Veleslavín	50	112	Kolín	237	175	Dux	47
50	Zlíchov	15	113	Boskovice	245	176	Český Brod	1
51	Kobylisy	49	114	Brno-město	2,655	177	Beroun	22
52	Strašnice	44	115	Brno-venkov	531	178	Prachatice	2
53	Troj-Podhoř	37	116	Dačice	95	179	Týn n/Vlt.	[illegible]
54	Krč	25	117	Jihlava	455	180	Kaplice	1
55	Ruzýň	42	118	Hustopeč	118	181	Blatno	2
56	Uhřiněves	37	119	Kyjov	122	182	Krumlov	3
57	Praha II	206	120	Mikulov	92	183	Jindřichův Hradec	2
58	Žižkov	120	121	Krumlov	96	184	Zbraslav	[illegible]
59	Vinohrady	599	122	Nové Město	56	185	Písek	1
60	Praha II a VI	346	123	Tišnov	97	186	Praha II	[illegible]
61	Žižkov	378	124	Třebíč	102	187	Bečov	[illegible]
62	Karlín	100	125	Uherské Hradiště	109	188	Jablonné	3
63	Praha VII	491	126	Velké Meziříčí	20	189	Rakovník	3

.R.A.-European Children's Fund

utfits—Reconstruction Period, 1919–1924

ceipt o.	Local Committee (Mistni Komitét)	Number of Clothing Outfits	Receipt No.	Local Committee (Mistni Komitét)	Number of Clothing Outfits	Receipt No.	Local Committee (Mistni Komitét)	Number of Clothing Outfits
90	Ústí n/L.	1,160	243	Semily	8	296	Lanškroun	168
91	Dvůr Králové	119	244	Slaný	100	297	Neveklov	39
92	Teplice	1,469	245	Děčín	1,333	298	Praha	141
93	Litoměřice	150	246	Ledeč	76	299	Bratislava	4,000
94	Mělník	48	247	Praha	14	300	Milevsko	216
95	Říčany	35	248	Pardubice	100	301	Nýdek	22
96	Klatovy	110	249	Vinohrady	41	302	Polička	140
97	Sušice	692	250	Ml. Boleslav	96	303	Sobotka	22
98	Sedlčany	78	251	Louny	2	304	Jičín	524
99	Plzeň	1,423	252	Tábor	164	305	Praha	620
00	Rokycany	513	253	Chrudim	100	306	Chrudim	178
01	Hořovice	169	254	Praha VII	17	307	Nymburk	54
02	Jablonec	830	255	Staňkov	35	308	Hořice	50
03	Nymburk	81	256	Mor. Ostrava	3,097	309	Praha	50
04	Ml. Boleslav	242	257	Brno	1,329	310	Praha	1,500
05	Turnov	473	258	Nová Paka	93	311	Praha	409
06	Tachov	119	259	Praha VIII	15	312	Karlín	100
07	Ústí n/Orl.	73	260	Dol. Velenice	40	313	Praha	60
08	Vysoké Mýto	935	261	Rychnov	44	314	Vinohrady	100
09	Nová Paka	288	262	Teplice	255	315	Prachatice	359
10	Jilemnice	766	263	Hořice	106	316	Pardubice	50
11	Roketnice	170	264	Benešov	90	317	Praha	50
12	Vrchlabí	697	265	Kácov n. S.	16	318	Nový Bydžov	26
13	Nové Strašecí	180	266	Košíře	101	319	Místek	700
14	Semily	333	267	Jílemnice	12	320	Hnojník	300
15	Železný Brod	310	268	Jablonec	193	321	Hlučín	520
16	Lomnice n. P.	204	269	Poděbrady	60	322	Mor. Ostrava	300
17	Nové Město n. M.	350	270	Praha III	70	323	Beroun	20
18	Broumov	340	271	Rakovník	9	324	Ketten	58
19	Nový Bydžov	130	272	Praha	400	325	Litomyšl	250
20	Vinohrady	41	273	Blovice	79	326	Nové Město n/M.	36
21	Frýdland	291	274	Benešov	9	327	Frýdlant	600
22	Praha	52	275	Hodonín	347	328	Nusle	100
23	Ledeč	114	276	Hranice	161	329	Vysoké Mýto	50
24	Trutnov	1,309	277	Jihlava	57	330	Ústí/Schönwald/	9
25	Česká Lípa	614	278	Šternberk. Medlov	30	331	Svatobořice	92
26	Praha	30	279	Uh. Hradiště	11	332	Jílové	10
27	Kralupy	20	280	Brno-venkov	402	333	Košíře	50
28	Kutná Hora	184	281	Šternberk	119	334	Kraslice	99
29	Pardubice	304	282	Mor. Třebová	198	335	Praha	24
30	Chotěboř	701	283	Svitavy	287	336	Prachatice	100
31	Loket	631	284	Mor. Budějovice	15	337	Vinohrady	100
32	Liberec	2,906	285	Královské Pole	25	338	Praha	120
33	Smíchov	491	286	Dašice	3	339	Velké Brno	141
34	Dubé	11	287	Zábřeh	71	340	Bruntál	281
35	Kouty	48	288	Prostějov	100	341	Bruntál	67
36	Most	1,333	289	Olomouc-Křelov	30	342	Velké Brno	60
37	Praha	9	290	Nový Jičín	61	343	Rychnov	19
38	Dejvice	65	291	Znojmo	33	344	Trutnov	55
39	Jílové	145	292	Prostějov	78	345	Mariánské Lázně	3
40	Jáchymov	140	293	Velké Brno	6,950	346	Praha	11
41	Praha	6	294	Štěrboholy	10	347	Praha	91
42	Praha	110	295	Opočno	31			
							Total Number Outfits	**98,299***

[*Continued on next page*]

* Each outfit consisted of 1 pair shoes, 1 pair stockings, and 1 overcoat or dress.

	Total as above, shoes (pairs)	98,299
48	Prague	1,248
49	Prague	1
50	Prague	1
..	Sundry	112
..	P.O.D.	1,635
	Total	**101,296**

	Total as above, stockings (pairs)	98,299
348		...
349	Prague	1
350	Prague	1
...	Sundry	278
...	P.O.D.	909
	Total	**99,488**

	Total as above, overcoats and dresses (each)	98,299
348	Prague	1,248
349	Prague	1
350	Prague	1
...	Prague	987
...	Prague	186
	Total	**100,722**

This final total is forwarded to Table 255 B.

CZECHO-SLOVAKIA—A.R.A.-European Children's Fund

B. Detail of Internal Deliveries of Overcoats, for Boys and Girls

Table 255—*Continued* Reconstruction Period, 1919–1924

Receipt No.	Local Committee (Mistni Komitét)	Number of Overcoats
1	Prague I	300
2	Rodiny Personálu	14
3	Praha	320
4	Vinohrady	750
5	Karlín	550
6	Sobotka	260
7	Vinohrady	600
8	Karlín	160
9	Vrchlabí	250
10	Zlíchov	90
11	Břevnov	320
12	Frýdlant	600
13	Liberec	200
14	Jílové	330
15	Hodkovičky	24
16	Podbaba	24
17	Lysoleje	10
18	Kbely	24
19	Jinonice	163
20	Pardubice	84
21	Žižkov	240
22	Vokovice	30
23	Nusle	90
24	Ruzýň	40
25	Vršovice	130
26	Libšice	65
27	Keje	85
28	Střešovice	17
29	Chuchle	40
30	Hlubočepy	130
31	Bohnice	1
32	Uhřineves	29
33	Česká Třebová	64
34	Střešovice	50
35	Podolí	70
36	Košiře	180
37	Brno	700
38	Záběhlice	14
39	Teplice	165
40	Lysoleje	10
41	Praha I.–V	80
42	Vokovice	55
43	Radlice	58
44	Bratislava	500
45	Smíchov	260
46	Michle	130
47	Kbely	6
48	Sukdol	46
49	Hradec Králové	270
50	Bráník	23
51	Smíchov	10
52	Česká Třebová	30
53	Ruzýň	
54	Vysočany	
55	Velká Praha	
56	Polička	4
57	Náchod	25
58	Mariánské Lázně	10
59	Stříbro	20
60	Ruzýň	1
61	Praha	5,00
62	Praha	1
63	Praha	
64	Mariánské Lázně	5
65	Karlín	
66	Praha I	3
	Total	**14,42**
	Forwarded from Table 255 A	100,72
	Grand Total All Overcoats and Dresses	**115,14**

CZECHO-SLOVAKIA—A.R.A. and A.R.A.-European Children's Fund

Detail of Internal Deliveries by Receipt Number, Local Committee, and Zone Warehouses—Reconstruction Period, 1919–1924

Tables 256–279, Inclusive

Table 256 Internal Deliveries from BRATISLAVA Warehouse

Receipt No.	Local Committee (Mistni Komitét)	Date	Flour	Rice	Beans, Peas	Pork Products	Milk Evap.	Milk Cond.	Cocoa	Sugar	Misc.*	No. of Biscuits
			Commodities in Net Metric Tons of 1,000 Kilograms or 2,204.6 Pounds									
Series 1		1919										
356	Užhorod	Nov. 4	2.424	.606	.606	2.424	2.424	4.040	.816	....	....	...
357	(J. Kořen)	Nov. 13	.....	.....	.....	.021	.....	.....	....	....	....	...
358	Zvoleň	Nov. 8	.....	.....	.....	.168	.....	.....	.050	....	....	...
359	Zvoleň	Nov. 8	2.000	.500	.500	2.000	2.000	2.003	.404	....	....	...
360	Žilina	Nov. 11	1.920	.480	.480	1.920	1.920	1.908	.385	....	....	...
361	Lipt. Sv. Mikuláš	Nov. 11	.640	.160	.160	.640	.640	.826	.168	....	....	...
487	Košice	Nov. 11	3.200	.800	.800	3.200	3.200	3.177	.641	....	....	...

* Detail of miscellaneous commodities indicated by the following indexes: [b], biscuits; [c], codliver oil; [e], oatmeal; [d], soap. See end of Table 256 (page 488) for complete detail.

CZECHO-SLOVAKIA

Internal Deliveries, BRATISLAVA Warehouse

Table 256—*Continued*

eipt o.	Local Committee (Mistni Komitét)	Date	Commodities in Net Metric Tons of 1,000 Kilograms or 2,204.6 Pounds									
			Flour	Rice	Beans, Peas	Pork Products	Milk Evap.	Milk Cond.	Cocoa	Sugar	Misc.	No. of Biscuits
es 1		1920										
23	Velké Topolčany	Mar. 20	.093	.....	.186	.040	.087	.036	.006	.006	....	.....
24	Košice	Mar. 27	.671	.671	.690	.450	.676	1.080	.276	.216	....	.....
25	Komárno	Mar. 15	.100	.....	.200	.067	.109	.250	.050	.050	.107[e]	.....
26	Užhorod	Mar. 13	1.360	.800	1.906	.902	1.353	2.096	.408	.419	.095[e]	.....
27	Košice	Mar. 1	.582	.582	.582	.388	.588	.933	.187	.187	.048[e]	.....
28	Lipt. Sv. Mikuláš	Mar. 30	.358	.358	.358	.238	.349	.306	.060	.060	....	.....
29	Turč. Sv. Martin	Mar. 30	.334	.334	.334	.223	.334	.474	.095	.095	....	.....
30	Čaca	Mar. 16	.827	.....	1.670	.600	.830	1.045	.204	.209	....	.....
31	Žilina	Mar. 30	.453	.453	.453	.302	.458	.568	.114	.114	....	.....
32	Užhorod	Mar. 27	1.514	1.514	1.530	1.010	1.505	2.412	.481	.481	....	.....
33	Nové Zámky	Apr. 17	.242	.235	.235	.150	.690	.....	.091	.737	.061[e]	.....
34	Zvoleň	Apr. 17	1.705	1.705	1.710	1.137	3.772	.....	.413	.619	....	.....
35	Mukačévo	Apr. 23	3.000	3.000	3.000	2.000	8.001	.....	1.000	....	....	.....
36	Košice	Apr. 26	1.025	1.025	1.035	.683	2.475	.....	.290	.435	....	.....
37	Bratislava	Apr. 4	.689	.....	.....	.....	1.112	.....	....	.075	....	.....
38	Bratislava	Apr. 9	.667	1.350	1.350	.900	1.352	.....	.225	.225	.091[e]	.....
39	Lipt. Sv. Mikuláš	May 18	.291	.317	.317	.211	.715	.....	.080	.120	....	.....
40	Žilina	May 18	.883	.883	.883	.597	1.724	.....	.169	.254	....	.....
41	Bratislava	May 17	1.130	1.100	1.129	.750	2.288	.....	.238	.356	....	.....
42	Velké Topolčany	May 6	.089	.089	.091	.059	.115	.....	.005	.008	....	.....
43	Bratislava	Mar. 5	1.360	.....	2.700	.900	1.352	1.125	.225	.225	....	.....
44	Čadca	May 6	1.750	1.750	1.750	1.182	3.008	.....	.250	.375	....	.....
45	Zvoleň	May 28	.701	.701	.701	.468	1.691	.....	.198	.297	.250[b]	10,000
46	Turč. Sv. Martin	May 28	.354	.354	.354	.236	.858	.....	.102	.157	....	.....
47	Komárno	June 1	.120	.120	.120	.080	.370	.....	.050	.075	....	.....
48	Uh. Skalice	May 20	.073	.073	.073	.049	.283	.....	.042	.063	....	.....
49	Košice	June 2	1.244	1.238	1.238	.825	2.727	.....	.306	.450	....	.....
50	Velké Topolčany	June 15	.089	.074	.048	.049	.094	.....	.005	.008	....	.....
51	Bratislava	June 23	3.510	2.010	5.010	2.339	3.510	3.575	.715	.715	....	.....
52	Dolní Smokovec	June 11	.033	.033	.033	.022	.033	.081	.016	.016	.224[cd]	.....
		1919										
82	Bratislava	Oct. 15	1.700	1.350	1.350	.900	1.350	1.125	.225	.225	.200[e]	.....
83	Žilina	Nov. 31	.850	.650	.650	.434	.650	.594	.119	.119	.100[e]	.....
84	Turč. Sv. Martin	Nov. 10	.334	.334	.334	.234	.334	.474	.095	.095	....	.....
85	Zvoleň	Nov. 11	1.530	1.530	1.530	1.071	1.530	1.875	.375	.375	.100[e]	.....
86	Bratislava	Nov. 24	.820	.205	.205	.820	.820	2.703	.546	....	.200[e]	.....
87	Turzovka Čaca	Nov. 28	.040	.010	.010	.040	.044	.079	.816	....	....	.....
88	Užhorod	Nov. 4	2.424	.605	.606	2.424	2.424	4.040	.616	....	....	.....
89	Žilina	Nov. 11	1.920	.480	.480	1.950	1.920	1.908	.385	....	....	.....
90	Zvoleň	Nov. 8	.....	.....	.....	.168	.....	.....	.050	....	....	.....
91	Zvoleň	Nov. 8	2.000	.500	.500	2.000	2.000	2.003	.404	....	....	.....
92	Bardiov	Nov. 25	.069	.017	.017	.069	.069	.097	.020	....	....	.....
93	Bratislava	Nov. 24	.....	.....	.....	.....	.....	.....	....	....	.100[e]	.....
94	Zvoleň	Sept. 5	1.530	1.530	1.530	1.071	1.530	1.875	.375	.375	.100[e]	.....
		1920										
95	Krompach	Jan. 19	.....	.....	.....	.....	.....	.....	....	....	.050[e]	.....
96	Čaca	Jan. 29	.830	.830	.830	.581	.830	1.042	.209	.209	....	.....
97	Turč. Sv. Martin	Feb. 11	.334	.334	.334	.234	.334	.474	.095	.095	....	.....
98	Žilina	Feb. 14	.850	.650	.650	.434	.650	.594	.119	.119	.100[e]	.....
99	Dolní Smokovec	Feb. 24	.720	.720	.720	.252	.720	.225	.045	....	.050[e]	.....
00	Bratislava	Feb. 7	1.700	1.350	1.350	.900	1.350	1.125	.225	.225	.200[e]	.....
01	Užhorod	Mar. 3	1.360	.800	1.906	.902	1.353	2.096	.408	.419	.095[e]	.....

[*Concluded on next page*]

CZECHO-SLOVAKIA

Table 256—*Concluded* Internal Deliveries, BRATISLAVA Warehouse

Receipt No.	Local Committee (Mistni Komitét)	Date	Commodities in Net Metric Tons of 1,000 Kilograms or 2,204.6 Pounds									
			Flour	Rice	Beans, Peas	Pork Products	Milk		Cocoa	Sugar	Misc.	No. of Biscuit
							Evap.	Cond.				
Series 1		1920										
2402	Čaca	Mar. 18	.827	.....	1.670	.600	.830	1.045	.209	.209	....	...
2403	Vel. Topolčany	Mar. 23	.093	.....	.186	.040	.087	.036	.006	.006	....	...
2404	Komárno	Mar. 4	.100	.....	.200	.067	.109	.250	.050	.050	.107[e]	...
2405	Brátislava	Feb. 15	1.360	.....	2.709	.900	1.352	1.125	.225	.225	....	...
2406	Brátislava	May 17	1.130	1.100	1.129	.750	2.289	.....	.238	.356	....	...
2407	Zvoleň	May 28	.....	.....	.....	.....	.....	.....	.035	....	....	...
2408	Brátislava	June 23	3.510	2.010	5.010	2.339	3.510	3.575	.715	.715	....	...
2409	Uh. Skalice	June 25	.190	.190	.190	.126	.190	.543	.111	.111	....	...
2410	Brátislava	July 5	.....	.....	.....	.....	.....	.....	....	....	.751[ce]	...
2411	Košice	July 2	1.890	1.880	1.880	1.253	1.880	2.923	.582	.582	.962[ce]	...
2412	Sv. Mikuláš	July 2	.820	.817	.811	.545	.817	.880	.176	.176	.368[ce]	...
2413	Rim. Sobota	July 1	1.517	1.517	1.517	1.012	1.518	2.081	.416	.416	.200[e]	...
2414	Bystřice	July 1	2.091	2.053	2.107	1.383	2.080	2.717	.543	.543	.700[be]	16,0
2415	Sv. Martin	July 1	.314	.514	.517	.343	.514	1.007	.204	.202	.790[cbe]	8,0
2416	Komárno	July 9	.325	.312	.310	.208	.312	.650	.130	.130	.631[bc]	20,0
2417	Velké Topolčany	July 12	.142	.142	.142	.095	.142	.042	.008	.008	.500[b]	20,0
2418	Žilina	July 7	1.362	1.340	1.349	.930	1.352	1.787	.357	.352	.894[bc]	20,0
2419	Čadca	July 8	2.007	2.000	2.006	1.344	2.005	2.508	.510	.500	....	...
2420	Nové Zámky	July 8	.....	.....	.023	.....	.....	.....	....	....	....	...
	Total	....	**72.320**	**49.085**	**66.990**	**53.649**	**89.538**	**69.433**	**17.607**	**13.889**	**8.074***	**94,0**

* Detail of miscellaneous commodity total: [b], weight of 94,000 biscuits, 2.350; [c], codliver oil, 2.743; [e], oatmeal, 2.969; [d], soap, .012.

CZECHO-SLOVAKIA

Table 257 Internal Deliveries from (1) BRNO, (2) OLOMOUC, (3) MEZIŘÍČÍ, (4) FRÝDEK MÍSTEK Warehouses

Receipt No.	Local Committee (Mistni Komitét)	Date	Commodities in Net Metric Tons of 1,000 Kilograms or 2,204.6 Pounds									
			Flour	Rice	Beans, Peas	Pork Products	Milk		Cocoa	Sugar	Misc.*	No. o Biscui
							Evap.	Cond.				
Series 1		1919										
119	Nové Město	Sept. 30	.160	.040	.040	.160	.160	.477	.096	....	....	..
120	Hodonín	Sept. 22	.680	.170	.170	.680	.680	1.272	.257	....	....	..
121	Boskovice	Sept. 10	.400	.100	.100	.400	.400	1.113	.225	....	....	..
122	Mor. Krumlov	Sept. 29	.240	.060	.060	.240	.240	.477	.096	....	....	..
123	Zábřeh	Sept. 23	1.200	.300	.300	1.200	1.200	2.862	.578	....	....	..
124	Kroměříž	Sept. 27	.280	.070	.070	.280	.280	.716	.144	....	....	..
126	Brno	Oct. 6	5.120	1.280	1.280	5.120	5.120	10.971	2.215	....	....	..
127	Olomouc	Oct. 1	.960	.240	.240	.960	.960	1.908	.385	....	....	..
128	Brno	Oct. 24	1.580	.395	.395	1.580	1.580	4.691	.947	....	....	..
129	Kyjov	Oct. 21	.240	.060	.060	.240	.240	.477	.096	....	....	..
130	Uherské Hradiště	Oct. 13	.200	.050	.050	.200	.200	.477	.096	....	....	..
131	Vyškov	Oct. 12	.380	.095	.095	.380	.380	.716	.145	....	....	..
139	Nový Jičín	Oct. 10	.960	.240	.240	.960	.960	1.749	.353	....	....	..
166	Rýmařov	Oct. 7	.440	.110	.110	.440	.440	.954	.193	....	....	..
167	Mähr Schönberg	Oct. 15	1.040	.260	.260	1.040	1.040	2.226	.450	....	....	..
168	Litovel	Oct. 13	.280	.070	.070	.280	.280	.716	.144	....	....	..
169	Hranice	Oct. 4	.260	.065	.065	.260	.260	.557	.112	....	....	..
170	Prostějov	Oct. 6	1.320	.330	.330	1.320	1.320	3.180	.642	....	....	..
171	Přerov	Oct. 21	.920	.230	.230	.920	.920	1.908	.385	....	....	..
172	Stomberg	Oct. 13	.960	.240	.240	.960	.960	1.908	.385	....	....	..

* Detail of miscellaneous commodities indicated by the following indexes: [a], powdered milk; [b], biscuits; [c], codliver oil; [d], soap. See end of Table 257 (page 497) for complete detail.

CZECHO-SLOVAKIA

Internal Deliveries, (1) BRNO, (2) OLOMOUC, (3) MEZIŘÍČÍ, (4) FRÝDEK MÍSTEK Warehouses

[T]able 257—*Continued*

[Recei]pt	Local Committee (Mistni Komitét)	Date	Commodities in Net Metric Tons of 1,000 Kilograms or 2,204.6 Pounds				Milk					
			Flour	Rice	Beans, Peas	Pork Products	Evap.	Cond.	Cocoa	Sugar	Misc.	No. of Biscuits
1		1919										
3	Val. Meziříčí	Oct. 10	.520	.130	.130	.520	.520	.795	.161	....	....	.....
	Místek	Oct. 6	1.000	.250	.250	1.000	1.000	2.385	.482	....	....	.....
	Všetín	Oct. 8	.920	.230	.230	.920	.920	1.749	.353	....	....	.....
	Frýdek	Oct. 10	.960	.240	.240	.960	.960	1.908	.385	....	....	.....
	Brno	Oct. 22	5.120	1.280	1.280	5.120	5.120	10.971	2.215	....	....	.....
	Hodonín	Oct. 31	.680	.170	.170	.680	.680	1.272	.257	....	....	.....
2	Beroun	Oct. 31	.440	.110	.110	.440	.440	.954	.193	....	....	.....
7	Rožnov	Oct. 20	.400	.100	.100	.400	.400	1.113	.225	....	....	.....
4	Boskovice	Nov. 10	.350	.088	.088	.350	.350	.949	.191	....	....	.....
5	Val. Meziříčí	Nov. 6	.100	.025	.025	.100	.100	.318	.064	....	....	.....
6	Kyjov	Nov. 28	.240	.060	.060	.240	.240	.477	.096	....	....	.....
7	Dačice	Dec. 4	.280	.070	.070	.280	.280	.318	.064	....	....	.....
8	Mor. Budějovice	Nov. 11	.042	.011	.011	.042	.042	.151	.031	....	....	.....
	Mor. Krumlov	Nov. 7	.240	.060	.060	.240	.240	.477	.096	....	....	.....
	Tišnov	Nov. 2	.280	.070	.070	.280	.280	.636	.128	....	....	.....
1	Třebíč	Nov. 12	.380	.095	.095	.380	.380	.875	.177	....	....	.....
2	Jihlava	Nov. 8	.960	.240	.240	.960	.960	2.226	.450	....	....	.....
3	Vyškov	Nov. 14	.076	.019	.019	.076	.076	.....	....	....	....	.....
4	Znojmo	Nov. 14	.320	.080	.080	.320	.320	1.113	.225	....	....	.....
5	Nový Jičín	Nov. 12	.960	.240	.240	.960	.960	1.749	.353	....	....	.....
6	Olomouc	Dec. 1	.960	.240	.240	.960	.960	1.908	.385	....	....	.....
7	Litovel	Nov. 27	.280	.070	.070	.280	.280	.716	.144	....	....	.....
8	Šumperk	Nov. 24	....	.260	.260	1.040	1.040	2.226	.450	....	....	.....
9	Šternberk	Nov. 19	.960	.240	.240	.960	.960	1.908	.385	....	....	.....
0	Hranice	Nov. 9	.260	.065	.065	.260	.260	.557	.112	....	....	.....
1	Kroměříž	Nov. 6	.280	.070	.070	.280	.280	.716	.144	....	....	.....
2	Přerov	Nov. 26	.920	.230	.230	.920	.920	1.908	.385	....	....	.....
3	Prostějov	Nov. 14	1.320	.330	.330	1.320	1.320	3.180	.642	....	....	.....
4	Zábřeh	Nov. 8	1.200	.300	.300	1.200	1.200	2.862	.578	....	....	.....
5	Wagstadt	Nov. 24	.382	.095	.095	.382	.382	.927	.187	....	....	.....
5	Nové Město na Moravě	Nov. 15	.200	.200	.200	.140	.200	.250	.050	.050	....	.....
6	Tišnov	Dec. 2	.420	.420	.420	.294	.420	.600	.120	.120	....	.....
7	Třebíč	Dec. 3	.527	.527	.527	.369	.527	.825	.165	.165	....	.....
8	Boskovice	Dec. 19	.547	.547	.547	.383	.547	.811	.162	.162	....	.....
9	Jihlava	Dec. 19	1.200	1.200	1.200	.840	1.200	1.750	.350	.350	....	.....
0	Uh. Brod	Dec. 1	.240	.240	.240	.168	.240	.300	.060	.060	....	.....
1	Litovel	Dec. 20	.350	.350	.350	.245	.350	.563	.113	.113	....	.....
2	Prostějov	Dec. 20	1.650	1.650	1.650	1.158	1.650	2.500	.500	.500	....	.....
3	Hranice	Dec. 4	.390	.390	.390	.273	.390	.525	.105	.105	....	.....
0	Hnojník	Dec. 31	1.200	1.200	1.200	.840	1.200	1.000	.200	.200	....	.....
1	Beroun	Dec. 12	.660	.660	.660	.462	.660	.900	.180	.180	....	.....
2	Šumperk	Dec. 20	....	1.300	1.300	.910	1.300	1.750	.350	....	....	.....
8	Hnojník	Nov. 19	.560	.140	.140	.560	.560	1.272	.257	....	....	.....
9	Všetín	Dec. 1	.920	.230	.230	.920	.920	1.749	.353	....	....	.....
0	Val. Meziříčí	Dec. 1	.520	.130	.130	.520	.520	.795	.161	....	....	.....
1	Rožňov	Dec. 2	.400	.100	.100	.400	.400	1.113	.225	....	....	.....
2	Místek	Nov. 22	.978	.244	.244	.978	.978	2.263	.456	....	....	.....
3	Brno	Nov. 8	.830	.395	.395	1.580	1.580	4.691	.947	....	....	.....
4	Nové Město na Moravě	Nov. 8	.160	.040	.040	.160	.160	.318	.064	....	....	.....
5	Uh. Hradiště	Nov. 25	.200	.050	.050	.200	.200	.477	.096	....	....	.....
0	Mor. Budějovice	Dec. 9	.063	.063	.063	.044	.063	.143	.029	.029	....	.....
1	Velké Meziříčí	Dec. 9	.125	.125	.125	.088	.125	.250	.050	.050	....	.....
2	Brno	Dec. 12	2.231	2.243	2.238	1.190	....	....	....	....	....	.....
3	Kroměříž	Dec. 5	.420	.420	.420	.294	.420	.675	.135	.135	....	.....
4	Zábřeh	Dec. 5	1.800	1.800	1.800	1.260	1.800	2.700	.540	.540	....	.....
4	Frenštát	Dec. 6	.400	.100	.100	.400	.400	.795	.161	....	....	.....

[*Continued on next page*]

CZECHO-SLOVAKIA

Internal Deliveries, (1) BRNO, (2) OLOMOUC, (3) MEZIŘÍČÍ, (4) FRÝDEK MÍSTEK Warehouses

Table 257—*Continued*

Receipt No.	Local Committee (Mistni Komitét)	Date	Commodities in Net Metric Tons of 1,000 Kilograms or 2,204.6 Pounds									
			Flour	Rice	Beans, Peas	Pork Products	Milk		Cocoa	Sugar	Misc.	No. of Biscuit
							Evap.	Cond.				
Series 1		1919										
515	Frýdek	Dec. 4	.960	.240	.240	.960	.960	1.908	.385	....	....	...
516	Mikulov	Dec. 3	....	.060	.060	.240	.240	.636	.128	....	....	...
517	Rýmařov	Dec. 2	.440	.110	.110	.440	.440	.954	.193	....	....	...
523	Znojmo	Dec. 2	.480	.480	.480	.336	.480	1.050	.210	....	....	...
524	Holešov	Nov. 25	.800	.200	.200	.800	.800	1.431	.280	....	....	...
		1920										
526	Dačice	Jan. 21	.630	.175	.350	.245	.350	.250	.050	.050	....	...
527	Mikulov	Jan. 12	.540	.150	.300	.210	.300	.500	.100	....	....	...
528	Hustopeč	Jan. 24	.300	.300	.300	.210	.300	.375	.075	.075	....	...
531	Kyjov	Jan. 14	.540	.150	.300	.210	.300	.375	.075	.075	....	...
532	Uh. Hradiště	Jan. 10	.450	.125	.250	.175	.250	.375	.075	.075	....	...
533	Brno	Jan. 17	1.975	1.975	1.975	1.383	1.975	3.810	.762	.762	....	...
534	Přerov	Jan. 17	2.070	.575	1.150	.805	1.150	1.500	.300	.300	....	...
535	Nový Jičín	Jan. 5	2.160	.600	1.200	.840	1.200	1.375	.275	.275	....	...
713	Boskovice	Mar. 20	.235	....	.235	.165	.235	.275	.055	.055	....	...
714	Znojmo	Mar. 4	.267	....	.267	.187	.267	.584	.117	.117	....	...
715	Prostějov	Mar. 4	....	....	....	....	....	1.975	.395	.395	....	...
716	Zábřeh	Mar. 18	1.500	....	1.500	1.050	1.500	2.250	.450	.450	....	...
717	Znojmo venkov	Mar. 4	.125	.031	.125	.088	.125	.250	.050	.050	....	...
718	Tišňov	Mar. 1	.331	....	.331	.232	.331	.487	.097	.097	....	..
719	Mikulov	Mar. 19	.300	....	.300	.210	.300	.500	.100	.100	.744[b]	24,
720	Všetín	Mar. 17	1.150	....	1.150	.805	1.150	1.375	.275	.275	....	...
721	Šumperk	Apr. 3	1.040	.520	1.040	.728	1.039	1.406	.280	.280	....	...
722	Rožnov	Mar. 23	.500	.500	1.000	.350	.500	.875	.175	.175	1.057[b]	34,
723	Brno venkov	Mar. 21	1.500	.750	1.500	1.050	1.500	2.875	.575	.575	2.976[b]	96,
724	Kroměříž	Mar. 20	.350	.175	.350	.245	.350	.563	.113	.113	....	..
725	Nový Jičín	Mar. 27	1.000	.500	1.000	.700	1.000	1.250	.250	.250	....	..
726	Olomouc	Mar. 24	.950	.475	.950	.665	.950	1.375	.275	.275	2.294[b]	74,
727	Jihlava	Mar. 20	.900	....	.900	.630	.900	1.250	.250	.250	....	..
728	Třebíč	Mar. 24	.400	.200	.400	.280	.400	.625	.125	.125	.868[b]	28,
729	Mor. Třebová	Mar. 20	.150	....	.299	.105	.150	.388	.078	.078	....	..
730	Svitavy	Mar. 19	1.088	....	2.176	.762	1.088	1.408	.281	.281	....	..
731	Beroun na Moravě	Mar. 11	1.210	.138	.550	.385	.750	.550	.150	.150	....	..
732	Hranice	Mar. 28	.325	.163	.325	.228	.325	.438	.088	.088	.744[b]	24,
733	Litovel	Mar. 27	.333	.333	.665	.233	.333	.525	.105	.105	.806[b]	26,
734	Val. Meziříčí	Mar. 23	.650	.325	.650	.455	.650	.625	.125	.125	1.364[b]	44,
930	Nové Město	Apr. 26	.125	.156	.156	.094	.156	.203	.037	.031	....	..
931	Zábřeh	Apr. 19	.890	1.113	1.113	.668	1.113	1.786	.330	.275	1.800[b]	72,
932	Beroun na Moravě	Apr. 30	.283	.354	.354	.212	.354	.452	.084	.070	.525[b]	21,
933	Boskovice	Apr. 27	.317	.396	.396	.238	.396	.530	.098	.082	....	..
934	Brno Město	May 3	2.558	3.212	3.140	1.910	3.028	7.597	1.319	1.263	6.664[cb]	265,
935	Brno venkov	Apr. 15 May 15	.861	.962	.962	.645	.944	2.148	.399	.340	1.575[b]	62,
936	Dačice	Apr. 15	.216	.270	.270	.162	.270	.187	.035	.029	.350[b]	14,
937	Frenštát	Apr. 26	.336	.420	.420	.252	.420	.546	.101	.084	.650[b]	26,
938	Hranice	Apr. 27	.199	.249	.249	.149	.249	.335	.062	.052	.375[b]	15,
939	Jihlava	Apr. 20	.530	.663	.633	.398	.663	1.006	.186	.155	1.050[b]	42,
940	Kroměříž	Apr. 27	.192	.240	.240	.144	.240	.390	.072	.060	.400[b]	15,
941	Kyjov	Apr. 26	.192	.240	.240	.144	.240	.312	.058	.048	....	..
942	Litovel	Apr. 21	.234	.292	.292	.167	.292	.473	.087	.073	.150[b]	6,
943	Mikulov	Apr. 21	.192	.240	.240	.144	.240	.390	.072	.060	.400[b]	16,
944	Mor. Třebová	Apr. 21	.144	.179	.179	.108	.179	.487	.090	.075	.200[b]	8,
945	Olomouc	Apr. 22	.588	.735	.735	.441	.735	1.131	.209	.174	.925[b]	37,
946	Prostějov	Apr. 15	....	....	....	....	....	1.560	.288	.240	1.125[b]	45,
947	Přerov	Apr. 20	.449	.561	.561	.337	.561	.959	.177	.148	.950[b]	37,
948	Rožnov	Apr. 27	.336	.420	.420	.252	.420	.780	.144	.120	....	..
949	Svitavy	Apr. 15	.792	.990	.990	.594	.990	1.357	.251	.209	1.525[b]	61,
950	Šumperk	May 5	.768	.960	.960	.576	1.276	1.087	.259	.216	1.500[b]	60,
951	Tišnov	Apr. 24	.211	.264	.264	.158	.264	.406	.075	.062	.425[b]	17,

CZECHO-SLOVAKIA

Internal Deliveries, (1) BRNO, (2) OLOMOUC, (3) MEZIŘÍČÍ, (4) FRÝDEK MÍSTEK Warehouses

Table 257—*Continued*

eipt o.	Local Committee (Mistni Komitét)	Date	Flour	Rice	Beans, Peas	Pork Products	Milk Evap.	Milk Cond.	Cocoa	Sugar	Misc.	No. of Biscuits
es 1		1920										
52	Třebíč	Apr. 15	....	....	....	....	....	.577	.107	.089	.450[b]	18,000
53	Uh. Brod	Apr. 26	.114	.143	.143	.086	.143	.203	.037	.031	.220[b]	8,800
54	Uh. Hradiště	May 2	.223	.279	.279	.167	.279	.351	.065	.054	.425[b]	17,000
55	Val. Klobouky	Apr. 15	.060	.076	.076	.045	.076	.156	.029	.024	.125[b]	5,000
56	Val. Meziříčí	Apr. 22	.367	.459	.459	.275	.459	.523	.097	.080	.300[b]	12,000
57	Val. Meziříčí	Apr. 15	.058	.072	.072	.043	.072	.156	.029	.024	.150[b]	6,000
58	Všetín	Apr. 20	.710	.888	.888	.533	.888	1.123	.207	.173	1.308[b]	52,320
59	Vyškov	Apr. 27	.149	.186	.186	.112	.186	.156	.029	.024	.250[b]	10,000
60	Znojmo město	Apr. 19	.159	.198	.198	.119	.198	.421	.078	.065	.350[b]	14,400
61	Znojmo venkov	Apr. 19	.096	.120	.120	.072	.120	.335	.062	.052	.250[b]	9,960
35	Holešov	May 4	.576	.720	.720	.432	.720	.906	.167	.139	1.075[b]	43,000
36	Všetín	May 20	.710	.888	.888	.533	.888	1.123	.207	.173	1.300[b]	52,320
37	Val. Meziříčí	May 24	.367	.459	.459	.275	.459	.523	.097	.080	.650[b]	36,400
38	Uh. Hradiště	June 3	.190	.237	.237	.142	.237	.257	.048	.040	.350[b]	14,000
39	Přerov	May 20	.276	.345	.345	.207	.345	.647	.120	.100	.600[b]	24,000
40	Prostějov	May 20	.408	.510	.510	.306	.510	1.560	.288	.240	1.225[cb]	45,000
41	Nový Jičín	June 1	.624	.780	.780	.468	.780	1.357	.251	.209	.900[b]	36,000
42	Jihlava	May 2	.444	.545	.545	.333	.545	.850	.157	.131	....	.....
43	Brno venkov	June 2	.705	.865	.779	.529	2.672	....	.329	.274	1.550[b]	61,740
44	Brno město	June 2	2.683	3.514	3.531	2.033	9.939	....	1.214	1.006	5.706[cb]	227,356
45	Val. Klobouky	June 1	.048	.060	.060	.036	.060	.156	.029	.024	.125[b]	5,000
46	Hustopeč	June 1	.194	.243	.243	.146	.243	.242	.045	.037	.200[b]	14,000
47	Litovel	June 1	.214	.267	.267	.160	.267	.429	.079	.066	.450[b]	18,000
48	Kyjov	June 5	.192	.240	.240	.144	.270	.312	.058	.048	....	.....
49	Třebíč	June 1	....	....	....	....	.240	.577	.107	.089	.450[b]	18,000
50	Val. Meziříčí	June 1	.058	.072	.072	.043	.072	.156	.029	.024	.150[b]	6,000
51	Hranice	May 30	.199	.249	.249	.149	.279	.335	.062	.052	.375[b]	15,000
52	Zábřeh	May 20	.890	1.113	1.113	.668	1.113	1.786	.330	.275	1.800[b]	72,000
53	Rožňov	May 21	.336	.420	.420	.252	.420	.780	.144	.120	.800[cb]	28,800
54	Boskovice	May 20	.212	.264	.264	.158	.748	....	.089	.074	.575[b]	23,000
55	Tišňov	May 30	.211	.264	.264	.158	.264	.406	.075	.062	.425[b]	17,000
56	Rýmařov	May 25	.307	.384	.384	.230	.384	.624	.115	.096	.625[b]	25,000
57	Mor. Krumlov	May 30	.173	.216	.216	.130	.216	.281	.052	.043	.325[b]	13,000
58	Vyškov	May 29	.149	.186	.186	.112	.186	.156	.029	.024	.250[b]	10,000
59	Znojmo město	May 27	.159	.138	.138	.119	.198	.421	.078	.065	.350[b]	14,000
60	Šumperk	May 23	.768	.960	.960	.576	.960	1.404	.259	.216	1.500[b]	60,000
61	Mor. Třebová	June 10	.144	.179	.179	.108	.179	.487	.090	.075	.375[b]	15,000
62	Frenštát	May 12	.336	.420	.420	.252	.420	.546	.101	.084	.650[b]	26,000
63	Mor. Budějovice	June 2	.048	.060	.060	.036	.060	.187	.035	.029	.150[b]	6,000
64	Mikulov	June 2	.192	.240	.240	.144	.240	.390	.072	.060	.400[b]	16,000
65	Hodonín	May 21	.384	.480	.480	.288	.480	.577	.107	.089	.700[b]	28,000
66	Dačice	June 2	.216	.270	.270	.162	.270	.187	.035	.029	.350[b]	14,000
67	Beroun	June 2	.283	.354	.354	.212	.354	.452	.084	.070	.525[b]	21,000
68	Kroměříž	June 5	.192	.240	.240	.144	.240	.390	.072	.060	.400[b]	16,000
69	Olomouc	May 23	.588	.735	.735	.441	.735	1.131	.209	.174	.925[b]	37,000
70	Znojmo venkov	May 29	.096	.120	.120	.072	.120	.335	.062	.052	.250[b]	9,960
71	Svitavy	May 17	.792	.990	.990	.594	.990	1.357	.251	.209	1.525[b]	61,000
72	Nov. Město	June 2	.125	.156	.156	.094	.156	.203	.037	.031	.....	.....
34	Nov. Město	June 15	.125	.156	.156	.094	.156	.203	.037	.031	.250[b]	10,000
45	Prostějov	June 11	1.020	1.275	1.275	.765	1.275	3.900	.720	.600	2.775[b]	111,000
46	Olomouc	June 20	.600	.750	.750	....	.750	1.170	.260	.180	1.200[b]	48,000
47	Šumperk	June 26	.768	.960	.960	.576	.960	1.404	.259	.217	1.500[b]	60,000
48	N. Jičín	June 19	.429	.775	.637	.346	.573	1.240	.236	.196	.....	.....
49	Třebíč	June 25	....	....	....	....	.240	.577	.107	.089	.450[b]	18,000
50	Mor. Budějovice	June 30	.048	.060	.060	.036	.060	.187	.035	.029	.150[b]	6,000
51	Jihlava	June 26	.487	.609	.609	.365	.609	.928	.171	.143	.975[b]	39,000
52	Vyškov	June 28	.120	.150	.150	.090	.150	.133	.024	.020	.225[b]	9,000

Commodities in Net Metric Tons of 1,000 Kilograms or 2,204.6 Pounds

[*Continued on next page*]

CZECHO-SLOVAKIA

Internal Deliveries, (1) BRNO, (2) OLOMOUC, (3) MEZIŘÍČÍ, (4) FRÝDEK MÍSTEK Warehouses

Table 257—*Continued*

Receipt No.	Local Committee (Mistni Komitét)	Date	Commodities in Net Metric Tons of 1,000 Kilograms or 2,204.6 Pounds									
			Flour	Rice	Beans, Peas	Pork Products	Milk		Cocoa	Sugar	Misc.	No. o Biscuit
							Evap.	Cond.				
Series 1		1920										
1353	Mor. Krumlov	June 28	.173	.216	.216	.130	.216	.246	.052	.043	.325[b]	13,0
1354	Hustopeč	June 28	.194	.243	.243	.146	.243	.272	.045	.037	.350[b]	14,0
1355	Svitavy	June 18	.672	.840	.840	.504	.870	.936	.173	.144	1.200[b]	48,0
1356	Hodonín	June 28	.408	.510	.510	.306	.510	.624	.115	.096	.750[b]	30,0
1357	Uher. Hradiště	June 20	.240	.300	.300	.180	.300	.390	.072	.060	.450[b]	18,0
1358	Boskovice	June 30	.269	.336	.336	.202	.336	.343	.063	.053	.475[b]	19,0
1359	Rýmařov	July 1	.307	.384	.384	.230	.384	.624	.115	.096	.625[b]	25,0
1360	Znojmo město	June 15	.139	.198	.198	.119	.198	.421	.078	.065	.375[b]	15,0
1361	Val. Klobouky	July 1	.048	.060	.060	.036	.060	.156	.029	.024	.125[b]	5,0
1362	Litovel	June 30	.224	.280	.280	.168	.280	.451	.083	.069	.475[b]	19,0
1363	Dačice	July 1	.163	.204	.204	.122	.204	.109	.020	.017	.250[b]	10,0
1364	Val. Meziříčí	July 1	.058	.072	.072	.043	.072	.156	.029	.024	.150[b]	6,0
1365	Zábřeh	June 20	.890	1.113	1.113	.668	1.113	1.786	.330	.275	1.800[b]	72,0
1366	Val. Meziříčí	July 1	.384	.480	.480	.288	.480	.624	.115	.096	.725[b]	29,0
1367	Šternberk	June 22	.595	.744	.744	.446	.744	1.030	.190	.158	1.150[b]	46,0
1368	Rožňov	June 17	.480	.600	.600	.360	.600	1.092	.202	.168	1.025[b]	41,0
1369	Kroměříž	July 2	.192	.240	.240	.144	.240	.390	.072	.060	.400[b]	16,0
1370	Znojmo venkov	June 24	.096	.120	.120	.072	.120	.335	.062	.052	.250[b]	10,0
1371	Hranice	July 2	.199	.249	.249	.149	.249	.335	.662	.052	.375[b]	15,0
1372	Frenštát	June 26	.432	.540	.540	.324	.540	.702	.130	.108	.825[b]	33,0
1373	Beroun-Morava	June 30	.283	.354	.354	.212	.354	.452	.084	.070	.525[b]	21,0
1374	Tišňov	July 2	.211	.264	.264	.158	.264	.406	.075	.062	.425[b]	17,0
1375	Mor. Třebová	July 3	.144	.180	.180	.108	.180	.315	.066	.055	.325[b]	13,0
1376	Kyjov	June 26	.153	.228	.214	.111	.203	.189	.036	.040	.375[b]	15,0
1377	Holešov	June 26	.576	.720	.720	.432	.720	.906	.167	.139	1.075[b]	43,0
1378	Brno venkov	June 26	.931	1.199	1.199	.719	1.110	2.374	.403	.367	2.100[b]	84,0
1379	Brno město	June 30	2.951	3.499	3.481	2.154	3.726	6.751	1.301	1.105	6.250[b]	251,9
1380	Mikulov	June 30	.013	.110	.023	.006	.023	.128	.023	.014	.100[b]	4,0
1462	Šternberk	July 7	.067	.084	.084	.050	.084	.094	.017	.014	.060[b]	2,4
		1919										
2275	Znojmo	Sept. 25	.320	.080	.080	.320	.320	1.113	.225	....	.....	..
2276	Kroměříž	Sept. 23	.280	.070	.070	.280	.280	.716	.144	....	.....	..
2277	Brno	Sept. 27	5.120	1.280	1.280	5.120	5.120	10.971	2.215	....	.....	..
2278	Krumlov	Sept. 29	.240	.060	.060	.240	.240	.477	.096	....	.....	..
2279	Jihlava	Sept. 25	.960	.240	.240	.960	.960	2.226	.450	....	.....	..
2280	Boskovice	Sept. 23	.400	.100	.100	.400	.400	1.113	.225	....	.....	..
2281	Hodonín	Sept. 26	.680	.170	.170	.680	.680	1.272	.257	....	.....	..
2282	Nové Město	Sept. 23	.160	.040	.040	.160	.160	.477	.096	....	.....	..
2283	Zábřeh	Sept. 23	1.200	.300	.300	1.200	1.200	2.862	.578	....	.....	..
2284	Brno	Oct. 27	5.120	1.280	1.280	5.120	5.120	10.971	2.215	....	.....	..
2285	Hodonín	Oct. 31	.680	.170	.170	.680	.680	1.272	.257	....	.....	..
2286	Hustopeč	Oct. 31	.240	.060	.060	.240	.240	.477	.096	....	.....	..
2287	Kyjov	Oct. 21	.240	.060	.060	.240	.240	.477	.096	....	.....	..
2288	Uh. Hradiště	Oct. 13	.200	.050	.050	.200	.200	.477	.096	....	.....	..
2289	Vyškov	Oct. 7	.380	.095	.095	.380	.380	.716	.144	....	.....	..
2290	Mähr Schönberg	Oct. 15	1.040	.260	.260	1.040	1.040	2.226	.449	....	.....	..
2291	Šternberg	Oct. 13	.960	.240	.240	.960	.960	1.908	.385	....	.....	..
2292	Rýmařov	Oct. 1	.440	.110	.110	.440	.440	.954	.193	....	.100[c]	..
2293	Přerov	Oct. 21	.920	.230	.230	.920	.920	1.908	.385	....	.....	..
2294	Prostějov	Oct. 6	1.320	.330	.330	1.320	1.320	3.180	.642	....	.....	..
2295	Olomouc	Oct. 26	.960	.240	.240	.960	.960	1.908	.385	....	.....	..
2296	Nový Jičín	Oct. 10	.960	.240	.240	.960	.960	1.749	.353	....	.....	..
2297	Litovel	Oct. 13	.280	.070	.070	.280	.280	.716	.144	....	.....	..
2298	Hranice	Oct. 4	.260	.065	.065	.260	.260	.557	.112	....	.....	..
2299	Beroun	Oct. 31	.440	.110	.110	.440	.440	.954	.195	....	.....	..
2300	Tišňov	Oct. 27	.280	.070	.070	.280	.280	.636	.128	....	.....	..
2301	Kroměříž	Oct. 21	.280	.070	.070	.280	.280	.716	.144	....	.....	..
2302	Nové Meziříčí	Oct. 6	.100	.025	.025	.100	.100	.318	.064	....	.....	..

CZECHO-SLOVAKIA

Internal Deliveries, (1) BRNO, (2) OLOMOUC, (3) MEZIŘÍČÍ, (4) FRÝDEK MÍSTEK Warehouses

Table 257—*Continued*

Receipt No.	Local Committee (Mistni Komitét)	Date	Flour	Rice	Beans, Peas	Pork Products	Milk Evap.	Milk Cond.	Cocoa	Sugar	Misc.	No. of Biscuits
			Commodities in Net Metric Tons of 1,000 Kilograms or 2,204.6 Pounds									
Series 1		1919										
2303	Mor. Krumlov	Nov. 7	.240	.060	.060	.240	.240	.477	.096	....	....	.....
2304	Zábřeh	Nov. 8	1.200	.300	.300	1.200	1.200	2.862	.578	....	....	.....
2305	Nové Město na Moravě	Nov. 8	.160	.040	.040	.160	.160	.795	.064	....	....	.....
2306	Jihlava	Nov. 8	.960	.240	.240	.960	.960	2.226	.450	....	....	.....
2307	Hranice	Nov. 9	.260	.065	.065	.260	.260	.557	.112	....	....	.....
2308a	Boskovice	Nov. 10	.025	.006	.006	.025	.025	.082	.017	....	....	.....
2308b	Boskovice	Nov. 10	.350	.088	.088	.350	.350	.949	.191	....	....	.....
2309	Nový Jičín	Nov. 12	.960	.240	.240	.960	.960	1.749	.353	....	....	.....
2310	Třebíč	Nov. 12	.380	.095	.095	.380	.380	.875	.177	....	....	.....
2311	Prostějov	Nov. 14	1.320	.330	.330	1.320	1.320	3.180	.642	....	....	.....
2312	Vyškov	Nov. 14	.076	.019	.019	.076	.076	....	....	....	....	.....
2313	Šternberk	Nov. 19	.960	.240	.240	.960	.960	1.908	.385	....	....	.....
2314	Holešov	Nov. 25	.800	.200	.200	.800	.800	1.431	.289	....	....	.....
2315	Uh. Hradiště	Nov. 25	.200	.050	.050	.200	.200	.477	.096	....	....	.....
2316	Přerov	Nov. 26	.920	.230	.230	.920	.920	1.908	.385	....	....	.....
2317	Brno venkov	Nov. 8	.380	.395	.395	1.580	1.580	4.691	.947	....	....	.....
2318	Beroun	Dec. 15	.660	.660	.660	.462	.660	.900	.180	.180	....	.....
2319	Šumperk	Dec. 16	....	.260	.260	1.040	1.040	2.226	.450	....	....	.....
2320	Litovel	Nov. 27	.280	.070	.070	.280	.280	.716	.144	....	....	.....
2321	Kyjov	Nov. 28	.240	.060	.060	.240	.240	.477	.096	....	....	.....
322	Olomouc	Dec. 1	.960	.240	.240	.960	.960	1.908	.385	....	....	.....
323	Uh. Brod	Dec. 1	.240	.240	.240	.168	.240	.300	.060	.060	....	.....
324	Znojmo	Dec. 2	.480	.480	.480	.336	.480	1.050	.210	.210	....	.....
325	Tišnov	Dec. 2	.420	.420	.420	.294	.420	.600	.120	.120	....	.....
326	Mikulov	Dec. 3	....	.060	.060	.240	.240	.636	.128	....	....	.....
327	Třebíč	Dec. 3	.527	.527	.527	.368	.527	.825	.165	.165	....	.....
328	Rýmařov	Dec. 4	.440	.110	.110	.440	.440	.954	.693	....	....	.....
329	Dačice	Dec. 4	.280	.070	.070	.280	.280	.318	.064	....	....	.....
330	Hranice	Dec. 4	.390	.390	.390	.273	.390	.525	.105	.105	....	.....
331	Kroměříž	Dec. 5	.420	.420	.420	.294	.420	.675	.135	.135	....	.....
332	Zábřeh	Dec. 5	1.800	1.800	1.800	1.260	1.800	2.700	.540	.540	....	.....
333	Hodonín	Dec. 6	1.020	1.020	1.020	.714	1.020	1.200	.240	.240	....	.....
334	Mor. Budějovice	Dec. 9	.063	.063	.063	.044	.063	.143	.029	.029	....	.....
335	Vel. Meziřičí	Dec. 9	.125	.125	.125	.088	.125	.250	.050	.050	....	.....
336	Brno Město	Dec. 10	2.251	2.243	2.238	1.189	....	....	....	....	....	.....
337	Nové Město na Moravě	Dec. 15	.200	.200	.200	.140	.200	.250	.050	.050	....	.....
338	Brno venkov	Dec. 17	1.975	1.975	1.975	1.383	1.975	3.810	.762	.762	....	.....
339	Boskovice	Dec. 19	.547	.547	.547	.383	.547	.811	.162	.162	....	.....
340	Jihlava	Dec. 19	1.200	1.200	1.200	.840	1.200	1.750	.350	.350	....	.....
341	Šumperk	Dec. 20	....	1.300	1.300	.910	1.300	1.750	.350	....	....	.....
342	Prostějov	Dec. 20	1.650	1.650	1.650	1.158	1.650	2.500	.500	.500	....	.....
343	Litovel	Dec. 20	.350	.350	.350	.245	.350	.563	.113	.113	....	.....
344	Sternberg	Dec. 21	2.160	.600	1.200	.840	1.200	1.500	.300	.300	....	.....
345	Hustopeč	Dec. 24	.300	.300	.300	.210	.300	.375	.075	.075	....	.....
		1920										
346	Nový Jičín	Jan. 1	2.160	.600	1.200	.840	1.200	1.375	.275	.275	....	.....
347	Brno	Jan. 26	3.638	1.721	3.047	1.992	2.840	5.520	1.087	1.241	....	.....
348	Všetín	Jan. 27	1.150	.575	1.150	.805	1.150	1.375	.275	.275	....	.....
349	Znojmo	Jan. 27	.400	.200	.400	.280	.400	.875	.175	.175	....	.....
350	Tišňov	Jan. 28	.350	.175	.350	.245	.350	.500	.100	.100	....	.....
351	Meziříčí	Jan. 28	.661	.330	.661	.462	.661	.625	.125	.125	....	.....
352	Brno venkov	Jan. 29	1.975	.988	1.975	1.383	1.975	3.810	.762	.762	....	.....
353	Zábřeh	Jan. 29	1.500	.750	1.500	1.050	1.500	2.250	.450	.450	....	.....
354	Rožňov	Jan. 29	.500	.250	.500	.350	.500	.875	.175	.175	....	.....
355	Frenštát	Jan. 29	.500	.250	.500	.350	.500	.625	.125	.125	....	.....
356	Boskovice	Feb. 2	1.445	.137	.548	.383	.548	.811	.162	.162	....	.....
357	Rýmařov	Feb. 2	.990	.275	.550	.385	.550	.750	.150	.150	....	.....
358	Litovel	Feb. 2	.980	.688	.350	.245	.350	.563	.113	.113	....	.....

[*Continued on next page*]

CZECHO-SLOVAKIA

Internal Deliveries, (1) BRNO, (2) OLOMOUC, (3) MEZIŘÍČÍ, (4) FRÝDEK MÍSTEK Warehouses

Table 257—*Continued*

Receipt No.	Local Committee (Mistni Komitét)	Date	Commodities in Net Metric Tons of 1,000 Kilograms or 2,204.6 Pounds									
			Flour	Rice	Beans, Peas	Pork Products	Milk Evap.	Milk Cond.	Cocoa	Sugar	Misc.	No. of Biscuits
Series 1		1920										
2359	Kroměříž	Feb. 2	.770	.138	.350	.245	.350	.563	.113	.113	....	....
2360	Jihlava	Feb. 3	3.360	.600	1.200	.840	1.200	1.750	.350	.350	....	....
2361	Hranice	Feb. 5	.715	.081	.325	.228	.325	.438	.088	.088	....	....
2362	Vyškov	Feb. 6	.361	.143	.285	.199	.285	.238	.048	.048	....	....
2363	Prostějov	Feb. 12	1.650	.825	1.650	1.155	1.650	2.500	.500	.500	....	....
2364	Velké Meziříčí	Feb. 13	.250	.113	.125	.088	.125	.250	.050	.050	....	....
2365	Mor. Krumlov	Feb. 14	.300	.075	.300	.210	.300	.375	.075	.075	....	....
2366	Nové Město na Moravě	Feb. 17	.400	.050	.200	.140	.200	.250	.050	.050	....	....
2367	Mor. Budějovice	Feb. 20	.053	.013	.053	.037	.053	.119	.024	.024	....	....
2368	Šternberk na Moravě	Feb. 17	1.200	.300	1.200	.840	1.200	1.500	.300	.300	....	....
2369	Přerov	Feb. 18	1.176	.294	1.176	.823	1.176	1.553	.311	.311	....	....
2370	Kyjov	Feb. 19	.300	.075	.300	.210	.300	.375	.075	.075	....	....
2371	Třebíč	Feb. 10	.439	.110	.439	.307	.439	.688	.138	.138	....	....
2372	Dačice	Feb. 21	.350	.088	.350	.245	.350	.250	.050	.050	....	....
2373	Uh. Hradište	Feb. 21	.250	.063	.250	.175	.250	.375	.075	.075	....	....
2374	Šumperk	Feb. 22	1.300	.325	1.300	.910	1.300	1.750	.350	.350	....	....
2375	Hranice	Feb. 18	....	....	....	....	....	....	....	....	.100[c]	....
2376	Prostějov	Feb. 25	....	....	....	....	....	....	.050	....	....	....
2377	Olomouc	Feb. 26	1.200	.600	1.200	.840	1.200	1.500	.300	.300	....	....
2378	Třebíč	Feb. 28	....	....	....	....	....	.688	....	....	....	....
2379	Beroun	Feb. 5	1.210	.138	.550	.385	.550	.750	.150	.150	....	....
2380	Velké Brno	Feb. 15	6.156	.962	6.198	4.383	10.913	9.852	2.518	2.673	.078[c]	...
2381	Velké Brno	Apr. 1–15	1.075	.506	1.208	.770	.891	2.698	.496	.500	.025[c]	...
2422	Uh. Hradiště	Feb. 12	....	....	....	....	....	....	....	....	.100[c]	...
2423	Boskovice	Feb. 15	....	....	....	....	....	....	....	....	.100[c]	...
2424	Vel. Meziříčí	Apr. 6	....	....	....	....	....	....	....	....	.100[c]	...
2425	Znojmo	Apr. 7	....	....	....	....	....	....	....	....	.100[c]	...
2426	Mor. Budějovice	Apr. 10	....	....	....	....	....	....	....	....	.100[c]	...
2427	Blánsko	Apr. 7	....	....	....	....	....	....	....	....	.031[c]	...
2428	Křilov u Olomouce	Apr. 1	....	....	....	....	....	....	....	....	.031[c]	...
2429	Prostějov	Apr. 29	....	....	....	....	....	....	....	....	.100[c]	...
2431	Brno město	May 1	....	....	....	....	....	....	....	....	.116[c]	...
2435	Nový Jičín	May 10	....	....	....	....	....	....	....	....	.100[c]	...
2436	Troppau	May 2	....	....	....	....	....	....	....	....	.100[c]	...
2440	Vyškov	June 10	....	....	....	....	....	....	....	....	.060[c]	...
2441	Karvín	May 5	....	....	....	....	....	....	....	....	.160[b c]	4,0
2442	Tišnov	June 8	....	....	....	....	....	....	....	....	.100[c]	...
2443	Brno	June 16	....	....	....	....	....	....	....	....	.200[c]	...
2444	Šternberk	June 9	....	....	....	....	....	....	....	....	.060[c]	...
2452	Brno	July 15	....	....	....	....	....	....	....	....	.100[c]	...
2453	Mor. Ostrava	July 24	....	....	....	....	....	....	....	....	.093[c]	...
2454	Prostějov	July 23	....	....	....	....	....	....	....	....	.100[c]	...
2455	Slezská Ostrava	July 7	....	....	....	....	....	....	....	....	.092[c]	...
2638	Brno	July 22	....	....	....	....	....	....	....	....	.125[d]	...
2648	Brno	July 21	....	....	....	....	....	....	....	....	.125[d]	...
Series 2		1921										
128	Kroměříž	Apr. 26	.666	.180	.225	.117	.360	....	.045	.207	....	...
129	Litovel	Apr. 26	.666	.180	.225	.117	.360	....	.045	.207	....	...
130	Jihlava	Apr. 26	2.886	.780	.975	.507	1.560	....	.195	.897	....	...
131	Boskovice	Apr. 26	.888	.240	.300	.156	.480	....	.060	.276	....	...
132	Mor. Třebová	Apr. 26	.888	.240	.300	.156	.478	....	.060	.276	....	...
133	Svitavy	Apr. 26	1.332	.360	.450	.234	.720	....	.090	.414	....	...
134	Třebíč	Apr. 26	1.110	.300	.375	.195	.600	....	.075	.345	....	...
135	Frenštát	Apr. 26	1.110	.300	.375	.195	.600	....	.075	.345	....	...
136	Prostějov	Apr. 26	3.108	.840	1.050	.546	1.680	....	.210	.966	....	...
137	Přerov	Apr. 26	2.997	.810	1.013	.527	1.620	....	.203	.932	....	...
138	Šumperk	Apr. 28	2.220	.600	.750	.390	1.200	....	.150	.690	....	...
139	Val. Meziříčí	Apr. 26	2.498	.675	.844	.439	1.349	....	.169	.776	....	...

CZECHO-SLOVAKIA

Internal Deliveries, (1) BRNO, (2) OLOMOUC, (3) MEZIŘÍČÍ, (4) FRÝDEK MÍSTEK Warehouses

Table 257—*Continued*

eipt o.	Local Committee (Mistni Komitét)	Date	Flour	Rice	Beans, Peas	Pork Products	Milk Evap.	Milk Cond.	Cocoa	Sugar	Misc.	No. of Biscuits
			Commodities in Net Metric Tons of 1,000 Kilograms or 2,204.6 Pounds									
es 2		1921										
40	Sternberk	Apr. 26	2.775	.750	.938	.488	1.500	....	.188	.863	....	.....
41	Velké Brno	Apr. 26	17.760	4.800	6.000	3.120	9.600	....	1.200	5.520	....	.....
42	Val. Klobouky	Apr. 16	.444	.120	.150	.078	.240	....	.030	.138	....	.....
43	Hranice	Apr. 28	1.110	.300	.375	.195	.600	....	.075	.345	....	.....
44	Rožnov pod Radhoštěm	Apr. 27	2.220	.600	.750	.390	1.200	....	.150	.690	....	.....
45	Zábřeh	Apr. 26	2.442	.660	.825	.429	1.319	....	.165	.759	....	.....
46	Olomouc	Apr. 14	3.663	.990	1.238	.644	1.980	....	.248	1.139	....	.....
47	Teleč	Apr. 16	.355	.096	.120	.062	.191	....	.024	.110	....	.....
48	Holešov	Apr. 26	.888	.240	.300	.150	.480	....	.060	.276	....	.....
49	Nový Jičín	Apr. 26	2.553	.690	.863	.449	1.380	....	.173	.794	....	.....
50	Beroun	Apr. 26	1.110	.300	.375	.195	.600	....	.075	.345	....	.....
51	Velké Meziříčí	May 11	.222	.060	.075	.039	.120	....	.015	.069	....	.....
52	Rýmařov	Apr. 26	2.220	.600	.750	.390	1.200	....	.150	.690	....	.....
53	Znojmo	May 25	.444	.270	....	.078	....	....	.030	.138	.240[a]	.....
54	Medvědice	May 11	.333	.090	.113	.059	.180	....	.023	.104	....	.....
89	Brno	May 9	.185	.050	.063	.033	.100	....	.013	.058	....	.....
90	Morkovice	May 19	.111	.068	....	.020	....	....	.008	.035	.060[a]	.....
91	Nová Říšeu Telče	May 25	.148	.090	....	.026	....	....	.010	.046	.080[a]	.....
92	Hustopeč	May 25	.074	.045	....	.013	....	....	.005	.023	.040[a]	.....
93	Lomnice	May 21	.056	.034	....	.010	....	....	.004	.018	.030[a]	.....
94	Brno	May 6	.370	.100	.125	.065	.200	....	.025	.115	....	.....
95	Brno	May 6	.148	.040	.050	.026	.080	....	.010	.046	....	.....
96	Brno	May 6	.370	.100	.125	.065	.200	....	.025	.115	....	.....
97	Brno	Apr. 21	.185	.050	.063	.033	.100	....	.013	.058	....	.....
98	Brno	May 6	.259	.070	.088	.046	.140	....	.018	.081	....	.....
99	Brno	Apr. 21	2.220	.600	.750	.390	1.200	....	.150	.690	....	.....
00	Jundrov	May 1	.185	.050	.063	.033	.100	....	.013	.058	....	.....
01	Brno	Apr. 23	.295	.080	.100	.052	.160	....	.020	.092	....	.....
02	Brno	Apr. 23	.148	.040	.050	.026	.080	....	.010	.046	....	.....
03	Střelice-Brno	Apr. 27	.296	.080	.100	.052	.160	....	.020	.092	....	.....
04	Brno	May 24	....	....	....	....	....	....	....	....	.011[a]	.....
05	Mor. Krumlov	May 19	.333	.203	....	.059	....	....	.023	.104	.180[a]	.....
06	Vel. Meziříčí	May 25	.037	.023	....	.007	....	....	.003	.012	.020[a]	.....
07	Svitavy	May 19	.111	.068	....	.020	....	....	.008	.035	.060[a]	.....
08	Vranov	May 19	.185	.113	....	.033	....	....	.013	.058	.100[a]	.....
09	Rajhrad u Hustopeče	May 23	.278	.169	....	.049	....	....	.019	.086	.150[a]	.....
10	Kunštát u Boskovic	May 19	.074	.045	....	.013	....	....	.005	.023	.040[a]	.....
11	Brno	May 12	.074	.020	.025	.013	.040	....	.005	.023	....	.....
12	Brno	May 14	.259	.070	.088	.046	....	....	.018	.081	.140[a]	.....
13	Brno	May 19	.222	.135	....	.039	....	....	.015	.069	.120[a]	.....
14	Mor. Budějovice	May 19	.740	.200	.250	.130	.399	....	.050	.230	....	.....
15	Boskovice	May 19	.056	.034	....	.010	....	....	.014	.018	.030[a]	.....
16	Boskovice	May 19	.222	.135	....	.039	....	....	.015	.069	.120[a]	.....
17	Jihlava	May 25	.185	.113	....	.033	....	....	.013	.058	.100[a]	.....
18	Třebíč	May 25	.204	.124	....	.036	....	....	.014	.063	.110[a]	.....
19	Znojmo	May 19	.111	.068	....	.020	....	....	.008	.035	.060[a]	.....
20	Znojmo	May 19	.111	.068	....	.020	....	....	.008	.035	.060[a]	.....
21	Liptál	June 1	.185	.113	....	.033	.100	....	.013	.058	....	.....
22	Lukov u Holešova	May 23	.056	.034	....	.010	....	....	.004	.018	.030[a]	.....
23	Val. Meziříčí	May 23	.092	.056	....	.016	....	....	.006	.029	.050[a]	.....
24	Čeladná u Frenštátu	May 23	.111	.068	....	.020	....	....	.008	.035	.060[a]	.....
25	Nezamyslice	May 23	.185	.050	.063	.033	....	....	.013	.058	.100[a]	.....
26	Novosady	May 13	.185	.050	.063	.033	....	....	.013	.058	.100[a]	.....
27	Olomouc	May 13	.092	.025	.031	.016	....	....	.006	.029	.050[a]	.....
28	Olomouc	May 13	.185	.050	.063	.033	....	....	.013	.058	.100[a]	.....
29	Přerov	May 13	.185	.050	.063	.033	....	....	.013	.058	.100[a]	.....
30	Litovel	May 13	.185	.050	.063	.033	....	....	.013	.058	.100[a]	.....

[*Continued on next page*]

CZECHO-SLOVAKIA

Internal Deliveries, (1) BRNO, (2) OLOMOUC, (3) MEZIŘÍČÍ, (4) FRÝDEK MÍSTEK Warehouses

Table 257—*Continued*

Receipt No.	Local Committee (Mistni Komitét)	Date	Commodities in Net Metric Tons of 1,000 Kilograms or 2,204.6 Pounds									
			Flour	Rice	Beans, Peas	Pork Products	Milk Evap.	Milk Cond.	Cocoa	Sugar	Misc.	No. of Biscuit
Series 2		1921										
331	Holešov	May 21	.185	.113	....	.033	....	....	.013	.058	.100[a]	...
332	Olomouc	May 13	.185	.050	.063	.033	....	....	.013	.058	.100[a]	...
333	Přerov	May 13	.174	.047	.059	.031	....	....	.012	.054	.094[a]	...
334	Týn u Lipníka	May 21	.056	.034	....	.010	....	....	.004	.018	.030[a]	...
335	Hranice	May 21	.185	.113	....	.033	....	....	.013	.058	.100[a]	...
336	Lipník	May 19	.296	.080	.100	.052	....	....	.020	.092	.160[a]	...
337	Prostějov	May 21	.259	.158	....	.046	....	....	.018	.081	.140[a]	...
338	Val. Meziříčí	May 21	.222	.135	....	.039	....	....	.015	.069	.130[a c]	...
339	Zábřeh	May 13	.185	.050	.063	.033	....	....	.013	.058	.100[a]	...
340	Val. Meziříčí	May 19	.370	.100	.125	.065	....	....	.025	.115	.200[a]	...
341	Prostějov	May 19	.370	.225	....	.065	....	....	.025	.115	.200[a]	...
342	Nový Jičín	May 21	.092	.056	....	.016	....	....	.006	.029	.050[a]	...
343	Kelč u Hranic	May 21	.056	.034	....	.010	....	....	.004	.018	.030[a]	...
344	Prostějov	May 11	1.073	.290	.363	.189	.579	....	.073	.335	....	...
345	Frýštát	May 21	.156	.034	....	.010	....	....	.004	.018	.030[a]	...
346	Nový Jičín	May 21	.092	.056	....	.016	....	....	.006	.029	.050[a]	...
347	Šternberk	May 19	.185	.113	....	.033	....	....	.013	.058	.100[a]	...
368	Košice	May 30	.148	.090	....	.026	....	....	.010	.046	.080[a]	...
369	Báňská Bystrica	June 21	.463	.281	....	.081	.250	....	.031	.144	....	...
370	Slovenská Lupča	June 27	.370	.225	....	.065	.200	....	.025	.115	....	...
371	Kláštor p. Znievom	June 21	.400	.243	....	.070	.215	....	.027	.124	....	...
372	Žilina	June 1	.222	.135	....	.039	.120	....	.015	.069	....	...
373	Košice	May 30	.740	.450	....	.130	.400	....	.050	.230	....	...
374	Košice	May 30	.629	.383	....	.111	.340	....	.043	.196	....	...
375	Trenčín	June 1	.296	.180	....	.052	.160	....	.020	.092	....	...
376	Žilina	June 1	.185	.113	....	.033	.100	....	.013	.058	....	...
377	Modrá	May 30	.278	.169	....	.049	....	....	.019	.086	.150[a]	...
378	Radvan	May 30	.130	.079	....	.023	....	....	.009	.040	.070[a]	...
379	Trnava	May 30	.148	.090	....	.026	....	....	.010	.046	.080[a]	...
380	Ružomberk	May 30	.148	.090	....	.026	....	....	.010	.046	.080[a]	...
381	Trstená	May 30	.074	.045	....	.013	....	....	.005	.023	.040[a]	...
382	Lučenec	May 30	.148	.090	....	.026	....	....	.010	.046	.080[a]	...
383	Nové Město n/Vahem	May 30	.074	.045	....	.013	....	....	.005	.023	.040[a]	...
384	Kremnice	June 1	.370	.225	....	.065	.200	....	.025	.115	....	...
385	Liptav. Sv. Mikuláš	May 30	.148	.090	....	.026	....	....	.010	.046	.080[a]	...
386	Turč. Sv. Martin	May 30	.148	.090	....	.026	....	....	.010	.046	.080[a]	...
387	Dolní Smokovec	June 21	.666	.405	....	.117	.360	....	.045	.207	....	...
388	Rimavská Sobota	June 21	.444	.270	....	.078	.240	....	.030	.138	....	...
389	Trenč. Slávnice	July 16	.600	....	....	....	....	....	....	....	....	...
390	Trenčín-Slávnice	July 16	.296	.180	....	.052	.160	....	.020	.092	....	...
468	Hranice	July 25	.592	.360	....	.104	.320	....	.040	.184	....	...
469	Beroun	July 28	1.480	.400	.500	.260	.800	....	.100	.460	....	...
470	Litovel	July 2	.296	.180	....	.052	.160	....	.020	.092	....	...
471	Val. Meziříčí	July 2	1.036	.630	....	.182	.560	....	.070	.322	....	...
472	Rožňov	July 2	.296	.180	....	.052	.160	....	.020	.092	....	...
473	Zábřeh	July 4	1.637	.443	.553	.288	.885	....	.111	.509	....	...
474	Jihlava	July 25	.533	.324	....	.094	.288	....	.036	.166	....	...
475	Třebíč	July 2	.444	.270	....	.078	.240	....	.030	.138	....	...
476	Mor. Šumperk	July 28	1.480	.400	.500	.260	.800	....	.100	.460	....	...
477	Nosislava	Aug. 11	.028	.018	....	.005	.015	....	.002	.008	....	...
478	Jundrov	Aug. 10	.071	.045	....	.013	.037	....	.005	.021	....	...
479	Veveří	Aug. 8	.071	.045	....	.013	.037	....	.005	.030	....	...
480	Mor. Šumperk	July 28	2.960	.800	.950	.520	1.600	....	.200	.920	....	...
481	Mor. Šumperk	July 28	....	....	....	....	1.633	....	....	....	....	...
482	Olomouc	July 26	.592	.360	....	.104	.320	....	.040	.184	....	...
483	Olomouc	July 26	.296	.180	....	.052	.160	....	.020	.092	....	...
484	Brno	July 2	4.032	2.452	....	.709	2.180	....	.273	1.253	....	...
485	Velké Brno	July 16	.740	.450	....	.130	.400	....	.050	.230	....	...
486	Svitavy	July 26	.888	.540	....	.156	.479	....	.060	.276	....	...
487	Nový Jičín	July 28	2.368	1.440	....	.416	1.280	....	.160	.736	....	...
596	Litovel	June 24	.111	.063	....	.020	.050	....	.008	.035	....	...
597	Nový Jičín	June 25	.851	.518	....	.150	.460	....	.058	.265	....	...

CZECHO-SLOVAKIA

Table 257—*Concluded*

Internal Deliveries, (1) BRNO, (2) OLOMOUC, (3) MEZIŘÍČÍ, (4) FRÝDEK MÍSTEK Warehouses

ceipt No.	Local Committee (Mistni Komitét)	Date	Commodities in Net Metric Tons of 1,000 Kilograms or 2,204.6 Pounds									
			Flour	Rice	Beans, Peas	Pork Products	Milk Evap.	Milk Cond.	Cocoa	Sugar	Misc.	No. of Biscuits
ries 2		1921										
598	Šternberk	June 24	.463	.281	....	.081	.300	....	.031	.144	....	.....
599	Zábřeh	June 25	.814	.495	....	.143	.440	....	.055	.253	....	.....
600	Přerov	June 28	.999	.608	....	.176	.540	....	.068	.311	....	.....
601	Rýmařov	June 25	.740	.450	....	.130	.400	....	.050	.230	....	.....
602	Svitava	June 24	.222	.135	....	.039	.120	....	.015	.069	....	.....
603	Beroun	June 24	.185	.113	....	.033	.100	....	.013	.058	....	.....
604	Olomouc	June 22	1.832	1.114	....	.322	.990	....	.124	.570	....	.....
605	Velké Brno	May 21	17.760	7.612	3.187	3.120	9.600	....	1.200	5.520	....	.....
606	Hranice	June 26	.370	.225	....	.065	.200	....	.025	.115	....	.....
607	Kroměříž	June 24	.111	.063	....	.020	.050	....	.008	.035	....	.....
608	Telč	June 24	.178	.108	....	.031	.096	....	.012	.055	....	.....
609	Frenštát	June 24	.185	.113	....	.033	.100	....	.013	.058	....	.....
610	Val. Meziříčí	June 25	.833	.506	....	.146	.450	....	.056	.259	....	.....
611	Val. Klobouky	June 24	.222	.135	....	.039	.120	....	.015	.069	....	.....
612	Rožňov pod Rad.	June 24	.370	.225	....	.065	.200	....	.025	.115	....	.....
613	Třebíč	June 24	.185	.113	....	.033	.100	....	.013	.058	....	.....
614	Jihlava	June 25	.962	.585	....	.169	.520	....	.065	.299	....	.....
615	Šumperk	June 24	.370	.225	....	.065	.200	....	.025	.115	....	.....
616	Holešov	June 24	.148	.090	....	.026	.080	....	.010	.046	....	.....
	Total	....	**342.048**	**168.692**	**186.065**	**195.616**	**295.023**	**389.776**	**88.791**	**76.978**	**101.467***	**3,683,983**

* Detail of miscellaneous commodity total: [a], powdered milk, 4.825; weight of 3,683,983 biscuits, 93.996; [c], codliver oil, 2.396; [d], soap, .250.

CZECHO-SLOVAKIA

Table 258

Internal Deliveries from CHOMŮTOV (Komotau) Warehouse

ceipt No.	Local Committee (Mistni Komitét)	Date	Commodities in Net Metric Tons of 1,000 Kilograms or 2,204.6 Pounds									
			Flour	Rice	Beans, Peas	Pork Products	Milk Evap.	Milk Cond.	Cocoa	Sugar	Misc.*	No. of Biscuits
ries 1		1919										
21	Bilina	Sept. 11	.400	.100	.100	.400	.400	.954	.193	....	....	.....
138	Most	Oct. 18	3.440	.860	.860	3.440	3.440	6.996	1.412	....	....	.....
195	Teplice	Oct. 26	2.760	.690	.690	2.760	2.760	5.247	1.060	....	....	.....
196	Duchcov	Oct. 23	....	.400	.400	1.600	1.600	3.975	.803	....	....	.....
197	Litoměřice	Nov. 2	.400	.100	.100	.400	.400	.636	.128	....	....	.....
198	Děčín	Oct. 17	2.700	.700	.700	2.800	2.800	....	1.152	....	....	.....
199	Bilina	Oct. 27	.400	.100	.100	.400	.400	.954	.192	....	....	.....
200	Ústí n/Labem	Oct. 23	2.960	.740	.740	2.960	2.960	5.883	1.188	....	....	.....
278	Žatec	Nov. 11	.054	.014	.014	.054	.054	.246	.050	....	....	.....
279	Chomutov	Nov. 11	1.350	.322	.322	1.308	1.308	3.048	.617	....	....	.....
280	Most	Nov. 16	....	.860	.860	3.440	3.440	6.996	1.412	....	....	.....
395	Bilina	Dec. 12	....	.600	.600	.420	.600	.900	.180	....	....	.....
396	Ústí n/Labem	Dec. 4	....	4.440	4.440	3.108	4.440	5.550	1.110	....	....	.....
397	Teplitz	Dec. 4	4.140	4.140	4.140	2.898	4.140	4.950	.990	.990	....	.....
398	Děčín	Dec. 3	....	4.200	4.200	2.940	4.200	5.400	1.080	....	....	.....
399	Žatec	Dec. 3	....	.179	.179	.125	.179	.397	.079	....	....	.....
400	Leitmeritz	Dec. 10	....	.600	.600	.420	.600	.600	.120	....	....	.....
401	Duchcov	Dec. 2	....	2.400	2.400	1.680	2.400	3.750	.750	....	....	.....
		1920										
394	Bilina	June 17	.245	.311	.332	.284	.305	.646	.119	.100	.600[b]	24,000
395	Děčín	June 22	2.496	3.137	3.125	1.929	3.117	4.522	.835	.709	4.900[b]	196,000
396	Duchcov	June 18	.784	.978	.996	.584	.981	1.672	.305	.267	1.650[b]	66,000
397	Chomůtov	June 18	1.326	1.623	1.659	1.043	1.613	2.964	.547	.466	2.800[b]	112,000
398	Litoměřice	June 18	.606	.721	.748	.457	.719	.779	.144	.120	1.050[b]	42,000

* Detail of miscellaneous commodities indicated by the following in-
xes: [b], biscuits; [d], soap. See end of Table 258 (page 499) for complete
ail.

[*Continued on next page*]

CZECHO-SLOVAKIA

Internal Deliveries, CHOMŮTOV (Komotau) Warehouse

Table 258—*Continued*

Receipt No.	Local Committee (Mistni Komitét)	Date	Flour	Rice	Beans, Peas	Pork Products	Milk Evap.	Milk Cond.	Cocoa	Sugar	Misc.	No. of Biscuits
			Commodities in Net Metric Tons of 1,000 Kilograms or 2,204.6 Pounds									
Series 1		1920										
1399	Most	June 15	1.186	1.440	1.437	.895	1.438	2.033	.374	.318	2.250[b]	90,00
1400	Rumburk	June 18	.734	.922	.902	.547	.894	1.254	.230	.198	1.400[b]	56,00
1401	Šluknov	June 16	1.490	1.878	1.861	1.261	1.875	2.660	.490	.406	2.900[b]	116,00
1402	Warnsdorf	June 18	.784	.987	.959	.583	.959	1.254	.230	.201	1.450[b]	58,00
1403	Teplice	June 15	2.656	3.303	3.305	2.052	3.292	6.232	1.152	.966	5.700[b]	228,00
1404	Ústí n/Labem	June 15	2.762	3.457	3.522	2.079	3.466	6.162	1.138	.949	5.850[b]	234,00
1405	Žatec	June 17	.263	.312	.317	.232	.305	.418	.077	.066	.500[b]	20,00
2590	Teplitz	Aug. 23	.014	.018	.018	.011	.022	.046	.068	.007	....	....
2591	Kralup b. Platz	Aug. 23	.320	.360	.365	.218	.576	.722	.168	.145	....	....
Series 2		1921										
1	Děčín a Podmokly	Apr. 3	3.441	.925	1.165	.604	1.860	....	.233	1.069	....	....
2	Rumburk	Apr. 2	2.109	.570	.713	.370	1.140	....	.143	.656	....	....
3	Teplice	Apr. 6	4.662	1.260	1.581	.821	2.520	....	.315	1.449	....	....
4	Čes. Kamenice	Apr. 5	1.776	.480	.600	.310	.960	....	.120	.552	....	....
5	Šluknov	Apr. 1	3.774	1.020	1.278	.664	2.040	....	.255	1.174	....	....
6	Warnsdorf	Mar. 24	2.775	.753	.938	.490	1.500	....	.188	.863	....	....
7	Ústí n/Labem	Apr. 20	10.878	2.940	3.672	1.909	5.880	....	.735	3.385	....	....
8	Duchcov	Apr. 3	....	.454	....	.294	.900	....	.113	.522	....	....
9	Chomůtov	Apr. 29	2.442	.660	.825	.430	1.320	....	.165	.759	....	....
Series 1		1919										
141	Rumburk	Oct. 22	2.840	7.710	.710	2.840	2.840	5.445	1.100	....	....	....
		1920										
792	Bilin	Mar. 22	.175	.086	.186	.153	.174	.304	.058	.068	....	....
793	Bostenbach	Mar. 17	2.814	....	2.865	2.024	2.812	3.610	.723	.732	....	....
794	Komotau	Mar. 22	.825	.410	.828	.564	.828	1.349	.273	.275	....	....
795	Leitmeritz	Mar. 22	.238	.120	.237	.151	.239	.247	.048	.055	....	....
796	Rumburg	Mar. 22	.341	.176	.364	.302	.348	.437	.088	.093	....	....
797	Warnsdorf	Mar. 22	.360	.187	.382	.308	.370	.494	.105	.105	....	....
798	Schluckenau-Hainspach	Mar. 18	1.276	....	1.298	.894	1.286	1.748	.348	.359	....	....
799	Teplitz	Mar. 19	1.556	.802	1.596	1.236	1.569	2.470	.517	.510	....	....
800	Aussig	Mar. 20	1.646	.843	1.660	1.196	1.635	2.622	.526	.529	....	....
801	Saatz	Mar. 28	.048	.023	.048	.150	.065	.133	.024	.026	....	....
889	Bilina	Apr. 12	.266	.155	.340	.157	.523	.247	.102	.081	.500[b]	20,0
890	Tetschen	Apr. 7	2.726	3.113	3.433	2.100	6.540	1.558	.864	.373	5.650[b]	209,0
891	Duchcov	Apr. 8	.939	.621	1.231	.776	2.441	.627	.344	.145	1.950[b]	77,0
892	Komotau	Apr. 14	1.496	1.805	1.820	1.031	3.880	1.045	.598	.402	3.000[b]	120,0
893	Leitmeritz	Apr. 13	.590	.730	.708	.443	1.068	.437	.144	.123	1.050[b]	41,0
894	Brüx	Apr. 8	1.166	.814	1.464	.871	2.790	.684	.374	.317	2.250[b]	89,0
895	Rumburg	Apr. 22	.717	.910	.942	.580	1.526	.627	.230	.178	1.400[b]	56,0
896	Schluckenau	Apr. 8	1.485	1.058	1.884	1.171	2.986	1.729	.490	.410	2.900[b]	115,0
897	Teplitz	Apr. 2	2.680	1.684	3.291	2.067	7.412	2.071	1.148	.450	5.700[b]	228,0
898	Aussig	Apr. 17	2.911	3.613	3.632	2.209	9.832	....	1.152	.481	....	....
899	Warnsdorf	Apr. 9	.798	.478	.993	.612	1.591	.627	.230	.200	1.450[b]	58,0
900	Saaz	Apr. 12	.278	.153	.332	.146	.610	.323	.115	.094	.550[b]	22,0
1129	Děčín	Apr. 26	2.750	3.420	3.430	2.034	8.110	....	.864	.726	5.650[b]	226,0
1130	Komotau	Apr. 19	1.445	1.835	1.830	1.027	4.925	....	.576	.485	3.000[b]	120,0
1131	Most	Apr. 20	1.152	1.440	1.471	.906	3.488	....	.374	.309	2.250[b]	90,0
1132	Žatec	Apr. 21	.240	.309	.319	.157	.523	....	.039	.039	.400[b]	16,0
1133	Bilin	Apr. 21	.240	.310	.326	.159	.763	....	.088	.080	.500[b]	20,0
1134	Duchcov	Apr. 15	.410	1.219	....	.465	1.809	....	.156	.293	1.950[b]	78,0
1135	Litoměřice	Apr. 18	.573	.723	.738	.450	1.504	....	.144	.126	1.050[b]	42,0
1136	Šluknov	Apr. 15	1.498	1.860	1.867	1.179	4.512	....	.512	.401	2.900[b]	116,0
1137	Teplice	Apr. 14	2.655	3.300	3.317	1.958	9.548	....	1.152	.966	5.700[b]	228,0
1138	Rumburg	Apr. 10	.043	.891	.854	.440	.900	1.244	.211	.191	1.150[b]	46,0
1139	Ústí n/Labem	Apr. 11	2.891	3.600	3.584	2.257	9.831	....	1.152	.967	6.000[b]	240,0
1140	Warnsdorf	Apr. 14	.758	.960	.967	.618	2.201	....	.230	.194	1.450[b]	58,0
Series 2		1921										
208	Komotau	June 14	.111	.030	.038	.020	.060	....	.008	.035	....	...
209	Litoměřice	May 11	.185	.050	.063	.033	.100	....	.013	.058	....	...
210	Chomůtov	May 2	.278	.075	.094	.049	.150	....	.019	.086	....	...
211	Osek-Duchcov	May 11	.148	.040	.050	.025	.080	....	.010	.046	....	...
212	Žatec	May 11	.111	.030	.038	.022	.060	....	.008	.035	.031[d]	...
213	Žatec	May 11	.111	.030	.038	.022	.060	....	.008	.035	....	...
214	Horšovice-Podbořany	May 11	.037	.010	.013	.005	.020	....	.003	.012	....	...
215	Ústí n/L.	May 12	.092	.025	.031	.016	.050	....	.006	.029	....	...
216	Warnsdorf	May 11	.092	.025	.031	.016	.050	....	.006	.030	....	...
217	Most	May 11	.185	.050	.063	.033	.100	....	.013	.058	....	...

CZECHO-SLOVAKIA

Internal Deliveries, CHOMŮTOV (Komotau) Warehouse

Table 258—*Concluded*

ceipt No.	Local Committee (Mistni Komitét)	Date	Commodities in Net Metric Tons of 1,000 Kilograms or 2,204.6 Pounds									
			Flour	Rice	Beans, Peas	Pork Products	Milk Evap.	Milk Cond.	Cocoa	Sugar	Misc.	No. of Biscuits
ies 2		1921										
218	Ústí n/L.	May 12	.092	.025	.031	.016	.050	....	.006	.029	....	.....
219	Pokaŭ-Ústí n/L.	May 11	.092	.025	.031	.016	.050	....	.006	.029	....	.....
220	Spiegelsberg	May 12	.185	.050	.063	.033	.100	....	.013	.058	....	.....
221	Teplice	May 11	.148	.040	.050	.025	.080	....	.010	.046	....	.....
222	Bilina	May 12	.111	.030	.038	.022	.060	....	.008	.035	....	.....
223	Ústí n/L.	May 12	.111	.030	.038	.022	.060	....	.008	.035	....	.....
224	Rumburg	May 11	.111	.030	.038	.022	.060	....	.008	.035	....	.....
225	Georgswalde-Šluknov	May 11	.222	.060	.075	.038	.120	....	.015	.070	....	.....
226	Most	May 11	.185	.050	.063	.033	.100	....	.013	.058	....	.....
413	Chomůtov	July 9	2.664	1.001	.613	.468	1.429	.010	.180	.830	....	.....
414	Děčín Podmokly	July 4	2.901	.784	.980	.510	1.568	....	.196	.904	....	.....
415	Teplice-Šanov	June 30	.089	.024	.030	.016	.048	....	.006	.028	....	.....
416	Teplice-Šanov	June 30	.758	.205	.256	.134	.410	....	.051	.236	....	.....
417	Teplice-Šanov	June 30	5.032	1.360	1.710	.900	2.720	....	.340	1.565	....	.....
418	Šluknov	June 28	3.256	.880	1.100	.575	1.760	....	.220	1.013	....	.....
419	Warnsdorf	June 28	3.108	.840	1.050	.546	1.679	....	.210	.966	....	.....
420	Ústí n/L.	July 4	2.797	.756	.945	.491	1.512	....	.189	.869	....	.....
515	Chomůtov	June 15	.814	.220	.275	.144	.440	....	.055	.253	....	.....
516	Děčín Podmokly	June 14	.310	.387	.200	1.147	.620	....	.077	.356	....	.....
517	Warnsdorf	June 9	2.775	.750	.938	.488	1.500	....	.188	.863	....	.....
518	Česká Kamenice	June 10	1.480	.405	.495	.260	.800	....	.100	.460	....	.....
519	Ústí n/L.	June 9	3.626	.980	1.125	.637	1.962	....	.245	1.127	....	.....
520	Šluknov	June 8	3.774	1.020	1.275	.663	2.040	....	.256	1.174	....	.....
521	Teplice	June 8	3.885	1.050	1.314	.675	2.100	....	.262	1.207	....	.....
522	Duchcov	June 11	.832	.225	.281	.146	.450	....	.056	.259	....	.....
	Total	....	**149.661**	**99.904**	**114.183**	**91.119**	**197.730**	**117.934**	**38.571**	**40.049**	**89.481***	**3,557,000**

* Detail of miscellaneous commodity total: [b], weight of 3,557,000 bis-its, 89.450; [d], soap, .031.

CZECHO-SLOVAKIA

Internal Deliveries from BUDWEIS (České-Budějovice) Warehouse

Table 259

ceipt No.	Local Committee (Mistni Komitét)	Date	Commodities in Net Metric Tons of 1,000 Kilograms or 2,204.6 Pounds							
			Flour	Rice	Beans, Peas	Pork Products	Milk Evap.	Milk Cond.	Cocoa	Misc.*
ies 1		1919								
36	Jindřichuv Hradec	Sept. 5	.680	.170	.170	.680	.680	1:590	.321	....
52	České Budějovice	Oct. 18	1.400	.350	.350	1.400	1.400	2.385	.482	....
53	Krumlov	Oct. 1	.560	.140	.140	.560	.560	1.590	.321	....
54	Třeboň	Oct. 10	.240	.060	.060	.240	.240	.636	.128	....
55	České Budějovice	Oct. 8	1.400	.350	.350	1.400	1.400	2.385	.482	....
09	České Budějovice	Oct. 16	1.400	.350	.350	1.400	1.400	2.385	.482	....
93	Kamenice n/Lipou	Nov. 5	.660	.165	.165	.660	.660	1.544	.312	....
94	Krumlov	Nov. 3	.560	.140	.140	.563	.560	1.590	.321	....
95	Třeboň	Nov. 5	.240	.060	.060	.281	.240	.636	.128	....
96	Jindřichuv Hradec	Nov. 5	.680	.170	.170	.679	.680	1.590	.321	....
97	Tábor	Nov. 8	.400	.100	.100	.397	.400	1.273	.257	....
98	Písek	Nov. 3	.329	.083	.083	.331	.329	.576	.119	....
41	Jindřichuv Hradec	Nov. 6	.680	.170	.170	.683	.680	1.590	.306	.102
42	Krumlov	Nov. 10	.560	.140	.140	.560	.560	1.590	.321	.096
43	Tábor	Nov. 20	.400	.100	.100	.397	.400	1.273	.257	....
45	Jindřichuv Hradec	Nov. 20	.680	.170	.170	.680	.680	1.590	.321	....
46	Třeboň	Nov. 5	.240	.060	.060	.481	.240	.636	.128	....
47	Krumlov	Nov. 3	.560	.140	.140	.563	.560	1.590	.321	....
48	Písek	Nov. 3	.329	.088	.083	.331	.329	.576	.119	....
49	Kamenice n/Lipou	Nov. 5	.660	.165	.156	.660	.660	1.544	.312	....
	Total	....	**12.658**	**3.171**	**3.157**	**12.946**	**12.658**	**28.569**	**5.759**	**.198**

* Codliver oil.

CZECHO-SLOVAKIA

Table 260 — Internal Deliveries from DEJVICE Warehouse

Receipt No.	Local Committee (Mistni Komitét)	Date	Flour	Rice	Beans, Peas	Pork Products	Milk: Evap.	Milk: Cond.	Cocoa	Sugar	Misc.*	No. of Biscuits
			Commodities in Net Metric Tons of 1,000 Kilograms or 2,204.6 Pounds									
Series 1		1919										
65	Břevnov	Sept. 9	.400	.100	.100	.400	.400	1.451	.292	....	....	....
66	Keje	Sept. 9	.029	.007	.007	.033	.029	.115	.019	....	....	....
67	Kbely	Sept. 24	.048	.012	.012	.048	.048	.127	.025	....	....	....
68	Malešice	Sept. 12	.018	.005	.005	.017	.018	.153	.029	....	....	....
69	Prosek	Sept. 12	.056	.014	.014	.055	.056	.238	.048	....	....	....
70	Zlíchov	Sept. 16	.033	.008	.008	.033	.033	.133	.028	....	....	....
71	Žalov	Sept. 9	.018	.005	.005	.028	.018	.063	.013	....	....	....
72	Troj-Podhoř	Sept. 13	.044	.011	.011	.044	.044	.182	.037	....	....	....
73	Uhřiněves	Sept. 13	.068	.017	.017	.071	.068	.110	.024	....	....	....
74	Žižkov	Sept. 13	.875	.218	.218	.875	.875	3.243	.618	....	....	....
75	Záběhlice	Sept. 13	.081	.020	.020	.082	.081	.147	.030	....	....	....
76	Vokovice	Sept. 12	.134	.033	.034	.136	.134	.297	.056	....	....	....
77	Střešovice	Sept. 12	.045	.011	.011	.044	.045	.191	.038	....	....	....
78	Selce	Sept. 12	.020	.005	.005	.028	.020	.071	.014	....	....	....
79	Radlice	Sept. 12	.164	.041	.041	.163	.164	.270	.054	....	....	....
80	Prague VII	Sept. 12	.710	.177	.177	.713	.710	1.351	.272	....	....	....
81	Prague III	Sept. 12	.320	.080	.080	.320	.320	.715	.144	....	....	....
82	Roztoky	Sept. 13	.024	.006	.006	.024	.024	.049	.009	....	....	....
83	Radotín	Sept. 12	.052	.013	.013	.054	.052	.190	.039	....	....	....
84	Košiře	Sept. 10	.400	.100	.100	.400	.400	1.303	.204	....	....	....
85	Lisoleje	Sept. 15	.025	.006	.006	.027	.025	.063	.012	....	....	....
86	Strášnice	Sept. 12	.124	.031	.031	.126	.124	.313	.063	....	....	....
87	Prague I	Sept. 12	.580	.145	.145	.580	.580	1.160	.234	....	....	....
88	Nusle	Sept. 9	.582	.140	.136	.582	.582	2.232	.450	....	....	....
89	Bráník	Sept. 10	.108	.027	.027	.109	.108	.254	.051	....	....	....
90	Michle	Sept. 11	.280	.070	.070	.219	.281	.269	.056	....	....	....
91	Karlín	Sept. 11	.384	.096	.096	.385	.384	.954	.193	....	....	....
92	Bubeneč	Sept. 13	.310	.078	.078	.310	.310	.637	.128	....	....	....
93	Podbaba	Sept. 17	....	....	....	....	....	.063	.012	....	....	....
94	Hlubočepy	Sept. 10	.087	.021	.021	.087	.087	.162	.032	....	....	....
95	Libšice	Sept. 12	.056	.014	.014	.054	.056	.136	.027	....	....	....
96	Vinohrady	Sept. 25	.768	.192	.192	.768	.768	1.876	.378	....	....	....
97	Hloubětin	Sept. 26	.096	.024	.024	.098	.096	.182	.036	....	....	....
98	Sukdol	Sept. 17	.024	.006	.006	.027	.024	.143	.029	....	....	....
99	Stříškov	Sept. 17	.012	.003	.003	.011	.012	.048	.010	....	....	....
100	Smíchov	Sept. 12	.634	.158	.158	.637	.634	2.051	.414	....	....	....
101	Vršovice	Sept. 12	.610	.152	.152	.610	.610	1.709	.346	....	....	....
102	Chuchle	Sept. 20	.028	.007	.007	.028	.028	.076	.015	....	....	....
103	Podolí	Sept. 13	.080	.020	.020	.082	.080	.254	.051	....	....	....
104	Prague II	Sept. 20	.008	.002	.002	.008	.008	....	....	....	....	....
105	Prague VI	Sept. 20	.012	.003	.003	.012	.012	....	....	....	....	....
106	Prague II	Sept. 9	....	....	....	....	....	.159	.032	....	....	....
107	Říčany	Sept. 20	.024	.006	.006	.028	.024	....	....	....	....	....
108	Břevnov	Sept. 20	.012	.003	.003	.012	.012	....	....	....	....	....
109	Prague	Sept. 19	.004	.001	.001	.006	.004	....	....	....	....	....
110	Horní Černošice	Sept. 25	.008	.002	.002	.008	.008	....	....	....	....	....
111	Praha	Sept. 21	.012	.003	.003	.012	.012	....	....	....	....	....
112	Praha III	Sept. 20	....	....	....	....	....	.015	.003	....	....	....
113	Praha	Sept. 20	.031	.008	.008	.031	.031	....	....	....	....	....
114	Prague II	Sept. 25	.016	.004	.004	.017	.016	.031	.006	....	....	....
115	Chvaly	Sept. 26	....	.002	.002	.008	.008	....	....	....	....	....
116	Prague III	Sept. 19	.012	.003	.003	.011	.012	....	....	....	....	....
117	Karlín	Sept. 20	.044	.011	.011	.044	.044	.031	.006	....	....	....
118	Praha	Sept. 20	.014	.004	.003	.014	.014	....	....	....	....	....
132	Praha	Sept. ..	....	....	....	....	....	....	....	....	.026[c]	....
133	Chvaly	Oct. 6	....	....	....	....	....	....	....	....	.009[c]	....

* Detail of miscellaneous commodities indicated by the following indexes: [b], biscuits; [c], codliver oil; [d], soap. See end of Table 260 (page 519) for complete detail.

CZECHO-SLOVAKIA

Table 260—*Continued*

Internal Deliveries, DEJVICE Warehouse

eipt o.	Local Committee (Mistni Komitét)	Date	Commodities in Net Metric Tons of 1,000 Kilograms or 2,204.6 Pounds									
			Flour	Rice	Beans, Peas	Pork Products	Milk		Cocoa	Sugar	Misc.	No. of Biscuits
							Evap.	Cond.				
es 1		1919										
34	Praha	Oct. 9	.012	.003	.003	.012	.012	....	....	....	....	.....
58	Jinonice	Oct. 8	.056	.014	.014	.055	.056	....	....	....	....	.....
59	Dobrovíz	Oct. 8	.028	.007	.007	.028	.028	....	....	....	....	.....
60	Bohnice	Oct. 10	.028	.007	.007	.028	.028	.238	.048	....	....	.....
61	Strášnice	Oct. 15	.124	.031	.031	.126	.124	.313	.063	....	....	.....
62	Praha	Oct. 6	.024	.006	.006	.024	.024	....	....	....	....	.....
63	Prague	Oct. 3	....	....	....	....	....	.095	.010	....	....	.....
64	Prague	Oct. 3	.026	.007	.006	.026	.026	.019	.004	....	....	.....
65	Prague	Oct. 3	.012	.003	.003	.012	.012	....	....	....	....	.....
11	Krč	Oct. 10	.040	.003	.003	.040	.040	.186	.038	....	....	.....
12	Sukdol	Oct. 15	.024	.006	.006	.024	.024	.134	.029	....	....	.....
13	Vinoř	Oct. 13	.056	.014	.014	.056	.056	....	....	....	....	.....
14	Keje	Oct. 14	.029	.007	.007	.029	.029	.115	.019	....	....	.....
15	Zlíchov	Oct. 16	.033	.008	.008	.033	.033	.138	.028	....	....	.....
16	Kobylisy	Oct. 15	.120	.030	.030	.120	.120	.333	.067	....	....	.....
17	Vokovice	Oct. 15	.067	.017	.017	.067	.067	.149	.030	....	....	.....
18	Vršovice	Oct. 15	.305	.076	.076	.305	.305	.855	.173	....	....	.....
19	Liboce	Sep. 11	.032	.008	.008	.033	.032	.160	.032	....	....	.....
20	Vršovice	Oct. 15	.203	.051	.051	.205	.203	.569	.115	....	....	.....
21	Lisoleje	Oct. 15	.025	.006	.006	.025	.025	.063	.012	....	....	.....
22	Záběhlice	Oct. 13	.081	.020	.020	.082	.081	.147	.030	....	....	.....
23	Praha IV	Oct. 23	.128	.033	.033	.128	.128	.397	.080	....	....	.....
24	Dejvice	Oct. 31	.232	.058	.058	.232	.232	.533	.107	....	....	.....
25	Bráník	Oct. 14	.109	.027	.027	.109	.109	.254	.051	....	....	.....
26	Vinohrady	Oct. 18	....	....	....	....	....	1.876	.378	....	....	.....
27	Podbaba	Oct. 16	....	....	....	....	....	.063	.040	....	....	.....
28	Střížkov	Oct. 20	.012	.003	.003	.012	.012	.048	.010	....	....	.....
29	Radlice	Oct. 17	.164	.041	.041	.164	.164	.270	.054	....	....	.....
30	Prosek	Oct. 13	.056	.014	.014	.056	.056	.238	.043	....	....	.....
31	Vysočany	Oct. 14	.120	.030	.030	.120	.120	.450	.091	....	....	.....
32	Vysočany	Oct. 10	.120	.030	.030	.120	.120	.450	.091	....	....	.....
33	Prague I	Oct. 20	.399	....	....	....	....	....	....	....	....	.....
34	Smíchov	Oct. 21	.317	.079	.079	.317	.317	1.027	.206	....	....	.....
35	Bubeneč	Oct. 15	.310	.078	.078	.309	.310	....	....	....	....	.....
36	Střešovice	Oct. 16	.022	.006	.006	.022	.022	.095	.010	....	....	.....
37	Hlubočepy	Oct. 13	.087	.021	.021	.087	.087	.162	.032	....	....	.....
38	Roztoky	Oct. 15	....	....	....	....	....	.049	.009	....	....	.....
39	Libšice n/Vlt.	Oct. 17	.056	.014	.014	.056	.056	.136	.027	....	....	.....
40	Bohnice	Oct. 10	.028	.007	.007	.028	.028	.238	.048	....	....	.....
41	Selce	Oct. 16	.020	.005	.005	.020	.020	.071	.014	....	....	.....
42	Chuchle	Oct. 18	.028	.007	.007	.028	.028	.076	.015	....	....	.....
43	Žalov	Oct. 15	.018	.005	.005	.018	.018	.063	.013	....	....	.....
44	Podol	Oct. 17	.080	.020	.020	.080	.080	.254	.051	....	....	.....
45	Radotín	Oct. 16	.052	.013	.013	.052	.052	.190	.039	....	....	.....
46	Michle	Oct. 15	.340	.070	.070	.340	.340	.278	.056	....	....	.....
47	Hodkovičky	Oct. 31	.010	.003	.003	.010	.010	.024	.005	....	....	.....
48	Modřany	Oct. 18	.046	.011	.011	.044	.046	.140	.028	....	....	.....
49	Praha	Oct. 22	.012	.003	.003	.012	.012	....	....	....	....	.....
50	Chvaly	Oct. 22	....	....	....	....	....	.018	.004	....	....	.....
51	Praha	Oct. 15	....	....	....	....	....	.159	.032	....	....	.....
52	Praha	Oct. 15	.024	.006	.006	.024	.024	....	....	....	....	.....
53	Prague	Oct. 17	....	....	....	....	....	.015	.003	....	....	.....
54	Prague II	Oct. 15	.016	.004	.004	.016	.016	.031	.006	....	....	.....
55	Chvaly	Oct. 15	.008	.002	.002	.008	.008	....	....	....	....	.....
56	Praha	Oct. 16	.012	.003	.003	.012	.012	....	....	....	....	.....
57	na Kopě	Oct. 15	.008	.002	.002	.008	.008	....	....	....	....	.....
58	Karlín	Oct. 15	.044	.011	.011	.044	.044	.031	.006	....	....	.....
59	Praha	Oct. 15	....	.100	....	....	.100	.200	....	....	....	.....

[*Continued on next page*]

CZECHO-SLOVAKIA

Table 260—*Continued* Internal Deliveries, DEJVICE Warehouse

Receipt No.	Local Committee (Mistni Komitét)	Date	Flour	Rice	Beans, Peas	Pork Products	Milk Evap.	Milk Cond.	Cocoa	Sugar	Misc.	No. of Biscuits
			Commodities in Net Metric Tons of 1,000 Kilograms or 2,204.6 Pounds									
Series 1		1919										
260	Prague VI	Oct. 15	.012	.003	.003	.012	.012	....	....	....	....	...
261	Prague	Oct. 15	.031	.008	.008	.033	.031	....	....	....	....	...
262	Hor. Černošice	Oct. 8	....	....	....	....	....	....	....	....	.009[c]	...
263	Prague	Oct. 23	....	....	....	....	....	.159	.032	....	....	...
264	Prague	Oct. 23	....	....	....	....	....	.095	.019	....	....	...
265	Prague	Oct. 23	.026	.007	.006	.026	.026	.019	.004	....	....	...
266	Prague	Oct. 23	.012	.003	.003	.012	.012	....	....	....	....	...
267	Prague	Oct. 27	.014	.003	.004	.014	.014	....	....	....	....	...
268	Prague	Oct. 15	....	....	....	....	....	.318	.064	....	....	...
269	Černošice	Oct. 15	.008	.002	.002	.008	.008	....	....	....	....	...
326	Troj-Podhoř	Nov. 16	.055	.055	.055	.039	.055	.173	.035	....	....	...
327	Radlice	Nov. 8	.123	.492	.062	.123	.123	.409	.051	.143	....	...
328	Prague VII	Nov. 15	.355	.089	.089	.355	.355	.665	.136	....	....	...
329	Roztoky	Nov. 3	.007	.002	.002	.007	.007	....	....	....	....	...
330	Kbely	Nov. 3	.048	.012	.012	.048	.048	.127	.025	....	....	...
331	Prague	Oct. 20	....	....	....	....	....	.048	.010	....	....	...
332	Žamberk	Nov. 7	.300	.120	.120	.120	.120	.420	.057	....	.270[cd]	...
333	Prague	Nov. 15	.010	.003	.003	.010	.010	....	....	....	....	...
362	Nová Paka	Nov. 15	.975	.976	.976	.683	.976	2.100	.420	....	....	...
363	Nové Strašecí	Nov. 15	.704	.700	.710	.490	.697	2.257	.450	.450	....	...
364	Ml. Boleslav	Nov. 15	.800	.800	.800	.560	.800	1.650	.330	.330	....	...
374	Prague	Dec. 19	....	....	....	....	....	....	....	....	.032[c]	...
375	Prague	Dec. 19	....	....	....	....	....	.152	.030	.030	....	...
376	Prague VII	Dec. 3	....	....	....	....	....	....	....	....	.031[c]	...
383	Slaný	Dec. 12	.850	.850	.850	.595	.850	1.800	.360	.360	....	...
384	Český Brod	Dec. 11	.115	.334	.334	....	.115	....	....	.128	....	...
385	Příbram	Dec. 14	.600	.600	.600	.420	.610	1.050	.210	.210	....	...
386	Kutná Hora	Dec. 10	.500	.500	.500	.348	.500	1.050	.210	.210	....	...
387	Rakovník	Dec. 12	.857	.998	.998	.700	1.000	1.500	.300	.300	....	...
388	Dobříš	Dec. 15	.303	.307	.307	.208	.307	.496	.100	.100	....	...
389	Brandýs n/L.	Dec. 13	.448	.454	.454	.321	.450	.750	.150	.150	....	...
390	Říčany	Nov. 18	.140	.140	.140	.095	.140	.230	.046	....	....	...
391	Beroun	Dec. 14	.550	.550	.550	.381	.544	.744	.150	.150	....	...
392	Sedlčany	Dec. 10	.250	.250	.250	.175	.250	.300	.060	.060	....	...
393	Kolín	Dec. 11	.550	.550	.550	.385	.550	.900	.180	.180	....	...
394	Benešov	Dec. 13	.250	.250	.250	.175	.250	.150	.060	.060	....	...
437	Chuchle	Nov. 20	.035	.035	.035	.025	.035	.072	.014	....	....	...
438	Dejvice	Nov. 15	.292	.292	.292	.204	.292	.502	.100	....	....	...
439	Hostivař	Nov. 20	.080	.080	.080	.056	.080	.261	.052	....	....	...
440	Karlín	Nov. 24	.480	.480	.480	.336	.480	.900	.180	....	....	...
441	Prague I	Nov. 18	.390	.520	.505	.132	.071	.821	.156	....	....	...
442	Prosek	Nov. 15	.070	.070	.070	.049	.070	.225	.045	....	....	...
443	Troj-Podhoř	Nov. 15	.055	.055	.055	.039	.055	.173	.035	....	....	...
444	Záběhlice	Nov. 20	.102	.102	.102	.071	.102	.140	.028	....	....	...
445	Žižkov	Nov. 13	1.094	1.094	1.094	.765	1.094	3.080	.612	....	....	...
446	Radotín	Nov. 21	.066	.066	.066	.046	.066	.180	.036	....	....	...
447	Bubeneč	Nov. 21	.425	.425	.425	.300	.425	.600	.120	....	....	...
448	Košíře	Nov. 15	.484	.365	.499	.307	.421	1.230	.097	....	....	...
449	Malešice	Nov. 15	.023	.023	.023	.017	.023	.135	.027	....	....	...
450	Hlubočepy	Nov. 29	.109	.109	.109	.077	.109	.153	.030	....	....	...
451	Prague IV	Nov. 25	.160	.160	.160	.112	.160	.375	.075	....	....	...
452	Hradčany-Prague	Nov. 25	.025	.025	.025	.018	.025	....	....	....	....	...
453	Hradčany-Prague	Nov. 25	.015	.015	.015	.011	.015	....	....	....	....	...
454	Hradčany-Prague	Nov. 25	....	....	....	....	....	.090	.018	....	....	...
455	Hradčany-Prague	Nov. 25	....	....	....	....	....	.150	.030	....	....	...
456	Zlíchov	Nov. 7	.078	.078	.039	.055	.078	.180	.036	....	....	...
457	Strášnice	Nov. 26	.160	.160	.160	.108	.160	.295	.059	....	....	...
458	Keje	Nov. 18	.037	.037	.037	.026	.037	.090	.018	.018	....	...

CZECHO-SLOVAKIA

Table 260—*Continued* Internal Deliveries, DEJVICE Warehouse

ipt .	Local Committee (Mistni Komitét)	Date	Flour	Rice	Beans, Peas	Pork Products	Milk: Evap.	Milk: Cond.	Cocoa	Sugar	Misc.	No. of Biscuits
			Commodities in Net Metric Tons of 1,000 Kilograms or 2,204.6 Pounds									
es 1		1919										
59	Sukdol	Nov. 19	.030	.030	.030	.022	.030	.135	.027	....	....	.....
60	Prague VIII	Nov. 22	.832	.832	....	.582	.832	2.663	.533	....	....	.....
61	Roztoky	Nov. 18	.030	.030	.030	.022	.030	.040	.009	....	....	.....
62	Střešovice	Nov. 21	.056	.056	.056	.039	.056	.180	.036	....	....	.....
63	Vinohrady	Nov. 21	....	....	....	....	....	1.770	.354	....	....	.....
64	Vršovice	Nov. 20	.763	.763	.763	.534	.763	1.613	.323	....	....	.....
65	Břevnov	Nov. 20	.500	.499	.499	.156	....	.407	.009	....	....	.....
66	Dobrovíz	Nov. 15	.028	.007	.007	.028	.028	....	....	....	....	.....
67	Jinonice	Nov. 15	.070	.070	.070	.050	.070	....	....	....	....	.....
68	Kobylisy	Nov. 24	.150	.150	.150	.095	.150	.315	.063	....	....	.....
69	Bráník	Nov. 22	.135	.135	.135	.094	.135	.240	.048	....	....	.....
70	Liboce	Nov. 18	.041	.041	.041	.023	.041	.151	.030	....	....	.....
71	Praha	Nov. 22	.015	.015	.015	.011	.015	....	....	....	....	.....
72	Prosek	Nov. 17	....	....	....	....	.004	.003	....	....	....	.....
73	Černošice	Nov. 22	.010	.010	.010	.007	.010	.009	.002	....	....	.....
74	Praha	Nov. 22	.015	.015	.015	.011	.015	....	....	....	....	.....
75	Praha	Nov. 24	.015	.015	.015	.011	.015	....	....	....	....	.....
76	Praha	Nov. 25	.018	.018	.018	.012	.018	....	....	....	....	.....
77	Praha	Nov. 22	....	....	....	....	....	.015	.003	....	....	.....
78	Karlín	Nov. 11	....	....	....	....	....	....	....	....	.030[c]	.....
79	Prague	Nov. 22	.012	.003	.003	.012	.012	....	....	....	....	.....
80	Karlín	Nov. 15	.055	.055	.055	.039	.055	.030	.006	....	....	.....
81	Praha	Nov. 15	....	....	....	....	....	.045	.009	....	....	.....
82	Chvaly	Nov. 22	.010	.010	.015	.011	.010	....	.002	....	....	.....
85	Střížkov	Nov. 25	.015	.015	.015	.011	.015	.045	.009	.009	....	.....
99	Břevnov	Dec. 29	.015	.015	.015	.011	.015	....	....	....	....	.....
06	Praha	Dec. 19	.033	.033	.033	.023	.033	.018	.004	.004	....	.....
07	Hořovice	Dec. 15	.500	.499	.499	.351	.500	.744	.150	.150	....	.....
29	Nusle	Dec. 13	.703	.703	.703	.492	.703	2.106	.412	....	....	.....
30	Nová Paka	Dec. 13	.975	.976	.976	.679	.976	2.100	.420	.420	....	.....
76	Prague II	Nov. 19	....	....	....	....	....	.318	.064	....	....	.....
77	Hlubočepy	Nov. 29	....	....	....	....	....	....	....	....	.023[c]	.....
78	Selce	Dec. 11	.025	.025	.025	....	.025	.072	.014	.014	....	.....
80	Praha	Nov. 20	.020	.020	.020	.009	.020	.030	.006	.006	....	.....
81	Uhřiněves	Nov. 30	.085	.091	.091	.061	.085	.114	.023	....	....	.....
82	Hlubočepy	Dec. 30	....	....	.109	....	....	....	....	.030	....	.....
84	Bubeneč	Dec. 20	.213	.213	.213	.148	.213	.300	.060	.180	....	.....
85	Černošice	Dec. 15	.005	.005	.005	.004	.005	.005	.001	.001	....	.....
86	Dobrovíz	Dec. 18	.018	.018	.018	.012	.018	....	....	....	....	.....
87	Chvaly	Dec. 18	.008	.008	.008	.006	.008	.005	.001	.001	....	.....
88	Praha	Dec. 19	.008	.008	.008	.006	.008	....	....	....	....	.....
89	Karlín	Dec. 16	.300	.300	.300	.210	.300	.450	.090	.090	....	.....
90	Keje	Dec. 23	.019	.019	.019	.013	.019	.045	.009	.027	....	.....
91	Liboce	Dec. 20	.022	.022	.022	.011	.022	.125	.015	.015	....	.....
92	Praha	Dec. 17	....	....	....	....	....	.008	.002	.002	....	.....
93	Kobylisy	Dec. 22	.075	.075	.075	.048	.075	.156	.032	.032	....	.....
94	Košíře	Dec. 15	.180	.225	.205	.143	.218	.296	.092	.123	....	.....
		1920										
02	Břevnov	Apr. 2	.100	.050	.100	.072	.109	.382	.075	.075	.300[b]	12,000
03	Bráník	Apr. 1	.045	.022	.045	.033	.044	.058	.011	.011	....	.....
04	Bubeneč	Mar. 31	.212	.106	.212	.149	.212	.250	.050	.050	.450[b]	18,000
05	Bohnice	Apr. 4	.018	.009	.018	.013	.022	.096	.038	.038	.150[b]	6,000
06	Dobrovíz	Mar. 30	.014	.007	.014	.009	.014	....	....	....	....	.....
07	Hlubočepy	Apr. 1	.064	.033	.065	.046	.066	.077	.015	.015	.131[bc]	4,000
08	Košíře	Apr. 2	.200	.102	.200	.140	.196	.344	.070	.070	....	.....
09	Libšice	Apr. 1	.042	.021	.045	.033	.044	.076	.013	.013	.100[b]	4,000
10	Lisoleje	Mar. 30	.019	.010	.019	.013	.022	.058	.012	.012	.050[b]	2,000
11	Michle	Mar. 19	.128	.063	.125	.089	.131	.229	.045	.045	.250[b]	10,000
12	Malešice	Mar. 13	.023	.012	.023	.017	.022	.115	.023	.023	.020[d]	.....

[*Continued on next page*]

CZECHO-SLOVAKIA

Table 260—*Continued* Internal Deliveries, DEJVICE Warehouse

Receipt No.	Local Committee (Mistni Komitét)	Date	Commodities in Net Metric Tons of 1,000 Kilograms or 2,204.6 Pounds									
			Flour	Rice	Beans, Peas	Pork Products	Milk		Cocoa	Sugar	Misc.	No. of Biscuits
							Evap.	Cond.				
Series 1		1920										
813	Modřany	Mar. 30	.023	.011	.023	.017	.023	.040	.008	.008	....	...
814	Nusle	Apr. 6	.300	.150	.300	.244	.305	.897	.180	.180	....	...
815	Prague I	Mar. 23	.237	.119	.237	.165	.240	.554	.111	.111	.300[b]	12,[illegible]
816	Podbaba	Mar. 26	....	....	....	....	....	.050	.010	.010	....	...
817	Prosek	Mar. 30	.042	.021	.042	.029	.044	.114	.023	.023	.100[b]	4,[illegible]
818	Radlice	Mar. 30	.128	.061	.123	.082	.123	.127	.026	.026	.262[bc]	8,[illegible]
819	Ruzýň	Apr. 2	.010	.005	.010	.007	.010	.038	.007	.007	....	...
820	Radotín	Apr. 1	.033	.017	.033	.022	.033	.077	.015	.015	....	...
821	Střešovice	Apr. 9	.015	.007	.015	.009	.015	.040	.008	.008	.002[d]	...
822	Smíchov	Mar. 19	....	....	....	....	....	1.622	.322	.322	1.300[b]	52,[illegible]
823	Sukdol	Mar. 16	....	.015	.030	.022	.030	.113	.022	.022	....	..
824	St. Strášnice	Mar. 27	.093	.046	.091	.066	.093	.153	.030	.030	.200[b]	8,[illegible]
825	Vinoř	Apr. 7	.042	.021	.042	.029	.044	....	....	....	.100[b]	4,[illegible]
826	Vinohrady Prague	Apr. 2	.384	.192	.384	.269	.392	.554	.114	.114	....	...
827	Vysočany Prague	Mar. 30	.090	.045	.090	.063	.090	.212	.042	.042	.250[b]	10,[illegible]
828	Zbraslav	Apr. 8	.033	.017	.033	.023	.033	.066	.013	.013	....	..
829	Zlíchov	Apr. 12	.025	.013	.025	.018	.022	.076	.016	.016	....	..
830	Benešov	Mar. 27	.186	.093	.182	.730	.196	.153	.031	.031	....	..
831	Boleslav	Mar. 23	.638	.320	.638	.455	.632	1.107	.220	.220	....	..
832	Hořovice	Apr. 1	.376	.188	.377	.266	.370	.401	.081	.081	....	..
833	Hořice	Mar. 27	.564	.395	.564	.277	.566	.725	.145	.145	....	..
834	Kralupy	Mar. 12	.473	.237	.473	.331	.479	.706	.140	.140	....	..
835	Louny	Mar. 30	.200	.100	.200	.146	.196	.305	.060	.060	....	..
836	Bydžov	Mar. 27	.328	.164	.328	.229	.327	.343	.068	.068	....	..
837	Paka	Mar. 26	.600	.300	.596	.420	.610	1.107	.220	.220	....	..
838	Příbram	Mar. 18	.600	.300	.594	.420	.588	.878	.175	.175	....	..
839	Roudnice	Apr. 1	.240	.120	.240	.168	.240	.248	.050	.050	....	..
840	Slaný	Mar. 30	.680	.340	.680	.478	.675	1.202	.240	.240	.092[c]	..
841	Sedlčany	Mar. 27	.200	.100	.200	.140	.196	.210	.040	.040	....	..
842	Karlín Prague	Mar. 30	.028	.014	.028	.022	.028	.013	.003	.003	.050[b]	2,[illegible]
843	Prague III	Mar. 31	.009	.005	.009	.006	.009	....	....	....	....	..
844	Prague	Mar. 27	....	....	....	....	....	.744	.150	.150	....	..
845	Prague	Mar. 30	....	....	....	....	....	.153	.030	.030	....	..
964	Prague	Mar. 4	....	....	....	....	.195	....	.036	.030	....	..
965	na Kopě	Apr. 30	.005	.012	.012	.006	.022	....	.004	.003	.024[c]	..
966	Prague IV	Apr. 13	.030	.015	.030	.022	.030	....	....	....	....	..
967	Dobřichovice	May 5	.054	.136	.136	.040	.068	....	....	....	.100[b]	4,[illegible]
968	Něm. Brod	Apr. 16	.960	2.400	2.404	.720	1.199	....	....	....	1.200[b]	48,[illegible]
969	Prague VII	Apr. 30	....	....	....	....	.058	....	.011	.009	....	..
970	Prague	Apr. 5	.005	.012	.012	.006	.006	....	....	....	....	..
971	Karlín	Apr. 20	.066	.033	.066	.046	.096	....	.006	.010	....	..
972	Prague IV	Apr. 14	.007	.004	.007	.006	.007	.096	.019	.019	.060[cd]	..
973	Prague III	Apr. 23	.013	.007	.013	.009	.013	....	....	....	....	..
974	Prague	Apr. 24	.033	.078	.078	.029	.039	....	....	....	.050[b]	2,[illegible]
975	Chvaly	Apr. 23	.012	.030	.030	.009	.027	....	.002	.002	.050[b]	2,[illegible]
976	Prague	Apr. 15	.018	.044	.045	.014	.022	....	....	....	.050[b]	2,[illegible]
977	Prague	Apr. 15	.018	.046	.046	.014	.023	....	....	....	.050[b]	2,[illegible]
978	Prague	Apr. 17	.017	.042	.042	.013	.022	....	....	....	.050[b]	2,[illegible]
979	Prague IV	Apr. 16	.014	.036	.036	.011	.022	....	....	....	....	..
980	Prague	Apr. 17	.018	.046	.046	.017	.023	....	....	....	.050[b]	2,[illegible]
981	Prague IV	Apr. 15	....	....	....	....	.015	....	.003	.010	....	..
982	Břevnov	Apr. 30	.013	.034	.034	.011	.033	....	.003	.005	.050[b]	2,[illegible]
983	Chvaly	Apr. 7	.006	.003	.006	.006	.006	.004	.001	.001	....	..
984	Prague	Apr. 1	.008	.004	.008	.005	.008	....	....	....	....	..
985	Prague	Apr. 2	.009	.005	.009	.006	.009	....	....	....	....	..
986	Prague	Apr. 7	.007	.004	.007	.006	.007	....	....	....	....	..
987	Prague	Apr. 3	....	....	....	....	....	.008	.002	.002	....	..
988	Benešov	Apr. 15	.072	.090	.091	.055	.087	.229	.043	.036	.200[b]	8[illegible]

CZECHO-SLOVAKIA

Table 260—*Continued* Internal Deliveries, DEJVICE Warehouse

eipt o.	Local Committee (Mistni Komitét)	Date	Commodities in Net Metric Tons of 1,000 Kilograms or 2,204.6 Pounds									
			Flour	Rice	Beans, Peas	Pork Products	Milk		Cocoa	Sugar	Misc.	No. of Biscuits
							Evap.	Cond.				
ies 1		1920										
89	Beroun	Apr. 14	.216	.270	.270	.243	.262	.477	.086	.072	.450[b]	18,000
90	Brandýs n/L.	Apr. 12	.144	.180	.180	.110	.175	.382	.072	.060	.350[b]	14,000
91	Dobříš	Apr. 19	.095	.120	.120	.072	.130	.400	.072	.060	.350[b]	14,000
92	Hořice	Apr. 15	.541	.677	.677	....	.675	.897	.166	.133	1.000[b]	40,000
93	Hořice	Apr. 15	.217	.272	.272	.165	.262	.382	.069	.058	.400[b]	16,000
94	Kladno	Apr. 20	.968	1.210	1.210	.726	1.219	1.564	.288	.240	1.800[b]	72,000
95	Kralupy	Apr. 20	.240	.306	.300	.180	.304	.553	.102	.084	.500[b]	20,000
96	Kolín	Apr. 15	.173	.216	.216	.141	.218	.477	.086	.072	.400[b]	16,000
97	Kutná Hora	Apr. 16	.206	.258	.258	.155	.261	.630	.115	.096	.500[b]	20,000
98	Louny	Apr. 16	.084	.102	.105	.066	.338	....	.043	.036	.200[b]	8,000
99	Mělník	Apr. 12	.066	.083	.083	.050	.087	.209	.037	.031	.150[b]	6,000
00	Ml. Boleslav	Apr. 15	.297	.372	.372	.223	.370	.935	.173	.146	.750[b]	30,000
01	N. Bydžov	Apr. 15	.153	.192	.192	.115	.196	.325	.060	.050	.300[b]	12,000
02	N. Paka	Apr. 15	.282	.352	.352	.211	.349	.935	.172	.144	.700[b]	28,000
03	Příbram	Apr. 15	.336	.420	.420	.252	1.044	....	.115	.096	.650[b]	26,000
04	Rakovník	Apr. 15	.306	.383	.383	.230	1.250	....	.159	.132	.700[b]	28,000
05	Roudnice	Apr. 12	.091	.114	.114	.072	.109	.306	.058	.048	.250[b]	10,000
06	Sedlčany	Apr. 15	.082	.102	.102	.061	.108	.229	.043	.036	.200[b]	8,000
07	Slaný	Apr. 15	.326	.408	.408	.243	1.291	....	.161	.134	.750[b]	30,000
08	Nymburk	Apr. 15	.175	.220	.220	.140	.218	.400	.072	.060	.350[b]	14,000
09	Malešice	Apr. 15	.014	.018	.018	.011	.109	....	.017	.014	.050[b]	2,000
10	Hodkovičky	Apr. 15	.013	.017	.017	.011	.051	....	.006	.015	.050[b]	2,000
11	Hostivař	Apr. 15	.037	.047	.046	.028	.044	.190	.034	.028	.150[b]	6,000
12	Břevnov	Apr. 13	.084	.103	.105	.066	.109	.600	.110	.092	.350[b]	14,000
13	Bubeneč	Apr. 12	.204	.255	.255	.153	.261	.400	.072	.060	.400[b]	16,000
14	Bohnice	Apr. 12	.019	.024	.024	.014	.024	.159	.029	.024	.100[b]	4,000
15	Bráník	Apr. 13	.070	.087	.091	.055	.087	.153	.027	.023	.150[b]	6,000
16	Černošice	Apr. 9	.012	.006	.012	.008	.012	.009	.002	.002	....	.....
17	Chuchle	Apr. 13	.021	.027	.027	.017	.027	.057	.010	.008	.050[b]	2,000
18	Dobrovíz	Apr. 14	.020	.026	.026	.015	.026	.047	.008	.007	.050[b]	2,000
19	Dejvice	Apr. 12	.143	.180	.180	.117	.180	.335	.062	.051	.300[b]	12,000
20	Hlubočepy	Apr. 12	.052	.066	.066	.040	.066	.114	.020	.017	.100	4,000
21	Hloubětín	Apr. 14	.064	.081	.081	.050	.196	....	.023	.019	.150	6,000
22	Keje	Apr. 12	.020	.026	.026	.015	.026	.062	.011	.010	.100	4,000
23	Kbely	Apr. 15	.037	.046	.046	.028	.138	....	.017	.014	.100	4,000
24	Kobylisy	Apr. 13	.080	.102	.100	.061	.100	.229	.042	.034	.200	8,000
25	Krč	Apr. 20	.027	.033	.033	.022	.164	....	.024	.020	.200	8,000
26	Karlín	Apr. 13	.321	.408	.408	.240	.401	.687	.126	.105	.700	28,000
27	Košíře	Apr. 15	.348	.435	.435	.216	1.263	....	.152	.127	.750	30,000
28	Lisoleje	Apr. 15	.019	.023	.023	.014	.073	....	.009	.018	.050	2,000
29	Liboce	Apr. 14	.023	.029	.029	.017	.029	.106	.020	.011	.050	2,000
30	Libšice	Apr. 14	.033	.042	.042	.025	.044	.090	.016	.014	.100	4,000
31	Modřany	Apr. 13	.031	.039	.039	.023	.039	.095	.017	.014	.100	4,000
32	Michle	Apr. 15	.075	.096	.091	.055	.283	....	.034	.028	.200	8,000
33	Nusle Prague	Apr. 15	.285	.357	.357	.214	1.764	....	.260	.216	.900	36,000
34	Podbaba	Apr. 23	....	....	....	....	....	.047	.009	.007	.050	2,000
35	Prosek	Apr. 15	.033	.042	.042	.025	.196	....	.029	.024	.100	4,000
36	Prague I and V	Apr. 15	.192	.240	.240	.144	.719	....	.089	.074	.450	18,000
37	Podolí	Apr. 16	.056	.071	.071	.042	.240	....	.032	.026	.150	6,000
38	Prague III	Apr. 16	.215	.269	.269	.159	.659	....	.072	.060	.463[bc]	16,000
39	Prague VIII	Apr. 16	.352	.440	.440	.291	2.286	....	.342	.285	1.150	46,000
40	Prague VII	Apr. 16	.375	.470	.470	.286	1.250	....	.144	.120	.800	32,000
41	Prague IV	Apr. 16	.074	.093	.093	.056	.093	.218	.040	.034	.200	8,000
42	Prague II and III	Apr. 15	.472	.590	.590	.351	1.460	....	.161	.134	.900	36,000
43	Prague I	Apr. 13	.024	.012	.024	.017	.024	.030	.006	.006	....	.....
44	Troj Podhoř	Apr. 17	.033	.042	.042	.025	.163	....	.022	.018	.100	4,000
45	Radotín	Apr. 16	.036	.045	.046	.028	.174	....	.023	.019	.100	4,000
46	Roztoky	Apr. 14	.015	.018	.018	.011	.044	....	.005	.004	.050	2,000

[*Continued on next page*]

CZECHO-SLOVAKIA

Table 260—*Continued* Internal Deliveries, DEJVICE Warehouse

Receipt No.	Local Committee (Mistni Komitét)	Date	Commodities in Net Metric Tons of 1,000 Kilograms or 2,204.6 Pounds									
			Flour	Rice	Beans, Peas	Pork Products	Milk		Cocoa	Sugar	Misc.	No. of Biscuit
							Evap.	Cond.				
Series 1		1920										
1047	Radlice	Apr. 16	.114	.142	.142	.084	.348	....	.038	.032	.250	10,0
1048	Ruzýň	Apr. 16	.012	.015	.015	.009	.058	....	.008	.016	.050	2,0
1049	Smíchov	Apr. 14	.161	.201	.201	.174	.201	1.318	.245	.202	.700	28,0
1050	Sukdol	Apr. 14	.014	.018	.018	.011	.109	....	.018	.015	.050	2,0
1051	Selce	Apr. 21	.013	.016	.016	.011	.070	....	.010	.008	.050	2,0
1052	Střešovice	Apr. 13	.028	.036	.036	.022	.036	.134	.024	.020	.100	4,0
1053	Strášnice	Apr. 17	.080	.102	.100	.061	.313	....	.039	.032	.150	6,0
1054	Uhřiněves	Apr. 15	.040	.051	.051	.030	.138	....	.016	.013	.100	4,0
1055	Vršovice	Apr. 14	.419	.524	.524	.314	1.611	....	.204	.168	.900	36,0
1056	Vinoř	Apr. 15	.043	.054	.054	.033	.054	....	....	....	.050	2,0
1057	Vokovice	Apr. 14	.075	.102	.105	.066	.305	....	.036	.030	.150	6,0
1058	Vinohrady Prague	Apr. 16	.500	.648	.648	.389	1.677	....	.191	.159	1.113[bc]	42,0
1059	Vysočany Prague	Apr. 14	.091	.114	.114	.066	.109	.305	.055	.046	.200	8,0
1060	Záběhlice	Apr. 15	.063	.076	.076	.045	.076	.098	.018	.015	.100	4,0
1061	Zbraslav	Apr. 16	.032	.040	.040	.024	.131	....	.017	.014	.050	2,0
1062	Zlíchov	Apr. 15	.036	.045	.045	.028	.183	....	.025	.021	.100	4,0
1063	Žižkov Prague	Apr. 30	.537	.672	.680	.403	2.722	....	.379	.316	1.450	58,0
1141	Říčany	May 10	.029	.072	.072	.022	.036	....	....	....	.050[b]	2,0
1142	Prague	May 11	.072	.180	.182	.054	.184	....	.018	.014	.150[b]	6,0
1143	Prague	May 22	....	....	....	....	.588	....	.108	.100	....	...
1144	Prague III	May 20	.013	.007	.013	.011	.013	....	....	....	....	...
1145	Břevnov	May 17	.013	.034	.034	.011	.017	.016	.003	.003	.050[b]	2,0
1146	Karlín	May 15	.064	.166	.166	.050	.113	....	.006	.010	.050[b]	2,0
1147	Prague	May 15	.017	.042	.046	.017	.022	....	....	....	.052[bd]	2,0
1148	Prague	May 20	....	....	....	....	....	.078	.014	.012	....	...
1149	Černošice	May 12	.012	.030	.030	.011	.027	....	.002	.006	....	...
1150	Prague	May 21	.012	.030	.030	.011	.015	....	....	....	.050[b]	2,0
1151	Prague	May 17	.018	.044	.044	.017	.022	....	....	....	.050[b]	2,0
1152	Prague IV	May 21	.033	.078	.078	.029	.044	....	....	....	.050[b]	2,0
1153	Prague IV	May 17	.033	.078	.078	.022	.044	.019	.003	.003	.050[b]	2,0
1154 A	Prague	May 18	.018	.046	.046	.017	.022	....	....	....	.050[b]	2,0
1154 B	Prague	May 14	.018	.046	.046	.017	.023	....	....	....	.050[b]	2,0
1155	Prague IV	May 28	.014	.036	.036	.011	.018	....	....	....	.050[b]	2,0
1156	Prague	May 6	.030	.076	.076	.022	.044	....	....	....	.050[b]	2,0
1157	Žamberk	May 31	.078	.204	.192	.061	.088	.058	.011	.010	.150[b]	6,0
1158	Prague	May 11	....	....	....	....	....	.019	.003	.003	....	...
1159	Prague	May 18	.019	.048	.046	.016	.055	....	.006	.005	.050[b]	2,
1161	Vokovice	May 21	.084	.103	.105	.066	.305	....	.036	.030	.150[b]	6,
1162	Žižkov Prague	May 25	.537	.672	.680	.429	2.721	....	.379	.316	1.450[b]	58,
1163	Troj-Podhoř	May 20	.033	.042	.042	.028	.163	....	.022	.018	.100[b]	4,
1164	Střešovice	May 19	.028	.036	.036	.022	.174	....	.024	.020	.100[b]	4,
1165	Strášnice	May 14	.080	.102	.100	.061	.313	....	.039	.032	.150[b]	6,
1166	Selce	May 20	.013	.016	.016	.011	.016	.057	.010	.008	.050[b]	2,
1167	Ruzýň	May 14	.012	.015	.015	.011	.058	....	.008	.006	.050[b]	2,
1168	Radotín	May 18	.036	.045	.045	.028	.173	....	.023	.019	.100[b]	4,
1169	Prague VII	May 18	.376	.470	.470	.290	1.243	....	.144	.120	.900[b]	36,
1170	Prague IV	May 17	....	....	....	....	....	.327	.060	.051	.150[b]	6,
1171	Prague II	May 25	.472	.590	.590	.354	1.464	....	.161	.134	.900[b]	36,
1172	Podolí	May 11	.056	.071	.071	.044	.240	....	.032	.026	.150[b]	6,
1173	Podbaba	May 18	....	....	....	....	....	.057	.009	.007	....	..
1174	Nusle	May 15	.285	.357	.363	.214	1.765	....	.260	.216	.900[b]	36,
1175	Modřany	May 12	.031	.039	.039	.022	.131	....	.017	.014	.100[b]	4,
1176	Michle	May 15	.076	.102	.091	.055	.283	....	.034	.028	.200[b]	8,
1177	Libšice	May 14	.033	.042	.046	.028	.131	....	.016	.014	.100[b]	4,
1178	Liboce	May 15	.023	.029	.029	.017	.135	....	.020	.011	.050[b]	2,
1179	Krč	May 15	.027	.033	.033	.022	.164	....	.024	.020	.200[b]	8,
1180	Košíře	May 15	.348	.435	.435	.268	1.263	....	.152	.127	.750[b]	30,
1181	Keje	May 14	.020	.026	.026	.017	.088	....	.011	.010	.100[b]	4,

CZECHO-SLOVAKIA

Table 260—*Continued* Internal Deliveries, DEJVICE Warehouse

eipt o.	Local Committee (Mistni Komitét)	Date	Commodities in Net Metric Tons of 1,000 Kilograms or 2,204.6 Pounds									
			Flour	Rice	Beans, Peas	Pork Products	Milk		Cocoa	Sugar	Misc.	No. of Biscuits
							Evap.	Cond.				
es 1		1920										
82	Kbely	May 14	.037	.046	.046	.028	.138	....	.017	.014	.100[b]	4,000
83	Karlín	May 14	.320	.408	.408	.235	1.086	....	.126	.105	.700[b]	28,000
84	Jinonice	May 12	.043	.054	.054	.023	.109	....	.010	.018	.119[bd]	4,000
85	Hodkovičky	May 15	.013	.017	.017	.011	.017	.038	.006	.005	.050[b]	2,000
86	Hlubočepy	May 11	.052	.066	.066	.039	.175	....	.020	.017	.100[b]	4,000
87	Hloubětín	May 14	.064	.081	.081	.050	.206	....	.023	.019	.150[b]	6,000
88	Dobrovíz	May 11	.020	.026	.026	.017	.073	....	.008	.007	.050[b]	2,000
89	Břevnov	May 10	.084	.103	.105	.063	.705	....	.110	.092	.350[b]	14,000
90	Prague III	May 18	.215	.269	.269	.161	.269	.390	.072	.060	.400[b]	16,000
91	Dejvice	May 18	.143	.180	.182	....	.523	....	.062	.051	.350[b]	14,000
92	Prosek	June 29	.033	.042	.042	.028	.044	.157	.029	.024	.100[b]	4,000
93	Hostivař	June 29	.037	.047	.046	.028	.047	.185	.034	.028	.150[b]	6,000
94	Prague VIII	May 18	.352	.440	.440	.266	2.286	....	.342	.285	1.150[b]	46,000
95	Roztoky	June 22	.015	.018	.018	.011	.018	.029	.005	.004	.057[bd]	2,000
96	Sukdol	June 29	.014	.018	.018	.011	.018	.101	.018	.015	.050[b]	2,000
97	Bráník	May 11	.070	.087	.090	.052	.239	....	.027	.023	.150[b]	6,000
98	Zbraslav	May 28	.032	.040	.040	.022	.133	....	.017	.014	.100[b]	4,000
99	Záběhlice	June 5	.064	.076	.076	.044	.076	.096	.018	.015	.100[b]	4,000
00	Radlice	May 16	.114	.142	.142	.084	.142	.206	.038	.032	.250[b]	10,000
01	Vršovice	May 31	.419	.524	.524	.313	1.611	....	.204	.168	.900[b]	36,000
02	Vinoř	May 19	.043	.054	.054	.032	.054	....	....	....	.050[b]	2,000
03	Vinohrady Prague	May 14	.512	.648	.648	.371	1.678	....	.191	.159	1.050[b]	42,000
04	Uhřiněves	May 21	.040	.051	.051	.033	.131	....	.016	.013	.100[b]	4,000
05	Smíchov	May 16	.161	.204	.201	.136	1.524	....	.245	.202	.700[b]	28,000
06	Lisoleje	May 14	.019	.023	.023	.017	.073	....	.009	.008	.050[b]	2,000
07	Chuchle	May 12	.021	.027	.027	.017	.087	....	.010	.018	.050[b]	2,000
08	Bubeneč	May 10	.204	.255	.255	.156	.654	....	.072	.060	.400[b]	16,000
09	Bohnice	May 10	.019	.024	.024	.014	.183	....	.029	.024	.100[b]	4,000
10	Zlíchov	May 22	.036	.045	.045	.027	.183	....	.025	.021	.100[b]	4,000
11	Kobylisy	May 12	.080	.102	.100	.061	.327	....	.042	.034	.200[b]	8,000
12	Prague I	May 17	.192	.240	.240	.145	1.208	....	.089	.074	.450[b]	18,000
13	Vysočany	May 19	.091	.114	.114	.066	.414	....	.055	.046	.200[b]	8,000
14	Malešice	May 15	.014	.018	.018	.011	.111	....	.017	.014	.050[b]	2,000
15	Nový Bydžov	June 19	.153	.192	.192	.139	.196	.325	.060	.050	.300[b]	12,000
16	Hořovice	June 8	.217	.272	.272	.163	.262	.382	.069	.058	.400[b]	16,000
17	Nová Paka	June 3	.282	.352	.352	.214	.349	.935	.172	.144	.700[b]	28,000
18	Dobříš	June 8	.095	.120	.120	.072	.130	.400	.072	.060	.350[b]	14,000
19	Kralupy	June 1	.240	.306	.300	.180	.305	.535	.102	.084	.500[b]	20,000
20	Roudnice	June 1	.091	.114	.114	.072	.109	.306	.058	.048	.250[b]	10,000
21	Ml. Boleslav	June 7	.279	.372	.372	.221	.371	.936	.173	.146	.750[b]	30,000
22	Sedlčany	June 1	.082	.102	.102	.060	.109	.229	.043	.036	.200[b]	8,000
23	Slaný	May 31	.320	.408	.408	.242	.414	.878	.161	.134	.750[b]	30,000
24	Rakovník	May 21	.306	.383	.383	.231	1.241	....	.159	.132	.700[b]	28,000
25	Příbram	May 26	.336	.420	.420	.287	1.045	....	.115	.100	.650[b]	26,000
26	Louny	May 31	.084	.103	.105	.066	.109	.229	.043	.036	.200[b]	8,000
27	Mělník	June 1	.064	.083	.083	.050	.087	.210	.037	.031	....	.....
28	Kutná Hora	May 27	.206	.258	.258	.154	.871	....	.115	.096	.500[b]	20,000
29	Brandýs	June 1	.144	.180	.181	.108	.175	.382	.072	.060	.350[b]	14,000
30	Hořice	June 3	.541	.677	.680	.441	.675	.897	.166	.138	1.064[bc]	40,000
31	Benešov	June 1	.072	.090	.091	.055	.087	.229	.043	.036	.200[b]	8,000
32	Kolín	May 27	.173	.216	.216	.732	.675	....	.082	.072	.400[b]	16,000
33	Jičín	May 22	.128	.306	.318	.120	.306	....	.028	.024	.210[bc]	6,000
34	Kladno	May 22	.960	1.224	1.225	.728	2.765	....	.280	.240	1.900[bc]	72,000
06	Karlín Prague	June 15	.482	.602	.602	.364	.610	1.030	.189	.158	1.050[b]	42,000
07	Podolí	June 17	.084	.106	.106	.066	.109	.256	.048	.039	.250[b]	10,000
08	Vysočany	June 17	.136	.171	.171	.105	.174	.458	.083	.069	.300[b]	12,000
09	Zlíchov	June 22	.054	.067	.067	.096	.065	.210	.037	.031	.150[b]	6,000
10	Kbely	July 14	.055	.069	.069	.044	.069	.138	.025	.021	.150[b]	6,000

[*Continued on next page*]

CZECHO-SLOVAKIA

Table 260—*Continued* Internal Deliveries, DEJVICE Warehouse

Receipt No.	Local Committee (Mistni Komitét)	Date	Commodities in Net Metric Tons of 1,000 Kilograms or 2,204.6 Pounds									
			Flour	Rice	Beans, Peas	Pork Products	Milk		Cocoa	Sugar	Misc.	No. of Biscuit
							Evap.	Cond.				
Series 1		1920										
1411	Chuchle	June 21	.032	.041	.041	.028	.044	.080	.015	.012	.100[b]	4,0
1412	Praha II	July 12	.704	.885	.900	.528	.893	1.317	.242	.201	1.350[b]	54,0
1413	Uhřiněves	June 24	.064	.076	.076	.045	.076	.130	.024	.020	.150[b]	6,0
1414	Žižkov Praha	July 14	.805	1.008	1.008	.605	1.008	3.072	.568	.474	2.150[b]	86,0
1415	Břevnov	June 15	.128	.157	.157	.099	.157	.900	.165	.138	.500[b]	20,0
1416	Dobřichovice	June 18	.086	.108	.108	.066	.109	....	....	....	.150[b]	6,0
1417	Bohnice	June 19	.030	.036	.036	.022	.036	.240	.045	.036	.150[b]	6,0
1418	Bráník	June 22	.105	.130	.136	.077	.131	.229	.050	.035	.250[b]	10,0
1419	Dobrovíz	June 27	.030	.040	.040	.022	.044	.076	.012	.010	.100[b]	4,0
1420	Dejvice	June 17	.214	.270	.272	.163	.270	.502	.093	.076	.500[b]	20,0
1421	Hlubočepy	June 15	.078	.102	.099	.066	.099	.163	.030	.025	.150[b]	6,0
1422	Jinonice	June 15	.064	.081	.081	.044	.081	.081	.015	.012	.150[b]	6,0
1423	Kobylisy	June 15	.128	.150	.150	.099	.152	.343	.063	.051	.300[b]	12,0
1424	Prague VIII	June 4	....	....	....	....	....	1.854	....	....	....	...
1425	Krč	June 17	.041	.050	.050	.033	.050	.305	.036	.030	.300[b]	12,0
1426	Keje	June 14	.030	.039	.039	.022	.044	.095	.017	.015	.150[b]	6,0
1427	Praha I and V	July 28	.288	.360	.363	.215	1.088	....	.134	.111	.650[b]	26,0
1428	Libšice	June 17	.050	.063	.063	.039	.065	.134	.024	.021	.150[b]	6,0
1429	Praha III	June 16	.323	.404	.404	.242	.404	.585	.108	.090	.600[b]	24,0
1430	Záběhlice	June 18	.095	.114	.114	.068	.114	.147	.027	.023	.150[b]	6,0
1431	Modřany	June 12	.046	.058	.058	.033	.058	.140	.026	.021	.150[b]	6,0
1432	Nusle	June 21	.428	.536	.536	.322	.549	2.118	.390	.324	1.350[b]	54,0
1433	Prosek	June 19	.050	.063	.063	.039	.065	.229	.044	.036	.250[b]	10,0
1434	Praha VIII	June 23	.528	.660	.660	.394	.654	2.786	.510	.427	1.750[b]	70,0
1435	Praha VII	June 18	.564	.705	.705	.441	.697	1.164	.216	.180	1.200[b]	48,0
1436	Radlice	June 16	.171	.213	.213	.138	.218	.306	.057	.048	.350[b]	14,0
1437	Radotín	June 21	.054	.067	.067	.044	.066	.191	.034	.039	.150[b]	6,0
1438	Praha IV	June 15	....	....	....	....	....	.496	.090	.076	.281[b]	10,0
1439	Selce	June 18	.019	.024	.024	.017	.024	.081	.015	.012	.100[b]	4,0
1440	Smíchov	June 15	.242	.300	.303	.179	.305	1.984	.367	.303	1.050[b]	42,0
1441	Střešovice	June 15	.042	.054	.054	.033	.054	.191	.036	.030	.200[b]	8,0
1442	Strášnice	June 18	.120	.150	.150	.088	.152	.324	.059	.048	.250[b]	10,0
1443	Troj Podhoř	June 22	.050	.063	.063	.037	.065	.182	.033	.027	.150[b]	6,0
1444	Košiře	June 16	.522	.653	.653	.325	.653	1.241	.228	.191	1.150[b]	46,
1445	Vršovice	June 17	.640	.786	.786	.469	.784	1.641	.306	.252	1.350[b]	54,
1446	Hodkovičky	June 15	.020	.026	.026	.017	.026	.051	.009	.008	.100[b]	4,
1447	Vokovice	June 18	.128	.158	.158	.099	.158	.197	.054	.045	.250[b]	10,
1448	Vinohrady-Praha	June 16	.768	.972	.972	.580	.980	1.546	.286	.238	1.550[b]	62,
1449	Ruzýň	June 17	.018	.022	.022	.017	.022	.064	.012	.009	.100[b]	4,
1450	Brandýs n/L.	July 13	.216	.270	.272	.165	.261	.592	.108	.090	.550[b]	22,
1451	Roztoky	July 22	.022	.027	.027	.017	.027	.043	.009	.006	.100[b]	4,
1452	Vinoř	July 22	.064	.081	.081	.050	.081	....	....	....	.100[b]	4,
1453	Zbraslav	July 22	.048	.060	.060	.039	.060	.140	.025	.021	.100[b]	4,
1454	Bubeneč	June 16	.306	.383	.383	.242	.392	.591	.102	.090	.600[b]	24,
1455	Praha IV	June 16	....	....	....	....	.327	....	.060	.051	.150[b]	6,
1456	Michle	June 17	.114	.144	.144	.088	.152	.268	.051	.042	.300[b]	12,
1457	Podbaba	June 24	....	....	....	....	....	.076	.014	.010	.050[b]	2,
1458	Hloubětín	July 22	.093	.121	.121	.077	.121	.190	.035	.029	.250[b]	10,
1459	Liboce	July 22	.035	.044	.045	.028	.044	.159	.030	.017	.100[b]	4,
1460	Lysoleje	June 15	.030	.039	.039	.022	.039	.095	.017	.015	.150[b]	6,
1461	Malešice	July 2	.021	.027	.027	.017	.027	.140	.026	.021	.100[b]	4,
1463	Prague IX	July 10	....	....	....	....	....	.591	.108	.090	....	..
1464	Třebovice	July 7	.960	1.200	1.224	.726	1.197	....	....	....	1.475[bd]	48,
1465	Praha	June 17	.018	.023	.023	.017	.022	.038	.007	.006	.050[b]	2,
1466	Praha III	June 8	.013	.007	.013	.011	.013	....	....	....	.050[b]	2,
1467	Praha	June 10	.030	.038	.038	.022	.038	.031	.006	.006	.050[b]	2,
1468	na Kopě	June 1	.005	.006	.006	.006	.006	.016	.004	.003	.050[b]	2,
1469	Praha	June 25	.072	.090	.090	.054	.090	.098	.018	.014	.150[b]	6,

CZECHO-SLOVAKIA

'able 260—*Continued* Internal Deliveries, DEJVICE Warehouse

t	Local Committee (Mistni Komitét)	Date	Flour	Rice	Beans, Peas	Pork Products	Milk Evap.	Milk Cond.	Cocoa	Sugar	Misc.	No. of Biscuits
			Commodities in Net Metric Tons of 1,000 Kilograms or 2,204.6 Pounds									
1		1920										
	Praha IV	June 14	.033	.039	.039	.022	.039	.081	.015	.013	.100[b]	4,000
	Praha	June 21	.019	.024	.024	.022	.024	.062	.012	.010	.050[b]	2,000
	Chvaly	July 2	.012	.015	.015	.011	.015	.012	.002	.002	.050[b]	2,000
	Černošice	June 7	.012	.015	.015	.011	.015	.012	.002	.002	.050[b]	2,000
	Říčany	June 16	.029	.036	.036	.022	.036	.062	.012	.012	.050[b]	2,000
	Praha	June 17	.018	.023	.023	.017	.022	.038	.007	.006	.050[b]	2,000
	Břevnov	June 16	.013	.017	.017	.011	.017	.016	.003	.003	.050[b]	2,000
	Karlín Praha	June 15	.052	.066	.066	.044	.066	.095	.017	.014	.100[b]	4,000
	Uh. Hradiště	July 7	.024	.030	.030	.018	.030	....	....	....	.030[b]	1,200
	Praha	June 16	....	....	....	....	....	.046	.009	.007	....	.....
	Praha	June 23	.010	.012	.012	.011	.012	.153	.029	.024	.050[b]	2,000
	Praha	June 22	.012	.015	.015	.011	.015	....	....	....	....	.....
	Praha	June 4	.012	.015	.015	.009	.015	....	....	....	....	.....
	Praha	June 5	.018	.022	.022	.017	.022	.038	.007	.006	.050[b]	2,000
	Praha IV	June 21	.014	.018	.018	.011	.018	....	....	....	.050[b]	2,000
	Dobřichovice	June 18	.086	.108	.108	.066	.109	....	....	....	.150[b]	6,000
	Vel-Meziříčí	July 3	.048	.060	.060	.039	.065	....	....	....	.100[b]	4,000
	Praha IX	June 26	.096	.120	.120	.066	.120	....	....	....	.150[b]	6,000
	Praha IV	May 28	.014	.036	.036	.011	.018	....	....	....	.050[b]	2,000
	Praha	May 31	....	....	....	....	....	.191	.036	.030	.100[b]	4,000
	Praha	May 28	....	....	....	....	....	.058	.011	.009	....	.....
	(See No. 1492)	....	....	....	....	....	....	....	....	....	....	.....
2	Praha	June 15	.017	.042	.045	.017	.022	....	....	....	.050[b]	2,000
3	Praha II	June 25	.027	.034	.034	.022	.034	.016	.003	.002	.050[b]	2,000
4	Praha VII	June 25	....	....	....	....	....	.078	.014	.012	.050[b]	2,000
5	Vlašim	June 17	.048	.060	.060	.039	.065	....	....	....	.100[b]	4,000
6	Praha	June 26	.022	.028	.028	.017	.028	.374	.069	.058	.150[b]	6,000
7	Prague I	June 30	.144	.180	.180	.110	.175	.477	.086	.072	.433[b,d]	14,000
8	Praha	June 25	.082	.120	.120	.071	.120	....	....	....	.200[b]	8,000
9	Praha	July 2	.960	1.200	1.224	.720	1.197	....	....	....	1.475[b]	48,000
0	Chvaly	June 7	.012	.015	.015	.011	.015	.012	.002	.002	.050[b]	2,000
1	Kutná Hora	July 20	.309	.387	.387	.331	.392	.935	.172	.144	.750[b]	30,000
2	Kralupy	July 15	.360	.450	.453	.270	.457	.820	.150	.126	.750[b]	30,000
3	Beroun	July 28	.320	.405	.408	.363	1.110	....	.129	.108	.700[b]	28,000
4	Kolín	July 20	.256	.324	.318	.198	.327	.706	.129	.108	.600[b]	24,000
5	Jičín	July 9	.192	.225	.227	.132	.218	.229	.042	.036	.200[b]	8,000
6	Selčany	July 20	.123	.153	.153	.099	.522	....	.065	.054	.300[b]	12,000
7	Dobříš	July 16	.143	.180	.181	.110	.174	.591	.108	.090	.500[b]	20,000
8	N. Paka	July 15	.423	.528	.528	.363	.523	1.412	.258	.216	1.050[b]	42,000
9	Brandýs	July 13	.216	.270	.272	.165	.262	.591	.102	.090	.550[b]	22,000
0	Benešov	June 20	.108	.135	.135	.081	.135	.361	.064	.054	.300[b]	12,000
1	N. Bydžov	July 16	.230	.288	.288	.176	.283	.591	.090	.075	.450[b]	18,000
2	Hořice	July 13	.811	1.015	1.015	.594	1.023	1.355	.249	.207	1.500[b]	60,000
3	Kladno	July 9	1.452	1.815	1.814	1.089	1.807	2.347	.432	.360	2.700[b]	108,000
4	Ml. Boleslav	June 18	.445	.558	.558	.334	.558	1.404	.259	.219	1.100[b]	44,000
5	Louny	July 12	.128	.157	.157	.099	.153	.344	.064	.054	.300[b]	12,000
6	Mělník	July 13	.100	.125	.125	.077	.131	.305	.045	.046	.250[b]	10,000
7	Hořovice	July 28	.320	.408	.408	.242	.980	....	.102	.087	.600[b]	24,000
8	Příbram	July 10	.512	.630	.635	.379	.631	.935	.173	.144	1.000[b]	40,000
9	Roudnice	July 15	.136	.171	.171	.110	.174	.477	.087	.072	.400[b]	16,000
0	Č. Brod	June 16	.192	.261	.261	.149	.261	.401	.076	.063	.850[b]	34,000
1	Rakovník	July 15	.459	.575	.575	.347	.566	1.297	.239	.198	1.050[b]	42,000
2	Slaný	July 12	.489	.612	.612	.363	.610	1.317	.242	.201	1.100[b]	44,000
1	Písek	Mar. 18	....	....	....	....	....	....	....	....	.030[c]	.....
3	Černovice u Tábora	Mar. 19	....	....	....	....	....	....	....	....	.031[c]	.....
		1919										
4	Zbraslav	Sept. 20	.286	.040	.040	.158	.160	.286	.058	....	....	.....
5	Kralupy	Nov. 10	.480	.120	.120	.480	.480	1.113	.225	....	....	.....
6	Louny	Oct. 26	.200	.050	.050	.250	.200	.477	.096	....	....	.....

[*Continued on next page*]

CZECHO-SLOVAKIA

Table 260—*Continued* Internal Deliveries, DEJVICE Warehouse

Receipt No.	Local Committee (Mistni Komitét)	Date	Flour	Rice	Beans, Peas	Pork Products	Milk Evap.	Milk Cond.	Cocoa	Sugar	Misc.	No. of Biscuit
			Commodities in Net Metric Tons of 1,000 Kilograms or 2,204.6 Pounds									
Series 1		1919										
1977	Roudnice	Dec. 10	.300	.300	.300	.209	.300	.375	.075	.075	....	...
1978	Kralupy	Dec. 10	.600	.600	.600	.424	.600	1.050	.210	.210	....	...
1979	Louny	Dec. 14	.250	.250	.250	.175	.250	.450	.090	.090	....	...
1980	Kladno	Dec. 21	1.516	2.250	1.658	1.575	2.242	.420	.092	.540	....	...
1981	Zbraslav	Dec. 22	.064	.067	.067	.050	.067	.159	.032	.032	....	...
		1920										
1982	Roudnice	Jan. 10	.300	.750	.300	.208	.305	.382	.075	.075	.100[d]	...
1983	Louny	Jan. 10	.256	.125	.250	.175	.261	.458	.090	.090	.100[d]	...
1984	Kralupy	Jan. 10	.600	.300	.600	.419	.670	1.050	.210	.950	....	...
1985	Benešov	Jan. 11	.256	.125	.250	.174	.267	.305	.060	.060	.086[d]	...
1986	Slaný	Jan. 12	.850	.425	.850	.594	.849	1.794	.360	.360	.362[d]	...
1987	Sedlčany	Jan. 12	.256	.125	.250	.174	.267	.305	.060	.060	.087[d]	...
1988	Bydžov	Jan. 12	.492	.246	.499	.312	.501	.520	.102	.700	.145[d]	...
1989	Č. Brod	Jan. 12	.465	.240	.488	.343	.501	.640	.128	.128	.154[d]	...
1990	Zbraslav	Jan. 1	.064	.033	.067	.050	.065	.153	.032	.032	.030[d]	...
1991	Paka	Jan. 13	.750	.375	.750	.523	.750	1.640	.330	.330	.075[d]	...
1992	Brandýs n/L.	Jan. 13	.450	.225	.454	.315	.457	.744	.150	.150	.175[d]	...
1993	Kladno	Jan. 13	2.250	1.125	2.250	1.575	2.242	2.709	.540	.540	.662[d]	...
1994	Kolín	Jan. 13	.550	.272	.544	.385	.544	.897	.180	.180	.212[d]	...
1995	Příbram	Jan. 14	.600	.300	.600	.420	.670	1.050	.210	.210	.237[d]	...
1996	Kutná Hora	Jan. 14	.600	.250	.499	.350	.507	1.050	.210	.210	.062[d]	...
1997	Dobříš	Jan. 15	.309	.154	.305	.216	.305	.515	.102	.100	.107[d]	...
1998	Rakovník	Jan. 15	1.000	.449	.998	.700	1.007	1.507	.300	.300	.375[d]	...
1999	N. Strašecí	Jan. 15	.704	.350	.700	.490	.697	2.257	.450	.450	.462[d]	...
2000	Mělník	Jan. 15	.174	.067	.174	.121	.174	.401	.081	.081	.070[d]	...
2001	Boleslav	Jan. 19	.800	.400	.800	.560	.805	1.660	.330	.330	.337[d]	...
2002	N. Paka	Feb. 4	1.171	.590	1.171	.823	1.175	2.099	.420	.420	....	...
2003	Slaný	Feb. 13	1.020	.510	1.033	.715	1.023	1.794	.360	.360	....	...
2004	Sedlčany	Feb. 21	.300	.150	.302	.208	.305	.305	.060	.060	....	...
2005	Benešov	Feb. 21	.279	.136	.280	.193	.283	.382	.047	.047	....	...
2006	Roudnice	Feb. 22	.360	.182	.360	.257	.370	.382	.075	.075	....	...
2007	Hořovice	Feb. 22	.572	.283	.566	.395	.566	.595	.119	.119	....	..
2008	Č. Brod	Feb. 20	.339	.169	.339	.336	.348	.515	.102	.100	....	..
2009	Louny	Feb. 22	.300	.150	.308	.210	.305	.458	.090	.090	....	..
2010	Ml. Boleslav	Feb. 22	.961	.480	.960	.670	.958	1.641	.330	.330	....	..
2011	N. Bydžov	Feb. 20	.492	.246	.403	.346	.501	.515	.102	.100	....	..
2012	Rakovník	Mar. 6	.920	.454	.920	.642	.914	1.182	.235	.235	....	..
2013	Brandýs	Mar. 13	.343	.172	.343	.244	.349	.630	.125	.125	....	..
2014	Mělník	Mar. 14	.174	.191	.174	.125	.175	.401	.081	.081	....	..
2015	Kladno	Mar. 22	....	....	....	....	....	....	....	....	.042[d]	..
		1919										
2016	Praha VIII	Sept 9	.665	.166	.166	.664	.665	2.822	.569	....	....	..
2017	Praha IV	Sept. 11	.128	.033	.033	.130	.128	.397	.080	....	....	..
2018	Modřany	Sept. 11	.046	.011	.011	.049	.046	.140	.028	....	....	..
2019	Praha II	Sept. 11	.642	.160	.160	.643	.642	1.431	.288	....	....	..
2020	Praha VIII	Sept. 25	....	....	....	....	....	....	....	....	.315[c]	..
2021	Hodkovičky	Sept. 27	.020	.005	.005	.020	.020	.047	.009	....	....	..
2022	Hloubětín	Sept. 15	....	....	....	....	....	.182	.036	....	....	..
2023	Praha VIII	Nov. 1	.333	.083	.083	.333	.333	1.411	.249	....	....	..
2024	Vysočany	Nov. 14	.150	.150	.150	.105	.150	.374	.084	....	....	..
2025	Praha II	Nov. 15	.950	.950	.953	.665	.955	1.350	.270	....	....	..
2026	Smíchov Praha	Nov. 15	.793	.793	.793	.554	.793	2.379	.387	....	....	..
2027	Bohnice	Nov. 15	.035	.035	.035	.025	.035	.235	.045	....	....	..
2028	Hloubětín	Nov. 15	.121	.121	.121	.084	.121	.172	.035	.771	....	..
2029	Hodkovičky	Nov. 15	.025	.025	.025	.018	.025	.045	.009	....	....	..
2030	Modřany	Nov. 15	.058	.058	.058	.040	.058	.132	.026	....	....	..
2031	Uhřiněves	Nov. 30	.085	.091	.091	.061	.085	.114	.023	.023	....	..
2032	Dejvice	Dec. 12	....	....	....	....	....	....	....	....	.030[c]	..
2033	Smíchov Praha	Dec. 15	.346	.366	.346	.230	.348	.820	.194	.580	....	..
2034	Lisoleje	Dec. 15	.016	.016	.016	.011	.016	.030	.006	.006	....	..

CZECHO-SLOVAKIA

Table 260—*Continued*

Internal Deliveries, DEJVICE Warehouse

eceipt No.	Local Committee (Mistni Komitét)	Date	Commodities in Net Metric Tons of 1,000 Kilograms or 2,204.6 Pounds									
			Flour	Rice	Beans, Peas	Pork Products	Milk		Cocoa	Sugar	Misc.	No. of Biscuits
							Evap.	Cond.				
eries 1		1919										
2035	Radlice	Dec. 12	....	....	....	....	....	....	....	.100	.031[c]	.....
2036	Strášnice	Dec. 16	.080	.080	.080	.055	.080	.148	.029	.029	....	.....
2037	Vysočany	Dec. 16	.075	.075	.075	.055	.075	.187	.042	.042	.006[d]	.....
2038	Praha III	Dec. 11	....	....	....	....	....	....	....	....	.060[c]	.....
2039	Chuchle	Dec. 17	.018	.018	.018	.012	.018	.036	.007	.021	....	.....
2040	Libšice	Dec. 17	.035	.035	.035	.025	.035	.065	.013	.039	....	.....
2041	Vokovice	Dec. 17	.168	.168	.168	.115	.168	.280	.056	.056	....	.....
2042	Podbaba	Dec. 17	....	....	....	....	....	.030	....	.006	....	.....
2043	Podolí	Dec. 18	.050	.050	.050	.033	.050	.120	.024	.024	....	.....
2044	Zlíchov	Dec. 18	.033	.033	.032	.018	.033	.090	.018	.018	....	.....
2045	Vinohrady Praha	Dec. 18	.336	.336	.411	.336	.336	.935	.177	.177	....	.....
2046	Střešovice	Dec. 19	.028	.028	.028	.020	.028	.090	.018	.018	....	.....
2047	Bohnice	Dec. 20	.018	.018	.018	.012	.018	.118	.022	.012	....	.....
2048	Praha III	Dec. 20	.140	.140	.200	.143	.140	.337	.067	.067	....	.....
2049	Vinoř	Dec. 20	.035	.035	.035	.025	.035	....	....	....	....	.....
2050	Praha VIII	Dec. 21	.416	.416	.410	.291	.416	1.331	.266	.266	....	.....
2051	Radotín	Dec. 22	.033	.033	.033	.023	.033	.090	.018	.018	....	.....
2052	Ruzýň	Dec. 22	.006	.007	.007	.004	.008	.023	.004	.029	....	.....
2053	Sukdol	Dec. 22	.015	.015	.015	.011	.015	.067	.014	.014	....	.....
2054	Hostivař	Dec. 23	.040	.040	.040	.028	.040	.130	.026	.026	....	.....
2055	Hlubočepy	Dec. 30	.109	.109	.109	.077	.109	.127	.026	.026	....	.....
2056	Strášnice	Dec. 31	.155	.155	.155	.110	.155	.248	.049	.049	....	.....
2057	Karlín Praha	Dec. 31	.600	.600	.600	.417	.600	.878	.175	.175	....	.....
2058	Žižkov Praha	Dec. 31	.704	....	.510	.751	.941	2.199	.510	.510	....	.....
2059	Radlice	Dec. 31	.205	.205	.205	.143	.205	.216	.042	.042	....	.....
2060	Vršovice	Dec. 31	....	....	....	....	.210	....	.005	.161	....	.....
		1920										
061	Košíře	Jan. 1	.480	.430	.430	.334	.491	.181	.154	.154	....	.....
062	Dejvice	Jan. 15	.146	.146	.146	.102	.146	.257	.050	.250	....	.....
063	Libšice	Jan. 2	.070	.070	.070	.050	.070	.107	.022	.022	....	.....
064	Lisoleje	Jan. 2	.032	.032	.032	.024	.032	.050	.009	.022	....	.....
065	Dobrovíz	Jan. 3	.035	.035	.035	.025	.035	....	....	....	....	.....
066	Bohnice	Jan. 3	.035	.035	.035	.024	.035	.138	.038	.038	....	.....
067	Nusle Praha	Jan. 5	.121	.157	.372	.405	....	....	.148	.351	....	.....
068	Podbaba	Jan. 5	....	....	....	....	.050	....	....	.010	....	.....
069	Praha III	Jan. 5	.400	.400	.400	.280	.400	.562	.112	.112	....	.....
070	Ruzýň	Jan. 5	.020	.020	.020	.068	.020	.020	.014	.014	....	.....
071	Modřany	Jan. 5	.058	.058	.058	.040	.058	.123	.026	.026	....	.....
072	Zlíchov	Jan. 5	.075	.075	.075	.044	.075	.150	.030	.030	....	.....
073	Vysočany	Jan. 5	.150	.150	.050	.105	.150	.353	.070	.070	....	.....
074	Zlíchov	Jan. 5	....	....	....	....	....	....	....	.036	....	.....
075	Malešice	Jan. 7	.023	.023	.023	.017	.022	.114	.013	.013	....	.....
076	Troj Podhora	Jan. 7	.055	.055	.055	.038	.055	.144	.029	.064	....	.....
077	Sukdol	Jan. 9	.064	.015	.030	.021	.030	.103	.023	.023	....	.....
078	Podolí	Jan. 9	.100	.050	.100	.070	.100	.190	.040	.040	....	.....
079	Michle	Jan. 9	.237	.118	.237	.165	.237	.418	.043	.095	....	.....
080	Hloubětín	Jan. 9	.116	.055	.120	.081	.113	.261	.031	.034	....	.....
081	Roztoky	Jan. 9	.030	.030	.030	.022	.030	.039	.008	.008	....	.....
082	Chuchle	Jan. 10	.035	.035	.035	.025	.035	.060	.012	.012	....	.....
083	Liboce	Jan. 10	.041	.020	.041	.029	.043	.153	.030	.030	....	.....
084	Prosek	Jan. 10	.030	.035	.045	.011	.022	....	....	.021	.036	.....
085	Záběhlice	Jan. 10	.102	.051	.102	.072	.102	.116	.023	.023	....	.....
086	Keje	Jan. 10	.037	.037	.037	.022	.037	.076	.015	.075	....	.....
087	Vršovice	Jan. 10	.763	.191	.771	.534	.763	1.612	.322	.322	....	.....
088	Střešovice	Jan. 12	.056	....	.013	.029	.056	.150	.013	.020	....	.....
089	Kobylisy	Jan. 12	.150	.075	.150	.105	.150	.263	.053	.053	....	.....
090	Radotín	Jan. 13	.064	.065	.065	.046	.065	.150	.030	.030	....	.....
091	Vinohrady	Jan. 14	.960	.480	.960	.671	.960	1.475	.295	.295	....	.....
092	Hodkovičky	Jan. 15	.025	.013	.025	.017	.025	.042	.012	.012	....	.....

[*Continued on next page*]

CZECHO-SLOVAKIA

Table 260—*Continued* Internal Deliveries, DEJVICE Warehouse

Receipt No.	Local Committee (Mistni Komitét)	Date	Flour	Rice	Beans, Peas	Pork Products	Milk Evap.	Milk Cond.	Cocoa	Sugar	Misc.	No. of Biscuits
			Commodities in Net Metric Tons of 1,000 Kilograms or 2,204.6 Pounds									
Series 1		1920										
2093	Praha I	Jan. 15	.550	.272	.550	.385	.550	.787	.137	.137	....	....
2094	Smíchov	Jan. 15	.793	.793	.793	.555	.793	1.613	.323	.323	....	....
2095	Hostivař	Jan. 16	.080	.040	.080	.055	.080	.217	.043	.043	....	....
2096	Praha II	Jan. 17	....	....	....	....	....	....	....	.270	....	....
2097	Dejvice	Jan. 18	.282	.146	.282	.204	.282	.481	.084	.084	....	....
2098	Uhřiněves	Jan. 18	.085	.042	.085	.060	.085	.095	.019	.019	....	....
2099	Kbely	Jan. 19	.064	.030	.060	.044	.060	.100	.020	.020	....	....
2100	Břevnov	Jan. 19	.100	.050	.100	.072	.100	.375	.075	.075	....	....
2101	Praha	Jan. 13	....	....	....	....	....	....	....	.009	....	....
2102	Prague	Jan. 17	.009	.009	.009	.006	.009	....	....	....	....	....
2103	Prague	Jan. 17	....	....	....	....	.150	....	.030	.030	....	....
2104	Prague	Jan. 5	.008	.008	.008	.006	.008	....	....	....	....	....
2105	Prague III	Jan. 5	.015	.008	.015	.009	.015	....	....	....	....	....
2106	Prague	Jan. 5	....	....	....	....	....	.015	.003	.003	....	....
2107	na Kopě	Jan. 7	.005	.005	.005	.004	.005	.012	.003	.003	....	....
2108	Prague, Karlín	Jan. 7	.055	.055	.055	.039	.055	.025	.007	.007	....	....
2109	Prague	Jan. 7	....	....	....	....	....	....	....	.006	....	....
2110	Hradčany Praha	Jan. 8	.025	.012	.025	.018	.025	....	....	....	....	....
2111	Chvaly	Jan. 9	.010	.005	.010	.007	.010	.008	.002	.002	....	....
2112	Prague	Jan. 9	.015	.008	.015	.017	.015	....	....	....	....	....
2113	Černošice	Jan. 14	.005	.003	.005	.004	.005	.005	.001	.001	....	....
2114	Prague IX	Jan. 23	.020	.010	.020	.017	.020	.025	.005	.005	....	....
2115	Prague IX	Jan. 24	.018	.009	.018	.012	.018	....	....	....	....	....
2116	Prague	Jan. 28	....	....	....	.450	....	....	.090	.090	....	....
2117	Prague-Hradčany	Jan. 28	....	....	....	....	....	.150	.030	.030	....	....
2118	Hradčany-Prague	Jan. 28	.015	.007	.015	.011	.015	....	....	....	....	....
2119	Prague	Jan. 28	....	....	....	....	....	.090	.015	.018	....	....
2120	Prague	Feb. 5	.015	.008	.015	.011	.015	....	....	....	....	....
2121	Prague III	Feb. 5	.018	.009	.018	.013	.018	....	....	....	....	....
2122	Prague II	Feb. 5	.021	.010	.021	.015	.021	....	....	....	....	....
2123	Prague	Feb. 5	.018	.009	.018	.013	.018	....	....	....	....	....
2124	Černošice	Feb. 6	.012	.006	.012	.009	.012	.009	.002	.002	....	....
2125	Chvaly	Feb. 6	.012	.006	.012	.009	.012	.009	.002	.002	....	....
2126	Hradčany-Prague	Feb. 9	.030	.075	.030	.022	.030	....	....	....	....	....
2127	Karlín	Feb. 11	.055	.028	.055	.039	.055	.025	.005	.005	....	....
2128	Praha	Feb. 13	....	....	....	....	....	.150	.030	.030	....	....
2129	Praha	Feb. 19	.020	.010	.020	.017	.020	.025	.005	.005	....	....
2130	Praha	Feb. 21	....	....	....	....	....	.375	.075	.075	....	....
2131	Praha	Mar. 9	....	....	....	....	....	.250	.050	.050	....	....
2132	Praha III	Mar. 1	.018	.009	.018	.013	.018	....	....	....	....	....
2133	Praha Karlín	Mar. 2	.055	.028	.055	.040	.055	.025	.005	.005	....	....
2134	Praha	Mar. 2	....	....	....	....	....	.075	.003	.003	....	....
2135	Chvaly	Mar. 4	.012	.006	.012	.009	.012	.009	.002	.002	....	....
2136	Černošice	Mar. 4	.012	.006	.012	.008	.012	.009	.002	.002	....	....
2137	Praha III	Mar. 4	.015	.008	.015	.011	.015	....	....	....	.012[c]	....
2138	Praha Karlín	Mar. 6	....	....	....	....	....	....	....	....	.026[c]	....
2139	Praha	Mar. 9	.018	.009	.018	.013	.018	....	....	....	....	....
2140	Praha IV	Mar. 11	.030	.015	.030	.022	.030	....	....	....	....	....
2141	Praha IV	Mar. 15	....	....	....	....	....	.150	.030	.030	....	....
2142	Praha IV	Mar. 15	....	....	....	....	....	.090	.018	.018	....	....
2143	na Kopě	Mar. 17	.006	.003	.006	.006	.006	.015	.003	.003	....	....
2144	Praha	Mar. 24	.020	.010	.020	.017	.020	.025	.005	.005	....	....
2145	Chuchle	Feb. 14	.035	.018	.035	.025	.035	.060	.012	.012	.015[d]	....
2146	Příbram	Feb. 15	.420	.210	.425	.296	.414	1.794	.360	.360	....	....
2147	Hloubětín	Feb. 17	.120	.060	.120	.084	.120	.145	.029	.029	.045[d]	....
2148	Hlubočepy	Feb. 18	.109	.055	.109	.077	.109	.197	.025	.025	.087[d]	....
2149	Dejvice	Feb. 18	.292	.146	.292	.205	.292	.420	.083	.083	.250[d]	....
2150	Zlíchov	Feb. 19	....	....	....	....	....	.076	....	....	....	....

CZECHO-SLOVAKIA

Table 260—*Continued* Internal Deliveries, DEJVICE Warehouse

ot	Local Committee (Mistni Komitét)	Date	Flour	Rice	Beans, Peas	Pork Products	Milk Evap.	Milk Cond.	Cocoa	Sugar	Misc.	No. of Biscuits
			Commodities in Net Metric Tons of 1,000 Kilograms or 2,204.6 Pounds									
1		1920										
1	Praha III	Feb. 20	....	....	....	....	....	.562	.112	.112	....	....
2	Praha Smíchov	Feb. 20	.300	.150	.300	.211	.300	1.612	.322	.322	.257[d]	....
3	Michle	Feb. 21	.125	.063	.125	.088	.125	.225	.045	.045	.060[d]	....
4	Selce	Feb. 21	.025	.013	.025	.018	.025	.057	.011	.011	.014[d]	....
5	Košíře	Feb. 23	....	....	....	....	....	....	....	....	.092[d]	....
6	Praha I	Feb. 24	.237	....	....	.164	.239	.553	.111	.111	.125[d]	....
7	Vokovice	Feb. 24	.168	.084	.168	.116	.174	.229	.047	.047	.074[d]	....
8	Radlice	Feb. 26	.205	.102	.203	.146	.205	.210	.042	.042	.112[cd]	....
9	Prosek	Feb. 25	.070	.035	.070	.050	.070	.191	.037	.037	....	....
0	Lisoleje	Feb. 26	.032	.016	.032	.022	.032	.050	.010	.010	.016[d]	....
1	Kbely	Feb. 27	.060	.030	.060	.044	.060	.100	.020	.020	.029[d]	....
2	St. Strášnice	Feb. 28	.155	.077	.155	.111	.152	.248	.049	.049	.070[d]	....
3	Troj Podhora	Feb. 28	.055	.028	.055	.039	.055	.144	.029	.029	.033[d]	....
4	Vinohrady, Praha	Feb. 28	....	....	....	....	....	....	....	....	.060[c]	....
5	Podbaba	Feb. 28	....	....	....	....	....	.050	.010	.010	.007[d]	....
6	Břevnov	Feb. 28	.200	.100	.200	.144	.200	.750	.150	.150	....	....
7	Hostivař	Mar. 1	....	....	....	....	....	.103	....	....	....	....
8	Vysočany	Mar. 1	.150	.075	.150	.106	.150	.354	.071	.071	....	....
9	Ruzýň	Mar. 1	.027	.020	.010	.020	.014	.068	.014	.014	.015[d]	....
0	Karlín	Mar. 1	....	....	....	.420	....	.877	....	.099	....	....
1	Košíře	Mar. 1	.448	.250	.496	.349	.500	.875	.175	.175	....	....
2	Hostivař	Mar. 1	.080	.040	.080	.055	.080	.217	.043	.043	....	....
3	Vinoř	Mar. 1	.070	.035	.070	.050	.070	....	....	....	.021[d]	....
4	Libšice	Mar. 2	.070	.035	.070	.044	.070	.107	.022	.022	.033[d]	....
5	Žižkov	Mar. 2	1.000	.499	1.000	.697	1.001	2.500	.500	.500	....	....
6	Nusle	Mar. 2	.703	.351	.709	.492	.703	1.755	.351	.351	....	....
7	Dobrovíz	Mar. 3	.035	.018	.035	.024	.035	....	....	....	.011[d]	....
8	Praha II	Mar. 4	.950	.475	.950	.665	.958	1.126	.225	.225	....	....
9	Praha Karlín	Mar. 12	....	....	....	....	....	.668	....	....	.258[d]	....
0	Radotín	Mar. 8	.064	.033	.065	.046	.065	.152	.030	.030	....	....
1	Zlíchov	Mar. 8	.051	.025	.051	.035	.051	.152	.031	.031	....	....
2	Bubeneč	Mar. 5	.425	.213	.425	.298	.425	.501	.102	.100	.172[d]	....
3	Liboce	Mar. 5	.041	.021	.041	.022	.041	.126	.025	.025	....	....
4	Bráník	Mar. 6	....	....	....	....	....	....	....	....	.039[d]	....
5	Bráník	Mar. 6	.090	.045	.090	.066	.087	.114	.023	.023	....	....
6	Vršovice	Mar. 3	.768	.382	.763	.534	.762	1.354	.269	.269	....	....
7	Modřany	Mar. 3	.058	.029	.058	.040	.058	.114	.022	.022	....	....
8	Selce	Jan. 23	.025	.013	.025	....	.025	.056	.011	.011	....	....
9	Prosek	Jan. 25	.035	.035	.035	.025	.043	.114	.023	.023	....	....
0	Bráník	Jan. 25	.135	.067	.135	.095	.133	.200	.037	.037	....	....
1	Praha VIII	Jan. 26	.832	.416	.831	.582	.831	2.219	.444	.447	....	....
2	Praha VII	Jan. 28	.396	....	.268	....	....	.150	....	.177	....	....
3	Radlice	Jan. 28	.205	.102	.205	.143	.205	.212	.042	.042	....	....
4	Prosek	Jan. 29	.070	.035	.070	.050	.070	.187	.038	.038	....	....
5	Podbaba	Jan. 30	....	....	....	....	....	....	....	....	.054[c]	....
6	Žižkov	Jan. 31	.906	.458	.909	.648	.906	2.300	.500	.500	....	....
7	Libšice n/Vl.	Feb. 1	.071	.035	.071	.042	.081	.108	.022	.022	....	....
8	Dobrovíz	Feb. 4	.035	.018	.035	.025	.035	....	....	....	....	....
9	Modřany	Feb. 4	.058	.029	.058	.040	.058	.057	.022	.022	....	....
0	Karlín	Feb. 4	.600	.300	.596	.429	.600	.191	.155	.155	....	....
1	Hlubočepy	Feb. 5	.109	.055	.109	.077	.109	.057	.026	.026	....	....
2	Zlíchov	Feb. 5	.048	.024	.046	.033	.048	.057	.028	.028	.030[c]	....
3	Vysočany	Feb. 5	.150	.075	.150	.105	.150	.095	.071	.071	....	....
4	Vršovice	Feb. 5	.763	.382	.763	.536	.762	.191	.269	.269	....	....
5	Nusle	Feb. 5	.700	.351	.703	.488	.703	.191	.351	.351	....	....
6	Malešice	Feb. 5	.023	.012	.023	.017	.023	.125	.023	.023	....	....
7	Košíre	Feb. 4	.430	.250	.454	.302	.472	.191	.174	.175	....	....
8	Jinonice	Feb. 6	.070	.035	.070	.050	.070	....	....	....	....	....

[*Continued on next page*]

CZECHO-SLOVAKIA

Table 260—*Continued* Internal Deliveries, DEJVICE Warehouse

Receipt No.	Local Committee (Mistni Komitét)	Date	Commodities in Net Metric Tons of 1,000 Kilograms or 2,204.6 Pounds									
			Flour	Rice	Beans, Peas	Pork Products	Milk		Cocoa	Sugar	Misc.	No. of Biscuit
							Evap.	Cond.				
Series 1		1920										
2209	Bubeneč	Feb. 6	.425	.212	.425	.297	.425	.191	.102	.100	....	...
2210	Břevnov	Feb. 6	.127	.072	.127	.072	.136	.153	.118	.105	....	...
2211	Roztoky	Feb. 6	.030	.015	.030	.022	.030	.038	.008	.008	.014[d]	...
2212	Liboce	Feb. 7	.041	.020	.041	.022	.041	.126	.025	.025	.027[d]	...
2213	Podbaba	Feb. 7	....	....	....	....	....	.050	.010	.010	....	...
2214	Hostivař	Feb. 9	.080	.040	.080	.055	.080	.115	.043	.043	....	...
2215	Bohnice	Feb. 9	.035	.018	.035	.024	.035	.188	.038	.038	....	...
2216	Sukdol	Feb. 10	.030	.015	.030	.022	.030	.114	.023	.023	.022[d]	...
2217	Vršovice	Feb. 10	....	....	....	....	....	1.152	....	....	....	...
2218	Lisoleje	Feb. 10	.032	.016	.032	.022	.032	.050	.010	.010	.005[c]	...
2219	Praha VII	Feb. 11	.539	.422	.855	.018	.174	1.019	.128	.118	.356[d]	...
2220	Keje	Feb. 11	.037	.018	.037	.026	.037	.075	.015	.015	.020[d]	...
2221	Vokovice	Feb. 11	.015	.008	.033	.006	.025	....	....	.024	....	...
2222	Záběhlice	Feb. 11	.102	.056	.102	.072	.102	.116	.023	.023	.042[d]	...
2223	Radotín	Feb. 11	.064	.033	.065	.046	.065	.150	.030	.030	.036[d]	...
2224	Žižkov	Feb. 12	....	....	....	....	....	1.851	....	....	.574[cd]	...
2225	Nusle	Feb. 13	....	....	....	....	....	1.565	....	....	....	...
2226	Praha	Feb. 13	....	....	....	....	....	....	....	....	.379[d]	...
2227	Hodkovičky	Feb. 13	.025	.013	.025	.018	.025	.038	.008	.008	.011[d]	...
2228	Vinohrady	Feb. 13	.960	.480	.960	.672	.958	1.469	.295	.295	.420[d]	...
2229	Podolí	Feb. 12	.025	.013	.025	.018	.025	.200	.040	.040	.044[d]	...
2230	Bohnice	Mar. 8	.035	.018	.035	.024	.035	.190	.038	.038	....	...
2231	Jinonice	Mar. 8	.070	.035	.070	.050	.070	....	....	....	....	...
2232	Střešovice	Mar. 9	.056	.028	.056	.039	.056	.152	.030	.030	....	...
2233	Praha VII	Mar. 9	....	....	....	....	....	1.068	.212	.212	....	...
2234	Keje	Mar. 10	.036	.018	.036	.026	.036	.077	.015	.015	....	...
2235	Hodkovičky	Mar. 12	.025	.013	.025	.018	.025	.039	.007	.007	....	...
2236	Vinohrady	Mar. 13	.480	.240	.480	.334	.478	.744	.148	.148	.800[b]	32,
2237	Podolí	Mar. 11	.075	.038	.075	.055	.075	.200	.040	.040	....	...
2238	Kobylisy	Mar. 11	.100	.050	.100	.072	.100	.262	.052	.052	.300[b]	12,
2239	Chuchle	Mar. 12	.035	.018	.035	.024	.035	.060	.012	.012	....	...
2240	Záběhlice	Mar. 12	.102	.056	.102	.072	.102	.115	.023	.023	....	...
2241	Dejvice	Mar. 13	.146	.073	.046	.104	.146	.210	.041	.041	.300[b]	12,
2242	Hloubětín	Mar. 18	.120	.060	.120	.085	.120	.153	.029	.029	.250[b]	10,
2243	Selce	Mar. 23	.025	.013	.025	.018	.025	.058	.011	.011	....	...
2244	Košíře	Mar. 26	....	....	....	....	....	....	....	....	1.033[bd]	32,
2430	Gablonz	May 20	....	....	....	....	....	....	....	....	.060[c]	..
2432	Gablonz	May 12	....	....	....	....	....	....	....	....	.060[c]	..
2433	Karlín	May 6	....	....	....	....	....	....	....	....	.092[c]	..
2434	Děčín	May 25	....	....	....	....	....	....	....	....	.092[c]	..
2437	Vys. Mýto	May 25	....	....	....	....	....	....	....	....	.062[c]	..
2438	Bubeneč	June 4	....	....	....	....	....	....	....	....	.032[c]	..
2439	Eger	May 29	....	....	....	....	....	....	....	....	.096[c]	..
2445	Trutnov	May 30	....	....	....	....	....	....	....	....	.030[c]	..
2446	Kutná Hora	June 22	....	....	....	....	....	....	....	....	.111[c]	..
2509	Praha	Sept. 2	....	....	....	....	....	.591	.108	.090	....	..
2510	Praha	Sept. 2	.022	.028	.028	.022	.028	.382	.069	.058	.150[b]	6,
2511	Praha	Aug. 31	.010	.012	.012	.011	.168	....	.029	.024	.050[b]	2,
2512	Praha	Aug. 21	.012	.015	.015	.011	.015	....	....	....	....	..
2513	Praha VII	Aug. 26	....	....	....	....	....	.078	.014	.012	.050[b]	2,
2514	Praha	Aug. 18	.027	.034	.034	.022	.034	.016	.003	.002	.050[b]	2,
2515	Praha	Aug. 23	.033	.039	.039	.022	.044	.077	.015	.012	.050[b]	2,
2516	Praha	Aug. 23	.018	.023	.023	.017	.023	.039	.007	.006	.050[b]	2,
2517	Praha	Aug. 18	.018	.022	.022	.017	.022	.038	.007	.006	.050[b]	2,
2518	Praha	Aug. 18	.018	.023	.023	.017	.022	.038	.007	.006	.050[b]	2,
2519	Chvaly	Aug. 20	.024	.030	.030	.022	.030	.024	.004	.003	.050[b]	2,
2520	na Kopě	Aug. 17	.005	.006	.006	.006	.006	.019	.004	.003	.050[b]	2,
2521	Praha	Aug. 17	.017	.021	.021	.017	.022	....	....	....	.050[b]	2,

CZECHO-SLOVAKIA

Table 260—*Continued*

Internal Deliveries, DEJVICE Warehouse

ceipt No.	Local Committee (Mistni Komitét)	Date	Commodities in Net Metric Tons of 1,000 Kilograms or 2,204.6 Pounds				Milk					
			Flour	Rice	Beans, Peas	Pork Products	Evap.	Cond.	Cocoa	Sugar	Misc.	No. of Biscuits
ries 1		1920										
522	Praha IV	Aug. 21	.014	.018	.018	.011	.018	....	....	....	.050[b]	2,000
523	Praha II	Aug. 27	.012	.015	.015	.009	.015	....	....	....	.050[b]	2,000
524	Hor. Krňsko	Aug. 17	.024	.030	.030	.022	.030	....	....	....	.050[b]	2,000
525	Břevnov	Aug. 27	.013	.017	.017	.011	.017	.050	.009	.010	.050[b]	2,000
526	Karlín	Aug. 15	.052	.066	.066	.050	.066	.095	.017	.014	.100[b]	4,000
527	Praha IV	Aug. 17	.030	.038	.038	.028	.069	....	.006	.007	.050[b]	2,000
528	Praha	Aug. 20	.007	.013	.013	.011	.013	.038	.006	.005	.050[b]	2,000
529	Kobylisy	Sept. 2	.080	.100	.100	.061	.100	.229	.042	.034	.200[b]	8,000
530	Bubeneč	Aug. 9	.204	.255	.255	.154	.261	.391	.072	.060	.400[b]	16,000
531	Bráník	Aug. 12	.070	.087	.087	.055	.087	.153	.027	.023	.150[b]	6,000
532	Strášnice	Aug. 24	.080	.100	.100	.061	.100	.210	.039	.032	.150[b]	6,000
533	Bohnice	Aug. 11	.019	.024	.024	.017	.024	.159	.029	.024	.100[b]	4,000
534	Břevnov	Aug. 12	.084	.105	.105	.066	.109	.610	.110	.092	.350[b]	14,000
535	Dobroviz	Aug. 9	.020	.026	.026	.017	.026	.047	.008	.007	.050[b]	2,000
536	Hloubětín	Aug. 1	.064	.081	.081	.050	.081	.125	.023	.019	.150[b]	6,000
537	Hlubočepy	Aug. 19	.052	.066	.066	.044	.066	.114	.020	.017	.100[b]	4,000
538	Jinonice	Aug. 9	.043	.054	.054	.033	.054	.057	.010	.008	.100[b]	4,000
539	Karlín	Aug. 10	.320	.400	.408	.242	.401	.687	.126	.105	.700[b]	28,000
540	Košíře	Aug. 9	.348	.435	.435	.215	.435	.839	.152	.127	.750[b]	30,000
541	Krč	Aug. 9	.027	.033	.033	.022	.033	.131	.024	.020	.200[b]	8,000
542	Malešice	Aug. 27	.014	.018	.018	.011	.018	.093	.017	.014	.050[b]	2,000
543	Michle	Aug. 11	.076	.096	.096	.061	.096	.190	.034	.028	.200[b]	8,000
544	Nusle	Aug. 17	.285	.357	.363	.215	.357	1.412	.260	.216	.900[b]	36,000
545	Podolí	Aug. 11	.056	.071	.071	.044	.071	.171	.032	.026	.150[b]	6,000
546	Praha II	Sept. 1	.472	.590	.590	.363	.588	.878	.161	.134	.900[b]	36,000
547	Praha IV	Aug. 9	....	....	....	....	....	.327	.060	.051	.150[b]	6,000
548	Praha VII	Aug. 20	.384	.470	.470	.297	.479	.782	.144	.120	.800[b]	32,000
549	Prosch	Aug. 18	.033	.042	.042	.028	.044	.157	.029	.024	.100[b]	4,000
550	Ruzyň	Aug. 9	.012	.015	.015	.011	.015	.043	.008	.006	.050[b]	2,000
551	Radotín	Aug. 9	.036	.045	.045	.028	.044	.133	.023	.019	.100[b]	4,000
552	Smíchov	Aug. 11	.161	.200	.201	.121	.201	1.317	.245	.202	.700[b]	28,000
553	Střešovice	Aug. 9	.028	.036	.036	.022	.036	.134	.024	.020	.100[b]	4,000
554	Troj Podhoř	Aug. 14	.033	.042	.042	.028	.044	.121	.022	.018	.100[b]	4,000
555	Vršovice	Aug. 24	.419	.524	.524	.314	.523	1.092	.204	.168	.900[b]	36,000
556	Vinohrady	Aug. 27	.512	.648	.648	.396	.653	1.045	.191	.159	1.050[b]	42,000
557	Zlíchov	Aug. 11	.036	.045	.045	.028	.044	.134	.025	.021	.100[b]	4,000
558	na Kopě	July 1	.005	.006	.006	.066	.006	.016	.004	.003	.050[b]	2,000
559	Praha	July 12	.013	.007	.013	.011	.013	.031	.006	.005	.050[b]	2,000
560	Praha	July 14	.018	.023	.023	.017	.022	.038	.007	.006	.050[b]	2,000
561	Dianaberk	July 15	.013	.017	.017	.011	.022	....	....	....	....	.....
562	Břevnov	July 5	.014	.018	.018	.011	.018	....	....	....	....	.....
563	Praha IV	July 2	.030	.038	.038	.033	.038	.031	.006	.006	.050[b]	2,000
564	Karlín	July 10	.052	.066	.066	.050	.065	.095	.017	.014	.100[b]	4,000
565	Praha	July 15	.018	.023	.023	.017	.023	.039	.006	.007	.050[b]	2,000
566	Praha IV	July 15	.014	.018	.018	.011	.018	....	....	....	.050[b]	2,000
567	Praha	July 13	.019	.024	.024	.022	.024	.062	.012	.010	.050[b]	2,000
568	Praha IV	July 26	.033	.039	.039	.022	.120	....	.015	.012	.100[b]	4,000
569	Praha II	July 21	.027	.034	.034	.022	.034	.016	.003	.002	.050[b]	2,000
570	Břevnov	July 15	.013	.017	.017	.011	.017	.050	.009	.008	.050[b]	2,000
571	Bělá-Techemek-Lavan	July 20	.010	.012	.012	.005	.012	....	....	....	.050[b]	2,000
572	Praha	July 14	.018	.022	.022	.017	.022	.038	.067	.006	.050[b]	2,000
574	Praha	July 20	.017	.021	.021	.017	.022	.019	.003	.002	.050[b]	2,000
575	Rožmitál	July 13	.014	.018	.018	.011	.018	.047	.009	.007	.050[b]	2,000
576	A.R.C.-Prague	July 5	.019	.024	.024	.011	.024	.030	.006	.005	.059[bd]	2,000
578	Praha	July 24	....	....	....	....	....	.591	.108	.090	....	.....
579	Praha	July 21	.012	.015	.015	.011	.015	....	....	....	.050[b]	2,000
580	Roztoky	July 31	.028	.036	.036	.022	.036	....	....	....	.050[b]	2,000
581	Praha	July 27	.010	.012	.012	.011	.168	....	.029	.024	.050[b]	2,000

[*Continued on next page*]

CZECHO-SLOVAKIA

Table 260—*Continued* Internal Deliveries, DEJVICE Warehouse

Receipt No.	Local Committee (Mistni Komitét)	Date	Flour	Rice	Beans, Peas	Pork Products	Milk Evap.	Milk Cond.	Cocoa	Sugar	Misc.	No. of Biscui[ts]
			Commodities in Net Metric Tons of 1,000 Kilograms or 2,204.6 Pounds									
Series 1		1920										
2582	Chvaly	July 26	.024	.030	.030	.022	.054	....	.004	.004	.050[b]	2,[illegible]
2583	Říčany	July 29	.029	.036	.036	.022	.098	....	.012	.011	.050[b]	2,[illegible]
2584	Praha VII	July 28	....	....	....	....	.078	....	.014	.012	.050[b]	2,[illegible]
2586	Praha II	July 5	.012	.015	.015	.009	.015	....	....	....	....	..
2587	Praha	Aug. 17	.022	.028	.028	.017	.028	.374	.069	.058	.150[b]	6,[illegible]
2588	Praha	Aug. 17	.072	.090	.090	.054	.179	....	.018	.014	.150[b]	6,[illegible]
2589	Praha	July 28	.024	.030	.030	.022	.030	....	....	....	.028[d]	..
2592	Praha	Oct. 30	....	....	....	....	....	....	....	....	.022[d]	..
2593	Praha II	Oct. 30	....	....	....	....	....	....	....	....	.009[d]	..
2595	Praha IV	May 3	....	....	....	....	....	....	....	....	.028[d]	..
2596	Praha	Apr. 13	....	....	....	....	....	....	....	....	.200[d]	..
2597	Praha	May 28	....	....	....	....	....	....	....	....	.004[d]	..
2598	Bubeneč	May 6	....	....	....	....	....	....	....	....	.014[d]	..
2599	Brünn	May 25	....	....	....	....	....	....	....	....	.170[d]	..
2600	Brüx	May 25	....	....	....	....	....	....	....	....	.017[d]	..
2601	Prague	May 14	....	....	....	....	....	....	....	....	.170[d]	..
2602	Brno	June 12	....	....	....	....	....	....	....	....	.009[d]	..
2629	Praha	July 14	....	....	....	....	....	....	....	....	.154[d]	..
2630	Praha	July 14	....	....	....	....	....	....	....	....	.154[d]	..
2637	Brod	July 8	....	....	....	....	....	....	....	....	.032[d]	..
2649	Něm. Brod	Aug. 10	....	....	....	....	....	....	....	....	.563[bd]	20,[illegible]
Series 2		1921										
49	Vinohrady Praha	Mar. 31	.056	.080	.100	.022	.153	....	.020	.072	....	..
50	Strášnice	Mar. 31	.014	.020	.025	.006	.044	....	.005	.018	....	..
51	Vršovice	Mar. 26	.105	.150	.188	.044	.300	....	.038	.135	....	..
52	Prague VIII	Mar. 26	.098	.150	.175	.044	.280	....	.035	.126	....	..
53	Žižkov	Mar. 26	.112	.160	.200	.050	.320	....	.040	.144	....	..
54	Nusle	Mar. 26	.056	.080	.100	.022	.160	....	.020	.072	....	..
55	Prague VII	Mar. 26	.084	.120	.150	.039	.240	....	.030	.108	....	..
56	Klecany	Mar. 22	.011	.015	.019	.006	.030	....	.004	.014	....	..
57	Prague II	Mar. 22	.105	.150	.188	.044	.305	....	.038	.135	....	..
58	Radlice	Mar. 22	.021	.030	.038	.011	.065	....	.008	.027	....	..
59	Prague IV	Apr. 5	.014	.020	.025	.006	.044	....	.005	.018	....	..
60	Prague III	Mar. 19	.028	.040	.050	.011	.080	....	.010	.036	....	..
61	Košiře	Mar. 22	.098	.150	.175	.044	.283	....	.035	.126	....	..
62	Michle	Apr. 2	.028	.040	.050	.011	.087	....	.010	.036	....	..
63	Břevnov	Mar. 31	.028	.040	.050	.011	.087	....	.010	.036	....	..
64	Hlubočepy	Mar. 26	.014	.020	.025	.006	.040	....	.005	.018	....	..
65	Bubeneč	Apr. 9	.028	.040	.050	.011	.087	....	.010	.036	....	..
66	Bohnice	Apr. 5	.007	.010	.013	.005	.022	....	.003	.010	....	..
67	Michle	Apr. 2	.140	.200	.252	.061	.392	....	.052	.180	....	..
68	Klecany	Apr. 5	.053	.075	.091	.022	.152	....	.019	.068	....	..
69	Bohnice	Apr. 5	.035	.050	.063	.017	.108	....	.013	.045	....	.
70	Vinohrady	Apr. 3	.140	.200	.252	.061	.392	....	.052	.180	....	.
71	Nusle	Apr. 7	.280	.400	.500	.121	.805	....	.102	.360	....	.
72	Košiře	Apr. 7	.490	.700	.875	.203	1.393	....	.175	.630	....	.
73	Bubeneč	Apr. 9	.140	.200	.252	.061	.392	....	.052	.180	....	.
74	Hlubočepy	Apr. 9	.070	.100	.126	.033	.196	....	.026	.090	....	.
75	Vysočany	Apr. 9	.106	.150	.182	.044	.305	....	.038	.160	....	.
76	Strášnice	Apr. 9	.070	.100	.126	.033	.196	....	.026	.090	....	.
77	Vršovice	Apr. 9	.525	.750	.938	.220	1.502	....	.188	.675	....	.
78	Radlice	Apr. 9	.106	.150	.182	.044	.305	....	.038	.136	....	.
79	Prague VIII	Apr. 13	.490	.700	.875	.204	1.393	....	.175	.630	....	.
80	Prague VII	Apr. 7	.420	.600	.750	.176	1.197	....	.150	.540	....	.
81	Prague I and V	Apr. 13	.280	.400	.500	.121	.805	....	.102	.360	....	.
82	Prague IV	Apr. 5	.070	.100	.126	.033	.196	....	.026	.090	....	.
83	Prague III	Apr. 7	.140	.200	.252	.060	.392	....	.052	.180	....	.
84	Prague II	Apr. 2	.525	.750	.938	.220	1.502	....	.188	.675	....	.
85	Karlín	Apr. 30	.147	.210	.263	.058	.420	....	.053	.189	....	.

CZECHO-SLOVAKIA

Table 260—*Continued*

Internal Deliveries, DEJVICE Warehouse

ceipt No.	Local Committee (Mistni Komitét)	Date	Commodities in Net Metric Tons of 1,000 Kilograms or 2,204.6 Pounds									
			Flour	Rice	Beans, Peas	Pork Products	Milk		Cocoa	Sugar	Misc.	No. of Biscuits
							Evap.	Cond.				
ies 2		1921										
86	Prague	Apr. 7	10.112	....	....	1.200	....	....	....	1.000	....	....
87	Prague	Apr. 30	10.048	....	....	1.200	....	....	....	1.000	....	....
88	Prague	May 28	9.984	....	....	1.200	....	....	....	1.000	....	....
89	Žižkov	Apr. 27	.576	1.808	....	.240	1.610	....	.208	.720	....	....
90	Břevnov	Apr. 27	.140	.455	....	.058	.400	....	.052	.180	....	....
91	Smíchov	Mar. 15	.504	.840	1.050	.236	1.676	....	.210	.756	....	....
55	Hořovice	Apr. 20	.444	.273	....	.080	.240	....	.032	.138	....	....
56	Příbram	Apr. 23	1.776	.480	.600	.315	.958	....	.128	.550	....	....
57	Nová Paka	Apr. 23	.888	.546	....	.157	.479	....	.064	.276	....	....
58	Stará Paka	Apr. 23	.444	.120	.150	.083	.240	....	.032	.138	....	....
59	Ml. Boleslav	Apr. 23	.888	.546	....	.157	.479	....	.064	.276	....	....
60	Kladno	Apr. 20	3.996	1.080	1.350	.702	2.155	....	.270	1.242	....	....
61	Louny	Apr. 23	.666	.409	....	.116	.370	....	.045	.207	....	....
62	Rakovník	Apr. 20	.666	.182	.228	.116	.370	....	.045	.207	....	....
63	Beroun Podčaply	Apr. 23	.888	.546	....	.158	.479	....	.064	.276	....	....
64	Slaný	Apr. 23	.888	.546	....	.157	.479	....	.064	.276	....	....
65	Hořice Miletín	Apr. 23	1.110	.300	.375	.199	.609	....	.075	.350	....	....
66	Kutná Hora	Apr. 20	.888	.240	.300	.157	.479	....	.064	.276	....	....
67	Benešov	Apr. 20	.444	.120	.150	.078	.240	....	.032	.138	....	....
81	Ml. Boleslav	May 11	.185	.050	.063	.033	.108	....	.013	.058	....	....
82	Krabčice	May 11	.111	.030	.038	.022	.065	....	.008	.035	....	....
83	Lobeč	May 11	.111	.030	.038	.022	.065	....	.008	.035	....	....
84	Ml. Boleslav	May 4	.111	.030	.038	.025	.065	....	.008	.035	....	....
85	Toušeň	Apr. 30	.148	.046	.046	.025	.087	....	.010	.050	....	....
86	Roudnice	Apr. 30	.148	.046	.046	.025	.087	....	.010	.050	....	....
87	Krňsko	Apr. 30	.148	.046	.046	.025	.087	....	.010	.050	....	....
88	Příbram	Apr. 30	.148	.046	.046	.025	.087	....	.010	.050	....	....
89	Kralupy	Apr. 27	.111	.030	.038	.022	.065	....	.008	.035	....	....
90	Benešov	May 4	.111	.030	.038	.025	.065	....	.008	.035	....	....
91	Jičín	May 4	.222	.060	.075	.042	.130	....	.015	.069	....	....
92	Hořovice	May 4	.259	.070	.091	.047	.152	....	.018	.081	....	....
93	Slaný	May 4	.222	.060	.075	.042	.130	....	.015	.069	....	....
94	Rozdělov	May 11	.111	.030	.038	.022	.065	....	.008	.035	....	....
95	Buštěhrad	May 11	.185	.050	.063	.033	.108	....	.013	.058	....	....
96	Nový Bydžov	Apr. 30	.148	.046	.046	.025	.087	....	.010	.050	....	....
97	Kolín	Apr. 30	.148	.046	.046	.025	.087	....	.010	.050	....	....
98	Nymburk	Apr. 30	.148	.046	.046	.025	.087	....	.010	.050	....	....
99	Březové Hory	Apr. 23	.074	.045	....	.017	.044	....	.005	.024	....	....
00	Lubno u Rakovníka	May 7	.111	.030	.038	.022	.065	....	.008	.035	....	....
01	na Kopě	Apr. 23	.074	.045	....	.011	.044	....	.005	.023	....	....
02	Sternberk	May 4	.185	.050	.063	.036	.108	....	.013	.058	....	....
03	Lovčen	May 11	.074	.020	.025	.016	.044	....	.005	.023	....	....
04	Dubé u Kladna	May 11	.111	.030	.038	.022	.065	....	.008	.035	....	....
05	Pecka	Apr. 30	.148	.045	.045	.025	.087	....	.010	.050	....	....
06	Kročehlavy	Apr. 30	.148	.045	.045	.025	.087	....	.010	.050	....	....
07	Vraně n/Vlt.	May 7	.216	.058	.073	.038	.130	....	.015	.067	....	....
66	Prague VII	June 25	.074	.020	.025	.017	.044	....	.005	.023	....	....
67	Vysočany	May 31	.056	.080	.100	.025	.122	.038	.020	.070	....	....
68	Prague VII	May 7	.035	.050	.063	.016	.108	....	.013	.050	....	....
69	Říčany	May 4	.021	.030	.038	.011	.065	....	.008	.027	....	....
70	Prague I	Apr. 30	.042	.060	.075	.025	.130	....	.015	.050	....	....
71	Prague III	Apr. 27	.021	.068	....	.011	.065	....	.008	.027	....	....
72	Vinohrady	Apr. 23	.028	.040	.043	.011	.087	....	.010	.036	....	....
73	Prague II	Apr. 23	.018	.025	.031	.006	.050	....	.006	.023	....	....
74	Žižkov	Apr. 23	.053	.075	.082	.022	.152	....	.019	.068	....	....
75	Vinohrady	Apr. 23	.018	.025	.031	.007	.050	....	.006	.023	....	....
76	Karlín	Apr. 16	.035	.050	.063	.015	.108	....	.013	.050	....	....
77	Prague II	Apr. 16	.018	.025	.031	.007	.050	....	.006	.023	....	....

[*Continued on next page*]

CZECHO-SLOVAKIA

Table 260—*Continued* Internal Deliveries, DEJVICE Warehouse

Receipt No.	Local Committee (Mistni Komitét)	Date	Commodities in Net Metric Tons of 1,000 Kilograms or 2,204.6 Pounds									
			Flour	Rice	Beans, Peas	Pork Products	Milk Evap.	Milk Cond.	Cocoa	Sugar	Misc.	No. of Biscuit
Series 2		1921										
278	Prague III	Apr. 16	.028	.040	.050	.011	.087	....	.010	.036	....	...
279	Prague III	Apr. 16	.021	.030	.038	.009	.065	....	.008	.027	....	...
280	Prague IV	Apr. 16	.063	.090	.113	.025	.174	....	.023	.081	....	...
281	Vinohrady	Apr. 20	.018	.025	.031	.007	.050	....	.006	.023	....	...
282	Prague II	Apr. 20	.018	.025	.031	.007	.050	....	.006	.023	....	...
283	Prague	Apr. 20	.025	.035	.044	.010	.070	....	.019	.032	....	...
284	Chvaly u Počernic	Apr. 20	.014	.020	.025	.006	.044	....	.005	.018	....	...
285	Prague VI	Apr. 20	.027	.038	.048	.011	.076	....	.010	.034	....	...
286	Prague IV	Apr. 20	.028	.040	.050	.011	.087	....	.010	.036	....	...
287	Prague III	Apr. 20	.021	.030	.038	.011	.065	....	.008	.027	....	...
288	Břevnov	Apr. 20	.021	.030	.038	.011	.065	....	.008	.027	....	...
391	Prague II	July 23	3.552	1.183	.965	.627	1.002	.916	.240	.800	....	...
392	Dianaberg	July 9	.370	.228	....	.066	.196	....	.025	.115	....	...
393	Karlín	July 27	.266	.162	....	.047	.152	....	.018	.083	....	...
394	Krušovice	June 28	.133	.081	....	.022	.072	....	.009	.041	....	...
395	Prague II	July 13	.888	.546	....	.150	....	.477	.064	.200	....	...
396	Košíře	July 5	.592	.364	....	.100	.327	....	.040	.184	.063[d]	...
397	Zbraslavice	July 5	.089	.054	....	.017	.048	....	.006	.028	....	...
398	Mor. Třebová	July 5	2.960	1.800	....	.520	1.611	....	.204	.920	....	...
399	Beroun	July 5	.355	.216	....	.062	.196	....	.024	.110	....	...
400	Prague II	June 28	.178	.108	....	.033	.096	....	.012	.055	....	...
401	Prague III	June 28	.102	.062	....	.022	.055	....	.007	.032	....	...
402	Žižkov	July 2	.592	.364	....	.105	.327	....	.040	.184	....	...
403	Nusle	July 2	.414	.252	....	.078	.258	....	.032	.129	....	...
404	Kladno	July 9	.296	.182	....	.050	.152	....	.020	.100	....	...
405	Choceň	June 2	1.110	.300	.375	.200	.600	....	.075	.350	....	...
406	Vlašim	June 25	.148	.091	....	.028	.087	....	.010	.050	....	...
407	Prague	June 22	3.712	2.275	....	.680	2.003	....	.250	1.150	....	...
408	Prague	June 22	.592	.364	....	.105	.327	....	.040	.184	....	...
409	Prague VII	June 22	.207	.126	....	.039	.109	....	.014	.064	....	...
410	Prague	June 18	.768	.455	....	.132	.414	....	.050	.230	....	...
411	Lubná u Rakov	July 30	.533	.324	....	.100	....	.286	.036	.111	....	...
412	Roudnice n/L.	July 9	.074	.046	....	.016	.044	....	.005	.023	....	...
502	Kutná Hora	June 11	.444	.273	....	.077	.240	....	.032	.138	....	...
503	Benešov	June 15	.222	.137	....	.039	.131	....	.015	.069	....	...
504	Nová Paka	June 11	.444	.273	....	.077	.240	....	.032	.138	....	...
505	Stará Paka	June 15	.222	.137	....	.038	.131	....	.015	.069	....	...
506	Louny	June 15	.333	.203	....	.061	.174	....	.023	.100	....	...
507	Rakovník	June 15	.333	.203	....	.060	.174	....	.023	.100	....	...
508	Hořice Miletín	June 15	.555	.338	....	.099	.305	....	.038	.173	....	...
509	Slaný	June 11	.444	.273	....	.077	.240	....	.032	.138	....	...
510	Příbram	June 15	.888	.546	....	.159	.479	....	.064	.276	....	...
511	Beroun Podčáply	June 11	.444	.273	....	.077	.240	....	.032	.138	....	...
512	Kladno	June 18	1.998	1.229	....	.363	1.089	....	.134	.621	....	...
513	Ml. Boleslav	June 11	.444	.273	....	.077	.240	....	.032	.138	....	...
514	Hořovice	June 15	.222	.060	.075	.039	.120	....	.015	.069	....	...
577	Prague II	June 25	.210	.300	.375	.088	.610	....	.075	.270	....	...
578	Prague VII	June 17	.168	.546	....	.072	.479	....	.064	.216	....	...
579	Prague VIII	June 2	.392	.560	.700	.166	.929	.191	.140	.500	....	...
580	Prague I and V	June 4	.224	.720	....	.094	....	.649	.080	.250	....	...
581	Prague III	May 31	.112	.160	.200	.050	.225	.095	.040	.150	....	...
582	Bubeneč	May 31	.140	.200	.252	.058	.400	....	.052	.180	....	...
583	Vysočany	May 31	.106	.150	.188	.047	.205	.095	.038	.130	....	...
584	Vinohrady	May 31	.280	.410	.328	.125	.800	....	.102	.360	....	...
585	Nusle	May 28	.224	.319	.400	.092	.632	....	.080	.288	....	...
586	Michle	May 25	.168	.546	....	.072	.479	....	.064	.216	....	...
587	Bohnice	May 21	.042	.060	.075	.017	.130	....	.015	.054	....	...
588	Strášnice	May 21	.084	.120	.150	.033	.240	....	.032	.108	....	...

CZECHO-SLOVAKIA

'able 260—*Concluded* Internal Deliveries, DEJVICE Warehouse

t	Local Committee (Mistni Komitét)	Date	Flour	Rice	Beans, Peas	Pork Products	Milk Evap.	Milk Cond.	Cocoa	Sugar	Misc.	No. of Biscuits
2		1921										
	Hlubočepy	May 21	.084	.120	.150	.033	.240	....	.032	.108	....	.....
	Klecany	May 21	.064	.091	.113	.025	.180	....	.023	.081	....	.....
	Radlice	May 21	.128	.182	.228	.050	.370	....	.045	.162	....	.....
	Prague IV	May 21	.084	.120	.150	.033	.240	....	.032	.108	....	.....
	Prague	May 28	.098	.140	.182	.042	.283	....	.035	.126	....	.....
	Prague	May 28	.024	.040	.050	.011	.087	....	.010	.034	....	.....
	Prague	May 28	.540	....	....	.069	....	....	....	.054	....	.....
	Total	....	**226.036**	**159.023**	**165.309**	**124.992**	**245.513**	**285.911**	**68.709**	**77.844**	**131.943***	**4,791,200**

Detail of miscellaneous commodity total: [b], weight of 4,791,200
ts, 119.780; [c], codliver oil, 2.305; [d], soap, 9.858.

CZECHO-SLOVAKIA

'able 261 Internal Deliveries from JABLONEC (Gablonz) Warehouse

t	Local Committee (Mistni Komitét)	Date	Flour	Rice	Beans, Peas	Pork Products	Milk Evap.	Milk Cond.	Cocoa	Sugar	Misc.*	No. of Biscuits
1		1919										
7	Jablonec	Sept. 28	1.840	.460	.460	1.840	1.840	3.657	.738	....	....	.....
8	Česká Lípa	Sept. 10	1.600	.400	.400	1.600	1.600	3.180	.642	....	....	.....
9	Jablonné	Sept. 10	1.360	.340	.340	1.360	1.360	2.702	.340	....	....	.....
0	Liberec	Sept. 10	2.160	.540	.540	2.160	2.160	4.292	.867	....	....	.....
1	Jilemnice	Sept. 12	1.600	.400	.400	1.600	1.600	3.180	.642	....	....	.....
2	Frýdland	Sept. 10	.800	.200	.200	.800	.800	1.590	.321	....	....	.....
3	Semily	Sept. 15	1.280	.320	.320	1.280	1.280	2.544	.514	....	....	.....
4	Turnov	Sept. 10	.560	.140	.140	.560	.560	1.112	.225	....	....	.....
9	Frýdland	Nov. 22	.800	.200	.200	.800	.800	1.590	.321	....	....	.....
0	Jablonné	Nov. 17	.891	.223	.223	.891	.891	2.330	.471	....	....	.....
1	Jilemnice	Nov. 14	1.600	.400	.400	1.600	1.600	3.180	.642	....	....	.....
2	Jablonec n/N.	Nov. 22	2.760	2.760	2.760	1.932	2.760	3.450	.690	.690	....	.....
3	Semily	Nov. 4	1.280	.320	.320	1.280	1.280	2.850	.575	....	....	.....
4	Jablonec	Nov. 4	1.840	.460	.460	1.840	1.840	3.657	.738	....	....	.....
5	Turnov	Nov. 3	.344	.086	.086	.344	.344	.796	.161	....	....	.....
1	Turnov	Dec. 5	.678	.678	.678	.475	.678	.900	.180	.180	....	.....
a	Semily	Dec. 6	1.920	1.920	1.920	1.344	1.920	2.689	.537	.537	....	.....
2	Jilemnice	Dec. 4	2.400	2.400	2.400	1.680	2.400	3.000	.600	.600	....	.....
3	Jablonec	Dec. 4	2.760	2.760	2.760	1.932	2.760	3.450	.690	.690	....	.....
5	Jablonec	Dec. 4	1.337	1.337	1.337	.936	1.337	2.197	.439	.439	....	.....
7	Friedland	Dec. 7	1.200	1.200	1.200	.840	1.200	1.500	1.500	.300	....	.....
		1920										
5	Gablonz	Feb. 22	1.104	.552	1.104	.810	1.104	1.380	.276	.276	....	.....
6	Friedland	Mar. 20	.800	.400	.800	.621	.800	.....	....	....	....	.....
7	Reichenberg	Mar. 22	1.296	.648	1.296	.886	1.296	1.620	.324	.324	....	.....
8	Jilemnice	Mar. 23	1.680	.840	1.680	1.220	1.680	2.100	.420	.420	....	.....
9	Dauba	Mar. 31	.145	.073	.145	.102	.145	.227	.045	.045	....	.....
0	Semily	Mar. 31	.768	.384	.768	.609	.768	1.076	.215	.215	....	.....
1	Deutsch Gabel	Mar. 29	.844	.422	.844	.615	.844	1.392	.278	.278	....	.....
2	Turnov	Mar. 31	.452	.226	.452	.310	.452	.600	.120	.091	....	.....
0	Böhm. Leipa	Mar. 9	.960	1.200	1.200	.777	1.200	1.560	.288	.240	1.800	72,000
1	Friedland	Mar. 12	1.344	1.680	1.680	.962	1.680	2.184	.408	.336	2.550	102,000
12	Gablonz	May 6,10	.552	2.760	2.760	1.702	6.348	....	.662	.552	4.400	156,000
13	Gablonz	Apr. 13	.960	1.200	1.200	.783	1.200	1.716	.317	.264	1.850	74,400
14	Semily	Apr. 13	1.200	1.500	1.500	.938	1.500	1.872	.346	.288	2.225	89,000
15	Turnov	Apr. 14	.480	.600	.600	.318	.600	.780	.144	.120	.900	36,000

* Biscuits.

[*Continued on next page*]

CZECHO-SLOVAKIA

Internal Deliveries, JABLONEC (Gablonz) Warehouse

Table 261—*Continued*

Receipt No.	Local Committee (Mistni Komitét)	Date	Commodities in Net Metric Tons of 1,000 Kilograms or 2,204.6 Pounds									
			Flour	Rice	Beans, Peas	Pork Products	Milk		Cocoa	Sugar	Misc.	No. Biscu
							Evap.	Cond.				
Series 1		1920										
926	Liberec	Apr. 12,15,23	2.736	3.420	3.420	2.137	4.774	3.795	.950	.792	5.400	216,
928	Jilemnice	Apr. 14, 17	1.824	2.280	2.280	1.373	2.280	2.964	.547	.456	.900	36,
929	Dauba	Apr. 14	.162	.203	.203	.141	.203	.368	.069	.057	.350	14,
1066	Semily	May 14, 25	1.200	1.500	1.500	.933	3.372	....	.346	.294	2.225	89,
1067	Gablonz	Apr. 14	3.864	2.240	2.760	1.655	2.760	3.588	.662	.562	4.150	166,
1068	Deutsch Gabel	May 14, 20	.960	1.200	1.200	.757	2.976	....	.317	.268	1.850	74,
1069	Friedland	May 19, 28	1.344	1.680	1.680	1.112	3.864	....	....	.335	2.550	102,
1070	Jilemnice	May 14, 18	1.824	2.280	2.280	1.407	5.244	....	.547	.456	3.425	137,
1071	Turnov	May 10	.480	.600	.600	.465	1.380	....	.144	.120	.900	36,
1072	Böhm. Leipa	May 14, 20	.546	.613	.640	.112	.....	....	.126	....	1.800	72,
1073	Liberec	May 11, 27	2.736	3.420	3.420	2.097	8.568	....	.950	.793	5.400	216,
1074	Dauba	May 19	.162	.203	.203	.122	.571	....	.069	.057	.350	14,
1326	Friedland	July 1	1.152	1.440	1.440	.927	1.440	2.028	....	.328	2.250	89,
1327	Jablonec	July 7	1.073	3.280	2.760	1.660	2.760	3.588	.662	.556	4.150	166,
1328	Č. Lípa	June 23	1.086	1.357	1.357	.920	.066	.312	.306	.181	2.000	80,
1329	Semily	June 24	.960	1.200	1.200	.767	1.200	1.560	.288	.250	1.800	72,
1330	Jablonné	June 23	.775	.941	1.015	.580	1.023	....	.148	.125	2.000	80,
1331	Jilemnice	June 24	1.824	2.280	2.280	1.368	2.280	2.964	.547	.456	3.450	136,
1332	Liberec	June 22	2.400	3.000	3.000	1.802	3.000	4.272	.778	.653	4.650	186,
1333	Turnov	June 28	.720	.900	.900	.540	.900	.780	.744	.125	1.200	48,
2456	Č. Lípa	Aug. 17	1.086	1.357	1.357	.814	1.357	1.277	.306	.255	2.100	84,
2457	Frýdland	Aug. 20	.984	1.277	1.230	.738	1.230	1.320	....	.278	1.900	76,
2458	Něm. Jablonné	Aug. 17	.960	1.200	1.200	.720	1.200	1.320	.317	.264	2.025	82,
2459	Jilemnice	Aug. 24	1.678	.....	2.097	1.258	.....	2.074	.510	.417	....	..
2460	Liberec	Aug. 29	2.376	2.970	2.970	1.781	2.970	3.204	.769	.630	4.650	185,
2461	Turnov	Aug. 18	.480	.600	.600	.360	.600	.600	.744	.125	.900	36,
2462	Semily	Aug. 20	.862	1.077	1.077	.646	1.077	1.068	.256	.214	1.625	64,
2463	Frýdland	Aug. 30	.....	.....	.....	....	.....	....	.317	....	....	..
2464	Jablonec	Sept. 23	3.677	2.352	2.352	1.477	2.352	2.376	.570	.487	3.550	142,
Series 2		1921										
40	Liberec	Apr. 30	9.502	2.595	3.244	1.687	5.190	....	.649	2.991	....	..
41	Jilemnice	Apr. 5	2.720	.735	.919	.482	1.470	....	.184	.845	....	..
42	Jablonné	Apr. 11	.093	.025	.032	.016	.050	....	.006	.029	....	..
43	Jablonné	Apr. 11	1.554	.420	.525	.276	.840	....	.105	.485	....	..
44	Frýdland	Apr. 22, 27	3.552	.960	1.200	.625	1.920	....	.240	1.170	....	..
45	Jablonec	Apr. 5, 28	8.880	2.400	3.000	1.575	4.800	....	.612	2.767	....	..
46	Č. Lípa	Apr. 20, 27	2.775	.750	.938	.500	1.500	....	.188	.863	....	..
47	Turnov	Apr. 13, 27	1.776	.480	.600	.312	.960	....	.120	.552	....	..
48	Semily	Apr. 16	.555	.150	.....	....	.300	....	.038	.173	....	..
262	Jilemnice	Apr. 24	.185	.050	.063	.033	.100	....	.013	.058	....	..
263	Mimoň u Č. Lípy	May 20	1.110	.300	.375	.195	.600	....	.075	.345	....	..
264	Liberec	Apr. 29	.185	.050	.063	.033	.100	....	.013	.058	....	..
265	Jablonné	Apr. 20	.185	.050	.063	.033	.100	....	.013	.058	....	..
459	Liberec	July 6, 11	15.066	4.072	5.090	2.662	8.144	....	1.020	4.992	....	..
460	Liberec	July 8	3.271	.884	1.105	.575	1.768	....	.227	1.017	....	..
461	Jablonec n/N.	July 19	7.122	3.538	.....	1.250	3.850	....	.481	2.208	....	..
462	Něm. Jablonné	June 28	.140	.038	.047	.025	.076	....	.009	.043	....	..
463	Česka Lípa	July 11	3.410	.922	1.152	.600	1.843	....	.230	1.065	....	..
464	Něm. Jablonné	July 7	1.480	.400	.500	.125	.800	....	.102	.460	....	..
465	Jilemnice	June 28	1.844	.499	.623	.325	.997	....	.125	.573	....	..
466	Frýdland	June 28	.089	.024	.030	.025	.048	....	.006	.028	....	..
467	Něm. Jablonné	July 7	.....	.....	.....	.125	.....	....	....	....	....	..
569	Něm. Jablonné	June 10	1.036	.280	.350	.200	.560	....	.070	.322	....	..
570	Turnov	June 7	.888	.240	.300	.156	.480	....	.060	.276	....	..
571	Č. Lípa	June 10	.463	.125	.156	.100	.250	....	.031	.148	....	..
572	Jablonec	June 8	2.960	.800	1.000	.525	1.600	....	.204	.920	....	..
573	Semily	June 7	.185	.050	.063	.050	.100	....	.013	.058	....	..
574	Liberec	June 6	3.167	.865	1.081	.575	1.730	....	.216	1.000	....	..
575	Jilemnice	June 7	2.266	.613	.766	.400	1.225	....	.153	.704	....	..
576	Frýdland	June 9	1.184	.320	.400	.200	.640	....	.080	.368	....	..
	Total		**161.169**	**97.534**	**101.309**	**80.101**	**152.115**	**109.811**	**32.948**	**40.995**	**81.275***	**3,227,**

* Weight of 3,227,800 biscuits.

CZECHO-SLOVAKIA

Internal Deliveries from KARLSBAD (Karlovy Vary) Warehouse

Table 262

ceipt No.	Local Committee (Mistni Komitét)	Date	Flour	Rice	Beans, Peas	Pork Products	Milk Evap.	Milk Cond.	Cocoa	Sugar	Misc.*	No. of Biscuits
			Commodities in Net Metric Tons of 1,000 Kilograms or 2,204.6 Pounds									
ries 1		1919										
1	Kraslice	Sept. 5	1.200	.300	.300	1.200	1.200	3.498	.706	....	....	.....
22	Jáchymov	Sept. 18	.720	.180	.180	.720	.720	1.431	.289	....	....	.....
23	Falknov	Sept. 17	1.600	.400	.400	1.600	1.600	4.134	.835	....	....	.....
24	Aš	Sept. 6	2.240	.510	.510	2.240	2.240	3.498	.706	....	....	.....
25	Cheb	Sept. 22	1.040	.260	.260	1.040	1.040	2.146	.433	....	....	.....
26	Nýdek	Sept. 22	1.120	.280	.280	1.120	1.120	2.385	.481	....	....	.....
27	Vildstein	Sept. 9	.880	.220	.220	.880	.880	1.113	.225	....	....	.....
28	Loket	Sept. 6	1.480	.370	.370	1.480	1.480	3.339	.674	....	....	.....
29	Blatno	Sept. 5	.760	.190	.190	.760	.760	1.272	.257	....	....	.....
30	Bečov	Sept. 6	.160	.040	.040	.160	.160	.318	.064	....	....	.....
35	Karlovy Vary	Oct. 3	2.000	.400	.400	2.000	2.000	4.452	.899	....	....	.....
37	Výprty	Oct. 2	.760	.190	.190	.760	.760	1.113	.225	....	....	.....
46	Přísečnice	Oct. 12	.680	.170	.170	.680	.680	1.113	.225	....	....	.....
201	Wildstein	Oct. 25	.864	.220	.214	.880	.880	1.105	.225	....	....	.....
202	Karlovy Vary	Oct. 17	2.000	.500	.500	2.000	2.000	4.452	.899	....	....	.....
281	Bečov	Nov. 19	.160	.040	.035	.157	.146	.318	.055	....	....	.....
282	Marienbad	Nov. 19	.611	.132	.132	.597	.382	1.008	.194	....	....	.....
283	Nýdek	Nov. 19	1.120	.280	.280	1.120	1.120	2.385	.482	....	....	.....
284	Blatno	Nov. 18	.752	.153	.190	.724	.757	1.272	.208	....	....	.....
285	Přísečnice	Nov. 20	.680	.170	.170	.680	.680	1.113	.225	....	....	.....
286	Kadaň	Nov. 17	.176	.044	.044	.176	.176	.333	.090	....	....	.....
287	Jáchymov	Dec. 20	.145	.108	.108	.145	.145	.839	.109			
288	Cheb	Nov. 20	1.040	.260	.260	1.040	1.040	2.147	.433	....	....	.....
402	Graslitz	Dec. 14	1.800	1.800	1.800	1.260	1.800	3.300	.660	....	....	.....
403	Asch	Dec. 14	3.360	3.360	3.360	2.352	3.360	3.300	.660	.660	....	.....
404	Platten	Dec. 14	1.140	1.140	1.140	.798	1.140	1.200	.240	.660	....	.....
405	Wildstein	Dec. 14	1.320	1.320	1.320	.924	1.320	1.050	.210	.240	....	.....
84	Aš	Dec. 27	2.240	.594	.594	2.227	2.225	3.498	.698	.210	....	.....
86	Weipert	Nov. 17	1.140	2.280	....	.798	1.140	1.050	.210	.... .210	....	.....
96	Loket	Nov. 19	1.424	.370	.370	1.480	1.480	3.339	.634			
97	Kraslice	Nov. 30	1.184	.300	.300	1.200	1.180	3.498	.698	....	....	.....
08	Falkenau	Dec. 29	2.400	2.400	2.400	1.680	2.400	3.900	.780	....	....	.....
09	Karlsbad	Dec. 30	3.000	3.000	3.000	2.100	3.000	4.200	.840	.780	....	.....
10	Elbogen	Dec. 29	2.220	2.220	2.220	1.554	2.220	3.150	.630	.840	....	.....
		1920								.630		
18	Kaaden	Jan. 12	.282	.282	.282	.107	.282	.420	.084	.084	....	.....
19	Marianské Lázně	Jan. 5	....	....	....	.131	....	....	....	....	....	.....
20	Marienbad	Jan. 5	.988	.988	.988	.692	.988	.982	.196	.196	....	.....
21	Petschau	Jan. 12	.240	.240	.240	.168	.240	.300	.060	.060	....	.....
22	Pressnitz	Jan. 12	1.020	1.020	1.020	.714	1.020	1.050	.210	.210	....	.....
79	Neudek	Jan. 24	....	3.360	....	1.176	1.680	2 250	.450	.450	....	.....
78	Karlsbad	Apr. 10	1.018	.509	.998	.683	.981	1.417	.310	....	1.924	76,968
79	Kaaden	Apr. 7	.184	.103	.136	.164	.152	.171	.035	....	.277	11,100
80	Falkenau	Apr. 1	.968	.520	.952	.622	.959	1.558	.306	....	1.980	79,200
81	Asch	Apr. 7	1.352	.731	1.360	.964	1.351	1.330	.306	....	2.340	93,600
82	Platten	Mar. 22	.729	....	.453	.313	.458	.494	.103	.305	.810	32,400
83	Joachimsthal	Mar. 23	1.562	....	.318	.241	.327	.399	.103	.242	.585	23,400
84	Graslitz	Mar. 23	1.099	....	.726	.621	.719	1.330	.312	.426	....	.....
85	Elbogen	Mar. 24	.946	.510	.907	.605	.893	1.273	.312	.251	1.740	69,600
86	Marienbad	Mar. 27	.736	.316	.680	.479	.654	.665	.177	....	1.151	46,040
87	Neudek	Mar. 22	1.332	....	.862	.637	.850	1.121	.311	.608	1.612	64,500
88	Prissnitz	Mar. 25	.718	.409	.680	.479	.698	.703	.153	....	....	.....
89	Eger	Mar. 18	.884	.442	.884	.619	.884	1.147	.230	.230	1.679	67,150
90	Výprty	Mar. 25	....	....	....	....	....	.399	.102	....	.210	8,400
91	Wildstein	Mar. 30	.668	.310	.680	.469	.654	.532	.102	....	1.088	43,500
75	Asch	Apr. 8	2.475	3.153	3.130	1.884	3.117	3.117	.612	....	4.320	172,800
76	Platten	Apr. 24	.975	1.236	1.179	.759	1.199	1.242	.205	....	1.250	67,200
77	Falkenau	Apr. 13	1.404	1.768	1.814	1.087	1.809	2.812	.615	....	2.900	115,200
78	Eger	Apr. 7	.425	.523	.544	.313	.545	.627	.102	....	.800	31,300
79	St. Joachimsthal	Apr. 14	.558	.719	.725	.438	.719	.937	.205	....	1.200	43,200
80	Kaaden	Apr. 7	.193	.208	.227	.155	.239	.304	.067	....	.350	14,000

* Biscuits.

[*Continued on next page*]

CZECHO-SLOVAKIA

Internal Deliveries, KARLSBAD (Karlovy Vary) Warehouse

Table 262—*Continued*

Receipt No.	Local Committee (Mistni Komitét)	Date	Commodities in Net Metric Tons of 1,000 Kilograms or 2,204.6 Pounds									
			Flour	Rice	Beans, Peas	Pork Products	Milk		Cocoa	Sugar	Misc.	No. o[f] Biscu[its]
							Evap.	Cond.				
Series 1		1920										
881	Karlsbad	Apr. 10	1.692	2.133	2.177	1.362	2.158	2.812	.510	....	3.250	129,
882	Graslitz	Apr. 23,29	1.575	1.924	1.905	1.205	1.918	3.597	.615	....	....	..
883	Elbogen	Apr. 9,10	2.699	2.151	2.086	1.228	2.092	3.117	.612	....	3.300	132,
884	Marienbad	Apr. 13	.557	.709	.680	.491	.654	.937	.205	....	1.000	40,
885	Neudek	Apr. 28	1.203	1.485	1.496	.900	3.205	.323	.411	....	....	..
886	Pressnitz	Apr. 17	.750	.977	.952	.568	.959	.937	.205	....	1.350	52,
887	Weipert	Apr. 22	.900	1.110	1.089	.590	2.463	....	.205	....	1.550	62,
888	Wildstein	Apr. 8	.972	1.177	1.179	.783	1.200	1.330	.204	....	1.700	68,
1115	Loket	May 26	1.728	1.832	2.086	1.205	2.092	3.116	.620	.960	3.300	132,
1116	Kar. Vary	May 27	1.731	2.148	2.177	1.268	4.970	....	.517	.432	3.250	130,
1117	Asch	May 15, 21	2.496	3.174	3.129	1.867	6.234	....	.619	.485	4.350	173,
1118	Výprty	May 18	.900	1.123	1.088	.626	2.441	....	.207	.182	1.850	62,
1119	Přísečnice	May 19	.704	.872	.907	.602	1.874	....	.206	.144	1.300	52,
1120	Mar. Lázně	May 26	.448	....	.705	.445	.654	.931	.102	.144	1.050	42,
1121	Blatno	May 18	.962	1.228	1.179	.745	2.441	....	.205	.197	1.700	68,
1122	Falknov	May 15	1.379	1.842	1.814	1.101	4.599	....	.517	.438	2.900	116,
1123	Kadaň	May 18	.193	.209	.226	.151	.545	....	....	.038	.350	14,
1124	Kraslice	May 14,15	1.533	1.853	1.905	1.041	5.515	....	.621	1.000	6.600	264,
1125	Eger	May 12	.432	.540	.540	.324	.540	.624	.115	.096	.800	32,
1126	Jáchymov	May 20	....	.714	.720	.467	1.635	....	.104	....	....	..
1127	Wildstein	May 21	.960	1.176	1.200	.777	2.528	....	.205	.206	1.750	70,
1128	Nýdek	May 18	1.216	1.534	1.497	.934	3.510	....	.309	....	2.300	92,
1381	Karlovy Vary	July 1	1.580	1.947	1.931	1.154	1.918	2.660	.510	.411	2.950	118,
1382	Asch	July 14	2.496	3.127	3.155	1.849	3.117	3.116	.612	.480	4.350	174,
1383	Platten	June 30	.960	1.180	1.198	.719	1.199	1.254	.204	.195	1.700	68,
1384	Falkenau	June 17	1.337	1.652	1.663	1.066	1.656	2.660	.510	.415	2.700	108,
1385	Eger	June 17	.566	.708	.701	.441	.675	.760	.102	.118	1.000	40,
1386	Joachimsthal	June 21	.576	.708	.723	.477	.719	.931	.204	.157	1.100	44,
1387	Kaaden	June 30	.192	.236	.235	.163	.240	.304	.102	.058	.400	16,
1388	Kraslice	June 17	1.552	1.947	1.912	1.203	1.918	3.591	.714	.651	3.500	132,
1389	Loket	June 17	1.665	2.124	2.119	1.222	2.093	3.116	.612	.480	3.300	132,
1390	Mar. Lázně	June 30	.512	.649	.660	.441	.654	.931	.204	.147	1.050	42,
1391	Nýdek	June 18	1.205	1.475	1.506	.870	1.504	2.014	.408	.319	2.300	92,
1392	Výprty	June 19	.877	1.062	1.057	.589	1.090	1.178	.204	.188	1.550	62,
1393	Wildstein	June 24	.945	1.198	1.209	.780	1.199	1.330	.306	.207	1.750	70,
2488	Falkenau	Aug. 14	1.344	1.640	1.678	.816	1.679	2.052	.511	.414	2.700	108,
2489	Asch	Aug. 11	2.496	3.127	3.130	1.862	2.136	2.394	.612	.480	4.350	174,
2490	Blatno	Aug. 16	.960	1.200	1.225	.719	....	.969	.205	.192	1.700	68,
2491	Elbogen	Aug. 13	1.536	2.087	1.860	1.143	....	....	.512	.433	2.950	118,
2492	Karlsbad	Sept. 18	1.536	1.928	1.905	1.143	1.536	2.040	.511	.450	2.950	118,
2493	Eger	Aug. 10	.576	.649	.680	.392	.654	.589	.204	.126	1.000	40,
2494	Kaaden	Aug. 18	.192	.284	.227	.163	....	.247	.102	.053	.400	16,
2495	Kraslice	Aug. 12	1.536	1.947	1.905	1.143	....	2.242	.715	.552	3.300	132,
2496	Joachimsthal	Aug. 20	.512	.617	.635	.392	.654	.684	.205	.140	1.000	40,
2497	Marienbad	Aug. 18	.448	.544	.544	.327	....	.618	.204	.123	.850	34,
2498	Neudek	Aug. 14	1.216	1.536	1.497	.914	....	....	.409	.318	2.300	91,
2499	Weipert	Aug 18	.320	.363	.408	.229	....	.247	.102	.054	.550	22,
2500	Wildstein	Aug. 16	.960	1.234	1.225	.719	....	1.026	.306	.293	1.750	70,
2501	Elbogen	Aug. 31	....	....	....	....	1.875	2.166	....	....	....	..
2502	Asch	Sept. 7	....	....	....	....	.981	....	....	....	....	..
2503	Wildstein	Sept. 6	....	....	....	....	1.199	....	....	....	....	..
2504	Neudek	Sept. 1	....	....	....	....	1.504	1.577	....	....	....	..
2505	Platten	Sept. 1	....	....	....	....	1.199	....	....	....	....	..

CZECHO-SLOVAKIA

Internal Deliveries, KARLSBAD (Karlovy Vary) Warehouse

able 262—*Concluded*

Local Committee (Mistni Komitét)	Date	Flour	Rice	Beans, Peas	Pork Products	Milk Evap.	Milk Cond.	Cocoa	Sugar	Misc.	No. of Biscuits
		Commodities in Net Metric Tons of 1,000 Kilograms or 2,204.6 Pounds									
	1920										
Graslitz	Sept. 1	....	....	....	....	1.918	.513	....	....	....	.....
Kaaden	Sept. 13	....	....	....	....	.240	....	....	....	....	.....
Weipert	Sept. 15	....	....	....	....	.392	....	....	....	....	.....
	1921										
Karl. Vary	Apr. 26	4.032	1.092	1.365	.718	2.177	....	.309	1.242	....	.....
Výprty	Apr. 26	3.520	.955	1.228	.625	1.915	....	.234	1.100	....	.....
Kraslice	Apr. 2	5.112	1.365	1.729	.895	2.765	....	.339	1.587	....	.....
Nýdek	May 2	....	....	....	....	....	....	.117	....	....	.....
Jáchymov	Apr. 1	1.472	.409	.500	.261	.784	....	.103	.449	....	.....
Přísečnice	Apr. 2	4.672	1.274	1.592	.807	2.526	....	.309	1.444	....	.....
Mar. Lázně	Apr. 27	1.344	.364	.455	.250	.718	....	.103	.400	....	.....
Nýdek	Apr. 1	5.376	1.456	1.820	.947	2.895	....	.309	1.656	....	.....
Falknov	Apr. 1	1.536	.910	1.138	.588	1.807	....	.225	1.096	....	.....
Aš	Mar. 30	7.680	2.093	2.594	1.339	4.136	....	.515	2.377	....	.....
Wildstein	Mar. 30	1.984	.546	.683	.359	1.089	....	.135	.625	....	.....
Cheb	Apr. 23	4.032	1.092	1.365	.700	2.155	....	.306	1.242	....	.....
Pressnitz	May 2	....	....	....	....	....	....	.040	....	....	.....
Falknov	May 7	....	....	....	....	....	....	.045	....	....	.....
Blatno	Apr. 26	3.712	1.001	1.229	.650	1.981	....	.248	1.140	....	.....
Loket	Apr. 26	2.240	.637	.773	.400	1.200	....	.204	.700	....	.....
Schlackenwerth	May 1	.370	.100	.125	.065	.200	....	.025	.115	....	.....
Kadaň	May 2	.222	.060	.075	.039	.120	....	.015	.069	....	.....
Einsiedel	May 2	.092	.025	.031	.016	.050	....	.006	.029	....	.....
Karl. Vary	May 1	.092	.025	.031	.016	.050	....	.006	.029	....	.....
Falkenau	May 6	.092	.025	.031	.016	.050	....	.006	.029	....	.....
Karl. Vary	May 1	.148	.040	.050	.026	.080	....	.010	.046	....	.....
Rodisdorf	Apr. 26	.192	.050	.091	.033	.100	....	.013	.058	....	.....
Loket	Aug. 13	2.304	.635	.771	.408	.870	.358	.205	.699	....	.....
Nýdek	June 24	5.780	1.588	1.950	1.025	2.983	.134	.410	1.795	....	.....
Aš	July 11	.128	.045	.045	.024	.065	....	.008	.038	....	.....
Aš	July 23	2.304	.635	.771	.408	.196	1.050	.196	.708	....	.....
Wildstein	July 23	2.688	.725	.907	.480	....	1.470	.205	.837	....	.....
Blatno	July 11	4.013	1.088	1.361	.700	2.177	....	.307	1.243	....	.....
Cheb	July 16	.768	.226	.272	.150	....	.400	.102	.230	....	.....
Falknov	July 15	2.112	.590	.725	.384	....	1.126	.204	.644	....	.....
Přísečnice	July 15	3.904	1.043	1.315	.696	....	2.100	.306	1.206	....	.....
Mar. Lazně	July 16	1.344	.362	.453	.250	....	.706	.102	.405	....	.....
Kraslice	June 24	6.868	1.860	2.313	1.200	3.701	....	.510	2.126	....	.....
Karl. Vary	June 24	2.360	.680	.815	.425	1.284	....	.206	.739	....	.....
Kraslice	June 9	.888	.229	.318	.150	.478	....	.057	.264	....	.....
Aš	June 8	7.680	2.086	2.631	1.350	3.896	.228	.510	2.381	....	.....
Výprty	June 9	1.224	.318	.408	.225	.653	....	.080	.368	....	.....
Wildstein	June 8	2.040	.545	.680	.350	1.089	....	.135	.621	....	.....
Nýdek	June 9	2.416	4.488	1.244	1.542	.800	....	.306	1.380	....	.....
Loket	June 9	1.020	.272	.362	.175	.544	....	.068	.311	....	.....
Falknov	June 7	2.992	.816	1.043	.525	1.611	....	.204	.920	....	.....
Přísečnice	June 7	3.904	1.043	1.315	.700	2.111	....	.306	1.207	....	.....
Cheb	June 10	.680	.181	.227	.125	.370	....	.045	.207	....	.....
Jáchymov	June 8	1.224	.325	.408	.225	.653	....	.102	.373	....	.....
Mar. Lázně	June 10	.476	.136	.181	.075	.239	....	.030	.138	....	.....
Blatno	June 10	1.224	.362	.408	.225	.675	....	.102	.379	....	.....
Karlovy Vary	June 7	3.328	.907	1.134	.600	1.807	....	.204	1.035	....	.....
Total	....	**228.886**	**141.332**	**146.419**	**113.835**	**205.825**	**169.354**	**46.003**	**54.755**	**123.316***	**4,921,358**

* Weight of 4,921,358 biscuits.

CZECHO-SLOVAKIA

Internal Deliveries from (1) SMÍCHOV, (2) DEJVICE Warehouses

Table 263

Receipt No.	Local Committee (Mistní Komitét)	Date	Commodities in Net Metric Tons of 1,000 Kilograms or 2,204.6 Pounds						
			Flour	Rice	Beans, Peas	Pork Products	Milk		Cocoa
							Evap.	Cond.	
Series 1		1919							
538	Kladno	May 2	1.079	....	....	....	....	.740	..
539	Kladno	May 6	....	....	....	.754	....	....	..
540	Kladno	May 13	.889	....	.182	.754	....	....	..
541	Prague VIII	May 12	....	....	.136	....	....	....	..
542	Prague Libeň	May 8	.635	....	....	.442	....	.435	..
543	Prague-Košíře	May 15	.825	....	.273	.910	....	.781	..
544	Prague	May 15	1.270	....	.273	.952	....	.833	..
545	Asch	May 28	2.349	....	.500	1.675	....	1.657	..
546	Mor. Ostrava	May 20	10.541	....	2.184	8.996	....	7.849	..
547	Kladno	May 23	....	....	....	....	....	.495	.1
548	Záběhlice	May 22	.317	....	.061	.260	....	.244	..
549	Bratislava	May 23	2.405	.600	.590	2.395	2.417	9.564	1.9
550	Hlubočepy	May 23	.063	....	....	.043	.043	.076	.0
551	Prague	May 22	....	.001	.001	....	.005	.005	.0
552	Prague IV	May 23	.205	.052	.045	.286	.326	.484	.1
553	Prague VIII-Libeň	May 23	.952	.300	.091	.906	.980	....	..
554	Most	May 24	1.140	.285	.273	1.135	1.140	.708	.1
555	Košíře	May 23	....	....	....	....	....	1.086	.1
556	Liberec	May 24	2.826	.700	.725	.415	2.819	5.342	1.0
557	Duchcov	May 24	.484	.120	.136	.480	.484	.710	.1
558	Kralupy	May 26	.254	.100	.045	.286	.275	.381	.0
559	Jablonec	May 27	4.338	1.100	1.088	4.248	4.333	4.830	.9
560	Břevnov	May 28	.571	.100	.212	.600	.598	....	..
561	Strašnice	May 28	....	....	....	.025	....	....	..
562	Luž	May 28	.114	.022	.022	.090	.090	.658	.0
563	Luž	May 28	....	....	....	.333	....	.798	.1
564	Žamberk	May 28	....	....	....	.217	....	.479	.0
565	Říčany	May 28	.072	.036	....	.072	.072	....	..
566	Břevnov	May 29	....	....	....	....	....	.764	.1
567	Kladno	May 29	....	....	....	....	.740	....	..
568	Kraslice	May 29	....	.200	.272	.896	.936	4.134	.8
569	Platten	May 29	1.225	.300	.318	1.178	1.219	1.433	.2
570	Výprty	June 4	1.152	.300	.272	1.119	1.154	1.114	.2
571	Jáchymov	June 4	.922	.200	.272	.921	.920	1.091	.2
572	Falknov	June 2	2.520	.700	.590	2.524	2.525	4.781	.9
573	Karlovy Vary	June 2	3.000	.800	.726	2.996	2.983	4.781	.9
574	Cheb	June 4	1.260	.400	.227	1.208	1.263	1.677	.3
575	Jablonec	June 6	3.430	.900	.816	3.384	3.418	2.762	.8
576	Záběhlice	June 4	....	....	....	....	....	.147	.0
577	Zlíchov	June 6	.050	.013	.013	.050	.050	....	..
578	Bilina	June 7	.280	.070	.070	.287	.283	.370	.0
579	Prague VIII-Libeň	June 7	....	....	....	....	....	2.191	.4
580	Příbram	June 1	.091	.023	.023	.090	.090	.679	.1
581	Březové Hory	June 1	.120	.030	.030	.120	.120	.316	.0
582	Líboce	June 6	.059	.014	.014	.105	.065	.152	.0
583	Plzeň	July 18	9.600	3.000	1.800	9.598	9.578	....	..
584	Frýdek-Místek	July 19	6.819	2.500	.907	6.819	6.814	....	..
585	Mor. Ostrava	July 18	10.432	3.400	1.814	10.432	10.406	....	..
586	Beroun	July 22	.661	.165	.165	.665	.653	.800	.1
587	Slaný	July 26	.730	.182	.182	.689	.827	1.715	.3
588	Mělník	Aug. 1	.028	.007	.007	.028	.033	.190	.0
589	Brno	June 13	2.400	.600	.599	2.400	2.394	2.286	.4
590	Radotín	June 13	.078	....	.039	.080	.087	.158	.0
591	Prague II	June 13	....	....	....	....	....	.158	.0
592	Prague II	June 20	....	....	....	.120	....	.324	.0
593	Prague VI	June 14	.018	.005	.005	.018	.018	....	..

CZECHO-SLOVAKIA

Internal Deliveries, (1) SMÍCHOV, (2) DEJVICE Warehouses

Table 263—*Continued*

eipt o.	Local Committee (Mistni Komitét)	Date	Commodities in Net Metric Tons of 1,000 Kilograms or 2,204.6 Pounds						
			Flour	Rice	Beans, Peas	Pork Products	Milk		Cocoa
							Evap.	Cond.	
ies 1		1919							
94	Jilemnice	June 8	1.800	.400	.499	1.800	1.785	3.353	.674
95	Kladno	June 11	3.600	.096	1.704	3.600	3.592	....	....
96	Olomouc	June 10	1.800	.492	.408	1.801	1.785	2.381	.472
97	Opava	June 11	1.660	.400	.430	1.663	1.654	2.134	.426
98	Místek	June 10	....	....	....	....	....	.716	.145
99	Mor. Ostrava	June 17	....	....	....	....	....	7.963	1.605
00	Prague II	June 13	.963	.300	.182	1.263	.958	....	....
01	Kladno	June 13	....	....	....	....	....	1.600	.321
)2	Záběhlice	June 3	....	.031	....	....	....	....	....
)3	Prague VII	June 3	....	....	....	....	....	.048	.010
)4	Prague-Bubeneč	June 13	.336	....	.168	.336	.326	....	....
)5	Prague-Libeň	June 13	....	....	....	.048	....	....	....
)6	Prague-Nusle	June 13	.843	....	.405	.534	.850	2.324	.451
)7	Velká Praha-Brod	June 4	.480	....	.235	.480	.479	....	....
)8	Bráník	June 4	.102	....	.051	.120	.109	....	....
)9	Ústí n/L.	June 12	1.080	.300	.226	1.080	1.067	1.600	.321
10	Praha I	June 12	.896	....	.405	.870	.870	....	....
11	Slaný	June 8	1.232	.300	.317	1.299	1.219	2.572	.434
12	Plzeň	June 11	9.600	2.400	2.385	9.600	9,579	12.744	2.568
13	Zlíchov	June 11	....	....	....	....	....	.135	.027
14	Vokovice	June 6	.201	....	.100	.201	.200	....	....
15	Vršovice	June 11	....	....	....	....	....	1.714	.345
16	Vokovice	June 6	....	....	....	....	....	.184	.037
17	Bubeneč	June 18	.128	.033	.032	.130	.130	....	....
8	Žižkov	June 5	....	....	....	....	....	3.238	.655
9	Prague III	June 11	.015	....	.008	.015	.015	....	....
0	Prague III	June 16	.018	.005	.004	.018	.018	....	....
1	Prague III	June 12	....	....	....	.030	....	....	....
2	Prague III	June 16	.046	.012	.011	.050	.044	....	....
3	Prague III	June 16	....	....	....	....	....	.016	.004
4	Říčany	June 5	....	.036	....	....	....	....	....
5	Teplice	June 13	1.558	.300	.227	1.558	1.545	1.390	.282
6	Strašnice	June 10	.194	....	.054	.186	.174	.309	.061
7	Karlín	June 11	.576	....	.287	.577	.566	....	....
8	Louny	June 14	.480	.200	.045	.480	.479	.637	.128
9	Opava	June 6	....	....	....	....	....	1.066	.214
0	Mor. Ostrava	June 15	....	....	....	....	....	3.638	.734
1	Aš	June 13	1.104	.200	.363	1.101	1.088	3.429	.690
2	Loket	June 13	2.040	.400	.635	2.040	2.055	2.629	.530
3	Dejvice	June 10	....	.100	.100	.400	....	.533	.108
4	Ruzyň	June 10	.024	....	.012	.025	.024	.083	.017
5	Karlín	June 13	....	....	....	....	....	.953	.193
6	Bránik	June 13	....	....	....	....	....	.254	.051
7	Dejvice	June 13	.400	....	....	....	....	....	....
8	Ústí n/L.	June 17	1.800	.500	.415	1.800	1.785	2.057	.417
9	Teplice	June 15	3.168	.600	.997	3.168	3.157	3.867	.780
0	Karlín	June 12	.064	.017	.016	.066	.065	.031	.006
1	Náchod	June 17	1.216	.300	.317	1.200	1.197	1.600	.321
2	Prague VII	June 13	....	....	....	....	....	1.352	.273
3	Smíchov	June 12	.960	.200	.272	.952	.958	2.057	.414
4	Prague	July 1	....	9.529	....	....	....	....	....
5	Chuchle	June 13	.042	.011	.010	.042	.044	.076	.016
6	Žižkov	June 13	....	....	....	.700	....	....	....
7	Brno	June 21	4.800	1.200	1.224	4.807	4.789	6.381	1.284
8	Olomouc	June 20	4.800	1.200	1.224	4.800	4.789	6.381	1.284
9	Radotín	June 15	....	....	....	....	....	.031	.006

[*Concluded on next page*]

CZECHO-SLOVAKIA

Internal Deliveries, (1) SMÍCHOV, (2) DEJVICE Warehouses

Table 263—*Concluded*

Receipt No.	Local Committee (Mistni Komitét)	Date	Flour	Rice	Beans, Peas	Pork Products	Milk Evap.	Milk Cond.	Cocoa
			Commodities in Net Metric Tons of 1,000 Kilograms or 2,204.6 Pounds						
Series 1		1919							
650	Prague	June 19	.036	.009	.009	.036	.036	....	..
651	Prague IV	June 16	....	....	....	....	.044	....	..
652	Prague II	June 16	.036	.009	.009	.036	.036	....	..
653	Prague II	June 16	.042	.013	.013	.042	.044	....	..
654	Střešovice	June 18	.067	.016	.016	.067	.065	.190	.0
655	Nýdek	June 27	1.620	.400	.415	1.620	1.611	2.381	.4
656	Hlubočepy	June 17	.128	.036	.033	.131	.130	.162	.0
657	Prague II	June 18	....	....	....	....	....	1.434	.2
658	Česká Lípa	June 28	2.002	.500	.495	2.010	2.003	3.943	.7
659	Budějovice	June 26	7.200	2.600	.990	7.200	7.184	6.382	1.2
660	Břevnov	June 18	....	....	....	....	....	.362	.0
661	Prague	June 18	.984	.300	.090	.984	.980	....	..
662	Karlovy Vary	June 20	28.800	1.700	....	12.225	28.758	32.756	6.0
663	Chomůtov	June 29	....	....	....	10.245	....	....	..
664	Jablonec	June 28	16.800	5.000	3.401	9.788	16.831	22.307	4.4
665	Král. Vinohrady-Praha	June 20	....	....	....	....	....	1.505	.[illegible]
666	Prague II	June 23	.054	.014	.014	.054	.054	....	..
667	Selce	June 26	.030	.008	.007	.030	.030	.072	.0
668	Kbely	June 23	.072	.018	.018	.072	.070	.127	.[illegible]
669	Radlice	June 22	.256	.067	.045	.246	.245	.270	.0
670	Nové Strašecí	June 26	.682	.335	....	.682	.674	2.381	.4
671	Kobylisy	June 24	.180	.045	.045	.180	.180	.344	.[illegible]
672	Střížkov	June 26	.027	.013	....	.030	.026	.095	.[illegible]
673	Vršovice	June 23	.896	.300	.180	.916	.914	....	..
674	Opava	July 5, 6	3.600	.900	.907	3.600	3.592	4.781	.[illegible]
675	Místek	July 9	3.600	.900	.907	3.600	3.592	4.781	.[illegible]
	Total	....	**191.342**	**49.970**	**37.360**	**174.635**	**174.652**	**235.927**	**44.[illegible]**

CZECHO-SLOVAKIA

Table 264

Internal Deliveries from UŽHOROD Warehouse

Receipt No.	Local Committee (Mistni Komitét)	Date	Flour	Rice	Beans, Peas	Corn Grits	Pork Products	Milk Evap.	Milk Cond.	Cocoa	Sugar	Misc
			Commodities in Net Metric Tons of 1,000 Kilograms or 2,204.6 Pounds									
Series 1		1920										
1799	Užhorod	May 19	.003	.030	.009	....	.015	.023	.016	.003	.002	.0
1800	Užhorod	May 21	.039	.049	.049	....	.029	.049	.029	.005	.005	..
1801	Užhorod	May 27	.021	.026	.026	....	.016	.026	.021	.004	.003	..
1802	Užhorod	June 2	.097	.121	.121	.015	.073	....	.211	.016	.013	..
1803	Užhorod	June 10	.034	.070	....	....	.026	.043	....	....	....	..
1804	Vel. Berezna	Jan. 15	.140	.092	.092	....	.097	.440	....	.027	....	..
1805	Užhorod	Jan. 20	....	....	....	....	....	1.100	....	....	....	..
1806	Užhorod	Jan. 20	.130	.202	.202	....	.063	.184	....	.011	....	..
1807	Užhorod	Jan. 20	....	....	....	....	....	1.100	....	....	....	..
1808	Volovca	Jan. 20	.600	.138	.322	....	.600	....	4.642	.496	....	..
1809	Užhorod	Jan. 20	....	....	....	....	....	1.100	....	....	....	..
1810	Mukačevo	Jan. 20	....	....	....	....	....	2.200	....	....	....	..
1811	Užhorod	Jan. 20	....	....	....	....	....	1.100	....	....	....	..
1812	Kóstrine	Jan. 21	.170	.138	.138	....	.097	....	.550	.054	....	..
1813	Vel. Berezna	Jan. 21	.170	.138	.138	....	.097	.550	....	.054	....	..

* All soap.

CZECHO-SLOVAKIA

Table 264—*Continued*   Internal Deliveries, UŽHOROD Warehouse

Receipt No.	Local Committee (Mistni Komitét)	Date	Flour	Rice	Beans, Peas	Corn Grits	Pork Products	Milk: Evap.	Milk: Cond.	Cocoa	Sugar	Misc.
			Commodities in Net Metric Tons of 1,000 Kilograms or 2,204.6 Pounds									
Series 1		1920										
1814	Perečín	Jan. 27	.170	.138	.138	....	.126	....	.270	.018	....	....
1815	Dubrinic	Jan. 27	.170	.184	.184	....	.151	.351	....	.027	....	....
1816	Turja Bystra	Jan. 27	.255	.230	.230	....	.189	....	.495	.045	....	....
1817	Porosko	Jan. 28	.255	.230	.230	....	.189	.495	....	.045	....	....
1818	Turja Remety	Jan. 28	.170	.138	.138	....	.126	.270	....	.018	....	....
1819	Antaloce	Jan. 29	....	....	....	....	....	....	....	.025	....	....
1820	Užhorod	Jan. 31	.255	.138	.138	....	.032	....	....	....	....	....
1821	Užhorod	Feb. 22	.180	.100	.260	....	.160	....	.367	.037	....	....
1822	Užhorod	Feb. 1	.085	.092	.092	....	.045	.066	.044	.009	....	....
1823	Šeredná	Feb. 14	....	.046	.092	....	....	....	....	....	....	....
1824	Mukačevo	Feb. 16	.300	.184	.368	....	.160	.270	.607	.122	....	....
1825	Abranka	Feb. 13	.150	.046	.092	....	.097	.144	.090	.018	....	....
1826	Užhorod	Feb. 24	.036	.046	....	....	.025	.046	.068	.014	....	....
1827	Štavná	Feb. 25	.396	.268	.524	....	.277	.936	....	.122	....	....
1828	Antaloce	Feb. 25	.162	.100	.224	.010	.113	.478	....	.063	....	....
1829	Vološanka	Mar. 10	.075	.050	.100	....	.050	.262	....	.037	....	.012
1830	Beregszasz	Mar. 15	.026	.026	.026	....	.018	....	.026	....	....	....
1831	Šeredná	Mar. 16	.050	.078	.124	....	.040	.112	....	.013	....	....
1832	Užhorod	Mar. 19	.023	.023	.023	....	.016	.023	.045	.003	....	....
1833	Užhorod	Mar. 19	.033	.033	.033	....	.023	.033	.026	.005	.005	....
1834	Užhorod	Mar. 19	.030	.030	.030	.005	.021	.030	.075	.002	.002	....
1835	Ljuta	Mar. 21	.360	.180	.540	.025	.252	.360	....	....	....	.025
1836	Užhorod	Mar. 31	.003	.003	.003	....	.002	.003	....	....	....	.001
1837	Mukačevo	Apr. 3	.262	.602	.602	....	.342	.602	1.330	.266	.262	....
1838	Perečín	Apr. 6	.362	.362	.362	....	.241	.326	.375	.075	....	....
1839	Užhorod	Apr. 14	.018	.018	.018	....	.012	.018	.014	.003	.003	....
1840	Užhorod	Apr. 14	.031	.031	.031	....	.022	.031	....	....	....	....
1841	Užhorod	Apr. 14	.090	.090	.090	....	.063	.090	.063	.013	.013	....
1842	Užhorod	Apr. 14	.033	.033	.033	....	.023	.033	.026	.005	.005	....
1843	Štavná	Apr. 16	.110	.110	.110	.011	.073	.110	.150	.030	.030	....
1844	Vološanka	Apr. 16	.019	.019	.019	....	.013	.019	.037	.007	.007	....
1845	Užhorod	May 5	.034	.043	.043	....	.026	.047	....	....	....	....
		1919										
1846	Užhorod	Aug. 27	.013	.003	.003	....	.015	.013	.024	.005	....	....
1847	Užhorod	Aug. 27	.010	.003	.003	....	.015	.010	.011	.002	....	....
1848	Užhorod	Aug. 27	.005	.002	.002	....	.001	.005	.010	.002	....	....
1849	Perečín	Sept. 1	.064	.058	.045	....	.081	.109	.076	.025	....	....
1850	Revhely	Sept. 20	.006	.005	.005	....	.016	....	.098	.016	....	....
1851	Vel. Berezna	Sept. 4	.016	.012	.012	....	.015	.016	.045	.009	....	....
1852	Užhorod	Sept. 13	.020	.005	.005	....	.016	....	.088	.006	....	....
1853	Vološanka	Sept. 20	.006	.005	.005	....	.016	....	.098	.016	....	....
1854	Užhorod	Sept. 20	....	....	....	....	....	....	2.200	....	....	....
1855	Užhorod	Sept. 23	.014	.009	.009	....	.016	....	....	....	....	....
1856	Užhorod	Sept. 30	.005	.005	.005	....	.016	.518	....	.005	....	....
1857	Užhorod	Oct. 2	.022	.005	.005	....	.016	....	.088	.006	....	....
1858	Užhorod	Oct. 3	.015	.005	.005	....	.016	....	.110	.005	....	....
1859	Ljuta	Oct. 6	.006	.005	.005	....	....	....	.098	.016	....	....
1860	Vel. Berezna	Oct. 6	....	....	....	....	....	.098	....	....	....	....
1861	Užhorod	Oct. 8	.170	....	....	....	....	....	2.200	....	....	....
1862	Mukačevo	Oct. 10	.170	....	....	....	.064	2.750	....	.050	....	....
1863	Antaloce	Nov. 2	.170	.045	.047	....	.175	.162	.333	.012	....	....
1864	Užhorod	Nov. 10	.030	.030	.030	....	.025	.044	.044	.003	....	....
1865	Vološanka	Nov. 11	.025	.019	.030	....	.021	.140	.040	.003	....	....
1866	Užhorod	Nov. 14	.030	.025	.025	....	.030	.072	....	.005	....	....
1867	Vel. Berezna	Nov. 17	.036	.009	.009	....	.036	.036	.096	.002	....	....
1868	Užhorod	Nov. 20	....	....	....	....	....	1.100	....	....	....	....
1869	Svalyava	Nov. 20	.170	.047	.045	....	.170	1.430	....	.125	....	....
1870	Mukačevo	Nov. 20	.340	.094	.090	....	.350	2.860	....	.250	....	....
1871	Užhorod	Nov. 21	....	.005	.005	....	.006	.006	....	.006	.022	....
1872	Užhorod	Nov. 21	.139	.051	.045	....	.138	....	....	....	....	....

[*Concluded on next page*]

CZECHO-SLOVAKIA

Table 264—*Concluded* Internal Deliveries, UŽHOROD Warehouse

Receipt No.	Local Committee (Mistni Komitét)	Date	Flour	Rice	Beans, Peas	Corn Grits	Pork Products	Milk Evap.	Milk Cond.	Cocoa	Sugar	Misc.
			Commodities in Net Metric Tons of 1,000 Kilograms or 2,204.6 Pounds									
Series 1		1919										
1873	Vološanka	Dec. 9	.048	.028	.030	....	.021	.135	.054	.031	....	....
1874	Ljuta	Dec. 2	.180	.045	.045	....	.180	.630	....	.090	....	....
1875	Užhorod	Dec. 11	.108	.036	.036	....	.076	.108	.090	.018	....	....
1876	Užhorod	Dec. 10	....	....	....	....	.044	....	....	....	....	....
1877	Užhorod	Dec. 11	.125	.126	.126	....	.095	.218	....	.021	....	....
1878–9	Revhely-Šeredná	Dec. 13	.097	.066	.022	....	.022	.047	.066	.019	....	....
1880	Mukačevo	Dec. 15	.255	.270	.270	....	.164	.585	.234	.125	....	....
1881	Užhorod	Dec. 15	.066	.054	.018	....	.018	.038	....	....	....	....
1882	Užhorod	Dec. 29	.097	.012	.012	....	.009	....	.036	.006	....	....
1883	Užhorod	Dec. 30	.015	.015	.015	....	.011	.015	....	....	....	....
		1920										
1884	Vološanka	Jan. 2	.068	.058	.058	....	.048	.068	.135	.027	....	....
1885	Varpalanka	Jan. 2	.085	.092	.092	....	.050	.242	....	.031	....	....
1886	Oroszveg	Jan. 2	.170	.184	.184	....	.106	....	.352	.030	....	....
1887	Užhorod	Jan. 3	.039	.039	.039	....	.028	.039	....	....	....	....
1888	Antaloce	Jan. 6	....	....	....	....	....	....	....	.014	....	....
	Total	....	**8.382**	**6.147**	**7.376**	**.066**	**6.166**	**24.564**	**16.203**	**2.673**	**.372**	**.040***

* All soap.

CZECHO-SLOVAKIA

Table 265 Internal Deliveries from TÁBOR Warehouse

Receipt No.	Local Committee (Mistni Komitét)	Date	Flour	Rice	Beans, Peas	Pork Products	Milk Evap.	Milk Cond.	Cocoa	Sugar	Misc.*	No. of Biscuits
			Commodities in Net Metric Tons of 1,000 Kilograms or 2,204.6 Pounds									
Series 1		1919										
412	Čes. Budějovice	Dec. 2	2.500	2.500	2.500	1.750	2.500	2.500	.500	.500	....	....
413	Písek	Dec. 3	.400	.400	.400	.280	.400	.686	.137	.137	....	....
414	Třeboň	Dec. 3	.300	.300	.300	.210	.300	.500	.100	.100	....	....
415	Tábor	Dec. 13	.500	.500	.268	.350	.500	1.000	.200	.200	....	....
416	Prachatice	Dec. 1	.650	.650	.650	.445	.650	1.063	.213	.213	....	....
417	Kaplice	Dec. 10	.250	.250	.250	.175	.250	.313	.063	.063	....	....
418	Týn n/Vlt.	Dec. 2	.200	.200	.200	.140	.200	.250	.050	.050	....	....
		1920										
759	Tábor	Apr. 15	.342	.171	.342	.236	.348	.475	.096	.096	....	....
760	Čes. Budějovice	Mar. 22	1.600	.803	1.606	1.120	1.613	1.729	.346	.346	....	....
761	Jindř. Hradec	Mar. 10	.704	.369	.738	.513	.741	1.026	.204	.200	....	....
762	Kaplice	Mar. 16	.128	.074	.149	.099	.153	.190	.039	.039	....	....
763	Kamenice	Mar. 19	.320	.177	.354	.259	.348	.456	.092	.092	....	....
764	Krumlov	Mar. 23	.320	.163	.325	.226	.327	.589	.102	.119	....	....
765	Písek	Mar. 16	.192	.109	.218	.160	.218	.399	.036	.078	....	....
766	Prachatice	Mar. 19	.256	.133	.266	.193	.261	.304	.062	.062	....	....
767	Týn n/Vlt.	Mar. 20	.192	.080	.160	.099	.153	.190	.040	.040	....	....
768	Třeboň	Mar. 20	.192	.109	.218	.160	.218	.361	.073	.073	....	....
868	Čes. Budějovice	Apr. 3	.832	1.002	1.002	.612	1.002	1.976	.360	.300	1.850[b]	70,0
869	Hradec Jindřichuv	Apr. 3	.320	.435	.435	.259	.436	1.292	.249	.199	.950[b]	38,0
870	Písek	Apr. 3	.098	.100	.100	.066	.109	.380	.070	.058	.300[b]	12,0
871	Prachatice	Apr. 3	.256	.361	.361	.226	.370	.741	.136	.114	.650[b]	26,0
872	Tábor	Apr. 15	.186	.233	.233	.143	.240	.532	.098	.078	.450[b]	18,0
873	Třeboň	Apr. 3	.192	.194	.194	.115	.196	.532	.102	.083	.400[b]	16,0
874	Týn n/Vlt.	Apr. 3	.064	.090	.090	.066	.087	.190	.039	.032	.200[b]	8,0
927	Č. Krumlov	Apr. 3	.256	.295	.298	.171	.283	1.064	.204	.165	.750[b]	29,0
1064	Kamenice n/L.	Apr. 3	.192	.200	.200	.121	.196	.475	.091	.074	.400[b]	16,0
1065	Kaplice	Apr. 3	.064	.078	.078	.044	.087	.190	.033	.028	.150[b]	6,0

* Detail of miscellaneous commodities indicated by the following indexes: [b], biscuits; [c], codliver oil; [d], soap. See end of Table 265 (page 530) for complete detail.

CZECHO-SLOVAKIA

Table 265—*Continued*

Internal Deliveries, TÁBOR Warehouse

ceipt No.	Local Committee (Mistni Komitét)	Date	Flour	Rice	Beans, Peas	Pork Products	Milk Evap.	Milk Cond.	Cocoa	Sugar	Misc.	No. of Biscuits
			Commodities in Net Metric Tons of 1,000 Kilograms or 2,204.6 Pounds									
ries 1		1920										
098	Třeboň	June 5	.028	.035	.035	.017	.043	.076	.016	.013	.050[b]	2,000
099	Čes. Budějovice	May 15	.826	1.030	1.033	.640	1.874	1.330	.408	.336	1.900[b]	76,000
100	Kamenice	May 22	.172	.202	.200	.132	.392	.285	.102	.074	.400[b]	16,000
101	Písek	May 15	.098	.110	.110	.066	.305	.190	.070	.058	.300[b]	12,000
102	Kaplice	May 15	.062	.078	.078	.044	.087	.190	.033	.028	.150[b]	6,000
103	Český Krumlov	May 15	.237	.295	.295	.177	.741	.570	.204	.165	.700[b]	28,000
104	Prachatice	May 15	.289	.361	.361	.210	.566	.570	.136	.114	.650[b]	26,000
105	Týn n/Vlt.	May 15	.072	.090	.090	.055	.087	.209	.039	.032	....	.....
106	Třeboň	May 15	.167	.206	.212	.132	.414	.380	.102	.088	.450[b]	18,000
160	Černovice	May 15	.024	.030	.030	.017	.031	.057	.014	.012	.050[b]	2,000
306	Kamenice n/L.	June 17	.128	.167	.167	.899	.174	.323	.060	.050	.300[b]	12,000
307	Jindř. Hradec	June 19	.343	.425	.428	.259	.436	1.273	.235	.200	.900[b]	36,000
308	Pelhřimov	June 12	.360	.459	.459	.320	.457	.855	.158	.129	.800[b]	32,000
309	Čes. Budějovice	June 16	.826	1.032	1.030	.640	1.046	2.185	.408	.336	1.875[b]	75,000
310	Kaplice	June 12	.062	.078	.078	.044	.087	.133	.025	.021	.150[b]	6,000
311	Č. Krumlov	June 19	....	.095	.050	....	....	....	....	.055	.700[b]	28,000
312	Písek	June 16	.098	.104	.110	.066	.109	.380	.070	.058	.300[b]	12,000
313	Prachatice	June 19	.283	.361	.361	.226	.371	.722	.136	.114	.650[b]	26,000
314	Černovice (Children's Camp)	June 21	.024	.030	.030	.017	.022	.076	.014	.012	.050[b]	2,000
315	Týn n/Vlt.	June 12	.090	.090	.054	....	.087	.209	.039	.032	....	.....
316	Třeboň	June 16	.195	.244	.244	.160	.240	.551	.113	.100	.500[b]	20,000
44	Jindřichuv Hradec	Dec. 18	.900	.900	.900	.630	.900	1.250	.250	.250	....	.....
50	Třeboň	Jan. 17	.300	.300	.300	.210	.300	.500	.100	....	....	.....
51	Třeboň	Jan. 18	....	....	....	....	....	....	....	....	.102[c]	.....
52	Čes. Budějovice	Jan. 15	2.372	1.186	2.372	1.660	2.372	2.472	.494	.994	....	.....
53	Jindř. Hradec	Jan. 17	.878	.878	.878	.015	.878	1.222	.249	.244	....	.....
54	Kamenice n/L.	Jan. 16	.412	.825	.579	....	.832	1.216	.243	.828	....	.....
55	Kaplice	Jan. 26	.174	.087	.174	.122	.174	.235	.047	.047	....	.....
56	Čes. Krumlov	Jan. 22	.617	.309	.617	.432	.617	1.106	.221	.221	....	.....
57	Písek	Jan. 3	.426	.426	.426	.298	.426	.750	.150	.150	....	.....
58	Prachatice	Jan. 31	.577	.289	.577	.404	.577	.644	.129	....	.129[d]	.....
59	Týn n/Vlt.	Jan. 3	.200	.200	.200	.140	.200	.250	.050	.015	....	.....
60	Týn n/Vlt.	Feb. 18	.192	.100	.200	.132	.196	.247	.050	.050	.400[b]	16,000
61	Třeboň	Feb. 19	.256	.136	.279	.193	.283	.456	.102	.100	.600[b]	24,000
62	Tábor	Feb. 23	.256	.131	.262	.193	.262	.437	.102	.087	....	.....
63	Čes. Budějovice	Feb. 7	2.048	1.024	2.047	1.440	2.049	2.185	.437	.437	3.650[b]	146,000
64	Jindř. Hradec	Feb. 8	.896	.439	.878	.612	.872	1.216	.244	.244	1.750[b]	70,000
65	Kamenice n/L.	Feb. 18	.448	.221	.443	.320	.436	.570	.115	.115	....	.....
66	Kaplice	Feb. 20	.011	.005	.011	....	.011	.008	.002	.002	.350[b]	14,000
68	Krumlov	Feb. 20	.128	.076	.153	.099	.153	.266	.055	.055	.350[b]	14,000
69	Prachatice	Mar. 2	.768	.340	.737	.513	.741	.855	.172	.172	1.350[b]	45,000
70	Černovice u Tábora	Mar. 1	.030	.015	.030	.022	.030	....	....	....	....	.....
72	Kaplice	Mar. 20	.128	.074	.149	.099	.153	.190	.039	.039	....	.....
48	Luž	July 9	....	....	....	....	....	....	....	....	.215[c]	.....
49	Praha	July 3	....	....	....	....	....	....	....	....	.109[c]	.....
50	Košiře-Praha	July 22	....	....	....	....	....	....	....	....	.111[c]	.....
51	Praha	July 16	....	....	....	....	....	....	....	....	.060[c]	.....
73	Tábor	July 12	....	....	....	....	....	.129	.023	.019	....	.....
85	Tábor	July 29	.010	.012	.012	.011	.012	....	....	....	.050[b]	2,000
05	Černovice	Aug. 12	....	....	....	....	....	....	....	....	.025[d]	.....
06	Jindř. Hradec	Aug. 12	....	....	....	....	....	....	....	....	.025[d]	.....
08	Kamenice	Aug. 12	....	....	....	....	....	....	....	....	.025[d]	.....
09	Třeboň	Aug. 12	....	....	....	....	....	....	....	....	.025[d]	.....
10	Čes. Krumlov	Aug. 14	....	....	....	....	....	....	....	....	.025[d]	.....
11	Čes. Krumlov	Aug. 12	....	....	....	....	....	....	....	....	.075[d]	.....
17	Kaplice	Aug. 12	....	....	....	....	....	....	....	....	.025[d]	.....
47	Čes. Budějovice	Aug. 14	....	....	....	....	....	....	....	....	.025[d]	.....

[*Concluded on next page*]

CZECHO-SLOVAKIA

Table 265—*Concluded* Internal Deliveries, TÁBOR Warehouse

Receipt No.	Local Committee (Mistni Komitét)	Date	Flour	Rice	Beans, Peas	Pork Products	Milk Evap.	Milk Cond.	Cocoa	Sugar	Misc.	No. of Biscuits
			Commodities in Net Metric Tons of 1,000 Kilograms or 2,204.6 Pounds									
Series 2		1921										
20	Týn n/Vlt.	Apr. 30	.222	.060	.075	.025	.109	....	.015	.069	....	....
21	Kaplice	Apr. 30	.222	.060	.075	.025	.109	....	.015	.069	....	....
22	Jindř. Hradec	Apr. 30	.666	.183	.224	.125	.348	....	.045	.200	....	....
23	Prachatice	Apr. 30	.555	.150	.181	.100	.283	....	.038	.171	....	....
24	Třeboň	Apr. 30	.222	.060	.075	.025	.109	....	.015	.069	....	....
25	Pelhřimov	Apr. 30	.999	.274	.338	.175	.523	....	.073	.311	....	....
26	Kaplice (Heilbrun)	Apr. 30	.126	.036	.045	.025	.065	....	.009	.048	....	....
27	Kaplice (Hohenfurth)	Apr. 30	.089	.024	.031	.025	.021	....	.006	.027	....	....
28	Čes. Budějovice	Apr. 30	3.545	.961	1.224	.625	1.918	....	.240	1.100	....	....
29	Třeboň	Apr. 30	1.554	.410	.525	.275	.828	....	.102	.482	....	....
244	Čes. Budějovice	Apr. 30	.426	.115	.136	.075	.218	....	.029	.132	....	....
245	Černovice u Tábora	Apr. 30	.045	.056	.025	.162	.087	....	.011	.052	....	....
246	Hrabice u Vimperka	Apr. 30	.111	.030	.038	.025	.043	....	.008	.035	....	....
247	Prachatice	Apr. 22	.148	.040	.050	.026	.080	....	.010	.046	....	....
438	Čes. Budějovice	June 28	.120	.032	.045	.025	.065	....	.008	.037	....	....
439	Třeboň	June 28	.297	.090	.090	.050	.152	....	.020	.100	....	....
543	Jindř. Hradec	June 9	.222	.060	.075	.025	.109	....	.015	.065	....	....
544	Prachatice	June 9	.185	.046	.063	.025	.109	....	.013	.050	....	....
545	Pelhřimov	June 9	.333	.090	.113	.050	.196	....	.024	.100	....	....
546	Kaplice	June 9	.074	.020	.025	.025	.044	....	.005	.023	....	....
547	Třeboň	June 9	.510	.135	.175	.100	.283	....	.035	.150	....	....
548	Čes. Budějovice	June 11	....	....	....	....	.567	....	.102	....	....	....
549	Čes. Budějovice	June 9	1.184	.322	.410	.200	.632	....	.077	.350	....	....
550	Týn n/Vlt.	June 9	.074	.020	.025	.025	.044	....	.005	.023	....	....
	Total	....	**39.846**	**26.745**	**33.677**	**21.942**	**39.171**	**46.171**	**10.311**	**13.344**	**26.451***	**1,005,0**

* Detail of miscellaneous commodity total: [b], weight of 1,005,000 biscuits, 25.475; [c], codliver oil, .597; [d], soap, .379.

CZECHO-SLOVAKIA

Table 266 Internal Deliveries from PRAGUE (Praha) Warehouse

Receipt No.	Local Committee (Mistni Komitét)	Date	Flour	Rice	Beans, Peas	Pork Products	Milk Evap.	Milk Cond.	Cocoa
			Commodities in Net Metric Tons of 1,000 Kilograms or 2,204.6 Pounds						
Series 1		1919							
2	Příbram	Sept. 5	.480	.120	.120	.479	.480	1.113	[illegible]
3	Zbraslav	Sept. 13	.160	.040	.040	.159	.160	.286	[illegible]
4	Kolín	Sept. 15	.440	.110	.110	.441	.440	.954	[illegible]
5	Hořovice	Sept. 15	.400	.100	.100	.397	.400	.795	[illegible]
6	Kladno	Sept. 13	1.800	.450	.450	1.796	1.800	2.862	[illegible]
7	Sedlčany	Sept. 5	.200	.050	.050	.196	.200	.318	[illegible]
8	Roudnice	Sept. 22	.240	.060	.060	.240	.240	.398	[illegible]
9	Beroun	Sept. 18	.440	.110	.110	.441	.440	.795	[illegible]
10	Benešov	Sept. 5	.200	.050	.050	.196	.200	.318	[illegible]
11	Slaný	Sept. 15	.680	.170	.170	.680	.680	1.908	[illegible]
12	Kutná Hora	Sept. 28	.400	.100	.100	.403	.400	1.113	[illegible]
13	Nová Paka	Sept. 12	.600	.150	.150	.599	.600	1.749	[illegible]
14	Louny	Sept. 29	.200	.050	.050	.201	.200	.477	[illegible]

CZECHO-SLOVAKIA

Table 266—*Continued* Internal Deliveries, PRAGUE (Praha) Warehouse

ceipt No.	Local Committee (Mistni Komitét)	Date	Commodities in Net Metric Tons of 1,000 Kilograms or 2,204.6 Pounds						
			Flour	Rice	Beans, Peas	Pork Products	Milk		Cocoa
							Evap.	Cond.	
ries 1		1919							
15	Kralupy	Sept. 5	.480	.120	.120	.479	.480	1.113	.225
16	Český Brod	Sept. 5	.400	.100	.090	.397	.400	.795	.161
17	Rakovník	Sept. 5	.800	.200	.200	.800	.800	1.590	.321
18	Rumburk	Sept. 12	2.600	.650	.650	2.600	2.600	5.247	1.059
19	Duchcov	Sept. 27	1.193	.300	.304	1.303	1.447	2.706	.580
20	Ústí	Sept. 5	2.960	.740	.740	2.960	2.960	5.883	1.188
40	Dobříš	Oct. 27	.212	.052	.052	.212	.212	.428	.088
42	Mělník	Oct. 27	.160	.040	.040	.160	.160	.477	.096
43	Brandýs n/L.	Oct. 25	.360	.090	.091	.360	.360	.795	.161
44	Nové Strašecí	Oct. 23	.560	.140	.140	.560	.560	2.385	.481
45	Mladá Boleslav	Oct. 24	.640	.160	.160	.640	.640	1.749	.353
82	Slaný	Oct. 24	.680	.170	.170	.680	.680	1.908	.385
83	Kutná Hora	Oct. 26	.400	.100	.100	.400	.400	1.113	.225
84	Kladno	Oct. 21	1.800	.450	.450	1.822	1.800	2.863	.578
85	Český Brod	Oct. 24	.400	.100	.100	.400	.400	.795	.161
86	Sedlčany	Oct. 25	.200	.050	.050	.200	.200	.318	.064
87	Benešov	Oct. 25	.200	.050	.050	.200	.200	.318	.064
88	Kolín	Oct. 24	.440	.110	.110	.440	.440	.954	.193
89	Roudnice	Oct. 27	.240	.060	.060	.240	.240	.398	.080
90	Rakovník	Oct. 24	.800	.200	.200	.798	.800	1.590	.321
91	Hořovice	Oct. 27	.400	.100	.100	.400	.400	.795	.161
92	Beroun	Oct. 27	.440	.110	.110	.440	.440	.795	.161
93	Louny	Oct. 26	.200	.050	.050	.200	.200	.477	.096
94	Nová Paka	Oct. 25	.600	.150	.150	.602	.600	1.749	.353
	Total	....	**23.405**	**5.852**	**5.847**	**23.521**	**23.659**	**50.327**	**10.199**

CZECHO-SLOVAKIA

Table 267 Internal Deliveries from PILSEN (Plzeň) Warehouse

ceipt o.	Local Committee (Mistni Komitét)	Date	Commodities in Net Metric Tons of 1,000 Kilograms or 2,204.6 Pounds									
			Flour	Rice	Beans, Peas	Pork Products	Milk		Cocoa	Sugar	Misc.*	No. of Biscuits
							Evap.	Cond.				
ies 1		1919										
31	Královice	Sept. 6	.318	.080	.080	.318	.318	.927	.187	....	....	.....
32	Plzeň	Sept. 5	2.453	.813	.613	2.453	2.453	5.705	1.172	....	....	.....
33	Sušice	Sept. 5	.670	.168	.168	.670	.670	1.776	.359	....	....	.....
34	Klatovy	Sept. 5	.426	.107	.107	.426	.426	1.129	.228	....	....	.....
35	Strakonice	Sept. 6	.737	.182	.184	.737	.737	1.952	.394	....	....	.....
47	Rokycany	Oct. 6	.842	.210	.210	.842	.842	1.952	.450	....	....	.....
48	Dobřany	Oct. 16	.578	.144	.144	.578	.578	2.161	.436	....	....	.....
49	Stříbro	Oct. 22	.452	.113	.113	.452	.452	.568	.115	....	....	.....
50	Tachov	Oct. 21	.288	.072	.072	.288	.288	.763	.072	....	....	.....
51	Domažlice	Nov. 11	.288	.072	.072	.288	.288	.763	.154	....	....	.....
03	Plzeň	Oct. 24	2.453	.613	.613	2.453	2.453	5.805	1.172	....	....	.....
04	Sušice	Oct. 24	.670	.168	.168	.670	.670	1.776	.359	....	....	.....
05	Strakonice	Oct. 15	.746	.187	.187	.746	.746	1.943	.395	....	....	.....

* Detail of miscellaneous commodities indicated by the following in-
es: [b], biscuits; [c], codliver oil; [d], soap. See end of Table 267 (page 533)
complete detail.

[*Continued on next page*]

CZECHO-SLOVAKIA

Table 267—*Continued* Internal Deliveries, PILSEN (Plzeň) Warehouse

Receipt No.	Local Committee (Mistni Komitét)	Date	Flour	Rice	Beans, Peas	Pork Products	Milk Evap.	Milk Cond.	Cocoa	Sugar	Misc.	No. of Biscuits
			Commodities in Net Metric Tons of 1,000 Kilograms or 2,204.6 Pounds									
Series 1		1919										
206	Královice	Oct. 15	.318	.080	.080	.318	.318	.927	.187	....	....	...
207	Tachov	Oct. 21	.288	.072	.072	.288	.288	.763	.154	....	....	...
208	Dobřany	Oct. 16	.578	.144	.144	.578	.578	2.161	.436	....	....	...
289	Rokycany	Nov. 12	.842	.210	.210	.842	.842	2.289	.842	....	....	...
290	Klatovy	Nov. 5	.430	.107	.107	.430	.430	1.129	.228	....	....	...
291	Domažlice	Nov. 5	.288	.072	.072	.288	.288	.763	.154	....	....	...
292	Stříbro	Nov. 6	.452	.113	.113	.452	.452	.568	.115	....	....	...
406	Dobřany	Dec. 1	.704	.720	.720	.544	.722	1.699	.306	....	....	...
407	Karlovice	Dec. 20	.398	.398	.398	.278	.398	.729	.146	....	....	...
408	Rokycany	Dec. 18	....	1.080	....	.712	1.067	1.890	.408	....	....	...
409	Strakonice	Dec. 10	....	.945	....	.623	.958	1.737	.322	....	....	...
410	Sušice	Dec. 6	....	1.125	....	.813	1.132	1.699	.306	....	....	...
411	Plzeň	Dec. 5	1.280	3.060	1.620	2.035	3.067	4.564	.918	....	....	...
		1920										
769	Domažlice	Apr. 12	.196	.100	.186	.138	.195	....	.102	.200	....	...
770	Dobřany	Mar. 30	.635	.300	.545	.471	.588	1.278	.306	.300	....	...
771	Klatovy	Mar. 24	.126	.045	.123	.150	.108	.229	.044	.044	....	...
772	Plzeň	Mar. 23	1.880	.945	1.918	1.362	1.894	2.500	.510	.500	....	...
773	Rokycany	Mar. 24	.380	.190	.371	.300	.392	.840	.102	.200	....	...
774	Strakonice	Mar. 26	.634	.345	.659	.448	.675	.735	.204	.200	....	...
775	Stříbro	Apr. 7	.158	.045	.180	.153	.152	.115	.022	.022	....	...
776	Sušice	Mar. 30	.626	.300	.610	.444	.610	.935	.204	.200	....	...
777	Tachov	Mar. 24	.127	.065	.134	.151	.130	.019	.019	.019	....	...
861	Klatovy	Apr. 4	.066	.103	.107	.151	.087	....	.055	.026	.250[b]	9,0
862	V. Kdýne	Apr. 13	.125	.145	.137	.149	.152	.019	.005	.004	.150[b]	6,0
863	Plzeň	Apr. 8	1.243	1.545	1.542	.916	1.545	3.741	.714	.600	3.000[b]	119,0
864	Strakonice	Apr. 16	.321	.400	.371	.319	.392	....	.204	....	.850[b]	33,0
865	Stříbro	Apr. 7	.150	.200	.160	.140	.196	.248	.044	.037	.250[b]	9,0
866	Sušice	Apr. 7	.433	.500	.513	.301	.501	1.603	.306	.200	1.150[b]	45,0
867	Tachov	May 3	.100	.145	.149	.136	.327	....	.033	.033	.200[b]	8,0
962	Rokycany	May 3	.308	.357	.361	.316	1.197	....	.204	.100	.700[b]	28,0
963	Domažlice	Apr. 12	.120	.200	.186	.167	.196	.458	.102	.045	.400[b]	16,0
1107	Strakonice	June 16	.301	.413	.412	.302	.391	1.087	.204	.200	.850[b]	34,0
1108	Klatovy	May 17	.064	.103	.096	....	.391	....	.055	.046	....	...
1109	Dobřany	May 14	.325	.412	.390	.302	1.545	....	.204	.200	.850[b]	34,
1110	Stříbro	May 27	.175	.206	.184	.145	.195	.229	.044	.037	.300[b]	12,
1111	Plzeň	May 15	1.251	1.584	1.544	.925	5.638	....	.714	.600	3.150[b]	126,
1112	Tachov	May 21	.111	.150	.138	.164	.305	....	.033	.027	.200[b]	8,
1113	Rokycany	May 13	.423	.515	.514	.295	1.806	....	.204	.200	1.050[b]	42,
1114	Nová Kdýně	May 13	.126	.148	.191	.153	.217	....	.008	.007	.200[b]	8,
1283	Dobřany	June 10	.332	.408	.400	.324	.392	1.146	.204	.200	.850[b]	34,
1284	Nová Kdýně	June 11	.128	.148	.158	.171	.174	.038	.008	.007	.200[b]	8,
1285	Klatovy	June 14	.110	.102	.103	....	.109	.305	.055	.046	.250[b]	10,
1286	Plzeň	June 16	1.264	1.580	1.584	1.028	1.589	4.103	.714	.600	3.200[b]	127,
1287	Rokycany	June 16	.433	.507	.515	.312	.522	1.279	.204	.200	1.050[b]	42,
1288	Strakonice	June 15	.301	.413	.412	.302	.391	1.087	.204	.200	.850[b]	34,
1289	Stříbro	June 16	.168	.206	.197	.162	.195	.248	.044	.037	.300[b]	12,
1290	Sušice	June 15	.444	.502	.515	.317	.500	1.603	.306	.248	1.150[b]	46,
1291	Tachov	June 12	....	.103	.039	....	.022	.134	.026	.020	.200[b]	8,
1889	Sušice	Jan. 1	2.304	.585	2.374	.796	1.132	1.698	.306	.600	....	..
1890	Plzeň	Jan. 20	3.130	1.575	3.139	2.215	3.135	4.561	.868	.900	....	..
1891	Stříbro	Jan. 28	.192	.090	.182	.155	.196	.115	.021	.021	....	..
1892	Strakonice	Jan. 16	1.746	.405	1.774	.490	.718	1.164	.204	.500	....	..
1893	Domažlice	Jan. 14	.448	.135	.455	.284	.435	.687	.102	.100	....	..
1894	Klatovy	Jan. 21	.128	.059	.136	.164	.109	.134	.028	.028	....	..
1895	Tachov	Jan. 20	.128	.090	.182	.158	.152	.172	.032	.100	....	..
1896	Dobřany	Jan. 16	.704	.360	.728	.475	.718	1.604	.306	.600	....	..
1897	Sušice	Feb. 8	1.141	.540	1.092	.756	1.110	1.641	.306	.300	....	..
1898	Plzeň	Feb. 27	2.876	1.440	2.903	1.963	2.895	3.836	.816	.700	....	..
1899	Plzeň	Feb. 18	1.264	1.580	1.580	1.028	1.589	4.096	.714	.600	....	..
1900	Rokycany	Feb. 24	1.066	.540	1.056	.777	1.067	2.328	.510	.400	....	..

CZECHO-SLOVAKIA

Table 267—*Concluded* Internal Deliveries, PILSEN (Plzeň) Warehouse

Receipt No.	Local Committee (Mistni Komitét)	Date	Flour	Rice	Beans, Peas	Pork Products	Milk Evap.	Milk Cond.	Cocoa	Sugar	Misc.	No. of Biscuits
			Commodities in Net Metric Tons of 1,000 Kilograms or 2,204.6 Pounds									
Series 1		1920										
1901	Domažlice	Feb. 8	.442	.225	.446	.300	.435	.687	.102	.078	....	.....
1902	Klatovy	Feb. 18	.253	.135	.227	.158	.239	.344	.102	.100	....	.....
1903	Klatovy	Feb. ..	.064	.103	.096	....	.034	....	.055	.046	....	.....
1904	Dobřany	Feb. 20	.719	.752	.360	.728	.458	1.603	.306	.300	....	.....
2421	Stříbro	Jan. 28	....	....	....	....	....	....	....	....	.050[c]	.....
2447	Plzeň	Aug. 20	....	....	....	....	....	....	....	....	.098[c]	.....
2480	Nová Kdýně	Aug. 17	.178	.180	.209	.157	.174	.038	.011	.009	.250[b]	10,000
2481	Domažlice	Aug. 17	.128	.120	.138	.157	.131	.344	.102	.100	.350[b]	14,000
2482	Plzeň	Aug. 10	1.265	1.591	1.571	.897	1.567	....	.714	.600	3.200[b]	128,000
2483	Rokycany	Aug. 12	.284	.480	.492	.288	.500	....	.204	.200	1.000[b]	40,000
2484	Strakonice	Aug. 16	.317	.420	.378	.280	.301	.877	.204	.200	.850[b]	34,000
2485	Stříbro	Aug. 16	.144	.180	.209	.139	.195	.185	.044	.037	.300[b]	12,000
2486	Sušice	Aug. 13	.385	.480	.523	.290	.501	....	.306	.248	1.150[b]	46,000
2487	Tachov	Aug. 13	.127	.120	.142	.141	.131	....	.033	.027	.200[b]	8,000
2577	Staňkov	July 22	.048	.060	.060	....	.065	.153	.029	.024	.050[b]	2,000
2603	Rokycany	Aug. 12	....	....	....	....	....	....	....	....	.150[d]	.....
2604	Rokycany	Aug. 12	....	....	....	....	....	....	....	....	.050[d]	.....
2607	Sušice	Aug. 10	....	....	....	....	....	....	....	....	.025[d]	.....
2612	Klatovy	Aug. 12	....	....	....	....	....	....	....	....	.025[d]	.....
2613	Strakonice	Aug. 16	....	....	....	....	....	....	....	....	.125[d]	.....
2618	Sušice	Aug. 13	....	....	....	....	....	....	....	....	.175[d]	.....
2619	Staňkov	Aug. 13	....	....	....	....	....	....	....	....	.037[d]	.....
627	Stříbro	Aug. 16	....	....	....	....	....	....	....	....	.025[d]	.....
639	Plzeň	Aug. 17	....	....	....	....	....	....	....	....	.475[d]	.....
645	Domažlice	Aug. 17	....	....	....	....	....	....	....	....	.050[d]	.....
646	Tachov	Aug. 13	....	....	....	....	....	....	....	....	.025[d]	.....
Series 2		1921										
102	Stříbro	Apr. 29	.960	.274	.312	.176	.544	....	.102	.300	....	.....
103	Strakonice	Apr. 29	.896	.230	.267	.150	.479	....	.102	.300	....	.....
104	Sušice	May 3	2.880	.782	.966	.500	1.567	....	.204	.900	....	.....
105	Domažlice	Apr. 4	.888	.242	.308	.156	.479	....	.060	.265	....	.....
106	Plzeň	Apr. 25	12.943	3.467	4.351	2.275	6.989	....	.918	2.613	....	.....
107	Tachov	May 11	1.088	.322	.368	.200	.609	....	.102	.350	....	.....
108	Nová Kdýně	May 4	.254	.070	.090	.050	.130	....	.017	.100	....	.....
109	Eisenstein	May 7	.128	.046	.046	.025	.065	....	.008	.050	....	.....
110	Rokycany	May 3	1.792	.506	.598	.325	.958	....	.120	.550	....	.....
111	Líny	May 10	.704	.184	.230	.125	.370	....	.047	.200	....	.....
234	Sušice	Apr. 28	.064	.046	.046	.025	.022	....	.003	.021	....	.....
235	Plzeň	May 5	.064	.046	.042	.025	.044	....	.005	.050	....	.....
236	Touškov	May 3	.064	.046	.046	.025	.044	....	.005	.025	....	.....
237	Plzeň	Apr. 27	.128	.046	.045	.025	.087	....	.010	.055	....	.....
238	Domažlice	Apr. 27	.128	.045	.046	.025	.065	....	.008	.035	....	.....
239	Plzeň	Apr. 29	.064	.020	.045	.025	.044	....	.005	.023	....	.....
240	Plzeň	May 7	.256	....	....	....	....	....	....	....	....	.....
241	Čer. Dvorce Sušice	May 3	.128	.046	.046	.025	.065	....	.008	.050	....	.....
242	Nová Kdýně	May 5	.190	.046	.046	.025	.087	....	.011	.050	....	.....
243	Volšov Sušice	May 11	.064	.046	.046	.025	.044	....	.005	.025	....	.....
33	Plzeň	July 9	.384	.092	....	.075	.217	....	.026	.120	....	.....
34	Plzeň	July 5	.710	.192	....	.125	.392	....	.048	.220	....	.....
35	Sušice	July 5	3.648	.966	1.242	.650	1.960	....	.204	1.150	....	.....
36	Rokycany	July 4	1.536	.414	.500	.275	.806	....	.102	.450	....	.....
37	Tachov	July 5	1.152	.322	.192	.200	.610	....	.102	.350	....	.....
36	Nová Kdýně	July 8	.063	.011	....	....	.022	....	.003	.015	....	.....
37	Plzeň	July 5	6.471	1.749	....	1.150	3.484	....	.462	2.010	....	.....
38	Stříbro	July 5	.320	.092	....	.050	.196	....	.023	.100	....	.....
39	Eisenstein	June 24	.019	.005	.006	.003	.022	....	.002	.005	....	.....
40	Rokycany	June 15	.317	.092	.091	.050	.174	....	.020	.100	....	.....
41	Sušice	June 17	.960	.276	.322	.175	.523	....	.102	.300	....	.....
42	Strakonice	June 13	.320	.092	.092	.050	.174	....	.020	.100	....	.....
	Total	....	**89.147**	**47.543**	**52.752**	**50.042**	**84.439**	**98.384**	**25.705**	**23.305**	**30.260***	**1,152,000**

* Detail of miscellaneous commodity total: [b], weight of 1,152,000 biscuits, 28.950; [c], codliver oil, .148; [d], soap, 1.162.

CZECHO-SLOVAKIA

Table 268 — Internal Deliveries from PARDUBICE Warehouse

Receipt No.	Local Committee (Mistni Komitét)	Date	Commodities in Net Metric Tons of 1,000 Kilograms or 2,204.6 Pounds									
			Flour	Rice	Beans, Peas	Pork Products	Milk		Cocoa	Sugar	Misc.*	No. of Biscuits
							Evap.	Cond.				
Series 1		1919										
37	Rychnov	Sept. 27	.614	.157	.157	.614	.614	2.343	.474	....	....	...
38	Humpolec	Sept. 19	.467	.116	.117	.467	.467	1.342	.271	....	....	...
39	Čáslav	Sept. 19	.260	.065	.065	.260	.260	.577	.117	....	....	...
40	Vysoké Mýto	Sept. 16	.840	.210	.210	.840	.840	3.992	.806	....	....	...
41	Ustí nad Orlici	Sept. 20	.130	.033	.033	.130	.130	.318	.064	....	....	...
42	Německý Brod	Sept. 18	.756	.189	.189	.756	.756	2.279	.458	....	....	...
43	Čes. Třebová	Sept. 20	.872	.218	.218	.872	.872	2.365	.476	....	....	...
44	Pelhřimov	Sept. 18	.598	.150	.150	.598	.598	1.970	.398	....	....	...
45	Chotěboř a Chrudim	Sept. 22	.540	.135	.135	.540	.540	1.460	.295	....	....	...
46	Chrudim	Sept. 22	.416	.104	.104	.416	.416	1.425	.288	....	....	...
47	Litomyšl	Sept. 27	.564	.141	.141	.564	.564	1.826	.368	....	....	...
48	Pardubice	Sept. 18	.576	.143	.143	.576	.573	2.465	.500	....	....	...
49	Polička	Sept. 28	.547	.137	.137	.547	.547	1.869	.376	....	....	...
50	Ústí n/O.	Sept. 20	.130	.033	.033	.130	.130	.318	.064	....	....	...
136	Ledeč	Oct. ..	.203	.051	.051	.203	.203	1.282	.259	....	....	...
210	Chotěboř	Oct. 26	.524	.131	.131	.524	.524	.642	.129	....	....	...
299	Německý Brod	Nov. 8	.666	.167	.167	.666	.666	.859	.176	....	....	...
300	Chrudim	Nov. 20	.386	.096	.096	.386	.386	.771	.024	....	....	...
301	Humpolec	Nov. 7	.467	.117	.117	.467	.467	1.341	.271	....	....	...
302	Čáslav	Nov. 29	.260	.065	.065	.260	.260	.133	.061	....	....	...
303	Pardubice	Nov. 9	.573	.143	.143	.573	.573	1.983	.390	....	....	...
304	Ustí n/O.	Nov. 6	.130	.033	.033	.130	.130	.318	.064	....	....	...
305	Česká Třebová	Nov. 3	.558	.140	.140	.558	.558	1.297	.262	....	....	...
306	Litomyšl	Nov. 13	.552	.137	.137	.552	.552	1.749	.354	....	....	...
307	Rychnov	Nov. 18	.636	.159	.159	.636	.636	2.439	.492	....	....	...
308	Polička	Nov. 19	.547	.137	.137	.547	.547	1.860	.376	....	....	...
309	Vysoké Mýto	Nov. 13	.840	.210	.210	.840	.840	.368	.074	....	....	...
419	Ustí n/O.	Dec. 6	.163	.163	.163	.114	.163	.250	.050	.050	....	...
420	Česká Třebová	Dec. 4	.803	.803	.803	.562	.803	1.140	.228	.228	....	...
421	Pelhřimov	Dec. 18	.744	.744	.744	.521	.744	1.625	.325	.325	....	...
422	Chrudim	Dec. 13	.520	.520	.520	.364	.520	1.125	.225	.225	....	...
423	Německý Brod	Dec. 13	.889	.889	.889	.622	.889	1.234	.247	.247	....	...
424	Pardubice	Dec. 13	.716	.716	.716	.501	.716	1.730	.346	.346	....	..
425	Vysoké Mýto	Dec. 11	1.051	1.051	1.051	.736	1.051	1.714	.343	.343	....	...
426	Litomyšl	Dec. 12	.739	.739	.739	.517	.739	1.415	.283	.283	....	...
427	Chotěboř	Dec. 14	.666	.666	.666	.466	.666	.826	.165	.165	....	...
436	Ledeč	Nov. 30	.249	.249	.249	.174	.249	1.020	.204	.204	....	...
683	Polička	Dec. 19	.684	.684	.684	.479	.684	1.463	.293	.293	....	...
		1920										
744	Pelhřimov	Apr. 26	.320	.200	.360	.240	.872	....	.038	.053	....	..
745	Chotěboř	Apr. 7	.350	.202	.340	.250	.349	.456	.102	.090	....	..
746	Pardubice	Apr. 17	.064	.104	.110	.067	.392	....	.102	.050	....	..
747	Vysoké Mýto	Apr. 12	.290	.150	.290	.230	.284	.418	.102	.100	....	..
748	Ledeč	Mar. 30	.192	.096	.192	.134	.192	.329	.066	.066	....	..
749	Humpolec	Apr. 12	.180	.102	.190	.130	.196	.318	.102	.050	....	..
750	Chrudim	Apr. 7	.315	.160	.320	....	.305	.665	.102	.130	....	..
751	Lanškroun	Apr. 12	.110	.100	.112	....	.262	....	.102	.050	....	..
752	Německý Brod	Apr. 12	.328	.210	.320	.230	.327	.570	.102	.115	....	..
753	Polička	Mar. 27	.309	.155	.309	.216	.309	.559	.112	.112	....	..
754	Litomyšl	Apr. 12	.600	.250	.490	.315	.480	.665	.102	.100	....	..
755	Čáslav	Mar. 27	.469	.104	.148	.048	.240	.019	....	....	....	..
756	Čes. Třebová	Mar. 20	.489	.252	.493	.312	.480	.874	.204	.168	....	..
757	Ústí n/O.	Mar. 23	.473	.207	.455	.219	.458	.646	.102	.117	....	..
758	Skuteč	Apr. 1	.102	.102	.099	....	.087	.135	....	.028	....	..
846	Čáslav	Apr. 15	.372	.158	.153	.158	.371	....	.102	.050	.250[b]	10,
847	Čes. Třebová	Apr. 23	.320	.312	.342	.295	.015	....	.204	.177	.800[b]	32,
848	Humpolec	Apr. 12	.206	.267	.272	.163	.284	.670	.102	.100	.550[b]	22,
849	Chotěboř	Apr. 7	.211	.307	.318	.209	.349	.741	.102	.092	.600[b]	24,
850	Chrudim	Apr. 7	.612	.497	.663	.297	.654	1.691	.306	.299	.750[b]	30,

* Detail of miscellaneous commodities indicated by the following indexes: [b], biscuits; [c], codliver oil; [d], soap. See end of Table 268 (page 537) for complete detail.

CZECHO-SLOVAKIA

Table 268—Continued — Internal Deliveries, PARDUBICE Warehouse

Local Committee (Mistni Komitét)	Date	Commodities in Net Metric Tons of 1,000 Kilograms or 2,204.6 Pounds									
		Flour	Rice	Beans, Peas	Pork Products	Milk Evap.	Milk Cond.	Cocoa	Sugar	Misc.	No. of Biscuits
	1920										
Lanškroun	Apr. 12	.338	.314	.396	.306	1.024	....	.102	.100	.650[b]	26,000
Ledeč	Apr. 15	.192	.174	.152	.153	.807	....	.102	.100	.450[b]	18,000
Litomyšl	Apr. 12	.236	.461	.471	.290	.479	....	.204	.150	.900[b]	36,000
Něm. Brod	Apr. 12	.233	.303	.328	.255	.327	.741	.102	.112	.650[b]	26,000
Pardubice	Apr. 17	.128	.104	.187	.157	.807	....	.102	.100	.450[b]	18,000
Pelhřimov	Apr. 20	.384	.392	.446	.295	1.243	....	.102	.200	.800[b]	32,000
Polička	Apr. 12	.285	.315	.271	.180	.349	.665	.204	.115	.600[b]	24,000
Skuteč	Apr. 1	.287	.312	.262	.153	.305	.456	.076	.050	.350[b]	14,000
Ústí n/O.	Apr. 6	.251	.308	.304	.312	.262	.665	.204	.102	.600[b]	24,000
Vys. Mýto	Apr. 12	.414	.446	.471	.232	.501	1.007	.102	.150	.900[b]	36,000
Chotěboř	May 31	.192	.246	.298	.152	.981	....	.204	.118	....	.....
Chrudim	May 26	.256	.351	.366	.280	1.374	....	.204	.145	....	.....
Vys. Mýto	June 2	.392	.520	.512	.342	1.483	....	.204	.145	....	.....
Humpolec	May 26	.256	.286	.311	.146	.916	....	.102	.106	.525[b]	21,000
Lanškroun	June 3	.320	.467	.423	.225	1.177	....	.102	.117	.750[b]	30,000
Litomyšl	June 2	.392	.461	.460	.282	1.352	....	.204	.144	.850[b]	33,000
Něm. Brod	May 6	.264	.329	.329	.198	.329	.741	.137	.114	.650[b]	26,000
Pardubice	May 22	.192	.206	.160	.151	1.046	....	.102	.133	....	.....
Polička	May 31	.256	.280	.321	.155	1.112	....	.102	.120	....	.....
Skuteč	May 31	.128	.146	.236	.159	.632	....	.102	.080	.400[b]	16,000
Čáslav	May 27	.139	.173	.173	.104	.173	.187	.035	.029	....	.....
Ledeč	May 13	.142	.178	.178	.107	.178	.641	.118	.098	.450[b]	18,000
Čes. Třebová	May 20	.256	.395	.355	.158	1.483	....	.204	.173	.800[b]	32,000
Ústí n/O.	May 27	.256	.277	.250	.108	1.134	....	.102	.143	....	.....
Ústí n/O.	May 14	.192	.274	.305	.154	.283	.855	.102	.120	.650[b]	26,000
Čáslav	July 1	....	.163	....	.108	.109	....	....	....	.250[b]	10,000
Chotěboř	July 2	.256	.374	.379	.200	.392	.817	.102	.100	.400[b]	16,000
Polička	July 12	.384	.474	.455	.288	.458	1.121	.204	.168	....	.....
Vys. Mýto	July 8	.256	.368	.370	.153	.371	.627	.102	.096	.600[b]	24,000
Ledeč	July 7	.128	.153	.190	.096	.174	.646	.102	.095	.900[b]	36,000
Litomyšl	July 8	.384	.475	.510	.300	.523	.912	.102	.138	1.700[b]	68,000
Pardubice	July 8	.384	.548	.560	.313	.567	1.349	.306	.200	1.650[b]	66,000
Skuteč	July 2	.256	.209	.210	.108	.196	.513	.102	.076	.400[b]	16,000
Něm. Brod	July 2	.384	.515	.515	.324	.501	1.026	.204	.150	1.300[b]	52,000
Humpolec	July 2	.192	.268	.283	....	.305	.513	.102	.100	.550[b]	22,000
Chrudim	July 2	.448	.571	.560	.317	.545	1.349	.204	.200	1.100[b]	44,000
Lanškroun	June 10	.316	.416	.456	.314	.458	.741	.102	.114	.750[b]	30,000
Čes. Třebová	June 15	.256	.359	.334	.161	.349	1.140	.204	.168	.800[b]	32,000
	1919										
Rychnov	June 24	.805	.202	.202	.805	.805	1.442	.291	....	....	.....
Hradec Králové	July 5	.978	.244	.244	.977	.978	1.641	.331	....	....	.....
Rychnov	July 24	.805	.202	.202	.805	.805	2.008	.291	....	....	.....
Rychnov	Aug. 25	.614	.157	.157	.614	.614	2.343	.474	....	.100[c]	.....
Pelhřimov	Mar. 9	.704	.450	.702	.496	.698	1.083	.204	.250	....	.....
Polička	June 30	.820	.205	.205	.899	1.609	1.393	.262	....	....	.....
Polička	July 8	.820	.205	.205	.820	.733	.551	.062	....	....	.....
Něm. Brod	July 12	2.269	.567	.567	2.305	2.269	....	....	....	....	.....
Polička	July 15	....	....	....	....	.739	3.306	.312	....	....	.....
Něm. Brod	Sept. 15	.756	.189	.189	.757	.756	2.219	.464	....	.100[c]	.....
Polička	Sept. 27	.547	.137	.137	.547	.547	1.860	.376	....	....	.....
Pardubice	Oct. 6	.576	.143	.143	.576	.573	2.465	.507	....	.100[c]	.....
Chrudim	Nov. 7	.416	.104	.104	.416	.416	1.425	.288	....	....	.....
Ústí n/O.	Dec. 4	....	.180	.180	.114	.176	.266	.050	....	....	.....
Něm. Brod	Dec. 10	.889	.900	.900	.622	.933	1.927	.408	....	....	.....
Humpolec	Dec. 16	....	.585	.585	.434	.589	1.045	.204	....	....	.....
Čáslav	Dec. 17	....	.315	.315	.301	.327	.342	.102	....	....	.....
	1920										
Čes. Třebová	Jan. 1	.768	.405	.810	.634	.807	1.140	.306	.250	....	.....
Německý Brod	Jan. 8	....	.900	.900	.675	.938	1.438	.408	....	....	.....

[*Continued on next page*]

CZECHO-SLOVAKIA

Table 268—*Continued* Internal Deliveries, PARDUBICE Warehouse

Receipt No.	Local Committee (Mistni Komitét)	Date	Flour	Rice	Beans, Peas	Pork Products	Milk: Evap.	Milk: Cond.	Cocoa	Sugar	Misc.	No. of Biscuits
			Commodities in Net Metric Tons of 1,000 Kilograms or 2,204.6 Pounds									
Series 1		1920										
2259	Chotěboř	Jan. 15	.666	.666	.666	.466	.666	.826	.165	.165	....	...
2260	Čáslav	Jan. 18	.320	.135	.315	.305	.327	.247	.102	.100	....	...
2261	Humpolec	Jan. 19	.576	.270	.540	.457	.545	.968	.204	.260	....	...
2262	Chrudim	Jan. 20	.386	.096	.096	.386	.286	.771	.024	....	....	...
2263	Německý Brod	Jan. 18	.896	.450	.900	.644	.894	1.235	.204	.250	....	...
2264	Pardubice	Jan. 26	.704	.360	.720	.548	.720	1.729	.408	.350	....	...
2265	Polička	Jan. 18	.547	.137	.137	.547	.547	1.860	.376	....	....	...
2266	Čes. Třebová	Feb. 17	.512	.262	.523	.139	.501	.665	.037	.200	1.229[b]	49,1
2267	Lanškroun	Feb. 21	.730	.365	.730	.509	.730	1.048	.209	.209	....	...
2268	Čáslav	Feb. 28	.192	.090	.158	.144	.153	.266	.510	.500	....	...
2269	Něm. Brod	Mar. 3	.300	....	.048	.067	.131	.304	.020	.100	....	...
2270	Chotěboř	Mar. 7	.464	.232	.464	.324	.464	.597	.120	.120	....	...
2271	Humpolec	Mar. 10	.448	.225	.417	.299	.414	.703	.102	.150	....	...
2272	Něm. Brod	Mar. 10	.320	....	.045	.067	.131	.304	....	.100	....	...
2273	Čes. Třebová	Mar. 12	.490	.252	.493	.312	.480	.874	.204	.168	1.050[b]	42,0
2274	Něm. Brod	Mar. 2	.916	....	....	....	....	....	....	....	....	...
2466	Chotěboř	Aug. 27	.192	.245	.225	.144	....	....	.102	.050	.350[b]	13,0
2467	Lanškroun	Sept. 1	.256	.285	.300	.180	....	....	.102	.100	.550[b]	21,0
2468	Čes. Třebová	Sept. 10	.128	.142	.142	.099	.153	....	.102	.100	.400[b]	16,0
2469	Čáslav	Aug. 12	.041	.051	.051	.031	.051	.034	.008	.007	.075[b]	3,0
2470	Něm. Brod	Aug. 18	.384	.523	.503	.324	....	.798	.204	.160	.950[b]	37,0
2471	Chrudim	Aug. 13	.448	.662	.549	.324	.567	....	.204	.205	1.100[b]	44,0
2472	Vys. Mýto	Aug. 17	.384	.539	.518	.288	.371	.950	.204	.195	1.000[b]	40,0
2473	Skuteč	Aug. 27	.128	.170	.170	.108	....	....	.102	.100	.350[b]	14,0
2474	Humpolec	Aug. 18	.256	.305	.318	.180	....	.475	.102	.098	.550[b]	23,0
2475	Litomyšl	Aug. 14	.320	.436	.454	.252	.436	.590	.102	.110	.750[b]	30,0
2476	Pardubice	Aug. 12	.320	.397	.404	.252	.392	....	.204	.137	.750[b]	30,0
2477	Polička	Aug. 24	.320	.370	.404	.252	....	.437	.204	.127	1.650[b]	66,0
2478	Čes. Třebová	Aug. 30	.256	.363	.362	.216	.327	.912	.204	.176	.800[b]	32,0
2479	Ústí n/O.	Aug. 18	.256	.306	.330	.180	....	1.140	.204	.135	.650[b]	26,0
2594	Chrudim	Feb. 18	....	....	....	....	....	....	....	....	.240[d]	...
2614	Humpolec	Aug. 10	....	....	....	....	....	....	....	....	.025[d]	...
2615	Humpolec	Aug. 10	....	....	....	....	....	....	....	....	.025[d]	...
2616	Humpolec	Aug. 10	....	....	....	....	....	....	....	....	.025[d]	...
2620	Pardubice	Aug. 12	....	....	....	....	....	....	....	....	.250[d]	..
2621	Pardubice	Aug. 12	....	....	....	....	....	....	....	....	.075[d]	..
2622	Helice-Pardubice	Aug. 12	....	....	....	....	....	....	....	....	.025[d]	..
2623	Ústí n/O.	Aug. 18	....	....	....	....	....	....	....	....	.175[d]	..
2624	Ústí n/O.	Aug. 18	....	....	....	....	....	....	....	....	.025[d]	..
2625	Litomyšl	Aug. 17	....	....	....	....	....	....	....	....	.025[d]	..
2626	Litomyšl	Aug. 17	....	....	....	....	....	....	....	....	.175[d]	..
2631	Čes. Třebová	July 30	....	....	....	....	....	....	....	....	.030[d]	..
2634	Čes. Třebová	July 30	....	....	....	....	....	....	....	....	.330[d]	..
2640	Rychnov n/K.	Aug. 11	....	....	....	....	....	....	....	....	.025[d]	..
2641	Telecí. Polička	Aug. 24	....	....	....	....	....	....	....	....	.025[d]	..
2642	Polička	Aug. 24	....	....	....	....	....	....	....	....	.025[d]	..
2643	Polička	Aug. 24	....	....	....	....	....	....	....	....	.200[d]	..
2650	Humpolec	Aug. 10	....	....	....	....	....	....	....	....	.050[d]	..
Series 2		1921										
92	Pardubice	Apr. 29	2.432	.658	.817	.425	1.320	....	.174	.760	....	..
93	Ústí n/O.	Apr. 29	1.600	.451	.525	.275	.850	....	.102	.483	....	..
94	Litomyšl	Apr. 18,30	1.324	.364	.452	.250	.720	....	.090	.414	....	..
95	Chrudim	May 5	1.256	.367	.433	.225	.654	....	.080	.383	....	..
96	Čes. Třebová	Apr. 29	1.792	.529	.630	.325	.960	....	.102	.528	....	..
97	Lanškroun	Apr. 30	.896	.276	.315	.150	.480	....	.053	.282	....	..
98	Humpolec	May 5	.321	.366	.200	1.152	.589	....	.080	.345	....	..
99	Vys. Mýto	Apr. 30	1.152	.321	.405	.200	.610	....	.075	.344	....	..
100	Skuteč	May 3	.448	.138	.183	.075	.240	....	.030	.132	....	..
101	Polička	May 3	.832	.227	.276	.150	.458	....	.053	.266	....	..

CZECHO-SLOVAKIA

Table 268—*Concluded* Internal Deliveries, PARDUBICE Warehouse

...pt	Local Committee (Mistni Komitét)	Date	Flour	Rice	Beans, Peas	Pork Products	Milk Evap.	Milk Cond.	Cocoa	Sugar	Misc.	No. of Biscuits
			Commodities in Net Metric Tons of 1,000 Kilograms or 2,204.6 Pounds									
2		1921										
3	Čáslav	Apr. 7	.255	.092	.090	.050	.131	....	.015	.066	....	.....
[illegible]	Pardubice	Apr. 27	.256	.092	.091	.050	.140	....	.018	.081	....	.....
[illegible]	Helice u Pardubice	Apr. 20	.256	.090	.090	.050	.153	....	.018	.081	....	.....
[illegible]	Černá u Ustí n/O.	Apr. 29	.448	.137	.136	.075	.218	....	.027	.132	....	.....
2	Ústí n/O.	Apr. 29	.128	.046	.046	.025	.088	....	.010	.049	....	.....
3	Polička	May 3	.256	.092	.092	.050	.130	....	.015	.067	....	.....
4	Polička	May 3	.256	.092	.091	.050	.130	....	.015	.067	....	.....
5	Luž u Vys. Mýta	Apr. 30	.576	.184	.183	.100	.305	....	.038	.174	....	.....
6	Luž u Vys. Mýta	Apr. 30	.960	.268	.364	.175	.545	....	.078	.311	....	.....
0	Pardubice	July 12	.207	.056	.090	.050	.066	.029	.014	.064	....	.....
1	Pardubice	July 8	.148	.046	.046	.025	.087	....	.010	.050	....	.....
2	Lanškroun	July 15	.098	.027	.033	.017	.053	....	.007	.030	....	.....
3	Litomyšl	July 11	.128	.029	.044	.025	.066	....	.007	.039	....	.....
4	Lanškroun	July 11	.384	.095	.146	.075	.240	....	.025	.113	....	.....
5	Skuteč	July 11	.576	.160	.201	.100	.262	....	.040	.185	....	.....
6	Vys. Mýto	June 28	.320	.091	.092	.050	.175	....	.020	.092	....	.....
7	Humpolec	June 28	1.152	.312	.406	.200	.654	....	.102	.374	....	.....
8	Ústí n/O.	June 28	2.112	.550	.676	.375	1.134	....	.140	.648	....	.....
9	Čes. Třebová	June 28	.448	.137	.136	.075	.240	....	.030	.134	....	.....
1	Lanškroun	June 10	.320	.092	.100	.050	.153	....	.020	.092	....	.....
2	Humpolec	June 7	.192	.046	.063	.025	.109	....	.013	.052	....	.....
3	Polička	June 8	.128	.046	.044	.025	.087	....	.009	.040	....	.....
4	Chrudim	June 10	.384	.117	.137	.075	.218	....	.028	.131	....	.....
5	Vys. Mýto	June 8	.384	.092	.136	.075	.196	....	.026	.120	....	.....
6	Skuteč	June 8	.064	.046	.046	.025	.044	....	.005	.026	....	.....
7	Pardubice	June 10	.832	.231	.272	.150	.436	....	.055	.251	....	.....
8	Litomyšl	June 8	.640	.184	.228	.125	.371	....	.046	.215	....	.....
9	Ústí n/O.	June 8	.512	.138	.181	.100	.284	....	.035	.160	....	.....
0	Čes. Třebová	June 8	.576	.176	.224	.100	.327	....	.040	.184	....	.....
	Total	....	**86.185**	**49.072**	**55.354**	**56.392**	**91.005**	**124.257**	**29.728**	**22.062**	**39.029***	**1,476,160**

Detail of miscellaneous commodity total: [b], weight of 1,476,160 [bisc]uits, 36.979; [c], codliver oil, .300; [d], soap, 1.750.

CZECHO-SLOVAKIA

Table 269 Internal Deliveries from (1) OPAVA (Troppau), (2) MOR. OSTRAVA (Mährisch Ostrav) Warehouses

...ipt ...	Local Committee (Mistni Komitét)	Date	Flour	Rice	Beans, Peas	Pork Products	Milk Evap.	Milk Cond.	Cocoa	Sugar	Misc.*	No. of Biscuits
			Commodities in Net Metric Tons of 1,000 Kilograms or 2,204.6 Pounds									
...es 1		1919										
25	Freiwaldau	Oct. 13	.787	.198	.198	.787	.787	1.113	.225	....	....	.....
73	Mor. Ostrava	Oct. 2	7.752	3.174	....	6.970	7.050	19.022	3.817	....	....	.....
74	Opava	Oct. 14	1.467	.367	.367	1.467	1.467	3.180	.643	....	....	.....
75	Bruntál	Oct. 14	.869	.218	.218	.869	.869	2.544	.514	....	....	.....
76	Jägerndorf	Oct. 1	.878	.219	.219	.878	.878	1.908	.385	....	....	.....
77	Wagstadt	Oct. 1	.400	.100	.100	.400	.400	.795	.161	....	....	.....
73	Mor. Ostrava	Oct. 20	7.200	1.800	1.800	7.200	7.200	21.306	4.301	....	....	.....
74	Jägerndorf	Oct. 24	.878	.219	.219	.878	.878	1.908	.385	....	....	.....
78	Bruntál	Oct. 30	.869	.218	.218	.869	.869	2.544	.514	....	....	.....
76	Frývaldov	Oct. 31	.786	.196	.196	.786	.786	1.113	.224	....	....	.....
77	Frývaldov	Dec. 13	.983	.983	.983	.688	.983	.875	.175	.175	....	.....
78	Krňov	Dec. 5	1.098	1.098	1.098	.769	1.098	1.500	.300	.300	....	.....

* Biscuits.

[*Continued on next page*]

CZECHO-SLOVAKIA

Internal Deliveries, (1) OPAVA (Troppau), (2) MOR. OSTRAVA (Mährisch Ostrav) Warehouses

Table 269—*Continued*

Receipt No.	Local Committee (Mistni Komitét)	Date	Commodities in Net Metric Tons of 1,000 Kilograms or 2,204.6 Pounds									
			Flour	Rice	Beans, Peas	Pork Products	Milk		Cocoa	Sugar	Misc.	No. of Biscuit
							Evap.	Cond.				
Series 1		1919										
379	Bruntál	Dec. 13	1.086	1.086	1.086	.760	1.086	2.000	.400	.400	....	...
483	Opava	Nov. 27	1.832	1.832	1.832	1.283	1.832	2.500	.500	.500	....	...
498	Místek	Dec. 30	1.236	1.236	1.236	.865	1.236	1.828	.366	.366	....	...
505	Opava	Dec. 2	1.832	1.832	1.832	1.283	1.832	2.500	.500	.500	....	...
		1920										
703	Opava	Mar. 20	1.742	.871	1.742	1.219	1.742	2.354	.471	.471	....	...
704	Mor. Ostrava	Mar. 18	9.270	4.635	9.270	6.489	9.270	16.750	3.350	3.350	24.180	780,0
705	Bílovec	Mar. 12	.500	.250	.500	.350	.500	.625	.125	.125	....	...
706	Frývaldov	Mar. 24	.986	.493	.986	.690	.986	.900	.180	.180	....	...
707	Freudenthal	Mar. 5	.670	.335	.670	.469	.670	1.299	.260	.260	....	...
708	Hlučín	Mar. 2	1.250	.625	1.250	.875	1.250	1.875	.375	.375	....	...
709	Místek	Mar. 13	1.236	.618	1.236	.865	1.236	1.828	.366	.366	3.038	98,0
710	Krňov	Mar. 26	1.098	.549	1.098	.769	1.098	1.500	.300	.300	2.604	84,0
711	Frýdek	Mar. 22	1.391	.696	1.391	.974	1.391	1.500	.300	.300	3.038	98,0
712	Hnojník	Mar. 29	1.075	.538	1.075	.753	1.075	.808	.162	.162	....	...
901	Bílovec	Apr. 24	.336	.420	.420	.252	.420	.546	.101	.084	.650	26,0
902	Bruntál	Apr. 12	.480	.600	.600	.360	.600	1.248	.230	.192	.150	6,0
903	Frýdek	Apr. 27	.816	1.020	1.020	.612	1.020	1.404	.259	.216	1.600	64,0
904	Frývaldov	Apr. 26	.624	.780	.780	.468	.780	.780	.144	.120	1.100	44,0
905	Hnojník	Apr. 27	1.032	1.290	1.290	.774	1.290	1.014	.187	.156	1.700	68,0
906	Krňov	Apr. 26	.576	.720	.720	.432	.720	1.404	.259	.216	1.300	51,0
907	Místek	Apr. 21	.720	.900	.900	.540	.900	1.560	.288	.240	1.500	60,0
908	Mor. Ostrava	Apr. 30	6.024	7.530	7.530	4.578	7.530	16.302	3.010	2.508	13.800	552,0
909	Opava	Apr. 26	1.104	1.380	1.380	.828	1.380	2.028	.374	.312	2.150	86,0
1273	Bílovec	May 17	.336	.420	.420	.252	.420	.546	.101	.084	.650	26,0
1274	Freudenthal	May 15	.480	.600	.600	.360	.600	1.248	.230	.192	1.100	44,0
1275	Frýdek	May 17	.816	1.020	1.020	.612	1.020	1.404	.259	.216	1.600	64,0
1276	Frývaldov	May 25	.624	.780	.780	.468	.780	.780	.144	.120	1.100	44,0
1277	Hlučín	May 11	.960	1.200	1.200	.720	1.200	3.120	.576	.480	2.400	96,0
1278	Hnojník	May 27	1.032	1.290	1.290	.774	1.290	1.014	.187	.156	1.700	68,0
1279	Krňov	May 15	.576	.720	.720	.432	.720	1.404	.259	.216	1.300	51,0
1280	Místek	May 15	.720	.900	.900	.540	.900	1.560	.288	.240	1.500	60,0
1281	Mor. Ostrava	May 31	6.024	7.530	7.530	4.518	7.530	16.302	3.010	2.508	13.800	552,0
1282	Opava	May 17	1.104	1.380	1.380	.828	1.380	2.028	.374	.312	2.200	88,0
1335	Bílovec	June 6	.336	.420	.420	.252	.420	.546	.101	.084	.650	26,0
1336	Freudenthal	June 19	.480	.600	.600	.360	.600	1.248	.230	.192	1.100	44,0
1337	Frýdek	June 24	.816	1.020	1.020	.612	1.020	1.404	.259	.216	1.600	64,0
1338	Frývaldov	June 26	.624	.780	.780	.468	.780	.780	.144	.120	1.100	44,0
1339	Hlučín	June 15	.960	1.200	1.200	.720	1.200	3.120	.576	.480	2.400	96,0
1340	Hnojník	June 30	1.032	1.290	1.290	.774	1.290	1.014	.187	.156	1.700	68,0
1341	Krňov	June 14	.576	.720	.720	.432	.720	1.404	.259	.216	1.250	50,0
1342	Místek	June 24	.720	.900	.900	.540	.900	1.560	.288	.240	1.500	60,0
1343	Mor. Ostrava	June 30	6.024	7.530	7.530	4.518	7.530	16.302	3.010	2.508	13.800	552,0
1344	Opava	June 23	1.104	1.380	1.380	.828	1.380	2.028	.374	.312	2.160	86,4
1700	Mor. Ostrava	Jan. 15	9.000	4.500	9.000	6.300	9.000	16.750	3.350	3.350	....	...
1701	Opava	Jan. 26	1.742	.871	1.742	1.219	1.742	2.354	.477	.471	....	...
1702	Hnojník	Jan. 26	1.200	.600	1.200	.840	1.200	1.000	.200	.200	....	...
1703	Místek	Feb. 9	1.236	.618	1.236	.866	1.236	1.828	.365	.366	....	...
1704	Krňov	Feb. 4	1.638	.545	1.098	.767	1.092	1.500	.300	.390	....	...
1705	Bílovec	Feb. 5	.500	.250	.500	.350	.500	.625	.125	.125	....	...
1706	Opava	Feb. 26	1.742	.871	1.742	1.219	1.742	2.354	.471	.471	....	...
Series 2		1921										
10	Krňov	Apr. 21	1.998	.540	.675	.351	1.080	....	.135	.621	....	...
11	Opava	Apr. 22	2.331	.630	.788	.410	1.260	....	.158	.725	....	...
12	Bílovec	Apr. 22	.666	.180	.225	.117	.360	....	.045	.207	....	...

CZECHO-SLOVAKIA

Internal Deliveries, (1) OPAVA (Troppau), (2) MOR. OSTRAVA (Mährisch Ostrav) Warehouses

Table 269—*Concluded*

eipt o.	Local Committee (Mistni Komitét)	Date	Commodities in Net Metric Tons of 1,000 Kilograms or 2,204.6 Pounds									
			Flour	Rice	Beans, Peas	Pork Products	Milk Evap.	Milk Cond.	Cocoa	Sugar	Misc.	No. of Biscuits
ies 2		1921										
13	Místek	Apr. 18	2.420	.660	.825	.429	1.320	....	.165	.759	....	.....
14	Hlučín	Apr. 18	1.443	.390	.488	.254	.780	....	.098	.449	....	.....
15	Hnojník	Apr. 20	2.775	.750	.938	.488	1.500	....	.188	.863	....	.....
16	Frývaldov	Apr. 20	3.275	.885	1.106	.575	1.770	....	.221	1.018	....	.....
17	Bruntál	Apr. 21	2.553	.690	.863	.449	1.380	....	.173	.794	....	.....
18	Frýdek	Apr. 21	1.776	.480	.600	.312	.960	....	.120	.552	....	.....
19	Vel. Ostrava	Apr. 23	17.682	4.779	5.974	3.106	9.558	....	1.195	5.496	....	.....
48	Orlová	Apr. 23	.111	.030	.038	.020	.060	....	.008	.035	....	.....
49	Mor. Ostrava	Apr. 23	.111	.030	.038	.020	.060	....	.008	.035	....	.....
50	Zábřeh n/O.	Apr. 23	.111	.030	.038	.020	.060	....	.008	.035	....	.....
51	Slezská Ost.	Apr. 23	.092	.025	.031	.016	.050	....	.006	.029	....	.....
52	Karvín	Apr. 23	.078	.021	.026	.014	.042	....	.005	.024	....	.....
53	Vítkovice	Apr. 23	.074	.020	.025	.013	.040	....	.005	.023	....	.....
54	Slezská Ost.	Apr. 27	.130	.035	.044	.023	.070	....	.009	.040	....	.....
55	Slezská Ost.	Apr. 23	.056	.015	.019	.010	.030	....	.004	.018	....	.....
56	Zábřeh n/O.	Apr. 23	.037	.010	.013	.007	.020	....	.003	.012	....	.....
57	Mor. Ostrava	Apr. 23	.030	.008	.010	.005	.016	....	.002	.019	....	.....
58	Marianské Hory	Apr. 23	.163	.044	.055	.029	.088	....	.011	.051	....	.....
59	Mor. Ostrava	Apr. 23	.370	.100	.125	.065	.200	....	.025	.115	....	.....
60	Mor. Ostrava	Apr. 23	1.850	.500	.625	.325	1.000	....	.125	.575	....	.....
61	Opava	Apr. 22	.185	.050	.063	.033	.100	....	.013	.058	....	.....
62	Opava	Apr. 22	.555	.150	.188	.098	.300	....	.038	.173	....	.....
63	Krňov	Apr. 21	.370	.100	.125	.065	.200	....	.025	.115	....	.....
64	Würbenthal	May 12	.148	.040	.050	.026	.080	....	.010	.046	....	.....
65	Würbenthal	May 12	.074	.020	.025	.013	.040	....	.005	.023	....	.....
66	Einsiedel	May 12	.155	.042	.053	.027	.084	....	.011	.048	....	.....
67	Opava	May 25	.592	.160	.200	.104	.320	....	.040	.184	....	.....
488	Hnojník	July 26	.296	.080	.100	.052	....	.125	.020	.092	....	.....
489	Hlučín	July 26	1.924	.635	.535	.338	....	1.040	.130	.598	....	.....
490	Krňov	July 28	2.664	1.070	.550	.468	1.440	....	.180	.898	....	.....
491	Místek	July 26	.444	.120	.150	.078	....	.240	.030	.138	....	.....
492	Mor. Ostrava	July 25	.340	....	.207	.060	....	.184	.023	.106	....	.....
493	Mor. Ostrava	July 25	5.506	....	3.348	.967	.574	2.402	.372	1.711	....	.....
494	Slezská Ostrava	July 25	.611	....	.371	.107	....	.330	.041	.190	....	.....
495	Opava	July 2	.148	.090	....	.026	.080	....	.010	.046	....	.....
496	Frýdek	July 26	.770	.208	.260	.135	....	.416	.052	.239	....	.....
497	Frýdek	July 26	.059	.016	.020	.010	....	.032	.004	.018	....	.....
498	Frývaldov	June 18	3.848	1.520	.820	.676	2.080	....	.260	1.196	....	.....
499	Bruntál	June 28	3.108	1.260	.630	.546	1.680	....	.210	.966	....	.....
500	Bílovec	June 30	.178	.108	....	.031	.096	....	.012	.055	....	.....
501	Bílovec	June 30	.888	.335	.205	.156	.480	....	.060	.276	....	.....
617	Hnojník	June 10	1.387	.375	.469	.244	.750	....	.094	.431	....	.....
618	Mor. Ostrava	June 15	8.841	5.376	....	1.553	4.779	....	.597	2.748	....	.....
619	Krňov	June 10	.999	.270	.338	.176	.540	....	.068	.311	....	.....
620	Bruntál	June 11	1.276	.345	.431	.224	.690	....	.086	.397	....	.....
621	Frývaldov	June 11	1.638	.443	.553	.288	.885	....	.111	.509	....	.....
622	Opava	June 11	1.110	.300	.375	.195	.600	....	.075	.345	....	.....
623	Místek	June 13	.440	.550	.286	1.628	.880	....	.110	.506	....	.....
624	Frýdek	June 13	.888	.240	.300	.156	.480	....	.060	.276	....	.....
625	Bílovec	June 14	.333	.090	.113	.058	.180	....	.023	.104	....	.....
626	Opava	June 16	.666	.180	.225	.117	.360	....	.045	.207	....	.....
627	Hlučín	June 18	.962	.260	.325	.169	.520	....	.065	.299	....	.....
	Total	....	**194.820**	**104.246**	**118.542**	**95.500**	**151.223**	**212.353**	**45.892**	**52.399**	**111.420***	**4,200,400**

* Weight of 4,200,400 biscuits.

CZECHO-SLOVAKIA

Internal Deliveries from MUKAČEVO (Munkács) Warehouse

Table 270

Receipt No.	Local Committee (Mistni Komitét)	Date	Commodities in Net Metric Tons of 1,000 Kilograms or 2,204.6 Pounds										
			Flour	Rice	Beans, Peas	Corn Grits	Pork Products	Milk: Evap.	Milk: Cond.	Cocoa	Sugar	Misc.*	Number of Biscuits
Series 1		1920											
1707	Komluš-Volovica	June 14	.033	....	.042	.033	.025	.325	....	.017	.028	.090[bf]	3,0
1708	Bogorevica	June 14	.026	....	.032	.033	.018	.275	....	.015	.025	.078[bf]	2,5
1709	Verecki	June 16	.065	....	.090	.082	.050	.613	....	.030	.050	.165[bf]	5,7
1710	Mukačevo	June 17	....	....	.050	.033	....	....	....	....	....	.083[bf]	3,0
1711	N. Verecka	June 16	.285	....	.370	.343	.213	2.240	....	.102	.170	.650[bf]	22,7
1712	Midanice	June 16	.050	....	.065	.060	.037	.388	....	.018	.030	.115[bf]	4,0
1713	V. Vyznica	June 21	.105	....	.137	.126	.079	.801	....	.036	.060	.200[b]	8,2
1714	Rozvigovo, Podmonastir	June 23	.158	....	.205	.190	.118	2.290	....	.081	.135	.480[bdf]	14,6
1715	Lalovo	June 23	.018	....	.023	.021	.013	.150	....	.008	.013	.042[bf]	1,5
1716	Baranka	June 24	.020	....	.026	.024	.015	.225	....	.012	.020	.055[bf]	2,0
1717	Kušnice	June 24	.030	....	.039	.036	.022	.338	....	.018	.030	.080[bf]	3,0
1718	Bogorevica	June 26	.019	....	.025	.023	.014	.061	....	....	....	.032[bdf]	9
1719	Luka u Bilki	June 26	....	....	....	....	....	.005	.005	.001	.005	.001[d]	...
1720	Mukačevo	June 26	.010	....	....	....	....	....	....	.001	.005	....	...
1721	Lisičevo	June 24	.038	....	.047	.045	.028	.425	....	.023	.038	.105[bf]	3,7
1722	Suzkovo	June 27	.025	....	.033	.032	.019	.138	....	.005	.008	.043[bf]	1,6
1723	Mukačevo	June 30	.100	....	.130	.131	.075	.901	....	.045	.075	.250[bf]	8,7
1724	Mukačevo	June 30	.087	....	.054	.065	.047	....	....	.003	.017	.140[bf]	5,2
1725	Mukačevo	June 28	....	....	....	....	....	.375	....	.027	.050	.050[b]	2,2
1726	Mukačevo	June 27	.320	....	.400	.386	....	2.328	....	.108	.180	.675[bf]	25,0
1727	Pistrlajovo	June 24	.028	....	.036	.033	.021	.175	....	.008	.013	.055[bf]	2,0
1728	Brestov	July 2	.035	....	.046	4.896	.027	.238	....	.009	.015	.072[bf]	2,5
1729	Mukačevo	July 3	....	....	....	....	....	4.800	....	.100	....	.250[b]	10,0
1730	Ilnica	June 30	.100	....	.135	.131	.089	.701	....	.030	.050	.230[bf]	7,5
1731	B. Remete	July 5	.035	....	.046	.049	.027	.225	....	.009	.015	.062[b]	2,5
1732	Pudhorod	July 7	.060	....	.062	.082	.045	.363	....	.014	.023	.100[b]	4,1
1733	Klačanovo	July 7	.058	....	.078	.065	.043	.397	....	.018	.030	.100[b]	4,3
1734	Lohovo	July 7	.034	....	.038	.049	.026	.172	....	.005	.009	.125[b]	2,8
1735	Dunkovici	July 7	.035	....	.046	.049	.026	.400	....	.021	.035	.080[b]	3,5
1736	Svaljava	July 7	.525	....	.675	.669	.380	3.593	....	.155	.257	.950[b]	38,1
1737	Perečín	July 9	.693	....	.901	.914	.573	5.155	....	.230	.382	1.350[b]	54,0
1738	Mukačevo	July 12	.063	....	....	....	....	....	.048	.010	.010	....	...
1739	Mukačevo	July 12	....	....	....	....	....	.600	....	.042	.070	.106[bd]	3,5
1740	Beregsazs	July 7	.233	....	.303	.147	.175	.652	.750	.053	.044	.400[b]	16,0
1741	V. Berezná	July 9	.557	....	.720	.702	.539	3.529	....	.136	.228	1.000[b]	40,0
1742	Užhorod	July 9	....	....	.500	.506	....	....	....	....	....	....	...
1743	Verecki	July 12	.282	....	.365	.372	.197	2.214	....	.102	.168	.550[b]	22,6
1744	Komluš	July 19	.049	....	.123	....	.037	.494	....	.025	.021	.125[b]	4,9
1745	Mukačevo	July 20	....	....	....	....	....	.164	....	.030	.025	.062[b]	2,5
1746	Silce	July 20	.042	....	.105	....	.031	.101	....	.009	.008	.062[b]	2,8
1747	Lalovo	July 28	.022	....	.054	....	.016	.098	....	.009	.008	.052[bd]	1,8
1748	Polanka	July 28	.120	....	.299	....	.090	.299	....	.028	.023	.200[b]	8,2
1749	Kivjazd	July 19	.056	....	.140	....	.042	.480	....	.024	.020	.127[bd]	4,8
1750	Pudhorod	July 23	.048	....	.135	....	.036	.125	....	.012	.010	.100[b]	4,0
1751	V. Vyznica	July 19	.138	....	.347	....	.104	1.056	....	.017	.039	.275[b]	10,8
1752	Pistrlajovo	July 19	.036	....	.090	....	.027	.225	....	.009	.015	.062[b]	2,5
1753	V. Berezná	July 23	.335	....	.855	....	.337	.867	....	.083	.070	.600[b]	24,0
1754	Bogorevica	July 29	.045	....	.112	....	.034	.350	....	.017	.014	.085[b]	3,6
1755	Midanice	July 10	.075	.090	.098	....	.057	.593	....	2.750	.045	.175[b]	7,1
1756	N. Verecka	Apr. 16	.510	.500	.450	....	.396	.392	.476	.100	.100	.872[bf]	30,0
1757	Volovoji	Apr. 16	.510	.500	.450	....	.380	.392	.476	.100	.100	.870[bf]	30,0
1758	Bogorevica	Apr. 21	....	.060	.060	....	.030	.044	.191	.480	.030	.165[bf]	6,0
1759	Beregsazs	Apr. 26	.480	.250	.500	....	.170	.392	.476	.100	.100	.800[bf]	30,0

* Detail of miscellaneous commodities indicated by the following indexes: [b], biscuits; [d], soap; [f], salt. See end of Table 270 (page 541) for complete detail.

CZECHO-SLOVAKIA

Internal Deliveries, MUKAČEVO (Munkács) Warehouse

Table 270—*Continued*

Receipt No.	Local Committee (Mistni Komitét)	Date	Commodities in Net Metric Tons of 1,000 Kilograms or 2,204.6 Pounds										
			Flour	Rice	Beans, Peas	Corn Grits	Pork Products	Milk		Cocoa	Sugar	Misc.	Number of Biscuits
								Evap.	Cond.				
Series 1		1920											
760	Dolha	Apr. 26	.240	.250	.450	....	.150	.327	.381	.100	.100	.750[b]	30,000
761	Kivjazd.	Apr. 28	....	.060	.060	....	.030	.044	.076	.010	.010	.150[b]	6,000
762	V. Berezná	May 3	.480	.900	.765	....	.390	1.481	....	.200	.200	1.250[b]	50,000
763	Perečín	May 3	.465	.750	.675	....	.340	.697	.572	.100	.100	.300[bf]	4,200
764	Silce	May 6	.030	.035	.035	....	.025	.065	....	.008	.050	.080[bf]	2,000
765	Svaljava	May 7	.480	.700	.657	....	.300	1.089	....	.100	.300	1.200[bf]	40,000
766	Bogorevica	May 7	.090	.100	.045	....	.030	.044	....	.010	....	....	.....
767	Midanice	May 11	.060	.100	.050	....	.025	.044	....	....	....	.015[f]	.....
768	Mukačevo	May 11	.060	....	....	....	....	....	....	.030	....	.167[bf]	6,000
769	Mukačevo	May 11	.060	.100	....	....	....	....	....	.020	.100	.167[bf]	6,000
770	Kivjazd	May 12	.020	.050	.050	....	....	.044	....	.013	.012	.015[f]	.....
771	Palanka	May 12	.050	.050	.050	....	....	.174	....	.020	.020	.115[bf]	4,000
772	Mukačevo	May 17	....	....	....	....	....	....	.191	.034	.028	.100[b]	4,000
773	Midanice	May 17	....	....	....	....	....	....	....	.016	.027	.050[b]	2,000
774	Komluš	May 26	.032	.039	.042	....	.025	.152	....	.017	.028	.100[bf]	2,750
775	Bogorevica	May 26	....	....	....	....	....	.044	....	....	....	....	.....
776	Pistrlajovo	May 26	.022	.027	.030	....	.017	.054	....	.005	.008	.037[bf]	1,500
777	Mukačevo	May 29	....	....	....	....	.025	.130	.019	....	.034	....	.....
778	Dunkovice	June 5	.035	....	.091	....	.026	.185	....	.021	.035	.085[b]	3,500
779	Mukačevo	June 5	....	....	....	....	....	....	....	.012	.010	....	.....
780	Svdljava	June 5	.361	....	.450	.408	.251	1.023	....	.100	.160	.600[b]	24,000
781	Kerecká	June 5	.100	....	.250	....	.075	.327	....	.030	.025	.185[b]	7,500
782	Berezinka	June 5	.075	....	.200	....	.105	.383	....	.030	.025	.150[b]	6,500
783	Beregsazs	June 6	.050	....	.045	.050	.027	.144	....	....	....	.050[b]	2,000
784	Palanka	June 6	.065	....	.085	.080	.050	.174	....	.015	.025	.085[b]	4,500
785	Lohová	June 7	.013	....	.017	.015	.009	.044	....	.003	.005	.027[bf]	875
786	Lalovo	June 7	.013	....	.016	.015	.010	.044	....	.005	.008	.027[bf]	1,000
787	Mukačevo	June 8	.110	....	.143	.132	....	.348	....	.033	.055	.203[bf]	8,250
788	Breštov	June 9	.023	....	.029	.033	.017	.065	....	.075	.013	.052[bf]	1,750
789	Mukačevo	June 10	.092	....	....	....	.070	....	....	....	.025	.002[b]	.....
790	Podhorod	June 11	.040	....	.052	....	.030	.109	.019	.009	.015	.075[bf]	2,750
791	Dubina	June 11	.030	....	.039	.036	.023	.065	....	.003	.005	.052[bf]	1,750
792	Mukačevo	June 11	.073	....	.101	....	.036	.174	....	.020	....	.110[bf]	4,000
793	Kivjazd	June 11	.035	....	.046	.042	.026	.300	....	.015	.025	.085[bf]	3,000
794	Rozvigovo	June 12	.100	....	.130	.131	.075	....	....	.030	.050	.195[bf]	7,500
795	Silce	June 12	.136	....	.170	.164	.100	.776	....	.030	.050	.240[bf]	9,250
796	Perečín	June 12	.700	....	.910	.832	.525	5.107	....	.235	.362	.850[bf]	28,000
797	V. Berezná	June 12	.470	....	.380	.272	....	1.740	....	....	.200	.350[bf]	10,000
798	Beregsazs	June 12	.187	....	.244	.228	.140	1.040	....	.036	.060	.350[bf]	12,375
Series 2		1921											
168	Mukačevo	Apr. 12	....	10.010	....	....	....	....	....	....	....	....	.....
169	Mukačevo	Apr. 12	....	....	....	....	....	10.015	....	....	....	....	.....
170	Mukačevo	Apr. 13	....	....	10.018	....	....	....	....	....	....	....	.....
171	Mukačevo	Apr. 13	....	....	....	....	....	10.015	....	....	....	....	.....
172	Mukačevo	Apr. 12	30.180	....	....	....	....	....	....	....	....	....	.....
173	Mukačevo	Apr. 15	....	....	....	....	....	....	....	6.120	....	....	.....
174	Mukačevo	May 1	....	....	....	....	10.000	....	....	....	....	....	.....
175	Mukačevo	May 5	10.035	....	....	....	....	....	....	....	....	10.000[b]	400,000
176	Mukačevo	May 7	....	15.002	....	....	....	....	....	....	....	....	.....
177	Mukačevo	May 9	....	....	....	....	....	10.015	....	....	....	....	.....
178	Mukačevo	May 9	10.050	....	....	....	....	....	....	....	....	....	.....
179	Mukačevo	May 11	10.000	....	....	....	....	....	....	....	....	....	.....
180	Mukačevo	July 19	....	....	....	....	....	....	....	....	1.100	....	.....
	Total	....	**71.655**	**29.573**	**25.862**	**12.765**	**17.680**	**87.646**	**3.680**	**12.790**	**6.186**	**31.665***	**1,201,955**

* Detail of miscellaneous commodities total: [b], weight of 1,201,955 scuits, 29.958; [d], soap, .133; [f], salt, 1.574.

CZECHO-SLOVAKIA

Internal Deliveries from HRADEC KRÁLOVÉ Warehouse

Table 271

Receipt No.	Local Committee (Mistní Komitét)	Date	Commodities in Net Metric Tons of 1,000 Kilograms or 2,204.6 Pounds									
			Flour	Rice	Beans, Peas	Pork Products	Milk		Cocoa	Sugar	Misc.*	No. of Biscuit
							Evap.	Cond.				
Series 1		1919										
51	Hradec Králové	Sept. 5	.652	.163	.163	.652	.652	1.237	.254	....	....	...
52	Náchod	Sept. 5	1.520	.380	.380	1.520	1.520	2.776	.560	....	....	...
53	Nové Město	Sept. 7	.520	.130	.130	.522	.520	1.235	.249	....	....	...
54	Trutnov	Sept. 10	1.900	.475	.475	1.903	1.900	3.045	.615	....	....	...
55	Vrchlabí	Sept. 12	1.280	.319	.320	1.287	1.280	2.355	.475	....	....	...
56	Kralové Dvůr	Sept. 13	.686	.172	.172	.687	.686	1.205	.243	....	....	...
156	Broumov	Oct. 17	.855	.131	.131	.858	.855	2.082	.420	....	....	...
157	Žamberk	Oct. 17	.960	.340	.340	1.359	1.360	2.715	.548	....	....	...
310	Broumov	Nov. 9	.855	.131	.131	.856	.855	2.082	.420	....	....	...
311	Dvůr Králové	Nov. 15	.686	.172	.172	.688	.686	1.205	.243	....	....	...
312	Králové Hradec	Nov. 15	.652	.163	.163	.652	.652	1.237	.250	....	....	...
313	Náchod	Nov. 21	1.520	.380	.380	1.523	1.520	2.776	.560	....	....	...
314	Nové Město	Nov. 8	.934	.234	.234	.934	.934	2.253	.455	....	....	...
315	Trutnov	Nov. 15	1.902	.476	.476	1.903	1.902	3.037	.613	....	....	...
316	Vrchlabí	Nov. 9	1.280	.320	.320	1.280	1.280	2.355	.475	....	....	...
317	Žamberk	Nov. 7	1.360	.340	.340	1.360	1.360	2.716	.548	....	....	...
318	Žamberk	Nov. 7	.120	.120	.120	.120	.120	.420	.060	....	....	...
428	Vrchlabí	Dec. 12	1.600	1.600	1.600	1.120	1.600	1.851	.370	.370	....	...
429	Hradec Králové	Dec. 10	....	.069	.815	.561	.807	.969	.200	.195	....	...
430	Žamberk	Dec. 11	1.700	1.700	1.700	1.176	1.700	2.128	.400	.426	....	...
431	Kralové Dvůr	Dec. 11	.988	.988	.988	.705	.981	1.064	.200	.211	....	...
432	Rychnov n/Kněžnou	Dec. 11	.795	.795	.795	.561	.785	1.919	.400	.384	....	...
433	Náchod	Dec. 12	1.900	1.900	1.900	1.320	1.897	2.185	.400	.437	....	...
434	Nové Město	Dec. 11	.650	.650	.650	.468	.654	.969	.200	.194	....	...
435	Trutnov	Dec. 11	2.378	2.378	2.378	1.677	2.376	2.394	.500	.478	....	...
		1920										
735	Žamberk	Mar. 31	.490	.245	.495	.363	.501	.608	.100	.121	....	...
736	Vrchlabí	Mar. 30	.216	.108	.225	.142	.218	.228	.100	.046	....	...
737	Trutnov	Mar. 30	.433	.217	.450	.250	.436	.437	.100	.088	....	...
738	Rychnov	Mar. 31	.439	.219	.450	.436	.248	.969	.200	.195	....	...
739	Náchod	Mar. 31	.775	.388	.765	.564	.785	1.026	.200	.207	....	...
740	Nové Město	Mar. 31	.363	.181	.360	.310	.370	.399	.100	.080	....	...
741	Hradec Králové	Mar. 29	.128	.332	.135	.150	.131	.190	.100	.039	....	...
742	Dvůr Králové	Mar. 30	.245	.122	.225	.153	.239	.361	.100	.074	....	...
743	Broumov	Mar. 20	.263	.132	.270	.135	.261	.342	.100	.067	....	...
916	Broumov	Apr. 13	.856	1.070	1.080	.732	1.068	2.090	.400	.322	....	...
917	Dvůr Králové	May 3	.557	.697	.675	.473	.697	1.273	.200	.196	1.250[b]	49,6
918	Hradec Králové	Apr. 8	.515	.643	.630	.298	.632	.608	.200	.156	....	...
919	Nové Město	May 5	.824	1.030	1.035	.594	1.024	....	.200	.212	.975[b]	39,0
920	Náchod	May 5	.849	1.061	1.080	.602	1.068	....	.200	.355	....	...
921	Rychnov	May 4	.608	.760	.765	.462	.763	....	.200	.334	1.877[b]	64,0
922	Vrchlabí	May 3	.720	.900	.900	.451	.894	1.786	.300	.274	....	...
923	Trutnov	Apr. 30	.665	.831	.855	.452	.828	2.261	.400	.420	....	...
924	Žamberk	May 4	.646	.810	.810	.531	.806	.551	.200	.221	1.400[b]	53,0
925	Trutnov	Apr. 30	....	....	....	....	....	.475	.100	.072	....	...
1075	Hradec Králové	May 28	.515	.643	.643	.316	1.962	....	.200	.203	....	...
1076	Broumov	May 28	.831	1.070	1.066	.667	3.161	....	.400	.322	....	...
1077	Vrchlabí	May 29	.720	.900	.900	.463	2.681	....	.300	.274	....	...
1078	Nové Město n/Metují	May 28	.827	1.024	1.030	.608	2.441	....	.300	.217	....	...
1079	Dvůr Králové	May 10	.532	.665	.665	.399	.680	1.280	.236	.196	1.175[b]	47,0
1080	Náchod	May 28	.875	1.093	1.093	.606	3.553	....	.500	.379	....	...
1081	Žamberk	May 29	.646	.808	.808	.476	2.419	....	.300	.249	....	...
1082	Trutnov	May 29	.665	.828	.831	.485	3.858	....	.600	.466	2.000[b]	80,0
1083	Rychnov	May 29	.639	.760	.760	.479	2.921	....	.400	.334	1.600[b]	64,0
1317	Rychnov	July 1	.788	.985	.985	....	.981	2.185	.300	.337	....	...
1318	Trutnov	July 5	.758	.948	.948	.494	.937	3.211	.600	.498	....	...

* Detail of miscellaneous commodities indicated by the following indexes: [b], biscuits; [c], codliver oil; [d], soap. See end of Table 271 (page 544) for complete detail.

CZECHO-SLOVAKIA

Internal Deliveries, HRADEC KRÁLOVÉ Warehouse

'able 271—*Continued*

ot	Local Committee (Mistni Komitét)	Date	Flour	Rice	Beans, Peas	Pork Products	Milk Evap.	Milk Cond.	Cocoa	Sugar	Misc.	No. of Biscuits
			Commodities in Net Metric Tons of 1,000 Kilograms or 2,204.6 Pounds									
1		1920										
	Trutnov	July 20	.443	.732	.732	.455	.741	.209	.100	.033	....	.....
	Hradec Králové	July 5	.637	.797	.797	.493	.789	1.311	.300	.203	....	.....
	Nové Město	July 2	.946	1.183	1.183	.640	1.177	1.444	.300	.222	....	.....
2	Náchod	July 3	1.660	2.075	2.075	1.296	2.075	2.869	.500	.440	....	.....
3	Vrchlabí	July 3	.720	.900	.900	.486	.894	1.786	.300	.274	....	.....
4	Broumov	July 2	.879	1.099	1.099	.617	1.090	2.128	.400	.326	....	.....
5	Žamberk	July 1	.853	1.066	1.066	.652	1.068	1.615	.300	.249	....	.....
		1919										
6	Náchod	June 10	1.216	.300	.315	1.200	.926	1.886	.306	....	....	.....
7	Broumov	July 12	1.283	.321	.321	1.287	1.285	1.186	.241	....	....	.....
	Vrchlabí	July 11	1.081	.270	.270	1.017	1.081	....	....	....	....	.....
1	Žamberk	July 11	2.002	.500	.500	2.023	2.004	1.186	.241	....	....	.....
3	Náchod	Aug. 4	1.202	.300	.300	1.197	.571	1.815	.321	....	....	.....
4	Broumov	Aug. 5	1.200	.300	.300	1.174	1.201	1.186	.562	....	....	.....
5	Vrchlabí	Aug. 5	.060	.030	....	.060	.060	....	.199	....	....	.....
6	Žamberk	Aug. 6	1.800	.900	....	1.804	1.793	1.186	.401	....	....	.....
7	Hradec Králové	Sept. 19	....	.163	.163	.652	.652	1.237	.254	....	....	.....
8	Dvůr Králové	Sept. 25	.686	.172	.172	.687	.686	1.205	.243	....	.102[c]	.....
9	Náchod	Sept. 23	1.520	.380	.380	1.520	1.520	2.776	.560	....	....	.....
	Nové Město n/M.	Oct. 24	.520	.130	.130	.522	.520	1.235	.249	....	....	.....
1	Trutnov	Sept. 25	1.900	.475	.475	1.902	1.900	3.645	.615	....	....	.....
2	Nové Město n/M.	Oct. 16	....	.234	.234	.934	.934	2.253	.455	....	....	.....
3	Žamberk	Oct. 17	.960	.340	.340	1.359	1.360	2.715	.548	....	.100[c]	.....
4	Dvůr Králové	Nov. 6	.686	.172	.172	.688	.686	1.205	.243	....	....	.....
5	Hradec Králové	Nov. 4	1.304	.163	.163	.652	.652	1.237	.250	....	....	.....
6	Náchod	Nov. 18	1.520	.380	.380	1.522	1.520	2.776	.560	....	....	.....
7	Město n/M.	Nov. 9	1.454	.234	.234	.934	.934	2.253	.455	....	....	.....
8	Trutnov	Nov. 5	1.902	.476	.476	1.902	1.902	3.037	.613	....	....	.....
9	Žamberk	Nov. 7	1.761	.340	.340	1.361	1.370	2.716	.544	....	....	.....
0	Dvůr Králové	Dec. 8	....	.988	.988	.705	.981	1.064	.200	....	....	.....
1	Hradec Králové	Dec. 10	....	.069	.875	.561	.807	.969	.200	....	....	.....
2	Náchod	Dec. 19	....	....	....	1.320	1.896	2.185	.400	....	....	.....
3	Nové Město n/M.	Dec. 8	....	....	....	.468	.654	.969	.200	....	....	.....
4	Trutnov	Dec. 8	....	2.378	2.378	1.677	2.376	2.394	.500	....	....	.....
5	Vrchlabí	Dec. 8	....	1.600	1.600	1.122	1.591	1.843	.400	....	....	.....
6	Žamberk	Dec. 3	....	....	....	1.176	1.700	2.128	.400	....	....	.....
		1920										
7	Náchod	Jan. 16	1.920	.945	1.890	1.344	1.896	2.166	.400	.437	....	.....
8	Nové Město n/M.	Jan. 16	1.152	.585	1.170	.814	1.155	1.767	.400	.354	....	.....
9	Vrchlabí	Jan 20	1.600	....	....	....	....	....	....	....	....	.....
0	Dvůr Králové	Mar. 3	.704	.340†	.675	.412	.675	1.026	.200	.205	....	.....
5	Hradec Králové	Aug. 12	.637	.355	1.199	.462	1.785	1.007	.300	.203	....	.....
8	Žamberk	Aug. 5	....	....	....	....	....	....	....	....	.025[d]	.....
3	Žamberk	Aug. 5	....	....	....	....	....	....	....	....	.375[d]	.....
4	Žamberk	Aug. 5	....	....	....	....	....	....	....	....	.150[d]	.....
5	Rychnov	Aug. 5	....	....	....	....	....	....	....	....	.375[d]	.....
6	Náchod	Aug. 5	....	....	....	....	....	....	....	....	.750[d]	.....
4	Nové Město n/M.	Aug. 5	....	....	....	....	....	....	....	....	.400[d]	.....
s 2		1921										
0	Vrchlabí	Apr. 29	2.664	.720	.900	.468	1.440	....	.180	.828	....	.....
1	Dvůr Králové	Apr. 27	2.997	.810	1.013	.528	1.620	....	.204	.932	....	.....
2	Nové Město	Apr. 29	2.220	.600	.750	.391	1.200	....	.150	.690	....	.....
3	Žamberk	May 7	1.332	.360	.450	.231	.720	....	.090	.414	....	.....
4	Broumov	Apr. 29	2.220	.600	.750	.391	1.200	....	.150	.690	....	.....
5	Hradec Králové	Apr. 27	1.887	.510	.637	.330	1.020	....	.127	.586	....	.....
6	Hradec Králové	Apr. 20	.064	....	....	....	.100	....	.190	.102	....	.....

† Corn grits.

[*Concluded on next page*]

CZECHO-SLOVAKIA

Internal Deliveries, HRADEC KRÁLOVÉ Warehouse

Table 271—*Concluded*

Receipt No.	Local Committee (Mistni Komitét)	Date	Commodities in Net Metric Tons of 1,000 Kilograms or 2,204.6 Pounds									
			Flour	Rice	Beans, Peas	Pork Products	Milk		Cocoa	Sugar	Misc.	No. of Biscuits
							Evap.	Cond.				
Series 2		1919										
37	Rychnov n/Kněžnou	May 10	4.399	1.200	.982	.781	1.613	....	.204	1.380	....	...
38	Trutnov	Apr. 27	4.107	1.110	1.380	.720	2.220	....	.278	1.277	....	...
39	Náchod	Apr. 2	4.662	1.260	1.575	.820	2.520	....	.315	1.440	....	...
257	Opočno u Nov. Města	May 11	.259	.070	.088	.044	.140	....	.018	.081	....	...
258	Kostelec n/Orlicí	May 11	.185	.050	.063	.033	.100	....	.013	.058	....	...
259	Hostinné n/L.	May 11	.074	.020	.032	.011	.040	....	.005	.023	....	...
260	Náchod	May 11	.185	.050	.063	.033	.100	....	.013	.058	....	...
261	Žamberk	May 11	.555	.150	.188	.099	.300	....	.038	.173	....	...
450	Nové Město n/M.	July 27	1.095	.296	.370	.154	.268	.323	.074	.340	....	...
451	Josefov	July 29	.065	.018	.022	.012	.036	....	.005	.020	....	...
452	Trutnov	July 26	....	....	....	....	.210	.190	.080	.160	....	...
453	Náchod	July 26	4.144	1.120	1.400	.758	1.100	1.140	.280	1.288	....	...
454	Rychnov n/K.	July 26	.044	.012	.015	.006	.024	....	.003	.014	....	...
455	Rychnov n/K.	July 26	.488	.132	.165	.082	.112	.152	.033	.060	....	...
456	Žamberk	July 26	.444	.120	.150	.158	.145	.095	.030	.138	....	...
457	Trutnov	July 26	.814	.220	.275	.155	.212	.228	.055	.253	....	...
458	Dvůr Králové n/L.	July 27	3.996	1.080	1.350	.764	1.096	1.064	.270	1.242	....	...
		1921										
561	Hrad. Králové	July 19	.994	.255	.319	.149	.510	....	.064	.293	....	...
562	Rychnov n/K.	July 26	....	....	....	....	....	....	.012	....	....	...
563	Náchod	June 11	3.885	1.050	1.313	.681	2.100	....	.263	1.208	....	...
564	Žamberk	June 11	.222	.060	.075	.033	.120	....	.015	.069	....	...
565	Vrchlabí	June 11	.888	.240	.300	.156	.480	....	.060	.276	....	...
566	Broumov	June 11	.740	.200	.250	.162	.400	....	.050	.230	....	...
567	Trutnov	June 11	1.369	.370	.463	.243	.740	....	.093	.426	....	...
568	Dvůr Králové	June 11	.999	.270	.338	.167	.540	....	.068	.311	....	...
	Total	....	**129.286**	**68.641†**	**76.178**	**85.440**	**134.778**	**137.297**	**34.384**	**27.648**	**12.554***	**396,**

† Of this total, 68.301 is rice and .340 is corn grits.

* Detail of miscellaneous commodities total: [b], weight of 396,620 biscuits, 10.277; [c], codliver oil, .202; [d], soap, 2.075.

CZECHO-SLOVAKIA

Internal Deliveries of Soap* from DEJVICE Warehouse, Province of Bohemia

Table 272

Receipt No.	Local Committee (Mistni Komitét)	Date	Soap No. of Pieces	Soap Total Tons
Series 1		1919		
1553	Benešov	Oct. 26	500	.136
1554	Něm Brod	Nov. 10	544	.140
1555	Užhorod	Nov. 19	34	.010
1556	Košice	Nov. 19	34	.010
1557	Benešov	Dec. 11	344	.095
1558	Smíchov	Oct. 20	201	.090
1559	Prague	Oct. 20	50	.012
1560	Prague	Oct. 20	99	.045
1561	Prague	Oct. 20	200	.032
1562	Prague	Oct. 20	100	.045
1563	Prague	Oct. 20	200	.090
1564	Prague VII	Oct. 20	200	.090
1565	Prague	Oct. 20	100	.045
1566	Vinohrady Praha	Oct. 20	100	.045
Series 1		1919		
1567	Prague	Oct. 20	100	.0
1568	Prague	Oct. 20	200	.0
1569	Prague	Oct. 20	198	.0
1570	Prague	Oct. 20	100	.0
1571	Prague VII	Oct. 20	100	.0
1572	Prague	Oct. 20	200	.0
1573	Prague	Oct. 20	200	.0
1574	Hobšovice	Oct. 20	50	.0
1575	Prague	Oct. 17	300	.1
1576	Prague	Oct. 20	100	.0
1577	Prague	Oct. 20	100	.0
1578	Prague	Oct. 20	100	.0
1579	Prague	Oct. 20	200	.0
1580	Prague	Oct. 20	200	.0

* In net metric tons of 1,000 kilograms or 2,204.6 pounds.

CZECHO-SLOVAKIA

Table 272—*Continued*

Internal Deliveries of Soap, DEJVICE Warehouse, Province of Bohemia

[Receip]t	Local Committee (Mistni Komitét)	Date	Soap No. of Pieces	Soap Total Tons	Receipt No.	Local Committee (Mistni Komitét)	Date	Soap No. of Pieces	Soap Total Tons
1		1919			Series 1		1920		
	Prague	Oct. 20	300	.135	1644	Kladno	Jan. ..	2,650	.716
2	Prague	Oct. 20	100	.045	1645	Prosek	Jan. ..	145	.039
3	Prague	Oct. 20	100	.045	1646	Ml. Boleslav	Jan. ..	1,350	.365
4	Prague	Oct. 20	200	.090	1647	Nové Strašecí	Jan. ..	1,850	.500
5	Prague	Oct. 20	100	.045	1648	Rakovník	Jan. ..	1,500	.405
6	Prague	Oct. 20	100	.045	1649	Říčany	Jan. ..	213	.036
7	Břevnov	Oct. 20	50	.009	1650	Prague VII	Jan. ..	2,000	.540
8	Prague	Oct. 20	200	.090	1651	Zlíchov	Feb. 5	111	.030
9	Prague	Oct. 20	300	.135	1652	Krč	Feb. 7	223	.063
0	Prague	Oct. 20	300	.135	1653	Roztoky	Feb. 6	52	.014
2	Prague	Oct. 20	100	.040	1654	Liboce	Feb. 7	98	.027
3	Prague I	Oct. 20	50	.009	1655	Sukdol	Feb. 10	81	.022
4	Prague	Oct. 21	...	.025	1656	Střešovice	Feb. 9	128	.033
5	Prague	Oct. 30	50	.009	1657	Záběhlice	Feb. 11	155	.042
6	Prague III	Oct. 23	100	.025	1658	Radotín	Feb. 11	132	.036
7	Prague II	Oct. 30	50	.009	1659	Keje	Feb. 11	73	.020
8	Prague II	Oct. 30	50	.012	1660	Kobylisy	Feb. 13	211	.057
9	Vinohrady Prague	Oct. 30	....	.017	1661	Žižkov-Prague	Feb. 12	2,006	.542
0	Karlín	Oct. 30	200	.034	1662	Karlín-Prague	Feb. 12	956	.258
1	Prague VII	Oct. 30	200	.034	1663	Prague VII	Feb. 11	1,319	.356
2	Prague II	Oct. 30	50	.009	1664	Podolí	Feb. 12	161	.044
3	Prague II	Oct. 24	....	.017	1665	Hodkovičky	Feb. 13	46	.013
4	Cities in Bohemia	Oct. 24	400	.068	1666	Prague II	Feb. 13	1,403	.379
5	Prague	Oct. 31	350	.060	1667	Vinohrady-Prague	Feb. 13	1,556	.420
6	Chvaly	Oct. 31	100	.017	1668	Chuchle	Feb. 11	74	.016
7	Prague IV	Oct. 24	100	.017	1669	Břevnov	Feb. 14	512	.138
8	Prague	Oct. 17	50	.009	1670	Libeň	Feb. 15	837	.469
9	Prague	Oct. 17	150	.024	1671	Vysočany	Feb. 15	303	.082
0	Prague III	Oct. 17	50	.009	1672	Dejvice	Feb. 18	924	.250
1	Prague	Oct. 18	300	.051	1673	Hlubočepy	Feb. 18	326	.088
		1920							
2	Sedlčany	Jan. 12	350	.095	1674	Hloubětín	Feb. 18	182	.049
3	Prague	Jan. 12	1,300	.351	1675	Modřany	Feb. 19	108	.029
4	Prague	Jan. 12	580	.157	1676	Smíchov	Feb. 20	951	.257
5	Prague	Jan. 12	950	.250	1677	Selce	Feb. 21	55	.015
6	Roudnice	Jan. 10	400	.108	1678	Michle	Feb. 21	221	.060
7	Louny	Jan. 10	400	.108	1679	Prague I	Feb. 24	465	.125
8	Slaný	Jan. 12	1,450	.391	1680	Vokovice	Feb. 24	273	.074
9	Český Brod	Jan. 12	618	.167	1681	Radlice	Feb. 26	296	.080
0	Kolín	Jan. 13	647	.230	1682	Lisoleje	Feb. 26	58	.016
1	Beroun	Jan. 12	800	.216	1683	Kbely	Feb. 27	106	.029
2	Hořovice	Jan. 13	720	.203	1684	Podbaba	Feb. 28	26	.007
3	Radotín	Jan. 14	126	.034	1685	Troj-Podhoř	Feb. 28	119	.033
4	Příbram	Jan. 14	950	.257	1686	St. Strášnice	Feb. 28	259	.070
5	Kutná Hora	Jan. 14	850	.229	1687	Ruzýn	Mar. 1	59	.015
6	Brandýs n/L.	Jan. 13	700	.189	1688	Libšice	Mar. 2	120	.033
7	Mělník	Jan. 15	280	.076	1689	Vinoř	Feb. 26	76	.021
1	Užhorod	Jan. 15	1,417	.315	1690	Dobrovíz	Mar. 3	41	.011
5	Cities supplied from				1691	Bubeneč	Mar. 5	632	.172
	Pardubice	Jan. ..	14,150	3.124	1692	Kladno	Mar. 6	500	.136
6	Hradec Král.	Jan. ..	17,700	3.909	1693	Bráník	Mar. 6	141	.038
7	Jablonec	Jan. ..	21,420	4.755	1694	Malešice	Mar. 6	74	.020
8	Tábor	Jan. ..	11,100	2.437	1695	Prague III	Mar. 20	331	.090
9	Plzeň	Jan. ..	14,736	3.526	1696	Uhřiněves	Feb. 18	123	.033
0	Chomůtov	Jan. ..	35,850	7.893	1697	Kladno	Mar. 22	155	.042
1	Karl. Vary	Jan. ..	27,602	7.540	1698	Košice	Mar. 25	856	.233
2	Kraslice	Jan. ..	120	.032	1699	Hostivař	Mar. 30	173	.047
3	Dobříš	Jan. ..	429	.116					

[*Concluded on next page*]

CZECHO-SLOVAKIA

Internal Deliveries of Soap, DEJVICE Warehouse, Province of Bohemia

Table 272—*Concluded*

Receipt No.	Local Committee (Mistni Komitét)	Date	Soap	
			No. of Pieces	Total Tons
Series 2		1921		
628	Duchcov	May 3	...	.062
629	Chomůtov	May 4	...	.124
630	Duchcov	Feb. 26	...	.204
631	Warnsdorf	May 10	...	.062
632	Most	May 10	...	.155
633	Žatec	May 11	...	.034
634	Ústí n/L.	May 11	...	.186
635	Rumburk	May 10	...	.031
636	Šluknov	May 10	...	.124
637	Teplice	May 11	...	.093
638	Žatec	May 11	...	.031
639	Haber	May 11	...	.031
640	Falknov	Apr. 26	...	.031
641	Mar. Lázně	Apr. 26	...	.025
642	Kadaň	Apr. 26	...	.062
643	Karlovy Vary	Apr. 26	...	.204
644	Tetschen	Feb. 16	...	.034
645	Dux	Mar. 1	...	.186
646	Sušice	May 3	...	.028
647	Plzeň	Apr. 24	...	.056
		1921		
648	Žamberk	May 7	...	.14
649	Rychnov	May 10	...	.05
650	Nové Město	May 4	...	.05
651	Náchod	May 4	...	.05
652	Jablonné	Apr. 25	...	.08
653	Liberec	Apr. 25	...	.08
654	Lomnice n/Pop.	Dec. 15	...	.11
655	Jilemnice	Apr. 25	...	.08
656	Jilemnice	Nov. 23	...	.19
657	Trutnov	June 20	...	.03
658	Olomouc	Feb. 3	...	.05
659	Vys. Mýto	Feb. 9	...	.02
660	Chomůtov	Mar. 1	...	.02
661	Chvaly-Počernice	Mar. 5	...	.02
662	Hořice	Jan. 18	...	.19
663	Prague	Apr. 15	...	.03
664	Prague II	May 28	...	.14
	Total	....	....	**50.70**

CZECHO-SLOVAKIA

Internal Deliveries of Soap* from BRATISLAVA Warehouse for Province of Slovakia

Table 273

Receipt No.	Local Committee (Mistni Komitét)	Date	Soap	
			No. of Pieces	Total Tons
Series 1		1920		
1628	Cities in Slovakia	Jan. ..	1,085	.217
1629	Košice	Jan. ..	1,666	.367
1630	Bardiov	Jan. ..	277	.048
1633	Cities Supplied from Ostrava	Jan. 12	15,000	3.350
667	Rimavská Sobota	Apr. 27	200	.056
668	Slovenská Lup.	Apr. 27	200	.056
669	Báňská Bystrica	Apr. 27	200	.056
670	Bratislava	Apr. 27	200	.056
671	Mukačevo	Apr. 30	...	.136
672	Rozvigovo	Apr. 30	...	.102
673	Užhorod	Apr. 30	...	.136
674	Priachevo	Apr. 30	...	.170
675	Žilina	Apr. 27	...	.055
676	Kremnica	Apr. 17	...	.055
677	Dolný Smokovec	Apr. 27	...	.055
678	Košice	Apr. 27	...	.081
	Total	....	...	**4.996**

* In net metric tons of 1,000 kilograms or 2,204.6 pounds.

CZECHO-SLOVAKIA

Internal Deliveries of Soap* from OPAVA Warehouse for Province of Silesia

Table 274

Receipt No.	Local Committee (Mistni Komitét)	Date	Soap	
			No. of Pieces	Total Tons
Series 1		1920		
1632	Cities supplied from Opava	Jan. 12	17,100	3.7
	Total	....	...	**3.7**

* In net metric tons of 1,000 kilograms or 2,204.6 pounds.

CZECHO-SLOVAKIA

[Int]ernal Deliveries of Soap* from BRNO Warehouse for Province of Moravia

[T]able 275

[Recei]pt [No.]	Local Committee (Mistni Komitét)	Date	Soap No. of Pieces	Soap Total Tons
[Serie]s 1		1920		
4 5 6	Cities supplied from Brno	Jan. .. / Feb. 26 / Nov. 22	41,960 / 200 / 500	9.240 / .056 / .140
	Total	....	...	**9.436**

[*] In net metric tons of 1,000 kilograms or 2,204.6 pounds.

CZECHO-SLOVAKIA

[Int]ernal Deliveries of Special Milk Ration* from BRNO Warehouse for Province of Moravia

[T]able 276

[Recei]pt [No.]	Local Committee (Mistni Komitét)	Date	Milk Total Tons
[Serie]s 2		1921	
[illegible]	Dol. Smokov	June 10	.065
[illegible]	Brno	June 16	.370
[illegible]	Brno	June 15	.261
[illegible]	Prostějov	June 22	.065
[illegible]	Telče	June 10	.065
1	Rýmařov	June 10	.370
2	Olomouc	June 10	.610
3	Beroun	June 10	.174
4	Val. Klobouky	June 10	.065
5	Hranice	June 24	.414
6	Hranice	June 24	.174
7	Přerov	June 10	.501
8	Velké Brno	June 10	3.048
9	Litovel	June 10	.109
0	Rožnov p/Radhoštěm..	June 10	.370
1	Šumperk	June 10	.370
2	Nový Jičín	June 10	.435
3	Šternberg	June 10	.457
4	Mor. Třebová	June 10	.152
5	Třebíč	June 10	.174
6	Boskovice	June 10	.152
7	Jihlava	June 10	.479
8	Frenštát	June 10	.174
9	Prostějov	June 10	.522
0	Zábřeh	June 10	.414
1	Medvědice	June 10	.043
2	Znojmo	June 10	.065
3	Svitavy	June 10	.218
4	Kroměříž	June 10	.109
5	Velké Meziříčí	June 10	.043
6	Holešov	June 10	.152
	Total	....	**10.620**

* In net metric tons of 1,000 kilograms or 2,204.6 pounds.

CZECHO-SLOVAKIA

Internal Deliveries of Special Milk Ration* from OPAVA Warehouse for Province of Silesia

Table 277

Receipt No.	Local Committee (Mistni Komitét)	Date	Milk Total Tons
Series 2		1921	
902	Mor. Ostrava	June 15	.153
903	Opava	May 25	.261
904	Zábřeh n/Odrou	June 16	.043
905	Slezská Ostrava	June 15	.087
906	Karvín	June 15	.109
907	Slezská Ostrava	June 15	.130
908	Orlová	June 15	.153
920	Velká Ostrava	June 15	2.960
921	Opava	May 25	.392
922	Krňov	June 10	.327
923	Hlučín	June 5	.239
924	Bruntál	June 11	.435
925	Hnojník	June 10	.457
926	Frývaldov	June 11	.544
927	Frýdek	June 13	.305
928	Místek	June 13	.414
929	Bílovec	June 14	.109
	Total	....	**7.118**

* In net metric tons of 1,000 kilograms or 2,204.6 pounds.

CZECHO-SLOVAKIA

Internal Deliveries of Special Milk Ration* from DEJVICE Warehouse for Province of Moravia

Table 278

Receipt No.	Local Committee (Mistni Komitét)	Date	Milk Total Tons	Receipt No.	Local Committee (Mistni Komitét)	Date	Milk Total Tons
Series 2		1921		Series 2		1921	
909	Jablonné	May 18	.261	1000	Třeboň	May 9	.262
910	Žamberk	May 20	.044	1001	Kaplice	May 9	.043
911	Vys. Mýto	May 23	1.459	1002	Čes. Budějovice	May 9	.614
912	Karlovy Vary	May 17	.218	1003	Pelhřimov	May 9	.153
913	Teplice	May 13	.218	1004	Týn n/Vlt.	May 9	.044
914	Ústí n/O.	May 13	.130	1005	Čes. Krumlov	May 9	.174
915	Prague VII	May 18	.261	1006	Strakonice	May 30	.152
916	Prague II	May 18	1.089	1007	Líny	May 10	.109
917	Prague II	May 25	1.089	1008	Tachov	May 11	.174
918	Prague II	June 28	.544	1009	Plzeň	May 10	2.221
957	Hlubočepy	June 28	.065	1010	Eisenstein	May 21	.022
958	Prague II	June 22	.566	1011	Rokycany	May 20	.305
959	Košíře	June 15	.523	1012	Sušice	May 25	.479
960	Prague III	June 15	.152	1013	Domažlice	May 30	.152
961	Karlín	June 11	.131	1014	Stříbro	May 30	.152
962	Smíchov	May 25	.522	1015	Nová Kdýně	May 30	.043
963	Vršovice	June 7	.382	1016	Kraslice	May 18	.872
964	Prague I and V	June 4	.305	1017	Karl. Vary	May 18	.675
965	Vinohrady-Prague	May 31	.305	1018	Aš	May 18	1.308
966	Žižkov-Prague	May 31	.610	1019	Přísečnice	May 18	.784
967	Prague VII	May 18	.457	1020	Falknov	May 18	.566
968	Bohnice	May 28	.044	1021	Wildstein	May 18	.327
969	Nusle-Prague	May 28	.305	1022	Loket	May 18	.370
970	Hradec Králové	May 20	.305	1023	Nýdek	May 18	.915
971	Nové Město	May 20	.371	1024	Blatno	May 18	.610
972	Vrchlabí	May 20	.458	1025	Cheb	May 18	.675
973	Dvůr Králové	May 20	.501	1026	Jáchymov	May 18	.239
974	Rychnov n/Kněžnou	May 20	.763	1027	Mar. Lázně	May 18	.218
975	Trutnov	May 20	.698	1028	Výprty	May 18	.610
976	Náchod	May 20	.785	1029	Hořovice	May 14	.065
977	Žamberk	May 20	.218	1030	Příbram	May 14	.305
978	Broumov	May 20	.371	1031	Rakovník	May 14	.109
979	Liberec	June 14	1.632	1032	Louny	May 14	.109
980	Frýdland	May 9	.610	1033	Kladno	May 14	.675
981	Jilemnice	May 9	.457	1034	Beroun-Podčáply	May 14	.153
982	Jablonec	May 10	1.523	1035	Slaný	May 14	.153
983	Semily	May 9	.087	1036	Kutná Hora	May 14	.153
984	Něm. Jablonné	May 9	.261	1037	Stará Paka	May 14	.065
985	Turnov	May 9	.305	1038	Hořice-Miletín	May 14	.174
986	Liberec	May 9	1.632	1039	Nová Paka	May 14	.153
987	Čes. Lípa	May 9	.457	1040	Ml. Boleslav	May 14	.153
988	Lanškroun	May 17	.153	1041	Benešov	May 14	.065
989	Pardubice	May 23	.414	1042	Chomůtov	May 10	.349
990	Vys. Mýto	May 17	.174	1043	Duchcov	May 11	.283
991	Humpolec	May 17	.174	1044	Warnsdorf	May 10	.480
992	Čes. Trebová	May 17	.305	1045	Šluknov	May 10	.654
993	Chrudim	May 17	.196	1046	Teplice	May 11	.806
994	Polička	May 17	.130	1047	Chomutov	May 13	.414
995	Skuteč	May 17	.065	1048	Dečín-Podmokly	May 10	.589
996	Ústí n/O.	May 17	.261	1049	Ústí n/L.	May 11	1.874
997	Litomyšl	May 17	.218	1050	Česká Kamenice	May 10	.305
998	Prachatice	May 9	.087				
999	Jindř. Hradec	May 9	.109		Total	....	**44.754**

* In net metric tons of 1,000 kilograms or 2,204.6 pounds.

CZECHO-SLOVAKIA

Internal Deliveries of Chocolate* from AUSSIG (Ústí n/Labem) Warehouse

Table 279

Receipt No.	Local Committee (Mistni Komitét)	Date	Chocolate Total Tons	Receipt No.	Local Committee (Mistni Komitét)	Date	Chocolate Total Tons
Series 2		1921		Series 2		1921	
	Šternberk Slaný	June 29	.041	736	Sušice	June 29	.040
	Kralupy	June 30	.041	737	Plzeň	June 29	.041
	Březové Hory Příbram	July 1	.041	738	Domažlice	June 29	.041
	Toušeň	July 1	.041	739	Nov. Kdýně	June 29	.041
	Hořovice	July 1	.040	740	Prachatice	June 29	.040
	Příbram	June 30	.041	741	Černovice u Tábora	July 1	.042
	Kolín	July 1	.041	742	Čes. Budějovice	July 1	.041
	Benešov	July 1	.041	743	Vimperk	June 29	.041
	Buštěhrad u Kladna	June 29	.041	744	Čáslav	July 2	.041
	Kralupy	June 30	.041	745	Pardubice	June 30	.040
	Ml. Boleslav	July 1	.041	746	Pardubice	June 30	.041
	Ml. Boleslav	June 30	.041	747	Ústí n/O.	June 30	.041
	Kladno	June 29	.040	748	Polička	June 30	.041
	Nová Paka	June 30	.041	749	Luž	July 1	.041
	Rozdělov u Kladna	June 29	.041	750	Polička	June 30	.040
	Slaný	June 29	.041	751	Ústí n/O.	July 1	.041
	Roudnice n/L.	June 30	.041	752	Luž u Vys. Mýta	July 1	.041
	Roudnice n/L.	June 30	.040	753	Hostinné n/L.	July 1	.041
	Jičín	July 1	.041	754	Nov. Město n/M.	July 1	.041
	Nový Bydžov	July 1	.041	755	Kostelec n/O.	July 1	.040
	Lubno u Rakovníka	June 30	.041	756	Žamberk	July 1	.082
	Nymburk	July 1	.041	757	Náchod	July 1	.041
	Dubá u Kladna	June 29	.040	758	Liberec	June 29	.041
	Ml. Boleslav	July 1	.041	759	Něm. Jablonné	June 29	.040
	Kostelec n/L.	June 30	.041	760	Jilemnice	July 1	.041
	Vrané n/Vlt.	July 1	.041	761	Čes. Lípa	June 29	.041
	Loučeň	July 1	.041	762	Prague II	June 30	.041
	Pokau-Ústí n/L.	June 29	.040	763	Prague	June 30	.041
	Duchcov	June 29	.041	764	Prague	July 1	.040
	Warnsdorf	July 1	.041	765	Prague VII	June 30	.041
	Ústí n/L.	June 29	.041	766	Prague	June 30	.041
	Ústí n/L.	June 29	.041	767	Prague	July 1	.041
	Ústí n/L.	June 29	.040	768	Prague	July 1	.041
	Šluknov	July 1	.041	769	Prague II	June 30	.040
	Ústí n/L.	June 29	.041	770	Prague VII	June 30	.041
	Chomůtov	June 29	.041	771	Prague II	June 30	.041
	Teplice	June 29	.041	772	Prague IV	June 30	.041
	Podbořany	June 29	.040	773	Vinohrady, Prague	June 30	.041
	Bilina	June 29	.041	774	Prague VI	June 30	.040
	Žatec	June 29	.041	775	Prague II	June 30	.041
	Most	June 29	.041	776	Prague III	June 30	.041
	Rumburk	July 1	.041	777	Prague II	July 1	.042
	Žatec	June 29	.040	778	Prague IV	June 30	.041
	Most	June 29	.041	779	Břevnov	July 1	.040
	Haber u Litoměřic	June 29	.041	780	Prague I	June 30	.041
	Karlovy Vary	July 1	.041	781	Prague III	June 30	.041
	Karlovy Vary	June 29	.041	782	Prague IV	June 30	.041
	Karlovy Vary	June 20	.040	783	Prague III	June 30	.041
	Karlsbad	June 30	.041	784	Prague II	June 30	.040
	Marianské Lázně	June 29	.041	785	Chvaly u Počernic	July 1	.041
	Kadaň	June 29	.041	786	Řicany	June 30	.041
	Falknov	July 1	.041	787	Brno	June 30	.041
	Sušice	June 29	.040	788	Brno	June 30	.041
	Plzeň	June 29	.041	789	Brno	July 1	.040
	Plzeň	June 29	.041	790	Kunštát	June 30	.041
	Stříbro	June 29	.041	791	Boskovice	June 30	.041
	Sušice	June 30	.041	792	Jevišovice	July 1	.041

*In net metric tons of 1,000 kilograms or 2,204.6 pounds.

[*Continued on next page*]

CZECHO-SLOVAKIA

Internal Deliveries of Chocolate, AUSSIG (Ústí n/Labem) Warehouse

Table 279—*Continued*

Receipt No.	Local Committee (Mistni Komitét)	Date	Chocolate Total Tons	Receipt	Local Committee (Mistni Komitét)	Date	Chocolate Total Tons
Series 2		1921		Series 2		1921	
793	Lomnice	June 30	.041	820	Hranice na Moravě	June 30	.040
794	Svitavy	June 30	.041	821	Hranice na Moravě	June 30	.041
795	Střelice u Brna	June 30	.041	822	Frenštát	June 30	.041
796	Rajhrad	June 30	.040	823	Šternberk	June 30	.041
797	Ivančice u Brna	June 30	.040	824	Přerov	June 30	.041
798	Moravský Krumlov	June 30	.041	825	Holešov	June 30	.040
799	Brno	June 30	.041	826	Hranice	June 30	.041
800	Cirkvenice-Brno	June 30	.041	827	Litovel	June 30	.041
801	Jundrov	June 30	.041	828	Val. Meziříčí	June 30	.041
802	Třebíč na Moravě	July 1	.040	829	Nový Jičín	June 30	.041
803	Telce	June 30	.041	830	Olomouc	June 30	.040
804	Brno	June 30	.041	831	Val. Meziříčí	July 1	.041
805	Brno	June 30	.041	832	Olomouc	June 30	.041
806	Vranov u Znojma	July 1	.040	833	Olomouc	June 30	.041
807	Jihlava	July 1	.042	834	Prostějov	June 30	.041
808	Brno	June 30	.041	835	Hranice	June 30	.040
809	Brno	June 30	.041	836	Zábřeh	June 30	.041
810	Hustopeč na Moravě	June 30	.041	837	Přerov	June 30	.041
811	Kuřim	June 30	.041	838	Meziříčí	June 30	.041
812	Boskovice	June 30	.041	839	Holešov	June 30	.041
813	Brno	June 30	.040	840	Prostějov	June 30	.040
814	Brno	July 1	.041	841	Prostějov	June 30	.040
815	Brno	June 30	.041	842	Holešov	June 30	.041
816	Znojmo	July 1	.041	843	Šumperk	June 30	.041
817	Meziřiči	July 1	.041	844	Nový Jičín	July 1	.041
818	Tasovice	July 1	.041	845	Přerov	June 30	.041
819	Brno	July 1	.041	846	Olomouc	June 30	.040

CZECHO-SLOVAKIA

Table 279—*Concluded*

Internal Deliveries of Chocolate, AUSSIG (Ústí n/Labem) Warehouse

eipt o.	Local Committee (Mistni Komitét)	Date	Chocolate Total Tons	Receipt No.	Local Committee (Mistni Komitét)	Date	Chocolate Total Tons
ies 2		1921		Series 2		1921	
47	Mor. Ostrava	June 30	.041	874	Ružomberk	June 30	.040
48	Karvin	June 30	.041	875	Košice	June 30	.041
49	Slezská Ostrava	June 30	.041	876	Žilina	June 30	.041
50	Mor. Ostrava	June 30	.041	877	Košice	June 30	.041
51	Mor. Ostrava	June 30	.040	878	Kláštor p. Znievom	June 30	.041
52	Mor. Ostrava	June 30	.041	879	Liptov. sv. Mikuláš	July 1	.040
53	Mar. Hory Slezsko	July 1	.041	880	Kremnice	June 30	.041
54	Zábřeh n/Odrou	June 30	.041	881	Dolný Smokovec	June 30	.041
55	Zábřeh n/Odrou	July 1	.041	882	Lupča	June 30	.041
56	Vítkovice	June 30	.040	883	Trstená	June 30	.041
57	Slezská Ostrava	June 30	.041	884	Bán. Bystrica	June 30	.040
58	Orlová-Slezsko	July 1	.041	885	Košice	June 30	.041
59	Slezská Ostrava	June 30	.041	886	Radvan	June 30	.041
60	Krňov	July 1	.041	887	Turč. Sv. Martin	June 30	.041
61	Opava	July 1	.040	888	Prague I	June 30	.041
62	Einsiedel	June 30	.041	889	Jasina	July 7	.040
63	Würbenthal	June 30	.041	890	Užhorod	July 7	.041
64	Opava	June 19	.041	891	Užhorod	July 7	.040
65	Karlsbrun, Würbenthal	July 1	.041	892	Mukačevo	June 30	.041
66	Opava	June 30	.041	893	Užhorod	July 7	.041
67	Lučenec Slovensko	June 30	.041	894	Beregsazs	July 7	.041
68	Stará Tura	June 30	.040	895	Vel. Sevljuš	July 7	.041
69	Trnava	July 1	.041	896	Mukačevo	June 30	.040
70	Rimavská Sobota	June 30	.041	897	Beregsazs	July 7	.041
71	Modrá, Slovensko	July 1	.041	898	Mukačevo	July 7	.041
72	Trenčín	June 30	.041				
73	Žilina	June 30	.041		Total		**9.020**

Table 280

THE FREE CITY OF DANZIG-

Operation	Table No.	Flour	Grain	Rice	Beans, Peas
A.R.A.-European Children's Fund	281, 286	.8	....	20.3	25.1
Danzig Free City, Government Donation	282, 286	51.1	....	....	....
American Friends Service Committee	283, 287	.4	....	30.4	40.3
Total Children's Relief	163	**52.3**	....	**50.7**	**65.4**
A.R.A. Warehouses—Food Drafts and Bulk Sales	284, 288–9	79.4	....	18.5	13.2
Grand Total, Net*	102	**131.7**	....	**69.2**	**78.6**

* This represents relief supplies used in Danzig area, and excludes bulk sale of flour to Poland.

THE FREE CITY OF DANZIG-

Table 281

Detail by Steamers of Arrivals for Childre

Steamer or Source	Port of Sailing	Date of Arrival	Port of Arrival	Transshipped on
		1921		
Donated by A.F.S.C., subject to replacement in kind or payment in cash	(U.S.A.)	....	Danzig	....
American, II	New York	Jan. 12	Hamburg	Echo, III
		1920		
Cornish City	New York	Dec. 31	Danzig	....
		1921		
Ipswich	New York	Jan. 25	Hamburg	Progress, IV
Ipswich	New York	Jan. 25	Hamburg	Progress, IV
Watsness, II	New York	May 13	Danzig	....
Watsness, II	New York	May 13	Danzig	....
Michigan	New Orleans	July 20	Bremen	Sea Lighter 164
Westbrook, II	New York	July 12	Danzig	....
Croxteth Hall	New York	July 6	Hamburg	Smolensk
Hawaiian, III	New York	July 4	Hamburg	Naval, III
West Kedron	San Francisco	Aug. 19	Danzig	....
Kielhaven	New Orleans	Aug. 24	Hamburg	Weichsel, VIII
Westbrook, II	New York	July 12	Danzig	....
Clarksburg, IV	New York	Oct. 8	Hamburg	Weichsel, IX
Clarksburg, IV	New York	Oct. 8	Hamburg	Weichsel, IX
Kielhaven	New Orleans	Aug. 24	Hamburg	Weichsel, VIII
Panama	San Francisco	Aug. 13	Danzig	....
Hawaiian, V	New York	Oct. 10	Hamburg	Etzel, II
Hawaiian, V	New York	Oct. 10	Hamburg	Weichsel, IX
Potomac, II	New York	Oct. 12	Danzig	....
Packing Room	(U.S.A.)	....	Danzig	....
Hawaiian, V	New York	Oct. 10	Hamburg	Weichsel, IX
Kielhaven	New Orleans	Aug. 24	Hamburg	Weichsel, VIII
Hudson	New York	Nov. 3	Bremerhaven	Moewe, I
Mexico, III	New Orleans	Nov. 5	Hamburg	Echo, V
Clarksburg, V	Norfolk	Dec. 12	Hamburg	Norma, I
		1922		
Gasconier	New York	Jan. 26	Hamburg	Hansa, V
Warehouse Overage	(U.S.A.)	....	Danzig	....
Total	....	....	....	....

* Shipments from Danzig Port to Danzig Mission, where relief supplies were issued to local committees.

† Sold to Danzig Free City Government.

nmary of Relief Deliveries

orn rits	Pork Products	Milk	Cocoa	Sugar	Misc. Food	Forage	Soap	Medical and Hospital Supplies	Misc.	Total Tons	Total Value
Commodities in Net Metric Tons of 1,000 Kilograms or 2,204.6 Pounds											
ONSTRUCTION PERIOD, 1919–1924											
...	12.8	43.7	5.3	....	...	....	....	....	...	108.0	$ 17,749.51
...	....	....	...	22.9	...	....	....	....	...	74.0	8,574.44
...	20.1	58.2	8.9	....	...	....	....	....	...	158.3	30,291.26
...	**32.9**	**101.9**	**14.2**	**22.9**	**...**	**....**	**....**	**....**	**...**	**340.3**	**$ 56,615.21**
2.8	16.9	89.9	2.5	5.6	2.5	....	....	....	1.6	232.9	71,085.48
2.8	**49.8**	**191.8**	**16.7**	**28.5**	**2.5**	**....**	**....**	**....**	**1.6**	**573.2**	**$127,700.69**

R.A.-European Children's Fund

ief—Reconstruction Period, 1919–1924

Port of Sailing	Port of Arrival	Shipment Number*	Date of Delivery	Flour	Rice	Beans, Peas	Pork Products	Milk	Cocoa	Total Tons	Total Value
			Contents of Cargoes in Net Metric Tons of 1,000 Kilograms or 2,204.6 Pounds								
			1921								
....	....	...	Apr. 9–15	...	2.9	4.6	2.5	7.8	1.1	18.9	$ 3,554.26
amburg	Danzig	424	May 18	...	...	...	...	7.4	...	7.4	1,804.51
....	....	424	May 18	...	...	4.8	2.5	...	.9	8.2	1,113.16
amburg	Danzig	424	May 18	...	3.7	...	...	...	...	3.7	219.77
amburg	Danzig	568	June 22	...	.4	...	...	...	...	.4	23.76
....	....	568	June 22	...	...	...	...	.1	.1	.2	34.34
....	....	657	Aug. 2	...	...	...	.2	4.6	.5	5.3	1,213.70
remen	Danzig	657	Aug. 2	...	2.0	...	...	...	...	2.0	118.80
....	....	657	Aug. 2	...	...	1.8	...	...	...	1.8	186.00
amburg	Danzig	657	Aug. 2	...	...	...	.5	...	...	.5	105.51
amburg	Danzig	769	Oct. 15	...	...	...	...	...	.7	.7	69.68
....	....	769	Oct. 15	...	...	3.7	...	...	...	3.7	339.03
amburg	Danzig	769	Oct. 15	...	2.8	...	...	...	...	2.8	166.31
....	....	769	Oct. 15	...	...	...	...	6.0	...	6.0	1,382.78
amburg	Danzig	782	Oct. 29	...	...	...	2.0	...	...	2.0	470.91
amburg	Danzig	825	Dec. 30	...	...	...	3.5	...	...	3.5	824.08
amburg	Danzig	825	Dec. 30	...	6.0	...	...	...	...	6.0	368.20
....	....	825	Dec. 30	...	...	7.7	...	...	...	7.7	705.54
lamburg	Danzig	825	Dec. 30	...	...	...	...	11.2	...	11.2	2,581.20
lamburg	Danzig	825	Dec. 30	...	...	...	...	1.2	...	1.2	276.56
....	....	825	Dec. 30	...	...	...	...	...	1.5	1.5	164.09
....	....	825	Dec. 30	.2	...	...	...	...	...	.2	18.96
			1922								
lamburg	Danzig	848	June 10	...	...	...	...	5.4	...	5.4	1,000.17
lamburg	Danzig	848	June 10	...	1.3	...	...	...	...	1.3	62.99
remerhaven	Danzig	848	June 10	...	...	...	...	...	.5	.5	22.96
lamburg	Danzig	848	June 10	...	1.2	...	...	...	...	1.2	58.15
lamburg	Danzig	848	June 10	...	...	...	1.6	...	...	1.6	599.74
lamburg	Danzig	848	June 10	...	...	2.5	...	...	...	2.5	264.35
....	....	855	July 28	.6	...	...	...	...	...	.6	......†
....	....	....	....	**.8**	**20.3**	**25.1**	**12.8**	**43.7**	**5.3**	**108.0**	**$17,749.51**

THE FREE CITY OF DANZIG—A.R.A.-European Children's Fund

Detail of Danzig Government Donations for Child Feeding

Table 282 — Reconstruction Period, 1919–1924

Time of Delivery	Commodities in Net Metric Tons of 1,000 Kilograms or 2,204.6 Pounds								Total Value
	Flour	Rice	Beans, Peas	Pork Products	Milk	Cocoa	Sugar	Total Tons	
Commencement to June 30, 1921	23.5	....	....	....	....	....	10.0	33.5	$4,329
July 1, 1921 to June 30, 1922	27.0	....	....	....	....	....	12.9	39.9	4,204
July 1, 1922 to end of operation	0.6	....	....	....	....	....	....	0.6	40
Total	**51.1**	....	....	....	....	....	**22.9**	**74.0**	**$8,574**

THE FREE CITY OF DANZIG—American Friends Service Committee

Detail of Deliveries by European Children's Fund ex-European Stocks

Table 283 — Reconstruction Period, 1919–1924

Steamer or Source	Transshipping Steamer, Hamburg to Danzig	Origin of Cargo	Date of Arrival	First Port of Arrival	Contents of Cargoes in Net Metric Tons of 1,000 Kilograms or 2,204.6 Pounds							Total Value
					Flour	Rice	Beans, Peas	Pork Products	Milk	Cocoa	Total Tons	
			1920									
Kermoor, II	Suzanne, II	New York	Apr. 11	Hamburg	....	....	....	....	5.0	...	5.0	$ 1,562
Mar Blanco, I	Aller I, II	New York	July 2	Hamburg	....	....	7.2	....	....	...	7.2	664
Mar Caspio, II	Saale, I	New York	July 16	Hamburg	....	....	....	....	22.2	...	22.2	5,835
Mar Mediterraneo, II	Saale, I	New York	July 22	Hamburg	....	....	....	5.7	5.0	2.4	13.1	3,847
Paul Stuppel Purchase	Fanal, I	Hamburg	July 27	Hamburg	....	....	9.9	....	....	...	9.9	874
Herefordshire	Progress, III	Rangoon	Aug. 18	Hamburg	....	4.4	....	....	....	...	4.4	577
Thorn Evacuations	....	U.S.A.	Nov. ..	Danzig	....	4.3	....	....	....	...	4.3	505
Cornish City, I	....	New York	Dec. 31	Danzig	....	....	28.0	16.9	....	6.3	51.2	9,270
			1921									
American, II	Echo, III	New York	Jan. 12	Hamburg	....	....	....	....	21.0	...	21.0	5,133
Ipswich	Progress, IV	New York	Jan. 25	Hamburg	....	16.3	....	....	....	...	16.3	1,917
Pomona	Romera	Portland	Mar. 28	Hamburg	18.6	....	....	....	....	...	18.6	2,868
Westbrook	Adele, II	New Orleans	Apr. 9	Hamburg	....	8.5	....	....	....	...	8.5	661
Watsness, II	....	New York	May 13	Danzig	....	....	....	....	23.6	.2	23.8	5,887
Michigan	Sea Lighter 164	New Orleans	July 20	Bremen	....	3.5	....	....	....	...	3.5	199
Total	....	....	....	....	**18.6**	**37.0**	**45.1**	**22.6**	**76.8**	**8.9**	**209.0**	**$39,806**
Returned to E.C.F. Stock, Danzig	....	....	....	....	18.2	6.6	4.8	2.5	18.6	...	50.7	9,514
Balance Exchanged for Cottonseed Meal *	....	....	....	....	**.4**	**30.4**	**40.3**	**20.1**	**58.2**	**8.9**	**158.3**	**$30,291**

* When the European Children's Fund took charge of child feeding in the Danzig area, the A.F.S.C. was given credit for feeding already accomplished. An equivalent amount of money, representing the cost of food supplies actually fed, was released to the A.F.S.C. The E.C used this money to purchase cottonseed meal for the A.F.S.C. Po program.

THE FREE CITY OF DANZIG—American Relief Administration Warehouses

Summary of Arrivals—Reconstruction Period, 1919–1924

Table 284

Source	Commodities in Net Metric Tons of 1,000 Kilograms or 2,204.6 Pounds											Total Value
	Flour	Rice	Beans, Peas	Corn Grits	Pork Products	Milk	Cocoa	Sugar	Misc. Food	Misc.	Total Tons	
t and Mission Stocks.......	**7,799.7**	**18.5**	**13.2**	**2.8**	**16.9**	**89.9**	**2.5**	**5.6**	**2.5**	**1.6**	**7,953.2**	**$935,647.88**

THE FREE CITY OF DANZIG—A.R.A.-European Children's Fund

Summary of Internal Deliveries by Operations Reconstruction Period, 1919–1924

Table 285

Operation	Table No.	Commodities in Net Metric Tons of 1,000 Kilograms or 2,204.6 Pounds										
		Flour	Rice	Beans, Peas	Corn Grits	Pork Products	Milk	Cocoa	Sugar	Misc. Food	Misc.	Total Tons
R.A.-European Children's Fund......	286	.8	20.3	25.1	...	12.8	43.7	5.3	....	...	...	108.0
nzig Government Donation..........	286	51.1	....	....	...	....	....	...	22.9	...	...	74.0
erican Friends Service Committee...	287	.4	30.4	40.3	...	20.1	58.2	8.9	....	...	...	158.3
R.A. Warehouses, Food Drafts......	288	30.5	5.4	6.3	...	8.6	9.5	.4	1.0	1.1	.8	63.6
R.A. Warehouses, Bulk Sales (net).	289	48.9	13.1	6.9	2.8	8.3	80.4	2.1	4.6	1.4	.8	169.3
Total	280	**131.7**	**69.2**	**78.6**	**2.8**	**49.8**	**191.8**	**16.7**	**28.5**	**2.5**	**1.6**	**573.2**

THE FREE CITY OF DANZIG—A.R.A.-European Children's Fund

Detail of Internal Deliveries, for Child Feeding—Reconstruction Period, 1919–1924

Table 286

Receipt No.	Local Committees	Date of Receipt	Flour	Rice	Beans, Peas	Pork Products	Milk	Cocoa	Sugar	Total Tons
			Commodities in Net Metric Tons of 1,000 Kilograms or 2,204.6 Pounds							
		1921								
1	Danzig and Environs	Aug. 13	....	2.940	4.580	2.532	7.752	1.109	.....	18.91
2	Danzig and Environs	Aug. 13	....	3.673	4.826	2.471	7.425	.914	.....	19.30
3	Danzig and Environs	Aug. 13	....	.372	.....	.....	.109	.102	.....	.58
4	Danzig and Environs	Aug. 13	....	1.994	1.765	.612	4.616	.544	.....	9.53
		1922								
5	Danzig and Environs	Feb. 23	....	2.845	3.650	2.040	6.009	.711	.....	15.25
6	Danzig and Environs	Feb. 23	....	6.033	7.655	3.452	12.432	1.524	.....	31.09
7	Danzig and Environs	June 4	.234	2.421	2.605	1.680	5.350	.422	.....	12.71
	Total	....	**.234**	**20.278**	**25.081**	**12.787**	**43.693**	**5.326**	.....	**107.39**
	Sale to Danzig Government	....	.600	.....	.....	.....	.....	.....	.....	.60
	Total	....	**.834**	**20.278**	**25.081**	**12.787**	**43.693**	**5.326**	.....	**107.99**
	Receipts to Danzig Government	....	51.100	.....	.....	.....	.....	.....	22.900	74.00
	Total	....	**51.934**	**20.278**	**25.081**	**12.787**	**43.693**	**5.326**	**22.900**	**181.99**

* Cf. Table 281. † Cf. Table 282.

THE FREE CITY OF DANZIG—American Friends Service Committee

Detail by Steamers of Deliveries to Cities from Danzig Warehouse, 1920, 1921

able 287

Steamer or Source	Delivered to	Commodities in Net Metric Tons of 1,000 Kilograms or 2,204.6 Pounds						
		Flour	Rice	Beans, Peas	Pork Products	Milk	Cocoa	Total Tons
noor, II.	Danzig	....	....	....	....	5.0	...	5.0
Blanco, I.	Danzig	....	....	7.2	....	....	...	7.2
Caspio, II.	Danzig	....	....	....	....	10.2	...	10.2
Caspio, II.	Koenigsberg	....	....	....	....	8.0	...	8.0
Caspio, II.	Elbing	....	....	....	....	4.0	...	4.0
Mediterraneo, II.	Danzig	....	....	....	5.7	5.0	2.4	13.1
Stuppel Purchase	Danzig	....	....	7.2	....	....	...	7.2
Stuppel Purchase	Elbing	....	....	2.7	....	....	...	2.7
·fordshire	Danzig	....	4.4	....	....	....	...	4.4
rn Evacuations	Danzig	....	4.3	....	....	....	...	4.3
ıish City, I.	Berlin	....	....	4.0	2.0	....	.8	6.8
ıish City, I.	Elbing	....	....	1.1	1.9	....	.7	3.7
ıish City, I.	Koenigsberg	....	....	22.9	13.0	....	4.8	40.7
rican, II.	Berlin	....	....	....	....	6.0	...	6.0
rican, II.	Koenigsberg	....	....	....	....	15.0	...	15.0
vich	Koenigsberg	....	11.3	....	....	....	..	11.3
vich	Berlin	....	3.0	....	....	....	..	3.0
vich	Elbing	....	2.0	....	....	....	..	2.0
ona	Danzig	18.6	....	....	....	....	..	18.6
tbrook	Koenigsberg	....	7.0	....	....	....	...	7.0
tbrook	Elbing	....	1.5	....	....	....	...	1.5
sness, II.	Elbing	....	....	....	....	1.5	...	1.5
sness, II.	Koenigsberg	....	....	....	....	22.1	.2	22.3
ıigan	Danzig	....	3.5	....	....	....	...	3.5
Total	....	**18.6**	**37.0**	**45.1**	**22.6**	**76.8**	**8.9**	**209.0***
s Amount Returned to E.C.F. Stock	....	18.2	6.6	4.8	2.5	18.6	...	50.7
Net Deliveries	....	**.4**	**30.4**	**40.3**	**20.1**	**58.2**	**8.9**	**158.3**

Total to Danzig, 73.5; Berlin, 15.8; Elbing, 15.4; Koenigsberg, 104.3.

THE FREE CITY OF DANZIG—

Detail by Months of Food Draft Deliveries*

Table 288

Time of Delivery	Number of Drafts Delivered				Unit	Flour	Rice	Beans, Peas	Bacon	
	A $10.00	B $50.00	C $10.00	D $50.00		M.T.	M.T.	M.T.	8-Lb. Piece	16-Lb. Piece
1920										
May	26	5	6	..	....	.673	.....	.239	26	5
June	69	10	4	1	....	1.509	.....	.577	69	10
July	266	49	26	2	....	6.480	.....	2.508	266	49
August	172	30	13	2	....	4.086	.....	1.554	172	30
September	154	30	11	1	....	3.800	.....	1.441	154	30
October	114	18	15	1	....	2.639	1.009	....	114	18
November	92	7	10	1	....	1.640	.639	....	92	7
December	132	8	11	..	....	2.095	.802	.023	118	15
1921										
January	124	11	10	2	....	2.313	.898	....	124	11
February	64	7	10	..	....	1.319	.509	....	64	8
March	70	21	7	2	....	2.316	.867	....	90	11
April	37	1	3	..	....	.454	.185	....	37	..
May	42	4	6	..	....	.787	.307	....	42	4
June	11	..	..	..	....	.122	.051	....	11	..
July	2	4	..	..	....	.277	.100	....	10	..
Total in Units	**1,375**	**205**	**132**	**12**	Unit	**30.510**	**5.367**	**6.342**	**1,389**	**198**
Total in Metric Tons	....	....	....	....	M.T.	**30.510**	**5.367**	**6.342**	**5.040**	**1.437**

* Taken from the records of the Danzig Mission.

THE FREE CITY OF DANZIG—

Detail by Months of Bulk Sale Deliveries

Table 289

Time of Delivery	Unit	Flour M.T.	Rice M.T.	Beans, Peas M.T.	Corn Grits M.T.	Bacon 8-Lb. Piece	Bacon 16-Lb. Piece
1920							
July	...	1,016.000	....	.....	.....	.....	....
December	...	.111	.020	.....	.....	.....	....
1921							
January	...	......	....	.....	.....	.....	....
February	...	1,700.863	....	.....	.....	.....	....
March	...	11.044	2.225	3.578	.....	.....	....
April	...	3,732.415	....	.....	.....	.....	....
May	...	629.486	....	.....	.....	.....	....
June	...	662.284	5.902	.....	1.101	478	21
July–October	...	......	....	.....	.....	.....	....
December	...	......	....	.....	.....	.....	....
1922							
February	...	......	....	1.940	.....	.....	....
September	...	16.953	4.937	1.344	1.689	.....	....
Total Deliveries in Units	Unit	**7,769.156**	**13.084**	**6.862**	**2.790**	**478**	**21**
Total Deliveries in Metric Tons	M.T.	**7,769.156**	**13.084**	**6.862**	**2.790**	**1.735**	**.152**
Deduct Deliveries to Polish Government	M.T.	7,720.300	....	.....	.....	.....	....
Total	M.T.	**48.856**	**13.084**	**6.862**	**2.790**	**1.735**	**.152**

.R.A. Warehouses and A.R.A.-European Children's Fund

econstruction Period, 1919–1924

Lard		Oil		Milk		Cocoa	Sugar	Corned Beef	Misc. (Sacks)	Total Metric Tons	Total Value
5-Lb. Tin	10-Lb. Tin	1-Gal. Tin	5-Gal. Tin	Cond. Case	Evap. Case	M.T.	M.T.	Case	No.		
5	5	6	..	8	3	....	....	1	65	......	......
10	10	5	1	17	6	....	....	2	157	......	......
49	49	28	2	76	25	....	....	8	635	......	......
30	30	15	2	48	16	....	....	5	402	......	......
30	30	12	1	45	14	....	....	5	361	......	......
18	18	16	1	29	12	....	....	3	277	......	......
7	7	11	1	16	10	.063	.150	1	...	......	......
8	8	11	..	20	12	.084	.191	1	...	......	......
11	11	12	2	25	12	.087	.212	2	...	......	......
8	8	9	..	14	8	.049	.121	1	533	......	......
21	21	9	2	28	9	.073	.215	3	177	......	......
..	..	3	..	4	4	.021	.041	..	490	......	......
4	4	6	..	7	5	.030	.072	1	100	......	......
..	..	..	..	1	1	.007	.011	..	22	......	......
4	4	..	..	4	..	.008	.026	1	8	......	......
205	**205**	**143**	**12**	**342**	**137**	**.422**	**1.039**	**34**	**3,227**	......	......
.465	**.930**	**.487**	**.204**	**6.509**	**2.976**	**.422**	**1.039**	**1.119**	**.786**	**63.633**	**$25,920.00**

.R.A. Warehouses and A.R.A.-European Children's Fund

econstruction Period, 1919–1924

Lard Substitute	Oil Bulk	Milk		Cocoa	Sugar	Corned Beef	Misc. (Sacks)	Total Metric Tons	Total Value
M.T.	M.T.	Evap. Case	Cond. Case	M.T.	M.T.	Case	No.		
....	.....	...	...	....	.....	..	...	......	......
....	.....	1	25	....	.....	..	...	......	......
....	.....	...	2,446	....	.....	..	...	......	......
....	.....	...	...	....	.....	..	...	......	......
1.489	.....	115	132	.609	.....	..	4	......	......
....	.....	...	...	....	.....	..	...	......	......
....	.....	...	...	....	.....	..	...	......	......
.780	.....	321	...	.390	1.560	43	3,600	......	......
....	.....	426	...	....	.....	..	...	......	......
....	.....	...	108	....	.....	..	...	......	......
....	.....	...	...	....	.....	..	...	......	......
2.829	1.360	369	104	1.055	3.061	..	...	......	......
5.098	**1.360**	**1,232**	**2,815**	**2.054**	**4.621**	**43**	**3,604**	......	......
5.098	**1.360**	**26.825**	**53.628**	**2.054**	**4.621**	**1.415**	**.817**	**7,889.597**	**$909,727.88**
....	.....	...	...	....	.....	..	...	7,720.300	864,562.40
5.098	**1.360**	**26.825**	**53.628**	**2.054**	**4.621**	**1.415**	**.817**	**169.297**	**$ 45,165.48**

DENMARK—Summary of Relief Deliveries

Table 290

Operation	Table No.	Commodities in Net Metric Tons of 1,000 Kilograms or 2,204.6 Pounds			Total Value
		Flour	Grain	Total Tons	
American Relief Administration—Cash Settlement	291	....	19,912.0	19,912.0	$2,147,059.[illegible]
Grand Total	102	....	**19,912.0**	**19,912.0**	**$2,147,059.[illegible]**

DENMARK—American Relief Administration

Table 291 Detail by Steamers of Commodities Sold for Cash—Armistice Period, 1919

Steamer	Port of Sailing	Date of Arrival	Port of Arrival	Contents of Cargoes in Net Metric Tons of 1,000 Kilograms or 2,204.6 Pounds			Total Value
				Rye Grain	Barley Grain	Total Tons	
		1919					
kembang	New York	Mar. 18	Copenhagen	7,747.0	......	7,747.0	$ 884,475.00
artensdijk	New York	Mar. 18	Copenhagen	2,253.0	......	2,253.0	257,225.00
labot *	Newport News	May 31	Copenhagen	......	9,912.0	9,912.0	1,005,359.30
Total Sales, to Table 120	....	....	....	**10,000.0**	**9,912.0**	**19,912.0**	**$2,147,059.30**

* This cargo handled direct by New York office, Food Administration in Corporation.

Table 292

ESTHONIA-

Operation	Table No.	Flour	Grain	Rice	Beans, Peas
A.R.A.—Congressional Appropriation, $100,000,000 Fund	293	15,649.9	4,466.5	91.6	.....
A.R.A.—Cash Settlement	294	......	862.0	....	.....
A.R.A.—Freight on Charity Shipments	143	......	.....	....	.....
A.R.A.—Freight, Ins., etc., on U.S. Liq. Com. Supplies	144	......	.....	....	.....
U.S. Liquidation Commission (War Dept.)	122	......	.....	....	.....
American Red Cross	126	......	.....	....	.....
Total American Relief	....	**15,649.9**	**5,328.5**	**91.6**	.....
United Kingdom	295	4,600.0	671.0	....	303.0
United Kingdom—Finance on Freight	295n	......	.....	....	.....
Denmark	136	......	462.6	....	.....
Total by Countries Other than U.S	132	**4,600.0**	**1,133.6**	....	**303.0**
Total Relief, Armistice Period	108	**20,249.9**	**6,462.1**	**91.6**	**303.0**
A.R.A.—Congressional Appropriation, $100,000,000 Fund	296, 302	288.0	.....	250.1	222.4
A.R.A.-European Children's Fund	296, 302	551.3	.....	266.7	225.1
Esthonian Government Donation*	296, 302	1,504.0	.....	15.0	.....
Total Children's Relief	163	**2,343.3**	.....	**531.8**	**447.5**
A.R.A.-European Children's Fund—Bulk Sales	296, 302	3.7	.....	1.5	1.9
Total Relief, Reconstruction Period	149	**2,347.0**	.....	**533.3**	**449.4**
Grand Total Relief Deliveries	102	**22,596.9**	**6,462.1**	**624.9**	**752.4**

* In addition to these supplies used in Esthonia, the Esthonian Government donated warehouse space for storage of supplies enroute Russia, valued at $1,102.94.

ESTHONIA-

Table 293

Detail by Steamers of Relief Deliveries Paid for by Funds fro

Arrival No.*	Steamer or Source	Port of Sailing	Date of Arrival	Port of Arrival	Wheat Flour	Cereal Flour
			1919			
73	Maartensdijk †	New York	Mar. 23	Copenhagen	.....	.....
156	Mirach and Besoeki †	New York	Apr. 30	Copenhagen	.....	.....
215	Lake Dancey, III ‡	Cardiff	May 21	Reval	1,360.6	.....
239	Lake Wimico, IV §	Bordeaux	May 31	Reval	1,409.0	.....
285	Lake Strabo	Montreal	June 16	Reval	2,059.7	.....
342	Lake St. Clair, V §	Bordeaux	July 10	Reval	.....	102.5
359	Theresa Horn	New York	July 20	Reval	4,572.0	.....
368	Slavonia	New York	Aug. 2	Reval	4,108.6	853.4
388	Lake Dancey, V	Danzig	Aug. 31	Reval	1,184.1	.....
...	Danish Seed Grain **	(U.S.A.)	....	Reval	.....	.....
	Total	....	....	....	**14,694.0**	**955.9**

* From Table 111.
† Transshipped from Copenhagen to Reval.
‡ From U.S. Navy stocks at Cardiff, England. Purchased by A.R.A.

ımmary of Relief Deliveries

Commodities in Net Metric Tons of 1,000 Kilograms or 2,204.6 Pounds											
Corn Grits	Pork Products	Milk	Cocoa	Sugar	Misc. Food	Forage	Soap	Medical and Hospital Supplies	Clothing and Misc.	Total Tons	Total Value
ᴇMISTICE PERIOD											
.....	725.3	127.5	.....	55.0	14.1	.....	....	.....	.....	21,129.9	$ 4,299,650.87
.....	.....	.....	.....	.....	.....	.....	....	.....	.....	862.0	116,371.62
.....	.....	.....	.....	.....	.....	.....	....	.....	.....	.....	50,490.62
.....	.....	.....	.....	.....	.....	.....	....	.....	.....	.....	151,113.05
.....	.....	.....	.....	.....	26,000.0	.....	....	.....	4,120.0	30,120.0	12,262,818.99
.....	.....	.....	.....	.....	.....	.....	....	312.3	.....	312.3	89,800.00
.....	**725.3**	**127.5**	.....	**55.0**	**26,014.1**	.....	....	**312.3**	**4,120.0**	**52,424.2**	**$16,970,244.55**
.....	.....	.....	.....	900.0	1,750.0	.....	....	.....	400.0	8,624.0	$ 2,032,960.00
.....	.....	.....	.....	.....	.....	.....	....	.....	.....	.....	309,400.00
.....	.....	.....	.....	.....	.....	.....	....	.....	.....	462.6	35,207.92
.....	.....	.....	.....	**900.0**	**1,750.0**	.....	....	.....	**400.0**	**9,086.6**	**$ 2,377,567.92**
.....	**725.3**	**127.5**	.....	**955.0**	**27,764.1**	.....	....	**312.3**	**4,520.0**	**61,510.8**	**$19,347,812.47**
CONSTRUCTION PERIOD											
.....	61.6	787.7	104.4	284.6	.....	.....	31.1	.....	.....	2,029.9	$ 701,520.82
.....	169.0	408.0	39.4	104.6	.....	.....	7.3	.....	59.9	1,831.3	522,929.39
.....	1.0	153.0	.....	10.0	10.0	.....	....	.....	.....	1,693.0	298,444.64
.....	**231.6**	**1,348.7**	**143.8**	**399.2**	**10.0**	.....	**38.4**	.....	**59.9**	**5,554.2**	**$ 1,522,894.85**
.....	76.3	209.0	.2	.9	.....	.....	....	.....	.....	293.5	146,556.24
.....	**307.9**	**1,557.7**	**144.0**	**400.1**	**10.0**	.....	**38.4**	.....	**59.9**	**5,847.7**	**$ 1,669,451.09**
.....	**1,033.2**	**1,685.2**	**144.0**	**1,355.1**	**27,774.1**	.....	**38.4**	**312.3**	**4,579.9**	**67,358.5**	**$21,017,263.56**

nerican Relief Administration

ɜ Congressional Appropriation for Relief—Armistice Period, 1919

Contents of Cargoes in Net Metric Tons of 1,000 Kilograms or 2,204.6 Pounds									
Rye Grain	Rice	Pork Products	Lard	Lard Substitute	Milk	Sugar	Misc. Food	Total Tons	Total Value
2,000.0	....	....	....	....	....	....	....	2,000.0	$ 270,000.00
.....	....	147.7	10.0	....	....	....	....	157.7	116,592.28
.....	27.2	334.3	....	....	45.5	55.0	14.1¶	1,836.7	609,006.70
.....	....	56.7	....	....	.5	....	....	1,466.2	351,301.16
.....	....	....	....	....	....	....	....	2,059.7	401,648.13
.....	....	....	....	....	81.5	....	....	184.0	54,809.91
945.6	....	....	....	....	....	....	....	5,517.6	1,019,195.06
.....	....	....	....	....	....	....	....	4,962.0	950,520.64
.....	64.4	....	....	176.6§§	....	....	....	1,425.1	410,829.01
1,520.9	....	....	....	....	....	....	....	1,520.9	115,747.98
4,466.5	**91.6**	**538.7**	**10.0**	**176.6**	**127.5**	**55.0**	**14.1**	**21,129.9**	**$4,299,650.87**

] Prunes
§ From U.S. Army stocks in France, purchased from the U.S. ıidation Commission by the A.R.A.

§§ Ex-S.S. Tyr loaded at Libau.
** Replaced to Denmark by deliveries from A.R.A. stocks.

ESTHONIA—American Relief Administration

Detail by Steamers of Commodities Sold for Cash
Armistice Period, 1919

Table 294

Arrival No.*	Steamer	Port of Sailing	Date of Arrival	Port of Discharge	Rye Grain†	Total Value
			1919			
71	Tjikembang	New York	Mar. 18	Copenhagen	520.0	$ 70,200.
73	Maartensdijk	New York	Mar. 23	Copenhagen		
73	Maartensdijk	New York	Mar. 23	Copenhagen	342.0	46,171.
	Total Sales				**862.0**	**$116,371.**

* Arrival numbers from Table 111.

† Contents of cargoes in net metric tons of 1,000 kilograms or 2,20 pounds.

ESTHONIA-

Summary of Arrivals by Operations

Table 296

Operation	Table No.	Flour	Rice	Beans, Peas	Pork Products
A.R.A.—Congressional Appropriation, $100,000,000 Fund	297	288.0	250.1	222.4	61.6
A.R.A.-European Children's Fund—Food	298	555.0	268.2	227.0	245.3
A.R.A.-European Children's Fund—Clothing	299	.....	.....	.....	.....
Esthonian Government Donation	300	1,504.0	15.0	.....	1.0
Total	......	**2,347.0**	**533.3**	**449.4**	**307.9**

ESTHONIA-

Detail by Steamers of Children's Relief Arrivals Paid for by Funds from t

Table 297

Steamer or Source	Port of Sailing	Date of Arrival	Port of Arrival	Flour	Rice
		1919			
Regulus and C.R.B. Stock *	(U.S.A.)	March	Rotterdam	....	10.0
C.R.B. Stock †	(U.S.A.)	April	Rotterdam	....	....
C.R.B. Stock ‡	(U.S.A.)	April	Rotterdam	....	....
Tyr	(U.S.A.)	June 12	Libau	....	....
Dio	Montreal	June 22	Viborg	....	....
Lake Traverse, IV	St. Nazaire	July 1	Reval	....	....
Lake St. Clair, V	Bordeaux	July 10	Reval	....	....
Theresa Horn	(U.S.A.)	July 20	Reval	147.0	....
Lake Dancey, V	Danzig	Aug. 1	Reval	60.0	103.0
Schwarzenfels and Danzig Stock §	(U.S.A.)	Aug. 1	Danzig	....	160.2
Total (1)	....	....	....	**207.0**	**273.2**
		1920			
Ranko, from Finland Stock	Helsingfors	Feb.	Reval	60.0	....
Frithiof, from Finland Stock	Hango	Mar. 17	Reval	....	....
Rail, from N.W.R. Stock	Reval	Mar. 17	Reval	21.0	242.9
Total Transfers to Esthonia (2)	....	....	....	**81.0**	**242.9**
Saratov, from Esthonian Stock **	Reval	....	Riga	....	150.0
Edjern, from Esthonian Stock ††	Reval	....	Danzig	....	116.0
Total Transfers from Esthonia (3)	....	....	....	....	**266.0**
Net Arrivals, (1) plus (2) minus (3)	....	....	....	**288.0**	**250.1**

* Shipped on Alwina from Rotterdam to Helsingfors, arriving May 20, 1919.

† Shipped on Orangepolder from Rotterdam to Helsingfors, arriving April 23, 1919.

‡ Shipped on Yssel, II from Rotterdam to Helsingfors, arriving 5, 1919.

ESTHONIA

Detail by Steamers of Relief Deliveries by the United Kingdom*

able 295

Armistice Period, 1919

Steamer	Port of Sailing	Date of Arrival	Port of Arrival	Contents of Cargoes in Net Metric Tons of 1,000 Kilograms or 2,204.6 Pounds								Total Value
				Wheat Flour	Cereal Flour	Wheat Grain	Beans	Sugar	Misc. Foods	Misc. Non-Foods	Total Tons	
		1919										
ɔnia	Leith	Feb. ..	Reval	1,400.0	......	671.0	.....	.....	.....	.....	2,071.0	$ 389,000.00
x	Liverpool	Apr. 1	Reval	......	2,000.0	.....	303.0	.....	.....	.....	2,303.0	404,000.00
·ge Fisher..	Hull	Apr. 8	Reval	......	1,200.0	.....	.....	.....	.....	.....	1,200.0	210,000.00
....	....	....	Reval	......	......	.....	.....	900.0	1,750.0	400.0	3,050.0	1,029,960.00
Total Deliveries	....	....	....	**1,400.0**	**3,200.0**	**671.0**	**303.0**	**900.0**	**1,750.0**	**400.0**	**8,624.0**	**$2,032,960.00**

United Kingdom, finance on freight (in addition to value above),
)0.00.

R.A.-European Children's Fund

onstruction Period, 1919–1924

Commodities in Net Metric Tons of 1,000 Kilograms or 2,204.6 Pounds							Total Value
Milk	Cocoa	Sugar	Miscellaneous Food	Soap	Clothing	Total Tons	
787.7	104.4	284.6	....	31.1	....	2,029.9	$ 701,520.82
617.0	39.6	105.5	....	7.3	....	2,064.9	463,880.84
.....	.....	.....	....	....	59.9	59.9	199,352.44
153.0	.....	10.0	10.0	....	....	1,693.0	298,444.64
1,557.7	**144.0**	**400.1**	**10.0**	**38.4**	**59.9**	**5,847.7**	**$1,663,198.74**

ıerican Relief Administration

ıgressional Appropriation for Relief—Reconstruction Period, 1919–1924

Contents of Cargoes in Net Metric Tons of 1,000 Kilograms or 2,204.6 Pounds									Total Value
Beans, Peas	Pork Products	Milk	Cocoa	Sugar	Misc. Food	Soap	Clothing, Misc.	Total Tons	
10.0	....	....	....	....	....	....	....	20.0	$ 5,361.88
....	....	60.0	20.0	....	....	....	....	80.0	27,200.00
....	....	....	....	40.0	....	....	....	40.0	8,600.00
....	32.9	....	....	....	....	....	....	32.9	22,634.79
71.7	....	25.0	....	....	....	....	....	96.7	32,807.00
....	20.0	115.2	....	....	....	....	....	135.2	63,287.50
....	....	184.3	....	....	....	....	....	184.3	74,060.00
....	....	....	....	....	....	....	....	147.0	28,665.00
34.0	....	....	42.7	123.6	....	....	....	363.3	106,838.03
36.1	....	59.3	26.7	42.0	....	20.8	....	345.1	111,927.59
151.8	**52.9**	**443.8**	**89.4**	**205.6**	....	**20.8**	....	**1,444.5**	**$481,381.79**
....	8.7	....	....	....	....	....	....	68.7	$ 17,836.88
....	....	....	....	35.0	....	....	....	35.0	8,400.00
176.6	....	446.9	40.0	44.0	....	10.3	....	981.7	346,281.15
176.6	**8.7**	**446.9**	**40.0**	**79.0**	....	**10.3**	....	**1,085.4**	**$372,518.03**
106.0	....	103.0	25.0	....	....	....	....	384.0	$122,219.00
....	....	....	....	....	....	....	....	116.0	30,160.00
106.0	....	**103.0**	**25.0**	....	....	....	....	**500.0**	**$152,379.00**
222.4	**61.6**	**787.7**	**104.4**	**284.6**	....	**31.1**	....	**2,029.9**	**$701,520.82**

§ Shipped on Lake Fray, III from Danzig to Reval, arriving Octo- 1919.

** Commodities used for Latvian child feeding.
†† Commodities used for Polish child feeding.

ESTHONIA-

Table 298

Detail by Steamers of Arrivals*-

Steamer or Source	Transshipped via	Port of Sailing	Date of Arrival	Port of Arrival
			1919	
Comité National	E. H. Stinnes to Wasa, I.	Antwerp	November	Rotterda
			1920	
Vardulia, II	Hela	New York	Mar. 15	Danzig
Mar Mediterraneo, II	Saale to Hela	New York	July 22	Hamburg
Herefordshire	Progress, III to Siedler	Rangoon	Aug. 18	Hamburg
Westford	Weichsel and Martha to Siedler	New Orleans	Sept. 13	Hamburg
American, I	Mineral to Hela	New York	Nov. 15	Hamburg
Cornish City, I	Siedler, Torfrid, Neva	New York	Dec. 31	Danzig
Thorn Evacuations	Siedler and Hela	U.S.A.	....	Danzig
Rail	Transfer from Northwest Russia Stocks †	Reval	....	Reval
			1921	
American, II	Echo, III to Hela	New York	Jan. 12	Hamburg
Modlin Purchase	Siedler and Torfrid	Poland	Jan. 13	Danzig
Leeds City, I	Torfrid	New York	Feb. 7	Danzig
Phoenix Bridge	Johanna and August to Echo, IV	New Orleans	Feb. 21	Hamburg
Homer City, II	Progress, V to Torfrid	New York	Feb. 25	Hamburg
Bradclyde, II	Torfrid	New Orleans	Apr. 2	Danzig
Westbrook	Adele, II to Torfrid	New Orleans	Apr. 9	Hamburg
Watsness, II	Echo, IV	New York	May 13	Danzig
Cornish City, II	Progress, VII to Neva	New York	May 14	Hamburg
Nemaha	Progress, VII to Neva	Philadelphia	May 15	Hamburg
Delevan	Echo, IV	New York	May 17	Danzig
Warsaw Mission	Torfrid	U.S.A.	Prior June	Danzig
Warsaw Mission	Echo, IV	Poland	Prior June	Danzig
Hawaiian, III	Sensal, IV to Neva	New York	July 4	Hamburg
Oregonian, IV	Hansa, IV to Neva	New York	July 11	Hamburg
Ipswich, II	Imperial, III to Neva	New York	July 28	Hamburg
Panama, I	Neva	San Francisco	Aug. 13	Danzig
Guernsey, I	Planet to Wasa, II	New York	Aug. 16	Danzig
Estonia	Ulrikka	New York	Aug. 30	Danzig
			1922	
Dallas	Strassburg, VI to Redondo to Mars	New York	Feb. 9	Hamburg
Nobles, II	Christel Salling, II to Redondo to Mars	New Orleans	Apr. 15	Hamburg
Western Scout	Strassburg, VI to Redondo to Mars	New York	Apr. 26	Hamburg
Chappaqua, II	Coblenz, III to Belvidere	Norfolk	Apr. 28	Hamburg
Sapinero, I	Coblenz, III to Belvidere	New Orleans	May 14	Hamburg
Transit Stocks ‡	....	U.S.A.	....	Reval
Total Arrivals	....	....	....	....

* These arrivals include supplies for children's relief and bulk sales.

† From Comité National, arrival Wasa, I.

ESTHONIA

Table 299

Detail by Steamers of Arrivals of Clothi

Steamer or Source	Ex	Port of Sailing	Date of Arrival	Port of Arrival
Kajak	....	London	Jan., 1920	Reval
Lackawanna Valley	....	New York	Sept., 1921	Reval
Rail	Oronoke	Riga	Dec., 1921	Reval
Total Arrivals	....	....	....	....
Transfers to Northwest Russia *	....	....	....	....
Transfers to Soviet Russia †	....	....	....	....
Total Transfers	....	....	....	....
Total Net Arrivals	....	....	....	....

* Ex-Kajak.

† Ex-Lackawanna Valley.

.R.A.-European Children's Fund

ɐconstruction Period, 1919–1924

Flour	Rice	Beans, Peas	Pork Products	Milk	Cocoa	Sugar	Misc. Food	Soap	Clothing, Misc.	Total Tons	Total Value
Contents of Cargoes in Net Metric Tons of 1,000 Kilograms or 2,204.6 Pounds											
....	....	....	87.9	....	....	....	....	....	....	87.9	$ 36,856.91
....	....	....	69.5	....	....	....	....	....	....	69.5	44,923.72
....	....	....	....	....	(.015)	....	....	....	....	(.015)	3.59
....	55.8	....	....	....	....	....	....	....	....	55.8	7,327.66
232.0	....	....	....	....	....	....	....	....	....	232.0	35,352.44
....	....	....	....	94.0	....	....	....	....	....	94.0	58,723.86
....	....	152.2	49.3	130.0	14.0	....	....	....	....	345.5	88,009.76
....	4.4	....	....	....	....	....	....	....	....	4.4	577.81
....	....	....	17.0	....	....	....	....	....	....	17.0	7,114.96
....	....	....	....	.2	....	....	....	....	....	.2	127.74
....	....	....	....	....	....	55.0	....	....	....	55.0	9,799.41
115.0	....	....	....	....	....	....	....	....	....	115.0	11,197.43
....	72.3	....	....	....	....	....	....	....	....	72.3	6,005.96
....	....	....	....	....	7.9	....	....	....	....	7.9	789.57
....	....	....	....	64.0	....	....	....	7.3	....	71.3	16,996.16
....	32.0	....	....	....	....	....	....	....	....	32.0	2,492.16
....	....	....	9.0	51.2	4.1	....	....	....	....	64.3	15,062.76
....	....	....	....	105.6	....	....	....	....	....	105.6	25,317.66
....	....	....	....	21.6	....	....	....	....	....	21.6	5,992.37
93.9	....	....	....	....	....	....	....	....	....	93.9	7,850.32
....	....	....	6.3	....	....	....	....	....	....	6.3	4,072.22
....	....	....	....	....	....	16.1	....	....	....	16.1	2,815.39
....	....	....	....	....	10.0	....	....	....	....	10.0	970.80
....	....	....	....	19.7	....	....	....	....	....	19.7	4,701.80
....	....	....	....	17.3	....	....	....	....	....	17.3	4,101.86
....	33.0	74.8	....	....	....	....	....	....	....	107.8	8,106.54
....	....	....	....	113.4	....	....	....	....	....	113.4	35,590.16
....	....	....	....	....	....	25.0	....	....	....	25.0	2,755.18
....	....	....	....	....	....	9.4	....	....	....	9.4	694.44
....	26.9	....	....	....	....	....	....	....	....	26.9	1,339.31
....	....	....	....	....	3.6	....	....	....	....	3.6	240.40
....	....	....	6.3	....	....	....	....	....	....	6.3	1,401.98
....	20.2	....	....	....	....	....	....	....	....	20.2	1,117.42
114.1	23.6	....	....	....	....	....	....	....	....	137.7	15,451.09
555.0	**268.2**	**227.0**	**245.3**	**617.0**	**39.6**	**105.5**	....	**7.3**	....	**2,064.9**	**$463,880.84**

‡ Shipments en route Soviet Russia.

.R.A.-European Children's Fund

d Accessories—Reconstruction Period, 1919–1924

Shoes (Pairs)	Laces (Pairs)	Stockings (Pairs)	Woolens (Yards)	Thread (Pounds)	Needles (No.)	Buttons (No.)	Total Metric Tons	Total Value
40,635	43,200	43,014	60,346	842	35,000	144,000	47.0	$186,323.21
10,737	.....	20,636	.....	...	.....	......	15.0	17,529.84
.....	.....	.....	1,915	...	.....	......	1.1	1,850.37
51,372	**43,200**	**63,650**	**62,261**	**842**	**35,000**	**144,000**	**63.1**	**$205,703.42**
1,360	1,360	1,224	1,625	24	.....	4,400	2.3	$ 4,965.06
.....	.....	10,000	.....	...	.....	......	0.9	1,385.92
1,360	**1,360**	**11,224**	**1,625**	**24**	.....	**4,400**	**3.2**	**$ 6,350.98**
50,012	**41,840**	**52,426**	**60,636**	**818**	**35,000**	**139,600**	**59.9**	**$199,352.44**

ESTHONIA-

Table 300

Detail by Months of Supplies Donated by the Esthonian Governme[n]

Month	Flour	Rice	Pork Products	Milk	Sugar	Misc. Food	Total Tons	Total Value
	Commodities in Net Metric Tons of 1,000 Kilograms or 2,204.6 Pounds							
1919								
Commencement to August 1	300.0	....	...	....	....	....	300.0	$ 67,500.
August	.....	15.0	...	25.0	10.0	10.0*	60.0	23,773.
November	208.0	....	...	....	....	....	208.0	35,361.
December	109.0	....	...	....	....	....	109.0	18,354.
1920								
January	84.0	....	...	....	....	....	84.0	14,267.
February	50.0	....	...	....	....	....	50.0	8,498.
March	110.0	....	...	....	....	....	110.0	18,695.
April	308.0	....	...	....	....	....	308.0	52,415.
1921								
January to August	335.0	....	1.0	122.0	....	....	458.0	57,321.
October	.....	....	...	6.0	....	....	6.0	2,257.
Total	**1,504.0**	**15.0**	**1.0**	**153.0**	**10.0**	**10.0**	**1,693.0**	**$298,444.**

* Prunes.

ESTHONIA-

Table 301

Detail of the Movement of Supplies, by Steame[r]

Transshipped via	Source and Retransshipping Steamer	Date of Arrival
Northwest Russia Stock		1920
Soviet Russia, Transit Stock		1922
Total		
E. H. Stinnes	Comité National—Wasa, I	1919
		1920
Saale, I	Mar Mediterraneo—Hela	August
Progress, III	Herefordshire—Siedler	Decembe[r]
Mineral	American, I—Hela	Decembe[r]
		1921
Weichsel, II and Martha, II	Westford—Siedler	January
Echo, III	American, II—Hela	January
Progress, V	Homer City, II—Torfrid	Apr. 8
Adele, II	Westbrook—Torfrid	April
Johanna and August	Phoenix Bridge—Echo, IV	May
Progress, VII	Cornish City, II, Nemaha—Neva	May
Sensal, IV	Hawaiian, III—Neva	July
Hansa, IV	Oregonian, IV—Neva	July
Imperial, III	Ipswich, II—Neva	August
Total		
		1922
Christel Salling, II	Nobles, II—Redondo—Mars	May 9
Strassburg, VI	Dallas and Western Scout—Redondo—Mars	May 10
Coblenz, III	Chappaqua, II and Sapinero, I—Belvidere	May 26
Total		

* Cf. Table 298.

..R.A.-European Children's Fund

r Children's Relief—Reconstruction Period, 1919–1924

..R.A.-European Children's Fund

r Ports*—Reconstruction Period, 1919–1924

Contents of Cargoes in Net Metric Tons of 1,000 Kilograms or 2,204.6 Pounds

Flour	Rice	Beans, Peas	Pork Products	Milk	Cocoa	Sugar	Soap	Total Tons
			A. DIRECT ARRIVALS					
.....	....	....	17.0	....	....	...	...	17.0
114.1	23.6	....	....	....	....	...	...	137.7
114.1	**23.6**	....	**17.0**	....	....	...	...	**154.7**
			B. ROTTERDAM—DANZIG					
.....	....	....	**87.9**	....	....	...	...	**87.9**
			C. HAMBURG—DANZIG					
.....	....	....	....	....	(.015)	...	...	(.015)
.....	55.8	....	....	....	....	...	...	55.8
.....	....	....	....	94.0	....	...	...	94.0
232.0	....	....	....	....	....	...	...	232.0
.....	....	....	....	.2	....	...	...	.2
.....	....	....	....	....	7.9	...	...	7.9
.....	32.0	....	....	....	....	...	...	32.0
.....	72.3	....	....	....	....	...	...	72.3
.....	....	....	....	127.2	....	...	...	127.2
.....	....	....	....	....	10.0	...	...	10.0
.....	....	....	....	19.7	....	...	...	19.7
.....	....	....	....	17.3	....	...	...	17.3
232.0	**160.1**	....	....	**258.4**	**17.9**	...	...	**668.4**
			D. HAMBURG—RIGA					
.....	26.9	....	....	....	....	...	...	26.9
.....	....	....	....	....	3.6	9.4	...	13.0
.....	20.2	....	6.3	....	....	...	...	26.5
.....	**47.1**	....	**6.3**	....	**3.6**	**9.4**	...	**66.4**

[*Continued on next page*]

Table 301—*Continued*

Detail of the Movement

Transshipped via	Source and Retransshipping Steamer	Date of Arrival
Redondo	Christel Salling, II and Strassburg, VI	1922 May 15
Planet	Guernsey, I—Wasa, II	1921 Sept. 15
Wasa, I	E. H. Stinnes	1919 Dec. 2
Siedler	Cornish City, I; Progress, III; Weichsel, II; Martha, II; Thorn Evac.; Modlin Purchase	1921 Jan. 2
Torfrid	Cornish City, I; Leeds City, I; Progress, V; Bradclyde, II; Adele, II; Modlin Purchase; Warsaw Mission	Apr. 2
Hela	Echo, III; Thorn Evac.; Vardulia; Royal; Saale, I; Mineral	Mar. 1
Echo, IV	Johanna; August; Watsness, II; Delevan; Warsaw Mission	June 2
Neva	Cornish City, I; Progress, VII; Sensal, IV; Hansa, IV; Imperial, III; Panama, I	Sept. [illegible]
Wasa, II	Planet	Sept. ..
Ulrikka	Estonia	Oct. [illegible]
Total	....	....
Belvidere	Coblenz, III	1922 July 7
Mars	Redondo	1922 May 2
Total Shipments Handled	....	....
Less B, C, D, E, and F	....	....
Net Arrivals	....	....

ESTHONIA—A.R.A. and A.R.A.-European Children's Fund

Summary of Internal Deliveries by Operations*

Reconstruction Period, 1919–1924

Table 302

Operation	Table No.	Commodities in Net Metric Tons of 1,000 Kilograms or 2,204.6 Pounds										
		Flour	Rice	Beans, Peas	Pork Products	Milk	Cocoa	Sugar	Misc. Food	Soap	Clothing	Tota[l] Ton[s]
Bulk Sales	303	3.7	1.5	1.9	76.3	209.0	.2	.9	....	....	....	29
Clothing	304	....	....	....	....	.....	....	....	....	....	59.9	5
Child Feeding	305	2,343.3	531.8	447.5	231.6	1,348.7	143.8	399.2	10.0	38.4	....	5,49
Total	292	**2,347.0**	**533.3**	**449.4**	**307.9**	**1,557.7**	**144.0**	**400.1**	**10.0**	**38.4**	**59.9**	**5,84**

* For division to organizations and value of relief applied see Table 292.

R.A.-European Children's Fund

pplies, by Steamers, by Ports

Flour	Rice	Beans, Peas	Pork Products	Milk	Cocoa	Sugar	Soap	Total Tons
			Contents of Cargoes in Net Metric Tons of 1,000 Kilograms or 2,204.6 Pounds					
			E. RIGA—HELSINGFORS					
.....	**26.9**	....	....	....	**3.6**	**9.4**	...	**39.9**
			F. DANZIG—RIGA					
.....	....	....	....	**113.4**	....	...	...	**113.4**
			G. DANZIG—REVAL					
.....	....	....	87.9	....	....	...	...	87.9
232.0	60.2	102.0	23.2	130.0	14.0	37.0	...	598.4
115.0	32.0	50.2	17.4	64.0	7.9	18.0	7.3	311.8
.....	....	....	69.5	94.2	....	...	...	163.7
93.9	72.3	....	9.0	51.2	4.1	16.1	...	246.6
.....	33.0	74.8	15.0	164.2	10.0	...	...	297.0
.....	....	....	....	113.4	....	...	...	113.4
.....	....	....	....	....	....	25.0	...	25.0
440.9	**197.5**	**227.0**	**222.0**	**617.0**	**36.0**	**96.1**	**7.3**	**1,843.8**
			H. RIGA—REVAL					
.....	**20.2**	....	**6.3**	....	....	...	...	**26.5**
			I. HELSINGFORS—REVAL					
.....	**26.9**	....	....	....	**3.6**	**9.4**	...	**39.9**
787.0	**502.3**	**227.0**	**339.5**	**988.8**	**64.7**	**124.3**	**7.3**	**3,040.9**
232.0	234.1	....	94.2	371.8	25.1	18.8	...	976.0
555.0	**268.2**	**227.0**	**245.3**	**617.0**	**39.6**	**105.5**	**7.3**	**2,064.9**

ESTHONIA—A.R.A.-European Children's Fund

Detail of Bulk Sale Deliveries, by Institutions and Organizations
Reconstruction Period, 1919–1924

Table 303

ceipt o.	Source	Date	Flour	Rice	Beans, Peas	Pork Products	Milk Evap. Cond.	Cocoa	Sugar	Total Tons
			Commodities in Net Metric Tons of 1,000 Kilograms or 2,204.6 Pounds							
	Institutions—Student Feeding	1921								
1	Tartu University	Apr. 1	1.701	.486	.891	.243	.648	.113	.405	4.487
2	Tartu University	May 1	1.953	.558	1.023	.279	.744	.131	.465	5.153
3	Tartu University	July 1	....	.420	....	....	....	....	....	.420
..	Total Deliveries for Student Feeding	....	**3.654**	**1.464**	**1.914**	**.522**	**1.392**	**.244**	**.870**	**10.060**
	Organizations									
..	Friends' Emergency and War Victims' Relief Committee	May 25	....	....	....	75.796	94.234	....	....	170.030
..	Friends' Emergency and War Victims' Relief Committee	Sept. 1	....	....	....	....	113.357	....	....	113.357
..	Total Deliveries to F.E. and W.V.R.C.	....	....	....	....	**75.796**	**207.591**	....	....	**283.387**
	Grand Total	....	**3.654**	**1.464**	**1.914**	**76.318**	**208.983**	**.244**	**.870**	**293.447**

ESTHONIA—A.R.A.-European Children's Fund

Detail of Internal Deliveries of Clothing, by Committees—Reconstruction Period, 1919–1924

Table 304

Receipt No.	District Committees	Date	Shoes (Pairs)	Laces (Pairs)	Stockings (Pairs)	Woolens (Yards)	Thread (Spools)	Needles (No.)	Buttons (No.)
		1920							
1	Paide	Feb. 12	184	184	184	252	28	....	70
2	Walk	Feb. 16	780	780	780	864	100	....	2,40
3	Werro	Feb. 16	1,510	1,510	1,510	2,174	252	....	6,04
4	Tartu	Feb. 16	3,000	3,000	3,000	4,320	500	....	12,00
5	Petchory	Feb. 16	1,751	1,751	1,751	2,454	284	....	6,81
6	Nömme	Feb. 14	120	120	120	173	20	....	48
7	Sindi	Feb. 12	145	145	145	209	24	....	58
8	Karu	Feb. 9	25	25	25	36	4	....	10
9	Kärdla	Feb. 26	175	175	175	252	29	....	70
10	Lehtse	Feb. 27	62	62	62	89	11	....	24
	Total for February	....	**7,752**	**7,752**	**7,752**	**10,823**	**1,252**	....	**30,06**
11	Pernau	Mar. 1	1,500	1,500	1,500	2,160	250	....	6,00
12	Fellin	Mar. 1	1,310	1,310	1,310	1,886	218	....	5,24
13	Arensburg	Mar. 1	1,215	1,215	1,215	1,750	203	....	4,80
14	Keila	Mar. 2	175	175	175	209	24	....	58
15	Tapa	Mar. 5	138	138	138	199	23	....	55
16	Wesenburg	Mar. 8	1,850	1,850	1,850	2,880	333	....	8,00
17	Hapsal	Mar. 8	1,500	1,500	1,500	2,304	267	....	6,40
18	Baltiski Port	Mar. 2	100	100	100	216	25	....	60
19	Johwi	Mar. 8	100	100	100	144	17	....	40
20	Paide	Mar. 8	1,616	1,616	1,616	3,348	388	....	9,30
21	Harju	Mar. 22	1,500	1,500	1,500	2,160	250	....	6,00
22	Tartu	Mar. 22	1,500	1,500	1,500	2,160	250	....	6,00
23	Walk	Mar. 22	300	300	300	432	50	....	1,20
24	Narva	Mar. 22	500	500	500	720	84	....	2,00
25	Pernau	Mar. 26	400	400	400	1,152	134	....	3,20
26	Werro	Mar. 26	400	400	400	1,480	184	....	4,00
27	Petchory	Mar. 26	400	400	400	1,480	184	....	4,00
28	Fellin	Mar. 26	400	400	400	1,480	184	....	4,00
29	Nömme	Mar. 31	100	65	100	144	17	....	4
30	Kärdla	Mar. 31	100	72	100	144	17	....	4
31	Rakwere	Mar. 31	250	170	250	360	42	....	1,0
32	Arensburg	Mar. 31	300	300	300	432	50	....	1,2
33	Vardi	Mar. 31	55	55	55	79	9	....	2
40	Narva	Mar. 31	2,400	2,400	2,400	3,456	400	....	9,6
	Total for March	....	**18,109**	**17,966**	**18,109**	**30,775**	**3,603**	....	**85,1**
34	Karu	Apr. 7	10	10	10	14	2	....	[illegible]
35	Rakwere	Apr. 7	500	500	500	1,440	167	....	4,0
36	Paide	Apr. 4	100	100	100	144	17	....	4
37	Narva-Hapsal	Apr. 4	96	96	96	138	16	....	3
38	Sindi	Apr. 4	100	100	100	144	17	....	4
39	Tartu	Apr. 4	500	432	500	...	...	....	..
41	Narva	Apr. 23	250	250	...	...	...	....	..
42	Hapsal	Apr. 23	250	250	...	...	...	....	..
43	Petchory	Apr. 23	500	500	...	288	34	....	8
44	Vöru	Apr. 26	250	200	200	...	...	....	..
45	Baltiski Port	Apr. 26	50	50	50	72	8	....	2
46	Fellin	Apr. 26	250	250	100	...	...	....	..
47	Reval	Apr. 27	10,558	13,384	14,268	14,885	1,683	35,000	18,1
	Total for April	....	**13,414**	**16,122**	**15,924**	**17,125**	**1,944**	**35,000**	**24,3**
		1921							
1	Werro	Oct. ..	1,000	...	1,000	...	...	....	..
2	Narva	Oct. ..	800	...	800	...	...	....	..
3	Tartu	Oct. ..	1,000	...	1,000	...	...	....	..
4	Petchory	Oct. ..	2,200	...	2,200	...	...	....	..
5	Vöru	Oct. ..	500	...	500	...	...	....	..

ESTHONIA

'able 304—*Continued* — Detail of Internal Deliveries, by Committees

pt	District Committees	Date	Shoes (Pairs)	Laces (Pairs)	Stockings (Pairs)	Woolens (Yards)	Thread (Spools)	Needles (No.)	Buttons (No.)
		1921							
	Paide	Oct. ..	500	...	500	...	...	....	....
	Pernau	Oct. ..	500	...	500	...	...	....	....
	Sindi	Oct. ..	50	...	50	...	...	....	....
	Fellin	Oct. ..	250	...	250	...	...	....	....
	Nömme	Oct. ..	100	...	100	...	...	....	....
	Baltiski Port	Oct. ..	50	...	50	...	...	....	....
	Kärdla	Oct. ..	100	...	100	...	...	....	....
	Hapsal	Oct. ..	200	...	200	...	...	....	....
	Arensburg	Oct. ..	200	...	200	...	...	....	....
	Reval	Oct. ..	2,530	...	2,530	...	...	....	....
	Total for October	....	**9,980**	...	**9,980**	...	...	....	....
	Total per Receipts	....	**49,255**	**41,840**	**51,765**	**58,723**	**6,799**	**35,000**	**139,600**
	Transferred from Latvia	....	757	...	661	1,915	...	....	....
	Total Deliveries *	....	**50,012**	**41,840**	**52,426**	**60,638**	**6,799†**	**35,000**	**139,600**

Total clothing deliveries equivalent to 59.9 metric tons.

† Equivalent to 818 pounds.

ESTHONIA—A.R.A. and A.R.A.-European Children's Fund

Detail of Internal Deliveries for Child Feeding by Districts and Kitchens, by Months—Reconstruction Period, 1919–1924

Table 305

...ipt	Districts and Kitchens	Flour	Rice	Beans, Peas	Pork Products	Milk Evap. Cond.	Cocoa	Sugar	Misc. Food*	Soap	Total Tons
		Commodities in Net Metric Tons of 1,000 Kilograms or 2,204.6 Pounds									
	June, 1919										
1	Reval	14.400	2.400	....	....	12.000	....	2.400	.480	....	31.680
2	Narva	6.000	1.000	....	....	4.202	....	1.000	....	....	12.202
3	Rakvere	10.800	1.400	....	....	1.064	....	1.800	....	....	15.064
4	Nömme	.540	.020	....	....	.532	....	.020	....	....	1.112
5	Fellin	5.040	.640	....	....	.672	....	.680	....	....	7.032
6	Pernau	7.800	1.060	....	....	1.652	....	1.304	....	....	11.816
7	Harju	6.000	.750	....	....	....	....	1.000	....	....	7.750
8	Harju	....	....	....	....	.280	....	....	....	....	.280
9	Jamburg	.114	.019	....	....	....	....	.019	....	....	.152
0	Werro	10.680	1.370	....	....	1.092	....	1.700	....	....	14.842
1	Dorpat	13.200	1.850	....	....	3.920	....	2.200	....	....	21.170
2	Paide	4.680	.580	....	....	.392	....	.780	....	....	6.432
3	Hapsal	8.400	.500	....	....	.532	....	1.400	....	....	10.832
4	Arensburg	8.280	1.055	....	....	.420	....	1.380	....	....	11.135
5	Walk	2.400	.400	....	....	1.960	....	.400	....	....	5.160
	Total for June	**98.334**	**13.044**	....	....	**28.718**	....	**16.083**	**.480**	....	**156.659**
	July, 1919										
6	Reval	27.925	1.854	3.600	2.400	15.271	4.800	5.454	2.400	....	63.704
7	Nömme	.910	....	....	....	.240	.232	.197	....	....	1.579
8	Arensburg	19.000	.320	....	.100	.326	.160	2.760	.075	....	22.741
9	Rakvere	21.200	.400	.400	.200	.768	.400	3.600	.226	....	27.194
20	Werro	1.200	.480	....	.120	.450	.240	.240	.120	....	2.850
20	Werro	18.720	....	....	....	....	....	3.120	....	....	21.840
21	Petchory	1.000	.400	....	.100	.400	.200	.200	.100	....	2.400
22	Paide	.800	.320	....	.080	.320	.160	.160	.080	....	1.920
23	Fellin	1.400	.560	....	.140	.560	.280	.280	.140	....	3.360
24	Hapsal	1.000	.416	....	.100	.400	.200	.200	.075	....	2.391

* All prunes.

[*Continued on next page*]

ESTHONIA

Table 305—*Continued* Detail of Internal Deliveries for Child Feeding

Receipt No.	Districts and Kitchens	Flour	Rice	Beans, Peas	Pork Products	Milk Evap. Cond.	Cocoa	Sugar	Misc. Food	Soap	Total Tons
		Commodities in Net Metric Tons of 1,000 Kilograms or 2,204.6 Pounds									
	July, 1919										
25	Walk	4.000	.800	.800	.400	1.500	.800	.800	.400	....	9.5
26	Pernau	3.400	1.360	....	.340	1.360	.680	.680	.340	....	8.1
27	Narva	10.000	2.000	2.000	1.000	3.768	2.000	2.000	.970	....	23.7
28	Dorpat (Tartu)	8.000	1.600	1.600	.800	3.000	1.600	1.600	.800	....	19.0
	Total for July	**118.555**	**10.510**	**8.400**	**5.780**	**28.363**	**11.752**	**21.291**	**5.726**	....	**210.3**
	August, 1919										
29	Reval	19.600	5.800	5.466	.800	12.852	.668	4.800	1.334	....	51.3
30	Rannamoise	....	....	....	.008	.085	.020	....	....	....	.1
31	Harju	8.000	2.000	....	....	....	....	2.000	....	....	12.0
32	Baltiski Port	.240	.060	.060	....	.112	....	.060	....	....	.5
33	Nömme	.720	.180	.180	....	.280	....	.180	....	....	1.5
34	Petchory	.816	.240	.228	.032	.504	.028	.200	....	....	2.0
35	Arensburg	.652	.190	.180	.024	.420	.020	.160	....	....	1.6
35	Arensburg	10.400	2.600	....	....	....	....	2.600	....	....	15.6
36	Paide	.652	.190	.180	.024	.420	.020	.160	....	....	1.6
37	Werro	.976	.280	.268	.048	.588	.028	.240	....	....	2.4
37	Werro	12.480	3.120	....	....	....	....	3.120	....	....	18.7
38	Fellin	1.136	.320	.308	.032	.644	.028	.280	....	....	2.7
39	Hapsal	.804	.250	.234	.040	.588	.034	.200	....	....	2.1
39	Hapsal	3.200	.800	....	....	....	....	.800	....	....	4.8
40	Rakvere	1.148	.350	.320	.056	.840	.047	.280	....	....	3.0
40	Rakvere	8.800	2.200	....	....	....	....	2.200	....	....	13.2
41	Walk	3.248	.920	.880	.144	1.876	.080	.800	....	....	7.9
42	Pernau	2.736	.720	.708	.032	1.064	.028	.680	....	....	5.9
42	Pernau	6.400	1.600	....	....	....	....	1.600	....	....	9.6
43	Narva	8.192	2.480	2.320	.384	5.740	.320	2.000	....	....	21.4
44	Tartu	6.504	1.860	1.774	.208	3.864	.172	1.600	....	....	15.9
	Total for August	**96.704**	**26.160**	**13.106**	**1.832**	**29.877**	**1.493**	**23.960**	**1.334**	....	**194.4**
	September, 1919										
45	Nömme	.720	.180	.180	....	.675	.090	.180	....	....	2.0
46	Hapsal	.804	.250	.234	.080	.750	.084	.200	....	....	2.4
46	Hapsal	3.200	.800	....	....	....	....	.800	....	....	4.8
47	Walk	3.248	.920	.880	.190	3.000	.360	.800	....	....	9.3
48	Reval	19.600	5.800	5.466	1.600	18.000	2.048	4.800	.284	....	57.5
49	Pernau	2.736	.720	.708	.064	2.550	.328	.680	....	....	7.7
49	Pernau	6.400	1.600	....	....	....	....	1.600	....	....	9.6
50	Rakvere	1.148	.350	.320	.112	1.050	.117	.280	....	....	3.3
50	Rakvere	8.800	2.200	....	....	....	....	2.200	....	....	13.2
51	Tartu	6.504	1.860	1.774	.416	6.000	.712	1.600	....	....	18.8
52	Fellin	1.136	.320	.308	.064	1.050	.128	.280	....	....	3.2
53	Narva	8.192	2.480	2.320	.768	7.500	.840	2.000	....	....	24.1
54	Werro	.976	.280	.268	.064	.900	.108	.240	....	....	2.8
54	Werro	12.480	3.120	....	....	....	....	3.120	....	....	18.7
55	Paide	.652	.190	.180	.048	.600	.070	.160	....	....	1.
56	Arensburg	.652	.190	.180	.048	.600	.070	.160	....	....	1.
56	Arensburg	10.400	2.600	....	....	....	....	2.600	....	....	15.
57	Rannamoise	.080	.024	.016	.016	.075	.020	.016	....	....	.
58	Petchory	.816	.240	.228	.064	.750	.088	.200	....	....	2.
59	Baltiski Port	.240	.060	.060	....	.225	.030	.060	....	....	.
	Total for September	**88.784**	**24.184**	**13.122**	**3.534**	**43.725**	**5.093**	**21.976**	**.284**	....	**200.**
	October, 1919										
60	Rannamoise	.080	.024	.016	.008	.075	.020	.016	....	....	.
61	Baltiski Port	.240	.060	....	....	.225	.030	.060	....	....	.
62	Nömme	.744	.244	.140	.054	.693	.120	.180	....	....	2.
63	Petchory	.816	.240	....	.058	.762	.108	.200	....	....	2.
64	Arensburg	.652	.190	....	.024	.600	.070	.160	....	....	1.
64	Arensburg	10.400	2.600	....	....	....	....	2.600	....	....	15.

ESTHONIA

Table 305—*Continued* Detail of Internal Deliveries for Child Feeding

eipt o.	Districts and Kitchens	Commodities in Net Metric Tons of 1,000 Kilograms or 2,204.6 Pounds									
		Flour	Rice	Beans, Peas	Pork Products	Milk Evap. Cond.	Cocoa	Sugar	Misc. Food	Soap	Total Tons
	October, 1919										
5	Paide	.652	.190	....	.064	.600	.096	.160	....	....	1.762
6	Werro	.976	.280	....	.058	.900	.133	.240	....	....	2.587
6	Werro	12.480	3.120	....	....	....	....	3.120	....	....	18.720
7	Pernau	2.736	.720	....	.056	2.550	.400	.680	....	....	7.142
7	Pernau	3.664	1.600	....	....	....	....	1.600	....	....	6.864
8	Fellin	1.136	.320	....	.056	1.050	.168	.280	....	....	3.010
9	Hapsal	.842	.250	.034	.040	.756	.100	.200	....	....	2.222
9	Hapsal	3.200	.800	....	....	....	....	.800	....	....	4.800
0	Rakvere	1.148	.350	.054	.120	1.050	.168	.280	....	....	3.170
0	Rakvere	8.800	2.200	....	....	....	....	2.200	....	....	13.200
1	Walk	3.248	.920	....	....	3.000	.464	.800	....	....	8.432
2	Narva	8.192	2.480	.240	.814	7.500	1.100	2.320	....	....	22.646
3	Tartu	6.504	1.860	....	.096	6.000	.964	1.600	....	....	17.024
4	Reval	19.600	5.800	....	1.600	18.000	2.068	4.800	....	....	51.868
	Total for October	**86.110**	**24.248**	**.484**	**3.048**	**43.761**	**6.009**	**22.296**	....	....	**185.956**
	November, 1919										
5	Arensburg	6.399	1.000	1.200	1.298	4.400	.501	1.399	....	....	16.197
6	Arensburg	55.766	8.710	....	....	....	....	12.195	....	....	76.671
7	Rannamoise	.246	.061	.016	.016	.240	.020	.061	....	....	.660
8	Harju	19.656	3.276	2.457	....	....	1.638	4.914	....	....	31.941
9	Baltiski Port	.737	.187	.094	....	.675	.062	.187	....	.045	1.987
0	Nömme	2.297	.768	.635	.364	2.025	.184	.246	....	.115	6.634
1	Petchory	2.531	.798	.614	.295	2.250	.205	.614	....	.150	7.457
A	Petchory	9.828	1.638	1.228	....	....	.819	2.457	....	....	15.970
2	Paide	2.015	.606	.450	.196	1.800	.164	.491	....	.120	5.842
3	Werro	3.022	.921	.676	.295	2.700	.246	.737	....	.170	8.767
3	Werro	38.329	6.388	4.791	....	....	3.194	9.582	....	....	62.284
4	Fellin	3.514	7.041	.737	.295	3.150	.287	.860	....	.210	16.094
5	Hapsal	2.518	.766	.563	.145	2.250	.195	.614	....	.731	7.782
5	Hapsal	9.828	1.638	1.229	....	....	.819	2.457	....	....	15.971
6	Walk	9.975	2.826	1.843	.589	9.000	.819	2.457	....	.517	28.026
7	Pernau	8.403	2.203	1.248	.196	7.650	.696	2.088	....	.511	22.995
7	Pernau	19.656	3.276	2.457	....	.480	1.638	4.914	....	.041	32.462
8	Tartu	20.983	6.020	4.013	1.376	18.900	1.720	5.760	....	1.261	60.033
8	Tartu	24.570	4.095	3.070	....	....	2.047	6.142	....	....	39.924
9	Rakvere	3.526	1.069	.787	.417	3.150	.287	.860	....	.178	10.274
9	Rakvere	27.027	4.504	3.378	....	....	2.252	6.757	....	....	43.918
0	Narva	25.160	7.617	5.528	2.902	22.500	2.048	6.143	....	1.278	73.176
1	Reval	20.066	5.938	4.163	1.638	18.000	1.639	4.914	....	1.638	57.996
	Total for November	**316.052**	**71.346**	**41.177**	**10.022**	**99.170**	**21.480**	**76.849**	....	**6.965**	**643.061**
	December, 1919										
2	Reval	20.066	5.938	4.163	1.638	18.000	1.639	4.914	2.176	1.470	60.004
3	Pernau	....	.016	.016	....	.420	.016	.323	....	....	.791
4	Taps	.823	.129	.154	.167	.563	.064	.179	....	....	2.079
	Total for December	**20.889**	**6.083**	**4.333**	**1.805**	**18.983**	**1.719**	**5.416**	**2.176**	**1.470**	**62.874**
	January, 1920										
5	Reval	25.691	....	4.022	10.090	9.259	2.072	4.566	....	1.320	57.020
6	Harju	9.598	1.293	3.031	....	....	....	1.383	....	....	15.305
7	Narva	11.408	....	1.332	4.524	2.644	.814	1.854	....	.550	23.126
8	Arensburg	1.594	....	.173	.623	.370	.114	.260	....	.077	3.211
9	Arensburg	13.198	2.779	4.168	8.168	27.658	.896	2.039	....	.605	59.511
00	Tartu	9.734	....	1.750	4.862	2.221	.684	1.558	....	.462	21.271
01	Partumaa	11.998	1.617	3.789	7.426	25.144	.814	1.854	....	.550	53.192
02	Pernau	4.030	....	1.083	2.328	.899	.280	.630	....	.187	9.437
03	Pernau	9.598	1.294	3.031	5.940	20.115	.651	1.483	....	.440	42.552
04	Hapsal	1.138	....	.123	.497	.264	.091	.185	....	.055	2.353

[*Continued on next page*]

ESTHONIA

Table 305—*Continued* Detail of Internal Deliveries for Child Feeding

Receipt No.	Districts and Kitchens	Commodities in Net Metric Tons of 1,000 Kilograms or 2,204.6 Pounds									
		Flour	Rice	Beans, Peas	Pork Products	Milk Evap. Cond.	Cocoa	Sugar	Misc. Food	Soap	Total Tons
	January, 1920										
105	**Hapsal**	4.799	.647	1.515	2.970	9.857	.326	.741	....	.220	21.0
106	**Fellin**	1.606	....	.223	.745	.370	.114	.260	....	.077	3.3
107	**Fellin**	19.198	2.998	4.802	3.898	13.200	1.502	4.198	....	.385	50.1
108	**Paide**	.911	....	.098	.387	.212	.065	.148	....	.044	1.8
109	**Paide**	17.964	2.814	4.570	3.648	12.356	1.406	2.529	....	.364	45.6
110	**Taps**	.411	.064	.077	.083	.281	.032	.089	....	.021	1.0
111	**Nömme**	.994	....	....	.324	.237	.073	.473	....	.050	2.1
112	**Baltiski Port**	.360	....	.112	.223	.079	.024	.053	....	.017	.8
113	**Rannamoise**	.120	....	.052	.058	.011	.008	.040	....	.005	.2
	Total for January	**144.350**	**13.506**	**33.951**	**56.794**	**125.177**	**9.966**	**24.343**	....	**5.429**	**413.5**
	February, 1920										
114	**Narva**	9.142	....	1.715	....	....	1.230	....	....	....	12.0
115	**Dorpat**	7.679	....	1.441	....	....	.994	....	....	....	10.1
115	**Dorpat**	6.782	....	.476	....	....	1.170	....	....	....	8.4
116	**Walk**	3.309	....	.201	2.381	1.058	.326	.742	....	.220	8.2
116	**Walk**	....	.200	.240	.260	.880	.100	.277	....	....	1.9
117	**Werro**	....	....	.148	.596	.317	.098	.223	....	.066	1.4
117	**Werro**	....	2.522	5.910	9.584	39.225	1.270	2.893	....	.858	62.2
118	**Petchory**	1.638	....	.072	.448	.264	.081	.185	....	.055	2.7
118	**Petchory**	....	1.617	3.788	7.426	25.144	.814	1.854	....	.550	41.1
119	**Kärdla**	.917	.143	.172	.186	.629	.071	.200	....	.055	2.3
120	**Sindi**	1.466	.228	.274	.297	1.006	.114	.319	....	.044	3.7
121	**Reval**	21.941	1.833	4.116	4.455	15.086	1.717	4.798	....	1.320	55.2
	Total for February	**52.874**	**6.543**	**18.553**	**25.633**	**83.609**	**7.985**	**11.491**	....	**3.168**	**209.8**
	March, 1920										
171	**Reval**	22.398	3.499	4.202	....	15.401	1.753	4.898	....	1.348	53.4
122	**Harju**	7.314	1.142	1.372	....	5.029	.572	1.599	....	.440	17.4
123	**Narva**	10.056	1.571	1.886	....	6.912	.787	2.199	....	.605	24.0
124	**Rakvere**	1.280	.200	.240	....	.880	.100	.280	....	.077	3.0
125	**Rakvere**	18.284	2.856	3.430	.400	12.568	1.431	3.998	....	1.100	44.0
126	**Tartu**	7.679	1.200	1.440	....	5.280	.601	1.679	....	.462	18.3
127	**Tartu**	9.142	1.428	1.715	....	6.286	.715	1.999	....	.550	21.8
128	**Pernau**	3.108	.486	.583	....	2.137	.244	.680	....	.187	7.4
129	**Pernau**	7.314	1.142	1.372	....	5.028	.572	1.599	....	.440	17.4
130	**Walk**	3.657	.571	.686	....	2.514	.286	.800	....	.220	8.7
131	**Walk**	1.280	.200	.240	....	.880	.100	.280	....	.077	3.[illegible]
132	**Hapsal**	.914	.143	.172	....	.629	.072	.200	....	.055	2.1
133	**Hapsal**	4.571	.714	.858	....	3.143	.358	1.000	....	.275	10.9
134	**Fellin**	1.280	.200	.240	....	.880	.100	.280	....	.077	3.[illegible]
135	**Fellin**	6.399	1.000	1.201	....	4.400	.501	1.339	....	.385	15.[illegible]
136	**Werro**	1.280	.200	.240	....	.880	.100	.280	....	.077	3.[illegible]
137	**Werro**	14.262	2.227	2.675	....	9.806	1.116	3.119	....	.858	34.[illegible]
138	**Paide**	.731	.114	.137	....	.503	.057	.160	....	.044	1.7
139–42	**Paide**	7.313	1.142	1.715	....	5.029	.572	1.599	....	.440	17.8
143	**Petchory**	1.097	.171	.206	....	.754	.086	.240	....	.066	2.[illegible]
144	**Petchory**	9.142	1.428	1.715	....	6.286	.715	1.999	....	.550	21.8
145	**Arensburg**	1.279	.200	.240	....	.880	.100	.280	....	.077	3.[illegible]
146	**Arensburg**	11.157	1.742	2.092	....	7.669	.773	2.439	....	.671	26.[illegible]
172	**Nömme**	1.646	.129	.154	....	.566	.064	.180	....	.050	2.[illegible]
173	**Baltiski Port**	.274	.043	.051	....	.188	.021	.060	....	.017	[illegible]
174	**Rannamoise**	.091	.014	.017	....	.063	.007	.020	....	.006	.[illegible]
147	**Kärdla**	.914	.143	.172	....	.629	.072	.200	....	.055	2.[illegible]
148	**Sindi**	.549	.086	.103	....	.377	.043	.120	....	.033	1.[illegible]
	Total for March	**154.411**	**23.991**	**29.154**	**.400**	**105.597**	**11.918**	**33.526**	....	**9.242**	**368.[illegible]**
	April and May, 1920										
149	**Reval**	44.796	7.997	9.349	4.455	30.802	5.645	5.817	....	1.347	110.[illegible]

ESTHONIA

Table 305—*Continued* Detail of Internal Deliveries for Child Feeding

ipt .	Districts and Kitchens	Flour	Rice	Beans, Peas	Pork Products	Milk Evap. Cond.	Cocoa	Sugar	Misc. Food	Soap	Total Tons
		Commodities in Net Metric Tons of 1,000 Kilograms or 2,204.6 Pounds									
	April and May, 1920										
9	Harju	14.627	2.285	3.744	1.455	10.058	1.045	1.599	....	....	34.813
1	Narva	20.112	3.141	3.773	1.856	13.825	1.574	2.199	....	.302	46.782
-53	Rakvere	39.128	....	7.340	1.699	....	3.062	4.278	....	.588	56.095
4	Tartu	33.643	2.916	6.311	2.600	13.728	2.633	3.679	....	.231	65.741
5	Pernau	20.844	3.255	4.910	.631	14.332	1.632	2.279	....	.093	47.976
6	Walk	9.873	1.542	2.352	1.002	6.789	.772	1.080	....	.110	23.520
7	Hapsal	10.970	1.714	2.058	1.371	18.858	.858	1.200	....	.104	37.133
8	Fellin	15.359	2.399	2.881	.260	6.160	1.202	1.679	....	.218	30.158
9	Werro	31.082	4.855	5.830	.260	21.372	2.432	3.399	....	.438	69.668
0	Paide	14.262	2.228	2.675	.149	9.806	1.116	1.559	....	.224	32.019
1	Taps	.914	.143	.172	....	6.286	.072	.100	....	.027	7.714
2	Karu	.365	.057	.069	.039	.251	.029	.040	....	.011	.861
3	Lehtse	.549	.086	.103	.056	.377	.043	.060	....	.016	1.290
4	Petchory	20.478	3.199	3.842	4.509	14.081	1.602	2.238	....	.341	50.290
5	Arensburg and Islands	24.862	3.884	4.665	....	8.676	1.746	2.719	....	....	46.552
6	Nomme	3.291	.257	.309	.167	1.131	.129	.180	....	.049	5.513
7	Baltiski Port	.549	.086	.103	.056	.377	.043	.060	....	.016	1.290
8	Rannamoise	.183	.029	.034	.019	.126	.014	.020	....	.005	.430
9	Kärdla	1.828	.286	.344	.628	1.257	.143	.200	....	.027	4.713
0	Sindi	1.097	.171	.206	.037	.754	.086	.120	....	.032	2.503
	Totals, April and May	**308.812**	**40.530**	**61.070**	**21.249**	**179.046**	**25.878**	**34.505**	....	**4.179**	**675.269**
	February, 1921										
1	Harju	2.729	.762	1.205	.270	1.533	.164	.434	....	....	7.097
2	Narva	3.538	.988	1.562	.350	1.987	.212	.563	....	....	9.200
3	Rakvere	6.571	1.834	2.901	.651	3.690	.394	1.045	....	....	17.086
4	Tartu	5.054	1.411	2.231	.501	2.838	.303	.804	....	....	13.142
5	Parnu	3.033	.847	1.339	.301	1.703	.182	.482	....	....	7.887
6	Walk	1.516	.423	.669	.150	.851	.091	.241	....	....	3.941
7	Hapsal	1.516	.423	.669	.150	.851	.091	.241	....	....	3.941
8	Fellin	2.022	.564	.893	.200	1.135	.121	.322	....	....	5.257
9	Werro	4.043	1.129	1.785	.401	2.271	.243	.643	....	....	10.515
0	Paide	2.022	.564	.893	.200	1.135	.121	.322	....	....	5.257
1	Petchory	3.538	.988	1.562	.350	1.987	.212	.563	....	....	9.200
2	Saaremaa Isles	3.538	.988	1.562	.350	1.987	.212	.563	....	....	9.200
3	Baltiski Port	.081	.023	.036	.008	.045	.005	.013	....	....	.211
4	Nömme	.202	.056	.089	.020	.114	.012	.032	....	....	.525
5	Sindi	.202	.056	.089	.020	.114	.012	.032	....	....	.525
6	Kärdla	.303	.085	.134	.030	.170	.018	.048	....	....	.788
7	Reval	6.591	1.840	2.910	.652	3.701	.396	1.049	....	....	17.139
	Total for February	**46.499**	**12.981**	**20.529**	**4.604**	**26.112**	**2.789**	**7.397**	....	....	**120.911**
	March, 1921										
8	Harju	4.977	1.389	2.197	.493	2.795	.299	.792	....	....	12.942
9	Narva	6.451	1.801	2.848	.639	3.623	.387	1.027	....	....	16.776
0	Rakvere	11.981	3.345	5.289	1.187	6.728	.719	1.906	....	....	31.155
1	Tartu	9.216	2.573	4.069	.913	5.175	.553	1.466	....	....	23.965
2	Pernau	5.530	1.544	2.441	.548	3.105	.332	.880	....	....	14.380
3	Walk	2.765	.772	1.221	.274	1.553	.166	.440	....	....	7.191
4	Hapsal	2.765	.772	1.221	.274	1.553	.166	.440	....	....	7.191
5	Fellin	3.687	1.029	1.628	.365	2.070	.221	.586	....	....	9.586
6	Werro	7.373	2.058	3.255	.730	4.140	.443	1.173	....	....	19.172
7	Paide	3.687	1.029	1.628	.365	2.070	.221	.586	....	....	9.586
8	Petchory	6.451	1.801	2.848	.639	3.623	.387	1.027	....	....	16.776
9	Saaremaa Isles	6.451	1.801	2.848	.639	3.623	.387	1.027	....	....	16.776
0	Baltiski Port	.147	.041	.065	.015	.083	.008	.023	....	....	.382
1	Nomme	.369	.103	.163	.037	.207	.022	.059	....	....	.960
2	Sindi	.369	.103	.163	.037	.207	.022	.059	....	....	.960
3	Kärdla	.553	.154	.244	.055	.311	.033	.088	....	....	1.438
4	Reval	12.018	3.355	5.306	1.191	6.749	.722	1.912	....	....	31.253
	Total for March	**84.790**	**23.670**	**37.434**	**8.401**	**47.615**	**5.088**	**13.491**	....	....	**220.489**

[*Continued on next page*]

ESTHONIA

Table 305—*Continued* Detail of Internal Deliveries for Child Feeding

Receipt No.	Districts and Kitchens	Flour	Rice	Beans, Peas	Pork Products	Milk Evap. Cond.	Cocoa	Sugar	Misc. Food	Soap	Total Tons
		Commodities in Net Metric Tons of 1,000 Kilograms or 2,204.6 Pounds									
	April, 1921										
35	Harju	4.816	1.345	2.126	.477	2.705	.289	.766	....	....	12.
36	Narva	6.457	1.803	2.851	.640	3.626	.388	1.027	....	....	16.
37	Rakvere	13.379	3.735	5.906	1.325	7.513	.803	2.129	....	....	34.
38	Tartu	8.919	2.490	3.938	.884	5.008	.536	1.419	....	....	23.
39	Pernau	4.460	1.245	1.969	.442	2.504	.368	.710	....	....	11.
40	Walk	2.676	.747	1.181	.265	1.503	.161	.426	....	....	6.
41	Hapsal	2.676	.747	1.181	.265	1.503	.161	.426	....	....	6.
42	Fellin	3.568	.996	1.575	.353	2.003	.214	.568	....	....	9.
43	Werro	7.135	1.992	3.150	.707	4.007	.428	1.135	....	....	18.
44	Paide	3.568	.996	1.575	.353	2.003	.214	.568	....	....	9.
45	Petchory	6.243	1.743	2.756	.618	3.506	.375	.993	....	....	16.
46	Arsenburg	5.351	1.494	2.363	.530	3.005	.321	.851	....	....	13.
47	Baltiski Port	.143	.040	.063	.014	.080	.009	.023	....	....	.
48	Nömme	.357	.100	.158	.035	.200	.021	.057	....	....	.
49	Sindi	.357	.100	.158	.035	.200	.021	.057	....	....	.
50	Kärdla	.535	.149	.236	.053	.301	.032	.085	....	....	1.
51	Reval	11.416	3.187	5.040	1.131	6.411	.685	1.816	....	....	29.
	Total for April	**82.056**	**22.909**	**36.226**	**8.127**	**46.078**	**5.026**	**13.056**	....	....	**213.**
	May, 1921										
52	Reval	12.995	3.628	5.737	1.287	7.297	.780	2.067	....	.423	34.
53	Harju	1.843	.515	.814	.183	1.035	.111	.293	....	.060	4.
54	Arensburg	4.608	1.287	2.034	.456	2.588	.277	.733	....	.150	12.
55	Petchory	6.451	1.801	2.848	.639	3.623	.387	1.026	....	.210	16.
56	Paide	3.687	1.029	1.628	.365	2.070	.221	.857	....	.120	9.
57	Werro	5.530	1.544	2.441	.548	3.105	.332	.880	....	.180	14.
58	Hapsal	2.396	.669	1.058	.237	1.345	.144	.381	....	.078	6.
59	Pernau	4.608	1.287	2.034	.456	2.588	.277	.733	....	.150	12.
60	Tartu	8.295	2.316	3.662	.822	4.658	.498	1.320	....	.270	21.
61	Walk	1.843	.515	.814	.183	1.035	.111	.293	....	.060	4.
62	Fellin	2.765	.772	1.221	.274	1.553	.166	.440	....	.090	7.
63	Kärdla	.737	.206	.326	.073	.414	.044	.117	....	.024	1.
64	Sindi	.553	.154	.244	.055	.311	.033	.088	....	.018	1.
65	Nömme	.553	.154	.244	.055	.311	.033	.088	....	.018	1.
66	Baltiski Port	.276	.077	.122	.027	.155	.017	.044	....	.009	.
67	Rakvere	8.663	2.496	3.947	.886	5.020	.570	1.422	....	.291	23.
68	Narva	7.926	2.136	3.377	.758	4.296	.459	1.217	....	.249	20.
	Total for May	**73.729**	**20.586**	**32.551**	**7.304**	**41.404**	**4.460**	**11.999**	....	**2.400**	**194.**
	June, 1921										
69	Kärdla	.535	.149	.236	.053	.301	.032	.085	....	.024	1.
70	Sindi	.535	.223	.139	.053	.301	.032	.085	....	.018	1.
71	Paide	3.568	1.488	.929	.353	2.003	.214	.568	....	.120	9.
72	Tartu	8.027	3.347	2.090	.795	4.508	.482	1.277	....	.270	20.
73	Rakvere	8.651	3.607	2.253	.857	4.858	.519	1.376	....	.291	22.
74	Harju	1.784	.744	.465	.177	1.002	.107	.284	....	.060	4.
75	Narva	7.135	2.975	1.858	.707	4.007	.428	1.135	....	.240	18.
76	Fellin	2.676	1.116	.697	.265	1.503	.161	.426	....	.090	6.
77	Pernau	4.460	1.859	1.161	.442	2.504	.268	.710	....	.150	11.
78	Petchory	6.243	2.603	1.626	.618	3.506	.375	.993	....	.210	16.
79	Werro	5.351	2.231	1.394	.530	3.005	.321	.851	....	.180	13.
80	Hapsal	2.676	1.116	.697	.265	1.503	.161	.426	....	.090	6.
81	Arensburg and Islands	4.460	1.859	1.161	.442	2.504	.268	.710	....	.150	11.
82	Reval	12.487	5.341	3.074	1.237	7.012	.750	1.987	....	.420	32.
83	Reval	14.984	6.357	3.756	1.484	8.414	.900	2.384	....	.498	38.
84	Baltiski Port	.268	.075	.118	.027	.150	.016	.043	....	.009	.
	Total for June	**83.840**	**35.090**	**21.654**	**8.305**	**47.081**	**5.034**	**13.340**	....	**2.820**	**217.**

ESTHONIA

able 305—*Continued* Detail of Internal Deliveries for Child Feeding

pt	Districts and Kitchens	Flour	Rice	Beans, Peas	Pork Products	Milk Evap. Cond.	Cocoa	Sugar	Misc. Food	Soap	Total Tons
		Commodities in Net Metric Tons of 1,000 Kilograms or 2,204.6 Pounds									
	July, 1921										
	Kärdla	.695	.529	....	.073	.180	.073	.104	....	.031	1.685
	Sindi	.521	.397	....	.055	.298	.032	.078	....	.023	1.404
	Paide	3.476	2.647	....	.366	1.988	.213	.518	....	.154	9.362
	Tartu	7.821	5.955	....	.823	4.474	.479	1.166	....	.346	21.064
	Rakvere	8.430	6.418	....	.887	4.821	.516	1.257	....	.372	22.701
	Harju	2.259	1.720	....	.238	.060	.138	.337	....	.100	4.852
	Narva	6.952	5.293	....	.731	3.977	.426	1.037	....	.307	18.723
	Fellin	2.607	1.985	....	.274	1.491	.160	.389	....	.115	7.021
	Pernau	4.345	3.308	....	.457	2.485	.266	.648	....	.192	11.701
	Petchory	6.083	4.632	....	.640	3.480	.373	.907	....	.269	16.384
	Werro	5.224	3.970	....	.549	2.983	.319	.778	....	.230	14.053
	Hapsal	2.597	1.985	....	.274	1.491	.160	.389	....	.115	7.011
	Arensburg and Islands	4.345	3.308	....	.457	2.485	.266	.648	....	.192	11.701
	Reval	13.903	10.586	....	1.463	.368	.852	2.074	....	.614	29.860
	Baltiski Port	.261	.198	....	.027	.006	.016	.039	....	.012	.559
	Total for July	**69.519**	**52.931**	....	**7.314**	**30.587**	**4.289**	**10.369**	....	**3.072**	**178.081**
	August, 1921										
	Kärdla	.348	.206	....	.037	.200	.021	.052	....	....	.864
	Sindi	.348	.206	....	.037	.200	.021	.052	....	....	.864
	Paide	2.607	1.544	....	.274	1.502	.160	.389	....	....	6.476
	Tartu	5.214	3.088	....	.549	3.005	.319	.777	....	....	12.952
	Viru	5.562	3.293	....	.585	3.201	.350	.829	....	....	13.820
	Harju	.695	.411	....	.073	.392	.043	.104	....	....	1.718
	Narva	5.214	3.088	....	.549	3.005	.320	.778	....	....	12.954
	Fellin	1.738	1.029	....	.183	1.002	.107	.259	....	....	4.318
	Pernau	3.476	2.058	....	.366	2.003	.213	.518	....	....	8.634
	Petchory	5.214	3.088	....	.549	3.005	.320	.778	....	....	12.954
	Nömme	.348	.206	....	.037	.200	.021	.052	....	....	.864
	Werro	3.476	2.058	....	.366	2.003	.213	.518	....	....	8.634
	Hapsal	1.738	1.029	....	.183	1.002	.107	.259	....	....	4.318
	Arensburg and Islands	3.476	2.058	....	.366	2.003	.213	.518	....	....	8.634
	Baltiski Port	.174	.103	....	.018	.098	.011	.026	....	....	.430
	Reval	5.562	3.293	....	.585	3.222	.341	.829	....	....	13.832
	Total for August	**45.190**	**26.758**	....	**4.757**	**26.043**	**2.780**	**6.738**	....	....	**112.266**
	September, 1921										
	Kärdla	.178	.050	.079	.018	.102	.011	.028	....	....	.466
	Sindi	.178	.050	.079	.018	.102	.011	.028	....	....	.466
	Paide	.892	.249	.394	.088	.503	.054	.142	....	....	2.322
	Tarlu	1.783	.498	.788	.177	1.007	.107	.284	....	....	4.644
	Viro Disti	2.675	.747	1.181	.265	1.513	.161	.426	....	....	6.968
	Narva	2.675	.747	1.181	.265	1.513	.161	.426	....	....	6.968
	Fellin	1.783	.249	.394	.088	.503	.054	.142	....	....	3.213
	Pernau	1.783	.249	.394	.088	.503	.054	.142	....	....	3.213
	Petchory	3.566	.996	1.575	.353	2.014	.214	.568	....	....	9.286
	Nömme	.357	.100	.158	.035	.201	.021	.057	....	....	.929
	Werro	.892	.249	.394	.088	.501	.054	.142	....	....	2.320
	Hapsal	.892	.249	.394	.088	.501	.054	.142	....	....	2.320
	Baltiski Port	.178	.050	.079	.018	.102	.011	.028	....	....	.466
	Reval	5.349	1.494	2.363	.524	3.019	.321	.851	....	....	13.921
	Total for September	**23.181**	**5.977**	**9.453**	**2.113**	**12.084**	**1.288**	**3.406**	....	....	**57.502**
	October, 1921										
0	Baltiski Port	.184	.051	.081	.018	.103	.011	.029	....	....	.477
1	Sindi	.184	.051	.081	.018	.103	.011	.029	....	....	.477
2	Nömme	.369	.103	.163	.036	.207	.022	.059	....	....	.959
3	Kärdla	.460	.129	.203	.046	.260	.028	.073	....	....	1.199
4	Fellin	.922	.257	.407	.091	.522	.055	.147	....	....	2.401
5	Arensburg and Islands	.922	.257	.407	.091	.522	.055	.147	....	....	2.401

[*Continued on next page*]

ESTHONIA

Table 305—*Continued* **Detail of Internal Deliveries for Child Feeding**

Receipt No.	Districts and Kitchens	Commodities in Net Metric Tons of 1,000 Kilograms or 2,204.6 Pounds									
		Flour	Rice	Beans, Peas	Pork Products	Milk Evap. Cond.	Cocoa	Sugar	Misc. Food	Soap	Tota[l] Ton[s]
	October, 1921										
106	Hapsal	1.290	.360	.570	.128	.730	.077	.205	....	....	3.
107	Paide	1.843	.515	.814	.183	1.045	.111	.293	....	....	4.
108	Walk	1.843	.515	.814	.183	1.045	.111	.293	....	....	4.
109	Pernau	1.843	.515	.814	.183	1.045	.111	.293	....	....	4.
110	Tartu	3.687	1.029	1.628	.365	2.091	.221	.587	....	....	9.
111	Narva	3.687	1.029	1.628	.365	2.091	.221	.587	....	....	9.
112	Werro	4.608	1.287	2.034	.457	2.613	.277	.733	....	....	12.
113	Petchory	7.373	2.058	3.255	.730	4.180	.443	1.173	....	....	19.
114	Reval	7.650	2.136	3.377	.758	4.241	.459	1.217	....	....	19.
	Total for October	**36.865**	**10.292**	**16.276**	**3.652**	**20.798**	**2.213**	**5.865**	....	....	**95.**
	November, 1921										
115	Baltiski Port	.143	.040	.063	.014	.080	.009	.023	....	....	.
116	Sindi	.178	.050	.079	.018	.101	.011	.028	....	....	.
117	Nömme	.357	.100	.158	.035	.201	.021	.057	....	....	.
118	Kärdla	.267	.075	.118	.027	.152	.016	.043	....	....	.
119	Fellin	.446	.125	.197	.044	.250	.027	.071	....	....	1.
120	Hapsal	.446	.125	.197	.044	.250	.027	.071	....	....	1.
121	Werro	.535	.150	.236	.053	.305	.032	.085	....	....	1.
122	Paide	.892	.249	.394	.088	.501	.054	.142	....	....	2.
123	Pernau	.892	.249	.394	.088	.501	.054	.142	....	....	2.
124	Tartu	1.784	.498	.788	.177	1.006	.107	.284	....	....	4.
125	Narvia	1.784	.498	.788	.177	1.006	.107	.284	....	....	4.
126	Virumaa	2.141	.598	.945	.212	1.208	.129	.341	....	....	5.
127	Petchory	3.568	.996	1.575	.353	2.014	.214	.577	....	....	9.
128	Reval	4.407	1.230	1.945	.436	2.514	.265	.701	....	....	11.
	Total for November	**17.840**	**4.983**	**7.877**	**1.766**	**10.089**	**1.073**	**2.849**	....	....	**46.**
	December, 1921										
129	Baltiski Port	.147	.041	.065	.015	.083	.008	.023	....	....	
130	Sindi	.184	.051	.081	.018	.103	.011	.029	....	....	.
131	Nömme	.369	.103	.163	.037	.206	.022	.059	....	....	.
132	Kärdla	.276	.077	.122	.027	.157	.017	.044	....	....	
133	Fellin	.461	.129	.203	.046	.260	.028	.073	....	....	1.
134	Hapsal	.461	.129	.203	.046	.260	.028	.073	....	....	1
135	Werro	.553	.154	.244	.055	.310	.033	.088	....	....	1
136	Paide	.922	.257	.407	.091	.522	.055	.147	....	....	2
137	Pernau	.922	.257	.407	.091	.522	.055	.147	....	....	2
138	Tartu	1.843	.515	.814	.183	1.045	.111	.293	....	....	4
139	Virumaa	2.212	.618	.977	.219	1.252	.133	.352	....	....	5
140	Petchory	3.687	1.029	1.628	.365	2.091	.221	.587	....	....	9
141	Reval	4.553	1.271	2.010	.451	2.542	.274	.724	....	....	11
142	Narva	1.843	.515	.814	.183	1.045	.111	.293	....	....	4
	Total for December	**18.433**	**5.146**	**8.138**	**1.827**	**10.398**	**1.107**	**2.932**	....	....	**47**
	January, 1922										
143	Baltiski Port	.147	.041	.065	.015	.076	.009	.023	....	....	
144	Sindi	.184	.051	.081	.018	.103	.011	.029	....	....	
145	Nömme	.369	.103	.163	.037	.207	.022	.059	....	....	
146	Kärdla	.276	.077	.122	.027	.156	.017	.044	....	....	
147	Fellin	.461	.129	.203	.046	.193	.028	.073	....	....	1
148	Hapsal	.461	.129	.203	.046	.241	.028	.073	....	....	1
149	Werro	.553	.154	.244	.055	.309	.033	.088	....	....	1
150	Paide	.922	.257	.407	.091	.455	.055	.147	....	....	2
151	Pernau	.922	.257	.407	.091	.455	.055	.147	....	....	2
152	Tartu	1.843	.515	.814	.183	.977	.111	.293	....	....	4
153	Narva	1.843	.515	.814	.183	.977	.111	.293	....	....	4
154	Virumaa	2.212	.618	.977	.219	1.245	.133	.352	....	....	5
155	Petchory	3.687	1.029	1.628	.365	2.090	.221	.587	....	....	9
156	Reval	4.553	1.271	2.010	.451	2.591	.274	.724	....	....	11
	Total for January	**18.433**	**5.146**	**8.138**	**1.827**	**10.075**	**1.108**	**2.932**	....	....	**47**

ESTHONIA

able 305—*Continued* **Detail of Internal Deliveries for Child Feeding**

Districts and Kitchens	Flour	Rice	Beans, Peas	Pork Products	Milk Evap. Cond.	Cocoa	Sugar	Misc. Food	Soap	Total Tons
	Commodities in Net Metric Tons of 1,000 Kilograms or 2,204.6 Pounds									
February, 1922										
Baltiski Port	.133	.037	.059	.013	.075	.008	.021	....	....	.346
Sindi	.166	.046	.074	.016	.093	.010	.026	....	....	.431
Turi-Alliku	.166	.046	.074	.016	.093	.010	.026	....	....	.431
Nömme	.333	.093	.147	.034	.187	.020	.053	....	....	.867
Kärdla	.250	.070	.110	.025	.140	.015	.040	....	....	.650
Fellin	.416	.116	.184	.041	.234	.025	.066	....	....	1.082
Hapsal	.416	.116	.184	.041	.234	.025	.066	....	....	1.082
Werro	.500	.139	.221	.049	.280	.030	.080	....	....	1.299
Paide	.666	.186	.294	.066	.374	.040	.106	....	....	1.732
Pernau	.832	.232	.368	.082	.467	.050	.132	....	....	2.163
Tartu	1.665	.465	.735	.165	.935	.100	.265	....	....	4.330
Narva	1.665	.465	.735	.165	.935	.100	.265	....	....	4.330
Viru	1.998	.558	.882	.198	1.121	.120	.318	....	....	5.195
Petchory	3.330	.930	1.470	.330	1.870	.200	.530	....	....	8.660
Reval	4.112	1.148	1.815	.407	2.309	.247	.654	....	....	10.692
Total for February	**16.648**	**4.647**	**7.352**	**1.648**	**9.347**	**1.000**	**2.648**	....	....	**43.290**
March, 1922										
Baltiski Port	.179	.020	.065	.015	.083	.009	.023	....	....	.394
Sindi	.224	.023	.081	.018	.104	.011	.029	....	....	.490
Turi-Alliku	.224	.023	.081	.018	.104	.011	.029	....	....	.490
Nömme	.449	.046	.163	.037	.207	.022	.059	....	....	.983
Kärdla	.336	.035	.122	.027	.155	.017	.044	....	....	.736
Fellin	.561	.058	.203	.046	.259	.028	.073	....	....	1.228
Hapsal	.561	.058	.203	.046	.259	.028	.073	....	....	1.228
Werro	.673	.070	.244	.055	.311	.033	.088	....	....	1.474
Paide	.897	.093	.326	.073	.414	.044	.117	....	....	1.964
Pernau	1.122	.116	.407	.091	.518	.055	.147	....	....	2.456
Tartu	2.243	.232	.814	.183	1.035	.111	.293	....	....	4.911
Narva	2.243	.232	.814	.183	1.035	.111	.293	....	....	4.911
Viru	2.692	.279	.977	.219	1.242	.133	.352	....	....	5.894
Petchory	4.487	.465	1.628	.365	2.070	.221	.587	....	....	9.823
Reval	5.541	.573	2.010	.451	2.557	.274	.724	....	....	12.130
Total for March	**22.432**	**2.323**	**8.138**	**1.827**	**10.353**	**1.108**	**2.931**	....	....	**49.112**
April, 1922										
Baltiski Port	.143	.040	.063	.014	.080	.009	.023	....	....	.372
Sindi	.178	.050	.079	.018	.100	.011	.028	....	....	.464
Turi-Alliku	.178	.050	.079	.018	.100	.011	.028	....	....	.464
Nömme	.357	.100	.158	.035	.200	.021	.057	....	....	.928
Kärdla	.267	.075	.118	.027	.150	.016	.043	....	....	.696
Fellin	.446	.124	.197	.044	.250	.027	.071	....	....	1.159
Hapsal	.446	.124	.197	.044	.250	.027	.071	....	....	1.159
Werro	.535	.149	.236	.053	.301	.032	.085	....	....	1.391
Paide	.714	.199	.315	.071	.401	.043	.114	....	....	1.857
Pernau	.892	.249	.394	.088	.501	.054	.142	....	....	2.320
Tartu	1.784	.498	.788	.177	1.002	.107	.284	....	....	4.640
Narva	1.784	.498	.788	.177	1.002	.107	.284	....	....	4.640
Viru	2.141	.598	.945	.212	1.202	.129	.341	....	....	5.568
Petchory	3.568	.996	1.575	.353	2.003	.214	.568	....	....	9.277
Reval	4.407	1.230	1.945	.436	2.474	.265	.701	....	....	11.458
Total for April	**17.840**	**4.980**	**7.877**	**1.767**	**10.016**	**1.073**	**2.840**	....	....	**46.393**
May, 1922										
Baltiski Port	.147	.041	.065	.015	.083	.009	.023	....	....	.383
Sindi	.184	.051	.081	.018	.104	.011	.029	....	....	.478
Turi-Alliku	.184	.051	.081	.018	.104	.011	.029	....	....	.478
Kärdla	.276	.077	.122	.027	.155	.017	.044	....	....	.718
Nömme	.369	.103	.163	.037	.207	.022	.059	....	....	.960
Fellin	.461	.129	.203	.046	.259	.028	.073	....	....	1.199

[*Continued on next page*]

ESTHONIA

Table 305—*Continued* Detail of Internal Deliveries for Child Feeding

Receipt No.	Districts and Kitchens	Commodities in Net Metric Tons of 1,000 Kilograms or 2,204.6 Pounds									
		Flour	Rice	Beans, Peas	Pork Products	Milk Evap. Cond.	Cocoa	Sugar	Misc. Food	Soap	Total Tons
	May, 1922										
193	Hapsal	.461	.129	.203	.046	.259	.028	.073	....	....	1.
194	Werro	.553	.154	.244	.055	.311	.033	.088	....	....	1.
195	Paide	.737	.206	.326	.073	.414	.044	.117	....	....	1.
196	Pernau	.922	.257	.407	.091	.518	.055	.147	....	....	2.
197	Tartu	1.843	.515	.814	.183	1.035	.111	.293	....	....	4.
198	Narva	1.843	.515	.814	.183	1.035	.111	.293	....	....	4.
199	Viru	2.212	.618	.977	.219	1.242	.133	.352	....	....	5.
200	Petchory	3.687	1.029	1.628	.365	2.070	.221	.587	....	....	9.
201	Reval	4.553	1.271	2.010	.451	2.557	.274	.724	....	....	11.
	Total for May	**18.432**	**5.146**	**8.138**	**1.827**	**10.353**	**1.108**	**2.931**	....	....	**47.**
	June, 1922										
202	Baltiski Port	.143	.040	.063	.014	.080	.009	.023	....	....	.
203	Sindi	.178	.050	.079	.018	.100	.011	.028	....	....	.
204	Turi-Alliku	.178	.050	.079	.018	.100	.011	.028	....	....	.
205	Kärdla	.267	.075	.118	.026	.150	.016	.043	....	....	.
206	Nömme	.357	.100	.158	.035	.200	.021	.057	....	....	.
207	Fellin	.446	.125	.197	.044	.250	.027	.071	....	....	1.
208	Hapsal	.446	.125	.197	.044	.250	.027	.071	....	....	1.
209	Werro	.535	.149	.236	.053	.301	.032	.085	....	....	1.
210	Paide	.714	.199	.315	.071	.401	.043	.114	....	....	1.
211	Pernau	.892	.249	.394	.088	.501	.054	.142	....	....	2.
212	Tartu	1.784	.498	.788	.177	1.002	.107	.284	....	....	4.
213	Narva	1.784	.498	.788	.177	1.002	.107	.284	....	....	4.
214	Viru	2.141	.598	.945	.212	1.202	.129	.341	....	....	5.
215	Petchory	3.568	.996	1.575	.353	2.003	.214	.568	....	....	9.
216	Reval	4.407	1.230	1.945	.436	2.474	.265	.701	....	....	11.
	Total for June	**17.840**	**4.982**	**7.877**	**1.766**	**10.016**	**1.073**	**2.840**	....	....	**46.**
	July, 1922										
217	Baltiski Port	.148	.106	....	.015	.083	.009	.023	....	....	.
218	Turi-Alliku	.184	.133	....	.018	.104	.011	.029	....	....	.
219	Kärdla	.276	.199	....	.027	.155	.017	.044	....	....	.
220	Hapsal	.461	.332	....	.046	.259	.028	.073	....	....	1.
221	Fellin	.461	.332	....	.046	.259	.028	.073	....	....	1.
222	Werro	.553	.398	....	.055	.311	.033	.088	....	....	1.

ESTHONIA

Table 305—*Concluded* Detail of Internal Deliveries for Child Feeding

Receipt No.	Districts and Kitchens	Commodities in Net Metric Tons of 1,000 Kilograms or 2,204.6 Pounds									
		Flour	Rice	Beans, Peas	Pork Products	Milk Evap. Cond.	Cocoa	Sugar	Misc. Food	Soap	Total Tons
223	Paide	.737	.531	....	.073	.414	.044	.117	....	....	1.916
224	Pernau	.922	.664	....	.091	.518	.055	.147	....	....	2.397
225	Narva	1.843	1.328	....	.183	1.035	.111	.293	....	....	4.793
226	Tartu	1.843	1.328	....	.183	1.035	.111	.293	....	....	4.793
227	Viru	2.212	1.594	....	.219	1.242	.133	.352	....	....	5.752
228	Petchory	3.687	2.657	....	.365	2.070	.221	.587	....	....	9.587
229	Reval	5.106	1.425	2.254	.506	2.867	.307	.812	....	....	13.277
	Total for July	**18.433**	**11.027**	**2.254**	**1.827**	**10.352**	**1.108**	**2.931**	....	....	**47.932**
	August, 1922										
230	Baltiski Port	.147	.106	....	.015	.083	.009	.023	....	....	.383
231	Turi-Alliku	.184	.133	....	.018	.104	.011	.029	....	....	.479
232	Kärdla	.276	.199	....	.027	.155	.017	.044	....	....	.718
233	Hapsal	.461	.332	....	.046	.259	.028	.073	....	....	1.199
234	Fellin	.461	.332	....	.046	.259	.028	.073	....	....	1.199
235	Werro	.553	.398	....	.055	.311	.033	.088	....	....	1.438
236	Paide	.737	.531	....	.073	.414	.044	.117	....	....	1.916
237	Pernau	.922	.664	....	.091	.518	.055	.147	....	....	2.397
238	Narva	1.843	1.328	....	.183	1.035	.111	.293	....	....	4.793
239	Tartu	1.843	1.328	....	.183	1.035	.111	.293	....	....	4.793
240	Virumaa	2.212	1.594	....	.219	1.242	.133	.352	....	....	5.752
241	Petchory	3.687	1.922	.735	.365	2.070	.221	.587	....	....	9.587
242	Reval	5.106	3.680	....	.506	2.867	.307	.812	....	....	13.278
	Total for August	**18.432**	**12.547**	**.735**	**1.827**	**10.352**	**1.108**	**2.931**	....	....	**47.932**
	Total per District Committee Receipts	**2,216.307**	**532.266**	**463.997**	**202.583**	**1,185.179**	**147.126**	**406.162**	**10.000**	**38.745**	**5,202.365**
	Turned over to Central Committee	127.000	....	....	29.000	163.500	....	....	....	....	319.500
	Total	**2,343.307**	**532.266**	**463.997**	**231.583**	**1,348.679**	**147.126**	**406.162**	**10.000**	**38.745**	**5,521.865**
	Deduct Duplications †	....	.500	16.500	....	....	3.300	7.000	....	.300	27.600
	Total Child Feeding	**2,343.307**	**531.766**	**447.497**	**231.583**	**1,348.679**	**143.826**	**399.162**	**10.000**	**38.445**	**5,494.265**

† Stock returned to Central Committee and re-issued.

Table 306

Operation	Table No.	Flour	Grain	Rice	Beans, Peas
					ARMISTI[CE PERIOD]
A.R.A.—Congressional Appropriation, $100,000,000 Fund	307	20,970.7	43,880.6	.....	121.5
A.R.A.—Cash Settlement	308	38,346.8	59,158.4	.....	1,685.5
A.R.A.—Freight on Charity Shipments	143	.....	......	.....	.....
American Red Cross	126	.....	......	.....	.....
Total American Relief	....	**59,317.5**	**103,039.0**	.....	**1,807.0**
United Kingdom	133	.....	......	.....	1,170.0
Denmark	136	.....	10,000.0	.....	.....
Norway	136	.....	......	.....	4,442.0
Total Relief by Other Countries	132B	.....	**10,000.0**	.....	**5,612.0**
Total, Armistice Period	108	**59,317.5**	**113,039.0**	.....	**7,419.0**
					RECONSTRUCTI[ON PERIOD]
A.R.A.—Congressional Appropriation, $100,000,000 Fund	310, 316	700.0	......	221.9	253.9
A.R.A.-European Children's Fund—Local Purchase	311, 316	350.1	......	.....	.....
A.R.A.-European Children's Fund	309, 316	.....	......	9.5	2.4
Finland Government Donation	313, 316	888.4	......	.....	.....
Total, Reconstruction Period	149	**1,938.5**	......	**231.4**	**256.3**
Deduct Sale at Local Market	316	.....	......	.....	.....
Net Deliveries for Children's Relief	163	**1,938.5**	......	**231.4**	**256.3**
Grand Total Relief Deliveries	102	**61,256.0**	**113,039.0**	**231.4**	**7,675.3**

FINLAND—American Relief Administration

Detail by Steamers of Relief Deliveries, Paid for by Funds from the Congressional Appropriation for Relief—Armistice Period, 1919

Table 307

Arrival No.*	Steamer	Port of Sailing	Date of Arrival	Port of Arrival	Contents of Cargoes in Net Metric Tons of 1,000 Kilograms or 2,204.6 Pounds: Wheat Flour	Cereal Flour	Rye Grain	Beans, Peas	Lard	Milk	Total Tons	Total Value
			1919									
56	Bali	New York	Mar. 7	Copenhagen	5,398.6	2,134.5	......	121.5	.....	....	7,654.6	$1,378,686
61,2	Mirach & Besoeki	New York	Mar. 13	Copenhagen	503.2	5,012.4	......	.....	714.1	38.8	6,268.5	1,514,487
78	Dubhe	Philadelphia	Mar. 20	Helsingfors	....	.....	4,070.0	.....	.....	....	4,070.0	496,710
107	Lake Yelverton	Philadelphia	Apr. 6	Helsingfors	....	.....	2,995.1	.....	.....	....	2,995.1	365,530
111	Wierington	New York	Apr. 8	Helsingfors	....	.....	4,074.3	.....	.....	....	4,074.3	497,230
143	Bussum	Baltimore	Apr. 21	Helsingfors	....	.....	4,906.3	.....	.....	....	4,906.3	598,769
257	Woonsocket	New York	June 4	Hango	....	.....	7,496.5	.....	.....	....	7,496.5	930,882
282	Westford	New York	June 15	Abo	....	.....	7,214.0	.....	.....	....	7,214.0	895,807
288	Sahale	Philadelphia	June 17	Mantyluto	....	.....	6,256.5	.....	.....	....	6,256.5	776,903
366	Hannau	New York	July 31	Helsingfors	....	3,023.6	3,224.7	.....	.....	....	6,248.3	964,458
380	Rudelsburg	New York	Aug. 25	Helsingfors	4,054.1	844.3	3,643.2	.....	.....	....	8,541.6	1,430,120
	Total	....	....	....	**9,955.9**	**11,014.8**	**43,880.6**	**121.5**	**714.1**	**38.8**	**65,725.7**	**$9,849,587**

* Arrival numbers from Table 111.

ummary of Relief Deliveries

Commodities in Net Metric Tons of 1,000 Kilograms or 2,204.6 Pounds										
Corn Grits	Pork Products	Milk	Cocoa	Sugar	Misc. Food	Forage	Soap	Clothing and Misc.	Total Tons	Total Value
ERIOD										
.....	714.1	38.8	....	.....	.....	.....	.....	.....	65,725.7	$ 9,849,587.73
.....	1,926.3	....	....	.....	.....	.....	.....	.....	101,117.0	16,004,404.13
.....	.....	....	....	.....	.....	.....	.....	.....	......	22,584.24
.....	.....	....	....	.....	.....	.....	.....	282.0	282.0	56,400.00
.....	**2,640.4**	**38.8**	....	.....	.....	.....	.....	**282.0**	**167,124.7**	**$25,932,976.10**
.....	.....	40.0	....	1,415.0	842.0	.....	.....	.....	3,467.0	$ 920,250.00
.....	.....	....	....	.....	.....	.....	.....	.....	10,000.0	1,141,700.00
.....	.....	....	....	.....	.....	.....	.....	.....	4,442.0	1,177,130.00
.....	.....	**40.0**	....	**1,415.0**	**842.0**	.....	.....	.....	**17,909.0**	**$ 3,239,080.00**
.....	**2,640.4**	**78.8**	....	**1,415.0**	**842.0**	.....	.....	**282.0**	**185,033.7**	**$29,172,056.10**
ERIOD										
.....	95.3	658.3	10.0	169.9	.....	.....	.....	.....	2,109.3	$ 660,175.34
.....	.....	....	....	.....	.....	.....	.....	.....	350.1	37,662.13
.....	.....	18.3	....	5.2	.....	.....	.....	56.0	91.4	216,205.33
.....	12.0	36.0	....	.....	.....	.....	.....	.....	936.4	195,949.00
.....	**107.3**	**712.6**	**10.0**	**175.1**	.....	.....	.....	**56.0**	**3,487.2**	**$ 1,109,991.80**
.....	.....	54.1	9.6	48.5	.....	.....	.....	.....	112.2	37,662.13
.....	**107.3**	**658.5**	**.4**	**126.6**	.....	.....	.....	**56.0**	**3,375.0**	**$ 1,072,329.67**
.....	**2,747.7**	**791.4**	**10.0**	**1,590.1**	**842.0**	.....	.....	**338.0**	**188,520.9**	**$30,282,047.90**

FINLAND-

Table 308 **Detail by Steamers of Commoditi**

Arrival No.*	Steamer	Port of Sailing	Date of Arrival	Port of Arrival
			1919	
34	Merfax	Rotterdam	Feb. 20	Helsingfors
35	Vesta	Rotterdam	Feb. 20	Helsingfors
38	Markab	Rotterdam	Feb. 22	Helsingfors
41	Hero	Rotterdam	Feb. 24	Helsingfors
48	Hollandish Diep	Rotterdam	Feb. 28	Helsingfors
58	Tjisondari	Philadelphia	Mar. 10	Copenhagen
61-2	Mirach and Besoeki	New York	Mar. 13	Copenhagen
64	Leda	Rotterdam	Mar. 14	Helsingfors
82	Yssel, I	Rotterdam	Mar. 22	Helsingfors
81	Lahta	Rotterdam	Mar. 22	Helsingfors
85	Alkaid	Baltimore	Mar. 25	Helsingfors
86	Garfield	Baltimore	Mar. 25	Helsingfors
89	Bjarmia	Rotterdam	Mar. 26	Helsingfors
94	Sapinero	(U.S.A.)	Mar. 28	Plymouth
103	Sverre	New York	Apr. 2	Helsingfors
104	Melang	New York	Apr. 3	Helsingfors
137	Sicilia	Rotterdam	Apr. 17	Helsingfors
138	Orangepolder	Rotterdam	Apr. 18	Helsingfors
149	Yssel, II	Rotterdam	Apr. 23	Helsingfors
158	Agnes, I	Rotterdam	May 1	Helsingfors
209	Mystic	Philadelphia	May 20	Helsingfors
207	Groenloo †	Rotterdam	May 20	Helsingfors
213	Ceres	Rotterdam	May 21	Helsingfors
218	Alwina †	Rotterdam	May 24	Helsingfors
289	Western Plains, II	Philadelphia	June 17	Hango
307	West Durfee	Boston	June 25	Mantyluoto
332	Pasadena	Philadelphia	July 5	Helsingfors
346	Lake Hemlock	New York	July 12	Hango
351	Jadden	(U.S.A.)	....	Helsingfors
365	Wolfsburgh	Baltimore	July 26	Helsingfors
	Total	....	....	....

* Arrival numbers from Table 111.

‡ Barley grain.

FINLAND—A.R.A. and A.R.A.-European Children's Fund

Table 309 **Summary of Arrivals, by Operations—Reconstruction Period, 1919–1924**

Operation	Table No.	Commodities in Net Metric Tons of 1,000 Kilograms or 2,204.6 Pounds										Total Value
		Wheat Flour	Cereal Flour	Rice	Beans, Peas	Pork Products	Milk	Cocoa	Sugar	Clothing	Total Tons	
A.R.A.—Congressional Appropriation, $100,000,000 Fund	310	560.0	140.0	221.9	253.9	95.3	658.3	10.0	169.9	....	2,109.3	$ 660,175
European Children's Fund—Food	311	.....	.....	9.5	2.4	....	18.3	....	5.2	....	35.4	14,378
European Children's Fund—Clothing	312	.....	.....	.....	.....	....	.....	....	.....	56.0	56.0	201,826
European Children's Fund—Local Purchase	311	350.1	.....	.....	.....	....	.....	....	.....	....	350.1	37,662
Finnish Government Donation	313	.....	888.4	.....	.....	12.0	36.0	....	.....	....	936.4	195,949
Total	306	**910.1**	**1,028.4**	**231.4**	**256.3**	**107.3**	**712.6**	**10.0**	**175.1**	**56.0**	**3,487.2**	**$1,109,991**

nerican Relief Administration

ld for Cash—Armistice Period, 1919

Wheat Flour	Cereal Flour	Rye Grain	Beans, Peas	Pork Products	Lard	Total Tons	Total Value
Contents of Cargoes in Net Metric Tons of 1,000 Kilograms or 2,204.6 Pounds							
1,414.2	283.3	......	.....	.....	73.6	1,771.1	$ 368,665.78
881.7	176.6	......	.....	.....	.....	1,058.3	194,429.08
1,108.6	222.1	......	.....	6.5	251.4	1,588.6	442,825.46
1,391.1	278.7	......	.....	.....	78.9	1,748.7	367,631.53
1,211.0	83.5	......	.....	22.1	292.0	1,608.6	481,141.58
6,797.6	1,230.7	......	.....	.....	.....	8,028.3	1,455,150.50
.....	.....	......	.....	715.5	.....	715.5	546,014.02
1,416.3	.....	......	.....	.....	16.2	1,432.5	277,917.95
1,383.3	56.3	......	.....	.....	106.4	1,546.0	346,988.83
2,233.1	310.1	......	127.9	.....	82.4	2,753.5	561,581.16
.....	.....	3,986.6	.....	.....	.....	3,986.6	486,526.62
.....	.....	2,898.3	.....	.....	.....	2,898.3	353,710.00
1,090.5	193.2	......	.....	.....	69.4	1,353.1	287,522.47
.....	.....	5,597.3	.....	.....	.....	5,597.3	643,689.16
.....	.....	5,116.8	.....	.....	.....	5,116.8	624,459.57
.....	.....	3,713.2	.....	.....	.....	3,713.2	453,161.10
1,729.4	350.8	......	.....	.....	104.5	2,184.7	459,268.31
410.0	87.1	......	.....	.....	.....	497.1	91,230.96
1,448.1	85.9	......	.....	.....	80.8	1,614.8	345,221.42
622.0	132.1	......	.....	.....	1.3	755.4	139,351.90
.....	.....	7,532.4‡	.....	.....	.....	7,532.4	902,946.35
1,373.6	238.3	......	.....	.....	25.3	1,637.2	315,469.42
549.5	88.3	......	.....	.....	.....	637.8	117,573.82
917.7	139.7	......	.....	.....	.....	1,057.4	195,056.16
.....	.....	7,145.7	.....	.....	.....	7,145.7	887,325.46
.....	.....	6,953.2	.....	.....	.....	6,953.2	863,424.12
.....	.....	7,729.8	.....	.....	.....	7,729.8	959,853.69
.....	181.8	......	1,557.6	.....	.....	1,739.4	437,070.29
8,230.6	.....	......	.....	.....	.....	8,230.6	1,345,548.64
.....	.....	8,485.1	.....	.....	.....	8,485.1	1,053,648.78
34,208.3	**4,138.5**	**59,158.4§**	**1,685.5**	**744.1**	**1,182.2**	**101,117.0**	**$16,004,404.13**

† These are Finnish boats, used in transporting supplies sold to Fin-

‡ ex-Rotterdam stock.

§ Rye grain, 51,626.0; barley grain, 7,532.4.

FINLAND-

Table 310 **Detail by Steamers of Children's Relief Arrivals, Paid for by Funds from th**

Steamer or Source	Transshipped via	Port of Sailing	Date of Arrival	Port of Arrival
			1919	
Mirach and Besoeki	Ceres, Mercur	(U.S.A.)	Mar. 13	Copenhage
Rotterdam Stock	Orangepolder	(U.S.A.)	Apr. 23	Rotterdam
Rotterdam Stock	Yssel	(U.S.A.)	May 3	Rotterdam
Rotterdam Stock	Alwina	(U.S.A.)	May 24	Rotterdam
Schwarzenfels, Danzig and C.R.B. Stock	Sture, Lake Fray	(U.S.A.)	Aug. ..	Danzig
Total				
Less Transfers to:				
Esthonia—via S.S. Ranko and Frithiof				
Northwest Russia—via S.S. Ranko and Frithiof				
Reduce Gross to Net Weight—Tare				
Total				
Total, Net Arrivals				

* Gross weight.

† Includes 76.0 metric tons milk ex-C.R.B. stock.

FINLAND-

Table 311 **Detail by Steamers and Local Purchase of Fo**

Steamer or Source	Transshipped via	Port of Sailing	Date of Arrival
			1920
Mar Caspio, II	Saale, I to Poseidon	New York	July 16
			1921
Modlin Purchase	Poseidon	(Poland)	Jan. 13
American, II	Echo, III to Poseidon	New York	Jan. 12
Ipswich	Progress, IV to Poseidon	New York	Jan. 25
Miscellaneous Charges			
Warehouse Adjustment, Overages			
Total			
Finland Market			

* Cf. Table 316, commodities sold.

FINLAND-

Table 312 **Detail by Steamers of Arrival of Clothing a**

Steamer or Source	Port of Sailing	Date of Arrival	Port of Arrival	Shoes (Pairs)	Laces (Pairs)
		1919			
Leda, I	London	Nov. 30	Danzig	30,936	36,000
		1920			
Pollux	London	Jan. 25	Helsingfors	245	....
Vesta	London	Jan. 27	Helsingfors	5,009	....
Leda, II	London	Jan. 28	Helsingfors	....	....
Capella, I	London	Feb. 5	Helsingfors	11,081	7,200
Capella, II	London	Mar. 26	Helsingfors	....	....
Total				**47,271**	**43,200**

* Total shipments equivalent to 2,640,000 yards.

† Shipped in 396 bales. Cf. Table 319 A.

erican Relief Administration

gressional Appropriation for Relief—Reconstruction Period, 1919–1924

heat Flour	Cereal Flour	Rice	Beans, Peas	Pork Products	Milk	Cocoa	Sugar	Total Tons	Total Value
Contents of Cargoes in Net Metric Tons of 1,000 Kilograms or 2,204.6 Pounds									
560.0	200.0	....	....	104.0	7.6	....	....	871.6	$219,701.90
....	....	....	....	....	107.7*	40.0*	....	147.7	50,487.92
....	....	....	....	....	32.4*	....	84.9	117.3	28,622.96
....	....	75.0	75.0	....	....	....	....	150.0	40,138.54
....	....	146.9	178.9	....	539.7†	....	120.0	985.5	357,460.90
560.0	**200.0**	**221.9**	**253.9**	**104.0**	**687.4**	**40.0**	**204.9**	**2,272.1**	**$696,412.22**
....	60.0	....	....	8.7	....	....	35.0	103.7	$ 26,236.88
....	....	....	....	....	....	25.0	....	25.0	10,000.00
....	....	....	....	....	29.1	5.0	....	34.1	......
....	**60.0**	**....**	**....**	**8.7**	**29.1**	**30.0**	**35.0**	**162.8**	**$ 36,236.88**
560.0	**140.0**	**221.9**	**253.9**	**95.3**	**658.3**	**10.0**	**169.9**	**2,109.3**	**$660,175.34**

R.A.-European Children's Fund

ivals—Reconstruction Period, 1919–1924

Port of Arrival	Flour	Rice	Beans, Peas	Pork Products	Milk	Cocoa	Sugar	Total Tons	Total Value
	Contents of Cargoes in Net Metric Tons of 1,000 Kilograms or 2,204.6 Pounds								
	BY STEAMERS								
Hamburg	.....	...	...	....	18.0	....	...	18.0	$10,510.00
Danzig	.....	...	...	....	....	....	5.2	5.2	1,056.67
Hamburg	.....	...	...	....	.3	....	...	.3	73.72
Hamburg	.....	9.1	...	....	....	....	...	9.1	1,579.75
....	.....	...	...	....	....	....	...	....	1,158.20
....	.....	.4	2.4	....	....	....	...	2.8	....
....	.....	**9.5**	**2.4**	....	**18.3**	....	**5.2**	**35.4**	**$14,378.34**
	BY LOCAL PURCHASE*								
....	**350.1**	...	...	....	....	....	...	**350.1**	**$37,662.13**

R.A.-European Children's Fund

cessories—Reconstruction Period, 1919–1924

Stockings (Pairs)	Woolens (Yards)	Thread* (Pounds)	Thread* (Reels)	Needles (Number)	Buttons (Number)	Total Metric Tons	Total Value
.....	41,265	...	...	.....	.....	33.0	$121,858.69
21,726	17,681	...	...	5,000	.....	11.0	32,180.23
.....	4,398	570	720	35,000	172,800	5.0	19,009.02
8,022	.....	...	...	.....	.....	1.0	3,934.51
.....	.....	...	...	.....	.....	5.0	21,834.95
10,254	.....	...	...	.....	.....	1.0	3,009.59
40,002	**63,344†**	**570**	**720**	**40,000**	**172,800**	**56.0**	**$201,826.99**

FINLAND—A.R.A.-European Children's Fund

Table 313 — Detail by Months of Supplies Donated by the Finnish Government for Children's Relief—Reconstruction Period, 1919–1924

Time of Delivery	Commodities in Net Metric Tons of 1,000 Kilograms or 2,204.6 Pounds				Total Value
	Cereal Flour	Pork Products	Milk	Total Tons	
1919					
August	188.0	6.0	2.0	196.0	$ 41,576.
September	100.0	...	34.2	134.0	33,185.
October	24.8	...	....	24.8	4,836.
November	447.8	6.0	....	453.8	91,431.
December	127.8	...	....	127.8	24,921.
Total	**888.4**	**12.0**	**36.0**	**936.4**	**$195,949.**

FINLAND—American Relief Administration

Table 314 — Detail by Steamers and Ports of Transshipments*

Steamer	Ex	Date of Arrival	Contents of Cargoes in Net Metric Tons of 1,000 Kilograms or 2,204.6 Pounds								Total Tons
			Wheat Flour	Cereal Flour	Rice	Beans, Peas	Pork Products	Milk	Cocoa	Sugar	
			A. TRANSSHIPMENTS—ROTTERDAM TO ABO AND HELSINGFORS								
		1919									
Orangepolder †	Rotterdam Stock	Apr. 30	....	.....	....	....	....	87.0	35.0	....	122
Yssel †	Rotterdam Stock	May 6	....	.....	....	....	....	24.0	....	84.9	108
Alwina ‡	Rotterdam Stock	June 3	....	.....	75.0	75.0	....	....	....	....	150
Total			....	.....	**75.0**	**75.0**	....	**111.0**	**35.0**	**84.9**	**380**
			B. TRANSSHIPMENTS—COPENHAGEN TO HANGO								
Ceres	Mirach and Besoeki	May 12	70.6	200.0	....	....	28.0	7.6	....	....	306
Mercur	Mirach and Besoeki	July 21	489.4	.....	....	....	76.0	....	....	....	565
Total			**560.0**	**200.0**	....	....	**104.0**	**7.6**	....	....	**871**
			C. TRANSSHIPMENTS—DANZIG TO HANGO								
Sture	Schwarzenfels and Danzig Stock	Sept. 16	....	.....	80.0	80.1	....	15.0	....	120.0	295
Lake Fray	Schwarzenfels and Danzig Stock	Oct. 4	....	.....	66.9	98.8	....	524.7	....	....	690
Total			....	.....	**146.9**	**178.9**	....	**539.7**	....	**120.0**	**985**
Total			**560.0**	**200.0**	**221.9**	**253.9**	**104.0**	**658.3**	**35.0**	**204.9**	**2,238**
Less Transfers			....	60.0	....	....	8.7	....	25.0	35.0	128
Total Net Arrivals			**560.0**	**140.0**	**221.9**	**253.9**	**95.3**	**658.3**	**10.0**	**169.9**	**2,109**

* Cf. Table 310.
† Arrivals at port of Abo.
‡ Arrival at port of Helsingfors.

FINLAND—A.R.A.-European Children's Fund

'able 315

Detail by Steamers and Ports of Transshipments

Steamer	Ex	Table No.	Date of Arrival	Contents of Cargoes in Net Metric Tons of 1,000 Kilograms or 2,204.6 Pounds							
				Cereal Flour	Rice	Beans, Peas	Pork Products	Milk	Sugar	Clothing	Total Tons
				A. TRANSSHIPMENTS—HAMBURG TO DANZIG							
e, I.	Mar Caspio, II	311	1920 Aug. 14	.....	...	...	....	18.0	...	....	18.0
o, III	American, II	311	1921 Jan. ..	.....	...	...	....	.3	...	....	.3
gress, IV	Ipswich	311	Feb. ..	.....	9.1	...	....	....	...	....	9.1
Total				.....	**9.1**	...	....	**18.3**	...	....	**27.4**
				B. TRANSSHIPMENTS—DANZIG TO HANGO							
eidon ... :	Modlin Purchase; Saale, I; Echo, III; Progress, IV	...	Mar. 9	.....	**9.1**	...	....	**18.3**	**5.2**	....	**32.6**
irect Arrivals—											
Clothing		312	......	.....	...	...	....	....	...	56.0	56.0
ocal Purchase		311	......	350.1	...	...	....	....	...	....	350.1
overnment Donation		313	......	888.4	...	...	12.0	36.0	...	....	936.4
djustments		311	......	.....	.4	2.4	....	....	...	....	2.8
Total				**1,238.5**	**.4**	**2.4**	**12.0**	**36.0**	...	**56.0**	**1,345.3**
Total Commodities Handled				**1,238.5**	**18.6**	**2.4**	**12.0**	**72.6**	**5.2**	**56.0**	**1,405.3**
s Retransshipments, ection "A"				.....	9.1	...	....	18.3	...	....	27.4
Total Net Arrivals				**1,238.5**	**9.5**	**2.4**	**12.0**	**54.3**	**5.2**	**56.0**	**1,377.9**

FINLAND—A.R.A. and A.R.A.-European Children's Fund

Summary of Internal Deliveries by Operations—Reconstruction Period, 1919–1924

Table 316

Operation	Table No.	Commodities in Net Metric Tons of 1,000 Kilograms or 2,204.6 Pounds									
		Wheat Flour	Cereal Flour	Rice	Beans, Peas	Pork Products	Milk	Cocoa	Sugar	Clothing	Total Tons
R.A.-European Children's Fund—Child Feeding	317	577.7	1,010.7	231.4	256.3	107.3	658.5	.4	126.6	....	2,968.9
R.A.-European Children's Fund—Local Purchase for Child Feeding	318	.....	350.1	.....	.....	.....	.....	...	.....	....	350.1
ropean Children's Fund—Clothing	319	.....	.....	.....	.....	.....	.....	...	.....	56.0	56.0
Total Children's Relief	...	**577.7**	**1,360.8**	**231.4**	**256.3**	**107.3**	**658.5**	**.4**	**126.6**	**56.0**	**3,375.0**
mmodities Sold *	...	.....	.....	.....	.....	.....	54.1	9.6	48.5	....	112.2†
Total Deliveries	306	**577.7**	**1,360.8**	**231.4**	**256.3**	**107.3**	**712.6**	**10.0**	**175.1**	**56.0**	**3,487.2‡**

* Cf. Table 311, commodities purchased.
† Value $37,662.13.
‡ For segregation to organization and value, see Table 306.

FINLAND—A.R.A.-European Children's Fund

Detail of Internal Deliveries for Child Feeding, by Districts and Kitchens, by Months

Table 317

Receipt No.	Districts and Kitchens	Wheat Flour	Cereal Flour	Rice	Beans, Peas	Pork Products	Milk: Evap.	Milk: Cond.	Sugar	Total Tons
	Commodities in Net Metric Tons of 1,000 Kilograms or 2,204.6 Pounds									
	May, 1919									
1–2	Eno	1.000	1.900	....	....	.360	....	.590	.184	4.0
3	Enontekio	.900	2.000	....	....	.332	....	....	....	3.2
4–6	Espoo and Alberga	2.200	.....	....	....	.260	....	.571	.091	3.1
7–8	Espoo and Alberga	....	.....	.183	.326	....	....	.571	.091	1.1
9–10	Juuka	2.500	5.450	....	....	.884	....	1.581	.407	10.8
11–12	Joutseno	.350	.700	....	....	.128	....	.171	.045	1.3
13–14	Kajaani	.800	1.900	....	....	.304	....	.819	.132	3.9
15–16	Kiihtelysvaara	.600	1.300	....	....	.236	....	.476	.132	2.7
17–18	Kolari	1.238	2.681	....	....	.460	....	.410	.180	4.9
19–20	Kontiolahti	5.400	12.200	....	....	2.028	....	2.381	.855	22.8
21–22	Kuolajarvi	1.600	3.400	....	....	.592	....	.410	.275	6.2
23–24	Kymi	5.600	12.400	....	....	.406	....	1.943	.810	21.1
25–26	Lappee	1.200	3.000	....	....	.444	....	.800	.183	5.6
27–28	Muonio	.800	1.650	....	....	.276	....	.209	.136	3.0
29–30	Nilsia	.450	1.000	....	....	.164	....	.400	.045	2.0
31–32	Nuermes	1.900	4.350	....	....	.700	....	1.681	.319	8.9
33–34	Paltamo	1.600	3.400	....	....	.566	....	.800	.272	6.6
35–36	Pielisjarvi	2.700	5.200	....	....	.992	....	1.981	.413	11.2
37–38	Pudasjarvi	....	.....	....	....	.640	....	2.438	.487	3.5
39–40	Rautavaara	.900	2.000	....	....	.332	....	.648	.130	4.0
41–42	Rautu	.400	.800	....	....	.184	....	1.981	.091	3.4
43	Ristijarvi	1.100	2.300	....	....	.438	....	....	....	3.8
44	Sodankyla	.800	1.800	....	....	.232	....	.419	.137	3.3
45	Sotkamo	3.000	6.900	....	....	1.104	....	....	....	11.0
46–47	Saraisniemi	.900	2.000	....	....	.432	....	.495	.090	3.9
48–49	Terijoki	1.200	2.700	....	....	.440	....	.590	.183	5.1
50	Uusikirrkko	1.800	3.746	....	....	.730	....	....	....	6.2
51–52	Valtimo	.600	1.250	....	....	.212	....	.228	.091	2.3
53	Viipurin	19.000	40.000	....	....	5.984	....	....	....	64.9
54–55	Vuolijoki	.900	2.000	....	....	.332	....	.800	.136	4.1
	Total for May, 1919	**61.438**	**128.027**	**.183**	**.326**	**20.192**	....	**23.393**	**5.915**	**239.4**
	June, July, Aug., 1919									
56–58	Alberg	.540	.....	.046	.079	.065	....	.326	.045	1.1
59–61	Malm	.792	.....	.136	.122	.125	....	1.088	.045	2.3
62–64	Eno	2.900	.....	.272	.272	.270	....	.247	.230	4.1
65–67	Enonkoski	1.860	.....	.194	.195	.185	....	.076	.138	2.6
68–69	Enontekio	1.100	.....	.124	.126	.120	....	.857	.222	2.5
72–74	Esbo	.540	.....	.045	.081	.065	....	.326	.045	1.1
75–77	Hankasalmi	1.400	.....	.148	.140	.147	....	.133	.135	2.1
78–80	Hankipudas	6.800	.....	.749	.742	.733	....	.361	.505	9.8
81–84	Haukivuori	.412	.....	.100	.100	.050	....	.218	.045	.9
85–90	Heinola	1.200	.....	.127	.127	.126	....	.190	.091	1.8
91–96	Helsingfors	10.560	.....	1.793	3.549	1.425	....	5.850	.889	24.0
97–99	Hyrynsalmi	2.100	.....	.232	.232	.230	....	.114	.138	3.0
100–2	Hyvinkaa	4.800	.....	.504	.504	.502	....	.324	.312	6.9
103–5	Ii	9.500	.....	.889	.890	.880	....	.914	.865	13.9
106–8	Ilomantsi	2.700	.....	.280	.280	.280	....	.190	.227	3.9
109–11	Imphilahti	7.700	.....	.792	.792	.790	....	.590	.625	11.2
111–14	Joensuu	.900	.....	.096	.096	.090	....	.038	.046	1.2
115–17	Joutseno	.900	.....	.096	.196	.100	....	.076	.092	1.4
118–20	Juuka	6.101	.....	....	....	.620	....	.762	.592	8.0
120–22	Jappila	1.400	.....	.152	.152	.156	....	.190	.092	2.1
123–25	Kaavi	4.068	.....	.450	.460	.440	....	4.681	.674	10.7
126–28	Kajaani	2.300	.....	.224	.224	.220	....	.324	.224	3.5
129–31	Kangasniemi	.750	.....	.076	.076	.075	....	.152	.091	1.2

FINLAND

Table 317—*Continued* **Detail of Internal Deliveries for Child Feeding**

Receipt No.	Districts and Kitchens	Commodities in Net Metric Tons of 1,000 Kilograms or 2,204.6 Pounds								
		Wheat Flour	Cereal Flour	Rice	Beans, Peas	Pork Products	Milk		Sugar	Total Tons
							Evap.	Cond.		
	June, July, Aug., 1919									
132-34	Kemijarven	6.300	....	.670	.673	.664	....	.895	.530	9.732
135-36	Kestila	....	....	.036	.036	....	....	.038	.046	.156
137-39	Kiihtelysvaara	1.600	....	.160	.160	.160	....	.218	.138	2.436
140-42	Kiimingi	3.500	....	.360	.370	.368	....	.342	.319	5.259
143-45	Kinnula	.350	....	.034	.035	.033	....	.076	.046	.574
146-47	Kittila	5.300	1.800	.407	.410	.840	....	2.019	.546	11.322
148-51	Kivennapa	8.000	....	.768	.768	.771	....	1.009	.699	12.015
152	Kivijarven	2.500	....	.260	.260	.260	....	.266	.311	3.857
153-54	Kolari	3.029	....	.353	.349	.340	....	.171	.219	4.461
155-57	Konginkangas	.871	....	.088	.080	.095	....	.348	.046	1.528
158-60	Kontiolahti	7.200	....	.720	.720	.720	....	.610	.681	10.651
161-63	Korpiselka	3.900	....	.511	.512	.510	....	.324	.360	6.117
164-67	Kotka	6.400	....	.683	.682	.685	....	1.486	.501	10.437
168-70	Konvola	1.116	....	.116	.129	.115	....	.370	.046	1.892
171-73	Kuhmoniemi	6.828	....	.751	.760	.760	....	.361	.493	9.952
174-75	Kuivaniemi	2.200	....	.238	.236	.233	....	.095	.330	3.332
176-79	Kuolajarvi	4.100	....	.441	.433	.430	....	.210	.304	5.919
180-82	Kuopio	1.700	....	.180	.180	.192	....	.479	.045	2.776
183	Kuusamon	....	....	2.000	2.000	....	....	....	....	4.000
184-86	Kuusankoski	1.700	....	.180	.166	.192	....	.319	.044	2.601
87-89	Kuusjarvi	.900	....	.088	.088	.088	....	.181	.088	1.433
90-92	Kymi	14.700	....	1.440	1.440	1.440	....	1.543	1.366	21.929
93-95	Kymintehdas	4.977	....	.541	.547	.541	....	.457	.045	7.108
96-98	Kyyrola	.900	....	.096	.096	.096	....	.038	.046	1.272
9-201	Lappee	3.400	....	.352	.352	.350	....	.361	.318	5.133
202-4	Leivonmaki	.330	....	.034	.040	.050	....	.130	.046	.630
205-8	Lempaala	1.200	....	.120	.123	.120	....	.544	.046	2.153
09-11	Leppavirta	.996	....	.120	.120	.120	....	.133	.230	1.719
11-13	Lestijarvi	1.123	....	.116	.120	.111	....	.370	.045	1.885
14-16	Liperi	5.500	....	.520	.520	.520	....	2.095	.902	10.057
17-19	Muola	1.200	....	.020	.120	.120	....	.228	.138	1.826
20-21	Muonio	....	....	.257	.253	....	....	.152	.181	.843
22-24	Nilsia	1.200	....	.120	.120	.120	....	.133	.130	1.823
25-27	Nurmes	8.200	....	.880	.880	.880	....	.362	.586	11.788
28-30	Oulujoki	6.336	....	.672	.603	.663	....	1.633	.182	10.089
31-33	Paavola	4.200	....	.447	.447	.438	....	.288	.272	6.092
34-36	Paltamo	4.100	....	.416	.416	.420	....	.324	.321	5.997
37-39	Parikkala	1.853	....	.228	.228	.219	....	.133	.137	2.798
240	Pelkosenniemi	2.000	....	.195	.195	.191	....	.342	.230	3.153
41-43	Perho	1.500	....	.136	.140	.135	....	.342	.229	2.482
44-46	Pieksamaki	2.700	....	.280	.280	.280	....	.324	.275	4.139
47-49	Pielisjarvi	8.000	....	.880	.880	.880	....	1.390	1.002	13.032
50-51	Pihtipudas	4.700	....	.484	.484	.129	....	.590	.415	6.802
52-54	Polvijarvi	3.900	....	.408	.408	.407	....	.590	.413	6.126
55-57	Pudasjarvi	10.700	....	1.075	1.068	1.060	....	1.009	.937	15.849
58-60	Puolanko	9.700	....	1.018	.999	.990	....	.648	.764	14.119
61-63	Puumala	2.300	....	.248	.248	.248	....	.190	.181	3.415
64-66	Pyhanto	1.800	....	.182	.185	.184	....	.210	.172	2.733
267	Pylkonmaki	1.100	....	.108	.107	.106	....	.133	.091	1.645
68-70	Ranua	3.800	....	.404	.395	.390	....	.248	.363	5.600
71-73	Rautavaara	5.000	....	.496	.496	.500	....	.514	.453	7.459
74-76	Rautu	1.800	....	.200	.200	.225	....	.762	.321	3.508
77-79	Ristijarvi	2.700	....	.280	.280	.280	....	.666	.407	4.613
81-84	Rovaniemi	13.950	....	1.560	1.540	1.527	....	.781	.943	20.301
85-87	Ruokolahti	3.050	....	.324	.321	.319	....	.588	.046	4.648
88-90	Raakkyla	4.100	....	.440	.440	.440	....	.305	.307	6.032
291	Salmi	....	....	1.440	1.440	....	....	....	....	2.880
92-93	Savonlinna	1.340	....	.144	.166	.144	....	.196	.046	2.036

[*Continued on next page*]

FINLAND

Table 317—*Continued* Detail of Internal Deliveries for Child Feeding

Receipt No.	Districts and Kitchens	Commodities in Net Metric Tons of 1,000 Kilograms or 2,204.6 Pounds								
		Wheat Flour	Cereal Flour	Rice	Beans, Peas	Pork Products	Milk		Sugar	Total Tons
							Evap.	Cond.		
	June, July, Aug., 1919									
294–97	Savukoski	.432	....	.045	.045	.030	....	.806	.090	1.4
298–300	Simo	1.300	....	.136	.134	.131	....	.229	.136	2.0
301–3	Soanlahti	3.400	....	.360	.360	.360	....	.190	.228	4.8
304–8	Sodankyla	2.200	....	.235	.236	.230	....	.686	.320	3.9
309	Kuolajarvi	....	....	1.200	1.200	....	....	....	....	2.4
310–12	Suistamo	6.000	....	.624	.624	.630	....	.362	.446	8.6
313–14	Sotkano	8.500	....	.896	.896	.890	....	2.743	1.191	15.1
315–17	Suojarvi	5.800	....	.509	.560	.519	....	.762	.605	8.7
318–20	Suomussalmi	2.200	....	.240	.240	.240	....	.133	.181	3.2
321–23	Sakkijarvi	.950	....	.104	.104	.105	....	.057	.091	1.4
324–26	Saraisniemi	3.960	....	.400	.560	.320	....	.210	.183	5.6
327–28	Taivalkoski	....	....	.720	.727	....	....	.914	.683	3.0
329–31	Terijoki	3.100	....	.320	.320	.320	....	.248	.274	4.5
332–34	Tervola	1.150	....	.117	.114	.111	....	.229	.137	1.8
335–37	Turtola	2.400	....	.260	.260	.255	....	.152	.184	3.5
338–40	Tohmajarvi	2.400	....	.240	.240	.240	....	.152	.182	3.4
341–43	Tuupovaara	1.200	....	.120	....	....	....	.076	.092	1.4
344	Utajarvi	3.700	....	.400	.403	.400	....	.324	.322	5.5
345–47	Uuraansaari	4.000	....	.440	.440	.440	....	.152	.229	5.7
348–51	Uusikirkko	4.200	....	.460	.460	.460	....	1.124	.501	7.2
352–54	Valkjarvi	1.500	....	.160	.160	.160	....	.038	.091	2.1
355–57	Valtimo	1.500	....	.160	.160	.160	....	.114	.139	2.2
358–60	Vammala	.300	....	.035	.036	.033	....	.038	.046	.4
360–62	Varkaus	2.400	....	.260	.260	.260	....	.179	.182	3.5
363–65	Vesanto	1.300	....	.134	.144	.137	....	.114	.092	1.9
366–68	Vesilahti	3.400	....	.363	.318	.366	....	.190	.451	5.0
369–71	Huopalahti	.372	....	.089	.080	.065	....	.544	.025	1.1
372–74	Vihanti	.800	....	.087	.084	.080	....	.171	.092	1.3
375–79	Viipuri	48.000	....	4.800	4.800	4.931	....	20.261	7.147	89.9
380–82	Vilyakkala	1.310	....	.142	.166	.145	....	.171	.045	1.9
383–85	Voikaa	4.780	....	.520	.524	.528	....	.391	.045	6.7
386–88	Vuolijoki	1.600	....	.160	.160	.160	....	.210	.136	2.4
389–91	Ylikiiminki	1.600	....	.147	.172	.145	....	1.306	.138	3.5
392	Espoo	....	....	.094	....	....	....	....	....	.0
393	Haukivuori	.534	....	....	....	.050	....	....	....	.5
394–96	Dickursby	.792	....	.137	.123	.105	....	1.452	.045	2.6
397–98	Helsingfors	....	....	....	....	.900	....	5.837	....	6.7
399	Juuka	....	....	.578	.616	....	....	....	....	1.1
400	Kestila	.356	....	....	....	.007	....	....	....	.3
401	Kittee	2.600	....	.273	.273	.272	....	.332	.226	3.9
402–3	Kuusamo	18.000	....	.160	....	2.000	....	1.235	1.794	23.1
404	Muonio	2.300	....	....	....	.250	....	....	....	2.5
405–6	Salmi	14.000	....	....	....	1.440	....	1.484	1.101	18.0
407	Taivalkoski	....	....	....	....	.720	....	....	....	.7
408–10	Huopalahti	1.080	....	.182	.165	.195	....	2.190	.092	3.9
	Total for June, July, Aug., 1919	**448.588**	**1.800**	**49.557**	**51.343**	**48.583**	....	**92.402**	**42.708**	**734.9**
	Sept., 1919									
411–14	Alatornio	.218	11.648	.404	.777	.776	....	....	.142	13.9
415	Antrea	.080	7.532	.530	.530	.530	....	....	.036	9.2
416–18	Isalmi	.240	5.760	.640	.640	.640	....	....	.160	8.0
419–21	Viipuri	.216	3.816	.424	.424	.425	....	....	.144	5.[illegible]
422–24	Jaaski	.042	1.532	.170	.170	.170	....	....	.018	2.1
425–27	Kaarina	.120	2.232	.248	.222	.250	....	....	.072	3.1
428–30	Kangaslampi	.048	1.676	.184	.185	.194	....	....	.028	2.3
431–33	Karttula	.518	7.422	.822	.824	.824	....	....	.258	10.0
434–36	Kesalahti	.042	.668	.100	.100	.100	....	....	.024	1.0
438–41	Koivisto	.144	5.472	.608	.608	.608	....	....	.104	7.5

FINLAND

Table 317—*Continued* Detail of Internal Deliveries for Child Feeding

Receipt No.	Districts and Kitchens	Wheat Flour	Cereal Flour	Rice	Beans, Peas	Pork Products	Milk Evap.	Milk Cond.	Sugar	Total Tons
		Commodities in Net Metric Tons of 1,000 Kilograms or 2,204.6 Pounds								
	Sept., 1919									
2-44	Kuokkala	.050	2.016	.224	.225	.150	....	....	.028	2.693
6-48	Kuolemajarvi	.036	1.476	.164	.160	.164	....	....	.020	2.020
9-51	Kuopio	.216	4.680	.520	.520	.520	....	....	.128	6.584
2-54	Lahti	.024	1.310	.144	.145	.144	....	....	.020	1.787
5-57	Lapinlahti	.060	1.440	.160	.160	.160	....	....	.040	2.020
8-60	Maaria	.156	5.220	.580	.580	.580	....	....	.088	7.204
1-63	Mikkeli	.089	4.032	.448	.448	.448	....	....	.044	5.509
4-66	Mantyharju	.288	7.560	.840	.456	.842	....	....	.192	10.178
7-69	Rihimaki	.096	1.980	.220	.220	.220	....	....	.060	2.796
0-73	Sortavala	.926	4.135	.568	.570	.322	....	....	.108	6.629
4-76	Sulkava	.090	3.620	.402	.402	.402	....	....	.060	4.976
7-79	Suonenjoki	.072	2.698	.300	.400	.300	....	....	.056	3.826
0-82	Saaksmaki	.048	2.664	.296	.296	.300	....	....	.026	3.630
3-86	Tohmajarvi	.318	5.738	.636	.636	.636	....	....	.202	8.166
7-89	Tuusula	.072	2.736	.304	.304	.304	....	....	.040	3.760
0-92	Vekkalahti	.062	1.288	.142	.145	.142	....	....	.028	1.807
3-95	Viitasaari	.060	2.052	.228	.328	.228	....	....	.034	2.930
6-98	Virtasalmi	.050	1.188	.132	.140	.132	....	....	.026	1.668
-501	Vuoksela	.036	1.936	.214	.115	.214	....	....	.018	2.533
02-4	Vartsila	.126	6.198	.688	.688	.628	....	....	.082	8.410
06-8	Ylitornio	.056	.....	.422	.431	.428	....	....	.050	1.387
	Total for Sept., 1919	**4.599**	**111.725**	**11.762**	**11.849**	**11.781**	....	....	**2.336**	**154.052**
	Oct., 1919 to Jan., 1920, Incl.									
9-10	Alatornio	.150	.....	.970	1.160	....	....	1.562	.385	4.227
511	Alberga	....	.....	....	....	....	....	.283	.046	.329
2-13	Antrea	.060	.....	.575	.690	....	....	.437	.230	1.992
4-15	Eno	.140	.....	.568	.670	.090	4.441	....	.332	6.241
6-17	Enonkoski	.098	.840	.675	.825	....	1.110	.310	.350	4.208
...	Enontekio	....	2.520	....	....	....	....	....	....	2.520
8-19	Haapajarvi	.140	3.180	.670	.804	....	....	.990	.268	6.052
520	Hankasalmi	.042	1.800	.375	.450	.045	1.262	.267	.151	4.392
521	Haukipudas	.140	5.940	1.250	1.475	.115	2.547	....	.630	12.097
22-23	Haukivuori	.020	1.200	.245	.294	.025	.571	.152	.098	2.605
524	Heinola	.020	.600	.135	.145	....	....	.191	.049	1.140
525	Heinola Mlk.	.056	.950	.200	.230	....	....	.305	.079	1.820
526	Hirvensalmi	.070	1.320	.270	.320	....	....	.495	.108	2.583
527	Hollola	.280	3.700	.770	.920	....	....	2.210	.308	8.188
28-29	Hyrynsalmi	.056	7.140	.440	.540	.367	.261	.323	.176	9.303
30-31	Hyvinkaa	.084	4.637	.966	1.160	.100	3.026	.343	.386	10.702
32-33	Ii	.280	6.720	1.400	1.750	.075	7.147	....	.840	18.212
34-35	Iisalmi	.200	4.800	1.000	1.200	....	....	2.217	.400	9.817
36-37	Ilomantsi	.280	17.520	2.275	2.730	1.417	1.707	....	1.260	27.189
538	Impilahti	.840	24.120	2.100	2.520	1.291	....	3.334	.840	35.045
539	Joensuu	.012	.480	.208	.265	....	.261	....	.100	1.326
40-41	Johannes	.180	1.920	.400	.450	....	....	2.000	.160	5.110
42-43	Juuka	.280	.....	1.500	1.800	.090	6.335	....	.800	10.805
544	Jappala	.030	1.200	.263	.350	....	....	.229	.105	2.177
45-46	Jaaski	.030	1.500	.300	.405	....	....	.267	.125	2.627
47-48	Kaarina	.060	2.100	.430	.505	....	....	.627	.170	3.892
...	Jontseno	....	1.560	....	....	....	....	....	....	1.560
49-50	Kaavi	.420	4.200	.875	1.050	.150	4.442	2.762	.350	14.249
51-52	Kajaani	.140	2.940	.612	.734	.020	.304	.972	.245	5.967
53-54	Kangaslampi	.030	1.300	.270	.335	....	....	.305	.110	2.350
555	Kangasniemi	.070	.800	.170	.220	.020	....	.495	.067	1.842
556	Karinainen	.042	.840	.175	.210	....	....	.267	.070	1.604
557	Karttula	....	4.500	....	....	....	....	1.029	....	5.529
558	Karungin	.140	1.920	.675	.810	....	....	.819	.270	4.634
559	Kemi	.120	5.880	1.225	1.490	....	....	.686	.490	9.891

[*Continued on next page*]

FINLAND

Table 317—*Continued* **Detail of Internal Deliveries for Child Feeding**

Receipt No.	Districts and Kitchens	Commodities in Net Metric Tons of 1,000 Kilograms or 2,204.6 Pounds								
		Wheat Flour	Cereal Flour	Rice	Beans, Peas	Pork Products	Milk		Sugar	Total Tons
							Evap.	Cond.		
	Oct., 1919 to Jan., 1920, Incl.									
560	Kemijarvi	.140	4.800	1.000	.600	....	3.157	....	.570	10.2
561	Kestila	.014	.360	.080	.096	....	....	.114	.080	.7
562–63	Kesalahti	.040	.900	.190	.185	....	....	.514	.075	1.9
564–65	Kiihtelysvaara	.140	5.040	1.050	1.260	.080	2.220	1.105	.420	11.3
566	Kiiminki	.115	3.360	.700	.840	.055	1.764	....	.420	7.2
567	Kinnula	.030	.420	.075	.080	....	.566	....	.050	1.2
568	Kitee	.110	2.880	.599	.677	.115	....	.876	.235	5.4
569–70	Kittila	.210	3.360	.700	.860	.035	4.095	....	.450	9.7
571–72	Kiuruvesi	.280	5.460	1.137	1.364	.150	4.311	2.209	.455	15.3
573–74	Kivennapa	.098	4.800	1.000	1.200	.060	1.655	.610	.400	9.8
575	Kivijarvi	.085	2.700	.560	.650	.020	1.764	....	.320	6.
576–77	Koivisto	.100	4.200	.875	1.050	....	....	1.160	.350	7.7
578	Kolari	.070	3.360	.700	.880	.020	1.240	....	.385	6.
579	Konginkanges	.084	.660	.140	.168	....	....	.667	.056	1.7
580–81	Kontiolahti	.140	6.300	1.300	1.560	.200	5.704	1.676	.525	17.4
582–83	Korpiselan	.084	9.300	.788	.944	.401	1.763	.553	.315	14.1
584	Kotka	.140	6.300	1.300	1.580	....	....	1.105	.525	10.9
585	Kuovola	.040	1.180	.240	.294	....	....	.323	.097	2.1
586–87	Kuhmoniemi	.280	22.927	1.531	1.836	1.259	1.894	1.943	.613	32.2
588	Kuivaniemi	.050	2.340	.500	.580	....	.510	....	.220	4.2
589–90	Kuokkla	.030	1.650	.350	.420	....	....	.286	.140	2.8
591	Kuolajarvi	.170	4.500	.930	1.100	....	2.024	....	.520	9.
592–93	Kuolemjarvi	.030	2.706	.250	.290	....	....	.267	.100	3.
594	Kuopio	.088	1.740	.350	.450	....	....	.476	.140	3.
595–96	Kuopio Mlk.	.180	3.480	.725	.855	....	....	1.752	.290	7.
597	Kuusamo	.240	28.500	2.257	2.676	1.363	....	....	1.171	36.
598	Kuusankoski	.056	1.770	.370	.440	....	....	.323	.147	3.
599–600	Kuusjarvi	.056	.960	.193	.230	.020	.370	.438	.077	2.
601–2	Kymi	1.120	7.150	1.500	1.800	.200	5.705	6.667	.595	24.
603	Kymitehtaan	.070	5.170	1.080	1.300	....	....	.438	.431	8.
604	Kyrola	.017	1.000	.210	.230	....	....	.114	.084	1.
605–6	Lahti	.030	1.000	.200	.290	....	....	.286	.085	1.
607–8	Lapinlahti	.050	1.185	.250	.290	....	....	.533	.100	2.
609–10	Lapee	.280	8.600	1.800	2.160	.080	2.220	1.943	.717	17.
611	Leivonmaki	.014	.360	.074	.115	....	....	1.332	.022	1.
612–13	Lempaala	.056	1.180	.250	.280	.020	.305	.533	.098	2.
614	Leppaverta	.084	2.100	.438	.524	.070	1.894	.533	.175	5.
615	Liperi	.210	4.860	1.000	1.200	....	....	1.943	.403	9.
616	Lestijarvi	.040	.840	.175	.220	.025	.610	....	.100	2.
617	Luumaki	.112	1.500	.315	.360	....	....	.724	.126	3.
618–19	Maaria	.060	3.300	.700	.820	....	....	.629	.275	5.
620	Messukyla	.140	2.500	.525	.630	....	....	1.047	.210	5.
621–22	Mikkeli	.070	3.200	.660	.830	....	....	.552	.265	5.
623	Muolaa	.070	1.200	.250	.300	.045	....	.610	.102	2.
624	Muonio	.088	2.340	.480	.560	.035	.893	....	.248	4.
625–26	Mantyharju	.140	4.700	.975	1.370	....	....	1.333	.390	8.
627	Nilsia	.056	4.020	.840	1.000	.115	....	.323	.336	6.
628	Nurmeksen	.420	.....	2.180	2.650	....	6.357	....	1.325	12.
629–30	Oulujoki	.197	11.760	.951	1.434	.135	6.946	....	.635	22.
631–32	Paavola	.140	4.440	.919	1.100	.070	3.679	....	.440	10.
633–34	Paltamo	.140	4.440	.919	1.104	.070	1.916	.836	.368	9.
635	Parikkala	.056	2.520	.525	.630	....	....	.438	.210	4.
636	Pelkosenniemi	.140	1.620	.330	.430	....	1.916	....	.240	4.
637	Perho	.140	1.020	.210	.265	.025	2.024	....	.200	3.
638	Pieksamaki	.140	2.700	.560	.672	.025	....	.876	.224	5.
639–40	Pielisjarvi	.560	.900	2.275	2.730	.125	8.578	....	1.190	16.
641	Pihtipudas	.210	4.200	.875	1.050	.065	3.091	....	.520	10.

FINLAND

'able 317—*Continued* **Detail of Internal Deliveries for Child Feeding**

eipt).	Districts and Kitchens	Wheat Flour	Cereal Flour	Rice	Beans, Peas	Pork Products	Milk: Evap.	Milk: Cond.	Sugar	Total Tons
	Oct., 1919 to Jan., 1920, Incl.									
642	Pirkkala	.280	3.360	.700	.840	....	....	1.943	.280	7.403
-44	Polvijarvi	.140	.....	.700	.855	.025	3.676	....	.448	5.844
645	Porin Mlk.	.084	3.360	.700	.840	....	....	.495	.280	5.759
646	Posio	.044	2.160	.450	.537	....	1.524	....	.236	4.951
7-48	Pudasjarvi	.420	26.820	1.800	2.200	.070	5.704	....	.945	37.959
...	Puolanga	....	16.680	....	....	.708	....	....	....	17.388
649	Puumala	.080	2.580	.540	.640	.080	2.220	.628	.214	6.982
650	Pyhanta	.040	1.440	.300	.370	.045	.762	....	.160	3.117
651	Pylkonmaki	.060	1.140	.230	.230	.025	1.002	....	.140	2.827
2-53	Ranua	.180	9.760	.550	.650	.416	1.959	....	.300	13.815
654	Rautavaari	.110	3.360	.578	.700	.070	1.785	....	.330	6.933
655	Rautu	.280	1.550	.320	.400	....	....	1.391	.129	4.070
6-57	Riihimaki	.060	1.560	.325	.410	....	....	.439	.130	2.924
658	Ristijarvi	.140	2.580	.484	.660	.030	....	.723	.218	4.835
659	Rovaniemi	.170	9.240	2.225	2.600	.120	3.309	4.724	.900	23.288
660	Ruokolahti	.098	3.360	.700	.840	....	....	.553	.280	5.831
1-62	Raakyla	.088	4.320	.900	1.080	.045	1.263	.779	.360	8.835
...	Ruskeala	....	1.450	....	....	....	....	....	....	1.450
663	Saaryarvi	.210	3.360	.700	.840	....	....	1.105	.280	6.495
664	Salmi	1.050	33.240	3.200	3.800	.331	....	4.153	1.260	47.034
665	Saloinen	.084	1.260	.265	.320	....	....	.552	.105	2.586
6-67	Savonranta	.028	1.440	.300	.330	.025	.631	.191	.122	3.067
668	Savukoski	.112	.300	.061	.080	....	1.894	1.567	.128	4.142
9-70	Simo	.115	1.380	.290	.325	.055	3.463	....	.220	5.848
1-72	Soaulahti	.056	5.880	.490	.588	.239	1.894	.323	.196	9.666
3-74	Sodanlyka	.126	2.880	.580	.700	.025	2.024	....	.315	6.650
5-77	Sortavala	.230	2.520	1.415	1.690	....	....	2.095	.565	8.515
8-79	Suistamo	.210	19.560	1.270	1.520	.210	6.009	1.372	.508	30.659
680	Sulkava	....	2.400	....	....	....	....	.171	....	2.571
...	Sotkamo	....	8.220	....	....	.055	....	....	....	8.275
681	Suojarvi	.280	19.980	1.444	1.732	.200	5.705	1.943	.578	31.862
682	Suomussalmi	.420	27.076	2.000	2.400	1.186	....	2.762	.805	36.649
3-84	Suonenjoki	.050	2.200	.460	.555	....	....	.590	.185	4.040
685	Sakkijarvi	.056	1.000	.200	.245	.040	....	.324	.083	1.948
6-87	Saraisniemi	.084	3.780	.780	.936	.025	.566	.495	.312	6.978
8-89	Saakamaki	.100	2.100	.450	.520	....	....	.476	.175	3.821
0-91	Taivalkoski	.140	10.620	.750	.895	.543	2.655	....	.412	16.015
2-94	Tampere	....	8.400	3.500	4.200	.450	25.409	....	1.400	43.359
5-96	Terijoki	.082	2.500	.525	.635	.090	2.525	.247	.200	6.804
697	Tervola	.170	1.800	.375	.435	....	2.526	....	.290	5.596
698	Tohmajarvi	....	3.700	....	....	....	....	.800	....	4.500
699	Tornio	.070	.840	.175	.210	....	....	.438	.070	1.803
700	Turku	....	8.400	3.500	4.200	.450	25.408	....	1.400	43.358
701	Turtola	.060	2.280	.460	.550	....	.871	....	.236	4.457
702-4	Tuupovaara	.060	10.260	.875	1.040	.583	2.220	.343	.350	15.731
705-6	Tuusula	.060	2.280	.475	.560	....	....	.380	.196	3.951
707	Utajarvi	.170	4.380	.900	1.110	.080	2.177	....	.483	9.300
708	Uuransaari	.042	2.300	.480	.580	....	....	.267	.193	3.862
709	Uusikirkko	.140	4.970	1.030	1.240	.135	....	.836	.414	8.765
710	Utajarvi	....	.....	....	....	....	2.220	....	....	2.220
711	Valkjarvi	.017	1.680	.320	.376	....	....	.114	.140	2.647
712	Valtimo	.070	.....	.435	.520	.035	1.284	....	.245	2.589
713	Vammala	.014	.336	.070	.084	....	....	.114	.028	.646
714	Varkaus	.025	1.620	.340	.400	....	....	.133	.135	2.653
715	Varpaisjarvi	.210	3.360	.700	.840	....	....	1.390	.280	6.780
16-17	Vehkalahti	.030	1.000	.225	.280	....	....	.343	.090	1.968
18-19	Vesanto	.056	1.440	.300	.356	.045	1.263	.323	.120	3.903

Commodities in Net Metric Tons of 1,000 Kilograms or 2,204.6 Pounds

[*Continued on next page*]

FINLAND

Table 317—*Continued* **Detail of Internal Deliveries for Child Feeding**

Receipt No.	Districts and Kitchens	Commodities in Net Metric Tons of 1,000 Kilograms or 2,204.6 Pounds								
		Wheat Flour	Cereal Flour	Rice	Beans, Peas	Pork Products	Milk		Sugar	Total Tons
							Evap.	Cond.		
	Oct., 1919 to Jan., 1920, Incl.									
720–21	Vesilahti	.140	3.570	.740	.892	.025	.631	.836	.297	7.1
722–23	Vihanti	.030	1.140	.236	.335	.025	1.023	....	.115	2.9
724	Viipurin	....	51.000	10.630	12.756	....	....	....	4.250	78.6
725–26	Viitassaari	.036	1.620	.340	.420	....	....	.380	.135	2.9
727	Viljakkala	.028	1.490	.309	.370	....	....	.171	.123	2.4
728	Virtasalmi	.050	1.050	.220	.255	....	....	.133	.085	1.7
729–30	Voikaa	.084	3.700	.770	.920	....	....	.438	.308	6.2
731–32	Vuoksela	.020	1.000	.210	.255	....	....	.114	.085	1.6
733–34	Vuolijoki	.056	2.280	.460	.560	.035	.958	.381	.185	4.9
735–36	Vartsila	.040	2.250	.470	.560	....	....	.609	.190	4.1
737–38	Ylikiiminki	.225	1.500	.315	.405	.025	3.679	....	.294	6.4
739–40	Ylitornio	.050	7.152	1.080	.800	....	....	.381	.275	9.7
741–43	Helsingfors	....	7.980	5.250	6.289	.300	32.485	....	1.648	53.9
	Total for Oct., 1919 to Jan., 1920	**20.120**	**735.079**	**125.215**	**149.777**	**15.534**	**265.309**	**100.929**	**55.117**	**1,467.0**
	Feb. 1, 1920 to June 30, 1920, Incl.									
744–45	Alatornio	.075	.....	....	.535	.160	....	.953	.213	1.9
746	Eno	.150	.....	.550	.300	.080	....	.781	.100	1.9
747	Enontekio	.025	.....	.370	.174	.045	....	.267	.060	.9
748	Hankipudas	.075	.....	.910	.446	.135	....	.800	.180	2.5
749	Maisteri B. Nyberg—Helsingfors	....	.....	....	....	.367	....	....	....	.3
750	Hyrnsalmi	.050	.....	....	.180	.050	....	.210	.060	.5
751	Ii	.040	.....	.910	.546	.135	....	.381	.180	2.1
752	Iisalmi	.300	.....	....	1.000	.170	....	1.581	.330	3.3
753	Ilomantsi	.300	.....	1.350	.800	.200	....	1.905	.270	4.8
754–56	Impilahti	....	.....	1.000	....	.110	....	7.577	.200	8.8
757–58	Johannes	....	.....	.315	....	.040	....	....	.060	.
759–61	Joutseno	.025	.....	.225	.160	.030	....	.133	.040	.
762	Joutseno	.056	.....	.330	.370	....	....	.210	.130	1.
763	Junka	.200	.....	....	.700	.180	....	.953	.240	2.
764	Kaavi	.300	.....	....	.360	....	....	1.581	.120	2.
765	Kajaani	.050	.....	....	.570	.080	....	.533	.100	1.
766–67	Kartula	.450	.....	.930	1.420	....	....	1.810	.475	5.
768	Karunki	.045	.....	.320	.227	.050	....	.517	.066	1.
769	Kemi	.075	.....	1.300	.780	.200	....	.800	.260	3.
770	Kemijarvi	.075	.....	.730	.455	.115	....	.800	.150	2.
771–72	Kestila	.010	.....	.090	.045	.049	....	.076	.015	.
773–75	Kestilahti	.020	.....	.135	.080	.020	....	.190	.030	.
776	Kiihtelysvaara	.080	.....	....	.500	.100	....	.800	.160	1.
777–78	Kiiminki	.025	.....	.225	.136	.030	....	1.795	.040	2.
779–81	Kitee	.040	.....	.270	.226	.050	....	.438	.060	1.
782–84	Kivennapa	.045	.....	.585	.400	.100	....	.305	.120	1.
785–87	Koivisto	.040	.....	.540	.320	.080	....	.324	.110	1.
788	Kolari	....	.....	....	....	....	....	.305	....	.
789	Kontiolahti	.100	.....	.750	.450	.100	....	.629	.150	2.
790–91	Korpiselka	.075	.....	....	.302	.070	....	.762	.100	1.
792	Kuhmoniemi	.300	.....	....	1.030	.150	....	1.581	.200	3.
793	Kiuvaniemi	.020	.....	.275	.174	.045	....	.152	.055	.
794–96	Kuolemajarvi	.025	.....	.225	.160	.030	....	.152	.040	.
797	Kuopio	.200	.....	....	.580	....	....	1.105	.190	2.
798	Kuusjarvi	.050	.....	.300	.180	.050	....	.248	.060	.
799	Lapinlahti	.050	.....	....	.180	....	....	.304	.060	.
800	Liperi	.150	.....	.500	.300	.080	....	1.104	.100	2.
801–3	Muolaa	.025	.....	.090	.080	.020	....	.152	.020	.
804	Nurmes	.300	.....	....	.850	.200	....	1.581	.280	3.
805–6	Oulum	.610	.....	1.225	1.490	....	....	2.496	.490	6.
807	Oulunjoki	.050	.....	.590	.364	.090	....	.628	.120	1.

FINLAND

Table 317—*Continued* **Detail of Internal Deliveries for Child Feeding**

Receipt No.	Districts and Kitchens	Wheat Flour	Cereal Flour	Rice	Beans, Peas	Pork Products	Milk Evap.	Milk Cond.	Sugar	Total Tons
		Commodities in Net Metric Tons of 1,000 Kilograms or 2,204.6 Pounds								
	Feb. 1, 1920 to June 30, 1920, Incl.									
808	Paavola	.050	....	....	.174	.045	....	.476	.060	.805
809	Paltamo	.330	....	.515	.360	.100	....	1.257	.120	2.682
810	Pieksamaki	.150	....	....	.270	....	....	.781	.090	1.291
811	Pielisjarvi	.250	....	1.350	.950	.250	....	1.257	.300	4.357
2–13	Pirkkala	.250	....	.360	.180	.050	....	.628	.060	1.528
814	Polvijarvi	.050	....	.400	.650	.060	....	1.238	.080	2.478
5–16	Pudasjarvi	.075	....	1.000	.242	.150	....	.800	.200	2.467
817	Puolanga	.252	....	1.295	2.554	....	....	1.621	.518	6.240
818	Pyhanta	.025	....	.320	....	.090	1.132	.248	.060	1.875
9–21	Palkjarvi	.030	....	....	.226	.050	....	.304	.060	.670
823	Ranua	.050	....	.450	.260	.065	....	.438	.086	1.349
4–25	Rautalampi	.600	....	.700	1.320	....	....	4.338	.400	7.358
826	Rautavaara	.100	....	....	.500	.130	....	.628	.170	1.528
7–28	Rautu	.075	....	.180	.080	.020	....	.572	.040	.967
830	Ristyarvi	.080	....	....	.220	.050	....	.305	.065	.720
831	Rovaniemio	.080	....	1.200	....	.180	....	.895	.240	2.595
832	Ruskela	.080	....	.300	.360	....	....	.572	.120	1.432
833	Raakyla	.025	....	....	.318	.070	....	.228	.100	.741
4–36	Salmi	.125	....	1.400	.160	.200	5.705	1.238	.274	9.102
837	Savukoski	.010	....	.090	.045	.020	....	.095	.015	.275
838	Simo	.040	....	.180	.091	.025	....	.476	.032	.844
9–40	Soanlahti	.025	....	....	.226	....	....	....	....	.251
841	Sotkamo	.400	....	....	.900	.200	....	2.477	.300	4.277
842	Sotkamo	.210	....	1.706	2.050	....	....	1.372	.683	6.021
843	Suomussalmi	.300	....	....	.850	.200	....	1.581	.280	3.211
4–45	Suistamo	.050	....	.616	.370	....	....	....	....	1.036
846	Sulkava	.100	....	.500	.615	....	....	.762	.200	2.177
7–50	Suojarvi	.075	....	.906	.606	.300	5.705	.537	.180	8.309
851	Saraisniemi	.060	....	....	.450	.070	....	.476	.090	1.146
852	Taivalkoski	.050	....	.455	.318	.070	....	.495	.092	1.480
853	Tampere	....	....	....	....	.263	....	....	....	.263
4–56	Terijoki	.025	....	.405	.240	.060	....	.190	.080	1.000
7–58	Tohmajarvi	.150	....	.780	1.380	.100	....	1.066	.460	3.936
859	Turtola	.040	....	.500	.318	.075	....	.400	.100	1.433
0–61	Tuupovaara	.040	....	....	.469	.070	....	.438	.100	1.117
862	Utajarvi	.080	....	.540	.318	.080	....	.705	.106	1.829
3–66	Usiskirkko	.050	....	.585	.400	.100	4.001	.572	.120	5.828
867	Valtimo	.060	....	....	.180	.050	....	.247	.060	.597
868	Varpaisjarvi	.150	....	....	.300	....	....	.781	.100	1.331
869	Vihanti	.020	....	.180	.087	.025	....	.191	.030	.533
870	Viipurin	....	....	....	....	1.140	12.084	....	....	13.224
871	Vuolijoki	.100	....	....	.450	.060	....	1.143	.080	1.833
2–73	Vartsila	.050	....	....	.151	.030	....	.476	.040	.747
874	Ylikiiminka	.080	....	.225	.136	.030	....	.762	.040	1.273
875	Ylitornio	.050	....	....	.364	.090	....	.572	.120	1.196
876	Kusamon	....	....	....	....	....	9.147	....	....	9.147
877	Impahahti	.160	....	....	.640	....	....	1.690	....	2.490
886	Rovaniemi	.075	....	.500	.608	.075	....	1.086	.100	2.444
879	Kiuruvesi	.200	....	....	.500	.170	....	1.448	.170	2.488
880	Kolari	.030	....	.400	.260	.060	....	.247	.080	1.077
1–82	Muonio	.030	....	.275	.174	.045	....	1.248	.055	1.827
883	Nilsia	.130	....	....	.500	....	....	.920	.160	1.710
884	Pelkosenniemi	.015	....	.120	.087	.020	....	.209	.025	.476
885	Puolanka	.250	....	.800	.500	.100	....	1.257	.160	3.067
887	Soanlahti	....	....	....	....	.050	....	.700	.060	.810
888	Sodankyla	.050	....	.500	.318	.045	....	.643	.100	1.656
889	Siustamo	....	....	....	....	.100	....	.700	.120	.920

[*Concluded on next page*]

FINLAND

Table 317—*Concluded* Detail of Internal Deliveries for Child Feeding

Receipt No.	Districts and Kitchens	Commodities in Net Metric Tons of 1,000 Kilograms or 2,204.6 Pounds								
		Wheat Flour	Cereal Flour	Rice	Beans, Peas	Pork Products	Milk: Evap.	Milk: Cond.	Sugar	Total Tons
	Feb. 1, 1920 to June 30, 1920, Incl.									
890	Tervola	.060	.....	.360	.227	.050	....	.853	.070	1.6
891	Johannes	.071	.....	.315	.141	....	....	.762	....	1.2
892	Sovajarvi	.030	.720	.150	.115	....	....	.392	.080	1.4
893	Ylitorio	....	.....	....	....	....	....	.195	....	.1
894	Kuusamo	....	.....	....	....	....	....	.324	....	.3
	Total for Feb. 1, 1920 to June 30, 1920, Incl.	**10.499**	**.720**	**35.598**	**41.078**	**8.694**	**37.774**	**83.231**	**13.165**	**230.7**
	Total, per District Receipts	**545.244**	**977.351**	**222.315**	**254.373**	**104.784**	**303.083**	**299.955**	**119.241**	**2,826.3**
	Turned Over to Local Committees	....	33.300	....	....	....	....	....	.400†	33.7
	Receipts Turned Over to Finnish Government	....	.....	....	....	....	36.000	....	....	36.0
	Final Distribution, Government Commodities, June, 1921*	32.460	.....	....	1.867	2.500	....	....	....	36.8
	Final Distribution, E.C.F. Commodities, June, 1921	....	.....	9.060	....	....	19.546	....	7.360	35.9
	Total	**577.704**	**1,010.651**	**231.375**	**256.240**	**107.284**	**358.629**	**299.955**	**127.001‡**	**2,968.8**

* Per report of Bertyl Nyberg, Secretary of Central Committee for Finnish Child Feeding, August 31, 1921.

† Cocoa.
‡ Of the total, 126.601 is sugar and .400 is cocoa.

FINLAND—A.R.A.-European Children's Fund

Table 318 Internal Deliveries of Commodities Purchased by Funds from Sale of A.R.A.-European Children's Fund Supplies*

Receipt No.	Districts and Kitchens	Commodities in Net Metric Tons of 1,000 Kilograms or 2,204.6 Pounds			
		Oatmeal	Rye Flour	Graham Flour	Total Tons
	May, 1920				
895–96	Alatornio	5.300	.....	1.560	6.
897–99	Eno	2.200	2.730	.750	5.
900–1	Enontekio	1.200	.....	.480	1.
902	Haukipudas	.....	.....	1.320	1.
903–4	Hyrynsalmi	1.500	.....	.400	1.
905–6	Ii	3.600	.....	1.380	4.
907–8	Iisalmi	8.300	.....	2.500	10.
909–11	Ilomahtsi	5.400	10.900	2.000	18.
912–13	Impilahti	5.000	.....	1.500	6.
914–15	Johannes	1.300	.500	.....	1.
916–17	Joutseno	.800	.....	.300	1.
918–20	Juuka	6.000	7.150	1.800	14.
921–22	Kaavi	3.000	.....	.900	3.
923–24	Kajaani	2.750	.....	.800	3.
925–26	Karttula	2.700	.....	.750	3.
927–28	Karunki	1.300	.....	.480	1.
929–30	Kemi	5.200	.....	1.980	7.
931–32	Kemijarvi	3.000	.....	1.080	4.
933–34	Kestila	.300	.....	.120	.
935–36	Kesalahti	.600	.....	.250	.
937–38	Kiihtelysvaara	3.200	.....	1.200	4.
939–40	Kiiminki	.800	.....	.300	1.
941–42	Kittee	1.400	.....	.450	1.
943–44	Kivennappa	2.400	.....	.900	3.
945–46	Koivisto	2.200	.....	.800	3.
947–48	Kolari	.....	.....	.600	.

* There was a surplus of condensed milk, cocoa, and sugar in Finland with a shortage in flour. The Finnish Children's Relief Committee was authorized by the European Children's Fund to dispose of the sur commodities, providing the proceeds be used to purchase the needed fl

FINLAND

Table 318—*Continued* Internal Deliveries of Commodities

Receipt No.	Districts and Kitchens	Commodities in Net Metric Tons of 1,000 Kilograms or 2,204.6 Pounds			
		Oatmeal	Rye Flour	Graham Flour	Total Tons
	May, 1920				
48-49	Kontiolahti	3.000	.....	1.150	4.150
50-51	Korpiselka	2.500	.....	.750	3.250
52-53	Kuhmoniemi	5.000	.....	1.450	6.450
54-55	Kuivaniemi	1.100	.....	.480	1.580
56-57	Kuolemjarvi	.800	.....	.300	1.100
58-59	Kuopio	4.750	.....	1.400	6.150
60-61	Kuusjarvi	1.200	.....	.450	1.650
62-63	Lapinlahti	1.500	.....	.400	1.900
64-65	Liperi	2.000	.....	.750	2.750
66-67	Muolaa	.400	.....	.150	.550
68-69	Muonio	1.100	.....	.420	1.520
70-72	Nurmes	7.000	10.500	2.100	19.600
73-74	Oulunjoki	2.400	.....	.900	3.300
75-76	Paavola	1.500	.....	.480	1.980
77-78	Paltamo	3.000	.....	.900	3.900
79-80	Pieksamaki	2.350	.....	.700	3.050
81-83	Pielisjarvi	6.400	10.000	2.300	18.700
84-85	Pirkkala	1.200	.....	.480	1.680
86-88	Polvijarvi	1.600	3.350	.600	5.550
89-90	Pudasjarvi	4.000	.....	1.500	5.500
991	Pyhanto	.....	.....	.480	.480
92-93	Palkijarvi	2.000	.....	.450	2.450
94-95	Ranua	1.700	.....	.660	2.360
96-97	Rautalamen	3.000	.....	.900	3.900
8-1000	Rautavaara	4.250	2.770	1.250	8.270
1001-2	Rautu	.750	.....	.300	1.050
1003-4	Ristijarvi	1.600	.....	.500	2.100
1005-6	Rovaniemi	4.800	.....	1.800	6.600
1007-8	Raakyla	2.000	.....	.750	2.750
009-10	Salmi	6.000	.....	2.100	8.100
1011	Savukosken	.....	.....	.120	.120
2, 1068	Simo	.700	.....	.240	.940
013-14	Soanlahti	2.000	.....	.450	2.450
015-16	Sotkamo	7.500	.....	2.300	9.800
017-18	Suistamo	2.300	.....	.900	3.200
019-20	Suojarvi	4.600	.....	1.350	5.950
021-22	Suomussalmi	7.000	.....	2.100	9.100
023-24	Saraisniemi	2.250	.....	.750	3.000
5, 1071	Taivalkosken	1.900	.....	.720	2.620
1026	Terijoki	.....	.....	.600	.600
027-28	Tohmajarvi	3.100	.....	1.100	4.200
029-30	Turtola	2.000	.....	.720	2.720
031-33	Toupovaara	2.000	.....	.750	2.750
034-35	Utajarvi	2.100	.....	.780	2.880
036-37	Uudenkirkou	2.400	.....	.900	3.300
038-40	Valtimo	1.500	2.100	.450	4.050
041-42	Varpaisjarvi	2.500	.....	.750	3.250
043-44	Vihanti	.600	.....	.240	.840
045-46	Vuolijoki	2.000	.....	.600	2.600
047-48	Vartsila	.750	.....	.300	1.050
049-50	Ylikiiminki	.800	.....	.300	1.100
051-52	Ylitornio	3.000	.....	.900	3.900
1053	Haukipudas	3.600	.....	....	3.600
1054	Johannes	.....	.....	.500	.500
055-56	Kittila	2.000	.....	.720	2.720
057-58	Kiuruvesi	4.250	.....	1.250	5.500
1059	Kolari	1.600	.....	....	1.600
060-61	Nilsia	4.000	.....	1.200	5.200
062-63	Pelkosenniemi	.500	.....	.240	.740
064-65	Puolauka	3.200	.....	1.200	4.400
1066	Pyhanta	1.200	.....	....	1.200
1067	Savukoski	.300	.....	....	.300
069-70	Sodankyla	2.000	.....	.720	2.720
1072	Terijoki	1.600	.....	....	1.600
073-74	Tervola	1.400	.....	.480	1.880
	Total	**225.000**	**50.000**	**75.080**	**350.080**

FINLAND—A.R.A.-European Children's Fund

Detail of Internal Deliveries of Children's Clothing, By Districts or Communes*—Reconstruction Period, 1919–1924

Table 319† Distribution from January to May, 1920

Districts or Communes	Shoes (Pairs)	Laces (Pairs)	Stockings (Pairs)	Boys' Coats (Each)	Boys' Pants (Pairs)	Girls' Dresses (Each)
Ahlainen	55	45	...	...	..	...
Alajarvi	135	135	...	120	20	120
Alatornio	316	267	335	139	100	100
Alavieska	52	39	...	50	10	50
Alberga	17	...	17	10	..	7
Antrea	248	210	145	90	40	60
Anttola	70	66	75	60	10	60
Assikkala	105	100	...	...	..	...
Borga Landskom	290	280	...	...	..	...
Elimaki	88	83	...	...	..	...
Eno	355	339	196	100	80	140
Enonkoski	75	55	60	40	40	40
Enontekio	39	37	145	50	100	50
Espoo	111	101	...	75	75	75
Eura	68	45	...	...	..	...
Evijarvi	75	67	...	60	10	60
Haapajarvi	151	70	200	100	20	100
Haapavesi	135	123	250	100	20	99
Hailuoto	52	23	60	50	..	50
Halsua	55	44	...	50	10	50
Hamina	90	90	...	40	20	40
Hangon Mlk.	40	40	...	...	..	...
Hankasalmi	152	130	...	75	75	75
Haukipudas	214	206	295	105	125	115
Haukivuori	52	47	65	60	40	80
Heinjoki	45	45	60	40	10	40
Heinolan Mlk.	45	45	...	...	..	...
Heinavesi	214	93	115	160	20	150
Hleisngin Mlk.	174	174	175	66	50	74
Helsingfors	1,479	1,371	1,360	500	100	500
Hiitola	340	280	320	200	20	200
Himanka	70	60	...	...	..	...
Hirvensalmi	55	...	75	60	10	60
Hollola	187	200	200	160	20	160
Hyrnsalmi	124	117	80	80	100	144
Hyvinkka	135	138	...	60	60	60
Hameenlinnen	70	60	...	...	..	...
Ii	183	180	350	122	102	149
Iissalmi	82	80	...	...	..	...
Iisalmen Mlk.	376	363	725	180	250	220
Ilomantsi	253	189	550	150	150	100
Impilaliti	550	418	300	306	200	200
Jaakkima	255	241	175	200	20	200
Joensnu	80	77	100	30	20	30
Johannes	179	162	110	60	40	60
Joroinen	75	65	100	60	10	60
Joutseno	42	28	50	60	40	60
Junka	410	375	474	105	39	75
Junpajoki	165	85	200	...	..	...
Juva	124	100	100	80	10	80
Jyvaskyla	100	100	...	40	20	40
Jyvaskylan Mlk.	158	...	...	...	..	...
Jappila	57	57	100	50	40	80
Jaaski	144	140	75	90	50	100
Kaarina	50	34	..	30	..	30
Kaavi	411	461	170	150	150	200
Kajaani	80	70	100	30	20	30

* Per statement of Finnish Children's Relief Bureau, signed by Aarne Linko, May 21, 1920.

† Cf. Table 312.

FINLAND

'able 319—*Continued* Detail of Internal Deliveries of Children's Clothing

Districts or Communes	Shoes (Pairs)	Laces (Pairs)	Stockings (Pairs)	Boys' Coats (Each)	Boys' Pants (Pairs)	Girls' Dresses (Each)
aanin Mlk.	205	184	195	95	75	150
ajoki	120	110	...	100	20	100
gasala	44	40	...	50	10	50
gaslampi	82	23	100	40	30	60
gasniemi	103	98	...	75	75	75
nus	105	99	155	100	20	100
is	70	66	...	...	..	...
stula	143	145	...	120	20	120
tula	239	220	250	95	75	150
unki	90	80	100	...	..	...
via	60	45	...	...	..	...
pola	130	101	170	120	20	120
ele	156	147	200	120	20	120
i	194	180	200	75	20	75
i Mlk.	354	347	415	390	40	390
ijarvi	247	243	170	100	150	180
pele	70	66	90	59	10	60
maki	182	175	145	110	20	90
tila	279	261	250	200	50	200
alahti	73	64	80	51	61	80
telysvaara	340	330	270	120	50	180
ninka	130	116	210	40	90	40
nula	53	50	...	20	20	25
vu	120	89	80	80	10	80
e	283	275	145	100	100	100
tila	128	125	300	...	..	...
ruvesi	496	452	330	180	230	180
ennapa	107	85	80	50	25	50
ijarvi	55	50	...	40	10	35
visto	93	64	58	35	35	40
ari	70	70	175	50	40	50
ginkangas	89	49	100	35	35	40
tiolahti	437	403	340	150	150	150
piselka	215	198	225	75	50	74
tesjarvi	121	100	...	100	10	100
ka	405	375	250	175	40	175
vola	45	35	...	35	..	35
moinen	111	111	150	...	..	...
moniemi	419	388	235	150	200	150
vaniemi	93	81	115	40	40	40
kkala	68	68	...	50	50	50
lajarvi	130	100	...	130	..	130
lemajarvi	57	39	50	25	25	25
pio	298	263	298	120	30	120
pion Mlk.	431	374	510	150	150	150
revesi	136	96	...	...	..	...
rkijoki	224	210	200	157	20	160
usamo	605	546	620	450	50	450
usijarvi	186	182	85	60	..	65
mi	320	315	300	200	100	200
mija Kunsankosken	128	125	...	100	50	100
kisalmi	90	90	104	40	20	40
kisalmen Mlk.	75	40	50	80	10	70
lvia	105	96	...	...	..	...
rsamaki	70	66	100	60	10	60
nti	115	115	125	50	20	54
inlahti	184	155	190	60	..	60
pajarvi	119	110	...	100	20	100
pee	303	270	300	200	50	200
vonmaki	32	32	...	40	..	40

[*Continued on next page*]

FINLAND

Table 319—*Continued* Detail of Internal Deliveries of Children's Clothing

Districts or Communes	Shoes (Pairs)	Laces (Pairs)	Stockings (Pairs)	Boys' Coats (Each)	Boys' Pants (Pairs)	Girls' Dresses (Each)
Lemi	58	55	...	50	10	50
Lappavirta	243	223	245	160	20	160
Lestijarvi	50	42	...	...	..	...
Liminka	52	45	69	40	10	40
Liperi	402	375	330	60	..	60
Lumijoki	52	49	75	50	10	50
Luumaki	90	73	80	80	10	80
Maanika	140	132	175	120	20	120
Maaria	113	110	...	45	..	45
Merijarvi	59	56	...	50	10	50
Messukyla	90	80	...	100	20	200
Metsapirtta	145	142	90	120	20	120
Miehikkala	80	76	85	80	10	80
Muhos	167	157	195	100	..	100
Multia	200	200	...	160	20	160
Muolaa	140	112	90	30	..	30
Muonio	55	54	150	...	..	...
Muuruvesi	235	214	190	140	20	140
Nilsia	337	326	245	60	20	60
Nivala	200	188	216	140	20	140
Nuijamaa	50	46	50	50	10	50
Nurmes	109	106	...	...	..	...
Nurmeksen Mlk.	579	473	525	90	30	90
Oulainen	145	137	145	100	20	100
Oulu	420	375	425	170	30	170
Oulunjoki	167	159	370	35	30	40
Oulunsalo	110	85	145	60	10	60
Paavola	123	120	100	30	..	30
Paltamo	280	270	425	45	25	45
Parainen	125	125	...	...	..	...
Parikkala	229	226	220	60	..	60
Pattijoki	70	66	100	60	10	60
Pelkosenniemi	47	41	...	25	..	20
Perho	56	56	...	...	..	...
Petajavesi	149	150	...	120	10	120
Pieksamaki	229	204	260	200	20	200
Pielavesi	258	245	240	200	20	200
Pielisjarvi	716	679	804	100	..	100
Pihtipudas	175	165	200	140	20	140
Piippola	85	83	85	50	10	50
Pirkkala	70	...	...	171	20	190
Polvijarvi	232	218	245	45	..	45
Pori	400	370	...	150	41	150
Porin Mlk.	115	105	...	...	..	...
Pudasjarvi	629	572	325	200	..	210
Pulkkila	137	132	100	60	10	60
Puolamka	184	160	350	30	..	30
Puumala	69	62	85	60	10	60
Pyhajoki	110	90	110	100	20	100
Pyhajarvi	235	204	330	398	40	400
Pyhanta	77	41	90	20	..	20
Pylkonmaki	88	82	...	33	..	28
Palkjarvi	128	83	150	200	20	200
Raahe	85	85	...	40	10	39
Rautasalmi	260	235	300	200	..	200
Rautsila	212	194	185	180	30	180
Ranua	142	70	85	25	20	25
Rautalampi	262	181	...	440	30	440
Rautavaara	134	110	80	20	..	20

FINLAND

Table 319—*Continued* Detail of Internal Deliveries of Children's Clothing

Districts or Communes	Shoes (Pairs)	Laces (Pairs)	Stockings (Pairs)	Boys' Coats (Each)	Boys' Pants (Pairs)	Girls' Dresses (Each)
tio	52	45	...	46	10	50
tjarvi	126	120	160	200	40	200
tu	100	65	60	20	..	20
jarvi	95	95	...	160	20	160
onlahti	50	25	80	100	10	100
imaki	80	80	...	20	..	20
iina	50	47	75	60	10	60
ijarvi	180	160	85	20	..	20
aniemi	365	295	550	100	..	100
kolahti	150	165	120	35	..	35
vesi	70	70	...	...	..	...
keala	330	142	185	320	30	320
sala	185	181	120	140	30	140
kkyla	225	218	220	35	..	35
rijarvi	149	160	...	...	..	...
kkola	80	74	85	160	10	160
mi	493	453	275	100	50	100
oinen	70	66	100	60	10	60
itaipali	50	47	75	160	20	160
onranta	144	130	140	19	..	20
ukoski	40	40	...	30	..	30
vi	122	115	100	100	20	100
ajoki	80	80	100	70	10	70
o	113	78	185	30	20	30
pola	185	175	...	...	..	...
nlahti	120	116	115	30	30	30
ankyla	141	143	500	75	50	75
ni	110	100	...	100	20	200
tavala	110	100	100	50	20	50
tavalan Mlk.	351	316	325	60	20	60
kamo	476	419	750	80	40	80
stamo	290	272	175	100	75	100
kava	104	69	100	...	..	...
niainen	129	130	125	100	20	100
jarvi	412	390	235	100	50	100
minniemi	39	30	53	100	10	100
mussalmi	300	292	575	100	50	100
nenjoki	121	80	100	...	..	...
kijarvi	40	36	50	20	..	20
aisniemi	146	140	160	20	..	20
aksmaki	71	61	...	20	..	20
aminki	332	313	175	260	40	260
palsaari	70	60	100	120	10	120
valkosiki	120	109	85	20	..	20
nmela	149	135	...	...	..	...
mpere	1,675	1,500	1,650	447	127	538
nmes	75	51	100	60	10	60
ijoki	97	79	60	25	..	25
vola	95	51	185	20	..	20
hamjarvi	150	132	240	30	30	30
holampi	70	66	...	60	10	60
vakka	69	70	...	60	10	60
rnio	100	95	145	50	20	90
rku	686	595	300	300	50	300
rtola	50	50	85	20	..	20
upovaara	145	130	135	40	30	40
usniemi	140	140	140	160	10	160
usula	117	114	100	...	..	...
rnava	115	95	115	100	20	100

[*Concluded on next page*]

FINLAND

Table 319—*Concluded* Detail of Internal Deliveries of Children's Clothing

Districts or Communes	Shoes (Pairs)	Laces (Pairs)	Stockings (Pairs)	Boys' Coats (Each)	Boys' Pants (Pairs)	Girls' Dresses (Each)
Ullava	...	...	...	100	15	100
Ulvila	90	75	...	...	..	...
Utajarvi	223	207	377	40	..	40
Uukunieme	127	133	135	80	20	80
Uurainen	70	...	...	60	10	60
Uuras	80	70	...	30	..	30
Uusikkirko	300	286	185	75	..	75
Valkeala	73	74	...	...	..	...
Valkjarvi	103	75	70	20	..	20
Valtimo	138	144	85	25	..	25
Varkaus	39	42	...	...	..	...
Varpaisjarvi	164	151	175	150	30	150
Vehkalahti	50	40	50	20	..	20
Vesanto	117	90	100	30	..	30
Vesalhti	136	130	...	40	..	40
Veteli	105	99	...	80	10	80
Vihanti	101	86	100	20	..	20
Viipuri	200	176	200	150	40	150
Viipurin Mlk.	1,815	1,379	1,675	200	100	200
Viitasaari	235	225	...	50	..	50
Viljakkala	46	40	...	...	..	...
Vimpeli	70	...	...	100	..	100
Virtasalmi	49	49	60	20	..	20
Vaikkaan	118	116	...	75	30	75
Vuoksela	88	82	70	20	..	20
Vuolijoki	135	73	165	30	..	30
Vartsila	226	218	225	40	10	30
Ylikiiminki	178	174	150	30	..	30
Ylitornio	136	133	250	78	100	90
Ylivieska	280	255	191	100	45	200
Ylojarvi	70	...	...	70	30	100
Aanekoski	120	113	138	100	..	100
Total	**47,264**	**41,736**	**39,280**	**21,927**	**7,000**	**22,741**

FINLAND—A.R.A.-European Children's Fund

Detail by Shops of Woolens and Accessories Turned Over to, and Garments Received from, Manufacturers—Reconstruction Period, 1919–1924

able 319 A

Location of Shops Receiving Goods	Material Acknowledged by Manufacturers — Woolens — Meters	Bales	Number of Garments Manufactured — Boys' Coats (Each)	Boys' Pants (Pairs)	Girls' Dresses (Each)
ˌ Street, Helsingfors	22,479.25	163 }			
·y Street, Helsingfors	2,311.25	21 }	12,211	4,010	13,180
ander Street, Helsingfors	5,468.30	50 }			
·ari Street in Abo	2,704.59	18	1,360	456	704
io Street in Abo	1,902.80	11	671	168	767
org	7,377.78	50	3,426	866	2,930
i	4,178.46	25	1,608	321	2,090
borg	1,313.50	9	500	187	503
a	1,534.55	9	587	151	569
mene	3,502.72	25	1,250	315	1,460
manstrand	628.00	4	701	84	226
merfors	341.00	2	130	37	129
.K. (Co-operative)	1,715.00	9	387	390	391
otal	**55,457.20**	**396***	**22,831**	**6,985**	**22,949**

	Thread (Yards)	Needles (Each)	Buttons (Each)
otal Furnished the Manufacturers by E.C.F.	**2,640,000**	**40,000**	**172,800**

Cf. arrivals, Table 312. The shops acknowledged receipt of the number of bales that were shipped. The receipt signed by Aarne) states: "No evidence of pilferage."

Table 320

Operation	Table No.	Flour	Grain	Rice	Beans, Peas
					COMMISSIO
C.R.B.—Northern France	103	75,788.0	508,861.0	102,030.0	49,312.
C.R.B.—French Refugees, etc., in Holland	103	25.0	150.0	14.0	17.(
Total, C.R.B. Period	103	**75,813.0**	**509,011.0**	**102,044.0**	**49,329.**
					U.S. FOO
Sales Financed by U.S. Treasury Credit	106	**1,738,079.8**	**1,549,746.1**	**104,589.9**	**78,625.**
					ARMISTIC
A.R.A.—President's National Security and Defense Fund	321	959.6	.....	.....	....
A.R.A.—Cash Settlement	322	31,106.1	.....	.....	....
U.S. Liquidation Commission (War Department)	122	.....	.....	.....	....
Total, Armistice Period	108	**32,065.7**	.....	.....	....
Grand Total Relief Deliveries	102	**1,845,958.5**	**2,058,757.1**	**206,633.9**	**127,954.**

FRANCE—American Relief Administration

Detail of Relief Deliveries to Russian Prisoners of War in Germany, Paid for from the President's National Security and Defense Fund—Armistice Period, 1919†

Table 321

Quartermaster Invoice No.*	Date of Delivery	Commodities in Net Metric Tons of 1,000 Kilograms or 2,204.6 Pounds					Total Value
		Flour	Sugar	Misc. Food		Total Tons	
				Tea	Hard Bread		
	1919						
40	Mar. 17	288.0	45.4	6.1	127.1	466.6	$111,290
34	Mar. 18	84.9	44.9	2.3	109.4	241.5	60,612
65	Mar. 18	562.7	90.7	6.1	54.6	714.1	161,642
68	Mar. 19	....	....	6.1	....	6.1	5,347
33	Mar. 19	24.0	.3	2.3	167.1	193.7	51,316
	Total	**959.6**	**181.3**	**22.9**	**458.2**	**1,622.0**	**$390,209**

† Although these supplies were paid for by the President's National Security and Defense Fund, the A.R.A. received notes from the Government of France which were turned over to the United States Government. At the time of writing, France has reimbursed the United States Government for the major portion of the value of these deliveries.

* Supplies purchased by A.R.A. from U.S. Army quartermaster France.

ımary of Relief Deliveries

ᵓork oducts	Milk	Cocoa	Sugar	Misc. Food	Forage	Soap	Clothing and Misc.	Total Tons	Total Value
Commodities in Net Metric Tons of 1,000 Kilograms or 2,204.6 Pounds									
. RELIEF IN BELGIUM PERIOD									
,380.0	53,731.0	6,988.0	49,505.0	65,009.0	.....	24,621.0	18,355.0	1,091,580.0	$ 220,203,521.62
29.0	21.0	.....	2.0	5.0	.....	18.0	18.0	299.0	80,028.90
,409.0	**53,752.0**	**6,988.0**	**49,507.0**	**65,014.0**	.....	**24,639.0**	**18,373.0**	**1,091,879.0**	**$ 220,283,550.52**
IINISTRATION PERIOD									
,290.4	**235,657.7**	.....	**378,018.0**	**389,594.7**	**2,042,715.2**	.....	.....	**6,781,317.6**	**$ 850,715,632.84**
:IOD									
.....	.....	.....	181.3	481.1	.....	.....	.....	1,622.0	$ 390,209.03
.....	.....	.....	.....	.....	.....	.....	.....	31,106.1	5,031,830.08
.....	.....	.....	.....	370,285.0	.....	.....	149,490.0	519,775.0	213,067,400.00
.....	.....	.....	**181.3**	**370,766.1**	.....	.....	**149,490.0**	**552,503.1**	**$ 218,489,439.11**
,699.4	**289,409.7**	**6,988.0**	**427,706.3**	**825,374.8**	**2,042,715.2**	**24,639.0**	**167,863.0**	**8,425,699.7**	**$1,289,488,622.47**

FRANCE—

American Relief Administration

tail by Source of Commodities Sold for Cash Armistice Period, 1919

ʻable 322

val .	Q.M.C. Invoice No.	Wheat Flour *	Total Value
	Paris Division	A. Sales of U.S. Army Surplus Flour from French Warehouses	
7	12	6,797.844	$1,087,655.04
7	17	2,587.142	413,942.72
7	25	1,877.756	300,440.96
7	28	1,177.472	188,395.55
7	29	2,851.039	456,166.24
7	30	360.737	57,717.92
7	43	536.001	85,760.16
7	44	67.668	10,826.88
7	45	451.441	72,230.56
7	71	336.804	53,888.64
7	56	1,905.647	304,903.52
7	57	2,370.896	379,343.36
7	58	2,125.842	340,134.72
7	60	286.029	45,764.64
7	61	715.689	114,510.24
7	62	345.142	55,222.72
7	63	4,721.453	755,432.45
7	64	684.336	109,493.76
	Total	**30,198.938†**	**$4,831,830.08†**
	Constantinople	B. Sales of U.S. Army Surplus Flour at Constantinople	
13	37 ‡	907.194	$ 200,000.00
	Grand Total §	**31,106.132**	**$5,031,830.08**

* Commodities in net metric tons of 1,000 kilograms or 2,204.6 pounds.
† Detail by warehouse of deliveries of U.S. Army surplus flour:

Location of Warehouse	Total Tons	Total Value
St. Nazaire	2,098.244	$ 335,719.04
Bordeaux	16,250.130	2,600,020.80
Marseilles	1,853.900	296,604.52
Interior Warehouses	9,996.664	1,599,485.72
Total	**30,198.938**	**$4,831,830.08**

‡ Ex-Maine which sailed from New York, arriving January 28, 1919, at Constantinople.
§ To Table 120.

Table 323

GERMANY-

Operation	Table No.	Flour	Grain	Rice	Beans, Peas
					ARMISTIC
A.R.A.—Cash Settlement	324	241,865.1	131,748.3	9,209.6	42,200.0
A.R.A.—Cash Settlement, American Friends Service Committee	325	......	......	......	......
Commission for Relief in Belgium—Cash Settlement	326	16,065.0	44,581.0	21,245.0	19,567.0
Total American Relief	......	**257,930.1**	**176,329.3**	**30,454.6**	**61,767.0**
United Kingdom—Cash Settlement	327	21,045.0	......	37,658.0	......
France	328	1,402.0	......	......	......
Argentina	329	......	135,000.0	......	......
Netherlands	329	......	......	......	......
Switzerland	329	......	......	......	......
Total Other than American Relief	132	**22,447.0**	**135,000.0**	**37,658.0**	......
Total Relief, Armistice Period	108	**280,377.1**	**311,329.3**	**68,112.6**	**61,767.0**
					RECONSTRUCTIC
American Friends Service Committee	330	4,863.0	......	4,341.9	5,426.
German Government—Donation	161	12,663.0	......	......	......
Total Children's Relief	163	**17,526.0**	......	**4,341.9**	**5,426.**
A.R.A. Warehouses—Food Drafts and Bulk Sales	332–33	4,020.7	......	1,166.7	801.
Sundry Sales—Liquidation Hamburg Port Warehouses	...	2,099.0	......	33.0	......
Total Other than Children's Relief	......	**6,119.7**	......	**1,199.7**	**801.**
Total Relief, Reconstruction Period	......	**23,645.7**	......	**5,541.6**	**6,227.**
Deduct Duplication—Warehouse Bulk Sales, Incl. Children's Relief	...	......	......	400.1	179.
Net Relief, Reconstruction Period	149	**23,645.7**	......	**5,141.5**	**6,047.**
Grand Total Relief Deliveries	102	**304,022.8**	**311,329.3**	**73,254.1**	**67,814.**

GERMANY

Table 324

Detail by Steamers of Commodit

Arrival No.*	Steamer	Port of Sailing	Date of Arrival	Port of Arrival	Wheat Flour	Cereal Flour
88	West Carnifax	Norfolk	1919 Mar. 25	Hamburg	**6,626.7**	.....
101	West Wauna	Norfolk	Apr. 1	Hamburg	7,218.8	.....
115	Oostdijk	Philadelphia	Apr. 10	Amsterdam	1,404.4	2,175.8
118	Franklin	Philadelphia	Apr. 12	Bremerhaven	255.5	5,978.9
119	Lambs	New York	Apr. 12	Bremerhaven	6,002.3	.....
120	Victorious	New York	Apr. 12	Hamburg	.....	.....
121	Cape Henry	New York	Apr. 13	Danzig	.....	.....
128	Merauke	Philadelphia	Apr. 15	Hamburg	.....	.....
127	Constantia	Boston	Apr. 15	Stettin	414.3	2,324.8
140	Thordis	New York	Apr. 20	Hamburg	3,121.1	.....
141	Waalhaven	New Orleans	Apr. 20	Stettin	1,487.1	3,406.8
152	Gorontalo	New York	Apr. 27	Hamburg	4,581.7	1,070.0
	Rotterdam Stock, Ex:					
99	Lake Eckhart, II	Rotterdam	Apr. 1	Hamburg	.....	.....
	Total Deliveries during April	....	....	....	**31,111.9**	**14,956.3**

* Arrival numbers from Table 111.

ummary of Relief Deliveries

Corn Grits	Pork Products	Milk	Cocoa	Sugar	Misc. Food	Forage	Soap	Clothing and Misc.	Total Tons	Total Value
Commodities in Net Metric Tons of 1,000 Kilograms or 2,204.6 Pounds										
RIOD										
......	46,956.1	11,115.8	....	.....	.....	.....	....	.....	483,094.9	$113,728,950.49
......	10.0	26.7	13.2	.....	.....	.....	....	11.0	60.9	29,687.25
......	32,995.0	......	....	.....	527.0	.....	....	.....	134,980.0	44,350,810.47
......	**79,961.1**	**11,142.5**	**13.2**	.....	**527.0**	.....	....	**11.0**	**618,135.8**	**$158,109,448.21**
......	49,228.0	17,018.0	....	.....	145,699.0	.....	....	28,496.0	299,144.0	$ 75,653,861.00
......	6,488.0	......	....	.....	6,514.0	.....	....	55,000.0	69,404.0	16,262,889.00
......	......	......	....	.....	.....	.....	....	20,000.0	155,000.0	16,774,000.00
......	13,650.0	......	....	.....	24,695.0	.....	....	6,303.0	44,648.0	9,784,989.00
......	......	......	....	.....	28,886.0	.....	....	.....	28,886.0	5,825,812.00
......	**69,366.0**	**17,018.0**	....	.....	**205,794.0**	.....	....	**109,799.0**	**597,082.0**	**$124,301,551.00**
......	**149,327.1**	**28,160.5**	**13.2**	.....	**206,321.0**	.....	....	**109,810.0**	**1,215,217.8**	**$282,410,999.21**
RIOD										
......	2,797.6	9,225.8	983.4	908.0	115.0	.....	50.0	9.0	28,720.1	$ 6,728,989.92
......	......	......	....	4,170.0	.....	.....	....	.....	16,833.0	2,392,021.25
......	**2,797.6**	**9,225.8**	**983.4**	**5,078.0**	**115.0**	.....	**50.0**	**9.0**	**45,553.1**	**$ 9,121,011.17**
......	864.7	2,154.6	43.6	107.1	84.8	.....	....	104.2	9,347.4	$ 2,820,420.47
,149.0	177.0	595.0	....	.....	.....	.....	....	.....	4,053.0	362,571.27
,149.0	**1,041.7**	**2,749.6**	**43.6**	**107.1**	**84.8**	.....	....	**104.2**	**13,400.4**	**$ 3,182,991.74**
,149.0	**3,839.3**	**11,975.4**	**1,027.0**	**5,185.1**	**199.8**	.....	**50.0**	**113.2**	**58,953.5**	**$ 12,304,002.91**
......	176.2	478.1	3.0	.....	.....	.....	....	.....	1,237.2	341,309.37
,149.0	**3,663.1**	**11,497.3**	**1,024.0**	**5,185.1**	**199.8**	.....	**50.0**	**113.2**	**57,716.3**	**$ 11,962,693.54**
,149.0	**152,990.2**	**39,657.8**	**1,037.2**	**5,185.1**	**206,520.8**	.....	**50.0**	**109,923.2**	**1,272,934.1**	**$294,373,692.75**

nerican Relief Administration

d for Cash—Armistice Period, 1919

Grain	Beans	Rice	Pork Products	Lard	Lard Substitute	Milk	Total Tons	Total Value
Contents of Cargoes in Net Metric Tons of 1,000 Kilograms or 2,204.6 Pounds								
DIRECT DELIVERIES								
.....	.....	.....	.....	.....	.....	.....	**6,626.7**	**$ 1,325,340.00**
.....	.....	.....	.....	.....	.....	.....	7,218.8	$ 1,443,754.40
.....	.....	.....	.....	.....	.....	.....	3,580.2	652,891.37
.....	.....	.....	.....	.....	.....	.....	6,234.4	1,127,298.90
.....	1,447.1	.....	255.6	106.8	.....	255.3	8,067.1	2,009,616.82
10,020.5	.....	.....	.....	.....	.....	.....	10,020.5	1,202,459.64
.....	.....	.....	1,055.0	.....	.....	.....	1,055.0	885,321.97
7,248.4	.....	.....	.....	.....	.....	.....	7,248.4	869,812.92
.....	.....	.....	.....	.....	.....	.....	2,739.1	501,324.08
.....	1,017.3	.....	613.1	.....	239.5	266.0	5,257.0	1,707,940.07
.....	.....	.....	.....	.....	.....	.....	4,893.9	910,635.50
.....	.....	1,353.0	.....	.....	.....	.....	7,004.7	1,494,566.11
.....	.....	.....	.....	63.5	.....	.....	63.5	47,727.38
17,268.9	**2,464.4**	**1,353.0**	**1,923.7**	**170.3**	**239.5**	**521.3**	**70,009.3**	**$ 14,178,689.16**

[*Continued on next page*]

Table 324—*Continued*

Detail by Steamers of Commoditi

Arrival No.	Steamer	Port of Sailing	Date of Arrival	Port of Arrival	Wheat Flour	Cereal Flour
			1919			
157	Absaroka, II	New York	May 1	Rotterdam	1,938.6	1,456.3
165	Bjornefjord	New York	May 5	Rotterdam	3,354.1	.....
166	Volunteer	New York	May 5	Hamburg	1.6	9,954.6
168	Ingold	New York	May 6	Rotterdam	1,095.9	.....
175	August	New York	May 9	Hamburg	758.7	3,201.9
176	Galesburg	Philadelphia	May 9	Rotterdam	3,575.2	1,126.9
177	Jethou	New York	May 9	Rotterdam	892.9	211.5
179	Thorjerd	New York	May 10	Hamburg	.....	.....
182	Agwidale	New York	May 11	Rotterdam	4,053.5	60.5
184	New Windsor	New York	May 11	Hamburg	3,225.6	.....
185	West Armagosa	Newport News	May 11	Rotterdam	2,220.1	4,528.7
187	West Humhau, II	New York	May 11	Hamburg	.....	.....
189	Ardgroom	St. Johns	May 13	Hamburg	581.4	.....
194	Hatteras	Philadelphia	May 15	Rotterdam	2,110.9	59.4
196	Masuda	New York	May 15	Hamburg	1,095.4	.....
198	Balli, II	New York	May 16	Hamburg	1,612.7	140.1
201	Guardo	New York	May 19	Bremerhaven	.....	.....
204	Ternate	New York	May 19	Emden	3,757.8	29.7
205	West Loquassuck	Boston	May 19	Rotterdam	7,146.5	.....
208	Mirach, II	Philadelphia	May 20	Brake	3,077.6	635.9
222	Winnebago	New Orleans	May 24	Hamburg	2,013.4	27.2
226	Chimo	Norfolk	May 26	Hamburg	.....	.....
230	Santa Cruz	Norfolk	May 27	Rotterdam	.....	.....
232	Williamantic, II	New York	May 27	Hamburg	1,387.2	.....
233	Western Maid, II	Baltimore	May 29	Rotterdam	128.9	1,633.8
234	Kronenfels	Philadelphia	May 30	Hamburg	.....	.....
	Rotterdam Stock, Ex:					
4	Absaroka, I	New York	Jan. 14*	Rotterdam	828.6	591.2
8	Nantasket	New York	Jan. 21*	Rotterdam	24.7	.2
12	Western Sea	New York	Jan. 25*	Rotterdam	5,570.9	1,184.9
17	Morristown	New York	Feb. 3*	Rotterdam	669.6	398.1
66	Edgecombe	Norfolk	Mar. 17*	Rotterdam	17.8	.....
67	Edgefield	Norfolk	Mar. 17*	Rotterdam	11.0	.....
	Total Deliveries during May				**51,150.6**	**25,240.9**
250	Calvert	Baltimore	June 4	Rotterdam	5,169.3	.....
252	Decatur Bridge	New York	June 4	Hamburg	852.5	167.6
254	Edgecombe, II	New Orleans	June 4	Hamburg	8,480.8	.....
256	Weissenfels	New York	June 4	Hamburg	2,302.0	.....
261	Clio	New York	June 6	Rotterdam	1,325.8	.....
264	Wondrichen	Baltimore	June 9	Bremerhaven	3,870.0	.....
272	Coperas	Montreal	June 12	Rotterdam	2,552.8	.....
275	West Kyska, II	New York	June 12	Hamburg	2,136.3	.....
287	Solfels	Philadelphia	June 16	Bremerhaven	1,709.2	.....
294	Python	Montreal	June 20	Hamburg	2,540.8	.....
305	Lake Gravity	Montreal	June 25	Bremerhaven	3,107.3	.....
309	Lake Foxboro	Montreal	June 26	Stettin	2,991.5	.....
311	Gertrud	Baltimore	June 27	Emden	.....	.....
313	Lake Corapeak	Montreal	June 28	Hamburg	2,520.9	.....
314	Artemisia	Philadelphia	June 29	Hamburg	.....	1,667.9
316	Franziska	New York	June 29	Hamburg	559.8	1,059.1
318	Altenfels	New York	June 30	Hamburg	.....	362.5
	Rotterdam Stock, Ex:					
247	Maine, II	Baltimore	June 1	Rotterdam	.....	.....
	Total Deliveries during June				**40,119.0**	**3,257.1**

* Delivered in May.

merican Relief Administration

old for Cash—Armistice Period, 1919

Contents of Cargoes in Net Metric Tons of 1,000 Kilograms or 2,204.6 Pounds								
Grain	Beans	Rice	Pork Products	Lard	Lard Substitute	Milk	Total Tons	Total Value
DIRECT DELIVERIES—*Continued*								
.....	954.5	.....	1,224.9	115.0	.....	346.7	6,036.0	$ 2,083,468.42
.....	.....	.....	332.5	51.3	234.1	721.9	4,693.9	1,378,052.60
.....	.....	.....	.....	.....	.....	.....	9,956.2	1,792,153.34
.....	.....	.....	.....	.....	.....	2,111.0	3,206.9	1,036,930.58
.....	937.1	.....	909.8	605.5	809.5	.....	7,222.5	2,681,678.75
.....	664.5	.....	.....	.....	.....	.....	5,366.6	1,006,559.91
.....	2,570.0	2,597.5	.....	.....	.....	.....	6,271.9	1,623,103.30
.....	.....	.....	1,466.2	644.3	52.6	.....	2,163.1	1,624,947.09
.....	875.9	.....	.....	.....	974.1	.....	5,964.0	1,623,105.16
.....	.....	.....	175.0	151.0	977.9	1,902.8	6,432.3	2,347,508.37
.....	.....	.....	.....	.....	.....	.....	6,748.8	1,124,205.10
.....	.....	.....	.....	.....	4,692.4	.....	4,692.4	3,143,890.58
6,039.7	.....	.....	.....	.....	.....	.....	6,621.1	922,917.39
.....	.....	.....	.....	.....	1,705.0	812.0	4,687.3	1,833,506.94
.....	2,607.4	783.9	852.6	376.1	22.8	.....	5,738.2	2,168,787.36
.....	257.7	.....	666.9	92.4	2,506.3	.....	5,276.1	2,596,315.09
.....	.....	.....	.....	.....	2,272.4	.....	2,272.4	1,522,494.60
.....	.....	.....	.....	.....	1,276.8	955.2	6,019.5	1,980,777.70
.....	.....	.....	.....	.....	.....	.....	7,146.5	1,286,370.36
.....	.....	.....	104.3	1,116.0	.....	.....	4,933.8	1,613,617.66
.....	2,840.7	918.1	.....	.....	.....	.....	5,799.4	1,429,418.45
.....	.....	2,742.6	.....	.....	.....	.....	2,742.6	685,657.25
6,493.8	.....	.....	.....	.....	.....	.....	6,493.8	746,789.53
.....	517.4	.....	1,058.1	.....	1,733.7	.....	4,696.4	2,386,359.26
5,265.3	.....	.....	.....	.....	.....	.....	7,028.0	886,382.87
10,745.2	.....	.....	.....	.....	.....	.....	10,745.2	1,289,425.20
.....	.....	.....	.....	.....	.....	.....	1,419.8	270,573.88
.....	.....	.....	.....	.....	.....	.....	24.9	4,977.34
.....	.....	.....	.....	.....	.....	.....	6,755.8	1,324,686.72
.....	.....	.....	.....	.....	.....	.....	1,067.7	204,910.94
.....	.....	.....	.....	.....	.....	.....	17.8	3,297.48
.....	.....	.....	.....	.....	.....	.....	11.0	2,127.40
28,544.0	**12,225.2**	**7,042.1**	**6,790.3**	**3,151.6**	**17,257.6**	**6,849.6**	**158,251.9**	**$ 44,624,996.62**
.....	.....	.....	.....	.....	.....	.....	5,169.3	$ 930,479.04
.....	.....	.....	157.5	161.3	1,839.8	.....	3,178.7	1,672,429.47
.....	.....	.....	.....	.....	.....	.....	8,480.8	1,568,943.74
.....	.....	.....	6,487.6	.....	123.0	.....	8,912.6	5,901,270.59
.....	.....	.....	.....	.....	1,271.4	.....	2,597.2	1,077,755.22
.....	.....	.....	.....	.....	.....	.....	3,870.0	715,944.82
.....	.....	.....	.....	.....	.....	.....	2,552.8	459,500.58
.....	1,094.0	222.1	1,683.5	65.8	718.5	536.6	6,456.8	2,933,825.74
.....	.....	.....	4,605.6	41.0	.....	.....	6,355.8	4,225,845.36
.....	.....	.....	.....	.....	.....	.....	2,540.8	470,054.11
.....	.....	.....	.....	.....	.....	.....	3,107.3	574,846.06
.....	.....	.....	.....	.....	.....	.....	2,991.5	553,420.66
6,772.9	.....	.....	.....	.....	.....	.....	6,772.9	812,753.16
.....	.....	.....	.....	.....	.....	.....	2,520.9	466,365.21
5,815.9	.....	.....	.....	.....	.....	.....	7,483.8	973,110.47
5,040.1	279.6	.....	13.8	.....	.....	221.0	7,173.4	1,080,567.61
8,019.9	.....	.....	39.5	.....	.....	792.8	9,214.7	1,432,348.71
7,190.7	.....	.....	.....	.....	.....	.....	7,190.7	882,900.14
32,839.5	**1,373.6**	**222.1**	**12,987.5**	**268.1**	**3,952.7**	**1,550.4**	**96,570.0**	**$ 26,732,360.69**

[*Concluded on next page*]

Detail by Steamers of Commoditi

Table 324—*Concluded*

Arrival No.	Steamer	Port of Sailing	Date of Arrival	Port of Arrival	Wheat Flour	Cereal Flour
			1919			
323	Augsburg	New York	July 2	Bremerhaven	.....	548.5
328	Lake Foxcroft	Montreal	July 2	Hamburg	2,985.7	.....
330	Greiffenfels	New York	July 3	Bremerhaven	13.4	172.9
331	Lake Grampian	Montreal	July 3	Emden	3,099.9	.....
333	Hornfels	Philadelphia	July 6	Stettin	1,495.6	2,117.9
337	Kybfels	Philadelphia	July 8	Bremerhaven	3,670.8	2,859.4
338	Gundomar	New York	July 9	Hamburg	1,682.5	28.4
340	Lippe	Philadelphia	July 9	Bremerhaven	2,080.6	427.6
341	Dessau	Boston	July 10	Bremerhaven	1,943.7	969.5
344	Lake Gravella	Montreal	July 11	Bremerhaven	3,126.7	.....
345	Gallipoli	Philadelphia	July 12	Hamburg	637.6	36.0
348	Waldenburg	Philadelphia	July 12	Hamburg	4,593.7	3,791.0
354	Isis	New York	July 18	Hamburg	474.6	1,841.5
358	Meiningen	Philadelphia	July 20	Bremerhaven	7,825.8	1,902.6
360	Lake Connoton	New York	July 21	Hamburg	2,624.1	.....
364	Mannheim	Philadelphia	July 26	Hamburg	3,762.2	.....
	Rotterdam Stock, Ex:					
5	Western Hero	New York	Jan. 14†	Rotterdam	425.2	.....
106	Regulus	New Orleans	Apr. 4†	Rotterdam	.....	.....
251	Challenger	Baltimore	June 4†	Rotterdam	9,953.7	210.8
	Total Deliveries during July				**50,395.8**	**14,906.1**
370	Wolfram	New York	Aug. 7	Hamburg	541.7	.....
372	Wachtfels	New York	Aug. 12	Hamburg	537.4	.....
373	Ehrenfels	New York	Aug. 13	Hamburg	1,850.2	.....
374	Belgravia	New York	Aug. 18	Rotterdam	3,444.6	.....
377	Remschied	New York	Aug. 21	Rotterdam	1,275.7	.....
379	Plitvice	New York	Aug. 25	Hamburg	2,567.8	206.2
382	Kagera	New York	Aug. 30	Hamburg	.....	.....
	Total Deliveries during August				**10,217.4**	**206.2**
	Total Direct Deliveries				**182,994.7**	**58,566.6**
7	Indianapolis	Philadelphia	Jan. 16	Rotterdam	**303.8**	.....
	Total				**183,298.5**	**58,566.6**

† Delivered in July.

‡ For total value of commodities sold to Germany for cash, value of commodities, Table 325.

GERMANY—American Relief Administration

Detail by Steamers of Commodities Sold for Cash to American Friends Service Committee—Armistice Period, 1919

Table 325

Arrival No.	Steamer	Port of Sailing	Date of Arrival	Port of Arrival	Contents of Cargoes in Net Metric Tons of 1,000 Kilograms or 2,204.6 Pounds					Total Value
					Pork Products	Milk	Cocoa	Clothing	Total Tons	
			1919							
354	Isis	New York	July 18	Hamburg	....	26.7	....	....	26.7	$12,156.
377	Remschied	New York	Aug. 21	Rotterdam	....	....	13.2	....	13.2	8,276.
378	Lake Fray	St. Nazaire	Aug. 25	Hamburg	10.0	....	....	....	10.0	8,344.
381	Huberfels	New York	Aug. 30	Hamburg	....	....	....	11.0	11.0	910.
	Total				**10.0**	**26.7**	**13.2**	**11.0**	**60.9**	**$29,687.**

* Freight only.

† For total value of commodities sold to Germany for cash, value of commodities in Table 324.

erican Relief Administration

l for Cash—Armistice Period, 1919

Contents of Cargoes in Net Metric Tons of 1,000 Kilograms or 2,204.6 Pounds								
rain	Beans	Rice	Pork Products	Lard	Lard Substitute	Milk	Total Tons	Total Value
IRECT DELIVERIES—*Concluded*								
7,426.8	1,973.6	.....	177.5	16.9	.....	184.6	10,327.9	$ 1,723,009.04
.....	.....	.....	.....	.....	.....	.....	2,985.7	552,351.54
6,918.6	.....	.....	.....	.....	.....	458.5	7,563.4	1,075,813.62
.....	.....	.....	.....	.....	.....	.....	3,099.9	573,474.84
1,651.1	.....	.....	.....	.....	.....	.....	5,264.6	824,265.87
.....	.....	.....	.....	.....	.....	.....	6,530.2	1,150,892.82
3,037.5	.....	.....	.....	20.4	.....	179.0	4,947.8	781,925.62
7,074.5	.....	.....	.....	.....	.....	.....	9,582.7	1,304,403.02
6,865.0	.....	.....	.....	.....	.....	.....	9,778.2	1,343,328.32
.....	.....	.....	.....	.....	.....	.....	3,126.7	578,432.47
5,061.8	.....	.....	.....	.....	.....	.....	5,735.4	731,306.89
.....	.....	.....	.....	.....	.....	.....	8,384.7	1,475,346.16
6,066.9	824.2	.....	.....	.....	.....	1,372.4	10,579.6	1,997,291.47
.....	.....	.....	.....	.....	.....	.....	9,728.4	1,761,701.36
.....	.....	.....	.....	.....	.....	.....	2,624.1	485,450.92
3,556.2	.....	.....	.....	.....	.....	.....	7,318.4	1,122,743.91
.....	.....	.....	.....	.....	.....	.....	425.2	84,441.60
.....	.....	592.4	.....	.....	.....	.....	592.4	150,319.22
.....	.....	.....	.....	.....	.....	.....	10,164.5	1,825,391.34
7,658.4	**2,797.8**	**592.4**	**177.5**	**37.3**	.....	**2,194.5**	**118,759.8**	**$ 19,541,890.03**
.....	7,735.9	.....	.....	.....	.....	.....	8,277.6	$ 2,111,563.55
.....	6,996.3	.....	.....	.....	.....	.....	7,533.7	1,918,450.30
.....	4,265.1	.....	.....	.....	.....	.....	6,115.3	1,451,202.19
5,437.5	.....	.....	.....	.....	.....	.....	8,882.1	1,245,343.74
.....	.....	.....	.....	.....	.....	.....	1,275.7	229,623.48
.....	2,076.3	.....	.....	.....	.....	.....	4,850.3	1,048,911.24
.....	2,265.4	.....	.....	.....	.....	.....	2,265.4	588,999.84
5,437.5	**23,339.0**	.....	.....	.....	.....	.....	**39,200.1**	**$ 8,594,094.34**
1,748.3	**42,200.0**	**9,209.6**	**21,879.0**	**3,627.3**	**21,449.8**	**11,115.8**	**482,791.1**	**$113,672,030.84**
ELIVERIES TO KURT RABBOW FOR GERMAN GOVERNMENT								
.....	.....	.....	.....	.....	.....	.....	**303.8**	**$ 56,919.65**
1,748.3	**42,200.0**	**9,209.6**	**21,879.0**	**3,627.3**	**21,449.8**	**11,115.8**	**483,094.9**	**$113,728,950.49‡**

GERMANY-

Detail of Commodities So
Sold to the German Government under t
A. Detail by Steame

Table 326

Invoice No.	Steamer or Lighter	Port of Sailing	Date of Arrival	Port of Arrival	Wheat Flour	Cereal Flour
			1919			
175	Elisabeth Maersk	New Orleans	Apr. 6	Rotterdam	106.7	931.
1	Remier, X.	New Orleans	Apr. 16	Rotterdam	.....	....
1	Herm, VI	Philadelphia	Apr. 18	Stettin	.....	....
37	Leopold, II.	New York	Apr. 23	Rotterdam	.....	....
46	Storviken, V.	New York	Apr. 30	Rotterdam	.....	....
	Total for April	....	....	....	**106.7**	**931.**
45	Danebrog, II.	New York	May 1	Rotterdam	.....	....
39	Calabria, III	Philadelphia	May 1	Rotterdam	.....	....
44	Hwah Jah, II.	Baltimore	May 5	Rotterdam	.....	....
36	Nippon, II.	Baltimore	May 6	Hamburg	.....	....
38	Josey	Philadelphia	May 8	Hamburg	.....	....
195	Natal, III (Drughorn 34 and 35; Duisberger Lloyd; Fred Drughorn 3)	New York	May 11	Rotterdam	.....	....
196, 196A	Pacific, V (Nassau; Maria; Anna Cornelia; Agatha; Anna II; Arnoldus-Elisabeth; Rotterdam 78; Rotterdam 67; 71; 87; 60; and Rotterdam 76; Hollandia; Senior; Pieter Bernard)	Baltimore	May 12	Rotterdam	.....	....
	Total for May	....	....	....	**106.7**	**....**
	Total Direct Deliveries	....	....	....	**106.7**	**931.**

GERMANY

Detail of Commodities S
B. Detail by Lighters

Table 326—*Continued*

Invoice No.	Lighter	Port of Sailing	Date of Invoice	Port of Arrival	Wheat Flour	Cereal Flour
			1919			
2	Barendina, I.	Antwerp	May 6	Rotterdam	29.0	364
3	Eugene Edouard	Antwerp	May 6	Rotterdam	61.7	201
6	Frathea	Antwerp	May 6	Rotterdam	.....	486
7	San Jose	Antwerp	May 6	Rotterdam	3.4	654
18	Agnes, II.	Antwerp	May 6	Rotterdam	.....	...
19	Wilhelmina	Antwerp	May 6	Rotterdam	.....	...
20	Sacre Coeur	Antwerp	May 6	Rotterdam	.....	...
24	Gambia	Antwerp	May 6	Rotterdam	.....	...
25	Mercator	Antwerp	May 6	Rotterdam	55.5	824
26	W. Kevelman	Antwerp	May 6	Rotterdam	89.8	998
27	Adeline	Antwerp	May 6	Rotterdam	.....	...
28	Manitoba	Antwerp	May 6	Rotterdam	.....	...
29	San Antonio, ex: Adma; Torpilleur	Antwerp	May 6	Coblenz	.....	1,400
30	Rosa Kate	Antwerp	May 6	Rotterdam	.....	319
4	Vredenburg, I.	Antwerp	May 7	Rotterdam	.....	373
5	Wilhelmina	Antwerp	May 7	Rotterdam	.....	321
8	St. Antoine	Antwerp	May 7	Rotterdam	.....	1,145
9	Dana	Antwerp	May 7	Rotterdam	.....	1,080
10	Successeur	Antwerp	May 7	Rotterdam	.....	1,263
11	St. Joseph	Antwerp	May 7	Rotterdam	.....	852

ommission for Relief in Belgium

r Cash—Armistice Period, 1919

rms of the Brussels Agreement of March 14, 1919

Direct Deliveries

Contents of Cargoes in Net Metric Tons of 1,000 Kilograms or 2,204.6 Pounds										
Wheat Grain	Corn Grain	Rye Grain	Rice	Beans, Peas	Pork Products	Lard Substitute	Misc. Food	Total Tons	Total Value	Credits
......	......	......	......	100.3	.....	.....	.....	1,138.7	$ 211,424.93	$ 163.73
......	......	......	4,268.2	.....	.....	.....	.....	4,268.2	828,024.79	.....
3,650.5	1,996.9	......	......	.....	.....	.....	.....	5,647.4	715,781.02	.....
......	......	4,140.2	......	.....	.....	.....	.....	4,140.2	476,121.16	.....
......	......	......	......	.....	259.3	3,329.0	.....	3,588.3	2,399,392.56	.....
3,650.5	**1,996.9**	**4,140.2**	**4,268.2**	**100.3**	**259.3**	**3,329.0**	.....	**18,782.8**	**$ 4,630,744.46**	**$ 163.73**
221.7	......	2,142.5	......	.....	.....	.....	.....	2,364.2	$ 275,210.23	.....
2,009.3	......	......	......	.....	.....	.....	.....	2,009.3	261,204.06	.....
6,765.9	......	......	......	.....	.....	.....	.....	6,765.9	879,560.89	.....
5,932.9	......	......	......	.....	.....	.....	.....	5,932.9	800,941.37	.....
3,517.8	......	......	......	.....	.....	.....	.....	3,517.8	474,904.08	.....
6,135.4	......	......	......	.....	.....	.....	.....	6,135.4	889,629.81	.....
......	......	6,245.8	......	.....	.....	.....	.....	6,245.8	811,955.30	.....
4,583.0	......	**8,388.3**	......	.....	.....	.....	.....	**32,971.3**	**$ 4,393,405.74**	.....
8,233.5	**1,996.9**	**12,528.5**	**4,268.2**	**100.3**	**259.3**	**3,329.0**	.....	**51,754.1**	**$ 9,024,150.20**	**$ 163.73**

ommission for Relief in Belgium

r Cash—Armistice Period, 1919

liveries from C.R.B. and C.N. Stock

Contents of Cargoes in Net Metric Tons of 1,000 Kilograms or 2,204.6 Pounds										
Wheat Grain	Corn Grain	Rye Grain	Rice	Beans, Peas	Pork Products	Lard Substitute	Misc. Food	Total Tons	Total Value	Credits
......	......	......	......	.....	.....	.....	.....	393.0	$ 74,798.67	.....
......	......	......	......	.....	.....	.....	.....	263.5	50,366.90	.....
......	......	......	......	.....	.....	.....	.....	486.6	92,452.10	.....
......	......	......	......	.....	.....	.....	.....	657.7	124,979.25	.....
......	......	......	......	1,084.8	.....	.....	.....	1,084.8	320,016.59	.....
......	......	......	......	1,024.9	.....	.....	.....	1,024.9	302,347.27	.....
......	......	......	41.3	1,430.5	.....	.....	.....	1,471.8	432,933.02	.....
......	......	......	......	329.1	.....	.....	.....	329.1	97,085.39	.....
......	......	......	......	.....	.....	.....	.....	879.8	167,443.56	.....
......	......	......	......	.....	.....	.....	.....	1,087.9	207,150.74	.....
......	......	......	......	281.4	.....	.....	.....	281.4	83,023.92	.....
......	......	......	......	137.7	.....	.....	.....	137.7	40,630.35	.....
......	......	......	......	.....	.....	.....	.....	1,400.0	266,000.38	.....
......	......	......	......	.....	.....	.....	.....	319.3	60,671.94	.....
......	......	......	......	.....	.....	.....	.....	373.9	71,048.98	.....
......	......	......	......	.....	.....	.....	.....	321.7	61,127.75	.....
......	......	......	......	.....	.....	.....	.....	1,145.1	217,570.33	.....
......	......	......	......	.....	.....	.....	.....	1,080.0	205,203.80	.....
......	......	......	......	.....	.....	.....	.....	1,263.9	240,134.92	.....
......	......	......	......	.....	.....	.....	.....	852.1	161,903.56	.....

[*Continued on next page*]

Table 326—*Continued*

B. Detail by Lighters

Invoice No.	Lighter	Port of Sailing	Date of Invoice	Port of Arrival	Wheat Flour	Cereal Flour
			1919			
12	Sarto	Antwerp	May 7	Rotterdam	.....	751.
32	Ostria	Antwerp	May 7	Mayence	300.0	....
33	Jacoba	Antwerp	May 7	Crefeld, Ludwigshafen	300.1	....
34	Orange	Antwerp	May 7	Neuss	255.4	....
35	Arundo	Antwerp	May 7	Neuss	.....	....
13	Stephanie	Antwerp	May 8	Rotterdam	.....	....
14	Jamais Pense	Antwerp	May 8	Rotterdam	.....	....
15	Scaldis	Antwerp	May 8	Rotterdam	.....	....
16	Belgenland	Antwerp	May 8	Rotterdam	.....	....
22	Minister Paul Segers	Antwerp	May 8	Rotterdam	.....	....
23	Kapitein Bulcke	Antwerp	May 8	Rotterdam	.....	....
31	Univers	Antwerp	May 8	Rotterdam	.....	....
43	De Vrede	Antwerp	May 12	Rotterdam	.....	....
41	Ibis	Antwerp	May 13	Rotterdam	.....	....
42	Juene Pierre	Antwerp	May 13	Rotterdam	.....	....
56	Scheldevry	Antwerp	May 16	Rotterdam	1.0	399.
47	Flandria	Antwerp	May 17	Rotterdam	.....	....
48	Maria Francisca	Antwerp	May 17	Rotterdam	.....	....
49	Memling	Antwerp	May 17	Rotterdam	.....	....
50	Leopold	Antwerp	May ..	Rotterdam	.....	....
51	Mechtilde	Antwerp	May 26	Rotterdam	.....	....
52	Marie Elisabeth	Antwerp	May 26	Rotterdam	.....	536.
53	Prior	Antwerp	May 26	Rotterdam	.....	185.
54	Japa, Ex: Espérance; Bentyn; Josephine	Antwerp	May 26	Rotterdam	.....	....
55	Alice, Ex: Mercator; Oshkook	Antwerp	May 26	Rotterdam	.....	....
57	Moretus, Ex: Bentyn; Jeannette; Rep. Argentinia; Ontario	Antwerp	May 26	Rotterdam	.....	....
60	Jonge Bruno	Antwerp	May 26	Rotterdam	.....	403
61	Ludovica	Antwerp	May 26	Rotterdam	.....	...
62	Filia Rheni	Antwerp	May 26	Rotterdam	.....	...
63	Confidence	Antwerp	May 26	Rotterdam	.....	...
64	Emmy	Antwerp	May 26	Rotterdam	.....	...
65	San Jose	Antwerp	May 26	Rotterdam	.....	...
59	Excelsior, Ex: Grinthandel; Clara; Wilhelmina	Antwerp	May 27	Rotterdam	.....	1,369
66	Barendina, II	Antwerp	May 27	Rotterdam	.....	...
67	Marie Virginie, Ex: Remier; Dirksland; Rep. Argentinia	Antwerp	May 27	Rotterdam	.....	...
68	Stephenson	Antwerp	May 27	Rotterdam	.....	...
69	Johanna Maria	Antwerp	May 27	Rotterdam	.....	...
70	Cisrhenan	Antwerp	May 27	Rotterdam	.....	...
71	Infatigable	Antwerp	May 27	Rotterdam	.....	...
72	Anna, Ex: Oshkook; Rep. Argentinia; Jelling; Myn Goesting	Antwerp	May 27	Rotterdam	.....	...
73	Sirius, Ex: Oshkook; Rep. Argentinia; Jelling	Antwerp	May 27	Rotterdam	.....	...
74	Grinthandel	Antwerp	May 27	Rotterdam	.....	...
75	Stephanie	Antwerp	May 30	Rotterdam	.....	...
78	Mechelen	Antwerp	May 30	Rotterdam	.....	...
81	Henri	Antwerp	May 30	Rotterdam	.....	...
82	Deo Juvante	Antwerp	May 30	Rotterdam	.....	...
	Total for May	....	....	....	**1,095.9**	**13,929**
83	St. Maria	Antwerp	June 2	Rotterdam	.....	...
85	Fraternite	Antwerp	June 2	Rotterdam	.....	...
86	Ludovicus	Antwerp	June 2	Rotterdam	.....	...
87	Twee Zusters	Antwerp	June 2	Rotterdam	.....	...
79	Ostara	Antwerp	June 2	Rotterdam	.....	...
77	L'Avenir	Antwerp	June 4	Rotterdam	.....	...
80	Dana	Antwerp	June 6	Rotterdam	.....	...
90	Charbonnierre	Antwerp	June 6	Rotterdam	.....	...

nmission for Relief in Belgium

veries from C.R.B. and C.N. Stock

Contents of Cargoes in Net Metric Tons of 1,000 Kilograms or 2,204.6 Pounds										
heat rain	Corn Grain	Rye Grain	Rice	Beans, Peas	Pork Products	Lard Substitute	Misc. Food	Total Tons	Total Value	Credits
.....	.....	.....	.....	.....	.....	.....	.....	751.2	$ 142,733.13	.....
.....	.....	.....	176.4	300.1	.....	.....	.....	776.5	193,786.85	$ 3.84
.....	.....	.....	200.1	280.9	.....	.....	.....	781.1	194,402.65	.....
.....	.....	.....	100.0	.....	.....	.....	.....	355.4	76,317.29	.....
.....	.....	.....	100.0	210.0	.....	.....	.....	310.0	88,453.84	.....
.....	.....	.....	.....	512.6	.....	.....	.....	512.6	140,954.28	.....
.....	.....	.....	.....	295.3	.....	.....	.....	295.3	81,201.18	.....
.....	.....	.....	.....	368.1	.....	.....	.....	368.1	101,218.43	.52
.....	.....	.....	.....	773.3	.....	.....	.....	773.3	212,664.10	7.80
.....	.....	.....	.....	200.0	.....	.....	.....	200.0	54,989.28	.....
.....	.....	.....	.....	247.5	.....	.....	.....	247.5	68,074.33	17.68
.....	.....	.....	22.9	215.0	.....	.....	.....	237.9	64,953.03	16.38
.....	.....	.....	701.0	.....	.....	.....	.....	701.0	185,743.01	4.24
.....	.....	.....	.....	303.8	.....	.....	.....	303.8	83,543.35	100.36
.....	.....	.....	.....	308.5	.....	.....	.....	308.5	84,848.23	46.80
.....	.....	.....	.....	.....	.....	.....	.....	400.1	76,012.54	699.58
.....	.....	.....	787.3	.....	.....	.....	.....	787.3	104,314.20	.....
.....	.....	.....	.....	.....	.....	266.1	.....	266.1	199,607.25	.....
.....	.....	.....	.....	.....	.....	142.9	.....	142.9	107,178.00	.....
.....	.....	.....	1,987.6	.....	.....	.....	.....	1,987.6	263,358.72	.....
.....	.....	.....	645.2	.....	.....	.....	.....	645.2	170,981.71	.....
.....	.....	.....	.....	.....	.....	.....	.....	536.8	101,985.54	304.57
.....	.....	.....	.....	.....	.....	.....	.....	185.1	35,162.54	.....
.....	.....	.....	.....	256.0	.....	.....	.....	256.0	75,518.23	.....
.....	.....	.....	.....	1,433.4	.....	.....	.....	1,433.4	422,855.07	.....
.....	.....	.....	.....	280.7	.....	.....	.....	280.7	82,798.54	.....
.....	.....	.....	.....	.....	.....	.....	.....	403.3	76,619.40	.....
.....	.....	.....	.....	289.0	.....	.....	.....	289.0	85,253.53	.....
.....	.....	.....	989.3	.....	.....	.....	.....	989.3	131,086.36	.....
.....	.....	.....	804.2	23.5	.....	.....	.....	827.7	211,540.71	8.25
.....	.....	.....	913.9	.....	.....	.....	.....	913.9	242,191.98	1,142.79
.....	.....	.....	685.7	.....	.....	.....	.....	685.7	181,723.49	18.55
.....	.....	.....	.....	.....	.....	.....	.....	1,369.0	260,113.42	577.03
.....	.....	.....	489.0	.....	.....	.....	.....	489.0	129,572.55	.....
.....	.....	.....	.....	248.1	.....	.....	.....	248.1	73,184.49	.....
.....	.....	.....	497.9	.....	.....	.....	.....	497.9	65,970.56	.....
.....	.....	.....	622.6	.....	.....	.....	.....	622.6	164,979.46	507.10
.....	.....	.....	1,190.3	.....	.....	.....	.....	1,190.3	315,429.50	1,087.35
.....	.....	.....	285.6	.....	.....	.....	.....	285.6	75,672.34	38.16
.....	.....	.....	.....	738.1	.....	.....	.....	738.1	217,746.29	.....
.....	.....	.....	.....	1,116.7	.....	.....	.....	1,116.7	329,424.44	.....
.....	.....	.....	801.7	.....	.....	.....	.....	801.7	106,226.18	.....
.....	.....	.....	.....	.....	259.7	.....	.....	259.7	146,599.36	.....
.....	.....	.....	.....	.....	93.8	.....	.....	93.8	55,146.48	.....
.....	.....	.....	798.1	.....	.....	.....	.....	798.1	211,483.78	.....
.....	.....	.....	869.0	.....	.....	.....	.....	869.0	230,285.80	.....
.....	.....	.....	**13,709.1**	**12,689.0**	**353.5**	**409.0**	.....	**42,186.1**	**$10,000,794.86**	**$ 4,581.00**
.....	.....	.....	.....	.....	310.6	.....	.....	310.6	$ 246,897.59	.....
.....	.....	.....	1,449.5	.....	.....	.....	.....	1,449.5	384,125.72	$ 294.68
.....	.....	.....	.....	.....	865.7	.....	.....	865.7	688,236.27	.....
.....	.....	.....	708.7	.....	.....	.....	.....	708.7	187,792.52	.....
.....	.....	.....	.....	.....	248.6	.....	.....	248.6	139,199.76	.....
.....	.....	.....	.....	.....	82.8	53.0	17.9	153.7	104,573.79	.....
.....	.....	.....	.....	.....	565.7	.....	.....	565.7	317,315.04	508.48
.....	.....	.....	.....	.....	165.8	.....	.....	165.8	131,783.18	.....

[*Continued on next page*]

Table 326—*Continued*

B. Detail by Lighters

Invoice No.	Lighter	Port of Sailing	Date of Invoice	Port of Arrival	Wheat Flour	Cereal Flour
			1919			
21	Grinthandel	Antwerp	June 7	Rotterdam	.....	....
76	Got Met Ons	Antwerp	June 7	Rotterdam	.....	....
89	Belgenland	Antwerp	June 7	Rotterdam	.....	....
91	Andrea	Antwerp	June 7	Rotterdam	.....	....
92	Prisa	Antwerp	June 7	Rotterdam	.....	....
93	Successeur	Antwerp	June 7	Rotterdam	.....	....
94	Cornelia	Antwerp	June 7	Rotterdam	.....	....
95	Charbonnierre	Antwerp	June 7	Rotterdam	.....	....
97	Deux Freres	Antwerp	June 10	Rotterdam	.....	....
98	Edouard	Antwerp	June 10	Rotterdam	.....	....
100	Zeebrauw	Antwerp	June 10	Rotterdam	.....	....
101	Sophia	Antwerp	June 10	Rotterdam	.....	....
102	Pauline	Antwerp	June 10	Rotterdam	.....	....
103	Albert, I.	Antwerp	June 10	Rotterdam	.....	....
104	Edelweiss	Antwerp	June 10	Rotterdam	.....	....
105	Louise	Antwerp	June 10	Rotterdam	.....	....
106	Wilson	Antwerp	June 10	Rotterdam	.....	....
108	Grinthandel, I	Antwerp	June 10	Rotterdam	.....	....
110	Deux Freres	Antwerp	June 10	Rotterdam	.....	....
111	Agile	Antwerp	June 10	Rotterdam	.....	....
112	Emile	Antwerp	June 10	Rotterdam	.....	....
115	Harry	Antwerp	June 10	Rotterdam	.....	....
116	Helena	Antwerp	June 10	Rotterdam	.....	....
117	Intrepide	Antwerp	June 10	Rotterdam	.....	....
119	Trois Freres	Antwerp	June 10	Rotterdam	.....	....
120	Irma	Antwerp	June 10	Rotterdam	.....	....
121	Kaba, II	Antwerp	June 10	Rotterdam	.....	....
122	Rosa	Antwerp	June 10	Rotterdam	.....	....
123	Charbonnierre, XXV	Antwerp	June 10	Rotterdam	.....	....
124	Silo	Antwerp	June 10	Rotterdam	.....	....
126	Vredenburg, II	Antwerp	June 10	Rotterdam	.....	....
127	Mentor	Antwerp	June 10	Rotterdam	.....	....
129	Therese	Antwerp	June 10	Rotterdam	.....	....
134	Gounod	Antwerp	June 10	Rotterdam	.....	....
135	Dymphna	Antwerp	June 10	Rotterdam	.....	....
136	Louise	Antwerp	June 10	Rotterdam	.....	....
139	Rosalie	Antwerp	June 10	Rotterdam	.....	....
107	Morgendster	Antwerp	June 11	Rotterdam	.....	....
109	Martha	Antwerp	June 11	Rotterdam	.....	....
114	Perspectif	Antwerp	June 11	Rotterdam	.....	....
118	Maria	Antwerp	June 11	Rotterdam	.....	....
133	Avonteur, II	Antwerp	June 11	Rotterdam	.....	....
125	Tyd Zal Leeren	Antwerp	June 13	Rotterdam	.....	....
128	Vrede	Antwerp	June 13	Rotterdam	.....	....
131	Roger	Antwerp	June 13	Rotterdam	.....	....
132	Mit	Antwerp	June 13	Rotterdam	.....	....
137	Rival	Antwerp	June 13	Rotterdam	.....	....
138	Memling	Antwerp	June 13	Rotterdam	.....	....
141	Hendrika	Antwerp	June 13	Rotterdam	.....	....
142	Maasstroom 29	Antwerp	June 13	Rotterdam	.....	....
143	Bon Credit	Antwerp	June 13	Rotterdam	.....	....
144	Amsterdam, VI	Antwerp	June 13	Rotterdam	.....	....
146	Anvers	Antwerp	June 13	Rotterdam	.....	....
147	Elisa	Antwerp	June 13	Rotterdam	.....	....
148	Van Eyck	Antwerp	June 13	Rotterdam	.....	....
194	Yildum,* Ex: Memento; Anna; Geertruida	Rotterdam	June 13	Rotterdam	.....	....
152	Monargue	Antwerp	June 14	Rotterdam	.....	....
155	Marconi	Antwerp	June 14	Rotterdam	.....	....
157	Mechelen	Antwerp	June 16	Rotterdam	.....	....

* Yildum cargo is replacement of loan by Netherlands.

nmission for Relief in Belgium

veries from C.R.B. and C.N. Stock

Contents of Cargoes in Net Metric Tons of 1,000 Kilograms or 2,204.6 Pounds									Total Value	Credits
heat rain	Corn Grain	Rye Grain	Rice	Beans, Peas	Pork Products	Lard Substitute	Misc. Food	Total Tons		
.....	.....	.....	.....	.....	.....	31.4	321.9	353.3	$ 176,484.95	.....
.....	.....	.....	.....	.....	556.2	87.4	.....	643.6	377,027.81	.....
.....	.....	.....	.....	.....	385.7	.....	.....	385.7	215,998.08	.....
.....	.....	.....	.....	.....	181.8	.....	.....	181.8	113,580.64	.....
.....	.....	.....	.....	.....	155.8	.....	.....	155.8	123,871.34	.....
.....	.....	.....	.....	.....	702.8	.....	.....	702.8	558,710.10	.....
.....	.....	.....	.....	.....	140.6	.....	.....	140.6	111,766.67	.....
.....	.....	.....	.....	.....	153.8	.....	.....	153.8	122,296.44	.....
.....	.....	.....	.....	.....	151.1	.....	.....	151.1	120,142.79	.....
.....	.....	.....	.....	.....	160.6	.....	.....	160.6	131,655.92	.....
.....	.....	.....	.....	.....	152.7	.....	.....	152.7	121,392.53	.....
.....	.....	.....	.....	.....	106.4	.....	.....	106.4	108,309.21	$ 23,737.11
.....	.....	.....	.....	.....	148.4	.....	.....	148.4	121,690.46	.....
.....	.....	.....	.....	.....	151.3	.....	.....	151.3	120,266.81	.....
.....	.....	.....	.....	.....	147.4	.....	.....	147.4	117,187.77	.....
.....	.....	.....	.....	.....	154.5	.....	.....	154.5	122,809.22	.....
.....	.....	.....	.....	.....	144.2	.....	.....	144.2	114,643.77	.....
.....	.....	.....	.....	.....	336.3	.....	.....	336.3	267,377.58	.....
.....	.....	.....	.....	.....	140.1	.....	.....	140.1	111,404.15	.....
.....	.....	.....	.....	.....	142.2	.....	.....	142.2	113,077.62	.....
.....	.....	.....	.....	.....	100.8	.....	.....	100.8	80,108.18	.....
.....	.....	.....	.....	.....	863.0	.....	.....	863.0	686,088.97	.....
.....	.....	.....	.....	.....	653.2	.....	.....	653.2	519,302.75	.....
.....	.....	.....	.....	.....	143.4	.....	.....	143.4	117,547.82	.....
.....	.....	.....	.....	.....	166.8	.....	.....	166.8	136,802.24	.....
.....	.....	.....	.....	.....	604.5	.....	.....	604.5	480,575.91	.....
.....	.....	.....	.....	.....	447.7	.....	.....	447.7	355,882.55	.....
.....	.....	.....	.....	.....	164.1	.....	.....	164.1	130,469.84	.....
.....	.....	.....	.....	.....	157.5	.....	.....	157.5	125,271.31	.....
.....	.....	.....	.....	.....	142.9	.....	.....	142.9	117,185.38	.....
.....	.....	.....	.....	.....	192.0	.....	.....	192.0	157,418.68	.....
.....	.....	.....	.....	.....	127.5	.....	.....	127.5	104,563.94	.....
.....	.....	.....	.....	.....	121.5	.....	.....	121.5	99,593.92	.....
.....	.....	.....	.....	.....	118.8	.....	.....	118.8	127,206.36	32,790.57
.....	.....	.....	.....	.....	132.9	.....	.....	132.9	113,356.66	7,714.68
.....	.....	.....	.....	.....	174.2	.....	.....	174.2	138,521.60	.....
.....	.....	.....	.....	.....	141.3	.....	.....	141.3	112,358.94	.....
.....	.....	.....	.....	.....	122.9	.....	.....	122.9	100,787.84	.....
.....	.....	.....	.....	.....	115.2	.....	.....	115.2	91,556.97	.....
.....	.....	.....	.....	.....	141.4	.....	.....	141.4	115,942.26	.....
.....	.....	.....	.....	.....	141.1	.....	.....	141.1	115,400.81	.....
.....	.....	.....	.....	.....	890.6	.....	.....	890.6	713,693.84	.....
.....	.....	.....	.....	.....	147.0	.....	.....	147.0	117,968.03	.....
.....	.....	.....	.....	.....	326.4	.....	.....	326.4	260,292.79	.....
.....	.....	.....	.....	.....	286.7	.....	.....	286.7	229,888.77	.....
.....	.....	.....	.....	.....	152.8	.....	.....	152.8	123,831.42	.....
.....	.....	.....	.....	.....	464.9	.....	.....	464.9	274,103.28	.....
.....	.....	.....	.....	.....	135.7	.....	.....	135.7	110,877.73	.....
.....	.....	.....	.....	.....	293.3	.....	.....	293.3	240,477.30	.....
.....	.....	.....	.....	.....	366.5	.....	.....	366.5	300,564.44	.....
.....	.....	.....	.....	.....	142.1	.....	.....	142.1	116,537.58	.....
.....	.....	.....	.....	.....	126.4	.....	.....	126.4	100,525.37	.....
.....	.....	.....	.....	.....	273.4	.....	.....	273.4	217,322.79	.....
.....	.....	.....	.....	.....	161.5	.....	.....	161.5	132,447.22	.....
.....	.....	.....	.....	.....	132.2	.....	.....	132.2	105,938.71	.....
,823.0	.....	.....	.....	.....	.....	.....	.....	1,823.0	264,337.18	.....
.....	.....	.....	.....	.....	138.6	.....	.....	138.6	113,658.56	.....
.....	.....	.....	.....	.....	99.3	.....	.....	99.3	81,435.84	.....
.....	.....	.....	.....	.....	177.4	.....	.....	177.4	145,475.38	.....

[*Continued on next page*]

B. Detail by Lighters

Table 326—*Continued*

Invoice No.	Lighter	Port of Sailing	Date of Invoice	Port of Arrival	Wheat Flour	Cereal Flour
			1919			
167	Jules Verne	Antwerp	June 16	Rotterdam	.....	....
170	Brabo	Antwerp	June 16	Rotterdam	.....	....
171	Cordula	Antwerp	June 16	Rotterdam	.....	....
172	Gladiateur	Antwerp	June 16	Rotterdam	.....	....
151	Jocko	Antwerp	June 16	Rotterdam	.....	....
150	L'Aurore	Antwerp	June 17	Rotterdam	.....	....
153	Dumas	Antwerp	June 17	Rotterdam	.....	....
154	Maria Francisca	Antwerp	June 17	Rotterdam	.....	....
156	Scaldis	Antwerp	June 17	Rotterdam	.....	....
158	Prior	Antwerp	June 17	Rotterdam	.....	....
159	Antoine Joseph	Antwerp	June 17	Rotterdam	.....	....
160	Marie	Antwerp	June 17	Rotterdam	.....	....
161	Jeannette	Antwerp	June 17	Rotterdam	.....	....
162	Flandria	Antwerp	June 17	Rotterdam	.....	....
163	Emma 3	Antwerp	June 17	Rotterdam	.....	....
164	Grinthandel, II	Antwerp	June 17	Rotterdam	.....	....
165	Stad Amsterdam, VII	Antwerp	June 17	Rotterdam	.....	....
166	Leontine	Antwerp	June 17	Rotterdam	.....	....
169	Elisa Hendrika	Antwerp	June 17	Rotterdam	.....	....
173	Santiago	Antwerp	June 17	Rotterdam	.....	....
58	Marie Serena	Antwerp	June 18	Rotterdam	.....	....
88	W. van Driel 63	Antwerp	June 18	Rotterdam	.....	....
96	Adoust	Antwerp	June 18	Rotterdam	.....	....
113	Repos Ailleur	Antwerp	June 18	Rotterdam	.....	....
140	Drie Gezusters	Antwerp	June 18	Rotterdam	.....	....
149	W. van Driel 43	Antwerp	June 18	Rotterdam	.....	....
184	Marie	Antwerp	June 18	Rotterdam	.....	....
17A	Ewin	Antwerp	June 19	Rotterdam	.....	....
17B	Pacificateur	Antwerp	June 19	Rotterdam	.....	....
168	Mercator	Antwerp	June 19	Rotterdam	.....	....
174	Therese	Antwerp	June 19	Rotterdam	.....	....
177	Vredenburg, I	Antwerp	June 19	Rotterdam	.....	....
178	Helene	Antwerp	June 19	Rotterdam	.....	....
179	Rynvaart	Antwerp	June 19	Rotterdam	.....	....
181	Jeune Cecile	Antwerp	June 19	Rotterdam	.....	....
182	Esperanto	Antwerp	June 19	Rotterdam	.....	....
183	Garcia Marena	Antwerp	June 19	Rotterdam	.....	....
187	Elbe	Antwerp	June 19	Rotterdam	.....	....
188	De Toekomst	Antwerp	June 19	Rotterdam	.....	....
189	Barendina, III	Antwerp	June 19	Rotterdam	.....	....
191	Moretus	Antwerp	June 19	Rotterdam	.....	....
84	St. Joseph	Antwerp	June 20	Rotterdam	.....	....
99	Kevelman	Antwerp	June 20	Rotterdam	.....	....
145	Sarto	Antwerp	June 20	Rotterdam	.....	....
176	Margaretha	Antwerp	June 20	Rotterdam	.....	....
185	Nenuphar	Antwerp	June 20	Rotterdam	.....	....
197	Fluviale 4	Antwerp	June 26	Rotterdam	.....	....
198	Fluviale 47	Antwerp	June 26	Rotterdam	.....	....
	Total for June	....	....	....	.....	....
201	Johanna Maria	Antwerp	July 1	Rotterdam	.....	....
202	Risquons Tout	Antwerp	July 1	Rotterdam	.....	....
203	St. Marie	Antwerp	July 1	Rotterdam	.....	....
204	Christiaan Johanna	Antwerp	July 1	Rotterdam	.....	....
205	Knaps, IV	Antwerp	July 3	Rotterdam	.....	....
193	Local Delivery	Rotterdam	July 15	Rotterdam	1.9	....
206	Anna	Antwerp	July 15	Rotterdam	.....	....
130	Arnold	Antwerp	July 22	Rotterdam	.....	....

ommission for Relief in Belgium

eliveries from C.R.B. and C.N. Stock

Contents of Cargoes in Net Metric Tons of 1,000 Kilograms or 2,204.6 Pounds										
Wheat Grain	Corn Grain	Rye Grain	Rice	Beans, Peas	Pork Products	Lard Substitute	Misc. Food	Total Tons	Total Value	Credits
......	......	......	......	.....	216.5	.....	.....	216.5	$ 177,537.38	.....
......	......	......	......	.....	150.9	.....	.....	150.9	123,770.80	.....
......	......	......	......	.....	142.9	.....	.....	142.9	117,150.12	.....
......	......	......	......	.....	146.0	.....	.....	146.0	119,719.18	.....
......	......	......	......	.....	54.9	.....	.....	54.9	112,656.52	$ 67,643.44
......	......	......	......	.....	147.4	.....	.....	147.4	117,150.41	.....
......	......	......	......	.....	139.8	.....	.....	139.8	114,602.38	.....
......	......	......	......	.....	259.4	.....	.....	259.4	212,741.62	.....
......	......	......	......	.....	199.5	.....	.....	199.5	163,587.54	.....
......	......	......	......	.....	139.1	.....	.....	139.1	114,078.40	.....
......	......	......	......	.....	227.2	.....	.....	227.2	186,330.24	.....
......	......	......	......	.....	142.5	.....	.....	142.5	116,872.14	.....
......	......	......	......	.....	145.6	.....	.....	145.6	119,362.48	.....
......	......	......	......	.....	398.8	.....	.....	398.8	326,982.38	.....
......	......	......	......	.....	624.4	.....	.....	624.4	512,016.20	.....
......	......	......	......	.....	422.9	.....	.....	422.9	346,797.68	.....
......	......	......	......	.....	109.3	.....	.....	109.3	89,632.56	.....
......	......	......	......	.....	617.8	.....	.....	617.8	653,718.76	147,124.40
......	......	......	......	.....	215.4	.....	.....	215.4	176,588.64	.....
......	......	......	......	.....	127.6	.....	.....	127.6	104,633.64	.....
......	......	......	......	.....	419.7	.....	.....	419.7	235,039.28	.....
......	......	......	......	394.5	.....	.....	.....	394.5	116,384.88	.....
......	......	......	......	.....	134.5	.....	.....	134.5	106,902.06	.....
......	......	......	......	.....	125.2	13.8	.2	139.2	91,275.13	.....
......	......	......	......	1,375.6	.....	.....	.....	1,375.6	405,808.20	3,651.81
......	......	......	......	1,309.3	.....	.....	.....	1,309.3	386,253.53	.....
......	......	......	......	331.5	.....	.....	.....	331.5	97,803.42	.....
......	......	......	224.0	.....	.....	.....	.....	224.0	57,130.71	.....
......	......	......	149.0	.....	.....	.....	.....	149.0	37,990.41	.....
......	......	......	......	.....	642.9	.....	.....	642.9	527,196.86	.....
......	......	......	......	473.7	.....	.....	.....	473.7	139,739.14	.....
......	......	......	......	.....	198.9	.....	.....	198.9	163,112.76	.....
......	......	......	......	441.4	.....	.....	.....	441.4	130,226.87	8,249.38
......	......	......	......	662.0	.....	.....	.....	662.0	195,287.64	.....
......	......	......	......	.....	146.9	.....	.....	146.9	120,452.26	.....
......	......	......	......	.....	142.2	.....	.....	142.2	116,640.90	.....
......	......	......	......	.....	138.2	.....	.....	138.2	113,313.34	.....
......	......	......	......	.....	136.9	.....	.....	136.9	112,237.50	.....
......	......	......	......	.....	153.1	.....	.....	153.1	125,532.16	.....
......	......	......	......	.....	210.2	.....	.....	210.2	172,378.76	.....
......	......	......	......	.....	150.7	.....	.....	150.7	123,537.92	.....
......	......	......	......	.....	.....	404.0	187.0	591.0	391,792.58	.....
......	......	......	......	.....	585.3	.....	.....	585.3	341,816.28	.....
......	......	......	......	.....	464.3	.....	.....	464.3	248,881.20	.....
......	......	......	......	.....	283.0	.....	.....	283.0	232,078.04	.....
......	......	......	......	.....	572.3	.....	.....	572.3	307,279.16	.....
......	......	......	......	.....	156.9	.....	.....	156.9	128,673.58	.....
......	......	......	......	.....	161.8	.....	.....	161.8	132,698.14	.....
1,823.0	......	......	**2,531.2**	**4,988.0**	**25,189.5**	**589.6**	**527.0**	**35,648.3**	**$22,608,328.67**	**$296,295.55**
......	......	......	......	.....	309.6	.....	.....	309.6	$ 253,896.60	.....
......	......	......	......	.....	600.8	.....	.....	600.8	492,661.74	.....
......	......	......	......	.....	292.7	.....	.....	292.7	240,046.80	.....
......	......	......	......	.....	328.2	.....	.....	328.2	269,115.80	.....
......	......	......	......	.....	194.4	.....	.....	194.4	159,376.84	.....
......	......	......	3.4	5.5	1.1	.....	.....	11.9	3,019.38	.....
......	......	......	......	.....	404.5	.....	.....	404.5	331,662.94	.....
......	......	......	209.0	491.3	.....	.....	.....	700.3	198,224.81	$ 32.31

[*Concluded on next page*]

Table 326—*Concluded*

B. Detail by Lighters o

Invoice No.	Lighter	Port of Sailing	Date of Invoice	Port of Arrival	Wheat Flour	Cereal Flour
			1919			
180	Fairaka	Antwerp	July 22	Rotterdam	.....	.....
186	Spa	Antwerp	July 22	Rotterdam	.....	.....
190	Jeanne	Antwerp	July 22	Rotterdam	.....	.....
192	Jonge Bruno	Antwerp	July 22	Rotterdam	.....	.....
208	Marcel	Antwerp	July 28	Rotterdam	.....	.....
199	Confidence	Antwerp	July 30	Rotterdam	.....	.....
200	Gambia	Antwerp	July 30	Rotterdam	.....	.....
207	Baris	Antwerp	July 30	Rotterdam	.....	.....
209	Grinthandel	Antwerp	July 30	Rotterdam	.....	.....
210	Johanna Maria	Antwerp	July 31	Rotterdam	.....	.....
	Total for July				1.9	.....
	Total Ex Stock (Section B)				1,097.8	13,929.6
	Total All Deliveries (Sections A and B)				1,204.5	14,861.3
	Adjustment to Settlement Basis — Add				.....	.....
	Adjustment to Settlement Basis — Deduct				.5	.3
	Total Net Deliveries †				1,204.0	14,861.0

† These figures are carried to the summary, Table 323, in even metric tons; see "The Commission for Relief in Belgium—Statistical Review of Relief Operations," George I. Gay, Stanford University Press, 1925.

GERMANY—Countries Other than United States

Table 327 Monthly Deliveries by the United Kingdom—Armistice Period, 1919

Month	Commodities in Net Metric Tons of 1,000 Kilograms or 2,204.6 Pounds									Total Value
	Cereal Flour	Rice, Beans, Peas	Pork, Beef	Lard	Lard Substitute	Milk	Miscellaneous Foods	Miscellaneous Non-Foods	Total Tons	
1919										
April	......	......	6,753.0	618.0	463.0	2,510.0	36,561.0	1,961.0	48,866.0	$10,443,793.
May	......	......	13,807.0	1,235.0	928.0	5,083.0	73,122.0	3,922.0	98,097.0	20,930,677.
June	9,192.0	......	5,161.0	.....	1,404.0	6,253.0	21,976.0	5,280.0	49,266.0	10,148,509.
July	......	1,604.0	3,121.0	.....	167.0	1,622.0	8,011.0	3,004.0	17,529.0	5,191,604.
——*	......	......	......	.....	.....	......	6,029.0	......	6,029.0	3,678,081.
August	11,835.0	36,054.0	15,522.0	.....	38.0	1,550.0	......	14,329.0	79,657.0	25,261,197.
Total	**21,045.0**	**37,658.0**	**44,375.0**	**1,853.0**	**3,000.0**	**17,018.0**	**145,699.0**	**28,496.0**	**299,144.0**	**$75,653,861.**

* Various dates. Deliveries ex–British War office surplus stocks.

GERMANY—Countries Other than United States

Table 328 Monthly Deliveries by France—Armistice Period, 1919

Month	Commodities in Net Metric Tons of 1,000 Kilograms or 2,204.6 Pounds						Total Value
	Wheat Flour	Cereal Flour	Pork, Beef	Miscellaneous Foods	Miscellaneous Non-Foods	Total Tons	
1919							
May	......	....	......	......	2,691.0	2,691.0	$ 522,615.
——*	1,318.0	84.0	283.0	6,514.0	......	8,199.0	1,142,400.
June	......	....	988.0	......	11,211.0	12,199.0	2,958,221.
July	......	....	1,535.0	......	4,907.0	6,442.0	1,899,487.
August	......	....	3,682.0	......	36,191.0	39,873.0	9,740,166.
Total	**1,318.0**	**84.0**	**6,488.0**	**6,514.0**	**55,000.0**	**69,404.0**	**$16,262,889.**

* Various dates. Deliveries ex–French Army surplus stocks.

nmission for Relief in Belgium

iveries from C.R.B. and C.N. Stock

heat rain	Corn Grain	Rye Grain	Rice	Beans, Peas	Pork Products	Lard Substitute	Misc. Food	Total Tons	Total Value	Credits
Contents of Cargoes in Net Metric Tons of 1,000 Kilograms or 2,204.6 Pounds										
.....	......	......	......	313.0	.....	.....	.....	313.0	$ 87,914.41	$ 2,412.11
.....	......	......	......	341.2	.....	.....	.....	341.2	93,816.53	.....
.....	......	......	......	319.3	.....	.....	.....	319.3	87,796.50	9,814.20
.....	......	......	......	344.3	.....	.....	.....	344.3	94,678.10	11,081.40
.....	......	......	500.0	.....	.....	.....	.....	500.0	127,494.39	1,499.91
.....	......	......	......	.....	264.8	.....	.....	264.8	152,142.70	.....
.....	......	......	......	.....	139.1	.....	.....	139.1	77,412.84	.....
.....	......	......	......	.....	99.5	.....	.....	99.5	55,930.20	.....
.....	......	......	......	.....	331.3	.....	.....	331.3	271,693.88	.....
.....	......	......	......	.....	62.4	.....	.....	62.4	51,128.64	.....
.....	......	......	**712.4**	**1,814.6**	**3,028.4**	.....	.....	**5,557.3**	**$ 3,048,013.10**	**$ 24,839.93**
,823.0	......	......	**16,952.7**	**19,491.6**	**28,571.4**	**998.6**	**527.0**	**83,391.7**	**$35,657,136.63**	**$321,135.48**
,056.5	**1,996.9**	**12,528.5**	**21,220.9**	**19,591.9**	**28,830.7**	**4,327.6**	**527.0**	**135,145.8**	**$44,681,286.83**	**$321,299.21**
.....	.1	......	24.1	.....	.....	.....	.....	24.2	......	$ 9,177.15
.5	......	.5	......	24.9	163.3	.....	.....	190.0	......	
,056.0	**1,997.0**	**12,528.0**	**21,245.0**	**19,567.0**	**28,667.4**	**4,327.6**	**527.0**	**134,980.0**	**$44,350,810.47**	.....

GERMANY—Countries Other than United States
(Exclusive of Three Major Allies)

Table 329 Monthly Deliveries from Neutral Countries—Armistice Period, 1919

Month	Wheat	Pork, Beef	Lard	Miscellaneous * Foods	Miscellaneous * Non-Foods	Total Tons	Total Value
	Commodities in Net Metric Tons of 1,000 Kilograms or 2,204.6 Pounds						
	DELIVERIES FROM ARGENTINA						
1919							
e	9,433.0	.....	......	......	......	9,433.0	$ 990,000.00
y	88,913.0	.....	......	......	1,367.0	90,280.0	9,513,000.00
gust	36,654.0	.....	......	......	18,633.0	55,287.0	6,271,000.00
Total	**135,000.0**	.....	......	......	**20,000.0**	**155,000.0**	**$16,774,000.00**
	DELIVERIES FROM NETHERLANDS						
e	......	**981.0**	**12,669.0**	**24,695.0**	**6,303.0**	**44,648.0**	**$ 9,784,989.00**
	DELIVERIES FROM SWITZERLAND						
y	......	.....	......	**28,886.0**	......	**28,886.0**	**$ 5,825,812.00**

* Tonnage partly estimated.

GERMANY-

Table 330

Summary of Arrivals of Relief Supplie

Operation	Table No.	Flour	Rice	Beans, Peas	Corn Grits
American Friends Service Committee—Direct Arrivals	167	4,863.0	1,958.0	2,617.0	......
American Friends Service Committee—E.C.F. Stock	331	......	2,383.9	2,809.4	......
German Government Donation	...*	12,663.0	......	......	......
A.R.A. Warehouses and European Children's Fund	...†	6,119.7	1,199.7	801.0	1,149.0
Total	......	**23,645.7**	**5,541.6**	**6,227.4**	**1,149.0**
Deduct Duplication ‡	......	......	400.1	179.8	......
Total Net Arrivals	323	**23,645.7**	**5,141.5**	**6,047.6**	**1,149.0**

§ The American Friends Service Committee received supplies from organizations other than the European Children's Fund, which makes it impossible to trace these specific commodities (by internal delivery receipts) to their final destination.

* Data supplied by the American Friends Service Committee. further detail available.

GERMANY-

Table 331

Detail by Steamers of Deliveries by European Children's Fun

Steamer or Source	Port of Sailing	Date of Arrival	Port of Arrival	Flour	Rice
		1920			
Clauseus	San Francisco	Mar. 2	Hamburg	....	.....
Bridges Stock	Hamburg	Mar. 11	Hamburg	....	.....
Gerrat	London	June 28	Hamburg	....	10.0
Minnekahda	New York	July 31	Hamburg	....	.....
Herefordshire	Rangoon	Aug. 18	Hamburg	....	319.6
Mette Jensen, I	New York	Aug. 22	Hamburg	....	.....
Mar Blanco, II	New York	Aug. 24	Hamburg	....	.....
Mar Rojo	New York	Sept. 16	Hamburg	....	.....
Sugar Ex-Czecho-Slovakia	Prague	Dec. 6	Hamburg	....	.....
Phillipi Purchase, I	Hamburg	Dec. 22	Hamburg	....	.....
Mar Del Norte	New York	Dec. 22	Hamburg	....	.....
Beursplein, II	New York	Dec. 27	Hamburg	....	.....
		1921			
Roath	New Orleans	Jan. 5	Hamburg	....	329.0
Paz de Epalza	New York	Jan. 9	Hamburg	....	.....
Norwich City	New York	Jan. 11	Hamburg	....	.....
Breiz Izel	New Orleans	Jan. 17	Hamburg	....	16.4
Clarksburg, I	New York	Jan. 18	Hamburg	....	.....
Mount Sterling *	Philadelphia	Jan. 22	Hamburg	....	.....
Leeds City, I	New York	Jan. 26	Hamburg	....	.....
Staude Bean Purchase	Hamburg	Jan. 31	Hamburg	....	.....
Bradford City, I	New York	Feb. 7	Hamburg	....	.....
Abraham Bean Purchase	Hamburg	Feb. 14	Hamburg	....	.....
Borga Bean Purchase	Hamburg	Feb. 24	Hamburg	....	.....
Homer City, II	New York	Feb. 25	Hamburg	....	.....
Haimon	New York	Feb. 25	Hamburg	....	.....
Sophie Rickmers	New Orleans	Feb. 26	Hamburg	....	107.0
Bradavon	New York	Mar. 3	Hamburg	....	.....
Mount Clay, II	New York	Mar. 5	Hamburg	....	.....
Andrea F. Luckenbach	New York	Mar. 12	Hamburg	....	.....
Marcus Bean Purchase, 1A	Hamburg	Mar. 19	Hamburg	....	.....
Kenowis	New Orleans	Mar. 21	Hamburg	....	198.8
Bradclyde, II	New Orleans	Mar. 23	Hamburg	....	.....
Harry Luckenbach	New York	Mar. 23	Hamburg	....	.....
Eastern City, II	New York	Mar. 27	Hamburg	....	.....

* Formerly S.S. Kerowlee.

nmary of Arrivals

)perations—Reconstruction Period, 1919–1924

·mmodities in Net Metric Tons of 1,000 Kilograms or 2,204.6 Pounds								Total Value
Pork ·roducts	Milk	Cocoa	Sugar	Misc. Food	Soap	Misc.	Total Tons	
,362.0	4,726.0	550.0	308.0	115.0	50.0	9.0	16,558.0	$ 4,526,624.76§
,435.6	4,499.8	433.4	600.0	.....	....	.....	12,162.1	2,202,365.16§
.....	.....	.....	4,170.0	.....	....	.....	16,833.0	2,392,021.25
,041.7	2,749.6	43.6	107.1	84.8	....	104.2	13,400.4	2,542,743.09
,839.3	**11,975.4**	**1,027.0**	**5,185.1**	**199.8**	**50.0**	**113.2**	**58,953.5**	**$11,663,754.26**
176.2	478.1	3.0	......	.....	....	.....	1,237.2	341,309.37
,663.1	**11,497.3**	**1,024.0**	**5,185.1**	**199.8**	**50.0**	**113.2**	**57,716.3**	**$11,322,444.89**

These commodities arrived on steamers listed in Tables 165 and 166.
·ries were made against food drafts, bulk sales, and sundry sales.

‡ This duplication is caused by giving the A.R.A. Warehouses full credit for all bulk sales and the American Friends Service Committee credit for delivery of same commodities in the child-feeding program.

ıerican Friends Service Committee

·European Stock—Reconstruction Period, 1919–1924

Contents of Cargoes in Net Metric Tons of 1,000 Kilograms or 2,204.6 Pounds									Total Value
Beans, Peas	Pork Products	Milk, Evap. and Cond.	Cocoa	Sugar	Corned Beef	Cotton Seed Meal	Soap	Total Tons	
738.3	.....	.....	....	.....	....	.....	....	738.3	$ 162,840.36
.....	.....	38.1	....	.....	....	.....	....	38.1	18,809.02
.....	.....	.....	....	.....	....	.....	....	10.0	2,026.82
.....	63.1	.....	....	.....	....	.....	....	63.1	37,519.58
.....	.....	.....	....	.....	....	.....	....	319.6	44,171.71
.....	15.8	.....	....	.....	....	.....	....	15.8	9,378.03
.....	.....	43.0	....	.....	....	.....	....	43.0	13,285.37
.....	.....	13.5	....	.....	....	.....	....	13.5	4,055.29
.....	.....	.....	....	600.0	....	.....	....	600.0	196,139.59
105.7	.....	.....	....	.....	....	.....	....	105.7	7,030.00
157.4	54.9	.....	39.4	.....	....	.....	....	251.7	34,077.23
.....	.....	42.8	....	.....	....	.....	....	42.8	10,707.74
.....	.....	.....	....	.....	....	.....	....	329.0	42,675.25
.....	29.9	.....	....	.....	....	.....	....	29.9	9,494.15
45.1	.....	.....	39.4	.....	....	.....	....	84.5	7,570.74
.....	.....	.....	....	.....	....	.....	....	16.4	2,442.73
.....	.....	214.5	....	.....	....	.....	....	214.5	49,381.98
.....	10.7	.....	....	.....	....	.....	....	10.7	3,988.99
.....	160.2	.....	41.0	.....	....	.....	....	201.2	44,773.51
10.0	.....	.....	....	.....	....	.....	....	10.0	701.70
.....	.....	435.5	....	.....	....	.....	....	435.5	98,415.84
90.4	.....	.....	....	.....	....	.....	....	90.4	6,500.93
274.6	.....	.....	....	.....	....	.....	....	274.6	19,399.90
54.2	.....	.....	....	.....	....	.....	....	54.2	5,572.55
.....	200.1	432.5	69.0	.....	....	.....	....	701.6	152,560.07
.....	.....	.....	....	.....	....	.....	....	107.0	7,437.16
.....	19.5	64.4	....	.....	....	.....	....	83.9	19,317.30
.....	.....	107.9	....	.....	....	.....	....	107.9	23,433.20
21.5	.....	.....	....	.....	....	.....	....	21.5	1,724.93
64.4	.....	.....	....	.....	....	.....	....	64.4	4,373.52
.....	.....	.....	....	.....	....	.....	....	198.8	10,178.50
.....	.....	108.6	....	.....	....	.....	....	108.6	23,608.52
.....	.....	107.5	....	.....	....	.....	....	107.5	24,876.40
.....	207.7	488.8	80.9	.....	....	.....	....	777.4	164,881.51

[*Continued on next page*]

Table 331—*Continued*

Detail by Steamers of Deliveries b

Steamer or Source	Port of Sailing	Date of Arrival	Port of Arrival	Flour	Rice
		1921			
Marcus Bean Purchase, 1B	Hamburg	Mar. 29	Hamburg	....	.....
Marcus Bean Purchase, 1C	Hamburg	Apr. 2	Hamburg	....	.....
Staude Bean Purchase, 3A	Hamburg	Apr. 9	Hamburg	....	.....
Staude Bean Purchase, 3B	Hamburg	Apr. 9	Hamburg	....	.....
Leeds City, II	New York	Apr. 12	Hamburg	....	.....
Minnekahda, III	Boston	Apr. 12	Hamburg	....	.....
Bradford City, II	New York	Apr. 23	Hamburg	....	.....
West Raritans	New Orleans	Apr. 25	Hamburg	....	618.0
King City	Galveston	Apr. 29	Hamburg	....	175.9
Ipswich Bean Purchase	Hamburg	Apr. 30	Hamburg	....	.....
Geron Bean Purchase, 7H—London	Hamburg	May 10	Hamburg	....	.....
Strathlorne	New Orleans	May 14	Hamburg	....	.....
Nemaha	Philadelphia	May 15	Hamburg	....	.....
West Camak	San Francisco	June 24	Hamburg	....	.....
Mexico, II	New Orleans	June 25	Hamburg	....	.....
Mount Clay, III	New York	July 5	Hamburg	....	.....
Oregonian, IV	New York	July 11	Hamburg	....	.....
Mount Carroll, II	New York	July 12	Hamburg	....	.....
Clarksburg, III	New York	Aug. 9	Hamburg	....	.....
Mystic, VI	New York	Aug. 15	Hamburg	....	.....
Noruega	New York	Sept. 15	Hamburg	....	.....
West Norranus	New Orleans	Sept. 23	Hamburg	....	258.5
Mongolia, V	New York	Dec. 12	Hamburg	....	.....
Westbrook, IV	New York	Dec. 22	Hamburg	....	.....
		1922			
Orleans	New Orleans	Jan. 8	Hamburg	....	177.8
Corson, IV	New York	Jan. 13	Hamburg	....	.....
Mount Clay, VI	New York	Feb. 7	Hamburg	....	.....
Mount Clinton, IV	New York	Mar. 7	Hamburg	....	.....
Oregonian, VIII	New York	Mar. 23	Hamburg	....	.....
City of Flint, III	Norfolk	Mar. 26	Hamburg	....	.....
Various Cargoes	U.S.A.	....	Hamburg	....	.....
Various Cargoes	U.S.A.	....	Hamburg	30.0	.....
Various Cargoes	U.S.A.	....	Danzig	16.4	15.3
King City, Alness, and Hans †	Galveston	....	Hamburg	....	.....
Various Cargoes	U.S.A.	....	Hamburg	....	173.0
Various Cargoes	U.S.A.	....	Hamburg	....	.....
Various Cargoes	U.S.A.	....	Hamburg	....	98.9
Total Deliveries				**46.4**	**2,498.2**
Less Deliveries to Other Countries ‡				46.4	114.3
Total Net Deliveries Used in Germany				....	**2,383.9**

* Shipped to Austria. Recorded as Bulk Sale No. 1082 to Vienna.

† Transshipped to Danzig on Mottlau, Aeolus, VIII; and Adele, I

erican Friends Service Committee

opean Children's Fund, Ex-European Stock

Contents of Cargoes in Net Metric Tons of 1,000 Kilograms or 2,204.6 Pounds

Beans, Peas	Pork Products	Milk, Evap. and Cond.	Cocoa	Sugar	Corned Beef	Cotton Seed Meal	Soap	Total Tons	Total Value
31.7	.....	.....	....	.....	....	.....	....	31.7	$ 2,355.77
43.3	.....	.....	....	.....	....	.....	....	43.3	2,692.06
10.4	.....	.....	....	.....	....	.....	....	10.4	473.01
55.7	.....	.....	....	.....	....	.....	....	55.7	2,988.44
355.2	253.8	467.9	43.0	.....	....	.....	....	1,119.9	205,234.45
.....	.....	.....	66.0	.....	....	.....	....	66.0	6,359.71
367.4	64.9	324.4	....	.....	....	.....	....	756.7	122,039.84
.....	.....	.....	....	.....	....	.....	....	618.0	38,152.79
.....	.....	.....	....	.....	....	.....	....	175.9	11,013.78
106.9	.....	.....	....	.....	....	.....	....	106.9	6,547.67
100.0	.....	.....	....	.....	....	.....	....	100.0	3,296.96
15.7	.....	.....	....	.....	....	.....	....	15.7	1,592.86
.....	.....	64.9	....	.....	....	.....	....	64.9	16,097.80
168.9	.....	.....	....	.....	....	.....	....	168.9	15,104.00
.2	.....	.....	....	.....	....	.....	....	.2	14.84
.....	.....	87.0	....	.....	....	.....	....	87.0	20,397.15
.....	.....	206.8	....	.....	....	.....	....	206.8	46,300.35
.....	.....	43.4	....	.....	....	.....	....	43.4	9,852.66
.....	.....	.....	85.6	.....	....	.....	....	85.6	8,104.35
.....	253.3	.....	....	.....	....	.....	....	253.3	58,536.06
.....	.....	797.1	....	.....	....	.....	....	797.1	159,262.17
.....	.....	.....	....	.....	....	.....	....	258.5	20,360.52
.....	74.8	86.7	....	.....	....	.....	....	161.5	45,356.25
.....	.....	135.0	....	.....	....	.....	....	135.0	34,421.41
.....	.....	.....	....	.....	....	.....	....	177.8	8,582.44
.....	.....	.....	....	.....	....	.....	13.6	13.6	3,976.10
.....	.....	117.5	....	.....	....	.....	....	117.5	29,959.45
.....	.....	13.2	....	.....	....	.....	....	13.2	3,365.66
.....	2.7	.....	....	.....	....	.....	....	2.7	616.36
.....	.2	.....	....	.....	....	.....	....	.2	45.17
.....	.....	15.4	....	49.0	....	.....	....	64.4	12,112.08*
.....	.....	84.2	....	30.0	....	.....	....	144.2	39,280.40
.....	35.5	.....	....	.....	10.6	.....	....	77.8	42,062.38
.....	.....	.....	....	.....	....	633.3	....	633.3	30,291.26
.....	.....	68.5	....	.....	....	.....	....	241.5	66,315.29
.....	169.0	.....	....	.....	....	.....	....	169.0	92,071.03
.....	.....	220.7	....	.....	....	.....	10.4	330.0	112,857.54
2,817.0	**1,616.1**	**4,829.8**	**464.3**	**679.0**	**10.6**	**633.3**	**24.0**	**13,618.7**	**$2,541,440.18§**
7.6	180.5	330.0	30.9	79.0	10.6	633.3	24.0	1,456.6	339,075.02
2,809.4	**1,435.6**	**4,499.8**	**433.4**	**600.0**	....	.....	....	**12,162.1**	**$2,202,365.16**

This is the net value. Insurance claims collected in the amount of 73.98 have been credited to above cargoes.

‡ Included in bulk sales to Russia, 468.0 M.T., value, $196,672.20; Poland, 740.0 M.T., value, $80,290.74; Austria, 248.6 M.T., value, $62,112.08.

Table 332

Detail by Months of Food Draft Deliveries

Time of Delivery	Number of Drafts Delivered A $10.00	B $50.00	C $10.00	D $50.00	Unit	Flour M.T.	Rice M.T.	Beans, Peas M.T.	Bacon 8-Lb. Piece	Bacon 16-Lb. Piece
1920										
March	212	41	13	..	....	5.174	......	1.933	209	41
April	5,099	721	343	49	....	109.696	......	41.797	5,036	741
May	7,331	1,388	933	92	....	185.709	......	70.737	7,336	1,389
June	6,430	1,072	812	188	....	160.396	......	61.065	5,003	1,786
July	10,382	1,810	1,207	123	....	251.383	53.335	42.501	10,616	1,693
August	10,092	1,542	1,063	150	....	231.262	88.436	......	10,332	1,422
September	7,523	1,413	1,099	99	....	191.716	72.971	......	7,523	1,413
October	7,499	1,200	1,171	78	....	187.715	69.339	1.556	7,499	1,200
November	7,170	1,193	1,492	94	....	177.874	67.943	.123	7,170	1,193
December	15,647	1,581	2,378	104	....	307.076	119.167	.060	15,647	1,581
1921										
January	9,028	1,005	1,853	84	....	189.931	73.521	.069	9,028	1,005
February	6,050	754	1,336	74	....	134.563	51.887	.069	6,050	754
March	5,978	565	1,025	58	....	117.295	45.558	.036	5,978	565
April	4,574	426	885	51	....	90.884	35.304	.040	4,574	426
May	3,733	420	714	50	....	79.207	30.611	.023	3,733	420
June	1,031	181	310	18	....	30.061	10.531	......	1,031	181
July	558	67	191	1	....	12.607	4.912	......	559	67
Grand Total in Units	**109,356**	**15,379**	**16,825**	**1,313**	Unit	**2,462.549**	**723.515**	**220.009**	**107,324**	**15,877**
Grand Total in Metric Tons	....	....	....	....	M.T.	**2,462.549**	**723.515**	**220.009**	**389.457**	**115.229**

* Detail from records of Hamburg Mission.

† Value of drafts or commodities delivered, $2,096,410.00.

Table 333

Detail by Months of Bulk Sa

Time of Delivery	Unit	Flour M.T.	Rice M.T.	Beans, Peas M.T.	Bacon A 8-Lb. Piece	Bacon B 16-Lb. Piece	Lard A 5-Lb. Tin	Lard B 10-Lb. Tin
1920								
February	....	.....	....	.....	...	..	..	..
April	....	.....	....	.....	...	..	..	..
May	....	1.000	....	.....	...	..	..	..
June	....	5.620	....	.....	...	..	..	1
July	....	1,502.338	....	.....	...	..	..	..
August	....	20.200	.900	575.000	...	..	..	..
October	....	9.899	.009	.100	202	22	5	280
November	....	5.232	.300	2.206	3	22	3	11
December	....	1.577	....	.....	12	11	4	..
1921								
January	....	.544	....	.....	9	..	2	..
February	....	.122	....	.....	2	..	..	..
March	....	1.907	.018	.....	12	1	15	3
April	....	19.832	....	.....	...	..	..	..
May	....	1.103	.080	.....	...	2	6	4
June	....	2.541	1.301	2.567	17	7	25	2
July–October	....	*—16.970*†	.005	.....	21	..	7	1
November–January, 1922	....	1.343	440.045	.....	...	3	10,739	12,860
1922								
February	....	1.847	.521	1.189	...	..	..	..
March	....	.....	....	.....	...	..	..	..
Total in Units	Unit	**1,558.135**	**443.179**	**581.062**	**278**	**68**	**10,806**	**13,162**
Total in Metric Tons	M.T.	**1,558.135**	**443.179**	**581.062**	**1.009**	**.494**	**24.508**	**59.704**

* Detail from records of Hamburg Port and Mission.

† Returned to stock.

.R.A. Warehouses and A.R.A.-European Children's Fund

Reconstruction Period, 1919–1924

Lard 5-Lb. Tin	Lard 10-Lb. Tin	Oil 1-Gal. Tin	Oil 5-Gal. Tin	Milk Cond. Case	Milk Evap. Case	Cocoa M.T.	Sugar M.T.	Corned Beef Case	Misc. Sacks Containers No.	Total Tons
41	41	13	..	80	...	.....	.....	7	713	.....
721	721	392	49	1,708	...	.....	.....	122	19,883	.....
1,388	1,388	1,025	92	2,935	...	.....	.....	232	33,107	.....
1,072	1,072	1,000	188	2,160	375	.....	.....	179	23,585	.....
1,810	1,810	1,330	123	159	3,806	.....	.....	302	33,552	.....
1,542	1,542	1,213	150	...	3,640	.....	.....	257	29,354	.....
1,413	1,413	1,198	99	1	3,040	.....	.....	235	24,668	.....
1,200	1,200	1,249	78	42	2,779	.....	.....	200	21,168	.....
1,193	1,193	1,586	94	63	2,792	5.986	15.654	199	.....	.....
1,581	1,581	2,457	104	289	4,598	11.541	28.135	263	.....	.....
1,005	1,005	1,962	84	103	2,954	7.075	17.415	168	.....	.....
754	754	1,410	74	72	2,098	4.936	12.354	126	92,632	.....
565	565	1,083	58	92	1,784	4.437	10.741	94	.....	.....
426	426	936	51	225	1,235	3.445	8.321	71	33,410	.....
420	420	764	50	111	1,159	2.928	7.267	70	9,365	.....
181	181	328	18	205	243	.969	.....	30	2,881	.....
70	67	191	1	206	...	.477	1.206	11	1,564	.....
15,382	**15,379**	**18,137**	**1,313**	**8,451**	**30,503**	**41.794**	**101.093**	**2,566**	**325,882**	.....
34.886	**69.759**	**61.702**	**22.334**	**161.082**	**664.132**	**41.794**	**101.093**	**83.808**	**91.433**	**5,242.782†**

R.A. Warehouses and A.R.A.-European Children's Fund

liveries*—Reconstruction Period, 1919–1924

Lard Substitute M.T.	Oil A 5-Gal. Tin	Oil B 10-Gal. Tin	Milk Evap. Case	Milk Cond. Case	Cocoa M.T.	Sugar M.T.	Misc. Food Case	Misc. Sacks Containers No.	Total Tons
......	..	..	11,285	...	....	....	..	.....	......
......	..	..	...	651	....	....	..	.....	......
......	..	..	80	10	....	....	..	.....	......
......	..	..	1	16,260	....	....	..	.....	......
......	..	..	...	...	....	....	..	.....	......
......	..	..	633	3	....	....	..	.....	......
......	9	..	67	44	....	....	28	.....	......
......	1	..	61	4	.113	.402	..	.....	......
......	1	..	41	17	.055	.260	..	.....	......
......	1	..	7	...	.054	.243	..	.....	......
......	..	..	3	...	....	.030	..	.....	......
......	5	..	24	7	.211	1.042	..	.....	......
......	1	..	6	2	.298	.673	..	.....	......
......	5	1	16	1	.135	.938	2 tins	.....	......
......	7	..	23	3	.784	1.177	..	28,170	......
......	5	..	...	3	.103	.636	6 tins	16	......
85.475	..	..	28,527	7	.030	.399	..	.....	......
......	..	..	...	...	....	.234	..	.....	......
......	..	..	5,396	...	....	....	..	.....	......
85.475	**35**	**1**	**46,170**	**17,012**	**1.783**	**6.034**	**29**	**28,186**	......
85.475	**.119**	**.017**	**1,005.252**	**324.103**	**1.783**	**6.034**	**.957‡**	**12.782**	**4,104.613§**

Soup, 1 case, .022; corned beef, .935.

§ Value of bulk sales or commodities delivered, $724,010.47.

Table 334

GREECE-

Operation	Table No.	Commodit-				
		Flour	Grain	Rice	Beans, Peas	Corn Grits
		RECONSTRUCTIC				
American Red Cross	335	**12,886.0**	**2,451.0**	**203.0**	**1,269.0**	**2,642.0**

GREECE-

Detail by Steamers of Relief Supplies Furnished by t (cf. Table 158)

Table 335

Arrival No.	Steamer	Port of Sailing	Date of Arrival	Port of Arrival	Flour	Wheat Grain	Rice
			1922				
1	Coeur d'Alene	New York	Dec. 3	Piraeus	140.0	.....	199.0
2	Stuyvesant	New York	Dec. 4	Piraeus	555.0	.....	.....
3	Hog Island, I.	New York	Dec. 5	Piraeus	1,731.0	.....	.....
4	Manhattan Island, I.	New York	Dec. 20	Piraeus	490.0	.....	4.0
			1923				
5	Maid of Psara	New York	Jan. 10	Piraeus	998.0	.....	.....
6	Manitowac	New York	Jan. 15	Piraeus	1,455.0	981.0	.....
7	Sabotawan, I.	New York	Feb. 1	Piraeus	.....	1,470.0	.....
8	Abron	New York	Feb. 13	Piraeus	4,908.0	.....	.....
9	West Gotomska	New York	Mar. 24	Piraeus	2,138.0	.....	.....
10	Corson	New York	Apr. 3	Piraeus	367.0	.....	.....
11	Hog Island, II.	New York	Apr. 18	Piraeus	32.0	.....	.....
12	Cohasset	New York	May 14	Piraeus	72.0	.....	.....
13	Sabotawan, II	New York	May 14	Piraeus	.....	.....	.....
14	Ossa	New York	May 28	Piraeus	.....	.....	.....
15	Manhattan Island, II.	New York	May 31	Piraeus	.....	.....	.....
16	Winona	New York	May 31	Piraeus	.....	.....	.....
	Value of Commodities				.....	.....	.....
	Freight †				.....	.....	.....
	Miscellaneous Expense †				.....	.....	.....
	Total				**12,886.0**	**2,451.0**	**203.0**

* Value of cargoes all quoted f.o.b. New York. All insurance, balance of freight, and miscellaneous expenses were handled directly by the American Red Cross, Washington, D.C.

† Paid from funds held by the European Children's Fund.

ummary of Relief Deliveries

Net Metric Tons of 1,000 Kilograms or 2,204.6 Pounds							
Pork Products	Milk	Cocoa	Sugar	Misc. Food	Soap	Total Tons	Total Value
ERIOD							
102.0	**162.0**	**409.0**	**203.0**	**45.0**	**2.0**	**20,374.0**	**$1,211,949.95**

merican Red Cross

merican Red Cross in Co-operation with the A.R.A.-E.C.F.
econstruction Period, 1919–1924

Contents of Cargoes in Net Metric Tons of 1,000 Kilograms or 2,204.6 Pounds									
Beans, Peas	Corn Grits	Pork Products	Milk	Cocoa	Sugar	Misc. Food	Soap	Total Tons	Total Value *
608.0	41.0	102.0	....	60.0	203.0	4.0	...	1,357.0	$ 120,823.55
451.0	.....	....	....	1.0	.....	....	...	1,007.0	68,620.32
210.0	.....	....	....	307.0	.....	41.0	...	2,289.0	157,958.88
.....	61.0	....	....	41.0	.....	....	...	596.0	36,613.90
.....	.....	....	....	....	.....	....	...	998.0	69,633.87
.....	.....	....	....	....	.....	....	2.0	2,438.0	150,377.72
.....	.....	....	....	....	.....	....	...	1,470.0	73,575.00
.....	.....	....	....	....	.....	....	...	4,908.0	233,582.00
.....	766.0	....	....	....	.....	....	...	2,904.0	129,269.58
.....	.....	....	....	....	.....	....	...	367.0	16,867.17
.....	701.0	....	....	....	.....	....	...	733.0	30,531.05
.....	.....	....	....	....	.....	....	...	72.0	3,645.00
.....	847.0	....	39.0	....	.....	....	...	886.0	42,873.81
.....	.....	....	46.0	....	.....	....	...	46.0	14,592.00
.....	226.0	....	39.0	....	.....	....	...	265.0	17,200.00
.....	.....	....	38.0	....	.....	....	...	38.0	12,000.00
.....	.....	....	....	....	.....	....	...	.....	**$1,178,163.85**
.....	.....	....	....	....	.....	....	...	.....	32,070.95
.....	.....	....	....	....	.....	....	...	.....	1,715.15
1,269.0	**2,642.0**	**102.0**	**162.0**	**409.0**	**203.0**	**45.0**	**2.0**	**20,374.0**	**$1,211,949.95**

Table 336

HUNGARY-

Operation	Table No.	Flour	Rice	Beans, Peas	Corn Grits
					ARMISTIC
A.R.A.—Cash Settlement	337	.....	.....	.....	....
					RECONSTRUCTIO
A.R.A.—President's National Security and Defense Fund	339, 345	98.0	.....	.....	....
A.R.A.-European Children's Fund	340, 344	459.2	430.2	326.9	23.4
Hungarian Government Donation	342, 345	1,441.0	.....	242.0	....
Total Children's Relief	163	**1,998.2**	**430.2**	**568.9**	**23.4**
U.S. Grain Corporation (Act of Congress, March 30, 1920)	343	14,114.0	.....	.....	....
United Kingdom—Finance on Freight, Insurance, etc.	343n	.....	.....	.....	....
A.R.A.W. and A.R.A.-E.C.F.—Food Drafts and Bulk Sales	349–50	672.3	208.4	73.5	....
A.R.A.-European Children's Fund—Sale of Surplus Clothing	346	.....	.....	.....	....
Commonwealth Fund—Intelligentsia Clothing	346	.....	.....	.....	....
Total Other than Children's Relief	...	**14,786.3**	**208.4**	**73.5**	....
Total Deliveries, Reconstruction Period	149	**16,784.5**	**638.6**	**642.4**	**23.4**
Grand Total Relief Deliveries	102	**16,784.5**	**638.6**	**642.4**	**23.4**

HUNGARY-

Table 337

Detail by Source of Commodities Sold for Cash

Arrival No.*	Source	Point of Origin	Date of Arrival	Port of Arrival	Contents of Cargoes in Net Metric Tons of 1,000 Kilograms or 2,204.6 Pound: Pork Products	Lard	Lard Substitute	Total Tons	Total Value
			1919						
319	Q.M. Inv. 32 †	(U.S.A.)	April	Trieste	98.7	192.2	8.1	299.0	$230,792.
319	Q.M. Inv. 47 †	(U.S.A.)	April	Trieste	16.0	4.1	...	20.1	14,727.
	Total Sales—to Table 120	....	....	....	**114.7**	**196.3**	**8.1**	**319.1**	**$245,519.**

* Arrival numbers from Table 111.

† Purchased from U.S. Army stock.

HUNGARY-

Table 338

Summary of Arrivals by Operations

Operation	Table No.	Flour	Rice	Beans, Peas
A.R.A.—President's National Security and Defense Fund	339	98.0	.....	.....
A.R.A.-European Children's Fund	340	1,131.5	638.6	400.4
A.R.A.-European Children's Fund, Clothing	341	......	.....	.....
Hungarian Government Donation	342	1,441.0	.....	242.0
U.S. Grain Corporation (Act of Congress, March 30, 1920)	343	14,114.0	.....	.....
United Kingdom—Freight, Insurance, Misc. Charges	343n	......	.....	.....
Total	......	**16,784.5**	**638.6**	**642.4**

* Cf. Table 336. These items total 4,940.4 metric tons. Deliveries made by European Children's Fund, for children's relief, 3,298.1; American Relief Administration Warehouses, for food drafts and bulk sa 1,629.6; clothing deliveries other than children's relief, 12.7.

mmary of Relief Deliveries

ommodities in Net Metric Tons of 1,000 Kilograms or 2,204.6 Pounds

Pork Products	Milk	Cocoa	Sugar	Misc. Food	Soap	Clothing and Misc.	Total Tons	Total Value
RIOD								
319.1	.....	....	.....	....	....	.....	**319.1**	**$ 245,519.96**
RIOD								
.....	95.0	27.0	30.0	....	37.0	.....	287.0	$ 101,325.00
135.0	1,049.0	125.6	476.3	55.2	....	217.3	3,298.1	1,190,832.53
50.0	.....	....	.....	....	....	.....	1,733.0	265,806.84
185.0	**1,144.0**	**152.6**	**506.3**	**55.2**	**37.0**	**217.3**	**5,318.1**	**$1,557,964.37**
.....	.....	....	.....	....	....	.....	14,114.0	$1,685,835.61
.....	.....	....	.....	....	....	.....	......	564,561.60
173.9	297.9	20.4	121.6	50.6	....	11.0	1,629.6	527,939.41
.....	.....	....	.....	....	....	.2	.2	790.83
.....	.....	....	.....	....	....	12.5	12.5	24,527.59
173.9	**297.9**	**20.4**	**121.6**	**50.6**	....	**23.7**	**15,756.3**	**$2,803,655.04**
358.9	**1,441.9**	**173.0**	**627.9**	**105.8**	**37.0**	**241.0**	**21,074.4**	**$4,361,619.41**
678.0	**1,441.9**	**173.0**	**627.9**	**105.8**	**37.0**	**241.0**	**21,393.5**	**$4,607,139.37**

nerican Relief Administration

mistice Period, 1919

mmary of Arrivals

construction Period, 1919–1924

Commodities in Net Metric Tons of 1,000 Kilograms or 2,204.6 Pounds

Corn Grits	Pork Products	Milk	Cocoa	Sugar	Misc. Food	Soap	Clothing and Misc.	Total Tons	Total Value
....	.....	95.0	27.0	30.0	.....	37.0	.....	287.0	$ 101,325.00
23.4	308.9	1,346.9	146.0	597.9	105.8	....	11.0	4,710.4*	1,181,864.84
....	.....	......	.....	.....	.....	....	230.0	230.0*	449,665.62
....	50.0	......	.....	.....	.....	....	.....	1,733.0	265,806.84
....	.....	......	.....	.....	.....	....	.....	14,114.0	1,685,835.61
....	.....	......	.....	.....	.....	....	.....	......	564,561.60
23.4	**358.9**	**1,441.9**	**173.0**	**627.9**	**105.8**	**37.0**	**241.0**	**21,074.4**	**$4,249,059.51**

HUNGARY—

Table 339

Detail by Steamers of Children's Relief Arrivals Paid for from th

Steamer	Port of Sailing	Date of Arrival	Port of Arrival	Flour	Rice	Beans, Peas	Corn Grits
		1919					
Neuse	New York	Apr. 24	Trieste	98.0	....	....	....
Sonnenfels	New York	Aug. 25	Trieste	....	....	....	....
Brisgravia	New York	Aug. 27	Trieste	....	....	....	....
Total				**98.0**	....	....	....

* Cf. Table 116.

HUNGARY—

Table 340

Detail by Steamers or Source of Arrivals

Steamer or Source *	Port of Sailing	Date of Arrival	Port of Arrival	Flour
		1919		
Stock	(Vienna)	Oct. 31	(Budapest)	....
Stock	(Vienna)	Dec. 8	(Budapest)	....
Stock	(Vienna)	Dec. 31	(Budapest)	....
		1920		
Cripple Creek	New York	Jan. 4	Hamburg	700.5
Inverawe	Liverpool	Jan. 23	Hamburg	....
Stock (Ex-Rotterdam)	(Vienna)	Feb. 7	(Budapest)	....
Stock (Ex-Antwerp)	(Vienna)	Feb. 7	(Budapest)	....
Stock (Ex-Suffolk, arr. Rotterdam, Jan. 9)	(Vienna)	Feb. 7	(Budapest)	....
Stock (Ex-Morlais, arr. Hamburg, Dec. 29, 1919)	(Vienna)	Feb. 7	(Budapest)	....
Zealand	Liverpool	Feb. 10	Hamburg	....
Stock (Ex-Suffolk, arr. Rotterdam, Jan. 9)	(Vienna)	Feb. 21	(Budapest)	....
Manchuria, I	New York	Feb. 26	Hamburg	....
Keresan, II	New York	Feb. 27	Hamburg	....
Stock (Ex-Rotterdam)	(Vienna)	Feb. 29	(Budapest)	....
Stock (Ex-Morlais, arr. Hamburg, Dec. 29, 1919)	(Vienna)	Feb. 29	(Budapest)	....
Clauseus	San Francisco	Mar. 2	Hamburg	....
Mar Caspio	New York	Mar. 7	Hamburg	....
Mongolia	New York	Mar. 10	Hamburg	....
Bridges Stock Purchase	Hamburg	Mar. 11	Hamburg	....
Stock	(Vienna)	Mar. 14	(Budapest)	....
Kerowlee	New York	Mar. 29	Hamburg	....
Stock	(Vienna)	Mar. 31	(Budapest)	....
Stock	(Vienna)	Apr. 7	(Budapest)	....
Stock	(Vienna)	Apr. 21	(Budapest)	....
Stock	(Vienna)	Apr. 30	(Budapest)	....
Carib, III	New York	May 23	Hamburg	....
West Isleta	Boston	June 18	Hamburg	....
Bellerose	Philadelphia	Aug. 2	Hamburg	....
Herefordshire	Rangoon	Aug. 18	Hamburg	....
Stock	(Vienna)	Nov. 7	(Budapest)	....
Stock, V.B. 1	(Vienna)	Nov. 14	(Budapest)	....
Stock, V.B. 2	(Vienna)	Dec. 21	(Budapest)	....
		1921		
Stock, V.B. 3	(Vienna)	Jan. 14	(Budapest)	....
Stock, V.B. 6	(Vienna)	Feb. 18	(Budapest)	....
Stock, V.B. 7	(Vienna)	Feb. 25	(Budapest)	....
Stock, V.B. 8	(Vienna)	Mar. 18	(Budapest)	93.
Stock, V.B. 9	(Vienna)	Mar. 25	(Budapest)	....
Stock, —	(Vienna)	Mar. ..	(Budapest)	....
Eemdijk (forwarded from Vienna)	Seattle	Apr. 22	Hamburg	....

* Stock shipments are ex-various cargoes that sailed from the United States and were allocated to Austria.
V. B. designates Vienna to Budapest shipments.

** Detail of miscellaneous food indicated by the following inde
[a], corned beef; [b], salmon; [c], chocolate, ex–S.S. Naamhok; [d], herring

erican Relief Administration

ident's National Security and Defense Fund*—Reconstruction Period, 1919–1924

nts of Cargoes in Net Metric Tons of 1,000 Kilograms or 2,204.6 Pounds								Total Value
Pork roducts	Milk	Cocoa	Sugar	Misc. Food	Soap	Clothing and Misc.	Total Tons	
....	95.0	27.0	....	....	....	....	220.0	$ 82,910.00
....	....	....	30.0	....	....	....	30.0	7,500.00
....	....	....	....	....	37.0	....	37.0	10,915.00
....	**95.0**	**27.0**	**30.0**	**....**	**37.0**	**....**	**287.0**	**$101,325.00**

.A.-European Children's Fund

ef Commodities—Reconstruction Period, 1919–1924

Contents of Cargoes in Net Metric Tons of 1,000 Kilograms or 2,204.6 Pounds											Total Value
ice	Beans, Peas	Corn Grits	Pork Products	Milk	Cocoa	Sugar	Misc. Food **	Soap	Misc. Sacks, Containers, etc.	Total Tons	
0.0	65.0	....	15.0	104.0	15.0	40.0	....	...	...	289.0	$ 99,775.10
...	....	....	....	116.0	....	40.0	....	...	...	156.0	68,287.60
0.0	....	....	....	....	....	....	....	...	...	50.0	12,525.00
...	....	....	....	....	....	....	....	...	.7	701.2	102,000.37
...	....	....	....	....	....	....	18.8[a]	...	...	18.8	10,940.99
...	....	....	....	....	10.0	....	....	...	...	10.0	4,760.00
...	....	....	....	....	....	66.0	....	...	...	66.0	16,017.50
...	14.0	....	....	....	....	....	....	...	...	14.0	2,107.00
6.0	....	....	....	....	....	....	....	...	...	16.0	4,008.00
...	....	....	....	....	....	....	13.9[a]	...	...	13.9	8,106.88
...	30.0	....	....	....	....	....	....	...	...	30.0	4,515.00
...	....	....	61.8	....	....	....	....	...	...	61.8	41,668.62
...	....	....	....	....	....	....	....	...	1.8	1.8	882.36
....	....	....	....	99.0	14.0	....	....	...	...	113.0	56,659.00
29.0	....	....	....	....	....	....	....	...	...	29.0	7,264.50
....	250.1	....	....	....	....	....	....	...	...	250.1	48,991.59
....	....	....	....	....	....	....	....	...	.4	.4	542.04
....	....	....	47.8	....	....	....	....	...	...	47.8	37,636.28
....	....	....	....	171.5	....	....	....	...	...	171.5	84,665.26
39.0	30.0†	....	....	....	....	....	....	...	...	69.0	14,284.50
....	....	....	23.1	....	....	....	....	...	...	23.1	15,617.41
....	30.0‡	....	....	....	....	....	....	...	...	30.0	4,515.00
51.0	51.0	....	....	88.0	....	....	....	...	...	190.0	64,891.00
46.0	100.0	....	....	136.0	17.0	57.0	....	...	...	356.0	117,178.30
....	....	....	20.0	....	....	....	....	...	...	20.0	10,800.00
....	....	....	....	....	....	....	....	...	.6	.6	958.60
....	....	....	7.6	....	....	....	....	...	...	7.6	6,153.61
....	....	....	14.8	....	....	....	....	...	...	14.8	11,967.22
25.0	....	....	....	....	....	....	....	...	...	25.0	3,255.05
....	....	....	....	....	1.8	5.0	....	...	...	6.8	1,298.22
30.1	....	....	7.4	32.7	....	....	....	...	...	70.2	17,720.93
5.8	....	....	....	21.6	3.4	13.9	....	2.7	...	47.4	10,340.97
12.2	....	....	12.3	22.0	2.3	10.1	....	...	...	58.9	13,551.70
25.5	....	....	10.0	43.5	5.0	40.8	....	...	...	124.8	26,511.31
16.2	....	....	7.0	27.2	2.3	35.7	....	...	...	88.4	18,912.38
....	....	....	....	....	....	....	....	...	...	93.6	13,670.47
20.4	....	....	9.4	65.3	15.2	35.6	....	...	...	145.9	31,198.46
....	....	....	....	....	....	....	5.0[a]	...	...	5.0	2,912.50
....	....	....	....	....	....	....	50.0[b]	...	...	50.0	7,967.25

All bean flour.

‡ Includes 16 metric tons of bean flour.

[*Continued on next page*]

HUNGARY-

Table 340—*Continued*

Detail by Steamers or Source c

Steamer or Source	Port of Sailing	Date of Arrival	Port of Arrival	Flour
		1921		
Local Purchase	(Budapest)	Apr. 22	(Budapest)	29.0
Stock, V.B. 11	(Vienna)	Apr. 22	(Budapest)	....
Stock, V.B. 12	(Vienna)	May 13	(Budapest)	59.6
Stock, V.B. 15	(Vienna)	May 27	(Budapest)	....
Stock, V.B. 16	(Vienna)	May 27	(Budapest)	98.4
Stock, V.B. 19	(Vienna)	June 24	(Budapest)	....
Stock, V.B. 20	(Vienna)	June 24	(Budapest)	62.3
Stock, V.B. 21	(Vienna)	June 24	(Budapest)	....
Stock, V.B. 24	(Vienna)	July 22	(Budapest)	32.0
Stock, V.B. 26	(Vienna)	Aug. 12	(Budapest)	....
Local Purchase	(Budapest)	Aug. 19	(Budapest)	10.2
Stock, V.B. 28	(Vienna)	Aug. 26	(Budapest)	....
Local Purchase	(Budapest)	Aug. 26	(Budapest)	10.2
Stock, V.B. 30	(Vienna)	Aug. 31	(Budapest)	....
Stock, V.B. 31	(Vienna)	Sept. 16	(Budapest)	35.7
Stock, V.B. 36	(Vienna)	Nov. 4	(Budapest)	....
Stock, V.B. 37	(Vienna)	Nov. 4	(Budapest)	....
Stock, V.B. 39	(Vienna)	Nov. 19	(Budapest)	....
Stock, V.B. 46	(Vienna)	Dec. 23	(Budapest)	....
		1922		
Stock, V.B. 47	(Vienna)	Jan. 6	(Budapest)	....
Donation	(U.S.A.)	......	(Budapest)	....
Outturn Overages	....	......	(Budapest)	....
Local Purchase	(Budapest)	......	(Budapest)	....
Total	....	....	....	**1,131.5**
Deduct Transfers:				
To Austria §	....	....	....	.....
To Jugoslavia ††	....	....	....	.....
Total Transfers	....	....	....	.....
Total Net Arrivals	....	....	....	**1,131.5**

§ Cf. Table 213.

†† Cf. Table 359, page 662.

HUNGARY-

Table 341*

Detail by Steamers or Source of Clothi

Steamer or Source	Port of Sailing	Date of Arrival	Port of Arrival	Shoes (Pairs)	Laces (Pairs)	Stockings (Pairs)	Woolens (Yards)
		1919					
Batavier 3, I	London	Nov. 30	Rotterdam	....	21,600	....	.....
Batavier 6, II	London	Dec. 9	Rotterdam	....	32,400	....	7,726.5
Batavier 3, III	London	Dec. 14	Rotterdam	8,682	.....	....	.....
Batavier 6, III	London	Dec. 18	Rotterdam	27,754	.....	....	16,497.5
Batavier 3, IV	London	Dec. 21	Rotterdam	....	.....	....	3,996.5
Batavier 6, IV	London	Dec. 25	Rotterdam	2,890	.....	11,520	.....
Julia Luckenbach	New York	Dec. 28	Rotterdam	....	.....	....	94,998.7
Continental Purchase	Antwerp	Dec. 29	Rotterdam	....	.....	12,000	.....
		1920					
Batavier 6, V	London	Jan. 1	Rotterdam	....	.....	2,910	.....
Maine	New York	Jan. 6	Rotterdam	192	192	....	.....
Batavier 6, VI	London	Jan. 8	Rotterdam	....	.....	....	2,116.5
Bellingham	New York	Jan. 13	Rotterdam	11,808	11,808	....	.....
Continental Purchase	Antwerp	Jan. 20	Rotterdam	....	.....	15,368	.....
Batavier 6, VII	London	Jan. 29	Rotterdam	....	.....	2,370	.....
Batavier 4, III	London	Feb. 8	Rotterdam	....	.....	5,832	.....

* Cf. Table 346.

R.A.-European Children's Fund

ivals of Relief Commodities

Contents of Cargoes in Net Metric Tons of 1,000 Kilograms or 2,204.6 Pounds

Rice	Beans, Peas	Corn Grits	Pork Products	Milk	Cocoa	Sugar	Misc. Food	Soap	Misc. Sacks, Containers, etc.	Total Tons	Total Value
....	....	....	....	....	....	....	....	...	...	29.0	$ 1,740.00
0.8	....	....	....	152.4	15.2	81.3	....	...	...	299.7	62,586.57
15.4	....	....	5.1	10.9	3.0	5.1	4.5[c]	...	...	103.6	18,115.67
25.3	....	....	18.1	43.5	2.0	30.4	....	...	...	119.3	25,696.43
....	....	....	....	....	....	....	....	...	...	98.4	14,371.52
....	....	....	....	....	....	....	13.3[d]	...	...	13.3	2,261.76
33.1	....	....	....	54.4	6.1	....	....	...	...	155.9	26,672.33
....	....	....	....	....	....	25.4	....	...	...	25.4	4,671.05
12.2	....	....	....	21.8	7.1	31.9	....	...	...	105.0	12,942.76
20.1	....	....	....	32.7	20.3	20.0	....	...	...	93.1	13,283.03
....	....	....	....	....	....	....	....	...	...	10.2	819.37
....	....	....	....	....	....	8.9	....	...	...	8.9	1,100.16
....	....	....	....	....	....	....	....	...	...	10.2	819.37
20.0	....	....	....	65.3	5.1	21.0	....	...	...	111.4	19,020.56
....	....	....	....	....	....	....	....	...	...	35.7	2,867.78
....	....	....	.6	....	....	....	....	...	...	.6	114.75
....	....	....	1.4	....	....	....	....	...	...	1.4	267.76
....	....	....	8.1	....	....	....	....	...	...	8.1	1,549.18
17.5	....	17.4	10.2	54.4	....	30.0	....	...	...	129.5	19,941.32
7.1	....	6.0	11.0	43.5	1.2	7.6	....	...	...	76.4	13,689.39
....	....	....	18.1	....	....	....	....	...	...	18.1	......
....	....	....	.1	....	....	....	.3	...	7.5	7.9	......
26.6	....	....	....	....	....	....	....	...	...	26.6	3,999.05
44.3	**570.1**	**23.4**	**308.9**	**1,405.7**	**146.0**	**605.7**	**105.8**	**2.7**	**11.0**	**4,955.1**	**$1,251,587.78**
....	169.7	....	....	57.2	....	....	....	...	...	226.9	$ 62,509.06
5.7	....	....	....	1.6	....	7.8	....	2.7	...	17.8	7,213.88
5.7	**169.7**	....	....	**58.8**	....	**7.8**	....	**2.7**	...	**244.7**	**$ 69,722.94**
38.6	**400.4**	**23.4**	**308.9**	**1,346.9**	**146.0**	**597.9**	**105.8**	...	**11.0**	**4,710.4**	**$1,181,864.84**

R.A.-European Children's Fund

rivals—Reconstruction Period, 1919–1924

Thread (Yards)	Thread (Spools)	Needles (No.)	Buttons (No.)	Blouses (No.)	Linings (Yards)	Underwear (Garments)	Total Metric Tons	Total Value
......	....	....	......	....	.....	....	.3	$ 239.01
......	....	....	......	....	.....	....	4.2	11,404.41
......	....	....	......	....	.....	....	4.5	16,573.31
......	....	....	......	....	.....	....	21.2	77,881.87
......	....	....	......	....	.....	....	1.3	5,679.12
......	....	....	......	....	.....	....	2.3	9,349.67
9,808,000	....	50,000	264,384	....	.....	....	45.2	116,437.98
......	....	....	......	....	.....	....	1.0	5,551.80
......	....	....	......	....	.....	....	.2	1,401.09
......	....	....	......	....	.....	....	.1	482.92
......	....	....	......	....	.....	....	.9	3,027.55
......	....	....	......	....	.....	....	16.0	30,107.46
......	....	....	......	....	.....	....	1.4	7,043.38
......	....	....	......	....	.....	....	.1	1,185.28
......	....	....	......	....	.....	....	.6	2,027.17

[*Continued on next page*]

Table 341—*Continued*

Detail by Steamers or Sourc

Steamer or Source	Port of Sailing	Date of Arrival	Port of Arrival	Shoes (Pairs)	Laces (Pairs)	Stockings (Pairs)	Woolens (Yards)
		1921					
Oregonian, II	New York	Apr. 5	Hamburg	....	.....	....	......
Mount Carroll, I	New York	May 30	Hamburg	....	.....	....	58,668.50
Clarksburg, II	New York	June 13	Hamburg	....	.....	....	58,559.00
Mount Clinton, I	New York	July 19	Hamburg	....	.....	....	6,824.00
Hawaiian, IV	New York	Aug. 22	Hamburg	15,500	.....	....	......
Oregonian, V (Vienna Stock)	New York	Aug. 28	Hamburg	....	.....	....	......
Mount Carroll, III	New York	Aug. 30	Hamburg	7,583	.....	....	......
King City, II †	New York	Sept. 1	Hamburg	2,500	.....	....	......
Sudburg, II	New York	Sept. 13	Hamburg	26,888	.....	....	......
Ipswich, III †	New York	Sept. 19	Hamburg	....	.....	4,984	9,391.00
Dakotan	New York	Sept. 24	Hamburg	....	.....	48,653	......
Orla †	New York	Sept. 29	Hamburg	....	.....	....	......
Virginian †	New York	Oct. 1	Hamburg	....	.....	....	......
Total Arrivals	....	....	....	**103,797**	**66,000**	**103,637**	**258,778.25**
Deduct Delivery to Dr. Reeder, Belgrade	....	....	....	....	.....	....	......
Total Net Arrivals	....	....	....	**103,797**	**66,000**	**103,637**	**258,778.25**

† Steamers carrying clothing for Intelligentsia, purchased by Commonwealth Fund, New York.

HUNGARY—A.R.A.-European Children's Fund

Detail by Months of Hungarian Government Donations for Child Feeding Reconstruction Period, 1919–1924

Table 342

Date of Delivery	Commodities in Net Metric Tons of 1,000 Kilograms or 2,204.6 Pounds				Total Value
	Flour	Beans, Peas	Pork Products	Total Tons	
1919					
Commencement to December	155.0	....	....	155.0	$ 24,793.
1920					
January–February	338.0	....	39.0	377.0	74,190.
March	155.0	....	4.0	159.0	26,857.
April	84.0	....	7.0	91.0	17,048.
May–July	74.0	....	....	74.0	11,837.
August	262.0	....	....	262.0	41,971.
September–November	149.0	....	....	149.0	22,994.
December	1.0	....	....	1.0	136.
1921					
January	.....	10.0	....	10.0	744.
February	.....	41.0	....	41.0	3,631.
March	.....	18.0	....	18.0	1,552.
April	.....	40.0	....	40.0	3,975.
May	.....	36.0	....	36.0	5,764.
June	.....	19.0	....	19.0	2,109.
July	25.0	31.0	....	56.0	5,576.
August	3.0	....	....	3.0	230.
September	98.0	6.0	....	104.0	11,147.
October	.....	18.0	....	18.0	1,586.
November	97.0	5.0	....	102.0	8,063.
December	.....	18.0	....	18.0	1,595.
Total	**1,441.0**	**242.0**	**50.0**	**1,733.0**	**$265,806.**

R.A.-European Children's Fund

Clothing Arrivals

Thread (Yards)	Thread (Spools)	Needles (No.)	Buttons (No.)	Blouses (No.)	Linings (Yards)	Underwear (Garments)	Total Metric Tons	Total Value
......	....	....	......	4,940	.....	....	8.2	$ 4,155.33
......	....	....	......	....	.....	....	31.6	21,553.01
......	....	....	......	....	.....	....	31.1	22,615.72
......	....	....	......	....	.....	....	4.0	2,667.41
......	....	....	......	....	.....	....	13.3	22,657.20
......	7,648	5,000	672,912	....	.....	....	1.6	3,575.11
......	....	....	......	....	.....	....	5.3	10,180.37
......	....	....	......	....	.....	....	4.4	6,090.91
......	....	....	......	....	.....	....	20.3	41,679.08
......	....	....	......	....	15,707	....	6.7	14,807.26
......	....	....	......	....	.....	....	4.4	6,965.90
......	....	....	......	....	.....	3,400	.8	2,242.05
......	....	....	......	....	.....	1,600	.6	1,387.37
,808,000	**7,648**	**55,000**	**937,296**	**4,940**	**15,707**	**5,000**	**231.6**	**$450,968.74**
......	....	....	......	1,000	.....	....	1.6	1,303.12
,808,000	**7,648**	**55,000**	**937,296**	**3,940**	**15,707**	**5,000**	**230.0**	**$449,665.62**

HUNGARY—U.S. Grain Corporation†

Detail by Steamers of Flour Deliveries under Act of Congress, March 30, 1920

Table 343

Reconstruction Period, 1919–1924

Steamer	Date of Sailing	Flour Barrels	Flour Pounds	Total Tons *	Total Value
	1920				
enstone	May 6	53,875	...	4,789.7	$ 578,944.81
anga	May 15	50,002	28	4,445.4	537,334.92
estone	May 30	54,876	84	4,878.9	569,555.88
Total Deliveries	....	**158,753**	**112**	**14,114.0**	**$1,685,835.61‡**

Cf. Table 157.

* Contents of cargoes in net metric tons of 1,000 kilograms or 2,204.6 nds.

‡ Value quoted, f.o.b. U.S.A. ports. Freight and other transportation charges were paid by the United Kingdom in the amount of $564,561.60.

HUNGARY-

Table 344*

Summary by Operations of Reli

Operation	Table No.	Flour	Rice	Beans, Peas	Corn Grits
A.R.A.-European Children's Fund—Child Feeding	345	1,998.2	430.2	568.9	23.4
A.R.A.-European Children's Fund—Clothing	346	.....	.....	.....	....
A.R.A.W. and A.R.A.-E.C.F.—Food Drafts	349	452.7	89.3	73.5	....
A.R.A.W. and A.R.A.-E.C.F.—Bulk Sales	350	219.6	119.1	.....	....
U.S. Grain Corporation (Act of Congress, March 30, 1920)	...†	14,114.0	.....	.....	....
United Kingdom—Freight, Insurance, etc	...	.....	.....	.....	....
Total	......	**16,784.5**	**638.6**	**642.4**	**23.4**

* For division to organizations supplying the finance, cf. Table 336.

† Delivered f.o.b. U.S.A. ports, therefore no detail of internal liveries is available.

HUNGARY-

Table 345

Detail by Months, by Districts or Kitchens, of Internal Deliveri

Receipt No.	District or Kitchen	Date	Flour	Rice	Beans, Peas
Series 1		1919			
1	Budapest and Environs	Nov. 15	.....	50.000	65.000
		1920			
2	Budapest and Environs	Jan. 13	.....	50.000	....
3	Budapest and Environs	Mar. 10	.....	45.000	44.000
4	Budapest and Environs	Apr. 9	.....	90.000	111.000
6	Budapest and Environs	May 5	.....	46.000	100.000
Series 2		1921			
1	Budapest and Environs	Jan. 28	46.880	6.215	....
2	Budapest and Environs	Jan. 31	2.675	1.292	8.879
	Total for January	....	**49.555**	**7.507**	**8.879**
3	Budapest and Environs	Feb. 4	11.560	4.464	5.707
4	Budapest and Environs	Feb. 11	7.905	3.393	3.226
5	Budapest and Environs	Feb. 18	6.015	2.301	2.800
6	Budapest and Environs	Feb. 25	22.442	4.566	5.570
7	Budapest and Environs	Feb. 28	5.633	1.755	2.097
	Total for February	....	**53.555**	**16.479**	**19.400**
8	Budapest and Environs	Mar. 4	3.385	1.200	1.101
9	Budapest and Environs	Mar. 11	3.745	3.929	5.256
10	Budapest and Environs	Mar. 18	15.356	1.606	1.557
11	Budapest and Environs	Mar. 25	12.862	2.632	3.682
12	Budapest and Environs	Mar. 31	8.596	3.679	4.763
	Total for March	....	**43.944**	**13.046**	**16.359**
13	Budapest and Environs	Apr. 1	1.774	.959	1.227
14	Budapest and Environs	Apr. 8	30.854	4.454	5.580
15	Budapest and Environs	Apr. 15	30.290	4.939	8.406
16	Budapest and Environs	Apr. 22	17.314	2.463	3.061
17	Budapest and Environs	Apr. 29	24.351	8.417	8.911
18	Budapest and Environs	Apr. 30	8.848	1.196	.896
	Total for April	....	**113.431**	**22.428**	**28.081**
19	Budapest and Environs	May 6	16.401	5.283	5.190
20	Budapest and Environs	May 13	19.768	1.070	1.503
21	Budapest and Environs	May 20	4.006	1.354	1.493
22	Budapest and Environs	May 27	15.910	5.604	4.732
23	Budapest and Environs	May 31	15.861	2.248	2.858
	Total for May	....	**71.946**	**15.559**	**15.776**

ummary of Relief Deliveries

eliveries—Reconstruction Period, 1919–1924

Commodities in Net Metric Tons of 1,000 Kilograms or 2,204.6 Pounds								
Pork Products	Milk	Cocoa	Sugar	Misc. Food	Soap	Clothing and Misc.	Total Tons	Total Value
185.0	1,144.0	152.6	506.3	55.2	37.0	....	5,100.8	$1,133,617.17
.....	.....	.....	.....	....	....	230.0	230.0	449,665.62
120.8	142.6	3.1	7.6	15.3	....	7.8	912.7	373,850.00
53.1	155.3	17.3	114.0	35.3	....	3.2	716.9	154,089.41
.....	.....	.....	.....	....	....	....	14,114.0	1,685,835.61
.....	.....	.....	.....	....	....	....	.....	564,561.60
358.9	**1,441.9**	**173.0**	**627.9**	**105.8**	**37.0**	**241.0**	**21,074.4**	**$4,361,619.41**

.R.A.-European Children's Fund

r Children's Relief—Reconstruction Period, 1919–1924

Commodities in Net Metric Tons of 1,000 Kilograms or 2,204.6 Pounds									
Corn Grits	Pork Products	Milk	Cocoa	Sugar	Miscellaneous Food			Soap	Total Tons
					Chocolate	Salmon	Herring		
....	15.000	104.000	15.000	40.000	....	....	....	......	289.000
....	....	116.000	....	40.000	....	....	....	20.000	226.000
....	....	98.000	24.000	66.000	....	....	....	17.000	294.000
....	....	88.000	....	....	....	....	....	......	289.000
....	20.000	136.000	17.000	57.000	....	....	....	......	376.000
....	2.973	10.930	1.417	3.393	....	....	....	......	71.808
....	.769	4.594	.389	1.679	....	....	....	......	20.277
....	**3.742**	**15.524**	**1.806**	**5.072**	....	....	....	......	**92.085**
....	2.716	7.402	1.051	5.717	....	....	....	......	38.617
....	1.854	11.823	.235	3.223	....	....	....	......	31.659
....	.971	3.612	.365	3.942	....	....	....	......	20.006
....	4.086	8.844	.783	8.209	....	....	....	......	54.500
....	.591	3.048	.402	3.461	....	....	....	......	16.987
....	**10.218**	**34.729**	**2.836**	**24.552**	....	....	....	......	**161.769**
....	.617	2.007	.226	.445	....	....	....	......	8.981
....	1.709	6.771	.905	5.377	....	....	....	......	27.692
....	.525	9.667	.296	2.251	....	....	....	......	31.258
....	1.317	5.813	.740	4.408	....	....	....	......	31.454
....	1.294	18.049	3.457	9.632	....	....	....	......	49.470
....	**5.462**	**42.307**	**5.624**	**22.113**	....	....	....	......	**148.855**
....	.345	2.569	.518	1.698	....	....	....	......	9.090
....	1.789	17.157	2.270	8.317	....	....	....	......	70.421
....	1.916	8.775	1.744	8.059	....	....	....	......	64.129
....	1.329	2.156	.562	2.753	....	....	....	......	29.638
....	2.823	22.524	2.398	11.534	....	....	....	......	80.958
....	.699	9.732	.578	1.972	....	....	....	......	23.921
....	**8.901**	**62.913**	**8.070**	**34.333**	....	....	....	......	**278.157**
....	2.009	13.346	1.645	8.924	....	....	....	......	52.798
....	.367	5.900	1.133	3.153	....	....	....	......	32.894
....	.447	4.376	.730	2.732	....	....	....	......	15.138
....	1.374	18.093	1.812	7.511	....	....	....	......	55.036
....	.504	9.160	1.525	4.777	....	....	....	......	36.933
....	**4.701**	**50.875**	**6.845**	**27.097**	....	....	....	......	**192.799**

[*Continued on next page*]

Table 345—*Continued*

Detail by Months, by Districts or Kitchen

Receipt No.	District or Kitchen	Date	Flour	Rice	Beans, Peas
Series 2		1921			
24	Budapest and Environs	June 3	21.789	3.371	4.849
25	Budapest and Environs	June 10	11.470	2.397	3.308
26	Budapest and Environs	June 17	29.433	4.031	5.397
27	Budapest and Environs	June 24	29.126	1.509	1.604
28	Budapest and Environs	June 30	20.498	1.394	3.439
	Total for June	....	**112.316**	**12.702**	**18.597**
29	Budapest and Environs	July 8	28.139	3.564	3.852
30	Budapest and Environs	July 15	9.345	2.887	3.570
31	Budapest and Environs	July 22	3.519	.079	.093
32	Budapest and Environs	July 29	1.942	.017	.080
33	Budapest and Environs	July 31	2.777	.220	.467
	Total for July	....	**45.722**	**6.767**	**8.062**
34	Budapest and Environs	Aug. 5	18.968	2.517	1.585
35	Budapest and Environs	Aug. 12	5.499	1.470	1.396
36	Budapest and Environs	Aug. 19	3.556	.497	.667
37	Budapest and Environs	Aug. 26	.....	....	....
38	Budapest and Environs	Aug. 31	14.027	.204	.194
	Total for August	....	**42.050**	**4.688**	**3.842**
39	Országos Liga Budapest	Sept. 9	8.044	....	....
40	Csepel	Sept. 9	.624	.225	.20
41	Rakosliget	Sept. 9	.211	.076	.067
42	Budafok	Sept. 9	.288	.105	.09
43	Wekerletelep	Sept. 9	.970	.346	.307
44	Ujpest	Sept. 14	1.152	.408	.36
45	Free Milk Institute, Budapest	Sept. 14	.....	....	....
46	Kispest	Sept. 14	.432	.153	.13
47	M.Á.V. Istvantelki	Sept. 14	.432	.153	.137
48	Pestszentlőrincz	Sept. 14	.432	.153	.13
49	Erzsébetfalva	Sept. 14	.535	.179	.16
50	Hámor Közseg	Sept. 14	.134	.048	.04
51	Pereczesbánya Közseg	Sept. 14	.288	.102	.09
52	Diósgyőr Közseg	Sept. 14	.346	.122	.10
53	Diósgyőr Vasgyár	Sept. 14	1.008	.357	.31
54	Baja, Bács Bodrog vm.	Sept. 19	.336	.119	.10
55	Miskolcz	Sept. 19	1.440	.510	.45
56	Sátoraljaujhely	Sept. 20	.384	.136	.12
57	Budapest	Sept. 30	.....	8.182	7.31
58	A.R.A.-Budapest (Special)	Sept. 30	.352	.151	.07
59	Rákosliget	Sept. 28	.253	.079	.07
60	Wekerletelep	Sept. 28	1.000	.362	.32
61	Erzsébetfalva	Sept. 30	.531	.191	.17
	Total for September	....	**19.192**	**12.157**	**10.80**
62	Országos Liga Budapest	Oct. 7	.....	....	...
63	Csepel	Oct. 7	.....	.223	.22
64	Budafok	Oct. 7	.321	.135	.09
65	Free Milk Institute, Budapest	Oct. 11	.....	....	...
66	Ujpest	Oct. 11	1.174	.410	.36
67	Diósgyőr	Oct. 13	1.010	.359	.33
68	Miskolcz	Oct. 13	1.512	.519	.47
69	M.Á.V. Istvántelek	Oct. 13	.481	.179	.13
70	Hámor	Oct. 13	.....	.049	.05
71	Pereczesbánya	Oct. 13	.....	.104	.09
72	Diósgyőr Község	Oct. 13	.....	.135	.12
73	Pestszentlorincz	Oct. 14	.....	.180	.15
74	Pécs	Oct. 20	.....	.272	.24
75	Rákosliget	Oct. 27	.....	.075	.06
76	Országos	Oct. 28	.....	....	...
77	City of Budapest	Oct. 28	.....	7.178	6.19
78	Wekerletelep	Oct. 28	.....	.360	.31
79	Kispest	Oct. 28	.....	.181	.13
	Total for October	....	**4.498**	**10.359**	**9.00**

R.A.-European Children's Fund

Internal Deliveries for Children's Relief

Commodities in Net Metric Tons of 1,000 Kilograms or 2,204.6 Pounds

Corn Grits	Pork Products	Milk	Cocoa	Sugar	Miscellaneous Food			Soap	Total Tons
					Chocolate	Salmon	Herring		
....	1.239	12.062	1.598	4.892	.204	....	....	......	50.004
....	.639	10.167	1.442	4.650	....	....	....	......	34.073
....	1.826	16.210	2.671	10.047	....	....	....	......	69.615
....	.803	6.314	.868	3.737	....	....	....	......	43.961
....	1.329	8.622	1.506	5.988	....	.287	.448	......	43.511
....	**5.836**	**53.375**	**8.085**	**29.314**	**.204**	**.287**	**.448**	......	**241.164**
....	1.426	13.782	2.043	8.268	.087	.177	.347	......	61.685
....	1.277	16.373	2.335	7.960	.315	.857	1.296	......	46.215
....	.037	1.742	.347	1.628	.403	.882	1.378	......	10.108
....	.033	9.047	2.113	5.663	.023	.040	.081	......	19.039
....	.203	5.487	.955	1.607	....	....	....	......	11.716
....	**2.976**	**46.431**	**7.793**	**25.126**	**.828**	**1.956**	**3.102**	......	**148.763**
....	.529	5.966	2.584	12.835	1.680	.766	1.250	......	48.680
....	.675	8.404	.519	2.699	.464	.257	.382	......	21.765
....	.237	8.709	.456	1.518	....	.003	....	......	15.643
....	.020	1.175	.077	5.124	....	....	....	......	6.396
....	.147	.784	.126	5.480	....	.039	....	......	21.001
....	**1.608**	**25.038**	**3.762**	**27.656**	**2.144**	**1.065**	**1.632**	......	**113.485**
....	....	7.970	1.992	4.020	....	....	....	......	22.026
....	.083	.169	.017	.125	....	.117	....	......	1.560
....	.028	.058	.006	.042	....	.039	....	......	.527
....	.038	.078	.008	.057	....	.054	....	......	.721
....	.128	.260	.026	.190	....	.180	....	......	2.407
....	.153	.312	.031	.226	....	.216	....	......	2.862
....	....	2.613	....	....	....	....	....	......	2.613
....	.058	.117	.012	.085	....	.081	....	......	1.074
....	.058	.117	.012	.085	....	.081	....	......	1.075
....	.058	.117	.012	.085	....	.081	....	......	1.075
....	.064	.143	.014	.102	....	.099	....	......	1.301
....	.018	.037	.004	.026	....	.025	....	......	.335
....	.038	.078	.008	.058	....	.054	....	......	.717
....	.046	.093	.009	.068	....	.065	....	......	.858
....	.134	.273	.027	.198	....	.189	....	......	2.505
....	.045	.091	.009	.066	....	.063	....	......	.835
....	.192	.270	.039	.283	....	.390	....	......	3.580
....	.051	.104	.010	.076	....	.072	....	......	.955
....	3.078	6.253	.631	4.541	....	4.366	....	......	34.365
....	.084	.182	.013	.094	....	.061	....	......	1.012
....	.028	.058	.006	.046	....	.040	....	......	.582
....	.162	.260	.026	.198	....	.180	....	......	2.511
....	.086	.143	.015	.136	....	.099	....	......	1.373
....	**4.630**	**19.796**	**2.927**	**10.807**	....	**6.552**	....	......	**86.869**
....	....	7.970	1.992	3.984	....	....	....	......	13.946
....	.087	.169	.018	.145	....	.117	....	......	.983
....	.040	.078	.008	.065	....	.054	....	......	.797
....	....	2.613	....	....	....	....	....	......	2.613
....	.154	.312	.039	.238	....	.216	....	......	2.909
....	.171	.273	.027	.195	....	.189	....	......	2.555
....	.200	.390	.039	.298	....	.270	....	......	3.700
....	.058	.117	.012	.099	....	.081	....	......	1.164
....	.018	.037	.004	.027	....	.025	....	......	.216
....	.038	.078	.008	.068	....	.054	....	......	.441
....	.082	.094	.009	.091	....	.065	....	......	.603
....	.064	.117	.012	.086	....	.081	....	......	.697
....	.102	.208	.021	.151	....	.144	....	......	1.141
....	.028	.058	.006	.042	....	.040	....	......	.316
....	....	7.968	1.992	3.984	....	....	....	......	13.944
....	2.207	4.835	.384	3.616	....	3.655	....	......	28.068
....	.137	.260	.026	.198	....	.180	....	......	1.471
....	.057	.117	.012	.100	....	.081	....	......	.684
....	**3.443**	**25.694**	**4.609**	**13.387**	....	**5.252**	....	......	**76.248**

[*Concluded on next page*]

Table 345—*Concluded*

Detail by Months, by Districts or Kitchen

Receipt No.	District or Kitchen	Date	Flour	Rice	Beans, Peas
Series 2		1921			
80	Csepel	Nov. 2	.....	.225	.205
81	Budafok	Nov. 4	.....	.136	.100
82	Erzsébetfalva	Nov. 8	.....	.194	.170
83	Ujpest	Nov. 9	.....	.406	.169
84	Free Milk Institute, Budapest	Nov. 10	.....	....	....
85	Miskolcz	Nov. 11	.....	1.021	.945
86	Diósgyőr Vasgyár	Nov. 11	.....	.758	.364
87	Diósgyőr Község	Nov. 11	.....	.207	.181
88	Hámor-Község	Nov. 11	.....	.084	.071
89	Pereczesbánya	Nov. 11	.....	.204	.164
90	M.Á.V. Főmühelytelep	Nov. 15	.....	.179	.166
91	Wekerletelep	Nov. 18	.....	.269	.230
92	Országos Liga	Nov. 24	.....	....	....
93	Baja	Nov. 24	.....	.179	.167
94	Pestszentlorincz	Nov. 24	.....	.109	.124
95	Kispest	Nov. 25	.....	.048	....
96	Csepel	Nov. 25	.....	.198	.230
97	Rákosliget	Nov. 25	.....	.089	.113
98	Budafok	Nov. 28	.....	.045	.130
99	Free Milk Institute, Budapest	Nov. 28	.....	....	....
100	Erzsebet Falva	Nov. 30	.....	.281	.256
101	Budapest	Nov. 30	.....	10.507	10.420
102	Ujpest	Nov. 30	.....	.612	.548
103	A.R.A. (Special)	Nov. 30	.378	.126	.095
	Total for November	....	**.378**	**15.877**	**14.848**
104	Pécs Baranya	Dec. 12	.....	....	.504
105	Wekerletelep	Dec. 23	.....	.340	.302
106	Baja	Dec. 23	.....	.090	.084
107	M.Á.V. Főmühelytelep	Dec. 23	.....	.157	.139
108	Pestszentlőrincz	Dec. 23	.....	.154	.131
109	Free Milk Institute, Budapest	Dec. 23	.....	....	....
110	Free Milk Institute, Budapest	Dec. 23	.....	....	....
111	City of Budapest	Dec. 31	.....	....	....
112	A.R.A. (Special)	Dec. 31	.195	.078	.059
113	Orszagos Liga, Budapest	Dec. 30	.....	....	....
	Total for December	....	**.195**	**.819**	**1.219**
		1922			
114	Pécs Baranya	Jan. 3	.....	.764	.455
115	Sátoraljaujhely	Jan. 3	.....	.164	.172
116	Russian School, Budapest	Jan. 9	.....	.022	.038
117	Rákosliget	Jan. 12	.....	.145	.141
118	Diósgyőr Község	Jan. 12	.....	.130	.230
119	Diósgyőr Vasgyár	Jan. 12	.....	.386	.689
120	Perecesbánya	Jan. 12	.....	.108	.192
121	Hámor	Jan. 12	.....	.051	.090
122	Miskolcz	Jan. 12	.....	.540	.964
55–74	Local Committee, Budapest	Jan. 20	.390	6.059	9.401
55–75	Local Committee, Budapest	Jan. 27	.....	8.108	4.575
	Total for January	....	**.390**	**16.477**	**16.947**
	Other Relief Organizations,* for Child Feeding	....	.....	....	77.100
	Hungarian Government Donations (Receipts Turned Over to Government)	....	1,441.000	....	....
	Warehouse Adjustments	....	.....	....	....
	Total Deliveries	....	**1,998.172**	**435.865**	**568.924**
	Deduct Delivery to Jugo-Slavia	....	.....	5.700	....
	Total Net Deliveries for Child Feeding	....	**1,998.172**	**430.165**	**568.924**

* International Red Cross and other relief organizations (deliveries other than bulk sales).

† Ex-Hungarian Government donation.

R.A.-European Children's Fund

nternal Deliveries for Children's Relief

Commodities in Net Metric Tons of 1,000 Kilograms or 2,204.6 Pounds									
					Miscellaneous Food				
Corn Grits	Pork Products	Milk	Cocoa	Sugar	Chocolate	Salmon	Herring	Soap	Total Tons
....	.083	.169	.018	.131	....	.117	....	......	.948
....	.038	....	.008	.055	....	.054	....	......	.391
....	.070	.143	.015	.104	....	.099	....	......	.795
....	.100	.218	.016	.181	....	.218	....	......	1.308
....	....	2.613	....	....	....	....	....	......	2.613
....	.388	.780	.076	.583	....	.540	....	......	4.333
....	.191	....	....	.104	....	.425	....	......	1.842
....	.068	.151	.014	.073	....	.144	....	......	.838
....	.031	.050	.005	.039	....	.050	....	......	.330
....	.071	.125	.009	.078	....	.122	....	......	.773
....	.051	.161	.016	.113	....	.102	....	......	.788
....	.052	.166	.021	.114	....	.167	....	......	1.019
....	....	7.346	1.886	3.700	....	....	....	......	12.932
....	.075	.136	.015	.099	....	.095	....	......	.766
....	.012	.133	.008	.099	....	.075	....	......	.560
....	.091	....	....	....	....	.131	....	......	.270
....	.130	.294	.015	.180	....	.178	....	......	1.225
....	.044	.093	.010	.071	....	.069	....	......	.489
....	.061	....	.008	.082	....	.095	....	......	.421
....	....	2.613	....	....	....	....	....	......	2.613
....	.105	.215	.022	.156	....	.149	....	......	1.184
....	4.763	9.050	.960	6.760	....	6.289	....	......	48.749
....	.231	.468	.047	.341	....	.324	....	......	2.571
....	.063	.171	.013	.076	....	.057	....	......	.979
....	**6.718**	**25.095**	**3.182**	**13.139**	**....**	**9.500**	**....**	**......**	**88.737**
....	.209	.218	.046	.298	....	.275	....	......	1.550
....	.138	.260	.026	.190	....	.180	....	......	1.436
....	.034	.068	.007	.052	....	.048	....	......	.383
....	.058	.117	.013	.087	....	.081	....	......	.652
....	.062	.117	.014	.086	....	.081	....	......	.645
....	....	.109	....	....	....	....	....	......	.109
....	....	2.613	....	....	....	....	....	......	2.613
....	....	....	....	....	1.808	....	....	......	1.808
....	.039	.106	.008	.047	....	.035	....	......	.567
....	....	7.970	1.992	3.984	....	....	....	......	13.946
....	**.540**	**11.578**	**2.106**	**4.744**	**1.808**	**.700**	**....**	**......**	**23.709**
.224	.272	.490	.026	.220	....	.252	....	......	2.703
.084	.156	.158	.004	.090	....	.145	....	......	.973
.016	.019	.028	.002	.019	....	.022	....	......	.166
.058	.071	.102	.009	.068	....	.079	....	......	.673
.095	.117	.166	.014	.112	....	.130	....	......	.994
.286	.358	.483	.042	.340	....	.378	....	......	2.962
.079	.097	.138	.012	.099	....	.108	....	......	.833
.037	.046	.064	.005	.044	....	.051	....	......	.388
.415	.483	.690	.075	.476	....	.540	....	......	4.183
3.956	4.649	26.425	2.573	5.669	....	5.216	....	......	64.338
17.717	16.177	56.370	8.575	34.718	....	12.803	....	......	159.043
22.967	**22.445**	**85.114**	**11.337**	**41.855**	**....**	**19.724**	**....**	**......**	**237.256**
....	18.800	105.100	27.700	24.100	....	....	....	......	252.800
....	50.000	....	....	....	....	....	....	......	1,491.000
.400	....	....	....	....	....	....	....	......	.400
23.367	**185.020**	**1,145.569**	**152.682**	**506.295**	**4.984**	**45.036**	**5.182**	**37.000**	**5,108.096**
....	....	1.600	....	....	....	....	....	......	7.300
23.367	**185.020**	**1,143.969**	**152.682**	**506.295**	**4.984**	**45.036**	**5.182**	**37.000**	**5,100.796**

Table 346

Summary by Operations of Clothing Deliveries

Operation	Shoes (Pairs)	Laces (Pairs)	Stockings (Pairs)	Woolens (Yards)
A.R.A.-European Children's Fund—Children's Relief*	101,261	66,000	98,426	248,975.75
A.R.A.-E.C.F.—Sale of Surplus and Warehouse Adjustment	36	.....	227	411.50
Commonwealth Fund—Intelligentsia Relief	2,500	.....	4,984	9,391.00
Total	**103,797**	**66,000**	**103,637**	**258,778.25**

* See Table 347.

HUNGARY—A.R.A.-European Children's Fund

Detail of Clothing Deliveries per Receipts of Hungarian Central Committee, Budapest

Table 347*

Date of Receipt	Shoes (Pairs)	Laces (Pairs)	Stockings (Pairs)	Woolens (Yards)	Thread (Yards)	Thread (Spools)	Needles (No.)	Buttons (No.)	Blouses (No.)
1920									
January 1—March 21	15,245	....	....	54,481	.....	....	....	....	....
March 22—March 31	4,579	....	....	23,755	.....	....	....	....	....
April 1—April 7	9,013	....	13,675	3,133	.....	....	....	....	....
April 8—April 14	4,324	....	8,862	14,551	.....	....	....	....	....
April 15—April 21	1,239	34,000	24,434	4,411	7,668,260	....	....	261,072	....
April 22—April 30	95	....	759	14,069	33,682	....	....	....	....
May 1—May 7	5,066	9,280	687	....	2,106,058	....	50,000	....	....
May 8—May 15	367	....	15	10,805	.....	....	....	....	....
May 16—May 22	5,690	22,720	....	....	.....	....	....	....	....
May 23—May 31	2,516	....	1,568	131	.....	....	....	....	....
June 1—June 7	3,192	....	....	....	.....	....	....	3,312	....
1921									
September 30	....	....	....	123,640	.....	....	....	....	....
December 21	....	....	....	....	.....	....	....	....	3,926
1922									
January 24	....	....	....	....	.....	7,052	3,000	495,216	....
January 31	49,935	....	48,426	....	.....	....	....	....	....
Total	**101,261**	**66,000**	**98,426**	**248,976**	**9,808,000**	**7,052**	**53,000**	**759,600**	**3,926**

* The woolens and clothing accessories listed in this table were used in the manufacture of suits for boys and girls, overcoats for boys. For detail of Internal Deliveries, cf. Table 348.

.A.-European Children's Fund
onstruction Period, 1919–1924

Thread (Yards)	Thread (Spools)	Needles (No.)	Buttons (No.)	Blouses (No.)	Linings (Yards)	Underwear (Garments)	Total Metric Tons	Total Value
808,000	7,052	53,000	759,600	3,926	.....	....	217.3	$424,347.20
......	596	2,000	177,696	14	.....	....	.2	790.83
......	...	....	......	...	15,707	5,000	12.5	24,527.59
808,000	**7,648**	**55,000**	**937,296**	**3,940**	**15,707**	**5,000**	**230.0**	**$449,665.62**

HUNGARY—A.R.A.-European Children's Fund
Detail by Local Committees of Internal Deliveries of Clothing
'able 348
Reconstruction Period, 1919–1924

Local Committee	Shoes * (Pairs)	Stockings (Pairs)	Girls' Suits (Each)	Boys' Suits (Each)	Overcoats (Each)	Blouses (Each)
apest and Suburbs	51,338	48,503	13,999	18,556	28,652	....
apest	29,747	29,747	8,715	10,893	12,684	3,926
urbs—						
ıdafok	203	203	39	96	90	....
sepel	1,580	1,580	266	377	446	....
rzsébetfalva	1,471	1,471	359	541	595	....
ispest	1,937	1,937	439	651	752	....
estszentlőrincz	1,208	1,208	231	358	391	....
estujhely	901	901	193	218	253	....
tvántelek	484	484	115	236	225	....
jpest	2,536	2,536	422	453	627	....
vinces—						
ákosliget	220	220	93	139	155	....
iósgyőr Község	565	565	142	212	236	....
iósgyőr Vasgyár	1,587	1,587	393	742	751	....
ámor	145	145	33	68	46	....
erecesbánya	470	470	102	192	194	....
iskolcz	4,048	4,048	902	1,164	1,483	....
yör	1,505	1,505	249	318	378	....
ítoraljaujhely	318	318	95	142	158	....
zolnok	798	798	104	138	156	....
zegléd	200	200	48	72	80	....
Total	**101,261**	**98,426**	**26,939**	**35,566**	**48,352**	**3,926**

ncludes shoe laces.

HUNGARY—

Table 349

Detail by Months of Food Draft Deliveries—

Time of Delivery	Number of Drafts Delivered * A $10.00	B $50.00	C $10.00	D $50.00	Unit	Flour M.T.	Rice M.T.	Beans, Peas M.T.	Bacon 8-Lb. Piece	Bacon 16-Lb. Piece
1920										
March	459	172	284	27	....	22.928	.....	.....	....	..
April	2,719	518	1,149	119	....	94.324	.....	32.954	3,920	..
May	2,411	350	747	56	....	60.835	.....	23.387	2,699	206
June	1,458	194	558	37	....	37.047	.....	14.293	1,458	194
July	975	99	404	15	....	22.546	6.071	2.712	975	99
August	1,029	107	1,008	11	....	30.105	11.718	.117	1,029	107
September	565	403	163	10	....	34.036	12.610	.....	565	403
October	498	160	210	7	....	18.734	6.960	.....	498	160
November	3,407	66	846	8	....	51.907	20.811	.....	3,407	66
December	1,693	206	283	54	....	38.444	14.768	.....	1,693	206
1921										
January	995	65	194	7	....	17.769	6.979	.....	995	65
February	320	32	69	9	....	6.922	2.678	.....	320	32
March	379	27	107	4	....	7.363	2.887	.....	379	27
April	277	23	45	5	....	5.352	2.082	.....	277	23
May	85	16	16	3	....	2.329	.884	.....	101	8
June	132	4	14	..	....	1.874	.746	.....	140	..
July	13	..	3	..	....	.177	.072	.....	13	..
Grand Total in Units	**17,415**	**2,442**	**5,900**	**372**	Unit	**452.692**	**89.266**	**73.463**	**18,469**	**1,596**
Grand Total in Metric Tons	....	....	....	....	M.T.	**452.692**	**89.266**	**73.463**	**67.020**	**11.583**

* Value of food drafts and commodities delivered, $373,850.00.

HUNGARY—

Table 350

Detail by Months of Bulk Sale Deliveries—

Time of Delivery	Unit	Flour M.T.	Rice M.T.	Bacon 8-Lb. Piece	Lard 5-Lb. Tin	Lard 10-Lb. Tin	Lard Substitute M.T.	Oil 1-Gal. Tin
1920								
October	....	.064	.....	...	...	...	.....	....
December	....	.228	2.000	...	...	...	.....	....
1921								
February	....	3.000	8.998	...	...	...	4.786	....
March	....	198.025	13.365	132	...	200	5.017	4,000
April	....	33.182	18.096	161	...	240	2.175	225
May	....	51.351	23.277	118	753	662	5.504	160
June	....	38.111	18.683	104	1,882	...	1.607	802
July—October	....	49.402	27.963	405	2,654	41	2.590	1,440
November—January, 1922	....	20.230	9.460	...	4	...	1.688	....
June, 1922	....	......	*—2.700**	...	...	...	.....	....
Total in Units	Unit	**393.593**	**119.142**	**920**	**5,293**	**1,143**	**23.367**	**6,627**
Total in Metric Tons	M.T.	**393.593**	**119.142**	**3.339**	**12.004**	**5.185**	**23.367**	**22.545**
Less Food Accounted for in Child Feeding Program	Unit	......	.....	...	...	...	.....	4,000
	M.T.	173.995	.....	...	...	...	.454	13.608
Total Net Bulk Sales in Units	Unit	**219.598**	**119.142**	**920**	**5,293**	**1,143**	**22.913**	**2,627**
Total Net Bulk Sales in Metric Tons	M.T.	**219.598**	**119.142**	**3.339**	**12.004**	**5.185**	**22.913**	**8.937**

* All (—) minus quantities were returned to stock.

.A. Warehouses and A.R.A.-European Children's Fund

onstruction Period, 1919–1924

Lard		Oil		Milk		Cocoa	Sugar	Corned Beef	Misc. Sacks, Containers	Total Metric Tons
Lb. Tin	10-Lb. Tin	1-Gal. Tin	5-Gal. Tin	Evap. Case	Cond. Case	M.T.	M.T.	Case	No.	
..	..	...	..	255	..	....	....	58	....	......
596	596	1,117	119	1,513	..	....	....	118	....	......
350	350	803	56	995	..	....	....	58	1,257	......
194	194	595	37	614	..	....	....	32	3,093	......
99	99	419	15	378	..	....	....	17	2,899	......
107	107	1,019	11	541	..	....	....	18	4,200	......
403	403	173	10	548	..	....	....	67	1,570	......
160	160	217	7	302	..	....	....	27	1,582	......
66	66	854	8	758	95	.155	.424	11	....	......
206	206	337	54	...	613	1.318	3.410	34	....	......
65	65	201	7	...	286	.701	1.618	11	....	......
32	32	78	9	...	112	.251	.623	5	16,063	......
27	27	111	4	...	121	.284	.654	4	1,004	......
23	23	50	5	...	85	.202	.490	4	704	......
16	16	19	3	...	37	.077	.215	3	225	......
4	4	14	..	...	30	.080	.170	1	296	......
..	..	3	..	...	3	.008	.016	..	32	......
,348	**2,348**	**6,010**	**345**	**5,904**	**1,382**	**3.076**	**7.620**	**468**	**32,925**	......
.325	**10.650**	**20.445**	**5.869**	**112.479**	**30.085**	**3.076**	**7.620**	**15.279**	**7.776**	**912.628***

.A. Warehouses and A.R.A.-European Children's Fund

onstruction Period, 1919–1924

Oil 5-Gal. Tin	Milk Evap. Case	Cocoa M.T.	Sugar M.T.	Miscellaneous Food: Corned Beef Case	Miscellaneous Food: Salmon Case	Miscellaneous Food: Herring Keg	Misc. Sacks, Containers No.	Total Metric Tons	Total Value
..	...	....	.....	183	..	...	3,500	......	......
..	372	.300	2.000	...	..	...	....	......	......
..	699	2.178	9.966	...	..	...	....	......	......
18	937	3.620	20.524	37	..	...	....	......	......
..	1,082	4.810	22.451	67	..	...	....	......	......
..	1,607	2.708	21.293	47	..	...	....	......	......
1	1,079	.805	13.144	173	71	...	....	......	......
21	1,364	2.478	21.954	179	99	200	7,332	......	......
..	222	.898	6.102	...	68	2	....	......	......
..	*—228*	*—.522*	*—3.478*	...	..	...	....	......	......
40	**7,134**	**17.275**	**113.956**	**686**	**238**	**202**	**10,832**	......	......
.680	**155.333**	**17.275**	**113.956**	**22.391**	**5.189**	**7.788**	**3.250**	**905.037**	**$199,902.64**
..	...	....	.....	...	..	...	....	......	......
..	...	....	.....	...	..	...	....	188.057	$ 45,813.23
40	**7,134**	**17.275**	**113.957**	**686**	**238**	**202**	**10,832**	......	......
.680	**155.333**	**17.275**	**113.956**	**22.391**	**5.189**	**7.788**	**3.250**	**716.980**	**$154,089.41**

Table 351 — Detail of Internal Deliveries, by Institutions, by Month

Receipt No.	Institution	Date of Delivery	Flour	Rice
		1921		
1	Mensa Technica, Budapest	Mar. 11	1.780	.812
2	Veterinary Surgeons, Students' Mensa, Budapest	Mar. 11	.193	.091
3	Mensa Academica, Budapest	Mar. 11	1.082	.504
4	Mensa Medica, Budapest	Mar. 11	1.715	.716
5	Mensa E.M.K.E. College, Budapest	Mar. 12	.191	.103
6	Mensa Pozsony-Kolozsvár University, Budapest	Mar. 12	.383	.160
7	Jewish Students Mensa, Budapest	Mar. 30	1.888	.450
	Total for March	....	**7.232**	**2.836**
8	Mensa E.M.K.E. College, Budapest	Apr. 12	.191	.103
9	Mensa Academica, Budapest	Apr. 12	1.463	.608
10	Eötvös College Mensa, Budapest	Apr. 13	.190	.092
11	Mensa Medica, Budapest	Apr. 20	.893	.510
12	Mensa Pozsony-Kolozsvár University, Budapest	Apr. 20	.286	.134
13	Mensa Technica, Budapest	Apr. 20	.843	.350
14	Mensa Ferencz József Tanitók Háza, Budapest	Apr. 20	.282	.144
15	Mensa Veterinary Surgeons' High School	Apr. 27	.110	.050
16	Mensa High School for Forestry and Mining, Sopron	Apr. 27	.864	.432
	Total for April	....	**5.122**	**2.423**
17	School for Applied Arts, Budapest	May 3	.147	.072
18	Mensa Academica, Budapest	May 9	.443	.320
19	Mensa Academica, Debreczen	May 9	.180	.090
20	Eötvös College, Budapest	May 11	.063	.050
21	Mensa Medica, Budapest	May 9	.872	.450
22	E.M.K.E. College, Budapest	May 26	.111	.020
23	Ferencz József Tanitók Háza, Budapest	May 26	.250	.125
24	Mensa Pozsony-Kolozsvár University, Budapest	May 26	.276	.150
25	Mensa Technica, Budapest	May 26	1.050	.506
26	School for Applied Arts, Budapest	May 26	.277	.138
	Total for May	....	**3.669**	**1.921**
27	Mensa Academica, Budapest	June 3	.887	.455
28	Mensa Medica, Budapest	June 3	.903	.455
29	Mensa Medica, Budapest	June 10	.432	.216
30	E.M.K.E. College, Budapest	June 10	.125	.065
31	O.M.I.K.E. Mensa, Budapest	June 10	....	....
32	Ferencz József Tanitók Háza, Budapest	June 10	.100	.045
33	Mensa Technica, Budapest	June 10	.750	.300
34	Mensa Pozsony-Kolozsvár University, Budapest	June 10	.275	.125
	Total for June	....	**3.472**	**1.661**
35	High School for Forestry and Mining, Sopron	July 15	.288	.142
36	Mensa Medica, Budapest	July 15	1.480	.748
37	Superseded	July 30	....	....
	Total for July	....	**1.768**	**.890**
38	Bányászati és Erdészeti Föiskola, Sopron	Sept. 9	.113	.057
39	Mensa Technica, Budapest	Sept. 9	.274	.140
40	Ferencz József Tanitók Háza, Budapest	Sept. 9	.400	.204
41	Mensa Medica, Budapest	Sept. 9	.483	.257
42	Mensa E.M.K.E., Budapest	Sept. 9	.037	.019
43	Mensa Technica, Budapest	Sept. 14	1.008	.336
44	Mensa Medica, Budapest	Sept. 14	1.728	.576
45	Mensa Iparmüvészeti, Budapest	Sept. 14	.173	.058
46	Ferencz József Tanitók Háza, Budapest	Sept. 14	.266	.133
47	Mensa E.M.K.E., Budapest	Sept. 14	.173	.086
48	Mensa Eötvös, Budapest	Sept. 14	.154	.053
49	Mensa Veterinary, Budapest	Sept. 15	.173	.057
50	Mensa Academica, Budapest	Sept. 15	.864	.288
51	Mensa O.M.I.K.E., Budapest	Sept. 15	.864	.288
	Total for September	....	**6.710**	**2.552**

* These deliveries are included in bulk sale deliveries, Table 350.

R.A.-European Children's Fund

Student Feeding*—Reconstruction Period, 1919–1924

Commodities in Net Metric Tons of 1,000 Kilograms or 2,204.6 Pounds

Pork Products	Bacon	Milk Evap.	Cocoa	Sugar	Misc. Food	Total Tons
.130	.162	.414	....	.400	.403	4.101
.016	.018	.044	....	.040	.041	.443
.110	.101	.239	....	.262	.245	2.543
.162	.144	.370	....	.395	.391	3.893
.018	.018	.044	....	.050	.041	.465
.032	.032	.087	....	.101	.082	.877
.305	....	....	.204	.251	....	3.098
.773	**.475**	**1.198**	**.204**	**1.499**	**1.203**	**15.420**
.018	.018	.044	....	.050	.041	.465
.128	.130	.320	....	.300	.321	3.270
.016	.018	.044	....	.040	.041	.441
.115	.130	.305	....	.250	.457	2.660
.032	.032	.087	....	.080	.122	.773
.165	.108	.130	....	.200	.359	2.155
.032	.032	.087	....	.080	.122	.779
.015	.015	.029	....	.036	.063	.318
.096	.098	.241	....	.240	.367	2.338
.617	**.581**	**1.287**	....	**1.276**	**1.893**	**13.199**
.016	.018	.044	....	.040	.063	.400
.060	.066	.152	....	.200	.421	1.662
.020	.021	.051	....	.050	.082	.494
.012	.018	.031	....	.035	.063	.272
.075	.094	.196	....	.400	.245	2.332
.012	.015	.022	....	.020	.065	.265
.025	.029	.065	....	.070	.103	.667
.032	.033	.044	....	.065	.122	.722
.082	.102	.261	....	.300	.261	2.562
.027	.032	.070	....	.073	.108	.725
.361	**.428**	**.936**	....	**1.253**	**1.533**	**10.101**
.112	.109	.207	....	.200	.395	2.365
.097	.058	.270	....	.100	.376	2.259
.048	.050	.120	....	.120	.179	1.165
.013	.011	.029	....	.032	.030	.305
....	....	....	....	.085	....	.085
.015	.011	.036	....	.030	.038	.275
.070	.105	.181	....	.215	.272	1.893
.028	.033	.074	....	.072	.109	.716
.383	**.377**	**.917**	....	**.854**	**1.399**	**9.063**
.032	.036	.080	....	.079	.122	.779
.169	.189	.414	....	.420	.585	4.005
....	....	....	....	....	....	....
.201	**.225**	**.494**	....	**.499**	**.707**	**4.784**
.013	.015	.032	....	.032	.049	.311
.031	.032	.076	....	.077	.114	.744
.045	.047	.111	....	.112	.168	1.087
.056	.058	.141	....	.141	.212	1.348
.004	.004	.010	....	.010	.016	.100
.112	....	.280	.056	.322	1.716	3.830
.192	....	.480	.096	.552	2.886	6.510
.019	....	.048	.010	.055	.312	.675
.030	.033	.074	....	.074	.112	.722
.019	.022	.048	....	.048	.073	.469
.018	....	.044	.009	.051	.273	.602
.019	....	.048	.010	.055	.312	.674
.096	....	.240	.048	.276	1.443	3.255
.041	....	.240	.048	.276	.819	2.576
.695	**.211**	**1.872**	**.277**	**2.081**	**8.505**	**22.903**

[*Continued on next page*]

Table 351—*Continued*

Detail of Internal Deliveries, by Institution

Receipt No.	Institution	Date of Delivery	Flour	Rice
		1921		
52	Mensa Iparmüvészeti, Budapest	Oct. 13	.174	.060
53	Mensa Academica, Budapest	Oct. 14	.876	.314
54	Mensa Eötvös, Budapest	Oct. 14	.044	.013
55	Mensa E.M.K.E., Budapest	Oct. 20	.174	.090
56	Mensa Medica, Budapest	Oct. 20	1.743	.594
57	Mensa Eötvös, Budapest	Oct. 21	.125	.045
58	Mensa Technica, Budapest	Oct. 24	1.047	.363
59	Erzsébet Mensa-Pozsony, Budapest	Oct. 24	.247	.081
60	Mensa Állatorvosi, Budapest	Oct. 24	.178	.063
	Total for October	....	**4.608**	**1.623**
61	Mensa Academica, Budapest	Nov. 9	.877	.290
62	Mensa Iparmüvészeti, Budapest	Nov. 9	.104	.090
63	Mensa E.M.K.E., Budapest	Nov. 11	.071	.032
64	Mensa Erzsébet, Budapest	Nov. 11	.024	.084
65	Mensa Academica, Budapest	Nov. 11	....	.127
66	Mensa Eötvös, Budapest	Nov. 15	.084	.090
67	Mensa Ferencz József Tanitók Háza, Budapest	Nov. 15	.164	.090
68	Mensa Medica, Budapest	Nov. 15	.209	.668
69	Mensa Veterinary Surgeons, Budapest	Nov. 22	....	.060
70	Mensa Technica, Budapest	Nov. 24	.754	.447
71	Mensa E.M.K.E., Budapest	Nov. 24	.250	.144
72	Mensa High School Forestry and Mining, Sopron	Nov. 24	.125	.069
73	Mensa Eötvös, Budapest	Nov. 28	.186	.037
74	Mensa Ferencz József Tanitók Háza, Budapest	Nov. 28	.372	.045
75	Mensa Academica, Budapest	Nov. 28	1.063	.146
76	Mensa Medica, Budapest	Nov. 28	2.181	.234
77	Mensa Iparmüvészeti, Budapest	Nov. 28	.251	.142
78	Mensa Veterinary, Budapest	Nov. 30	.251	.144
79	Mensa Erzsébet, Budapest	Nov. 30	.288	.180
80	Mensa Technica, Budapest	Nov. 30	1.260	.840
	Total for November	....	**8.514**	**3.959**
81	High School Forestry and Mining, Sopron	Dec. 27	.064	.034
82	Mensa Medica, Budapest	Dec. 29	.864	1.783
83	Mensa Ferencz József Tanitók Háza, Budapest	Dec. 29	.133	.269
84	Mensa Erzsébet, Budapest	Dec. 29	.126	.082
85	Mensa High School Applied Arts, Budapest	Dec. 30	.086	.058
86	Mensa Eötvös, Budapest	Dec. 30	.079	.100
87	Mensa Veterinary Surgeons, Budapest	Dec. 31	.086	.057
88	Mensa Academica, Budapest	Dec. 31	.432	.863
89	Mensa E.M.K.E., Budapest	Dec. 31	.086	.057
90	Mensa Technica, Budapest	Dec. 31	.504	.336
	Total for December	....	**2.460**	**3.639**
		1922		
91	Mensa Medica, Budapest	Jan. 10	1.200	....
92	Mensa Erzsébet, Budapest	Jan. 10	.150	....
93	Mensa Ferencz József Tanitók Háza, Budapest	Jan. 10	.185	....
94	Mensa Veterinary Surgeons, Budapest	Jan. 10	.120	....
95	Mensa Technica, Budapest	Jan. 10	.700	....
96	Mensa Academica, Budapest	Jan. 10	.600	....
97	Mensa School Applied Arts, Budapest	Jan. 10	.120	....
98	Mensa E.M.K.E., Budapest	Jan. 10	.120	....
99	Mensa O.M.I.K.E., Budapest	Jan. 10	.600	....
100	High School Forestry and Mining, Sopron	Jan. 10	.070	....
101	Mensa Eötvös, Budapest	Jan. 10	.110	....
	Total for January	....	**3.975**	**....**
	Total Student Feeding †	....	**47.530**	**21.504**

† Cf. Special Program. Value of these deliveries, $28,300.16.

‡ Composed of corned beef, 7.576; herring, 7.833; salmon, 1.395.

A.R.A.-European Children's Fund

y Months, for Student Feeding

Commodities in Net Metric Tons of 1,000 Kilograms or 2,204.6 Pounds

Pork Products	Bacon	Milk Evap.	Cocoa	Sugar	Misc. Food	Total Tons
.019	....	.048	.010	.068	....	.379
.103	....	.240	.049	.286	....	1.868
.004	....	.011	.002	.014	....	.088
.019	.022	.049	....	.050	.076	.480
.192	....	.480	.099	.596	....	3.704
.014	....	.033	.007	.046	....	.270
.161	....	.280	.104	.344	....	2.299
.024	....	.062	.012	.076	.072	.574
.019	....	.049	.010	.058	....	.377
.555	**.022**	**1.252**	**.293**	**1.538**	**.148**	**10.039**
.096	....	.239	.056	.342	....	1.900
.010	.058	.025	.005	.020	....	.312
.006	.022	.008	....	.021	.021	.181
.003	.036	.007	.002	.010	....	.166
....	.145	....	....	....	....	.272
.010	.011	.025	.005	.025	....	.250
.017	.025	.041	.007	.046	....	.390
.050	.192	....	.043	.090	....	1.252
....	.022	....	....	....	....	.082
....	....	.056	....	.071	....	1.328
.024	.051	.060	.012	.069	....	.610
.011	.025	....	.006	.034	....	.270
.018	.044	.048	.010	.063	....	.406
.037	.076	.092	.019	.105	....	.746
.133	....	.300	.061	.337	.243	2.283
.229	.093	.600	.107	.689	.388	4.521
.024	.051	.060	.012	.072	....	.612
.024	.031	.060	.012	.072	....	.594
.030	.062	.082	.015	.090	....	.747
.140	....	.350	.070	.402	.225	3.287
.862	**.944**	**2.053**	**.442**	**2.558**	**.877**	**20.209**
.006	....	.012	.003	.017	.011	.147
.096	....	.240	.048	.276	.192	3.499
.015	....	.037	.007	.043	.030	.534
.012	....	.029	.006	.036	.024	.315
.010	....	.024	.005	.028	.019	.230
.008	....	.022	.004	.025	.017	.255
.010	....	.024	.005	.027	.019	.228
.048	....	.120	.024	.138	.096	1.721
.010	....	.024	.005	.027	.019	.228
.056	....	.140	.028	.161	.112	1.337
.271	**....**	**.672**	**.135**	**.778**	**.539**	**8.494**
....	....	....	....	....	....	1.200
....	....	....	....	....	....	.150
....	....	....	....	....	....	.185
....	....	....	....	....	....	.120
....	....	....	....	....	....	.700
....	....	....	....	....	....	.600
....	....	....	....	....	....	.120
....	....	....	....	....	....	.120
....	....	....	....	....	....	.600
....	....	....	....	....	....	.070
....	....	....	....	....	....	.110
....	....	....	....	....	....	**3.975**
4.718	**3.263**	**10.681**	**1.351**	**12.336**	**16.804‡**	**118.187**

Table 352

Operation	Table No.	Flour	Grain	Rice
				U.S. FOO
Sales—Financed by U.S. Treasury Credits	106	1,804,252.8	5,039,879.8	14,634.7
				ARMISTIC
A.R.A.—Cash Settlement	353	15,031.1	....	....
Grand Total Relief Deliveries	102	**1,819,283.9**	**5,039,879.8**	**14,634.7**

ITALY—American Relief Administration

Detail by Steamers or Source of Commodities Sold for Cash

Armistice Period, 1919

Table 353

Arrival No.*	Steamer or Source	Port of Sailing	Date of Arrival	Port of Arrival	Contents of Cargoes in Net Metric Tons of 1000 Kilograms or 2,204.6 Pounds			Total Value
					Wheat Flour	Cereal Flour	Total Tons	
			1919					
90	Callabasas †	Norfolk	Mar. 27	Messina	2,914.4	......	2,914.4	$ 543,087.
95	Watonwah †	Philadelphia	Mar. 28	Genoa	2,894.1	4,222.6	7,116.7	1,200,631.
270	West Togus	Norfolk	June 11	Trieste	313.6	......	313.6	69,136.
271	Q.M. Inv. 22 ‡	(U.S.A.)	June ..	Trieste	4,686.4	......	4,686.4	1,033,158.
	Total—to Table 120				**10,808.5**	**4,222.6**	**15,031.1**	**$2,846,014.**

* Arrival numbers from Table 111.
† These cargoes handled direct by New York office, Food Administration Grain Corporation.
‡ Quartermaster invoice, purchased from U.S. Army.

ummary of Relief Deliveries

Beans, Peas	Pork Products	Milk	Sugar	Misc. Food	Forage	Total Tons	Total Value
Commodities in Net Metric Tons of 1,000 Kilograms or 2,204.6 Pounds							
DMINISTRATION PERIOD							
6,355.7	141,867.9	13,152.7	30,682.1	93,341.9	320,582.0	7,464,749.6	$796,762,249.59
ERIOD							
......	....	....	....	....	....	15,031.1	$ 2,846,014.42
6,355.7	**141,867.9**	**13,152.7**	**30,682.1**	**93,341.9**	**320,582.0**	**7,479,780.7**	**$799,608,264.01**

Table 354

Operation	Table No.	Flour	Grain	Rice
				ARMISTIC
A.R.A.—U.S. Treasury Loan	355	50,199.4	......	58.2
U.S. Liquidation Commission (War Dept.), Sales	122	......	......	....
American Red Cross	126–27	......	......	....
A.R.A.—Freight on Charity Shipment	143	......	......	....
Total American Relief	...	**50,199.4**	......	**58.2**
United Kingdom	356	10,197.0	4,116.0	....
United Kingdom—Finance on Freight	133	......	......	....
Total Relief by United Kingdom	132	**10,197.0**	**4,116.0**	....
Total Relief, Armistice Period	108	**60,396.4**	**4,116.0**	**58.2**
				RECONSTRUCTIC
A.R.A.—Congressional Appropriation, $100,000,000 Fund	357,364	......	......	477.3
A.R.A.-European Children's Fund	357,364	......	......	5.7
Jugoslavian Government Donation	363	2,551.0	......	58.0
Total Children's Relief	163	**2,551.0**	......	**541.0**
Serbian Child Welfare Association of America	361	......	......	....
Dr. Reeder (Serbian Child Welfare Association of America)	361	......	......	....
American Women's Hospital, Serbia	362	......	......	....
Total Other than Children's Relief	...	......	......	....
Total Relief, Reconstruction Period	149	**2,551.0**	......	**541.0**
Grand Total Relief Deliveries	102	**62,947.4**	**4,116.0**	**599.2**

JUGOSLAVIA

Table 355

Detail by Steamers of Relief Deliveries Paid for by Fun

Arrival No.*	Steamer	Port of Sailing	Date of Arrival	Port of Arrival	Wheat Flour
			1919		
6	Western Plains (Q.M. 8, 12) †	New York	Jan. 14	Cattaro	598.1
14	Western Plains (Q.M. 41)	New York	Jan. 28	Zeleneke	190.1
16	Western Hope (Q.M. 46)	New York	Feb. 2	Gravosa	7,319.9
20	Durham (Q.M. 53)	New York	Feb. 6	Zeleneke	.....
22	Nantahala (Q.M. 38)	New York	Feb. 10	Fiume	7,146.8
37	Williamantic (Q.M. 38)	New York	Feb. 21	Fiume	5,446.0
52	Durham (Q.M. 53)	New York	Mar. 5	Spalato	.....
57	Durham (Q.M. 53)	New York	Mar. 10	Gravosa	.....
80	Edenton	Baltimore	Mar. 22	Spalato	3,859.8
83	Orion	New York	Mar. 23	Salonica	4,435.9
97	Canoga, II (Q.M. 50)	New York	Mar. 31	Trieste	.....
150	Tordenskjold	Baltimore	Apr. 26	Gravosa	4,747.3
148	Neuse	New York	Apr. 23	Trieste	.....
193	Eastern Sun	Philadelphia	May 15	Constantinople	600.0
214	Ida	New York	May 21	Gravosa	3,910.4
237	Quistconck	Norfolk	May 30	Salonica	6,285.0
47	West Kyska, I (Q.M. 16)	New York	Feb. 27	Trieste	433.4
276	Ocland	New York	June 13	Salonica	.....
270	West Togus	Norfolk	June 11	Ex-Trieste to Spalato	428.6
292	West Togus	Norfolk	June 18	Gravosa	4,798.1
	Total	....	....	....	**50,199.4**

* Arrival numbers from Table 111.

† Q.M. refers to quartermaster invoice number, on commodities chased and transported by the U.S. Army.

nmary of Relief Deliveries

Beans, Peas	Pork Products	Milk	Cocoa	Sugar	Misc. Food	Soap	Clothing and Misc.	Total Tons	Total Value
Commodities in Net Metric Tons of 1,000 Kilograms or 2,204.6 Pounds									
RIOD									
469.9	2,714.0	469.8	.....	.....	.....	....	165.9	55,077.2	$13,191,246.46
.....	.....	.....	.....	.....	16,300.0	....	15,550.0	31,850.0	20,464,191.25
.....	.....	.....	.....	.....	.....	....	667.6	667.6	224,800.00
.....	.....	.....	.....	.....	.....	....	.....	.....	81,140.98
469.9	**2,714.0**	**469.8**	.....	.....	**16,300.0**	....	**16,383.5**	**87,594.8**	**$33,961,378.69**
788.0	985.0	381.0	.....	52.0	48.0	....	14,088.0	33,655.0	$ 9,261,532.00
.....	.....	.....	.....	.....	.....	....	.....	.....	373,660.00
788.0	**985.0**	**381.0**	.....	**52.0**	**48.0**	....	**14,088.0**	**33,655.0**	**$ 9,635,192.00**
257.9	**3,699.0**	**850.8**	.....	**52.0**	**16,348.0**	....	**30,471.5**	**121,249.8**	**$43,596,570.69**
RIOD									
287.9	30.0	1,623.3	239.0	327.7	.....	69.1	.....	3,054.3	$ 1,164,617.41
.....	.....	1.6	.....	127.8	.....	2.7	180.0	317.8	490,705.04
5.0	20.0	.....	.....	.....	.....	....	.....	2,634.0	533,677.16
292.9	**50.0**	**1,624.9**	**239.0**	**455.5**	.....	**71.8**	**180.0**	**6,006.1**	**$ 2,188,999.61**
.....	.....	.....	.....	.....	.....	....	77.7	77.7	$ 76,566.82
.....	.....	.....	.....	.....	.....	....	1.6	1.6	1,303.12
.....	.....	.....	.....	.....	.....	....	23.8	23.8	35,211.19
.....	.....	.....	.....	.....	.....	....	**103.1**	**103.1**	**$ 113,081.13**
292.9	**50.0**	**1,624.9**	**239.0**	**455.5**	.....	**71.8**	**283.1**	**6,109.2**	**$ 2,302,080.74**
550.8	**3,749.0**	**2,475.7**	**239.0**	**507.5**	**16,348.0**	**71.8**	**30,754.6**	**127,359.0**	**$45,898,651.43**

ierican Relief Administration

ined by the United States Treasury—Armistice Period, 1919

Rice	Beans, Peas	Pork Products	Lard	Lard Substitute	Milk	Misc.	Total Tons	Total Value
Contents of Cargoes in Net Metric Tons of 1,000 Kilograms or 2,204.6 Pounds								
....	......	.....	.....	.....	.....	.....	598.1	$ 131,855.47
....	......	.....	.....	.....	.....	.....	190.1	41,912.60
....	......	.....	.....	.....	.....	.....	7,319.9	1,613,739.40
....	......	.....	301.0	.....	27.0	.....	328.0	240,539.90
....	......	.....	.....	.....	.....	.....	7,146.8	1,572,009.30
....	......	.....	.....	.....	.....	.....	5,446.0	1,197,901.40
....	......	19.0	.....	.....	.....	.....	19.0	12,417.00
....	......	1,031.7	1,002.5	.....	294.9	.....	2,329.1	1,558,289.87
....	......	.....	.....	.....	.....	.....	3,859.8	808,391.49
....	......	.....	.....	.....	.....	.....	4,435:9	929,058.20
....	......	144.6	.....	137.9	.....	.....	282.5	187,909.66
....	......	.....	.....	.....	.....	.....	4,747.3	994,282.38
....	......	.....	.....	.....	.....	165.9‡	165.9	31,950.00
....	......	.....	.....	.....	.....	.....	600.0	132,000.00
....	1,469.9	.....	.....	.....	.....	.....	5,380.3	1,193,650.08
....	......	.....	.....	.....	.....	.....	6,285.0	1,225,568.76
....	......	.....	.....	.....	.....	.....	433.4	95,544.00
58.2	......	.....	.....	77.3	147.9	.....	283.4	147,683.79
....	......	.....	.....	.....	.....	.....	428.6	92,158.24
....	......	.....	.....	.....	.....	.....	4,798.1	984,384.92
58.2	**1,469.9**	**1,195.3**	**1,303.5**	**215.2**	**469.8**	**165.9**	**55,077.2**	**$13,191,246.46**

1,050 barrels of oil.

JUGOSLAVIA-

Table 356*

Detail by Steamers of Relief Deliveries b

Steamer	Port of Sailing	Date of Arrival	Port of Arrival	Wheat Flour
		1919		
Saint Patrick	London	January	Fiume	......
War Redcap	Portland	March	Fiume	5,018.0
Dunclutha	New York	April	Fiume	3,047.0
Abaris	London	May	Fiume	......
Sea Glory	London	May	Fiume	......
War Swan	Colombo	May	Salonica	2,132.0
British Stock	....	......	....	......
Total				**10,197.0**

* Cf. Table 133A for value of these supplies and finance on freight.

JUGOSLAVIA-

Table 357

Summary of Arrivals of Relief Suppli

Operation	Table No.	Flour	Rice	Beans, Peas
A.R.A.—Congressional Appropriation, $100,000,000 Fund	358	......	477.3	287.9
A.R.A.-European Children's Fund—Food	359	......	5.7	.....
A.R.A.-European Children's Fund—Clothing	360	......	.....	.....
Serbian Child Welfare Association—Clothing	361	......	.....	.....
American Women's Hospital, Serbia—Clothing	362	......	.....	.....
Jugoslavian Government Donation—Food	363	2,551.0	58.0	5.0
Total	...	**2,551.0**	**541.0**	**292.9**

JUGOSLAVIA-

Table 358

Detail by Steamers of Children's Relief Arrivals Paid for fr

Steamer or Source	Port of Sailing	Date of Arrival	Port of Arrival	Rice
		1919		
Sudbury, Q.M. 51	Philadelphia	Feb. 4	Trieste	....
Sudbury, Q.M. 54	Philadelphia	Feb. 4	Trieste	....
Lake Farge	New York	Apr. 23	Trieste	53.3
Neuse	New York	Apr. 23	Trieste	....
Ida	New York	May 21	Gravosa	....
West Lashaway, II	New York	May 24	Trieste	....
Siretul	London	May 27	Salonica	27.5
Agwistar	New York	June 6	Trieste	....
Ocland	New York	June 13	Salonica	50.0
Lake Clear, V	Bordeaux	July 2	Hamburg	100.0
Augusta Foherczegno	New York	July 29	Trieste	....
Szent Istvan	New York	Aug. 8	Trieste	....
Marianne	New York	Aug. 10	Trieste	....
Remschied *	New York	Aug. 21	Rotterdam	....
Sonnenfels	New York	Aug. 25	Trieste	....
Frederica	New York	Aug. 15	Trieste	....
Brisgravia	New York	Aug. 27	Trieste	246.5
Total				**477.3**
Less Transfers to Austria				
Jugoslavia Stock				....
Remschied				....
Total Transfers				....
Total Net Arrivals				**477.3**

* Commodities shipped from Rotterdam to Mannheim in February, 1920, via Lighter Anna Jacobus.

ıntries Other than the United States

United Kingdom—Armistice Period, 1919

Contents of Cargoes in Net Metric Tons of 1,000 Kilograms or 2,204.6 Pounds

Rye	Beans, Peas	Lard	Milk	Sugar	Miscellaneous: Foods	Miscellaneous: Non-Foods	Total Tons
.....	......	.....	.....	....	....	6,040.0	6,040.0
1,695.0	......	.....	.....	....	....	......	6,713.0
2,421.0	......	.....	.....	....	....	......	5,468.0
......	1,043.0	985.0	381.0	52.0	48.0	1,874.0	4,383.0
......	2,745.0	.....	.....	....	....	2,300.0	5,045.0
......	......	.....	.....	....	....	1,348.0	3,480.0
......	......	.....	.....	....	....	2,526.0	2,526.0
4,116.0	**3,788.0**	**985.0**	**381.0**	**52.0**	**48.0**	**14,088.0**	**33,655.0**

R.A. and A.R.A.-European Children's Fund

Operations—Reconstruction Period, 1919–1924

Commodities in Net Metric Tons of 1,000 Kilograms or 2,204.6 Pounds

Pork Products	Milk	Cocoa	Sugar	Soap	Clothing and Misc.	Total Tons	Total Value
30.0	1,623.3	239.0	327.7	69.1	.....	3,054.3	$1,164,617.41
....	1.6	.....	127.8	2.7	.....	137.8	31,926.20
....	.....	.....	.....	....	180.0	180.0	458,778.84
....	.....	.....	.....	....	79.3	79.3	77,869.94
....	.....	.....	.....	....	23.8	23.8	35,211.19
20.0	.....	.....	.....	....	.....	2,634.0	533,677.16
50.0	**1,624.9**	**239.0**	**455.5**	**71.8**	**283.1**	**6,109.2**	**$2,302,080.74**

ıerican Relief Administration

ıgressional Appropriation for Relief—Reconstruction Period, 1919–1924

Contents of Cargoes in Net Metric Tons of 1,000 Kilograms or 2,204.6 Pounds

Beans, Peas	Pork Products	Milk	Cocoa	Sugar	Soap	Total Tons	Total Value
....	....	107.6	....	....	....	107.6	$ 46,692.45
....	....	92.7	....	....	....	92.7	40,238.10
....	....	211.6	69.8	....	....	334.7	137,069.65
....	....	.....	8.7	....	....	8.7	3,757.38
60.0	....	.....	....	....	....	60.0	16,800.00
....	....	.....	50.3	....	....	50.3	21,626.76
....	....	216.5	27.4	55.9	....	327.3	121,490.31
....	....	297.3	33.0	....	....	330.3	178,828.32
197.2	30.0	90.0	50.8	101.6	....	519.6	181,945.86
....	....	.....	....	....	....	100.0	25,004.50
....	....	.....	18.5	....	....	18.5	11,742.42
....	....	266.8	....	....	....	266.8	110,268.00
....	....	340.8	....	....	....	340.8	140,859.00
....	....	276.8	20.3	128.5	....	425.6	164,173.63
....	....	.....	....	....	2.3	2.3	612.36
....	....	.....	....	....	58.0	58.0	22,628.03
30.7	....	.....	16.5	99.7	8.8	402.2	112,046.59
287.9	**30.0**	**1,900.1**	**295.3**	**385.7**	**69.1**	**3,445.4**	**$1,335,783.36**
....	....	.....	36.0	....	....	36.0	$ 22,860.00
....	....	276.8	20.3	58.0	....	355.1	148,305.95
....	....	**276.8**	**56.3**	**58.0**	....	**391.1**	**$ 171,165.95**
287.9	**30.0**	**1,623.3**	**239.0**	**327.7**	**69.1**	**3,054.3**	**$1,164,617.41**

JUGOSLAVIA–

Table 359

Detail by Source of Arrivals for Chil

Source	Date of Delivery	Commodities in Net Metric Tons of 1,000 Kilograms or 2,204.6 Pounds					Total Value
		Rice	Milk	Sugar	Soap	Total Tons	
	1920						
Czecho-Slovakian Purchase	June 10	...	...	120.0	...	120.0	$24,712.
Austrian Stock Shipped via Hungary	Dec. 22–31	5.7	1.6	7.8	2.7	17.8	7,213.
Total		**5.7**	**1.6**	**127.8**	**2.7**	**137.8**	**$31,926.**

JUGOSLAVIA–

Table 360

Detail by Steamers of Arrivals of Clothing f

Steamer	Port of Sailing	Date of Arrival	Port of Arrival	Shoes (Pairs)	Laces (Pairs)
		1920			
River Orontes	Boston	Jan. 19	Salonica	.....	.....
Romeo	New York	Feb. 10	Salonica	26,136	26,136
Indianola	London	Feb. 17	Salonica	.....	.....
Aleppo	New York	Mar. 9	Salonica	43,796	43,796
Claro	London	Apr. 12	Salonica	.....	.....
Total Deliveries				**69,932**	**69,932**

JUGOSLAVIA-

Table 361

Detail by Steamers of Arrivals of Clothing in Co-operation wi

Steamer	Port of Sailing	Date of Arrival	Port of Arrival	Shoes (Pairs)	Cloth for Suits (Yards)	Lining (Yards
		1921				
Massillon Bridge	New York	May 23	Salonica	15,000	70,058¼	4,364
Blair	New York	July 9	Salonica	.....	.....	4,160
Chester Valley	New York	Nov. 7	Salonica	4,000	.....	12,661
Charges per New York Accounts				.....	.....	.....
Total				**19,000**	**70,058¼**	**21,186**
Hungarian Stock ex-Oregonian, II (for Dr. Reeder)				.....	.....	.....
Grand Total				**19,000**	**70,058¼**	**21,186**

* Detail of internal deliveries not available. Receipts in hands of Serbian Child Welfare Association.

JUGOSLAVIA

Table 362

Detail by Steamers of Arrivals of Clothing in Co-operati

Steamer	Port of Sailing	Date of Arrival	Port of Arrival	Shoes (Pairs)	Stockings (Pairs)	Cloth f Suits (Yard
		1921				
Crewe Hall	New York	Sept. 14	Salonica	7,700	.....	20,051
Chester Valley	New York	Nov. 7	Salonica	2,291	10,000	30,561
Total				**9,991**	**10,000**	**60,612**

* Detail of internal deliveries not available. Receipts in hands of American Women's Hospital.

R.A.-European Children's Fund

ding—Reconstruction Period, 1919–1924

R.A.-European Children's Fund

ldren's Relief—Reconstruction Period, 1919–1924

Stockings (Pairs)	Woolens (Yards)	Thread (Yards)	Needles (No.)	Buttons (No.)	Overcoats (No.)	Sewing Machines (No.)	Total Metric Tons	Total Value
.....	43,347.75	....	30,000	......	....	30	39.0	$100,663.83
.....	114,940.25	13,776,000	36,000	390,528	4,030	..	78.0	207,133.26
37,818	....	....	.....	......	....	..	4.0	21,647.60
.....	....	....	.....	......	....	..	56.0	116,697.68
32,544	....	....	.....	......	....	..	3.0	12,636.47
70,362	**158,288.00**	**13,776,000**	**66,000**	**390,528**	**4,030**	**30**	**180.0**	**$458,778.84**

rbian Child Welfare Association of America*

R.A.-European Children's Fund—Reconstruction Period, 1919–1924

Muslin (Yards)	Thread (Cops)	Woolen Yarn (Lbs.)	Needles (No.)	Buttons (No.)	Sewing Machines (No.)	Leather (Lbs.)	Blouses (No.)	Total Metric Tons	Total Value
94,000	14,400	5,710	100,000	94,608	...	716	....	65.2	$63,733.30
.....	.....	1,214	.....	.....	100	...	....	6.1	3,942.52
.....	.....	.....	.....	.....	...	...	....	6.4	8,047.92
.....	.....	.....	.....	.....	...	...	....	...	843.08
94,000	**14,400**	**6,924**	**100,000**	**94,608**	**100**	**716**	....	**77.7**	**$76,566.82**
.....	.....	.....	.....	.....	...	...	1,000	1.6	1,303.12
94,000	**14,400**	**6,924**	**100,000**	**94,608**	**100**	**716**	**1,000**	**79.3**	**$77,869.94**

nerican Women's Hospital, Serbia*

th A.R.A.-E.C.F.—Reconstruction Period, 1919–1924

Lining (Yards)	Muslin (Yards)	Thread (Cops)	Woolen Yarn (Lbs.)	Needles (No.)	Buttons (No.)	Sewing Machines (No.)	Leather (Lbs.)	Total Metric Tons	Total Value
....	....	...	....	....	......	....	....	12.3	$18,760.27
....	....	312	....	....	250,128	....	....	11.5	16,450.92
....	....	**312**	....	....	**250,128**	....	....	**23.8**	**$35,211.19**

JUGOSLAVIA–

Table 363

Detail of Jugoslavian Government Donatior

Time of Delivery	Commodities in Net Metric Tons of 1,000 Kilograms or 2,204.6 Pounds					Total Value
	Flour	Rice	Beans, Peas	Pork Products	Total Tons	
To July, 1919	2,400.0	58.0	...	20.0	2,478.0	$509,560.
August, 1919, to August, 1920	151.0	....	5.0	....	156.0	24,117.
Total	**2,551.0**	**58.0**	**5.0**	**20.0**	**2,634.0**	**$533,677.**

JUGOSLAVIA–

Table 364

Summary of Internal Deliveries b

District	Table No.	Flour	Rice	Beans, Peas
I. Southern Serbia—Food	365	......	78.7	181.6
II. Southwestern Serbia—Food	366	......	322.6	54.0
III. Northern Serbia—Food	367	......	139.7	52.3
All Districts—Jugoslavian Donations, Food *	...	2,551.0	.....	5.0
All Districts—A.R.A.-E.C.F.—Clothing	368	......	.....	.....
Total	...	**2,551.0**	**541.0**	**292.9**
Less Errors in Receipts †	...	......	.....	.....
Total Net Internal Deliveries—Children's Relief	...	**2,551.0**	**541.0**	**292.9**
Receipts to Co-operating Organizations—Clothing ‡	...	......	.....	.....
Grand Total	...	**2,551.0**	**541.0**	**292.9**

* Receipts turned over to Jugoslavian Government, after being verified by E.C.F. representative.

† 23,440 cases of condensed milk were receipted as evaporated m difference is 63.8 metric tons. The tare on milk receipted as gross inst of net amounts to 75.3 metric tons.

JUGOSLAVIA—A.R.A. and A.R.A.-European Children's Fund

Detail by Districts and by Months of Internal Deliveries for Child Feeding
Reconstruction Period, 1919–1924

Table 365

I. Southern Serbia

Receipt No.	District	Date	Commodities in Net Metric Tons of 1,000 Kilograms or 2,204.6 Pounds							
			Rice	Beans, Peas	Pork Products	Milk Evap., Cond.	Cocoa	Sugar	Soap	Tota Ton
		1919								
1366–71	Monastir	August	3.091	9.137	.....	15.568	2.222	7.090	....	37.
1372–74	Monastir	September	.182	.318	.....	.630	.202	.273	....	1.
1375	Monastir	October	2.909	15.226	.....	15.784	2.727	7.363	....	44.
1376–88	Monastir	Nov. 19–May 20	4.547	18.644	.....	18.704	3.232	8.044	....	53.
	Total to Monastir	....	**10.729**	**43.325**	.....	**50.686**	**8.383**	**22.770**	....	**135.**
		1919								
1346–65	Nish	June 24–July 28	**3.818**	.....	.....	**69.142**	**8.787**	**14.908**	....	**96.**
		1919								
1220–36	Skoplje	June	8.435	.....	.....	61.722	7.496	19.651	....	97.
1237–61	Skoplje	July	15.545	39.400	.....	75.674	11.765	34.161	....	176.
1262–88	Skoplje	August	10.338	42.467	5.000	44.234	6.567	17.284	....	125.

R.A.-European Children's Fund

Children's Relief—Reconstruction Period, 1919–1924

R.A. and A.R.A.-European Children's Fund

tricts—Reconstruction Period, 1919–1924

Commodities in Net Metric Tons of 1,000 Kilograms or 2,204.6 Pounds							
Pork Products	Milk	Cocoa	Sugar	Soap	Clothing and Misc.	Total Tons	Total Value
11.5	453.4	60.8	150.2	.3	.....	936.5	$1,730,220.77
17.0	789.1	105.8	176.6	45.1	.....	1,510.2	
1.5	521.5	72.4	128.7	26.4	.....	942.5	
20.0	.....	.....	....	....	.....	2,576.0	
....	.....	.....	....	....	180.0	180.0	458,778.84
50.0	**1,764.0**	**239.0**	**455.5**	**71.8**	**180.0**	**6,145.2**	....
....	139.1	.....	....	....	.....	139.1	....
50.0	**1,624.9**	**239.0**	**455.5**	**71.8**	**180.0**	**6,006.1**	**$2,188,999.61**
....	.....	.....	....	....	103.1	103.1	113,081.13
50.0	**1,624.9**	**239.0**	**455.5**	**71.8**	**283.1**	**6,109.2**	**$2,302,080.74**

See Table 354 for organizations.

JUGOSLAVIA

Detail by Districts and by Months of Internal Deliveries for Child Feeding

I. Southern Serbia

Table 365—*Continued*

eceipt No.	District	Date	Rice	Beans, Peas	Pork Products	Milk Evap., Cond.	Cocoa	Sugar	Soap	Total Tons
		1919								
9–1309 34–45,	Skoplje	September	4.241	26.307	3.400	16.709	2.520	3.290	....	56.467
10–45	Skoplje	October	3.877	.348	.045	13.695	1.639	.970	....	20.574
46–79	Skoplje	November	2.592	1.215	.600	6.827	.970	.739	....	12.943
0–1117	Skoplje	December	3.207	3.285	.232	16.436	1.845	3.522	.060	28.587
		1920								
17–58	Skoplje	January	3.910	8.249	.136	17.368	1.664	6.083	.005	37.415
59–96	Skoplje	February	6.663	11.117	1.461	56.166	5.932	18.251	.072	99.662
6–1219	Skoplje	March	5.356	5.858	.620	24.765	3.207	8.611	.184	48.601
	Total to Skoplje........	....	**64.164**	**138.246**	**11.494**	**333.596**	**43.605**	**112.562**	**.321**	**703.988**
	Total to Southern Serbia	....	**78.711**	**181.571**	**11.494**	**453.424**	**60.775**	**150.240**	**.321**	**936.536**

JUGOSLAVIA—A.R.A. and A.R.A.-European Children's Fund

Detail by Districts and by Months of Internal Deliveries for Child Feeding

Reconstruction Period, 1919–1924

Table 366

II. Southwestern Serbia

Receipt No.	District	Date	Commodities in Net Metric Tons of 1,000 Kilograms or 2,204.6 Pounds							
			Rice	Beans, Peas	Pork Products	Milk Evap., Cond.	Cocoa	Sugar	Soap	Total Tons
R12–17, R39	Dalmatia	Sept., 1919–Apr., 1920	**5.000**	....	....	.....	....	....	....	**5.0**
		1919								
386–88	Montenegro	July	....	....	....	2.808	.202	.200	....	3.2
389	Montenegro	August	....	....	....	.653	....	....	....	.6
390–93	Montenegro	September	....	....	....	2.068	.100	.253	....	2.4
394, R15, 16	Montenegro	October	24.000	....	....	1.088	....	....	3.570	28.6
395–99	Montenegro	November	.186	.468	....	.300	.024	....	....	.9
400–25	Montenegro	December	.180	....	....	2.770	.182	.125	....	3.2
		1920								
426–61	Montenegro	January	.174	.025	....	1.200	.064	.107	....	1.5
462–88	Montenegro	February	12.981	.450	....	30.058	2.486	7.158	....	53.1
489–508	Montenegro	March	7.605	1.842	....	8.678	1.208	3.978	....	23.3
509–13	Montenegro	April	2.158	....	....	2.784	.556	.815	....	6.3
513–19	Montenegro	May	2.163	....	....	3.786	.646	.707	....	7.3
520–28, 530–33	Montenegro	July	.995	....	....	12.194	2.546	3.653	....	19.3
529–34, 535	Montenegro	August	.682	.100	....	13.060	1.825	3.216	....	18.8
	Total to Montenegro		**51.124**	**2.885**	....	**81.447**	**9.839**	**20.212**	**3.570**	**169.0**
		1919								
536–37	Trebinje	July	.100	....	....	.653	.100	.197	....	1.0
538–45, D5	Trebinje	August	.100	....	....	.934	5.100	....	....	6.1
546–51	Trebinje	September	....	.182	....	1.769	.603	.099	....	2.6
552–60, R7, 8	Trebinje	October	4.000	....	....	.818	.072	.112	.570	5.5
561–67	Trebinje	November	....	....	....	.712	.059	.140	....	.9
568–73	Trebinje	December	....	....	....	.915	.079	.112	....	1.1
		1920								
574–81	Trebinje	January	....	....	....	.633	.252	.132	....	1.0
582–89	Trebinje	February	.384	.056	....	3.853	.252	.646	....	5.1
590–96	Trebinje	March	.172	.193	....	1.186	.093	.166	.051	1.8
597–607	Trebinje	April	.584	.198	....	2.274	.217	.559	.124	3.9
608–11	Trebinje	June	.407	....	....	6.052	.812	.906	....	8.1
	Total to Trebinje		**5.747**	**.629**	....	**19.799**	**7.639**	**3.069**	**.745**	**37.6**
		1919								
612–23	Mostar	July	.005	....	....	8.350	.674	2.285	....	11.3
624–40, D5	Mostar	August	.018	....	....	4.707	6.719	1.631	....	13.0
641–53	Mostar	September	1.156	....	....	8.917	.822	.396	....	11.2
654–56	Mostar	October	.162	....	....	.697	.076	....	....	.9
657–68, R18–20, 45	Mostar	November	12.000	....	....	5.976	.591	.773	....	19.3
669–77	Mostar	December	.580	....	....	14.286	1.002	3.357	....	19.2
		1920								
678	Mostar	January	....	....	....	.635	.045	.130	....	.8
679–84	Mostar	February	1.001	....	....	3.265	.280	1.251	.225	6.
685–93	Mostar	March	1.914	....	....	6.359	.673	1.547	.429	10.
694–706	Mostar	April	2.318	....	....	4.747	.291	1.485	.734	9.
707–716	Mostar	May	5.734	....	....	5.977	.378	2.203	1.529	15.
	Total to Mostar		**24.888**	....	....	**63.916**	**11.551**	**15.058**	**2.917**	**118.**
		1919								
717–25, 727–31	Spalato	June	1.883	....	....	21.933	2.933	5.836	....	32.
726, 763–71	Spalato	July	.498	....	....	5.173	.767	1.481	....	7.
748–49	Spalato	September	....	....	....	.087	.051	.013	....	.
733, 737, 744–47, 750–62	Spalato	October	....	2.873	....	20.945	3.793	3.443	....	31.
738–43	Spalato	November	....	.094	....	8.987	.632	.299	....	10.
732, 734–36	Spalato	December	.180	1.167	....	13.038	.885	1.677	....	16.
		1920								
R9–11	Spalato	January–April	15.000	....	....	.....	....	....	....	15.
	Total to Spalato		**17.561**	**4.134**	....	**70.163**	**9.061**	**12.749**	....	**113.**

JUGOSLAVIA

Detail by Districts and by Months of Internal Deliveries for Child Feeding

Table 366—*Continued* II. Southwestern Serbia

Receipt No.	District	Date	Rice	Beans, Peas	Pork Products	Milk Evap., Cond.	Cocoa	Sugar	Soap	Total Tons
		Commodities in Net Metric Tons of 1,000 Kilograms or 2,204.6 Pounds								
		1919								
D5	Sarajevo	August	14.936	....	....	.....	6.000	....	....	20.936
772-73, 775-78	Sarajevo	September	....	....	....	7.433	2.586	....	....	10.019
, R21-22, R44-45	Sarajevo	October	35.000	....	....	.218	.102	....	8.160	43.480
780-86, PD9	Sarajevo	November	.101	3.319	....	8.505	2.037	.101	....	14.063
787-816	Sarajevo	December	.147	.180	....	48.683	9.266	10.813	....	69.089
		1920								
817-25, 866-87	Sarajevo	January	3.309	1.075	....	39.780	3.970	6.047	1.271	55.452
.....	Sarajevo	February	6.474	....	....	21.382	1.526	4.022	.858	34.262
.....	Sarajevo	March	2.994	....	....	12.118	1.906	2.823	.796	20.637
.....	Sarajevo	April	7.977	.653	....	53.559	3.820	8.925	2.382	77.316
950-64	Sarajevo	March-April	.428	....	....	13.566	1.630	4.002	....	19.626
965-67	Sarajevo	May	11.988	.272	....	141.676	15.240	29.159	....	198.335
	Total to Sarajevo		**83.354**	**5.499**	....	**346.920**	**48.083**	**65.892**	**13.467**	**563.215**
		1919								
D-4	Ragusa	May	1.016	....	....	.....	....	....	....	1.016
968-78	Ragusa	June	.045	....	....	1.568	.282	.883	....	2.778
PD1-5, PD7	Ragusa	July	....	10.653	....	2.025	.245	.505	....	13.428
968-78	Ragusa	August	.100	.100	....	2.482	.301	.667	....	3.650
R1-6, 23-44	Ragusa	September	5.950	....	....	2.221	.264	.590	....	9.025
968-78	Ragusa	October	....	....	....	.980	.285	.536	....	1.801
968-78	Ragusa	November	....	....	....	2.439	.308	.585	....	3.332
968-78	Ragusa	December	....	....	....	2.700	.319	.613	....	3.632
		1920								
968-78	Ragusa	January	....	....	....	2.678	.329	.617	....	3.624
968-78	Ragusa	February	....	....	....	2.678	.328	.616	....	3.622
968-78	Ragusa	March	....	....	....	2.787	.330	.360	....	3.477
968-78	Ragusa	April	.146	.430	....	2.722	.326	.245	....	3.869
	Total to Ragusa		**7.257**	**11.183**	....	**25.280**	**3.317**	**6.217**	....	**53.254**
		1919								
D2, 3, 7	Cattaro	July	7.925	....	....	.....	....	....	....	7.925
979-1033	Cattaro	September	.557	.405	....	9.512	1.728	1.550	....	13.752
979-1033	Cattaro	October	....	.085	....	1.349	.097	.300	....	1.831
979-1033	Cattaro	November	....	....	....	.925	....	.240	....	1.165
979-1033	Cattaro	December	....	....	....	4.505	.490	1.317	....	6.312
	Total to Cattaro		**8.482**	**.490**	....	**16.291**	**2.315**	**3.407**	....	**30.985**
		1919								
D 1	Visegrad	June	.711	....	....	.....	....	....	....	.711
PD 6-8	Visegrad	August	....	2.857	....	.....	....	....	....	2.857
	Total to Visegrad		**.711**	**2.857**	....	.....	....	....	....	**3.568**
			RECEIPTS FROM OUTLYING POINTS							
R 41-43	Programs I, II, and III Miscellaneous	May, 1919–April, 1920	5.649	....	5.100	.....	....	....	....	10.749
		1920								
1384-88	Trebinje	May	.160	.156	....	.894	.069	.240	.040	1.559
1389-1419	Cattaro	February-May	3.725	....	....	3.948	1.272	1.795	.795	11.535
1420-60	Spalato	March-May	14.358	....	....	19.308	2.762	3.609	2.367	42.404
1484-1527	Montenegro	March-May	3.189	.450	....	7.715	1.146	2.628	1.027	16.155
1528-34	Trebinje	May-June	.672	.138	....	2.326	.070	.381	....	3.587
1535-47	Mostar	June	1.077	....	....	8.902	.436	.515	.776	11.706
1547-57	Spalato	Nov.-Dec., 1919–Jan., 1920	....	....	....	8.541	1.428	1.187	....	11.156
		1920								
1558-72	Sarajevo	July	.386	.236	....	4.145	.305	8.062	.057	13.191
1573-81	Ragusa	July	4.959	.107	....	4.457	.003	1.089	.674	11.289
1582-83	Cattaro	June	.190	....	....	.108	.050	.100	.040	.488

[*Concluded on next page*]

JUGOSLAVIA

Detail by Districts and by Months of Internal Deliveries for Child Feeding

Table 366—*Concluded*

II. Southwestern Serbia

Receipt No.	District	Date	Rice	Beans, Peas	Pork Products	Milk Evap., Cond.	Cocoa	Sugar	Soap	Total Tons
			Commodities in Net Metric Tons of 1,000 Kilograms or 2,204.6 Pounds							
			RECEIPTS FROM OUTLYING POINTS—Cont.							
	Program IV	1920								
1584–87	Sarajevo	June 10–July 15	38.530	15.635	9.615	52.119	2.055	15.288	11.042	144.2
1596, 1599	Cattaro	June 26–July 31	6.900	....	.480	9.280	.900	.909	1.400	19.8
1597	Spalato	June 26	6.900	....	....	9.280	.900	2.865	1.400	21.3
1598	Mostar	June 26	11.590	....	....	.....	....	4.700	1.716	18.0
1600–2	Zelenika	June 26–July 31	20.178	....	1.830	34.277	2.600	6.544	3.030	68.4
1603–4	Ragusa	Aug. 12–13	....	9.575	....	.....	....	.045	....	9.6
	Total to Outlying Points	....	**118.463**	**26.297**	**17.025**	**165.300**	**13.996**	**49.957**	**24.364**	**415.4**
	Total to Southwestern Serbia	....	**322.587**	**53.974**	**17.025**	**789.116**	**105.801**	**176.561**	**45.063**	**1,510.1**

JUGOSLAVIA—A.R.A. and A.R.A.-European Children's Fund

Detail by Districts and by Months of Internal Deliveries for Child Feeding

Reconstruction Period, 1919–1924

Table 367

III. Belgrade and Northern Serbia

Receipt No.	District	Date	Rice	Beans, Peas	Pork Products	Milk Evap., Cond.	Cocoa	Sugar	Soap	Total Tons
			Commodities in Net Metric Tons of 1,000 Kilograms or 2,204.6 Pounds							
		1919								
1–5	Belgrade Warehouse	June	5.845	....	....	11.360	5.830	2.535	....	25.5
6–19	Belgrade Warehouse	July	5.876	....	....	52.947	5.671	5.519	....	70.0
20–38	Belgrade Warehouse	August	5.885	3.420	....	27.643	2.726	2.745	....	42.4
39–50	Belgrade Warehouse	September	1.313	.765	....	3.511	.579	1.505	....	7.6
51–76	Belgrade Warehouse	October	5.490	6.535	....	32.890	3.532	10.730	....	59.1
77–96	Belgrade Warehouse	November	3.285	3.330	....	15.566	1.624	3.870	1.550	29.2
97–107	Belgrade Warehouse	December	1.800	1.440	....	5.573	.856	.360	1.870	11.8
		1920								
108–12	Belgrade Warehouse	January	1.980	.540	....	5.861	.466	.135	.480	9.4
113–42	Belgrade Warehouse	February	5.202	2.320	....	8.297	1.013	5.381	2.635	24.8
143–84	Belgrade Warehouse	March	32.473	4.256	....	54.036	5.392	18.010	9.678	123.8
185–214	Belgrade Warehouse	April	3.473	.648	....	5.851	.605	.762	.516	11.8
215–18	Belgrade Warehouse	May	.101	....	....	.277	.023	.025	.060	.4
207	Belgrade Warehouse	June	.540	.855	....	18.226	1.415	2.300	....	23.3
208	Belgrade Warehouse	August	.270	.270	....	4.942	.909	.900	....	7.2
	Total to Belgrade Kitchens	....	**73.533**	**24.379**	....	**246.980**	**30.641**	**54.777**	**16.789**	**447.0**
		1919								
223	Croatia Warehouse	December	.....	....	....	.218	....	....	....	.2
		1920								
222	Croatia Warehouse	February	.086	.024	....	.152	.014	.045	....	.3
209–18	Croatia Warehouse	April	2.669	3.203	....	5.416	.472	1.437	....	13.1
1461–74	Croatia Warehouse	May	1.367	....	....	2.562	.248	.738	....	4.9
247	Croatia Warehouse	May	2.931	....	....	6.758	.509	1.641	....	11.8
X41–1	Lika, ex-Zagreb	May	2.880	.365	....	4.800	.480	1.520	.348	10.3
X41–2	Zagorje, ex-Zagreb	May	2.880	....	....	4.800	.480	1.520	....	9.6
X41–3	Zumberak, ex-Zagreb	May	1.440	....	....	2.400	.240	.760	....	4.8
X41–4	Catholic Ladys, ex-Zagreb	May	1.400	.400	....	2.400	.240	.760	.300	5.5
X41–5	Committee for Children, ex-Zagreb	May	1.440	.400	....	2.400	.240	.760	1.152	6.3
X41–6	Institutions of Zagreb	May	1.152	....	....	1.920	.192	.608	....	3.8
X41–7	Children's Home Agram and Susak, ex-Zagreb	May	.604	.168	....	1.008	.100	.322	.504	2.7
X41–8	Local Committee Croatia, ex-Zagreb	May	.720	....	....	1.200	.120	.380	....	2.4
	Total to Croatia	....	**19.609**	**4.560**	....	**36.034**	**3.335**	**10.491**	**2.304**	**76.3**

JUGOSLAVIA

Detail by Districts and by Months of Internal Deliveries for Child Feeding

'able 367—*Continued* III. Belgrade and Northern Serbia

ceipt No.	District	Date	Rice	Beans, Peas	Pork Products	Milk Evap., Cond.	Cocoa	Sugar	Soap	Total Tons
			Commodities in Net Metric Tons of 1,000 Kilograms or 2,204.6 Pounds							
		1919								
6-61	Slovenia	June	12.103	....	....	98.320	12.641	25.000	....	148.064
8-55	Slovenia	July–August	2.700	9.620	....	86.580	19.560	28.589	....	147.049
		1920								
75-83	Slovenia (Program III)........	April	1.274	.249	....	2.156	.224	.658	.603	5.164
	Total to Slovenia...........	....	16.077	9.869	....	187.056	32.425	54.247	.603	300.277
		1919								
374-76	Croatian Coast	December	.096	.127	....	.098	.012	....	.064	.397
		1920								
....	Croatian Coast	January	4.517	2.872	....	5.122	.439	.153	1.441	14.544
....	Croatian Coast	February	1.630	2.192	....	2.446	.213	.510	.652	7.643
....	Croatian Coast	March	.775	1.198	....	1.794	.221	.443	.281	4.712
....	Croatian Coast	April	1.710	2.250	....	5.879	.631	.803	.600	11.873
....	Croatian Coast	May	.180	.225	....	.500	.052	.090	.080	1.127
	Total to Croatian Coast.....	....	**8.908**	**8.864**	....	**15.839**	**1.568**	**1.999**	**3.118**	**40.296**
	Program IV	1920								
88-90	Cirkvenika	June 6–July 15	5.400	1.500	.482	9.812	1.942	2.973	1.390	23.499
91-92	Ljubljana	June 10–July 15	5.400	1.500	.482	9.280	.900	2.865	....	20.427
1593	Belgrade	June 10	5.320	....	....	7.200	.720	.820	.800	14.860
94-95	Zagreb	June 10–July 15	5.400	1.602	.482	9.280	.900	.573	1.400	19.637
	Total, Program IV..........	....	**21.520**	**4.602**	**1.446**	**35.572**	**4.462**	**7.231**	**3.590**	**78.423**
	Total to Northern Serbia....	....	**139.647**	**52.274**	**1.446**	**521.481**	**72.431**	**128.745**	**26.404**	**942.428**

JUGOSLAVIA—A.R.A.-European Children's Fund

Detail by Districts of Internal Deliveries of Children's Clothing Outfits

Table 368* Reconstruction Period, 1919–1924

District	Shoes (Pairs)	Laces (Pairs)	Stockings (Pairs)	Overcoats (Each)	Suits Boys (Each)	Dresses Girls (Each)	Caps Boys (Each)
nastir	6,000	6,000	6,000	3,000	1,500	1,500	3,000
plje	6,000	6,000	6,000	3,000	1,500	1,500	3,000
h	8,000	8,000	8,000	4,000	2,000	2,000	4,000
grade	13,932	13,932	14,362	11,030	3,500	3,500	11,030
visad	3,000	3,000	3,000	1,500	750	750	1,500
otica	3,000	3,000	3,000	1,500	750	750	1,500
greb	7,000	7,000	7,000	3,500	1,750	1,750	3,500
bljana	4,000	4,000	4,000	2,000	1,000	1,000	2,000
ajevo	8,000	8,000	8,000	4,000	2,000	2,000	4,000
inje	6,000	6,000	6,000	3,000	1,500	1,500	3,000
lato	5,000	5,000	5,000	2,500	1,250	1,250	2,500
Total †	**69,932**	**69,932**	**70,362**	**39,030**	**17,500**	**17,500**	**39,030**

See Table 360, the woolens, thread, needles, buttons, and sewing hines were used in the manufacture of 70,000 garments, i.e., 35,000 coats for boys and girls, 17,500 suits for boys, and 17,500 dresses for s. From the remnants 39,030 caps were made.

† The total clothing is equivalent to 180.0 metric tons.

Table 369

LATVIA—

Operation	Table No.	Flour	Rice	Beans, Peas
				ARMISTIC
A.R.A.—Congressional Appropriation, $100,000,000 Fund	370	11,244.6	233.5	564.3
A.R.A.—Freight on Charity Shipment	143	......	.....	.....
U.S. Liquidation Commission (War Dept.)	122	......	.....	.....
Total American Relief	...	**11,244.6**	**233.5**	**564.3**
United Kingdom—Finance on Freight	133	......	.....	.....
Total Relief, Armistice Period	108	**11,244.6**	**233.5**	**564.3**
				RECONSTRUCTIO
A.R.A.—Congressional Appropriation, $100,000,000 Fund	371, 377	260.2	310.0	447.0
A.R.A.-European Children's Fund	371, 377	2,114.3	505.9	205.9
Latvian Government Donation *	371, 377	......	28.9	342.0
Norwegian Government Donation	371, 377	......	.....	.....
Total Children's Relief	380, 381	**2,374.5**	**844.8**	**994.9**
A.R.A.-E.C.F.—Sale to Latvian Government	377	2.3	29.9	.9
A.R.A.-E.C.F.—Food Drafts and Bulk Sales (Net) †	378	15.7	3.9	5.7
Total Other than Children's Relief	...	**18.0**	**33.8**	**6.6**
Total, Reconstruction Period	149	**2,392.5**	**878.6**	**1,001.5**
Grand Total Relief Deliveries	102	**13,637.1**	**1,112.1**	**1,565.8**

* In addition to these supplies used in Latvia, the Latvian government donated warehouse space for the storage of transit supplies, en route Russia, in the amount of $24,257.69.

† Commodities used for student feeding in Lithuania have been deducted from Latvian bulk sales. Cf. Table 391.

LATVIA-

Table 370

Detail by Steamers of Relief Deliveries, Paid for by Funds from t

Arrival No.	Steamer	Port of Sailing	Date of Arrival	Port of Arrival	Wheat Flour	Cereal Flour
			1919			
108	Mirach, Besoeki	New York	Apr. 8	Copenhagen	.....	500.0
112	Lake Wimico, III *	Rotterdam	Apr. 9	Libau	1,166.3	.....
228	Lake Wimico, IV †	Bordeaux	May 26	Libau	462.2	.....
235	Lake Mary, IV †	Bordeaux	May 30	Libau	1,151.5	.....
236	Lake Mary, IV †	Bordeaux	May 30	Riga	847.5	.....
273	Tyr	New York	June 12	Libau	397.9	.....
322	Lake Tulare, V †	Bordeaux	July 1	Riga	1,465.3	.....
325	Charlot	New York	July 2	Riga	2,525.8	.....
363	Lake Dancey, IV	Danzig	July 25	Libau	228.1	.....
376	Kagera	New York	Aug. 21	Danzig	2,500.0	.....
	Total	....	....	....	**10,744.6**	**500.0**

* Rotterdam transshipment ex-Eastern Light.

† From U.S. Army stocks in France.

nmary of Relief Deliveries

Pork Products	Milk	Cocoa	Sugar	Misc. Food	Soap	Clothing and Misc.	Total Tons	Total Value
Commodities in Net Metric Tons of 1,000 Kilograms or 2,204.6 Pounds								
RIOD								
771.1	500.2	....	.....	.....	....	....	13,313.7	$3,323,818.79
.....	.....	....	.....	.....	....	....	......	159.72
.....	.....	....	.....	5,378.0	....	918.0	6,296.0	2,556,952.84
771.1	**500.2**	....	....	**5,378.0**	....	**918.0**	**19,609.7**	**$5,880,931.35**
.....	.....	....	.....	.....	....	....	......	80,920.00
771.1	**500.2**	....	.....	**5,378.0**	....	**918.0**	**19,609.7**	**$5,961,851.35**
RIOD								
43.3	814.0	83.2	147.9	.....	36.7	....	2,142.3	$ 753,774.72
122.7	670.7	71.4	263.8	.....	7.9	57.7	4,020.3	752,076.08
76.5	31.2	....	.....	.....	....	....	478.6	60,879.55
.....	.....	....	.....	6.6	....	....	6.6	3,960.00
242.5	**1,515.9**	**154.6**	**411.7**	**6.6**	**44.6**	**57.7**	**6,647.8**	**$1,570,690.35**
.1	.....	....	.3	.....	....	....	33.5	$ 2,720.62
25.6	19.6	1.1	3.7	.3	....	....	75.6	14,759.37
25.7	**19.6**	**1.1**	**4.0**	**.3**	....	....	**109.1**	**$ 17,479.99**
268.2	**1,535.5**	**155.7**	**415.7**	**6.9**	**44.6**	**57.7**	**6,756.9**	**$1,588,170.34**
1,039.3	**2,035.7**	**155.7**	**415.7**	**5,384.9**	**44.6**	**975.7**	**26,366.6**	**$7,550,021.69**

nerican Relief Administration

ngressional Appropriation for Relief—Armistice Period, 1919

Rice	Beans, Peas	Pork	Lard	Lard Substitute	Milk	Total Tons	Total Value
Contents of Cargoes in Net Metric Tons of 1,000 Kilograms or 2,204.6 Pounds							
.....	.....	65.0	20.0	.....	4.8	589.8	$ 140,458.44
.....	.....	.....	....	.....	.....	1,166.3	247,707.91
.....	.....	.....	....	.....	.....	462.2	97,066.62
.....	.....	.....	....	.....	.....	1,151.5	241,812.27
.....	.....	132.4	....	.....	104.0	1,083.9	336,575.88
.....	149.2	.....	....	15.3	.....	562.4	131,388.86
161.2	.....	127.5	....	.....	55.5	1,809.5	487,620.56
.....	415.1‡	.....	....	410.9	335.9	3,687.7	1,057,548.94
72.3	.....	.....	....	.....	.....	300.4	71,139.31
.....	.....	.....	....	.....	.....	2,500.0	512,500.00
233.5	**564.3**	**324.9**	**20.0**	**426.2**	**500.2**	**13,313.7**	**$3,323,818.79**

28.1 tons delivered at Libau.

LATVIA—

Table 371

Summary by Operations of Arrivals of Reli[e]

Operation	Table No.	Flour	Rice	Beans, Peas
A.R.A.—Congressional Appropriation, $100,000,000 Fund	372	260.2	310.0	447.0
A.R.A.-European Children's Fund—Food	373	2,135.5	540.5	214.1
A.R.A.-European Children's Fund—Clothing	374	.....	.....	.....
Latvian Government Donation—Food	375	.....	28.9	342.0
Norwegian Government Donation—Food *	...	.....	.....	.....
Total †	...	**2,395.7**	**879.4**	**1,003.1**

* Shipped via Lake Dancey, V, Danzig to Riga, arrived July 15, 1919.

† This total includes 8.4 metric tons, value $926.78, which represe[n] a Latvian bulk sale, delivered to Lithuania for student feeding.

LATVIA-

Table 372*

Detail by Steamers of Arrivals for Children's Relief, Paid for by Fun[d]

Steamer	Port of Sailing	Date of Arrival	Port of Arrival	Flour
		1919		
Lake Wimico, IV	Rotterdam	May 26	Libau	....
Lake Wimico, IV	Bordeaux	May 26	Libau	....
Lake Mary, IV	Bordeaux	May 30	Libau	1.6
Lake Mary, IV	Rotterdam	May 30	Libau	....
Tyr	(U.S.A.)	June 12	Libau	108.6
Lake Tulare, V	Bordeaux	July 1	Riga	90.0
Charlot	(U.S.A.)	July 2	Libau	....
Charlot	(U.S.A.)	July 9	Riga	....
Lake Dancey, V	Danzig	July 15	Riga	....
Lake Dancey, V	Danzig	July 25	Libau	60.0
Remschied †	New York	Aug. 21	Rotterdam	....
Schwarzenfels and Danzig Stock ‡	(U.S.A.)	Aug. ..	Danzig	....
Total				**260.2**
Saratov (Transferred from Northwest Russia and Esthonia Stock)	Reval	....	Riga	....
Total				**260.2**
Less Transfers to Lithuania				....
Grand Total				**260.2**

* Cf. Table 376 for shipments to final port of discharge.

† Transshipped via Bavaria, I.

.R.A. and A.R.A.-European Children's Fund

upplies—Reconstruction Period, 1919–1924

Commodities in Net Metric Tons of 1,000 Kilograms or 2,204.6 Pounds								
Pork Products	Milk	Cocoa	Sugar	Misc. Food	Soap	Clothing and Misc.	Total Tons	Total Value
43.3	814.0	83.2	147.9	...	36.7	....	2,142.3	$ 753,774.72
149.0	691.5	72.7	268.6	.3	7.9	....	4,080.1	571,562.35
....	....	....	.....	...	....	57.7	57.7	198,763.64
76.5	31.2	....	.....	...	....	....	478.6	60,879.55
....	....	....	.....	6.6	....	....	6.6	3,960.00
268.8	**1,536.7**	**155.9**	**416.5**	**6.9**	**44.6**	**57.7**	**6,765.3**	**$1,588,940.26‡**

‡ Total $1,588,940.26 less $926.78 (value of bulk sale delivered to huania) plus $156.86 (surplus derived from Latvian bulk sales) leaves 588,170.34, or net value of relief deliveries per Table 369.

merican Relief Administration

om the Congressional Appropriation for Relief—Reconstruction Period, 1919–1924

Contents of Cargoes in Net Metric Tons of 1,000 Kilograms or 2,204.6 Pounds								
Rice	Beans, Peas	Pork Products	Milk	Cocoa	Sugar	Soap	Total Tons	Total Value
8.0	25.0	....	....	3.1	....	....	36.1	$ 11,168.57
....	....	15.2	29.6	....	....	....	44.8	24,687.63
....	....	.1	....	....	....	....	1.7	452.78
....	....	....	....	....	14.0	....	14.0	3,788.64
....	9.3	....	183.7	....	....	....	301.6	121,632.94
41.0	....	20.0	20.0	....	....	....	171.0	55,031.45
....	....	....	6.9	....	....	....	6.9	2,756.25
....	15.0	2.0	....	....	....	....	17.0	5,431.94
....	....	6.0	....	19.2	....	....	25.2	13,278.05
30.0	40.1	....	....	24.2	36.3	....	190.6	54,138.37
....	....	....	273.8	....	....	....	273.8	120,383.25
81.0	251.6	....	197.0	11.7	97.6	41.7	680.6	220,077.03
160.0	**341.0**	**43.3**	**711.0**	**58.2**	**147.9**	**41.7**	**1,763.3**	**$632,826.90**
150.0	106.0	....	103.0	25.0	....	....	384.0	122,219.00
310.0	**447.0**	**43.3**	**814.0**	**83.2**	**147.9**	**41.7**	**2,147.3**	**$755,045.90**
....	....	....	....	....	....	5.0	5.0	1,271.18
310.0	**447.0**	**43.3**	**814.0**	**83.2**	**147.9**	**36.7**	**2,142.3**	**$753,774.72**

‡ Transshipped via Lake Fray.

Table 373*

Detail by Steamers of Arrivals of Reli

Steamer	Transshipped via	Port of Sailing	Date of Arrival	Port of Arrival
			1919	
Comité National, Belgium........	E. H. Stinnes to St. Croix..........	Antwerp	Nov. 30	Rotterda
			1920	
St. Thomas, I...................	....	(United Kingdom)	Jan. 19	Riga
Comité National, Belgium........	Bavaria, I	Antwerp	Feb. ..	Rotterda
Frazier & Company Purchase.....	St. Thomas, II..............	London	Feb. 22	Riga
Frazier & Company Purchase.....	Reval, IV	London	Mar. 6	Libau
Willdomino	Elin	New York	Mar. 20	Danzig
A.R.A.W. Stock, Danzig..........	St. Thomas, III.............	(U.S.A.)	May ..	Danzig
Herefordshire	Mineral, II	Rangoon	Aug. 18	Hamburg
Westford	Echo, II and Martha, I to Meitzung...	New Orleans	Sept. 13	Hamburg
Cornish City	Meitzung and Torfrid	New York	Dec. 31	Danzig
			1921	
Modlin Purchase	Meitzung and Torfrid..............	(Poland)	Jan. 13	Danzig
Ipswich, I......................	Progress, IV to Stadt Memel.........	New York	Jan. 25	Hamburg
Leeds City, I...................	Torfrid	New York	Feb. 7	Danzig
Phoenix Bridge	Johanna and August to Echo, IV.....	New Orleans	Feb. 21	Hamburg
Homer City, II..................	Progress, V to Torfrid	New York	Feb. 25	Hamburg
Bradclyde, II	Torfrid	New Orleans	Apr. 2	Danzig
Westbrook	Adele, II to Torfrid	New Orleans	Apr. 9	Hamburg
Watsness, II	Echo, IV	New York	May 13	Danzig
Nemaha	Progress, VII to Wasa.............	Philadelphia	May 15	Hamburg
Delevan	Echo, IV	New York	May 17	Danzig
Warsaw Purchase	Echo, IV and Stadt Memel...........	(Poland)	May 30	Danzig
Walter Luckenbach	Kellersee, IV to Stadt Memel........	Philadelphia	June 12	Hamburg
Warsaw Purchase	Wotan	(Poland)	June 30	Danzig
Hawaiian, III	Sensal, IV to Stadt Memel and Neva..	New York	July 4	Hamburg
Orbita, II	Adele, III to Neva................	New York	July 14	Hamburg
Mount Clinton, I................	Imperial, II to Neva..............	New York	July 19	Hamburg
Michigan	Sea Lighter 164 to Stadt Memel......	New Orleans	July 20	Hamburg
Ipswich, II	Imperial, III to Neva.............	New York	July 28	Hamburg
Panama, I.......................	Neva	San Francisco	Aug. 13	Danzig
Estonia	Ulrikka	New York	Aug. 30	Danzig
Hawaiian, V	Weichsel, IX to Bolten............	New York	Oct. 10	Hambur
Glentworth	Guenther Russ	New Orleans	Nov. 1	Hambur
Panola	....	Philadelphia	Nov. 5	Riga
Mount Clay, V...................	Martha Russ	New York	Dec. 19	Hambur
Gdansk	Rimfakse	New York	Dec. 23	Danzig
			1922	
Texan, II	Norderney, III	Portland	Jan. 19	Hambur
Gasconier	Hansa, V to Bolten...............	New York	Jan. 26	Hambur
Local Purchase	....	Riga	Jan. 31	Riga
Wachsmuth Purchase 2 and 3....	Norderney, III	(Czecho-Slovakia)	Jan. 31	Hambur
Dallas	Strassburg, VI	New York	Feb. 9	Hambur
Mount Carroll, VII	Gotenhof	New York	Feb. 15	Hambur
Georgian	Gotenhof	New York	Feb. 21	Hambur
Potomac, IV.....................	Moewe, III to Bolten..............	New York	Mar. 3	Hambur
Mount Clinton, IV...............	Strassburg, VI, Marathon...........	New York	Mar. 7	Hambur
Mount Clinton, IV...............	Marathon	New York	Mar. 7	Hambur
Western Ocean	Bolama	New Orleans	Mar. 7	Hambur
Peninsular State	Moewe, IV to Bolten..............	New York	Mar. 10	Hambur
Morristown, I	Bolama	Philadelphia and New York	Mar. 12	Hambur
Nobles, II	Christel Salling, II..............	New Orleans	Apr. 15	Hambur
Western Scout	Strassburg, VI	New York	Apr. 26	Hambur
Chappaqua, II	Coblenz, III	Norfolk	Apr. 28	Hambur
Minnekahda, VI	Strassburg, VI and Coblenz, III.....	New York	Apr. 30	Hambur
Sapinero	Coblenz, III	New Orleans	May 14	Hambur
Ex-Port Stock	....	(U.S.A.)	......	Riga
Sundry Transportation Charges..	....	....	......	....
Total	....	....	......	....
Less Transfers to Lithuania......	....	....	......	....
Total	....	....	......	....

* Cf. Table 376 for shipments to final port of discharge.

† Corned beef.

..R.A.-European Children's Fund

upplies—Reconstruction Period, 1919–1924

Contents of Cargoes in Net Metric Tons of 1,000 Kilograms or 2,204.6 Pounds										
Wheat Flour	Rice	Beans, Peas	Pork Products	Milk	Cocoa	Sugar	Misc. Food	Soap	Total Tons	Total Value
....	....	....	42.1	....	....	....	...	....	42.1	$ 17,648.64
....	103.3	....	....	....	....	....	...	....	103.3	11,070.31
686.1	....	....	....	....	....	....	...	....	686.1	74,443.63
....	....	54.6	....	....	....	....	...	....	54.6	9,455.37
....	....	25.8	....	....	....	....	...	....	25.8	4,527.19
....	....	....	41.6	....	....	74.9	...	....	116.5	47,317.38
250.0	....	....	....	....	....	....	...	....	250.0	25,626.00
....	100.2	....	....	....	....	....	...	....	100.2	13,154.00
164.3	....	....	....	....	....	....	...	....	164.3	25,036.23
....	....	135.2	31.0	112.0	11.9	....	...	....	290.1	72,807.15
....	....	....	....	....	....	47.9	...	....	47.9	8,534.39
....	....	....	....	108.0	....	....	...	....	108.0	24,793.57
107.0	....	....	....	....	....	....	...	....	107.0	10,418.48
....	47.3	....	....	....	....	....	...	....	47.3	3,929.21
....	....	....	....	....	7.0	....	...	....	7.0	699.62
....	....	....	....	90.0	....	....	...	7.9	97.9	22,965.26
....	30.0	....	....	....	....	....	...	....	30.0	2,336.40
....	....	....	10.9	41.2	6.0	....	...	....	58.1	13,172.48
....	....	....	....	12.1	....	....	...	....	12.1	3,001.28
143.8	....	....	....	....	....	....	...	....	143.8	12,022.11
....	....	....	....	....	....	54.0	...	....	54.0	11,213.60
100.0	....	....	....	....	....	....	...	....	100.0	8,156.00
....	....	....	....	....	....	10.0	...	....	10.0	1,612.80
....	....	....	....	....	28.5	....	...	....	28.5	2,766.78
....	....	....	....	27.2	....	....	...	....	27.2	6,648.60
....	....	....	....	26.2	....	....	...	....	26.2	6,074.76
....	60.0	....	....	....	....	....	...	....	60.0	3,415.67
....	....	....	....	72.1	....	....	...	....	72.1	17,095.05
269.8	60.0	....	....	....	....	....	...	....	329.8	24,191.31
....	....	....	....	....	....	35.0	...	....	35.0	3,857.24
....	....	....	....	16.7	....	....	...	....	16.7	4,178.17
....	28.0	....	....	....	....	....	...	....	28.0	1,802.26
117.0	....	....	....	....	....	....	...	....	117.0	9,121.32
....	....	....	....	....	1.0	....	...	....	1.0	78.79
....	....	....	....	47.0	....	....	...	....	47.0	9,423.64
32.6	....	....	....	....	....	....	...	....	32.6	1,818.80
....	....	....	....	....	11.0	....	...	....	11.0	945.14
....	....	....	....	....	.8	....	...	....	.8	89.15
....	....	....	....	....	....	32.5	...	....	32.5	2,563.66
84.4	....	....	....	....	....	13.5	...	....	97.9	5,715.71
....	....	....	....	....	....	1.5	...	....	1.5	107.18
....	....	....	1.4	....	....	....	...	....	1.4	314.29
....	....	....	....	21.0	....	....	...	....	21.0	5,266.40
183.4	....	....	....	38.3	....	....	...	....	221.7	16,790.30
....	....	....	15.5	....	....	....	...	....	15.5	3,497.58
....	60.0	....	....	....	....	....	...	....	60.0	2,784.00
....	....	....	....	80.6	....	....	...	....	80.6	14,265.47
....	....	....	....	....	2.0	....	...	....	2.0	133.66
....	23.6	....	....	....	....	....	...	....	23.6	1,175.00
....	....	....	....	....	4.7	....	...	....	4.7	313.85
....	....	....	6.9	....	....	....	...	....	6.9	1,535.51
....	....	....	....	13.3	....	....	...	....	13.3	2,847.87
....	28.9	....	....	....	....	....	...	....	28.9	1,598.69
....	....	....	....	....	....	....	.3	....	.3	195.53
....	....	....	....	....	....	....	...	....	....	4,317.72
138.4	**541.3**	**215.6**	**149.4**	**705.7**	**72.9**	**269.3**	**.3**	**7.9**	**4,100.8**	**$578,870.20**
2.9	.8	1.5	.4	14.2	.2	.7	...	....	20.7	7,307.85
135.5	**540.5**	**214.1**	**149.0**	**691.5**	**72.7**	**268.6**	**.3†**	**7.9**	**4,080.1**	**$571,562.35**

Table 374*

Detail by Steamers of Arrivals of Clothing ar

Steamer	Port of Sailing and Call	Date of Arrival	Port of Arrival	Shoes (Pairs)	Laces (Pairs)
		1919			
St. Croix, II	London—Danzig	Dec. 10	Riga	13,477	21,600
Reval, II	London	Dec. 19	Libau	.....	3,600
		1920			
St. Thomas, I	London—Danzig	Jan. 16	Riga	23,005	10,008
Reval, III	London	Feb. 6	Libau	2,288	.....
St. Thomas, II	London—Danzig	Feb. 22	Riga	.....	.....
Reval, IV	London	Mar. 6	Libau	.....	.....
		1921			
Oronoke	New York—Danzig	Aug. 22	Riga	9,966	.....
Total				**48,736**	**35,208**
Deduct Transfers to					
Soviet Russia				.....	.....
Esthonia				.....	.....
Total Transfers				.....	.....
Total Net Arrivals				**48,736**	**35,208**

* Cf. Table 381.

LATVIA—A.R.A.-European Children's Fund

Detail by Months of Latvian Government Donations for Child Feeding
Reconstruction Period, 1919–1924

Table 375

Deliveries per Receipts		Date of Delivery	Commodities in Net Metric Tons of 1,000 Kilograms or 2,204.6 Pounds					Total Value
Receipt No. from Latvian Government	Receipt No. from Minister of Interior		Rice	Beans, Peas	Pork Products	Milk	Total Tons	
		1920						
....	....	June	....	25.4	....	31.2	56.6	$11,162
		1921						
1	7	September	....	33.2	9.8	....	43.0	5,183
2	11	October	....	9.3	3.0	....	12.3	5,889
3	12	October	....	41.1	3.0	....	44.1	
4	13	November	....	15.1	14.7	....	29.8	4,885
5	14	December	....	15.8	....	....	15.8	5,833
6	15	December	....	46.5	....	....	46.5	
		1922						
7	16	January	....	3.3	6.9	....	10.2	1,977
8	18	February	....	44.4	15.3	....	59.7	7,892
9	19	March	....	21.1	....	....	21.1	5,856
10	20	March	....	....	16.9	....	16.9	
11	21	April	....	16.4	....	....	16.4	4,198
12	22	April	....	24.6	....	....	24.6	
13	24	May	....	15.5	....	....	15.5	1,587
14	25	June	28.9	4.9	6.9	....	40.7	3.811
15	27	July	....	25.4	....	....	25.4	2,601
Total			**28.9**	**342.0**	**76.5**	**31.2**	**478.6**	**$60,879**

..R.A.-European Children's Fund

.ccessories—Reconstruction Period, 1919–1924

Stockings (Pairs)	Woolens (Yards)	Thread (Yards)	Thread (Pounds)	Needles (No.)	Buttons (No.)	Total Metric Tons	Total Value
.....	23,342	......	...	.....	......	12.2	$ 61,011.75
.....	28,565	......	...	.....	......	12.7	45,631.85
15,702	885	......	800	35,000	100,944	13.0	54,101.67
6,096	.....	......	...	.....	......	1.6	6,782.46
8,304	.....	......	...	.....	......	.7	4,350.74
5,862	.....	......	...	.....	......	.5	1,874.85
19,085	29,687	1,000,000	...	15,000	39,888	19.0	28,291.09
55,049	**82,479**	**1,000,000**	**800**	**50,000**	**140,832**	**59.7**	**$202,044.41**
10,000	.....	......	...	.....	......	.9	$ 1,430.40
.....	1,915	......	...	.....	......	1.1	1,850.37
10,000	**1,915**	......	...	.....	......	**2.0**	**$ 3,280.77**
45,049	**80,564**	**1,000,000**	**800**	**50,000**	**140,832**	**57.7**	**$198,763.64**

Table 376

Detail by Steamers of Transshipments

Transshipping Steamer	Ex-Steamers (Tables 372, 373)	Port of Sailing	Date of Arrival
			1919
E. H. Stinnes	Comité National-Belgium	Rotterdam	Nov. 3
			1920
Bavaria, I	Comité National-Belgium and Remschied	Rotterdam	Feb.
Echo, II	Westford	Hamburg	Decemb
Martha, I	Westford	Hamburg	Decemb
			1921
Progress, IV	Ipswich, I	Hamburg	Februa
Johanna, August	Phoenix Bridge	Hamburg	May
Progress, V	Homer City, II	Hamburg	April
Adele, II	Westbrook	Hamburg	April
Progress, VII	Nemaha	Hamburg	May
Kellersee, IV	Walter Luckenbach and Hamburg Stock	Hamburg	July
Sensal, IV	Hawaiian, III	Hamburg	July
Adele, III	Orbita, II	Hamburg	July
Imperial, II	Mount Clinton, I	Hamburg	July
Sea Lighter 164	Michigan	Hamburg	July
Imperial, III	Ipswich, II	Hamburg	July
Weichsel, IX	Hawaiian, V	Hamburg	Octobe
			1922
Hansa, V	Gasconier	Hamburg	Januar
Moewe, III	Potomac, IV	Hamburg	Februa
Moewe, IV	Peninsular State	Hamburg	March
Total, C			
			1921
Mineral, II	Herefordshire	Hamburg	Jan.
Guenther Russ	Glentworth	Hamburg	Nov.
			1922
Martha Russ	Mount Clay, V	Hamburg	Jan.
Norderney, III	Texan, II, and Wachsmuth Purchase	Hamburg	Mar.
Gotenhof	Georgian and Mount Carroll, VII	Hamburg	Mar.
Marathon	Mount Clinton, IV	Hamburg	Mar.
Bolama	Western Ocean and Morristown, I	Hamburg	Mar.
Christel Salling, II	Nobles, II	Hamburg	May
Strassburg, VI	Minnekahda, VI; Western Scout; Mount Clinton, IV; Dallas	Hamburg	May
Coblenz, III	Minnekahda, VI; Sapinero; Chappaqua, II	Hamburg	May
Total, D			
			1919
Lake Fray	Schwarzenfels and Danzig Stock	Danzig	Augus
St. Croix	E. H. Stinnes	Danzig	Dec.
			1920
Elin	Willdomino	Danzig	Apr.
St. Thomas, III	A.R.A.W. Stock, Danzig	Danzig	May
			1921
Meitzung	Echo, II; Martha; Modlin Purchase; Cornish City	Danzig	Jan.
Torfrid	Bradclyde, II; Progress, V; Leeds City, I; Cornish City, I; Adele, II; Modlin Purchase	Danzig	Apr.
Echo, IV	Johanna; August; Warsaw Purchase; Watsness, II; Delevan	Danzig	June
Stadt Memel	Sea Lighter 164; Progress, IV; Kellersee, IV; Sensal, IV; Warsaw Purchase	Danzig	Aug.
Wasa, II	Nemaha	Danzig	Aug.
Neva	Sensal, IV.; Adele, III; Imperial, II and III; Panama	Danzig	Aug.
Ulrikka, I	Estonia	Danzig	Oct.
Wotan	Warsaw Purchase	Danzig	Nov.

.A. and A.R.A.-European Children's Fund

ief Supplies—Reconstruction Period, 1919–1924

ort of rrival	Contents of Cargoes in Net Metric Tons of 1,000 Kilograms or 2,204.6 Pounds									
	Wheat Flour	Rice	Beans, Peas	Pork Products	Milk	Cocoa	Sugar	Misc. Food	Soap	Total Tons
					A. TRANSSHIPMENTS					
anzig	.....	....	....	**42.1**	....	....	....	....	....	**42.1**
					B. TRANSSHIPMENTS					
bau	**686.1**	....	....	....	**273.8**	....	....	....	....	**959.9**
					C. TRANSSHIPMENTS					
anzig	157.5	....	....	....	....	....	....	....	....	157.5
anzig	6.8	....	....	....	....	....	....	....	....	6.8
anzig	.....	....	....	....	108.0	....	....	....	....	108.0
anzig	.....	47.3	....	....	....	....	....	....	....	47.3
anzig	.....	....	....	....	....	7.0	....	....	....	7.0
anzig	.....	30.0	....	....	....	....	....	....	....	30.0
anzig	.....	....	....	....	12.1	....	....	....	....	12.1
anzig	100.0	....	....	....	....	....	....	....	....	100.0
anzig	.....	....	....	....	....	28.5	....	....	....	28.5
anzig	.....	....	....	....	27.2	....	....	....	....	27.2
anzig	.....	....	....	....	26.2	....	....	....	....	26.2
anzig	.....	60.0	....	....	....	....	....	....	....	60.0
anzig	.....	....	....	....	72.1	....	....	....	....	72.1
anzig	.....	....	....	....	16.7	....	....	....	....	16.7
anzig	.....	....	....	....	....	11.0	....	....	....	11.0
anzig	.....	....	....	....	21.0	....	....	....	....	21.0
anzig	.....	....	....	....	80.6	....	....	....	....	80.6
....	**264.3**	**137.3**	....	....	**363.9**	**46.5**	....	....	....	**812.0**
					D. TRANSSHIPMENTS					
bau	.....	100.2	....	....	....	....	....	....	....	100.2
iga	.....	28.0	....	....	....	....	....	....	....	28.0
iga	.....	....	....	....	....	1.0	....	....	....	1.0
indau	32.6	....	....	....	....	....	32.5	....	....	65.1
indau	.....	....	....	1.4	....	....	1.5	....	....	2.9
indau	183.4	....	....	15.5	....	....	....	....	....	198.9
indau	.....	60.0	....	....	....	2.0	....	....	....	62.0
iga	.....	23.6	....	....	....	....	....	....	....	23.6
iga	84.4	....	....	....	45.1	4.7	13.5	....	....	147.7
iga	.....	28.9	....	6.9	6.5	....	....	....	....	42.3
....	**300.4**	**240.7**	....	**23.8**	**51.6**	**7.7**	**47.5**	....	....	**671.7**
					E. TRANSSHIPMENTS					
iga	.....	81.0	251.6	....	197.0	11.7	97.6	....	41.7	680.6
iga	.....	....	....	42.1	....	....	....	....	....	42.1
iga	.....	....	....	41.6	....	....	74.9	....	....	116.5
iga	250.0	....	....	....	....	....	....	....	....	250.0
ibau	164.3	....	88.2	19.9	112.0	11.9	31.9	....	....	428.2
iga	107.0	30.0	47.0	11.1	90.0	7.0	16.0	....	7.9	316.0
iga	143.8	47.3	....	10.9	41.2	6.0	19.0	....	....	268.2
iga	100.0	60.0	....	....	108.0	14.5	35.0	....	....	317.5
iga	.....	....	....	....	12.1	....	....	....	....	12.1
iga	269.8	60.0	....	....	125.5	14.0	....	....	....	469.3
iga	.....	....	....	....	....	....	35.0	....	....	35.0
iga	.....	....	....	....	....	....	10.0	....	....	10.0

[*Continued on next page*]

LATVIA-

Table 376—*Continued*

Detail by Steamers

Transshipping Steamer	Ex-Steamers (Tables 372, 373)	Port of Sailing	Date of Arrival
			1922
Rimfakse	Gdansk	Danzig	Jan. 1
Bolten	Weichsel, IX; Hansa, V; Moewe, III and IV	Danzig	Mar. 1
Total, E			
Total Direct Arrivals, Tables 372, 373			
Total Commodities Handled			
Deduct Duplications:			
Retransshipments, A			
Retransshipments, C			
Transfers, Table 372			
Transfers, Table 373			
Total Duplications			
Total Net Arrivals			

* Corned beef.

LATVIA

Table 377

Summary of Internal Deliveries,

Operation	Table No.	Flour	Rice	Beans, Peas
A.R.A.—Congressional Appropriation, $100,000,000 Fund	380	260.2	310.0	447.0
A.R.A.-European Children's Fund—Food	380	2,114.3	505.9	205.9
A.R.A.-European Children's Fund—Clothing	381	.....	....	....
E.C.F., Latvian Government Donation—Food	380	.....	28.9	342.0
E.C.F., Norwegian Government Donation—Food	380	.....	....	....
Total Children's Relief	369	**2,374.5**	**844.8**	**994.9**
A.R.A.-E.C.F.—Food Drafts and Bulk Sales, Total Deliveries	378	18.9	4.7	7.3
A.R.A.-E.C.F.—Sale to Latvian Government	...	.....	28.8	....
A.R.A.-E.C.F.—Sale to Latvian Government (through Minister of Interior)	...	2.3	1.1	.9
Total Other than Children's Relief	....	**21.2**	**34.6**	**8.2**
Total Deliveries, Reconstruction Period *	....	**2,395.7**	**879.4**	**1,003.1**

* A bulk sale of 8.4 metric tons, value $926.78, was delivered to Lithuania for student feeding. Therefore net deliveries in Latvia amount to 6,756.9 metric tons, value $1,588,170.34. Cf. Table 371 surplus of $156.86 was derived from bulk sales.

R.A. and A.R.A.-European Children's Fund

ansshipments of Relief Supplies

Port of Arrival	Contents of Cargoes in Net Metric Tons of 1,000 Kilograms or 2,204.6 Pounds									Total Tons
	Wheat Flour	Rice	Beans, Peas	Pork Products	Milk	Cocoa	Sugar	Misc. Food	Soap	
					E. TRANSSHIPMENTS (*Continued*)					
iga	....	....	....	....	47.0	....	....	....	....	47.0
'indau	....	....	....	....	118.3	11.0	....	....	....	129.3
....	**1,034.9**	**278.3**	**386.8**	**125.6**	**851.1**	**76.1**	**319.4**	....	**49.6**	**3,121.8**
					F. DIRECT ARRIVALS					
....	**377.2**	**332.3**	**275.8**	**43.3**	**343.2**	**72.3**	**50.3**	**.3**	....	**1,494.7**
....	**2,662.9**	**988.6**	**662.6**	**234.8**	**1,883.6**	**202.6**	**417.2**	**.3**	**49.6**	**7,102.2**
....	....	....	....	42.1	....	....	....	....	....	42.1
....	264.3	137.3	....	....	363.9	46.5	....	....	....	812.0
....	....	....	....	....	....	....	....	....	5.0	5.0
....	2.9	.8	1.5	.4	14.2	.2	.7	....	....	20.7
....	**267.2**	**138.1**	**1.5**	**42.5**	**378.1**	**46.7**	**.7**	....	**5.0**	**879.8**
....	**2,395.7**	**850.5**	**661.1**	**192.3**	**1,505.5**	**155.9**	**416.5**	**.3***	**44.6**	**6,222.4**

R.A. and A.R.A.-European Children's Fund

erations—Reconstruction Period, 1919–1924

Commodities in Net Metric Tons of 1,000 Kilograms or 2,204.6 Pounds								Total Value
Pork Products	Milk	Cocoa	Sugar	Misc. Food	Soap	Clothing and Misc.	Total Tons	
43.3	814.0	83.2	147.9	...	36.7	....	2,142.3	$ 753,774.72
122.7	670.7	71.4	263.8	...	7.9	....	3,962.6	553,312.44
....	....	....	....	...	....	57.7	57.7	198,763.64
76.5	31.2	....	....	...	....	....	478.6	60,879.55
....	....	....	....	6.6	....	....	6.6	3,960.00
242.5	**1,515.9**	**154.6**	**411.7**	**6.6**	**44.6**	**57.7**	**6,647.8**	**$1,570,690.35**
26.2	20.8	1.3	4.5	.3	....	....	84.0	$ 15,686.15
....	....	....	....	...	....	....	28.8	2,136.37
.1	....	....	.3	...	....	....	4.7	584.25
26.3	**20.8**	**1.3**	**4.8**	**.3**	....	....	**117.5**	**$ 18,406.77**
268.8	**1,536.7**	**155.9**	**416.5**	**6.9**	**44.6**	**55.7**	**6,765.3**	**$1,589,097.12**

LATVIA—A.R.A.-European Children's Fund

A. Detail of Food Draft Deliveries, by Beneficiaries—Reconstruction Period, 1919–1924

Table 378

Receipt No.	Beneficiary	Date	Flour	Rice	Beans, Peas	Pork Products	Milk Evap.	Milk Cond.	Cocoa	Sugar	Misc. Food	Total Tons	Total Value
			Commodities in Net Metric Tons of 1,000 Kilograms or 2,204.6 Pounds										
		1921											
1	E. Zvitkov	Feb.	.011	....	.005	....	....	.007	.001	.001	....	.025	$10.
24	E. Jende Foodst.	Feb.	.011	....	.005	....	....	.007	.001	.001	....	.025	10
	Total *	....	**.022**	....	**.010**	....	....	**.014**	**.002**	**.002**	....	**.050**	**$20**

* Fractional part of kilograms increase total over amount shown in summary Table 154.

LATVIA—A.R.A.-European Children's Fund

B. Detail of Bulk Sale Deliveries—Reconstruction Period, 1919–1924

Table 378—*Continued*

Time of Delivery	Unit	Flour M.T.	Rice M.T.	Beans, Peas M.T.	Pork Products M.T.	Milk Evap. (Case)	Milk Cond. (Case)	Cocoa M.T.	Sugar M.T.	Misc. Food (Case)	Total Metric Tons	Total Value
1921												
April	...	7.498	2.142	3.927	1.071	744	...	.499	1.785	...	......	......
July–October	...	1.470	.....	.770	.210	33	...	....	.350	...	......	......
November–December	...	9.932	2.520	2.608	1.419	178	...	.798	2.365	9	......	......
1922												
June	...	.....	.....	.....	23.513	...	...	....	.....	...	......	......
Total in Units	Unit	**18.900**	**4.662**	**7.305**	**26.213**	**955**	...	**1.297**	**4.500**	**9**	......	......
Total in Metric Tons	M.T.	**18.900**	**4.662**	**7.305**	**26.213**	**20.783**	...	**1.297**	**4.500**	**.299**	**83.959**	**$15,666**
Deduct Bulk Sale for Lithuania Students	....	3.2	.8	1.7	.5	1.3	...	.2	.7	...	8.4	926
Total Bulk Sales Used in Latvia *	....	**15.7**	**3.9**	**5.6**	**25.7**	**19.5**	...	**1.1**	**3.8**	**.3†**	**75.6**	**$14,739**

* Of these deliveries 39.5 metric tons were used in Riga student kitchens. Cf. Table 379.

† Corned beef.

LATVIA

Table 380

Detail of Internal Deliveries for Child Feeding, by Distri

Receipt No.	Districts or Kitchens	Date of Delivery †	Flour	Rice	Beans, Peas
		1919			
43	Latvia—Not Segregated	To Sept.	....	....	...
1	Libau	September	11.851	6.073	3.467
2	Libau outside Towns	September	9.059	3.177	1.853
3	Riga outside Kitchens	September	9.776	7.977	6.479
4	Riga City Kitchens	September	75.514	35.173	26.771
	Total for September	....	**106.200**	**52.400**	**38.570**

* Except as noted. Starting in April, 1921, milk is quoted in cans and in May, 1921, soap is quoted in pieces. In these instances the total tons per receipt exclude milk and soap. The monthly totals, however, include all commodities in net metric tons.

† Receipts are tabulated according to months in which food was u Where delivery date differs from the tabulated month, it indicates the food was delivered on that date but was held over to the follow month for child feeding. See Receipts 59, 60, May, 1921, for example.

LATVIA—A.R.A.-European Children's Fund

Detail of Deliveries, by Receipt Number, to Riga Student Kitchens†

'able 379 Reconstruction Period, 1919–1924

Date	Flour	Rice	Beans, Peas	Pork Products	Milk Evap. (Cans)	Milk Cond. (Cans)	Cocoa	Sugar	Misc. Food ‡ (Tins)	Total
1921										
April 11	1.470	.420	.770	.210	....	1,589	.098	.350	..	3.318
April 26	1.470	.420	.770	.210	1,589	....	.098	.350	..	3.318
May 19	1.260	.360	.660	.180	1,361	....	.084	.300	..	2.844
September 17	1.470	.420	.770	.210	1,588	....	....	.350	..	3.220
October 8	1.470	.420	.770	.210	1,588	....	.098	.350	18	3.318
October 22	1.470	.420	.452	.210	1,588	....	.098	.350	18	3.000
November 3	1.470	.420	.452	.210	1,588	....	.098	.350	18	3.000
November 19	1.470	.420	....	.210	945	....	.098	.350	18	2.548
December 5	1.470	.420	....	.210	945	....	.098	.350	18	2.548
December 20	1.470	.420	.352	.210	946	....	.098	.350	20	2.900
1922										
January 27	1.112	.318	.582	.159	933	....	.210	.265	..	2.646
Total Cans of Milk, Tins of Corned Beef	.....	....	....	....	**13,071**	**1,589**	....	....	**110**	6.859
Total Metric Tons	**15.602**	**4.458**	**5.578**	**2.229**	**5.929**	**.631**	**1.078**	**3.715**	**.299**	**39.519**

Commodities in Net Metric Tons of 1,000 Kilograms or 2,204.6 Pounds *

'hese deliveries are included in bulk sales. Cf. Table 378.

* Except as noted. Milk in cans and corned beef in tins are not included in monthly total tons column; however, all commodities are converted and included in final total.

‡ All corned beef.

R.A. and A.R.A.-European Children's Fund

Kitchens, by Months—Reconstruction Period, 1919–1924

Commodities in Net Metric Tons of 1,000 Kilograms or 2,204.6 Pounds *

Pork Products	Milk Evap.	Milk Cond.	Cocoa	Sugar	Misc. Food ‡	Soap	Total Tons
17.000	**92.000**	....	**15.000**	**35.000**	....	....	**159.000**
1.400	11.140	....	.423	.617	....	....	34.971
....	6.360	....	.565	.683	....	....	21.697
2.763	6.183	....	.920	1.893	....	....	35.991
7.723	25.727	....	3.980	10.817	....	....	185.705
11.886	**49.410**	....	**5.888**	**14.010**	....	....	**278.364**

Codliver oil.

[*Continued on next page*]

Table 380—*Continued*

Detail of Internal Deliveries for Chi

Receipt No.	Districts or Kitchens	Date of Delivery	Flour	Rice	Beans, Peas
		1919			
5	Libau	October	12.900	3.765	5.660
6	Libau outside Towns	October	19.520	6.400	6.138
7	Riga outside Kitchens	October	6.051	5.148	4.445
8	Riga City Kitchens	October	63.379	19.472	28.655
	Total for October		**101.850**	**34.785**	**44.898**
9	Libau	November	15.451	4.354	6.304
10	Libau outside Towns	November	2.857	.861	2.646
11	Riga outside Kitchens	November	58.089	16.214	29.180
12	Riga City Kitchens	November	10.723	3.583	5.942
	Total for November		**87.120**	**25.012**	**44.072**
13	Libau outside Towns	December	6.670	1.870	3.058
14	Libau City	December	20.842	4.844	7.993
15	Riga outside Kitchens	December	20.808	6.148	9.573
16	Riga City Kitchens	December	54.382	16.549	25.108
	Total for December		**102.702**	**29.411**	**45.732**
		1920			
17	Libau outside Towns	January	3.254	5.389	8.620
18	Libau City	January	2.988	13.876	16.052
19	Riga City	January	59.156	16.809	25.967
20	Riga outside Kitchens	January	37.337	14.051	22.172
	Total for January		**102.735**	**50.125**	**72.811**
21	Riga City Kitchens	February	57.102	16.249	25.037
22	Riga outside Kitchens	February	54.861	13.269	19.541
23	Libau City	February	18.504	7.154	8.792
24	Libau outside Towns	February	25.455	4.768	7.525
	Total for February		**155.922**	**41.440**	**60.895**
25	Libau City	March	21.164	6.090	10.111
26	Libau outside Towns	March	10.150	2.774	4.644
27	Riga outside Kitchens	March	45.034	13.840	21.560
28	Riga City Kitchens	March	69.007	17.410	26.934
	Total for March		**145.355**	**40.114**	**63.249**
29	Libau outside Towns	April	14.828	4.008	6.656
30	Libau City	April	15.630	3.685	6.725
31	Riga City Kitchens	April	54.603	14.000	21.563
32	Riga outside Kitchens	April	54.163	16.169	24.910
	Total for April		**139.224**	**37.862**	**59.854**
33	Libau City	May	18.819	4.801	7.882
34	Libau outside Towns	May	9.432	2.298	4.289
35	Riga City Kitchens	May	35.214	12.400	18.607
36	Riga outside Kitchens	May	28.144	8.434	13.146
	Total for May		**91.609**	**27.933**	**43.924**
37	Libau City	June	16.311	4.525	6.586
38	Libau outside Towns	June	10.191	3.004	4.939
39	Riga City Kitchens	June	35.579	9.798	15.109
40	Riga outside Kitchens	June	51.327	15.583	23.600
	Total for June		**113.408**	**32.910**	**50.234**
41	Libau and outside Towns	July	7.396	10.825	13.059
42	Riga and outside Towns	July	43.511	61.559	....
	Total for July		**50.907**	**72.384**	**13.059**

.A. and A.R.A.-European Children's Fund

ling, by Districts or Kitchens, by Months

Commodities in Net Metric Tons of 1,000 Kilograms or 2,204.6 Pounds *

Pork Products	Milk		Cocoa	Sugar	Misc. Food	Soap	Total Tons
	Evap.	Cond.					
1.700	9.905	....	.484	.703	....	....	35.117
....	13.060	....	.404	1.131	....	....	46.653
1.836	4.682	....	.628	.393	....	....	23.183
6.312	34.938	....	3.442	.707	.245	....	157.150
9.848	**62.585**	....	**4.958**	**2.934**	**.245**	....	**262.103**
1.262	13.100	....	.853	1.169	....	.231	42.724
....	1.459	....	.125	.311	....	.....	8.259
2.715	31.583	....	3.258	12.466	.368	2.014	155.887
.538	7.652	....	.727	2.383	....	.279	31.827
4.515	**53.794**	....	**4.963**	**16.329**	**.368**	**2.524**	**238.697**
1.111	4.600	....	.388	.670	....	....	18.367
1.657	15.317	....	.972	1.563	....	.230	53.418
1.318	12.659	....	1.285	3.853	....	.657	56.301
2.531	37.918	....	3.718	8.073	1.228	2.377	151.884
6.617	**70.494**	....	**6.363**	**14.159**	**1.228**	**3.264**	**279.970**
1.730	9.850	....	.800	1.453	....	....	31.096
2.285	13.145	....	.937	1.520	.522	.225	51.550
5.284	33.341	....	3.431	8.104	1.474	2.227	155.793
4.521	28.962	....	2.841	7.624	.368	2.049	119.925
13.820	**85.298**	....	**8.009**	**18.701**	**2.364**	**4.501**	**358.364**
5.240	32.840	....	2.427	7.771	.245	2.309	149.220
4.582	23.276	....	2.687	7.326	.123	2.170	127.835
1.593	15.195	....	1.010	1.544	.245	1.400	55.437
1.601	9.591	....	.836	1.642	.010	....	51.428
13.016	**80.902**	....	**6.960**	**18.283**	**.623**	**5.879**	**383.920**
1.895	15.782	....	1.041	1.601	.245	.956	58.885
1.067	6.127	....	.372	1.017	.010	....	26.161
4.215	27.970	....	2.965	3.594	.744	1.974	121.896
4.513	44.027	....	3.816	3.923	.372	7.155	177.157
11.690	**93.906**	....	**8.194**	**10.135**	**1.371**	**10.085**	**384.099**
.980	9.034	....	.078	.156	....	....	35.740
1.379	11.518	....	.694	1.067	.013	1.635	42.346
4.348	33.356	....	2.822	6.897	.061	1.955	139.605
4.763	32.236	....	2.804	7.532	.248	1.451	144.276
11.470	**86.144**	....	**6.398**	**15.652**	**.322**	**5.041**	**361.967**
1.543	13.806	....	.888	1.557	....	.288	49.584
.756	5.106	....	.525	.653	....	.007	23.066
3.802	27.166	....	2.779	7.176	....	1.745	108.889
3.046	21.310	....	1.840	4.526	....	1.061	81.507
9.147	**67.388**	....	**6.032**	**13.912**	....	**3.101**	**263.046**
1.315	11.666	....	.831	1.269	....	.885	43.388
.922	5.143	....	.538	.790	....	.027	25.554
3.224	27.575	....	1.502	5.127	....	.028	97.942
5.420	31.378	....	2.901	8.470	....	1.054	139.733
10.881	**75.762**	....	**5.772**	**15.656**	....	**1.994**	**306.617**
3.543	8.451	....	2.622	1.976	.052	.067	47.991
2.654	....	....	....	35.928	....	....	143.652
6.197	**8.451**	....	**2.622**	**37.904**	**.052**	**.067**	**191.643**

[*Continued on next page*]

Table 380—*Continued*

Detail of Internal Deliveries for Chi

Receipt No.	Districts or Kitchens	Date of Delivery	Flour	Rice	Beans, Peas
Series 2		1921			
1	Riga	February	12.486	3.486	5.512
2	Riga	February	2.294	.632	1.013
3	Saldus	February	.333	.093	.147
4	Rezekne	February	3.163	.883	1.397
5	Rezekne	February	.166	.046	.074
6	Jelgava	February	3.330	.930	1.470
7	Krustpils	February	.333	.093	.147
8	Livani	February	.333	.093	.147
9	Sloka	February	.333	.093	.147
10	Limbazi	February	.333	.093	.147
11	Smiltene	February	.333	.093	.147
12	Ilukste	February	.416	.116	.184
13	Tukums	February	.499	.139	.219
14	Jaun Jelgava	February	.500	.139	.221
15	Kuntesburg	February	.167	.047	.074
16	Livani	February	.167	.047	.074
17	Cesis	February	.916	.256	.404
18	Valmeera	February	.916	.256	.404
19	Ventspils	February	1.998	.558	.882
20	Milgravis	February	.583	.163	.257
21	Daugavpils (Dvinsk)	February	5.827	1.627	2.573
22	Naukseni	February	.166	.046	.074
23	Schognova	February	.083	.023	.037
24	Silupe	February	.250	.070	.110
25	Riga	February	.499	.139	.220
26	Riga	February	.472	.232	.368
27	Riga outside Kitchens	February	14.600	4.065	6.448
	Total for February	....	**51.496**	**14.458**	**22.897**
28	Riga	March	45.181	10.199	16.330
29	Mitau	March	....	....	....
30	Solitude	March	.022	....	....
31	Bolderaja	March	.666	.174	.290
32	Dobele	March	.566	.156	.247
33	Limbazi	March	.333	.092	.147
34	Ventspils	March	....	....	....
35	Riga Jurmala	March	.764	.213	.338
36	Milgravis	March	.707	.163	.294
37	Kreslava	March	.666	.186	.285
	Total for March	....	**48.905**	**11.183**	**17.931**
New Series					
1	Liepaja (Libau)	Apr. 1	9.152	2.551	4.047
2	Kuldiga	Apr. 7	1.828	.508	.810
3	Rezekne	Apr. 7	3.439	.928	1.472
4	Saldus	Apr. 7	.664	.185	.294
5	Ventspils	Apr. 7	2.163	.603	.956
6	Jelgava	Apr. 7	3.328	.928	1.471
8	Riga City Asylum	Apr. 8	.224	.166	.265
9	Riga City Asylum	Apr. 8	.340	.251	.401
10	Sloka	Apr. 8	.416	.116	.183
11	Riga City Asylum	Apr. 8	.297	.219	.348
12	Riga City Asylum	Apr. 8	.328	.243	.386
13	Riga City Asylum	Apr. 8	.149	.108	.172
14	Riga City Asylum	Apr. 8	.427	.300	.504
15	Riga	Apr. 9	.531	.393	.626
16	Kreslava	Apr. 11	.832	.232	.368
18	Riga	Apr. 11	.380	.290	.427
19	Riga	Apr. 11	.243	.232	.318

A.R.A. and A.R.A.-European Children's Fund

Feeding, by Districts or Kitchens, by Months

Commodities in Net Metric Tons of 1,000 Kilograms or 2,204.6 Pounds *

Pork Products	Milk		Cocoa	Sugar	Misc. Food	Soap	Total Tons
	Evap.	Cond.					
1.237	5.008	2.305	.750	1.986	....	....	32.770
.227	.693	.619	.138	.365	....	....	5.981
.033	.070	.117	.020	.053	....	....	.866
.313	.665	1.109	.190	.503	....	....	8.223
.016	.035	.058	.010	.026	....	....	.431
.330	.701	1.167	.200	.530	....	....	8.658
.033	.070	.117	.020	.053	....	....	.866
.033	.070	.117	.020	.053	....	....	.866
.033	.070	.117	.020	.053	....	....	.866
.033	.070	.117	.020	.053	....	....	.866
.033	.070	.117	.020	.053	....	....	.866
.041	.088	.146	.025	.066	....	....	1.082
.051	.305	....	.030	.079	....	....	1.322
.049	.105	.175	.030	.079	....	....	1.298
.017	.035	.058	.010	.026	....	....	.434
.017	.035	.058	.010	.026	....	....	.434
.091	.193	.321	.055	.146	....	....	2.382
.091	.193	.321	.055	.146	....	....	2.382
.198	.420	....	.120	.318	....	....	4.494
.058	.122	.204	.035	.093	....	....	1.515
.577	1.227	2.043	.350	.927	....	....	15.151
.016	.035	.058	.010	.026	....	....	.431
.008	.018	.029	.005	.013	....	....	.216
.025	.053	.087	.015	.040	....	....	.650
.050	.105	.175	.030	.079	....	....	1.297
.068	.175	.292	.050	.132	....	....	1.789
1.550	3.681	4.452	.876	2.322	....	....	37.994
5.228	**14.312**	**14.379**	**3.114**	**8.246**	....	....	**134.130**
4.460	13.596	8.352	2.224	6.397	....	....	106.739
....	....	1.167	....	....	....	....	1.167
.003	.038	.033	.004	.009	....	....	.109
.066	.141	.233	.040	.105	....	....	1.715
.056	.185	.140	.034	.074	....	....	1.458
.033	.066	.117	.020	.053	....	....	.861
....	....	.700	....	....	....	....	.700
.075	.161	.268	.055	.120	....	....	1.994
.068	.149	.218	.040	.101	....	....	1.740
.023	.407	....	.039	.105	....	....	1.711
4.784	**14.743**	**11.228**	**2.456**	**6.964**	....	....	**118.194**
	(Cans)	(Cans)					
.901	4,250	8,085	.549	1.452	....	....	18.652
.078	950	1,616	.109	.289	....	....	3.622
.328	1,535	2,940	.200	.528	....	....	6.895
.065	310	588	.040	.105	....	....	1.353
.213	1,004	1,911	.129	.343	....	....	4.407
.328	1,545	2,940	.199	.528	....	....	6.782
.043	278	528	.036	.072	....	....	.806
.065	420	800	.055	.143	....	....	1.255
.041	193	367	.025	.066	....	....	.847
.057	328	644	.047	.125	....	....	1.093
.063	405	722	.052	.138	....	....	1.210
.028	171	345	.024	.052	....	....	.533
.082	528	1,020	.069	.180	....	....	1.562
.102	663	1,249	.085	.224	....	....	1.961
.125	....	735	.050	.132	....	....	1.739
.067	....	1,256	.042	.166	....	....	1.372
.060	....	982	.043	.129	....	....	1.025

[*Continued on next page*]

Table 380—*Continued*

Detail of Internal Deliveries for Chil

Receipt No.	Districts or Kitchens	Date of Delivery	Flour	Rice	Beans, Peas
New Series		1921			
20	Riga	Apr. 11	.203	.154	.242
21	Jekabmiests	Apr. 15	.832	.231	.368
22	Ludza	Apr. 14	2.663	.743	1.177
23	Riga	Apr. 11	.562	.418	.663
24	Riga	Apr. 11	.562	.418	.663
25	Talsi	Apr. 12	.499	.139	.221
26	Riga Children's Hospital	Apr. 12	.188	.136	.220
27	Jaun Jelgava	Apr. 11	.582	.162	.258
28	Riga	Apr. 11	.542	.430	.636
29	Riga	Apr. 11	.273	.216	.329
30	Riga	Apr. 12	.591	.442	.697
31	Riga	Apr. 12	.282	.216	.309
32	Wolmar's Asylum	Apr. 11	.070	.020	.033
33	Riga	Apr. 11	.618	.423	.668
34	Riga	Apr. 13	.278	.209	.315
35	Riga Women's Corps Asylum	Apr. 12	....	.036	.046
36	Tukums	Apr. 11	.600	.172	.272
37	Valmeera	Apr. 14	.924	.255	.404
38	Cesis	Apr. 14	.999	.278	.441
39	Riga	Apr. 14	.178	.088	.133
40	Bolderaja	Apr. 14	.666	.186	.294
41	Riga City Children's Bakery	Apr. 14	4.680	....	....
42	Smiltene	Apr. 18	.333	.093	.147
43	Riga City Asylum	Apr. 18	.016	.010	.017
44	Daugavpils (Dvinsk)	Apr. 19	9.734	2.714	4.306
45	Riga	Apr. 18	9.257	1.213	.369
47	Rujene	Apr. 23	.666	.186	.293
48	Riga Jurmala	Apr. 23	.716	.196	.312
49	Naukseni Asylum	Apr. 25	.167	.047	.073
50	Veselauskas Asylum	Apr. 25	.133	.037	.059
51	Zogovas Refugee Committee	Apr. 25	.083	.023	.037
52	Silupes Refugee Committee	Apr. 25	.252	.070	.111
53	Rezekne Refugee Committee	Apr. 25	.499	.139	.221
55	Milgravis	Apr. 27	.707	.197	.311
56	Korsovka	Apr. 27	.357	.099	.158
57	Riga City Asylum	Apr. 15	.067	.018	.029
58	Riga Refugee Committee	Apr. 15	.382	.107	.170
	Total Cans of Milk	....	....	....	....
	Total for April (All Metric Tons)	....	**64.902**	**18.774**	**28.050**
59	Riga	Apr. 24	2.593	3.652	5.963
60	Lives District	Apr. 24	.258	.072	.114
61	Ogre	May 2	.191	.054	.083
62	Riga Children's Bakery	May 2	6.399	....	....
63	Riga Children's Bakery	May 3	6.650	....	....
64	Riga Children's Hospital	May 3	.718	.169	.318
65	Ventspils	May 3	2.163	.604	.957
66	Jelgava	May 3	3.328	.929	1.472
67	Riga Asylum	May 3	.087	.065	.102
68	Riga Asylum	May 3	.302	.225	.356
69	Riga Asylum	May 4	.365	.271	.430
70	Riga City Asylum	May 4	.134	.097	.158
71	Riga City Asylum	May 4	.322	.237	.379
72	Riga City Asylum	May 4	.247	.183	.302
73	Sloka	May 4	.416	.116	.184
74	Rezekne	May 6	3.686	1.030	1.628
75	Bolderaja	May 7	.737	.205	.325
76	Serenes	May 9	.110	.030	.048

R.A. and A.R.A.-European Children's Fund

ding, by Districts or Kitchens, by Months

Commodities in Net Metric Tons of 1,000 Kilograms or 2,204.6 Pounds *

Pork Products	Milk Evap.	Milk Cond.	Cocoa	Sugar	Misc. Food	Soap	Total Tons
	(Cans)	(Cans)					
.031	....	754	.033	.087	....	....	.750
.082	368	735	.050	.132	....	....	1.695
.263	....	3,588	.160	.423	....	....	5.429
.108	....	2,088	.090	.237	....	....	2.078
.085	....	2,048	.090	.237	....	....	2.055
.049	....	1,050	.032	.079	....	....	1.019
.036	....	672	.030	.079	....	....	.689
.035	....	784	.035	.093	....	....	1.165
.104	....	1,703	.094	.232	....	....	2.038
.062	....	1,029	.044	.124	....	....	1.048
.113	....	1,775	.094	.247	....	....	2.184
.050	....	895	.055	.138	....	....	1.050
.007	....	96	.004	.011	....	....	.145
.109	....	2,232	.091	.222	....	....	2.131
.052	....	1,008	.040	.105	....	....	.999
.002	....	167	.009	.021	....	....	.114
.061	....	826	.038	.097	....	....	1.240
.090	....	1,153	.055	.145	....	....	1.873
.098	....	1,345	.060	.158	....	....	2.034
.023	....	601	.024	.057	....	....	.503
.065	....	899	.040	.106	....	....	1.357
.198	....	....	....	.026	....	....	4.904
.033	155	294	.020	.053	....	....	.679
.003	17	33	.002	.006	....	....	.054
.959	4,540	8,599	.585	1.544	....	....	19.842
.293	1,716	3,308	.295	.540	....	....	11.967
.065	309	588	.040	.106	....	....	1.356
.070	317	590	.032	.112	....	....	1.438
.016	77	147	.010	.027	....	....	.340
.013	62	117	.008	.021	....	....	.271
.008	38	73	.005	.013	....	....	.169
.025	115	220	.015	.040	....	....	.513
.049	231	441	.030	.079	....	....	1.017
.069	328	624	.042	.112	....	....	1.438
.035	166	316	.022	.056	....	....	.727
.007	31	59	.004	.010	....	....	.135
.038	177	338	.023	.060	....	....	.780
....	**21,227**	**67,923**	....	....	....	....	36.587
6.052	**9.629**	**26.958**	**4.055**	**10.507**	....	....	**168.927**
.454	7,063	12,040	.823	1.933	....	....	15.418
.026	120	229	.016	.041	....	....	.527
.019	88	169	.012	.029	....	....	.388
.492	....	....	....	.537	....	....	7.428
.512	....	....	....	.558	....	....	7.720
.061	241	455	.040	.097	....	....	1.403
.213	1,004	1,911	.130	.343	....	....	4.410
.328	1,545	2,940	.200	.528	....	....	6.785
.016	108	205	.014	.037	....	....	.321
.058	374	712	.049	.128	....	....	1.118
.069	452	859	.059	.154	....	....	1.348
						(Pieces)	
.026	166	316	.022	.057	....	....	.494
.062	397	757	.059	.136	....	....	1.195
.047	305	580	.040	.104	....	....	.923
.041	193	367	.027	.066	....	....	.850
.368	1,545	2,940	.222	.586	....	2,000	7.520
.073	187	357	.044	.117	....	....	1.501
.010	28	52	.006	.018	....	60	.222

[*Continued on next page*]

Table 380—*Continued*

Detail of Internal Deliveries for Chil-

Receipt No.	Districts or Kitchens	Date of Delivery	Flour	Rice	Beans, Peas
New Series		1921			
77	Salaspils	May 7	.055	.015	.024
78	Tukums	May 9	.682	.191	.301
79	Riga Women's Corps Asylum	May 9	.073	.051	.081
80	Cesis	May 10	1.106	.309	.489
81	Valmiera	May 10	1.093	.305	.483
82	Riga City	May 10	5.515	4.473	7.076
83	Smiltene	May 10	.369	.103	.163
84	Limbazi	May 10	.369	.103	.163
85	Jaun Jelgava	May 11	.645	.180	.285
86	Krustpils	May 11	.645	.180	.285
87	Tome	May 11	.101	.028	.045
88	Jekabmiests	May 11	.922	.257	.407
89	Kreslava	May 12	.992	.257	.407
90	Riga Refugee Committee	May 13	.015	.010	.016
91	Riga Children's Bakery	May 18	5.930	....	....
92	Riga Children's Bakery	May 18	5.946	....	....
93	Kuldiga	May 19	1.014	.283	.454
95	Liepaja (Libau)	May 12	11.611	3.245	5.128
96	Saldus	May 19	.369	.103	.163
97	Ventspils	May 19	....	....	....
98	Jelgava	May 20	....	....	....
99	Valka	May 19	.184	.051	.081
100	Talsi	May 21	.553	.154	.244
101	Riga Jurmala	May 21	.847	.237	.374
102	Milgravis	May 23	.783	.219	.346
103	Daugavpils (Dvinsk)	May ..	3.568	.996	1.576
105	Eglaine	May 24	.323	.090	.143
106	Ilukste	May 24	.208	.058	.092
107	Zilanu	May 24	.737	.205	.325
108	Zogovas Refugee Committee	May 24	.092	.025	.041
109	Riga Refugee Committee	May ..	.074	.020	.032
110	Naukseni Refugee Committee	May 25	.184	.051	.081
111	Silupes Refugee Committee	May 24	.276	.077	.122
112	Korsovka	May 23	.396	.111	.175
113	Rezekne Refugee Committee	May 24	.553	....	.244
114	Spares Refugee Committee	May 25	.147	.041	.065
115	Olaine	May 24	.369	.103	.163
	Total Cans of Milk, Pieces of Soap	....	....	....	....
	Total for May, Metric Tons	....	**75.452**	**20.470**	**32.893**
104	Rujene	June 1	.737	.205	.325
116	Latvia Railroad Children's Sanatorium	June 1	.178	.050	.079
117	Riga	June 1	2.892	2.450	3.822
118	Ogre	June 2	.205	.057	.090
119	Bolderaja	June 2	.714	.166	.299
120	Sloka	June 3	.446	.124	.197
121	Dobele Ferienheim	June 1	.535	.149	.236
122	Latvian Red Cross Refugee Committee	June 4	1.843	.515	.814
123	Limbazi	June 6	.357	.095	.158
124	Tome	June 6	.145	.040	.064
125	Riga	June 7	.083	.093	.147
126	Riga City Asylum	June 7	....	.198	.314
127	Livani	June 8	.624	.174	.275
128	Plavinas	June 8	.421	.117	.185
129	Krustpils	June 8	.579	.174	.253
130	Riga City Asylum	June 9	....	.101	.159
131	Jaun Jelgava	June 9	.624	.174	.275
132	Bramberga	June 9	.107	.029	.047

R.A. and A.R.A.-European Children's Fund

ding, by Districts or Kitchens, by Months

Commodities in Net Metric Tons of 1,000 Kilograms or 2,204.6 Pounds *

Pork Products	Milk		Cocoa	Sugar	Misc. Food	Soap	Total Tons
	Evap.	Cond.					
	(Cans)	(Cans)				(Pieces)	
.005	14	26	.003	.009	....	30	.111
.068	173	330	.041	.108	....	370	1.391
.005	257	....	.011	.029	....	100	.250
.110	573	975	.066	.176	....	600	2.256
.108	567	965	.065	.174	....	593	2.228
.988	12,474	9,827	.970	2.550	....	17,965	21.572
.037	191	325	.022	.059	....	200	.753
.037	191	325	.022	.059	....	200	.753
.064	334	569	.039	.102	....	350	1.315
.064	334	569	.039	.102	....	350	1.315
.011	53	90	.006	.016	....	55	.207
.092	478	813	.056	.147	....	500	1.881
.092	1,291	....	.056	.147	....	500	1.951
.003	52	....	.002	.006	....	20	.052
.335	....	....	....	....	....	....	6.265
.335	....	....	....	....	....	....	6.281
.028	1,513	....	.061	.163	....	550	2.003
1.153	16,776	....	.699	1.846	....	6,300	23.682
.037	516	....	.022	.059	....	200	.753
....	....	....	....	....	....	1,300	....
....	....	....	....	....	....	2,000	....
.018	257	....	.011	.029	....	100	.374
.055	744	....	.033	.088	....	300	1.127
.084	1,142	....	.051	.134	....	460	1.727
.078	1,055	....	.047	.125	....	425	1.598
.352	4,806	....	.216	.568	....	4,000	7.276
.032	435	....	.019	.051	....	350	.658
.041	310	....	.014	.033	....	250	.446
.073	993	....	.044	.117	....	400	1.501
.009	124	....	.005	.015	....	50	.187
.007	99	....	.004	.008	....	40	.145
.018	248	....	.011	.029	....	100	.374
.027	372	....	.016	.044	....	150	.562
.039	534	....	.024	.063	....	215	.808
.055	744	....	.033	....	....	300	.885
.015	198	....	.008	.023	....	80	.299
.037	496	....	.022	.059	....	200	.753
....	**62,160**	**39,703**	....	....	....	**41,663**	46.502
7.387	**28.196**	**15.757**	**4.501**	**12.607**	....	**2.549**	**199.812**
.073	993	....	.044	.117	....	400	1.501
.017	240	....	.010	.029	....	100	.363
.584	10,989	44	.547	1.282	....	12,815	11.577
.020	276	....	.012	.032	....	115	.416
.071	961	....	.042	.113	....	400	1.405
.044	601	....	.027	.071	....	250	.909
.053	720	....	.032	.085	....	300	1.090
.183	2,483	....	.111	.293	....	1,000	3.759
.035	458	....	.019	.057	....	200	.721
.014	195	....	.009	.023	....	81	.295
.033	449	....	.020	.053	....	700	.429
.070	911	....	.043	.113	....	398	.738
.062	841	....	.037	.099	....	350	1.271
.041	567	....	.025	.067	....	236	.856
.059	629	....	.037	.099	....	350	1.201
.035	488	....	.032	.057	....	203	.384
.062	841	....	.037	.099	....	350	1.271
.010	144	....	.006	.017	....	60	.216

Table 380—*Continued*

Detail of Internal Deliveries for Chil

Receipt No.	Districts or Kitchens	Date of Delivery	Flour	Rice	Beans, Peas
New Series		1921			
133	Cesis	June 9	.940	.231	.370
134	Lives	June 9	.251	.070	.111
135	Valmiera	June 10	....	.283	.212
136	Riga City Asylum	June 11	....	.132	.185
137	Riga City Asylum	June 17	4.610	3.735	5.910
138	Riga City Asylum	June 18	.125	....	....
139	Riga Children's Hospital	June 20	.375	.083	.112
141	Jekabmiests	June 20	.629	.170	.270
142	Riga City Asylum	June 18	.244	....	....
143	Riga City Asylum	June 21	.182	.200	.316
144	Riga City Children's Bakery	June 22	.897	....	....
145	Riga City Children's Bakery	June 22	1.053	....	....
148	Riga Zoölogical Gardens	June 27	.100	.082	.130
149	Riga City Children's Bakery	June 27	2.249	....	....
150	Riga City Children's Bakery	June 27	2.250	....	....
151	Baltic Scandinavian Children's Colony	June 27	.055	.015	.024
152	Valmiera	June 27	1.058	....	....
153	Kreslava	June 29	.888	.249	.397
	Total Milk in Cans, Soap in Pieces	....	....	....	....
	Total for June, Metric Tons	....	**26.396**	**10.161**	**15.776**
146	Chief of Army Supply	June 29	8.229	....	....
140	Riga Russ Refugee Committee	June 20	.012	.026	....
147	Riga City Asylum	June 22	.341	.713	....
154	Riga Refugee Committee	June 28	.309	.193	....
155	Riga Women's Corps Asylum	June 28	....	.108	....
156	Dobele	June 27	.221	.161	....
158	Jelgava	June 30	3.318	.898	.972
159	Ventspils	June 30	1.654	.497	.810
160	Milgravis	June 30	.645	.177	.285
161	Tukums	July 1	.488	.384	....
162	Ogre	June 30	.251	.197	....
163	Daugavpils (Dvinsk)	July 1	9.216	6.217	....
165	Griva	July 1	1.684	1.227	....
166	Eglaine	July 1	.520	.381	....
167	Ilukste	July 1	.338	.238	....
168	Svente	July 1	.461	.332	....
169	Kalkuni	July 1	.553	.398	....
170	Subate	July 1	.276	.199	....
171	Latvian Railroad Children's Sanatorium	July 2	.181	.132	....
172	Naukseni Refugee Committee	July 2	.242	.178	....
173	Libau	July 1	1.475	1.063	....
174	Libau	July 1	9.216	6.642	....
175	Saldus	July 1	.276	.197	....
176	Kuldiga	July 1	.922	.664	....
177	Riga	June 29	4.451	4.202	5.118
178	Ludza	July 1	1.290	.894	....
179	Aizpute	July 1	.313	.225	....
180	Kurmene	July 5	.407	.366	....
181	Sloka	July 5	.414	.330	....
182	Riga City Children's Bakery	July 5	5.845	....	....
183	Riga City Children's Bakery	July 5	4.886	....	....
184	Bierini	July 5	.369	.266	....
185	Rezekne	July 2	3.318	2.140	....
186	Salaspils	July 6	.054	.037	....
187	Riga Refugee Committee	July 4	.069	.052	....
188	Spare	July 4	.146	.103	....
192	Jekabmiests	July 6	.857	.646	....

R.A. and A.R.A.-European Children's Fund

ding, by Districts or Kitchens, by Months

Commodities in Net Metric Tons of 1,000 Kilograms or 2,204.6 Pounds *

Pork Products	Milk Evap.	Milk Cond.	Cocoa	Sugar	Misc. Food	Soap	Total Tons
	(Cans)	(Cans)				(Pieces)	
.071	1,118	....	.051	.136	....	600	1.799
.024	338	....	.015	.040	....	141	.511
.096	1,397	....	.052	.164	....	593	.807
.072	684	....	.026	.122	....	470	.537
.990	18,022	....	.810	2.130	....	....	18.185
....	....	....	....	....	....	....	.125
.027	143	....	.009	.020	....	210	.626
.058	843	....	.036	.095	....	500	1.258
....	....	....	....	....	....	....	.244
.053	824	....	.022	....	....	373	.773
.152	....	....	....	....	....	....	1.049
.178	....	....	....	....	....	....	1.231
.021	397	....	.018	.047	....	160	.398
.095	....	....	....	....	....	....	2.344
.095	....	....	....	....	....	....	2.345
.005	74	....	.003	.009	....	30	.111
....	....	....	....	....	....	....	1.058
.061	1,141	....	.053	.142	....	500	1.790
....	**47,767**	**44**	....	....	....	**21,885**	23.023
3.464	**21.667**	**.017**	**2.185**	**5.611**	....	**1.339**	**86.616**
....	....	....	....	....	....	....	8.229
.003	48	....	.002	.006	....	20	.049
.073	1,333	....	.039	.158	....	555	1.324
.024	288	....	.015	.041	....	230	.582
.013	140	.....	.009	.016	....	100	.146
.022	298	....	.013	.035	....	120	.452
.329	4,099	....	.192	.514	....	1,800	6.223
.183	2,299	....	.107	.282	....	1,000	3.533
.064	869	....	.038	.097	....	350	1.306
.052	691	....	.032	.086	....	300	1.042
.027	340	....	.016	.041	....	150	.532
.913	12,031	....	.513	1.366	....	5,000	18.225
.155	2,483	....	.111	.293	....	1,000	3.470
.046	706	....	.022	.068	....	300	1.037
.032	474	....	.021	.058	....	200	.687
.046	621	....	.028	.073	....	250	.940
.055	745	....	.033	.088	....	300	1.127
.027	372	....	.017	.044	....	150	.563
.018	248	....	.011	.029	....	100	.371
.026	348	....	.014	.039	....	140	.499
.147	1,986	....	.089	.235	....	800	3.009
.913	12,416	....	....	1.466	....	5,000	18.237
.027	372	....	.017	.041	....	150	.558
.091	1,242	....	.055	.147	....	500	1.879
.798	17,421	....	.776	2.058	....	14,500	17.403
.128	1,738	....	.077	.205	....	700	2.594
.031	442	....	.019	.050	....	170	.638
.050	683	....	.030	.081	....	275	.934
.046	621	....	.026	.070	....	250	.886
.369	....	....	....	....	....	....	6.214
.276	....	....	....	....	....	....	5.162
.037	497	....	.022	.059	....	200	.753
.315	4,470	....	.185	.528	....	1,800	6.486
.005	75	....	.003	.009	....	30	.108
.006	99	....	.004	.012	....	40	.143
.015	188	....	.008	.023	....	80	.295
.088	1,242	....	.053	.189	....	500	1.833

[*Continued on next page*]

Table 380—*Continued*

Detail of Internal Deliveries for Chil

Receipt No.	Districts or Kitchens	Date of Delivery	Flour	Rice	Beans, Peas
New Series		1921			
193	Zilani	July 8	.424	.281	....
194	Jaun Jelgava	July 7	.550	.447	....
195	Krustpils	July 8	.592	.410	....
196	Livani	July 6	.645	.465	....
197	Riga City Asylum	July 8	.154	.421	....
198	Riga City Asylum	July 9	.289	.539	....
199	Cesis	July 11	.605	.510	....
200	Riga Women's Corps Asylum	July 11	.057	.041	....
201	Rujene	July 6	.530	.346	....
202	Valka	July 11	.276	.192	....
203	Valmiera	July 11	.922	.577	....
204	Riga City Asylum	July 11	.125	.246	....
205	Bolderaja	July 6	.588	.380	....
207	Ferienheim Dobele	July 12	.553	.398	....
209	Limbazi	July 6	.256	.192	....
210	Riga	July 13	3.091	9.072	....
188	Silupe	July 4	.245	.186	....
190	Zogova	July 6	.092	.067	....
191	Rezekne Refugee Committee	July 6	.387	.279	....
206	Korsovka	July 11	.304	.252	....
208	Talsi	July 11	.362	.265	....
211	Plavinas	July 6	.369	.253	....
212	Jekabmiests	July 6	....	....	....
213	Riga City Children's Bakery	July 14	6.045	....	....
214	Lives	July 6	.184	.121	....
215	Jelgava	July 15	....	.446	....
216	Riga City Children's Bakery	July 19	5.972	....	....
217	Grienvalde	July 20	.065	.047	....
218	Riga Children's Hospital	July 21	.453	.250	....
219	Riga Society "Kinderfreund"	July 21	.024	.067	....
220	Daudzeva	July 25	.323	.232	....
221	Nauksen	July 26	.323	.232	....
222	Nitauri	July 27	.111	.080	....
	Total Milk in Cans, Soap in Pieces	....	....	....	....
	Total for July, Metric Tons	....	**88.163**	**47.777**	**7.185**
223	Baltic-Seand Child Colony	July 26	.055	.039	....
224	Riga	July 27	1.896	8.149	....
225	Riga Russian Refugee Committee	July 30	.010	.026	....
226	Milgravis	Aug. 1	.645	.465	....
227	Riga Refugee Committee	July 30	.507	.366	....
228	Riga Refugee Committee	July 30	.138	.100	....
229	Tukums	Aug. 1	.553	.398	....
230	Jelgava	Aug. 2	3.041	2.192	....
231	Ventspils	Aug. 2	1.659	1.195	....
232	Ogre	Aug. 2	.221	.160	....
233	Riga City Children's Bakery	Aug. 2	5.496	....	....
234	Riga City Children's Bakery	Aug. 2	5.429	....	....
235	Spare	Aug. 3	.148	.106	....
236	Griva	Aug. 2	1.843	1.329	....
237	Latvia Railroad Children's Sanatorium	Aug. 3	.157	.103	....
238	Ilukste	Aug. 2	.369	.266	....
239	Eglaine	Aug. 2	.553	.398	....
240	Kalkuni	Aug. 2	.553	.398	....
241	Daugavpils (Dvinsk)	Aug. 2	9.032	6.509	....
242	Svente	Aug. 2	.415	.299	....
243	Salaspils	Aug. 4	.092	.067	....
244	Krustpils	Aug. 4	.599	.431	....

R.A. and A.R.A.-European Children's Fund

eding, by Districts or Kitchens, by Months

Commodities in Net Metric Tons of 1,000 Kilograms or 2,204.6 Pounds *

Pork Products	Milk Evap.	Milk Cond.	Cocoa	Sugar	Misc. Food	Soap	Total Tons
	(Cans)	(Cans)				(Pieces)	
.042	510	....	.023	.062	....	230	.832
.057	761	....	.031	.095	....	350	1.180
.063	869	....	.035	.103	....	350	1.203
.064	869	....	.037	.103	....	350	1.314
....	702	....	.038	.107	....	398	.720
.031	1,034	....	.050	.085	....	470	.994
.082	851	....	.051	.120	....	500	1.368
.006	77	....	.003	.009	....	31	.116
.005	745	....	.033	.086	....	300	1.000
.025	372	....	.017	.044	....	150	.554
.085	1,208	....	.051	.133	....	500	1.768
....	504	....	.015	.060	....	203	.446
.055	825	....	.036	.099	....	350	1.158
.055	744	....	.033	.088	....	300	1.127
.027	337	....	.016	.043	....	150	.534
.377	10,370	....	.573	1.490	....	....	14.603
.026	372	....	.017	.044	....	150	.518
.009	124	....	.006	.015	....	50	.189
.038	521	....	.023	.062	....	210	.789
.016	172	....	.021	.053	....	200	.646
.042	522	....	.024	.062	....	250	.755
.037	477	....	.022	.057	....	200	.738
....	....	....	....	.114	....	....	.114
.372	....	....	....	....	....	....	6.417
.018	248	....	.011	.029	....	100	.363
....	....	....	....	....	....	....	.446
.367	....	....	....	....	....	....	6.339
.006	87	....	.004	.010	....	35	.132
.032	455	....	.018	.061	....	300	.814
.005	124	....	.006	.015	....	50	.117
.032	435	....	.019	.051	....	175	.657
.032	435	....	.019	.051	....	175	.657
.011	149	....	.007	.018	....	60	.227
....	**96,824**	....	....	....	....	**43,647**	46.590
7.467	**43.920**	....	**3.836**	**11.876**	....	**2.670**	**212.894**
.005	74	....	.003	.009	....	30	.111
.449	13,970	....	.669	1.633	....	11,070	12.796
.002	50	....	.002	.006	....	20	.046
.064	664	....	.039	.103	....	350	1.316
.050	683	....	.030	.081	....	275	1.034
.014	186	....	.008	.022	....	75	.282
.055	745	....	.033	.088	....	300	1.127
.301	2,998	....	.183	.484	....	1,650	6.201
.164	2,235	....	.099	.264	....	900	3.381
.022	278	....	.013	.035	....	120	.451
.372	....	....	....	....	....	....	5.868
.367	....	....	....	....	....	....	5.796
.015	199	....	.009	.023	....	80	.301
.183	2,483	....	.111	.293	....	1,000	3.759
.011	119	....	.006	.019	....	65	.296
.037	497	....	.022	.059	....	200	.753
.055	745	....	.033	.088	....	300	1.127
.055	745	....	.033	.088	....	300	1.127
.895	9,404	....	.542	1.437	....	4,900	18.415
.041	559	....	.025	.066	....	225	.846
.009	124	....	.006	.015	....	50	.189
.059	807	....	.036	.095	....	....	1.220

[*Continued on next page*]

Table 380—*Continued*

Detail of Internal Deliveries for Chil

Receipt No.	Districts or Kitchens	Date of Delivery	Flour	Rice	Beans, Peas
New Series		1921			
245	Rezekne	Aug. 4	2.506	1.411	....
246	Riga City Asylum	Aug. 4	.268	.736	....
247	Riga Women's Corps Asylum	Aug. 12	.058	.047	....
248	Sloka	Aug. 4	.461	.332	....
249	Zilani	Aug. 4	.369	.266	....
250	Lives	Aug. 13	.184	.132	....
251	Kreslava	Aug. 4	.829	.598	....
252	Olaine	Aug. 5	.221	.160	....
253	Latvian Red Cross Hospital	Aug. 5	.074	.054	....
254	Riga Zoölogical Asylum	Aug. 6	.077	.212	....
255	Ludza	Aug. 6	.485	.321	....
256	Riga City Asylum	Aug. 19	.270	.485	....
257	Silupe	Aug. 8	.276	.199	....
258	Riga City Asylum	Aug. 20	.145	.181	....
259	Jekabmiests	Aug. 6	.347	.163	....
260	Jaun Jelgava	Aug. 9	.599	.431	....
261	Livani	Aug. 8	.302	.271	....
262	Grienvalde	Aug. 16	.065	.047	....
263	Kulduga	Aug. 16	.531	.387	....
264	Libau	Aug. 16	8.479	6.110	....
265	Saldus	Aug. 16	.046	.064	....
266	Aizputes	Aug. 16	.276	.199	....
267	Libau	Aug. 16	1.475	1.063	....
268	Bolderaja	Aug. 16	.645	.465	....
269	Rujene	Aug. 16	.298	.185	....
270	Bierini	Aug. 16	.369	.266	....
271	Daugavpils Refugee Committee	Aug. 18	.369	.266	....
272	Riga City Asylum	Aug. 8	.127	.270	....
273	Cesis	Aug. 16	.829	.435	....
274	Riga	Aug. 18	1.722	5.625	....
275	Riga Women's Corps Asylum	Aug. 9	.072	.199	....
276	Bulli Women's Corps Asylum	Aug. 19	....	....	....
277	Talsi	Aug. 16	.329	.173	....
278	Plavinas	Aug. 19	.126	.185	....
279	Lives	Aug. 19	....	....	....
280	Valka	Aug. 18	.276	.199	....
281	Dobele	Aug. 16	.222	.160	....
282	Livani	Aug. 19	....	....	....
283	Limbazi	Aug. 16	.184	.132	....
283B	Riga City Asylum	Aug. 19	.173	.369	....
284	Riga City Asylum	Aug. 24	.018	.044	....
285	Riga "Kinderfreund"	Aug. 23	.031	.067	....
286	Rezekne Refugee Committee	Aug. 24	.461	.332	....
287	Zogovas Refugee Committee	Aug. 24	.221	.160	....
288	Korsovka	Aug. 16	.369	.266	....
289	Riga City Children's Bakery	Aug. 26	3.867	....	....
290	Riga City Children's Bakery	Aug. 26	3.645	....	....
291	Riga Children's Hospital	Aug. 26	.553	.398	....
	Total Milk in Cans, Soap in Pieces	....	....	....	....
	Total for August, Metric Tons	....	**66.660**	**47.061**	....
292	Riga	Sept. ..	3.374	9.127	....
293	Russian Refugee Committee	Sept. 1	.036	.026	....
294	Jelgava	Sept. 2	2.943	2.121	....
295	Tukums	Sept. 1	.490	.353	....
296	Ventspils	Sept. 1	1.605	1.197	....
297	Olaine	Sept. 2	.214	.155	....
298	Eglaine	Sept. 2	.535	.385	....

R.A. and A.R.A.-European Children's Fund

ding, by Districts or Kitchens, by Months

Commodities in Net Metric Tons of 1,000 Kilograms or 2,204.6 Pounds *

Pork Products	Milk Evap.	Milk Cond.	Cocoa	Sugar	Misc. Food	Soap	Total Tons
	(Cans)	(Cans)				(Pieces)	
.198	2,144	....	.144	.175	....	....	4.434
.049	1,376	....	.042	.162	....	....	1.257
....	....	....	.004	.008	....	....	.117
.046	621	....	.028	.073	....	....	.940
.037	332	....	.022	.059	....	....	.753
.018	....	....	.011	.029	....	....	.374
....	1,117	....	.050	.132	....	....	1.609
.022	298	....	.013	.035	....	....	.451
.007	99	....	.004	.012	....	....	.151
.014	397	....	.018	.047	....	....	.368
.116	205	....	.033	....	....	....	.955
....	907	....	.040	.105	....	....	.900
....	372	....	.017	.044	....	....	.536
....	579	....	.026	.040	....	....	.392
.029	436	....	.027	.009	....	....	.575
....	807	....	.036	.095	....	....	1.161
.022	....	....	....	.057	....	....	.652
....	87	....	.004	.010	....	....	.126
....	694	....	.023	.094	....	....	1.035
.431	11,422	....	.509	1.349	....	....	16.878
....	89	....	.003	.016	....	....	.129
....	372	....	.017	.044	....	....	.536
....	1,986	....	.089	.235	....	....	2.862
....	869	....	.039	.103	....	....	1.252
....	103	....	.011	.031	....	....	.525
....	497	....	.022	.059	....	....	.716
....	497	....	.022	.059	....	....	.716
....	504	....	.022	.060	....	....	.479
....	1,050	....	.029	.085	....	....	1.378
....	9,411	....	.467	1.237	....	....	9.051
....	372	....	.017	.044	....	....	.332
....	84	....	....	....	....	....	....
....	139	....	.025	.055	....	....	.582
....	248	....	.012	.054	....	....	.377
....	248	....	....	....	....	....	....
....	372	....	.017	.044	....	....	.536
....	298	....	.013	.035	....	....	.430
....	681	....	.036	....	....	....	.036
....	248	....	.011	.029	....	....	.356
....	690	....	.031	.082	....	....	.655
....	82	....	.004	.010	....	....	.076
....	124	....	.006	.015	....	....	.119
....	621	....	.028	.073	....	....	.894
....	298	....	.013	.035	....	....	.429
....	497	....	.022	.059	....	....	.716
....	....	....	....	....	....	....	3.867
....	....	....	....	....	....	....	3.645
....	745	....	.033	.088	....	....	1.072
....	**80,583**	....	....	....	....	**21,910**	37.893
4.214	**36.553**	....	**3.942**	**9.995**	....	**1.340**	**169.765**
....	17,061	....	.760	2.015	....	....	15.276
.004	48	....	.002	.006	....	....	.074
.292	3,965	....	.177	.468	....	....	6.001
.049	661	....	.029	.078	....	....	.999
.159	2,163	....	.096	.255	....	....	3.312
.021	288	....	.013	.034	....	....	.437
.053	721	....	.032	.085	....	....	1.090

[*Continued on next page*]

Table 380—*Continued*

Detail of Internal Deliveries for Chi

Receipt No.	Districts or Kitchens	Date of Delivery	Flour	Rice	Beans, Peas
New Series		1921			
299	Kalkuni	Sept. 2	.535	.385	....
300	Svente	Sept. 2	.401	.289	....
301	Daugavpils (Dvinsk)	Sept. 2	8.740	6.299	....
302	Griva	Sept. 2	1.784	1.286	....
303	Ilukste	Sept. 2	.357	.258	....
304	Riga Asylum, Talsu St.	Sept. 2	.284	.584	....
305	Milgravis	Sept. 2	.624	.450	....
306	Jaun Jelgava	Sept. 5	.468	.373	....
307	Ogre	Sept. 5	.214	.155	....
308	Riga Bakery, Herrnberger	Sept. 5	5.528	....	....
309	Jekabmiests	Sept. 6	.802	.578	....
310	Silani	Sept. 6	.356	.258	....
311	Livani	Sept. 6	.580	.417	....
312	Krustpils	Sept. 6	.580	.343	....
313	Kurmene	Sept. 6	.356	.258	....
314	Plavinas	Sept. 6	.356	.258	....
315	Sloka	Sept. 7	.445	.322	....
316	Ludza	Sept. 7	1.159	.836	....
317	Rezekne	Sept. 7	2.943	2.121	....
318	Riga Bakery, Briedis	Sept. 7	5.056	....	....
319	Rujene	Sept. 8	.445	.125	.157
321	Valka	Sept. 8	.123	....	.106
322	Talsi	Sept. 9	.302	....	.197
323	Cesis	Sept. 8	.660	.224	.247
324	Valmiera	Sept. 7	.802	.224	.354
325	Lives	Sept. 5	.268	.075	.118
326	Limbazi	Sept. 12	.178	.050	.079
327	Zogova	Sept. 10	.223	.062	.098
328	Dobele	Sept. 10	.214	.060	.095
329	Naukseni	Sept. 10	.330	.092	.145
330	Saldus	Sept. 11	.268	.075	.118
331	Liepaja (Libau)	Sept. 12	8.205	2.291	3.623
332	Liepaja (Libau)	Sept. 12	1.427	.398	.630
333	Kuldiga	Sept. 12	.892	.249	.394
334	Aizpute	Sept. 12	....	....	.118
335	Salaspils	Sept. 13	.089	.025	.039
336	Nitaure	Sept. 13	.071	.020	.032
337	Grienvalde	Sept. 14	.098	.027	.043
338	Riga	Sept. 14	4.359	3.536	5.591
339	Bolderaja	Sept. 12	.624	.174	.276
341	Riga Asylum, Dunte St.	Sept. 10	.153	.122	.192
342	Daudzeva	Sept. 19	.312	.087	.138
343	Bierini	Sept. 19	.357	.100	.158
344	Riga Asylum, Miera St.	Sept. 10	.150	.120	.189
345	Riga Asylum, Matisa St.	Sept. 19	.268	.214	.339
346	Kreslava	Sept. 20	.802	.224	.354
347	Korsovka	Sept. 20	.357	.100	.158
348	Riga Asylum, Jekabmiesta St.	Sept. 21	.300	.239	.378
349	Rezekne and Silupe	Sept. 21	.535	.149	.236
350	Riga Refugee Committee	Sept. 22	.357	.100	.158
351	Spare	Sept. 22	.161	.045	.071
352	Riga Refugee Committee, Valmiera St.	Sept. 22	.089	.025	.039
353	Riga Bakery, Herrnberger	Sept. 22	4.975	....	....
354	Riga Bakery, Briedis	Sept. 22	4.533	....	....
355	Kinderfreund	Sept. 23	.031	.025	.039
356	Riga Asylum, Katelu St	Sept. 26	.021	.016	.026
	Total Milk in Cans	....	....	....	....
	Total for September, Metric Tons	....	**73.744**	**38.107**	**14.935**

.A. and A.R.A.-European Children's Fund

ding, by Districts or Kitchens, by Months

Commodities in Net Metric Tons of 1,000 Kilograms or 2,204.6 Pounds *

Pork Products	Milk		Cocoa	Sugar	Misc. Food	Soap	Total Tons
	Evap.	Cond.					
	(Cans)	(Cans)				(Pieces)	
.053	721	....	.032	.085	....	....	1.090
.040	541	....	.024	.064	....	....	.818
.866	11,775	....	.525	1.390	....	....	17.820
.177	2,403	....	.107	.284	....	....	3.638
.035	481	....	.021	.057	....	....	.728
.035	1,093	....	.049	.129	....	....	1.081
.062	841	....	.037	.099	....	....	1.272
.062	652	....	.037	.075	....	....	1.015
.021	288	....	.010	.034	....	....	.434
.374	....	....	....	....	....	....	5.902
.079	1,082	....	.048	.128	....	....	1.635
.035	481	....	.021	.057	....	....	.727
.057	781	....	.035	.092	....	....	1.181
.043	267	....	.035	.082	....	....	1.083
.035	481	....	.021	.057	....	....	.727
.035	481	....	.021	.057	....	....	.727
.039	601	....	.027	.071	....	....	.904
.115	1,562	....	.070	.184	....	....	2.364
.292	3,965	....	.117	.468	....	....	5.941
.342	....	....	....	....	....	....	5.398
.044	566	....	.027	.065	....	....	.863
.026	....	....	.008	.026	....	....	.289
.044	563	....	.016	.052	....	....	.611
.079	839	....	.045	.128	....	....	1.383
.079	1,082	....	.048	.128	....	....	1.635
.026	360	....	.016	.043	....	....	.546
.018	240	....	.011	.028	....	....	.364
.022	300	....	.013	.035	....	....	.453
.021	288	....	.013	.034	....	....	.437
.033	445	....	.020	.053	....	....	.673
.026	360	....	.016	.043	....	....	.546
.813	11,054	....	....	1.305	....	....	16.237
.141	1,922	....	.086	.227	....	....	2.909
.088	1,202	....	.054	.142	....	....	1.819
.027	....	....	....	....	....	....	.145
.009	120	....	.005	.014	....	....	.181
.007	96	....	.004	.011	....	....	.145
.010	132	....	.006	.015	....	....	.199
.781	17,061	....	.760	2.015	....	....	17.042
.062	841	....	.037	.099	....	....	1.272
.019	589	....	.026	.070	....	....	.582
.031	420	....	.019	.050	....	....	.637
.035	481	....	.021	.057	....	....	.728
.018	757	....	.026	.068	....	....	.571
.033	1,034	....	.046	.122	....	....	1.022
.079	1,082	....	.048	.128	....	....	1.635
.035	481	....	.021	.057	....	....	.728
.036	1,153	....	.051	.136	....	....	1.140
.053	721	....	.032	.085	....	....	1.090
.035	481	....	.021	.057	....	....	.728
.016	216	....	.010	.026	....	....	.329
.009	120	....	.005	.014	....	....	.181
.272	....	....	....	....	....	....	5.247
.248	....	....	....	....	....	....	4.781
.003	120	....	.005	.014	....	....	.117
.002	79	....	.004	.009	....	....	.078
....	**98,608**	....	....	....	....	....	44.729
6.655	**44.729**	....	**3.866**	**11.710**	....	....	**193.746**

[*Continued on next page*]

Table 380—*Continued*

Detail of Internal Deliveries for Chil

Receipt No.	Districts or Kitchens	Date of Delivery	Flour	Rice	Beans, Peas
New Series		1921			
357	Riga	Oct. ..	3.683	2.001	4.264
358	Latvian Red Cross Assari	Oct. 1	.092	.013	.054
359	Russian Refugee Committee, Gertrud St	Oct. 1	....	.010	.016
360	Krape	Oct. 1	.092	.013	.054
361	Malinova	Oct. 1	.184	.026	.106
362	Osunas	Oct. 1	.148	.021	.085
363	Uzvaldes	Oct. 1	.276	.039	.160
364	Liksnas	Oct. 1	.369	.052	.214
365	Riga Asylum, Talsu St	Oct. 1	.315	.130	.541
366	Jelgava	Oct. 4	3.041	.425	1.768
367	Kreslava	Oct. 4	.829	.116	.483
368	Daugavpils (Dvinsk)	Oct. 4	9.032	1.421	3.987
369	Eglaine	Oct. 4	....	....	.244
370	Kalkuni	Oct. 4	.412	.107	.244
371	Ilukste	Oct. 3	.369	.045	.214
372	Griva	Oct. 4	1.637	....	.814
373	Zilani	Oct. 4	.335	.052	.214
374	Krustpils	Oct. 4	.599	.082	.235
375	Jekabmiests	Oct. 4	.829	.116	.483
376	Livani	Oct. 4	.599	.084	.347
377	Svente	Oct. 7	.213	....	.183
378	Latvian Welfare Society	Oct. 4	.016	.006	.024
379	Tukums	Oct. 5	.497	....	.024
380	Rujene	Oct. 5	.412	.065	.267
381	Riga's Women's Corps Asylum	Oct. 5	.047	....	.061
382	Ventspils	Oct. 5	1.659	....	.732
383	Milgravis	Oct. 5	.645	.054	.375
384	Ogre	Oct. 5	.221	....	.098
385	Riga's City Children's Hospital	Oct. 5	.553	.087	.244
386	Sloka	Oct. 5	.461	.065	.267
387	Liepaja (Libau)	Oct. 11	8.479	1.184	4.921
389	Saldus	Oct. 11	.276	.039	.160
390	Aizpute	Oct. 11	.414	.058	.241
391	Kuldiga	Oct. 11	.829	.116	.483
392	Vec-Zvarde	Oct. 11	.092	.026	.041
393	Olaine	Oct. 12	.221	.031	.129
394	Naukseni	Oct. 12	.276	.047	.193
395	Riga	Oct. 13	3.143	2.929	4.965
396	Riga Bakery, Briedis	Oct. 13	5.131	....	....
397	Riga Bakery, Herrnberger	Oct. 13	5.307	....	....
398	Lives	Oct. 14	.276	.039	.160
399	Cesis	Oct. 14	.829	.116	.483
400	Jaun Jelgava	Oct. 14	.645	....	.375
401	Valka	Oct. 14	.267	.039	.160
402	Valmiera	Oct. 14	.503	.116	.483
403	Riga Asylum, Miera St	Oct. 17	.142	.068	.190
404	Riga Asylum, Dunte St	Oct. 17	.158	.065	.271
405	Bolderaja	Oct. 17	.645	.090	.375
406	Rezekne's Refugee Committee	Oct. 18	.461	.065	.267
407	Zogova	Oct. 18	.184	.051	.081
408	Silupe	Oct. 18	.111	.016	.064
409	Spare	Oct. 18	.148	.021	.085
410	Riga Refugee Committee, Valmiera St	Oct. 18	.092	.013	.054
411	Riga Refugee Committee, Kazaku St	Oct. 18	.424	.059	.246
412	Dobele	Oct. 18	.221	.031	.129
413	Plavinas	Oct. 18	.369	.052	.214
414	Talsi	Oct. 18	.461	.065	.267
415	Ludza	Oct. 18	.529	....	.496

A.R.A. and A.R.A.-European Children's Fund

Feeding, by Districts or Kitchens, by Months

Commodities in Net Metric Tons of 1,000 Kilograms or 2,204.6 Pounds *

Pork Products	Milk: Evap. (Cans)	Milk: Cond. (Cans)	Cocoa	Sugar	Misc. Food	Soap (Pieces)	Total Tons
.620	10,591	....	.626	1.718	....	....	12.912
.009	124	....	.006	.015	....	....	.189
....	50	....	.002	.006	....	....	.034
.009	124	....	.006	.015	....	....	.189
.018	248	....	.011	.029	....	....	.374
.015	199	....	.009	.023	....	....	.301
.027	372	....	.017	.044	....	....	.563
.037	497	....	.022	.059	....	....	.753
.051	1,227	....	.056	.148	....	....	1.241
.302	3,888	....	.183	.484	....	....	6.203
.082	1,117	....	.050	.132	....	....	1.692
.859	12,168	....	.542	1.437	....	....	17.278
....	....	....	....	....	....	....	.244
.041	706	....	.026	.075	....	....	.905
.037	412	....	.021	.059	....	....	.745
.142	2,167	....	.111	.293	....	....	2.997
.022	497	....	.016	.059	....	....	.698
.059	807	....	.036	.095	....	....	1.106
.082	1,117	....	.050	.132	....	....	1.692
.057	273	....	.011	.092	....	....	1.190
.018	599	....	.008	.053	....	....	.475
.003	56	....	.003	.007	....	....	.059
.016	580	....	.028	.077	....	....	.842
.035	528	....	.021	.073	....	....	.873
.003	....	....	.003	.015	....	....	.129
.164	1,057	....	.099	.264	....	....	2.918
.064	869	....	.039	.103	....	....	1.280
.022	298	....	.013	.035	....	....	.389
.055	745	....	.033	.088	....	....	1.060
.044	407	....	.027	.073	....	....	.937
.840	11,422	....	.509	1.349	....	....	17.282
.027	372	....	.017	.044	....	....	.563
.041	558	....	.025	.066	....	....	.845
.082	1,117	....	.050	.132	....	....	1.692
.009	124	....	.006	.015	....	....	.189
.022	298	....	.011	.035	....	....	.449
.033	355	....	.019	.041	....	....	.609
.739	13,262	....	.635	1.679	....	....	14.090
.253	....	....	....	....	....	....	5.384
.261	....	....	....	....	....	....	5.568
.027	372	....	.017	.044	....	....	.563
.082	1,033	....	.050	.128	....	....	1.688
.064	828	....	.039	.103	....	....	1.226
.022	372	....	.015	.035	....	....	.538
.065	541	....	.036	.114	....	....	1.317
.023	541	....	.026	.039	....	....	.488
.026	628	....	.028	.074	....	....	.622
.064	869	....	.039	.103	....	....	1.316
.046	621	....	.028	.073	....	....	.940
.018	248	....	.011	.029	....	....	.374
.011	149	....	.007	.018	....	....	.227
.015	199	....	.009	.023	....	....	.301
.009	124	....	.006	.015	....	....	.189
.042	633	....	.025	.068	....	....	.864
.022	298	....	.013	.035	....	....	.451
.037	497	....	.022	.059	....	....	.753
.046	621	....	.028	.073	....	....	.940
.002	1,614	....	.072	.119	....	....	1.218

[*Continued on next page*]

Table 380—*Continued*

Detail of Internal Deliveries for Chil[d]

Receipt No.	Districts or Kitchens	Date of Delivery	Flour	Rice	Beans, Peas
New Series		1921			
416	Rezekne	Oct. 19	3.041	....	1.766
417	Bierini	Oct. 19	.369	.052	.214
418	Salaspils	Oct. 20	.092	.013	.054
419	Latvian Welfare Society	Oct. 20	.164	....	....
420	Daudzeva	Oct. 21	.310	.045	.187
422	Ikskile	Oct. 21	.094	.013	.055
423	Kurmene	Oct. 21	.369	.052	.214
424	Korsovka	Oct. 21	.369	.052	.214
425	Grienvalde	Oct. 21	.101	.014	.059
426	Nitaure	Oct. 24	.074	.011	.043
427	Riga Asylum, Matisa St	Oct. 24	.261	.108	.447
428	Riga Asylum, Jekabmiesta St	Oct. 24	.273	.113	.468
429	Riga Asylum, Katolu St	Oct. 25	.021	.009	.035
	Total Milk in Cans	....	....	....	....
	Total for October, Metric Tons	....	**63.736**	**10.848**	**36.291**
430	Riga Bakery, Briedis	Nov. 1	4.618	....	....
431	Riga	Nov. 1	4.430	1.768	7.359
432	Riga Bakery, Herrnberger	Nov. 2	4.870	....	....
433	Russian Refugee Committee	Nov. 3	.012	.010	.016
434	Jelgava	Nov. 4	2.291	.411	1.224
436	Ventspils	Nov. 4	1.435	.224	.424
437	Tukums	Nov. 4	.327	.069	.284
438	Ogre	Nov. 5	.214	.030	.125
439	Riga Asylum, Talsu St	Nov. 7	.290	.116	.482
440	Sloka	Nov. 7	.446	.063	.259
441	Zilani	Nov. 8	.184	.050	.125
442	Rujene	Nov. 9	.332	.063	.127
443	Livani	Nov. 9	.548	.081	.276
444	Milgravis	Nov. 8	.624	.087	.363
445	Krustpils	Nov. 9	.580	.081	.366
446	Riga's Women's Corps Asylum	Nov. 9	.047	.019	.077
447	Jekabmiests	Nov. 9	.608	.112	.291
448	Svente	Nov. 10	.402	.056	.233
449	Eglaine	Nov. 10	.260	.130	.236
450	Daugavpils (Dvinsk)	Nov. 10	8.740	1.220	5.079
451	Griva	Nov. 10	1.784	.249	1.037
452	Krape	Nov. 10	.086	.018	.033
453	Ilukste	Nov. 11	.357	.050	.208
454	Salaspils	Nov. 11	.068	.015	.028
455	Kalkuni	Nov. 11	.535	.075	.310
456	Riga	Nov. 12	3.765	3.167	4.795
457	Valka	Nov. 14	.192	.038	.115
458	Cesis	Nov. 14	.686	.112	.290
459	Valmiera	Nov. 14	.803	.112	.289
460	Ludza	Nov. 15	1.050	.123	.394
461	Riga Bakery, Herrnberger	Nov. 15	5.411	....	....
462	Riga Bakery, Briedis	Nov. 15	5.095	....	....
463	Riga Refugee Committee, Valmiera St	Nov. 16	.134	.037	.059
464	Jaun Jelgava	Nov. 16	.469	.126	.219
465	Riga Asylum, Miera St	Nov. 16	.138	.055	.231
466	Liepaja (Libau)	Nov. 16	8.205	1.146	4.768
467	Saldus	Nov. 16	.170	.038	.052
468	Kuldiga	Nov. 16	.803	.112	.466
469	Aizpute	Nov. 16	.268	.038	.155
470	Rezekne	Nov. 17	2.943	.411	1.552
471	Latvian Welfare Society	Nov. 19	.016	.006	.025
472	Lives	Nov. 16	.121	.036	.084

.A. and A.R.A.-European Children's Fund

ding, by Districts or Kitchens, by Months

Commodities in Net Metric Tons of 1,000 Kilograms or 2,204.6 Pounds *

Pork Products	Milk Evap. (Cans)	Milk Cond. (Cans)	Cocoa	Sugar	Misc. Food	Soap (Pieces)	Total Tons
.308	4,097	....	.183	.484	....	....	5.782
.037	497	....	.022	.059	....	....	.753
.009	124	....	.006	.015	....	....	.189
....	....	....	....	....	....	....	.164
.028	379	....	.017	.051	....	....	.638
.009	127	....	.006	.015	....	....	.192
.037	497	....	.022	.059	....	....	.753
.037	497	....	.022	.059	....	....	.753
.010	137	....	.006	.016	....	....	.206
.007	99	....	.004	.012	....	....	.151
.042	1,038	....	.046	.123	....	....	1.027
.044	1,085	....	.048	.128	....	....	1.074
.003	83	....	.004	.010	....	....	.082
....	**88,079**	....	....	....	....	....	39.953
6.392	**39.953**	....	**4.204**	**11.247**	....	....	**172.671**
.189	....	....	....	....	....	....	4.807
.880	17,061	....	.760	2.015	....	....	17.212
.200	....	....	....	....	....	....	5.070
.002	48	....	.002	.006	....	....	.048
.209	2,430	....	.150	.396	....	....	4.681
.034	1,874	....	.084	.225	....	....	2.426
.042	661	....	.015	.049	....	....	.786
.021	288	....	.012	.032	....	....	.434
.047	1,117	....	.050	.132	....	....	1.117
.044	415	....	.024	.053	....	....	.889
.021	301	....	.007	.032	....	....	.419
.031	345	....	.020	.061	....	....	.634
.046	516	....	.034	.080	....	....	1.065
.062	841	....	.037	.099	....	....	1.272
.057	781	....	.035	.092	....	....	1.211
.005	170	....	.008	.021	....	....	.177
.029	679	....	.027	.090	....	....	1.157
.040	540	....	.020	.064	....	....	.815
.021	....	....	.023	.054	....	....	.724
.848	11,775	....	.525	1.390	....	....	17.802
.144	763	....	.094	.246	....	....	3.554
.008	110	....	.004	.011	....	....	.160
.035	481	....	.021	.057	....	....	.728
.011	49	....	.004	.011	....	....	.137
.053	721	....	.032	.085	....	....	1.090
.818	12,624	....	.681	1.751	....	....	14.977
.019	270	....	.011	.028	....	....	.403
.066	688	....	.033	.104	....	....	1.291
.080	992	....	.048	.128	....	....	1.460
.017	424	....	.024	.047	....	....	1.655
.266	....	....	....	.250	....	....	5.927
.251	....	....	....	.235	....	....	5.581
.013	180	....	.008	.021	....	....	.272
.057	709	....	.013	.076	....	....	.960
.022	533	....	.024	.063	....	....	.533
.813	11,054	....	.493	1.305	....	....	16.730
.016	....	....	.008	.018	....	....	.302
.080	1,081	....	.048	.128	....	....	1.637
.026	360	....	.016	.043	....	....	.546
.291	3,419	....	.177	.423	....	....	5.797
.003	60	....	.003	.007	....	....	.060
.027	251	....	.015	.041	....	....	.324

[*Continued on next page*]

Table 380—*Continued*

Detail of Internal Deliveries for Chi

Receipt No.	Districts or Kitchens	Date of Delivery	Flour	Rice	Beans, Peas
New Series		1921			
473	Plavinas	Nov. 19	.357	.029	.186
474	Riga Asylum, Dunte St	Nov. 17	.154	.062	.256
475	Naukseni	Nov. 17	.268	.038	.155
476	Kreslava	Nov. 19	.631	.112	.307
477	Riga's City Children's Hospital	Nov. 19	.535	.149	.236
478	Talsi	Nov. 22	.304	.062	....
479	Bolderaja	Nov. 21	.624	.087	.363
481	Riga Asylum, Jekabmiesta St	Nov. 21	.144	.074	.191
482	Riga Asylum, Matisa St	Nov. 22	.103	.040	.119
483	Riga Asylum, "Kinderfreund"	Nov. 23	.037	.015	.062
484	Latvian Red Cross, Erglu St	Nov. 23	.025	.010	.042
485	Daudzeva	Nov. 19	.312	.043	.180
486	Olaine	Nov. 23	.214	.030	.107
	Total Milk in Cans	....	....	....	....
	Total for November, Metric Tons	....	**68.065**	**11.305**	**34.660**
488	Riga Asylum, Katolu St	Dec. 1	.021	.009	.035
489	Riga Bakery, Herrnberger	Dec. 1	4.908	....	....
490	Riga	Dec. ..	4.345	3.536	5.592
491	Riga Refugee Committee, Gertrud St	Dec. ..	.019	.008	.031
492	Jumprava	Dec. 1	.111	.016	.064
493	Ogre	Dec. 1	.276	.039	.153
494	Jelgava	Dec. 1	2.426	.424	.758
495	Tukums	Dec. 2	.452	.071	.275
496	Ventspils	Dec. 2	1.659	.232	.963
497	Riga Bakery, Briedis	Dec. 2	4.510	....	....
498	Riga Asylum, Talsu St	Dec. 3	.296	.123	.509
499	Sloka	Dec. 3	.461	.064	.235
501	Rujene	Dec. 3	.461	.064	.267
502	Latvian Red Cross, Assari	Dec. 5	.110	.015	.015
503	Milgravis	Dec. 5	.645	.091	.331
504	Jekabmiests	Dec. 5	.510	.116	.116
505	Dobele	Dec. 2	.224	.039	.142
506	Zilani	Dec. 7	.303	.052	.128
507	Riga Women's Corps Asylum	Dec. 7	.047	.020	.080
508	Grienvalde	Dec. 6	.212	.030	.124
509	Krustpils	Dec. 5	.244	.103	.217
510	Livani	Dec. 7	.595	.084	.347
511	Daugavpils (Dvinsk)	Dec. 7	9.032	1.261	5.248
512	Eglaine	Dec. 8	.553	.077	.321
513	Ilukste	Dec. 8	.553	.077	.321
514	Kalkuni	Dec. 8	.553	.077	.321
515	Svente	Dec. 8	.415	.058	.241
516	Saldus	Dec. 8	.267	.039	.108
517	Liksnas	Dec. 8	.369	.052	.214
518	Griva	Dec. 6	1.591	.258	.774
519	Liepaja (Libau)	Dec. 8	1.475	.206	.857
520	Liepaja (Libau)	Dec. 8	8.563	1.196	4.977
521	Aizpute	Dec. 8	.204	.039	....
522	Valmiera	Dec. 9	.805	.116	.367
523	Cesis	Dec. 9	.829	.116	.483
524	Spare	Dec. 9	.157	.022	.092
525	Valka	Dec. 9	.225	.039	.071
526	Salaspils	Dec. 9	.106	.016	.064
527	Ludza	Dec. 12	.301	.129	.128
528	Plavinas	Dec. 12	.369	.052	.214
529	Korsova	Dec. 12	.369	.020	.183
530	Riga Asylum, Jekabmiesta St	Dec. 12	.284	.234	.370

R.A. and A.R.A.-European Children's Fund

ding, by Districts or Kitchens, by Months

Commodities in Net Metric Tons of 1,000 Kilograms or 2,204.6 Pounds *

Pork Products	Milk Evap. (Cans)	Milk Cond. (Cans)	Cocoa	Sugar	Misc. Food	Soap (Pieces)	Total Tons
.035	476	....	.021	.057	....	....	.685
.025	594	....	.027	.070	....	....	.594
.026	360	....	.016	.043	....	....	.546
.064	794	....	.030	.064	....	....	1.208
.053	721	....	.032	.085	....	....	1.090
.018	316	....	.022	.054	....	....	.460
.062	841	....	.037	.099	....	....	1.272
.033	407	....	.021	.058	....	....	.521
.016	251	....	.014	.043	....	....	.335
.006	144	....	.006	.017	....	....	.143
.004	96	....	.004	.011	....	....	.096
.031	421	....	.019	.050	....	....	.635
.020	289	....	.011	.026	....	....	.408
....	**80,321**	....	....	....	....	....	36.434
6.337	**36.434**	....	**3.850**	**10.646**	....	....	**171.297**
.003	82	....	.004	.010	....	....	.082
.268	....	....	....	....	....	....	5.176
.909	17,062	....	.758	2.014	....	....	17.154
.003	74	....	.003	.009	....	....	.073
.011	149	....	.007	.018	....	....	.227
.027	372	....	.017	.043	....	....	.555
.202	2,754	....	.127	.346	....	....	4.283
.050	484	....	.029	.076	....	....	.953
.164	1,951	....	.091	.247	....	....	3.356
.252	....	....	....	....	....	....	4.762
.048	1,179	....	.052	.139	....	....	1.167
.046	392	....	.022	.073	....	....	.901
.046	621	....	.028	.073	....	....	.939
.010	95	....	....	.012	....	....	.162
.046	869	....	.039	.103	....	....	1.255
.063	602	....	.022	.063	....	....	.890
.025	427	....	.013	.035	....	....	.478
.035	497	....	.022	.059	....	....	.599
.008	153	....	.008	.022	....	....	.185
.021	285	....	.012	.034	....	....	.433
.021	449	....	.015	.046	....	....	.646
.059	601	....	.018	.084	....	....	1.187
.895	12,168	....	.411	1.282	....	....	18.129
.055	745	....	.033	.088	....	....	1.127
.055	745	....	.033	.088	....	....	1.127
.055	745	....	.033	.088	....	....	1.127
.041	559	....	.025	.066	....	....	.846
.025	240	....	.011	.029	....	....	.479
.037	497	....	.022	.059	....	....	.753
.183	1,382	....	.072	.242	....	....	3.120
.146	1,986	....	.089	.235	....	....	3.008
.848	11,534	....	.514	1.362	....	....	17.460
.027	197	....	.011	.022	....	....	.303
.081	925	....	.046	.121	....	....	1.536
.082	1,117	....	.050	.132	....	....	1.692
.015	211	....	.010	.025	....	....	.321
.023	279	....	.013	.033	....	....	.404
.002	121	....	.006	.017	....	....	.211
.011	306	....	.015	.044	....	....	.628
.037	497	....	.019	.056	....	....	.747
.037	497	....	.022	.059	....	....	.690
.046	1,130	....	.050	.130	....	....	1.114

[*Continued on next page*]

Table 380—*Continued*

Detail of Internal Deliveries for Chil

Receipt No.	Districts or Kitchens	Date of Delivery	Flour	Rice	Beans, Peas
New Series		1921			
531	Riga	Dec. 13	4.206	3.508	5.766
532	Riga Asylum, Matisa St.	Dec. 13	.159	.131	.208
533	Rezekne	Dec. 13	1.697	.360	.360
534	Krape	Dec. 14	.092	.013	.053
535	Bolderaja	Dec. 14	.645	.180	.285
536	Talsi	Dec. 19	.458	.064	.215
537	Lives	Dec. 14	.276	.039	.160
538	Riga Bakery, Herrnberger	Dec. 14	1.691	....	....
539	Viskali	Dec. 15	.037	.010	.016
540	Pridruiska	Dec. 15	.184	.026	.106
541	Riga Bakery, Herrnberger	Dec. 15	4.467	....	....
542	Riga Bakery, Briedis	Dec. 15	1.691	....	....
543	Riga Bakery, Briedis	Dec. 15	3.994	....	....
544	Riga Asylum, Dunte St.	Dec. 15	.167	.137	.218
545	Dagda	Dec. 16	.092	.013	.054
546	Riga Asylum, Miera and Spitalu Sts.	Dec. 20	.064	.027	.112
547	Riga's City Children's Hospital	Dec. 16	.553	.154	.244
548	Latvian Welfare Society	Dec. 17	.016	.013	.020
549	Kuldiga	Dec. 17	.829	.116	.482
550	Kreslava	Dec. 17	.829	.116	.481
551	Jaun Jelgava	Dec. 17	.645	.090	.278
552	Riga Asylum, "Kinderfreund"	Dec. 19	.041	.033	.048
553	Tome	Dec. 19	.120	.033	.053
554	Riga Refugee Committee, Valmiera St.	Dec. 19	.138	.039	.061
555	Naukseni	Dec. 20	.276	.077	.122
557	Jaunciem	Dec. 21	.276	.077	.122
558	Olaine	Dec. 21	.221	.062	.097
	Total Milk in Cans	....	....	....	....
	Total for December, Metric Tons	....	**73.719**	**14.538**	**35.297**
		1922			
560	Riga Refugee Committee	Jan. ..	.019	.015	.024
561	Riga	Jan. 2	4.455	3.821	5.980
562	Latvian Red Cross, Erglu St.	Jan. 2	.074	.021	.033
563	Tukums	Jan. 4	.507	.142	.046
564	Ventspils	Jan. 4	1.799	.463	.732
565	Russian Society in Latvia	Jan. 3	.064	....	....
566	Katlakalns	Jan. 4	.193	.054	.085
567	Sloka	Jan. 4	.461	.129	....
568	Riga Bakery, Briedis	Jan. 4	5.257	....	....
569	Riga Women's Corps Asylum	Jan. 4	.050	.039	.029
570	Jelgava	Jan. 4	3.010	.849	.921
571	Riga Asylum, Talsu St.	Jan. 4	.288	.238	.349
572	Bierini	Jan. 4	.231	.077	.056
573	Riga Asylum, Matisu St.	Jan. 5	.158	.137	.176
575	Riga Bakery, Herrnberger	Jan. 4	5.607	....	....
574	Riga Asylum, Miera St.	Jan. 5	.115	.082	.144
577	Ogre	Jan. 5	.258	.072	.064
578	Griva	Jan. 7	1.843	.515	.577
579	Svente	Jan. 7	.402	.116	.054
580	Valka	Jan. 7	.267	.077	.060
581	Eglaine	Jan. 7	.529	.154	....
582	Kalkuni	Jan. 7	.521	.154	....
583	Riga Asylum, Katolu St.	Jan. 10	.021	.017	.017
584	Riga Asylum, Duntes St.	Jan. 14	.153	.126	.136
585	Daugavpils (Dvinsk)	Jan. 10	9.032	2.522	3.458
586	Zilani	Jan. 7	.369	.103	.112
587	Saldus	Jan. 10	.100	.086	.030
588	Milgravis	Jan. 9	.645	.180	.274

A.R.A. and A.R.A.-European Children's Fund
eeding, by Districts or Kitchens, by Months

Commodities in Net Metric Tons of 1,000 Kilograms or 2,204.6 Pounds *

Pork Products	Milk		Cocoa	Sugar	Misc. Food	Soap	Total Tons
	Evap.	Cond.					
	(Cans)	(Cans)				(Pieces)	
.857	16,467	....	.787	2.104	....	....	17.228
.026	633	....	.028	.075	....	....	.627
.101	685	....	.071	.112	....	....	2.701
.009	124	....	.006	.015	....	....	.188
.064	869	....	.039	.103	....	....	1.316
.046	621	....	.028	.073	....	....	.884
.017	372	....	.013	.044	....	....	.549
.132	275	....	....	.619	....	....	2.442
.004	50	....	.002	.006	....	....	.075
.018	248	....	.011	.029	....	....	.374
.120	....	....	....	....	....	....	4.587
.132	275	....	....	.619	....	....	2.442
.107	....	....	....	....	....	....	4.101
.027	665	....	.030	.079	....	....	.658
.009	124	....	.006	.015	....	....	.189
.012	261	....	.012	.031	....	....	.258
.026	745	....	.030	.088	....	....	1.095
.003	62	....	.003	.007	....	....	.062
.082	1,117	....	.050	.129	....	....	1.688
.082	1,117	....	.050	.132	....	....	1.690
.051	869	....	.035	.103	....	....	1.202
.007	161	....	.007	.019	....	....	.155
.012	161	....	.007	.019	....	....	.244
.014	186	....	.008	.022	....	....	.282
.027	372	....	.017	.044	....	....	.563
.027	372	....	.017	.044	....	....	.563
.022	292	....	.013	.035	....	....	.450
....	**92,102**	....	....	....	....	....	41.778
7.052	**41.778**	....	**4.042**	**12.250**	....	....	**188.676**
.003	75	....	.003	.009	....	....	.073
.917	18,095	....	.821	2.172	....	....	18.166
.007	99	....	.004	.012	....	....	.151
.050	683	....	.030	.081	....	....	.856
.164	1,847	....	.099	.264	....	....	3.521
....	48	....	.008	.020	....	....	.092
.019	260	....	.011	.031	....	....	.393
.046	180	....	.025	.073	....	....	.734
.249	....	....	....	....	....	....	5.506
.003	55	....	.003	.010	....	....	.134
.274	3,670	....	.180	.484	....	....	5.718
.043	727	....	.047	.127	....	....	1.092
.018	243	....	.013	.039	....	....	.434
.030	310	....	.023	.067	....	....	.591
.276	....	....	....	....	....	....	5.883
.018	246	....	.013	.049	....	....	.421
.025	347	....	.013	.041	....	....	.473
.174	1,725	....	.111	.293	....	....	3.513
.023	262	....	.017	.066	....	....	.678
.021	289	....	.013	.037	....	....	.475
.055	426	....	.027	.055	....	....	.820
.024	390	....	.014	.049	....	....	.762
.003	82	....	.002	.004	....	....	.064
.017	390	....	.027	.072	....	....	.531
.767	12,168	....	.442	1.262	....	....	17.483
.036	371	....	.020	.052	....	....	.692
.012	333	....	.009	.028	....	....	.265
.060	864	....	.039	.103	....	....	1.301

[*Continued on next page*]

Table 380—*Continued*

Receipt No.	Districts or Kitchens	Date of Delivery	Flour	Rice	Beans, Peas
New Series		1922			
589	Lielais	Jan. 10	.157	.044	.069
590	Riga	Jan. 11	4.425	3.602	5.749
591	Lives	Jan. 11	.276	.077	....
592	Refugee Committee, Velmiera St.	Jan. 11	.138	.039	.061
593	Spare	Jan. 11	.157	.044	.070
594	Jekabmiests	Jan. 14	.766	.232	.284
595	Riga Bakery, Herrnberger	Jan. 12	5.705	....	....
596	Rezekne	Jan. 12	.674	.618	....
597	Cesis	Jan. 12	.829	.232	.143
598	Riga Asylum, Strazdumuiza	Jan. 14	.012	.010	.016
599	Ludza	Jan. 12	.921	.257	.407
600	Talsi	Jan. 18	.460	.129	.203
601	Libau	Jan. 17	5.765	2.390	....
602	Latvian Red Cross, Assari	Jan. 12	.110	.031	.046
603	Riga Bakery, Briedis	Jan. 13	5.015	....	....
604	Jaun Jelgava	Jan. 14	.645	.180	.210
605	Rujene	Jan. 17	.460	.128	.105
606	Riga Asylum, Jekabmiests	Jan. 16	.221	.182	.280
607	Salaspils	Jan. 17	.055	.015	.024
608	Latvian Refugee Committee, Kazaku	Jan. 17	.369	.103	.103
609	Bolderaja	Jan. 18	.645	.180	.127
610	Livani	Jan. 18	.599	.167	.100
614	Krustpils	Jan. 19	.737	.205	.318
615	Valmiera	Jan. 20	.829	.232	.277
616	Korsowka	Jan. 20	.336	.088	.100
617	Riga Children's Hospital	Jan. 20	.514	.154	.244
618	Kurmene	Jan. 20	.368	.102	.163
619	Plavinas	Jan. 20	.013	.102	....
621	Ikskile	Jan. 23	.102	.028	.045
622	Grienvalde	Jan. 24	.197	.060	.077
623	Riga, Krimuldas St.	Jan. 24	....	....	.132
624	Riga Asylum, "Kinderfreund"	Jan. 24	.041	.033	.046
625	Latvian Welfare Society	Jan. 24	.016	.010	....
626	Jumprava	Jan. 24	.111	.031	.020
627	Olaine	Jan. 24	.057	.047	.018
628	Viskali	Jan. 25	.037	.010	.016
629	Skriveri	Jan. 27	.276	.077	.122
631	Jaunciem	Jan. 28	.276	.077	.122
	Total Milk in Cans	....	....	....	....
	Total for January, Metric Tons	....	**68.742**	**20.105**	**23.054**
633	Riga Asylum, Matisa St.	Feb. 1	.242	.183	.266
634	Riga Refugee Committee, Gertrud St.	Feb. ..	.019	.014	.022
635	Riga	Feb. ..	4.468	3.635	5.749
636	Riga Bakery, Herrnberger	Feb. ..	5.157	....	....
637	Sloka	Feb. ..	.416	.116	.184
638	Riga Bakery, Briedis	Feb. ..	4.626	....	....
639	Riga Asylum, Katolu St.	Feb. 1	.021	.015	.024
640	Naukseni	Feb. 1	.208	.058	.092
641	Riga Asylum, Miera St.	Feb. 1	.144	.081	.169
642	Riga Asylum, Talsu St.	Feb. 1	.312	.232	.368
643	Riga Refugee Committee, Valmiera St.	Feb. 2	.167	.047	.074
644	Riga Women's Corps Asylum	Feb. 2	.047	.035	.055
645	Jelgava	Feb. 3	2.294	.766	.925
646	Tukums	Feb. 3	.456	.128	.202
647	Bramberga	Feb. 3	.100	.028	.046
648	Ventspils	Feb. 3	1.498	.418	.660

.R.A. and A.R.A.-European Children's Fund

eeding, by Districts or Kitchens, by Months

Commodities in Net Metric Tons of 1,000 Kilograms or 2,204.6 Pounds *

Pork Products	Milk Evap.	Milk Cond.	Cocoa	Sugar	Misc. Food	Soap	Total Tons
	(Cans)	(Cans)				(Pieces)	
.016	211	....	.009	.025	....	....	.320
.797	17,088	....	.775	2.057	....	....	17.405
.017	285	....	.014	.044	....	....	.428
.007	57	....	.008	.022	....	....	.275
.015	211	....	.010	.025	....	....	.321
.054	898	....	.040	.132	....	....	1.508
.281	....	....	....	....	....	....	5.986
.076	692	....	.037	.134	....	....	1.539
.075	981	....	.029	.128	....	....	1.436
.002	50	....	.002	.006	....	....	.048
.091	1,242	....	.055	.147	....	....	1.878
.046	621	....	.028	.073	....	....	.939
.082	....	....	....	.774	....	....	9.011
.011	149	....	.007	.018	....	....	.223
.247	....	....	....	....	....	....	5.262
.063	863	....	.038	.102	....	....	1.238
.045	584	....	.024	.073	....	....	.835
.036	884	....	.035	.103	....	....	.857
....	40	....	.003	.009	....	....	.106
.037	120	....	.022	.059	....	....	.693
.064	869	....	.039	.103	....	....	1.158
.059	797	....	.035	.095	....	....	1.055
.071	993	....	.044	.117	....	....	1.492
.082	1,117	....	.050	.132	....	....	1.602
.028	496	....	.022	.058	....	....	.632
.028	745	....	.026	.088	....	....	1.054
.036	496	....	.022	.058	....	....	.749
....	162	....	.009	.008	....	....	.132
.010	137	....	.006	.016	....	....	.207
.021	259	....	.011	.033	....	....	.399
....	....	....	....	....	....	....	.132
.007	122	....	.006	.016	....	....	.149
.003	57	....	.003	.007	....	....	.039
.009	149	....	.007	.018	....	....	.196
.012	158	....	....	.012	....	....	.146
.004	50	....	.002	.006	....	....	.075
.027	372	....	.017	.044	....	....	.563
.027	372	....	.017	.044	....	....	.563
....	**96,512**	....	....	....	....	....	34.706
5.820	**34.106**	....	**3.466**	**10.286**	....	....	**166.179**
.033	639	....	.034	.097	....	....	.855
.003	67	....	.003	.008	....	....	.069
.818	17,341	....	.781	2.071	....	....	17.522
.282	....	....	....	....	....	....	5.439
.041	560	....	.018	.066	....	....	.841
.253	....	....	....	....	....	....	4.879
.003	74	....	.003	.009	....	....	.075
.022	153	....	.014	.033	....	....	.427
.023	516	....	.023	.061	....	....	.501
.050	1,044	....	.050	.132	....	....	1.144
.017	224	....	.010	.027	....	....	.342
.008	168	....	.007	.020	....	....	.172
.191	3,094	....	.152	.437	....	....	4.765
.045	611	....	.027	.073	....	....	.931
.010	135	....	.006	.016	....	....	.206
.148	1,651	....	.090	.238	....	....	3.052

[*Continued on next page*]

Table 380—*Continued*

Detail of Internal Deliveries for Chi

Receipt No.	Districts or Kitchens	Date of Delivery	Flour	Rice	Beans, Peas
New Series		1922			
649	Pope	Feb. 3	.058	.016	.026
650	Salaspils	Feb. 3	.100	.028	.035
651	Allazi	Feb. 4	.175	.049	.077
652	Malinova	Feb. 4	.166	.046	.074
653	Dundaga	Feb. 4	.077	.021	.034
654	Vec-Auce	Feb. 4	.333	.093	.147
655	Davgavpils (Dvinsk)	Feb. 6	8.158	2.277	2.459
656	Eglaine	Feb. 6	.420	.134	.135
567	Liksnas	Feb. 6	.333	.093	.147
658	Katlakalns	Feb. 6	.199	.055	.088
659	Ogre	Feb. 6	.233	.059	.103
660	Ilukste	Feb. 6	.416	.116	.184
661	Dobele	Feb. 6	.199	.055	.088
662	Svente	Feb. 6	.309	.070	.126
663	Kalkuni	Feb. 6	.449	.139	.220
664	Griva	Feb. 7	1.314	.416	.735
665	Zilani	Feb. 6	.285	.075	.077
666	Krape	Feb. 7	.083	.023	.023
667	Jekabmiests	Feb. 6	.748	.208	.331
668	Demene	Feb. 7	.324	.090	.143
669	Kreslava	Feb. 9	.499	.139	.220
670	Milgravis	Feb. 11	.508	.162	.210
671	Riga Asylum, Jekabmiesta St	Feb. 9	.290	.207	.237
672	Spare	Feb. 10	.142	.040	.062
673	Rezekne	Feb. 10	1.997	.557	.882
674	Ludza	Feb. 10	.640	.196	.022
675	Lives	Feb. 11	.249	.057	.110
676	Riga	Feb. 13	3.694	3.151	4.982
677	Riga	Feb. 13	.219	....	....
678	Valka	Feb. 13	.250	.070	.110
679	Cesis	Feb. 13	.749	.209	.330
680	Valmiera	Feb. 13	.742	.204	.213
681	Aizpute	Feb. 14	.250	.070	.019
682	Saldus	Feb. 14	.250	.070	.110
683	Libau	Feb. 15	7.492	2.091	3.308
684	Libau	Feb. 15	1.332	.372	.588
685	Daudzeva	Feb. 14	.199	.055	.088
686	Riga Asylum, Duntes St	Feb. 15	.159	.102	.187
687	Riga Bakery, Herrnberger	Feb. 15	4.610	....	....
688	Jaun Jelgava	Feb. 16	.582	.162	.257
689	Livani	Feb. 16	.541	.151	.152
690	Rujene	Feb. 16	.416	.116	.182
691	Kuldiga	Feb. 16	.749	.209	.098
692	Riga Bakery, Briedis	Feb. 16	4.086	....	....
693	Bolderaja	Feb. 16	.583	.162	.243
694	Bierini	Feb. 16	.250	.070	.110
695	Maz-Irbe	Feb. 17	.075	.021	.033
696	Lielais	Feb. 17	.129	.040	.053
697	Riga Asylum, "Strazdumuiza"	Feb. 18	.016	.012	.018
698	Plavinas	Feb. 20	.332	.093	.032
699	Tome	Feb. 20	.108	.030	.047
700	Korsova	Feb. 20	.243	.062	.104
701	Krustpils	Feb. 21	.651	.186	....
702	Riga Asylum, "Kinderfreund"	Feb. 21	.041	.021	.034
703	Silupe	Feb. 21	.142	.040	.062
704	Tukums	Feb. 23	.075	.021	.034
705	Kalnciems	Feb. 23	.200	.056	.088
	Total Milk in Cans	....	....	....	....
	Total for February, Metric Tons	....	**68.044**	**19.023**	**27.313**

R.A. and A.R.A.-European Children's Fund

ding, by Districts or Kitchens, by Months

Commodities in Net Metric Tons of 1,000 Kilograms or 2,204.6 Pounds *

Pork Products	Milk		Cocoa	Sugar	Misc. Food	Soap	Total Tons
	Evap.	Cond.					
	(Cans)	(Cans)				(Pieces)	
.006	79	....	.004	.009	....	....	.119
.010	135	....	.006	.016	....	....	.195
.023	235	....	.010	.028	....	....	.362
.016	224	....	.010	.026	....	....	.338
.008	103	....	.005	.012	....	....	.157
.033	448	....	.020	.053	....	....	.679
.608	9,404	....	.334	.957	....	....	14.793
.034	516	....	.007	.060	....	....	.790
.024	448	....	.020	.053	....	....	.670
.019	269	....	.012	.031	....	....	.404
.023	314	....	.010	.037	....	....	.465
041	561	....	.025	.066	....	....	.848
.019	269	....	.012	.031	....	....	.404
.034	364	....	.015	.035	....	....	.589
.049	673	....	.030	.079	....	....	.966
.134	1,300	....	.050	.200	....	....	2.849
.018	237	....	.014	.039	....	....	.508
.008	102	....	.005	.013	....	....	.155
.073	1,009	....	.045	.119	....	....	1.524
.031	437	....	.019	.051	....	....	.658
.049	673	....	.030	.079	....	....	1.016
.044	371	....	.029	.093	....	....	1.046
.047	539	....	.030	.089	....	....	.900
.014	177	....	.008	.023	....	....	.289
.197	2,691	....	.119	.317	....	....	4.069
.032	119	....	.025	.093	....	....	1.008
.020	274	....	.013	.037	....	....	.486
.759	13,651	....	.678	1.796	....	....	15.060
....	2,064	....	.219	.511	....	....	.949
.025	336	....	.015	.040	....	....	.510
.074	1,009	....	.045	.119	....	....	1.526
.039	740	....	.036	.067	....	....	1.301
.025	336	....	.013	.040	....	....	.417
.025	336	....	.015	.040	....	....	.510
.742	8,135	....	.386	1.192	....	....	15.211
.132	1,794	....	.080	.212	....	....	2.716
.019	269	....	.012	.031	....	....	.404
.026	572	....	.025	.055	....	....	.554
.213	....	....	....	....	....	....	4.823
.058	709	....	.024	.093	....	....	1.176
.050	583	....	.030	.086	....	....	1.010
.041	339	....	.014	.063	....	....	.832
.074	834	....	.045	.119	....	....	1.294
.188	....	....	....	....	....	....	4.274
.054	785	....	.035	.093	....	....	1.170
.025	336	....	.015	.040	....	....	.510
.007	101	....	.004	.012	....	....	.152
.014	135	....	.008	.022	....	....	.266
.003	56	....	.003	.007	....	....	.059
.020	381	....	.020	.053	....	....	.550
.010	145	....	.006	.017	....	....	.218
.021	339	....	.017	.041	....	....	.488
.020	86	....	.031	.081	....	....	.969
.007	146	....	.005	.016	....	....	.124
.014	191	....	.008	.023	....	....	.289
.007	101	....	.005	.012	....	....	.154
.020	269	....	.012	.032	....	....	.408
....	**83,026**	....	....	....	....	....	37.661
6.273	**37.661**	....	**3.931**	**10.847**	....	....	**173.092**

[*Continued on next page*]

Table 380—*Continued*

Detail of Internal Deliveries for Chi

Receipt No.	Districts or Kitchens	Date of Delivery	Flour	Rice	Beans, Peas
New Series		1922			
706	Riga	Mar. ..	4.406	3.586	5.670
707	Grienvalde	Mar. ..	.203	.056	.089
708	Riga Refugee Committee, Gertrud St	Mar. ..	.019	.015	.024
709	Riga Bakery, Briedis	Mar. ..	4.523	....	....
710	Riga Bakery, Herrnberger	Mar. ..	5.122	....	....
711	Kreslava	Mar. ..	.829	.231	.366
712	Milgravis	Mar. ..	.645	.180	.285
713	Selpils	Mar. ..	.148	.041	.065
714	Madliena	Mar. 1	.055	.015	.024
715	Assari	Mar. 1	.092	.026	.041
716	Jaunciem	Mar. 1	.276	.077	.122
717	Ogre	Mar. 2	.247	.069	.089
718	Riga Asylum, Miera St	Mar. 9	.110	.094	.139
719	Riga Asylum, Talsu St	Mar. 9	.309	.255	.403
720	Riga Women's Corps Asylum	Mar. 2	.047	.039	.061
721	Jaun Jelgava	Mar. 2	.645	.180	.285
722	Jekabmiests	Mar. 2	.829	.236	.366
723	Svente	Mar. 3	.336	.086	.128
724	Jelgava	Mar. 2	2.949	.823	1.302
725	Ventspils	Mar. 2	1.613	.451	.712
726	Tukums	Mar. 3	.507	.142	.224
727	Bramberga	Mar. 2	.111	.031	.049
728	Pope	Mar. 3	.065	.018	.029
729	Sloka	Mar. 2	.434	.121	.192
730	Viskali	Mar. 2	.046	.013	.020
731	Lives	Mar. 6	.266	.075	.118
732	Vec-Svarte	Mar. 6	.055	.015	.024
733	Katlakalns	Mar. 6	.221	.062	.098
734	Riga Asylum, Katolu St	Mar. 6	.021	.018	.027
735	Zilani	Mar. 6	.321	.088	.142
736	Jumprava	Mar. 6	.111	.031	.049
737	Naukseni	Mar. 6	.221	.062	.098
738	Spare	Mar. 6	.147	.041	.065
739	Demene	Mar. 6	.349	.097	.155
740	Eglaine	Mar. 6	.507	.123	.174
741	Kalkuni	Mar. 6	.553	.154	.244
742	Griva	Mar. 6	1.843	.515	.814
743	Ilukste	Mar. 6	.461	.129	.203
744	Liksnas	Mar. 6	.369	.103	.163
745	Ikskile	Mar. 6	.101	.028	.031
746	Daugavpils (Dvinsk)	Mar. 6	8.940	2.360	3.303
747	Kurmene	Mar. 7	.331	.092	.146
748	Riga Asylum, Matisa St	Mar. 9	.196	.198	.271
749	Skriveri	Mar. 6	.276	.077	.122
750	Riga Refugee Committee, "Valmiera"	Mar. 9	.138	.039	.053
751	Riga Children's Hospital	Mar. 9	.494	.140	.220
752	Salaspils	Mar. 9	.111	.031	.049
753	Riga Asylum, Jaroslava St	Mar. 9	.044	.038	.061
754	Olaine	Mar. 10	.313	.087	.138
755	Rujene	Mar. 10	.367	.084	.088
756	Riga Asylum, Krasta St	Mar. 14	.069	.056	.089
757	Cesis	Mar. 11	.790	.178	.312
758	Latvian Red Cross Hospital, Erglu St	Mar. 11	.074	.021	.029
759	Malinova	Mar. 11	.153	.042	.065
760	Valka	Mar. 11	.237	.064	.084
761	Rezekne	Mar. 13	2.211	.616	.976
762	Ludza	Mar. 13	.921	.257	.407
763	Riga	Mar. 13	4.334	3.824	6.048

..R.A. and A.R.A.-European Children's Fund

...eeding, by Districts or Kitchens, by Months

Commodities in Net Metric Tons of 1,000 Kilograms or 2,204.6 Pounds *

Pork Products	Milk Evap. (Cans)	Milk Cond. (Cans)	Cocoa	Sugar	Misc. Food	Soap (Pieces)	Total Tons
.806	16,890	....	.771	2.043	....	....	17.282
.020	273	....	.012	.032	....	....	.412
.003	74	....	.003	.009	....	....	.073
.185	....	....	....	....	....	....	4.708
.210	....	....	....	....	....	....	5.332
.082	775	....	.050	.132	....	....	1.690
.064	850	....	.038	.102	....	....	1.314
.015	199	....	.009	.023	....	....	.301
.005	74	....	.003	.009	....	....	.111
.009	124	....	.006	.015	....	....	.189
.027	372	....	.017	.044	....	....	.563
.019	267	....	.012	.034	....	....	.470
.018	452	....	.020	.063	....	....	.444
.050	1,210	....	.053	.145	....	....	1.215
.008	186	....	.008	.022	....	....	.185
.064	869	....	.038	.102	....	....	1.314
.082	1,117	....	.049	.131	....	....	1.688
.031	441	....	.022	.059	....	....	.662
.292	3,707	....	.117	.469	....	....	5.952
.161	2,114	....	.069	.257	....	....	3.263
.050	683	....	.030	.081	....	....	1.034
.011	149	....	.007	.018	....	....	.227
.006	87	....	.004	.010	....	....	.132
.033	584	....	.025	.069	....	....	.874
.005	62	....	.003	.007	....	....	.094
.026	341	....	.016	.042	....	....	.543
.005	74	....	.003	.009	....	....	.111
.022	298	....	.013	.035	....	....	.451
.003	82	....	.004	.010	....	....	.083
.030	396	....	.018	.051	....	....	.650
.011	149	....	.006	.018	....	....	.226
.022	298	....	.005	.035	....	....	.443
.015	199	....	.009	.023	....	....	.300
.035	471	....	.020	.055	....	....	.711
.030	603	....	.030	.081	....	....	.945
.055	745	....	.033	.088	....	....	1.127
.183	2,483	....	.111	.293	....	....	3.759
.046	621	....	.028	.073	....	....	.940
.037	497	....	.022	.059	....	....	.753
.010	115	....	.006	.016	....	....	.192
.827	10,678	....	.387	1.208	....	....	17.025
.033	445	....	.020	.052	....	....	.674
.034	870	....	.037	.106	....	....	.842
.027	372	....	.017	.044	....	....	.563
.014	182	....	.006	.022	....	....	.272
.025	670	....	.027	.079	....	....	.985
.011	149	....	.007	.018	....	....	.227
.008	186	....	.008	.022	....	....	.181
.031	380	....	.019	.044	....	....	.632
.024	379	....	.020	.051	....	....	.634
.011	260	....	.012	.032	....	....	.269
.064	890	....	.037	.111	....	....	1.492
.006	93	....	.004	.012	....	....	.146
.016	180	....	.009	.024	....	....	.309
.016	283	....	.013	.039	....	....	.453
.218	2,979	....	.132	.350	....	....	4.503
.091	1,241	....	.055	.146	....	....	1.877
.894	17,052	....	.823	2.179	....	....	18.102

[*Continued on next page*]

Table 380—*Continued*

Detail of Internal Deliveries for Chi

Receipt No.	Districts or Kitchens	Date of Delivery	Flour	Rice	Beans, Peas
New Series		1922			
764	Dobele	Mar. 16	.184	.051	.081
765	Riga Asylum, Moscow St	Mar. 15	.056	.046	.073
766	Lielais	Mar. 16	.157	.044	.069
767	Plavinas	Mar. 16	.307	.103	.134
768	Riga Asylum, Sarkana St	Mar. 16	.028	.024	.037
769	Riga Asylum, Jekabmiesta St	Mar. 16	.090	.075	.118
770	Riga Asylum, Duntes St	Mar. 16	.090	.075	.118
771	Riga Asylum, Patversmes St	Mar. 16	.072	.060	.094
772	Latvian Welfare Society, Riga	Mar. 16	.019	.015	.025
773	Bolderaja	Mar. 16	.645	.180	.285
774	Aizpute	Mar. 16	.276	.077	.122
775	Livani	Mar. 25	.553	.154	.244
776	Saldus	Mar. 16	.276	.077	.122
777	Allazi	Mar. 17	.193	.054	.085
778	Riga Bakery, Herrnberger	Mar. 17	5.710	....	....
779	Riga Bakery, Briedis	Mar. 18	5.006	....	....
780	Pridruiska	Mar. 16	.184	.051	.081
781	Tome	Mar. 20	.110	.026	.037
782	Vec-Auce	Mar. 20	.369	.103	.163
783	Libau	Mar. 22	8.294	2.315	3.661
	Total Milk in Cans	....	....	....	....
	Total for March, Metric Tons	....	**72.730**	**20.055**	**31.100**
784	Libau	Apr. ..	1.382	.386	.610
785	Valmiera	Apr. ..	.774	.228	.360
786	Krape	Apr. ..	.092	.026	.040
787	Riga Asylum, "Kinderfreund"	Apr. ..	.037	.031	.049
788	Korsova	Apr. ..	.357	.100	.158
789	Krustpils	Apr. ..	.714	.199	.315
790	Riga Bakery, Herrnberger	Apr. ..	10.249	....	....
791	Bierini	Apr. 3	.196	.055	.087
792	Grienvalde	Apr. 3	.196	.055	.087
793	Viskali	Apr. 3	.045	.012	.019
794	Tukums	Apr. 3	.080	.022	.035
795	Riga	Apr. ..	8.813	7.171	11.340
796	Riga Bakery, Briedis	Apr. 1	9.065	....	....
797	Spare	Apr. 3	.143	.040	.063
798	Russian Refugee Committee	Apr. 3	.019	.015	.024
799	Kalnciems	Apr. 3	.214	.041	.095
800	Riga Women's Corps Asylum	Apr. 3	.047	.037	.059
801	Kuldiga	Apr. ..	.753	.210	.335
802	Riga Asylum, Pioneru St	Apr. 3	.047	.037	.059
803	Riga Asylum, Kalnciem St	Apr. 3	.022	.017	.027
804	Riga Asylum, Hermana St.	Apr. 3	.081	.068	.102
805	Riga Asylum, Spitala St	Apr. 3	.062	.050	.079
806	Riga Asylum, Valmiera St.	Apr. 3	.132	.037	.059
807	Sloka	Apr. 3	.418	.117	.185
808	Riga Asylum, Suvorova St	Apr. 3	.031	.023	.030
809	Riga Asylum, Kandavas St	Apr. 3	.097	.077	.121
810	Riga Asylum, Katolu St.	Apr. 5	.021	.015	.026
811	Riga Asylum, Martinu St	Apr. 5	.019	.013	.019
812	Jelgava	Apr. 5	2.854	.797	1.148
813	Jumprava	Apr. 5	.107	.030	.047
814	Tukums	Apr. 5	.491	.055	.216
815	Riga Asylum, Miera St	Apr. 5	.034	.027	.043
816	Ventspils	Apr. 5	1.559	.435	.688
817	Bramberga	Apr. 5	.107	.030	.047
818	Pope	Apr. 5	.062	.017	.027

R.A. and A.R.A.-European Children's Fund

ding, by Districts or Kitchens, by Months

Commodities in Net Metric Tons of 1,000 Kilograms or 2,204.6 Pounds *

Pork Products	Milk Evap.	Milk Cond.	Cocoa	Sugar	Misc. Food	Soap	Total Tons
	(Cans)	(Cans)				(Pieces)	
.018	245	....	.011	.029	....	....	.374
.009	224	....	.010	.026	....	....	.220
.016	211	....	.009	.025	....	....	.320
.027	240	....	.022	.059	....	....	.652
.005	112	....	.005	.013	....	....	.112
.014	355	....	.016	.043	....	....	.356
.014	358	....	.016	.043	....	....	.356
.012	280	....	.012	.034	....	....	.284
.003	74	....	.003	.009	....	....	.074
.064	860	....	.039	.103	....	....	1.316
.027	370	....	.017	.044	....	....	.563
.048	514	....	.021	.085	....	....	1.105
.027	370	....	.017	.044	....	....	.563
.019	260	....	.012	.031	....	....	.394
.281	....	....	....	....	....	....	5.991
.246	....	....	....	....	....	....	5.252
.018	248	....	.011	.029	....	....	.374
.009	108	....	.006	.018	....	....	.206
.037	495	....	.022	.059	....	....	.753
.821	11,173	....	.498	1.319	....	....	16.908
....	**92,717**	....	....	....	....	....	42.057
6.851	**42.057**	....	**4.070**	**11.316**	....	....	**188.179**
.137	1,862	....	.083	.220	....	....	2.818
.070	952	....	.050	.122	....	....	1.604
.009	106	....	.005	.015	....	....	.187
.007	130	....	.007	.018	....	....	.149
.035	481	....	.021	.057	....	....	.728
.071	961	....	.043	.114	....	....	1.456
.420	....	....	....	....	....	....	10.669
.019	260	....	.012	.031	....	....	.400
.019	260	....	.012	.031	....	....	.400
.004	60	....	.003	.007	....	....	.090
.008	105	....	.005	.013	....	....	.163
1.613	31,738	....	1.542	4.087	....	....	34.566
.372	....	....	....	....	....	....	9.437
.014	190	....	.009	.023	....	....	.292
.003	72	....	.003	.009	....	....	.073
.021	288	....	.013	.034	....	....	.418
.008	174	....	.008	.021	....	....	.180
.075	1,008	....	.046	.120	....	....	1.539
.008	159	....	.008	.021	....	....	.180
.004	84	....	.004	.010	....	....	.084
.013	272	....	.014	.037	....	....	.315
.010	200	....	.011	.028	....	....	.240
.013	180	....	.008	.021	....	....	.270
.023	560	....	.025	.066	....	....	.834
.005	99	....	.005	.014	....	....	.108
.016	370	....	.017	.044	....	....	.372
.003	79	....	.004	.009	....	....	.078
.003	53	....	.003	.007	....	....	.064
.256	3,430	....	.171	.454	....	....	5.680
.011	134	....	.006	.017	....	....	.218
.034	525	....	.029	.078	....	....	.903
.006	130	....	.006	.015	....	....	.131
.154	1,900	....	.093	.248	....	....	3.177
.011	144	....	.006	.017	....	....	.218
.006	84	....	.004	.010	....	....	.126

[*Continued on next page*]

Table 380—*Continued*

Detail of Internal Deliveries for Chi[ld]

Receipt No.	Districts or Kitchens	Date of Delivery	Flour	Rice	Beans, Peas
New Series		1922			
819	Riga Asylum, Talsu St.	Apr. 6	.064	.075	.118
820	Riga Refugee Committee, Kazaku St	Apr. 6	.258	.072	.102
821	Naukseni	Apr. 6	.214	.059	.094
822	Latvian Red Cross Asylum, Assari	Apr. 7	.084	.024	.039
823	Daudzeva	Apr. 7	.178	.050	.079
824	Jaunciems	Apr. 8	.268	.075	.105
825	Selpils	Apr. 8	.143	.040	.063
826	Milgravis	Apr. 8	.624	.174	.276
827	Riga Asylum, Valmiera St	Apr. 8	.034	.027	.043
828	Riga Asylum, Suvorova St	Apr. 8	.047	.014	.045
829	Riga Asylum, Matisa St	Apr. 8	.057	.033	.057
830	Rujene	Apr. 10	.446	.077	.164
831	Ogre	Apr. 10	.230	.067	.106
832	Riga Asylum, Bruninieku St	Apr. 10	.028	.022	.035
833	Riga Asylum, Narva St	Apr. 10	.034	.027	.043
834	Svente	Apr. 10	.356	.090	.157
835	Griva	Apr. 10	1.784	.498	.721
836	Eglaine	Apr. 10	.491	.125	.207
837	Liksnas	Apr. 8	.231	.086	....
838	Daugavpils (Dvinsk)	Apr. 10	8.651	1.985	3.819
839	Ikskile	Apr. 11	.089	.025	.039
840	Riga Asylum, Kurmanov St	Apr. 11	.012	.010	.014
841	Cesis	Apr. 11	.803	.224	.354
842	Kalkuni	Apr. 10	.535	.149	.236
843	Katlakalns	Apr. 11	.214	.060	.095
844	Valka	Apr. 11	.255	.072	.103
845	Zilani	Apr. 11	.251	.061	.111
846	Malinova	Apr. 11	.268	.075	.118
847	Skriveri	Apr. 11	.256	.075	.116
848	Lives	Apr. 11	.267	.075	.118
849	Jekabmiests	Apr. 11	.803	.224	.354
850	Maz-Irbe	Apr. 11	.080	.022	.035
851	Kurmene	Apr. 11	.303	.085	.134
852	Jaun Jelgava	Apr. 11	.624	.174	.276
853	Riga Asylum, Jaroslavas St	Apr. 11	.033	.037	.059
854	Stradzmuiza, (Blind Institute)	Apr. 12	.016	.012	.019
855	Ludza	Apr. 19	.891	.249	.393
856	Dobele	Apr. 19	.178	.050	.079
857	Kreslava	Apr. 19	.803	.224	.354
858	Rezekne	Apr. 19	2.140	.597	.944
859	Plavinas	Apr. 22	.356	.080	.158
860	Salaspils	Apr. 19	.107	.030	.047
861	Lielais	Apr. 19	.205	.057	.091
862	Riga Asylum, Duntes St	Apr. 20	.162	.119	.205
863	Riga Asylum, Krasta St	Apr. 20	.069	.055	.087
864	Latvian Welfare Society, Riga	Apr. 20	.019	.015	.024
865	Libau	Apr. 21	8.027	2.241	3.544
866	Riga Children's Hospital	Apr. 21	.481	.135	.213
867	Riga Asylum, Jekabmiesta St	Apr. 21	.094	.075	.118
868	Talsi	Apr. 21	.321	.090	.142
869	Latvian Red Cross Hospital	Apr. 21	....	....	....
870	Riga Asylum, Sarkana St	Apr. 21	.028	.022	.035
871	Vec-Auce	Apr. 22	.446	.125	.197
872	Rezekne's Refugee Committee	Apr. 24	.098	.027	.043
873	Riga Refugee Committee, Valmiera	Apr. 24	.045	.012	.019
874	Flooded Regions (Dvinsk)	Apr. 26	8.919	2.490	3.937
875	Flooded Regions (Jekabmiests)	Apr. 28	1.784	.498	.787
	Total Milk in Cans	....	....	....	....
	Total for April, Metric Tons	....	**83.524**	**22.664**	**36.470**

A.R.A. and A.R.A.-European Children's Fund
Feeding, by Districts or Kitchens, by Months

Commodities in Net Metric Tons of 1,000 Kilograms or 2,204.6 Pounds *

Pork Products	Milk		Cocoa	Sugar	Misc. Food	Soap	Total Tons
	Evap.	Cond.					
	(Cans)	(Cans)				(Pieces)	
.015	360	....	.016	.043	....	....	.331
.025	345	....	.015	.038	....	....	.510
.010	230	....	.013	.034	....	....	.424
.008	90	....	.003	.014	....	....	.172
.018	230	....	.011	.028	....	....	.364
.022	280	....	.016	.042	....	....	.528
.013	190	....	.009	.023	....	....	.291
.062	840	....	.037	.099	....	....	1.272
.006	120	....	.006	.016	....	....	.132
.006	124	....	.007	.016	....	....	.135
.009	225	....	.009	.023	....	....	.188
.044	540	....	.024	.071	....	....	.826
.021	225	....	.012	.035	....	....	.471
.005	105	....	.005	.013	....	....	.108
.006	130	....	.006	.016	....	....	.132
.034	450	....	.020	.057	....	....	.714
.162	1,800	....	.086	.280	....	....	3.531
.041	565	....	.024	.078	....	....	.966
.020	230	....	.016	.051	....	....	.404
.857	10,620	....	.519	1.376	....	....	17.207
.008	96	....	.005	.014	....	....	.180
.002	48	....	.002	.006	....	....	.046
.080	1,080	....	.048	.128	....	....	1.637
.053	721	....	.032	.085	....	....	1.090
.021	288	....	.013	.034	....	....	.437
.021	315	....	.013	.037	....	....	.501
.019	290	....	.016	.043	....	....	.501
.021	360	....	.016	.043	....	....	.541
.023	300	....	.016	.043	....	....	.529
.027	360	....	.016	.042	....	....	.545
.080	660	....	.048	.128	....	....	1.637
.008	108	....	.005	.013	....	....	.163
.030	384	....	.018	.048	....	....	.618
.062	768	....	.037	.099	....	....	1.272
.008	165	....	.008	.021	....	....	.166
.003	60	....	.003	.007	....	....	.060
.088	1,200	....	.053	.141	....	....	1.815
.018	240	....	.011	.028	....	....	.364
.080	1,081	....	.048	.128	....	....	1.637
.211	2,784	....	.128	.340	....	....	4.360
.035	480	....	.015	.057	....	....	.701
.011	144	....	.006	.017	....	....	.218
.021	276	....	.012	.033	....	....	.419
.026	588	....	.028	.063	....	....	.603
.011	264	....	.012	.031	....	....	.265
.003	72	....	.003	.009	....	....	.073
.795	10,800	....	.482	1.277	....	....	16.366
.047	648	....	.027	.076	....	....	.979
.015	200	....	.016	.043	....	....	.361
.032	400	....	.019	.051	....	....	.655
....	....	....	....	.006	....	....	.006
.005	108	....	.005	.013	....	....	.108
.044	600	....	.027	.071	....	....	.910
.010	132	....	.006	.016	....	....	.200
.004	60	....	.003	.007	....	....	.090
.883	12,000	....	.535	1.419	....	....	18.183
.177	2,400	....	.107	.284	....	....	3.637
....	**105,229**	....	....	....	....	....	47.732
7.847	**47.732**	....	**4.969**	**13.272**	....	....	**216.478**

[*Continued on next page*]

Table 380—*Continued*

Receipt No.	Districts or Kitchens	Date of Delivery	Flour	Rice	Beans, Peas
New Series		1922			
876	Riga	May ..	3.517	3.586	5.670
877	Riga Bakery, Herrnberger	May ..	6.031	....	....
878	Riga Bakery, Briedis	May ..	4.512	....	....
879	Russian Refugee Committee	May 3	.019	.015	.024
880	Riga Women's Corps Asylum	May 3	.047	.039	.061
881	Sloka	May 3	.420	.117	.185
882	Riga Asylum, Kandavas St.	May 3	.100	.082	.130
883	Riga Asylum, Kalnciema St.	May 4	.022	.018	.029
884	Riga Asylum, Suvorova St.	May 4	.015	.010	.020
885	Riga Asylum, Talsu St.	May 4	.090	.075	.118
886	Riga Asylum, Moscow St.	May 4	.056	.046	.073
887	Plavinas	May 22	.368	.093	.149
888	Riga Refugee Committee, Valmiera St.	May 4	.202	.057	.089
889	Valmiera	May 4	.829	.232	.367
890	Riga Asylum, Valmiera St.	May 4	.034	.028	.045
891	Riga Asylum, Hermana St.	May 4	.078	.059	.102
892	Riga Asylum, Miera St.	May 4	.031	.026	.041
893	Tukums	May 5	.507	.132	.224
894	Ventspils	May 5	1.613	.451	.712
895	Jelgava	May 5	2.900	.823	1.302
896	Bramberga	May 5	.111	.031	.049
897	Riga Asylum, Martin St.	May 5	.016	.018	.029
898	Bierini	May 5	.203	.057	.090
899	Ogre	May 5	.240	.056	.110
900	Rujene	May 5	.440	.088	.203
901	Riga Asylum, Pioneru St.	May 5	.047	.039	.061
902	Riga Asylum, Katolu St.	May 5	.021	.017	.027
903	Milgravis	May 5	.645	.180	.285
904	Pridruiska	May 8	.183	.051	.081
905	Spare	May 8	.148	.041	.065
906	Naukseni	May 8	.202	.056	.090
907	Riga Asylum, Kurmanov St.	May 8	.008	.010	.012
908	Jekabmiests	May 8	.280	....	.091
909	Riga Asylum, "Kinderfreund"	May 8	.037	.031	.045
910	Dobele	May 8	.141	.042	.050
911	Cesis	May 8	.798	.081	.366
912	Krustpils	May 8	.092	.026	.041
913	Jaun Jelgava	May 10	.184	.051	.081
914	Jaunciems	May 8	.276	.060	.122
915	Riga Asylum, Suvorova St.	May 10	.042	.036	.043
916	Riga Asylum, Jaroslavas St.	May 10	.024	.039	.055
917	Riga Asylum, Spitalu St.	May 10	.062	.051	.081
918	Riga Asylum, Matisa St.	May 10	.043	.046	.049
919	Bolderaja	May 10	.645	.180	.285
920	Vec-Svarte	May 10	.055	.015	.024
921	Zilani	May 10	.239	.066	.105
922	Livani	May 10	.550	.154	.244
923	Korsova	May 10	.369	.103	.163
924	Valka	May 10	.276	.077	.122
925	Svente	May 10	.369	.103	.163
926	Eglaine	May 10	.507	.142	.224
927	Kalkuni	May 10	.553	.154	.244
928	Griva	May 10	1.843	.515	.814
929	Daugavpils (Dvinsk)	May 1	8.940	2.495	3.940
930	Riga	May 11	4.334	3.824	6.048
931	Liksna	May 11	.369	.103	.163
932	Ilukste	May 11	.461	.129	.203
933	Judovka	May 11	.790	.221	.350

.R.A. and A.R.A.-European Children's Fund

eeding, by Districts or Kitchens, by Months

Commodities in Net Metric Tons of 1,000 Kilograms or 2,204.6 Pounds *

Pork Products	Milk		Cocoa	Sugar	Misc. Food	Soap	Total Tons
	Evap.	Cond.					
	(Cans)	(Cans)				(Pieces)	
.806	13,968	....	.771	2.043	....	....	16.393
.281	....	....	....	....	....	....	6.312
.246	....	....	....	....	....	....	4.758
.003	50	24	.003	.009	....	....	.073
.008	100	60	.008	.022	....	....	.185
.042	376	188	.019	.067	....	....	.850
.016	264	132	.018	.047	....	....	.393
.004	58	29	.004	.010	....	....	.087
.005	20	41	.004	.009	....	....	.063
.015	240	120	.016	.043	....	....	.357
.009	148	74	.010	.025	....	....	.219
.032	336	144	.013	.059	....	....	.714
.020	182	91	.012	.032	....	....	.412
.082	744	372	.050	.132	....	....	1.692
.006	60	45	.006	.016	....	....	.135
.013	82	103	.014	.037	....	....	.303
.005	80	40	.006	.015	....	....	.124
.043	400	224	.030	.070	....	....	1.006
.161	1,150	722	.097	.257	....	....	3.291
.292	1,800	1,320	.177	.425	....	....	5.919
.011	98	49	.007	.018	....	....	.227
.004	58	29	.004	.010	....	....	.081
.020	182	91	.012	.032	....	....	.414
.021	214	106	.015	.037	....	....	.479
.043	321	207	.022	.063	....	....	.859
.008	82	62	.008	.022	....	....	.185
.003	54	28	.004	.010	....	....	.082
.062	580	289	.034	.103	....	....	1.309
.018	152	96	.011	.029	....	....	.373
.015	132	66	.009	.024	....	....	.302
.015	134	91	.010	.032	....	....	.405
.002	20	15	.002	.005	....	....	.039
....	48	361	....	.057	....	....	.428
.003	83	49	.007	.018	....	....	.141
.011	....	96	.011	.017	....	....	.272
.082	510	306	.038	.124	....	....	1.489
.009	82	42	.006	.015	....	....	.189
.018	....	....	....	.029	....	....	.363
.026	179	124	.013	.044	....	....	.541
.004	23	44	.006	.019	....	....	.150
.007	87	62	.008	.022	....	....	.155
.010	166	82	.011	.029	....	....	.244
.004	76	75	.009	.025	....	....	.176
.064	580	284	.039	.103	....	....	1.316
.005	48	26	.003	.008	....	....	.110
.023	210	105	.014	.038	....	....	.485
.055	466	234	.033	.088	....	....	1.124
.037	320	160	.022	.059	....	....	.753
.027	248	124	.017	.044	....	....	.563
.037	315	165	.022	.059	....	....	.753
.050	448	224	.030	.081	....	....	1.034
.020	152	298	.033	.065	....	....	1.069
.183	1,656	824	.111	.293	....	....	3.759
.885	8,000	4,000	.536	1.422	....	....	18.218
.894	11,568	5,808	.823	2.180	....	....	18.103
.037	320	160	.022	.059	....	....	.753
.046	414	206	.028	.073	....	....	.940
.078	710	355	.047	.125	....	....	1.611

[*Continued on next page*]

Table 380—*Continued*

Detail of Internal Deliveries for Chil

Receipt No.	Districts or Kitchens	Date of Delivery	Flour	Rice	Beans, Peas
New Series		1922			
934	Ribaki	May 11	.627	.175	.277
935	Rezekne	May 12	1.988	.618	.935
936	Ludza	May 12	.900	.189	.200
937	Lives	May 13	.275	.073	.122
938	Assari	May 13	.092	.026	.041
939	Riga Asylum, Narvas St.	May 16	.034	.028	.045
940	Riga Asylum, Jacobmiesta St.	May 16	.090	.075	.118
941	Riga Asylum, Duntes St.	May 16	.087	.072	1.114
942	Riga Bakery, Herrnberger	May 16	5.694	....	....
943	Riga Bakery, Briedis	May 16	5.020	....	....
944	Latvian Welfare Society	May 16	.025	.021	.033
945	Silupe	May 17	.221	.062	.098
946	Katlakalns	May 17	.075	.018	.030
947	Saldus	May 18	.276	.077	.122
948	Aizpute	May 18	.276	.077	.122
949	Riga Asylum, Krasta St.	May 18	.066	.054	.085
950	Riga Asylum, Brunneku St.	May 18	.028	.023	.037
951	Malinova	May 18	.276	.077	.122
952	Libau	May 18	8.200	2.300	3.650
953	Libau	May 18	1.300	.360	.600
954	Riga Asylum, Sarkana St.	May 18	.037	.023	.036
955	Kreslava	May 18	.830	.226	.110
956	Kuldiga	May 19	1.500	.400	.600
957	Olaine	May 22	.184	.051	.053
958	Riga Children's Hospital	May 24	.455	.138	.219
959	Riga Asylum, Patversmes St.	May 26	.069	.056	.082
960	Riga Refugee Committee	May 27	.264	.061	.089
	Total Milk in Cans	....	....	....	....
	Total for May, Metric Tons	....	**74.823**	**20.557**	**32.506**
961	Riga	June 1	8.813	12.839	5.672
962	Riga Bakery, Herrnberger	June ..	10.235	....	....
963	Riga Bakery, Briedis	June ..	9.028	....	....
964	Railway Men's Sanatorium, Bulduros	June 1	.178	.089	.040
965	Riga Asylum, Katolu St.	June 2	.021	.029	.013
966	Strazdmuiza (Blind Institute)	June 14	.016	.023	.010
967	Riga Asylum, Talsu St.	June 2	.087	.125	.055
968	Ogre	June 14	.220	.119	....
969	Assari	June 2	.535	.267	.118
970	Riga Women's Corps Asylum	June 2	.047	.066	.030
971	Riga Asylum, Kuldigas St.	June 2	.028	.039	.018
972	Russian Refugee Committee	June 2	.019	.027	.012
973	Jaun Jelgava	June 14	.600	.311	.137
974	Riga Asylum, Martin St.	June 2	.024	.034	.015
975	Riga Asylum, Pioneru St.	June 2	.044	.063	.028
976	Riga Asylum, Kandavas St.	June 2	.106	.152	.067
977	Riga Asylum, Kalnciema St.	June 7	.016	.023	.010
978	Riga Asylum, Suvorova St.	June 7	.031	.044	.020
979	Ventspils	June 7	1.561	.780	.345
980	Tukums	June 7	.491	.245	.108
981	Livani	June 8	.535	.267	.118
982	Jelgava	June 7	2.608	1.427	.630
983	Riga Asylum, Kurmanova St.	June 8	.013	.020	.009
984	Riga Asylum, Jaroslava St.	June 9	.044	.062	.003
985	Riga Asylum, Spitalu St.	June 8	.061	.081	.025
986	Riga Asylum, Miera St.	June 8	.017	.044	.006
987	Riga Asylum, Hermana St.	June 8	.072	.100	.045
988	Riga Asylum, Mascavas St.	June 8	.053	.075	.033

R.A. and A.R.A.-European Children's Fund

eding, by Districts or Kitchens, by Months

Commodities in Net Metric Tons of 1,000 Kilograms or 2,204.6 Pounds *

Pork Products	Milk Evap.	Milk Cond.	Cocoa	Sugar	Misc. Food	Soap	Total Tons
	(Cans)	(Cans)				(Pieces)	
.062	560	280	.037	.100	....	....	1.278
.210	1,440	672	.110	.209	....	....	4.070
.056	672	288	.042	.121	....	....	1.508
.027	276	96	.017	.044	....	....	.558
.009	76	48	.005	.015	....	....	.188
.006	90	45	.006	.016	....	....	.135
.015	138	119	.015	.043	....	....	.356
.014	232	115	.015	.041	....	....	.343
.280	....	....	....	....	....	....	5.947
.247	....	....	....	....	....	....	5.247
.004	60	30	.004	.012	....	....	.099
.022	198	100	.013	.035	....	....	.451
.008	....	12	.003	.012	....	....	.146
.027	248	124	.017	.044	....	....	.563
.027	248	124	.017	.044	....	....	.563
.011	174	86	.011	.031	....	....	.258
.005	74	38	.005	.013	....	....	.111
.027	248	124	.017	.044	....	....	.563
.800	7,200	3,024	.450	1.300	....	....	16.700
.130	1,248	576	.082	.200	....	....	2.672
.005	74	38	.005	.013	....	....	.119
.083	453	372	.043	.105	....	....	1.397
.150	1,248	672	.090	.230	....	....	2.970
.003	450	66	.003	.019	....	....	.313
.048	420	210	.027	.079	....	....	.996
.011	182	91	.012	.032	....	....	.269
.026	240	119	.015	.037	....	....	.492
....	**64,647**	**26,541**	....	....	....	....	39.858
7.239	**29.324**	**10.534**	**4.346**	**11.638**	....	....	**190.967**
1.613	23,058	11,529	1.542	4.087	....	....	34.566
.420	....	....	....	....	....	....	10.655
.370	....	....	....	....	....	....	9.398
.018	160	80	.011	.028	....	....	.364
.003	48	24	.004	.010	....	....	.080
.003	45	15	.003	.007	....	....	.062
.014	224	112	.015	.040	....	....	.336
.010	225	75	.012	.038	....	....	.399
.053	480	240	.032	.085	....	....	1.090
.008	120	60	.008	.021	....	....	.180
.005	72	36	.005	.013	....	....	.108
.003	48	24	.003	.009	....	....	.073
.061	624	192	.037	.099	....	....	1.245
.004	60	30	.005	.011	....	....	.093
.007	112	56	.007	.020	....	....	.169
.017	272	136	.018	.048	....	....	.408
.003	40	20	.003	.007	....	....	.062
.005	80	40	.005	.014	....	....	.119
.155	1,402	701	.093	.248	....	....	3.182
.049	440	220	.029	.078	....	....	1.000
.053	525	175	.032	.085	....	....	1.090
.283	2,505	835	.171	.419	....	....	5.538
.002	38	12	.002	.006	....	....	.052
.007	126	42	.008	.020	....	....	.144
.010	150	50	.010	.027	....	....	.214
.005	81	27	.002	.014	....	....	.088
.012	207	69	.010	.030	....	....	.269
.009	153	50	.009	.024	....	....	.203

[*Continued on next page*]

Table 380—*Continued*

Detail of Internal Deliveries for Chil

Receipt No.	Districts or Kitchens	Date of Delivery	Flour	Rice	Beans, Peas
New Series		1922			
989	Bilderlini	June 9	.016	.023	.010
990	Eglaine	June 8	.491	.237	.108
991	Kurmene	June 8	.303	.151	.067
992	Riga Asylum, "Kinderfreund"	June 8	.037	.053	.011
993	Rujene	June 8	.446	.223	.099
994	Ilukste	June 8	.446	.223	.099
995	Zilani	June 8	.232	.117	.052
996	Talsi	June 8	.322	.161	.071
997	Milgravis	June 8	.624	.312	.138
998	Riga Asylum, Suvorova St.	June 8	.050	.071	.032
999	Riga Refugee Committee, Valmiera	June 8	.223	.110	.049
1000	Bolderaja	June 9	.624	.212	.138
1001	Riga Asylum, Matisa St.	June 9	.054	.084	.028
1002	Sloka	June 9	.420	.209	.093
1003	Mazirbe	June 14	.080	.039	.018
1004	Daugavpils (Dvinsk)	June 9	8.651	4.324	1.910
1005	Griva	June 9	1.784	.695	.390
1006	Svente	June 9	.357	.179	.051
1007	Ribakova	June 9	.530	.303	.134
1008	Judovka	June 9	.196	.380	.170
1009	Kalkuni	June 9	.785	.392	.174
1010	Bierini	June 10	.196	.098	.028
1011	Valmiera	June 12	.803	.401	.177
1012	Cesis	June 12	.803	.401	.177
1013	Dobele	June 12	.178	.089	.040
1014	Valka	June 12	.268	.134	.059
1015	Korsova	June 12	.356	.179	.065
1016	Vecauce	June 12	.356	.179	.079
1017	Riga Asylum, Jekabmiesta St.	June 12	.097	.138	.061
1018	Riga Asylum, Narvas St.	June 12	.034	.048	.022
1019	Riga Asylum, Valmiera St.	June 12	.034	.048	.022
1020	Jekabmiests	June 12	.803	.401	.177
1021	Ludza	June 12	.891	.445	.196
1022	Rezekne	June 12	2.140	1.069	.472
1023	Krustpils	June 12	.602	.339	.115
1024	Malinova	June 12	.260	.134	.050
1025	Lives	June 13	.267	.133	.059
1026	Grienvalde	June 12	.196	.093	.044
1027	Kreslava	June 12	.800	.400	.015
1028	Naukseni	June 13	.169	.084	.038
1029	Spare	June 13	.142	.071	.032
1030	Libau	June 16	.891	.445	.196
1031	Saldus	June 16	.268	.134	.059
1032	Aizpute	June 16	.268	.134	.059
1033	Riga Asylum, Duntes St.	June 16	.087	.125	.056
1034	Latvian Red Cross Asylum, Assari	June 16	.089	.043	.020
1035	Libau	June 16	8.000	4.000	1.770
1036	Riga Asylum, Krasta St.	June 17	.066	.092	.042
1037	Riga Asylum, Sarakana St.	June 17	.019	.027	.012
	Total Milk in Cans	....	....	....	....
	Total for June, Metric Tons	....	**71.257**	**35.733**	**15.551**
1038	Jaunciems	July ..	.276	.138	.061
1039	Children's Summer Sanatorium, Vecaki	July ..	.368	.183	.081
1040	Riga	July ..	4.286	6.496	2.868
1041	Riga Bakery, Herrnberger	July 1	5.835	....	....
1042	Riga Bakery, Briedis	July 1	5.335	....	....
1043	Riga Asylum, Patversmes St	July 1	.069	.100	.045

A.R.A. and A.R.A.-European Children's Fund

Feeding, by Districts or Kitchens, by Months

Commodities in Net Metric Tons of 1,000 Kilograms or 2,204.6 Pounds *

Pork Products	Milk		Cocoa	Sugar	Misc. Food	Soap	Total Tons
	Evap. (Cans)	Cond. (Cans)				(Pieces)	
.003	45	15	.003	.007	....	....	.062
.049	495	165	.029	.078	....	....	.992
.030	288	96	.018	.048	....	....	.617
.006	85	35	.005	.017	....	....	.129
.044	450	150	.027	.071	....	....	.910
.044	450	150	.027	.071	....	....	.910
.023	234	78	.014	.037	....	....	.475
.031	246	82	.019	.052	....	....	.656
.062	630	210	.037	.099	....	....	1.272
.008	144	48	.009	.023	....	....	.193
.022	180	60	.013	.035	....	....	.452
.062	630	210	.037	.099	....	....	1.172
.010	160	40	.008	.025	....	....	.209
.042	423	141	.025	.067	....	....	.856
.008	60	48	.005	.012	....	....	.162
.857	8,250	2,750	.519	1.376	....	....	17.637
.115	591	197	.097	.284	....	....	3.365
.035	300	100	.017	.053	....	....	.692
.060	525	175	.036	.096	....	....	1.159
....	489	163	.034	.096	....	....	.876
.078	792	264	.047	.125	....	....	1.601
.020	156	54	.011	.031	....	....	.384
.080	810	270	.048	.128	....	....	1.637
.080	810	270	.048	.128	....	....	1.637
.018	180	60	.011	.028	....	....	.364
.026	270	90	.015	.043	....	....	.545
.035	336	114	.021	.057	....	....	.713
.035	360	120	.021	.057	....	....	.727
.016	279	93	.017	.044	....	....	.373
.006	75	25	.006	.016	....	....	.132
.006	75	25	.006	.016	....	....	.132
.080	810	270	.048	.128	....	....	1.637
.088	912	288	.053	.141	....	....	1.814
.211	2,160	720	.128	.340	....	....	4.360
.038	600	200	.014	.055	....	....	1.163
.022	240	80	.014	.038	....	....	.518
.026	264	96	.016	.042	....	....	.543
.020	123	41	.012	.031	....	....	.396
.077	675	225	.040	.128	....	....	1.460
.017	171	57	.010	.027	....	....	.345
.014	144	48	.009	.023	....	....	.291
.088	912	288	.053	.142	....	....	1.815
.026	210	90	.016	.043	....	....	.546
.026	270	90	.016	.043	....	....	.546
.014	252	82	.015	.039	....	....	.336
.009	90	30	.005	.014	....	....	.180
.795	7,248	2,400	.480	1.270	....	....	16.315
.011	216	36	.011	.030	....	....	.252
.003	72	....	.003	.009	....	....	.073
....	**65,482**	**26,189**	....	....	....	....	40.097
6.678	**29.703**	**10.394**	**4.249**	**11.350**	....	....	**184.915**
.027	372	....	.017	.044	....	....	.563
.036	496	....	.022	.058	....	....	.748
.662	12,572	....	.780	2.067	....	....	17.159
.416	....	....	....	....	....	....	6.251
.380	....	....	....	....	....	....	5.715
.011	150	....	.012	.030	....	....	.267

[*Continued on next page*]

Table 380—*Continued*

Detail of Internal Deliveries for Chil

Receipt No.	Districts or Kitchens	Date of Delivery	Flour	Rice	Beans, Peas
New Series		1922			
1044	Riga Asylum, Kalnciem St.	July 3	.016	.020	.010
1045	Riga Asylum, "Kinderfreund"	July 3	.040	.050	.025
1046	Riga Asylum, Miera St.	July 3	.025	.030	.021
1047	Riga Women's Corps Asylum	July 3	.047	.050	.030
1048	Riga Asylum, Maskavas St	July 3	.050	.045	.033
1049	Riga Asylum, Kandavas St	July 3	.100	.100	.066
1050	Sloka	July 3	.245	.124	.055
1051	Riga Asylum, Suvorova St	July 3	.028	.030	.019
1052	Riga Asylum, Katolu St	July 3	.021	.025	.014
1053	Riga Asylum, Spitalu St	July 3	.062	.040	.041
1054	Riga Asylum, Pioneru St	July 3	.035	.020	.027
1055	Griva	July 8	....	.290	.116
1056	Riga Asylum, Talsu St	July 3	.070	.080	.051
1057	Russian Refugee Committee	July 4	.019	.027	.012
1058	Jelgava	July 4	.296	.030	.078
1059	Krustpils	July 4	.370	.042	.102
1060	Riga Asylum, Kurmanova St	July 4	.014	.012	.009
1061	Riga Asylum, Hermana St	July 4	.060	.096	.043
1062	Ventspils	July 5	.800	.093	.084
1063	Tukums	July 6	.220	.043	.050
1064	Riga Women's Corps Sanatorium	July 6	.046	.023	.010
1065	Dubultos	July 6	.250	.138	.061
1066	Daugavpils (Dvinsk)	July 7	5.000	2.150	.580
1067	Liksnas	July 8	.140	.082	.037
1068	Spare	July 8	.148	.073	.033
1069	Riga Asylum, Valmiera St.	July 8	.037	.055	.018
1070	Riga Asylum, Martina St	July 8	.028	.041	.019
1071	Riga Asylum, Kuldigas St	July 8	.025	.031	.012
1072	Riga Asylum, Jaroslav St	July 8	.044	.036	.019
1073	Olaine	July 10	.047	.050	.023
1074	Silupe	July 10	.129	.064	.029
1075	Riga Children's Hospital	July 11	.470	.247	.099
1076	Riga Asylum, Matisa St	July 11	.060	.091	.034
1077	Milgravis	July 11	.074	....	.057
1078	Ludza	July 11	.400	.166	.105
1079	Rezekne	July 11	.800	.319	.219
1080	Riga Asylum, Suvorova St	July 12	.047	.069	.031
1081	Latvia Red Cross Sanatorium	July 12	.090	.045	.020
1082	Jaun Jelgava	July 13	.320	.193	.085
1083	Railwaymen's Sanatorium	July 15	.184	.091	.041
1084	Lives	July 15	.230	.118	.052
1085	Plavinas	July 15	.138	.085	.025
1086	Riga Asylum, Jekabmiesta St.	July 17	.094	.138	.061
1087	Jekabmiests	July 17	.354	.200	.092
1088	Rujene	July 17	.100	.018	.036
1089	Naukseni	July 17	.203	.100	.045
1090	Eglaine	July 17	.167	.110	....
1091	Latvian Red Cross Hospital, Riga	July 27	.037	.018	....
1092	Libau	July 20	.900	2.200	1.200
1093	Riga Asylum, Kazaku St	July 18	.150	.091	.020
1094	Riga Asylum, Duntes St	July 18	.084	.124	.055
1095	Cesis Asylum, Drabuzi	July 18	.166	.082	.037
1096	Riga Asylum, Narvas St	July 19	.034	.050	.023
1097	Riga Asylum, Sarkana St	July 20	.022	.032	.013
1098	Riga Asylum, Krasta St	July 20	.056	.082	.013
1099	Kalkuni	July 17	.254	.107	.019
1100	Korsova	July 20	.360	.184	.068
1101	Kreslava	July 20	.470	.250	.100

.R.A. and A.R.A.-European Children's Fund

eeding, by Districts or Kitchens, by Months

Commodities in Net Metric Tons of 1,000 Kilograms or 2,204.6 Pounds *

Pork Products	Milk		Cocoa	Sugar	Misc. Food	Soap	Total Tons
	Evap. (Cans)	Cond. (Cans)				(Pieces)	
.002	22	....	.002	.005	....	....	.055
.004	100	....	.006	.015	....	....	.140
.004	80	....	.005	.013	....	....	.098
.005	86	....	.006	.020	....	....	.158
.005	160	....	.009	.023	....	....	.165
.011	220	....	.012	.042	....	....	.331
.024	200	....	.010	.039	....	....	.497
.002	60	....	.005	.010	....	....	.094
.001	80	....	.004	.007	....	....	.072
.005	200	....	.011	.029	....	....	.188
.002	100	....	.007	.015	....	....	.106
....	400	....	....	.080	....	....	.486
.002	200	....	.014	.035	....	....	.252
.002	74	....	.003	.009	....	....	.072
.024	32	....	....	.002	....	....	.430
.041	140	....	.018	.045	....	....	.618
.001	55	....	.002	.004	....	....	.042
.007	250	....	.010	.026	....	....	.242
.078	....	....	.050	.132	....	....	1.237
....	80	....	.015	.016	....	....	.344
.005	62	....	.003	.007	....	....	.094
.027	372	....	.017	.035	....	....	.528
.320	2,740	....	.229	.440	....	....	8.719
....	180	....	.010	.022	....	....	.291
.011	197	....	.009	.024	....	....	.298
.002	140	....	.007	.018	....	....	.137
.003	112	....	.005	.013	....	....	.109
.002	99	....	.003	.011	....	....	.084
.005	170	....	.008	.021	....	....	.133
.010	100	....	.002	....	....	....	.132
.013	174	....	.008	.021	....	....	.264
.045	600	....	.030	.075	....	....	.966
.002	200	....	.011	.025	....	....	.223
....	182	....	.005	.033	....	....	.169
.033	288	....	.017	.043	....	....	.764
.095	144	....	.059	.140	....	....	1.632
.005	180	....	.008	.020	....	....	.180
.009	96	....	.006	.013	....	....	.183
.038	240	....	.023	.050	....	....	.709
.018	248	....	.011	.029	....	....	.374
.023	192	....	.014	.037	....	....	.474
.019	272	....	.012	.030	....	....	.309
.010	300	....	.017	.042	....	....	.362
.026	273	....	.012	.065	....	....	.749
.006	....	....	....	....	....	....	.160
.020	273	....	.012	.032	....	....	.412
....	98	....	.005	.034	....	....	.316
.004	37	....	.002	....	....	....	.061
.500	2,880	....	.300	.300	....	....	5.400
.016	200	....	.007	.018	....	....	.302
.009	335	....	.015	.030	....	....	.317
.016	224	....	.010	.026	....	....	.337
.003	130	....	.006	.010	....	....	.126
.003	87	....	.004	.010	....	....	.084
.001	220	....	.009	.020	....	....	.181
.011	222	....	.019	.056	....	....	.466
.037	480	....	.022	.050	....	....	.721
.035	740	....	.018	.028	....	....	.901

[*Continued on next page*]

Table 380—*Continued*

Detail of Internal Deliveries for Chi

Receipt No.	Districts or Kitchens	Date of Delivery	Flour	Rice	Beans, Peas
New Series		1922			
1102	Malinova	July 20	.100	.069	.031
1103	Riga Refugee Committee, Valmiera	July 25	.166	.082	.037
1104	Vec-Auce	July 25	.184	.091	.041
1105	Rezekne Refugee Committee	July 25	.184	.091	.041
1106	Ilukste	July 27	.120	.118	.053
1107	Grienvalde	July 27	.056	.055	.025
1108	Vec-Svarte	July 27	.030	.015	.024
	Total Milk in Cans	....	....	....	....
	Total for July, Metric Tons	....	**31.685**	**16.638**	**7.584**
		1922			
1109	Vecaki	Aug. ..	....	.090	.142
1110	Riga	Aug. 1	.147	.632	1.630
1111	Riga Asylum, Palversem St	Aug. 1	.069	.056	.089
1112	Bolderaja	Aug. 2	.157	.077	.113
1113	Riga Asylum, Pioneru St	Aug. ..	.038	.040	.033
1114	Riga Asylum, Kalnciem St	Aug. 1	.018	.015	.024
1115	Riga Asylum, Kuldigas St	Aug. 2	.028	.023	.037
1116	Riga Asylum, Talsu St	Aug. 2	.075	.066	.105
1117	Riga Asylum, Kurmanov St	Aug. 2	.012	.013	.017
1118	Riga Asylum, Kandavas St	Aug. 2	.090	.072	.118
1119	Riga Asylum, Spitalu St	Aug. 2	.060	.051	.081
1120	Riga Women's Corps Asylum	Aug. 2	.047	.039	.061
1121	Riga Asylum, "Kinderfreund"	Aug. 3	.040	.033	.053
1122	Russian Emigrants	Aug. 3	.019	.015	.024
1123	Riga Asylum, Katolu St	Aug. 3	.021	.017	.027
1124	Riga Asylum, Miera St	Aug. 3	.016	.010	.033
1125	Riga Asylum, Jaroslava St	Aug. 3	.024	.036	.057
1126	Milgravis	Aug. 3	.121	.077	.122
1127	Sloka	Aug. 3	.186	.077	.122
1128	Plavinas	Aug. 10	....	.030	.015
1129	Spare	Aug. 14	....	.036	.065
1130	Riga Asylum, Jekabmiesta St	Aug. 15	....	.077	.080
1131	Riga Asylum, Maskavas St	Aug. 5	.002	.016	.054
1132	Riga Asylum, Suvorova St	Aug. 5	.014	.021	.033
1133	Krustpils	Aug. 7	....	.075	.203
1134	Olaine	Aug. 9	.022	.028	.045
1135	Judovka	Aug. 7	....	.142	.075
1136	Cesis Asylum, Drabuzi	Aug. 7	.006	.025	.046
1137	Malinova	Aug. 7	....	.057	.098
1138	Ilukste	Aug. 7	....	.074	.203
1139	Jekabmiests	Aug. 8	....	.153	.284
1140	Rezekne	Aug. 8	....	....	.247
1141	Ludza	Aug. 8	....	.120	.240
1142	Riga Asylum, Hermana St	Aug. 9	.029	.056	.089
1143	Riga Asylum, Valmiera St	Aug. 9	.017	.031	.049
1144	Riga Asylum, Matisa St	Aug. 9	....	.025	.081
1145	Riga Asylum, Suvorova St	Aug. 9	.005	.036	.057
1146	Riga Women's Corps Sanatorium	Aug. 9	.043	.010	.020
1147	Griva	Aug. 9	.087	.199	.464
1148	Latvian Red Cross Assari	Aug. 10	.007	.017	.040
1149	Kreslava	Aug. 9	....	....	.244
1150	Valmiera	Aug. 9	....	.010	.097
1151	Kalkuni	Aug. 9	....	....	.158
1152	Korsova	Aug. 9	....	....	.158
1153	Rujene	Aug. 9	....	....	.085
1154	Valka	Aug. 9	....	.036	.050
1155	Daugavpils (Dvinsk)	Aug. 10	....	.340	1.806

.R.A. and A.R.A.-European Children's Fund

'eeding, by Districts or Kitchens, by Months

Commodities in Net Metric Tons of 1,000 Kilograms or 2,204.6 Pounds *

Pork Products	Milk		Cocoa	Sugar	Misc. Food	Soap	Total Tons
	Evap.	Cond.					
	(Cans)	(Cans)				(Pieces)	
.014	180	....	.008	.011	....	....	.233
.016	224	....	.010	.026	....	....	.337
.018	248	....	.011	.029	....	....	.374
.018	248	....	.011	.029	....	....	.374
.023	322	....	.014	.019	....	....	.347
.011	149	....	.007	.009	....	....	.163
.005	74	....	.003	.005	....	....	.082
....	**31,061**	....	....	....	....	....	14.088
3.239	**14.088**	....	**2.039**	**4.722**	....	....	**79.995**
.020	384	....	.022	.050	....	197	.324
.167	720	....	.295	.357	....	....	3.228
.007	273	....	.012	.032	....	....	.265
.008	186	....	.006	.020	....	....	.381
.005	172	....	.009	.023	....	....	.148
.002	74	....	.003	.008	....	....	.070
.003	114	....	.005	.010	....	....	.106
.009	322	....	.013	.031	....	....	.299
.002	50	....	.002	.005	....	....	.051
.010	360	....	.016	.032	....	....	.338
.007	240	....	.011	.022	....	....	.232
.005	186	....	.008	.018	....	....	.178
.007	160	....	.007	.012	....	....	.152
.003	74	....	.003	.007	....	....	.071
.003	80	....	.004	.005	....	....	.077
.004	65	....	.004	.007	....	....	.074
.007	120	....	.008	.014	....	....	.146
.027	186	....	.010	.020	....	....	.377
.027	370	....	.017	.034	....	....	.463
.012	....	....	.006	....	....	....	.063
.015	190	....	.009	.013	....	....	.138
.019	100	....	.005	.010	....	....	.191
.009	199	....	.009	.016	....	....	.106
.005	99	....	.004	.010	....	....	.087
.034	621	....	.028	.048	....	....	.388
.010	136	....	.004	....	....	....	.109
.017	580	....	.025	.020	....	....	.279
.013	140	....	.008	.008	....	....	.106
.022	150	....	.010	.018	....	....	.205
.040	380	....	.009	.042	....	....	.368
.064	778	....	.039	.068	....	....	.608
.012	960	....	.008	....	....	....	.267
.040	720	....	.030	.020	....	....	.450
.015	250	....	.012	.004	....	....	.205
.011	140	....	.006	.009	....	....	.123
.018	200	....	.007	.015	....	....	.146
.013	160	....	.004	.005	....	....	.120
.005	60	....	.002	.004	....	....	.084
.056	1,169	....	.044	.074	....	....	.924
.004	96	....	.003	.004	....	....	.075
.034	188	....	.024	.027	....	....	.329
....	400	....	....	....	....	....	.107
.023	130	....	.011	....	....	....	.192
.016	253	....	.011	....	....	....	.185
.008	96	....	....	....	....	....	.093
.007	20	....	.002	....	....	....	.095
....	....	....	.163	.193	....	....	2.502

[*Concluded on next page*]

Table 380—*Concluded*

Detail of Internal Deliveries for Chi

Receipt No.	Districts or Kitchens	Date of Delivery	Flour	Rice	Beans, Peas
New Series		1922			
1156	Jaun Jelgava	Aug. 10	....	....	.131
1157	Jelgava	Aug. 11	....	.463	.732
1158	Ventspils	Aug. 11	....	.257	.407
1159	Riga	Aug. 14	....	1.381	2.484
1160	Tukums	Aug. 15	....	.035	.122
1161	Riga Bakery Briedis	Aug. 15	....	....	....
1162	Railwaymen's Sanatorium	Aug. 15	....	.010	.030
1163	Riga Bakery Herrnberger	Aug. 15	....	....	....
1164	Vec-Auce	Aug. 16	....	.082	.130
1165	Eglaine	Aug. 16	....	.065	.102
1166	Riga Asylum, Sarkana St	Aug. 16	....	.018	.029
1167	Lives	Aug. 17	....	.016	.096
1168	Liksnas	Aug. 19	.002	.062	....
1169	Naukseni	Aug. 21	....	.056	.089
1170	Riga Asylum, Narvas St	Aug. 22	....	.028	.045
1171	Riga Asylum, Krasta St	Aug. 22	....	.047	.076
1172	Riga Asylum, Duntes St	Aug. 22	....	.069	.110
1173	Jaunciems	Aug. 22	....	.051	.084
1174	Rezekne Refugee Station	Aug. 23	....	....	....
1175	Riga Blind Institute	Aug. 23	....	.013	.020
....	Rice Receipted as Beans	....	....	4.768	4.768
....	Turnover	....	4.044	....	20.672
	Total Milk in Cans, Soap in Pieces		....	....	....
	Total for August, Metric Tons		**5.446**	**.938**	**38.101**
	Grand Total, Children's Relief §		**2,374.5**	**844.8**	**994.9**

§ Except clothing.

R.A. and A.R.A.-European Children's Fund

eding, by Districts or Kitchens, by Months

Commodities in Net Metric Tons of 1,000 Kilograms or 2,204.6 Pounds *

Pork Products	Milk		Cocoa	Sugar	Misc. Food	Soap	Total Tons
	Evap.	Cond.					
	(Cans)	(Cans)				(Pieces)	
.006	192	....	....	....	....	....	.137
.164	2,200	....	.099	.183	....	....	1.641
.091	1,242	....	.050	.116	....	....	.921
.248	4,500	....	.357	....	....	....	4.470
.024	250	....	.010	.019	....	....	.210
.216	....	....	....	....	....	....	.216
.003	73	....	.002	.008	....	....	.053
.118	....	....	....	....	....	....	.118
.002	340	....	.015	....	....	....	.229
.010	95	....	.009	.017	....	....	.203
.005	87	....	.004	.009	....	....	.065
.014	160	....	.007	....	....	....	.133
.022	290	....	.013	....	....	....	.099
.020	144	....	.011	....	....	....	.176
.007	136	....	.006	....	....	....	.086
.011	230	....	.011	....	....	....	.145
.016	286	....	.015	....	....	....	.210
.018	248	....	.011	....	....	....	.164
.031	422	....	....	....	....	....	.031
.003	62	....	.003	....	....	....	.039
....	....	....	....	....	....	....	....
5.600	50,174	....	4.711	12.262	....	793	47.289
....	**73,482**	....	....	....	....	**3,990**	33.575
7.474	**33.331**	....	**6.272**	**13.929**	....	**.244**	**105.735**
242.5	**1,426.6**	**89.3**	**154.6**	**411.7**	**6.6**	**44.6**	**6,590.1**

LATVIA—A.R.A.-European Children's Fund

Detail of Internal Deliveries of Clothing Outfits, by Local Committees

Table 381*

Reconstruction Period, 1919–1924

Receipt No.	Local Committee	Date of Delivery	Shoes (Pairs)†	Stockings (Pairs)	Suits (Each)
		1920			
14	Libau	Jan. 2	....	877	3,395
17	Cities on outside of Libau	Feb. 3	3,000	...	...
18	Libau	Feb. 3	5,655	3,480	590
19	Riga	Feb. 3	12,932	...	17,085
23	Libau	Mar. 12	....	4,175	...
25	Libau	Apr. 7	690	2,223	4,993
28	Riga	Apr. 9	15,539	22,204	8,935
30	Libau	May 3	197	2,344	...
		1921			
431	Riga	November	2,272	2,272	2,272
433	Russian Refugee Committee	November	10	10	10
434	Jelgava	November	360	360	360
436	Ventspils	November	158	158	158
437	Tukums	November	55	55	55
438	Ogre	November	24	24	24
440	Sloka	November	50	50	50
441	Zilani	November	24	24	24
442	Rujene	November	30	30	30
443	Livani	November	65	65	65
444	Milgravis	November	56	56	56
445	Krustpils	November	78	78	78
446	Riga Women's Corps Asylum	November	38	38	38
447	Jekabmiests	November	90	90	90
448	Svente	November	54	54	54
449	Eglaine	November	60	60	60
450	Daugavpils	November	1,130	1,130	1,130
451	Griva	November	200	200	200
452	Krape	November	10	10	10
453	Ilukste	November	48	48	48
454	Salaspils	November	10	10	10
455	Kalkuni	November	60	60	60
457	Valka	November	18	18	18
458	Cesis	November	74	74	74
459	Valmiera	November	87	87	87
460	Ludza	November	111	111	111
463	Refugee Committee, Valmiera Street	November	14	14	14
464	Jaun Jelgava	November	70	70	70
466	Libau	November	867	867	867
467	Saldus	November	18	...	18
468	Kuldiga	November	54	...	54
469	Aizpute	November	18	...	18
470	Rezekne	November	235	235	235
471	Latvian Welfare Society	November	9	9	9
472	Lives	November	30	30	30
473	Plavinas	November	40	40	40
475	Naukseni	November	100	100	100
476	Kreslava	November	72	72	72
478	Talsi	November	30	...	30
479	Bolderaja	November	56	56	56

* The woolens, thread, needles, and buttons listed in Table 374 were turned over to the clothing manufacturers in Riga, who returned 46,516 suits of clothing.

† Including laces.

LATVIA

Detail of Internal Deliveries of Clothing Outfits, by Local Committees

Table 381—*Continued*

Receipt No.	Local Committee	Date of Delivery	Shoes (Pairs)†	Stockings (Pairs)	Suits (Each)
		1921			
483	Riga Asylum "Kinderfreund"	November	20	20	20
485	Daudzeva	November	35	35	35
486	Olaine	November	24	24	24
487	Riga Asylums	November	883	883	883
	Total for November	....	**7,747**	**7,627**	**7,747**
488	Riga Asylum, Katolu Street	December	11	11	11
505	Dobele	December	20	20	20
508	Grienvalde	December	11	11	11
517	Liksnas	December	40	40	40
519	Libau District	December	96	...	96
524	Spare	December	90	90	90
529	Korsovka	December	24	24	24
540	Priduiska	December	14	14	14
553	Tome	December	5	5	5
559	Congress of the Devastated Districts of Latvia	December	446	446	446
	Total for December	....	**757**	**661**	**757**
		1922			
563	Tukums	January	20	20	50
564	Ventspils	January	50	30	100
567	Sloka	January	20	20	50
570	Jelgava	January	100	50	290
576	Riga Refugee Committee	January	300	300	400
581	Eglaine	January	20	...	50
582	Kalkuni	January	20	...	50
580	Valka	January	10	...	20
588	Milgravis	January	20	20	40
594	Jekabmiests	January	40	...	80
596	Rezekne	January	55	...	150
597	Cesis	January	20	...	40
599	Ludza	January	25	...	65
602	Latvian Red Cross at Assari	January	60	60	60
604	Jaun Jelgava	January	30	...	70
605	Rujene	January	10	...	25
609	Bolderaja	January	20	...	40
610	Livani	January	20	...	50
611	Vec Svarte	January	17	17	17
612	Libau	January	25	25	25
613	Dobele	January	10	...	20
614	Krustpils	January	30	20	75
615	Valmiera	January	30	10	60
616	Korsovka	January	10	...	20
620	Riga	January	254	...	473
631	Jaunciems	January	40	40	40
632	Congress of the Devastated Districts of Latvia	January	206	185	654
	Total for January	....	**1,462**	**797**	**3,014**
	Total ‡	....	**47,979**	**44,388**	**46,516**

‡ Equivalent to 57.7 metric tons.

Operation	Table No.	Flour	Rice	Beans, Peas
				ARMISTICE
A.R.A.—Congressional Appropriation, $100,000,000 Fund	383	2,565.9	84.2	185.1
A.R.A.—Finance on Freight, Insurance, etc., U.S. Liquidation Commission Supplies	144	.....	....	.....
U.S. Liquidation Commission (War Dept.)	122	.....	....	.....
Total American Relief	...	**2,565.9**	**84.2**	**185.1**
United Kingdom—Finance on Freight	133	.....	....	.....
Total Deliveries, Armistice Period	108	**2,565.9**	**84.2**	**185.1**
				RECONSTRUCTION
A.R.A.—Congressional Appropriation, $100,000,000 Fund	384, 388	351.0	83.0	77.8
A.R.A.-European Children's Fund	384, 388	42.6	15.9	25.4
Total Children's Relief	163	**393.6**	**98.9**	**103.2**
A.R.A.-E.C.F.—Student Relief *	384, 391	3.2	.8	1.7
Total Relief, Reconstruction Period	149	**396.8**	**99.7**	**104.9**
Grand Total Relief Deliveries	102	**2,962.7**	**183.9**	**290.0**

* Bulk sale, Latvia.

LITHUANIA—American Relief Administration

Detail by Steamers of Relief Deliveries Paid for by Funds from the Congressional Appropriation for Relief—Armistice Period, 1919

Table 383

Arrival No.	Steamer	Port of Sailing	Date of Arrival	Port of Arrival	Contents of Cargoes in Net Metric Tons of 1,000 Kilograms or 2,204.6 Pounds: Wheat Flour	Beans, Peas	Rice	Pork Products	Lard Substitute	Milk	Total Tons	Total Value
			1919									
126	Lake Wimico, III	Rotterdam	Apr. 15	Memel	1,078.5	....	....	.....	.....	....	1,078.5	$229,053.
154	Lake Eckhart, III	Rotterdam	Apr. 30	Memel	929.5	....	....	.....	.....	....	929.5	202,114.
274	Tyr	New York	June 12	Memel	551.6	1.1	....	.....	101.3	50.6	704.6	200,091.
326	Charlot	New York	July 2	Libau	.....	59.7	....	.....	.....	....	59.7	16,131.
343	Lake St. Clair, V *	Bordeaux	July 10	Libau	.....	....	....	278.2	.....	....	278.2	235,041.
347	Tyr	New York	July 12	Libau	6.3	124.3	....	.....	45.5	46.2	222.3	89,234.
363	Lake Dancey, IV †	Danzig	July 25	Libau	.....	....	84.2	.....	.....	....	84.2	24,427.
	Total				**2,565.9**	**185.1**	**84.2**	**278.2**	**146.8**	**96.8**	**3,357.0**	**$996,093.**

* Cargo from Army stocks in France purchased by American Relief Administration from U.S. Liquidation Commission.

† Delivery ex-Danzig stocks.

ummary of Relief Deliveries

Commodities in Net Metric Tons of 1,000 Kilograms or 2,204.6 Pounds								
Pork Products	Milk	Cocoa	Sugar	Misc. Food	Soap	Clothing and Misc.	Total Tons	Total Value
ERIOD								
425.0	96.8	....	....	......	...	.....	3,357.0	$ 996,093.08
.....	....	....	....	......	...	.....	......	48,930.00
.....	....	....	....	4,700.0	...	3,620.0	8,320.0	4,414,861.39
425.0	**96.8**	....	....	**4,700.0**	...	**3,620.0**	**11,677.0**	**$5,459,884.47**
.....	....	....	....	......	...	.....	......	57,120.00
425.0	**96.8**	....	....	**4,700.0**	...	**3,620.0**	**11,677.0**	**$5,517,004.47**
ERIOD								
28.0	307.5	57.2	95.9	......	5.0	.....	1,005.4	$ 351,789.53
19.1	58.2	3.4	9.3	......	...	13.0	186.9	111,060.61
47.1	**365.7**	**60.6**	**105.2**	......	**5.0**	**13.0**	**1,192.3**	**$ 462,850.14**
.5	1.3	.2	.7	......	...	......	8.4	926.78
47.6	**367.0**	**60.8**	**105.9**	......	**5.0**	**13.0**	**1,200.7**	**$ 463,776.92**
472.6	**463.8**	**60.8**	**105.9**	**4,700.0**	**5.0**	**3,633.0**	**12,877.7**	**$5,980,781.39**

LITHUANIA—A.R.A. and A.R.A.-European Children's Fund

Table 384 Summary of Arrivals by Operations—Reconstruction Period, 1919–1924

Operation	Table No.	Commodities in Net Metric Tons of 1,000 Kilograms or 2,204.6 Pounds										Total Value
		Flour	Rice	Beans, Peas	Pork Products	Milk	Cocoa	Sugar	Soap	Clothing	Total Tons	
R.A.—Congressional Appropriation, $100,000,000 Fund..........	385	351.0	83.0	77.8	28.0	307.5	57.2	95.9	5.0	....	1,005.4	$351,789.53
R.A.-European Children's Fund—Food*	386	45.8	16.7	27.1	19.6	59.5	3.6	10.0	...	....	182.3	50,521.81
R.A.-European Children's Fund—Clothing	387	.....	....	....	....	....	....	....	....	13.0	13.0	61,465.58
Total Arrivals*	....	**396.8**	**99.7**	**104.9**	**47.6**	**367.0**	**60.8**	**105.9**	**5.0**	**13.0**	**1,200.7**	**$463,776.92**

* 8.4 metric tons, value $926.78, included in Latvian arrivals and bulk
es.

LITHUANIA—

Table 385

Detail by Steamers of Arrivals for Children's Relief Paid for by Fund

Steamer	Port of Sailing	Date of Arrival	Port of Arrival	Wheat Flour	Rice
		1919			
Cape Henry	New York	Apr. 13	Pillau	....	....
Lake Eckhart, III (ex-Edgefield)	Rotterdam	Apr. 14	Pillau	90.0	....
Lake St. Regis, III	Rotterdam	Apr. 17	Pillau	....	....
Tyr	New York	June 12	Libau	201.0	....
Charlot	New York	July 2	Libau	....	....
Lake Dancey, IV	Danzig	July 25	Libau	60.0	83.0
Remschied *	New York	Aug. 21	Rotterdam	....	....
Stock †	(U.S.A.)	....	Riga	....	....
Total	....	....	....	**351.0**	**83.0**

* Transshipped on Bavaria—Rotterdam to Libau; arrived February 9, 1920.

† Transshipped via rail—Riga to Kovno; arrived 1921.

LITHUANIA—A.R.A.-European Children's Fund

Detail by Steamers or Source of Arrivals for Children's Relief Reconstruction Period, 1919–1924

Table 386

Steamer or Source	Port of Sailing	Date of Arrival	Port of Arrival	Commodities in Net Metric Tons of 1,000 Kilograms or 2,204.6 Pounds: Flour	Rice	Beans, Peas	Pork Products	Milk	Cocoa	Sugar	Total Tons	Total Value
		1919										
St. Croix, II *	Danzig	Dec. 12	Libau	...	...	...	13.5	...	...	...	13.5	$ 5,632.
		1921										
Riga Stock	Riga	Feb.	(Kovno)	...	15.1	...	...	...	...	...	15.1	2,014.
Warsaw Stock	(Warsaw)	Mar.	(Kovno)	...	...	23.9	5.2	44.0	3.2	8.6	84.9	27,024.
Riga Stock	Riga	Apr.	(Kovno)	2.9	.8	1.5	.4	14.2	.2	.7	20.7	7,307.
Latvian Bulk Sale ‡	Riga	....	(Kovno)	3.2	.8	1.7	.5	1.3	.2	.7	8.4	926.
Local Purchase †	(Kovno)	....	(Kovno)	39.7	...	...	...	...	...	...	39.7	7,548.
Removal of Warehouse	....	....	....	...	...	...	...	...	...	...	....	67.
Total	....	....	....	**45.8**	**16.7**	**27.1**	**19.6**	**59.5**	**3.6**	**10.0**	**182.3**	**$50,521.**

* Cargo purchased from Comité National, shipped from Rotterdam to Danzig via E. H. Stinnes.

‡ Included in Latvian arrivals. Cf. Tables 371, 377.

† Purchased from proceeds of sale of sugar. See Delive Table 389.

LITHUANIA-

Table 388

Summary of Internal Deliveries

Operation	Table No.	Flour	Rice	Beans, Peas
A.R.A.—Congressional Appropriation, $100,000,000 Fund	389	351.0	83.0	77.8
A.R.A.-European Children's Fund—Food	389	42.6	15.9	25.4
A.R.A.-European Children's Fund—Clothing	390	....	....	....
Total Children's Relief	....	**393.6**	**98.9**	**103.2**
A.R.A.-European Children's Fund—Student Feeding	391	3.2	.8	1.7
Total Relief, Reconstruction Period	382	**396.8**	**99.7**	**104.9**

merican Relief Administration

rom the Congressional Appropriation for Relief—Reconstruction Period, 1919–1924

Contents of Cargoes in Net Metric Tons of 1,000 Kilograms or 2,204.6 Pounds

Beans, Peas	Lard	Lard Substitute	Milk	Cocoa	Sugar	Soap	Total Tons	Total Value
8.0	12.0	....	45.6	....	1.9	...	67.5	$ 36,612.79
...	....	....	....	....	...	...	90.0	19,115.10
...	....	....	....	15.0	...	...	15.0	6,600.00
...	....	16.0	101.0	....	...	...	318.0	107,512.08
...	....	....	11.6	....	...	...	11.6	4,681.25
69.8	....	....	103.8	42.2	94.0	...	452.8	153,292.13
...	....	....	45.5	....	...	...	45.5	22,705.00
...	....	....	....	....	...	5.0	5.0	1,271.18
77.8	**12.0**	**16.0**	**307.5**	**57.2**	**95.9**	**5.0**	**1,005.4**	**$351,789.53**

LITHUANIA—A.R.A.-European Children's Fund

Detail by Steamers of Arrivals of Clothing and Accessories for Children's Relief—Reconstruction Period, 1919–1924

Table 387

Steamer	Port of Sailing and Call	Date of Arrival	Port of Arrival	Shoes (Pairs)	Laces (Pairs)	Stockings (Pairs)	Woolens (Yards)	Thread (Lbs.)	Needles (No.)	Buttons (No.)	Total Metric Tons	Total Value
		1919										
. Croix, II......	London, Danzig	Dec. 10	Riga	13,939	4,320	....	....	...	.....	.....	3.1	$26,218.27
eval, II	London	Dec. 19	Libau	.....	....	....	9,274	...	.....	.....	4.3	13,227.46
		1920										
. Thomas, I....	London, Danzig	Jan. 19	Riga	.....	1,008	4,992	8,704	350	15,000	49,680	3.7	16,895.43
eval, III	London	Feb. 6	Libau	.....	....	7,596	....	...	.....	.....	.7	3,458.56
. Thomas, II....	London, Danzig	Feb. 22	Riga	.....	7,200	....	1,066	...	.....	.....	1.2	1,665.86
Total	....	....	....	**13,939**	**12,528**	**12,588**	**19,044**	**350**	**15,000**	**49,680**	**13.0**	**$61,465.58**

.R.A. and A.R.A.-European Children's Fund

perations—Reconstruction Period, 1919–1924

Commodities in Net Metric Tons of 1,000 Kilograms or 2,204.6 Pounds

Pork Products	Milk	Cocoa	Sugar	Soap	Clothing	Total Tons	Total Value
28.0	307.5	57.2	95.9	5.0	....	1,005.4	$351,789.53
19.1	58.2	3.4	9.3	...	....	173.9	49,595.03
....	....	....	....	...	13.0	13.0	61,465.58
47.1	**365.7**	**60.6**	**105.2**	**5.0**	**13.0**	**1,192.3**	**$462,850.14**
.5	1.3	.2	.7	...	....	8.4	926.78
47.6	**367.0**	**60.8**	**105.9**	**5.0**	**13.0**	**1,200.7**	**$463,776.92**

LITHUANIA—A.R.A. and A.R.A.-European Children's Fund

Table 389 Detail of Internal Deliveries for Child Feeding, by Districts or Institutions, by Months—Reconstruction Period, 1919–1924

Receipt No.	District or Institution *	Date	Commodities in Net Metric Tons of 1,000 Kilograms or 2,204.6 Pounds									
			Flour	Rice	Beans, Peas	Pork Products	Milk Evap.	Milk Cond.	Cocoa	Sugar	Soap	Total Tons
		1919										
1	Kaunas (Kovno)	May 14	1.032	....	.164	.180	.212	....	.164	.410	....	2.16
2	Mariampolė	May 17	2.050	....	.328	.180	.600	....	.419	.410	....	3.98
3	Kaišedorys	May 17	1.228	....	.197	.180	.353	....	.222	.246	....	2.42
4	Šiauliai	May 17	3.080	....	.493	.180	.867	....	.480	.614	....	5.71
5	Taurage	May 17	2.050	....	.328	.180	.600	....	.307	.410	....	3.87
6	Priena	May 17	1.640	....	.263	.180	.427	....	.246	.328	....	3.08
7	Vilkaviškis	May 17	4.100	....	.657	.360	1.165	....	.687	.821	....	7.79
8	Jurbarkas	May 17	4.100	....	.657	.360	1.165	....	.687	.821	....	7.79
9	Ukmergė	May 21	2.050	....	.328	.180	.600	....	.307	.410	....	3.87
10	Alytus	May 22	1.640	....	.263	.180	.459	....	.246	.328	....	3.11
11	Kaunas (Kovno)	May 27	1.033	....	.164	.180	.211	....	.164	....	....	1.7
12	Kaunas (Kovno)	May 30	....	....	....	....	.283	....	....	....	....	.2
13	Kaunas (Kovno)	May 30	1.033	....	.164	.180	.468	....	.164	....	....	2.0
	Total for May	....	**25.036**	....	**4.006**	**2.520**	**7.410**	....	**4.093**	**4.798**	....	**47.8**
14	Panevėžys	June 2	4.100	....	.656	.360	1.138	....	.615	.820	....	7.6
15	Janava	June 3	1.033	....	.164	.180	.595	....	.154	....	....	2.1
16	Kaunas (Kovno)	June 6	2.050	....	.328	.180	1.120	....	.280	....	....	3.9
17	Kedainiai	June 6	1.230	....	.197	.180	.672	....	.168	....	....	2.4
18	Sėda	June 7	1.640	....	.263	.180	.853	....	.246	....	....	3.1
19	Telšiai	June 7	1.228	....	.197	.180	.706	....	.185	....	....	2.4
20	Kaunas (Kovno)	June 11	3.853	....	.606	.414	2.072	....	.518	....	....	7.4
21	Vilkija	June 11	.308	....	.050	.034	.168	....	.042	....	....	.6
22	Joniškis	June 12	.820	....	.131	.090	.448	....	.112	....	....	1.6
23	Pivašiūnai	June 13	.205	....	.033	....	.112	....	.024	....	....	.3
24	Rokiškis	June 13	3.085	....	.328	.336	1.678	....	.420	....	....	5.8
25	Raseiniai	June 13	....	....	....	....	.560	....	....	....	....	.5
26	Seinai	June 16	.513	....	.082	.056	.280	....	.070	....	....	1.0
27	Kupiškis	June 16	1.538	....	.246	.168	.840	....	.210	....	....	3.0
28	Veliuona	June 17	1.025	....	.164	.180	.560	....	.140	....	....	2.0
29	Pilviškiai	June 18	.103	....	.016	.011	.053	....	.014	....	....	.1
30	Utena	June 20	2.050	....	.328	.224	1.120	....	.280	....	....	4.0
31	Biržai	June 23	3.075	....	.492	.336	1.680	....	.420	....	....	6.0
32	Veiveriai	June 24	.513	....	.082	.056	.280	....	.070	....	....	1.0
33	Janava	June 27	.205	....	.033	.022	.112	....	.028	....	....	.4
34	Kaunas (Kovno)	June 30	4.818	....	....	.526	2.632	....	.658	....	....	8.6
35	Seinai	June 30	.410	....	....	.045	.219	....	.056	....	....	.7
36	Joniškis	June 30	....	....	....	.180	....	....	.112	....	....	.2
	Total for June	....	**33.802**	....	**4.396**	**3.938**	**17.898**	....	**4.822**	**.820**	....	**65.6**
37	Lapės	July 1	.072	....	....	.008	.039	....	.010	....	....	.1
38	Kedainiai	July 1	2.050	....	....	.224	1.120	....	.280	....	....	3.6
39	Vandziogala	July 3	.308	....	....	.034	.168	....	.042	....	....	.
40	Birštonis Sociales Apsargos	July 3	.205	....	....	.022	.106	....	.028	....	....	.
41	Garleva	July 3	.103	....	....	.011	.053	....	.014	....	....	.
42	Pakuonis	July 7	.103	....	....	.011	.053	....	.014	....	....	.
43	Skaudvilė	July 7	.205	....	....	.022	.106	....	.028	....	....	.
44	Janava	July 5	.615	....	....	....	.336	....	.084	....	....	1.
45	Balbieriškis	July 5	.410	....	....	.045	.228	....	.056	....	....	.
46	Pilviskiai	July 8	.820	....	....	.090	.425	....	.112	....	....	1.
47	Raseiniai	July 8	1.230	....	....	.137	.668	....	.168	....	....	2.
48	Vilkija	July 10	.308	....	....	....	.158	....	....	....	....	.
49	Vilkaviškis	July 11	1.640	....	....	.179	.896	....	.227	....	....	2.
50	Širvintai	July 14	.410	....	....	.045	.212	....	.056	....	....	.
51	Getvenu, Valsčiaus	July 14	.205	....	....	.023	.105	....	.028	....	....	.
52	Daršuniskis	July 15	.103	....	....	.011	.053	....	.014	....	....	.

* Spelling of cities revised in accordance with "Visa Lietuva," published by Central Statistical Bureau of Minister of Finance, Kovno, 1925.

LITHUANIA

Detail of Internal Deliveries for Child Feeding, by Districts or Institutions, by Months

Table 389—*Continued*

District or Institution *	Date	Flour	Rice	Beans, Peas	Pork Products	Milk Evap.	Milk Cond.	Cocoa	Sugar	Soap	Total Tons
		Commodities in Net Metric Tons of 1,000 Kilograms or 2,204.6 Pounds									
	1919										
Garleva	July 15	.153	....	....	.016	.070	....	.021	....	....	.260
Kaunas (Kovno)	July 16	2.562	....	....	.280	1.408	....	.420	....	....	4.670
Turžėnai	July 16	.103	....	....	.011	.053	....	.014	....	....	.181
Prienai	July 17	.512	....	....	.056	.281	....	.084	....	....	.933
Sėda	July 18	3.075	....	....	.336	2.068	....	.420	....	....	5.899
Mariampolė	July 19	2.050	....	....	.224	1.120	....	.252	....	....	3.646
Janava	July 21	.513	....	....	.056	.281	....	.084	....	....	.934
Tauraziai	July 21	.512	....	....	.056	.281	....	.084	....	....	.933
Lapės	July 21	.103	....	....	.011	.053	....	.014	....	....	.181
Kredrians	July 24	.615	....	....	.067	.336	....	.084	....	....	1.102
Pakuonis	July 25	.308	....	....	.034	.176	....	.042	....	....	.560
Kaunas (Kovno)	July 25	3.075	....	....	.220	1.689	....	.336	....	....	5.320
Ukmergė	July 25	2.050	....	....	.224	1.126	....	.252	....	....	3.652
Ministerci Tikeium	July 25	....	....	....	.127	....	....	....	....	....	.127
Kretinga	July 26	1.640	....	....	.116	.915	....	.168	....	....	2.839
Vilkija	July 29	.615	....	....	....	.350	....	.084	....	....	1.049
Raudonoaris	July 29	.154	....	....	.017	.088	....	.021	....	....	.280
Veliuona	July 30	.512	....	....	.056	.281	....	.070	....	....	.919
Kaunas (Kovno)	July 30	1.543	....	....	.232	.269	....	.252	....	....	2.296
Garleva	July 30	.102	....	....	.022	.017	....	.028	....	....	.169
Sialiai	July 30	.512	....	....	.116	.140	....	.100	....	....	.868
Prienai	July 30	.615	....	....	.116	.176	....	.168	....	....	1.075
Alytus	July 30	1.538	....	....	.232	.422	....	.252	....	....	2.444
Pilviškiai	July 30	.615	....	....	.062	.352	....	.084	....	....	1.113
Kaunas (Kovno)	July 31	....	....	....	....	....	....	....	.046	....	.046
Valdyba, Valgykles	July 9	.298	....	.049	.033	....	.167	.045	.002	....	.594
Panevėžys	July 10	.410	....	.066	.048	....	.329	.052	.001	....	.906
Raguva	July 20	.113	....	.016	.014	....	.066	.016	....	....	.225
Valdyba, Valgykles	July 25	.298	....	.049	.033	....	.167	.045	....	....	.592
Prieglauda	July 26	.045	....	.002	.002	....	.026	.003	....	....	.078
Panevėžys	July 26	.410	....	.066	.048	....	.230	.052	....	....	.806
Prieglauda	July 26	.015	....	.002	.001	....	.008	.002	....	....	.028
Panevėžys	July 28	.098	....	.016	.003	....	.052	.005	....	....	.174
Raguva	July 30	.113	....	.016	.014	....	.066	.016	....	....	.225
Panevėžys, Sabačius	July 31	.031	....	.002	.001	....	.016	.002	....	....	.052
Total for July	....	**34.095**	....	**.284**	**3.746**	**16.678**	**1.127**	**4.733**	**.049**	....	**60.712**
Seinai	Aug. 5	1.025	....	....	.112	.563	....	.140	....	....	1.840
Janava	Aug. 6	.513	....	....	.056	.281	....	.070	....	....	.920
Čekiškė	Aug. 8	.410	....	....	.044	.228	....	.056	....	....	.738
Vilkaviškis	Aug. 8	3.075	....	....	.336	1.689	....	.226	....	....	5.326
Raseiniai	Aug. 11	6.150	....	....	.672	3.379	....	.788	....	....	10.989
Turžėnai	Aug. 12	.205	....	....	.023	.105	....	.028	....	....	.361
Lapės	Aug. 12	.103	....	....	.013	.053	....	.017	....	....	.186
Kaunas (Kovno)	Aug. 16	10.250	....	....	1.120	5.632	....	1.260	2.050	....	20.312
Balbieriškis	Aug. 14	.512	....	....	.022	.387	....	.028	.164	....	1.113
Gudeliai	Aug. 16	.128	....	....	.014	.070	....	.018	.051	....	.281
Kaunas (Kovno)	Aug. 19	.717	....	.228	.157	.475	....	.098	.144	....	1.819
Janava	Aug. 19	1.025	....	....	.112	.563	....	.140	.205	....	2.045
Vilkaviškis	Aug. 21	3.075	....	....	.336	1.689	....	.336	.615	....	6.051
Kėdainiai	Aug. 22	6.150	....	....	.672	3.379	....	.756	1.230	....	12.187
Kaisedorys	Aug. 22	6.150	....	....	.672	3.379	....	.756	1.230	....	12.187
Prienai	Aug. 22	1.025	....	....	.056	.563	....	.084	.205	....	1.933
Lapės	Aug. 22	.205	....	....	.022	.124	....	.028	.041	....	.420
Panevėžys	Aug. 27	.512	....	....	.056	.281	....	.070	.102	....	1.021
Veliuona	Aug. 28	1.025	....	....	.112	.563	....	.140	.205	....	2.045

[*Continued on next page*]

LITHUANIA

Detail of Internal Deliveries for Child Feeding, by Districts or Institutions, by Months

Table 389—*Continued*

Receipt No.	District or Institution *	Date	Flour	Rice	Beans, Peas	Pork Products	Milk Evap.	Milk Cond.	Cocoa	Sugar	Soap	Total Tons
		Commodities in Net Metric Tons of 1,000 Kilograms or 2,204.6 Pounds										
		1919										
98	Vainatrakiu, Mazasniams Komitetui	Aug. 28	.205	....	....	.022	.123	....	.028	.041	....	.4
391	Panevėžys	Aug. 2	.200	....	.033	.024	....	.114	.030	....	....	.4
393	Prieglauda	Aug. 9	.015	....	.002	.001	....	.002	.002	.001	....	.0
383	Valdyba, Valgykles	Aug. 12	.298	....	.049	.033	....	.167	.044	.118	....	.7
378	Panevėžys	Aug. 13	.410	....	.066	.009	....	.330	.052	.134	....	1.0
384	Prieglauda	Aug. 13	.049	....	.003	.002	....	.030	.003	.001	....	.0
379	Surdegis	Aug. 18	.027	....	.002	....	....	.016	.002	.005	....	.0
318	Zagarė	Aug. 21	.196	.010	.066	....	....	.120	.012	....	....	.4
319	Mažeikiai	Aug. 22	.426	....	.066	....	....	.240	....	....	....	.7
320	Kretinga	Aug. 22	4.100	....	.650	....	....	2.500	.609	....	....	7.8
321	Kuršėnai	Aug. 24	.524	....	.085	....	....	.300	.070	....	....	.9
322	Šiauliai, Lopšelis	Aug. 24	.656	.098	.410	....	....	....	....	....	....	1.1
323	Pasiausis	Aug. 24	.400	....	.051	....	....	.169	.038	....	....	.6
314	Šiauliai, Jewish Charity Society	Aug. 26	1.049	....	.164	....	....	.600	.147	....	....	1.9
315	Radviliškis	Aug. 26	1.246	....	.196	.196	....	.720	.180	....	....	2.5
316	Mažeikiai	Aug. 26	1.115	....	.149	....	....	.590	....	....	....	1.8
317	Tauragė	Aug. 28	2.755	....	.422	....	....	1.656	.442	....	....	5.2
394	Panevėžys	Aug. 28	.395	....	.065	....	....	.828	.057	.198	....	1.5
395	Panevėžys	Aug. 30	.164	....	.246	....	....	.740	.183	.526	....	1.8
	Total for August	....	**56.485**	**.108**	**2.953**	**4.894**	**23.526**	**9.122**	**6.938**	**7.266**	....	**111.2**
99	Rumsiskės	Sept. 2	.308	....	....	.034	....	.176	.042	....	....	.5
100	Kruonis	Sept. 2	.564	....	....	.062	....	.334	.077	....	....	1.0
101	Viliampolio	Sept. 2	.308	....	....	.034	....	.176	.042	....	....	.5
102	Raudondvaris	Sept. 2	.512	....	....	.056	....	.281	.070	....	....	.9
103	Vikija	Sept. 2	.615	....	....	.068	....	.352	.084	....	....	1.1
104	Balbieriškis	Sept. 2	.820	....	....	.090	....	.357	.112	....	....	1.3
105	Panevėžys	Sept. 4	.513	....	....	.056	....	.281	.082	....	....	.9
106	Jurbarkas	Sept. 4	1.230	....	....	.134	....	.704	.168	....	....	2.2
107	Čekiškė	Sept. 5	.410	....	....	.045	....	.228	.056	....	....	.7
108	Seredžius	Sept. 5	.615	....	....	.067	....	.352	.084	....	....	1.1
110	Alytus	Sept. 15	5.125	....	....	.696	....	2.816	.672	....	....	9.3
111	Janava	Sept. 15	.820	....	....	....	....	.563	.140	....	....	1.5
112	——————§	Sept. 16	.475	.262	.262	....	....	....	.112	....	....	1.1
113	Kaunas (Kovno)	Sept. 16	5.125	1.640	.820	....	....	5.632	1.260	....	....	14.4
114	Gudeliai	Sept. 15	.205	....	....	....	....	.105	.028	....	....	[illegible]
115	Ukmergė	Sept. 19	2.050	....	....	....	....	1.126	.280	....	....	3.4
116	Lapės	Sept. 25	.123	....	.037	....	....	....	.018	....	....	[illegible]
117	Paežerėliai	Sept. 25	.281	....	.080	....	....	....	.140	....	....	[illegible]
118	Rumsiskės	Sept. 30	....	.049	.099	....	....	.176	.042	....	....	[illegible]
396	N. Radviliskis	Sept. 1	....	....	.082	....	....	.098	.065	.180	....	[illegible]
397	Surdegis	Sept. 2	....	....	....	....	....	.003	....	.002	....	[illegible]
398	Panevėžys	Sept. 6	....	....	.004	....	....	.007	.002	.004	....	[illegible]
399	Raguva	Sept. 9	....	....	.050	....	....	.069	.035	.115	....	[illegible]
400	Panevėžys	Sept. 12	....	....	.002	....	....	.012	.003	.017	....	[illegible]
401	Panevėžys	Sept. 12	....	....	.069	....	....	.090	.052	.134	....	[illegible]
402	Panevėžys, Jewish Children	Sept. 12	....	....	.052	....	....	.826	.057	.132	....	1.
324	Mažeikiai	Sept. 12	15.744	30.600	15.750	....	....	....	....	....	....	62.
403	Panevėžys	Sept. 16	....	....	.004	....	....	.052	.006	.033	....	[illegible]
325	Šiauliai	Sept. 16	.459	....	.135	.027	....	.120	....	.045	....	[illegible]
326	Šiauliai	Sept. 16	1.246	....	.215	....	....	.380	....	.090	....	1.
404	Surdegis, Panevėžys	Sept. 18	....	....	.001	....	....	.008	.002	.007	....	[illegible]
405	Panevėžys	Sept. 20	....	....	....	....	....	.005	.001	.004	....	[illegible]
327	Šiauliai	Sept. 20	.656	....	.135	....	....	.180	....	.045	....	1.
406	Panevėžys, Jewish Society	Sept. 22	....	....	.001	....	....	.008	.002	.004	....	[illegible]
328	Šiauliai	Sept. 26	.459	....	....	....	....	.120	....	.045	....	[illegible]
329	Mažeikiai	Sept. 27	3.148	....	....	....	....	.615	....	.450	....	4.
330	Pašiaušis, Šiauliai	Sept. 30	.361	....	.067	....	....	.984	....	.067	....	1.
	Total for September	....	**42.172**	**32.551**	**17.865**	**1.369**	....	**17.236**	**3.734**	**1.374**	....	**116.**

§ Name of local committee listed on this receipt is illegible.

LITHUANIA

Detail of Internal Deliveries for Child Feeding, by Districts or Institutions, by Months

Table 389—*Continued*

Receipt No.	District or Institution *	Date	Flour	Rice	Beans, Peas	Pork Products	Milk Evap.	Milk Cond.	Cocoa	Sugar	Soap	Total Tons
		1919										
9	Panevėžys	Oct. 2	....	.017	.132	....	....	.246	.056	....	....	.451
0	Prienai	Oct. 6	....	.066	.525	....	....	.915	.224	....	....	1.730
1	Čekiškė	Oct. 6	....	.066	.130	....	....	.228	.056	.032	....	.512
2	Viliampolio	Oct. 6	....	.016	.098	....	....	.176	.042	.041	....	.373
3	Balbieriškis	Oct. 8	....	.032	.228	....	....	.422	.098	....	....	.780
4	Vilkija	Oct. 8	....	.033	.196	....	....	.352	.084	....	....	.665
5	Seredžius	Oct. 11	....	.066	.130	....	....	.246	.056	.029	....	.527
6	Paežerėliai	Oct. 15	....	.066	.328	....	....	.563	.140	....	....	1.097
7	Panevėžys	Oct. 15	13.120	....	....	....	....	....	....	....	....	13.120
8	Jurbarkas	Oct. 17	.820	.033	.392	....	....	.686	.168	.082	....	2.181
9	Kaunas (Kovno)	Oct. 17	.308	.016	.098	....	....	.176	.042	.041	....	.681
0	Kaunas (Kovno)	Oct. 20	.205	.012	.064	....	....	.105	.028	.014	....	.428
1	Janava	Oct. 20	.820	.164	.820	....	....	1.584	.252	.164	....	3.804
2	Kaunas (Kovno)	Oct. 21	4.100	.820	4.100	....	....	7.920	1.500	.820	....	19.260
3	Kaunas (Kovno)	Oct. 21	.820	.164	.820	....	....	1.584	.300	.164	....	3.852
4	Lapės	Oct. 24	.164	.033	.164	....	....	.316	.060	.033	....	.770
5	Veliuona	Oct. 24	.820	.164	.820	....	....	1.800	.300	.164	....	4.068
6	Kruonis	Oct. 28	.410	.082	....	....	....	.900	.150	.082	....	1.624
7	Raudondvaris	Oct. 28	.410	.082	.410	....	....	.900	.150	.082	....	2.034
1	Taurage	Oct. 2	2.427	....	.400	....	....	1.560	....	....	....	4.387
2	Šiauliai, Lopŝelis	Oct. 2	.656	.900	.135	.054	....	....	....	.090	....	1.835
3	Šiauliai	Oct. 3	.656	....	.135	....	....	.220	....	.045	....	1.056
4	Kuršėnai	Oct. 7	.525	....	.090	....	....	.300	....	....	....	.915
5	Šiauliai	Oct. 10	.656	....	.135	....	....	.180	....	.045	....	1.016
6	Šiauliai	Oct. 10	.196	.050	.090	....	....	.160	....	.045	....	.541
7	Šiauliai, Lopŝelis	Oct. 11	....	....	....	....	....	....	....	.092	....	.092
8	Mažeikiai	Oct. 14	....	.215	....	....	....	....	....	.230	....	.445
9	Zagarė	Oct. 23	.394	....	.090	....	....	.160	....	....	....	.644
0	Šiauliai	Oct. 23	.787	....	....	....	....	.340	....	.138	....	1.265
1	Telšiai	Oct. 24	3.280	....	....	....	....	1.340	....	.046	....	4.666
2	Šiauliai	Oct. 24	.328	.135	.135	....	....	.180	....	....	....	.778
4	Šiauliai, Jewish Charity Society	Oct. 25	2.361	.215	.360	....	....	.680	....	....	....	3.616
5	Šiauliai	Oct. 27	....	.045	....	....	....	....	....	....	....	.045
6	Šiauliai, Jewish Society	Oct. 28	.131	.045	....	....	....	.060	....	....	....	.236
7	Šiauliai	Oct. 29	.590	....	.215	.135	....	.420	....	....	....	1.360
	Total for October	....	**34.984**	**3.537**	**11.240**	**.189**	....	**24.719**	**3.706**	**2.479**	....	**80.854**
8	Balbieriškis	Nov. 3	.328	.066	.328	....	....	....	.120	.066	....	.908
9	Alytus	Nov. 4	.246	.049	.246	....	....	....	.090	.049	....	.680
0	Panevėžys	Nov. 5	.246	.049	.246	....	....	....	.090	.049	....	.680
1	Kėdainiai	Nov. 5	3.280	.656	3.280	....	....	....	1.200	.656	....	9.072
2	Paežerėliai	Nov. 5	.492	.098	.492	....	....	....	.180	.098	....	1.360
3	Ukmergė	Nov. 9	.984	.197	.984	....	....	....	.360	.197	....	2.722
4	Kaunas (Kovno)	Nov. 10	.197	.039	.197	....	....	.216	.072	.039	....	.760
5	Čekiškė	Nov. 11	.164	.033	.164	....	....	....	.060	.033	....	.454
6	Rumšiškės	Nov. 11	.246	.049	.246	....	....	....	.090	.049	....	.680
7	Daršuniskis	Nov. 13	.492	.049	....	....	....	....	.090	.049	....	.680
8	Vilkija	Nov. 13	.492	.049	....	....	....	....	.090	.049	....	.680
9	Seredžius	Nov. 15	.328	.033	....	....	....	....	.060	.033	....	.454
0	Kaunas (Kovno)	Nov. 17	.492	.098	.492	....	....	.640	.180	.098	....	2.000
1	Čekeškė	Nov. 20	.328	.033	.328	....	....	....	.060	.033	....	.782
2	Garleva	Nov. 22	.016	.008	....	.004	....	.004	.002	.008	....	.042
3	Kaunas (Kovno)	Nov. 24	4.100	1.845	2.050	....	....	....	1.500	2.050	....	11.545
4	Kaunas (Kovno)	Nov. 24	.820	.272	.205	....	....	....	.300	.205	....	1.802
5	Panevėžys	Nov. 28	.246	.049	.246	....	....	....	.090	.123	....	.754
6	Alytus	Nov. 29	1.025	.369	.697	....	....	....	.375	.513	....	2.979
8	Šiauliai	Nov. 2	.393	....	....	....	....	....	....	....	....	.393

Commodities in Net Metric Tons of 1,000 Kilograms or 2,204.6 Pounds

[*Continued on next page*]

LITHUANIA

Detail of Internal Deliveries for Child Feeding, by Districts or Institutions, by Months

Table 389—*Continued*

Receipt No.	District or Institution *	Date	Commodities in Net Metric Tons of 1,000 Kilograms or 2,204.6 Pounds									
			Flour	Rice	Beans, Peas	Pork Products	Milk: Evap.	Milk: Cond.	Cocoa	Sugar	Soap	Total Tons
		1919										
349	Telšiai	Nov. 2	1.640	....	....	....	....	.660	....	.344	....	2.6
350	Pašiaušis	Nov. 5	.393	....	.090	....	....	.260	....	....	....	.7
343	Šiauliai, Lopšelis	Nov. 6	.656	....	....	....	....	....	....	....	....	.6
351	Šiauliai	Nov. 6	.393	.090	....	....	....	....	....	....	....	.4
352	Joniškis	Nov. 6	.131	.045	.045	....	....	.080	....	....	....	.3
	Total for November	....	**18.128**	**4.176**	**10.336**	**.004**	**....**	**1.860**	**5.009**	**4.741**	**....**	**44.2**
157	Gustaičio	Dec. 2	.820	....	....	.180	....	.211	.016	.820	....	2.0
158	Prienai	Dec. 3	....	.394	....	....	....	....	.120	.164	....	.6
159	Kaunas (Kovno)	Dec. 3	.328	.033	....	.016	....	.360	....	.328	....	1.0
160	Gustaičio	Dec. 4	.164	.656	....	....	....	....	.164	.045	....	1.0
161	Balbieriškis	Dec. 5	....	.394	....	....	....	....	.120	.164	....	.6
162	Čekiškė	Dec. 10	....	.197	....	....	....	....	.060	.082	....	.3
163	Vilkaviškis	Dec. 11	....	1.476	....	....	....	....	.459	.615	....	2.5
164	Gustaičio	Dec. 12	....	....	....	....	....	.053	.164	.664	....	.8
353	Mažeikiai	Dec. 16	.820	.180	....	....	....	.650	....	.132	....	1.7
354	Šiauliai	Dec. 17	1.115	.270	....	....	....	.560	....	....	....	1.9
165	Vilkija	Dec. 16	....	.295	....	....	....	....	.092	....	....	[illegible]
166	Seredzius	Dec. 16	....	.197	....	....	....	....	.062	....	....	[illegible]
167	Veliuona	Dec. 17	....	.820	....	....	....	....	.119	.039	....	[illegible]
168	Kaunas (Kovno)	Dec. 18	.127	.262	....	....	....	....	.090	.086	....	[illegible]
169	Kaunas (Kovno)	Dec. 31	.312	.295	....	....	....	....	....	.443	....	1.
	Total for December	....	**3.686**	**5.469**	**....**	**.196**	**....**	**1.834**	**1.466**	**3.582**	**....**	**16.**
		1920										
170	Kaunas (Kovno)	Jan. 2	.246	.246	....	....	....	.479	....	.123	....	1.
171	Kaunas (Kovno)	Jan. 2	.328	.082	....	....	....	.158	.060	.082	....	[illegible]
172	Rumšiškės	Jan. 7	....	.164	....	....	....	....	.060	.041	....	[illegible]
173	Zasliai	Jan. 7	.164	.164	....	....	....	....	....	.041	....	[illegible]
174	Panevėžys	Jan. 8	....	.246	....	....	....	....	.090	.123	....	[illegible]
175	Ukmergė	Jan. 8	....	.656	....	....	....	....	.246	.164	....	1.
176	Daršuniskis	Jan. 8	....	.205	....	....	....	....	.075	.098	....	[illegible]
177	Pivašiūnai	Jan. 9	....	.205	....	....	....	....	....	....	....	[illegible]
178	Kaunas (Kovno)	Jan. 10	....	.205	....	....	....	....	.075	.103	....	[illegible]
179	Kaunas (Kovno)	Jan. 13	.410	4.510	....	....	....	....	1.691	.820	....	7.
180	Rumšiškės	Jan. 15	....	.098	....	.036	....	....	.036	....	....	[illegible]
181	Čekiškė	Jan. 15	....	.164	....	.060	....	....	.060	....	....	[illegible]
182	Kaunas (Kovno)	Jan. 15	....	....	....	1.650	....	....	....	....	....	1.
183	Lekėčiai	Jan. 16	....	.246	....	.090	....	....	.090	....	....	[illegible]
184	Kaunas (Kovno)	Jan. 16	....	.057	....	.021	....	....	.021	....	....	[illegible]
185	Alytus	Jan. 16	.082	.082	....	.060	....	....	.030	.041	....	[illegible]
186	Lapės	Jan. 17	....	.082	....	.030	....	....	.030	....	....	[illegible]
187	Kaunas (Kovno)	Jan. 21	....	....	....	.072	....	....	....	....	....	[illegible]
188	Pakuonis	Jan. 21	....	....	....	.120	....	....	....	....	....	[illegible]
189	Vilkija	Jan. 22	....	.246	....	.090	....	....	.090	....	....	[illegible]
190	Vilkaviškis	Jan. 22	....	1.230	....	.450	....	....	.450	....	....	2.
191	Ukmergė	Jan. 23	....	....	....	.240	....	....	....	....	....	[illegible]
192	Veiveriai	Jan. 26	....	.062	....	.021	....	....	.021	....	....	[illegible]
193	Seredzius	Jan. 30	....	.164	....	.060	....	....	.060	....	....	[illegible]
194	Balbieriskis	Jan. 30	....	.328	....	.120	....	....	.120	....	....	[illegible]
195	Prienai	Jan. 31	....	.410	....	.150	....	....	.150	....	....	[illegible]
	Total for January	....	**1.230**	**9.852**	**....**	**3.270**	**....**	**.637**	**3.455**	**1.636**	**....**	**20**
196	Rumšiškės	Feb. 3	....	.246	....	.090	....	....	.090	....	....	
197	Kaunas (Kovno)	Feb. 3	.246	.246	....	.090	....	....	.090	.123	....	
198	Garleva	Feb. 3	....	.098	....	.036	....	....	.036	....	....	
199	Kaunas (Kovno)	Feb. 4	.197	.197	....	.072	....	.088	.072	.098	....	
200	Girkalnis	Feb. 5	....	.071	....	.026	....	....	.026	....	....	

LITHUANIA

Detail of Internal Deliveries for Child Feeding, by Districts or Institutions, by Months

Table 389—*Continued*

Receipt No.	District or Institution *	Date	Flour	Rice	Beans, Peas	Pork Products	Milk Evap.	Milk Cond.	Cocoa	Sugar	Soap	Total Tons
		1920										
201	Paežerėliai	Feb. 5	....	.410	....	.150	....	....	.150	....	....	.710
202	Raudondvaris	Feb. 10	....	.205	....	.075	....	....	.075	....	....	.355
203	Panevėžys	Feb. 10	....	.328	....	.120	....	....	.120	....	....	.568
204	Kretinga	Feb. 10	....	.205	....	.075	....	....	.075	....	....	.355
205	Daršuniskis	Feb. 10	....	.205	....	.075	....	....	.075	....	....	.355
206	Alytus	Feb. 10	....	.082	....	.030	....	....	.030	....	....	.142
207	Kaišedorys	Feb. 11	....	.820	....	.300	....	....	.300	....	....	1.420
208	Čekiškė	Feb. 11	....	.164	....	.060	....	....	.060	....	....	.284
209	Rumšiškės	Feb. 12	....	.197	....	.072	....	....	.072	....	....	.341
210	Mariampolė	Feb. 13	....	....	....	.900	....	....	.900	....	....	1.800
211	Kaunas (Kovno)	Feb. 13	6.150	2.666	....	1.560	....	3.280	1.845	2.665	....	18.166
212	Raudondvaris	Feb. 17	....	.205	....	.075	....	....	.075	....	....	.355
213	Kretinga	Feb. 19	....	.820	....	.300	....	....	.300	....	....	1.420
214	Seinai	Feb. 20	....	.164	....	.060	....	....	.060	....	....	.284
215	Lekečiai	Feb. 20	....	.246	....	.090	....	....	.090	....	....	.426
216	Raseiniai	Feb. 20	....	.082	.082	.060	....	....	.060	.041	....	.325
217	Vilkija	Feb. 21	....	.246	....	.090	....	....	.090	....	....	.426
218	Janava	Feb. 23	....	....	....	.600	....	.350	.750	....	....	1.700
219	Vilkaviškis	Feb. 23	....	1.230	....	.450	....	....	.450	....	....	2.130
220	Seinai	Feb. 23	....	....	....	.960	....	....	1.200	....	....	2.160
221	Utena	Feb. 23	....	....	....	.240	....	....	.300	....	....	.540
222	Seredzius	Feb. 27	....	.164	....	.045	....	.264	.060	....	....	.533
223	Balbieriškis	Feb. 28	....	....	....	.122	....	.528	.016	....	....	.666
224	Lapes	Feb. 28	....	....	....	.024	....	.158	.030	....	....	.212
99	Panevėžys, Mrs. Netenburg	Feb. 1	.001	....	....	....	....	....	....	....	....	.001
00	Panevėžys, Polish Shelter	Feb. 3	....	....	.004	....	....	....	.003	.002	....	.009
01	Panevėžys, Surdegiu Shelter	Feb. 4	.033	....	.005	....	....	....	.004	.020	....	.062
02	Panevėžys, Catholic Shelter	Feb. 4	....	....	.020	....	....	....	.017	.051	....	.088
03	Panevėžys, Jewish Poor, Kupiškis	Feb. 5	....	....	.050	....	....	....	.035	.101	....	.186
04	Panevėžys, War Sufferers' Relief Organization	Feb. 6	....	....	.002	....	....	....	.002	.004	....	.008
05	Panevėžys, Jewish Committee of Raguva	Feb. 9	....	....	.036	....	....	....	.020	.084	....	.140
06	Panevėžys, Catholic Shelter	Feb. 14	....	....	.017	....	....	....	.016	.050	....	.083
07	Panevėžys, Polish Stelter	Feb. 14	....	....	.004	....	....	....	.003	.018	....	.025
08	Panevėžys, Jewish Children	Feb. 17	....	....	.082	....	....	....	.067	.198	....	.347
09	Panevėžys, 1,000 Christian Children	Feb. 17	....	....	.164	....	....	....	.136	.426	....	.726
10	Panevėžys, Jewish Orphans	Feb. 18	....	....	.033	....	....	....	.021	.082	....	.136
11	Panevėžys, Jewish Children, Kupiškis	Feb. 24	....	....	.050	....	....	....	.036	.103	....	.189
12	Panevėžys, Jewish Children	Feb. 24	....	....	.066	....	....	....	.069	.213	....	.348
13	Panevėžys, Christian Children	Feb. 1	....	....	.200	....	....	....	.150	.429	....	.779
55	Kaunas (Kovno)	Feb. 2	6.544	....	....	4.920	....	1.200	....	....	....	12.664
56	Šiauliai	Feb. 13	1.460	....	.131	....	....	.900	....	....	....	2.491
57	Raudėnai	Feb. 19	.757	.757	.131	....	....	.540	....	....	....	2.185
58	Pasiausis	Feb. 23	.378	.396	.265	....	....	....	....	....	....	1.039
59	Kretinga	Feb. 23	.822	.672	.806	....	....	....	....	....	....	2.300
60	Kuršėnai	Feb. 23	1.643	1.624	.265	....	....	....	....	....	....	3.532
61	Šiauliai	Feb. 25	3.300	4.923	....	....	....	....	....	....	....	8.223
62	Tauragė	Feb. 27	1.643	.396	2.067	....	....	....	....	....	....	4.106
63	Šiauliai, Kurtavėnai	Feb. 27	.659	.495	.265	....	....	....	....	....	....	1.419
64	Šiauliai Užventis	Feb. 27	.120	....	.034	....	....	....	....	....	....	.154
65	Stačiūnai	Feb. 27	.755	.543	.265	....	....	....	....	....	....	1.563
	Total for February		**24.708**	**19.103**	**5.044**	**11.767**	....	**7.308**	**8.076**	**4.708**	....	**80.714**

Commodities in Net Metric Tons of 1,000 Kilograms or 2,204.6 Pounds

[*Continued on next page*]

LITHUANIA

Detail of Internal Deliveries for Child Feeding, by Districts or Institutions, by Months

Table 389—*Continued*

Receipt No.	District or Institution *	Date	Flour	Rice	Beans, Peas	Pork Products	Milk Evap.	Milk Cond.	Cocoa	Sugar	Soap	Total Tons
			Commodities in Net Metric Tons of 1,000 Kilograms or 2,204.6 Pounds									
		1920										
225	Rumšiškės	Mar. 1	.042	.216	....	.093	....	.475	.093	.013	....	.9[illegible]
226	Kaunas (Kovno)	Mar. 1	.164	.123	....	.176	....	.704	.120	....	....	1.2[illegible]
227	Kedainiai	Mar. 1	....	.820	....	.480	....	2.220	.600	.328	....	4.4[illegible]
228	Sėda	Mar. 2	.164	....	.082	.060	....	.316	.060	.043	....	.7[illegible]
229	Šiauliai	Mar. 2	....	.164	....	.048	....	.316	.060	.016	....	.6[illegible]
230	Kaunas (Kovno)	Mar. 3	.164	.197	....	.029	....	.387	.074	.098	....	.9[illegible]
231	Panevėžys	Mar. 3	....	....	....	.480	....	2.220	.600	....	....	3.3[illegible]
232	Panevėžys	Mar. 8	....	.410	....	.120	....	.900	.150	.082	....	1.6[illegible]
233	Naumiestis	Mar. 9	....	....	....	....	....	.100	....	.066	....	.1[illegible]
234	Daršuniskis	Mar. 10	....	.205	....	.060	....	.450	.075	....	....	.7[illegible]
235	Kaunas (Kovno)	Mar. 9	....	....	....	....	....	.020	....	....	....	.0[illegible]
236	Kaunas (Kovno)	Mar. 10	.310	4.920	....	1.558	....	7.035	1.845	2.665	....	18.3[illegible]
237	Kruonis	Mar. 10	....	.102	....	.060	....	.320	.075	....	....	.5[illegible]
238	Pakuonis	Mar. 10	....	.082	....	.048	....	.240	.060	....	....	.4[illegible]
239	Paežerėliai	Mar. 11	....	....	....	.120	....	.620	.150	....	....	.8[illegible]
240	Alytus	Mar. 11	....	....	....	.300	....	1.560	....	....	....	1.8[illegible]
241	Girkalnis	Mar. 15	.033	.066	....	....	....	.140	.024	....	....	.2[illegible]
242	Čekiškė	Mar. 15	.082	....	....	.048	....	.240	.060	.016	....	.4[illegible]
243	Seinai	Mar. 17	.123	....	....	.072	....	.300	.090	.025	....	.6[illegible]
244	Rumšiškės	Mar. 17	.049	....	....	....	....	.140	....	.010	....	.1[illegible]
245	Telšiai	Mar. 17	.041	....	....	.024	....	.120	.050	.008	....	.2[illegible]
246	Sėda	Mar. 18	.070	....	....	.041	....	.220	.051	.014	....	.[illegible]
247	Veliuona	Mar. 18	.205	....	....	.120	....	.620	.150	.041	....	1.1[illegible]
248	Kaišedorys	Mar. 20	.205	....	....	.120	....	.620	.150	.041	....	1.1[illegible]
249	Raudondvaris	Mar. 22	.205	....	....	.120	....	.620	.150	.041	....	1.1[illegible]
250	Janava	Mar. 23	.049	....	....	.014	....	.060	.009	.025	....	.1[illegible]
251	Raseiniai	Mar. 23	.205	....	....	.120	....	.620	.150	.041	....	1.1[illegible]
252	Mariampolė	Mar. 23	.205	....	....	.120	....	.620	.150	.041	....	1.1[illegible]
253	Vilkaviškis	Mar. 24	.205	....	....	....	....	1.240	.300	.041	....	1.[illegible]
254	Kupiškis	Mar. 24	.033	....	....	....	....	.160	.240	.008	....	.4[illegible]
255	Veiveriai	Mar. 24	.082	....	....	....	....	.380	.060	.016	....	.[illegible]
256	Pakruojis	Mar. 26	.049	....	....	....	....	.140	.036	.010	....	.[illegible]
257	Kalvarija	Mar. 26	.246	....	....	....	....	1.120	.180	.049	....	1.5[illegible]
258	Bukanėiškes	Mar. 26	.082	.082	....	.060	....	.540	.030	.041	....	.[illegible]
259	Vandžiogola	Mar. 29	....	....	....	....	....	.360	.087	....	....	.[illegible]
260	Seredzius	Mar. 29	....	....	....	....	....	.240	.060	....	....	.[illegible]
261	Kaunas (Kovno)	Mar. 30	.246	....	....	.072	....	.560	.090	.123	....	1.[illegible]
262	Kaunas (Kovno)	Mar. 30	.197	.098	....	.029	....	.440	....	.098	....	.[illegible]
263	Lietuviu Moteru Globos	Mar. 30	.164	.082	....	.048	....	.360	.060	.082	....	.[illegible]
264	Bukanėiškes	Mar. 30	.082	....	....	....	....	.180	.030	.041	....	.[illegible]
265	Lapės	Mar. 30	....	....	....	....	....	.180	.030	....	....	.[illegible]
266	Rumšiškės	Mar. 31	....	....	....	....	....	.560	.090	....	....	.[illegible]
267	Kaunas (Kovno)	Mar. 31	....	....	....	....	....	.160	.026	....	....	.[illegible]
268	Seinai	Mar. 31	....	....	....	....	....	.240	.038	....	....	.[illegible]
269	Garleva	Mar. 31	....	....	....	....	....	.360	.060	....	....	.[illegible]
270	Kaunas (Kovno)	Mar. 31	....	....	....	....	....	.140	.022	....	....	.[illegible]
377	Šiauliai	Mar. 1	5.136	.935	3.017	....	....	.820	....	....	....	9.[illegible]
366	Šiauliai	Mar. 5	....	.630	.630	....	....	....	....	....	....	1.[illegible]
367	Lygumai	Mar. 8	....	.395	.395	....	....	....	....	....	....	.[illegible]
368	Šiauliai, Lopšelis	Mar. 11	.262	.180	.180	....	....	.200	....	....	....	.[illegible]
369	Lygumai	Mar. 15	....	1.125	1.125	....	....	....	....	....	....	2.[illegible]
370	Zagare	Mar. 31	....	.446	.446	....	....	....	....	....	....	.[illegible]
371	Pakruojis	Mar. 31	....	.360	.360	....	....	....	....	....	....	.[illegible]
372	Šiauliai	Mar. 31	....	.213	.213	....	....	....	....	....	....	.[illegible]
373	Šiauliai, Kurtavėnai	Mar. 31	....	2.430	.541	....	....	....	....	....	....	2.[illegible]
374	Měskučiai	Mar. 31	....	.360	....	....	....	....	....	....	....	.[illegible]
375	Saukėnai	Mar. 31	....	2.525	....	....	....	....	....	....	....	2.[illegible]
	Total for March	....	**9.100**	**17.166**	**6.989**	**4.640**	....	**30.583**	**6.435**	**4.123**	....	**79.**[illegible]

LITHUANIA

Detail of Internal Deliveries for Child Feeding, by Districts or Institutions, by Months

Table 389—*Continued*

Receipt No.	District or Institution *	Date	Flour	Rice	Beans, Peas	Pork Products	Milk Evap.	Milk Cond.	Cocoa	Sugar	Soap	Total Tons
		1920										
271	Kaunas (Kovno)	Apr. 1	.082	....	....	....	....	.140	....	....	....	.222
272	Sėda	Apr. 1	....	....	....	....	....	1.180	.191	....	....	1.371
273	Rokiškis	Apr. 10	....	....	....	....	....	.100	.014	.025	....	.139
274	Sėda	Apr. 20	....	....	....	....	....	.600	.096	....	....	.696
275	Utena	Apr. 21	....	....	....	....	....	.080	.012	.021	....	.113
276	Girkalnis	Apr. 23	....	....	....	....	....	.120	.019	....	....	.139
277	Seredžius	Apr. 23	....	....	....	....	....	.140	.040	....	....	.180
278	Lietuviu Mission	Apr. 24	....	....	....	....	....	1.260	....	....	....	1.260
279	Zagarė	Apr. 26	....	....	....	....	....	.300	.048	.082	....	.430
280	Zagarė	Apr. 26	....	....	....	....	....	1.320	....	....	....	1.320
281	Lietuviu, Jewish Society	Apr. 29	....	....	....	....	....	.100	.015	.026	....	.141
282	Vilkija	Apr. 29	....	....	....	....	....	.400	....	....	....	.400
283	Janava	Apr. 30	....	....	....	....	....	.060	.007	.025	....	.092
76	Papiles Society	Apr. 2	....	.630	....	....	....	....	....	....	....	.630
	Total for April	....	**.082**	**.630**	....	....	....	**5.800**	**.442**	**.179**	....	**7.133**
284	Kaunas (Kovno)	May 3	.492	....	....	.054	....	.440	.072	.123	....	1.181
285	Utena	May 4	.164	....	....	.018	....	.060	.024	.041	....	.307
286	Kaunas (Kovno)	May 5	.197	....	....	.022	....	.180	.029	.049	....	.477
ap.	Pasvalio Apsk. Vald.	May	....	....	....	....	....	....	....	....	.115	.115
87	Žalioji	May 11	....	....	....	....	....	.540	....	....	....	.540
88	Kaunas (Kovno)	May 23	.131	....	....	.108	....	.340	.082	.246	....	.907
89	Kaunas (Kovno)	May 23	.131	....	....	.432	....	.360	.057	.098	....	1.078
90	Prieglauda	May 23	.131	....	....	.036	....	.320	.049	.082	....	.618
91	Žalioji	May 23	....	....	....	.182	....	....	.228	312	....	.722
92	Lietuviu Komitetin	May 23	....	....	....	.180	....	.400	.180	.082	....	.842
93	Utena	May 23	....	....	....	....	....	.200	.072	.049	....	.321
94	Kalvarija	May 23	....	....	....	....	....	.200	.360	....	....	.560
95	Garleva	May 23	....	....	....	....	....	.100	.040	.049	....	.189
96	Zagarė	May 23	....	....	....	....	....	.100	.040	.066	....	.206
97	Aleksotas	May 23	....	....	....	....	....	....	.060	....	....	.060
98	Seinais	May 23	....	....	....	.012	....	....	.063	....	....	.075
99	Sakiai	May 12	....	....	....	....	....	....	....	....	.115	.115
10	Mažeikiai	May 17	....	....	....	....	....	....	....	....	.115	.115
11	Tauragė	May 17	....	....	....	....	....	....	....	....	.115	.115
12	Seinai	May 18	....	....	....	....	....	....	....	....	.115	.115
13	Kretinga	May 16	....	....	....	....	....	....	....	....	.115	.115
14	Mariampolė	May 17	....	....	....	....	....	....	....	....	.115	.115
15	Utena	May 17	....	....	....	....	....	....	....	....	.115	.115
16	Kedainiai	May 18	....	....	....	....	....	....	....	....	.115	.115
17	Vilkaviškis	May 22	....	....	....	....	....	....	....	....	.115	.115
18	Šiauliai	May 22	....	....	....	....	....	....	....	....	.115	.115
19	Ukmergė	May 22	....	....	....	....	....	....	....	....	.115	.115
20	Panevėžys	May 22	....	....	....	....	....	....	....	....	.115	.115
21	Ežerėnai	May 22	....	....	....	....	....	....	....	....	.115	.115
22	Kaunas (Kovno)	May 22	....	....	....	....	....	....	....	....	1.099	1.099
23	Telšiai	May 22	....	....	....	....	....	....	....	....	.115	.115
24	Raseiniai	May 22	....	....	....	....	....	....	....	....	.115	.115
25	Traku Apsk. Vald.	May 22	....	....	....	....	....	....	....	....	.115	.115
26	Rokiškis	May 21	....	....	....	....	....	....	....	....	.115	.115
27	Alytus	May 21	....	....	....	....	....	....	....	....	.115	.115
28	Valstybinie Vaiku Prieg.	May 24	....	....	....	....	....	....	....	....	.246	.246
29	Macekevicians No. 2 Prieg.	May 24	....	....	....	....	....	....	....	....	.246	.246
30	Sanciai	May 24	....	....	....	....	....	....	....	....	.164	.164
31	Utena	May 24	....	....	....	....	....	....	....	....	.082	.082
32	Mariampolė	May 24	....	....	....	....	....	....	....	....	.049	.049
33	Zagarė	May 24	....	....	....	....	....	....	....	....	.033	.033
	Total for May	....	**1.246**	....	....	**1.044**	....	**3.240**	**1.356**	**1.197**	**4.104**	**12.187**

Commodities in Net Metric Tons of 1,000 Kilograms or 2,204.6 Pounds

[*Continued on next page*]

LITHUANIA

Detail of Internal Deliveries for Child Feeding, by Districts or Institutions, by Months

Table 389—*Continued*

Receipt No.	District or Institution *	Date	Commodities in Net Metric Tons of 1,000 Kilograms or 2,204.6 Pounds									
			Flour	Rice	Beans, Peas	Pork Products	Milk		Cocoa	Sugar	Soap	Total Tons
							Evap.	Cond.				
		1921										
1	Kaunas (Kovno) Institution	Mar. 3	1.098	.423	.669	.150	....	1.702	.091	.241	....	4.3[illegible]
2	Šančiai Institution	Mar. 3	1.196	.755	1.194	.268	....	3.038	.162	.430	....	7.0[illegible]
3	Lopšelis Institution	Mar. 3	.599	.227	.358	.080	....	.912	.049	.129	....	2.3[illegible]
4	Kaunas (Kovno) Institution	Mar. 3	.998	.378	.597	.134	....	1.518	.081	.215	....	3.9[illegible]
5	Kaunas (Kovno) Institution	Mar. 16	.699	.272	.430	.096	....	1.094	.058	.155	....	2.8[illegible]
6	Kaunas (Kovno) Institution	Mar. 1	....	.211	.334	.075	....	.850	.045	.121	....	1.6[illegible]
7	Kaunas (Kovno) Institution	Mar. 6	.649	.242	.382	.086	....	.972	.052	.138	....	2.5[illegible]
8	Salako Mustas Kaunas (Kovno) Institution	Mar. 19	.899	.332	.525	.118	....	1.336	.071	.189	....	3.4[illegible]
9	Kaunas (Kovno) Institution	Mar. 6	.449	.196	.311	.070	....	.790	.042	.112	....	1.9[illegible]
10	Kaunas (Kovno)	Mar. 6	.998	.378	.597	.134	....	1.518	.081	.215	....	3.9[illegible]
11	Panevėžys, Panemunis Institution	Mar. 7	.449	.196	.311	.070	....	.790	.042	.112	....	1.9[illegible]
12	Mariampolė Institution	Mar. 14	.699	.272	.430	.096	....	1.094	.058	.155	....	2.8[illegible]
13	Mariampolė Institution	Mar. 14	.449	.196	.311	.070	....	.790	.042	.112	....	1.9[illegible]
14	Kaunas (Kovno) Institution	Mar. 21	.599	.227	.358	.080	....	.910	.049	.129	....	2.[illegible]
15	Sanciai	Mar. 14	.599	.227	.358	.080	....	.910	.049	.129	....	2.[illegible]
16	Naumiestis	Mar. 14	.749	.287	.464	.102	....	1.154	.062	.164	....	2.9[illegible]
17	Naumiestis	Mar. 31	....	.211	.334	.075	....	.850	.045	.121	....	1.[illegible]
18	Virbalis	Mar. 31	.300	.121	.191	.043	....	.486	.026	.069	....	1.[illegible]
19	Alytaus	Mar. 15	.899	.332	.525	.118	....	1.336	.071	.189	....	3.[illegible]
20	Žasliai	Mar. 21	.819	.302	.478	.107	....	1.216	.065	.172	....	3.[illegible]
21	Šiauliai	Mar. 24	.449	.166	.263	.059	....	.668	.038	.095	....	1.[illegible]
22	Joniškis	Mar. 24	.329	.121	.191	.043	....	.486	.026	.069	....	1.[illegible]
	Total for March	....	**13.925**	**6.072**	**9.611**	**2.154**	....	**24.420**	**1.305**	**3.461**	....	**60.[illegible]**
23	Merkine Alytaus	Apr. 8	.898	.272	.430	.096	....	1.094	.058	.155	....	3.[illegible]
24	Zagarė	Apr. 16	1.927	.725	1.146	.257	....	2.916	.156	.413	....	7.[illegible]
25	Panevėžys	Apr. 17	1.080	.574	.908	.204	....	2.308	.123	.327	....	5.[illegible]
26	Panevėžys, Surdegis	Apr. 17	.328	.151	.239	.054	....	.608	.032	.086	....	1.[illegible]
27	Utena	Apr. 16	1.398	.529	.836	.188	....	2.126	.114	.301	....	5.[illegible]
28	Rokiškis	Apr. 16	.499	.196	.311	.070	....	.790	.042	.112	....	2.[illegible]
29	Ežerėnai	Apr. 19	1.198	.453	.716	.160	....	1.822	.097	.258	....	4.[illegible]
30	Antalieptė	Apr. 19	.800	.302	.478	.107	....	1.216	.065	.172	....	3.[illegible]
31	Telšiai	Apr. 2	.649	.242	.382	.086	....	.972	.052	.138	....	2.[illegible]
32	Kaunas (Kovno)—Bebavars Children's Asylum	Apr. 19	.244	.091	.143	.032	....	.364	.019	.052	....	.[illegible]
33	Kretinga	Apr. 20	.669	.257	.406	.091	....	1.034	.055	.146	....	2.[illegible]
34	Tauragė	Apr. 7	.820	.453	.717	.161	....	1.824	.097	.258	....	4.[illegible]
35	Kaunas (Kovno) Institution	Apr. 7	....	.076	.119	.027	....	.304	.016	.043	....	.[illegible]
36	Kaunas (Kovno) Institution	Apr. 2	.399	.121	.191	.043	....	.486	.026	.069	....	1.[illegible]
37	Jurbarkas	Apr. 2	1.198	.453	.717	.161	....	1.824	.097	.258	....	4.[illegible]

LITHUANIA

Detail of Internal Deliveries for Child Feeding, by Districts or Institutions, by Months

Table 389—*Concluded*

District or Institution *	Date	Flour	Rice	Beans, Peas	Pork Products	Milk Evap.	Milk Cond.	Cocoa	Sugar	Soap	Total Tons
	1921										
Mažeikiai	Apr. 24	.300	.121	.191	.043	....	.486	.026	.069	....	1.236
Kaunas (Kovno) Institution	Apr. 16	.799	.242	.382	.086	....	.972	.052	.138	....	2.671
Ukmergės Place	Apr. 13	.369	.121	.191	.043	....	.486	.026	.069	....	1.305
Jurbarkas	Apr. 13	.799	.242	.382	.086	....	.972	.052	.138	....	2.671
Kaunas (Kovno) Benedyklym Institution	Apr. 13	.599	.227	.358	.080	....	.912	.049	.129	....	2.354
Kaunas (Kovno)	Apr. 15	.998	.377	.597	.134	....	1.520	.081	.215	....	3.922
Kaunas (Kovno) Children's Kitchen	Apr. 15	.839	.302	.478	.107	....	1.216	.065	.172	....	3.179
Kaunas (Kovno)	Apr. 15	.749	.287	.474	.102	....	1.154	.062	.164	....	2.992
Kaunas (Kovno)	Apr. 15	.449	.166	.263	.059	....	.668	.036	.095	....	1.736
Kaunas (Kovno)	Apr. 15	.668	.257	.406	.091	....	1.034	.055	.146	....	2.657
Kaunas (Kovno)	Apr. 15	.230	.091	.143	.032	....	.364	.019	.052	....	.931
Sanciai	Apr. 15	.399	.121	.191	.043	....	.486	.026	.069	....	1.335
Kaunas (Kovno)	Apr. 15	.549	.211	.334	.075	....	.850	.045	.121	....	2.185
Kaunas (Kovno)	Apr. 15	.399	.121	.191	.043	....	.486	.026	.069	....	1.335
Kaunas (Kovno) Institution	Apr. 15	.200	.076	.119	.027	....	.304	.016	.043	....	.785
Kaunas (Kovno) Institution	Apr. 15	.200	.076	.119	.027	....	.304	.016	.043	....	.785
Kaunas (Kovno) Institution	Apr. 15	.200	.076	.119	.027	....	.304	.016	.043	....	.785
Kaunas (Kovno) Institution	Apr. 15	.749	.287	.464	.102	....	1.154	.062	.164	....	2.982
Palanga	Apr. 20	1.198	.453	.717	.160	....	1.824	.097	.258	....	4.707
Kaunas (Kovno)—Uytanta Deutsches Waisenhaus	Apr. 25	.250	.076	.119	.027	....	.304	.016	.043	....	.835
Miskug Kaunas (Kovno)	Apr. 25	.160	.060	.096	.021	....	.244	.013	.034	....	.628
Rokiškis	Apr. 25	.599	.166	.263	.059	....	.668	.036	.095	....	1.886
Total for April	....	**23.809**	**9.051**	**14.336**	**3.211**	....	**36.400**	**1.941**	**5.157**	....	**93.905**
Total to Districts and Institutions	....	**322.488**	**107.715**	**87.060**	**42.942**	**65.512**	**164.286**	**57.511**	**45.570**	**4.104**	**897.188**
City of Memel	May ..	2.400	.700	1.300	....	.800	....	.200	.500	....	5.900
Repatriated Children	June ..	.400	.300	.200	.400	.900	....	.100	.100	....	2.400
Local Sale †	....	....	....	....	....	....	....	....	30.900	....	30.900
Turned over to Local Committees	July ..	.100	1.600	10.800	....	13.900	....	2.800	.100	.900	30.200
Invoiced Lithuanian Government	1920 Aug. ..	68.200	....	3.800	8.700	....	120.300	....	28.000	....	229.000
Total	....	**393.588**	**110.315**	**103.160**	**52.042**	**81.112**	**284.586**	**60.611**	**105.170**	**5.004**	**1,195.588**
Deduct:											
Credit Lithuanian Government (Overages)	....	....	11.400	....	....	....	....	....	....	....	11.400
Tare on Weight, Lard Substitute	....	....	....	....	4.900	....	....	....	....	....	4.900
Total Deductions	....	....	**11.400**	....	**4.900**	....	....	....	....	....	**16.300**
Total Net Deliveries ‡	....	**393.588**	**98.915**	**103.160**	**47.142**	**81.112**	**284.586**	**60.611**	**105.170**	**5.004**	**1,179.288**

Commodities in Net Metric Tons of 1,000 Kilograms or 2,204.6 Pounds

† Proceeds used to purchase flour. See arrival Table 386. Handled by ...operative Radzyilishki and Lithuanian Government.

‡ Cf. Table 390. For total children's relief add the 13.0 metric tons of clothing.

LITHUANIA—A.R.A.-European Children's Fund

Table 390 Detail of Internal Deliveries of Clothing and Accessories to Local Committees—Reconstruction Period, 1919–1924

Receipt No.	Local Committee	Date	Shoes (Pairs)	Laces (Pairs)	Stockings (Pairs)	Woolens (Yards)	Overcoats (Each)	Thread (Spools)	Needles (No.)	Buttons (No.)
		1920								
1	Kovno Miesto Vald.	Jan. 16	...	...	...	2,986.5	...	...	...	...
48	Kovno Miesto Vald.	Feb. 14	4,000	...	...	...	...	...	...	...
49	Seinu Apsk. Vald.	Feb. 14	200	...	...	...	...	...	...	...
50	Kretingos Apsk. Vald.	Feb. 14	400	...	...	...	...	...	...	...
2	Kovno Miesto Vald.	Feb. 21	...	...	...	1,453.2	...	...	...	...
59	Tauragės Apsk. Kom.	Feb. 23	400	...	...	...	200	...	...	...
60	Ežerėnu Apsk. Kom.	Feb. 23	2,900	...	...	...	...	...	...	...
3	Kovno Miesto Vald.	Feb. 26	...	...	...	3,132	750	...	...	...
51	Saulės School	Mar. 3	60	...	...	...	...	...	...	...
6	Saulės Draugijai	Mar. 3	...	...	...	466	...	...	...	...
R	Kauno Miesto Vald.	Mar. 6	...	...	...	...	...	2,560	5,000	...
85	Panevezio Apsk. Vald.	Mar. 6	...	358	...	...	...	22	...	520
86, 54	Raseiniu Apsk. Vald.	Mar. 6	300	288	...	...	120	20	...	480
87, 53	Kedainiu Apsk. Vald.	Mar. 6	250	244	...	...	120	20	...	480
88	Kovno Miesto Vald.	Mar. 6	...	...	...	...	...	...	...	7,000
52	Rokiskio Apsk. Vald.	Mar. 6	600	...	...	...	...	...	...	...
55	Telsiu Apsk. Vald.	Mar. 6	330	...	...	...	150	...	...	...
61, 89	Utenos Apsk. Vald.	Mar. 6	500	432	150	...	240	33	...	720
7	Valstybinei Prieg.	Mar. 8	...	144	300	252	...	40	...	400
90	Ežerėnu Apsk. Kom.	Mar. 8	...	2,160	200	...	...	35	...	2,560
R	Bukanciskes Prieg.	Mar. 8	...	...	100	...	...	...	...	...
92	Moteru Globos Kom.	Mar. 8	8	144	120	...	...	...	...	204
93	Kauno Miesto Vald.	Mar. 9	...	...	1,000	...	...	...	...	...
56	Sakiu Apsk. Vald.	Mar. 10	240	...	...	...	90	...	...	...
57	Alytaus Apsk. Vald.	Mar. 10	380	...	...	...	150	...	...	...
58	Vilkaviskio Apsk. Vald.	Mar. 10	240	...	...	...	100	...	...	...
62	Panevezio Apsk. Vald.	Mar. 10	300	...	...	...	130	...	...	...
8	Tremtinio Gamisausko	Mar. 12	4	...	...	12	...	...	...	...
9	Bukauciskes Vaiku Prieg.	Mar. 15	40	...	...	155	...	...	...	30[illegible]
63	Mazeikiu Apsk. Virsin.	Mar. 15	330	660	...	...	180	...	...	54[illegible]
66	Kaisedorin Apsk. Kom.	Mar. 20	380	...	...	...	150	...	...	...
67	Pavargelio Ganzeno Vaiku	Mar. 22	6	...	13	...	...	...	...	...
R	Pavargelio E. Nomeikienei	Mar. 22	2	...	4	...	...	...	...	...
68	Kauno Apsk. Kom.	Mar. 22	200	...	...	...	200	...	...	...
10	Moteru Globos Kom.	Mar. 22	...	...	...	163	...	30	...	30[illegible]
70	Mariampol Apsk. Kom.	Mar. 23	330	...	...	...	150	...	...	...
11	Pralato Janusev. Prieg.	Mar. 26	...	...	...	39	...	10	...	9[illegible]
12	Padegelio Kakuno Vaiku	Mar. 26	...	...	1	4	...	...	...	...
4	Kauno Miesto Vald.	Mar. 27	...	...	...	249	...	...	...	...
70	Ukmergai Apsk. Vald.	Mar. 29	430	...	...	...	140	...	...	...
72	Pasvalio Apsk. Vald.	Mar. 29	240	...	...	...	100	...	...	...
R	Kauno Rusu Mokyklai	Mar. 29	60	120	...	250	...	...	...	...
13	Moksleiviai Onai Astra	Mar. 29	...	...	...	2	...	...	...	...
14	Zofijai Prezvanai	Mar. 29	...	...	3	4	...	...	...	...
16	Juozui Skulevieiu	Mar. 30	...	...	1	2	...	...	...	...
21	Seinu Apsk. Kom.	Apr. 4	...	...	...	78	...	...	...	...
22	Pasvalio Apsk. Vald.	Apr. 5	...	...	...	250	...	...	...	...
23	Kretingos Apsk. Vald.	Apr. 6	...	...	...	250	...	...	...	...
24	Juozui Kalinauskui	Apr. 6	...	...	...	1	...	...	...	...
17	Lenku Vaiku Prieg.	Apr. 8	...	...	...	58	...	10	...	9[illegible]
25	Padauguvos Padegeliems	Apr. 10	...	...	38	58	...	...	...	10[illegible]
26	Valstybines Prieg.	Apr. 10	...	...	...	117	...	...	...	...
27	Sakui Apsk. Vald.	Apr. 12	...	...	...	250	...	30	...	45[illegible]
R	Moksleiviui Praniu. Jan.	Apr. 24	1	...	...	...	...	...	...	...
18	Zagares Vaiku Prieg.	Apr. 26	30	144	200	117	...	30	...	30[illegible]
19	Juzefos Davidaetis	Apr. 26	...	...	...	6	...	...	...	...
5	Kauno Miesto Vald.	Apr. 1	...	144	3,000	1,138	...	...	5,000	6,90[illegible]
20	Lepunu Zydu Bedno	Apr. 29	...	...	100	39	...	12	...	9[illegible]
31	Vaiku Prieg. Mick.	Apr. 27	...	144	100	8	...	40	...	20[illegible]
32	Nasles Marles Galauvenes	Apr. 27	...	...	...	4	...	...	...	...
81	R. L. Simpson	Apr. 27	21	...	...	...	...	...	...	...
21	Seinu Apsk. Kom.	May 4	...	...	100	...	...	16	...	15[illegible]
106	Kretingos Apsk. Kom.	May 6	...	...	150	...	...	16	...	45[illegible]

LITHUANIA

Detail of Internal Deliveries of Clothing and Accessories to Local Committees

Table 390—*Continued*

Receipt No.	Local Committee	Date	Shoes (Pairs)	Laces (Pairs)	Stockings (Pairs)	Woolens (Yards)	Overcoats (Each)	Thread (Spools)	Needles (No.)	Buttons (No.)
		1920								
28	Taurages Apsk. Kom.	May 17	...	...	...	250	...	20	...	450
29	Mazeiku Apsk. Kom.	May 17	...	...	...	250	...	20	...	450
33	Seinu Apsk. Vald.	May 18	...	...	250	172	...	20	...	342
34	Mariampoli Apsk. Vald.	May 18	...	...	75	300	...	30	...	600
37	Kedainiam Apsk. Vald.	May 18	...	...	110	250	...	20	...	450
32	Kauno Miesto Apsk. Vald.	May 17	...	4,880	...	2,000	1,300	840	...	15,000
35	Utenoa Apsk. Vald.	May 17	...	...	...	350	...	30	...	660
37	Rokiskio Apsk. Vald.	May 18	...	300	200	300	...	20	...	450
47	Alytaus Apsk. Vald.	May 21	150	...	...	350	230	50	125	1,215
8, 109	Traku Apsk. Vald.	May 22	...	160	160	400	...	20	125	600
9, 110	Raseiniu Apsk. Vald.	May 22	...	...	...	300	...	20	125	450
0, 111	Telsu Apsk. Vald.	May 22	...	120	300	300	...	20	125	450
1, 112	Kauno Apsk. Vald.	May 22	...	...	100	200	...	20	125	300
2, 113	Ežerėnu Apsk. Vald.	May 22	...	300	2,100	600	...	20	1,125	900
3, 114	Panevezui Apsk. Vald.	May 22	...	...	250	250	...	20	125	375
4, 115	Ukmergai Apsk. Vald.	May 22	...	...	120	250	...	20	125	375
116, 83	Siauliu Apsk. Vald.	May 22	430	200	300	450	...	20	2,000	675
6, 117	Vilkaviskio Apsk. Vald.	May 22	...	200	150	200	...	20	...	300
30	Moteru Globos Kom.	May 22	8	...	...	...	...	...	1,000	...
124	Saulės Draugijai	May 24	...	120	90	...	...	180	...	2,400
125	Valstybinei Vaiku Prieg.	May 24	...	400	...	...	...	400	...	500
126	Vaiku Prieg. Mick.	May 24	...	338	...	...	...	300	...	397
100	Sanciu Vauku Darzelim	May 24	...	...	315	...	...	...	...	...
83	Joniskio Vauku Prieg.	May 24	33	...	...	...	...	...	...	...
80	Alex. Sandelio	May 24	18	...	...	...	...	...	...	...
R	Naslaiciai Aniuleuuiu	May 27	1	...	...	...	...	...	...	...
R	Naslaiciai Kacinauskui	May 27	1	...	...	...	...	...	...	...
..	Kaunas, Central Committee	June 1	116	528	2,488	328	...	...	...	5
	Total *	...	**13,939**	**12,528**	**12,588**	**19,044**	**4,500†**	**5,034‡**	**15,000**	**49,680**

* Equivalent to 13.0 metric tons; value, $61,465.58.
† Yard goods all receipted for by committees and tailors. In some ances committees also receipted for overcoats when received for dis- ution—hence overcoat column.
‡ Equivalent to 350 pounds.

LITHUANIA—A.R.A.-European Children's Fund

Detail of Internal Deliveries, by Receipt Number, for Student Feeding Reconstruction Period, 1919–1924

Table 391

Receipt No.	Student Kitchen or Institution	Date	Commodities in Net Metric Tons of 1,000 Kilograms or 2,204.6 Pounds							
			Flour	Rice	Beans, Peas	Pork Products	Milk Evap., Cond.	Cocoa	Sugar	Total Tons
		1921								
1	Kaunas—Saulės, Normal	April 15 to May 15	.659	.094	.345	.188	.251	.044	.157	1.738
2	Kaunas—Didzivji Vil. Gve. No. 2	April 15 to May 15	.185	.053	.097	.026	.070	.012	.044	.487
3	Jewish Teachers' Seminary	April 15 to May 15	.130	.037	.068	.019	.050	.009	.031	.344
4	Kaunas—Praneiškonu 4, Teachers' Seminary	April 15 to May 15	.092	.026	.048	.013	.035	.006	.023	.243
5	Panevėžys—Marijos Gve., Teachers' Seminary	April 15 to May 15	.256	.073	.134	.037	.098	.017	.062	.677
6	Panevėžys—Marijos Teachers' Seminary	April 15 to May 15	.105	.030	.055	.015	.040	.007	.025	.277
7	Mariampolė—Teachers' Seminary	April 15 to May 15	.307	.088	.161	.044	.117	.020	.073	.810
8	Mariampolė—Teachers' Seminary	April 15 to May 15	.097	.028	.051	.014	.037	.006	.023	.256
9	Šiauliai—Teachers' Seminary	April 15 to May 15	.223	.064	.117	.032	.085	.015	.053	.589
10	Šiauliai—Teachers' Seminary	April 15 to May 15	.176	.050	.092	.025	.067	.012	.042	.464
11	Rokiškis—Teachers' Seminary	April 15 to May 15	.088	.025	.046	.013	.034	.006	.021	.233
12	Telsiai—Teachers' Seminary	April 15 to May 15	.109	.031	.057	.016	.042	.007	.026	.288
13	Tauragė—Student Kitchens	April 15 to May 15	.155	.044	.081	.059	.059	.010	.037	.445
14	Kaunas—Mickevičians No. 2	April 15 to May 15	.375	.107	.196	.054	.143	.025	.089	.989
15	Kaunas—Student Kitchens	April 15 to May 15	.195	.056	.102	.028	.074	.013	.047	.515
	Total	...	**3.152**	**.806**	**1.650**	**.583**	**1.202**	**.209**	**.753**	**8.355**

Table 392

THE NETHERLANDS—Summary of Relief Deliveries

Operation	Flour	Total Metric Tons	Total Value
American Relief Administration—Cash Settlement	25,027.4	25,027.4	$4,219,498.4

THE NETHERLANDS—American Relief Administration

Detail by Steamers of Commodities Sold for Cash

Table 393

Armistice Period, 1919

Arrival No.	Steamer	Port of Sailing	Date of Arrival	Port of Arrival	Contents of Cargoes in Net Metric Tons of 1,000 Kilograms or 2,204.6 Pounds			Total Value
					Wheat Flour	Cereal Flour	Total Tons	
			1919					
2	West Shore	New York	Jan. 4	Rotterdam	3,793.7	2,687.9	6,481.6	$1,091,011.[illegible]
3	Ossineke	New York	Jan. 5	Rotterdam	2,442.6	3,451.7	5,894.3	982,713.[illegible]
5	Western Hero	New York	Jan. 14	Rotterdam	3,491.7	1,632.3	5,124.0	874,772.[illegible]
15	Eastern Star	Philadelphia	Jan. 31	Rotterdam	2,985.8	1,686.1	4,671.9	792,996.[illegible]
23	Western Light	New York	Feb. 10	Rotterdam	1,190.8	1,181.3	2,372.1	401,790.[illegible]
27	Pequot	New York	Feb. 18	Rotterdam	13.0	251.4	264.4	40,474.[illegible]
26	Newburg	New York	Feb. 18	Rotterdam	......	219.1	219.1	35,738.[illegible]
	Total—(To Table 120)				**13,917.6**	**11,109.8**	**25,027.4**	**$4,219,498.[illegible]**

Map of Poland showing principal warehouses and cities where A.R.A. carried on child-feeding operations

Table 394 **POLAND—**

Operation	Table No.	Flour	Grain	Rice	Beans, Peas
					ARMISTIC
A.R.A.—Congressional Appropriation, $100,000,000 Fund	395	132,619.5	81,871.5	8,041.2	8,586.3
A.R.A.—Freight on Charity Supplies	143	......	......	......	......
A.R.A.—Freight on U.S. Liquidation Commission Supplies	144	......	......	......	......
A.R.A.—Freight, Insurance, etc., on Liquidation Commission Supplies (through J.D.C.)	146	......	......	......	......
U.S. Liquidation Commission (War Dept.)	122	......	......	......	......
Joint Distribution Committee	124	3,663.0	......	......	......
American Red Cross	126	......	......	......	......
Total American Relief	....	**136,282.5**	**81,871.5**	**8,041.2**	**8,586.3**
United Kingdom	133, 396	3,239.0	5,813.0	......	1,362.0
United Kingdom—Finance on Freight	133, 396	......	......	......	......
Polish League of Women	136	......	......	......	......
Russo-Carpathian Commission	136	......	......	......	......
Total Other than American Relief	132B	**3,239.0**	**5,813.0**	......	**1,362.0**
Total, Armistice Period	108	**139,521.5**	**87,684.5**	**8,041.2**	**9,948.3**
					RECONSTRUCTIO
A.R.A.—Congressional Appropriation, $100,000,000 Fund	397, 406	858.2	......	2,193.3	2,898.2
A.R.A.-European Children's Fund	397, 406	3,652.6	......	10,247.2	15,952.9
Polish Government Donation	397, 406	41,253.0	......	531.0	728.0
Joint Distribution Committee	397, 406	......	......	......	......
Other Polish Donations	397, 406	......	......	......	......
Total Children's Relief	163	**45,763.8**	......	**12,971.5**	**19,579.1**
A.R.A. Warehouses—Food Draft and Bulk Sales	400, 406	4,965.2	......	516.1	570.9
A.R.A. Warehouses, Danzig—Bulk Sale to Polish Government	406	7,720.3	......	......	......
Polish Government Donation (Adult Relief)	404n	7,072.7	......	......	......
Commonwealth Fund—Intelligentsia Clothing	403	......	......	......	......
U.S. Grain Corporation (Act of Congress, March 30, 1920)	405	202,564.0	......	......	......
United Kingdom—Finance on Freight	405n	......	......	......	......
American Friends Service Committee	331n	......	......	......	......
Total Other than Children's Relief	....	**222,322.2**	......	**516.1**	**570.9**
Total, Reconstruction Period	149	**268,086.0**	......	**13,487.6**	**20,150.0**
Grand Total Relief Deliveries	102	**407,607.5**	**87,684.5**	**21,528.8**	**30,098.3**

nmary of Relief Deliveries

orn rits	Pork Products	Milk	Cocoa	Sugar	Misc. Food	Forage	Soap	Medical and Hospital Supplies	Clothing and Misc.	Total Tons	Total Value
	Commodities in Net Metric Tons of 1,000 Kilograms or 2,204.6 Pounds										
RIOD											
....	21,797.3	2,100.8	47.6	1.6	.....	.....	.....	.....	5,777.4	260,843.2	$ 63,191,316.61
....	......	......	....	....	.....	.....	.....	.....	.....	......	149,063.99
....	......	......	....	....	.....	.....	.....	.....	.....	......	328,607.29
....	......	......	....	....	.....	.....	.....	.....	.....	......	66,364.12
....	......	......	....	....	44,360.0	.....	.....	.....	62,766.0	107,126.0	59,365,111.97
....	2,267.0	1,707.0	....	....	90.2	.....	75.0	525.6	1,378.0	9,705.8	3,412,497.00
....	......	......	....	....	.....	.....	.....	2,592.6	1,450.0	4,042.6	813,800.00
....	**24,064.3**	**3,807.8**	**47.6**	**1.6**	**44,450.2**	.....	**75.0**	**3,118.2**	**71,371.4**	**381,717.6**	**$127,326,760.98**
....	1,255.0	......	....	....	541.0	.....	568.0	370.0	8,314.0	21,462.0	$ 6,304,620.00
....	......	......	....	....	.....	.....	.....	.....	.....	......	1,389,920.00
....	......	......	....	....	.....	.....	.....	.....	4.1	4.1	1,640.00
....	......	......	....	....	.....	.....	.....	.....	.5	.5	200.00
....	**1,255.0**	**......**	**....**	**....**	**541.0**	.....	**568.0**	**370.0**	**8,318.6**	**21,466.6**	**$ 7,696,380.00**
....	**25,319.3**	**3,807.8**	**47.6**	**1.6**	**44,991.2**	.....	**643.0**	**3,488.2**	**79,690.0**	**403,184.2**	**$135,023,140.98**
RIOD											
....	765.0	6,284.2	766.3	1,647.1	20.3	.....	441.6	.....	826.7	16,700.9	$ 6,055,842.03
57.8	4,475.4	14,399.1	1,155.9	5,217.4	305.0	.....	263.7	.....	1,915.5	59,242.5	16,769,322.10
....	852.0	......	....	1,205.9	.....	.....	.....	.....	.....	44,569.9	6,702,221.02
....	......	506.0	....	....	.....	.....	31.0	.....	.....	537.0	273,555.00
....	......	......	31.4	95.8	913.7	.....	.....	.....	.....	1,040.9	40,094.51
57.8	**6,092.4**	**21,189.3**	**1,953.6**	**8,166.2**	**1,239.0**	.....	**736.3**	.....	**2,742.2**	**122,091.2**	**$ 29,841,034.66**
31.6	527.9	722.6	78.2	218.0	166.6	.....	.....	.....	42.4	7,839.5	$ 1,675,087.41
....	......	......	....	....	.....	.....	.....	.....	.....	7,720.3	864,562.40
....	......	......	....	....	.....	.....	.....	.....	.....	7,072.7	917,059.24
....	......	......	....	....	.....	.....	.....	.....	30.4	30.4	57,532.49
....	......	......	....	....	.....	.....	.....	.....	.....	202,564.0	24,353,590.97
....	......	......	....	....	.....	.....	.....	.....	.....	......	8,102,558.32
....	......	......	....	....	.....	633.3	.....	.....	.....	633.3	30,291.26
31.6	**527.9**	**722.6**	**78.2**	**218.0**	**166.6**	**633.3**	.....	.....	**72.8**	**225,861.2**	**$ 36,000,682.09**
89.4	**6,620.3**	**21,911.9**	**2,031.8**	**8,384.2**	**1,405.6**	**633.3**	**736.3**	.....	**2,815.0**	**347,951.4**	**$ 65,841,716.75**
89.4	**31,939.6**	**25,719.7**	**2,079.4**	**8,385.8**	**46,396.8**	**633.3**	**1,379.3**	**3,488.2**	**82,505.0**	**751,135.6**	**$200,864,857.73**

POLAND-

Table 395 **Detail by Steamers of Relief Deliveries, Paid for by Funds from th**

Arrival No.*	Steamer or Source	Port of Sailing	Date of Arrival	Port of Arrival	Wheat Flour	Cereal Flour	Wheat Grain
			1919				
19	Purchase from Red Cross (via Rail)....	(Berne)	Feb. 5	(Lemberg)	......	.....	.....
31	Lake Dancey, I........................	Rotterdam	Feb. 19	Danzig	2,646.8	.....	.....
33	Lake Wimico, I........................	Rotterdam	Feb. 19	Danzig	1,995.3	.....	.....
32	Lake Mary, I..........................	Rotterdam	Feb. 19	Danzig	2,448.6	.....	.....
43	Lake Eckhart, I.......................	Rotterdam	Feb. 25	Danzig	2,352.6	.....	.....
42	Lake Clear, I.........................	Rotterdam	Feb. 25	Danzig	1,452.6	.....	.....
46	Lake St. Regis, I.....................	Rotterdam	Feb. 27	Danzig	2,068.4	.....	.....
49	Lake St. Clair, I.....................	Rotterdam	Mar. 2	Danzig	793.5	.....	.....
54	Lake Catherine, I.....................	Rotterdam	Mar. 6	Danzig	1,447.4	.....	.....
59	Lake Tulare, I........................	Rotterdam	Mar. 11	Danzig	1,623.4	.....	.....
65	Via Rail (to Polish White Cross)......	(Paris)	Mar. 15	(Warsaw)	......	.....	.....
69	Lake Mary, II.........................	Rotterdam	Mar. 18	Danzig	1,460.2	.....	.....
70	Lake Wimico, II.......................	Rotterdam	Mar. 18	Danzig	1,169.0	.....	.....
75	Lake Traverse, I......................	Rotterdam	Mar. 19	Danzig	1,450.5	.....	.....
74	Lake Dancey, II.......................	Rotterdam	Mar. 19	Danzig	1,954.5	.....	.....
79	Lake Clear, II........................	Rotterdam	Mar. 20	Danzig	1,291.0	.....	.....
78	Lake St. Clair, II....................	Rotterdam	Mar. 25	Danzig	2,393.5	.....	.....
91	Democracy, I..........................	Rotterdam	Mar. 27	Danzig	3,077.6	.....	.....
92	Lake Catherine, II....................	Rotterdam	Mar. 27	Danzig	2,211.5	.....	.....
93	Lake St. Regis, II....................	Rotterdam	Mar. 27	Danzig	2,397.2	.....	.....
53	West Humhaw, I	New York	Mar. 5	Danzig	......	.....	.....
68	West Cobalt	Norfolk	Mar. 17	Danzig	7,086.2	.....	.....
77	Zaca	Norfolk	Mar. 19	Danzig	7,996.1	.....	.....
84	Arakan, I	New York	Mar. 24	Danzig	......	.....	.....
100	Manitowoc, I.........................	New York	Apr. 1	Danzig	......	.....	.....
113	Selandia, I	New York	Apr. 9	Danzig	3,839.7	.....	.....
117	Canton, I............................	Baltimore	Apr. 12	Danzig	......	.....	.....
122	Cape Henry, I	New York	Apr. 13	Danzig	1,690.7	.....	.....
125	Lake Tulare, III	Rotterdam	Apr. 14	Danzig	2,229.3	.....	.....
124	Lake Traverse, II....................	Rotterdam	Apr. 14	Danzig	2,188.5	.....	.....
132	Lake Mary, III.......................	Rotterdam	Apr. 16	Danzig	2,397.8	.....	.....
131	Lake Clear, III......................	Rotterdam	Apr. 16	Danzig	2,257.9	.....	.....
130	Lake Catherine, III..................	Rotterdam	Apr. 16	Danzig	2,245.4	.....	.....
136	Lake St. Regis, III..................	Rotterdam	Apr. 17	Danzig	2,156.1	.....	.....
135	Lake Eckhart, III....................	Rotterdam	Apr. 17	Danzig	884.7	.....	.....
153	Jan Van Nassau	Boston	Apr. 27	Danzig	3,271.0	.....	.....
155	Lake Tulare, IV	Rotterdam	Apr. 30	Danzig	......	.....	.....
167	Democracy, II ‡	St. Nazaire	May 6	Danzig	4,312.7	.....	.....
170	Lake Traverse, III...................	Rotterdam	May 7	Danzig	......	.....	.....
178	Lake Dancey, III **..................	Cardiff	May 9	Danzig	108.0	.....	.....
181	Wico	Philadelphia	May 10	Danzig	3,835.3	.....	.....
186	Western Chief	Baltimore	May 11	Danzig	7,133.1	.....	.....
183	Lake St. Regis, IV...................	Copenhagen	May 11	Danzig	......	.....	.....
190	Kerowlee, I ‡	St. Nazaire	May 13	Danzig	4,339.9	.....	.....
191	Lake Clear, IV ‡	St. Nazaire	May 13	Danzig	153.6	.....	.....
192	Navarino ††	Canada	May 14	Danzig	6,142.1	.....	.....
200	Eastern Queen	Baltimore	May 18	Danzig	7,345.0	.....	.....
203	Saco	Philadelphia	May 19	Danzig	......	.....	.....
219	Athenic ††	St. John	May 24	Danzig	......	.....	6,167.
224	Queen Alexandra ††	Portland	May 25	Danzig	......	.....	6,226.
227	Lake Larga	Philadelphia	May 26	Danzig	......	.....	.....
246	Lake Eckhart, IV ‡	St. Nazaire	June 1	Danzig	111.0	.....	.....
248	Wakanna	Newport News	June 1	Danzig	......	.....	.....
243	Forster	Norfolk	June 1	Danzig	......	.....	.....
266	Panola	New York	June 10	Danzig	......	.....	.....
267	West Erral	New York	June 10	Danzig	......	.....	.....
268	Catawba	L'Havre	June 11	Danzig	......	.....	.....
278	Yakima	Baltimore	June 13	Danzig	80.0	.....	.....
277	Sacandago	New Orleans	June 13	Danzig	1,900.1	.....	.....
279	Westward Ho, II......................	New York	June 14	Danzig	......	.....	.....
280	Western Belle, II....................	New York	June 14	Danzig	......	.....	.....
291	Schodack	Philadelphia	June 18	Danzig	......	.....	.....

* Arrival numbers from Table 111.
† Beef.

‡ Cargo ex-Army stocks in France purchased by A.R.A. from U.S. Liquidation Commission.

merican Relief Administration

ongressional Appropriation for Relief—Armistice Period, 1919

Contents of Cargoes in Net Metric Tons of 1,000 Kilograms or 2,204.6 Pounds										
Rye Grain	Beans, Peas	Rice	Pork Products	Lard	Lard Substitute	Milk	Sugar, Cocoa	Misc.	Total Tons	Total Value
......	.....	.....	.....	.....	.....	38.0	....	2.0	40.0	$ 14,709.49
......	.....	.....	.....	.....	.....	.....	....	.....	2,646.8	554,348.73
......	.....	.....	.....	.....	.....	.....	....	.....	1,995.3	417,887.46
......	.....	.....	.....	.....	.....	.....	....	.....	2,448.6	512,840.44
......	.....	.....	.....	143.2	.....	.....	....	.....	2,495.8	606,432.50
......	.....	.....	.....	339.2	.....	.....	....	.....	1,791.8	573,467.78
......	.....	.....	37.4†	275.5	.....	.....	....	.....	2,381.3	675,703.10
......	.....	.....	214.6	928.1	.....	197.9	....	.....	2,134.1	1,158,510.70
......	.....	.....	351.8	99.2	.....	.....	....	.....	1,898.4	634,440.26
......	.....	.....	304.2	54.2	.....	.....	....	.....	1,981.8	607,446.22
......	.....	54.4	.....	.....	.....	.....	....	.....	54.4	11,297.56
......	.....	.....	615.9	19.2	.....	.....	....	.....	2,095.3	745,364.81
......	.....	.....	571.3	.....	.....	.....	....	.....	1,740.3	664,363.31
......	.....	.....	355.3	.....	.....	.....	....	.....	1,805.8	548,572.19
......	.....	.....	366.6	259.3	.....	.....	....	.....	2,580.4	928,292.01
......	.....	.....	271.8	276.1	.....	.....	....	.....	1,838.9	717,349.23
......	.....	.....	.....	.....	.....	.....	....	.....	2,393.5	501,288.15
......	.....	.....	232.8	412.7	.....	.....	....	.....	3,723.1	1,161,673.46
......	.....	.....	.....	.....	.....	.....	....	.....	2,211.5	463,184.52
......	.....	.....	.....	.....	.....	.....	....	.....	2,397.2	502,068.94
......	.....	.....	2,196.1	2,679.5	.....	457.6	....	.....	5,333.2	3,911,290.08
......	.....	.....	.....	.....	.....	.....	....	.....	7,086.2	1,269,346.17
......	.....	.....	.....	.....	.....	.....	....	.....	7,996.1	1,432,345.33
......	.....	.....	2,364.4	1,722.9	.....	861.1	....	.....	4,948.4	3,500,577.33
6,299.2	.....	.....	.....	.....	.....	.....	....	.....	6,299.2	744,000.00
......	846.7	.....	687.5	32.2	.....	212.4	....	.....	5,618.5	1,612,629.32
2,804.2	.....	.....	.....	.....	.....	.....	....	.....	2,804.2	347,743.63
829.4	.....	.....	19.1	359.2	.....	333.8	48.4	.....	3,280.6	993,607.58
......	.....	.....	.....	.....	.....	.....	....	.....	2,229.3	466,900.19
......	.....	.....	.....	.....	.....	.....	....	.....	2,188.5	458,366.77
......	.....	.....	.....	.....	.....	.....	....	.....	2,397.8	502,188.11
......	.....	.....	.....	.....	.....	.....	....	.....	2,257.9	472,887.04
......	.....	.....	.....	.....	.....	.....	....	.....	2,245.4	470,273.02
......	.....	.....	.....	.....	.....	.....	....	.....	2,156.1	451,579.03
......	.....	.....	.....	.....	.....	.....	....	.....	884.7	185,286.12
......	.....	.....	.....	.....	.....	.....	....	.....	3,271.0	585,934.23
......	.....	1,645.3	.....	.....	.....	.....	....	.....	1,645.3	460,693.52
......	.....	.....	.....	.....	.....	.....	....	.....	4,312.7	884,093.25
......	.....	1,941.0	.....	.....	.....	.....	....	.....	1,941.0	543,482.24
......	.....	.....	.....	.....	.....	.....	....	.....	108.0	20,520.00
......	.....	.....	.....	.....	.....	.....	....	.....	3,835.3	728,706.62
......	29.0	.....	.....	.....	.....	.....	....	.....	7,162.1	1,363,118.68
2,400.0	.....	.....	.....	.....	.....	.....	....	.....	2,400.0	372,000.00
......	.....	.....	.....	.....	.....	.....	....	.....	4,339.9	889,682.78
......	.....	.....	282.7	.....	.....	.....	....	.....	436.3	268,979.95
......	.....	.....	.....	.....	.....	.....	....	.....	6,142.1	921,310.05
......	.....	.....	.....	.....	.....	.....	....	.....	7,345.0	1,395,552.85
6,127.5	.....	.....	.....	.....	.....	.....	....	.....	6,127.5	796,576.95
......	.....	.....	.....	.....	.....	.....	....	.....	6,167.1	616,710.50
......	.....	.....	.....	.....	.....	.....	....	.....	6,226.4	933,959.85
2,924.6	.....	.....	.....	.....	.....	.....	....	.....	2,924.6	380,226.99
......	.....	.....	217.1	.....	.....	.....	....	.....	328.1	205,112.37
......	618.6	.....	.....	.....	.....	.....	....	.....	618.6	167,031.99
......	.....	2,788.7	.....	.....	.....	.....	....	.....	2,788.7	725,065.90
3,810.2	.....	.....	.....	.....	.....	.....	....	.....	3,810.2	495,327.95
6,667.8	.....	.....	.....	.....	.....	.....	....	265.8	6,933.6	1,075,479.56
......	.....	.....	.....	.....	.....	.....	....	1,281.7	1,281.7	1,148,851.21
......	1,909.4	115.8	.....	.....	.....	.....	....	.....	2,105.2	560,823.85
......	4,400.6	.....	.....	.....	.....	.....	....	.....	6,300.7	1,549,196.75
4,063.6	.....	.....	.....	.....	.....	.....	....	.....	4,063.6	528,266.05
......	.....	.....	.....	.....	4,688.8	.....	....	.....	4,688.8	3,188,360.20
6,140.7	82.2	.....	.....	.....	.....	.....	....	.....	6,222.9	820,493.97

* Cargo ex-U.S. naval stocks in England purchased by the A.R.A. the U.S. Navy.

†† Value includes cost of cargo only. Freight paid by the United Kingdom; cf. Table 396 B.

[*Continued on next page*]

Table 395—*Continued*

Detail by Steamers of Relief Deliveries, Paid for by Fun(

Arrival No.	Steamer or Source	Port of Sailing	Date of Arrival	Port of Arrival	Wheat Flour	Cereal Flour	Wheat Grain
			1919				
300	Shooters Island	Philadelphia	June 23	Danzig	2,998.0	67.5	.....
301	West Cressy, II	New York	June 23	Danzig	......	.....	.....
298	Lake Licoco	Montreal	June 23	Danzig	2,754.3	.....	.....
296	Coquinor	Montreal	June 23	Danzig	2,520.1	.....	.....
302	West Chester	New York	June 24	Danzig	......	.....	.....
308	Ceralvo	Montreal	June 26	Danzig	1,272.3	.....	.....
310	Phoenix Bridge	Philadelphia	June 26	Danzig	......	.....	.....
320	Lake Lilicusum	Montreal	July 1	Danzig	2,781.3	.....	.....
329	Lipsos	Rotterdam	July 2	Danzig	......	.....	.....
335	Hilda	Rotterdam	July 7	Danzig	......	.....	.....
349	Garabaldi	Liverpool	July 14	Danzig	......	.....	.....
350	Hansa	Liverpool	July 25				
355	Faraby	New York	July 19	Danzig	......	.....	.....
371	Schwarzenfels	New York	Aug. 12	Danzig	......	266.0	.....
375	Gerfreid	New York	Aug. 19	Danzig	284.4	8,012.2	.....
376	Kagera	New York	Aug. 21	Danzig	2,866.2	.....	.....
...	Ex-Danzig Stock	(U.S.A.)	....	....	859.4	.....	.....
	Total				**124,273.8**	**8,345.7**	**12,393.**

§ Cocoa 47.6, sugar 1.6.

POLAND—Countries Other than United States

A. Detail by Steamers of Relief Deliveries by the United Kingdom

Table 396

Armistice Period, 1919

Steamer or Source	Port of Sailing	Date of Arrival	Port of Arrival	Contents of Cargoes in Net Metric Tons of 1,000 Kilograms or 2,204.6 Pounds: Cereal Flour	Grain	Beans	Pork Products	Misc. Food	Soap	Clothing and Medical Supplies	Misc. Non-Foods	Tota Ton
		1919										
Rex	London	Apr. 24	Danzig	702.0	......	413.0	.....	100.0	48.0	370.0*	......	1,63
Marnetown	Liverpool	Apr. 24	Danzig	1,526.0	......	288.0	106.0	224.0	59.0	.....	......	2,20
Peveril	London	May 5	Danzig	556.0	......	661.0	640.0	10.0	461.0	1.0	......	2,32
Thagra	Liverpool	June 8	Danzig	.....	4,096.0	.....	.....	.....	.....	.....	......	4,09
Miscellaneous	(U.K.)	....	Danzig	455.0	1,717.0	.....	509.0	207.0	.....	1,053.0	7,260.0	11,20
Total †				**3,239.0**	**5,813.0**	**1,362.0**	**1,255.0**	**541.0**	**568.0**	**1,424.0***	**7,260.0**	**21,46**

* Medical supplies. Of the total, 1,054.0 is clothing and 370.0 medical supplies.

† Cf. Table 133 A for value of these supplies.

POLAND

Table 397

Summary of Arrivals by Operations

Operation	Table No.	Flour	Rice	Beans, Peas	Corn Grits
A.R.A.—Congressional Appropriation, $100,000,000 Fund—Food	398	858.2	2,193.3	2,898.2	.....
A.R.A.—Congressional Appropriation, $100,000,000 Fund—Clothing	399	......	......	......	.....
A.R.A.-European Children's Fund—Food	400, 401	8,617.8	10,763.3	16,523.8	1,689.
A.R.A.-European Children's Fund—Clothing	402	......	......	......	.....
Polish Government Donation—Food	404	48,325.7	531.0	728.0	.....
Other Polish Donations—Food	...	......	......	......	.....
Joint Distribution Committee—Children's Relief	...	......	......	......	.....
Commonwealth Fund—Intelligentsia Clothing	403	......	......	......	.....
U.S. Grain Corporation (Act of Congress, March 30, 1920)	405	202,564.0	......	......	.....
United Kingdom—Finance on Freight	405n	......	......	......	.....
American Friends Service Committee	331n	......	......	......	.....
A.R.A.W.—Danzig Bulk Sale to Polish Government	289	7,720.3	......	......	.....
Total		**268,086.0**	**13,487.6**	**20,150.0**	**1,689.**

merican Relief Administration

om the Congressional Appropriation for Relief

Rye Grain	Beans, Peas	Rice	Pork Products	Lard	Lard Substitute	Milk	Sugar, Cocoa	Misc.	Total Tons	Total Value
Contents of Cargoes in Net Metric Tons of 1,000 Kilograms or 2,204.6 Pounds										
......	699.8	744.8	.....	.....	419.4	.....	....	.....	4,929.5	$ 1,250,367.70
5,751.8	.....	.....	.....	.....	.....	.....	....	1,007.7	6,759.5	1,538,776.68
......	.....	.....	.....	.....	.....	.....	....	.....	2,754.3	523,324.79
......	.....	.....	.....	.....	.....	.....	....	.....	2,520.1	478,826.60
6,198.0	.....	.....	.....	.....	.....	.....	....	913.9	7,111.9	1,523,141.08
......	.....	.....	.....	.....	.....	.....	....	.....	1,272.3	241,737.76
4,334.0	.....	.....	.....	.....	.....	.....	....	.....	4,334.0	563,419.09
......	.....	.....	.....	.....	.....	.....	....	.....	2,781.3	528,452.70
5,341.2	.....	.....	.....	.....	.....	.....	....	.....	5,341.2	827,890.81
5,785.8	.....	.....	.....	.....	.....	.....	....	.....	5,785.8	896,804.27
......	.....	.....	.....	.....	.....	.....	....	1,002.0	1,002.0	986,150.90
......	.....	751.2	.....	.....	.....	.....	....	415.2	1,166.4	521,235.84
......	.....	.....	.....	.....	.....	.....	....	889.1	1,155.1	743,202.38
......	.....	.....	.....	.....	.....	.....	....	.....	8,296.6	1,416,107.51
......	.....	.....	.....	.....	.....	.....	....	.....	2,866.2	544,586.36
......	.....	.....	.....	.....	.....	.....	.8	.....	860.2	163,473.30
9,478.0	**8,586.3**	**8,041.2**	**9,088.6**	**7,600.5**	**5,108.2**	**2,100.8**	**49.2§**	**5,777.4**	**260,843.2**	**$63,191,316.61**

POLAND

B. Detail by Steamers of Freight Finance, Paid by the United Kingdom

Table 396—*Continued*

Armistice Period, 1919

ival .*	Steamer or Source	Port of Sailing	Date of Arrival	Port of Arrival	Contents of Cargoes in Net Metric Tons of 1,000 Kilograms or 2,204.6 Pounds: Wheat Flour	Wheat	Total Tons	Finance on Freight only
			1919					
92	Navarino	Canada	May 14	Danzig	6,142.1	......	6,142.1	$ 225,610.00
19	Athenic	St. John	May 24	Danzig	......	6,167.1	6,167.1	226,520.00
24	Queen Alexandria	Portland	May 25	Danzig	......	6,226.4	6,226.4	228,550.00
..	U.S. Liquidation Supplies †	....	......	....	......	......	......	709,240.00
	Total	....	....	....	**6,142.1**	**12,393.5**	**18,535.6**	**$1,389,920.00**

Arrival numbers from Table 395.

† Cf. Table 122. Detail of tonnage handled by U.K. not available.

mmary of Arrivals

construction Period, 1919–1924

Pork Products	Milk	Cocoa	Sugar	Misc. Food	Forage	Soap	Clothing and Misc.	Total Tons	Total Value
Commodities in Net Metric Tons of 1,000 Kilograms or 2,204.6 Pounds									
765.0	6,284.2	766.3	1,647.1	20.3	.....	441.6	.....	15,874.2	$ 5,863,141.40
.....	.....	.....	......	.....	.....	.....	826.7	826.7	192,700.63
,003.3	15,121.7	1,234.1	5,435.4	471.6	.....	263.7	42.4	65,166.5	13,395,341.82
.....	.....	.....	......	.....	.....	.....	1,915.5	1,915.5	4,689,625.07
852.0	.....	.....	1,205.9	.....	.....	.....	.....	51,642.6	7,619,280.26
.....	.....	31.4	95.8	913.7	.....	.....	.....	1,040.9	40,094.51
.....	506.0	.....	......	.....	.....	31.0	.....	537.0	273,555.00
.....	.....	.....	......	.....	.....	.....	30.4	30.4	57,532.49
.....	.....	.....	......	.....	.....	.....	.....	202,564.0	24,353,590.97
.....	.....	.....	......	.....	.....	.....	.....	......	8,102,558.32
.....	.....	.....	......	.....	633.3	.....	.....	633.3	30,291.26
.....	.....	.....	......	.....	.....	.....	.....	7,720.3	864,562.40
,620.3	**21,911.9**	**2,031.8**	**8,384.2**	**1,405.6**	**633.3**	**736.3**	**2,815.0**	**347,951.4**	**$65,482,274.13**

Table 398

Detail by Steamers of Children's Relief Arrivals Paid for by Funds from th

Steamer	Port of Sailing	Date of Arrival	Port of Arrival	Flour
		1919		
Cape Henry	New York	Apr. 13	Danzig	.....
Lake St. Regis, III	Rotterdam	Apr. 17	Danzig	.....
Lake Tulare, IV	Rotterdam	Apr. 30	Danzig	.....
Lake St. Regis, IV	Rotterdam	May 5	Danzig	.....
Democracy, II	St. Nazaire	May 6	Danzig	858.2
Lake Traverse, III	Rotterdam	May 7	Danzig	.....
Lake Clear, IV	St. Nazaire	May 13	Danzig	.....
Wakanna	Newport News	June 1	Danzig	.....
Lake Eckhart, IV	St. Nazaire	June 1	Danzig	.....
Yakima	Baltimore	June 13	Danzig	.....
Westward Ho, II	New York	June 14	Danzig	.....
Shooters Island	Philadelphia	June 23	Danzig	.....
West Cressey, II	New York	June 23	Danzig	.....
Faraby	New York	July 19	Danzig	.....
Yssel †	Rotterdam	Oct. 14	Danzig	.....
E. H. Stinnes †	Rotterdam	Nov. 30	Danzig	.....
Admiral †	Rotterdam	Dec. 31	Danzig	.....
Schwarzenfels and Danzig Stocks ‡	New York	....	Danzig	.....
Freight, Insurance, and Sundry Charges	....	....	....	.....
Total	....	....	....	**858.2**
Edjern, Ex-Esthonia Stock	Reval	....	Danzig	.....
Grand Total	....	....	....	**858.2**

* Codliver oil.

† Ex-Remschied, which sailed from New York, arrived Rotterda August 21, 1919.

POLAND—American Relief Administration

Detail by Steamers of Clothing Arrivals, Paid for by Funds from the Congressional Appropriation for Relief—Reconstruction Period, 1919–1924

Table 399

Steamer	Port of Sailing	Date of Arrival	Port of Arrival	Shoes (Pairs)	Garments (Single)	Total Metric Tons	Total Value
		1919					
Democracy, I	Rotterdam	Mar. 27	Danzig	57,636	1,069,060	460.3	$ 98,201.
Lake Traverse, III	Rotterdam	May 7	Danzig	14,413	267,263	125.5	33,817
Lake St. Regis, V	Rotterdam	June 10	Danzig	28,818	534,530	240.9	60,681
Total *	....	....	....	**100,867**	**1,870,853**	**826.7**	**$192,700**

* Purchased from the C.R.B. by the A.R.A. Cf. "Commission for Relief in Belgium, Statistical Review of Relief Operations," George I. Gay. The Polish Central Committee receipted for these supplies. A.R.A. supervised the internal distribution. No further detail availa

ıerican Relief Administration

.gressional Appropriation for Relief—Reconstruction Period, 1919–1924

Rice	Beans, Peas	Pork Products	Milk	Cocoa	Sugar	Misc. Foods *	Soap	Total Tons	Total Value
Contents of Cargoes in Net Metric Tons of 1,000 Kilograms or 2,204.6 Pounds									
.....	.....	.....	.....	54.0	199.2	....	.....	253.2	$ 69,794.35
.....	.....	.....	.....	126.0	.....	....	.....	126.0	52,920.00
400.6	.....	.....	.....	.....	.....	....	.....	400.6	112,179.48
.....	.....	.....	.....	.....	.....	20.3	.....	20.3	12,884.15
.....	.....	.....	.....	.....	.....	....	.....	858.2	175,927.51
.....	57.2	.....	.....	.....	.....	....	.....	57.2	17,726.11
.....	.....	.....	474.1	.....	.....	....	.....	474.1	185,104.50
778.6	1,263.0	.....	.....	.....	.....	....	.....	2,041.6	543,451.14
.....	.....	765.0	274.0	.....	.....	....	.....	1,039.0	749,572.50
551.0	.....	.....	.....	.....	.....	....	.....	551.0	143,260.00
.....	.....	.....	.....	274.5	101.6	....	.....	376.1	134,169.44
.....	.....	.....	784.9	.....	.....	....	.....	784.9	393,550.00
.....	.....	.....	.....	81.2	.....	....	.....	81.2	32,473.20
.....	.....	.....	.....	45.6	.....	....	.....	45.6	18,248.40
.....	.....	.....	845.1	.....	600.0	....	.....	1,445.1	522,832.50
.....	.....	.....	935.7	.....	246.3	....	218.8	1,400.8	520,438.56
.....	.....	.....	1,102.3	.....	.....	....	.....	1,102.3	487,310.00
347.1	1,578.0	.....	1,868.1	185.0	500.0	....	222.8	4,701.0	1,639,136.56
.....	.....	.....	.....	.....	.....	....	.....	......	22,003.00
,077.3	**2,898.2**	**765.0**	**6,284.2**	**766.3**	**1,647.1**	**20.3**	**441.6**	**15,758.2**	**$5,832,981.40**
116.0	.....	.....	.....	.....	.....	....	.....	116.0	30,160.00
:,193.3	**2,898.2**	**765.0**	**6,284.2**	**766.3**	**1,647.1**	**20.3**	**441.6**	**15,874.2**	**$5,863,141.40**

Schwarzenfels arrived August 12, 1919; Danzig stock taken from
›us cargoes arriving various dates.

Table 400†

Detail by Steamers of Arrivals of Reli

Steamer or Source	Transshipped via	Port of Sailing	Date of Arrival	Port of Arrival
			1919	
E. H. Stinnes, Ex-Comité National Purchase		Rotterdam	Nov. 30	Danzig
Commercial, Ex-Comité National Purchase		Rotterdam	Dec. 4	Danzig
National, Ex-Comité National Purchase		Rotterdam	Dec. 5	Danzig
Admiral, Ex-Comité National Purchase		Rotterdam	Dec. 31	Danzig
Barmen, Ex-Comité National Purchase		Antwerp	Dec. 31	Danzig
Purchase, Ex-Czecho-Slovakian Government		(Prague)	Dec. ..	(Warsaw)
Total for December				
			1920	
Amsteldijk	Frederich Karl to Agnes	New Orleans	Jan. 13	Rotterda
Bonn, III, Ex-Comité National Purchase		Antwerp	Jan. 13	Danzig
St. Thomas, I		London	Jan. 16	Danzig
Jolly George		(United Kingdom)	Jan. 17	Danzig
Total for January				
Shortsville		New York	Feb. 9	Danzig
Wisla		New York	Feb. 16	Danzig
Agnes, Ex-Bridges & Company Purchase		Hamburg	Feb. 16	Danzig
St. Thomas, II		London	Feb. 19	Danzig
Pawnee		Philadelphia	Feb. 28	Danzig
Total for February				
Krakow		New York	Mar. 3	Danzig
Ina Blumenthal		Liverpool	Mar. 4	Danzig
Clauseus		San Francisco	Mar. 9	Danzig
Vardulia, Ex-A.R.A.W. Arrivals		New York	Mar. 15	Danzig
Echo, I, Ex-Antwerp Purchase		Antwerp	Mar. 15	Danzig
Vardulia		New York	Mar. 15	Danzig
Willdomino		New York	Mar. 20	Danzig
Carib, II	Bertha	New York	Mar. 26	Hamburg
Kerowlee		New York	Mar. 29	Hamburg
Local Purchase, Ex-Polish Government		(Poland)	Mar. 31	(Poland)
Total for March				
Kermanshah	Kellersee, I; Progress, I	New York	Apr. 3	Hamburg
Valacia		New York	Apr. 5	Danzig
Vasconia		New York	Apr. 5	Danzig
Kermoor, II	Haval, I; Suzanne, I	New York	Apr. 11	Hamburg
Mexico, I		New York	Apr. 14	Danzig
Ozaukee, II		New York	Apr. 24	Danzig
Total for April				
Warszawa, I, Ex-London Purchase		(United Kingdom)	May 4	Danzig
Kersan, III	Reval, V	New York	May 27	Hamburg
Total for May				
Kermit, I	Normal, I	New York	June 5	Hamburg
Corson, I		New York	June 10	Danzig
Kerlew, II	Kellersee, II	Norfolk	June 24	Hamburg
Bird City		New York	June 26	Danzig
Total for June				

† Cf. Table 401 for transshipments.
* Detail of miscellaneous commodities indicated by the following indexes: [a], auto parts; [b], corned beef; [c], whalemeat; [d], salmon; [e], soup; [f], codliver oil; [g], soap; [s], sacks. See end of Table 400 (page 766) complete detail.

R.A.-European Children's Fund

pplies—Reconstruction Period, 1919–1924

Contents of Cargoes in Net Metric Tons of 1,000 Kilograms or 2,204.6 Pounds											Total Value
								Miscellaneous *			
Flour	Rice	Beans, Peas	Corn Grits	Pork Products	Milk	Cocoa	Sugar	Food	Soap, etc.	Total Tons	
.....	.....	.....	.....	**121.7**	.....	.....	.....	....	....	**121.7**	**$ 51,045.35**
.....	.....	1,166.1	.....	247.3	.....	.....	.....	....	....	1,413.4	206,265.95
.....	.....	233.9	.....	243.4	.....	.....	.....	....	....	477.3	119,943.77
.....	.....	.....	.....	427.8	.....	.....	.....	....	....	427.8	176,278.36
994.1	.....	.....	.....	.....	.....	.....	.....	....	....	1,994.1	190,691.49
.....	.....	.....	.....	.....	.....	.....	443.0	....	....	443.0	90,221.38
,994.1	.....	**1,400.0**	.....	**918.5**	.....	.....	**443.0**	....	....	**4,755.6**	**$ 783,400.95**
.....	158.0	.....	.....	.....	.....	.....	.....	....	....	158.0	$ 47,430.67
,985.7	.....	.....	.....	.....	.....	.....	.....	....	....	1,985.7	195,773.59
.....	146.8	.....	.....	.....	.....	.....	.....	....	....	146.8	14,808.34
.....	250.1	.....	.....	.....	.....	.....	.....	....	....	250.1	26,440.56
,985.7	**554.9**	.....	.....	.....	.....	.....	.....	....	....	**2,540.6**	**$ 284,453.16**
.....	.....	588.0	.....	.....	.....	.....	.....	....	1.1[a]	589.1	$ 123,615.24
.....	.....	.....	.....	.....	158.7	.....	.....	....	5.8[as]	164.5	73,041.51
.....	.....	.....	.....	.....	380.1	.....	.....	....	....	380.1	189,675.66
.....	76.4	.....	.....	.....	.....	.....	.....	....	....	76.4	8,246.77
336.9	.....	.....	.....	.....	.....	.....	.....	....	....	336.9	52,429.39
336.9	**76.4**	**588.0**	.....	.....	**538.8**	.....	.....	....	**6.9**	**1,547.0**	**$ 447,008.57**
.....	.....	.....	.....	.....	37.0	.....	.....	....	....	37.0	$ 12,393.03
.....	.....	.....	.....	.....	.....	.....	.....	41.4[b]	....	41.4	24,093.14
.....	.....	4,089.0	.....	.....	.....	.....	.....	....	....	4,089.0	851,217.76
326.3	.....	.....	.....	225.3	.....	.....	.....	....	....	551.6	225,178.88
.....	400.3	.....	.....	.....	.....	.....	.....	....	....	400.3	109,410.78
.....	868.6	.....	.....	.....	1,776.4	50.8	.....	....	15.0[a]	2,710.8	1,065,474.38
.....	1,706.8	2,044.2	.....	304.1	430.8	.....	378.8	....	....	4,864.7	1,387,683.88
.....	.....	.....	.....	.....	84.9	.....	.....	....	....	84.9	27,394.67
.....	.....	.....	.....	13.6	.....	.....	.....	....	....	13.6	8,531.29
.....	.....	.....	.....	.....	.....	.....	1,001.5	....	....	1,001.5	250,364.25
326.3	**2,975.7**	**6,133.2**	.....	**543.0**	**2,329.1**	**50.8**	**1,380.3**	**41.4**	**15.0**	**13,794.8**	**$ 3,961,742.06**
.....	.....	.....	.....	.....	100.1	.....	.....	....	....	100.1	$ 32,252.46
.....	.....	239.6	.....	219.2	1,014.8	151.4	.....	....	7.1[as]	1,632.1	688,553.00
.....	.....	.....	.....	.....	275.9	.....	.....	....	....	275.9	98,226.42
.....	.....	.....	.....	.....	238.5	101.6	.....	....	....	340.1	113,259.86
.....	.....	.....	.....	.....	85.7	.....	.....	....	12.0[a]	97.7	56,847.44
.....	.....	.....	.....	.....	.....	.....	.....	....	.1[a]	.1	75.92
.....	.....	**239.6**	.....	**219.2**	**1,715.0**	**253.0**	.....	....	**19.2**	**2,446.0**	**$ 989,215.10**
.....	345.5	.....	.....	.....	.....	.....	.....	....	....	345.5	$ 66,245.48
.....	.....	105.4	.....	.....	.....	.....	.....	....	....	105.4	17,960.98
.....	**345.5**	**105.4**	.....	.....	.....	.....	.....	....	....	**450.9**	**$ 84,206.46**
.....	.....	63.0	.....	44.8	122.5	.....	.....	....	....	230.3	$ 72,488.43
.....	.....	775.9	.....	87.6	814.9	.....	.....	....	3.0[a]	1,681.4	418,057.82
.....	.....	178.9	.....	.....	75.7	.....	.....	....	....	254.6	57,350.60
.....	.....	.....	.....	.....	.....	.....	.....	....	4.0[a]	4.0	9,405.39
.....	.....	**1,017.8**	.....	**132.4**	**1,013.1**	.....	.....	....	**7.0**	**2,170.3**	**$ 557,302.24**

[*Continued on next page*]

Table 400—*Continued*

Detail by Steamers o

Steamer or Source	Transshipped via	Port of Sailing	Date of Arrival	Port of Arrival
			1920	
Mar Blanco, I	Aller, I	New York	July 2	Hamburg
Kermoor, III	Haval, II	New York	July 3	Hamburg
Monticello, I	Saale, I	New York	July 9	Hamburg
Poznan, I	....	New York	July 13	Danzig
Mar Caspio, II	Saale, I	New York	July 16	Hamburg
Wheeling Mold	....	New York	July 22	Danzig
Mar Mediterraneo, II	Saale, I	New York	July 22	Hamburg
Fraser & Company Purchase	Alster to Pregel, I	Rotterdam	July 27	Rotterdam
Paul Stuppel Purchase	Fanal, I	Hamburg	July 27	Hamburg
Total for July	....	....	....	....
Verbania, I	....	New York	Aug. 1	Danzig
Herefordshire	Progress, III	Rangoon	Aug. 18	Hamburg
Kermit, II	Kellersee, III	New York	Aug. 21	Hamburg
Mette Jensen, I	Progress, II	New York	Aug. 22	Hamburg
Mette Jensen, I	Pregel, I	New York	Aug. 22	Hamburg
Susquehanna	....	New York	Aug. 23	Danzig
Mar Blanco, II	Progress, II	New York	Aug. 24	Hamburg
Monticello, II	Suzanne, II	New York	Aug. 28	Hamburg
Warszawa, III	....	Philadelphia	Aug. 30	Danzig
Total for August	....	....	....	....
Mar Rojo	Weichsel, I	New York	Sept. 16	Hamburg
Corson, II	Normal, II	Philadelphia	Sept. 19	Hamburg
Total for September	....	....	....	....
Susquehanna, II	....	New York	Oct. 13	Danzig
Mystic, I	Naval	New York	Oct. 26	Hamburg
Total for October	....	....	....	....
Danzig Stock	....	(U.S.A.)	Nov. 1	Danzig
Beursplein, I	Hammonia, I	New York	Nov. 1	Hamburg
Iowan, I	Hammonia, I	New York	Nov. 6	Hamburg
American, I	Mineral, I	New York	Nov. 15	Hamburg
Texan	Progress, III	New York	Nov. 22	Hamburg
Susquehanna, III	....	New York	Nov. 26	Danzig
Orlando	....	(United Kingdom)	Nov. 26	Danzig
Total for November	....	....	....	....
Homer City, I	Weichsel, II	New York	Dec. 19	Hamburg
Cornish City, I	....	New York	Dec. 31	Danzig
Local Purchase, Ex-Polish Government	....	(Poland)	Dec. ..	(Poland)
Total for December	....	....	....	....
			1921	
Paz de Epalza	Aeolus, VI	New York	Jan. 9	Hamburg
American, II	Echo, III	New York	Jan. 12	Hamburg
Clarksburg	Fanal, II	New York	Jan. 18	Hamburg
Susquehanna, IV	....	New York	Jan. 18	Danzig
Eastern City	....	New York	Jan. 25	Danzig
Ipswich	Progress, IV	New York	Jan. 25	Hamburg
Hamburg Stock	Royal	New York	....	Hamburg
Local Purchase, Ex-Polish Government	....	(Poland)	Jan. ..	(Poland)
Total for January	....	....	....	....

A.R.A.-European Children's Fund

Arrivals of Relief Supplies

Flour	Rice	Beans, Peas	Corn Grits	Pork Products	Milk	Cocoa	Sugar	Miscellaneous: Food	Miscellaneous: Soap, etc.	Total Tons	Total Value
	Contents of Cargoes in Net Metric Tons of 1,000 Kilograms or 2,204.6 Pounds										
.....	.....	28.2	.....	.....	201.1	.....	.....	1.5[c]	....	230.8	$ 85,314.38
.....	.....	294.0	.....	.....	105.3	.....	.....	....	....	399.3	74,414.10
.....	.....	.....	.....	.....	28.6	.....	.....	....	....	28.6	11,895.38
.....	.....	.....	.....	.....	.....	152.4	.....	....	....	152.4	41,987.22
.....	.....	.....	.....	104.8	21.4	.....	.....	....	....	126.2	58,137.60
.....	.....	.....	.....	.....	.....	.....	.....	....	4.0[a]	4.0	7,027.59
.....	.....	.....	.....	198.6	59.1	150.4	.....	....	....	408.1	174,365.83
.....	.....	286.6	.....	.....	.....	.....	.....	....	....	286.6	29,836.19
.....	.....	396.0	.....	.....	.....	.....	.....	....	....	396.0	34,965.00
.....	.....	**1,004.8**	.....	**303.4**	**415.5**	**302.8**	.....	**1.5**	**4.0**	**2,032.0**	**$ 517,943.29**
.....	.....	.....	.....	17.3	117.6	.....	.....	....	.4[a]	135.3	$ 75,492.48
.....	739.9	.....	.....	.....	.....	.....	.....	....	....	739.9	97,163.67
.....	.....	.....	.....	27.3	.....	.....	.....	....	....	27.3	17,252.04
.....	.....	.....	.....	16.7	74.3	.....	.....	....	....	91.0	48,618.19
.....	.....	.....	.....	.....	9.4	.....	.....	....	....	9.4	4,885.04
.....	.....	.....	.....	.....	.....	.....	.....	....	2.4[s]	2.4	937.81
.....	.....	.....	.....	193.1	.....	.....	.....	....	....	193.1	88,018.57
.....	.....	.....	.....	.....	122.8	.....	.....	....	....	122.8	68,442.12
.....	.....	70.9	.....	89.1	.....	.....	.....	....	....	160.0	55,458.78
.....	**739.9**	**70.9**	.....	**343.5**	**324.1**	.....	.....	....	**2.8**	**1,481.2**	**$ 456,268.70**
.....	.....	.....	.....	.....	156.2	.....	.....	....	....	156.2	$ 86,263.41
.....	.....	61.2	.....	.....	.....	.....	.....	....	....	61.2	8,890.62
.....	.....	**61.2**	.....	.....	**156.2**	.....	.....	....	....	**217.4**	**$ 95,154.03**
.....	.....	.....	.....	.....	.....	.....	.....	....	.7[a]	.7	$ 2,076.78
.....	.....	.....	.....	.....	228.5	.....	.....	....	....	228.5	140,509.01
.....	.....	.....	.....	.....	**228.5**	.....	.....	....	**.7**	**229.2**	**$ 142,585.79**
.....	.....	.....	.....	239.7	250.7	.....	.....	60.6[b]	....	551.0	$ 259,919.05
.....	.....	.....	.....	.....	165.5	.....	.....	....	....	165.5	101,634.96
.....	.....	.....	.....	.....	148.9	.....	.....	....	....	148.9	91,432.93
.....	.....	.....	.....	.....	60.5	.....	.....	....	....	60.5	37,280.37
.....	.....	.....	.....	.....	.....	.....	.....	....	3.4[a]	3.4	1,879.90
.....	.....	.....	.....	.....	.....	.....	.....	....	.3[a]	.3	218.56
.....	.....	.....	.....	.....	.....	.....	.....	10.0[f]	....	10.0	3,963.14
.....	.....	.....	.....	**239.7**	**625.6**	.....	.....	**70.6**	**3.7**	**939.6**	**$ 496,328.91**
.....	.....	.....	.....	.....	.....	.....	.....	....	19.3[a]	19.3	$ 21,979.29
.....	.....	2,718.2	.....	242.0	1,227.9	93.8	.....	....	....	4,281.9	661,386.61
.....	.....	.....	.....	.....	.....	.....	264.9	....	....	264.9	48,997.23
.....	.....	**2,718.2**	.....	**242.0**	**1,227.9**	**93.8**	**264.9**	....	**19.3**	**4,566.1**	**$ 732,363.13**
170.4	.....	.....	.....	.....	.....	.....	.....	....	....	170.4	$ 16,397.20
.....	.....	.....	.....	.....	194.7	.....	.....	....	....	194.7	55,151.69
.....	80.0	.....	.....	.....	.....	.....	.....	....	....	80.0	8,723.81
.....	.....	.....	.....	.....	.....	.....	.....	....	.6[a]	.6	1,508.70
2,929.2	.....	.....	.....	.....	394.4	.....	.....	6.0[e]	....	3,329.6	403,028.88
.....	196.1	.....	.....	.....	1.4	.....	.....	....	....	197.5	21,649.94
.....	.....	.....	.....	59.9	.....	.....	.....	....	....	59.9	39,523.64
.....	.....	.....	.....	.....	.....	.....	373.5	....	....	373.5	69,084.43
3,099.6	**276.1**	.....	.....	**59.9**	**590.5**	.....	**373.5**	**6.0**	**.6**	**4,406.2**	**$ 615,068.29**

[*Continued on next page*]

Table 400—*Continued*

Detail by Steamers o

Steamer or Source	Transshipped via	Port of Sailing	Date of Arrival	Port of Arrival
			1921	
Moerdijk	Aeolus, VI	Portland	Feb. 6	Hamburg
Phoenix Bridge	Aeolus, II; Weichsel, III; Johanna; August, II	New Orleans	Feb. 21	Hamburg
Sophie Rickmers	Imperial, I; Weichsel, IV	New Orleans	Feb. 26	Hamburg
Oregonian, I	Hammonia, II	New York	Feb. 28	Hamburg
Hawaiian, I	Hammonia, II	New York	Feb. 28	Hamburg
Alexa		London	Feb. ..	Danzig
Local Purchase, Ex-Polish Government		(Poland)	Feb. ..	(Poland)
Total for February				
Borga	Aeolus, III	New York	Mar. 4	Hamburg
Watsness, I		New York	Mar. 5	Danzig
Bradclyde, II		New Orleans	Mar. 23	Hamburg
Pomona	Aeolus, IV	Portland	Mar. 28	Hamburg
Local Purchase	Paul	Hamburg	Mar. ..	Hamburg
Local Purchase, Ex-Polish Government		(Poland)	Mar. ..	(Poland)
Total for March				
Oregonian, II	Mineral, III	New York	Apr. 5	Hamburg
Westbrook	Adele, II; August, I	New Orleans	Apr. 9	Hamburg
Leeds City, II		New York	Apr. 12	Hamburg
Eemdijk	Weichsel, V	Seattle	Apr. 22	Hamburg
Bradford City, II	Hansa, III	New York	Apr. 23	Hamburg
Schoharie, II	Mottlau; Pregel, III; Weichsel, V; Sensal, II	New Orleans	Apr. 27	Hamburg
King City	Hansa, III; Mottlau; Pregel, III	Galveston	Apr. 29	Hamburg
Hamburg Stock	Progress, VI	(U.S.A.)	Apr. 29	Hamburg
Local Purchase, Ex-Polish Government		(Poland)	Apr. ..	(Poland)
Total for April				
East Cape		New York	May 2	Danzig
West Katan	Aeolus, VI	Portland	May 12	Hamburg
Watsness, II		New York	May 13	Danzig
Cornish City, II	Progress, VII	New York	May 14	Hamburg
Nemaha	Sea Lighter, R.W. 36; Progress, VII; Signal	Philadelphia	May 15	Hamburg
Hawaiian, II	Elina	New York	May 17	Hamburg
Vittorio Emmanuelle, IV		New York	May 24	Danzig
Chile	Arnold Koepke, Pomerania, Spitzberg	San Francisco	May 26	Danzig
Amassia	Sensal, III	New Orleans	May 27	Hamburg
American, IV	Fanal, III	New York	May 27	Hamburg
Oregonian, III	Hammonia, III; Alesia	New York	May 29	Hamburg
Norrtelje		London	May ..	Danzig
Suzanne	Naval, II	(United Kingdom)	May ..	Hamburg
Local Purchase, Ex-Polish Government		(Poland)	May ..	(Poland)
Total for May				
Orbita	Hinrich, I	New York	June 2	Hamburg
Walter Luckenbach	Hammonia, III	Philadelphia	June 12	Hamburg
Oropesa	Weichsel, VII	New York	June 17	Hamburg
Ruurlo	Weichsel, VI	New York	June 18	Hamburg
Mexico, II	Weichsel, VII	New Orleans	June 25	Hamburg
Hamburg Stock	Etzel, I	(U.S.A.)	June ..	Hamburg
Total for June				

R.A.-European Children's Fund

rivals of Relief Supplies

Flour	Rice	Beans, Peas	Corn Grits	Pork Products	Milk	Cocoa	Sugar	Miscellaneous Food	Miscellaneous Soap, etc.	Total Tons	Total Value
Contents of Cargoes in Net Metric Tons of 1,000 Kilograms or 2,204.6 Pounds											
83.2	.....	.....	.....	.....	.....	.....	.....	....	....	83.2	$ 7,956.17
.....	1,333.1	.....	.....	.....	.....	.....	.....	....	....	1,333.1	113,517.76
.....	412.1	.....	.....	.....	.....	.....	.....	....	....	412.1	32,027.85
406.0	.....	.....	.....	.....	.....	.....	.....	....	....	406.0	23,217.29
414.3	.....	.....	.....	.....	.....	.....	.....	....	....	414.3	23,607.91
.....	.....	.....	.....	.....	.....	.....	.....	....	1 Case[a]	.....	16.59
.....	.....	.....	.....	.....	.....	.....	587.9	....	....	587.9	108,740.92
903.5	**1,745.2**	.....	.....	.....	.....	.....	**587.9**	....	....	**3,236.6**	**$ 309,084.49**
195.3	.....	.....	.....	.....	.....	.....	.....	....	....	195.3	$ 10,808.42
.....	.....	.....	.....	203.1	176.0	.....	.....	....	....	379.1	92,566.95
.....	.....	.....	.....	.....	693.3	.....	.....	....	55.2[g]	748.5	175,225.31
108.4	.....	.....	.....	.....	.....	.....	.....	....	....	108.4	14,676.83
.....	.....	.....	.....	.....	.....	.....	.....	....	1.0[s]	1.0	1,311.10
.....	.....	.....	.....	.....	.....	.....	623.5	....	....	623.5	115,325.68
303.7	.....	.....	.....	**203.1**	**869.3**	.....	**623.5**	....	**56.2**	**2,055.8**	**$ 409,914.29**
.....	.....	.....	50.8	.....	.....	.....	.....	....	....	50.8	$ 2,760.18
.....	282.8	.....	.....	.....	.....	.....	.....	....	....	282.8	22,024.46
.....	.....	52.7	.....	357.4	302.3	127.0	.....	....	17.9[g]	857.3	165,280.52
.....	.....	.....	.....	.....	.....	.....	.....	300.2[d]	....	300.2	47,787.00
.....	.....	.....	.....	.....	227.6	.....	.....	....	....	227.6	72,404.88
.....	817.1	.....	.....	.....	.....	.....	.....	....	....	817.1	48,256.21
.....	257.2	.....	.....	.....	.....	.....	.....	....	....	257.2	22,019.91
.....	.....	.....	.....	62.2	.....	.....	.....	....	....	62.2	55,533.40
.....	.....	.....	.....	.....	.....	.....	1,317.3	....	....	1,317.3	243,654.39
.....	**1,357.1**	**52.7**	**50.8**	**419.6**	**529.9**	**127.0**	**1,317.3**	**300.2**	**17.9**	**4,172.5**	**$ 679,720.95**
.....	.....	140.7	88.4	114.2	346.2	.....	.....	....	53.3[g]	742.8	$ 140,248.27
.....	.....	.....	.....	.....	.....	.....	.....	57.8[d]	....	57.8	9,141.10
.....	.....	368.2	318.1	183.1	458.4	31.4	.....	....	....	1,359.2	210,296.43
.....	.....	.....	.....	.....	90.9	.....	.....	....	....	90.9	21,771.46
.....	.....	.....	.....	.....	255.3	.....	.....	....	....	255.3	64,590.02
.....	.....	.....	.....	.....	.....	.....	.....	....	20.4[g]	20.4	5,227.15
.....	.....	.....	.....	.....	655.9	84.7	.....	....	60.9[g]	801.5	186,695.43
.....	.....	1,290.9	.....	.....	.....	.5	.....	....	....	1,291.4	124,743.92
.....	212.0	.....	.....	.....	.....	.....	.....	....	....	212.0	13,644.36
.....	.....	.....	.....	.....	.....	.....	.....	....	30.4[g]	30.4	8,098.21
418.1	.....	.....	209.6	249.0	.....	.....	.....	....	30.3[g]	907.0	103,054.30
.....	.....	.....	.....	.....	.....	.....	.....	....	4 Cases[a]	.....	1,724.44
.....	.....	.....	.....	.....	.....	.....	.....	13.1[b]	....	13.1	7,823.24
.....	.....	.....	.....	.....	.....	.....	357.7	....	....	357.7	66,161.98
418.1	**212.0**	**1,799.8**	**616.1**	**546.3**	**1,806.7**	**116.6**	**357.7**	**70.9**	**195.3**	**6,139.5**	**$ 963,220.31**
.....	.....	.....	.....	103.3	61.7	76.2	.....	....	....	241.2	$ 48,899.81
25.2	.....	.....	.....	.....	.....	.....	.....	....	....	25.2	2,055.31
.....	.....	.....	.....	.....	257.0	.....	.....	....	....	257.0	77,587.30
.....	136.1	.....	.....	.....	.....	.....	.....	....	....	136.1	6,442.26
.....	171.1	.....	.....	.....	.....	.....	.....	....	....	171.1	8,316.42
56.8	.....	.....	.....	.....	.....	.....	.....	....	....	56.8	4,418.14
82.0	**307.2**	.....	.....	**103.3**	**318.7**	**76.2**	.....	....	....	**887.4**	**$ 147,719.24**

[*Continued on next page*]

Table 400—*Continued*

Detail by Steamers o

Steamer or Source	Transshipped via	Port of Sailing	Date of Arrival	Port of Arrival
			1921	
Orduna, I	Emma, I; Kaethe	New York	July 1	Hamburg
Hawaiian, III	Naval, III; Sensal, IV	New York	July 4	Hamburg
Bradclyde, III		New York	July 5	Danzig
Croxteth Hall	Smolensk, I	New York	July 6	Hamburg
Potomac, I		New York	July 6	Danzig
Oregonian, IV	Hansa, IV	New York	July 11	Hamburg
Westbrook, II		New York	July 12	Danzig
Michigan	Sea Lighter 164	New Orleans	July 20	Bremen
Jacques Cartier, II	Pologne	New Orleans	July 20	Le Havre
Ipswich, II	Imperial, III	New York	July 28	Hamburg
Vienna Stock		(U.S.A.)	July ..	Warsaw
Total for July				
Panama, I		San Francisco	Aug. 13	Danzig
West Kedron		San Francisco	Aug. 14	Hamburg
Guernsey, I		New York	Aug. 16	Danzig
Keilehaven	Weichsel, VIII	New Orleans	Aug. 24	Hamburg
Galileo	Smolensk, II	New York	Aug. 24	Hull
Adalia	Progress, VIII	New Orleans	Aug. 29	Hamburg
Estonia, I		New York	Aug. 30	Danzig
A.R.A.W. Stock		(U.S.A.)	Aug. ..	Danzig
Total for August				
Chile, II	Elsa, Greta, Progress, IX	San Francisco	Sept. 8	Hamburg
Noruega	Kaethe, II	New York	Sept. 15	Hamburg
Idefjord		Philadelphia	Sept. 18	Danzig
Ipswich, III	Greta	New York	Sept. 19	Hamburg
Total for September				
Virginian	Suzanne, VI	New York	Oct. 1	Hamburg
Latvia, II		New York	Oct. 5	Danzig
Clarksburg, IV	Weichsel, IX	Baltimore	Oct. 8	Hamburg
Hawaiian, V	Weichsel, IX; Etzel, II	New York	Oct. 10	Hamburg
Potomac, II		New York	Oct. 12	Danzig
Estonia, II		New York	Oct. 18	Danzig
Hamburg Sweepings	Pregel, IV	(U.S.A.)		Hamburg
Hamburg Stock	Signal	(U.S.A.)		Hamburg
Total for October				
Polonia, II		New York	Nov. 2	Danzig
Hudson	Moewe, I	New York	Nov. 3	Bremerhaven
Mexico, III	Aeolus, VIII; Echo, V	New Orleans	Nov. 3	Hamburg
Lituania, II		New York	Nov. 15	Danzig
Samnanger	Emma, III	New Orleans	Nov. 25	Hamburg
Local Purchase, Ex-Polish Government		(Poland)	Nov. ..	(Poland)
Total for November				
Mt. Clinton, II	Norma, I	New York	Dec. 7	Hamburg
Clarksburg, V	Norma, I	Norfolk	Dec. 12	Hamburg
Polonia, III		New York	Dec. 20	Danzig
Gdansk		New York	Dec. 23	Danzig
Total for December				

R.A.-European Children's Fund

rivals of Relief Supplies

Contents of Cargoes in Net Metric Tons of 1,000 Kilograms or 2,204.6 Pounds											Total Value
								Miscellaneous			
'lour	Rice	Beans, Peas	Corn Grits	Pork Products	Milk	Cocoa	Sugar	Food	Soap, etc.	Total Tons	
....	....	....	....	....	462.6	....	....	....	....	462.6	$ 112,992.42
....	....	....	....	....	....	103.8	....	....	....	103.8	10,076.91
....	....	120.5	....	....	205.5	....	....	....	....	326.0	79,865.62
....	....	....	....	151.3	....	....	....	....	....	151.3	31,637.79
....	....	....	351.4	64.4	....	....	....	....	....	415.8	30,972.10
....	....	....	410.4	....	....	....	....	....	....	410.4	37,884.43
....	....	352.8	....	....	184.5	....	....	....	....	537.3	88,110.68
....	488.1	....	....	....	....	....	....	....	....	488.1	27,787.53
....	373.8	....	....	....	....	....	....	....	....	373.8	21,837.15
....	....	....	....	....	3.2	....	....	....	....	3.2	753.94
....	....	....	....	....	....	....	....	15.3[b]	....	15.3	9,017.72
....	**861.9**	**473.3**	**761.8**	**215.7**	**855.8**	**103.8**	....	**15.3**	....	**3,287.6**	**$ 450,936.29**
962.5	780.4	670.2	....	....	....	....	....	....	....	2,413.1	$ 172,596.21
34.8	....	257.6	....	....	....	....	....	....	....	292.4	24,811.99
....	....	....	....	....	26.4	....	....	....	....	26.4	5,915.90
....	330.5	....	....	....	....	....	....	....	....	330.5	21,472.10
....	....	....	....	69.1	....	....	....	....	....	69.1	14,356.22
....	....	16.2	....	....	....	....	....	....	....	16.2	1,808.98
....	....	....	....	....	32.8	....	....	....	....	32.8	10,285.38
5.8	.2	....	....	.9	1.4	.1	....	....	....	8.4	2,287.54
003.1	**1,111.1**	**944.0**	....	**70.0**	**60.6**	**.1**	....	....	....	**3,188.9**	**$ 253,534.32**
....	....	11.5	....	....	....	....	....	....	....	11.5	$ 1,026.49
....	....	....	....	....	6.3	....	....	....	.6[a]	6.9	2,908.51
659.7	....	....	....	....	....	....	....	....	....	659.7	49,860.13
....	....	....	....	....	....	....	....	....	.3[a]	.3	450.34
659.7	....	**11.5**	....	....	**6.3**	....	....	....	**.9**	**678.4**	**$ 54,245.47**
....	....	....	....	....	78.7	....	....	....	....	78.7	$ 18,485.70
....	....	....	260.7	....	....	....	....	....	4.0[a]	264.7	27,381.39
....	....	....	....	273.8	....	....	....	....	....	273.8	67,023.50
....	....	....	....	....	648.3	....	....	....	....	648.3	162,198.18
....	....	....	....	....	....	95.1	....	....	....	95.1	9,405.39
....	....	....	....	....	....	....	....	....	1.6[a]	1.6	2,143.70
....	....	.6	....	....	....	....	....	....	....	.6	30.00
....	....	....	....	....	.6	....	....	....	....	.6	149.00
....	....	**.6**	**260.7**	**273.8**	**727.6**	**95.1**	....	....	**5.6**	**1,363.4**	**$ 286,816.86**
....	....	....	....	....	....	....	....	....	.8[a]	.8	$ 1,618.38
....	....	....	....	....	....	15.5	....	....	....	15.5	1,539.77
....	71.7	....	....	....	....	....	....	....	....	71.7	5,830.64
....	....	....	....	....	....	....	....	....	1.9[a]	1.9	4,390.24
....	145.8	....	....	....	....	....	....	....	....	145.8	10,068.95
....	....	....	....	....	....	....	301.1	....	....	301.1	55,692.96
....	**217.5**	....	....	....	....	**15.5**	**301.1**	....	**2.7**	**536.8**	**$ 79,140.94**
....	....	....	....	....	90.8	....	....	....	....	90.8	$ 18,251.46
....	....	....	....	48.2	....	....	....	....	....	48.2	11,195.90
....	....	....	....	....	....	....	....	....	.8[a]	.8	81.64
....	....	....	....	....	195.2	....	....	....	....	195.2	39,150.38
....	....	....	....	**48.2**	**286.0**	....	....	....	**.8**	**335.0**	**$ 68,679.38**

[*Concluded on next page*]

Table 400—*Concluded*

Detail by Steamers o

Steamer or Source	Transshipped via	Port of Sailing	Date of Arrival	Port of Arrival
			1922	
Gasconier	Hansa, V	New York	Jan. 26	Hamburg
Sapinero	Nuernberg	New Orleans	May 14	Hamburg
Minnekahda, VII	Elsfleth	New York	June 3	Hamburg
Manchuria, VII	Elsfleth, Brake	New York	June 11	Hamburg
St. Paul, II	Brake	New York	June 18	Hamburg
Total for June				
Warehouse Overages				
Total Gross Arrivals				
Deduct Transfers, Adjustments, etc.:				
Transferred to Danzig, for Other Destinations				
Transferred to Czecho-Slovakia				
Transferred to Hamburg				
Weight and Value of Auto Parts, Handled under General and Administrative Expense Account				
Port Adjustments, Shortages				
Total Deductions				
Total Net Arrivals §				

‡ There are 5 cases of auto parts, additional to metric tons as listed.
§ Includes 57,327.0 metric tons for children's relief and 7,839.5 metric tons for food drafts and bulk sales.

* Total 471.6 metric tons composed of: [b], corned beef, 96.1; [c], wha meat, 1.5; [d], salmon, 358.0; [e], soup, 6.0; [f], codliver oil, 10.0. Of t total 306.1 metric tons, 263.7 is soap and 42.4 sacks and containers. T latter were used in food draft and bulk sale deliveries.

POLAND—

Table 401*

Detail by Steamers of Transshipments to Fin

Transshipping Steamer	Source	Port of Sailing	Date of Arrival	Port of Arrival
			1920	
Frederich Karl	Amsteldijk	Rotterdam	Feb. 8	Hambur
Agnes	Frederich Karl	Hamburg	Feb. 16	Danzig
Bertha	Carib, II	Hamburg	Apr. 4	Danzig
Kellersee, I	Kermanshah	Hamburg	Apr. 13	Danzig
Progress, I	Kermanshah	Hamburg	Apr. 20	Danzig
Haval, I	Kermoor, II	Hamburg	Apr. 30	Danzig
Suzanne, I	Kermoor, II	Hamburg	May 9	Danzig
Reval, V	Kersan, III	Hamburg	June 11	Danzig
Normal, I	Kermit, I	Hamburg	June 13	Danzig
Kellersee, II	Kerlew, II	Hamburg	July 2	Danzig
Aller, I	Mar Blanco, I	Hamburg	July 14	Danzig
Haval, II	Kermoor, III	Hamburg	July 14	Danzig
Alster	Fraser & Company Purchase	Rotterdam	July 20	Hambur
Fanal, I	Paul Stuppel Purchase	Hamburg	July 30	Danzig
Saale, I	Monticello, I	Hamburg	Aug. 14	Danzig
Saale, I	Mar Caspio	Hamburg	Aug. 14	Danzig
Saale, I	Mar Mediterraneo, II	Hamburg	Aug. 14	Danzig
Progress, II	Mette Jensen, I	Hamburg	Sept. 4	Danzig
Progress, II	Mar Blanco, II	Hamburg	Sept. 4	Danzig
Normal, II	Corson, II	Hamburg	Sept. 19	Danzig
Weichsel, I	Mar Rojo	Hamburg	Sept. 30	Danzig
Suzanne, II	Monticello, II	Hamburg	Oct. 4	Danzig

* Cf. Table 400.

R.A.-European Children's Fund

rivals of Relief Supplies

Contents of Cargoes in Net Metric Tons of 1,000 Kilograms or 2,204.6 Pounds											Total Value
								Miscellaneous			
'lour	Rice	Beans, Peas	Corn Grits	Pork Products	Milk	Cocoa	Sugar	Food	Soap, etc.	Total Tons	
.....	.....	**213.2**	.....	.....	**28.5**	.....	.....	....	....	**241.7**	**$ 31,131.28**
64.9	.....	.....	.....	.....	.....	.....	.....	....	....	**64.9**	**$ 3,861.55**
.....	.....	.....	.....	.....	108.8	.....	.....	....	....	108.8	$ 18,488.74
.....	.....	.....	.....	.....	250.4	.....	.....	....	....	250.4	42,497.29
.....	.....	.....	.....	.....	119.8	.....	.....	....	....	119.8	20,340.24
.....	.....	.....	.....	.....	**479.0**	.....	.....	....	....	**479.0**	**$ 81,326.27**
.....	.....	.....	.....	.....	.....	.....	.....	....	**31.0**	**31.0**	....
,177.6	**10,780.5**	**16,834.2**	**1,689.4**	**5,003.3**	**15,132.7**	**1,234.7**	**5,649.2**	**505.9**	**389.6‡**	**68,397.1**	**$14,033,417.67**
,559.8	.....	.....	.....	.....	.....	.....	209.7	....	....	2,769.5	$ 434,045.88
.....	.....	300.0	.....	.....	.....	.....	.....	....	....	300.0	45,141.12
.....	.....	.....	.....	.....	.....	.....	.....	34.3[b]	....	34.3	19,961.22
.....	.....	.....	.....	.....	.....	.....	.....	....	78.8‡	78.8	107,496.49
.....	17.2	10.4	.....	.....	11.0	.6	4.1	....	4.7[g]	48.0	31,431.14
,559.8	**17.2**	**310.4**	.....	.....	**11.0**	**.6**	**213.8**	**34.3**	**83.5‡**	**3,230.6**	**$ 638,075.85**
,617.8	**10,763.3**	**16,523.8**	**1,689.4**	**5,003.3**	**15,121.7**	**1,234.1**	**5,435.4**	**471.6***	**306.1***	**65,166.5**	**$13,395,341.82**

R.A.-European Children's Fund

rt of Discharge—Reconstruction Period, 1919–1924

Contents of Cargoes in Net Metric Tons of 1,000 Kilograms or 2,204.6 Pounds											
Flour	Rice	Beans, Peas	Corn Grits	Pork Products	Milk	Cocoa	Sugar	Misc. Food	Soap	Misc.	Total Tons
.....	158.0	.....	.....	.....	.....	....	....	....	....	....	158.0
.....	158.0	.....	.....	.....	.....	....	....	....	....	....	158.0
.....	.....	.....	.....	.....	84.9	....	....	....	....	....	84.9
.....	.....	.....	.....	.....	94.6	....	....	....	....	....	94.6
.....	.....	.....	.....	.....	5.5	....	....	....	....	....	5.5
.....	.....	.....	.....	.....	220.5	101.6	....	....	....	....	322.1
.....	.....	.....	.....	.....	18.0	....	....	....	....	....	18.0
.....	.....	105.4	.....	.....	.....	....	....	....	....	....	105.4
.....	.....	63.0	.....	44.8	122.5	....	....	....	....	....	230.3
.....	.....	178.9	.....	.....	75.7	....	....	....	....	....	254.6
.....	.....	28.2	.....	.....	201.1	....	....	1.5	....	....	230.8
.....	.....	294.0	.....	.....	105.3	....	....	....	....	....	399.3
.....	.....	286.6	.....	.....	.....	....	....	....	....	....	286.6
.....	.....	396.0	.....	.....	.....	....	....	....	....	....	396.0
.....	.....	.....	.....	.....	28.6	....	....	....	....	....	28.6
.....	.....	.....	.....	104.8	21.4	....	....	....	....	....	126.2
.....	.....	.....	.....	198.6	59.1	150.4	....	....	....	....	408.1
.....	.....	.....	.....	16.7	74.3	....	....	....	....	....	91.0
.....	.....	.....	.....	193.1	....	....	....	....	....	....	193.1
.....	.....	61.2	.....	.....	.....	....	....	....	....	....	61.2
.....	.....	.....	.....	.....	156.2	....	....	....	....	....	156.2
.....	.....	.....	.....	.....	122.8	....	....	....	....	....	122.8

[*Continued on next page*]

Table 401—*Continued*

Detail by Steamers of Transshipment

Transshipping Steamer	Source	Port of Sailing	Date of Arrival	Port of Arrival
			1920	
Pregel, I	Alster	Hamburg	Oct. 20	Danzig
Pregel, I	Mette Jensen, I	Hamburg	Oct. 20	Danzig
Naval, I	Mystic, I	Hamburg	Nov. 8	Danzig
Hammonia, I	Bursplein, I	Hamburg	Nov. 16	Danzig
Hammonia, I	Iowan, I	Hamburg	Nov. 16	Danzig
Mineral, I	American, I	Hamburg	Dec. 1	Danzig
Progress, III	Herefordshire	Hamburg	Dec. 8	Danzig
Progress, III	Texan	Hamburg	Dec. 8	Danzig
			1921	
Weichsel, II	Homer City, I	Hamburg	Jan. 8	Danzig
Echo, III	American, II	Hamburg	Jan. 11	Danzig
Fanal, II	Clarksburg	Hamburg	Jan. 25	Danzig
Progress, IV	Ipswich	Hamburg	Feb. 8	Danzig
Kellersee, III	Kermit, II	Hamburg	Feb. 14	Danzig
Aeolus, II	Phoenix Bridge	Hamburg	Feb. 15	Danzig
Weichsel, III	Phoenix Bridge	Hamburg	Feb. 21	Danzig
Hammonia, II	Oregonian, I	Hamburg	Feb. 28	Danzig
Hammonia, II	Hawaiian, I	Hamburg	Feb. 28	Danzig
Royal	Hamburg Stock	Hamburg	Mar. 2	Danzig
Aeolus, III	Borga	Hamburg	Mar. 4	Danzig
Weichsel, IV	Sophie Rickmers	Hamburg	Mar. 9	Danzig
Imperial, I	Sophie Rickmers	Hamburg	Mar. 11	Danzig
Paul	Local Purchase	Hamburg	Mar. 29	Danzig
Aeolus, IV	Pomona	Hamburg	Apr. 5	Danzig
Adele, II	Westbrook	Hamburg	Apr. 9	Danzig
August, I	Westbrook	Hamburg	Apr. 11	Danzig
Mineral, III	Oregonian, II	Hamburg	Apr. 19	Danzig
Progress, VI	Hamburg Stock	Hamburg	Apr. 26	Danzig
Aeolus, VI	Paz de Epalza	Hamburg	Apr. 28	Danzig
Aeolus, VI	Moerdijk	Hamburg	Apr. 28	Danzig
Weichsel, V	Eemdijk	Hamburg	May 2	Danzig
Weichsel, V	Schoharie, II	Hamburg	May 2	Danzig
Pregel, III	Schoharie, II	Hamburg	May 3	Danzig
Pregel, III	King City	Hamburg	May 3	Danzig
Hansa, III	King City	Hamburg	May 5	Danzig
Hansa, III	Bradford City	Hamburg	May 5	Danzig
Sensal, II	Schoharie, II	Hamburg	May 7	Danzig
Mottlau	Schoharie, II	Hamburg	May 10	Danzig
Mottlau	King City	Hamburg	May 10	Danzig
August, II	Phoenix Bridge	Hamburg	May 14	Danzig
Johanna	Phoenix Bridge	Hamburg	May 17	Danzig
Fanal, III	American, IV	Hamburg	May 17	Danzig
Aeolus, VI	West Katan	Hamburg	May 24	Danzig
Elina	Hawaiian, II	Hamburg	May 26	Danzig
Spitzberg	Chile	Hamburg	May 26	Danzig
Sensal, III	Amassia	Hamburg	May 27	Danzig
Pomerania	Chile	Hamburg	May 28	Danzig
Arnold Koepke	Chile	Hamburg	May 28	Danzig
Progress, VII	Cornish City, II	Hamburg	May 30	Danzig
Progress, VII	Nemaha	Hamburg	May 30	Danzig
Sea Lighter R.W. 36	Nemaha	Hamburg	June 2	Danzig
Alesia	Oregonian, III	Hamburg	June 7	Danzig
Naval, II	Suzanne	Hamburg	June 7	Danzig
Hinrich, I	Orbita	Hamburg	June 14	Danzig
Weichsel, VI	Ruurlo	Hamburg	June 18	Danzig
Hammonia, III	Oregonian, III	Hamburg	June 26	Danzig
Hammonia, III	Walter Luckenbach	Hamburg	June 26	Danzig
Etzel, I	Hamburg Stock	Hamburg	June 28	Danzig
Weichsel, VII	Oropesa	Hamburg	July 4	Danzig
Weichsel, VII	Mexico, II	Hamburg	July 4	Danzig

A.R.A.-European Children's Fund

Final Port of Discharge

Contents of Cargoes in Net Metric Tons of 1,000 Kilograms or 2,204.6 Pounds											
Flour	Rice	Beans, Peas	Corn Grits	Pork Products	Milk	Cocoa	Sugar	Misc. Food	Soap	Misc.	Total Tons
....	....	286.6	....	....	....	....	....	....	....	....	286.6
....	....	....	....	....	9.4	....	....	....	....	....	9.4
....	....	....	....	....	228.5	....	....	....	....	....	228.5
....	....	....	....	....	165.5	....	....	....	....	....	165.5
....	....	....	....	....	148.9	....	....	....	....	....	148.9
....	....	....	....	....	60.5	....	....	....	....	....	60.5
....	739.9	....	....	....	....	....	....	....	....	....	739.9
....	....	....	....	....	....	....	....	....	....	3.4	3.4
....	....	....	....	....	....	....	....	....	....	19.3	19.3
....	....	....	....	....	194.7	....	....	....	....	....	194.7
....	80.0	....	....	....	....	....	....	....	....	....	80.0
....	196.1	....	....	....	1.4	....	....	....	....	....	197.5
....	....	....	....	40.9	....	....	....	....	....	....	40.9
....	371.7	....	....	....	....	....	....	....	....	....	371.7
....	610.8	....	....	....	....	....	....	....	....	....	610.8
406.0	....	....	....	....	....	....	....	....	....	....	406.0
414.3	....	....	....	....	....	....	....	....	....	....	414.3
....	....	....	....	59.9	....	....	....	....	....	....	59.9
195.3	....	....	....	....	....	....	....	....	....	....	195.3
....	175.7	....	....	....	....	....	....	....	....	....	175.7
....	236.4	....	....	....	....	....	....	....	....	....	236.4
....	....	....	....	....	....	....	....	....	....	1.0	1.0
108.4	....	....	....	....	....	....	....	....	....	....	108.4
....	75.4	....	....	....	....	....	....	....	....	....	75.4
....	207.4	....	....	....	....	....	....	....	....	....	207.4
....	....	....	50.8	....	....	....	....	....	....	....	50.8
....	....	....	....	62.2	....	....	....	....	....	....	62.2
170.4	....	....	....	....	....	....	....	....	....	....	170.4
83.2	....	....	....	....	....	....	....	....	....	....	83.2
....	....	....	....	....	....	....	....	300.2	....	....	300.2
....	199.0	....	....	....	....	....	....	....	....	....	199.0
....	77.5	....	....	....	....	....	....	....	....	....	77.5
....	38.9	....	....	....	....	....	....	....	....	....	38.9
....	51.2	....	....	....	....	....	....	....	....	....	51.2
....	....	....	....	....	227.6	....	....	....	....	....	227.6
....	67.1	....	....	....	....	....	....	....	....	....	67.1
....	473.5	....	....	....	....	....	....	....	....	....	473.5
....	167.1	....	....	....	....	....	....	....	....	....	167.1
....	268.7	....	....	....	....	....	....	....	....	....	268.7
....	81.9	....	....	....	....	....	....	....	....	....	81.9
....	....	....	....	....	....	....	....	....	30.4	....	30.4
....	....	....	....	....	....	....	57.8	....	....	....	57.8
....	....	....	....	....	....	....	....	....	20.4	....	20.4
....	....	303.1	....	....	....	.5	....	....	....	....	303.6
....	212.0	....	....	....	....	....	....	....	....	....	212.0
....	....	128.6	....	....	....	....	....	....	....	....	128.6
....	....	859.2	....	....	....	....	....	....	....	....	859.2
....	....	....	....	....	90.9	....	....	....	....	....	90.9
....	....	....	....	....	18.7	....	....	....	....	....	18.7
....	....	....	....	....	217.7	....	....	....	....	....	217.7
....	....	....	209.6	249.0	....	....	....	....	30.3	....	488.9
....	....	....	....	....	....	....	....	13.1	....	....	13.1
....	....	....	....	103.3	61.7	76.2	....	....	....	....	241.2
....	136.1	....	....	....	....	....	....	....	....	....	136.1
418.1	....	....	....	....	....	....	....	....	....	....	418.1
25.2	....	....	....	....	....	....	....	....	....	....	25.2
56.8	....	....	....	....	....	....	....	....	....	....	56.8
....	....	....	....	....	257.0	....	....	....	....	....	257.0
....	171.1	....	....	....	....	....	....	....	....	....	171.1

[*Concluded on next page*]

Table 401—*Concluded*

Detail by Steamers of Transshipment

Transshipping Steamer	Source	Port of Sailing	Date of Arrival	Port of Arrival
			1921	
Smolensk, I	Croxteth Hall	Hamburg	July 6	Danzig
Pologne	Jacques Cartier, II	Hamburg	July 6	Danzig
Sea Lighter 164	Michigan	Hamburg	July 9	Danzig
Kaethe	Orduna	Hamburg	July 11	Danzig
Sensal, IV	Hawaiian, III	Hamburg	July 12	Danzig
Emma, I	Orduna, I	Hamburg	July 12	Danzig
Naval, III	Hawaiian, III	Hamburg	July 18	Danzig
Smolensk, II	Galileo	Hamburg	July 19	Danzig
Hansa, IV	Oregonian, IV	Hamburg	July 21	Danzig
Weichsel, VIII	Kielhaven	Hamburg	July 26	Danzig
Imperial, III	Ipswich, II	Hamburg	Aug. 15	Danzig
Progress, VIII	Adalia	Hamburg	Aug. 22	Danzig
Elsa	Chile, II	Hamburg	Sept. 23	Danzig
Kaethe	Noruega	Hamburg	Sept. 24	Danzig
Progress, IX	Chile, II	Hamburg	Sept. 24	Danzig
Greta	Chile, II	Hamburg	Oct. 1	Danzig
Greta	Ipswich, III	Hamburg	Oct. 1	Danzig
Signal	Nemaha	Hamburg	Oct. 10	Danzig
Signal	Hamburg Stock	Hamburg	Oct. 10	Danzig
Suzanne	Virginian	Hamburg	Oct. 15	Danzig
Etzel, II	Hawaiian, V	Hamburg	Oct. 21	Danzig
Weichsel, IX	Clarksburg, IV	Hamburg	Oct. 26	Danzig
Weichsel, IX	Hawaiian, V	Hamburg	Oct. 26	Danzig
Moewe, I	Hudson	Bremerhaven	Nov. 3	Danzig
Aeolus, VIII	Mexico, III	Hamburg	Nov. 15	Danzig
Pregel, IV	Hamburg Sweepings	Hamburg	Nov. 17	Danzig
Echo, V	Mexico, III	Hamburg	Nov. 18	Danzig
Emma, III	Samnanger	Hamburg	Dec. 5	Danzig
Norma, I	Mt. Clinton, II	Hamburg	Dec. 22	Danzig
Norma, I	Clarksburg, V	Hamburg	Dec. 22	Danzig
			1922	
Hansa, V	Gasconier	Hamburg	Jan. 19	Danzig
Nuernberg	Sapinero	Hamburg	June 2	Danzig
Elsfleth	Minnekahda, VII	Hamburg	June 26	Danzig
Elsfleth	Manchuria, VII	Hamburg	June 26	Danzig
Brake	Manchuria, VII	Hamburg	June 26	Danzig
Brake	St. Paul, II	Hamburg	June 26	Danzig
Total Shipments				
Deduct Re-Transshipments				
Total Net Transshipments				

R.A.-European Children's Fund

Final Port of Discharge

Contents of Cargoes in Net Metric Tons of 1,000 Kilograms or 2,204.6 Pounds											
Flour	Rice	Beans, Peas	Corn Grits	Pork Products	Milk	Cocoa	Sugar	Misc. Food	Soap	Misc.	Total Tons
.....	.....	.....	.....	151.3	.....	....	....	....	....	....	151.3
.....	373.8	.....	.....	.....	.....	....	....	....	....	....	373.8
.....	488.1	.....	.....	.....	.....	....	....	....	....	....	488.1
.....	.....	.....	.....	.....	334.7	....	....	....	....	....	334.7
.....	.....	.....	.....	.....	.....	32.6	....	....	....	....	32.6
.....	.....	.....	.....	.....	334.7	....	....	....	....	....	334.7
.....	.....	.....	.....	.....	.....	71.2	....	....	....	....	71.2
.....	.....	.....	.....	69.1	.....	....	....	....	....	....	69.1
.....	.....	.....	410.4	.....	.....	....	....	....	....	....	410.4
.....	330.5	.....	.....	.....	.....	....	....	....	....	....	330.5
.....	.....	.....	.....	.....	3.2	....	....	....	....	....	3.2
.....	.....	16.2	.....	.....	.....	....	....	....	....	....	16.2
.....	.....	2.4	.....	.....	.....	....	....	....	....	....	2.4
.....	.....	.....	.....	.....	6.3	....	....	....	....	....	6.3
.....	.....	3.2	.....	.....	.....	....	....	....	....	....	3.2
.....	.....	5.9	.....	.....	.....	....	....	....	....	....	5.9
.....	.....	.....	.....	.....	.....	....	....	....	....	.3	.3
.....	.....	.....	.....	.....	18.9	....	....	....	....	....	18.9
.....	.....	.....	.....	.....	.6	....	....	....	....	....	.6
.....	.....	.....	.....	.....	78.7	....	....	....	....	....	78.7
.....	.....	.....	.....	.....	361.7	....	....	....	....	....	361.7
.....	.....	.....	.....	273.8	.....	....	....	....	....	....	273.8
.....	.....	.....	.....	.....	286.6	....	....	....	....	....	286.6
.....	.....	.....	.....	.....	.....	15.5	....	....	....	....	15.5
.....	4.8	.....	.....	.....	.....	....	....	....	....	....	4.8
.....	.....	.6	.....	.....	.....	....	....	....	....	....	.6
.....	66.9	.....	.....	.....	.....	....	....	....	....	....	66.9
.....	145.8	.....	.....	.....	.....	....	....	....	....	....	145.8
.....	.....	.....	.....	.....	90.8	....	....	....	....	....	90.8
.....	.....	.....	.....	48.2	.....	....	....	....	....	....	48.2
.....	.....	213.2	.....	.....	28.5	....	....	....	....	....	241.7
64.9	.....	.....	.....	.....	.....	....	....	....	....	....	64.9
.....	.....	.....	.....	.....	108.8	....	....	....	....	....	108.8
.....	.....	.....	.....	.....	70.5	....	....	....	....	....	70.5
.....	.....	.....	.....	.....	179.9	....	....	....	....	....	179.9
.....	.....	.....	.....	.....	119.8	....	....	....	....	....	119.8
,942.6	**6,363.4**	**3,232.3**	**670.8**	**1,615.7**	**5,096.7**	**448.0**	**57.8**	**314.8**	**81.1**	**24.0**	**19,847.2**
.....	158.0	286.6	.....	.....	.....	....	....	....	....	....	444.6
,942.6	**6,205.4**	**2,945.7**	**670.8**	**1,615.7**	**5,096.7**	**448.0**	**57.8**	**314.8**	**81.1**	**24.0**	**19,402.6**

Table 402

Detail by Steamers of Arrivals of Clothing an

Steamer or Source	Transshipped via *	Port of Sailing	Date of Arrival	Port of Arrival	Shoes (Pairs)	Laces (Pairs)	Stockin (Pairs
			1919				
Lita, I		London	Nov. 15	Danzig	90,557	36,000	43,11
Reval, I		London	Nov. 18	Danzig	15,507	7,200	49,65
St. Croix, I		London	Nov. 19	Danzig	21,961	.....	....
Akershus, I		London	Nov. 24	Danzig	38,060	.....	11,05
Ozaukee, I		New York	Dec. 8	Danzig	13,780	13,780	....
St. Croix, II		London	Dec. 10	Danzig	.....	.....	16,96
Jolly Kate		London	Dec. 24	Danzig	75,036	388,800	103,46
			1920				
Kosciuszko		Philadelphia	Jan. 3	Danzig	.....	.....	....
St. Croix, III		London	Jan. 10	Danzig	8,538	.....	....
St. Thomas, I		London	Jan. 16	Danzig	672	.....	....
Jolly George, I		London	Jan. 17	Danzig	198,499	293,833	50,38
Akershus, II		London	Jan. 20	Danzig	87,491	57,600	44,95
Angelica Maersk		Liverpool	Jan. 26	Danzig	.....†	.....	....
Shortsville		New York	Feb. 9	Danzig	50,140	50,140	....
Local Purchase		(Warsaw)	Feb. 14	(Warsaw)	.....	.....	....
Wisla		New York	Feb. 16	Danzig	24,192	24,191	....
Jolly George, II		London	Feb. 16	Danzig	52,089	14,401	177,11
Local Purchase		(Warsaw)	Feb. 27	(Warsaw)	.....	.....	....
Local Purchase		(Warsaw)	Mar. 2	(Warsaw)	.....	.....	....
Krakow		New York	Mar. 3	Danzig	8,064	8,064	....
Neptune, I		London	Mar. 8	Danzig	596	.....	70,2
Neptune, II		London	Apr. 4	Danzig	.....	.....	135,3
Valacia		New York	Apr. 5	Danzig	19,512	19,512	...
Poznan, I		New York	July 13	Danzig	.....	.....	14,6
Susquehanna, I		New York	Aug. 23	Danzig	.....	.....	...
Mar Blanco, II	Hansa, II	New York	Aug. 24	Hamburg	.....	.....	...
Akershus, III		London	Sept. 29	Danzig	.....	.....	...
Hansa, I		London	Oct. 6	Danzig	.....	.....	...
Hermodia		London	Oct. 18	Danzig	.....	.....	...
Stonehenge		London	Oct. 24	Danzig	.....	.....	...
Hulda Maersk		London	Oct. 28	Danzig	.....	.....	...
Susquehanna, III		New York	Nov. 26	Danzig	.....	.....	...
Manhattan	Courrier, London to Warsaw	New York	Dec. 31	London	21	.....	...
			1921				
Clarksburg	Fanal, II	New York	Jan. 18	Hamburg	.....	.....	...
Ipswich	Progress, IV	New York	Jan. 25	Hamburg	9,101	.....	...
Leeds City, II		New York	Apr. 19	Danzig	200	.....	...
Hawaiian, III	Naval, III	New York	July 4	Hamburg	.....	.....	...
Oregonian, IV	Weichsel, VIII	New York	July 11	Hamburg	.....	.....	...
Mt. Clinton, I	Imperial, II	New York	July 19	Hamburg	.....	.....	...
Oronoke		New York	Aug. 14	Danzig	36,000	.....	...
Guernsey		New York	Aug. 16	Danzig	36,000	.....	...
Latvia, I		New York	Aug. 19	Danzig	53,400	.....	...
Estonia, I		New York	Aug. 30	Danzig	.....	.....	112,0
Sudbury, II	Elsa	New York	Sept. 13	Hamburg	.....	.....	98,5
Noruega	Kaethe, II	New York	Sept. 15	Hamburg	91,800	.....	...
Lituania, I		New York	Sept. 21	Danzig	36,000	.....	138,0
Latvia, II		New York	Oct. 5	Danzig	92,600	.....	...
Port overages and accounting adjustments		....	......	....	546	.....	...
Total Gross Arrivals					**1,060,362**	**913,521**	**1,065,3**
Deduct Transfers and Adjustments:							
Shipped Danzig for Russia		....	......	....	.....	.....	...
Warsaw Warehouse Adjustments		....	......	....	2,225	.....	6,2
Total Deductions					**2,225**	.....	**6,2**
Total Net Arrivals **					**1,058,137**	**913,521**	**1,059,1**

* All transshipping steamers sailed from Hamburg to Danzig, arriving as follows: Hansa, II, October 29, 1920; Fanal, II, January 25, 1921; Progress, IV, February, 1921; Naval, III, July, 1921; Weichsel, VIII, July, 1921; Imperial, II, July, 1921; Elsa, September, 1921; Kaethe, II, September, 1921.

† Leather for shoes.

‡ In addition to the number listed, 1 case of needles is included in total gross arrivals. This is canceled by the deduction as given.

.R.A.-European Children's Fund

ccessories—Reconstruction Period, 1919–1924

Woolens (Yards)	Underwear (Suits)	Flannelette (Yards)	Blankets (No.)	Thread (Yards)	Thread (Reels)	Thread (Lbs.)	Needles (No.)	Buttons (No.)	Overcoats (No.)	Tape (Yards)	Total Metric Tons	Total Value
87,600	.....	.....	13	......	5,003	572	150,000	115,200	.....	.....	83.0	$ 324,976.42
36,905	.....	.....	..	......	3,024	216	.....	48,936	.....	.....	25.0	105,074.78
.....	.....	.....	..	......	....	...	.....	.....	.....	.....	10.0	44,072.95
91,241	.....	.....	..	......	....	...	.....	.....	.....	.....	59.0	198,613.06
784,205⅞	.....	.....	..	32,956,800	....	...	225,200	1,036,800	.....	.....	339.8	820,952.31
.....	.....	.....	..	......	....	...	.....	.....	.....	.....	1.7	7,829.24
71,895¼	.....	.....	..	5,400,000	....	...	.....	28,800	.....	.....	80.4	285,618.02
144,420⅝	.....	.....	..	18,928,000	....	...	.....	.....	.....	.....	104.7	230,187.32
11,400¾	.....	.....	..	......	....	...	.....	.....	.....	.....	9.4	33,889.58
.....	.....	.....	..	......	....	...	.....	.....	.....	.....	.3	1,549.69
7,000¼	.....	.....	..	1,800,000	....	...	.....	.....	.....	.....	94.2	460,492.83
63,943¾	.....	.....	..	......	....	...	.....	61,776	.....	.....	74.5	287,184.17
.....	.....	.....	..	......	....	...	.....	.....	.....	.....	.7	1,259.36
.....	.....	.....	..	28,680,000	....	...	484,000	2,628,288	32,931	.....	98.6	244,342.57
.....	.....	.....	..	......	....	...	28,800	.....	.....	.....	....	144.26
.....	.....	.....	..	20,104,000	....	...	.....	.....	.....	.....	31.2	54,562.65
75,671½	.....	.....	..	......	....	...	.....	.....	.....	.....	77.6	298,100.88
.....	.....	.....	..	......	....	...	.....	142,560	.....	.....	.3	165.65
.....	.....	.....	..	......	....	...	.....	115,200	.....	.....	.2	133.86
.....	.....	.....	..	......	....	...	.....	.....	.....	.....	9.8	15,615.34
32,366	.....	.....	..	......	....	...	.....	.....	.....	.....	22.6	65,065.85
15,110	.....	.....	..	......	....	...	.....	.....	.....	.....	27.0	74,143.52
.....	.....	.....	..	10,640,000	....	...	.....	.....	.....	.....	24.9	40,586.50
.....	20,978	.....	..	......	....	...	.....	.....	.....	.....	27.9	27,979.45
.....	34,820	.....	..	......	....	...	.....	.....	.....	.....	16.8	22,769.83
18,869	.....	.....	..	......	....	...	.....	.....	.....	.....	9.5	16,585.69
.....	.....	220,432	..	14,700,000	....	...	300,000	1,044,165	.....	30,000	34.4	64,741.04
.....	.....	171,741	..	5,600,000	....	...	.....	.....	.....	.....	25.7	45,127.66
.....	.....	58,335	..	......	....	...	.....	.....	.....	.....	8.6	15,317.78
.....	.....	42,189	..	......	....	...	.....	.....	.....	.....	6.3	9,884.45
.....	.....	7,121	..	2,000,000	....	...	50,000	190,080	.....	.....	1.4	2,524.10
.....	.....	171,457½	..	......	....	...	.....	.....	.....	.....	16.7	41,599.43
.....	.....	.....	..	......	....	...	.....	.....	.....	.....	....	41.27
50,000	.....	.....	..	......	....	...	.....	.....	.....	.....	21.0	23,331.99
.....	.....	.....	..	......	....	...	.....	.....	.....	.....	9.0	17,871.19
.....	.....	.....	..	......	....	...	.....	.....	.....	.....	.4	833.16
45,100	.....	.....	..	......	....	...	.....	.....	.....	.....	12.1	13,368.64
41,709	.....	.....	..	......	....	...	.....	.....	.....	.....	23.8	15,633.12
12,001	.....	.....	..	......	....	...	.....	.....	.....	.....	7.2	4,824.00
105,387	.....	.....	..	......	....	...	.....	.....	.....	.....	72.1	93,885.29
411,171	.....	.....	..	......	....	...	.....	.....	.....	.....	152.7	188,698.29
133,463	.....	.....	..	5,000,000	....	...	1 case	19 cases	.....	.....	91.7	133,791.51
.....	.....	.....	..	......	....	...	.....	.....	.....	.....	9.4	15,166.98
.....	.....	.....	..	......	....	...	.....	.....	.....	.....	8.5	13,653.46
.....	.....	.....	..	......	....	...	.....	.....	.....	.....	87.1	133,224.39
.....	.....	.....	..	......	....	...	.....	.....	.....	.....	46.4	70,667.25
.....	.....	.....	..	......	....	...	.....	.....	.....	.....	87.4	133,733.17
2.233	.....	.....	..	......	....	...	.....	.....	.....	.....	1.7	26,615.66
241,693	**55,798**	**671,275½**	**13**	**145,808,800**	**8,027**	**788**	**1,238,000‡**	**5,411,805§**	**32,931**	**30,000**	**1,952.7**	**$4,726,429.61**
87,500	.....	.....	..	......	....	...	1 case	8 cases	.....	.....	36.0	$ 34,173.23
.....	.....	.....	..	......	....	...	.....	.....	.....	.....	1.2	2,631.31
87,500	.....	.....	..	......	....	...	**1 case**	**8 cases**	.....	.....	**37.2**	**$ 36,804.54**
154,193	**55,798**	**671,275½**	**13**	**145,808,800**	**8,027**	**788**	**1,238,000**	**5,411,805§**	**32,931**	**30,000**	**1,915.5**	**$4,689,625.07**

In addition to the number listed, 19 cases of buttons are included he total gross arrivals. Allowing for the deduction of 8 cases, 11 s must be added to the total net arrivals.

** Woolens, flannelette, and accessories were used in the manufacture of the following: Overcoats, 929,312; caps, 70,091; dresses, trousers, aprons, etc., 61,743 pieces; underwear, 235,902 suits. These articles are in addition to ready-made garments included in total above.

Table 403

Detail by Steamers of Arrivals of Clothing and Accessori

Steamer	Transshipped via	Port of Sailing	Date of Arrival	Port of Arrival	Shoes (Pairs)
			1921		
Noruega	Ferdinand	New York	Sept. 15	Hamburg	5,800
Ipswich, III	Greta	New York	Sept. 19	Hamburg	....
Latvia, II		New York	Oct. 5	Hamburg	....
Total *					**5,800**

* For detail of deliveries, cf. Special Programs, page 104.

POLAND—A.R.A. and A.R.A.-European Children's Fund

Detail by Months of Supplies Donated by the Polish Government for Children's Relief—Reconstruction Period, 1919–1924

Table 404

Time of Delivery	Commodities in Net Metric Tons of 1,000 Kilograms or 2,204.6 Pounds: Flour	Rice	Beans, Peas	Pork Products	Sugar	Total Tons	Total Value
1919							
To July 1	5,472.0	65.0	601.0	587.0	.....	6,725.0	$1,682,580
August, September	......	466.0	127.0	265.0	.....	858.0	236,076
October, 1919, to March, 1920	3,810.0	.....	.....	.....	.....	3,810.0	592,988
1920							
April	6,057.0	.....	.....	.....	.....	6,057.0	942,711
June	3,034.4	.....	.....	.....	.....	3,034.4	472,211
July	7,001.9	.....	.....	.....	.....	7,001.9	1,089,480
November	2,598.1	.....	.....	.....	.....	2,598.1	400,923
December	2,373.2	.....	.....	.....	.....	2,373.2	365,971
1921							
January	575.3	.....	.....	.....	.....	575.3	88,719
February	1,386.6	.....	.....	.....	.....	1,386.6	136,493
March	732.9	.....	.....	.....	.....	732.9	72,457
April	2,354.1	.....	.....	.....	.....	2,354.1	231,560
May	2,467.9	.....	.....	.....	.....	2,467.9	283,193
June	667.6	.....	.....	.....	.....	667.6	73,313
July	1,484.1	.....	.....	.....	.....	1,484.1	119,466
August	830.2	.....	.....	.....	.....	830.2	66,834
September	902.7	.....	.....	.....	.....	902.7	108,329
October	411.3	.....	.....	.....	.....	411.3	26,812
November	2,503.9	.....	.....	.....	.....	2,503.9	176,773
December	1,002.0	.....	.....	.....	.....	1,002.0	102,815
1922							
January	15.3	.....	.....	.....	.....	15.3	1,569
March	640.2	.....	.....	.....	.....	640.2	51,741
April	1,947.9	.....	.....	.....	403.0	2,350.9	202,269
June	57.6	.....	.....	.....	802.9	860.5	93,986
Total *	**48,325.7**	**531.0**	**728.0**	**852.0**	**1,205.9**	**51,642.6**	**$7,619,280**

* Of this total, 7,072.7 metric tons of flour valued at $917,059.24 was used for adult feeding; the balance, 44,569.9 metric tons, valued at $6,702,221.02, was used for child feeding.

POLAND—U.S. Grain Corporation

Detail by Steamers of Deliveries, under Act of Congress, March 30, 1920 Reconstruction Period, 1919–1924

Table 405†

Steamer	Date of Sailing	Flour: Barrels	Flour: Pounds	Total Tons *	Total Value **
	1919				
Kosciuszko, I	Nov. 29	13,965	...	1,241.6	$ 146,632
Ophis	Dec. 1	64,966	84	5,775.8	682,147
	1920				
Krakow	Feb. 10	11,012	168	979.1	116,461

† Cf. Table 157.
* Contents of cargoes in net metric tons of 1,000 kilograms or 2,204.6 pounds.

** Value quoted f.o.b. U.S.A. ports. In addition to this v[illegible] freight and other transportation charges were paid by the United [illegible]dom in the amount of $8,102,558.32.

A.R.A.-European Children's Fund

Handled for Commonwealth Fund—Reconstruction Period, 1919–1924

Stockings (Pairs)	Woolens (Yards)	Underwear (Garments)	Thread (Yards)	Needles (No.)	Lining (Yards)	Buttons (No.)	Hooks and Eyes (No.)	Total Metric Tons	Total Value
.....	.....	.....	......	....	.....	.....	.....	9.9	$13,693.71
11,600	20,938⅝	.....	3,333,334	5,000	26,755	82,800	86,400	14.7	32,911.91
.....	.....	13,600	......	....	.....	.....	.....	5.8	10,926.87
11,600	**20,938⅝**	**13,600**	**3,333,334**	**5,000**	**26,755**	**82,800**	**86,400**	**30.4**	**$57,532.49**

POLAND

Detail by Steamers of Deliveries, under Act of Congress, March 30, 1920

Table 405—*Continued*

Steamer	Date of Sailing	Flour Barrels	Flour Pounds	Total Tons	Total Value
	1920				
axilby	Feb. 12	63,962	28	5,686.6	$ 687,250.20
'oodmansie	Feb. 12	22,481	84	1,998.7	241,211.63
ardulia, I	Feb. 21	20,557	168	1,827.7	220,055.10
'arszawa	Mar. 6	50,452	168	4,485.5	541,665.90
ikespool	Mar. 9	61,950	...	5,507.7	665,925.43
ılsam	Mar. 12	31,685	...	2,817.0	339,894.98
ılacia	Mar. 13	27,650	...	2,458.2	296,050.46
ısconia	Mar. 16	73,687	28	6,551.2	790,972.09
›espool	Mar. 17	75,862	168	6,744.6	814,692.97
‹mouth	Mar. 20	61,693	152	5,484.9	662,919.32
exico	Mar. 24	36,402	168	3,236.4	391,214.34
zaukee, I	Mar. 28	19,138	112	1,701.5	195,069.22
›znan	Mar. 28	29,232	168	2,599.0	313,952.37
'abana	Mar. 31	74,887	168	6,657.9	804,591.99
›zciuszko, II	Apr. 1	41,165	...	3,659.8	442,370.45
ıstern Moon	Apr. 7	77,082	28	6,853.0	828,633.04
›und Brook	Apr. 10	46,907	168	4,170.3	483,892.20
akemoor	Apr. 12	63,900	...	5,681.0	663,427.14
;sa	Apr. 25	70,617	28	6,278.2	759,134.29
agpool	Apr. 30	75,175	...	6,683.4	806,841.44
ıstern Belle	May 1	42,421	84	3,771.5	455,966.98
ırliness	May 2	48,161	84	4,281.8	517,367.26
vingstonia	May 4	68,872	168	6,123.1	739,069.63
andby	May 5	62,511	84	5,557.6	671,712.11
ıeafdart	May 8	48,320	140	4,296.0	519,270.25
earpool	May 11	69,873	112	6,212.1	749,536.26
ırkestan	May 11	64,550	140	5,738.9	693,196.68
.eaflance	May 12	47,588	112	4,230.9	511,333.62
rdulia, II	May 13	27,846	84	2,475.7	297,644.55
rginia	May 14	41,735	...	3,710.5	448,331.49
›mera	May 15	79,572	168	7,074.4	854,900.58
ookvale	May 18	48,645	140	4,324.9	522,779.13
rborough	May 25	46,350	140	4,120.8	498,165.97
zelside	June 4	44,955	...	3,996.7	483,048.01
lantic	June 9	50,435	...	4,483.9	541,884.82
beck	June 9	67,760	...	6,024.2	727,953.37
ristan	June 14	70,115	140	6,233.6	753,472.77
ha Rickmers	June 15	56,747	168	5,045.2	586,280.72
›st Zeda	June 15	6,379	56	567.2	68,553.18
esbridge	June 19	61,321	84	5,451.8	640,160.11
.tra	June 26	54,707	168	4,863.8	585,653.77
ergreen City	July 5	4,407	168	391.8	47,377.06
ıisboffin	July 12	42,059	56	3,739.3	452,008.70
lfarli	July 15	5,790	...	514.8	62,196.98
aukee, II	July 19	2,861	84	254.4	30,720.85
Total	....	**2,278,428**	**152‡**	**202,564.0**	**$24,353,590.97**

Flour in pounds converted to barrels at 196 pounds per barrel.

Table 406

Summary of Internal Deliveries, b

Operation	Table No.	Flour	Rice	Beans, Peas	Corn Grits
A.R.A.—Congressional Appropriation, $100,000,000 Fund—Food	411	858.2	2,193.3	2,898.2	....
A.R.A.—Congressional Appropriation, $100,000,000 Fund—Clothing	399n	.....	.....	.....	....
A.R.A.-European Children's Fund—Food	411	3,652.6	10,247.2	15,952.9	1,657.8
A.R.A.-European Children's Fund—Clothing	407	.....	.....	.....	....
Poland Government Donation—Children's Relief	411	41,253.0	531.0	728.0	....
Joint Distribution Committee—Children's Relief	411	.....	.....	.....	....
Other Polish Donations—Children's Relief	411	.....	.....	.....	....
A.R.A.W.—Food Drafts	408	721.7	203.5	89.1	....
A.R.A.W.—Bulk Sales	409	4,243.5	312.6	481.8	31.6
A.R.A.W. Danzig—Bulk Sale to Polish Government	289	7,720.3	.....	.....	....
Polish Government Donation—Adult Relief	404n	7,072.7	.....	.....	....
Commonwealth Fund—Intelligentsia Clothing	403n	.....	.....	.....	....
U.S. Grain Corporation (Act of Congress, March 30, 1920)	405	202,564.0	.....	.....	....
United Kingdom—Finance on Freight	405n	.....	.....	.....	....
American Friends Service Committee	331n	.....	.....	.....	....
Total	394	**268,086.0**	**13,487.6**	**20,150.0**	**1,689.4**

POLAND—A.R.A.-European Children's Fund

Detail of Internal Deliveries of Clothing Outfits to Local Committees
Reconstruction Period, 1919–1924

Table 407

A. From the Beginning to July 22, 1920

Receipt No.	Local Committee	Overcoats (Each)	Shoes (Pairs)	Stockings (Pairs)
		DELIVERIES FROM BIAŁYSTOK WAREHOUSE		
1	Augustow	1,254	1,277	1,242
2	Białystok	13,421	12,801	11,802
3	Baranowicze	2,622	2,684	2,720
4	Brzostowica W.	1,121	1,198	1,176
5	Grajewo	1,201	1,221	1,053
6	Grodno	4,598	4,727	4,486
7	Nowogródek	5,519	5,145	4,190
8	Slonim	5,605	5,116	5,292
9	Sokolka	1,504	2,077	3,215
10	Suwalki	2,427	2,481½	2,160
11	Wolkowysk	1,971	1,867	2,986
	Total	**41,243**	**40,594½**	**40,322**
		DELIVERIES FROM BREST WAREHOUSE		
1	Bielsk	5,551	5,015	3,527
2	Biala	5,842	5,820	5,701
3	Brest	5,906	5,937	5,605
4	Bialowieża	493	505	453
5	Kobryń	5,635	5,750	590
6	Janow	5,408	4,986	5,000
7	Pińsk	6,305	6,000	6,000
8	Pružany	5,848	5,523	5,764
	Total	**40,988**	**39,536**	**32,640**
		DELIVERIES FROM CHELM WAREHOUSE		
1	Chelm	4,703	4,644	4,057
2	Hrubieszow	1,950	1,896	1,854
3	Krasnystaw	979	992	909
4	Lubartów	980	983	918

A.R.A. and A.R.A.-European Children's Fund

Operations—Reconstruction Period, 1919–1924

Pork Products	Milk	Cocoa	Sugar	Misc. Food	Forage	Soap	Clothing and Misc.	Total Tons	Total Value
Commodities in Net Metric Tons of 1,000 Kilograms or 2,204.6 Pounds									
765.0	6,284.2	766.3	1,647.1	20.3	.....	441.6	....	15,874.2	$ 5,863,141.40
.....	.....	....	.....	.....	.....	.....	826.7	826.7	192,700.63
4,475.4	14,399.1	1,155.9	5,217.4	305.0	.....	263.7	....	57,327.0	12,079,697.03
.....	.....	....	.....	.....	.....	.....	1,915.5	1,915.5	4,689,625.07
852.0	.....	....	1,205.9	.....	.....	.....	....	44,569.9	6,702,221.02
.....	506.0	....	.....	.....	.....	31.0	....	537.0	273,555.00
.....	.....	31.4	95.8	913.7	.....	.....	....	1,040.9	40,094.51
213.6	231.7	16.4	38.0	15.0	.....	.....	42.4	1,571.4	624,910.00
314.3	490.9	61.8	180.0	151.6	.....	.....	....	6,268.1	1,050,177.41
.....	.....	....	.....	.....	.....	.....	....	7,720.3	864,562.40
.....	.....	....	.....	.....	.....	.....	....	7,072.7	917,059.24
.....	.....	....	.....	.....	.....	.....	30.4	30.4	57,532.49
.....	.....	....	.....	.....	.....	.....	....	202,564.0	24,353,590.97
.....	.....	....	.....	.....	.....	.....	....	.....	8,102,558.32
.....	.....	....	.....	.....	633.3	.....	....	633.3	30,291.26
6,620.3	**21,911.9**	**2,031.8**	**8,384.2**	**1,405.6**	**633.3**	**736.3**	**2,815.0**	**347,951.4**	**$65,841,716.75**

POLAND

Detail of Internal Deliveries of Clothing Outfits to Local Committees

A. From the Beginning to July 22, 1920—*Continued*

Table 407—*Continued*

Receipt No.	Local Committee	Overcoats (Each)	Shoes (Pairs)	Stockings (Pairs)
5	Lublin	2,473	2,841	2,340
6	Parczew	2,560	2,300	2,508
7	Pulawy	744	744	744
8	Tomaszow	2,321	2,310	2,134
9	Wlodawa	7,661	7,664	7,462
10	Zamość	393	406	394
11	Zwierzyniec	767	708	800
12	Bilgoraj	1,073	1,008	913
13	Janow	505	503	503
14	Ostrow	1,690	1,680	1,668
	Total	**28,799**	**28,679**	**27,204**
		DELIVERIES FROM CZĘSTOCHOWA WAREHOUSE		
1	Bendzin	1,903	1,685	2,269
2	Częstochowa	6,187	5,886	5,800
3	Dombrowa	2,130	2,134	1,976
4	Katowice	3,070	3,225	3,050
5	Miechow	100	100	100
6	Olkusz	490	525	246
7	Radomsk	1,656	1,423	1,571
8	Sosnowiec	2,950	2,885	2,688
9	Zawiercie	200	207	200
	Total	**15,686**	**18,070**	**17,900**
		DELIVERIES FROM KOWEL WAREHOUSE		
1	Dubno	3,033	2,965	2,976
2	Kowel	5,885	5,977	5,757
3	Krzemieniec	2,552	2,602	2,560
4	Luck	5,575	5,615	5,568
5	Olyka	2,806	2,799	2,712
6	Ostrog	2,505	2,455	2,865

[*Continued on next page*]

POLAND

Detail of Internal Deliveries of Clothing Outfits to Local Committees

A. From the Beginning to July 22, 1920—*Continued*

Table 407—*Continued*

Receipt No.	Local Committee	Overcoats (Each)	Shoes (Pairs)	Stockings (Pairs)
		DELIVERIES FROM KOWEL WAREHOUSE—*Cont.*		
7	Rowno	3,031	3,236	2,652
8	Wlodzimierz	10,275	9,268	8,160
9	Zwiahel	1,476	1,490	1,540
10	Zaslaw	2,882	2,837	2,718
	Total	**40,020**	**39,244**	**37,508**
		DELIVERIES FROM KRAKOW WAREHOUSE		
1	Krakow Committees	**27,118**	**27,131**	**32,188**
1	Lwow Committees *	**108,069**	**107,908**	**82,450**
		DELIVERIES FROM ŁÓDŹ WAREHOUSE		
1	Aleksandrow	784	676	652
2	Kalisz	1,328	1,461	1,393
3	Kolo	510	515	516
4	Lenczica	963	934	1,003
5	Łódź	19,510	8,980	10,128
6	Ozorkow	1,181	1,088	1,129
7	Sieradz	1,524	1,507	1,017
8	Łódź District	5,133	4,742	4,576
9	Tomaszow	2,321	2,310	2,134
10	Wieluń	491	515	483
11	Zduńska Wola	603	640	450
	Total	**34,348**	**23,368**	**23,481**
		DELIVERIES FROM MIŃSK WAREHOUSE		
1	Bobrujsk	3,140	3,007	3,108
2	Mińsk	17,545	17,471	16,825
	Total	**20,685**	**20,478**	**19,933**
		DELIVERIES FROM PŁOCK WAREHOUSE		
1	Ciechanow	563	525	630
2	Gostynin	1,178	1,251	1,220
3	Kutno	1,885	1,857	1,920
4	Lipno	879	884	900
5	Rypin	895	835	784
6	Makow	1,000	1,000	1,000
7	Mlawa	1,330	1,697	1,656
8	Płock	2,585	2,472	2,501
9	Przasnysz	826	733	862
10	Pultusk	724	597	750
11	Nasielsk	467	502	504
12	Wyszkow	1,603	1,602	1,550
13	Wloclawek	1,996	1,939	1,816
	Total	**15,931**	**15,894**	**16,093**
		DELIVERIES FROM RADOM WAREHOUSE		
1	Busk	3,607	3,638	3,617
2	Borkowice	300	296	300
3	Jendrzejow	1,438	1,549	1,231

* 21,950 caps furnished.

POLAND

Detail of Internal Deliveries of Clothing Outfits to Local Committees

A. From the Beginning to July 22, 1920—*Continued*

Table 407—*Continued*

Receipt No.	Local Committee	Overcoats (Each)	Shoes (Pairs)	Stockings (Pairs)
4	Kielce	2,567	2,549	2,632
5	Kozienice	853	751	684
6	Końskie	1,165	1,174	1,045
7	Ostrowiec	2,208	1,951	2,021
8	Opoczno	800	711	565
9	Pinczow	1,450	1,435	1,468
10	Piotrkow	1,805	1,820	1,830
11	Radom	2,129	1,978	1,980
12	Sandomierz	1,044	1,193	1,161
13	Wloszczowa	953	1,125	940
14	Ilza	799	821	800
15	Przedborz	100	100	100
	Total	**21,218**	**21,091**	**20,374**
		DELIVERIES FROM SIEDLCE WAREHOUSE		
1	Garwolin	5,358	5,358	4,300
2	Kolno	1,089	1,099	1,149
3	Łomża	2,988	2,835	3,437
4	Łukow	1,790	1,779	1,736
5	Miendzyrzec	280	292	291
6	Radzyn	150	150	114
7	Ostrow	2,437	2,431	2,437
8	Ostrolenka	984	1,091	969
9	Siedlce	4,454	4,956	4,490
10	Wysoko Mazow	2,871	2,206	2,200
11	Wengrow	2,562	2,534	2,401
12	Sokolow	1,016	1,116	926
	Total	**25,979**	**25,775**	**24,450**
		DELIVERIES FROM WARSAW WAREHOUSE†		
1	Grodzisk	2,494	2,517	2,352
2	Gora Kalwarja	1,899	1,931	1,981
3	Lowicz	1,099	1,270	1,366
4	Minsk Mazow	1,424	1,680	2,748
5	Rawa	1,800	1,800	1,800
6	Skierniewice	827	921	767
7	Sochaczew	697	692	627
1	Radzymin Warsaw	13,381	13,381	13,381
2	Warsaw City	17,441	17,264	17,264
	Total	**41,062**	**41,456**	**42,286**
		DELIVERIES FROM WILNO WAREHOUSE		
1	Lida	2,905	2,944	2,877
2	Wilejka	3,207	2,779	3,860
3	Wilno	19,656	20,159	20,286
	Total	**25,768**	**25,882**	**27,023**
		DELIVERIES FROM ZONE WAREHOUSES		
	Institutions, Etc.	**6,043**	**18,028½**	**20,639**
	Total	**492,957**	**493,135**	**464,491**

† 32,697 caps furnished.

[*Continued on next page*]

POLAND—A.R.A.-European Children's Fund

Detail of Internal Deliveries of Clothing Outfits, by Districts
Reconstruction Period, 1919–1924

Table 407—*Continued* B. August 1, 1920, to January 1, 1921

District	Overcoats (Each)	Shoes (Pairs)	Stockings (Pairs)
Lemberg	47,252	47,377	47,226
Brest–Pinsk	13,994	15,093	15,010
Warsaw	10,445	29,939	41,441
Kraków	12,249	12,227	12,238
Łódź	7,507	8,878	8,007
Kowel	23,086	23,213	23,205
Białystok	13,972	14,336	14,392
Wilno	2,988	3,025	2,964
Lublin	15,182	15,416	15,475
Częstochowa	3,490	3,521	3,484
Radom	5,228	6,054	5,974
Siedlce	11,018	12,416	12,055
Płock	3,806	4,536	4,409
Mazowieck	2,405	2,553	2,470
Total	**172,622**	**198,584**	**208,350**

POLAND—A.R.A.-European Children's Fund

Detail by Months of Internal Deliveries of Clothing Outfits for Refugee Children—Reconstruction Period, 1919–1924

Table 407—*Continued* C. October, 1921, to May, 1922

Month	Overcoats	Shoes	Stockings
1921			
October	....	5,560	13,176
November	42	5,490	13,200
December	9	2,840	6,565
1922			
January	6,111	6,111	6,111
February	4,774	4,774	4,774
March	5,895	5,895	5,895
April	7,272	7,272	7,272
May	7,646	7,646	7,646
Total	**31,749**	**45,588**	**64,639**

POLAND—A.R.A.-European Children's Fund

Detail of Internal Deliveries from Warsaw Warehouse

Reconstruction Period, 1919–1924

Table 407—*Continued*

D. October and November, 1921

Receipt No.	Local Committee	Overcoats (Each)	Shoes (Pairs)	Stockings (Pairs)
1	Baranowicze	15,580	19,320	19,480
2	Białystok	3,360	4,190	4,190
3	Białowieza	2,240	2,800	2,800
4	Biała Krak	690	870	870
5	Bielsk	2,410	3,020	3,020
6	Biłgoraj	900	1,120	1,120
7	Borysław	1,300	1,500	1,500
8	Brody	900	1,000	1,000
9	Brzesko	760	950	950
10	Brzeziny, Koluszki	270	340	340
11	Brzesc Biała	7,020	8,780	8,780
12	Brzezany	1,000	1,200	....
13	Buczacz	1,000	1,200	1,200
14	Cieszanow	500	600	600
15	Cieszyn	720	890	890
16	Częstochowa	3,170	3,870	3,870
17	Chełm, Hrub. Krasne	2,370	2,910	2,960
18	Czortkow	560	600	600
19	Chrzanow	760	950	950
20	Chyrow	200	200	200
21	Dabrowa Gorn	2,630	3,270	3,290
22	Dubno	1,520	1,930	1,960
23	Garwolin	670	840	840
24	Głebokie	1,570	1,970	1,970
25	Gostynin	670	840	840
26	Grodno	3,580	4,470	4,470
27	Grodzisk	840	1,030	1,030
28	Grojec	640	800	800
29	Jarosław	800	900	900
30	Jaworow	260	300	....
31	Jedrzejow	1,650	2,020	2,020
32	Kalisz	900	1,120	1,120
33	Kałusz	700	900	900
34	Kielce	1,340	1,680	1,680
35	Koło Konin	310	390	390
36	Konskie	1,340	1,927	1,675
37	Kołomyja	1,300	1,400	2,100
38	Kosow	600	1,000	1,000
39	Kopyczynce	800	1,000	....
40	Kobryn	2,410	3,020	3,020
41	Kowel	6,580	8,220	8,390
42	Krakow	5,180	6,480	6,480
43	Krosno	270	310	340
44	Krzemieniec	1,720	2,160	2,240
45	Kutno	670	840	840
46	Łapy	940	1,170	1,170
47	Lida	3,130	3,920	3,920
48	Liskow	270	330	330
49	Łódź	8,050	9,660	9,860
50	Łomza	1,620	2,010	2,010
51	Łowicz	800	1,000	1,000
52	Lublin	2,330	2,680	2,400
53	Łuck	1,780	2,160	2,350
54	Łukow	1,575	1,723	3,360
55	Luboml	2,000	2,520	2,520
56	Lwow City	10,860	13,600	13,600
57	Minsk-Mazow	710	890	890
58	Nadworna	800	1,000	....
59	Nieswiez	890	1,120	1,120
60	Nowogrodek	3,130	3,910	3,910
61	Nowy Sacz	1,570	1,960	1,960
62	Nowy Targ	1,250	1,570	1,570
63	Olkusz, Miechow	1,350	1,680	1,680
64	Ołyka	780	1,000	1,010
65	Ostrog	1,290	1,480	1,670
66	Ostrowiec	2,380	2,950	2,960
67	Ostrołeka	450	560	560
68	Ostrow Łomz.	1,160	1,450	1,450
69	Oswiecim	1,100	1,370	1,370
70	Oszmiany	2,540	3,160	3,360
71	Ozorkow	360	450	450
72	Pabjanice	1,070	1,340	1,340
73	Parczew	530	670	670
74	Peczynizyn	400	700	....
75	Pinsk	8,040	9,860	9,860
76	Piotrkow	1,120	1,400	1,400
77	Płock	890	1,120	1,200
78	Podhajce	500	600	....
79	Poznan	520	900	1,400
80	Przasnysz	450	560	560
81	Przemysl	2,000	2,500	2,500
82	Pruzany	3,030	3,790	3,930
83	Puławy	900	1,120	1,120
84	Pułtusk	890	1,120	1,120
85	Radom	2,450	3,070	3,075
86	Radomsk	890	1,120	1,120
87	Radziechow	300	400	....
88	Rawa-Mazow	560	960	880
89	Rawa-Ruska	400	500	500
90	Rowne	3,580	4,320	4,460
91	Rowne for refugees	4,000	5,000	5,000
92	Rohatyn	500	600	600
93	Rzeszow	1,340	1,680	1,680
94	Sambor	1,660	2,100	2,100
95	Sanok	750	870	....
96	Sarny	5,600	6,990	7,250
97	Siedlce	1,340	1,680	1,680
98	Sieradz	760	950	950
99	Skirniewice	590	740	740
100	Skole	600	700	....

[*Continued on next page*]

POLAND

Detail of Internal Deliveries from Warsaw Warehouse

D. October and November, 1921—*Continued*

Table 407—*Continued*

Receipt No.	Local Committee	Overcoats (Each)	Shoes (Pairs)	Stockings (Pairs)
101	Słonim	3,580	4,470	4,470
102	Sochaczew	580	730	730
103	Sokołow	1,210	1,510	1,510
104	Sosnowice	2,850	3,550	3,580
105	Stanislawow	2,900	3,500	3,500
106	Stryj	1,300	1,600	1,600
107	Stołpce	1,120	1,400	1,400
108	Suwałki	1,340	1,680	1,680
109	Tarnopol	2,000	2,300	2,300
110	Tarnow	1,740	2,180	2,180
111	Tomaszow	1,550	1,960	1,940
112	Torun	1,650	2,090	2,090
113	Turka	1,000	1,200	....
114	Wadowice	720	890	890
115	Warsaw	21,920	27,370	27,400
116	Włocławek	1,120	1,400	1,400
117	Włodawa	2,000	2,520	2,520
118	Włodzimierz W.	3,100	3,860	3,910
119	Wołkowysk	1,790	2,240	2,240
120	Wyszkow	450	560	560
121	Zaleszczyki	240	300	300
122	Zawiercie	930	1,160	1,160
123	Zborow	1,200	1,400	....
124	Zgierz	1,030	1,290	1,290
125	Zywiec	450	560	560
	Total	**241,205**	**299,530**	**294,440**

POLAND—

Detail by Months of Food Draft Deliveries—

Table 408

Time of Delivery	Number of Drafts Delivered: A $10.00	B $50.00	C $10.00	D $50.00	Unit	Flour M.T.	Rice M.T.	Beans, Peas M.T.
1920								
April	42	5	45	4	....	1.456	.....	.597
May	559	106	808	71	....	26.475	.....	10.234
June	800	181	2,144	83	....	49.609	.....	19.386
July	4,318	518	1,555	149	....	107.622	.....	41.768
August	545	20	117	13	....	9.452	1.736	2.037
September	2,046	153	788	25	....	42.659	11.401	5.585
October	3,721	183	1,175	37	....	68.318	24.184	2.800
November	1,740	198	1,034	89	....	49.050	19.096	.....
December	2,115	249	975	17	....	51.230	30.046	.....
1921								
January	1,524	174	371	19	....	33.290	12.910	.....
February	3,285	234	493	21	....	58.129	18.239	4.500
March	2,849	202	447	23	....	50.873	17.645	2.250
April	2,169	193	299	21	....	41.098	16.017	.....
May	1,678	94	341	30	....	30.285	11.889	.....
June	3,620	85	195	11	....	48.442	19.336	.....
July	2,781	161	602	93	....	53.681	20.967	.....
Grand Total in Units	**33,792**	**2,756**	**11,389**	**706**	Unit	**721.669**	**203.466**	**89.157**
Grand Total in Metric Tons*	.....	....	.....	...	M.T.	**721.669**	**203.466**	**89.157**

* Value of food drafts and commodities delivered, $624,910.00. Weight of commodities, 1,571.351 net metric tons.

POLAND—A.R.A.-European Children's Fund

Detail of Internal Deliveries of Clothing from Warsaw Warehouse to Local Committees—Reconstruction Period, 1919–1924

Table 407—*Concluded*

E. January, 1922

eceipt No.	Local Committee	Overcoats (Each)	Shoes (Pairs)	Stockings (Pairs)
1	Baranowicze	7,500	9,500	9,000
2	Białystok	1,800	700	500
3	Brzešč	1,800	700	500
4	Brzeżany	...	...	1,200
5	Brody	300	300	300
6	Husiatyn	...	...	1,000
7	Jarosław	50	100	100
8	Kalisz	50	50	50
9	Kowel	1,600	800	800
10	Nadwórna	...	...	1,000
11	Pinsk	700	700	700
12	Przemyšl	50	100	100
13	Podhajce	...	...	600
14	Radom	160	100	100
15	Radziechów	...	...	400
16	Równe	2,750	3,500	3,250
17	Sarny	2,000	2,500	2,500
18	Stryj	50	100	100
19	Skole	...	...	700
20	Tarnopol	100	200	200
21	Turka	...	...	1,200
22	Vilno	2,800	1,000	600
23	Zborów	...	...	1,400
24	Warsaw	2,000	950	950
	Total	**23,710**	**21,300**	**27,250**
	Grand total * of A, B, C, D, and E.	**962,243**	**1,058,137**	**1,059,170**

* In addition to the above outfits of clothing, 291,700 suits of under-ar were distributed during the winter of 1920–21; 15,444 caps, winter of 1–22, making total caps, 70,091; and miscellaneous articles of clothing, 3,040, winter of 1919–20; 58,703, winter of 1920–21; total miscellaneous articles 61,743, each. All clothing is equivalent to 1,915.5 metric tons.

.R.A. Warehouses and A.R.A.-European Children's Fund

econstruction Period, 1919–1924

Bacon		Lard		Lard Substitute	Oil		Milk		Cocoa	Sugar	Corned Beef	Misc.
A Lb. Piece	B 16-Lb. Piece	A 5-Lb. Tin	B 10-Lb. Tin	M.T.	A 1-Gal. Tin	B 5-Gal. Tin	Cond. Case	Evap. Case	M.T.	M.T.	Case	Sacks, etc.
84	10	9	9	....	49	4	27	...	.....	.....	1	270
563	106	106	106	....	857	76	473	...	.....	.....	18	4,278
800	181	181	181	....	2,229	72	935	...	.....	.....	30	9,096
2,508	1,428	518	518	....	1,309	122	1,748	...	.....	.....	86	18,286
345	120	20	20	....	130	13	153	...	.....	.....	3	2,019
1,991	147	145	145	.322	546	25	715	...	.....	.....	25	8,680
3,617	235	183	183	....	1,212	37	1,134	...	.....	.....	30	14,908
1,052	542	198	198	....	1,068	102	...	...	1.818	4.496	33	....
1,907	353	249	249	....	992	17	...	862	1.944	4.686	41	....
1,524	174	174	174	....	390	19	540	...	1.238	3.053	29	....
1,212	928	282	895	....	474	29	926	...	2.272	5.308	39	34,612
2,445	154	202	702	....	470	23	1,648	...	1.985	4.646	34	11,113
2,115	50	473	399	....	320	21	651	...	1.558	3.758	32	7,636
1,712	12	436	53	....	371	30	489	...	1.197	2.763	16	6,181
3,693	...	263	93	....	221	8	748	...	2.052	4.391	14	11,541
3,098	...	273	110	....	694	93	32	836	2.330	4.907	27	9,720
28,666	**4,440**	**3,712**	**4,035**	**.322**	**11,332**	**691**	**10,219**	**1,698**	**16.394**	**38.008**	**458**	**138,340**
04.023	**32.224**	**8.419**	**18.303**	**.322**	**38.551**	**11.754**	**194.686**	**36.971**	**16.394**	**38.008**	**14.968**	**42.436**

POLAND–

Table 409 **Detail by Months of Bulk Sale Deliveries–**

Time of Delivery	Unit	Flour M.T.	Rice M.T.	Beans, Peas M.T.	Corn Grits M.T.	Bacon 8-Lb. Piece	Bacon 16-Lb. Piece	Lard 5-Lb. Tin	Lard 10-Lb. Tin
1920									
April	....	63.774	.....	22.991	.....	....	973	1,000	1,000
July	....	45.890	2.770	18.534	.....	11	320	120	120
August	....	40.155	1.620	20.938	.....	1	341	217	....
September	....	244.809	42.264	128.819	.....	318	2,614	214	828
October	....	152.232	27.518	53.243	.....	9	853	8	538
November	....	40.906	.670	15.259	.....	2	19	2	42
December	....	26.546	2.230	12.357	.....	1	51	21	61
1921									
January	....	72.561	12.233	32.237	.....	1	109	220	36
February	....	1,434.928	3.330	3.122	.....	209	118	98	532
March	....	1,250.475	13.749	13.821	.....	675	10	3	341
April	....	114.380	9.093	7.563	.....	292	....	358	120
May	....	85.031	18.517	15.250	3.164	1,181	....	1,355	1
June	....	75.529	26.320	17.853	5.480	7,193	....	4,810	....
July–October	....	121.575	18.790	20.456	5.977	3,096	....	227	414
November–January, 1922	....	10.125	7.145	*—3.891*	*—2.343*	....	5	17	1,418
1922									
February	....	......	4.897	2.524	.005	*—4*	....	....	....
March	....	39.115	7.884	8.573	.....	....	....	....	....
April	....	41.913	13.767	18.286	.....	....	....	....	....
May	....	35.275	9.607	4.196	1.058	....	....	....	....
June	....	62.669	17.402	21.969	.....	170	....	....	....
July	....	59.877	18.857	20.799	.....	....	....	....	....
November–December	....	19.538	1.378	4.979	7.891	....	....	....	....
1923									
January	....	35.971	1.538	1.327	3.866	....	....	....	....
February	....	13.483	3.587	4.884	.....	....	....	....	....
March	....	51.370	14.221	9.939	.....	....	....	....	....
April	....	33.257	9.372	5.725	.....	....	....	....	....
May	....	64.522	22.455	.....	5.815	....	....	....	....
June	....	7.642	1.389	.....	.690	....	....	....	....
Total in Units	**Unit**	**4,243.548**	**312.603**	**481.753**	**31.603**	**13,155**	**5,413**	**8,670**	**5,451**
Total in Metric Tons	**M.T.**	**4,243.548**	**312.603**	**481.753**	**31.603**	**87.022**		**44.391**	
Less Food Included in Child Feeding Program ex-A.R.A.W. surplus	....	......	.....	.....	.....	......		......	
Total Net Bulk Sale Deliveries	....	**4,243.548**	**312.603**	**481.753**	**31.603**	**87.022**		**44.391**	

POLAND–

Table 410 **Summary by Months and Districts of the Number of Childre**

Month	Białystok	Brest-Pinsk	Częstochowa	Kowel	Kraków	Łódź
1919						
May	.....	.....	.....	.....	.....	.....
June	.....	.....	.....	.....	.....	.....
July	.....	.....	.....	.....	.....	.....
August	.....	.....	.....	.....	.....	.....
September	.....	.....	.....	.....	.....	.....
October	.....	.....	.....	.....	.....	.....
November	.....	.....	.....	.....	.....	.....
December	.....	.....	.....	.....	.....	.....
1920						
January	87,533	118,330	60,392	77,878	95,605	68,496
February	89,887	112,036	65,576	76,965	96,973	71,112
March	100,835	90,248	66,962	103,217	101,172	78,802
April	97,191	63,587	72,102	103,130	107,073	83,851

* Detailed data by districts not available previous to fixation of districts in January, 1920.

R.A. Warehouses and A.R.A.-European Children's Fund

onstruction Period, 1919–1924

rd and ard stitute .T.	Oil Bulk M.T.	Oil 1-Gal. Tin	Oil 5-Gal. Tin	Milk Cond. Case	Milk Evap. Case	Cocoa M.T.	Sugar M.T.	Miscellaneous Food Corned Beef Case	Miscellaneous Food Salmon Case	Total Metric Tons	Total Value
....	.....	...	....	1,000	....	.....	.....	167	...	....	....
....	.....	382	62	352	....	.....	.....	101	...	....	....
....	.....	...	199	341	....	.....	.....	17	...	....	....
.803	.....	851	1,620	1,391	495	.....	.....	172	...	....	....
.187	.....	21	700	1,042	....	.....	.....	160	...	....	....
.200	.....	...	100	327	....	.004	.016	15	...	....	....
....	.....	...	54	159	154	.740	2.471	18	...	....	....
.200	.....	...	558	692	49	2.211	2.920	21	...	....	....
....	.....	...	48	472	82	.927	3.323	41	...	....	....
.472	.....	12	42	7,613	89	1.844	7.478	466	...	....	....
.957	.....	25	26	534	157	1.040	10.431	59	...	....	....
.562	.831	...	97	388	1,300	2.766	12.076	217	...	....	....
.354	.154	132	226	804	681	13.209	12.215	512	750	....	....
.180	.701	860	....	390	1,135	3.628	19.815	88	270	....	....
.983	1.667	49	10	315	601	3.087	6.557	302	873	....	....
.477	1.188	...	....	221	545	1.786	4.786	34	184	....	....
.058	.....	...	....	109	510	2.197	11.578	21	532	....	....
.787	1.835	...	16	263	782	3.332	11.622	...	231	....	....
.054	.941	...	....	162	293	1.998	5.940	...	169	....	....
.871	1.237	34	20	147	1,089	4.463	18.245	...	323	....	....
.201	4.417	...	....	464	927	4.417	12.616	...	16	....	....
.677	.....	...	....	81	435	1.426	3.547	...	...	....	....
.311	.....	...	....	50	237	1.433	4.474	...	...	....	....
.620	.....	...	....	223	180	1.368	2.813	...	...	....	....
.628	.....	...	....	346	682	3.065	9.545	...	...	....	....
.271	.....	...	....	214	448	2.139	6.035	...	...	....	....
....	11.484	...	....	499	1,329	4.333	10.990	...	...	....	....
.206	.073	...	....	44	442	.417	.511	...	...	....	....
.059	**24.528**	**2,366**	**3,778**	**18,643**	**12,642**	**61.830**	**180.004**	**2,411**	**3,348**	....	....
.059	**24.528**	**72.313**		**355.175**	**275.250**	**61.830**	**180.004**	**78.727**	**72.885**	**6,407.691**	**$1,131,091.93**
....	......	......		139.503	......	......	......	......	......	139.503	80,914.52
.059	**24.528**	**72.313**		**215.672**	**275.250**	**61.830**	**180.004**	**78.727**	**72.885**	**6,268.188**	**$1,050,177.41**

R.A. and A.R.A.-European Children's Fund

Nursing Mothers Fed—Reconstruction Period, 1919–1924

Districts * ublin	Lwów	Mazowsze	Minsk	Płock	Radom	Siedlce	Warsaw	Wilno	Total
.....	.....	.....	.....	.....	.....	.....	.....	.....	125,000
.....	.....	.....	.....	.....	.....	.....	.....	.....	300,000
.....	.....	.....	.....	.....	.....	.....	.....	.....	400,000
.....	.....	.....	.....	.....	.....	.....	.....	.....	525,000
.....	.....	.....	.....	.....	.....	.....	.....	.....	600,000
.....	.....	.....	.....	.....	.....	.....	.....	.....	700,000
.....	.....	.....	.....	.....	.....	.....	.....	.....	900,000
.....	.....	.....	.....	.....	.....	.....	.....	.....	975,000
56,386	200,485	19,316	33,499	23,392	48,778	46,298	94,724	49,610	1,080,722
65,823	202,974	22,633	37,158	29,650	47,402	50,194	98,163	62,272	1,128,818
81,327	207,140	25,656	50,228	35,016	57,738	59,122	113,153	52,054	1,222,680
86,123	221,392	29,451	61,479	38,326	58,431	63,878	118,733	63,566	1,268,313

[*Continued on next page*]

Table 410—*Continued*

Summary by Months and Districts of th

Month	Białystok	Brest-Pinsk	Częstochowa	Kowel	Kraków	Łódź
1920						
May	99,654	67,974	74,519	100,972	113,748	82,430
June	94,432	70,145	70,736	.....†	115,002	76,056
July	.....†	.....†	51,430	.....	87,758	50,363
August	.....	.....	41,822	.....	66,049	35,241
September	.....	.....	43,837	.....	62,308	34,091
October	5,678	.....	43,960	19,416	66,173	34,926
November	22,938	36,673	27,007	38,758	52,441	38,615
December	30,837	49,481	30,524	63,659	63,378	44,056
1921						
January	56,933	66,641	40,555	74,927	75,078	58,518
February	79,760	83,806	48,075	97,530	88,230	64,853
March	84,599	94,265	53,180	111,356	102,545	71,978
April	95,489	98,479	55,418	114,225	107,763	69,394
May	92,532	90,416	52,579	94,257	109,305	67,075
June	92,585	90,137	52,823	83,200	104,051	64,673
July	78,027	83,494	42,258	62,818	69,007	52,591
August	53,574	70,342	28,713	52,274	57,527	40,018
September	45,728	52,408	21,250	41,883	41,804	23,492
October	59,538	51,436	24,128	41,142	37,085	26,621
November	46,906	60,342	24,239	44,668	35,328	27,254
December	42,479	59,672	24,371	41,035	29,097	23,349
1922						
January	40,688	65,780	23,011	38,040	26,412	20,090
February	42,403	67,540	20,915	36,568	25,657	20,331
March	40,457	64,880	20,226	39,312	24,383	20,757
April	45,454	58,406	18,160	33,191	23,684	17,989
May	31,837	50,303	18,657	32,913	22,565	18,213
June §	.....	.....	.....	.....	.....	.....
July §	.....	.....	.....	.....	.....	.....

† Feeding stopped on account Bolshevik invasion.
‡ Ceded to Russia.

§ P.A.K.P.D. did not segregate deliveries to districts.

Table 411

Summary of Internal Deliveries for Child Feeding, by Mont

Zone Warehouse	Table No.	Time of Delivery	Flour	Rice	Beans, Peas	Corn Grits	Pork Products	Vegetable Oil
Białystok	412	1920 To Oct. 31	**1,456.550**	**451.970**	**735.213**	......	**138.802**	**74.58**
Brest-Pinsk	413	1920 To Oct. 31	2,333.744	662.690	1,110.377	......	246.130	66.25
Brest	432	December	263.485	....	50.975	......	8.247	3.35
Brest	437	1921 January	379.016	120.367	212.098	......	31.394	15.38
Brest	442	February	641.069	66.401	434.290	......	53.497	28.22
Brest	446	March	635.656	225.715	337.026	.175	39.550	13.40
Brest	450	April	355.264	141.026	229.028	......	67.504	33.48
Brest	454	May	640.561	410.484	68.598	......	66.935	33.61
Brest	458	June	555.646	111.648	357.333	......	43.613	38.56
Brest	462	July	400.852	155.345	182.104	91.090	55.623	18.73
Brest	466	August	260.122	96.161	116.305	137.531	32.191	14.60
Brest	470	September	371.681	94.716	92.719	107.500	28.713	11.31
Brest	473	October	426.764	129.285	165.295	91.204	46.263	11.90
Brest	476	November	272.504	85.120	6.939	136.479	30.493	8.14
Brest	479	December	316.923	105.630	111.531	30.849	35.999	6.87
Brest	485	1922 April	29.407	21.026	28.147	......	10.480	2.24
Total Ex-Brest	....	....	**7,882.694**	**2,425.614**	**3,502.765**	**594.828**	**796.632**	**306.12**

R.A. and A.R.A.-European Children's Fund

mber of Children and Nursing Mothers Fed

Districts									Total
Lublin	Lwów	Mazowsze	Minsk	Płock	Radom	Siedlce	Warsaw	Wilno	
78,780	254,447	31,235	59,520	38,819	59,047	60,956	140,503	52,886	1,315,490
75,354	115,280	29,606	45,407	37,173	53,381	64,724	122,000	28,056	997,352
37,767	115,280	20,206	.....‡	24,844	39,496	41,070	77,111	.....†	545,325
18,785	58,508	15,971	.....	13,304	18,883	4,734	77,572	.....	350,869
12,500	46,548	14,065	.....	12,159	18,872	8,558	74,120	.....	327,058
32,453	52,093	14,622	.....	16,457	22,515	19,494	79,407	.....	407,194
49,506	75,221	15,194	.....	22,115	23,763	32,147	94,640	.....	529,018
48,815	98,146	18,792	.....	26,651	32,452	40,995	96,407	28,865	673,058
65,073	150,825	21,975	.....	32,694	42,043	48,719	78,069	51,494	863,544
67,050	184,103	25,991	.....	38,252	47,745	57,352	92,882	65,140	1,040,769
88,365	233,193	31,170	.....	42,532	55,096	68,166	109,361	75,915	1,221,721
89,208	235,386	30,532	.....	41,931	58,683	69,463	113,239	67,711	1,246,921
71,089	237,092	28,621	.....	44,821	61,475	69,720	109,000	59,337	1,187,319
64,625	230,305	24,826	.....	42,345	63,029	63,000	91,084	66,626	1,133,309
55,338	197,574	17,745	.....	34,888	51,822	48,163	71,416	57,821	922,962
42,835	130,411	13,382	.....	30,266	41,015	39,878	46,427	48,692	695,354
22,543	81,804	9,568	.....	23,071	21,446	18,813	38,111	46,302	488,223
22,169	81,459	9,798	.....	16,690	19,220	18,102	42,591	49,074	499,053
25,441	78,882	9,684	.....	16,618	18,278	18,713	39,817	52,886	499,056
24,594	69,478	6,672	.....	16,323	15,502	20,613	40,907	46,663	460,755
23,741	63,431	6,407	.....	16,033	15,392	18,689	39,279	40,408	437,401
21,178	62,824	5,913	.....	16,716	17,490	14,905	34,542	37,942	424,924
20,584	63,360	5,882	.....	15,877	16,793	15,407	32,516	36,808	417,242
16,788	59,110	5,499	.....	14,713	15,873	13,698	26,051	35,614	384,230
18,026	59,090	5,215	.....	14,511	16,513	14,542	27,101	34,309	363,795
.....	.....	.....	.....	.....	.....	.....	.....	.....	176,647
.....	.....	.....	.....	.....	.....	.....	.....	.....	197,155

R.A. and A.R.A.-European Children's Fund

l by Zone Warehouses—Reconstruction Period, 1919–1924

modities in Net Metric Tons of 1,000 Kilograms or 2,204.6 Pounds

Milk, Evap. and Cond.	Cocoa	Sugar	Miscellaneous Food						Soap	Total Tons
			Corned Beef	Salmon and Whalemeat	Soup	Codliver Oil	Hard Bread	Salt		
762.072	**64.760**	**163.874**	....	.....	.....	.....	**21.052**	**45.154**	**24.372**	**3,938.406**
111.166	74.494	266.280	....	.....	.....	.....	28.038	68.503	40.096	6,007.777
41.300	4.387	14.803	....	.....	.....	.....	......	......	.400	386.955
183.650	17.835	58.347	....	.....	.....	.600	......	11.138	10.080	1,039.911
291.578	21.789	102.689	....	.....	.....	.360	......	20.606	......	1,660.502
249.342	29.221	94.216	....	.....	.....	.160	......	......	......	1,624.470
229.471	17.551	152.915	....	.....	.....	.....	......	38.451	......	1,264.692
234.252	32.829	152.191	....	.....	.....	.....	......	37.308	......	1,676.774
243.706	27.594	114.210	....	.....	.....	.....	......	34.192	27.384	1,553.889
179.085	19.539	75.018	....	.....	.....	.....	......	15.117	16.835	1,209.342
122.859	13.015	58.152	....	.....	.....	.....	......	14.205	11.308	876.453
105.727	17.177	56.258	....	8.978	.....	.....	......	3.135	8.335	906.252
162.002	17.398	83.820	....	13.362	.....	.....	......	5.115	22.942	1,175.359
98.150	11.599	65.548	....	3.015	.....	.....	......	9.580	.410	727.986
96.879	13.210	70.126	....	10.874	.....	.....	......	8.326	.400	807.621
18.668	2.322	10.100	....	.....	.....	.....	......	......	......	122.396
367.835	**319.960**	**1,374.673**	....	**36.229**	.....	**1.120**	**28.038**	**265.676**	**138.190**	**21,040.379**

[*Continued on next page*]

Table 411—*Continued*

Summary of Internal Deliveries for Chi

Zone Warehouse	Table No.	Time of Delivery	Flour	Rice	Beans, Peas	Corn Grits	Pork Products	Vegetable Oil
Częstochowa	414	1920 To Oct. 31	**1,273.233**	**393.906**	**644.127**	......	**157.096**	**34.78**
Kowel	415	1920 To Oct. 31	**1,424.955**	**409.374**	**723.542**	......	**147.710**	**30.21**
Kraków	416	1920 To Oct. 31	1,686.269	507.878	815.227	......	236.380	18.67
Kraków	426	November	86.698	29.702	34.216	......	9.501	1.13
Kraków	433	December	194.803	58.644	100.527	......	22.160	4.38
Kraków	438	1921 January	203.986	51.010	130.376	......	23.076	6.36
Kraków	443	February	266.668	26.533	154.958	......	20.076	10.98
Kraków	447	March	282.607	107.067	123.940	......	30.845	3.73
Kraków	451	April	262.626	43.523	92.994	......	25.275	5.66
Kraków	455	May	277.575	80.206	2.258	19.398	30.209	8.90
Kraków	459	June	161.506	31.160	27.198	121.083	7.636	15.07
Kraków	463	July	123.836	61.322	58.173	49.192	23.649	2.63
Kraków	467	August	151.631	45.274	30.411	41.828	7.215	4.75
Total Ex-Kraków	......	....	**3,698.205**	**1,042.319**	**1,570.278**	**231.501**	**436.022**	**82.29**
Łódź	417	1920 To Oct. 31	1,842.061	464.650	817.018	......	181.787	43.84
Łódź	427	November	32.040	....	18.097	......	3.004	1.00
Total Ex-Łódź	......	....	**1,874.101**	**464.650**	**835.115**	......	**184.791**	**44.85**
Lublin	418	1920 To Oct. 31	**1,245.069**	**347.023**	**620.279**	......	**113.233**	**34.93**
Lwów	419	1920 To Oct. 31	3,866.058	1,078.044	1,862.228	......	453.768	74.37
Lwów	428	November	122.194	39.217	51.999	......	11.167	3.92
Lwów	434	December	338.234	27.617	166.995	......	23.890	3.48
Lwów	439	1921 January	357.352	114.475	156.732	......	31.854	13.77
Lwów	444	February	509.303	48.989	311.567	......	48.210	16.73
Lwów	448	March	369.812	157.960	212.081	......	37.972	10.64
Lwów	452	April	535.971	87.857	115.385	1.040	55.464	12.90
Lwów	456	May	521.699	134.049	....	89.482	29.617	19.32
Lwów	460	June	244.680	95.323	136.375	61.276	34.201	10.98
Lwów	464	July	123.181	59.278	44.176	185.676	26.631	7.40
Lwów	468	August	224.786	66.949	33.868	55.928	22.420	6.06
Lwów	471	September	108.731	40.359	....	67.809	10.662	3.42
Lwów	474	October	167.937	56.060	28.758	32.780	16.977	3.71
Lwów	477	November	131.064	46.283	29.911	30.139	8.289	6.10
Lwów	480	December	123.767	40.769	35.355	27.920	21.873	3.84
Lwów	486	1922 April	43.900	17.949	14.618	2.510	5.218	1.18
Total Ex-Lwów	......	....	**7,788.669**	**2,111.178**	**3,200.048**	**554.560**	**838.213**	**197.91**
Mazowieck	420	1920 To Oct. 31	**414.006**	**117.007**	**192.584**	......	**41.931**	**11.63**
Modlin	429	1920 November	439.560	154.428	211.106	......	2.790	58.51
Modlin	435	December	525.485	30.754	311.353	......	36.317	49.15
Modlin	440	1921 January	631.855	286.071	353.079	......	50.836	21.34
Total Ex-Modlin	......	....	**1,596.900**	**471.253**	**875.538**	......	**89.943**	**129.01**
Płock	421	1920 To Oct. 31	**588.208**	**158.436**	**274.518**	......	**62.270**	**12.65**
Radom	422	1920 To Oct. 31	**973.071**	**258.833**	**403.214**	......	**106.499**	**22.44**
Siedlce	423	1920 To Oct. 31	**749.893**	**189.206**	**351.652**	......	**64.663**	**22.67**
Sosnowiec	430	1920 November	**68.809**	**27.911**	**51.405**	......	**8.363**	....

R.A. and A.R.A.-European Children's Fund

eding, by Months and by Zone Warehouses

nmodities in Net Metric Tons of 1,000 Kilograms or 2,204.6 Pounds

Milk, Evap. and Cond.	Cocoa	Sugar	Miscellaneous Food: Corned Beef	Miscellaneous Food: Salmon and Whalemeat	Miscellaneous Food: Soup	Miscellaneous Food: Codliver Oil	Miscellaneous Food: Hard Bread	Miscellaneous Food: Salt	Soap	Total Tons
602.093	**65.419**	**206.323**	....	.....	.....	.....	......	**12.026**	**40.814**	**3,429.824**
670.668	**66.727**	**166.433**	....	.....	.....	.....	**18.276**	**36.964**	**18.410**	**3,713.269**
828.304	87.932	239.745	....	.....	.....	.....	......	32.454	40.028	4,492.888
43.288	3.903	14.043	....	.....	.....	.....	......	......	......	222.486
114.694	5.880	25.994	....	.....	.....	.....	......	......	5.950	533.032
95.425	11.768	38.146	....	.....	.....	.....	......	2.265	.100	562.518
97.917	12.294	41.804	....	.....	.....	.....	......	.450	.125	631.808
121.600	10.891	51.606	....	.....	.....	.....	......	1.200	.150	733.637
101.348	12.715	42.551	....	.....	.....	.....	......	3.150	.150	589.993
113.226	12.847	55.296	....	.....	.....	.....	......	1.955	.375	602.247
89.082	9.181	34.257	....	.....	.....	.....	......	.700	8.410	505.284
91.375	8.898	40.690	....	.....	.....	.....	......	4.525	5.172	469.469
51.790	4.562	16.698	....	.....	.....	.....	......	2.851	4.161	361.175
,748.049	**180.871**	**600.830**	....	.....	.....	.....	......	**49.550**	**64.621**	**9,704.537**
771.939	68.019	210.162	....	.....	.....	.....	......	21.182	29.799	4,450.462
14.993	......	....	....	.....	.....	.....	......	2.500	......	71.642
786.932	**68.019**	**210.162**	....	.....	.....	.....	......	**23.682**	**29.799**	**4,522.104**
528.319	**58.592**	**163.438**	....	.....	.....	.....	......	......	**24.627**	**3,135.518**
,765.715	194.799	586.407	....	.....	.....	.....	......	27.874	43.125	9,952.396
55.186	5.309	19.422	....	.....	.....	.....	......	8.186	......	316.601
129.047	14.538	29.612	....	.....	.....	.....	......	......	2.975	736.396
163.316	15.837	40.974	....	.....	.....	.....	......	1.040	4.675	900.030
208.249	11.553	73.697	....	.....	.....	.....	......	2.335	1.170	1,231.810
201.729	20.525	102.986	....	.....	.....	.....	......	3.300	......	1,117.014
160.708	7.298	102.834	....	.....	.....	.....	......	3.860	......	1,083.322
160.403	20.005	74.158	....	.....	.....	.....	......	3.400	......	1,052.137
124.126	9.493	61.173	....	.....	.....	.....	......	3.150	12.847	793.632
95.939	13.404	45.523	....	.....	.....	.....	......	2.500	7.838	611.555
82.282	10.053	39.051	....	.....	.....	.....	......	1.500	4.596	547.495
59.133	5.595	24.678	....	.....	.....	.....	......	2.420	3.596	326.406
92.553	6.837	32.378	....	74.344	.....	.....	......	1.330	12.968	526.636
52.919	6.640	30.316	....	19.242	.....	.....	......	1.773	1.254	363.938
70.106	5.192	26.837	....	.013	.....	.....	......	......	......	355.681
34.528	1.863	10.544	....	.....	.....	.....	......	1.000	......	133.313
,455.939	**348.941**	**1,300.590**	....	**93.599**	.....	.....	......	**63.668**	**95.044**	**20,048.362**
195.171	**21.426**	**66.588**	....	.....	.....	.....	......	**5.943**	**7.025**	**1,073.312**
240.056	22.798	77.223	....	.....	.....	.....	......	16.633	.084	1,223.192
316.840	33.612	115.539	....	.....	.....	.....	......	5.643	20.007	1,444.707
301.239	25.090	92.321	....	.....	.....	1.700	......	4.158	.300	1,767.989
858.135	**81.500**	**285.083**	....	.....	.....	**1.700**	......	**26.434**	**20.391**	**4,435.888**
275.868	**30.250**	**89.444**	....	.....	.....	.....	......	**11.761**	**8.950**	**1,512.362**
412.843	**51.136**	**149.575**	....	.....	.....	.....	......	**11.817**	**11.300**	**2,400.730**
389.010	**37.885**	**123.714**	....	.....	.....	.....	......	**16.068**	**13.525**	**1,958.286**
31.079	**4.281**	**13.376**	....	.....	.....	.....	......	......	......	**205.224**

[*Concluded on next page*]

Table 411—*Concluded*

Summary of Internal Deliveries for Chil

Zone Warehouse	Table No.	Time of Delivery	Flour	Rice	Beans, Peas	Corn Grits	Pork Products	Vegetable Oil
		1920						
Warsaw	424	To Oct. 31	2,044.449	575.868	966.513	......	229.348	131.929
Warsaw	431	November	68.033	50.510	88.520	......	2.418	6.096
Warsaw	436	December	199.223	66.807	148.720	......	26.394	6.037
		1921						
Warsaw	441	January	354.824	47.569	210.502	......	35.208	9.675
Warsaw	445	February	983.886	84.620	605.236	......	80.519	31.349
Warsaw	449	March	622.491	328.633	456.037	......	97.462	38.864
Warsaw	453	April	588.589	327.882	243.284	......	93.092	37.074
Warsaw	457	May	951.842	242.528	102.402	......	92.262	36.750
Warsaw	461	June	853.346	289.308	380.253	......	78.051	36.753
Warsaw	465	July	658.032	224.803	372.404	......	91.644	23.522
Warsaw	469	August	374.814	116.824	229.376	......	24.752	9.986
Warsaw	472	September	188.415	46.157	84.947	......	19.704	8.296
Warsaw	475	October	426.464	132.340	179.513	32.241	40.841	11.142
Warsaw	478	November	199.205	58.983	53.272	49.975	21.969	4.460
Warsaw	481	December	120.936	33.999	33.278	24.978	18.005	2.788
		1922						
Warsaw	482	January	614.978	306.588	142.610	35.230	72.869	18.910
Warsaw	483	February	630.704	267.642	194.143	45.189	71.731	16.663
Warsaw	484	March	1,083.086	481.870	408.614	47.089	121.911	38.255
Warsaw	487	April	99.331	14.497	13.255	.687	4.667	.166
Warsaw	488	May	.468	3.112	.196	......	.468	......
Warsaw	489	June	1,051.434	43.473	....	24.922	.405	......
Warsaw	490	July	1,159.985	165.275	146.388	13.415	34.389	16.553
Warsaw—by P.U.Z.A.P.P.	...	....	....	....	124.500	3.200	......	......
Warsaw—Sundry	...	....	....	....	....	......	43.911	25.876
Total Ex-Warsaw	......	....	**13,274.535**	**3,909.288**	**5,183.963**	**276.926**	**1,302.020**	**511.144**
		1920						
Wilno	425	To Oct. 31	**1,454.851**	**284.462**	**414.810**	......	**99.096**	**14.534**
Total Gross	......	....	**45,763.749**	**13,062.430**	**19,579.051**	**1,657.815**	**4,587.284**	**1,529.793**
Deduct Duplications *	...	....	....	90.900	....	......	24.700	......
Total Net	......	....	**45,763.749**	**12,971.530**	**19,579.051**	**1,657.815**	**4,562.584**	**1,529.793**

* Internal shipments, receipted by more than one warehouse.

.R.A. and A.R.A.-European Children's Fund

eeding, by Months and by Zone Warehouses

ommodities in Net Metric Tons of 1,000 Kilograms or 2,204.6 Pounds

			Miscellaneous Food							
Milk, Evap. and Cond.	Cocoa	Sugar	Corned Beef	Salmon and Whalemeat	Soup	Codliver Oil	Hard Bread	Salt	Soap	Total Tons
1,642.203	111.691	307.249	....	.....	.....	23.334	......	49.349	53.475	6,135.408
58.532	7.580	25.302	....	.....	.....	.....	......	10.950	......	317.941
117.100	9.911	45.480	....	.....	.....	.....	......	4.133	1.200	625.005
194.518	11.866	53.638	....	.....	.....	3.500	......	12.760	1.406	935.466
412.162	35.572	149.192	....	.....	.....	.200	......	11.870	1.150	2,395.756
436.084	41.702	214.826	....	.....	.....	.150	......	30.526	1.601	2,268.376
359.235	37.360	203.334	.865	.....	.....	.300	......	20.807	.929	1,912.751
409.492	40.431	193.248	....	.....	.....	.....	......	17.093	2.050	2,088.098
352.147	35.885	175.597	....	.....	.....	.....	......	12.020	33.115	2,246.475
289.919	21.899	121.446	....	.....	.....	.....	......	14.546	19.574	1,837.789
119.399	14.730	46.069	....	.....	5.238	.....	......	14.375	11.788	967.351
85.767	10.315	48.609	....	40.035	.....	.....	......	8.053	9.248	549.546
205.795	16.346	83.505	....	55.796	.....	.....	......	3.221	24.962	1,212.166
81.308	7.266	32.953	1.404	21.378	.....	.....	......	2.086	......	534.259
67.662	4.293	20.993	....	8.534	.....	.....	......	2.788	......	338.254
269.285	28.004	139.318	....	31.696	.....	.....	......	......	.200	1,659.688
304.671	28.494	144.598	....	.131	.....	.....	......	......	......	1,703.966
546.002	49.328	262.118	....	.....	.....	.....	......	......	......	3,038.273
15.798	1.461	7.224	....	.....	.....	.....	......	......	.500	157.586
1.546	.016	.123	....	.....	.....	.....	......	......	.022	5.951
39.299	1.010	2.159	....	1.649	.....	.....	......	......	......	1,164.351
683.096	17.511	840.385	....	24.832	.070	.....	......	......	42.307	3,144.206
......	......	....	....	.....	.....	.....	......	......	19.200	146.900
......	......	....	....	.....	.....	.....	......	......	......	69.787
6,691.020	**532.671**	**3,117.366**	**2.269**	**184.051**	**5.308**	**27.484**	......	**214.577**	**222.727**	**35,455.349**
448.879	**50.456**	**134.754**	....	.....	.....	.....	**49.428**	**13.560**	**16.464**	**2,981.294**
[illegible],223.912	**1,982.894**	**8,166.223**	**2.269**	**313.879**	**5.308**	**30.304**	**116.794**	**796.880**	**736.259**	**119,554.844**
34.700	29.200	....	....	26.500	.....	.....	......	......	......	206.000
[illegible],189.212	**1,953.694**	**8,166.223**	**2.269**	**287.379**	**5.308**	**30.304**	**116.794**	**796.880**	**736.259**	**119,348.844**

POLAND—A.R.A.-European Children's Fund

Detail of Internal Deliveries from Zone Warehouses to Local Committees (Kitchens), by Receipt Numbers—Reconstruction Period, 1919–1924
Tables 412 to 490, Inclusive

Table 412
Deliveries from BIAŁYSTOK WAREHOUSE, from the Beginning to October 31, 1920

Receipt No.	Local Committee	Commodities in Net Metric Tons of 1,000 Kilograms or 2,204.6 Pounds										
		Flour	Milk	Beans, Peas	Rice	Sugar	Cocoa	Pork Products	Vegetable Oil	Soap	Salt	Hard Bread
1	Augustów	41.304	19.030	23.042	11.613	6.379	1.859	3.006	1.907	.875	1.591	.....
2	Białystok	475.884	246.709	228.599	139.147	49.133	21.381	52.361	41.415	4.125	12.585	.....
3	Baranowicze	108.702	55.246	59.949	36.491	9.180	4.207	8.243	3.511	2.449	3.925	.....
4	Brzostowica	44.178	32.148	25.797	14.532	4.732	3.041	5.144	1.783	.932	1.402	.....
5	Grajewo-Szczuczyn	39.206	19.981	20.748	11.246	5.898	1.916	3.504	.729	.775	1.350	.....
6	Grodno	198.309	102.446	104.952	64.980	26.088	10.199	14.579	10.754	3.366	4.900	.....
7	Nowogródek	94.498	47.032	44.811	30.992	9.400	4.252	8.588	1.202	2.692	3.881	.....
8	Słonim	240.975	120.433	104.836	72.650	21.636	7.801	23.986	6.876	4.080	9.547	21.05
9	Sokółka	51.310	21.774	22.730	15.462	5.069	1.260	5.136	1.988	.799	1.332	.....
10	Suwałki	75.145	41.805	41.919	21.799	11.038	3.512	7.244	2.062	2.025	2.536	.....
11	Wołkowysk	66.766	40.301	42.134	25.618	10.309	4.579	6.093	2.187	1.765	1.305	.....
12	Mołodeczno	14.450	13.935	14.762	6.500	4.541	.495	.902	.171	.489	.800	.....
13	Białystok (gimnazjum)	.100	.054	.034	.033	.017	.008	.016	....	....	....	.....
14	Białystok R.G.O.	3.000	.....	....	....	....	....	....	....	....	....	.....
15	Sopockinie	2.723	1.176	.900	.907	.454	.250	....	....	....	....	.....
	Total	**1,456.550**	**762.072**	**735.213**	**451.970**	**163.874**	**64.760**	**138.802**	**74.587**	**24.372**	**45.154**	**21.05**

POLAND

Table 413
Deliveries from Brest—Pinsk Warehouse, from the Beginning to October 31, 1920

Receipt No.	Local Committee	Commodities in Net Metric Tons of 1,000 Kilograms or 2,204.6 Pounds										
		Flour	Milk	Beans, Peas	Rice	Sugar	Cocoa	Pork Products	Vegetable Oil	Soap	Salt	Hard Bread
1	Biała Podlaska	86.191	33.388	48.835	26.562	13.706	3.369	7.007	1.063	1.458	4.814	...
2	Bielsk	249.653	129.762	127.158	75.388	37.641	10.105	29.907	7.203	4.028	8.597	...
3	Brześć Litewski	433.489	193.028	185.317	116.549	46.825	12.389	46.976	10.769	4.789	11.612	2.2
4	Białowieża	8.626	5.861	8.694	3.690	1.608	.269	1.496	.174	.082	.590	...
5	Kobryń	358.004	167.687	135.897	117.390	24.504	8.931	41.141	13.712	2.966	6.248	3.0
6	Pińsk	355.534	159.983	164.382	105.867	38.095	11.613	33.718	15.914	3.946	12.783	18.5
7	Prużany	250.342	125.244	130.836	60.872	27.421	7.356	30.594	8.074	2.967	7.091	4.2
8	Łuniniec	6.276	3.624	2.484	2.784	1.000	.281	.388	.174	....	....	...
9	Janów	13.671	7.894	8.027	4.289	3.197	.545	1.802	....	.299	.800	...
10	Bobrujsk	62.708	34.745	36.478	17.488	8.221	2.086	5.708	....	2.400	3.120	...
11	Chołuj	.564	.196	.315	.182	.091	.....	.....	....	....	....	...
12	Ihumeń	4.736	....	1.575	1.544	.728	.....	.297	....	....	.378	...
13	Lepel	3.608	1.855	2.215	1.164	.582	.203	.306	....	.210	....	...
14	Mińsk Litewski	480.602	240.853	248.474	122.473	60.819	17.062	46.008	9.176	16.600	12.470	...
15	Nowo Borysów	5.779	1.704	3.483	1.846	.500	.102	.307	....	.150	....	...
16	Osipowicze	3.059	1.242	1.894	.984	.240	.....	.153	....	.100	....	...
17	Smolewicze	6.092	2.789	1.260	1.967	.323	.101	.153	....	.100	....	...
18	Słuck	3.136	.400	1.973	1.015	.510	.....	.....	....	....	....	...
19	Swisłocz	1.674	.892	1.080	.536	.269	.082	.153	....	....	....	...
20	Drohiczyn	.....	.019	.....	.090	....	.....	.016	....	....	....	...
	Total	**2,333.744**	**1,111.166**	**1,110.377**	**662.690**	**266.280**	**74.494**	**246.130**	**66.259**	**40.096**	**68.503**	**28.0**

POLAND

Deliveries from CZĘSTOCHOWA Warehouse, from the Beginning to October 31, 1920

Table 414

eipt o.	Local Committee	Commodities in Net Metric Tons of 1,000 Kilograms or 2,204.6 Pounds									
		Flour	Milk	Beans, Peas	Rice	Sugar	Cocoa	Pork Products	Vegetable Oil	Soap	Salt
1	Będzin	13.016	20.672	22.546	10.968	7.104	2.059	1.602	3.105	1.605	....
2	Częstochowa	344.372	146.551	177.872	108.544	55.886	17.653	35.225	17.159	24.570	4.110
3	Dąbrowa	84.843	40.049	42.795	46.819	13.702	4.216	11.794	1.186	1.080	....
4	Miechów	33.738	17.009	17.065	10.246	5.786	1.904	3.871	1.218	.509	.578
5	Olkusz	67.872	32.645	32.059	22.103	10.631	4.267	7.817	2.843	.450	.626
6	Radomsk	86.031	34.541	39.841	22.169	12.355	3.578	8.711	1.544	1.350	2.456
7	Sosnowiec	313.701	135.387	149.058	74.128	46.215	14.284	34.006	7.043	4.850	1.556
8	Zawiercie	16.892	8.333	9.275	2.887	2.542	.856	1.682	.170	.400	....
9	Katowice	312.768	166.906	153.616	96.042	52.102	16.601	52.388	.519	6.000	2.700
	Total	**1,273.233**	**602.093**	**644.127**	**393.906**	**206.323**	**65.419**	**157.096**	**34.787**	**40.814**	**12.026**

POLAND

Deliveries from KOWEL Warehouse, from the Beginning to October 31, 1920

Table 415

eipt o.	Local Committee	Commodities in Net Metric Tons of 1,000 Kilograms or 2,204.6 Pounds										
		Flour	Milk	Beans, Peas	Rice	Sugar	Cocoa	Pork Products	Vegetable Oil	Soap	Salt	Hard Bread
1	Dubno	61.884	27.937	35.996	15.131	6.033	2.882	4.272	1.577	1.900	2.989	......
2	Kowel	463.269	224.534	242.360	114.954	60.335	24.265	46.805	11.488	5.500	8.924	18.276
3	Krzemieniec	86.796	40.007	37.179	19.698	7.109	3.622	3.954	1.808	1.550	.267	......
4	Łuck	156.958	78.602	91.567	53.132	20.422	7.272	14.061	2.421	2.350	3.052	......
5	Ołyka	51.648	24.311	27.044	13.680	4.352	2.556	6.059	.091	.400	1.311	......
6	Ostróg	50.758	18.391	17.231	17.055	10.170	2.297	9.423	1.519	.610	1.473	......
7	Równo	121.299	58.918	66.554	41.284	16.565	5.403	10.223	3.319	1.200	3.865	......
8	Sarny	10.006	5.710	6.056	3.228	1.614	.484	.897	....	....	.403	......
9	Włodzimierz Wołyński	334.197	143.117	144.175	100.883	28.036	12.887	43.419	5.959	3.500	8.244	......
10	Kijów	7.440	2.621	4.200	2.400	1.200	.326	.765	.180	.400	.600	......
11	Kijów Polski Czerw. Krzyż	24.181	12.681	13.290	7.496	3.960	1.109	2.555	.732	....	1.650	......
12	Starokonstantynów	3.422	1.790	2.028	1.104	.552	.276	.336	....	....	.276	......
13	Zasław	23.064	11.705	11.087	7.440	2.067	1.292	1.307	.447	.500	1.132	......
14	Zwiahel	16.089	13.615	16.900	7.384	1.767	1.357	2.497	....	.300	1.653	......
15	Żytomierz	13.944	6.728	7.875	4.505	2.250	.699	1.137	.668	.200	1.125	......
	Total	**1,424.955**	**670.668**	**723.542**	**409.374**	**166.433**	**66.727**	**147.710**	**30.210**	**18.410**	**36.964**	**18.276**

POLAND

Deliveries from KRAKÓW Warehouse, from the Beginning to October 31, 1920

Table 416

Receipt No.	Local Committee	Commodities in Net Metric Tons of 1,000 Kilograms or 2,204.6 Pounds									
		Flour	Milk	Beans, Peas	Rice	Sugar	Cocoa	Pork Products	Vegetable Oil	Soap	Salt
1	Biała	43.101	21.032	20.830	14.117	6.879	2.156	5.549	....	1.116	1.000
2	Brzesko	30.406	16.445	16.457	10.783	4.834	1.662	4.151	.515	.958	.350
3	Okocim	5.274	3.244	1.013	1.894	.581	.296	.635	....	.100	....
4	Wojnicz	6.012	2.997	1.737	1.843	.731	.367	.847	.046	.200	....
5	Bochnia	14.034	5.968	7.031	4.173	1.963	.641	1.117	.328	.435	.350
6	Niepołomice	4.822	2.667	2.223	1.737	.925	.239	.709	.058	.191	.100
7	Chrzanów	29.724	12.484	11.151	8.383	3.719	1.503	3.396	.735	.517	.200
8	Jaworzno	4.399	2.201	1.488	1.487	.585	.292	.997	....	....	....
9	Trzebinia	3.619	1.184	2.086	1.179	.613	.171	.294	.178	.109	.200
10	Szczakowa	4.445	2.211	2.631	1.497	.725	.218	.443	.074	.272	.100
11	Dębica	17.166	8.615	9.129	5.443	2.748	.936	1.868	.414	.844	.500
12	Pilzno	1.759	.825	.732	.563	.157	.071	.337	....	....	....
13	Mielec	17.077	8.051	8.001	4.508	2.284	.859	1.787	.191	.489	.350
14	Gorlice	45.992	23.733	21.985	9.329	6.014	1.915	7.008	.616	.681	.550
15	Jasło	24.848	11.185	11.975	7.453	2.902	1.182	3.268	.402	.463	.250
16	Żmigród	.930	.464	.310	.310	.155	.078	.232	....	....	....
17	Krośno	44.361	19.624	22.332	13.578	6.241	2.229	5.213	.911	.871	1.250
18	Krościenko	.744	.372	.248	.248	.124	.062	.186	....	....	....
19	Dukla	5.022	2.511	1.674	1.674	.837	.418	1.256	....	....	....
20	Miejsce Piaskowe	2.286	1.156	.772	.461	.291	.147	.593	....	....	....
21	Jordanów	48.737	23.459	24.238	12.125	7.714	2.560	6.286	.203	2.052	.900
22	Myślenice	36.740	21.287	15.931	12.024	5.881	2.307	5.771	.344	1.798	.700
23	Maków	13.369	7.105	7.863	4.688	2.235	.763	1.803	.063	.381	.550
24	Kraków	419.679	213.569	208.581	132.104	61.557	21.399	64.578	3.086	10.061	6.600
25	Skawina	5.524	2.804	2.813	1.587	.726	.285	.782	.062	.163	.050
26	Wieliczka	12.573	4.977	7.393	3.539	2.114	.607	1.008	.146	.218	.300
27	Nowy Sącz	133.270	67.475	59.889	35.515	18.961	6.497	13.999	1.832	2.313	2.050
28	Stary Sącz	4.763	2.397	1.588	1.588	.816	.398	.768	.162	.025	....
29	Grybów	3.406	1.974	1.614	1.178	.544	.229	.684	.174	....	....
30	Muszyna	39.080	22.692	20.745	12.761	6.083	2.413	5.908	.369	.816	.700
31	Limanowa	8.417	4.071	5.352	2.948	1.601	.442	1.098	.183	.218	.300
32	Mszana Dolna	1.846	1.318	.907	.227	.318	.030	.326	....	....	....
33	Nowy Targ	44.552	22.538	21.265	13.145	4.786	1.935	6.033	.336	.898	.450
34	Zakopane	32.393	17.704	15.722	7.734	4.859	1.186	5.108	.137	.435	.550
35	Nisko	39.196	17.141	16.708	12.263	6.347	2.220	5.749	.364	1.735	.750
36	Oświęcim	49.024	17.426	25.639	16.022	7.189	2.354	5.085	1.078	.819	.900
37	Rzeszów	70.397	26.561	36.878	20.496	7.687	3.236	8.484	.978	1.007	1.450
38	Łańcut	20.733	9.752	8.648	6.551	3.280	1.228	2.952	.323	.353	.300
39	Leżajsk	21.039	9.269	10.161	6.078	3.793	1.029	1.579	.476	.381	.700
40	Tarnobrzeg	21.634	9.075	10.069	5.942	1.722	.889	3.015	.243	.445	4.200
41	Rozwadów	25.025	13.565	14.303	8.634	4.813	1.450	3.587	.453	.626	.600
42	Tarnów	90.669	49.522	48.601	30.769	13.235	4.749	10.641	1.889	2.715	1.800
43	Wadowice	37.251	18.945	19.119	10.372	4.469	1.711	4.335	.412	.680	.653
44	Kalwarja	8.866	4.822	4.310	2.905	1.206	.393	.787	.099	.285	.351
45	Żywiec	38.106	19.069	16.440	10.317	5.694	1.715	5.757	.112	.871	.450
46	Sucha	8.279	4.372	3.441	2.851	1.387	.609	1.808	.041	.482	.250
47	Cieszyn	102.531	48.009	44.064	30.307	10.254	5.850	20.138	....	1.007	1.500
48	Krzeszowice	12.638	6.122	6.998	4.140	2.029	.871	2.200	.155	.326	.150
49	Miłówka	14.135	7.066	4.712	4.712	2.356	1.178	3.476	.058	1.520	....
50	Pawlikowice	.381	.182	.136	.136	.063	.030	.071	....	....	....
51	Staniątka	.127	.060	.045	.045	.018	.009	.027	....	....	....
52	Żółkiew	15.114	6.575	6.975	3.444	2.551	.913	2.489	.426	.150	....
53	Zbylitowska Góra	.487	.304	.136	....	.091	.992	.131	....	....	....
54	Igołomnia	.266	.127	.136	.069	.057	.012	.030	....	....	.050
	Total	**1,686.269**	**828.304**	**815.227**	**507.878**	**239.745**	**87.932**	**236.380**	**18.671**	**40.028**	**32.45[illegible]**

POLAND

Deliveries from ŁÓDŹ Warehouse, from the Beginning to October 31, 1920

Table 417

Receipt No.	Local Committee	Commodities in Net Metric Tons of 1,000 Kilograms or 2,204.6 Pounds									
		Flour	Milk	Beans, Peas	Rice	Sugar	Cocoa	Pork Products	Vegetable Oil	Soap	Salt
1	Aleksandrów i Konst.	22.606	9.989	11.397	6.769	3.209	1.078	2.357	.630	.337	.426
2	Brzeziny i Koluszki	31.816	11.639	16.764	8.748	4.592	1.204	2.292	1.804	.641	1.251
3	Kalisz i Turek	68.845	27.557	33.733	21.695	11.285	3.758	6.411	2.792	2.267	.500
4	Koło	22.840	11.576	11.919	6.176	3.799	1.136	2.390	.462	.645	.419
5	Konin	3.423	1.774	1.976	1.100	.552	.184	.283	.180	....	.138
6	Łęczyca	32.307	13.776	14.044	10.257	5.158	1.984	3.849	1.050	.625	.704
7	Łask i Zelów	30.743	15.296	14.117	8.924	3.803	1.402	3.513	1.381	.104	.527
8	Łódź Miasto	1,046.747	392.851	430.104	253.347	86.802	30.770	92.422	17.674	11.638	5.529
9	Łódź Okręg	116.742	72.791	55.717	11.174	23.230	6.338	12.898	3.480	4.704	....
10	Rzgów i Tuszyn	18.163	8.379	8.857	5.154	2.679	.889	2.360	.558	.281	.391
11	Ozorków	41.599	19.211	20.143	10.918	4.862	1.623	3.492	1.748	1.393	1.128
12	Pabjanice i Folwark	82.842	42.909	41.838	24.893	11.129	2.411	11.685	.871	1.547	3.069
13	Ruda Pabjanicka	9.061	5.024	5.188	2.713	2.123	.406	1.035	.054	....	.401
14	Sieradz	39.537	15.952	18.490	12.144	5.307	1.879	3.658	2.371	.949	.291
15	Stryków i Główno	24.061	11.106	12.148	7.582	3.359	1.040	2.376	.808	.501	.895
16	Tomaszów	39.751	16.806	21.545	12.461	6.617	2.044	4.152	1.182	.746	1.102
17	Wieluń	33.425	12.126	16.004	10.859	5.809	1.626	3.168	2.604	.370	1.169
18	Zduńska Wola	47.441	17.432	20.335	10.697	5.249	1.760	4.696	1.403	.986	.518
19	Zgierz	77.357	40.992	40.547	24.067	12.075	3.256	9.601	2.418	1.164	1.999
20	Bruś	35.901	19.176	15.309	9.498	5.508	1.936	6.538	.375	.764	.393
21	Jeżów	.768	.330	.273	.227	.124	.006	.164	....	.024	....
22	Chojny	1.214	.636	.409	.364	.228	.111	.264	....	.025	....
23	Łagiewniki	4.980	.674	.910	1.729	1.001	.649	.726	....	.024	....
24	Radogoszcz	.320	.152	.182	.046	.046	.102	.066	....	....	....
25	Łódź (Kolonje Letnie)	1.081	.588	.364	.364	.046	....	.262	....	....	....
26	Lisków	8.491	3.197	4.704	2.744	1.571	.428	1.128	....	.053	.332
	Total	**1,842.061**	**771.939**	**817.018**	**464.650**	**210.162**	**68.019**	**181.787**	**43.845**	**29.799**	**21.182**

POLAND

Deliveries from LUBLIN Warehouse, from the Beginning to October 31, 1920

Table 418

Receipt No.	Local Committee	Commodities in Net Metric Tons of 1,000 Kilograms or 2,204.6 Pounds									
		Flour	Milk	Beans, Peas	Rice	Sugar	Cocoa	Pork Products	Vegetable Oil	Soap	Salt
1	Biłgoraj	30.720	14.986	17.387	9.890	3.862	1.401	2.478	1.195	.175	1.824
2	Chełm	348.593	137.850	161.260	91.931	40.788	15.909	36.757	6.357	3.000	16.925
3	Hrubieszów	50.073	22.998	28.746	15.078	6.806	2.721	5.013	1.444	.690	1.980
4	Krasnystaw	38.839	18.843	21.702	11.451	4.587	1.870	3.139	1.508	.500	1.594
5	Lublin	231.627	90.996	113.360	64.383	32.804	11.454	21.090	8.476	12.800	8.019
6	Lubartów	22.181	9.757	12.245	6.864	2.580	1.089	1.659	.909	.260	.721
7	Luboml	34.918	17.180	19.987	10.906	5.608	1.458	3.021	.668	.762	1.999
8	Parczew	77.775	28.645	36.764	22.708	12.246	2.550	7.233	2.208	.500	2.865
9	Puławy	30.698	15.304	17.276	8.874	4.674	1.266	2.377	.759	.450	1.159
10	Tomaszów Lubelski	99.535	42.993	45.927	30.671	12.287	5.356	7.344	4.282	1.050	5.182
11	Włodawa	193.589	86.514	103.961	49.456	25.618	9.414	15.511	5.058	2.800	7.290
12	Zamość	28.712	13.406	13.325	8.388	4.454	1.506	2.758	.728	.240	.929
13	Ostrów Lubelski	19.515	9.193	7.948	5.276	2.175	.829	1.181	.657	.650	1.162
14	Janów Lubelski	20.595	10.533	11.823	6.250	2.799	.859	1.826	.516	.300	1.107
15	Zwierzyniec	14.635	7.498	6.832	3.907	1.655	.761	1.450	.172	.450	....
16	Werbkowice	3.064	1.622	1.733	.990	.495	.149	.396	....	....	.248
	Total	**1,245.069**	**528.319**	**620.279**	**347.023**	**163.438**	**58.592**	**113.233**	**34.938**	**24.627**	**53.004**

POLAND

Deliveries from LWÓW Warehouse, from the Beginning to October 31, 1920

Table 419

Receipt No.	Local Committee	Commodities in Net Metric Tons of 1,000 Kilograms or 2,204.6 Pounds									
		Flour	Milk	Beans, Peas	Rice	Sugar	Cocoa	Pork Products	Vegetable Oil	Soap	Salt
1	Bóbrka	7.796	3.672	4.641	2.824	1.187	.444	.739	.172	.025	.142
2	Bohorodczany	31.864	14.880	10.561	4.842	4.724	1.615	3.522	.697	.275	....
3	Borszczów	4.489	2.685	1.905	1.598	.999	.203	.874	.174	.100	....
4	Borvsław	116.686	49.807	56.266	37.091	15.121	5.181	14.334	1.598	.725	....
5	Brody	139.120	63.279	54.716	25.138	24.629	9.132	18.640	4.295	1.175	....
6	Brzeżany	108.086	42.481	49.848	26.637	15.369	4.286	10.189	1.219	1.075	1.110
7	Brzozów	53.684	23.704	24.344	13.426	7.401	2.446	5.159	1.423	.675	.768
8	Buczacz	108.951	39.029	41.100	23.703	15.124	4.764	11.825	1.744	2.650	1.100
9	Cieszanów	21.813	10.001	13.163	7.102	3.596	.925	1.503	.352	.125	.600
10	Czortków	23.501	8.664	9.753	4.333	3.174	1.016	1.789	.341	.275	....
11	Dolina	43.129	21.633	18.553	13.300	6.384	2.729	6.582	.857	.275	....
12	Drohobycz	50.861	26.884	30.657	18.539	10.072	3.165	4.572	.807	.325	.624
13	Gródek Jagielloński	35.027	17.646	18.621	11.338	5.590	1.672	4.714	.422	.175	.061
14	Halicz	12.041	4.508	6.147	2.970	2.150	.508	1.439	.348	.250	....
15	Horodenka	1.022	.517	.610	.364	.200	.203	.153	....	....	....
16	Husiatyn	23.638	11.745	13.884	5.772	3.736	1.023	2.158	....	....	....
17	Jarosław	168.608	75.042	78.846	39.730	24.914	7.021	16.895	3.036	.975	1.201
18	Janów	7.424	3.347	4.376	2.670	1.298	.329	.779	.172	....	.260
19	Jaworów	25.197	8.858	12.681	7.636	3.454	1.168	1.689	.159	.150	....
20	Kałusz	44.486	22.099	22.855	13.970	6.585	2.365	3.795	1.523	.350	.300
21	Kamionka Strumił.	14.495	5.561	8.291	4.244	2.239	.711	1.433	.175	.100	....
22	Kołomyja	118.472	54.427	58.517	39.007	20.216	6.195	13.656	2.429	.975	1.300
23	Kosów	74.612	37.555	37.550	25.984	11.265	4.166	6.670	2.156	1.175	....
24	Lisko	41.041	17.995	23.348	13.726	6.440	2.258	4.096	.776	.300	.661
25	Lwów (Powiat)	82.756	29.864	34.435	20.548	13.133	4.156	10.729	.870	1.825	.863
26	Lwów	396.827	267.053	238.545	160.401	62.042	31.215	75.895	4.222	7.100	6.858
27	Nadworna	107.267	44.733	49.964	28.851	15.952	3.554	9.848	2.101	1.150	2.181
28	Otynja	17.508	7.573	8.380	5.202	1.934	.597	1.100	.171	.150	.309
29	Peczeniżyn	24.789	8.483	13.228	6.412	2.956	.921	1.587	.874	.700	....
30	Podhajce	49.231	16.391	25.888	13.082	7.643	2.453	5.844	.343	.200	.860
31	Przemyśl	270.596	95.612	104.240	63.530	41.964	11.816	30.019	2.751	1.500	.650
32	Przemyślany	11.112	4.046	4.111	3.312	1.600	.508	1.267	.345	.150	....
33	Przeworsk	85.228	29.811	36.357	26.264	11.353	4.501	11.350	2.475	1.710	....
34	Radziechów	23.049	5.859	11.233	6.400	3.707	1.118	1.580	.337	.100	....
35	Rawa Ruska	91.263	35.532	46.794	28.422	15.351	4.639	10.306	2.238	.700	1.285
36	Rohatyn	32.576	13.124	18.235	8.453	5.309	1.473	2.469	....	.175	.278
37	Rudki	19.240	10.619	11.404	4.806	2.963	1.212	2.553	.429	.125	....
38	Sambor	71.737	32.850	37.969	19.460	10.882	3.849	8.548	1.975	....	.450
39	Skole	63.564	23.945	27.781	15.184	8.971	2.359	5.531	1.192	.500	.902
40	Sniatyn	4.179	1.907	1.681	.944	.474	.305	.305	.172	....	....
41	Sokal	59.824	30.044	31.375	19.118	9.640	3.019	6.039	2.789	.650	....
42	Stanisławów	295.156	150.544	146.584	85.119	45.605	12.747	38.318	7.560	3.550	.675
43	Stary Sambor	55.808	22.893	31.793	15.099	9.875	3.149	5.208	1.203	.625	.343
44	Stryj	103.619	45.641	43.169	25.636	13.352	4.665	11.158	2.072	1.250	.300
45	Skałat	6.017	1.886	3.248	1.580	1.080	.203	.465	.173	.100	....
46	Tarnopol	57.228	23.553	27.965	15.205	8.250	2.667	6.549	1.683	....	.887
47	Tłumacz	90.697	45.326	34.183	23.919	12.849	4.150	11.223	2.070	1.200	.418
48	Trombowla	16.329	7.373	7.549	3.056	2.319	.711	1.633	.169	.200	....
49	Turka	61.973	20.355	28.157	15.132	8.215	2.644	4.837	1.124	.325	.855
50	Zaleszczyki	20.755	13.778	12.289	6.698	2.615	1.118	1.792	1.031	.325	....
51	Zbaraż	20.342	10.589	10.272	4.140	3.711	1.321	3.038	.506	.250	....
52	Zborów	148.296	61.758	72.257	31.233	20.789	7.160	18.278	2.091	1.825	....
53	Złoczów	60.263	33.842	26.789	18.393	9.615	2.929	7.110	1.553	.350	....
54	Żydaczów	25.424	12.766	11.338	4.978	3.981	1.016	1.878	.694	.300	....
55	Sanok	104.647	38.176	46.888	24.392	16.176	4.712	8.673	2.129	1.000	.95[illegible]
56	Wycofany	.....	.....	.....	.....	.....	.....	.....	....	....	....
57	Lwów Biały Krzyż	.....	1.074	.726	.726	.....	.....	.555	....	....	....

POLAND

Deliveries from LWÓW Warehouse, from the Beginning to October 31, 1920

Table 419—*Continued*

ceipt No.	Local Committee	Commodities in Net Metric Tons of 1,000 Kilograms or 2,204.6 Pounds									
		Flour	Milk	Beans, Peas	Rice	Sugar	Cocoa	Pork Products	Vegetable Oil	Soap	Salt
58	Ustrzyki	1.778	.892	1.179	.....	.....	.102	.359	.086	....	....
59	Dobromil	20.654	7.191	10.152	4.476	3.027	.864	1.438	.520	.150	....
60	Kamieniec Podol.	21.031	10.926	12.536	7.015	3.525	1.016	1.703	.518	2.500	.675
61	Płoskirów	5.832	2.949	3.169	1.809	.891	.305	.418	.348	....	....
62	Mościska	28.539	11.494	13.810	6.463	4.244	1.049	2.031	.689	.300	....
63	Rymanów	8.958	4.317	3.084	.589	1.089	.....	1.959	....	....	....
64	Żegiestów	2.376	1.439	.726	.454	.408	.....	.653	....	....	....
65	Kostrzyń	.....	.628	.....	.272	.181	.....	.294	....	....	....
66	Brzuchowice	8.085	3.425	2.177	.771	.589	.102	1.273	....	....	....
67	Gniewczyń	.366	.284	.091	.....	.091	.....	.131	....	....	....
68	Cięcina	.318	.162	.135	.....	.....	.....	.065	....	....	....
69	Dydnia	1.488	.527	.272	.....	.045	.047	.229	....	....	....
70	Komarno	6.159	2.621	3.391	1.854	.645	.305	.323	....	....	....
71	Subkomitet Żydowski	7.129	5.838	5.443	2.700	1.497	.595	.....	....	....	....
	Total	**3,866.058**	**1,765.715**	**1,862.228**	**1,078.044**	**586.407**	**194.799**	**453.768**	**74.378**	**43.125**	**27.874**

POLAND

Deliveries from MAZOWIECK Warehouse, from the Beginning to October 31, 1920

Table 420

ceipt No.	Local Committee	Commodities in Net Metric Tons of 1,000 Kilograms or 2,204.6 Pounds									
		Flour	Milk	Beans, Peas	Rice	Sugar	Cocoa	Pork Products	Vegetable Oil	Soap	Salt
1	Grodzisk	104.165	40.679	42.064	28.412	15.521	4.983	9.779	2.065	1.100	.959
2	Grójec	44.546	30.472	23.860	19.421	8.637	2.940	5.467	3.946	1.375	.310
3	Łowicz	40.145	19.049	20.079	11.365	6.491	2.004	4.317	1.182	.575	.810
4	Mińsk Mazowiecki	59.527	26.899	24.009	13.638	9.051	2.503	6.153	1.128	1.100	1.518
5	Rawa Mazowiecka	57.472	27.780	25.006	13.015	9.722	3.191	7.388	.988	.925	....
6	Skierniewice	41.127	17.620	22.341	11.635	6.556	2.104	3.416	.470	.550	.345
7	Sochaczew	41.848	21.660	22.950	11.627	6.868	2.274	3.483	1.336	.675	.998
8	Góra Kalwarja	25.176	11.012	12.275	7.894	3.742	1.427	1.928	.516	.725	1.003
	Total	**414.006**	**195.171**	**192.584**	**117.007**	**66.588**	**21.426**	**41.931**	**11.631**	**7.025**	**5.943**

POLAND

Deliveries from PŁOCK Warehouse, from the Beginning to October 31, 1920

Table 421

Receipt No.	Local Committee	Commodities in Net Metric Tons of 1,000 Kilograms or 2,204.6 Pounds									
		Flour	Milk	Beans, Peas	Rice	Sugar	Cocoa	Pork Products	Vegetable Oil	Soap	Salt
1	Ciechanów	24.056	12.426	13.147	6.705	3.198	1.116	2.499	.604	.275	.305
2	Gostynin	48.895	23.661	21.339	11.905	8.146	2.584	4.883	1.620	.650	1.389
3	Kutno	108.571	50.115	49.474	29.406	17.789	5.728	9.714	2.231	1.100	2.862
4	Maków	25.077	11.740	13.651	6.885	3.656	1.226	2.137	.747	.475	.744
5	Mława	41.132	18.808	21.498	11.192	6.154	1.874	4.608	.605	.525	.670
6	Płock	89.904	43.384	36.216	25.412	14.586	4.927	10.378	2.179	1.900	2.657
7	Płońsk	16.463	7.683	7.359	4.691	2.076	.890	1.915	.503	.325	.082
8	Pomorze	14.880	7.190	7.200	3.600	2.640	.480	2.645	....	....	....
9	Gniew	1.333	.476	.765	.432	.225	.064	.162	....	....	....
10	Przasnysz	29.921	13.918	14.467	7.205	3.944	1.454	2.961	.634	.350	.802
11	Pułtusk	34.810	16.625	13.796	10.509	4.761	1.823	3.746	.739	.550	.657
12	Sierpc	7.991	3.994	3.255	2.649	.400	.552	1.462	.122	....	....
13	Wyszków	36.238	15.860	18.096	9.465	5.512	1.741	3.664	.973	.450	.670
14	Włocławek	61.000	25.590	32.996	16.096	9.396	2.822	6.688	.926	1.500	....
15	Ciechocinek	1.841	.914	.708	.720	.350	.170	.528	....	....	....
16	Lipno	21.891	11.022	7.693	6.030	2.659	1.203	2.006	.336	.200	.761
17	Rypin	12.170	6.257	6.193	2.295	1.998	.943	1.269	.347	.400	....
18	Nieszawa	1.488	.533	.878	.480	.240	.072	.155	....	....	....
19	Nasielsk	10.361	5.595	5.682	2.699	1.684	.572	.817	.092	.250	.162
20	Lubocześnica	.186	.076	.105	.060	.030	.009	.033	....	....	....
	Total	**588.208**	**275.868**	**274.518**	**158.436**	**89.444**	**30.250**	**62.270**	**12.657**	**8.950**	**11.761**

POLAND

Deliveries from RADOM Warehouse, from the Beginning to October 31, 1920

Table 422

Receipt No.	Local Committee	Commodities in Net Metric Tons of 1,000 Kilograms or 2,204.6 Pounds									
		Flour	Milk	Beans, Peas	Rice	Sugar	Cocoa	Pork Products	Vegetable Oil	Soap	Salt
1	Jędrzejów	39.691	16.010	13.969	10.862	6.558	2.133	4.714	1.086	....	....
2	Kielce	172.439	79.176	72.771	51.536	32.666	10.198	23.984	4.655	1.900	1.17
3	Końskie	58.055	22.114	23.623	17.783	9.488	2.847	7.056	1.201	1.000	.05
4	Kozienice	46.567	22.634	21.232	12.151	6.775	2.114	3.474	1.789	.800	.92
5	Opoczno	35.694	15.357	16.750	8.837	4.618	1.429	3.596	.785	.400	.56
6	Ostrowiec	110.753	37.289	42.114	30.745	16.662	5.404	10.919	1.471	1.300	3.86
7	Pińczów	46.296	20.886	17.233	14.700	7.300	1.819	4.723	1.124	.300	.42
8	Piotrków	104.615	38.902	44.215	23.657	13.995	4.506	9.204	1.582	1.150	1.18
9	Radom	107.966	43.589	46.917	26.285	14.323	4.901	9.568	1.474	1.000	.30
10	Sandomierz	30.692	13.896	13.770	7.454	3.532	1.471	2.858	1.146	.475	.28
11	Wierzbnik	46.092	21.282	18.075	15.149	7.077	3.196	7.191	.335	.275	.69
12	Włoszczowa	47.043	20.873	18.982	12.221	6.196	2.654	4.228	1.426	.400	...
13	Opatów	13.323	6.915	6.582	1.819	1.297	.862	1.700	.524	....	...
14	Szydłowiec	1.820	.800	.645	.635	.315	.152	.467	....	....	...
15	Suchedniówn	3.108	1.378	.726	.681	.363	.991	.621	....	....	...
16	Iłża	9.031	4.706	2.325	....	1.449	.451	.953	....	.300	...
17	Busk	99.886	47.036	43.285	24.318	16.961	6.008	11.243	3.844	2.000	2.36
	Total	**973.071**	**412.843**	**403.214**	**258.833**	**149.575**	**51.136**	**106.499**	**22.442**	**11.300**	**11.81**

POLAND

Deliveries from SIEDLCE Warehouse, from the Beginning to October 31, 1920

Table 423

eipt o.	Local Committee	Commodities in Net Metric Tons of 1,000 Kilograms or 2,204.6 Pounds									
		Flour	Milk	Beans, Peas	Rice	Sugar	Cocoa	Pork Products	Vegetable Oil	Soap	Salt
1	Kolno	23.746	10.513	8.932	5.491	3.083	1.273	1.928	1.166	.325	.217
2	Garwolin	123.317	61.839	67.112	34.531	20.329	5.868	10.420	3.780	2.075	2.106
3	Łomża	85.885	43.709	37.472	17.735	14.091	4.261	8.674	2.664	1.550	.375
4	Łuków, Międzyrzec	48.814	23.884	21.168	14.608	6.635	2.199	3.660	2.064	.750	2.534
5	Ostrów Łomżyński	63.698	40.284	41.352	18.728	13.097	4.127	7.704	3.167	1.600	2.655
6	Ostrołęka	29.105	14.378	14.115	7.487	4.761	1.348	1.778	1.060	.450	.333
7	Siedlce	168.078	80.929	60.052	38.077	27.769	8.829	12.153	4.413	2.900	5.101
8	Węgrów	55.185	37.980	20.865	18.659	8.719	2.856	6.299	.870	1.225	1.235
9	Sokołów	33.710	16.604	15.874	9.492	5.496	1.643	2.473	1.230	.300	.627
0	Wysoko Mazowieck	64.377	30.981	34.249	14.958	10.660	2.912	5.240	1.092	.900	.696
1	Sobienie Jeziory	21.762	11.641	10.680	5.482	3.886	1.361	2.198	.523	.275	.189
2	Żelechów	9.354	4.490	5.792	1.016	1.508	.303	.440	.245	.375	....
3	Łaskarzew	5.880	3.024	3.572	.589	.948	.204	.420	.090	.225	....
4	Sobolew	2.264	1.129	1.464	.230	.363	.109	.099	.060	.100	....
5	Ryki	10.512	5.508	6.438	1.619	1.689	.399	.773	.185	.300	....
6	Stężyca	1.599	.792	.928	.228	.260	.068	.181	....	.075	....
7	Maciejowice	2.607	1.325	1.587	.276	.420	.125	.223	.061	.100	....
	Total	**749.893**	**389.010**	**351.652**	**189.206**	**123.714**	**37.885**	**64.663**	**22.670**	**13.525**	**16.068**

POLAND

Deliveries from WARSAW Warehouse, from the Beginning to October 31, 1920

Table 424

eipt o.	Local Committee	Commodities in Net Metric Tons of 1,000 Kilograms or 2,204.6 Pounds										
		Flour	Milk	Beans, Peas	Rice	Sugar	Cocoa	Pork Products	Vegetable Oil	Soap	Salt	Codliver Oil
1	Warsaw (City)	1,402.145	653.822	592.990	374.930	188.865	73.200	130.511	12.251	17.925	35.233	......
2	Warsaw Radzymin	522.089	282.906	322.213	168.593	91.521	34.939	73.376	6.021	20.550	14.044	......
3	Feeding Stations	74.500	36.002	34.800	18.005	13.600	2.439	13.533	.....	.....	....	......
4	Warsaw	45.215	47.387	16.510	14.340	7.502	1.113	11.206	.....	.....	.072	......
5	Sanitary Approvisation Department	....	......	......	......	.....	.....	.722	.....	15.000	....	23.334
6	Dr. Bogen (J.D.C.)	.500	619.588	......	......	5.761	.....	....	113.657	.....	....	......
7	American Red Cross	....	2.498	......	......	.....	.....	....	.....	.....	....	......
	Total	**2,044.449**	**1,642.203**	**966.513**	**575.868**	**307.249**	**111.691**	**229.348**	**131.929**	**53.475**	**49.349**	**23.334**

POLAND

Deliveries from WILNO Warehouse, from the Beginning to October 31, 1920

Table 425

eipt o.	Local Committee	Commodities in Net Metric Tons of 1,000 Kilograms or 2,204.6 Pounds										
		Flour	Milk	Beans, Peas	Rice	Sugar	Cocoa	Pork Products	Vegetable Oil	Soap	Salt	Hard Bread
1	Bogdanów	29.205	13.224	17.260	9.350	4.625	.288	2.429	....	.....	.132	......
2	Lida	210.671	95.177	99.490	61.241	34.310	11.649	25.974	5.353	1.575	2.460	15.422
3	Oszmiany	124.794	56.323	58.055	37.606	16.945	6.494	16.406	.347	1.200	4.380	......
4	Swięciany	15.600	6.836	9.344	5.000	2.430	.722	1.669	....	.....	.690	......
5	Wilejka	18.091	8.354	6.854	5.631	1.141	.845	2.039	....	.600	.800	......
6	Głebokie Dziska	3.422	1.789	2.110	1.104	.552	.166	.264	....	.....	....	......
7	Wilno	1,049.088	265.117	219.326	163.291	74.100	30.107	49.908	8.834	13.089	4.822	34.006
8	Bracław	3.980	2.059	2.371	1.239	.651	.184	.407	....	.....	.276	......
	Total	**1,454.851**	**448.879**	**414.810**	**284.462**	**134.754**	**50.456**	**99.096**	**14.534**	**16.464**	**13.560**	**49.428**

POLAND

Table 426 — Deliveries from KRAKÓW Warehouse, Month of November, 1920

Receipt No.	Local Committee	Commodities in Net Metric Tons of 1,000 Kilograms or 2,204.6 Pounds								
		Cocoa	Sugar	Milk		Flour	Beans, Peas	Rice	Pork Products	Vegetable Oil
				Evap.	Cond.					
1	Cieszyn	....	.451	....	....	2.921	....	1.978	....	....
2	Chrzanow	.072	.240	.544	....	1.461	....	.480	....	....
3	Debica	....	.195	.436	.305	1.209	.689	.406	.152	.031
4	Gorlice	....	.189	.435	.438	1.143	....	.390	.166	....
5	Kalwarja	....	.042	.109	.267	.063	....	.078	.015	....
6	Krzeszowice	.037	.135	.174	....	.635	.497	.200	.054	....
7	Kraków	1.100	3.562	7.663	3.239	21.547	12.247	7.023	2.823	....
8	Limanowa	.055	.181	.414	.172	1.143	....	.358	.151	.030
9	Lezajsk	.101	.210	.479	....	1.334	.738	.430	.163	....
10	Lancut	.059	.195	.348	.191	1.079	.514	.400	.163	.168
11	Muszyna	.047	.225	.501	.114	1.397	....	.458	.147	....
12	Miêlec	.043	.135	.261	.281	.952	.550	.317	.150	....
13	Myslenice	.032	.109	.239	.191	.635	.368	.216	.050	....
14	Nowy Sacz	.299	.985	2.134	1.372	5.969	....	1.901	.621	.151
15	Oswiecim	.190	.575	1.263	.324	3.556	....	1.136	.473	.171
16	Rzêszow	.322	1.026	2.308	....	6.541	3.286	2.000	.709	.175
17	Szczakowa	....	....	....	....	.....	.315	....	....	....
18	Tarnow	.322	1.445	3.200	2.381	9.017	4.840	2.997	1.001	.162
19	Tarnobrezeg	.111	.046	.566	.515	.270	1.048	.543	....	.174
20	Wadowice	.101	.335	.762	.629	2.032	1.143	.653	.266	....
21	Zywiec	.101	.270	.609	....	1.651	.948	.541	.197	....
22	Biala	.102	.393	.958	.171	2.680	1.522	.851	.309	....
23	Bochnia	.053	.177	.392	.229	1.097	.620	.354	.142	....
24	Brzesko	.101	.338	.806	.629	2.286	....	.734	.128	....
25	Igolomja	.005	.015	.043	....	.093	.053	.030	.012	....
26	Jordanow	.023	.075	.174	....	.444	....	.150	.055	....
27	Krosno	....	.420	....	....	2.540	.998	.862	.294	.030
28	Makow	.040	.135	.305	....	.826	....	.272	.099	....
29	Nowy Targ	.132	.448	.979	.496	2.739	1.519	.906	.294	....
30	Niepolomoce	.015	.047	.109	.095	.321	.135	.089	.038	....
31	Nisko	.064	.214	.479	.324	1.334	....	.427	.164	....
32	Okocim	.018	.060	.152	....	.381	....	.120	.021	....
33	Rozwadow	.090	.300	.675	....	1.842	....	.595	....	....
34	Skawina	.018	.060	.152	....	.318	.179	.136	.034	.012
35	Szczakowa	.026	.092	.218	....	.571	....	.182	.065	....
36	Sucha	.027	.086	....	....	.572	....	.177	....	....
37	Trzêbinia	.026	.065	....	....	.508	....	.138	.054	....
38	Wieliczka	.079	.264	.588	.076	1.623	.934	.544	.188	.031
39	Zakopane	.092	.303	.697	1.677	1.968	1.073	.630	.303	....
	Total	**3.903**	**14.043**	**29.172**	**14.116**	**86.698**	**34.216**	**29.702**	**9.501**	**1.135**

POLAND

Table 427 — Deliveries from ŁÓDŹ Warehouse, Month of November, 1920

Receipt No.	Local Committee	Commodities in Net Metric Tons of 1,000 Kilograms or 2,204.6 Pounds									
		Flour	Milk	Beans, Peas	Rice	Sugar	Cocoa	Pork Products	Vegetable Oil	Soap	Salt
1	Region of Łódź	**32.040**	**14.993**	**18.097**	......	......	......	**3.004**	**1.008**	......	**2.50**

POLAND

Table 428 — Deliveries from LWÓW Warehouse, Month of November, 1920

ceipt No.	Local Committee	Commodities in Net Metric Tons of 1,000 Kilograms or 2,204.6 Pounds									
		Cocoa	Sugar	Milk		Flour	Beans, Peas	Rice	Pork Products	Vegetable Oil	Salt
				Evap.	Cond.						
1	Grodek Jagiellonski	.101	.290	.327	.343	1.905	.....	.591	.155	.170	.150
2	Kolomyja	.303	1.260	1.959	1.885	7.810	.....	2.508	.753	.323	.630
3	Lwów	....	.....	.....	7.049	.....	.....	.....	....	....	....
4	Prezemysl	.802	2.870	4.028	4.191	18.859	10.080	5.754	1.565	.680	1.403
5	Stryj	.301	1.152	1.589	1.524	7.176	.....	2.304	.595	.376	.584
6	Sambor	.109	.680	1.219	1.048	4.318	.253	1.521	.442	.174	.350
7	Stanislawow	.733	1.989	2.330	1.905	12.573	6.885	4.073	1.204	.682	.895
8	Turka	....	.....	.761	.572	.....	.....	.....	....	....	....
9	Trembowla	.200	.834	1.394	1.181	5.143	2.599	1.629	.463	.172	.416
10	Złoczow	.200	.850	1.306	1.181	5.271	.....	1.598	.459	.361	.411
11	Zborow	.401	1.423	2.025	1.714	9.017	5.090	2.899	.948	.171	.738
12	Boryslaw	.424	1.600	.....	1.714	9.969	4.581	3.190	.927	....	....
13	Brody	.501	1.690	2.721	1.296	10.478	5.919	3.363	.747	....	.840
14	Dolina	....	.578	.653	.648	3.725	2.102	1.215	.307	.173	....
15	Lisko	.180	.473	.653	.667	2.731	1.899	1.100	.314	....	.300
16	Nadworna	.893	3.193	3.221	2.591	19.790	10.650	6.388	1.996	.470	1.300
17	Skalat	.161	.540	.958	.533	3.429	1.941	1.084	.292	.169	.169
	Total	**5.309**	**19.422**	**25.144**	**30.042**	**122.194**	**51.999**	**39.217**	**11.167**	**3.921**	**8.186**

POLAND

Table 429 — Deliveries from MODLIN Warehouse, Month of November, 1920

ceipt o.	Local Committee	Commodities in Net Metric Tons of 1,000 Kilograms or 2,204.6 Pounds										
		Cocoa	Sugar	Milk		Flour	Beans, Peas	Rice	Pork Products	Vegetable Oil	Salt	Soap
				Evap.	Cond.							
1	Baranowicze	.341	1.145	.....	3.448	3.160	4.000	2.286	....	.905	....	....
2	Biala Podlaska	.325	1.110	2.460	1.086	6.875	3.885	2.220	....	.891	.555	....
3	Białystok	.961	3.210	7.075	3.239	19.902	11.219	6.420	....	2.563	1.063	....
4	Bilgoraj	.255	.893	.....	3.048	5.417	1.510	1.770	....	.694	....	....
5	Bogdanow	.404	1.393	.....	3.677	8.635	4.858	2.793	....	1.105	....	....
6	Brzesc Litewski	.940	3.099	.....	9.049	19.335	5.445	6.240	....	2.495	....	....
7	Brzostowica	.074	.276	.....	.895	1.710	.458	.539	....	.213	....	....
8	Chelm	.909	3.052	.....	9.620	18.964	.....	6.105	....	2.441	....	....
9	Dubno	.485	1.645	.....	4.363	10.230	5.770	3.293	....	1.322	.828	....
0	Garwolin	.369	1.230	2.721	1.086	7.626	4.300	2.460	....	.986	....	....
1	Gostynin	.332	1.110	2.438	1.105	6.892	3.884	2.223	....	.783	.277	....
2	Grajewo	.153	.506	.....	1.486	2.650	1.774	1.023	....	.409	.122	....
3	Grodno	.518	1.716	.....	5.201	5.010	5.990	3.420	....	1.372	.243	....
4	Grodzisk	.215	.955	.....	.....	.....	3.344	1.911	....	.754	....	....
5	Hrubieszow	.222	.738	.....	2.267	4.703	1.305	1.511	....	.610	....	....
6	Kobryn	.412	1.380	.....	4.477	7.718	4.830	2.730	....	1.102	.200	....
7	Kowel	1.742	5.794	.....	15.259	35.891	.....	11.573	....	4.629	2.887	....
8	Krasnystaw	.139	.468	.....	1.448	2.860	.800	.932	....	.368	....	....
9	Krzemieniec	.218	.729	.....	2.038	4.538	2.453	1.447	....	.583	.360	....
0	Kutno	.234	.780	1.720	.724	4.836	2.730	1.560	....	.620	....	....
1	Lida	.339	1.146	2.482	.838	7.008	3.958	2.268	.608	.268	.566	....
2	Lubomla	.505	1.678	.....	4.991	10.471	2.005	3.372	....	1.358	....	....
3	Lublin	.486	1.620	.....	5.734	6.355	5.655	3.225	....	1.289	....	....
4	Lomza	.374	1.255	.....	3.562	7.812	4.410	2.526	....	1.006	....	....
5	Luck	.594	1.980	.....	5.429	12.276	4.620	3.960	....	1.579	.987	....

[*Continued on next page*]

POLAND

Deliveries from MODLIN Warehouse, Month of November, 1920

Table 429—*Continued*

Receipt No.	Local Committee	Cocoa	Sugar	Milk: Evap.	Milk: Cond.	Flour	Beans, Peas	Rice	Pork Products	Vegetable Oil	Salt	Soap
		Commodities in Net Metric Tons of 1,000 Kilograms or 2,204.6 Pounds										
26	Lukow	.248	.840	1.850	.724	5.211	2.940	1.680	....	.678	.420	....
27	Nowogrodek	.342	1.140	.....	3.600	7.044	3.986	2.260	....	.906	....	....
28	Olyka	.126	.405	.....	1.295	2.604	1.466	.835	....	.326	.203	....
29	Ostrog	.208	.720	.....	2.305	4.464	2.500	1.440	....	.580	....	....
30	Ostrowiec	.248	.855	.....	.553	2.993	1.995	1.705	....	.678	....	....
31	Ostroleka	.172	.576	1.263	.286	3.570	2.016	1.152	....	.463	.288	....
32	Ostrow Lomzynski	.321	1.065	2.351	.724	6.603	3.727	2.122	....	.795	....	....
33	Oszmiana	.422	1.408	.....	4.191	8.722	4.915	2.821	....	1.126	.700	....
34	Parczew	.288	.960	.....	2.838	5.952	1.010	1.928	....	.763	....	....
35	Pinsk	.596	1.980	.....	5.791	12.271	6.907	3.974	....	1.582	....	....
36	Piotrkow	.233	.851	.....	.....	.....	2.940	1.677	....	.672	....	....
37	Płock	.296	.990	.....	2.896	5.138	3.440	1.977	....	.789	....	....
38	Poznan	.216	.720	.....	1.943	4.464	2.520	1.445	....	.577	....	....
39	Pruzany	.585	1.978	.....	5.791	9.000	6.903	3.984	....	1.577	.693	....
40	Pulawy	.117	.395	.....	1.239	2.422	.....	.772	....	.304	....	.084
41	Pultusk	.189	.625	.....	1.753	3.000	2.205	1.260	....	.500	.276	....
42	Radom	.345	1.128	2.482	.857	4.000	3.945	2.256	....	.898	....	....
43	Rowno	.584	1.980	.....	5.791	12.263	6.922	3.951	....	1.576	.966	....
44	Sarny	.270	.885	.....	2.665	5.497	.....	1.775	....	.705	....	....
45	Siedlce	.464	1.560	3.439	1.086	9.672	5.460	3.120	....	1.239	....	....
46	Sierpce	.226	.765	1.698	.553	4.743	2.677	1.530	....	.586	....	....
47	Sokolow	.162	.496	.....	1.315	2.773	.821	1.002	....	.410	....	....
48	Suwalki	.337	1.125	2.482	.914	6.975	3.937	2.250	....	.910	.562	....
49	Swieciany	.255	.840	.....	2.381	5.316	2.996	1.710	....	.674	.405	....
50	Tomaszow	.306	1.009	.....	3.105	6.231	3.539	1.991	....	.803	....	....
51	Torun	.216	.720	.....	1.943	4.486	2.530	1.430	....	.570	....	....
52	Warszawa J.D.C.	....	....	11.974	10.478	.....	.....	.....	....	....	....	....
53	Wegrow	.226	.750	.....	2.019	4.007	1.000	1.500	....	.598	....	....
54	Wilejka	.289	.964	.....	2.781	5.980	3.375	1.929	....	.769	.486	....
55	Wilno	1.313	4.342	9.579	1.810	26.950	15.215	8.694	2.182	1.320	2.175	....
56	Wloclawek	.260	.853	.....	1.333	3.509	1.485	1.722	....	.515	....	....
57	Wlodawa	.462	1.555	.....	4.515	9.690	5.443	3.126	....	1.238	....	....
58	Wlodzimierz W.	.621	2.758	.....	7.525	16.500	9.660	5.480	....	2.213	1.371	....
59	W. Mazowiecki	.132	.474	.....	1.486	2.920	1.659	.933	....	.371	....	....
60	Wyszkow	.125	.417	.914	.....	2.580	1.459	.834	....	.321	....	....
61	Zamosc	.052	.186	.....	.572	1.136	.310	.356	....	.137	....	....
	Total	**22.798**	**77.223**	**56.928**	**183.128**	**439.560**	**211.106**	**154.428**	**2.790**	**58.514**	**16.633**	**.084**

POLAND

Table 430 Deliveries from SOSNOWIEC Warehouse, Month of November, 1920

Receipt No.	Local Committee	Cocoa	Sugar	Milk: Evap.	Milk: Cond.	Flour	Beans, Peas	Rice	Pork Products
		Commodities in Net Metric Tons of 1,000 Kilograms or 2,204.6 Pounds							
1	Bedzin	.315	.796	.....	.572	4.006	3.191	1.885	.159
2	Czestochowa	.837	2.411	2.177	2.286	.....	9.619	5.100	.768
3	Dabrowa Gornicza	.106	.484	.....	.762	5.952	2.894	.969	.326
4	Katowice	1.788	6.000	.....	13.201	37.200	21.000	12.000	4.826
5	Miechow	.210	.548	.989	.571	3.935	2.000	1.000	.131
6	Olkusz	.200	.636	.653	.953	3.951	2.515	1.273	.299
7	Radomsk	.209	.500	1.088	1.143	.....	2.690	1.484	.440
8	Sosnowiec	.616	2.000	2.874	3.810	13.764	7.496	4.200	1.414
	Total	**4.281**	**13.376**	**7.781**	**23.298**	**68.809**	**51.405**	**27.911**	**8.363**

POLAND

Deliveries from WARSAW Warehouse, Month of November, 1920

Table 431

pt.	Local Committee	Cocoa	Sugar	Milk: Evap.	Milk: Cond.	Flour	Beans, Peas	Rice	Pork Products	Vegetable Oil	Salt
		Commodities in Net Metric Tons of 1,000 Kilograms or 2,204.6 Pounds									
	Grojec	.171	.570	1.219	.362	3.534	1.995	1.140	.302	.168	.....
	Minsk Mazowiecki	.239	.798	1.263	.991	4.947	2.793	1.596	.341	.350	.....
	Rawa	.214	.714	.....	....	4.427	2.499	.878	....	.188	.....
	Skierniewice	.145	.485	.....	....	3.007	1.697	.970	.261	.184	.....
	Sochaczew	.236	.825	1.829	.533	5.116	2.887	1.650	.338	.347	.....
	Warsaw, Przejazd 5	1.396	4.654	10.232	....	28.856	16.289	9.308	....	.877	2.327
	Warsaw, Przejazd	.450	1.500	3.309	....	9.300	5.250	3.000	1.176	....	.750
	Warsaw City	4.729	15.746	32.720	1.905	7.624	55.110	31.492	....	3.451	7.873
	Warsaw City	.....	.010	.087	....	1.222	.....	.476	....	.531	.....
	Dr. Bogen J.D.C.	.....	....	2.177	1.905	.....	.....	....	....	....	.....
	Total	**7.580**	**25.302**	**52.836**	**5.696**	**68.033**	**88.520**	**50.510**	**2.418**	**6.096**	**10.950**

POLAND

Deliveries from BREST Warehouse, Month of December, 1920

Table 432

pt.	Local Committee	Cocoa	Sugar	Milk: Evap.	Milk: Cond.	Flour	Beans, Peas	Rice	Pork Products	Vegetable Oil	Soap
		Commodities in Net Metric Tons of 1,000 Kilograms or 2,204.6 Pounds									
	Biala Podlaska	....	.....	.....	.....	13.335	.....	.....	.....	....	....
	Bielsk	.610	1.970	.....	5.791	12.653	6.936	.....	1.029	.532	....
	Brzesc Litewski	....	.....	.....	.....	29.302	.....	.....	.....	....	....
	Chelm	....	.....	.....	.....	16.367	.....	.....	.....	....	....
	Dubno	....	.....	.....	.....	13.018	.....	.....	.....	....	....
	Kobryn	.616	2.261	.....	6.858	13.008	7.823	.....	1.205	.528	....
	Kowel	....	.....	.....	.....	41.265	.....	.....	.....	....	....
	Krzemieniec	.410	1.194	.....	2.096	8.763	2.970	.....	.681	.354	....
	Luboml	....	.....	.....	.....	11.280	.....	.....	.....	....	....
	Luck	....	.....	.....	.....	14.542	.....	.....	.....	....	....
	Ostrog	.202	.776	.....	2.819	4.906	2.783	.....	.413	.173	....
	Pinsk	....	.....	.....	.....	17.453	.....	.....	.....	....	....
	Prozany	.599	1.980	.....	5.791	12.525	7.033	.....	1.126	.358	.400
	Rowno	.928	3.181	.....	9.220	19.918	11.235	.....	1.566	.879	....
	Wlodawa	....	.....	.....	.....	11.098	.....	.....	.....	....	....
	Wlodzimierz Wol.	1.022	3.441	.....	8.725	24.050	12.195	.....	2.227	.534	....
	Total	**4.387**	**14.803**	.....	**41.300**	**263.485**	**50.975**	.....	**8.247**	**3.358**	**.400**

POLAND

Table 433 — Deliveries from KRAKÓW Warehouse, Month of December, 1920

Receipt No.	Local Committee	Commodities in Net Metric Tons of 1,000 Kilograms or 2,204.6 Pounds									
		Cocoa	Sugar	Milk		Flour	Beans, Peas	Rice	Pork Products	Vegetable Oil	Soa
				Evap.	Cond.						
1	Bedzin	....	1.389	3.135	.914	8.827	5.029	2.855	....	.699	.30
2	Biala	....	.857	1.960	1.124	5.397	3.030	1.722	.744	....	.17
3	Brzesko	.193	.507	1.045	.972	3.301	1.874	1.089	.308	.184	.1
4	Bochnia	....	.326	.718	.400	2.032	1.164	.670	.200	.061	...
5	Bytom	3.048	....	....	26.879	38.100	8.152	5.445	6.644	....	...
6	Chrzanow	....	.402	.871	.686	2.447	1.394	.782	.293	.091	.1
7	Cieszyn	....	.902	....	....	5.426	3.084	1.783	.774	....	.1
8	Dabrowa	....	1.006	....	3.048	.....	4.731	2.718	....	.304	.3
9	Debica	.102	.300	.653	.457	1.825	1.029	.620	.150	....	.07
10	Gorlice	....	.195	.501	.553	1.461	.804	.458	....	.031	.0
11	Jaslo	....	.201	....	....	.889	.545	.360	....	.030	.0
12	Jordanow	....	.201	.283	.114	1.091	.628	.357	.152	.015	.0
13	Kalwarja	....	.094	.152	.457	.433	.258	.136	....	.015	.0
14	Kraków	1.513	4.851	10.928	8.534	30.099	16.983	9.700	3.448	.517	1.1
15	Krosno	....	.606	1.328	....	3.747	2.102	1.239	.437	.091	.1
16	Lancut	....	.607	.566	.419	1.921	1.091	.609	.154	.061	.0
17	Lezajsk	.101	.302	.610	.133	2.049	1.136	.679	.142	.015	.0
18	Makow	....	.202	.414	....	1.154	.621	.358	.154	.015	.0
19	Mielec	....	.295	.522	.419	1.461	.847	.494	.151	.030	.0
20	Muszyna	....	.202	.522	.133	1.460	.817	.476	.152	.030	.0
21	Myslenice	....	.131	.283	.229	.956	.479	.272	.151	.015	.0
22	Niepolomice	....	.100	.174	.152	.498	.270	.179	.056	.015	.0
23	Nisko	....	.504	.958	.209	3.072	1.736	.999	.358	.031	.1
24	Olkusz	.304	.979	2.046	.362	5.808	3.265	1.874	.470	.522	.2
25	Oswiecim	....	1.070	1.524	1.333	6.825	3.762	2.195	.729	.091	.2
26	Rozwadow	....	.493	1.001	....	2.817	1.557	.910	.303	.137	.1
27	Rzeszow	....	1.142	2.656	....	7.470	4.240	2.437	.736	.213	.2
28	Krzeszowice	....	.246	.479	.076	1.543	.850	.504	.144	.030	.0
29	Nowy Sacz	....	1.369	2.961	1.905	8.303	4.710	2.695	.889	.213	.3
30	Sosnowice	....	1.593	....	10.535	13.988	6.990	4.006	.884	.695	.6
31	Sucha	....	.101	....	....	.769	.461	.264	.144	....	.0
32	Skawina	....	.090	.218	....	.578	.310	.181	.060	.015	.0
33	Szczakowa	....	.190	.348	....	.992	.540	.319	.142	.015	.0
34	Tarnow	.619	1.676	3.723	3.067	10.511	5.942	3.414	1.239	....	.4
35	N. Targ	....	.594	1.219	.610	3.429	1.918	1.095	.461	.061	.1
36	Tarnobrzeg	....	.395	.740	1.010	2.044	1.243	.796	....	....	.1
37	Trzebinia	....	.150	.348	....	.952	.545	.323	.148	.030	.0
38	Wadowice	....	.403	.893	1.067	2.925	1.663	.960	.304	.046	.1
39	Wieliczka	....	.323	.719	.095	2.032	1.253	.648	.292	.031	.0
40	Zakopane	....	.399	.871	2.096	2.413	1.370	.810	.303	....	.1
41	Zywiec	....	.601	.936	.400	3.758	2.104	1.213	.444	.030	.1
	Total	**5.880**	**25.994**	**46.305**	**68.389**	**194.803**	**100.527**	**58.644**	**22.160**	**4.380**	**5.9**

POLAND

Table 434 Deliveries from LWÓW Warehouse, Month of December, 1920

Receipt No.	Local Committee	Cocoa	Sugar	Milk Evap.	Milk Cond.	Flour	Beans, Peas	Rice	Pork Products	Vegetable Oil	Soap
		Commodities in Net Metric Tons of 1,000 Kilograms or 2,204.6 Pounds									
1*											
2	Bełz	.101	.240	....	.781	2.222	1.374	.736	.097	....	.025
3	Bohorodczany	.203	.832	....	2.629	5.490	3.748	....	.198	.182	.100
4	Bobrka	.204	.384	.414	1.124	4.723	2.152	....	.441	....	.050
5	Borysław	.309	.050	....	4.438	9.840	4.457	....	.746	....	.100
6	Brody	.410	.950	1.502	2.533	11.685	5.383	....	.947	....	.150
7	Brzezany	.402	.888	....	2.953	9.017	5.630	1.370	.490	....	.125
8	Brzozow	.284	.750	....	2.477	6.975	3.937	2.229	.391	.152	.075
10	Buczacz	.411	....	1.502	2.533	11.686	5.276	....	.753	....	.150
11	Chyrow	.103	.144	....	.476	1.774	.774	....	.146	....	.025
12	Cieszanow	.304	.565	....	2.629	4.636	2.863	1.660	.196	.243	.050
13	Czortkow	.204	.250	....	1.638	4.660	2.625	.501	.301	.180	....
14	Dolina	.306	.591	.131	1.848	6.477	.....	....	.458	....	.100
15	Drohobycz	.303	.966	....	3.372	6.794	2.821	1.948	.327	....	.075
16	Grodek Jagiellonski	.204	.299	....	.914	2.984	.500	.597	.306	....	.050
17	Halicz	.103	.450	....	.991	3.240	2.025	....	.131	.091	.050
18	Jaworow	.304	.600	....	1.981	6.480	4.050	....	.196	.182	.050
19	Janow	.102	.200	....	.648	2.160	1.050	....	.146	....	.025
20	Jarosław	.202	.887	....	....	11.057	3.931	....	....	....	.125
21	Kałisz	.101	.335	....	1.638	3.726	1.411	....	.146	....	.075
22	Kamionka Strumił	.196	.450	....	1.486	4.189	2.362	1.369	.235	.213	.075
23	Kołomyja	.408	1.378	....	4.477	9.398	6.440	1.098	.727	....	.025
24	Kopyczynce	.412	.854	....	3.619	9.208	4.488	....	.763	....	.075
25	Kosow	.484	1.155	....	4.610	13.462	6.063	....	.905	....	.100
26	Lisko	.304	....	....	2.228	6.096	3.607	.653	.456	.273	.125
27	Lwów, Town	.412	1.332	....	12.858	5.914	3.771	3.300	.741	.456	....
28	Lwów, District	.569	1.375	.980	4.077	15.812	7.465	.962	1.584	.030	.125
29	Nadworna	.410	.802	....	2.667	10.604	6.690	....	.522	....	.150
30	Peczynizyn	.096	.300	....	.914	2.603	1.375	.842	.131	.091	.025
31	Podhajce	.406	.584	....	3.315	3.068	.591	.848	.602	....	.125
32	Przemyslany	.100	.225	....	.991	3.239	2.025	....	.131	.121	.025
33	Przemysl	.714	1.694	....	7.258	18.483	8.963	....	2.838	....	.250
34	Radziechow	.498	1.200	....	3.943	11.176	6.300	3.602	.326	.152	.100
35	Rawa Ruska	.417	.803	.653	1.981	8.636	4.225	....	.582	....	.025
36	Rohatyn	.204	.336	....	.667	3.175	1.865	1.072	.196	....	.050
37	Rudki	.101	.272	.348	.686	3.365	1.593	....	.142	....	.050
38	Sambor	.299	.449	....	2.172	4.383	3.654	1.392	.274	.152	.050
39	Sanok	.613	.981	....	4.343	11.288	5.747	....	.616	.180	.100
40	Sniatyn	.101	.245	....	.991	3.240	2.025	....	.131	.091	.050
41	Sokal	.201	.595	....	1.829	5.996	4.016	....	.327	....	.050
42	Stanisławow	.613	....	1.502	3.848	16.573	7.595	....	1.332	....	.200
43	Stryj	.204	.426	....	.857	2.730	3.321	.881	.229	....	.075
44	Tarnopol	.403	.729	....	2.172	5.954	3.214	2.141	.618	.395	.125
45	Tłumacz	.203	.304	....	.629	2.731	.....	....	.297	....	.075
46	Trembowla	.102	.199	....	1.009	2.223	1.365	....	.308	....	.050
47	Turka	.306	.700	....	2.458	8.100	5.304	....	.228	....	.075
48	Zaleszczyki	.183	.200	....	1.314	2.720	2.100	.416	.298	.121	....
49	Zborow	.513	1.287	....	4.991	13.970	.....	....	1.191	....	.125
50	Złoczow	.305	.688	....	2.534	8.382	3.787	....	.614	....	.100
51	Zydaczow	.201	.668	....	1.486	4.889	3.037	....	.131	.182	.075
	Total	**14.538**	**29.612**	**7.032**	**122.015**	**338.234**	**166.995**	**27.617**	**23.890**	**3.488**	**2.975**

* Receipt No. 1 cancelled.

POLAND

Deliveries from MODLIN Warehouse, Month of December, 1920

Table 435

Receipt No.	Local Committee	Commodities in Net Metric Tons of 1,000 Kilograms or 2,204.6 Pounds										
		Cocoa	Sugar	Milk		Flour	Beans, Peas	Rice	Pork Products	Vegetable Oil	Salt	Soap
				Evap.	Cond.							
1	Aleksandrowo	.163	.435	.....	1.257	2.588	1.920	.....	.305	.091	....	.10
2	Augustow	.296	.610	.....	2.553	4.515	3.014	.....	....	.689	.424	.17
3	Baranowicze	.419	1.800	.....	5.601	13.080	.....	.....	.909	....	....	.40
4	Białystok	....	4.087	.....	12.497	29.166	.....	.....	1.812	....	....	.17
5	Bogdanow	.402	1.401	.....	4.039	7.915	.....	.....	.786	.279	....	.30
6	Brzesc Litewski	1.376	4.482	.....	13.640	.....	20.190	.....	2.230	1.352	....	...
7	Brzostowica	.100	.404	.....	1.181	2.986	.....	.....	.142	....	....	.07
8	Brzezina	.210	.593	.....	1.676	1.023	2.710	.....	.307	.274	....	.12
9	Busk	.205	.827	.....	2.552	5.226	3.766	.....	.452	.228	....	.17
10	Ciechanow	.109	.404	.....	1.333	2.584	1.858	.....	.257	.106	....	.10
11	Częstochowa	1.015	3.409	.....	9.677	21.233	11.965	6.855	....	2.754	....	.72
12	Garwolin	.621	1.997	.....	5.848	14.225	.....	.....	....	1.594	....	.40
13	Gostynin	.100	.240	.....	.552	1.460	.820	.470	.060	.182	....	.16
14	Grajewo	.207	.679	.....	2.057	5.582	.....	.....	....	.552	.340	.15
15	Grodno	.863	2.811	.....	8.725	17.463	12.700	.....	1.328	.972	....	.61
16	Grodzisk	.410	1.432	.....	3.943	8.872	6.452	.....	.754	.395	....	.30
17	Jedrzejow	.206	.594	.....	1.676	3.713	2.710	.....	.299	.137	....	.12
18	Kalisz	.425	1.384	.....	3.696	4.035	6.075	.....	.755	.304	....	.28
19	Kielce	.203	....	.....	.....	.....	6.037	3.439	....	1.382	....	.35
20	Kolo	.101	.346	.....	.991	2.103	.....	.....	.157	.106	....	.07
21	Kolno	.215	.870	.....	2.496	.....	3.812	.....	.302	.395	....	.17
22	Konin	.101	.403	.....	1.219	2.668	.....	.....	.309	.091	....	.10
23	Konskie	.306	.948	.....	2.972	6.755	4.245	.....	.....	.328	....	.20
24	Kowel	2.151	7.228	.....	21.126	.....	22.449	.....	.....	5.781	....	...
25	Kozienice	.257	.909	.....	2.476	5.510	3.130	1.767	.....	.708	.430	.1
26	Kutno	.303	1.004	.....	3.010	6.274	3.549	2.028	.....	.811	....	.21
27	Lapy	.205	.836	.....	2.496	5.230	3.818	.....	.444	.243	....	.17
28	Lida	.645	1.985	.....	6.210	1.935	9.050	.....	.902	.683	....	.4
29	Lubartow	.180	.710	.....	2.286	5.186	.....	.....	....	.572	.360	.1
30	Lublin	.490	2.280	.....	7.163	16.430	.....	.....	1.194	.699	....	.4
31	Leczyca	.104	.338	.....	.991	2.103	1.535	.....	.149	.091	....	.0
32	Lask	.210	.589	.....	1.657	1.525	2.535	.....	.301	.121	....	.1
33	Łódź	2.547	8.604	.....	.....	.....	4.220	.....	....	1.792	....	1.8
34	Lomza	.707	2.277	.....	6.686	16.282	.....	.....	.923	.760	....	.4
35	Lukow (Miedzyrzecz)	.478	1.390	.....	4.172	9.118	6.369	.....	....	1.120	....	.3
36	Makow	.104	.431	.....	1.410	2.732	1.995	.....	.255	.106	....	.1
37	Mlawa	.100	.404	.....	1.276	3.030	1.898	.....	....	.328	....	.0
38	Miechow	.211	.685	.....	1.886	4.025	2.953	.....	.377	.137	....	.1
39	Nowogrodek	.520	1.654	.....	5.201	10.361	7.516	.....	.770	.562	....	.2
40	Opoczno	.200	.605	.....	1.734	3.678	.....	.....	.429	.123	....	.1
41	Ostroleka	.198	.705	.....	2.076	4.371	2.467	1.410	....	.577	.352	.1
42	Ostrowiec Lomzynski	.507	1.692	.....	5.010	12.177	5.982	.....	....	1.329	....	.3
43	Ostrowiec	.435	1.490	.....	3.677	3.970	6.579	.....	1.020	.334	....	.3
44	Oszmiany	.600	2.191	.....	6.629	15.754	.....	.....	1.270	....	....	.4
45	Ozorkow	.200	.502	.....	1.486	3.712	.....	.....	.304	.107	....	.1
46	Pabjanice	.401	1.440	.....	4.096	9.005	5.088	.....	1.027	.106	....	.3
47	Parczew	.303	.990	.....	3.105	7.236	.....	.....	....	.802	....	.2
48	Piotrkow	.524	1.550	.....	4.496	.....	7.030	.....	.976	.289	....	.3
49	Płock	.459	1.540	.....	4.801	9.478	5.355	3.060	....	1.216	....	.3
50	Plonsk	.100	.433	.....	1.276	3.050	1.888	.....	....	.338	....	.0
51	Poznan	.206	.700	.....	2.229	4.958	.....	.....	.593	....	....	..
52	Prasnysz	.202	.563	.....	1.676	3.527	2.533	.....	.311	.182	....	.1
53	Pultusk	.308	.953	.....	2.762	2.023	4.329	.....	....	.759	....	.2
54	Radom	.630	1.901	.....	4.877	4.002	8.525	.....	1.036	.501	....	.3
55	Radomsk	.410	1.289	.....	.....	5.745	.....	.....	....	1.010	.637	.2
56	Ruda Pabjanicka	.218	.506	.....	1.581	3.464	2.495	.....	.387	.106	....	.1
57	Rzgow	.103	.294	.....	.838	1.795	1.260	.....	.163	.076	....	.0
58	Sandomierz	.150	.540	.....	1.600	3.306	1.869	1.068	....	.422	....	.1
59	Siedlce	.734	2.540	.....	7.525	18.230	11.468	.....	....	2.032	....	.5

POLAND

Table 435—*Continued*

Deliveries from MODLIN Warehouse, Month of December, 1920

eipt o.	Local Committee	Cocoa	Sugar	Milk Evap.	Milk Cond.	Flour	Beans, Peas	Rice	Pork Products	Vegetable Oil	Salt	Soap
		Commodities in Net Metric Tons of 1,000 Kilograms or 2,204.6 Pounds										
0	Sieradz	.105	.485	.....	1.448	3.079	2.227	.....	.169	.152	....	.102
1	Sierpc	....	.996	.....	2.991	6.285	3.549	2.034	....	.816	....	.200
2	Slonim	.827	2.670	.....	7.925	19.161	7.513	.....	....	2.119	1.337	.550
3	Sokolka	.103	.490	.....	1.543	3.650	.....	.....	.301	....	....	.100
4	Sokolow	.192	.613	.....	1.829	3.850	2.822	.....	.152	.289	....	.127
5	Strykow	.106	.422	.....	1.219	2.626	1.930	.....	.289	.091	....	.076
6	Suwalki	.590	1.918	.....	5.906	11.868	6.680	3.823	....	1.527	.966	.400
7	Swieciany	.401	1.400	.....	4.324	8.041	.....	.....	.885	....	....	.300
8	Tomaszow	.414	1.230	.....	3.429	3.032	5.535	.....	.578	.288	....	.255
9	Torun	.200	.690	.....	2.229	4.968	.....	.....	.588	....	....	....
0	Wegrow	.416	1.219	.....	3.600	3.507	5.428	.....	.580	.349	....	.252
1	Wierzbnik	.210	.625	.....	1.886	3.773	2.750	.....	.312	.152	....	.127
2	Wielun	.215	.400	.....	1.219	2.630	1.905	.....	.169	.152	....	.102
3	Wilno	3.678	12.230	.....	38.882	45.413	24.907	.....	6.184	3.543	....	1.198
4	Wilejka	.403	1.355	.....	4.324	7.995	.....	.....	.702	....	....	.300
5	Wolkowysk	.504	1.585	.....	4.953	9.956	5.623	3.070	....	1.279	.797	.350
6	Wyszkow	.208	.530	.....	1.657	3.473	2.538	.....	.295	.228	....	.127
7	Wloclawek	.304	.853	.....	2.419	5.310	2.992	1.730	....	.680	....	.175
8	Zdunska Wola	.107	.500	.....	1.467	1.520	2.315	.....	.300	.152	....	.102
9	Zgierz	.536	1.424	.....	3.886	8.934	6.480	.....	.879	.304	....	.306
	Total	**33.612**	**115.539**	.....	**316.840**	**525.485**	**311.353**	**30.754**	**36.317**	**49.157**	**5.643**	**20.007**

POLAND

Table 436

Deliveries from WARSAW Warehouse, Month of December, 1920

eipt o.	Local Committee	Cocoa	Sugar	Milk Evap.	Milk Cond.	Flour	Beans, Peas	Rice	Pork Products	Vegetable Oil	Salt	Soap
		Commodities in Net Metric Tons of 1,000 Kilograms or 2,204.6 Pounds										
1	Biała Podlaska	.579	1.956	.....	4.305	1.956	8.802	.....	1.054	....	....	....
2	Biłgoraj	.305	1.110	2.438	1.086	6.882	3.885	2.220	.570	.355	....	....
3	Chełm	1.016	2.237	1.089	9.944	2.917	15.044	.....	1.960	....	....	....
4	Dubno	.610	2.010	2.612	3.315	.....	7.035	4.020	1.155	....	....	....
5	Grojec	.305	1.089	2.395	.609	6.750	3.812	2.178	.617	.358	....	.225
6	Hrubieszow	.289	.840	1.829	.724	5.208	2.940	1.680	.459	.169	.420	....
7	Krasnystaw	.203	.833	.740	1.905	5.995	3.746	.....	.447	.183	.416	....
8	Luboml	.508	1.815	2.808	2.800	.....	6.353	3.630	.904	.495	.908	....
9	Łódź	1.626	5.475	.....	11.621	33.846	.....	16.095	3.299	1.212	....	....
0	Łowicz	.....	.600	1.306	.362	3.720	2.100	1.200	.405	.172	....	.125
1	Łuck	.812	2.820	.....	6.839	2.820	12.690	.....	1.473	.178	....	....
2	Minsk Mazowiecki	.406	1.275	1.959	1.733	7.905	4.463	2.550	.691	.368	.637	.275
3	Ołyka	.305	1.110	.....	2.439	7.992	4.995	.....	.606	....	.555	....
4	Pinsk	1.118	3.675	.....	7.620	3.675	16.538	.....	1.961	1.019	....	....
5	Rawa	.203	.978	1.393	.....	6.064	3.423	1.956	.465	.149	....	.200
6	Sarny	.305	.975	.....	1.962	7.020	4.388	.....	.592	....	.488	....
7	Skierniewice	.203	.506	1.198	1.143	5.357	3.024	1.728	.484	.173	....	.175
8	Sochaczew	.203	.900	1.524	1.181	5.580	3.150	1.800	.473	.171	....	.200
9	Tomaszow Lubelski	.406	1.418	3.113	.991	10.206	6.379	.....	.574	.527	.709	....
)	Warszawa, Przejazd 5	.....	3.582	.....	2.438	24.038	15.960	.....	....	....	....	....
1	Warszawa, Punkty Odzywcze (Feeding Points)	.....	.....	.....	.....	11.862	.....	24.300	....	....	....	....
2	Włodawa	.508	1.725	2.395	3.010	.....	6.030	3.450	.934	.508	....	....
3	Warsaw-Radzymin	.....	8.551	14.368	9.906	39.430	13.963	.....	7.271	....	....	....
	Total	**9.911**	**45.480**	**41.167**	**75.933**	**199.223**	**148.720**	**66.807**	**26.394**	**6.037**	**4.133**	**1.200**

POLAND

Deliveries from BREST Warehouse, Month of January, 1921

Table 437

Receipt No.	Local Committee	Commodities in Net Metric Tons of 1,000 Kilograms or 2,204.6 Pounds										
		Cocoa	Sugar	Milk		Flour	Beans, Peas	Rice	Pork Products	Vegetable Oil	Soap	Misc. Food *
				Evap.	Cond.							
1	Bilgoraj	.305	.943	2.721	.....	5.346	4.480	1.707	.655	....	.225	....
2	Biala Podlaska	.717	2.512	.....	7.525	15.692	8.865	5.076	1.346	.707	.450	....
3	Bielsk	.714	1.856	.....	7.715	15.586	6.811	5.040	1.172	.713	.450	....
4	Brzesc Litewski	1.618	5.514	3.984	13.335	34.537	19.542	11.084	2.852	1.691	1.000	....
5	Chelm	1.321	4.530	9.905	3.543	27.918	15.700	8.026	1.754	.878	.650	....
6	Dubno	.640	2.004	4.419	2.057	12.462	7.035	4.045	1.079	.525	.350	1.009
7	Hrubieszow	.307	.898	1.089	1.905	5.952	3.368	1.960	.288	.348	.175	....
8	Kobryn	1.018	3.308	.....	9.963	21.035	10.008	6.714	1.678	1.042	.600	....
9	Kowel	2.558	8.379	18.178	4.763	51.990	29.404	16.791	4.957	1.583	1.450	4.830
10	Krasnystaw	.205	.896	2.112	.400	5.045	2.956	1.868	.455	.353	.175	....
11	Krzemieniec	.406	1.410	3.113	1.086	8.763	4.905	2.842	.690	.351	.250	.705
12	Luboml	.711	2.400	5.290	1.791	14.843	8.415	4.814	1.188	.705	.425	....
13	Luck	.813	2.967	6.531	1.962	17.442	10.280	6.001	1.746	.533	.450	1.316
14	Olyka	.406	1.353	3.048	1.352	8.600	4.850	2.701	.449	.359	.200	.530
15	Ostrog	.305	1.084	2.395	1.391	6.720	3.768	2.148	.611	.354	.150	.418
16	Pinsk	1.210	4.020	9.230	3.581	26.010	14.642	7.481	2.339	1.211	.750	....
17	Pruzany	.823	2.819	.....	8.382	17.519	9.870	5.000	1.189	.879	.100	....
18	Rowno	.914	3.209	7.053	2.096	19.840	11.225	6.462	1.359	.865	.550	....
19	Sarny	.406	1.507	.....	5.143	9.589	5.407	3.084	1.069	.176	.275	.793
20	Tomaszow	.407	1.658	3.614	1.791	10.251	5.757	3.339	.818	.532	.300	....
21	Wlodawa	.813	2.820	6.226	2.057	17.460	9.910	5.687	1.169	.889	.350	....
22	Wlodzimierz Wol.	1.218	2.260	9.013	3.890	26.416	14.900	8.497	2.531	.692	.755	2.137
	Total	**17.835**	**58.347**	**97.921**	**85.729**	**379.016**	**212.098**	**120.367**	**31.394**	**15.386**	**10.080**	**11.738**

* Detail of miscellaneous food indicated by the following indexes: [a], salt; [c], codliver oil. Of the total, 11.738, 11.138 is salt and .600 is codliver oil.

POLAND

Deliveries from KRAKÓW Warehouse, Month of January, 1921

Table 438

Receipt No.	Local Committee	Commodities in Net Metric Tons of 1,000 Kilograms or 2,204.6 Pounds										
		Cocoa	Sugar	Milk		Flour	Beans, Peas	Rice	Pork Products	Vegetable Oil	Soap	Salt
				Evap.	Cond.							
1	Biala	.305	.970	1.089	2.038	6.034	3.428	1.949	....	....	....	...
2	Bochnia	.203	.583	.....	1.676	3.520	2.005	1.394	....	.174	.100	...
3	Brzesko	.203	.555	.....	2.153	3.436	1.460	1.128	.158	.171	....	...
4	Bedzin	.609	2.018	.....	5.505	.....	5.020	....	.512	.889	....	...
5	Cieszyn	.305	1.175	.....	.....	7.330	4.110	.495	1.023	....	....	...
6	Chrzanow	.203	.805	.....	2.381	4.652	2.642	1.511	.502	.176	....	...
7	Dembica	.101	.298	.....	1.219	1.988	1.137	.641	.255	....	....	...
8	Dabrowa	.609	2.009	.....	5.505	5.990	7.037	....	.515	.532	....	...
9	Gorlice	.102	.300	.....	1.296	1.945	1.103	.621	.169	.084	....	...
10	Jordanow	.102	.219	.....	.514	1.399	.805	.457	.161	....	....	...
11	Jaslo	.102	.204	.....	.....	.....	.752	.433	....	.085	....	...
12	Krzeszowice	.102	.290	.....	.609	.448	.956	.120	.167	....	....	.02
13	Krosno	.203	.691	.....	1.067	4.105	2.321	1.337	.501	.174	....	...
14	Kalwarja	.035	.101	.....	.362	.702	.402	.225	.161	.014	....	...
15	Kraków	2.018	6.598	14.586	.....	40.960	23.104	13.214	5.246	....	....	...
16	Lezajšk	.102	.406	.....	.953	2.613	1.476	....	.335	.172	....	...
17	Lancut	.101	.404	.....	1.181	2.498	1.378	.152	.168	.167	....	...
18	Myslenice	.102	.246	.....	.743	1.373	.799	.485	.172	....	....	...
19	Muszyna	.068	.248	.....	.648	1.470	.800	.457	.165	.037	....	...

POLAND

Deliveries from KRAKÓW Warehouse, Month of January, 1921

Table 438—*Continued*

[Re]ceipt [N]o.	Local Committee	Commodities in Net Metric Tons of 1,000 Kilograms or 2,204.6 Pounds										
		Cocoa	Sugar	Milk		Flour	Beans, Peas	Rice	Pork Products	Vegetable Oil	Soap	Salt
				Evap.	Cond.							
20	Makow	.101	.348	.....	.762	2.043	1.169	.681	.174	....	....	....
21	Mielec	.102	.300	.....	1.105	1.851	1.034	.578	.178	....	....	.290
22	Miechow	.203	.596	1.524	.362	.....	2.135	.411	.341	.346	....	....
23	Nisko	.203	.633	.....	2.210	3.866	1.994	.204	.446	.174	....	.300
24	Nowy Targ	.305	1.008	.....	.....	6.307	3.567	2.034	.834	....	....	....
25	Nowy Sacz	.609	1.933	.....	6.649	12.169	7.874	3.907	1.375	.311	....	....
26	Niepolomice	.040	.144	.....	.514	.831	.480	.272	.169	....	....	....
27	Oswiecim (Baraki)	.135	.450	.....	1.143	2.790	1.575	.900	.342	....	....	....
28	Oswiecim	.170	.697	.....	1.905	4.281	2.432	1.373	.511	.175	....	....
29	Olkusz	.407	1.486	3.309	.724	9.303	5.251	3.006	.686	.534	....	....
30	Rozwadow	.203	.583	.....	1.143	3.702	2.106	.311	.326	.171	....	....
31	Rzeszow	.610	1.895	.....	3.219	11.740	6.629	....	1.187	.354	....	.250
32	Skawina	.045	.147	.....	.343	1.026	.532	.318	.169	.008	....	....
33	Sucha	.102	.246	.....	.553	1.512	.840	.495	.169	....	....	....
34	Szczakowa	.048	.202	.....	.476	1.348	.754	.434	.170	.018	....	....
35	Sosnowiec	1.129	3.803	5.442	7.620	16.980	12.012	2.003	2.027	.860	....	....
36	Tarnobrzeg	.203	.585	.....	.....	3.639	2.068	.208	.171	.173	....	....
37	Tarnow	.711	2.240	.....	8.077	13.180	7.096	4.529	1.559	.356	....	1.200
38	Trzebinia	.054	.202	.....	.400	1.092	.633	.367	.170	.030	....	....
39	Wieliczka	.203	.403	.....	1.009	2.612	1.444	.842	.347	....	....	....
40	Wadowice	.203	.700	.....	1.733	4.281	2.438	1.393	.508	.180	....	....
41	Zywiec	.203	.741	.....	1.677	4.665	2.653	.748	.502	....	....	....
42	Zakopane	.203	.684	.....	.....	4.305	2.425	1.377	.504	....	....	.200
	Total	**11.768**	**38.146**	**25.950**	**69.475**	**203.986**	**130.376**	**51.010**	**23.076**	**6.366**	**.100**	**2.265**

POLAND

Table 439

Deliveries from LWÓW Warehouse, Month of January, 1921

[Re]ceipt [N]o.	Local Committee	Commodities in Net Metric Tons of 1,000 Kilograms or 2,204.6 Pounds										
		Cocoa	Sugar	Milk		Flour	Beans, Peas	Rice	Pork Products	Vegetable Oil	Salt	Soap
				Evap.	Cond.							
1	Bohorodczany	.205	.403	.871	.876	3.404	1.945	1.129	.352	.173	....	.050
2	Busk	.103	.303	.414	.419	2.306	1.288	.779	.174	.176	....	.025
3	Bobrka	.205	.796	.827	.836	5.271	2.975	2.295	.668	.175	....	....
4	Brody	.409	1.063	2.003	2.019	6.477	4.463	2.800	.702	.334	.500	.150
5	Boryslaw	.409	.903	.435	.....	7.429	4.233	2.103	.682	.363	....	.175
6	Brzozow	.310	.783	....	1.543	4.318	2.465	1.415	.508	.360	....	.075
7	Belz	.104	.227	....	.648	1.842	1.066	.614	.166	.180	....	.025
8	Brzezany	.714	1.411	....	3.962	23.304	.....	3.600	1.959	.359	....	.200
9	Cieszanow	.207	.604	1.089	1.086	5.322	3.012	1.671	.516	.183	....	.100
10	Czortkow	.305	.450	....	1.981	8.763	.....	1.800	.496	.175	....	.100
11	Dolina	.209	.517	.653	.952	3.810	3.184	1.820	.339	.183	....	....
12	Drohobycz	.305	.504	....	2.381	6.159	3.551	1.999	.672	.173	....	....
13	Grodek Jagiellon	.101	.302	....	.991	5.525	.....	1.205	.156	.176	....	.050
14	Halicz	.212	.405	.653	.648	3.737	2.225	1.200	.316	.177	....	.050
15	Janow	.102	.202	.348	.324	1.864	1.058	.612	.158	.125	....	.025
16	Jaworow	.210	.620	.980	.990	5.580	2.028	1.742	.507	.187	....	.050
17	Jaroslaw	.494	1.280	....	5.182	10.548	5.993	3.414	.996	.359	....	.175
18	Kamionka Strum.	.201	.563	.631	.629	3.556	2.030	1.125	.497	.175	....	.050
19	Kalusz	.207	.448	....	1.391	4.445	2.515	1.584	.506	.168	....	.025
20	Kossow	.311	1.041	....	2.210	4.826	3.209	2.926	.340	.348	....	.050
21	Kolomyja	.310	1.008	....	4.134	7.346	3.224	2.744	.989	.351	....	.125

[*Continued on next page*]

POLAND

Deliveries from LWÓW Warehouse, Month of January, 1921

Table 439—*Continued*

Receipt No.	Local Committee	Commodities in Net Metric Tons of 1,000 Kilograms or 2204.6 Pounds										
		Cocoa	Sugar	Milk		Flour	Beans, Peas	Rice	Pork Products	Vegetable Oil	Salt	Soap
				Evap.	Cond.							
22	Lwów (Miasto)	....	....	....	.....	.....	7.000	.....	....	.341	....	....
23	Lwów (Miasto)	.832	2.927	13.302	13.278	24.180	13.650	7.800	1.347	.682	....	.375
24	Lwów (Miasto)	....	1.300	....	.....	.....	.....	4.000	....	....	....	....
25	Lwów (Miasto)	1.190	....	3.309	23.241	24.180	.....	.....	3.057	....	....	.375
26	Lwów (Powiat)	.302	1.003	.979	.991	8.370	3.214	2.700	.727	.159	....	.125
27	Lisko	.205	.605	....	1.409	5.017	1.562	1.952	.302	.176	....	.100
28	Nadworna	.411	1.036	....	4.286	8.594	3.094	3.882	.833	.350	....	.175
29	Otynia	.205	.386	....	1.048	3.226	1.607	.980	.384	.174	....	.100
30	Podhajce	.412	1.019	1.371	1.372	7.620	4.633	2.456	.836	.350	....	.125
31	Przemysl	.408	1.209	2.721	.....	5.707	3.982	4.963	....	.347	....	....
32	Peczeniczyn	.206	.468	....	1.314	3.757	2.093	1.214	.334	.177	....	.050
33	Przemyslany	.203	.608	....	1.009	4.127	.....	1.819	.308	.175	....	.075
34	Rawa Ruska	.204	.891	.784	.800	4.763	2.140	2.389	.337	.353	....	.100
35	Rohatyn	.210	.535	....	2.362	3.874	2.217	1.250	.323	.180	....	.025
36	Radziechow	.310	.916	....	2.629	7.429	4.186	2.435	.675	.339	....	.100
37	Stary Sambor	.204	.460	.653	.667	3.746	2.133	1.200	.339	.183	....	.050
38	Sanok	.409	1.006	....	3.562	8.819	4.777	2.836	.751	.343	....	.025
39	Stryj	.305	.769	....	2.534	6.350	3.009	2.008	.684	.178	....	.100
40	Sokal	.200	.750	....	1.467	3.303	1.221	1.512	.330	.166	....	.075
41	Stanislawow	.410	1.513	....	5.353	8.064	6.300	4.063	.642	.535	....	....
42	Sniatyn	.205	.592	....	1.276	4.636	.....	1.500	.604	.178	....	.050
43	Skole	.205	.776	....	2.477	10.992	.....	2.250	.574	.361	....	.100
44	Sambor	.339	.865	....	4.153	12.255	2.073	2.828	1.098	.358	.200	.150
45	Stary Sambor	.204	....	....	1.314	4.953	2.244	.....	.305	....	....	.050
46	Trembowla	.197	.405	.871	.876	3.596	1.982	1.097	.335	.178	....	.050
47	Tlumacz	.104	.583	.871	.876	3.900	2.855	1.626	.358	.174	....	.025
48	Tarnopol	.511	1.844	....	4.191	11.366	6.183	3.312	.839	.834	....	.175
49	Turka	.202	.750	....	1.848	5.334	3.681	2.850	.754	.183	....	.100
50	Zaleszczyki	.207	.563	.827	.819	4.636	2.639	1.529	.518	.170	....	.075
51	Zloczow	.307	.981	.936	.933	4.898	3.734	2.882	.493	.350	....	.050
52	Zydaczow	.208	.450	....	1.314	3.747	2.100	1.216	.310	.179	....	.050
53	Zborow	.516	1.111	....	2.477	8.826	5.248	3.026	.984	.175	....	.150
54	Zborow	....	.215	....	.648	1.842	1.067	.605	....	.176	....	.025
55	Zbaraz	.203	.605	....	2.419	5.334	3.019	1.718	.489	.178	....	.075
56	Zaleszczyki	.171	....	....	1.639	4.150	2.625	.....	.284	.173	.340	.075
	Total	**15.837**	**40.974**	**35.529**	**127.787**	**357.352**	**156.732**	**114.475**	**31.854**	**13.775**	**1.040**	**4.675**

POLAND

Deliveries from MODLIN Warehouse, Month of January, 1921

Table 440

Receipt No.	Local Committee	Commodities in Net Metric Tons of 1,000 Kilograms or 2,204.6 Pounds										
		Cocoa	Sugar	Milk		Flour	Beans, Peas	Rice	Pork Products	Vegetable Oil	Soap	Misc. Food
				Evap.	Cond.							
1	Aleksandrow	.105	.565	.....	1.771	3.417	1.465	1.918	.296	.178	....	....
2	Augustow	.404	1.408	.....	4.191	8.692	4.924	4.516	.622	.535	....	....
3	Bogdanow	.510	1.716	3.788	.895	10.716	6.024	6.337	1.029	.356	....	....
4	Busk	....	.998	.....	2.896	6.140	2.664	3.607	.592	....	....	....
5	Brzeziny	.206	.805	1.676	.895	6.110	3.468	.....	.322	.364	....	....
6	Bialystok	1.535	1.010	7.184	7.696	27.537	17.872	18.295	2.418	1.621	....	1.510
7	Baranowicze	.712	2.260	4.942	1.791	17.118	7.351	.....	1.043	....	....	....
8	Brzostowice	.307	.808	1.850	.724	4.809	2.926	2.533	.421	.175	....	....
9	Ciechanowice	.210	.552	.....	1.772	3.430	1.500	1.985	.312	.171	....	....
10	Dzisna	.500	1.709	3.701	1.448	12.102	7.580	.....	.892	.432	....	....
11	Garwolin	.720	2.425	.....	6.915	12.965	8.465	8.801	.894	1.060	....	.450
12	Gostyn	.306	1.110	.....	3.238	6.595	3.665	2.144	.470	.355	....	....
13	Grajewo	.307	1.133	2.482	.895	5.738	3.900	3.635	.526	.340	....	....

* Detail of miscellaneous food indicated by the following indexes: [a], salt; [c], codliver oil. Of the total, 5.858, 4.158 is salt and 1.700 is codliver oil.

POLAND

Deliveries from MODLIN Warehouse, Month of January, 1921

Table 440—*Continued*

Receipt No.	Local Committee	Cocoa	Sugar	Milk: Evap.	Milk: Cond.	Flour	Beans, Peas	Rice	Pork Products	Vegetable Oil	Soap	Misc. Food
		Commodities in Net Metric Tons of 1,000 Kilograms or 2,204.6 Pounds										
14	Grodno	1.138	.....	8.643	3.239	24.380	10.926	13.423	1.822	1.246	....	.666[a]
15	Jedrzejow	.307	1.008	2.242	.362	7.340	3.990	.....	.627	.071	....	....
16	Kolno	....	1.427	.....	4.039	8.855	4.790	4.535	.452	....	....	....
17	Kozienice	....	.909	.....	2.476	5.475	3.420	1.800	.310	....	....	....
18	Konskie	.414	1.414	.....	3.886	8.700	3.544	4.788	.750	.365	....	....
19	Kielce	.525	1.818	.....	3.238	6.037	6.562	3.720	1.059	....	....	....
20	Kutno	.300	1.140	.....	3.372	6.982	3.944	2.260	.426	.533	....	....
21	Konin	.100	.436	1.045	.533	2.863	1.680	1.808	.152	.180	....	....
22	Kolo	.100	.400	.....	1.276	2.575	1.473	.795	.151	.179	....	....
23	Kalusz	.610	1.963	4.289	1.791	12.110	5.433	6.635	.961	.531	....	....
24	Lida	.714	2.313	5.072	1.791	16.605	9.403	.....	1.107	....	....	....
25	Lukow	....	1.849	.....	5.334	11.063	5.683	5.146	.869	....	....	....
26	Lask	.204	.550	1.088	.724	3.363	1.322	2.195	.294	.177	....	....
27	Leczyca	.102	.330	.784	.362	2.225	.835	1.380	.163	.182	....	....
28	Lublin	1.130	3.775	8.360	4.839	28.829	13.287	.....	2.126	.888	....	2.085[ac]
29	Lapy	.410	1.359	.....	3.696	8.377	3.880	4.348	.590	.530	....	.295[a]
30	Lomza	.815	.....	.....	8.058	15.338	9.940	10.257	1.137	1.066	....	....
31	Mlawa	....	.542	.....	1.676	3.080	1.690	2.007	.250	....	....	....
32	Makow	....	.721	.....	2.096	4.365	2.224	2.342	.361	....	....	....
33	Nowy Dwor	.032	.104	.....	.324	1.480	.858	.439	....	.178	....	.052[a]
34	Nowogrodek	.609	1.985	4.332	1.619	15.818	8.835	.....	.855	.711	....	....
35	Oszmiany	.715	2.498	5.464	1.790	14.530	11.216	.....	1.444	....	....	....
36	Ostroleka	....	1.032	.....	2.876	6.622	4.090	2.091	.451	....	....	....
37	Ostrow	....	1.987	.....	5.867	10.785	7.829	7.400	.759	....	....	....
38	Ostrowiec	.502	1.771	.....	4.343	10.917	4.698	6.493	.908	.525	....	....
39	Opoczno	.203	.883	1.916	.362	6.862	4.545	.....	.441	.177	....	....
40	Ozorkow	.103	.538	.....	1.753	2.886	1.960	2.119	....	.181	....	....
41	Piotrkow	.510	1.882	.....	.....	11.544	4.185	6.872	1.155	.353	....	....
42	Pinczow	.207	.876	1.894	.438	5.337	3.030	1.679	.458	.176	....	....
43	Plonsk	.200	.535	.....	1.714	2.872	1.548	1.938	.238	.175	....	....
44	Poznanskie	.204	.706	.....	2.096	3.702	2.450	2.731	.548	....	.150	....
45	Prasnysz	.210	.705	.....	2.153	4.550	2.155	2.613	.282	.189	....	....
46	Pultusk	.304	1.175	.....	3.505	7.345	3.206	4.340	.713	.361	....	....
47	Płock	....	1.832	.....	5.467	11.342	6.880	3.664	.973	....	....	....
48	Pabjanice	.505	1.713	.....	5.639	10.682	6.030	6.317	1.185	.176	....	....
49	Parczew	....	2.344	.....	7.658	13.475	8.990	6.707	1.117	....	....	....
50	Pulawy	....	.800	.....	2.858	5.045	3.155	1.625	.290	....	....	....
51	Rzgow	.101	.407	.914	.362	2.590	1.200	1.425	.279	.181	....	....
52	Ruda Pabjanska	.204	.540	1.219	.724	3.433	1.375	2.184	.443	.176	....	....
53	Radom	.609	2.205	.....	5.524	13.595	5.710	8.204	1.164	.532	....	.200[c]
54	Swieciany	.510	1.703	3.723	1.257	10.517	5.928	6.180	1.066	.358	....	....
55	Sokolow	.307	.896	.....	2.553	5.702	.....	3.025	.302	....	....	....
56	Siedlce	....	3.015	.....	8.553	14.923	9.102	11.632	1.203	....	....	....
57	Sandomierz	....	.605	.....	1.810	3.850	2.315	1.207	.317	....	....	....
58	Sierpc	.414	1.299	.....	3.772	8.110	4.504	2.620	.606	....	....	....
59	Strykow	.204	.598	.....	1.886	3.827	1.735	2.120	.268	.175	....	....
60	Sieradz	.216	.561	.....	1.753	3.411	1.480	2.121	.292	.181	....	....
61	Slonim	.923	3.110	6.858	2.153	16.826	10.900	11.568	1.495	1.069	....	....
62	Sokolka	.205	.853	1.829	.705	4.625	2.909	2.683	.408	.357	....	....
63	Suwalki	.510	1.708	3.701	.....	8.712	5.870	3.423	.848	.540	....	....
64	Tomaszowice	.405	1.312	2.895	1.086	10.788	5.911	.....	.723	.353	....	....
65	Torun	.205	.710	.....	2.095	3.682	2.480	2.776	.599	....	.150	.100[c]
66	Wilno	....	.....	.....	.....	.....	19.198	14.572	....	....	....	.500[c]
67	Wilejka	.510	1.703	.....	4.991	9.857	.....	3.375	.826	.532	....	....
68	Wegrow	.408	1.650	.....	4.705	10.265	.....	5.742	.688	....	....	....
69	Wloszczowa	.203	.807	.....	2.133	4.798	2.720	1.561	.398	.189	....	....
70	Wierzbnik	.308	.858	4.289	1.791	5.327	2.370	2.957	.542	.179	....	....
71	Wloclawek	.210	.600	.....	1.352	4.005	3.412	1.924	.282	.177	....	....
72	Wyszkow	.204	.648	.....	2.591	4.017	.....	2.479	.293	.358	....	....
73	Wielun	.208	.606	.....	1.962	3.989	1.860	2.112	.302	.182	....	....
74	Wolkowysk	.511	1.698	3.701	1.429	10.390	5.877	3.348	.754	.529	....	....
75	Zdunska Wola	.205	.603	.....	2.096	3.927	.....	2.235	.303	.176	....	....
76	Zgierz	.515	1.807	.....	5.696	10.964	4.733	6.380	1.174	.359	....	....
	Total	**25.090**	**92.321**	**99.881**	**201.358**	**631.855**	**353.079**	**286.071**	**50.836**	**21.340**	**.300**	**5.858***

POLAND

Deliveries from WARSAW Warehouse, Month of January, 1921

Table 441

Receipt No.	Local Committee	Cocoa	Sugar	Milk Evap.	Milk Cond.	Flour	Beans, Peas	Rice	Pork Products	Vegetable Oil	Soap	Misc. Food *
		Commodities in Net Metric Tons of 1,000 Kilograms or 2,204.6 Pounds										
1	Częstochowa	1.931	6.930	6.161	12.287	43.712	26.395	9.240	4.048	1.597	.....	.800[c]
2	Grodzisk	.508	1.710	3.614	....	11.288	7.181	.....	1.029	.528	.....	.855[a]
3	Grojec	.406	1.479	3.244	.972	10.649	6.656	.....	.839	.356	.....	....
4	Łódź	1.626	5.475	16.719	2.115	33.021	19.880	5.805	3.184	1.242	.....	1.200[c]
5	Lowicz	.102	.600	1.328	.362	4.320	2.700	.....	.175	.178	.....	....
6	Lukow	.406	1.925	4.376	1.257	14.369	8.972	.....	.718	.601	.....	.186[a]
7	Minsk	.406	1.560	3.417	1.086	9.672	5.460	3.120	.837	.359	.....	....
8	Rawa	.305	1.419	3.113	.972	10.217	6.386	.....	.684	.355	.....	....
9	Radomsk	.508	1.830	2.721	2.743	9.540	6.405	3.660	1.034	....	.....	....
10	Skierniewice	.203	.864	1.894	.438	6.221	3.888	.....	.518	.175	.....	....
11	Sochaczew	.203	.900	1.981	.704	5.600	3.144	1.800	.508	.181	.....	....
12	Siedlce	.711	2.841	6.575	1.905	21.507	13.417	.....	1.025	1.231	.....	....
13	Wilno	1.016	7.960	18.483	7.811	60.480	37.774	.....	5.171	2.088	.....	....
14	Warszawa	3.535	18.145	33.629	54.611	114.228	62.244	23.944	15.438	.784	1.406	13.219[c]
	Total	**11.866**	**53.638**	**107.255**	**87.263**	**354.824**	**210.502**	**47.569**	**35.208**	**9.675**	**1.406**	**16.260***

* Detail of miscellaneous food indicated by the following indexes: [a], salt; [c], codliver oil. Of the total, 16.260, 12.760 is salt and 3.500 is codliver oil.

POLAND

Deliveries from BREST Warehouse, Month of February, 1921

Table 442

Receipt No.	Local Committee	Cocoa	Sugar	Milk Evap.	Milk Cond.	Flour	Beans, Peas	Rice	Pork Products	Vegetable Oil	Salt	Codliver Oil
		Commodities in Net Metric Tons of 1,000 Kilograms or 2,204.6 Pounds										
1	Augustow	.408	1.607	3.549	1.067	11.680	7.297	.....	1.007	.526	.....	....
2	Bilgoraj	....	1.407	.....	.....	8.747	5.383	.....	.701	.529	.....	....
3	Brzostowice	....	1.000	.....	2.858	6.954	4.637	.....	.439	.354	.....	....
4	Brezesc Litewski	1.618	6.418	11.821	7.334	33.896	23.611	11.160	3.274	1.935	.....	....
5	Bielsk	.613	2.509	5.551	2.153	15.633	8.822	5.047	1.234	.708	1.260	.072
6	Biala Podlaska	.711	2.549	5.573	1.943	15.722	8.877	5.071	1.314	.694	1.272	.072
7	Białystok	1.709	5.865	12.888	3.600	42.228	26.392	.....	2.733	1.953	.....	....
8	Baranowicze	.813	2.606	5.682	1.809	18.650	11.579	.....	1.230	.872	.....	....
9	Chelm	1.323	4.530	1.589	11.297	.....	15.921	9.081	2.399	.529	.....	....
10	Dubno	.715	2.311	5.094	2.343	16.645	11.382	.....	1.226	.524	1.005	....
11	Grajewo	.403	1.244	2.830	.896	9.234	5.817	.....	.645	.354	.....	....
12	Grodno	1.117	3.913	8.643	3.238	24.375	13.762	6.780	1.843	1.227	.....	....
13	Hrubieszow	....	1.407	3.178	1.067	10.414	6.942	.....	.643	.530	.....	....
14	Kobryn	1.016	3.390	7.446	2.514	21.014	11.888	6.737	1.767	1.051	1.704	.096
15	Krasnystaw	....	1.100	2.438	1.067	7.944	4.298	.....	.509	.354	.....	....
16	Krzemieniec	.409	1.609	3.570	1.067	11.674	7.295	.....	.856	.360	.725	....
17	Kowel	1.619	10.061	22.162	4.324	72.569	45.308	.....	5.994	1.928	4.192	....
18	Loboml	....	3.952	.....	11.525	28.561	19.021	.....	2.144	.894	.....	....
19	Luck	....	3.309	.....	9.011	23.591	15.685	.....	1.783	.704	1.320	....
20	Nowogrodek	.583	2.244	4.963	1.638	16.284	10.165	.....	.974	.697	.....	....
21	Olyka	....	1.269	.....	3.372	9.184	6.120	.....	.793	.348	.555	....
22	Ostrog	....	1.300	2.808	1.067	9.186	6.105	.....	.628	.344	.420	....
23	Pruzany	1.224	4.106	9.034	2.153	25.392	14.378	8.196	2.143	1.229	1.394	....
24	Pinsk	1.524	5.109	11.212	3.600	31.649	17.840	10.200	2.495	1.406	2.100	.120
25	Rowno	1.224	4.014	8.839	2.153	29.070	18.186	.....	1.922	1.234	1.605	....
26	Suwałki	....	1.911	4.289	1.429	12.000	8.250	.....	.989	.527	.152	....
27	Sarny	.610	2.211	4.920	1.809	16.160	10.080	.....	1.214	.531	.772	....
28	Sokolka	.306	.966	2.133	.705	6.926	4.321	.....	.529	.354	.....	....
29	Stopce	.678	2.226	4.963	1.619	16.270	10.142	.....	1.082	.699	.....	....
30	Slonim	1.027	3.500	7.881	2.153	25.385	16.132	.....	1.609	1.329	.....	....

POLAND

Table 442—*Continued*

Deliveries from BREST Warehouse, Month of February, 1921

Receipt No.	Local Committee	Cocoa	Sugar	Milk: Evap.	Milk: Cond.	Flour	Beans, Peas	Rice	Pork Products	Vegetable Oil	Salt	Codliver Oil
		Commodities in Net Metric Tons of 1,000 Kilograms or 2,204.6 Pounds										
31	Tomaszow	.611	2.059	4.615	1.810	9.407	7.225	4.129	1.052	.698	....	....
32	Wlodawa	1.016	3.415	5.443	3.943	.....	15.505	.....	1.869	1.045	.....	....
33	Wlodzimierz	....	5.213	.....	14.668	37.348	24.944	.....	3.264	.883	2.130	....
34	Wolkowysk	.511	1.909	4.245	1.429	13.916	8.660	.....	.867	.698	.....	....
35	Zamosc	....	.450	1.023	.533	3.360	2.320	.....	.326	.175	.....	....
	Total	**21.789**	**102.689**	**178.383**	**113.195**	**641.069**	**434.290**	**66.401**	**53.497**	**28.223**	**20.606**	**.360**

POLAND

Table 443

Deliveries from KRAKÓW Warehouse, Month of February, 1921

Receipt No.	Local Committee	Cocoa	Sugar	Milk: Evap.	Milk: Cond.	Flour	Beans, Peas	Rice	Pork Products	Vegetable Oil	Salt	Soap
		Commodities in Net Metric Tons of 1,000 Kilograms or 2,204.6 Pounds										
1	Brzesko	.203	.752	.....	2.972	5.437	3.412	.....	.504	.171	....	....
2	Biala	.406	1.193	.....	3.676	8.732	5.475	.....	.993	....	....	....
3	Bochnia	.203	.768	.....	2.515	5.479	3.434	.....	.510	.178	....	....
4	Bedzin	.610	2.031	.....	5.505	14.449	9.054	.....	.680	1.059	....	....
5	Chrzanow	.203	.751	.....	2.877	5.505	3.448	.....	.338	.185	....	....
6	Cieszyn	....	1.356	.....	.....	9.698	6.067	.....	....	1.063	....	....
7	Dembica	.102	.403	.....	1.410	2.902	1.795	.....	....	.358	....	....
8	Dabrowa	.711	2.307	.....	6.325	14.367	8.100	4.622	1.358	.531	....	....
9	Gorlice	.102	.330	.....	1.619	2.486	1.571	.....	.169	.087	....	....
10	Jordanow	.102	.300	.....	.686	2.255	1.380	.....	.165	.079	....	....
11	Jaslo	.102	.300	.....	.705	2.221	1.383	.....	.169	.088	....	....
12	Kalwarja	.102	.146	.....	.229	1.142	.742	.....	.173	.036	....	....
13	Krosno	.305	.747	.....	1.238	5.145	3.383	.....	.175	.179	....	....
14	Krzeszowice	.101	.349	.....	.762	2.475	1.544	.....	.172	.177	....	....
15	Krakow	1.829	6.158	.....	18.898	38.178	21.644	12.310	4.798	.347	....	....
16	Lezajsk	.203	.495	.....	1.143	3.770	2.185	.....	.323	.181	....	....
17	Lancut	.203	.501	.....	1.238	3.434	2.219	.....	.341	....	....	....
18	Myslenice	.102	.252	.....	.914	1.527	.870	.500	....	.166	....	....
19	Muszyna	.102	.257	.....	.705	1.685	.943	.550	....	.180	....	....
20	Mielec	.102	.349	.....	.933	2.361	1.481	.....	.170	.183	....	.075
21	Makow	.102	.296	.....	.....	2.234	1.391	.....	.167	.097	....	....
22	Miechow	.406	1.331	.....	3.810	10.225	6.375	.....	.505	.346	....	....
23	Nowy Targ	.305	.984	.....	3.048	7.012	3.017	.....	.686	.....	....	....
24	Nowy Sacz	.711	2.418	.....	7.506	17.552	10.966	.....	....	1.784	....	....
25	Niepolomice	.102	.145	.....	.591	1.066	.678	.....	....	.178	....	....
26	Nisko	.203	.794	.....	2.800	4.939	2.800	1.608	.519	.175	....	....
27	Oswiecim (Baraki)	.203	.506	.....	1.162	3.753	2.336	.....	.343	....	....	....
28	Oswiecim	.203	.773	.....	2.172	5.695	3.563	.....	.513	.179	....	....
29	Olkusz	.508	1.716	.....	4.610	10.730	6.013	3.485	.686	.704	....	....
30	Rzeszow	.305	2.057	.....	1.714	7.546	3.626	.....	.699	.166	.400	....
31	Rozwadow	.203	.690	.....	1.200	4.329	2.692	1.382	.336	.180	....	....
32	Szczakowa	.102	.292	.....	.610	1.984	1.240	.....	....	.177	....	....
33	Skawina	.101	.188	.....	.381	1.282	.762	.....	....	.177	....	....
34	Sosnowiec	1.118	3.853	.....	1.905	14.546	4.525	.....	1.538	....	....	....
35	Trzebinia	.101	.291	.....	.305	1.986	1.257	.....	....	.177	.050	....
36	Tarnobrzeg	.305	.678	.....	1.143	4.432	3.003	.....	....	.535	....	....
37	Tarnow	.609	1.880	.....	4.305	12.443	7.040	.....	1.018	.361	....	....
38	Wieliczka	.203	.540	.....	1.314	3.886	2.438	.....	.172	.180	....	.050
39	Wadowice	.203	.803	.....	.....	5.694	3.548	.....	.499	.140	....	....
40	Zywiec	.305	1.032	.....	2.248	6.482	4.068	2.076	.669	.179	....	....
41	Zakopane	.203	.792	.....	2.743	5.604	3.490	.....	.688	....	....	....
	Total	**12.294**	**41.804**	.....	**97.917**	**266.668**	**154.958**	**26.533**	**20.076**	**10.983**	**.450**	**.125**

POLAND

Table 444 Deliveries from LWÓW Warehouse, Month of February, 1921

Receipt No.	Local Committee	Commodities in Net Metric Tons of 1,000 Kilograms or 2,204.6 Pounds										
		Cocoa	Sugar	Milk		Flour	Beans, Peas	Rice	Pork Products	Vegetable Oil	Salt	Soap
				Evap.	Cond.							
1	Belz	.036	.404	.762	....	2.409	1.550	.152	.163	.178	....	....
2	Bohorodczany	.063	.604	1.415	.534	4.436	2.720	.315	.521	.181	....	....
3	Boryslaw	.104	1.386	3.048	1.810	9.628	5.871	.705	1.143	.362	....	....
4	Borszczow	.194	.597	1.324	.819	3.766	2.148	1.244	.377	.175	....	.075
5	Brody	.351	1.638	3.614	.895	11.412	6.952	.819	.859	.533	1.000	....
6	Brzezany	.409	2.427	5.311	....	16.801	10.551	1.219	1.520	.351	....	....
7	Brzozow	....	1.380	3.048	....	9.595	6.072	.640	1.037	.351	....	....
8	Buczacz	.410	3.060	6.748	1.791	20.212	12.197	3.704	2.030	.713	....	.150
9	Czortkow	.120	1.202	2.656	....	8.634	5.136	.597	.682	.350	....	....
10	Chyrow	.044	.305	.653	....	2.085	1.260	.150	.185	....	....	....
11	Dobromil	.103	.338	.762	....	2.402	1.486	.147	.198	.175	....	....
12	Dolina	.401	1.367	3.047	....	9.915	6.199	....	.966	.359	....	....
13	Drohobycz	.173	1.607	3.527	1.257	11.155	6.832	.795	1.201	.340	....	....
14	Grodek Jagiel	.112	.614	1.328	....	3.641	2.104	1.214	.356	.178	....	.050
15	Halicz	.031	.698	1.763	....	4.826	2.935	.375	.383	.178	....	....
16	Janow	.034	.345	.762	....	2.464	1.494	.172	.194	.175	....	....
17	Jaroslaw	.360	2.284	5.007	1.448	15.843	10.019	1.138	1.445	.357	....	....
18	Jaworow	.211	.916	1.981	....	5.554	3.128	1.753	.535	.179	....	.075
19	Kalusz	.143	1.278	2.895	.724	9.125	5.567	.622	1.130	.173	....	....
20	Kolomyja	.413	1.823	4.071	2.496	11.995	7.011	3.004	1.091	.356	....	.150
21	Kosow	....	1.962	4.354	.895	13.776	8.845	.973	1.335	.532	....	....
22	Kopyczynce	.101	.927	2.177	.533	6.834	4.182	.477	.832	.181	....	....
23	Lisko	.208	1.003	2.286	....	7.213	4.446	.502	.628	.182	....	....
24	Lwów (Miasto)	1.345	4.485	9.862	18.002	31.173	19.061	2.242	2.976	.909	....	....
25	Lwów (Powiat)	.517	1.725	3.788	....	11.989	7.330	.862	1.378	.178	....	....
26	Nadworna	.785	2.823	6.226	....	19.650	12.067	1.414	1.814	.538	....	....
27	Otynia	.135	.910	1.894	....	5.976	3.784	.431	.548	.171	....	....
28	Podhajce	.136	1.803	3.962	1.029	11.955	7.036	.467	1.195	.371	.450	.150
29	Peczeniczyn	.102	1.020	2.286	....	7.177	4.586	.510	.689	.182	....	....
30	Przemyslany	.102	.729	1.524	....	4.755	3.068	.365	.356	.181	....	....
31	Przemysl	.283	2.904	6.379	2.153	20.703	12.286	1.461	2.029	.533	....	....
32	Przeworsk	.310	.910	1.916	.362	5.397	3.074	1.744	.502	.173	....	.075
33	Rawa Ruska	.332	1.723	3.810	....	10.886	6.240	2.992	.913	.540	....	....
34	Rohatyn	.105	1.299	2.851	.838	9.028	5.824	.650	.861	.352	....	....
35	Rudki	.102	.468	1.045	.152	2.908	1.644	.875	.179	.178	....	....
36	Sambor	.305	1.906	4.158	1.905	13.401	8.041	.944	1.183	.353	.300	....
37	Stary Sambor	.067	.691	1.524	....	4.790	3.078	.310	.365	.175	....	.145
38	Sanok	.516	1.949	4.289	1.257	13.536	8.281	.975	1.019	.350	....	....
39	Skalat	....	.979	2.177	.571	6.823	4.331	.490	.840	.168	....	....
40	Skole	.225	1.201	2.656	....	8.426	5.283	.606	.697	.355	....	....
41	Sokal	.104	1.173	2.591	....	8.378	4.985	.586	.672	.371	....	....
42	Sniatyn	.198	1.009	2.286	....	7.177	4.525	.495	.575	.177	....	....
43	Stanislawow	.484	2.621	5.791	1.334	18.298	11.483	1.314	1.445	.531	....	....
44	Stryj	.102	1.427	3.592	1.048	11.306	6.885	.767	1.334	.534	.185	.125
45	Tarnopol	.206	2.027	4.419	1.086	12.512	7.055	1.597	1.184	.533	....	....
46	Tlumacz	....	1.233	2.895	.724	9.146	5.694	.625	.999	.533	.400	....
47	Trembowla	.079	.638	1.415	.533	4.448	2.847	.304	.346	.185	....	....
48	Turka	.172	1.727	3.788	....	11.989	7.338	.848	1.341	.351	....	....
49	Zaleszczyki	.085	1.035	2.285	....	7.193	4.658	.518	.683	.181	....	....
50	Zborow	.312	2.369	5.312	....	16.793	10.695	1.224	1.523	.358	....	....
51	Zloczow	.255	1.717	3.853	.648	10.831	6.109	2.012	1.001	.363	....	.150
52	Zolkiew	.029	.....	.....	....	1.758	1.008	.123	.172	.178	....	.025
53	Zydaczow	.139	1.031	2.286	....	7.180	4.566	.521	.580	.176	....	....
	Total	**11.553**	**73.697**	**163.405**	**44.844**	**509.303**	**311.567**	**48.989**	**48.210**	**16.737**	**2.335**	**1.170**

POLAND

Table 445 Deliveries from WARSAW Warehouse, Month of February, 1921

eipt o.	Local Committee	Commodities in Net Metric Tons of 1,000 Kilograms or 2,204.6 Pounds										
		Cocoa	Sugar	Milk		Flour	Beans, Peas	Rice	Pork Products	Vegetable Oil	Salt	Misc.*
				Evap.	Cond.							
1	Aleksandrow	.203	.562	1.393	....	4.594	2.871	.....	.307	....	....	....
2	Bogdanow	.305	2.319	5.094	.991	16.684	10.429	.....	1.194	.538	....	....
3	Brzeziny	.203	.724	1.328	.362	4.242	2.404	1.367	.310	.179	....	....
4	Busk	.406	1.530	2.634	.209	8.556	4.830	2.756	.887	.181	....	....
5	Ciechanow	....	.636	1.415	.533	4.595	2.871	.....	.310	.176	....	....
6	Chelm	....	....	.....	....	28.222	.....	.....	....	....	....	....
7	Czestochowa	.610	7.020	15.435	2.153	50.545	31.590	.....	3.726	1.771	....	....
8	Glebokie	.300	1.932	4.245	1.448	13.910	8.514	.....	1.016	.532	....	....
9	Garwolin	.813	1.813	6.096	1.619	19.985	12.518	.....	1.165	1.076	....	....
0	Grojec	.508	1.699	3.744	.972	12.394	7.653	.....	.918	.539	.795	....
1	Grodziska	.610	1.937	4.332	1.067	14.149	8.825	.....	1.101	.535	....	....
2	Gostynin	.300	1.224	2.699	1.067	8.817	5.510	.....	.655	.352	....	....
3	Jedrzejow	.406	1.380	2.634	.....	8.556	4.830	2.760	.861	.186	....	....
4	Kolno	.500	1.576	3.592	.895	11.827	7.353	.....	.605	.718	....	....
5	Konskie	.508	1.696	3.461	.724	10.262	5.835	3.334	....	.354	....	....
6	Kielce	.305	2.040	3.157	.895	12.208	8.112	.....	1.231	.182	....	....
7	Kozienica	....	1.035	2.482	1.257	7.454	4.646	.....	.467	.352	....	....
8	Kutno	.203	1.090	2.482	.895	8.100	5.062	.....	.348	.528	....	....
9	Konin	.102	.302	.588	.362	1.912	1.073	.638	.131	.181	....	....
0	Kolo	.304	1.287	2.460	.248	7.094	4.166	1.200	7.014	.353	.241	....
1	Kalisz	.610	1.918	3.636	1.086	11.751	6.648	3.745	1.003	.532	....	....
2	Lida	.406	2.935	6.466	1.791	29.178	13.157	.....	1.275	.895	....	....
3	Lapy	.406	1.553	3.418	.724	11.178	7.110	.....	.727	.537	....	....
4	Lomza	1.016	3.259	6.270	1.810	20.105	11.442	6.570	1.435	1.239	....	....
5	Lowicz	.203	.704	1.328	.362	4.267	2.416	1.364	.305	.180	....	....
6	Lublin	.508	3.808	8.447	4.324	27.648	17.280	.....	2.031	1.059	....	....
7	Lubartow	.100	.404	.892	.533	2.881	1.619	.934	.309	.181	....	....
8	Łódź	3.759	12.560	27.691	5.810	90.555	56.702	.....	7.380	2.671	....	....
9	Lask	.203	.656	1.263	.362	4.054	2.294	1.311	.294	.176	....	....
0	Leczyca	.102	.402	.784	.362	2.579	1.435	.857	.152	.184	.240	....
1	Minsk Mazow.	.508	1.794	3.940	1.067	12.916	8.073	.....	.930	.538	....	....
2	Mlawa	.102	.648	1.415	.438	4.673	2.922	.....	.323	.175	....	....
3	Makow	.203	.781	1.546	.533	5.041	2.817	1.641	.432	.176	....	....
4	Oszmiany	.406	2.932	6.444	1.791	21.114	13.196	.....	1.630	.712	....	....
5	Ostroleka	.203	1.155	2.525	.534	8.316	5.197	.....	.514	.353	.352	....
6	Ostrow	....	2.616	5.769	1.448	18.876	11.778	.....	1.039	1.027	.405	....
7	Opoczno	.203	.833	1.589	.362	5.149	2.901	1.645	.446	.179	....	....
8	Ostrowiec	.610	2.180	4.833	.457	15.811	9.889	.....	....	....	....	....
9	Ozorkow	.203	.638	1.219	.533	3.957	2.233	1.276	.302	.181	....	....
0	Pinczow	.302	1.008	1.894	.438	6.164	3.493	1.990	.463	.357	....	....
1	Piotrkow	.610	2.176	.....	....	14.986	9.652	.....	1.313	.301	....	....
2	Pultusk	.406	1.328	3.004	.895	9.836	6.156	.....	.726	.351	....	....
3	Przasnysz	.305	.844	1.611	.533	5.273	2.960	1.708	.347	.178	....	.100[c]
4	Poznanskie	.203	.810	1.785	.533	5.958	3.647	.....	.595	....	....	....
5	Plonsk	.203	.614	1.176	.438	3.806	2.149	1.228	.293	.181	....	....
6	Plock	.406	1.830	4.027	1.448	13.181	8.235	.....	.997	.532	....	.100[c]
7	Pabjanice	.406	1.206	3.853	1.791	12.696	7.955	.....	1.217	.179	.398	....
8	Pulawy	.261	1.035	2.286	1.067	7.447	4.663	.....	.308	.526	....	....
9	Parczew	....	2.706	5.921	2.515	19.386	12.111	.....	1.212	.896	.583	....
0	Radom	.808	2.691	5.442	.705	19.374	12.109	.....	1.478	.702	....	....
1	Rawa Mazow.	.508	1.632	3.113	.972	10.117	5.710	3.263	.842	.348	....	....
2	Ruda Pabjanska	.102	.500	1.088	.457	3.601	2.250	.....	.308	....	....	....
3	Rzgow	.102	.483	1.089	....	3.477	2.173	.....	.280	.177	....	....
4	Radomsk	.610	2.059	4.615	1.429	15.151	9.478	.....	1.205	.534	....	....
5	Swieciany	.305	2.414	5.377	1.448	17.678	11.036	.....	1.516	.358	....	....

* Detail of miscellaneous commodities indicated by the following in- es: [c], codliver oil; [d], soap. Of the total, 1.350, .200 is codliver oil 1.150 is soap.

[*Continued on next page*]

POLAND

Table 445—*Continued*

Deliveries from WARSAW Warehouse, Month of February, 1921

Commodities in Net Metric Tons of 1,000 Kilograms or 2,204.6 Pounds

Receipt No.	Local Committee	Cocoa	Sugar	Milk Evap.	Milk Cond.	Flour	Beans, Peas	Rice	Pork Products	Vegetable Oil	Salt	Misc.
56	Sokolow	.406	1.334	2.917	.533	9.563	5.951	.....	.427	.567	....	....
57	Sochaczew	.203	1.022	2.286	.705	6.399	3.636	2.054	.569	.179	....	....
58	Sandomierz	.102	.994	.457	....	7.153	4.471	.....	.598	.181	....	....
59	Skierniewice	.305	.994	1.894	.438	6.159	3.478	1.987	.556	.175	....	....
60	Strykow	.203	.706	1.546	.533	5.091	3.181	.....	.440	.177	....	....
61	Sierpc	.203	.700	2.874	....	9.396	5.872	.....	.602	.349	....	....
62	Sieradz	.203	.669	1.480	....	4.854	3.040	.....	.277	.179	....	....
63	Torun	.406	1.327	3.048	....	9.958	6.237	.....	1.061	....	....	....
64	Tomaszow	.405	1.406	2.765	.724	8.983	5.061	2.887	.771	.356	.500	....
65	Wegrow	.500	1.783	4.180	1.067	13.662	8.538	.....	.907	.521	....	....
66	Wloszczowa	.203	.864	1.894	.419	6.220	3.880	.....	.159	.175	....	....
67	Wierzbnik	.305	1.107	.....	....	8.208	5.145	.....	.413	.178	....	....
68	Wloclawek	.305	1.075	2.156	....	6.801	3.944	2.235	.598	.359	....	....
69	Wyszkow	.203	.752	1.654	1.143	5.413	3.384	.....	.309	.356	....	....
70	Wielun	.102	.741	1.633	....	5.340	3.337	.....	.302	.181	....	....
71	Wilejka	.702	2.415	5.072	1.619	17.388	10.868	.....	1.141	.680	....	....
72	Wilno	3.200	8.610	6.858	37.090	.....	23.899	.....	5.183	....	....	....
73	Warsaw Child. Inst.	3.510	12.453	25.899	22.493	106.157	46.351	28.400	10.713	1.213	8.356	1.15
74	Warsaw Feeding Point	1.521	10.907	10.864	.191	5.249	20.728	7.470	4.637	....	....	....
75	Zgierz	.609	2.056	4.485	....	14.638	9.152	.....	1.295	.175	....	....
76	Zdunsk	.102	.363	1.524	....	4.968	3.105	.....	....	....	....	....
	Total	**35.572**	**149.192**	**290.514**	**121.648**	**983.886**	**605.236**	**84.620**	**80.519**	**31.349**	**11.870**	**1.35**

* See previous page.

POLAND

Table 446

Deliveries from BREST Warehouse, Month of March, 1921

Commodities in Net Metric Tons of 1,000 Kilograms or 2,204.6 Pounds

Receipt No.	Local Committee	Cocoa	Sugar	Milk Evap.	Milk Cond.	Flour	Beans, Peas	Rice	Corn Grits	Pork Products	Vegetable Oil	Misc.
1	Augustow	.510	1.807	....	5.315	11.650	6.468	3.915	....	.834	.693	....
2	Bilgoraj	.413	1.206	....	4.134	7.876	4.320	2.705	....	.593	.348	....
3	Białystok	1.189	2.300	....	16.383	13.023	7.516	11.865	.175	.692	....	2.79
4	Baranowicze	.813	2.703	....	8.249	17.109	10.198	5.723	....	1.341	.104	....
5	Brzostowica	.306	1.000	....	2.896	6.270	3.962	2.112	....	....	.345	....
6	Biala Podlaska	.816	2.826	....	8.211	26.486	.....	7.344	....	2.309	....	1.45
7	Bielsk	.819	2.149	....	8.515	17.781	9.846	6.000	....	2.184	.673	1.44
7	Bielsk	.306	.900	....	1.981	5.580	3.161	1.824	....	....	....	....
8	Bialowieza	.306	1.108	....	3.524	7.062	4.105	2.394	....	.651	....	....
9	Brzesc Litewski	1.790	6.057	....	19.812	38.655	23.133	13.224	....	2.879	....	3.36
10	Chelm	1.223	2.973	....	9.525	25.974	17.123	8.400	....	....	.863	....
11	Dobno	.305	1.098	....	2.876	7.149	1.310	5.042	....	1.511	....	....
12	Grodno	1.320	4.422	....	13.792	27.944	17.812	10.071	....	....	1.513	....
13	Grajewo	.305	1.105	....	3.372	7.138	3.922	2.424	....	.646	.346	....
14	Hrubieszow	.406	1.200	....	.....	8.000	4.387	2.711	....	.670	.429	....
15	Kowel	3.065	10.149	....	27.014	62.932	37.609	21.212	....	3.257	2.041	....
16	Kobryn	.711	1.100	....	3.371	17.846	10.625	6.010	....	1.450	....	1.94
17	Krasnystaw	.274	.960	....	3.200	6.138	3.662	2.112	....	.479	....	....
18	Krzemieniec	.503	1.806	....	5.010	11.271	6.710	3.766	....	1.017	....	....
19	Luck	1.006	3.450	....	9.392	21.690	12.803	7.200	....	2.017	....	....

* Detail of miscellaneous commodities indicated by the following indexes: [a], salt; [c], codliver oil. Of the total, 15.999, 15.839 is salt and .160 is codliver oil.

POLAND

Deliveries from BREST Warehouse, Month of March, 1921

Table 446—*Continued*

eceipt No.	Local Committee	Cocoa	Sugar	Milk Evap.	Milk Cond.	Flour	Beans, Peas	Rice	Corn Grits	Pork Products	Vegetable Oil	Misc.*
		Commodities in Net Metric Tons of 1,000 Kilograms or 2,204.6 Pounds										
20	Luboml	1.034	3.612	....	.....	28.689	17.351	7.780	....	....	.860	....
21	Ostrog	.508	1.703	....	4.839	10.781	6.934	3.593	....	....	.532	....
22	Olyka	.625	2.179	....	.....	16.473	11.787	4.515	....	....	.345	....
23	Pruzany	.608	2.100	.588	5.810	13.316	10.836	4.532	....	1.244	.520	.....
23	Pruzany	1.205	4.184	....	12.837	26.643	12.065	8.999	....	2.420	....	2.052[a]
24	Pinsk	1.601	5.310	....	16.364	42.998	.....	18.003	....	4.294	....	2.932[a]
25	Rowno	1.480	4.780	....	13.144	29.989	17.048	9.935	....	2.539	....	....
26	Suwalki	.610	1.980	....	5.791	12.510	6.930	4.189	....	.995	.523	....
27	Sarny	.611	2.115	....	.....	16.765	11.937	4.190	....	....	.521	....
28	Slonim	1.098	3.716	....	10.344	23.437	14.250	7.804	....	1.829	....	....
29	Tomaszow	.514	1.900	....	6.668	12.065	6.615	4.200	....	.862	.680	....
30	Wlodawa	.813	2.970	....	8.687	18.800	10.363	6.325	....	1.506	.854	....
31	Wlodzimierz	1.416	4.831	....	.....	19.627	13.396	10.200	....	....	.354	....
32	Wolkowysk	.610	1.962	....	5.944	12.456	6.885	4.200	....	1.011	.693	....
33	Zamosc	.102	.555	....	1.753	3.533	1.957	1.196	....	.320	.172	....
	Total	**29.221**	**94.216**	**.588**	**248.754**	**635.656**	**337.026**	**225.715**	**.175**	**39.550**	**13.409**	**15.999***

POLAND

Table 447

Deliveries from KRAKÓW Warehouse, Month of March, 1921

eceipt No.	Local Committee	Cocoa	Sugar	Milk Evap.	Milk Cond.	Flour	Beans, Peas	Rice	Pork Products	Vegetable Oil	Salt	Soap
		Commodities in Net Metric Tons of 1,000 Kilograms or 2,204.6 Pounds										
1	Biala	.406	1.261	1.393	....	4.486	2.474	2.515	1.020	....	....	....
2	Bedzin	.305	....	.435	5.220	12.533	.....	4.223	....	.535	.600	....
3	Bochnia	.203	.686	....	....	4.433	1.773	1.459	.676	....	....	....
4	Bytom	2.438	11.468	20.050	....	37.274	12.990	9.939	6.453	....	....	....
5	Brzesko	.305	.799	.914	1.581	5.040	2.848	1.635	.511	....	....	....
6	Cieszyn	....	1.421	1.872	2.153	9.043	3.990	2.984	1.198	....	....	....
7	Chrzanow	.103	.923	1.198	....	4.514	3.226	1.928	.508	....	....	....
8	Dabrowa	.406	2.011	.370	3.048	8.484	4.014	2.701	.343	.352	....	....
9	Debica	.101	.399	.653	.229	2.601	1.110	.921	.174	....	....	....
10	Gorlice	.102	.393	....	....	2.275	1.347	.780	.337	....	....	....
11	Jaslo	....	.302	....	....	1.082	.816	.646	....	.179	....	....
12	Kalwarja	....	.147	.218	.267	.928	.538	.322	.168	....	....	....
13	Kraków	2.235	7.330	8.055	13.868	49.000	29.185	7.292	5.536	.354	....	....
14	Krosno	....	.739	.849	....	3.525	2.018	1.511	.341	....	....	....
15	Krzeszowice	....	.298	.392	.381	2.120	.805	.688	.346	....	....	....
16	Lancut	....	.100	.696	....	1.579	1.697	1.049	....	....	.300	.050
17	Lezajsk	....	.520	.588	.590	3.275	1.830	1.065	.353	....	....	.050
18	Makow	....	.334	.370	.381	1.577	.612	.647	.337	....	....	....
19	Mielec	.102	.388	.435	....	2.402	....	2.004	.177	....	....	.050
20	Myslenice	.101	.245	.392	.476	1.589	.863	.546	.166	.178	....	....
21	Muszyna	.101	.269	.348	.381	1.623	....	1.411	.168	.178	....	....
22	Niepolomice	....	.201	.196	.191	1.017	.587	.320	.164	....	....	....
23	Nisko	....	.601	1.306	....	5.034	2.488	1.790	.336	....	.300	....
24	Nowy Sacz	.508	2.520	3.549	4.324	15.008	.....	14.008	1.535	....	....	....
25	Nowy Targ	....	1.020	1.502	....	3.979	2.986	2.390	.681	....	....	....
26	Olkusz	.305	1.501	3.483	....	5.014	4.806	3.130	.682	....	....	....

[*Continued on next page*]

POLAND

Deliveries from KRAKÓW Warehouse, Month of March, 1921

Table 447—*Continued*

Receipt No.	Local Committee	Cocoa	Sugar	Milk Evap.	Milk Cond.	Flour	Beans, Peas	Rice	Pork Products	Vegetable Oil	Salt	Soap
		Commodities in Net Metric Tons of 1,000 Kilograms or 2,204.6 Pounds										
27	Oswiecim Baraki	.101	.444	.523	1.162	2.479	1.384	.909	.327	....	....	....
28	Oswiecim	.203	.833	.914	1.162	5.086	2.870	1.656	.510	.177	....	....
29	Rozwadow	....	.590	.762	....	3.914	2.096	1.395	.165	....	....	....
30	Rzeszow	.623	1.507	2.351	2.400	5.990	6.015	4.001	1.167	.353	....	....
31	Skawina	....	.124	....	....	.383	.....	.650	.161	....	....	....
32	Sosnowiec	.914	3.981	1.350	11.735	25.982	8.983	8.801	2.232	.532	....	....
33	Szczakowa	....	.303	.305	.305	1.697	.976	.545	.172	....	....	....
34	Sucha	.102	.175	.196	.190	1.018	.594	.321	.171	....	....	....
35	Tarnobrzeg	....	.502	.806	....	2.998	1.507	1.381	.335	....	....	....
36	Tarnow	.102	2.491	3.962	....	13.957	4.965	5.697	1.024	.355	....	....
37	Trzebinia	....	.194	.305	.153	1.209	.520	.553	.170	....	....	....
38	Wadowice	.203	.828	1.154	1.600	5.265	2.204	1.790	.513	....	....	....
39	Wieliczka	.102	.541	.609	.610	3.433	1.953	1.096	.328	....	....	....
40	Zakopane	.203	.852	1.024	....	5.021	2.804	1.587	.517	....	....	....
41	Zawiercie	.312	1.150	2.721	.286	7.306	4.066	2.381	....	.359	....	....
42	Zywiec	.305	1.215	1.328	1.334	7.425	.....	6.400	.844	.178	....	....
	Total	**10.891**	**51.606**	**67.575**	**54.025**	**282.607**	**123.940**	**107.067**	**30.845**	**3.731**	**1.200**	**.150**

POLAND

Deliveries from LWÓW Warehouse, Month of March, 1921

Table 448

Receipt No.	Local Committee	Cocoa	Sugar	Milk Evap.	Milk Cond.	Flour	Beans, Peas	Rice	Pork Products	Vegetable Oil	Salt
		Commodities in Net Metric Tons of 1,000 Kilograms or 2,204.6 Pounds									
1	Brzozow	.305	1.896	2.765	.724	7.821	1.855	3.520	.150	....	...
2	Belz	.102	.505	.718	....	2.066	1.290	.647	.185	....	...
3	Buczacz	.407	2.322	3.461	.895	9.755	5.477	3.158	.687	.170	...
4	Bobrka	.136	.856	1.263	.286	1.849	2.038	1.142	.374	.174	...
5	Bohorodczany	.103	.806	1.219	.533	1.215	1.947	1.110	.340	.180	...
6	Boryslaw	.403	1.813	3.244	2.058	8.401	3.171	3.359	....	....	...
7	Brody	.504	2.362	3.462	.895	9.764	5.932	3.180	1.109	....	2.00
8	Brzezany	.703	3.594	5.289	....	18.189	1.829	8.127	1.834	.531	...
9	Borszczow	.204	.814	1.219	.533	3.461	1.923	1.103	.462	.178	.40
10	Busk	.072	.309	.522	....	.769	.883	.483	.196	....	...
11	Cieszanow	.311	1.326	2.025	.534	5.679	3.222	1.808	.549	.352	...
12	Czortkow	.302	1.610	2.308	....	1.251	3.673	2.095	.812	.358	...
13	Drohobycz	.507	2.413	3.527	1.257	9.947	5.595	3.213	1.099	.362	...
14	Dolina	.306	1.815	2.634	....	1.026	4.219	2.399	.871	.181	...
15	Dobromil	.103	.517	.762	.114	2.148	1.305	.690	.124	....	...
16	Grodek Jagiellonski	.188	1.035	1.524	....	4.278	2.415	1.380	.410	.179	...
17	Halicz	.180	.918	1.328	....	1.170	2.100	1.208	.450	.177	...
18	Jaroslaw	.608	3.195	4.681	1.448	9.266	7.446	4.267	1.574	.530	...
19	Janow	.103	.507	.762	....	2.142	1.189	.690	.359	.182	...
20	Jaworow	.310	1.800	2.634	....	7.105	4.199	2.418	.864	.366	...
21	Kolomyja	.515	2.812	4.158	.724	11.734	6.615	3.773	1.505	.530	...
22	Kalusz	.406	1.935	3.070	.953	8.119	4.875	2.736	.323	....	...
23	Kosow	.502	2.609	4.093	.610	10.842	6.524	3.623	.766	....	...
24	Kamionka Strumilowa	.208	.919	1.328	....	3.692	2.137	1.213	.470	.182	...
25	Lisko	.308	1.412	2.112	....	3.545	3.372	1.929	.667	.353	...
26	Lwow, District	.505	2.560	3.788	....	10.683	6.292	3.460	....	....	...
27	Lwow, City	1.352	6.834	9.884	18.002	23.423	15.807	12.006	3.356	.691	...

POLAND

Deliveries from LWÓW Warehouse, Month of March, 1921

Table 448—*Continued*

eceipt No.	Local Committee	Cocoa	Sugar	Milk Evap.	Milk Cond.	Flour	Beans, Peas	Rice	Pork Products	Vegetable Oil	Salt
		Commodities in Net Metric Tons of 1,000 Kilograms or 2,204.6 Pounds									
28	Nadworna	.637	3.378	4.942	1.905	17.784	.267	8.308	.293	....	....
29	Otynia	.202	1.126	1.655	.419	4.691	2.810	1.524	.170	....	....
30	Przemysl	.816	4.320	6.335	2.172	13.134	10.076	5.752	2.218	.532	....
31	Peczenizyn	.203	1.347	1.981	....	4.084	3.126	1.800	.670	.170	....
32	Przeworsk	.309	1.435	2.090	....	5.772	3.332	1.859	.675	.185	....
33	Podhajce	.510	2.587	3.788	.895	10.653	6.037	3.450	1.319	.357	....
34	Rohatyn	.307	.808	2.830	....	.....	.....	2.563	.196	.179	....
35	Radziechow	.410	2.244	3.309	....	9.350	5.267	3.025	1.144	.360	.300
36	Rawa Ruska	.518	2.433	3.636	....	3.080	5.751	3.289	.340	.536	....
37	Sanok	.509	2.967	4.398	2.400	12.553	5.233	4.205	.374	....	.200
38	Sambor	.611	2.906	4.267	2.534	12.379	6.806	4.213	.906	.171	.300
39	Stary Sambor	.203	1.011	1.459	....	4.080	2.310	1.328	.296	.171	....
40	Sniatyn	.203	1.350	1.981	....	5.550	3.150	1.800	.698	.178	....
41	Stryj	.408	2.116	3.135	.895	7.179	4.984	2.853	.768	.355	.100
42	Stanislawow	.709	3.658	5.355	3.048	15.126	9.293	4.886	....	....	....
43	Skole	.307	1.627	2.308	.476	6.487	3.979	2.117	.131	....	....
44	Skalat	.203	1.265	1.872	.572	5.499	2.976	1.935	.623	....	....
45	Sokal	.395	1.707	2.438	....	.593	3.935	2.243	.838	.357	....
46	Turka	.508	2.419	3.636	....	10.200	5.766	3.300	1.217	.354	....
47	Tarnopol	.507	.210	.....	....	2.862	.699	3.103	.314	....	....
48	Tlumacz	.303	1.682	2.743	1.333	7.202	4.304	2.393	....	....	....
49	Trembowla	.201	.926	1.348	.533	1.020	2.166	1.242	.536	.176	....
50	Zydaczow	.299	1.425	2.112	....	5.925	3.356	1.940	.679	.178	....
51	Zaleszczyki	.306	1.487	1.263	.800	.....	.....	1.994	.614	....	....
52	Zborow	.595	3.150	4.615	....	16.706	.....	7.871	1.813	....	....
53	Zbaraz	.185	1.057	1.546	.533	.833	2.465	1.428	.151	.183	....
54	Zloczow	.508	2.851	4.180	.648	7.730	6.663	3.802	1.453	.531	....
	Total	**20.525**	**102.986**	**152.999**	**48.730**	**369.812**	**212.081**	**157.960**	**37.972**	**10.649**	**3.300**

POLAND

Deliveries from WARSAW Warehouse, Month of March, 1921

Table 449

ceipt No.	Local Committee	Cocoa	Sugar	Milk Evap.	Milk Cond.	Flour	Beans, Peas	Rice	Pork Products	Vegetable Oil	Salt	Misc.*
		Commodities in Net Metric Tons of 1,000 Kilograms or 2,204.6 Pounds										
1	Aleksandrow	.102	.776	1.393	.362	.....	.970	1.200	.319	.179	....	....
2	Bogdanow	.610	2.992	4.811	.838	12.532	6.982	4.200	1.391	.539	1.050	....
3	Busk	.406	1.900	3.135	.724	.....	4.415	2.707	.888	.348	....	....
4	Brzeziny	.203	1.100	1.829	.248	4.541	2.500	1.510	.444	.354	.200	....
5	Ciechanow	.203	1.057	1.742	....	3.931	1.828	1.500	.459	.180	....	....
6	Częstochowa	1.881	7.651	.....	....	21.106	.....	13.200	1.346	....	4.987	....
7	Glebokie	.508	2.721	4.507	.953	11.600	6.410	3.894	1.356	.505	....	....
8	Garwolin	.914	4.489	7.206	1.200	18.902	10.510	6.319	1.514	1.582	.521	....
9	Gostynin	.406	2.114	3.462	.724	8.963	4.925	3.000	.873	.525	....	....
10	Grodziska	.524	2.905	4.659	....	.....	1.601	4.065	1.395	.516	....	....
11	Jedrzejow	.406	1.898	3.135	.724	.....	4.428	2.703	.906	.338	....	....
12	Kielce	.610	3.040	2.395	.476	7.585	4.335	4.216	1.403	.356	....	....
13	Kutno	.305	1.654	2.373	.610	5.505	2.814	3.000	.288	.721	....	....
14	Konskie	.508	2.610	4.071	.476	.....	6.090	3.600	1.173	.518	....	....
15	Kozienice	.305	1.665	2.809	.724	7.060	3.883	2.400	.636	.389	....	....

* Detail of miscellaneous commodities indicated by the following in- ces: c, codliver oil; d, soap. Of the total, 1.751, .150 is codliver oil d 1.601 is soap.

[*Continued on next page*]

POLAND

Deliveries from WARSAW Warehouse, Month of March, 1921

Table 449—*Continued*

Receipt No.	Local Committee	Commodities in Net Metric Tons of 1,000 Kilograms or 2,204.6 Pounds										
		Cocoa	Sugar	Milk		Flour	Beans, Peas	Rice	Pork Products	Vegetable Oil	Salt	Misc.
				Evap.	Cond.							
16	Liskow	.203	.718	1.589	....	6.966	.....	1.443	.613	....	....	....
17	Lida	.813	4.410	6.923	2.281	18.758	9.907	6.180	2.123	.888	1.800	....
18	Lomza	1.016	4.921	8.098	1.676	.....	11.546	7.003	1.593	1.716	....	....
19	Lukow	.711	3.391	5.552	1.200	14.230	7.879	4.800	1.071	1.071	....	....
20	Lapy	.406	2.389	3.788	.724	.....	5.465	3.300	.791	.860	....	....
21	Lowicz	.305	1.596	2.547	.476	3.315	3.675	2.196	.843	.167	.204	.050
22	Lubartow	.203	.810	1.437	.476	3.468	1.890	1.200	.314	.177	....	....
23	Lublin	1.219	5.942	6.096	....	7.783	9.871	9.000	2.863	1.250	....	....
24	Łódź	.203	14.836	19.419	5.772	.....	18.807	23.998	5.605	....	.315	....
25	Lask	.203	1.100	1.698	.248	.....	1.608	1.507	.447	.315	....	....
26	Makow	.203	1.003	1.742	.362	.....	2.463	1.500	.406	.172	....	....
27	Minsk Mazowiecki	.508	2.526	4.115	.838	10.637	5.846	3.552	1.126	.537	....	....
28	Mlawa	.203	1.057	1.742	.362	4.461	2.467	1.500	.413	.178	....	....
29	Ostrow Lomzynski	.712	3.885	6.204	....	16.146	8.953	5.421	1.186	1.416	....	....
30	Ostroleka	.305	1.701	2.722	.362	7.260	4.042	2.409	.571	.537	.407	....
31	Opoczno	.302	1.302	2.025	.248	.....	.....	1.783	.600	.344	....	....
32	Ostrowiec	.406	3.711	5.726	.476	.....	5.420	5.098	1.148	.356	.308	....
33	Ozorkow	.203	.793	1.393	.362	.....	1.902	1.185	.415	.147	....	....
34	Oszmiany	.803	4.217	6.923	1.448	17.830	9.879	5.989	2.004	.711	....	....
35	Piotrkow	.508	2.510	4.115	.724	10.787	5.994	3.596	1.208	.536	....	....
36	Pultusk	.406	2.002	3.244	.610	.....	4.672	2.820	.765	.340	....	....
37	Przasnysz	.203	1.291	2.133	.362	.....	3.101	1.872	.600	.349	....	....
38	Poznanskie	.203	1.010	1.742	.362	4.448	2.457	1.508	.713	....	....	....
39	Plonsk	.204	1.204	1.916	.286	.....	2.814	1.694	.461	.338	....	....
40	Plock	.609	3.160	5.160	.953	13.468	7.446	4.521	1.498	.726	....	....
41	Parczew	.813	4.189	6.988	.114	17.710	9.775	6.006	1.652	1.064	....	....
42	Pulawy	.305	1.665	2.808	.724	7.062	3.885	2.400	.745	.355	....	....
43	Pabjanice	.406	2.475	4.223	....	.....	3.334	3.600	1.396	.175	....	....
44	Pinczow	.305	1.700	2.722	.362	.....	.....	2.424	.802	.342	....	....
45	Rawa Mazowiecka	.406	2.313	4.027	1.200	.....	.....	3.437	1.179	.339	....	....
46	Ruda Pabjanska	....	.153	.240	....	.....	.....	.411	.....	....	....	...
47	Rzgow	.203	.855	1.372	.248	.....	1.126	1.200	.312	.166	.655	...
48	Radomsk	.406	2.079	3.505	.914	8.831	4.810	3.014	.843	.537	....	...
49	Radom	.813	4.318	6.770	.724	.....	10.171	5.991	1.817	1.059	....	...
50	Swieciany	.711	3.393	5.530	1.143	14.272	7.906	4.810	1.769	.537	.485	...
51	Sokolow	.305	1.706	2.721	.362	7.280	4.041	2.398	.563	.529	2.382	.10
52	Siedlce	1.016	4.912	8.338	2.153	.....	11.555	7.136	1.637	1.699	....	...
53	Sierpc	.508	2.538	4.115	.724	10.764	5.977	3.604	1.070	.530	....	...
54	Sochaczew	.508	2.520	4.180	.953	10.636	5.887	3.600	1.175	.527	....	...
55	Skierniewice	.406	2.012	3.266	.610	.....	4.745	2.827	1.064	.345	....	...
56	Sieradz	.203	1.000	1.742	.362	.....	2.468	1.490	.459	.173	....	...
57	Strykow	.203	1.004	1.742	.362	.....	2.477	1.497	.593	.164	....	...
58	Sandomierz	.305	1.710	2.743	.476	7.188	4.008	2.400	.895	.184	....	...
59	Tomaszow	.305	2.003	3.135	.476	.....	4.651	2.745	.919	.358	....	...
60	Torun (Pomorze)	.305	1.813	2.634	....	7.416	4.198	2.379	1.176	....	....	...
61	Wlodawa	....	.....	.....	....	21.396	.....	.....	.....	....	4.530	...
62	Wilno	2.743	13.094	29.977	13.791	55.902	30.772	19.575	6.029	2.646	1.142	...
63	Wilejka	.610	3.176	5.203	1.086	13.384	7.389	4.522	1.540	.533	....	...
64	Wegrow	.508	2.512	3.984	.724	.....	5.791	3.484	.907	.679	....	...
65	Wierzbnik	.610	2.115	3.418	.476	.....	5.025	3.014	1.064	.368	....	...
66	Wloszczowa	.305	1.445	2.416	.438	6.268	3.459	2.111	.651	.355	....	...
67	Wyszkow	.203	1.206	1.829	.762	.....	2.289	1.503	.302	.337	....	...
68	Wloclawek	.407	1.867	3.048	.610	.....	4.357	2.640	.856	.339	....	...
69	Wielun	.203	1.000	1.742	.362	.....	2.471	1.500	.447	.337	10.169	...
70	Warsaw Child. Inst.	5.070	17.512	39.267	30.633	178.272	64.072	37.403	12.607	2.584	1.371	1.60
71	Warsaw Feeding Stat.	2.946	12.901	19.375	2.191	10.304	31.084	21.819	7.820	.879	....	...
72	Zgierz	.508	2.502	4.115	....	.....	5.998	3.604	1.356	.373	....	...
73	Zdunska Wola	.203	1.080	1.698	....	4.524	2.520	1.500	.152	.170	....	...
	Total	**41.702**	**214.826**	**344.439**	**91.645**	**622.491**	**456.037**	**328.633**	**97.462**	**38.864**	**30.526**	**1.75**

* See previous page.

POLAND

Deliveries from BREST Warehouse, Month of April, 1921

Table 450

Local Committee	Cocoa	Sugar	Milk Evap.	Milk Cond.	Flour	Beans, Peas	Rice	Pork Products	Vegetable Oil	Salt
	Commodities in Net Metric Tons of 1,000 Kilograms or 2,204.6 Pounds									
Augustow	.190	2.761	2.830	.....	7.343	2.403	2.771	1.051	.....	.700
Bilgoraj	....	1.404	.....	.....	.....	.....	.....	.295	.....	.....
Bialowieza	1.894	9.565	16.153	4.324	27.530	22.274	13.800	3.786	2.563	3.030
Brzesc Litewski	.305	1.667	2.786	.724	7.071	3.900	2.427	.918	.335	.555
Bielsk	1.120	6.013	5.399	5.639	10.028	13.877	8.383	2.416	1.545	1.402
Biala Podlaska	....	4.699	4.006	.....	6.016	5.465	2.973	2.021	1.035	1.417
Brzostowice	.101	2.176	3.157	.....	6.853	3.981	2.346	.925	.348	.....
Baranowicze	.617	2.615	5.551	1.200	10.019	6.835	3.829	1.366	.856	.....
Bialystok	1.188	8.348	.....	8.992	15.550	15.848	2.890	3.343	2.417	1.410
Chelm	....	.693	.....	.....	12.012	1.180	.....	2.753	1.210	2.700
Dubno	.599	3.480	5.029	.....	2.020	7.346	4.904	1.377	.683	1.155
Grajewo	.203	1.602	.....	2.496	1.350	2.046	1.227	.457	.527	.400
Grodno	.195	6.745	2.177	.....	11.230	5.612	.....	2.590	1.847	2.400
Hrubieszow	.402	1.907	3.113	.723	7.610	4.034	2.699	.731	.507	.....
Krashystaw	.303	1.400	2.460	.724	2.038	3.340	2.085	.605	.328	.....
Krzemieniec	.603	3.108	4.985	.953	2.011	7.175	4.354	1.396	.557	.780
Kowel	3.255	16.059	12.161	13.335	50.214	19.551	22.198	6.043	2.236	5.100
Kobryn	.995	5.132	.....	8.935	10.004	11.858	7.199	2.279	1.184	1.400
Luck	.304	5.208	5.203	.....	6.638	8.105	7.020	2.467	.854	1.725
Nieswierz	.566	2.985	4.833	.953	10.212	6.946	4.229	1.382	.599	.....
Nowogrodek	.585	3.194	5.203	1.200	13.307	7.353	4.515	1.211	.867	.....
Ostrog	....	2.970	4.115	.....	6.000	3.609	.598	1.407	.682	.705
Olyka	....	3.220	5.094	.724	6.728	1.218	.460	1.686	.621	.855
Pruzany	.101	8.333	9.971	.....	10.041	8.012	5.002	4.141	1.371	2.100
Pinsk	1.695	8.861	12.997	3.105	36.690	20.698	11.821	3.525	2.314	2.655
Rowno	....	6.464	2.025	1.619	6.502	1.286	1.467	2.792	1.527	1.897
Sarny	.201	3.064	3.157	3.524	10.419	4.525	3.780	1.547	.680	1.050
Suwalki	.709	3.786	6.204	1.200	10.158	8.920	5.402	1.683	.857	.....
Sokolka	.306	1.728	1.132	.....	7.216	3.979	2.420	.758	.467	.....
Slonim	....	5.577	9.775	.....	10.306	4.199	.....	2.280	1.539	1.600
Tomaszow	....	2.820	4.593	.....	9.679	.585	.....	1.075	.687	.....
Wlodawa	....	4.469	7.249	1.619	7.007	.905	.....	1.888	.697	.....
Wlodezimierz Wolynski	.912	7.830	.....	10.992	10.024	9.331	9.018	3.963	1.200	2.415
Wolkowysk	....	2.234	2.177	1.200	1.901	.680	.....	1.046	.168	1.000
Zamosc	.202	.798	1.393	.362	3.537	1.952	1.209	.301	.174	.....
Total	**17.551**	**152.915**	**154.928**	**74.543**	**355.264**	**229.028**	**141.026**	**67.504**	**33.482**	**38.451**

POLAND

Table 451 — Deliveries from KRAKÓW Warehouse, Month of April, 1921

Receipt No.	Local Committee	Commodities in Net Metric Tons of 1,000 Kilograms or 2,204.6 Pounds										
		Cocoa	Sugar	Milk		Flour	Beans, Peas	Rice	Pork Products	Vegetable Oil	Salt	Soap
				Evap.	Cond.							
1	Bochnia	.206	.651	....	....	4.090	.816	....	.452	....	....	....
2	Biala	.404	1.232	.239	3.219	4.417	4.390	2.610	1.074	....	....	....
3	Brzesko	.307	.831	.240	2.248	5.179	2.854	1.768	.451	....	....	....
4	Bedzin	.414	1.802	.501	....	10.000	2.500	....	.475	1.197	....	....
5	Cieszyn	.524	1.588	.327	4.096	9.911	1.997	....	1.245	....	....	....
6	Chrzanow	.305	.912	....	2.019	5.964	1.212	....	.793	....	....	....
7	Debica	.102	.273	.196	1.276	1.577	.805	.917	.161	....	....	....
8	Dabrowa Gorna	.515	2.411	.370	....	10.477	2.791	.183	.306	.174	1.050	....
9	Gorlice	.103	.398	.261	1.353	2.533	1.195	.919	.305	.052	....	....
10	Jaslo	.102	.323	....	.705	1.957	.800	.644	.156	.155	....	....
11	Jordanow	.104	.325	....	.724	2.028	1.150	.644	.148	....	....	....
12	Kalwarja	.104	.145	.065	.438	1.000	....	.230	....	....	....	....
13	Krosno	.305	....	.653	....	4.308	.694	....	.478	.177	....	....
14	Krzeszowice	.103	.325	....	.762	2.466	1.443	....	.158	....	....	....
15	Krakow Miasto	1.852	7.312	1.959	19.983	46.282	25.607	15.596	5.449	.346	....	....
16	Lancut	.305	.849	1.393	1.638	6.125	2.498	2.110	.484	.345	....	....
17	Lezajsk	.207	.546	....	1.200	3.361	1.872	1.058	.315	.101	....	....
18	Muszyna	.095	.268	.044	.667	1.659	.950	....	.158	....	....	....
19	Mielec	.101	.382	....	....	2.458	1.352	.594	.153	....	....	....
20	Makow	.104	.366	....	.838	2.344	1.285	.737	.156	....	....	.100
21	Nowy Sacz	.819	2.494	....	5.525	15.896	2.990	....	1.553	.340	....	....
22	Niepolomice	.103	.096	....	.476	1.077	.577	.366	....	....	....	....
23	Nisko	.202	.437	....	....	4.188	....	1.601	.466	....	....	....
24	Nowy Targ	.304	.608	....	3.010	4.983	2.507	2.488	.313	....	....	....
25	Oswiecim	.206	.810	....	1.334	5.138	2.878	1.698	.300	....	....	....
26	Oswiecim Baraki	.102	.466	.218	1.429	2.946	1.629	1.035	.330	....	....	....
27	Olkusz	.421	2.254	.261	3.810	9.420	1.984	....	.767	.706	....	....
28	Rzeszow	.609	....	.087	1.905	7.018	.935	2.978	.301	.168	....	....
29	Rozwadow	.203	.487	....	1.524	3.014	....	1.403	.310	....	.600	....
30	Szczakowa	.102	.271	....	.610	1.956	1.214	....	.155	....	....	....
31	Sucha	.101	.406	....	.876	2.401	1.377	.784	.306	....	....	....
32	Skawina	....	.147	....	.419	1.007	.600	.185	....	....	....	....
33	Sosnowice	.737	4.949	3.070	9.087	26.025	6.051	.775	2.022	.864	....	....
34	Tarnobrzeg	.207	.601	....	1.581	4.227	.939	....	.300	.179	....	....
35	Trzebinia	.104	.168	....	.610	1.522	1.010	....	.146	....	....	....
36	Tarnow	.818	2.437	....	7.944	13.824	2.639	....	1.690	.352	1.000	.050
37	Wadowice	.206	.835	.348	2.477	5.250	1.016	.506	.631	....	....	....
38	Wieliczka	.206	.564	....	1.219	3.906	2.389	....	.465	.169	....	....
39	Zywiec	.406	1.334	....	2.972	8.377	1.807	....	1.068	....	.500	....
40	Zawiercie	.399	1.742	.152	2.381	7.255	1.604	....	.769	.336	....	....
41	Zakopane	.202	.507	....	.610	5.060	2.637	1.694	.465	....	....	....
	Total	**12.715**	**42.551**	**10.384**	**90.964**	**262.626**	**92.994**	**43.523**	**25.275**	**5.661**	**3.150**	**.150**

POLAND

Table 452 — Deliveries from LWÓW Warehouse, Month of April, 1921

Receipt No.	Local Committee	Commodities in Net Metric Tons of 1,000 Kilograms or 2,204.6 Pounds										
		Cocoa	Sugar	Milk		Flour	Beans, Peas	Rice	Corn Grits	Pork Products	Vegetable Oil	Salt
				Evap.	Cond.							
1	Borszczow	.040	.706	.588	.....	2.378	.....	.849	1.040	.150	....	....
2	Brzozow	....	1.905	3.156	.....	14.752	.....	....	.....	.147	....	....
3	Boryslaw	....	2.022	4.115	.....	2.204	1.611	.512	.....	1.342	.168	....
4	Bobrka	....	1.224	....	1.753	6.070	3.735	....	.....	.765	.168	....
5	Brody	....	2.857	....	4.401	10.896	7.354	1.278	.....	1.526	.675	1.000
6	Brzezany	....	3.587	.196	4.763	17.197	3.831	6.736	.....	2.580	.511	....
7	Buczacz	....	3.473	....	3.886	18.815	3.980	2.400	.....	1.530	.335	....
8	Busk	.102	.360	.501	.....	1.532	.877	.489	.....	.163	.171	....
9	Belz	....	.685	....	.762	3.001	.....	.910	.....	.297	.175	....
10	Bohorodczany	....	1.800	....	2.305	11.139	.....	2.381	.....	1.230	.099	....
11	Czortkow	....	.900	....	1.143	5.820	.....	1.200	.....	.435	.345	....
12	Cieszanow	.103	1.372	2.090	.....	4.164	1.938	1.480	.....	.618	.347	....
13	Chyrow	.104	.675	.980	.....	2.788	1.585	.900	.....	.399	....	....
14	Dolina	....	.950	....	.....	5.667	.....	.415	.....	.150	.168	.500
15	Dobromil	....	.517	....	.667	3.329	.....	.692	.....	.310	.170	....
16	Drohobycz	.411	2.107	2.569	.686	6.489	1.996	3.118	.....	1.347	....	....
17	Grodek Jagiellonski	.304	1.439	2.112	.....	5.979	3.364	1.913	.....	.757	.174	....
18	Halicz	....	.900	....	.457	5.630	....	....	.....	.763	....	....
19	Jaworow	....	1.980	2.895	.....	8.152	4.616	3.029	.....	1.098	.337	....
20	Jaroslaw	.512	1.280	4.898	.....	13.447	7.459	4.500	.....	1.603	.506	....
21	Janow	.090	.450	.653	.....	1.852	.750	.603	.....	.241	....	....
22	Kolomyja	.103	2.760	2.525	.....	12.811	.....	5.671	.....	1.227	....	....
23	Kopyczynce	.204	1.282	2.046	.....	2.178	.....	1.794	.....	.323	.170	....
24	Kalusz	....	1.247	.435	.591	6.255	.....	....	.....	.155	.159	....
25	Kosow	....	1.466	2.460	.....	13.408	.....	....	.....	.307	....	....
26	Lisko	....	1.800	....	2.629	11.070	2.036	1.193	.....	.757	.338	....
27	Lwow City	1.752	8.541	19.745	8.583	35.971	.....	....	.....	2.527	.179	....
28	Lwow District	....	2.291	....	1.200	15.310	.....	....	.....	1.962	....	....
29	Nadworna	....	1.892	....	4.858	24.423	.....	5.052	.....	2.627	.516	....
30	Podhajce	....	1.926	....	2.267	8.388	4.973	....	.....	1.062	.169	....
31	Przemysl	....	4.602	....	7.982	19.780	10.704	5.591	.....	3.270	.679	....
32	Przemyslany	.203	.965	1.306	.....	3.054	2.100	1.212	.....	.476	.173	....
33	Peczenizyn	....	.996	....	1.028	5.320	.....	1.616	.....	.304	.173	....
34	Przeworsk	.209	1.321	.544	.....	5.514	2.096	1.837	.....	.619	.173	....
35	Radziechow	.409	2.250	3.287	.....	9.304	5.259	2.993	.....	1.154	.341	.500
36	Rudki	....	.444	....	.724	3.448	1.057	....	.....	.150	.179	....
37	Rohatyn	....	1.712	....	1.105	6.294	.....	....	.....	.588	.338	....
38	Rawa Ruska	.078	1.025	....	.....	8.120	.....	.800	.....	.774	.174	....
39	Sniatyn	....	1.555	....	2.305	12.078	.....	....	.....	.900	.168	....
40	Stary Sambor	....	1.800	2.504	.457	14.044	.....	....	.....	1.222	.171	....
41	Stanislawow	....	3.874	....	6.267	18.978	11.812	....	.....	2.899	.682	....
42	Sokal	....	1.933	....	2.838	9.230	5.797	....	.....	1.368	.338	....
43	Sambor	.611	3.130	5.225	1.257	13.208	7.338	4.507	.....	1.666	.514	....
44	Sanok	....	2.400	....	4.400	14.077	.....	....	.....	.466	.343	1.000
45	Skole	....	.860	.588	.076	5.540	.....	....	.....	.151	....	....
46	Stryj	.310	1.919	1.372	1.390	9.457	.....	4.430	.....	.932	.169	.210
47	Tlumacz	....	1.433	....	1.067	9.236	.....	....	.....	1.051	.173	....
48	Trembowla	....	.732	....	.895	6.132	.....	....	.....	.459	....	....
49	Tarnopol	.508	2.854	4.615	.286	12.267	5.962	3.926	.....	1.534	.172	.250
50	Turka	.522	2.891	4.289	.....	12.058	4.196	3.899	.....	1.501	.504	....
51	Zydaczow	....	1.350	....	2.191	8.324	.....	....	.....	.429	.179	....
52	Zbaraz	.206	1.048	1.742	.....	8.023	2.303	1.500	.....	.768	.176	.400
53	Zloczow	.517	2.896	4.376	.419	11.876	6.656	3.866	.....	1.338	.523	....
54	Zborow	....	3.129	....	1.524	20.706	.....	2.405	.....	2.131	.340	....
55	Zolkiew	....	1.322	....	1.734	8.788	.....	1.800	.....	.916	.343	....
	Total	**7.298**	**102.834**	**81.812**	**78.896**	**535.971**	**115.385**	**87.857**	**1.040**	**55.464**	**12.905**	**3.860**

POLAND

Deliveries from WARSAW Warehouse, Month of April, 1921

Table 453

Receipt No.	Local Committee	Commodities in Net Metric Tons of 1,000 Kilograms or 2,204.6 Pounds										
		Cocoa	Sugar	Milk		Flour	Beans, Peas	Rice	Pork Products	Vegetable Oil	Salt	Misc.*
				Evap.	Cond.							
1	Aleksandrow	.203	.795	1.393	.362	1.768	.....	2.153	.312	.192	....	....
2	Bogdanow	.203	2.977	4.811	.838	12.549	.....	3.385	1.436	.514	....	....
3	Chmielnik	.203	1.080	1.981	....	3.996	.....	1.361	.....	.338	....	....
4	Ciechanow	.203	1.059	1.720	....	2.854	1.469	1.494	.289	.177	....	....
5	Czestochowa	1.829	5.606	8.991	2.648	.....	.....	19.797	2.610	1.313	....	....
6	Grojec	.610	2.891	5.007	1.257	12.443	6.827	4.244	1.340	.662	.975	....
7	Gostynin	.406	1.969	3.461	.248	.....	.....	4.491	1.035	.518	.614	....
8	Garwolin	.383	4.500	7.206	1.200	18.894	.....	3.143	.920	....	....	....
9	Glebokie	.....	2.736	4.506	.953	11.584	.....	3.894	1.360	.500	.829	....
10	Jedrzejow	.407	1.895	3.135	.724	3.993	.....	4.895	.940	.341	....	....
11	Kolno	.407	1.947	3.178	.590	.....	4.577	2.601	.681	.683	....	....
12	Kozienice	.406	2.122	3.461	.724	8.922	4.938	3.017	.838	.518	....	....
13	Konskie	.508	2.636	4.071	.476	3.993	.....	6.659	1.049	.674	....	....
14	Kielce	.711	3.469	5.443	.724	.....	.....	8.740	1.661	.662	....	....
15	Kutno	.711	4.255	6.879	1.219	8.995	.....	5.501	1.257	1.692	....	....
16	Konin	.093	.540	.914	.248	2.294	.....	.780	.148	.168	....	....
17	Kolo	.203	.904	1.372	.248	3.575	1.995	1.186	.447	.167	....	....
18	Kalisz	.102	2.553	.....	....	.....	.....	.822	1.288	....	....	....
19	Lida	.914	4.882	.....	1.448	3.982	5.519	6.600	2.097	1.027	....	....
20	Lapy	.508	2.334	3.788	.724	9.843	5.472	3.282	.758	.845	....	....
21	Lukow	1.118	6.751	11.103	2.400	14.227	.....	8.736	2.464	2.054	....	.100
22	Lomza	1.016	4.950	8.098	1.676	20.874	11.542	7.018	1.683	1.708	....	.100
23	Lowicz	.305	1.549	2.547	.476	.....	3.690	2.210	.878	....	....	....
24	Łódź	1.627	7.945	12.126	1.429	.....	30.456	23.994	5.019	.343	....	....
25	Laski	.203	1.108	1.698	.248	4.551	.....	2.748	.442	.336	....	....
26	Leczyca	.102	.602	1.045	.248	2.658	.....	.....	.311	.168	....	....
27	Lubartow	.203	.810	1.437	.476	1.734	.....	2.145	.310	.170	....	....
28	Minsk Mazowiecka	.508	2.504	4.115	.209	.....	.....	6.360	1.217	.344	....	....
29	Mlawa	.203	1.000	1.720	....	.....	.....	2.123	.502	.171	....	....
30	Makow	.203	1.100	1.720	.324	4.472	2.485	1.515	.441	.175	....	....
31	Opoczno	.102	1.148	1.154	....	2.789	.....	3.466	.147	.348	....	....
32	Ostrowiec	.813	4.134	6.422	.724	17.277	9.657	5.708	1.834	.845	....	....
33	Ostroleka	.305	1.732	2.721	.362	.....	4.044	2.413	.613	.510	....	....
34	Ostrow	.813	1.809	4.506	....	3.016	.....	5.716	.917	1.145	....	....
35	Oszmiany	.406	4.242	6.923	1.429	17.870	.....	5.988	1.894	.694	1.504	....
36	Pinczow	.305	1.685	2.721	.362	3.622	.....	4.400	.860	.343	....	....
37	Piotrkow	.592	2.773	1.850	.724	.....	6.384	3.713	1.230	.647	.972	....
38	Pultusk	.406	2.025	3.244	.590	8.414	4.630	2.817	.918	.345	....	....
39	Poznanskie	.609	2.619	4.289	.609	11.201	1.672	3.654	1.788	....	....	.817
40	Plonsk	.204	1.195	1.916	.286	5.154	2.815	1.622	.453	.345	....	....
41	Płock	.610	3.161	5.159	.953	13.419	7.446	4.511	1.390	.670	....	....
42	Pabjanice	.508	2.457	3.396	1.200	10.351	5.798	3.603	1.173	.172	....	....
43	Pulawy	.305	1.665	2.808	.629	3.534	.....	4.342	.602	.502	....	....
44	Parczew	.813	3.786	.....	....	4.984	.....	9.331	1.660	.866	.521	....
45	Radom	.891	4.398	6.770	.724	23.282	.....	11.093	1.891	1.049	....	....
46	Rawa Mazowiecka	.102	1.185	.....	....	9.978	4.785	1.619	.630	.169	....	.04[illegible]
47	Ruda Pabjanska	.102	.673	1.132	.362	1.384	.....	1.728	.381	.164	....	....
48	Rzgow	.149	.805	1.372	.248	1.818	.....	2.206	.429	.172	....	....
49	Radomsk	....	.622	1.589	.171	.....	.....	2.995	.299	.179	....	....
50	Swieciany	.813	4.230	6.923	1.429	17.848	.....	.....	2.204	.689	1.200	....
51	Sokolow	.305	1.725	2.896	.362	.....	.....	4.437	.619	.658	....	....
52	Siedlce	1.016	3.438	7.663	....	21.000	11.553	7.130	1.688	1.537	....	....
53	Sandomierz	.406	1.935	.....	....	.....	2.253	4.941	1.027	.336	....	....
54	Sierpc	.508	2.565	4.115	.724	10.753	5.988	3.608	1.081	.685	.060	....
55	Sochaczew	.508	2.535	3.766	.972	.....	.....	3.323	1.210	.343	....	....
56	Strykow	.203	1.048	1.720	.362	4.451	2.476	1.525	.434	.172	....	....
57	Sieradz	.203	1.057	1.720	.362	4.457	2.467	1.500	.452	.171	....	....
58	Torun	.406	1.812	1.306	....	3.022	.....	4.481	1.219	....	....	....
59	Tomaszow	.406	1.998	3.135	.476	5.000	.....	5.074	.949	.341	....	....

* Detail of miscellaneous commodities indicated by the following indexes: [b], corned beef; [c], codliver oil; [d], soap. Of the total, 2.094, .865 is corned beef, .300 is codliver oil, and .929 is soap.

POLAND

Deliveries from WARSAW Warehouse, Month of April, 1921

Table 453—*Continued*

Receipt No.	Local Committee	Cocoa	Sugar	Milk Evap.	Milk Cond.	Flour	Beans, Peas	Rice	Pork	Vegetable	Salt	Misc.
		Commodities in Net Metric Tons of 1,000 Kilograms or 2,204.6 Pounds										
60	Wierzbnik	.406	2.129	3.396	.476	9.048	5.003	2.987	1.082	.343	....	....
61	Wielun	.203	1.048	1.720	.362	4.441	2.468	1.515	.449	.332	....	....
62	Wyszkow	.203	.988	1.829	.762	4.250	2.266	1.504	.300	.342	....	....
63	Wloclawek	.398	1.905	3.048	.609	7.840	4.365	2.626	.912	.336	....	....
64	Wilno	1.524	11.431	15.892	....	48.234	.678	.366	5.126	2.317	4.530	.100[c]
65	Wegrow	.508	2.475	3.984	.724	10.436	5.775	3.486	.905	.831	....	....
66	Wloszczowa	.203	1.708	2.743	.476	.....	.....	4.397	.....	.363	....	....
67	Warsaw Child. Inst.	4.068	21.672	32.463	21.673	120.274	40.443	28.078	12.258	1.486	6.518	.929[d]
68	Warsaw Feeding Stat.	2.337	13.192	20.355	2.096	10.482	31.348	17.485	7.862	....	3.084	....
69	Zgierz	.203	2.860	2.308	....	10.759	.....	3.600	.473	.167	....	....
	Total	**37.360**	**203.334**	**295.880**	**63.355**	**588.589**	**243.284**	**327.882**	**93.092**	**37.074**	**20.807**	**2.094***

POLAND

Table 454

Deliveries from BREST Warehouse, Month of May, 1921

Receipt No.	Local Committee	Cocoa	Sugar	Milk Evap.	Milk Cond.	Flour	Beans, Peas	Rice	Pork Products	Vegetable Oil	Salt
		Commodities in Net Metric Tons of 1,000 Kilograms or 2,204.6 Pounds									
1	Augustow	.508	.906	.893	....	6.995	.....	.....	.964	.....	.....
2	Baranowicze	1.141	5.898	9.709	2.153	15.370	.....	22.155	2.101	1.715	.....
3	Biala Podlaska	.922	4.676	4.920	....	19.685	.....	16.926	1.899	1.182	1.560
4	Bialowieza	.529	2.547	4.180	.953	10.645	.....	4.996	1.348	.340	.555
5	Bialystok	.712	5.798	.....	....	26.946	.....	21.365	1.430	1.194	.....
6	Bielsk	1.222	5.911	9.665	....	24.632	.....	19.230	1.396	1.527	1.972
7	Bilgoraj	.404	1.850	3.178	.953	7.885	4.309	.574	.....	1.182	.....
8	Brzesc Litewski	1.944	9.527	16.044	....	40.510	.....	17.397	2.643	1.183	3.180
9	Brzostowica	.413	2.003	3.418	.610	8.964	.....	5.486	.960	.510	.....
10	Chelm	1.221	1.788	8.664	....	23.011	.....	22.257	2.729	1.201	.....
11	Dubno	.405	3.343	3.549	....	14.118	.....	.....	1.612	.508	1.200
12	Grajewo	.302	1.294	2.046	.362	6.297	3.001	.....	.....	.835	.....
13	Grodno	1.249	5.829	6.226	....	27.432	13.558	4.791	1.917	.853	2.400
14	Hrubieszow	.406	1.887	3.135	....	8.012	.....	7.123	.797	.508	.....
15	Kobryn	1.001	5.078	4.136	....	21.439	.....	7.097	1.808	1.214	1.695
16	Kowel	3.183	16.063	11.995	....	45.185	.....	59.698	8.170	2.205	5.500
17	Krasnystaw	.305	1.400	2.112	....	6.124	.....	5.443	.635	.342	.....
18	Krzemieniec	.391	3.018	5.072	....	12.671	.....	4.208	1.383	.682	1.050
19	Luboml	1.533	7.655	12.409	2.400	32.189	17.858	10.829	3.204	1.717	.....
20	Luck	1.027	5.134	6.509	....	21.673	.....	10.281	2.560	.859	1.800
21	Nieswierz	.611	2.970	4.833	.953	12.518	.....	4.186	1.253	.680	.....
22	Nowogrodek	.396	3.146	1.154	....	4.934	.....	4.664	1.276	.....	.....
23	Olyka	.607	1.466	4.659	.705	11.817	.....	11.245	1.590	.....	1.050
24	Ostrog	.606	2.988	1.306	....	12.545	.....	8.890	1.267	.676	1.050
25	Pinsk	1.660	8.357	13.889	3.105	35.581	19.646	12.011	3.353	2.369	2.955
26	Pruzany	1.533	7.205	12.235	....	33.684	.....	11.401	4.017	1.189	2.790
27	Rowno	1.285	4.983	4.985	1.429	18.350	.....	21.123	2.741	1.528	2.250
28	Sarny	.815	4.009	6.575	....	16.897	.....	15.027	1.931	.835	1.425
29	Slonim	1.118	1.534	8.904	1.429	18.592	.....	20.810	2.060	1.520	1.860
30	Sokolka	.102	1.308	1.480	....	......	.....	.....	.316	.....	.....
31	Stolpce	.603	2.968	4.833	.953	12.508	.....	4.214	1.374	.670	.....
32	Suwalki	.708	2.383	3.940	....	13.372	.....	4.871	1.280	.....	.391
33	Tomaszow Lubelski	.606	2.822	4.985	1.676	10.470	6.634	4.198	.....	1.831	.....
34	Wlodawa	.913	4.401	7.249	1.429	18.778	.....	16.716	1.932	.847	.....
35	Wlodzimierz	1.534	7.535	8.839	....	31.646	.....	28.122	4.026	1.027	2.625
36	Wolkowysk	.711	1.708	5.660	....	5.530	3.592	.....	.966	.520	.....
37	Zamosc	.203	.803	1.393	.362	3.556	.....	3.150	.....	.167	.....
	Total	**32.829**	**152.191**	**214.783**	**19.469**	**640.561**	**68.598**	**410.484**	**66.935**	**33.616**	**37.308**

POLAND

Table 455 Deliveries from KRAKÓW Warehouse, Month of May, 1921

Receipt No.	Local Committee	Commodities in Net Metric Tons of 1,000 Kilograms or 2,204.6 Pounds										
		Cocoa	Sugar	Milk		Flour	Beans, Peas	Rice	Corn Grits	Pork Products	Vegetable Oil	Misc.*
				Evap.	Cond.							
1	Będzin	.500	2.983	4.811	....	12.367	.....	2.094	.....	.647	1.198	....
2	Biała	.412	1.884	3.004	.457	7.911	.....	2.620	4.283	.920	.341	....
3	Bochnia	.206	1.144	1.763	....	6.279	.....	.....	.....	.793	....	....
4	Brzesko	.207	.812	2.264	.457	5.163	.....	1.732	2.828	.481	.168	....
5	Cieszyn	.524	2.367	3.788	.648	9.881	.....	6.683	2.007	.636	.872	....
6	Chrzanów	.306	1.400	2.264	....	5.852	.....	1.961	.....	.959	....	....
7	Dabrowa Górnicza	.516	.974	5.182	....	12.374	.....	4.502	.....	1.261	.325	....
8	Dębica	.103	.535	1.088	.400	1.570	.....	.....	.....	.322	....	....
9	Gorlice	.205	.609	1.132	....	2.608	.....	.912	.....	.329	....	....
10	Grzybów	.206	1.099	1.676	....	4.632	.....	1.518	.....	.637	.168	....
11	Jasło	.101	.487	.697	....	1.909	.....	.644	.....	.305	....	....
12	Jordanów	.103	.494	.718	....	1.978	.....	1.747	.....	.154	.169	....
13	Kalwarja	....	.245	.457	.114	.955	.....	.....	.....	.166	....	....
14	Kraków	2.161	9.739	16.763	3.886	51.309	2.258	23.314	9.995	6.589	.347	....
15	Krosno	.208	1.224	1.829	....	4.128	.....	1.632	.....	.643	.180	....
16	Krzeszowice	.102	.444	.675	....	1.611	.....	.....	.....	.317	....	....
17	Leżajsk	.103	.822	1.198	....	3.336	.....	1.055	.....	....	.168	....
18	Maków	.104	.582	.....	....	2.289	.....	.736	.....	....	....	....
19	Mielec	.101	.552	.871	.019	2.391	.....	.....	.....	.326	.168	.375[d]
20	Miechów	.204	1.217	2.133	.724	7.981	.....	1.787	.....	.162	.698	....
21	Muszyna	....	.366	.632	....	1.693	.....	.228	.....	.168	....	....
22	Myślenice	.104	.489	.871	....	2.291	.....	.735	.285	.317	.167	....
23	Niepołomice	.102	.243	.392	....	1.067	.....	.....	.....	.156	....	....
24	Nisko	.201	1.156	2.177	.876	5.610	.....	1.283	.....	....	.684	....
25	Nowy Sącz	.514	2.724	6.531	....	11.586	.....	3.997	.....	1.457	.336	1.155
26	Nowy Targ	.309	1.707	3.004	....	5.503	.....	2.099	.....	1.129	.172	....
27	Olkusz	.411	2.272	3.549	....	8.989	.....	2.994	.....	.788	.692	....
28	Oświęcim	.308	1.323	2.046	.171	7.785	.....	1.823	.....	.638	....	....
29	Oświęcim (Baraki)	.199	.774	1.132	....	3.198	.....	.....	.....	.480	....	....
30	Rzeszów	.625	3.190	4.746	.114	13.259	.....	.....	.....	1.612	.521	....
31	Skawina	.101	.243	.....	....	.574	.....	.....	.....	.156	....	....
32	Sosnowice	1.248	....	10.363	.743	24.996	.....	.....	.....	1.609	....	....
33	Sucha	....	.036	.....	....	2.030	.....	.....	.....	....	....	....
34	Tarnobrzeg	.206	1.024	1.546	....	3.736	.....	1.394	.....	.647	.169	....
35	Tarnów	.824	3.984	6.988	....	15.036	.....	5.841	.....	2.212	.511	.300
36	Trzebinia	.197	.830	1.219	....	3.435	.....	.621	.....	.308	.340	....
37	Wadowice	.203	1.224	2.177	.686	5.336	.....	.....	.....	.799	.169	....
38	Wieliczka	.208	.852	1.263	....	3.545	.....	1.137	.....	.481	....	....
39	Zawiercie	.307	1.217	.....	....	3.009	.....	2.411	.....	.313	.339	....
40	Zywiec	.409	2.029	2.982	....	8.373	.....	2.706	.....	1.281	....	.500
	Total	**12.847**	**55.296**	**103.930**	**9.296**	**277.575**	**2.258**	**80.206**	**19.398**	**30.209**	**8.902**	**2.330**

* Detail of miscellaneous commodities indicated by the following indexes: [a], salt; [d], soap. Of the total, 2.330, 1.955 is salt and .375 is soap.

POLAND

Table 456 — Deliveries from LWÓW Warehouse, Month of May, 1921

Receipt No.	Local Committee	Cocoa	Sugar	Milk: Evap.	Milk: Cond.	Flour	Corn Grits	Rice	Pork Products	Vegetable Oil	Salt
		Commodities in Net Metric Tons of 1,000 Kilograms or 2,204.6 Pounds									
1	Belz	.102	.603	.718	....	2.744	.....	.718	.161	.168	....
2	Boryslaw	.408	.484	1.742	....	12.631	5.786	5.076	.142	.170	....
3	Bobrka	.207	.437	.....	.533	6.710	.....	2.272	.149	.167	....
4	Busk	.090	.427	.631	....	2.290	.....	1.070	.162	....	....
5	Buczacz	.616	.533	1.110	.552	3.304	6.640	4.232	.396	.846	....
6	Brody	.513	.202	3.483	.572	8.071	3.061	3.599	....	.543	1.000
7	Brzozow	.307	1.888	2.678	....	8.138	4.440	2.526	.156	.523	....
8	Brzezany	.710	3.602	5.377	....	25.262	.....	.....	1.904	.511	....
9	Cieszanow	.204	1.052	1.089	....	4.128	2.393	1.346	.162	.172	....
10	Czortkow	.308	....	.....	.895	5.969	.....	.....	....	.173	....
11	Dobromil	.103	.500	.762	....	3.375	.....	.690	.164	.170	....
12	Dolina	.307	1.206	.740	....	5.471	.....	3.373	.447	.169	....
13	Drohobycz	.186	.368	....	.190	4.014	.....	....	....	.170	....
14	Grodek Jagiellonski	.306	1.586	2.308	....	10.207	.....	2.099	.790	.167	....
15	Halicz	.205	1.103	1.655	....	7.340	.....	1.500	.810	....	....
16	Janow	.104	.540	.784	....	2.244	1.288	.722	.313	....	....
17	Jaroslaw	.613	3.168	5.638	....	21.162	.....	4.549	1.726	....	....
18	Jaworow	.410	1.418	2.525	....	11.480	.....	2.418	.951	.173	....
19	Kolomyja	.614	2.415	4.572	.095	20.275	.....	....	.605	.346	....
20	Kamionka Strumilowa	....	.456	.283	....	.813	.364	.275	....	....	....
21	Kalusz	.306	1.815	1.067	....	5.214	3.565	2.136	.149	.341	....
22	Kosow	.513	1.346	3.919	.114	9.407	5.098	3.615	.316	1.206	....
23	Lwów City	1.332	8.062	20.398	14.402	36.074	40.937	30.612	2.767	5.145	1.000
23b	Lwów District	.512	2.699	9.361	1.200	11.516	.....	3.884	2.032	.512	....
24	Lisko	.305	1.007	1.742	....	2.879	.....	3.931	.420	.172	....
25	Nadworna	.717	1.784	.218	....	24.030	.....	....	.471	....	....
26	Peczenizyn	.308	1.304	1.328	.648	9.604	.....	....	.314	.344	....
27	Podhajce	.405	1.487	2.874	1.429	8.399	3.686	3.234	.515	.339	....
28	Przemysl	.921	2.391	8.186	....	32.290	.....	7.343	.950	....	....
29	Przemyslany	.102	.303	.479	....	1.145	.....	1.772	.156	.166	....
30	Przeworsk	.204	.742	....	....	8.446	.....	1.716	.651	.170	....
31	Radziechow	.410	1.426	2.220	....	10.740	.....	2.089	.320	.511	....
32	Rawa Ruska	.411	1.548	1.959	....	12.267	.....	....	.297	.350	....
33	Rohatyn	.310	.....	.....	.838	.463	2.838	1.986	....	.165	....
34	Rudki	.210	.910	.697	.343	3.708	2.098	1.211	.129	.339	.100
35	Sanok	.513	2.552	4.267	....	21.942	.....	....	.636	.510	....
36	Sambor	.613	3.117	6.618	....	21.490	.....	4.062	1.573	.327	1.000
37	Skalat	.205	.863	.....	....	.....	1.010	1.163	....	.171	....
38	Skole	.203	1.308	1.981	....	5.603	3.154	1.792	.461	.344	....
39	Sniatyn	.307	1.581	2.112	....	2.859	.....	3.944	.287	.168	....
40	Sokal	.313	....	2.177	....	1.146	.....	1.976	....	.174	....
41	Stary Sambor	.311	1.710	2.525	....	10.512	.....	2.400	.959	.171	....
42	Stanislawow	.820	2.307	7.119	....	26.606	.....	2.194	1.598	.507	....
43	Stryj	.418	.723	3.440	....	13.926	.....	....	.643	.168	....
44	Tarnopol	.411	1.873	2.721	....	15.705	.....	....	.937	.342	.300
45	Tlumacz	.317	....	....	....	3.360	.....	2.541	.317	.169	....
46	Trembowla	.204	.906	.283	....	7.028	.....	....	.161	.175	....
47	Turka	.617	2.915	4.289	....	14.053	3.124	5.679	1.435	.512	....
48	Zaleszczyki	.041	.427	.435	1.334	1.192	.....	1.229	....	.338	....
49	Zborow	.511	.910	2.329	....	9.135	.....	....	.326	.171	....
50	Zloczow	.511	2.710	4.789	....	18.322	.....	3.875	1.464	.343	....
51	Zolkiew	.206	.404	.784	.781	5.604	.....	....	....	.336	....
52	Zydaczow	.205	1.040	.065	....	1.406	.....	3.200	.293	.170	....
	Total	**20.005**	**74.158**	**136.476**	**23.927**	**521.699**	**89.482**	**134.049**	**29.617**	**19.324**	**3.400**

POLAND

Deliveries from WARSAW Warehouse, Month of May, 1921

Table 457

Receipt No.	Local Committee	Commodities in Net Metric Tons of 1,000 Kilograms or 2,204.6 Pounds										
		Cocoa	Sugar	Milk		Flour	Beans, Peas	Rice	Pork Products	Vegetable Oil	Salt	Soap
				Evap.	Cond.							
1	Aleksandrow	....	.....	.....	....	3.591	.....	.....	....	....	....	.....
2	Bogdanow	.610	2.962	4.811	.838	12.579	3.514	4.184	1.431	.670	....	.....
3	Brzeziny	.203	1.080	1.948	....	4.524	2.510	1.500	.315	.346	....	.....
4	Chmielnik	.305	1.350	2.395	....	7.914	1.437	.644	....	.342	....	.....
5	Ciechanow	.203	.513	1.089	.362	1.815	1.019	.503	.325	.171	....	.....
6	Czestochowa	1.524	5.088	12.452	2.629	38.792	.....	6.619	2.878	1.355	....	.....
7	Garwolin	.902	2.173	4.637	1.200	13.810	.....	6.298	1.540	1.520	....	.....
8	Glebokie	.508	2.738	5.508	.953	11.586	.....	3.902	1.451	.342	....	.....
9	Gostynin	.305	1.308	3.004	.190	7.465	.....	1.054	.624	.341	....	.....
10	Grodziska	.610	2.910	4.659	....	12.294	3.392	1.002	1.274	.514	....	.....
11	Grojec	.610	2.914	5.007	1.429	12.450	.....	4.263	1.400	.680	1.030	.....
12	Jedrzejow	.406	1.665	2.808	.724	7.045	3.706	2.395	.822	.341	....	.....
13	Kielce	.711	3.454	5.443	.724	14.452	.....	2.017	1.690	.681	....	.....
14	Kolo	.203	.942	1.742	....	3.948	.....	1.235	.466	.173	....	.....
15	Kalisz	.203	1.612	3.701	....	10.925	.....	2.528	1.106	....	....	.....
16	Kolno	.305	1.455	2.177	.286	7.551	.....	2.520	.421	.516	.139	.....
17	Konskie	.508	2.610	4.071	.476	10.890	.....	3.620	1.100	.679	....	.....
18	Konin	.101	.540	.914	....	2.287	.....	.550	.161	.096	....	.....
19	Kozienice	.406	2.060	3.461	.724	8.910	.....	3.004	.796	.510	.430	.....
20	Lapy	.406	2.341	3.788	.724	9.853	.....	3.315	.761	.849	....	.....
21	Lida	1.016	5.130	8.251	1.429	21.574	.....	7.183	2.346	1.186	1.650	.....
22	Leczyca	....	.621	.....	....	.753	.....	1.640	....	....	....	.....
23	Lomza	.610	1.406	.....	....	20.876	3.591	.....	.392	....	....	.....
24	Lodz	1.829	5.670	17.351	....	63.822	.....	.....	3.565	.664	....	.....
25	Lask	.305	1.309	2.090	.362	5.482	.....	1.803	.644	.336	.617	.....
26	Lowicz	.305	1.560	2.547	.476	6.612	.....	1.135	.908	.167	.300	.....
27	Lubartow	.203	.340	1.415	.476	3.480	.....	.453	.312	.165	....	.....
28	Lublin	1.219	6.075	9.644	3.600	26.010	.....	8.984	2.859	1.205	....	.....
29	Makow	.203	1.237	2.003	.362	5.205	.....	1.740	.598	.153	....	.....
30	Mlawa	.203	1.057	1.720	.362	4.461	.....	1.421	.473	.166	....	.....
31	Minsk Mazowiecki	.406	1.888	4.115	.419	3.627	5.863	1.597	.943	.342	1.069	.....
32	Opoczno	.305	1.521	2.373	.248	6.413	.....	2.092	.626	.346	....	.....
33	Ostrowiec	.406	.924	6.422	.724	17.303	2.801	3.325	.163	....	....	.....
34	Ostrow	.711	3.817	6.204	1.200	16.105	.....	5.402	1.268	1.354	.209	.....
35	Ostroleka	.305	1.620	2.504	.248	6.756	.....	1.110	.466	.494	.400	.....
36	Oszmiany	.813	4.193	6.923	1.429	17.863	.....	6.008	2.099	.700	.810	.....
37	Pabjanice	.480	2.474	4.223	1.200	5.251	.....	3.311	1.433	.174	....	.....
38	Parczew	.813	2.493	3.875	1.676	17.731	.....	1.514	1.538	.698	....	.....
39	Piotrkow	.508	2.787	5.268	.....	11.712	.....	1.950	1.277	.677	....	.....
40	Pinczow	.305	1.722	2.721	.362	7.219	.....	2.413	.790	.336	....	.....
41	Plonsk	.102	.889	1.023	.286	5.022	.....	1.440	.316	.176	....	.....
42	Plock	.610	3.183	6.117	....	13.440	3.722	4.522	1.445	.684	....	.....
43	Poznanskie	.406	1.898	3.091	.610	4.026	.....	2.553	1.296	....	....	.....
44	Pomorze	.406	1.813	2.634	....	3.729	.....	2.424	1.241	....	....	.....
45	Pulawy	.305	1.663	2.787	.724	3.523	.....	2.185	.763	.340	....	.....
46	Pultusk	.305	1.794	2.961	.610	7.694	4.238	2.598	.780	.341	....	.....
47	Przasnysz	.102	1.193	2.133	....	5.577	.635	.370	.475	.169	....	.....
48	Radom	.900	4.353	7.467	....	18.227	.....	.....	1.934	1.021	....	.....
49	Radomsk	.102	1.614	2.721	.972	.....	.....	2.622	.318	.674	....	.....
50	Rawa Mazowiecka	.406	1.690	5.225	....	8.683	.....	2.224	.408	.343	....	.....
51	Ruda Pabjanska	....	.....	.....	....	2.718	.....	.....	....	....	....	.....
52	Rzgow	....	.....	.....	....	3.600	.....	.....	....	....	....	.....
53	Sandomierz	.305	1.696	2.743	.476	7.167	.....	2.388	.788	.332	....	.....
54	Siedlce	1.016	3.789	7.750	2.400	21.617	.....	7.371	1.602	1.678	....	.....
55	Sierpc	.508	2.511	4.115	.724	10.761	.....	3.594	1.054	.669	....	.....
56	Sieradz	.203	1.047	1.720	.362	4.455	.....	1.473	.330	.171	....	.....
57	Sochaczew	.406	1.000	2.177	.952	10.645	.....	2.431	1.097	.345	....	.....
58	Sokolow	.406	1.845	2.939	.476	7.743	2.010	2.607	.631	.686	....	.....
59	Skiermiewice	.406	2.019	1.023	.590	8.496	.....	1.408	9.137	....	....	.....
60	Strykow	.203	1.010	1.720	.362	4.359	.....	1.419	.457	.173	....	.....
61	Swiecany	.813	4.210	6.923	1.448	17.820	45.151	5.983	2.307	.674	....	.....
62	Tomaszow	.102	2.000	3.984	....	12.188	4.383	2.356	.481	.511	....	.....

POLAND

Deliveries from WARSAW Warehouse, Month of May, 1921

Table 457—*Continued*

Receipt No.	Local Committee	Cocoa	Sugar	Milk Evap.	Milk Cond.	Flour	Beans, Peas	Rice	Pork Products	Vegetable Oil	Salt	Soap
		Commodities in Net Metric Tons of 1,000 Kilograms or 2,204.6 Pounds										
63	Wegrow	....	.....	3.418	....	10.390	.....	.....	....	....	....	.....
64	Wielun	.203	1.025	1.720	.362	4.441	.....	1.420	.311	.338	....	.....
65	Wilejka	.385	4.680	7.576	1.429	19.704	.....	6.600	2.129	1.002	....	.....
66	Wilno	2.337	11.917	19.876	4.801	50.510	.....	17.095	5.416	2.354	....	.....
67	Wirzbnik	.305	2.307	1.284	....	10.919	.....	3.603	1.070	.344	....	.....
68	Wloszczowa	.203	1.680	2.264	....	7.186	.....	.364	.786	.338	....	.....
69	Wloclawek	....	1.254	1.502	....	7.836	.....	1.593	.856	....	....	.....
70	Warsaw City	4.845	24.323	39.396	20.486	166.001	23.907	32.740	12.381	3.754	9.001	2.050
71	Warsaw Feeding Sta.	3.454	15.881	27.321	1.524	8.134	28.003	17.532	7.699	....	1.955	.....
72	Zdunska Wola	.203	1.080	1.938	....	4.524	2.520	1.425	.476	.174	.100	.....
73	Zgierz	.508	.324	3.265	....	9.771	.....	3.950	1.240	.169	....	.....
	Total	**40.431**	**193.248**	**344.067**	**65.425**	**951.842**	**102.402**	**242.528**	**92.262**	**36.750**	**17.093**	**2.050**

POLAND

Deliveries from BREST Warehouse, Month of June, 1921

Table 458

Receipt No.	Local Committee	Cocoa	Sugar	Milk Evap.	Milk Cond.	Flour	Beans, Peas	Rice	Pork Products	Vegetable Oil	Soap	Salt
		Commodities in Net Metric Tons of 1,000 Kilograms or 2,204.6 Pounds										
1	Augustow	.375	.788	1.154	....	5.441	4.456	2.561	.102	.533	.300	....
2	Baranowicze	1.186	5.880	9.709	2.153	24.851	13.740	1.457	2.153	1.783	.980	....
3	Biala Podlaska	.765	2.888	6.117	....	16.045	8.956	.643	.323	.706	.735	1.560
4	Bialowieza	.602	2.962	3.157	....	12.490	6.907	.....	1.834	.....	.490	.840
5	Bialystok	.764	2.537	9.949	1.829	25.918	14.377	.....	.....	2.130	1.190	....
6	Bielsk	1.211	4.711	9.775	2.400	24.800	13.640	.....	2.758	.686	.989	1.980
7	Brzesc Litewski	1.507	8.520	13.976	....	40.515	22.260	13.806	4.014	2.469	1.610	3.180
8	Brzostowica	.388	1.247	2.460	.514	6.195	4.243	.....	.....	1.010	.350	....
9	Chelm	1.404	6.210	8.643	....	30.237	16.917	9.902	3.085	1.728	1.155	1.371
10	Dubno	.184	2.307	3.418	....	12.053	5.674	3.590	.....	1.186	.490	1.050
11	Grajewo	.198	1.092	1.763	.305	3.604	2.526	1.533	.496	.183	.210	....
12	Grodno	.954	4.291	6.117	....	22.651	12.595	8.098	.....	2.208	1.050	....
13	Hrubieszow	.296	1.765	3.004	.800	4.900	4.106	.280	.830	.344	.350	.432
14	Kobryn	1.031	5.154	7.641	1.200	21.693	12.062	7.192	2.143	1.226	.840	1.695
15	Kowel	2.120	4.910	21.356	....	27.107	31.917	.....	.668	6.927	2.590	5.550
16	Krasnystaw	.288	1.406	2.373	.610	5.992	3.279	.323	.....	.996	.280	....
17	Krzemieniec	.653	2.865	3.374	....	12.675	7.033	4.209	1.395	.674	.490	1.050
18	Luboml	1.135	5.742	9.927	2.038	15.000	14.113	8.133	2.506	1.256	1.210	....
19	Luck	.878	1.879	3.810	....	18.449	10.264	3.764	1.469	.531	.840	1.800
20	Nieswierz	.467	2.266	4.833	.952	11.671	6.916	3.099	.914	.706	.490	....
21	Nowogrodek	.560	3.689	6.858	.324	15.367	8.479	5.080	.151	1.921	.595	....
22	Olyka	.375	.545	.588	.610	.....	5.078	.....	.839	.....	.420	.900
23	Pinsk	1.818	8.863	14.847	2.457	37.450	20.673	.....	4.154	1.861	1.470	2.805
24	Pruzany	1.401	7.571	11.974	1.772	31.517	17.500	10.502	4.158	.356	1.225	2.655
25	Rowno	1.264	6.022	10.210	1.429	27.724	15.115	7.836	2.463	1.258	1.050	2.250
26	Sarny	.931	4.688	7.554	.666	19.688	10.927	3.380	1.532	1.608	.770	1.650
27	Slonim	.656	1.776	.....	1.219	17.403	10.169	.....	.632	.....	.840	....
28	Sokolka	.277	.876	2.112	....	4.059	3.555	2.403	.464	.....	.280	....
29	Stolpy	.188	2.517	3.701	....	11.624	5.946	3.550	.....	1.710	.490	....
30	Suwalki	.295	1.741	3.048	....	6.158	5.177	1.827	.....	.683	.630	.254
31	Tomaszow Lubelski	.976	.890	3.984	....	.....	5.628	3.539	.486	.347	.490	....
32	Wlodawa	.754	1.790	6.161	1.219	15.028	8.856	.414	.617	.681	.735	....
33	Wlodzimierz Wolynski	1.313	2.613	10.406	....	11.938	15.433	.....	2.777	.182	1.260	2.700
34	Wolkowysk	.280	.304	4.550	.895	11.552	6.721	4.205	.318	.341	.490	.470
35	Zamosc	.100	.905	1.459	.305	3.801	2.095	.322	.332	.333	....	....
	Total	**27.594**	**114.210**	**220.008**	**23.698**	**555.646**	**357.333**	**111.648**	**43.613**	**38.563**	**27.384**	**34.192**

POLAND

Table 459 — Deliveries from KRAKÓW Warehouse, Month of June, 1921

Receipt No.	Local Committee	Commodities in Net Metric Tons of 1,000 Kilograms or 2,204.6 Pounds										
		Cocoa	Sugar	Milk		Flour	Beans, Peas	Rice	Pork Products	Vegetable Oil	Corn Grits	Misc.*
				Evap.	Cond.							
1	Bedzin	.522	2.420	2.003	.819	8.772	....	....	....	.865	8.745	.900[ad]
2	Biala	.410	1.256	1.655	1.867	8.074	....	....	....	1.046	7.159	.300[d]
3	Bochnia	.105	.439	.914	.972	3.806	....	.645	....	.173	2.757	.100[d]
4	Brzesko	.206	.821	1.132	1.372	5.216	....	1.792	....	.528	2.792	.200[d]
5	Chrzanow	.181	1.035	2.242	....	.....	2.268	1.357	....	.852	.....	.200[d]
6	Cieszyn	.515	1.666	2.112	2.419	10.265	....	....	....	1.196	9.136	.400[d]
7	Dabrowa Gorna	.454	1.217	2.221	....	.....	5.971	3.418	....	1.010	.....	.425[d]
8	Dembica	.091	....	....	....	.....	.491	....	....	....	.127	.050[d]
9	Gorlice	....	.195	....	....	1.367	....	....	....	....	1.234	.050[d]
10	Grzybow	.204	.609	1.110	.229	3.718	....	....	....	.681	3.305	.150[d]
11	Jaslo	.105	.100	.348	.343	1.511	....	....	.150	.172	1.366	.050[d]
12	Jordanow	.104	.299	....	.381	1.876	....	....	....	.171	1.027	.075[d]
13	Kalwarja	.103	.122	....	.248	.608	....	....	....	....	.797	.035[d]
14	Krakow	2.261	7.897	10.646	12.592	50.006	....	16.787	2.806	3.438	27.898	1.950[d]
15	Krosno	.181	.906	1.328	....	.....	2.194	1.195	....	.682	.....	.150[d]
16	Kszeszowice	.106	.202	.348	.343	1.549	....	....	.158	....	1.305	.050[d]
17	Makow	....	.200	.348	.381	1.866	....	....	....	.338	.985	.075[d]
18	Miechow	.207	.818	2.177	....	3.221	....	....	.458	.170	1.621	.200[a]
19	Mielec	.103	.122	.566	....	1.396	.840	....	....	.173	.500	.075[d]
20	Muszyna	.103	....	....	....	1.139	....	....	....	....	.936	.050[d]
21	Myslenice	.091	.366	.936	....	1.394	.765	.495	....	.175	.....	.070[d]
22	Niepolomice	....	....	.239	.305	1.080	....	....	....	.169	.964	.050[d]
23	Nowy Targ	.306	....	1.415	1.524	2.409	....	....	....	....	3.734	.200[d]
24	Nowy Sacz	.407	1.455	2.177	2.667	9.051	....	....	....	1.187	7.220	.375[d]
25	Olkusz	.363	1.782	2.852	....	3.017	4.172	2.516	.625	....	.....	.305[d]
26	Oswiecim Baraki	....	.165	....	.571	2.458	....	....	....	.344	2.258	.100[d]
27	Rzeszow	.308	1.459	2.612	....	3.963	4.189	....	....	.683	2.649	.300[d]
28	Skawina	....	....	.174	....	.320	....	.180	....	....	.....	.050[d]
29	Sosnowiec	.720	4.876	6.096	2.686	15.994	....	....	2.201	.166	17.697	.800[d]
30	Sucha	.103	.201	.218	.209	1.149	....	....	.153	....	.976	.050[d]
31	Szczakowa	.199	.488	.566	.534	2.881	....	....	....	.338	2.583	.050[d]
32	Tarnow	....	....	3.788	....	.....	3.060	....	....	....	.....	.280[d]
33	Wadowice	.309	.831	1.241	1.562	5.198	....	.900	.625	....	2.862	.400[ad]
34	Wieliczka	.102	.445	.610	.610	2.631	....	....	.313	....	2.389	.100[d]
35	Zakopane	.103	.245	....	....	.....	....	....	.148	.174	1.116	.075[d]
36	Zawiercie	....	.710	2.242	....	.....	3.248	1.875	....	.340	.....	.220[d]
37	Zywiec	.209	.910	2.133	....	5.571	....	....	....	....	4.945	.200[d]
	Total	**9.181**	**34.257**	**56.449**	**32.633**	**161.506**	**27.198**	**31.160**	**7.636**	**15.071**	**121.083**	**9.110***

* Detail of miscellaneous commodities indicated by the following indexes: [a], salt; [d], soap. Of the total, 9.110, .700 is salt and 8.410 is soap.

POLAND

Table 460 — Deliveries from LWÓW Warehouse, Month of June, 1921

eipt o.	Local Committee	Commodities in Net Metric Tons of 1,000 Kilograms or 2,204.6 Pounds										
		Cocoa	Sugar	Milk		Flour	Beans, Peas	Rice	Pork Products	Vegetable Oil	Corn Grits	Misc.*
				Cond.	Evap.							
1	Belz	.094	.378	....	.784	2.236	1.288	.594	.174	.189	.....	.105[d]
2	Borszczow	.109	.685	....	.....	2.793	.....	.761	.165	.176	1.656	.129[d]
3	Boryslaw	.373	1.028	....	.....	4.787	3.810	1.726	.846	.171	.....	.352[d]
4	Bobrka	.189	.903	....	1.197	2.904	2.300	.872	.455	.148	.....	.192[d]
5	Brody	.375	.516	....	2.046	4.895	4.807	2.402	.640	.162	.....	1.400[da]
6	Brzezany	....	.500	....	1.067	.....	6.726	2.976	....	.182	.....	.567[d]
7	Brzozow	.288	1.512	....	2.221	6.290	3.544	2.010	.774	.340	.....	.294[d]
8	Buczacz	.467	1.861	....	3.070	5.007	3.274	.....	1.338	....	2.440	.472[d]
9	Busk	....	.342	....	.501	1.402	.804	.456	.154	.166	.068	.200[a]
0	Chyrow	.055	.217	....	.414	1.122	.....	.363	.159	....	.640	....
1	Cieszanow	.198	1.085	.286	1.742	4.614	2.564	.119	.461	.177	1.400	.213[d]
2	Czortkow	....	.362	....	1.045	1.266	1.395	1.500	....	.175	1.620	.277[d]
3	Dolina	.169	.196	....	1.067	3.661	2.087	.889	.303	....	.....	.170[d]
4	Drohobycz	....	1.528	.400	1.676	3.719	3.614	1.955	....	....	.234	.282[d]
5	Grodek Jagiellonski	.291	1.255	....	1.850	5.250	1.454	1.678	.756	.171	1.480	.275[d]
6	Halicz	.047	1.019	....	.936	.....	1.030	1.183	.152	....	1.151	....
7	Janow	.050	.457	....	.631	1.779	.....	.576	.152	.164	1.055	....
8	Jaroslaw	....	2.199	.952	.392	1.714	5.991	2.541	.312	....	.397	.494[d]
9	Jaworow	....	1.594	....	2.395	6.542	3.698	2.097	.778	.344	.307	....
0	Kalusz	.276	.525	....	1.916	5.443	1.651	1.929	.680	.349	1.761	.282[d]
1	Kamionka Strumilowa	....	.275	....	.392	1.130	.655	.367	.151	....	.052	....
2	Kolomyja	.464	2.371	.381	3.788	12.760	5.712	3.366	1.678	.344	.....	.476[d]
3	Kopyczynce-Husiatyn	....	.887	....	.....	3.386	2.388	1.440	.305	.168	.209	.199[d]
4	Kosow	.390	1.221	.438	2.591	6.779	.....	2.295	.999	.165	3.913	.399[d]
5	Lisko	.278	1.165	....	1.850	5.219	2.938	.075	.606	.177	.....	.245[d]
6	Lwów (District)	.285	2.015	.953	.609	3.105	4.604	2.249	1.229	.164	.....	.411[d]
7	Lwów (City)	.748	3.812	10.992	13.911	15.053	1.580	1.200	3.768	....	.....	1.868[da]
8	Nadworna	....	1.345	.838	5.921	1.000	.....	5.254	1.216	....	9.357	....
9	Peczenizyn	.186	.638	....	1.306	4.474	2.520	1.534	.466	.157	.095	.210[d]
0	Podhajce	.372	1.301	....	2.896	7.869	.....	1.186	.495	.342	4.902	.360[d]
1	Przemysl	1.116	5.187	1.353	7.554	20.508	6.504	6.815	2.293	.501	6.484	.864[d]
2	Przeworsk	....	.734	....	.762	1.009	2.498	.150	.148	.172	.....	....
3	Radziechow	....	.389	....	.435	.699	2.647	.870	.158	.346	.....	.500[a]
4	Rawa Ruska	....	1.126	....	1.219	2.901	3.769	2.172	.567	.350	.219	....
5	Rohatyn	.095	.587	....	2.155	3.423	1.252	1.107	.170	.355	.694	.263[d]
6	Sambor	....	2.500	1.029	4.267	10.680	1.960	3.604	1.368	.343	3.933	.300[a]
7	Sanok	.474	1.000	.057	3.592	9.266	5.167	3.142	1.068	.358	.....	.430[d]
8	Skole	.186	1.035	....	1.458	4.301	2.497	1.466	.513	.358	.....	.212[d]
9	Sniatyn	.260	.599	....	1.720	5.204	2.980	1.665	.616	.175	.....	.245[d]
0	Stanislawow	.660	3.200	.895	4.485	13.706	7.656	4.350	1.385	.853	.....	.634[d]
1	Stary Sambor	....	1.445	....	2.112	5.957	.....	1.930	.784	.338	3.648	....
2	Stryj	....	1.577	.457	1.916	5.839	3.994	2.605	.771	.172	2.307	.300[a]
3	Sokal	....	.....	....	.....	4.051	.389	1.590	....	.339	.248	.235[d]
4	Tarnopol	....	1.657	....	2.525	2.528	5.637	3.359	.770	.343	.375	.820[da]
5	Tlumacz	.280	1.070	....	1.328	1.162	3.080	1.253	.784	.181	.....	.255[d]
6	Trembowla	....	....	.286	2.373	2.508	1.812	1.101	.313	.175	.161	.153[d]
7	Turka	....	2.909	....	4.289	12.101	.....	3.905	1.400	.499	7.402	....
8	Zaleszczyki	....	.143	....	.958	2.202	1.685	.775	....	....	.061	.141[d]
9	Zborow	.376	.....	....	.544	.....	5.046	2.876	.330	.347	.....	.420[d]
0	Zloczow	....	1.347	.248	.239	3.591	5.268	2.453	.916	....	.487	.353[d]
1	Zolkiew	.187	.407	....	.827	2.354	2.100	.915	.165	.180	.....	....
2	Zydaczow	.155	1.069	....	1.589	4.491	.....	1.447	.473	.172	2.520	....
	Total	**9.493**	**61.173**	**19.565**	**104.561**	**244.680**	**136.375**	**95.323**	**34.201**	**10.988**	**61.276**	**15.997***

* Detail of miscellaneous commodities indicated by the following in-
es: [a], salt; [d], soap. Of the total, 15.997, 3.150 is salt and 12.847 is
p.

POLAND

Deliveries from WARSAW Warehouse, Month of June, 1921

Table 461

Receipt No.	Local Committee	Commodities in Net Metric Tons of 1,000 Kilograms or 2,204.6 Pounds										
		Cocoa	Sugar	Milk		Flour	Beans, Peas	Rice	Pork Products	Vegetable Oil	Soap	Salt
				Evap.	Cond.							
1	Aleksandrow	.102	.906	1.567	.476	3.861	2.105	1.355	.465	.177	.141	...
2	Bogdanow	.610	2.990	4.811	.838	12.603	.....	4.183	1.372	.533	.500	...
3	Brzeziny	.178	.902	1.524	.362	3.929	2.175	1.316	.312	.348	.124	...
4	Chmielnik	.091	.801	.697	....	6.400	3.545	1.018	.467	.176	.315	...
5	Ciechanow	.187	.802	1.480	.362	3.523	1.898	1.410	.156	.171	.141	...
6	Częstochowa	1.309	6.614	11.974	2.096	27.876	14.879	9.346	3.035	1.410	1.075	...
7	Garwolin	.726	3.584	5.769	....	15.455	8.409	5.039	1.213	1.172	.700	...
8	Glebokie	.406	1.920	3.070	.476	8.150	.....	2.700	.917	.346	.325	...
9	Gostynin	.181	.789	1.154	....	7.105	3.948	1.098	.331	.167	.350	...
10	Grodzisk	.286	2.856	3.440	....	11.838	6.626	3.903	1.365	....	.419	...
11	Grojec	.453	2.306	3.962	....	.....	5.369	3.357	.463	.679	.495	...
12	Jedrzejow	.272	1.305	2.242	.571	7.034	3.113	1.923	....	.164	.293	...
13	Kalisz	.363	1.804	2.874	....	7.836	4.121	2.490	.826	.345	.360	...
14	Kielce	....	.599	1.437	....	11.582	6.461	1.521	.771	....	.560	...
15	Kolno	.272	1.464	2.308	....	6.056	3.365	2.010	.456	.418	.293	...
16	Kolo	.203	1.083	1.698	.248	4.506	2.509	1.492	.452	.343	.165	...
17	Konskie	.363	2.040	3.266	....	8.714	4.867	2.875	.819	.511	.420	...
18	Kozienice	.363	1.664	2.765	....	7.149	3.937	2.391	.660	.506	.338	...
19	Kutno	....	.....	.....	....	8.940	4.505	3.001	....	....	....	...
20	Lida	1.016	5.089	8.250	1.429	21.575	.....	7.215	2.314	1.203	.850	...
21	Lubartow	.181	.865	1.459	.381	3.663	2.021	1.251	.306	.174	.180	...
22	Lublin	1.016	2.507	.....	....	16.565	12.422	7.802	.459	1.059	.908	...
23	Lapy	.373	1.906	3.026	.591	9.852	4.376	3.321	.772	.676	.277	...
24	Lask	.181	1.044	1.720	.381	4.410	2.431	1.491	....	.166	.203	...
25	Leczyca	.094	.585	.980	.248	2.466	1.355	.860	.313	.168	.071	...
26	Łódź	2.054	8.127	12.409	8.401	69.978	38.325	23.985	4.826	.922	2.790	...
27	Lomza	.711	3.940	6.487	1.333	16.498	9.233	5.284	1.333	1.209	.698	...
28	Lowicz	.305	1.605	2.547	.476	6.655	3.662	2.227	.767	.168	.255	...
29	Lukow	.711	3.364	5.551	1.200	14.251	.....	4.789	1.253	1.005	.550	...
30	Makow	.280	1.178	2.003	.362	5.196	2.885	1.730	.630	.172	.205	...
31	Minsk Mazowiecki	.363	1.719	3.004	.209	4.987	5.592	8.397	1.076	.180	.478	...
32	Mlawa	.203	1.005	1.633	.362	4.466	2.461	1.335	.447	.171	.163	...
33	Opoczno	.280	1.209	1.894	.191	6.351	2.885	1.678	....	.347	.207	...
34	Ostroleka	.283	1.624	2.504	.248	6.740	3.783	2.231	.616	.529	.281	...
35	Ostrowiec Radomski	.454	2.099	5.138	.572	13.840	3.873	2.817	.466	.166	.630	...
36	Ostrow Lomzynski	.400	3.180	4.746	.953	12.280	7.140	4.331	.915	1.063	.499	...
37	Oszmiany	.813	4.222	6.923	1.428	17.838	.....	6.017	2.157	.698	.700	.76
38	Pabjanice	.372	2.178	2.460	1.200	10.679	5.852	2.544	.928	....	.400	.41
39	Parczew	.635	3.240	5.704	....	6.931	7.549	4.816	1.341	.864	.704	...
40	Piotrkow	.508	2.813	.....	.724	11.724	6.496	3.901	1.251	.676	.420	.46
41	Płock	.610	3.190	5.159	.953	13.445	7.455	4.502	1.391	.521	.513	...
42	Plonsk	.187	.705	.675	.229	4.026	2.235	1.261	.303	.179	.203	...
43	Poznan	.406	.....	3.113	.610	8.044	4.458	2.730	....	....	.280	...
44	Pulawy	.406	1.801	3.004	.724	7.620	4.201	2.580	.621	.514	.298	...
45	Pultusk	.272	1.489	2.373	....	6.575	3.401	2.045	.658	.334	.293	...
46	Radom	.406	1.751	.....	....	18.223	10.181	6.023	.521	.916	.694	...
47	Radomsk	.610	2.995	4.833	.953	12.835	.....	4.210	.966	1.017	.500	.29
48	Rawa Mazowiecka	.406	2.392	4.093	1.200	10.155	5.584	3.483	1.280	.338	.408	...
49	Ruda Pabjanska	....	.597	1.067	.362	2.593	1.447	.912	.463	.015	.093	...
50	Rzgow	.102	.563	.893	.133	2.352	1.330	.780	.295	.086	.094	.09
51	Sandomierz	.280	.599	2.177	....	5.732	3.181	....	.311	.171	.274	...
52	Siedlce	.816	3.431	6.923	1.924	17.330	9.481	5.891	1.210	1.341	.840	1.83
53	Sieradz	.187	1.107	1.807	.152	4.760	2.634	1.580	.450	.337	.278	...
54	Sokolow	.272	1.507	2.351	.381	6.154	3.444	2.077	.463	.535	.315	...
55	Strykow	.181	.800	1.393	.286	3.587	1.987	1.191	.449	.166	.159	...
56	Swieciany	.813	4.198	6.923	1.429	17.836	.....	5.997	2.183	.676	.690	...

POLAND

Deliveries from WARSAW Warehouse, Month of June, 1921

Table 461—*Continued*

Receipt No.	Local Committee	Cocoa	Sugar	Milk: Evap.	Milk: Cond.	Flour	Beans, Peas	Rice	Pork Products	Vegetable Oil	Soap	Salt
		Commodities in Net Metric Tons of 1,000 Kilograms or 2,204.6 Pounds										
57	Tomaszow	.272	1.588	2.416	....	6.594	3.701	2.160	.653	.340	.280	....
58	Torun	.305	1.785	2.634	....	7.450	4.206	2.414	1.223	....	.275	....
59	Sierpc	.374	1.120	3.287	.572	4.300	4.805	7.200	.919	.519	.418	....
60	Sochaczew	.374	1.888	3.048	....	7.820	4.313	2.618	.915	.354	.383	....
61	Wegrow	.363	1.992	3.178	....	8.328	4.631	2.788	.782	.511	.420	....
62	Wielun	.292	1.282	2.025	.248	5.431	3.038	1.812	.614	.358	.183	....
63	Wierzbnik	.374	1.102	1.785	....	8.718	4.864	2.788	.609	.355	.280	....
64	Wilejka	1.118	5.601	8.904	1.429	23.407	13.100	7.791	2.620	1.197	.910	....
65	Wilno	2.337	11.874	19.876	4.801	50.502	.....	17.132	5.508	2.372	1.971	....
66	Wloclawek	.272	1.475	.....	....	6.296	3.503	2.099	.603	.342	.280	....
67	Wloszczowa	.272	1.353	2.199	....	5.769	3.194	1.925	.661	.332	.270	....
68	Wyszkow	.186	.978	1.829	.762	4.240	2.307	1.311	.320	.353	.142	....
69	Warsaw (Small Del.)	4.107	19.934	36.967	19.388	132.961	40.069	28.985	9.638	3.323	2.439	6.733
70	Warsaw (Feeding Sta.)	1.233	7.493	15.892	2.762	5.081	18.050	10.327	4.560	....	....	1.428
71	Zgierz	.454	1.079	1.437	....	5.680	5.295	2.246	.612	.169	.449	....
	Total	**35.885**	**175.597**	**286.734**	**65.413**	**853.346**	**380.253**	**289.308**	**78.051**	**36.753**	**33.115**	**12.020**

POLAND

Table 462

Deliveries from BREST Warehouse, Month of July, 1921

Receipt No.	Local Committee	Cocoa	Sugar	Milk: Evap.	Milk: Cond.	Flour	Beans, Peas	Rice	Pork Products	Vegetable Oil	Corn Grits	Misc.*
		Commodities in Net Metric Tons of 1,000 Kilograms or 2,204.6 Pounds										
1	Augustow	.169	.....	.806	.267	3.370	2.490	1.510	....	....	.....	.175[d]
2	Białystok	1.490	7.329	8.708	1.543	16.014	.....	10.201	4.003	.877	.....	....
2a	Białystok	.378	.361	5.464	1.905	.....	2.314	.....	.610	....	3.015	.700[d]
3	Baranowicze	.500	2.250	3.309	....	9.300	5.250	3.000	1.050	.450	.....	....
3a	Baranowicze	1.020	4.876	8.229	1.429	21.607	11.970	3.388	2.508	....	.....	.840[d]
8	Biała Podlska	.474	.800	.....	....	15.324	5.571	2.404	....	.524	1.984	....
8a	Biała Podlska	....	.....	.....	....	.....	4.989	3.004	....	....	2.396	2.025[da]
9	Białowieza	.555	2.846	4.354	.305	11.819	6.691	3.889	1.349	.517	.....	1.445[da]
10	Bielsk	.565	3.728	5.921	2.934	16.304	5.693	1.189	2.161	.348	.....	2.615[da]
10a	Bielsk	.192	.....	.....	....	.....	.....	4.534	....	....	2.999	....
24	Biłgoraj	.281	1.308	2.025	....	.....	1.543	1.825	.634	....	1.499	.210[d]
11	Brzesc n/Bugiem	1.407	10.100	11.712	3.048	15.292	10.889	10.203	.823	1.751	3.024	4.370[da]
11a	Brzesc n/Bugiem	....	4.014	11.974	.991	15.740	15.130	15.015	11.050	4.917	6.025	....
11b	Brzesc n/Bugiem	....	.973	5.987	....	15.007	4.991	5.023	1.537	1.035	.....	....
11c	Brzesc n/Bugiem	....	.....	.....	....	15.180	.....	.....	....	....	.....	....
25	Chełm	.659	.....	.....	....	15.172	5.284	3.016	....	....	5.004	.700[d]
15	Dubno	.099	.909	3.353	.229	9.181	3.173	.319	.951	.353	.....	....
15a	Dubno	.377	1.256	.....	....	.....	.....	2.670	....	....	2.012	.350[d]
4	Grodno	.185	.401	1.372	....	.....	.....	3.706	1.332	....	.....	.700[d]
26	Hrubieszow	.282	1.262	2.112	.572	5.306	1.873	1.811	.311	.321	1.014	.210[d]
17	Krzemieniec	....	.528	2.699	....	7.296	1.024	1.533	....	.173	1.035	.280[d]
16	Kowel	1.412	.....	8.708	1.562	30.770	8.018	4.022	3.901	....	5.012	1.190[d]
16a	Kowel	....	.....	.....	....	.....	.....	.....	....	....	4.748	....
12	Kobryn	.186	2.680	.....	....	9.405	8.272	4.785	1.068	.866	.....	2.312[da]
27	Krasnystaw	.186	1.074	1.742	.476	4.393	1.615	1.500	4.575	....	.809	.175[d]
28	Luboml	.594	1.486	4.811	.838	12.576	4.983	4.191	1.408	.655	1.985	.490[d]

* Detail of miscellaneous commodities indicated by the following indexes: [a], salt; [d], soap. Of the total, 31.952, 15.117 is salt and 16.835 is soap.

[*Continued on next page*]

POLAND

Deliveries from BREST Warehouse, Month of July, 1921

Table 462—*Continued*

Receipt No.	Local Committee	Cocoa	Sugar	Milk Evap.	Milk Cond.	Flour	Beans, Peas	Rice	Pork Products	Vegetable Oil	Corn Grits	Misc.
		Commodities in Net Metric Tons of 1,000 Kilograms or 2,204.6 Pounds										
18	Łuck	.658	.....	.....	....	6.322	4.770	1.607	.169	....	3.024	.525
18a	Łuck	....	.....	.....	....	.....	1.984	2.015	....	....	2.496	....
19	Ołyka	.298	1.736	2.699	.286	7.270	2.078	2.400	.924	.170	1.996	.280
20	Ostrog	.182	.....	.....	....	5.467	2.026	.....	....	....	1.006	.210
14	Pruzany	.895	1.455	3.222	.838	12.973	10.127	5.986	1.508	.358	.....	3.490
14a	Pruzany	....	2.882	3.570	....	5.213	.....	.....	1.072	....	.....	....
13	Pinsk	1.787	9.032	1.524	3.010	23.430	14.277	12.889	3.805	2.116	7.018	4.460
13a	Pinsk	....	.....	13.345	....	14.993	.....	.....	....	....	.....	....
21	Rowno	.939	.302	1.850	.476	20.088	7.327	3.083	.459	.864	3.992	.770
21a	Rowno	....	1.969	6.509	....	.....	.....	3.510	1.988	....	.....	....
22	Sarny	.882	4.240	6.923	1.429	16.450	5.870	5.163	2.338	.181	4.042	.700
5	Słonim	.894	2.023	7.532	1.200	6.279	11.028	12.594	2.234	.857	7.566	.770
6	Stołpcy	.279	1.395	1.263	.476	4.391	2.403	2.081	.609	....	.999	.245
29	Tomaszow	....	.....	.....	....	.....	.....	.....	....	....	2.414	.175
23	Włodzimierz Wołynski	.280	.....	2.634	.591	15.170	.....	5.091	.914	.534	3.845	.595
23a	Włodzimierz Wołynski	.470	.....	2.373	.610	.....	.....	.....	....	....	4.526	....
30	Włodawa	.594	1.175	2.199	1.181	12.391	3.838	2.004	.332	.345	2.995	.490
7	Wołkowyski	.286	.455	2.308	.838	1.359	3.265	2.990	....	.522	1.602	.350
31	Zamosc	.084	.173	.588	.229	.....	1.348	1.194	....	....	1.008	.105
	Total	**19.539**	**75.018**	**151.824**	**27.261**	**400.852**	**182.104**	**155.345**	**55.623**	**18.734**	**91.090**	**31.952**

* See previous page.

POLAND

Deliveries from KRAKÓW Warehouse, Month of July, 1921

Table 463

Receipt No.	Local Committee	Cocoa	Sugar	Milk Evap.	Milk Cond.	Flour	Beans, Peas	Rice	Pork Products	Vegetable Oil	Corn Grits	Misc.*
		Commodities in Net Metric Tons of 1,000 Kilograms or 2,204.6 Pounds										
1	Bedzin	....	....	2.504	.686	....	3.377	1.930	.163	....	....	.246
13	Biała	....	.447	2.830	....	3.044	1.474	2.403	.332	....	2.591	.210
26	Bochnia	.363	1.376	.827	.895	....	.781	.970	.663	....	1.569	.160
11	Brzesko	.181	.848	1.698	....	1.017	.579	1.196	.340	.180	1.386	.140
34	Bytom	2.449	11.454	20.028	....	37.284	12.976	9.934	6.470	....	....	....
38	Chrzanow	.102	.854	1.611	.229	3.002	.641	1.196	.637	....	1.334	.542
17	Cieszyn	.305	1.616	2.961	....	2.595	1.213	2.254	1.137	....	2.535	.280
2	Dabrowa	.305	1.445	2.373	.514	6.086	3.379	2.061	.658	.349	....	1.364
12	Dembica	....	....	....	....	....	.229	.368	....	.175	.385	.071
40	Gorlice	....	.139	....	....	.552	.093	.229	.163	....	.211	.025
27	Grybow	.203	1.073	1.655	.057	....	.792	1.425	.677	....	1.712	.156
20	Jordanow	.102	.264	.414	....	.318	.226	.368	.165	....	.439	.056
16	Kalwarja	....	.101	.370	....	....	.142	.230	....	....	.257	.028
33	Kraków	1.179	5.970	10.254	1.619	24.980	5.000	6.000	2.477	.358	10.013	....
39	Krosno	.102	.811	1.197	....	3.342	.637	1.088	.322	....	1.254	.126
37	Krzeszowice	....	.282	.414	....	....	.230	.365	....	.168	.426	.042
8	Łancut	....	.501	1.045	....	1.011	.411	.645	.166	.182	.762	.070
9	Lezajsk	.091	....	.827	....	1.211	.417	.727	.336	....	.849	.192
21	Makow	.091	.221	....	....	.392	.241	.415	.162	....	.480	.149
3	Miechow	.203	1.076	1.872	.572	4.560	2.511	1.601	.338	.354	....	.183
10	Mielec	.091	.254	.414	....	.749	.228	.371	.166	....	.439	.372

* Detail of miscellaneous commodities indicated by the following indexes: [a], salt; [d], soap. Of the total, 9.697, 4.525 is salt and 5.172 is soap.

POLAND

Deliveries from KRAKÓW Warehouse, Month of July, 1921

Table 463—*Continued*

eipt o.	Local Committee	Commodities in Net Metric Tons of 1,000 Kilograms or 2,204.6 Pounds										
		Cocoa	Sugar	Milk		Flour	Beans, Peas	Rice	Pork Products	Vegetable Oil	Corn Grits	Misc.
				Evap.	Cond.							
5	Muszyna	.102	.223	.392	....	....	.375	.323	.169	....	.162	.035[d]
8	Myslenice	.102	.244	....	.571	....	.560	.365	.164	....	1.079	.042[d]
8	Niepołomice	....	.122	.283	....	.303	.097	.183	....	....	.189	.021[d]
4	Nowy Sacz	.363	1.868	3.331	1.143	....	1.402	2.749	.837	.351	2.909	.322[d]
0	Nowy Targ	.102	.710	....	....	....	.814	1.350	.342	....	1.598	.213[d]
4	Olkusz	....	....	1.850	....	2.029	2.518	1.422	.473	....	....	.165[d]
5	Oswiecim (Baraks)	.102	.403	.435	.495	....	.453	.786	.319	....	.926	.105[d]
6	Oswiecim (City)	.181	.679	1.459	....	....	.679	1.194	.230	....	1.359	.142[d]
2	Rzeszow	.406	1.783	3.374	....	....	1.801	3.060	1.155	....	3.555	.655[da]
2	Skawina	....	....	.283	....	....	.137	....	....	....	.297	.028[d]
5	Sosnowice	.454	....	4.136	3.277	12.613	2.380	4.058	.993	....	4.759	1.568[da]
9	Sucha	....	.223	.348	....	.384	.146	.320	.167	....	.380	.035[d]
4	Tarnobrzeg	.102	....	....	....	3.680	2.079	1.227	....	....	....	.070[d]
7	Tarnow	.406	1.322	4.267	....	7.847	4.263	2.707	.817	.174	....	1.000[a]
5	Wadowice	.203	1.022	2.329	....	2.002	.809	1.519	.654	....	1.569	.340[da]
3	Wieliczka	.102	.669	1.001	....	1.011	.584	.896	.481	....	1.011	.105[d]
9	Zakopane	.102	.522	.827	....	....	.408	.415	.333	....	.797	.084[d]
6	Zawiercie	.203	.904	1.437	.171	3.824	2.141	1.286	.326	.346	....	.142[d]
1	Zywiec	.203	1.263	1.850	.248	....	.950	1.686	.818	....	1.960	.213[d]
	Total	**8.898**	**40.690**	**80.897**	**10.478**	**123.836**	**58.173**	**61.322**	**23.649**	**2.637**	**49.192**	**9.697***

POLAND

Deliveries from LWÓW Warehouse, Month of July, 1921

Table 464

eipt o.	Local Committee	Commodities in Net Metric Tons of 1,000 Kilograms or 2,204.6 Pounds										
		Cocoa	Sugar	Milk		Flour	Beans, Peas	Rice	Pork Products	Vegetable Oil	Corn Grits	Misc.*
				Evap.	Cond.							
6	Borysław	.353	1.591	1.241	....	4.361	1.876	1.135	.962	....	4.960	.275[d]
7	Brody	.414	1.732	2.721	.343	2.474	.....	2.400	1.010	.341	8.845	.072[d]
7	Brzezany	.414	1.808	2.699	....	.....	1.508	1.348	.664	.177	4.546	.225[d]
7a	Brzezany	.566	.....	.....	....	.....	.....	.....	....	....	.....	....
2	Brzozow	.207	.905	1.306	....	1.245	.....	1.216	.504	.164	2.982	.140[d]
7	Buczacz	.205	.....	1.045	.267	3.630	.....	2.415	.331	.344	7.656	....
4	Dolina	.136	.675	1.001	....	1.320	.804	.452	.354	....	2.622	.105[d]
5	Grodek Jagiellonski	.207	.917	1.328	....	3.698	2.081	1.200	.493	.178	.....	.140[d]
6	Halicz	.297	.675	1.001	....	.926	.791	.300	.329	....	2.648	.105[d]
9	Jarosław	.347	1.680	2.765	.610	3.552	2.637	.800	.825	.345	6.455	.233[d]
9	Jaworow	.306	1.350	1.981	....	2.810	1.044	.880	.671	.169	5.822	.211[d]
0	Kałusz	.204	.445	.718	....	1.038	.....	.725	....	....	3.018	....
6	Kołomyja	.312	1.485	2.416	.476	3.108	.444	2.107	.834	.165	6.114	.216[d]
2	Kossow	.207	.743	1.742	.400	.....	.....	1.501	.688	....	5.466	.163[d]
5	Lisko	.188	.906	1.306	....	1.860	1.045	.585	.502	.164	3.507	.140[d]
9	Lwów (District)	.204	.667	1.916	.724	2.475	.....	.959	.336	....	4.453	....
4	Lwów (City)	.873	3.216	10.363	7.277	24.709		10.045	3.501	....	8.230	1.124[d]
4	Nadworna	.354	1.234	2.678	.191	7.368	4.122	1.483	1.157	....		.253[d]
2	Ottynia	.195	.126	.....	....	.819	.146	.460	.327	.173	1.407	.106[d]
3	Peczynizyn	.132	.452	.958	....	2.543	1.615	.895	.332	.171	.....	.070[d]
3	Podhajce	.103	.661	.958	....	.....	.798	.492	.338	.176	2.749	....

* Detail of miscellaneous commodities indicated by the following in- ·es: [a], salt; [d], soap. Of the total, 10.338, 2.500 is salt and 7.838 is ·p.

[*Continued on next page*]

POLAND

Deliveries from LWÓW Warehouse, Month of July, 1921

Table 464—*Continued*

Receipt No.	Local Committee	Commodities in Net Metric Tons of 1,000 Kilograms or 2,204.6 Pounds										
		Cocoa	Sugar	Milk		Flour	Beans, Peas	Rice	Pork Products	Vegetable Oil	Corn Grits	Misc.
				Evap.	Cond.							
20	Przemysl	.748	3.626	5.856	1.086	7.609	4.226	2.550	1.920	.507	14.388	.563
8	Przemyslany	.208	.676	.980	....	2.802	1.550	.907	.333	.172	.....	.106
28	Radziechow	.207	.496	1.633	....	1.635	.....	1.043	.335	.345	3.569	.175
21	Rawa Ruska	.218	1.137	1.655	....	2.550	2.604	.774	.479	.172	3.086	.17
22	Rohatyn	.104	.668	.370	.095	.....	.782	.452	.169	....	.....	....
13	Rudki-Komarno	.415	1.919	2.787	....	3.935	1.505	1.270	.849	.536	8.171	.294
11	Sambor	.385	2.310	3.527	.972	4.969	.840	2.513	1.336	.368	4.515	.329
2	Sambor	.502	....	....	....	.....	.....	.....	....	....	.....	....
38	Sanok	.346	....	2.787	.629	4.095	3.922	2.408	.883	.174	2.931	.26
43	Skole	.208	....	....	....	.....	.....	.360	.171	....	.677	.04
33	Sokal	.208	.301	.414	....	.....	.....	.684	....	.170	3.922	.12
24	Stanisławow	.480	2.590	4.115	.667	5.389	3.013	1.796	1.318	.503	10.213	2.70
41	Stary Sambor	.207	1.125	1.655	....	1.559	.....	1.506	....	.170	5.729	.17
18	Stryj	.413	1.725	2.743	.438	.229	1.353	1.217	1.006	.341	10.887	.27
30	Tarnopol	.410	1.029	1.415	.248	1.744	.....	2.444	.489	.337	3.832	.37
36	Trembowla	.207	.500	.327	.362	1.052	.....	1.051	.331	.172	3.737	.09
7	Turka	.504	.903	1.001	....	3.943	2.700	1.139	....	....	8.690	.21
10	Zaleszczyki	.208	.675	1.001	....	2.790	.....	.906	....	.169	.....	.10
14	Zbaraz	.207	.904	.806	....	1.590	.714	.593	.505	.178	1.899	.14
31	Zborow	.310	.827	2.155	....	2.003	.....	1.964	.844	....	7.492	.17
15	Złoczow	.308	1.268	2.068	.438	2.696	1.001	.905	.666	.179	5.533	.20
29	Zołkiew	.185	.668	1.001	....	2.795	.....	.905	.332	.176	1.595	.10
35	Zydaczow	.192	.908	1.328	....	1.860	1.055	.493	.508	.173	3.330	.14
45	Reverand Lucyniak	....	....	....	.953	.....	.....	.....	....	....	.....	...
	Total	**13.404**	**45.523**	**79.765**	**16.174**	**123.181**	**44.176**	**59.278**	**26.631**	**7.409**	**185.676**	**10.33**

* See previous page.

POLAND

Deliveries from WARSAW Warehouse, Month of July, 1921

Table 465

Receipt No.	Local Committee	Commodities in Net Metric Tons of 1,000 Kilograms or 2,204.6 Pounds										
		Cocoa	Sugar	Milk		Flour	Beans, Peas	Rice	Pork Products	Vegetable Oil	Soap	Sa
				Evap.	Cond.							
7	Aleksandrow	....	....	.....	....	.....	1.156	.....	....	....	.022	..
74	Bohdanow	.406	2.003	3.266	.476	8.676	4.830	2.886	1.178	.163	.338	1.0
8	Brzeziny	.102	.540	.849	.114	2.240	1.250	.765	.166	.172	.090	..
31a	Ciechanow	....	....	.....	.057	.....	.....	.....	....	....	.090	..
44	Chmielnik	....	.641	.....	.248	.253	1.848	.....	....	.358	.140	..
1	Częstochowa	.813	4.020	6.596	1.410	11.911	1.578	5.721	1.814	.870	.790	..
1	Częstochowa	.508	1.985	3.004	....	5.088	7.792	2.985	.984	.492	.203	3.0
79	Częstochowa	....	....	.....	....	9.009	5.022	.....	....	....	....	..
69	Feeding Points	.907	4.765	10.450	4.191	4.267	12.495	5.171	3.247	....	....	1.0
57	Garwolin	.542	3.060	4.724	.476	12.768	7.140	4.184	.962	1.030	.490	1.3
76	Głębokie	.181	1.096	1.698	.210	4.551	2.515	1.500	.678	.169	.138	..
32	Gostynin	....	....	.....	....	4.415	2.141	.....	....	....	....	..
25	Grodzisk	....	....	.....	....	1.445	3.647	1.725	.530	....	.280	..
26	Grojec	....	.272	.218	.629	5.475	3.032	1.868	....	.345	.204	.3
45	Jedrzejow	....	....	.....	....	2.946	1.921	.....	....	.181	.140	..
9	Kalisz	.272	1.279	2.025	.248	5.466	3.037	1.805	.677	.520	.210	..
46	Kielce	.385	1.920	3.091	.533	8.069	4.486	2.706	1.007	.352	.315	..
58	Kolno	.203	.826	1.372	.248	3.594	1.995	1.223	.350	.329	.135	..
10	Kolo	.091	.598	.893	.114	2.352	1.308	.773	.166	.170	.071	..
11	Konin	.091	.274	.479	.114	1.220	.688	.408	.167	.163	.069	..
47	Konskie	....	....	.....	....	6.305	3.545	.....	....	....	.210	..
48	Kozienice	.181	....	.631	.381	6.310	3.195	.937	.346	.169	.157	..
33	Kutno	.181	.360	.327	.476	4.425	2.420	.499	.162	....	.141	..
71	Lida	.657	3.286	5.247	.476	13.690	7.678	4.500	1.546	.672	.517	..

POLAND

Deliveries from WARSAW Warehouse, Month of July, 1921

Table 465—*Continued*

eipt o.	Local Committee	Cocoa	Sugar	Milk Evap.	Milk Cond.	Flour	Beans, Peas	Rice	Pork Products	Vegetable Oil	Soap	Salt
		Commodities in Net Metric Tons of 1,000 Kilograms or 2,204.6 Pounds										
4	Lubartow	.091	.806	.....	....	3.355	1.952	1.220	....	.175	.140	....
3	Lublin	.636	3.087	5.268	1.448	9.768	.317	2.630	1.393	.700	.486	....
3	Lublin	....	....	.....	....	3.450	6.927	1.869	....	....	....	....
1	Lapy	.363	1.796	3.004	.724	7.630	4.202	2.564	.642	.517	.280	....
3	Lask	.091	.640	1.045	.248	2.653	1.449	.908	.359	.174	.069	....
2	Lęczyce	.091	.163	.109	....	1.773	1.009	.227	.169	.170	.068	....
4	Łódź	1.909	9.573	15.783	3.600	26.867	.....	.....	....	....	....	....
4	Łódź	....	....	.....	....	13.465	22.270	13.599	5.038	1.361	1.598	....
7	Łódź	1.016	5.000	7.990	1.010	22.000	12.044	7.000	2.496	.494	....	....
9	Lomza	.689	2.600	5.878	1.200	15.142	8.416	5.100	1.178	1.212	.559	....
7	Lowicz	....	....	.....	.076	3.703	1.729	1.378	....	....	.135	.300
0	Lukow	.635	3.384	5.551	1.200	14.246	7.884	4.824	1.152	1.063	.563	....
8	Minsk Mazowiecki	....	....	.....	....	6.445	1.542	.....	....	....	....	....
4	Mlawa	....	....	.....	.095	1.588	.899	.116	....	.167	.090	....
9	Opoczno	.181	.811	1.372	.248	3.569	2.000	1.231	.332	.162	.135	....
3	Ostrolęka	.091	....	.....	.248	.....	.....	.544	....	.176	.136	.303
0	Ostrowiec	....	....	1.829	.248	9.106	.....	.....	....	....	.210	....
2	Ostrow Lomz	.726	3.608	5.638	.724	15.060	8.410	4.982	1.131	1.136	.560	....
2	Osmiany	.091	....	.....	....	2.032	6.209	1.608	1.319	....	.090	....
6	Ozorkow	.091	.302	.544	.191	1.322	.705	.456	.168	.161	.070	....
7	Pabjanice	....	.040	.....	....	6.219	3.689	1.042	....	....	.210	....
5	Parczew	....	....	.....	.229	8.945	2.494	1.215	....	....	....	.610
1	Pinczow	.203	1.106	1.785	.305	4.688	2.607	1.548	.525	.338	.180	....
2	Piotrkow	....	....	3.461	....	8.944	3.815	2.827	.504	....	.281	....
5	Plock	.203	.220	2.090	.476	.....	2.935	1.177	.499	....	.200	....
6	Plonsk	....	....	.370	.248	2.451	.713	.....	....	....	....	....
8	Poznan	.272	1.202	1.807	.610	5.284	2.882	1.680	.856	....	.211	....
9	Przasnysz	.102	.600	1.067	.362	2.602	1.406	.908	.169	.172	.112	....
6	Pulawy	.363	1.710	2.743	....	7.175	3.970	2.370	.826	.342	.274	....
0	Pultusk	....	....	.....	....	1.907	.....	.498	....	....	.135	....
3	Radom	.091	....	.631	....	8.507	6.599	3.898	.161	.134	.494	....
2	Radomsk	....	....	.....	.800	.....	2.835	1.031	.492	....	.210	.720
9	Rawa Mazowiecka	....	....	.479	.933	.....	.588	.....	....	.176	.070	....
5	Rzgow	.102	.304	.697	.057	1.270	.708	.410	.174	.169	.045	....
8	Ruda Pabjanicka	....	....	.....	.114	.....	.....	.....	....	....	.045	....
4	Sandomierz	.203	.857	1.372	.248	3.570	1.995	1.129	.470	.159	.135	....
4	Siedlce	.816	2.169	6.662	1.200	16.495	9.651	5.820	....	1.856	.675	....
9	Sieradz	.181	.894	1.023	.190	3.613	2.039	1.212	.168	.166	.140	....
1	Sierpe	.102	....	.849	.476	5.328	2.938	.....	....	....	.210	....
0	Skierniewice	.102	.670	1.132	.305	2.831	1.563	.967	.499	....	.140	....
8	Small Delivery	3.277	15.812	30.898	16.818	107.797	37.980	23.172	7.411	3.018	2.142	5.248
1	Sochaczew	.181	1.005	1.938	.857	4.439	2.405	1.586	.338	.308	.202	....
5	Sokolow	.091	.603	.762	.248	3.844	2.085	1.208	.172	....	....	....
8	Sokolow	.102	.135	.196	....	.545	.310	.182	....	.176	.070	....
0	Strykow	.091	.158	.065	.095	2.217	1.481	.075	....	.169	.023	....
3	Swieciany	....	....	.....	....	3.522	5.465	3.275	....	....	.350	....
1	Tomaszow Rawski	.203	1.079	1.698	.248	4.511	2.513	1.513	.500	.185	.210	....
7	Torun Nabrzezie	.272	1.343	1.981	....	5.616	3.151	1.802	.874	....	.203	....
7	Rejon Warszawski	....	20.000	31.000	24.994	70.000	50.000	50.000	20.033	....	....	....
6	Wegrow	.203	1.291	2.025	.248	5.460	3.055	1.795	.498	.334	.210	....
2	Wielun	....	....	.....	....	2.721	1.539	.912	....	....	.140	....
5	Wierzbnik	....	1.440	.....	.324	5.996	3.350	2.003	....	.165	.210	....
5	Wilejka	.454	....	.....	....	14.064	4.933	4.547	22.295	....	.280	....
0	Wilno	1.524	7.650	12.648	2.877	32.307	17.848	10.920	3.637	1.340	1.260	....
9	Wloclawek	.091	.151	1.959	....	4.961	2.736	.195	....	....	.070	....
6	Wloszczowa	.181	.881	1.459	.286	3.778	2.069	1.280	.336	.329	.135	....
8	Wolomin	....	.101	.144	.288	.072	.....	.072	....	....	....	....
2	Wyszkow	....	....	.....	....	1.488	1.270	.135	....	....	.070	.630
3	Zdunska Wola	....	....	.....	....	1.328	.792	.596	.159	....	.068	....
4	Zgierz	.272	1.420	2.242	.362	5.885	3.312	1.891	.694	.163	.225	....
	Total	**21.899**	**121.446**	**214.063**	**75.856**	**658.032**	**372.404**	**224.803**	**91.644**	**23.522**	**19.574**	**14.546**

POLAND

Table 466 — Deliveries from BREST Warehouse, Month of August, 1921

Receipt No.	Local Committee	Cocoa	Sugar	Milk (Cases) Evap.	Milk (Cases) Cond.	Flour	Beans, Peas	Rice	Pork Products	Vegetable Oil	Corn Grits	Misc.*
		Commodities in Net Metric Tons of 1,000 Kilograms or 2,204.6 Pounds										
1	Augustów	.099	....	94	...	2.663	1.464	1.596	....	.336	.505	.630
2	Biała	.406	1.891	134	21	.....	.....	.....	.818	.496	.....	1.426
3	Bielsk	.396	....	146	63	2.493	3.707	4.359	.984	....	4.288	1.73
4	Białowieża	.398	1.959	136	12	8.657	2.532	3.045	1.011	.178	4.018	1.283
5	Baranowicze	.596	3.006	220	38	12.668	3.011	4.228	1.343	.540	4.061	2.17
6	Brzostowica	.100	.601	48	12	2.638	1.464	.917	.343	.165	.....	.10
7	Brześć	.400	....	135	84	8.318	2.949	2.831	.508	.684	1.992	3.46
8	Białystok	....	....	...	105	.....	5.015	.....	....	....	5.984	....
9	Biłgoraj	.202	.875	62	7	3.620	.979	1.196	.350	.179	1.038	.14
10	Chełm	.301	....	135	...	7.446	2.079	2.503	.810	.304	1.985	.294
11	Dubno	.305	1.761	...	...	3.370	3.122	2.409	.978	.345	1.998	.28
12	Grodno	.508	2.577	190	...	12.170	.....	6.025	1.239	.530	8.969	.42
13	Grajewo	.184	.854	65	20	3.552	.937	1.210	.357	.172	1.017	.14
14	Hrubieszów	.199	.829	65	20	3.527	.924	1.189	.322	.176	.999	.07
15	Krasnystaw	.187	.668	53	20	2.753	1.036	.985	.347	.173	.996	.11
16	Kobryń	.099	1.904	135	9	8.119	2.022	2.648	.826	.495	2.559	1.50
17	Kowel	....	4.501	328	...	19.429	4.017	.....	2.070	....	6.481	.73
18	Kobryń	.201	....	...	...	2.515	2.016	1.806	....	.844	2.987	...
19	Krzemieniec	.403	1.756	123	...	.....	5.632	4.405	.888	.347	8.308	.28
20	Luboml	.403	2.202	156	20	9.125	2.090	3.001	1.006	.352	3.029	.35
21	Łuck	.403	....	138	...	8.286	2.680	2.701	1.056	.345	4.023	.31
22	Nieśwież	....	....	...	25	1.185	1.996	1.231	.506	.180	2.043	.14
23	Nowogródek	.298	1.710	126	25	7.211	2.006	2.386	.842	.351	1.988	.28
24	Nowogródek	.202	.824	72	16	3.608	1.976	1.229	.490	.346	2.007	...
25	Ostróg	.203	....	...	...	.....	2.068	1.200	.490	.169	3.643	.14
26	Ołyka	.203	.863	59	7	.....	2.114	.....	.501	....	3.601	.14
27	Pińsk	1.187	6.913	444	102	25.057	13.001	10.424	2.656	1.198	6.828	4.20
28	Pińsk	.609	4.002	207	53	.....	10.021	6.518	1.142	.858	10.002	...
29	Prużany	.298	....	...	...	9.969	3.022	3.295	....	.340	4.569	1.88
30	Równe	.704	3.607	253	25	15.700	4.004	4.933	1.923	.676	4.433	.57
31	Słonim	.610	3.011	220	38	12.660	5.013	2.009	1.403	.625	6.023	.49
32	Sarny	.696	2.175	261	50	13.571	5.509	4.531	1.615	.496	7.023	.52
33	Stołpce	.198	1.066	79	15	4.520	2.493	1.817	.491	.334	.996	.17
34	Sokołka	.300	1.277	96	25	5.353	1.239	1.811	.499	.334	1.736	.10
35	Suwałki	.203	....	63	...	3.611	.....	1.230	.488	....	2.019	.14
36	Tomaszów	.099	.498	39	13	2.075	1.158	.723	.172	.181	.....	.08
37	Włodawa	.405	2.231	163	...	9.137	2.073	3.022	1.053	.494	3.975	.35
38	Wołkowysk	.199	.732	97	32	5.266	.997	1.789	.669	.172	1.882	.21
39	Wołkowysk	.101	....	...	31	3.802	2.018	.....	.343	.181	2.496	...
40	Włodzimierz	.610	3.146	229	38	13.200	7.353	.....	1.479	.659	6.015	.51
41	Zamość	.099	.713	51	12	2.848	.568	.959	.173	.350	1.015	.11
	Total	**13.015**	**58.152**	**4,822†**	**938‡**	**260.122**	**116.305**	**96.161**	**32.191**	**14.604**	**137.531**	**25.51**

* Detail of miscellaneous commodities indicated by the following indexes: [a], salt; [d], soap. Of the total, 25.513, 14.205 is salt and 11.308 is soap.

† 4,822 cases evaporated milk are equivalent to 104.989 metric tons.

‡ 938 cases condensed milk are equivalent to 17.870 metric tons. To milk, 122.859 metric tons.

POLAND

Table 467 — Deliveries from KRAKÓW Warehouse, Month of August, 1921

Receipt No.	Local Committee	Cocoa	Sugar	Milk (Cases) Evap.	Milk (Cases) Cond.	Flour	Beans, Peas	Rice	Pork Products	Vegetable Oil	Corn Grits	Misc.*
		Commodities in Net Metric Tons of 1,000 Kilograms or 2,204.6 Pounds										
1	Biała	....	....	..	..	1.943	....	.136	....	....	....	.105[d]
2	Brzesko	....	.051	22	..	3.494	.087	1.044	....	.356	.315	.140[d]
3	Bochnia	....	....	..	..	.....	.091	.132	....	....	....	....
4	Będzin	.203	.963	83	42	4.182	2.218	1.500	.332	.346	....	.173[d]
5	Cieszyn	.102	.101	14	..	5.291	.574	1.727	....	....	2.021	.076[d]
6	Chrzanow	....	....	..	10	.....	....	....	....	....	.078	1.060[a]
7	Dębica	....	....	10	..	.125	....	.078	....	....	....	.119[a]
8	Dąbrowa Górnicza	.203	1.006	77	20	4.226	2.359	1.452	....	....	....	.167[d]
9	Grybow	....	.202	36	..	2.143	.284	.733	....	....	1.004	....
10	Jordanow	....	....	18	..	.252	.137	.042	....	....	.312	....
11	Krzeszowice	....	....	16	..	.509	....	.136	....	....	.120	....
12	Kraków	....	.093	6	4	.251	....	.090	....	....	.121	....
13	Kraków	1.626	7.641	814	185	37.118	2.698	11.364	5.019	.332	15.756	1.470[d]
14	Kalwarja	....	....	..	6	.569	.267	.180	....	....	.306	.021[d]
15	Kielce	....	....	20	..	1.502	.223	.450	....	....	.650	.029[d]
16	Myślenice	.048	.223	16	7	1.039	.140	.365	....	.171	.413	....
17	Muszyna	....	.170	11	..	2.590	.373	.732	....	.162	.985	.084[d]
18	Makow	....	....	..	..	1.013	.274	....	....	....	.311	.218[d]
19	Miechow	.203	1.062	86	33	4.533	2.465	1.577	.181	.514	....	.183[d]
20	Nisko	.101	....	..	..	.....	....	....	....	....	....	....
21	Niepołomice	....	.037	..	3	.491	.135	.054	....	....	....	.007[d]
22	Nowy Targ	.044	....	10	..	1.899	....	.665	....	.325	....	....
23	Nowy Sącz	.406	.399	160	49	13.181	3.013	3.898	....	.870	4.290	.300[d]
24	Olkusz	.203	1.134	82	11	7.127	2.650	1.561	.484	.173	....	.182[d]
25	Oświęcim	....	....	..	7	3.566	....	....	....	....	.298	.386[da]
26	Oświęcim Baraki	.203	.523	37	..	4.871	....	1.197	....	.501	1.973	.210[d]
27	Rzeszow	.102	....	..	..	12.660	.993	3.621	....	....	5.590	.410da
28	Skawina	....	....	..	..	.....	....	....	....	....	.248	....
29	Sucha	....	.034	4	..	1.135	.138	.367	....	....	.186	....
30	Sosnowiec	.406	1.928	170	88	8.425	4.528	3.026	.849	.324	....	.350[d]
31	Tarnów	.102	....	23	45	9.917	2.153	3.910	....	.332	3.497	1.000[a]
32	Wieliczka	.102	....	..	..	1.180	....	.318	....	....	.423	.036[d]
33	Wadowice	.203	....	52	49	6.195	1.955	2.184	....	....	1.936	.112[d]
34	Zakopane	....	....	5	..	2.811	....	.667	....	....	....	....
35	Żywiec	.203	.477	68	..	4.671	1.124	1.192	....	.173	.995	.070[d]
36	Zawiercie	.102	.654	46	4	2.722	1.532	.876	.350	.175	....	.104[d]
	Total	**4.562**	**16.698**	**1,886†**	**563‡**	**151.631**	**30.411**	**45.274**	**7.215**	**4.754**	**41.828**	**7.012***

* Detail of miscellaneous commodities indicated by the following indexes: [a], salt; [d], soap. Of the total, 7.012, 2.851 is salt and 4.161 is soap.

† 1,886 cases evaporated milk are equivalent to 41.064 metric tons.

‡ 563 cases condensed milk are equivalent to 10.726 metric tons. Total milk, 51.790 metric tons.

POLAND

Table 468 Deliveries from LWÓW Warehouse, Month of August, 1921

Commodities in Net Metric Tons of 1,000 Kilograms or 2,204.6 Pounds

Receipt No.	Local Committee	Cocoa	Sugar	Milk (Cases)		Flour	Beans, Peas	Rice	Pork Products	Vegetable Oil	Corn Grits	Misc.*
				Evap.	Cond.							
1	Buczacz	.209	1.059	170	22	8.101	....	1.282	.496	.165	1.005	.186[d]
2	Brody	.209	.606	116	10	9.299	.968	1.608	.170	.166	.....	.054[d]
3	Brzeżany	.209	1.109	76	..	4.644	....	1.496	.662	.169	2.638	.175[d]
4	Borysław	.145	.718	49	..	2.980	1.680	.967	.348	....	.....	.112[d]
5	Bóbrka	.075	.357	26	1	1.571	.886	.503	.177	.110	.....	.063[d]
6	Brzozów	.282	.360	..	56	4.705	....	2.041	.519	.284	3.128	....
7	Chyrów	.090	.448	31	..	1.865	1.053	.606	.300	....	.....	.070[d]
8	Czortków	.208	.765	52	..	3.168	....	1.022	.339	.174	1.770	.119[d]
9	Cieszanów	.131	.258	..	11	1.772	....	1.866	.353	.338	.....	.052[d]
10	Dolina	.076	.379	29	..	3.357	.414	.319	.169	.090	.442	.070[d]
11	Drohobycz	.104	.494	38	9	2.156	....	.733	.335	.172	1.199	.079[d]
12	Gródek Jagielloński	.206	1.299	70	..	4.555	....	1.344	.662	.168	2.876	.084[d]
13	Halicz	.045	.050	15	..	3.359	2.037	1.261	.174	.160	.....	.028[d]
14	Jarosław	.313	.726	73	16	8.172	....	2.127	.521	....	.....	....
15	Jaworów	.207	.510	55	..	3.334	....	1.085	.492	.156	.....	.126[d]
16	Janów	.027	.135	9	..	.558	.315	.180	.060	....	.....	.021[d]
17	Kałusz	.045	.537	35	..	4.109	....	.692	.307	....	.....	.043[d]
18	Kołomyja	.162	.899	48	12	5.081	1.009	1.124	.361	.113	.....	....
19	Kopyczyńce	.415	.465	50	..	4.329	.957	.593	.341	.166	1.133	.115[d]
20	Kosów	.163	.130	29	24	1.053	.244	1.303	.690	....	1.466	.161[d]
21	Lisko	.188	.957	72	..	4.981	.897	1.499	.351	....	.....	.010[d]
22	Lwów City	....	....	38	125	.....	....	.....	....	....	.....	....
23	Nadworna	.710	2.734	229	28	15.311	....	4.493	.984	....	7.373	.113[d]
24	Nadworna	.193	1.163	83	9	4.865	2.736	1.613	.679	....	.....	....
25	Przemyśl	1.038	5.072	361	63	20.329	6.333	7.500	2.840	.881	6.364	....
26	Podhajce	.103	.432	26	9	3.376	....	1.100	.496	....	.....	....
27	Peczeniżyn	.309	1.254	85	..	5.197	1.251	1.686	.673	.171	1.696	.196[d]
28	Przemyślany	.104	.403	28	..	1.672	....	.558	.166	....	.935	.072[d]
29	Radziechów	.309	1.353	94	..	5.989	....	1.868	.503	.347	2.785	.136[d]
30	Rohatyn	.104	.600	37	27	3.744	.898	.459	.330	.170	.....	.070[d]
31	Rawa Ruska	.126	.630	43	..	2.608	1.470	.843	.342	.147	.....	.098[d]
32	Rudki	.014	.072	5	..	.317	....	.096	.048	....	.168	.011[d]
33	Skole	.248	.120	64	..	1.497	1.671	2.037	.540	.131	1.686	.233
34	Sanok	.207	1.330	89	30	5.755	....	1.607	.503	....	2.617	.113[d]
35	Stanisławów	.666	3.207	275	36	15.359	3.605	5.194	1.583	.377	3.614	.265
36	Sniatyń	.104	.438	30	..	1.845	....	.592	.332	....	1.015	.066
37	Stryj	.175	.880	67	19	1.662	2.036	1.262	.413	....	.....	.147
38	Sambor	.296	1.204	101	50	10.163	....	1.780	.666	.174	2.763	1.710
39	Stary Sambor	.103	.540	36	..	2.232	....	.726	.326	.162	1.254	.084
40	Sokal	.206	.522	87	..	4.927	....	.695	....	.160	1.065	.138
41	Trembowla	.045	.517	56	2	3.941	....	.724	.321	....	.930	.116
42	Turka	.270	1.262	85	..	5.212	1.335	1.691	.659	.159	.....	.196
43	Tarnopol	.208	....	33	23	1.867	....	1.208	.667	.165	1.623	.210
44	Złoczów	.370	1.709	101	..	7.626	....	2.386	.669	.337	3.568	.135
45	Zaleszczyki	.099	.340	30	..	3.243	2.073	.912	.176	.088	.....	.103
46	Zborów	.312	.447	72	..	7.694	....	1.242	.341	....	.....	.160
47	Żydaczów	.225	.563	38	39	5.206	....	1.026	.333	.162	.815	.156
	Total	**10.053**	**39.051**	**3,236†**	**621‡**	**224.786**	**33.868**	**66.949**	**22.420**	**6.062**	**55.928**	**6.096**

* Detail of miscellaneous commodities indicated by the following indexes: [a], salt; [d], soap. Of the total, 6.096, 1.500 is salt and 4.596 is soap.

† 3,236 cases of evaporated milk are equivalent to 70.451 metric tons.

‡ 621 cases of condensed milk are equivalent to 11.831 metric tons. Total milk, 82.282 metric tons.

POLAND

Table 469 **Deliveries from WARSAW Warehouse, Month of August, 1921**

Receipt No.	Local Committee	Commodities in Net Metric Tons of 1,000 Kilograms or 2,204.6 Pounds										
		Cocoa	Sugar	Milk (Cases)		Flour	Beans, Peas	Rice	Pork Products	Vegetable Oil	Soap	Salt
				Evap.	Cond.							
1	Bogdanów	.102	....	19	19	4.592	3.595	.752	1.002	....	.248	....
2	Brzeziny	....	....	..	..	1.071	.584	.886	....	....	.202	....
3	Chmielnik	.203	.989	72	..	4.714	2.710	1.412	.178	.346	.112	....
4	Ciechanów	.091	.542	42	13	2.303	1.271	.775	.178	.174	.069	....
5	Częstochowa	....	....	..	..	.....	1.665	....	....	....	.070	....
6	Feeding Stations	2.836	7.397	269	430	32.396	17.387	10.779	3.936	1.664	1.903	4.986
7	Głębokie	....	....	..	..	.....	3.053	1.746	....	....	.293	....
8	Gostynin	.050	.116	7	9	.....	1.967	....	....	.280	.070	....
9	Grójec	....	.200	9	20	2.729	1.099	.765	....	.174	.139	....
10	Grójec	.102	.641	49	18	5.411	1.506	1.028	....	.343	....	....
11	Garwolin	....	....	..	25	.....	3.539	.501	....	....	....	....
12	Jędrzejów	....	.163	..	..	2.180	1.174	....	....	.332	.225	....
13	Kozienice	.363	1.369	147	30	3.502	3.489	2.177	.507	.530	.139	....
14	Kutno	.102	.327	23	1	2.023	1.467	.449	.164	....	.140	....
15	Koło	.102	....	..	11	.641	.919	.452	....	....	.070	....
16	Konin	.102	.048	..	..	1.127	.739	....	....	....	.070	....
17	Kielce	.508	2.210	190	27	14.744	8.180	4.922	1.210	....	.338	....
18	Lublin	....	....	..	..	9.666	5.325	3.233	1.009	.494	....	....
19	Lubartów	.102	.201	3	..	2.788	1.142	.689	.168	.164	....	....
20	Lisków	.153	.765	51	..	3.162	1.785	1.020	.495	....	.067	....
21	Lida	....	....	..	..	14.499	8.618	4.177	....	....	.210	....
22	Łuków	.406	....	..	..	7.310	4.091	2.400	....	....	.113	....
23	Łuków	.305	....	11	..	11.470	6.203	3.666	....	....	.293	....
24	Łapy	.304	.597	68	22	6.561	5.430	1.126	....	.487	....	....
25	Łowicz	....	....	26	18	4.760	2.483	1.489	.188	....	.135	....
26	Łęczyca	.101	.183	11	7	.895	.893	.272	.164	....	.067	....
27	Łask	....	....	..	..	.105	1.393	.200	....	.152	.070	....
28	Maków	.102	....	..	13	3.026	1.671	1.020	.347	.171	.112	....
29	Mława	.102	.396	18	7	2.472	1.313	.805	.164	.165	.140	....
30	Mińsk Mazowiecki	....	....	..	..	6.482	1.111	....	....	....	.045	....
31	Nowo-Radomsk	.091	.852	20	33	4.728	3.075	2.686	.695	....	.212	.605
32	Oszmiany	.453	2.317	..	..	9.639	5.402	3.176	1.385	....	.349	....
33	Ostrów	.272	....	..	..	3.223	2.553	.224	....	....	.278	....
34	Ostrołęka	.102	....	..	12	2.434	.527	.903	....	.332	.135	....
35	Ostrowiec	.305	....	182	20	.....	3.389	2.072	.483	....	.262	....
36	Płońsk	....	.175	6	..	.....	.800	....	....	....	.071	....
37	Płock	.101	.674	96	25	2.311	1.999	1.132	.322	.166	.225	....
38	Piotrków	.136	.703	3	3	3.914	2.144	1.262	....	.332	.090	....
39	Pułtusk	....	....	30	..	4.573	.530	.836	....	....	.135	....
40	Płock	.203	.810	66	25	3.458	1.893	1.181	.318	.154	.135	....
41	Pabjanice	.181	1.408	50	25	7.720	3.279	1.908	.680	....	.070	....
42	Parczew	....	....	..	6	3.639	2.045	1.226	....	....	.135	....
43	Puławy	.305	1.225	47	10	8.859	4.155	2.962	....	.668	.216	....
44	Poznań	....	1.195	..	26	4.718	5.690	2.370	1.004	....	.280	....
45	Radom	.102	.617	5	..	.295	3.917	.847	.159	....	....	....
46	Swięciany	....	.879	..	..	4.339	2.666	1.749	.162	....	.420	....
47	Station Milk	4.136	11.408	1,910	869	75.243	36.477	24.221	5.798	1.197	1.627	6.449
48	Siedlce	.203	1.226	77	24	6.819	8.032	4.325	.356	.674	.090	1.833
49	Sierpc	.305	.121	61	26	6.105	3.785	.244	.824	.163	....	.202
50	Sieradz	.102	.598	27	18	4.448	2.651	1.251	.173	.174	....	.300
51	Stryków	.050	.456	32	..	2.337	1.508	.818	.167	....	....	....
52	Sokołów	.101	.617	46	11	4.099	2.821	1.670	.161	.176	.070	....
53	Toruń	....	....	..	..	6.770	3.918	.337	....	....	.090	....
54	Wilno	.610	....	..	..	28.419	14.291	3.922	....	....	.632	....
55	Wilejka	.610	2.622	..	..	12.166	6.868	3.919	1.656	....	.399	....
56	Wyszków	....	....	32	..	2.737	1.820	1.318	....	....	....	....

[*Continued on next page*]

POLAND

Deliveries from WARSAW Warehouse, Month of August, 1921

Table 469—*Continued*

Receipt No.	Local Committee	Cocoa	Sugar	Milk (Cases)		Flour	Beans, Peas	Rice	Pork Products	Vegetable Oil	Soap	Salt
				Evap.	Cond.							
57	Włocławek	.203	.880	64	..	2.939	2.417	1.172	.519	....	.068	....
58	Włoszczowa	....	.302	83	28	4.503	3.107	1.142	....	.158	.135	....
59	Wierzbnik	....	.840	..	14	1.384	.444	....	....	.316	.100	....
60	Zduńska Wola	.025	....	..	..	2.366	1.371	1.210	.180	....	.067	....
61	Zgierz	....	....	..	20	.....	....	....	....	....	.157	....
	Total	**14.730**	**46.069**	**3,852***	**1,865†**	**374.814**	**229.376**	**116.824**	**24.752**	**9.986**	**11.788**	**14.375**

Commodities in Net Metric Tons of 1,000 Kilograms or 2,204.6 Pounds

* 3,852 cases of evaporated milk are equivalent to 83.875 metric tons.
† 1,865 cases of condensed milk are equivalent to 35.524 metric tons.
Total milk, 119.399 metric tons.

‡ In addition to above quantities, 5.238 metric tons of soup were delivered but not segregated to districts.

POLAND

Deliveries from BREST Warehouse, Month of September, 1921

Table 470

Commodities in Net Metric Tons of 1,000 Kilograms or 2,204.6 Pounds

Receipt No.	Local Committee	Cocoa	Sugar	Milk (Cases)		Flour	Beans, Peas	Rice	Pork Products	Vegetable Oil	Corn Grits	Misc.*
				Evap.	Cond.							
1	Bielsk	....	....	225	60	.....	2.033	.....	.977	.142	3.971	1.222[d]
2	Bielsk	....	.458	31	9	14.087	.....	.274	.338	....	1.459	.070[d]
3	Bogdanów	.305	....	134	26	7.749	2.142	2.558	....	....	2.024	.362[d]
4	Białowieża	.303	.495	134	..	15.808	9.024	5.235	2.122	....	.....	.270[d]
5	Brześć n/Bugiem	2.119	....	580	99	26.677	1.074	.....	1.583	1.870	.....	....
6	Brześć n/Bugiem	.090	.515	..	..	22.314	5.094	.743	....	.352	15.263	2.364[e]
7	Brześć n/Bugiem	....	6.809	40	10	2.692	12.491	10.541	.156	.165	.....	2.020[e]
8	Białystok	....	....	79	..	9.727	.844	.....	....	....	.....	.535[e]
9	Baranowicze	.102	.697	45	56	15.849	4.020	.519	2.125	....	4.804	.501[e]
10	Baranowicze	.275	1.700	126	25	.....	.....	2.401	1.003	....	3.993	.280[e]
11	Głębokie	.609	2.825	203	32	.....	3.634	3.895	1.704	.176	2.932	.455[e]
12	Grodno	.192	.843	176	13	3.086	.....	.497	.470	....	1.982	....
13	Grodno	.203	1.469	76	..	.....	2.014	.....	1.128	....	2.665	....
14	Krzemieniec	.204	.886	..	..	12.799	.....	.....	.308	.182	.....	.500
15	Kobryń	.304	1.146	75	..	10.437	1.428	1.736	.334	.333	.....	.143
16	Kowel	1.321	.951	..	..	22.580	.....	.....	.650	....	.....	.435
17	Łuck	....	....	..	..	11.370	.....	.....	....	.330	.....	.370
18	Nowogródek	.303	1.277	95	19	5.412	.....	1.795	.624	.341	3.016	.210
19	Nowogródek	.505	1.939	49	24	8.031	1.828	2.014	.837	.351	2.024	.292
20	Nieśwież	.201	1.108	..	12	4.143	.932	.....	....	.176	1.445	....
21	Oszmiany	.403	.205	..	..	12.622	3.753	4.559	.158	....	4.006	....
22	Ostróg	.301	1.571	94	..	9.602	.....	.....	....	.615	1.510	.453
23	Pińsk	2.319	10.103	809	115	43.410	7.972	12.003	5.758	2.160	10.016	.975
24	Prużany	.498	....	12	11	14.319	3.665	3.507	....	.679	3.987	.377
25	Równe	.586	....	..	..	10.945	3.026	1.099	....	....	4.669	.167
26	Stołpce	.302	.971	71	..	3.757	3.529	1.817	.503	.337	.....	.600
27	Swięciany	.365	2.110	20	..	8.482	1.996	2.747	.320	....	2.838	....
28	Słonim	.247	....	54	50	10.422	.....	.....	....	....	.....	....
29	Sarny	1.406	3.718	269	99	27.858	7.746	9.602	2.677	.872	8.016	.689
30	Wilejka	.995	4.341	..	21	21.374	5.000	6.530	1.604	....	6.883	.764
31	Włodzimierz	....	....	..	..	7.652	.....	.....	....	....	.....	.251
32	Wołkowysk	.101	.192	11	12	5.078	.....	.....	....	....	1.324	.078
33	Wilno	2.618	9.827	574	176	.....	8.450	19.105	3.334	1.528	15.030	6.065
34	Włodawa	....	.101	89	28	3.399	1.024	1.539	....	.704	3.643	....
	Total	**17.177**	**56.258**	**4,071†**	**897‡**	**371.681**	**92.719**	**94.716**	**28.713**	**11.313**	**107.500**	**20.448**

* Detail of miscellaneous commodities indicated by the following indexes: [a], salt; [d], soap; [e], salmon. Of the total, 20.448, 3.135 is salt, 8.335 is soap, and 8.978 is salmon.

† 4,071 cases of evaporated milk are equivalent to 88.638 metric tons.
‡ 897 cases of condensed milk are equivalent to 17.089 metric tons.
Total milk, 105.727 metric tons.

POLAND

Deliveries from LWÓW Warehouse, Month of September, 1921

Table 471

Receipt No.	Local Committee	Cocoa	Sugar	Milk (Cases) Evap.	Milk (Cases) Cond.	Flour	Rice	Pork Products	Vegetable Oil	Corn Grits	Soap	Salt
		Commodities in Net Metric Tons of 1,000 Kilograms or 2,204.6 Pounds										
1	Buczacz	.302	.992	23	..	2.790	2.075	.465	.174	4.853	.219	1.000
2	Brzeżany	....	.501	106	9	.878	2.051	....	.349	.....	.159	....
3	Borysław	.310	1.568	103	9	6.422	2.047	.479	.173	3.288	.084	....
4	Borysław	.209	.827	49	..	6.539	2.313	.483	.348	1.706	.112	....
5	Brody	.208	.905	98	23	3.109	1.309	.651	....	3.674	.135	....
6	Cieszanów	.104	.568	29	13	3.370	.....	.134	....	2.510	....	....
7	Czortków	.031	....	41	..	.....	.....	....	....	.127	....	....
8	Gródek	.268	1.218	84	..	5.143	1.656	.616	.172	2.716	.216	.400
9	Jarosław	.314	.943	63	10	.679	.547	.490	....	3.509	....	....
10	Kołomyja	.137	.600	73	14	1.581	1.015	.469	.178	1.563	.061	....
11	Kosów	.064	.201	19	8	4.390	.604	....	....	.....	.037	....
12	Kałusz	.377	2.305	121	..	5.609	2.689	.765	.315	5.762	.247	....
13	Lwów (City)	.742	3.843	555	509	15.378	5.009	2.038	.424	8.780	.581	.260
14	Lwów (District)	.229	1.133	102	58	5.000	1.802	.652	.106	2.677	.066	.110
15	Lisko	.208	1.159	76	..	4.356	1.641	.627	.175	2.895	.191	....
16	Nadworna	.283	.537	78	15	5.465	1.597	.154	....	2.030	.193	....
17	Przemyśl	.144	1.057	77	1	7.671	1.554	....	.154	.....	.371	....
18	Rohatyn	.059	.324	33	..	2.015	.720	.163	.181	1.502	.034	....
19	Stanisławów	.347	1.600	67	3	4.626	1.548	.667	.149	3.583	.267	....
20	Stryj	.208	1.087	68	8	2.988	1.921	.488	....	3.217	....	.050
21	Sanok	.209	.685	71	7	4.189	1.360	.319	....	2.328	.206	.600
22	Sambor	.306	.586	65	32	7.804	3.178	.498	.175	3.526	.249	....
23	Turka	.284	1.174	86	..	5.618	2.415	.503	.350	5.557	.168	....
24	Tarnopoł	.252	.865	..	..	3.111	1.308	....	....	2.006	....	....
	Total	**5.595**	**24.678**	**2,087***	**718†**	**108.731**	**40.359**	**10.662**	**3.423**	**67.809**	**3.596**	**2.420**

* 2,087 cases of evaporated milk are equivalent to 45.443 metric tons.

† 718 cases of condensed milk are equivalent to 13.690 metric tons. Total milk, 59.133 metric tons.

POLAND

Deliveries from WARSAW Warehouse, Month of September, 1921

Table 472

Receipt No.	Local Committee	Cocoa	Sugar	Milk (Cases) Evap.	Milk (Cases) Cond.	Flour	Beans, Peas	Rice	Pork Products	Vegetable Oil	Soap	Misc. Food *
		Commodities in Net Metric Tons of 1,000 Kilograms or 2,204.6 Pounds										
1	Beuthen Society of Friends	.813	11.453	920	..	34.326	2.010	9.941	5.163	....	....	....
2	Biała	.102	.200	..	..	2.826	2.240	.853	.348	....	.070	....
3	Brzesko	.203	1.324	56	..	4.969	3.331	1.494	.803	....	.247	....
4	Częstochowa	.508	2.326	202	101	.....	5.453	3.596	1.125	.505	.427	....
5	Chrzanów	.101	.563	40	5	2.358	1.313	.775	.325	.099	.090	....
6	Dąbrowa	....	....	..	11	5.894	.....	.236	.344	....	....	1.023[e]
7	Gostynin	.101	.500	32	..	.563	1.031	.444	.065	....	....	....
8	Jędrzejów	....	.945	..	..	3.734	1.697	....	....	.174	.140	....
9	Krosno	.101	.041	..	5	3.094	1.927	.979	.202	....	.070	....
10	Końskie	....	....	..	..	2.261	2.958	....	.641	....	....	.326[e]
11	Kutno	.080	.274	26	14	1.136	.447	.453	.151	....	....	.327[e]
12	Kielce	.203	1.290	95	19	.....	3.000	1.800	.771	.170	.210	....
13	Lublin	....	....	..	..	.....	2.307	....	....	....	....	....
14	Łukôw	.203	....	62	13	4.503	2.796	1.570	....	....	.190	....
15	Łowicz	.102	.460	53	..	3.234	1.841	1.075	.505	....	.140	....

* Detail of miscellaneous food indicated by the following indexes: salt; [e], salmon. Of the total, 48.088, 8.053 is salt and 40.035 is salmon.

[*Continued on next page*]

POLAND

Deliveries from WARSAW Warehouse, Month of September, 1921

Table 472—*Continued*

Receipt No.	Local Committee	Commodities in Net Metric Tons of 1,000 Kilograms or 2,204.6 Pounds										
		Cocoa	Sugar	Milk (Cases)		Flour	Beans, Peas	Rice	Pork Products	Vegetable Oil	Soap	Misc. Food
				Evap.	Cond.							
16	Nowy Sącz	.304	2.707	137	23	6.724	4.635	....	1.162	.313	.350	....
17	Nowy Targ	.406	1.124	90	..	5.227	4.871	1.896	.657	....	.157	....
18	Olkusz	....	.192	8	..	4.788	1.332	.634	.672	....	.131	....
19	Ostrowiec	.406	.384	126	22	8.786	4.869	3.212	1.362	.276	.350	....
20	Ostrołęka	.102	....	..	7	2.173	1.282	.661	....	.290	....	.203[a]
21	Płock	.102	.418	11	1	1.573	.957	.448	.171	.158	....	....
22	Piotrków	.086	.167	116	..	1.220	.740	.393	.828	....	....	....
23	Pabjanice	.101	.522	54	21	2.276	1.261	.750	.329	.167	.140	.022[e]
24	Puławy	.091	.300	42	31	1.394	1.672	.590	....	.160	.059	....
25	Parczew	....	....	..	..	3.239	.960	.315	....	....	....	....
26	Radomsk	.102	.274	16	..	1.132	.846	....	....	....	.053	....
27	Rawa	....	.168	47	..	.....	1.916	....	.161	.032	....	....
28	Radom	.610	3.456	240	..	14.354	8.073	4.637	1.584	.425	.350	....
29	Siedlce	.203	1.178	101	50	.....	2.776	1.805	.449	.333	.210	....
30	Sosnowiec	.406	....	85	83	3.867	3.342	1.633	.346	....	....	....
31	Sierpc	....	.201	21	12	2.440	1.055	....	....	....	....	....
32	Sokołów	.102	.671	49	6	2.853	1.526	.954	.357	....	.070	.065[e]
33	Tarnów	.406	1.364	..	..	7.819	4.037	2.541	.663	.311	.315	.588[e]
34	Toruń	....	.443	30	..	3.402	1.117	1.035	....	....	.203	1.589[e]
35	Włocławek	.203	.767	52	14	5.157	2.124	1.437	.166	.335	.280	.980[e]
36	Warszawa	4.166	14.897	700	145	39.041	2.097	....	.195	4.547	4.995	42.965[e]
37	Zawiercie	....	....	18	..	2.052	1.108	....	.156	....	....	....
	Total	**10.315**	**48.609**	**3,429†**	**583‡**	**188.415**	**84.947**	**46.157**	**19.704**	**8.296**	**9.248**	**48.088***

* See previous page.
† 3,429 cases of evaporated milk are equivalent to 74.660 metric tons.
‡ 583 cases of condensed milk are equivalent to 11.107 metric tons. Total milk, 85.767 metric tons.

POLAND

Table 473 Deliveries from BREST Warehouse, Month of October, 1921

Receipt No.	Local Committee	Commodities in Net Metric Tons of 1,000 Kilograms or 2,204.6 Pounds										
		Cocoa	Sugar	Milk (Cases)		Flour	Beans, Peas	Rice	Pork Products	Vegetable Oil	Corn Grits	Misc.*
				Evap.	Cond.							
1	Baranowicze	.898	4.717	364	142	20.889	7.148	6.717	2.952	.....	3.046	1.230[d]
2	Białowieża	.609	3.764	187	4	11.441	6.439	3.719	1.486	.362	.....	1.653[d]
3	Brześć	.809	4.519	387	..	5.706	.564	2.920	1.208	1.636	.....	1.441[d]
4	Brześć	....	.....	...	..	12.153	.....	.....	.....	....	.....	....
5	Białystok	.392	2.611	278	49	16.295	4.000	.....	1.362	....	3.684	2.103[d]
6	Bohdanów	.388	1.489	135	23	7.603	3.152	2.514	1.670	....	1.100	.677[d]
7	Bielsk	.102	1.409	92	38	4.222	4.482	3.706	.696	.335	.....	.576[d]
8	Chełm	.759	2.587	489	..	15.000	4.718	4.546	1.195	.172	.....	.621[e]
9	Dubno	.402	1.623	194	..	7.509	8.991	3.314	.906	.355	.....	.444[d]
10	Grodno	.606	3.309	251	..	11.272	5.009	4.660	1.426	.521	4.161	1.132[e]
11	Kowel	1.012	7.773	505	..	48.003	32.521	13.245	5.873	1.369	14.996	1.009[d]
12	Kobryń	.503	2.795	172	21	12.256	4.154	3.940	1.053	.787	3.000	1.155[d]
13	Krzemieniec	.305	1.039	46	..	1.645	.....	.838	.324	.177	.....	1.134[e]
14	Lida	1.410	.....	553	..	34.231	18.186	11.434	2.262	1.531	.996	1.185[d]
15	Łuck	.200	1.785	183	..	3.878	.....	.....	.....	.537	.....	.438[e]
16	Nieśwież	.305	1.588	106	23	7.404	1.511	2.913	.184	.337	1.674	.337[d]
17	Nowogródek	.402	2.226	163	52	4.160	.....	3.140	1.153	.273	10.020	1.532[d]

* Detail of miscellaneous commodities indicated by the following indexes: [a], salt; [d], soap; [e], salmon. Of the total, 41.419, 5.115 is salt, 22.942 is soap, and 13.362 is salmon.

POLAND

Deliveries from BREST Warehouse, Month of October, 1921

Table 473—*Continued*

Receipt No.	Local Committee	Cocoa	Sugar	Milk (Cases) Evap.	Milk (Cases) Cond.	Flour	Beans, Peas	Rice	Pork Products	Vegetable Oil	Corn Grits	Misc.
		Commodities in Net Metric Tons of 1,000 Kilograms or 2,204.6 Pounds										
18	Oszmiany	.711	3.440	56	..	14.120	5.810	4.006	1.731	.349	6.019	.692[de]
19	Ostróg	.399	2.301	177	13	8.759	4.544	4.019	.649	.498	.....	.309[de]
20	Pińsk	.506	2.034	229	..	15.494	4.007	4.997	1.030	....	4.008	5.924[dea]
21	Prużany	.711	3.352	243	26	14.165	4.012	4.782	1.641	.515	3.441	1.458[de]
22	Równe	.806	2.415	166	..	15.162	3.196	5.960	.....	....	4.976	1.681[dea]
23	Słonim	.506	1.869	210	81	10.990	3.277	4.374	1.536	....	1.013	3.370[dea]
24	Swięciany	.711	2.651	181	..	11.018	2.998	3.596	2.753	.178	2.709	1.176[de]
25	Stołpce	.300	1.473	110	5	6.188	2.406	2.079	.480	.511	1.029	.399[de]
26	Sarny	1.315	5.027	511	169	30.074	10.738	10.160	3.392	1.127	.168	1.654[de]
27	Swięciany dla Dukszty	.203	.804	65	19	2.704	1.952	1.199	.495	.170	.....	....
28	Suwałki	.201	1.594	51	..	.....	.....	1.683	1.359	....	2.930	.811[de]
29	Wołkowysk	.501	2.203	176	64	11.440	4.768	3.336	1.208	....	1.991	.472[de]
30	Wilejka	1.216	5.990	323	37	25.996	9.292	9.509	4.617	....	5.241	1.136[de]
31	Włodawa	.210	2.811	148	22	11.143	.....	1.979	.757	.169	.....	.736[de]
32	Wilno	....	2.622	...	..	25.844	7.420	.....	.864	....	15.002	4.934[de]
	Total	**17.398**	**83.820**	**6,751†**	**788‡**	**426.764**	**165.295**	**129.285**	**46.263**	**11.909**	**91.204**	**41.419***

† 6,751 cases evaporated milk are equivalent to 146.990 metric tons.

‡ 788 cases condensed milk are equivalent to 15.012 metric tons. Total milk, 162.002 metric tons.

POLAND

Deliveries from LWÓW Warehouse, Month of October, 1921

Table 474

Receipt No.	Local Committee	Cocoa	Sugar	Milk (Cases) Evap.	Milk (Cases) Cond.	Flour	Beans, Peas	Rice	Pork Products	Vegetable Oil	Corn Grits	Misc.*
		Commodities in Net Metric Tons of 1,000 Kilograms or 2,204.6 Pounds										
1	Borszczów	.050	.....	..	..	.....	.....	.....	....	....	.....	.....
2	Brzeziny	.203	1.502	82	..	2.718	3.610	1.879	.934	.173	.....	5.941[de]
3	Chyrów	.101	.635	..	27	2.245	1.202	.794	.455	....	.....	1.161[de]
4	Jarosław	.192	1.506	130	4	8.738	.....	2.730	1.080	.175	3.721	2.488[de]
5	Jaworów	.102	.....	56	..	5.002	.....	1.820	....	....	3.160	2.072[de]
6	Kopyczyńce	....	.400	20	..	2.911	1.686	.963	.326	....	.....	2.837[dea]
7	Kołomyja	.406	1.206	120	27	8.844	4.909	2.950	.621	.170	.....	3.223[de]
8	Lwów	2.055	10.452	1,249	1,204	50.596	2.267	20.125	5.235	.847	11.185	27.903[de]
9	Nadworna	.406	1.204	119	3	7.108	4.435	2.952	.902	.174	.....	5.335[de]
10	Podhajce	.305	1.257	96	27	5.350	1.677	1.829	.608	.298	.....	2.925[de]
11	Przemyśl	.387	2.128	143	12	8.953	.....	2.801	1.399	.172	.....	4.820[de]
12	Peczeniżyn	.102	.698	24	29	3.591	1.835	1.147	....	.179	.....	1.202[de]
13	Rohatyn	.203	.606	54	23	1.841	.....	.560	.173	....	.693	1.397[de]
14	Radziechów	.203	.835	39	..	3.787	.....	1.098	.303	.225	2.797	2.286[dea]
15	Sambor	.479	2.718	227	84	13.750	.....	3.498	1.384	.162	2.177	4.280[de]
16	Stryj	....	.151	55	..	3.985	.....	.....	.150	....	.....	2.053[dea]
17	Skole	.203	.302	..	65	3.890	2.084	1.221	.304	.159	.....	1.906[de]
18	Sanok	.059	.....	20	..	5.705	.....	.522	....	....	.....	4.495[de]
19	Turka	.574	2.586	178	..	11.661	.....	3.211	1.222	.356	5.502	3.282[de]
20	Tarnopol	.406	2.285	170	..	9.214	.....	2.973	.617	.327	2.255	4.281[dea]
21	Zborów-Złoczów	.305	1.303	115	..	5.747	5.053	2.191	.951	.150	.....	3.610[dea]
22	Żydaczów	.095	.604	37	..	2.301	.....	.796	.311	.146	1.290	1.145[de]
	Total	**6.837**	**32.378**	**2,934†**	**1,505‡**	**167.937**	**28.758**	**56.060**	**16.977**	**3.714**	**32.780**	**88.642***

* Detail of miscellaneous commodities indicated by the following indexes: [a], salt; [d], soap; [e], salmon. Of the total, 88.642, 1.330 is salt, 12.968 is soap, and 74.344 is salmon.

† 2,934 cases of evaporated milk are equivalent to 63.879 metric tons.

‡ 1,505 cases of condensed milk are equivalent to 28.674 metric tons. Total milk, 92.553 metric tons.

POLAND

Deliveries from WARSAW Warehouse, Month of October, 1921

Table 475

Receipt No.	Local Committee	Cocoa	Sugar	Milk (Cases) Evap.	Milk (Cases) Cond.	Flour	Beans, Peas	Rice	Pork Products	Vegetable Oil	Corn Grits	Misc.*
		Commodities in Net Metric Tons of 1,000 Kilograms or 2,204.6 Pounds										
1	Brzesko	.406	1.485	111	28	9.942	4.665	3.366	.946	.248	....	.832[de]
2	Biała	.305	1.096	78	19	5.518	.....	1.855	.833	....	....	.476[de]
3	Cieszyn	.203	1.380	91	3	5.791	1.526	2.022	.647	....	1.457	1.045[de]
4	Chrzanów	.102	.703	53	6	3.092	.888	1.025	.507	.154	.872	.350[d]
5	Częstochowa	....	....	..	..	4.527	2.450	.....	....	....	2.425	2.532[dea]
6	Dąbrowa Górnicza	.203	....	..	41	14.012	7.040	4.410	.451	....	....	.768[de]
7	Gostynin	.203	1.053	84	27	4.458	2.013	1.710	.333	.295	....	.381[de]
8	Grodzisk	....	....	..	6	2.349	.570	.775	.302	....	.535	....
9	Grójec	.203	.493	36	..	2.120	.565	.553	....	.159	.562	.520[de]
10	Jędrzejów	....	.649	..	..	.....	.....	.....	....	....	....	.280[d]
11	Kraków	.305	3.061	216	261	8.338	.....	3.558	1.061	.170	....	4.850[de]
12	Kutno	.203	.976	79	45	4.270	2.357	1.515	.159	.071	....	.156[de]
13	Kalisz	....	....	27	..	.....	2.804	.....	....	....	....	.544[e]
14	Koło	....	.494	28	19	1.509	.308	.546	.172	.136	.305	.537[de]
15	Kraków	1.016	7.557	603	463	26.263	6.436	10.413	3.760	.336	....	16.367[de]
16	Krosno	.102	.442	17	1	1.835	.534	.600	.319	....	....	1.023[e]
17	Kielce	.203	1.410	111	54	4.792	1.005	1.758	.860	.120	1.010	1.577[de]
18	Końskie	....	.274	77	..	5.038	1.483	.....	.643	....	1.473	.330[d]
19	Łowicz	.203	.803	59	6	3.481	.838	1.103	.513	.122	.802	.955[de]
20	Lisków	.102	.540	32	5	2.232	1.260	.720	.350	....	....	.293da
21	Łódź	....	....	..	432	31.927	3.535	4.066	....	....	3.505	5.727[de]
22	Łapy	.203	.908	56	..	3.782	1.145	2.201	....	.629	1.062	.110[de]
23	Łuków	.102	....	22	25	2.014	.311	.418	....	....	.288	.249[de]
24	Lublin	.102	.503	..	..	....	1.869	1.100	....	.333	1.910	2.155[e]
25	Mińsk Mazowiecki	.102	....	..	..	1.862	.491	.....	....	....	.566	.467[de]
26	Nowy Sącz	.609	3.147	243	63	13.299	7.126	4.280	1.497	.477	....	.926[de]
27	Nowy Targ	.304	2.136	145	11	10.560	4.118	3.816	1.414	....	....	.754[de]
28	Olkusz	.101	.776	63	..	2.633	1.798	1.145	.452	....	....	.476[de]
29	Oświęcim	.610	2.014	198	94	11.356	2.766	3.690	1.550	....	2.934	2.097[de]
30	Ostrowiec	.395	2.192	112	74	8.863	2.101	3.135	.154	.297	2.127	1.944[de]
31	Ostrołęka	.101	.453	34	12	3.359	.907	1.092	....	.220	.960	....
32	Ostrów	.203	.597	88	..	4.938	.951	1.727	....	.633	.953	2.362[de]
33	Ozorków	....	....	5	6	.....	.....	.....	....	....	....	.050[d]
34	Płońsk	....	....	2	2	.....	.....	.....	....	....	....	....
35	Pułtusk	.305	1.366	131	50	6.937	3.717	2.179	.153	.506	....	1.090[de]
36	Pabjanice	.102	.455	24	13	.....	.575	.645	.168	....	.562	.372[de]
37	Płock	.304	1.554	124	43	6.701	3.302	2.427	.615	.463	....	1.773[de]
38	Puławy	.102	.863	62	9	3.876	1.770	1.187	.154	.333	....	.362[de]
39	Piotrków	.102	.805	66	..	3.541	.749	1.419	.329	....	.915	.467[de]
40	Poznań	....	....	..	50	.....	.....	.....	....	....	....	....
41	Radomsk	.102	.884	59	19	3.724	1.867	1.158	.137	.154	....	.639[de]
42	Rawa Mazowiecka	.102	.695	46	..	2.402	.815	.863	.451	.169	.814	.025[d]
43	Rzesów	.609	1.249	82	..	11.524	6.011	4.012	1.382	....	....	1.407[de]
44	Radom	.508	2.336	184	..	9.826	2.546	3.374	1.063	.787	2.549	1.173[de]
45	Sieradz	....	....	..	..	.369	.....	.....	....	....	....	.421[de]
46	Sochaczew	....	....	..	28	.....	.....	.....	....	....	....	....
47	Sosnowiec	.609	2.086	248	153	13.019	2.533	4.224	1.508	....	....	1.919[de]
48	Sokołów	.203	1.210	85	13	5.083	1.452	1.693	.493	.331	1.445	.677[de]
49	Siedlce	....	....	..	51	.....	.....	.....	....	....	....	....
50	Tarnów	.508	2.420	..	82	11.783	5.998	4.361	1.899	.322	....	1.727[de]
51	Toruń	.305	1.502	54	..	6.250	1.910	2.122	.678	....	1.825	2.544[de]
52	Wadowice	.305	1.507	139	44	7.213	3.601	2.528	.686	.150	....	.576[de]
53	Włocławek	.305	1.715	81	39	5.292	3.492	1.869	.454	.372	....	.210[d]
54	Wyszków	....	....	46	..	2.730	1.869	.582	.360	....	....	.022[e]

* Detail of miscellaneous commodities indicated by the following indexes: [a], salt; [d], soap; [e], salmon. Of the total, 83.979, 3.221 is salt, 24.962 is soap, and 55.796 is salmon.

POLAND

Deliveries from WARSAW Warehouse, Month of October, 1921

Table 475—*Continued*

Receipt No.	Local Committee	Cocoa	Sugar	Milk (Cases) Evap.	Milk (Cases) Cond.	Flour	Beans, Peas	Rice	Pork Products	Vegetable Oil	Corn Grits	Misc.
		Commodities in Net Metric Tons of 1,000 Kilograms or 2,204.6 Pounds										
55	Warsaw	4.978	25.864	2,181	1,157	111.762	68.093	32.329	12.119	3.155	....	15.960[de]
56	Zgierz	....	....	..	27	.....	.398	.....	....	....	.385	.654[de]
57	Zawiercie	.101	.792	61	..	4.709	2.569	1.229	.437	....	....	.345[de]
58	Zywiec	.203	1.060	63	..	5.563	2.386	1.540	.832	....	....	.483[de]
	Total	**16.346**	**83.505**	**6,406†**	**3,481‡**	**426.464**	**179.513**	**132.340**	**40.841**	**11.142**	**32.241**	**83.979***

† 6,406 cases of evaporated milk are equivalent to 139.478 metric tons.

‡ 3,481 cases of condensed milk are equivalent to 66.317 metric tons. Total milk, 205.795 metric tons.

POLAND

Deliveries from BREST Warehouse, Month of November, 1921

Table 476

Receipt No.	Local Committee	Cocoa	Sugar	Milk (Cases) Evap.	Milk (Cases) Cond.	Flour	Beans, Peas	Rice	Pork Products	Vegetable Oil	Corn Grits	Misc.*
		Commodities in Net Metric Tons of 1,000 Kilograms or 2,204.6 Pounds										
1	Brześć	.193	.709	35	..	1.700	.....	.504	.637	....	1.594	....
2	Brześć	1.057	5.865	445	61	24.996	.....	8.586	1.461	1.917	14.063	2.383[ea]
3	Brześć	.102	.608	42	5	2.500	.....	.806	.306	.146	1.391	.220[a]
4	Brześć	....	.506	25	..	2.504	.....	.680	....	....	.947	....
5	Brześć	.199	....	...	..	.....	.....	.....	1.008	....	.....	....
6	Bohdanów	.644	3.220	230	33	13.638	.....	4.525	1.562	....	7.605	.024[e]
7	Baranowicze	.301	1.293	96	25	5.325	.....	1.811	.796	....	2.960	....
8	Bielsk	.302	1.995	188	58	8.640	.....	2.966	1.541	.357	4.564	.970[ea]
9	Dubno	....	....	...	..	.....	.....	.....	....	....	.....	.087[e]
10	Grodno	.092	.203	...	..	3.463	.....	1.423	.356	.159	2.682	....
11	Kowel	....	3.910	140	..	.....	.....	1.858	....	....	.....	.455[e]
12	Kobryń	.397	2.103	140	..	8.700	.....	2.818	1.208	.336	4.937	.660[a]
13	Krzemieniec	....	.595	7	..	.....	.....	.810	.179	.172	1.771	....
14	Luboml	.419	....	155	44	14.434	.....	4.575	....	....	.....	.410[d]
15	Lida	....	4.050	...	..	.....	.....	.....	....	....	.....	....
16	Łuck	.185	1.000	74	..	4.100	.....	1.142	....	.213	.125	.109[e]
17	Nieśwież	.302	1.106	50	21	4.624	.....	1.412	.628	.140	2.823	....
18	Nowogródek	.183	1.105	92	36	9.700	.....	1.503	.952	....	.....	....
19	Oszmiany	.837	4.518	206	..	19.304	.....	6.314	2.613	.180	7.310	....
20	Pińsk	.204	1.267	83	..	4.960	.....	1.572	.461	.411	2.837	.521[ea]
21	Pińsk	2.218	11.049	665	..	32.700	.....	13.483	5.762	2.425	29.008	2.497[ea]
22	Prużany	.608	3.121	214	21	12.900	.....	4.318	1.702	.316	7.724	.070[e]
23	Równe	.406	2.815	166	..	9.124	.....	2.332	1.286	.351	6.909	....
24	Sarny	....	.800	...	..	.....	.....	.....	....	....	3.633	.087[e]
25	Swięciany	1.215	6.051	416	69	24.680	6.939	8.162	2.235	.527	6.920	.276[e]
26	Słonim	.471	1.694	175	80	8.537	.....	2.928	1.720	....	8.277	1.200[a]
27	Stołpce	.202	1.111	58	17	4.900	.....	1.571	.694	....	2.701	....
28	Suwałki	....	....	...	..	3.944	.....	.....	....	....	.....	....
29	Wilno	....	....	...	..	24.647	.....	.....	.333	....	.....	2.679[ea]
30	Włodawa	.203	.707	107	22	3.652	.....	2.374	.636	.329	6.081	.035[e]
31	Włodzimierz	.361	2.047	14	..	7.558	.....	2.122	1.032	....	4.120	.228[e]
32	Wołkowysk	.498	2.000	194	69	11.274	.....	4.525	1.385	.170	5.497	.094[e]
33	Wilejka	....	.100	...	..	.....	.....	.....	....	....	.....	....
	Total	**11.599**	**65.548**	**4,017†**	**561‡**	**272.504**	**6.939**	**85.120**	**30.493**	**8.149**	**136.479**	**13.005***

* Detail of miscellaneous commodities indicated by the following in-
es: [a], salt; [d], soap; [e], salmon. Of the total, 13.005, 9.580 is salt,
0 is soap, and 3.015 is salmon.

† 4,017 cases of evaporated milk are equivalent to 87.462 metric tons.

‡ 561 cases of condensed milk are equivalent to 10.688 metric tons. Total milk, 98.150 metric tons.

POLAND

Table 477 — Deliveries from LWÓW Warehouse, Month of November, 1921

Receipt No.	Local Committee	Cocoa	Sugar	Milk (Cases) Evap.	Milk (Cases) Cond.	Flour	Beans, Peas	Rice	Pork Products	Vegetable Oil	Corn Grits	Misc.*
		Commodities in Net Metric Tons of 1,000 Kilograms or 2,204.6 Pounds										
1	Borysław	.102	.805	7	..	2.845	.266	1.101	.456	....	....	.609
2	Buczacz	.102	.101	..	18	2.708	.....	1.115	.152	....	....	3.136
3	Brody	.302	1.504	80	..	6.841	1.620	2.346	.776	.346	....	4.584
4	Czortków	.203	.892	7	..	2.883	1.194	.962	....	....	....	1.132
5	Cieszanów	.101	.123	9	9	1.523	.....	.495	.156	....	....	1.719
6	Drohobycz	....	.202	15	27	.632	.300	.231	.166	....	....	.43[illegible]
7	Jarosław	.102	.805	62	12	4.303	1.652	1.144	.510	....	....	.....
8	Kołomyja	.102	.755	124	..	2.203	1.196	1.810	....	.532	....	.....
9	Kosów	.102	.502	48	11	2.303	.....	.138	....	....	....	1.00[illegible]
10	Kałusz	.203	.444	60	..	3.724	.....	1.065	.319	.174	....	3.24[illegible]
11	Lwów (City)	2.544	11.815	1,045	..	47.258	.....	16.203	.234	2.154	29.517	1.77[illegible]
12	Lwów (City)	....	.....	..	..	.....	.....	.....	.142	.335	....	.....
13	Nadworna	.305	1.004	74	..	7.311	3.931	2.502	....	.708	....	.....
14	Przemyśl	.406	1.498	101	25	5.511	3.890	2.252	.642	....	....	.....
15	Rohatyn	.031	.394	32	..	1.958	2.088	.649	....	.161	....	.....
16	Rawa Ruska	....	.....	..	..	.....	.....	.....	....	....	....	1.13[illegible]
17	Sanok	.203	1.187	80	..	3.294	2.234	1.655	....	.743	.622	.27[illegible]
18	Stanisławów	.711	2.796	249	50	12.411	6.471	5.724	1.803	.326	....	3.22[illegible]
19	Stryj	.305	1.800	73	..	8.130	.....	2.204	1.002	.170	....	....
20	Sambor	.305	1.610	116	42	6.188	1.587	2.246	.775	.172	....	....
21	Tarnopol	.305	1.072	..	..	4.556	2.435	1.559	.524	.287	....	....
22	Turka	.203	1.007	68	..	4.482	1.047	1.422	.631	....	....	....
23	Złoczów	....	.....	..	10	.....	.....	.....	....	....	....	....
24	Złoczów	....	.....	..	2	.....	.....	.....	....	....	....	....
	Total	**6.640**	**30.316**	**2,250†**	**206‡**	**131.064**	**29.911**	**46.283**	**8.289**	**6.108**	**30.139**	**22.26[illegible]**

* Detail of miscellaneous commodities indicated by the following indexes: [a], salt; [d], soap; [e], salmon. Of the total, 22.269, 1.773 is salt, 1.254 is soap, and 19.242 is salmon.

† 2,250 cases of evaporated milk are equivalent to 48.994 metric to[illegible]
‡ 206 cases of condensed milk are equivalent to 3.925 metric to[illegible]
Total milk, 52.919 metric tons.

POLAND

Table 478 — Deliveries from WARSAW Warehouse, Month of November, 1921

Receipt No.	Local Committee	Cocoa	Sugar	Milk (Cases) Evap.	Milk (Cases) Cond.	Flour	Beans, Peas	Rice	Pork Products	Vegetable Oil	Corn Grits	Misc Foo[illegible]
		Commodities in Net Metric Tons of 1,000 Kilograms or 2,204.6 Pounds										
1	Benthen, Society of Friends	.470	4.140	362	..	16.334	3.937	3.976	1.507	....	....	...
2	Brzesko	....	....	..	10	.....	....	....	....	....	....	...
3	Cieszyn	.102	.303	23	..	1.224	.230	.463	.351	.017	.252	.39[illegible]
4	Chrzanów	....	....	142	..	1.550	1.194	.505	....	....	1.270	.72[illegible]
5	Częstochowa	....	....	..	..	10.209	1.623	....	....	....	1.556	1.03[illegible]
6	Dąbrowa	.305	....	..	..	8.960	1.175	2.265	.497	....	1.211	2.39[illegible]
7	Grodzisk	....	.202	12	..	2.224	.486	.783	.329	....	.497	.78[illegible]
8	Gostynin	.102	.704	44	2	2.752	.839	.869	.327	.166	.822	.02[illegible]
9	Kielce	.102	....	21	..	4.784	.133	....	....	....	.125	...
10	Końskie	....	.808	46	..	3.356	1.581	.880	.337	....	1.578	...
11	Kraków (City)	.914	4.544	391	201	19.535	4.885	6.951	3.518	.153	4.887	2.92[illegible]
12	Kraków (City)	....	....	70	..	.....	....	....	....	....	....	...
13	Kutno	.102	.503	44	17	2.058	.400	.690	.306	.169	.437	.39[illegible]
14	Kalisz	.102	.540	36	..	2.238	.625	.735	.380	....	.630	...
15	Lublin	.305	1.818	..	..	4.028	3.732	3.270	.486	.505	3.716	1.95[illegible]

* Detail of miscellaneous food indicated by the following indexes: [a], salt; [b], corned beef; [e], salmon. Of the total, 24.868, 2.086 is salt, 1.404 is corned beef, and 21.378 is salmon.

POLAND

Deliveries from WARSAW Warehouse, Month of November, 1921

Table 478—*Continued*

Receipt No.	Local Committee	Cocoa	Sugar	Milk (Cases) Evap.	Milk (Cases) Cond.	Flour	Beans, Peas	Rice	Pork Products	Vegetable Oil	Corn Grits	Misc. Food
		Commodities in Net Metric Tons of 1,000 Kilograms or 2,204.6 Pounds										
16	Łapy	.101	1.014	73	..	4.099	1.110	1.425	.347	.343	1.106	.043[e]
17	Łódź	.711	....	456	..	16.009	4.455	6.858	1.621	....	4.427	....
18	Łuków	.203	.202	100	..	4.579	1.212	1.713	.647	.271	1.265	.152[e]
19	Mińsk Mazowiecki	.101	.403	18	..	2.374	.744	....	.321	....	.754	.022[e]
20	Nowy Targ	.102	....	..	..	2.798	.570	....	.174	....	.622	.305[e]
21	Ostrowiec	....	....	2	..	2.990	1.510	....	....	....	1.495	....
22	Oświęcim	.305	1.615	109	..	7.810	1.188	2.499	.902	....	1.167	....
23	Ostrów	.294	1.101	84	..	4.583	1.578	1.420	.477	.313	1.560	....
24	Ostrołęka	.102	.404	33	..	1.570	.406	.598	.174	.171	.407	.326[ea]
25	Olkusz	.203	.907	65	..	3.630	.723	1.235	.489	.065	.801	1.067[e]
26	Puławy	.102	.905	71	..	3.632	1.050	1.226	.295	.170	1.077	....
27	Piotrków	.203	1.214	85	..	4.610	1.321	1.745	.831	....	1.317	.450[a]
28	Poznań	.406	2.116	206	..	8.802	1.355	3.010	1.327	....	1.400	4.136[e]
29	Pabjanice	....	.053	..	..	3.391	.475	.458	....	.016	.831	.022[e]
30	Pułtusk	.203	.803	70	20	4.750	1.075	1.501	.313	.049	1.085	.392[e]
31	Płock	.203	.905	125	..	3.840	.580	1.358	.499	.174	.555	1.851[e]
32	Płock	....	....	28	..	.....	....	....	....	....	....	....
33	Radom	.406	2.219	92	..	9.185	3.487	3.037	.805	.686	3.512	.980[e]
34	Radomsk	.203	.707	54	22	3.008	.934	1.020	.332	.078	.934	.065[e]
35	Sokołów	.102	....	..	..	1.296	.670	.231	.167	.240	.685	....
36	Siedlce	....	....	3	61	1.249	....	....	....	....	....	....
37	Skierniewice	....	....	..	..	2.360	.737	.677	....	....	.727	.631[e]
38	Sosnowiec	.203	1.218	156	..	8.236	2.330	2.678	1.189	....	2.328	.305[e]
39	Sochaczew	....	....	..	..	.....	.800	....	....	....	.820	.152[e]
40	Toruń	.203	1.313	135	..	5.187	1.206	1.638	.984	....	1.205	2.460[e]
41	Włocławek	.203	.978	112	..	3.795	.926	1.470	.494	.356	.935	.588[e]
42	Wadowice	.102	.505	99	..	1.760	.677	.645	.334	....	.635	.196[e]
43	Warsaw	....	....	..	..	.....	....	....	1.372	....	....	....
44	Zgierz	....	....	22	..	.950	.510	....	....	.180	.507	....
45	Zawiercie	.102	.809	54	..	3.460	.803	1.154	.517	.338	.837	.087[e]
	Total	**7.266**	**32.953**	**3,443†**	**333‡**	**199.205**	**53.272**	**58.983**	**21.969**	**4.460**	**49.975**	**24.868***

† 3,443 cases of evaporated milk are equivalent to 74.964 metric tons.

‡ 333 cases of condensed milk are equivalent to 6.344 metric tons. Total milk, 81.308 metric tons.

POLAND

Deliveries from BREST Warehouse, Month of December, 1921

Table 479

Receipt No.	Local Committee	Cocoa	Sugar	Milk (Cases) Evap.	Milk (Cases) Cond.	Flour	Beans, Peas	Rice	Pork Products	Vegetable Oil	Corn Grits	Misc.*
		Commodities in Net Metric Tons of 1,000 Kilograms or 2,204.6 Pounds										
1	Biłgoraj	.201	.303	40	..	5.924	2.356	1.522	.306	....	.....	.994[de]
2	Białystok	.198	1.091	162	..	10.227	2.910	.492	1.114	....	1.885	.858[ea]
3	Bielsk	.611	3.104	231	58	12.940	3.990	4.354	.850	.439	2.999	.899[ea]
4	Baranowicze	.705	3.530	291	130	20.568	8.418	5.666	2.255	.471	.....	.288[e]
5	Brześć	....	7.898	581	30	30.790	.....	.....	1.274	....	.....	2.355[a]
6	Brześć	1.626	.....	...	..	2.208	14.013	15.090	2.784	1.350	.....	.803[e]
7	Chełm	....	.....	...	..	8.850	3.988	2.896	....	....	2.243	....
8	Dubno	.203	.707	46	..	2.720	1.567	.903	.517	....	.....	.185[e]
9	Grodno	.201	1.205	101	26	5.050	1.827	1.820	.704	....	.....	.789[e]

* Detail of miscellaneous commodities indicated by the following in-
xes: [a], salt; [d], soap; [e], salmon. Of the total, 19.600, 8.326 is salt,
0 is soap, and 10.874 is salmon.

[*Continued on next page*]

POLAND

Table 479—*Continued*

Deliveries from BREST Warehouse, Month of December, 1921

Receipt No.	Local Committee	Commodities in Net Metric Tons of 1,000 Kilograms or 2,204.6 Pounds										
		Cocoa	Sugar	Milk (Cases)		Flour	Beans, Peas	Rice	Pork Products	Vegetable Oil	Corn Grits	Misc.
				Evap.	Cond.							
10	Kobryń	.710	5.116	209	..	12.979	4.011	4.246	1.407	.477	2.852	1.019[ea]
11	Kowel	1.016	7.173	239	..	22.761	5.316	8.301	2.934	.851	3.000	.359[e]
12	Łuck	.301	1.314	94	..	5.578	2.714	1.888	.472	.347	.....	.144[e]
13	Nowogródek	.405	2.001	145	27	8.300	2.288	2.771	.962	.172	.....	.040[e]
14	Nieśwież	.203	.703	47	8	2.441	2.297	.543	.322	.127	.....	.021[e]
15	Prużany	1.011	5.764	394	..	24.006	8.032	7.906	3.602	.338	5.313	1.500[ea]
16	Pińsk for Luniniec	.585	3.118	216	..	13.157	5.034	4.263	1.270	.938	2.468	.879[ea]
17	Pińsk	1.107	5.438	378	18	22.083	8.022	7.195	3.412	.338	4.170	3.074[ea]
18	Równe	.406	1.917	142	..	14.023	3.833	2.622	1.040	.257	.....	....
19	Słonim	.604	2.100	212	20	12.530	7.423	4.445	2.063	....	.....	.676[e]
20	Suwalki	.297	1.417	...	..	7.302	2.471	2.140	.349	....	.770	.602[e]
21	Stołpce	.303	1.286	125	20	5.460	3.017	1.893	.951	....	.....	.038[e]
22	Sarny	.102	2.521	4	..	2.419	4.152	2.278	.637	.096	1.022	.191[e]
23	Swięciany	.102	.607	41	..	2.580	.785	1.375	.341	....	.430	....
24	Tomaszów	....	.....	...	..	3.853	.....	.....	.....	....	.....	.364[e]
25	Wołkowysk	.404	2.704	136	31	9.150	5.037	3.338	1.440	.169	.....	.050[e]
26	Wilno	1.108	5.386	...	..	31.395	4.020	10.781	3.092	....	3.055	3.472[e]
27	Włodawa	.801	3.723	269	28	17.629	4.010	6.902	1.901	.503	.642	....
	Total	**13.210**	**70.126**	**4,103†**	**396‡**	**316.923**	**111.531**	**105.630**	**35.999**	**6.874**	**30.849**	**19.600***

* See previous page.
† 4,103 cases of evaporated milk are equivalent to 89.335 metric tons.
‡ 396 cases of condensed milk are equivalent to 7.544 metric tons
Total milk, 96.879 metric tons.

POLAND

Table 480

Deliveries from LWÓW Warehouse, Month of December, 1921

Receipt No.	Local Committee	Commodities in Net Metric Tons of 1,000 Kilograms or 2,204.6 Pounds										
		Cocoa	Sugar	Milk (Cases)		Flour	Beans, Peas	Rice	Pork Products	Vegetable Oil	Corn Grits	Salmon
				Evap.	Cond.							
1	Buczacz	.188	1.119	87	...	5.238	1.862	1.646	.613	.176	1.705	....
2	Brzeżany	.102	.774	50	...	3.523	....	.137	....	.148	1.751	....
3	Chyrów	.102	.449	46	...	2.040	....	.658	.320	....	.818	.013
4	Cieszanów	.203	.582	45	...	2.749	1.470	.870	.305	.179	.757	....
5	Czortków	.169	1.008	100	...	5.360	1.807	1.685	.646	.337	1.023	....
6	Husiatyn	.190	.076	26	...	3.586	1.209	1.325	.478	....	2.285	....
7	Jarosław	.305	1.210	128	...	4.246	1.962	1.684	.638	.280	.318	....
8	Kosów	.305	1.275	125	...	6.201	2.695	1.827	.796	.141	.899	....
9	Lwów	....	6.206	138	200	26.842	14.535	9.560	3.182	.863	....	....
10	Lwów	1.219	.....	404	607	.....	....	.....	6.293	....	....	....
11	Nadworna	.305	2.390	237	...	12.073	.180	3.967	2.082	....	4.320	....
12	Podhajce	.189	.846	80	...	3.544	1.117	1.234	.489	.166	.826	....
13	Przemyśl	.203	1.280	132	...	6.274	.092	1.804	.632	.397	2.460	....
14	Radziechów	.225	1.067	70	...	4.337	1.218	1.412	.477	.356	.128	....
15	Rohatyn	.189	.892	115	...	3.370	....	2.142	.466	....	.444	....
16	Stanisławów	.508	3.036	285	...	13.236	4.883	3.331	1.597	.474	5.354	....
17	Sambor	.203	.800	104	...	3.300	2.233	1.242	.611	....	....	....
18	Stryj	.102	.300	80	...	3.000	.092	1.101	.487	....	....	....
19	Tarnopol	.203	1.891	131	...	8.457	....	2.949	1.123	.128	2.866	....
20	Zborów	.282	1.636	122	10	6.391	....	2.195	.638	.204	1.966	....
	Total	**5.192**	**26.837**	**2,505***	**817†**	**123.767**	**35.355**	**40.769**	**21.873**	**3.849**	**27.920**	**.013**

* 2,505 cases of evaporated milk are equivalent to 54.541 metric tons.
† 817 cases of condensed milk are equivalent to 15.565 metric tons
Total milk, 70.106 metric tons.

POLAND

Deliveries from WARSAW Warehouse, Month of December, 1921

Table 481

Receipt No.	Local Committee	Cocoa	Sugar	Milk (Cases) Evap.	Milk (Cases) Cond.	Flour	Beans, Peas	Rice	Pork Products	Vegetable Oil	Corn Grits	Misc. Food *
		Commodities in Net Metric Tons of 1,000 Kilograms or 2,204.6 Pounds										
1	Bytom	.330	1.590	98	..	1.566	.....	.994	1.363	....	....	....
2	Chrzanów	....	....	..	68	1.700	.....	.782	....	....	....	.327[e]
3	Cieszyn	....	.182	17	21	.800	.023	.321	....	....	.017	.239[e]
4	Częstochowa	....	....	..	..	9.416	1.635	.090	....	.169	1.229	....
5	Dąbrowa	.406	.875	151	31	9.250	3.015	2.939	.763	.179	2.255	.888[e]
6	Gostynin	.102	.602	45	2	2.700	1.205	.917	.164	.170	.925	.022[e]
7	Koło	....	.605	66	17	3.152	.998	.860	.154	....	.750	.131[e]
8	Kalisz	.102	.550	68	6	4.145	1.036	.872	.620	....	.788	1.219[e]
9	Kielce	....	....	..	27	.....	.....	....	....	....	....	....
10	Lublin	.305	1.111	88	..	9.735	1.480	1.865	.768	....	1.125	....
11	Łódź	....	....	..	230	.....	.....	....	....	....	....	....
12	Łuków	.102	.500	67	1	3.079	1.085	1.150	.159	.174	.811	.065[e]
13	Łapy	.305	.850	63	25	3.595	1.118	1.240	.157	.334	.818	.044[e]
14	Mińsk Mazowiecki	.101	.705	48	..	3.042	.920	....	.343	....	.690	....
15	Nowy Sącz	.397	1.965	124	52	5.788	1.662	1.478	.797	.332	1.247	.305[e]
16	Ozorków	....	.029	42	14	2.073	.229	....	....	....	.189	.544[e]
17	Ostrów	.101	.403	42	3	1.836	.625	.830	....	.059	.470	....
18	Oświęcim	.022	.201	37	60	1.554	.772	.500	.166	....	.615	....
19	Olkusz	....	....	..	3	2.754	1.774	1.971	.159	....	1.350	.522[e]
20	Pabjanice	....	.524	52	34	2.243	.490	.784	....	.169	.375	.600[a]
21	Pułtusk	.102	....	..	..	1.630	1.495	1.603	....	....	1.120	.174[e]
22	Puławy	.286	.710	48	38	3.192	1.003	1.106	.313	.162	.754	.044[e]
23	Płock	.102	.942	53	50	3.540	.809	1.208	.305	.174	.623	1.132[e]
24	Płock Milk Station	....	....	14	31	.....	.....	....	....	....	....	....
25	Radomsk	.101	.833	58	15	3.413	1.041	1.185	.473	.173	.793	.109[e]
26	Rzeszów	....	.099	71	..	.....	1.088	....	....	....	.803	.300[a]
27	Sokołów	.108	.303	..	..	2.647	.718	.972	.300	.168	.522	.305[e]
28	Sieradz	....	....	..	..	1.694	.537	.355	....	....	.393	.370[e]
29	Sochaczew	....	....	..	36	.....	.....	....	....	....	....	....
30	Siedlce	....	....	65	44	3.400	.....	.138	....	....	....	....
31	Sosnowiec	.508	2.265	197	206	9.355	2.877	3.007	1.265	.181	2.156	.261[e]
32	Toruń	.203	1.312	87	..	5.258	.....	1.653	....	....	....	2.046[e]
33	Tarnów	.101	.807	36	33	2.980	.453	1.052	....	....	.320	1.327[ea]
34	Wyszków	....	....	54	..	2.448	.950	.960	....	....	.690	.022[e]
35	Włocławek	.204	1.011	70	24	4.567	1.288	1.380	.477	.169	.935	.261[e]
36	Warszawa	....	....	..	272	.....	.....	....	8.764	....	....	....
37	Zgierz	.102	1.209	94	13	5.018	1.635	1.332	.189	....	1.215	....
38	Zawiercie	.203	.810	60	7	3.366	1.317	.455	.305	.175	1.000	.065[e]
	Total	**4.293**	**20.993**	**1,915†**	**1,363‡**	**120.936**	**33.278**	**33.999**	**18.005**	**2.788**	**24.978**	**11.322***

* Detail of miscellaneous food indicated by the following indexes: salt; [e], salmon. Of the total, 11.322, 2.788 is salt and 8.534 is salmon.

† 1,915 cases of evaporated milk are equivalent to 41.695 metric tons.

‡ 1,363 cases of condensed milk are equivalent to 25.967 metric tons. Total milk, 67.662 metric tons.

POLAND

Deliveries from WARSAW Warehouse, Month of January, 1922

Table 482

Receipt No.	Central Committee	Flour	Rice	Beans, Peas	Corn Grits	Pork Products	Vegetable Oil	Milk Evap.	Cocoa	Sugar	Salmon and Whalemeat	Soap
		Commodities in Net Metric Tons of 1,000 Kilograms or 2,204.6 Pounds										
...	P.A.K.P.D.	**614.978**	**306.588**	**142.610**	**35.230**	**72.869**	**18.910**	**269.285**	**28.004**	**139.318**	**31.696**	**.200**

POLAND

Deliveries from WARSAW Warehouse, Month of February, 1922

Table 483

Receipt No.	Central Committee	Flour	Rice	Beans, Peas	Corn Grits	Pork Products	Vegetable Oil	Milk Evap.	Cocoa	Sugar	Salmon and Whalemeat	Soap
		Commodities in Net Metric Tons of 1,000 Kilograms or 2,204.6 Pounds										
...	P.A.K.P.D.	**630.704**	**267.642**	**194.143**	**45.189**	**71.731**	**16.663**	**304.671**	**28.494**	**144.598**	**.131**	....

POLAND

Table 484 — Deliveries from WARSAW Warehouse, Month of March, 1922

Receipt No.	Central Committee	Flour	Rice	Beans, Peas	Corn Grits	Pork Products	Vegetable Oil	Milk Evap.	Cocoa	Sugar	Salmon and Whalemeat	Soap
		Commodities in Net Metric Tons of 1,000 Kilograms or 2,204.6 Pounds										
...	P.A.K.P.D.	**1,083.086**	**481.870**	**408.614**	**47.089**	**121.911**	**38.255**	**546.002**	**49.328**	**262.118**	......	....

POLAND

Table 485 — Deliveries from BREST Warehouse, Month of April, 1922

Receipt No.	Local Committee	Flour	Rice	Beans, Peas	Corn Grits	Pork Products	Vegetable Oil	Milk Evap.	Milk Cond.	Cocoa	Sugar	Salt
		Commodities in Net Metric Tons of 1,000 Kilograms or 2,204.6 Pounds										
130	Biłgoraji	.....	.....	.....	.....	.....	.....	.....	.....	.049	.....	.....
131	Barańowicki	.....	.....	3.795	.....	1.380	.....	.....	.....	.410	.....	.....
132	Tomaszowie	4.661	1.659	2.243	.....	.417	.....	.....	.....	.105	.....	.....
133	Stolpce	.....	.....	.759	.....	.276	.....	.....	.....	....	.....	.....
134	Chełiński	.....	.....	.....	.....	1.167	.....	2.300	.....	.516	.....	.....
135	Slonim	.....	.....	.....	.....	.....	.....	.752	.624	....	.....	.....
138	Brzéścic Ñ/Bugiem'	.....	4.024	14.974	.....	.....	.....	.....	.....	....	10.100	.....
139	Brzéścic Ñ/Bugiem'	24.746	15.343	6.376	.....	4.213	2.246	13.940	1.052	.837	.....	.....
140	Lucki	.....	.....	.....	.....	.543	.....	.....	.....	.305	.....	.....
141	Kowelski	.....	.....	.....	.....	2.484	.....	.....	.....	.100	.....	.....
	Total	**29.407**	**21.026**	**28.147**	.....	**10.480**	**2.246**	**16.992**	**1.676**	**2.322**	**10.100**	.....

POLAND

Table 486 — Deliveries from LWÓW Warehouse, Month of April, 1922

Receipt No.	Local Committee	Flour	Rice	Beans, Peas	Corn Grits	Pork Products	Vegetable Oil	Milk Evap.	Milk Cond.	Cocoa	Sugar	Salt
		Commodities in Net Metric Tons of 1,000 Kilograms or 2,204.6 Pounds										
1	Búczacz	2.975	1.302	.329	.....	.353	....	1.207	....	.123	.708	.....
2	Chyrów	1.052	.447	.453	.....	.208	....	.390	....	.043	.261	.....
3	Cieszanów	.982	.340	1.109	.....	.158	....	.353	....	.035	.225	.....
4	Czortków	2.265	.531	.316	.....	.104	....	.628	....	.043	.405	.....
5	Jarosław	.188	.071	.....	.....	....	.022	.054	.075	....	.063	.....
6	Kołomyja	3.951	1.453	1.579	.....	.474	.099	2.056	....	.206	.974	.....
7	Kosów	.321	.015	.....	.....	.012	....	.027	....	....	.089	.....
8	Lwów	29.992	12.859	9.889	2.510	3.684	.926	17.229	11.021	1.330	7.391	.....
9	Stryj	2.174	.931	.943	.....	.225	.136	1.488	....	.083	.428	1.000
	Total	**43.900**	**17.949**	**14.618**	**2.510**	**5.218**	**1.183**	**23.432**	**11.096**	**1.863**	**10.544**	**1.000**

POLAND

Table 487 — Deliveries from WARSAW Warehouse, Month of April, 1922

eceipt No.	Local Committee	Flour	Rice	Beans, Peas	Corn Grits	Pork Products	Vegetable Oil	Milk Evap.	Milk Cond.	Cocoa	Sugar	Soap
		Commodities in Net Metric Tons of 1,000 Kilograms or 2,204.6 Pounds										
1	Brześcic Lit.	.....	2.000	....	....	....	....	2.504	....	....	....	....
2	Kuta Królewska	6.448	2.860	2.860	....	1.040	....	2.888	....	.313	1.560	....
3	Katowice Magistrat Rezsow	1.240	.550	.550	....	.201	....	.400	....	.060	.300	....
4	Katowice Magistrat ...	9.920	4.400	4.400	....	1.600	....	3.520	....	.480	2.400	....
5	Katowice dla doz dzieci	4.960	2.200	2.200	....	.800	....	1.760	....	.240	1.200	....
6	Katowice dla dzieci...	13.659	1.992	2.750	.687	.846	.166	3.167	.462	.314	1.494	....
7	Tarnowski Góvy dla doz dzieci	1.116	.495	.495	....	.180	....	.396	....	.054	.270	....
8	Rejon Wam Rodk Grojecki	61.988	....	....	....	....	....	.002	....	....	....	....
9	Rejon Warszawski	.....	....	....	....	....	....	....	1.259	....	....	.500
	Total	**99.331**	**14.497**	**13.255**	**.687**	**4.667**	**.166**	**14.077**	**1.721**	**1.461**	**7.224**	**.500**

POLAND

Table 488 — Deliveries from WARSAW Warehouse, Month of May, 1922

eceipt No.	Local Committee	Flour	Rice	Beans, Peas	Corn Grits	Pork Products	Vegetable Oil	Milk Evap.	Milk Cond.	Cocoa	Sugar	Soap
		Commodities in Net Metric Tons of 1,000 Kilograms or 2,204.6 Pounds										
1	Kraków	....	3.000	....	.....	....	.....	....	.....	....	....	....
2	Lublin Milk Station...	....	....	....	.....	....	.....	.762	.....	....	....	....
3	Poznan	.275	....	....	.....	.037	.....	.051	.....	....	.037	....
4	Strzałkow	.193	.112	.196	.....	.058	.....	.733	.....	.016	.086	....
5	Warsaw	....	....	....	.....	.373	.....	....	.....	....	....	.022
	Total	**.468**	**3.112**	**.196**	.....	**.468**	.....	**1.546**	.....	**.016**	**.123**	**.022**

POLAND

Table 489 — Deliveries from WARSAW Warehouse, Month of June, 1922

eceipt No.	Central Committee	Flour	Rice	Beans, Peas	Corn Grits	Pork Products	Vegetable Oil	Milk Evap.	Cocoa	Sugar	Salmon and Whalemeat	Soup	Soap
		Commodities in Net Metric Tons of 1,000 Kilograms or 2,204.6 Pounds											
..	P.A.K.P.D. .	**1,051.434**	**43.473**	....	**24.922**	**.405**	......	**39.299**	**1.010**	**2.159**	**1.649**	....	....

POLAND

Table 490 — Deliveries from WARSAW Warehouse, Month of July, 1922

eceipt No.	Central Committee	Flour	Rice	Beans, Peas	Corn Grits	Pork Products	Vegetable Oil	Milk Evap.	Cocoa	Sugar	Salmon and Whalemeat	Soup	Soap
		Commodities in Net Metric Tons of 1,000 Kilograms or 2,204.6 Pounds											
..	P.A.K.P.D. .	**1,159.985**	**165.275**	**146.388**	**13.415**	**34.389**	**16.553**	**683.096**	**17.511**	**840.385**	**24.832**	**.070**	**42.307**

Table 491

ROUMANIA—

Operation	Table No.	Flour	Grain	Rice
		ARMISTIC		
A.R.A.—U.S. Treasury Loan	492	90,644.8	5,545.3	374.3
U.S. Liquidation Commission (War Dept.)	122	......	......	.....
Jewish Joint Distribution Committee	124	......	......	.....
Total American Relief	....	**90,644.8**	**5,545.3**	**374.3**
United Kingdom	493	22,643.0	21,911.0	.....
United Kingdom—Finance on Freight	493	......	......	.....
Canada	493	7,702.0	26,382.0	.....
Newfoundland	....	......	......	.....
Total British Empire Relief	133	**30,345.0**	**48,293.0**	.....
Total Relief, Armistice Period	108	**120,989.8**	**53,838.3**	**374.3**
		RECONSTRUCTIO		
A.R.A.—Congressional Appropriation, $100,000,000 Fund	494–95	250.0	......	170.0
Roumanian Government Donation	494n	492.0	......	.....
Total Children's Relief	163	**742.0**	......	**170.0**
Grand Total Relief Deliveries	102	**121,731.8**	**53,838.3**	**544.3**

ROUMANIA—

Table 492

Detail by Steamers of Relief Deliveries Paid for b

Arrival No.*	Steamer	Port of Sailing	Date of Arrival	Port of Arrival	Wheat Flour
			1919		
9	Western Plains	New York	Jan. 21	Constanza	6,637.6
25	West Mohamet	New York	Feb. 17	Constanza	7,053.5
55	West Zeda	New York	Mar. 7	Constanza	6,681.2
60	West Cressy	Norfolk	Mar. 11	Constanza	7,117.7
63	Eastern Shore	New York	Mar. 14	Constanza	8,298.3
76	Lydia	Baltimore	Mar. 19	Constanza	4,963.7
29	Bucegi, I, Ex-Western Belle	Derindje	....	Galatz	2,326.0
142	West Corum	New York	Apr. 20	Constanza	7,352.6
144	Englewood	New York	Apr. 21	Constanza	......
134	East Cape	Norfolk	Apr. 17	Constanza	7,300.2
159	Coastwise	Philadelphia	May 1	Constanza	......
162	Everett	New York	May 3	Constanza	3,870.6
172	Western Ally	Norfolk	May 8	Sulina	6,666.3
174	Absecon	New York	May 9	Constanza	2,329.2
211	Saucon	Philadelphia	May 20	Constanza	6,288.3
199	West Harcuvar	Newport News	May 16	Constanza	7,551.4
265	Milcovul ‡	Marseilles	June 10	Galatz	5,386.1
299	Regele Carol	Montreal	June 23	Galatz	300.7
356	Bucegi, II ‡	Marseilles	July 20	Braila	......
361	Constanza ‡	Marseilles	July 25	Galatz	......
	Total	....	....	....	**90,123.4**

* Arrival numbers from Table 111.
† Corn, 2,977.8; rye, 2,567.5.
‡ Purchased by A.R.A. from U.S. Army stocks in France.

ummary of Relief Deliveries

Beans, Peas	Pork Products	Milk	Cocoa	Sugar	Misc. Food	Soap	Clothing and Misc.	Total Tons	Total Value
Commodities in Net Metric Tons of 1,000 Kilograms or 2,204.6 Pounds									
ERIOD									
684.1	2,919.1	2,774.9	.....	.....	......	....	......	102,942.5	$23,438,339.29
.....	.....	.....	.....	.....	17,596.0	....	4,735.0	22,331.0	13,012,689.00
100.0	100.0	50.0	.....	.....	25.0	25.0	82.0	382.0	256,000.00
784.1	**3,019.1**	**2,824.9**	.....	.....	**17,621.0**	**25.0**	**4,817.0**	**125,655.5**	**$36,707,028.29**
1,892.0	562.0	.....	.....	.....	5,240.0	....	7,000.0	59,248.0	$10,004,628.00
.....	.....	.....	.....	.....	......	....	......	......	21,420.00
.....	.....	.....	.....	.....	......	....	4,100.0	38,184.0	3,836,600.00
.....	.....	.....	.....	.....	2,356.0	....	......	2,356.0	1,566,040.00
1,892.0	**562.0**	.....	.....	.....	**7,596.0**	....	**11,100.0**	**99,788.0**	**$15,428,688.00**
2,676.1	**3,581.1**	**2,824.9**	.....	.....	**25,217.0**	**25.0**	**15,917.0**	**225,443.5**	**$52,135,716.29**
ERIOD									
130.0	70.0	185.0	220.9	406.4	......	....	......	1,432.3	$ 477,272.76
492.0	161.0	1,090.0	.....	.....	92.0	....	......	2,327.0	1,024,322.26
622.0	**231.0**	**1,275.0**	**220.9**	**406.4**	**92.0**	....	......	**3,759.3**	**$ 1,501,595.02**
3,298.1	**3,812.1**	**4,099.9**	**220.9**	**406.4**	**25,309.0**	**25.0**	**15,917.0**	**229,202.8**	**$53,637,311.31**

merican Relief Administration

unds Loaned by U.S. Treasury—Armistice Period, 1919

Cereal Flour	Grain	Beans, Peas	Rice	Pork Products	Lard	Milk	Total Tons	Total Value
Contents of Cargoes in Net Metric Tons of 1,000 Kilograms or 2,204.6 Pounds								
....	......	.....	.....	......	.....	.....	6,637.6	$ 1,390,187.74
....	......	.....	.....	......	.....	.....	7,053.5	1,477,301.38
....	......	.....	.....	......	.....	.....	6,681.2	1,399,302.36
....	......	.....	.....	......	.....	.....	7,117.7	1,490,725.22
....	......	.....	.....	......	.....	.....	8,298.3	1,738,001.19
....	......	.....	.....	......	.....	.....	4,963.7	1,039,596.07
....	......	.....	.....	......	.....	217.8	2,543.8	606,220.00
....	......	.....	.....	......	.....	.....	7,352.6	1,539,922.68
....	......	.....	.....	1,932.2	986.9	962.0	3,881.1	2,732,860.90
....	......	.....	.....	......	.....	.....	7,300.2	1,528,962.06
....	5,545.3†	.....	.....	......	.....	.....	5,545.3	774,291.59
22.2	......	501.4	.....	......	.....	590.8	4,985.0	1,224,443.37
....	......	.....	.....	......	.....	.....	6,666.3	1,399,932.66
....	......	.....	.....	......	.....	1,004.3	3,333.5	923,666.89
....	......	.....	.....	......	.....	.....	6,288.3	1,320,532.92
....	......	.....	.....	......	.....	.....	7,551.4	1,585,788.96
....	......	.....	.....	......	.....	.....	5,386.1	969,502.14
....	......	.....	.....	......	.....	.....	300.7	66,151.58
481.3	......	156.8	363.8	......	.....	.....	1,001.9	218,364.68
17.9	......	25.9	10.5	......	.....	.....	54.3	12,584.90
521.4	**5,545.3†**	**684.1**	**374.3**	**1,932.2**	**986.9**	**2,774.9**	**102,942.5**	**$23,438,339.29**

Table 493

Detail by Steamers of Relie

Steamer	Port of Sailing	Date of Sailing	Port of Arrival	Date of Arrival	Wheat Flour
		1918		1919	
Leucadia	Freemantle	Dec. 5	Constanza	Feb. ..	5,910.0
		1919			
War Tulip	New Orleans	Jan. 3	Constanza	Feb. ..	7,290.0
Pengreep	Geelong	Mar. 20	Constanza	May 13	......
Constanza	Liverpool	....	Constanza	Apr. 23	......
Tregarthen	Freemantle	Mar. 29	Constanza	May 17	......
Ferngarth	Melbourne	Mar. 15	Constanza	May 20	......
Oltul	Liverpool	May 14	Constanza	June 2	......
Sirtul	London	May 10	Constanza	June 4	......
War Pike	Basra	....	Constanza	....	......
Cranmore	Salonica	May 6	Galatz	June 6	......
Total					**13,200.0**
War Syren	Portland	Mar. 11	Constanza	Apr. 14	832.0
Germania	Portland	Apr. 23	Constanza	May 22	1,233.0
Baron Edmund Vay	Portland	Apr. 22	Constanza	June 2	335.0
Absirtea	Portland	Apr. 30	Constanza	June 6	1,938.0
Burma	Portland	May 9	Constanza	June 3	......
Principessa-Christiana	Montreal	May 15	Constanza	June ..	3,364.0
Tudor Prima	Montreal	May 30	Constanza	July ..	......
Juil	Montreal	July 5	Constanza	Aug. ..	......
Total					**7,702.0**
Eskaloni			Constanza		......
Grand Total, British Empire *					**20,902.0**

* For value of above deliveries, Cf. Table 133.

ROUMANIA—American Relief Administration

Detail by Steamers of Children's Relief Arrivals, Paid for by Funds from the Congressional Appropriation for Relief—Reconstruction Period, 1919–1924

Table 494*

Steamer	Port of Sailing	Date of Arrival	Port of Arrival	Contents of Cargoes in Net Metric Tons of 1,000 Kilograms or 2,204.6 Pounds									Total Value
				Wheat Flour	Rice	Beans, Peas	Pork Products: Meat	Pork Products: Lard	Milk	Cocoa	Sugar	Total Tons	
		1919											
Englewood	New York	Apr. 21	Constanza	.....	.....	.....	30.0	10.0	.....	.....	.....	40.0	$ 28.750.
Point Bonita	New York	Apr. 25	Braila	.....	.....	.....	....	....	.....	116.9	203.2	320.1	102,536.
Everett	New York	May 3	Constanza	250.0	.....	30.0	....	....	185.0	104.0	203.2	772.2	252,996.
Bucegi, II.	Marseilles	July 20	Braila	.....	170.0	100.0	30.0	....	.....	.....	.....	300.0	92,989.
Total †				**250.0**	**170.0**	**130.0**	**60.0**	**10.0**	**185.0**	**220.9**	**406.4**	**1,432.3**	**$477,272.**

* In addition to the supplies listed in this table, the Roumanian government made a donation to the child feeding program. This donation consisted of 2,327.0 metric tons, valued at $1,024,322.26. The commodities in metric tons were flour, 492.0 (including 79.0, oatmeal); beans, 492.0; bacon, 161.0; milk, 1,090.0; and veal loaf and potatoes, 92.0. Receipts showing internal delivery were turned over to the government. This da from "Certificate furnished by Chairman of Roumanian Children's Rel Association."

† For detail of internal deliveries, cf. Table 495.

Countries Other Than United States

Deliveries—Armistice Period, 1919

Cereal Flour	Wheat	Beans	Lard Substitute	Meat	Miscellaneous Foods	Miscellaneous Non-Foods	Total Tons
Contents of Cargoes in Net Metric Tons of 1,000 Kilograms or 2,204.6 Pounds							
A. BY UNITED KINGDOM							
......	......	.....	.....	.....	......	......	5,910.0
......	......	.....	.....	.....	......	......	7,290.0
......	7,360.0	.....	.....	.....	......	......	7,360.0
1,987.0	......	268.0	.....	.....	......	......	2,255.0
......	7,267.0	.....	.....	.....	......	......	7,267.0
......	7,284.0	.....	.....	.....	......	......	7,284.0
2,819.0	......	1,198.0	262.0	.....	......	6,178.0	10,457.0
4,637.0	......	426.0	.....	.....	......	822.0	5,885.0
......	......	.....	.....	.....	4,900.0	......	4,900.0
......	......	.....	.....	300.0	340.0	......	640.0
9,443.0	**21,911.0**	**1,892.0**	**262.0**	**300.0**	**5,240.0**	**7,000.0**	**59,248.0**
B. BY CANADA							
......	4,940.0	.....	.....	.....	......	......	5,772.0
......	5,717.0	.....	.....	.....	......	......	6,950.0
......	3,668.0	.....	.....	.....	......	......	4,003.0
......	4,360.0	.....	.....	.....	......	......	6,298.0
......	6,466.0	.....	.....	.....	......	......	6,466.0
......	......	.....	.....	.....	......	......	3,364.0
......	217.0	.....	.....	.....	......	......	217.0
......	1,014.0	.....	.....	.....	......	4,100.0	5,114.0
......	**26,382.0**	.....	.....	.....	......	**4,100.0**	**38,184.0**
C. BY NEWFOUNDLAND							
......	......	.....	.....	.....	**2,356.0**	......	**2,356.0**
9,443.0	**48,283.0**	**1,892.0**	**262.0**	**400.0**	**7,596.0**	**11,100.0**	**99,788.0**

ROUMANIA—American Relief Administration

Detail of Internal Deliveries, by Receipt Numbers and Committees

Reconstruction Period, 1919–1924

Table 495

Receipt No.	District and Local Committee	Date	Flour	Rice	Beans, Peas	Pork Products	Milk	Cocoa	Sugar	Total Tons
			Commodities in Net Metric Tons of 1,000 Kilograms or 2,204.6 Pounds							
		1919								
1	Arges	May 25	8.000	.....	2.000	6.000	4.000	.....	.....	20.000
4	Sud Muscel	May 26	8.000	.....	2.000	6.000	4.000	.....	.....	20.000
5	Dâmbovița, Targoviște	May 25	8.000	.....	2.000	6.000	4.000	.....	.....	20.000
6	Slatina, Olt	May 26	8.000	.....	2.000	6.000	4.000	.....	.....	20.000
7	Teleorman	May 26	8.000	.....	2.000	6.000	4.000	.....	.....	20.000
	Total for May	....	**40.000**	.....	**10.000**	**30.000**	**20.000**	.....	.....	**100.000**
2	Buzeu	June 3	8.000	.....	.....	6.000	4.000	.....	.....	18.000
3	Călărași	June 2	8.000	.....	.....	6.000	4.000	.....	.....	18.000
8	Prahova	June 3	8.000	.....	.....	6.000	4.000	.....	.....	18.000
9	Cernauți	June 30	8.000	.....	.....	2.000	4.000	2.101	2.000	18.101
10	R.-Sarat	June 2	8.000	.....	.....	6.000	4.000	.....	.....	18.000
11	Vlașca	June ..	8.000	.....	.....	.....	4.000	.....	.....	12.000
12	Sud Ilfov, Bucharest	June 10	.....	.....	.530	.....	.712	.054	.075	1.371
13	Sud Ilfov	June 10	.....	.....	.....	.....	.....	.128	.045	.173

[*Continued on next page*]

ROUMANIA

Detail of Internal Deliveries, by Receipt Numbers and Committees

Table 495—*Continued*

Receipt No.	District and Local Committee	Date	Flour	Rice	Beans, Peas	Pork Products	Milk	Cocoa	Sugar	Total Tons
			Commodities in Net Metric Tons of 1,000 Kilograms or 2,204.6 Pounds							
		1919								
14	Sud Vlașca	June 9	8.000	.....	2.000	.....	4.000	2.000	2.000	18.000
15	R.-Sarat	June 23	8.000	.....	.....	.....	4.000	2.121	1.990	16.111
16	Ploesti, Prahova	June 22	12.000	.....	.....	.....	12.000	3.139	3.154	30.293
17	Teleorman	June 18	8.000	.....	2.000	.....	4.000	2.000	2.000	18.000
18	Slatina, Olt	June ..	8.000	.....	2.000	2.000	4.000	2.000	2.000	20.000
19	Targoviște	June 9	8.000	.....	2.000	2.000	2.000	2.000	2.000	18.000
20	Câmpu-Lung	June 9	8.000	.....	2.000	.....	4.000	2.000	2.000	18.000
21	Călărași	June 24	4.000	.....	.....	.....	2.000	1.047	.981	8.028
22	Buzeu	June 20	8.000	.....	.....	.....	4.000	2.109	1.999	16.108
23	Sud Ilfov, Bucharest	June 30	.....	.....	.630	.....	.264	.132	.090	1.116
	Total for June	....	**120.000**	.....	**11.160**	**30.000**	**64.976**	**20.831**	**20.334**	**267.301**
24	Ploesti, Prahova	July ..	.....	.....	5.250	.....	4.944	1.820	1.940	13.954
25	Targoviște	July 10	.....	.....	5.250	.....	4.944	1.820	1.985	13.99
26	Buzeu	July 12	.....	.....	5.250	.....	4.944	1.820	1.979	13.99
27	Teleorman	July 19	.....	.....	5.250	.....	4.944	1.820	1.971	13.98
28	Brașov	July 20	.....	.....	5.250	.....	4.944	1.820	1.951	13.96
29	Călărași	July 13	.....	.....	5.250	.....	4.944	1.820	1.979	13.99
30	Giurgiu	July 11	.....	.....	5.250	.....	4.944	1.820	2.001	14.01
31	Muscel	July 31	.....	.....	.315	.....	.....	.130	.090	.53
32	Bucharest	July 8	8.010	.....	2.730	.....	8.688	.....	.....	19.42
32A	Copăciósa	July 13	.....	.....	.210	.....	.....	.....	.....	.21
33	Drăgănesci	July 16	.....	.....	.....	.....	.....	.040	.030	.07
34	Bucharest	July 20	25.219	.....	.....	.....	.....	.....	.....	25.21
35	Buzeu	July 20	23.664	.....	.....	.....	.....	.....	.....	23.66
36	Dâmbovița	July 20	27.179	.....	.....	.....	.....	.....	.....	27.17
37	Giurgiu, Vlasca	July 20	5.929	.....	.....	.....	.....	.....	.....	5.92
38	Dr. Pop, Institution *	July 18	.....	.....	.....	.....	.672	.108	.136	.91
39	Alex Istrati, Institution *	July 18	.....	.....	.....	.....	.984	.305	.682	1.97
40	Joe Mesan, Institution *	July 27	.....	.....	.....	.....	.168	.108	.045	.32
41	Ilfov	July 22	.....	.....	.....	.....	.288	.....	.....	.28
42	Ilfov	July 30	.....	.....	.....	.....	.....	3.024	2.730	5.75
43	Maria I. Pillat, Institution *	July 28	.....	.....	.....	.....	.168	.108	.046	.32
44	Preot Paunesai, Institution*	July 31	.....	.....	.....	.....	.504	.216	.136	.85
65	Brăila	July 7	.....	.....	6.760	.....	4.506	1.321	1.814	14.40
66	Chișinău	July 21	.....	.....	5.824	.....	8.380	3.048	2.540	19.79
67	Cernauți, Brăila	July 22	.....	.....	9.152	.....	6.285	2.844	4.082	22.36
68	Covurlui, Brăila	July 5	.....	.....	.....	.....	.....	1.727	2.313	4.04
69	Teleorman	July 22	.....	.....	3.952	.....	.....	2.032	1.995	7.97
70	Botosani	July 23	.....	.....	1.456	.....	1.502	.609	.589	4.15
71	Bacău, Brăila	July 21	.....	.....	2.912	.....	3.004	1.117	1.224	8.25
77	Iași, Brăila	July 11	.....	.....	.....	.....	.....	.813	1.134	1.94
78	Tulcea	July 18	.....	.....	.....	.....	.....	.....	3.175	3.17
83	Ploesti, Brăila	July 19	.....	.....	.....	.....	.....	2.743	2.268	5.01
87	Constanza	July 31	.....	.....	.....	1.326	.....	3.162	4.595	9.08
105	Chișinău	July 20	.....	.....	.....	.....	.....	.....	1.134	1.13
106	Brăila	July 20	.....	.....	.....	.....	.....	.....	.454	.45
107	Brăila	July 28	.....	.....	.....	.....	.....	3.759	.....	3.75
	Total for July	....	**90.001**	.....	**70.061**	**1.326**	**69.757**	**39.954**	**45.018**	**316.11**
45	Slatina, Olt	Aug. 5	.....	.....	.....	.....	2.400	.756	.557	3.71
46	Ton P. Scolea, Institution *	Aug. 5	.....	.....	.....	.....	1.728	.432	.364	2.52
47	Bucharest	Aug. 7	.....	.....	.....	.....	3.744	.972	.773	5.48
48	Vlașca	Aug. 5	.....	.....	.....	.....	2.400	.756	.592	3.74
49	Bucharest	Aug. 13	.....	.....	.....	.....	.198	.108	.045	.35
50	Mia Levesu, Institution *	Aug. 14	.....	.....	8.000	.....	.....	.....	.....	8.00
51	Sud Ilfov	Aug. 15	.....	.....	20.000	.....	.....	.....	.....	20.00
52	Dr. Valerie Pop, Institution *	Aug. 15	.....	.....	2.000	.....	.....	.....	.....	2.00

* Name of city written on this receipt is illegible.

ROUMANIA

Detail of Internal Deliveries, by Receipt Numbers and Committees

Table 495—*Continued*

Receipt No.	District and Local Committee	Date	Commodities in Net Metric Tons of 1,000 Kilograms or 2,204.6 Pounds							
			Flour	Rice	Beans, Peas	Pork Products	Milk	Cocoa	Sugar	Total Tons
		1919								
53	Bucharest	Aug. 19	.....	.....	.....	.....	.195	.105	.046	.346
54	Bucharest	Aug. 25	.....	.....	.....	.....	.....	.....	.834	.834
55	Călărași	Aug. 29	.....	.....	.....	.....	.....	.012	.015	.027
56	Dr. Bratianu, Institution *	Aug. 26	.....	.....	.....	.....	.....	.037	.045	.082
57	Coralie Pavlo, Institution *	Aug. 25	.....	.....	.....	.....	.075	.025	.030	.130
58	Bucharest	Aug. 29	.....	.....	.....	.....	.075	.025	.030	.130
59	Bucharest	Aug. 29	.....	.....	.105	.....	.....	.....	.022	.127
60	Pia Bratianu, Institution *	Aug. 29	.....	.....	.105	.....	.....	.....	.022	.127
61	Zudistabil, Institution *	Aug. 25	.....	1.400	.....	.....	.....	.610	.907	2.917
72	Ialomița, Brăila	Aug. 4	.....	.....	.....	.....	.....	.....	1.814	1.814
73	Bacău, Brăila	Aug. 4	.....	.....	.....	.....	.....	.610	.590	1.200
74	Suceava, Brăila	Aug. 4	.....	.....	.....	.....	3.004	1.118	1.225	5.347
75	Brăila	Aug. 11	.....	.....	7.999	.....	11.278	2.743	2.268	24.288
76	Dâmbovița, Targoviște	Aug. 15	.....	.....	.....	.....	5.713	3.455	2.858	12.026
79	Suceava, Brăila	Aug. 26	.....	.....	.....	.....	.....	.203	1.360	1.563
80	Cernauți, Brăila	Aug. 29	.....	.....	.....	.....	.....	1.930	.....	1.930
82	Cernauți, Brăila	Aug. 16	.....	.....	.....	.....	.....	.....	2.721	2.721
84	Buzeu, Brăila	Aug. 23	.....	.....	.....	.....	.....	2.032	1.725	3.757
85	Silistra	Aug. 23	.....	.....	.....	.....	.....	.406	.273	.679
86	Constanza	Aug. 31	.....	.....	.....	2.407	.....	1.632	1.957	5.996
95	Suceava, Brăila	Aug. 20	.....	.....	.....	.....	.....	1.321	.454	1.775
96	Brăila	Aug. 25	.....	.....	.....	.....	.....	.508	.453	.961
97	Galatz, Brăila	Aug. 25	.....	.....	.....	.....	.....	2.032	1.732	3.764
	Total for August	....	.....	**1.400**	**38.209**	**2.407**	**30.810**	**21.828**	**23.712**	**118.366**
62	"Barmesa" *	Sept. 4	.....	.....	.420	.....	.....	.102	.019	.541
63	"Israelite Institution" *	Sept. 4	.....	.....	.150	.....	.....	.025	.030	.205
64	Gradina	Sept. 5	.....	.....	.....	.....	.048	.012	.009	.069
81	Golesci, Bucharest	Sept. 26	.....	.....	.....	.....	.....	.510	.591	1.101
88	Bucharest	Sept. 5	.....	.....	.....	.....	.....	.025	.030	.055
89	Comitetul Central de Ajutor *	Sept. 10	.....	.....	.....	.....	.....	.013	.009	.022
90	Vlașca, Bucharest	Sept. 14	.....	.....	.....	.....	.....	1.632	1.956	3.588
91	Olt, Bucharest	Sept. 5	.....	.....	.....	.....	.....	.918	1.118	2.036
92	Bucharest	Sept. 15	.....	.....	.....	.....	.....	.102	.182	.284
93	Muscel, Bucharest	Sept. 14	.....	.....	.....	.....	.....	.510	.592	1.102
94	Coralie Pavlon, Institution *	Sept. 22	.....	.....	.....	.....	.....	.025	.030	.055
98	R.-Sarat	Sept. 3	.....	2.100	.....	.....	.....	.508	.632	3.240
99	R.-Sarat, Brăila	Sept. 3	.....	2.100	.....	.....	.....	.508	.632	3.240
100	Tulcea, Brăila	Sept. 4	.....	6.000	.....	.....	.....	2.540	3.221	11.761
101	Bucharest	Sept. 26	.....	.....	.....	.....	.....	.037	.045	.082
102	Bucharest	Sept. 29	.....	.....	.....	.....	.....	.012	.015	.027
103	Bucharest	Sept. 25	.....	.....	.....	.....	.....	.510	.591	1.101
104	Bucharest	Sept. 16	.....	.....	.....	.....	.....	.007	.009	.016
108	Chișinău, Brăila	Sept. 9	.....	.....	.....	.....	.....	1.424	.902	2.326
109	Cernauți, Brăila	Sept. 11	.....	.....	.....	.....	.....	.....	3.301	3.301
110	Cernauți, Brăila	Sept. 11	.....	.....	.....	.....	.....	.....	1.134	1.134
	Total for September	....	.....	**10.200**	**.570**	.....	**.048**	**9.420**	**15.048**	**35.286**
111	Constanza	Oct. 1	.....	.....	.....	6.267	.....	.....	.....	6.267
112	Constanza	Oct. 1	.....	.....	.....	.....	.....	.....	1.365	1.365
113	Bucharest and Ilfov	Oct. 1	.....	.....	.....	.....	.....	.037	.046	.083
114	Bucharest and Ilfov	Oct. 2	.....	.....	.....	.....	.....	.204	.136	.340
115	Bucharest and Ilfov	Oct. 11	.....	.150	.....	.....	.....	.025	.045	.220
116	Bucharest and Ilfov	Oct. 16	.....	.150	.....	.....	.....	.070	.156	.376
117	Bucharest and Ilfov	Oct. ..	.....	.100	.....	.....	.....	.070	.156	.326
118	Bucharest and Ilfov	Oct. 20	.....	.500	.....	.....	.....	.042	.300	.842
119	Bucharest and Ilfov	Oct. 20	.....	.500	.....	.....	.....	.042	.300	.842
120	Bucharest and Ilfov	Oct. 21	.....	.500	.....	.....	.....	.300	.300	1.100

[*Concluded on next page*]

ROUMANIA

Detail of Internal Deliveries, by Receipt Numbers and Committees

Table 495—*Concluded*

Receipt No.	District and Local Committee	Date	Commodities in Net Metric Tons of 1,000 Kilograms or 2,204.6 Pounds							
			Flour	Rice	Beans, Peas	Pork Products	Milk	Cocoa	Sugar	Tons Total
		1919								
121	Bucharest and Ilfov........	Oct. ..	.....	.230	.....	.....	.....	.105	.230	.565
122	Bucharest and Ilfov........	Oct. 23	.....	.090	.....	.....	.....	.042	.093	.225
123	Bucharest and Ilfov........	Oct. ..	.....	.100	.....	.....	.....	.070	.156	.326
124	Bucharest and Ilfov........	Oct. 25	.....	.300	.....	.....	.....	.200	.300	.800
125	Bucharest and Ilfov........	Oct. 25	.....	.100	.....	.....	.....	.070	.156	.326
126	Bucharest and Ilfov........	Oct. 27	.....	.075	.....	.....	.....	.035	.075	.185
127	Bucharest and Ilfov........	Oct. 24	.....	.300	.....	.....	.....	.200	.200	.700
128	Bucharest and Ilfov........	Oct. 25	.....	.300	.....	.....	.....	.200	.300	.800
129	Bucharest and Ilfov........	Oct. 27	.....	.300	.....	.....	.....	.200	.300	.800
130	Bucharest and Ilfov........	Oct. 27	.....	.300	.....	.....	.....	.200	.300	.800
131	Bucharest and Ilfov........	Oct. 25	.....	.300	.....	.....	.....	.200	.300	.800
132	Bucharest and Ilfov........	Oct. 20	.....	.150	.....	.....	.....	.100	.200	.450
133	Bucharest and Ilfov........	Oct. 16	.....	.750	.....	.....	.....	.350	.780	1.880
134	Bucharest and Ilfov........	Oct. 27	.....	.900	.....	.....	.....	.500	.600	2.000
135	Bucharest and Ilfov........	Oct. 27	.....	.300	.....	.....	.....	.200	.300	.800
136	Bucharest and Ilfov........	Oct. 27	.....	.300	.....	.....	.....	.200	.300	.800
137	Bucharest and Ilfov........	Oct. ..	.....	.300	.....	.....	.....	.204	.300	.804
138	Bucharest and Ilfov........	Oct. ..	.....	.100	.....	.....	.....	.070	.156	.326
139	Bucharest and Ilfov........	Oct. 24	.....	.075	.....	.....	.....	.035	.075	.185
140	Bucharest and Ilfov........	Oct. ..	.....	.150	.....	.....	.....	.070	.150	.370
141	Bucharest and Ilfov........	Oct. 24	.....	.300	.....	.....	.....	.204	.300	.804
142	Bucharest and Ilfov........	Oct. 25	.....	.075	.....	.....	.....	.035	.075	.185
143	Bucharest and Ilfov........	Oct. 19	.....	.900	.....	.....	.....	.400	.780	2.080
144	Bucharest and Ilfov........	Oct. 29	.....	3.000	.....	.....	.....	2.100	3.500	8.600
145	Bucharest and Ilfov........	Oct. 29	.....	3.000	.....	.....	.....	2.100	3.500	8.600
146	Bucharest and Ilfov........	Oct. 29	.....	3.000	.....	.....	.....	2.100	3.500	8.600
147	Bucharest and Ilfov........	Oct. 29	.....	3.000	.....	.....	.....	3.462	7.725	14.187
148	Bucharest and Ilfov........	Oct. 29	.....	7.550	.....	.....	.....	3.500	7.800	18.850
149	Bucharest and Ilfov........	Oct. 29	.....	.050	.....	.....	.....	.017	.045	.112
150	Bucharest and Ilfov........	Oct. 29	.....	3.020	.....	.....	.....	.700	1.560	5.280
151	Bucharest and Ilfov........	Oct. 29	.....	.900	.....	.....	.....	.500	.600	2.000
152	Bucharest and Ilfov........	Oct. 29	.....	.300	.....	.....	.....	.200	.300	.800
153	Bucharest and Ilfov........	Oct. 29	.....	.075	.....	.....	.....	.035	.075	.185
154	Bucharest and Ilfov........	Oct. 29	.....	2.500	.....	.....	.....	2.000	3.000	7.500
155	Bucharest and Ilfov........	Oct. 29	.....	2.500	.....	.....	.....	1.500	2.000	6.000
156	Bucharest and Ilfov........	Oct. 29	.....	1.500	.....	.....	.....	1.000	2.000	4.500
157	Bucharest and Ilfov........	Oct. 29	.....	23.742	.....	.....	.....	45.939	105.303	174.984
158	Brăila to Various Committees	Oct. 25	.....	103.000	.....	.....	.....	35.500	94.500	233.000
159	Constanza, Debrogia	Oct. ..	.....	.....	.....	.....	.....	21.824	49.276	71.100
	Total for October........	....	.....	**165.732**	.....	**6.267**	.....	**127.157**	**293.914**	**593.070**
...	Port and Warehouse Shortages (Plus)	....	.....	.....	.....	.....	.....	1.700	8.400	10.100
...	Port and Warehouse Overages (Minus)	....	.....	*7.300*	.....	.....	*.600*	.....	.....	*7.900*
	Grand Total †	....	**250.001**	**170.032**	**130.000**	**70.000**	**184.991**	**220.890**	**406.426**	**1,432.340**

† Cf. Table 494.

Accounts	Table No.	Commodities in Net					
		Flour	Grain	Rice	Beans, Peas	Corn Grits	Pork Products
Northwest Russia	497	14,323.1	......	64.0	407.7	......	2,289.9
Kouban	507	.....	......	.....	.....	......	......
Siberia	510	.....	......	.....	.....	......	......
Soviet Republics	511	134,781.2	386,556.1	18,914.6	7,895.5	96,202.3	12,425.5
Ukraine	537	.....	......	.....	.....	......	......
Volunteer Army	538	394.0	......	.....	.....	......	......
Grand Total Relief Deliveries	...	**149,498.3**	**386,556.1**	**18,978.6**	**8,303.2**	**96,202.3**	**14,715.4**

RUSSIA (NORTHWEST RUSSIA)

Table 497 Summary of Relief Deliveries

Operation	Table No.	Commodities in Net Metric Tons of 1,000 Kilograms or 2,204.6 Pounds										Total Value
		Flour	Rice	Beans, Peas	Pork Products	Milk	Cocoa	Sugar	Soap	Clothing and Misc.	Total Tons	
		ARMISTICE PERIOD										
A.R.A.—Congressional Appropriation, $100,000,000 Fund	498	14,248.4	....	379.8	2,266.6	1,055.6	...	...	....	....	17,950.4	$5,285,380.17
A.R.A.—Finance on Freight	144	......	....	....	......	.....	...	...	....	....	.....	52,188.1
U.S. Liquidation Commission (War Dept.)	122	......	....	....	......	.....	...	...	....	710.0	710.0	428,299.4
Total American Relief	108	**14,248.4**	**....**	**379.8**	**2,266.6**	**1,055.6**	**...**	**...**	**....**	**710.0**	**18,660.4**	**$5,765,867.8**
		RECONSTRUCTION PERIOD										
A.R.A.—Congressional Appropriation, $100,000,000 Fund	499, 504	39.4	64.0	27.9	20.0	129.4	5.0	9.0	10.5	....	305.2	$ 111,705.1
A.R.A.-European Children's Fund	499, 504	3.3	....	....	3.0	3.9	.2	.1	....	2.3	12.8	6,223.6
Northwest Russian Government Donation	499, 504	32.0	....	....	.3	.....	...	...	....	....	32.3	6,280.0
Total Children's Relief	163	**74.7**	**64.0**	**27.9**	**23.3**	**133.3**	**5.2**	**9.1**	**10.5**	**2.3**	**350.3**	**$ 124,208.7**
Grand Total Relief Deliveries	102	**14,323.1**	**64.0**	**407.7**	**2,289.9**	**1,188.9**	**5.2**	**9.1**	**10.5**	**712.3**	**19,010.7**	**$5,890,076.5**

ummary of Relief Deliveries

etric Tons of 1,000 Kilograms or 2,204.6 Pounds									Total Value
Milk	Cocoa	Sugar	Misc. Food	Forage	Soap	Medical and Hospital Supplies	Clothing and Misc.	Total Tons	
1,188.9	5.2	9.1	.....	.....	10.5	.....	712.3	19,010.7	$ 5,890,076.54
......	.....	.....	.....	.....	.....	577.0	1,015.5	1,592.5	578,490.50
......	.....	.....	.....	.....	.....	.....	40.0	40.0	75,000.00
43,362.6	3,945.0	21,555.9	1,351.5	2,501.0	599.8	8,281.9	3,199.8	741,572.7	63,174,848.78
......	.....	.....	.....	.....	.....	.....	5,550.0	5,550.0	8,500,222.67
......	.....	.....	.....	.....	.....	.....	.....	394.0	86,680.00
44,551.5	**3,950.2**	**21,565.0**	**1,351.5**	**2,501.0**	**610.3**	**8,858.9**	**10,517.6**	**768,159.9**	**$78,305,318.49**

RUSSIA (NORTHWEST RUSSIA)—American Relief Administration

Detail by Steamers of Relief Deliveries Paid for by Funds from the Congressional Appropriation for Relief

Table 498

Armistice Period, 1919

rival o.*	Steamer	Port of Sailing	Date of Arrival	Port of Arrival	Contents of Cargoes in Net Metric Tons of 1,000 Kilograms or 2,204.6 Pounds						Total Value
					Wheat Flour	Cereal Flour	Beans, Peas	Pork Products	Milk	Total Tons	
			1919								
283	Lake Strabo	Montreal	June 16	Reval	633.7	.....	.....	.....	.....	633.7	$ 123,573.84
284	Lake Charlottesville..	Montreal	June 16	Hungerburg	2,774.3	.....	.....	.....	.....	2,774.3	540,984.80
295	Dio	New York	June 22	Viborg	3,973.9	57.9	379.8	420.7†	364.3	5,196.6	1,373,227.60
303	Democracy, III ‡	St. Nazaire	June 25	Viborg	3,381.1	.....	.....	498.7	450.3	4,330.1	1,331,826.86
304	Lake Calvenia	Montreal	June 25	Reval	2,731.7	.....	.....	.....	.....	2,731.7	532,688.13
321	Lake Traverse, IV ‡..	St. Nazaire	July 1	Reval	.....	.....	.....	961.8	.....	961.8	817,514.45
342	Lake St. Clair, V ‡...	Bordeaux	July 10	Reval	.....	280.2	.....	385.4	241.0	906.6	484,516.64
368	Slavonia	New York	Aug. 2	Reval	415.6	.....	.....	.....	.....	415.6	81,047.85
	Total	....	....	....	**13,910.3**	**338.1**	**379.8**	**2,266.6**	**1,055.6**	**17,950.4**	**$5,285,380.17**

* Arrival numbers from Table 111.
† Lard substitute.

‡ Cargo ex-Army stocks in France purchased by the A.R.A. from U.S. Liquidation Commission.

RUSSIA (NORTHWEST RUSSIA)—A.R.A. and A.R.A.-European Children's Fund

Table 499 **Summary of Arrivals, by Operations—Reconstruction Period, 1919–1924**

Operation	Table No.	Commodities in Net Metric Tons of 1,000 Kilograms or 2,204.6 Pounds										Total Value
		Flour	Rice	Beans, Peas	Pork Products	Milk	Cocoa	Sugar	Soap	Clothing	Total Tons	
R.A.—Congressional Appropriation, $100,000,000 Fund.......	500	39.4	64.0	27.9	20.0	129.4	5.0	9.0	10.5	...	305.2	$111,705.13
R.A.-European Children's Fund—Food	501	3.3	....	....	3.0	3.9	.2	.1	....	...	10.5	1,258.54
R.A.-European Children's Fund—Clothing	502	....	....	....	....	....	...	...	....	2.3	2.3	4,965.06
rthwest Russian Government Donation	503	32.0	....	....	.3	....	...	...	....	...	32.3	6,280.00
Total	...	**74.7**	**64.0**	**27.9**	**23.3**	**133.3**	**5.2**	**9.1**	**10.5**	**2.3**	**350.3**	**$124,208.73**

RUSSIA (NORTHWEST RUSSIA)—

Table 500

Detail by Steamers of Arrivals for Children's Relief Paid for by Funds

Steamer or Source	Ex	Port of Sailing	Date of Arrival
			1919
Lake Strabo		Montreal	June 16
Lake Traverse, IV	U.S. Army Stock, France	St. Nazaire	July 1
Sture, Lake Fray	Schwarzenfels and Danzig Stock	Danzig	Aug., Sept.
Total			
Add Transfer from Finland:			1920
Ranko, Frithiof	Orangepolder (Cf. Table 310)	Helsingfors, Hango	Feb., Mar. 17
Total Arrivals, Gross			
Deduct Transfers to Esthonia:			1920
Rail (Cf. Table 297)	Above-Listed Steamers	(Narva)	Mar. 17
Total Arrivals, Net			

RUSSIA (NORTHWEST RUSSIA)—

Table 501

Detail by Steamers or Source of Arrivals fo

Steamer or Source	Ex	Port of Sailing	Date of Arrival
			1919
E. H. Stinnes	Comité National Stock	Rotterdam	Dec. 22
Warehouse Adjustments	Port Overages		
Total			
			1920
Deduct Transfer to Esthonia *	E. H. Stinnes	Reval	
Total Arrivals, Net			

* Cf. Table 298.

RUSSIA (NORTHWEST RUSSIA)—A.R.A.-European Children's Fund

Table 502

Detail by Steamer of Arrival of Clothing and Accessories for Children's Relief—Reconstruction Period, 1919–1924

Steamer	Port of Sailing	Date of Arrival	Port of Arrival	Shoes (Pairs)	Laces (Pairs)	Stockings (Pairs)	Woolens (Yards)	Thread (Pounds)	Buttons (No.)	Total Metric Tons	Total Value
		1920									
Kajak	London	Jan. 10	Reval	1,360	1,360	1,224	1,625	24	4,400	2.3	$4,965.(

.merican Relief Administration

om the Congressional Appropriation for Relief—Reconstruction Period, 1919–1924

Port of Arrival	Contents of Cargoes in Net Metric Tons of 1,000 Kilograms or 2,204.6 Pounds									Total Value
	Wheat Flour	Rice	Beans, Peas	Pork Products	Milk	Cocoa	Sugar	Soap	Total Tons	
Reval	60.4	.....	.....	....	.....	....	....	....	60.4	$ 11,775.47
Reval	....	.....	.....	20.0	240.3	....	....	....	260.3	113,556.25
Reval	....	306.9	204.5	....	336.0	20.0	53.0	20.8	941.2	322,654.56
....	**60.4**	**306.9**	**204.5**	**20.0**	**576.3**	**20.0**	**53.0**	**20.8**	**1,261.9**	**$447,986.28**
Reval	....	.....	.....	....	.....	25.0	....	....	25.0	10,000.00
....	**60.4**	**306.9**	**204.5**	**20.0**	**576.3**	**45.0**	**53.0**	**20.8**	**1,286.9**	**$457,986.28**
Reval	21.0	242.9	176.6	....	446.9	40.0	44.0	10.3	981.7	346,281.15
....	**39.4**	**64.0**	**27.9**	**20.0**	**129.4**	**5.0**	**9.0**	**10.5**	**305.2**	**$111,705.13**

.R.A.-European Children's Fund

iild Feeding—Reconstruction Period, 1919–1924

Port of Arrival	Commodities in Net Metric Tons of 1,000 Kilograms or 2,204.6 Pounds									Total Value
	Wheat Flour	Rice	Beans, Peas	Pork Products	Milk	Cocoa	Sugar	Soap	Total Tons	
Reval	....	.....	.....	20.0	...	...	...	...	20.0	$8,373.50
Reval	3.3	.....	.....	....	3.9	.2	.1	...	7.5	....
....	**3.3**	.....	.....	**20.0**	**3.9**	**.2**	**.1**	...	**27.5**	**$8,373.50**
Reval	....	.....	.....	17.0	...	...	...	...	17.0	7,114.96
....	**3.3**	.....	.....	**3.0**	**3.9**	**.2**	**.1**	...	**10.5**	**$1,258.54**

RUSSIA (NORTHWEST RUSSIA)—A.R.A.-European Children's Fund

Detail by Months of Northwest Russian Government Donations for Children's Relief—Reconstruction Period, 1919–1924

Table 503

Date of Delivery	Flour	Pork Products	Total Tons	Total Value
1919				
cember	....	.3	.3	$ 125.60
1920				
uary	10.0	..	10.0	1,962.50
ruary	22.0	..	22.0	4,191.90
Total	**32.0**	**.3**	**32.3***	**$6,280.00**

* Commodities in net metric tons of 1,000 kilograms or 2,204.6 Pounds.

RUSSIA (NORTHWEST RUSSIA)—A.R.A. and A.R.A.-European Children's Fund

Summary of Internal Deliveries by Operations

Table 504 — Reconstruction Period, 1919–1924

Operation	Table No.	Commodities in Net Metric Tons of 1,000 Kilograms or 2,204.6 Pounds										Total Value
		Flour	Rice	Beans, Peas	Pork Products	Milk	Cocoa	Sugar	Soap	Clothing	Total Tons	
A.R.A.—Congressional Appropriation, $100,000,000 Fund......	505	39.4	64.0	27.9	20.0	129.4	5.0	9.0	10.5	...	305.2	$111,705.1
A.R.A.-European Children's Fund	505	3.3	....	....	3.0	3.9	.2	.1	....	...	10.5	1,258.5
Northwest Russian Government Donation	505	32.0	....	....	.3	....	...	...	....	...	32.3	6,280.0
Total Child Feeding...........	...	**74.7**	**64.0**	**27.9**	**23.3**	**133.3**	**5.2**	**9.1**	**10.5**	...	**348.0**	**$119,243.6**
A.R.A.-European Children's Fund	506	....	....	....	....	....	...	...	....	2.3	2.3	4,965.0
Total Relief	497	**74.7**	**64.0**	**27.9**	**23.3**	**133.3**	**5.2**	**9.1**	**10.5**	**2.3**	**350.3**	**$124,208.7**

RUSSIA (NORTHWEST RUSSIA)—A.R.A. and A.R.A.-European Children's Fund

Detail of Internal Deliveries, by Local and District Committees, by Months

Table 505 — Reconstruction Period, 1919–1924

Receipt No.	Local and District Committees	Date of Delivery	Commodities in Net Metric Tons of 1,000 Kilograms or 2,204.6 Pounds								Total Tons
			Flour	Rice	Beans, Peas	Pork Products	Milk	Cocoa	Sugar	Soap	
		1919									
1	Pskov	July	9.852	....	....	3.934	12.016	....	....	....	25.80
2	Gdov	July	4.951	....	....	1.967	8.738	....	....	....	15.65
	Total for July	....	**14.803**	....	....	**5.901**	**20.754**	....	....	....	**41.45**
3	Pskov	August	3.229	....	....	....	9.623	....	....	....	12.85
4	Yamburg	August	3.006	....	....	2.279	7.557	....	....	....	12.84
	Total for August	....	**6.235**	....	....	**2.279**	**17.180**	....	....	....	**25.6[illegible]**
5	Yamburg	September	**10.021**	....	....	**4.935**	**32.722**	....	....	....	**47.67**
6	Luga	October	1.828	.284	.342	.370	1.356	.142	.400	....	4.7[illegible]
7	Gatchina (Gatsina)	October	2.593	.205	.264	.523	1.770	.155	.381	....	5.8[illegible]
8	Gdov	October	7.984	.183	.237	1.380	3.055	....	....	....	12.8[illegible]
9	Yamburg	October	7.137	.295	.244	3.049	3.934	....	....	....	14.65
	Total for October	....	**19.542**	**.967**	**1.087**	**5.322**	**10.115**	**.297**	**.781**	....	**38.1[illegible]**
11	Jeve	November	.653	.102	.123	.133	.449	.051	.143	....	1.65
12	Narva, Station II.............	November	.059	.010	.011	.011	.040	.006	.013	....	.15
13	Narva, Station II.............	November	.104	.016	.020	.021	.072	.009	.023	....	.2[illegible]
14	Narva, Village Krionchi (Krivouski)	November	....	.033	....	.055	.046	....	....	....	.1[illegible]
15	Jeve	November	1.175	.184	.221	.239	.808	.092	.257	....	2.9
16	Narva, Station II.............	November	1.175	.012	.221	.239	.054	.006	.017	....	1.7[illegible]
17	Narva, Station II.............	November	....	....	....	....	.004	.004	.011	....	.0[illegible]
	Total for November.........	....	**3.166**	**.357**	**.596**	**.698**	**1.473**	**.168**	**.464**	....	**6.9[illegible]**
18	Narva, Station I..............	December	.007	.001	.001	.001	.005	.001	.001	....	.0[illegible]
19	Narva, Station I..............	December	.007	.001	.001	.001	.005	.001	.001	....	.0[illegible]
20	Narva, Station I..............	December	.013	.002	.003	.003	.009	.001	.003	....	.0[illegible]
21	Narva, Station I..............	December	.026	.004	.005	.005	.018	.002	.006	....	.0[illegible]

RUSSIA (NORTHWEST RUSSIA)

Detail of Internal Deliveries, by Local and District Committees, by Months

Table 505—*Continued*

Receipt No.	Local and District Committees	Date of Delivery	Flour	Rice	Beans, Peas	Pork Products	Milk	Cocoa	Sugar	Soap	Total Tons
		Commodities in Net Metric Tons of 1,000 Kilograms or 2,204.6 Pounds									
		1919									
22	Jeve	December	.783	.122	.147	.159	.539	.061	.171	....	1.982
23	Village Venkull	December	.130	.020	.025	.027	.090	.010	.029	....	.331
24	Narva	December	.007	.001	.001	.001	.005	.001	.001	....	.017
25	Isenhof	December	1.306	.204	.245	.265	.898	.102	.286	.075	3.381
26	Jeve	December	1.306	.204	.245	.265	.898	.102	.286	.075	3.381
27	Jeve	December	1.959	.306	.367	.397	1.347	.153	.429	.075	5.033
	Total for December	....	**5.544**	**.865**	**1.040**	**1.124**	**3.814**	**.434**	**1.213**	**.225**	**14.259**
		1920									
28	Isenhof	January	1.959	.306	.368	.398	1.347	.153	.428	....	4.959
29	Isenhof	January	1.959	.306	.368	.398	1.347	.153	.428	....	4.959
30	Isenhof	January	1.306	.204	.245	.265	.898	.102	.286	....	3.405
31	Isenhof	January	.653	.102	.123	.133	.449	.051	.143	.099	1.654
32	Jeve	January	1.306	.204	.245	.265	.898	.102	.286	.075	3.381
33	Narva	January	.131	.020	.025	.027	.090	.010	.029	....	.332
	Total for January	....	**7.314**	**1.142**	**1.374**	**1.486**	**5.029**	**.571**	**1.600**	**.174**	**18.690**
34	Narva	February	.065	.010	.012	.013	.045	.005	.014	....	.164
35	Asserin	February	1.959	.306	.368	.398	1.347	.153	.428	.051	5.010
36	Isenhof	February	1.959	.306	.368	.398	1.347	.153	.428	.051	5.010
37	Rarrits	February	.002	....	....	.001	.002	....	.001	....	.006
38	Waikull	February	.006	.001	.001	.001	.005	.001	.001	....	.016
39	Welts	February	.014	.002	.003	.003	.010	.001	.003	....	.036
40	Jeve	February	.653	.102	.123	.133	.449	.051	.143	....	1.654
41	Jeve	February	.653	.102	.123	.133	.449	.051	.143	.040	1.694
42	Jeve	February	1.959	.313	.367	.406	1.328	.140	.425	....	4.938
43	Wesenburg (Rakvere)	February	.017	.003	.003	....	.012	.001	.004	....	.040
44	Wesenburg (Rakvere)	February	.013	.002	.003	.003	.009	.001	.003	....	.034
45	Wesenburg (Rakvere)	February	.013	.002	.003	.003	.009	.001	.003	....	.034
46	Wesenburg (Rakvere)	February	.013	.002	.002	.003	.009	.001	.003	....	.033
47	Wesenburg (Rakvere)	February	.013	.002	.002	.003	.009	.001	.003	....	.033
48	Wesenburg (Rakvere)	February	.001	....	....	....	.001	....	....	....	.002
49	Wesenburg (Rakvere)	February	.004	.001	.001	.001	.003	....	.001	....	.011
50	Wesenburg (Rakvere)	February	.006	.001	.001	.001	.005	.001	.001	....	.016
51	Wesenburg (Rakvere)	February	.010	.002	.002	.002	.007	.001	.002	....	.026
52	Wesenburg (Rakvere)	February	.012	.002	.002	.002	.008	.001	.003	....	.030
53	Wesenburg (Rakvere)	February	.014	.002	.003	.003	.010	.001	.003	....	.036
54	Wesenburg (Rakvere)	February	.016	.002	.003	....	.011	.001	.003	....	.036
55	Wesenburg (Rakvere)	February	.017	.003	.003	.003	.012	.001	.004	....	.043
56	Wesenburg (Rakvere)	February	.060	.009	.011	.012	.041	.005	.013	....	.151
	Total for February	....	**7.479**	**1.175**	**1.404**	**1.522**	**5.128**	**.571**	**1.632**	**.142**	**19.053**
	Turned Over to Central Committee	March	.....	.750	.400	....	....	....	....	.900	2.050
10	Loss to Red Army at Luga	1919 November	.653	.102	.123	.133	.449	.051	.143	....	1.654
57	Russian Refugees	1920 January	....	....	....	....	....	....	....	.548	.548
58	Russian Refugees	February	....	....	....	....	....	....	....	.551	.551
..*	Warehouse Destroyed by Fire—Loss	....	.....	58.600	21.900	....	36.600	3.000	3.300	8.000	131.400
	Total Miscellaneous	....	**.653**	**59.452**	**22.423**	**.133**	**37.049**	**3.051**	**3.443**	**9.999**	**136.203**
	Grand Total	....	**74.757**	**63.958**	**27.924**	**23.400**	**133.264**	**5.092**	**9.133**	**10.540**	**348.068**

* Taken from correspondence and commodity reports. No receipt for s item.

RUSSIA (NORTHWEST RUSSIA)—A.R.A.-European Children's Fund

Detail of Internal Deliveries of Clothing to Local Committees

Table 506

Reconstruction Period, 1919–1924

Receipt No.	Local Committee	Date of Delivery	Shoes (Pairs)	Laces (Pairs)	Stockings (Pairs)	Woolens (Yards)	Thread (Spools)	Buttons (No.)
		1920						
1	Jeve	February	1,000	1,000	1,000	1,480	184	4,000
2	Jeve	February	360	360	224	145	17	400
	Total *		**1,360**	**1,360**	**1,224**	**1,625**	**201†**	**4,400**

* Equivalent to 2.3 metric tons.

† Equivalent to 24 pounds.

RUSSIA (KOUBAN)

Table 507

Summary of Relief Deliveries

Operation	Table No.	Commodities in Net Metric Tons of 1,000 Kilograms or 2,204.6 Pounds			Total Value
		Medical and Hospital Supplies	Clothing and Miscellaneous	Total Tons	
A.R.A.—Cash Settlement	508	.....	915.5	915.5	$444,718.
American Red Cross	509	577.0	.....	577.0	123,300.
Total American Relief	......	**577.0**	**915.5**	**1,492.5**	**$568,018.**
United Kingdom	133	.....	100.0	100.0	10,472.
Grand Total Relief Deliveries	102	**577.0**	**1,015.5**	**1,592.5**	**$578,490.**

RUSSIA (KOUBAN)—American Relief Administration

Detail by Steamer of Commodities Sold for Cash

Table 508 Armistice Period, 1919

Arrival No.	Steamer	Port of Sailing	Date of Arrival	Port of Arrival	Miscellaneous Supplies *	Total Value
383	Kickapoo	Marseilles	1919 Aug. 30	Novorossisk	915.5	$444,718.50

* These supplies were bartered for wheat that was shipped to Armenia. Cf. Table 201. Stated in net metric tons.

RUSSIA (KOUBAN)—American Red Cross

Table 509* Detail by Steamer of Relief Deliveries—Armistice Period, 1919

Steamer	Port of Sailing	Date of Arrival	Port of Arrival	Medical and Hospital Supplies	Total Value
Kickapoo	Marseilles	1919 Aug. 30	Novorossisk	577.0†	$123,300.00

* Cf. Table 126.

† Net metric tons.

RUSSIA (SIBERIA)—Jewish Joint Distribution Committee

Table 510* Detail by Steamer of Relief Deliveries—Armistice Period, 1919

Steamer	Port of Sailing	Date of Arrival	Port of Arrival	Clothing	Total Value
Tenyo Maru	....	1919 July	Vladivostok	40.0†	$75,000.00

* Cf. Table 124.

† Net metric tons.

RUSSIA (SOVIET REPUBLICS)—

Table 511

Summary of Relief Deliveries, by Operations—

Operation	Table No.	Flour	Grain	Rice	Beans, Peas
A.R.A.—Children's Relief, Food	513, 527	85,923.6	......	7,291.5	3,221.2
Soviet Government Donation, Food	520, 527	64.0	......	.....	.....
A.R.A.—U.S. Grain Corporation $20,000,000 Appropriation	517, 530	......	214,710.4	.....	.....
A.R.A.—Clothing	513, 528	......	......	.....	.....
A.R.A.—Paioks (Employees Pay)	513, 532	1,603.5	......	693.2	10.0
U.S. Grain Corporation $20,000,000 Appropriation—Near East Relief	517, 530	......	4,927.9	.....	.....
A.R.A. Medical Supplies:					
U.S. Government Surplus, American Red Cross	521, 523, 531	......	......	.....	.....
U.S. Government Surplus—Near East Relief	521, 531	......	......	.....	.....
American Friends Service Committee	525	3,037.3	......	71.9	90.6
Total Child and Adult Relief	163	**90,628.4**	**219,638.3**	**8,056.6**	**3,321.8**
U.S. Grain Corporation $20,000,000 Appropriation	517, 530	......	54,007.6	.....	.....
Soviet Gold—(R.S.F.S.R. and U.S.R.)	519	......	105,135.3	.....	4,229.6
Total Seed Grain	....	......	**159,142.9**	.....	**4,229.6**
A.R.A.—Food Remittances	513, 533	27,199.1	......	6,690.0	.....
A.R.A.—Bulk, Eurelcon, and Internal Sales	513, 534–36	15,783.3	......	3,716.9	249.5
A.R.A.—Clothing Remittances, Bulk Sales, etc.	513, 528	......	......	.....	.....
Total Sales, Food and Clothing	....	**42,982.4**	......	**10,406.9**	**249.5**
Total Sale of Damaged Commodities and Other Adjustments ‡	....	**1,170.4**	**7,774.9**	**451.1**	**94.6**
Esthonian Government Donation (Warehouse Facilities for Russian Supplies)	....	......	......	.....	.....
Latvian Government Donation (Warehouse Facilities for Russian Supplies)	....	......	......	.....	.....
Poland Government Donation (Railway Transportation for Russian Supplies)	....	......	......	.....	.....
Total Donations by Countries Other than U.S.	....	......	......	.....	.....
Grand Total Relief Deliveries	102	**134,781.2**	**386,556.1**	**18,914.6**	**7,895.5**

* This represents A.R.A. clothing, 1,447.8 metric tons; bags used for food remittances, bulk sales, etc., 119.4 metric tons; auto parts, 156.2 metric tons.

† Weight of sacks and containers included with 1,723.4 metric to[ns] clothing and miscellaneous above.

RUSSIA (SOVIET REPUBLICS)—

Table 512

Summary of Arrivals by Operations—

Operation	Table No.	Flour	Grain	Rice	Beans, Peas	Corn Grits
American Relief Administration	513	131,679.9	......	18,842.7	3,575.3	11,324.1
U.S. Grain Corporation $20,000,000 Fund	517	......	281,420.8	....	....	83,960.4
R.S.F.S.R. and U.S.R., Gold Account	519	......	105,135.3	....	4,229.6	.....
Soviet Government Donation	520	64.0	......	....	....	.....
U.S. Government Surplus Medical Supplies	521	......	......	....	....	.....
American Red Cross Medical Supplies	523	......	......	....	....	.....
American Friends Service Committee	525	3,037.3	......	71.9	90.6	917.8
Total	......	**134,781.2**	**386,556.1**	**18,914.6**	**7,895.5**	**96,202.3**

American Relief Administration
Reconstruction Period, 1919–1924

Corn Grits	Pork Products	Milk	Cocoa	Sugar	Misc. Food	Forage	Soap	Medical and Hospital Supplies	Clothing and Misc.	Total Tons	Total Value
Commodities in Net Metric Tons of 1,000 Kilograms or 2,204.6 Pounds											
928.4	7,687.7	9,459.9	3,325.4	12,890.4	114.9	......	569.6	.....	.....	131,412.6	$12,347,924.55
.....	.....	.....	.....	.....	464.0	......	....	.....	26.0	554.0	30,026.64
76,415.0	.....	19,548.3	.....	.....	.....	......	....	.....	.....	310,673.7	14,865,303.45
.....	.....	.....	.....	.....	.....	......	....	.....	1,723.4*	1,723.4	1,700,795.00
273.8	278.5	345.6	66.1	373.8	15.2	......	27.8	.....	.....	3,687.5	375,312.38
6,103.9	.....	.....	.....	.....	.....	......	....	.....	.....	11,031.8	557,874.95
.....	.....	.....	.....	.....	.....	......	....	8,066.7	.....	8,066.7	7,862,524.40
.....	.....	.....	.....	.....	.....	......	....	215.2	.....	215.2	209,731.63
917.8	16.6	.....	.....	67.6	.....	......	....	.....	.4	4,202.2	267,394.24
84,638.9	**7,982.8**	**29,353.8**	**3,391.5**	**13,331.8**	**594.1**	......	**597.4**	**8,281.9**	**1,749.8**	**471,567.1**	**$38,216,887.24**
.....	.....	.....	.....	.....	.....	......	....	.....	1,100.0	55,107.6	$ 2,948,485.24
.....	.....	.....	.....	.....	.....	2,501.0	....	.....	.....	111,865.9	7,034,874.30
.....	.....	.....	.....	.....	.....	**2,501.0**	....	.....	**1,100.0**	**166,973.5**	**$ 9,983,359.54**
3,737.1	2,741.0	8,428.5	69.2	4,919.1	532.1	......	.2	.....	.....†	54,316.3	$ 9,305,300.00
4,237.3	1,701.7	5,347.0	484.3	2,906.8	141.5	......	2.2	.....	.....†	34,570.5	4,374,893.28
.....	.....	.....	.....	.....	.....	......	....	.....	350.0	350.0	737,317.12
7,974.4	**4,442.7**	**13,775.5**	**553.5**	**7,825.9**	**673.6**	......	**2.4**	.....	**350.0**	**89,236.8**	**$14,417,510.40**
3,589.0	.....	**233.3**	.....	**398.2**	**83.8**	......	....	.....	.....	**13,795.3**	**$ 441,730.97**
.....	.....	.....	.....	.....	.....	......	....	.....	.....	......	$ 1,102.94
.....	.....	.....	.....	.....	.....	......	....	.....	.....	......	24,257.69
.....	.....	.....	.....	.....	.....	......	....	.....	.....	......	90,000.00
.....	.....	.....	.....	.....	.....	......	....	.....	.....	......	**$ 115,360.63**
96,202.3	**12,425.5**	**43,362.6**	**3,945.0**	**21,555.9**	**1,351.5**	**2,501.0**	**599.8**	**8,281.9**	**3,199.8**	**741,572.7**	**$63,174,848.78**

‡ Handled by Grain Corporation: grain, 7,774.9; corn grits, 1,441.5; lk, 41.3; total, 9,257.7, value $290,516.36. The balance, 4,537.6, value 51,214.61 was handled by A.R.A.

American Relief Administration
Reconstruction Period, 1919–1924

Pork Products	Milk	Cocoa	Sugar	Misc. Food	Forage	Soap	Medical and Hospital Supplies	Clothing and Misc.	Total Tons	Total Value
Commodities in Net Metric Tons of 1,000 Kilograms or 2,204.6 Pounds										
12,408.9	23,773.0	3,945.0	21,488.3	887.5	......	599.8	......	2,073.4	230,597.9	$24,211,460.16
....	19,589.6	......	....	.....	......	.....	......	1,100.0	386,070.8	18,662,180.00
....	......	......	....	.....	2,501.0	.....	......	....	111,865.9	7,034,874.30
....	......	......	....	464.0	......	.....	......	26.0	554.0	30,026.64
....	......	......	....	.....	......	.....	3,107.6	....	3,107.6	4,267,392.88
....	......	......	....	.....	......	.....	5,174.3	....	5,174.3	3,804,863.15
16.6	......	......	67.6	.....	......	.....	......	.4	4,202.2	267,394.24
12,425.5	**43,362.6**	**3,945.0**	**21,555.9**	**1,351.5**	**2,501.0**	**599.8**	**8,281.9**	**3,199.8**	**741,572.7**	**$58,278,191.37**

Table 513

Detail by Steamers of Arrivals of Relief

Steamer by No.	Steamer or Source	Transshipping Steamer by Number *	Port of Sailing	Date of Arrival	Port of Arrival
1	St. Croix, II	522	London	1919 Dec. 10	Danzig
2	Wisla	513	New York	1920 Feb. 16	Danzig
3	Ina Blumenthal	301, 420	Liverpool	Mar. 4	Danzig
4	Vardulia	513	New York	Mar. 15	Danzig
	Total for March				
5	Valacia	513	New York	Apr. 5	Danzig
6	Bellerose	402, 420	Philadelphia	Aug. 2	Hamburg
7	Susquehanna	513	New York	Aug. 23	Danzig
8	Mongolia, IV	420	New York	Aug. 26	Hamburg
9	Hamburg Stock	401, 402, 420, 403, 429	(U.S.A.)	....	Hamburg
	Total for August				
10	Hamburg Stock	306 : 509	(U.S.A.)	Prior Nov.	Hamburg
11	Bradclyde	402, 420	New York	1921 Jan. 15	Hamburg
12	Homer City, II	401, 402, 420, 403	New York	Feb. 25	Hamburg
13	Leeds City, II	420	New York	Apr. 12	Hamburg
14	Vittorio Emmanuelle, IV	420	New York	Apr. 15	Hamburg
15	Bradford City, II	401, 420	New York	Apr. 23	Hamburg
16	King City	402	Galveston	Apr. 29	Hamburg
	Total for April				
17	East Cape	512	New York	May 2	Danzig
18	Nemaha	307 : 507	Philadelphia	May 15	Hamburg
	Total for May				
19	Walter Luckenbach	311 : 505, 506, 508	Philadelphia	June 12	Hamburg
20	Warsaw, V to X, Inclusive	515	(Poland)	June 30	Danzig
21	Warsaw	504, 509	(Poland)	June 30	Danzig
	Total for June				
22	Orduna	402	New York	July 1	Hamburg
23	Mystic, V	401, 420	New York	July 2	Hamburg
24	Hawaiian, III	308 : 505, 508. 309 : 508	New York	July 4	Hamburg
25	Mount Clay, III	401, 420	New York	July 5	Hamburg
26	Potomac, I	512, 522, Rail	New York	July 6	Danzig
27	Oregonian, IV	310 : 509. 401, 403	New York	July 11	Hamburg
28	Mount Carroll, II	312 : 507, 509. 401, 402, 420, 403, 422	New York	July 12	Hamburg
29	Orbita, II	401, 402	New York	July 14	Hamburg
30	Mount Clinton, I	313 : 507, 509. 420, 403	New York	July 19	Hamburg
31	Sudbury, I	314 : 509. 401, 402, 420, 422	New York	July 24	Hamburg
32	Ipswich, II	314 : 509	New York	July 28	Hamburg
	Total for July				
33	Panama, I	401, 402, 403	San Francisco	Aug. 7	Hamburg
34	Clarksburg, III	420	New York	Aug. 9	Hamburg
35	Panama, I	505, 506, 511, 507, 504	San Francisco	Aug. 13	Danzig
36	West Kedron, I	401, 402, 420, 403	San Francisco	Aug. 14	Hamburg
37	Guernsey, I	505, 506, 508, 509, 507	New York	Aug. 16	Danzig
38	West Kedron, I	507, 508, 505, 509, 511	San Francisco	Aug. 19	Danzig

† This organization is not to be confused with the A.R.A. that handled the U.S. Congressional Appropriation, $100,000,000 fund. The E.C.F. has been dropped from Russian tables because all Russian relief was handled under the Riga Agreement, dated August 20, 1921, by a between the A.R.A. and the Russian Socialist Federative Soviet Repub (R.S.F.S.R.). Cf. pages 926-27.

American Relief Administration†

Supplies—Reconstruction Period, 1919–1924

Contents of Cargoes in Net Metric Tons of 1,000 Kilograms or 2,204.6 Pounds													
Flour	Rice	Beans, Peas	Corn Grits	Pork Products	Milk	Cocoa	Sugar	Misc. Food	Clothing and Misc.	Soap	Total Tons		Total Value
.....	.....	....	.....	....	....	....	....	...	**.3**	....	**.3**	**$**	**547.03**
.....	.....	....	.....	....	....	....	....	...	**.0**	....	**.0**	**$**	**32.12**
.....	.....	....	.....	....	....	....	....	.8	...	....	.8	$	4,655.68
.....	.....	....	.....	41.8	....	....	....	...	...	....	41.8		28,361.30
.....	.....	....	.....	**41.8**	....	....	....	**.8**	...	....	**42.6**	**$**	**33,016.98**
.....	.....	....	.....	**10.4**	....	....	....	...	**3.7**	....	**14.1**	**$**	**9,753.23**
.....	.....	....	.....	21.1	....	....	....	...	...	....	21.1	$	17,061.38
.....	.....	....	.....	....	....	....	....	...	.5	....	.5		197.56
.....	.....	....	.....	2.0	....	....	....	...	...	....	2.0		1,370.37
61.0	35.1	.2	.....	17.9	2.7	3.6	6.9	3.1	2.7	....	133.2		33,928.74
61.0	**35.1**	**.2**	.....	**41.0**	**2.7**	**3.6**	**6.9**	**3.1**	**3.2**	....	**156.8**	**$**	**52,558.05**
.....	.....	....	.....	**9.0**	....	....	....	...	...	....	**9.0**	**$**	**7,130.97**
.....	.....	....	.....	....	....	**2.9**	....	...	...	....	**2.9**	**$**	**359.81**
.....	.....	....	.....	**28.1**	....	**39.5**	....	...	...	....	**67.6**	**$**	**18,311.20**
.....	.....	....	.....	150.8	....	8.3	....	...	...	....	159.1	$	73,955.36
.....	.....	....	.....	48.5	....	....	....	...	...	....	48.5		26,402.62
.....	.....	....	.....	49.0	6.7	....	....	...	...	....	55.7		27,829.01
.....	35.2	....	.....	....	....	....	....	...	...	....	35.2		2,875.49
.....	**35.2**	....	.....	**248.3**	**6.7**	**8.3**	....	...	...	....	**298.5**	**$**	**131,062.48**
.....	.....	....	.....	41.9	....	....	....	...	...	....	41.9	$	7,445.36
.....	.....	....	.....	....	9.7	....	....	...	...	....	9.7		2,405.99
.....	.....	....	.....	41.9	9.7	....	....	...	...	....	**51.6**	**$**	**9,851.35**
98.3	.....	....	.....	....	....	....	....	...	...	....	98.3	$	8,041.82
.....	.....	....	.....	....	....	....	712.1	...	...	....	712.1		114,847.49
.....	.....	....	.....	....	....	....	219.6	...	...	....	219.6		38,401.23
98.3	.....	....	.....	....	....	....	**931.7**	...	...	....	**1,030.0**	**$**	**161,290.54**
.....	.....	....	.....	28.6	....	....	....	...	...	....	28.6	$	5,676.69
.....	.....	....	.....	....	22.3	....	....	...	...	....	22.3		7,600.61
.....	.....	....	.....	....	....	111.0	....	...	...	....	111.0		10,775.88
.....	.....	....	.....	....	21.8	....	....	...	...	....	21.8		7,243.79
.....	.....	....	.....	129.9	....	....	....	...	...	....	129.9		23,712.77
.....	.....	....	.....	....	196.6	....	....	...	...	....	196.6		58,601.88
.....	.....	....	.....	....	504.7	....	....	...	7.9	....	512.6		142,796.10
.....	.....	....	.....	49.5	....	....	....	...	...	....	49.5		10,001.66
.....	.....	....	.....	....	62.2	....	....	...	...	....	62.2		14,438.93
107.1	.....	....	232.6	....	65.3	....	....	...	10.2	....	415.2		44,602.08
.....	.....	....	.....	....	106.6	....	....	...	...	....	106.6		25,275.04
107.1	.....	....	**232.6**	**208.0**	**979.5**	**111.0**	....	...	**18.1**	....	**1,656.3**	**$**	**350,725.43**
543.1	.....	....	.....	....	....	....	....	...	...	....	543.1	$	42,508.74
.....	.....	....	.....	....	....	19.1	....	...	...	....	19.1		1,836.70
749.0	1,142.0	2.7	.....	....	....	....	....	...	...	....	1,893.7		116,620.80
.....	.....	858.9	.....	....	....	....	....	...	...	....	858.9		72,505.39
.....	.....	....	253.6	....	968.7	....	....	...	...	....	1,222.3		247,071.85
.....	308.9	759.4	.....	....	....	....	....	...	...	....	1,068.3		79,448.67

* For the 300 series, cf. Tables 514 and 515. For 401 and up, cf. Table 516. Table 513 quotes original steamers or source by numbers 1 to 286, inclusive. Table 514 quotes transshipping steamers by numbers 301 to 352, inclusive. These supplies must be retransshipped to reach Russia.

All steamer numbers or rail following a colon indicate that transshipments come from steamers preceding the colon. Table 515 shows retransshipments via rail from Danzig to Stolpce. Table 516 quotes transshipping steamers 401 to 522, inclusive.

[*Continued on next page*]

Table 513—*Continued*

Detail by Steamers of

Steamer by No.	Steamer or Source	Transshipping Steamer	Port of Sailing	Date of Arrival	Port of Arrival
				1921	
39	Galileo	302 : 505, 507	New York	Aug. 24	Hull
40	Keilehaven	312 : Rail	New Orleans	Aug. 24	Hamburg
41	Wachsmuth Purchase, I	401	(Czecho-Slovakia)	Aug. 26	Hamburg
42	Lizzie	420, 403	Amsterdam	Aug. 29	Hamburg
43	Estonia, I	510, 512	New York	Aug. 30	Danzig
	Total for August	....	....	....	....
44	Samland, I	511, 514	Philadelphia	Sept. 7	Danzig
45	Polonia, I	510, 512, 519, 521	New York	Sept. 7	Danzig
46	Chile, II	315 : 512, 514. 316, 317 : 512	San Francisco	Sept. 8	Hamburg
47	Noruega	318 : 510, 522. 423, 424, 425	New York	Sept. 15	Hamburg
48	Idefjord	511, 512, 514, 515	Philadelphia	Sept. 18	Danzig
49	Lituania, I	512	New York	Sept. 21	Danzig
50	Werra	422	London	Sept. 21	Hamburg
51	West Norranus, I	425, 431	New Orleans	Sept. 23	Hamburg
52	Dakotan, I	421, 422, 425, 426, 427	New York	Sept. 24	Hamburg
53	Mount Clay, IV	421	New York	Sept. 26	Hamburg
54	Vienna Stock	420, 431	(U.S.A.)	Sept. ..	Hamburg
	Total for September	....	....	....	....
55	Virginian, I	319 : 522. 425	New York	Oct. 1	Hamburg
56	Massick	....	New York	Oct. 3	Riga
57	Moravia Bridge	....	Philadelphia	Oct. 3	Riga
58	Latvia, II	512	New York	Oct. 5	Danzig
59	Clarksburg, IV	424, 427, 429	Baltimore	Oct. 8	Hamburg
60	Hawaiian, V	321 : 522. 426, 427, 430	New York	Oct. 10	Hamburg
61	Mount Carroll, IV	321 : 513	New York	Oct. 11	Hamburg
62	Winfried	430	New York	Oct. 12	Hamburg
63	City of Flint, II	430, 428	Philadelphia	Oct. 12	Hamburg
64	Westbrook, III	426	New York	Oct. 13	Hamburg
65	Tonesit	303 : 513	Baltimore	Oct. 13	Copenhagen
66	Estonia, II	513	New York	Oct. 18	Danzig
67	Tordenskjold	320 : 513	New York	Oct. 19	Hamburg
68	Bayern	430	New York	Oct. 19	Hamburg
69	Oregonian, VI	322 : 514. 430	New York	Oct. 19	Hamburg
70	Manchuria, V	323 : 513. 324 : 515	New York	Oct. 23	Hamburg
71	New England	304 : 514, 515	Baltimore	Oct. 25	Copenhagen
72	Bradford City, III	325, 324 : 515, 431	New York	Oct. 26	Hamburg
73	Guernsey, II	430	Norfolk	Oct. 26	Hamburg
74	Orla	431	New York	Oct. 29	Hamburg
75	Deutschfeld	326, 327 : 517. 326 : 515	Norfolk	Oct. 29	Hamburg
76	Samland, II	514, 515	Philadelphia	Oct. 31	Danzig
	Total for October	....	....	....	....
77	Warsaw, XI, XII, XIII	Rail : 515	(U.S.A.)	Nov. ..	Danzig
78	Glentworth	431	New Orleans	Nov. 1	Hamburg
79	Mexico, III	328 : 515. 432, 431, 433	New Orleans	Nov. 3	Hamburg
80	Hudson	305 : Rail	New York	Nov. 3	Bremerhaven
81	William A. McKenney	431	New York	Nov. 5	Hamburg
82	Panola	513	Philadelphia	Nov. 5	Riga
83	Guernsey, II	....	Norfolk	Nov. 9	Riga
84	Buchanness	433, 434	New York	Nov. 10	Hamburg
85	Lituania, II	515	New York	Nov. 15	Danzig
86	Mount Carroll, V	437	New York	Nov. 21	Hamburg
87	Manitowac	517, 518, 519, 521	New York	Nov. 22	Danzig
88	Elzasier, I	517, 516	New York	Nov. 23	Danzig
89	Sachsenwald	329 : 517	New Orleans	Nov. 25	Hamburg
90	Samnanger	330 : 517, 522	New Orleans	Nov. 25	Hamburg
91	Tancred	436	New York	Nov. 25	Hamburg

American Relief Administration

Arrivals of Relief Supplies

Flour	Rice	Beans, Peas	Corn Grits	Pork Products	Milk	Cocoa	Sugar	Misc. Food	Clothing and Misc.	Soap	Total Tons	Total Value
Contents of Cargoes in Net Metric Tons of 1,000 Kilograms or 2,204.6 Pounds												
....	....	....	....	161.2	....	....	....	...	...	....	161.2	$ 32,487.47
....	170.2	....	....	....	....	....	....	...	...	....	170.2	11,032.90
....	....	....	....	....	....	....	65.0	...	...	....	65.0	5,102.32
....	....	....	....	....	....	....	101.8	...	...	....	101.8	10,230.00
22.2	....	....	....	....	....	....	145.2	...	...	....	167.4	17,676.00
1,314.3	**1,621.1**	**1,621.0**	**253.6**	**161.2**	**968.7**	**19.1**	**312.0**	...	...	....	**6,271.0**	**$ 636,520.84**
1,016.1	....	....	....	....	....	....	....	...	...	....	1,016.1	$ 77,685.79
248.7	....	....	....	....	....	....	496.5	...	...	....	745.2	74,362.22
....	....	567.1	....	....	....	....	....	...	...	....	567.1	50,539.53
....	....	....	....	....	271.6	....	....	...	16.0	....	287.6	74,343.83
864.7	....	....	....	....	....	....	....	...	...	....	864.7	65,596.49
....	....	....	....	....	....	....	304.8	...	...	....	304.8	33,940.81
....	....	....	....	....	....	....	....	...	.2	....	.2	1,009.00
....	183.2	....	....	....	....	....	....	...	...	....	183.2	14,423.98
....	....	....	....	....	256.6	209.8	312.1	...	...	....	778.5	112,775.51
....	....	....	....	150.1	....	....	....	...	...	....	150.1	36,869.61
....	....	....	....	68.7	....	....	....	...	5.7	....	74.4	48,638.13
2,129.5	**183.2**	**567.1**	....	**218.8**	**528.2**	**209.8**	**1,113.4**	...	**21.9**	....	**4,971.9**	**$ 590,184.90**
....	....	....	....	49.8	349.4	....	90.0	...	...	....	489.2	$ 107,524.98
....	....	....	....	....	....	....	....	.9	...	....	.9	30.69
2,032.6	....	....	....	....	....	....	....	...	...	....	2,032.6	157,088.88
....	....	....	....	....	....	....	....	...	4.0	....	4.0	6,107.45
1,345.1	....	....	....	....	....	....	....	...	...	....	1,345.1	102,443.18
....	....	....	....	....	427.8	....	....	...	...	....	427.8	107,406.47
....	....	....	....	....	21.8	....	....	...	...	....	21.8	5,218.59
....	....	....	260.7	....	....	....	....	...	...	....	260.7	12,440.19
394.8	....	....	....	....	....	....	....	...	...	....	394.8	29,561.55
535.3	....	....	....	....	....	....	....	...	...	....	535.3	40,495.06
186.7	....	....	....	....	....	....	....	...	...	....	186.7	13,937.30
....	....	....	....	....	....	....	....	...	19.1	....	19.1	29,824.37
....	....	....	....	....	....	....	....	...	11.3	....	11.3	17,749.28
....	....	....	....	....	200.1	....	....	...	...	....	200.1	47,166.61
....	....	....	....	....	329.6	....	....	...	...	....	329.6	80,678.07
308.4	....	....	190.5	....	....	....	....	...	...	....	498.9	31,725.39
438.2	....	....	....	....	....	....	....	...	...	....	438.2	32,914.72
378.1	....	....	595.9	....	....	....	....	...	11.7	....	985.7	71,831.10
80.1	....	....	....	....	....	....	....	...	...	....	80.1	5,966.23
....	....	....	....	....	....	....	....	...	1.1	....	1.1	2,001.35
511.2	....	....	....	....	....	....	....	...	...	....	511.2	39,211.03
1,016.1	....	....	....	....	....	....	....	...	...	....	1,016.1	76,715.78
7,226.6	....	....	**1,047.1**	**49.8**	**1,328.7**	....	**90.0**	**.9**	**47.2**	....	**9,790.3**	**$ 1,018,038.27**
....	....	....	....	....	....	....	....	...	29.9	....	29.9	$ 34,173.23
....	436.6	....	....	....	....	....	....	...	...	....	436.6	28,102.45
....	928.1	....	....	....	....	....	....	...	...	....	928.1	69,182.78
....	....	....	....	....	....	4.8	....	...	...	....	4.8	476.81
....	....	....	....	....	....	....	....	...	4.2	....	4.2	5,408.51
1,496.0	....	....	....	....	....	....	....	...	...	....	1,496.0	116,634.37
....	....	....	....	590.1	....	....	....	...	...	....	590.1	165,175.03
....	....	....	101.3	....	....	....	449.5	...	...	....	550.8	43,080.16
106.7	....	....	....	....	....	....	....	...	...	....	106.7	8,148.76
....	....	....	....	....	108.9	....	....	...	...	....	108.9	21,633.51
427.5	....	103.5	441.8	....	169.3	11.5	....	...	...	....	1,153.6	100,329.76
....	....	56.4	....	....	1,158.1	86.9	....	...	...	....	1,301.4	268,645.53
....	309.7	....	....	....	....	....	....	...	...	....	309.7	20,282.87
....	111.2	....	....	....	....	....	....	...	...	....	111.2	7,678.75
....	....	....	....	....	....	....	....	...	...	57.3	57.3	12,083.97

[*Continued on next page*]

Table 513—*Continued*

Detail by Steamers of

Steamer by No.	Steamer or Source	Transshipping Steamer	Port of Sailing	Date of Arrival	Port of Arrival
				1921	
92	Manitowac		New York	Nov. 27	Riga
93	Hogstadt ‡		London	Nov. 30	Riga
94	Polish Repayment	517	Posen	Nov. 30	Danzig
95	Warsaw Purchase	514	Warsaw	Nov. ..	Danzig
	Total for November				
96	Elzasier, I		New York	Dec. 1	Riga
97	Chickasaw, I	437	New York	Dec. 4	Hamburg
98	Natirar		New York	Dec. 5	Riga
99	Mount Clinton, II	331 : 519, 521	New York	Dec. 7	Hamburg
100	Floridian	439, 438, 441, 440	Portland	Dec. 11	Hamburg
101	Clarksburg, V	331 : 518, 522, Rail. 440, 441	Norfolk	Dec. 12	Hamburg
102	Mount Clay, V	441, 473	New York	Dec. 19	Hamburg
103	Westbrook, IV	441	New York	Dec. 22	Hamburg
104	Gdansk	518, 519, 521, 522	New York	Dec. 23	Danzig
105	Edna		London	Dec. 25	Riga
106	Minnekahda, III	474	New York	Dec. 26	Hamburg
107	Eastport, I		New York	Dec. 24	Riga
	Total for December				
				1922	
108	Mount Carroll, VI	473, 474	New York	Jan. 3	Hamburg
109	Mercator		London	Jan. 6	Riga
110	City of Weatherford	475, 404	New Orleans	Jan. 10	Hamburg
111	Auk	441	Hamburg	Jan. 13	Hamburg
112	Corson, IV	475, 478	New York	Jan. 13	Hamburg
113	Mount Clinton, III	477	New York	Jan. 17	Hamburg
114	Texan, II	478, 476, 477, 480, 484	Portland	Jan. 19	Hamburg
115	Potomac, III	322 : 522	New York	Jan. 20	Hamburg
116	Conejos, I		New York	Jan. 22	Reval
117	Oregonian, VII	495, 485	New York	Jan. 24	Hamburg
118	Eastern Coast	522	New York	Jan. 26	Danzig
119	Gasconier	333 : 522. Rail, 479	New York	Jan. 26	Hamburg
120	Mongolia, VI	481	New York	Jan. 29	Hamburg
121	Hickman	481	New York	Jan. 31	Hamburg
122	Wachsmuth Purchase 2 and 3	484, 495	(Czecho-Slovakia)	Jan. 31	Hamburg
123	European Purchase			Jan. 31	Riga
	Total for January				
124	Ara ‡		London	Feb. 3	Windau
125	Dakotan, II	482, 483. 336 : Rail	Portland	Feb. 6	Hamburg
126	Mount Clay, VI	334 : 522. 337 : 520, Rail	New York	Feb. 7	Hamburg
127	Minnekahda, IV	419. 335 : Rail. 489	New York	Jan. 8	Hamburg
128	Dallas	404, 445, 407, 408	New York	Feb. 9	Hamburg
129	Sudbury, III	334 : Rail	Norfolk	Feb. 9	Hamburg
130	Nobles, I	404, 413	New Orleans	Feb. 9	Hamburg
131	Bayern, II	346 : Rail. 490	New York	Feb. 11	Hamburg
132	Mount Carroll, VII	486. 336 : Rail	New York	Feb. 15	Hamburg
133	Minnesotan	493, 503. 338, 342 : Rail	Portland	Feb. 19	Hamburg
134	Hansa	490. 339 : Rail	New York	Feb. 20	Hamburg
135	Chappaqua	489	Norfolk	Feb. 21	Hamburg
136	Georgian	486. 336 : Rail	New York	Feb. 21	Hamburg
137	Stonewall		Baltimore	Feb. 21	Novorossisk
138	Haverford	492. 340 : Rail	New York	Feb. 23	Hamburg
139	Chickasaw, II	488, 489, 494, 496	New York	Feb. 24	Hamburg
140	Waxahachie	408	Galveston	Feb. 25	Hamburg
	Total for February				

‡ Ex-European purchases.

American Relief Administration

Arrivals of Relief Supplies

Contents of Cargoes in Net Metric Tons of 1,000 Kilograms or 2,204.6 Pounds												Total Value
Flour	Rice	Beans, Peas	Corn Grits	Pork Products	Milk	Cocoa	Sugar	Misc. Food	Clothing and Misc.	Soap	Total Tons	
2,263.9	478.4	183.5	311.1	247.2	832.2	100.3	....	...	...	20.4	4,437.0	$ 501,221.54
.....	.....	....	.....	....	....	....	....	30.0	...	....	30.0	7,784.73
651.9	.....	....	.....	....	....	....	....	...	...	....	651.9	49,860.13
.....	.....	....	.....	....	....	....	....	...	.0	....	.0	3.00
4,946.0	**2,264.0**	**343.4**	**854.2**	**837.3**	**2,268.5**	**203.5**	**449.5**	**30.0**	**34.1**	**77.7**	**12,308.2**	**$ 1,459,905.89**
.....	.....	....	.....	....	....	....	....	...	...	123.1	123.1	$ 31,315.63
.....	.....	....	.....	....	108.9	....	....	...	...	....	108.9	21,581.52
.....	.....	....	.....	....	....	....	....	...	10.9	....	10.9	16,374.95
.....	.....	....	.....	....	152.0	....	....	...	...	....	152.0	30,578.78
2,011.8	.....	....	.....	....	....	....	....	...	...	....	2,011.8	133,837.18
.....	.....	....	.....	306.4	....	....	....	...	...	....	306.4	70,623.17
.....	.....	....	.....	....	90.4	49.8	....	...	64.1	....	204.3	102,336.41
.....	.....	....	.....	....	....	....	....	...	18.7	....	18.7	21,511.55
.....	.....	....	.....	....	484.5	....	....	...	140.1	....	624.6	290,547.39
.....	.....	....	.....	....	....	....	....	49.0	...	....	49.0	1,326.00
.....	.....	....	.....	90.6	130.6	....	....	...	...	....	221.2	47,902.70
.....	.....	....	.....	....	....	127.0	....	...	...	....	127.0	10,252.49
2,011.8	.....	....	.....	**397.0**	**966.4**	**176.8**	....	**49.0**	**233.8**	**123.1**	**3,957.9**	**$ 778,187.77**
.....	.....	153.0	.....	....	....	70.1	....	...	62.6	....	285.7	$ 101,370.56
.....	.....	....	.....	....	....	....	....	105.7	...	....	105.7	16,508.95
.....	514.7	....	.....	....	....	....	....	...	...	....	514.7	24,756.32
.....	.....	....	.....	....	28.5	....	....	...	...	....	28.5	7,764.75
.....	.....	....	.....	....	....	50.8	501.6	.8	...	....	553.2	45,126.73
.....	.....	27.4	.....	....	....	....	....	...	107.1	1.7	136.2	93,249.11
2,567.4	.....	....	.....	....	....	....	....	...	...	....	2,567.4	143,238.56
.....	.....	164.2	.....	....	....	....	....	...	109.0	....	273.2	174,169.80
.....	.....	....	.....	....	....	49.8	....	...	...	....	49.8	3,768.00
.1	.....	320.3	.....	....	....	....	....	...	18.3	.5	339.2	42,768.38
.....	.....	137.2	.....	....	....	....	....	...	88.7	....	225.9	138,524.81
.....	.....	58.4	.....	....	....	34.2	....	...	...	126.1	218.7	41,541.09
.....	.....	....	.....	....	....	....	....	...	17.7	....	17.7	6,980.72
.....	.....	....	.....	....	....	....	....	...	3.0	....	3.0	4,168.20
.....	.....	....	.....	....	....	....	468.9	...	...	....	468.9	36,482.91
.....	.....	....	.....	....	....	....	....	50.0	...	....	50.0	2,191.43
2,567.5	**514.7**	**860.5**	.....	....	**28.5**	**204.9**	**970.5**	**156.5**	**406.4**	**128.3**	**5,837.8**	**$ 882,610.32**
.....	.....	....	.....	....	....	....	....	84.1	...	....	84.1	$ 28,168.85
3,767.7	.....	....	.....	....	....	....	....	...	...	....	3,767.7	212,742.54
26.6	.....	71.9	.....	203.3	....	99.6	....	.7	27.9	....	430.0	81,378.34
1,467.1	.....	....	.....	....	....	181.9	....	...	...	....	1,649.0	93,082.66
714.4	.....	....	.....	....	....	....	488.9	...	...	....	1,203.3	76,056.54
.....	.....	....	.....	171.3	....	....	....	...	...	....	171.3	38,892.05
.....	313.3	....	.....	....	....	....	....	...	...	....	313.3	13,795.00
508.6	.....	....	.....	....	....	....	....	...	...	....	508.6	28,354.16
71.7	.....	....	.....	....	....	....	845.3	...	...	11.1	928.1	67,095.76
1,843.6	.....	....	.....	....	....	....	....	...	...	....	1,843.6	103,835.69
296.4	.....	....	.....	....	....	....	204.7	...	...	....	501.1	31,159.26
.....	.....	....	.....	585.6	....	....	....	...	...	....	585.6	132,061.91
527.9	.....	....	.....	59.6	....	....	....	...	23.4	11.4	622.3	50,659.50
.....	.....	....	.....	....	....	....	....	...	.1	....	.1	334.41
1,469.7	.....	....	.....	....	....	....	....	...	...	....	1,469.7	115,093.20
2,432.2	.....	....	.....	....	....	....	266.2	...	35.7	....	2,734.1	191,576.56
.....	25.8	....	.....	....	....	....	....	...	...	....	25.8	1,255.37
13,125.9	**339.1**	**71.9**	.....	**1,019.8**	....	**281.5**	**1,805.1**	**84.8**	**87.1**	**22.5**	**16,837.7**	**$ 1,265,541.80**

[*Continued on next page*]

Table 513—*Continued*

Detail by Steamers of

Steamer by No.	Steamer or Source	Transshipping Steamer	Port of Sailing	Date of Arrival	Port of Arrival
				1922	
141	West Neris		Baltimore	Mar. 1	Libau
142	Bradford City, IV	489	New York	Mar. 7	Hamburg
143	Lloyd		Boston	Mar. 7	Novorossisk
144	Western Ocean	496. 341, 343 : Rail	New Orleans	Mar. 7	Hamburg
145	Mount Clinton, IV	487, 491, 493, 498	New York	Mar. 7	Hamburg
146	Württemberg	493	New York	Mar. 9	Hamburg
147	Morristown, I	496, 404. 342 : Rail	N. Y., Phila.	Mar. 12	Hamburg
148	Mira	341	Bergen	Mar. 13	Hamburg
149	Orduna, II	496. 342, 341, 344 : Rail	New York	Mar. 15	Hamburg
150	Alaskan	341 : Rail. 497	Portland	Mar. 16	Hamburg
151	Huronian	343, 345 : Rail	New York	Mar. 18	Hamburg
152	Cody, I	498, 404. 344, 346, 347, 345 : Rail	New Orleans	Mar. 23	Hamburg
153	Oregonian, VIII	500. 346 : Rail	New York	Mar. 23	Hamburg
154	West Norranus, II	497, 499	Galveston	Mar. 25	Hamburg
155	Minnekahda, V	499. 343 : Rail	New York	Mar. 26	Hamburg
156	Siam City	404. 342 : Rail	New York	Mar. 26	Hamburg
157	Mount Carroll, VIII	499. 345 : Rail	New York	Mar. 26	Hamburg
158	City of Flint, III	344 : Rail	Norfolk	Mar. 26	Hamburg
159	Clontarf		New York	Mar. 27	Odessa
160	Cragness	346 : Rail	New York	Mar. 28	Hamburg
161	Noccalula, I	502. 346, 347 : Rail	New Orleans	Mar. 30	Hamburg
162	Corson, V	499, 500. 347 : Rail	New York	Mar. 31	Hamburg
	Total for March				
163	Schoharie, III	502, 500. 348 : Rail	New York	Apr. 1	Hamburg
164	Gaffney, I		New York	Apr. 3	Odessa
165	Hawaiian, VI	501, 443	New York	Apr. 5	Hamburg
166	Haverford, II	442	New York	Apr. 7	Hamburg
167	Jacona		New York	Apr. 12	Odessa
168	Mount Clinton, V	501, 502	New York	Apr. 12	Hamburg
169	Nobles, II	502, 444. 348 : Rail	New Orleans	Apr. 15	Hamburg
170	Georgian, II	405	New York	Apr. 20	Hamburg
171	Saugus		New York	Apr. 22	Odessa
172	Chickasaw, III	446, 406	Philadelphia	Apr. 25	Hamburg
173	Western Scout	445, 406, 407, 408, 450, 414	New York	Apr. 26	Hamburg
174	Chappaqua, II	446, 405, 406, 407, 447, 408	Norfolk	Apr. 28	Hamburg
175	Sunewco		New York	Apr. 29	Odessa
176	Sunewco (for J.D.C.)		New York	Apr. 29	Odessa
177	Mount Clay, VII	405, 407, 447	New York	Apr. 29	Hamburg
178	Chester Valley	446, 405, 413	Beaumont	Apr. 30	Hamburg
	Total for April				
179	Emergency Aid, I	349, 350, 351, 352 : Rail	New Orleans	May 1	Hamburg
180	Redondo		New York	May 5	Riga
181	Manchuria, VI	414	New York	May 8	Hamburg
182	Schmidt Purchase 1A	405	Hamburg	May 11	Hamburg
183	Sunewco		New York	May 12	Novorossisk
184	Sutransco		New York	May 13	Odessa
184	Sutransco (for J.D.C.)		New York	May 13	Odessa
185	Bremerton		New York	May 14	Riga
186	St. Paul	449	New York	May 14	Hamburg
187	Sapinero	447, 408, 414	New Orleans	May 14	Hamburg
188	Virgianian, II	447, 454	Portland	May 14	Hamburg
189	Surico		Boston	May 16	Petrograd
190	Schmidt Purchase 1B	407	Hamburg	May 18	Hamburg
191	Sutorpco		New York	May 19	Odessa
192	Sunelseco		New York	May 19	Petrograd
193	City of Flint, IV	449	Norfolk	May 21	Hamburg
194	Suholco		Newark	May 22	Odessa
195	Suholco (for J.D.C.)		Newark	May 22	Odessa
196	Mount Clinton, VI	448	New York	May 23	Hamburg
197	Menominee	409	New York	May 23	Hamburg

American Relief Administration

Arrivals of Relief Supplies

Contents of Cargoes in Net Metric Tons of 1,000 Kilograms or 2,204.6 Pounds												Total Value
Flour	Rice	Beans, Peas	Corn Grits	Pork Products	Milk	Cocoa	Sugar	Misc. Food	Clothing and Misc.	Soap	Total Tons	
.....	.....	....	.....	....	....	....	....	...	.1	....	.1	$ 504.17
.....	.....	....	.....	....	....	155.0	....	...	...	....	155.0	9,517.45
.....	.....	....	.....	....	....	....	....	...	1.5	....	1.5	1,177.82
.....	770.9	....	.....	....	....	....	....	...	...	....	770.9	35,769.75
484.0	.....	84.2	.....	26.6	16.7	....	346.5	...	10.3	47.2	1,015.5	89,205.89
266.8	.....	....	.....	....	....	....	....	...	...	....	266.8	14,926.15
933.3	.....	....	.....	....	....	199.1	490.9	...	2.0	11.7	1,637.0	106,918.42
.....	.....	....	.....	....	....	....	....	53.0	...	....	53.0	7,799.04
1,000.0	.....	....	.....	....	....	....	....	...	...	....	1,000.0	$ 54,497.73
1,016.1	.....	....	.....	....	....	....	....	...	...	....	1,016.1	57,157.79
1,475.2	.....	....	.....	....	....	....	....	...	...	....	1,475.2	78,607.41
.....	1,195.5	....	.....	76.7	....	....	....	...	...	....	1,272.2	77,247.48
313.0	.....	....	.....	698.2	....	....	255.9	...	7.4	28.3	1,302.8	199,432.12
270.3	308.8	....	.....	....	....	....	....	...	...	....	579.1	31,225.44
1,582.3	.....	....	.....	....	....	....	....	...	.1	30.6	1,613.0	91,322.47
868.6	.....	....	.....	....	....	....	....	...	...	....	868.6	48,162.73
.....	.....	27.0	.....	....	....	....	481.1	...	...	51.0	559.1	52,449.76
.....	.....	....	.....	294.6	....	....	....	...	...	....	294.6	66,531.18
448.6	.....	....	.....	....	108.8	25.4	273.3	81.2	1.5	....	938.8	98,944.95
1,036.8	.....	....	.....	....	....	....	....	...	...	....	1,036.8	56,592.43
.....	464.4	....	.....	137.0	....	....	....	...	...	....	601.4	53,316.78
1,330.0	.....	....	.....	....	....	....	255.9	...	...	....	1,585.9	94,996.16
11,025.0	**2,739.6**	**111.2**	.....	**1,233.1**	**125.5**	**379.5**	**2,103.6**	**134.2**	**22.9**	**168.8**	**18,043.4**	**$ 1,326,303.12**
1,631.3	.....	....	.....	....	....	128.5	....	...	...	71.4	1,831.2	$ 120,192.42
2,248.6	475.4	....	.....	....	....	15.2	244.6	...	28.0	....	3,011.8	209,110.53
.....	.....	....	.....	508.0	....	....	....	...	...	....	508.0	114,718.22
172.9	.....	....	.....	....	....	....	....	...	...	....	172.9	10,238.36
.....	.....	....	.....	304.7	283.0	20.3	....	...	...	....	608.0	114,111.23
201.7	.....	....	.....	....	....	....	511.8	...	...	....	713.5	51,801.85
.....	1,261.8	....	.....	....	....	....	....	...	...	....	1,261.8	62,822.85
.....	.....	....	.....	....	....	....	502.9	...	...	....	502.9	39,349.04
154.4	147.9	....	.....	96.0	152.4	....	....	...	...	....	550.7	76,321.14
93.4	.....	....	.....	....	....	.8	....	...	...	....	94.2	5,642.14
3,152.8	.....	....	.....	....	56.0	86.7	....	1.8	4.2	64.4	3,365.9	218,219.95
.....	.....	....	.....	722.7	....	....	....	...	...	....	722.7	174,987.92
260.3	.....	....	.....	....	....	....	....	...	...	....	260.3	17,459.76
1,513.5	.....	....	.....	....	43.5	....	972.6	...	15.7	....	2,545.3	235,330.72
.....	.....	....	.....	....	....	146.3	254.9	...	...	....	401.2	30,579.95
.....	619.9	....	.....	....	....	....	....	...	...	....	619.9	33,444.22
9,428.9	**2,505.0**	....	.....	**1,631.4**	**534.9**	**397.8**	**2,486.8**	**1.8**	**47.9**	**135.8**	**17,170.3**	**$ 1,514,330.30**
1,284.6	1,134.7	....	.....	....	....	....	395.3	...	...	....	2,814.6	$ 162,429.84
.....	.....	....	.....	....	....	....	309.9	...	...	....	309.9	25,947.79
.....	.....	....	.....	....	13.9	....	....	...	...	....	13.9	2,350.34
.....	.....	....	.....	....	....	....	....	16.2	...	....	16.2	7,850.42
7.1	.....	....	.....	....	....	....	....	...	...	....	7.1	520.91
.....	.....	....	.....	105.2	....	....	102.3	...	...	....	207.5	40,830.26
1,365.3	.....	....	380.6	482.9	....	120.9	....	...	...	....	2,349.7	285,116.53
.....	.....	....	.....	....	....	....	597.2	...	...	....	597.2	50,009.02
98.6	.....	....	.....	....	....	....	....	...	...	....	98.6	6,283.70
397.4	69.0	....	.....	.9	....	....	....	...	...	....	467.3	27,841.33
426.8	.....	....	.....	....	....	....	....	...	...	....	426.8	25,442.24
953.5	.....	....	.....	....	....	....	....	...	.5	....	954.0	59,472.53
.....	.....	....	.....	....	....	....	....	12.7	...	....	12.7	6,154.30
1,619.3	.....	....	396.3	50.4	1,174.7	....	....	...	7.0	....	3,247.7	385,268.13
2,396.2	.....	....	.....	....	....	101.6	....	...	20.9	....	2,518.7	173,810.95
.....	.....	....	.....	249.9	....	....	....	...	...	....	249.9	75,652.63
.....	.....	....	.....	....	....	....	....	30.8	1.0	....	31.8	1,458.32
1,524.1	.....	....	347.6	....	746.2	119.9	....	...	...	....	2,737.8	281,932.19
232.9	.....	....	.....	....	....	....	....	...	...	....	232.9	14,602.59
338.4	.....	....	.....	....	....	....	....	...	...	....	338.4	20,265.21

[*Continued on next page*]

Table 513—*Continued*

Detail by Steamers of

Steamer by No.	Steamer or Source	Transshipping Steamer	Port of Sailing	Date of Arrival	Port of Arrival
				1922	
198	Mailand		Copenhagen	May 25	Riga
199	Casey, I		New Orleans	May 25	Odessa
200	Casey, I (for J.D.C.)		New Orleans	May 25	Odessa
201	Dakotan, III	409	New York	May 26	Hamburg
202	Sutransco		New York	May 27	Novorossisk
202	Sutransco (for J.D.C.)		New York	May 27	Novorossisk
203	Morristown, II	411, 414	Philadelphia	May 28	Hamburg
204	Cody, II	411, 451	New Orleans	May 31	Hamburg
205	Local Purchase 44A	Rail	Danzig	....	Danzig
	Total for May				
206	Conejos, II		New York	June 1	Odessa
207	Conejos, II (for J.D.C.)		New York	June 1	Odessa
208	Texan, III	450, 451, 410	Tacoma	June 1	Hamburg
209	Casey, I		New Orleans	June 5	Novorossisk
210	Corson, VI	451	Philadelphia	June 7	Hamburg
211	Suholco		Newark	June 9	Novorossisk
212	Noccalula, II	412, 413, 452	New York	June 9	Hamburg
213	Manchuria, VII	414	New York	June 11	Hamburg
214	Eastport, II		New York	June 16	Riga
215	Gaffney, II		New York	June 19	Odessa
216	Mount Carroll, IX	414	New York	June 20	Hamburg
217	Belvidere, II		New York	June 24	Riga
218	West Helix	414	Norfolk	June 24	Hamburg
219	Saturn, II		London	June 25	Riga
220	Clontarf, II		New York	June 29	Constantinople
	Total for June				
221	Emergency Aid, II	453, 414	New Orleans	July 9	Hamburg
222	Clontarf, II		New York	July 10	Odessa
223	Allaguash, I		New York	July 25	Petrograd
224	Saugus, II		New York	July 26	Odessa
225	Irene		New York	July 29	Odessa
226	Irene (for J.D.C.)		New York	July 29	Odessa
	Total for July				
227	Nevadan	415	Norfolk	Aug. 6	Hamburg
228	George W. Allen		New York	Aug. 13	Odessa
229	George W. Allen (for J.D.C.)		New York	Aug. 13	Odessa
230	Manitowac, I		New York	Aug. 22	Petrograd
231	Eastern Star		New York	Aug. 31	Petrograd
	Total for August				
232	Conejos, III		New York	Sept. 7	Odessa
233	Chebaulip		New York	Sept. 10	Petrograd
234	Norlina		New York	Sept. 11	Petrograd
235	Norlina ‡		New York	Sept. 11	Petrograd
236	Sagaporack		New York	Sept. 21	Odessa
237	Eastern Coast, III		New York	Sept. 26	Petrograd
238	Emergency Aid, III	416	New Orleans	Sept. 28	Hamburg
239	James B. Duke		New York	Sept. 29	Petrograd
	Total for September				
240	Western Scout	416	Norfolk	Oct. 9	Hamburg
241	West Islay		New York	Oct. 16	Petrograd
242	West Hematite	417	New Orleans	Oct. 18	Hamburg
243	Orient		New York	Oct. 29	Odessa
	Total for October				
244	Cliffwood	418	New Orleans	Nov. 11	Hamburg
245	Helmo Hemsoth		London	Nov. 18	Petrograd
246	Allaguash, II		New York	Nov. 24	Petrograd
247	Aquarius	455	New Orleans	Nov. 26	Hamburg
	Total for November				

‡ For Central Volga Relief Society.

merican Relief Administration

rrivals of Relief Supplies

Flour	Rice	Beans, Peas	Corn Grits	Pork Products	Milk	Cocoa	Sugar	Misc. Food	Clothing and Misc.	Soap	Total Tons	Total Value
				Contents of Cargoes in Net Metric Tons of 1,000 Kilograms or 2,204.6 Pounds								
.....	.....	....	.....	....	....	....	....	8.6	...	....	8.6	1,183.96
.....	154.5	....	.....	....	....	....	....	...	...	....	154.5	9,543.10
.....	1,341.4	....	.....	....	....	....	....	...	...	....	1,341.4	86,765.05
889.1	.....	....	.....	....	....	....	....	...	...	....	889.1	58,946.14
133.3	.....	....	.....	268.9	....	120.0	486.1	...	...	....	1,008.3	145,064.76
.....	.....	....	.....	....	65.3	....	....	...	...	....	65.3	11,607.08
.....	.....	....	.....	....	....	209.7	....	...	...	....	209.7	14,159.31
1,141.6	.....	....	.....	....	....	....	....	...	...	....	1,141.6	73,139.47
.....	.....	....	.....	....	....	....	....	20.3	...	....	20.3	6,535.74
2,808.2	**2,699.6**	....	**1,124.5**	**1,158.2**	**2,000.1**	**672.1**	**1,890.8**	**88.6**	**29.4**	....	**22,471.5**	**$ 2,060,183.84**
.....	77.2	....	.....	....	....	....	....	...	...	....	77.2	$ 4,897.00
.....	.....	....	803.9	....	138.8	....	....	...	16.8	....	959.5	85,362.59
2,222.6	.....	....	.....	....	....	....	....	...	...	....	2,222.6	148,947.87
1,860.6	.....	....	.....	....	....	....	....	...	...	....	1,860.6	145,832.19
.....	.....	....	.....	....	....	76.2	....	...	...	....	76.2	5,322.19
18.2	.....	....	.....	....	....	....	....	...	...	....	18.2	12,294.26
1,650.1	.....	....	.....	....	....	....	....	...	...	....	1,650.1	115,604.61
.....	.....	....	.....	....	83.3	....	49.3	...	...	....	132.6	22,940.85
284.9	.....	....	.....	....	.6	....	....	...	5.0	....	290.5	21,793.81
637.4	.....	....	.....	136.2	272.2	....	138.2	40.8	15.0	....	1,239.8	178,060.48
.....	.....	....	.....	....	83.8	....	....	...	3.3	....	87.1	14,596.44
654.3	.....	....	.....	....	....	....	....	...	2.0	....	656.3	46,190.88
.....	.....	....	.....	33.1	....	....	....	...	...	....	33.1	8,977.98
.....	.....	....	.....	....	....	....	....	31.3	...	....	31.3	8,583.27
159.4	78.3	....	.....	20.3	71.1	8.1	44.1	...	...	....	381.3	42,263.84
7,487.5	**155.5**	....	**803.9**	**189.6**	**649.8**	**84.3**	**231.6**	**72.1**	**42.1**	....	**9,716.4**	**$ 861,668.26**
.....	393.6	....	.....	....	....	....	....	...	...	....	393.6	$ 22,393.81
983.6	.....	....	.....	....	....	....	....	...	...	....	983.6	75,430.88
1,935.8	.....	....	.....	269.7	557.4	101.6	990.0	53.4	13.1	....	3,921.0	451,136.84
31.1	922.4	....	.....	185.2	....	....	248.3	...	12.5	....	1,399.5	151,824.32
1,541.8	.....	....	243.5	86.1	566.1	20.3	101.0	81.8	...	....	2,640.6	302,832.82
.....	.....	....	.....	....	....	....	....	...	3.3	....	3.3	2,508.01
4,492.3	**1,316.0**	....	**243.5**	**541.0**	**1,123.5**	**121.9**	**1,339.3**	**135.2**	**28.9**	....	**9,341.6**	**$ 1,006,126.68**
.....	.....	....	.....	236.8	....	....	....	...	...	....	236.8	$ 65,888.51
6,900.8	.....	....	.....	39.7	142.8	....	....	...	...	....	7,083.3	532,464.36
.....	.....	....	.....	44.2	....	....	....	...	1.0	....	45.2	12,239.04
4,831.7	.....	....	.....	....	405.5	211.3	487.3	...	...	....	5,935.8	482,420.17
370.7	.....	....	.....	....	....	....	....	...	...	....	370.7	26,548.27
2,103.2	.....	....	.....	**320.7**	**548.3**	**211.3**	**487.3**	...	**1.0**	....	**13,671.8**	**$ 1,119,560.35**
334.0	.....	....	.....	....	....	....	....	...	...	....	334.0	$ 23,730.20
587.7	.....	....	.....	....	....	....	....	...	...	....	587.7	41,644.58
3,647.8	.....	....	.....	....	....	....	573.3	...	...	....	4,221.1	312,124.00
.....	.....	....	.....	....	....	....	....	...	33.2	....	33.2	2,832.27
.....	.....	....	.....	....	398.4	....	....	...	...	....	398.4	76,640.85
165.4	.....	....	.....	....	65.3	....	....	...	...	....	230.7	23,559.98
.....	466.1	....	.....	....	....	....	....	...	...	....	466.1	24,045.09
4,645.5	.....	....	.....	....	834.4	117.4	1,504.1	16.2	...	....	7,117.6	631,857.80
9,380.4	**466.1**	....	.....	....	**1,298.1**	**117.4**	**2,077.4**	**16.2**	**33.2**	....	**13,388.8**	**$ 1,136,434.77**
.....	.....	....	.....	359.7	....	....	....	...	...	....	359.7	$ 82,593.42
4,377.2	126.0	....	404.7	374.1	1,313.3	54.9	....	...	18.7	....	6,668.9	657,271.69
.....	103.4	....	.....	....	....	....	....	...	...	....	103.4	5,321.40
1,132.6	3.0	....	733.7	158.5	1,050.1	108.3	870.1	15.7	8.8	....	4,080.8	449,070.31
5,509.8	**232.4**	....	**1,138.4**	**892.3**	**2,363.4**	**163.2**	**870.1**	**15.7**	**27.5**	....	**11,212.8**	**$ 1,194,256.82**
.....	76.4	....	.....	....	....	....	....	...	...	....	76.4	$ 3,326.02
.....	.....	....	.....	....	....	....	....	5.0	...	....	5.0	2,573.82
3,769.4	52.8	....	485.3	144.2	670.9	....	....	6.8	35.8	....	5,165.2	455,636.91
.....	883.1	....	.....	....	....	....	....	...	...	....	883.1	44,275.80
3,769.4	**1,012.3**	....	**485.3**	**144.2**	**670.9**	....	....	**11.8**	**35.8**	....	**6,129.7**	**$ 505,812.55**

[*Concluded on next page*]

Table 513—*Concluded*

Detail by Steamers c

Steamer by No.	Steamer or Source	Transshipping Steamer	Port of Sailing	Date of Arrival	Port of Arrival
				1922	
248	Emergency Aid, IV	456	New Orleans	Dec. 17	Hamburg
249	Mount Clinton, VII	457	New York	Dec. 20	Hamburg
250	Mount Clinton, VII	457	New York	Dec. 20	Hamburg
251	Muskegon		New York	Dec. 22	Odessa
252	Stuyvesant		New York	Dec. 24	Odessa
253	Winnebago		New York	Dec. 25	Riga
254	Winnebago (Clothing Rem. Acct.)		New York	Dec. 25	Riga
	Total for December				
				1923	
255	Mount Clay, X	457, 458	New York	Jan. 1	Hamburg
256	Mount Clay, X (Clothing Rem. Acct.)	460	New York	Jan. 1	Hamburg
257	Mount Carroll, XI	459	New York	Jan. 25	Hamburg
258	Manitowac, II		New York	Jan. 28	Odessa
259	Belvidere (Clothing Rem. Acct.)		New York	Jan. 29	Riga
	Total for January				
260	West Maximus		New York	Feb. 17	Riga
261	Saugus		N.Y., Norfolk	Feb. 26	Odessa
262	West Ira	461, 463	New Orleans	Feb. 28	Hamburg
	Total for February				
263	Tomalva	462	Galveston	Mar. 3	Hamburg
264	Winneconne		New York	Mar. 10	Odessa
265	Emergency Aid, V	462	New Orleans	Mar. 14	Hamburg
266	Allaguash, III		New York	Mar. 24	Windau
267	Allaguash, III (Old Clothing)		New York	Mar. 24	Windau
268	Rockaway Park		New York	Mar. 28	Windau
	Total for March				
269	Mount Carroll, XII	467	New York	Apr. 2	Hamburg
270	Cold Water	464, 465, 466	Norfolk	Apr. 5	Hamburg
271	Eastern Star		New York	Apr. 11	Windau
272	Reliance	467	New York	Apr. 11	Hamburg
273	Eastern Coast		New York, Phila.	Apr. 14	Riga
274	President Harding	469	New York	Apr. 16	Hamburg
275	Hansa	467	New York	Apr. 17	Hamburg
276	Springfield	468, 470, 471, 472	Norfolk	Apr. 18	Hamburg
277	Conejos, IV		New York	Apr. 24	Odessa
278	Coeur d'Alene		New York	Apr. 24	Odessa
279	George Washington	469	New York	Apr. 24	Bremen
280	Local Purchase		Riga	Apr. 24	Riga
281	Satsuma		New York	Apr. 26	Libau
282	Local Purchase		Riga	Apr. 30	Riga
	Total for April				
283	Suruga		New York	May 3	Riga
284	Local Purchase		Riga	May 4	Riga
285	Local Purchase		Riga	May 25	Riga
286	Baltannic		London	May 28	Libau
	Total for May				
	Arrival Adjustments, Overages				
	Total, Gross				
	Deduct Duplication: Included in Medical Arrivals				
	Total, Net **				

** This table includes 57,823.0 metric tons of relief supplies, value $4,322,450.83 (Cf. Table 165), delivered to Soviet Republics and paid for by gold deposited by R.S.F.S.R. and U.S.R. These supplies are in addition to those quoted in Table 519.

§ Tea, 669.8; corned beef, 3.9; dehydrated potatoes, .9; salt, 148.0; cuits, 20.1; dates, .7; rice and milk, 42.3; dried milk, 1.8. All net m tons.

merican Relief Administration

rivals of Relief Supplies

Flour	Rice	Beans, Peas	Corn Grits	Pork Products	Milk	Cocoa	Sugar	Misc. Food	Clothing and Misc.	Soap	Total Tons	Total Value
Contents of Cargoes in Net Metric Tons of 1,000 Kilograms or 2,204.6 Pounds												
.....	309.2	....	.....	....	....	....	....	...	...	....	309.2	$ 16,808.67
.....	.....	....	.....	....	....	....	....	...	46.8	....	46.8	69,925.87
.....	.....	....	.....	....	....	....	....	...	1.0	....	1.0	1,472.94
1,486.7	289.5	....	.....	640.4	525.3	107.7	888.5	54.6	11.4	....	4,004.1	515,729.43
22.2	826.2	....	.....	379.3	661.6	....	....	...	...	....	1,889.3	260,500.47
2,083.9	34.6	....	149.7	217.8	522.6	....	789.3	32.2	199.2	....	4,029.3	682,862.68
.....	.....	....	.....	....	....	....	....	...	273.3	....	273.3	407,079.05
3,592.8	**1,459.5**	....	**149.7**	**1,237.5**	**1,709.5**	**107.7**	**1,677.8**	**86.8**	**531.7**	....	**10,553.0**	**$ 1,954,379.11**
.....	.....	....	.....	....	....	....	....	...	63.7	....	63.7	$ 85,789.87
.....	.....	....	.....	....	....	....	....	...	136.7	....	136.7	149,091.41
.....	.....	....	.....	....	217.7	....	....	...	...	91.5	309.2	69,446.85
1,107.1	259.2	....	.....	....	396.2	....	....	...	101.4	....	1,863.9	184,168.33
.....	.....	....	.....	....	....	....	....	...	80.2	....	80.2	158,007.26
1,107.1	**259.2**	....	.....	....	**613.9**	....	.....	...	**382.0**	**91.5**	**2,453.7**	**$ 646,503.72**
.....	.....	....	.....	....	140.3	....	....	...	...	42.4	182.7	$ 40,478.86
.....	.....	....	.....	596.3	296.1	....	....	...	...	....	892.4	240,500.77
.....	701.7	....	.....	....	....	....	....	...	...	....	701.7	34,167.35
.....	**701.7**	....	.....	**596.3**	**436.4**	....	.....	...	...	**42.4**	**1,776.8**	**$ 315,146.98**
.....	103.5	....	.....	....	....	....	....	...	...	....	103.5	$ 4,958.75
3,002.6	.....	....	.....	....	489.9	....	350.5	...	...	....	3,843.0	368,420.78
.....	199.9	....	.....	....	....	....	....	...	...	....	199.9	9,702.80
4,132.8	.....	....	.....	....	796.5	....	512.5	...	...	81.0	5,522.8	537,214.06
.....	.....	....	.....	....	....	....	....	...	27.8	....	27.8	5,128.03
4,089.1	.....	....	.....	....	339.0	382.5	176.3	...	1.0	....	4,987.9	412,190.30
1,224.5	**303.4**	....	.....	....	**1,625.4**	**382.5**	**1,039.3**	...	**28.8**	**81.0**	**14,684.9**	**$ 1,337,614.72**
268.2	.....	....	117.4	....	170.4	....	....	...	...	....	556.0	$ 61,865.66
.....	.....	....	.....	754.1	....	....	....	...	...	....	754.1	211,864.32
2,072.8	.....	....	31.8	....	....	....	....	...	...	....	2,104.6	145,038.39
.....	.....	....	158.3	....	192.9	....	....	...	...	....	351.2	50,059.66
198.8	.....	....	749.1	....	700.0	13.6	568.8	...	5.2	....	2,235.5	282,285.93
76.1	.....	....	358.0	....	....	....	....	...	...	....	434.1	21,724.92
26.7	.....	....	256.9	....	65.3	....	....	...	...	....	348.9	28,730.51
.....	.....	....	.....	388.2	....	....	....	...	...	....	388.2	113,925.83
.....	.....	....	.....	....	21.8	....	....	...	...	....	21.8	5,039.61
.....	.....	....	.....	....	214.9	....	....	...	...	....	214.9	51,197.40
.....	.....	....	269.6	....	....	....	....	...	...	....	269.6	12,645.21
.....	.....	....	.....	....	....	....	304.6	...	...	....	304.6	45,880.05
2,825.9	.....	....	2,012.0	....	1,297.1	....	22.7	...	.2	....	6,157.9	581,461.07
.....	.....	....	.....	....	....	....	155.0	...	...	....	155.0	20,428.38
5,468.5	.....	....	**3,953.1**	**1,142.3**	**2,662.4**	**13.6**	**1,051.1**	...	**5.4**	....	**14,296.4**	**$ 1,632,146.94**
694.3	.....	....	1,038.2	....	323.3	....	258.7	...	...	....	2,314.5	$ 208,244.29
.....	.....	....	.....	....	....	....	195.4	...	...	....	195.4	29,431.93
.....	.....	....	.....	....	....	....	100.0	...	...	....	100.0	15,062.41
.....	.....	....	.....	....	....	....	....	...	1.0	....	1.0	420.00
694.3	.....	....	**1,038.2**	....	**323.3**	....	**554.1**	...	**1.0**	....	**2,610.9**	**$ 253,158.63**
.....	.....	....	.....	9.9	....	32.8	....	...	...	....	42.7	....
,679.9	**18,842.7**	**3,575.3**	**11,324.1**	**12,408.9**	**23,773.0**	**3,945.0**	**21,488.3**	**887.5**	**2,073.4**	**871.1**	**230,869.2**	**$24,269,255.77**
.....	.....	....	.....	....	....	....	....	...	...	271.3	271.3	$ 57,795.61
,679.9	**18.842.7**	**3,575.3**	**11,324.1**	**12,408.9**	**23,773.0**	**3,945.0**	**21,488.3**	**887.5§**	**2,073.4¶**	**599.8**	**230,597.9**	**$24,211,460.16**

Of this total, 1,797.8 metric tons are clothing; 156.2, auto parts;
4, bags and containers.

Table 514 Detail by Steamers of the Transshipment of Relief Supplies

Steamer No.	Steamer	Original Steamer by Number (Cf. Table 513)	Retransshipping Steamer by Number (Cf. Tables 515–16)	Date of Arrival Week Ending
				1920
301	Suzanne	3	420	Nov. 1
				1921
302	Smolensk, II	39	505, 507	July 22
				1921
303	Horst	65	513	Oct. 28
304	Torborg	71	514, 515	Nov. 4
	Total Copenhagen to Danzig			
				1921
305	Moewe, I	80	Rail	Nov. 11
				1921
306	Progress, VI	10	509	Apr. 29
307	Progress, VII	18	507	May 31
308	Sensal, IV	24	505, 508	July 15
309	Naval, III	24	508	July 22
310	Hansa, IV	27	509	July 22
311	Kellersee, IV	19	505, 506, 508	July 29
312	Weichsel, VIII	28, 40	507, 509, Rail	July 29
313	Imperial, II	30	507, 509	July 29
	Total for July			
314	Imperial, III	31, 32	509	Aug. 12
315	Progress, IX	46	512, 514	Sept. 23
316	Elsa, I	46	512	Sept. 23
317	Greta, I	46	512	Sept. 23
318	Kaethe, II	47	510, 522	Sept. 30
	Total for September			
319	Suzanne, VI	55	522	Oct. 14
320	Mietzung, II	67	513	Oct. 21
321	Weichsel, IX	60, 61	513, 522	Oct. 28
322	Elsa, II	69	514	Oct. 28
323	Hinrich, III	70	513	Oct. 28
	Total for October			
324	Doris	70, 72	431, 515	Nov. 4
325	Emma, II	72	431, 515	Nov. 4
326	Pregel, IV	75	515, 517	Nov. 18
327	Echo, V	75	517	Nov. 18
328	Aeolus, VIII	79	515	Nov. 18
329	Fanal, IV	89	517	Nov. 30
330	Emma, III	90	517, 522	Nov. 30
	Total for November			
331	Norma, I	99, 101	518, 519, 522, Rail	Dec. 23
				1922
332	Moewe, II	115	522	Jan. 27
333	Hansa, V	119	522, Rail	Jan. 27
	Total for January			

American Relief Administration

to and from Danzig Port—Reconstruction Period, 1919–1924

Flour	Rice	Beans, Peas	Corn Grits	Pork Products	Milk	Cocoa	Sugar	Misc. Food	Clothing and Misc.	Total Tons
Contents of Cargoes in Net Metric Tons of 1,000 Kilograms or 2,204.6 Pounds										
DANZIG TO HAMBURG										
....	.....	....	.....	....	....	....	.....	**.8**	....	**.8**
HULL TO DANZIG										
....	.....	....	.....	**161.2**	....	....	.....	....	....	**161.2**
COPENHAGEN TO DANZIG										
186.7	.....	....	.....	....	....	....	.....	....	....	186.7
438.2	.....	....	.....	....	....	....	.....	....	....	438.2
624.9	.....	....	.....	....	....	....	.....	....	....	**624.9**
BREMERHAVEN TO DANZIG										
....	.....	....	.....	....	....	**4.8**	.....	....	....	**4.8**
HAMBURG TO DANZIG										
....	.....	....	.....	**9.0**	....	....	.....	....	....	**9.0**
....	.....	....	.....	....	**9.7**	....	.....	....	....	**9.7**
....	.....	....	.....	....	....	81.3	.....	....	....	81.3
....	.....	....	.....	....	....	29.7	.....	....	....	29.7
....	.....	....	.....	....	45.2	....	.....	....	....	45.2
98.3	.....	....	.....	....	....	....	.....	....	....	98.3
....	170.2	....	.....	....	206.8	....	.....	....	....	377.0
....	.....	....	.....	....	38.3	....	.....	....	....	38.3
98.3	**170.2**	....	.....	....	**290.3**	**111.0**	.....	....	....	**669.8**
....	.....	....	.....	....	**171.9**	....	.....	....	....	**171.9**
....	.....	215.2	.....	....	....	....	.....	....	....	215.2
....	.....	199.4	.....	....	....	....	.....	....	....	199.4
....	.....	141.0	.....	....	....	....	.....	....	....	141.0
....	.....	....	.....	....	14.7	....	.....	....	16.0	30.7
....	.....	**555.6**	.....	....	**14.7**	....	.....	....	**16.0**	**586.3**
....	.....	....	.....	....	56.4	....	.....	....	....	56.4
....	.....	....	.....	....	....	....	.....	....	11.3	11.3
....	.....	....	.....	....	280.6	....	.....	....	....	280.6
....	.....	....	.....	....	94.2	....	.....	....	....	94.2
308.4	.....	....	.....	....	....	....	.....	....	....	308.4
308.4	.....	....	.....	....	**431.2**	....	.....	....	**11.3**	**750.9**
70.0	.....	....	280.0	....	....	....	.....	....	....	350.0
305.8	.....	....	488.1	....	....	....	.....	....	....	793.9
359.7	.....	....	.....	....	....	....	.....	....	....	359.7
151.5	.....	....	.....	....	....	....	.....	....	....	151.5
....	251.5	....	.....	....	....	....	.....	....	....	251.5
....	309.7	....	.....	....	....	....	.....	....	....	309.7
....	111.2	....	.....	....	....	....	.....	....	....	111.2
887.0	**672.4**	....	**768.1**	....	....	....	.....	....	....	**2,327.5**
....	.....	....	.....	**99.6**	**152.0**	....	.....	....	....	**251.6**
....	.....	164.2	.....	....	....	....	.....	....	109.0	273.2
....	.....	58.4	.....	....	....	34.2	.....	....	....	92.6
....	.....	**222.6**	.....	....	....	**34.2**	.....	....	**109.0**	**365.8**

[*Continued on next page*]

Table 514—*Continued*

Detail by Steamers of the Transshipment of

Steamer No.	Steamer	Original Steamer by Number (Cf. Table 513)	Retransshipping Steamer by Number (Cf. Tables 515–16)	Date of Arrival Week Ending
				1922
334	Gerrat	126, 129	522, Rail	Mar. 10
335	Hentsch	127	Rail	Mar. 10
336	Gottefried Poppe	125, 132, 136	Rail	Mar. 17
337	Stella Wega	126	520, Rail	Mar. 17
338	Marathon, III	133	Rail	Mar. 24
339	Neutral	134	Rail	Mar. 24
340	Aval	138	Rail	Mar. 24
341	Frankfurt, III	144, 148, 149, 150	Rail	Mar. 31
342	Hannah Blumenthal	133, 147, 149, 156	Rail	Mar. 31
	Total for March	....	....	....
343	Fricka	144, 151, 155	Rail	Apr. 7
344	Bonus, I	149, 152, 158	Rail	Apr. 7
345	Elina	151, 152, 157	Rail	Apr. 14
346	Erda	131, 152, 153, 160, 161	Rail	Apr. 14
347	Aeolus, IX	152, 161, 162	Rail	Apr. 14
348	Weichsel, X	163, 169	Rail	Apr. 28
	Total for April	....	....	....
349	Bonus, II	179	Rail	May 5
350	Progress, X	179	Rail	May 5
351	Hammonia, III	179	Rail	May 12
352	Weichsel, XI	179	Rail	May 19
	Total for May	....	....	....
	Total Hamburg to Danzig	....	....	....
	Grand Total	....	....	....

American Relief Administration

Relief Supplies to and from Danzig Port

Contents of Cargoes in Net Metric Tons of 1,000 Kilograms or 2,204.6 Pounds

Flour	Rice	Beans, Peas	Corn Grits	Pork Products	Milk	Cocoa	Sugar	Misc. Food	Clothing and Misc.	Total Tons
				HAMBURG TO DANZIG—*Continued*						
26.5	.....	71.0	.....	328.5	....	....	.....	....	....	426.0
14.6	.....	....	.....	....	....	181.9	.....	....	....	196.5
2,431.6	.....	....	.....	....	....	....	201.9	....	....	2,633.5
....	.....	....	.....	45.9	....	99.6	.....	.7	27.9	174.1
645.7	.....	....	.....	....	....	....	.....	....	....	645.7
143.6	.....	....	.....	....	....	....	202.2	....	....	345.8
207.1	.....	....	.....	....	....	....	.....	....	....	207.1
643.6	433.5	....	.....	....	....	....	.....	52.9	....	1,130.0
961.5	.....	....	.....	....	....	26.6	.....	....	....	988.1
5,074.2	**433.5**	**71.0**	.....	**374.4**	....	**308.1**	**404.1**	**53.6**	**27.9**	**6,746.8**
2,928.7	9.7	....	.....	....	....	....	.....	....	....	2,938.4
449.6	43.5	....	.....	294.1	....	....	.....	....	....	787.2
124.1	85.7	27.0	.....	....	....	....	481.1	....	....	717.9
1,349.6	571.8	....	.....	695.5	....	....	252.7	....	....	2,869.6
454.8	79.2	....	.....	66.3	....	....	.....	....	....	600.3
1,289.4	217.2	....	.....	....	....	....	.....	....	....	1,506.6
6,596.2	**1,007.1**	**27.0**	.....	**1,055.9**	....	....	**733.8**	....	....	**9,420.0**
225.5	723.0	....	.....	....	....	....	.....	....	....	948.5
620.3	406.8	....	.....	....	....	....	192.3	....	....	1,219.4
379.9	.....	....	.....	....	....	....	202.3	....	....	582.2
59.2	.....	....	.....	....	....	....	1.1	....	....	60.3
1,284.9	**1,129.8**	....	.....	....	....	....	**395.7**	....	....	**2,810.4**
14,249.0	**3,413.0**	**876.2**	**768.1**	**1,538.9**	**1,069.8**	**453.3**	**1,533.6**	**53.6**	**164.2**	**24,119.7**
14,873.9	**3,413.0**	**876.2**	**768.1**	**1,700.1**	**1,069.8**	**458.1**	**1,533.6**	**54.4**	**164.2**	**24,911.4**

RUSSIA (SOVIET REPUBLICS)—American Relief Administration

Detail by Shipment Numbers (Train No.) of Retransshipment of Relief Supplies, via Rail—Reconstruction Period, 1919–1924

Table 515

D.S.R. No.*	Transshipping Steamer by Number (Cf. Table 514)	Original Steamer by Number (Cf. Table 513)	Date of Shipment	Commodities in Net Metric Tons of 1,000 Kilograms or 2,204.6 Pounds							
				Flour	Rice	Beans, Peas	Pork Products	Cocoa	Sugar	Misc. Food	Total Tons
			1922								
9	334	129	March	....	....	....	19.6	....	....	....	19.6
9	334	126	March	....	....	....	69.7	....	....	....	69.7
12	334	126	March	....	....	....	60.6	....	....	....	60.6
12	334	129	March	....	....	....	128.2	....	....	....	128.2
15	336	125, 132, 136	March	91.0	....	....	....	....	....	....	91.0
16	336	125, 132, 136	March	404.0	....	....	....	....	....	....	404.0
16	339	134	March	45.8	....	....	....	....	122.0	....	167.8
17	339	134	March	75.7	....	....	....	....	....	....	75.7
17	336	125, 132, 136	March	375.0	....	....	....	....	....	....	375.0
18	336	125, 132, 136	March	347.6	....	....	....	....	37.1	....	384.7
18	339, 338	134, 133	March	187.6	....	....	....	....	....	....	187.6
19	338	133	March	469.0	....	....	....	....	....	....	469.0
19	336	125, 132, 136	March	72.2	....	....	....	....	45.0	....	117.2
20	336	125, 132, 136	March	460.3	....	....	....	....	....	....	460.3
20	340	138	March	53.9	....	....	....	....	....	....	53.9
20	338	133	March	4.7	....	....	....	....	....	....	4.7
20	339	134	March	....	....	....	....	....	14.8	....	14.8
20	335	127	March	....	....	....	....	32.5	....	....	32.5
21	334	129	March	....	....	....	23.3	....	....	....	23.3
21	334	126	March	....	....	....	27.7	....	....	....	27.7
21	337	126	March	....	....	....	....	30.1	....	....	30.1
21	340	138	March	52.7	....	....	....	....	....	....	52.7
21	339	134	March	....	....	....	....	....	65.4	....	65.4
21	336	125, 132, 136	March	280.4	....	....	....	....	27.9	....	308.
22	336	125, 132, 136	March	245.1	....	....	....	....	73.2	....	318.
22	337	126	March	....	....	....	....	32.4	....	....	32.4
22	340	138	March	89.8	....	....	....	....	....	....	89.8
22	339	134	March	8.0	....	....	....	....	....	....	8.0
	Total for March	....	....	**3,262.8**	....	....	**329.1**	**95.0**	**385.4**	....	**4,072.**
23	336	125, 132, 136	April	156.0	....	....	....	....	17.4	....	173.
23	341	144, 148, 149, 150	April	236.9	27.2	....	....	....	....	52.9	317.
23	340	138	April	12.6	....	....	....	....	....	....	12.
25	344	149, 152, 158	April	205.6	43.2	....	74.2	....	....	....	323.
25	342	133, 147, 149, 156	April	146.4	....	....	....	....	....	....	146.
25	337	126	April	....	....	....	45.4	....	....	....	45.
25	335	127	April	....	....	....	....	25.9	....	....	25.
26	344	149, 152, 158	April	233.9	....	....	131.6	....	....	....	365.
26	335	127	April	....	....	....	....	48.2	....	....	48.
26	342	133, 147, 149, 156	April	106.9	....	....	....	26.5	....	....	133.
26	341	144, 148, 149, 150	April	5.3	....	....	....	....	....	....	5.
27	342	133, 147, 149, 156	April	286.3	....	....	....	....	....	....	286.
27	335	127	April	....	....	....	....	62.7	....	....	62.
27	344	149, 152, 158	April	10.1	....	....	88.3	....	....	....	98.
27	337	126	April	....	....	....	....	37.1	....	....	37.
27	341	144, 148, 149, 150	April	45.9	....	....	....	....	....	....	45.
28	341	144, 148, 149, 150	April	76.1	183.4	....	....	....	....	....	259.
28	342	133, 147, 149, 156	April	137.1	....	....	....	....	....	....	137.
28	343	144, 151, 155	April	179.9	....	....	....	....	....	....	179.
28	335	127	April	....	....	....	....	12.4	....	....	12.
29	343	144, 151, 155	April	464.5	....	....	....	....	....	....	464.
29	341	144, 148, 149, 150	April	25.4	45.2	....	....	....	....	....	70.
29	335	127	April	14.5	....	....	....	....	....	....	14.
30	343	144, 151, 155	April	429.0	....	....	....	....	....	....	429.
30	341	144, 148, 149, 150	April	116.8	25.3	....	....	....	....	....	142.
31	347	152, 161, 162	April	455.1	79.1	....	66.6	....	....	....	600.
32	343	144, 151, 155	April	400.2	....	....	....	....	....	....	400.
32	341	144, 148, 149, 150	April	30.4	15.2	....	....	....	....	....	45.
32	346	131, 152, 153, 160, 161	April	....	....	....	12.7	....	....	....	12.
33	343	144, 151, 155	April	269.7	....	....	....	....	....	....	269.

* Designates shipments from Danzig to Stolpce for Russia.

RUSSIA (SOVIET REPUBLICS)

Detail by Shipment Numbers (Train No.) of Retransshipment of Relief Supplies, via Rail

Table 515—*Continued*

D.S.R. No.*	Transshipping Steamer by Number (Cf. Table 514)	Original Steamer by Number (Cf. Table 513)	Date of Shipment	Commodities in Net Metric Tons of 1,000 Kilograms or 2,204.6 Pounds							
				Flour	Rice	Beans, Peas	Pork Products	Cocoa	Sugar	Misc. Food	Total Tons
			1922								
33	346	131, 152, 153, 160, 161	April	....	97.6	....	88.2	....	....	....	185.8
34	342	133, 147, 149, 156...	April	6.9	....	....	....	....	....	....	6.9
34	343	144, 151, 155	April	223.5	....	....	....	....	....	....	223.5
34	341	144, 148, 149, 150...	April	....	76.1	....	....	....	....	....	76.1
34	346	131, 152, 153, 160, 161	April	....	70.1	....	148.1	....	....	....	218.2
35	343	144, 151, 155	April	50.5	....	....	....	....	....	....	50.5
35	345	151, 152, 157	April	52.6	....	26.2	....	....	186.6	....	265.4
35	341	144, 148, 149, 150...	April	108.7	60.9	....	....	....	....	....	169.6
35	342	133, 147, 149, 156...	April	45.6	....	....	....	....	....	....	45.6
35	346	131, 152, 153, 160, 161	April	....	10.0	....	....	....	14.2	....	24.2
37	342	133, 147, 149, 156...	April	232.4	....	....	....	....	....	....	232.4
37	343	144, 151, 155	April	23.4	....	....	....	....	....	....	23.4
37	346	131, 152, 153, 160, 161	April	15.2	29.8	....	10.3	....	90.0	....	145.3
37	345	151, 152, 157	April	....	85.7	....	....	....	106.5	....	192.2
38	346	131, 152, 153, 160, 161	April	242.4	88.0	....	47.2	....	65.0	....	442.6
38	343	144, 151, 155	April	58.2	....	....	....	....	....	....	58.2
39	345	151, 152, 157	April	71.4	....	....	....	....	181.8	....	253.2
39	346	131, 152, 153, 160, 161	April	191.9	....	....	28.7	....	....	....	220.6
40	346	131, 152, 153, 160, 161	April	312.8	75.2	....	12.4	....	....	....	400.4
40	343	144, 151, 155	April	115.9	....	....	....	....	....	....	115.9
41	343	144, 151, 155	April	174.7	....	....	....	....	....	....	174.7
41	346	131, 152, 153, 160, 161	April	117.9	105.8	....	152.7	....	....	....	376.4
42	343	144, 151, 155	April	230.5	....	....	....	....	....	....	230.5
42	346	131, 152, 153, 160, 161	April	....	76.4	....	184.6	....	....	....	261.0
44	346	131, 152, 153, 160, 161	April	301.9	....	....	11.7	....	61.3	....	374.9
44	343	144, 151, 155	April	160.6	....	....	....	....	....	....	160.6
45	343	144, 151, 155	April	139.5	9.6	....	....	....	....	....	149.1
45	346	131, 152, 153, 160, 161	April	163.9	15.1	....	....	....	21.0	....	200.0
	Total for April			**7,085.0**	**1,218.9**	**26.2**	**1,102.7**	**212.8**	**743.8**	**52.9**	**10,442.3**
46	348	163, 169	May	447.7	141.0	....	....	....	....	....	588.7
47	348	163, 169	May	436.3	75.6	....	....	....	....	....	511.9
48	348	163, 169	May	404.4	.1	....	....	....	....	....	404.5
49	350	179	May	209.8	216.3	....	....	....	55.1	....	481.2
51	350	179	May	153.1	66.4	....	....	....	90.1	....	309.6
51	349	179	May	100.2	90.1	....	....	....	....	....	190.3
53	350	179	May	213.1	54.1	....	....	....	....	....	267.2
53	349	179	May	30.8	139.2	....	....	....	....	....	170.0
53	351	179	May	41.4	....	....	....	....	29.9	....	71.3
55	350	179	May	42.4	69.0	....	....	....	44.8	....	156.2
55	351	179	May	....	....	....	....	....	114.4	....	114.4
55	348	163, 169	May	....	1.0	....	....	....	....	....	1.0
55	349	179	May	27.4	320.3	....	....	....	....	....	347.7
56	351	179	May	335.5	....	....	....	....	55.0	....	390.5
56	349	179	May	66.7	172.9	....	....	....	....	....	239.6
56	348	163, 169	May	....	1.2	....	....	....	....	....	1.2
56	350	179	May	.7	2.3	....	....	....	....	....	3.0
58	....	205	May	....	....	....	....	....	....	20.3	20.3
	Total for May			**2,509.5**	**1,349.5**	....	....	....	**389.3**	**20.3**	**4,268.6**
59	312	40	June	....	170.2	....	....	....	....	....	170.2
59	352	179	June	56.1	....	....	....	....	1.1	....	57.2
59	305	80	June	....	....	....	....	4.3	....	....	4.3
59	331	101	June	....	....	....	17.6	....	....	....	17.6
59	....	26	June	....	....	....	9.1	....	....	....	9.1
59	333	119	June	....	....	58.4	....	....	....	....	58.4
59	Stock, Sweepings	....	June	....	....	.8	....	....	....	....	.8
	Total for June			**56.1**	**170.2**	**59.2**	**26.7**	**4.3**	**1.1**	....	**317.6**
	Grand Total			**12,913.4**	**2,738.6**	**85.4**	**1,458.5**	**312.1**	**1,519.6**	**73.2**	**19,100.8**

Table 516

Detail by Steamers of Transshipments from Hamburg,

Steamer No.	Transshipping Steamer	Original and Transshipping Steamer by Number (Cf. Tables 513, 514)	Date of Arrival
			1921
401	Phoenix	9, 12, 15, 23, 25, 27, 28, 29, 31, 33, 36, 41	Sept. 1
402	Goeteborg	6, 9, 11, 12, 16, 22, 28, 29, 31, 33, 36	Sept. 6
403	Stella	9, 12, 27, 28, 30, 33, 36, 42	Sept. 13
			1922
404	Electra	110, 128, 130, 147, 152, 156	May 15
405	Ina Lotte Blumenthal	170, 174, 177, 178, 182	May 20
406	Lotte Reith	172, 173, 174	May 24
407	Alesia, II	128, 173, 174, 177, 190	May 24
408	Cordelia	128, 140, 173, 174, 187	June 2
409	Carsten Russ, II	197, 201	June 8
410	Wilhelm Russ, I	208	June 14
411	Wiedau	203, 204	June 16
412	Andalusia, I	212	June 27
413	Johannes C. Russ, III	130, 178, 212	July 4
414	Norwegian Solhaug	173, 181, 187, 203, 213, 216, 218, 221	Aug. 8
415	Martha Russ, II	227	Aug. 23
416	Andalusia, II	238, 240	Oct. 26
417	Alesia, V	242	Nov. 7
418	Duisburg	244	Nov. 25
	Total, Hamburg to Petrograd		
			1922
419	Gasconier	127	Mar. 10
			1921
420	Hamburg	3 : 301. 6, 8, 9, 11, 12, 13, 14, 15, 23, 25, 28, 30, 31, 34, 36, 42, 54	Sept. 11
421	Pentelikon, I	52, 53	Oct. 10
422	Sunion, I	28, 31, 50, 52	Oct. 12
423	Hebron	47	Oct. 20
424	Helikon, I	47, 59	Oct. 23
425	Carsten Russ, I	47, 51, 52, 55	Oct. 24
426	Coblenz, I	52, 60, 64	Oct. 28
427	Libianon, III	52, 59, 60	Oct. 28
428	Sunion, II	63	Oct. 29
429	Mannheim, I	9, 59	Oct. 30
430	Frankfurt, I	60, 62, 63, 68, 69, 73	Nov. 11
431	Guenther Russ	51, 54, 72, 74, 78, 79, 81	Nov. 20
432	Libianon, IV	79	Nov. 21
433	Helikon, III	79, 84	Nov. 23
434	Pentelikon, II	84	Nov. 27
435	Mannheim, II	Purchase No. 6	Dec. 6
436	Strassburg, I	91	Dec. 12
437	Sunion, III	86, 97	Dec. 16
438	Greta, II	100	Dec. 24
439	Renate	100	Dec. 24
440	Norderney, I	100, 101	Dec. 25
			1922
441	Martha Russ	100, 101, 102, 103, 111	Jan. 10
442	Marathon, IV	166	May 5
443	Frankfurt, V	165	May 7
444	Christel Salling, II	169	May 9
445	Strassburg, VI	128, 173	May 10
446	Mannheim, IV	172, 174, 178	May 16
447	Coblenz, III	174, 177, 187, 188	May 26
448	Karlsruhe, V	196	June 4
449	Gertrud Salling	186, 193	June 7
450	Mannheim, V	173, 208	June 7

American Relief Administration

Retransshipments from Danzig—Reconstruction Period, 1919–1924

Contents of Cargoes in Net Metric Tons of 1,000 Kilograms or 2,204.6 Pounds

Flour	Rice	Beans, Peas	Corn Grits	Pork Products	Milk	Cocoa	Sugar	Misc. Food	Clothing and Misc.	Soap	Total Tons
					HAMBURG TO PETROGRAD						
160.5	35.1	67.0	74.0	39.0	121.3	13.5	64.9	...	...	....	575.3
461.3	35.2	150.0	95.9	57.9	44.5	22.9	6.9	...	...	....	874.6
86.6	.....	218.0	....	....	169.4	.1	71.4	...	...	....	546.5
269.5	165.7	.....	....	76.1	.....	34.5	....	...	9.0	....	554.8
.....	217.7	.....	....	153.8	.....	79.4	497.7	16.2	3.0	....	967.8
1,574.1	.....	.....	....	230.4	.....	....	....	...	...	64.4	1,868.9
1,052.8	.....	.....	....	41.7	.....	....	252.3	12.7	1.0	....	1,360.5
1,315.6	91.8	.....	....	154.3	.....	84.4	221.6	...	4.2	....	1,871.9
1,220.2	.....	.....	....	....	.....	....	....	...	1.4	....	1,221.6
1,273.9	.....	.....	....	....	.....	....	....	...	...	....	1,273.9
872.1	.....	.....	....	....	.....	174.1	....	...	...	....	1,046.2
836.0	.....	.....	....	....	.....	....	....	...	...	....	836.0
302.2	381.1	.....	....	....	.....	....	....	...	...	....	683.3
.....	116.9	.....	....	33.7	233.6	35.2	49.3	...	...	....	468.7
.....	.....	.....	....	236.8	.....	....	....	...	...	....	236.8
.....	464.5	.....	....	359.7	.....	....	....	...	...	....	824.2
.....	102.0	.....	....	....	.....	....	....	...	...	....	102.0
.....	69.2	.....	....	....	.....	....	....	...	...	....	69.2
9,424.8	**1,679.2**	**435.0**	**169.9**	**1,383.4**	**569.8**	**444.1**	**1,164.1**	**28.9**	**18.6**	**64.4**	**15,382.2**
					HAMBURG TO REVAL						
1,448.2	.....	.....	....	....	.....	....	....	...	...	....	**1,448.2**
					HAMBURG TO RIGA						
.....	.....	424.1	61.5	366.1	178.6	36.9	29.6	3.9	...	....	1,100.7
.....	.....	.....	....	150.1	.....	50.0	....	...	...	....	200.1
.....	.....	.....	....	....	.....	69.6	....	...	18.3	....	87.9
.....	.....	.....	....	....	185.2	....	....	...	...	....	185.2
241.4	.....	.....	....	....	67.8	....	....	...	...	....	309.2
.....	170.2	.....	....	45.9	394.2	....	397.4	...	...	....	1,007.7
533.7	.....	.....	....	....	128.7	89.3	....	...	...	....	751.7
262.2	.....	.....	....	....	63.1	....	....	...	...	....	325.3
324.3	.....	.....	....	....	.....	....	....	...	...	....	324.3
829.9	.....	.....	....	....	.....	....	....	...	...	....	829.9
147.3	.....	.....	260.6	....	557.8	....	....	...	...	....	965.7
.....	637.4	.....	....	....	.....	....	....	...	22.9	....	660.3
.....	399.4	.....	....	....	.....	....	....	...	...	....	399.4
.....	101.1	.....	....	....	.....	....	266.8	...	...	....	367.9
.....	.....	.....	101.3	....	.....	....	182.7	...	2.8	....	286.8
.....	.....	.....	....	....	.....	....	....	...	.6	....	.6
.....	.....	.....	....	....	.....	....	....	...	...	57.3	57.3
.....	.....	.....	....	....	213.9	....	....	...	...	....	213.9
749.0	.....	.....	....	....	.....	....	....	...	...	....	749.0
1,059.1	.....	.....	....	....	.....	....	....	...	...	....	1,059.1
80.1	.....	.....	....	198.1	.....	....	....	...	.2	....	278.4
123.1	.....	.....	....	3.7	117.6	49.7	....	...	80.5	....	374.6
172.4	.....	.....	....	....	.....	....	....	...	...	....	172.4
.....	.....	.....	....	63.7	.....	....	....	...	...	....	63.7
.....	723.7	.....	....	....	.....	....	....	...	...	....	723.7
169.5	.....	.....	....	....	.....	1.9	261.8	...	...	....	433.2
.....	146.5	.....	....	94.5	.....	.8	....	...	...	....	241.8
446.8	.....	.....	....	51.0	.....	66.7	....	...	...	....	564.5
232.9	.....	.....	....	....	.....	....	....	...	...	....	232.9
98.6	.....	.....	....	249.9	.....	....	....	...	...	....	348.5
619.4	.....	.....	....	....	.....	....	....	2.1	...	....	621.5

[*Continued on next page*]

Table 516—*Continued*

Detail by Steamers of Transshipments from

Steamer No.	Transshipping Steamer	Original and Transshipping Steamer by Number (Cf. Tables 513, 514)	Date of Arrival
			1922
451	Laura, IV	204, 208, 210	June 18
452	Christel Salling, III	212	July 4
453	Norwegian Cygnus	221	July 24
454	Wilhelm Russ, II	188	Aug. 30
455	Strassburg, VIII	247	Dec. 10
			1923
456	Tillie Russ, IV	248	Jan. 3
457	Erna	249, 250, 255	Jan. 10
458	Karlsruhe, VII	255	Jan. 14
459	Coblenz, IV	257	Feb. 3
460	Alesia, VI	256	Feb. 28
461	Uranus, III	262	Mar. 7
462	Minos, I	263, 265	Mar. 19
463	Uranus, IV	262	Apr. 2
464	Minos, II	270	Apr. 11
465	Uranus, V	270	Apr. 17
466	Victoria	270	Apr. 23
467	Andalusia, III	269, 272, 275	Apr. 25
468	Vulkan	276	Apr. 28
469	Najade	274, 279	May 2
470	Venus	276	May 8
471	Uranus, VI	276	May 11
472	Phaedra	276	May 19
	Total Hamburg to Riga		
			1922
473	Strassburg, II	102, 108	Jan. 17
474	Norderney, II	106, 108	Jan. 18
475	Tillie Russ, I	110, 112	Jan. 23
476	Phaleron, I	114	Jan. 29
477	Frankfurt, II	113, 114	Jan. 29
478	Coblenz, II	112, 114	Feb. 1
479	Tiber	119	Feb. 2
480	Strassburg, III	114	Feb. 6
481	Johannes C. Russ, I	120, 121	Mar. 1
482	Karlsruhe, I	125	Mar. 3
483	Aeolus, I	125	Mar. 3
484	Norderney, III	114, 122	Mar. 4
485	Tillie Russ, II	117	Mar. 4
486	Gotenhof	132, 136	Mar. 11
487	Marathon, II	145	Mar. 12
488	Borkum, I	139	Mar. 13
489	Christel Salling, I	127, 135, 139, 142	Mar. 14
490	Wilhelm Biesterfeld	131, 134	Mar. 15
491	Strassburg, IV	145	Mar. 16
492	Johannes C. Russ, II	138	Mar. 17
493	Karlsruhe, II	133, 145, 146	Mar. 19
494	Tillie Russ, III	139	Mar. 19
495	Laura, I	117, 122	Mar. 20
496	Bolama	139, 144, 147, 149	Mar. 27
497	Strassburg, V	150, 154	Apr. 4
498	Karlsruhe, III	145, 152	Apr. 7
499	Frankfurt, IV	154, 155, 157, 162	Apr. 19
500	Norderney, IV	153, 162, 163	Apr. 23
501	Laura, III	165, 168	Apr. 23
502	Borkum, II	161, 163, 168, 169	Apr. 25
503	Karlsruhe, IV	133	Apr. 25
	Total Hamburg to Windau		

American Relief Administration

Hamburg, Retransshipments from Danzig

Contents of Cargoes in Net Metric Tons of 1,000 Kilograms or 2,204.6 Pounds

Flour	Rice	Beans, Peas	Corn Grits	Pork Products	Milk	Cocoa	Sugar	Misc. Food	Clothing and Misc.	Soap	Total Tons
HAMBURG TO RIGA—*Continued*											
584.6	....	....	....	....	....	76.2	....	...	...	....	660.8
498.8	....	....	....	....	....	....	....	...	...	....	498.8
....	276.7	....	....	....	....	....	....	...	...	....	276.7
.7	....	....	....	....	....	....	....	...	...	....	.7
....	878.0	....	....	....	....	....	....	...	...	....	878.0
....	300.8	....	....	....	....	....	....	...	...	....	300.8
....	....	....	....	....	....	....	....	...	50.2	....	50.2
....	....	....	....	....	....	....	....	...	61.3	....	61.3
....	....	....	....	....	217.7	....	....	...	...	91.5	309.2
....	....	....	....	....	....	....	....	...	136.7	....	136.7
....	688.4	....	....	....	....	....	....	...	...	....	688.4
....	302.7	....	....	....	....	....	....	...	...	....	302.7
....	1.4	....	....	....	....	....	....	...	...	....	1.4
....	....	....	....	132.4	....	....	....	...	...	....	132.4
....	....	....	....	515.9	....	....	....	...	...	....	515.9
....	....	....	....	105.5	....	....	....	...	...	....	105.5
294.9	....	....	532.6	....	428.6	....	....	...	...	....	1,256.1
....	....	....	....	102.1	....	....	....	...	...	....	102.1
76.1	....	....	621.9	....	....	....	....	...	...	....	698.0
....	....	....	....	91.7	....	....	....	...	...	....	91.7
....	....	....	....	81.6	....	....	....	...	...	....	81.6
....	....	....	....	112.8	....	....	....	...	...	....	112.8
7,544.8	**4,626.3**	**424.1**	**1,577.9**	**2,365.0**	**2,553.2**	**441.1**	**1,138.3**	**6.0**	**373.5**	**148.8**	**21,199.0**
HAMBURG TO WINDAU											
....	....	151.6	....	....	....	69.9	....	...	61.1	....	282.6
....	....	....	....	91.3	130.2	....	....	...	.8	....	222.3
....	510.4	....	....	....	....	50.8	500.5	...	...	....	1,061.7
332.9	....	....	....	....	....	....	....	...	...	....	332.9
178.9	....	27.1	....	....	....	....	....	...	107.1	1.7	314.8
886.0	....	....	....	....	....	....	....	.8	...	....	886.8
....	....	....	....	....	....	....	....	...	...	126.1	126.1
809.3	....	....	....	....	....	....	....	...	...	....	809.3
....	....	....	....	....	....	....	....	...	20.3	....	20.3
716.5	....	....	....	....	....	....	....	...	.5	....	717.0
630.0	....	....	....	....	....	....	....	...	...	....	630.0
351.6	....	....	....	....	....	....	219.9	...	...	....	571.5
....	....	138.6	....	....	....	....	....	...	...	....	138.6
575.0	....	....	....	59.8	....	....	634.5	...	...	22.5	1,291.8
435.3	....	83.8	....	42.2	....	....	....	...	1.0	....	562.3
686.3	....	....	....	....	....	....	....	...	...	....	686.3
650.1	....	....	....	583.8	....	154.8	3.0	...	35.7	....	1,427.4
660.8	....	....	....	....	....	....	....	...	...	....	660.8
219.7	....	....	....	....	....	....	150.4	...	...	....	370.1
1,262.6	....	....	....	....	....	....	....	...	...	....	1,262.6
459.0	....	....	....	....	....	....	190.5	...	10.0	47.2	706.7
1,026.9	....	....	....	....	....	....	262.6	...	...	....	1,289.5
.1	....	177.6	....	....	....	....	249.0	...	18.3	.5	445.5
1,201.7	321.1	....	....	....	....	137.6	486.5	...	2.0	11.7	2,160.6
877.5	....	....	....	....	....	....	....	...	...	....	877.5
....	865.3	....	....	....	16.7	....	....	...	1.0	....	883.0
418.3	308.4	....	....	....	....	....	249.9	...	.1	81.6	1,058.3
808.6	....	....	....	....	....	....	....	...	7.3	28.3	844.2
201.2	....	....	....	444.3	....	....	154.9	...	...	....	800.4
....	307.5	....	....	70.1	....	127.5	352.5	...	...	71.4	929.0
939.7	....	....	....	....	....	....	....	...	...	....	939.7
14,328.0	**2,312.7**	**578.7**	....	**1,291.5**	**146.9**	**540.6**	**3,454.2**	**.8**	**265.2**	**391.0**	**23,309.6**

[*Concluded on next page*]

RUSSIA (SOVIET REPUBLICS)—

Table 516—*Concluded*

Detail by Steamers of Transshipments from

Steamer No.	Transshipping Steamer	Original and Transshipping Steamer by Number (Cf. Tables 513, 514)	Date of Arrival
			1921
504	Motor Sailer Annen	21, 35	Aug. 28
505	Bolores	19 : 311. 24 : 308. 39 : 302. 35, 38, 37	Sept. 3
506	Planet	19 : 311. 35, 37	Sept. 5
507	Ober Praesident Delbruck	18 : 307. 28 : 312. 30 : 313. 39 : 302. 35, 37, 38	Sept. 8
508	Windau	19 : 311. 24 : 308. 24 : 309. 37, 38	Sept. 16
509	Adrana	10 : 306. 27 : 310. 28 : 312. 30 : 313. 31 : 314. 32 : 314. 21, 37, 38	Sept. 17
510	Southerner	47 : 318. 43, 45	Oct. 1
511	Ulrikka	35, 38, 44, 48	Oct. 2
512	Georg Kimme	46 : 315. 46 : 316. 46 : 317. 17, 26, 43, 45, 48, 49, 58	Oct. 21
513	Panola	2, 4, 5, 7, 66, 82. 61 : 321. 65 : 303. 67 : 320. 70 : 323	Nov. 5
514	Jacob Schroeder	44, 48, 76, 95. 46 : 315. 69 : 322. 71 : 304	Nov. 14
515	Wotan	20, 48, 76, 77, 85. 70 : 324. 71 : 304. 72 : 325. 72 : 324. 75 : 326. 79 : 328	Nov. 22
516	Elzasier, I	88	Dec. 1
517	Gustave Fischer	87, 88, 94. 75 : 326. 75 : 327. 89 : 329. 90 : 330	Dec. 23
			1922
518	Greta, III	101 : 331. 87, 104	Jan. 8
519	Rimfakse	99 : 331. 45, 87, 104	Jan. 13
520	Bolsta	126 : 337	Apr. 28
	Total Danzig to Riga		
			1922
521	Rimfakse	99 : 331. 45, 87, 104	Jan. 18
522	Bolten	47 : 318. 55 : 319. 60 : 321. 90 : 330. 101 : 331. 119 : 333. 126 : 334. 115 : 332. 1, 26, 104, 118	Mar. 17
	Total Danzig to Windau		
	Grand Total		

Table 517

RUSSIA (SOVIET REPUBLICS)—

Detail by Steamers of Relief Supplies Purchased and Shipped by the U.S. Grain Corporation,

Arrival No.	Steamer	Port of Sailing	Date of Arrival	Port of Arrival	Contents of Cargoes: No. 2 Amber Durum Seed Wheat	Seed Corn	No. 2 Mixed Corn
			1922				
1	Mount Carroll, VI	New York	Jan. 3	Hamburg	......	......	......
2	Corson, III	New York	Jan. 13	Hamburg	......	......	......
3	Mount Clinton, III	New York	Jan. 17	Hamburg	......	......	......
4	Conejos	New York	Jan. 22	Reval	......	......	......
5	Oregonian, VII	New York	Jan. 24	Hamburg	......	......	......
6	Eastern Coast	New York	Jan. 26	Danzig	......	......	......
7	Mongolia, VI	New York	Jan. 29	Hamburg	......	......	......
8	Hickman	New York	Jan. 31	Hamburg	......	......	......
	Total for January				......	......	......
9	Winnebago	Baltimore	Feb. 6	Novorossisk	......	......	5,951.6
10	Honolulu	Baltimore	Feb. 10	Novorossisk	......	......	6,726.3
11	Northern Star	New York	Feb. 15	Novorossisk	......	......	5,876.2
12	Mount Carroll, VII	New York	Feb. 15	Hamburg	......	......	......
13	Stonewall, I	Baltimore	Feb. 21	Novorossisk	......	......	7,007.2
14	Georgian	New York	Feb. 21	Hamburg	......	......	......
15	American Star	Baltimore	Feb. 26	Theodosia	......	......	5,927.3
16	Effna	Baltimore	Feb. 26	Odessa	......	......	7,000.7
17	Eastern Ocean	Philadelphia	Feb. 26	Novorossisk	6,988.1	......	......
18	Deepwater	Baltimore	Feb. 26	Odessa	......	......	10,234.6
19	Clairton	Baltimore	Feb. 27	Novorossisk	......	......	8,262.8
20	Norlina	Baltimore	Feb. 27	Novorossisk	......	......	5,839.4
	Total for February				**6,988.1**	......	**62,826.1**

* All commodities purchased and shipped by the U.S. Grain Corporation, applying against the U.S. Government $20,000,000 appropriation, were sold f.o.b. U.S. ports. Freight, insurance, etc. (comprising c.i.f. charges), were charged separately against the same appropriation.

American Relief Administration

Hamburg, Retransshipments from Danzig

Contents of Cargoes in Net Metric Tons of 1,000 Kilograms or 2,204.6 Pounds

Flour	Rice	Beans, Peas	Corn Grits	Pork Products	Milk	Cocoa	Sugar	Misc. Food	Clothing and Misc.	Soap	Total Tons
DANZIG TO RIGA											
.....	408.0	.....	....	....	.....	....	192.0	...	...	....	600.0
601.4	.....	253.8	....	105.0	38.2	48.0	....	...	...	....	1,046.4
232.1	.....	.....	....	....	281.1	....	....	...	...	....	513.2
.....	776.2	.....	145.5	56.1	375.0	....	....	...	...	....	1,352.8
13.8	.....	275.4	106.6	....	5.5	63.0	....	...	...	....	464.3
.....	.....	229.2	....	9.0	736.1	....	27.6	...	...	....	1,001.9
.....	.....	.....	....	....	.....	....	620.9	...	16.0	....	636.9
691.3	265.5	.....	....	....	.....	....	....	...	...	....	956.8
350.0	.....	343.9	....	78.8	.....	....	315.7	...	4.0	....	1,092.4
1,989.5	.....	.....	....	52.2	21.5	....	....	...	34.3	....	2,097.5
2,139.5	.....	211.7	....	....	92.8	....	....	...	.0	....	2,444.0
1,075.4	250.3	.....	768.5	....	.....	....	712.1	...	29.9	....	2,836.2
.....	.....	51.0	....	....	744.5	27.3	....	...	...	....	822.8
966.3	315.2	5.1	437.7	....	454.6	71.0	....	...	...	....	2,249.9
426.5	.....	103.5	....	69.7	.....	....	....	...	33.8	....	633.5
.6	.....	.....	....	....	589.8	....	....	...	50.1	....	640.5
.....	.....	.....	....	....	.....	....	....	.7	28.1	....	28.8
8,486.4	**2,015.2**	**1,473.6**	**1,458.3**	**370.8**	**3,339.1**	**209.3**	**1,868.3**	**.7**	**196.2**	....	**19,417.9**
DANZIG TO WINDAU											
.....	.....	.....	....	....	173.9	....	....	...	54.7	....	228.6
26.5	100.2	368.3	....	95.3	330.2	44.5	....	...	201.6	....	1,166.6
26.5	**100.2**	**368.3**	....	**95.3**	**504.1**	**44.5**	....	...	**256.3**	....	**1,395.2**
41,258.7	**10,733.6**	**3,279.7**	**3,206.1**	**5,506.0**	**7,113.1**	**1,679.6**	**7,624.9**	**36.4**	**1,109.8**	**604.2**	**82,152.1**

American Relief Administration

Applying against the U.S. Government $20,000,000 Appropriation*—Reconstruction Period, 1919–1924

n Net Metric Tons of 1,000 Kilograms or 2,204.6 Pounds

Corn Grits	No. 2 Seed Rye	Milk		Misc.	Total Tons	F.O.B. Value	Freight	Insurance	Miscellaneous Charges	Total C.I.F. Value
		Evap.	Cond.							
427.8	......	496.9	106.4	.....	1,031.1	$ 132,324.57	$ 7,161.39	$ 5,437.80	$ 232.95	$ 145,156.71
.....	......	.....	89.9	.....	89.9	24,071.15	792.72	964.60	32.00	25,860.47
514.6	......	478.8	55.8	.....	1,049.2	117,358.79	6,886.58	2,964.50	198.28	127,408.15
993.5	......	258.4	38.1	.....	1,290.0	87,227.35	9,890.53	3,566.27	163.90	100,848.05
459.1	......	490.2	119.0	.....	1,068.3	134,390.58	7,294.25	3,160.82	192.42	145,038.07
.....	......	65.5	.....	.....	65.5	12,024.00	640.08	498.59	309.56	13,472.23
.....	......	118.2	57.1	.....	175.3	35,519.29	1,518.54	1,038.31	54.00	38,130.14
.....	......	359.5	87.8	.....	447.3	88,349.90	3,869.04	1,837.71	148.41	94,205.06
2,395.0	......	**2,267.5**	**554.1**	.....	**5,216.6**	**$ 631,265.63**	**$ 38,053.13**	**$ 19,468.60**	**$ 1,331.52**	**$ 690,118.88**
.....	......	.....	....	.....	5,951.6	$ 151,080.48	$ 44,610.69	$ 2,671.33	$ 6,946.85	$ 205,309.35
.....	......	.....	....	.....	6,726.3	168,111.39	60,150.87	3,138.21	9,027.45	240,427.92
.....	......	.....	....	.....	5,876.2	147,764.43	50,663.16	3,636.99	7,476.03	209,540.61
.....	......	130.6	89.6	.....	220.2	46,692.00	1,905.52	918.74	68.50	49,584.76
.....	......	.....	....	.....	7,007.2	173,064.99	58,702.40	3,108.49	3,265.00	238,140.88
.....	......	65.3	....	.....	65.3	11,700.00	567.00	261.69	21.00	12,549.69
.....	......	.....	....	.....	5,927.3	146,858.23	49,656.08	2,622.51	4,060.40	203,197.22
.....	......	.....	....	.....	7,000.7	175,350.50	58,647.68	3,160.28	4,950.48	242,108.94
.....	......	.....	....	.....	6,988.1	326,355.80	59,034.36	5,311.63	16,221.69	406,923.48
.....	......	.....	....	.....	10,234.6	252,989.37	88,452.82	4,977.75	9,625.78	356,045.72
.....	......	.....	....	.....	8,262.8	206,884.08	69,221.14	3,996.52	5,383.06	285,484.80
.....	......	.....	....	.....	5,839.4	143,339.04	48,918.92	2,826.40	7,112.40	202,196.76
.....	......	**195.9**	**89.6**	.....	**70,099.7**	**$ 1,950,190.31**	**$ 590,530.64**	**$ 36,630.54**	**$ 74,158.64**	**$ 2,651,510.13**

[*Continued on next page*]

Table 517—*Continued* Detail by Steamers of Relief Supplies Purchased and Shipped by the U.S.

Arrival No.	Steamer	Port of Sailing	Date of Arrival	Port of Arrival	Contents of Cargoes		
					No. 2 Amber Durum Seed Wheat	Seed Corn	No. 2 Mixed Corn
			1922				
21	West Neris	Baltimore	Mar. 1	Libau	......	......	6,126.7
22	Ward	New Orleans	Mar. 1	Odessa	......	......	7,696.7
23	West Chatala	Baltimore	Mar. 1	Danzig	......	......	6,361.6
24	Absaroka	Baltimore	Mar. 2	Libau	......	......	6,551.9
25	Western Maid	Baltimore	Mar. 3	Reval	......	......	6,328.9
26	John Stevens	New Orleans	Mar. 3	Reval	......	......	6,274.2
27	Argus	Philadelphia	Mar. 3	Reval	7,266.0	......	......
28	Aquarius	Philadelphia	Mar. 4	Reval	7,362.7	......	......
29	Brave Coeur	New Orleans	Mar. 5	Novorossisk	......	......	7,071.8
30	Carolinian	Baltimore	Mar. 5	Theodosia	......	......	6,096.4
31	Eastern Exporter	New Orleans	Mar. 5	Novorossisk	......	......	7,406.4
32	Mount Clinton, IV	New York	Mar. 7	Hamburg	......	......	......
33	Belvidere	New Orleans	Mar. 9	Theodosia	......	......	5,022.2
34	Eastern Cross	New York	Mar. 10	Reval	......	......	2,237.2
35	Eastern Glade	New York	Mar. 11	Novorossisk	4,445.2	......	2,150.8
36	Narcissus	Baltimore	Mar. 12	Libau	......	......	4,572.3
37	Muskegon	New Orleans	Mar. 14	Theodosia	......	......	4,647.6
38	Duquesne	Baltimore	Mar. 15	Odessa	......	......	6,925.7
39	West Munham	Newport News	Mar. 15	Hamburg	......	......	7,379.1
40	Western Glen	New Orleans	Mar. 16	Odessa	......	......	6,655.2
41	Oregonian, VIII	New York	Mar. 23	Hamburg	......	......	......
42	Eastern Crown	Philadelphia	Mar. 27	Reval	5,149.8	......	......
43	Clontarf	New York	Mar. 27	Odessa	......	......	......
44	West Bridge	Baltimore	Mar. 30	Reval	......	......	3,567.0
45	Natirar	New York	Mar. 31	Libau	......	......	......
46	Eastern Admiral	Philadelphia	Mar. 31	Novorossisk	......	......	......
	Total for March	....	....	....	**24,223.7**	......	**103,071.7**
47	Eastern Star	New York	Apr. 1	Libau	......	......	......
48	Bellingham	New Orleans	Apr. 2	Theodosia	......	......	5,538.4
49	Rockaway Park	New York	Apr. 5	Libau	......	......	......
50	Eastern Breeze	New York	Apr. 7	Libau	......	......	1,928.5
51	Manitowoc	New Orleans	Apr. 11	Novorossisk	......	......	6,670.4
52	Jacona	New York	Apr. 11	Odessa	......	......	......
53	New Britain	Baltimore	Apr. 11	Theodosia	......	3,216.3	......
54	Santa Oliva	Baltimore	Apr. 12	Reval	......	......	......
55	Aledo	Baltimore	Apr. 12	Reval	5,726.8	......	......
56	Orient	Baltimore	Apr. 16	Novorossisk	......	5,638.0	......
57	Saugus	New York	Apr. 22	Odessa	......	......	......
58	Santa Clara	Baltimore	Apr. 24	Reval	......	......	7,410.1
59	Chebaulip	New York	Apr. 25, May 1	Libau, Reval	......	......	......
60	Santa Malta	Baltimore	Apr. 26	Reval	......	......	2,612.7
61	J. R. Gordon	Baltimore	Apr. 27	Novorossisk	......	6,901.9	......
62	Glen White	Baltimore	Apr. 27	Novorossisk	......	1,434.2	......
63	Northern Star, II	Baltimore	Apr. 27	Reval	......	......	6,123.3
	Total for April	....	....	....	**5,726.8**	**17,190.4**	**30,283.4**
64	Redondo	New York	May 5	Riga	......	......	......
65	Sunewco	New York	May 13	Novorossisk	......	1,219.6	......
66	Bremerton	New York	May 14	Riga	......	......	......
67	Suboatco	New York	May 16	Petrograd	......	......	......
68	Surico	Boston	May 16	Petrograd	......	......	......
69	American Star, II	Baltimore	May 18	Petrograd	......	......	6,105.8
70	Ausable	Baltimore	May 18	Petrograd	......	......	4,666.6
71	Sunelsco	New York	May 19	Petrograd	......	......	......
72	Winding Gulf	Baltimore	May 20	Odessa	......	......	......
73	Honolulu, II	Baltimore	May 21	Petrograd	......	......	......
74	Mount Clinton, III	New York	May 23	Riga	......	......	......
75	Casey	New Orleans	May 25	Odessa	......	......	......
76	Surichco	New York	May 26, June 2	Reval, Riga	......	......	......
77	Norlina, II	Baltimore	May 27	Odessa	......	......	......
	Total for May	....	....	....	......	**1,219.6**	**10,772.4**

American Relief Administration

Grain Corporation, Applying against the U.S. Government $20,000,000 Appropriation

in Net Metric Tons of 1,000 Kilograms or 2,204.6 Pounds										
Corn Grits	No. 2 Seed Rye	Milk		Misc.	Total Tons	F.O.B. Value	Freight	Insurance	Miscellaneous Charges	Total C.I.F. Value
		Evap.	Cond.							
.....	......	.....	....	.....	6,126.7	$ 153,660.68	$ 47,274.15	$ 2,704.56	$ 3,557.50	$ 207,196.89
.....	......	.....	....	.....	7,696.7	187,860.00	72,967.21	3,800.48	7,741.44	272,369.13
.....	......	.....	....	.....	6,361.6	155,844.22	49,086.83	2,978.69	4,703.12	212,612.86
.....	......	.....	....	.....	6,551.9	163,465.74	50,555.09	3,120.54	5,574.50	222,715.87
.....	......	.....	....	.....	6,328.9	156,339.10	48,834.38	3,562.96	3,140.13	211,876.57
.....	......	.....	....	.....	6,274.2	151,565.00	55,703.64	3,641.63	6,449.02	217,359.29
.....	......	.....	....	.....	7,266.0	339,334.82	56,512.97	7,929.93	16,548.32	420,326.04
.....	......	.....	....	.....	7,362.7	343,851.89	57,297.35	8,041.89	17,315.45	426,506.58
.....	......	.....	....	.....	7,071.8	166,342.63	67,500.12	3,410.11	7,352.63	244,605.49
.....	......	.....	....	.....	6,096.4	149,950.00	51,072.00	2,892.35	2,669.26	206,583.61
.....	......	.....	....	.....	7,406.4	175,462.50	70,210.40	3,485.10	262.63	249,420.63
.....	......	87.1	....	.....	87.1	15,800.00	756.00	316.08	20.00	16,892.08
.....	......	.....	....	.....	5,022.2	121,550.42	47,609.60	2,406.21	662.59	172,228.82
895.9	......	.....	....	.....	3,133.1	82,920.34	17,564.77	1,905.94	74.31	102,465.36
.....	......	.....	....	.....	6,596.0	261,682.41	55,524.94	5,186.30	17,226.69	339,620.34
3,375.1	......	.....	....	.....	7,947.4	209,874.99	61,572.72	3,931.95	4,757.05	280,136.71
.....	......	.....	....	.....	4,647.6	110,115.75	40,617.78	2,208.90	5,270.00	158,212.43
505.7	......	.....	....	.....	7,431.4	187,047.36	62,835.43	3,697.52	7,635.69	261,216.00
.....	......	.....	....	.....	7,379.1	180,110.00	56,938.00	4,146.46	5,626.88	246,821.34
.....	......	.....	....	.....	6,655.2	155,562.50	63,632.65	3,210.75	8,013.39	230,419.29
.....	......	21.8	....	.....	21.8	3,950.00	189.00	73.82	......	4,212.82
1,492.4	......	.....	....	.....	6,642.2	285,481.18	51,592.78	6,658.84	15,788.66	359,521.46
.....	......	87.1	....	.....	87.1	14,970.00	1,717.64	348.27	11.60	17,047.51
1,867.8	......	.....	....	.....	5,434.8	144,345.15	42,146.18	3,258.83	4,119.83	193,869.99
.....	......	2,393.1	....	.....	2,393.1	410,810.21	28,077.58	7,983.46	483.82	447,355.07
334.5	......	.....	....	.....	334.5	10,085.81	2,802.64	170.71	14.80	13,073.96
8,471.4	......	**2,589.1**	....	.....	**138,355.9**	**$ 4,337,982.70**	**$1,160,591.85**	**$ 91,072.28**	**$145,019.31**	**$ 5,734,666.14**
.....	......	800.8	....	.....	800.8	$ 137,094.73	$ 9,241.69	$ 2,662.55	$ 204.00	$ 149,202.97
304.6	......	.....	....	.....	5,843.0	138,172.24	56,161.37	2,861.28	8,010.63	205,205.52
.....	......	2,571.2	....	.....	2,571.2	439,727.18	29,857.74	8,546.74	498.83	478,630.49
.....	......	.....	....	.....	1,928.5	48,494.54	10,203.78	843.82	248.86	59,791.00
.....	......	.....	....	.....	6,670.4	172,583.93	57,759.59	3,389.02	8,591.39	242,323.93
.....	......	457.2	....	.....	457.2	74,896.00	8,948.08	1,749.84	99.27	85,693.19
.....	......	.....	....	.....	3,216.3	121,722.79	27,653.52	1,969.50	258.16	151,603.97
6,738.1	......	.....	....	.....	6,738.1	210,679.40	50,506.42	3,454.39	1,028.11	265,668.32
.....	......	.....	....	.....	5,726.8	267,452.80	44,188.27	6,233.13	12,350.52	330,224.72
.....	......	.....	....	.....	5,638.0	218,746.38	47,240.75	3,517.67	162.58	269,667.38
.....	......	65.3	....	.....	65.3	10,440.00	1,268.97	244.33	24.00	11,977.30
.....	......	.....	....	.....	7,410.1	212,144.34	55,543.66	3,648.48	8,173.67	279,510.15
.....	1,625.6	1,086.6	....	.....	2,712.2	256,436.92	24,274.09	4,715.38	3,500.34	288,926.73
.....	4,697.6	.....	....	.....	7,310.3	293,514.02	54,907.79	4,790.96	13,822.18	367,034.95
.....	......	.....	....	.....	6,901.9	283,502.73	57,833.94	4,047.20	303.87	345,687.74
5,016.6	......	.....	....	.....	6,450.8	232,599.81	54,042.39	3,408.65	911.82	290,962.67
.....	......	.....	....	.....	6,123.3	175,154.37	43,197.76	2,720.86	10,230.30	231,303.29
12,059.3	**6,323.2**	**4,981.1**	....	.....	**76,564.2**	**$ 3,293,362.18**	**$ 632,829.81**	**$ 58,803.80**	**$ 68,418.53**	**$ 4,053,414.32**
.....	......	1,951.3	....	.....	1,951.3	$ 313,972.24	$ 22,661.71	$ 5,223.49	$ 151.20	$ 342,008.64
.....	......	.....	....	.....	1,219.6	54,734.55	12,603.35	800.55	140.75	68,279.20
.....	......	654.5	....	.....	654.5	104,022.87	7,572.93	1,737.54	113.50	113,446.84
38.0	2,252.1	989.2	....	.....	3,279.3	263,363.17	27,238.41	4,294.15	6,082.43	300,978.16
784.7	......	1,101.4	....	.....	1,886.1	203,249.48	17,167.85	3,274.38	622.07	224,313.78
.....	......	.....	....	.....	6,105.8	174,870.11	43,074.53	3,013.46	9,743.69	230,701.79
.....	......	.....	....	.....	4,666.6	133,652.16	34,149.19	2,283.69	8,018.68	178,103.72
114.3	......	506.0	....	.....	620.3	85,202.78	5,973.85	1,396.92	130.25	92,703.80
6,177.2	535.1	.....	....	.....	6,712.3	251,405.26	51,792.89	3,621.06	2,202.11	309,021.32
2,027.2	5,080.3	.....	....	.....	7,107.5	308,842.15	53,468.97	4,929.06	10,801.45	378,041.63
.....	......	196.0	....	.....	196.0	31,387.50	1,897.50	560.94	57.00	33,902.94
2,843.1	......	.....	....	.....	2,843.1	100,886.70	27,992.60	1,532.18	244.23	130,655.71
.....	......	254.9	....	.....	254.9	40,438.32	2,601.83	725.59	55.00	43,820.74
6,277.7	......	.....	....	.....	6,277.7	236,686.95	48,439.04	3,389.72	803.32	289,319.03
18,262.2	**7,867.5**	**5,653.3**	....	.....	**43,775.0**	**$ 2,302,714.24**	**$ 356,634.65**	**$ 36,782.73**	**$ 39,165.68**	**$ 2,735,297.30**

[*Concluded on next page*]

Table 517—*Concluded* Detail by Steamers of Relief Supplies Purchased and Shipped by the U.S.

Arrival No.	Steamer	Port of Sailing	Date of Arrival	Port of Arrival	Contents of Cargoes: No. 2 Amber Durum Seed Wheat	Seed Corn	No. 2 Mixed Corn
			1922				
78	Westport	Philadelphia	June 3	Petrograd	......	......	......
79	Stonewall, II	Baltimore	June 4	Theodosia	......	......	......
80	Sutorpsco	New York	June 6	Novorossisk	......	......	......
81	Deepwater, II	Baltimore	June 6	Batoum	......	......	......
82	Suholco	New York	June 9	Novorossisk	......	......	......
83	Noccalula	New Orleans	June 9	Hamburg	......	......	......
84	Eastern Coast, II	Philadelphia	June 10	Petrograd	......	......	......
85	Carolinian, II	Baltimore	June 14	Petrograd	......	......	......
86	Eastport	New York	June 16	Riga	......	......	......
87	Belvidere, II	New York	June 24	Riga	......	......	......
	Total for June	....	....	....	......	......	......
88	Winnebago, II	Baltimore	July 6	Petrograd	......	......	......
89	Allaguash	New York	July 25	Petrograd	......	......	......
	Total for July	....	....	....	......	......	......
90	Muskegon, II	Philadelphia	Aug. 3	Petrograd	......	......	......
91	Chebaulpis II	Philadelphia	Aug. 8	Petrograd	......	......	......
	Total for August	....	....	....	......	......	......
92	Norlina, III	New York	Sept. 11	Petrograd	......	......	......
93	Eastport, II	New York	Sept. 21	Petrograd	......	......	......
94	Eastern Coast, III	New York	Sept. 26	Petrograd	......	......	......
	Ex-Above Steamers	....	....	....	......	......	......
	Total for September	....	....	....	......	......	......
	Grand Total	....	....	....	**36,938.6**	**18,410.0**	**206,953.6**

† Bags, 3,725,316; lumber, 483,566 board feet; twine, 10,787¼ pounds; nails, 33 kegs; needles, 1,452; slings and tarpaulins, 30. Estimated 1,100.0 net metric tons.

RUSSIA (SOVIET REPUBLICS)—American Relief Administration

Detail by Steamers of Transshipments of Relief Supplies Shipped by U.S.G.C.—Reconstruction Period, 1919–1924

Table 518*

Transshipping Steamer	Original Steamer	Port of Sailing	Date of Arrival	Port of Arrival	Commodities in Net Metric Tons of 1,000 Kilograms or 2,204.6 Pounds: No. 2 Mixed Corn	Corn Grits	Milk: Evap.	Milk: Cond.	Total Tons
			1922						
Strassburg, II	Mount Carroll, VI	Hamburg	Jan. 17	Windau	......	425.0	....	....	425.
Norderney, II	Mount Carroll, VI	Hamburg	Jan. 18	Windau	......	.....	359.0	105.5	464.
Tillie Russ, I	Corson, III	Hamburg	Jan. 23	Windau	......	.....	....	59.5	59.
Frankfurt, II	Mount Clinton, III	Hamburg	Jan. 29	Windau	......	31.8	477.9	55.2	564.
Total for January	....	....	....	....	......	**456.8**	**836.9**	**220.2**	**1,513.**
Coblenz, II	Corson, III	Hamburg	Feb. 1	Windau	......	.....	....	30.1	30.
Marathon, I	Mount Carroll, VI; Mount Clinton, III	Hamburg	Feb. 3	Windau	......	477.4	135.6	....	613
Total for February	....	....	....	....	......	**477.4**	**135.6**	**30.1**	**643**
Johannus C. Russ, I	Mongolia, VI; Hickman	Hamburg	Mar. 1	Windau	......	.....	475.6	143.1	618
Tillie Russ, II	Oregonian, VII	Hamburg	Mar. 4	Windau	......	301.9	426.2	114.9	843.
Gotenhof	Mount Carroll, VII; Georgian	Hamburg	Mar. 11	Windau	......	.....	193.5	87.5	281
Bolten	Eastern Coast	Danzig	Mar. 17	Windau	......	.....	65.3	....	65

* Cf. Table 517.

American Relief Administration

Grain Corporation, Applying against the U.S. Government $20,000,000 Appropriation

Corn Grits	No. 2 Seed Rye	Milk Evap.	Milk Cond.	Misc.	Total Tons	F.O.B. Value	Freight	Insurance	Miscellaneous Charges	Total C.I.F. Value
in Net Metric Tons of 1,000 Kilograms or 2,204.6 Pounds										
2,547.7	......	.....	....	.....	2,547.7	$ 91,776.25	$ 19,770.75	$ 1,461.71	$ 778.36	$ 113,787.07
7,078.3	......	.....	....	.....	7,078.3	266,977.22	54,616.49	4,253.35	846.38	326,693.44
.....	......	364.6	....	.....	364.6	57,318.55	5,025.45	1,039.74	76.00	63,459.74
6,103.9	4,927.9	.....	....	.....	11,031.8	437,420.38	94,850.82	6,461.29	12,917.75	551,650.24
.....	......	717.1	....	.....	717.1	111,934.65	10,009.96	1,957.28	132.00	124,033.89
708.7	......	.....	....	.....	708.7	26,478.87	5,156.26	371.27	55.82	32,062.22
3,385.3	......	.....	....	.....	3,385.3	129,021.52	26,270.60	2,020.98	323.16	157,636.26
6,066.5	......	.....	....	.....	6,066.5	232,552.76	40,122.60	3,561.83	720.21	276,957.40
836.8	......	.....	....	.....	836.8	32,359.82	5,168.08	394.75	171.18	38,093.83
629.6	......	.....	....	.....	629.6	24,555.66	3,886.37	297.62	12.69	28,752.34
27,356.8	**4,927.9**	**1,081.7**	....	.....	**33,366.4**	**$ 1,410,395.68**	**$ 264,877.38**	**$ 21,819.82**	**$ 16,033.55**	**$ 1,713,126.43**
5,839.4	......	.....	....	.....	5,839.4	$ 221,895.20	$ 41,195.73	$ 3,436.63	$ 1,516.76	$ 268,044.32
.....	......	1,088.7	....	.....	1,088.7	175,003.50	11,250.27	3,986.00	245.00	190,484.77
5,839.4	......	**1,088.7**	....	.....	**6,928.1**	**$ 396,898.70**	**$ 52,446.00**	**$ 7,422.63**	**$ 1,761.76**	**$ 458,529.09**
4,474.2	......	.....	....	.....	4,474.2	$ 167,629.22	$ 37,482.10	$ 2,411.88	$ 1,153.13	$ 208,676.33
28.6	......	.....	....	.....	28.6	1,108.22	176.31	16.78	10.19	1,311.50
4,502.8	......	.....	....	.....	**4,502.8**	**$ 168,737.44**	**$ 37,658.41**	**$ 2,428.66**	**$ 1,163.32**	**$ 209,987.83**
.....	......	1,001.5	....	.....	1,001.5	$ 165,132.82	$ 9,572.88	$ 3,645.23	$ 194.00	$ 178,544.93
2,831.0	......	.....	....	.....	2,831.0	104,358.17	17,475.49	1,592.97	361.68	123,788.31
2,242.5	......	87.1	....	.....	2,329.6	95,556.96	14,675.34	1,573.10	391.24	113,196.64
.....	......	.....	....	1,100.0†	1,100.0	......	......	......	.....	....
5,073.5	......	**1,088.6**	....	**1,100.0**	**7,262.1**	**$ 366,047.95**	**$ 41,723.71**	**$ 6,811.30**	**$ 946.92**	**$ 415,529.88**
83,960.4	**19,118.6**	**18,945.9**	**643.7**	**1,100.0**	**386,070.8**	**$14,857,594.83**	**$3,175,345.58**	**$281,240.36**	**$347,999.23**	**$18,662,180.00**

RUSSIA (SOVIET REPUBLICS)

Detail by Steamers of Transshipments of Relief Supplies Shipped by U.S.G.C.

Table 518—*Continued*

Transshipping Steamer	Original Steamer	Port of Sailing	Date of Arrival	Port of Arrival	No. 2 Mixed Corn	Corn Grits	Milk Evap.	Milk Cond.	Total Tons
					Commodities in Net Metric Tons of 1,000 Kilograms or 2,204.6 Pounds				
			1922						
arlsruhe, II	Mount Clinton, IV...	Hamburg	Mar. 19	Windau	......	.....	86.0	....	86.0
aura, I	Oregonian, VII	Hamburg	Mar. 20	Windau	......	153.1	62.2	2.9	218.2
ail	West Chatala	Danzig	Mar. 20	Stolpce	6,361.6	.....	....	....	6,361.6
Total for March.....	....	....	....	....	**6,361.6**	**455.0**	**1,308.8**	**348.4**	**8,473.8**
ea Lighter Elbe......	West Munham	Hamburg	Apr. 12	Libau	1,015.0	.....	....	....	1,015.0
ea Lighter Fulda.....	West Munham	Hamburg	Apr. 12	Libau	1,015.1	.....	....	....	1,015.1
ea Lighter Oder......	West Munham	Hamburg	Apr. 26	Libau	1,020.0	.....	....	....	1,020.0
rda	Oregonian, VIII	Hamburg	Apr. 14	Danzig	......	.....	21.4†	....	21.4
ea Lighter Lahn.....	West Munham	Hamburg	Apr. 26	Libau	1,135.0	.....	....	....	1,135.0
ea Lighter Clara.....	West Munham	Hamburg	Apr. 26	Libau	154.1	.....	....	....	154.1
Total for April......	....	....	....	....	**4,339.2**	.....	**21.4**	....	**4,360.6**
ansa	West Munham	Hamburg	May 11	Libau	**67.1**	.....	....	....	**67.1**
aura, IV	Noccalula	Hamburg	June 18	Riga	......	**250.0**	....	....	**250.0**
annheim, VI	Noccalula	Hamburg	July 5	Riga	......	**459.4**	....	....	**459.4**
Total Transshipments	....	....	....	....	**10,767.9**	**2,098.6**	**2,302.7**	**598.7**	**15,767.9**

† Retransshipments from Danzig to Stolpce via rail, April 22.

Table 519

Detail by Steamers of Direct Arrivals of Relief Supplies Paid for by

Steamer or Source	Port of Sailing	Date of Arrival	Port of Arrival	Contents of Cargoes in Wheat (Seed)	Corn (Seed)	Rye (Seed)
		1922				
Castellano	Philadelphia	Mar. 1	Reval	6,896.7	.....	.....
Lloyd	Boston	Mar. 7	Novorossisk	4,021.7	.....	.....
Gasconier, II	New York, Hamburg	Mar. 10	Reval	5,606.0	.....	.....
Eastern Glade	New York	Mar. 11	Novorossisk	225.9	.....	.....
Tenafly	Boston	Mar. 14	Reval	5,528.3	.....	.....
Braddock	Boston	Mar. 16	Theodosia	7,702.1	.....	.....
Eastern City	Philadelphia	Mar. 25	Reval	8,024.0	.....	.....
Haugarland	New York	Mar. 26	Reval	9,783.0	.....	.....
Meanticut	Boston	Mar. 26	Reval	7,664.8	.....	.....
Narbo	Philadelphia	Mar. 26	Novorossisk	7,197.9	.....	.....
Hinckley	Boston	Mar. 28	Reval	5,612.2	.....	.....
Westmead	Portland	Mar. 30	Reval	6,531.8	.....	.....
Westbridge	Baltimore	Mar. 30	Reval	1,424.6	.....	.....
Eastern Admiral	Philadelphia	Mar. 31	Novorossisk	8,369.0	.....	.....
Hampstead Heath	New York	Apr. 3	Novorossisk	7,999.9	.....	.....
New Britain	Baltimore	Apr. 11	Theodosia	2,371.6	.....	.....
Exmouth	New York	Apr. 12	Reval	6,123.1	.....	.....
Santa Olivia	Baltimore	Apr. 12	Reval	.....	.....	.....
Santa Clara	Baltimore	Apr. 24	Reval	.....	.....	.....
Glen White	Baltimore	Apr. 27	Novorossisk	.....	.....	.....
Sunewco	New York	Apr. 29	Odessa	.....	.....	.....
Suricho	New York	Apr. 29	Reval	.....	1.1	.....
Surico	Boston	May 16	Petrograd	238.4	.....	.....
Sunelsco	New York	May 19	Petrograd	.....	3.0	.....
Vikfred	Oxelösund	Apr. 7	Windau	.....	.....	.....
Cimbria	Oxelösund	Apr. 15	Windau	.....	.....	.....
Local Purchase, Esthonia	Reval	Jan. 25–May 13	Reval	.....	.....	.....
Winnecone	Baltimore	July 25	Petrograd	.....	.....	3,810.2
Total ‡				**101,321.0**	**4.1**	**3,810.2**

* The gold was turned over to the U.S. Grain Corporation by the R.S.F.S.R. and U.S.R.

‡ These same quantities are carried as deliveries, but internal deliveries are not segregated to districts.

† In addition to these direct arrivals, 57,823.0 metric tons, valu[e] $4,322,450.83, from arrivals quoted in Tables 165 and 513, were turne[d] over to the Soviet Republics. The total arrivals paid from Soviet gol[d] account was 169,688.9 metric tons, value $11,357,325.13.

RUSSIA (SOVIET REPUBLICS)—American Relief Administration

Detail by Date of Delivery of Supplies Donated by Soviet Government for Children's Relief—Reconstruction Period, 1919–1924

Table 520

Date of Delivery	Commodities in Net Metric Tons of 1,000 Kilograms or 2,204.6 Pounds: Flour	Miscellaneous Food	Miscellaneous	Total Tons	Total Value
1922					
June 30	....	123.0	....	123.0	$ 5,577.6
September 7	64.0	.....	26.0*	90.0	11,688.7
October 25	....	134.0	....	134.0	4,976.9
1923					
May 31	....	180.0	....	180.0	6,733.8
July 11	....	21.0	....	21.0	848.9
September 18	....	4.0	....	4.0	150.0
September 27	....	2.0	....	2.0	50.4
Total	**64.0**	**464.0†**	**26.0**	**554.0**	**$30,026.6**

* 65,000 empty fourteen-ounce bags.

† Salt.

American Relief Administration

Gold Supplied by Soviet Republics*—Reconstruction Period, 1919–1924

Net Metric Tons of 1,000 Kilograms or 2,204.6 Pounds									
Oats (Forage)	Grass (Seed)	Beans, Peas	Total Tons	F.O.B. Value	Freight	Insurance	Miscellaneous Charges	Total C.I.F. Value
.....	.....	.....	6,896.7	$ 342,885.12	$ 45,613.14	$ 7,993.09	$ 18,560.04	$ 415,051.39
.....	.....	.....	4,021.7	194,642.32	27,616.51	3,681.92	8,078.70	234,019.45
.....	.....	.....	5,606.0	271,320.31	34,545.91	6,118.28	12,013.55	323,998.05
.....	.....	.....	225.9	10,932.78	1,901.33	216.12	764.38	13,814.61
.....	.....	.....	5,528.3	269,401.45	42,656.64	6,123.00	11,938.11	330,119.20
.....	.....	.....	7,702.1	382,928.49	64,837.50	7,401.92	18,570.81	473,738.72
.....	.....	.....	8,024.0	388,347.33	54,143.45	8,951.58	22,393.42	473,835.78
.....	.....	.....	9,783.0	484,246.69	66,495.94	11,008.66	20,765.97	582,517.26
.....	.....	.....	7,664.8	381,072.67	59,141.99	8,681.70	17,338.52	466,234.88
.....	.....	.....	7,197.9	348,364.91	60,815.91	6,738.21	19,315.95	435,234.98
.....	.....	.....	5,612.2	279,024.00	43,304.17	6,451.09	13,670.75	342,450.01
.....	.....	.....	6,531.8	316,129.00	50,400.00	7,450.92	23,656.05	397,635.97
.....	.....	.....	1,424.6	69,607.93	11,060.13	1,613.61	3,262.15	85,543.82
.....	.....	.....	8,369.0	405,045.53	70,680.59	7,949.51	23,647.73	507,323.36
.....	.....	.....	7,999.9	393,549.89	62,003.06	7,416.12	14,665.85	477,634.92
.....	.....	.....	2,371.6	114,779.84	20,044.20	1,993.00	6,225.48	143,042.52
.....	.....	.....	6,123.1	300,733.59	40,681.47	6,080.43	11,450.36	358,945.85
.....	.....	725.2	725.2	113,508.76	5,435.97	1,556.57	212.66	120,713.96
.....	.....	87.0	87.0	13,622.05	652.32	186.47	63.12	14,523.96
.....	.....	203.0	203.0	31,782.06	1,701.01	393.63	129.15	34,005.85
.....	9.1	.....	9.1	970.00	94.69	12.51	8.67	1,085.87
.....	132.9	3,187.2	3,321.2	459,296.11	21,987.27	6,357.48	813.11	488,453.97
.....	.....	27.2	265.6	15,445.27	2,359.09	234.37	881.10	18,919.83
.....	.....	.....	3.0	360.00	66.50	3.24	444.17	873.91
393.2	.....	.....	393.2 }					
458.2	.....	.....	458.2 }	100,268.46	......	......	......	100,268.46
1,507.6	.....	.....	1,507.6 }					
.....	.....	.....	3,810.2	165,000.00	26,880.00	3,007.72	......	194,887.72
2,359.0	**142.0**	**4,229.6**	**111,865.9†**	**$5,853,264.56**	**$815,118.79**	**$117,621.15**	**$248,869.80**	**$7,034,874.30†**

Table 521

Detail by Steamers or Source of Arrivals of Surplus Medical and Hospital

Steamer or Source	Transshipping Steamer	Port of Sailing	Date of Arrival	Port of Arrival
			1922	
Mount Carroll, VIII	Frankfurt, IV	New York	Mar. 26	Hamburg
Hawaiian, VI	Frankfurt, V	New York	Apr. 5	Hamburg
Georgian, II	Ina Lotte Blumenthal	New York	Apr. 20	Hamburg
Surico	....	New York	May 16	Petrograd
Suboatco	....	New York	May 16	Petrograd
Sunelsco	....	New York	May 19	Petrograd
Surichco	....	New York	May 26	Riga
Eastport, II	....	New York	June 16	Riga
Belvidere, II	....	New York	June 24	Riga
Winnebago, III	....	New York	Dec. 25	Riga
Total from New York	....	....	....	....
Total from Coblenz Stock	Andalusia, I; Karlsruhe, VI; Bianca	Coblenz	....	Hamburg
Delivered Near East Relief in New York for Distribution in Southern Russia	....	....	....	....
Warehousing, Inland Freight, etc.	....	....	....	....
Grand Total *	....	....	....	....

* For detail of internal deliveries in Russia by A.R.A., see pages 946 to 976; and detail of deliveries to N.E.R., see pages 977 to 986.

† Freight, insurance, handling charges, and miscellaneous expenses paid from funds contributed especially for that purpose.

RUSSIA (SOVIET REPUBLICS)—American Relief Administration

Detail by Steamers of Transshipments of Surplus Medical and Hospital Supplies, Donated by the U.S. Government

Reconstruction Period, 1919–1924

Table 522

Transshipping Steamer	Original Steamer	Port of Sailing	Date of Arrival	Port of Arrival	Number of Packages	Total Metric Tons
			1922			
Frankfurt, IV	Mount Carroll, VIII	Hamburg	Apr. 19	Windau	436	17.
Frankfurt, V	Hawaiian, VI	Hamburg	May 7	Riga	7,356	485.
Ina Lotte Blumenthal	Georgian, II	Hamburg	May 20	Petrograd	12,823	583.
Andalusia, I	Coblenz Stock	Hamburg	June 27	Petrograd	363	24.
Karlsruhe, VI	Coblenz Stock	Hamburg	Aug. 4	Petrograd	7,771	304.
Bianca	Coblenz Stock	Hamburg	Aug. 15	Petrograd	338	18.
Total	....	....	....	....	**29,087**	**1,432.**

American Relief Administration

Supplies, Donated by the U.S. Government—Reconstruction Period, 1919–1924

Number of Packages	Total Metric Tons	U.S. Government F.O.B. Value	Freight	Insurance	Miscellaneous Expenses	Total Expenses	Total C.I.F. Value
436	17.0	....					
7,356	485.0	....					
12,823	583.0	....					
5,478	266.0	....	$66,110.89	$38,043.46	....	$104,154.35	....
3,837	176.0	....					
8,169	319.0	....					
5,931	233.0	....					
3,601	182.0	....	4,321.20	2,884.79	....	7,205.99	....
8,959	460.0	....	11,993.71	8,365.97	....	20,359.68	....
482	39.0	....	1,006.95	1,702.66	....	2,709.61	....
57,072	**2,760.0**	**$3,442,862.87**	....	....	....	....	....
8,475	347.6	347,405.50	....	....	....	....	....
....	.....	209,731.63	....	....	....	....	....
....	.....	....	....	....	$132,963.25	132,963.25	....
65,547	**3,107.6**	**$4,000,000.00**	**$83,432.75**	**$50,996.88**	**$132,963.25**	**$267,392.88†**	**$4,267,392.88**

Table 523 Detail by Steamers of Arrivals of Medical and Hospital Supplies,

Arrival No.	Steamer or Source	Transshipping Steamer	Port of Sailing	Date of Arrival
				1921
1	Oregonian, VI	Mannheim, I	New York	Oct. 19
2	Elzasier, I		New York	Dec. 1
3	Natirar, I		New York	Dec. 5
4	Mount Clay, V	Strassburg, II; Martha Russ	New York	Dec. 19
5	Westbrook, IV	Martha Russ	New York	Dec. 22
6	Eastport, I		New York	Dec. 24
				1922
7	Mount Carroll, VI	Strassburg, II; Norderney, II	New York	Jan. 3
8	Barbadian, I	Tillie Russ	New York	Jan. 11
9	Corson, IV	Tillie Russ; Coblenz, II	New York	Jan. 13
10	Mount Clinton, III	Frankfurt, II	New York	Jan. 17
11	Oregonian, VII	Laura	New York	Jan. 24
12	Mongolia, VI	Johannes C. Russ	New York	Jan. 29
13	Hickman, I	Johannes C. Russ	New York	Jan. 31
14	Mount Clay, VI	Stella Wega: Bolsta, Bolten	New York	Feb. 7
15	Minnekahda, IV	Hentsch: Bolsta	New York	Feb. 8
16	Mount Carroll, VII	Gotenhof	New York	Feb. 15
17	Georgian, I	Gotenhof	New York	Feb. 21
18	Mount Clinton, IV	Marathon, II; Karlsruhe, II	New York	Mar. 7
19	Morristown, I	Tillie Russ, III; Bolama	New York	Mar. 12
20	Oregonian, VIII	Norderney, IV	New York	Mar. 23
21	Minnekahda, V	Frankfurt, IV	New York	Mar. 26
22	Mount Carroll, VIII	Frankfurt, IV	New York	Mar. 26
23	Schoharie, III	Borkum, II	Philadelphia	Apr. 1
24	Hawaiian, VI	Frankfurt, V	New York	Apr. 5
25	Merry Mount	Borkum, II	Portland	Apr. 10
26	Georgian, II	Ina Lotte Blumenthal	New York	Apr. 20
27	Chickasaw, III	Mannheim, IV	Philadelphia	Apr. 25
28	Western Scout, I	Alesia, II	New York	Apr. 26
29	Mount Clay, VII	Alesia, II	New York	Apr. 29
30	Minnekahda, VI	Cordelia	New York	Apr. 30
31	Manchuria, VI	Ina Lotte Blumenthal	New York	May 8
32	Mount Clinton, VI	Karlsruhe, V	New York	May 23
33	Reliance, I	Strassburg, VII	New York	May 26
34	Mount Clay, VIII	Coblenz, IV	New York	June 5
35	Manchuria, VII	Uranus, I	New York	June 11
36	Eastport, II		New York	June 16
37	Mount Carroll, IX	Mannheim, VI, VII	New York	June 20
38	Reliance, II	Mannheim, VII	New York	June 23
39	Belvidere, II		New York	June 24
40	Mount Clay, IX	Martha Russ, II	New York	July 17
41	Allaguash, I		New York	July 25
42	Mongolia, VII	Alesia, IV	New York	Aug. 8
43	Minnekahda, VIII	Alesia, IV	New York	Aug. 13
44	Manitowoc		New York	Aug. 22
45	Norlina, III		New York	Sept. 11
46	Mongolia, VIII	Andalusia, II	New York	Sept. 11
47	J. B. Duke		New York	Oct. 4
48	West Islay		New York	Oct. 16
49	Allaguash, II		New York	Nov. 24
50	Mount Clinton, VII	Erna	New York	Dec. 20
51	Winnebago		New York	Dec. 25
				1923
52	Mount Clay, X	Erna, Karlsruhe, VI	New York	Jan. 1
53	Mount Carroll, XI	Coblenz, IV	New York	Jan. 25
54	Belvidere		New York	Jan. 29
55	West Maximus		New York	Feb. 17
56	Allaguash, III		New York	Mar. 24
57	Rockaway Park		New York	Mar. 28
58	Eastern Coast		New York	Apr. 14
59	Satsuma		New York	Apr. 26
	Total, A			

American Relief Administration

Donated by the American Red Cross—Reconstruction Period, 1919–1924

Port of Arrival	Number of Packages	Total Metric Tons	F.O.B. Value	Freight	Insurance	Miscellaneous Charges	Total C.I.F. Value
			A. SHIPMENTS FROM THE UNITED STATES				
Hamburg	148	11.1	$ 7,801.75	$ 1,004.00	$ 345.58	.....	$ 9,151.33
Riga	566	27.6	34,026.36	114.38	1,234.54	.....	35,375.28
Riga	1,269	71.1	63,846.10	3,014.00	2,391.02	$ 210.69	69,461.81
Hamburg	2,455	121.5	108,338.27	6,639.75	3,264.19	3,375.72	121,617.93
Hamburg	56	9.1	469.02	186.90	14.15	.....	670.07
Riga	986	63.4	31,772.74	1,794.80	1,159.17	90.44	34,817.15
Hamburg	537	32.2	33,289.04	2,067.79	1,012.20	99.97	36,469.00
Hamburg	400	21.2	3,564.00	660.00	123.05	.....	4,347.05
Hamburg	1,091	24.7	6,830.88	551.56	209.09	25.00	7,616.53
Hamburg	113	5.7	8,393.97	629.10	130.42	.....	9,153.49
Hamburg	60	2.1	2,513.52	83.25	37.53	31.59	2,665.89
Hamburg	213	13.9	4,389.74	379.65	68.99	.....	4,838.38
Hamburg	160	14.4	5,760.17	260.55	87.08	25.00	6,132.80
Hamburg	594	43.6	54,630.25	2,190.15	824.79	11.14	57,656.33
Hamburg	2,069	78.9	37,983.21	1,969.79	471.19	25.00	40,449.19
Hamburg	1,260	47.3	14,360.75	950.08	181.50	35.50	15,527.83
Hamburg	666	54.5	11,485.86	1,148.62	147.27	155.40	12,937.15
Hamburg	1,403	56.8	37,489.47	1,514.88	520.41	198.71	39,723.47
Hamburg	1,911	62.5	6,145.77	972.43	85.37	321.18	7,524.75
Hamburg	2,059	111.7	65,575.36	3,937.05	823.13	191.55	70,527.09
Hamburg	95	8.3	11,242.09	583.50	139.70	10.93	11,976.22
Hamburg	1,092	69.4	47,764.71	3,160.50	683.94	564.64	52,173.79
Hamburg	180	15.8	20,404.50	647.63	261.00	.....	21,313.13
Hamburg	760	65.7	83,986.30	2,630.40	1,135.50	733.93	88,486.13
Hamburg	200	25.1	5,000.00	618.30	66.17	.....	5,684.47
Hamburg	100	10.4	12,871.95	310.50	155.16	.....	13,337.61
Hamburg	120	6.3	11,265.40	527.28	139.26	.....	11,931.94
Hamburg	635	69.9	80,596.75	2,060.30	976.81	24.41	83,658.27
Hamburg	216	16.5	5,688.66	577.50	73.76	868.68	7,208.60
Hamburg	99	5.1	2,723.64	285.15	35.70	1.80	3,046.29
Hamburg	1	0.1	960.40	4.20	11.61	.....	976.21
Hamburg	40	4.3	6,950.00	148.75	119.70	.....	7,218.45
Hamburg	61	6.5	6,642.90	254.25	116.24	.....	7,013.39
Hamburg	117	9.4	12,575.00	378.00	219.00	.....	13,172.00
Hamburg	189	16.5	21,633.36	473.14	373.59	.....	22,480.09
Riga	3,071	125.3	40,151.27	1,933.51	715.02	75.00	42,874.80
Hamburg	299	22.2	35,706.02	720.25	618.35	.....	37,044.62
Hamburg	562	28.6	24,690.66	881.25	432.89	60.75	26,065.55
Riga	4,000	219.0	22,192.04	2,103.00	383.07	150.00	24,828.13
Hamburg	178	20.3	29,266.00	558.25	662.24	.....	30,486.49
Petrograd	1,109	85.3	100,396.01	2,970.62	2,214.30	84.81	105,665.74
Hamburg	335	40.8	55,208.86	1,010.29	1,248.42	.....	54,467.57
Hamburg	230	25.7	43,209.38	929.79	980.44	.....	45,119.61
Petrograd	312	34.7	61,025.69	1,272.67	1,366.94	.....	63,665.30
Petrograd	5,773	528.6	246,447.84	8,597.40	5,324.48	268.50	260,638.22
Hamburg	394	42.1	68,206.95	1,296.14	1,544.11	.....	71,047.20
Petrograd	127	13.6	21,762.11	412.10	461.18	.....	22,635.39
Petrograd	157	18.2	22,075.63	493.59	471.02	.....	23,040.24
Petrograd	1,792	155.3	60,110.54	2,204.57	1,550.91	157.00	64,023.02
Hamburg	192	6.1	9,119.20	329.65	247.82	162.49	9,859.16
Riga	2,502	152.2	177,448.12	4,449.67	3,308.02	15.98	185,221.79
Hamburg	2,221	109.8	49,119.28	2,115.76	1,352.77	102.02	52,689.83
Hamburg	555	33.4	28,913.79	636.24	566.49	23.63	30,140.15
Riga	920	73.4	42,815.73	1,390.80	789.46	.....	44,995.99
Reval	1,855	64.6	19,600.79	629.17	370.81	50.00	20,650.77
Windau	643	21.2	9,938.22	179.64	184.41	.....	10,302.27
Windau	3,390	145.7	69,319.82	1,941.11	1,274.71	75.00	72,610.64
Riga	202	16.8	22,754.65	754.17	418.03	.....	23,926.85
Libau	96	7.3	28,932.59	228.48	573.03	.....	29,734.10
....	**52,836**	**3,192.8**	**$2,157,383.08**	**$80,766.25**	**$44,696.75**	**$ 8,226.46**	**$2,291,072.54**

[*Continued on next page*]

Table 523—*Continued*

Detail by Steamers of Arrivals of Medical and

Arrival No.	Steamer or Source	Transshipping Steamer	Port of Sailing	Date of Arrival
				1922
60	Foyna	....	Bergen	Mar. 7
..	New York Warehouse and Washington Office Expenses	....	....	....
	Total, B	....	....	....
				1921
61	A.R.C. Donation	Overland	Riga	Sept. 3
62	A.R.C. Donation	Overland	Riga	Sept. 9
63	A.R.C. Donation	Overland	Riga	Sept. 14
64	A.R.C. Donation	Rail	Paris	Oct. 8
65	A.R.C. Donation	Rail	Paris	Oct. 14
66	A.R.C. and Y.M.C.A. Donation	Overland and Rail	Paris Coblenz	Oct. 17
67	J. C. Jacobson	....	Copenhagen	Nov. 4
68	A.R.C. Donation	Rail	Paris	Nov. 26
69	A.R.C. Donation	....	Riga	Dec. 7
70	Juno, II	Norderney	Hull	Dec. 12
71	Ilmar	Norderney	London	Dec. 13
				1922
72	Otto, II	Norderney	London	Jan. 2
73	Saturn	....	Hamburg	Jan. 8
74	Werner	....	Hamburg	Jan. 25
75	Saturn	....	London	Jan. 29
76	Ora	....	London	Feb. 3
77	Aeolus	....	Hamburg	Mar. 3
78	Edna	....	Bergen	Mar. 4
79	Karlsruhe, II	....	Hamburg	Mar. 19
80	Martha Halm	....	London	Apr. 4
81	A.R.C. Donation	....	Paris	Apr. 5
82	Malaga	Karlsruhe, III	....	......
83	Balbeck	....	London	Apr. 19
84	Claro	....	Liverpool	June 17
85	Tommeliten	....	Dunkirk	June 29
86	Terneskjaer	....	Calais	Aug. 6
87	Corvus	....	....	Aug. 15
88	Halfdan	....	....	Aug. 22/31
89	Trudwang	....	London	Sept. 15
90	Alesia, IV	....	Antwp. Hmbg	Sept. 19
91	Halfdan, II	....	Hamburg	Oct. 24
92	Minos	....	....	Nov. 25
				1923
93	A.R.C. Donation	Rail	Paris	Jan. 29
94	Coblenz	....	Hamburg	Feb. 3/9
95	Cygnus	....	....	Mar. 3
96	Uranus, III	....	Hamburg	Mar. 3
97	Caster	....	....	Mar. 24/30
98	Uranus, V	....	Hamburg	Apr. 17
99	Venus	....	Hamburg	May 8
100	Uranus, III	....	Hamburg	May 11
101	Seine	....	Hamburg	May 12/18
102	Halfdan, III	....	....	June 9/22
...	Value of Arrivals, 61–102, Inclusive	....	....	....
	Total, C	....	....	....
	Grand Total	....	....	....

* $3,754,587.38, funds appropriated by A.R.C.; $50,275.77, funds supplied by A.R.A. from insurance recoveries made on Government surplus and A.R.C. shipments.

American Relief Administration

Hospital Supplies, Donated by the American Red Cross

Port of Arrival	Number of Packages	Total Metric Tons	F.O.B. Value	Freight	Insurance	Miscellaneous Charges	Total C.I.F. Value
			B. PURCHASED IN NEW YORK				
Riga	1,334	163.4	$ 28,661.15	......	$ 91.81	.....	$ 28,752.96
....	....	....	....	......	......	$ 1,836.61	1,836.61
....	**1,334**	**163.4**	**$ 28,661.15**	......	**$ 91.81**	**$ 1,836.61**	**$ 30,589.57**
			C. PURCHASES AND DONATIONS IN EUROPE				
Riga	10	15.0	....	.....	.....	.....	....
Riga	5	7.5	....	.....	.....	.....	....
Riga	5	7.5	....	.....	.....	.....	....
Riga	1,996	114.7	....	.....	.....	.....	....
Riga	1,092	62.7	....	.....	.....	.....	....
Riga	236	53.9	....	.....	.....	.....	....
Riga	148	20.3	....	.....	.....	.....	....
Riga	368	21.1	....	.....	.....	.....	....
Riga	7	10.5	....	.....	.....	.....	....
Hamburg	101	12.1	....	.....	.....	.....	....
Hamburg	400	38.6	....	.....	.....	.....	....
Hamburg	101	12.0	....	.....	.....	.....	....
Petrograd	909	110.5	....	.....	.....	.....	....
Windau	1	.1	....	.....	.....	.....	....
Windau	7	.4	....	.....	.....	.....	....
Windau	13	.7	....	.....	.....	.....	....
Windau	3	.2	....	.....	.....	.....	....
Windau	333	40.0	....	.....	.....	.....	....
Windau	1	.1	....	.....	.....	.....	....
Windau	916	70.0	....	.....	.....	.....	....
Windau	1,764	101.3	....	.....	.....	.....	....
Hamburg	300	30.3	....	.....	.....	.....	....
Windau	1	.1	....	.....	.....	.....	....
Petrograd	3,050	327.2	....	.....	.....	.....	....
Petrograd	1,821	200.8	....	.....	.....	.....	....
Petrograd	3,187	338.7	....	.....	.....	.....	....
Riga	62	3.6	....	.....	.....	.....	....
Riga	87	5.0	....	.....	.....	.....	....
Petrograd	40	3.0	....	.....	.....	.....	....
Petrograd	110	6.5	....	.....	.....	.....	....
Riga	34	2.0	....	.....	.....	.....	....
Riga	2,000	114.9	....	.....	.....	.....	....
Riga	4	.2	....	.....	.....	.....	....
Riga	555	31.9	....	.....	.....	.....	....
Riga	60	3.4	....	.....	.....	.....	....
Riga	11	.6	....	.....	.....	.....	....
Riga	840	48.3	....	.....	.....	.....	....
Riga	5	.3	....	.....	.....	.....	....
Riga	3	.2	....	.....	.....	.....	....
Riga	6	.3	....	.....	.....	.....	....
Riga	16	.9	....	.....	.....	.....	....
Riga	13	.7	....	.....	.....	.....	....
....	....	....	$1,483,201.04	.....	.....	.....	$1,483,201.04
....	**20,621**	**1,818.1**	**$1,483,201.04**	.....	.....	.....	**$1,483,201.04**
....	**74,791**	**5,174.3**	**$3,669,245.27**	**$80,766.25**	**$44,788.56**	**$10,063.07**	**$3,804,863.15***

RUSSIA (SOVIET REPUBLICS)—American Relief Administration

Detail by Steamers of Transshipments from Hamburg and Retransshipments from Danzig of A.R.C. Medical and Hospital Supplies

Table 524 — Reconstruction Period, 1919–1924

Transshipping Steamer	Original Steamer by Number	Port of Sailing	Date of Arrival	Port of Arrival	Number of Packages	Total Metric Tons
			1922			
Hentsch	15	Hamburg	Mar. 10	Danzig	2,069	78.9
Stella Wega	14	Hamburg	Mar. 13	Danzig	594	43.6
Total					**2,663**	**122.5**
			1921			
Mannheim, I	1	Hamburg	Oct. 30	Riga	**148**	**11.1**
			1922			
Martha Russ, I	4, 5	Hamburg	Jan. 10	Riga	2,466	128.8
Strassburg, II	4, 7	Hamburg	Jan. 17	Riga	344	16.9
Norderney, II	7	Hamburg	Jan. 18	Windau	238	18.7
Tillie Russ	8, 9	Hamburg	Jan. 23	Windau	1,046	42.9
Frankfurt, II	10	Hamburg	Jan. 29	Windau	113	5.7
Total					**4,207**	**213.0**
Coblenz, II	9	Hamburg	Feb. 1	Windau	**15**	**3.2**
Johannus C. Russ	12, 13	Hamburg	Mar. 1	Windau	373	28.3
Gotenhof	16, 17	Hamburg	Mar. 11	Windau	1,926	102.6
Marathon, II	18	Hamburg	Mar. 12	Windau	329	15.3
Bolten	14: Stella Wega	Danzig	Mar. 17	Windau	52	3.6
Karlsruhe	18	Hamburg	Mar. 19	Windau	1,069	41.7
Tillie Russ, III	19	Hamburg	Mar. 19	Windau	298	8.3
Laura, I	11	Hamburg	Mar. 20	Windau	60	2.1
Bolama	19	Hamburg	Mar. 27	Windau	1,607	52.7
Total					**5,714**	**254.6**
Frankfurt, IV	21, 22	Hamburg	Apr. 19	Windau	1,187	77.7
Norderney, IV	20	Hamburg	Apr. 23	Windau	2,059	110.6
Borkum, II	23, 25	Hamburg	Apr. 25	Windau	380	40.9
Bolsta	15: Hentsch; 14: Stella Wega	Danzig	Apr. 28	Riga	2,611	118.7
Total					**6,237**	**347.9**

RUSSIA (SOVIET REPUBLICS)

Detail by Steamers of Transshipments from Hamburg and Retransshipments from Danzig of A.R.C. Medical and Hospital Supplies

Table 524—*Continued*

Transshipping Steamer	Original Steamer by Number	Port of Sailing	Date of Arrival	Port of Arrival	Number of Packages	Total Metric Tons
			1922			
rankfurt, V	24	Hamburg	May 7	Riga	760	65.7
annheim, IV	27	Hamburg	May 16	Riga	120	6.3
na Lotte Blumenthal	26, 31	Hamburg	May 20	Petrograd	101	10.5
lesia, II	28, 29	Hamburg	May 24	Petrograd	851	86.4
Total					**1,832**	**168.9**
ordelia	30	Hamburg	June 2	Petrograd	99	5.1
arlsruhe, V	32	Hamburg	June 4	Riga	40	4.3
trassburg, VII	33	Hamburg	June 6	Riga	61	6.5
oblenz, IV	34	Hamburg	June 16	Riga	117	9.4
ranus, I	35	Hamburg	June 29	Riga	189	16.5
Total					**506**	**41.8**
Iannheim, VI	37	Hamburg	July 5	Riga	**194**	**11.9**
Iannheim, VII	37, 38	Hamburg	Aug. 7	Riga	667	38.7
Iartha, Russ, II	40	Hamburg	Aug. 23	Petrograd	178	20.3
Total					**845**	**59.0**
lesia, IV	42, 43	Hamburg	Sept. 19	Petrograd	**565**	**66.5**
ndalusia, II	46	Hamburg	Oct. 26	Petrograd	**394**	**42.1**
			1923			
rna	50, 52	Hamburg	Jan. 10	Riga	1,873	97.7
arlsruhe, VI	52	Hamburg	Jan. 14	Riga	540	18.4
Total					**2,413**	**116.1**
oblenz, IV	53	Hamburg	Feb. 3	Riga	**555**	**33.4**
Total Transshipments Handled					**26,288**	**1,492.0**
educt Retransshipments					2,663	122.5
Total Net					**23,625**	**1,369.5**

Table 525

Detail by Steamers of Supplies Forwarded

Transshipping Steamer	Origin of Cargo	Port of Sailing	Date of Arrival	Port of Arrival
			1922	
Helikon	Stock *	Hamburg	Jan. 17	Windau
Mannheim, III	Stock *	Hamburg	Jan. 24	Windau
Coblenz, I	Callisto	Hamburg	Feb. 1	Windau
Johannus C. Russ	Hickman	Hamburg	Mar. 1	Windau
Norderney, III	Orla, II	Hamburg	Mar. 4	Windau
Gottfried Poppe	Themisto	Hamburg	Mar. 17	Danzig †
Karlsruhe, II	Wuerttemberg	Hamburg	Mar. 19	Windau
Bolama	Morristown, I	Hamburg	Mar. 27	Riga
Laura, II	Stock ††	Hamburg	Apr. 5	Riga
Erda	Wuerttemberg	Hamburg	Apr. 14	Danzig †
Borkum, II	Noccalula	Hamburg	Apr. 25	Windau
Borkum, II	Schoharie, III	Hamburg	Apr. 25	Windau
Borkum, II	Union City	Hamburg	Apr. 25	Windau
Bolsta	——— ‡	Danzig	Apr. 28	Riga
Bonus, II	Emergency Aid, I	Hamburg	May 5	Danzig †
Progress, X	Emergency Aid, I	Hamburg	May 5	Danzig †
Frankfurt, V	Adalia, II	Hamburg	May 7	Riga
Christel Salling, II	Schoharie, III	Hamburg	May 9	Riga
Christel Salling, II	Tomalva	Hamburg	May 9	Riga
Strassburg, VI	Adalia, II	Hamburg	May 10	Riga
Electra	Orla, I	Hamburg	May 15	Petrograd
Mannheim, IV	Chickasaw, III	Hamburg	May 16	Riga
Weichsel, XI	Emergency Aid, I	Hamburg	May 19	Danzig †
Coblenz, III	Einfeld	Hamburg	May 26	Riga
Mannheim, V	Chickasaw, III	Hamburg	June 7	Riga
Mannheim, V	Morristown, II	Hamburg	June 7	Riga
Mannheim, V	Schoharie, III	Hamburg	June 7	Riga
Mannheim, V	Westerwald	Hamburg	June 7	Riga
Eastport		New York	June 16	Riga
Belvidere		New York	June 24	Riga
Mannheim, VI	Stock *	Hamburg	July 5	Riga
Uranus, II	Stock *	Hamburg	Aug. 14	Riga
Alesia, III	Stock *	Hamburg	Aug. 20	Riga
Total Commodities Forwarded by A.R.A. for A.F.S.C.				
Estimated Value of Commodities				

* A.F.S.C. arrivals, Hamburg.
† Shipped Russia via rail through Stolpce.
†† Ex-Dallas, Auk, Modig, and Otto Hugo Stinnes.
‡ Ex-Minnesotan, U.S.A. to Hamburg; Marathon, III, Hamburg to Danzig.

American Relief Administration

for A.F.S.C.—Reconstruction Period, 1919–1924

Contents of Cargoes in Net Metric Tons of 1,000 Kilograms or 2,204.6 Pounds

Flour	Rice	Beans, Peas	Corn Grits	Vegetable Oil	Sugar	Clothing	Total Tons
....	22.0	....	....	....	....	..	22.0
....	49.0	....	....	....	....	..	49.9
79.4	....	....	....	....	....	..	79.4
76.1	....	....	....	....	....	..	76.1
227.9	....	90.6	....	....	66.7	..	385.2
122.8	....	....	....	....	....	..	122.8
17.5	....	....	....	....	....	..	17.5
115.3	....	....	....	....	....	..	115.3
302.7	....	....	....	....	....	..	302.7
1.2	....	....	....	....	....	..	1.2
39.4	....	....	....	....	....	..	39.4
83.6	....	....	20.0	....	....	..	103.6
80.1	....	....	....	....	....	..	80.1
....	....	....	....	....	....	.4‡‡	.4
....	....	....	95.8	....	....	..	95.8
....	....	....	49.6	....	....	..	49.6
33.8	....	....	....	....	....	..	33.8
189.2	....	....	....	....	....	..	189.2
18.5	....	....	....	....	....	..	18.5
260.8	....	....	....	....	....	..	260.8
....	....	....	....	16.6	.9	..	17.5
444.2	....	....	184.0	....	....	..	628.2
....	....	....	13.1	....	....	..	13.1
270.0	....	....	....	....	....	..	270.0
....	....	....	20.0	....	....	..	20.0
48.9	....	....	....	....	....	..	48.9
92.6	....	....	....	....	....	..	92.6
76.2	....	....	....	....	....	..	76.2
44.3	....	....	58.8	....	....	..	103.1
207.7	....	....	415.5§	....	....	..	623.2
37.6	....	....	61.0	....	....	..	98.6
145.6	....	....	....	....	....	..	145.6
21.9	....	....	....	....	....	..	21.9
3,037.3¶	**71.9**	**90.6**	**917.8**	**16.6**	**67.6**	**.4**	**4,202.2**
$198,489.68	$4,176.02	$9,065.80	$44,589.48	$3,283.65	$6,789.61	$1,000.00	$267,394.24

‡‡ Eight bales of clothing.
§ Corn flour, corn meal, and hominy, mixed, not segregated.

¶ 101.0 metric tons is corn flour; balance, 2,936.3 metric tons is wheat flour.

Table 526

Summary of Relief Deliveries by Districts—

Districts	Commodities in Net							
	Flour	Wheat	No. 2 Mixed Corn	Seed Corn	Rye	Rice	Beans, Peas	Corn Grits
Alexandrovsk	2,826.681	....	....	....	....	409.305	16.775	4,255.323
Batoum	....	....	....	255.500	....	....	.....	....
Ekaterinoslav	6,004.419	....	....	....	....	943.445	1.457	4,242.742
Elizabethgrad	870.607	....	....	....	....	216.306	.....	133.115
Gomel	1,588.668	....	....	....	....	378.528	5.365	253.189
Kazan	17,944.424	....	37,389.600	....	3,908.100	817.666	556.970	11,173.826
Kharkov	2,529.202	....	....	....	....	731.202	17.306	867.502
Kiev	7,589.206	....	....	....	....	1,906.347	1.992	2,270.221
Mariupol	446.161	....	....	....	....	13.548	.....	1,278.602
Minsk	2,990.783	....	....	....	....	657.384	50.007	656.992
Moscow	7,493.179	....	....	....	....	1,395.832	149.125	2,078.216
Nijni-Novgorod	....	....	....	....	....	....	.129	....
Nikolaiev	1,145.562	....	....	....	....	....	.....	2,815.888
Novorossisk	16.221	....	....	938.900	....	4.565	.....	22.682
Odessa	11,559.862	....	....	....	....	1,629.211	1.753	7,050.368
Orenburg	5,402.718	15,734.900	13,394.900	....	1,026.200	712.952	250.206	10,293.510
Petrograd	4,638.892	....	....	....	....	774.675	269.130	1,274.250
Rostov/Don	796.690	4,098.400	....	9,332.000	....	232.555	1.230	47.232
Rostov/Don-Tzaritzin	2,102.811	....	....	....	....	250.642	.....	257.186
Samara	11,271.432	....	13,745.300	....	1,235.000	2,079.994	948.015	4,984.181
Sanitary Train No. 1	....	....	....	....	....	....	.....	....
Sanitary Train No. 2	....	....	....	....	....	....	.....	....
Saratov	12,209.804	7,389.100	32,047.600	1,951.600	1,825.500	1,730.297	421.156	8,358.309
Simbirsk	10,006.782	....	14,583.400	....	1,641.100	1,046.965	419.935	7,419.734
Simferopol	3,892.952	....	....	....	....	489.272	.....	513.135
Theodosia	....	....	1,642.500	2,877.900	....	....	.....	2,947.900
Tiflis	....	....	....	2,576.200	....	....	.....	....
Tzaritzin	5,161.113	4,756.100	61,598.100	362.200	461.000	354.709	179.100	6,184.910
Ufa	9,937.072	3,734.800	22,881.900	....	1,573.200	1,131.636	186.016	5,805.230
Vitebsk	2,148.284	....	....	....	....	484.530	5.132	407.373
Soviet R.R. Workers	....	....	4,112.000	....	1,645.000	....	.....	....
Near East Relief-Caucasus	....	....	....	....	4,927.900	....	.....	6,103.900
Not Segregated	3,037.300	101,321.000	....	4.100	3,810.200	71.900	4,320.200	917.800
Adjustments	1,170.400	1,225.300	5,558.300	115.700	875.600	451.100	94.600	3,589.000
Total	**134,781.225**	**138,259.600**	**206,953.600**	**18,414.100**	**22,928.800**	**18,914.566**	**7,895.599**	**96,202.316**

* Of the total, 2,359.0 tons are oats; 142.0 tons are grass seed.

† Of the total, 1,510.6 tons are not segregated to districts. This represents 1,100.0 tons of Grain Corporation shipping material; 254.0 tons of A.R.A. clothing; 156.2 tons of auto parts; .4 ton of A.F.S.C. clothing. The balance, 1,689.2 tons, represents 350.0 tons of A.R.A. clothing used in clothing remittances and bulk sales; 1,193.8 tons of child and adult clothing; 119.4 tons of A.R.A., and 26.0 tons of Soviet bags and containers used for food remittances, bulk sales, etc.

American Relief Administration

Reconstruction Period, 1919–1924

Metric Tons of 1,000 Kilograms or 2,204.6 Pounds

Pork Products	Milk	Cocoa	Sugar	Misc. Food	Soap	Medical and Hospital Supplies	Forage	Clothing and Other Misc.	Total Tons	Total Value
209.830	1,004.550	94.262	408.842	......	......	....	....	20.152	9,245.720	$ 790,769.83
....	....	......	....	......	......	....	....	......	255.500	12,774.14
581.733	1,923.463	136.080	974.659	53.217	31.472	484.000	....	88.847	15,465.534	2,211,424.78
75.814	254.115	5.334	158.534	5.708	.699	....	....	16.927	1,737.159	278,755.92
150.145	466.164	16.305	275.218	17.608	.499	....	....	23.037	3,174.726	518,308.12
1,587.142	4,837.664	607.199	3,075.448	57.115	127.481	484.000	....	180.697	82,747.332	5,769,277.85
349.109	783.548	36.156	430.120	32.297	......	484.000	....	39.703	6,300.145	1,286,135.58
812.223	2,398.961	98.187	1,404.882	111.681	......	645.300	....	90.138	17,329.138	3,168,592.35
32.695	134.151	14.670	62.388	......	......	....	....	.375	1,982.590	133,979.66
339.441	968.987	40.386	547.588	47.386	1.899	484.000	....	39.759	6,824.612	1,464,754.15
940.351	2,666.543	264.278	1,314.816	104.737	39.946	887.300	....	176.951	17,511.274	3,257,283.24
....	....	......	....	......	......	....	....	......	.129	12.83
101.140	382.285	46.035	174.879	......	......	....	....	.368	4,666.157	334,068.50
63.839	.914	......	19.891	.690	......	....	....	.910	1,068.612	68,148.06
917.722	3,285.933	178.915	1,761.455	103.103	22.972	484.000	....	105.355	27,100.649	3,749,081.02
374.221	2,070.303	231.333	662.644	56.539	54.084	161.300	....	75.168	50,500.978	3,189,230.61
515.437	1,779.885	103.801	912.230	60.776	13.757	726.000	....	109.981	11,178.814	2,267,012.73
52.719	220.081	1.256	104.285	14.880	......	645.400	....	......	15,546.728	1,564,328.03
200.559	624.072	70.093	333.570	4.309	57.793	....	....	111.915	4,012.950	594,609.50
1,208.415	4,596.421	489.568	2,092.793	225.014	121.398	484.000	....	151.200	43,632.731	4,030,787.91
....	....	......	....	......	......	121.000	....	......	121.000	117,937.87
....	....	......	....	......	......	121.000	....	......	121.000	117,937.86
1,171.629	3,977.022	454.724	1,885.666	76.419	......	484.000	....	172.891	74,155.717	5,427,400.49
828.805	3,173.853	332.052	1,357.111	98.577	.026	484.000	....	96.201	41,488.541	3,302,245.53
372.734	1,223.837	132.944	603.013	9.903	14.384	....	....	39.320	7,291.494	920,878.14
....	....	......	....	......	......	161.300	....	......	7,629.600	493,601.55
....	....	......	....	......	......	....	....	......	2,576.200	129,048.81
372.060	2,236.558	162.873	674.904	72.150	39.729	161.400	....	9.994	82,786.900	3,926,518.69
915.014	3,444.772	406.573	1,458.957	81.255	73.564	564.700	....	107.505	52,302.194	3,952,794.51
236.179	675.198	21.928	396.219	34.296	......	....	....	31.806	4,440.945	749,015.26
....	....	......	....	......	......	....	....	......	5,757.000	238,009.33
....	....	......	....	......	......	215.200	....	......	11,247.000	767,606.58
16.600	....	......	67.600	......	......	....	2,501.000	1,510.600	117,578.300	7,900,788.38
....	233.300	......	398.200	83.800	......	....	....	......	13,795.300	441,730.97
12,425.556	**43,362.580**	**3,944.952**	**21,555.912**	**1,351.460**	**599.703**	**8,281.900**	**2,501.000***	**3,199.800†**	**741,572.669**	**$63,174,848.78**

Table 527

Detail of Internal Deliveries for Child Feeding,

Districts	Flour	Rice	Beans, Peas	Corn Grits
				A. DISTRIBUTION
Alexandrovsk	2,061.004	258.484	......	.....
Ekaterinoslav	2,895.434	35.719	......	.....
Elizabethgrad	118.083	17.497	......	.505
Gomel	76.218	......	1.985	.....
Kazan	17,460.658	745.640	552.443	139.944
Kharkov	439.881	19.012	......	.....
Kiev	1,057.257	2.419	......	2.468
Mariupol	439.547	12.399	......	.....
Minsk	499.296	21.023	28.445	.....
Moscow	1,794.836	224.912	117.652	17.486
Nijni-Novgorod	......	......	.129	.....
Nikolaiev	1,137.345	......	......	.....
Novorossisk	......	......	......	20.436
Odessa	4,434.665	.833	......	.....
Orenburg	4,773.321	429.240	241.988	58.619
Petrograd	1,771.064	152.421	258.829	86.058
Rostov/Don-Tzaritzin	1,123.194	......	......	39.384
Samara	9,662.532	1,701.701	839.791	86.670
Saratov	9,177.625	1,034.169	403.065	190.858
Simbirsk	9,761.862	966.742	417.414	77.304
Simferopol	2,098.356	6.565	......	.....
Tzaritzin	4,963.136	321.938	178.907	.....
Ufa	9,549.404	1,018.187	180.581	101.988
Vitebsk	77.738	......	......	.....
Colton Account (Y.M.C.A.)	......	......	......	.....
Total, A	**85,372.456**	**6,968.901**	**3,221.229**	**821.720**
				B. COMMODITIES TURNED
Ekaterinoslav	40.100	28.304	......	.....
Elizabethgrad	1.203	.849	......	.....
Gomel	58.945	28.589	......	13.018
Kazan	2.246	1.586	......	.....
Kharkov	62.815	36.468	......	6.085
Kiev	103.055	42.340	......	28.017
Minsk	73.784	43.581	......	8.489
Moscow	28.681	11.692	......	9.265
Odessa	73.585	28.919	......	23.807
Orenburg	10.403	......	......	7.250
Petrograd	16.039	11.316	......	.....
Samara	13.881	8.707	......	.....
Saratov	7.615	5.381	......	.....
Simferopol	40.898	27.864	......	.....
Ufa	4.812	.566	......	2.829
Vitebsk	76.995	46.411	......	7.922
Total, B	**615.057**	**322.573**	......	**106.682**
Grand Total	**85,987.513**	**7,291.474**	**3,221.229**	**928.402**

* This total includes 1.687 tons of powdered milk, delivered to Orenburg district.

† This total comprises 89.064 tons of rice and milk; 471.072 tons of salt; 15.485 tons of biscuits; 1.159 tons of tea; 1.084 tons of dehydrated potatoes; and 1.000 tons of dates.

American Relief Administration

by Districts—Reconstruction Period, 1919–1924

Commodities in Net Metric Tons of 1,000 Kilograms or 2,204.6 Pounds

Pork Products	Milk	Cocoa	Sugar	Misc. Food	Soap	Total Tons	Total Value
SUPERVISED BY A.R.A.							
152.629	714.785	68.161	291.938	......	......	3,547.001	$ 379,907.46
270.042	983.110	108.142	434.811	......	31.472	4,758.730	535,199.89
16.224	43.252	4.641	23.252	......	.699	224.153	25,575.69
18.262	23.607	4.976	11.421	......	.499	136.968	16,698.22
1,530.136	526.271	596.329	2,978.140	48.583	125.562	24,703.706	2,138,044.10
36.598	140.926	16.639	69.081	......	......	722.137	78,471.17
100.231	380.494	48.604	167.502	.022	......	1,758.997	198,650.61
32.046	133.367	14.670	61.203	......	......	693.232	74,219.36
54.272	18.600	22.895	73.321	.194	1.899	719.945	66,143.90
325.754	342.587	120.640	286.490	23.128	13.960	3,267.445	352,691.00
......	......	......	......	......	......	.129	12.83
99.904	380.783	45.664	173.374	......	......	1,837.070	204,192.02
62.206	......	......	.760	......	......	83.402	16,807.90
336.360	1,257.777	147.521	559.186	.110	22.972	6,759.424	726,324.90
312.293	147.178	209.152	563.639	54.526	53.819	6,845.462	581,201.38
155.720	181.392	68.610	256.542	2.942	13.757	2,947.335	282,210.61
80.688	269.391	38.936	141.900	.106	57.793	1,751.392	187,454.22
1,004.878	767.553	424.739	1,707.110	195.938	121.398	16,512.310	1,525,217.64
821.072	598.612	387.884	1,351.251	12.981	......	13,977.517	1,264,272.53
796.584	485.766	325.361	1,307.139	96.889	......	14,235.061	1,236,768.60
193.297	651.165	84.787	300.060	.533	14.384	3,349.147	370,181.47
353.507	36.988	161.293	647.704	67.899	39.631	6,771.003	561,426.82
856.243	1,171.653	395.120	1,386.047	75.013	71.722	14,805.958	1,407,347.42
18.944	14.751	7.140	12.926	......	......	131.499	15,150.40
......	......	......	......	......	......	....	6,476.05
7,627.890	**9,271.695***	**3,301.904**	**12,804.797**	**578.864†**	**569.567**	**130,539.023**	**$12,250,646.19**
OVER TO AND DISTRIBUTED BY J.D.C.							
3.797	12.065	1.500	5.500	......	......	91.266	$ 8,291.06
.114	.362	.045	.165	......	......	2.738	248.73
5.583	17.736	2.205	8.085	......	......	134.161	12,187.85
.208	.675	.086	.318	......	......	5.119	465.03
5.915	19.699	2.468	8.937	......	......	142.387	12,935.14
9.701	32.043	4.006	14.535	......	......	233.697	21,230.20
9.792	22.201	2.758	10.118	......	......	170.723	15,509.32
2.668	8.609	1.082	3.919	......	......	65.916	5,988.13
6.910	23.191	2.894	10.494	......	......	169.800	15,425.47
.975	3.118	.400	1.400	......	......	23.546	2,139.03
1.518	4.826	.601	2.205	......	......	36.505	3,316.30
1.301	4.436	.554	2.004	......	......	30.883	2,805.56
.721	2.288	.285	1.047	......	......	17.337	1,574.97
2.875	12.307	1.531	5.612	......	......	91.087	8,274.80
.456	1.448	.180	.660	......	......	10.951	994.83
7.293	23.165	2.880	10.562	......	......	175.228	15,918.58
59.827	**188.169**	**23.475**	**85.561**	......	......	**1,401.344**	**$ 127,305.00**
7,687.717	**9,459.864**	**3,325.379**	**12,890.358**	**578.864**	**569.567**	**131,940.367‡**	**$12,377,951.19**

‡ This includes 64.0 tons of flour and 464.0 tons of miscellaneous food donated by the Soviet government.

Table 528

Summary of Internal Deliveries of Clothing, by

Account	Table No.	Shoes (Pairs)	Stockings (Pairs)	Woolens (Yards)	Linings (Yards)	Flannel (Yards)
Remittances and Bulk Sales	529	......	......	191,561	163,800	327,600
General Relief	529	......	......	117,585	153,298	311,796
Children's Relief	529	586,991	771,827	......	.....	.....
Institutions	...	......	......	637,107	.....	.....
Sale at Riga	...	......	......	255	.....	.....
Handling, Outturn, Cutting, and other Shortages..	...	......	......	3,195	9,870	11,565
Total	...	**586,991**	**771,827**	**949,703**	**326,968**	**650,961**

* Value of 40,950 packages, divided between clothing remittances, 14,943 packages, value $298,860.00; and 26,007 packages, bulk sales, value $438,140.00.

† Thirty-three cases of buttons in addition to figures above.

RUSSIA (SOVIET REPUBLICS)—American Relief Administration

Detail of Internal Deliveries of Clothing, by Districts and Accounts

Reconstruction Period, 1919–1924

Table 529†

Account	No. of Packages	Shoes (Pairs)	Stockings (Pairs)	Woolens (Yards)	Linings (Yards)	Flannel (Yards)	Muslin (Yards)	Buttons (No.)	Thread (Yards)	Total Value
					EKATERINOSLAV					
Remittances and Bulk Sales...	2,445	...	...	11,453	9,780	19,560	39,120	117,360	1,956,000	$ 44,004.03
General Relief	....	...	...	5,549	11,417	24,029	29,689	148,220	2,352,000	16,496.99
Children's Relief	....	28,000	25,391	....	....	....	.....	.....	......	44,643.90
Total for Ekaterinoslav	....	**28,000**	**25,391**	**17,002**	**21,197**	**43,589**	**68,809**	**265,580**	**4,308,000**	**$ 105,144.92**
					ELIZABETHGRAD					
Remittances and Bulk Sales...	922	...	...	4,320	3,688	7,376	14,752	44,256	737,600	$ 16,593.75
General Relief	....	...	...	869	1,499	2,889	5,025	16,698	228,800	2,370.72
Children's Relief	....	669	615	....	....	....	.....	.....	......	1,067.90
Total for Elizabethgrad	....	**669**	**615**	**5,189**	**5,187**	**10,265**	**19,777**	**60,954**	**966,400**	**$ 20,032.37**
					GOMEL					
Remittances and Bulk Sales...	1,263	...	...	5,903	5,052	10,104	20,208	60,624	1,010,400	$ 22,730.92
General Relief	....	...	...	1,342	1,573	4,039	8,350	13,553	221,800	3,493.13
Children's Relief	....	650	605	....	....	....	.....	.....	......	1,038.69
Total for Gomel	....	**650**	**605**	**7,245**	**6,625**	**14,143**	**28,558**	**74,177**	**1,232,200**	**$ 27,262.74**
					KAZAN					
Remittances and Bulk Sales...	1,154	...	...	5,407	4,616	9,232	18,464	55,392	923,200	$ 20,769.18
General Relief	....	...	...	5,766	10,262	22,291	42,090	129,168	2,052,800	17,933.29
Children's Relief	....	106,693	130,412	....	....	....	.....	.....	......	175,141.00
Total for Kazan	....	**106,693**	**130,412**	**11,173**	**14,878**	**31,523**	**60,554**	**184,560**	**2,976,000**	**$ 213,843.47**
					KHARKOV					
Remittances and Bulk Sales...	2,158	...	...	10,121	8,632	17,264	34,528	103,584	1,726,400	$ 38,838.73
General Relief	....	...	...	2,451	3,183	6,989	16,250	26,392	428,400	6,555.28
Children's Relief	....	990	989	....	....	....	.....	.....	......	1,592.10
Total for Kharkov	....	**990**	**989**	**12,572**	**11,815**	**24,253**	**50,778**	**129,976**	**2,154,800**	**$ 46,986.11**
					KIEV					
Remittances and Bulk Sales...	4,663	...	...	21,765	18,652	37,304	74,608	223,824	3,730,400	$ 83,922.63
General Relief	....	...	...	5,408	8,295	16,486	33,057	102,816	1,813,600	14,760.73
Children's Relief	....	4,970	4,938	....	....	....	.....	.....	......	7,988.67
Total for Kiev	....	**4,970**	**4,938**	**27,173**	**26,947**	**53,790**	**107,665**	**326,640**	**5,544,000**	**$ 106,672.03**

† Cf. Table 528 for total per account.

Muslin (Yards)	Buttons (No.)	Thread (Yards)	Needles (No.)	Blankets (Bales)	Old Clothing (Bales)	Overcoats (Barrels)	Total Value
655,202	1,965,606	32,760,000	.....	....	....	...	$ 737,000.00*
638,559	1,808,889	30,329,200	.....	....	....	...	301,758.79
.....	......	......	.....	....	....	...	971,670.96
.....	......†	6,600,000‡	20,736§	2,149**	2,890	180	427,365.25
.....	......	......	.....	....	....	...	317.12
2,847	156,705	3,150,800	.....	....	....	...	12,686.01
1,296,608	**3,931,200†**	**72,840,000‡**	**20,736§**	**2,149****	**2,890††**	**180††**	**$2,450,798.13**

‡ Seventeen cases of thread in addition to figures above.
§ Two cases of needles in addition to figures above.

** Equivalent to 9,920 overcoats.
†† Contents not itemized.

RUSSIA (SOVIET REPUBLICS)

Detail of Internal Deliveries of Clothing, by Districts and Accounts

Table 529—*Continued*

Account	No. of Packages	Shoes (Pairs)	Stockings (Pairs)	Woolens (Yards)	Linings (Yards)	Flannel (Yards)	Muslin (Yards)	Buttons (No.)	Thread (Yards)	Total Value
						MINSK				
Remittances and Bulk Sales...	1,792	...	...	8,357	7,168	14,336	28,672	86,016	1,433,600	$ 32,251.63
General Relief	....	...	...	3,488	5,385	12,823	25,156	35,248	576,400	10,244.25
Children's Relief	....	3,002	1,183	....	....	....	.....	.....	......	4,556.57
Total for Minsk	....	**3,002**	**1,183**	**11,845**	**12,553**	**27,159**	**53,828**	**121,264**	**2,010,000**	**$ 47,052.45**
						MOSCOW				
Remittances and Bulk Sales...	7,416	...	...	34,965	29,664	59,328	118,658	355,974	5,932,800	$ 133,469.90
General Relief	....	...	...	25,769	9,356	28,765	81,675	280,104	4,973,800	47,965.59
Children's Relief	....	15,897	32,018	....	....	....	.....	.....	......	27,975.01
Total for Moscow	....	**15,897**	**32,018**	**60,734**	**39,020**	**88,093**	**200,333**	**636,078**	**10,906,600**	**$ 209,410.50**
						ODESSA				
Remittances and Bulk Sales...	3,542	...	...	16,517	14,168	28,336	56,672	170,016	2,833,600	$ 63,747.36
General Relief	....	...	...	6,968	12,777	25,880	51,031	67,065	1,096,400	21,015.77
Children's Relief	....	24,820	24,815	....	....	....	.....	.....	......	39,918.27
Total for Odessa	....	**24,820**	**24,815**	**23,485**	**26,945**	**54,216**	**107,703**	**237,081**	**3,930,000**	**$ 124,681.40**
						ORENBURG				
Remittances and Bulk Sales...	444	...	...	2,069	1,776	3,552	7,104	21,312	355,200	$ 7,990.92
General Relief	....	...	...	2,109	3,952	6,289	13,357	42,650	820,000	6,099.85
Children's Relief	....	46,081	51,114	....	....	....	.....	.....	......	74,865.60
Total for Orenburg.........	....	**46,081**	**51,114**	**4,178**	**5,728**	**9,841**	**20,461**	**63,962**	**1,175,200**	**$ 88,956.37**
						PETROGRAD				
Remittances and Bulk Sales...	4,685	...	...	21,868	18,740	37,480	74,960	224,880	3,748,000	$ 84,318.48
General Relief	....	...	...	6,783	12,308	18,801	48,654	68,667	1,124,400	19,387.92
Children's Relief	....	14,889	31,645	....	....	....	.....	.....	......	26,448.99
Total for Petrograd	....	**14,889**	**31,645**	**28,651**	**31,048**	**56,281**	**123,614**	**293,547**	**4,872,400**	**$ 130,155.39**
						TZARITZIN AND ROSTOV-TZARITZIN				
Children's Relief*	....	31,450	49,615	....	....	....	.....	.....	......	$ 53,295.15
Remittances and Bulk Sales...	2,295	...	...	10,707	9,180	18,360	36,720	110,160	1,836,000	41,304.40
General Relief	....	...	...	5,471	12,021	21,784	41,004	138,288	2,344,800	17,740.22
Children's Relief	....	12,500	12,500	....	....	....	.....	.....	......	20,104.26
Total for Tzarintzin and Rostov-Tzaritzin	....	**43,950**	**62,115**	**16,178**	**21,201**	**40,144**	**77,724**	**248,448**	**4,180,800**	**$ 132,444.03**

* These supplies all delivered Tzaritzin.

[*Concluded on next page*]

RUSSIA (SOVIET REPUBLICS)

Detail of Internal Deliveries of Clothing, by Districts and Accounts

Table 529—*Concluded*

Account	No. of Packages	Shoes (Pairs)	Stockings (Pairs)	Woolens (Yards)	Linings (Yards)	Flannel (Yards)	Muslin (Yards)	Buttons (No.)	Thread (Yards)	Total Value
					SAMARA					
Remittances and Bulk Sales...	1,045	...	...	4,887	4,180	8,360	16,720	50,160	836,000	$ 18,807.45
General Relief	....	...	...	3,781	7,613	12,586	24,218	77,388	1,248,800	11,190.16
Children's Relief	....	92,783	90,852	....	....	....	.....	.....	......	148,938.31
Total for Samara..........	....	**92,783**	**90,852**	**8,668**	**11,793**	**20,946**	**40,938**	**127,548**	**2,084,800**	**$ 178,935.92**
					SARATOV					
Remittances and Bulk Sales...	1,986	...	...	9,255	7,944	15,888	31,776	95,328	1,588,800	$ 35,743.15
General Relief	....	...	...	5,044	8,958	15,124	33,839	103,520	1,892,000	14,648.64
Children's Relief	....	91,709	136,667	....	....	....	.....	.....	......	154,213.54
Total for Saratov	....	**91,709**	**136,667**	**14,299**	**16,902**	**31,012**	**65,615**	**198,848**	**3,480,800**	**$ 204,605.33**
					SIMBIRSK					
Remittances and Bulk Sales...	804	...	...	3,753	3,216	6,432	12,864	38,592	643,200	$ 14,470.04
General Relief	....	...	...	2,808	5,175	11,258	21,045	65,708	956,800	8,870.95
Children's Relief	....	50,526	112,421	....	....	....	.....	.....	......	90,506.68
Total for Simbirsk	....	**50,526**	**112,421**	**6,561**	**8,391**	**17,690**	**33,909**	**104,300**	**1,600,000**	**$ 113,847.67**
					SIMFEROPOL					
Remittances and Bulk Sales...	1,213	...	...	5,661	4,852	9,704	19,408	58,224	970,400	$ 21,831.04
General Relief	....	...	...	334	280	560	1,120	3,360	56,000	585.25
Children's Relief	....	12,500	39,368	....	....	....	.....	.....	......	24,116.83
Total for Simferopol	....	**12,500**	**39,368**	**5,995**	**5,132**	**10,264**	**20,528**	**61,584**	**1,026,400**	**$ 46,533.12**
					UFA					
Remittances and Bulk Sales...	1,296	...	...	6,039	5,184	10,368	20,736	62,208	1,036,800	$ 23,324.84
General Relief	....	...	...	8,854	17,560	36,904	74,168	223,052	3,659,200	29,686.33
Children's Relief	....	48,202	26,029	....	....	....	.....	.....	......	74,214.08
Total for Ufa..............	....	**48,202**	**26,029**	**14,893**	**22,744**	**47,272**	**94,904**	**285,260**	**4,696,000**	**$ 127,225.25**
					VITEBSK					
Remittances and Bulk Sales...	1,821	...	...	8,486	7,284	14,568	29,136	87,408	1,456,800	$ 32,773.56
General Relief	....	...	...	1,491	1,684	4,299	8,831	26,992	483,200	3,820.92
Children's Relief	....	650	650	....	....	....	.....	.....	......	1,045.41
Total for Vitebsk	....	**650**	**650**	**9,977**	**8,968**	**18,867**	**37,967**	**114,400**	**1,940,000**	**$ 37,639.89**
					JOINT DISTRIBUTION COMMITTEE					
General Relief	....	...	...	**23,300**	**20,000**	**40,000**	**80,000**	**240,000**	**4,000,000**	**$ 48,892.80**
					HAMBURG, LONDON, PARIS, RIGA, VIENNA, AND WARSAW					
Remittances and Bulk Sales...	6	...	...	**28**	**24**	**48**	**96**	**288**	**4,800**	**$ 107.99**
Grand Total	**40,950**	**586,991**	**771,827**	**309,146**	**317,098**	**639,396**	**1,293,761**	**3,774,495**	**63,089,200**	**$2,010,429.75**

RUSSIA (SOVIET REPUBLICS)—American Relief Administration

Table 530 — Detail of Internal Deliveries, by Districts, of Commodities Received from the U.S. Grain Corporation—Reconstruction Period, 1919–1924

Districts	Wheat No. 2 Amber Durum	Corn No. 2 Mixed	Corn Seed	Corn Grits	Rye	Milk Evap. Cond.	Misc.	Total Tons	Total Value
	Commodities in Net Metric Tons of 1,000 Kilograms or 2,204.6 Pounds								
A. CHILD AND ADULT RELIEF									
Alexandrovsk	......	......	.....	3,974.6	......	.....	......	3,974.6	$ 181,216.27
Ekaterinoslav	......	......	.....	3,834.3	......	.....	......	3,834.3	174,788.22
Elizabethgrad	......	......	.....	60.4	......	.....	......	60.4	2,735.34
Gomel	......	......	.....	50.0	......	.....	......	50.0	2,279.45
Kazan	......	37,389.6	.....	10,896.1	3,908.1	4,153.7	......	56,347.5	2,798,227.70
Kharkov	......	......	.....	743.5	......	.....	......	743.5	33,918.22
Kiev	......	......	.....	1,518.4	......	.....	......	1,518.4	69,204.10
Mariupol	......	......	.....	1,271.0	......	.....	......	1,271.0	57,943.62
Minsk	......	......	.....	240.8	......	140.8	......	381.6	36,061.98
Moscow	......	......	.....	765.6	......	602.6	......	1,368.2	143,515.92
Nicolaiev	......	......	.....	2,811.5	......	.....	......	2,811.5	128,150.67
Odessa	......	......	.....	5,929.6	......	.....	......	5,929.6	270,342.76
Orenburg	......	13,394.9	.....	10,165.6	1,026.2	1,733.9	......	26,320.6	1,301,268.40
Petrograd (Leningrad)	......	......	.....	616.4	......	697.8	......	1,314.2	164,713.49
Samara	......	13,745.3	.....	4,248.6	1,235.0	3,117.6	......	22,346.5	1,302,962.13
Saratov	......	32,047.6	.....	7,310.1	1,825.5	2,263.9	......	43,447.1	1,977,021.00
Simbirsk	......	14,583.4	.....	7,309.8	1,641.1	2,617.2	......	26,151.5	1,409,771.86
Theodosia	......	1,642.5	.....	2,947.9	......	.....	......	4,590.4	192,168.65
Tzaritzin	......	61,598.1	.....	6,151.8	461.0	2,139.9	......	70,350.8	2,860,366.97
Ufa	......	22,881.9	.....	5,522.0	1,573.2	2,068.2	......	32,045.3	1,516,182.80
Vitebsk	......	......	.....	47.0	......	12.7	......	59.7	4,454.57
Soviet Railway Workers	......	4,112.0	.....	......	1,645.0	.....	......	5,757.0	238,009.33
Total	......	**201,395.3**	.....	**76,415.0**	**13,315.1**	**19,548.3**	......	**310,673.7**	**$14,865,303.45**
B. SEED PLANTING									
Batoum	......	......	255.5	......	......	.....	......	255.5	$ 12,774.14
Novorossisk	......	......	938.9	......	......	.....	......	938.9	47,038.87
Orenburg	15,734.9	......	.....	......	......	.....	......	15,734.9	895,297.99
Rostov	4,098.4	......	9,332.0	......	......	.....	......	13,430.4	700,683.20
Saratov	7,389.1	......	1,951.6	......	......	.....	......	9,340.7	518,213.08
Theodosia	......	......	2,877.9	......	......	.....	......	2,877.9	144,182.41
Tiflis	......	......	2,576.2	......	......	.....	......	2,576.2	129,048.81
Tzaritzin	4,756.1	......	362.2	......	......	.....	......	5,118.3	288,740.84
Ufa	3,734.8	......	.....	......	......	.....	......	3,734.8	212,505.90
Total	**35,713.3**	......	**18,294.3**	......	......	.....	......	**54,007.6**	**$ 2,948,485.24**
C. NEAR EAST RELIEF DISTRIBUTION									
The Caucasus	......	......	.....	**6,103.9**	**4,927.9**	.....	......	**11,031.8**	**$ 557,874.95**
D. PACKING AND SHIPPING MATERIAL*									
All Districts	......	......	.....	......	......	.....	**1,100.0**	**1,100.0**	....
E. SHORTAGES, DAMAGED, PILFERAGE, ETC.									
Adjustments	**1,225.3**	**5,558.3**	**115.7**	**1,441.5**	**875.6**	**41.3**	......	**9,257.7**	**$ 290,516.36†**
Grand Total	**36,938.6**	**206,953.6**	**18,410.0**	**83,960.4**	**19,118.6**	**19,589.6**	**1,100.0**	**386,070.8**	**$18,662,180.00**

* This represents bags, lumber, twine, nails, needles, slings, and tarpaulins used in shipping to interior. Value prorated to districts above.

† Collected from insurance underwriters and ocean carriers. Cf. "The Grain Trade during the World War," by F. M. Surface (MacMillan, 1928), page 422.

RUSSIA (SOVIET REPUBLICS)—

Table 531*

Summary of Internal Deliveries of Medical and Hospital Supplies,†

District	Metric Tons	Value	District	Metric Tons	Value
Ekaterinoslav	484.0	$ 471,751.46	Sanitary Train No. 2	121.0	117,937.86
Kazan	484.0	471,751.46	Saratov	484.0	471,751.46
Kharkov	484.0	471,751.47	Simbirsk	484.0	471,751.47
Kiev	645.3	629,001.95	Theodosia	161.3	157,250.49
Minsk	484.0	471,751.46	Tzaritzin	161.4	157,250.49
Moscow	887.3	864,877.68	Ufa	564.7	550,376.71
Odessa	484.0	471,751.46			
Orenberg	161.3	157,250.49	Total	**8,066.7**	**$7,862,524.40**
Petrograd	726.0	707,627.20			
Rostov/Don	645.4	629,001.95	Caucasus	215.2‡	209,731.63‡
Samara	484.0	471,751.47			
Sanitary Train No. 1	121.0	117,937.87	Grand Total	**8,281.9**	**$8,072,256.03**

* For complete detail of internal deliveries to districts, see pages 935–86.

† These supplies were a donation from the U.S. Government surplus medical and hospital supplies and the American Red Cross. The tonnage and value, per district, have been made on a percentage basis, in accordance with the figures contained in "A.R.A. Bulletin," Series 2, No. 45, April 1926, by Henry Beeuwkes, M.D., Table 20, pages 89–90.

‡ These figures are based upon the actual weight and value of supplies turned over to the Near East Relief in New York City.

RUSSIA (SOVIET REPUBLICS)—

Table 532

Detail of Paiok (Employees Pay) Deliveries, by

District	Commodities in Net Metric Tons of					
	Flour	Rice	Beans, Peas	Corn Grits	Pork Products	Milk
Alexandrovsk	17.315	4.703	....	5.192	3.539	30.047
Ekaterinoslav	54.631	13.656	....	21.432	10.241	13.695
Elizabethgrad	12.011	4.689	....	2.220	2.117	2.373
Gomel	14.455	3.433	....	3.728	2.419	2.199
Kazan	95.516	42.949	3.446	10.915	17.646	22.716
Kharkov	23.541	11.230	....	1.598	3.854	4.921
Kiev	112.546	45.185	....	12.328	18.411	22.252
Mariupol	5.705	1.103	....	1.667	.501	.784
Minsk	29.240	12.390	....	.....	4.210	5.182
Moscow	305.601	222.580	.194	50.471	65.640	61.052
Nikolaiev	8.217	.....	....	4.388	1.236	1.502
Novorossisk	11.109	4.565	....	1.153	1.633	.914
Odessa	294.303	76.480	....	81.492	39.017	46.072
Orenburg	50.691	20.753	....	7.063	8.782	8.996
Petrograd	60.134	25.353	.025	12.591	11.704	15.140
Rostov	15.457	5.505	....	2.099	1.468	2.765
Samara	174.424	59.777	.149	13.927	15.857	35.845
Saratov	67.243	26.069	3.798	8.619	12.840	15.297
Simbirsk	74.023	37.919	.002	5.035	14.403	16.189
Simferopol	40.168	10.716	....	16.613	8.574	8.883
Ufa	73.642	36.038	2.399	4.015	22.384	15.440
Vitebsk	20.479	8.530	....	1.381	2.963	3.680
Tzaritzin	15.419	3.856	....	3.415	2.907	3.506
Tzaritzin-Rostov	27.655	15.683	....	2.485	6.115	6.118
Total Deliveries	**1,603.525**	**693.162**	**10.013**	**273.827**	**278.461†**	**345.568**

* Detail of miscellaneous food indicated by the following indexes: [a], tea and [b], salt. Of the total metric tons, 14.987 is tea and .196 is salt.

† See right of table for detail. This total is composed of lard substitute, 192.155 metric tons; bacon, 14.263 metric tons (3,930 8-pound pieces) and lard, 72.043 metric tons (31,764 5-pound tins).

American Relief Administration

by Districts—Reconstruction Period, 1919–1924

American Relief Administration

Districts—Reconstruction Period, 1919–1924

1,000 Kilograms or 2,204.6 Pounds					Total Value	Detail of Pork Products		
Cocoa	Sugar	Misc. Food *	Soap	Total Tons		Lard 5-Lb. Tin	Bacon 8-Lb. Piece	Lard Substitute M.T.
1.057	3.496	....	....	65.349	$ 6,700.20	...	...	3.539
2.491	12.084	.628[a]	....	128.858	13,298.86	1,078	180	7.143
.631	2.361	....	....	26.402	2,740.99	192	...	1.682
1.853	2.809	.204[a]	....	31.100	3,045.54	298	25	1.652
6.408	20.606	.124[b]	1.208	221.534	22,537.00	1,152	...	15.033
.710	4.630	.491[a]	....	50.975	5,380.45	645	3	2.380
2.825	25.258	2.831[a]	....	241.636	24,567.46	4,550	206	7.344
....	1.053	....	....	10.813	1,218.22	...	...	.501
.947	5.754	.298[a]	....	58.021	5,786.53	1,060	13	1.759
12.068	110.590	2.120[a]	24.873	855.189	86,899.51	6,558	1,754	44.402
.371	1.505	....	....	17.219	1,725.81	...	...	1.236
....	2.290	.690[a]	....	22.354	2,334.91	720	...	.....
7.165	58.036	4.531[a]	....	607.096	61,621.53	8,659	515	17.509
2.634	10.035	....	.251	109.205	11,166.98	...	...	8.782
3.516	13.974	.113[a]	....	142.550	14,517.07	1,168	135	8.565
.076	2.758	.622[a]	....	30.750	3,248.58	547	...	.227
6.973	27.187	1.304[ab]	....	335.443	34,008.53	1,380	547	10.742
3.474	13.912	....	....	151.252	15,329.22	1,167	...	10.193
3.548	16.662	....	.026	167.807	17,055.02	271	...	13.788
1.885	10.263	.381[a]	....	97.483	9,948.76	862	...	6.617
4.684	15.611	.611[ab]	1.398	176.222	18,070.20	...	326	21.201
.657	3.734	.235[a]	....	41.659	4,263.76	281	39	2.184
1.045	3.032	....	....	33.180	3,248.58	...	187	2.228
1.079	6.115	....	....	65.250	6,598.67	1,176	...	3.448
66.097	**373.755**	**15.183***	**27.756**	**3,687.347**	**$375,312.38**	**31,764**	**3,930**	**192.155**

RUSSIA (SOVIET REPUBLICS)—

Table 533

Detail of Food Remittance (Food Draft) Deliveries*

District	Commodities in Net Metric Tons of 1,000 Kilograms or						
	Flour	Rice	Beans, Peas	Corn Grits	Pork Products	Milk	Cocoa
Alexandrovsk	131.176	5.907	....	27.554	......	26.781	....
Ekaterinoslav	1,796.487	578.327	....	119.316	186.832	549.485	.308
Elizabethgrad	656.351	162.475	....	60.027	43.931	177.885	....
Gomel	1,291.493	318.176	....	148.514	106.868	371.186	3.063
Kazan	209.768	10.682	....	65.938	17.410	61.365	.082
Kharkov	1,379.710	451.289	....	60.814	124.367	407.887	2.554
Kiev	4,951.130	1,510.160	....	468.031	564.362	1,583.115	23.686
Minsk	1,995.998	498.078	....	306.150	227.668	645.462	3.092
Moscow	2,713.966	418.258	.012	627.722	273.772	834.385	8.390
Odessa	4,871.811	1,130.137	....	639.052	421.211	1,477.799	....
Orenburg	67.414	10.862	....	11.475	4.487	17.876	.101
Petrograd	2,145.896	454.891	....	424.530	251.764	701.918	14.693
Rostov/Don	612.102	172.302	....	30.303	33.666	162.100	....
Tzaritzin	81.946	14.447	....	14.860	7.400	23.689	....
Tzaritzin-Rostov	220.128	56.831	....	36.882	29.906	74.834	1.013
Samara	159.990	25.410	....	34.759	22.815	6.054	....
Saratov	1,440.168	341.319	....	262.932	174.948	547.634	5.563
Simbirsk	49.856	5.804	....	11.540	3.498	13.238	.096
Simferopol	503.183	107.459	....	77.803	48.743	151.932	....
Ufa	152.986	40.403	....	19.676	15.757	47.944	1.156
Vitebsk	1,767.539	376.820	....	289.204	181.589	545.893	5.411
Total Deliveries	**27,199.098**	**6,690.037**	**.012**	**3,737.082**	**2,740.994†**	**8,428.462**	**69.208**

* All food remittances were sold for $10.00 per package. Delivery was effected on 98.72 per cent of food draft sales.

† See right of table for detail. Of the total metric tons, 116.954 is lard substitute; 288.781 is bacon (79,576 8-pound pieces); and 2,335.259 is lard (1,029,656 5-pound tins).

RUSSIA (SOVIET REPUBLICS)—

Table 534

Detail of Bulk Sale Deliveries, by Districts—

District	Commodities in Net Metric Tons of 1,000 Kilograms or					
	Flour	Rice	Beans, Peas	Corn Grits	Pork Products	Milk
Alexandrovsk	21.151	.591	....	4.804	......	4.311
Ekaterinoslav	668.855	200.624	....	47.379	61.469	196.893
Elizabethgrad	82.535	30.748	....	7.080	13.354	30.199
Gomel	89.001	20.145	....	17.717	11.986	30.286
Kazan	129.485	14.831	....	42.420	18.682	45.810
Kharkov	358.061	132.961	....	9.126	156.038	115.375
Kiev	1,084.088	267.592	....	123.639	90.558	313.183
Minsk	142.813	35.842	....	24.791	24.602	48.554
Moscow	1,122.366	325.437	.091	190.660	147.470	364.328
Odessa	1,234.511	278.638	....	130.777	67.542	320.020
Orenburg	53.984	15.344	....	6.811	6.502	17.963
Petrograd	373.380	98.300	.049	72.568	59.566	136.778
Rostov/Don	141.487	52.292	....	3.684	15.078	44.787
Tzaritzin	90.493	13.618	....	10.865	6.676	19.770
Tzaritzin-Rostov	117.137	44.182	....	12.143	21.124	45.048
Samara	135.044	31.998	....	26.536	17.121	49.680
Saratov	482.677	130.349	.008	90.054	72.243	176.404
Simbirsk	83.278	28.118	....	6.347	10.599	27.183
Simferopol	126.809	36.056	....	15.819	17.984	41.499
Ufa	100.380	28.637	....	27.537	17.778	38.865
Vitebsk	103.044	40.261	....	23.710	16.849	37.907
Total Deliveries	**6,740.579**	**1,826.564**	**.148**	**894.467**	**853.221***	**2,104.843**

* See right of table for detail. Of the total metric tons, 29.716 is lard substitute; 68.452 is bacon (18,864 8-pound pieces); and 755.053 is lard (332,917 5-pound tins).

† All tea.

‡ The surplus, or difference between cost and selling price of commodities, was used to purchase more child-feeding supplies.

American Relief Administration

by Districts—Reconstruction Period, 1919–1924

2,204.6 Pounds				Total Value (Cost Price)	Total Value (Sales Price)	Detail of Pork Products		
Sugar	Misc. Food	Soap	Total Tons			Lard 5-Lb. Tin	Bacon 8-Lb. Piece	Lard Substitute M.T.
13.385	......	....	204.803	$ 18,302.74	$ 29,510.00	.....	....	.....
318.427	41.174	....	3,590.356	380,164.89	612,950.00	76,475	3,689	.....
110.878	4.372	....	1,215.919	121,582.06	196,030.00	19,370	....	.....
223.559	16.350	....	2,479.209	254,768.47	410,770.00	36,326	2,060	17.005
33.828	4.247	....	403.320	41,970.40	67,670.00	5,798	1,174	.....
231.036	26.835	....	2,684.492	279,676.57	450,930.00	47,026	3,478	5.090
960.519	95.553	....	10,156.556	1,082,047.56	1,744,620.00	220,946	9,139	30.091
385.995	44.870	....	4,107.313	440,903.20	710,880.00	68,092	6,304	50.358
493.859	51.753	....	5,422.117	571,844.41	922,000.00	105,036	9,796	.....
840.756	87.842	....	9,468.608	1,010,353.55	1,629,200.00	172,544	8,234	.....
9.438	.930	....	122.583	12,218.37	19,600.00	404	167	2.965
420.521	49.648	....	4,463.861	478,631.29	771,710.00	89,878	13,205	.....
75.803	10.560	....	1,096.836	112,598.45	181,550.00	11,871	1,858	.....
11.848	1.077	....	155.267	15,844.67	25,550.00	1,930	833	.....
52.194	2.725	....	474.513	49,142.96	79,240.00	13,186	....	.....
26.178	5.258	....	280.464	45,394.03	73,190.00	4,218	3,651	.....
255.756	45.005	....	3,073.325	329,908.33	531,920.00	60,860	10,173	.....
7.338	.816	....	92.186	9,303.33	14,900.00	1,044	253	.212
95.008	6.933	....	991.061	110,455.28	178,090.00	20,734	....	1.718
26.363	3.694	.215	308.194	32,778.72	52,850.00	4,088	1,386	1.455
326.425	32.451	....	3,525.332	373,460.30	602,140.00	69,830	4,176	8.060
4,919.114	**532.093‡**	**.215**	**54,316.315**	**$5,771,349.58**	**$9,305,300.00§**	**1,029,656**	**79,576**	**116.954**

‡ All tea.

§ The surplus, or difference between cost and selling price of commodities, was used to purchase more child-feeding supplies.

American Relief Administration

Reconstruction Period, 1919–1924

2,204.6 Pounds				Total Value (Cost Price)	Total Value (Sales Price)	Detail of Pork Products		
Cocoa	Sugar	Misc. Food	Total Tons			Lard 5-Lb. Tin	Bacon 8-Lb. Piece	Lard Substitute M.T.
.....	2.165	......	33.022	$ 2,852.92	$ 4,265.06	.....	...	....
.794	117.169	11.234	1,304.417	139,530.74	208,595.76	26,434	418	....
.....	21.765	1.329	187.010	20,827.24	31,136.32	5,888	...	....
1.947	19.987	1.054	192.123	20,545.99	30,715.86	4,567	158	1.055
1.048	28.633	3.173	284.082	31,189.15	46,627.18	6,528	767	1.093
3.389	74.735	4.962	854.647	78,596.38	117,400.07	67,558	112	2.410
4.643	189.229	12.893	2,085.825	211,334.51	315,941.01	36,859	277	5.957
.831	33.125	2.014	312.572	32,869.68	49,139.54	7,782	40	6.807
12.675	229.324	22.258	2,414.609	248,165.31	371,102.34	56,828	5,121	....
.....	188.043	9.210	2,228.741	217,876.52	325,721.19	28,851	581	....
.759	10.816	.980	113.159	11,946.69	17,860.07	546	223	4.455
7.708	90.775	6.869	845.993	93,495.10	139,773.37	23,618	1,648	.023
.....	21.095	3.697	282.120	28,512.75	42,626.01	6,554	59	....
.002	9.910	2.174	153.508	18,054.50	26,991.13	1,590	841	.018
1.952	33.091	1.459	276.136	27,907.97	41,721.88	9,314	...	....
15.754	28.677	3.270	308.080	31,377.13	46,908.20	4,204	1,600	1.780
3.927	99.614	18.418	1,073.694	121,150.39	181,117.49	22,155	6,041	.073
1.401	17.431	.872	175.229	18,937.03	28,310.49	4,062	292	.326
.....	27.331	2.054	267.552	29,354.59	43,884.55	7,638	...	.663
4.066	23.355	1.792	242.410	26,524.88	39,654.18	5,339	654	3.296
1.656	26.268	1.582	251.277	26,064.27	38,965.58	6,602	32	1.760
62.552	**1,292.538**	**111.294†**	**13,886.206**	**$1,437,113.74**	**$2,148,457.28‡**	**332,917**	**18,864**	**29.716**

RUSSIA (SOVIET REPUBLICS)—

Table 535

Detail of Eurelcon* Sale Deliveries, by

District	Commodities in Net Metric Tons of				
	Flour	Rice	Beans, Peas	Corn Grits	Pork Products
Alexandrovsk	594.001	139.388	16.775	221.560	53.442
Ekaterinoslav	362.149	50.575	1.457	162.324	32.958
Gomel	56.156	7.458	3.380	17.592	4.955
Kazan	1.117	.605	.037	.088	.102
Kharkov	258.081	78.342	17.306	44.561	22.006
Kiev	239.342	38.558	.....	96.450	11.260
Minsk	248.333	46.348	21.557	72.427	18.596
Moscow	742.647	118.045	15.574	359.775	70.538
Odessa	227.974	55.655	.980	93.067	19.910
Orenburg	441.298	234.309	7.911	30.719	40.351
Petrograd	28.466	5.962	.543	8.921	2.503
Rostov/Don	27.004	2.400	1.230	11.135	2.421
Tzaritzin	1.790	.240	.131	.605	.148
Tzaritzin-Rostov	411.558	103.892	.....	166.236	38.523
Samara	1,117.570	251.202	107.686	572.800	145.685
Saratov	896.111	146.989	14.166	451.183	76.577
Simbirsk	32.935	5.933	1.653	9.149	2.775
Simferopol	907.152	243.733	.....	344.222	85.340
Ufa	22.687	3.904	2.267	6.185	1.924
Vitebsk	101.656	12.343	5.132	38.094	8.416
Total Deliveries	**6,718.027**	**1,545.881**	**217.785**	**2,707.093**	**638.430†**

* Eurelcon refers to organizations belonging to the European Relief Council.

† See right of table for detail. Of the total metric tons, 595.736 is lard substitute; .148 is vegetable oil; and 42.546 is lard (18,759 5-pound tins).

RUSSIA (SOVIET REPUBLICS)—

Table 536

Detail of Internal Sale Deliveries, by

District	Commodities in Net Metric Tons of 1,000 Kilograms or						
	Flour	Rice	Beans, Peas	Corn Grits	Pork Products	Milk	Cocoa
Alexandrovsk	2.034	.232	....	21.613	.220	.762	.063
Ekaterinoslav	186.763	36.240	....	57.991	16.394	39.409	7.149
Elizabethgrad	.424	.048	....	2.883	.074	.044	.017
Gomel	2.400	.727	....	2.620	.072	.936	.067
Kazan	45.634	1.373	1.044	18.421	2.958	26.757	3.202
Kharkov	7.113	1.900	....	1.818	.331	1.372	.042
Kiev	41.788	.093	1.992	20.888	17.700	.218	4.768
Mariupol	.909	.046	....	5.935	.148	....	....
Minsk	1.319	.122	.005	4.335	.301	.544	.029
Moscow	785.082	74.908	15.602	57.237	54.509	206.624	55.098
Novorossisk	5.112	......	....	1.093	......	....	....
Odessa	423.013	58.549	.773	152.573	26.772	78.013	11.824
Orenburg	5.607	2.444	.307	5.973	.831	1.319	.318
Petrograd	243.913	26.432	9.684	53.182	32.662	32.790	7.536
Rostov/Don	.540	.056	....	.011	.086	.566	....
Samara	7.991	1.199	.389	.889	.758	15.075	.485
Saratov	138.365	46.021	.119	44.563	13.228	45.685	5.356
Simbirsk	4.828	2.449	.866	.559	.946	2.411	.245
Simferopol	176.386	56.879	....	58.678	15.921	60.442	7.561
Ufa	33.161	3.901	.769	121.000	.472	93.133	.460
Vitebsk	.833	.165	....	.062	.125	.457	.021
Tzaritzin	8.329	.610	.062	3.365	1.422	12.052	.461
Tzaritzin-Rostov	203.139	30.054	....	.056	24.203	86.700	10.519
Total Deliveries	**2,324.683**	**344.448**	**31.612**	**635.745**	**210.133†**	**705.309**	**115.221**

* Detail of miscellaneous food indicated by the following indexes: [a], tea; [b], salt; [c], corned beef; [d], oil. Of the total metric tons, 5.246 is tea; 4.649 is salt; 1.153 is corned beef; and .041 is oil.

† See right of table for detail. Of the total metric tons, 184.454 is lard substitute; 3.285 is bacon (904 8-pound pieces); and 22.394 is lard (9,874 5-pound tins).

American Relief Administration

Districts—Reconstruction Period, 1919–1924

1,000 Kilograms or 2,204.6 Pounds					Total Value (Cost price)	Total Value (Sales Price)	Detail of Pork Products	
Milk	Cocoa	Sugar	Misc. Food	Total Tons			Lard 5-Lb. Tin	Lard Substitute M.T.
227.864	24.981	97.354	....	1,375.365	$ 158,318.41	$ 186,947.98	...	53.442
128.806	15.696	58.556	....	812.521	42,076.99	49,686.00	...	32.958
20.214	2.194	8.972	....	120.921	12,491.16	14,750.00	...	4.955
.370	.044	.162	....	2.525	237.12	280.00	...	.102
93.368	10.354	41.276	....	565.294	57,024.88	67,337.00	...	22.006
67.656	9.655	37.008	....	499.929	42,546.99	50,240.99	...	11.260
87.644	9.834	38.820	....	543.559	52,434.06	61,916.00	88	18.396
246.358	54.325	91.985	....	1,699.247	156,556.10	184,866.98	18,671	28.192
83.061	9.511	36.224	....	526.382	45,433.93	53,649.99	...	19.910
138.266	17.969	65.743	....	976.566	95,653.46	112,950.99	...	40.351
9.241	1.137	3.983	....	60.756	6,356.52	7,506.00	...	2.503
9.863	1.180	4.405	....	59.638	5,968.07	7,047.31	...	2.421
.653	.072	.288	....	3.927	465.77	550.00	...	.148
141.981	16.594	63.345	....	942.129	96,234.14	113,636.68	...	38.523
600.178	41.063	298.859	19.134	3,154.177	332,416.45	392,529.11	...	145.685
327.202	48.235	143.167	.003	2,103.633	198,799.92	234,750.00	...	76.577
11.866	1.401	5.203	....	70.915	7,247.41	8,558.00	...	2.775
297.609	37.180	136.060	....	2,051.296	194,218.41	229,340.00	...	85.340
8.089	.907	3.599	....	49.562	4,899.92	5,786.00	...	1.924
36.645	4.163	16.030	....	222.479	25,741.94	30,396.99	...	8.416
2,536.934	**306.495**	**1,151.039**	**19.137‡**	**15,840.821**	**$1,535,121.65**	**$1,812,726.02§**	**18,759**	**595.884¶**

‡ Of the total metric tons, 19.134 is salt and .003 tea.
§ The surplus, or difference between cost and selling price of commodities, was used to purchase more child-feeding supplies.

¶ Of the total metric tons, .148 is vegetable oil.

American Relief Administration

Districts—Reconstruction Period, 1919–1924

2,204.6 Pounds				Total Value (Cost price)	Total Value (Sales Price)	Detail of Pork Products		
Sugar	Misc. Food *	Soap	Total Tons			Lard 5-Lb. Tin	Bacon 8-Lb. Piece	Lard Substitute M.T.
.504	....	....	25.428	$ 2,146.63	$ 2,222.86	..	..	.220
28.112	.181[a]	....	372.239	30,630.79	31,718.61	77	4	16.204
.113	.007[a]	....	3.610	247.68	256.48	8	..	.056
.385	....	....	7.207	577.94	598.46	..	2	.065
13.761	.988[abc]	.711	114.849	9,494.72	9,831.91	4	4	2.934
.425	.009[a]	....	13.010	990.76	1,025.95	58	50	.018
10.831	.382[a]	....	98.660	8,173.72	8,464.00	592	5	16.339
.132	....	....	7.170	577.94	598.46	..	..	.148
.455	.010[a]	....	7.120	495.38	512.97	107	3	.047
98.649	5.478[abc]	1.113	1,354.300	111,955.21	115,931.18	8,777	186	33.928
16.841	....	....	23.046	1,898.94	1,966.38	..	..	......
68.716	1.410[a]	....	821.643	67,949.18	70,362.32	109	25	26.431
1.573	.103[b]	.014	18.489	1,486.13	1,538.91	..	..	.831
124.230	1.204[ac]	....	531.633	43,923.41	45,483.30	53	591	30.397
.224	.001[a]	....	1.484	165.12	170.98	20	..	.041
2.778	.110[ab]	....	29.674	2,394.32	2,479.35	..	..	.758
20.919	.012[a]	....	314.268	25,924.72	26,845.41	6	17	13.152
3.338	....	....	15.642	1,238.44	1,282.42	..	..	.946
28.679	.002[a]	....	404.548	33,437.93	34,625.44	..	..	15.921
3.322	.145[ab]	.229	256.592	21,053.52	21,801.22	..	10	.436
.274	.028[a]	....	1.965	82.56	85.49	32	3	.042
2.122	1.000[abd]	.098	29.521	2,311.76	2,393.86	..	4	1.407
36.925	.019[a]	....	391.615	32,364.62	33,514.02	31	..	24.133
463.308	**11.089***	**2.165**	**4,843.713**	**$399,521.42**	**$413,709.98‡**	**9,874**	**904**	**184.454**

‡ The surplus, or difference between cost and selling price of commodities, was used to purchase more child-feeding supplies.

RUSSIA (UKRAINE)—
American Organizations Other Than A.R.A.

Table 537 Summary of Relief Deliveries—Armistice Period, 1919

Organization	Clothing	Other Miscellaneous	Total Tons *	Total Value
U.S. Liquidation Commission †—Sales	4,000.0	1,550.0	5,550.0	$8,500,222.67

* Commodities in net metric tons of 1,000 kilograms or 2,204.6 pounds.

† For total deliveries by U.S. Liquidation Commission, cf. Table 122.

RUSSIA (VOLUNTEER ARMY)—
American Relief Administration

Table 538 Detail by Steamers of Relief Deliveries, Paid for by Funds from the Congressional Appropriation for Relief—Armistice Period, 1919

Arrival No.*	Steamer	Port of Sailing	Date of Arrival	Port of Arrival	Wheat Flour	Total Tons †	Total Value
13	Maine ‡	New York	1919 Jan. 28	Constantinople	394.0	394.0	$86,680.00

* Arrival number from Table 111.

† Contents of cargo in net metric tons of 1,000 kilograms or 2,204.6 pounds.

‡Transshipped on British transport War Pointer.

RIGA AGREEMENT

Agreement between the American Relief Administration and the Russian Socialist Federative Soviet Republic

Whereas, a famine condition exists in parts of Russia, and

Whereas, Mr. Maxim Gorky, with the knowledge of the Russian Socialist Federative Soviet Republic, has appealed through Mr. Hoover to the American people for assistance to the starving and sick people, more particularly the children, of the famine stricken parts of Russia, and

Whereas, Mr. Hoover and the American people have read with great sympathy this appeal on the part of the Russian people in their distress and are desirous, solely for humanitarian reasons, of coming to their assistance, and

Whereas, Mr. Hoover, in his reply to Mr. Gorky, has suggested that supplementary relief might be brought by the American Relief Administration to up to a million children in Russia;

Therefore, it is agreed between the American Relief Administration, an unofficial volunteer American charitable organization under the chairmanship of Mr. Herbert Hoover, hereinafter called the A.R.A., and the Russian Socialist Federative Soviet Republic, hereinafter called the Soviet Authorities,

That the A.R.A. will extend such assistance to the Russian people as is within its power, subject to the acceptance and fulfillment of the following conditions on the part of the Soviet Authorities who hereby declare that there is need of this assistance on the part of the A.R.A.

The Soviet Authorities agree:

First: That the A.R.A. may bring into Russia such personnel as the A.R.A. finds necessary in the carrying out of its work and the Soviet Authorities guarantee them full liberty and protection while in Russia. Non-Americans and Americans who have been detained in Soviet Russia since 1917 will be admitted on approval by the Soviet Authorities.

Second: That they will, on demand of the A.R.A., immediately extend all facilities for the entry into and exit from Russia of the personnel mentioned in (1) and while such personnel are in Russia the Soviet Authorities shall accord them full liberty to come and go and move about Russia on official business and shall provide them with all necessary papers such as safe-conducts, laissez passer, etcetera, to facilitate their travel.

Third: That in securing Russian and other local personnel the A.R.A. shall have complete freedom as to selection and the Soviet Authorities will, on request, assist the A.R.A. in securing same.

Fourth: That on delivery by the A.R.A. of its relief supplies at the Russian ports of Petrograd, Murmansk, Archangel, Novorossisk, or other Russian ports as mutually agreed upon, or the nearest practicable available ports in adjacent countries, decision to lie with the A.R.A., the Soviet Authorities will bear all further costs such as discharge, handling, loading, and transportation to interior base points in the areas where the A.R.A. may operate. Should demurrage or storage occur at above ports mutually agreed upon as satisfactory such demurrage and storage is for the account of the Soviet Authorities. For purposes of this agreement the ports of Riga, Reval, Libau, Hango, and Helsingfors are also considered satisfactory ports. Notice of at least five days will be given to Soviet representatives at respective ports in case the Soviet Authorities are expected to take c.i.f. delivery.

Fifth: That they will at their own expense supply the necessary storage at interior base points mentioned in paragraph (4) and handling and transportation from same to all such other interior points as the A.R.A. may designate.

Sixth: That in all above storage and movement of relief supplies they will give the A.R.A. the same priority over all other traffic as the Soviet Authorities give their own relief supplies, and on demand of the A.R.A. will furnish adequate guards and convoys.

Seventh: That they will give free import and re-export and guarantee freedom from requisition to all A.R.A. supplies of whatever nature. The A.R.A. will repay the Soviet Authorities for expenses incurred by them on re-exported supplies.

Eighth: That the relief supplies are intended only for children and the sick, as designated by the A.R.A. in accordance with paragraph (24), and remain the property of the A.R.A. until actually consumed by these children and the sick, and are to be distributed in the name of the A.R.A.

Ninth: That no individual receiving A.R.A. rations shall be deprived of such local supplies as are given to the rest of the population.

Tenth: That they will guarantee and take every step to insure that relief supplies belonging to the A.R.A. will not go to the general adult population nor to the Army, Navy, or Government employees but only to such persons as designated in paragraphs (8) and (24).

Eleventh: The Soviet Authorities undertake to reimburse the A.R.A. in dollars at c.i.f. cost or replace in kind any misused relief supplies.

Twelfth: That the A.R.A. shall be allowed to set up the necessary organizations for carrying out its relief work free from governmental or other interference. The Central and Local Soviet Authorities have the right of representation thereon.

Thirteenth: That the Soviet Authorities will provide:

A. The necessary premises for kitchens, dispensaries and, in as far as possible, hospitals.

B. The necessary fuel and, when available, cooking, distributing, and feeding equipment for the same.

C. The total cost of local relief administration, food preparation, distribution, etc., themselves are in conjunction with local authorities. Mode of payment to be arranged at later date.

D. On demand of the A.R.A. such local medical personnel and assistance, satisfactory to the A.R.A., as are needed to efficiently administer its relief.

E. Without cost railway, motor, water or other transportation for movement of relief supplies and of such personnel as may be necessary to efficiently control relief operations. The Soviet Authorities will for the duration of the A.R.A. operations assign to the A.R.A. for the sole use of its personnel, and transport free of cost, such railway carriages as the A.R.A. may reasonably request.

Fourteenth: In localities where the A.R.A. may be operating and where epidemics are raging, the A.R.A. shall be empowered by the Soviet Authorities to take such steps as may be necessary towards the improvement of sanitary conditions, protection of water supply, etc.

Fifteenth: That they will supply free of charge the necessary offices, garages, storerooms, etc., for the transaction of the A.R.A. business and when available heat, light, and water for same. Further that they will place at the disposal of the A.R.A. adequate residential quarters for the A.R.A. personnel in all localities where the A.R.A. may be operating. All such above premises to be free from seizure and requisition. Examination of above premises will not be made except with knowledge and in presence of the chief of the A.R.A. operations in Russia or his representative and except in case of *flagrant delit,* when examiner will be held responsible in case examination unwarranted.

Sixteenth: That they will give to the A.R.A. complete freedom and priority without cost in the use of existing radio, telegraph, telephone, cable, post, and couriers in Russia and will provide the A.R.A., when available and subject to the consent of competent authorities, with private telegraph and telephone wires and maintenance free of cost.

Seventeenth: To accord the A.R.A. and its American representatives and its couriers the customary diplomatic privileges as to passing the frontiers.

Eighteenth: To supply the A.R.A. free of cost with the necessary gasoline and oil to operate its motor transportation and to transport such motor transportation by rail or otherwise as may be necessary.

Nineteenth: To furnish at the request of the competent A.R.A. Authorities all A.R.A. personnel, together with their impediments and supplies, free transportation in Russia.

Twentieth: To permit the A.R.A. to import and reexport free of duty and requisition such commissary, transport, and office supplies as are necessary for its personnel and administration.

Twenty-first: That they will acquaint the Russian people with the aims and methods of the relief work of the A.R.A. in order to facilitate the rapid development of its efficiency and will assist and facilitate in supplying the American people with reliable and non-political information of the existing conditions and the progress of the relief work as an aid in developing financial support in America.

Twenty-second: That they will bear all expenses of the relief operation other than:

A. Cost of relief supplies at port (see paragraph 4).

B. Direct expenses of American control and supervision of relief work in Russia with exceptions as above. In general they will give the A.R.A. all assistance in their power toward the carrying out of its humanitarian relief operations.

The A.R.A. agrees:

Twenty-third: Within the limits of its resources and facilities, to supply, as rapidly as suitable organization can be effected, food, clothing, and medical relief to the sick and particularly to the children within the age limits as decided upon by the A.R.A.

Twenty-fourth: That its relief distribution will be to the children and sick without regard to race, religion, or social or political status.

Twenty-fifth: That its personnel in Russia will confine themselves strictly to the ministration of relief and will engage in no political or commercial activity whatever. In view of paragraph (1) and the freedom of American personnel in Russia from personal search, arrest, and detention, any personnel contravening this will be withdrawn or discharged on the request of the Central Soviet Authorities. The Central Soviet Authorities will submit to the chief officer of the A.R.A. the reasons for this request and the evidence in their possession.

Twenty-sixth: That it will carry on its operations where it finds its relief can be administered most efficiently and to secure best results. Its principal object is to bring relief to the famine stricken areas of the Volga.

Twenty-seventh: That it will import no alcohol in its relief supplies and will permit customs inspection of its imported relief supplies at points to be mutually agreed upon.

The Soviet Authorities having previously agreed as the absolute *sine qua non* of any assistance on the part of the American people to release all Americans detained in Russia and to facilitate the departure from Russia of all Americans so desiring, the A.R.A. reserves to itself the right to suspend temporarily or terminate all of its relief work in Russia in case of failure on the part of the Soviet Authorities to fully comply with this primary condition or with any condition set forth in the above agreement. The Soviet Authorities equally reserve the right of cancelling this agreement in case of non-fulfillment of any of the above clauses on the part of the A.R.A.

Made in Riga, August Twentieth, Nineteen Hundred and Twenty-one.

On behalf of Council of Peoples Commissaries of the Russian Socialist Federative Soviet Republic.

(*Signed*) MAXIM LITVINOFF
Assistant Peoples Commissary for Foreign Affairs

On behalf of the American Relief Administration.

(*Signed*) WALTER LYMAN BROWN
Director for Europe

Operation	Table No.	Flour	Grain	Rice	Beans, Peas
		ARMISTICE			
Commission for Relief in Belgium, Sales, etc.	103	618.0	19,496.0	975.0	1,498.0
A.R.A.—Cash Settlement	540	1,682.1	....	.....	43.8
Total American Relief	...	**2,300.1**	**19,496.0**	**975.0**	**1,541.8**
France—Russian Prisoners of War in Germany	134	959.6	....	.....	......
Total Relief, Armistice Period	108	**3,259.7**	**19,496.0**	**975.0**	**1,541.8**
		RECONSTRUCTION			
Laura Spelman Rockefeller Memorial through A.R.A.-E.C.F., Russian Refugees, Constantinople	...*	257.0	....	55.0	38.0
Grand Total Relief Deliveries	102	**3,516.7**	**19,496.0**	**1,030.0**	**1,579.8**

* Commodities from Clontarf, Orient, and local purchases. Cf. Special Programs, pages 106–8. C.I.F. value of food was $62,957.64.

SUNDRY ACTIVITIES—American Relief Administration

Table 540 Detail of Deliveries for Cash, by Steamer or Source—Armistice Period, 1919

Arrival No.*	Steamer or Source	Point of Origin	Date of Arrival	Port of Arrival	Contents of Cargoes in Net Metric Tons of 1,000 Kilograms or 2,204.6 Pounds: Wheat Flour	Cereal Flour	Beans, Peas	Pork Products	Lard	Lard Substitute	Milk	Total Tons	Total Value
					A. BELGIUM, C.R.B.								
233	Western Maid, II.	Baltimore	1919 May 29	Rotterdam	**551.2**	**117.1**	....	.....	....	....	...	**668.3**	**$122,638.77**
					B. JADRANSKA BANK								
352	Q.M. Invoices 20, 31	(U.S.A.)	......	Trieste	**160.6**	.....	....	**109.0**	**39.6**	**17.1**	...	**326.3**	**$156,975.28**
					C. MISCELLANEOUS SALES †								
352	Sundry Invoices	(U.S.A.)	......	All Ports	**512.7**	.....	....	.....	....	....	**5.5**	**518.2**	**$ 99,315.69**
					D. U.S. NAVY IN ADRIATIC								
352	Q.M. Invoices 30, 58	(U.S.A.)	......	Gravosa, Trieste	**10.6**	.....	....	**.9**	....	**.7**	**4.5**	**16.7**	**$ 6,325.33**
					E. VIBORG SALES								
303	Democracy, III	St. Nazaire	June 25	Viborg	167.5	.....	....	.....	....	....	...	167.5	$ 36,022.18
295	Dio	New York	June 22	Viborg	162.4	.....	43.8	.....	....	....	...	206.2	43,492.83
	Total				**329.9**	.....	**43.8**	.....	....	....	...	**373.7**	**$ 79,515.01**
	Total Sundry Cash Sales—To Table 120				**1,565.0**	**117.1**	**43.8**	**109.9**	**39.6**	**17.8**	**10.0**	**1,903.2**	**$464,770.08**

* From Table 111.

† The detail of miscellaneous sales, showing source, port of arrival, and total value, is as follows:

	Total Value
Magazzini Generali (Trieste)	$ 8,895.86
American Red Cross (Gravosa)	449.31
Officers Mess at Gravosa (Gravosa)	2,316.25
Services Paid for in Commodities (Gravosa)	4,343.82
Sales Locally for Cash (All Ports)	74,889.12
Sales of Damaged Commodities (All Ports)	8,421.33
Total	$99,315.69

Summary of Relief Deliveries

Corn Grits	Pork Products	Milk	Cocoa	Sugar	Misc. Food	Soap	Clothing and Misc.	Total Tons	Total Value
Commodities in Net Metric Tons of 1,000 Kilograms or 2,204.6 Pounds									
PERIOD									
....	2,845.0	756.0	261.0	220.0	347.0	11.0	24,365.0	51,392.0	$21,990,430.40
....	167.3	10.0	.....	.....	.....	....	....	1,903.2	464,770.08
....	**3,012.3**	**766.0**	**261.0**	**220.0**	**347.0**	**11.0**	**24,365.0**	**53,295.2**	**$22,455,200.48**
....	1,050.0	.....	.....	181.3	481.1	....	....	2,672.0	$ 1,100,917.00
....	**4,062.3**	**766.0**	**261.0**	**401.3**	**828.1**	**11.0**	**24,365.0**	**55,967.2**	**$23,556,117.48**
PERIOD									
23.0	28.0	122.0	11.0	19.0	9.0	....	....	562.0	$ 98,622.59
23.0	**4,090.3**	**888.0**	**272.0**	**420.3**	**837.1**	**11.0**	**24,365.0**	**56,529.2**	**$23,654,740.07**

Table 541

TURKEY—Summary of Relief Deliveries

Operation	Table No.	Commodities in Net Metric Tons of 1,000 Kilograms or 2,204.6 Pounds			Total Value
		Wheat Flour	Cereal Flour	Total Tons	
A.R.A.—Cash Sales to J. W. Whittall & Company	542	17,812.0	2,466.3	20,278.3	$4,369,404.30

TURKEY—American Relief Administration

Detail by Steamers of Relief Deliveries Paid for by J. W. Whittall & Company—Armistice Period, 1919

Table 542

Arrival No.*	Steamer	Port of Sailing	Date of Arrival	Port of Arrival	Contents of Cargoes in Net Metric Tons of 1,000 Kilograms or 2,204.6 Pounds			Total Value
					Wheat Flour	Cereal Flour	Total Tons	
			1919					
13	Maine	New York	Jan. 28	Constantinople	4,069.4	......	4,069.4	$ 985,325.00
36	West Mount	New York	Feb. 21	Derindje	4,521.7	......	4,521.7	1,098,112.80
193	Eastern Sun	Philadelphia	May 15	Constantinople	5,244.3	......	5,244.3	1,002,178.83
357	Elbing	Philadelphia	July 20	Constantinople	3,976.6	2,466.3	6,442.9	1,283,787.67
	Total Sales—To Table 120				**17,812.0**	**2,466.3**	**20,278.3**	**$4,369,404.30**

* From Table 111.

Operation	Table No.	Flour	Grain	Rice
				U.S. FOOD
Sales—Financed by U.S. Treasury Credits	106	1,350,580.8	3,274,037.9	24,289.4
				ARMISTICE
A.R.A.—Cash Settlement*	131	46,283.9	....	....
Grand Total Relief Deliveries	...	**1,396,864.7**	**3,274,037.9**	**24,289.4**

* This sale to the United Kingdom was for delivery to Austria under the Joint Allied Finance (Table 131) and hence represents a duplication. For purposes of the summary of all relief deliveries this transaction is deducted, and the total sales to the United Kingdom are taken as those made under the United States Food Administration only, viz., $1,375,484,734.33.

Summary of Relief Deliveries

Beans, Peas	Pork Products	Milk	Sugar	Misc. Food	Forage	Total Tons	Total Value
Commodities in Net Metric Tons of 1,000 Kilograms or 2,204.6 Pounds							
ADMINISTRATION PERIOD							
23,878.9	957,641.3	181,886.2	1,539,236.7	439,799.9	813,945.6	8,605,296.7	$1,375,484,734.33
PERIOD							
....	....	1,088.0	....	....	....	47,371.9	$ 10,618,045.72
23,878.9	**957,641.3**	**182,974.2**	**1,539,236.7**	**439,799.9**	**813,945.6**	**8,652,668.6**	**$1,386,102,780.05**

APPENDIX III

MEDICAL TABLES 1, 2

The spelling of the names of three cities or district headquarters have been changed to conform with the spelling adopted by the A.R.A. Accounting Department in food deliveries: Cherkov to Kharkov, Kief to Kiev, and Simpheropol to Simferopol.

MEDICAL TABLES 2, 3

The captions of the original reports submitted to the President and filed with the Congress of the United States read:

"AMERICAN RELIEF ADMINISTRATION Report on The Distribution in Russia of Army Surplus Medical Supplies under the Authorization of Congress, 1922–1923."

"AMERICAN RELIEF ADMINISTRATION Supplementary Report on the Delivery in the United States to The Near East Relief of Army Surplus Medical Supplies under the Authorization of Congress for Distribution in Southern Russia by the Near East Relief, 1922–1923."

The captions on these reports have been changed to conform with the Act of Congress of January 20, 1922, and the Executive Order of January 24, 1922, to wit:

Medical Table 2

"American Relief Administration Report of the Distribution in Russia of the United States Government Surplus Medical and Hospital Supplies, 1922–1923."

Medical Table 3

"American Relief Administration Detail of Deliveries of the U.S. Government Surplus Medical and Hospital Supplies to the Near East Relief for Distribution in Southern Russia, 1922–1923."

AMERICAN RELIEF ADMINISTRATION

Detail by Districts of the Distribution in Russia of Medical and Hospital Supplies Donated by the American Red Cross,* 1921–1923

Medical Table 1†

DRUGS AND MEDICINES

Commodity and Unit	Shortage	Detail of Deliveries by Districts																	Total
		1 Alexandrovsk-Ekaterinoslav	2 Kharkov	3 Kazan	4 Kiev	5 Minsk	6 Moscow	7 Odessa	8 Orenburg	9 Petrograd	10 Rostov	11 Samara	12 Sanitary Trains, Nos. 1 and 2	13 Saratov	14 Simbirsk	15 Theodosia-Simferopol	16 Tzaritzin	17 Ufa	
Acacia, ½ lb	......	200	100	200	......	......	1,000	200	......	......	300	200	1,300	200	......	......	......	300	4,000
Acacia, 1 lb	18	95	100	17	......	3	720	100	117	17	150	167	......	117	117	6	117	139	2,000
Acetanilidum, 4 oz	......	400	350	420	50	50	919	350	100	400	400	470	600	300	350	......	100	421	5,680
Acetphenetidinum, ¼ lb	14	964	1,214	1,484	1,104	892	2,303	850	356	1,175	1,000	1,000	2,060	1,239	920	301	370	1,022	18,268
Acid, boricum, ½ lb	15	20	800	3,800	800	836	421	800	2,000	3,600	......	3,800	8	2,600	2,600	100	2,200	1,600	26,000
Acid, boricum, 1 lb	......	800	1,300	800	1,000	1,000	2,400	800	......	400	800	800	1,900	800	800	400	......	1,000	15,000
Acid, hydrochloric, ½ lb	......	152	225	282	175	245	769	225	6	212	300	322	400	137	187	65	25	193	3,920
Acid, salicylic, 3 oz	......	6	200	307	200	276	56	200	230	230	25	240	2	230	230	12	230	260	2,934
Acid, salicylic, 4 oz	3	400	800	800	600	200	497	800	200	400	2,250	850	800	800	200	200	400	600	10,800
Acid, salicylic, ½ lb	......	......	50	100	50	50	250	50	......	100	100	100	......	100	......	......	......	50	1,000
Acid, tannic, 3 oz	......	300	220	260	280	206	297	180	140	460	240	260	8	260	160	10	140	263	3,684
Acid, tannic, 4 oz	......	390	......	700	40	40	1,448	740	40	700	700	1,090	1,400	40	390	40	40	740	8,538
Acid, tannic, 10 lb	18	30	10	10	10	10	10	20	......	10	30	10	12	40	20	10	......	20	270
Acid, tartaric, lbs	24	150	200	150	200	175	226	125	100	......	200	150	250	150	150	......	50	200	2,500
Adrenalin chloride, 20 and 25 tabs., tubes	80	2,100	2,150	3,300	2,750	2,260	6,339	3,150	350	3,480	3,600	3,350	15,200	2,800	2,196	1,000	450	3,055	57,610
Alcohol, absolute and ethyl, qts	306	648	722	1,610	650	652	1,865	1,130	510	150	1,537	1,110	1,440	1,110	1,014	778	......	1,470	21,262
Ammonia chloride, ¼ lb	9	450	725	991	325	561	1,117	625	182	691	1,025	1,141	817	491	666	130	250	584	10,780
Ammonia chloride troches, 250 tabs	169	......	100	240	100	100	144	100	180	270	......	280	47	180	180	......	180	180	2,450
Aqua hydrogen dioxide, 1 lb	21	150	75	215	150	200	462	150	15	265	50	265	100	140	90	50	50	202	2,650
Argyrol, 1 oz	18	2,020	1,440	2,260	1,440	1,440	2,912	1,200	480	1,600	1,350	2,020	1,590	1,060	1,780	702	240	1,200	24,752
Argenti Nitras crystals, 1 oz	......	......	30	88	30	43	63	30	88	88	......	88	......	88	88	6	80	100	910
Arsenic trioxide, 250 tabs	124	......	58	330	40	64	168	40	10	10	40	370	662	300	260	60	10	250	2,796
Arsenic trioxide, 500 tabs	......	300	232	100	300	400	718	250	......	500	650	650	1,600	......	200	100	......	......	6,000
Aspirin powder, 1 oz	......	......	......	......	......	10	54	......	......	......	......	......	......	......	......	......	......	......	64
Aspirin powder, 4 oz	123	1,240	1,000	1,000	500	924	1,763	1,100	......	700	1,375	1,200	3,100	1,250	1,000	100	......	475	16,850
Aspirin tablets, 250 tabs	......	......	200	......	......	200	400	......	......	200	200	200	400	......	200	......	......	......	2,000
Aspirin tablets, 500 tabs	433	300	400	1,000	500	210	706	400	700	1,000	200	1,100	4	1,100	900	100	700	600	10,353
Atropine sulphate, 20 tabs., tubes	137	600	50	50	50	125	490	50	......	50	380	50	900	550	50	1,000	50	50	4,632
Balsam peru, ½ lb	102	300	250	400	350	149	1,396	350	50	100	400	450	3	100	150	50	50	350	5,000
Balsam peru, lbs	......	50	50	50	50	25	50	......	......	50	50	50	50	......	50	......	......	50	575
Barium sulphate, 1 lb	......	......	......	......	......	12	73	......	......	......	......	......	......	......	......	20	......	......	105
Barbital, 100 tabs	......	100	10	......	......	......	390	100	......	......	200	......	......	......	......	......	......	200	1,000
Barbital, 1 oz	......	......	......	250	......	......	......	......	......	......	......	250	500	......	......	......	......	......	1,000
Bismuth subnitrate, ½ lb	87	1,238	1,238	1,634	1,383	593	2,611	1,044	535	835	1,044	1,878	2,040	1,323	729	224	510	1,358	20,304
Bismuth subnitrate, lbs	......	100	300	300	200	200	500	300	......	300	......	200	......	200	200	......	......	200	3,000
Cannabis indica, ¼ lb	......	50	......	20	......	25	73	......	20	20	......	20	......	20	20	12	......	20	300
Caffeine citrate, ½ oz	48	......	200	1,665	200	108	495	300	45	845	......	815	908	1,615	337	820	30	45	8,476
Caffeine citrate, 1 oz	......	200	200	700	500	500	1,500	600	......	500	800	700	2,900	500	700	......	......	700	11,000
Caffeine citrate, lbs	23	......	......	6	......	......	7	......	25	13	......	15	......	30	25	......	25	......	169
Caffeine sodii benzoate, 2 oz	2	988	500	790	400	......	1,235	150	......	150	1,380	1,130	451	800	384	......	......	640	9,000
Caffeine sodii benzoate, lbs	......	......	100	50	50	100	......	100	......	50	50	50	300	50	50	......	......	50	1,000
Caffeine sodii benzoate, 500 tabs	......	400	200	200	......	......	200	......	......	400	......	......	......	200	......	200	......	200	2,000
Caffeine sodii salicylate, 250 tabs	......	300	......	300	......	......	......	300	......	......	300	300	600	300	300	......	......	300	3,000
Caffeine sodii salicylate, 500 tabs	16	......	85	75	295	335	1,120	85	66	23	95	318	......	318	279	60	20	43	3,233

Commodity and Unit	Shortage	Detail of Deliveries by Districts 1	2	3	4	5	6	7	8	9	10	11	12	13	14	15	16	17	Total
Calcium glycerophosphate, ½ lb.	......	350	200	250	225	125	600	225	......	200	350	350	375	325	100	......	......	325	4,000
Calcium glycerophosphate, 1 lb.	......	50	50	183	100	65	158	50	83	58	150	133	1	183	83	12	58	83	1,500
Camphor, 1 lb.	......	350	100	110	100	110	399	......	10	10	100	210	151	210	10	10	10	210	2,100
Cathartic compound pills, 1,000 tabs.	7	5	......	......	......	35	14	......	30	......	......	......	2	......	40	20	40	6	199
Chloretone capsules, 500 tabs.	18	......	200	25	100	28	51	20	100	15	......	200	2	50	100	6	100	40	1,055
Chloroform, ¼ lb.	86	1,280	2,540	3,460	2,840	2,300	5,452	2,160	1,800	4,460	2,160	4,480	2,760	3,860	3,820	200	1,600	3,860	49,118
Chloroform, 2 lb.	......	160	140	120	160	160	660	160	......	120	140	100	120	120	200	40	......	100	2,500
Cocaine hydrochloride, ¼ oz.	......	50	60	95	60	106	200	60	50	90	60	75	70	......	40	......	50	50	1,116
Cocaine hydrochloride, ⅛ oz.	......	......	20	20	20	20	26	20	......	......	......	20	8	20	......	58	......	12	244
Cocaine hydrochloride, 25 oz.	......	......	......	......	1	......	4	......	......	......	......	......	......	......	......	......	......	......	5
Cocaine hydrochloride, tubes.	10	......	......	300	......	......	80	......	......	......	312	60	......	100	100	......	......	......	962
Codeine sulphate, 1 oz.	......	100	200	415	200	224	552	300	260	460	100	365	2	355	260	48	200	260	4,301
Collodion, 1 oz.	70	250	......	240	......	60	403	......	250	240	......	200	1,510	200	250	12	250	25	3,960
Creosote, 1 oz.	......	450	72	132	72	124	488	72	80	870	72	152	1,202	252	145	58	80	89	4,410
Creosote, 8 oz.	......	200	400	250	400	400	700	400	......	......	600	400	400	450	600	200	......	600	6,000
Creta praeparata, ⅛ lb.	......	200	240	165	240	254	364	135	64	285	200	185	505	165	265	106	140	267	3,780
Creta praeparata, 1 lb.	......	250	......	500	......	......	250	......	......	......	250	250	250	250	......	......	......	......	2,000
Digitalis folio capsules, 250 tabs.	......	......	......	500	500	......	500	......	......	......	......	......	......	......	......	......	......	500	2,000
Digitalis folio capsules, 500 tabs.	102	100	100	350	100	124	783	100	300	110	......	400	303	800	210	48	200	800	4,930
Digitalin, H.T., tubes.	100	2,780	5,000	6,000	10,500	5,000	9,120	5,000	......	5,000	6,000	5,000	22,500	6,000	5,000	2,000	......	5,000	100,000
Emetine hydrochloride, H.T., tubes.	......	10	......	5	......	20	50	......	5	5	......	5	......	5	5	24	......	17	151
Emplastrum Sinapis, rolls.	1	215	240	250	240	186	344	140	85	75	180	195	101	295	280	150	90	85	3,152
Emplastrum Sinapis, 100 in box, bxs.	......	......	......	......	......	......	117	......	......	......	......	250	......	......	8	......	......	125	500
Ether, ¼ lb.	4	1,600	2,450	4,800	1,400	1,900	9,161	2,450	2,000	4,350	2,600	2,500	4,598	4,600	2,000	800	2,000	1,800	51,013
Eserine salicylas, ⅛ oz.	......	25	10	24	10	21	26	10	......	10	......	24	......	30	25	12	10	5	242
Extractum belladonnae foliorum, 1 oz.	......	650	400	707	411	290	1,391	290	37	257	200	707	121	307	307	250	40	787	7,152
Extractum rhamni purschiannae, 250 tabs.	......	150	150	779	750	198	663	150	20	620	300	870	3,602	170	70	648	20	20	9,180
Extract thyroid gland, 250 tabs.	15	50	......	50	......	......	485	......	......	......	100	......	250	50	50	......	......	......	1,050
Ferri et quininae, soluble, 3 oz.	4	44	350	450	350	324	590	350	90	450	450	400	2	710	190	36	140	440	5,370
Fluid extract ipecac, ½ lb.	......	344	560	285	558	340	758	460	164	87	488	416	150	560	316	228	216	480	6,410
Glycerine, 1 lb.	......	350	200	440	225	235	622	275	90	315	425	440	450	390	240	18	25	390	5,130
Glycerine, 1 qt.	19	125	125	125	150	100	331	125	......	......	125	125	150	125	125	50	......	125	1,925
Guaiacol carbonate, 1 lb.	2	150	278	260	178	183	642	228	36	308	228	314	421	314	236	103	33	286	4,200
Gum opium, lbs.	......	......	15	15	15	15	395	15	......	......	......	15	......	15	......	......	......	......	500
Hexamethylenamine, 1 oz.	......	250	830	430	620	83	803	620	140	180	200	480	502	210	184	3	100	120	5,755
Hydrargyri chloridum mite, 2 oz.	16	850	486	310	500	......	493	500	40	60	800	350	2,603	740	265	1	40	40	8,094
Hydrargyri chloridum mite, 250 tabs.	......	820	2,440	100	1,000	888	288	1,720	......	150	1,440	150	4,240	250	285	12	60	160	14,003
Hydrargyri chloridum mite, 500 tabs.	11	......	......	400	......	20	10	......	315	330	......	230	......	315	327	......	327	15	2,300
Hydrargyri iodidum flavum, 1,000 tabs.	......	2	......	145	20	31	50	20	20	83	......	125	2	50	50	10	50	10	668
Hydrargyri iodidum flavum, 250 tabs.	......	75	75	75	100	75	226	175	......	......	175	175	600	75	75	......	......	100	2,001
Hydrargyri salicylas, 1 oz.	......	200	210	350	260	178	385	200	200	310	200	680	120	550	400	4	175	230	4,652
Ichthyol, ¼ lb.	......	50	606	50	406	242	297	606	206	50	806	417	1,630	216	392	414	206	206	6,800
Ichthyol, ½ lb.	......	200	200	200	200	200	300	......	......	......	......	200	......	200	100	......	......	200	2,000
Ichthyol, 1 lb.	6	......	4	6	4	5	19	4	6	6	......	6	......	6	6	......	6	16	100
Ichthyol, 2 lb.	41	38	......	......	......	......	......	......	......	......	......	......	......	......	......	......	......	21	100
Iodoform, 1 oz.	......	......	45	45	20	25	30	20	45	45	......	45	......	45	45	......	45	45	500
Iodoform, ¼ lb.	......	50	......	......	......	......	197	......	......	......	......	......	3	......	......	......	......	......	250
Iodine swabs, 6 in box, bxs.	15	......	2,800	11,200	2,800	280	8,825	2,800	9,800	11,200	......	12,600	......	11,200	9,800	280	9,800	7,000	100,400
Iodine, 1 oz.	97	96	860	621	1,060	848	580	460	368	615	400	791	1,867	550	531	200	416	410	10,770
Iodine, 2 oz.	7	1,000	478	999	500	100	1,045	610	35	800	650	909	832	650	450	70	465	900	10,500
Liquid wax, gals.	......	......	36	30	36	6	48	36	30	60	6	30	......	36	30	......	30	12	426
Magnesium sulphate, 4 lb.	......	......	96	970	96	3	196	96	530	1,020	......	970	......	970	970	10	50	770	6,747
Magnesium sulphate, 5 lb.	1	280	200	240	......	......	640	240	......	200	320	240	1,039	240	160	......	......	200	4,000
Menthol, 1 oz.	......	......	......	......	......	......	444	......	......	......	100	100	256	100	......	......	......	......	1,000
Mistura glycyrrhizae, tabs.	164,000	......	450,000	650,000	450,000	466,400	191,600	450,000	690,000	708,000	......	720,000	5,000	472,000	1,080,000	24,000	1,080,000	560,000	8,161,000
Morphine sulphate, ¼ oz.	195	30	77	117	77	65	271	77	27	107	60	67	......	57	27	222	27	57	1,560

[Continued on next page]

Commodity and Unit	Shortage	Detail of Deliveries by Districts																	Total
		1	2	3	4	5	6	7	8	9	10	11	12	13	14	15	16	17	
Morphine sulphate, ¼ oz	......	......	80	80	80	176	182	80	25	......	......	94	......	105	25	......	15	14	956
Morphine sulphate, 33,000 tabs., bags	......	......	......	......	½	......	......	½	......	......	......	......	......	......	......	......	......	......	1
Morphine sulphate, tubes	140	1,000	1,100	1,300	1,100	280	2,641	1,100	160	160	1,000	1,160	50	1,160	160	500	160	1,135	14,306
Morphine sulphate, 100 tabs	......	......	......	......	......	......	7	......	......	......	......	......	......	......	......	......	......	......	7
Morphine sulphate, 500 tabs	......	......	......	......	......	......	6	......	......	......	......	......	......	......	......	......	......	......	6
Morphine sulphate, 1,000 tabs	......	......	......	......	......	......	18	......	......	......	......	......	......	......	......	......	......	......	18
Morphine hydrochloride, .4 gr. sol., amp	......	......	......	......	......	......	435	......	......	......	......	......	......	......	......	......	......	......	435
Natrii chloride, amp	8	......	......	24	18	......	16	......	6	24	......	30	......	30	......	......	......	24	180
Naphthalene, 1 lb	14	......	102	400	50	100	803	100	100	......	100	300	201	100	100	130	100	300	3,000
Neosalvarsan, amps	2,582	49,500	30,750	44,285	26,750	29,400	80,099	50,750	2,345	40,285	59,414	38,285	98,200	41,785	44,785	22,795	3,725	33,315	699,050
Nitroglycerine, 25 tabs., amps	......	200	1,350	5,350	1,350	1,450	2,375	1,350	3,350	3,350	......	5,350	20	2,350	3,550	100	2,550	3,350	37,395
Normal saline, tabs	24,000	2,000	60,000	175,000	60,000	25,800	107,400	60,000	115,000	175,000	10,000	135,000	......	155,000	148,000	4,800	105,000	425,000	1,787,000
Novocaine, 1 oz	......	160	67	167	82	77	357	67	7	207	160	167	102	167	167	36	7	47	2,044
Oleoresina aspidii, 1 oz	2	......	126	36	16	32	318	26	26	36	100	136	2	136	26	20	26	126	1,190
Oleum morrhuae, 1 qt	......	1,200	1,425	1,825	1,525	1,225	2,874	1,425	25	1,100	1,600	1,225	580	1,200	800	275	1,125	1,475	20,904
Oleum morrhuae, lbs	2,000	......	10,000	20,600	10,000	10,000	8,400	10,000	6,000	15,400	6,000	20,600	......	17,000	8,000	9,000	......	7,000	160,000
Oleum morrhuae, gal	390	4,050	4,200	5,280	5,400	2,300	7,170	3,600	......	5,730	5,700	5,460	720	4,050	3,900	1,950	......	5,730	66,630
Oleum olivae, pts	......	240	320	496	320	410	893	320	10	576	240	484	......	336	335	160	10	340	5,490
Oleum olivae, gal	......	......	6	4	6	6	......	6	4	8	......	6	1	2	6	......	5	5	65
Oleum olivae, 2 gal	......	3	8	8	8	14	12	8	8	8	5	8	......	7	8	4	8	8	125
Oleum ricini, 1 qt	46	2,125	2,625	3,975	3,750	2,162	5,769	2,875	1,350	3,075	3,000	3,475	2,135	2,825	1,775	1,013	1,425	3,100	46,500
Oleum terebinthinal, 1 pt	......	200	100	200	200	200	300	200	......	......	250	250	400	200	200	100	......	200	3,000
Oleum terebinthinal, 1 qt	1	75	175	215	125	155	542	75	133	243	125	217	327	166	159	75	109	133	3,050
Opii pulvis, 2 oz	......	......	40	20	40	32	18	100	40	......	40	70	2	50	40	28	40	40	600
Pepsin, ¼ lb	1	......	......	50	......	......	247	......	......	......	50	......	......	60	......	......	......	......	408
Petrolatum, 3 lb	......	......	300	780	300	60	242	300	650	800	......	880	......	650	750	18	50	720	6,500
Petrolatum, 5 lb	......	500	900	1,020	1,040	1,140	1,730	940	500	440	1,580	1,060	250	1,580	540	400	540	840	15,000
Petrolatum liquidum, 1 qt	......	50	125	175	125	125	251	125	75	124	125	150	......	200	75	75	75	125	2,000
Phenylis salicylas, 3 oz	7	50	......	......	......	26	297	......	......	......	50	......	1,196	......	......	24	......	......	1,650
Phenylis salicylas, tabs	......	......	......	300,000	......	......	......	......	250,000	350,000	......	350,000	......	250,000	300,000	......	300,000	150,000	2,250,000
Phenylis salicylas, 250 tabs	......	200	200	200	200	......	400	200	......	......	200	200	200	......	......	......	......	......	2,000
Picis liquid, 1 lb	8	697	706	645	706	562	1,603	606	120	649	654	638	1,002	591	220	112	220	570	10,309
Pilocarpine hydrochloride, H.T., tubes	......	100	300	450	300	240	195	435	50	110	250	360	......	360	100	60	50	250	3,610
Pills, aloin compound, 500 tabs	227	......	300	400	300	260	377	200	500	800	100	400	111	500	600	200	600	100	5,975
Pills, ferri compound, 80 tabs	106	350	420	550	350	500	284	450	200	300	350	550	5,503	450	200	120	200	300	11,183
Pills, ipecacuanhae et opii, 500 tabs	306	......	......	200	......	......	42	......	200	100	......	200	2	100	400	......	......	250	2,000
Plaster of Paris, 1 lb	......	100	......	100	......	100	400	100	......	400	100	100	500	......	......	......	......	100	2,000
Potassium bromide, 1 lb	7	102	300	150	300	162	291	300	100	400	100	350	277	150	150	12	200	200	3,551
Potassium iodide, ½ lb	3	100	290	190	540	215	988	315	255	640	270	490	2	847	455	......	195	455	6,250
Potassium iodide, 1 lb	303	200	300	260	100	102	320	200	100	100	260	160	340	100	......	5	100	300	3,250
Potassium iodide, 5 lb	......	......	1	2	1	1	1	1	......	2	......	2	......	1	......	......	......	......	12
Pulvis ipecacuanhae et opii, 500 tabs	......	200	200	400	......	200	950	200	......	......	450	400	400	400	......	......	......	400	4,200
Pulvis ipecacuanhae et opii, ¼ lb	59	100	200	240	100	140	253	200	40	240	100	284	......	140	100	12	......	190	2,398
Quinine hydrochloride and dihydrochl., 5 oz	38	100	......	1,000	......	100	1,612	200	......	100	2,900	1,500	300	2,000	500	50	......	400	10,800
Quinine hydrochloride, 500 tabs	......	......	......	750	......	......	10,995	......	......	750	......	......	......	......	750	......	......	750	13,995
Quinine sulphate, 5 oz	159	200	100	1,100	......	......	1,379	......	......	120	2,400	1,700	1,040	1,500	1,000	......	......	500	11,198
Quinine sulphate, 25 oz	19	180	380	210	297	302	203	317	135	122	656	663	414	366	302	164	135	255	5,120
Quinine sulphate, 32 oz	......	......	......	25	......	......	30	......	25	25	......	25	......	25	25	......	......	35	215
Quinine sulphate, 500 tabs	349	975	1,225	1,742	1,020	620	3,352	864	800	1,150	2,885	2,610	902	2,496	1,200	310	1,150	1,400	25,050
Quinine hydrochloride and dihydrochl., tubes	53	250	1,250	2,075	1,750	1,950	1,160	1,450	1,825	1,125	15,950	9,375	......	9,580	1,825	1,000	1,500	3,075	55,193
Santonin, 250 tabs	100	50	90	127	180	119	187	130	42	7	90	197	1	137	27	24	25	117	1,650
Sodium bicarbonate, 1 lb	148	1,700	3,400	2,772	3,200	3,224	5,096	2,550	922	1,842	2,800	3,352	1,710	3,290	1,792	498	842	2,358	41,496
Sodii carbonas, 1 lb	150	......	......	......	......	50	......	......	......	......	......	......	......	......	......	......	......	......	200
Sodii carbonas monohydratus, 1 lb	......	......	......	......	......	......	55	......	......	......	......	......	......	......	......	45	......	......	100
Sodii salicylas, 6 oz	......	210	325	550	550	237	638	325	125	600	325	450	229	650	225	137	225	445	6,246
Sodii salicylas, 1 lb	......	......	......	40	......	......	......	......	......	......	......	40	......	20	50	......	50	......	200

Commodity and Unit	Shortage	Detail of Deliveries by Districts																	Total
		1	2	3	4	5	6	7	8	9	10	11	12	13	14	15	16	17	
Strophanthinum, H.T., tubes	525	400	400	3,300	400	700	5,706	600	2,000	600	600	5,660	1,010	400	2,000	500	2,000	900	27,701
Strychnine sulphate, tabs	100,000	......	166,750	650,000	200,750	650,000	1,800,000	166,750	300,000	350,000	......	666,050	......	650,000	350,000	100,000	300,000	150,000	6,600,300
Strychnine sulphate, tubes	10	2,000	......	2,000	......	300	3,323	......	500	1,500	......	1,000	......	1,120	1,002	150	500	500	13,905
Strychnine sulphate, 250 tabs	......	......	......	......	......	......	123	......	......	......	......	......	3	......	......	24	......	......	150
Sulphur lotum, 1 lb	......	......	......	12	......	......	11	......	12	12	......	12	......	12	12	5	......	12	100
Syrup ferrous iodide, ½ lb	......	444	807	885	963	569	1,420	663	288	954	763	853	805	879	716	268	194	832	12,303
Tincture aconite, 1 oz	14	260	350	313	325	325	546	325	161	275	475	463	503	295	381	78	171	320	5,580
Tincture of digitalis, ½ lb	......	844	788	869	888	654	1,700	788	169	375	988	807	1,861	1,008	519	146	144	1,013	13,561
Tincture of iodine, 1 qt	......	......	24	......	......	......	5	......	......	......	......	......	......	......	10	......	......	......	39
Tincture of nux vomica, ½ lb	11	144	340	174	360	166	288	360	216	102	144	136	603	360	216	156	144	360	4,280
Tincture of opium, 1 lb	23	25	162	150	137	162	418	107	100	125	88	185	128	175	112	25	112	120	2,354
Tincture of opium, camphorated, 1 lb	21	97	745	307	362	522	633	203	141	194	313	504	507	350	358	292	204	343	6,096
Tincture of valerian, ½ lb	......	500	300	500	400	200	1,100	400	......	300	500	100	600	400	300	......	......	400	6,000
Tincture of valerian, 1 lb	22	150	100	150	150	200	475	100	50	200	200	350	3	150	200	250	50	200	3,000
Thymol, 1 oz	47	180	324	340	300	334	28	500	360	140	390	520	502	570	411	274	360	520	6,100
Unguentum hydrargyri oxidi flavi, ⅛ oz	......	......	200	300	300	300	667	300	......	......	300	300	300	300	433	......	......	300	4,000
Unguentum hydrargyri oxidi flavi, ¼ oz	177	24	96	96	96	120	476	96	192	96	......	19	......	288	96	36	96	......	2,004
Unguentum hydrargyri oxidi flavi, ½ oz	100	200	......	400	......	......	1,600	200	......	......	300	300	1,300	300	......	......	......	300	5,000
Unguentum hydrargyri, 5 lb	......	12	24	60	24	33	103	21	12	60	12	36	1	24	12	36	24	26	520
Zinc oxide, 1 lb	......	14	25	120	50	87	89	50	50	31	31	50	4	25	100	24	50	60	860
Zinc sulphate, 1 lb	10	......	......	10	......	......	20	......	10	10	......	10	......	10	10	......	......	10	100

LABORATORY SUPPLIES

Commodity and Unit	Shortage	1	2	3	4	5	6	7	8	9	10	11	12	13	14	15	16	17	Total
Acetone, 1 lb	......	6	6	6	8	6	15	8	......	12	6	6	......	6	6	3	......	6	100
Acid, acetic, 1 lb	......	27	27	22	27	27	76	27	......	52	22	22	......	22	22	5	......	22	400
Agar agar, lbs	......	73	73	73	85	73	687	85	......	162	73	73	......	73	73	24	......	73	1,700
Alcohol, methyl, lbs	19	30	65	85	73	36	85	48	......	95	51	65	......	65	36	25	......	32	810
Ammonia hydroxide, lbs	5	18	24	26	28	18	99	22	......	46	24	24	......	24	18	6	......	18	400
Aniline oil, 1 lb	......	24	24	24	26	24	66	28	......	56	24	24	......	24	24	10	......	22	400
Arthur H. Thomas catalogues, ea	......	......	......	......	......	......	2	......	......	......	......	......	......	......	......	......	......	......	2
Autoclave, vertical, ea	......	......	......	......	......	......	......	......	......	......	......	1	......	......	......	......	......	......	1
Ampules, 1 ml., ea	......	......	......	......	......	......	......	......	......	......	......	10,000	......	......	......	......	......	......	10,000
Ampules, 10 ml., ea	......	......	......	......	......	......	......	......	......	......	......	10,000	......	......	......	......	......	......	10,000
Ampules, 25 ml., ea	......	......	......	......	......	......	......	......	......	......	......	8,000	......	......	......	......	......	......	8,000
Azur II-eosin, 1 gm., vials	......	2	3	3	3	......	18	2	......	6	1	1	......	1	......	......	......	......	40
Bismarck brown, 10 gm., vials	7	24	24	24	28	20	566	28	......	56	24	24	......	24	24	3	......	24	900
Beef extract, 4 oz	......	72	72	72	72	72	228	72	......	168	......	72	72	72	84	......	......	72	1,200
Bottles, nm. ½ gal., ea	......	......	......	......	......	......	......	......	......	......	......	24	......	......	......	......	......	......	24
Cedar oil for immersion, 1 oz	......	24	24	24	28	24	66	28	......	56	24	24	......	24	24	6	......	24	400
Cotton, non-absorbent, lbs	......	120	124	135	175	100	325	160	......	325	110	110	......	90	100	26	......	100	2,000
Copper sulphate, 1 lb	......	12	12	19	14	12	37	14	......	35	12	19	......	19	19	3	......	13	240
Cylinders, graduated, 10 ml., ea	......	24	24	24	24	24	64	24	......	48	24	24	......	24	24	24	......	24	400
Cylinders, graduated, 100 ml., ea	......	24	24	24	24	24	76	24	......	60	24	24	......	48	......	......	......	24	400
Cylinders, graduated, 1,000 ml., ea	......	......	......	......	......	......	......	......	......	......	......	6	......	......	......	......	......	......	6
Culture dishes, ea	2	240	230	234	296	252	1,630	296	......	509	235	234	......	234	240	124	......	260	5,016
Culture slides, ea	20	107	139	114	139	102	335	139	......	303	164	114	......	64	114	32	......	114	2,000
Dropping bottles, with rubber bulbs, ea	......	114	114	114	132	82	306	120	......	264	102	102	......	102	114	20	......	114	1,800
Eosin, alcohol soluble, 10 gm	......	6	6	6	8	6	565	8	......	12	6	6	......	6	6	3	......	6	650
Eosin, water soluble, 10 gm	......	24	30	30	34	24	574	28	......	62	30	30	......	30	24	6	......	24	950
Flasks, Kolle culture, ea	......	......	......	......	......	......	......	......	......	......	......	100	......	......	......	......	......	......	100
Flasks, Erlenmeyer, 1,000 ml., ea	......	......	......	......	......	......	......	......	......	......	......	20	......	......	......	......	......	......	20
Flasks, Erlenmeyer, 2,000 ml., ea	......	......	......	......	......	......	......	......	......	......	......	20	......	......	......	......	......	......	20
Fuchsin, acid, 10 gm	......	36	36	36	42	36	599	42	......	84	36	36	......	36	36	9	......	36	1,100
Fuchsin, basic, 10 gm	......	44	49	49	57	44	635	52	......	123	49	49	......	49	44	12	......	44	1,300

[*Continued on next page*]

Medical Table 1—(*Continued*)

LABORATORY SUPPLIES

Commodity and Unit	Shortage	Detail of Deliveries by Districts 1	2	3	4	5	6	7	8	9	10	11	12	13	14	15	16	17	Total
Funnels, glass, 3 in., ea.	......	52	50	10	50	12	40	52	......	35	35	10	......	10	12	20	......	12	400
Funnels, glass, 8¾ in., ea.	......	18	......	......	......	......	10	......	......	60	......	......	......	......	......	......	......	......	88
Funnels, glass, 10¾ in., ea.	......	4	32	102	32	31	151	32	......	146	8	86	......	36	26	......	......	26	712
Galactose, 1 oz.	......	10	10	12	10	8	32	10	......	24	10	10	......	10	6	......	......	8	160
Gelatine, 1 lb.	......	24	24	24	32	24	260	32	......	48	24	24	......	24	24	12	......	24	600
Gentian violet, 10 gm.	......	60	60	60	70	60	1,160	70	......	140	60	60	......	60	60	20	......	60	2,000
Giemsa's Stain, 500 of 100 gm. and 400 4 oz.	......	24	24	24	28	24	566	28	......	56	24	24	......	24	24	6	......	24	900
Glucose, 1 lb.	......	12	12	12	14	12	233	14	......	28	12	12	......	12	12	3	......	12	400
Haemoglobin scale, Talliquist, ea.	......	34	11	11	13	31	60	34	......	57	11	11	......	11	32	2	......	32	350
Haemacytometer, ea.	......	54	33	38	44	54	125	60	......	116	33	38	......	38	54	9	......	54	750
Iron wire gauze, pcs.	......	50	50	75	50	50	100	50	......	100	50	50	......	50	50	25	......	50	800
Iodine re-sublimated, 1 oz.	4	28	24	20	24	24	78	24	......	60	24	24	......	20	20	6	......	20	400
Leischman's stain, 10 gm.	1	12	12	12	16	12	530	16	......	24	12	12	......	12	12	5	......	12	700
Lactose, lbs.	......	60	55	55	80	60	275	70	......	145	55	55	......	55	60	15	......	60	1,100
Levulose, 1 lb.	......	4	4	4	4	......	10	4	......	8	4	4	......	4	......	......	......	......	50
Litmus paper, blue, vials.	2	48	44	48	56	42	140	54	......	114	48	48	......	48	48	12	......	48	800
Litmus paper, red, vials.	2	48	49	48	56	42	134	54	......	114	49	48	......	48	48	12	......	48	800
Maltose, 1 oz.	......	20	20	24	20	16	64	20	......	48	20	20	......	20	12	......	......	16	320
Mannite, 1 lb.	......	3	......	2	3	......	8	3	......	4	......	......	......	2	......	......	......	......	25
Mortars and pestles, ea.	374	30	35	65	35	35	63	32	2	65	35	32	213	65	63	2	2	32	1,180
Methylene blue, 10 gm.	5	60	60	60	70	55	1,165	70	......	140	60	60	......	60	60	15	......	60	2,000
Microscope cover glasses, ea.	......	44	49	49	57	44	125	72	......	110	49	49	......	49	44	15	......	44	800
Microscope slides, ½ gross in box, bxs.	......	135	150	100	160	110	300	135	......	300	125	100	......	125	110	40	......	110	2,000
Microscopes, ea.	2	8	......	8	6	6	21	8	......	8	8	8	......	8	5	......	......	4	100
Paper, filter, 150 mm., pkgs.	......	178	214	214	303	178	680	326	......	879	214	214	......	214	119	89	......	178	4,000
Paper, filter, 330 mm., pkgs.	......	126	127	124	188	125	250	219	......	187	127	124	......	124	92	63	......	125	2,001
Peptone, 1 lb.	......	21	27	28	26	23	560	28	......	62	27	28	......	27	18	10	......	21	906
Petri culture dishes, ea.	......	100	124	120	120	100	456	100	......	320	120	120	......	120	100	......	......	100	2,000
Phenolphthalein indicator, ¼ oz.	......	20	28	20	32	16	78	24	......	72	24¼	20	......	20	20	6	......	20	400¼
Pipettes, volumetric, 25 ml., ea.	......	......	......	......	......	......	......	......	......	......	......	20	......	......	......	......	......	......	20
Potassium hydroxide, 1 lb.	66	48	49	49	53	48	125	56	......	113	49	49	......	49	48	20	......	44	866
Potassium iodide, 4 oz.	1	24	24	24	28	24	66	28	......	56	24	24	......	24	24	5	......	24	400
Romansky's Stain, 1/10 gm.	......	117	135	135	135	104	1,324	117	......	264	150	135	......	135	117	30	......	102	3,000
Saccharose, 1 lb.	......	12	12	12	14	12	133	14	......	28	12	12	......	12	12	3	......	12	300
Safranine, 10 gm.	......	24	24	24	28	24	66	28	......	56	24	24	......	24	24	6	......	24	400
Sodium chloride, 1 lb.	......	......	......	......	......	......	......	......	......	......	......	10	......	......	......	......	......	......	10
Sodium hydroxide, 4 oz.	......	24	24	24	28	24	66	28	......	56	24	24	......	24	24	6	......	24	400
Sodium hydroxide, 1 lb.	......	12	12	......	12	12	......	12	......	......	12	......	......	12	......	10	......	......	94
Sodium potassium tartrate, 1 lb.	......	24	24	24	24	24	76	24	......	56	24	22	......	24	24	8	......	22	400
Starch, soluble, 1 lb.	......	24	24	24	24	24	56	28	......	66	24	24	......	24	24	10	......	24	400
Test tube, thin wall, 75x11, ea.	......	500	500	1,000	500	500	2,000	1,000	......	2,000	......	500	......	500	500	......	......	500	10,000
Test tube, thick and thin wall, 150x60 mm., ea.	......	2,300	2,700	2,700	2,700	2,000	5,200	2,700	......	8,600	1,900	1,900	......	2,700	2,300	......	......	2,300	40,000
Tubing, rubber, ft.	......	75	55	80	100	25	200	75	......	140	65	80	......	80	100	25	......	100	1,200
Thermometers, 0–100 degrees, ea.	......	......	......	......	......	......	......	......	......	......	......	5	......	......	......	......	......	......	5
Thermometers, 0–200 degrees, ea.	......	......	......	......	......	......	......	......	......	......	......	3	......	......	......	......	......	......	3
Urinometers, Squibb, ea.	20	27	22	27	31	27	90	38	......	84	22	22	......	22	34	......	......	34	500
Wright's Stain solution, 10 gm. and 1 oz.‡	......	24	24	24	28	24	1,063	28	......	56	27	24	......	24	24	6	......	24	1,400
Wright's Stain solution, 1 gm., amps.	......	......	......	60	60	......	68	......	......	72	......	60	......	60	......	......	......	......	380
Xylene, 1 lb.	......	20	30	30	30	20	66	20	......	42	30	30	......	30	18	18	......	16	400

DISINFECTANTS

Commodity and Unit	Shortage	1	2	3	4	5	6	7	8	9	10	11	12	13	14	15	16	17	Total
Aluminum sulphate, lbs.	......	......	......	......	......	......	......	......	67,200	......	......	......	......	......	......	......	......	......	67,200
Calx chlorinata, lbs.	93	......	950	3,000	950	850	1,057	950	4,150	9,500	750	3,000	......	3,000	2,750	500	750	2,750	35,000
Calx chlorinata, lbs.	......	53,800	21,000	21,000	21,000	21,000	7,600	21,000	42,000	525,149	54,200	37,695	......	74,800	86,600	......	21,000	21,000	1,028,844

DISINFECTANTS

Commodity and Unit	Shortage	1	2	3	4	5	6	7	8	9	10	11	12	13	14	15	16	17	Total
		Detail of Deliveries by Districts																	
Hydrargyri chloridum corrosivum, 250 tabs., bot.	106	200	1,050	3,050	1,050	1,150	710	1,050	2,300	2,550	50	3,050	25	2,700	2,250	100	2,050	1,050	24,491
Liquor cresolis compositus, 1 pt.	172	......	......	471	......	......	117	......	60	288	......	471	......	570	360	......	360	176	3,045
Liquor cresolis compositus, 1 qt.	......	......	50	75	54	33	71	50	225	175	......	175	5	175	175	12	......	225	1,500
Liquor cresolis compositus, 1 gal.	......	40	60	40	20	20	60	20	......	20	160	60	360	20	60	40	......	20	1,000
Liquor formaldehydi, 1 qt.	......	10	1,025	1,500	1,025	972	910	400	1,125	1,500	......	1,500	25	1,000	1,000	25	1,250	1,175	14,442
Liquor formaldehydi, lbs.	......	2,800	2,880	3,200	1,600	3,200	4,040	1,600	......	3,200	3,600	1,720	4,800	1,600	1,840	1,200	......	2,400	39,680
Lye, tins	55	1,248	1,392	1,872	1,632	1,848	3,905	1,152	720	2,016	1,248	2,352	......	2,208	2,352	1,104	816	2,928	28,848
Phenol, ½ lb.	......	100	50	325	50	299	464	300	150	300	250	250	4	250	100	48	150	150	3,240
Phenol, 1 lb.	135	......	100	250	100	......	......	......	200	300	......	300	......	100	200	......	200	200	2,085
Potassium permanganate, 1 lb.	12	1,950	850	3,900	1,150	874	1,190	850	1,800	3,450	2,250	3,900	150	3,450	2,550	324	2,550	2,700	33,900
Soap, common, lbs.	3,270	96,812	89,560	88,100	108,866	106,440	126,753	90,148	19,500	105,996	106,368	113,314	78,192	128,636	93,380	62,120	49,020	92,916	1,559,391
Soap, toilet, lbs.	12,207	37,130	40,584	69,858	44,264	41,390	81,947	46,414	27,110	60,430	38,074	86,974	62,896	49,450	44,780	27,650	30,270	68,685	870,113
Sulphur roll, lbs.	720	28,757	40,839	59,636	40,839	46,854	47,979	40,839	24,466	57,167	39,399	48,332	69,263	53,548	48,130	18,619	23,605	50,139	739,131

WATER PURIFICATIONS

Commodity and Unit	Shortage	1	2	3	4	5	6	7	8	9	10	11	12	13	14	15	16	17	Total
Bags, water sterilizing, ea.	......	11	1	20	1	2	18	......	10	10	21	40	......	20	10	5	10	25	204
Chlorinated lime, tubes	167	4,040	4,000	13,936	120	420	193	......	4,320	9,952	16,000	23,952	......	8,320	4,320	320	4,320	6,880	101,260
Chlorine control unit, compl. with spare pts., ea.	......	......	......	......	......	......	......	......	......	......	......	2	......	......	......	......	......	......	2
Chlorine gas in tank, ea.	......	......	......	......	......	......	......	......	......	......	......	120	......	......	......	......	......	......	120

VACCINES

Commodity and Unit	Shortage	1	2	3	4	5	6	7	8	9	10	11	12	13	14	15	16	17	Total
Anticholera tablets, 50 tabs., bots.	10	......	......	......	......	......	12	26	......	......	26	......	......	......	......	26	......	......	100
Anticholera vaccine, 20 cc., amps.	......	......	3,000	10,000	3,000	3,000	1,010	3,000	3,000	......	3,000	10,000	......	3,000	3,000	......	2,000	3,000	50,010
Antidysentery tablets, 50 tabs., bots.	......	......	......	......	......	......	6	32	......	......	32	......	......	......	......	32	......	......	102
Antidysentery serum, 10, 15, and 20 cc., vials	232	550	1,662	1,116	1,672	622	1,748	772	564	2,748	1,612	1,060	......	1,860	1,534	256	564	1,664	20,236
Antidiphtheria serum, 500, 2,000, 2,500, 5,000 u., vs.	20	1,050	1,910	1,805	2,210	1,680	4,929	1,060	695	2,615	1,080	1,595	5,100	2,225	1,861	480	763	1,125	32,203
Antimeningococcic serum, 10, 15, and 50 cc., vials.	48	200	840	672	940	790	2,603	622	258	944	336	612	2,439	362	900	4	258	458	13,286
Antitetanic serum, 1,500, 5,000, 8,000 units, vials.	......	275	342	289	342	307	678	342	124	414	292	289	......	209	219	......	191	249	4,562
Antityphoid, 50 tabs., bots.	10	......	......	......	......	......	......	30	......	......	30	......	......	......	......	30	......	......	100
Triple vaccine, 1, 10, 20, and 50 cc., amps.	......	......	1,520	1,875	1,515	1,615	3,132	1,515	1,595	1,575	1,515	1,875	......	1,795	1,675	......	3,090	1,585	25,877
Tetra vaccine, 10 and 20 cc., amps.	......	27,000	10,160	51,300	14,160	13,160	9,390	2,160	22,000	4,500	39,660	53,500	800	38,000	20,600	18,500	24,500	62,160	411,550
Bubonic plague vaccine, 25 and 50 cc., vials.	......	......	......	......	......	......	128	......	......	......	......	......	......	50	10	......	50	......	238
Smallpox vaccine, 20 doses, amps.	......	1,200	2,650	12,650	1,250	1,250	6,300	6,050	5,000	5,750	3,650	11,350	12,000	8,700	14,800	......	5,000	2,400	100,000
Smallpox vaccine, 50 doses, amps.	......	4,500	3,300	7,000	4,300	4,800	3,654	3,800	4,000	2,500	4,300	5,521	......	8,000	4,000	1,000	4,350	6,000	71,025
Syringes, glass, Luer type, 2, 5, and 10 cc., ea.	313	1,410	1,955	2,400	1,840	1,463	3,781	1,255	960	1,642	1,840	2,538	2,598	1,978	1,520	597	879	2,273	31,242

HOSPITAL SUPPLIES

Commodity and Unit	Shortage	1	2	3	4	5	6	7	8	9	10	11	12	13	14	15	16	17	Total
Abdominal bandages, cs.	......	......	......	1	......	......	1	......	1	1	......	1	......	......	1	......	1	......	7
Anklets, cs.	......	......	......	1	......	......	......	......	1	1	......	1	......	2	......	......	......	1	7
Applicators, wood, 500 in ctn., ctn.	......	48	48	48	48	......	96	......	......	......	......	......	......	......	......	......	......	......	288
Atomizers, hand, metal, ea.	10	252	144	96	24	12	259	144	132	120	24	132	7	132	252	12	132	132	2,016
Baby outfits, ea.	3,284	4,400	5,200	5,400	5,200	5,800	8,356	6,580	400	6,000	5,780	5,600	5,000	5,600	5,800	3,400	1,200	6,200	89,200
Bags, rubber, hot water, ea.	260	1,047	1,042	1,184	1,321	1,069	3,672	980	408	2,239	856	1,159	2,504	1,050	968	569	717	1,062	22,107
Bags, rubber, ice, ea.	48	465	366	646	363	288	3,088	432	136	1,410	439	420	364	420	693	290	136	372	10,376
Bandages, gauze, compresses, gross	......	......	2	64	......	......	32½	......	48	64	......	64	......	48	48	......	48	16	434½
Bandages, foot, slipper, cs.	......	......	......	1	......	......	......	......	......	......	......	......	......	......	......	......	......	......	1
Bandages, kneecap, cs.	......	......	......	1	......	......	......	......	......	......	......	......	......	......	......	......	......	......	1
Bandages, manytailed, cs.	......	......	......	5	......	......	......	......	5	5	......	5	......	2	3	......	3	......	28
Basins, pus, ea.	......	211	316	520	521	418	690	342	12	224	313	636	1,845	402	5	12	12	267	6,746
Beakers, glass, grad., 2 oz., ea.	......	......	192	......	......	......	192	......	......	......	192	......	......	......	......	......	......	......	576

[*Continued on next page*]

Medical Table 1—(*Continued*)

HOSPITAL SUPPLIES

Commodity and Unit	Shortage	Detail of Deliveries by Districts 1	2	3	4	5	6	7	8	9	10	11	12	13	14	15	16	17	Total
Beakers, glass, grad., 4 oz., ea.	.....	.....	.....	96	96	.....	96	.....	96	96	.....	96	.....	.....	.....	.....	.....	.....	576
Beakers, glass, grad., 6 oz., ea.	.....	60	.....	.....	60	.....	.....	48	.....	60	60	60	60	60	.....	.....	48	60	576
Bed pans, ea.	.....	926	994	927	1,042	813	1,574	931	116	942	765	733	1,296	745	1,101	745	384	909	14,943
Blankets, cotton wool, ea.	288	18,800	27,650	29,356	30,824	30,581	36,583	22,386	10,860	31,246	27,110	30,040	6,562	27,404	29,485	15,749	10,170	28,089	413,183
Bedsacks, ea.	398	3,050	3,520	4,520	3,760	3,850	7,040	3,520	160	4,432	4,042	4,720	.....	4,000	4,480	2,057	320	1,600	56,269
Books:																			
A Textbook of Bacteriology, ea.	.....	1	.....	1	.....	.....	2	.....	1	1	.....	1	.....	1	1	.....	1	1	11
Diseases of Infancy and Childhood, ea.	.....	1	.....	1	.....	.....	2	.....	1	1	.....	1	.....	1	1	.....	1	1	11
Preventative Medicine and Hygiene, ea.	.....	1	.....	1	.....	.....	2	.....	1	1	.....	1	.....	1	1	.....	1	1	11
Pharmacology and Therapeutics, ea.	.....	1	.....	1	.....	.....	2	.....	1	1	.....	1	.....	1	1	.....	1	1	11
Principles and Practice of Medicine, ea.	.....	1	.....	1	.....	.....	2	.....	1	1	.....	1	.....	1	1	.....	1	1	11
Bottles, glass, ea.	69	1,872	3,168	6,480	3,888	3,024	29,861	4,176	2,304	7,344	2,880	4,464	.....	6,336	4,608	2,304	3,888	4,464	91,130
Bottles, nursing, 8 oz., ea.	162	1,152	1,440	1,584	1,296	1,188	3,798	1,152	.....	1,008	1,296	1,296	288	1,584	1,008	612	144	1,008	20,016
Boxes, folding, for tablets, ea.	1,800	27,000	7,000	42,500	34,000	12,000	102,700	34,000	9,000	14,000	27,000	42,500	.....	36,000	9,000	5,000	9,000	36,000	448,500
Boxes, ointment, doz.	12	924	240	1,200	1,272	1,404	5,779	240	156	396	.....	1,176	.....	1,608	1,098	120	1,008	1,008	17,641
Bowls, soup, ea.	.....	.....	.....	210	.....	.....	.....	.....	.....	.....	.....	.....	.....	.....	.....	.....	.....	.....	210
Capsules, gelatine, 100 in box, bxs.	1,438	48	4,048	2,860	2,200	3,344	2,132	2,200	4,500	2,632	2,000	5,200	15	6,676	5,742	2,000	3,000	4,500	54,535
Cases, surgical, pocket, ea.	.....	4	2	6	2	11	45	2	.....	8	2	.....	.....	2	6	8	2	.....	100
Catheters, rubber, ea.	14	400	628	596	716	622	906	688	352	1,282	460	320	10	512	460	474	508	220	9,168
Clippers, hair, ea.	14	75	198	152	49	222	583	45	28	255	176	217	.....	108	237	36	34	55	2,484
Comforts, ea.	101	504	120	312	656	385	557	218	192	240	360	150	1	96	120	216	240	485	4,953
Corks, assorted, ea.	2,584	.....	.....	30,000	.....	5,000	22,916	.....	14,000	30,000	.....	30,000	.....	32,000	30,000	.....	.....	14,000	210,500
Corks, assorted, 500 in bag, bags	.....	170	159	123	100	130	399	84	45	135	62	80	.....	142	83	42	53	93	1,900
Compresses, 4x4, 9x9, cs.	.....	.....	2	46	2	.....	8	2	18	41	.....	46	.....	29	18	.....	18	20	250
Cotton, absorbent, 1 lb., pkgs.	27	1,500	3,834	4,780	2,840	2,863	10,230	3,444	1,646	10,643	2,100	3,600	11,660	2,488	2,482	564	1,450	1,931	68,082
Cotton, absorbent, 5 lb., pkgs.	.....	.....	.....	.....	.....	.....	.....	.....	100	.....	100	100	.....	100	100	.....	100	100	700
Cotton, absorbent, 100 lbs. per case	.....	.....	.....	3	.....	.....	.....	.....	2	3	.....	3	.....	2	2	.....	2	.....	17
Cotton batting, 150 lbs., per case	.....	.....	.....	.....	.....	.....	.....	.....	.....	.....	.....	3	.....	2	1	.....	1	.....	7
Cotton cellulose, cs.	1	.....	.....	.....	.....	.....	.....	.....	.....	.....	.....	.....	.....	.....	.....	.....	.....	.....	1
Contagious face masks, cs.	.....	.....	.....	5	.....	.....	.....	.....	2	5	.....	5	.....	2	2	.....	2	.....	23
Crutch pads, cs.	.....	.....	.....	1	.....	.....	.....	.....	.....	.....	.....	.....	.....	.....	.....	.....	.....	.....	1
Cushions, rubber, circular, ea.	16	.....	55	25	55	57	91	30	25	25	30	25	84	25	25	53	25	25	671
Disinfectors, French type, ea.	.....	.....	.....	.....	.....	6	.....	.....	.....	.....	.....	.....	.....	.....	.....	.....	.....	.....	6
Douche pans, ea.	14	.....	.....	.....	.....	.....	.....	.....	.....	.....	.....	.....	.....	.....	.....	.....	.....	.....	14
Elbow traction bands, cs.	.....	.....	.....	.....	.....	.....	.....	.....	1	1	.....	.....	.....	1	.....	.....	.....	.....	3
Emplastrum cantharides, ea.	.....	6	.....	.....	.....	13	35	.....	50	20	.....	20	.....	20	50	6	30	20	270
Etherizing apparatus, McKesson, ea.	.....	1	2	2	2	2	4	2	.....	3	.....	2	.....	2	1	.....	.....	1	24
Flannel traction bands, cs.	.....	.....	.....	1	.....	.....	.....	.....	1	.....	.....	1	.....	2	.....	.....	.....	.....	5
Forceps, surgical, assorted, ea.	.....	.....	250	811	250	347	1,458	250	255	1,131	300	355	.....	355	255	272	255	355	6,899
Forceps, tissue, ea.	.....	.....	75	268	75	132	522	75	118	418	75	118	.....	118	118	102	118	118	2,450
Front line packets, cs.	.....	.....	.....	1	.....	.....	.....	.....	.....	.....	.....	1	.....	.....	2	.....	2	.....	6
Gauze, plain, yds.	.....	37,600	23,142	115,400	26,578	31,881	97,785	22,131	3,200	77,900	62,400	112,000	26,000	101,100	99,000	14,438	31,500	57,800	968,655
Gauze, plain, 25 yds., in rl.	.....	.....	.....	.....	50	50	.....	50	.....	.....	50	.....	.....	.....	.....	50	.....	.....	250
Gloves, rubber, prs.	104	599	550	1,398	250	586	5,373	850	1,000	3,022	200	1,550	1,444	1,402	1,548	224	500	1,400	22,000
Graduates, 250 cc., ea.	64	25	49	36	49	49	22	49	24	.....	15	24	121	15	.....	.....	12	36	590
Graduates, 500 cc., ea.	160	25	49	36	49	78	34	49	24	.....	15	24	72	15	.....	.....	12	36	673
Hospital garments, ea.	.....	.....	.....	.....	.....	.....	.....	.....	628	.....	.....	.....	.....	.....	.....	.....	.....	.....	628
Infusion apparatus, ea.	.....	.....	.....	.....	.....	.....	12	.....	.....	.....	.....	.....	.....	.....	.....	.....	.....	.....	12
Irrigators, ea.	2	.....	.....	12	.....	.....	13	.....	.....	24	.....	12	.....	.....	.....	15	.....	40	118
Knives, surgical, ea.	.....	.....	50	250	60	50	372	60	50	280	60	100	.....	60	50	50	50	50	1,592
Lamps, Coleman, ea.	.....	.....	.....	.....	.....	.....	3	.....	.....	.....	.....	.....	.....	.....	.....	.....	.....	.....	3
Lamps, electric, ea.	62	.....	500	500	500	.....	2,386	500	.....	1,124	500	550	2,248	500	.....	.....	.....	688	10,058
Lanterns, Coleman, ea.	.....	.....	.....	.....	.....	.....	3	.....	.....	.....	.....	.....	.....	.....	.....	.....	.....	.....	3
Medicine droppers, ea.	.....	3,888	3,228	4,728	3,528	3,912	4,057	3,888	500	2,640	3,528	4,608	5,556	4,908	3,144	2,664	1,500	4,008	60,285
Medicine glasses, doz.	11	.....	30	78	30	30	81	30	30	78	78	126	418	52	78	.....	30	78	1,258
Muslin bags, cs.	1	.....	.....	1	.....	.....	.....	.....	.....	.....	.....	1	.....	.....	.....	.....	.....	.....	3

Commodity and Unit	Shortage	Detail of Deliveries by Districts 1	2	3	4	5	6	7	8	9	10	11	12	13	14	15	16	17	Total
Needles, aneurism, ea	......	......	30	35	30	30	70	30	30	45	30	30	......	30	30	20	30	30	500
Needles, infusion, ea	46	......	100	286	100	106	443	100	136	236	100	136	......	136	136	67	136	136	2,400
Needles, surgical, and ex/for Hypo. syr., ea	2,688	996	2,700	3,480	1,776	2,892	8,752	1,380	1,224	1,764	2,256	2,268	5,220	2,940	2,256	1,920	1,224	1,824	47,560
Nipples for nursing bottles, ea	510	4,888	3,168	5,679	2,160	3,384	6,918	4,032	288	1,512	3,816	4,248	2,640	5,678	2,730	1,188	288	5,400	58,527
Oakum pads, cs	......	......	......	......	......	......	......	......	......	......	......	......	......	......	1	......	......	1	2
Operating masks, cs	......	......	......	......	......	......	......	......	......	......	......	......	......	1	......	......	......	......	1
Pajamas, ea	481	14,580	17,571	15,423	24,474	17,369	17,724	15,264	2,593	22,672	22,776	17,752	8,520	16,895	17,973	7,474	3,317	17,091	259,949
Pillows, ea	......	......	......	......	......	......	135	......	......	......	......	......	......	......	......	......	......	......	135
Pillowcases, ea	1,702	1,800	4,500	......	4,500	900	2,803	3,600	......	......	5,400	2,700	8,191	900	2,214	2,970	......	......	42,180
Pillowsacks, ea	15,205	......	1,825	2,400	2,400	......	11	......	......	3,000	3,000	2,400	4,759	2,400	1,800	......	......	......	39,200
Pins, common, papers of 200, pkgs	......	800	600	1,300	700	......	1,996	500	200	800	600	860	1,500	600	7,800	......	300	220	18,776
Pins, safety, gro	140	35	......	10	......	......	375	30	......	......	50	30	100	......	30	......	......	30	830
Plaster, adhesive, spls	257	1,280	2,736	3,790	3,392	2,904	3,990	3,380	828	3,468	2,588	4,080	2,930	2,604	1,902	528	2,304	2,388	45,349
Plates, X-Ray, doz	5	25	21	96	37	21	193	22	......	92	101	104	......	94	78	......	......	44	933
Razors, ea	......	110	60	210	70	60	412	60	60	255	110	100	203	60	108	20	30	70	1,998
Rectal tubes, ea	......	180	180	180	210	180	518	150	60	240	180	180	1,505	180	235	100	60	210	4,548
Retractors, ea	......	30	50	122	50	50	248	50	20	146	30	50	4	50	30	20	20	30	1,000
Scales, balance with pincets, ea	......	5	7	8	8	......	16	7	3	12	7	7	......	5	7	......	3	5	100
Scissors, bandage, ea	......	50	40	210	40	40	462	40	50	180	40	60	48	60	50	40	40	50	1,500
Scissors, str., surgical, ea	1	......	50	209	......	86	293	40	75	333	50	75	......	75	75	72	75	75	1,584
Scultetus bandages, cs	......	......	......	1	......	......	......	......	1	1	......	1	......	2	1	......	1	1	9
Sheets, cotton, ea	8,553	29,245	32,944	37,706	39,090	35,125	58,518	32,820	4,830	47,100	40,838	39,038	27,056	37,038	35,913	17,000	4,341	46,007	573,162
Sheets, dwight anchor, ea	......	......	......	192	......	......	......	......	......	432	......	......	......	......	......	......	......	......	624
Sheeting, rubber, yds	5	......	......	100	......	......	342	......	......	196	......	113	396	......	......	......	......	200	1,352
Sheet, wadding, cs	......	......	......	......	......	......	1	......	......	......	......	1	....	1	1	......	......	......	4
Slippers, hospital, pr	97	960	1,419	900	1,286	1,361	2,186	1,260	700	1,180	869	900	50	1,000	800	510	700	1,100	17,278
Speculum, nasal, ea	......	......	10	65	10	......	145	10	20	120	10	30	......	20	20	......	20	20	500
Splint straps, cs	1	......	......	......	......	......	......	......	......	......	......	......	......	......	......	......	......	......	1
Splints, wire, ea	......	......	......	......	......	......	......	......	......	......	......	......	......	250	......	......	......	......	250
Sprays, vermin, ea	......	......	2	3	2	6	4	2	3	2	2	3	2	3	7	3	3	3	50
Sputum cups, ea	16	18	18	83	24	24	1,020	18	6	37	12	84	......	84	......	10	6	12	1,472
Stoppers, rubber, ea	......	......	......	......	......	3,072	38	......	......	......	......	......	......	......	......	72	......	......	3,182
Stump pads, cs	......	......	......	1	......	......	......	......	......	......	......	......	......	......	......	......	......	......	1
Sutures, surgical, asst., tubes	2,600	1,008	900	2,450	1,000	850	6,810	3,780	700	2,900	400	1,750	5,760	1,100	2,008	368	800	3,780	38,964
Sutures, catgut, chromic, tubes	......	......	320	600	320	410	607	320	220	808	20	520	......	420	350	250	220	220	5,695
Sutures, silk, pkg	......	2,200	5,500	2,732	500	550	6,115	2,500	400	1,194	2,200	5,200	9,827	5,100	1,400	1,300	400	4,900	52,018
Sutures, silkworm gut, tubes	10	12	50	110	50	74	374	50	50	304	50	158	......	50	50	37	25	50	1,504
Surgical dressings, cs	......	......	......	25	......	......	......	......	......	20	......	25	......	4	......	......	......	......	74
Syringes, fountain, ea	56	383	288	531	578	298	3,294	432	298	773	522	543	532	443	196	145	324	554	10,190
Syringes, male, ea	......	204	108	108	120	216	427	108	24	144	108	60	12	84	60	132	60	60	2,035
Taps for codliver oil, ea	......	......	2	2	2	1	1	2	2	2	......	2	......	2	2	......	2	2	24
Thermometers, asst., ea	54	2,244	2,250	2,600	1,650	1,900	5,873	2,050	400	2,100	2,500	1,650	3,860	2,300	2,222	720	700	2,600	37,673
Tongue depressors, 500 in box, bxs	......	......	24	50	......	......	202	......	......	......	......	......	......	......	25	......	......	......	301
Towels, bath, ea	4,214	19,784	26,590	27,109	30,296	28,000	52,838	29,064	3,576	35,234	28,968	24,103	21,764	26,423	28,048	13,160	4,117	32,836	436,124
Towels, hand, ea	5,021	12,960	14,400	16,645	14,064	8,379	22,217	12,192	3,346	17,141	13,680	22,180	12,340	12,600	16,986	10,800	3,600	12,274	230,825
Tubing, rubber, ft	......	50	300	750	300	450	......	300	......	750	......	750	700	500	400	150	300	200	5,900
Tool chests, cs	......	......	......	......	......	......	1	......	......	......	......	......	......	......	......	......	......	......	1
Tubes, X-Ray, ea	......	6	6	6	8	6	20	6	......	10	8	6	......	6	6	......	......	6	100
Urinals, ea	156	821	1,132	963	1,177	939	1,779	796	203	674	781	1,237	1,834	738	648	475	109	756	15,218

CLOTHING

Commodity and Unit	Shortage	1	2	3	4	5	6	7	8	9	10	11	12	13	14	15	16	17	Total
Aprons, women's, ea	......	......	......	......	......	......	223	......	......	......	......	......	......	223	......	......	......	......	446
Bed jackets, ea	......	......	......	251	......	......	......	......	60	......	......	212	......	......	......	......	......	......	523
Bed shirts, ea	......	......	......	215	......	......	......	......	......	......	......	......	......	......	......	......	......	......	215

[*Continued on next page*]

Medical Table 1—(*Continued*)

CLOTHING

Commodity and Unit	Shortage	Detail of Deliveries by Districts																	Total
		1	2	3	4	5	6	7	8	9	10	11	12	13	14	15	16	17	
Bedside bags, ea.									1,004										1,004
Bed socks, cs.				3					2			3		2	3		3		16
Bloomers, girls', ea.	300						600												900
Blue scarfs, shawls, and mufflers, cs.							1												1
Blouses, girls, ea.				100															100
Chemises, girls', cs.				5					2	3		5		2	3		1	2	23
Chemises, women's, ea.												767							767
Coats, women's, ea.												175						49	224
Comfort bags, empty, ea.				1,040															1,040
Comfort bags, complete, cs.				12			10		10	10		12		8	10		7	7	86
Comfort kits, Colgate's empty, ea.									2,500										2,500
Drawers, boys' and girls', ea.	1,219	3,777	2,477	4,951	3,319	3,262	3,192	3,612		2,904	3,780	4,212		3,728	4,188	2,213		6,415	53,249
Drawers, girls', cs.				4								3						1	8
Drawers, men's, ea.	548	2,700	2,346	2,928	2,400	2,568	2,407	2,700		1,176	2,400	2,739		2,952	2,604	1,176		3,876	35,520
Drawers, women's, ea.												324							324
Gowns, hospital, and operating, ea.	920	412	400	200	400	400	495	200		400	200	200	20	200	400		200	400	5,447
Helmets, knitted, cs.				2			1		1	2		2		1	1		1		11
Holdalls, cs.				2			1		2	1		2			3				11
Helpless case shirts, cs.									5					4	6		6		21
Housegowns, women's, cs.				1			2				1	1							5
Housewives, complete, cs.				2					2	3		2		5	2		2		18
Housewives, empty, cs.														2					2
Handkerchiefs, cs.							1			1									2
Morning blouses, women's, ea.				121															121
Morning jackets, women's, ea.				134								150							284
Mufflers, cs.	4			8			4		2	5		8		4	2		2	1	40
Nightdresses, children's, cs.				2								2			1				5
Nightgowns, girls', cs.				4					2	4		5		1	2		2	2	22
Nightgowns, women's, cs.	1			2					2			3		1	2		2	1	14
Old clothing, babies', cs.							1		1										2
Old clothing, boys', cs.	1			1															2
Old clothing, children's, cs.	1											7							8
Old clothing, girls', cs.														1				1	2
Old clothing, men's, cs.									1										1
Old clothing, women's, cs.									1					1					2
Overcoats, cs.														9					9
Pants, women's, asst., ea.	668	2,334	1,691	2,760	1,932	1,380	2,012	1,656		552	1,932	2,484		2,208	2,940	1,380		2,454	28,383
Petticoats, ea.												200							200
Petticoats, children's, cs.				4			2		2	3		4		3	2		2	1	23
Petticoats, girls', cs.	1			3			4		2	3		6		3	2		2	3	29
Petticoats, girls', knitted, ea.												140							140
Petticoats, women's, ea.												586						165	751
Shawls, knitted, cs.				1			2		1			1		1			2		8
Shirt binders, French, ea.									320										320
Shirts, boys', ea.																	50		50
Shirts, boys' and girls', ea.	884	4,197	2,491	4,690	3,325	3,225	3,180	3,468		2,868	4,596	5,748		3,592	4,500	2,141		6,271	55,176
Shirts, men's, ea.																	69		69
Shirts, men's, ea.	1,451	3,060	2,208	3,432	1,514	2,576	2,385	3,084		1,152	3,084	3,257		2,804	2,484	1,104		4,140	37,735
Skirts, women's, ea.				100															100
Skirts, women's, ea.										225									225
Sleeping suits, ea.												200							200
Socks, cs.	3			60			36		13	22		55					30	11	285
Socks, Red Cross, cs.									1					30	25				1
Socks, salvage, cs.									3										3
Stockings, children's, cs.				10			12		1	4		10		4	4		3	3	51
Suits, blouses, girls', cs.												1							1

CLOTHING

Commodity and Unit	Shortage	Detail of Deliveries by Districts																	Total
		1	2	3	4	5	6	7	8	9	10	11	12	13	14	15	16	17	
Sweaters, cotton, cs									1										1
Sweaters, knitted,									3										3
Sweaters, Red Cross, cs									1										1
Sweaters, sleeveless, cs	1			49			39		15	23		50		20	19		17	5	238
Tents, complete, ea							8												8
Tights, ladies', cs												1							1
Underdrawers, boys', ea							120		147									164	431
Underdrawers, men's, ea							69												69
Underdrawers, men's, summer, ea												474							474
Undershirts, cotton flannel, cs														2					2
Undershirts, boys', cs									1									1	2
Undershirts, hospital, French, ea									550										550
Undershirts, men's, ea							3												3
Undershirts, men's, winter, ea														36					36
Underwear, men's, winter, cs				3								2			2		1	1	9
Underwear, men's, cs				1															1
Underwear, ladies', cs				1															1
Uniform pants, ea				57														60	117
Union suits, women's, cs							1					2						1	4
Vests, aviators', ea									75										75
Vests, khaki, ea														210					210
Vests, paper, ea				443															443
Vests, women's, ea	1,291	2,304	1,656	3,400	1,508	1,380	1,932	1,656		552	2,484	3,312		2,117	2,484	1,380		3,180	30,636
Waists, boys', ea																	100		100
Waists, women's, ea												214							214
Wristlets, cs.				8			4		2	5		8		4	4		3	1	39
Children's nightdresses, (child's gowns), (children's night gowns), ea	3,071	10,362	11,616	11,400	13,616	10,872	22,922	12,720	984	12,180	15,531	12,642	8,484	13,080	12,336	6,636	1,564	15,492	195,508
Women's nightdresses, (ladies' gowns), (ladies' nightgowns), ea	6,177	3,675	5,616	4,884	5,614	4,587	11,354	4,800	252	6,420	5,964	4,228	2,510	4,104	3,864	1,968	1,524	2,988	80,529

AMERICAN RELIEF ADMINISTRATION

Detail by Districts of the Distribution in Russia of the United States Government Surplus Medical and Hospital Supplies,* 1922–1923

Medical Table 2†

DRUGS, CHEMICALS, AND REAGENTS

Commodity and Unit	Shortage	1 Alexandrovsk-Ekaterinoslav	2 Kharkov	3 Kazan	4 Kiev	5 Minsk	6 Moscow	7 Odessa	8 Orenburg	9 Petrograd	10 Rostov	11 Samara	12 Sanitary Trains, Nos. 1 and 2	13 Saratov	14 Simbirsk	15 Theodosia-Simferopol	16 Tzaritzin	17 Ufa	Total
Acacia powder, lbs.	179	290	125	215	235	424	298	175		416	238	136		200	85	255	30	125	3,426
Acetanilid, ¼ lb.					13		288			18	36							6	361
Acetanilid, ½ lb.		50	93	50	203		234	100	98	294		43	250	100	250		50	59	1,874
Acetanilid, 1 lb.	37		32	120	102	164	19	106		50	50	162	32	18	88	45		75	1,100
Acetphenetidin, ¼ lb.	86				250		102									48			486
Acetphenetidin, 1 lb.	44			25			6					44		50				60	229
Acetphenetidin, 500 tabs.					50	120	4	120		50	60							50	454
Acid, acetic, 1 lb.	18		25	24										25		19			111
Acid, acetylsalicylic, 1 lb.	97	100	121	159	213		241	100		499		136		100	216	100	36	36	2,154
Acid, acetylsalicylic, 500 tabs.	151	600	1,300	750	1,350	1,200	2,077	736	228	1,100	1,000	1,000		600	727	400	200	988	14,407
Acid, benzoic, 2 oz.				4															4
Acid, benzoic, ½ lb.					4														4
Acid boric, 1 lb.		648	917	889	745	696	1,575	648	288	1,723	700	677		649	653	360	384	816	12,368
Acid, boric, 250 tabs.												21							21
Acid, boric, 500 tabs.	104	350	404	200	500	350	1,023	573	50	1,452	250	925		550	1,535	200	100	450	9,016
Acid, boric, 700 tabs.							8												8
Acid, chromic, 1 oz.							42												42
Acid, citric, ¼ lb.	1																		1
Acid, citric, ½ lb.		100		126	100		1					119		38	27	40			551
Acid, citric, crystals, 1 lb.	181		70	126	210	200	851	115		440	200	351		20	400		92	200	3,456
Acid, hydrobromic, 1 oz.							19												19
Acid, hydrochloric, 1 lb.		75	125	75	145	95	302	72	25	150	100	250	150	150	240	25	25	110	2,114
Acid, hydriodic, 1 oz.							13												13
Acid, lactic, 1 oz.							55												55
Acid, nitric, 1 lb.			9		50	6	160			84									309
Acid, oxalic, ¼ lb.	822						46			20	16								904
Acid, oxalic, ½ lb.			50				25			145		150							370
Acid, oxalic, 1 lb.					25	14	14	25											78
Acid, phosphoric, ¼ lb.										43									43
Acid, phosphoric, ½ lb.							2												2
Acid, picramic, 1 oz.										16									16
Acid, pyrogallic, 1 oz.							90												90
Acid, rosalic, 10 gm.							9												9
Acid, salicylicum, 3 oz.		150	150	50	50	100	51	151		150	50	432		50	150	135		275	1,944
Acid, salicylicum, ¼ lb.	567					500	56								133				1,256
Acid, salicylic, 400 tabs.				35			2												37
Acid, salicylic, 500 tabs.			2	592	100	100	1,305	95		1,382	100		526		600	200	100		5,102
Acid, sulphanilic,							18												18
Acid, sulphuric, 1 lb.	126						48							50				50	274
Acid, tannic, 3 oz.			40	8		50	50			50	50				100	140		50	538
Acid, tannic, ¼ lb.	302		50		50		119				50	50				188		50	859
Acid, tannic, ½ lb.				97	22	128					100	150							497
Acid, tannic, 1 lb.	90			6	24	51		48						48					267

* Deliveries represent the amounts of each item forwarded to each district. Receipts signed by district physicians, substantiating all shipments made, were filed with Congress.

Commodity and Unit	Shortage	Detail of Deliveries by Districts																	Total
		1	2	3	4	5	6	7	8	9	10	11	12	13	14	15	16	17	
Acid, tannic, 500 tabs		60		200			317	3		152				110	90	50			982
Acid, tartaricum, ½ lb				50			3			25			2		50		89		219
Acid, tartaricum, 1 lb	16	100		158	279	100	173	136		100		200		90	24	100			1,476
Acid, trichloracetic, 1 oz			53			100	25												178
Aconite root, powdered, 1 oz				8			8												16
Adeps lanae, ¼ lb			250		250		250				250								1,000
Adeps lanae, ½ lb					21		18												39
Adrenalin hydrochloride, tubes		100			100		194	100	100	1,000					100	100	100		1,894
Adrenalin hydrochloride, 100 tabs							2						2						4
Aethyl chloride, 3 oz					100		200			200		100						100	700
Agar agar, ½ lb	346		12	14	20	14	4	4		4	12	44		10	164			22	670
Agar agar, 1 lb		50	25	74	100	50	116	50	50	222	50	65		83					935
Alcohol, 3 pt										4,260									4,260
Alcohol, ethyl, absolute, 1 lb				28			34			34									96
Alcohol, ethyl, 1 qt	417		2				10			20					48				497
Alcohol, ethyl, 50 gal		5	5	6	6	5	18	5	2	7	6	5		6	5	1	2	6	90
Alcohol, denatured, 2 qts					6		10						10						26
Alcohol, octyl, 1 oz							30												30
Alcohol, methyl, 1 lb							54								60				114
Alcohol, methyl, 1 qt				60								60					36	60	216
Alcohol, denatured, 2 lb				40	20	40	44	20			40	40		30	63	20		40	397
Alcohol, solidified, tins			140	140	210	210	280	70			140	140		140					1,470
Alizarin, C.P., 10 gm							41												41
Aloes pulvis, 1 oz							80			250									330
Aloes pulvis, 2 oz				170			302			400		200		114	200			200	1,586
Aloes pulvis, ¼ lb							76												76
Aluminum ammonium sulphate, 1 lb	24		25		50	25	73	18		25	26	25			25			27	343
Aluminum potassium sulphate, ½ lb	233	50	81	50				50			50					50		36	600
Aluminum potassium sulphate, 1 lb		25			100	25	55		33	48	48								334
Ambrine, ½ lb., cakes			950	470				900		200	310			450	545				3,825
Ambrine, 1 lb., cakes		300	199	250	397	657	229	190		310	200	383		238				50	3,403
Ammonia, aromatic spirits, ½ lb	298	221	508	150	298	150	146	432	6	420	269	300		288	160	100	100	400	4,246
Ammonia, aromatic spirits, 1 lb		73	48	203	359	142	485	48	96	232		144	1	98	50	48			2,027
Ammonia, aromatic spirits, 2 lb						45										50			95
Ammonia, aromatic spirits, 5 gal							1				6								7
Ammonia, acetate, ¼ lb					84														84
Ammonium bromide, 185 gm					1														1
Ammonium bromide, 250 gm					4														4
Ammonium bromide, ½ lb					99		279		200						45				623
Ammonium carbonate, 15 oz				12	4													29	45
Ammonium carbonate ½ lb			75	130	353		515	205		424	126	120		150		50	60	50	2,258
Ammonium carbonate, 1 lb		125	125	100		125	128	49	25	148	50	75		25	86	49	35	25	1,170
Ammonium carbonate, 500 tabs															48				48
Ammonium chloride, ¼ lb							49											167	216
Ammonium chloride, 1 lb			42			48	73	100		199	106		352	127	75				1,122
Ammonium hydroxide, 1 lb	19	24		24								25							92
Ammonium hydroxide, 1 qt	40	24		61			30			96		24							275
Ammonium molybdate, 1 oz							43												43
Ammonium oxalate, ¼ lb							10												10
Ammonium phosphate, 5 lb	1																		1
Ammonium potassium phosphate, 1 lb	2			7															9
Ammonium sulphate, 10 gm							4												4
Ammonium sulphate, 1 lb							14					25			25			25	89
Ammonium sulphate, 1,000 tabs			50																50
Amyl nitrate, 5 M amp., 12 in box			3				285												288
Amyl nitrate, 5 drop spirits, box							8	2											10

[Continued on next page]

Medical Table 2—(*Continued*)

DRUGS, CHEMICALS, AND REAGENTS

Commodity and Unit	Shortage	Detail of Deliveries by Districts																	Total
		1	2	3	4	5	6	7	8	9	10	11	12	13	14	15	16	17	
Aniline green, 10 gm	......	......	......	......	......	......	25	......	......	......	......	......	......	......	......	......	......	......	25
Aniline green, 4 oz	......	......	......	......	......	......	......	33	......	......	......	......	......	......	......	......	......	......	33
Aniline green, S.M., 1 oz	......	......	......	......	......	......	54	......	......	......	......	......	......	......	......	......	......	......	54
Antiformin, 1 lb	......	......	......	24	25	......	22	......	......	......	......	......	......	24	......	......	......	......	95
Antimony and potassium tartrate, 1 oz	134	......	......	......	......	......	309	93	......	......	......	......	......	......	......	......	......	......	536
Antipyrene, 1 oz	......	......	......	......	131	......	26	......	......	......	......	......	......	......	......	......	......	......	157
Antipyrene, 75 gm	......	......	......	......	......	......	196	......	......	......	......	......	......	......	......	......	......	......	196
Antipyrene, 125 gm	9	......	......	100	4	......	50	......	......	33	100	......	......	35	......	......	......	......	331
Antipyrene, 500 tabs	......	......	......	......	......	......	2	......	......	......	......	......	1	......	......	......	......	......	3
Aqua ammonia, 1 qt	224	......	......	......	......	......	1	......	......	......	......	......	......	......	......	50	......	......	275
Aqua ammonia, 1 lb	......	100	50	100	......	175	162	150	46	175	100	50	......	100	125	......	25	50	1,408
Aqua ammonia, 4 lb	......	......	18	......	24	......	......	......	......	......	......	12	......	......	......	......	......	......	54
Apomorphine hydrochloride, tubes	580	80	100	......	......	100	2,014	106	......	100	......	100	......	......	100	......	......	100	3,380
Arecoline hydrobromide, tubes	......	......	......	......	......	......	44	120	......	......	......	......	......	......	......	......	......	......	164
Arsenic trioxide, 125 tabs	......	......	......	......	......	......	8	......	......	......	......	......	......	......	......	......	......	......	8
Arsenic trioxide, 250 tabs	......	62	......	......	264	......	132	......	......	......	......	......	......	154	107	......	......	......	719
Arsenic trioxide, 500 tabs	......	100	200	300	279	200	510	350	......	542	100	399	1,300	1,000	200	......	......	500	5,980
Arsenic trioxide, 875 tabs	......	......	......	......	......	......	......	......	......	54	......	......	......	......	......	......	......	......	54
Arsenic and mercuric oxide ½ lb	......	......	......	......	......	......	1	......	......	......	......	......	......	......	......	......	......	......	1
Asafetida, ½ oz	......	......	......	......	......	......	249	......	......	......	......	......	......	......	......	......	......	......	249
Asafetida, ¼ lb	......	......	......	......	......	......	99	......	......	......	......	......	......	......	......	......	......	......	99
Atropine sulphate, ⅛ oz	......	......	......	......	......	......	......	......	......	87	......	76	......	......	......	......	17	......	180
Atropine sulphate, 1 oz	......	13	......	......	......	......	11	......	......	......	......	......	......	......	......	......	......	......	24
Atropine sulphate, tubes	......	849	1,400	......	2,000	4,000	4,713	2,394	......	6,000	1,000	1,000	......	2,000	2,702	......	......	2,500	30,558
Atropine sulphate, 100 tabs	......	......	......	764	......	......	......	......	......	......	......	......	......	......	......	......	......	......	764
Atropine sulphate, 250 tabs	169	......	......	......	399	50	206	......	......	......	......	300	......	......	......	......	......	399	1,523
Balsam canada, 1 oz	......	......	......	......	......	......	78	......	......	......	......	......	......	......	......	......	......	......	78
Balsam copaiba, ½ lb	99	164	50	208	150	215	132	50	150	249	50	148	......	100	265	176	......	50	2,256
Balsam copaiba, 1 lb	......	......	......	......	65	11	78	......	......	23	50	70	......	49	......	50	87	74	557
Balsam copaiba, 200 gm	......	......	......	......	......	......	14	......	......	......	......	......	......	......	......	......	......	......	14
Balsam peru, ¼ lb	......	......	......	......	......	......	1	......	......	......	......	......	......	......	......	......	......	......	1
Balsam peru, ½ lb	......	......	......	50	48	......	53	......	......	......	......	......	2	......	23	......	......	......	176
Balsam peru, 1 lb.	75	......	......	......	......	......	......	......	......	......	......	......	......	......	......	......	......	......	75
Balsam tolu, 4 oz	......	......	......	......	30	......	193	36	......	31	......	......	2	......	......	......	......	......	292
Balsam tolu, ½ lb	......	......	......	......	......	......	23	......	......	43	......	......	......	......	......	......	......	......	66
Barbital, 100 tabs	......	250	......	280	736	......	972	......	......	......	......	......	......	......	360	......	......	......	2,598
Barbital, 500 tabs	151	......	200	100	299	300	160	100	55	200	200	132	......	......	......	100	100	355	2,452
Barium chloride, ¼ lb.	......	......	......	......	......	......	76	......	......	......	......	......	......	......	......	......	......	......	76
Barium hydroxide, 1 lb	......	......	......	......	......	......	10	......	......	......	......	......	......	......	......	......	......	......	10
Barium nitrate, ¼ lb	......	......	......	......	......	......	38	......	......	......	......	......	......	......	......	......	......	......	38
Barium sulphate, 1 oz	......	......	......	......	......	......	......	......	......	50	......	......	......	......	......	......	......	......	50
Barium sulphate, 1 lb	......	......	......	......	......	......	150	......	......	......	......	......	......	......	......	......	......	......	150
Beef extract, 4 oz	904	4,100	4,300	4,100	4,500	4,652	5,208	4,100	2,000	4,844	4,580	2,500	13,200	4,020	4,720	3,414	2,000	4,600	77,742
Belladonna root, powder, ½ lb	38	......	......	......	......	......	......	......	......	......	......	......	......	......	......	......	......	......	38
Benzene, ¼ lb	......	......	......	......	......	......	10	......	......	......	......	......	......	......	......	......	......	......	10
Benzidine, 10 gm	......	......	......	......	......	......	666	......	......	......	......	......	......	......	......	......	......	......	666
Bile for culture media, 1 lb	......	25	......	......	......	36	......	......	......	......	......	......	......	21	......	......	......	......	82
Bismuth subcarbonate, 1 lb	51	......	100	......	25	......	49	......	......	......	25	25	......	......	......	......	......	25	300
Bismuth subcarbonate, 500 tabs	......	100	......	......	149	44	231	100	......	200	......	......	......	......	100	200	......	200	1,324
Bismuth subgallas, 2 oz	......	......	......	......	......	......	......	......	......	......	12	......	......	......	......	......	......	......	12
Bismuth subgallas, ¼ lb	......	......	......	......	......	4	......	......	......	......	......	......	......	......	......	......	......	......	4
Bismuth subgallas, ½ lb	583	18	......	58	......	85	57	50	......	119	25	75	25	47	......	25	......	71	1,238
Bismuth subgallas, 1 lb	73	100	......	......	36	3	2	30	......	......	25	......	......	99	29	53	......	......	450
Bismuth subgallas, 250 gm	......	......	100	......	100	......	75	50	......	50	105	50	50	50	125	100	......	......	805
Bismuth subnitrate, ½ lb	......	......	......	......	......	......	......	......	......	60	......	......	......	......	......	......	......	......	60
Bismuth subnitrate, 1 lb	......	......	......	......	......	......	25	......	......	......	......	......	......	......	......	......	......	......	25

Commodity and Unit	Shortage	Detail of Deliveries by Districts																	Total
		1	2	3	4	5	6	7	8	9	10	11	12	13	14	15	16	17	
Bismuth subnitrate, 250 tabs.						50								50					100
Bismuth subnitrate, 500 tabs.	69				138		3			133			2		55				400
Bismuth subnitrate, 700 tabs.							49			57									106
Bismuth subnitrate, 1,200 tabs.			1																1
Brilliant green, 10 gm.							65												65
Bromine, 1 oz.							25			92				52					169
Caffeine citrate, ¼ oz.										200									200
Caffeine citrate, ½ oz.	242	100				190	58				250	100							940
Caffeine citrate, 1 oz.		528	252	390	718	720	1,001	288	264	1,170	480	480	1,680		24	24	264	440	8,733
Caffeine citrate, ½ lb.			33																33
Caffeine citrate, 250 tabs.			100		150		200			100		100			200				850
Caffeine citrate, 500 tabs.														74	100	100			274
Caffeine sodii benzoate, amps.					316		39												355
Caffeine sodii benzoate, 7½ gr., amps.							932	84											1,016
Calamine, ¼ lb.				1															1
Calamine, 1 lb.				3															3
Camphorated oil, 5 cc., amps.	17,271			2,369	2,245		5,752				190			825					28,652
Carlsbad salts, 4 lbs.				8			36												44
Calcium carbonate, 1 oz.							4												4
Calcium carbonate, ½ lb.							4												4
Calcium carbonate, 1 lb.										2									2
Calcium chloride, 1 lb.										16				50					66
Calcium hydroxide, ¼ lb.	39																		39
Calcium hypophosphate, ½ lb.	1																		1
Calcium lactate, ¼ lb.										40									40
Calcium lactate, 500 tab.										10									10
Calcium oxide, ½ lb.							3												3
Calcium oxide, 1 lb.				30			238	50											318
Calcium oxide, 10 lb.							1												1
Calcium phosphide, 1 lb.							3												3
Calcium sulphate, 1 oz.	3																		3
Calcium sulphate, 1 lb.	1																		1
Calcium sulphate, 3 lb.	1																		1
Calx chlorinata, amps.							240												240
Camphora, ½ lb.	202	237	100	100	183	434	503	120	50	311	48	161		150	229	249	50	150	3,277
Camphor, 1 lb.	19	265	38	73	210	313	148	113	40	136	76	38	80	126	76	71		88	1,910
Camphor pulvis, lbs.		40	400	240	440		400	200		320	400	480	100	200	280		120	360	3,980
Cannabis indica, ¼ lb.							95												95
Cantharides, 1 oz.			200	200	300		250	100		523	200	200		230	198				2,401
Cantharides plaster, tins.			100	100	100		413			154	121			121	87			106	1,302
Capsicum powder, ½ oz.	241			250		14				78								77	660
Capsicum powder, 1 oz.							200											74	274
Capsicum powder, 1 lb.					32					14		30							76
Capsicum, 500 tabs.		100	5	100		71	226	1		250	100							6	859
Capsicum, 600 tabs.							91												91
Carbo ligni, ½ lb.	391	150	150	175	150	150	85	125	25	250	175	125		159	125	50	50	150	2,485
Carbo ligni, 1 lb.							377	25	25	40					51	50			568
Carbon tetrachloride, ½ lb.							6												6
Cascara tonic pwd., 1 lb.					50														50
Cataplasma of kaolin, 1 lb.								125											125
Cereline, ½ lb.						14													14
Chalk, prepared, ½ lb.							78	50						50				100	278
Chalk, prepared, 1 lb.	537						53	29		70		19				90		240	1,038
Chalk prepared, 2 lb.				100			34			100				20					254
Chloral hydrate, ¼ lb.	137				48	125	142												452
Chloral hydrate, 1 lb.	24	50	22	22	16	61			25	20			4		100	17		9	370

[*Continued on next page*]

Commodity and Unit	Shortage	Detail of Deliveries by Districts																	Total
		1	2	3	4	5	6	7	8	9	10	11	12	13	14	15	16	17	
Chloral hydrate, 400 tabs			2				15	2											19
Chloral hydrate, 500 tabs	304	947	921	650	915	1,190	1,679	1,025	100	1,463	800	1,159		950	910	200	427	1,150	14,790
Cement, crown and bridge, 1 oz		40	60	40	50	50	65	82		65	45	40		65	40	50		40	732
Chlorazene, 500 tabs														56					56
Chloesterol, 8 gms							27												27
Chloretone tabs., 100 tabs		250	681	500		250	657	300	500	950	46	1,050	500	355	1,082	200	650	750	8,721
Chloretone tabs, 500 tabs	50			300		115	17				250								732
Chloroform, ¼ lb	232	900	900	1,400	1,268	1,200	3,477	1,021		3,680	1,000	715	30	800	900	400	64	800	18,787
Chloroform, ½ lb														399					339
Chlorocosane, 4 lbs	4														48				52
Chlorocosane, 5 lbs	8	12	12	48	48	47	138	12		132	42	18		18	44	12		12	603
Chloramine, 100 tabs					186														186
Chrome alum, 1 lb				25			14												39
Chrysarobin, 25 gms				57			1	60		200				125	104		80		627
Chrysarobin, ½ oz				84	101		333								11				529
Cinchona powder, 1 lb							1												1
Cinchophenealco, 1 oz							69												69
Cocaine alkaloid, 1 oz	8			8															16
Cocaine hydrochloride, ¼ oz	745	914	604	480	418	240	775	496	16	474	240	480		480	331	16	16	416	7,141
Cocaine hydrochloride, 5 cc., amps							156												156
Cocaine hydrochloride, tubes		1,200	1,000	1,000	1,700	400	5,196	100	1,100	3,006		1,000		1,000	3,275	521	1,100	1,000	22,598
Cocaine hydrochloride, tubes	10		1,000	1,500			5						5,000						7,515
Cocaine hydrochloride, 250 tabs	72	202	450	200		200	250	200	130			50	450	200	200			398	3,002
Cocaine hydrochloride, 500 tabs					40			400		80	34					400			954
Cocaine, powdered, 6 grams	1																		1
Codeine, 50 gms							2												2
Codeine sulphate, 1 oz					100														100
Codeine, 500 tabs	22	400	601	645	1,193	400	1,093	300		1,297	800	800	883	1,100	300	100		490	10,424
Collodium, 1 oz	133	6,076	4,722	3,960	6,791	4,220	10,810	4,286	548	6,984	5,600	5,080	4,500	4,805	4,996	1,468	1,848	5,570	82,397
Copper foil, 1 oz							6			13									19
Copper oxide, 1 lb	684	100		43		100	400	100	6	72	100			100	100	100	50	40	1,995
Copper sulphate, 1 oz									12										12
Copper sulphate, ¼ lb			100	236	400		100	112	1	200	400	468		616	120			501	3,254
Copper sulphate, 1½ lb									1										1
Copper sulphate, 3 lbs									1										1
Creoline, 1 lb					25		25				75					25			150
Cresol, 1 pt	992	20	100	20	40	80	868	100		410	40	20	95	20	130	20		120	3,075
Creosote, 1 oz	85		240			239	57			366		36			100			240	1,363
Dextrose, 10 gms								25											25
Dextrose, ¼ lb				76			105												181
Diacetyl morphine hydrochloride, amps		10			6		22	6											44
Dichloramine, 4 oz	66	62		72	299		68			544	78	150		60	100			100	1,599
Digalen, 1 cc., amps					148		62												210
Digalen, 1 cc., ½ oz					26			30											56
Dichloramine, ½ lb							50												50
Dichloramine, 1 lb						25	50	50											125
Digitalinum, 25 tab., tubes							5												5
Digitalis pwd., ½ lb	50						40							50					140
Digitalis, 500 tabs	539		200	183	300		534		42	400	300		1	125	200	100			2,924
Digitalis, 800 tabs				108			82	200											390
Digitalin H.T., tubes	450	750			970		1,545	750	750						750	750	750		7,465
Digipuratum, 12 tab., tubes							11	751											762
Digitalinum, 100 tabs							4												4
Dimethylaminoazo-benzene, 10 gms							44												44
Emetine hydrochloride, 20 tabs., tube		75		1,074	50		4,179	50	40	1,500	1,500			666	75	75	75		9,359
Emetine hydrochloride, 100 tabs												174						820	994

Commodity and Unit	Shortage	Detail of Deliveries by Districts																	Total
		1	2	3	4	5	6	7	8	9	10	11	12	13	14	15	16	17	
Emetine hydrochloride, 10 tabs., tubes							9												9
Emetine hydrochloride, 25 tabs, tubes				180															180
Emetine hydrochloride, 1/3 gr							190												190
Emplastrum belladonnae, tins	16		102	100	223		160	251		200	100	300		100	139			100	1,791
Emplastrum capsici, tins		711					630	350											1,691
Emplastrum sinapis, tins		59	100	116	150	250	284	50	100	292	150	192		173	150	100	50	130	2,346
Eosin, pure, 10 gms				47															47
Eosin, alcohol-soluble, 10 gms							42												42
Eosin, water-soluble, 10 gms							6												6
Ergotin, 50 tabs										2									2
Ergotin, 100 tabs										4									4
Ergotin, 200 tabs	62						26			97									185
Ergotin, ½ lb							50												50
Erythrosin, 10 gms							1												1
Eucainae hydrochloride, 1 oz							13												13
Eucalyptol, 1 oz	272						128												400
Eucalyptol, ¼ lb	84		85			40	96	94		255		50						50	754
Eugenol, 1 oz							55												55
Ether, ¼ lb	605	8,900	8,360	10,200	9,700	11,130	15,404	7,400	2,500	10,900	9,700	9,275	3,960	8,500	10,236	3,900	2,600	8,920	142,190
Ether, ½ lb		300					175			1,000		22			700				2,197
Ether, 1 lb			70		500	36		36		250						108			1,000
Extract cascara sagrada, 500 tabs							300	100		144		100		100					744
Extract of glycyrrhiza, ¼ lb	577	187	100		100	296	194	136		319		64		50		108		37	2,168
Extract of glycyrrhiza, 1 lb		48	107	114	24	91	120	84		96	96	37		48		120		48	1,033
Extract of hyoscyamus, 1 oz							124							168					292
Ferric ammonium protosulphate, ¼ lb							10												10
Ferric ammonium sulphate, ¼ lb							58												58
Ferric chloride, ¼ lb	1,759					96													1,855
Ferric phosphate, soluble, ¼ lb											92								92
Ferric phosphate, soluble, 1 lb		570	712	650	804	649	1,390	740	245	1,210	518	721	660	574	684	350	250	662	11,389
Ferri et potassium tartrate, ¼ lb							3												3
Ferrous sulphate, dried, ¼ lb		99					329	81		182									691
Ferrous sulphate, dried, 1 lb					97	27	77	48							5				254
Ferrous sulphate, dried, 2 lb			12		12		3			12	12	12						12	75
Ferrous sulphide, fused sticks, 1 lb							31												31
Ferri et quininae citras, soluble, 3 oz					74	400	14	62				50							600
Ferri et quininae citras, soluble, 1 lb					2														2
Fluid extract of aconite, ¼ lb		30					1			17									48
Fluid extract of aconite, ½ lb							21												21
Fluid extract of aconite, 1 lb										28									28
Fluid extract of belladona, 1 oz							11												11
Fluid extract of belladona, 4 oz		90					6						249						345
Fluid extract of belladona, 8 oz										19		19							38
Fluid extract of belladona, 1 lb										31		31							62
Fluid extract of buchu, 1 lb							20												20
Fluid extract of cannibis indica, ¼ lb		200		80	100	100	100	100		168									848
Fluid extract of cannibis indica, ½ lb					72		45					61							178
Fluid extract of cannibis indica, 1 lb				10	163	25	179			90									467
Fluid extract of cinchona, 1 lb							2												2
Fluid extract of colchicum seed, ½ lb		25					59												84
Fluid extract of digitalis, 2 oz					50	50					36					9			145
Fluid extract of digitalis, 4 oz		150		103			303		120	257	270	53		120	150	146		150	1,822
Fluid extract of digitalis, 8 oz							40									102			142
Fluid extract of digitalis, 1 lb		18						50				22							90
Fluid extract of echinoca, 1 lb							2												2
Fluid extract of ergot, ½ lb	50																		50

[*Continued on next page*]

DRUGS, CHEMICALS, AND REAGENTS

Commodity and Unit	Shortage	Detail of Deliveries by Districts																	Total
		1	2	3	4	5	6	7	8	9	10	11	12	13	14	15	16	17	
Fluid extract of ipecac, ½ lb.							103	97		162									362
Fluid extract of nux vomica, ½ lb.												69							69
Fluid extract of nux vomica, 1 lb.				21	54		4			64	9								152
Fluid extract of stramonium, ½ lb.							118												118
Fluid extract of wild cherry, 1 lb.				25	75	25	31	50			50			50	75				381
Fluid extract of ginger, ¼ lb.								120			55								175
Fluid extract of ginger, ½ lb.						9	56												65
Fluid extract of ginger, 1 lb.		50	25		50	43	50				45	25	25	25					338
Fluorescein, 1 oz.			10																10
Foot powder, ¼ lb.	125		420	200	1,000	561	666	532	2,300	200	400	200		200		1,200	200	1,800	10,004
Formaldehyde solution, 1 pt.		100	298		369		49	336		12		180			396	60		1,224	3,024
Formaldehyde solution, 1 qt.		216	95	136	354	144	369	126	720	3,015	24	72		312	497	396	1,080	576	8,132
Formaldehyde solution, 1 lb.	1,234				40		1,085												2,359
Formaldehyde solution, ½ lb.							1												1
Formaldehyde solution, 1 gal.							2											1	3
Formaldehyde solution, 5 gal.		180	180	210	218	180	365	183		75	180	181		156	42			153	2,303
Gelatin powder, ¼ lb.							33												33
Gentian powder, 1 lb.		72	60	72	40	124	198	57		92	148	72		72	96	36			1,099
Gentian violet, 1 gm.							25												25
Gentian violet, 10 gm.							244												244
Glass wool, ½ lb.							10												10
Glycozone, 1 lb.							25	23											48
Gold chloride, 1 grm.							14												14
Glycerine, 2 oz.												150							150
Glycerine, 4 oz.											110								110
Glycerine, 1 lb.		75	214	100	416	105	151	155		130	210	338	162	160	140	80		160	2,596
Glycerine, 3 pts.			1				9	1											11
Glycerine, 1 gal.			20	10	50	10	10	10			20	40	20	20	10	10		20	250
Glycyrrhiza extract (extract of glycyrrhiza) ½ lb.							1												1
Greely unit, morphine sulphate, 16 mm., clips.		1,335					10,802			1,000				4,032					17,169
Greely unit strychnine sulphate, clips.										2,232									2,232
Haematoxylin, light, 10 gms.													100						100
Haematoxylin, dark, 10 gms.							240												240
Heroin hydrochloride, 5 gms.				8															8
Heroin hydrochloride, 10 gms.										3									3
Heroin hydrochloride, 1 oz.	467		1				137			52									657
Heroin hydrochloride, 500 tabs.		21		76	20	10	345	21	16	100		33				20			662
Heroin hydrochloride, 1,500 tabs.							66												66
Hexamethylenamine, 10 gms.							49												49
Hexamethylenamine, ¼ lb.	252		234	100	636	100	224	236	100	492		328	100	400		320	100	180	3,802
Hexamethylenamine, 250 tabs.								1											1
Hexymethylenamine, 500 tabs.		400	150	299	200	227	755	200		350	200	250	400	50	400			606	4,487
Hexamethylenamine, 600 tabs.							2												2
Holocaine hydrochloride, 100 tabs.							24												24
Homatropine hydrobromide, 15 gm.							69												69
Hydrargyri chloridum corrosivum, 3 oz.	58						21				133	74		116					402
Hydrargyri chloridum corrosivum, 100 gm.							1	25											26
Hydrargyri chloridum corrosivum, ¼ lb.	18	180		120		99	525						500	200	400	120			2,162
Hydrargyri chloridum corrosivum, 1 lb.	44		135	34	175	182	50	129		194	150	56	361	25	150	57		100	1,842
Hydrargyri chloridum corrosivum, 250 tabs.	998	2,997	1,628	957	1,374	1,545	2,669	1,708	460	1,575	1,455	894	3,349	1,258	1,265	1,188	600	2,579	28,489
Hydrargyri chloridum mite, 1 lb.			50	75		25	75	25		111	50	100			75	50		25	661
Hydrargyri chloridum mite, 500 tabs.		150	2			200	591				100	200			25	245			1,513
Hydrargyri chloridum mite, 1,000 tabs.	160	1,328	751	1,100	625	600	2,010	327	350	900	1,007	675	1,100	410	1,100	75	200	1,950	14,668
Hydrargyri mass, 3 oz.							111							18					129
Hydrargyri iodidum flavum, 1 oz.				81	10		7	2				200							300
Hydrargyri iodidum flavum, 250 tabs.				300			411			446	150				590	145		200	2,242

Commodity and Unit	Shortage	Detail of Deliveries by Districts																	Total
		1	2	3	4	5	6	7	8	9	10	11	12	13	14	15	16	17	
Hydrargyri iodidum flavum, 500 tabs.						14	65					100		250	53				482
Hydrargyri iodidum flavum, 750 tabs.							8												8
Hydrargyri iodidum flavum, 1,000 tabs.		107	204	100	390		203	395	40	150	96	138	558	108	200	40	40		2,769
Hydrargyri iodidum rubrum, 1 oz.							32			112					24				168
Hydrargyri iodidum rubrum, ¼ lb.					14		94								42				150
Hydrargyri iodidum rubrum, 1 lb.			25	30	11	25	95	25		50	9	25		30	27			19	371
Hydrargyri oxidum flavum, 25 gm.							511												511
Hydrargyri oxidum flavum, 1 oz.							78	50		250			49	50					477
Hydrargyri oxidum flavum, 250 tabs.					32														32
Hydrargyri oxidum flavum, 1,000 tabs.													175						175
Hydrargyri iodidum flavum, 1 lb.							19												19
Hydrargyri salicylate, 1 oz.				250	629		766	329		240				320		240		240	3,014
Hyoscine hydrochloride, tubes	2,524	300			300		2,485	300	10	2,000	2,000			490	300	300	300		11,309
Hyoscine hydrochloride, 100 tabs.		20			11			10	20						20	10	20		111
Hyoscine hydrochloride, 250 tabs.							240							9					249
Hyoscine hydrochloride, 500 tabs.							1												1
Hyoscine hydrochloride, 1,000 tabs.							30												30
Ichthyol, 3 oz.		26	140	250	76	100	430	176	26	100		250			276	26	26	135	2,037
Ichthyol, ¼ lb.	1,586		25		388	111	270	202			260			346		192			3,380
Ichthyol, 1 lb.		50	50	50			2	100		50		50			100	50	50		552
Iodine, 1 oz.			240	240	240		481	280			230	230		131		240		230	2,542
Iodine, 2 oz.						100		60								70		100	330
Iodine potassium iodide, tubes		27,200	33,960		3,500	45,300	42,143	37,500		20,000	30,000	5,000	196,085	25,000	15,000	30,000	10,000	40,730	561,418
Iodine potassium iodide, bxs.			10					10											20
Iodine swabs, 6 in box		6,344	7,531	8,162	4,650	6,000	21,620	6,420	2,150	24,500	6,451	14,925		13,300	14,465	5,875	65	11,200	153,658
Iodoform, ¼ lb.				116	10		151	10						18		9			314
Iodoform, ½ lb.												20							20
Ipecac powder, 3 oz.			96	32			50												178
Ipecac powder, ¼ lb.	849	56					21						400						1,326
Ipecac powder, ½ lb.					65									149					214
Ipecac, 875 tabs.							10												10
Ipecac root, ½ lb.							50												50
Ipecac et opii, powdered, ¼ lb.			450	100	350	100	106	195			233	950	1,122	175	545			300	4,626
Ipecac et opii, powdered, ½ lb.	250					3													253
Ipecac et opii, powdered, 12 oz.							2												2
Ipecac et opii, powdered, 500 tabs.	60	240	100	380	196	100	1,041	215	100	502	476	160		440	284	179	284	220	4,977
Ipecac et opii, powdered, 700 tabs.							142												142
Ipecac et opii, powdered, 1,000 tabs.							1												1
Ipecac et opii, powdered, 1,200 tabs.		81						2											83
Laxarettes, 12 tabs., bxs.				84			16	900											1,000
Lead acetate, ¼ lb.							81												81
Lead acetate, 6 oz.				187			190			112									489
Lead acetate, ½ lb.					50		118	93											261
Lead acetate, 1 lb.		100	276	88	276	376	238	376		553	226	220			190			100	3,119
Lead acetate, 2 lb.		60	50	46			132	20		90	65			20					483
Lead acetate, 500 tabs.				200	100						200			200	269	100			1,069
Lead acetate, 600 tabs.							3	1											4
Lead acetate, 875 tabs.																130			130
Licorice compound, powdered, 4 oz.					150		50												200
Licorice compound, powdered, 1 lb.							7			24									31
Licorice compound, mixture, 500 tabs.							199												199
Licorice compound, mixture, 1,000 tabs.		2,653	3,278	3,743	3,175	3,075	8,671	4,226	1,000	6,626	3,425	3,552	400	3,105	2,565	725	1,600	3,600	55,419
Linum pulvis, 5 lbs.							18												18
Linum pulvis, 10 lbs.							1												1
Linimentum rubefacient, 250 tabs.	3	396	114	120	572	110	730	268	206	543	338	120		166	487	286	59	150	4,668
Liquor cresol, solution compound, 1 pt.	320		125			150	400	350				290			38	105		400	2,178

[Continued on next page]

Medical Table 2—(*Continued*)

DRUGS, CHEMICALS, AND REAGENTS

Commodity and Unit	Shortage	Detail of Deliveries by Districts																	Total
		1	2	3	4	5	6	7	8	9	10	11	12	13	14	15	16	17	
Liquor cresol solution compound, 1 qt.							22			12			8		35				77
Liquor cresol solution compound, 1 gal.		1,036	900	1,120	1,240	880	2,402	1,000	440	1,710	1,050	200	100	1,070	949	190	646	890	15,823
Liquor cresol solution compound, 5 gal.					20		6					130			30				186
Liquor cresol solution compound, 10 gal.															300				300
Liquor cresol solution compound, 50 gal.							2												2
Liquor hydrogen dioxide, 1 lb.		5	50	25	32		78	75	25	25		25	304	5	55		25		729
Liquor potassii arsenitis, ½ lb.							50	135							41				226
Lithii citras, effervescent, 25 tabs.	6			100			583	200				12							901
Litmus paper, blue and red, vials							778												778
Lycopodium, ¼ lb.										36									36
Magnesia carbonas pulvis, 2 oz.					25		8			50									83
Magnesia carbonas pulvis, ½ lb.	90																		90
Magnesia carbonas pulvis, 1 lb.					60		135	10		81				50					336
Magnesium oxide, 1 lb.				16			4												20
Manganese sulphate, 1 oz.								112											112
Magnesium sulphate, 1 lb.		440	455	470	110	110	345	450	110	710	440	550	283	250	465	40	110	410	5,748
Magnesium sulphate, 4 lbs.		1,296	1,014	1,577	1,341	1,342	2,489	1,321	432	3,069	1,204	1,366	1,959	1,243	961	390	504	813	22,321
Magnesium sulphate, 3 lbs.					5		5						24						34
Magnesium sulphate, 25 lbs.													12						12
Menthol, 1 oz.							240												240
Methylene blue, 10 gms.							200												200
Methyl salicylate, 1 lb.					20	31	16												67
Mixture senna compound, 1 lb.							1												1
Mixt. chlor. et opium (pill chlor. et opii), 60 tabs.		50		66		120	2			58						120			416
Morphine and atropine, tubes.		30			200			200	100						100	100	100		830
Morphine sulphate, ¼ oz.			100				800					100	4,100		300				5,400
Morphine sulphate, tubes	1,116	9,500	17,000	7,500	6,337		18,884	2,500	1,250				6,730		7,400	1,250	1,250	8,175	88,892
Morphine sulphate, 500 tabs.	1,308	410	103	400	220	300	400	430	20	529	100	200	1,400	547	74	20	20	335	7,116
Morphine sulphate, 600 tabs.							4												4
Morphine sulphate, 3 oz.							137												137
Morphine sulphate, 100 tabs.							1												1
Morphine hydrochloride, amps.										40									40
Mustard, lbs.							31												31
Naphthaline, 1 lb.					145		60			60				100	200	80			645
Naphthaline, 5 lb.	3	27	25	51	25	25	42	25		25	25	25	10	50		3		60	421
Nitroglycerine, tubes				25			9,586	2,797		1,486				50					13,944
Nitroglycerine, 100 tabs.							662												662
Nitroglycerine, 500 tabs.							1												1
Nitroglycerine, 250 tabs.							28												28
Nitrous ether, spirits, 1 oz.							355												355
Nitrous ether, spirits, ½ lb.	1,978	50	22	50	100	85	13	121			80	100		50		50			2,699
Nitrous ether, spirits, 1 lb.			75	25	49	75	50			50	75	75		25	325			25	849
Normal saline solution, 100 tabs.		200	451	250	393	280	500	430		425	249	419		440	316	420	100	685	5,558
Normal saline solution, 200 tabs.		400	221	200	120	317	451	300	50	400		100	1	400	416		49	50	3,475
Normal saline solution, 150 tabs.					180		4	1			540								725
Normal saline solution, 500 tabs.	750						50	100											900
Nux vomica powder, ¼ lb.										76									76
Nux vomica powder, 1 lb.			12				115												127
Oil, castor, 1 lb.			31				1												32
Oil, castor, 1 qt.			51	40	40			7				40		31	60				269
Oil, castor, 3 pt.					31	8	28					31			8				106
Oil, castor, 4 lb.		96	195	120		192	367	192		392	233	286		452	336	96		275	3,232
Oil, castor, 1 gal.	27				70					9									106
Oil, castor, 40 lb.										8					122				130
Oil, chenopodium, 1 lb.				20			16												36
Oil, chenopodium, 100 tabs.		100	100	200	499	100	1,382	50		900					100			214	3,645

Commodity and Unit	Shortage	Detail of Deliveries by Districts 1	2	3	4	5	6	7	8	9	10	11	12	13	14	15	16	17	Total
Oil of cloves, 1 oz.	......	......	......	......	......	......	2	......	......	......	......	......	......	......	......	......	......	......	2
Oil of cloves, 4 oz.	......	......	100	......	......	......	......	......	......	......	......	......	......	......	......	......	......	......	100
Oil of cloves, ½ lb.	7	......	27	250	100	90	191	50	50	100	100	50	......	50	150	......	50	150	1,415
Oil of cod liver, 1 lb.	12	......	50	45	50	74	91	50	......	......	98	50	......	......	100	......	......	50	670
Oil of cottonseed, 1 qt.	......	132	80	20	......	28	158	92	......	83	40	57	......	92	40	40	......	8	870
Oil of cottonseed, 3 pt.	......	......	60	......	......	60	......	......	......	......	......	......	40	......	40	......	......	......	200
Oil of cottonseed, 1 gal.	11	......	......	35	50	......	40	54	......	185	......	......	192	10	35	......	1	40	653
Oil of cottonseed, 5 gal.	......	......	......	4	......	......	8	2	......	2	......	8	......	4	......	2	......	......	30
Oil of eucalyptus, ¼ lb.	......	......	......	85	......	......	......	......	......	8	......	100	......	......	......	......	......	......	193
Oil of linseed, 1 qt.	......	......	......	......	......	......	48	24	......	......	......	......	......	......	12	......	......	......	84
Oil of linseed, ½ gal.	......	20	80	181	14	87	21	......	......	108	80	40	......	120	80	40	......	200	1,071
Oil of linseed, 1 gal.	......	......	......	......	......	......	8	......	......	......	......	......	......	......	......	......	......	......	8
Oil of orange, 1 oz.	111	......	24	......	60	19	597	......	......	24	24	24	......	24	......	......	......	......	907
Oil of orange, 8 oz.	......	......	......	50	......	......	52	......	......	......	......	......	......	......	......	......	......	......	102
Oil of peppermint, 1 oz.	107	......	249	......	......	......	83	13	......	......	......	......	......	......	......	......	......	......	452
Oil, santal, 1 oz.	60	......	......	......	......	......	3	......	......	......	......	......	......	......	......	......	......	13	76
Oil, santal, 8 oz.	......	......	......	......	......	......	55	......	......	......	......	......	......	......	......	......	......	......	55
Oil of theobroma, ¼ lb.	90	......	......	321	......	......	461	176	......	180	......	147	......	......	......	......	......	......	1,375
Oil of theobroma, ½ lb.	......	......	......	......	......	......	......	......	......	......	......	21	......	......	......	......	......	......	21
Oil of theobroma, 12 oz.	......	......	......	......	......	......	......	......	......	......	......	89	......	......	......	......	......	......	89
Oleum tiglii, 1 oz.	......	......	......	......	......	......	244	......	......	......	......	......	......	......	......	......	......	......	244
Oil of turpentine, ½ lb.	......	......	......	......	......	......	25	......	......	......	......	......	......	......	......	......	......	......	25
Oil of turpentine, 1 lb.	......	......	......	......	......	......	1	......	......	......	......	......	......	......	......	......	......	......	1
Oil of turpentine, 2 lb.	29	228	170	156	312	204	217	145	84	558	252	360	......	184	268	153	48	120	3,488
Oil of turpentine, 3 pts.	......	......	......	......	......	......	2	......	......	......	......	......	......	......	......	......	......	......	2
Oil of turpentine, 1 gal.	......	......	30	30	......	......	120	84	......	40	......	......	......	......	48	......	......	30	382
Oil of turpentine, 5 gal.	......	......	......	......	......	......	30	2	......	......	......	16	60	......	2	......	......	......	110
Oleoresin of aspidium, 1 oz.	61	......	240	240	......	......	454	88	1,200	323	46	150	......	......	......	......	......	240	3,042
Oleoresin of aspidium, 50 gms.	......	......	......	......	......	......	......	......	......	......	......	50	......	200	......	......	......	......	250
Oil of cedarwood, 1 oz.	......	......	......	......	......	......	......	......	......	57	......	......	......	......	......	......	......	......	57
Oil of cedarwood, ¼ lb.	......	......	......	......	......	......	4	......	......	......	......	......	......	......	......	......	......	......	4
Opii pulvis, 2 oz.	......	12	100	268	160	40	250	240	......	250	240	......	......	......	......	......	......	......	1,560
Opii pulvis, 100 gms.	25	......	......	......	......	......	40	......	......	......	......	33	......	50	......	......	......	50	198
Opii pulvis, 100 tabs.	......	4	......	......	......	......	2	......	......	......	......	......	......	......	......	......	......	......	6
Opii pulvis, 200 tabs.	......	......	......	......	......	......	3	......	......	......	......	......	......	......	......	......	......	......	3
Opium and lead, 100 tabs.	......	......	......	......	81	......	......	......	......	......	......	......	......	......	......	......	......	......	81
Opium hydrochloride, 20 tabs., tubes	......	......	......	......	......	......	612	......	......	......	......	......	......	......	......	......	......	......	612
Pancreatin, 100 gms.	......	......	......	......	......	9	......	42	......	......	......	......	......	......	......	......	......	......	51
Paraffin, hard, 1 lb.	......	......	......	......	......	......	75	20	......	......	......	......	......	......	......	......	......	......	95
Paraffin, oil, 1 qt.	......	......	......	......	......	......	7	......	......	......	......	......	......	......	......	......	......	......	7
Paralodin, 1 oz.	......	......	......	70	......	......	10	......	......	......	......	......	......	......	......	......	......	......	80
Pepsin, 1 oz.	9	......	......	......	......	......	54	9	......	36	......	......	......	......	......	......	......	......	108
Pepsin, 3 oz.	......	......	......	12	......	......	25	......	......	200	26	13	2	......	22	......	......	......	300
Pepsin powder, 50 gms.	......	......	......	......	......	......	47	......	......	......	......	88	......	......	......	100	......	......	235
Pepsin, ½ lb.	......	185	250	195	400	200	600	200	50	300	200	200	550	249	100	100	50	250	4,079
Pepsin, 500 tabs.	......	......	......	......	......	......	......	......	......	141	......	......	......	......	77	......	......	......	218
Peptonizing tabs., 100 tabs.	45	12	......	200	32	......	270	12	12	......	28	56	......	91	12	12	12	......	794
Petrolatum, 1 lb.	3,995	2,144	4,607	1,761	3,810	3,720	5,795	1,574	688	9,394	787	4,269	3,500	3,074	2,398	1,440	582	5,045	58,583
Petrolatum, 1 oz.	......	......	......	......	......	......	......	......	......	......	......	......	......	......	70	......	......	......	70
Petrolatum, 3 lb.	324	2,076	1,145	972	648	2,258	1,569	771	108	1,176	1,764	1,246	......	664	2,093	569	216	666	18,265
Petrolatum, 40 lb.	......	......	......	......	60	......	......	......	......	6	......	8	......	......	......	......	......	......	74
Petrolatum, 2 lb.	......	......	136	......	......	......	......	......	......	......	......	......	......	......	......	......	......	......	136
Petrolatum, liquid, 1 lb.	73	3,400	440	500	1,170	474	7,096	1,305	1,780	900	1,744	618	1,045	1,000	3,054	1,005	6,000	800	32,404
Petrolatum, liquid, 1 gal.	......	......	......	......	......	......	......	2	......	......	......	......	......	......	......	......	......	......	2
Phenol, camphorated, ¼ lb.	......	......	......	......	94	......	35	......	......	......	......	......	......	......	......	......	......	......	129
Phenol, crude, ½ gal.	......	......	......	......	......	......	......	......	......	......	......	......	......	......	......	10	......	......	10

[Continued on next page]

	Shortage	Detail of Deliveries by Districts																	Total
		1	2	3	4	5	6	7	8	9	10	11	12	13	14	15	16	17	
Phenol, crude, 1 gal							6					23				71			100
Phenol crystals, ¼ lb				50										80					130
Phenol crystals, ½ lb		1,494	928	2,690	560	2,080	2,979	3,458	888	2,285	2,079	2,335	1,206	1,058	1,823	2,019	2,600	1,842	32,324
Phenol crystals, 1 lb		2,925	2,830	2,250	3,735	2,310	3,762	1,675	650	3,100	2,625	2,000		2,650	1,250	120	250	3,850	35,982
Phenol crystals, 6 lb	11																		11
Phenolphthalein, 100 tabs							5												5
Phenolsulphonephthalein, 6 mgm., 10 tabs							122												122
Phenylhydrazine hydrochloride, 1 oz							2												2
Phenyl salicylate, 1 oz																		100	100
Phenyl salicylate, 3 oz			50	158		16	1						40			35			300
Phenyl salicylate, ¼ lb	769	50	100	160		387	302	375		84				172	60	15		100	2,574
Phenyl salicylate, ½ lb			200	50	100	50	203			295	50	50	328		200	150	50	100	1,826
Phenyl salicylate, 500 tab		150	24	22	35	88	98	151	50	124	86	300	220	100	270	148		224	2,090
Phloroglucinol, 8 gms								16											16
Physostigminae sulphas, 50 tabs					330														330
Philocarpine hydrochloride, 20 tabs., tubes							1,045					100							1,145
Pills, aloin compound, 100 tabs	360									100	600				200			40	1,300
Pills, aloin compound, 350 tabs								1,875			375								2,250
Pills, aloin compound, 500 tabs	202	463	701	698	1,000	616	909	664	300	600	100	800	300	650	200	665	1,701	100	10,669
Pills, aloin compound, 750 tabs	655		1			100	3	1											760
Pills, aloin compound, 1,000 tabs							1			134					50	50			235
Pills, aloin compound, 1,200 tabs	137															50			189
Pills, camphor and opium, 500 tabs	59		53	27			351	382		100				361		104			1,437
Pills, camphor and opium, 1,200 tabs				137												52			189
Pills, carminative, with opium, 200 tabs	98		200	250		250	46	206		200	250								1,500
Pills, cathartic compound, 100 tabs								100											100
Pills, cathartic compound, 500 tabs	158		172	40										40	142				552
Pills, cathartic compound, 1,000 tabs		3,945	4,747	3,184	5,450	4,113	5,486	3,490	2,191	4,006	3,965	5,150		4,150	2,354	2,050	2,130	2,350	58,761
Pills, cathartic compound, 1,200 tabs			110				9	54		17									190
Pills, copaiba compound, 100 tabs							6												6
Pills, copaiba compound, 250 tabs		100	82	100		100	35			100	116			33		60		100	826
Pills, copaiba compound, 500 tabs		100	558	100	400	200	728	350		400	500	200		299	542	79	50	200	4,706
Pills, ferric arsenic, quinine, strychnine, 500 tabs.			73							15									88
Pills, ferri compound, 1,000 tabs			2		66		141	1		50					200	50			510
Pills, ferri compound, 12 oz							1												1
Pills, ferrous carbonate, 1,000 tabs		150	100	100	150	100	250	100	50	150	150	100		100	100		50	121	1,771
Pills, ferrous carbonate, 1,200 tabs							38												38
Pills, hyoscyamus compound, 100 tabs							200												200
Pills, hyoscyamus compound, 200 tabs							100		272										372
Pills, hyoscyamus compound, 1,200 tabs									35										35
Pills, ferric quinine and strychnine, 1200 tabs							32												32
Potassium acetate, 1 oz										48									48
Potassium acetate, 6 oz							205							85					290
Potassium acetate, 1 lb							63									55		7	125
Potassium bicarbonate, 1 lb.	73						17							33					123
Potassium bicarbonate, 1,200 tabs.							5												5
Potassium bromide, 500 tabs.			28	102	258		554	2				208		28		172			1,352
Potassium bromide, ¼ lb.					156		20												176
Potassium bromide, 1 lb.	166	210	25	142	60	58	129	85	13	100	272	100		100	50	60		76	1,646
Potassium bromide, 5 lb.				2															2
Potassium bromide, 500 tab.			28	102	258		554	2				208		28		172			1,352
Potassium carbonate, ¼ lb.					72														72
Potassium carbonate, 1 lb.				16	22					16									54
Potassium carbonate, 500 tab.			2																2
Potassium chlorate, 1 lb.		36	81	231	75	50	233	25		476	25	115		32	100	75		26	1,580
Potassium chlorate, 200 tab.					71	200						280							551

Commodity and Unit	Shortage	Detail of Deliveries by Districts																	Total
		1	2	3	4	5	6	7	8	9	10	11	12	13	14	15	16	17	
Potassium chlorate, 500 tab.	7		16	14	70	47	13			71					19		14		271
Potassium chlorate, 1,000 tab.		50	42	62	50		71	57		92	100	90		100	135			140	989
Potassium chlorate, 1,200 tab.							3												3
Potassium chlorate and borax, 100 tab.												40		117					157
Potassium chloride, 1 oz.							2	1										2	5
Potassium ferricyanide, 1 oz.							50												50
Potassium hydroxide, 1 oz.								14											14
Potassium hydroxide, ¼ lb.								7											7
Potassium hydroxide, ½ lb.				26		17	68	48											159
Potassium hydroxide, 1 lb.								12		144									156
Potassium iodate, 1 oz.									26										26
Potassium iodide, ¼ lb.									116										116
Potassium iodide, ½ lb.	87			100			17		10			50		49		50			363
Potassium iodide, 1 lb.		75	25	25	50		155			100	200	75	175	45	75	25		25	1,050
Potassium iodide, 500 tab.		92	2	1,000			503	2		1,755		800		200	1,400				5,754
Potassium nitrate, ¼ lb.		7																	7
Potassium nitrate, 1 lb.		125	170	84	85	101	91	106	10	278	125	104	48	106	58	62	8		1,561
Potassium nitrate, 4 lb.			49																49
Potassium nitrate, 100 tab.					43														43
Potassium permanganate, 1 lb.		150	226	50	50	25	54	227		50	50	25		35	225	25		169	1,361
Potassium permanganate, 1,000 tab.																		30	30
Potassium permanganate, 1,200 tab.							3												3
Potassium phosphate, 1 oz.				48															48
Potassium phosphate, ¼ lb.							11												11
Potassium and sodium tartrate, 1 lb.	94		50		50		19		15		50	50							328
Potassium and sodium tartrate, 3 lb.			109	42			32	24		176	75	168		112	24			24	786
Potassium and sodium tartrate, 5 lb.				24			51							10					85
Potassium sulphate, ¼ lb.									72										72
Procaine, 1 oz.	107		40			40	274			40	40	40		40					621
Procaine, tubes	5	1,750	1,695	1,200	950	1,750	2,935	1,750		4,025	700	2,200	407	1,200	2,200	400	400	1,400	24,967
Protargol, 1 oz.		1,296	1,968	805	1,518	720	531	820	37	1,760	1,470	940	2,650	729	1,751	504	24	490	18,013
Protargol, 2 oz.							200												200
Protargol, 4 oz.							61												61
Pumice powder, 1 lb.				5			35			5				5	2			5	57
Pumice powder, 4 lb.							24												24
Quinine chlorohydrosulphate, tubes			500	500		500	1,403	20		1,000	50	3,800	1,000	3,408				450	12,361
Quinine chlorohydrosulphate, 100 tab.							15						705					100	820
Quinine chlorohydrosulphate, 250 tab.	171		435	236	200	36	467	200	200	450	40	36	400	620	400		200	400	4,491
Quinine chlorohydrosulphate, 25 tabs., tube			20			100	1,684				500								2,304
Quinine dihydrochlorate, 50 gms.							7												7
Quinine dihydrochlorate, 1 oz.			20	63							20	20		36					159
Quinine dihydrochlorate, 1 lb.																		1	1
Quinine dihydrochlorate, tubes	1,000																		1,000
Quinine dihydrochlorate, amps.											60								60
Quinine dihydrochloride, 250 tab.	200						4				100	200		200					704
Quinine hydrochlorosulphas, 1 oz.			29				2											25	56
Quinine sulphate, 100 tab.							100												100
Quinine sulphate, 350 tab.							1												1
Quinine sulphate, 500 tab.			12	24	41		68	17			136			86	24		12	100	520
Quinine sulphate, 30 gr., 500 tab.				72	428	231	75	144	12	128	36	186		12		50		28	1,402
Quinine sulphate, 200 mgm., 1,000 tab.		890	810	362	739	775	2,219	588	253	1,697	1,850	1,600	300	1,730	1,210	766	629	1,711	18,129
Quinine and camphor pills, 100 tab.							1											30	31
Resina podophylii, 10 gms.					4														4
Resina podophylii, 25 gms.					3														3
Resina podophylii, ½ oz.					172		18												190
Saccharose, 1 lb.							5												5

[Continued on next page]

Medical Table 2—(*Continued*)

DRUGS, CHEMICALS, AND REAGENTS

Commodity and Unit	Shortage	Detail of Deliveries by Districts 1	2	3	4	5	6	7	8	9	10	11	12	13	14	15	16	17	Total
Salicin, 10 gms.							26												26
Santonin tabs., 100 tabs.					10														10
Santonin tabs., 250 tabs.	200						55												255
Sapo mollis, 1 lb.		25	65	175	25	75	255	78		150	25	50		125	150	25		100	1,323
Scarlet red, 10 gms.							20												20
Scopalamine hydrobromide, tubes			500	500	2,000	500	1,479	500		10	500	500		500				500	7,489
Scopalamine hydrobromide, 100 tabs.							87												87
Scopalamine hydrobromide, 250 tabs.										533									533
Silver nitrate crystals, 1 oz.		216	432	879	863	575	1,983	902	381	929	1,070	240	750	490	240	90		125	10,165
Silver nitrate fused, 1 oz.	13	280	650	580		406	844	520	40	90	250	240	12	200	290	390	40	240	5,085
Silver nitrate, formalin compound, bxs.							346												346
Silver nucleinate, 1 oz.			150	462	1,707		1,356			125		480		500	480	297		210	5,767
Sodium acetate, 1 lb.					25		75	25		50		50		50	50	25			350
Sodium bicarbonate, ¼ lb.					100		39									100			239
Sodium bicarbonate, 1 lb.		180	126	100		100	100	200		200		100		100	600			200	2,006
Sodium bicarbonate, 500 tabs.			3				83							85				11	182
Sodium bicarbonate, 1,000 tabs.		173	250	345	270	250	162	101	50	350	100	250		268	270	70	77	300	3,286
Sodium bicarbonate and peppermint, 100 tabs.								120											120
Sodium bicarbonate and peppermint, 500 tabs.				65				115		175									355
Sodium bicarbonate and peppermint, 1,000 tabs.		350	438	340	700	550	392	500	148	543	625	500		450	492	270	136	510	6,944
Sodium bisulphate, 1 lb.							6												6
Sodium borate, 1 lb.	64	400	200	121	350	224	480	391	100	338	300	50		150	541	625		350	4,684
Sodium borate, 500 tabs.															115				115
Sodium bromide, 6 oz.			58	50											61			40	209
Sodium bromide, ½ lb.								50		296									346
Sodium bromide, 1 lb.		400	200	94	325	211	501	169	25	225	175	100		125	350	75	50	150	3,175
Sodium bromide, 500 tabs.		400	200	200	400	400	407	200	200	800	600	200			400	108	200	400	5,115
Sodium carbonate monohydrated, ½ lb.				80			6	25											111
Sodium carbonate monohydrated, 1 lb.	2,047	75	75	123	125	75	277	78		250	25	92		86	75	75		123	3,601
Sodium chloras, 1 lb.				50		25	150			329	25	150		125					854
Sodium chloride, 1 lb.										50									50
Sodium citrate, 1 lb.	64	25		25	25	25	10	25		75		50		50		25			399
Sodium fluoride, 5 lb.			60	80	60	60	80			81	60	80		60					621
Sodium hydroxide, ½ lb.										125									125
Sodium hydroxide, 5 lb.								4											4
Sodium oleate, ¼ lb.							10												10
Sodium oxalate, 1 oz.							45					180							225
Sodium oxalate, 2 oz.												2							2
Sodium oxalate, ¼ lb.												1							1
Sodium oxalate, 1 lb.												2							2
Sodium phosphate, 3 oz.		257					350			480				250	230				1,567
Sodium phosphate, exsiccated, ½ lb.				100		150	369								200				819
Sodium phosphate, monobasic, ½ lb.							5												5
Sodium phosphate, 1 lb.										149									149
Sodium and potassium, tubes							1,151												1,151
Sodium salicylate, 1 oz.							13												13
Sodium salicylate, ¼ lb.		400																	400
Sodium salicylate, 6 oz.			45													40			85
Sodium salicylate, ½ lb.			39		34		200						200	136					609
Sodium salicylate, 1 lb.		200			100	328	900		100		100	100		85				169	2,082
Sodium salicylate, 500 tabs.	819	700	1,349	419	550	550	561	700	100	900	900	829	1,150	527	850	550	99	649	12,201
Sodium salicylate, 600 tabs.							6	2											8
Sodium salicylate, 1,000 tabs.					22									250					272
Sodium stearate, 1 lb.								18											18
Sodium sulphate, ¼ lb.	48					93		24											165
Sodium sulphite, ½ lb.								125											125

Commodity and Unit	Shortage	Detail of Deliveries by Districts																	Total
		1	2	3	4	5	6	7	8	9	10	11	12	13	14	15	16	17	
Sodium sulphite, 1 lb				25															25
Solution of potassium arsenitis, ½ lb	235																		235
Stannous chloride, 1 oz	18																		18
Strophanthin, tubes							3,633	1,750						3,250					8,633
Strophanthin, 500 tabs			10	10		10	20			40	10	10		5				40	155
Strychnine powder, ¼ oz	36		250	214			554	25											1,079
Strychnine sulphate, tubes		5,000	40		1,400	3,355	9,873	5,300		650	4,000		2,500	2,500	5,000	2,315			41,923
Strychnine sulphate, 25 tab., tubes	3,223	1,000	4,076	1,000	3,800	1,715	15,322	5,575		5,574	5,820	5,000	3,508	5,789	4,000	2,000			67,402
Strychnine sulphate, 100 tabs	100																		100
Strychnine sulphate, 250 tabs		2,045	2,399	2,700	2,000	3,199	2,019	400	400	4,199	1,300	1,400	1,600	1,200	3,690	1,350	600	3,003	33,504
Strychnine sulphate, 500 tabs										100	100		100						300
Strychnine sulphate, 1,000 tabs		50																	50
Sphenamine, 1 gr., tubes							700												700
Strychnine sulphate, 120 tabs						490													490
Sulphonal, 200 tabs			181	35	342	191	4	80			284								1,117
Sugar, 1 lb		72	216				288	288	240	1,400		480		144	24		216		3,368
Sugar, 4 lb		72	82	168	162	108	96	42	24	66	126	96		54	144	158	72	72	1,542
Spiritus glycerylis nitratis, 1 oz							200												200
Sulphonethylemthane, 725 tabs												21							21
Sulphur, roll, 1 lb		760	2,820	360	1,400	2,500			4,000			4,000		2,600	3,000				21,440
Sulphur, washed, ½ lb		1,100		200	50	98	139	50	168	150	750	300	159	100	600	250	300	50	4,464
Sulphur, washed, 1 lb		726	1,818	1,205	2,225	1,974	2,795	1,827	300	1,860	975	1,165	730	1,733	1,800	840	800	1,200	23,973
Sulphur, washed, 5 lb							3												3
Syrup of ferrous iodide, 1 lb				25			25							4					54
Syrup of hypophosphite, 1 lb					27	42	398			250		56		50					823
Syrup sarsaparilla, 1 lb			4																4
Syrupus scillae, 1 lb			4	44	36		165			19		50		50					368
Talcum, purified, ½ lb							1												1
Talcum, purified, 1 lb										12									12
Talcum, purified, 2 lb							10					10							20
Talcum, purified, 5 lb				20	20		7		20					20					87
Thorium nitrate, 1 lb							1												1
Thymol iodide, 1 oz			204		200		891	102	100	200	100			300					2,097
Thymol, 1 oz							100	60		170									330
Thyroid glands, desiccated, 1 oz							39												39
Tincture of aconite, 1 oz						125		125								75		175	500
Tincture of belladonna, 1 lb							9												9
Tincture of benzoin, compound, 1 lb					50		100	137				20			25			25	357
Tincture of cantharides, 4 oz							28			90		40							158
Tincture of capsicum, ¼ lb	51		9	30		6	1			112	17	20		30					276
Tincture of cardamom, compound, 1 lb	56																		56
Tincture of cinchona, compound, 1 lb	95	25	50	60	16	32	247	50		156	50	25		25	56	21		25	949
Tincture of digitalis, ½ lb	48		132	78	50		147			6		50	500	38	75		50		1,174
Tincture of digitalis, 1 lb							25												25
Tincture of digitalis, 225 tabs											800								800
Tincture of digitalis, 500 tabs	199	39				200	78	200		100		452			100	100		800	2,268
Tincture of digitalis, 800 tabs			2					1		4									7
Tincture of ferric chloride, 1 lb			20	66			5	25		212	30	16	87	16	30			130	637
Tincture of ferric chloride, 2 lb					15					4									19
Tincture of gentian, compound, 1 lb		26	25	25	25	45	189	48		25	25	25		25	25	25		25	558
Tincture of iodine ½ lb							7					18							25
Tincture of lavender, compound, 1 lb					6	25						26							57
Tincture of lavender, ½ lb							30	40											70
Tincture of lobelia, 1 lb							2												2
Tincture of myrrh, ½ lb					100														100
Tincture of myrrh, 1 lb							13												13

[*Continued on next page*]

Commodity and Unit	Shortage	Detail of Deliveries by Districts																	Total
		1	2	3	4	5	6	7	8	9	10	11	12	13	14	15	16	17	
Tincture of nux vomica, 1 lb	......	......	......	25	......	......	50	......	......	......	......	......	......	25	......	......	......	......	100
Tincture of opium, ¼ lb	......	......	......	......	......	......	......	......	......	......	......	......	......	......	2	......	......	......	2
Tincture of opium, ½ lb	......	150	147	100	100	75	473	152	50	243	240	186	400	75	150	135	50	265	2,991
Tincture of opium, 1 lb	......	579	575	449	775	525	1,060	575	......	776	475	464	171	602	553	425	248	625	8,877
Tincture of opium, 2 lb	......	......	......	......	......	......	......	......	125	......	55	......	......	......	......	......	......	......	180
Tincture of opium, camphorated, 1 lb	......	......	48	......	......	150	28	......	......	......	24	25	......	......	......	24	......	......	299
Tincture of opium, compound, 200 tabs	......	......	......	......	......	......	45	......	......	......	......	......	......	......	......	......	......	......	45
Tincture of stramonium, ¼ lb	......	......	......	......	......	......	72	......	......	......	......	......	......	......	......	......	......	......	72
Tincture of strophanthus, 100 cc	......	......	......	......	......	......	1	......	......	......	......	......	......	......	......	......	......	......	1
Tincture of strophanthus, 1 oz	......	......	25	......	......	......	15	......	......	......	25	......	......	......	119	......	......	......	184
Tincture of valerian, 1 lb	......	......	......	......	......	......	......	......	......	......	30	......	......	......	......	......	......	......	30
Tincture Warburg, 1 lb	......	......	......	......	......	......	19	......	......	......	......	......	......	......	......	......	......	......	19
Troches, ammonia chloride, 100 tabs	......	200	......	33	......	150	......	150	......	......	......	50	......	......	50	50	......	......	683
Troches, ammonia chloride, 250 tabs	......	1,350	408	1,636	300	1,104	3,014	1,154	250	1,750	1,050	1,250	......	1,350	1,600	700	450	800	18,166
Troches, ammonia chloride, 500 tabs	......	......	......	......	......	......	......	......	......	......	400	......	......	......	......	......	32	......	432
Tumeric paper, 100 strips in vial	......	......	......	......	......	......	......	......	......	210	......	......	......	......	......	......	......	......	210
Unguentum, antiseptic, 1 lb	......	75	235	460	500	275	880	350	50	700	300	306	......	300	225	100	125	125	5,006
Unguentum, capsici, ½ oz	......	......	......	......	......	199	395	......	......	1,200	......	......	......	798	......	......	......	......	2,592
Unguentum hydrargyri, ½ lb	......	260	522	328	150	410	454	1	......	290	250	550	883	1,000	1,315	600	......	250	7,263
Unguentum hydrargyri, 1 lb	4	75	60	60	......	36	38	40	......	20	57	......	60	150	......	......	......	......	600
Unguentum hydrargyri, 2 lb	427	180	162	144	216	188	384	216	......	76	68	192	152	135	12	36	......	192	2,780
Unguentum hydrargyri, 5 lb	......	......	......	......	......	......	4	12	......	40	......	......	......	......	12	......	......	......	68
Unguentum hydrargyri chloride, mite, ½ lb	......	......	140	110	200	134	12	300	......	150	110	270	......	298	240	......	......	290	2,254
Unguentum hydrargyri chloride, mite, 1 lb	......	......	......	125	......	......	243	2	48	16	......	......	......	......	......	......	......	......	434
Unguentum hydrargyri chloride, mite, 2 lb	7	384	432	640	648	480	701	492	144	971	522	600	360	546	528	108	276	648	8,487
Unguentum hydrargyri chloride, mite, 5 lb	6	48	24	12	24	12	72	......	12	24	24	18	......	......	12	12	12	72	384
Unguentum hydrargyri oxidi, ¼ oz. tube	......	......	......	......	......	......	93	......	......	......	......	......	......	......	......	......	......	......	93
Unguentum hydrargyri nitras, 3 oz	......	......	......	......	12	......	......	......	......	......	......	......	......	......	......	......	......	......	12
Uranium acetate, 1 oz	......	......	......	......	......	......	15	......	......	......	......	......	......	......	......	......	......	......	15
Urea, 1 oz	......	......	......	......	......	......	......	......	......	5	......	......	......	......	......	......	......	......	5
Urease, pure, 100 tabs	......	......	......	......	......	......	......	......	......	24	......	......	......	......	......	......	......	......	24
Vanillin, refined, 1 oz	......	......	......	......	......	......	8	......	......	......	......	......	......	......	......	......	......	......	8
Wax, white, ½ lb	183	......	......	......	......	......	242	......	......	......	......	......	......	......	......	......	......	......	425
Xylene, 1 lb	......	......	......	20	......	......	55	......	......	......	......	......	......	......	......	......	......	......	75
Zinc chloride, ¼ lb	......	......	......	100	......	......	578	20	......	100	......	100	......	100	79	......	......	......	1,077
Zinc oxide,¼ lb	......	......	......	......	......	......	36	......	......	......	......	......	......	......	......	......	......	......	36
Zinc oxide, ½ lb	......	1,500	2,101	1,200	2,300	1,060	3,610	2,010	270	3,110	2,210	1,630	5	1,510	1,300	700	1,050	1,600	27,166
Zinc oxide, 1 lb	313	90	136	729	45	439	100	151	200	74	100	59	200	200	68	150	......	160	3,214
Zinc oxide, tabs., 12 oz	......	......	......	......	......	......	25	......	......	......	......	......	......	......	......	......	......	......	25
Zinc stearate, 1 lb	......	......	......	3	......	......	18	......	......	......	......	......	......	......	......	......	......	......	21
Zinc sulphate, ¼ lb	1,087	......	402	......	......	......	120	......	......	......	......	......	......	......	......	......	......	......	1,610
Zinc sulphate, ½ lb	......	......	55	50	......	50	50	......	......	96	110	175	1	124	100	50	......	......	761
Zinc sulphate, 1 lb	8	25	......	19	36	30	......	132	......	......	......	......	......	87	......	......	......	19	356
Zinc sulphate, 250 tab	......	......	......	......	......	......	2	......	......	......	......	......	......	......	......	......	......	......	2
Zinc in sheets	......	25	......	......	......	25	......	25	......	......	......	......	......	......	......	25	......	......	100
Zinc ingots, ½ lb	......	......	......	......	......	......	150	......	......	......	......	......	......	......	......	......	......	......	150
Zingiberis, pulvis, 1 lb	......	18	......	50	32	......	149	......	......	......	......	......	......	......	......	......	......	......	249
Soap, castile, mottled, 4 lbs. in bars	......	160	160	160	192	160	207	192	......	192	160	128	......	160	288	160	......	184	2,503
Soap, common, lbs	......	......	......	......	......	......	104	......	......	......	......	......	......	......	......	......	......	......	104
Soap, Ivory, cks	......	18	12	......	......	......	260	......	......	......	......	......	......	......	......	......	......	......	290
Soap, scouring, cks	......	300	300	300	400	300	700	300	100	400	300	......	......	400	400	100	200	461	4,961
Soap, toilet, ½ lb	......	......	6	......	......	......	1	......	......	......	......	......	......	......	......	......	......	......	7

Commodity and Unit	Shortage	Detail of Deliveries by Districts																	Total
		1	2	3	4	5	6	7	8	9	10	11	12	13	14	15	16	17	
Acetylene heating and lighting outfit, ea		3	3	3	3		3	3			3	3		3	3			8	38
Adapter, glass, ea	196																		196
Air compressor, unit, dental asstd., ea			1	1															2
Air compressor unit, electric, with tank, ea					1		1	1		1				1					5
Air compressor unit, terminal cock for, ea							45			45									90
Adding machine, ea							2												2
Ambulance Co., Par. 874, ea			1	3	2		4	1			2	2		2		2			19
Ambulance Co., mixed cases of medicine, ea							1								6				7
Ampule, 25 cc., ea							3,800												3,800
Animal cages, ea							6												6
Anvil, cast base, ea		2	5	3	2	2		3		3	3	3		3	2	2		3	36
Apparatus, bone extension, ea		10	20	20	20	10	20	20		20	20	10		20	10			10	210
Apparatus, compressed air, ea		3	2	3	2	2	7	2	1	2	2	2		2	2	2	2	3	39
Apparatus, electric, ea	14				4		8			8		4		1	4			10	53
Apparatus, chloride of silver, ea						4	4			19									27
Apparatus, chloride of silver, cells for, ea	20																		20
Apparatus, infusion, ea	50		10	20			75				9	35		36				15	250
Apparatus, infusion, glass connection, ea							33	29		13									75
Apparatus, infusion, punch forceps for, ea	11		6		8		16	6		12	7								66
Apparatus, infusion, tubing and connection, ea	11																		11
Air compressor unit, automatic, electric, ea														1					1
Apparatus, oxygen inhalation, ea			2	4	2		5			6	3	2		2	2			2	30
Apparatus, restraint, ea			1	12	3		37	1		34	1	26							115
Apparatus, salvarsan, ea		2	22	3	30	1	5	3	1	19	8	3		3	3	1	1	1	106
Apparatus, salvarsan, wall bracket for, ea							6												6
Apparatus, salvarsan, graduated reservoir, ea							2												2
Apparatus, transfusion, tubing, connection, ea							3												3
Apparatus, filter, bougie for, ea							25												25
Appliances, soldering, ea			3							8	3			3				3	20
Aprons, lead, X-Ray, ea	4		1		2	2					1			2	2			2	16
Aprons, rubber, ea			39	150	125		287				1								602
Aprons, laboratory, ea				102						18									120
Atomizers, hand, ea	86	55	119	143	222	225	432	109	55	141	117	105		35	60	9	3	154	2,070
Atomizers, extra bulbs for, ea							153												153
Atomizers, paraffin, ea		2	2	3	2	2	11	2	2	3	2	2	2	1	1	2	2	2	43
Atomizers, physician, set of four, ea			12				17							4					33
Autoclave, complete, ea										1									1
Autoclave, dressing sterilizer, copper, stand, ea														1					1
Autoclave, small, ea															1				1
Autoclave, vertical copper, ea			1	1		1				1		1						1	6
Autoclave, sterilizer, bockel, ea		1																	1
Autoclave, dressing sterilizer, gas burner, tank					1						1								2
Axe, short handled, ea		1	1	1	1	1	37	1	1	15				1	1	1	1	2	66
Bags, canvas packsaddle, ea		4	1	56	1	1	22	1	1	1	4	4		1	1	1	1	2	102
Bags, obstetrical, ea							2												2
Bags, politzer, ea	128	17	17	17	25	17	161	17	12	36	17	17	15	17	15	10	12	6	556
Bags, rubber, hot water, ea		338	702	687	553	144	795	432	16	591	615	830		501	579	250		465	7,498
Bags, rubber, ice, ea					174	10	19		28	209	578	155		100	59	30	15	43	1,420
Bags, hot water, and syringe, ea				41	72	100	123			27			1,644						2,007
Bags, saddle, veterinary, ea		20		23		4	40				20	26		30	11	23			197
Bags, water, sterilizing, ea		1	3				52	4		1	1	1		1	1			2	67
Balance, Harvard trip, ea		1	1	1			1	2		3	1	1			2	2		1	16
Balance, laboratory, ea		2	1	1	2	2	3			1		1		2					15
Bags, canvas, ea							76												76
Balkan frame, complete, ea				12			12			12		12		12					60
Bandages, abdominal, ea			749				639	773				639		639	2,408				5,847

[*Continued on next page*]

Medical Table 2—(*Continued*)

HOSPITAL SUPPLIES

Commodity and Unit	Shortage	Detail of Deliveries by Districts																	Total
		1	2	3	4	5	6	7	8	9	10	11	12	13	14	15	16	17	
Bandages, abdominal, rubber, ea							12			5									17
Bandages, canton flannel, doz				120			139	20	300	120		120			120				939
Bandages, crinolin, doz		288	336	384	336	240	720	240	144	480	288	1,384			144	96	144	288	5,512
Bandages, gauze, assorted, gro		4,008	3,645	4,077	3,498	2,720	6,939	2,879	1,156	4,875	3,975	4,042	3,940	3,280	3,626	2,006	2,352	1,600	58,618
Bandages, gauze, roller, ctn		360	78				3		120	1,272									1,833
Bandages, muslin, doz		2	917	955	836	644	436	485	300	1,265	1,009	880		798	1,230	663		795	11,215
Bandages, plaster of paris, doz	47		12	42	15		27			111								15	269
Bandages, rubber, doz					356		12												368
Bandages, suspensory, doz			2		23		2	2											29
Bandages, triangular, doz										150		97		298		76			621
Bandages, winder, ea							68												68
Bands, traction, ea	24																		24
Basins, w.e. for sponges, ea		1,430	1,378	1,428	1,800	1,447	2,400	1,140	440	1,775	1,479	1,488		1,320	1,421	440	640	1,520	21,546
Basins, w.e. for O.R., ea		1,500	1,571	1,660	2,118	1,550	2,985	1,439	250	2,700	1,573	1,750	557	1,915	1,800	605	900	2,096	26,969
Basins, hand, w.e., ea		175	100				78	233			197	100						105	988
Basins, hand, w.e., 2½ qt., ea			13	240	200	10	259	21		520	70	239		225	200	79		116	2,192
Basins, pus, ea				123			144			200		180							647
Basins, rubber, hand, ea	397		400		150	600	1				600	400		453		600		400	4,001
Baskets, wire, ea							61			60		60							181
Bath robes, ea							7		34			275							316
Beakers, glass, assorted sizes, ea			80	121	91	60	131	38		54	38	45		148	36			96	938
Bed caps, outing flannel, ea							326												326
Bed pans, box of, ea		2	3	4	2	4	3	3		3	2	2		2	2	2		2	36
Bed pans, w.e., ea		70	316	313	190	226	141	118		360	200	171	60	186	193	95		117	2,756
Bedsacks, M.D.'s, ea	58	398	401	719	385	520	1,098	180	761	605	433	475		470	700	703	308	410	8,624
Bedsocks, wool, ea							25								22				47
Bed, fracture, ea	3	7	6	12	10	7	7	8	6	9	8	10	13	9	6	5	10	8	144
Bell, call, ea		4	4	6	4	4	9	4		6	4	4		4	4	4		4	65
Blankets, wool, ea		7,571	400	1,173	5,310	7	6,919	3,382	1,906	2,000	5,422	1,738	9,998	1,310	1,594	1,848	1,104	4,780	56,462
Blankets, rubber, ea		975	1,002	1,406	1,276	1,111	1,379	1,055	350	1,620	432	902	240	1,451	1,324	711	498	1,050	16,782
Blowers, powder, ea							5												5
Boats, gravy, ea		33	54	100	38	32	252	46		68	32	189		40	24			100	1,008
Boilers, coffee, ea				74			46					46		20		19			205
Boilers, double for cooking, ea				8			113			16	24			20	12	21	6	24	244
Boilers, instrument, assorted, ea	22	18	20	22	34	4	69	3		26	26	41		10	48			23	366
Boilers, tin, copper bottom, ea		9	5	13	9	9	27	9		9		9			9	1			109
Books, note manifolding, binder for, ea		15	20	20	30	20	105	20		15	30	20		20	20	92		20	447
Books, note manifolding, filler for, ea		30	567	300	1,350	200	1,746	200		30	300	200		456	200	176		200	5,955
Books, prescription, ea							59		35									16	110
Bottles, assorted, not vials, ea	26	44	475	92	14	310	1,752	386		313	98	264		151					3,925
Bowls, g.e., ea							25												25
Bowls, soup, aluminum, ea	105				240							75				245			665
Bowls, soup, china, ea	237	325		450	200	100	990	595		220	710	750		400	325			250	5,552
Bowls, soup, w.e., ea	128	1,050	10	1,259		10	12		1,250	464		1,000		999	1,000	400		1,000	8,582
Bowls, sugar, china, ea			309	340	500	368	440	240		444	298	364						230	3,533
Bowls, sugar, w.e., ea		300				100		200			100			370	400			29	1,499
Bowls, w.e., 2 qt., ea.	22																		22
Bowls, w.e., 3 pt., ea			93															38	131
Boxes, combat equipment, empty, ea.		1					2			1									4
Boxes, folding for tab., doz.			1,245	120	1,354	508	4,254	10		2,541	480								10,512
Boxes, folding fracture, ea.			46				1	11				5							63
Boxes, ointment, metal, ea.				5,184			9,420			487									15,091
Boxes, impervious, 3 in nest, doz.		400	680	564	972	800	1,536	575		2,193	564	564		400				1,044	10,292
Boxes, pill, ea.	23,412	6,048	26,064				31,680					8,640			15,360				111,204
Boxes, powder, 3 in nest, doz.		480	960	972	960	606	2,042	480		1,440	960	480	250	480	1,038	432		480	12,060
Boxes, soap, metal, ea.				172			16			150		100							438

HOSPITAL SUPPLIES

Commodity and Unit	Shortage	1	2	3	4	5	6	7	8	9	10	11	12	13	14	15	16	17	Total
		Detail of Deliveries by Districts																	
Bradfords frame, ea.	.....	.....	.....	.....	.....	.....	15	.....	.....	.....	.....	.....	.....	.....	.....	.....	.....	.....	15
Brushes, hand, fiber, ea.	.....	120	72	72	340	120	3,140	60	120	1,872	72	216	.....	72	1,472	48	96	60	7,952
Brushes, flask, ea.	.....	.....	436	.....	.....	.....	300	.....	.....	100	.....	.....	.....	.....	.....	.....	.....	.....	836
Brushes, laboratory, ea.	.....	.....	.....	.....	.....	.....	67	.....	.....	.....	.....	.....	.....	.....	.....	.....	.....	.....	67
Brushes, shaving, ea.	141	7	6	12	12	6	12	12	.....	12	12	12	.....	12	6	6	.....	6	274
Brushes, test tube, ea.	.....	.....	.....	2,500	.....	.....	2	.....	.....	.....	.....	.....	.....	700	.....	.....	.....	.....	3,202
Buckets, G.I., ea.	.....	1	1	1	1	1	26	1	33	1	1	.....	62	1	1	1	1	2	135
Buckets, metal, covered, ea.	.....	.....	96	.....	.....	.....	136	.....	.....	.....	107	.....	.....	122	.....	.....	.....	.....	461
Buckets, w.e., ea.	.....	32	.....	.....	193	48	186	136	.....	208	.....	170	234	.....	.....	.....	90	86	1,383
Buckets, w.e., 3 in nest, ea.	49	.....	.....	168	.....	.....	2	.....	.....	.....	.....	.....	.....	6	.....	.....	.....	.....	225
Buckets, w.e., 2 qt., ea.	.....	.....	.....	.....	.....	.....	.....	.....	.....	.....	.....	.....	.....	.....	144	.....	.....	.....	144
Bulbs, electric carbon, ea.	144	.....	.....	130	.....	.....	18	.....	.....	109	.....	157	.....	.....	180	.....	.....	97	835
Burettes, assorted, ea.	.....	.....	.....	64	50	.....	131	.....	.....	20	.....	.....	.....	.....	.....	.....	.....	.....	265
Burette support, Chaddock, ea.	.....	.....	.....	.....	.....	.....	25	10	.....	38	.....	.....	.....	.....	.....	.....	.....	.....	73
Burners, alcohol stove, ea.	11	.....	18	3	.....	30	24	10	12	15	9	9	3	28	4	.....	.....	.....	176
Burners, gas, ea.	.....	.....	12	.....	28	.....	93	.....	.....	50	12	.....	.....	12	.....	.....	.....	10	217
Burners, kerosene, ea.	.....	.....	.....	.....	8	.....	.....	.....	.....	.....	12	.....	.....	12	.....	.....	.....	20	52
Buttons, Murphy, size 2, ea.	.....	20	20	11	20	20	20	20	.....	20	20	20	.....	20	50	11	.....	20	292
Cabinet, for medicine ward, ea.	.....	.....	2	2	2	.....	9	2	.....	.....	1	2	.....	2	.....	.....	.....	.....	22
Camp Infirm., compl. ¶869, and reserve, ea.	.....	3	3	3	4	3	5	3	.....	3	4	3	.....	3	3	2	.....	3	45
Candles, lbs.	.....	94	111	222	196	81	250	86	.....	200	288	90	.....	184	90	.....	.....	170	2,062
Can openers, ea.	44	.....	24	24	24	10	121	24	.....	24	24	24	.....	24	24	.....	.....	24	415
Caps, operating, linen, ea.	.....	.....	.....	.....	.....	.....	.....	.....	.....	.....	.....	.....	.....	.....	.....	53	.....	.....	53
Capsules, gelatine, assorted sizes, bxs.	.....	1,530	2,495	2,712	2,500	1,531	5,614	2,500	1,500	5,306	2,441	2,000	5,112	2,531	2,531	1,301	1,000	2,000	44,604
Carriage dressing, ea.	.....	.....	.....	1	2	1	2	1	.....	.....	1	1	.....	1	.....	1	.....	.....	11
Carrier, ligature, ea.	.....	.....	.....	.....	.....	.....	2	.....	.....	.....	.....	.....	.....	.....	.....	.....	.....	.....	2
Case bedding, ea.	.....	.....	.....	.....	.....	.....	.....	.....	39	71	.....	.....	.....	.....	.....	.....	.....	.....	110
Case, empty, for folding field furniture, ea.	.....	.....	16	30	.....	21	42	.....	23	.....	.....	.....	.....	.....	.....	.....	.....	.....	138
Canvas for cots, ea.	.....	.....	6	.....	.....	.....	.....	.....	.....	.....	.....	76	.....	.....	198	.....	.....	.....	280
Cautery paquelin, ea.	.....	.....	1	.....	2	2	2	2	1	2	1	1	1	1	1	.....	1	1	19
Centrifuge, hand, ea.	10	.....	.....	.....	.....	16	43	.....	.....	20	.....	.....	.....	.....	6	.....	.....	.....	95
Centrifuge, water, ea.	.....	.....	1	2	5	.....	3	2	.....	2	1	1	.....	1	1	.....	.....	1	20
Centrifuge tubes, ea.	124	.....	144	144	288	288	1,019	144	.....	.....	144	144	.....	144	288	72	.....	288	3,231
Chest, commode, ea.	.....	.....	3	20	.....	15	.....	23	20	20	.....	1	.....	20	.....	2	20	.....	144
Chest, cooking utensil, ea.	.....	13	11	11	10	1	28	12	5	10	12	12	6	12	12	11	3	11	180
Chest, detached service, ea.	.....	5	.....	10	.....	.....	.....	.....	.....	6	.....	.....	.....	.....	.....	.....	.....	.....	21
Chest, field laboratory, incomplete, ea.	.....	.....	.....	.....	.....	.....	.....	.....	.....	.....	2	1	.....	.....	.....	.....	.....	.....	3
Chest, instrument, empty, ea.	.....	.....	1	2	2	.....	3	.....	.....	2	1	1	7	2	1	.....	.....	.....	22
Chest, dental supplies, incomplete, ea.	.....	.....	.....	.....	.....	.....	.....	.....	.....	1	.....	.....	.....	.....	.....	.....	.....	.....	1
Chest, medical and surgical, ea.	.....	6	6	11	4	8	10	8	3	6	8	7	7	7	8	8	10	9	126
Chest, medical and surgical, incomplete, ea.	.....	24	15	21	31	25	40	25	17	42	40	40	41	18	14	15	28	10	446
Chest, mess, ea.	.....	8	7	15	6	6	9	6	.....	6	12	11	.....	10	16	4	10	8	134
Chest, sterilizing, ea.	.....	9	9	8	9	8	11	7	5	9	8	8	.....	12	8	6	7	7	131
Chest, tableware, incomplete, ea.	14	6	8	12	9	12	11	8	.....	6	11	9	.....	10	7	5	.....	10	138
Chest, tool, ea.	.....	.....	1	1	1	.....	1	1	.....	.....	1	.....	.....	1	.....	.....	.....	1	8
Chest, tool, orthopedic, ea.	.....	.....	.....	.....	.....	.....	1	.....	.....	1	.....	.....	.....	.....	.....	.....	.....	.....	2
Clothes line, cotton, yds.	274	1,960	.....	2,160	.....	.....	2,226	.....	.....	2,160	2,160	2,160	.....	2,160	1,620	.....	.....	2,160	19,240
Color comparison tubes, 50 cc., ea.	.....	.....	.....	.....	.....	.....	.....	.....	.....	48	.....	.....	.....	.....	.....	.....	.....	.....	48
Color comparison tubes, 100 cc., ea.	.....	.....	.....	.....	.....	.....	48	.....	.....	.....	.....	.....	.....	.....	.....	.....	.....	.....	48
Collander, ea.	.....	.....	.....	18	.....	.....	.....	.....	.....	.....	19	.....	.....	.....	.....	.....	.....	.....	37
Combat equipment, Par. 866, incomplete, ea.	.....	.....	1	7	6	.....	7	1	.....	.....	6	7	.....	6	.....	6	.....	.....	47
Condenser, assorted, ea.	.....	.....	.....	.....	.....	.....	58	.....	.....	21	.....	.....	.....	.....	.....	.....	.....	.....	79
Control, galvanic with meter, ea.	.....	.....	.....	.....	.....	.....	1	.....	.....	.....	.....	.....	.....	.....	.....	.....	.....	.....	1
Corks, assorted sizes, bags	.....	.....	62	1	.....	.....	1,139	1	.....	.....	.....	.....	.....	12	12	38	.....	.....	1,265
Cork borer, sets	.....	.....	.....	.....	.....	.....	.....	.....	.....	25	.....	.....	.....	.....	.....	.....	.....	.....	25
Corkscrews, ea.	.....	20	23	28	20	20	35	23	20	25	20	20	.....	20	20	23	20	20	357

[Continued on next page]

Medical Table 2—(*Continued*)

HOSPITAL SUPPLIES

Commodity and Unit	Shortage	Detail of Deliveries by Districts																	Total
		1	2	3	4	5	6	7	8	9	10	11	12	13	14	15	16	17	
Cots, folding, ea.	22	......	......	400	......	373	93	......	......	......	......	300	......	300	150	300	......	300	2,238
Cotton, absorbent, 1 oz., pkg.	......	4,000	9,189	1,000	19,001	1,200	2,145	1,775	850	1,997	800	7,645	4,400	2,400	4,386	5,917	......	6,727	73,432
Cotton, absorbent, lbs.	......	11,044	9,500	10,970	13,460	10,198	30,962	9,749	3,043	14,843	8,995	9,702	3,000	11,561	10,065	4,604	4,900	14,242	180,838
Cotton batting, lbs.	6,311	1,002	690	820	520	360	955	100	16	620	420	2,205	......	900	200	264	120	800	16,303
Cover glasses, assorted, bxs.	......	4	10	20	10	......	20	4	......	20	10	20	......	10	20	......	......	20	168
Covers, paper, aseptic, bxs.	......	......	......	......	......	150	50	100	......	50	......	......	......	......	......	......	......	......	350
Cradles, bed, ea.	......	......	25	75	87	48	232	75	9	131	25	25	......	25	25	25	56	17	880
Crinolin, 6 yds., pcs.	......	......	......	......	......	......	268	......	......	......	......	......	......	......	......	......	......	......	268
Crutches, prs.	......	44	......	85	12	100	185	87	......	126	25	6	......	2	8	52	......	50	782
Crutches, tips for, ea.	......	55	55	55	1,210	55	4,253	55	55	110	55	55	......	55	55	24	55	55	6,257
Cups, delft, ea.	......	100	50	......	......	......	1,480	600	......	220	......	220	......	220	......	......	......	220	3,110
Cups, drinking, w.e., ea.	......	......	200	233	400	......	415	107	......	155	541	100	......	102	......	......	......	......	2,253
Cups, aluminum, ea.	......	......	......	......	......	112	......	......	......	......	......	......	......	......	......	......	......	......	112
Cups, feeding, ea.	......	......	......	389	342	......	183	288	......	365	......	476	727	272	300	56	......	100	3,498
Cups, feeding, w.e., ea.	......	......	300	......	......	200	......	......	......	......	300	......	......	......	......	......	......	......	800
Cups, spit, metal frame for, ea.	......	......	100	339	......	622	622	100	......	200	239	100	......	239	100	......	100	100	2,861
Cups, spit, w.e., ea.	......	2,200	3,000	3,139	3,867	3,849	5,612	2,300	600	4,000	3,322	3,000	3,226	3,007	3,130	1,223	800	3,122	49,397
Cups, w.e., ea.	......	174	272	244	258	200	354	260	100	492	367	186	157	144	144	232	100	100	3,684
Cups, paper, nickel holder for, ea.	......	2	2	2	2	2	2	2	......	2	2	......	......	2	......	......	......	1	21
Cups, tin, 2 in nest, ea.	......	......	......	......	......	......	......	......	......	136	......	36	......	......	......	......	......	......	172
Cushions, rubber, open center, ea.	......	......	30	21	29	2	48	3	36	25	14	4	......	3	4	......	......	1	220
Cushion, rubber, air, ea.	......	......	26	142	......	......	144	......	......	166	......	245	503	......	216	......	......	......	1,442
Cushions, surgical, Kelley, ea.	......	......	17	72	76	10	53	......	......	37	72	72	72	10	72	......	......	......	563
Cuspidor, n.p., ea.	......	......	......	......	......	......	3	3	......	103	......	......	......	......	......	......	......	......	109
Cylinders, glass, assorted, ea.	153	......	......	23	48	......	120	38	......	80	24	25	......	113	......	......	......	50	674
Dark-room equipment, ea.	......	......	......	......	......	1	2	......	......	......	......	......	......	......	......	......	......	......	3
Desk, field, large, ea.	......	1	......	......	1	......	1	1	......	1	......	1	......	......	......	......	......	......	6
Dish, culture, ea.	......	12	84	87	156	75	264	162	......	444	162	12	......	144	......	......	......	144	1,746
Dish, evaporating, ea.	......	......	......	......	......	26	168	......	......	66	......	......	......	10	......	......	......	26	296
Dish, meat, assorted, ea.	......	300	200	850	300	200	300	650	150	300	450	800	......	250	700	250	100	400	6,200
Dish, oatmeal, ea.	......	238	......	288	50	......	119	363	......	100	......	......	......	......	238	......	......	......	1,396
Dish, petri, ea.	......	......	......	......	......	......	100	......	......	......	......	......	......	......	......	......	......	......	100
Dish, pickle, ea.	......	......	......	......	80	......	......	......	......	......	......	......	......	......	120	......	......	......	200
Dish, stender, ea.	440	......	......	20	180	......	380	......	......	20	180	200	......	180	......	......	......	20	1,620
Dish, vegetable, assorted, ea.	......	250	250	250	250	150	688	......	......	250	175	135	......	150	250	......	......	25	2,823
Dippers, w.e., ea.	......	45	100	100	176	......	300	100	......	428	100	100	......	100	100	100	......	100	1,849
Disinfector, cog gear, with pump, ea.	......	......	......	......	......	......	1	......	......	......	......	......	......	......	......	......	......	......	1
Disinfector, hand spray, ea.	......	......	......	6	......	......	5	......	......	......	......	17	......	6	......	24	......	6	64
Dispensing set, ea.	......	1	......	1	......	......	......	1	......	......	1	......	......	......	......	......	......	1	5
Distributor, Carrel-Dakin, ea.	......	......	36	......	196	......	2,477	......	......	2,448	......	......	......	......	......	......	......	......	5,157
Drawers, boys' winter, ea.	......	......	......	......	......	......	......	......	......	......	......	......	......	......	......	404	......	......	404
Drums for sterilizing dressings, ea.	......	......	......	......	......	......	84	......	......	31	......	4	......	13	4	......	......	......	136
Egg beater, ea.	......	......	......	......	......	......	32	......	......	......	......	......	......	......	......	......	......	......	32
Esophagoscope, extra lamp for, ea.	......	......	......	......	......	......	......	......	......	......	......	22	......	......	......	......	......	......	22
Envelope openers, ea.	......	......	......	......	......	......	2	......	......	......	......	......	......	......	......	......	......	......	2
Eye shades, ea.	556	136	100	396	500	110	2,136	200	......	144	500	352	......	350	200	220	......	100	6,000
Eye spud, ea.	......	5	......	10	10	......	......	......	......	10	10	10	......	10	......	......	......	......	65
Felt, assorted, yds.	......	103	276	242	276	103	324	103	......	552	103	103	414	190	103	69	......	379	3,340
Field Hospital, Par. 879, incomplete, ea.	......	......	......	......	......	......	4	......	......	......	......	......	......	......	......	......	......	......	4
Files, Shannon, ea.	......	......	......	20	......	......	20	......	......	......	20	......	......	20	......	20	......	......	100
Filter apparatus, glass cylinder for, ea.	......	......	......	......	......	......	25	......	......	......	......	......	......	......	......	......	......	......	25
First-aid packets, assorted, ea.	......	10,400	17,500	25,000	19,432	16,804	17,624	16,810	15,000	34,760	19,300	30,061	......	23,050	23,250	9,360	7,500	14,411	300,262
Flasks, Kjeldahl, ea.	......	......	......	......	......	......	31	......	......	......	......	......	......	......	......	......	......	......	31
Flask, Erlenmeyer, ea.	82	......	......	12	135	......	171	......	......	145	73	800	......	105	32	......	......	......	1,555
Flask, for belt, ea.	......	......	285	693	520	238	918	......	......	533	730	283	......	533	1,193	210	......	865	7,001
Fly tent, with rope, ea.	......	1	3	......	......	......	4	3	......	1	1	1	......	1	1	......	......	2	18

Commodity and Unit	Shortage	Detail of Deliveries by Districts 1	2	3	4	5	6	7	8	9	10	11	12	13	14	15	16	17	Total
Flashlights, ea.							7												7
Food, amb., box of, ea.			2	75		75	150	75	75	59				75					586
Food boxes, Par. 948, ea.		3	8		3	3	37	8			18	3	8	23	23	2	20	3	162
Forks, meat, large, ea.							580												580
Forks, table, ea.	231	120		201			1,400								60			1,632	3,644
Flashlights, extra lamps for, ea.							10												10
Frame, heating and wire, ea.				1			1			1	1	1		1	1			1	8
Front-line packets, assorted, ea.		3,443	3,065	4,575	3,234	6,109	4,091	3,205	1,650	9,129	3,811	2,699		5,271	4,992	1,802	2,250	2,977	62,303
Funnels, glass, assorted, ea.	28	99		200	175	95	555	145		485	498					57		141	2,478
Funnels, assorted, w.e., ea.		24	50	217	48	87	37	22	67	100		152		99	184		27	248	1,362
Gasoline engine, with dynamo, ea.					1	1	5												7
Gauze, compressed, ea.					5,760				1,000			4,275			1,000			1,440	13,475
Gauze, iodoform, tubes,			64				28				14								106
Gauze, packing, pkgs.,							2,500								2,400				4,900
Gauze, plain, assorted, yds.		134,627	132,482	127,007	209,956	196,340	357,441	99,258	30,200	203,515	136,030	101,983	165,921	145,812	155,206	52,633	54,929	84,600	2,387,940
Gauze, sublimated, 2½ yd. pc. in, pkg.		87,020	104,811	102,180	109,383	104,691	223,125	107,565	58,790	319,281	91,155	111,580	60,000	81,862	108,065	46,185	40,980	129,835	1,886,508
Gauze, rolls, ea.	192																		192
Gauze wipes, ea.				21,000										40,000	20,000				81,000
Gauze rolls, 4 inch by 3 inch, ea.								935											935
Generator, gasoline, ea.				6								6						6	18
Generator, violet ray, ea.										1									1
Glass rods, assorted, lbs.				270			53	149	20										492
Glass tubing, lbs.					160									48					208
Gloves, rubber, prs.	191		46		447		749			250	250	86	837	482	152	250		2	3,742
Gowns, operating ea.		440	573	1,090	970	490	3,008	625	400	1,579	1,531	838	2,378	700	650	400	286	1,089	17,047
Graduates, aluminum, ea.							818												818
Graduates, glass, ea.	655		126	217	365	122	196	82		288	143	95		177	234		9	200	2,909
Graduates, w.e., ea.			11																11
Graters, large, ea							4			34									38
Hammocks, ea.							11			10									21
Headlight, Murphy, electric, ea.							9												9
Headpieces, ea.	14		10	10	10	6	15	10		45	10	10		10				10	160
Heaters, electric cutoff, ea.	100		3	3	3		3	1		3									116
Heaters, electric, with 3 spray bottles, ea.		1	1	1	1	1	16	1		7	1	1		1	1	1		1	35
Haemoglobinometer, Tallquist scale, ea.		7	7	7	7	7	11	7		11	7	7		7	7	7		7	106
Hook, eye, foreign body, ea.						1													1
Hones, oil, ea.	94	26	23	127	21	24	22	26	9	23	23	18	5	23	21	17	8	16	526
Individual dressing packets, ea.		14,250	18,814	13,370	17,001	13,800	18,450	10,250		20,500	12,350	5,393		22,150	13,950	5,850	6,000	10,900	203,028
Inhaler, chloroform, with drop bottles, ea.		6	4	5	6	8	14	1	6	6	4	4		4	3	8	10	9	98
Inhaler, chloroform, drop bottle, for, ea.					24		92												116
Inhaler, metal, Yankhauer, ea.		20	20	40	35	10	132	20		20	45	40		40	11	20		20	473
Irrigation appar. Valentines, extra glass jars, ea.							6												6
Irrigation apparatus, tubing clip for, ea.		5	5		5	5	10	5	5	10	5	5			5	5	5	5	80
Irrigator, metal, seamless, ea.				180															180
Irrigator, nasal, glass, ea.										90									90
Irrigator, urethral, nozzle for, ea.		144	144		180	144	180	144	72	180	144	144		144	72	55	40	108	1,895
Irrigator, metal, 2 qt., ea.		25	24	32	6	6				20		17		12	31			22	195
Irrigator, anterior chamber, ea.							82												82
Irrigation apparatus, wall bracket for, ea.		3	5	5	5	3	5	5		5	5	5		5	5			5	61
Jackets, pneumonia, ea.		1,314	3,205	4,006	2,980	2,791	3,714	3,795	1,247	4,171	2,984	2,939	1,508	2,459	2,589	1,823	779	2,772	45,076
Jackknives, with sawblade, ea.							131												131
Jars, w.e., for dressing, ea.		12	46	152	41	39	195	72		157	24	83	193	73	48	15		37	1,187
Jars, coplin, ea.	137						65												202
Jars, glass-covered, for sutures, ea.			20	50			110			110									290
Jars, specimen, ea.				9	56		57			58				56					236

[Continued on next page]

Medical Table 2—(*Continued*)

HOSPITAL SUPPLIES

Commodity and Unit	Short-age	Detail of Deliveries by Districts																	Total
		1	2	3	4	5	6	7	8	9	10	11	12	13	14	15	16	17	
Kettles, tea, ea	.....	.....	.....	.....	30	.....	2	.....	.....	28	.....	.....	.....	30	.....	.....	.....	30	120
Kettles, stew, ea	.....	.....	.....	.....	.....	.....	.....	.....	.....	.....	.....	.....	.....	.....	.....	.....	.....	14	14
Knives, table, s.p., ea	93	540	.....	325	.....	.....	2,100	.....	.....	.....	.....	168	.....	.....	264	594	.....	.....	4,084
Knives, butcher, ea	36	.....	.....	216	.....	.....	.....	.....	.....	.....	.....	.....	.....	396	144	.....	.....	.....	792
Knives, bread, ea	.....	.....	.....	.....	78	.....	268	.....	.....	.....	.....	.....	.....	.....	.....	.....	.....	.....	346
Labels for vials, gro	.....	7,750	7,502	9,091	7,800	4,450	28,187	7,452	1,500	14,625	6,000	9,025	.....	6,750	4,700	8,100	1,500	6,000	130,432
Labels for vials, "poison," ea	.....	16,800	24,000	14,400	55,200	32,400	64,700	31,200	.....	8,400	7,200	12,000	.....	31,200	31,200	.....	.....	32,400	361,100
Ladles, melting, assorted, ea	.....	4	5	9	43	5	6	45	.....	9	5	9	.....	5	9	5	.....	5	164
Ladles, melting, handles for, ea	.....	2	1	2	1	1	2	1	.....	2	1	2	.....	3	2	1	.....	2	23
Ladles, pickling, copper, ea	.....	.....	1	1	1	1	5	1	.....	1	1	1	.....	1	1	.....	.....	1	16
Lamps, spirit, ea	.....	7	8	133	205	194	253	23	.....	305	94	319	.....	70	62	73	.....	8	1,754
Lamps, carbide, ea	.....	.....	.....	.....	.....	.....	17	.....	.....	.....	.....	.....	.....	.....	.....	.....	.....	.....	17
Lamps, diagnostic, Cameron, ea	.....	1	1	1	1	1	2	2	.....	1	.....	.....	.....	.....	.....	.....	.....	.....	10
Lamps, therapeutic, radio vibrant, ea	.....	.....	.....	.....	.....	.....	1	.....	.....	1	.....	.....	.....	.....	.....	.....	.....	.....	2
Lamps, hand, ea	.....	.....	.....	50	.....	.....	1	84	.....	.....	.....	.....	.....	.....	.....	36	.....	50	221
Lamps, hand, wicks for, ea	.....	.....	.....	.....	.....	.....	.....	.....	.....	.....	.....	.....	.....	.....	.....	3	.....	.....	3
Lamps, hand, chimney for, ea	144	.....	.....	122	.....	.....	64	144	.....	34	15	50	.....	.....	.....	64	.....	102	739
Lamps, alcohol, extra wicks for, ea	.....	144	144	288	288	288	1,288	288	.....	288	144	144	.....	144	144	144	.....	144	3,880
Lamps, head, ea	.....	9	.....	.....	.....	.....	.....	.....	.....	12	.....	15	.....	.....	.....	.....	.....	.....	36
Lamp, shade for, ea	.....	.....	.....	.....	.....	.....	.....	.....	.....	30	44	.....	.....	.....	.....	.....	.....	.....	74
Lanterns, folding, ea	64	56	112	108	58	130	192	58	2	106	108	76	300	58	60	52	2	132	1,674
Lanterns, complete, with globes, ea	.....	.....	12	36	12	23	12	95	.....	17	12	12	.....	15	11	11	.....	8	276
Lanterns, extra globes for, ea	.....	.....	10	24	18	.....	31	19	.....	.....	15	45	.....	18	.....	17	.....	26	223
Linen, white, yds	.....	.....	.....	.....	.....	.....	18	.....	.....	.....	.....	.....	.....	.....	.....	.....	.....	.....	18
Litters, extra canvas for, ea	.....	25	120	362	220	359	459	160	24	436	180	180	.....	364	174	115	.....	312	3,490
Litters, snowshoe, ea	.....	.....	.....	.....	.....	.....	20	.....	.....	.....	.....	.....	.....	.....	.....	.....	.....	.....	20
Litters, studs for, ea	.....	.....	.....	.....	.....	.....	1,424	.....	.....	.....	.....	.....	.....	.....	.....	.....	.....	.....	1,424
Litters, tacks for, pkg	.....	.....	.....	2,000	1,000	.....	3,087	.....	48	1,000	21	.....	.....	1,000	.....	.....	.....	.....	8,156
Litters, with slings, ea	.....	62	70	90	70	70	110	70	.....	90	110	90	.....	70	90	46	.....	110	1,148
Localizer, parallax, ea	.....	.....	.....	.....	.....	.....	1	.....	.....	.....	.....	.....	.....	.....	.....	.....	.....	.....	1
Localizer, Sweet's eye, ea	.....	.....	.....	.....	.....	.....	1	.....	.....	.....	.....	.....	.....	.....	.....	.....	.....	.....	1
Machine for diathermy, ea	.....	.....	.....	.....	.....	.....	.....	.....	.....	1	.....	.....	.....	.....	.....	.....	.....	.....	1
Machine, galvanizing, with motor, ea	.....	.....	.....	.....	.....	.....	1	.....	.....	.....	.....	.....	.....	.....	.....	.....	.....	.....	1
Mailing cases, ea	.....	.....	100	.....	15	20	115	288	.....	.....	65	250	.....	15	.....	.....	.....	.....	868
Manta, canvas, ea	.....	.....	.....	.....	.....	.....	9	.....	.....	.....	.....	.....	.....	.....	.....	.....	.....	.....	9
Matches, safety, boxes, doz	.....	.....	5	600	684	.....	28,847	503	.....	600	720	348	.....	600	640	.....	.....	.....	33,547
Mattress cover, ea	.....	.....	.....	509	912	924	117	113	.....	.....	20	451	.....	.....	440	262	.....	111	3,859
Mattress pads for cots, ea	.....	.....	7	100	.....	99	114	.....	98	.....	.....	418	.....	110	100	100	.....	103	1,249
Mattress, rubber, ea	.....	.....	1	.....	.....	.....	.....	.....	.....	.....	.....	.....	.....	.....	1	.....	.....	1	3
Measure for Seidletz powder, ea	.....	.....	.....	.....	.....	.....	.....	.....	.....	.....	.....	.....	.....	.....	.....	.....	.....	6	6
Measure, metal, 1 gal., ea	.....	3	.....	.....	.....	.....	.....	.....	.....	.....	.....	.....	.....	.....	.....	.....	.....	.....	3
Mechanical dam, ea	.....	1	2	77	2	2	7	2	.....	7	2	7	.....	2	6	1	.....	2	120
Mechanical dam, automatic, ea	.....	1	1	1	1	1	2	1	.....	2	1	1	.....	1	1	1	.....	1	16
Medicine droppers, doz	.....	12	589	25	24	162	261	163	.....	481	1,476	24	24	3	.....	150	.....	204	3,598
Medicine glasses, ea	.....	.....	12	124	467	467	13	479	.....	483	467	.....	.....	.....	.....	.....	.....	.....	2,512
Metal, fusible, Mellott's, ea	.....	10	10	10	10	25	10	10	.....	10	10	10	.....	10	10	.....	.....	10	145
Microscope, mechanical stage, ea	.....	.....	.....	.....	.....	.....	14	.....	.....	.....	.....	.....	.....	.....	.....	.....	.....	.....	14
Microscopical supply cases, ea	.....	.....	.....	5	8	.....	16	2	.....	7	2	.....	.....	3	.....	.....	.....	.....	43
Mills, coffee, ea	.....	.....	.....	.....	.....	.....	18	.....	2	3	.....	1	.....	1	1	.....	.....	.....	26
Mimeograph, ea	.....	.....	.....	.....	.....	.....	1	.....	.....	.....	.....	.....	.....	.....	.....	.....	.....	.....	1
Moccasins, prs	16	.....	.....	40	.....	.....	144	.....	.....	46	.....	.....	.....	.....	.....	44	.....	.....	290
Mortars and pestles, assorted, ea	.....	12	33	97	103	119	478	248	.....	50	96	344	58	43	157	7	.....	17	1,862
Muslin, yds	6,600	9,180	12,446	29,908	12,928	10,663	35,068	16,040	11,496	46,984	22,167	22,313	.....	19,761	19,655	2,220	11,100	15,790	304,319
Nightingale scarf, ea	.....	.....	.....	.....	.....	.....	152	.....	.....	.....	.....	.....	.....	.....	.....	.....	.....	.....	152
Oakum, lbs	.....	.....	567	54	94	76	146	.....	.....	139	81	810	.....	54	167	.....	.....	120	1,808
Overshoes, prs	93	257	252	340	380	348	637	288	.....	392	360	280	.....	296	256	168	.....	280	4,627

HOSPITAL SUPPLIES

Commodity and Unit	Shortage	Detail of Deliveries by Districts																	Total
		1	2	3	4	5	6	7	8	9	10	11	12	13	14	15	16	17	
Packers, gauze, uterine, ea.							2												2
Pads, absorbent and dressing, assorted, ea.		1,030	1,631	2,042	1,327	928	4,810	1,824		2,317	1,649	2,910	6,979	51,873	1,131	2,024		1,613	84,088
Pail, commode, ea.		60	66	170	82	70	161	83	44	81	166	104	47	92	88	25	64	66	1,469
Pail, w.e., 10 qt., ea.	367			16			20		6	45	12	81			132			10	689
Pajama coats, ea.							268												268
Pajama trousers, ea.							38												38
Pajama suits, ea.		922	1,184	500		941	980	430	533	732	2,219	500		1,323	1,171	1,135	344	2,499	15,413
Pans, dish, ea.		13	25	25	25	25	80	26		25	13	72		61	36			25	451
Pans, frying, ea.				60		51	50	50		60	12	50		50	50			50	483
Pans, sauce, enamel, ea.		250	36		32	57	250												625
Pans, dust, ea.			100	43			25			26									194
Pans, muffin, ea.		50																	50
Pans, w.e., 4 qt., ea.							4							200					204
Paper, filter, assorted, pkg.							213												213
Paper, filter, 20 x 20 in., shts.		500	500	1,000	1,000	500	1,117	1,000		1,000	500	1,000		500	506	500		500	10,123
Paper lens, Japanese, pkgs.							87												87
Paper, carbon, pkgs.							1												1
Paper, manifolding, 100 sheets in, pkgs.							1												1
Paper, manifolding, 500 sheets in pkgs.							3												3
Paper, oiled, 1,700 yards in roll							6				3	6							15
Paper, typewriting, 250 sheets in pkg.							2												2
Paper, typewriting, 500 sheets in pkg.							2												2
Pencils, lead, ea.																		428	428
Pencils, wax, red and blue, ea.				72		72	730	72		72	72	72		72	72			72	1,378
Percolator, glass, ea.	24						59												83
Perimeter, cabinet, ea.							1												1
Pillow cases, ea.	3,000	6,688	4,100	8,162	5,780	4,117	10,329	6,548	1,200	17,441	4,152	3,988	6,014	7,886	4,409	2,300	1,800	7,278	105,192
Pillow sacks, ea.	811	800	400	400	800	400	2,449	1,832	600	1,000		641		600	1,400	832	400	2,992	16,357
Pill machine, ea.							10												10
Pill tile, assorted, ea.	68	28	21	21	21	21	321	21		30	21	21		21	21	34		21	691
Pinchcock for rubber tubing, ea.	6																		6
Pins, common, papers			24			600		919	624							200		700	3,067
Pins, safety, doz.	499		2,374	3,420	1,400	1,072	2,044	1,476		2,880	3,800	5,112		8,028	2,880	1,400		3,420	39,805
Pipettes, assorted, ea.			100				128			141	100	75		75		35			654
Pipette box, ea.	310						100			100					80				590
Pitchers, delft, 4 qt., ea.	63		2																65
Pitchers, 1 pt., ea.	71																		71
Pitchers, w.e., assorted, ea.	93	102	228	235	270	213	521	221	24	572	477	463	429	447	356	96		416	5,163
Plaster, adhesive, spls.			636	600	983	276	1,278	36		1,200	600		3,600	600	600				10,409
Plaster, moleskin, 5 yds. in roll				105															105
Plaster of paris, 4 lbs.	39	48	120	40	48	48	116	93		150	72	90		200	89	60		48	1,261
Plastic instrument, special filling, ea.	4																		4
Plates, dessert, ea.				300			324			300		300							1,224
Plates, dinner, delft, ea.		500	436	1,530	509	2,020	2,628	600		700		1,144		1,224	1,200	150		900	13,541
Plates, pie, ea.		472	400		237		1,000	139				497							2,745
Plates, soup, enamel, ea.						400					2,115								2,515
Plates, soup, delft, ea.	150	92		150	150			150		300		150		150	570	150		150	2,162
Plates, X-Ray, German, doz.					10	9	28									9			56
Platters, meat, assorted, ea.		200	200	130	250	600	258	200		450	1,000	100		200	720	50		200	4,558
Pockets, bed, ea.				626			300		270						307				1,503
Pots, chamber, ea.			3				31												34
Pot, coffee, individual, ea.	55	5	5	89	5	4	411	5		374	5	4		4	4	4		4	978
Pots, stock, assorted, ea.		24	54	36	94	24	128	24		60	66	48		24	48		12	32	674
Pots, dappen, green and white, ea.		30	30	66	30	1	116	30		116	30	66		30	66	26		50	687
Pots, tea, assorted, ea.	10	48	24		48	10	96	24		24	24	24		24		24			380
Pouches, M.D., with sling, ea.		262	212	338		486	83			169	445	343		641	594	133		185	3,891

[Continued on next page]

Medical Table 2—(*Continued*)

HOSPITAL SUPPLIES

Commodity and Unit	Short-age	Detail of Deliveries by Districts																	Total
		1	2	3	4	5	6	7	8	9	10	11	12	13	14	15	16	17	
Pouches, orderly incomplete, ea	......	......	20	20	......	30	4	8	......	......	48	10	......	119	......	112	......	10	381
Pumps, rectal, double section, ea	18	......	......	......	......	......	......	......	......	......	......	......	......	......	......	......	......	......	18
Regimental combat equipment, incomplete, ea	......	......	10	......	......	......	10	5	......	......	9	8	1	......	......	2	......	5	50
Rheostat, ea	24	......	......	......	3	......	4	......	......	4	......	......	......	......	......	......	......	......	35
Rubber tubing, and drainage, assorted, yds	......	......	288	1,000	87	......	2,656	923	......	177	......	......	......	291	......	......	......	......	5,422
Rubber stoppers, ea	......	......	20	60	100	60	150	60	......	1,400	100	60	......	60	42	50	......	100	2,262
Ruler, refraction, Prime, ea	......	......	......	......	1	......	1	......	......	1	......	......	......	......	......	......	......	......	3
Sandpaper grits, shts	500	......	1,000	1,000	1,000	1,000	1,000	1,000	......	1,000	1,000	1,000	......	1,000	500	500	......	1,000	12,500
Sanitary train, headgear equipment, ea	......	......	......	......	......	......	......	......	......	......	......	......	1	......	......	......	......	......	1
Saucers, w.e., ea	308	720	1,220	......	1,440	600	4,221	720	......	580	1,322	1,440	......	920	720	......	......	720	14,931
Scales, weights, apothecary, balance, asstd., ea	......	4	2	3	7	10	15	4	......	4	5	2	......	5	3	3	......	3	70
Screwdriver, ea	......	......	......	......	......	......	3	......	......	......	......	......	......	......	......	......	......	......	3
Shakers, salt and pepper, ea	......	......	......	......	526	......	9	......	......	312	150	......	......	60	......	......	......	......	1,057
Shade, with cord, ea	......	......	......	......	......	1	......	......	1	1	......	......	......	1	......	1	1	......	6
Sheets, cotton, ea	......	......	133	1,791	......	530	......	......	......	650	717	23	......	......	......	870	......	991	5,705
Sheets, impervious, ea	91	......	280	......	630	210	1,565	210	......	......	1,532	280	......	......	70	210	......	840	5,918
Sheeting, rubber, yds	341	180	219	54	......	145	625	136	......	265	......	267	......	......	180	20	......	80	2,512
Shellac, dry, white, lbs	......	......	......	......	......	......	22	......	......	......	......	......	......	......	......	......	......	......	22
Shirts, cotton, ea	413	10,413	8,820	6,513	10,264	5,210	9,846	6,381	1,603	7,734	9,280	6,192	31,160	7,560	6,543	6,749	720	9,072	144,473
Slides, microscope, ea	......	......	8	10	7	......	15	5	......	......	10	......	......	50	5	5	......	7	122
Slippers, prs	......	4,925	4,820	5,503	6,809	4,727	7,793	3,521	1,100	6,989	6,641	5,946	5,504	5,024	4,644	3,031	3,400	6,853	87,230
Splints, assorted	......	263	420	3,108	936	1,622	8,642	1,210	131	1,199	222	1,874	......	2,199	824	371	117	3,394	26,532
Sponges, animal, large, ea	......	......	1,102	......	305	......	......	2,936	......	......	......	......	......	......	......	......	......	......	4,343
Sponges, gauze, assorted, ea	......	20,500	1,342	42,000	305	5,000	67	5,814	......	226,000	......	......	......	......	20,000	20,000	......	5,960	346,988
Spoons, lens, wire loop, ea	......	......	......	......	......	......	201	......	......	......	......	......	......	......	......	......	......	......	201
Spoons, table, ea	......	1,000	1,000	1,808	1,000	1,808	1,000	1,000	......	1,808	1,000	1,000	......	2,072	1,248	......	......	2,258	18,002
Sprinklers, powder, hard rubber, ea	......	......	......	......	......	......	728	......	......	......	......	......	......	......	......	......	......	......	728
Sterilizer, electric, asbestos, ea	......	......	......	......	1	......	1	......	......	1	......	......	......	......	......	......	......	......	3
Sterilizer, hot air, ea	......	1	1	1	2	2	2	2	......	2	2	2	......	2	2	1	1	2	25
Sterilizer, hot air, 12 x 18 x 9, ea	......	1	1	1	......	......	......	......	......	1	1	......	......	......	......	......	......	......	5
Sterilizer, autoclave, ea	......	......	......	1	......	1	1	1	......	1	......	......	......	......	......	......	......	......	5
Sterilizer set, 2-25 gal. hot and cold water tanks	......	......	1	1	......	......	......	......	......	1	......	1	......	......	......	......	......	......	4
Sterilizer set, Scanlon Morris, 2-25 gal. h. and c.	......	......	......	......	......	......	1	......	......	......	......	......	......	......	......	......	......	......	1
Sterilizing set, Kny Scheerer, 2-6 gal. h. and c.	......	......	......	......	......	......	......	......	......	......	......	......	......	......	......	......	......	1	1
Sterilizer, electric, assorted, ea	......	1	2	2	......	......	4	......	......	2	1	......	......	......	1	......	......	1	14
Sterilizer, hypo, all glass, ea	......	......	......	......	......	......	3	......	......	2	......	......	......	......	......	......	......	......	5
Sterilizer, steam, Arnold, ea	......	11	9	11	10	9	19	8	4	12	11	10	......	8	9	7	6	10	154
Stands, portable, table, dental, ea	1	......	10	10	5	1	12	2	......	10	1	......	......	2	......	......	......	......	54
Stand, portable, complete, less table, ea	......	......	......	......	......	......	......	......	......	......	......	7	......	......	......	......	......	1	8
Stool, folding, canvas, ea	1	......	......	......	......	......	36	......	......	12	......	......	......	......	......	......	......	......	49
Stool, revolving, w.e., ea	......	......	......	......	6	......	22	......	......	......	......	......	......	......	......	......	......	......	28
Stone, artificial for models, 3 lb	......	......	6	......	6	6	......	6	......	......	......	......	......	......	......	......	......	......	24
Stove, coal oil, 1 and 2 burner, ea	......	43	42	62	36	56	36	28	24	67	20	62	30	40	43	32	20	61	702
Stretcher, top and frame, ea	......	......	......	......	1	1	3	......	......	......	......	......	......	......	......	......	......	......	5
Suit, convalescent, ea	278	......	120	234	105	......	458	130	......	382	91	291	......	198	316	......	......	218	2,821
Suit, operating, ea	......	......	......	......	......	......	......	......	......	174	......	......	......	......	......	......	......	......	174
Supports, leg, ea	......	......	4	......	......	......	......	......	......	......	......	......	......	......	......	......	......	......	4
Supports, perineal, ea	......	......	4	......	......	......	......	......	......	......	......	......	......	......	......	......	......	......	4
Support, abdominal, ea	......	......	......	......	......	......	29	......	......	......	......	......	......	......	......	......	......	......	29
Surgical dressings, ambulance box, Par. 954, ea	......	107	278	228	353	182	153	189	126	327	221	372	......	232	106	94	252	433	3,653
Surgical dressings, box of Par. 955, ea	163	191	89	175	103	91	222	168	17	192	100	157	251	162	217	116	23	131	2,568
Sutures, surgical, assorted, ea	......	36,241	47,334	71,955	51,500	39,636	98,147	46,671	7,072	57,306	44,680	53,493	85,644	43,702	45,648	15,500	10,445	34,086	789,060
Table, aseptic, bracket to fit arm chair, ea	1	......	......	......	......	......	......	......	......	......	......	......	......	......	......	......	......	......	1
Table, aseptic, gas attachment for spider, ea	3	......	......	......	......	......	2	......	......	5	......	......	......	......	......	......	......	......	10
Table, bedside, folding iron, ea	......	......	......	37	11	11	22	11	6	11	......	36	......	2	24	......	......	36	207
Table, bedside, folding top for, ea	......	......	......	......	......	50	......	......	......	......	......	......	......	......	......	......	......	......	50

Commodity and Unit	Shortage	1	2	3	4	5	6	7	8	9	10	11	12	13	14	15	16	17	Total
		Detail of Deliveries by Districts																	
Table, bedside folding shelves for, ea						50													50
Table, bedside folding, legs for, ea						200													200
Table, dressing, glass top, ea.		2		2			6	1		1		1							13
Table, dressing, instrument, w.e., ea.					1		15				1								17
Table, fracture, Howley, ea.				1			1	1							1				4
Table, instrument, ea.		1	1			3	15	1				1							22
Table, instrument, aluminum w. wall bracket, ea.							1												1
Tables, operating, field folding, ea.	12	12	11	24	13	14	25	8	1	21	10	16	12	14	14	4	4	9	224
Tables, operating, post, ea.		3	3	7	3	5	5	3	5	5	4	5		4	1		3	9	65
Tables, orthopedic, metal, ea.							1												1
Table, pressed steel, white, Harvard, ea.		3	2	3	2		6	1		2	1	2		2	2		2	1	29
Table, portable, X-ray, ea.					1	1	3												5
Table, portable, accessories, boxes of, ea.					1	1	3												5
Tanks, developing X-ray, ea.							2												2
Tape, cotton, rolls and yards,							1,400											280	1,680
Telatherm, portable, with motor, 110 volt, ea.							1												1
Tent pins, small, ea		6	12				6	18		6	6	6		6	6			12	84
Test glasses, ungraduated, 200 cc., ea.	299									54									353
Test tubes, assorted, ea.	4,753	14,907	1,928	24,051	4,635	3,310	29,686	3,969		23,008	10,187	2,551		12,689	11,640	1,550		2,509	151,373
Test tubes, supports, ea.				5	62														67
Test tube support, Wasserman rack, ea				27			2	33											62
Test tubes, 3 in nest, nest											57								57
Thread, cotton, spl.			2,406	4,800	3,216	2,400	1,722	2,405		2,460	4,800	2,400		4,800	4,800		2,400	2,400	41,009
Tin, 6 in. square, shts.							25			25									50
Tongue depressors, metal, assorted, ea.		77	1,370	321	77	77	191	77	50	77	77	77		77	77	77	50	77	2,829
Tongue depressors, wood, gross		200	200	800	166	200	600	200		404	200	200		400	800			400	4,770
Tools, universal, ea.		10			10		30	6	6	97					6	6	6		177
Towel, dish and hand, ea.	431	14,420	11,854	13,756	12,248	15,972	24,257	12,828		7,451	18,388	13,678	16,200	18,216	13,800	5,141		21,396	220,036
Towel, paper, 100 in rl.		100				100	29									50			279
Tractor, postatic, Young, ea.							4			4									8
Transportable laboratory, ea.				1			1												2
Transformer, electric, with switch, ea.					1	1	5												7
Trays, instrument, ea.	115		64	123	50	181	107	318	79	332	50	120	300	70	112			60	2,081
Trays, serving, ea.	138						1												139
Tripod, iron, ea.	27						50												77
Tub, bath, folding,				4			2	4	4		4			4	6		4	1	33
Tub, bath, portable, ea.		3	2	3		3		4	2	2	2	3	6		1	1		2	34
Tub, foot, ea.		24	23	37	72	30	76	38		81	49	25		37	46	24	24	54	640
Tube, Pelon X-ray, ea.							14									2			16
Tube, rectal, ea.				66	14		115	150		12						104		129	590
Tube, stomach, ea.		128	224	250	533	313	711	456	6	744	417	41		53	53	9	3	321	4,262
Tube, tracheotomy, ea		2	13	3	13	3	18	13		13	2	3		3	2	2		3	93
Tube, valve, French, ea.	1				3	3					1								8
Tube, rubber, stomach, vet., 10-ft. lengths, ea.																5			5
Tumblers, w.e., ea.			375	1,057		360	100			792		116		982			300		4,082
Tumblers, glass, ea.			210		420		530	312			420	210			400	210		210	2,922
Twine, coarse, lbs.			2	2															4
Typewriters, Royal, ea.		1	1	1	1	1	22				2	1		1	1	1	1	1	35
Urinals, glass and w.e., ea.			48	268		69	215	100	100	732	65			178	517	65		274	2,631
Vials, assorted, gro	100	147	210	294	159	189	681	237	101	261	206	158	371	221	150	54	120	205	3,864
Vision test set, cards for, ea.		13	10	12	10	12	15	10		14	10	12		10	12	10		10	160
Vision test set, color for, ea.							6												6
Venereal prophylaxis unit, Par. 958, ea.			4	4	6		7	2		6	1	1		2	1	2			36
Wasserman bath, ea.							2			1									3
Wash bottle, 1,000 c.c., ea.							25												25
Water bath, copper, ea.	1																		1

[Continued on next page]

Medical Table 2—(*Continued*)

HOSPITAL SUPPLIES

Commodity and Unit	Shortage	Detail of Deliveries by Districts 1	2	3	4	5	6	7	8	9	10	11	12	13	14	15	16	17	Total
Webster's dictionary, English, ea.	4																		4
Wheel brush laboratory lathe, ea.		5	6	6	6	6	12	6		12	6	6		6	6	6		6	95
Wire, German silver, 4 ft. lengths, ea.							35												35
Wire, binding, spls.		3	5	5	5	5	12	5		10	5	5		5	5	5		5	80
Wire ligature, Angle's, bxs.		4	2	3	47	3	127	203		104	3	3		2	2	7		2	512
Wire, nichrome, ft.	23																		23
Wrenches, bone plate, ea.							10												10

SURGICAL INSTRUMENTS AND APPLIANCES, INCLUDING DENTAL INSTRUMENTS, APPLIANCES, AND SUPPLIES

Commodity and Unit	Shortage	1	2	3	4	5	6	7	8	9	10	11	12	13	14	15	16	17	Total
Albumenometer, ea.				5			5			5	2	5		5	5			5	37
Alcohol burner, ea.							11					3						2	16
Alloy balance, ea.		1	1	1	1	1	2	1		2	1	1		1	1	1		2	17
Apparatus, nit. ox. and oxyg., Heidbrink, ea.	1																		1
Applicators, surgical, assorted, ea.		200	150	282	300	150	1,036	150	28	400	200	271	408	200	200	79	100	200	4,354
Applicators, portable, light, ea.	5																		5
Applicators, radio, ea.	2																		2
Articulators, crown and bridge, ea.		6	6	6	6	6	14	6		14	6	6		6	6	6		6	100
Asbestos board, ea.		5	6	110	6	5	113	6		10	6	8		107	8	5		6	401
Asbestos mat, ea.				42															42
Axe heads, ea.	5																		5
Axe, helves for, ea.	60																		60
Bags, canvas, for buckshot, ea.	76																		76
Balance, analytical, ea.					1										1			1	3
Bands, fracture, assorted, ea.		90	152	208	128	128	1,385	128		310	228	228		129	178	120		228	3,640
Bellows, foot, ea.	4																		4
Bench, combination, ea.				1			2							1					4
Bench, combination, extra bellows for, ea.							5												5
Bistoury, probe pointed, straight and curved, ea.		100	50	100	75	84	171	75		100	74	75		50	50	50		50	1,104
Blood lancet, automatic, ea.	3				5	2	5	2		5									22
Blower, chip, bulb, for, ea.		7	7	7	7	7	23	7		8	7	7		7	7	7		7	115
Blower, chip, assorted		10	10	10	10	10	50	10		36	10	10		10	10	10		10	206
Blower, foot-power, ea.					1		1			2									4
Blow pipe for gas, ea.							2												2
Bougies, assorted, ea.	600	1,468	2,639	2,881	3,391	1,620	5,562	3,013	876	4,554	2,265	2,150	864	2,207	1,626	1,078	432	1,776	39,002
Bowls, plaster, assorted, ea.	15	9	7	7	7	7	1	7		13	7	7		7	7	7		7	115
Bridge repair set, ea.		3	4	4	4	4	10	4		10	4	4		4	4	3		4	66
Bronchoscope, incomplete, ea.					1		1			1									3
Brush, tooth-polishing, ea.		144	72	144	144	144	144	144		144	144	144		144		144			1,656
Burnishers, assorted, ea.		15	15	15	15	15	30	15		20	15	15		15	15	15		15	230
Burs, dental, assorted, ea.		2,172	2,670	3,231	2,670	2,814	4,776	2,886		4,590	2,744	2,892		2,526	2,244	1,230		2,094	39,539
Cabinet, dental, ea.			1		1		3	1						1					7
Carborundum stone, ea.				5		2	7	2			3	3		3					25
Carrier, amalgam, assorted, ea.		2	2	2	2	2	6	2		5	2	2		2	2	1		2	34
Carver, amalgam, Frahm's, ea.			3	3			3			3	3	3		3				3	24
Case, aspirating, ea.		2	1	2	1	1	13	2		2	1	2		1	1	1		1	31
Case, bedding, ea.			5				110		30	12	1					3			161
Case, 3 lens, hooks, and dilator, ea.												1							1
Case, diagnostic, ea.												6							6
Case, ear, nose and throat, ea.		14	12	7	15	4	22	16	4	12	13	3	17	4	3	4	2	5	157
Case, eye, incomplete, ea.		10	10	8	8	9	68	11	4	8	8	7	2	8	9	4	2	7	183
Case, eye, incomplete, ea.	3	5	7	3	9	6	10	9	2	8	8	10	38	4	3	3	3	6	137
Case, foot, ea.							6												6
Case, forceps, incomplete, ea.							1												1

SURGICAL INSTRUMENTS AND APPLIANCES, INCLUDING DENTAL INSTRUMENTS, APPLIANCES, AND SUPPLIES

Commodity and Unit	Shortage	Detail of Deliveries by Districts																	Total
		1	2	3	4	5	6	7	8	9	10	11	12	13	14	15	16	17	
Case, forceps, haemostatic, ea.		19	24	20	20	24	136	20		20	15	15		15	10	10		19	367
Case, general operating, ea.		48	47	47	38	25	32	36	19	27	42	49	68	54	35	44	19	31	661
Case, genito-urinary, ea.		15	25	16	27	15	42	23	8	28	23	22	32	12	14	7	12	15	336
Case, instrument for privates, ea.							11												11
Case, instrument for Medical Officers, ea.							435												435
Case, medicine, incomplete, ea.			11																11
Case, office preparation, ea.				3	3		2			6	2	4		3	5			4	32
Case, pocket, incomplete, ea.							1			1									2
Case, pocket, Medical Officers', ea.	6			1								1							8
Case, post mortem, incomplete, ea.							7												7
Case, tooth extracting, ea.	9	2	2	5	2	1	4	3		6	2	1		2	3	1		4	47
Case, treatment for eye, ea.							1												1
Case, trial lenses, ea.							5					5							10
Case, ward, dressing, ea.							53												53
Casserole, 125 cc., ea.	63																		63
Catheters, assorted, ea.		105	100	126	100	496	1,125	520		173	100	145		100	89	280		100	3,550
Cautery, electric, ea.												1							1
Cautery, handle, all metal, ea.												2							2
Cautery, handle plain for eye and ear, ea.							1												1
Cautery, iron, copper point, ea.		5	5	4	5	5	10	5		5	5	5		5	2	1		5	67
Cautery, paquelin, ea.				2			20									1			23
Cautery, paquelin, extra tips for, ea.												22							22
Cautery, veterinary, in case, incomplete, ea.							9												9
Cautery, paquelin, incomplete, ea.		2					23												25
Cautery, paquelin, extra bulbs for, ea.			10	10		11	65			15	10	10		10				10	151
Cement, dental, assorted, bxs.		361	888	1,112	793	580	1,453	429		2,130	1,320	302		658	717	135		190	11,068
Cement, rubber, tubes							300												300
Chair, dental, portable, ea.		3	4	6	5	3	8	3		6	5	3		4	3	1		3	57
Chair, dental, operating, ea.				1			3							1				1	6
Chest, supply, ea.	2	1	2	3	3	1	4	2		3	3	2	6	3	2	1		2	40
Chest, instrument, dental, ea.		2	2	2	2	2	3	1		3	3	3	10	2	3	2		4	44
Chisels, surgical and dental, assorted, ea.		25	45	50	50	50	775	50		100	45	61		45	45	25		45	1,411
Clamps, surgical, assorted, ea.		119	60	60	62	81	163	60		102	80	61		60	60	80		60	1,108
Clamps, rubber-dam, ea.		3	11	15	9	6	21	9		19	11	13		11	10	2		11	151
Clamps, for test tubes, ea.			35	124	35	21	105	30		258	15	60		30	55	10		30	808
Cleaners, root, canal, ea.		10	8	12	8	8	12	8		12	8	2		8	12	5		12	125
Clippers, hair, ea.	86		50	22	452	50	80	50		19	400	10			12	3		50	1,284
Clippers, horse, hand, ea.		3	12	4	4	9	4	3	4	5	3	2		3	2	11	4	4	77
Clips, wound, assorted, ea.		250	500	1,000	1,000	500	17,461	1,400		7,000	500	1,000		1,000	1,000	250		1,000	33,861
Composition, modeling, ½ lb., Kerr type, ea.		5	5	5	5	5	5	5		5	5	5		5				5	60
Compressor unit, air, with 8-gal. tank, ea.							1			1									2
Cones, felt, dental, assorted, ea.		25	50	50	50	50	75	50		75	50	50		50	25	25		50	675
Cotton rolls, dental, bxs.		100	2	15	2	102	443	2		107	3	3		15	305	24		3	1,126
Cotton absorbent, ¼ oz., pkg.							24												24
Counting apparatus, ea.							1												1
Counting chamber, ea.	10						3												13
Coupler, joining, Luer syringe, ea.			12	12	12		28	12		12	12	12		12	10			7	141
Crown remover, Johnson, ea.			1	1			3			1	1	1							8
Crowns, assorted, ea.																		1	1
Crucible, Gooch, rubber tubing for, ea.	145						177												322
Crucible, porcelain, ea.							32												32
Cups, polishing, bxs.	36	37	50	65	50	45	75	45		70	55	57		55	35	15		50	740
Curette, assorted, ea.		39	51	39	54	39	326	51	12	81	51	49		39	27	39	24	39	960
Cuspidor, fountain, ea.						1	1			2									4
Cuspidor, fount., met. saliva eject. mouthpiece,							10	5		10									25

[*Continued on next page*]

Medical Table 2—(*Continued*)

SURGICAL INSTRUMENTS AND APPLIANCES, INCLUDING DENTAL INSTRUMENTS, APPLIANCES, AND SUPPLIES

Commodity and Unit	Shortage	Detail of Deliveries by Districts																	Total
		1	2	3	4	5	6	7	8	9	10	11	12	13	14	15	16	17	
Cuspidor, fountain, incomplete, ea.	......	......	......	......	5	......	......	......	......	......	......	......	......	......	......	......	......	......	5
Cuspidor, fountain, extra bowls for, ea.	......	......	......	......	4	......	......	......	......	......	......	......	......	......	......	......	......	......	4
Cystoscope, Brown & Burger, ea.	25	......	1	3	4	......	15	1	......	......	3	2	......	2	1	2	......	1	60
Cystoscope, extra cord for, ea.	......	......	......	......	......	......	......	......	......	......	......	15	......	......	......	......	......	......	15
Cystotome, Graefe, ea.	150	10	10	12	10	10	15	10	......	15	10	12	......	10	10	6	......	10	300
Dark ground illuminator, ea.	......	......	......	......	......	......	......	......	......	......	......	2	......	......	......	......	......	......	2
Dentimeter, metal handle, ea.	......	4	4	4	4	4	12	4	......	5	4	4	......	4	4	4	......	4	65
Depressor, vaginal, ea.	......	......	......	......	......	......	4	......	......	......	......	......	......	......	......	......	......	......	4
Desk, field, dental, empty, ea.	......	5	3	4	5	3	5	4	......	4	3	3	1	3	4	3	......	4	54
Desiccator, Scheibler, ea.	......	......	......	......	......	......	1	......	......	......	......	......	......	......	......	......	......	......	1
Die holder and 1 tap, ea.	......	......	......	......	......	......	3	......	......	3	......	......	......	......	......	......	......	......	6
Die plate, cusp, ea.	......	......	......	......	......	......	50	......	......	17	......	......	......	......	......	......	......	......	67
Die plate and tops, Guilford's, sets	2	......	......	......	......	......	......	......	......	......	......	......	......	......	......	......	......	......	2
Dilator, jaw, ea.	......	......	......	......	......	......	1	......	......	......	......	......	......	......	......	......	......	......	1
Dilator, jaw, Blair, ea.	......	......	......	......	......	......	1	......	......	3	......	......	......	......	......	......	......	......	4
Dilator, lachrymal, ea.	......	......	......	......	......	......	264	......	......	......	......	......	......	......	......	......	......	......	264
Directors, grooved, ea.	81	120	96	96	144	96	244	120	36	192	96	96	250	96	72	21	72	72	2,000
Directors, perineal, assorted, ea.	......	......	......	......	5	......	12	......	......	6	......	......	......	......	......	......	......	......	23
Directors, probe, pointed, ea.	156	150	100	100	150	100	22	100	100	300	100	100	......	100	70	100	100	162	2,010
Dishes, soap, metal, ea.	......	......	......	100	......	......	......	......	......	131	......	......	......	......	......	......	......	......	231
Disks, dental, assorted, ea.	......	200	472	2,318	336	300	645	300	......	2,656	396	396	......	1,440	396	136	......	688	10,679
Disks, dental, assorted, bxs	6,950	1,196	1,198	2	1,080	1,188	2,459	1,022	......	3	1,118	1,186	......	144	978	504	......	500	19,528
Dissector, tonsil, ea.	......	......	3	......	......	4	6	4	......	4	......	......	......	......	......	......	......	......	21
Drills, assorted, ea.	......	54	228	162	216	132	432	216	......	216	118	150	......	180	140	48	......	162	2,454
Drills, bone, 3 point, ea.	......	......	......	......	......	......	6	......	......	......	......	......	......	......	......	......	......	......	6
Drill, bone, 3 point detachable, ea.	......	......	......	......	......	......	5	......	......	5	......	......	......	......	......	......	......	......	10
Drill set, ea.	......	......	......	......	......	......	5	......	......	......	......	......	......	......	......	......	......	......	5
Ear hook and spoon, ea.	19	......	......	......	......	......	......	1	......	......	......	......	......	......	......	......	......	......	20
Engine bit holder, revolving head, ea.	......	......	1	1	1	1	1	1	......	1	1	1	......	1	1	......	......	1	12
Elevators, surgical, assorted, ea.	......	6	10	16	10	10	78	10	......	26	13	18	......	10	10	6	......	10	233
Engine, dental, cable for, ea.	......	2	2	3	2	......	3	......	......	3	2	2	......	2	3	1	......	2	27
Engine, dental cable, sheath for, ea.	......	......	......	......	......	......	3	......	......	......	......	......	......	......	......	......	......	......	3
Engine, dental cord for, ea.	......	100	100	200	100	100	300	102	......	237	100	100	......	100	100	100	......	100	1,839
Engine, dental, sheath, for, ea.	......	......	......	10	......	......	16	......	......	15	......	10	......	......	10	......	......	......	61
Engine, dental, electric top for switch, ea.	......	......	......	......	......	......	2	......	......	......	......	......	......	......	......	......	......	......	2
Engine, dental, ea.	......	......	......	......	......	......	......	......	......	......	......	......	......	2	......	......	......	......	2
Engine, dental, handpiece, str. for HP 7, ea.	......	......	......	4	......	1	3	1	......	4	3	1	......	4	4	......	......	4	29
Engine, dental for HP "M", ea.	......	......	1	2	1	......	1	......	......	1	......	......	......	......	1	1	......	......	8
Engine, dental, lubricating oil for, ea.	4	20	18	24	18	16	24	18	......	24	18	24	......	24	24	20	......	24	300
Engine, dental, oil can for, ea.	......	......	......	......	......	......	15	......	......	12	......	......	......	......	......	......	......	......	27
Engine, dental, portable, ea.	......	1	1	1	1	1	2	1	......	8	2	8	......	4	1	......	......	1	32
Engine, dental, screwdriver for, ea.	1	......	1	2	1	1	2	1	......	2	1	1	......	2	2	1	......	2	20
Engine, dental slip joint connection for 2O, ea.	......	2	3	2	2	2	5	2	......	4	3	6	......	3	2	2	......	3	41
Engine, dental slip joint connection 2F, ea.	......	2	2	2	2	2	5	2	......	4	2	2	......	2	2	2	......	2	33
Engine, dental, wall bracket for, w.e., ea.	......	......	......	......	......	......	1	......	......	......	......	......	......	......	......	......	......	......	1
Excavators, dental, assorted, ea.	......	300	400	400	400	300	700	400	......	500	400	400	......	300	300	200	......	300	5,300
Explorers, assorted, ea.	......	100	100	150	100	100	200	100	......	150	100	99	......	100	100	50	......	100	1,549
Facers, root, assorted, ea.	2	48	50	50	100	50	100	100	......	100	50	25	......	50	25	22	......	50	822
Fiber, devitalizing, jars	55	25	25	57	25	25	50	25	......	50	25	25	......	25	25	12	......	25	474
Files, assorted, dental, ea.	......	10	10	......	10	10	30	10	......	30	10	10	......	10	5	5	......	......	150
Files, assorted, dental, pkg.	......	14	7	20	7	7	10	10	......	10	7	7	......	7	7	7	......	17	137
Finisher and scraper, bxs.	7	......	......	......	......	......	......	......	......	......	......	......	......	......	......	......	......	......	7
Flask, vulcanizer for bolts, ea.	......	5	5	5	5	5	8	5	......	32	5	5	......	5	5	5	......	5	100
Forceps, surgical, assorted, ea.	3,050	2,048	2,345	1,885	3,379	1,528	7,186	2,447	546	3,654	1,837	1,750	2,237	1,627	1,463	1,156	586	1,501	40,225
Forceps, tooth extracting, ea.	89	50	100	100	150	100	175	150	......	154	100	100	......	100	52	26	......	85	1,531

SURGICAL INSTRUMENTS AND APPLIANCES, INCLUDING DENTAL INSTRUMENTS, APPLIANCES, AND SUPPLIES

Commodity and Unit	Shortage	Detail of Deliveries by Districts																	Total
		1	2	3	4	5	6	7	8	9	10	11	12	13	14	15	16	17	
Forceps, tooth extracting, rolls, ea	......	......	......	......	......	......	......	......	......	......	......	3	......	......	......	......	......	......	3
Forks, tuning, sets	......	......	......	......	......	......	......	......	......	......	6	......	......	......	......	......	......	......	6
Funnels, rubber, ea	......	......	......	......	......	......	30	......	......	14	......	......	......	......	......	......	......	......	44
Gags, mouth, assorted, ea	3	2	2	2	2	2	3	2	......	2	2	2	......	2	2	2	......	2	32
Gouges, surgical, assorted, ea	120	59	25	25	62	50	171	52	......	62	25	54	......	25	10	26	......	27	793
Gauze, plate and wire, ea	8	......	......	......	......	......	4	......	......	......	......	......	......	......	......	......	......	......	12
Gutta percha, bxs	......	200	200	300	735	225	926	225	......	450	225	250	......	300	250	100	......	200	4,586
Hammer, steel, ea	......	......	......	......	......	......	1	......	......	......	......	......	......	......	......	......	......	......	1
Hammer, swaging, 1½ lb., ea	......	1	1	1	1	1	2	1	......	2	1	1	......	1	1	1	......	1	16
Handle, universal, cone socket, ea	......	7	5	10	5	6	14	6	......	13	5	9	......	6	7	6	......	5	104
Headband, folding, metal, ea	......	......	12	13	9	......	42	......	......	12	6	5	......	12	6	......	......	5	122
Headgear, angular, ea	......	2	5	3	3	2	5	3	......	5	3	3	......	3	2	3	......	3	45
Hemacytometer, red, white corp. pipette for, ea	1	......	......	......	......	......	182	......	......	......	......	......	......	......	......	......	......	......	183
Holders, for cotton, ea	......	6	7	7	7	7	8	7	......	9	7	7	......	7	7	7	......	7	100
Holders, crown, ivory, ea	......	......	......	3	......	......	3	......	......	3	......	......	......	......	3	......	......	......	12
Holders, glass, cheek and tongue, ea	......	......	......	......	......	......	2	......	......	......	......	......	......	......	......	......	......	......	2
Holders, needle, assorted, ea	50	73	96	59	96	71	330	108	24	134	10	58	3	56	56	34	61	68	1,387
Holders, nerve broach, ea	10	3	3	3	3	3	3	3	......	3	3	3	......	3	3	3	......	3	52
Holders, mercury, ea	......	1	2	4	2	1	5	1	......	5	1	4	......	1	4	1	......	4	36
Holders, rubber dam, ea	......	......	1	1	1	1	1	1	......	1	1	1	......	1	1	......	......	1	12
Holders, sponge, assorted, ea	......	12	12	12	24	12	38	12	12	24	12	115	......	12	12	12	12	12	345
Hooks, surgical, assorted, ea	......	......	......	11	2	......	185	......	......	4	......	2	......	......	......	......	......	......	204
Incubator, bacteria, field laboratory, ea	......	......	......	......	......	......	......	......	......	......	1	......	......	......	......	......	......	......	1
Incubator, bacteria, kerosene, ea	......	......	1	1	......	......	2	......	......	1	......	......	......	......	......	......	......	......	5
Incubator, bacteria, oil heated, ea	......	......	1	1	1	......	2	1	......	1	1	......	......	1	......	......	......	1	10
Investment compound, 4 lb., tins	13	......	......	......	......	......	......	......	......	......	......	11	......	11	......	......	......	......	35
Instrument cabinets, ea	......	......	......	......	2	......	......	1	......	......	......	......	......	1	......	......	......	......	4
Jars, slop, w.e., ea	......	......	......	2	......	......	......	......	......	......	......	......	......	......	......	......	......	......	2
Keratome, angular, needle, ea	......	5	20	10	20	20	20	20	......	20	20	10	......	10	10	5	......	10	200
Knives, surgical, assorted, ea	96	392	640	618	884	456	2,499	526	123	1,239	622	635	1,800	571	469	148	126	331	12,175
Knife, plaster, ea	......	37	60	60	60	25	105	35	......	60	35	35	......	60	35	25	......	25	657
Lamp, op., Shanberg, w. adj. wall bracket, ea	1	......	1	1	1	1	1	1	......	1	1	1	......	1	1	1	......	1	14
Lancets, surgical, assorted, ea	......	17	14	15	14	14	20	14	......	20	14	14	......	14	14	14	......	14	212
Lathe, dental, electric, extra chucks for, ea	8	......	......	......	......	......	......	......	......	......	......	......	......	......	......	......	......	......	8
Lathe, head driving wheel for, ea	......	......	......	......	......	......	2	......	......	1	......	......	......	......	......	......	......	......	3
Lead, ½ lb. ingot, ea	......	......	......	......	......	......	300	......	......	......	......	......	......	......	......	......	......	......	300
Lens, condensing, 2 in. broad, h.r. rings, ea	......	......	......	......	......	......	187	......	......	......	......	......	......	......	......	......	......	......	187
Lingual bars, w.m. platinoid, ea	10	......	......	......	......	......	......	......	......	......	......	......	......	......	......	......	......	......	10
Local anesth. dent., Fisher & Reidmuller, ea	1	......	......	1	......	......	1	......	......	1	......	......	......	......	......	......	......	......	4
Mallets, surgical, assorted, ea	......	8	6	10	6	6	39	7	2	16	6	8	......	8	10	3	......	6	141
Mandrels, surgical, assorted, ea	......	200	100	200	200	41	450	100	......	300	200	150	......	200	150	51	......	150	2,492
Mandrins, assorted, ea	4	1	2	2	2	2	13	2	......	2	2	1	......	2	1	......	......	2	38
Mats, rubber, for dental chairs, ea	......	......	......	......	......	......	17	......	......	2	......	......	......	......	......	......	......	......	19
Microscopes, Bausch & Lomb, ea	......	......	......	......	......	......	32	......	......	......	......	......	......	......	......	......	......	......	32
Microscope, field, with access. case, incompl., ea	1	......	......	......	......	......	......	......	......	......	......	......	......	......	......	......	......	......	1
Microscope, Spencer, ea	......	......	......	......	......	......	3	......	......	......	......	......	......	......	......	......	......	......	3
Mirrors, hand, ea	......	......	......	1	......	......	3	......	......	1	......	......	......	......	......	......	......	......	5
Mirrors, laryngeal, ea	......	2	2	......	2	2	28	2	2	......	2	6	......	......	......	2	2	4	56
Mirrors, mouth, extra glasses for, ea	......	130	50	100	50	60	100	50	......	100	50	100	......	50	60	60	......	50	1,010
Mirrors, mouth, with aluminum handle, ea	......	5	6	6	6	6	10	6	......	10	6	6	......	6	6	5	......	4	88
Mirrors, head, ea	......	50	79	62	55	62	241	55	20	112	66	62	......	37	45	41	25	44	1,056
Napkins, dental, aseptic, 500 in bx	......	......	......	50	100	......	......	......	......	50	50	50	......	......	......	......	......	50	350
Needles, aneurism, ea	......	12	15	15	200	10	99	20	......	48	15	10	2	15	10	13	......	15	499
Needles, hypodermic, ea	......	1,020	1,308	480	1,128	1,032	1,284	1,128	......	1,094	1,008	1,128	......	996	936	612	576	792	14,522
Needles, infusion, ea	......	60	60	60	60	60	60	60	......	60	60	60	......	60	60	60	60	60	900

[*Continued on next page*]

Medical Table 2—(*Continued*)

SURGICAL INSTRUMENTS AND APPLIANCES, INCLUDING DENTAL INSTRUMENTS, APPLIANCES, AND SUPPLIES

Commodity and Unit	Shortage	Detail of Deliveries by Districts																	Total
		1	2	3	4	5	6	7	8	9	10	11	12	13	14	15	16	17	
Needles, surgical, assorted, ea	......	672	1,010	990	1,265	972	6,106	1,094	660	1,702	986	14,102	600	984	1,044	702	540	684	34,113
Nuts, gold, ea	......	10	10	10	10	10	10	10	......	10	10	10	......	10	......	......	......	10	120
Opthalmoscope, ea	......	5	7	5	8	5	16	7	......	12	5	5	......	5	4	3	2	5	94
Operating set, bone electric, ea	7	2	2	4	5	2	16	3	......	7	2	2	......	2	3	......	......	2	59
Operating set, cranial, ea	......	......	1	1	1	......	3	1	......	3	1	1	......	1	1	......	......	1	15
Osteotomes, assorted, ea	35	......	12	......	......	24	......	8	10	......	......	......	......	12	12	......	......	......	113
Paper, articulating, thin, in books, bks	......	15	15	15	15	15	35	15	......	35	15	15	......	15	15	15	......	15	250
Periosteotomes, assorted, ea	......	14	18	13	15	9	172	15	......	22	16	14	......	14	9	22	12	14	379
Pins, transfusion, ea	......	......	......	......	......	......	2	......	......	......	......	......	......	......	......	......	......	......	2
Plates, bone, assorted, ea	5	50	50	50	50	50	328	50	......	200	50	50	......	50	50	50	......	50	1,133
Plates, brush, bone handle, ea	......	2	5	5	5	5	5	5	......	5	5	5	......	5	5	3	......	5	65
Plates, liberty, silver, ea	11	4	10	5	10	5	15	......	......	15	10	10	......	10	5	5	......	10	125
Plate lid, hard rubber, ea	......	......	......	......	......	......	100	......	......	......	......	......	......	......	......	......	......	......	100
Pliers, assorted, ea	47	43	100	200	100	75	200	100	......	200	100	51	......	100	50	30	......	50	1,446
Pluggers, dental, assorted, ea	36	83	100	150	200	60	200	100	......	200	50	141	......	......	100	60	......	50	1,530
Points, aseptic, absorbent, 100 in bx	......	35	50	......	50	50	250	150	......	390	50	50	......	50	50	25	......	50	1,250
Points, dental, assorted, ea	......	288	240	386	288	288	687	338	......	149	336	386	......	336	336	288	......	336	4,682
Plaster of Paris for modeling, tins	149	......	......	......	......	......	......	......	......	......	......	......	......	......	......	......	......	......	149
Port polishers, contra angle, ea	......	......	......	......	......	......	3	......	......	2	......	......	......	......	......	......	......	......	5
Points, root canal, gutta percha, bxs	22	53	100	150	100	100	......	......	......	100	100	50	......	100	25	50	......	50	1,000
Points, rubber dam, ea	......	......	......	3	......	......	3	......	......	......	......	3	......	......	3	......	......	......	12
Portable dental outfits, ea	......	......	1	1	1	......	......	......	......	......	......	35	......	......	......	......	......	......	38
Post puller, Little Giant, ea	......	1	1	1	1	1	......	1	......	......	1	1	......	1	1	1	......	1	12
Press flask, Wilson, ea	......	......	......	......	......	......	25	......	......	8	......	......	......	......	......	......	......	......	33
Probes, surgical, assorted, ea	......	642	406	458	526	406	2,262	501	106	708	406	466	......	408	308	306	106	313	8,328
Proctoscope, Kelly, ea	......	......	1	......	1	......	1	6	......	1	......	3	......	......	1	......	......	......	14
Pulp preserver and copper, ea	3	......	......	......	......	......	2	......	......	......	......	......	......	......	......	......	......	......	5
Punch, tonsil, ea	......	......	......	......	......	......	7	......	......	......	......	......	......	......	......	......	......	......	7
Punch, rubber dam, ea	......	......	......	......	......	......	1	......	......	......	......	......	......	......	......	......	......	......	1
Raspatory, periosteal, Ballinger, ea	......	......	......	......	......	......	......	......	......	......	......	1	......	......	......	......	......	......	1
Razors, assorted, ea	40	20	20	20	10	70	562	80	......	20	10	17	......	10	10	30	......	80	999
Razors, skin, grafting, ea	......	......	......	5	......	......	......	......	......	......	......	......	......	......	......	......	......	......	5
Razors, strops for, ea	53	102	212	96	96	96	712	96	......	96	240	96	......	96	48	48	......	48	2,135
Reamers, dental, assorted, pkg	71	68	100	200	150	......	300	150	......	300	100	150	......	100	100	50	......	100	1,939
Repositor, iris, ea	......	13	10	25	15	10	29	15	......	25	10	10	......	10	10	10	......	10	202
Repositor, uterine, ea	......	......	......	......	......	......	6	......	......	......	......	......	......	......	......	......	......	......	6
Retainer, matrix, ea	......	......	......	5	......	......	5	......	......	5	......	12	......	......	12	......	......	12	51
Retractors, assorted, ea	......	82	73	67	122	81	566	97	6	122	49	139	......	37	62	43	1	25	1,572
Rings, molding, 2 in set	......	......	......	......	......	......	......	20	......	......	......	......	......	......	......	......	......	......	20
Root driers, ea	......	......	......	......	......	......	1	......	......	1	......	......	......	......	......	......	......	......	2
Rubber dam, rls	......	10	10	10	10	10	70	10	......	10	10	10	......	10	10	10	......	10	200
Rubber dam, weights for, ea	......	2	2	2	2	2	7	2	......	6	2	2	......	2	2	2	......	2	37
Rubber, red, ½ lb., bxs	......	25	25	25	25	25	248	25	......	50	25	25	......	25	25	20	......	25	593
Rubber, white, base plate, ½ lb., bxs	......	......	......	......	......	......	......	......	......	105	......	......	......	......	......	......	......	......	105
Saliva ejector, hand, ea	......	......	......	......	3	......	3	5	......	3	......	......	......	......	......	......	......	......	14
Saws, surgical, assorted, ea	623	57	188	211	236	75	663	124	3	302	204	212	......	204	229	84	3	224	3,642
Saw frames, ea	4	2	4	4	4	4	4	4	......	4	4	4	......	4	4	2	......	4	56
Saws, Gigli, handles for, ea	......	......	......	......	102	......	104	104	......	104	......	......	......	......	102	......	......	102	618
Saws, Gigli, guide for, ea	......	......	......	......	4	......	4	4	......	4	......	......	......	......	2	......	......	4	22
Scalers, dental, assorted, ea	......	250	200	400	300	200	628	300	......	500	200	300	12	100	100	100	......	209	3,799
Scalers, dental, sets	......	43	......	......	......	......	......	......	......	......	......	......	......	......	......	......	......	......	43
Scalpel, assorted, ea	54	......	......	......	......	......	......	......	......	......	......	......	......	......	......	......	......	......	54
Scissors, surgical, assorted, ea	747	410	630	621	723	390	2,718	566	118	812	527	490	891	486	328	310	184	334	11,285
Scoop, gall bladder, ea	......	......	......	......	2	......	2	24	......	2	......	3	......	......	......	1	......	2	36

SURGICAL INSTRUMENTS AND APPLIANCES, INCLUDING DENTAL INSTRUMENTS, APPLIANCES, AND SUPPLIES

Commodity and Unit	Shortage	Detail of Deliveries by Districts																	Total
		1	2	3	4	5	6	7	8	9	10	11	12	13	14	15	16	17	
Screws, surgical, assorted, ea.	......	......	12	2,036	14	......	5,058	2,010	......	4,541	12	12	......	12	12	......	......	12	13,731
Screwports, ea.	......	......	......	......	......	......	4	......	......	......	......	......	......	......	......	......	......	......	4
Screw, ivory, taps for, ea.	......	......	......	......	......	......	......	......	......	......	......	2	......	......	......	......	......	......	2
Screw, ivory, small taps for, ea.	......	......	......	......	......	......	......	......	......	......	......	2	......	......	......	......	......	......	2
Screw, ivory, large, drill for, ea.	......	......	......	......	......	......	......	......	......	......	......	2	......	......	......	......	......	......	2
Screw, ivory, small, drill for, ea.	......	......	......	......	......	......	......	......	......	......	......	2	......	......	......	......	......	......	2
Searcher, stone, ea.	1	......	......	......	1	......	......	......	......	......	......	1	......	......	......	......	......	......	3
Separatory, adjustable, assorted, ea.	3	......	1	2	1	1	4	2	......	2	1	2	......	2	1	1	......	1	24
Shears, surgical, assorted ea.	128	4	6	6	7	4	10	4	3	8	6	115	......	5	4	2	4	6	322
Silicate cement, shade guide for, ea.	......	......	......	......	......	......	......	30	......	......	......	......	......	......	......	......	......	......	30
Slab, glass, ea.	......	3	4	3	4	4	114	4	......	114	4	4	......	4	4	3	......	3	272
Snares, assorted, ea.	2	2	2	2	2	2	2	2	2	2	2	2	......	2	2	2	3	2	35
Snares, wire, assorted, spl.	2	......	......	......	24	......	36	......	......	36	......	......	......	......	......	......	......	......	98
Soldering and heating outfit, gas., incom., ea.	......	......	......	1	......	......	1	......	......	1	1	1	......	1	1	......	......	1	8
Solder, silver, pcs.	......	2	4	4	2	2	5	4	......	5	4	4	......	4	4	2	......	4	50
Sounds, surgical, assorted, ea.	19	......	......	......	......	......	6	......	......	2	......	......	......	47	......	......	......	......	74
Spatula, assorted, ea.	696	70	49	112	77	49	287	55	24	227	74	124	......	74	62	49	36	76	2,141
Spectroscope, ea.	2	......	......	......	......	......	......	......	......	......	......	......	......	......	......	......	......	......	2
Speculum, assorted, ea.	......	27	26	27	29	27	379	21	15	69	25	239	4	26	22	21	20	26	1,003
Sphygnomamometer, ea.	38	2	2	2	2	2	5	2	......	2	2	2	......	2	2	1	......	2	68
Stereoscope, pocket, ea.	3	......	......	......	......	......	......	......	......	......	......	......	......	......	......	......	......	......	3
Stethoscope, ea.	......	50	50	50	60	50	84	50	25	60	50	50	41	50	50	20	30	50	820
Stool, revolving, dental, ea.	......	......	......	......	......	......	1	......	......	......	......	......	......	......	......	......	......	......	1
Strips, dental, bxs.	......	100	100	100	100	100	1,283	100	......	256	100	172	......	100	100	52	......	100	2,763
Swager, metal, ea.	......	5	5	5	5	5	5	5	......	5	5	5	......	5	1	1	......	5	62
Switchboard, electric type, ea.	......	......	1	1	1	......	......	......	......	1	......	......	......	1	......	......	......	......	5
Synthetic porcelain, caulks, 10 shades, bxs.	......	......	......	......	......	......	2	......	......	2	......	......	......	......	......	......	......	......	4
Synthetic porcelain, caulks, guide for, bot.	......	12	17	19	17	12	38	17	......	25	16	19	......	16	17	16	......	16	257
Syringe, aseptic, irrigating, ea.	......	......	......	1	1	......	......	......	......	......	......	......	......	......	......	......	......	......	2
Syringe, bulb, rubber, alpha, ea.	......	......	......	......	......	......	151	......	......	132	......	15	......	......	......	......	......	......	298
Syringe, deep, urethral, ea.	......	......	2	1	2	2	2	2	......	2	2	2	......	......	......	......	......	2	19
Syringe, ear and ulcer, ea.	......	96	60	108	72	132	204	87	......	360	96	72	......	96	60	72	......	72	1,587
Syringe, fountain, rubber, ea.	......	......	30	100	225	221	92	......	......	495	154	50	......	193	381	129	......	......	2,070
Syringes, Luer type, ea.	868	221	247	377	330	232	1,597	236	58	566	385	277	......	276	254	199	62	334	6,419
Syringes, Keyes-Ultzman, extra canula for, ea.	......	......	......	......	......	8	35	......	......	10	......	......	......	......	......	......	......	......	53
Syringes, hypodermic, wires for, bdls.	......	......	102	......	......	......	78	......	......	......	102	......	......	......	......	......	......	......	282
Syringes, metal, 2 oz., ea.	......	......	15	......	21	15	19	25	......	19	......	......	......	......	......	......	......	......	114
Syringes, metal, extra pipes for, ea.	......	......	......	......	......	......	379	672	......	912	......	......	......	......	......	......	......	......	1,963
Syringes, hypodermic, short hubs for, ea.	......	15	15	15	15	15	15	15	......	15	23	23	......	28	15	15	......	34	258
Syringe needles, canula, ea.	......	7	8	8	10	612	15	10	......	......	......	......	......	......	8	6	......	......	684
Syringe, penis, glass, ea.	......	864	224	324	209	......	3,024	24	......	3,838	1,272	296	......	2,000	272	572	......	134	13,053
Syringe, dental, extra pipes for, ea.	......	......	......	......	......	......	1,068	......	......	......	600	......	......	......	......	......	......	......	1,668
Syringe, fountain, rubber, rectal, tips for, ea.	......	......	......	......	......	......	......	63	......	......	......	......	......	......	......	......	......	......	63
Syringe, penis, hard rubber, ea.	......	......	102	......	72	72	20	......	......	......	......	......	......	......	......	......	......	......	266
Syringe, hard rubber, ea.	......	42	6	30	162	42	802	48	4	55	136	37	......	36	30	4	4	36	1,474
Syringe, urethral, Chetwood, ea.	......	1,914	2,050	2,100	2,990	1,100	3,100	4,684	1,000	2,100	1,528	1,050	......	1,050	2,050	1,124	1,240	1,000	30,080
Syringe, urethral, rubber tips for, ea.	......	......	......	......	......	......	50	......	......	......	......	......	......	......	......	......	......	......	50
Syringe, water, self-filling, ea.	......	5	6	10	6	4	24	4	......	20	6	6	......	6	6	......	......	6	109
Syringe, water, self-filling, extra pipes for, ea.	......	600	40	612	691	......	40	......	......	20	20	552	......	620	552	336	......	......	4,083
Syringe, water, curved point, ea.	......	......	......	118	15	......	......	......	......	......	20	......	......	......	......	......	......	......	153
Syringe, water, Moffet, ea.	......	1	1	......	......	1	......	1	......	10	1	......	......	1	......	1	......	......	17
Syringe, water, rubber bulb for, ea.	......	10	......	......	6	......	20	......	......	10	32	......	......	10	......	......	......	......	88
Table, portable, dental, ea.	......	......	......	......	......	......	......	......	......	2	......	......	......	......	......	......	......	......	2
Teeth shade, guide for, ea.	......	1	2	1	2	1	2	2	......	2	1	1	......	1	1	1	......	1	19
Tenaculum, assorted, ea.	5	......	......	......	......	......	......	......	......	......	......	......	......	......	......	......	......	......	5

[*Concluded on next page*]

Medical Table 2—(*Concluded*)

SURGICAL INSTRUMENTS AND APPLIANCES, INCLUDING DENTAL INSTRUMENTS, APPLIANCES, AND SUPPLIES

Commodity and Unit	Shortage	Detail of Deliveries by Districts																	Total
		1	2	3	4	5	6	7	8	9	10	11	12	13	14	15	16	17	
Tenotome, ea.	36	......	......	......	2	......	3	2	......	2	......	......	......	......	......	......	......	......	45
Thermometers, chemical assorted, ea.	22	......	10	10	......	10	50	......	......	23	10	......	......	10	......	......	......	10	155
Thermometers, clinical, ea.	......	......	30	......	14	800	30	630	......	8	......	580	......	......	......	352	......	1,000	3,444
Tissue, gutta percha, sht.	......	......	......	......	......	......	23	......	......	......	......	......	......	......	......	......	......	......	23
Tongs, flask, ea.	......	......	......	......	......	......	1	......	......	1	......	......	......	......	......	......	......	......	2
Tongs, soldering, ea.	1	2	3	3	3	3	6	3	......	6	3	3	......	3	3	3	......	3	48
Tourniquets, assorted, ea.	......	144	916	2,666	762	144	316	132	84	228	2,033	161	......	213	120	109	84	168	8,280
Torch, 5 lbs., automatic reducing valve, ea.	......	......	......	......	......	......	1	......	......	......	......	......	......	......	......	......	......	......	1
Transilluminator, lamps for, ea.	19	......	......	......	......	......	......	......	......	......	......	......	......	......	......	......	......	......	19
Trays, dental impression, assorted, ea.	......	16	14	14	14	15	25	14	......	25	14	14	......	14	14	14	......	14	221
Trephine, assorted, ea.	......	7	7	6	8	8	20	6	1	10	7	10	......	7	6	7	1	7	118
Trimmer, pyorrhea, ea.	3	......	......	......	......	......	......	......	......	......	......	......	......	......	......	......	......	......	3
Trimmer, vulcanite, ea.	4	......	......	......	......	......	......	......	......	......	......	......	......	......	......	......	......	......	4
Trocar and canula, assorted, ea.	110	10	10	10	10	10	12	10	......	10	10	10	......	10	10	......	......	6	238
Tube, abdominal, suction, ea.	......	......	......	......	2	......	3	......	......	3	......	......	......	......	......	......	......	......	8
Tube, diagnostic, ea.	9	......	......	......	......	......	200	......	......	......	......	......	......	......	......	......	......	......	209
Tweezers, dental, assorted, ea.	......	5	9	10	10	5	20	10	......	15	5	5	......	5	5	5	......	5	114
Urethroscope, Young, ex. l. car. for l'mp h'd, ea.	......	......	......	......	......	......	20	......	......	......	......	......	......	......	......	......	......	......	20
Urethroscope, Young, extra pair cords for, ea.	......	......	......	......	......	......	17	......	......	......	......	......	......	......	......	......	......	......	17
Urethrotome, assorted, ea.	......	5	10	5	10	5	24	10	......	13	10	5	......	5	2	3	......	10	117
Urinometer, with and without thermometer, ea.	......	......	6	6	......	6	26	......	......	12	5	6	......	5	......	......	......	6	78
Vise, bench, jeweler's, ea.	3	......	......	......	......	......	9	......	......	......	......	......	......	......	......	......	......	......	12
Vein stripper, small, ea.	......	......	......	......	......	......	2	......	......	......	......	......	......	......	......	......	......	......	2
Vulcanizer, scraper and finisher, ea.	......	2	3	6	3	3	11	3	......	11	3	3	......	3	3	3	......	3	60
Vulcanizer, anchor flask, wrenches for, ea.	......	1	1	1	1	1	1	1	......	6	......	1	......	1	......	......	......	1	16
Vulcanizer, cross bar for, ea.	......	......	......	......	......	......	1	......	......	......	......	......	......	......	......	......	......	......	1
Vulcanizer, with flask and kero. heat. appar., ea.	......	......	1	......	1	......	......	1	......	......	......	......	......	......	......	......	......	......	3
Vulcanizer, 3 flasks, gas or kerosene, ea.	......	......	......	......	......	......	......	......	......	......	1	1	......	1	1	......	......	1	5
Vulcanizer, packing for, ea.	3	......	1	......	1	......	......	1	......	......	1	2	......	2	3	......	......	2	16
Vulcanizer, thermometer for, ea.	1	1	1	2	1	......	2	1	......	2	2	2	......	2	2	1	......	2	22
Vulcanizer, universal wrench for, ea.	......	1	1	1	1	1	3	1	......	3	1	1	......	1	1	1	......	1	18
Wax base-plate, ½ lb. in bx.	33	22	60	35	60	25	190	50	......	60	60	35	......	35	35	25	......	35	760
Wax, crown, sticky, bx.	......	......	......	......	12	......	12	......	......	......	......	......	......	......	......	......	......	......	24
Wax, bone, jar	......	......	7	......	......	......	12	12	......	12	......	......	......	......	......	......	......	......	43
Wax, bone, tubes	......	......	......	......	......	......	36	......	......	10	......	......	......	......	......	......	......	......	46
Wax, inlay, bxs.	81	5	10	20	10	10	18	10	......	18	10	15	......	15	14	5	......	15	256
Wheel, carborundum, ea.	......	5	5	5	5	5	15	5	......	20	5	5	......	5	5	5	......	5	95
Wire cutters, ea.	......	1	1	1	1	1	129	1	1	1	4	......	......	4	1	1	1	5	153
Wood, orange stick, bdls.	......	......	50	575	50	......	100	......	......	100	50	25	......	25	25	25	......	25	1,050

AMERICAN RELIEF ADMINISTRATION

Detail of Deliveries of the United States Government Surplus Medical and Hospital Supplies to the Near East Relief for Distribution in Southern Russia,* 1922–1923

Medical Table 3

Commodity and Unit	Quantity
Acacia powder, lbs	32
Acetanilid, ¼ lb., bot	40
Acetanilid, ½ lb., bot	47
Acetanilid, 1 lb., bot	1
Acetanilid, 30 gr. tabs., 100 in box	3
Acetphenetidum, 1 lb., lbs.	4
Acid, acetic, ¼ lb., bot	6
Acid, acetic, 1 lb., USP., bot	22
Acid, acetic, glacial, 1 lb., bot	48
Acid, acetysalicylic, 1 lb., lbs	6
Acid, boric, 1 lb., lbs	4
Acid, boric, 324 mgm. tabs., 500 in bot	165
Acid, citric, crystals, lbs	7
Acid, hydrochloric, USP., ½ lb., bot	25
Acid, hydrochloric, SM., 1 lb., bot	40
Acid, hydrochloric, USP., 1 lb., bot	91
Acid, nitric, ½ lb., bot	7
Acid, nitric, lbs	21
Acid, oxalic, ¼ lb., SM., bot	15
Acid, oxalic, ½ lb., USP., bot	14
Acid, oxalic, 1 lb., bot	17
Acid, pyrogallic, bot	8
Acid, gylicilicum, ¼ lb., USP., bot	78
Acid, gylicilicum, ½ lb., bot	10
Acid, gylicilicum, 1 lb., bot	7
Acid, gylicilicum, 5 gr. tabs., 500 in bot	335
Acid, sulphuric, ½ lb., bot	12
Acid, sulphuric, 1 lb., SM., bot	3
Acid, sulphuric, 1 lb., USP., bot	3
Acid, sulphuric, aromatic, ½ lb., bot	20
Acid, tannic, ¼ lb., USP., bot	110
Acid, tannic, 1 lb., bot	26
Acid, tartaricum, ½ lb., bot.	115
Acid, trichloracetic, oz	22
Adeps lanae hydrosus, ½ lb., jar	**35**
Adrenalin hydrochloridum, 3/200 gr. tabs., 23 in tube	100
Agar agar, ½ lb., pkg	15
Agar agar, 1 lb., pkg	25
Alcohol, 12 oz., bot	9
Alcohol, 3 pts., tin	130
Aloes, pulverized, USP., 1 oz., bot	8
Aloes, pulverized, USP., 2 oz., bot	62
Alumen powder, ½ lb., bot	5
Alumen powder, 1 lb., bot	26
Ambrine, 1 lb., cake	6
Ammonia, aromatic spirits, ½ lb., bot	8
Ammonia, aromatic spirits, 1 lb., bot	4
Ammonia, bromide, ½ lb., bot	31
Ammonia, carbonate, ½ lb., USP., bot	41
Ammonia, carbonate, 1 lb., bot	1
Ammonia, chloride, ½ lb., bot	57
Ammonia, chloride, 1 lb., bot	6
Ammonia, chloride, 60 gr. tabs., 100 in bot	14
Ammonia, persulphate, 1 lb., bot	7
Anilin, 10 gms., vial	14
Apomorphine, hydrochloride, 6 mgm., 20 in tube	169
Apomorphine, hydrochloride, 6 mgm., 25 in tube	25
Antimony and potassium tartrate, 1 oz., bot	24
Arecoline hydrobromide, ½ gr. H.T., 10 in tube	20
Arecoline hydrobromide, 1 gr., H.T., 10 in tube	4
Arseni trioxidum, 1 oz., bot	2
Arseni trioxidum, 1 mgm. tabs., 250 in bot	5
Arseni trioxidum, 1 mgm. tabs., 500 in bot	1
Asafetida, 2 oz., bot	1
Atropine sulphate, ⅛ oz., bot	5
Atropeine sulphate, .65 mgm. H.T., 20 in tube	168
Bacto, dextrose, 1 lb., bot	16
Bacto, gelatine, ¼ lb., bot	72
Bacto, lactose, 1 lb., bot	25
Bacto, peptone, ½ lb., bot	54
Bacto, peptone, 1 lb., bot	26
Balsam copaiba, ½ lb., bot	87
Balsam copaiba, 1 lb., bot	3
Balsam peru, ½ lb., bot	37
Barbital tabs., 324 mgm., 500 in bot	3
Barium sulphate, CP., 1 oz., bot	1
Barium sulphate, lbs	2
Beef extract, ¼ lb., tin	300
Bismuth, subcarbonate, 1 lb., bot	33
Bismuth, subcarbonate, 324 mgm. tabs., 500 in bot	2
Bismuth, subgallas, 1 lb., bot	16
Bismuth, subgallas, 250 gm., bot	15
Bismuth, subnitras, ½ lb., bot	4
Bismuth, subnitras, 5 gr. tabs., 500 in bot	1
Brilliant green, 10 gms., vial	5
Caffeine citrate, tabs., 65 mgm., 250 in bot	5
Camphor, 1 lb., bot	11
Camphor, opium tabs., hard rub. bot. for case emerg., bot.	10
Cantharides, 1 oz., USP., bot	8
Capsicum powder, ½ oz., bot	10
Capsicum tabs., 32 mgm., 600 in bot	32
Carmine powder, 1 oz., bot	1
Carium oxalate, ¼ lb., bot	2
Chalk, prepared, ½ lb., bot	44
Chloral hydrate, ¼ lb., bot	2
Chloral hydrate, 1 lb., bot	3
Chloral hydrate, 324 mgm. tabs., 400 in bot	6
Chloral hydrate, 324 mgm. tabs., 500 in bot	67
Chlorazene tabs., N.R., 100 in bot	5
Chloroform, ¼ lb., tin	100
Chrome alum, lbs.	5
Chrysarobinum, ½ oz., bot	5
Cocaine hydrochloride, ¼ oz., bot	27
Cocaine hydrochloride, 10 mgm. H.T., 20 in tube	555
Cocaine hydrochloride, 10 mgm. H.T., 25 in tube	55
Cocaine hydrochloride, 1/6 gr. tabs., 100 in bot	1
Cocaine hydrochloride, 2 gr. H.T., 10 in tube	95
Codeine sulphas, 32 mgm., 500 in bot	17
Codeine sulphas, 32 mgm., 600 in bot	14
Codeine sulphas, 1 oz., bot	23
Congo red, 10 gm., vial	12
Copper sulphate, 1 oz., bot	35
Copper sulphate, ¼ lb., bot	8
Creosote, 1 oz., USP., bot	92
Dextrose, ¼ lb., bot	45
Dextrose, ½ lb., bot	1
Elan, 1 oz., bot	44
Eosine, pure, alcohol soluble, 10 gm., vial	1
Eucalyptol, 1 oz., bot	11
Eugenol, ½ oz., bot	27
Extractum belladonnae, 1 oz., bot	18
Extract cascara sagrada tabs., 250 in 130 mgm., bot	5
Extract cascara sagrada tabs., 500 in 130 mgm., bot	3
Extractum glycyrrhizae, ¼ lb., bot	4
Extractum glycyrrhizae, 1 lb., jar	34
Extractum hyoscamus, 1 oz., bot	13
Ferric phosphate, 1 lb., bot	51
Ferrous sulphate, dried, ¼ lb., bot.	2
Ferri et quinae citrate sol., 3 oz., bot	110
Fluid extractum, belladonnae, 1 oz., bot	2
Fluid extractum, belladonnae leaves, 1 pt., bot	2
Fluid extractum, colchican, 1 oz., bot	9
Fluid extractum, ergot, ½ lb., bot	14
Fluid extractum, gentian, 1 lb., bot	14
Fluid extractum, gelsomium, 1 lb., bot	2
Fluid extractum, ipecac, ⅛ lb., bot	48
Fluid extractum, mucis vomica, bot	12
Fluid extractum, wild cherry, 1 lb., bot	23
Fluid extractum, zingeberris, ¼ lb., bot	7
Foot powder, ¼ lb., tin	20,692
Formin, 1 oz., bot	6
Gelatine powder, ¼ lb., bot	50
Glycerine, 1 lb., bot	3
Guiac rosin, ½ lb., bot	2
Hematoxylin, light, 10 gm., vial	2
Heroin tabs., hard rubber bot. for case emerg., bot	3
Hexamethylenamine, 1 oz., bot	6
Hexamethylenamine, 1 lb. bot	7
Hexamethylenamine, 324 mgm., 500 in bot	139
Hometropinae hydrobromide, 15 gr., vial	24
Hydrargyri, chlor. corros., 500 gm., bot	1
Hydrargyri, chlor. corros., S.M., ¼ lb., bot	49
Hydrargyri, chlor. corros., S.M., ½ lb., bot	1
Hydrargyri, chlor. corros., comm., 1 lb., bot	22
Hydrargyri, chlor. corros., tabs., 250 in bot	28
Hydrargyri, chlor. mite, 2 oz., bot	20
Hydrargyri, chloride, 6.5 mgm. tabs., 250 in bot	12
Hydrargyri, chloride, mite, 65 mgm. tabs., 500 in bot	12
Hydrargyri, chloride, mite, 65 mgm., tabs., 1,000 in bot	7
Hydrargyri, chloride, mite, 32 mgm., tabs., 1,000 in bot	50
Hydrargyri, chloride, mite, 30 mgm., tabs., 100 in bot	5
Hydrargyri, chloride, mite, 32 mgm., tabs., 500 in bot	24
Hydrargyri, iodide flavum, 10 mgm., 500 in bot	11
Hydrargyri, iodide rubium, 1 lb., bot	87
Hydrargyri, massa, ¼ lb., bot	4

* These supplies were turned over to the Near East Relief in New York City. Transportation and distribution in Russia handled by the Near East Relief.

[*Continued on next page*]

AMERICAN RELIEF ADMINISTRATION

Detail of Deliveries of the United States Government Surplus Medical and Hospital Supplies to the Near East Relief for Distribution in Southern Russia, 1922–1923

Medical Table 3—(*Continued*)

Commodity and Unit	Quantity	Commodity and Unit	Quantity	Commodity and Unit	Quantity
Hydrargyri, oxidum flavum, 10 mgm., 250 in bot	30	Oleum chenopodi, 1,000 in box	6	Potassium iodide, ½ lb., bot	3
Hydrargyri redistilled, 5 lbs., jar	1	Oil, cod liver, 1 lb., bot	29	Potassium iodide, 324 mgm., 500 in bot	26
Hydrargyri salicylate, oz	37	Oil, cottonseed, 1 qt., bot	88	Potassium nitrate, ¼ lb.,	2
Hydroxide powder, 1 lb., tin	23	Oil, linseed, ½ gal., tin	12	Potassium nitrate, powder, 1 lb., bot	10
Hydroquinine, ¼ lb., bot	4	Oil, orange, 1 oz., bot	9	Potassium nitrate, 4 gm., compressed tabs., 100 in bot	55
Hyoscine hydrobromide, 65 mgm. tabs., 20 in tube	137	Oil, peppermint, 1 oz., bot	7	Potassium oxalate, ¼ lb., bot	1
Ichthyol or equivalent, 1 lb., tin	99	Oil, mantali, 1 oz., bot	2	Potassium permanganate, 324 mgm., 8,400 in tin	1
Iodine swabs, 6 in box	271	Oil, theobroma, ¼ lb., bot	26	Potassium permanganate, 1 lb., bot	8
Ipecac powder, ¼ lb., bot	45	Oil, tigli, ½ oz., bot	3	Potassium et sodium tartrate, 3 lb., bot	7
Ipecac et opii powder, 2 oz., bot	1	Oleoresin aspidium, 1 oz., bot	6	Procaine, 1 oz., bot	2
Ipecac et opii powder, 3 oz., bot	1	Pepsin, gran., 3 oz., bot	1	Protargol, 1 oz., bot	68
Ipecac et opii powder, ¼ lb., bot	16	Peptone, ½ lb., bot	54	Pyrethrum, 8 oz., tin	200
Ipecac et opii, 324 mgm., 500 in bot	47	Peptone, 1 lb., bot	11	Quinine dihydrochlorate, 32 mgm., 20 in tube	100
Ipecac et opii, 324 mgm., 700 in bot	28	Peptonizing tabs., 100 in bot	17	Quinine chlorohydrosulphate, 32 mgm., 20 in tube	318
Lactose, ¼ lb., bot	10	Petrolatum, 1 lb., tin	1	Rosinae podophylli, ½ oz., bot	18
Lead acetate, 6 oz., bot	8	Petrolatum, 3 lb., tin	1	Rheum powder, 2 oz., bot.	16
Lead acetate, ½ lb., USP., bot	4	Phenol, camphorated, 4 oz., bot	5	Saccharum lactis, ¼ lb., bot.	7
Lead acetate, 1 lb., bot	1	Phenol, crystals, ½ lb., bot	43	Saccharum lactis, 1 lb., bot.	1
Lead acetate, 2 lb., bot	9	Phenolphthalein, 130 mgm., 100 in bot	3	Santonin tabs., 250 in bot.	1
Lead acetate, 130 gm., 500 in bot	9	Phenyl salicylate, ¼ lb., bot	35	Sapo mollis, ½ lb., jar	4
Lead acetate, 130 gm., 600 in bot	40	Phenyl salicylate, ½ lb., bot	21	Sapo mollis, 1 lb., jar	41
Licorice comp. powder, 1 lb., bot	9	Phenyl salicylate, 1 lb., bot	8	Silver nitrate crystals, 1 oz., bot	22
Licorice comp. mixture, 1,000 in bot	12	Phenyl salicylate, 324 mgm., 500 in bot	11	Silver nitrate fused, 1 oz., bot.	2
Liquor potassium arsenide, ½ lb., bot	14	Physostigma sulphate, 1 gm., 10 in bot	9	Sodium bicarbonate, 1 lb., bot.	1
Lithii citros, efferves., 325 tabs., 25 in bot	14	Physostigma sulphate, 6 gm., vial	3	Sodium bicarbonate, tabs., 1000 in bot.	2
Litmus paper, red, 100 strips in vial	165	Ipecac and opium tabs., h. rub., bot. for case emer., bot	11	Sodium bicarbonate, menthae pip., 250 in bot.	2
Litmus paper, blue, 100 strips in vial	12	Morphine sulphate, tabs., bot. for case emer., bot	11	Sodium borate, 1 lb., bot.	101
Litmus powder, 4 oz., bot	1	Pill, aloin comp., 200 in bot	2	Sodium bromide, 6 oz., bot.	6
Lycopodium, 100 gm., bot	10	Pill, aloin comp., 12 in pkg	10	Sodium bromide, 1 lb., bot.	18
Lycopodium, ¼ lb., bot	11	Pill, camphor and opii, 200 in bot	1	Sodium carbonate, 1 lb., bot.	2
Magnesia carbonas, 2 oz., bot	102	Pill, camphor and opii, 500 in bot	21	Sodium carbonate monohydrated, ½ lb., bot	78
Menthol crystals, 1 oz., bot	50	Pill, camphor and opii, 875 in tin	67	Sodium carbonate monohydrated, ¼ lb., bot	40
Methylene blue, S.M., 10 mgm., vial	34	Pill, cathartic comp., 200 in pkg	2	Sodium carbonate monohydrated, 1 lb., bot.	4
Methyl salicylate, 1 lb., bot	2	Pill, copaiba comp., 500 in bot	19	Sodium carbonate, sal soda crystals, 1 lb., bot.	20
Methyl violet, 10 gm., bot	1	Pill, ferri comp., 100 in bot	6	Sodium chlorate, 1 lb., bot	527
Morphine sulphas, ¼ oz., bot	6	Pill, ferri comp., 80 in bot	200	Sodium chlorate, 1 lb., bot	100
Morphine sulphas, ¼ gr. H.T., 500 in bot	28	Pill, ferri comp., 100 in bot	1	Sodium hydroxide, ¼ lb., bot	35
Morphine sulphas, 8 mgm., H.T., 25 in tube	277	Pill, ferri carb., 200 in bot	1	Sodium hydroxide, 1 lb., bot.	4
Morphine sulphas, 8 mgm., 3 oz., tin	21	Pill, ferri carb., 500 in bot	1	Sodium hyposulphate, lbs.	120
Morphine sulphas, 8 mgm., 20 in tube	1,923	Pill, ferri carb., 500 in 324 mgm. tabs., bot	5	Sodium phosphate, 3 oz., bot.	61
Morphine sulphas, 8 mgm., 500 in bot	61½	Pilocarpine hydrochloride, 1 gr., 10 in tube	12	Sodium phosphate, exsiccated, ½ lb., bot.	11
Morphine sulphas, 8 mgm., 600 in bot	25	Pilocarpine hydrochloride, 20 in tube	40	Sodium salicylate, 6 oz., bot.	53
Mustard, ground, 5 lb., pkg	1	Pix liquida, 1 lb., tin	8	Sodium salicylate, tabs., 500 in bot.	113
Naphthalene, 1 lb., bot	175	Pix liquida, 1 gal., tin	1	Sodium salicylate, 1 lb., bot.	99
Naphthalene, 5 lb., cart	2	Potassium acetate, 1 lb., bot	17	Sodium sulphate, ½ lb., bot.	59
Nitroglycerine, .65 mgm., H.T., 20 in tube	53	Potassium acetate, 6 oz., bot	73	Sodium sulphite crystals, 1 lb., bot.	45
Nitroglycerine, spirits of, 1 oz., bot	28	Potassium arsenate tabs., 100 in bot	8	Spirits of aether compound, ½ lb., bot.	8
Nitrous ether, spirits of, ½ lb., bot	23	Potassium bicarbonate, 1 lb., bot	34	Strychnine sulphate, H.T., 1 mgm., 20 in tube	405
Nitrous ether, spirits of, 1 lb., bot	28	Potassium bromide, 1 lb., bot	20	Strychnine sulphate, H.T., 1 mgm., 100 in bot.	5
Normal saline solution, tabs., 100 in bot	92	Potassium bromide, 324 mgm., 500 in bot	75	Strychnine sulphate, H.T., 1 mgm., 250 in bot.	2
Novocaine, 1 oz., bot	1	Potassium chlorate, 1 lb., bot	106	Strychnine sulphate, H.T., 1 mgm., 500 in bot	4
Novocaine, 35 gr., cart	7	Potassium chlorate, 324 mgm., 500 in bot	55	Sudan, 10 gm., vial	1
Novocaine, 1 per cent solution, bot	9	Potassium chlorate, 324 mgm., 1,000 in bot	21	Sulphonal tabs., 1,000 in bot.	1
Nux vomica powder, 1 lb., bot	20	Potassium hydroxide, 1 oz., bot	21	Sulphur, lotum, ½ lb., bot.	28
Oil of castor, 1 qt., bot	16	Potassium iodide, 1 lb., bot	10	Sulphur, roll, lbs.	70

Item	Quantity
Sulphur, sublimated, lbs.	2,000
Pulvis, glycerrhizae compound, lbs.	9
Sodium bromide tabs., 500 in bot.	11
Unguentum hydrargyri, 10 per cent., lbs.	9
Wright's stain, powder, 2 gm., amp.	56
Apparatus, compressed air, each	2
Unguentum hydrargyri, ½ lb., bot.	216
Syrupus ferrous iodide, ½ lb., bot.	10
Syrupus ferrous iodide, 1 lb., bot.	102
Sulphocarbonate, 30 gr. tabs., 100 in bot.	50
Syrup hypophosphite, 1 lb., bot.	6
Syrup scillae, lbs.	26
Syrup, wild cherry and turpentine, compound, 1 lb., bot.	2
Talcum purified, USP., 2 lb., tin	1
Thymol, 1 oz., bot.	136
Thyroid gland, desiccated, 1 oz., vial	7
Tincture aconite, 1 oz., bot.	26
Tincture benzoin, compound, ½ lb., bot.	22
Tincture cantharides, 4 oz., bot.	4
Tincture capsici, ¼ lb., bot.	4
Tincture cinchona compound, 1 lb., bot.	7
Tincture digitalis, ½ lb., bot.	58
Tincture digitalis, .3 cc. tabs., 500 in bot.	7
Tincture ferric chloride, 1 lb., bot.	51
Tincture gentian compound, 1 lb., bot.	22
Tincture myrrhae, ½ lb., bot.	10
Tincture mucis vomica, 1 lb., bot.	13
Tincture opii, ½ lb., bot.	83
Tincture opii, lbs.	29
Tincture opii, camphor, 1 lb., bot.	41½
Tincture stroplantris, 1 oz., bot.	15
Troches of ammonium chloride, 250 in bot.	9
Unguentum hydrargyri chloridum, mite, ½ lb., bot.	30
Whiskey, ½ pt., bot.	42
Whiskey, 1 qt., bot.	42
Zinc chloride, ¼ lb., USP., bot.	23
Zinc oxide, heavy, ¼ lb., bot.	25
Zinc oxide, heavy, ½ lb., bot.	1
Zinc sulphas, ½ lb., bot.	35
Zinc sulphas, 1 lb., bot.	13
Zinc sulphas, tabs., 500 in bot.	4
"Accessory Sinuses of the Nose," Skillon, ea.	1
Acetylene outfit, burner outfit tips for, 927, 6 in., set	3
Acolite, 1 oz., pkg.	3
"Agricultural Bacteriology," Conn, ea.	1
Air service, medical, ea.	1
Alloy, balances, ea.	15
Alloy, copper, 1 oz., box	20
Alloy, Crandall's, 1 oz., bot.	12
Alloy, S. S. White's, 1 oz., bot.	12
Aluminum ingots for casting, ea.	3
Amalgam carriers, double end, No. 5, ea.	10
Ambulance Company, Par. 874, ea.	4
"Anatomy," Gray's, ea.	2
"Anatomy and Kinesiology Applied," Bowan-Kinzle, ea.	1
"Anatomy and Physiology," 5th Edition, Kimber, ea.	23
"Anatomy, Text Book of," Cunningham, 3rd Edition, ea.	1
Anesthetizer, gas complete, with fixtures, ea.	2
Animal cages, 14x14x16, Phipps, ea.	22
Antium and Simms illum., Jackson's lamp for, ea.	3
Anvils, cast base, ea.	5
Anvils, swaging, ea.	4

Item	Quantity
Apparatus, bone extension, ea.	2
Apparatus, compressed air, tankless, electric, ea.	3
Apparatus, infusion, commercial, ea.	15
Apparatus, compressed air, "903," DeVillbis, 4 in set	5
Apparatus, fat extraction, Sorhlett, ea.	2
Apparatus, N.O. and O., Heidbrink, stand for, ea.	1
Apparatus, restraint, ea.	5
Apparatus, filtering, glass, ea.	2
Appliances, soldering, Mellott's, complete, ea.	2
Applicator, laryngeal, ea.	4
Applicator, throat, metal, ea.	12
Applicator, wood, gross	4
"Applied Biology," Biglow, ea.	1
Apron, rubber, 50-inch, ea.	25
Apron, rubber, ea.	111
Apron, rubber, waterproof, ea.	88
Apron, rubber, laboratory, ea.	4
Articulators, anatomical, with snow face bow, Gysi type, ea.	3
Articulators, crown and bridge, ea.	7
Articulators, plain lines, ea.	18
Articulators, outfit, Gysi, simplex, complete, ea.	1
Asbestos, ½ lb., box	1
Atomizers, DeVillbis, for appar. comp. air, Sorensen, set	3
Atomizers, hand, ea.	245
Atomizers, paraffin, ea.	1
Autoclave, vertical copper, ea.	1
Axes, with helves, ea.	2
Back rests for bed, canvas on wood frame, ea.	9
"Bacteriology for Nurses," Cary, ea.	1
"Bacteriology, General," Jordon, ea.	1
"Bacteriology," Stitt, ea.	1
"Bacteriology, Textbook of," Hiss & Zinser, 4th Edition, ea.	1
Bacteria, yeasts and molds, in home, ea.	1
Bag, oxygen, ea.	1
Bag, Politzer, ea.	6
Bag, rubber, Hildbrink's gas and anaesth. appar., ea.	2
Bag, rubber, hot water, ea.	12
Bag, ice, ea.	35
Bag, throat and spinal, screw top, ea.	5
Bag, water sterilizing, ea.	3
Balance, analytical, in glass case, ea.	2
Bandages, flannel, 3x4 in., doz.	516
Bandages, flannel, rolls 3 in. x 4 yds., doz.	22
Bandages, flannel, rolls 4 in. x 4 yds., doz.	18
Bandages, muslin, 4 in., ea.	10
Bandages, rubber, ea.	33
Bandages, suspensories, assorted sizes, ea.	103
Bandages, winder, ea.	2
Bandages, triangular, ea.	62
"Bandaging, Practical," Eleason, 1914, ea.	1
Band, fracture angles, set	60
Band, seamless copper, Ramson & Randolph, 100 in box	1
Bars, mosquito, Medical Dispensary Service, ea.	104
Base plate, perfection for trial denture, Kerr's, ea.	12
Basin, white enamel, assorted sizes, ea.	82
Basin, white enamel, for sponges, ea.	21
Basin, white enamel and agate hand, ea.	274
Basin, white enamel, 2½ qt., hand, ea.	25
Basin, kidney, ea.	36
Basin, pus, ea.	347
Basin, rubber, hand, ea.	165
Bath bricks, ea.	24

Item	Quantity
Bath robes, ea.	1,014
Bed pans, agate, ea.	19
Bed pans, white enamel, ea.	631
Bed fracture, ea.	2
Bedstead, white enamel, ea.	3,635
Bells, call, ea.	9
Bells, glass, ground flanges, 5x5, ea.	11
Bellows, foot, ea.	5
Benches, combination, No. 17, ea.	5
Binder, loose leaf, Par. 412, ea.	1
Bistoury, S.P., 2 in., curved, ea.	5
Bistoury, p.p., 2 in., curved, ea.	8
Blankets, gray, ea.	1,469
Blank books, cap., 250 pages, ea.	8
Blower, chip and hot air syringe, ea.	74
Blower, insect powder, ea.	5
Blow pipe, automaton, ea.	5
Blow pipe, pad, ea.	2
Blow pipe, for gas, Mellott's, ea.	1
"Body Changes in Hunger, Fear and Rage," Cannon, ea.	1
Boilers, double, for cooking, assorted, ea.	2
Boilers, instrument "B," ea	67
Boilers, instrument, electric, 11x5x3, ea.	13
"Bones and Joints, Deformities, Including Diseases," ea.	1
Books, prescription, ea.	3
Bottles, empty, 5 gal., ea.	1
Bottles, empty, 3 gal., ea.	1
Bottles, graduated, for Dakin's solution, ea.	3
Bottles, hard rubber, in case emergency, ea.	35
Bottles, hot water, Thomas, ea.	10
Bottles, medicine, ½ oz., ea.	60
Bottles, narrow, 120 cc., flint glass, ea.	110
Bottles, office, preparation, extra, 1 oz., for, ea.	36
Bottles, office, preparation, extra, ½ oz., for, ea.	18
Bottles, office, preparation, No. 6, ea.	88
Bottles, sample, 4 oz., ea.	250
Bottles, w.m., 250 cc., ea.	172
Bottles, Wolfe, 250 cc., ea.	4
Bougies a boule, assorted, ea.	6
Bougies, flax, ea.	2
Bowls, plaster, ea.	8
Bowls, plaster, "A," small rubber, S.S.W. type, ea.	4
Bowls, plaster, "B," medium rubber, ea.	3
Boxes, ambulance, empty, ea.	94
Boxes, fracture, folding, ea.	2
Boxes, ointment, tin, ½ gross in pkg.	5
Boxes, ointment, imperv., tin, 1 gross in pkg.	20
Boxes, pack mule, empty, ea.	24
Boxes, pill, assorted, nested, doz.	96
Boxes, powder, 3 in nest	2
Boxes, twine, conical, iron, ea.	1
Boiler, instrument, 20 in., ea.	10
Broach, reamers, 6 in., pkg.	12
Brackets, for table to fit chair arm, dental, ea.	15
Bradford frame, ea.	2
Bridge repair set, set,	1
"Bronchi, Lungs and Plurae, Disease of," Lord, ea.	1
Brush, hand, ea.	59
Brush, lab., stiff, ea.	2
Brush, lab., stiff, plain, ⅞ inch wide, ea.	4
Brush, test tube, ea.	200
Buckets, white enamel, assorted sizes, ea.	1

[*Continued on next page*]

AMERICAN RELIEF ADMINISTRATION

Detail of Deliveries of the United States Government Surplus Medical and Hospital Supplies to the Near East Relief for Distribution in Southern Russia, 1922–1923

Medical Table 3—(*Continued*)

Commodity and Unit	Quantity
Burette, 25 cc., ea.	12
Burette, 50 cc., ea.	7
Burette, 50 cc., with stopcock, ea.	1
Bowls, soup, Delft, ea.	974
Box, soap, metal, ea.	2
Burner, Bunsen, assorted, ea.	15
Burner, Bunsen, dental, No. 12, with spider, ea.	2
Burner, Bunsen, gas, Scimataco patent, ea.	3
Burner, Bunsen, gas, blast, ea.	1
Burner, Bunsen, gas, micro., ea.	2
Burner, Terrill, gas, wing top for, ea.	9
Burnisher, l.b., assorted, ea.	80
Burnisher, l.b., No. 29, ea.	18
Burnisher, tantalum, No. 1, ea.	20
Burs, dentate, for H.P., No. 7, No. 359, ea.	210
Burs, dentate, for H.P., No. 568, ea.	198
Burs, bone, Friedman's, No. 27, ea.	3
Burs, invert cone for, HP., "M," ea.	216
Burs, invert cone for, HP., No. 7 No. 33½, ea.	180
Burs, invert cone for, HP., No. 7 No. 34, ea.	240
Burs, invert cone for, HP., No. 7 No. 35, ea.	240
Burs, invert cone for, HP., No. 7 No. 41, ea.	180
Burs, round HP., "M," No. ½, ea.	300
Burs, round HP., "M," No. 1, ea.	200
Burs, round HP., "M," No. 2, ea.	300
Burs, round HP., "M," No. 3, ea.	240
Burs, round HP., "M," No. 6, ea.	198
Burs, round HP., "M," No. 8, ea.	240
Burs, round HP., "M," No. 9, ea.	198
Cabinet, dental, ea.	3
Cabinet, dental, aseptic pressed, No. 610, ea.	25
Cabinet, file, wood, 4 drawers, "B," ea.	9
Cabinet, file, wood, 5 drawers, "B," ea.	1
Cabinet, for medicine ward, ea.	39
Cabinet, large, for dressing and instrument, ea.	4
Cabinet, metal, for blanks and documents, "B," ea.	3
Cabinet, small, for dressing and instrument, ea.	11
Cake turner, ea.	8
Calcar molding sand, 3 lbs., tin	5
Camp, infirmary, Par. 869, ea.	5
Camp, infirmary, reserve, ea.	7
Candles, 6 in., lb.	60
Can opener, ea.	1
Canvas for litter, ea.	113
Caps, operating, paper, ea.	100
Capsules, 100 in box	216
Capsules, size 00, 100 in box	115
Capsules, size 0, 100 in box	200
Carriages, dressing, ea.	2
Carrier, amalgam, double end, No. 5, ea.	4
Carvers, amalgam, Frahm's, ea.	24
Carvers, amalgam, ea.	9
Carvers, wax suction, Rooch, ea.	1
Case, aspirating, 910, complete, ea.	9
Case, bedding, large, empty, ea.	2

Commodity and Unit	Quantity
Case, canvas, with instrument, ea.	151
Case, canvas, for instrument, assorted, ea.	9
Case, ear, nose, and throat, 912, ea.	2
Case, emergency, 1913–1916, ea.	14
Case, eye, incomplete, ea.	2
Case, field dressing, veterinary, empty, ea.	23
Case, field, incomplete, veterinary, ea.	12
Case, foot, ea.	1
Case, forceps, haem., ea.	13
Case, general operating, complete, ea.	8
Case, general operating, incomplete, ea.	3
Case, G.U., Par. 917 (1 syringe short), ea.	2
Case, G.O., Par. 971, veterinary, ea.	1
Case, gynecological, ea.	1
Case, heater, ea.	2
Case, hoof knives, "B," ea.	1
Case, for hoof knives, "B," ea.	2
Case, hoof, veterinary, contains 3 knives and 1 handle, ea.	1
Case, hoof, veterinary, contains 5 knives and 1 handle, ea.	1
Case, instrument, ea.	1
Case, instrument, for M.O., 919, ea.	12
Case, instrument, for M.O., incomplete, ea.	1
Case, instrument, for E.M., web belts, with contents, ea.	24
Case, office prep., extra, ½ oz. bot. for, ea.	2
Case, office prep., oak, empty, ea.	14
Case, office prep., oak, ea.	3
Case, operating, small canvas, ea.	1
Case, operating, small rosewood box, ea.	6
Case, operating, small incomp., ea.	8
Case, pocket, 923, ea.	1
Case, pocket, complete, ea.	3
Case, pocket, incomp., ea.	18
Case, post mortem, 924, ea.	1
Case, post mortem, incomp., ea.	1
Case, rubber gloves, empty, ea.	52
Case, rubber gloves, filled, ea.	3
Case, surgical, small, ea.	2
Case, thermo, cautery, ea.	4
Case, tooth extracting, 925 MMD., 1916, ea.	2
Case, tooth extracting, 3 in., ea.	8
Case, tooth extracting, forceps, 6 in., roll	7
Case, trial lenses, 926, ea.	4
Case, veterinary dental, "B," roll	1
Case, veterinary foot, "B," ea.	1
Case, veterinary general oper., "B," ea.	1
Case, veterinary post mortem, "B," ea.	1
Case, ward dressing, ea.	3
Casting machine, ea.	4
Casting machine, elgin, extra rings for casting inlay, lge, ea.	2
Casting machine, elgin, extra rings for casting inlay, sml., ea.	2
Catheters, Gouley, grooved and tunneled, 14 F, ea.	1
Catheters, horse, rubber, ea.	5
Catheters, metal, ea.	1
Catheters, metal, mare, "B," ea.	1
Catheters, rubber, American, size 28, ea.	264

Commodity and Unit	Quantity
Cautery, Paquelin, ea.	1
Cautery, Paquelin, extra bulbs for, ea.	3
Cautery, points No. 1, with handle, ea.	3
Cellu, cotton, lbs.	575
Cement, anes crown and bridge colors, pkg.	90
Cement, dark brown, box.	100
Cement, pearl gray, box.	100
Cement, small, tube.	1
Cement, yellow, box.	100
Centrifuge, elec., 110 v., with rheostat, ea.	1
Centrifuge, elec., 110 v., without rheostat, ea.	2
Centrifuge, hand, ea.	2
Centrifuge, tube, grad., 15 cc., ea.	50
Centrifuge, tube, grad., 50 cc., ea.	20
Centrifuge, tube, ungrad., 15 cc., ea.	100
Chairs, barony, w.e., ea.	1
Chairs, dental, Columbia, ea.	5
Chairs, dental, portable, in chests, ea.	14
Chairs, dental, portable, in chests, crates for, ea.	5
Chairs, invalid, rolling, ea.	11
Chairs, operating, dental, ea.	4
Chairs, specialist, ea.	1
Chairs, wood seat and back, ea.	56
"Chemistry," Simon, ea.	1
"Chemistry, Blood and Urine, New Methods," C. & B., ea.	1
"Chemistry, Elementary," Chemot, ea.	1
Chest, with dental engine, complete, ea.	15
Chest, field lab., No. 1, Par. 930, ea.	1
Chest, field lab., No. 2, Par. 931, ea.	1
Chest, field lab., not listed, contains 1 inc. oil heater, ea.	1
Chest, field veterinary, ea.	9
Chest, instrument, empty, No. 1, ea.	18
Chest, instrument, empty, No. 2, ea.	14
Chest, instrument, ea.	3
Chest, localizing, ea.	1
Chest, supplementary med. and surg., 933, ea.	3
Chest, supplementary med. and surg., 933, incomp., ea.	25
Chest, supplementary med. and surg., 933, incomp., ea.	70
Chest, supply, dental, ea.	20
Chest, supply, empty, ea.	15
Chest, tool, No. 1, incomplete, 837, ea.	2
Chest, veterinary, officers, ea.	2
Chisel, bone, 18 mm., ea.	1
Chisel, Buckley, ea.	8
Chisel, c.s. points, ea.	2
Chisel, labyrinth, ea.	2
Chisel, l.h., assorted, ea.	366
Chucks, "D," for Schimmel dental needles, ea.	1
Clamp, bone plating, Bowman, ea.	3
Clamp, hemorroidal, Kelsey, ea.	1
Clamp, rubber dam, Ivory's, ea.	50
Cleaners, root canal, S.S.W., No. 0, 12 in pkg.	12
"Clinical Diagnosis," Simon, ea.	1
Clipper, hair, B. & S., No. 1, ea.	2
Clocks, "B," ea.	10

Item	Quantity
Cabinets, materia medica with 288 drugs, ea	1
Capsules, gelatine, No. 10, 1 oz., 100 in box	3
Clocks, wall, ea	2
Coats, white, ea	8
Comforters, ea	405
Condenser, electric, with stand, ea	2
Cones, felt, large, blunt, ea	22
Conveyor, for soiled linen, without canvas bags, ea	3
Corks, assorted, 300 in bag	7
Cork borer, h. brass, 12 in set	3
Cots, finger, rubber, ea	298
Cotton, absorbent, 1 oz., pkg	80
Cotton batting, 1 lb., roll	559
Cotton, rolls, 100 in box	100
Counting apparatus, Wolfhuegal, ea	1
Coupler joining lueria syringe, ea	2
Cover glasses, round, box	50
Covers for ward tents, ea	30
Cradle bed, ea	18
Cresol form. Caulk's, box	1
Crinolin, 25 yds. in piece	3
"Crown and Bridge Work," Poeso, ea	1
Crowns, assortment, No. 10, ea	1
Crowns, assortment, No. 10, incomplete, ea	1
Crowns, remover, Johnson, ea	4
Crucible, filtering, pore, 25 cc., ea	9
Crucible, Gootch, 25 cc., porc., without cover, ea	14
Cruets, vinegar and oil, ea	12
Crutches, pr	108
Cups, china, ea	356
Cups, Delft, ea	122
Cups, feeding, w.e., ea	3
Cups, polishing, soft rubber, small, 72 in box	49
Cups, spit, metal frame for, ea	448
Cups, spit, paper, ea	57,500
Cups, spit, w.e., ea	380
Cups, w.e., ea	31
Cups, w.e., small, ea	5
Cups, w.e., for fountain cuspidors, ea	63
Curette, apex, extra fine, 6 in box, ea	24
Curette, bone, ea	2
Curette, bone, assorted, ea	1
Curette, metal handle, right angle, ea	2
Curette, metal handle, left angle, ea	3
Curette, metal handle, straight, ea	2
Curette, metal handle, No. 3-24-25, ea	9
Curette, mastoid, assorted, ea	3
Cushions, air, rubber, small, ea	37
Cuspidor, fountain, ea	2
Cuspidor, metal, ea	7
Cuspidor, w.e., ea	49
Cylinder, nitrous oxide, "F," ea	5
Cystoscope, lamps for, ea	7
"Dental Materia, Medica and Therapeutics," ea	1
"Dental Pathology and Therapeutics," Buchard & Ingis, ea.	1
"Dental Pathology, Therapeutics Prescription Writing," ea.	1
Dentimeters, Kirk's, No. 2, ea	15
Desk, field dental, empty, ea	14
Desk, field dental, ea	46
Desiccator, Scheible, 150 mm., ea	4
"Determination of Hydrogen," Clark, ea	1
"Diagnosis, Clinical and Microscopical," Wood, 3d Ed., 1917	1
"Diagnosis, Clinical," Simon, 8th Ed., 1914, ea	1
Dictionary, American Medical, Darland, 9th Ed., 1918, ea	1
Die cusp plate, No. 5, ea	7
"Dietetics, Essentials of," Pope & Carpenter, 1917, ea	1
"Dietetics, Practical," Pattee, ea	2
"Digestive Organs, Diseases of," Aaron, ea	1
Dilator, uterine, ea	1
Dippers, assorted, ea	6
Directors, grooved, ea	9
"Diseases of the Ear, Nose and Throat," Ballenger, ea	1
Director, probe pointed, 5 in., silver, Arnott, ea	6
"Diseases, Infancy and Childhood," ea	1
"Diseases of the Eye," De Schweinitis, ea	1
"Diseases of the Skin," Stellawayan, ea	1
"Diseases of Voca. and Occupa. Hyg.," Kober & Hanson, ea.	1
Dish, evaporating, porc., 100 cc., ea	4
Dish, petri, pr	4,664
Dish, soap with cover, ea	9
Dish, vegetable, w.e., ea	2
Disinfector, hand spray, ea	5
Disinfector, hand spray, on skids, ea	1
Disks in boxes of 100, box	396
Case, veterinary officers, ea	2
Catheters, urethral, flexible rubber, assorted, ea	22
Centrifuge, hand, high speed, ea	3
"Chemical Annual," Von Ostrand-Olsen, ea	1
Chisels, beveled, carpenter's, assorted, ea	4
Disks, bristle, 9-11, and cup-shaped, assorted, ea	198
Disks, carborundum, knife-edge, assorted, ea	78
Disks, garnet, ⅜, ½ grit, 100 to box	12
Disks, separating, carborundum, cup-shaped, ½ in. diam., ea.	42
Disks, separating, thin, vulcarbol ½ in. diameter, ea	500
Disks, separating, thin, vulcarbol ⅝ in. diameter, ea	50
Dispensing set, 942, incomplete, ea	3
Distillery, Silverman's, complete, ea	1
Dividers, ea	10
Division medical supply, Unit group, ea	1
Division surgeon's office, Par. 854, ea	1
Douche, large uterine, ea	2
Douche, medium uterine, ea	2
Douche, small uterine, ea	1
Drill bone, 3 point, No. 32, ea	1
Drums for sterilized dressings, 9 in., ea	4
Electrode disk, with handle, ea	1
Electrode, with handles surface, ea	1
Electrode round, sponge or asbestos, ea	10
Elevator, Dodel type, set of 4 in handle, ea	1
Elevator, Le Cluse, ea	4
Elevator, No. 3, metal handle, ea	10
Elevator, No. 3, Knott's, metal handle, right and left, ea	25
Elevator, No. 1, Knott's, metal handle, right and left, ea	20
Elevator, No. 2, Knott's, metal handle, right and left, ea	8
Engines, dental, all cords, with K-3 attach. for HP, No. 7, ea.	1
Engines, dental, all cords, Ritter's electric, ea	2
Engines, dental, cord for, ea	44
Engines, dental, electric belts for, Ritter, ea	103
Engines, dental, handpiece str. for, HP, No. 7, ea	10
Engines, dental, for HP "M," ea	5
Engines, dental, handpiece for "H" contra angle for s.j. 2, ea	5
Engines, dental, wrists and s.j. conn. for attachment K-3, ea.	1
Engines, instrument HP No. 7, drills No. 100-102, ea	42
Engines, instrument for HP No. 7, box	30
Envelope openers, ea	2
"Epidemiology Tubercule," Bushnell, ea	1
Examination blanks, No. 2, dental, pads	30
Excavators, c.s. points, assorted, ea	50
Excavators, L.H., No. 23, ea	10
Excavators, L.H., No. 37, ea	22
Excavators, L.H., No. 49, ea	10
Excavators, L.H., No. 57, ea	20
Excavators, L.H., No. 63, ea	15
Excavators, L.H., Black's assorted, ea	50
Explorer's c.s. points, assorted, ea	4
Explorer's L.H., ea	50
Eyes, artificial reform, ea	1,500
Eyes, artificial, shell, ea	1,500
Eye shades, single, ea	107
Eye shades, double, ea	110
Facers, Root, safe side, No. 8, for HP No. 7, ea	3
Facings, U.S. Army, assortment No. 21, set	2
Fans, electric, ea	10
"Feeding the Family," Rose, ea	2
Fibre, devitalizing, arsenical, jars	43
Field Hospital, Par. 879, ea	4
Files, gold, ea	15
Files, gold, flat, 6 in., ea	3
Files, gold, half round, No. 6, ea	4
Files, gold, half round, 7 in., ea	1
Files, gold, round, ea	4
Files, gold, round, 6 in., ea	9
Files, rattail, 6 in., ea	2
Files, root canal, Kerr's, No. 4, style "D," 6 in pkg	3
Files, saw, steel, 8 inch, ea	1
Files, saw, tapered, 6 inch, ea	1
Files, triangular, 8 inch, ea	9
Files, vulcanite, ea	11
Files, vulcanite, half round, ea	1
Files, vulcanite, round, 8 inch, ea	3
Files, wall, No. 3 finish, Cleve-Dent, pkg	6
Files, wall, No. 4 finish, Cleve-Dent, pkg	6
Finisher plate, Ideal emery arbor to fit Ritter lathe, ea	5
Finisher plate, Ideal extra bands for, 100 in box	1
First-aid packet, ea	35,207
First-aid packet, Par. 945, ea	50,418
Flask, Kjeldald, 500 cc., ea	39
Flask, bolts, sets	5
Flask, box, ea	7
Flask, distilling, with tube in middle, 500 cc., ea	4
Flask, Erlenmeyer, 500 cc., ea	25
Flask, Erlenmeyer, 1,000 cc., ea	4
Flask, flat bottom, 1,000 cc., ea	2
Flask, for spirits of aromatic ammonia, with cup, ea	214
Flask, glass, 2 gal., heavy glass, ea	1
Flask, molding, Bailey, ea	14
Flask, press, ea	6
Flask, Pyrex, 500 cc., ea	6
Flask, Pyrex, 1,000 cc., ea	8
Flask, volumetric, 1,000 cc., with stopper, ea	1
Flask, vulcanite, ea	12
Flask, Whiting, ea	18
Floss silk, waxed, 24 yds. in spool	450
Flys for tent, hosp. trop., ea	16
"Food & Cooking for the Sick & Convalescent," Frazer, ea.	1
Food carts, Dear model, ea	23

[*Continued on next page*]

AMERICAN RELIEF ADMINISTRATION

Detail of Deliveries of the United States Government Surplus Medical and Hospital Supplies to the Near East Relief for Distribution in Southern Russia, 1922–1923

Medical Table 3—(*Continued*)

Commodity and Unit	Quantity
Food carts, metal frame, ea	2
Forceps, No. 65, ea	1
Forceps, artery, 3,153, ea	16
Forceps, bone cutting, heavy, 10 inch, ea	3
Forceps, bone cutting, curved, s.l., ea	1
Forceps, crown slitting, ea	10
Forceps, dressing spring, 5½ inch, ea	11
Forceps, dressing spring, straight, 10 inch, ea	9
Forceps, dressing spring, 12 inch, ea	4
Forceps, dressing spring, handle, ea	6
Forceps, dressing angular, "B," ea	2
Forceps, haemostatic, assorted, ea	20
Forceps, haemostatic, assorted, 5½ inch, ea	1
Forceps, haemostatic, 5½ inch, str. s.l., ea	19
Forceps, haemostatic, small, ea	6
Forceps, haemostatic, Halstead, mosquito, ea	13
Forceps, haemostatic, Kelly & Dean, 6¼ inch, ea	19
Forceps, haemostatic, Kelly & Dean, cvd., flat shk., CND 119	12
Forceps, haemostatic, Kocher, straight, 5½ inch, ea	11
Forceps, haemostatic, Oschner, 7 inch, ea	14
Forceps, haemostatic, Pean, curved, 8½ inch, ea	3
Forceps, haemostatic, Pean, straight, 8½ inch, ea	5
Forceps, intestinal, curved, Doyen, 8 inch, ea	6
Forceps, intestinal, straight, Doyen, 8 inch, ea	6
Forceps, mechanical clasp bending, ea	1
Forceps, mouse-toothed, C.N.D., 130-B, ea	13
Forceps, nasal dressing, Kny-Scheerer, ea	3
Forceps, needle, Heager, C.N.D., 133, 7½ inches, ea	7
Forceps, obstetrical, Sampson, ea	1
Forceps, placenta, Kelly, ea	1
Forceps, Rouguer, ea	4
Forceps, Rouguer, bone, C.N.D., 175 and 176, ea	6
Forceps, Rouguer, bone, De Villbis, ea	1
Forceps, rubber dam, clamp, Brewer, ea	10
Forceps, rubber dam, punch, perfected, ea	10
Forceps, screw holding, Lane, ea	1
Forceps, sequestum, ea	6
Forceps, straight, medium fine, ea	3
Forceps, sterilizer, ea	1
Forceps, suture, Michel, ea	2
Forceps, tenaculum, ea	6
Forceps, tissue, mouse tooth, extra heavy, 5½ inches, ea	6
Forceps, haemostatic, Halstead, 5 inches, ea	21
Forceps, Rouguer, bone, CND., 176-1, ea	3
First-aid packets, for instruction, ea	1,878
Flask, distilling, 1,000 cc., ea	4
Forceps, tissue, 6 inches, Allis, ea	8
Forceps, tongue, 5½ inches, ea	1
Forceps, tooth extracting, assorted, ea	149
Forceps, tooth extracting, No. 10, ea	16
Forceps, tooth extracting, No. 15, ea	16
Forceps, tooth extracting, No. 18-L, ea	17
Forceps, tooth extracting, No. 18-R, ea	16
Forceps, tooth extracting, No. 65, ea	8
Forceps, tooth extracting, No. 150, ea	16
Forceps, tooth extracting, No. 151, ea	10
Forceps, tooth extracting, No. 222, ea	10
Forceps, towel, 5 in., ea	39
Forceps, towel, Backhaus, 3 inches, ea	3
Forceps, wedge cutting, ea	2
Forks, table, silver plated, ea	2,575
Fracture appliances outfit, No. 3, ea	1
"Fractures and Dislocations," Scudder, ea	2
Frames, Gotch, adjustable spring, ea	25
Freezer, ice cream, ea	1
Front-line packet, No. 2, white label, ea	50
Funnel, glass, 25 cc., ea	3
Funnel, glass, 250 cc., ea	27
Funnel, glass, 500 cc., ea	32
Funnel, glass, 1,000 cc., ea	4
Funnel, porc, 65 mm., ea	1
Funnel, porc., 100 mm., ea	1
Gag, mouth, Denhart, ea	3
Gauge, plate and wire, B. & L., ea	9
Gauge, with attachment for gas oxygen machine, ea	2
Gauze, packer, slight curve, No. 2, Cleveland Mfg. Co., ea	1
Gauze, sublimated, 1 yd. in pkg., ea	680
Generator, kerosene, ea	1
Glass rods, assorted, ea	5
Gloves, rubber, pr	4
Glue, Dennison, 1 pt., can	1
Gouges, C.N.D. mastoid, 508, ea	1
Gowns, delousing, ea	50
Gowns, operating, ea	258
Graduate, glass, 10 cc., ea	10
Graduate, glass, 60 cc., ea	2
Graduate, glass, 100 cc., ea	35
Graduate, glass, 250 cc., ea	10
Graduate, glass, 500 cc., ea	1
Graters, large, ea	3
Graters, small, ea	3
Guns, balling, Class B, ea	5
"Gunshot Wounds, Their Therapeutic Orthopedic Treatment," Moyer, ea	1
Gutta Percha stopping, temporary 1 oz. in box	131
Gutta Percha stopping, excelsior sticks ½ oz. in box	138
"Gynecology," Graves, Second Edition, 1918, ea	1
Hammer, reflex, ea	1
Hammer, steel, post-mortem, ea	1
Hammer, swaging, 1½ lb., ea	7
Hammer, swaging, 2 lb., ea	1
"Hand Book for Sanitary Troops," Mason, ea	31
Handles, c.s. points, ea	120
Handles, metal tube 18 x ½ in., ea	1
Handles, special type, vac. electrode, ea	1
Hardware, for Balkan frame, sets	5
Harness casting, ½ in. rope, ea	32
Heater, elec. cut-off, No. 4 opr. spray bottle, ea	10
Heater, elec. with 3-spray bottles and water glasses, ea	7
Heater, Petan-Krane, extra bottle for, ea	15
Hobbles, rope, ea	4
Holders, cotton, aseptic, heavy glass, ea	2
Holders, cotton, Methot's type, ea	22
Holders, needle, Hegar, 7½ in., ea	3
Holders, nerve broach, No. 6, ea	24
Holders, mercury, ebony, No. 1, ea	26
Holders, rubber dam, anatinik, ea	10
Holders, sponge, oval blades, 9½ in., ea	15
Hones, Arkansas stone, ea	44
Hones, oil, ea	8
"Housecleaning, Municipal," Cooper and Carpenter, 1918, ea	1
"House Sanitation," Albert, ea	1
"Household Economics," Campbell, ea	1
"House on Henry Street," ea	1
"Household Chemistry," Vulte, ea	1
"Hygiene and Sanitation for Nurses," ea	13
"Hygiene for Nurses," McIsaac, ea	1
"Hygiene, Meat," Edelman, Mohler, and Eichorn, ea	1
"Hygiene, Principles of," Bergey, ea	1
"Hygiene, Military, and Sanitation," Kaefer, 1914, ea	1
"Hygiene, Military," Ashburn, 1917, ea	1
"Hygiene, Milk, Principles and Practice of," Klein, 1917	1
"Hygiene of the Mind," McClauston, ea.	1
Hypodermic tablets, assorted, tins	4
"Immediate Care of the Injured," Morrow, ea	1
Incubator, Bact. C.S. & E., No. 2 Thermo., 56, ea	1
Incubator, oil, complete, ea	1
Individual dressing packets, 949, ea	2,710
"Infections and Resistance," Zinsser, ea	1
"Infections of the Hand," Kanavel, ea	1
Inhaler, chloroform drop bottle, Esmarch, ea	3
Inhaler, chloroform drop bottle for, ea	29
Inhaler, masks, Yankners, ea	42
Inhaler, gas, ether, ea	2
Inhaler, oxygen, with 3 cylinders, ea	1
Inhaler, oxygen, No. 3127, Bennet, ea	1
Instruments, eye, ea	24
"Invalid Occupation," Tracy, ea	1
Investment compound, crown and bridge, tins	6
Irrigator, glass tips for, ea	24
Irrigator, metal, seamless, ea	4
Irrigator, Valentines, shields for, ea	9
Irrigator, Valentines, tubes, holders for, ea	13
Irrigator, w.e., 2 qt., ea	29
Irrigation apparatus, wall bracket for, ea	5
Jackknives, with saw blade, ea	7
Jar, large, w.e., dressing, ea	40
Jar, ointment, 125 cc., ea	2
Jar, ointment, 250 cc., ea	2
Jar, Coplin, ea	20
Jar, small, for dressing, ea	3
Jar, small, glass covered, for sutures, ea	20
Kettle, croup, ea	40
Knives, carving, ea	8

Item	Quantity
Knives, M.O., 103, ea	6
Knives, operating, ea	6
Knife, operating, 2 in., ea	37
Knife, plaster, ea	16
Knives, table, silver plated, ea	302
Labels, for vials, sheet	129
Labels, dispensing, set	10
Lactometers, ea	2
Ladles, melting, No. 6, without handles, ea	12
Ladles, melting, No. 8, ea	9
Ladles, melting, handles for, ea	6
Lamp, alcohol, No. 1, with flame shield, ea	10
Lamp, alcohol, No. 26, with flame shield, ea	5
Lamp, alcohol, No. 1, extra wicks for, ea	1
Lamp, alcohol, No. 26, with nealing tray, No. 9, ea	3
Lamp, alcohol, large, Purdy, ea	10
Lamp, diagnostic, lamps for straight, Cameron, ea	6
Lamp, large, extra wicks for, ea	7
Lamp, spirit, brass, ea	19
Lamp, spirit, glass, ea	48
Lamp, stand, ea	2
Lancets, 3 blades, ea	2
Lancets, abscess and gum, ea	20
Lancets, abscess, metal handle, octagon, No. 5, ea	30
Lancets, gun-metal handle, octagon, No. 2, ea	20
Lanterns, folding, ea	38
Lanterns, with globes, ea	102
Lathe, dental electric, with 8 chucks, ea	5
Lens, measure, ea	1
Litters, with slings, ea	1,645
Localizer, eye, incomplete, ea	1
Looking glasses, 12 x 18, ea	46
Machine, galvanic-faradic, with pole charger, ea	1
"Malarial fever," Craig, ea	1
"Malingering," Lane, ea	1
Mallets, metal case, No. 11-12-15, ea	10
Mallet, plugging, ea	15
Mallet, round, No. 3, Lig-Vitae, ea	2
Mallet, swaging, horn, ea	5
Mallet, wooden, ea	2
Mandrels, No. 303, for HP, "M", ea	12
Mandrels, No. 303, for HP, No. 7, ea	24
Mandrels, Morgan-Maxfield, for HP, No. 7, ea	4
Mandrels, Morgan-Maxfield, for HP, "M," ea	39
Mandrin, with spring handle, Conde beak, ea	2
"Manual, Bacteriology Determination," Chester, ea	1
"Manual of Ethics," McKinzie, ea	1
"Manual, for the Medical Dept.," ea	1
Knives, M.O., 102, ea	6
Litters, canvas for, ea	113
Manual, military urology, ea	1
Manometer, mercury (blood pressure instr.), ea	1
"Materia Medica," Blumgarten, ea	8
"Materia Medica for Nurses," ea	1
"Materia Medica and Therapeutics," Potter, ea	1
"Materia Medica, Therapeutics for Nurses," Parker, ea	1
Matrix retainers, Ivory's, No. 1, ea	15
Matrix spring synthetic, Caulk's, ea	2
Mattress cover, ea	2,543
Mattress, hair, ea	100
Mattress, cotton, hospital, ea	65
Measures, metal assorted, ea	3

Item	Quantity
Mechanical dam automatum, ea	10
"Medical Dictionary," Gould, ea	1
"Medical and Surgical Therapy," Vols. 1, 3, 4, 5, ea	2
"Medicine and Hygiene, Preventive," Rosenau, ea	1
Medicine dropper, doz	12
Medicine glass, ea	112
Microscope, Field, B. & L. with access. case inc., ea	2
Microscope, M. M. D., B. & L., 951, ea	12
Microscope, Spencer, ea	5
Microscope, Spencer, mechan. stage in case, ea	3
Microtome auto. Minot, ea	1
Military hygiene, ea	1
"Military Medical Administration," Ford, ea	2
Mimeograph, No. 78, ea	1
Mirrors, hand, beveled edge, 5 in., ea	4
Mirrors, laryngeal, size 3, ea	24
Mirrors, laryngeal, size 5, ea	4
Mirrors, laryngeal, boil., size 3, ea	1
Mirrors, laryngeal, boil., size 4, ea	1
Mirrors, mouth, alum., size 4, ea	25
Mirrors, mouth, metal, ea	4
Mirrors, head, ea	12
"Modern Methods of Nursing," Saunders, ea	1
"Modern Otology," Barnhill, ea	1
Modeling compound, lbs	5
Modeling composition perfection, Detroit, ½ lbs	30
Mortar and pestle, ww., 8 cm., ea	43
Mortar and pestle, ww., 20 cm., ea	10
Mortar and pestle, ww., 30 cm., ea	5
Mortar and pestle, ww., 65 cm., ea	2
Mortar and pestle, glass, No. 3, ea	20
Mortar and pestle, glass, 10 cm., ea	4
"Mosquito Control in Panama," LaPrince, ea	1
Motor generator for operat., 110 v., ea	1
Motor generator, small set, ea	1
Muslin, unbleached, yds	300
Needle, aneurism, Deschamps, ea	6
Needle, hypo., ea	234
Needle, lumbar puncture, ea	16
Needle, Schimmel, assort. sizes, 1 in., ea	3
Needle, Seton, ea	1
Needle, utricle, Silver, ea	1
Needle, Wasserman, ea	2
"Neurasthenia," Bollet, ea	1
"New and Non-Official Remedies," 1916, ea	1
"Notes, Nurses," Nightingale, ea	1
"Nursing Ethics," Robbs, ea	2
"Nurses' Handbook of Drugs and Sol.," Stinson, ea	1
"Nursing Problems and Obligations," Parson, ea	1
"Nursing the Insane," Barnes, ea	1
"Nutrition and Dietetics," Hill, ea	1
Nuts, gold, Bryant's, No. 5, ea	12
Oakum, 1 lb., pkg	543
"Occupat. Therapy and Manual for Nurses," Dunton, ea	1
"Operative Dentistry," Black, ea	1
Operating tables, small, ea	2
Opthalmoscope elec., DeZang, ea	1
Opthalmoscope elec., DeZang, extra lamps for, ea	10
Opthalmoscope, Loring, ea	6
"Oral Diseases and Malformations," ea	2
"Organic Chemistry," Holen, Perkins, and Kibben, ea	1
"Orthopedic Surgery," Whitman, ea	1

Item	Quantity
Osteotome, square handle, ea	2
Oven for 110 v., No. 100, Freas, ea	1
Ox para, box	2
Pads, interlaced, curled hair, ea	8
Pail, commode, ea	72
Pail, ww 10 qt., ea	30
Pajama coats, ea	957
Pajama trousers, ea	1,815
Mastoid gouges, assort., ea	3
Mortar and pestle, porcelain, 20 cc., ea	1
Pajama suits, ea	620
Pans, dust, ea	1
Pants, white, ea	5
Paper, articulating, thin, in books, book	24
Paper, oiled, roll	18
Paper, toilet, roll	195
"Pathology," McCall, ea	1
Periosteotome, narrow, ea	2
Periosteotome, plain, ea	2
"Physics and Chemistry for Nurses," Pope, ea	24
"Physiology," Howell, ea	1
Pick axes, with helves, ea	6
Pillows, feather, ea	174
Pillows, hair, M.D.S., ea	28
Pill tile, glass, 5x8 in., ea	4
Pill tile, H.R., ea	17
Pipette, 1 cc., ea	200
Pipette, 5 cc., ea	200
"Pipette, Milk Testing," Babcock, ea	25
Pipette, volume of transfer, 5 cc., ea	50
Pipette, volume of transfer, 10 cc., ea	200
Pipette, box, ea	1
Pitchers, Delft, large, ea	12
Pitchers, w.e., 2 qt., ea	1
Pitchers, w.e., 4 qt., ea	5
Pitchers, w.e., 6 qt., ea	8
Plaster, adhesive, 1 in. x 5 yd., spool	1,800
Plaster of Paris, French impression, lbs	110
Plaster of Paris, for models, tins	27
Plates, dinner, Delft, ea	476
Plates, silver, 30 ga., ea	10
Pliers, cone socket, No. 102, ea	1
Pliers, contouring, No. 115, ea	4
Pliers, contour., chain nose, office, smooth beak, No. 322, ea.	40
Pliers, dressing, No. 2, ea	80
Pliers, dressing, No. 17, ea	3
Pliers, laboratory, universal, ea	5
Pliers, Lane, ea	1
Pliers, office, smooth beak, No. 122, ea	23
Pliers, pin roughening and binding, ea	2
Pliers, round nose, etc., assorted, ea	6
Pluggers, amalgam., Black's s.h., No. 1, ea	4
Pluggers, amalgam, Black's s.h., No. 3, ea	4
Pluggers, amalgam., Black's s.h., No. 4, ea	12
Pluggers, amalgam., Black's l.h., No. 5, ea	12
Pluggers, plastic, ea	31
Pluggers, root canal, Donaldson, ea	25
Pluggers, Woodson's amalgam., ea	25
Points, root canal, gutta-percha, ea	14
Points, root canal, gutta-percha, No. 12, pink, round, ea	2
Points, soft rubber, corrugated, in box, G.L., box	30
Polishers, rubber cups, Young's, 12 in box	4

[*Continued on next page*]

AMERICAN RELIEF ADMINISTRATION

Detail of Deliveries of the United States Government Surplus Medical and Hospital Supplies to the Near East Relief for Distribution in Southern Russia, 1922–1923

Medical Table 3—(*Continued*)

Commodity and Unit	Quantity
Portable dental outfit, complete, 854, ea	26
Portable polishers, contra angle, ea	2
Post puller, Little Giant, ea	1
Pots, medicine, glass, Dappens, ea	39
Pots, coffee, w.e., ea	2
Pouches, for diagnosis tags and instruments, empty, ea	299
"Practical Methods, Electro-Chemistry," Perkins, ea	1
"Practical Nursing," Maxwell and Pope, ea	21
"Practice of Medicine," ea	1
"Principles and Practice of Milk Hygiene," ea	1
"Principles of Sanitary Tactics," Munson, ea	1
Probes, assorted, ea	4
Probes, C.N.D., Fig. 156–3, ea	2
Probes, copper plated, ea	1
Probes, jointed, ea	3
Probes, mastoid, Kny-Scheerer, ea	2
Probes, plated, asstd., ea	10
Probes, pliable, copper, ea	1
Probes, silver, ea	15
Probes, silver, in case, telescopic S.S.W. type, ea	10
Probes, straight 5 in., ea	3
Probes, straight, silver plated, double, ea	1
Probes, straight, silver plated, single, ea	2
"Pulmonary Tuberculosis," Norris and Fishberg, ea	1
Punch, Marvel, ea	2
Punch, nasal, Stykeus, ea	1
Punch, for punching Dakin's tube, ea	2
Pupil lights (pocket flashlights), ea	1
Probe, straight, 8 inch, ea	3
Racks, metal for test tubes, ea	4
Rakes, steel, ea	8
Razor, hone, ea	1
Razor, Rippenhagen, ea	10
Razor, strop for, ea	5
Reamer, broach, Kerr's, 6 in pkg	12
Reamer, root, Peeso's, for HP., No. 7, ea	10
Receptacles for waste, with covers, 15x24, ea	4
Refrigerators, small, ea	10
Regulators, thermo-electric, with cond. current, ea	1
Retainers, matrix, Ivory's, extra bands, ea	9
Retort stands, with 3 rings, ea	6
Retractor, 4 prong, ea	2
Retractor, abdominal, Belfour, ea	1
Retractor, army type, sizes nest, ea	2
Retractor, double-end comb., Rich and Eastman, ea	2
Retractor, flexible, copper, ea	3
Retractor, Buckley, tissue, ea	2
Retractor, tissue, Thoma, No. 1, ea	2
Retractor, tissue, Thoma, No. 2, ea	2
Retractor, vaginal, Kelly, ea	2
Rheostat, E.S.T. lamp socket type, bulbs broken, ea	1
Roller, gold, No. 3, S.A.C.Co., type, ea	1
Root driers, ea	2
Rubber dam, medium, 18 foot x 5 inch roll, roll	2
Rubber, red, for pressure, anaesthesia, vulcanite, sheets	23
Rubber, pink, vulcanite, ½ lb. in box	15
Ruler, assorted, ea	4
Saccharometer, Einhorn, ea	2
Saddle bags, veterinary, complete, ea	22
Saddle bags, veterinary, empty, ea	12
Saddle, pack, 953, Texas style, ea	45
Safe, iron, ea	2
Sandarac gum, ea	12
Sandarac varnish, in bot	10
"Sanitary Science and Public," Sedgwick's, ea	1
Saucers, china, ea	388
Saw, butcher, ea	4
Saw, dental, Gordon-White, complete, ea	25
Saw, mechanical, extra blades for, ea	48
Saw, frames, extra blades for, ea	24
Saw frames, mechanical, ea	12
Saw, metacarpal, ea	2
Saw, plain frame for, Gigli, ea	1
Saw, tracheotomy, with dbl. blade and guide handle, ea	1
Saw, separating, assortment, 12 in pkg	12
Scalers, c.s. point, ea	21
Scalers, dentinol, ea	10
Scalers, l.h., ea	25
Scalers, pyorrhea, McCall's, 12 in set	25
Scale, examination, recruits, Fairbanks, ea	1
Scale and weights, apoth., metric, ea	8
Scale and weights, balance in glass case, metric, ea	14
Scale and weights, grocer, ea	1
Scale and weights, Troomer, ea	1
Scale, small, Fairbanks, Class B, ea	1
Scalpels, ea	6
Scalpels, medium, ea	2
Scalpels, small, ea	4
Scissors, assorted, ea	2
Scissors, bandage, ea	22
Scissors, bandage, C.N.D., 115, ea	14
Scissors, dissecting, medium, ea	7
Scissors, dissecting, Mayo, C.N.D., 108, ea	22
Scissors, double blunt, 5 inch and 6 inch, ea	4
Scissors, gum, curved on flat, No. 22, ea	19
Scissors, Iris, ea	1
Scissors, long blade, ea	4
Scissors, Mayo, curved, 5½, ea	4
Scissors, nasal, R. and L., Kny-Scheerer, ea	2
Scissors, nasal, Watson, ea	1
Scissors, straight, 1 point sharp, 5½, ea	13
Scissors, straight, double blunt, assorted, ea	4
Scissors, straight, for port. dent. unit, ea	2
Scissors, straight, sharp pointed, ea	4
Scoops, ea	8
Screens, for bed, folding frames for, w.e., ea	67
Screw driver, comb., M.D., model, ea	1
Screw driver, Lane, 10 inch, ea	1
Screw driver, Sherman, ea	1
Screw, oral, hard rubber, ea	1
Screw, post, platenoid, gold plated, asstd., 12 in box, BTC	6
Screwportes, Morrison's improved, No. 2, ea	32
Screwpost wrenches, ea	4
Scythes, ea	6
Searcher, flat end, Thompson, ea	1
Separatory, adjustable, Ivory's, ea	10
"Sewage, Disposal of," Fuller, 1912, ea	1
Shade bars, ea	14
Shade guide, S.S.W., ea	7
Shears, No. 32, ea	15
Shears, assorted dental, ea	1
Shears, for fixed bandages, ea	1
Shears, gold, ea	1
Shears, laboratory, ea	1
Shears, plaster, ea	2
Shears, straight, small, crown and bridge, 10 inch, asst., ea	35
Shakers, pepper, glass, ea	97
Shakers, salt, glass, ea	94
Sheets, cotton, MDS, ea	7,790
Shellac, gum, 2 oz., cart	6
Shirt, cotton, ea	563
Silicate, synthetic extra liquid, bot	24
Silicate, synthetic extra powder, box	18
Silk, oiled, 5 yds. in roll	3
Slab, glass, No. 6, ea	30
Slicers, meat, "B", ea	2
Slides, glass, doz	50
Slings, suspending, ea	1
Slippers, pr	2,052
"Social Work in Hospitals," Cannon, ea	2
Soldering and heating, gas outfit, less blow-pipe stand, ea	1
Soldering iron, copper, 2 oz., ea	1
Solder, silver, in squares, ¼ oz. in piece	30
Solder soft form, ¼ lb., coil	1
Sounds, tunneled, Gouley, 8-F, ea	1
Sounds, tunneled, Gouley, 14-F, ea	1
Sounds, uterine, Simpson, ea	3
"Source and Mode of Infection," Chopin, ea	1
Spatula, 8 inch, ea	2
Spatula, 10 inch, ea	2
Spatula, Nos. 22 and 24, ea	25
Spatula, agate or bone, ea	32
Spatula, cement, ea	8
Spatula, cocoa wood handle, ea	1
Spatula, double end, ea	2
Spatula, ebony handle, ea	1
Spatula, plaster, No. 4, ea	15
Spatula, wax, ea	7
Spatula, with steel blade and cocoa wood handle, ea	1
Spatula, wood, handle, 6 inch, ea	6
Specula, ear, 3 in set	9
Specula, ear, Erhardt, 3 in set	23
Specula, mouth, horse, "B", ea	1
Specula, nasal, Bosworth, ea	2
Specula, nasal, Hartman, ea	1

Item	Quantity
Specula, rectal, ea.	38
Sphygmomanometer, ea.	5
Splints, arm extension, large, ea.	10
Splints, arm, Jones, CND, 709, ea.	2
Splints, coaptation, 5 in set	10
Splints, foot support, Thomas, ea.	20
Splints, foot and ankle, Jones, comb., 707, ea.	10
Splints, abduction, universal, No. 709, ea.	20
Splints, foot rest, Jones, ea.	10
Splints, hand, short, Jones, ea.	10
Splints, Hodgins, with rope and pulley, ea.	7
Splints, elbow, Jones, 712, ea.	10
Splints, humur., Jones, exter., ea.	8
Splints, simple, Jones, straight, No. 700, 4 in set	20
Splints, long handle, 715, ea.	45
Splints, long handle, 716, with thumb piece, Jones, ea.	20
Splints, simple, straight, 20 in., ea.	10
Splints, skeleton dorsiflex, Jones, ea.	10
Splints, straight, assorted, ea.	20
Splints, traction, leg, Thomas, ea.	4
Splints, veneer, doz.	3
Splints, wire gauze for, 1 yd. in roll	373
Splints, wood, straight, ea.	10
Sponges, animal, piece	61
Spools, Holstead, ea.	45
Spoons, tea, s.p., No. 7280, ea.	107
Spoons, sugar, s.p., ea.	23
Spoons, table, No. 7279, ea.	506
Spray pumps, New Misty, ea.	66
Sprinkler powder, h.r., ea.	141
Stand, blow pipe, ea.	3
Stand, for 3 basins, w.e., ea.	1
Stand, for Heidbrink machine (nitrous oxide appar.), ea.	1
Stand, port., Clark's type without table, for field use, ea.	10
Standard curriculum, school for nurses, ea.	1
Sterilizer, Down's, ea.	2
Sterilizer, boiler, with alcohol stove, ea.	8
Sterilizer, comb., steam boiler, ea.	1
Sterilizer, elec., large, dental, ea.	3
Sterilizer, high pressure, with 2 gasburners, National, ea.	1
Sterilizer, hot air, ea.	2
Sterilizer, hypo., all glass, Hood's, ea.	6
Sterilizer, steam, Arnold's, ea.	1
Sterilizer, veterinary, ea.	1
Sterilizer outfit, ea.	2
Stethescope, ea.	25
Still, water, ea.	2
Stone, artificial, for models, 3 lbs., tin	1
Stone, carborundum, ea.	1
Stools, ea.	9
Stools, operating, ea.	1
Stools, revolving, w.e., ea.	23
Stopcock, brass, ⅛ inch, ea.	2
Stopcock, 3-way, for admission of serum, ea.	10
Stove, alcohol, for boilers, ea.	8
Stove, alcohol, ea.	25
Stove, gas-O-pipe, ea.	6
Stove, kerosene, ea.	1
Stretcher, wheel, ea.	10
Strips, celluloid, thin, pkg.	50
Strips, polishing, assorted, grits, box	131
Strips, copper, soft, ½ inch, 36-gauge matrix, ea.	80
"Study of Gases," Travers, ea.	1
Suit, convalescent, ea.	1,143
Suit, convalescent coats, ea.	41
Suit, convalescent pants, ea.	33
Support, burette, with double chain, 3 rings, ea.	7
Support, burette, wood, ea.	2
Suppository mold, ea.	4
"Surgery and Diseases of Mouth and Jaw," Blair, ea.	1
"Surgery, General, Modern and Operative," DeCosta, 1918, ea.	1
"Surgery, Operative Manual of," Binney, 7th Ed., 1916, ea.	1
"Surgery, Practice of," 1910, ea.	1
"Surgery, Principles and Practice," Ashurst, 1914, ea.	1
"Surgery, System of," Kean, 4 vols., ea.	1
"Surgical After Treatment," Crandon, ea.	1
Surgical dressings, amb. box of, 454, ea.	76
Surgical dressings, Par. 955, MMD, incomp., ea.	41
Sutures, aseptic, 3 sizes, 20 pkgs. in box	10
Sutures, aseptic, 2 sizes, 70 pkgs. in linen, box	4
Sutures, aseptic, 3 sizes, 100 pkgs. in silk, box	8
Sutures, catgut, chromic, assorted, ea.	233
Sutures, catgut, chromic, size 2, 10 tubes in pkg.	24
Sutures, catgut, chromic, size 1, 100 tubes in med. hard box.	27
Sutures, catgut, plain, in tubes, ea.	300
Sutures, catgut, plain, 3 in pkg., gross	11
Sutures, catgut, plain, 10 tubes in box	13
Sutures, silk braided, 3 sizes in pkg.	191
Sutures, silk, surgeon's, spool	4
Sutures, silk, surgeon's, No. 9, spool	1
Sutures, silk, surgeon's, No. 4, spool	15
Swager, metal, ea.	7
Synthetic porcelain, Caulk's guide for, ea.	11
Synthetic porcelain, Caulk's, 10 shades, cabinets for, ea.	98
Syringes, champion, veterinary, ea.	2
Syringes, dose, veterinary, all metal, ea.	1
Syringes, ear and bladder, 2 oz., ea.	1
Syringes, ear and bladder ulcer, ea.	1
Syringes, fountain, metal, ea.	3
Syringes, fountain, rubber, ea.	106
Syringes glass, 100 cc., asbestos, pkg.	2
Syringes, hot air, elec., with 8 foot silk-covered tubing, ea.	5
Syringes, hypo., complete, ea.	39
Syringes, hypo., complete, 956, ea.	53
Syringes, hypo., dental, all metal, 172-A, ea.	17
Syringes, hypo., dental, extra needles for, ea.	45
Syringes, hypo., dental, extra needles for s&c 24 ga., ea.	36
Syringes, hypo., dent., ex needles for, cond. steel 23 mm., ea.	34
Syringes, hypo., dent., ex. need. for razor edge, p. 24 ga., ea.	92
Syringes, hypo., dental, Fischer type, ea.	4
Syringes, Luer type, extra needles for, assorted, ea.	216
Syringes, Schimmel, needles for 26 ga., ea.	12
Syringes, Keyes-Ultman, with extra canula for, ea.	1
Syringes, Luer, glass, 1 cc., ea.	3
Syringes, Luer, glass, 30 cc., ea.	6
Syringes, hard rubber, ea.	10
Syringes, metal, veterinary, dose 2 oz., ea.	20
Syringes, metal, veterinary, dose 4 oz., ea.	4
Syringes, metal, veterinary, dose, 6 oz., ea.	5
Syringes, metal, veterinary, dose 10 cc., ea.	6
Syringes, metal, veterinary, dose 30 cc., ea.	4
Syringes, needles, canula, 2 inch, No. 18, ea.	144
Syringes, post-nasal, all metal, 2 oz., ea.	2
Syringes, hypo., 5 cc., in canvas case, Quitman, ea.	22
Syringes, hypo., 10 cc., Quitman, ea.	3
Syringes, extra needles for, Quitman, ea.	108
Syringes, record, metal case, 1 cc., ea.	1
Syringes, rectal, hard rubber, 6 oz., ea.	12
Syringes, vesical, large, ea.	1
Syringes, water, No. 39, ea.	3
Syringes, water, No. 21, A. Moffatt, ea.	66
Syringes, water, self filling, all metal, ea.	11
Tables, aseptic, ea.	10
Tables, bedroom, ea.	83
Tables, bedside, folding iron, ea.	3
Tables, bedside, folding wood, ea.	504
Tables, dining extension, MDS., ea.	17
Tables, fracture, Howley, ea.	2
Tables, instrument, w.e., ea.	27
Tables, opalite, 14 inch, ea.	11
Tables, operating, complete, ea.	11
Tables, operating, castors for, large, ea.	31
Tables, pressed steel, K.D., ea.	4
Tables, reception room, ea.	2
Tables, top for, ea.	100
Tables, typewriter, ea.	8
Tables, w.e., ea.	75
Tags, diagnosis, book	210
Tanks, connection for, style No. 1, ea.	1
Tanks, connection for, with double valve, ea.	2
Tape, 1 inch x 36 yards, roll	119
Tape measure, 60 inch, ea.	15
Teeth, U.S. Army, assorted, No. 1, set	4
Tenaculum, ea.	3
Tents, hospital, tropical, ea.	16
Tents, wall, small, ea.	2
Test glasses, footed urinary, ea.	8
Test, malingering, Snelling, ea.	1
Test tubes, assorted, ea.	17,886
Test tubes, large, ea.	14
Test tubes, medium wall, without lip, 150x10 mm., ea.	500
Test tubes, thin wall, with lip, 125x16 mm., ea.	500
Test tubes, support wood, ea.	6
Test tubes, Wassermann rack, ea.	4
Tester, hoof, "B", ea.	1
"The Labyrinth," Brown and Treisner, ea.	1
Thermometer, bath, ea.	25
Thermometer, chemical, 360 degrees, cent., ea.	16
Tin foil, thin, roll	(
Tongs, soldering, 7 in., No. 4, ea.	9
Tongue depressor, Farlow, ea.	3
Tongue depressor, metal, ea.	29
Tongue depressor, wood, gross	80
Tongue depressor, wood, ea.	150
Tools, universal, ea.	3
Tourniquet, field, ea.	2
Tourniquet and bandage rubber, ea.	76
Torch attachment for Bunsen burner, ea.	3
Torch, blow pipe, Prestolite D, ea.	4
Torch, 5 lb. auto reduc. valve for Prestolite, ea.	2
Towels, bath, ea.	656
Towels, hand, "B", ea.	975
Towels, paper, ea.	4,000
Towels, paper, 100 in roll	5
Transilluminator, cat. No. 5714, ea.	1
Traps, mouse, ea.	3
Trays, bed, with legs, ea.	247

[*Concluded on next page*]

AMERICAN RELIEF ADMINISTRATION

Detail of Deliveries of the United States Government Surplus Medical and Hospital Supplies to the Near East Relief for Distribution in Southern Russia, 1922–1923

Medical Table 3—(*Concluded*)

Commodity and Unit	Quantity
Trays, butler, ea.	181
Trays, crown and bridge, Universal, No. 43, ea.	2
Trays, upper and lower impression, ea.	4
Trays, lower impression, ea.	25
Trays, lower impression, No. 5, ea.	3
Trays, lower and upper impression, crown and bridge, ea.	25
Trays, lower and upper impression, ea.	25
Trays, upper impression, No. 1, ea.	1
Trays, instrument, with stand, ea.	2
Trays, instrument, w.e., ea.	67
Trays, porcelain, ea.	1
Trays, splint hinge, Roach, 4 in set	6
Trephine, plain ¾ inch, for ear and throat, case	5
Trephine, with 3 bits, ea.	1
Trimmer, Pearson, No. 25, ea.	3
Trimmer, Pearson, No. 26, ea.	3
Tripods for water baths, ea.	5
Trocar and canula, ea.	1
Trocar and canula, with handle, ea.	1
Trucks, food, comp., with trays and contain., 6-gal. type, ea.	14
Tub, bath, portable, ea.	4
Tub, foot, ea.	41
Tube, rectal, ea.	8
Tube, rubber stomach, veterinary, 10 foot, ea.	19
Tube, stomach, stylet for, ea.	11
Tube, stomach, ea.	31
Tube, trachea, Bevette, ea.	1
Tube, trachea, veterinary, ea.	4
Tube, tracheotomy, Class B, ea.	6
Tubing, glass, assorted, lbs.	25
Tubing, rubber for catheters, etc., feet	15
Tubing, rubber, for saliva ejector, ea.	1
Tumblers, w.e., ea.	185
Tumblers, glass, ea.	100
Tweezers, ea.	14

Commodity and Unit	Quantity
Tweezers, "B", soldering, ea.	3
Tweezers, "C", soldering, ea.	3
Tweezers, "D", soldering, ea.	3
Tweezers, "E", soldering, ea.	3
Tweezers, "F", soldering, ea.	3
Tweezers, "L", soldering, ea.	3
Typewriter, Remington, on Class B, ea.	1
Typewriter, Royal, No. 5, ea.	1
Typewriter, Royal, ea.	3
"Uncinariasis, Hookworm Diseases in Porto Rico," Ashford, 1911, ea.	1
Ureometer, Doremus Hinds, ea.	1
Ureometer, Squibb, M.D., model, ea.	1
Urethroscope, No. 225, ea.	1
Urinals, glass, ea.	20
Urinals, w.e., ea.	424
Venereal prophylactic unit, No. 958, Class B, ea.	30
Vials, 1 oz., doz.	93
Vials, 2 oz., doz.	24
Vials, 4 oz., doz.	35
Vials, 6 oz., doz.	115
Vials, 32 oz., ea.	160
Vials, 8 oz., gross	52
Vials, 12 oz., gross	1
Vials, 16 oz.	110
Vials, 16 oz., gross	10
Vials, plain ovals, 3 oz., gross	12
Vibrator, mechanical, without pedestal, motor for, ea.	1
Vibrator, mechanical, with pedestal, ea.	1
Vise bench, jeweler's, ea.	6
Vulcanite scrapers and finishers, Nos. 3, 6, 7, 8, 27, ea.	35
Vulcanizer, with flask and ker. heat appar., Lewis' C.B., ea.	2
Vulcanizer, 3 flasks, gas or kerosene, ea.	2
Wallets, veterinary, farrier's, ea.	8
Wallets, veterinary officer's, Class B, ea.	8

Commodity and Unit	Quantity
Wasserman bath, ea.	1
Waste receivers, can type with foot device, w.e., ea.	12
Water baths, polished copper, ea.	1
Water baths, inoculating, polished copper, ea.	1
Water baths, seriological, ea.	2
"Water Purification," Elms, ea.	1
Wax, base plate, pink, lbs.	6
Wax, bone, aseptic, box,	6
Wax, crown, sticky, box	14
Wax, impression, yellow, ½ lb. in cart.	19
Wax, inlay, box	21
Webster's Dictionary, English, ea.	4
Wheel brush, No. 3, laboratory lathe, ea.	20
Wheel brush, No. 26, laboratory lathe, ea.	7
Wheel brush, assorted, ea.	11
Wheel, carborund., med. grit., 3-16 in. x 1 in., L.S. edge, ea.	12
Wheel, carborundum, coarse grit., ea.	12
Wheel, carborundum, L.S. edge 1 and 2x3-16 in., ea.	19
Wheel, carborundum, square edge, Nos. 301 and 302, ea.	5
Wheel, felt, K.E., ea.	3
Wheel, felt, round edge, No. 4, ea.	4
Wheel, polishing chamois, 3 inch, ea.	11
Whetstone, carborundum, 5 inch, ea.	2
Wicks, for vulcanizer, ea.	6
Wire cutters, ea.	9
Wire, bending, iron, 38-gauge, spool	4
Wire, copper, roll	5
Wire, ligature, angle, No. 187, box	4
Wood orange stick, 25 in bdl.	12
Wrenches, dental, ends, assorted, ea.	3
Wright's stain, 2-10 gm. amp.	56
"X-ray Technique, Manual of," ea.	1
Zinc, ½ lb. ingot	29
"Zoology, Practical," Parker, 4th Edition, 1916, ea.	2

BIBLIOGRAPHY

BIBLIOGRAPHY

I. COMMISSION FOR RELIEF IN BELGIUM

ALLEN, B. S. "Feeding Seven Million Belgians," in *World's Work* (London), 25 : 423–33. April, 1915.

"American Revival," in *New Republic*, 10 : 3–5. February 3, 1917.

"Belgian Fellowships," in *School and Society*, 21 : 463–64. April 18, 1925.

"Belgian Relief Work Transferred," in *Current History*, 6 : 237–38. May, 1917.

BICKNELL, E. P. "Helping the Belgians," in *Review of Reviews*, 52 : 705–15. December, 1915.

———. "Nation on Strike," in *Survey*, 36 : 558–64. September 2, 1916.

"Bread and Education," in *Survey*, 46 : 39–40. April 9, 1921.

C.R.B. Bulletin, No. 1–13. 15 October 1917—22 October 1930. New York, The Commission for Relief in Belgium, 1917–1930.

C.R.B. Educational Foundation, Inc. New York, 1920. 5 pages.

C.R.B. Educational Foundation, Inc. *Annual Reports*, 1920–1930. New York, [1921–1931] 10 volumes.

———. *Record of Belgian and American C.R.B. Fellows. 1920–1925.* New York, [1926] 68 pages.

Comité Provincial de Secours et d'Alimentation du Hainaut. Dept. "Alimentation." *Rapport du Conseil d'Administration à l'Assemblée Générale des Actionnaires du 20 Janvier 1919.* Mons, 1919. [166 pages]

Commission for Relief in Belgium. *Annual Report, 1st–4th: Nov. 1, 1914—Oct. 31, 1918.* [London, 1916–1919?]

———. *Calorie Production and C.R.B. Analyses of the Common Foods.* [London, n.d.] 4 pages.

———. *Executive Personnel; Balance Sheet and Accounts; French Government Accounts, Belgian Government Accounts, Supporting Schedules: Statistical Data, Covering Six Years from Commencement of Operations, October, 1914, to September 30, 1920.* [Deloitte, Plender, Griffiths & Company, Chartered Accountants and Auditors, London] New York, 1921. 157 pages.

———. *Special Departmental Reports (from October 26, 1914, to April 1, 1917).* [London, 1917?] 461 pages.

———. *Public Relations of the Commission for Relief in Belgium; Documents,* by George I. Gay with the collaboration of H. H. Fisher. Stanford University, 1919. 2 volumes.

———. *Statistical Review of Relief Operations,* by George I. Gay. Five years, November 1, 1914, to August 31, 1919, and to final liquidation. [Stanford University, 1925] 81+439 pages.

———. *Statistical Review of Relief Operations,* by George I. Gay. Five years, November 1, 1914, to August 31, 1919, and to final liquidation. (Abbreviated reprint) [Stanford University, 1925] 81+32 pages.

"Commission for Relief in Belgium Fellowships," in *School and Society*, 26 : 549–50. October 29, 1927.

"Diplomatic Correspondence between the United States and Belligerent Governments . . . [Belgian relief]" in *American Journal of International Law*, Vol. 9, Supplement Pt. 15, pages 314–36. July, 1917.

DOSCH-FLEUROT, A. W. "A Day in the Belgian Relief Stations," in *World's Work*, 29 : 551–57. March, 1915. *Ibid.* (London), 25 : 434–40. April, 1915.

EDGAR, W. C. *The Millers' Belgian Relief Movement, 1914–15, Conducted by the Northwestern Miller. Final Report.* Minneapolis, 1915. 72 pages.

"Educational Foundation of the Commission for Relief in Belgium," in *School and Society*, 17 : 487–88. May 5, 1923.

"Fellowships," in *Science*, N.S., 66 : 446. November 11, 1927.

"Fellowships for Belgian Students," in *School and Society*, 22 : 459. October 10, 1925.

"Fellowships of the Belgian Educational Foundation," in *School and Society*, 25 : 623. May 28, 1927.

"For Lack of Help," in *New Republic*, 9 : 202–4. December 23, 1916.

FREEMAN, L. R. "Hoover and the Belgians," in *Outlook*, 111 : 81–83. September 8, 1915.

GADE, J. A. "Belgium's Plight," in *National Geographic Magazine*, 31 : 433–39. May, 1917.

GAILOR, F. H. "A Rhodes Scholar in Belgium," in *Living Age* (reprinted from *Cornhill Magazine*), 285 : 717–27. 19 June 1915.

GALPIN, P. C. "The Rhodes Scholar and the C.R.B.," in *American Oxonian*, April, 1924.

GIBSON, HUGH. *A Journal from Our Legation in Belgium.* Garden City, 1917. 360 pages.

GOODE, W. A. M. "Relief Work in Belgium," in *Royal Society of Arts Journal*, 65 : 178–89. January 26, 1917.

"Graduate Fellowships for Belgian Universities," in *School and Society*, 20 : 585–86. November 8, 1924.

"Great Work of the Belgian Relief Commission," in *Current History*, 6 : 132–36. April, 1917.

GROMAIRE, GEORGES. "Commission for Relief in Belgium," in his *L'Occupation Allemande en France (1914–1918).* Paris, 1925. Pages 191–99.

HENRY, ALBERT. *L'Oeuvre du Comité National de Secours e d'Alimentation Pendant la Guerre.* Bruxelles, 1920. 377 pages.

I. COMMISSION FOR RELIEF IN BELGIUM (*Cont.*)

HENRY, ALBERT. *Le Ravitaillement de la Belgique Pendant l'Occupation Allemande.* Paris, 1924. 210 pages.

"Herbert Hoover," in *World's Work* (London), 25 : 408–13. April, 1915.

HOOVER, HERBERT. "Bind the Wounds of France," in *National Geographic Magazine,* 31 : 439–44. May, 1917.

HOUSE, R. T. "Schoolmaster in Belgium," in *School and Society,* 6 : 739–40. December 22, 1917.

HUNT, E. E. "Herbert Clark Hoover and the Commission for Relief in Belgium," in *New Republic,* 8 : 213–15. September 30, 1916.

———. "Hoover of the C.R.B.," in *World's Work,* 34 : 165–68. June, 1917.

———. *War Bread.* New York, 1916. 374 pages.

JESSE, F. T. "Relief in Belgium; A Report," in *English Review,* 20 : 215–24. May, 1915.

KELLOGG, CHARLOTTE. "A Cinema of the C.R.B.," in *Atlantic Monthly,* 119 : 535–45. April, 1917.

———. *Women of Belgium.* New York, 1917. 210 pages.

KELLOGG, VERNON. "The Authentic Story of Belgian Relief," in *World's Work,* 34 : 165–76, 264–85, 405–12. June–August, 1917.

———. "The Belgian Wilderness," in *Atlantic Monthly,* 117 : 407–17. March, 1916.

———. "Feeding Belgium via Canals," in *World's Work,* 35 : 92–98. November, 1917.

———. *Fighting Starvation in Belgium.* Garden City, 1918. 219 pages.

———. *Headquarters Nights.* Boston, 1917. 116 pages.

———. "How Belgium Was Fed," in *World's Work,* 34 : 528–41. September, 1917.

———. "How North France Has Been Fed," in *World's Work,* 35 : 299–305. January, 1918.

KIRK, LETA. *The Relations between the Commission for Relief in Belgium and the German Authorities in the Occupied Territories, 1914–1917.* [Stanford University] 1926. 126 pages. Thesis. Typewritten.

KITTREDGE, M. H. "Taking Care of Belgium," in *New Republic,* Vol. 3, Supplement. July 31, 1915.

"Lest We Forget," in *Bellman,* 22 : 400. April 14, 1917.

LEVY, R. C. "La Ravitaillement du Nord de la France et de la Belgique," in *Revue des Deux Mondes,* 42 : 417–44. 15 November 1917.

LUCAS, W. P. *The General Health Conditions of Belgium. Report of . . . August 14th, 1916.* London, Commission for Relief in Belgium, [1916?] 14 pages.

MAPES, L. D. "Accounting of the Commission for Relief in Belgium," in *Journal of Accountancy,* 27 : 1–16. January, 1919.

"Mr. Herbert C. Hoover, Unofficial Diplomat," in *World's Work,* 30 : 335–36. July, 1915.

OSKISON, JOHN. "How You Can Help Feed and Clothe the Belgians," in *World's Work,* 29 : 275–77. January, 1915.

POOLE, ERNEST. "Hoover of Belgium," in *Saturday Evening Post,* May 26, 1917.

PRICE, BURR. *Children's Work in Belgium during the War. Brussels,* 1919. 31 pages.

SAINT-RENÉ TAILLANDIER, MME. *The Soul of the "C.R.B."* New York, 1919. 233 pages.

"Saving Belgium by Yankee Business Wizardry," in *Literary Digest,* 50 : 1266. May 29, 1915.

SMITH, ROBINSON. *A Food Bibliography.* London, Commission for Relief in Belgium, [1917] 4 pages.

———. *Food Values and the Rationing of a Country.* 3 ed. rev. [London?] 1917. 23 pages.

———. *Rationing through Commercial Channels, Together with a Sample Bread-Card.* [London, Commission for Relief in Belgium?] 1918. 8 pages.

———. "Relief from Belgium: An Adventure in Socialism," in *World's Work* (London), 29 : 434–46. April, 1917.

———. "Snapshots of the Relief Work in Belgium," in *World's Work* (London), 30 : 509–19. November, 1917.

"Torpedoing Belgian Relief Ships; Commission's Formal Protest," in *Current History,* Vol. 7, Pt. 2, pages 167–68. January, 1918.

WHITE, F. M. "Charity's Great Adventure," in *Outlook,* 111 : 914–17. December 15, 1915.

WHITLOCK, BRAND. *Belgium; A Personal Narrative.* New York, 1920. 2 volumes.

WITHINGTON, ROBERT. *In Occupied Belgium,* with a Chapter by Prentiss N. Gray. Boston, [1921] 173 pages.

———. *That These May Eat.* New York, 1917. 11 pages.

II. FOOD ADMINISTRATION

An Act to Provide Further for the National Security and Defense by Encouraging the Production, Conserving the Supply, and Controlling the Distribution of Food Products and Fuel. [Washington, 1917] 13 pages. [Public—No. 41—65th Congress. H.R. 4961] [The Food Control (Lever) Act]

"Adventure in Democracy," in *Bellman,* 23 : 369–70. October 6, 1917.

"And They Did All Eat and Were Filled," in *Survey,* 38 : 142–43. May 12, 1917.

"As the Food Bill Stands Today," in *Survey,* 38 : 339–40. July 14, 1917.

BAKER, G. B. "Great Fat Fight," in *Saturday Evening Post,* 200 : 12–13. May 12, 1928. *Ibid.,* 200 : 33. May 19, 1928.

BARNES, J. H. *Conference of Trade Representatives with the United States Wheat Director; Introductory Address.* New York, 1919. 21 pages.

BARTLEY, J. C. *Study of Price Control by the United States Food Administration.* [Gettysburg, 1922] 139 pages.

"Beginning of Food Control," in *Survey,* 38 : 491–93. September 1, 1917.

BERNHARDT, JOSHUA. *Government Control of the Sugar Industry in the United States.* New York, 1920. 272 pages.

BLAKEY, R. G. "Sugar Prices and Distribution under Food Control," in *Quarterly Journal of Economics,* 32 : 567–96. August, 1918.

BROWN, E. S. "Archives of the Food Administration as Historical Sources," in *American Historical Association. Report, 1917,* pages 124–35.

CHASE, STEPHEN. *Production of Meat in the United States.* Washington, United States Food Administration, 1919. 85 pages.

Conference of Representatives of the Grain Trade of the United States, Washington, D. C., 10 o'clock A.M., *August 15th, 1917.* [Washington, 1917?] 57 pages.

COOKE, JAY. "The Work of the Federal Food Administration," in *Annals of the American Academy of Political and Social Science,* 78 : 175–84. July, 1918.

DICKINSON, T. H. "Lord Rhondda and British Food Control," in *Atlantic Monthly,* 123 : 221–26. February, 1919.

———. "The Problem of the Food Administration," in *World's Work,* 36 : 103–10. May, 1918.

———. "A Year of Food Administration," in *North American Review,* 208 : 111–21. July, 1918.

DUFFUS, W. M. "Government Control of the Wheat Trade in the United States," in *American Economic Review,* 8 : 62–87. March, 1918.

EDGAR, W. C. *Food Control and Food Fallacies.* Minneapolis, 1917. 89 pages.

ELDRED, WILFRED. "Grain Corporation and the Guaranteed Wheat Price," in *Quarterly Journal of Economics,* 34 : 698–719. August, 1920.

———. "Wheat and Flour Trade under Food Administration Control: 1917–18," in *Quarterly Journal of Economics,* 33 : 1–70. November, 1918.

"Farmers and Food Regulation," in *Outlook,* 116 : 51. May 9, 1917.

"Federal Food Control Proposed," in *Survey,* 38 : 38. April 14, 1917.

"Fighting over the Empty Sugar-Bowl," in *Literary Digest,* 55 : 17–18. December 29, 1917.

FITZGERALD, CLAUDIA. "Food Administration Cafeteria," in *Journal of Home Economics,* 10 : 411–13. September, 1918.

"The Food Administration. I. Strategy in Food," by Charles Merz; "II. The Control of Meat," by George Soule; "III. Wheat for the Allies," by Charles Merz; "IV. 'Natural Laws'," by George Soule; "V. Wasting Less Food," by Charles Merz; "VI. Instead of Revolution," by George Soule. *New Republic,* 13 : 377–79; 14 : 13–15, 52–54, 83–85, 107–8, 142–44. 26 January—2 March 1918.

"Food Administration at Work," in *Current History,* Vol. 7, Pt. 1, pages 236–37. November, 1917.

The Food Administration's Relations with Hog Producers. Reprinted from the Congressional Records of February 24–25, 1920. 15 pages.

"Food Bill Law at Last," in *Independent,* 91 : 249. August 18, 1917.

"Food Control and Lower Prices," in *Current History,* Vol. 7, Pt. 1, pages 428–29. December, 1917.

"Food Control Bill," in *Outlook,* 116 : 606–7. August 22, 1917.

"Food Control Enacted at Last," in *Survey,* 38 : 445–46. August 18, 1917.

"Food Control Muddle in New York," in *New Republic,* 12 : 65–67. August 18, 1917.

"Food Control Now!" in *Independent,* 90 : 527. June 23, 1917.

"Food Crisis in the United States," in *Current History,* Vol. 6, Pt. 2, pages 15–17. July, 1917.

"Food Dictator for the United States," in *Current History,* Vol. 6, Pt. 2, pages 389–92. September, 1917.

"Food for Ourselves and the Allies," in *Literary Digest,* 57 : 70–76. April 6, 1918.

GARRETT, P. W. "The Food Administration," in *Government Control Over Prices.* Washington, 1920. Pages 40–150. (W.I.B. Price Bulletin No. 3.)

GEPHART, W. F. "Perishable Produce under Food Regulation," in *Quarterly Journal of Economics,* 32 : 621–34. August, 1918.

———. "Provisions of the Food Act and Activities Which Should Be Made Permanent; With Discussion," in *American Economic Review,* Vol. 9, Supplement, pages 61–78. March, 1919.

GIBSON, HUGH. "Herbert C. Hoover," in *Century Magazine,* 94 : 508–17. August, 1917.

GOODE, W. A. M. "Herbert Hoover," in *The Teacher's World* (London), 19 : 260–61. June 19, 1918.

GRAY, L. C. "Price-Fixing Policies of the Food Administration," in *American Economic Review,* Vol. 9: Supplement, pages 252–71. March, 1919.

HARD, WILLIAM. "Mr. Henley and Mr. Hoover," in *New Republic,* 18 : 110–12. February 22, 1919.

HASKIN, F. J. *War Cook Book for American Women: Suggestions for Patriotic Service in the Home.* Issued by the United States Food Administration, [1917?] 30 pages.

HATCH, LEONARD. "Food Administration and the Nation's Response," in *Scientific American,* 119 : 390. November 16, 1918.

II. FOOD ADMINISTRATION (*Cont.*)

Heinz, Howard. "Some Factors To Be Considered in Connection with the Food Problem," in *Annals of the American Academy of Political and Social Science,* 74 : 119–23. November, 1917.

Hiatt, W. S. "World's Biggest Commissary Job," in *Technical World,* 23 : 138–43. April, 1915.

Holman, C. W. *Doubling the Wheat Dollar.* Washington, United States Food Administration, 1918. 16 pages. Reprinted from the *Country Gentleman,* 26 January 1918.

Hoover, Herbert. *America's Contribution through Food Administration:* A Letter to the President . . . July 11, 1918. Washington, 1918. 4 pages.

———. *America's Grain Trade.* New York, 1918. 21 pages.

———. *The Dairy and the World Food Problem.* An Address . . . at the National Milk and Dairy Farm Exposition, New York City, May 23, 1918. Washington, United States Food Administration, 1918. 13 pages.

———. "Food Administration," in *Independent,* 92 : 510. December 15, 1917.

———. "Food for All—A Fundamental War Problem," in *Scientific American,* 118 : 310–11. April 6, 1918.

———. "Food for Our Allies in 1919," in *National Geographic Magazine,* 34 : 242–44. September, 1918.

———. "Food Future," in *Forum,* 61 : 210–18. February, 1919.

———. *"Food in War,* with an Introduction by the Right Honorable J. R. Clynes. London, [1918?] 16 pages. [This is a reprint of the Pittsburg Press Club address, 18 April 1918, which appeared as Food Administration Press Release 868 and in Food Administration Bulletins 15 and 16]

———. [*Report to the President on the Chicago Packing Industry*] *September 11, 1918.* Washington, United States Food Administration. [Press Release] 1386, February 19, 1919.

———. *Preface to a Report of the United States Food Administration.* [New York] 1920. 50 pages.

"Hoover Mobilizes Food Control Forces for Embargo and for War on Profiteers," in *Current Opinion,* 63 : 149–51. September, 1917.

Houston, D. F. "Steps to Victory," in *Academy of Political Science Proceedings,* 7 : 673–97. February, 1918.

"How Hoover Will Help Win," in *Literary Digest,* 54 : 1689. June 2, 1917.

Inter-Allied Food Council. Committee of Representatives. *Minutes of Proceedings.* I–IV. July–December, 1918. [London, 1918?]

Irwin, Will. "Autocrat of the Dinner Table," in *Saturday Evening Post,* June 23, 1917. p. 26+

Kellogg, Vernon. "Food Administration," in *Nation,* 107 : 142–44. August 10, 1918.

———. *Patriotism and Sacrifice.* Washington, United States Food Administration, 1918. 8 pages. (Reprinted from the *North American Review,* June, 1918)

Kellogg, Vernon, and Taylor, A. E. *The Food Problem.* New York, 1917. 213 pages.

King, C. L. "The Trend in Wholesale Prices for the Products of American Farms during the War Period," in *Annals of the American Academy of Political and Social Science,* 89 : 44–50. May, 1920.

"Legislative Control of Food," in *Journal of Political Economy,* 25 : 846–47. October, 1917.

"Licensing of Food Importation," in *Survey,* 39 : 70. October 20, 1917.

Lippincott, Isaac. "War Control. (Food Products)," in his *Problems of Reconstruction.* New York, 1919. Pages 20–71.

Litman, Simon. *Prices and Price Control in Great Britain and the United States during the World War.* New York, 1920. 331 pages.

MacKinnon, J. G. "Office of Home Economics and the United States Food Administration," in *Journal of Home Economics,* 10 : 280–81. June, 1918.

McCain, G. N. *War Rations for Pennsylvanians. The Story of the Operations of the Federal Food Administration in Pennsylvania.* Philadelphia, 1920. 273 pages.

McCann, A. W. "Hoover Food-Control Failure," in *Forum,* 58 : 381–90. October, 1917.

Merritt, A. N. *War-Time Control of Distribution of Foods.* New York, 1920. 237 pages.

Mitchell, S. A. *"America Is Feeding the World,"* in *The Teacher's World* (London), 19 : 262–63. June 19, 1918.

"Mr. Hoover to Fight the Food-Pirates," in *Literary Digest,* 54 : 1975–77. July 30, 1917.

"Nation's Food as the Nation's Business," in *Literary Digest,* 55 : 9–11. August 18, 1917.

"New Food Control," in *Nation,* 105 : 502–3. November 8, 1917.

O'Brien, Charles. "Food-Preparedness for the United States," in *Atlantic Monthly,* 119 : 839–45. June, 1917.

"Our Food Problem," in *New Republic,* 11 : 290–92. July 14, 1917.

"Our National Wheat Corporation," in *Literary Digest,* 55 : 13. September 1, 1917.

Pearl, Raymond. *The Nation's Food; A Statistical Study of a Physiological and Social Problem.* Philadelphia, 1920. 274 pages.

———. *A New Price Index.* Washington, United States Food Administration, 1918. 7 pages.

Pearl, Raymond, and Matchett, E. P. *Reference Handbook of Food Statistics in Relation to the War.* Washington, 1918. 124 pages.

Phelan, J. D. *Conservation of Food: The Public Services of Herbert C. Hoover.* Speech . . . in the Senate of the United States, July 16, 1917. Washington, 1917. 16 pages.

Pollock, I. L. *Food Administration in Iowa.* Iowa City, 1923. 2 volumes.

Proclamations and Executive Orders by the President, under and by Virtue of the Food Control Act, of August 10, 1917. November 25, 1918. Washington, United States Food Administration, 1918. 31 pages.

Russell, A. L. *Supplement to Grain and Flour Statistics during the War.* [Washington?] United States Grain Corporation, 1920. 44 pages.

"Senate Begins an Inquiry," in *New Republic,* 13 : 253. December 29, 1917.

"Significance of Mr. Hoover," in *North American,* 206 : 357–60. September, 1917.

Surface, F. M. *American Pork Production in the World War.* Chicago, 1926. 217 pages.

———. *The Grain Trade during the World War.* New York, 1928. 679 pages.

———. *The Stabilization of the Price of Wheat during the War and Its Effects upon the Returns to the Producer.* Washington, [1925] 100 pages.

Sweet, L. D. "The War and Our Potato Industry," in *Annals of the American Academy of Political and Social Science,* 74 : 197–202. November, 1917.

Taft, W. N. "Hoover—Our New Food Controller," in *Illustrated World,* 28 : 37–41. September, 1917.

Taylor, A. E. *Human Factors in Food Supply.* Washington, United States Food Administration, 1918. 10 pages.

———. "International and National Food Control," in *Annals of the American Academy of Political and Social Science,* 78 : 149–56. July, 1918.

———. *War Bread.* New York, 1918. 99 pages.

———. *Wheat Needs of the World.* Washington, United States Food Administration, 1917. 8 pages.

"Truth at the Bottom of the Sugar-Barrel," in *Literary Digest,* 56 : 9–11. 5 January 1918.

United States Bureau of Foreign and Domestic Commerce (Department of Commerce). *Foreign Commerce and Navigation of the United States, 1917–1919.* Washington, 1918–1920. 3 volumes.

United States Food Administration. *Annual Report, 1917–1918.* Washington, 1918–1919. 2 volumes.

———. *Bulletin,* Nos. 1–17. Washington, 1917–1918.

———. *The Day's Food in War and Peace.* United States Department of Agriculture. Woman's Committee, Council of National Defense. [Washington, 1918?] 108 pages.

———. *Enlisting the Food Merchants; A Campaign to Win the Voluntary Support of Retailers and Wholesalers. The Method of Democracy.* Washington, 1917. 7 pages.

———. *Food Conservation Bibliography.* February, 1918. Washington, 1918. 8 pages.

———. *Food Guide for War Service at Home.* New York, [1918] 67 pages.

United States Food Administration. *Food Saving and Sharing.* Garden City, 1918. 102 pages.

———. *Graphic Exhibits on Food Conservation at Fairs and Expositions.* Washington, [1917] 52 pages.

———. *List of Most Important Occupations & Employments in Food Producing Industries under the Supervision of the United States Food Administration.* Washington, 1918. 58 pages.

———. *Official Statement,* Nos. 1–18. June 6, 1918—September 2, 1919. Washington, 1918–1919.

———. *Policies and Plan of Operation. Wheat, Flour, and Bread.* December 1, 1917. [Washington?] 1917. 171 pages.

———. [*Press Releases*] 1–1400. [Washington] 1917–1919.

———. *Provisional Statistical Statement of the Operations of the American Relief Administration and United States Food Administration Grain Corporation.* Nos. 1–2. January 1–March 31, 1919. Paris, 1919.

———. *Report of Federal Trade Commission on Bakery Business in United States;* Report of Bakery Section of Food Administration, November, 1917. Washington, 1917. 23 pages.

———. *War Economy in Food, with Suggestions and Recipes for Substitutions in the Planning of Meals.* Washington, 1918. 30 pages.

———. *War Program for Public Eating Places.* Washington, 1918. 11 pages.

———. *Purchases and Disbursements Made by the United States Food Administration and by the United States Fuel Administration. Letters from the United States Food Administrator Transmitting Itemized Statements of Purchases and Disbursements Made by the United States Food Administration and by the United States Fuel Administration for the Period from August 11 to December 31, 1917, Inclusive.* Washington, 1918. 116 pages. (65th Congress, 2d Session, House Doc. 890.)

———. *A Sugar Program: Household Conservation Policy to Meet the Sugar Situation for the Summer of 1918.* Washington, 1918. 4 pages.

———. Collegiate Section. *Food and the War.* Boston, [1918] 379 pages.

———. Grain Corporation. *Book of Information.* Issued March 15, 1919. [Washington?] 1919. 40 pages.

———. Grain Corporation. *Conference of Representatives of the Grain Trade of the United States, New York, April 30th, 1918.* [New York, 1918?] 251 pages.

———. Grain Corporation. *Policies and Plan of Operation. Food Administration Grain Corporation and Milling Division.* October 19, 1917. [Washington, 1917?] 42 pages.

II. FOOD ADMINISTRATION (*Cont.*)

United States Food Administration. International Sugar Committee. *Agreement as to Cuban Sugars, 1917–1918 Crop.* [New York, 1917?] 28 pages.

———. Milk Committee. *The Production, Distribution, and Food Value of Milk;* A Report to Herbert C. Hoover . . . by the Milk Committee, Clyde L. King, Chairman. Washington, 1918. 41 pages.

United States Grain Corporation. *Proceedings of Conference of Men Engaged in Grain Dust Explosion and Fire Prevention Campaign.* Conducted in Co-operation with the Bureau of Chemistry, 42 Broadway, New York, N.Y., April 22–24, 1920. New York, 1920. 159 pages.

———. *Report on Commodity Purchases and Sales, Reconciled with Monthly Reports to the Senate of the United States. September 1917 to January 31, 1921.* Prepared by Smart, Gore & Company, Public Accountants and Auditors. New York, [1925] [99 pages] Typed.

United States Sugar Equalization Board. *A Statistical Survey of the Sugar Industry and Trade of the United States.* By Joshua Bernhardt. [New York] 1920. 113 pages.

United States Treasury Department. *Annual Report of the Secretary of the Treasury on the State of the Finances . . .* [with accompanying documents], 1917–1920. Washington, 1918–1920. 4 volumes.

United States Wheat Director. *Conference of Grain and Flour Trade Representatives, Chicago, Ill., May 7, 1920.* [Chicago, 1920?] 96 pages.

———. *Official State.* Nos. 1–5. October 1, 1919—February 2, 1920. New York, 1919–1920.

Van Hise, C. R. *Conservation and Regulation in the United States during the World War.* Prepared for the United States Food Administration. [Part I] Washington, 1917. Part II, Madison, 1918.

Walcott, F. C. "Forerunners of Famine," in *National Geographic Magazine,* 33 : 336–47. April, 1918.

———. *The Prussian System.* Washington, United States Food Administration, 1917. 8 pages.

"War-Time Food Problems." Sixteen articles selected from a series prepared for The *Literary Digest* by the United States Food Administration and especially designed for use in high schools. New York, *Literary Digest,* [1918]

Watrous, R. B. "Food Situation," in *Outlook,* 116 : 323–25. June 27, 1917.

Weld, L. D. H. "The After-War Fall in Meat Prices," in *Annals of the American Academy of Political and Social Science,* 89 : 51–54. May, 1920.

———. "The Live-Stock and Meat Situation," in *Annals of the American Academy of Political and Social Science,* 78 : 168–75. July, 1918.

"What Has Mr. Hoover Really Done?" in *Ladies' Home Journal,* 35 : 33. May, 1918.

Wilbur, R. L. *Fighting with Food.* Washington, United States Food Administration, 1918. 8 pages.

Wildman, Edwin. "Our Daily Meat," in *Forum,* 60 : 581–91. November, 1918.

Wilhelm, Donald. "Hoover and His Food Organization," in *Review of Reviews,* 56 : 283–86. September, 1917.

"Work of the Food Administration," in *Journal of Home Economics,* 9 : 419–20. September, 1917.

III. AMERICAN RELIEF ADMINISTRATION

An Act Providing for the Relief of Populations in Europe and in Countries Contiguous Thereto Suffering for Want of Food. Approved March 30, 1920. (Public—No. 167—66th Congress) (H.R. 12954)

American Friends Service Committee. *Bulletins,* 1919–1923. Philadelphia.

The American Jewish Joint Distribution Committee in Russia. [New York] January, 1924. 83 pages.

American National Red Cross. *Annual Report,* 1919–1923. [Washington, 1919–1923] 5 volumes.

American Relief Administration. *Annual Report of the Executive Committee. Meeting of Trustees and Members, April 5th, 1922, April 4th, 1923.* New York, [1922–23] 2 volumes.

———. *Audited Accounts.* [Hyslop & McCallum, Accountants and Auditors, New York] [New York, 1921–1923] 3 volumes.

———. *Bulletin,* Nos. 1–22 and Index. 17 March—22 August 1919. Paris, 1919.

———. *Bulletin.* Second Series. Nos. 1–45. 1 October 1920—April 1926. [New York] 1920–1926.

———. *Incorporated under Membership Corporations Law of the State of New York, May 27, 1921. Constitution and By-Laws as adopted June 1, 1921.* [New York, 1921?]

American Relief Administration; Message from the President of the United States, Transmitting a Letter from the Secretary of Commerce Submitting a Report by the American Relief Administration of the Disposition of Certain Supplies for the Relief of the Famine-Stricken People of Russia. Washington, 1923. 8 pages. (67th Congress, 4th Session, Senate Document 307)

American Relief Administration. *Mitteilungen,* Nos. 1–198. July, 1920–August, 1922. Redigiert von Regierungs-Rat Friedrich Reischl. Wien, Amerikanische Kinderhilfsaktion für Österreich, 1920–1922.

———. *Receipts and Expenditures under the Act Approved February 25, 1919. Message from the President of the United States, Transmitting Preliminary Report Covering the Approximate Receipts and Expenditures Made under the Act of Congress Approved February 25, 1919, Appropriating $100,000,000 for Relief in Europe.* [Washington, 1919] 6 pages. (66th Congress, 2d Session, House Document 449)

American Relief Administration. *Report of Distribution in Russia under Congressional Act Public No. 117—67th Congress (H.R. 9548) for the Relief of the Distressed and Starving People of Russia.* To the President of the United States. December 15, 1922. [Hyslop & McCallum, Accountants and Auditors, New York] [New York, 1922?] 62 pages. Typed.

———. *Report on the Distribution in Russia of Army Surplus Medical Supplies under the Authorization of Congress.* 1922–1923. [New York, 1923?] 34 pages. Typed.

———. *Report on the Distribution in Russia of Medical Supplies Donated by the American Red Cross.* 1921–1923. [New York, 1923?] 17 pages. Typed.

———. *Summary Review of Financial Transactions Relating to European Relief Operations for Period from August, 1919, to December 31, 1924.* Prepared by Allen R. Smart & Company, Public Accountants and Auditors. New York, [1928] [11 pages] Typed.

———. *Supplementary Report of Distribution in Russia under Congressional Act Public No. 117—67th Congress (H.R. 9548) for the Relief of the Distressed and Starving People of Russia.* To the President of the United States. September 29, 1923. [Smart, Gore & Company, Accountants and Auditors] [New York, 1923?] 7 pages. Typed.

———. *Supplementary Report on the Delivery in the United States to the Near East Relief of Army Surplus Medical Supplies under the Authorization of Congress for Distribution in Southern Russia by the Near East Relief, 1922–1923.* [New York, 1923?] 8 pages. Typed.

American Relief Administration European Children's Fund. *List of Child-Feeding Stations in Austria.* Vienna, 1921. p. 75–106. (Mitteilungen Nr. 18–26) Text in English and German.

The American Relief Administration European Children's Fund in Austria. Ed. by the General-Commissariat of the Amerikanische Kinderhilfsaktion für Österreich. Based on scientific studies made and practical experiences gained by Dr. Clemens Pirquet and Dr. Ernst Mayerhofer. Tr. by H. W. Tschirf. Vienna, [1920?] 30 pages.

American Relief for Students. Wien, Amerikanische Kinderhilfsaktion für Österreich, 1921. 37 pages. (Mitteilungen, Nr. 133–42)

"America's Loaf in Russia," in *Literary Digest,* 78 : 30–31, August 18, 1923.

Die Amerikanische Kinderhilfsaktion in den Ländern Österreichs. Wien, 1921. 162 pages.

Die Amerikanische Kinderhilfsaktion in Wien. Wien, 1921. 148 pages.

"Austria's Rising Generation," in *Independent,* 105:122. January 29, 1921.

Baker, R. S. "American Attitude on Economic Questions at Paris toward Reparations and Debts. The Supreme Economic Council," in his *Woodrow Wilson and World Settlement,* Garden City, 1922. Vol. II, pages 314–67.

Barber, A. B. *Report of European Technical Advisers Mission to Poland, 1919–1922.* New York, 1923. 76 pages.

Barton, J. L. *Story of Near East Relief (1915–1930): an Interpretation.* New York, 1920. 479 pages.

Bernstein, Herman. *Herbert Hoover, the Man Who Brought America to the World.* [New York, 1928] 44 pages. Reprinted from *McClure's Magazine,* September–October, 1925.

Brooks, Sidney. *America and Germany, 1918–1925.* 2 ed. rev. New York, 1927. 167 pages.

Brown, E. S. "Some Unofficial Relations with Soviet Russia," in *Michigan Law Review,* Vol. 22, No. 5, pages 421–36. March, 1924.

Cary, R. L. "Child-Feeding Work in Germany under the American Friends' Service Committee Co-operating with the American Relief Administration and the European Children's Fund, Herbert C. Hoover, Chairman," in *Annals of the American Academy of Political and Social Science,* 92 : 157–62. November, 1920.

Dickinson, T. H. "The American Relief Administration," in *Atlantic Monthly,* 124 : 701–07. November, 1919.

———. "Learning the Tricks of the Revolution," in *Review,* 1 : 580–81. November 15, 1919.

Economic Conditions in Central Europe. Vols. I–II. London, 1920. (Misc. 1, 6. Cmd. 521, 641) [Signed: William Goode]

European Relief Council. *Final Report, May 31, 1922.* [Hyslop & McCallum, Accountants and Auditors, New York] New York, American Relief Administration, [1922] 9 pages.

———. *Interim Report, Including Statement of Contributions by States and Auditors' Preliminary Report on Accounts, May 31, 1921.* [Hyslop & McCallum, Chartered Accountants] [New York, 1921] 51 pages.

———. *Report on the National Collection by the Control Committee.* [New York, 1921] 31 pages.

Ferrière, Suzanne. *Les Etats-Unis au Secours de l'Europe 1918–1923; l'Oeuvre de Hoover en Europe depuis l'Armistice.* Genève, Union Internationale de Secours aux Enfants, 1923. 158 pages.

Fisher, H. H. "The Character of American Participation in European Affairs since the War." Reprinted from the *Proceedings of the Pacific Coast Branch of the American Historical Association,* 1926. Pages 73–83.

———. *The Famine in Soviet Russia,* 1919–1923. New York, 1927. 609 pages.

Fisher, H. H., and Brooks, Sidney. *America and the New Poland.* New York, 1928. 403 pages.

Fry, A. R. *A Quaker Adventure.* London, [1926] 389 pages.

Garvin, J. L. *The Economic Foundations of Peace.* Ch. iv, v, vi, pages 55–109. London, 1919.

III. AMERICAN RELIEF ADMINISTRATION (*Cont.*)

GOLDER, F. A. "Christmas, 1921, in Russia," in *Independent,* 119 : 626. December 24, 1927.

GOLDER, F. A., and HUTCHINSON, LINCOLN. *On the Trail of the Russian Famine.* Stanford University, 1927. 319 pages.

GREGORY, T. T. C. "Stemming the Red Tide," in *World's Work,* 41 : 608–13; 42 : 95–100; 153–64. April–June, 1921.

HARD, WILLIAM. *Who's Hoover?* New York, 1928. 274 pages.

HARRIS, H. W. "The Feeding of Europe," in his *The Peace in the Making.* London, [1919] Pages 179–90.

HOOVER, HERBERT. I. *Central European Relief.* II. *Relief for Europe . . .* New York, American Association for International Conciliation, No. 160, [1921] 24 pages.

———. "Announcement," in *Saturday Evening Post,* 193 : 25. November 20, 1920. Reprinted by the European Relief Council with the title: "Three and One-Half Million Children to Save: An Announcement."

———. "The Economic Administration during the Armistice," in E. M. House and Charles Seymour, *What Really Happened at Paris.* New York, 1921. Pages 336–47.

———. *Food Conservation for World Relief.* Washington, United States Food Administration, 1918. 8 pages.

———. "How America Helped Starving Europe," in *World Outlook,* 6 : 4–5. June, 1920.

———. "How Much Longer Must We Feed Europe," in *Forum,* 64 : 377–79. December, 1920.

———. *Organization of Child Relief in Europe.* [New York, 1920?] 7 pages.

———. "Three Million Starving Children Crying to America," in *Current Opinion,* 69 : 611–16. November, 1920.

HOYT, EDITH. "In the Hunger Districts," in *Yale Review,* N.S., 10 : 351–61. January, 1921.

IRWIN, WILL. *Herbert Hoover, a Reminiscent Biography.* New York, [1928] 315 pages.

———. "Hoover as an Executive," in *Saturday Evening Post,* 192 : 5+ March 27, 1920.

JONES, L. M. *Quakers in Action.* New York, 1929. 226 pages.

JONES, R. M. *Service of Love in War Time: American Friends Relief Work in Europe, 1917–1919.* New York, 1920. 284 pages.

KAHN, BERNHARD, and ROSEN, J. A. *Report on the Activities of the Joint Distribution Committee.* Constructive Relief Conference United Jewish Campaign and Joint Distribution Committee, Chicago, October 22–23, 1927. [New York, 1927?] 70 pages.

KELLOGG, VERNON. "Herbert Hoover, as Individual and Type," in *Atlantic Monthly,* 1921 : 375–85. March, 1918.

———. *Herbert Hoover, the Man and His Work.* New York, 1920. 375 pages.

———. "The Russian Famine Region," in *Annals of the American Academy of Political and Social Science,* 100 : 105–7. March, 1922.

———. "Story of Hoover," *Everybody's,* 42 : 18–22; 33–37; 33–38; 18–22; 32–36. February–June, 1920.

KEYNES, J. M. *The Economic Consequences of the Peace.* New York, 1920. Pages 273–74.

LANE, R. W. *The Making of Herbert Hoover.* New York, 1920. 356 pages.

"Life-Line of the A.R.A." in *Independent,* 107 : 206. November 26, 1921. *Ibid.,* 108 : 301. March 25, 1922.

League of Nations. *Report on Economic Conditions in Russia, with Special Reference to the Famine of 1921–1922 and the State of Agriculture.* [Geneva, 1922?] 164 pages.

MARCOSSON, I. F. "American Relief—and After," in *Saturday Evening Post,* 193 : 21–22. April 30, 1921.

MARTIN, WILLIAM. "Hoover" in his *Statesmen of the War in Retrospect, 1918–1928.* New York, 1928. Pages 195–206.

MATHEWS, PHILIP. "Efforts of the Soviet Government to Block American Aid to Russia," in *Annals of the American Academy of Political and Social Science,* 114 : 85–88. July, 1924.

Mennonite Central Committee. *Feeding the Hungry; Russian Famine 1919–1925.* Edited by P. C. Hiebert and O. O. Miller. Scottdale, 1929. 465 pages.

"Most Stupendous Act of Mercy," in *Literary Digest,* 74:36. August 26, 1922.

National Information Bureau, Inc. Commission on Russian Relief. *The Russian Famines, 1921–22, 1922–23.* Summary Report. New York, [1923] 40 pages.

OSKISON, J. M. "Back-Firing Against Bolshevism," in *Outlook,* 122 : 510+ July 30, 1919.

PENNYBACKER, MRS. P. V. "Salvaging the Children," in *Ladies' Home Journal,* 40 : 104. April, 1923.

PIRQUET, CLEMENS. *Die Amerikanische Kinder-Hilfsaktion in Österreich.* Sonderabdruck aus der "Österreichischen Rundschau," Band LXIII, Heft 6. 1920.

———. *An Outline of the Pirquet System of Nutrition.* Philadelphia, 1922. 96 pages.

POTTLE, EMERY. "Sketches for a Portrait of Herbert Hoover," in *The Touchstone,* 7 : 117–21, 152. May, 1920.

The Professor's Mess. Wien, Amerikanische Kinderhilfsaktion für Österreich, 1921. 20 pages. (Mitteilungen [unnumbered])

REEVES, EARL. *This Man Hoover.* New York, [1928] 255 pages.

ROUSE, RUTH. *Rebuilding Europe: The Student Chapter in Post-War Reconstruction.* London, 1925. 224 pages.

Russian Committee in Turkey. *Materials Concerning the Evacuation of Russian Refugees from Constantinople.* Constantinople, 1922. 76 pages. Text in Russian, French, and English.

Schülerspeisung in den Städten und Kleineren Orten Niederösterreichs. Organisation und Betrieb der Amerikanischen Kinderhilfsaktion. Wien, Amerikanische Kinderhilfsaktion, 1921. 84 pages. (Mitteilungen [unnumbered])

STROTHER, FRENCH. "Herbert Hoover, Representative American and Practical Idealist," in *World's Work,* 39 : 578–85. April, 1920.

Supreme Council of Supply and Relief, Paris. *Minutes and Documents.* [Paris, 1919]

Supreme Economic Council, Paris. *Minutes and Documents.* [Paris, 1919] 9 volumes and Index.

TAYLOR, A. E. "Hoover's Fifth Year," in *Sunset,* 44 : 28+ January, 1920.

———. "What the United States Has Done for Central Europe," in *Saturday Evening Post,* 193 : 6–7. July 17, 1920.

TEMPERLEY, H. W. V. "Executive Working of the Conference," in his *A History of the Peace Conference of Paris.* London, 1920. Volume I, pages 279–357.

THOMAS, EDWARD. *Quaker Adventures.* New York, [1928] 221 pages.

United States Congress. House Committee on Ways and Means. *Relief of European Populations;* Report to Accompany H.R. 12193. Washington, 1920. 4 pages (66th Congress, 2d Session, House Report 594)

United States Grain Corporation. *American Relief Administration. Fiscal Report and Audit of One Hundred Million Dollar Appropriation Submitted to the President of the United States by the United States Grain Corporation, Fiscal Agent of the American Relief Administration. September 25, 1920.* [Leslie, Banks & Company, Chartered Accountants] [New York?] 1920. 16 pages.

———. *Fiscal Report on European Relief Operations of the American Relief Administration, January–August, 1919.* [Leslie, Banks & Company, Chartered Accountants] [New York, 1920] 254+ pages. Typed.

———. *Purchasing Commission for Russian Relief. United States Grain Corporation, Fiscal Agent. Statement of Expenditures and Activities under Congressional Act Public No. 117—67th Congress (H.R. 9548) for the Relief of the Distressed and Starving People of Russia. To the President of the United States. December 15, 1922.* [Hyslop & McCallum, Accountants and Auditors] [New York, 1922] 247 pages. Typed.

———. London Office. *Fiscal Agent, American Relief Administration. Supplementary Accounting Report Covering Period from October 1, 1920, to August 31, 1922. Fiscal Report on European Relief Operations of the American Relief Administration—January to August, 1919—and on the Books as Adjusted to September 30, 1920. Submitted under Date of September 30, 1920.* [Hyslop & McCallum, Accountants and Auditors] [New York, 1922] 7+ pages. Typed.

WADE, M. H. "Herbert Clark Hoover," in her *Real Americans.* Boston, 1922. Pages 66–113.

WALDRON, WEBB. "About This Man Hoover," in *Collier's,* 65 : 15. April 3, 1920.

Wiens Kinder und Amerika. Die Amerikanische Kinderhilfsaktion, 1919. Hrsg. v. Deutschösterreichischen Jugendhilfswerk in Wien fur die Amerikanische Reife Jugend Verfasst von Friedrich Reischl. 2 aufl. Wien, 1920. 188 pages.

WILKINSON, LUPTON. "Feeding Hungry Europe," in *Current History,* 13 : 332–34. November, 1920.

Die II. Jahresfeier der Amerikanischen Kinderhilfsaktion. Das Fest im Park des Schlosses Schönbrunn. [Wien, 1921?] 16 pages.

IV. MISSION REPORTS

AUSTRIA

Three Years' Work of the American Relief Administration in Austria. Vienna, 1922. 57 pages.

A Review of the Work of the American Relief Administration in Austria. Year 1922–1923. Vienna, 1923.

A Review of the Work of the American Relief Administration in Austria. Vienna, 1921. 58 pages.

American Relief Administration European Children's Fund. *The Organization and Distribution System in Austria.* Vienna, 1920. 27 pages.

CZECHO-SLOVAKIA

The American Relief Administration in Czecho-Slovakia. A Sketch of the Child-Feeding Operations of the A.R.A. Mission to Czecho-Slovakia, 1919–1921. Prague, Czecho-Slovakia, December 1921. New York, [1922?] 16 pages.

DANZIG

American Relief Administration European Children's Fund. *Danzig Port Mission, 1919–1922.* [Warszawa, 1922?] 40 pages.

GERMANY

American Relief Administration European Children's Fund. *Germany, 1921–1922.* Hamburg, 1922. 2 volumes.

———. *Germany. Final Report Published at the Close of Operations of the Hamburg Office, July 1923.* Hamburg, 1923. 25 pages.

HUNGARY

Az Amerikai Gyermek Segélyzö Actió Magyarországon. The Work of the American Relief Administration Eu-

IV. MISSION REPORTS (*Cont.*)

ropean Children's Fund in Hungary, 1919 Nov. 2—1921 Dec. 31. Report of the Hungarian Executive Committee. Ed. by the American Relief Administration European Children's Fund. Budapest, 1920–1922. 2 volumes. Text in Hungarian and English.

American Relief Administration European Children's Fund. *An Account of the Work in Hungary.* Written by the Members of the American Child Welfare Mission. Budapest, 1920. 15 pages.

———. *Final Report of the Work in Hungary.* Written by the Members of the American Child Welfare Mission. Budapest, 1920. 27 pages.

JUGOSLAVIA

American Relief Administration European Children's Fund. *Final Report of the Work in Kingdom S.H.S.* Written by Members of A.R.A.E.C.F. Belgrade, Kingdom S.H.S., June 15th, 1920. 22 pages.

POLAND

American Relief Administration European Children's Fund Mission to Poland. Polsko-Amerykański Komitet Pomocy Dzieciom, 1919–1922. [Warsaw, 1922] 76 pages.

The American Relief Administration in Poland, 1922–1923. [Warszawa, 1923?] 39 pages.

INDEX

INDEX TO TEXT

(See page 1023 for Index to Tables)

INDEX TO TABLES

(See page 1001 for Index to Text)

STANFORD UNIVERSITY PRESS
STANFORD UNIVERSITY, CALIFORNIA

LONDON: HUMPHREY MILFORD
OXFORD UNIVERSITY PRESS

THE BAKER & TAYLOR COMPANY
55 FIFTH AVENUE, NEW YORK

MARTINUS NIJHOFF
9 LANGE VOORHOUT, THE HAGUE

THE MARUZEN COMPANY
TOKYO, OSAKA, KYOTO, SENDAI

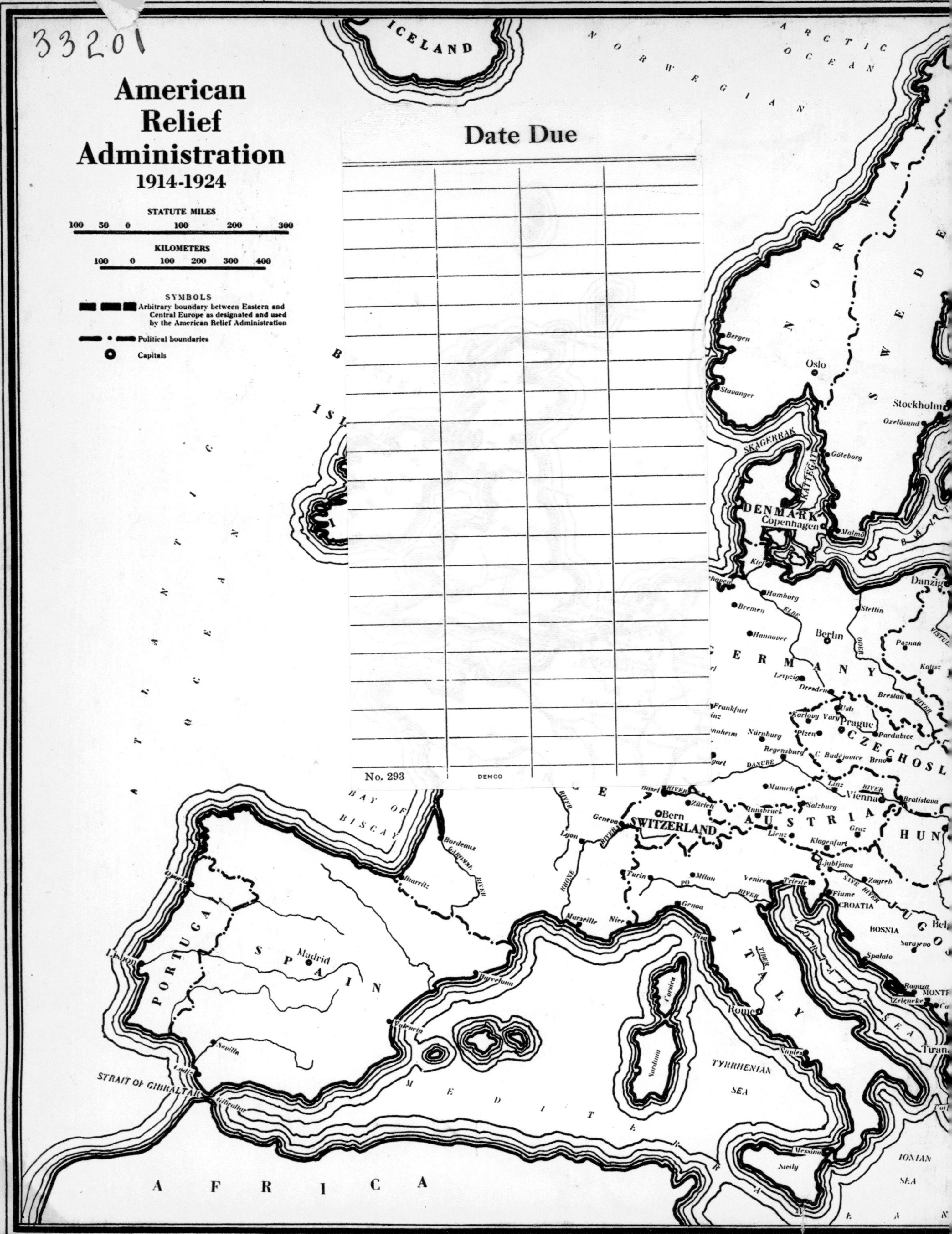

33201
American Relief Administration
1914-1924
STATUTE MILES
100 50 0 100 200 300
KILOMETERS
100 0 100 200 300 400
SYMBOLS
Arbitrary boundary between Eastern and Central Europe as designated and used by the American Relief Administration
Political boundaries
Capitals
Date Due
No. 293
DEMCO
ICELAND
NORWEGIAN
ARCTIC OCEAN
ATLANTIC OCEAN
NORWAY
SWEDEN
Bergen
Oslo
Stavanger
Stockholm
Oxelösund
SKAGERRAK
KATTEGAT
Göteborg
DENMARK
Copenhagen
Malmö
Kiel
Danzig
Hamburg
Bremen
ELBE
Stettin
Hannover
Berlin
ODER
Poznan
Kalisz
GERMANY
Leipzig
Dresden
Breslau
Frankfurt
Usti
Karlovy Vary
Prague
Nürnburg
Plzeň
Pardubice
CZECHOSL
Regensburg
Budějovice
Brno
DANUBE
Munich
Linz
Vienna
Bratislava
Basel
Zürich
Innsbruck
Salzburg
Bern
SWITZERLAND
AUSTRIA
Geneva
Graz
HUN
Lyon
Lienz
Klagenfurt
RHONE
Ljubljana
Turin
Milan
PO
Venice
Trieste
Zagreb
Fiume
CROATIA
Marseille
Nice
Genoa
BOSNIA
Sarajevo
Pisa
ITALY
TIBER
Spalato
Corsica
Rome
Ragusa
Zelenike
Sardinia
Naples
TYRRHENIAN SEA
Tirana
Messina
Sicily
IONIAN SEA
BAY OF BISCAY
Bordeaux
GARONNE RIVER
Biarritz
Oporto
PORTUGAL
SPAIN
Madrid
Lisbon
Barcelona
Valencia
Sevilla
Cadiz
STRAIT OF GIBRALTAR
Gibraltar
MEDITERRANEAN
AFRICA